2017-2018

OFFICIAL CONGRESSIONAL DIRECTORY

115TH CONGRESS

CONVENED JANUARY 3, 2017

JOINT COMMITTEE ON PRINTING
UNITED STATES CONGRESS

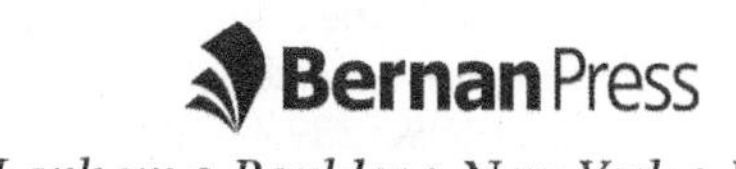

Lanham • Boulder • New York • London

Published by Bernan Press
An imprint of The Rowman & Littlefield Publishing Group, Inc.
4501 Forbes Boulevard, Suite 200, Lanham, Maryland 20706
www.rowman.com

6 Tinworth Street, London SE11 5AL, United Kingdom

Library of Congress Cataloging-in-Publication Data Available

ISBN 13 hardback: 978-1-59888-978-9
ISBN 13 paperback: 978-1-59888-979-6

∞™ The paper used in this publication meets the minimum requirements of American National Standard for Information Sciences—Permanence of Paper for Printed Library Materials, ANSI/NISO Z39.48-1992.

Printed in the United States of America

NOTES

Closing date for compilation of the Congressional Directory was July 27, 2018.

[Republicans in roman, Democrats in *italic*.]

The following changes have occurred in the membership of the 115th Congress since the election of November 8, 2016:

Name	Resigned, [Died], **[**Term Ended**]**, or (Interim Vacant Status)	Successor	Elected or [Appointed]	Sworn in
SENATORS				
Luther Strange, AL	**[**Jan. 3, 2018**]**	*Doug Jones*	Dec. 12, 2017 ..	Jan. 3, 2018
Al Franken, MN	Jan. 2, 2018	*Tina Smith*	Jan. 3, 2018	Jan. 3, 2018
Thad Cochran, MS	Apr. 1, 2018	Cindy Hyde-Smith	Apr. 2, 2018	Apr. 9, 2018
REPRESENTATIVES				
Mike Pompeo,[1] 4th KS	Jan. 23, 2017	Ron Estes	Apr. 11, 2017 ..	Apr. 25, 2017
Xavier Becerra, 34th CA	Jan. 24, 2017	*Jimmy Gomez*	June 6, 2017	July 11, 2017
Tom Price,[2] 6th GA	Feb. 10, 2017	Karen C. Handel	June 20, 2017 ..	June 26, 2017
Mick Mulvaney,[3] 5th SC	Feb 16, 2017	Ralph Norman	June 20, 2017 ..	June 26, 2017
Ryan K. Zinke,[4] 2nd MT	Mar. 1, 2017	Greg Gianforte	May 25, 2017 ..	June 21, 2017
Jason Chaffetz, 3rd UT	June 30, 2017	John R. Curtis	Nov. 7, 2017	Nov. 13, 2017
Tim Murphy, 18th PA	Oct. 21, 2017	*Conor Lamb*	Mar. 13, 2018 ..	Apr. 12, 2018
John Conyers, Jr.,[5] 13th MI	(Dec. 5, 2017)	....	....	
Trent Franks, 8th AZ	Dec. 8, 2017	Debbie Lesko	Apr. 24, 2018 ..	May 7, 2018
Patrick J. Tiberi,[6] 12th OH	(Jan. 15, 2017)	....	....	
Louise McIntosh Slaughter,[7] 25th NY	[Mar. 16, 2018]	....	....	
Blake Farenthold 27th TX	Apr. 6, 2018	Michael Cloud	June 30, 2018 ..	July 10, 2018
Jim Bridenstine,[8] 1st OK	(Apr. 23, 2018)	....	....	
Patrick Meehan,[9] 7th PA	(Apr. 27, 2018)	....	....	
Charles W. Dent,[10] 15th PA	(May 12, 2018)	....	....	

[1] Mike Pompeo resigned to become Director of the Central Intelligence Agency.

[2] Tom Price resigned to become Secretary of the Department of Health and Human Services.

[3] Mick Mulvaney resigned to become Director of the Office of Management and Budget.

[4] Ryan K. Zinke resigned to become Secretary of the Department of the Interior.

[5] This seat is in interim vacant status. A special election for a new U.S. Representative will be held on November 6, 2018.

[6] This seat is in interim vacant status. A special election for a new U.S. Representative will be held on August 7, 2018, to serve the remainder of Representative Tiberi's term until January 3, 2019.

[7] This seat is in interim vacant status. Louise Slaughter died on March 16, 2018. A special election, concurrent with the general election, will be held on November 6, 2018, for a new U.S. Representative to serve the remainder of Representative Slaughter's term.

[8] Jim Bridenstine resigned to become Administrator of the National Aeronautics and Space Administration.

[9] This seat is in interim vacant status. A special election for a new U.S. Representative for the 7th District will be held on November 6, 2018. The special election coincides with the general election for the newly redrawn 7th District made up of the old 15th, 17th, and 10th Districts. The old 7th District will no longer exist on December 31, 2018.

[10] This seat is in interim vacant status. The Supreme Court of Pennsylvania redrew the district in February 2018. Boundaries of the old 15th District will be compressed, becoming the 7th District. The old 5th District will have its boundaries adjusted to become the 15th district for the 2018 election.

[Republicans in roman, Democrats in *italic*.]

The following changes have occurred in the membership of the 114th Congress since the election of November 4, 2014:

Name	Resigned, [Died] or (Interim Vacant Status)	Successor	Elected or [Appointed]	Sworn in
REPRESENTATIVES				
John A. Boehner,[1] 8th OH	Oct. 31, 2015	....	....	
Aaron Schock, 18th IL	Mar. 31, 2015	Darin LaHood	Sept. 10, 2015	Sept. 17, 2015
Alan Nunnelee, 1st MS	[Feb. 6, 2015]	Trent Kelly	June 2, 2015	June 9, 2015
Michael G. Grimm, 11th NY	Jan. 5, 2015	Daniel M. Donovan, Jr.	May 5, 2015	May 12, 2015

[1] Honorable John A. Boehner served as the 53rd Speaker of the United States House of Representatives from 2011 to 2015. The Washington, DC, office and the district offices of former Representative John A. Boehner will continue to serve the people of the Eighth Congressional District of Ohio under the supervision of the Clerk of the House of Representatives. Representative Boehner resigned from Congress effective October 31, 2015.

FOREWORD

The *Congressional Directory* is one of the oldest working handbooks within the United States Government. While there were unofficial directories for Congress in one form or another beginning with the 1st Congress in 1789, the *Congressional Directory* published in 1847 for the 30th Congress is considered by scholars and historians to be the first official edition because it was the first to be ordered and paid for by Congress. With the addition of biographical sketches of legislators in 1867, the *Congressional Directory* attained its modern format.

The *Congressional Directory* is published by the United States Congress in partnership with the Government Publishing Office, at the direction of the Joint Committee on Printing under the authority of Title 44, Section 721 of the U.S. Code.

JOINT COMMITTEE ON PRINTING

Roy Blunt, Senator from Missouri, *Chair*

Rodney Davis, Representative from Illinois, *Vice Chair*

Senate

Pat Roberts, of Kansas.
Roger F. Wicker, of Mississippi.
Amy Klobuchar, of Minnesota.
Tom Udall, of New Mexico.

House

Gregg Harper, of Mississippi.
Mark Walker, of North Carolina.
Robert A. Brady, of Pennsylvania.
Jamie Raskin, of Maryland.

The 2017–2018 *Congressional Directory* was compiled by the Government Publishing Office, under the direction of the Joint Committee on Printing by:

Project Manager.—Mary C. Forschler.

Editors: Jacqueline Henderson; Heather M. Lawson; Lisa Lewis.

Typographer/Editor.—Eve M. Hiers.

Proofreader/Editor.—Eleanor F. Umali.

State District Maps.—Election Data Services, Inc.

Representatives' Zip Codes.—House Office of Mailing Services/U.S. Postal Service.

For sale by the Superintendent of Documents, U.S. Government Publishing Office

Internet: bookstore.gpo.gov; Phone: toll free (866) 512–1800; DC area (202) 512–1800

Fax: (202) 512–2250; Mail: Stop SSOP, Washington, DC 20402–0001

Paper Cover ISBN–978–0–16–094208–2

Casebound ISBN–978–0–16–094209–9

CONTENTS

Name Index on page 1151

	Page
The Vice President	1
Members of Congress, biographies, office listings, district descriptions—arranged by State	
Alabama	2
Alaska	7
Arizona	9
Arkansas	15
California	19
Colorado	46
Connecticut	51
Delaware	55
Florida	57
Georgia	75
Hawaii	83
Idaho	85
Illinois	88
Indiana	99
Iowa	105
Kansas	108
Kentucky	112
Louisiana	117
Maine	121
Maryland	123
Massachusetts	129
Michigan	135
Minnesota	143
Mississippi	149
Missouri	153
Montana	159
Nebraska	161
Nevada	164
New Hampshire	167
New Jersey	169
New Mexico	177
New York	180
North Carolina	195
North Dakota	203
Ohio	205
Oklahoma	215
Oregon	219
Pennsylvania	223
Rhode Island	235
South Carolina	237
South Dakota	242
Tennessee	244
Texas	250
Utah	271
Vermont	274
Virginia	276
Washington	284
West Virginia	290
Wisconsin	293
Wyoming	298
American Samoa	300
District of Columbia	300
Guam	301
Members of Congress, biographies, office listings, district descriptions—arranged by State—Continued	
Northern Mariana Islands	302
Puerto Rico	302
Virgin Islands	303
State Delegations	305
Alphabetical List of Members—Senate	317
Alphabetical List of Members—House	318
Senate, House—Nine-Digit Postal Zip Codes	323
Terms of Service	327
Standing Committees of the Senate	345
Agriculture, Nutrition, and Forestry	345
Subcommittees:	
Commodities, Risk Management, and Trade	345
Conservation, Forestry, and Natural Resources	345
Livestock, Marketing, and Agriculture Security	346
Nutrition, Agricultural Research, and Specialty Crops	346
Rural Development and Energy	346
Appropriations	347
Subcommittees:	
Agriculture, Rural Development, Food and Drug Administration, and Related Agencies	347
Commerce, Justice, Science, and Related Agencies	347
Defense	348
Energy and Water Development	348
Financial Services and General Government	348
Homeland Security	348
Interior, Environment, and Related Agencies	348
Labor, Health and Human Services, Education, and Related Agencies	349
Legislative Branch	349
Military Construction, Veterans Affairs, and Related Agencies	349
State, Foreign Operations, and Related Programs	349
Transportation, Housing and Urban Development, and Related Agencies	349
Armed Services	352

	Page
Armed Services—Continued	
Subcommittees:	
Airland	352
Cybersecurity	352
Emerging Threats and Capabilities	352
Personnel	353
Readiness and Management Support	353
Seapower	353
Strategic Forces	353
Banking, Housing, and Urban Affairs	359
Subcommittees:	
Economic Policy	359
Financial Institutions and Consumer Protection	359
Housing, Transportation, and Community Development	359
National Security and International Trade and Finance	359
Securities, Insurance, and Investment	360
Budget	361
No Subcommittees.	
Commerce, Science, and Transportation	362
Subcommittees:	
Aviation Operations, Safety, and Security	362
Communications, Technology, Innovation, and the Internet	362
Consumer Protection, Product Safety, Insurance, and Data Security	363
Oceans, Atmosphere, Fisheries, and Coast Guard	363
Space, Science, and Competitiveness	363
Surface Transportation and Merchant Marine Infrastructure, Safety and Security	363
Energy and Natural Resources	365
Subcommittees:	
Energy	365
National Parks	365
Public Lands, Forests, and Mining	365
Water and Power	366
Environment and Public Works	367
Subcommittees:	
Clean Air and Nuclear Safety	367
Fisheries, Water, and Wildlife	367
Superfund, Waste Management, and Regulatory Oversight	367
Transportation and Infrastructure	368
Finance	369
Subcommittees:	
Energy, Natural Resources, and Infrastructure	369
Fiscal Responsibility and Economic Growth	369
Health Care	369
International Trade, Customs, and Global Competitiveness	370
Social Security, Pensions, and Family Policy	370
Taxation and IRS Oversight	370
Foreign Relations	372
Subcommittees:	
Africa and Global Health Policy	372
East Asia, the Pacific, and International Cybersecurity Policy	372

	Page
Foreign Relations—Continued	
Subcommittees—Continued	
Europe and Regional Security Cooperation	372
Multilateral International Development, Multilateral Institutions, and International Economic, Energy, and Environmental Policy	372
Near East, South Asia, Central Asia, and Counterterrorism	373
State Department and USAID Management, International Operations, and Bilateral International Development	373
Western Hemisphere, Transnational Crime, Civilian Security, Democracy, Human Rights, and Global Women's Issues	373
Health, Education, Labor, and Pensions	374
Subcommittees:	
Children and Families	374
Employment and Workplace Safety	374
Primary Health and Retirement Security	374
Homeland Security and Governmental Affairs	377
Subcommittees:	
Federal Spending Oversight and Emergency Management	377
Permanent Subcommittee on Investigations	377
Regulatory Affairs and Federal Management	377
Judiciary	379
Subcommittees:	
Antitrust, Competition Policy and Consumer Rights	379
Border Security and Immigration	379
Constitution	379
Crime and Terrorism	379
Oversight, Agency Action, Federal Rights and Federal Courts	380
Privacy, Technology and the Law	380
Rules and Administration	382
No Subcommittees.	
Small Business and Entrepreneurship	383
No Subcommittees.	
Veterans' Affairs	384
No Subcommittees.	
Select and Special Committees of the Senate	385
Committee on Indian Affairs	385
Select Committee on Ethics	386
Select Committee on Intelligence	386
Special Committee on Aging	387
Democratic Senatorial Campaign Committee	387
Democratic Policy and Communications Center	388
Democratic Steering and Outreach Committee	388
Senate Democratic Conference	388
Senate Democratic Media Center	389
National Republican Senatorial Committee	389
Senate Republican Policy Committee	389
Senate Republican Conference	390

	Page
Officers and Officials of the Senate	391
President of the Senate	391
President Pro Tempore	391
Majority Leader	391
Office of the Majority Whip	392
Democratic Leader	392
Democratic Whip	392
Assistant Democratic Leader	393
Office of the Secretary	393
Office of the Chaplain	394
Office of the Sergeant at Arms	394
Office of the Secretary for the Majority	397
Office of the Secretary for the Minority	397
Office of the Legislative Counsel	397
Office of Senate Legal Counsel	398
Standing Committees of the House	399
Agriculture	399
Subcommittees:	
Biotechnology, Horticulture, and Research	400
Commodity Exchanges, Energy, and Credit	400
Conservation and Forestry	400
General Farm Commodities and Risk Management	400
Livestock and Foreign Agriculture	400
Nutrition	401
Appropriations	402
Subcommittees:	
Agriculture, Rural Development, Food and Drug Administration, and Related Agencies	402
Commerce, Justice, Science, and Related Agencies	402
Defense	403
Energy and Water Development, and Related Agencies	403
Financial Services and General Government	403
Homeland Security	403
Interior, Environment, and Related Agencies	403
Labor, Health and Human Services, Education, and Related Agencies	404
Legislative Branch	404
Military Construction, Veterans Affairs, and Related Agencies	404
State, Foreign Operations, and Related Programs	404
Transportation, Housing and Urban Development, and Related Agencies	404
Armed Services	406
Subcommittees:	
Emerging Threats and Capabilities	406
Military Personnel	407
Oversight and Investigations	407
Readiness	407
Seapower and Projection Forces	407
Strategic Forces	407
Tactical Air and Land Forces	408
Budget	409
No Subcommittees.	
Education and the Workforce	410
Education and the Workforce—Continued	
Subcommittees:	
Early Childhood, Elementary, and Secondary Education	410
Health, Employment, Labor, and Pensions	410
Higher Education and Workforce Development	411
Workforce Protections	411
Energy and Commerce	413
Subcommittees:	
Communications and Technology	413
Digital Commerce and Consumer Protection	414
Energy	414
Environment	414
Health	415
Oversight and Investigations	415
Ethics	417
No Subcommittees.	
Financial Services	418
Subcommittees:	
Capital Markets, Securities, and Investments	418
Financial Institutions and Consumer Credit	419
Housing and Insurance	419
Monetary Policy and Trade	419
Oversight and Investigations	419
Terrorism and Illicit Finance	420
Foreign Affairs	421
Subcommittees:	
Africa, Global Health, Global Human Rights, and International Organizations	421
Asia and the Pacific	421
Europe, Eurasia, and Emerging Threats	422
The Middle East and North Africa	422
Terrorism, Nonproliferation, and Trade	422
The Western Hemisphere	422
Homeland Security	424
Subcommittees:	
Border and Maritime Security	424
Counterterrorism and Intelligence	424
Cybersecurity and Infrastructure Protection	424
Emergency Preparedness, Response, and Communications	424
Oversight and Management Efficiency	425
Transportation and Protective Security	425
House Administration	427
No Subcommittees.	
Judiciary	428
Subcommittees:	
The Constitution and Civil Justice	428
Courts, Intellectual Property, and the Internet	428
Crime, Terrorism, Homeland Security, and Investigations	429
Immigration and Border Security	429
Regulatory Reform, Commercial and Antitrust Law	429
Natural Resources	431
Subcommittees:	
Energy and Mineral Resources	431
Federal Lands	432

	Page
Natural Resources—Continued	
Subcommittees—Continued	
Indian, Insular and Alaska Native Affairs	432
Oversight and Investigations	432
Water, Power and Oceans	432
Oversight and Government Reform	434
Subcommittees:	
Government Operations	434
Health Care, Benefits, and Administrative Rules	434
Information Technology	435
Intergovernmental Affairs	435
Interior, Energy, and Environment	435
National Security	435
Rules	437
Subcommittees:	
Legislative and Budget Process	437
Rules and Organization of the House	437
Science, Space, and Technology	438
Subcommittees:	
Energy	438
Environment	438
Oversight	439
Research and Technology	439
Space	439
Small Business	441
Subcommittees:	
Agriculture, Energy, and Trade	441
Contracting and Workforce	441
Economic Growth, Tax, and Capital Access	441
Health and Technology	442
Investigations, Oversight, and Regulations	442
Transportation and Infrastructure	443
Subcommittees:	
Aviation	444
Coast Guard and Maritime Transportation	444
Economic Development, Public Buildings, and Emergency Management	444
Highways and Transit	445
Railroads, Pipelines, and Hazardous Materials	445
Water Resources and Environment	446
Veterans' Affairs	448
Subcommittees:	
Disability Assistance and Memorial Affairs	448
Economic Opportunity	448
Health	448
Oversight and Investigations	448
Ways and Means	450
Subcommittees:	
Health	450
Human Resources	450
Oversight	451
Social Security	451
Tax Policy	451
Trade	451
Select and Special Committees of the House	453
Permanent Select Committee on Intelligence	453
Permanent Select Committee on Intelligence—Continued	
Subcommittees:	
Central Intelligence Agency	453
Department of Defense Intelligence and Overhead Architecture	453
Emerging Threats	453
National Security Agency and Cybersecurity	454
National Republican Congressional Committee	454
House Republican Policy Committee	455
House Republican Conference	455
Democratic Congressional Campaign Committee	455
Democratic Steering and Policy Committee	456
Democratic Caucus	456
Officers and Officials of the House	459
Office of the Speaker	459
Office of the Majority Leader	459
Office of the Majority Whip	460
Office of the Democratic Leader	460
Democratic Leader's Press Office	460
Democratic Leader's Floor Office	461
Office of the Democratic Whip	461
Office of the Assistant Democratic Leader	461
Office of the Clerk	461
Chief Administrative Officer	462
Chaplain	463
Office of the House Historian	463
Office of Interparliamentary Affairs	463
Office of Attending Physician	463
Office of Inspector General	463
Office of the Law Revision Counsel	464
Office of the Legislative Counsel	464
Office of the Parliamentarian	464
Office of the Sergeant at Arms	465
Joint Committees	467
Joint Economic Committee	467
Joint Committee on the Library of Congress	468
Joint Committee on Printing	468
Joint Committee on Taxation	469
Joint Select Committee on Budget and Appropriations Process Reform	470
Joint Select Committee on Solvency of Multiemployer Pension Plans	470
Assignments of Senators to Committees	473
Assignments of Representatives to Committees	483
Congressional Advisory Boards, Commissions, and Groups	501
United States Air Force Academy Board of Visitors	501
United States Military Academy Board of Visitors	501
United States Naval Academy Board of Visitors	502
United States Coast Guard Academy Board of Visitors	502
British-American Parliamentary Group	502
Canada-United States Interparliamentary Group	502
China-United States Interparliamentary Group	503

	Page
Korea-United States Interparliamentary Group	503
Mexico-United States Interparliamentary Group	503
NATO Parliamentary Assembly	503
Commission on Congressional Mailing Standards	503
Commission on Security and Cooperation in Europe	504
Congressional Award Foundation	505
Congressional Club	505
Congressional Executive Commission on China	506
House Democracy Partnership	506
House Office Building Commission	507
Japan-United States Friendship Commission	507
Migratory Bird Conservation Commission	507
Permanent Committee for the Oliver Wendell Holmes Devise Fund	508
United States-China Economic and Security Review Commission	508
Senate National Security Working Group	508
United States Association of Former Members of Congress	509
U.S. Capitol Historical Society	509
U.S. Capitol Preservation Commission	510
U.S. House of Representatives Fine Arts Board	510
U.S. Senate Commission on Art	511
Other Congressional Officials and Services	513
Architect of the Capitol	513
Capitol Telephone Exchange	514
Child Care Centers	514
House of Representatives Child Care Center	514
Senate Employees' Child Care Center	514
Combined Airlines Ticket Offices (CATO)	514
Congressional Record Daily Digest	514
Congressional Record Index Office	515
Office of Congressional Accessibility Services	515
Liaison Offices:	
Air Force	515
Army	515
Coast Guard	515
Navy/Marine Corps	516
Government Accountability Office	516
Office of Personnel Management	516
Social Security Administration	516
State Department Liaison Offices	517
Veterans' Affairs	517
United States Senate Page School	517
U.S. Capitol Police	517
Statistical Information	521
Votes Cast for Senators	521
Votes Cast for Representatives, Resident Commissioner, and Delegates	522
Sessions of Congress	530
Joint Sessions and Meetings, Addresses to the Senate or the House, and Inaugurations	549
Representatives Under Each Apportionment	565
Impeachment Proceedings	567
Representatives, Senators, Delegates, and Resident Commissioners Serving in the 1st–115th Congresses	568
Political Divisions of the Senate and House from 1855 to 2017	570
Governors of the States, Commonwealth, and Territories—2017	571
Presidents and Vice Presidents and the Congresses Coincident With Their Terms	572
Capitol Buildings and Grounds	573
Legislative Branch	583
Congressional Budget Office	583
Government Accountability Office	583
U.S. Government Publishing Office	584
Library of Congress	588
U.S. Copyright Office	588
United States Botanic Garden	590
The Cabinet	591
Executive Branch	593
The President	593
Executive Office of the President	593
Office of the Vice President	593
Council of Economic Advisers	593
Council on Environmental Quality	594
President's Intelligence Advisory Board	594
National Security Council	594
Office of Administration	595
Office of Management and Budget	595
Office of National Drug Control Policy	595
Office of Science and Technology Policy	596
Office of the United States Trade Representative	596
The White House Office	596
Cabinet Affairs	596
Chief of Staff	596
Communications and Press	597
Office of Digital Strategy	597
Office of American Innovation	597
Domestic Policy Council	597
Office of the Senior Advisor for Policy	597
Office of Economic Initiatives and Entrepreneurship	597
Office of the First Lady	597
Office of Legislative Affairs	597
Office of Management and Administration	597
National Economic Council	598
Presidential Personnel Office	598
Office of Intergovernmental Affairs	598
Office of Political Affairs	598
Office of Public Liasion	598
Office of Presidential Appointments and Scheduling	598
Office of Presidential Advance	598
Office of the Senior Counselor	598
Office of the Staff Secretary	598
White House Counsel	598
Special Counsel	599
Department of State	601
Office of the Secretary	601
Deputy Secretary for Management and Resources	601

	Page
Department of State—Continued	
Office of the Secretary—Continued	
Ambassador-at-Large for Global Criminal Justice	601
Office of the Chief of Protocol	601
Office of Civil Rights	601
Bureau of Counterterrorism	601
Bureau of Conflict and Stabilization Operations	601
Executive Secretariat	601
Office of the Inspector General	602
Bureau of Intelligence and Research	602
Office of Legal Adviser	602
Bureau of Legislative Affairs	602
Policy Planning Staff	602
Office of the U.S. Global AIDS Coordinator	602
Under Secretary for Political Affairs	602
African Affairs	602
East Asian and Pacific Affairs	602
European and Eurasian Affairs	602
Near Eastern Affairs	603
South and Central Asian Affairs	603
Western Hemisphere Affairs	603
International Narcotics and Law Enforcement Affairs	603
International Organization Affairs	603
Under Secretary for Economic Growth, Energy, and the Environment	603
Economic and Business Affairs	603
Under Secretary for Arms Control and International Security	603
International Security and Nonproliferation	603
Political-Military Affairs	604
Arms Control, Verification and Compliance	604
Under Secretary for Public Diplomacy and Public Affairs	604
Educational and Cultural Affairs	604
International Information Programs	604
Public Affairs	604
Under Secretary for Management	604
Administration	604
Consular Affairs	604
Diplomatic Security	604
Director General of the Foreign Service and Director of Human Resources	605
Foreign Service Institute	605
Information Resource Management	605
Medical Services	605
Overseas Buildings Operations	605
Under Secretary of State for Civilian Security, Democracy, and Human Rights	605
Democracy, Human Rights, and Labor	605
Oceans and International Environmental and Scientific Affairs	605
Population, Refugees, and Migration	605
U.S. Mission to the United Nations	606
Office of U.S. Foreign Assistance Resources	606
United States Diplomatic Offices—Foreign Service	606
List of Chiefs of Mission	606
Department of State—Continued	
United States Permanent Diplomatic Missions to International Organizations	610
Department of the Treasury	611
Office of the Secretary	611
Office of the Deputy Secretary	611
Office of the Chief of Staff	611
Office of the General Counsel	611
Office of the Inspector General	612
Office of the Under Secretary for Domestic Finance	612
Office of the Assistant Secretary for Financial Institutions	612
Office of the Assistant Secretary for Financial Markets	612
Office of the Fiscal Assistant Secretary	612
Office of the Assistant Secretary for Financial Stability	613
Financial Stability Oversight Council	613
Financial Management Service	613
Bureau of the Fiscal Service	613
Office of the Under Secretary for International Affairs	613
Office of the Assistant Secretary for International Affairs	614
U.S. Banks	614
Overseas	615
Under Secretary for Terrorism and Financial Intelligence	615
Assistant Secretary for Terrorist Financing and Financial Crimes	615
Assistant Secretary for Intelligence and Analysis	615
Office of Foreign Assets Control	615
Executive Office for Asset Forfeiture	615
Financial Crimes Enforcement Network (FINCEN)	615
Office of the Assistant Secretary for Economic Policy	615
Office of the Assistant Secretary for Legislative Affairs	615
Office of the Assistant Secretary for Management	616
Office of the Assistant Secretary for Public Affairs	616
Office of the Assistant Secretary for Tax Policy	617
Bureau of Engraving and Printing	617
Office of the Comptroller of the Currency	617
Internal Revenue Service	618
Inspector General for Tax Administration (TIGTA)	618
Office of the Treasurer of the United States	618
United States Mint	619
Department of Defense	621
Office of the Secretary	621
Office of the Deputy Secretary	621
Executive Secretariat	621
General Counsel	621
Operational Test and Evaluation	621
Inspector General	622

	Page
Department of Defense—Continued	
Under Secretary of Defense for Acquisition, Technology, and Logistics	622
Joint Strike Fighter Program Office	622
Under Secretary of Defense (Comptroller) and Chief Financial Officer	622
Under Secretary of Defense for Personnel and Readiness	622
Under Secretary of Defense for Policy	622
Department of Defense Chief Information Officer (DoD CIO)	623
Assistant Secretary for Legislative Affairs	623
Assistant to the Secretary for Public Affairs	623
Office of the Chief Management Officer	623
Department of Defense Field Activities	623
Defense Media Activity	623
Department of Defense Education Activity	623
Department of Defense Human Resources Activity	623
Office of Economic Adjustment	623
Washington Headquarters Services	624
Joint Chiefs of Staff	624
Office of the Chair	624
Joint Staff	624
Defense Agencies	624
Missile Defense Agency	624
Defense Advanced Research Projects Agency	624
Defense Commissary Agency	625
Washington Office	625
Defense Contract Audit Agency	625
Defense Finance and Accounting Service	625
Defense Health Agency	625
Defense Information Systems Agency	625
Defense Intelligence Agency	625
Defense Legal Services Agency	625
Defense Logistics Agency	625
Defense POW/MIA Accounting Agency	626
Defense Security Cooperation Agency	626
Defense Security Service	626
Defense Threat Reduction Agency	626
National Geospatial-Intelligence Agency	626
National Security Agency/Central Security Service	626
Joint Service Schools	626
Defense Acquisition University	626
National Intelligence University	626
National Defense University	626
Capstone/Pinnacle/Keystone	627
College of International Security Affairs	627
College of Information and Cyberspace	627
Joint Forces Staff College	627
National War College	627
Dwight D. Eisenhower School for National Security and Resource Strategy	627
Uniformed Services University of the Health Sciences	627
Department of the Air Force	629
Secretary of the Air Force	629

	Page
Department of Defense—Continued	
Department of the Air Force—Continued	
SECAF/CSAF Executive Action Group	629
Under Secretary of the Air Force	629
Chief of Staff	629
Deputy Under Secretary for International Affairs	629
Assistant Secretary for Acquisition, Technology and Logistics	630
Deputy Assistant Secretary for Acquisition Integration	630
Deputy Assistant Secretary for Contracting	630
Deputy Assistant Secretary for Science, Technology and Engineering	630
Capability Directorate for Global Power Programs	630
Capability Directorate for Global Reach Programs	630
Capability Directorate for Information Dominance	630
Capability Directorate for Space Programs	630
Directorate for Special Programs	631
Directorate for Air Force Rapid Capabilities	631
Assistant Secretary for Financial Management and Comptroller of the Air Force (SAF/FM)	631
Principal Deputy Assistant Secretary for Financial Management	631
Deputy Assistant Secretary for Budget (SAF/FMB)	631
Deputy Assistant Secretary for Cost and Economics (SAF/FMC)	631
Deputy Assistant Secretary for Financial Operations (SAF/FMF)	631
Deputy Assistant Secretary for Programs (SAF/FMP)	632
Assistant Secretary for Installations, Environment, and Energy	632
Deputy Assistant Secretary for Installations (SAF/IEI)	632
Deputy Assistant Secretary for Environment, Safety and Infrastructure (SAF/IEE)	632
Deputy Assistant Secretary for Operational Energy (SAF/IEN)	633
Deputy Assistant Secretary for Reserve Affairs	633
Deputy Assistant Secretary for Strategic Diversity Integration	633
Air Force Review Boards Agency (SAF/MRB)	633
Air Force Civilian Appellate Review Office (AFCARO), SAF/MRBA	633
Air Force Security Protection Directorate, SAF/MRBA	633
Air Force Board for Correction of Military Records (AFB/CMR), SAF/MRBC	634
DoD Physical Disability Board of Review (PDBR), SAF/MRBD	634
Air Force Review Boards Agency Legal Directorate, SAF/MRBL	634

Page

Department of Defense—Continued
Department of the Air Force—Continued
Air Force Review Boards Agency Medical Support Directorate, SAF/MRBM 634
Secretary of the Air Force Personnel Council (SAFPC), SAF/MRBP 634
Mission Support Directorate, SAF/MRBX 634
Chief, Information Dominance and Chief Information Officer 634
Deputy Chief of Staff for Intelligence, Surveillance and Reconnaissance (ISR) 634
Deputy Chief of Staff for Logistics, Engineering and Force Protection 635
Deputy Chief of Staff for Manpower, Personnel and Services 635
Deputy Chief of Staff for Operations 635
Deputy Chief of Staff for Strategic Plans and Requirements 635
Directorate of Studies and Analysis and Assessments 635
Strategic Deterrence and Nuclear Integration (A10) 636
Administrative Assistant to the Secretary 636
Auditor General 636
Air Force Audit Agency 636
Chief of Chaplains 637
Air Force Chief of Safety 637
Air Force General Counsel 637
Air Force Historian 637
Inspector General 637
Judge Advocate General 638
Legal Operations 638
Directorate of Legislative Liaison 638
National Guard Bureau 638
Office of Public Affairs 638
Air Force Reserve 639
Scientific Advisory Board 639
Air Force Scientist 639
Air Force Office of Small Business Programs 639
Surgeon General 639
Directorate of Test and Evaluation 640
Army and Air Force Exchange Service 640
Washington Office/Office of the Board of Directors 640
Department of the Army 641
Secretary of the Army 641
Under Secretary of the Army 641
Chief of Staff of the Army (CSA) 641
Deputy Under Secretary of the Army (DUSA) 641
Assistant Secretary of the Army (Acquisition, Logistics, and Technology) (ASA(ALT)) 642
Assistant Secretary of the Army (Civil Works) (ASA(CW)) 642
Assistant Secretary of the Army (Financial Management and Comptroller) (ASA(FM&C)) 642
Assistant Secretary of the Army (Installations, Energy, and Environment) (ASA(IE&E)) 643

Page

Department of Defense—Continued
Department of the Army—Continued
Assistant Secretary of the Army (Manpower and Reserve Affairs) (ASA(M&RA)) 643
Army General Counsel (GC) 643
Administrative Assistant to the Secretary of the Army (AASA) 644
Army Auditor General 644
Army National Military Cemeteries (ANMC) 644
Assistant Chief of Staff for Installation Management (ACSIM) 644
Chief Army Reserve (CAR) 644
Chief Information Officer, G-6 (CIO, G-6) 645
Chief Legislative Liaison (CLL) 645
Chief National Guard Bureau (CNGB) 645
Chief of Chaplains (CCH) 645
Chief of Engineers (CoE) 646
Chief of Public Affairs (CPA) 646
Deputy Chief of Staff, G-1 (DCS, G-1) (Personnel) 646
Deputy Chief of Staff, G-2 (DCS, G-2) (Intelligence) 646
Deputy Chief of Staff, G-3 (DCS, G-3) (Operations) 647
Deputy Chief of Staff, G-4 (DCS, G-4) (Logistics) 647
Deputy Chief of Staff, G-8 (DCS, G-8) (Programs) 647
Director of the Army Staff (DAS) 648
Provost Marshal General (PMG) 648
Office of Small Business Programs (OSBP) 648
The Inspector General (TIG) 648
The Judge Advocate General (TJAG) 649
The Surgeon General (TSG) 649
Army Commands 649
U.S. Army Forces Command (FORSCOM) 649
U.S. Army Training and Doctrine Command (TRADOC) 649
U.S. Army Materiel Command (AMC) 650
Army Service Component Commands Liaison Offices 650
Joint Force Headquarters-National Capital Region and Military District of Washington (JFHQ–NCR/MDW) 650
U.S. Army Special Operations Command 650
Department of the Navy 651
Office of the Secretary of the Navy 651
Office of the Under Secretary of the Navy 651
General Counsel 651
Naval Inspector General 651
U.S. Navy Office of Information 651
Judge Advocate General 652
Legislative Affairs 652
Assistant Secretary for Financial Management and Comptroller 653
Assistant Secretary for Energy, Installations and Environment 653

Page

Department of Defense—Continued
Department of the Navy—Continued
Assistant Secretary for Manpower and Reserve Affairs ... 653
Secretary of the Navy Council of Review Boards ... 653
Assistant Secretary for Research, Development and Acquisition ... 653
Department of the Navy Chief Information Officer ... 654
Chief of Naval Operations ... 654
Bureau of Medicine and Surgery ... 654
Military Sealift Command ... 654
Walter Reed National Military Medical Center ... 655
Naval Air Systems Command ... 655
Naval Criminal Investigative Service Headquarters ... 655
Naval District of Washington ... 655
Naval Facilities Engineering Command . 655
Office of Naval Intelligence ... 655
Naval Sea Systems Command ... 655
Naval Supply Systems Command ... 655
Space and Naval Warfare Systems Command Space Field Activity ... 655
U.S. Naval Academy ... 655
U.S. Marine Corps Headquarters ... 656
Marine Barracks ... 656
Training and Education Command ... 656

Department of Justice ... 657
Office of the Attorney General ... 657
Office of the Deputy Attorney General ... 657
Office of the Associate Attorney General .. 658
Office of the Solicitor General ... 658
Antitrust Division ... 658
Field Offices ... 658
Bureau of Alcohol, Tobacco, Firearms, and Explosives (ATF) ... 659
Office of the Director ... 659
Office of Strategic Management ... 659
Office of Diversity and Inclusion (ODI) 659
Office of Chief Counsel ... 659
Office of Enforcement Programs and Services ... 659
Office of Equal Opportunity ... 659
Office of Field Operations ... 659
Office of Management ... 659
Office of Ombudsperson ... 659
Office of Professional Responsibility and Security Operations ... 659
Public and Governmental Affairs ... 660
Office of Science and Technology/CIO .. 660
Office of Strategic Intelligence and Information ... 660
Office of Human Resources and Professional Development ... 660
Civil Division ... 660
Appellate Staff ... 660
Commercial Litigation Branch ... 660
Consumer Litigation ... 661
Federal Programs Branch ... 661
Immigration Litigation ... 661
Management Programs ... 661
Torts Branch ... 661
Civil Rights Division ... 661

Page

Department of Justice—Continued
Office of Community Oriented Policing Services ... 662
Director's Office ... 662
Communications Division ... 662
Community Relations Service ... 662
Regional Directors ... 662
Criminal Division ... 663
Office of Dispute Resolution ... 663
Drug Enforcement Administration ... 663
Financial Management Division ... 664
Human Resources Division ... 664
Inspections Division ... 664
Intelligence Division ... 664
Operations Division ... 665
Operational Support Division ... 665
Field Offices ... 665
Other DEA Offices ... 666
Foreign Offices ... 666
Environment and Natural Resources Division ... 669
Executive Office for Immigration Review (EOIR) ... 669
Executive Office for United States Attorneys (EOUSA) ... 670
Executive Office for United States Trustees ... 671
U.S. Trustees ... 671
Federal Bureau of Investigation ... 673
Office of the Director/Deputy Director/ Associate Deputy Director ... 673
Information and Technology Branch ... 673
Criminal, Cyber, Response, and Services Branch ... 673
Human Resources Branch ... 674
National Security Branch ... 674
Science and Technology Branch ... 674
Intelligence Branch ... 674
Field Divisions ... 674
Federal Bureau of Prisons (BOP) ... 675
Foreign Claims Settlement Commission ... 676
Office of Information Policy ... 676
Office of the Inspector General ... 676
Regional Audit Offices ... 676
Regional Investigations Offices ... 676
INTERPOL-U.S. National Central Bureau . 677
Justice Management Division ... 677
Office of Justice Programs (OJP) ... 678
Office of the Assistant Attorney General ... 678
Bureau of Justice Assistance ... 678
Bureau of Justice Statistics ... 678
National Institute of Justice ... 678
Office of Juvenile Justice and Delinquency Prevention ... 678
Office for Victims of Crime ... 678
Office of Administration ... 679
Office of the Chief Financial Officer ... 679
Office of the Chief Information Officer . 679
Office for Civil Rights ... 679
Office of Communications ... 679
Office of the General Counsel ... 679
Office of Sex Offender Sentencing, Monitoring, Apprehending, Registering, and Tracking ... 679
Office of Legal Counsel ... 679

	Page
Department of Justice—Continued	
Office of Legal Policy	679
Office of Legislative Affairs (OLA)	680
National Security Division	680
Counterintelligence and Export Control Section	680
Counterterrorism Section	680
Foreign Investment Review Staff	680
Office of Intelligence	680
Office of Justice for Victims of Overseas Terrorism	680
Office of the Pardon Attorney	680
Office of Professional Responsibility	681
Professional Responsibility Advisory Office	681
Office of Public Affairs	681
Tax Division	681
United States Marshals Service (USMS)	682
Office of Equal Employment Opportunity	682
Office of the General Counsel	682
Office of Professional Responsibility	682
Judicial Security Division	682
Investigative Operations Division	682
Prisoner Operations Division	682
Justice Prisoner and Alien Transportation System (JPATS)	682
Asset Forfeiture Division	682
Witness Security Division	682
Tactical Operations Division	682
Financial Services Division	683
Human Resources Division	683
Information Technology Division	683
Management Support Division	683
Training Division	683
U.S. Parole Commission	683
Office on Violence Against Women (OVW)	683
Department of the Interior	685
Office of the Secretary	685
Executive Secretariat	685
Congressional and Legislative Affairs	685
Office of Communications	685
Office of the Deputy Secretary	685
Assistant Secretary for Fish and Wildlife and Parks	685
U.S. Fish and Wildlife Service	686
National Park Service	686
Assistant Secretary for Indian Affairs	687
Bureau of Indian Affairs	687
Bureau of Indian Education	687
Assistant Secretary for Land and Minerals Management	687
Bureau of Land Management	687
Bureau of Ocean Energy Management	688
Bureau of Safety and Environmental Enforcement	688
Office of Surface Mining Reclamation and Enforcement	689
Assistant Secretary for Policy, Management, and Budget	689
Assistant Secretary for Water and Science	689
U.S. Geological Survey	689
Bureau of Reclamation	690
Office of Inspector General	690
Department of the Interior—Continued	
Office of the Solicitor	690
Office of the Special Trustee for American Indians	690
Department of Agriculture	691
Office of the Secretary	691
Office of the Assistant Secretary for Administration	691
Office of Administrative Law Judges	691
Office of Human Resources Management	691
Office of the Judicial Officer	691
Office of Operations	692
Office of Procurement and Property Management	692
Office of Homeland Security	692
Office of Small and Disadvantaged Business Utilization	692
Assistant Secretary for Civil Rights	692
Office of Budget and Program Analysis	692
Office of the Chief Economist	693
Office of the Chief Financial Officer	693
Office of the Chief Information Officer	693
Office of Communications	693
Office of Congressional Relations	693
External and Intergovernmental Affairs	694
Office of Tribal Relations	694
Office of the Executive Secretariat	694
Office of the General Counsel	694
Office of the Inspector General	694
National Appeals Division	695
Under Secretary for Natural Resources and Environment	695
Forest Service	695
Business Operations	695
National Forest System	695
Research and Development	696
State and Private Forestry	696
Natural Resources Conservation Service	696
Office of the Chief Financial Officer	696
Deputy Chief for Programs	696
Chief Human Resources Officer	697
Deputy Chief of Science and Technology	697
Deputy Chief of Soil Survey and Resource Assessment	697
Deputy Chief of Strategic Planning and Accountability	697
Under Secretary for Farm Production and Conservation	697
Under Secretary for Trade and Foreign Agricultural Affairs	697
Farm Service Agency	697
Foreign Agricultural Service	698
Office of the Chief Operating Officer	698
Office of Capacity Building and Development	698
Office of Country and Regional Affairs	698
Office of Foreign Service Operations	699
Office of Global Analysis	699
Office of Agreements and Scientific Affairs	699
Office of Trade Programs	699
Risk Management Agency	699
Under Secretary for Rural Development	700

	Page
Department of Agriculture—Continued	
Business and Cooperative Programs	700
Rural Housing Service	700
Rural Utilities Service	700
Food, Nutrition, and Consumer Services	701
Food and Nutrition Service	701
Office of the Administrator	701
Office of Policy Support	701
Office of the Chief Communications Officer (OCCO)	701
Office of Management Technology and Finance	702
Management	702
Financial Management	702
Information Technology	702
Regional Operations and Support	702
Office of Supplemental Nutrition Assistance Program	702
Office of Special Nutrition Programs	703
Center for Nutrition Policy and Promotion	703
Under Secretary for Food Safety	703
Food Safety and Inspection Service	703
Office of Field Operations (OFO)	703
Office of Data Integration and Food Protection (ODIFP)	703
Office of International Coordination (OIC)	703
Office of Management (OM)	703
Office of Policy and Program Development (OPPD)	703
Office of Investigation, Enforcement and Audit (OIEA)	704
Office of Public Affairs and Consumer Education (OPACE)	704
Office of Public Health Science (OPHS)	704
Office of Outreach, Employee Education and Training (OOEET)	704
Under Secretary for Research, Education, and Economics	704
Agricultural Research Service	704
Area Offices	704
National Institute of Food and Agriculture	705
Economic Research Service	705
National Agricultural Statistics Service	705
Under Secretary for Marketing and Regulatory Programs	705
Agricultural Marketing Service	706
Animal and Plant Health Inspection Service (APHIS)	706
Office of the Administrator	706
Animal Care	706
Biotechnology Regulatory Services	706
International Services	706
Legislative and Public Affairs	706
Marketing and Regulatory Programs Business Services	707
Plant Protection and Quarantine	707
Policy and Program Development	707
Veterinary Services	707
Wildlife Services	707
Grain Inspection, Packers and Stockyards Administration	707

	Page
Department of Commerce	709
Office of the Secretary	709
General Counsel	709
Assistant Secretary for Legislative and Intergovernmental Affairs	709
Chief Financial Officer (CFO) and Assistant Secretary for Administration	709
Chief Information Officer	710
Inspector General	710
Economics and Statistics Administration	710
Bureau of Economic Analysis	710
The Bureau of the Census	711
Bureau of Industry and Security	712
Economic Development Administration	712
International Trade Administration	713
Administration	713
Global Markets and U.S. and Foreign Commercial Service	713
Assistant Secretary for Enforcement and Compliance	713
Assistant Secretary for Industry and Analysis	714
President's Export Council	714
Minority Business Development Agency	714
National Oceanic and Atmospheric Administration	714
National Marine Fisheries Service	715
National Ocean Service	715
National Environmental Satellite, Data, and Information Service	715
National Weather Service	716
Oceanic and Atmospheric Research	716
Program Planning and Integration	716
United States Patent and Trademark Office	717
Commissioner for Patents	717
Commissioner for Trademarks	718
Policy and External Affairs	718
Chief Financial Officer	719
Chief Performance Improvement Officer	719
Chief Administrative Officer	719
Director of the Office of Equal Employment Opportunity and Diversity	719
Office of General Counsel	719
Chief Information Officer	719
National Institute of Standards and Technology	720
National Technical Information Service	720
National Telecommunications and Information Administration	720
Department of Labor	721
Office of the Secretary	721
Office of Public Engagement	721
Administrative Law Judges	721
Administrative Review Board	721
Office of the Assistant Secretary for Administration and Management (OASAM)	721
Business Operations Center	721
Performance Management Center	722
Civil Rights Center	722
Emergency Management Center	722

Page

Department of Labor—Continued
Office of the Assistant Secretary for Administration and Management (OASAM)—Continued
Benefits.gov ... 722
Human Resources Center ... 722
Office of the Chief Information Officer . 722
Security Center ... 723
Assistant Secretary for Policy ... 723
Benefits Review Board ... 723
Bureau of Labor Statistics ... 723
Bureau of International Labor Affairs ... 723
Office of Child Labor, Forced Labor, and Human Trafficking ... 724
Office of Trade and Labor Affairs ... 724
Office of International Relations ... 724
Office of Economic and Labor Research ... 724
Office of the Chief Financial Officer ... 724
Office of Congressional and Intergovernmental Affairs ... 724
Secretary's Representatives in the Regional Offices ... 725
Office of Disability Employment Policy ... 725
Employee Benefits Security Administration ... 725
Employees' Compensation Appeals Board . 725
Employment and Training Administration . 726
DOL Center for Faith-Based and Neighborhood Partnerships ... 726
Office of the Inspector General ... 726
Mine Safety and Health Administration ... 726
Coal Mine Safety and Health ... 726
Metal and Nonmetal Mine Safety and Health ... 726
Educational Policy and Development ... 726
Occupational Safety and Health Administration ... 727
Office of Public Affairs ... 727
Regional Offices ... 727
Office of Small and Disadvantaged Business Utilization ... 727
Office of the Solicitor ... 727
Division of Black Lung and Longshore Legal Services ... 727
Division of Civil Rights and Labor-Management ... 728
Division of Employment and Training Legal Services ... 728
Division of Fair Labor Standards ... 728
Division of Federal Employee and Energy Workers Compensation ... 728
Division of Management and Administrative Legal Services ... 728
Division of Mine Safety and Health ... 728
Division of Occupational Safety and Health ... 729
Division of Plan Benefits Security ... 729
Office of Legal Counsel ... 729
Veterans' Employment and Training Service ... 729
Regional Offices ... 729
Women's Bureau ... 729
Office of Workers' Compensation Programs ... 729
Office of Labor-Management Standards ... 730
Wage and Hour Division ... 730

Page

Department of Labor—Continued
Office of Federal Contract Compliance Programs ... 730

Department of Health and Human Services ... 733
Office of the Secretary ... 733
Assistant Secretary for Administration and Management ... 733
Program Support Center ... 733
Assistant Secretary for Legislation ... 733
Assistant Secretary for Planning and Evaluation ... 734
Assistant Secretary for Public Affairs ... 734
Assistant Secretary for Preparedness and Response ... 734
Assistant Secretary for Financial Resources ... 734
Office for Civil Rights ... 734
Office of the General Counsel ... 734
Office of Global Affairs ... 735
Office of the Inspector General ... 735
Office of Medicare Hearings and Appeals . 735
Office of the National Coordinator for Health Information Technology ... 735
Office of the Assistant Secretary for Health ... 735
Administration for Community Living ... 736
Administration for Children and Families .. 736
Agency for Healthcare Research and Quality (AHRQ) ... 737
Agency for Toxic Substances and Disease Registry ... 737
Centers for Disease Control and Prevention ... 737
Center for Faith-Based and Neighborhood Partnerships ... 737
Centers for Medicare & Medicaid Services ... 738
Food and Drug Administration ... 738
Health Resources and Services Administration ... 739
Indian Health Service ... 739
National Institutes of Health ... 740
Substance Abuse and Mental Health Services Administration (SAMHSA) .. 741

Department of Housing and Urban Development ... 743
Office of the Secretary ... 743
Office of the Deputy Secretary ... 743
Assistant Secretary for Community Planning and Development ... 743
Assistant Secretary for Congressional and Intergovernmental Relations ... 743
Assistant Secretary for Fair Housing and Equal Opportunity ... 744
Assistant Secretary for Housing ... 744
Assistant Secretary for Policy Development and Research ... 744
Assistant Secretary for Public Affairs ... 744
Assistant Secretary for Public and Indian Housing ... 744
Office of Field Policy and Management ... 744
Government National Mortgage Association ... 744

	Page
Department of Housing and Urban Development—Continued	
Chief Financial Officer	745
Chief Information Officer	745
Chief Procurement Officer	745
General Counsel	745
Inspector General	745
Office of Departmental Equal Employment Opportunity	746
Office of the Chief Human Capital Officer	746
Office of Lead Hazard Control and Healthy Homes	746
Office of Small and Disadvantaged Business Utilization	746
HUD Regional Administrators	746
Department of Transportation	747
Office of the Secretary	747
Assistant Secretary for Administration	747
Assistant Secretary for Aviation and International Affairs	747
Assistant Secretary for Budget and Programs	748
Assistant Secretary for Governmental Affairs	748
Office of the Under Secretary of Transportation for Policy	748
General Counsel	748
Inspector General	748
Regional Audit Offices	748
Regional Investigations Offices	749
Office of Public Affairs	749
Federal Aviation Administration	749
Federal Highway Administration	751
Field Services	751
Federal Motor Carrier Safety Administration	751
Field Offices	752
Federal Railroad Administration	752
Regional Offices (Railroad Safety)	752
Federal Transit Administration	753
Maritime Administration	753
Field Activities	754
U.S. Merchant Marine Academy	754
National Highway Traffic Safety Administration	754
Regional Offices	754
Pipeline and Hazardous Materials Safety Administration	755
Hazardous Materials Safety Offices	755
Pipeline Safety Offices	755
Office of the Assistant Secretary for Research and Technology (OST–R)	756
Saint Lawrence Seaway Development Corporation–U.S. DOT	756
Seaway Operations	756
Surface Transportation Board	756
Department of Energy	759
Office of the Secretary	759
Under Secretary for Management and Performance	759
Under Secretary for Science	760
National Nuclear Security Administration	760
Major Field Organizations	760
Operations Offices	760
Department of Energy—Continued	
Major Field Organizations—Continued	
Integrated Support/Business Centers	760
Power Marketing Administrations	760
Petroleum Reserves	760
Federal Energy Regulatory Commission	760
Department of Education	763
Office of the Secretary	763
Office of the Deputy Secretary	763
Office of the Under Secretary	763
Office of the Chief Financial Officer	763
Office of the Chief Information Officer	763
Office of Management	764
Office for Civil Rights	764
Office of Career, Technical, and Adult Education	765
Office of Communications and Outreach	765
Office of Elementary and Secondary Education	765
Office of English Language Acquisition	765
Office of Federal Student Aid	765
Office of the General Counsel	766
Office of Innovation and Improvement	766
Office of Inspector General	766
International Affairs Office	766
Institute of Education Sciences	766
Office of Legislation and Congressional Affairs	767
Office of Planning, Evaluation, and Policy Development	767
Office of Postsecondary Education	767
Office of Special Education and Rehabilitative Services	767
Department of Veterans' Affairs	769
Office of the Secretary	769
Board of Veterans' Appeals	769
Office of General Counsel	769
Office of Inspector General	769
Office of Acquisitions, Logistics, and Construction	770
Assistant Secretary for Congressional and Legislative Affairs	770
Assistant Secretary for Public and Intergovernmental Affairs	770
Assistant Secretary for Enterprise Integration	770
Assistant Secretary for Operations, Security, and Preparedness	770
Assistant Secretary for Management	771
Assistant Secretary for Information and Technology	771
Assistant Secretary for Human Resources and Administration	771
National Cemetery Administration	771
Veterans Benefits Administration	772
Veterans Health Administration	772
Department of Homeland Security	775
Office of the Secretary	775
Citizenship and Immigration Services Ombudsman	775
Civil Rights and Civil Liberties	775
Executive Secretariat	775
Office of the General Counsel	775
Office of Inspector General	775

	Page
Department of Homeland Security—Continued	
Office of the Secretary—Continued	
Office of Intelligence and Analysis	776
Office of Partnership and Engagement	776
Office of Legislative Affairs	776
Military Advisor's Office	776
Privacy Office	776
Office of Public Affairs	776
National Protection and Programs Directorate	776
Science and Technology Directorate	776
Management Directorate	777
Office of Policy	777
Federal Emergency Management Agency (FEMA) Directorate	777
Countering Weapons of Mass Destruction (CWMD)	778
Transportation Security Administration (TSA)	778
United States Customs and Border Protection (CBP)	778
United States Immigration and Customs Enforcement (ICE)	779
Federal Law Enforcement Training Centers	780
United States Citizenship and Immigration Services	780
United States Coast Guard	780
United States Secret Service	780
Independent Agencies, Commissions, Boards	781
Advisory Council on Historic Preservation	781
American Battle Monuments Commission	781
American National Red Cross	782
Honorary Officers	782
Corporate Officers	782
Board of Governors	782
Executive Leadership	782
Governmental Relations	782
Appalachian Regional Commission	783
Armed Forces Retirement Home	783
Armed Forces Retirement Home—Washington	783
Armed Forces Retirement Home—Gulfport	783
Board of Governors of the Federal Reserve System	783
Office of Board Members	783
Division of Banking Supervision and Regulation	783
Division of Consumer and Community Affairs	784
Division of Federal Reserve Bank Operations and Payment Systems	784
Division of Information Technology	784
Division of International Finance	784
Division of Monetary Affairs	784
Division of Research and Statistics	784
Inspector General	785
Legal Division	785
Management Division	785
Office of the Secretary	785
Division of Financial Stability Policy and Research	785
Board of Governors of the Federal Reserve System—Continued	
Office of the Chief Operating Officer	785
Division of Financial Management	785
Broadcasting Board of Governors	786
International Broadcasting Bureau	786
Governors	786
Central Intelligence Agency	786
Commission of Fine Arts	786
Board of Architectural Consultants for the Old Georgetown Act	787
Committee for Purchase From People Who Are Blind or Severely Disabled	787
Commodity Futures Trading Commission	787
Regional Offices	788
Consumer Product Safety Commission	788
Corporation for National and Community Service	788
Defense Nuclear Facilities Safety Board	788
Delaware River Basin Commission	789
Federal Representatives	789
Staff	789
Delaware Representatives	789
New Jersey Representatives	789
New York Representatives	789
Pennsylvania Representatives	789
Environmental Protection Agency	790
Administration and Resources Management	790
Air and Radiation	790
Enforcement and Compliance Assurance	790
Office of Environmental Information	790
Chief Financial Officer	790
General Counsel	790
Inspector General	791
International Affairs	791
Chemical Safety and Pollution Prevention	791
Research and Development	791
Land and Emergency Response	791
Water	791
Regional Administration	791
Equal Employment Opportunity Commission	792
Export-Import Bank of the United States	792
Office of Inspector General	793
Farm Credit Administration	793
Federal Communications Commission	794
Office of Administrative Law Judges	794
Office of Communications Business Opportunities	794
Consumer and Governmental Affairs Bureau	794
Enforcement Bureau	794
Office of Engineering and Technology	795
Office of General Counsel	795
Office of Inspector General	795
International Bureau	795
Office of Legislative Affairs	795
Office of Managing Director	795
Media Bureau	795
Office of Media Relations	796
Office of Strategic Planning and Policy Analysis	796
Public Safety and Homeland Security Bureau	796
Wireless Telecommunications Bureau	796
Wireline Competition Bureau	796

	Page
Federal Communications Commission—Continued	
Office of Workplace Diversity	797
Regional and Field Offices	797
Federal Deposit Insurance Corporation	797
Federal Election Commission	797
Federal Housing Finance Agency	798
Office of Congressional Affairs and Communications	798
Federal Labor Relations Authority	798
Authority	798
General Counsel of the FLRA	799
Office of Administrative Law Judges	799
Federal Service Impasses Panel (FSIP)	799
Regional Offices	799
Federal Maritime Commission	799
Office of the Chair	799
Office of the Secretary	799
Office of Equal Employment Opportunity	800
Office of the General Counsel	800
Office of Consumer Affairs and Dispute Resolution	800
Office of Administrative Law Judges	800
Office of the Inspector General	800
Office of the Managing Director	800
Bureau of Certification and Licensing	800
Bureau of Enforcement	800
Bureau of Trade Analysis	800
Federal Mediation and Conciliation Service	801
Federal Mine Safety and Health Review Commission	801
Federal Retirement Thrift Investment Board	801
Federal Trade Commission	801
Regional Directors	802
Foreign-Trade Zones Board	802
General Services Administration	802
Office of the Administrator	802
National Services	802
Public Building Service	802
Federal Acquisition Service	803
Staff Offices	803
Office of the Chief Financial Officer	803
Office of Congressional and Intergovernmental Affairs	803
Office of Strategic Communications	803
Office of Governmentwide Policy	803
Office of the General Counsel	804
Office of the Chief Information Officer	804
Office of Small Business Utilization	804
Office of Human Resources Management	804
Office of Civil Rights	804
Office of Mission Assurance	804
Office of Administrative Services	804
Regional Offices	804
Independent Offices	805
Office of the Inspector General	805
Civilian Board of Contract Appeals	805
Harry S. Truman Scholarship Foundation	806
Board of Trustees	806
Inter-American Foundation	806
James Madison Memorial Fellowship Foundation	807
Board of Trustees	807
The John F. Kennedy Center for the Performing Arts	807
The John F. Kennedy Center for the Performing Arts—Continued	
Board of Trustees	807
Legal Services Corporation	808
Board of Directors	808
National Aeronautics and Space Administration	808
Office of the Administrator	808
Office of the General Counsel	809
Office of Inspector General	809
Office of Communications	809
Office of Diversity and Equal Opportunity Programs	809
Office of Education	809
Office of International and Interagency Relations	809
Office of Legislative and Intergovernmental Affairs	809
Office of Small Business Programs	809
Aeronautics Research Mission Directorate	809
Human Exploration and Operations Mission Directorate	809
Science Mission Directorate	809
Space Technology Mission Directorate	810
Mission Support Directorate	810
Office of Human Capital Management	810
Office of Procurement	810
Office of Protective Services	810
Office of Strategic Infrastructure	810
NASA Management Office	810
NASA National Offices	810
NASA Overseas Representatives	811
National Archives and Records Administration	811
Presidential Libraries	812
Administrative Committee of the Federal Register	812
National Archives Trust Fund Board	812
National Historical Publications and Records Commission	813
National Capital Planning Commission	813
Appointive Members	813
Executive Staff	814
National Council on Disability	814
National Credit Union Administration	814
Regional Offices	814
National Foundation on the Arts and the Humanities	815
National Endowment for the Arts	815
The National Council on the Arts	815
National Endowment for the Humanities	815
National Council on the Humanities	815
Federal Council on the Arts and the Humanities	816
Institute of Museum and Library Services	816
National Museum and Library Services Board	816
National Gallery of Art	817
Board of Trustees	817
National Labor Relations Board	817
Division of Judges	818
Division of Operations Management	818
Division of Advice	818
Division of Enforcement Litigation	818
Division of Legal Counsel	818
National Mediation Board	819

	Page
National Academies of Sciences, Engineering, and Medicine	819
National Academy of Sciences	819
National Academy of Engineering	819
National Academy of Medicine	819
National Science Foundation	819
National Science Board	820
Members	820
National Transportation Safety Board	820
Neighborhood Reinvestment Corporation	821
Board of Directors	821
Nuclear Regulatory Commission	821
Office of the Chair	821
Commissioners	821
Staff Offices of the Commission	821
Advisory Committee on Medical Uses of Isotopes	821
Advisory Committee on Reactor Safeguards	822
Atomic Safety and Licensing Board Panel	822
Office of the Executive Director for Operations	822
Regional Offices	822
Occupational Safety and Health Review Commission	822
Office of Government Ethics	823
Office of Personnel Management	823
Office of the Director	823
Office of the Executive Secretariat	823
Chief Financial Officer	823
Office of Communications	824
Congressional, Legislative and Intergovernmental Affairs (CLIA)	824
National Background (NBIB) Investigations Bureau	824
Merit System Accountability and Compliance	824
Chief Information Officer	824
Human Resources Solutions (HRS)	825
Retirement Services	825
Office of the General Counsel	825
Office of the Inspector General	825
Office of Small and Disadvantaged Business Utilization (OSDBU)	826
Office of Procurement Operations (OPO)	826
Facilities, Security, and Emergency Management (FSEM)	826
Equal Employment Opportunity	826
Human Resources	826
Diversity and Inclusion	826
Healthcare and Insurance	827
Planning and Policy Analysis	827
Employee Services	827
Office of the Special Counsel	827
Peace Corps	827
Office of the Director	827
Office of Victim Advocacy	828
Office of Civil Rights and Diversity	828
Office of Communications	828
Office of Congressional Relations	828
Office of the General Counsel	828
Office of Strategic Partnerships and Intergovernmental Affairs	828
Office of External Affairs	828
Office of Gifts and Grants Management	828
Office of Strategic Information, Research, and Planning	828
Peace Corps—Continued	
Office of the Director—Continued	
Office of Third Goal and Returned Volunteer Services	828
Office of Global Operations	828
Office of Overseas Programming and Training Support	829
Peace Corps Response	829
Office of Global Health and HIV	829
Office of Management	829
Office of Human Resource Management	829
Office of the Inspector General	829
Office of the Chief Financial Officer	829
Office of the Chief Information Officer	829
Office of Volunteer Recruitment and Selection	829
Regional Offices	829
Office of Safety and Security	830
Office of Health Services	830
Pension Benefit Guaranty Corporation	830
Board of Directors	830
Officials	830
Postal Regulatory Commission	830
Securities and Exchange Commission	831
The Commission	831
Office of the Secretary	831
Office of Legislative and Intergovernmental Affairs	831
Office of the Chief Operating Officer	831
Office of Investor Education and Advocacy	831
Office of Support Operations	831
Office of Equal Employment Opportunity	831
Office of Minority and Women Inclusion	831
Office of the Chief Accountant	831
Office of Compliance Inspections and Examinations	832
Division of Risk, Strategy, and Financial Innovation	832
Office of the General Counsel	832
Office of Ethics Counsel	832
Division of Investment Management	832
Division of Corporation Finance	832
Division of Enforcement	833
Division of Trading and Markets	833
Office of Credit Ratings	833
Office of Municipal Securities	833
Office of Administrative Law Judges	833
Office of International Affairs	833
Office of the Investor Advocate	833
Office of the Inspector General	833
Office of Public Affairs	833
Office of Financial Management	834
Office of Information Technology	834
Office of Administrative Services	834
Office of Human Resources	834
Regional Offices	834
Selective Service System	835
Smithsonian Institution	835
The Board of Regents	835
Office of the Secretary	836
Office of the Under Secretary for Finance and Administration	836
Office of the Provost	836
Smithsonian Enterprises	837

	Page
Social Security Administration	837
Office of the Commissioner	837
Office of the Chief Actuary	837
Office of the Chief Strategic Officer	837
Office of Communications	838
Office of Disability Adjudication and Review	838
Office of Retirement and Disability Policy	838
Office of Budget, Finance, Quality, and Management	839
Office of the General Counsel	839
Office of Human Resources	839
Office of the Inspector General	840
Office of Legislation and Congressional Affairs	840
Office of Operations	840
Office of Systems/Office of the Chief Information Officer	841
State Justice Institute	841
Board of Directors	841
Susquehanna River Basin Commission	842
Commissioners and Alternates	842
Staff	842
Tennessee Valley Authority	842
Board of Directors	842
Executive Officers	842
Washington Office	842
U.S. Advisory Commission on Public Diplomacy	843
U.S. Agency for International Development	843
U.S. Commission on Civil Rights	843
U.S. Election Assistance Commission	843
Office of the Executive Director	844
Office of the General Counsel	844
Office of National Clearinghouse on Elections	844
Office of the Inspector General	844
U.S. Holocaust Memorial Council	844
U.S. Institute of Peace	845
Board of Directors	845
U.S. International Trade Commission	845
Commissioners	845
U.S. Merit Systems Protection Board	846
Regional Offices	846
U.S. Overseas Private Investment Corporation	847
Board of Directors	847
U.S. Postal Service	847
Board of Governors	847
Officers of the Board of Governors	847
Officers of the Postal Service	847
U.S. Railroad Retirement Board	848
U.S. Sentencing Commission	849
U.S. Small Business Administration	849
U.S. Trade and Development Agency	850
Washington Metropolitan Area Transit Authority	850
Washington National Monument Society	850
Woodrow Wilson International Center for Scholars	851
Judicial Branch	853
Supreme Court of the United States	853
United States Courts of Appeals	857
United States Court of Appeals for the District of Columbia Circuit	859
United States Court of Appeals for the Federal Circuit	865
United States District Court for the District of Columbia	871
United States Court of International Trade	879
United States Court of Federal Claims	883
United States Tax Court	887
United States Court of Appeals for the Armed Forces	895
United States Court of Appeals for Veterans Claims	898
United States Judicial Panel on Multidistrict Litigation	901
Administrative Office of the United States Courts	903
Federal Judicial Center	903
District of Columbia Courts	904
District of Columbia Court of Appeals	904
Superior Court of the District of Columbia	904
Government of the District of Columbia	907
Council of the District of Columbia	907
Executive Office of the Mayor	907
Office of the City Administrator	908
Commissions	908
Departments	908
Offices	909
Independent Agencies	910
Other	912
Post Office Locations	912
Classified Stations	912
International Organizations	915
European Space Agency (E.S.A.)	915
Inter-American Defense Board	915
Chiefs of Delegation	915
Inter-American Defense College	916
Inter-American Development Bank	916
Officers	916
IDB Invest	917
Multilateral Investment Fund	917
Board of Executive Directors	917
Inter-American Tropical Tuna Commission	917
International Boundary and Water Commission, United States and Mexico	921
United States Section	921
Mexican Section	921
International Boundary Commission, United States and Canada	921
United States Section	921
Canadian Section	922
International Cotton Advisory Committee	922
Member Countries	922
International Joint Commission, United States and Canada	922
United States Section	922
Canadian Section	922
Great Lakes Regional Office	923
International Labor Organization	923
International Monetary Fund	923
Management and Senior Officers	923
Executive Directors and Alternates	924
International Organization for Migration	925
Headquarters	925
Member States	925

Page

International Organizations—Continued
International Organization for Migration—Continued
Observer States (10) 926
International Governmental and Non-Governmental Organizations 926
Organs and Organizations of the United Nations System 926
Other Organizations With Observer Status 927
Duty Stations 2015 927
International Pacific Halibut Commission, United States and Canada 931
Organization of American States 931
Permanent Missions to the OAS 931
General Secretariat 933
Organization for Economic Co-Operation and Development 933
Paris Headquarters 933
Washington Center 933
OECD Washington Center 933
Pan American Health Organization (PAHO) Regional Office of the World Health Organization 933
PAHO/WHO Field Offices, OPS/WHO Oficinas de los Representantes en los Paises 934
Centers 935
Permanent Joint Board on Defense, Canada-United States 936
Canadian Section 936
United States Section 936
Secretariat of the Pacific Community 936
Secretariat of the Pacific Regional Environmental Programme 937
United Nations 937
General Assembly 937
Security Council 938
Economic and Social Council 938
Trusteeship Council 938
International Court of Justice 938
United Nations Secretariat 939
Executive Office of the Secretary-General 939
Office of Internal Oversight Services 939
Office of Legal Affairs 939
Department of Political Affairs 939
Department for Disarmament Affairs 939
Department of Peace-Keeping Operations 939
Department of Field Support 939
Office for the Coordination of Humanitarian Affairs 939
Department of Economic and Social Affairs 940
Department of General Assembly and Conference Management 940
Department of Public Information 940
Department of Management 940
Office of the Special Representative of the Secretary-General for Children and Armed Conflict 940
United Nations Office for Partnerships 940
United Nations at Geneva (UNOG) 940
United Nations at Vienna (UNOV) 940
United Nations at Nairobi (UNON) 940

Page

International Organizations—Continued
United Nations Secretariat—Continued
United Nations Information Centre 940
Regional Economic Commissions 940
Funds and Programs 941
Other United Nations Entities 942
Research and Training Institutes 943
Specialized Agencies 943
Related Body 944
Special and Personal Representatives and Envoys of the Secretary-General 944
Africa 944
The Americas 946
Asia and the Pacific 946
Europe 947
Middle East 947
Other High Level Appointments 948
World Bank Group 949
International Bank for Reconstruction and Development 949
Other World Bank Offices 950
Board of Executive Directors 950
International Development Association 952
International Finance Corporation 952
Multilateral Investment Guarantee Agency 952

Foreign Diplomatic Offices in the United States 955

Press Galleries 985
Senate Press Gallery 985
House Press Gallery 985
Standing Committee of Correspondents 985
Rules Governing Press Galleries 985
Members Entitled to Admission 987
Newspapers Represented in Press Galleries 1000
Press Photographers' Gallery 1009
Standing Committee of Press Photographers 1009
Rules Governing Press Photographers' Gallery 1009
Members Entitled for Admission 1011
Services Represented 1014
Freelance 1015
White House News Photographers' Association 1017
Officers 1017
Executive Board 1017
Members Represented 1017
Radio and Television Correspondents' Galleries 1023
Senate Radio and Television Gallery 1023
House Radio and Television Gallery 1023
Executive Committee of the Radio and Television Correspondents' Galleries 1023
Rules Governing Radio and Television Correspondents' Galleries 1023
Members Entitled to Admission 1025
Networks, Stations, and Services Represented 1060
Freelance 1073
Periodical Press Galleries 1075
House Periodical Press Gallery 1075

Page

Press Galleries—Continued
- Senate Periodical Press Gallery 1075
- Executive Committee of Correspondents ... 1075
- Rules Governing Periodical Press Galleries 1075

Page

Press Galleries—Continued
- Members Entitled to Admission 1077
- Periodicals Represented in Press Galleries . 1086

Congressional District Maps 1093
Name Index 1151

115th Congress*

THE VICE PRESIDENT

MIKE PENCE, Republican, of Columbus, IN; born in Columbus, June 7, 1959; education: Hanover College, 1981; J.D., Indiana University School of Law, 1986; professional: former Republican nominee for the U.S. House of Representatives, 2nd District, 1988 and 1990; president, Indiana Policy Review Foundation, 1991–93; radio broadcaster: the Mike Pence Show, syndicated statewide in Indiana; married: Karen; children: Michael, Charlotte, and Audrey; elected to the 107th Congress on November 7, 2000; reelected to the 108th through 112th Congress, 2011–13; Governor, State of Indiana, 2013–17; elected 48th Vice President of the United States on November 8, 2016; took the oath of office on January 20, 2017.

The Office of the Vice President is S–212 in the Capitol. The Vice President has offices in the Dirksen Senate Office Building, the Eisenhower Executive Office Building (EEOB), and the White House (West Wing).

Assistant to the President and Chief of Staff to the Vice President.—Nick Ayers.

Assistant to the President and National Security Advisor to the Vice President.—Keith Kellogg.

Deputy Assistants to the President and Deputy Chiefs of Staff to the Vice President: Jarrod Agen, John Horne.

Deputy Assistant to the President and Chief of Staff to Mrs. Karen Pence.—Jana Toner.

Deputy Assistant to the President and Domestic Policy Director to the Vice President.—Steve Pinkos.

Deputy Assistant to the President and Director of Public Liaison and Intergovernmental Affairs for the Vice President.—Sarah Makin.

Special Assistant to the President and Deputy Director of Public Liaison and Intergovernmental Affairs.—Andeliz Castillo.

Special Assistant to the President and Director of External Affairs.—Billy Kirkland.

Special Assistant to the President and Director of Media Affairs.—Rebeccah Propp.

Special Assistant to the President and Press Secretary to the Vice President.—Alyssa Farah.

Assistant to the Vice President and Counsel.—Matt Morgan.

Assistant to the Vice President and Director of Legislative Affairs.—Jonathan Hiler.

Deputy Director of House Legislative Affairs.—Chris Hodgson.

Deputy Assistant to the Vice President and Director of Administration.—Katherine Purucker.

Director of Advance.—Saibatu Mansaray.

Deputy Assistant to the Vice President and Director of Scheduling.—Meghan Patenaude.

Special Assistant to the Vice President.—Zach Bauer.

Executive Assistant to the Vice President.—Heather Whitaker.

---

*Biographies are based on information furnished or authorized by the respective Senators and Representatives.

ALABAMA

(Population 2010, 4,779,736)

SENATORS

RICHARD C. SHELBY, Republican, of Tuscaloosa, AL; born in Birmingham, AL, May 6, 1934; education: attended the public schools; B.A., University of Alabama, 1957; LL.B., University of Alabama School of Law, 1963; professional: attorney; admitted to the Alabama Bar in 1961 and commenced practice in Tuscaloosa; member, Alabama State Senate, 1970–78; law clerk, Supreme Court of Alabama, 1961–62; city prosecutor, Tuscaloosa, 1963–71; U.S. Magistrate, Northern District of Alabama, 1966–70; Special Assistant Attorney General, State of Alabama, 1969–71; chairman, Legislative Council of the Alabama Legislature, 1977–78; former president, Tuscaloosa County Mental Health Association; member, Alabama Code Revision Committee, 1971–75; member, Phi Alpha Delta legal fraternity, Tuscaloosa County; Alabama and American Bar Associations; First Presbyterian Church of Tuscaloosa; Exchange Club; American Judicature Society; Alabama Law Institute; married: the former Annette Nevin in 1960; children: Richard C., Jr., and Claude Nevin; committees: chair, Appropriations; Banking, Housing, and Urban Affairs; Environment and Public Works; Joint Committee on the Library; Rules and Administration; elected to the 96th Congress on November 7, 1978; reelected to the three succeeding Congresses; elected to the U.S. Senate on November 4, 1986; reelected to each succeeding Senate term.

Office Listings

http://shelby.senate.gov twitter: @senshelby

304 Russell Senate Office Building, Washington, DC 20510 .... (202) 224–5744
Chief of Staff.—Katie Britt. FAX: 224–3416
Personal Secretary / Appointments.—Anne Caldwell.
Communications Director.—Blair Taylor.
The Federal Building, 2005 University Boulevard, Suite 2100, Tuscaloosa, AL 35401 .... (205) 759–5047
Vance Federal Building, Room 321, 1800 5th Avenue North, Birmingham, AL 35203 .... (205) 731–1384
John A. Campbell Federal Courthouse, Suite 445, 113 St. Joseph Street, Mobile, AL 36602 (251) 694–4164
Frank M. Johnson Federal Courthouse, Suite 208, 15 Lee Street, Montgomery, AL 36104 .. (334) 223–7303
Huntsville International Airport, 1000 Glenn Hearn Boulevard, Box 20127, Huntsville, AL 35824 .... (256) 772–0460

* * *

DOUG JONES, Democrat, of Birmingham, AL; born in Fairfield, AL, May 4, 1954; education: University of Alabama, Tuscaloosa, AL, 1976; Cumberland School of Law, 1979; honored for his work by the Southern Christian Leadership Conference, the NAACP, the Federal Bureau of Investigation, the SCLC/Women, Inc., and the Community Affairs Committee of Operation New Birmingham, among many others; religion: Christian; family: wife, Louise; children, Carson and Christopher; committees: Banking, Housing, and Urban Affairs; Health, Education, Labor, and Pensions; Homeland Security and Governmental Affairs; Special Committee on Aging; elected to the U.S. Senate, by special election, on December 12, 2017, to fill the vacancy caused by the resignation of Senator Jefferson Sessions for the term ending January 3, 2021, and took the oath of office on January 3, 2018.

Office Listings

http://jones.senate.gov

326 Russell Senate Office Building, Washington, DC 20510 .... (202) 224–4124
Chief of Staff.—Dana Gresham.
Scheduler.—Angelica Annino.
Special Assistant.—Garrett Stephens.
Press Secretary.—Sam Coleman.
341 Vance Federal Building, 1800 Fifth Avenue North, Birmingham, AL 35203 .... (205) 731–1500
BB&T Centre, Suite 2300–A, 41 West I-65 Service Road North, Mobile, AL 36608.
200 Clinton Avenue, NW., Suite 802, Huntsville, AL 35801.
1 Church Street, Suite 500B, Montgomery, AL 36104.

REPRESENTATIVES

FIRST DISTRICT

BRADLEY BYRNE, Republican, of Fairhope, AL; born in Mobile, AL, February 16, 1955; education: B.A. in public policy and history, Duke University, 1977; J.D., the University of Alabama, 1980; professional: Alabama State Board of Education; Chancellor of two-year college system, Alabama State Senate/Organizations: Leadership Alabama, Alabama PTA, U.S. Supreme Court Bar, Alabama State Workforce Planning Council; chair/awards: Council for Leaders in Alabama Schools Legislative Leadership Award, 2007; Alabama Wildlife Foundation Legislator of the Year Award, 2005; South Alabama Literacy Champion Award, 2006; religion: Episcopalian; wife: Rebecca; children: Patrick, Laura, Kathleen, and Colin; committees: Armed Services; Education and the Workforce; Rules; elected, by special election, to the 113th Congress on December 17, 2013, to fill the vacancy caused by the resignation of U.S. Representative Jo Bonner; reelected to each succeeding Congress.

Office Listings

http://byrne.house.gov

119 Cannon House Office Building, Washington, DC 20515 .... (202) 225–4931
Chief of Staff.—Alex Schriver. FAX: 225–0562
Legislative Director.—Chad Carlough.
Communications Director.—Seth Morrow.
Scheduler.—Holly Lewis.
11 North Water Street, Suite 15290, Mobile, AL 36602 .... (251) 690–2811
502 West Lee Street, Summerdale, AL 26580 .... (251) 989–2664

Counties: BALDWIN, CLARKE (part), ESCAMBIA, MOBILE, MONROE, AND WASHINGTON. Population (2010), 687,841.

ZIP Codes: 36420, 36425–27, 36432, 36439, 36441, 36444–46, 36451, 36460–62, 36470–71, 36475, 36480–83, 36502–05, 36507, 36509, 36511–13, 36518, 36521–30, 36532–33, 36535–36, 36538–39, 36541–45, 36547–51, 36553, 36555–56, 6558–62, 36564, 36567–69, 36571–72, 36575–85, 36587, 36590, 36601–13, 36615–19, 36628, 36633, 36640, 36652, 36660, 36663, 36670–71, 36685, 36688–89, 36691, 36693, 36695, 36768–69

* * *

SECOND DISTRICT

MARTHA ROBY, Republican, of Montgomery, AL; born in Montgomery, July 26, 1976; education: B.M., New York University, New York, NY, 1998; J.D., Cumberland School of Law at Samford University, Birmingham, AL, 2001; professional: attorney, Copeland, Franco, Screws, and Gill, P.A.; Councilor, District 7, City of Montgomery; awards: Alabama's Most Outstanding Minuteman (2014); Alabama Association of School Boards Legislative Award (2013); Running Start Women to Watch (2012); religion: Christian (Presbyterian); family: husband, Riley; children: Margaret and George; committees: Appropriations; Judiciary; elected to the 112th Congress on November 2, 2010; reelected to each succeeding Congress.

Office Listings

http://roby.house.gov http://twitter.com/repmartharoby

442 Cannon House Office Building, Washington, DC 20515 .... (202) 225–2901
Chief of Staff.—Torrie Matous.
Legislative Director.—Mike Albares.
Communications Director.—Todd Stacy.
Director of Scheduling.—Kate Hollis.
401 Adams Avenue, Suite 160, Montgomery, AL 36104 .... (334) 277–9113
217 Graceland Drive, Suite 5, Dothan, AL 36303 .... (334) 794–9680
505 East Three Notch Street, Andalusia City Hall, Room 322, Andalusia, AL 36420 .... (334) 428–1129

Counties: AUTAUGA, BARBOUR, BULLOCK, BUTLER, COFFEE, CONECUH, COVINGTON, CRENSHAW, DALE, ELMORE, GENEVA, HENRY, HOUSTON, MONTGOMERY (part), AND PIKE. Population (2010), 673,887.

ZIP Codes: 35010, 36003, 36005–06, 36009–10, 36016–17, 36020, 36022, 36024–30, 36032–38, 36041–43, 36046–49, 36051–54, 36064, 36066–67, 36069, 36071, 36078–82, 36089, 36091–93, 36104–13, 36115–17, 36301, 36303, 36305, 36310–14, 36316–23, 36330, 36340, 36343–46, 36350–53, 36360, 36362, 36370–71, 36373–76, 36401, 36420–21, 36426, 36432, 36442, 36453–56, 36460, 36467, 36471, 36473–77, 36483, 36502, 36703, 36749, 36758, 36860

* * *

THIRD DISTRICT

MIKE ROGERS, Republican, of Saks, AL; born in Hammond, IN, July 16, 1958; education: B.A., Jacksonville State University, 1981; M.P.A., Jacksonville State University, 1984; J.D., Birmingham School of Law, 1991; professional: attorney; awards: Anniston Star Citizen of the Year, 1998; public service: Calhoun County Commissioner, 1987–91; Alabama House of Representatives, 1994–2002; family: married to Beth; children: Emily, Evan, and Elliot; committees: Agriculture; Armed Services; Homeland Security; elected to the 108th Congress on November 5, 2002; reelected to each succeeding Congress.

Office Listings

http://mikerogers.house.gov twitter: @repmikerogersal

2184 Rayburn House Office Building, Washington, DC 20515 .... (202) 225–3261
Chief of Staff.—Chris Brinson. FAX: 226–8485
Legislative Director.—Whitney Verett.
Press Secretary.—Shea Miller.
Scheduler.—Alexis Barranca.
1129 Noble Street, 104 Federal Building, Anniston, AL 36201 .... (256) 236–5655
District Director.—Sheri Rollins.
G.W. Andrews Building, 701 Avenue A, Suite 300, Opelika, AL 36801 .... (334) 745–6221
Field Representatives: Alvin Lewis, Lee Vanoy.

Counties: CALHOUN, CHAMBERS, CHEROKEE, CLAY, CLEBURNE, LEE, MACON, MONTGOMERY (part), RANDOLPH, RUSSELL, ST. CLAIR, TALLADEGA, AND TALLAPOOSA. Population (2010), 682,819.

ZIP Codes: 30165, 31905, 35004, 35010, 35014, 35032, 35044, 35052, 35054, 35072, 35082, 35089, 35094, 35096, 35112, 35120–21, 35125, 35128, 35131, 35133, 35135, 35146, 35149–51, 35160, 35173, 35178, 35901, 35903, 35905, 35953, 35959–61, 35967, 35972–73, 35983, 35987, 36013, 36027, 36029, 36031, 36039, 36052, 36064, 36075, 36078, 36083, 36088–89, 36116–17, 36201, 36203, 36205–07, 36250–51, 36255–56, 36258, 36260, 36262–69, 36271–74, 36276–80, 36801, 36804, 36830, 36832, 36849–50, 36852–56, 36858–63, 36865–67, 36869–71, 36874–75, 36877, 36879

* * *

FOURTH DISTRICT

ROBERT B. ADERHOLT, Republican, of Haleyville, AL; born in Haleyville, July 22, 1965; education: graduate, Birmingham Southern University; J.D., Cumberland School of Law, Samford University; professional: attorney; assistant legal advisor to Governor Fob James, 1995–96; Haleyville municipal judge, 1992–96; George Bush delegate, Republican National Convention, 1992; Republican nominee for the 17th District, Alabama House of Representatives, 1990; married: Caroline McDonald; children: Mary Elliott and Robert Hayes; committees: Appropriations; elected to the 105th Congress; reelected to each succeeding Congress.

Office Listings

http://www.aderholt.house.gov twitter: @robert_Aderholt

235 Cannon House Office Building, Washington, DC 20515 .... (202) 225–4876
Chief of Staff.—Brian Rell. FAX: 225–5587
Legislative Director.—Mark Dawson.
Communications Director / Press Secretary.—Brian Rell, Carson Clark.
Administrative Director.—Chris Lawson.
Carl Elliott Building, 1710 Alabama Avenue, Room 247, Jasper, AL 35501 .... (205) 221–2310
District Field Director.—Paul Housel.
205 Fourth Avenue, Northeast, Suite 104, Cullman, AL 35055 .... (256) 734–6043
Director of Constituent Services.—Jennifer Taylor.
107 Federal Building, 600 Broad Street, Gadsden, AL 35901 .... (256) 546–0201
Field Representative.—James Manasco.
1011 George Wallace Boulevard, Suite 146, Tuscumbia, AL 35674 .... (256) 381–3450
Field Representative.—Kreg Kennedy.

Counties: BLOUNT (part), CHEROKEE (part), COLBERT, CULLMAN, DEKALB, ETOWAH, FAYETTE, FRANKLIN, JACKSON (part), LAMAR, LAWRENCE, MARION, MARSHALL, TUSCALOOSA (part), WALKER, AND WINSTON. Population (2010), 682,029.

ZIP Codes: 35006, 35013, 35016, 35019, 35031, 35033, 35049, 35053, 35055, 35057–58, 35062–63, 35070, 35077, 35079, 35083, 35087, 35097–98, 35121, 35126, 35130, 35133, 35146, 35172, 35175, 35179–80, 35447, 35461, 35481, 35501, 35503–04, 35540–46, 35548–50, 35552–55, 35563–65, 35570–72, 35574–82, 35584–87, 35592–94, 35601, 35603, 35619, 35621–22, 35640, 35653–54, 35670, 35673, 35747, 35754–55, 35760, 35765, 35769, 35771, 35775–76, 35901, 35903–07, 35950–54, 35956–57, 35961–64, 35966–68, 35971–72, 35974–76, 35978–81, 35984, 35986–90, 36272

* * *

FIFTH DISTRICT

MO BROOKS, Republican, of Huntsville, AL; born in Charleston, SC, April 29, 1954; education: B.A., Duke University, Durham, NC, 1975; J.D., University of Alabama School of Law, Tuscaloosa, AL, 1978; professional: lawyer, private practice, partner in Leo and Brooks law firm; prosecutor, Office of the District Attorney, Tuscaloosa County, AL, 1978–80; clerk, Circuit Court Judge John Snodgrass, 1980–82; member of the Alabama State House of Representatives, 1983–91; district attorney, Office of the District Attorney, Madison County, AL, 1991–93; special assistant attorney general, State of Alabama, 1995–2002; commissioner, Madison County, AL, board of commissions, 1996–2010; religion: Christian; married: Martha; four children; committees: Armed Services; Foreign Affairs; Science, Space, and, Technology; elected to the 112th Congress on November 2, 2010; reelected to each succeeding Congress.

Office Listings

http://brooks.house.gov https://twitter.com/repmobrooks

2400 Rayburn House Office Building, Washington, DC 20515 .... (202) 225–4801
Chief of Staff / Legislative Director.—Mark Pettitt.
Scheduler / Office Manager.—Kelly Zams.
2101 West Clinton Avenue, Suite 302, Huntsville, AL 35805 .... (256) 551–0190
District Director.—Tiffany Noel.
Field Representative and Grants Coordinator.—Kathy Murray.
Special Projects Coordinator and Caseworker.—Sandy Garvey.
Caseworkers: Debi Echols, Timothy Jackson.
302 Lee Street, Room 86, Decatur, AL 35601 .... (256) 355–9400
District Field Representative and Caseworker.—Johnny Turner.
102 South Court Street, Suite 310, Florence, AL 35630 .... (256) 718–5155
District Field Representative and Caseworker.—Laura Smith.

Counties: JACKSON, LAUDERDALE, LIMESTONE, MADISON, AND MORGAN. Population (2010), 718,724.

ZIP Codes: 35016, 35601–03, 35609–15, 35617, 35619–22, 35630–34, 35640, 35645, 35647–49, 35652, 35670–71,35673, 35677, 35699, 35739–42, 35744–46, 35748–52, 35754–69, 35756–63, 35767, 35771–76, 35801–16, 35824, 35893–94, 35896, 35898–99, 35958, 35966, 35978–79

* * *

SIXTH DISTRICT

GARY PALMER, Republican, of Hoover, AL; born in Hackleburg, AL, May 14, 1954; education: B.S., University of Alabama, Tuscaloosa, 1977; professional: president, Alabama Policy Institute; founding member, State Policy Network; member, Briarwood Presbyterian Church; spouse: Ann; children: Claire, Kathleen, and Rob; committees: Budget; Oversight and Government Reform; Science, Space, and Technology; elected to the 114th Congress on November 4, 2014; reelected to the 115th Congress on November 8, 2016.

Office Listings

https://palmer.house.gov https://www.facebook.com/CongressmanGaryPalmer
twitter: @usrepgarypalmer https://www.youtube.com/channel/ucyzfp-cnivljy3acac9oppq

206 Cannon House Office Building, Washington, DC 20515 .... (202) 225–4921
Chief of Staff.—William Smith. FAX: 225–2082
Communications Director.—Cate Cullen.
Legislative Director.—Cari Kelly.
Scheduler.—Nonie Brown.
3535 Grandview Parkway, Suite 525, Birmingham, AL 35243 .... (205) 968–1290
703 Second Avenue North, P.O. Box 502, Clanton, AL 35046 .... (205) 280–6846
202 3rd Avenue, East Oneonta, AL 35121 .... (205) 274–2136

Counties: BIBB, BLOUNT (part), CHILTON, COOSA (part), JEFFERSON (part), AND SHELBY. CITIES AND TOWNSHIPS: Adamsville, Allgood, Altoona, Argo, Bessemer, Birmingham, Blountsville, Brantleyville, Brent, Brook Highland, Brookside, Calera, Cardiff, Center Point, Centreville, Chelsea, Clanton, Clay, Cleveland, Columbiana, Concord, County Line, Dunnavant, Forestdale, Fultondale, Gardendale, Garden City, Goodwatter, Graysville, Harpersville, Hayden, Helena, Highland Lake, Hissop, Homewood, Hoover, Hueytown, Indian Springs Village, Irondale, Jemison, Kellyton, Kimberly, Leeds, Locust Fork, Maplesville, Maytown, McDonald Chapel, Meadowbrook, Montevallo, Morris, Mount Olive, Mountain Brook, Mulga, Nectar, North Johns, Oneonta, Pelham, Pinson, Pleasant Grove, Rock Creek, Rockford, Rosa, Shelby, Shoal Creek, Smoke Rise, Snead, Sterrett, Susan Moore, Sylvan Springs, Tarrant, Thorsby, Trafford, Trussville, Vance, Vandiver, Vestavia Hills, Vincent, Warrior, West Blocton, West Jefferson, Westover, Wilsonville, Wilton, and Woodstock. Population (2010), 682,819.

ZIP Codes: 35004–07, 35015, 35022–23, 35035, 35040, 35043, 35046, 35048, 35051–52, 35054, 35060, 35062–63, 35068, 35071, 35073–74, 35078–80, 35085, 35091, 35094, 35096, 35111–12, 35114–20, 35123–28, 35130–31, 35133, 35135, 35137, 35139, 35142–44, 35146–48, 35151, 35171–73, 35175–76, 35178, 35180–88, 35201–03, 35205–07, 35209–10, 35212–17, 35219, 35222–26, 35230, 35233, 35235–37, 35240, 35242–46, 35249, 35253–55, 35259–61, 35266, 35277–83, 35285, 35287–99, 35402–03, 35406–07, 35444, 35446, 35452, 35456–58, 35466, 35468, 35473, 35475–76, 35480, 35482, 35490, 35546, 35579, 35953, 35987, 36006, 36051, 36064, 36091, 36750, 36758, 36790, 36792–93

* * *

SEVENTH DISTRICT

TERRI A. SEWELL, Democrat, of Birmingham, AL; born in Selma, AL, January 1, 1965; education: graduated from Selma High School, Selma, AL; B.A., *cum laude*, Princeton University, Princeton, NJ, 1986; master's degree, first class honors, Oxford University, Oxford, UK, 1988; J.D., Harvard Law School, Cambridge, MA, 1992; professional: attorney; judicial law clerk to the Honorable Chief Judge U.W. Clemon, U.S. District Court, Northern District of Alabama, Birmingham; memberships and boards: treasurer of the board and chair of the finance committee, St. Vincent's Foundation; Girl Scouts of Cahaba Council; community advisory board for the DAB Minority Health and Research Center; governing board of the Alabama Council on Economic Education; Corporate Partners Council for the Birmingham Art Museum; Alpha Kappa Alpha Sorority, Inc.; professional affiliations: American Bar Association; National Bar Association; Alabama Bar Association; religion: African Methodist; Chief Deputy Whip; committees: Permanent Select Committee on Intelligence; Ways and Means; elected to the 112th Congress on November 2, 2010; reelected to each succeeding Congress.

Office Listings

http://sewell.house.gov facebook: https://www.facebook.com/repsewell
twitter: @repterrisewell

2201 Rayburn House Office Building, Washington, DC 20515 .... (202) 225–2665
Legislative Director.—Cachavious English.
Communications Director.—Christopher MacKenzie.
Legislative Assistant.—Hillary Beard.
Legislative Correspondent.—Robert Nuttall.
Executive Assistant.—Scott Harris.
Two 20th Street North, Suite 1130, Birmingham, AL 35203 .... (205) 254–1960
District Director.—Chasseny Lewis. FAX: 254–1974
Federal Building, 908 Alabama Avenue, Suite 112, Selma, AL 36701 .... (334) 877–4414
FAX: 877–4489
2501 7th Street, Suite 300, Tuscaloosa, AL 35401 .... (205) 752–5380
FAX: 752–5899
101 South Lawrence Street, Montgomery, AL 36104 .... (334) 262–1919
FAX: 262–1921

Counties: CHOCTAW, CLARKE (part), DALLAS, GREENE, HALE, JEFFERSON (part), LOWNDES, MARENGO, MONTGOMERY (part), PERRY, PICKENS (part), SUMTER, TUSCALOOSA (part), AND WILCOX. Population (2010), 682,742.

ZIP Codes: 35005–06, 35020–23, 35034, 35036, 35041–42, 35061, 35064, 35068, 35071, 35073–74, 35079, 35111, 35117, 35126–27, 35173, 35175, 35184, 35188, 35203–15, 35217–18, 35221–22, 35224, 35228–29, 35233–35, 35238, 35243, 35401, 35404–06, 35440–44, 35446–49, 35452–53, 35456, 35459–60, 35462–64, 35466, 35469–71, 35473–78, 35480–81, 35485–87, 35490–91, 35546, 35601, 35603, 35640, 35754, 36030, 36032, 36040, 36064, 36105, 36435–36, 36451, 36482, 36524, 36540, 36545, 36558, 36701–03, 36720, 36722–23, 36726–28, 36732, 36736, 36738, 36740–42, 36744–45, 36748–54, 36756, 36758–59, 36761–69, 36773, 36775–76, 36782–86, 36790, 36792–93, 36901, 36904, 36906–08, 36910, 36912–13, 36915–16, 36919, 36921–22, 36925

ALASKA

(Population 2010, 710,231)

SENATORS

LISA MURKOWSKI, Republican, of Anchorage, AK; born in Ketchikan, AK, May 22, 1957; education: Willamette University, 1975–77; Georgetown University, 1978–80, B.A., economics; Willamette College of Law, 1982–85, J.D.; professional: attorney; private law practice; Alaska and Anchorage Bar Associations; public service: Anchorage Equal Rights Commission; Anchorage District Court Attorney, 1987–89; Task Force on the Homeless, 1990–91; Alaska State Representative, 1998–2002; family: married to Verne Martell; children: Nicholas and Matthew; committees: chair, Energy and Natural Resources; Appropriations; Health, Education, Labor, and Pensions; Indian Affairs; appointed to the U.S. Senate on December 20, 2002; elected to the 109th Congress for a full Senate term on November 2, 2004; reelected as a write-in candidate to the 112th Congress on November 2, 2010; reelected to the 115th Congress on November 8, 2016.

Office Listings

http://murkowski.senate.gov https://www.facebook.com/senlisamurkowski
https://twitter.com/lisamurkowski

522 Hart Senate Office Building, Washington, DC 20510 .... (202) 224–6665
Chief of Staff.—Michael Pawlowski. FAX: 224–5301
Legislative Director.—Garrett Boyle.
Scheduler.—Kristen Daimler-Nothdurft.
510 L Street, Suite 550, Anchorage, AK 99501 .... (907) 271–3735
101 12th Avenue, Room 329, Fairbanks, AK 99701 .... (907) 456–0233
4079 Tongass Avenue, Suite 204, Ketchikan, AK 99901 .... (907) 225–6880
851 East Westpoint Drive, Wasilla, AK 99654 .... (907) 376–7665
805 Frontage Road, Suite 105, Kenai, AK 99611 .... (907) 283–5808
800 Glacier Avenue, Suite 101, Juneau, AK .... (907) 586–7277

* * *

DAN SULLIVAN, Republican, of Anchorage, AK; born in Fairview Park, OH, November 13, 1964; education: B.A., economics, Harvard University, 1987; joint masters of science in foreign service and J.D., Georgetown University, 1993; military: U.S. Marine Corps 1993–97; U.S. Marine Corps Reserve 1997–present, attaining rank of Colonel; professional: attorney, private law practice,1997–2001; public service: director, National Security Council Staff, 2002–04; U.S. Assistant Secretary of State for Economic, Energy and Business Affairs, 2006–09; Attorney General, State of Alaska, 2009–10; Commissioner, Alaska Department of Natural Resources, 2011–13; awards: National Security Council Outstanding Service Award; Defense Meritorious Service Medal; religion: Catholic; family: married to Julie Fate Sullivan; children: Meghan, Isabella, and Laurel; committees: Armed Services; Commerce, Science, and Transportation; Environment and Public Works; Veterans' Affairs; elected to the U.S. Senate on November 4, 2014.

Office Listings

http://sullivan.senate.gov https://www.facebook.com/SenDanSullivan
https://twitter.com/SenDanSullivan

702 Hart Senate Office Building, Washington, DC 20510 .... (202) 224–3004
Chief of Staff.—Larry Burton. FAX: 224–6501
Legislative Director.—Erik Elam.
Scheduling Director.—Avery Fogels.
510 L Street, Suite 750, Anchorage, AK 99501 .... (907) 271–5915
101 12th Avenue, Room 328, Fairbanks, AK 99701 .... (907) 456–0261
851 East Westpoint Drive, Suite 309, Wasilla, AK 99654 .... (907) 357–9956
800 Glacier Avenue, Suite 101, Juneau, AK 99801 .... (907) 586–7277
805 Frontage Road, Suite 101, Kenai, AK 99611 .... (907) 283–4000
1900 First Avenue, Suite 225, Ketchikan, AK 99901 .... (907) 225–6880

REPRESENTATIVE

AT LARGE

DON YOUNG, Republican, of Fort Yukon, AK; born in Meridian, CA, June 9, 1933; education: A.A., Yuba Junior College; B.A., Chico State College, Chico, CA; honorary doctorate of laws, University of Alaska, Fairbanks; professional: State House of Representatives, 1966–70; U.S. Army, 41st Tank Battalion, 1955–57; elected member of the State Senate, 1970–73; served on the Fort Yukon City Council for six years, serving four years as Mayor; educator for nine years; river boat captain; member: National Education Association, Elks, Lions, Jaycees; widowed: Lula Fredson of Fort Yukon; children: Joni and Dawn; committees: Natural Resources; Transportation and Infrastructure; elected to the 93rd Congress, by special election, on March 6, 1973, to fill the vacancy created by the death of Congressman Nick Begich; reelected to each succeeding Congress.

Office Listings

http://www.donyoung.house.gov facebook: https://www.facebook.com/RepDonYoung
twitter: https://twitter.com/DonYoungAK

2314 Rayburn House Office Building, Washington, DC 20515 .... (202) 225–5765
Chief of Staff.—Pamela Day. FAX: 225–0425
Executive Assistant / Office Manager.—Paula Conru.
Legislative Director.—Alex Ortiz.
4241 B Street, Suite 203, Anchorage, AK 99503 .... (907) 271–5978
FAX: 271–5950
100 Cushman Street, Suite 307, Fairbanks, AK 99707 .... (907) 456–0210
FAX: 456–0279

Population (2010), 710,231.

ZIP Codes: 99501–24, 99540, 99546–59, 99561, 99563–69, 99571–81, 99583–91, 99599, 99602–15, 99619–22, 99624–41, 99643–45, 99647–72, 99674–95, 99697, 99701–12, 99714, 99716, 99720–27, 99729–30, 99732–34, 99736–86, 99788–89, 99791, 99801–03, 99811, 99820–21, 99824–27, 99829–30, 99832–33, 99835–36, 99840–41, 99850

ARIZONA

(Population 2010, 6,392,017)

SENATORS

JOHN McCAIN, Republican, of Phoenix, AZ; born in the Panama Canal Zone, August 29, 1936; education: graduated, Episcopal High School, Alexandria, VA, 1954; graduated, U.S. Naval Academy, Annapolis, MD, 1958; National War College, Washington, DC, 1973; retired captain (pilot), U.S. Navy, 1958–81; military awards: Silver Star, Bronze Star, Legion of Merit, Purple Heart, and Distinguished Flying Cross; chair, International Republican Institute; married to the former Cindy Hensley; seven children: Doug, Andy, Sidney, Meghan, Jack, Jim, and Bridget; committees: chair, Armed Services; Homeland Security and Governmental Affairs; Indian Affairs; ex officio, Select Committee on Intelligence; elected to the 98th Congress in November, 1982; reelected to the 99th Congress in November, 1984; elected to the U.S. Senate in November, 1986; reelected to each succeeding Senate term.

Office Listings

http://mccain.senate.gov twitter: @senjohnmccain

218 Russell Senate Office Building, Washington, DC 20510 .... (202) 224–2235
Chief of Staff.—Truman Anderson. TDD: 224–7132
Legislative Director.—Joseph Donoghue.
Communications Director.—Julie Tarallo.
Scheduler.—Ellen Cahill.
2201 East Camelback Road, Suite 115, Phoenix, AZ 85016 .... (602) 952–2410
TDD: 952–0170
407 West Congress Street, Suite 103, Tucson, AZ 85701 .... (602) 670–6334

* * *

JEFFRY "JEFF" FLAKE, Republican, of Mesa, AZ; born in Snowflake, AZ, December 31, 1962; education: B.A., international relations, Brigham Young University, Provo, UT, 1986; M.A., political science, Brigham Young University, Provo, 1987; professional: executive director, Foundation for Democracy, Namibia, 1989–90; director, Interface Public Affairs, Washington, DC, 1990–92; executive director, Goldwater Institute, Phoenix, AZ, 1992–99; member, U.S. House of Representatives, 2001–13; religion: Church of Jesus Christ of Latter-Day Saints; family: wife, Cheryl; children: Ryan, Alexis, Austin, Tanner, and Dallin; committees: Energy and Natural Resources; Foreign Relations; Judiciary; Special Committee on Aging; elected to the U.S. Senate on November 6, 2012.

Office Listings

http://flake.senate.gov www.facebook.com/senatorjeffflake twitter: @jeffflake

S–413 Russell Senate Office Building, Washington, DC 20510 .... (202) 224–4521
Chief of Staff.—Chandler Morse.
Legislative Director.—Helen Heiden.
Administrative Director.—Celeste Gold.
Scheduler.—Meagan Shepherd.
2200 East Camelback Road, Suite 120, Phoenix, AZ 85016 .... (602) 840–1891
6840 North Oracle Road, Suite 150, Tucson, AZ 85704 .... (520) 575–8633

REPRESENTATIVES

FIRST DISTRICT

TOM O'HALLERAN, Democrat, of the Village of Oak Creek, AZ; born in Chicago, IL, January 24, 1946; education: graduated from St. Mel High School, Chicago, IL, 1964; attended Lewis University, Romeoville, IL, 1965–66; attended DePaul University, Chicago, 1991–92; professional: police officer, Chicago, 1966–79; bond trader; business owner; member of the Arizona House of Representatives, 2001–07; member of the Arizona Senate, 2007–09; religion: Catholic; family: spouse, Pat O'Halleran; caucuses: Congressional Native American Caucus; Labor and Working Families Caucus; Law Enforcement Caucus; Problem Solvers Caucus; committees: Agriculture; Armed Services; elected to the 115th Congress on November 8, 2016.

Office Listings

http://ohalleran.house.gov

126 Cannon House Office Building, Washington, DC 20515 .... (202) 225–3361
Chief of Staff.—Jeremy Nordquist. FAX: 225–3462
Legislative Director.—Xenia Ruiz.
Communications Director.—Cody Uhing.
Scheduler.—Willa Prescott.
Legislative Assistants.—Paul Babbitt.
405 North Beaver Street, Suite 6, Flagstaff, AZ 86001 .... (928) 286–5338
Deputy District Director.—Chip Davis.
Outreach Director.—Ryan Mulcahy.
Veterans Service Representative.—Steven Flanagan.
211 North Florence Street, Suite 1, Casa Grande, AZ 85122 .... (520) 316–0839
District Director.—Blanca Varela.
Veterans Services Manager.—Palmer Miller.
Special Projects Manager.—Zak Royse.
3037 West Ina Road, Suite 101, Oro Valley 85741 .... (928) 304–0131
Constituent Services Representative.—Max Dell'Oliver.
Mobile (202) 225–3361
Constituent Services Manager.—Judy Burns-Sulltrop.
Constituent Services Representative.—Keith Brekhus.
Tribal Outreach Director.—Jack Jackson.
Tribal Outreach and Constituent Services Representative.—Luther Lee.

Counties: APACHE, COCONINO (part), GILA (part), GRAHAM, GREENLEE, MARICOPA (part), NAVAJO, PIMA (part), PINAL (part), AND YAVAPAI (part). Population (2010), 724,868.

ZIP Codes: 85122–23, 85128, 85130–32, 85135, 85137–39, 85141–42, 85145, 85172–73, 85191–94, 85226, 85248, 85339, 85501–02, 85530–36, 85539–40, 85542–43, 85545–46, 85548, 85550–52, 85618, 85623, 85631, 85643, 85652–54, 85658, 85704, 85718, 85737, 85739, 85741–43, 85755, 85901–02, 85911–12, 85920, 85922–42, 86001–04, 86011, 86015, 86017–18, 86020, 86022–25, 86028, 86030–33, 86035–36, 86038–40, 86042, 86044–47, 86052–54, 86322, 86325–26, 86335–36, 86339–42, 86351, 86434–35, 86502–08, 86510–12, 86514–15, 86520, 86535, 86538, 86540, 86544–45, 86547, 86556

* * *

SECOND DISTRICT

MARTHA MCSALLY, Republican, of Tucson, AZ; born in Warwick, RI, March, 22, 1966; education: St. Mary Academy-Bay View, Riverside, RI, 1984; United States Air Force Academy, Colorado Springs, CO, 1988; master of public policy, Harvard, Cambridge, MA, 1990; master of strategic studies, United States Air War College, Montgomery, AL, 2007; professional: U.S. Air Force officer with various assignments, 1988–2010; T–37 Instructor Pilot, 1991–94; A–10 pilot / Instructor Pilot, 1994–99; Air Force Legislative Fellowship Program, 1999–2000; director of Joint Search and Rescue Center, 2000–01; Flight Commander / Operation Officer, 612th Combat Operations Squadron, 2002–04; 354th Fighter Squadron Commander, 2004–06; Chief of Current Operations, United States Africa Command, 2007–10; professor of national security studies, George C. Marshall European Center for Security Studies, 2010–12; leadership development and inspirational speaker, 2012–14; military: Bronze Star and six Air Medals; Defense Superior Service Medal; Defense and Air Force Meritorious Service Medal; Air Force Association David C. Schilling Award for the most outstanding contribution in the field of flight in 2006 (awarded to 354th Fighter Squadron under McSally's command); awards: Al Neuharth Free Spirit Award; Lifetime Achievement Award from the National Center on Women in Policing; Tucson YWCA Women on the Move Award; religion: Christian; committees: Armed Services; Homeland Security; elected to the 114th Congress on December 17, 2014; reelected to the 115th Congress on November 8, 2016.

Office Listings

https://mcsally.house.gov

510 Cannon House Office Building, Washington, DC 20515 .... (202) 225–2542
Chief of Staff.—Justin Roth. FAX: 225–0378
Scheduler.—Ashlee Bierworth.
Legislative Director.—Pace McMullan.
Communications Director.—Kelly Schibi.
4400 East Broadway Boulevard, Suite 510, Tucson, AZ 85711 .... (520) 881–3588
77 Calle Portal, Suite B–160, Sierra Vista, AZ 85635 .... (520) 459–3115

Counties: COCHISE AND PIMA (part). Population (2010), 713,631.

ZIP Codes: 85602–03, 85605–11, 85613–17, 85619–20, 85622, 85625–27, 85629–30, 85632, 85635–38, 85641, 85643–45, 85650, 85655, 85670, 85704–08, 85710–13, 85715–19, 85728, 85730–33, 85738, 85740–45, 85747–52

* * *

THIRD DISTRICT

RAÚL M. GRIJALVA, Democrat, of Tucson, AZ; born in Tucson, February 19, 1948; education: Sunnyside High School, Tucson, AZ; B.A., University of Arizona; professional: former Assistant Dean for Hispanic Student Affairs, University of Arizona; former Director of the El Pueblo Neighborhood Center; public service: Tucson Unified School District Governing Board 1974–86; Pima County Board of Supervisors, 1989–2002; family: married to Ramona; three daughters; committees: ranking member, Natural Resources; Education and the Workforce; elected to the 108th Congress on November 5, 2002; reelected to each succeeding Congress.

Office Listings

http://www.grijalva.house.gov www.facebook.com/Rep.Grijalva twitter: @RepRaulGrijalva

1511 Longworth House Office Building, Washington, DC 20515 .... (202) 225–2435
Chief of Staff.—Amy Emerick. FAX: 225–1541
Legislative Director.—Kelsey Mishkin.
Communications Director.—Dan Lindner.
Scheduler.—Cristina Villa.
101 West Irvington Road, Tucson, AZ 85705 .... (520) 622–6788
146 North State Avenue, Somerton, AZ 85350 .... (928) 343–7933
13065 West McDowell Road, Suite C–113, Avondale, AZ 85392 .... (623) 536–3388

Counties: LA PAZ (part), MARICOPA (part), PIMA (part), PINAL (part), SANTA CRUZ (part), and YUMA. Population (2010), 710,224.

ZIP Codes: 85033 (part), 85037 (part), 85043 (part), 85123 (part), 85139 (part), 85193 (part), 85305 (part), 85307 (part), 85321–22, 85323 (part), 85326 (part), 85333 (part), 85336–37, 85338–40 (part), 85341, 85343, 85347 (part), 85349–50, 85353 –54 (part), 85364–65 (part), 85392 (part), 85395 (part), 85396, 85601, 85611 (part), 85621, 85622 (part), 85624, 85629 (part), 85633–34, 85637 (part), 85640, 85645 (part), 85646, 85648, 85653 (part), 85701, 85705–06 (part), 85713–14 (part), 85719 (part), 85723–24, 85726, 85735–36, 85743 (part), 85745 (part), 85746, 85756 (part), 85757

* * *

FOURTH DISTRICT

PAUL GOSAR, Republican, of Prescott, AZ; born in Rock Springs, WY, November 27, 1958; education: graduated, Pinedale High School, Pinedale, WY; B.S., Creighton University, Omaha, NE, 1981; D.D.S., Creighton University, Omaha, 1985; religion: Catholic; family: wife, Maude; children: Elle, Gaston, and Isabelle; caucuses: chairman, Western Caucus; Coal Caucus; GOP Doctor's Caucus; Immigration Reform Caucus; committees: Natural Resources; Oversight and Government Reform; elected to the 112th Congress on November 2, 2010; reelected to each succeeding Congress.

Office Listings

http://www.gosar.house.gov https://www.facebook.com/repgosar twitter: @repgosar
https://www.youtube.com/repgosar https://www.flickr.com/photos/repgosar

2057 Rayburn House Office Building, Washington, DC 20515 .... (202) 225–2315
Chief of Staff.—Thomas Van Flein.
Legislative Director.—Trevor Pearson.
Press Secretary.—Vacant.
Scheduler / Office Manager.—Leslie Foti.
District Director.—Penny Pew.
6499 South Kings Ranch Road, #4, Gold Canyon, AZ 85118.
122 North Cortez Street, Suite 104, Prescott, AZ 86301.

Counties: GILA, LA PAZ, MARICOPA, MOHAVENUE, PINAL, YAVAPAI, AND YUMA. CITIES AND TOWNSHIPS: Ak-Chin Village, Apache Junction, Arcosanti, Arizona City, Arizona Village, Ash Fork, Bagdad, Beaver Dam, Big Park, Black Canyon City, Blackwater, Bouse, Buckeye, Bullhead City, Central Heights-Midland City, Chino Valley, Chloride, Chuichu, Cibola, Clarkdale, Claypool, Colorado City, Cordes Lakes, Cornville, Cottonwood-Verde Village, Desert Hills, Dewey-Humboldt, Dolan Springs, Dudleyville, Ehrenberg, Eloy, Florence, Fort MohAvenue, Fortuna Foothills, Gadsden, Gisela, Globe, Gold Canyon, Golden Valley, Hackberry, Hayden, Hope, Jerome, Kaibab, Kearny, Kingman, Kohls Ranch, Lake Havasu City, Lake Montezuma, Litchfield Park, Littlefield, Mammoth, Marana, Maricopa, Mayer, Meadview, Mesquite Creek, Mohave Valley, Mojave Ranch Estates, New Kingman-Butler, Nothing, Oatman, Oracle, Parker, Parker Strip, Paulden, Payson, Peach Springs, Peeples Valley, Peoria, Pine, Poston, Prescott Valley, Quartzsite, Queen Creek, Queen Valley, Sacaton, Salome, San Luis, San Manuel, San Tan Valley, Santan, Scenic, Seligman, Somerton, Spring Valley, Stanfield, Star Valley, Superior, Surprise, Tacna, Topock, Top-of-the-World, Valentine, Wellton, Wendon, Wickenburg, Wikieup, Wilhoit, Williamson, Willow Valley, Winkelman, Yarnell, Young, Yucca, and Yuma. Population (2010), 707,750.

ZIP Codes: 85118, 85140, 85142–43, 85173, 85324–26, 85328, 85334, 85340, 85344, 85346, 85348, 85352, 85356–60, 85362, 85364–65, 85367, 85371, 85383, 85387, 85390, 85541, 85544, 85547, 85554, 86021–22, 86305, 86312, 86314–15, 86320–21, 86323–27, 86331–34, 86337, 86401–06, 86409, 86411–13, 86426, 86431–33, 86436–38, 86440–42, 86444–46

* * *

FIFTH DISTRICT

ANDY BIGGS, Republican, of Gilbert, AZ; born in Tucson, AZ; education: B.A. in Asian studies, Brigham Young, Provo, UT, 1982; M.A. in political science, Arizona State University, Phoenix, AZ, 1999; J.D., Arizona State University, Phoenix, 1984; professional: licensed attorney; member of the Arizona Legislature, 1999–2016; president, Arizona State Senate, 2012–16; awards: ''Champion of the Taxpayer'' from Americans for Prosperity; ''Friend of Liberty'' from Goldwater Institute; religion: Church of Jesus Christ of Latter-Day Saints; family: wife, Cindy; six children; four grandchildren; committees: Judiciary; Science, Space, and Technology; elected to the 115th Congress on November 8, 2016.

Office Listings

http://biggs.house.gov facebook: https://www.facebook.com/RepAndyBiggs
twitter: @RepAndyBiggsAZ

1626 Longworth House Office Building, Washington, DC 20515 .... (202) 225–2635
Chief of Staff.—Deborah Weigel. FAX: 226–4386
Scheduler.—Abigail Groski.
Communications Director.—Daniel Stefanski.
2509 South Power Road, Suite 204, Mesa, AZ 85209 .... (480) 699–8239

Counties: MARICOPA (part) AND PINAL (part). CITIES AND TOWNSHIPS: Apache Junction, Chandler, Gilbert, Mesa, and Queen Creek. Population (2010), 710,224.

ZIP Codes: 85120–21, 85127, 85142, 85147, 85201, 85203–10, 85212–13, 85215–16, 85224–25, 85233–34, 85236, 85249, 85275, 85277, 85286, 85295–97

* * *

SIXTH DISTRICT

DAVID SCHWEIKERT, Republican, of Fountain Hills, AZ; born March 3, 1962; education: B.A., Arizona State University, Tempe, AZ, 1988; M.B.A., Arizona State University, Tempe, AZ, 2005; professional: business owner of a real estate company; realtor; financial consultant; member of the Arizona State House of Representatives, 1989–94; member of the Arizona State Board of Equalization, 1995–2003; former Treasurer, Maricopa County, AZ, 2004–06; religion: Catholic; married: Joyce Schweikert; committees: Ways and Means; Joint Economic Committee; elected to the 112th Congress on November 2, 2010; reelected to each succeeding Congress.

Office Listings

http://schweikert.house.gov twitter: @repdavid

2059 Cannon House Office Building, Washington, DC 20515 .... (202) 225–2190
Chief of Staff.—Oliver Schwab.
Scheduler.—Ashley Sylvester.
Legislative Director.—Katherina Dimenstein.
Communications Directors: Oliver Schwab, Ashley Sylvester.
10603 North Hayden Road, Suite 108, Scottsdale, AZ 85260 .... (480) 946–2411
FAX: 946–2446

Counties: MARICOPA (part). CITIES AND TOWNSHIPS: Carefree, Cave Creek, Fountain Hills, Paradise Valley, Phoenix (part), Rio Verde, Scottsdale, Salt River Pima Maricopa Indian Community, and Yavapai Nation. Population (2010), 754,482.

ZIP Codes: 85020, 85022–24, 85027–29, 85032, 85050, 85054, 85201, 85250–51, 85253–56, 85258–60, 85264, 85268

* * *

SEVENTH DISTRICT

RUBEN GALLEGO, Democrat, of Phoenix, AZ; born in Chicago, IL, November 20 1979; education: A.B., Harvard, Cambridge, MA, 2004; professional: delegate, Democratic National

Convention, 2008; Chief of Staff to Phoenix Councilman Michael Nowakowski, 2008–10; vicechair, Arizona Democratic Party, 2009; member of the Arizona House of Representatives, 2011–14; Assistant Democratic Leader for the Arizona House of Representatives, 2013–14; military: U.S. Marine Corps, 2000–06; awards: Combat Action Ribbon; religion: Catholic; caucuses: Congressional Hispanic Caucus; Congressional LGBT Equality Caucus; Congressional Progressive Caucus; Medicaid Expansion Caucus; Post 9/11 Veterans Caucus; Quiet Skies Caucus; committees: Armed Services; Natural Resources; elected to the 114th Congress on November 4, 2014; reelected to the 115th Congress on November 8, 2016.

Office Listings

https://rubengallego.house.gov www.facebook.com/reprubengallego twitter: @reprubengallego

1218 Longworth House Office Building, Washington, DC 20515 .... (202) 225–4065
Scheduler.—Abigail O'Brien.
411 North Central Avenue, Suite 150, Phoenix, AZ 85004 .... (602) 256–0551
District Director.—Luis Heredia.

Counties: MARICOPA (part). Population (2010), 725,197.

ZIP Codes: 85001–10, 85012–19, 85021, 85025–26, 85030–31, 85033–38, 85040–44, 85048, 85051, 85061–64, 85066–67, 85072, 85074–75, 85079, 85082, 85098, 85282–83, 85301, 85303, 85305, 85311, 85318, 85323, 85339, 85353

* * *

EIGHTH DISTRICT

DEBBIE LESKO, Republican, of Peoria, AZ; born November 14, 1958; education: B.B.A., University of Wisconsin, Madison, WI; professional/awards: business owner; Arizona State Representative, Legislative District 21, 2008–12 (Majority Whip, 2011–12; Arizona State Senator, Legislative District 21, 2015–18 (President Pro Tempore, 2017–18; Chair, Appropriations Committee); Republican Chairman, Legislative District 9; Voter Registration Chair, Maricopa County Republican Party; Senator of the Year Award, Arizona Chamber of Commerce; religion: Christian; married; three children; caucuses: Republican Study Committee; committees: Homeland Security; Science, Space, and Technology; elected to the 115th Congress, by special election, on April 24, 2018, to fill the vacancy caused by the resignation of Representative Trent Franks.

Office Listings

https://lesko.house.gov www.facebook.com/SenatorDebbieLesko twitter: @DebbieLesko

2435 Rayburn House Office Building, Washington, DC 20515 .... (202) 225–4576
Chief of Staff.—Abby Gunderson-Schwarz. FAX: 225–6328
Legislative Director.—Matt Simon.
7121 West Bell Road, Suite 200, Glendale, AZ 85308 .... (623) 776–7911
District Director.—Lisa Gray.

Counties: GLENDALE, MARICOPA, NEW RIVER, NEW VILLAGE, NORTH GATEWAY, PEORIA, SUN CITY, SUN CITY WEST, AND SURPRISE (part). Population (2014), 741,374.

ZIP Codes: 85083, 85085–87, 85301–10, 85312, 85318, 85331, 85335, 85338, 85340, 85345, 85351, 85361, 85363, 85372–76, 85378–83, 85385, 85387–88, 85395

* * *

NINTH DISTRICT

KYRSTEN SINEMA, Democrat, of Phoenix, AZ; born in Tucson, AZ, July 12, 1976; education: B.A., social work, Brigham Young University, Provo, UT, 1995; M.A., social work, Arizona State University, Tempe, AZ, 1999; J.D., Arizona State University, Tempe, AZ, 2004; Ph.D., social justice, social inquiry, Arizona State University, Tempe, 2012; professional: member of the Arizona House of Representatives, 2005–11; Aspen-Rodel Public Leadership Fellow, 2008; Assistant Minority Leader, Arizona House of Representatives, 2009–11; *Time* magazine's Top 40 Under 40, 2010; member of the Arizona State Senate, 2011–12; TED Fellow, 2012; committees: Financial Services; elected to the 113th Congress on November 6, 2012; reelected to each succeeding Congress.

Office Listings

http://sinema.house.gov twitter: @repsinema

1725 Longworth House Office Building, Washington, DC 20515 .... (202) 225–9888
Chief of Staff.—Meg Joseph. FAX: 225–9731
Deputy Chief of Staff, Legislative.—Michael Brownlie.
Legislative Director.—Alyssa Marois.
Communications Director.—Macey Matthews.
Scheduler.—Kate Gonzales.
2944 North 44th Street, Suite 150, Maricopa County, AZ 85018 .... (602) 956–2285
Deputy Chief of Staff, District.—Michelle Davidson.

Counties: MARICOPA COUNTY (part). CITIES: Ahwatukee, Chandler, Guadalupe, Mesa, Phoenix, and Tempe. Population (2010), 722,896.

ZIP Codes: 85008 (part), 85012–14 (part), 85016 (part), 85018 (part), 85020–21 (part), 85034 (part), 85040 (part), 85044 (part), 85045, 85048 (part), 85051 (part), 85201 (part), 85202, 85203–04 (part), 85210 (part), 85224–26 (part), 85233 (part), 85251 (part), 85253 (part), 85256–57 (part), 85281–83 (part), 85284

ARKANSAS

(Population 2010, 2,915,918)

SENATORS

JOHN NICHOLS BOOZMAN, Republican, of Rogers, AR; born in Shreveport, LA, December 10, 1950; education: Southern College of Optometry, Memphis, TN, 1977; also attended University of Arkansas, Fayetteville, AR; professional: doctor of optometry; business owner; rancher; religion: Southern Baptist; married: Cathy Boozman; children: three daughters; committees: Agriculture, Nutrition, and Forestry; Appropriations; Budget; Environment and Public Works; Veterans' Affairs; elected to the U.S. House of Representatives 2001–11; elected to the U.S. Senate on November 2, 2010; reelected to each succeeding Senate term.

Office Listings

http://boozman.senate.gov facebook: johnboozman twitter: @johnboozman

141 Hart Senate Office Building, Washington, DC 20510 .... (202) 224–4843
Chief of Staff.—Toni-Marie Higgins. FAX: 228–1371
Deputy Chief of Staff / Counsel.—Susan Olsen.
Legislative Director.—Mackenzie Burt.
Communications Director.—Sara Lasure.
Scheduler.—Kelsi Daniell.
Senior Communications Advisor.—Patrick Creamer.
106 West Main Street, Suite 104, El Dorado, AR 71730 870–863–4641
1120 Garrison Avenue, Suite 2B, Fort Smith, AR 72901 479–573–0189
Constituent Services Director.—Kathy Watson.
300 South Church Street, Suite 400, Jonesboro, AR 72401 870–268–6925
1401 West Capitol Avenue, Suite 155, Little Rock, AR 72201 501–372–7153
213 West Monroe, Suite N, Lowell, AR 72745 479–725–0400
State Director.—Stacey McClure.
1001 Hwy. 62 East, Suite 11, Mountain Home, AR 72653 870–424–0129
620 East 22nd Street, Suite 204, Stuttgart, AR 72160 870–672–6941

* * *

TOM COTTON, Republican, of Dardanelle, AR; born in Dardanelle, AR, May 13, 1977; education: graduated Dardanelle High School; B.A., Harvard University, 1999; J.D., Harvard University, 2002; professional: attorney; management consultant; military service: U.S. Army Infantry Officer, 2005–09; awards: graduated *magna cum laude*, Harvard University; Ranger Tab Recipient; Army Commendation Medal; Combat Infantryman Badge; Iraq Campaign Medal; Bronze Star Medal; committees: Armed Services; Banking, Housing, and Urban Affairs; Budget; Joint Economic Committee; Select Committee on Intelligence; elected to the 113th Congress on November 6, 2012; elected to the U.S. Senate on November 4, 2014.

Office Listings

http://cotton.senate.gov

124 Russell Senate Office Building, Washington, DC 20510 .... (202) 224–2353
Chief of Staff.—Doug Coutts. FAX: 228–0908
Legislative Director.—Joe Kraistol.
Communications Director.—Caroline Tabler.
11809 Hinson Road, Suite 100, Little Rock, AR 72212 .... (501) 223–9081
State Director.—Vanessa Moody.
1108 South Old Missouri Road, Suite B, Springdale, AR 72764 .... (479) 751–0879
300 South Church, Suite 338, Jonesboro, AR 72401 .... (870) 933–6223
106 West Main Street, Suite 410, El Dorado, AR 71730 .... (870) 864–8582

REPRESENTATIVES

FIRST DISTRICT

RICK CRAWFORD, Republican, of Jonesboro, AR; born in Homestead AFB, FL, January 22, 1966; education: graduated, Alvirne High School; B.A., agricultural business and economics, Arkansas State University, 1996; professional: U.S. Army—Bomb Disposal Technician, 1985–89; professional rodeo announcer; KAIT–TV Jonesboro—news anchor; KFIN–FM—farm director; Delta Farm Roundup TV Show—producer and anchor; Agwatch—owner and operator;

member: National Association of Farm Broadcasting; 4–H Foundation Board of Arkansas; recipient of the NAFB Newscast Award, 2006 and 2008; married: Stacy; children: Will and Delaney; caucuses: Republican Study Committee; committees: Agriculture; Permanent Select Committee on Intelligence; Transportation and Infrastructure; elected to the 112th Congress on November 2, 2010; reelected to each succeeding Congress.

Office Listings

http://crawford.house.gov https://www.facebook.com/reprickcrawford?ref=brltf
twitter: @reprickcrawford

2422 Rayburn House Office Building, Washington, DC 20515 .... (202) 225–4076
Chief of Staff.—Jonah Shumate. FAX: 225–5602
Press Secretary.—James Arnold.
Legislative Director.—Chris Jones.
112 South First Street, Cabot, AR 72023 .... (501) 843–3043
2400 East Highland Drive, Suite 300, Jonesboro, AR 72401 .... (870) 203–0540
1001 Highway 62 East, Suite 9, Mountain Home, AR 72653 .... (870) 424–2075

Counties: ARKANSAS, BAXTER, CHICOT, CLAY, CLEBURNE, CRAIGHEAD, CRITTENDEN, CROSS, DESHA, FULTON, GREENE, INDEPENDENCE, IZARD, JACKSON, JEFFERSON (part), LAWRENCE, LEE, LINCOLN, LONOKE, MISSISSIPPI, MONROE, PHILLIPS, POINSETT, PRAIRIE, RANDOLPH, SAINT FRANCIS, SEARCY, SHARP, STONE, AND WOODRUFF. Population (2015), 722,402.

ZIP Codes: 72003, 72005–07, 72014, 72017, 72020–21, 72023–24, 72026, 72029, 72031, 72036–38, 72040–44, 72046, 72048, 72051, 72055, 72059–60, 72064, 72067, 72069, 72072–76, 72083, 72086, 72101–02, 72108, 72112, 72121, 72123, 72130–31, 72134, 72137, 72139–40, 72142–43, 72153, 72160, 72165–66, 72169–70, 72175–76, 72179, 72189, 72301, 72303, 72310–13, 72315–16, 72319–22, 72324–33, 72335–36, 72338–42, 72346–48, 72350–55, 72358–60, 72364–70, 72372–74, 72376–77, 72383–84, 72386–87, 72389–92, 72394–96, 72401–04, 72410–17, 72419, 72421–22, 72424–45, 72447, 72449–51, 72453–62, 72464–67, 72469–76, 72478–79, 72482, 72501, 72503, 72512–13, 72515, 72517, 72519–34, 72536–40, 72542–46, 72550, 72553–56, 72560–62, 72564–69, 72571–73, 72575–79, 72581, 72583–85, 72587, 72610, 72613, 72617, 72623, 72626, 72629, 72631, 72633, 72635–36, 72639, 72642, 72645, 72650–51, 72653–54, 72658, 72663, 72669, 72675, 72679–80, 72685–86

* * *

SECOND DISTRICT

J. FRENCH HILL, Republican, of Little Rock, AR; born in Little Rock, December 5, 1956; education: B.S., economics, Vanderbilt University, Nashville, TN, 1979, graduated *magna cum laude*; professional: senior financial analyst, InterFirst Corporation, 1979–82; legislative assistant, assistant to the chairman, Subcommittee on Housing and Urban Development, the Honorable John Tower (R–TX), Senate Committee on Banking, Housing, and Urban Affairs, 1982–84; director, Mason Best Company, 1984–89; Deputy Assistant Secretary (Corporate Finance), U.S. Department of the Treasury, 1989–91; Special Assistant to the President, Executive Office of the White House, 1991–93; executive officer, Regions West, 1993–99; chief executive officer, Delta Trust & Banking Corp., 1999–2014; religion: Roman Catholic; family: married, two children; caucuses: Bipartisan Congressional Arts Caucus; Congressional Air Force Caucus; Congressional Army Caucus; Congressional Boating Caucus; Congressional Caucus on Fitness; Congressional Caucus on Foster Youth; Congressional Caucus on India and Indian-Americans; Congressional Chicken Caucus; Congressional Congenital Heart Caucus; Congressional Caucus on India and Indian-Americans; Congressional Diabetes Caucus; Congressional French Caucus; Congressional Historic Preservation Caucus; Congressional International Conservation Caucus; Congressional Israel Allies Caucus; Congressional Kidney Caucus; Congressional Missile Defense Caucus; Congressional Natural Gas Caucus; Congressional Prayer Caucus; Congressional Scouting Caucus; Congressional Sportsmen's Caucus; Congressional Wine Caucus; House Republican Israel Caucus; House Small Brewers Caucus; National Guard and Reserve Components Caucus (NGRCC); Science, Technology, Engineering, and Math (STEM) Education Caucus; U.S.-Japan Caucus; committees: Financial Services; elected to the 114th Congress on November 4, 2014; reelected to the 115th Congress on November 8, 2016.

Office Listings

http://www.hill.house.gov https://www.facebook.com/repfrenchhill
https://twitter.com/repfrenchhill https://www.youtube.com/channel/uct8uwrojtkwsscjlvg0ikvq

1229 Longworth House Office Building, Washington, DC 20515 .... (202) 225–2506
Chief of Staff.—A. Brooke Bennett. FAX: 225–5903
Communications Director.—Mike Siegel.
Legislative Director.—Peter Comstock.
Senior Legislative Assistants: Chip Bartlett, Dylan Frost.
Legislative Assistants / Legislative Correspondents: Lesley Hill, Matt Karvelas.
Executive Assistant.—Anna Wilbourn.
Staff Assistant.—Mary Katherine Barker.
1501 North University, Suite 150, Little Rock, AR 72207 .... (501) 324–5941

Office Listings—Continued

District Representatives: John Grove, Chloe Maxwell. FAX: 324–6029
District Representatives for Military / Veterans Affairs: David L. Carnahan, Richard E. Maxwell.
Staff Assistant.—Leigh Anna Gildner.
1105 Deer Street, Suite 12, Conway, AR 72032 .... (501) 358–3481
District Representative.—Anushree Jumde. FAX: 358-3494

Counties: CONWAY, FAULKNER, PERRY, PULASKI, SALINE, VAN BUREN, AND WHITE. Population (2010), 751,377.

ZIP Codes: 71772, 71909, 72001–02, 72010–13, 72015–18, 72020, 72022–23, 72025, 72027–28, 72030–35, 72039, 72045–47, 72052–53, 72057–61, 72063, 72065–68, 72070, 72076, 72078–82, 72085, 72087–89, 72099, 72102–04, 72106–08, 72110–11, 72113–22, 72124–27, 72131, 72135–37, 72139, 72141–43, 72145, 72149, 72153, 72156–57, 72164, 72167, 72173, 72178, 72180–81, 72183, 72190, 72199, 72201–07, 72209–12, 72214–17, 72219, 72221–23, 72225, 72227, 72231, 72260, 72295, 72419, 72568, 72629, 72645, 72679, 72823

* * *

THIRD DISTRICT

STEVE WOMACK, Republican, of Rogers, AR; born in Russellville, AR, February 18, 1957; education: Russellville High School, Russellville, AR; B.A., Arkansas Tech University, 1979; professional: radio station manager; financial consultant; Mayor of Rogers, AR; military: retired colonel, National Guard; awards: Legion of Merit; Meritorious Service Medal; Army Commendation Medal; Army Achievement Medal; Global War on Terror Expeditionary and Service Medals; religion: Southern Baptist; family: married the former Terri Williams of DeWitt, AR; three sons; caucuses: Congressional Chicken Caucus; committees: chair; Budget; Appropriations; elected to the 112th Congress on November 2, 2010; reelected to each succeeding Congress.

Office Listings

http://womack.house.gov

2412 Rayburn House Office Building, Washington, DC 20515 .... (202) 225–4301
Chief of Staff.—Beau Walker. FAX: 225–5713
Communications Director.—Claire Burghoff.
Scheduler.—Aimee Rosen.
Legislative Director.—Adrielle Churchill.
Legislative Assistant.—Jessica Powell.
Legislative Correspondents: Colin Hayes, Katie Morley.
Military Fellow.—Austin Booth.
Staff Assistant.—Hannah Shea.
3333 Pinnacle Hills, Suite 120, Rogers, AR 72758 .... (479) 464–0446
District Director.—Bootsie Ackerman. FAX: 464–0063
Constituent Service Manager.—Janet Foster.
Caseworker.—Gillie Brandolini.
Field Representative.—Jeff Thacker.
Projects Director.—Kyle Weaver.
423 North 6th Street, Fort Smith, AR 72902 .... (479) 424–1146
Field Representative / Military and Veterans Advisor.—Janice Scaggs. FAX: 424–2737
Caseworker.—Chris Bader.
303 North Main Street, Suite 102, Harrison, AR 72601 .... (870) 741–6900
Field Representative.—Teri Garrett. FAX: 741–7741

Counties: BENTON, BOONE, CARROLL, CRAWFORD, FRANKLIN, JOHNSON, MADISON, MARION, NEWTON, POPE, SEBASTIAN, AND WASHINGTON. Population (2010), 754,704.

ZIP Codes: 65729, 65733, 65761, 72063, 72080, 72601, 72611, 72616, 72619, 72624, 72630–34, 72638, 72640–41, 72644, 72648, 72653, 72655, 72660–62, 72668–69, 72672, 72675, 72677, 72679, 72682–83, 72685, 72687, 72701, 72703–04, 72712, 72714–15, 72717–19, 72722, 72727, 72729–30, 72732, 72734, 72736, 72738–40, 72744–45, 72747, 72749, 72751, 72753, 72756, 72758, 72761–62, 72764, 72768–69, 72773–74, 72801–02, 72823, 72837, 72839, 72843, 72846–47, 72856, 72858, 72901, 72903–04, 72908, 72916, 72921, 72923, 72927, 72932–34, 72936–37, 72940–41, 72945–46, 72948, 72952, 72955–56, 72959

* * *

FOURTH DISTRICT

BRUCE WESTERMAN, Republican, of Hot Springs, AR; born in Hot Springs, November 18, 1967; education: graduated, Fountain Lake High School, 1986; B.S., University of Arkansas, 1990; M.F., Yale University, 2001; professional: engineer; forester; past elected office: Arkansas

House of Representatives Majority Leader, 2013; Arkansas House of Representatives Minority Leader, 2012; Arkansas State Representative, 2011–15; Fountain Lake School Board President, 2009–10; Fountain Lake School Board, 2006–10; awards: University of Arkansas College of Engineering, Outstanding Young Alumni Award, 2005; University of Arkansas College of Engineering, Distinguished Alumni Award, 2012; Engineer of the Year by the Arkansas Society of Professional Engineers, 2013; committees: Budget; Natural Resources; Transportation and Infrastructure; elected to the 114th Congress on November 4, 2014; reelected to the 115th Congress.

Office Listings

http://westerman.house.gov

130 Cannon House Office Building, Washington, DC 20515 .... (202) 225–3772
FAX: 225–1314

Chief of Staff.—Vivian Moeglein.

Legislative Director.—Jefferson Deming.

Communications Director.—Ryan Saylor.

National Parks Service Headquarters, 101 Reserve Street, Suite 200, Hot Springs, AR 71901 .... (501) 609–9796

District Director.—Jason McGehee.

George Howard Jr. Federal Building, 100 East 8th Avenue, Room 2521, Pine Bluff, AR 71601 .... (870) 536–8178

Franklin County Courthouse, 211 West Commercial St, Ozark, AR 72949 .... (501) 295–9752

Union County Courthouse, 101 North Washington Street, Suite 406, El Dorado, AR 71730 (870) 864–8946

Counties: Ashley, Bradley, Calhoun, Clark, Cleveland, Columbia, Crawford, Dallas, Drew, Franklin, Garland, Grant, Hempstead, Hot Spring, Howard, Jefferson, Johnson, Lafayette, Little River, Logan, Madison, Miller, Montgomery, Nevada, Newton (part), Ouachita, Pike, Polk, Scott, Sebastian, Sevier, Union, and Yell. Population (2010), 717,926.

ZIP Codes: 71601–03, 71631, 71635, 71638, 71642, 71644, 71646–47, 71651–52, 71655, 71658–61, 71663, 71665, 71667, 71670–71, 71675–77, 71701, 71711, 71720, 71722, 71724–26, 71730, 71740, 71742–45, 71747, 71751–53, 71758–59, 71762–66, 71770, 71772, 71801, 71820, 71822–23, 71825–27, 71832–39, 71841–42, 71845–47, 71851–55, 71857–62, 71865–66, 71901, 71909, 71913, 71921–23, 71929, 71933, 71935, 71937, 71940–41, 71943–45, 71949–50, 71952–53, 71956–62, 71964–65, 71968–73, 71998–99, 72004, 72015, 72025, 72046, 72057, 72065, 72079, 72084, 72087, 72104, 72128–29, 72132, 72150, 72152, 72167–68, 72175, 72601, 72624, 72628, 72632, 72638, 72641, 72648, 72655, 72666, 72670, 72703, 72721, 72727, 72738, 72740, 72742, 72752, 72756, 72760, 72773, 72776, 72821, 72824, 72826–28, 72830, 72832–35, 72838–42, 72845–47, 72851–57, 72860, 72863, 72865, 72921, 72926–28, 72930, 72933–38, 72940–41, 72943–47, 72949–51, 72956, 72958–59

CALIFORNIA

(Population 2010, 37,253,956)

SENATORS

DIANNE FEINSTEIN, Democrat, of San Francisco, CA; born in San Francisco, June 22, 1933; education: B.A., Stanford University, 1955; professional: elected to San Francisco Board of Supervisors, 1970–78; president of Board of Supervisors, 1970–71, 1974–75, 1978; Mayor of San Francisco, 1978–88; candidate for governor of California, 1990; recipient: Distinguished Woman Award, *San Francisco Examiner*; Achievement Award, Business and Professional Women's Club, 1970; Golden Gate University, California, LL.D. (hon.), 1979; SCOPUS Award for Outstanding Public Service, American Friends of the Hebrew University of Jerusalem; University of Santa Clara, D.P.S. (hon.); University of Manila, D.P.A. (hon.), 1981; Antioch University, LL.D. (hon.), 1983; Los Angeles Anti-Defamation League of B'nai B'rith's Distinguished Service Award, 1984; French Legion d'Honneur from President Mitterand, 1984; Mills College, LL.D. (hon.), 1985; U.S. Army Commander's Award for Public Service, 1986; Brotherhood/Sisterhood Award, National Conference of Christians and Jews, 1986; Paulist Fathers Award, 1987; Episcopal Church Award for Service, 1987; U.S. Navy Distinguished Civilian Award, 1987; Silver Spur Award for Outstanding Public Service, San Francisco Planning and Urban Renewal Association, 1987; All Pro Management Team Award for No. 1 Mayor, *City and State* Magazine, 1987; Community Service Award Honoree for Public Service, 1987; American Jewish Congress, 1987; President's Award, St. Ignatius High School, San Francisco, 1988; Coro Investment in Leadership Award, 1988; President's Medal, University of California at San Francisco, 1988; University of San Francisco, D.H.L. (hon.), 1988; member: Coro Foundation, Fellowship, 1955–56; California Women's Board of Terms and Parole, 1960–66, executive committee; U.S. Conference of Mayors, 1983–88; Mayor's Commission on Crime, San Francisco; Bank of California, director, 1988–89; San Francisco Education Fund's Permanent Fund, 1988–89; Japan Society of Northern California, 1988–89; Inter-American Dialogue, 1988–present; Publius Award from the Center for the Study of the Presidency and Congress, 2009; chair, U.S. Senate Caucus on International Narcotics Control; married: Dr. Bertram Feinstein (dec.); married on January 20, 1980, to Richard C. Blum; children: one child; three stepchildren; religion: Jewish; committees: ranking member, Judiciary Committee; Appropriations; Rules and Administration; Select Committee on Intelligence; elected to the U.S. Senate, by special election, on November 3, 1992, to fill the vacancy caused by the resignation of U.S. Senator Pete Wilson; reelected to each succeeding Senate term.

Office Listings

http://feinstein.senate.gov twitter: @senfeinstein

331 Hart Senate Office Building, Washington, DC 20510 .... (202) 224–3841
Chief of Staff.—David Grannis. FAX: 228–3954
Legislative Director.—Roscoe Jones.
Director of Communications.—Tom Mentzer.
880 Front Street, Suite 3296, San Diego, CA 92101 .... (619) 231–9712
2500 Tulare Street, Suite 4290, Fresno, CA 93721 .... (559) 485–7430
One Post Street, Suite 2450, San Francisco, CA 94104 .... (415) 393–0707
11111 Santa Monica Boulevard, Suite 915, Los Angeles, CA 90025 .... (310) 914–7300

* * *

KAMALA D. HARRIS, Democrat, of Los Angeles, CA; born in Oakland, CA; October 20, 1964; education: B.A., Howard University, Washington, DC; J.D., University of California Hastings College of Law, San Francisco, CA; professional: attorney, Alameda County District Attorney's Office, 1990–98; attorney, San Francisco District Attorney's Office, 1998–2000; attorney, San Francisco City Attorney's Office, 2000–04; elected District Attorney, San Francisco, 2004–10; elected Attorney General, California, 2011–17; married: Douglas Emhoff, 2014; children: Cole and Ella; committees: Budget; Homeland Security and Governmental Affairs; Judiciary; Select Committee on Intelligence; elected to the U.S. Senate on November 8, 2016.

Office Listings

http://harris.senate.gov

112 Hart Senate Office Building, Washington, DC 20510 .... (202) 224–3553
Chief of Staff.—Nathan Barankin. FAX: 228–2382
Legislative Director.—Clint Odom.
Director of Scheduling.—Michelle Rothblum.
Communications Director.—Lily Adams.
333 Bush Street, Suite 3225, San Francisco, CA 94104 .... (415) 981–9369

Office Listings—Continued

11845 Olympic Boulevard, Suite 1250W, Los Angeles, CA 90064	(213) 894–5000
501 I Street, Suite 7–600, Sacramento, CA 95814	(916) 448–2787
600 B Street, Suite 2240, San Diego, CA 92101	(619) 239–3884
2500 Tulare Street, Suite 5290, Fresno, CA 93721	(559) 497–5109

REPRESENTATIVES

FIRST DISTRICT

DOUG LAMALFA, Republican, of Richvale, CA; born in Oroville, CA, July 2, 1960; education: graduated from Oroville High School; B.S., California Polytechnic State University, San Luis Obispo, CA, 1982; professional: rice farmer; California State Assemblyman, 2002–08; California State Senator, 2010–12; married: Jill; children: four; caucuses: Cement Caucus; Congressional Sportsmen's Caucus; Congressional Western Caucus; Congressional Wine Caucus; National Guard and Reserve Components Caucus; Natural Gas Caucus; PORTS Caucus; Prayer Caucus; Republican Study Committee; Rice CALIFORNIA 115th Congress 21 Caucus; Sikh Caucus; Small Business Caucus; Values Action Team; committees: Agriculture; Natural Resources; Transportation and Infrastructure; elected to the 113th Congress on November 6, 2012; reelected to each succeeding Congress.

Office Listings

http://lamalfa.house.gov twitter: @replamalfa

322 Cannon House Office Building, Washington, DC 20515	(202) 225–3076
Chief of Staff.—Mark Spannagel.	FAX: 226–0852
Scheduler.—Meredith Kroft.	
Legislative Director.—Kevin Eastman.	
Communications Director.—Parker Williams.	
2862 Olive Highway, Suite D, CA 95966	(530) 534–7100
	FAX: 534–7800
2885 Churn Creek Road, Suite C, Redding, CA 96002	(530) 223–5898
	FAX: 605–4342
2399 Rickenbacker Way, Auburn, CA 95602	(530) 878–5035
	FAX: 878–5037

Counties: BUTTE, GLENN, LASSEN, MODOC, NEVADA, PLACER, PLUMAS, SHASTA, SIERRA, SISKIYOU, AND TEHAMA. Population (2010), 702,905.

ZIP Codes: 95568, 95602–03, 95712–13, 95728, 95910, 95914–17, 95923–24, 95926–30, 95934, 95936, 95938, 95940–42, 95944–49, 95954, 95956–60, 95965–66, 95968–69, 95971, 95973–78, 95980, 95983–84, 95986, 96001, 96006–09, 96011, 96013–17, 96019–23, 96025, 96027–29, 96031–35, 96037–40, 96044, 96047, 96050–51, 96054–59, 96061–62, 96064–65, 96067–71, 96073–75, 96078–80, 96084–90, 96092, 96094–97, 96101, 96104–06, 96108–19, 96121–30, 96132, 96134–37, 96161, 97635

* * *

SECOND DISTRICT

JARED W. HUFFMAN, Democrat, of San Rafael, CA; born in Independence, MO, February 18, 1964; education: B.A., University of California, Santa Barbara, 1986; J.D., Boston College, 1990; professional: California Assembly, 2006–12; senior lawyer, Natural Resources Defense Council, 2001–06; board member, Marin Municipal Water District, 1994–2006; public interest attorney, 1990–2001; family: married, Susan Huffman; two children; caucuses: co-chair, Wild Salmon Caucus; Congressional Animal Protection Caucus; Congressional Labor and Working Families Caucus; Congressional Progressive Caucus; Congressional Rare Disease Caucus; Congressional Shellfish Caucus; Congressional Wine Caucus; House Rural Education Caucus; Native American Caucus; National Marine Sanctuary Caucus; Sensible Drug Policy Working Group; Sustainable Energy & Environment Coalition; committees: vice ranking member, Natural Resources; Transportation and Infrastructure; elected to the 113th Congress on November 6, 2012; reelected to each succeeding Congress.

Office Listings

http://huffman.house.gov twitter: @rephuffman https://www.facebook.com/rephuffman

1406 Longworth House Office Building, Washington, DC 20515	(202) 225–5161

Office Listings—Continued

Chief of Staff.—Benjamin Miller. FAX: 225–5163
Executive Assistant / Scheduler.—Miranda Dixon.
999 Fifth Avenue, Suite 290, San Rafael, CA 94901 .... (415) 258–9657
District Director.—Jeannine Callaway.
430 North Franklin Street, P.O. Box 2208, Fort Bragg, CA 95437 .... (707) 962–0933
Field Representative.—Heather Gurewitz.
317 Third Street, Suite 1, Eureka, CA 95501 .... (707) 407–3585
District Representative.—John Driscoll.

Counties: DEL NORTE, HUMBOLDT, MARIN, MENDOCINO, SONOMA (part), AND TRINITY. CITIES AND TOWNSHIPS: Arcata, Cloverdale, Crescent City, Eureka, Fort Bragg, Garberville, Healdsburg, Mendocino, Mill Valley, Novato, Petaluma, San Rafael, Sebastopol, Ukiah, Windsor, and Willits. Population (2010), 708,596.

ZIP Codes: 94946–50, 94952–54, 94956–57, 94960, 94963–66, 94970–79, 94998–99, 95401, 95403–04, 95410, 95412, 95415, 95417–18, 95420–21, 95425, 95427–30, 95432, 95436–37, 95441, 95444–46, 95448–51, 95454, 95456, 95459–60, 95462–63, 95465–66, 95468–73, 95480–82, 95486, 95488, 95490, 95492, 95494, 95497, 95501–03, 95511, 95514, 95518–19, 95521, 95524–28, 95531–32, 95534, 95536–38, 95540, 95542–43

* * *

THIRD DISTRICT

JOHN GARAMENDI, Democrat, of Walnut Grove, CA; born in Camp Blanding, FL, January 24, 1945; raised in Mokelumne Hill, CA; education: B.A., business, University of California-Berkeley, Berkeley, CA, 1966; M.B.A., Harvard University, Cambridge, MA, 1974; professional: small business owner; Peace Corps volunteer, 1966–68; California State Assembly member, 1974–76; member of the California State Senate, 1976–90; California Insurance Commissioner, 1991–94, and 2002–06; Deputy Secretary of the U.S. Interior Department, 1995–98; previously California Lieutenant Governor, 2007–09; regent, University of California; trustee, California State University; religion: Christian; family: married to Patricia Garamendi; six children; twelve grandchildren; caucuses: co-chair, American Sikh Caucus; co-chair, Coast Guard Caucus; co-chair, Mobility Air Forces Caucus; member of Make It in America Working Group; Deputy Whip; committees: Armed Services; Transportation and Infrastructure; elected, by special election, to the 111th Congress on November 3, 2009, to fill the vacancy caused by the resignation of U.S. Representative Ellen Tauscher; elected to each succeeding Congress.

Office Listings

http://garamendi.house.gov https://www.facebook.com/repgaramendi
https://twitter.com/RepGaramendi https://www.instagram.com/repgaramendi

2438 Rayburn House Office Building, Washington, DC 20515 .... (202) 225–1880
Chief of Staff.—Emily Burns. FAX: 225–5914
Legislative Director.—Garrett Durst.
District Director.—John Evalle.
Deputy District Director.—Debbi Gibbs.
Scheduler.—Jennifer Lee.
Communications Director.—Donald Lathbury.
795 Plumas Street, Yuba City, CA 95991 .... (530) 329–8865
FAX: 763–4248
412 G Street, Davis, CA 95616 .... (530) 753–5301
FAX: 753–5614
1261 Travis Boulevard, Suite 130, Fairfield, CA 94533 .... (707) 438–1822
FAX: 438–0523

Counties: COLUSA, GLENN (part), LAKE (part), SACRAMENTO (part), SOLANO (part), SUTTER, YOLO (part), AND YUBA. Population (2010), 712,075.

ZIP Codes: 94503, 94510, 94512, 94533–35, 94558, 94571, 94585, 94591, 95422–24, 95443, 95451, 95453, 95457–58, 95464, 95485, 95493, 95606–07, 95612, 95615–18, 95620, 95625–27, 95632, 95637, 95639, 95641, 95645, 95653–54, 95659–60, 95668, 95673–74, 95676, 95679–80, 95687–88, 95690–92, 95694–98, 95757–59, 95776, 95823, 95834–37, 95843, 95901, 95903, 95912–14, 95918–19, 95922, 95925, 95932, 95935, 95937, 95939, 95941, 95950–51, 95953, 95955, 95957, 95960–63, 95966, 95970, 95972, 95977, 95979, 95982, 95987–88, 95991–93

FOURTH DISTRICT

TOM McCLINTOCK, Republican, of Granite Bay, CA; born in Bronxville, NY, July 10, 1956; education: B.A., *cum laude,* political science, UCLA, Los Angeles, CA, 1978; professional: member, California State Assembly, 1982–92 and 1996–2000; member, California State Senate, 2000–08; director, Center for the California Taxpayer, National Tax Limitation Foundation, 1992–94; director, Economic and Regulatory Affairs, Claremont Institute, 1994–96; married: Lori; two children; committees: Budget; Natural Resources; elected to the 111th Congress on November 4, 2008; reelected to each succeeding Congress.

Office Listings

http://www.mcclintock.house.gov twitter: @repmcclintock

2312 Rayburn House Office Building, Washington, DC 20515 .... (202) 225–2511
FAX: 225–5444
Chief of Staff.—Igor Birman.
Scheduler.—Rachel Long.
Legislative Director.—Chris Tudor.
Legislative Assistants: Adam Pugh, Richard Stern.
Legislative Correspondent.—Taylor Bower.
2200A Douglas Boulevard, Suite 240, Roseville, CA .... (916) 786–5560
District Director.—Rocky Deal.

Counties: ALPINE, AMADOR, CALAVERAS, EL DORADO, FRESNO (part), MADERA (part), MARIPOSA, NEVADA (part), PLACER (part), AND TUOLUMNE. POPULATION (2010), 760,078.

ZIP Codes: 35251, 59223, 85252, 92532, 93601–02, 93604–05, 93610–11, 93614, 93619, 93621, 93623, 93626, 93628, 93633–34, 93636, 93638, 93641, 93643–45, 93649, 93651, 93653, 93657, 93664, 93667, 93669, 93675, 93701, 94248, 95147, 95221–26, 95228–30, 95232–33, 95236, 95245–49, 95251–52, 95254–57, 95305–06, 95309–11, 95318, 95321, 95325, 95327, 95329, 95333, 95335, 95338, 95345–47, 95364, 95369–70, 95372–73, 95379, 95383, 95389, 95601, 95603, 95613–14, 95619, 95623, 95626, 95629, 95631, 95633–36, 95640, 95642, 95644, 95646, 95648, 95650–51, 95656, 95658, 95661, 95663–69, 95672, 95675, 95678, 95681–82, 95684–85, 95689, 95699, 95709, 95713, 95715, 95720–21, 95724, 95726, 95728, 95735, 95746–47, 95762, 95765, 95945–46, 95949, 95959, 96120, 96140–43, 96145–46, 96148, 96150, 96161–62

* * *

FIFTH DISTRICT

MIKE THOMPSON, Democrat, of Napa Valley, CA; born in St. Helena, CA, January 24, 1951; education: graduated, St. Helena High School, St. Helena, CA; Purple Heart; B.A., Chico State University, 1982; M.A., Chico State University, 1996; professional: U.S. Army, 1969–72; teacher at San Francisco State University, and Chico State University; elected to the California State Senate, 2nd District, 1990–98; former chairman of the California State Senate Budget Committee; married to Janet; two children: Christopher and Jon; committees: Ways and Means; elected to the 106th Congress; reelected to each succeeding Congress.

Office Listings

http://mikethompson.house.gov http://www.house.gov/writerep twitter: @repthompson

231 Cannon House Office Building, Washington, DC 20515 .... (202) 225–3311
FAX: 225–4335
Chief of Staff.—Melanie Rhinehart Van Tassell.
Deputy Chief of Staff.—Jennifer Goedke.
Communications Director.—TJ Adams Falconer.
2751 Napa Valley Corporate Drive, Building 2, Napa, CA 94558 .... (707) 226–9898
1985 Walnut Avenue, Vallejo, CA 94592 .... (707) 645–1888
2300 County Center Drive, Suite A100, Santa Rosa, CA 95403 .... (707) 542–7182

Counties: CONTRA COSTA. CITIES AND TOWNSHIPS: Christie, Crockett, Glen Frazer, Hercules, Martinez, Pinole, Port Costa, Rodeo, Selby, Tara Hills, Tormey, and Vine Hill. LAKE COUNTY. CITIES AND TOWNSHIPS: Cobb, Kelseyville, Lakeport, and Middletown. SONOMA COUNTY. CITIES AND TOWNSHIPS: Boyes Hot Springs, Cotati, El Verano, Eldridge, Fetters Hot Springs, Fulton, Glen Ellen, Kenwood, Mark West, Rohnert Park, Santa Rosa, Sonoma, and Vineburg. NAPA COUNTY. CITIES AND TOWNSHIPS: American Canyon, Angwin, Aetna Springs, Calistoga, Deer Park, Oakville, Pope Valley, Rutherford, and St. Helena. SOLANO COUNTY. CITIES AND TOWNSHIPS: Benicia, Tiara, and Vallejo. Population (2011), 547,495.

ZIP Codes: 94508, 94510, 94515, 94525, 94547, 94553, 94558–59, 94562, 94564, 94567, 94569, 94572–74, 94576, 94581, 94587, 94589–92, 94599, 94806, 94926–28, 94931, 95401, 95409, 95416, 95426, 95431, 95433, 95435, 95439, 95442, 95451–53, 95461, 95476, 95492, 95621

* * *

SIXTH DISTRICT

DORIS OKADA MATSUI, Democrat, of Sacramento, CA; born in Poston, AZ, September 25, 1944; education: B.A., University of California, Berkeley, CA, 1966; professional: staff, White House, 1992–98; private advocate; previous organizations: Meridian International Center

Board of Trustees; Woodrow Wilson Center Board of Trustees; California Institute Board of Directors; current organizations: Smithsonian Institution Board of Regents; National Symphony Orchestra Board of Directors; married: Robert Matsui, 1966; children: Brian Robert; grandchildren: Anna Elizabeth and Robert Thomas; committees: Energy and Commerce; elected to the 109th Congress, by special election, on March 8, 2005, to fill the vacancy caused by the death of her husband, Representative Robert Matsui; reelected to each succeeding Congress.

Office Listings

http://www.matsui.house.gov https://www.facebook.com/doris.matsui/?ref=aymt_homepage_panel https://twitter.com/dorismatsui

2311 Rayburn House Office Building, Washington, DC 20515 .... (202) 225–7163
Chief of Staff.—Julie Eddy. FAX: 225–0566
Executive Assistant.—McKinley Krongaus.
Legislative Director.—Margaret McCarthy.
Press Secretary.—Lauren Dart.
501 I Street, 12–600, Sacramento, CA 95814 .... (916) 498–5600
District Director.—Sam Stefanki.

County: SACRAMENTO COUNTY (part) AND YOLO COUNTY (part). CITIES: Sacramento and West Sacramento. Population (2010), 702,905.

ZIP Codes: 95605, 95621, 95652, 95660, 95673, 95691, 95758, 95811, 95814–26, 95828–29, 95831–35, 95837–38, 95841–43, 95864

* * *

SEVENTH DISTRICT

AMI BERA, Democrat, of Elk Grove, CA; born in La Palma, CA, March 2, 1965; education: B.S., University of California, Irvine, CA; M.D., University of California, Irvine, CA, 1991; professional: military; awards: medical director for care management, Mercy Hospital, Sacramento, CA; chief medical officer, Sacramento, CA; associate dean of admissions for University of California, Davis Medical School, 2004–07; religion: Unitarian; married: Janine Bera (also a physician); children: Sydra; committees: Foreign Affairs; Science, Space, and Technology; elected to the 113th Congress on November 6, 2012; reelected to each succeeding Congress.

Office Listings

http://bera.house.gov https://twitter.com/repbera

1535 Longworth House Office Building, Washington, DC 20515 .... (202) 225–5716
Chief of Staff.—Chad Obermiller. FAX: 226–1298
Scheduler.—Marguerite Biagi.
Legislative Director.—Erin O'Quinn.
Press Secretary.—Annie Ellison.
11070 White Rock Road, Suite 195, Rancho Cordova, CA 95670 .... (916) 635–0505
District Director.—Faith Whitmore.

Counties: EASTERN HALF OF SACRAMENTO COUNTY. CITIES: Citrus Heights, Elk Grove, Folsom, and Rancho Cordova, as well as the unincorporated communities of, Carmichael, Fair Oaks, Orangevale, Rosemont, La Riviera, Sloughhouse, Rancho Murieta, Vineyard, Florin, Vintage Park, Wilton, Herald, and half of Arden Arcade. Population (2010), 710,607.

ZIP Codes: 95608–11, 95621, 95624, 95628, 95630, 95632, 95638, 95655, 95662, 95670, 95678, 95683, 95693, 95741–42, 95757–58, 95763, 95821, 95823, 95825–30, 95841–42, 95864–66 (Some of these zips are only partially in the District)

* * *

EIGHTH DISTRICT

PAUL COOK, Republican, of Yucca Valley, CA; born in Meriden, CT, March 3, 1943; education: B.S., Southern Connecticut University, New Haven, CT, 1966; M.P.A., California State University San Bernardino, San Bernardino, CA, 1996; M.A., University of California Riverside, Riverside, CA, 2000; professional: U.S. Marine Corps, 1966–92; professor; member, Yucca Valley California Town Council, 1998–2006; California State Assemblyman, 2006–12; married: Jeanne; committees: Armed Services; Foreign Affairs; Natural Resources; elected to the 113th Congress on November 6, 2012; reelected to each succeeding Congress.

Office Listings

http://cook.house.gov twitter: @RepPaulCook

1222 Longworth House Office Building, Washington, DC 20515 .... (202) 225–5861
Chief of Staff.—John Sobel. FAX: 225–6498
14955 Dale Evans Parkway, Apple Valley, CA 92307 .... (760) 247–1815
District Director.—Matthew Knox.

Counties: SAN BERNARDINO (part), MONO, AND INYO. CITIES AND TOWNSHIPS: Adelanto, Angelus Oaks, Apple Valley, Arrowbear, Arrowhead Farms, Baldy Mesa, Baker, Barstow, Bear Valley, Benton, Big Bear City, Big Bear Lake, Big Pine, Big River, Bishop, Bridgeport, Bums Canyon, Cartago, Cedar Glen, Cedar Pines Park, Coleville, Crestline, Daggett, Darwin, El Mirage, Erwin Lake, Fawnskin, Flamingo Heights, Forest Falls, Furnace Creek, Green Valley Lake, Helendale, Hesperia, Highland, Hinkley, Independence, Joshua Tree, June Lake, Lake Arrowhead, Keeler, Landers, Lenwood, Lee Vining, Lytle Creek, Mono City, Mount Baldy, Morongo Valley, Needles, Newberry Springs, Oak Glen, Oak Hills, Oro Grande, Paradise, Pioneertown, Pinon Hills, Phelan, Red Mountain, Rimrock, Running Springs, Skyforest, Sugarloaf, Topaz, Trona, Twentynine Palms, Twin Peaks, Victorville, Walker, Wrightwood, Yucca Valley, and Yucaipa. Population (2010), 708,578.

ZIP Codes: 91759, 92242, 92252, 92256, 92268, 92277–78, 92284–86, 92301, 92304–05, 92307–12, 92314–15, 92317, 92320–23, 92325, 92327–29, 92332–33, 92338–42, 92344–47, 92352, 92356, 29358–59, 92363–65, 92368–69, 92372, 92382, 92385–86, 92388–65, 92391–95, 92397–99, 92407, 93512–15, 93522, 93526, 93529–30, 93541, 93549, 93558, 93562–92, 95223, 95967, 95969, 96107, 96133

* * *

NINTH DISTRICT

JERRY MCNERNEY, Democrat, of Stockton, CA; born in Albuquerque, NM, June 18, 1951; education: attended the U.S. Military Academy, West Point, NY, 1969–71; B.S., University of New Mexico, Albuquerque, NM, 1973; M.S., University of New Mexico, 1975; Ph.D. in Mathematics, University of New Mexico, 1981; professional: wind engineer; entrepreneur; business owner; married: Mary; children: Michael, Windy, and Greg; committees: Energy and Commerce; Science, Space, and Technology; elected to the 110th Congress on November 7, 2006; reelected to each succeeding Congress.

Office Listings

http://mcnerney.house.gov twitter: @repmcnerney

2265 Rayburn House Office Building, Washington, DC 20515 .... (202) 225–1947
Chief of Staff.—Nicole Damasco Alioto. FAX: 225–4060
Scheduler.—Teresa Frison.
Communications Director.—Vacant.
Legislative Director.—Patrick Arness.
District Director.—Alisa Alva.
2222 Grand Canal Boulevard, #7, Stockton, CA 95207 .... (209) 476–8552
4703 Lone Tree Way, Antioch, CA 94531 .... (925) 754–0716

Counties: CONTRA COSTA (part), SACRAMENTO (part), AND SAN JOAQUIN (part). CITIES AND TOWNSHIPS: Antioch, Brentwood, Discovery Bay, Galt, Lathrop, Lodi, Oakley, and Stockton. Population (2010), 648,766.

ZIP Codes: 94505, 94509, 94511, 94513–14, 94531, 94548, 94561, 95201–15, 95219–20, 95227, 95230–31, 95234, 95236–37, 95240–42, 95253, 95258, 95267, 95269, 95296, 95304, 95320, 95330, 95336–37, 95361, 95366, 95391, 95632, 95686, 95690, 95757

* * *

TENTH DISTRICT

JEFF DENHAM, Republican, of Turlock, CA; born in Hawthorne, CA, July 29, 1967; education: A.A., Victor Valley Junior College, Victorville, CA, 1989; B.A., California Polytechnic State University, San Luis Obispo, CA, 1992; military: U.S. Air Force, 1984–88; U.S. Air Force Reserve, 1988–2000; professional: business owner; served in the California State Senate, 2002–10; religion: Christian; family: wife, Sonia; two children; committees: Agriculture; Natural Resources; Transportation and Infrastructure; elected to the 112th Congress on November 2, 2010; reelected to each succeeding Congress.

Office Listings

http://www.denham.house.gov twitter: @repjeffdenham https://facebook.com/repjeffdenham
https://www.youtube.com/repjeffdenham http://www.flickr.com/photos/59309318@No4/

1730 Longworth House Office Building, Washington, DC 20515 .... (202) 225–4540

Office Listings—Continued

Chief of Staff.—Jason Larrabee. FAX: 225–3402
Scheduler.—Carol Kresse.
4701 Sisk Road, Suite 202, Modesto, CA 95356 .... (209) 579–5458
District Director.—Mike Anderson.

Counties: SAN JOAQUIN COUNTY (part) AND STANISLAUS COUNTY (part). CITIES AND TOWNSHIPS: Airport, Bret Harte, Bystrom, Ceres, Cowan, Cowan Landing, Del Rio, Denair, Diablo Grande, East Oakdale, Empire, Escalon, Grayson, Hickman, Hughson, Keyes, Manteca, Modesto, Monterey Park Tract, Newman, Oakdale, Parklawn, Patterson, Ripon, Riverbank, Riverdale Park, Rouse, Salida, Shackelford, Tracy, Turlock, Valley Home, Waterford, West Modesto, Woodbridge, Westley, and Westport. Population (2010), 714,750.

ZIP Codes: 94550, 95230, 95304, 95307, 95313, 95316, 95319–20, 95322–23, 95326, 95328–30, 95336–37, 95350–51, 95354–58, 95360–61, 95363, 95366–68, 95376–77, 95380, 95382, 95385–87

* * *

ELEVENTH DISTRICT

MARK DESAULNIER, Democrat, of Concord, CA; born in Lowell, MA, March 31, 1952; education: B.A., history, College of the Holy Cross, Worcester, MA, 1974; professional: deputy probation officer, 1970–74; hotel service employee, 1975–76; restaurant general manager, 1978; restaurant owner, 1978–2006; Concord Mayor, 1993; Concord City Council, 1991–94; Contra Costa County Supervisor, 1994–2006; California Assembly, 2006–08; California Senate, 2008–15; religion: Catholic; children: Tristan and Tucker; committees: Education and the Workforce; Oversight and Government Reform; Transportation and Infrastructure; elected to the 114th Congress on November 4, 2014.

Office Listings

https://desaulnier.house.gov twitter: @repdesaulnier

115 Cannon House Office Building, Washington, DC 20515 .... (202) 225–2095
Chief of Staff.—Betsy Arnold Marr. FAX: 225–5609
Scheduler.—Alexandra Fox.
3100 Oak Road, Suite 110, Walnut Creek, CA 94597 .... (925) 602–1880
District Director.—Shanelle Scales Preston.
440 Civic Center Plaza, Second Floor, Richmond, CA 94804 .... (510) 262–6500
Outreach Coordinator.—Jessica Angulo.

Counties: CONTRA COSTA (part), SOLANO (part). CITIES AND TOWNSHIPS: Alomo, Antioch, Bay Point, Blackhawk, Clayton, Concord, El Cerrito, El Sobrante, Kensington, Lafayette, Martinez, Moraga, Orinda, Pittsburg, Pleasant Hill, Richmond, San Pablo, and Walnut Creek. Population (2014), 773,916.

ZIP Codes: 92526, 94506–07, 94509, 94517–24, 94527–30, 94549, 94553, 94556–57, 94563, 94565, 94595–98, 94708, 94801–08, 94820, 94850

* * *

TWELFTH DISTRICT

NANCY PELOSI, Democrat, of San Francisco, CA; born in Baltimore, MD, March 26, 1940; daughter of the late Representative Thomas D'Alesandro, Jr., of MD; education: graduated, Institute of Notre Dame High School, 1958; B.A., Trinity College, Washington, DC (major, political science; minor, history), 1962; professional: northern chair, California Democratic Party, 1977–81; state chair, California Democratic Party, 1981–83; chair, 1984 Democratic National Convention Host Committee; finance chair, Democratic Senatorial Campaign Committee, 1985–86; member: Democratic National Committee; California Democratic Party Executive Committee; San Francisco Library Commission; Board of Trustees, LSB Leakey Foundation; married: Paul F. Pelosi, 1963; children: Nancy Corinne, Christine, Jacqueline, Paul, Jr., and Alexandra; 9 grandchildren; elected by special election, June 2, 1987, to the 100th Congress to fill the vacancy caused by the death of U.S. Representative Sala Burton; reelected to each succeeding Congress; elected Democratic Whip in the 107th Congress; Democratic Leader in the 108th and 109th Congresses; elected Speaker of the House in the 110th and 111th Congresses; elected Democratic Leader in the 112th, 113th, 114th, and 115th Congresses.

Office Listings

http://www.pelosi.house.gov twitter: @nancypelosi

233 Cannon House Office Building, Washington, DC 20515 .... (202) 225–4965

Office Listings—Continued

Chief of Staff.—Robert Edmondson (California). FAX: 225–8259
90 7th Street, Suite 2–800, San Francisco, CA 94103 .... (415) 556–4862
District Chief of Staff.—Dan Bernal.

County: SAN FRANCISCO COUNTY (part). CITY: San Francisco. Population (2010), 702,905.

ZIP Codes: 94014, 94102–05, 94107–12, 94114–18, 94121–24, 94127, 94129–34, 94158, 94164

* * *

THIRTEENTH DISTRICT

BARBARA LEE, Democrat, of Oakland, CA; born in El Paso, TX, July 16, 1946; education: graduated, San Fernando High School; B.A., Mills College, 1973; MSW, University of California, Berkeley, 1975; professional: congressional aide and public servant; senior advisor and Chief of Staff to Congressman Ronald V. Dellums in Washington, DC, and Oakland, CA, 1975–87; California State Assembly, 1990–96; California State Senate, 1996–98; Assembly committees: Housing and Land Use; Appropriations; Business and Professions; Industrial Relations; Judiciary; Revenue and Taxation; board member, California State Coastal Conservancy, District Export Council, and California Defense Conversion Council; committees: Appropriations; Budget; elected to the 105th Congress on April 7, 1998, by special election, to fill the remaining term of retiring U.S. Representative Ronald V. Dellums; reelected to each succeeding Congress.

Office Listings

http://lee.house.gov twitter: @repbarbaralee

2267 Rayburn House Office Building, Washington, DC 20515 .... (202) 225–2661
Chief of Staff.—Julie Nickson. FAX: 225–9817
Scheduler.—Christopher Livingston.
Communications Director.—Emma Mehrabi.
Legislative Director.—Diala Jadallah.
1301 Clay Street, Suite 1000–N, Oakland, CA 94612 .... (510) 763–0370

Counties: ALAMEDA COUNTY. CITIES: Alameda, Albany, Berkeley, Emeryville, Oakland, Piedmont, and San Leandro. Population (2015), 755,776.

ZIP Codes: 994577–79, 94601–15, 94617–21, 94623–27, 94643, 94649, 94659–62, 94666, 94701–10, 94712, 94720

* * *

FOURTEENTH DISTRICT

JACKIE SPEIER, Democrat, of Hillsborough, CA; born in San Francisco, CA, May 14, 1950; education: B.A., University of California at Davis; J.D., University of California, Hastings College of the Law, 1976; professional: legislative council, Congressman Leo J. Ryan; member, San Mateo County Board of Supervisors; member, California State Assembly; senator, California State Senate; married: Barry Dennis; two children: Jackson Sierra and Stephanie Sierra; committees: Armed Services; Permanent Select Committee on Intelligence; elected, by special election, on April 8, 2008, to fill the vacancy caused by the death of U.S. Representative Thomas P. Lantos; elected to the 111th Congress on November 4, 2008; reelected to each succeeding Congress.

Office Listings

http://speier.house.gov https://www.facebook.com/jackiespeier twitter: @repspeier
https://www.youtube.com/user/jackiespeierCA12 instagram: @jackiespeier

2465 Rayburn House Office Building, Washington, DC 20515 .... (202) 225–3531
Chief of Staff.—Josh Connolly. FAX: 226–4183
Legislative Director.—Miriam Goldstein.
155 Bovet Road, Suite 780, San Mateo, CA 94402 .... (650) 342–0300
District Representative.—Brian Perkins. FAX: 375–8270

Counties: SAN MATEO COUNTY (part). CITIES: Belmont, Brisbane, Burlingame, Colma, Daly City, East Palo Alto, Foster City, Half Moon Bay, Hillsborough, Menlo Park, Millbrae, Montara, Moss Beach, Pacifica, Redwood City, San Bruno,

San Carlos, San Gregorio, San Mateo, South San Francisco, and Woodside. SAN FRANCISCO COUNTY (part). CITIES: San Francisco. Population (2012), 726,958.

ZIP Codes: 94002, 94005, 94010–11, 94013–15, 94019, 94025, 94030, 94038, 94044, 94061–66, 94070, 94074, 94080, 94083, 94099, 94112, 94116–17, 94127–28, 94131–32, 94134, 94143, 94303, 94401–04, 94497

* * *

FIFTEENTH DISTRICT

ERIC SWALWELL, Democrat, of Dublin, CA; born in Sac City, IA, November 16, 1980; education: graduated, Dublin High School, Dublin, CA, 1999; B.A., University of Maryland, College Park, College Park, MD, 2003; J.D., University of Maryland School of Law, Baltimore, MD, 2006; professional: former city councilman at City of Dublin City Council; former Deputy District Attorney at Alameda County District Attorney's Office; Planning Commissioner at City of Dublin; Heritage & Cultural Arts Commissioner at City of Dublin; law clerk at Alameda County District Attorney's Office; commission: Tom Lantos Human Rights; caucuses: Ad Hoc Congressional Committee for Irish Affairs; Congressional Anti-Bullying Caucus; Congressional Asian Pacific American Caucus; Congressional Caucus on India and Indian Americans; Congressional Cyber Security Caucus; Congressional Diabetes Caucus; Congressional Dyslexia Caucus; Congressional Friends of Ireland Caucus; Congressional High Tech Caucus; Congressional Internet Caucus; Congressional LGBT Equality Caucus; Congressional PORTS Caucus; Congressional Pro-Choice Caucus; Congressional Soccer Caucus; Congressional Victims' Rights Caucus; Congressional Wine Caucus; Democratic Whip's Task Force on Poverty and Opportunity; House Science and National Labs Caucus; International Religious Freedom Caucus; committees: Judiciary; Permanent Select Committee on Intelligence; elected to the 113th Congress on November 6, 2012; reelected to each succeeding Congress.

Office Listings

http://www.swalwell.house.gov twitter: @repswalwell

129 Cannon House Office Building, Washington, DC 20515 .... (202) 225–5065
Chief of Staff.—Ricky Le. FAX: 226–3805
3615 Castro Valley Boulevard, Castro Valley, CA 94546 .... (510) 370–3322

Counties: ALAMEDA COUNTY (part) AND CONTRA COSTA (part). CITIES AND TOWNSHIPS: Ashland, Castro Valley, Danville (part), Dublin, Fairview, Fremont (part), Hayward, Pleasanton, San Leandro (part), San Lorenzo, San Ramon, Sunol, and Union City. Population (2010), 732,515.

ZIP Codes: 94505–06, 94514, 94526, 94536, 94538–39, 94541–42, 94544–46, 94550–52, 94555, 94566, 94568, 94577–78

* * *

SIXTEENTH DISTRICT

JIM COSTA, Democrat, of Fresno, CA; born in Fresno, April 13, 1952; education: B.A., California State University, Fresno, 1974; professional: special assistant, Congressman John Krebs, 1975–76; administrative assistant, California Assemblyman Richard Lehman, 1976–78; California State Assembly, 1978–94; California State Senate, 1994–2002; Chief Executive Officer, Costa Group, 2002–03; religion: Catholic; committees: Agriculture; Natural Resources; elected to the 109th Congress on November 2, 2004; reelected to each succeeding Congress.

Office Listings

http://www.costa.house.gov https://twitter.com/repjimcosta
https://www.facebook.com/repjimcosta https://www.youtube.com/user/repjimcostaca20

2081 Rayburn House Office Building, Washington, DC 20515 .... (202) 225–3341
Chief of Staff.—Juan Lopez. FAX: 225–9308
Legislative Director.—Scott Petersen.
Communications Director.—Kristina Solberg (CA).
Schedulers: Christy Bourdon (CA), Claudia Santiago (DC).
District Director.—Gary Chahil.
855 M Street, Suite 940, Fresno, CA 93721 .... (559) 495–1620
2222 M Street, Suite 305, Merced, CA 95340 .... (209) 384–1620

Counties: FRESNO (part), MADERA (part), and MERCED. Population (2011), 714,214.

ZIP Codes: 93606, 93610 (part), 93620 (part), 93622 (part), 93626 (part), 93630 (part), 93635, 93636 (part), 93637, 93638 (part), 93639, 93661, 93665, 93701–03, 93704–06 (part), 93707–09, 93711 (part), 93712, 93714–18, 93721, 93722–23 (part), 93724, 93725–27 (part), 93728, 92741, 93744–45, 93747, 93750, 93755, 93760–61, 93764, 93771–79, 93786, 93790–94, 93844, 93888, 95301, 95303, 95312, 95315, 95316 (part), 95317, 95322 (part), 95324, 95333–34, 95340–41, 95343–44, 95348, 95356, 95360 (part), 95369 (part), 95374, 95380 (part), 95388

* * *

SEVENTEENTH DISTRICT

RO KHANNA, Democrat, of Fremont, CA; born in Philadelphia, PA, September 13, 1976; education: B.A., economics, University of Chicago, 1998; J.D., Yale Law, 2001; professional: taught economics at Stanford University, law at Santa Clara University, and American Jurisprudence at San Francisco State University; author, *Entrepreneurial Nation: Why Manufacturing is Still Key to America's Future*; lawyer, specializing in intellectual property law; Deputy Assistant Secretary at the U.S. Department of Commerce, 2009–11; appointed by California Governor Jerry Brown in 2012 to the California Workforce Investment Board; religion: Hindu; married: Ritu Ahuja Kanna; caucuses: vice chair, Progressive Caucus; committees: Armed Services; Budget; elected to the 115th Congress on November 8, 2016.

Office Listings

http://khanna.house.gov twitter: @RepRoKhanna

513 Cannon House Office Building, Washington, DC 20515–0517 .... (202) 225–2631
Chief of Staff.—Pete Spiro. FAX: 225–2699
Legislative Director.—Chris Schloesser.
Communications Director.—Liz Bartolomeo.
900 Lafayette Street, Suite 206, Santa Clara, CA 95050 .... (408) 436–2720
District Director.—Christopher Moylan. FAX: 436–2721

Counties: ALAMEDA (part), SANTA CLARA (part). CITIES AND TOWNSHIPS: Cupertino, Fremont, Milpitas, Newark, North San Jose, Santa Clara, and Sunnyvale. Population (2014), 724,244.

ZIP Codes: 94024, 94040, 94043, 94085–89, 94536, 94538–39, 94555, 94560, 95002, 95014–15, 95035–36, 95050–56, 95070, 95101, 95110, 95112, 95116–17, 95126–29, 95131–34, 95140

* * *

EIGHTEENTH DISTRICT

ANNA G. ESHOO, Democrat, of Menlo Park, CA; born in New Britain, CT, December 13, 1942; education: A.A., Cañada College, Redwood City, CA, 1975; professional: chairwoman, San Mateo County Democratic Party, 1978–82; chief of staff to Speaker of the California State Assembly, 1981–82; member of the Democratic National Commission on Presidential Nominations, 1982; member of the San Mateo County, California Board of Supervisors, 1983–92, president, 1986; committees: Energy and Commerce; elected on November 3, 1992, to the 103rd Congress; reelected to each succeeding Congresses.

Office Listings

http://www.eshoo.house.gov

241 Cannon House Office Building, Washington, DC 20515 .... (202) 225–8104
Executive Assistant / Scheduler.—Anna Perry. FAX: 225–8890
Legislative Director.—Matthew McMurray.
Press Secretary.—Emma Crisci.
698 Emerson Street, Palo Alto, CA 94301 .... (650) 323–2984
District Chief of Staff.—Karen Chapman.

Counties: SANTA CLARA, SANTA CRUZ, AND SAN MATEO. CITIES AND TOWNSHIPS: Atherton, Ben Lomond, Boony Doon, Boulder Creek, Brookdale, Campbell, Cambrian Park, Davenport, Felton, Fruitdale, La Honda, Ladera, Lexington Hills, Loma Mar, Lompico, Los Altos, Los Altos Hills, Los Gatos, Menlo Park, Monte Sereno, Mountain View, Palo Alto, Pescadero, Portola Valley, Redwood City, San Jose, Saratoga, Scotts Valley, Stanford, Woodside, and Zayante. Population (2010), 702,906.

ZIP Codes: 94020–28, 94035, 94039–43, 94060–63, 94074, 94301–06, 94309, 95005–09, 95011, 95014, 95017–18, 95026, 95030–33, 95041–42, 95044, 95050, 95060, 95065–67, 95070–71, 95073, 95076, 95117–18, 95120, 95123–26, 95128–30, 95141, 95154, 95157–58, 95160, 95170

* * *

NINETEENTH DISTRICT

ZOE LOFGREN, Democrat, of San Jose, CA; born in San Mateo, CA, December 21, 1947; education: graduated, Gunn High School, 1966; B.A., Stanford University, Stanford, CA, 1970; J.D., Santa Clara Law School, Santa Clara, CA, 1975; professional: admitted to the California Bar, 1975; District of Columbia Bar, 1981; Supreme Court, 1986; member: board of trustees, San Jose Evergreen Community College District, 1979–81; board of supervisors, Santa Clara County, CA, 1981–94; married: John Marshall Collins, 1978; children: Sheila and John; committees: House Administration; Joint Committee on the Library; Judiciary; Science, Space, and Technology; elected to the 104th Congress; reelected to each succeeding Congress.

Office Listings

http://www.lofgren.house.gov twitter: @repzoelofgren

1401 Longworth House Office Building, Washington, DC 20515 .... (202) 225–3072
Chief of Staff.—Stacey Leavandosky. FAX: 225–3336
Communications Director.—Peter Whippey.
Executive Assistant / Scheduler.—Andrew DeLuca.
635 North First Street, Suite B, San Jose, CA 95112 .... (408) 271–8700
District Chief of Staff.—Sandra Soto.

Counties: SANTA CLARA (part). CITIES AND TOWNSHIPS: San Jose, San Martin, Gilroy, and unincorporated portions of southern Santa Clara County. Population (2010), 702,904.

ZIP Codes: 94550, 95013, 95020, 95023, 95033, 95035, 95037–38, 95046, 95050, 95076, 95103, 95106, 95108–13, 95115–16, 95118–28, 95132–33, 95135–36, 95138–41, 95148, 95150–53, 95155–56, 95159, 95172–73, 95191–92, 95196

* * *

TWENTIETH DISTRICT

JIMMY PANETTA, Democrat, of Carmel Valley, CA; born in Washington, DC, October 1, 1969; education: bachelor's in international relations, University of California at Davis, Davis, CA, 1991; law degree, Santa Clara University, Santa Clara, CA, 1996; professional: Deputy District Attorney for Monterey County; U.S. Navy Reserve for 8 years; deployed to Afghanistan in support of Operation Enduring Freedom; medals: awarded Bronze Star for Meritorious Service, Joint Meritorious Unit Award Ribbon, Meritorious Unit Commendation Ribbon, National Defense Service Medal, Afghanistan Campaign Medal, Global War on Terrorism Expeditionary Medal, Global War on Terrorism Service Medal, Navy Armed Services Reserve Deployment Medal, Navy Expert Rifle Military Medal, Navy Expert Pistol Military Medal; religion: Catholic; married: Carrie McIntyre Panetta; two daughters; Siri and Gia; committees: Agriculture; Armed Services; elected to the 115th Congress on November 8, 2016.

Office Listings

http://panetta.house.gov

228 Cannon House Office Building, Washington, DC 20515 .... (202) 225–2861
Chief of Staff.—Tom Tucker.
Legislative Director.—Debbie Merrill.
Press Secretary.—Sarah Davey.
701 Ocean Avenue, Santa Cruz, CA 95060 .... (831) 429–1976
100 West Alisal Street, Salinas, CA 93901 .... (831) 424–2229

Counties: MONTEREY, SAN BENITO, SANTA CRUZ (southern half), AND SANTA CLARA (southern portion). Population (2010), 744,350.

ZIP Codes: 93426, 93450–51, 93901–02, 93905–08, 93912, 93915, 93920–28, 93930, 93932–33, 93940, 93942–44, 93950, 93953–55, 93960, 93962, 95001, 95003–04, 95010, 95012, 95019, 95020–21, 95023–24, 95039, 95043, 95045, 95060–65, 95073, 95075–77

* * *

TWENTY-FIRST DISTRICT

DAVID VALADAO, Republican, of Hanford, CA; born in Hanford, April 14, 1977; education: graduated from Hanford High School; attended College of the Sequoias in Visalia, CA.

professional: dairy farmer; leadership: member, California Milk Advisory Board, Western States Dairy Trade Association; elected as Regional Leadership Council Chairman for Land O' Lakes Inc., a Fortune 200 company; member of the California State Assembly, 2010–12; religion: Catholic; married: Terra Valadao; three children, Connor, Madeline, and Lucas; committees: Appropriations; elected to the 113th Congress on November 6, 2012; reelected to each succeeding Congress.

Office Listings

http://www.valadao.house.gov https://www.facebook.com/congressmandavidvaladao
https://twitter.com/repdavidvaladao

1004 Longworth House Office Building, Washington, DC 20515 .... (202) 225–4695
Chief of Staff.—Cole Rojewski. FAX: 225–3196
Scheduler.—Allison Rosa.
Legislative Director.—Kristina Dunklin.
101 Irwin Street, Suite 110B, Hanford, CA 93230 .... (559) 582–5526
District Director.—Justin Mendes.
2700 M Street, Suite 250B, Bakersfield, CA 93301 .... (661) 864–7736

Counties: KERN (part), KINGS, FRESNO (part), AND TULARE (part). Population (2010), 714,164.

ZIP Codes: 93201–04, 93206, 93210, 93212, 93215, 93218–19, 93227, 93230, 93234, 93237, 93239, 93241–43, 93245, 93249–51, 93256–57, 93261, 93263, 93266, 93270, 93272, 93274–75, 93278–80, 93290–91, 93304–07, 93311–12, 93314, 93607–09, 93616, 93620, 93622, 93624–25, 93627, 93631, 93640, 93648, 93652, 93654, 93656–57, 93660, 93662, 93668, 93706, 93723, 93725

* * *

TWENTY-SECOND DISTRICT

DEVIN NUNES, Republican, of Tulare, CA; born in Tulare County, CA, October 1, 1973; education: A.A., College of the Sequoias; B.S., agricultural business, and a master's degree in agriculture, from California Polytechnic State University, San Luis Obispo; graduate, California Agriculture Leadership Fellowship Program; professional: farmer and businessman; elected, College of the Sequoias Board of Trustees, 1996, reelected, 2000; appointed by President George W. Bush to serve as California State Director of the U.S. Department of Agriculture Rural Development Office, 2001; religion: Catholic; married: the former Elizabeth Tamariz, 2003; three children; committees: chair, Permanent Select Committee on Intelligence; Ways and Means; Joint Committee on Taxation; elected to the 108th Congress on November 5, 2002; reelected to each succeeding Congress.

Office Listings

http://www.nunes.house.gov

1013 Longworth House Office Building, Washington, DC 20515 .... (202) 225–2523
Chief of Staff.—Anthony Ratekin. FAX: 225–3404
Deputy Chief of Staff.—Caitlin Shannon.
Legislative Director.—Jilian Plank.
Communications Director.—Jack Langer.
Scheduler.—Jennifer Morrow.
113 North Church Street, Suite 208, Visalia, CA 93291 .... (559) 733–3861
264 Clovis Avenue, Suite 206, Clovis, CA 93612 .... (559) 323–5235

Counties: TULARE AND FRESNO (part). Population (2010), 702,904.

ZIP Codes: 93201, 93207–08, 93212, 93215, 93218–19, 93221, 93223, 93227, 93235, 93237, 93242, 93244, 93247, 93256–58, 93260–62, 93265, 93267, 93270–72, 93274–75, 93277–79, 93286, 93290–92, 93602–03, 93605, 93609, 93611–13, 93615–16, 93618, 93621, 93625–26, 93628, 93631, 93633–34, 93641–42, 93646–49, 93651, 93654, 93656–57, 93662, 93664, 93666–67, 93670, 93673, 93675, 93703, 93710, 93720, 93726–27, 93740, 93747

* * *

TWENTY-THIRD DISTRICT

KEVIN MCCARTHY, Republican, of Bakersfield, CA; born in Bakersfield, January 26, 1965; education: graduated, Bakersfield High School, 1983; B.S., business administration, CSU-Bakersfield, 1989; M.B.A., CSU-Bakersfield, 1994; professional: intern, worked up to District Director for U.S. Congressman Bill Thomas, 1987–2002; served as Trustee, Kern Community

College District, 2000–02; served in the California State Assembly, 2002–06; elected, California Assembly Republican Leader, 2003–06; married to the former Judy Wages, 1992; two children: Connor and Meghan; elected, House Majority Whip, 2011–14; elected, House Majority Leader, 2014–present; committees: Financial Services (on leave); elected to the 110th Congress on November 7, 2006; reelected to each succeeding Congress.

Office Listings

http://www.kevinmccarthy.house.gov twitter: @GOPleader

2421 Rayburn House Office Building, Washington, DC 20515 .... (202) 225–2915
Chief of Staff.—James Min. FAX: 225–2908
Scheduler.—Alexandra Gourdikian.
Legislative Director.—Kyle Lombardi.
Senior Legislative Assistant.—George Caram.
Press Secretary.—Matt Sparks.
4100 Empire Drive, Suite 150, Bakersfield, CA 93309 .... (661) 327–3611
District Administrator.—Robin Lake Foster.
District Scheduler.—Christiana Duncan.

Counties: KERN COUNTY (part). CITIES AND TOWNSHIPS: Arvin, Bakersfield, Bodfish, Boron, Caliente, California City, Cantil, China Lake, Edison, Edwards, Fellows, Frazier Park, Glennville, Havilah, Inyokern, Keene, Kernville, Lake Isabella, Lebec, Maricopa, McKittrick, MojAvenue, Monolith, North Edwards, Onyx, Randsburg, Ridgecrest, Rosamond, Taft, Tehachapi, Tupman, Weldon, Willow Springs, Wofford Heights, and Woody. TULARE COUNTY (part). CITIES AND TOWNSHIPS: Badger, California Hot Springs, Exeter, Lemon Cove, Lindsay, Orosi, Porterville, Posey, Springville, Strathmore, Terra Bella, Three Rivers, Visalia, and Woodlake. LOS ANGELES COUNTY (part). CITIES AND TOWNSHIPS: Lancaster. Population (2012), 707,345.

ZIP Codes: 93203, 93205, 93207–08, 93221–22, 93224–26, 93238, 93240, 93243–44, 93247, 93251–52, 93255, 93257, 93260, 93262, 93265, 93267–68, 93270–71, 93276, 93283, 93285–87, 93292, 93301, 93304–07, 93309, 93311–14, 93501, 93505, 93516, 93518–19, 93523, 93527–28, 93531, 93534, 93536, 93554–55, 93560–61, 93603, 93633, 93647

* * *

TWENTY-FOURTH DISTRICT

SALUD O. CARBAJAL, Democrat, of Santa Barbara, CA; born in Moroleón, Mexico, November 11, 1956; education: B.A., Iberian studies, University of California, Santa Barbara, 1990; military: U.S. Marine Corps Reserve veteran; religion: Catholic; wife: Gina Carbajal; children: Natasha and Michael; caucuses: Congressional Hispanic Caucus; New Democratic Coalition; committees: Armed Services; Budget; elected to the 115th Congress on November 8, 2016.

Office Listings

http://www.carbajal.house.gov

212 Cannon House Office Building, Washington, DC 20515 .... (202) 225–3601
Chief of Staff.—Jeremy Tittle.
Executive Assistant.—Erin Sandlin.
Legislative Director.—Nancy Juarez.
Communications Director.—Tess Whittlesey.
1411 Marsh Street, Suite 205, San Luis Obispo, CA 93401 .... (805) 546–8348
District Representatives: Whitney Gordon, Greg Haas, Erica Reyes.
360 South Hope Avenue, Suite C–301, Santa Barbara, CA 93101 .... (805) 730–1710
District Director.—Christopher Henson.
District Representatives: Elijah Ettenger, Blanca Figueroa, Wendy Motta.

Counties: SAN LUIS OBISPO COUNTY (all). CITIES AND TOWNSHIPS: Atascadero, Arroyo Grande, Baywood-Los Osos, Cambria, Cayucos, Grover Beach, Morro Bay, Nipomo, Oceano, Paso Robles, Pismo Beach, and San Luis Obispo. SANTA BARBARA COUNTY (all). CITIES AND TOWNSHIPS: Carpinteria, Goleta, Guadalupe, Isla Vista, Mission Canyon, Montecito, Santa Barbara, Santa Maria, Summerland, and Toro Canyon. VENTURA COUNTY (part). CITIES AND TOWNSHIPS: Ventura. Population (2010), 708,744.

ZIP Codes: 93001, 93013–14, 93067, 93101–21, 93130, 93140, 93150, 93160, 93190, 93199, 93254, 93401–12, 93420–24, 93427–30, 93432–37, 93440–49, 93451–58, 93460–61, 93463–65, 93475, 93483, 94338

* * *

TWENTY-FIFTH DISTRICT

STEVE KNIGHT, Republican, of Palmdale, CA; born at Edwards AFB, CA, December 17, 1966; professional: veteran, U.S. Army; married: Lily; children: Christopher and Michael; caucuses: Bipartisan Task Force to Combat the Heroin Epidemic; Congressional Caucus on Long Range Strike; Congressional Lupus Caucus; Congressional Military Family Caucus; Congressional Range and Testing Center; Congressional Recreational Vehicle Caucus; House Aerospace Caucus; Law Enforcement Caucus; Military Youth Programs Congressional Caucus; committees: Armed Services; Science, Space and Technology; Small Business; elected to the 114th Congress on November 4, 2014; reelected to the 115th Congress on November 8, 2016.

Office Listings

https://knight.house.gov twitter: @steveknight25

1023 Longworth House Office Building, Washington, DC 20515 .... (202) 225–1956
Chief of Staff.—Jeanette Whitener. FAX: 226–0683
Scheduler.—Andrea Grace.
District Director.—Lisa Moulton.
1008 West Avenue, M–14, Suite E, Palmdale, CA 93551 .... (661) 441–0320
1445 East Los Angeles Avenue, #206, Simi Valley, CA 93065 .... (805) 581–7130
26415 Carl Boyer Drive, Suite 220, Santa Clarita, CA 91350 .... (661) 255–5630

Counties: NORTHERN LOS ANGELES (part) AND VENTURA (part). CITIES: Lancaster, and Northern San Fernando Valley (part), Palmdale, Santa Clarita, and Simi Valley. Population (2010), 702,904.

ZIP Codes: 91304, 91311, 91321, 91326, 91344, 91350–51, 91354–55, 91381, 91384, 91387, 91390, 93063, 93065 93243, 93510, 93532, 93534–36, 93543–44, 93550–53, 93563, 93591

* * *

TWENTY-SIXTH DISTRICT

JULIA BROWNLEY, Democrat, of Westlake Village, CA; born in Aiken, SC, August 28, 1952; education: B.A., Mount Vernon College at George Washington University, 1975; M.B.A., American University, 1979; professional: product manager, Steelcase, 1984–92; sales manager, Pitney Bowes, 1981–84; sales manager, Burroughs Corporation, 1976–81; Santa Monica-Malibu School Board, 1994–2006; California State Assembly, 2007–12; chair of California State Assembly Committee on Education; children: Fred and Hannah; committees: Transportation and Infrastructure; Veterans' Affairs; elected to the 113th Congress on November 6, 2012; reelected in 2014 and 2016.

Office Listings

http://juliabrownley.house.gov

1019 Longworth House Office Building, Washington, DC 20515 .... (202) 225–5811
Chief of Staff.—Lenny Young. FAX: 225–5811
Legislative Director.—Sharon Wagener.
Communications Director.—Darwin Pham.
Scheduler.—Eva Gavrish.
300 East Esplanade Drive, Suite 470, Oxnard, CA 93036 .... (805) 379–1779
District Director.—Carina Armenta. FAX: 379–1799
223 East Thousand Oaks Boulevard, Suite 411, Thousand Oaks, CA 91360 .... (805) 379–1779
FAX: 379–1799

Counties: LOS ANGELES (part) AND VENTURA (part). Population (2010), 702,905.

ZIP Codes: 91320, 91360–62, 91377, 93003–04, 93010, 93012, 93015, 93021–23, 93030, 93033, 93035–36, 93040–41, 93060, 93065–66

* * *

TWENTY-SEVENTH DISTRICT

JUDY M. CHU, Democrat, of Pasadena, CA; born in Los Angeles, CA, July 7, 1953; education: B.A., math, UCLA, Los Angeles, CA, 1974; Ph.D., psychology, California School of Professional Psychology, 1979; professional: Garvey School District Board member, 1985–88; Monterey Park City Council and Mayor, 1988–2001; California State Assembly, 2001–06; California State Board of Equalization, 2006–09; first Chinese American woman elected to Congress; family: married to former Assemblymember Mike Eng in 1978; committees: Small Business; Ways and Means; elected to the 111th Congress on July 14, 2009, by special election, to fill the vacancy caused by the resignation of U.S. Representative Hilda Solis; reelected to each succeeding Congress.

Office Listings

http://www.chu.house.gov https://twitter.com/repjudychu

2423 Rayburn House Office Building, Washington, DC 20515 .... (202) 225–5464
Chief of Staff.—Linda Shim. FAX: 225–5467
Legislative Director.—Sonali Desai.
Congressional Asian Pacific American Caucus (CAPAC) Executive Director.—Krystal Ka'ai.
Congressional Asian Pacific American Caucus (CAPAC) Policy Advisor / Press Assistant.—Alton Wang.
Legislative Assistants: Ellen Hamilton, Dan Sahr.
Legislative Correspondent.—David Silberberg.
Communications Director.—Ben Suarato.
Scheduler.—Joanna Barrett.
Staff Assistant.—Vacant.
527 South Lake Avenue, Suite 106, Pasadena, CA 91101 .... (626) 304–0110
District Director.—Becky Cheng. FAX: 304–0132
Deputy District Director.—Enrique Robles.
Field Representative / Case Workers: Elizabeth Andalon, Anna Iskikian.
District Scheduler.—Lindsay Plake.
Staff Assistant.—Cindy Lee.

Counties: LOS ANGELES COUNTY (part). CITIES: Alhambra, Altadena (unincorporated), Arcadia, Bradbury, Claremont, Glendora, Monterey Park, Monrovia, Pasadena, Rosemead, South Pasadena, San Gabriel, San Marino, Sierra Madre, Temple City, Upland, San Antonio Heights (unincorporated), East Pasadena (unincorporated), and South San Gabriel (unincorporated). Population (2010), 684,496.

ZIP Codes: 91001, 91003, 91006–07, 91010, 91016–17, 91024–25, 91030–31, 91066–77, 91101–10, 91114–18, 91121, 91123–26, 91129, 91131, 91175, 91182, 91184–89, 91191, 91711, 91740–41, 91754–56, 91770–72, 91775–76, 91778, 91780, 91784–86, 91801–04, 91841, 91896, 91899

* * *

TWENTY-EIGHTH DISTRICT

ADAM B. SCHIFF, Democrat, of Burbank, CA; born in Framingham, MA, June 22, 1960; education: B.A., Stanford University, 1982; J.D., Harvard University, 1985; professional: attorney; U.S. Attorney's Office, served as a criminal prosecutor; public service: elected to the California State Senate, 1996; involved in numerous community service activities; family: married: Eve; children: Alexa and Elijah; committees: ranking member, Permanent Select Committee on Intelligence; on leave from Appropriations Committee; elected to the 107th Congress on November 7, 2000; reelected to each succeeding Congress.

Office Listings

http://www.schiff.house.gov twitter: @repadamschiff

2372 Rayburn House Office Building, Washington, DC 20515 .... (202) 225–4176
Chief of Staff.—Jeff Lowenstein. FAX: 225–5828
Communications Director.—Patrick Boland.
Executive Assistant.—Christopher Hoven.
245 East Olive Avenue, Burbank, CA 91502 .... (626) 304–2727
District Director.—Ann Peifer.

Counties: LOS ANGELES (part). CITIES: Burbank, Glendale, La Canada-Flintridge, La Crescenta, Los Angeles, Pasadena, and West Hollywood. Population (2010), 702,904.

ZIP Codes: 90004, 90026–29, 90031, 90036, 90038–39, 90046, 90048, 90068–69, 91011, 91020, 91040, 91042 (part), 91103, 91105, 91201–08, 91214, 91352 (part), 91501–02, 91504–06

* * *

TWENTY-NINTH DISTRICT

ANTONIO CÁRDENAS, Democrat, of San Fernando Valley, CA; born in Pacoima, CA, March 31, 1963; education: B.A., University of California at Santa Barbara, 1986; professional: businessman; public service: California State Assembly, 1996–2002; Los Angeles City Council, 2002–13; religion: Christian; family: married to Norma Sanchez; children: Andres, Alina, Vanessa, and Cristian; committees: Energy and Commerce; elected to the 113th Congress on November 6, 2012; reelected to each succeeding Congress.

Office Listings

http://www.cardenas.house.gov twitter: @repcardenas

1510 Longworth House Office Building, Washington, DC 20515 .... (202) 225–6131
Chief of Staff.—Miguel Franco. FAX: 225–0819
Legislative Director.—Jacqueline Usyk.
Communications Director.—Francesca Amodeo.
9612 Van Nuys Boulevard, Suite 201, Panorama City, CA 91402 .... (818) 221–3718
District Director.—Gabriela Marquez.

Counties: Los Angeles. Population (2010), 680,661.

ZIP Codes: 91040, 91321, 91331, 91340, 91342–45, 91352, 91387, 91401–02, 91405–06, 91411, 91504–05, 91601–02, 91605–07

* * *

THIRTIETH DISTRICT

BRAD SHERMAN, Democrat, of Sherman Oaks, CA; born in Los Angeles, CA, October 24, 1954; education: B.A., *summa cum laude,* UCLA, 1974; J.D., *magna cum laude,* Harvard Law School, 1979; professional: admitted to the California Bar in 1979 and began practice in Los Angeles; attorney, CPA, certified tax law specialist; elected to the California State Board of Equalization, 1990, serving as chairman, 1991–95; committees: Financial Services; Foreign Affairs; elected to the 105th Congress; reelected to each succeeding Congress.

Office Listings

facebook: congessmanbradsherman twitter: @bradsherman

2181 Rayburn House Office Building, Washington, DC 20515 .... (202) 225–5911
Chief of Staff.—Don MacDonald. FAX: 225–5879
5000 Van Nuys Boulevard, Suite 420, Sherman Oaks, CA 91403 .... (818) 501–9200
District Director.—Scott Abrams.

Counties: Los Angeles (part). Population (2013), 744,617.

ZIP Codes: 90046, 90049, 90068, 90077, 90210, 91302–04, 91306–07, 91311, 91316, 91324–26, 91330, 91335, 91342–44, 91356, 91364, 91367, 91371, 91401, 91403, 91406, 91411, 91423, 91436, 91505–06, 91601–02, 91604, 91607–08, 93064

* * *

THIRTY-FIRST DISTRICT

PETE AGUILAR, Democrat, of Redlands, CA; born in Fontana, San Bernardino County, CA, June 19, 1979; education: B.S., University of Redlands, Redlands, CA, 2001; professional: business owner; Interim Director and Deputy Director, Inland Empire Regional Office of the Governor of California, 2001; member of the Redlands, California City Council, 2006–14; Mayor of Redlands, CA, 2010–14; married: Alisha; children: Evan and Palmer; committees: Appropriations; elected to the 114th Congress on November 4, 2014.

Office Listings

https://aguilar.house.gov @reppeteaguilar

1223 Longworth House Office Building, Washington, DC 20515 .... (202) 225–3201
Chief of Staff.—Boris Medzhibovsky. FAX: 226–6962
Legislative Director.—Becky Cornell.
Communications Director.—Sarah Weinstein.
685 East Carnegie Drive, Suite 100, San Bernardino, CA 92408 .... (909) 890–4445
District Director.—Teresa Valdez. FAX: 890–9643

Counties: San Bernardino (part). Cities and Townships: Colton, Fontana, Upland, Grand Terrace, Loma Linda, Rancho Cucamonga, Redlands, Rialto, and San Bernardino. Population (2011) 727,523.

ZIP Codes: 91701, 91730, 91737, 91739, 91786, 92313, 92316, 92324, 92335–36, 92346, 92350, 92354, 92357, 92359, 92373–74, 92376–77, 92399, 92401, 92404–05, 92407–08, 92410–11, 92509

* * *

THIRTY-SECOND DISTRICT

GRACE F. NAPOLITANO, Democrat, of Los Angeles, CA; born in Brownsville, TX, December 4, 1936; education: Brownsville High School, Brownsville, TX; Cerritos College, Norwalk, CA; Texas Southmost College, Brownsville, TX; professional: Transportation Coordinator, Ford Motor Company; elected to Norwalk, California, City Council, 1986; became Mayor of Norwalk, 1989; elected to the California Assembly, 58th District, 1992–98; organizations: Norwalk Lions Club; Veterans of Foreign Wars (auxiliary); American Legion (auxiliary); Soroptimist International; past director, Cerritos College Foundation; director, Community Family Guidance Center; League of United Latin American Citizens; director, Los Angeles County Sanitation District; director, Los Angeles County Vector Control (Southeast District); director, Southeast Los Angeles Private Industry Council; director, Los Angeles County Sheriff's Authority; National Women's Political Caucus; past national board secretary, United States-Mexico Sister Cities Association; caucuses: co-chair, Congressional Mental Health Caucus; Congressional Hispanic Caucus; maiden name: Flores; married: Frank Napolitano; children: Yolanda Louwers (deceased), Fred Musquiz, Edward Musquiz, Michael Musquiz, and Cynthia Dowling; committees: Natural Resources; Transportation and Infrastructure; elected to the 106th Congress; reelected to each succeeding Congress.

Office Listings

http://www.napolitano.house.gov www.facebook.com/repgracenapolitano
https://www.youtube.com/repgracenapolitano https://www.twitter.com/gracenapolitano

1610 Longworth House Office Building, Washington, DC 20515 .... (202) 225–5256
Chief of Staff.—Daniel Chao. FAX: 225–0027
Legislative Director.—Joe Sheehy.
Press Secretary.—Jerry O'Donnell.
Scheduler.—Joseph Ciccone.
4401 Santa Anita Avenue, Suite 201, El Monte, CA 91731 .... (626) 350–0150
District Director.—Perla Hernandez.

Counties: LOS ANGELES (part). Population (2010), 702,905.

ZIP Codes: 91009–10, 91016–17, 91702, 91706, 91714–16, 91722–24, 91731–32, 91734–35, 91744, 91746–47, 91749–50, 91773, 91790–93, 91797

* * *

THIRTY-THIRD DISTRICT

TED LIEU, Democrat, of Torrance, CA; born in Taipei, Taiwan, March 29, 1969; education: B.A., political science, Stanford University, 1991; B.S., computer science, Stanford University, CA, 1991; J.D., Georgetown University Law Center, 1994; professional; admitted to the California State Bar, 1994; U.S. Air Force, 1995–1999; United States Air War College, 2012; U.S. Air Force Reserve, 2000–present; Air Force Humanitarian Service Medal; Air Force Commendation Medal; Air Force Meritorious Service Medal; Torrance City Council member, 2002–05; California State Assemblyman, 2005–10; California State Senator, 2011–14; married to Betty Chim; children: Brennan and Austin; elected as president of the Democratic Freshman Class, 2015–16; committees: Foreign Affairs; Judiciary; elected to the 114th Congress on November 4, 2014; reelected to the 115th Congress on November 8, 2016.

Office Listings

https://lieu.house.gov facebook: rep.tedlieu twitter: @reptedlieu

236 Cannon House Office Building, Washington, DC 20515 .... (202) 225–3976
Chief of Staff.—Marc Cevasco.
5055 Wilshire Boulevard, Suite 310, Los Angeles, CA 90036 .... (323) 651–1040
1600 Rosecrans Avenue, 4th Floor, Manhattan Beach, CA 90266 .... (310) 321–7664
District Director.—Nicolas Rodriquez.

Counties: LOS ANGELES COUNTY (part). CITIES AND TOWNSHIPS: Agoura Hills, Bel-Air, Beverly Hills, Brentwood, Calabasas, El Segundo, Hermosa Beach, Malibu, Manhattan Beach, Marina Del Rey, Pacific Palisades, Palos Verdes Estates, Rancho Palos Verdes, Redondo Beach, Rolling Hills, Rolling Hills Estates, Santa Monica, Topanga, Venice, and Vista Del Mar. The 33rd Congressional District also includes a portion of the communities of Hancock Park, Harbor City, San Pedro, Torrance, West Los Angeles, and Westwood. Population (2010), 707,854.

ZIP Codes: 90004 (part), 90020 (part), 90024 (part), 90036, 90048–49, 90073, 90077, 90095, 90209, 90211–13, 90245, 90254, 90263–67, 90272, 90274–75, 90277–78, 90290–95, 90401–08 (part), 90409–11, 90503 (part), 90505 (part), 90710 (part), 90731–32 (part), 90744 (part), 91301–02, 91376

* * *

THIRTY-FOURTH DISTRICT

JIMMY GOMEZ, Democrat, of Los Angeles, CA; born in Fullerton, CA, November 25, 1974; education: graduated, Ramona High School, Riverside, 1993; attended Riverside Community College, 1993–96; B.A., University of California Los Angeles, 1999; M.P.P., Harvard John F. Kennedy School of Government, Cambridge, MA, 2003; professional: Assemblyman, California State Legislature, Sacramento, CA, 2012–17; political director, United Nurses Association of California, Los Angeles, CA, 2009–12; political representative, American Federation of State, County and Municipal Employees, Los Angeles, 2006–09; field operations assistant, National League of Cities, Washington, DC, 2005–06; married to Mary Hodge; caucuses: Congressional Asian Pacific American Caucus; Congressional Hispanic Caucus; Congressional LGBT Equality Caucus; Congressional Progressive Caucus; Future Forum; committees: Natural Resources; Oversight and Government Reform; elected to the 115th Congress on June 6, 2017.

Office Listings

https://gomez.house.gov http://www.facebook.com/RepJimmyGomez @RepJimmyGomez

1226 Longworth House Office Building, Washington, DC 20515 .... (202) 225–6235
Chief of Staff.—Bertha Alisia Guerrero.
Legislative Director.—Andrew Noh.
Staff Assistant.—S. Ali Zaid.
350 South Bixel Street, #120, Los Angeles, CA 90017 .... (213) 481–1425
District Director.—Marcella Cortez. FAX: 481–1427

Counties: LOS ANGELES COUNTY (part). CITIES: Los Angeles. Population (2010), 698,741.

ZIP Codes: 90004–07, 90010, 90012–15, 90017–23, 90026, 90030–33, 90038, 90041–42, 90053, 90057, 90063, 90065, 90071, 90079, 90086, 90090

* * *

THIRTY-FIFTH DISTRICT

NORMA J. TORRES, Democrat, of Pomona, CA; born in Escuintla, Guatemala; education: B.A., labor studies, National Labor College, Silver Spring, MD, 2012; professional: 9-1-1 dispatcher; Pomona City Council, 2000–06; Mayor of Pomona, 2006–08; member of the California State Assembly, 2008–13; member of the California State Senate, 2013–14; married: Louis; children: Robert, Matthew, and Christopher; one grandchild; caucuses: chair, Central America Caucus; chair, New American Caucus; Ahmadiyya Caucus; Animal Protection Caucus; Arthritis Caucus; Cancer Prevention Caucus; Caucus for Effective Foreign Assistance; Congressional Hispanic Caucus; Congressional Human Trafficking Caucus; Congressional Law Enforcement Caucus; Congressional Native American Caucus; Diabetes Caucus; Former Mayor's Caucus; Foster Youth Caucus; Hospitality Caucus; Job Corps Caucus; Manufacturing Caucus; NextGen 9-1-1 Caucus; PORTS Caucus; Primary Care Caucus; Gun Violence Prevention Task Force; Poverty Income Inequality, and Opportunity Task Force; Tom Lantos Human Rights Commission; committees: Foreign Affairs; Rules; elected to the 114th Congress on November 4, 2014; reelected to the 115th Congress.

Office Listings

https://torres.house.gov twitter: @normajtorres https://www.facebook.com/repnormatorres

1713 Longworth House Office Building, Washington, DC 20515 .... (202) 225–6161
Chief of Staff.—Dara Postar Cohen. FAX: 225–8671
Legislative Director.—Justin Vogt.
Legislative Assistants: Clay Boggs, Rudy Soto.
Legislative Aide.—John Christie.
Communications Director.—Anna Gonzalez.
Executive Assistant/Scheduler.—Bambi Yingst.
Staff Assistant.—Edgar D. Rodriguez.
3200 Inland Empire Boulevard, Suite 200B, Ontario, CA 91764 .... (909) 481–6474
District Director.—Marc Hanson. FAX: 941–1362

Counties: SAN BERNARDINO COUNTY (part). CITIES: Bloomington, Chino, Fontana, Montclair, Ontario, and Rialto. LOS ANGELES COUNTY (part). CITIES: Pomona. Population (2015), 739,819.

ZIP Codes: 91708–11, 91730, 91739, 91743, 91750, 91752, 91758, 91761–69, 91786, 91789, 92316, 92324, 92331, 92334–37, 92509, 92880

* * *

THIRTY-SIXTH DISTRICT

RAUL RUIZ, M.D., Democrat, of Palm Springs, CA; born in Coachella, CA, August 25, 1972; education: B.S., University of California, Los Angeles, 1994; M.D., Harvard University, 2001; M.P.P., Harvard University, 2001; M.P.H., Harvard University, 2007; professional: emergency physician, Eisenhower Medical Center; founder, Coachella Valley Healthcare Initiative, 2010; senior associate dean, School of Medicine at University of California Riverside, 2011; caucuses: Friends of Canada Caucus; Government Efficiency Caucus; Law Enforcement Caucus; LGBT Caucus; Native American Caucus; No Labels-Problem Solvers; Renewable Energy Caucus; Seniors Task Force; Small Business Caucus; Specialty Crop Caucus; Veterans Job Caucus; committees: Energy and Commerce; elected to the 113th Congress on November 6, 2012; reelected to each succeeding Congress.

Office Listings

http://ruiz.house.gov

1319 Longworth House Office Building, Washington, DC 20515 .... (202) 225–5330
Chief of Staff.—Reed Adamson. FAX: 225–1238
Legislative Director.—Erin Doty.
Press Secretary.—Alex MacFarlane.
Scheduler.—Laura Heasley.
43875 Washington Street, Suite F, Palm Desert, CA 92211 .... (760) 424–8888
District Director.—Geno Sexton.

Counties: RIVERSIDE COUNTY. CITIES: Cathedral City, Coachella, Desert Hot Springs, Indian Wells, Indio, Palm Springs, Palm Desert, and Rancho Mirage. Population (2010), 714,975.

ZIP Codes: 92201–03, 92210–11, 92220, 92230, 92234, 92236, 92240–41, 92253–54, 92258, 92260, 92262, 92264, 92270, 92276, 92282, 92539, 92549, 92561, 92583

* * *

THIRTY-SEVENTH DISTRICT

KAREN R. BASS, Democrat, of Los Angeles, CA; born in Los Angeles, October 3, 1953; education: B.S., health sciences, California State University, Dominguez Hills, CA, 1990; Master of Social Work, USC, 2015; P.A., University of Southern California School of Medicine, Los Angeles; professional: elected first Democratic woman Speaker of the California Assembly; founded and served as Executive Director of the non-profit organization Community Coalition, Los Angeles; physician assistant, Los Angeles County General Hospital; religion: Baptist; family: daughter, Emilia Bass-Lechuga, son-in-law, Michael Wright; stepchildren: Scythia, Omar, and Yvette Lechuga; awards: JFK Profile in Courage Award; Congressional Black Caucus Phoenix Award; committees: Foreign Affairs; Judiciary; elected to the 112th Congress on November 2, 2010; reelected to each succeeding Congress.

Office Listings

http://www.bass.house.gov twitter: @repkarenbass

2241 Rayburn House Office Building, Washington, DC 20515 .... (202) 225–7084
Chief of Staff.—Carrie Kohns. FAX: 225–2422
Legislative Director.—Janice Bashford.
Scheduler/Executive Assistant.—Bridget Brenna.
Communications Director.—Zach Seidl.
4929 Wilshire Boulevard, Suite 650, Los Angeles, CA 90010 .... (323) 965–1422
District Director.—Maral Karaccusian.

Counties: LOS ANGELES (part). CITIES: Culver and Los Angeles. COMMUNITIES OF: Ladera Heights and View Park-Windsor Hills. Population (2010), 702,904.

ZIP Codes: 90004–08, 90010–11, 90016, 90018–20, 90022, 90026–29, 90033–39, 90043–45, 90047–48, 90053, 90056–58, 90062–64, 90066, 90068, 90070, 90078, 90083, 90093, 90099, 90103, 90230–33

* * *

THIRTY-EIGHTH DISTRICT

LINDA T. SÁNCHEZ, Democrat, of Lakewood, CA; born in Orange, CA, January 28, 1969; education: B.A., University of California, Berkeley; J.D., UCLA Law School; passed bar exam in 1995; professional: attorney; has practiced in the areas of appellate, civil rights, and employment law; International Brotherhood of Electrical Workers Local 441; National Electrical Contractors Association; Orange County Central Labor Council Executive Secretary, AFL–CIO; religion: Catholic; caucuses: chair, Congressional Hispanic Caucus; National Women's Political Caucus; Women in Leadership; committees: Ways and Means; elected to the 108th Congress on November 5, 2002; reelected to each succeeding Congress.

Office Listings

http://www.lindasanchez.house.gov twitter: @replindasanchez

2329 Rayburn House Office Building, Washington, DC 20515 .... (202) 225–6676
Chief of Staff.—Lea Sulkala. FAX: 226–1012
Legislative Director.—Melissa Kiedrowicz.
Communications Director.—Alex Nguyen.
12440 East Imperial Highway, Suite 140, Norwalk, CA 90650 .... (562) 860–5050
District Director.—Yvette Shahinian.

Counties: LOS ANGELES (part). Population (2010), 715,745.

ZIP Codes: 90601–06, 90623, 90638, 90701, 90703, 90706, 90716, 90712–13, 90715, 90640, 90650, 90660, 90670, 91733

* * *

THIRTY-NINTH DISTRICT

EDWARD R. ROYCE, Republican, of Fullerton, CA; born in Los Angeles, CA, October 12, 1951; education: B.A., California State University, Fullerton, 1977; professional: small business owner; controller; corporate tax manager; California State Senate, 1982–92; member: Fullerton Chamber of Commerce; board member, Literacy Volunteers of America; board of advisers, California Interscholastic Athletic Foundation; married: Marie Therese Porter, 1985; committees: chair, Foreign Affairs; Financial Services; elected on November 3, 1992, to the 103rd Congress; reelected to each succeeding Congress.

Office Listings

http://www.royce.house.gov twitter: @repedroyce

2310 Rayburn House Office Building, Washington, DC 20515 .... (202) 225–4111
Chief of Staff.—Amy Porter. FAX: 226–0335
Deputy Chief of Staff.—Peter Freeman.
Communications Director.—Steven D. Smith.
Scheduler.—Kate Barlow.
210 West Birch Street, Suite 201, Brea, CA 92821 .... (714) 255–0101
FAX: 225–0109
1380 South Fullerton Road, Suite 205, Rowland Heights, CA 91748 .... (626) 964–5123
District Director.—Sara Catalan. FAX: 810–3891

Counties: California's 39th District encompasses cities in northern ORANGE COUNTY, eastern LOS ANGELES COUNTY, and southwestern SAN BERNARDINO COUNTY. CITIES: Brea, Buena Park, Chino Hills, Diamond Bar, Fullerton, Hacienda Heights, La Habra, Placentia, Rosemead, Rowland Heights, Walnut, and Yorba Linda. Population (2013), 721,014.

ZIP Codes: 90603, 90620–22, 90624, 90631–33, 90638, 91709–10, 91745–46, 91748–49, 91765–66, 91768, 91788–89, 92801, 92806–07, 92811, 92817, 92821–23, 92831–38, 92865, 92867, 92870–71, 92885–87, 92899

* * *

FORTIETH DISTRICT

LUCILLE ROYBAL-ALLARD, Democrat, of Los Angeles, CA; born in Los Angeles, June 12, 1941; education: B.A., California State University, Los Angeles, 1965; professional: served in the California State Assembly, 1987–92; the first Mexican-American woman elected to Congress on November 3, 1992 to the 103rd Congress; the first woman to serve as the chair of the California Democratic Congressional Delegation in the 105th Congress; in the 106th Congress, she became the first woman to chair the Congressional Hispanic Caucus, and the first Latina in history to be appointed to the House Appropriations Committee; in the 114th Congress, she became the first Latina to serve as Ranking Member of a House Appropriations subcommittee; married: Edward T. Allard III; two children: Lisa Marie and Ricardo; two stepchildren: Angela and Guy Mark; committees: Appropriations; elected to the 103rd Congress; reelected to each succeeding Congress.

Office Listings

http://www.roybal-allard.house.gov https://twitter.com/reproybalallard
https://www.facebook.com/reproybalallard

2083 Rayburn House Office Building, Washington, DC 20515–0534 .... (202) 225–1766
Chief of Staff.—Victor G. Castillo. FAX: 226–0350
Legislative Director.—Joseph Racalto.
Executive Assistant.—Christine C. Ochoa.
500 Citadel Drive, Suite 320, Commerce, CA 90040–1572 .... (323) 721–8790
District Director.—Ana Figueroa. FAX: 721–8789

Counties: LOS ANGELES COUNTY (part). CITIES: Bell Gardens, Bellflower, Bill, Commerce, Cudahy, Downey, East Los Angeles, Florence-Graham, Huntington Park, Maywood, Paramount, South Los Angeles, Vernon, and Walnut Park. Population (2010), 694,514.

ZIP Codes: 90001, 90003, 90007, 90011, 90015, 90021–23, 90037, 90040, 90052, 90058–59, 90063, 90082, 90091, 90201–02, 90239–42, 90255, 90270, 90280, 90640, 90650, 90660, 90706, 90723, 91754

* * *

FORTY-FIRST DISTRICT

MARK TAKANO, Democrat, of Riverside, CA; born in Riverside, December 10, 1960; education: B.A. in government, Harvard College, 1983; M.A. in fine arts, University of California Riverside, 2010; professional: public school teacher; Riverside Community College District Board Trustee; awards: chairman of the Asian Pacific Islander Caucus of the California Democratic Party; charter member of the Association of Latino Community College Trustees; member of the Association of California Asian American Trustees; member of Asian Pacific Americans in Higher Education; recipient of Martin Luther King Visionaries Award; religion: Methodist; committees: Education and the Workforce; Science, Space, and Technology; Veterans' Affairs; elected to the 113th Congress on November 6, 2012; reelected to each succeeding Congress.

Office Listings

http://takano.house.gov http://twitter.com/repmarktakano

1507 Longworth House Office Building, Washington, DC 20515 .... (202) 225–2305
Chief of Staff.—Richard Kirk McPike. FAX: 225–7018
Deputy Chief of Staff/Legislative Director.—Yuri Beckelman.
3403 10th Street, Suite 610, Riverside, CA 92501 .... (951) 222–0203
District Director.—Rafael Elizalde.

Counties: RIVERSIDE (part). CITIES: Jurupa Valley, Moreno Valley, Perris, and Riverside. Population (2010), 797,133.

ZIP Codes: 91572, 92324, 92373, 92501, 92503–09, 92518, 92551, 92553, 92555, 92557, 92570–71, 92880

* * *

FORTY-SECOND DISTRICT

KEN CALVERT, Republican, of Corona, CA; born in Corona, June 8, 1953; education: A.A., Chaffey College, CA, 1973; B.A. in economics, San Diego State University, 1975; professional: congressional aide to Representative Victor V. Veysey, CA; general manager, Jolly Fox Restaurant, Corona, 1975–79; Marcus W. Meairs Co., Corona, 1979–81; president and general manager, Ken Calvert Real Properties, 1981–92; County Youth Chairman, Representative Veysey's District, 1970–72; Corona/Norco Youth Chairman for Nixon, 1968 and 1972; Reagan-Bush campaign worker, 1980; co-chairman, Wilson for Senate Campaign, 1982; chairman, Riverside Republican Party, 1984–88; co-chairman, George Deukmejian election, 1978, 1982, and 1986;

co-chairman, George Bush election, 1988; co-chairman, Pete Wilson Senate elections, 1982 and 1988; co-chairman, Pete Wilson for Governor election, 1990; chairman and charter member, Lincoln Club of Riverside County, 1986–90; past president, Corona Rotary Club; Corona Elks; Navy League of Corona / Norco; Corona Chamber of Commerce; past chairman, Norco Chamber of Commerce; County of Riverside Asset Leasing; past chairman, Corona / Norco Board of Realtors; Monday Morning Group; Corona Group; executive board, Economic Development Partnership; charter member, Corona Community Hospital Corporate 200 Club; Silver Eagles (March AFB Support Group); Corona Airport Advisory Commission; committees: Appropriations; elected on November 3, 1992 to the 103rd Congress; reelected to each succeeding Congress.

Office Listings

http://www.calvert.house.gov twitter: @kencalvert

2205 Rayburn House Office Building, Washington, DC 20515 .... (202) 225–1986
Chief of Staff.—Dave Kennett. FAX: 225–2004
Legislative Director.—Rebecca Keightley.
4160 Temescal Canyon Road, Suite 214, Corona, CA 92883 .... (951) 277–0042
District Director.—Jolyn Murphy.
Press Secretary.—Jason Gagnon.

Counties: RIVERSIDE COUNTY. CITIES AND TOWNSHIPS: Canyon Lake, Corona, Eastvale, Lake Elsinore, Menifee, Murrieta, Norco, a portion of Temecula, and Wildomar. Population (2010), 710,617.

ZIP Codes: 91752, 92028, 92223, 92503–04, 92506–08, 92530–32, 92536, 92544–45, 92548, 92555, 92562–63, 92567, 92570–71, 92582, 92584–87, 92590–92, 92595–96, 92860, 92877–83

* * *

FORTY-THIRD DISTRICT

MAXINE WATERS, Democrat, of Los Angeles, CA; born in St. Louis, MO, August 15, 1938; education: B.A., California State University; honorary degrees: Harris-Stowe State College, St. Louis, MO; Central State University, Wilberforce, OH; Spelman College, Atlanta, GA; North Carolina A&T State University; Howard University; Central State University; Bishop College; and Morgan State University; professional: elected to California State Assembly, 1976; reelected every two years thereafter; member: California State Assembly Democratic Caucus; Board of TransAfrica Foundation, National Women's Political Caucus; chair, Democratic Caucus Special Committee on Election Reform; chair, Ways and Means Subcommittee on State Administration; chair, Joint Committee on Public Pension Fund Investments; founding member, National Commission for Economic Conversion and Disarmament; member of the board, Center for National Policy; Clara Elizabeth Jackson Carter Foundation (Spelman College); Minority AIDS Project; married to Sidney Williams, former U.S. Ambassador to the Commonwealth of the Bahamas; two children: Karen and Edward; committees: ranking member, Financial Services; elected to the 102nd Congress on November 6, 1990; reelected to each succeeding Congress.

Office Listings

http://www.waters.house.gov twitter: @maxinewaters

2221 Rayburn House Office Building, Washington, DC 20515 .... (202) 225–2201
Chief of Staff.—Twaun Samuel. FAX: 225–7854
Legislative Director.—Jason Powell.
10124 South Broadway, Suite 1, Los Angeles, CA 90003 .... (323) 757–8900
District Director.—Blanca Jimenez.

Counties: LOS ANGELES COUNTY (part). CITIES: Gardena, Hawthorne, Inglewood, Lawndale, Lomita, Los Angeles, Playa Del Ray, and Torrance. Population (2010), 702,983.

ZIP Codes: 90007, 90009, 90044–45, 90047, 90052, 90056, 90059, 90061, 90066, 90082, 90094, 90189, 90247–51, 90260–61, 90293, 90301–13, 90397–98, 90504, 90506, 90717

* * *

FORTY-FOURTH DISTRICT

NANETTE DIAZ BARRAGÁN, Democrat, of San Pedro, CA; born in Harbor City, CA, September 15, 1976; education: J.D., University of Southern California, Los Angeles, CA, 2005;

caucuses: Congressional Hispanic Caucus; Congressional Progressive Caucus; committees: Homeland Security; Natural Resources; elected to the 115th Congress on November 8, 2016.

Office Listings

http://www.barragan.house

1320 Longworth House Office Building, Washington, DC 20515 .... (202) 225–8220
Chief of Staff.—Marsha Catron. FAX: 226–7290
Legislative Director.—Javier Gamboa.
Scheduler.—Jonathan Cousimano.
302 West 5th Street, San Pedro, CA 90731 .... (310) 831–1799
8650 California Avenue, South Gate, CA 90280 .... (323) 563–9562
701 East Carson Street, Carson, CA 90745 .... (310) 233–4811

Counties: Los Angeles (part). Cities and Communities: Carson, Compton, Lynwood, North Long Beach, Rancho Dominguez, San Pedro, South Gate, Walnut Park, Watts, Willowbrook, and Wilmington.

ZIP Codes: 90001–05 (part), 90007 (part), 90011 (part), 90015 (part), 90018 (part), 90020–23 (part), 90025–26 (part), 90031 (part), 90037–38 (part), 90058–59 (part), 90061 (part), 90063–64 (part), 90089 (part), 90220, 90221 (part), 90222, 90223 (part), 90230 (part), 90248 (part), 90255 (part), 90262 (part), 90280, 90291–92 (part), 90302 (part), 90405 (part), 90503–05 (part), 90631 (part), 90640 (part), 90706 (part), 90710 (part), 90712 (part), 90717 (part), 90731–32 (part), 90733–34, 90744 (part), 90746–48, 90802 (part), 90805 (part), 90810–11 (part), 90895, 91016 (part), 91030 (part), 91103 (part), 91105 (part), 91124 (part), 91321 (part), 91344 (part), 91505 (part), 91702 (part), 91711 (part), 91724 (part), 91731–32 (part), 91740 (part), 91745 (part), 91754 (part), 91768 (part), 91770 (part), 91773 (part), 91789 (part), 93550–51 (part)

* * *

FORTY-FIFTH DISTRICT

MIMI WALTERS, Republican, of Irvine, CA; born in Pasadena, CA, May 14, 1962; education: B.A., University of California, Los Angeles, CA; professional: member of Laguna Niguel City Council; member of the California State Assembly; member of the California State Senate; married: David; children: two daughters; two sons; committees: Energy and Commerce; Ethics; elected to the 114th Congress on November 4, 2014; reelected to the 115th Congress on November 8, 2016.

Office Listings

https://walters.house.gov facebook: https://www.facebook.com/RepMimiWalters
twitter: @repmimiwalters

215 Cannon House Office Building, Washington, DC 20515 .... (202) 225–5611
Chief of Staff.—Sam Oh. FAX: 225–9177
Deputy Chief of Staff.—Yvette Wissmann.
Office Manager.—Cody Laliberte.
Legislative Director.—Casey Fitzpatrick.
Communications Director.—T.W. Arrighi.
3333 Michelson Drive, Suite 230, Irvine, CA 92612 .... (949) 263–8703

Counties: Orange County (part). Cities: Anaheim Hills, Irvine, Laguna Hills, Lake Forest, Mission Viejo, North Tustin, Rancho Santa Margarita, Tustin, and Villa Park.

ZIP Codes: 92602–04, 92606, 92609–10, 92612, 92614, 92617–18, 92620, 92630, 92637, 92653, 92656, 92676–79, 92688, 92691–92, 92701, 92705, 92780, 92782, 92807–08, 92861, 92865, 92867, 92869, 92887

* * *

FORTY-SIXTH DISTRICT

J. LUIS CORREA, Democrat, of Santa Ana, CA; born in East Los Angeles, CA, January 24, 1958; education: graduate of California State University, Fullerton; J.D. and M.B.A., University of California Los Angeles; religion: member of Christ Cathedral Catholic Church; married: Esther Correa; four children; caucuses: Blue Dog Coalition; Congressional Hispanic Caucus; New Democrat Caucus; committees: Homeland Security; Veterans' Affairs; elected to the 115th Congress on November 8, 2016.

Office Listings

https://correa.house.gov facebook: https://www.facebook.com/RepLouCorrea
twitter: @reploucorrea

1039 Longworth House Office Building, Washington, DC 20515 .... (202) 225–2965
Chief of Staff.—Laurie Saroff. FAX: 225–5859
Scheduler.—Julia Kermott.
Legislative Director.—Alejandro Renteria.
Communications Director.—Andrew Scibetta.
Legislative Correspondent / Staff Assistant.—Valeria Sandoval.
2323 North Broadway, Third Floor, Santa Ana, CA 92706.
District Director.—Vacant.

Counties: ORANGE COUNTY (part). CITIES: Anaheim, Garden Grove, Orange, and Santa Ana. Population (2010), 648,663.

ZIP Codes: 90620–21, 92606, 92614, 92701, 92703–07, 92780, 92801–07, 92840, 92843, 92865–68, 92870

* * *

FORTY-SEVENTH DISTRICT

ALAN S. LOWENTHAL, Democrat, of Long Beach, CA; born in Manhattan, New York County, NY, March 8, 1941; education: Baldwin High School, Baldwin, NY, 1958; B.A., Hobart College, Geneva, NY, 1962; M.A., Ohio State University, Columbus, OH, 1965; Ph.D., Ohio State University, Columbus, OH, 1967; professional: psychology professor, California State University, Long Beach, 1969–98; president, Long Beach Area Citizens Involved 1989–92; member of the Long Beach, Calif., City Council, 1992–98; member of the California State Assembly, 1998–2004; member of the California State Senate, 2004–12; caucuses: chair, Congressional Safe Climate Caucus; chair, Green Schools Caucus; co-chair, Cambodia Caucus; co-chair, Congressional Caucus on Vietnam; co-chair, Ports Caucus; co-chair, STARBASE Caucus; vice-chair, House LGBT Equality Caucus; vice-chair, Sustainable Energy and Environment Coalition; committees: Natural Resources; Transportation and Infrastructure; elected to the 113th Congress on November 6, 2012; reelected to each succeeding Congress.

Office Listings

http://www.lowenthal.house.gov twitter: @replowenthal facebook: replowenthal

125 Cannon House Office Building, Washington, DC 20515 .... (202) 225–7924
Chief of Staff.—Tim Hysom. FAX: 225–7926
Legislative Director.—Rachel Gentile.
Communications Director.—Keith Higginbotham.
Scheduler.—Emily Strombom.
100 West Broadway Street, West Tower, Suite 600, Long Beach, CA 90802 .... (562) 436–3828
District Director.—Mark Pulido.

Counties: LOS ANGELES COUNTY (part). CITIES: Avalon, Lakewood, Long Beach, and Signal Hill. ORANGE COUNTY (part). CITIES: Anaheim, Buena Park, Cypress, Garden Grove, Los Alamitos, Midway City, Rossmoor, Stanton, and Westminster. Population (2013), 719,805.

ZIP Codes: 90620, 90623, 90630, 90680, 90704, 90712–13, 90716, 90720–21, 90731, 90740, 90744, 90755, 90801–10, 90813–15, 90831–35, 90840, 90842, 90844, 90846–48, 90853, 92647, 92655, 92683–85, 92703, 92801–02, 92804, 92840–46

* * *

FORTY-EIGHTH DISTRICT

DANA T. ROHRABACHER, Republican, of Costa Mesa, CA; born in Coronado, CA, June 21, 1947; education: graduated, Palos Verdes High School, CA, 1965; attended Los Angeles Harbor College, Wilmington, CA, 1965–67; B.A., Long Beach State College, CA, 1969; M.A., University of Southern California, Los Angeles, 1975; professional: writer/journalist; speechwriter and special assistant to the President, The White House, Washington, DC, 1981–88; assistant press secretary, Reagan/Bush Committee, 1980; reporter, City News Service/Radio News West, and editorial writer, *Orange County Register,* 1972–80; family: wife and triplets; committees: Foreign Affairs; Science, Space, and Technology; elected on November 8, 1988, to the 101st Congress; reelected to each succeeding Congress.

Office Listings

http://www.rohrabacher.house.gov

2300 Rayburn House Office Building, Washington, DC 20515 .... (202) 225–2415
Chief of Staff.—Rick Dykema.
Legislative Director.—Jeff Vanderslice.
Communications Director.—Ken Grubbs.
Senior Policy Advisor.—Tony DeTora.
Legislative Assistant.—Jessica Roxburgh.
Executive Assistant / Scheduler.—Justin Ahn.
101 Main Street, Suite 380, Huntington Beach, CA 92648 .... (714) 960–6483
District Director.—Kathleen Staunton.

Counties: ORANGE COUNTY (part). COMMUNITIES OF ALISO VIEJO, CORONA DEL MAR, COSTA MESA, FOUNTAIN VALLEY, GARDEN GROVE (part), HUNTINGTON BEACH, LAGUNA BEACH, LAGUNA NIGUEL, MIDWAY CITY (part), NEWPORT BEACH, SANTA ANA (part), SEAL BEACH, SUNSET BEACH, SURFSIDE, AND WESTMINSTER (part). Population (2010), 702,905.

ZIP Codes: 90740, 90742–43, 92625–27, 92646–49, 92651, 92655 (part), 92656–57, 92660–63, 92677, 92683 (part), 92703–04 (part), 92708, 92843–44 (part)

* * *

FORTY-NINTH DISTRICT

DARRELL E. ISSA, Republican, of Vista, CA; born in Cleveland, OH, November 1, 1953; education: Siena Heights College; military service: Captain U.S. Army; attended college on an ROTC scholarship; professional: businessman; founder and CEO of Directed Electronics, Inc.; past chairman, Consumer Electronics Association; previously on the Board of Directors, Electronics Industry Association; public service: co-chairman of the campaign to pass the California Civil Rights Initiative (Proposition 209); chairman of the Volunteer Committee for the 1996 Republican National Convention; chairman of the San Diego County Lincoln Club; candidate for the U.S. Senate in 1998; architect of 2003 California recall campaign of former Governor Gray Davis; married: Kathy; children: William; committees: Foreign Affairs; Judiciary; Oversight and Government Reform; elected to the 107th Congress on November 7, 2000; reelected to each succeeding Congress.

Office Listings

http://issa.house.gov twitter: @darrellissa

2269 Rayburn House Office Building, Washington, DC 20515 .... (202) 225–3906
Chief of Staff.—Veronica Wong. FAX: 225–3303
Legislative Director.—Tyler Grimm.
Communications Director.—Calvin Moore.
Scheduler.—Katie Weiss.
1800 Thibodo Road, Suite 310, Vista, CA 92081 .... (760) 599–5000

Counties: ORANGE (part) AND SAN DIEGO (part). Population (2010), 702,906.

ZIP Codes: 92003, 92007–14, 92018, 92023–24, 92028–29, 92037, 92049, 92051–52, 92054–58, 92067–69, 92075, 92078, 92081, 92083–85, 92091–93, 92121, 92127, 92130, 92624, 92629, 92672–75, 92677, 92688, 92690–94

* * *

FIFTIETH DISTRICT

DUNCAN HUNTER, Republican, of Lakeside, CA; born in San Diego, CA, December 7, 1976; education: graduated, Granite Hills High School; B.S., business administration, San Diego State University, San Diego, CA, 2001; professional: business analyst; military: captain, U.S. Marine Corps, 2002–05; U.S. Marine Corps Reserves, 2005–08; religion: Protestant; married: Margaret; children: Duncan, Elizabeth, and Sarah; committees: Armed Services; Education and the Workforce; Transportation and Infrastructure; elected to the 111th Congress on November 4, 2008; reelected to each succeeding Congress.

Office Listings

http://www.hunter.house.gov https://www.facebook.com/DuncanHunter
https://twitter.com/Rep_Hunter

2429 Rayburn House Office Building, Washington, DC 20515 .... (202) 225–5672

Office Listings—Continued

Chief of Staff / Communications Director.—Joe Kasper. FAX: 225–0235
Legislative Director.—Reed Linsk.
Scheduler / Legislative Assistant.—Kyle Egan.
Military Legislative Assistant.—Cassie Roper.
Legislative Correspondent.—Meghan Badame.
Staff Assistant.—Jonathan Kupperman.
Military Fellow.—Anthony Trevino.
1611 North Magnolia Avenue, Suite 310, El Cajon, CA 92020 .... (619) 448–5201
41000 Main Street, Temecula, CA 92590 .... (951) 216–2111

Counties: SAN DIEGO COUNTY (part). CITIES AND TOWNSHIPS: Alpine, Barona I.R., Borrego Springs, Bonsall, Boulevard, Descanso, El Cajon, Escondido, Fallbrook, Guatay, Jamul, Julian, Lakeside, La Mesa, Mount Laguna, Pala, Palamar Mountain, Pauma Valley, Pine Valley, Potrero, Poway, Ramona, Ranchita, San Marcos, Santa Ysabel, Santee, Spring Valley, Temecula, Valley Center, Vista, and Warner Springs. Population (2010), 724,472.

ZIP Codes: 91901, 91903, 91916, 91931, 91935, 91941, 91948, 91962, 91978, 92003–04, 92019–21, 92025–30, 92033, 92036, 92040, 92046, 92059–61, 92064–66, 92069–72, 92078–79, 92082, 92084, 92086, 92088, 92589–93

* * *

FIFTY-FIRST DISTRICT

JUAN VARGAS, Democrat, of San Diego, CA; born in National City, CA, March 7, 1961; education: B.A., University of San Diego, San Diego, CA, 1983; M.A., Fordham University, New York, NY, 1987; J.D., Harvard University, Cambridge, MA, 1991; professional: lawyer; business executive; member of the San Diego, California, City Council, 1993–2000; member of the California State Assembly, 2000–06; member of the California State Senate, 2010–12; religion: Roman Catholic; spouse: Adrienne Vargas; children: Rosa Celina Vargas and Helena Jeanne Vargas; committees: Financial Services; elected to the 113th Congress on November 6, 2012; reelected to each succeeding Congress.

Office Listings

http://vargas.house.gov https://twitter.com/repjuanvargas

1605 Longworth House Office Building, Washington, DC 20515 .... (202) 225–8045
Chief of Staff.—Tim Walsh. FAX: 225–2772
Scheduler/Executive Assistant.—Christina Reyes.
Legislative Director.—Scott Hinkle.
333 F Street, Suite A, Chula Vista, CA 91910 .... (619) 422–5963
District Director.—Janine Pairis. FAX: 422–7290
380 North 8th Street, Suite 14, El Centro, CA 92243 .... (760) 355–8800
Senior Field Representative.—Tomas Oliva. FAX: 312–9664

Counties: COUNTIES: SAN DIEGO (part), AND IMPERIAL COUNTY. CITIES: Bombay Beach, Bonita, Boulevard, Brawley, Calexico, Calipatria, Campo, Chula Vista, Desert Shores, Dulzura, El Centro, Heber, Holtville, Imperial, Imperial Beach, Jacumba, National City, Niland, Ocotillo, Palo Verde, Potrero, Salton City, Salton City Beach, San Diego, Seeley, Westmorland, and Winterhaven. Population (2010), 702,906.

ZIP Codes: 91901–02, 91905–06, 91909–12, 91915, 91917, 91932–35, 91945, 91950–51, 91962–63, 91980, 91987, 92019, 92101–02, 92104–05, 92113–15, 92136, 92139, 92143, 92153–54, 92158, 92165, 92170, 92173–74, 92179, 92222, 92225, 92227, 92231–33, 92243–44, 92249–51, 92257, 92259, 92266, 92273–74, 92281, 92283

* * *

FIFTY-SECOND DISTRICT

SCOTT PETERS, Democrat, of La Jolla, CA; born in Springfield, OH, June 17, 1958; education: *magna cum laude*, Phi Beta Kappa, Duke University; New York University School of Law; professional: Environmental lawyer; City Council President; San Diego Port Commissioner; religion: Lutheran; wife, Lynn; two children; committees: Energy and Commerce; Veterans' Affairs; elected to the 113th Congress on November 6, 2012; reelected to each succeeding Congress.

Office Listings

http://scottpeters.house.gov twitter: @repscottpeters

1122 Longworth House Office Building, Washington, DC 20515 .... (202) 225–0508

Office Listings—Continued

Chief of Staff.—Michelle Dorothy.
Scheduler.—Baillee Brown.
Legislative Director.—Daniel Zawitoski.
Communications Director.—Jacob Peters.
Digital Media Manager.—Quin LaCapra.
4350 Executive Drive, Suite 105, San Diego, CA 92121 .... (858) 455–5550
District Director.—MaryAnne Pintar.

Counties: SAN DIEGO COUNTY (part). CITIES AND TOWNSHIPS: Carmel Valley, Coronado, Downtown San Diego, La Jolla, Point Loma, and Poway. Population (2010), 704,565.

ZIP Codes: 92025, 92027, 92037, 92064, 92101, 92106–07, 92109–11, 92117–18, 92121–24, 92126–31, 92137, 92140, 92145, 92155

* * *

FIFTY-THIRD DISTRICT

SUSAN A. DAVIS, Democrat, of San Diego, CA; born in Cambridge, MA, April 13, 1944; education: B.S., University of California at Berkeley; M.A., University of North Carolina; public service: served three terms in the California State Assembly; served nine years on the San Diego City School Board; former president of the League of Women Voters of San Diego; awards: California School Boards Association Legislator of the Year; League of Middle Schools Legislator of the Year; family: married to Steve; children: Jeffrey and Benjamin; grandsons: Henry and Theo; granddaughter: Jane; committees: Armed Services; Education and the Workforce; elected to the 107th Congress on November 7, 2000; reelected to each succeeding Congress.

Office Listings

http://www.susandavis.house.gov https://www.facebook.com/RepSusanDavis
https://twitter.com/RepSusanDavis https://www.instagram.com/repsusandavis

1214 Longworth House Office Building, Washington, DC 20515 .... (202) 225–2040
Chief of Staff.—Lisa Sherman. FAX: 225–2948
Press Secretary.—Aaron Hunter.
Scheduler.—Cynthia Patton.
2700 Adams Avenue, Suite 102, San Diego, CA 92116 .... (619) 280–5353
District Director.—Jessica Poole. FAX: 280–5311

Counties: SAN DIEGO COUNTY (part). Population (2010), 639,008.

ZIP Codes: 91902, 91908, 91910–11, 91913–15, 91921, 91941–46, 91976–79, 92019–22, 92101–05, 92108, 92110–11, 92114–16, 92119–20, 92123–24, 92134, 92139, 92149, 92154, 92160, 92163–64, 92168, 92171, 92175–76, 92182, 92190, 92193, 92195

COLORADO

(Population 2010, 5,029,196)

SENATORS

* * *

MICHAEL F. BENNET, Democrat, of Denver, CO; born in New Delhi, India, November 28, 1964; education: B.A., Wesleyan University, 1987; J.D., Yale Law School, 1993; editor-in-chief of the *Yale Law Journal*; professional: Counsel to U.S. Deputy Attorney General, 1995–97; special assistant, U.S. Attorney, CT, 1997; managing director, Anschutz Investment Co., 1997–2003; Chief of Staff to Mayor of Denver, CO, 2003–05; superintendent, Denver Public Schools, 2005–09; married: Susan D. Daggett; children: Caroline, Halina, and Anne; committees: Agriculture, Nutrition, and Forestry; Finance; Health, Education, Labor, and Pensions; appointed January 21, 2009, to the U.S. Senate for the term ending January 3, 2011; elected for a full Senate term on November 2, 2010; reelected to the U.S. Senate on November 8, 2016.

Office Listings

http://bennet.senate.gov https://www.facebook.com/senbennetco
https://twitter.com/SenBennetCO

261 Russell Senate Office Building, Washington, DC 20510–0606 .... (202) 224–5852
Chief of Staff.—Jonathan Davidson.
Legislative Director.—Brian Appel.
Communications Director.—Samantha Slater.
Scheduler.—Kristin Mollet.
1127 Sherman Street, Suite 150, Denver, CO 80203 .... (303) 455–7600
FAX: 455–8851
129 West B Street, Pueblo, CO 81003 .... (719) 542–7550
FAX: 542–7555
609 Main Street, Suite 110, Alamosa, CO 81101 .... (719) 587–0096
FAX: 587–0098
409 North Tejon, Suite 107, Colorado Springs, CO 80903 .... (719) 328–1100
FAX: 328–1129
1200 South College Avenue, Suite 211, Fort Collins, CO 80524 .... (970) 224–2200
FAX: 224–2205
225 North 5th Street, Suite 511, Grand Junction, CO 81501 .... (970) 241–6631
FAX: 241–8313
835 East 2nd Avenue, Suite 206, Durango, CO 81301 .... (970) 259–1710
FAX: 259–9789

* * *

CORY GARDNER, Republican, of Yuma, CO; born in Yuma, August 22, 1974; education: B.A., political science, Colorado State University, Fort Collins, CO, 1997; J.D., University of Colorado, Boulder, CO, 2001; professional: agricultural advocate; staff, U.S. Senator Wayne Allard of Colorado, 2002–05; member of the Colorado State House of Representatives, 2005–10; member of the U.S. House of Representatives, 2011–14; committees: Budget; Commerce, Science, and Transportation; Energy and Natural Resources; Foreign Relations; elected to the U.S. Senate on November 4, 2014.

Office Listings

http://gardner.senate.gov https://facebook.com/sencorygardner
https://twitter.com/sencorygardner

354 Russell Senate Office Building, Washington, DC 20510 .... (202) 224–5941
Chief of Staff.—Natalie Rogers.
Legislative Director.—Curtis Swager.
Communications Director.—Alex Siciliano.
Director of Scheduling.—Amy Barrera.
1125 17th Street, Suite 525, Denver, CO 80202 .... (303) 391–5777
400 Rood Avenue, Suite 220, Grand Junction, CO 81501 .... (970) 245–9553
801 8th Street, Suite 140A, Greeley, CO 80631 .... (970) 352–5546
529 North Albany Street, Suite 1220, Yuma, CO 80759 .... (970) 848–3095
503 North Main Street, Suite 426, Pueblo, CO 81003 .... (719) 543–1324
2001 South Shields Street, Building H, Suite 104, Fort Collins, CO 80526 .... (970) 484–3502
329 South Camino Del Rio, Suite I, Durango, CO 81303 .... (970) 415–7416

REPRESENTATIVES

FIRST DISTRICT

DIANA DEGETTE, Democrat, of Denver, CO; born in Tachikawa, Japan, July 29, 1957; education: B.A., political science, *magna cum laude*, The Colorado College, 1979; J.D., New York University School of Law, 1982 (Root Tilden Scholar); professional: attorney with McDermott, Hansen, and Reilly; Colorado Deputy State Public Defender, Appellate Division, 1982–84; Colorado House of Representatives, 1992–96; board of directors, Planned Parenthood, Rocky Mountain Chapter; member and formerly on board of governors, Colorado Bar Association; member, Colorado Women's Bar Association; past memberships: board of trustees, The Colorado College; Denver Women's Commission; board of directors, Colorado Trial Lawyers Association; former editor, *Trial Talk* magazine; listed in 1994–96 edition of *Who's Who in America*; Chief Deputy Whip; committees: Energy and Commerce; elected to the 105th Congress; reelected to each succeeding Congress.

Office Listings

http://degette.house.gov www.facebook.com/DianaDeGette twitter: @RepDianaDeGette

2111 Rayburn House Office Building, Washington, DC 20515 .... (202) 225–4431
Chief of Staff.—Lisa B. Cohen. FAX: 225–5657
Scheduler.—Diana Gambrel.
Communications Director.—Lynne Weil.
600 Grant Street, Suite 202, Denver, CO 80203 .... (303) 844–4988
District Director.—Tom Kelly.

Counties: ARAPAHOE (part), DENVER, AND JEFFERSON (part). Population (2010), 718,457.

ZIP Codes: 80012, 80014, 80110–11, 80113, 80120–21, 80123, 80127–28, 80202–07, 80209–12, 80214–16, 80218–24, 80226–27, 80230–32, 80235–39, 80246–47, 80249, 80264, 80290, 80293–94

* * *

SECOND DISTRICT

JARED POLIS, Democrat, of Boulder, CO; born in Boulder, May 12, 1975; education: B.A., political science, Princeton University, Princeton, NJ, 1996; professional: Internet entrepreneur; founder of New America Schools; chair, Colorado State Board of Education; House Democratic Steering and Policy Committee; religion: Jewish; committees: Education and the Workforce; Rules; Select Committee on Ethics; elected to the 111th Congress on November 4, 2008; reelected to each succeeding Congress.

Office Listings

http://www.polis.house.gov

1727 Longworth House Office Building, Washington, DC 20515 .... (202) 225–2161
Chief of Staff.—Eve Lieberman.
Legislative Director.—Hilary Gawrilow.
1644 Walnut Street, Boulder, CO 80302 .... (303) 484–9596
Communications Director.—Jessica Bralish.
P.O. Box 1453, Frisco, CO 80443 .... (970) 409–7301
1220 South College Avenue, Fort Collins, CO 80525 .... (970) 226–1239

Counties: BOULDER, BROOMFIELD, CLEAR CREEK, EAGLE (part), GILPIN, GRAND, JEFFERSON (part), LARIMER, PARK (part), AND SUMMIT. Population (2010), 732,658.

ZIP Codes: 80007, 80020–21, 80023, 80025–28, 80135, 80228, 80234, 80301–05, 80310, 80401, 80403, 80419, 80421–25, 80427, 80433, 80435–36, 80438–39, 80442–44, 80446–48, 80451–55, 80457, 80459, 80465–66, 80468, 80470–71, 80475–76, 80478, 80481–82, 80497–98, 80503–04, 80510–13, 80515–17, 80521, 80524–26, 80528, 80532, 80534–38, 80540, 80544–45, 80547, 80549–50, 80612, 81620, 81632, 81645, 81649, 81655, 81657, 82063

* * *

THIRD DISTRICT

SCOTT TIPTON, Republican, of Cortez, CO; born in Espanola, NM, November 9, 1956; education: graduated, B.S., political science, Ft. Lewis College, Durango, CO, 1978; professional: owner/president of Mesa Verde Pottery, Cortez, CO; public service: elected to Colorado House of Representatives, 2008–10; religion: Anglican; married: Jean Tipton; children: Liesl (married to Chris Ross) and Elizabeth (married to Jace Weber); caucuses: chair, Congressional Small Business Caucus; vice chair, Congressional Western Caucus; Congressional Beef Caucus; Congressional Coal Caucus; Congressional Dairy Farmer Caucus; Congressional Natural Gas Caucus; Congressional Sportsmen's Caucus; House Republican Israel Caucus; committees: Financial Services; Natural Resources; elected to the 112th Congress on November 2, 2010; reelected to each succeeding Congress.

Office Listings

http://tipton.house.gov

218 Cannon House Office Building, Washington, DC 20515 .... (202) 225–4761
Chief of Staff.—Joshua Green. FAX: 226–9669
Legislative Director.—Dustin Sherer.
Executive Assistant.—Agustina Andisco.
225 North 5th Street, Suite 702, Grand Junction, CO 81501 .... (970) 241–2499
District Director.—Joshua Green.
609 Main Street, Suite 105, Box 11, Alamosa, CO 81101 .... (719) 587–5105
503 North Main Street, Suite 658, Pueblo, CO 81003 .... (719) 542–1073
835 East Second Avenue, Suite 230, Durango, CO 81301 .... (970) 259–1490

Counties: ALAMOSA, ARCHULETA, CONEJOS, COSTILLA, CUSTER, DELTA, DOLORES, EAGLE (part), GARFIELD, GUNNISON, HINSDALE, HUERFANO, JACKSON, LA PLATA, LAKE, MESA, MINERAL, MOFFAT, MONTEZUMA, MONTROSE, OURAY, PITKIN, PUEBLO, RIO BLANCO, RIO GRANDE, ROUTT, SAGUACHE, SAN JUAN, AND SAN MIGUEL. Population (2010), 718,457.

ZIP Codes: 80423, 80426, 80428, 80434, 80461, 80463, 80467, 80469, 80473, 80477, 80479–80, 80483, 80487–88, 81001, 81003–08, 81019, 81022–23, 81025, 81039–40, 81055, 81069, 81089, 81101, 81120–26, 81128–33, 81136–38, 81140–41, 81143–44, 81146–49, 81151–52, 81154–55, 81210, 81220, 81224–25, 81230–31, 81235, 81237, 81239, 81241, 81243, 81248, 81251–53, 81301, 81303, 81320–21, 81323–28, 81330–32, 81334–35, 81401, 81403, 81410–11, 81413, 81415–16, 81418–19, 81422–35, 81501, 81503–07, 81520–27, 81601, 81610–12, 81615, 81620–21, 81623–25, 81630–33, 81635, 81637–43, 81645–50, 81652–56

* * *

FOURTH DISTRICT

KEN BUCK, Republican, of Windsor, CO; born February 16, 1959; education: undergraduate, Princeton University, Princeton, NJ, 1980; J.D., University of Wyoming, Laramie, WY, 1983; professional: prosecutor; U.S. Department of Justice, Washington, DC, 1985–1995; U.S. Attorney's Office, CO, 1995–2000; District Attorney, Weld County, CO, 2004–14; Corporate Counsel, Hensel Phelps Construction, 2002–04; committees: Judiciary; Rules; elected to the 114th Congress on November 4, 2014.

Office Listings

http://www.buck.house.gov

1130 Longworth House Office Building, Washington, DC 20515 .... (202) 225–4676
Chief of Staff.—Ritika Robertson.
Legislative Director.—Garrett Bess.
Communications Director.—Kyle Huwa.
Scheduling/Office Administrator.—Carly Wortham.
1023 39th Avenue, Unit B, Greeley, CO 80634 .... (970) 702–2136
900 Castleton Road, Meadows Crossing, Suite 112, Castle Rock, CO 80109 .... (720) 639–9165

Counties: ADAMS (part), ARAPAHOE (part), BACA, BOULDER (part), BENT, CHEYENNE, CROWLEY, DOUGLAS (part), ELBERT, KIOWA, KIT CARSON, LAS ANIMAS, LINCOLN, LOGAN, MORGAN, OTERO, PHILLIPS, PROWERS, SEDGWICK, WASHINGTON, WELD, AND YUMA.

ZIP Codes: 80101–09, 80112, 80116–18, 80124–27, 80130–31, 80134–38, 80501–04, 80514, 80520, 80530, 80534, 80542–43, 80546, 80550–51, 80603, 80610–12, 80615, 80620–24, 80631–34, 80638–39, 80642–46, 80648–54, 80701, 80705, 80720–23, 80726–29, 80731–37, 80740–47, 80749–51, 80754–55, 80757–59, 80801–02, 80804–05, 80807, 80810, 80812, 80815, 80818, 80821–26, 80828, 80830, 80832–36, 80861–62, 81020–21, 81024, 81027, 81029–30, 81033–34, 81036, 81038–39, 81041, 81043–47, 81049–50, 81052, 81054, 81057–59, 81062–64, 81067, 81071, 81073, 81076–77, 81084, 81087, 81090–92

* * *

FIFTH DISTRICT

DOUG LAMBORN, Republican, of Colorado Springs, CO; born in Leavenworth, KS, May 24, 1954; education: B.S., University of Kansas, Lawrence, 1978; J.D., University of Kansas, Lawrence, 1985; professional: lawyer, private practice (business and real estate); Colorado State House of Representatives, 1995–98; Colorado State Senate, 1998–2006; married: Jeanie; five children; committees: Armed Services; Natural Resources; elected to the 110th Congress on November 7, 2006; reelected to each succeeding Congress.

Office Listings

http://www.lamborn.house.gov https://www.facebook.com/congressmandouglamborn

2402 Rayburn House Office Building, Washington, DC 20515 .... (202) 225–4422
Chief of Staff.—Adam Magary. FAX: 226–2638
Legislative Director.—James Thomas.
Director of Communications.—Jarred Rego.
Scheduler / Executive Assistant.—Alysa Davis.
1125 Kelly Johnson Boulevard, Suite 330, Colorado Springs, CO 80920 .... (719) 520–0055

Counties: CHAFFEE, EL PASO, FREMONT, PARK (part), AND TELLER. Population (2010), 718,457.

ZIP Codes: 80106, 80132–33, 80420–21, 80432, 80440, 80448–49, 80456, 80808–09, 80813–14, 80816–17, 80819–20, 80827, 80829, 80831–33, 80840, 80860, 80863–64, 80902–11, 80913–30, 80938–39, 80951, 81008, 81201, 81211–12, 81221–23, 81226–27, 81232–33, 81236, 81240, 81242, 81244, 81253

* * *

SIXTH DISTRICT

MIKE COFFMAN, Republican, of Aurora, CO; born in Fort Leonard Wood, MO, March 19, 1955; education: attended, Aurora Central High School; B.A., University of Colorado, Boulder, CO, 1979; military: U.S. Army, 1972–74; U.S. Army Reserve, 1975–78; U.S. Marine Corps, 1979–82; U.S. Marine Corps Reserve, 1983–94 and 2005–06; professional: business owner; elected to the Colorado State House of Representatives, 1989–94; elected to the Colorado State Senate, 1994–98; Colorado State Treasurer, 1999–2007; Colorado Secretary of State, 2007–08; religion: Methodist; married: Cynthia; committees: Armed Services; Veterans' Affairs; elected to the 111th Congress on November 4, 2008; reelected to each succeeding Congress.

Office Listings

http://www.coffman.house.gov

2443 Rayburn House Office Building, Washington, DC 20515 .... (202) 225–7882
Chief of Staff.—Ben Stein. FAX: 226–4623
Scheduler.—Michelle Patrick.
3300 South Parker Road, Suite 305, Aurora, CO 80014 .... (720) 748–7514

Counties: ADAMS (part), ARAPAHOE (part), AND DOUGLAS (part). Population (2010), 718,456.

ZIP Codes: 80013–19, 80040–42, 80044–46, 80102, 80111–12, 80120–26, 80128–30, 80137–38, 80160–61, 80163, 80165–66, 80231, 80247

* * *

SEVENTH DISTRICT

ED PERLMUTTER, Democrat, of Arvada, CO; born in Denver, CO, May 1, 1953; education: B.A., University of Colorado, 1975; J.D., University of Colorado, 1978; professional: former partner at the law firm Berenbaum Weinshienk, specializing in bankruptcy law; served as a member of the Board of Governors of the Colorado Bar Association; served on the Board of Trustees and Judicial Performance Commission for the First Judicial District; Trustee, Midwest Research Institute, the primary operator of the National Renewable Energy Laboratory; board member, National Jewish Medical and Research Center; elected to two 4-year terms to represent central Jefferson County as a Colorado State Senator, 1995–2003; served on numerous committees in the State Senate, including Water, Finance, Judiciary, Child Welfare, Telecommunication, Transportation, Legal Services, and Oil and Gas; also served as chair of the Public Policy and Planning Committee, chair of the Bi-Partisan Renewable Energy Caucus, and President Pro Tem (2001–02 session); married to Nancy Perlmutter; between them they have six adult children; committees: Financial Services; Science, Space, and Technology; elected to the 110th Congress on November 7, 2006; reelected to each succeeding Congress.

Office Listings

http://perlmutter.house.gov https://www.facebook.com/RepPerlmutter
https://twitter.com/RepPerlmutter

1410 Longworth House Office Building, Washington, DC 20515 .... (202) 225–2645
Chief of Staff.—Danielle Radovich Piper. FAX: 225–5278
Legislative Director.—Noah Marine.
Chief of Operations/Scheduler.—Alison Inderfurth.
Staff Assistant.—Tia Bogeljic.
12600 West Colfax Avenue, Suite B400, Lakewood, CO 80215 .... (303) 274–7944

Counties: Adams (part), Jefferson (part). Cities and Townships: Arvada, Commerce City, Edgewater, Golden, Lakewood, Wheat Ridge, Westminster, Thornton and Northglenn. Population (2010), 718,456.

ZIP Codes: 80001, 80002 (part), 80003–07, 80020–23 (part), 80024, 80030–31, 80033 (part), 80034–37, 80123 (part), 80212 (part), 80214 (part), 80215, 80216 (part), 80221 (part), 80225, 80226–27 (part), 80228–29, 80232 (part), 80233, 80234–35 (part), 80239 (part), 80241 (part), 80260, 80303 (part), 80401 (part), 80402, 80403 (part), 80419, 80465 (part), 80601–03 (part), 80614, 80640 (part), 80260, 80303 (part), 80614, 80640 (part)

CONNECTICUT

(Population 2010, 3,574,097)

SENATORS

RICHARD BLUMENTHAL, Democrat, of Greenwich, CT; born in Brooklyn, NY, February 13, 1946; son of Martin and Jane Rosenstock Blumenthal; education: graduated, Riverdale Country School, Riverdale, NY, 1963; B.A., government, Harvard College, Cambridge, MA, 1967; J.D., Yale Law School, New Haven, CT, 1973; professional: admitted to Connecticut Bar, 1976; admitted to District of Columbia Bar, 1977; appointed U.S. Attorney for the District of Connecticut, 1977–81; Connecticut State House of Representatives, 1984–87; Connecticut State Senate, 1987–90; elected Attorney General for the State of Connecticut, 1990, reelected in 1994, 1998, 2002, and 2006; military: served in the U.S. Marine Corps Reserves, 1970–76, honorably discharged as Sergeant; married: Cynthia M. Blumenthal; children: Matthew, Michael, David, and Claire; committees: Armed Services; Commerce, Science, and Transportation; Judiciary; Special Committee on Aging; Veterans' Affairs; elected to the U.S. Senate on November 2, 2010, reelected in 2016.

Office Listings

http://blumenthal.senate.gov

706 Hart Senate Office Building, Washington, DC 20510 .... (202) 224–2823
Chief of Staff.—Joel Kelsey. FAX: 224–9673
Legislative Director.—Colleen Bell.
Scheduling Director.—Michael Lawson.
Communications Director.—Maria McElwain.
90 State House Square, 10th Floor, Hartford, CT 06103 .... (860) 258–6940
FAX: 258–6958
915 Lafayette Boulevard, Room 330, Bridgeport, CT 06604 .... (203) 330–0598
FAX: 330–0608

* * *

CHRISTOPHER S. MURPHY, Democrat, of Cheshire, CT; born in White Plains, Westchester County, NY, August 3, 1973; education: attended Exeter College, Oxford, England, 1994–95; graduated with honors with double majors in history and political science, Williams College, Williamstown, MA, 1996; J.D., University of Connecticut, Hartford, CT, 2002; professional: lawyer, private practice; Southington, CT; planning and zoning commission, 1997–99; practiced real estate and banking law from 2002–06, with the firm of Ruben, Johnson & Morgan in Hartford; member of the Connecticut State House of Representatives, 1999–2003; member of the Connecticut State Senate, 2003–06; married: Cathy Holahan, a legal aid attorney who represents children in need in New Britain and Waterbury; children: Chris, Cathy, and their sons Owen and Rider; committees: Appropriations; Foreign Relations; Health, Education, Labor, and Pensions; elected as a Democrat to the 110th Congress and to the two succeeding Congresses, January 3, 2007–January 3, 2013; elected to the U.S. Senate on November 6, 2012.

Office Listings

http://www.murphy.senate.gov

136 Hart Senate Office Building, Washington, DC 20510 .... (202) 224–4041
Chief of Staff.—Allison Herwitt. FAX: 224–9750
Executive Assistant.—Misha Lehver.
Legislative Director.—David Bonine.
120 Huyshope Avenue, Suite 401, Hartford, CT 06106 .... (860) 549–8463
State Director.—Kenny Curran.

REPRESENTATIVES

FIRST DISTRICT

JOHN B. LARSON, Democrat, of East Hartford, CT; born in Hartford, July 22, 1948; education: Mayberry Elementary School, East Hartford, CT; East Hartford High School; B.A., Central Connecticut State University; Senior Fellow, Yale University, Bush Center for Child Development and Social Policy; professional: high school teacher, 1972–77; insurance broker, 1978–

98; president, Larson and Lyork; public service: Connecticut State Senate, 12 years, President Pro Tempore, 8 years; married: Leslie Larson; children: Carolyn, Laura, and Raymond; committees: Ways and Means; elected to the 106th Congress; reelected to each succeeding Congress.

Office Listings

http://www.larson.house.gov

1501 Longworth House Office Building, Washington, DC 20515 .... (202) 225–2265
Chief of Staff.—David Sitcovsky. FAX: 225–1031
Legislative Director.—Scott Stephanou.
221 Main Street, Hartford, CT 06106–1864 .... (860) 278–8888
District Director.—Maureen Moriarty.
Press Secretary.—Mary Yatrousis.

Counties: HARTFORD (part), LITCHFIELD (part), AND MIDDLESEX (part). Population (2010), 714,820.

ZIP Codes: 06002, 06010, 06013, 06016, 06021, 06023, 06026–27, 06033, 06035, 06037, 06040, 06042, 06052, 06057–63, 06065, 06067, 06073–74, 06088, 06090–91, 06095–96, 06098, 06103, 06105–12, 06114, 06117–20, 06160, 06416, 06444, 06451, 06457, 06467, 06479–80, 06489, 06759, 06790

* * *

SECOND DISTRICT

JOE COURTNEY, Democrat, of Vernon, CT; born in Hartford, CT, April 6, 1953; education: B.A., Tufts University, 1971–75; University of Connecticut Law School, 1975–78; public service: Connecticut State Representative, 1987–94; Vernon Town Attorney, 2003–06; professional: attorney, Courtney, Boyan, and Foran, LLC, 1978–2006; religion: Roman Catholic; married: Audrey Courtney; children: Robert and Elizabeth; committees: Armed Services; Education and the Workforce; elected to the 110th Congress on November 7, 2006; reelected to each succeeding Congress.

Office Listings

http://www.courtney.house.gov https://www.facebook.com/joecourtney
https://twitter.com/repjoecourtney

2348 Rayburn House Office Building, Washington, DC 20515 .... (202) 225–2076
Chief of Staff.—Neil McKiernan. FAX: 225–4977
Communications Director.—Tim Brown.
Scheduler.—Kathleen Corcoran.
Legislative Director.—Alexa Combelic.
55 Main Street, Suite 250, Norwich, CT 06360 .... (860) 886–0139
District Director.—Ayanti Grant. FAX: 886–2974
77 Hazard Avenue, Unit J, Enfield, CT 06082 .... (860) 741–6011
FAX: 741–6036

Counties: HARTFORD (part), MIDDLESEX (part), NEW HAVEN (part), NEW LONDON, TOLLAND, AND WINDHAM. Population (2010), 714,819.

ZIP Codes: 06029, 06033, 06043, 06066, 06071, 06076, 06078, 06082, 06084, 06093, 06226, 06231–32, 06234–35, 06237–39, 06241–43, 06247–50, 06254–56, 06259–60, 06262–64, 06266, 06268–69, 06277–82, 06320, 06330–36, 06339–40, 06350–51, 06353–55, 06357, 06359–60, 06365, 06370–71, 06373–80, 06382, 06384–85, 06387, 06389, 06409, 06412–15, 06417, 06419–20, 06423–24, 06426, 06438, 06441–43, 06447, 06456, 06469, 06475

* * *

THIRD DISTRICT

ROSA L. DELAURO, Democrat, of New Haven, CT; born in New Haven, March 2, 1943; education: graduated, Lauralton Hall High School; attended London School of Economics, Queen Mary College, London, 1962–63; B.A., *cum laude*, history and political science, Marymount College, NY, 1964; M.A., international politics, Columbia University, NY, 1966; professional: executive assistant to Mayor Frank Logue, city of New Haven, 1976–77; executive assistant/development administrator, city of New Haven, 1977–78; chief of staff, Senator Christopher Dodd, 1980–87; executive director, Countdown '87, 1987–88; executive director, Emily's List, 1989–90; religion: Catholic; family: married, Stanley Greenberg; children: Anna, Kathryn, and Jonathan; co-chair, Democratic Steering and Policy Committee; committees: Appropriations; elected to the 102nd Congress on November 6, 1990; reelected to each succeeding Congress.

Office Listings

http://www.delauro.house.gov

2413 Rayburn House Office Building, Washington, DC 20515 .... (202) 225–3661
Chief of Staff.—Beverly Pheto. FAX: 225–4890
Scheduler.—Ryann Kinney.
59 Elm Street, New Haven, CT 06510 .... (203) 562–3718
District Director.—Jennifer Lamb.

Counties: FAIRFIELD (part), MIDDLESEX (part), AND NEW HAVEN (part). CITIES AND TOWNSHIPS: Ansonia, Beacon Falls, Bethany, Branford, Derby, Durham, East Haven, Guilford, Hamden, Middlefield, Middletown (part), Milford, Naugatuck, New Haven, North Branford, North Haven, Orange, Prospect, Seymour, Shelton (part), Stratford, Wallingford, Waterbury (part), West Haven, and Woodbridge. Population (2011), 718,549.

ZIP Codes: 06401, 06403, 06405, 06410, 06418, 06422, 06437, 06450, 06455, 06457, 06460, 06471–73, 06477, 06481, 06483–84, 06492–94, 06501–21, 06524–25, 06530–38, 06540, 06607, 06614–15, 06706, 06708, 06712, 06762, 06770

* * *

FOURTH DISTRICT

JAMES A. HIMES, Democrat, of Cos Cob, CT; born in Lima, Peru, to American parents, July 5, 1966; education: B.A., Harvard University, Cambridge, MA, 1988; M.Phil, Oxford University, Oxford, England, 1990; professional: vice president, Goldman Sachs & Co., 1990–2002; vice president, Enterprise Community Partners, 2002–07; Commissioner, Greenwich Housing Authority; chair, Greenwich Democratic Town Committee; religion: Presbyterian; married: Mary Himes, 1994; children: Emma and Linley; committees: Financial Services; Permanent Select Committee on Intelligence; elected to the 111th Congress on November 4, 2008; reelected to each succeeding Congress.

Office Listings

http://www.himes.house.gov

1227 Longworth House Office Building, Washington, DC 20515 .... (202) 225–5541
Chief of Staff.—Mark Henson. FAX: 225–9629
Executive Aide.—Cara Pavlock.
888 Washington Boulevard, Stamford, CT 06901–2927 .... (866) 453–0028
211 State Street, 2nd Floor, Bridgeport, CT 06604–4223 .... (866) 453–0028
District Director.—Tyrone McClain.

Counties: FAIRFIELD (part) AND NEW HAVEN (part). CITIES AND TOWNSHIPS: Bridgeport, Darien, Easton, Fairfield, Greenwich, Monroe, New Canaan, Norwalk, Oxford, Redding, Ridgefield, Shelton, Stamford, Trumbull, Weston, Westport, and Wilton. Population (2010), 714,819.

ZIP Codes: 06468, 06478, 06604–08, 06610–12, 06807, 06820, 06824–25, 06830–31, 06840, 06850–51, 06853–56, 06870, 06877–78, 06880, 06883, 06890, 06896–97, 06901–03, 06905–07

* * *

FIFTH DISTRICT

ELIZABETH H. ESTY, Democrat, of Cheshire, CT; born August 25, 1959; education: graduated, A.B., Harvard College, Cambridge, MA, 1981; graduated, J.D., Yale University, New Haven, CT, 1985; professional: law clerk for a federal judge; a Supreme Court lawyer at Sidley Austin LLP in Washington, DC; professor at American University; former member, Cheshire Town Council, CT, 2005–08; member of the Connecticut State House of Representatives, 2008–10; caucuses: serves as vice chair on Gun Violence Prevention Task Force; committees: vice ranking member, Transportation and Infrastructure; Science, Space, and Technology; Veterans' Affairs; elected to the 113th Congress on November 6, 2012; reelected to each succeeding Congress.

Office Listings

http://esty.house.gov

221 Cannon House Office Building, Washington, DC 20515 .... (202) 225–4476

Office Listings—Continued

Chief of Staff.—Timothy Daly. FAX: (860) 223–8412
Communications Director.—Craig Frucht.
Scheduler.—Hilary Badger.
1 Grove Street, Suite 600, New Britain, CT 06053 .... (860) 223–8412
District Director.—Stephanie Podewell.

Counties: FAIRFIELD (part), HARTFORD (part), LITCHFIELD, AND NEW HAVEN (part). CITIES: Danbury, Meriden, New Britain, Torrington, and Waterbury. Population (2010), 714,820.

ZIP Codes: 06001, 06013, 06018–20, 06022, 06024, 06030–32, 06034, 06039, 06050–53, 06058–59, 06062, 06068–70, 06079, 06081, 06085, 06087, 06089, 06092, 06107, 06404, 06408, 06410–11, 06440, 06450–51, 06454, 06470, 06482, 06487–88, 06701–06, 06708, 06710, 06716, 06720–26, 06749–59, 06762–63, 06776–79, 06781–87, 06790–91, 06793–96, 06798, 06801, 06804, 06810–14, 06816–17

DELAWARE

(Population 2010, 897,934)

SENATORS

THOMAS R. CARPER, Democrat, of Wilmington, DE; born in Beckley, WV, January 23, 1947; education: B.A., Ohio State University, 1968; M.B.A., University of Delaware, 1975; military service: U.S. Navy, served during Vietnam War; public service: Delaware State Treasurer, 1977–83; U.S. House of Representatives, 1983–93; Governor of Delaware, 1993–2001; organizations: Third Way; New Democrat Network; former National Governors' Association chair; religion: Presbyterian; family: married to the former Martha Ann Stacy; children: Ben and Christopher; committees: ranking member, Environment and Public Works, Finance; Homeland Security and Governmental Affairs; elected to the U.S. Senate on November 7, 2000; reelected to each succeeding Senate term.

Office Listings

http://carper.senate.gov www.facebook.com/tomcarper twitter: @senatorcarper

513 Hart Senate Office Building, Washington, DC 20510 .... (202) 224–2441
Chief of Staff.—Bill Ghent. FAX: 228–2190
Legislative Director.—Emily Spain.
Administrative Director.—Madge Farooq.
500 West Loockerman Street, Suite 470, Dover, DE 19904 .... (302) 674–3308
301 North Walnut Street, Suite 102 L–1, Wilmington, DE 19801 .... (302) 573–6291
12 The Circle, Georgetown, DE 19947 .... (302) 856–7690

* * *

CHRISTOPHER A. COONS, Democrat, of Wilmington, DE; born in Greenwich, CT, September 9, 1963; education: B.A., Amherst College, 1985; M.A.R., Yale University, 1992; J.D., Yale University, 1992; professional: associate (legal counsel), W.L. Gore & Associates, 1996–2004; president of New Castle County Council, 2000–04; county executive, New Castle County, 2005–10; religion: Presbyterian; married: Annie; children: Michael, Jack, and Maggie; committees: vice chair, Select Committee on Ethics; Appropriations; Foreign Relations; Judiciary; Small Business and Entrepreneurship; elected on November 2, 2010, to the U.S. Senate to fill the remainder of the vacancy caused by the unfinished term of Joseph R. Biden, Jr., and took the oath of office on November 15, 2010; reelected to the U.S. Senate on November 4, 2014.

Office Listings

http://coons.senate.gov https://www.facebook.com/senatorchriscoons
https://www.twitter.com/sencoonsoffice

127A Russell Senate Office Building, Washington, DC 20510 .... (202) 224–5042
Chief of Staff.—Jonathan Stahler. FAX: 228–3075
Legislative Director.—Brian Winseck.
Communications Director.—Sean Coit.
Administrative Director.—Trinity Hall.
1105 North Market Street, Suite 100, Wilmington, DE 19801–1233 .... (302) 573–6345
State Director.—Jim Paoli.
500 West Loockerman Street, Suite 450, Dover, DE 19904 .... (302) 736–5601

REPRESENTATIVE

AT LARGE

LISA BLUNT ROCHESTER, Democrat, of Wilmington, DE; born in Philadelphia, PA, February 10, 1962; education: graduated from Padua Academy, Wilmington, DE, 1980; B.A., Fairleigh Dickinson University, Rutherford, NJ, 1985; M.A., University of Delaware, Newark, DE, 2003; professional: staff, U.S. Representative Thomas Richard Carper of Delaware; Deputy Secretary, Delaware Department of Health and Social Services, 1993–98; Delaware State Secretary of Labor, 1998–2001; Personnel Director, State of Delaware, 2001–04; chief executive officer, Metropolitan Wilmington Urban League, 2004–07; senior fellow, University of Massachusetts Boston, 2012–15; caucuses: Congressional Black Caucus; Congressional Progressive

Caucus; New Democrat Coalition; Equality Caucus; committees: Agriculture; Education and the Workforce; elected to the 115th Congress on November 8, 2016.

Office Listings

http://www.bluntrochester.house.gov

1123 Longworth House Office Building, Washington, DC 20515 .... (202) 225–4165
Chief of Staff.—Minh Ta.
Legislative Director.—Elizabeth Connolly.
DC Scheduler.—Kalila Hines.
1105 North Market Street, Suite 400, Wilmington, DE 19801 .... (302) 830–2330
State Director.—Sylvia Banks.
DE Scheduler.—Waynna Dobson.

Counties: KENT, NEW CASTLE, AND SUSSEX. CITIES AND TOWNSHIPS: Bethany Beach, Bethel, Bellefonte, Blades, Bowers, Bridgeville, Camden, Cheswold, Dagsboro, Delmar, Delaware City, Dewey Beach, Dover, Ellendale, Elsmere, Farmington, Felton, Fenwick Island, Frankford, Frederica, Georgetown, Greenwood, Harrington, Hartly, Henlopen Acres, Houston, Kenton, Laurel, Lewes, Little Creek, Leipsic, Magnolia, Middletown, Milford, Millsboro, Millville, Milton, New Castle, Newark, Newport, Ocean View, Odessa, Rehoboth Beach, Seaford, Selbyville, Slaughter Beach, South Bethany, Smyrna, Townsend, Viola, Wilmington, Woodside, and Wyoming. Population (2010), 897,934.

ZIP Codes: 19701–03, 19706–18, 19720–21, 19725–26, 19730–36, 19801–10, 19850, 19880, 19884–87, 19890–99, 19901–06, 19930–31, 19933–34, 19936, 19938–41, 19943–47, 19950–56, 19958, 19960–64, 19966–71, 19973, 19975, 19977, 19979–80

FLORIDA

(Population 2010, 18,801,310)

SENATORS

BILL NELSON, Democrat, of Orlando, FL; born in Miami, FL, September 29, 1942; education: Melbourne High School, 1960; B.A., Yale University, 1965; J.D., University of Virginia School of Law, 1968; professional: attorney; admitted to the Florida Bar, 1968; captain, U.S. Army Reserve, 1965–71; active duty, 1968–70; public service: Florida State House of Representatives, 1973–79; U.S. House of Representatives, 1979–91; Florida Treasurer, Insurance Commissioner, and State Fire Marshal, 1995–2001; Astronaut: payload specialist on the space shuttle *Columbia,* January, 1986; married: the former Grace Cavert; children: Bill Jr. and Nan Ellen; committees: ranking member, Commerce, Science, and Transportation; Armed Services; Finance; Special Committee on Aging; elected to the U.S. Senate on November 7, 2000; reelected to each succeeding Senate term.

Office Listings

http://billnelson.senate.gov twitter: @senbillnelson

716 Hart Senate Office Building, Washington, DC 20510 .... (202) 224–5274
Chief of Staff.—Susie Perez Quinn. FAX: 228–2183
Deputy Chief of Staff, Administration.—Brenda Strickland.
Communications Director.—Ryan Brown.
Legislative Director.—Carla McGarvey.
U.S. Courthouse Annex, 111 North Adams Street, Tallahassee, FL 32301 .... (850) 942–8415
801 North Florida Avenue, 4th Floor, Tampa, FL 33602 .... (813) 225–7040
2555 Ponce De Leon Boulevard, Suite 610, Coral Gables, FL 33134 .... (305) 536–5999
3416 South University Drive, Ft. Lauderdale, FL 33328 .... (954) 693–4851
413 Clematis Street, Suite 210, West Palm Beach, FL 33401 .... (561) 514–0189
225 East Robinson Street, Suite 410, Orlando, FL 32801 .... (407) 872–7161
1301 Riverplace Boulevard, Suite 2010, Jacksonville, FL 32207 .... (904) 346–4500
2000 Main Street, Suite 801, Ft. Myers, FL 33901 .... (239) 334–7760

* * *

MARCO A. RUBIO, Republican, of West Miami, FL; born in Miami, May 28, 1971; education: South Miami Senior High School, 1989; B.S., political science, University of Florida, 1993; J.D., *cum laude*, University of Miami, 1996; professional: Florida House of Representatives, 2000–08; served as Majority Whip, Majority Leader, and Speaker of the House; attorney, Broad and Cassel; Marco Rubio, P.A.; lecturer and senior fellow at Florida International University, 2009–present; Bob Dole for President, 1996, Miami-Dade County Director; religion: Roman Catholic; married: Jeanette; children: Amanda, Daniella, Anthony, and Dominick; committees: Appropriations; Foreign Relations; Select Committee on Intelligence; Small Business and Entrepreneurship; Special Committee on Aging; elected to the U.S. Senate on November 2, 2010; reelected on November 8, 2016.

Office Listings

http://rubio.senate.gov twitter: @senrubiopress
https://facebook.com/SenatorMarcoRubio

SR–284 Russell Building, Washington, DC 20510 .... (202) 224–3041
Chief of Staff.—Michael Needham. FAX: 228–0285
Legislative Director.—Lauren Reamy.
201 South Orange Avenue, Suite 350, Orlando, FL 32801 .... (407) 254–2573
700 South Palafox Street, Suite 125, Pensacola, FL 32502 .... (850) 433–2603
8669 Northwest 36th Street, Suite 110, Doral, FL 33166 .... (305) 418–8553
402 South Monroe Street, Suite 2105E, Tallahassee, FL 32399 .... (850) 599–9100
4580 PGA Boulevard, Suite 201, Palm Beach Gardens, FL 33418 .... (561) 775–3360

REPRESENTATIVES

FIRST DISTRICT

MATT GAETZ, Republican, of Fort Walton Beach, FL; born in Hollywood, FL, May 7, 1982; education: B.S., history/political science, Florida State University, Tallahassee, FL, 2003; J.D., College of William and Mary, Williamsburg, VA, 2007; professional: Florida House of Representatives, 2010–16; attorney with the Keefe, Anchors & Gordon law firm; religion: Baptist; family: Don Gaetz, father; Vicky Gaetz, mother; and Erin Gaetz, sister; committees: Armed Services; Budget; Judiciary; elected to the 115th Congress on November 8, 2016.

Office Listings

http://matt.gaetz.house.gov twitter: @Rep_Matt_Gaetz

507 Cannon House Office Building, Washington, DC 20515 .... (202) 225–4136
FAX: 225–3414
Chief of Staff.—Amanda Cogan.
Legislative Director.—Heather Ham-Warren.
Scheduler.—Kendall Kelley.
22 South Palafox Place, 6th Floor, Pensacola, FL 32502 .... (850) 479–1183
District Director.—Dawn McArdle.

Counties: ESCAMBIA (all). CITIES AND TOWNSHIPS: Bellview, Brent, Century, Ensley, Ferry Pass, Gonzalez, Goulding, Molino, Myrtle Grove, Pensacola, Warrington, and West Pensacola. HOLMES (part). CITIES AND TOWNSHIPS: Esto, Noma, Ponce de Leon, and Westville. OKALOOSA (all). CITIES AND TOWNSHIPS: Cinco Bayou, Crestview, Destin, Eglin, Fort Walton Beach, Lake Lorraine, Laurel Hill, Mary Esther, Niceville, Ocean City, Shalimar, Valparaiso, and Wright. SANTA ROSA (all). CITIES AND TOWNSHIPS: Allentown, Avalon, Bagdad, Berrydale, Brownsdale, Chumuckla, Cobbtown, Dickerson City, Dixonville, East Milton, Fidelis, Floridatown, Garcon Point, Gulf Breeze, Harold, Holley, Jay, Midway, Milton, Mount Carmel, Mulat, Munson, Navarre Beach, Navarre, Oriole Beach, Pace, Pea Ridge, Pine Level, Point Baker, Roeville, Springhill, Tiger Point, Wallace, and Woodlawn Beach. WALTON (all). CITIES AND TOWNSHIPS: De Funiak Springs, Freeport, Miramar Beach, and Paxton. Population (2010), 687,856.

ZIP Codes: 32413 (part), 32425 (part), 32433, 32435, 32439, 32440 (part), 32455, 32459, 32461, 32462 (part), 32464, 32501–09, 32511, 32514, 32526, 32530, 32531, 32533–36, 32539, 32541–42, 32544, 32547–48, 32550, 32561, 32563–71, 32577–80, 32583

* * *

SECOND DISTRICT

NEAL P. DUNN, Republican, of Panama City, FL; born in New Haven, CT, February 16, 1953; education: B.A., Washington and Lee University, Lexington, VA; M.D., George Washington University Medical School, Washington, DC; residency, Walter Reed Army Medical Center; professional: founding president, Advanced Urology Institute, Panama City, FL; founding chair, Summit Bank, Panama City, FL; member, board of governors, Florida Medical Association; military: Major, U.S. Army (ret.); religion: Roman Catholic; married, Leah Ott Dunn; three children; committees: Agriculture; Science, Space, and Technology; Veterans' Affairs; elected to the 115th Congress on November 8, 2016.

Office Listings

http://dunn.house.gov https: facebook.com/DrNealDunnFL2
https: twitter.com/DrNealDunnFL2

423 Cannon House Office Building, Washington, DC 20515 .... (202) 225–5235
Chief of Staff.—Brian Schubert.
Communications Director.—Shelby Hodgkins.
Legislative Director.—Evan Lee.
Legislative Assistant.—Courtney Veatch.
Legislative Correspondent.—Tyler Russell.
Scheduler.—Danielle Houser.
300 South Adams Street, Suite A–3, Tallahassee, FL 32301 .... (850) 891–8610
Deputy Chief of Staff and District Director.—Bret Prater.
Deputy District Director.—Will Kendrick.
840 West 11th Street, Suite 2250, Panama City, FL 32401 .... (850) 785–0812

Counties: BAY, CALHOUN, FRANKLIN, GADSDEN, GULF, HOLMES (part), JACKSON, JEFFERSON, LEON, LIBERTY, MADISON (part), TAYLOR, WAKULLA, AND WASHINGTON. Population (2010), 737,519.

ZIP Codes: 32008, 32024–25, 32038, 32055, 32060–62, 32064, 32066, 32071, 32094, 32096, 32301, 32303–05, 32308–12, 32317, 32320–23, 32327–28, 32331, 32334, 32336, 32344, 32346–48, 32355–56, 32358–59, 32361, 32399, 32401,

32403–05, 32407–10, 32413, 32420–21, 32423–28, 32430–32, 32437–38, 32440, 32442–49, 32456, 32460, 32462–63, 32465–66, 32618–19, 32621, 32625–26, 32628, 32639, 32643, 32648, 32668–69, 32680, 32683, 32692–93, 32696, 34431–32, 34449, 34474, 34476, 34481–82, 34498

* * *

THIRD DISTRICT

TED S. YOHO, D.V.M., Republican, of Gainesville, FL; born in Minneapolis, MN, April 13, 1955; education: graduated from Deerfield Beach High School, Deerfield Beach, FL, 1973; attended Florence State University (University of North Alabama), Florence, AL; A.A., Broward Community College, Fort Lauderdale, FL, 1977; B.S.A., University of Florida, Gainesville, FL, 1979; D.V.M., University of Florida, Gainesville, FL, 1983; professional: large animal veterinarian; religion: Christian; married: the former Carolyn Sue Marlin; children: Katie, Tyler, and Lauren; caucuses: Congressional Cystic Fibrosis Caucus; Congressional Sportsmen's Caucus; Florida Ports Caucus; Freshman Regulatory Reform Working Group; House Liberty Caucus; Republican Study Committee; Veterinary Medicine Caucus; committees: Agriculture; Foreign Affairs; elected to the 113th Congress on November 6, 2012; reelected to each succeeding Congress.

Office Listings

http://yoho.house.gov www.facebook.com/congressmantedyoho
twitter: @RepTedYoho instagram: @reptedyoho

511 Cannon House Office Building, Washington, DC 20515 .... (202) 225–5744
Chief of Staff.—Larry Calhoun. FAX: 225–3973
Scheduler.—Emily Scheinost.
Legislative Director.—James Walsh.
Communications Director.—Brian Kaveney.
5000 Northwest 27th Court, Suite A, Gainesville, FL 32606 .... (352) 505–0838
Deputy Chief of staff.—Kat Cammack.
District Director.—Jessica Norfleet.
35–1 Knight Boxx Road, Orange Park, FL 32065 .... (904) 276–9626
Deputy Staff Director.—Greg Rawson.
Constituent Advocacy Manager.—Dorothy Richardson.
2509 Crill Avenue, Suite 200, Palatka, FL 32177 .... (386) 326–7221

Counties: ALACHUA, BRADFORD, CLAY, MARION (part), AND PUTNAM. Population (2015), 726,720.

ZIP Codes: 32003, 32008, 32024–26, 32038, 32043–44, 32052–55, 32058–62, 32064–66, 32068, 32071, 32073, 32079, 32083, 32091, 32094, 32096, 32234, 32331, 32340, 32350, 32359, 32601, 32603, 32605–09, 32612, 32615–16, 32618–19, 32621–22, 32625–26, 32628, 32631, 32639–41, 32643, 32648, 32653, 32656, 32658, 32664, 32666–69, 32680, 32683, 32686, 32692–94, 32696–97, 34431–32, 34449, 34474–76, 34481–82, 34498

* * *

FOURTH DISTRICT

JOHN H. RUTHERFORD, Republican, of Jacksonville, FL; born in Omaha, NE, September 2, 1952; education: B.S., criminology, at Florida State University; FBI National Academy in Quantico, VA, graduated in session 171; professional: law enforcement officer with the Jacksonville Sheriff's office and Duval County Sheriff from 2003–2015; religion: Catholic; family, married: Patricia; children: Alicia and Michael; grandchildren: Michela, Hannah, Maria Vittoria, Kiera, and John-Carlo; committees: Appropriations; Homeland Security; Judiciary; elected to the 115th Congress on November 8, 2016.

Office Listings

http://www.rutherford.house.gov

230 Cannon House Office Building, Washington, DC 20515 .... (202) 225–2501
Chief of Staff.—Kelly Simpson.
Legislative Director.—Jenifer Nawrocki.
Communications Director.—Taryn Fenske.
4130 Salisbury Road, Suite 2500, Jacksonville, FL 32216 .... (904) 831–5205
District Director.—Jackie Smith.

Counties: Duval (part), NASSAU AND ST. JOHNS. CITIES AND TOWNSHIPS: Atlantic Beach, Callahan, Fernandina Beach, Jacksonville, Jacksonville Beach, Neptune Beach, and St. Augustine.

ZIP Codes: 32004, 32009, 32011, 32033 (part), 32034–35, 32040 (part), 32041, 32046, 32073 (part), 32080–82 (part), 32084 (part), 32085, 32086–87 (part), 32092 (part), 32095 (part), 32097 (part), 32099, 32145 (part), 32202 (part),

32204–05 (part), 32207 (part), 32209–12 (part), 32214, 32216–19 (part), 32220, 32221–22 (part), 32223, 32224–25 (part), 32226–29, 32233, 32234–35 (part), 32237, 32240–41, 32244–46 (part), 32250, 32254 (part), 32255–58, 32259 (part), 32260, 32266, 32277 (part)

* * *

FIFTH DISTRICT

AL LAWSON, JR., Democrat, of Tallahassee, FL; born in Midway, FL, September 23, 1948; education: B.S., Florida A&M University, 1970; M.P.A., Florida State University, 1973; professional: insurance executive, Northwestern Mutual; public service: former member, Florida House of Representatives and Florida State Senate; Dean, Florida Legislature, 2008–10; Senate Democratic Leader, 2008–10; chair, Environmental Preservation and Conservation Committee; chair, Florida Conference of Black State Legislators; chair, Government Oversight and Accountability Committee; chair, Health & Life Insurance and General Insurance Regulation Committee; vice-chair, General Government Appropriations; religion: Episcopal; married: Delores Brooks Lawson; committees: Agriculture; Small Business; elected to the 115th Congress on November 8, 2016.

Office Listings

http://www.lawson.house.gov twitter: @RepAlLawsonJr
facebook: RepAlLawsonJr

1337 Longworth House Office Building, Washington, DC 20515 .... (202) 225–0123
Chief of Staff.—Tola Thompson. FAX: 225–2256
Special Assistant / Scheduler.—Vincent Evans.
Legislative Director.—Margaret Franklin.
District Directors: Deborah Fairhurst (Tallahassee), Kortney Wesley (Jacksonville).
1010 North Davis Street, Suite 206, Jacksonville, FL 32209 .... (904) 354–1652
435 North Macomb Street, Tallahassee, FL 32301 .... (850) 558–9450

Counties: BAKER, COLUMBIA (part), DUVAL (part), GADSDEN, HAMILTON, JEFFERSON (part), LEON (part), AND MADISON. Population (2010), 696,345.

ZIP Codes: 32003 (part), 32043 (part), 32073 (part), 32102 (part), 32113 (part), 32134 (part), 32140 (part), 32148 (part), 32177 (part), 32202 (part), 32204–05 (part), 32206, 32207 (part), 32208–09, 32210–12 (part), 32216 (part), 32218–22 (part), 32244 (part), 32254 (part), 32277 (part), 32601 (part), 32609 (part), 32631 (part), 32640–41 (part), 32664 (part), 32666–67 (part), 32681, 32686 (part), 32702–03 (part), 32712 (part), 32736 (part), 32746 (part), 32751 (part), 32757 (part), 32767, 32771 (part), 32773 (part), 32776 (part), 32784 (part), 32798, 32801 (part), 32804–06 (part), 32808, 32809–32811 (part), 32818–19, 32835, 32839, 34734, 34761

* * *

SIXTH DISTRICT

RONALD "RON" DESANTIS, Republican, of Ponte Vedra Beach, FL; born in Jacksonville, FL, September 14, 1978; education: *magna cum laude* with a B.A. in history, Yale University, New Haven, CT, 2001; J.D., Harvard Law School, Cambridge University, MA, 2005; sworn into the Judge Advocate General Corps of the U.S. Navy, while still a student at the Harvard Law School; completed U.S. Naval Justice School in 2005; professional: served in the Trial Service Office Command South East at the Naval Station Mayport, FL, as a military prosecutor; promoted to Lieutenant (O–3) and worked for the Joint Task Force-Guantanamo Commander (JTF–GTMO), at the Guantanamo Bay Joint Detention Facility, 2006; assigned to SEAL Team One and deployed to Iraq with the troop surge as the Legal Advisor to the SEAL Commander, Special Operations Task Force-West in Fallujah, 2007; earned an appointment with the U.S. Department of Justice to serve as a federal prosecutor at the U.S. Attorney's Office in the Middle District of Florida, 2008; concurrently accepted a Reserve commission as a Lieutenant, Judge Advocate General Corps, in the U.S. Navy Reserve; currently a Lieutenant Commander; awards: Bronze Star Medal and Iraq Campaign Medal Award; authored a book titled *Dreams From Our Founding Fathers: First Principles in the Age of Obama*, which was published in 2011; religion: Roman Catholic; married: Casey Black DeSantis; children: daughter, Madison; committees: Foreign Affairs; Judiciary; Oversight and Government Reform; elected to the 113th Congress on November 6, 2012; reelected to each succeeding Congress.

Office Listings

http://desantis.house.gov https://www.facebook.com/repdesantis
https://twitter.com/repdesantis

1524 Longworth House Office Building, Washington, DC 20515 .... (202) 225–2706

Office Listings—Continued

Chief of Staff.—Dustin Carmack. FAX: 226–6299
Scheduler.—Mimi Rothfus.
Legislative Director.—John Maniscalco.
Communications Director.—Elizabeth Fusick.
1000 City Center Circle, 2nd Floor, Port Orange, FL 32129 .... (386) 756–9798
120 South Florida Avenue, Suite 324, DeLand, FL 32720 .... (386) 279–7343
31 Lupi Court, Suite 130, Palm Coast, FL 32137 .... (386) 302–0474

Counties: FLAGLER, ST. JOHNS, AND VOLUSIA (part). CITIES: Daytona Beach, Deltona, and Palm Coast. Population (2015), 755,981.

ZIP Codes: 32033, 32080–82, 32084, 32086, 32092, 32095, 32102 (part), 32110, 32112, 32114, 32117–19, 32124, 32127–32, 32134 (part), 32136–37, 32139, 32140 (part), 32141, 32145, 32147, 32148 (part), 32157, 32164, 32168 (part), 32169, 32174, 32176, 32177 (part), 32180–81, 32187, 32189–90, 32193, 32224 (part), 32259, 32640 (part), 32720 (part), 32724 (part), 32738 (part), 32744 (part), 32759, 32763–64 (part)

* * *

SEVENTH DISTRICT

STEPHANIE N. MURPHY, Democrat, of Winter Park, FL; born in Ho Chi Minh City, Vietnam, September 16, 1978; education: B.A., economics; B.A., international relations, College of William and Mary, Williamsburg, VA, 2000; M.S., foreign service, Georgetown University, Washington, DC, 2004; professional: strategy and operations consultant, Deloitte, 2000–02; national security specialist, Office of the Under Secretary of Defense for Policy, U.S. Department of Defense, 2004–08; executive, SunGate Capital LLC, 2008–16; instructor, Rollins College, 2014–16; awards: Secretary of Defense Medal for Exceptional Civilian Service; married: Sean Murphy; children: Liem and Maya; caucuses: Blue Dog Coalition; Congressional Asian Pacific American Caucus; Future Forum; Modeling, Simulation and Training Caucus; New Democrat Coalition; Problem Solvers Caucus; committees: Armed Services; Small Business; elected to the 115th Congress on November 8, 2016.

Office Listings

http://stephaniemurphy.house.gov

2137 Longworth House Office Building, Washington, DC 20515 .... (202) 225–4035
Chief of Staff.—Brad Howard. FAX: 226–0821
District Director.—Lauren Allen.
Deputy Chief of Staff/Legislative Director.—John Laufer.
Communications Director.—Roberto Valdez.
Scheduler.—Alli Everton.
225 East Robinson Street, Suite 525, Orlando, FL 32801 .... (888) 205–5421
110 West First Street, Suite 210, Sanford, FL 32725 .... (888) 205–5421

Counties: ORANGE COUNTY (part). CITIES AND TOWNSHIPS: Maitland, Orlando, and Winter Park. SEMINOLE COUNTY. CITIES AND TOWNSHIPS: Altamonte Springs, Casselberry, Lake Mary, Longwood, Oviedo, Sanford, and Winter Springs. Population (2010), 702,203.

ZIP Codes: 32168 (part), 32701, 32703 (part), 32707–08, 32712 (part), 32714, 32730, 32732, 32738 (part), 32744 (part), 32746 (part), 32750, 32751 (part), 32754 (part), 32765–66, 32771 (part), 32773 (part), 32779, 32789, 32792 (part), 32803–04 (part), 32807 (part), 32810 (part), 32814 (part), 32817 (part), 32820 (part), 32826 (part), 32833 (part)

* * *

EIGHTH DISTRICT

BILL POSEY, Republican, of Rockledge, FL; born in Washington, DC, December 18, 1947; education: graduated, Cocoa High School, 1966; A.A., Eastern Florida State College; professional: Realtor; Rockledge City Council (1976–86); Florida House of Representatives (1992–2000); Florida Senate (2000–08); National Legislator of the Year by the American Legislative Exchange Council; married: Katie Posey; children: Pamela and Catherine; caucuses: chair, Congressional Automotive Performance and Motorsports Caucus; chair, Congressional Estuary Caucus; chair, Congressional Motorsports Caucus; Congressional Autism Caucus; House Aerospace Caucus; Military Veterans Caucus; committees: Financial Services; Science, Space, and Technology; elected to the 111th Congress on November 4, 2008; reelected to each succeeding Congress.

Office Listings

http://www.posey.house.gov facebook: https://www.facebook.com/bill.posey15
twitter: @congbillposey

2150 Rayburn House Office Building, Washington, DC 20515 .... (202) 225–3671
Chief of Staff.—Marcus Brubaker. FAX: 225–3516
Legislative Director.—Patrick Deitz.
Communications Director / Deputy Chief of Staff.—George Cecala.
Scheduler.—Kyra Thomas.
2725 Judge Fran Jamieson Way, Building C, Melbourne, FL 32940 .... (321) 632–1776
Indian River County .... (772) 226–1701
Titusville .... (321) 383–6090
District Director.—Patrick Gavin.
Directors of Community Relations: David Jackson, Rob Medina, Cheryl Moore.

Counties: BREVARD, INDIAN RIVER, AND ORANGE (part). Population (2010), 696,344.

ZIP Codes: 32709, 32754 (part), 32780, 32796, 32820 (part), 32828 (part), 32831 (part), 32833 (part), 32901, 32903–05, 32907–09, 32920, 32922, 32925–27, 32931, 32934–35, 32937, 32940, 32948–53, 32955, 32958, 32960, 32962–63, 32966–68, 32970, 32976

* * *

NINTH DISTRICT

DARREN SOTO, Democrat, of Celebration, FL; born in Ringwood, NJ, February 25, 1978; education: B.A., economics, Rutgers University, New Brunswick, NJ, 2000; J.D., George Washington University Law School, Washington, DC, 2004; professional: founder of Darren Soto Law Firm; served for four years in the Florida Senate; served for five years in the Florida House of Representatives; former member of the Civil Service Board for the City of Orlando; former treasurer of the Orange County Democrats; former vice president of communications for the Orange County Young Democrats; awards: Champion of Northern Everglades, the Audobon Society of Florida; religion: Roman Catholic; married to Amanda Soto; leadership: Democratic Steering and Policy, Assistant Regional Whip; caucuses: chair, Civil Rights and Voting Rights Task Force; Congenital Heart Caucus; Congressional #FutureForum; Congressional Hispanic Caucus; Japan Caucus; New Democrat Coalition; Problem Solvers Caucus; Turkey Caucus; committees: Agriculture; Natural Resources; elected to the 115th Congress on November 8, 2016.

Office Listings

http://www.soto.house.gov

1429 Longworth House Office Building, Washington, DC 20515 .... (202) 225–9889
Chief of Staff.—Christine Biron. FAX: 225–9742
Legislative Director.—Mike Nichola.
Communications Director.—Oriana Pina.
Legislative Aides: Nicole McLaren, Martin Rivera.
Scheduler / Office Manager.—Liana Guerra.
Staff Assistant.—Bill Rockwood.
804 Bryan Street, Kissimmee, FL 34741 .... (407) 452–1171
District Director.—Alex Barrio.
Outreach Director.—Vivian Rodriguez.
6900 Lake Nona Boulevard, Suites #101A and #101B, Orlando, FL 32827 .... (407) 266–7161
Director of Constituent Services.—Shasta Shaffer.
620 East Main Street, Haines City, FL 33844 .... (202) 600–0843
(202) 615–1308
451 3rd Street, NW., Winter Haven, FL 33881 .... (202) 600–0843
(202) 615–1308

Counties: ORANGE (part), OSCEOLA, AND POLK (part). Population (2010), 753,549.

ZIP Codes: 32792 (part), 32803 (part), 32806–07 (part), 32809 (part), 32812 (part), 32814 (part), 32817 (part), 32821–22 (part), 32824–25, 32826 (part), 32827, 32828 (part), 32829, 32831 (part), 32832, 32837 (part), 33837–38 (part), 33844 (part), 33848, 33851, 33881 (part), 33896 (part), 34739, 34741, 34743–44, 34746, 34747 (part), 34758–59, 34769, 34771–73, 34972 (part)

* * *

TENTH DISTRICT

VAL BUTLER DEMINGS, Democrat, of Orlando, FL, born in Jacksonville, FL, March, 12, 1957; education: B.S., criminology, Florida State University; M.A., public administration, Webster University; professional: former Orlando Police Chief; caucuses: Congressional Black Caucus; Congressional Caucus on Black Women and Girls; Congressional Caucus for Women's Issues; Congressional Cybersecurity Caucus; Congressional Florida Ports Caucus; Congressional Pro-Choice Caucus; Congressional Progressive Caucus; Congressional Travel and Tourism Caucus; House Gun Violence Prevention Task Force; Law Enforcement Caucus; New Democrat Coalition; committees: Homeland Security; Judiciary; elected to the 115th Congress on November 8, 2016.

Office Listings

http://www.demings.house.gov twitter: @repvaldemings
facebook.com/usrepresentativevaldemings

238 Cannon House Office Building, Washington, DC 20515 .... (202) 225–2176
Chief of Staff.—Wendy Anderson.
Legislative Director.—Chris Wilcox.
Communications Director.—Caroline Rowland.
Senior Legislative Aide.—Aimee Collins-Mandeville.
Legislative Aide.—Maurice Velazco.
Legislative Correspondent.—Maximilian de Vreeze.
Staff Assistant.—Juan de la Vega.
Scheduler / Executive Assistant.—Wendy Featherson.
District Director.—Sonja White.
Director of Business and Economic Development.—Erin Waldron.
District Outreach Coordinator.—Jeff Branch.
Constituent Services.—Chester Glover.
Constituent Services Representative.—Gladys Morales Smith.
Staff Assistant.—Harrison Angelis.

Counties: ORANGE (part).

ZIP Codes: 32703 (part), 32704, 32710, 32712, 32751, 32757 (part), 32768, 32776–77, (part) 32789, 32798, 32801 (part), 32802, 32803–06 (part), 32808, 32809 (part), 32810, 32811–12 (part), 32815, 32818–19 (part), 32821–22 (part), 32824, 32827, 32830, 32835 (part), 32836, 32837 (part), 32839 (part), 32854–55, 32858–62, 32868–69, 32877, 32885–86, 32891, 32896, 34734 (part), 34736–37, 34740, 34744, 34747 (part), 34760, 34761 (part), 34777–78, 34786–87

* * *

ELEVENTH DISTRICT

DANIEL WEBSTER, Republican, of Clermon, FL; born in Charleston, WV, April 27, 1949; education: graduated from Evans High School, Orlando, FL; B.S., Georgia Institute of Technology, Atlanta, GA, 1971; professional: owner, Webster Air Conditioning & Heating, Inc., Orlando, FL; Florida House of Representatives, 1980–98; Speaker, Florida House of Representatives, 1996–98; Florida Senate, 1998–2008; Senate Majority Leader, Florida Senate, 2006–08; married: Sandy Jordan; father of six children and grandfather of fourteen; committees: Natural Resources; Science, Space, and Technology; Transportation and Infrastructure; elected to represent the 8th District in the 112th Congress on November 2, 2010; elected to represent the 10th District in the 113th Congress on November 6, 2012, and reelected on November 4, 2014; elected to represent the 11th District in the 115th Congress on November 8, 2016.

Office Listings

http://www.webster.house.gov twitter: @repwebster facebook.com/repwebster

1210 Longworth House Office Building, Washington, DC 20515 .... (202) 225–1002
Chief of Staff / Communications Director.—Jaryn Emhof. FAX: 226–6559
Legislative Director.—Steve Koncar.
Staff Attorney.—Emily Percival.
Communications Assistant.—Danny Jativa.
800 North U.S. Highway 27, Minneola, FL 34715 .... (352) 241–9220
Scheduler.—Natali Knight. FAX: 241–9181
Community Relations Representative.—Pam Jones.
Constituent Services Director / Office Manager.—Abigail Tyrrell.
Constituent Services Representatives: Sam Green, Stephen Shylkofski, Debbie Warren.
15 North Main Street, Suite B, Brooksville, FL 34601 .... (352) 241–9230

Office Listings—Continued

District Director.—Christa Pearson.
212 West Main Street, Suite 208A, Inverness, FL 34450 .... (352) 241–9204
Community Relations Associate.—Victoria White.
8015 E. County Road 466, Suite B, The Villages, FL 32162 .... (352) 383–3552
Community Relations Representative.—Cindy Brown.
Communications and Outreach Associate.—Laura Murtha.

Counties: CITRUS, HERNANDO, LAKE (part), MARION (part), AND SUMTER. CITIES AND TOWNSHIPS: Brooksville, Ocala, and The Villages. Population (2010), 696,345.

ZIP Codes: 32113 (part), 32133, 32134 (part), 32159 (part), 32162, 32179, 32195, 32617, 32686 (part), 32702 (part), 32784 (part), 33513–14, 33521, 33523 (part), 33538, 33585, 33597 (part), 34420, 34428–29, 34432 (part), 34433–34, 34436, 34442, 34445–46, 34448, 34449 (part), 34450, 34452–53, 34461, 34465, 34470–73, 34474–76 (part), 34479–80, 34481–82 (part), 34484, 34488, 34491, 34601–02, 34604, 34606–09, 34613–14, 34661, 34731 (part), 34785

* * *

TWELFTH DISTRICT

GUS M. BILIRAKIS, Republican, of Palm Harbor, FL; born in Gainesville, FL, February 8, 1963; raised in Tarpon Springs, FL; education: B.A., University of Florida, 1986; J.D., Stetson University, 1989; son of former Representative Michael Bilirakis (1983–2006); professional: volunteered on his father's congressional campaigns; interned for President Ronald Reagan and the National Republican Congressional Committee; worked for former Representative Don Sundquist (R-TN); ran the Bilirakis Law Group in Holiday, FL; taught government classes at St. Petersburg College; member of the Florida House of Representatives, 1998–2006; chaired several prominent panels in the State House, including Crime Prevention, Public Safety Appropriations, and the Economic Development, Trade, and Banking Committee; married: Eva; children: Michael, Teddy, Manuel, and Nicholas; committees: vice chair, Veterans' Affairs; Energy and Commerce; elected to the 110th Congress on November 7, 2006; reelected to each succeeding Congress.

Office Listings

http://bilirakis.house.gov https://www.facebook.com/gusbilirakis
https://twitter.com/repgusbilirakis

2112 Rayburn House Office Building, Washington, DC 20515 .... (202) 225–5755
Chief of Staff.—Elizabeth Hittos. FAX: 225–4085
Legislative Director.—Thomas Power.
Communications Director.—Elena Hernandez.
Director of Operations.—Samantha Gottshall.
Deputy Chief of Staff.—Summer Robertson.
7132 Little Road, New Port Richey, FL 34654 .... (727) 232–2921
FAX: 232–2923
600 Klosterman Road, Room BB–038, Tarpon Springs, FL 34689 .... (727) 940–5860
FAX: 940–5861

Counties: HILLSBOROUGH (part): Lutz and Odessa. PASCO: Aripeka, Bayonet Point, Crystal Springs, Dade City, Elfers, Holiday, Hudson, Lacoochee, Land O'Lakes, New Port Richey, Port Richey, San Antonio, Shady Hills, Spring Hill, St. Leo, Tilby, Trinity, Wesley Chapel, and Zephyrhills. PINELLAS (part): Dunedin, Clearwater, East Lake, Oldsmar, Ozona, Palm Harbor, Safety Harbor, and Tarpon Springs. POLK (part): Lakeland and Kathleen. SUMTER (part): Webster. Population (2015): 740,955.

ZIP Codes: 33523 (part), 33525, 33540 (part), 33541–45, 33548–49 (part), 33556, 33558, 33559 (part), 33574, 33576, 33597 (part), 33612–13 (part), 33618 (part), 33624–26 (part), 33647 (part), 33761 (part), 34610, 34637–39, 34652–55, 34667–69, 34677 (part), 34679 (part), 34681, 34683–84 (part), 34685, 34688–91, 34695 (part), 34698 (part)

* * *

THIRTEENTH DISTRICT

CHARLIE CRIST, Democrat, of St. Petersburg, FL; born in Altoona, PA, July 24, 1956; education: graduated from St. Petersburg High School, 1974; B.A., Florida State University, Tallahassee, FL, 1978; J.D., Samford University Cumberland School of Law, Birmingham, AL, 1981; professional: former Florida State Senator; former Education Commissioner of Florida; former Attorney General of Florida; Florida's 44th Governor; religion: Methodist; committees: Financial Services; Science, Space, and Technology; elected to the 115th Congress on November 8, 2016.

Office Listings

http://www.Crist.House.gov https://www.facebook.com/RepCharlieCrist/
twitter: @RepCharlieCrist

427 Cannon House Office Building, Washington, DC 20515 .... (202) 225–5961
Chief of Staff.—Austin Durrer. FAX: 225–9764
Legislative Director.—Christopher Fisher.
Communications Director.—Erin Moffet.
Legislative Counsel.—David Geller.
Legislative Assistant.—Sarah Hanson.
Legislative Correspondent.—Virginia Poe.
Scheduler.—Jonathan Pekkala.
Staff Assistant.—Victor Yang.
696 1st Avenue North, Suite #203, St. Petersburg, FL 33701 .... (727) 318–6770
District Director.—Steven Cary (acting). FAX: 623–0619
Outreach Director.—Gershom Faulkner.
Constituent Services Supervisor.—Michael Kenny.
Constituent Services Representatives: Michael Batista, John Foster, Dillion Stafford.
District Operations Manager.—Kendrick Lewis.

Counties: PINELLAS COUNTY (part). CITIES AND TOWNSHIPS: Bardmoor, Bay Pines, Bear Creek, Belleair, Belleair Beach, Belleair Bluffs, Belleair Shore, Clearwater, Dunedin, Feather Sound, Greenbriar, Gulfport, Harbor Bluffs, Indian Rocks Beach, Indian Shores, Kenneth City, Largo, Lealman, Madeira Beach, North Redington Beach, Olsmar, Pinellas Park, Redington Beach, Redington Shores, Ridgecrest, Safety Harbor, Seminole, South Highpoint, South Pasadena, St. Pete Beach, St. Petersburg, Tierra Verde, Treasure Island, and West Lealman. Population (2012), 702,203.

ZIP Codes: 33701 (part), 33702–03, 33704–05 (part), 33706, 33707 (part), 33708–09, 33710–11 (part), 33713 (part), 33714–16, 33744, 33755–56, 33759–60, 33761 (part), 33762–65, 33767, 33770–74, 33776–78, 33781–82, 33785–86, 34677 (part), 34683–84 (part), 34695 (part), 34698

* * *

FOURTEENTH DISTRICT

KATHY CASTOR, Democrat, of Tampa, FL; born in Miami, FL, August 20, 1966; education: B.A., political science, Emory University, 1988; J.D., Florida State University, 1991; professional: Assistant General Counsel, State of Florida, Department of Community Affairs, 1991–94; attorney, Icard Merrill, 1994–95; partner, Broad and Cassel, 1995–2000; ran for Florida State Senate, 2000; Hillsborough County Commissioner, 2002–06; religion: member of Palma Ceia Presbyterian Church; married: William Lewis; children: two; committees: Energy and Commerce; elected to the 110th Congress on November 7, 2006; reelected to each succeeding Congress.

Office Listings

http://castor.house.gov www.facebook.com/USRepKathyCastor
www.twitter.com/USRepKCastor

2052 Rayburn House Office Building, Washington, DC 20515 .... (202) 225–3376
Chief of Staff.—Clay Phillips. FAX: 225–5652
Deputy Chief of Staff / Scheduler.—Lara Hopkins.
Legislative Director.—Elizabeth Brown.
4144 North Armenia Avenue, Suite 300, Tampa, FL 33607 .... (813) 871–2817
District Director.—Marcia Mejia.
Press Secretary.—Steven Angotti.

Counties: HILLSBOROUGH. CITIES: East Lake-Orient Park, Egypt Lake-Leto, Gibsonton, Lake Magdalene, Northdale, Palm River-Clair Mel, Tampa, Town 'n' Country, University of South Florida, and Westchase. Population (2015), 757,440.

ZIP Codes: 33510–11 (part), 33534 (part), 33549 (part), 33570 (part), 33572, 33578 (part), 33584 (part), 33602–07, 33609, 33610 (part), 33611, 33612–13 (part), 33614–16, 33617–18 (part), 33619, 33621, 33624–26 (part), 33629, 33634–35, 33637 (part), 33701 (part), 33704–05 (part), 33707 (part), 33710–11 (part), 33712, 33713 (part)

* * *

FIFTEENTH DISTRICT

DENNIS A. ROSS, Republican, of Lakeland, FL; born in Lakeland, October 18, 1959; education: Lakeland Senior High School; B.S., organizational management, Auburn University, Auburn, AL, 1981; J.D., Cumberland School of Law at Samford University, Birmingham, AL, 1987; professional: attorney, Holland and Knight; attorney, Walt Disney World; founder and attorney, Ross Vecchio, PA, 1989–2010; awards: Workers Compensation Section, Appreciation Award, 2001; Florida Building Material Association, Legislator of the Year Award, 2001 and 2003; Florida Workers Advocate, Outstanding Freshman Representative Award, 2001; The Trust for Public Land, Legislative Leadership Award, 2001; Polk Community College, Outstanding Legislator, 2001; Florida Crane Owners Council, Representative of the Year, 2003; Florida Association of Roofing Professionals, Legislative Achievement Award, 2003; Florida Automotive Dealer Association, Legislator of the Year, 2003; Florida Retail Federation, Legislator of the Year, 2003; Florida Bankers Association, Outstanding Leadership Award, 2004; ARC Florida, Representative of the Year, 2004; YMCA of Florida, Outstanding Leadership Award, 2005; Florida League of Cities, Legislative Appreciation Award, 2005, 2006, and 2007; Florida Insurance Council, Harry G. Landrum Outstanding Legislative Leadership, 2005 and 2008; Florida Association of Counties, Champion Award, 2005; Florida Trucking Association, Legislator of the Year, 2005 and 2006; Associated Industries of Florida, Champion for Business Award, 2005; Florida Association of Insurance and Financial Advisors, Representative of the Year, 2005; Florida Association of Mortgage Brokers, Grateful Recognition Award, 2005; Florida Association of Insurance Agents, Legislator of the Year, 2006; Florida Chamber, Most Valuable Legislator, 2008; Governor's Hurricane Conference, Legislative Award, 2008; Associated Industries of Florida Financial Securities Council, Legislator of the Year, 2008; Florida Chamber Honor Roll 2001, 2002, 2003, 2004, 2005, 2007, and 2008; religion: member, First Presbyterian Church, Lakeland; married: Cindy; children: Shane and Travis; committees: Financial Services; Oversight and Government Reform; elected to the 112th Congress on November 2, 2010; reelected to each succeeding Congress.

Office Listings

http://www.dennisross.house.gov twitter: @repdennisross

436 Cannon House Office Building, Washington, DC 20515 .... (202) 225–1252
Chief of Staff.—Anthony Foti. FAX: 226–0585
Deputy Chief of Staff.—Kyle Glenn.
DC Scheduler.—Joni Shockey.
170 Fitzgerald Road, Suite 1, Lakeland, FL 33813 .... (863) 644–8215
FAX: 648–0749
110 West Reynolds Street, Suite 101, Plant City, FL 33563 .... (813) 752–4790
685 West Montrose Street, Clermont, FL 34711 .... (352) 727–2248
District Director.—Shelee Meeker.
Field Representative.—Stephen Gately.

Counties: HILLSBOROUGH (part). CITIES AND TOWNSHIPS: Bloomingdale, Brandon, Dover, East Lake-Orient Park, Fish Hawk, Lake Magdalene, Mango, Pebble Creek, Plant City, Riverview, Seffner, Tampa, Temple Terrace, Thonotosassa, and Valrico. POLK (part). CITIES AND TOWNSHIPS: Combee Settlement, Crystal Lake, Fussels Corner, Highland City, Kathleen, Lakeland Highlands, Lakeland, and Medulla. LAKE (part). CITIES AND TOWNSHIPS: Clermont, Four Corners, Groveland, Orange Mountain, Polk City, Skytop, and South Clermont. Population (2010), 813,570.

ZIP Codes: 33510–11 (part), 33527, 33540 (part), 33547–49 (part), 33559 (part), 33563, 33565–67, 33569 (part), 33578 (part), 33584 (part), 33592, 33594, 33596 (part), 33610 (part), 33612–13 (part), 33617–18 (part), 33620, 33637 (part), 33647 (part), 33801, 33803, 33805 (part), 33809 (part), 33810–13, 33815, 33823 (part), 33830 (part), 33849, 33860 (part), 33868 (part), 33880 (part)

* * *

SIXTEENTH DISTRICT

VERN BUCHANAN, Republican, of Longboat Key, FL; born in Detroit, MI, May 8, 1951; education: B.B.A., business administration, Cleary University; M.B.A., University of Detroit; honorary degree: Doctorate of Science in Business Administration, Cleary University; professional: founder and chairman, Buchanan Enterprises; founder and chairman, Buchanan Automotive Group, 1992; operations include Sarasota Ford and 18 auto franchises in the southeastern United States; experience in real estate including home building and property development and management; awards: One of America's Ten Outstanding Young Men, U.S. Jaycees; Entrepreneur of the Year, *Inc.* Magazine and Arthur Young; Entrepreneur of the Year, Harvard Business School, Club of Detroit; One of Michigan's Five Outstanding Young Men, Michigan Jaycees; President's Award, Ford Motor Company; Certified Retailer Award, J.D. Power and Associates; Outstanding Citizen Award, United Negro College Fund; Outstanding Philanthropic Corporation Award, National Society of Fund Raising Executives; Freedom Award for Business and Industry, NAACP; The American Jewish Committee Civic Achievement Award; Tampa Bay Business Hall of Fame Award; married: Sandy Buchanan; children: James and Matt; committees: Ways and Means; elected to the 110th Congress on November 7, 2006; reelected to each succeeding Congress.

Office Listings

http://www.buchanan.house.gov twitter: @vernbuchanan
https://www.facebook.com/congressmanbuchanan

2104 Cannon House Office Building, Washington, DC 20515 .... (202) 225–5015
FAX: 226–0828
Chief of Staff.—Dave Karvelas.
Deputy Chief of Staff.—Max Goodman.
Legislative Director.—Katie Wise.
Communications Director.—Vacant.
Scheduler.—Hobart Richey.
111 South Orange Avenue, Suite 200W, Sarasota, FL 34236 .... (941) 951–6643
District Director.—Sally Tibbetts.
Scheduler.—Sydney Gruters.
151 Manatee Avenue West, Suite 205, Bradenton, FL 34205 .... (941) 747–9081

Counties: MANATEE, SARASOTA. Population (2010), 639,345.

ZIP Codes: 33834, 34211–12, 34219, 34221, 34223, 34240–41, 34251, 34287–88, 34292–93

* * *

SEVENTEENTH DISTRICT

THOMAS J. ROONEY, Republican, of Okeechobee, FL; born in Philadelphia, PA, November 21, 1970; education: B.A., Washington and Jefferson, Washington, PA; M.A., University of Florida, Gainesville, FL; J.D., University of Miami, Coral Gables, FL; religion: member, Roman Catholic Church; married: Tara; children: Tommy, Sean, and Seamus; committees: Appropriations; Permanent Select Committee on Intelligence; elected to the 111th Congress on November 4, 2008; reelected to each succeeding Congress.

Office Listings

http://www.rooney.house.gov https://www.facebook.com/reptomrooney?ref=mf
https://twitter.com/tomrooney

2160 Rayburn House Office Building, Washington, DC 20515 .... (202) 225–5792
Chief of Staff.—Jessica Moore.
Deputy Chief of Staff.—Michelle Reinshuttle.
Legislative Director.—Andrew Callahan.
Communications Director.—Meghan Rodgers.
226 Taylor Street, Suite 230, Punta Gorda, FL 33950 .... (941) 575–9101
304 NW 2nd Street, Room 105, Okeechobee, FL 34972 .... (863) 402–9082
4507 George Boulevard, Sebring, FL 33875 .... (863) 402–9082

Counties: CHARLOTTE, DESOTO, GLADES, HARDEE, HIGHLANDS, LEE (part), OKEECHOBEE, POLK (part), AND SARASOTA (part). Population (2010), 696,344.

ZIP Codes: 33471, 33503, 33511 (part), 33534 (part), 33547 (part), 33569–70 (part), 33573, 33578 (part), 33579, 33596 (part), 33598 (part), 33825, 33827, 33830 (part), 33834, 33838 (part), 33839, 33841, 33843, 33844 (part), 33847, 33852–59, 33860 (part), 33865, 33867, 33870, 33872–73, 33875–77, 33880–81 (part), 33884 (part), 33890, 33898, 33903 (part), 33905 (part), 33917 (part), 33920, 33921 (part), 33935–36 (part), 33944, 33946–48, 33950, 33952–54, 33955 (part), 33960, 33971 (part), 33972, 33974 (part), 33980–83, 34219, (part), 34223–24 (part), 34251 (part), 34266 (part), 34268–69, 34972 (part), 34974 (part)

* * *

EIGHTEENTH DISTRICT

BRIAN J. MAST, Republican, of Palm City, FL; born in Grand Rapids, MI, July 10, 1980; education: bachelor's degree in extension studies with a concentration in economics and minors in government and environmental studies, Harvard Extension School, Cambridge, MA, 2016; professional: analyst in NA-42 Office of Emergency Response, National Nuclear Security Administration, Department of Energy; instructor in post blast analysis and homemade explosives, Bureau of Alcohol, Tobacco, and Firearms; explosive specialist under the Department of Homeland Security; military: 12-year Army veteran, including under the elite Joint Special Operations Command; awards: Bronze Star Medal; Army Commendation Medal for Valor; Purple Heart Medal; Defense Meritorious Service Medal; religion: Christian; family: wife, Brianna; children: Magnum, Maverick, and Madeline; committees: Foreign Affairs; Transportation and Infrastructure; Veterans' Affairs; elected to the 115th Congress on November 8, 2016.

Office Listings

http://www.mast.house.gov https://www.facebook.com/repbrianmast
twitter: @repbrianmast instagram: @repbrianmast

2182 Rayburn House Office Building, Washington, DC 20515 .... (202) 225–3026
Chief of Staff.—James Langenderfer. FAX: 225–3026
Director of Operations.—Caitlin McBride.
Communications Director.—Brad Stewart.
Legislative Director.—Barry Smith.
Legislative Assistant.—Wes Brooks.
Legislative Aide.—Michael Weglein.
Legislative Correspondent.—Sarah Miller.
Staff Assistant.—Hannah Hughes.
171 Southwest Flagler Avenue, Stuart, FL 34994 .... (772) 403–0901
Deputy Chief of Staff.—Stephen Leighton.
Constituent Services Representative.—Alex Melendez.
Field Representatives: Nick Ciotti, John Haddox.
121 Southwest Port St. Lucie Boulevard, Room 187, Port St. Lucie, FL 34984 .... (772) 336–2877
Constituent Services Representatives: Derek Hankerson, Kalene Rowley.

Counties: MARTIN, ST. LUCIE, AND PALM BEACH (northern part). CITIES: Eden, Fort Pierce, Hobe Sound, Hutchinson Island, Indian River Estates, Indiantown, Jensen Beach, Juno Beach, Jupiter, Jupiter Inlet Colony, Jupiter Island, Lakewood Park, Loxahatchee, North Palm Beach, Palm Beach Gardens, Palm Beach Shores, Port Salerno, Port St. Lucie, Riviera Beach, Royal Palm Beach, Sewall's Point, Singer Island (part), Stuart, Palm City, Tequesta, Tradition, and West Palm Beach (part). Population (2010), 696,345.

ZIP Codes: 33403–04, 33407–12, 33417–18, 33420, 33422, 33438, 33455, 33458, 33468–70, 33475, 33477–78, 34945–54, 34956–58, 34972, 34974, 34979, 34981–88, 34990–92, 34994–97

* * *

NINETEENTH DISTRICT

FRANCIS ROONEY, Republican, of Naples, FL; born in Tulsa, OK, December 4, 1953; education: A.B., English, Georgetown University, Washington, DC, 1975; J.D., Georgetown University, Washington, DC, 1978; professional: former CEO of an international investment company; U.S. Ambassador to the Holy See, 2005–08; religion: Catholic; family: wife, Kathleen C. Rooney; daughter, Kathleen; sons, Michael and Larry; daughter-in-law, Porshca; two grandchildren; committees: Education and the Workforce; Foreign Affairs; Joint Economic Committee; elected to the 115th Congress on November 8, 2016.

Office Listings

http://rooney.house.gov

228 Cannon House Office Building, Washington, DC 20515 .... (202) 225–2536
Chief of Staff.—Jessica Carter.
Legislative Director.—Corey Schrodt.
Communications Director.—Chris Berardi.
Scheduler.—Janae Cardinali.
3299 Tamiami Trail, Suite 105, Naples, FL 34112 .... (239) 252–6225
1039 SE., 9th Avenue, Suite 308, Cape Coral, FL 33990 .... (239) 599–6033

Counties: COLLIER (part) AND LEE (part). Population (2010), 696,345.

ZIP Codes: 33901, 33903 (part), 33904, 33905 (part), 33907–09, 33912–14, 33916, 33917 (part), 33919, 33921 (part), 33922, 33924, 33928, 33931, 33936 (part), 33945, 33955 (part), 33956–57, 33965–67, 33971 (part), 33973, 33974 (part), 33976, 33990–91, 33993, 34101–03, 34104–05 (part), 34108, 34109 (part), 34110, 34112 (part), 34113, 34114 (part), 34119 (part), 34134–35, 34140, 34145

* * *

TWENTIETH DISTRICT

ALCEE L. HASTINGS, Democrat, of Delray Beach, FL; born in Altamonte Springs, FL, September 5, 1936; education: graduated, Crooms Academy, Sanford, FL, 1954; B.A., Fisk University, Nashville, TN, 1958; Howard University, Washington, DC; J.D., Florida A&M University, Tallahassee, 1963; professional: attorney; admitted to the Florida bar, 1963; Circuit Judge, U.S. District Court for the Southern District of Florida; member: NAACP; Miami-Dade Chamber of Commerce; Family Christian Association; ACLU; Southern Poverty Law Center; National Organization for Women; Planned Parenthood; Women and Children First, Inc.; Sierra

Club; Cousteau Society; Broward County Democratic Executive Committee; Dade County Democratic Executive Committee; Lauderhill Democratic Club; Hollywood Hills Democratic Club; Pembroke Pines Democratic Club; Urban League; National Bar Association; Florida Chapter of the National Bar Association; T.J. Reddick Bar Association; National Conference of Black Lawyers; Simon Wiesenthal Center; The Furtivist Society; Progressive Black Police Officers Club; International Black Firefighters Association; co-chair, Florida Delegation; religion: member, African Methodist Episcopal Church; family: three children: Alcee Lamar II, Chelsea, and Leigh; ranking Democratic member, Helsinki Commission; Senior Democratic Whip; committees: Rules; elected on November 3, 1992, to the 103rd Congress; reelected to each succeeding Congress.

Office Listings

http://www.alceehastings.house.gov https://www.facebook.com/RepHastingsFL
https://twitter.com/RepHastingsFL

2353 Rayburn House Office Building, Washington, DC 20515 .... (202) 225–1313
Chief of Staff.—Lale Morrison. FAX: 225–1171
Legislative Director / Senior Counsel.—Tom Carnes.
Counsel / Rules Associate.—Matt Price.
Senior Legislative Assistant / Press Secretary.—Evan Polisar.
Director of Operations.—DeBorah Posey.
2701 West Oakland Park Boulevard, Suite 200, Ft. Lauderdale, FL 33311 .... (954) 733–2800
Chief of Staff.—Arthur W. Kennedy.
Palm Beach County Office, Town of Mangonia Park Municipal Center, 1755 East Tiffany Drive, Mangonia Park, FL 33407 .... (561) 469–7048

Counties: BROWARD (part) AND PALM BEACH (part). Population, 713,165.

ZIP Codes: 33060 (part), 33063–64 (part), 33066 (part), 33068, 33069 (part), 33071 (part), 33301 (part), 33304–05 (part), 33309 (part), 33311–12 (part), 33313, 33317 (part), 33319, 33321, 33322 (part), 33326–27 (part), 33334 (part), 33351, 33401 (part), 33403–11 (part), 33413–15 (part), 33417–18 (part), 33426 (part), 33428 (part), 33430, 33435 (part), 33438 (part), 33440–42 (part), 33449 (part), 33460 (part), 33462 (part), 33470 (part), 33472 (part), 33476, 33493, 34142 (part)

* * *

TWENTY-FIRST DISTRICT

LOIS FRANKEL, Democrat, of West Palm Beach, FL; born in New York City, NY, May 16, 1948; education: B.A., Boston University, Boston, MA, 1970; J.D., Georgetown University Law Center, Washington, DC, 1973; professional: elected State Representative in the 83rd District of the Florida House of Representatives, 1986; first female Florida House Minority Leader from 1995–2003; elected Mayor of West Palm Beach from 2003–11; religion: Jewish; caucuses: chair, Democratic Women's Working Group; co-chair, Congressional Caucus for Women's Issues; Bipartisan Task Force for Combating Anti-Semitism; Congressional Animal Protection Caucus; Congressional Arts Caucus; Congressional Boating Caucus; Congressional Everglades Caucus; Congressional Human Trafficking Caucus; Congressional LGBT Equality Caucus; Congressional Military Sexual Assault Prevention Caucus; Congressional Ports Caucus; Congressional Progressive Caucus; Congressional Pro-Choice Caucus; Bipartisan Congressional Task Force on Alzheimer's Disease; Congressional Travel and Tourism Caucus; Democratic Israel Working Group; Safe Climate Caucus; committees: Foreign Affairs; Transportation and Infrastructure; elected to the 113th Congress on November 6, 2012; reelected to each succeeding Congress.

Office Listings

http://frankel.house.gov https://www.facebook.com/reploisfrankel
https://twitter.com/reploisfrankel

1037 Longworth House Office Building, Washington, DC 20515 .... (202) 225–9890
Chief of Staff.—Jim Cho. FAX: 225–1224
Legislative Director / Deputy Chief of Staff.—Kelsey Moran.
Legislative Assistants: Aliyah Dash, Yana Mayayeva, Bradley Solyan.
Press Secretary.—Rachel Huxley-Cohen.
Communications and Media Director for Women's Issues.—Rosie Hilmer.
Scheduler.—Kate Regan.
Legislative Correspondent / Press Assistant.—Olivia Hodge.
2500 North Military Trail, Suite 490, Boca Raton, FL 33431 .... (561) 998–9045
District Director.—Felicia Goldstein. FAX: 998–9048

Counties: PALM BEACH. CITIES: Boynton Beach, Delray Beach, Greenacres, Lake Worth, Wellington, and West Palm Beach. Population (2010), 738,875.

ZIP Codes: 33400–01, 33411, 33414, 33422, 33424, 33426, 33435, 33437, 33444, 33448–49, 33460, 33467, 33472, 33474, 33482, 33484

* * *

TWENTY-SECOND DISTRICT

THEODORE DEUTCH, Democrat, of Fort Lauderdale, FL; born in Bethlehem, PA, May 7, 1966; education: graduate of Liberty High School; B.A., University of Michigan, Ann Arbor, MI, 1988; J.D., University of Michigan Law School, Ann Arbor, 1990; admitted to the Florida Bar, 1991; professional: attorney; Florida State Senator, 2006–10; member: Florida Bar Association; Jewish Federation of South Palm Beach County; League of Women Voters; married to the former Jill Weinstock; three children; committees: Foreign Affairs; Judiciary; Select Committee on Ethics; elected, by special election, to the 111th Congress on April 13, 2010, to fill the vacancy caused by the resignation of U.S. Representative Robert Wexler; reelected to each succeeding Congress.

Office Listings

http://deutch.house.gov www.facebook.com/congressmanteddeutch
twitter: @repteddeutch instagram: @repteddeutch

2447 Rayburn House Office Building, Washington, DC 20515 .... (202) 225–3001
Chief of Staff.—Joshua Rogin. FAX: 225–5974
Deputy Chief of Staff.—Ellen McLaren.
Press Secretary.—Jason Atterman.
7900 Glades Road, Suite 250, Boca Raton, FL 33434 .... (561) 470–5440
District Director.—Wendi Lipsich. FAX: 470–5446

Counties: BROWARD (part). CITIES: Broadview Park, Coconut Creek, Deerfield Beach, Fort Lauderdale, Hillsboro Beach, Lauderdale-by-the-Sea, Lighthouse Point, Oakland Park, Pompano Beach, Sea Ranch Lakes, and Wilton Manors. PALM BEACH (part). CITIES: Boca Raton and Highland Beach. Population (2010), 696,345.

ZIP Codes: 33060 (part), 33062, 33064 (part), 33069 (part), 33301 (part), 33304–05 (part), 33306, 33308, 33309 (part), 33311–12 (part), 33315–17 (part), 33322–25 (part), 33334 (part), 33401 (part), 33404–07 (part), 33415 (part), 33426 (part), 33431–32, 33433–36 (part), 33441 (part), 33444–45, 33460 (part), 33461, 33462–63 (part), 33480, 33483, 33484 (part), 33486–87, 33496 (part)

* * *

TWENTY-THIRD DISTRICT

DEBBIE WASSERMAN SCHULTZ, Democrat, of Weston, FL; born in Forest Hills, Queens County, NY, September 27, 1966; education: B.A., University of Florida, Gainesville, FL, 1988; M.A., University of Florida, FL, 1990; professional: public policy curriculum specialist, Nova Southeastern University; adjunct instructor, political science, Broward Community College; aide to Florida State House of Representatives member Peter Deutsch, 1989–92; member, Florida State House of Representatives, 1992–2000; member, Florida State Senate, 2000–04; organizations: board of trustees, Westside Regional Medical Center; Outstanding Freshman Legislator, Florida Women's Political Caucus; secretary; board of directors, American Jewish Congress; member, Broward National Organization for Women; board of directors, National Safety Council, South Florida Chapter; religion: Jewish; married: Steve; children: Rebecca, Jake, and Shelby; Chief Deputy Democratic Whip; chair, Democratic National Committee, 2011–16; committees: Appropriations; Budget; elected to the 109th Congress on November 2, 2004; reelected to each succeeding Congress.

Office Listings

http://wassermanschultz.house.gov twitter: @repDWStweets
facebook: https://www.facebook.com/RepDWS

1114 Longworth House Office Building, Washington, DC 20515 .... (202) 225–7931
Chief of Staff.—Tracie Pough. FAX: 226–2052
District Director.—Lori Green.
Communications Director.—David Damron.
Legislative Director / General Counsel.—Sarah Farhadian.
Scheduler / Executive Assistant.—Lauren Mylott.
777 Sawgrass Corporate Parkway, Sunrise, FL 33325 .... (954) 845–1179
19200 West Country Club Drive, Third Floor, Aventura, FL 33180 .... (305) 936–5724

Counties: BROWARD COUNTY (part). CITIES: Cooper City, Dania Beach, Davie, Fort Lauderdale, Hallandale Beach, Hollywood, Pembroke Pines, Plantation, Southwest Ranches, Sunrise, and Weston. MIAMI-DADE COUNTY (part). CITIES: Aventura,

Bal Harbour, Bay Harbor Islands, Golden Beach, Indian Creek, Sunny Isles Beach, and Surfside. Population (2010), 703,594.

ZIP Codes: 33004, 33009 (part), 33019–20, 33021 (part), 33023–25 (part), 33026, 33027 (part), 33028, 33029 (part), 33109 (part), 33132 (part), 33139 (part), 33140, 33141 (part), 33154 (part), 33160 (part), 33179–81 (part), 33312 (part), 33314, 33315–17 (part), 33323–27 (part), 33328, 33330–31, 33332 (part)

* * *

TWENTY-FOURTH DISTRICT

FREDERICA S. WILSON, Democrat, of Miami, FL; born in Miami, November 5; education: B.S., Fisk University; M.S., University of Miami; honorary doctorate of humane letters, Florida Memorial University and Bethune-Cookman University; professional: executive director, Office of Alternative Education and Dropout Prevention, Miami-Dade County Schools; member, Miami-Dade County School Board, 1992–98; Minority Whip, Florida State House of Representatives, 1998–2002; Democratic Whip, Florida State Senate, 2002–04; Minority Leader Pro Tempore, Florida State Senate, 2002–10; Minority Whip, Florida State Senate, 2008–10; organizations: regional director, Alpha Kappa Alpha Sorority, Inc., 1986–present; founder/member, 5000 Role Models of Excellence, Inc., 1993–present; founder, Stop Day Enough is Enough, 1996–present; Miami delegate, President's Summit for America's Future, 1997; State of Florida ''STOP DAY'', Enough is Enough, founder, 1996; President's Summit for America's Future, 1997; founder, Miami-Dade County ''Keep Me Safe'' summit, march, and candlelight vigil; board member, Women's Action for New Directions Educational Fund, 2004; current member, National Association of Black School Educators; current member, the Links, Inc.; honors and awards: Southern Living, Outstanding Southerner, May 1993; Macedonia Missionary Baptist Church, Image Maker, 1993; South Florida Association of Black Journalists, Kuumba Award, 1994; St. Petersburg Junior College, In Recognition, 1996; American Red Cross, Spectrum Award, 1998; African-American Achiever Award for Education, 1998; Peace Education Foundation, Peacemaker of the Year, 1998; Youth Crime Watch/Citizens Crime Watch, a Champion for All Poor and Minority Students, 1998; Imperial Daughters of Isis Miami Beach, Florida Hall of Fame, 1999; NAACP, Florida Chapter, Morris Milton Memorial Award, 2001; Zeta Phi Beta Sorority, Inc., Leadership Award, 2001; Florida A&M University, National Alumni Association Expresses Gratitude, 2001; The Florida HIV-AIDS Ministries, Inc., Honors State Representative Frederica S. Wilson, 2001; Florida AIDS Action, Outstanding Leadership and Support for HIV/AIDS and Health Care, 2002; Alpha Kappa Alpha Sorority, Inc., In Appreciation, 2002; Western Union, L'Union Fait la Force Award, 2003; Community Action Agency, Citizen of the Year Award, 2004; American Cancer Society, Florida Chapter, Legislative Leadership Award, 2004; Florida Education Association, Educator of the Year, 2004; Association of Black Health-System Pharmacists, Legislator Achievement Award, 2004; Easter Seals of Miami-Dade, Legislator of the Year Award, 2004; Northside Seventh Day Adventist Church (Miami), Distinguished Community Leader Award, 2004; The Black Archives, History and Research Foundation of South Florida, Inc., Chairman's Award, 2004; Sierra Club, Florida Chapter, Legislative Recognition Award, 2004; Network Miami Magazine, One of Miami's 50 Most Influential Black Business Professionals, 2004; Millennium Movers, Inc., Shaker Award, 2004; Alpha Kappa Alpha Sorority, Ft. Pierce, Florida Chapter, Soror of the Year, 2005; Alpha Kappa Alpha Sorority, Ft. Walton Beach, Florida Chapter, Soror of the Year, 2005; Alpha Kappa Alpha Sorority, Thomasville, GA Chapter, Soror of the Year, 2005; Carrie P. Meek Education Leadership Achievement Award, 2005; Miami Gardens Jaycees, Distinguished Service Award, 2005; Alpha Kappa Alpha, Inc., Emerald Service Award, 2005; The Links, Inc., Links of Gold Award, 2005; Belafonte TACOLCY Center, Inc., U.S. Department of Justice/Drug Enforcement Administration in Recognition of State Senator Frederica S. Wilson, 2005; SEIU Florida Healthcare Union, Legislative Hero Award, 2006; Barry University, SGA Acknowledgement of Florida's Residents Access Grant Award, 2006; City of Miami, Women Builders of Community Dreams Award, 2006; Florida Memorial University, SGA Leadership Character and Service Award, 2006; Holy Faith Missionary Baptist Church, Participation Award, 2006; Miami-Dade Police Department, Appreciation Award, 2006; The Historic St. Agnes Episcopal Church, 108th Anniversary Appreciation Award, 2006; FAU, Small Business Development Appreciation Award, 2006; Day of the Child, Mentoring Award, 2006; Project H.O.P.E., Katrina Humanitarian Award, 2006; South Florida Chapter of the Coalition of Black Trade Unionists, Audrey McCollum Scholarship Award, 2006; CEO Magazine, Legislative Action Recognition, 2006; Community Action Agency, Youth Leadership Award, 2006; I.B.P.O.E. of W., Antlers Temple #39, Legislative Excellence Award, 2006; Community Health of South Dade, Inc., Health Hero Award, 2006; Health Council of South Florida, Inc., Health Leadership Award, 2006; National Coalition of 100 Black Women, Inc., Greater Miami Chapter, Candace Award, 2006; Kiwanis Club of Miami Shores, North Dade Exemplary Service Award, 2006; Academy of Florida Trial Lawyers, Rosemary Barkett Award, 2006; National Pan Hellenic Council, Inc., Celebration of Excellence, 2006; NAACP Milton Morris Award, 2007; Jessie C. Trice Humanitarian Award, 2007; Liberty City's

Community Action Agency, Community Service Award, 2007; Miami Dade College, Pathway to Opportunity Appreciation Award, 2007; Florida Association of School Administrators, Legislator of the Year, 2007; Florida Association of Women Lawyers, Legislative Recognition Award, 2007; Florida Health Center, Jessie C. Trice Humanitarian Award, 2007; Miami Dade Community Action Agency, Liberty City Advisor Committee in Recognition of State Senator Frederica S. Wilson June 2007; The National Medical Association, Scroll of Merit for Public Education Advocacy, 2008; American School Health Association, Legislator of the Year, 2008; Alpha Kappa Alpha Sorority International, Rosa Parks Coretta Scott King Award, 2008; Florida Association of Counties (FAC), County Partner Award, 2008; Florida Cable Telecommunications Association, Leaders in Learning Award, 2008; AKA Educational Advancement Foundation, The Green Diamond Award, 2008; Bethune-Cookman University, In Tribute, 2009; Alpha Kappa Alpha Sorority, Inc., With Appreciation, 2009; The Links, Inc., In Appreciation, 2010 Alpha Kappa Alpha Sorority, Inc., Timeless Service to Mankind, 2011; Miami Dade Chamber of Commerce, H.T. Smith Lifetime Achievement Award, 2011; ICABA, Salutes South Florida's 100 Accomplished Caribbean Americans, 2012; TheGrio.com, The Grio's 100, 2012; Louie Bing Scholarship Fund, Inc., Award of Excellence, 2012; National Voices for Equality Education and Enlightenment Voices of Leadership Award, Congresswoman Wilson, April 2012; First Focus Campaign for Children, Defender of Children, 2012; Youth Power Movement, First Annual Humanitarian Award, 2012; I Am Empowered for Jobs Award, National Urban League, 2013; Broward Black Elected Officials Inaugural Lifetime Achievement Community Service Award; The Links, Inc., Services to Youth Award, 2013; City of North Miami, In Recognition, 2013; Honorary Nigerian Chieftaincy title of ''Jagunmolu,'' which means The People's Warrior in the Yoruba language, October 2016; Appreciation Trophy, City of Miami Gardens, 2016; Appreciation Trophy, City of North Miami, 2016; Visionary Honoree, Little Haiti Cultural Complex Women's International Month, 2016; Community Service Award, Word of life Bible Ministry, 2016; Matron, Word of life Bible Ministry, 2016; David Lawrence Jr. Champion for Children Award by The Children's Trust, July 2017; caucuses: founder and chair, Florida Ports Caucus; committees: Education and the Workforce; Transportation and Infrastructure; elected to the 112th Congress on November 2, 2010; reelected to each succeeding Congress.

Office Listings

http://wilson.house.gov twitter.com/repwilson https://www.facebook.com/repwilson
https://www.instagram.com/repwilson https://www.youtube.com/user/RepFredericaWilson

2445 Rayburn House Office Building, Washington, DC 20515 .... (202) 225–4506
Chief of Staff.—Chasseny Lewis. FAX: 226–0777
Legislative Director.—Lori Stith.
Communications Director.—Joyce Jones.
Legislative Assistants: Jean Roseme, David Simon.
Legislative Correspondent.—Phoenix Chi Wang.
Staff Assistant.—Gabrielle Miller.
Special Assistant / Scheduler.—Cheyenne Range.
18425 Northwest, 2nd Avenue, Suite 355, Miami, FL 33169 .... (305) 690–5905
District Chief of Staff.—Alexis Snyder.
District Office Director.—Joyce Postell.
Director of Field Operations.—Shirlee Moreau-Lafleur.
Deputy Communications Director.—Cheryl R. Waide.
Director of Special Community Relations.—Greg King.
Director of Special Community Outreach.—Charles C. Scott II.
District Policy Assistant.—Daphne Jean-Pierre, Esq.
Congressional Aide.—Vacant.
2600 Hollywood Boulevard, Old Library 1st Floor, Hollywood, FL 33020 .... (954) 921–3682
West Park City Hall, 1965 South State Road 7, West Park, FL 33023 .... (954) 989–2688

Counties: BROWARD (part) AND MIAMI-DADE (part). Population (2010), 725,282.

ZIP Codes: 33009, 33013–14, 33021, 33023–25, 33027, 33054–56, 33101, 33109, 33125, 33127–28, 33130–32, 33136–39, 33141–42, 33147, 33150, 33154, 33160–62, 33167–69, 33179–81

* * *

TWENTY-FIFTH DISTRICT

MARIO DIAZ-BALART, Republican, of Miami, FL; born in Ft. Lauderdale, FL, September 25, 1961; education: University of South Florida; professional: president, Gordon Diaz-Balart and Partners (public relations and marketing business); public service: administrative assistant to the Mayor of Miami, 1985–88; Florida House of Representatives, 1988–92, and 2000–02; Florida State Senate, 1992–2000; religion: Catholic; committees: Appropriations; Budget; elected Representative of the 25th District to the 108th Congress on November 5, 2002; reelected to each succeeding Congress; elected Representative of the 21st District to the 112th Congress on November 2, 2010; elected Representative of the 25th District to the 113th Congress on November 6, 2012; reelected to each succeeding Congress.

Office Listings

http://www.mariodiaz-balart.house.gov https://www.facebook.com/mdiazbalart
https://twitter.com/mariodb https://www.youtube.com/user/mariodiazbalart
http://instagram.com/repmariodb

440 Cannon House Office Building, Washington, DC 20515 .... (202) 225–4211
Chief of Staff.—Cesar A. Gonzalez. FAX: 226–8576
Deputy Chief of Staff / Legislative Director.—Miguel Mendoza.
8669 Northwest 36th Street, Suite 100, Doral, FL 33166 .... (305) 470–8555
Deputy Chief of Staff / District Director.—Miguel Otero. FAX: 470–8575
Deputy District Director.—Gloria Amor.
4715 Golden Gate Parkway, Suite 1, Naples, FL 34116 .... (239) 348–1620
Congressional Aide.—Enrique Padron. FAX: 348–3569

Counties: COLLIER (part). CITIES AND TOWNSHIPS: Chokoloskee, Everglades, Everglades City, Golden Gate, Immokalee, Island Walk, Orangetree, Plantation Island, Verona Walk, and Vineyards. HENDRY. CITIES AND TOWNSHIPS: Clewiston, Fort Denaud, LaBelle, Montura, Pioneer, and Port LaBelle. MIAMI-DADE COUNTY (part). CITIES AND TOWNSHIPS: Country Club, Doral, Fountainebleau, Hialeah, Hialeah Gardens, Medley, Miami Lakes, Palm Springs North, Sweetwater, Tamiami, Virginia Gardens, and West Little River. Population (2015), 754,595.

ZIP Codes: 33010 (part), 33012–14 (part), 33015–16, 33018, 33027 (part), 33029 (part), 33054 (part), 33122 (part), 33126 (part), 33147 (part), 33166 (part), 33172, 33174 (part), 33178, 33182, 33184 (part), 33194 (part), 33332 (part), 33440 (part), 33930, 33935–36 (part), 34104–05 (part), 34109 (part), 34112 (part), 34114 (part), 34116–17, 34119 (part), 34120, 34137–39, 34141, 34142 (part)

* * *

TWENTY-SIXTH DISTRICT

CARLOS CURBELO, Republican, of Miami, FL; born in Miami, March 1, 1980; education: B.A., business administration, University of Miami; M.P.A., University of Miami, 2011; professional: founder of Capitol Gains; State Director for U.S. Senator George LeMieux, 2009; member of Miami Dade County School Board, 2010; appointed to Miami-Dade Metropolitan Planning Organization (MPO), 2010; co-founder of Centre Court Charities; Governor's Education Transition Team; religion: Catholic; married with two children; committees: Ways and Means; elected to the 114th Congress on November 4, 2014; reelected to the 115th Congress on November 8, 2016.

Office Listings

http://www.curbelo.house.gov twitter: @repcurbelo

1429 Longworth House Office Building, Washington, DC 20515 .... (202) 225–2778
Chief of Staff.—Roy Schultheis. FAX: 226–0346
Legislative Director.—Adam Wolf.
Legislative Assistants: Hector Arguello, Ashley Rose.
Communications Assistant.—Joanna Rodriguez.
Scheduler.—Alex Cisneros.
12851 Southwest 42 Street, Suite 131, Miami, FL 33175 .... (305) 222–0160
District Director.—Chris Miles. FAX: 228–9397
Legislative Correspondent / Staff Assistant.—Charles Castagna.
404 West Palm Drive, Florida City, FL 33034 .... (305) 247–1234
1100 Simonton Street, Suite 1–213, Key West, FL 33040 .... (305) 292–4485
Monroe County Director.—Nicole Rapanos.

Counties: MIAMI-DADE (part). CITIES AND TOWNSHIPS: Country Walk, Florida City, Goulds, Homestead, Kendall, Kendale Lakes, Kendall West, Leisure City, Naranja, Olympia Heights, Palmetto Estates, Princeton, Richmond Heights, Richmond West, South Miami Heights, Sunset, Tamiami, The Crossings, The Hammocks, Three Lakes, University Park, West Perrine, Westchester, and Westwood Lakes. MONROE (all): Big Coppitt Key, Big Pine Key, Cudjoe Key, Duck Key, Islamorada, Village of Islands, Key Colony Beach, Key Largo, Key West, Layton, Marathon, North Key Largo, Stock Island, and Tavernier. Population (2014), 728,285.

ZIP Codes: 33001, 33030 (part), 33031, 33032–33 (part), 33034, 33035 (part), 330036–37, 33040, 33042–43, 33050–51, 33070, 33157, 33165, 33170, 33173 (part), 33175, 33176 (part), 33177, 33183, 33184 (part), 33185–87, 33189 (part), 33193, 33194 (part), 33196, 34141 (part)

* * *

TWENTY-SEVENTH DISTRICT

ILEANA ROS-LEHTINEN, Republican, of Miami, FL; born in Havana, Cuba, July 15, 1952; education: B.A., English, Florida International University; M.S., educational leadership, Florida International University; Ed.D., University of Miami, 2004; professional: certified Florida school teacher; founder and former owner, Eastern Academy; elected to the Florida House of Representatives, 1982; elected to the Florida State Senate, 1986; former president, Bilingual Private School Association; regular contributor to leading Spanish-language newspaper; during House tenure, married then-State Representative and former U.S. Attorney Dexter Lehtinen; four adult children and four grandchildren; committees: chairman emeritus, Foreign Affairs; Permanent Select Committee on Intelligence; elected, by special election, on August 29, 1989 to the 101st Congress; reelected to each succeeding Congress.

Office Listings

http://ros-lehtinen.house.gov https://twitter: @roslehtinen

2206 Rayburn House Office Building, Washington, DC .... (202) 225–3931
Chief of Staff.—Maytee Sanz. FAX: 225–5620
DC Chief of Staff.—Joshua Salpeter.
Legislative Director.—Gabriella Boffelli.
Communications Director.—Keith Fernandez.
4960 Southwest 72nd Avenue, Suite 208, Miami, FL 33155 .... (305) 668–2285

Counties: MIAMI-DADE (part). CITIES AND TOWNSHIPS: Coral Gables, Cutler Bay, Fountainebleau, Gladeview, Glenvar Heights, Kendall, Key Biscayne, Miami, Miami Beach, Olympia Heights, Palmetto Bay, Pinecrest, South Miami, Virginia Gardens, West Miami, Westchester, and West Little River. Population (2010), 696,345.

ZIP Codes: 33010 (part), 33012–13 (part), 33030 (part), 33032–33 (part), 33035 (part), 33039, 33109 (part), 33122 (part), 33125–26 (part), 33128 (part), 33129, 33130–31 (part), 33133–35, 33136 (part), 33142 (part), 33143–46, 33147 (part), 33149, 33155–56, 33157 (part), 33158, 33165–66 (part), 33170 (part), 33173–74 (part), 33176 (part), 33189 (part), 33190

GEORGIA

(Population 2010, 9,687,653)

SENATORS

JOHNNY ISAKSON, Republican, of Marietta, GA; born in Fulton County, GA, December 28, 1944; education: University of Georgia; professional: real estate executive; president, Northside Realty; public service: Georgia State House of Representatives, 1977–90; Georgia State Senate, 1993–96; appointed chairman of the Georgia Board of Education, 1997–99; awards: Republican National Committee ''Best Legislator in America,'' 1989; organizations: past board of directors, Metro Atlanta and Georgia Chambers of Commerce; past president, Cobb Chamber of Commerce; past executive committee, National Association of Realtors; past president, Realty Alliance; married: Dianne; children: John, Kevin, and Julie; religion: Methodist; committees: chair, Select Committee on Ethics; chair, Veterans' Affairs; Finance; Foreign Relations; Health, Education, Labor, and Pensions; elected to the 106th Congress on February 23, 1999, by special election; reelected to each succeeding Congress; elected to the U.S. Senate on November 2, 2004; reelected to each succeeding Senate term.

Office Listings

http://isakson.senate.gov twitter: @senatorisakson

131 Russell Senate Office Building, Washington, DC 20510 .... (202) 224–3643
Chief of Staff.—Joan Kirchner. FAX: 228–0724
Deputy Chief of Staff.—Edward Tate.
Scheduler.—Stefanie Mohler.
One Overton Park, 3625 Cumberland Boulevard, Suite 970, Atlanta, GA 30339 .... (770) 661–0999

* * *

DAVID PERDUE, Republican, of Glynn County, GA; born in Macon, GA, December 10, 1949; education: graduated, Northside High School, Warner Robins, GA, 1968; bachelor's degree in industrial engineering, Georgia Institute of Technology, 1972; master's degree in operations research, Georgia Institute of Technology, 1975; professional: senior vice president of operations for Sara Lee Corporation, 1992–94; senior vice president of Haggar Corporation, 1994–98; CEO of Reebok, 2001–02; CEO of Pillowtex, 2002–03; CEO of Dollar General, 2003–07; religion: United Methodist; married: the former Bonnie Dunn, 1972; children: David A. Perdue III and Blake Perdue; committees: Agriculture, Nutrition, and Forestry; Armed Services; Banking, Housing, and Urban Affairs; Budget; elected to the U.S. Senate on November 4, 2014.

Office Listings

http://perdue.senate.gov facebook: https://www.facebook.com/SenatorDavidPerdue
twitter: @sendavidperdue

383 Russell Senate Office Building, Washington, DC 20510 .... (202) 224–3521
Chief of Staff.—Derrick Dickey. FAX: 228–1031
Director of Operations.—Caleb Moore.
Deputy Chief of Staff / Legislative Director.—PJ Waldrop.
Deputy Chief of Staff / Communications Director.—Megan Whittemore.
191 Peachtree Street, NE., Suite 3250, Atlanta, GA 30303 .... (770) 661–0999
State Director.—Joyce White. FAX: 661–0768

REPRESENTATIVES

FIRST DISTRICT

EARL L. ''BUDDY'' CARTER, Republican, of Pooler, GA; born in Port Wentworth, GA, September, 6, 1957; education: Young Harris College, 1977; University of Georgia, 1980; professional: pharmacist; small business owner; Mayor of Pooler, GA, 1996–2004; Georgia State Legislature, 2006–14; married: Amy Carter, 1979; children: Joel, Barrett, and Travis; committees: Energy and Commerce; elected to the 114th Congress on November 4, 2014; reelected to the 115th Congress on November 8, 2016.

Office Listings

http://www.buddycarter.house.gov

432 Cannon House Office Building, Washington, DC 20515 .... (202) 225–5831
Chief of Staff.—Chris Crawford. FAX: 226–2269
Legislative Director.—Jordan See.
Legislative Assistants: Nick Schemmel, Hart Thompson.
Legislative Correspondent.—Vacant.
Communications Director.—Mary Carpenter.
Scheduler.—Brooke Miller.
Staff Assistant.—Caroline Holden.
6602 Abercorn Street, Suite 105–B, Savannah, GA 31405 .... (912) 352–0101
Casework Manager.—Trish DePriest.
Caseworker.—Bruce Bazemore.
Staff Assistant.—Tracy Dowdy.
Field Representative.—Hunter Hall.
1510 Newcastle Street, Suite 200, Brunswick, GA 31520 .... (912) 265–9010
District Director.—Jud Seymour.
Field Representative.—Emmitt Nolan.

Counties: BACON, BRANTLEY, BRYAN, CAMDEN, CHARLTON, CHATHAM, CLINCH, ECHOLS, EFFINGHAM (part), GLYNN, LIBERTY, LONG, LOWNDES (part), MCINTOSH, PIERCE, WARE, AND WAYNE. Population (2014), 703,020.

ZIP Codes: 30427–28, 31300–01, 31305, 31308–09, 31313–16, 31319–21, 31323–24, 31327–28, 31331–33, 31401–12, 31414–16, 31418–21, 31501–03, 31520–21, 31523–25, 31542, 31553, 31605–24, 31630–32, 31634–36

* * *

SECOND DISTRICT

SANFORD D. BISHOP, JR., Democrat, of Albany, GA; born in Mobile, AL, February 4, 1947; education: attended Mobile County public schools; B.A., Morehouse College, 1968; J.D., Emory University, 1971; professional: attorney; admitted to the Georgia and Alabama Bars; Georgia House of Representatives, 1977–91; Georgia Senate, 1991–93; former member: Executive Board, Boy Scouts of America; YMCA; Sigma Pi Phi Fraternity; Kappa Alpha Psi Fraternity; 32nd Degree Mason, Shriner; member: Mt. Zion Baptist Church, Albany, GA; married: Vivian Creighton Bishop; child: Aayesha Reese; committees: Appropriations; elected to the 103rd Congress; reelected to each succeeding Congress.

Office Listings

http://www.bishop.house.gov https://www.facebook.com/sanfordbishop
twitter: @SanfordBishop

2407 Rayburn House Office Building, Washington, DC 20515 .... (202) 225–3631
Chief of Staff.—Michael Reed. FAX: 225–2203
Scheduler / Executive Assistant.—Whitney Woods.
Legislative Director.—Jonathan Halpern.
Legislative Assistant / Social Media Manager.—Adilene Rosales.
Legislative Assistant / Office Manager.—Julian Johnson.
Communications Director.—Jonathan Black.
Albany Towers, 235 West Roosevelt Avenue, Suite 114, Albany, GA 31701 .... (229) 439–8067
District Director.—Kenneth Cutts.
Office Manager / Constituent Services.—Toni Pickel.
Field Representative.—Michael Bryant.
Constituent Services.—Tameka Wimbush.
Staff Assistant.—Jennifer Wells.
18 Ninth Street, Suite 201, Columbus, GA 31901 .... (706) 320–9477
Constituent Services: Arnez Cherry, Lenzie Jones, Peggy Sagul.
Field Representative.—Elaine Gillispie.
Staff Assistant.—Gerald Washington.
682 Cherry Street, Suite 302, Macon, GA 31201 .... (478) 803–2631
Deputy District Director.—Shavonda Hill.
Staff Assistant.—Christy Thompson.

Counties: BAKER, BIBB, CALHOUN, CHATTAHOOCHEE, CLAY, CRAWFORD, CRISP, DECATUR, DOOLY, DOUGHERTY, EARLY, GRADY, LEE, MACON, MARION, MILLER, MITCHELL, MUSCOGEE, PEACH, QUITMAN, RANDOLPH, SCHLEY, SEMINOLE, STEWART, SUMTER, TALBOT, TAYLOR, TERRELL, AND WEBSTER. Population (2010), 631,973.

ZIP Codes: 31006–08, 31015–16, 31020, 31030, 31039, 31041, 31050–52, 31057–58, 31063, 31066, 61068–70, 31072, 31076, 31078, 31081, 31091–92, 31201, 31204, 31206–07, 31210–11, 31213, 31216–17, 31220, 31701, 31705, 31707, 31709, 31711–12, 31716, 31719, 31721, 31730, 31735, 31743–44, 31763–65, 31773, 31779–80, 31784, 31787, 31791–92, 31801, 31803, 31805–06, 31810, 31812, 31814–16, 31820–21, 31824–27, 31829, 31831–32, 31836, 31901, 31903–

07, 31909, 39813, 39815, 39817, 39819, 39823–28, 39834, 39836–37, 39840–42, 39845–46, 39851, 39854, 39859, 39861–62, 39866–67, 39870, 39877, 39885–86, 39897

* * *

THIRD DISTRICT

A. DREW FERGUSON, IV, Republican, of West Point, GA; born in Langdale, AL, November 15, 1966; education: D.M.D., Medical College of Georgia, Augusta, GA, 1992; professional: dentist; public service: Mayor of West Point, 2008–16; religion: Christian; married: Buffy; children: Drew, Lucy, Mary Parks, and Thad; committees: Budget; Education and the Workforce; Transportation and Infrastructure; elected to the 115th Congress on November 8, 2016.

Office Listings

http://www.ferguson.house.gov

1032 Longworth House Office Building, Washington, DC 20515 .... (202) 225–5901
Chief of Staff.—Bobby Saparow. FAX: 225–2515
Communications Director.—Amy Timmerman.
Legislative Director.—Mary Dee Beal.
Office Manager.—Jenna Heard.
Scheduler.—Jenna Heard.
1601–East Highway 34, Suite B, Newnan, GA 30265 .... (770) 683–2033

Counties: CARROLL. CITIES AND TOWNSHIPS: Bowdon, Carrollton, Mount Zion, Roopville, Temple, Villa Rica, and Whitesburg. COWETA (part). CITIES AND TOWNSHIPS: Grantville, Haralson, Lone Oak, Luthersville, Meriwether, Moreland, Newnan, Palmetto, Senoia, Sharpsburg, and Turin. FAYETTE. CITIES AND TOWNSHIPS: Brooks, Fayetteville, Peachtree City, Tyrone, and Woolsey. HARRIS. CITIES AND TOWNSHIPS: Cataula, Ellerslie, Fortson, Hamilton, Midland, Pine Mountain, Pine Mountain Valley, Shiloh, Waverly Hall, and West Point. HENRY (part). CITIES AND TOWNSHIPS: Hampton, Locust Grove, McDonough, and Stockbridge. LAMAR. CITIES AND TOWNSHIPS: Aldora, Barnesville, Milner. MUSCOGEE (part). CITIES AND TOWNSHIPS: Columbus. PIKE. CITIES AND TOWNSHIPS: Concord, Meansville, Molena, Williamson, and Zebulon. SPALDING. CITIES AND TOWNSHIPS: Griffin, Orchard Hill, and Sunny Side. TROUP. CITIES AND TOWNSHIPS: Hogansville and LaGrange. UPSON. CITIES AND TOWNSHIPS: Thomaston and Yatesville. Population (2010), 757,344.

ZIP Codes: 30257–59, 30263, 30265, 30268–69, 30275–77, 30285–86, 30290, 30292–93, 30295, 31016, 31029, 31066, 31097, 31800, 31804, 31807–08, 31811, 31816, 31820, 31822–23, 31826, 31829–31, 31833, 31901, 31904, 31906, 31909

* * *

FOURTH DISTRICT

HENRY C. "HANK" JOHNSON, JR., Democrat, of Lithonia, GA; born in Washington, DC, October 2, 1954; education: B.A., Clark College (Clark Atlanta University), Atlanta, GA, 1976; J.D., Thurgood Marshall School of Law, Texas Southern University, Houston, TX, 1979; professional: partner, Johnson & Johnson Law Group LLC, 1980–2007; Judge, Magistrate Court, 1989–2001; DeKalb County Commissioner, 2001–06; married: Mereda, 1979; two children: Randi and Alex; committees: Judiciary; Transportation and Infrastructure; elected to the 110th Congress on November 7, 2006; reelected to each succeeding Congress.

Office Listings

http://www.hankjohnson.house.gov

2240 Rayburn House Office Building, Washington, DC 20515 .... (202) 225–1605
Chief of Staff.—Arthur D. Sidney. FAX: 226–0691
Legislative Director.—Robin Chand.
Office Manager / Scheduler.—Alem Tewoldeberhan.
5240 Snapfinger Park Drive, Suite 130, Decatur, GA 30035 .... (770) 987–2291
District Director.—Kathy Register.

Counties: DEKALB (part), GWINNETT (part), NEWTON (part), AND ROCKDALE. CITIES: Atlanta (part), Avondale Estates (part), Clarkston, Conyers, Covington, Decatur (part), Lilburn (part), Lithonia, Norcross, Pine Lake, Snellville, Stone Mountain, and Tucker (part). Population (2010), 691,976.

ZIP Codes: 30002–03, 30012–17, 30021, 30030–39, 30047, 30052, 30058, 30070, 30072, 30074, 30078–79, 30083–84, 30086–88, 30252, 30281, 30294, 30329, 30340, 30345, 30359

* * *

FIFTH DISTRICT

JOHN LEWIS, Democrat, of Atlanta, GA; born in Pike County, AL, February 21, 1940; education: graduated, Pike County Training School, Brundidge, AL, 1957; B.A., American Baptist Theological Seminary, Nashville, TN, 1961; B.A., Fisk University, Nashville, TN, 1963; professional: civil rights leader; Atlanta City Council, 1982–86; member: Martin Luther King Center for Social Change; African American Institute; Robert F. Kennedy Memorial; married the former Lillian Miles in 1968; one child, John Miles Lewis; appointed Senior Chief Deputy Democratic Whip for the 109th Congress; committees: Ways and Means; Joint Committee on Taxation; elected to the 100th Congress on November 4, 1986; reelected to each succeeding Congress.

Office Listings

http://www.johnlewis.house.gov www.facebook.com/repjohnlewis twitter: @repjohnlewis

343 Cannon House Office Building, Washington, DC 20515 .... (202) 225–3801
Chief of Staff.—Michael Collins. FAX: 225–0351
Office Manager / Scheduler.—David Bowan.
Director of Communications.—Brenda Jones.
Legislative Director.—Jamila Thompson.
100 Peachtree Street, NW., Suite 1920, Atlanta, GA 30303 .... (404) 659–0116
District Director.—Aaron Ward.

Counties: CLAYTON (part), DEKALB (part), AND FULTON (part). Population (2012), 691,975.

ZIP Codes: 30030 (part), 30032 (part), 30034 (part), 30236 (part), 30260 (part), 30273–74 (part), 30281 (part), 30288, 30294 (part), 30296–97 (part), 30303, 30305 (part), 30306–19 (part), 30322, 30324 (part), 30326–27 (part), 30331–32, 30334, 30336, 30337 (part), 30342 (part), 30344 (part), 30349 (part), 30354, 30363

* * *

SIXTH DISTRICT

KAREN C. HANDEL, Republican, of Roswell, GA; born in Washington, DC, April 18, 1962; professional: Deputy Chief of Staff to Georgia Governor Sonny Perdue, 2002–03; chair, Fulton County (GA) Board of Commissioners, 2003–06; Georgia Secretary of State, 2007–09; family: husband, Steve; committees: Education and the Workforce; Judiciary; Joint Economic Committee; elected to the 115th Congress, by special election, on June 20, 2017, to fill the vacancy caused by the resignation of U.S. Representative Tom Price.

Office Listings

https://handel.house.gov

1211 Longworth House Office Building, Washington, DC 20515 .... (202) 225–4501
Chief of Staff.—Muffy Day. FAX: 225–4656
District Director.—Ashley Jenkins.
85 Mill Street, Suite C–300, Roswell, GA 30075 .... (770) 998–0049

Counties: COBB (part), FULTON (part), AND DEKALB (part). CITIES AND TOWNSHIPS: Sandy Springs, Roswell, Johns Creek, Alpharetta, Milton, Dunwoody, Tucker, Doraville, Chamblee, and Brookhaven. Population (2010), 699,103.

ZIP Codes: 30004–07, 30009, 30022–24, 30033, 30062, 30065–68, 30075–77, 30084–85, 30092–93, 30097–98, 30102, 30144, 30188, 30319, 30324, 30326, 30328–29, 30338–42, 30345–46, 30350, 30356, 30358, 30360, 30362, 30366, 31119, 31141, 31145–46, 31150, 31156

* * *

SEVENTH DISTRICT

W. ROBERT WOODALL, Republican, of Lawrenceville, GA; born in Athens, GA, February 11, 1970; education: undergraduate, B.A., Furman University, Greenville, SC, 1992; J.D., University of Georgia, Athens, GA, 1997; awards: co-author of *The New York Times* bestselling book *Fair Tax: The Truth;* religion: Methodist; committees: Budget; Rules; Transportation and Infrastructure; elected to the 112th Congress on November 2, 2010; reelected to each succeeding Congress.

Office Listings

http://woodall.house.gov

1724 Longworth House Office Building, Washington, DC 20515 .... (202) 225–4272
Chief of Staff.—Derick Corbett. FAX: 225–4696
Legislative Director.—Janet Rossi.
District Director.—Debra Poirot.
75 Langley Drive, Lawrenceville, GA 30046 .... (770) 232–3005
(No mail accepted at this address.) FAX: 232–2909

Counties: FORSYTH (part) AND GWINNETT (part). Population (2010), 691,975.

ZIP Codes: 30004–05, 30017, 30019, 30024, 30040–41, 30043–49, 30052, 30071, 30078, 30091–93, 30095–97, 30099, 30340, 30360, 30518–19

* * *

EIGHTH DISTRICT

AUSTIN SCOTT, Republican, of Tifton, GA; born in Augusta, GA, December 10, 1969; education: B.B.A., University of Georgia, 1993; professional: business owner; member of the Georgia State House of Representatives, 1997–2010; member, National Association of Insurance and Financial Advisors; Coastal Plains Chapter of the American Red Cross; awards: American Cancer Society's Outstanding Legislative Leadership Award, 2003 and 2004; Georgia Association of Emergency Medical Services Star of Life Legislative Award, 2007 and 2008; religion: Southern Baptist; married: wife, Vivien; son, Wells; daughter, Carmen Gabriela; Republican Freshman Class President; committees: Agriculture; Armed Services; elected to the 112th Congress on November 2, 2010; reelected to each succeeding Congress.

Office Listings

http://austinscott.house.gov twitter: @austinscottga08
www.youtube.com/user/repaustinscott www.facebook.com/repaustinscott

2417 Rayburn House Office Building, Washington, DC 20515 .... (202) 225–6531
Chief of Staff.—Joby Young. FAX: 225–3013
Legislative Director.—Cameron Bishop.
Military Legislative Assistant.—Michael Tehrani.
Legislative Correspondent.—Mark Sanders.
Communications Director.—Ryann DuRant.
Legislative Assistant.—Craig Anderson.
Scheduler.—Haley Dorval.
127–B North Central Avenue, Tifton, GA 31794 .... (229) 396–5175
FAX: 396–5179
230 Margie Drive, Suite 500, Warner Robins, GA 31088 .... (478) 971–1776
FAX: 971–1778

Counties: ATKINSON, BEN HILL, BERRIEN, BIBB (part), BLECKLEY, BROOKS, COLQUITT, COOK, DODGE, HOUSTON, IRWIN, JONES, LANIER, LOWNDES (part), MONROE, PULASKI, TELFAIR, THOMAS, TIFT, TURNER, TWIGGS, WILCOX, WILKINSON, AND WORTH. Population (2011), 693,640

ZIP Codes: 30233, 31001, 31033–35, 31008, 31011–17, 31020–21, 31023, 31028–33, 31035–38, 31042, 31044, 31046–47, 31054–55, 31060–61, 31065–66, 31069, 31071–72, 31077, 31079, 31083–84, 31086, 31088, 31090–93, 31095, 31098–99, 31204, 31209–11, 31217, 31220–21, 31297, 31512, 31544, 31549, 31601–66, 31620, 31622, 31624–27, 31629, 31632, 31635–39, 31641–45, 31647, 31649–50, 31698, 31705, 31712, 31714, 31720, 31722, 31727, 31733, 31738, 31744, 31747, 31749–50, 31753, 31756–58, 31760, 31765, 31768–69, 31771–79, 31781, 31783–84, 31788–96, 31798–99

* * *

NINTH DISTRICT

DOUGLAS COLLINS, Republican, of Gainesville, GA; born in Gainesville, August 16, 1966; education: B.S., political science, criminal law, University of North Georgia, Dahlonega, GA, 1988; master of divinity, New Orleans Baptist Theological Seminary, New Orleans, LA, 1996; juris doctorate, John Marshall Law School, Atlanta, GA, 2008; professional: preacher; business owner; Chaplain, U.S. Air Force Reserve; lawyer; Georgia State House of Representatives, 2007–13; religion: Baptist; married: Lisa Collins; children: Jordan, Copelan, and Cameron; leadership: vice chair, House Republican Conference; committees: Judiciary; Rules; elected, by regular election, to the 113th Congress on November 6, 2012, to fill the vacancy caused by the redistricting of District 9; reelected to each succeeding Congress.

Office Listings

http://www.dougcollins.house.gov

1504 Longworth House Office Building, Washington, DC 20515 .... (202) 225–9893 FAX: 226–1224
Chief of Staff.—Brendan Belair.
Communications Director.—Jessica Andrews.
Legislative Director.—Sally Rose Larson.
Scheduler.—Erin Wall.
Counsel.—Jon Ferro.
Legislative Aide.—Dan Ashworth.
Legislative Aide / Legislative Correspondent.—Erica Barker.
Staff Assistant.—Cooper Mullinax.
210 Washington Street Northwest, Suite 202, Gainesville, GA 30501 .... (770) 297–3388

Counties: Banks, Clarke (part), Dawson, Elbert, Fannin, Forsyth (part), Franklin, Gilmer, Habersham, Hall, Hart, Jackson, Lumpkin, Madison, Pickens (part), Rabun, Stephens, Towns, Union, and White. Cities and Townships: Alto, Arcade, Baldwin, Blairsville, Blue Ridge, Bowersville, Bowman, Braselton, Canon, Carlton, Carnesville, Clarkesville, Clayton, Clermont, Cleveland, Colbert, Comer, Commerce, Cornelia, Cumming, Dahlonega, Danielsville, Dawsonville, Demorest, Dillard, Elberton, Elijay, Flowery Branch, Franklin Springs, Gainesville, Gillsville, Hartwell, Helen, Hiawassee, Homer, Hoschton, Hull, Ila, Jasper, Jefferson, Lavonia, Lula, Martin, McCaysville, Morganton, Mount Airy, Mountain City, Nelson, Nicholson, Oakwood, Pendergrass, Royston, Sky Valley, Talking Rock, Tallulah Falls, Talmo, Toccoa, and Young Harris. Population (2010), 691,975.

ZIP Codes: 30028 (part), 30040–41 (part), 30107 (part), 30143 (part), 30148, 30151, 30175 (part), 30177, 30501, 30504, 30506–07, 30510–13, 30516, 30517–19 (part), 30520–23, 30525, 30527–31, 30533, 30534 (part), 30535–38, 30540–43, 30545–47, 30548 (part), 30549, 30552–55, 30557–60, 30562–68, 30571–73, 30575–77, 30581–82, 30601 (part), 30605 (part), 30607 (part), 30622 (part), 30624, 30627–29 (part), 30633–35, 30643, 30646, 30662, 30666 (part), 30680 (part), 30683 (part)

* * *

TENTH DISTRICT

JODY B. HICE, Republican, of Greensboro, GA; born on April 22, 1960; grew up in Tucker, GA; education: B.A., ministry, Asbury University, Wilmore KY; professional: pastor; religion: Southern Baptist; married: Dee Dee Crocker Hice; children: Anna and Sara; grandchildren: Peter, Margaret, Alyssa, and Felix; committees: Armed Services; Natural Resources; Oversight and Government Reform: elected to the 114th Congress on November 4, 2014; reelected to 115th Congress on November 8, 2016.

Office Listings

http://www.hice.house.gov https://www.facebook.com/congressmanjodyhice
https://twitter.com/congressmanhice

324 Cannon House Office Building, Washington, DC 20515 .... (202) 225–4101
Chief of Staff.—David Sours.
Director of Scheduling and Operations.—Taylor Ford.
Communications Director.—Nadgey Louis-Charles.
Legislative Director.—Tim Reitz.
Military Legislative Assistant.—Caryn Hamner.
Legislative Assistant.—Nicholas R. Brown.
Legislative Correspondent / Press Assistant.—Elizabeth Genrty.
Staff Assistant.—Nathan Barker.

Counties: Baldwin, Barrow, Butts, Columbia (part), Clarke (part), Glascock, Greene, Gwinnett (part), Hancock, Henry (part), Jasper, Jefferson, Johnson, Lincoln, McDuffie, Morgan, Newton (part), Oconee, Oglethorpe, Putnam, Taliaferro, Walton, Warren, Washington, and Wilkes. Population (2010), 691,976.

ZIP Codes: 30011–12, 30014, 30016, 30019, 30025, 30043, 30045, 30052, 30054–56, 30216, 30233–34, 30248, 30252–53, 30413, 30434, 30477, 30517, 30519, 30548, 30601–02, 30605–07, 30609, 30619–23, 30625, 30627–31, 30641–42, 30648, 30650, 30655–56, 30660, 30663–69, 30773, 30677–78, 30680, 30683, 30802–03, 30807–10, 30814, 30816–18, 30820–21, 30823–24, 30828, 30833, 31002, 31018, 31024, 31029, 31031, 31033, 31035, 31038, 31045, 31049, 31061–62, 31064, 31067, 31082, 31085, 31087, 31089, 31094, 31096

* * *

ELEVENTH DISTRICT

BARRY LOUDERMILK, Republican, of Cassville, GA; born in Riverdale, GA, December 22, 1963; education: A.A. in Telecommunications Technology, Community College of the Air Force, Maxwell AFB, AL, 1987; B.S. in Occupational Education and Information Systems Technology, Wayland Baptist University, Plainview, TX, 1992; professional: former small business owner, Innovative Network Systems, Inc. and Freedom Flight Center; founder of non-profit, Firm Reliance; served in Georgia State House, 2005–10; Georgia State Senate, 2011–13; member, NRA; Aircraft Owners and Pilots Association; American Legion; served in the U.S. Air Force, 1984–92; Civil Air Patrol member, official auxiliary of the U.S. Air Force, 2005–present; religion: Protestant; married to Desiree since 1983; three grown children; committees: Financial Services; House Administration; Joint Committee on the Library; Science, Space, and Technology; elected to the 114th Congress on November 4, 2014; reelected to the 115th Congress on November 8, 2016.

Office Listings

http://www.loudermilk.house.gov twitter: https://twitter.com/reploudermilk
www.facebook.com/RepLoudermilk

329 Cannon House Office Building, Washington, DC 20515 .... (202) 225–2931
Chief of Staff.—Robert Adkerson. FAX: 225–2944
Legislative Director.—Colin Carr.
District Director.—Caric Martin.
9898 Highway 92, Suite 100, Woodstock, GA 30188 .... (770) 429–1776
135 West Cherokee Avenue, Suite 122, Cartersville, GA 30120 .... (770) 429–1776
600 Galleria Parkway, Suite 120, Atlanta, GA 30339 .... (770) 429–1776

Counties: BARTOW, CHEROKEE, COBB (part), AND FULTON (part). Population (2010), 794,969.

ZIP Codes: 30004, 30008, 30040, 30060, 30062, 30064, 30066–68, 30075, 30080, 30082, 30101–04, 30107, 30114–15, 30120–21, 30127, 30132, 30137, 30139, 30143–45, 30152–53, 30157, 30161, 30171, 30178, 30183–84, 30188–89, 30305, 30318–19, 30326–27, 30339, 30342

* * *

TWELFTH DISTRICT

RICK W. ALLEN, Republican, of Augusta, GA; born in Augusta, November 7, 1951; education: graduated, Evans High School, Evans, GA, 1969; B.S., in building construction, Auburn University, Auburn, AL, 1973; professional: founder and owner of R.W. Allen & Associates construction company, Augusta, GA, and Athens, GA, founded in 1976; awards: Augusta Metro Chamber of Commerce Small Business Person of the Year, 2008; CSRA Business Hall of Fame Inductee, 2011; religion: Methodist; married: wife, Robin; children: Jennifer Allen Green, Andy Allen, Molly Allen Hargather, and Robin Anne Allen Wills; grandchildren: Hadley Green, Wyche Green, Hutton Green, Collier Green, Hammond Hargather, Delle Hargather, Riley Kate Wills, and Ellis Wills; committees: Agriculture; Education and the Workforce; elected to the 114th Congress on November 4, 2014; reelected to the 115th Congress on November 8, 2016.

Office Listings

http://www.allen.house.gov https://www.facebook.com/CongressmanRickAllen
https://www.twitter.com/RepRickAllen

426 Cannon House Office Building, Washington, DC 20515 .... (202) 225–2823
Chief of Staff.—Tim Baker. FAX: 225–3377
Deputy Chief of Staff.—Lauren Swing.
Legislative Director.—Katie Hunter.
Communications Director.—Catherine Costakos.
2743 Perimeter Parkway, Building 200, Suite 225, Augusta, GA 30909 .... (706) 228–1980
Statesboro City Hall, 50 East Main Street, Statesboro, GA 30458 .... (912) 243–9452
100 South Church Street, Dublin, GA 31021 .... (478) 272–4030
Vidalia Community Center, 107 Old Airport Road, Suite A, Vidalia, GA 30475 .... (912) 403–3311

Counties: APPLING, BULLOCH, BURKE, CANDLER, COFFEE, COLUMBIA (part), EFFINGHAM (part), EMANUEL, EVANS, JEFF DAVIS, JENKINS, LAURENS, MONTGOMERY, RICHMOND, SCREVEN, TATTNALL, TOOMBS, TREUTLEN, AND WHEELER. Population (2010), 701,142.

ZIP Codes: 30401, 30410–12, 30415, 30417, 30420–21, 30423, 30425–29, 30434, 30436, 30438–39, 30441–42, 30445–46, 30448–58, 30460–61, 30464, 30467, 30470–71, 30473–75, 30802, 30805, 30809, 30812–16, 30822, 30830, 30901, 30903–07, 30909, 30912, 31002, 31009, 31019, 31021–22, 31027, 31037, 31049, 31065, 31075, 31083, 31303, 31308, 31312, 31321, 31326, 31329, 31510, 31512–13, 31518–19, 31532–33, 31535, 31539, 31549, 31552, 31554–55, 31563, 31567, 31624, 31650, 31798

* * *

THIRTEENTH DISTRICT

DAVID SCOTT, Democrat, of Atlanta, GA; born in Aynor, SC, June 27, 1945; education: Florida A&M University, graduated with honors, 1967; M.B.A., graduated with honors, University of Pennsylvania Wharton School of Finance, 1969; professional: businessman; owner and CEO, Dayn-Mark Advertising; public service: Georgia House of Representatives, 1974–82; Georgia State Senate, 1983–2002; married: Alfredia Aaron, 1969; children: Dayna and Marcye; committees: Agriculture; Financial Services; elected to the 108th Congress on November 5, 2002; reelected to each succeeding Congress.

Office Listings

http://davidscott.house.gov facebook: repdavidscott twitter: @repdavidscott

225 Cannon House Office Building, Washington, DC 20515 .... (202) 225–2939
Chief of Staff.—Gary Woodward. FAX: 225–4628
Scheduler and Office Manager.—Breanna Swims.
Legislative Director.—Ashley Smith.
173 North Main Street, Jonesboro, GA 30236 .... (770) 210–5073
888 Concord Road, Suite 100, Smyra, GA 30080 .... (770) 432–5405

Counties: CLAYTON, COBB, DOUGLAS, FAYETTE, FULTON, AND HENRY. Population (2010), 707,070.

ZIP Codes: 30252–53, 30260, 30268, 30273–74, 30281, 30290–91, 30294, 30296–97, 30331, 30337, 30344, 30349

* * *

FOURTEENTH DISTRICT

TOM GRAVES, Republican, of Ranger, GA; born in St. Petersburg, FL, February 3, 1970; education: B.A.A., finance, University of Georgia, Athens, GA, 1993; professional: business owner; Georgia State House of Representatives, 2003–10; religion: Baptist: married: Julie Howard Graves; children: JoAnn, John, and Janey; committees: Appropriations; elected to the 111th Congress on June 8, 2010, by special election, to fill the vacancy caused by the resignation of U.S. Representative John Nathan Deal; elected to the 112th Congress on November 2, 2010; reelected to each succeeding Congress.

Office Listings

http://www.tomgraves.house.gov https://www.facebook.com/reptomgraves
https://www.twitter.com/RepTomGraves

2078 Rayburn House Office Building, Washington, DC 20515 .... (202) 225–5211
Chief of Staff.—John Donnelly. FAX: 225–8272
Legislative Director.—Jason Murphy.
Communications Director.—Garrett Hawkins.
Scheduler.—Morgan Joyce.
702 South Thornton Avenue, Dalton, GA 30720 .... (706) 226–5320
FAX: 278–0840
600 East First Street, Suite 301, Rome, GA 30161 .... (706) 290–1776
FAX: 232–7864

Counties: CATOOSA, CHATTOOGA, DADE, FLOYD, GORDON, HARALSON, MURRAY, PAULDING, PICKENS (part), POLK, WALKER, AND WHITFIELD. Population (2010), 619,974.

ZIP Codes: 30101, 30103–05, 30110, 30113, 30120, 30124–25, 30127, 30129, 30132, 30134, 30138–41, 30143

HAWAII

(Population 2010, 1,360,301)

SENATORS

BRIAN SCHATZ, Democrat, of Hawaii; born in Ann Arbor, MI, October 20, 1972; education: graduated from Punahou School, Honolulu, HI, 1990; B.A., Pomona College, Claremont, CA, 1994; professional: chairman, Democratic Party of Hawaii, 2008–10; CEO, Helping Hands Hawaii, 2002–10; Hawaii House of Representatives, 1998–2006; Lieutenant Governor of Hawaii, 2010–12; married: Linda Schatz; committees: Appropriations; Banking, Housing, and Urban Affairs; Commerce, Science, and Transportation; Indian Affairs; Select Committee on Ethics; appointed to the U.S. Senate on December 26, 2012, and took the oath of office on December 27, 2012.

Office Listings

http://www.schatz.senate.gov twitter: @senbrianschatz
https://www.facebook.com/senbrianschatz

722 Hart Senate Office Building, Washington, DC 20510 .... (202) 224–3934
Chief of Staff.—Andrew Winer. FAX: 228–1153
Scheduler.—Diane Miyasato.
Legislative Director.—Arun Revana.
Communications Director.—Michael Inacay.
300 Ala Moana Boulevard, Room 7–212, Honolulu, HI 96850 .... (808) 523–2061
FAX: 523–2065

* * *

MAZIE HIRONO, Democrat, of Hawaii; born in Fukushima, Japan, November 3, 1947; education: graduated from Kaimuki High School, Honolulu, HI; B.A., University of Hawaii, Manoa, HI, 1970; J.D., Georgetown University, Washington, DC, 1978; professional: lawyer, private practice; member of the Hawaii State House of Representatives, 1981–94; Hawaii Lieutenant Governor, 1994–2002; elected to the U.S. House of Representatives as a Democrat to the 110th, 111th, and 112th Congresses; was not a candidate for reelection to the U.S. House of Representatives for the 113th Congress; committees: Armed Services; Energy and Natural Resources; Judiciary; Small Business and Entrepreneurship; Veterans' Affairs; elected to the U.S. Senate on November 6, 2012.

Office Listings

http://www.hirono.senate.gov facebook: facebook.com/senatorhirono
twitter: @maziehirono

730 Hart Senate Office Building, Washington, DC 20510 .... (202) 224–6361
Chief of Staff.—Alan Yamamoto. FAX: 224–2126
Prince Kuhio Federal Building, 300 Ala Moana Boulevard, Room 3–106, Honolulu, HI 96850 .... (808) 522–8970
District Director.—Alan Yamamoto.

REPRESENTATIVES

FIRST DISTRICT

COLLEEN HANABUSA, Democrat, of Waianae, HI; born in Honolulu, HI, May 4, 1951; education: graduated from St. Andrews Priory School, Honolulu, 1969; B.A., University of Hawaii, Honolulu, 1973; M.A., University of Hawaii, Manoa, HI, 1975; J.D., University of Hawaii, Manoa, 1977; professional: attorney, 1977–2010; Hawaii State Senate, 1998–2010; Hawaii State Senate President, 2006–10; lawyer, private practice, January 3, 2015 to November 6, 2016; religion: Buddhism; married: John Souza; caucuses: Congressional Asian Pacific American Caucus (CAPAC); Congressional Native American Caucus; Congressional Singapore Caucus; Gun Violence Prevention Task Force; LGBT Caucus; New Democrat Coalition; Shipbuilding Caucus; Sustainable Energy and Environment Coalition; committees: Armed Services; Natural Resources; Science, Space, and Technology; elected to the 112th Congress on November 2, 2010; reelected to the 113th Congress on November 6, 2012; elected to the 114th Congress, by special election, on November 8, 2016, serving through January 3, 2017, to fill the vacancy caused by the death of U.S. Representative Mark Takai; elected simultaneously to the 115th Congress on November 8, 2016.

Office Listings

http://www.hanabusa.house.gov

422 Cannon House Office Building, Washington, DC 20515 .... (202) 225–2726
Chief of Staff.—Michael D. Formby. FAX: 255–0688
District Director.—Ainoa Naniole.
1132 Bishop Street, Suite 1910, Honolulu, HI 96813 .... (808) 541–2570
(808) 533–0133

Counties: HONOLULU (part). CITIES AND TOWNSHIPS: Aiea, Ewa Beach, Honolulu, Kahala, Kaimuki, Kalihi, Kapolei (part), Manoa, Mililani, Palolo, Pearl City, Waikiki, and Waipahu. Population (2010), ~700,000.

ZIP Codes: 96701, 96706–07, 96782, 96789, 96797, 96813–19, 96821–22, 96825–26, 96850, 96853, 96859–60

* * *

SECOND DISTRICT

TULSI GABBARD, Democrat, of Hawaii; born in Leloaloa, American Samoa, April 12, 1981; education: Hawai'i Pacific University, Officer Candidate School, Army; professional: member of the Hawaii House of Representatives from the 42nd District, 2002–04; member of the Honolulu City Council from the 6th District, 2011–12; member of the Army National Guard, 2003–present; committees: Armed Services; Foreign Affairs; elected to the 113th Congress on November 6, 2012; reelected to each succeeding Congress.

Office Listings

http://gabbard.house.gov

1433 Longworth House Office Building, Washington, DC 20515 .... (202) 225–4906
Senior Advisor.—Adam Schantz.
300 Ala Moana Boulevard, 5–104 Prince Kuhio Federal Building, Honolulu, HI 96850 .... (808) 541–1986
Chief of Staff.—Kainoa Penaroza.

Counties: HAWAI'I. CITIES: Hawi, Hilo, Honoka'a, Kailua-Kona, Kealakekua, Na'alehu, Ocean View, Pahoa, Volcano, Waikoloa, and Waimea. HONOLULU COUNTY (part). CITIES: Hale'iwa, Honolulu, Kailua, Kane'ohe, Kapolei, La'ie, Makakilo, Nanakuli, Wahiawa, Waialua, Wai'anae, and Waimanalo. KALAWAO COUNTY. CITY: Kalaupapa. KAUA'I COUNTY. CITIES: Hanalei, Hanapepe, Kalaheo, Kapa'a, Kekaha, Kilauea, Koloa, Lihue, and Waimea. MAUI COUNTY. CITIES: Hana, Kahului, Kaunakakai, Lahaina, Lana'i City, Makawao, and Wailuku. NORTHWESTERN HAWAIIAN ISLANDS. Islands of: Becker, French Frigate Shoals, Gardener Pinnacles, Hermes and Kure Atolls, Laysan, Lisianski, Maro Reef, Nihoa, and Pearl. Population (2010), 679,805.

ZIP Codes: 96703–05, 96707–08, 96710, 96712–14, 96716–17, 96719–20, 96722, 96725–32, 96734, 96737–38, 96740–44, 96746–57, 96759–66, 96768–74, 96776–81, 96783, 96785–86, 96789–93, 96795–97, 96825, 96857, 96863

IDAHO

(Population 2010, 1,567,582)

SENATORS

MIKE CRAPO, Republican, of Idaho Falls, ID; born in Idaho Falls, May 20, 1951; education: graduated, Idaho Falls High School, 1969; B.A., Brigham Young University, Provo, UT, 1973; J.D., Harvard University Law School, Cambridge, MA, 1977; professional: attorney; admitted to the California Bar, 1977; admitted to the Idaho Bar, 1979; law clerk, Hon. James M. Carter, Judge of the U.S. Court of Appeals for the 9th Circuit, San Diego, CA, 1977–78; associate attorney, Gibson, Dunn, and Crutcher, San Diego, 1978–79; attorney, Holden, Kidwell, Hahn and Crapo, 1979–92; partner, 1983–92; Idaho State Senate, 1984–92; Assistant Majority Leader, 1987–89, President Pro Tempore, 1989–92; member: American Bar Association, Boy Scouts of America, Idaho Falls Rotary Club, 1984–88; married: the former Susan Diane Hasleton, 1974; children: Michelle, Brian, Stephanie, Lara, and Paul; caucuses: co-chair, COPD Caucus; co-chair, Western Water Caucus; Sportsmen's Caucus; Majority Chief Deputy Whip; committees: chair, Banking, Housing, and Urban Affairs; Budget; Finance; Indian Affairs; Joint Committee on Taxation; Judiciary; elected on November 3, 1992, to the 103rd Congress; reelected to each succeeding Congress; elected to the U.S. Senate on November 3, 1998; reelected to each succeeding Senate term.

Office Listings

http://www.crapo.senate.gov https://www.facebook.com/mikecrapo twitter: @mikecrapo

239 Dirksen Senate Office Building, Washington, DC 20510 .... (202) 224–6142
Chief of Staff.—Susan Wheeler. FAX: 228–1375
Legislative Director.—Ken Flanz.
251 East Front Street, Suite 205, Boise, ID 83702 .... (208) 334–1776
Chief of Staff.—John Hoehne.
Communications Director.—Lindsay Nothern.
610 Hubbard Street, Suite 209, Coeur d'Alene, ID 83814 .... (208) 664–5490
Director.—Karen Roetter.
313 D Street, Suite 105, Lewiston, ID 83501 .... (208) 743–1492
Director.—Tony Snodderly.
275 South 5th Avenue, Suite 225, Pocatello, ID 83201 .... (208) 236–9635
Director.—Farhanna Hibbert.
410 Memorial Drive, Suite 204, Idaho Falls, ID 83402 .... (208) 522–9779
Director.—Kathryn Hitch.
202 Falls Avenue, Suite 2, Twin Falls, ID 83301 .... (208) 734–2515
Director.—Samantha Marshall.

* * *

JAMES E. RISCH, Republican, of Boise, ID; born in Milwaukee, WI, May 3, 1943; education: St. Johns Cathedral High School, Milwaukee; B.S., forestry, University of Idaho, Moscow, ID, 1965; J.D., University of Idaho, Moscow, 1968; Law Review, College of Law Advisory Committee; professional: Ada County Prosecuting Attorney, 1970–74; president, Idaho Prosecuting Attorneys Association, 1973; Idaho State Senate, 1974–88, 1995–2003; Assistant Majority Leader, 1996; Majority Leader, 1976–82, 1997–2002; President Pro Tempore, 1983–88; Lieutenant Governor of Idaho, 2003–06, 2007–09; Governor of Idaho, 2006; small business owner; ranch / farmer; former partner, Risch, Goss, Insinger, Gustavel law firm; member, National Cattle Association; Idaho Cattle Association; American, Idaho and Boise Valley Angus Associations; National Rifle Association; Ducks Unlimited; Rocky Mountain Elk Foundation; married: Vicki; children: James, Jason, and Jordan; three daughters-in-law; eight grandchildren; caucuses: Congressional Youth Leadership Council; Impact Aid Coalition; National Guard Caucus; Recycling Caucus; Republican High Tech Task Force; Rural Education Caucus; Senate Rural Health Caucus; Sportsmen's Caucus; Western Caucus; WMD / Terrorism Caucus; committees: chair, Small Business and Entrepreneurship; Energy and Natural Resources; Foreign Relations; Select Committee on Ethics; Select Committee on Intelligence; elected to the U.S. Senate on November 4, 2008; reelected to the U.S. Senate on November 4, 2014.

Office Listings

http://risch.senate.gov twitter: @senatorrisch

483 Russell Senate Office Building, Washington, DC 20510 .... (202) 224–2752

Office Listings—Continued

Chief of Staff.—John Sandy. FAX: 224–2573
Communications Director.—Kaylin Minton.
Executive Assistant / Scheduler.—Alexa Green.
Legislative Director.—Darren Parker.
350 North Ninth Street, Suite 302, Boise, ID 83702 .... (208) 342–7985

REPRESENTATIVES

FIRST DISTRICT

RAÚL R. LABRADOR, Republican, of Eagle, ID; born in Carolina, PR, December 8, 1967; education: B.A., Brigham Young University, Provo, UT, 1992; J.D., University of Washington, Seattle, WA, 1995; professional: attorney; religion: The Church of Jesus Christ of Latter-Day Saints; married: Becca Labrador; five children; committees: Judiciary; Natural Resources; elected to the 112th Congress on November 2, 2010; reelected to each succeeding Congress.

Office Listings

http://labrador.house.gov facebook: https://www.facebook.com/raul.r.labrador
twitter: @Raul_Labrador

1523 Longworth House Office Building, Washington, DC 20515 .... (202) 225–6611
Chief of Staff.—Mike Cunnington. FAX: 225–3029
Legislative Director.—Aaron Calkins.
Scheduler.—Will Johnson.
33 East Broadway Avenue, Suite 251, Meridian, ID 83642 .... (208) 888–3188
1250 Ironwood Drive, Suite 241, Coeur d'Alene, ID 83814 .... (208) 667–0127
313 D Street, Suite 107, Lewiston, ID 83501 .... (208) 743–1388

Counties: ADA (part), ADAMS, BENEWAH, BOISE, BONNER, BOUNDARY, CANYON, CLEARWATER, GEM, IDAHO, KOOTENAI, LATAH, LEWIS, NEZ PERCE, OWYHEE, PAYETTE, SHOSHONE, VALLEY, AND WASHINGTON. Population (2010), 784,132.

ZIP Codes: 59847, 83302, 83316, 83501, 83520, 83522–26, 83530, 83533, 83535–37, 83539–49, 83552–55, 83602, 83604–05, 83607, 83610–12, 83615–17, 83619, 83622, 83624, 83626–29, 83631–32, 83634, 83636–39, 83641–46, 83650–51, 83654–57, 83660–61, 83666, 83669–72, 83676–77, 83686–87, 83702, 83705, 83709, 83713–14, 83716, 83801–06, 83808–15, 83821–27, 83830, 83832–37, 83839–52, 83854–58, 83860–61, 83864, 83866–74, 83876, 89832, 97910, 97913, 99128

* * *

SECOND DISTRICT

MICHAEL K. SIMPSON, Republican, of Blackfoot, ID; born in Burley, ID, September 8, 1950; education: graduated, Blackfoot High School, 1968; Utah State University, 1972; Washington University School of Dental Medicine, 1977; professional: dentist, private practice; Blackfoot, ID, City Council, 1981–85; Idaho State Legislature, 1985–98; Idaho Speaker of the House, 1992–98; married: Kathy Simpson; committees: Appropriations; elected to the 106th Congress; reelected to each succeeding Congress.

Office Listings

http://simpson.house.gov

2312 Rayburn House Office Building, Washington, DC 20515 .... (202) 225–5531
Chief of Staff.—Lindsay Slater. FAX: 225–8216
Scheduler.—Emilee Henshaw.
Legislative Director.—Nathan Greene.
Communications Director.—Nikki Wallace.
802 West Bannock, Suite 600, Boise, ID 83702 .... (208) 334–1953
1341 Fillmore, #202, Twin Falls, ID 83301 .... (208) 734–7219
410 Memorial Drive, Suite 203, Idaho Falls, ID 83402 .... (208) 523–6701
275 South Fifth Avenue, #275, Pocatello, ID 83201 .... (208) 233–2222

Counties: ADA (Part), BANNOCK, BEAR LAKE, BINGHAM, BLAINE, BONNEVILLE, BUTTE, CAMAS, CARIBOU, CASSIA, CLARK, CUSTER, ELMORE, FRANKLIN, FREMONT, GOODING, JEFFERSON, JEROME, LEMHI, LINCOLN, MADISON, MINIDOKA, ONEIDA, POWER, TETON, AND TWIN FALLS. Population (2010), 793,109.

ZIP Codes: 83201–06, 83209–15, 83217–18, 83220–21, 83223, 83226–30, 83232–39, 83241, 83243–46, 83250–56, 83261–63, 83271–72, 83274, 83276–78, 83281, 83283, 83285–87, 83301–03, 83311–14, 83316, 83318, 83320–25, 83327–28, 83330, 83332–38, 83340–44, 83346–50, 83352–55, 83401–06, 83415, 83420–25, 83427–29, 83431, 83433–36, 83438, 83440–46, 83448–52, 83454–55, 83460, 83462–69, 83601–02, 83604, 83623–24, 83627, 83633–34, 83647–48, 83701–09, 83712, 83714–17, 83720–33, 83735, 83744, 83756

ILLINOIS

(Population, 2010 12,830,632)

SENATORS

RICHARD J. DURBIN, Democrat, of Springfield, IL; born in East St. Louis, IL, November 21, 1944; son of William and Ann Durbin; education: graduated, Assumption High School, East St. Louis; B.S., foreign service and economics, Georgetown University, Washington, DC, 1966; J.D., Georgetown University Law Center, 1969; professional: attorney; admitted to the Illinois Bar in 1969; began practice in Springfield; legal counsel to Lieutenant Governor Paul Simon, 1969–72; legal counsel to Illinois Senate Judiciary Committee, 1972–82; parliamentarian, Illinois Senate, 1969–82; adjunct professor, Southern Illinois University School of Medicine; married: the former Loretta Schaefer, 1967; children: Christine (deceased), Paul, and Jennifer; committees: Appropriations; Judiciary; Rules and Administration; elected to the 98th Congress on November 2, 1982; reelected to each succeeding Congress; elected to the U.S. Senate on November 5, 1996; reelected to each succeeding Senate term; elected as Democratic Whip, 2004; reelected for each succeeding Congress.

Office Listings

http://durbin.senate.gov facebook.com/senatordurbin twitter.com/senatordurbin

711 Hart Senate Office Building, Washington, DC 20510 .... (202) 224–2152
Chief of Staff.—Patrick Souders. TTY: 224–8180
Legislative Director.—Corey Tellez.
Communications Director.—Emily Hampsten. VRS: 540–9872
Director of Scheduling.—Claire Reuschel.
230 South Dearborn, Kluczynski Building, 38th Floor, Chicago, IL 60604 .... (312) 353–4952
Chicago Director.—Clarisol Duque.
525 South Eighth Street, Springfield, IL 62703 .... (217) 492–4062
State Director.—Bill Houlihan.
1504 Third Avenue, Suite 227, Rock Island, IL 61201 .... (309) 786–5173
250 West Cherry Street, Suite 115D, Carbondale, IL 62901 .... (618) 351–1122

* * *

TAMMY DUCKWORTH, Democrat, of Hoffman Estates, IL; born in Bangkok, Thailand; education: B.A., political science, University of Hawaii, 1989; M.A., George Washington University, Washington, DC, 1992; Ph.D., in Human Services at Capella University, 2014; professional: Rotary International; Illinois Department of Veterans' Affairs; U.S. Department of Veterans' Affairs; military: Lt. Colonel, Illinois National Guard; combat veteran, Operation Iraqi Freedom; married: Bryan Bowlsbey; committees: Commerce, Science, and Transportation; Energy and Natural Resources; Environment and Public Works; Small Business and Entrepreneurship; elected to the 113th Congress on November 6, 2012; reelected to the 114th Congress on November 4, 2014; elected to the U.S. Senate on November 8, 2016.

Office Listings

http://duckworth.senate.gov https://www.twitter.com/SenDuckworth
https://www.facebook.com/SenDuckworth https://www.youtube.com/c/SenDuckworth
https://www.instagram.com/senduckworth/

524 Hart Senate Office Building, Washington, DC 20510 .... (202) 224–2854
Chief of Staff.—Kaitlin Fahey. FAX: 228–0618
Deputy Chief of Staff.—Kalina Bakalov.
Policy Director.—Ben Rhodeside.
Communications Director.—Ben Garmisa.
Administrative Director.—Paul Kohnstamm.
Scheduling Director.—Kelsey Becker.
230 South Dearborn Street, Suite 3900, Chicago, IL 60604 .... (312) 886–3506
Chicago Director.—Marina Faz-Huppert.
8 South Old State Capitol Plaza, Springfield, IL 62701.
State Director.—Cameron Joost.

REPRESENTATIVES

FIRST DISTRICT

BOBBY L. RUSH, Democrat, of Chicago, IL; born in Albany, GA; November 23, 1946; education: attended Marshall High School, Marshall, IL; B.A., Roosevelt University, Chicago,

IL, 1974; M.A., University of Illinois, Chicago, 1994; M.A., McCormick Theological Seminary, Chicago, 1998; professional: U.S. Army, 1963–68; insurance agent; alderman, Chicago, Illinois, City Council, 1983–93; deputy chairman, Illinois Democratic Party, 1990; unsuccessful candidate for Mayor of Chicago, 1999; minister; widower: Carolyn; five children; committees: Energy and Commerce; elected on November 3, 1992 to the 103rd Congress; reelected to each succeeding Congress.

Office Listings

http://www.rush.house.gov https://www.facebook.com/congressmanbobbyrush
https://twitter.com/RepBobbyRush

2188 Rayburn House Office Building, Washington, DC 20515 .... (202) 225–4372
Chief of Staff / Counsel.—Yardly Pollas. FAX: 226–0333
Legislative Director.—Nishith Pandya.
Director of Administration and Operations.—N. Lenette Myers.
Communications Director.—Debra Johnson.
11750 S. Western Avenue, Chicago, IL 60643 .... (773) 779–2400
District Director.—Robyn Wheeler Grange.

Counties: COOK COUNTY (part) AND WILL COUNTY (part). CITIES AND TOWNSHIPS: Alsip, Blue Island, Bremen Township, Calumet Park, Calumet Township, Chicago Country, Club Hills, Crestwood, Dixmoor, Elwood, Evergreen Park, Frankfort Square, Frankfort Township, Frankfort, Green Garden Township, Harvey, Jackson Township, Manhattan Township, Manhattan, Markham, Merrionette Park, Midlothian, Mokena, New Lenox Township, New Lenox, Oak Forest, Oak Lawn, Orland Hills, Orland Park, Orland Township, Palos Heights, Palos Township, Posen, Rich Township, Riverdale, Robbins, Thornton Township, Tinley Park, Will County, Worth, and Worth Township. Population (2012), 711,982.

ZIP Codes: 60406, 60421, 60423, 60426, 60428, 60442, 60445, 60448–49, 60451–53, 60462–64, 60467–69, 60472, 60477–78, 60482, 60487, 60609, 60615–17, 60619–21, 60628–29, 60636–37, 60643, 60649, 60652–53, 60655, 60803, 60805, 60827

* * *

SECOND DISTRICT

ROBIN L. KELLY, Democrat, of Matteson, IL; born in New York, NY, April 30, 1956; education: B.A. in psychology, Bradley University, IL, 1977; M.A., counseling, Bradley University, 1982; Ph.D., political science, Northern Illinois University, IL, 2004; professional: counselor; community affairs director, Matteson, IL, 1992–2006; member, Illinois State House of Representatives, 2003–07; Chief of Staff, Illinois State Treasurer, 2007–10; Chief Administrative Officer, Cook County, IL, 2010–12; caucuses: co-chair, Diversifying Tech Caucus; vice chair, Gun Violence Prevention Task Force; member, Congressional Black Caucus; Congressional Caucus on Black Women and Girls; married: Dr. Nathaniel Horn; two children; committees: Foreign Affairs; Oversight and Government Reform; elected to the 113th Congress on April 9, 2013, by special election, to fill the vacancy caused by the resignation of U.S. Representative Jesse L. Jackson, Jr.; reelected to each succeeding Congress.

Office Listings

http://www.robinkelly.house.gov www.facebook.com/reprobinkelly
https://twitter.com/reprobinkelly

1239 Longworth House Office Building, Washington, DC 20515 .... (202) 225–0773
Chief of Staff.—Brandon Webb.
Legislative Director.—Zachary Ostro.
Communications Director.—James Lewis.
Legislative Assistants: Jay Cho, Mia Keeys, Matt McMurray.
Director of Advance / Scheduler.—Tony Presta.
600 Holiday Plaza Drive, Suite 505, Matteson, IL 60443 .... (708) 679–0078
District Director.—Audra Wilson.

Counties: COOK (part), KANKAKEE, AND WILL (part). CITIES AND TOWNSHIPS: Beecher, Blue Island, Bonfield, Bourbonnais, Bradley, Buckingham, Cabery, Calumet City, Chebanse, Chicago, Chicago Heights, Country Club Hills, Crete, Custer Park, Dixmoor, Dolton, Essex, Flossmoor, Ford Heights, Frankfort, Gardner, Glenwood, Grant Park, Harvey, Hazel Crest, Herscher, Homewood, Hopkins Park, Kankakee, Lansing, Lynwood, Manhattan, Manteno, Markham, Matteson, Momence, Monee, Olympia Fields, Park Forest, Pembroke Township, Peotone, Phoenix, Reddick, Richton Park, Riverdale, Saint Anne, Sauk Village, South Chicago Heights, South Holland, Steger, Tinley Park, Thornton, Union Hill, University Park, and Wilmington. Population (2010), 718,507.

ZIP Codes: 60401, 60406, 60409, 60411–12, 60417, 60419, 60422–23, 60425–26, 60428–30, 60438, 60443, 60449, 60461, 60466, 60468, 60471, 60473, 60475–78, 60481, 60484, 60615, 60617, 60628, 60633, 60637, 60649, 60827, 60901, 60913–15, 60917, 60919, 60922, 60935, 60940–42, 60944, 60950, 60954, 60958, 60961, 60964, 60969

* * *

THIRD DISTRICT

DANIEL LIPINSKI, Democrat, of Chicago, IL; born in Chicago, July 15, 1966; son of former Congressman William Lipinski, 1983–2004; education: B.S., mechanical engineering, *magna cum laude*, Northwestern University, 1988; M.S., engineering-economic systems, Stanford University, 1989; Ph.D., political science, Duke University, 1998; professional: aide to U.S. Representative George Sangmeister, 1993–94; aide to U.S. Representative Jerry Costello, 1995–96; aide to U.S. Representative Rod Blagojevich, 1999–2000; professor, James Madison University Washington Program, Washington, DC, 2000; professor, University of Notre Dame, South Bend, IN, 2000–01; professor, University of Tennessee, Knoxville, TN, 2001–04; married: Judy; committees: Science, Space, and Technology; Transportation and Infrastructure; elected to the 109th Congress on November 2, 2004; reelected to each succeeding Congress.

Office Listings

http://www.lipinski.house.gov

2346 Rayburn House Office Building, Washington, DC 20515 .... (202) 225–5701
Chief of Staff.—Eric Lausten. FAX: 225–1012
Office Administrative.—Jennifer Sypolt.
Legislative Director.—Sofya Leonova.
6245 South Archer Avenue, Chicago, IL 60638 .... (312) 886–0481
District Chief of Staff.—Jerry Hurckes.
222 East 9th Street, Suite 109, Lockport, IL 60441 .... (815) 838–1990
Communications Director.—Isaac Sancken.
5210 West 95th Street, Suite 104, Oak Lawn, IL 60453 .... (708) 424–0853
14700 Ravinia Avenue, 1st Floor, Orland Park, IL 60462 .... (708) 403–4379

Counties: COOK (part), DUPAGE (part), AND WILL (part). CITIES AND TOWNSHIPS: Alsip, Bedford Park, Berwyn, Bridgeview, Brookfield, Burbank, Burr Ridge, Chicago, Chicago Ridge, Cicero, Countryside, Crest Hill, Forest Park, Forest View, Hickory Hills, Hillside, Hinsdale, Homer Glen, Hometown, Hodgkins, Indian Head Park, Justice Burbank, LaGrange, Lemont, Lockport, Lyons, McCook, Merrionette Park, North Riverside, Oak Lawn, Oak Park, Palos Heights, Palos Hills, Palos Park, Proviso, Riverside, Romeoville, Stickney, Summit Brookfield, Western Springs, Willow Springs, and Worth. Population (2012), 704,438.

ZIP Codes: 60402 (part), 60406, 60415, 60432 (part), 60435 (part), 60439 (part), 60441 (part), 60446 (part), 60448 (part), 60451 (part), 60463 (part), 60455, 60456 (part), 60457–58, 60459 (part), 60462–65 (part), 60467 (part), 60477 (part), 60480 (part), 60482 (part), 60501, 60513 (part), 60521 (part), 60425–26 (part), 60534 (part), 60544 (part), 60546 (part), 60558 (part), 60561 (part), 60608–09 (part), 60616 (part), 60620 (part), 60629 (part), 60632 (part), 60636 (part), 60638 (part), 60643 (part), 60652 (part), 60655 (part), 60803 (part), 60804 (part), 60805 (part)

* * *

FOURTH DISTRICT

LUIS V. GUTIÉRREZ, Democrat, of Chicago, IL; born in Chicago, December 10, 1953; education: B.A., Northeastern Illinois University, DeKalb, IL, 1974; professional: teacher; social worker, Illinois State Department of Children and Family Services; administrative assistant, Chicago, Mayor's office, Subcommittee on Infrastructure, 1984–85; co-founder, West Town–26th Ward Independent Political Organization, 1985; Alderman, Chicago, Illinois, City Council, 1986–93, President Pro Tem, 1989–92; Democratic National Committee, 1984; married: Soraida Arocho; children: Omaira and Jessica; committees: Judiciary; elected to the 103rd Congress on November 3, 1992; reelected to each succeeding Congress.

Office Listings

http://www.gutierrez.house.gov https://facebook.com/RepGutierrez
https://twitter.com/RepGutierrez

2408 Rayburn House Office Building, Washington, DC 20515 .... (202) 225–8203
Chief of Staff.—Susan Collins. FAX: 225–7810
Communications Director.—Douglas Rivlin.
3240 West Fullerton Avenue, Chicago, IL 60647 .... (773) 342–0774
FAX: 342–0776

Counties: COOK COUNTY (part). CITIES: Berkeley, Berwyn, Brookfield, Chicago, Cicero, Elmwood Park, Forest Park, Hillside, La Grange Park, Lyons, Maywood, Melrose Park, Northlake, North Riverside, Oak Park, Riverside, Stickney, Stone Park, and Westchester. Population (2012), 724,644.

ZIP Codes: 60126, 60154, 60160, 60162–64, 60304–05, 60402, 60513, 60546, 60608–09, 60616, 60618, 60622–23, 60625, 60629–30, 60632, 60634, 60639, 60641, 60647, 60651, 60707, 60804

* * *

FIFTH DISTRICT

MIKE QUIGLEY, Democrat, of Chicago, IL; born in Indianapolis, IN, October 17, 1958; education: B.A., political science, Roosevelt University, 1981; M.P.P., University of Chicago, 1985; J.D., Loyola University, 1989; professional: Chicago aldermanic aide, 1983–89; practicing attorney, 1990–2009; Cook County Commissioner, 1998–2009; adjunct professor, Roosevelt University, 2006–07; adjunct professor, Loyola University, 2002–09; married: Barbara; children: Meghan and Alyson; committees: Appropriations; Permanent Select Committee on Intelligence; elected to the 111th Congress on April 7, 2009, by special election, to fill the vacancy caused by the resignation of U.S. Representative Rahm Emanuel; reelected to the 112th Congress on November 2, 2010; reelected to each succeeding Congress.

Office Listings

http://www.quigley.house.gov https://www.facebook.com/repmikequigley
https://twitter.com/RepMikeQuigley

2458 Rayburn House Office Building, Washington, DC 20515 .... (202) 225–4061
Chief of Staff.—Juan Hinojosa. FAX: 225–5603
Communications Director.—Tara Vales.
Scheduler.—Haley Fulford.
Legislative Director.—Doug Lee.
4345 North Milwaukee Avenue, Chicago, IL 60641 .... (773) 267–5926
FAX: 267–6583
3223 North Sheffield Avenue, Chicago, IL 60657 .... (773) 267–5926

Counties: COOK COUNTY (part). Population (2010), 648,610.

ZIP Codes: 60018, 60106, 60126, 60131, 60154, 60160, 60162, 60164, 60171, 60176, 60181, 60191, 60521, 60523, 60525–26, 60558, 60610, 60612–14, 60618, 60622, 60625, 60630–31, 60634, 60640–42, 60645–47, 60656–57, 60659, 60706–07, 60714

* * *

SIXTH DISTRICT

PETER J. ROSKAM, Republican, of Wheaton, IL; born in Hinsdale, IL, September 13, 1961; education: B.A., University of Illinois, Urbana-Champaign, IL, 1983; J.D., Illinois Institute of Technology - Chicago-Kent College of Law, Chicago, IL, 1989; professional: lawyer, private practice; staff, U.S. Representative Tom DeLay of Texas, 1985–86; U.S. Representative Henry Hyde of Illinois, 1986–87; teacher; businessman; member, Illinois House of Representatives, 1993–99; member, Illinois Senate, 2000–06; married: Elizabeth; children: four; committees: Ways and Means; elected to the 110th Congress on November 7, 2006; reelected to each succeeding Congress.

Office Listings

http://roskam.house.gov

2246 Rayburn House Office Building, Washington, DC 20515 .... (202) 225–4561
Chief of Staff.—David Mork. FAX: 225–1166
Scheduler.—Mary Sobczak.
Legislative Director.—Joe Fawell.
Press Secretary.—David Pasch.
2700 International Drive, Suite 304, West Chicago, IL 60185 .... (630) 232–0006

Counties: COOK (part), DUPAGE (part), LAKE (part), AND MCHENRY (part). CITIES AND TOWNSHIPS: Algonquin, Barrington, Barrington Hills, Bartlett, Carol Stream, Carpentersville, Cary, Clarendon Hills, Crystal Lake, Darien, Deer Park, Downers Grove, Dundee, East Dundee, Elgin, Fox River Grove, Gilberts, Glen Ellyn, Hanover Park, Hawthorne Woods, Hinsdale, Hoffman Estates, Huntley, Inverness, Kildeer, Lake in the Hills, Lakewood, Lake Barrington, Lake Zurich, Lisle, Lombard, Long Grove, Naperville, North Barrington, Oak Brook, Oakwood Hills, Oakbrook Terrace, Palatine, Port Barrington, Rolling Meadows, Saint Charles, Schaumburg, Sleepy Hollow, South Barrington, South Elgin, Tower Lakes, Trout Valley, Warrenville, Wayne, West Chicago, West Dundee, Westmont, Wheaton, Willowbrook, and Winfield. Population (2010), 712,813.

ZIP Codes: 60008, 60010–11, 60013–14, 60021, 60039, 60047, 60055, 60060, 60067, 60074, 60078, 60094, 60102–03, 60107, 60110, 60118, 60120, 60122–24, 60133, 60136–39, 60142, 60148, 60156, 60169, 60173–75, 60177, 60179, 60181, 60184–85, 60187–90, 60192, 60195, 60197, 60199, 60514–16, 60521, 60523, 60527, 60532, 60540, 60555, 60559, 60561, 60563–65

* * *

SEVENTH DISTRICT

DANNY K. DAVIS, Democrat, of Chicago, IL; born in Parkdale, AR, September 6, 1941; education: B.A., Arkansas AM&N College, 1961; M.A., Chicago State University; Ph.D., Union Institute, Cincinnati, OH; professional: educator and health planner-administrator; board of directors, National Housing Partnership; Cook County Board of Commissioners, 1st District, 1990–96; Chicago City Council, 29th Ward, 1979–90; recipient of the Independent Voters of Illinois' Best Alderman Award for 1980–82 and 1989–90; co-chair, Clinton-Gore-Braun '92; founder and past president, Westside Association for Community Action; past president, National Association of Community Health Centers; recipient of the Leon M. Despres Award, 1987; married to Vera G. Davis; two sons: Jonathan and Stacey; committees: Ways and Means; elected to the 105th Congress; reelected to each succeeding Congress.

Office Listings

http://www.davis.house.gov facebook: www.facebook.com/CongressmanDKDavis
twitter: @RepDannyDavis

2159 Rayburn House Office Building, Washington, DC 20515 .... (202) 225–5006
Chief of Staff.—Yul Edwards. FAX: 225–5641
Deputy Chief of Staff.—Jill Hunter-Williams.
Director of Issues and Communications.—Ira Cohen.
2815 West 5th Avenue, Chicago, IL 60612 .... (773) 533–7520

Counties: COOK. CITIES AND TOWNSHIPS: Berwyn, Chicago, Oak Park, Proviso, River Forest, and Riverside. Population (2010), 712,812.

ZIP Codes: 60104, 60130, 60141, 60153–55, 60160, 60162–63, 60301–12, 60614–16, 60621–24, 60629, 60632, 60636–37, 60639, 60642, 60644, 60651, 60653–54, 60661, 60707, 60804

* * *

EIGHTH DISTRICT

RAJA KRISHNAMOORTHI, Democrat, of Schaumburg, IL; born in New Delhi, India, July 19, 1973; education: B.S.E., mechanical engineering and certificate in public policy, Princeton University, 1995; J.D., Harvard Law School, 2000; professional: private law practice; Special Assistant Illinois Attorney General; Deputy Illinois Treasurer; president of research-oriented small businesses; religion: Hindu; married to Priya; three children: Vijay, Vikram, and Sonia; committees: Education and the Workforce; Oversight and Government Reform; elected to the 115th Congress on November 8, 2016.

Office Listings

http://Krishnamoorthi.house.gov https://www.facebook.com/CongressmanRaja
https://twitter.com/congressmanraja https://www.instagram.com/congressmanraja
https://www.youtube.com/c/CongressmanRaja

515 Cannon House Office Building, Washington, DC 20515 .... (202) 225–3711
Chief of Staff.—Mark Schauerte. FAX: 225–7830
1701 East Woodfield Road, Suite 704, Schaumburg, IL 60173 .... (847) 413–1959
District Director.—Steven Baskin. FAX: 413–1965

Counties: COOK COUNTY (part). TOWNSHIPS: Arlington Heights, Barrington Hills, Buffalo Grove, Chicago (part), Des Plaines, Elk Grove, Hoffman Estates, Mount Prospect, Palatine, Rolling Meadows, Rosemont, Schaumburg, Streamwood, and Wheeling. DUPAGE COUNTY (part). TOWNSHIPS: Addison, Bartlett, Bensenville, Bloomingdale, Carol Stream, Elmhurst, Glen Ellyn, Glendale, Hanover Park, Itasca, Lombard, Oak Brook, Oakbrook Terrace, Roselle, Villa Park, and Wheaton. KANE COUNTY (part). TOWNSHIPS: Algonquin, Carpentersville, East Dundee, and Elgin. Population (2010), 726,418.

ZIP Codes: 60004–05, 60007–10, 60016, 60018, 60038, 60056, 60067, 60074, 60089–90, 60101–03, 60106–08, 60110, 60116–18, 60120–21, 60123–24, 60126, 60131–33, 60137, 60139, 60143, 60148, 60157, 60168–70, 60172–73, 60177, 60179, 60181, 60187–88, 60191–95, 60399, 60523

* * *

NINTH DISTRICT

JANICE D. SCHAKOWSKY, Democrat, of Evanston, IL; born in Chicago, IL, May 26, 1944; education: B.A., University of Illinois, 1965; professional: consumer advocate; program director, Illinois Public Action; executive director, Illinois State Council of Senior Citizens, 1985–90; State Representative, 18th District, Illinois General Assembly, 1991–99; served on Labor and Commerce, Human Service Appropriations, Health Care, and Electric Deregulation Committees; religion: Jewish; married: Robert Creamer; children: Ian, Mary, and Lauren; committees: Budget; Energy and Commerce; elected to the 106th Congress; reelected to each succeeding Congress.

Office Listings

http://www.schakowsky.house.gov https://www.facebook.com/janschakowsky
https://twitter.com/janschakowsky

2367 Rayburn House Office Building, Washington, DC 20515 .... (202) 225–2111
Chief of Staff.—Cathy Hurwit. FAX: 226–6890
Communications Director.—Jeronimo Anaya-Ortiz.
Legislative Director.—Matt Hayward.
Appointments Secretary.—Kim Muzeroll.
5533 Broadway, Chicago, IL 60640 .... (773) 506–7100
District Director.—Leslie Combs.
1852 Johns Drive, Glenview, IL 60025 .... (847) 328–3409

Counties: COOK COUNTY (part). CITIES: Arlington Heights, Chicago, Des Plaines, Evanston, Glenview, Golf, Kenilworth, Lincolnwood, Morton Grove, Mount Prospect, Niles, Northbrook, Northfield, Park Ridge, Prospect Heights, Skokie, Wheeling, Wilmette, and Winnetka. Population (2010), 712,813.

ZIP Codes: 60004–05, 60016, 60018–19, 60025–26, 60029, 60043, 60053, 60056, 60062, 60068, 60070, 60076–77, 60090–91, 60093, 60176, 60201–03, 60613, 60626, 60630, 60640, 60645–46, 60656–57, 60659–60, 60706, 60712, 60714

* * *

TENTH DISTRICT

BRADLEY SCOTT SCHNEIDER, Democrat, of Deerfield, IL; born in Denver, CO, August 20, 1961; education: Cherry Creek High School, Greenwood Village, CO, 1979; B.A., Northwestern University, Evanston, IL, 1983; M.B.A., Kellogg School of Management, Evanston, IL, 1988; professional: owner, Cadence Consulting Group, LLC; director of Family Business Center, Blackman Kallick, LLP; managing principal, Davis Dann Adler Schneider, LLC; family: wife, Julie Dann; children: Adam and Daniel; committees: Foreign Affairs; Judiciary; Small Business; elected to the 113th Congress on November 6, 2012; unsuccessful candidate for reelection to the 114th Congress in 2014; elected to the 115th Congress on November 8, 2016.

Office Listings

http://schneider.house.gov facebook: www.facebook.com/congressmanbradschneider
twitter: www.twitter.com/repschneider

1432 Longworth House Office Building, Washington, DC 20515 .... (202) 225–4835
Chief of Staff.—Ashley Jones. FAX: 225–0837
111 Barclay Boulevard, Suite 200, Lincolnshire, IL 60069 .... (847) 383–4870
District Director.—Magen Ryan. FAX: 793–0677

Counties: COOK (part) AND LAKE (part). Population (2010), 709,209.

ZIP Codes: 60004, 60015–16, 60020, 60022, 60025–26, 60030–31, 60035, 60037, 60040–41, 60044–48, 60050–51, 60053, 60056, 60060–62, 60064, 60068–70, 60073, 60081, 60083, 60085, 60087–90, 60093, 60096, 60099, 60714

* * *

ELEVENTH DISTRICT

BILL FOSTER, Democrat, of Naperville, IL; born in Madison, WI, October 7, 1955; education: B.S., University of Wisconsin-Madison, 1976; Ph.D., Harvard University, 1983; professional: small business owner, physicist; committees: Financial Services; Science, Space, and Technology; elected to the 113th Congress on November 6, 2012; reelected to the 114th Congress on November 4, 2014.

Office Listings

http://www.foster.house.gov https://twitter.com/repbillfoster
https://www.facebook.com/congressmanbillfoster?ref=hl

1224 Longworth House Office Building, Washington, DC 20515 .... (202) 225–3515

Office Listings—Continued

Chief of Staff.—Adam Elias. FAX: 225–9420
2711 East New York Street, Suite 204, Aurora, IL 60502 .... (630) 585–7672
195 Springfield Avenue, Suite 102, Joliet, IL 60435 .... (815) 280–5876
District Director.—Carole Cheney.

Counties: COOK (part), DUPAGE (part), KANE (part), KENDALL (part), AND WILL (part). Population (2010), 722,173.

ZIP Codes: 60403–04, 60410, 60421, 60431–36, 60439–42, 60446–48, 60451, 60480, 60490, 60502–06, 60512, 60515–17, 60519, 60525, 60527, 60532, 60538, 60540, 60542–44, 60559–65, 60586

* * *

TWELFTH DISTRICT

MIKE BOST, Republican, of Murphysboro, IL; born in Murphysboro, December 30, 1960; education: University of Illinois Certified Firefighter II Academy; professional: state representative, small business owner, firefighter; military: U.S. Marine Corps, 1979–82; religion: Christian, non-denominational; married: Tracy Stanton, 1980; children: Steven, Kasey, and Kaitlin; committees: Agriculture; Transportation and Infrastructure; Veterans' Affairs; elected to the 114th Congress on November 4, 2014.

Office Listings

http://www.bost.house.gov http://www.twitter.com/repbost http://www.facebook.com/repbost

1440 Longworth House Office Building, Washington, DC 20515 .... (202) 225–5661
Chief of Staff.—Matt McCullough. FAX: 225–0285
Scheduler.—Kristen Lebryk.
Legislative Director.—Mark Ratto.
Communications Director.—George O'Connor.
District Director.—Matt Rice.
103 North Oak Street, O'Fallon, IL 62269 .... (618) 233–8026
FAX: 233–8765
300 East Main Street, Suite 4, Carbondale, IL 62901 .... (618) 457–5787
FAX: 457–2990
1100 Main Street, Mt. Vernon, IL 62864 .... (618) 826–3043

Counties: ALEXANDER, FRANKLIN, JACKSON, JEFFERSON, MADISON (part), MONROE, PERRY, PULASKI, RANDOLPH, ST. CLAIR, UNION, AND WILLIAMSON. Population (2010), 712,813.

ZIP Codes: 62002, 62010, 62018, 62024–25, 62035, 62040, 62048, 62059–60, 62067, 62084, 62087, 62090, 62095, 62201, 62203–08, 62217, 62220–21, 62223, 62225–26, 62232–34, 62236–44, 62248, 62254–55, 62257–58, 62260–61, 62263–65, 62268–69, 62272, 62274, 62277–80, 62282, 62285–86, 62288–89, 62292–95, 62297–98, 62801, 62808, 62810, 62812, 62814, 62816, 62819, 62822, 62825, 62830–32, 62836, 62841, 62846, 62851, 62856, 62860, 62864–65, 62872, 62874, 62877, 62883–84, 62888–91, 62893–94, 62896–98, 62901–03, 62905–07, 62912, 62914–18, 62920–24, 62926–27, 62932–33, 62939–42, 62948–52, 62956–59, 62961–64, 62966, 62969–70, 62974–76, 62983, 62987–88, 62990, 62992, 62994, 62996–99

* * *

THIRTEENTH DISTRICT

RODNEY DAVIS, Republican, of Taylorville, IL; born in Des Moines, IA, January 5, 1970; education: graduated from Taylorville High School, 1988; B.A., Millikin University, IL, 1992; professional: congressional aide, 1999–2012; has served on numerous local civic and community organizations and groups; religion: Catholic; married: Shannon R. Davis; children: Toryn, Clark, and Griffin; committees: vice chair, Joint Committee on Printing; Agriculture; House Administration; Transportation and Infrastructure; elected to the 113th Congress on November 6, 2012; reelected to each succeeding Congress.

Office Listings

http://www.rodneydavis.house.gov https://www.facebook.com/reprodneydavis
twitter.com/rodneydavis

1740 Longworth House Office Building, Washington, DC 20515 .... (202) 225–2371
Chief of Staff.—Jen Daulby.
Legislative Director.—Miles Chiotti.
Scheduler / Director of Operations.—Brittany Randall.
Communications Director.—Ashley Phelps.
243 South Water Street, Suite 100, Decatur, IL 62523 .... (217) 791–6224

Office Listings—Continued

District Director.—Helen Albert.
2004 Fox Drive, Champaign, IL 61820 .... (217) 403–4690
2833 South Grand Avenue East, Springfield, IL 62703 .... (217) 791–6224
104 West North Street, Normal, IL 61761 .... (309) 252–8834
108 East Market Street, Taylorville, IL 62568 .... (217) 824–5117
15 Professional Park Drive, Maryville, IL 62062 .... (618) 205–8660

Counties: BOND (part), CALHOUN, CHAMPAIGN (part), CHRISTIAN, DEWITT, GREENE, JERSEY, MACON, MACOUPIN, MADISON (part), MCLEAN (part), MONTGOMERY, PIATT, AND SANGAMON (part). Population (2010), 710,784.

ZIP Codes: 60481, 61252, 61701–02, 61704–05, 61709–10, 61727, 61735, 61745, 61749, 61756, 61761, 61772, 61777–78, 61790–91, 61799, 61801–03, 61813, 61815, 61818, 61820–22, 61824, 61826, 61830, 61839, 61842, 61854–56, 61864, 61872, 61874, 61880, 61882, 61884, 61913, 61929, 61936, 62002, 62006, 62009, 62013–17, 61719, 61721–23, 61725–28, 62031–37, 62044–45, 62049–54, 62056, 62058, 62060, 62062–63, 62065, 62069–70, 62074–77, 62079, 62081–83, 62086, 62088–89, 62091–94, 62097, 62234, 62262, 62355, 62501, 62510, 62513, 62517, 62521–26, 62531, 62533, 62535, 62538, 62540, 62544–47, 62549–51, 62554–58, 62560, 62563, 62567–68, 62570, 62572–73, 62626, 62629–30, 62640, 62649, 62667, 62670, 62672, 62674, 62685–86, 62690, 62701–04, 62707, 62711–12

* * *

FOURTEENTH DISTRICT

RANDY HULTGREN, Republican, of Plano, IL; born in Park Ridge, IL, March 1, 1966; education: graduated, B.A., Bethel College, 1988; J.D., Chicago-Kent College of Law, 1993; professional: elected to the DuPage County Board and county Forest Preserve Board, 1994; elected to the Illinois House of Representatives, 1999; elected to the Illinois State Senate, 2007; married: wife, Christy; four children; committees: Financial Services; Science, Space, and Technology; elected to the 112th Congress on November 2, 2010; reelected to each succeeding Congress.

Office Listings

http://hultgren.house.gov facebook.com/rephultgren twitter: @rephultgren

2455 Rayburn House Office Building, Washington, DC 20515 .... (202) 225–2976
Chief of Staff.—Katherine McGuire. FAX: 225–0697
Deputy Chief of Staff.—Doug Thomas.
Communications Director.—Jameson Cunningham.
Special Projects.—Brandon McKee.
Senior Legislative Assistant.—Andrew Mooney.
Legislative Assistants: Bill Hulse, Elise Tollefson.
Executive Assistant / Scheduler.—Katie Hunt.
40W310 Lafox Road, Suite F2, Campton Hills, IL 60175 .... (630) 584–2734
Deputy District Director.—Beth Goncher. FAX: 584–2734
Coalitions Director.—Susan Russell.
Constituent Services: Joanna Annerino, Carol Berger.
1500 South State Route 31, Suite B, McHenry, IL 60050 .... (202) 503–7563
Deputy District Director.—Nick Provenzano. FAX: 584–2734

Counties: DEKALB (part), DUPAGE (part), KANE (part), KENDALL (part), LAKE (part), MCHENRY (part), AND WILL (part). CITIES AND TOWNSHIPS: Alden, Algonquin, Antioch, Aurora, Batavia, Beach Park, Big Grove, Big Rock, Blackberry, Bolingbrook, Boulder Hill, Bristol, Bull Valley, Burlington, Burton, Campton, Campton Hills, Channahon, Channel Lake, Chemung, Coral, Cortland, Crystal Lake, DeKalb, Dorr, Dunham, Elburn, Elgin, Fox, Fox Lake Hills, Fox Lake, Fremont, Geneva, Grafton, Grandwood Park, Greenwood, Gurnee, Hampshire, Hartland, Harvard, Hawthorn Woods, Hebron, Hinckley, Holiday Hills, Huntley, Island Lake, Johnsburg, Joliet, Kaneville, Kendall, Lake Barrington, Lake Catherine, Lake in the Hills, Lake Villa, Lakemoor, Lakewood, Lily Lake, Lindenhurst, Lisbon, Little Rock, Maple Park, Marengo, McCullom Lake, McHenry, Millbrook, Millington, Minooka, Montgomery, Mundelein, Na-Au-Say, Naperville, Newark, Newport, North Aurora, North Barrington, Nunda, Oakwood Hills, Old Mill Creek, Oswego, Pierce, Pingree Grove, Pistakee Highlands, Pittsfield, Plainfield, Plano, Plato, Plattville, Port Barrington, Prairie Grove, Prestbury, Richmond, Riley, Ringwood, Romeoville, Rutland, Sandwich, Seneca, Seward, Shorewood, Somonauk, Spring Grove, Squaw Grove, St. Charles, Sugar Grove, Sycamore, Troy, Union, Virgil, Volo, Wadsworth, Warren, Warrenville, Wauconda, Waukegan, West Chicago, Wheatland, Winfield, Wonder Lake, Woodstock, and Yorkville. Population (2010), 721,774.

ZIP Codes: 60001–02, 60010, 60012–14, 60020, 60030–31, 60033–34, 60042, 60046–48, 60050–51, 60060, 60071–73, 60075, 60081, 60083–84, 60087, 60097–99, 60102, 60109, 60112, 60115, 60119, 60124, 60134–36, 60140, 60142, 60144, 60147, 60151–52, 60156, 60174–75, 60178, 60180, 60183, 60185–86, 60189–90, 60404, 60410, 60431, 60447, 60450, 60490, 60502–03, 60506, 60510–12, 60520, 60536–39, 60541–45, 60548, 60552, 60554–56, 60560, 60563–65, 60585, 61012, 61038

* * *

FIFTEENTH DISTRICT

JOHN SHIMKUS, Republican, of Collinsville, IL; born in Collinsville, February 21, 1958; education: graduated from Collinsville High School; B.S., United States Military Academy, West Point, NY, 1980; teaching certificate, Christ College, Irvine, CA, 1990; M.B.A., Southern Illinois University, Edwardsville, IL, 1997; professional: U.S. Army, 1980–85; Reserves, 1985–2008; government and history teacher, Metro East Lutheran High School, Edwardsville; Collinsville Township trustee, 1989; Madison County Treasurer, 1990–96; married: the former Karen Muth, 1987; children: David, Daniel, and Joshua; committees: Energy and Commerce; elected to the 105th Congress; reelected to each succeeding Congress.

Office Listings

http://www.shimkus.house.gov https://www.facebook.com/repshimkus
https://twitter.com/repshimkus

2217 Rayburn House Office Building, Washington, DC 20515 .... (202) 225–5271
Chief of Staff.—Craig Roberts. FAX: 225–5880
15 Professional Park Drive, Maryville, IL 62062 .... (217) 492–5090
District Director.—Deb Detmers.
201 North Vermillion Street, Suite 218, Danville, IL 61832 .... (217) 446–0664
101 North 4th Street, Suite 303, Effingham, IL 62401 .... (217) 347–7947
110 East Locust Street, Room 12, Harrisburg, IL 62946 .... (618) 252–8271

Counties: BOND, CHAMPAIGN, CLARK, CLAY, COLES, CRAWFORD, CUMBERLAND, DOUGLAS (part), EDGAR, EDWARDS, EFFINGHAM, FAYETTE, FORD, GALLATIN, HAMILTON, HARDIN, JASPER, JOHNSON, LAWRENCE, MADISON (part), MARION, MASSAC, MOULTRIE, POPE, RICHLAND, SALINE (part), SHELBY, VERMILLION, WABASH, WASHINGTON, WAYNE, AND WHITE. Population (2011), 715,066.

ZIP Codes: 60932–33, 60936 (part), 60942 (part), 60949, 60957, 60960, 60963, 61802 (part), 61810–11, 61814, 61816–17, 61822 (part), 61832–34, 61840–41, 61843–44, 61845 (part), 61846–50, 61852, 61853 (part), 61857–59, 61863 (part), 61864 (part), 61865–66, 61870–73, 61875 (part), 61876–78, 61880 (part), 61883, 61910–12, 61913 (part), 61914 (part), 61917, 61919–20, 61924, 61925 (part), 61928, 61929 (part), 61930–33, 61937 (part), 61938, 61940–44, 61949, 61951, 61953, 61955–57, 62001 (part), 62002, 62011–12, 62025 (part), 62032 (part), 62034 (part), 62035, 62040, 62046, 62061–62, 62074 (part), 62075 (part), 62080 (part), 62086 (part), 62097 (part), 62214, 62231–32, 62234 (part), 62237 (part), 62246 (part), 62249, 62253, 62255 (part), 62257 (part), 62262 (part), 62263, 62265 (part), 62266, 62268 (part), 62271, 62273, 62275, 62281 (part), 62284 (part), 62292, 62293 (part), 62294 (part), 62401, 62410–11, 62414, 62417–22, 62424, 62426–28, 62431–33, 62435–36, 62439–43, 62445–52, 62454, 62458–68, 62471, 62473–76, 62479–81, 62510 (part), 62534, 62544 (part), 62550 (part), 62553 (part), 62557 (part), 62565, 62571, 62801 (part), 62803, 62806–07, 62808 (part), 62809, 62810 (part), 62811, 62814 (part), 62815, 62817–18, 62820–21, 62823–24, 62827–28, 62830 (part), 62831 (part), 62835, 62836 (part), 62837–39, 62842–44, 62848–50, 62851 (part), 62852–54, 62858–59, 62860 (part), 62861–63, 62867–71, 62875–76, 62877 (part), 62879–82, 62886–87, 62889 (part), 62890 (part), 62892, 62893 (part), 62895, 62899 (part), 62908, 62910 (part), 62912 (part), 62917 (part), 62919, 62922 (part), 62923 (part), 62928, 62930–31, 62934–35, 62938, 62939 (part), 62941 (part), 62946, 62953–54, 62956 (part), 62960, 62965, 62967, 62977, 62979, 62982, 62984–85, 62987 (part), 62995, 62215, 62216, 62218, 62219, 62230, 62231, 62245, 62250, 62253, 62265 (part), 62266, 62293 (part)

* * *

SIXTEENTH DISTRICT

ADAM KINZINGER, Republican, of Channahon, IL; born in Kankakee, IL, February 27, 1978; education: graduated, Normal Community West High School, 1996; B.S., Illinois State University, 2000; professional: McLean County Board, 1998–2003; Sales Representative, STL Technologies, 2000–03; U.S. Air National Guard, 2003–present, current rank: Major; religion: Protestant; single; Deputy Republican Whip; committees: Energy and Commerce; Foreign Affairs; elected to the 112th Congress on November 2, 2010; reelected to each succeeding Congress.

Office Listings

http://www.kinzinger.house.gov

1221 Longworth House Office Building, Washington, DC 20515 .... (202) 225–3635
Chief of Staff.—Austin Weatherford.
628 Columbus Street, Suite 507, Ottawa, IL 61350 .... (815) 431–9271
District Director.—Bonnie Walsh.
Deputy District Director.—Reed Wilson.
Legislative Director.—Josh Baggett.
Communications Director.—Catherine Gatewood.

Counties: BOONE, BUREAU, DEKALB (part), FORD (part), GRUNDY, IROQUOIS, LASALLE, LEE, LIVINGSTON, OGLE, PUTNAM, STARK (part), WILL (part), AND WINNEBAGO (part). Population (2010), 712,813.

ZIP Codes: 60033, 60111, 60113, 60115, 60129, 60135, 60140, 60145–46, 60150, 60152, 60178, 60407–08, 60410, 60416, 60420–21, 60424, 60437, 60442, 60444, 60447, 60450, 60460, 60470, 60474, 60479, 60481, 60518, 60520, 60530–31, 60537, 60541, 60548–53, 60556–57, 60911–12, 60917–22, 60924, 60926–31, 60934, 60936, 60938, 60941–42, 60945–46, 60948, 60950–53, 60955–56, 60959–62, 60964, 60966, 60968, 60970, 60973–74, 61006–08, 61010–12, 61015–16, 61019–21, 61024, 61030–31, 61038–39, 61042–43, 61047, 61049, 61051–52, 61054, 61057, 61061, 61063–65, 61068, 61071–73, 61078–81, 61084, 61088, 61091, 61101–04, 61107–09, 61111–12, 61114–15, 61283, 61301, 61310–38, 61340–42, 61344–46, 61348–50, 61353–54, 61356, 61358–64, 61367–68, 61370–74, 61376–79, 61421, 61443, 61483, 61491, 61537, 61560, 61726, 61731, 61739–41, 61743–44, 61764, 61769, 61773, 61775, 61845

* * *

SEVENTEENTH DISTRICT

CHERI BUSTOS, Democrat, of East Moline, IL; born in Springfield, IL, October 17, 1961; education: graduated B.A., University of Maryland, College Park, MD, 1983; M.A., University of Illinois at Springfield, 1985; religion: Roman Catholic; married: Gerry; children: Tony, Nick, and Joseph; committees: Agriculture; Transportation and Infrastructure; elected to the 113th Congress on November 6, 2012; reelected to each succeeding Congress.

Office Listings

http://bustos.house.gov twitter: @repcheri
facebook: rep.cheribustos

1009 Longworth House Office Building, Washington, DC 20515 .... (202) 225–5905
Chief of Staff.—Jon Pyatt.
Legislative Director.—Trevor Reuschel.
Communications Director.—Jared S. Smith.
Scheduler.—Laura Piccioli.
Legislative Assistants: Steffanie Bezruki, Alexandra ''Ally'' Fields.
Legislative Correspondent.—Mike Williams.
Staff Assistant.—Vacant.

2401 4th Avenue, Rock Island, IL 61201 .... (309) 786–3406
District Director.—Kate Jennings Gerber.
District Scheduler and Events Coordinator.—Lucie VanHecke.
Constituent Advocates: Miranda French, Ellie LaBotte.

3100 North Knoxville Avenue, Suite 205, Peoria, IL 61603 .... (309) 966–1813
Field Representative.—Josiah Williams.
Constituent Advocate.—Laura Rude.

119 North Church Street, Suites 207 and 208, Rockford, IL 61101 .... (815) 968–8011
Field Representative.—Ricardo Montoya-Picazo.
Constituent Advocate.—Tiana McCall.

Counties: CARROLL, FULTON, HENDERSON, HENRY, JO DAVIESS, KNOX, MERCER, PEORIA (part), ROCK ISLAND, STEPHENSON, TAZEWELL (part), WARREN, WHITESIDE, AND WINNEBAGO (part). Population (2010), 712,813.

ZIP Codes: 61001, 61007, 61013–14, 61018–20, 61025, 61027–28, 61032, 61036–37, 61039, 61041, 61044, 61046–48, 61050–51, 61053, 61059–60, 61062–64, 61067, 61070–71, 61074–75, 61077–78, 61081, 61084–85, 61087–89, 61101–10, 61125, 61201, 61204, 61230–44, 61250–52, 61254, 61256–66, 61270, 61272–79, 61281–85, 61299, 61344, 61361, 61401–02, 61410, 61412–15, 61417–19, 61422–23, 61425, 61427–28, 61430–37, 61439, 61441–43, 61447–50, 61453–54, 61458–60, 61462, 61465–78, 61480, 61482, 61484–86, 61488–90, 61501, 61519–20, 61524, 61529, 61531, 61533–34, 61536, 61539, 61542–47, 61553–55, 61558, 61563–64, 61569, 61572, 61601–07, 61610–11, 61613–16, 61625, 61629–30, 61633–34, 61636–37, 61641, 61650–56, 62330, 62644

* * *

EIGHTEENTH DISTRICT

DARIN LAHOOD, Republican, of Peoria, IL; born in Peoria, July 5, 1968; education: B.A. Loras College, Dubuque, IA, 1990; juris doctorate, John Marshall Law School, 1997; professional: Illinois State Senate, 2011–15; Miller, Hall, & Triggs, 2006–15; Assistant U.S. Attorney, 2001–06; religion: Roman Catholic; married: Kristen; children: McKay, Lucas, and Teddy; committees: Joint Economic Committee; Ways and Mean; elected, by special election, to the 114th Congress on September 10, 2015, to fill the vacancy caused by the resignation of U.S. Representative Aaron Schock; reelected to the 115th Congress on November 8, 2016.

Office Listings

http://www.lahood.house.gov https://www.facebook.com/replahood
https://www.twitter.com/replahood

1424 Longworth House Office Building, Washington, DC 20515 .... (202) 225–6201

Chief of Staff.—Steven Pfrang. FAX: 225–9249
Legislative Director.—Ashley Antoskiewicz.
Deputy Communication Director.—Luke Bunting.
Scheduler.—Rebekah Gudeman.
Legislative Assistant.—Mary Ellen Richardson.
Legislative Correspondent.—Samantha Dybas.
Staff Assistant.—Joey Kouri.

100 Northeast Monroe Street, Peoria, IL 61602 .... (309) 271–7027
District Director.—Brad Stotler.
Communications Director.—JD Dalfonso.
Office Manager.—Lester Davis.
Military Affairs Advisor.—Michael Gilmore.
Constituent Service Representatives: Lester Davis, Autum Greeson.
Staff Assistant.—Tanner Schutte.

201 West Morgan Street, Jacksonville, IL 62650 .... (309) 245–1431
Constituent Service Representative.—Barb Baker.

235 South 6th Street, Springfield, IL 62701 .... (217) 670–1653
Field Representative.—Hal Smith.

3004 G.E. Road, Suite 1B, Bloomington, IL 61704 .... (309) 205–9556

Counties: ADAMS, BROWN, CASS, HANCOCK, LOGAN, MASON, MARSHALL, MCDONOUGH, MCLEAN (part), MENARD, MORGAN, PEORIA (part), PIKE, SANGAMON (part), SCHUYLER, SCOTT, STARK (part), TAZEWELL (part), AND WOODFORD. Population (2010), 712,813.

ZIP Codes: 61321, 61358, 61369, 61375, 61377, 61411, 61415–16, 61420–22, 61424, 61426, 61434, 61438, 61440, 61449–52, 61455, 61459, 61470, 61473, 61475, 61479, 61482–84, 61489, 61491, 61516–17, 61523, 61525–26, 61528–37, 61540–41, 61545–48, 61550, 61552, 61554, 61559, 61561–62, 61565, 61567–71, 61603–04, 61607, 61610–12, 61614–16, 61635, 61638, 61643, 61701–02, 61704–05, 61709–10, 61720–26, 61728–34, 61736–38, 61742, 61744–45, 61747–49, 61751–55, 61758–61, 61770–71, 61774, 61776, 61791, 61799, 61842–43, 62082, 62301, 62305–06, 62311–14, 62316, 62319–21, 62323–26, 62329–30, 62334, 62336, 62338–41, 62343–49, 62351–63, 62365–67, 62370, 62373–76, 62378–80, 62512, 62515, 62518–20, 62530, 62536, 62539, 62541, 62543, 62545, 62548, 62558, 62561, 62563, 62601, 62610–13, 62615, 62617–18, 62621–22, 62624–25, 62627–29, 62631, 62633–35, 62638–39, 62642–44, 62650–51, 62655–56, 62659–68, 62670–71, 62673, 62675, 62677, 62681–82, 62684, 62688–95, 62702–04, 62707, 62711–12

INDIANA

(Population 2010, 6,483,802)

SENATORS

JOSEPH S. DONNELLY, Democrat, of Granger, IN; born in Queens, NY, September 29, 1955; education: graduated, B.A., University of Notre Dame, Notre Dame, IN, 1977; J.D., University of Notre Dame, Notre Dame, IN, 1981; religion: Roman Catholic; married: Jill Truitt, 1979; two children; committees: Agriculture, Nutrition, and Forestry; Armed Services; Banking, Housing, and Urban Affairs; Special Committee on Aging; elected to the U.S. Senate on November 6, 2012.

Office Listings

http://www.donnelly.senate.gov https://www.facebook.com/senatordonnelly
twitter.com/sendonnelly

720 Hart Senate Office Building, Washington, DC 20510 .... (202) 224–4814
Chief of Staff.—Joel Elliott. FAX: 224–5011
Scheduler.—Lynn Demos.
Legislative Director.—Andrew Lattanner.
Communications Director.—Sarah Rothschild.
115 North Pennsylvania Street, Suite 100, Indianapolis, IN 46204 .... (317) 226–5555
205 West Colfax Avenue, South Bend, IN 46601 .... (574) 288–2780
5400 Federal Plaza, Suite 3200, Hammond, IN 46320 .... (219) 852–0089
123 Northwest 4th Street, Suite 417, Evansville, IN 47708 .... (812) 425–5813
702 North Shore Drive, Suite LL–101, Jeffersonville, IN 47130 .... (812) 284–2027
203 East Berry Street, Suite 702B, Fort Wayne, IN 46802 .... (260) 420–4955

* * *

TODD C. YOUNG, Republican, of Bloomington, IN; born in Indianapolis, IN, August 24, 1972; education: B.S., political science, United States Naval Academy, Annapolis, MD, 1995; M.B.A., University of Chicago, Chicago, IL, 2000; M.A., American history, School of Advanced Study, University of London, UK, 2001; J.D., Indiana University, Bloomington, 2005; professional: legislative assistant, U.S. Senate, 2002–03; management consultant, Crowe Chizek, 2003–05; attorney, Tucker and Tucker, PC, in Paoli, IN, 2005–09; military: U.S. Navy, 1990–95; U.S. Marine Corps, 1995–2000; member: Sherwood Oaks Christian Church, Bloomington, IN; married: Jennifer Tucker Hill; children: Tucker, Annalise, Abigal, and Ava; committees: Commerce, Science, and Transportation; Foreign Relations; Health, Education, Labor, and Pensions; Small Business and Entrepreneurship; elected to the 112th Congress on November 2, 2010; reelected to each succeeding Congress; elected to the U.S. Senate on November 8, 2016.

Office Listings

http://toddyoung.senate.gov twitter: @sentoddyoung

B33 Russell Senate Office Building, Washington, DC 20510 .... (202) 224–5623
Chief of Staff.—John Connell. FAX: 226–6866
Legislative Director.—Adam Hechavarria.
Communications Director.—Amy Graham.
Scheduler.—Clay Helton.
11035 Broadway, Suite A, Crown Point, IN 46307 .... (219) 663–2595
FAX: 663–4586
101 Martin Luther King Jr. Boulevard, Suite 110, Evansville, IN 47708 .... (812) 465–6500
FAX: 465–6503
1300 South Harrison Street, Suite 3161, Fort Wayne, IN 46802 .... (260) 426–3151
FAX: 420–0060
46 East Ohio Street, Suite 462, Indianapolis, IN 46204 .... (317) 226–6700
FAX: 554–0760
121 West Spring Street, Suite 130-C & 225, New Albany, IN 47150 .... (812) 542–4820
FAX: 754–0539

REPRESENTATIVES

FIRST DISTRICT

PETER J. VISCLOSKY, Democrat, of Merrillville, IN; born in Gary, IN, August 13, 1949; education: graduated, Andrean High School, Merrillville, 1967; B.S., accounting, Indiana University Northwest, Gary, 1970; J.D., University of Notre Dame Law School, Notre Dame, IN, 1973; LL.M., international and comparative law, Georgetown University Law Center, Washington, DC, 1982; professional: attorney; admitted to the Indiana State Bar, 1974, the District of Columbia Bar, 1978, and the U.S. Supreme Court Bar, 1980; associate staff, U.S. House of Representatives, Committee on Appropriations, 1977–80; Committee on the Budget, 1980–82; practicing attorney, Merrillville law firm, 1983–84; wife: Joanne Royce; children: John Daniel and Timothy Patrick; committees: Appropriations; elected to the 99th Congress on November 6, 1984; reelected to each succeeding Congress.

Office Listings

http://www.visclosky.house.gov twitter: @repvisclosky
facebook: https://www.facebook.com/repvisclosky

2328 Rayburn House Office Building, Washington, DC 20515 .... (202) 225–2461
Chief of Staff.—Mark Lopez. FAX: 225–2493
Deputy Chief of Staff.—Joe DeVooght.
Executive Assistant.—Korry Baack.
Communications Director.—Kevin Spicer.
7895 Broadway, Suite A, Merrillville, IN 46410 .... (219) 795–1844
District Directors: Gregory Gulvas, Elizabeth Johnson. FAX: 795–1850
(888) 423–7383

Counties: LAKE, LAPORTE (part), PORTER. Population (2010), 720,422.

ZIP Codes: 46301–04, 46307–08, 46310–12, 46319–25, 46327, 46341–42, 46345, 46347–49, 46350, 46355–56, 46360, 46368, 46373, 46375–77, 46379–85, 46390, 46392–94, 46401–11

* * *

SECOND DISTRICT

JACKIE WALORSKI, Republican, of Elkhart, IN; born in South Bend, IN, August 17, 1963; education: B.A., communications, Taylor University, Upland, IN, 1985; professional: served in the Indiana General Assembly from 2005–10; religion: Christian; married: Dean; committees: Ways and Means; elected to the 113th Congress on November 6, 2012.

Office Listings

http://walorksi.house.gov https://www.facebook.com/repjackiewalorski
https://twitter.com/repwalorski

419 Cannon House Office Building, Washington, DC 20515 .... (202) 225–3915
Chief of Staff.—Ben Falkowski. FAX: 225–6798
Legislative Director.—Mike Dankler.
Scheduler.—Faith Ammen.
Communications Director.—Jack Morrissey.
202 Lincolnway East, Suite 101, Mishawaka, IN 46544 .... (574) 204–2645
709 Main Street, Rochester, IN 46975 .... (574) 223–4373

Counties: ELKHART, FULTON, KOSCIUSKO (part), LAPORTE (part), MARSHALL, MIAMI, PULASKI, ST. JOSEPH, STARKE, AND WABASH. CITIES: Elkhart, Goshen, Knox, La Porte, Mishawaka, Peru, Plymouth, Rochester, South Bend, Syracuse, Wabash, and Winamac. Population (2010), 718,237.

ZIP Codes: 46340, 46345–46, 46348, 46350, 46352, 46365–66, 46374, 46382, 46501–02, 46504, 46506–08, 46510–11, 46513–17, 46524, 46526–28, 46530–32, 46534, 46536–39, 46540, 46542–46, 46550, 46552–56, 46561, 46563, 46565, 46567, 46570, 46572–74, 46580, 46582, 46595, 46601, 46613–17, 46619, 46624, 46626, 46628, 46634–35, 46637, 46660, 46680, 46702, 46732, 46750, 46767, 46787, 46901, 46910–12, 46914, 46919, 46921–22, 46926, 46931–32, 46939, 46940–41, 46943, 46945–46, 46950–51, 46958–59, 46960, 46962, 46968, 46970–71, 46974–75, 46978, 46980, 46982, 46984–85, 46988, 46990, 46992, 46996, 47946, 47957, 47959, 47960

* * *

THIRD DISTRICT

JIM BANKS, Republican, of Columbia City, IN; born in Columbia City, July 16 1979; education: B.A., Indiana University, Bloomington, IN, 2004; M.B.A, Grace College, Winona Lake, IN, 2013; professional: commercial construction and real estate industry, 2008–10; member of the Whitley County Council, 2008–10; Indiana State Senate 2010–16; military: U.S. Navy Reserve, Supply Corps Officer, 2012–15; deployed to Afghanistan, 2014–15; awards: Defense

Meritorious Service Medal, Afghanistan Campaign Medal, ISAF NATO Medal, American Legion's Distinguished Public Service Award, 2013, 2014, and 2016; religion: Evangelical; family: wife, Amanda; daughters: Lillian, Elizabeth, and Joann; caucuses: 115th Class Caucus; Air Force Caucus; Army Caucus; Automotive Caucus; Caucus on Macedonia and Macedonian-Americans; Congressional Sportsmen's Caucus; Israel Caucus; Long Range Strike Caucus; Medical Technology Caucus; National Guard and Reserve Components Caucus; Navy–USMC Caucus; Pro-Life Caucus; Republican Study Committee; School Choice Caucus; Shipbuilding Caucus; Steel Caucus; Submarine Caucus; Taiwan Caucus; Warrior Caucus; committees: Armed Services; Education and the Workforce; Veterans' Affairs; elected to the 115th Congress on November 8, 2016.

Office Listings

http://banks.house.gov facebook: https://www.facebook.com/RepJimBanks
twitter: @RepJimBanks instagram: @repjimbanks

2418 Rayburn House Office Building, Washington, DC 20515 .... (202) 225–4436
Chief of Staff.—Matt Lahr.
Deputy Chief of Staff.—David Keller.
Legislative Director.—Brandt Anderson.
Scheduler.—Elizabeth Bettis.
Press Secretary.—Anna Swick.
1300 South Harrison, Fort Wayne, IN 46802 .... (260) 702–4750
District Director.—Paul Lagemann.

Counties: ADAMS, ALLEN, BLACKFORD (part), DEKALB, HUNTINGTON, JAY, KOSCIUSKO (part), LAGRANGE, NOBLE, STEUBEN, WELLS, AND WHITLEY. Population (2010), 723,633.

ZIP Codes: 46538, 46555, 46562, 46565, 46571, 46580, 46582, 46590, 46701–03, 46705–06, 46710–11, 46714, 46721, 46723, 46725, 46730–33, 46737–38, 46740–43, 46745–48, 46750, 46755, 46759, 46760, 46762–67, 46770, 46772–74, 46776–77, 46779, 46781, 46783–85, 46787–88, 46791–95, 46797–98, 46802–09, 46814–16, 46818–19, 46825, 46835, 46845, 47326, 47359, 47369, 47371, 47373, 47381

* * *

FOURTH DISTRICT

TODD ROKITA, Republican, of Indianapolis, IN; born in Munster, IN, February 9, 1970; education: graduated with a B.A., Wabash College, Crawfordsville, IN, 1992; J.D., Indiana University School of Law, Indianapolis, IN, 1995; professional: practicing attorney, 1995–97; general counsel at the Indiana Secretary of State's office, 1997–2000; Deputy Secretary of State, 2000–02; Secretary of State, 2002–10; president of the Association of Secretaries of State (NASS), 2007–08; awards: Indianapolis Choice Award, by the Indianapolis Chapter of the Association of Women Business Owners, 2008; Award of Merit, by the International Association of Commercial Administrators (IACA), 2008 and 2010; Friend of Foreign Service Medal, by the Taiwanese Government, 2010; religion: Roman Catholic; married: Kathy Rokita; children: Teddy and Ryan; committees: vice chair, Budget; Education and the Workforce; Transportation and Infrastructure; elected to the 112th Congress on November 2, 2010; reelected to each succeeding Congress.

Office Listings

http://www.rokita.house.gov twitter: @toddrokita instagram: @toddrokita

2439 Rayburn House Office Building, Washington, DC 20515 .... (202) 225–5037
Chief of Staff.—Mark Cruz. FAX: 226–0544
Legislative Director.—Parker Reynolds.
Communications Director.—Amy Hasenberg.
Scheduler.—Jessica Williams.
355 South Washington Street, Danville, IN 46122 .... (317) 718–0404
District Director.—Joseph McClain.
230 North 4th Street, Room 222, Lafayette, IN 47901 .... (765) 838–3930

Counties: BENTON, BOONE (part), CARROL, CASS, CLINTON, FOUNTAIN, HENDRICKS, HOWARD (part), JASPER, MONTGOMERY, MORGAN (part), NEWTON, PUTNAM, TIPPECANOE, WARREN, AND WHITE. Population (2010), 774,798.

ZIP Codes: 46035, 46039, 46041, 46049–50, 46052, 46057–58, 46065, 46069, 46071, 46075, 46077, 46103, 46105, 46112–13, 46118, 46120–23, 46125, 46128, 46135, 46147, 46149, 46151, 46157–58, 46165–68, 46171–72, 46175, 46180, 46231, 46234, 46278, 46310, 46349, 46374, 46379, 46381, 46392, 46901–02, 46913, 46915, 46917, 46920, 46923, 46926, 46929, 46932, 46947, 46950, 46961, 46967, 46970, 46978–79, 46985, 46988, 46994, 46996, 46998, 47456, 47840, 47868, 47872, 47901, 47904–07, 47909, 47916–18, 47920–26, 47929–30, 47932–33, 47940–44, 47946, 47948–52, 47954–55, 47957–60, 47963–65, 47967–71, 47975, 47977–78, 47980–83, 47987, 47989–95, 47997

* * *

FIFTH DISTRICT

SUSAN W. BROOKS, Republican, of Carmel, IN; born in Fort Wayne, IN, August 25, 1960; education: graduated, Homestead High School, 1978; Miami University, Oxford, OH 1982; J.D. from the Indiana University Robert H. McKinney School of Law, 1985; professional: criminal defense attorney, 1985–97; Deputy Mayor of Indianapolis, 1998–99; Ice Miller Government Affairs, 1999–2001; U.S. Attorney for the Southern District of Indiana, 2001–07; Ivy Tech Community College Senior Vice President and General Counsel, 2007–11; married: David; children: Jessica and Conner; committees: chair, Select Committee on Ethics; Energy and Commerce; elected to the 113th Congress on November 6, 2012; reelected to each succeeding Congress.

Office Listings

http://www.susanwbrooks.house.gov https://facebook.com/CongresswomanSusanWBrooks
https://twitter.com/susanwbrooks

1030 Longworth House Office Building, Washington, DC 20515 .... (202) 225–2276
Chief of Staff.—Megan Savage. FAX: 225–0016
Legislative Director.—Helen Dwight.
Communications Director.—Kristen Johnson.
Scheduler / Executive Assistant.—Jack Miles.
District Director.—Karen Glaser.
11611 North Meridian Street, Suite 415, Carmel, IN 46032 .... (317) 848–0201
120 East 8th Street, Anderson, IN 46016 .... (765) 640–5115

Counties: Blackford, Boone, Grant, Hamilton, Howard, Madison, Marion, and Tipton. Population (2010), 720,423.

ZIP Codes: 46001, 46011–13, 46016–17, 46030–34, 46036–38, 46040, 46044–45, 46047–52, 46055–56, 46060, 46062–64, 46068–70, 46072, 46074–77, 46112, 46205, 46208, 46216, 46220, 46226, 46228, 46234–36, 46240, 46250, 46254, 46256, 46260, 46268, 46278, 46280, 46290–02, 46919, 46928, 46930, 46933, 46936, 46938, 46940, 46952–53, 46957, 46986–87, 46989, 46991, 47336, 47348, 47356

* * *

SIXTH DISTRICT

LUKE MESSER, Republican, of Greensburg, IN; born in Evansville, IN, February 27, 1969; education: B.A., Wabash College, Crawfordsville, IN, 1991; J.D., Vanderbilt University, Nashville, TN, 1994; professional: attorney; religion: Presbyterian; wife, Jennifer Messer; children, Emma, Ava, and Hudson; committees: chair, Republican Policy Committee; Education and the Workforce; Financial Services; elected to the 113th Congress on November 6, 2012; reelected to each succeeding Congress.

Office Listings

http://www.messer.house.gov www.policy.house.gov twitter: @replukemesser
www.facebook.com/replukemesser www.youtube.com/user/replukemesser

1230 Longworth House Office Building, Washington, DC 20515 .... (202) 225–3021
Chief of Staff.—Doug Menorca. FAX: 225–3382
Legislative Director.—Jason Grassie.
Communications Director.—Molly Gillaspie.
Scheduler / Office Manager.—Amy Burke.
2 Public Square, Shelbyville, IN 46176 .... (317) 421–0704
Indiana Chief of Staff.—Jason Kneeland. FAX: 421–0739
Director of Constituent Services.—John Hatter.
107 West Charles Street, Muncie, IN 47305 .... (765) 747–5566
50 North 5th Street, Richmond, IN 47374 .... (765) 962–2883

Counties: Bartholomew, Dearborn, Decatur, Delaware, Fayette, Franklin, Hancock, Henry, Jefferson, Jennings, Ohio, Randolph, Ripley, Rush, Scott (part), Shelby, Switzerland, Union, and Wayne. Population (2010), 720,422.

ZIP Codes: 45003, 45030, 45053, 45056, 45347, 45390, 46001, 46012, 46017, 46040, 46055–56, 46064, 46070, 46104, 46110, 46115, 46117, 46124, 46126–27, 46130–31, 46133, 46140, 46144, 46146, 46148, 46150, 46154–56, 46161–63, 46173, 46176, 46182, 46186, 46229, 46235–36, 46239, 46259, 46725, 46989, 46994, 47001, 47003, 47006, 47010–12, 47016–18, 47020, 47022–25, 47030–32, 47034–38, 47040–43, 47060, 47102, 47138, 47141, 47147, 47170, 47177, 47201–03, 47223–27, 47229–32, 47234, 47236, 47240, 47243–47, 47250, 47261, 47263, 47265, 47270, 47272–74, 47280, 47282–83, 47302–05, 47307–08, 47320, 47322, 47324–25, 47327, 47330–31, 47334–42, 47344–46, 47351–58, 47360–62, 47366–68, 47370, 47373–75, 47380, 47382–88, 47390, 47392–94, 47396, 47448, 47546

* * *

SEVENTH DISTRICT

ANDRÉ CARSON, Democrat, of Indianapolis, IN; born in Indianapolis, October 16, 1974; education: graduated, Arsenal Technical High School, Indianapolis, IN; B.A. in Criminal Justice Management, Concordia University Wisconsin, Mequon, WI; M.B.A, Indiana Wesleyan University, Marion, IN; professional: Investigative Officer for the Indiana State Excise Police, 1997–2006; Indiana Department of Homeland Security's Intelligence Fusion Center, 2006; City County Councilor, Marion County, 2007; religion: Muslim; children: Salimah; senior whip; caucuses: first vice chair, Congressional Black Caucus; New Democrat Coalition; Progressive Caucus; committees: Permanent Select Committee on Intelligence; Transportation and Infrastructure; elected to the 110th Congress on March 11, 2008, by special election, to fill the vacancy caused by the death of U.S. Representative Julia Carson; reelected to each succeeding Congress.

Office Listings

http://www.carson.house.gov https://twitter.com/repandrecarson
www.facebook.com/congressmanandrecarson

2453 Rayburn House Office Building, Washington, DC 20515 .... (202) 225–4011
Chief of Staff.—Kim Rudolph. FAX: 225–5633
Legislative Director.—Nathan Bennett.
Legislative Assistants: Andrea Martin, Omair Mirza, Erica Powell.
Communications Director.—Jessica Gail.
Scheduler.—Cynthia Johnson.
300 East Fall Creek Parkway North Drive, Suite 300, Indianapolis, IN 46205 .... (317) 283–6516
District Director.—Megan Sims. FAX: 283–6567
Staff Assistant / Legislative Correspondent.—Sara Yaakoub.

Counties: MARION. City of Indianapolis, township of Center, parts of the townships of Decatur, Lawrence, Perry, Pike, Warren, Washington, and Wayne, included are the cities of Beech Grove and Lawrence. Population (2010), 676,351.

ZIP Codes: 46107, 46160, 46201–09, 46211, 46214, 46216–22, 46224–31, 46234–35, 46237, 46239–42, 46244, 46247, 46249, 46251, 46253–55, 46260, 46266, 46268, 46274–75, 46277–78, 46282–83, 46285, 46291, 46295–96, 46298

* * *

EIGHTH DISTRICT

LARRY BUCSHON, Republican, of Newburgh, IN; born in Kincaid, IL, May 31, 1962; education: graduated from South Fork High School, Kincaid, IL, 1980; B.S., with a concentration in chemistry, University of Illinois, Urbana-Champaign, IL, 1984; M.D., University of Illinois, Chicago, 1988; professional: residency, Medical College of Wisconsin in Milwaukee, 1988–95; cardiothoracic surgeon, 1995–2010; commissioned lieutenant, U.S. Navy Reserves, 1989; promoted, lieutenant commander, 1994; honorable discharge, 1998; married: Kathryn; children: Luke, Alec, Blair, and Zoe; committees: Energy and Commerce; elected to the 112th Congress on November 2, 2010; reelected to each succeeding Congress.

Office Listings

http://www.bucshon.house.gov twitter: @replarrybucshon

1005 Longworth House Office Building, Washington, DC 20515 .... (202) 225–4636
Chief of Staff.—Teresa Buckley. FAX: 225–3284
Press Secretary.—Nick McGee.
Legislative Director.—Sarah Killeen.
Executive Assistant.—Susey Davis.
420 Main Street, Suite 1402, Evansville, IN 47708 .... (812) 465–6484
District Director.—Carol Jones.
901 Wabash Avenue, Suite 140, Terre Haute, IN 47807 .... (812) 232–0523

Counties: CLAY, CRAWFORD (part), DAVIESS, DUBOIS, GIBSON, GREENE, KNOX, MARTIN, OWEN, PARKE, PERRY, PIKE, POSEY, SPENCER, SULLIVAN, VANDERBURGH, VERMILLION, VIGO, AND WARRICK. Population (2010), 694,398.

ZIP Codes: 46105, 46120–21, 46128, 46135, 46165–66, 46170–72, 46175, 47403–04, 47424, 47427, 47429, 47431–33, 47438–39, 47441, 47443, 47445–46, 47449, 47453, 47455–57, 47459–60, 47462, 47465, 47469–71, 47501, 47512, 47516, 47519, 47522–24, 47527–29, 47535, 47537, 47541–42, 47553, 47557–58, 47561–62, 47564, 47567–68, 47573, 47578, 47581, 47584–85, 47590–91, 47596–98, 47601, 47610–14, 47616, 47618–20, 47629–31, 47633, 47637–40, 47647–49, 47654, 47660, 47665–66, 47670, 47683, 47701–06, 47708, 47710–16, 47719–22, 47724–25, 47727–28, 47730–37, 47739–41, 47744, 47747, 47750, 47801–05, 47807–09, 47811–12, 47830–34, 47836–38, 47840–42, 47845–66, 47868–

72, 47874–76, 47878–82, 47884–85, 47917–18, 47921, 47928, 47932, 47952, 47966, 47969–70, 47974–75, 47982, 47987, 47989, 47991–93

* * *

NINTH DISTRICT

TREY HOLLINGSWORTH, Republican, of Jeffersonville, IN, born in Clinton, TN, September 12, 1983; education: business degree, Wharton School, University of Pennsylvania, Philadelphia, PA, 2004; master's degree, Georgetown University, Washington, DC, 2014; wife: Kelly; committees: Financial Services; elected to 115th Congress on November 8, 2016.

Office Listings

http://hollingsworth.house.gov

1641 Longworth House Office Building, Washington, DC 20515 .... (202) 225–5315
Washington, DC, Chief of Staff.—Rebecca Shaw. FAX: 226–6866
Communications Director.—Rob Burgess.
Legislative Director.—Connor Lentz.
Scheduler.—Marjorie Daily.
279 Quartermaster Drive, Jeffersonville, IN 47130 .... (812) 288–3999
Indiana Chief of Staff.—Rachel Jacobs.
720 Executive Park Drive, Suite 3000B, Greenwood, IN 47404 .... (317) 851–8710

Counties: BROWN, CLARK, CRAWFORD (part), FLOYD, HARRISON, JACKSON, JOHNSON, LAWRENCE, MONROE, MORGAN (part), ORANGE, SCOTT (part), AND WASHINGTON. Population (2010), 726,570.

ZIP Codes: 46106, 46110–11, 46113, 46124, 46131, 46140, 46142–43, 46151, 46158, 46160, 46162, 46164, 46166, 56181, 46184, 46229, 46259, 47019, 47021, 47033, 47039, 47102, 47104, 47106–08, 47110–12, 47114–20, 47122–26, 47129–38, 47140–47, 47150–51, 47160–67, 47170, 47172, 47175, 47177, 47190, 47199, 47201, 47220, 47228–29, 47235, 47249, 47260, 47264, 47274, 47281, 47401–08, 47420–21, 47426, 47429, 47432–37, 47446, 47448, 47451–52, 47454, 47458, 47460, 47462–64, 47467–70

IOWA

(Population 2010, 3,046,355)

SENATORS

CHUCK GRASSLEY, Republican, of New Hartford, IA; born in New Hartford, September 17, 1933; education: graduated, New Hartford Community High School, 1951; B.A., University of Northern Iowa, 1955; M.A., University of Northern Iowa, 1956; doctoral studies, University of Iowa, 1957–58; professional: farmer; member: Iowa State Legislature, 1959–74; Farm Bureau; State and County Historical Society; Masons; Baptist Church; and International Association of Machinists, 1962–71; co-chair, International Narcotics Control Caucus; married: the former Barbara Ann Speicher, 1954; children: Lee, Wendy, Robin Lynn, and Michele Marie; committees: chair, Judiciary; Agriculture, Nutrition, and Forestry; Budget; Finance; Joint Committee on Taxation; elected to the 94th Congress, November 5, 1974; reelected to the 95th and 96th Congresses; elected to the U.S. Senate, November 4, 1980; reelected to each succeeding Senate term.

Office Listings

http://grassley.senate.gov https://www.facebook.com/grassley
https://twitter.com/chuckgrassley

135 Hart Senate Office Building, Washington, DC 20510 .... (202) 224–3744
Chief of Staff.—Jill Kozeny. FAX: 224–6020
Legislative Director.—James Rice.
721 Federal Building, 210 Walnut Street, Des Moines, IA 50309 .... (515) 288–1145
State Administrator.—Aaron McKay.
111 7th Avenue, Southeast, Suite 6800, Cedar Rapids, IA 52404 .... (319) 363–6832
120 Federal Courthouse Building, 320 Sixth Street, Sioux City, IA 51101 .... (712) 233–1860
210 Waterloo Building, 531 Commercial Street, Waterloo, IA 50701 .... (319) 232–6657
201 West 2nd Street, Suite 720, Davenport, IA 52801 .... (563) 322–4331
307 Federal Building, 8 South Sixth Street, Council Bluffs, IA 51501 .... (712) 322–7103

* * *

JONI ERNST, Republican, of Red Oak, IA; born in Red Oak, July 1, 1970; education: graduated Stanton High School, Stanton, IA; B.S., Iowa State University, Ames, IA, 1992; M.P.A., Columbus State University, 1995; military service: U.S. Army Reserves, 1993–2001; Iowa Army National Guard, 1992–2015; auditor of Montgomery County, IA, 2005–11; member of the Iowa State Senate, 2011–14; married: Gail Ernst; children: Regina, Jennifer, and Elizabeth; committees: Agriculture, Nutrition, and Forestry; Armed Services; Environment and Public Works; Small Business and Entrepreneurship; elected to the U.S. Senate on November 4, 2014.

Office Listings

http://ernst.senate.gov

111 Russell Hart Senate Office Building, Washington, DC 20510 .... (202) 224–3254
Chief of Staff.—Lisa Goeas. FAX: 224–9369
Legislative Director.—Jena McNeil.
Communications Director.—Liz Bowman.
733 Federal Building, 210 Walnut Street, Des Moines, IA 50309 .... (515) 284–4574
111 7th Avenue Southeast, Suite 480, Cedar Rapids, IA 52401 .... (319) 365–4504
201 West Second Street, Suite 806, Davenport, IA 52801 .... (563) 322–0677
194 Federal Building, 320 Sixth Street, Room 110, Sioux City, IA 51101 .... (712) 252–1550
221 Federal Building, 8 South Sixth Street, Council Bluffs, IA 51501 .... (712) 352–0087

REPRESENTATIVES

FIRST DISTRICT

ROD BLUM, Republican, of Dubuque, IA; born in Dubuque, April 26, 1955; education: B.A., Loras College, 1977; M.B.A., University of Dubuque, 1989; professional: CyCare Systems Inc., 1978–88; Eagle Point Software Inc., chairman and CEO, 1989–2000; Digital Canal Inc., chairman and CEO, 2000–present; Salto de Fede, 2006–present; former Iowa Entrepreneur of the Year; student pilot; basketball coach; Dubuque Senior High School chair; married: Karen; five children; caucuses: chair, Congressional Term Limits Caucus; chair, Czech and Slovak Caucus; committees: Oversight and Government Reform; Small Business; elected to the 114th Congress on November 4, 2014; reelected to the 115th Congress on November 8, 2016.

Office Listings

http://www.blum.house.gov

1108 Longworth House Office Building, Washington, DC 20515 .... (202) 225–2911
Chief of Staff.—Paul Smith.
1050 Main Street, Dubuque, IA 52001 .... (563) 557–7789
District Director.—John Ferland.
515 Main Street, Suite D, Cedar Falls, IA 50613 .... (319) 266–6925
310 3rd Street, Southeast, Cedar Rapids, IA 52401 .... (319) 364–2288

Counties: ALLAMAKEE, BENTON, BLACK HAWK, BREMER, BUCHANAN, CLAYTON, DELAWARE, DUBUQUE, FAYETTE, HOWARD, IOWA, JACKSON, JONES, LINN, MARSHALL, MITCHELL, POWESHIEK, TAMA, WINNESHIEK, AND WORTH. Population (2010), 761,548.

ZIP Codes: 50005, 50027, 50051, 50078, 50106, 50112, 50120, 50136, 50141–42, 50148, 50153, 50157–58, 50162, 50171, 50173, 50206–07, 50234, 50239, 50242, 50247, 50258, 50434, 50440, 50444, 50446, 50448, 50450, 50454–56, 50458–61, 50464, 50466, 50471–72, 50476, 50603, 50606–07, 50609, 50612–13, 50621–22, 50626, 50628–30, 50632, 50634–35, 50641, 50643–45, 50647–48, 50650–52, 50654–55, 50662, 50664, 50666–71, 50674–77, 50681–82, 50701–03, 50707, 52001–03, 52030–33, 52035, 52037–50, 52052–54, 52057, 52060, 52064–66, 52068–70, 52072–74, 52076–79, 52101, 52132–36, 52140–42, 52144, 52146–47, 52151, 52154–66, 52168–72, 52175, 52201–03, 52205–25, 52227–29, 52232–33, 52236–37, 52249, 52251, 52253, 52257, 52301–02, 52305–16, 52318, 52320–21, 52323–26, 52328–30, 52332, 52334, 52336, 52338–39, 52341–42, 52345–49, 52351–52, 52354–56, 52361–62, 52401–05, 52411, 52731

* * *

SECOND DISTRICT

DAVID LOEBSACK, Democrat, of Iowa City, IA; born in Sioux City, IA, December 23, 1952; education: graduated, East High School, 1970; B.A., Iowa State University, 1974; M.A., Iowa State University, 1976; Ph.D., political science, University of California, Davis, 1985; professional: professor, political science, Cornell College, 1982–2006; married: Teresa Loebsack; four children; committees: Energy and Commerce; elected to the 110th Congress on November 7, 2006; reelected to each succeeding Congress.

Office Listings

http://www.loebsack.house.gov

1527 Longworth House Office Building, Washington, DC 20515 .... (202) 225–6576
Chief of Staff.—Eric Witte.
Office Manager / Scheduler.—Sam Ward.
209 West 4th Street, Suite 104, Davenport, IA 52801 .... (563) 323–5988
District Director.—Rob Sueppel. FAX: 323–5231
125 South Dubuque Street, Iowa City, IA 52240–4003 .... (319) 351–0789
(866) 914–4692

Counties: APPANOOSE, CEDAR, CLARKE, CLINTON, DAVIS, DECATUR, DES MOINES, HENRY, JASPER, JEFFERSON, JOHNSON, KEOKUK, LEE, LOUISA, LUCAS, MAHASKA, MARION, MONROE, MUSCATINE, SCOTT, VAN BUREN, WAPELLO, WASHINGTON, AND WAYNE. Population (2010), 761,624.

ZIP Codes: 50008, 50027–28, 50044, 50049, 50052, 50054, 50057, 50060, 50062, 50065, 50067–68, 50103–04, 50108, 50116, 50119, 50123, 50127, 50135–38, 50140, 50143–44, 50147, 50150–51, 50153, 50163, 50165, 50168, 50170, 50174, 50207–08, 50213–14, 50219, 50225, 50228, 50232, 50238, 50251–52, 50255–56, 50262, 50264, 50268, 50272, 50275, 52037, 52201, 52216, 52231, 52235, 52240–48, 52254–55, 52306, 52317, 52319, 52322, 52327, 52333, 52335, 52337–38, 52340, 52353, 52355–56, 52358–59, 52531, 52533–35, 52537–38, 52540, 52542–44, 52549–52, 52555–57, 52560–63, 52565, 52567–74, 52576–77, 52580–81, 52583–86, 52588, 52590–91, 52593–95, 52601, 52619–21, 52623–27, 52630–32, 52635, 52637–42, 52644–60, 52701, 52720–22, 52726–34, 52736–39, 52742, 52745–61, 52765–69, 52771–74, 52776–78, 52801–09

* * *

THIRD DISTRICT

DAVID YOUNG, Republican, of Van Meter, IA; born in Van Meter, May 11, 1968; education: graduated Johnston High School, 1986; attended Buena Vista College; bachelor of arts in English; Drake University, 1991; professional: manager loan trainee, Norwest Financial, 1992; legislative aide, U.S. Senator Hank Brown, 1993; legislative director, chief of staff, campaign manager, Senator Jim Bunning, 1998; chief of staff, Senator Chuck Grassley, 2006; committees: Appropriations; elected to the 114th Congress on November 4, 2014; reelected to the 115th Congress on November 8, 2016.

Office Listings

http://www.davidyoung.house.gov facebook: @RepDavidYoung twitter: @RepDavidYoung

240 Cannon House Office Building, Washington, DC 20515 .... (202) 225–5476
Chief of Staff.—James D. Carstensen.
400 East Court Avenue, Suite 346, Des Moines, IA 50309 .... (515) 282–1909
District Manager / Scheduler.—Eric Baker.
208 West Taylor Street, Creston, IA 50801 .... (641) 782–2495
Caseworker.—Laura Hartman.
501 5th Avenue, Council Bluffs, IA 51503 .... (712) 325–1404
Caseworker.—Charlie Johnson.

Counties: ADAIR, ADAMS, CASS, DALLAS, FREMONT, GUTHRIE, MADISON, MILLS, MONTGOMERY, PAGE, POLK, POTTAWATTAMIE, RINGGOLD, TAYLOR, UNION, AND WARREN. Population (2010), 761,612.

ZIP Codes: 50001–03, 50007, 50009, 50020–23, 50026, 50029, 50032–33, 50035, 50038–39, 50047–48, 50061, 50063, 50066, 50069–70, 50072–74, 50109, 50111, 50115, 50118, 50125, 50128, 50131, 50133, 50139, 50145–46, 50149, 50155, 50160, 50164, 50166–67, 50169, 50210–11, 50216, 50218, 50220, 50222, 50226, 50229, 50233, 50237, 50240–41, 50243, 50250, 50254, 50257, 50261, 50263, 50265–66, 50273–74, 50276–77, 50301–25, 50327–36, 50339–40, 50359–64, 50367–69, 50380–81, 50391–96, 50398, 50801, 50830–31, 50833, 50835–37, 50839–43, 50845–49, 50851, 50853–54, 50857–64, 50936, 50940, 50947, 50950, 50980–83, 51501–03, 51510, 51521, 51525–26, 51532–36, 51540–42, 51544, 51548–49, 51551–54, 51559–61, 51566, 51571, 51573, 51575–77, 51591, 51601, 51603, 51630–32, 51636–40, 51645–54, 51656

* * *

FOURTH DISTRICT

STEVE KING, Republican, of Kiron, IA; born in Storm Lake, IA, May 28, 1949; education: graduated, Denison Community High School; attended Northwest Missouri State University, Maryville, MO, 1967–70; professional: agri-businessman; owner and operator of King Construction Company; public service: Iowa State Senate, 1996–2002; religion: Catholic; family: married to Marilyn; children: David, Michael, and Jeff; committees: Agriculture; Judiciary; Small Business; elected to the 108th Congress on November 5, 2002; reelected to each succeeding Congress.

Office Listings

http://www.steveking.house.gov facebook: SteveKingIA twitter: SteveKingIA

2210 Rayburn House Office Building, Washington, DC 20515 .... (202) 225–4426
Chief of Staff.—Sarah Stevens. FAX: 225–3193
Legislative Director.—Jared Culver.
Scheduler.—Hunter King.
Communications Directors: Tori Beth Black, Sarah Stevens.
526 Nebraska Street, Sioux City, IA 51101 .... (712) 224–4692
202 1st Street, SE., Suite 126, Mason City, IA 50401 .... (641) 201–1624
723 Central Avenue, Fort Dodge, IA 50501 .... (515) 573–2738
306 North Grand Avenue, Spencer, IA 51301 .... (712) 580–7754
1421 South Bell Avenue, Suite 102, Ames, IA 50010 .... (515) 232–2885

Counties: AUDUBON, BOONE, BUENA VISTA, BUTLER, CALHOUN, CARROLL, CERRO GORDO, CHEROKEE, CHICKASAW, CLAY, CRAWFORD, DICKINSON, EMMET, FLOYD, FRANKLIN, GREENE, GRUNDY, HAMILTON, HANCOCK, HARDIN, HARRISON, HUMBOLDT, IDA, KOSSUTH, LYON, MONONA, O'BRIEN, OSCEOLA, PALO ALTO, PLYMOUTH, POCAHONTAS, SAC, SHELBY, SIOUX, STORY, WEBSTER, WINNEBAGO, WOODBURY, AND WRIGHT. Population (2010), 761,571.

ZIP Codes: 50006, 50010–12, 50014, 50020, 50022, 50025–26, 50029, 50034, 50036, 50040–42, 50046, 50050, 50055–56, 50058, 50064, 50071, 50075–76, 50101–02, 50105, 50107, 50117, 50122, 50124, 50126, 50128–30, 50132, 50134, 50154, 50156, 50161, 50201, 50206, 50212, 50217, 50220, 50223, 50227, 50230–31, 50235–36, 50243–44, 50246–49, 50258, 50269, 50271, 50276, 50278, 50401, 50420–21, 50423–24, 50428, 50430–36, 50438–39, 50441, 50444, 50446, 50449–53, 50457–58, 50460–61, 50464–65, 50467–71, 50473, 50475, 50477–80, 50482–84, 50501, 50510–11, 50514–25, 50527–33, 50535–36, 50538–46, 50548, 50551, 50554, 50556–63, 50565–71, 50573–79, 50581–83, 50585–86, 50588, 50590–95, 50597–99, 50601–05, 50609, 50611, 50613, 50616, 50619–21, 50624–25, 50627, 50630, 50633, 50636, 50638, 50642–43, 50645, 50653, 50657–60, 50665–66, 50669–70, 50672–74, 50680, 51001–12, 51014, 51016, 51018–20, 51022–31, 51033–41, 51044–56, 51058, 51060–63, 51101, 51103–06, 51108–09, 51111, 51201, 51230–32, 51234–35, 51237–50, 51301, 51331, 51333–34, 51338, 51340–43, 51345–47, 51350–51, 51354–55, 51357–58, 51360, 51363–66, 51401, 51430–31, 51433, 51436, 51439–55, 51458–59, 51460–63, 51465–67, 51520–21, 51523, 51527–31, 51537, 51543, 51545–46, 51550, 51552, 51555–59, 51562–65, 51570, 51572, 51577–79, 52154, 52171

KANSAS

(Population 2010, 2,853,118)

SENATORS

PAT ROBERTS, Republican, of Dodge City, KS; born in Topeka, KS, April 20, 1936; education: graduated, Holton High School, Holton, KS, 1954; B.S., journalism, Kansas State University, Manhattan, KS, 1958; professional: Captain, U.S. Marine Corps, 1958–62; editor and reporter, Arizona newspapers, 1962–67; aide to Senator Frank Carlson, 1967–68; aide to Representative Keith Sebelius, 1969–80; U.S. House of Representatives, 1980–96; married: the former Franki Fann, 1969; children: David, Ashleigh, and Anne-Wesley; committees: chair, Agriculture, Nutrition, and Forestry; Finance; Health, Education, Labor, and Pensions; Joint Committee on the Library; Joint Committee on Printing; Rules and Administration; Select Committee on Ethics; elected to the U.S. Senate in November, 1996; reelected to each succeeding Senate term.

Office Listings

http://roberts.senate.gov www.facebook.com/senpatroberts twitter: @senpatroberts

109 Hart Senate Office Building, Washington, DC 20510 .... (202) 224–4774
Chief of Staff.—Jackie Cottrell. FAX: 224–3514
Legislative Director.—Amber Kirchhoefer.
Scheduler.—Jensine Moyer.
Communications Director.—Sarah Little.
100 Military Plaza, P.O. Box 550, Dodge City, KS 67801 .... (620) 227–2244
District Director.—Martha Ruiz-Martinez.
125 North Market Street, Suite 1120, Wichita, KS 67202 .... (316) 263–0416
District Director.—Tamara Woods.
Frank Carlson Federal Building, 444 Southeast Quincy, Room 392, Topeka, KS 66683 .... (785) 295–2745
District Director.—Gilda Lintz.
11900 College Boulevard, Suite 203, Overland Park, KS 66210 .... (913) 451–9343
State Director.—Chad Tenpenny.

* * *

JERRY MORAN, Republican, of Manhattan, KS; born in Plainville, KS, May 29, 1954; education: B.S., University of Kansas, Lawrence, KS, 1976; J.D., University of Kansas School of Law, Lawrence, KS, 1981; M.B.A., candidate, Fort Hays State University, Hays, KS; professional: banker; attorney; U.S. House of Representatives, 1997–2010; Kansas State Senate, 1989–97, served as vice president, 1993–95, majority leader, 1995–97; Kansas State Special Assistant Attorney General, 1982–85; deputy attorney, Rooks County, KS, 1987–95; University of Kansas School of Law Board of Governors, served as vice president, 1993–94, president, 1994–95; volunteering: Fort Hays State University Endowment Foundation, Board of Trustees; Coronado Area Council of the Boy Scouts of America, Executive Committee; Eisenhower Foundation; former Trustee; Lions Club Member; Rotary Club Member; and Sons of The American Legion member; religion: Christian; family: married, Robba; two daughters, Kelsey and Alex; caucuses: co-founder, Economic Mobility Caucus; co-founder, Senate Community Pharmacy Caucus; co-founder, Senate Hunger Caucus; co-chair, Congressional Task Force on Down Syndrome; co-chair, Senate Aerospace Caucus; co-chair, Senate Defense Communities Caucus; committees: Appropriations; Banking, Housing, and Urban Affairs; Commerce, Science, and Transportation; Environment and Public Works; Indian Affairs; Veterans' Affairs; elected to the U.S. Senate on November 2, 2010.

Office Listings

http://moran.senate.gov https://www.facebook.com/jerrymoran
https://twitter.com/jerrymoran

521 Dirksen Senate Office Building, Washington, DC 20510 .... (202) 224–6521
Chief of Staff.—Brennen Britton. FAX: 228–6966
Legislative Director.—Will Ruder.
Scheduler.—Emily Whitfield.
Communications Director.—Katie Niederee.
1200 Main Street, Suite 402, Hays, KS 67601 .... (785) 628–6401
State Casework Director.—Chelsey Ladd. FAX: 628–3791
23600 College Boulevard, Suite 201, Olathe, KS 66061 .... (913) 393–0711
Kansas State Scheduler.—Lisa Dethloff. FAX: 768–1366
306 North Broadway, Suite 125, P.O. Box 1372, Pittsburg, KS 66762 .... (620) 232–2286
FAX: 232–2284
923 Westport Place, Suite 210, P.O. Box 067, Manhattan, KS 66502 .... (785) 539–8973

Office Listings—Continued

FAX: 587–0789

3450 North Rock Road, Building 200, P.O. Box 781753, Suite 209, Wichita, KS 67226 ..... (316) 631–1410
State Director.—Alex Richard. FAX: 631–1297
Deputy State Director.—Mike Zamrzla.

REPRESENTATIVES

FIRST DISTRICT

ROGER W. MARSHALL, Republican, of Great Bend, KS; born in El Dorado, KS, August 9, 1960; education: Butler Community College, El Dorado, 1980; biochemistry, Kansas State University, Manhattan, KS; M.D., University of Kansas School of Medicine, Kansas City, KS, 1980; professional: former board chairman of Great Bend Regional Hospital; board member of Farmers Bank and Trust; former Rotary district governor; military: Captain, U.S. Army Reserves; awards: Teacher of the Year during residency in St. Petersburg, FL; Resident Research Award in St. Petersburg; religion: Christian; family: wife; children: four; grandchildren: one and one grandchild on the way; committees: Agriculture; Science, Space, and Technology; Small Business; elected to the 115th Congress on November 8, 2016.

Office Listings

http://marshall.house.gov

312 Cannon House Office Building, Washington, DC 20515 .... (202) 225–2715
Chief of Staff.—Brent Robertson.
Legislative Director.—Dalton Henry.
Communications Assistant.—Eric Pahls.
Director of Operations.—Katie Moore.
200 East Iron Avenue, Salina, KS 67401 .... (785) 829–9000

Counties: Barber, Barton, Chase, Cheyenne, Clark, Clay, Cloud, Comanche, Decatur, Dickinson, Edwards, Ellis, Ellsworth, Finney, Ford, Geary (part), Gove, Graham, Grant, Gray, Greeley, Greenwood (part), Hamilton, Haskell, Hodgeman, Jewell, Kearny, Kiowa, Lane, Lincoln, Logan, Lyon, McPherson, Marion (part), Marshall, Meade, Mitchell, Morris, Morton, Nemaha (part), Ness, Norton, Osborne, Ottawa, Pawnee, Phillips, Pratt, Rawlins, Reno, Republic, Rice, Rooks, Rush, Russell, Saline, Scott, Seward, Sheridan, Sherman, Smith, Stafford, Stanton, Stevens, Thomas, Trego, Wabaunsee, Wallace, Washington, and Wichita. Population (2010), 713,278.

ZIP Codes: 66401, 66403 (part), 66406 (part), 66407, 66411–13 (part), 66422 (part), 66423, 66427 (part), 66431–32 (part), 66438 (part), 66441–42, 66449, 66501–03, 66506–07, 66508 (part), 66514, 66517–18, 66520, 66521 (part), 66523 (part), 66526, 66531, 66535, 66536 (part), 66547, 66548 (part), 66549, 66554, 66614–15 (part), 66801, 66830, 66833–35, 66838, 66840 (part), 66843, 66845–46, 66849–51, 66854 (part), 66858–59, 66860 (part), 66861–62, 66864 (part), 66865, 66866 (part), 66868 (part), 66869, 66872–73, 66901, 66930, 66932–33, 66935–46, 66948–49, 66951–53, 66955–56, 66958–60, 66962–64, 66966–68, 66970, 67020 (part), 67025 (part), 67035 (part), 67053, 67062 (part), 67063, 67068 (part), 67073, 67107–08 (part), 67114 (part), 67127 (part), 67151 (part), 67401, 67410, 67416–18, 67420, 67422–23, 67425, 67427–28, 67430–32, 67436–39, 67441–52, 67454–60, 67464, 67466–68, 67470, 7473–75, 67478, 67480–85, 67487, 67490–92, 67501–02, 67505, 67510–16, 67518, 67519 (part), 67520–21, 67522–23 (part), 67524–25, 67526 (part), 67529–30 (part), 67543–44, 67546, 67547 (part), 67548, 67550 (part), 67553–54, 67556, 67557 (part), 67559–61, 67563 (part), 67564–66, 67567 (part), 67568, 67570 (part), 67572–73, 67574 (part), 67575, 67579, 67581, 67583 (part), 67584, 67601, 67621–23, 67625–26, 67628–29, 67631–32, 67634–35, 67637–40, 67642–51, 67653–54, 67656–61, 67663–65, 67667, 67669, 67671–75, 67701, 67730–41, 67743–45, 67747–49, 67751–53, 67756–58, 67761–62, 67764, 67801, 67831, 67834–44, 67846, 67849–51, 67853–55, 67857, 67859–65, 67867–71, 67876–80, 67882, 67901, 67951–54

* * *

SECOND DISTRICT

LYNN JENKINS, Republican, of Topeka, KS; born in Topeka, June 10, 1963; education: A.A., Kansas State University, Manhattan, KS, 1985; B.S., accounting/economics, Weber State College, Ogden, UT, 1985; professional: certified public accountant; accountant, Braunsdorf, Carson, and Clinkinbeard; accountant, Baird, Kurtz and Dobson; certified public accountant, Public Accounting/Specialty Taxation, 1985–present; Representative, Kansas State House of Representatives, 1999–2000; Senator, Kansas State Senate, 2001–02; Treasurer, State of Kansas, 2003–08; children: Hayley and Hayden; caucuses: Community Pharmacy Caucus; Cystic Fibrosis Caucus; Defense Communities Caucus; Down Syndrome Caucus; Financial and Economic Literacy Caucus; House Army Caucus; House Hunger Caucus; Impact Aid Caucus; Military Veterans Caucus; No Labels Problem Solvers Caucus; Nursing Caucus; Yellow Pages Caucus; committees: Ways and Means; elected to the 111th Congress on November 4, 2008; reelected to each succeeding Congress.

Office Listings

http://lynnjenkins.house.gov

1526 Longworth House Office Building, Washington, DC 20515 .... (202) 225–6601
Chief of Staff.—Pat Leopold. FAX: 225–7986
Deputy Chief of Staff.—Colin Brainard.
Scheduler.—Roderick Patton.
Press Aide.—Michael Byerly.
3550 SW., 5th Street, Topeka, KS 66606 .... (785) 234–5966
1001 North Broadway, Suite C, Pittsburg, KS 66762 .... (620) 231–5966

Counties: ALLEN, ANDERSON, ATCHISON, BOURBON, BROWN, CHEROKEE, COFFEY, CRAWFORD, DONIPHAN, DOUGLAS, FRANKLIN, JACKSON, JEFFERSON, LABETTE, LEAVENWORTH, LINN, MARSHALL (part), MIAMI (part), MONTGOMERY, NEMAHA, NEOSHO, OSAGE, SHAWNEE, WILSON, AND WOODSON. Population (2010), 713,272.

ZIP Codes: 66002, 66006–08, 66010, 66012, 66014–17, 66020–21, 66023–27, 66032–33, 66035, 66039–50, 66052–54, 66056, 66058, 66060, 66064, 66066–67, 66070–73, 66075–76, 66078–80, 66083, 66086–88, 66090–95, 66097, 66109, 66402–04, 66406, 66408–09, 66411–19, 66422, 66424–25, 66427–29, 66431–32, 66434, 66436, 66438–40, 66451, 66508–10, 66512, 66515–16, 66521–24, 66527–28, 66532–34, 66536–44, 66546, 66548, 66550, 66552, 66603–12, 66614–19, 66621–22, 66701, 66710–14, 66716–17, 66720, 66724–25, 66728, 66732–36, 66738–41, 66743, 66746, 66748–49, 66751, 66753–58, 66760–63, 66767, 66769–73, 66775–83, 66839, 66852, 66854, 66856–57, 66864, 66868, 66871, 67047, 67301, 67330, 67332–33, 67335–37, 67340–42, 67344, 67347, 67351, 67354, 67356–57, 67363–64

* * *

THIRD DISTRICT

KEVIN YODER, Republican, of Overland Park, KS; born in Hutchinson, KS, January 8, 1976; education: B.A., University of Kansas, Lawrence, KS, 1999; J.D., University of Kansas College of Law, Lawrence, 2002; professional: attorney; admitted to the Kansas Bar, 2002; prior public service: Kansas House of Representatives, 20th District, 2003–11; serves on the Board of Trustees of Gallaudet University; married: Brooke Robinson Yoder; caucuses: co-chairman, Congressional Beef Caucus; Congressional Children's Caucus; Congressional Civility Caucus; Congressional Deaf Caucus; House Cancer Caucus; committees: Appropriations; Joint Committee on the Library; elected to the 112th Congress on November 2, 2010; reelected to each succeeding Congress.

Office Listings

http://www.yoder.house.gov

2433 Rayburn House Office Building, Washington, DC 20515 .... (202) 225–2865
Chief of Staff.—Dave Natonski.
Legislative Director.—Joe Eannello.
Scheduler.—Cate Duerst.
Communications Director.—CJ Grover.
7325 West 79th Street, Overland Park, KS 66204 .... (913) 621–0832
District Director.—Molly Haase. FAX: 621–1533
Constituent Services Director.—Cheyne Worley.

Counties: JOHNSON, MIAMI (part), AND WYANDOTTE. Population (2010), 713,272.

ZIP Codes: 66012–13, 66018–19, 66021, 66025, 66030–31, 66053, 66061–62, 66071, 66083, 66085, 66101–06, 66109, 66111–12, 66115, 66118, 66202–21, 66223–24, 66226–27

* * *

FOURTH DISTRICT

RON ESTES, Republican, of Wichita, KS; born in Topeka, KS; education: B.A., civil engineering, Tennessee Technological University, Cookville, TN, 1973; M.B.A., Tennessee Technological University, TN, 1983; professional: Procter & Gamble; Koch Industries; Bombardier Learjet; Sedgwick County Kansas Treasurer; Kansas State Treasurer; religion: Lutheran; married, Susan Estes; children: Brent, Laura, and Grace; committees: Education and the Workforce; Homeland Security; elected to the 115th Congress on April 11, 2017, by special election, to fill the vacancy caused by the resignation of U.S. Representative Mike Pompeo.

Office Listings

https://estes.house.gov

2452 Rayburn House Office Building, Washington, DC 20515 .... (202) 225–6216

Office Listings—Continued

Chief of Staff.—Josh Bell. FAX: 225–3489
Deputy Chief of Staff / Scheduler.—Lynn Haueter.
Legislative Director.—Nicholas O'Boyle.
Communications Director.—Robert Kuhlman.
Military Legislative Assistant.—Greg Baker.
Legislative Assistants.—Rebekah Geffert, Tanner Tempel.
Staff Assistant.—Chris Naylor.

7701 East Kellogg, Suite 510, Wichita, KS 67207 .... (316) 262–8992

Counties: BARBER, BUTLER, CHAUTAUQUA, COMANCHE, COWLEY, EDWARDS, ELK, GREENWOOD, HARPER, HARVEY, KINGMAN, KIOWA, PAWNEE (part), PRATT, SEDGWICK, STAFFORD, AND SUMNER. Population (2010), 715,456.

ZIP Codes: 66736 (part), 66777 (part), 66840 (part), 66842, 66852 (part), 66853, 66860 (part), 66863, 66866 (part), 66870, 67001–05, 67008–10, 67012–13, 67016–19, 67020 (part), 67021–24, 67025 (part), 67026, 67028–31, 67035 (part), 67036–39, 67041–42, 67045, 67047 (part), 67049–52, 67054–61, 67062 (part), 67065–67, 67068 (part), 67070–72, 67074, 67101, 67103–06, 67107–08 (part), 67109–12, 67114 (part), 67117–20, 67122–24, 67127 (part), 67131–35, 67137–38, 67140, 67142–44, 67146–47, 67149–50

KENTUCKY

(Population 2010, 4,339,367)

SENATORS

MITCH McCONNELL, Republican, of Louisville, KY; born in Colbert County, AL, February 20, 1942; education: graduated, Manual High School, Louisville, 1960, president of the student body; B.A. with honors, University of Louisville, 1964, president of the student council, president of the student body of the College of Arts and Sciences; J.D., University of Kentucky Law School, 1967, president of student bar association, outstanding oral advocate; professional: attorney, admitted to the Kentucky Bar, 1967; Chief Legislative Assistant to U.S. Senator Marlow Cook, 1968–70; Deputy Assistant U.S. Attorney General, 1974–75; Judge/Executive of Jefferson County, KY, 1978–84; chairman, National Republican Senatorial Committee, 1997–2000; chairman, Joint Congressional Committee on Inaugural Ceremonies, 1999–2001; Senate Majority Whip, 2002–06; Senate Republican Leader, 2007–14, Senate Majority Leader, 2015–present; married to Elaine L. Chao on February 6, 1993; children: Elly, Claire, and Porter; committees: Agriculture, Nutrition, and Forestry; Appropriations; Rules and Administration; ex officio, Select Committee on Intelligence; elected to the U.S. Senate on November 6, 1984; reelected to each succeeding Senate term.

Office Listings

http://mcconnell.senate.gov https://www.facebook.com/mitchmcconnell
https://twitter.com/mcconnellpress

317 Russell Senate Office Building, Washington, DC 20510 .... (202) 224–2541
Chief of Staff.—Phil Maxson.
Scheduler.—Laura Vincent.
Legislative Director.—Katelyn Conner.
Communications Director.—Robert Steurer.
601 West Broadway, Suite 630, Louisville, KY 40202 .... (502) 582–6304
State Director.—Terry Carmack.
Federal Building, 241 Main Street, Room 102, Bowling Green, KY 42101 .... (270) 781–1673
1885 Dixie Highway, Suite 345, Fort Wright, KY 41011 .... (859) 578–0188
771 Corporate Drive, Suite 108, Lexington, KY 40503 .... (859) 224–8286
300 South Main Street, Suite 310, London, KY 40741 .... (606) 864–2026
100 Fountain Avenue, Suite 300, Paducah, KY 42001 .... (270) 442–4554

* * *

RAND PAUL, Republican, of Bowling Green, KY; born in Pittsburgh, PA, January 7, 1963; education: undergraduate, Baylor University, Waco, Texas, 1981–84; M.D., Duke University School of Medicine, 1988; religion: Methodist; family: married to the former Kelley Ashby; three sons: William, Duncan, and Robert; committees: Foreign Relations; Health, Education, Labor, and Pensions; Homeland Security and Governmental Affairs; Small Business and Entrepreneurship; elected to the U.S. Senate on November 2, 2010.

Office Listings

http://paul.senate.gov https://www.facebook.com/senatorrandpaul twitter: @senrandpaul

167 Russell Senate Office Building, Washington, DC 20510 .... (202) 224–4343
Chief of Staff.—William Henderson.
Deputy Chief of Staff of Communications.—Sergio Gor.
Press Secretary.—Matthew Hawes.
Scheduler.—Drake Henle.
State Director.—Jim Milliman.
1029 State Street, Bowling Green, KY 42101 .... (270) 782–8303

REPRESENTATIVES

FIRST DISTRICT

JAMES COMER, Republican, of Tompkinsville, KY; born in Carthage, TN, August 19, 1972; education: B.S., agriculture, Western Kentucky University, Bowling Green, KY, 1993; professional: businessman; farmer; member, Kentucky House of Representatives, 2001–12; Kentucky Commissioner of Agriculture, 2012–15; religion: Baptist; spouse: Tamara Jo; children:

Reagan, Harlan, and Aniston; committees: Agriculture; Oversight and Government Reform; Small Business; elected simultaneously to the 114th and 115th Congresses, by special election, on November 8, 2016, to fill the vacancy caused by the resignation of U.S. Representative Ed Whitfield.

Office Listings

http://www.comer.house.gov

1513 Longworth House Office Building, Washington, DC 20515 .... (202) 225–3547
Chief of Staff.—Caroline Cash.
Scheduler / Office Manager.—Kaity Wolfe.
Legislative Director.—Jim Goldenstein.
Communications Director.—Michael Gossum.
200 North Main, Suite F, Tompkinsville, KY 42167 .... (270) 487–9509
District Director.—Sandy Simpson.
67 North Main Street, Madisonville, KY 42431 .... (270) 487–9509
Field Representative.—Amelia Wilson.
300 South 3rd Street, Paducah, KY 42001 .... (270) 408–1865
Field Representative.—Martie Wiles.

Counties: Adair, Allen, Ballard, Caldwell, Calloway, Carlisle, Casey, Christian, Clinton, Crittenden, Cumberland, Fulton, Graves, Henderson, Hickman, Hopkins, Livingston, Logan, Lyon, Marion, Marshall, McCracken, McLean, Metcalf, Monroe, Muhlenberg, Ohio, Russell, Simpson, Taylor, Todd, Trigg, Union, Washington, and Webster. Population (2010), 725,929.

ZIP Codes: 40009, 40033, 40037, 40040, 40049, 40052, 40060–63, 40069, 40078, 40119, 40328, 40330, 40437, 40442, 40448, 40464, 40468, 40484, 40489, 42001–03, 42020–25, 42027–29, 42031–33, 42035–41, 42044–45, 42047–51, 42053–56, 42058, 42060–61, 42063–64, 42066, 42069–71, 42076, 42078–79, 42081–88, 42101, 42104, 42120, 42122–24, 42129, 42133–35, 42140–41, 42150–51, 42153–54, 42164, 42166–67, 42170, 42201–04, 42206, 42209–11, 42214–17, 42219–21, 42223, 42232, 42234, 42236, 42240–41, 42251–52, 42254, 42256, 42262, 42265–67, 42274, 42276, 42280, 42283, 42286–88, 42301, 42320–28, 42330, 42332–34, 42337–38, 42344–45, 42347, 42349–50, 42352, 42354, 42356, 42361, 42367–69, 42370–72, 42374–76, 42378, 42402–04, 42406, 42408–11, 42413, 42419–20, 42431, 42436–37, 42440–42, 42444–45, 42450–53, 42455–64, 42516, 42528, 42539, 42541, 42544, 42565–67, 42602–03, 42629, 42642, 42711, 42715–16, 42718–20, 42728, 42731, 42733, 42735, 42740–43, 42746, 42749, 42753, 42758–59, 42786

* * *

SECOND DISTRICT

BRETT GUTHRIE, Republican, of Bowling Green, KY; born in Florence, AL, February 18, 1964; education: B.S., United States Military Academy, West Point, NY, 1987; M.P.M., Yale University, New Haven, CT, 1997; military service: U.S. Army, Field Artillery Office, 101st Airborne Division, 1987–90; professional: vice president, Trace Die Cast, 1991–2009; member: Kentucky Senate, 1998–2009; married: Beth; children: Caroline, Robby, and Elizabeth; committees: Education and the Workforce; Energy and Commerce; elected to the 111th Congress on November 4, 2008; reelected to each succeeding Congress.

Office Listings

http://www.guthrie.house.gov facebook: https://www.facebook.com/CongressmanGuthrie
twitter: @RepGuthrie

2434 Rayburn House Office Building, Washington, DC 20515 .... (202) 225–3501
Chief of Staff.—Eric Bergren.
Legislative Director.—Joel Miller.
Communications Director.—Lauren Gaydos.
Scheduler.—Jennifer Beil.
996 Wilkinson Trace, Suite B2, Bowling Green, KY 42103 .... (270) 842–9896
District Director.—Mark Lord.

Counties: Barren, Boyle, Breckinridge, Bullitt, Butler, Daviess, Edmonson, Garrard, Grayson, Green, Hancock, Hardin, Hart, Jessamine (part), Larue, Meade, Mercer, Nelson, Spencer (part), Warren, and Washington (part). Population (2010), 723,137.

ZIP Codes: 40004, 40008, 40012–13, 40020, 40037 (part), 40040, 40046 (part), 40047–48, 40051, 40052 (part), 40069 (part), 40071 (part), 40078, 40104, 40107–11, 40115, 40117, 40119 (part), 40121, 40140, 40142–46, 40150, 40152, 40155, 40157, 40160–62, 40165, 40170–71, 40175–76, 40177 (part), 40178, 40229 (part), 40272 (part), 40299, 40310, 40328 (part), 40330, 40339, 40356 (part), 40372 (part), 40383 (part), 40390 (part), 40403 (part), 40419 (part), 40422 (part), 40440 (part), 40444 (part), 40461 (part), 40464 (part), 40468 (part), 40484 (part), 42101–03, 42104 (part), 42122 (part), 42123, 42127, 42130, 42133 (part), 42141, 42154 (part), 42156, 42159–60, 42163, 42166 (part), 42170 (part), 42171, 42206 (part), 42207, 42210, 42214 (part), 42256 (part), 42259, 42261, 42273, 42274 (part), 42275, 42285, 42301 (part), 42303, 42320 (part), 42327 (part), 42333 (part), 42339 (part), 42343 (part), 42348, 42349 (part), 42351, 42355–56, 42361 (part), 42366 (part), 42368 (part), 42376 (part), 42378 (part), 42701, 42712–13, 42716 (part), 42718 (part), 42721–22, 42724, 42726, 42729, 42732, 42740, 42743 (part), 42746 (part), 42748, 42749 (part), 42754, 42757, 42762, 42764–65, 42776, 42782, 42784, 42788

* * *

THIRD DISTRICT

JOHN A. YARMUTH, Democrat, of Louisville, KY; born in Louisville, November 4, 1947; education: graduated, Atherton High School, Louisville, 1965; graduated, Yale University, New Haven, CT, 1969; professional: legislative aide for Kentucky Senator Marlow Cook, 1971–74; publisher, *Louisville Today Magazine*, 1976–82; Associate Vice President of University Relations at the University of Louisville, 1983–86; vice president of a local healthcare firm, 1986–90; founder, editor and writer *LEO Newsweekly*, 1990–2005; television host and commentator, 2003–05; awards: 2007 Spirit of Enterprise Award; Louisville Alzheimer's Association Person of the Year; named Outstanding New Member of Congress by the Committee for Education and Funding; 16 Metro Louisville Journalism Awards for editorial and column writing; married: Cathy Yarmuth, 1981; child: Aaron; committees: Budget; elected to the 110th Congress on November 7, 2006; reelected to each succeeding Congress.

Office Listings

http://www.yarmuth.house.gov facebook: https://www.facebook.com/RepJohnYarmuth
twitter: https://twitter.com/repjohnyarmuth

131 Cannon House Office Building, Washington, DC 20515 .... (202) 225–5401
Chief of Staff.—Julie Carr. FAX: 225–5776
Legislative Director.—Zack Marshall.
Press Secretary.—Christopher Schuler.
Scheduler.—Clair Elliott.
600 Martin Luther King Jr. Place, Suite 216, Louisville, KY 40202 .... (502) 582–5129
District Director.—Carolyn Tandy.

Counties: JEFFERSON. Population (2010), 741,096.

ZIP Codes: 40025, 40027, 40041, 40047, 40059 (part), 40118, 40177 (part), 40201–22, 40223 (part), 40224–25, 40228, 40229 (part), 40231–33, 40241 (part), 40242–43, 40245 (part), 40250–53, 40255–59, 40261, 40266, 40268–70, 40272 (part), 40280–83, 40285, 40289–90, 40291 (part), 40292–93, 40295, 40297–98, 40299 (part)

* * *

FOURTH DISTRICT

THOMAS MASSIE, Republican, of Garrison, KY; born in Huntington, WV, January 13, 1971; education: graduated from Lewis County High School; B.S., electrical engineering / economics, Massachusetts Institute of Technology, 1993; M.S., mechanical engineering, Massachusetts Institute of Technology, 1996; professional: inventor / engineer; founder of SensAble Devices, Inc.; farmer; Lewis County Judge Executive; married: Rhonda; four children; committees: Oversight and Government Reform; Science, Space, and Technology; Transportation and Infrastructure; elected simultaneously to the 112th and 113th Congresses on November 6, 2012, by special election, to fill the vacancy caused by the resignation of U.S. Representative Geoffrey C. (Geoff) Davis; reelected to each succeeding Congress.

Office Listings

http://massie.house.gov

2453 Rayburn House Office Building, Washington, DC 20515 .... (202) 225–3465
Chief of Staff.—Chris McCane. FAX: 225–0003
Legislative Director / Deputy Chief of Staff.—Seana Cranston.
Legislative Correspondent.—Jonathan Tkachuk.
Press Secretary.—Jennifer Kruntz.
Scheduler.—Mary Troutman.
Staff Assistant.—Jonathan Tkachuk.
541 Buttermilk Pike, Suite 208, Crescent Springs, KY 41017 .... (859) 426–0080
District Director.—Chris McCane. FAX: 426–0061
1700 Greenup Avenue, R–505, Ashland, KY 41101 .... (606) 324–9898
Eastern District Field Representative.—J.R. Reed.
108 West Jefferson Street, LaGrange, KY 40031 .... (502) 265–9119
Western District Field Representative.—Stacie Rockaway. FAX: 265–9126

Counties: BOYD, BOONE, BRACKEN, CARROLL, CAMPBELL, GREENUP, GALLATIN, GRANT, HENRY, HARRISON, JEFFERSON, KENTON, LEWIS, MASON, OLDHAM, OWEN, PENDLETON, SHELBY, SPENCER, AND TRIMBLE. Population (2010), 723,450.

ZIP Codes: 40003 (part), 40006–07, 40010–11, 40014, 40019, 40022–23, 40026, 40031, 40036, 40045, 40046 (part), 40050, 40055–58, 40059 (part), 40065, 40067–68, 40070, 40071 (part), 40075, 40076 (part), 40077, 40241 (part),

40245 (part), 40291 (part), 40299 (part), 40359, 40363, 40370 (part), 40379 (part), 40601 (part), 41001–03, 41004 (part), 41005–08, 41010 (part), 41011, 41014–18, 41030, 41031 (part), 41033–35, 41040, 41042–43, 41044 (part), 41045–46, 41048, 41051–52, 41055 (part), 41056, 41059, 41062–63, 41064 (part), 41071, 41073–76, 41080, 41083, 41085–86, 41091–92, 41093 (part), 41094–95, 41097–99, 41101, 41102 (part), 41121, 41129 (part), 41135, 41139, 41141, 41143 (part), 41144, 41164 (part), 41166, 41169, 41174–75, 41179, 41183, 41189

* * *

FIFTH DISTRICT

HAROLD ROGERS, Republican, of Somerset, KY; born in Barrier, KY, December 31, 1937; education: graduated, Wayne County High School, 1955; attended Western Kentucky University, 1956–57; A.B., University of Kentucky, 1962; LL.B., University of Kentucky Law School, 1964; professional: lawyer; admitted to the Kentucky State Bar, 1964; commenced practice in Somerset; member, North Carolina and Kentucky National Guard, 1957–64; associate, Smith and Blackburn, 1964–67; private practice, 1967–69; Commonwealth Attorney, Pulaski and Rockcastle Counties, KY, 1969–80; delegate, Republican National Convention, 1972, 1976, 1980, 1984, and 1988; Republican nominee for Lieutenant Governor, KY, 1979; past president, Kentucky Commonwealth Attorneys Association; member and past president, Somerset-Pulaski County Chamber of Commerce and Pulaski County Industrial Foundation; founder, Southern Kentucky Economic Development Council, 1986; member, Chowder and Marching Society, 1981–present; married: the late former Shirley McDowell, 1957; three children: Anthony, Allison, and John Marshall; married: the former Cynthia Doyle Stewart, 1999; committees: Appropriations; elected to the 97th Congress, November 4, 1980; reelected to each succeeding Congress.

Office Listings

http://halrogers.house.gov

2406 Rayburn House Office Building, Washington, DC 20515 .... (202) 225–4601
Chief of Staff.—Megan O'Donnell Bell. FAX: 225–0940
Office Manager.—Chelsea Jarrett.
Legislative Correspondent.—Clay Montgomery.
Staff Assistant.—Ellen DelCotto.
Legislative Assistants: Ashley Nichols, Alex Pinson.
Legislative Director.—Ryan Canfield.
District Director.—Karen Kelly. FAX: 439–4647
551 Clifty Street, Somerset, KY 42503 .... (606) 679–8346
48 South Kentucky Highway 15, Hazard, KY 41701 .... (606) 439–0794
110 Resource Court, Suite A, Prestonsburg, KY 41653–1842 .... (606) 886–0844
FAX: 889–0371

Counties: BELL, BOYD, BREATHITT, CARTER, CLAY, ELLIOTT, FLOYD, HARLAN, JACKSON, JOHNSON, KNOTT, KNOX, LAUREL, LAWRENCE, LEE, LESLIE, LETCHER, LINCOLN, MAGOFFLIN, MARTIN, MCCREARY, MORGAN, OWSLEY, PERRY, PIKE, PULASKI, ROCKCASTLE, ROWAN, WAYNE, AND WHITLEY. Population (2010), 723,228.

ZIP Codes: 40313, 40351, 40393, 40402, 40409, 40434, 40445, 40447–48, 40456, 40460, 40481, 40486, 40701, 40729, 40734, 40737, 40740–41, 40743–44, 40759, 40763, 40769, 40771, 40801, 40806–08, 40813, 40815–16, 40818–20, 40823–24, 40826–31, 40840, 40843–45, 40847, 40849, 40854–56, 40858, 40862–63, 40865, 40868, 40870, 40873–74, 40902–03, 40906, 40913–15, 40921, 40923, 40927, 40935, 40940–41, 40943, 40946, 40949, 40953, 40958, 40962, 40964–65, 40972, 40977, 40979, 40982–83, 40988, 40995, 40997, 41124, 41132, 41142, 41146, 41149, 41159, 41168, 41171, 41180, 41201, 41203–04, 41214, 41216, 41219, 41222, 41224, 41226, 41230–32, 41234, 41238, 41240, 41250, 41254–57, 41260, 41262–65, 41267–68, 41271, 41274, 41311, 41314, 41317, 41339, 41348, 41352, 41366–67, 41385, 41390, 41397, 41408, 41421, 41425, 41464–65, 41472, 41501, 41503, 41512–14, 41517, 41519, 41522, 41526, 41527–28, 41531, 41534–35, 41537–40, 41544, 41547–48, 41553–55, 41557–60, 41562–64, 41566–68, 41571, 41601–07, 41612, 41615–16, 41619, 41621–22, 41630–32, 41635–36, 41640, 41642–43, 41645, 41647, 41649–50, 41653, 41659–60, 41663, 41666–67, 41669, 41701, 41712–14, 41719, 41721–23, 41725, 41727, 41729, 41731, 41735, 41739–40, 41745–46, 41749, 41751, 41754, 41759–60, 41762–64, 41766, 41772–77, 41804, 41810, 41815, 41817, 41819, 41822, 41824–26, 41828, 41831–37, 41840, 41843–45, 41847–49, 41855, 41858, 41861–62, 42501, 42503, 42518–19, 42533, 42567, 42631, 42634–35, 42638, 42649, 42653

* * *

SIXTH DISTRICT

ANDY BARR, Republican, of Lexington, KY; born in Lexington, July 24, 1973; education: B.A. degree in government and philosophy from the University of Virginia in Charlottesville, VA, 1996, graduating with *magna cum laude* and *Phi Beta Kappa* honors; J.D., from the University of Kentucky College of Law, in Lexington, KY, 2001; religion: Episcopal; married to the former Eleanor Carol Leavell of Georgetown, Kentucky; together, they are the proud parents of two daughters; caucuses: chair of Congressional Horse Caucus; Bipartisan Prescription Drug Caucus; Can Caucus; Congressional Arthritis Caucus; Congressional Automotive Caucus; Congressional Bourbon Caucus; Congressional Coal Caucus; Congressional Diabetes Caucus; Congressional Down Syndrome Caucus; Congressional Kurdish American Caucus; Congressional Natural Gas Caucus; Congressional Peace Corps Caucus; Congressional Prayer Caucus; Congressional Recycling Caucus; Congressional Sportsmen's Caucus; Congressional United Solutions Caucus; Congressional Veterans Job Caucus; Historic Preservation Caucus; House Army Caucus; House Baltic Caucus; House General Aviation Caucus; House Manufacturing Caucus; House Military Depot, Arsenal, Ammunition Plant, and Industrial Facilities Caucus; Military Sexual Assault Prevention Caucus; National Guard and Reserves Components Caucus; National Guard Youth Challenge Caucus; Pro-Life Caucus; USO Congressional Caucus; US-Japan Caucus; Republican Study Committee; committees: Financial Services; elected to the 113th Congress on November 6, 2012; reelected to each succeeding Congress.

Office Listings

http://www.barr.house.gov www.facebook.com/repandybarr
www.twitter.com/repandybarr www.youtube.com/repandybarr

1427 Longworth House Office Building, Washington, DC 20515 .... (202) 225–4706
Chief of Staff.—Mary Rosado. FAX: 225–2122
Legislative Director.—Eric Bunning.
Communications Director.—Rick VanMeter.
Scheduler.—Gabriela Spence.
2709 Old Rosebud Road, Suite 100, Lexington, KY 40509 .... (859) 219–1366

Counties: Anderson, Bath, Bourbon, Clark, Estill, Fayette, Fleming, Franklin, Harrison (part), Jessamine (part), Madison, Menifee, Montgomery, Nicholas, Powell, Robertson, Scott, Wolfe, and Woodford. Population (2010), 723,203.

ZIP Codes: 40003, 40046, 40076, 40311–13, 40316, 40322, 40324, 40334, 40336–37, 40340, 40342, 40346–48, 40350, 40353, 40356, 40358, 40360–61, 40370–72, 40374, 40376, 40379–80, 40383, 40385, 40387, 40390–91, 40403–04, 40461, 40472, 40475, 40502–11, 40513–17, 40601, 40604, 41004, 41010, 41031, 41039, 41041, 41044, 41049, 41055, 41064, 41093, 41301, 41332, 41360, 41365

LOUISIANA

(Population 2010, 4,553,762)

SENATORS

BILL CASSIDY, Republican, of Baton Rouge, LA; born in Highland Park, IL, September 28, 1957; education: graduated, Tara High School; B.S., Louisiana State University, Baton Rouge, 1979; M.D., Louisiana State University Medical School, New Orleans, LA, 1983; professional: medical doctor, Baton Rouge; associate professor of medicine with LSU Health Sciences Center; member of the Louisiana State Senate; married: Laura Layden Cassidy, M.D.; children: Will, Meg, and Kate; committees: Energy and Natural Resources; Finance; Health, Education, Labor, and Pensions; Veterans' Affairs; Joint Economic Committee; elected to the 111th Congress; reelected to the 112th and 113th Congresses; won the runoff election to the U.S. Senate on December 6, 2014.

Office Listings

http://www.cassidy.senate.gov

520 Hart Senate Office Building, Washington, DC 20510 .... (202) 224–5824
Chief of Staff.—James Quinn. FAX: 224–9735
Deputy Chief of Staff.—Allison Kapsner.
Communications Director.—Matt Wolking.
5555 Hilton Avenue, Suite 100, Baton Rouge, LA 70808 .... (225) 929–7711
3421 North Causeway Boulevard, Suite 204, Metairie, LA 70002 .... (504) 838–0130
101 La Rue France, Suite 505, Lafayette, LA 70508 .... (337) 261–1400
1651 Louisville Avenue, Suite 123, Monroe, LA 71201.

* * *

JOHN KENNEDY, Republican, of Madisonville, LA; born in Centreville, MS, November 21, 1951; education: B.A., Vanderbilt University, Nashville, TN, 1973; J.D., University of Virginia, Charlottesville, VA, 1977; BCL, Magdalen College, Oxford University, 1979; professional: special counsel to Louisiana Governor Buddy Roemer, 1988–92; secretary in the governor's cabinet, 1990–92; secretary of the Louisiana Department of Revenue, 1996–99; Louisiana State Treasurer, 2000–17; religion: Methodist; wife: Rebecca Stulb; children: Preston; committees: Appropriations; Banking, Housing, and Urban Affairs; Budget; Judiciary; Small Business and Entrepreneurship; won the runoff election to the U.S. Senate on December 10, 2016.

Office Listings

http://www.kennedy.senate.gov twitter: https://twitter.com/SenJohnKennedy
https://www.facebook.com/SenatorJohnKennedy/?ref=bookmarks

383 Russell Senate Office Building, Washington, DC 20510 .... (202) 224–4623
Chief of Staff.—Preston Robinson. FAX: 228–5061

REPRESENTATIVES

FIRST DISTRICT

STEVE SCALISE, Republican, of Jefferson, LA; born in New Orleans, LA, October 6, 1965; education: B.S., Louisiana State University, Baton Rouge, LA, 1983; professional: computer programmer for technology company; Louisiana House of Representatives, 1995–2007; Louisiana Senate, 2007–08; awards: Spirit of Enterprise, U.S. Chamber of Commerce; religion: Catholic; married: former Jennifer LeTulle; children: Madison and Harrison; Majority Whip; committees: Energy and Commerce; elected to the 110th Congress, by special election, on May 4, 2008; reelected to each succeeding Congress.

Office Listings

http://www.scalise.house.gov www.facebook.com/repstevescalise
https://twitter.com/stevescalise

2338 Rayburn House Office Building, Washington, DC 20515 .... (202) 225–3015

Office Listings—Continued

Chiefs of Staff: Charles Henry, Brett Horton, Megan Miller. FAX: 226–0386
Legislative Director.—John Seale.
Scheduler.—Ellen Gosnell.
Communications Director.—Chris Bond.
110 Veterans Memorial Boulevard, Suite 500, Metaire, LA 70005 .... (504) 837–1259
21454 Koop Drive, Suite 1E, Mandeville, LA 70471 .... (985) 893–9064
112 South Cypress Street, Hammond, LA 70403 .... (985) 340–2185
8026 Main Street, Suite 700, Houma, LA 70360 .... (985) 879–2300

Parishes: All or parts of: JEFFERSON, LAFOURCHE, ORLEANS, PLAQUEMINES, ST. BERNARD, ST. TAMMANY, TANGIPAHOA, AND TERREBONNE. Population (2010), 758,994.

ZIP Codes: 70001–06, 70009–11, 70033, 70038, 70041, 70055–56, 70060, 70062, 70064–65, 70083, 70091, 70115, 70118–19, 70121–24, 70160, 70181, 70183–84, 70343–45, 70353–54, 70357–58, 70360–61, 70363–64, 70373–74, 70377, 70401–04, 70420, 70427, 70431, 70433–38, 70445, 70447–48, 70452, 70454–67, 70469–71, 70764–65

* * *

SECOND DISTRICT

CEDRIC L. RICHMOND, Democrat, of New Orleans, LA; born in New Orleans, September 13, 1973; education: B.A., Morehouse College, Atlanta, GA, 1995; J.D., Tulane School of Law, New Orleans, 1998; Harvard University Executive Education Program at the John F. Kennedy School of Government, Cambridge, MA; professional: member of the Louisiana State House of Representatives, 1999–2010; awards: *Time* magazine's 2010 40 Under 40; Innocence Project Legislative Champion Award; religion: Baptist; commissions, caucuses: Congressional Black Caucus; Gulf Coast Caucus; New Democrat Coalition; committees: Homeland Security; Judiciary; elected to the 112th Congress on November 2, 2010; reelected to each succeeding Congress.

Office Listings

http://www.richmond.house.gov twitter: @reprichmond
www.facebook.com/reprichmond

420 Cannon House Office Building, Washington, DC 20515 .... (202) 225–6636
Chief of Staff.—Virgil Miller. FAX: 225–1988
Director of Scheduling.—Kemah Dennis-Morial.
Legislative Director.—Peter Hunter.
Communications Director.—Brandon Gassaway.
2021 Lakeshore Drive, Suite 309, New Orleans, LA 70122 .... (504) 288–3777
District Director.—Enix Smith.
200 Derbigny Street, Suite 3200, Gretna, LA 70053 .... (504) 365–0390
1520 Thomas H. Delpit Drive, Suite 126, Baton Rouge, LA 70802 .... (225) 636–5600

Parishes: ASCENSION (part), ASSUMPTION (part), EAST BATON ROUGE (part), IBERVILLE (part), JEFFERSON (part), ORLEANS (part), ST. CHARLES (part), ST. JAMES, ST. JOHN THE BAPTIST (part), AND WEST BATON ROUGE (part). Population (2010), 755,538.

ZIP Codes: 70001, 70003, 70030, 70031, 70039, 70047, 70049, 70051–53, 70056–58, 70062, 70065, 70068, 70070–72, 70076, 70080, 70084, 70086, 70087, 70090, 70094, 70112–19, 70121–31, 70139, 70163, 70301, 70341, 70346, 70372, 70390, 70391, 70393, 70710, 70714, 70719, 70721, 70723, 70725, 70734, 70737, 70743, 70763, 70764, 70767, 70776, 70780, 70788, 70791, 70802, 70805–07, 70811, 70812, 70814, 70815

* * *

THIRD DISTRICT

CLAY HIGGINS, Republican, of Port Barre, LA; born in New Orleans, LA, August 24, 1961; education: Covington High School, Covington, LA; attended Louisiana State University, Baton Rouge, LA; professional: Lafayette City Marshal Deputy; Deputy Sheriff, St. Landry Parish; officer, Port Barre Police Department; reserve officer, Opelousas Police Department; manager, auto dealership; military: Military Police Corps, Louisiana National Guard; religion: Catholic; married, Rebecca; children: Daniella (deceased), Haley, Heather, and Joseph; committees: Homeland Security; Science, Space, and Technology; Veterans' Affairs; elected to the 115th Congress on December 10, 2016.

Office Listings

http://www.clayhiggins.house.gov

1711 Longworth House Office Building, Washington, DC 20515 .... (202) 225–2031
Chief of Staff.—Kathee Facchiano. FAX: 225–5724
Legislative Director.—Ward Cormier.
Scheduler.—Jordan Lane.
600 Jefferson Street, Suite 808, Lafayette, LA 70501 .... (337) 703–6105
One Lakeshore Drive, Suite 1670, Lake Charles, LA 70629 .... (337) 656–2833

Parishes: ACADIA, CALCASIEU, CAMERON, IBERIA, JEFFERSON DAVIS, LAFAYETTE, ST. MARTIN, ST. MARY, AND VERMILION.

ZIP Codes: 70339–40, 70342, 70380, 70392, 70501, 70503, 70506–08, 70510, 70512–20, 70523, 70525–26, 70528–29, 70531–35, 70537–38, 70542–44, 70546, 70548–49, 70552, 70555–56, 70558–60, 70563, 70575, 70578, 70581–84, 70591–92, 70601, 70605, 70607, 70611, 70615, 70630–33, 70640, 70643, 70645–48, 70650, 70657, 70661, 70663, 70665, 70668–69, 70757

* * *

FOURTH DISTRICT

MIKE JOHNSON, Republican, of Benton, LA; born in Shreveport, LA, January 30, 1972; education: juris doctorate from the Paul M. Hebert Law Center at Louisiana State University in Baton Rouge in 1998; religion: Southern Baptist; family: wife, Kelly; children: Hannah, Abigail, Jack, and Will; committees: Judiciary; Natural Resources; elected to the 115th Congress on December 10, 2016.

Office Listings

http://www.mikejohnson.house.gov facebook: facebook.com/RepMikeJohnson
twitter: @RepMikeJohnson

327 Cannon House Office Building, Washington, DC 20515 .... (202) 225–2777
Chief of Staff.—Hayden Haynes. FAX: 225–8039
Legislative Director.—Joshua Hodges.
Scheduler.—Ruth Ward.
Communications Director.—Ainsley Holyfield.
2250 Hospital Drive, Suite 248, Bossier City, LA 71111 .... (318) 840–0309
Deputy Chief of Staff.—Chip Layton.
3329 University Parkway, Building 552, Room 24, Leesville, LA 71446 .... (337) 392–3146
444 Caspari Drive, South Hall Room 224, Natchitoches, LA 71497 .... (318) 357–5731

Parishes: ALLEN, BEAUREGARD, BIENVILLE, BOSSIER, CADDO, CLAIBORNE, DESOTO, EVANGELINE, NATCHITOCHES, RED RIVER, SABINE, ST. LANDRY, UNION, VERNON, AND WEBSTER. Population (2010), 667,109.

ZIP Codes: 70515, 70524, 70535, 70541, 70570, 70576, 70584–86, 70589, 70634, 70637–39, 70644, 70648, 70651–60, 70662, 71001–09, 71016, 71018–19, 71021, 71023–24, 71027–34, 71037–40, 71043–52, 71055, 71058, 71060–61, 71063–73, 71075, 71078–80, 71082, 71101–13, 71115, 71118–20, 71129–30, 71133–38, 71148, 71156, 71161, 71163–66, 71171–72, 71222, 71234, 71241, 71256, 71260, 71277, 71403, 71406, 71411, 71414, 71416, 71419, 71426, 71429, 71434, 71438–39, 71443, 71446–47, 71449–50, 71456–63, 71468–69, 71474–75, 71486, 71496–97, 71526

* * *

FIFTH DISTRICT

RALPH LEE ABRAHAM, Republican, of Alto, LA; born in Monroe, LA, September 16, 1954; education: studied biochemistry as an undergraduate at Louisiana State University, Baton Rouge, LA, 1972–76; D.V.M., Louisiana State University School of Veterinary Medicine, Baton Rouge, 1980; M.D., Louisiana State University School of Medicine, Shreveport, LA, 1994; professional: general family practitioner; military: Army National Guard; religion: Baptist; married: Dianne; three children, nine grandchildren; committees: Agriculture; Armed Services; Science, Space, and Technology; elected to the 114th Congress on December 6, 2014 in a run-off election; reelected to the 115th Congress on November 8, 2016.

Office Listings

https://abraham.house.gov facebook: http://www.facebook.com/CongressmanRalphAbraham
twitter: https://twitter.com/repabraham

417 Cannon House Office Building, Washington, DC 20515 .... (202) 225–8490

Office Listings—Continued

Chief of Staff.—Luke Letlow. FAX: 225–5639
Legislative Director.—Ted Verrill.
Communications Director.—Cole Avery.
District Director.—Wyatt Lobrano.
Scheduler.—Emma Herrock.
North Louisiana Office, 426 DeSiard Street, Monroe, LA 71201 .... (318) 322–3500
Central Louisiana Office, 2003 MacArthur Drive, Building 5, Alexandria, LA 71301 .... (318) 445–0818

Parishes: AVOYELLES, CALDWELL, CATAHOULA, CONCORDIA, EAST CARROLL, EAST FELICIANA (part), FRANKLIN, JACKSON, LASALLE, LINCOLN, MADISON, MOREHOUSE, OUACHITA, RAPIDES, RICHLAND, ST. LANDRY (part), ST. HELENA (part), TANGIPAHOA (part), TENSAS, WASHINGTON, WEST CARROLL, WEST FELICIANA, AND WINN. Population (2010), 758,851.

ZIP Codes: 70401, 70422, 70426–27, 70431, 70435–38, 70441–44, 70446, 70450–51, 70455–56, 70465–66, 70512, 70570, 70577, 70589, 70656, 70712, 70722, 70730, 70748, 70750, 70761, 70775, 70782, 70787, 70789, 71001, 71031, 71201–03, 71209, 71219–20, 71223, 71225–27, 71229, 71232–35, 71237, 71238, 71243, 71245, 71247, 71250–51, 71253–54, 71259, 71261, 71263–64, 71266, 71268–70, 71272, 71275–76, 71279–80, 71282, 71286, 71291–92, 71295, 71301–03, 71316, 71322–23, 71325–28, 71331, 71333–34, 71336, 71339–43, 71345–46, 71350–51, 71353–58, 71360, 71362, 71366–69, 71371, 71373, 71375, 71377–78, 71401, 71404–05, 71407, 71409–10, 71417, 71418, 71422–25, 71427, 71430, 71432–33, 71435, 71438, 71441, 71447, 71454–55, 71457, 71463, 71465–67, 71472–73, 71479–80, 71483, 71485

* * *

SIXTH DISTRICT

GARRET GRAVES, Republican, of Baton Rouge, LA; born in Baton Rouge, January 31, 1972; education: graduated, Catholic High School; studied at Louisiana Tech, University of Alabama, and the American University; professional: coastal preservation; served as an aide for the U.S. Senate Committee on Commerce, Science, and Transportation; staff director for the U.S. Senate Subcommittee on Climate Change and Impacts; chief legislative aide to the U.S. Senate Committee on Environment and Public Works; served as the head of the Louisiana Coastal Protection and Restoration Authority; married: Carissa Vanderleest Graves; children: Ralston, Calla, and Kulshan; committees: Natural Resources; Transportation and Infrastructure; elected to the 114th Congress in a runoff election on December 6, 2014; reelected to the 115th Congress on November 8, 2016.

Office Listings

http://garretgraves.house.gov

430 Cannon House Office Building, Washington, DC 20515 .... (202) 225–3901
Chief of Staff.—Paul Sawyer. FAX: 225–7313
Press Secretary.—Kevin Roig.
2351 Energy Drive, Suite 1200, Baton Rouge, LA 70808 .... (225) 442–1731
29261 Frost Road, Livingston, LA 70753 .... (225) 686–4413
908 East 1st Street NSU, Candies Hall, Suite 405, Thibodaux, LA 70301 .... (985) 448–4103

Parishes: ASCENSION, ASSUMPTION, EAST BATON ROUGE, EAST FELICIANA, IBERVILLE, LAFOURCHE, LIVINGSTON, POINTE COUPEE, ST. CHARLES, ST. HELENA, ST. JOHN THE BAPTIST, TERREBONNE, AND WEST BATON ROUGE. Population (2010), 755,607.

ZIP Codes: 70030, 70047, 70068–69, 70079, 70087, 70301–02, 70339, 70341, 70352, 70356, 70359–61, 70364, 70371–72, 70375, 70380, 70390, 70394–95, 70403, 70422, 70436, 70441, 70443, 70449, 70453, 70456, 70462, 70466, 70704, 70706–07, 70710–11, 70714–15, 70718–19, 70722, 70725–30, 70732–34, 70736–37, 70739–40, 70744, 70747–49, 70752–57, 70759–60, 70762, 70764–65, 70767, 70769–70, 70772–74, 70777–78, 70783, 70785–86, 70788, 70791, 70801–02, 70806–11, 70814–21, 70825–27, 70831, 70835–37, 70874, 70879, 70884, 70893–96, 70898

MAINE

(Population, 2010 1,328,361)

SENATORS

SUSAN M. COLLINS, Republican, of Bangor, ME; born in Caribou, ME, December 7, 1952; education: graduated, Caribou High School, 1971; B.A., *magna cum laude*, Phi Beta Kappa, St. Lawrence University, Canton, NY, 1975; Outstanding Alumni Award, St. Lawrence University, 1992; professional: staff director, Senate Subcommittee on the Oversight of Government Management, 1981–87; for 12 years, principal advisor on business issues to former Senator William S. Cohen; Commissioner of Professional and Financial Regulation for Maine Governor John R. McKernan, Jr., 1987; New England administrator, Small Business Administration, 1992–93; appointed Deputy Treasurer of Massachusetts, 1993; executive director, Husson College Center for Family Business, 1994–96; committees: chair, Special Committee on Aging; Appropriations; Health, Education, Labor, and Pensions; Select Committee on Intelligence; elected to the U.S. Senate on November 5, 1996; reelected to each succeeding Senate term.

Office Listings

http://collins.senate.gov   www.facebook.com/susancollins   twitter: @senatorcollins

413 Dirksen Senate Office Building, Washington, DC 20510 .... (202) 224–2523
Chief of Staff.—Steve Abbott. FAX: 224–2693
Communications Director.—Annie Clark.
Legislative Director.—Olivia Kurtz.
202 Harlow Street, Suite 20100, Bangor, ME 04401 .... (207) 945–0417
State Representative.—Carol Woodcock.
68 Sewall Street, Room 507, Augusta, ME 04330 .... (207) 622–8414
State Representative.—Mark Winter.
160 Main Street, Biddeford, ME 04005 .... (207) 283–1101
State Representative.—Alex Pelczar.
55 Lisbon Street, Suite 1100, Lewiston, ME 04240 .... (207) 784–6969
State Representative.—Carlene Tremblay.
25 Sweden Street, Suite A, Caribou, ME 04736 .... (207) 493–7873
State Representative.—Trisha House.
One Canal Plaza, Suite 802, Portland, ME 04101 .... (207) 780–3575
State Representative.—Kate Simson.

* * *

ANGUS S. KING, Jr., Independent, of Brunswick, ME; born in Alexandria, VA, March 31, 1944; education: graduated, Dartmouth College, 1966; University of Virginia Law School, 1969; professional: Chief Counsel to U.S. Senate Subcommittee on Alcoholism and Narcotics for former Maine Senator William Hathaway; founded Northeast Energy Management, Inc., 1989; elected Maine's 71st Governor, 1994; reelected 1998 by one of the largest margins in Maine's history; Maine's first Independent U.S. Senator; committees: Armed Services; Budget; Energy and Natural Resources; Rules and Administration; Select Committee on Intelligence; elected to the U.S. Senate on November 6, 2012.

Office Listings

http://king.senate.gov   twitter: @senangusking
https://www.facebook.com/senatorangusskingjr

133 Hart Senate Office Building, Washington, DC 20510 .... (202) 224–5344
Chief of Staff.—Kay Rand. FAX: 224–1946
Personal Assistant / Legislative Aide.—Jacob ''Izzy'' Rosen.
DC Scheduler / Executive Assistant.—Claire Bridges.
Communications Director.—Kathleen Connery Dawe.
DC Scheduler.—Matt Liscovitz.
Legislative Director.—Chad Metzler.
Senior Policy Advisor.—Marge Kilkelly.
Administrative Director.—Patrick Doak.
4 Gabriel Drive, Suite F1, Augusta, ME 04330 .... (207) 622–8292
202 Harlow Street, Suite 20350, Bangor, ME 04401 .... (207) 945–8000
169 Academy Street, Suite A, Presque Isle, ME 04769 .... (207) 764–5124
383 U.S. Route 1, Suite 1C, Scarborough, ME 04074 .... (207) 883–1588
Regional Representatives: Sharon Campbell, Travis Kennedy, Gail Kezer, Elizabeth Schneider MacTaggart, Bonnie Pothier, Chris Rector, Edie Smith, Ben Tucker.

REPRESENTATIVES

FIRST DISTRICT

CHELLIE PINGREE, Democrat, of North Haven, ME; born in Minneapolis, MN, April 2, 1955; education: B.A., College of the Atlantic, Bar Harbor, ME, 1979; professional: farmer; businesswoman; religion: Lutheran; family: three children; caucuses: Bicycle Caucus; House Oceans Caucus; House Trade Working Group; Humanities Caucus; National Guard and Reserve Component Caucus; Philanthropy Caucus; Progressive Caucus; Sustainable Energy and Environment Coalition; Women's Caucus; committees: Appropriations; elected to the 111th Congress on November 4, 2008; reelected to each succeeding Congress.

Office Listings

http://pingree.house.gov

2162 Rayburn House Office Building, Washington, DC 20515 .... (202) 225–6116
Chief of Staff.—Jesse Connolly. FAX: 225–5590
Scheduler.—Karen Sudbay.
2 Portland Fish Pier, Suite 304, Portland, ME 04101 .... (207) 774–5019

Counties: CUMBERLAND, KENNEBEC (part), KNOX, LINCOLN, SAGADAHOC, AND YORK. Population (2010), 668,515.

ZIP Codes: 03901–11, 04001–11, 04013–15, 04017, 04019–21, 04024, 04027–30, 04032–34, 04038–40, 04042–43, 04046–50, 04053–57, 04061–64, 04066, 04069–79, 04082–87, 04090–98, 04101–10, 04112, 04116, 04122–24, 04259–60, 04265, 04284, 04287, 04330, 04332–33, 04336, 04338, 04341–55, 04357–60, 04363–64, 04530, 04541, 04543–44, 04547–48, 04551, 04553–56, 04558, 04562–65, 04567–68, 04570–76, 04578–79, 04841, 04843, 04846–56, 04858–65, 04901, 04910, 04917–18, 04922, 04926–27, 04935, 04937, 04941, 04949, 04952, 04962–63

* * *

SECOND DISTRICT

BRUCE POLIQUIN, Republican, of Maine; born in Waterville, Kennebec County, ME, November 1, 1953; education: graduated from Phillips Exeter Academy, Exeter, New Hampshire, 1972; A.B., Harvard University, Cambridge, MA, 1976; professional: businessman; State Treasurer of Maine, 2010–12; committees: Financial Services; Veterans' Affairs; elected to the 114th Congress on November 4, 2014; reelected to the 115th Congress on November 8, 2016.

Office Listings

https://poliquin.house.gov facebook: https://www.facebook.com/RepPoliquin
twitter: https://twitter.com/RepPoliquin

1208 Longworth House Office Building, Washington, DC 20515 .... (202) 225–6306
Chief of Staff.—Matt Hutson.
District Director.—Corenna O'Brien.
Legislative Director.—Philip Swatzfager.
Press Secretary.—Brendan Conley.
Scheduler.—Danielle Branz.
6 State Street, Suite 101, Bangor, ME 04401 .... (207) 942–0583
179 Lisbon Street, Ground Floor, Lewiston, ME 04240 .... (207) 784–0768
631 Main Street, Suite 2, Presque Isle, ME 04769 .... (207) 764–1968

Counties: ANDROSCOGGIN, AROOSTOOK, FRANKLIN, HANCOCK, KENNEBEC (part), OXFORD, PENOBSCOT, PISCATAQUIS, SOMERSET, WALDO, AND WASHINGTON. Population (2010), 664,180.

ZIP Codes: 04010, 04016, 04022, 04037, 04041, 04051, 04068, 04088, 04210–12, 04216–17, 04219–28, 04230–31, 04234, 04236–41, 04243, 04250, 04252–58, 04261–63, 04266–68, 04270–71, 04274–76, 04278, 04280–83, 04285–86, 04288–92, 04294, 04354, 04401–02, 04406, 04408, 04410–24, 04426–31, 04434–35, 04438, 04441–44, 04448–51, 04453–57, 04459–64, 04467–69, 04471–76, 04478–79, 04481, 04485, 04487–93, 04495–97, 04549, 04605–07, 04609, 04611–17, 04619, 04622–31, 04634–35, 04637, 04640, 04642–46, 04648–50, 04652–58, 04660, 04662, 04664, 04666–69, 04671–77, 04679–81, 04683–86, 04691, 04693–94, 04730, 04732–47, 04750–51, 04756–66, 04768–70, 04772–77, 04779–81, 04783, 04785–88, 04848–51, 04857, 04903, 04911–12, 04915, 04920–25, 04928–30, 04932–33, 04936–45, 04947, 04949–58, 04961, 04964–67, 04969–76, 04978–79, 04981–88, 04992

MARYLAND

(Population 2010, 5,773,552)

SENATORS

BENJAMIN L. ''BEN'' CARDIN, Democrat, of Baltimore, MD; born in Baltimore, October 5, 1943; education: graduated, City College High School, 1961; B.A., *cum laude*, University of Pittsburgh, 1964; L.L.B., 1st in class, University of Maryland School of Law, 1967; professional: attorney, Rosen and Esterson, 1967–78; elected to the Maryland House of Delegates in November 1966, served from 1967–87; Speaker of the House of Delegates, youngest Speaker at the time, 1979–87; elected to the U.S. House of Representatives in November 1986, Maryland 3rd Congressional District, served from 1987–2007; member: Associated Jewish Charities and Welfare Fund, 1985–89; trustee, Baltimore Council on Foreign Affairs, 1999–2007; trustee, Goucher College, 1999–2008; St. Mary's College, 1988–99; lifetime member, NAACP, since 1990; Board of Visitors, University of Maryland Law School, 1998–present; President's Board of Visitors, UMBC, 1993–present; Johns Hopkins University Institute for Policy Studies' National Advisory Board, 2003–present; Board of Visitors, U.S. Naval Academy, 2007–present; Board of Trustees, The James Madison Memorial Fellowship, 2010–present; awards: Congressional Award, Small Business Council of America, 1993, 1999, 2005; Public Sector Distinguished Award, Tax Foundation, 2003; Congressional Voice for Children Award, National PTA, 2009; Congressional Leadership Award, American College of Emergency Physicians, 2010; Whitney M. Young Award, Baltimore Urban League, 2011; Chesapeake Conservation Hero, Chesapeake Conservancy, 2012; commissioner, Commission for Security and Cooperation in Europe (CSCE), since 1993; co-chair, CSCE, 2007–08; chair, CSCE, 2009–10; co-chair, CSCE, 2011–13; chair, CSCE, 2013–14; vice president, Organization for Security and Cooperation in Europe (OSCE) Parliamentary Assembly, 2006–14; Special Representative on Anti-Semitism, Racism, and Intolerance for the OSCE Parliamentary Assembly, 2014–present; religion: Jewish; married: Myrna Edelman of Baltimore, 1964; two children (one deceased); two grandchildren; committees: ranking member, Small Business and Entrepreneurship; Environment and Public Works; Finance; Foreign Relations; elected to the U.S. Senate on November 7, 2006; reelected to the U.S. Senate on November 6, 2012.

Office Listings

http://cardin.senate.gov facebook: @SenatorBenCardin twitter: @SenatorCardin

509 Hart Senate Office Building, Washington, DC 20510 .... (202) 224–4524
Chief of Staff.—Chris Lynch. FAX: 224–1651
Floor Director.—Gray Maxwell.
Scheduler.—Debbie Yamada.
Communications Director.—Sue Walitsky.
100 South Charles Street, Tower I, Suite 1710, Baltimore, MD 21201 .... (410) 962–4436
State Director.—Carleton Atkinson. FAX: 962–4256
10201 Martin Luther King Jr Highway, Suite 210, Bowie, MD 20720 .... (301) 860–0414
451 Hungerford Drive, Suite 230, Rockville, MD 20850 .... (301) 762–2974
212 West Main Street, Suite 301C, P.O. Box 11, Salisbury, MD 21801 .... (410) 546–4250
13 Canal Street, Room 305, Cumberland, MD 21502 .... (301) 777–2957

* * *

CHRIS VAN HOLLEN, Democrat, of Kensington, MD; born in Karachi, Pakistan, January 10, 1959; education: B.A., Swarthmore College, 1982; master's in public policy, Harvard University, 1985; J.D., Georgetown University, 1990; professional: attorney; legislative assistant to former Senator Charles McC. Mathias, Jr., of Maryland; staff member, U.S. Senate Committee on Foreign Relations; senior legislative advisor to former Maryland Governor William Donald Schaefer; public service: elected, Maryland House of Delegates, 1990; elected, Maryland State Senate, 1994; married: Katherine; children: Anna, Nicholas, and Alexander; committees: Appropriations; Banking, Housing, and Urban Affairs; Budget; Environment and Public Works; elected to the 108th Congress on November 5, 2002; reelected to each succeeding Congress through 2016. Elected to the U.S. Senate on November 8, 2016.

Office Listings

http://www.vanhollen.senate.gov

110 Hart Senate Office Building, Washington, DC 20510 .... (202) 224–4654

Office Listings—Continued

Chief of Staff.—Karen Robb.
Legislative Director.—Sarah Schenning.
Communications Director.—Bridgett Frey.
State Director.—Joan Kleinman (301) 545–1500
111 Rockville Pike, Suite 960, Rockville, MD 20850 .... (301) 545–1500
32 West Washington Street, Suite 203, Hagerstown, MD 21740 .... (301) 797–2826

REPRESENTATIVES

FIRST DISTRICT

ANDY HARRIS, Republican, of Cockeysville, MD; born in Brooklyn, NY, January 25, 1957; education: B.S., Johns Hopkins University, Baltimore, MD, 1977; M.D., Johns Hopkins University, Baltimore, 1980; M.H.S., Johns Hopkins University, 1995; professional: anesthesiologist, as an associate professor of anesthesiology and critical care medicine; member of the Maryland State Senate, 1998–2010; Minority Whip, Maryland State Senate; military: Commander, Johns Hopkins Medical Naval Reserve Primus Unit P0605C; religion: Catholic; widowed; five children; four grandchildren; committees: Appropriations; elected to the 112th Congress on November 2, 2010; reelected to each succeeding Congress.

Office Listings

http://harris.house.gov

1533 Longworth House Office Building, Washington, DC 20515 .... (202) 225–5311
FAX: 225–0254
Chief of Staff.—John Dutton.
Legislative Director.—Tim Daniels.
Press Secretary.—Jacque Clark.
Scheduler.—Charlotte Heyworth.
100 Olde Point Village, Suite 101, Chester, MD 21619 .... (410) 643–5425
15 Churchville Road, Suite 102B, Bel Air, MD 21014 .... (410) 588–5670
100 East Main Street, Suite 702, Salisbury, MD 21801 .... (443) 944–8624

Counties: BALTIMORE (part), CAROLINE, CARROLL (part), CECIL, DORCHESTER, KENT, HARFORD (part), QUEEN ANNE'S, SOMERSET, TALBOT, WICOMICO, AND WORCESTER. Population (2010), 721,529.

ZIP Codes: 21001, 21009, 21013–15, 21018, 21023, 21028, 21030–32, 21034, 21040, 21047–48, 21050–51, 21053, 21057, 21074, 21078, 21082, 21084–85, 21087–88, 21102, 21111, 21120, 21128, 21131–32, 21136, 21154–57, 21160–62, 21234, 21236, 21286, 21601, 21606–07, 21609–10, 21612–13, 21617, 21619–20, 21622–29, 21631–32, 21634–36, 21638–41, 21643–45, 21647–73, 21675–79, 21681–85, 21687, 21690, 21757, 21784, 21787, 21791, 21801–04, 21810–11, 21813–14, 21817, 21821–22, 21824, 21826, 21829–30, 21835–38, 21840–43, 21849–53, 21856–57, 21861–67, 21869, 21871–72, 21874–75, 21890, 21901–04, 21911–22, 21930

* * *

SECOND DISTRICT

C. A. DUTCH RUPPERSBERGER, Democrat, of Cockeysville, MD; born in Baltimore, MD, January 31, 1946; education: Baltimore City College; University of Maryland, College Park; J.D., University of Baltimore Law School, 1970; professional: attorney; partner, Ruppersberger, Clark, and Mister (law firm); public service: Baltimore County Assistant State's Attorney; Baltimore County Council; Baltimore County Executive, 1994–2002; married: the former Kay Murphy; children: Cory and Jill; committees: Appropriations; elected to the 108th Congress on November 5, 2002; reelected to each succeeding Congress.

Office Listings

http://dutch.house.gov https://twitter.com/call_me_dutch
https://www.facebook.com/dutchrupp

2416 Rayburn House Office Building, Washington, DC 20515 .... (202) 225–3061
FAX: 225–3094
Chief of Staff.—Tara Oursler.
Deputy Chief of Staff.—Cori Duggins.
Communications Director.—Jaime Lennon.
Senior Policy Advisor.—Walter Gonzales.
The Atrium, 375 West Padonia Road, Suite 200, Timonium, MD 21093 .... (410) 628–2701
FAX: 628–2708
District Director.—Jennifer Riggs.
Scheduler.—Elliott Phaup.

Counties: ANNE ARUNDEL (part), BALTIMORE CITY (part), BALTIMORE COUNTY (part), HARFORD (part), AND HOWARD (part). Population (2016), 763,156.

ZIP Codes: 20701, 20723–24, 20755, 20763, 20794, 21001, 21005, 21009–10, 21015, 21017, 21022, 21027, 21030–31, 21040, 21043, 21052, 21057, 21062, 21071, 21075–78, 21085, 21090, 21093–94, 21113, 21117, 21128, 21130, 21133, 21136, 21139, 21144, 21162–63, 21204, 21206, 21208, 21212–14, 21219–22, 21224–27, 21230–31, 21234, 21236–37, 21239, 21240, 21244, 21252, 21281, 21284, 21286

* * *

THIRD DISTRICT

JOHN P. SARBANES, Democrat, of Baltimore, MD; born in Baltimore, May 22, 1962; education: A.B., *cum laude*, Woodrow Wilson School of Public and International Affairs; Princeton University, 1984; Fulbright Scholar, Greece, 1985; J.D., Harvard University School of Law, 1988; professional: law clerk to Judge J. Frederick Motz, U.S. District Court for the District of Maryland, 1988–89; admitted to Maryland Bar, 1988; member: American Bar Association; Maryland State Bar Association; attorney, Venable, LLP, 1989–2006 (chair, health care practice); founding member, board of trustees, Dunbar Project, 1990–94; board of directors, Public Justice Center, 1991–2006 (president, 1994–97); Institute for Christian and Jewish Studies, 1991–present (past chair, membership committee); Special Assistant to State Superintendent of Schools, State Department of Education, 1998–2005; awards: Unsung Hero Award, Maryland Chapter of the Association of Fundraising Professionals, 2006; Arthur W. Machen, Jr. Award, Maryland Legal Services Corp., 2006; married to Dina Sarbanes; three children; committees: Energy and Commerce; Oversight and Government Reform; elected to the 110th Congress on November 7, 2006; reelected to each succeeding Congress.

Office Listings

http://www.sarbanes.house.gov

2444 Rayburn House Office Building, Washington, DC 20510 .... (202) 225–4016
Chief of Staff.—Jason Gleason. FAX: 225–9219
Deputy Chief of Staff.—Dvora Lovinger.
Legislative Director.—Raymond O'Mara.
Scheduler.—Kate Gieron.
Legislative Assistants: Peter Gelman, Anna Killius.
Communications Director.—Daniel Jacobs.
600 Baltimore Avenue, Suite 303, Towson, MD 21204 .... (410) 832–8890
44 Calvert Street, Suite 349, Annapolis, MD 21401 .... (410) 295–1679

Counties: ANNE ARUNDEL (part), BALTIMORE (part), BALTIMORE CITY (part), HOWARD (part), AND MONTGOMERY (part). Population (2010), 720,094.

ZIP Codes: 20705, 20707, 20723–24, 20759, 20777, 20783, 20832–33, 20853, 20855, 20860–62, 20866, 20868, 20882, 20901, 20903–06, 21012, 21022, 21029, 21037, 21043–46, 21054, 21056, 21060–61, 21075–77, 21090, 21093, 21108, 21113, 21117, 21122, 21128, 21136, 21139, 21144, 21153, 21201–15, 21218, 21223–27, 21229–31, 21234, 21236–37, 21239, 21252, 21281–82, 21285–86, 21401–03, 21409, 21412, 21797

* * *

FOURTH DISTRICT

ANTHONY G. BROWN, Democrat, of Bowie, MD; born in Huntington, NY, November 21, 1961; education: A.B. in government, Harvard University, Cambridge, MA, 1984; J.D., Harvard University, Cambridge MA, 1992; professional: clerkship for Chief Judge Eugene Sullivan of the United States Courts of Appeals for the Armed Forces, 1992–94; associate attorney, Wilmer, Cutler & Pickering, Washington, DC, 1994–98; Of Counsel, Gibbs & Haller, 2000–07; delegate, Maryland House of Delegates, 1999–2007; Lt. Governor of Maryland, 2007–14; co-chair, Agency Review Team for U.S. Department of Veterans' Affairs, Obama-Biden Transition, 2008–09; chair, National Lieutenant Governors Association, 2010–11; military: U.S. Army, Commissioned Aviation Officer (Captain), 1984–89; U.S. Army Reserve, 1989–2014: Colonel in Judge Advocate General's Corps, 2007–14; served in Iraq with 353rd Civil Affairs Command as senior consultant to Iraqi Ministry of Displacement and Migration, 2004–05; Commander, 153rd Legal Support Organization, 2008–11; medals and honors (partial list): Bronze Star Medal; Legion of Merit; Meritorious Service Medal; Army commendation with 2 Oak Leaf Clusters; Iraq Campaign Medal; awards: Public Officials of the Year, *Governing* magazine, 2013; Nathan Davis Award, American Medical Association, 2013; Congressional Leadership Award, Congressional Black Caucus, 2012; Morris H. Blum Humanitarian Award, Dr. Martin Luther King, Jr., Committee, 2012; honorary doctor of laws, Hood College, 2011; Policymaker/Elected Official of the Year, Association of Defense Communities, 2011; Toll Fellow, Council of State Governments, 2000; religion: Catholic; member, St. Joseph Catholic Church, Largo, MD; family: married: Karmen Walker-Brown; three children; caucuses: Parliamentarian, Congressional Black Caucus; New Democrat Coalition; committees: Armed Services; Natural Resources; Select Committee on Ethics; elected to the 115th Congress on November 8, 2016.

Office Listings

http://www.anthonybrown.house.gov facebook.com/repanthonybrown
twitter.com/repanthonybrown

1505 Longworth House Office Building, Washington, DC 20515 .... (202) 225–8699
Chief of Staff.—Maia Estes.
Legislative Director.—Eric Delaney.
Communications Director.—Matthew Verghese.
District Director.—Nichelle Schoultz.
Director of Operations.—Ann Mathew.
Deputy District Director.— Ben Wolff.
9701 Apollo Drive, Suite 103, Largo, MD 20774 .... (301) 458–2600
2666 Riva Road, Suite 120, Annapolis, MD 21401 .... (410) 266–3249

Counties: ANNE ARUNDEL (part), PRINCE GEORGE'S (part). CITIES AND TOWNSHIPS: Andrews Air Force Base, Annapolis, Arnold, Beltsville, Bladensburg, Bowie, Brentwood, Capitol Heights, Clinton, College Park, Crofton, Crownsville, Davidsonville, District Heights, Edgewater, Fort Washington, Gambrills, Glen Burnie, Glenn Dale, Hyattsville, Lanham, Laurel, Millersville, Mount Rainier, Odenton, Oxon Hill, Pasadena, Riva, Riverdale, Severn, Severna Park, Sherwood Forest, Silver Spring, Suitland, Takoma Park, Temple Hills, and Upper Marlboro. Population (2010), 720,065.

ZIP Codes: 20705–08, 20710, 20712, 20720–22, 20724, 20735, 20737, 20740, 20743–48, 20762, 20769, 20772, 20774, 20781–85, 20903–04, 20912, 21012, 21032, 21035, 21037, 21054, 21061, 21108, 21113–14, 21122, 21140, 21144, 21146, 21401, 21405, 21409

* * *

FIFTH DISTRICT

STENY H. HOYER, Democrat, of Mechanicsville, MD; born in New York, NY, June 14, 1939; education: graduated, Suitland High School; B.S., University of Maryland, 1963; J.D., Georgetown University Law Center, 1966; honorary doctor of public service, University of Maryland, 1988; admitted to the Maryland Bar Association, 1966; professional: practicing attorney, 1966–90; Maryland State Senate, 1967–79; vice chairman, Prince George's County, MD, Senate delegation, 1967–69; chairman, Prince George's County, MD, Senate delegation, 1969–75; president, Maryland State Senate, 1975–79; member, State Board for Higher Education, 1978–81; married: Judith Pickett, deceased, February 6, 1997; children: Susan, Stefany, and Anne; Democratic Steering Committee; Democratic Whip, 108th and 109th Congresses; House Majority Leader, 110th and 111th Congresses; Democratic Whip, 112th, 113th, and 114th Congresses; elected to the 97th Congress on May 19, 1981, by special election; reelected to each succeeding Congress.

Office Listings

http://www.hoyer.house.gov www.facebook.com/whiphoyer twitter: @whiphoyer

1705 Longworth House Office Building, Washington, DC 20515 .... (202) 225–4131
Chief of Staff.—Alexis Covey-Brandt. FAX: 226–0663
Personal Office Director.—Jim Notter.
U.S. Federal Courthouse, Suite 310, 6500 Cherrywood Lane, Greenbelt, MD 20770 .... (301) 474–0119
4475 Regency Place, Suite 203, White Plains, MD 20695 .... (301) 843–1577

Counties: ANNE ARUNDEL (part), CALVERT, CHARLES, PRINCE GEORGE'S (part), AND ST. MARY'S. Population (2012), 721,529.

ZIP Codes: 20601–03, 20606–09, 20611–13, 20615–26, 20628–30, 20632, 20634, 20636–37, 20639–40, 20645–46, 20650, 20653, 20657–60, 20662, 20664, 20667, 20670, 20674–76, 20678, 20680, 20684–90, 20692–93, 20695, 20705–08, 20711, 20714–16, 20720–21, 20732–33, 20735–37, 20740, 20742, 20744, 20746, 20748, 20751, 20754, 20758, 20762, 20764–65, 20769–70, 20772, 20774, 20776, 20778–79, 20781–84, 21035, 21037, 21054, 21113–14

* * *

SIXTH DISTRICT

JOHN K. DELANEY, Democrat, of Potomac, MD; born in Wood-Ridge, NJ, April 16, 1963; education: B.A., Columbia University, 1985; J.D., Georgetown University Law School, 1988;

professional: former practicing attorney, Shaw, Pittman, Potts & Trowbridge; co-founder, chair, and chief executive officer, Health Care Financial Partners, Inc., 1993–99; co-founder and executive chair, Capital Source, 2000–12; awards: Ernst & Young Entrepreneur Of The Year®, 2005; *Fortune* Magazine, 50 World's Greatest Leaders, 2017; married: April; children: Summer, Brooke, Lily, and Grace; committees: Financial Services; Joint Economic Committee; elected to the 113th Congress on November 6, 2012; reelected to each succeeding Congress.

Office Listings

http://www.delaney.house.gov https://www.facebook.com/congressmanjohndelaney
https://twitter.com/repjohndelaney

1632 Longworth House Office Building, Washington, DC 20515 .... (202) 225–2721
Chief of Staff.—Xan Fishman.
Legislative Director.—Lauren Santabar.
Scheduler.—Elizabeth Virga.
9801 Washingtonian Boulevard, Suite 330, Gaithersburg, MD 20878 .... (301) 926–0300
38 South Potomac Street, Suite 205, Hagerstown, MD 21740 .... (301) 733–2900

Counties: ALLEGANY, FREDERICK (part), GARRETT, MONTGOMERY (part), AND WASHINGTON. CITIES AND TOWNSHIPS: Boonsboro, Boyds, Clarksburg, Cumberland, Darnestown, Frederick, Frostburg, Funkstown, Gaithersburg, Germantown, Hagerstown, Hancock, Montgomery Village, Oakland, Poolesville, Potomac, Rockville, Sharpsburg, Smithburg, Urbana, and Williamsport. Also includes Antietam National Battlefield. Population (2010), 728,400.

ZIP Codes: 20837–39, 20841–42, 20850, 20852–55, 20859, 20871–72, 20874–80, 20882, 20884–86, 20898–99, 20906, 21501–05, 21520–24, 21528–30, 21531–32, 21536, 21538–43, 21545, 21550, 21555–57, 21560–62, 21701–05, 21709–11, 21713, 21715–17, 21719–22, 21733–34, 21740–42, 21746–50, 21754–56, 21758, 21766–67, 21769, 21774, 21777, 21779–83, 21790, 21795

* * *

SEVENTH DISTRICT

ELIJAH E. CUMMINGS, Democrat, of Baltimore City, Baltimore County, and Howard County, MD; born in Baltimore, January 18, 1951; education: graduated, Baltimore City College High School, 1969; B.S., political science, Phi Beta Kappa, Howard University, Washington, DC, 1973; J.D., University of Maryland Law School, 1976; professional: attorney; admitted to the Maryland Bar in 1976; Delegate, Maryland State Legislature, 1982–96; chairman, Maryland Legislative Black Caucus, 1984; Speaker Pro Tempore, Maryland General Assembly, 1995–96; vice chairman, Constitutional and Administrative Law Committee; vice chairman, Economic Matters Committee; active in civic affairs, and recipient of numerous community awards; member, U.S. Naval Academy Board of Visitors, Morgan State University Board of Regents, University of Maryland Law School Board of Advisors; religion: member, New Psalmist Baptist Church, Baltimore, MD; married: Dr. Maya Rockeymoore; committees: ranking member, Oversight and Government Reform; Transportation and Infrastructure; elected to the 104th Congress, by special election, in April, 1996; reelected to each succeeding Congress.

Office Listings

http://www.cummings.house.gov https://www.facebook.com/elijahcummings
https://twitter.com/elijahecummings

2230 Rayburn House Office Building, Washington, DC 20515 .... (202) 225–4741
FAX: 225–3178
Chief of Staff.—Vernon Simms.
Legislative Director.—Suzanne Owen.
Legislative Assistants: Aaron Blacksberg, Marc Broady, Todd Phillips.
Communications Director.—Trudy Perkins.
1010 Park Avenue, Suite 105, Baltimore, MD 21201 .... (410) 685–9199
754 Frederick Road, Catonsville, MD 21228 .... (410) 719–8777
8267 Main Street, Room 102, Ellicott City, MD 21043 .... (410) 465–8259

Counties: BALTIMORE (part), HOWARD (part), AND BALTIMORE CITY (part). Population (2010), 660,523.

ZIP Codes: 21036, 21042, 21051, 21111, 21152, 21207, 21216–17, 21228, 21235, 21245, 21250–51, 21287, 21723, 21737–38, 21794, 20777, 20833, 21013, 21029–31, 21043–45, 21047, 21057, 21074–75, 21082, 21087, 21093, 21102, 21104, 21117, 21120, 21131, 21133, 21136, 21155, 21161

* * *

EIGHTH DISTRICT

JAMIE RASKIN, Democrat, of Takoma Park, MD; born in Washington, DC, December 13, 1962; education: B.A., *magna cum laude*, government, Harvard University, Cambridge, MA, 1983; J.D., *magna cum laude*, Harvard Law School, Cambridge, 1987; professional: teaching fellow, Harvard University Government Department, 1985–87; Assistant Attorney General, Commonwealth of Massachusetts, 1987–89; general counsel, National Rainbow Coalition, 1989–90; professor of law, Washington College of Law, American University, 1990–2016; founder, Marshall-Brennan Fellowship Program, American University, 1999–2016; Senator, Maryland State Legislature, 2007–16; religion: member, Temple Sinai; married: Sarah Bloom Raskin; children: Hannah, Tommy, and Tabitha; caucuses: Senior Democratic Whip, House Democratic Caucus; freshman Representative, House Democratic Steering and Policy Committee; Congressional Progressive Caucus; committees: vice ranking member, Judiciary; House Administration; Oversight and Government Reform; Joint Committee on Printing; elected to the 115th Congress on November 8, 2016.

Office Listings

http://www.raskin.house.gov facebook: repraskin twitter: @RepRaskin

431 Cannon House Office Building, Washington, DC 20515 .... (202) 225–5341
Chief of Staff.—Julie Tagen.
Legislative Director.—William Roberts.
Communications Director.—Lauren Doney.
51 Monroe Street, Suite 503, Rockville, MD 20850 .... (301) 424–3501
District Director.—Kathleen Connor.

Counties: CARROLL (part), FREDERICK (part), AND MONTGOMERY (part). Population (2015), 761,778.

ZIP Codes: 20810–11, 20812 (part), 20813–16, 20817 (part), 20818, 20824–25, 20827 (part), 20832–33 (part), 20847–49, 20850 (part), 20851, 20852–55 (part), 20857, 20859–60 (part), 20871–72 (part), 20877–78 (part), 20882 (part), 20889, 20894–96, 20901 (part), 20902, 20903–06 (part), 20907–08, 20910–11, 20912 (part), 20913, 20914 (part), 20915–16, 20918, 20993, 21048 (part), 21104 (part), 21157–58 (part), 21701–04 (part), 21713 (part), 21714, 21718, 21727, 21754–55 (part), 21757 (part), 21759, 21762, 21765 (part), 21769 (part), 21770, 21771 (part), 21773, 21774 (part), 21775–76, 21778, 21780 (part), 21788, 21791 (part), 21793, 21794 (part), 21797 (part), 21798

MASSACHUSETTS

(Population 2010, 6,547,629)

SENATORS

ELIZABETH WARREN, Democrat, of Cambridge, MA; born in Oklahoma City, OK, June 22, 1949; education: B.A., University of Houston, Houston, TX, 1970; J.D., Rutgers Law School, Newark, NJ, 1976; professional: Leo Gottlieb Professor of Law, Harvard Law School, 1995–2012; chief advisor, National Bankruptcy Review Commission, 1995–97; chair, Congressional Oversight Panel, 2008–10; Assistant to the President and Special Advisor to the Secretary of the Treasury for the Consumer Financial Protection Bureau, 2010–11; married: Bruce Mann; two children; three grandchildren; committees: Armed Services; Banking, Housing, and Urban Affairs; Health, Education, Labor, and Pensions; Special Committee on Aging; elected to the U.S. Senate on November 6, 2012.

Office Listings

http://warren.senate.gov facebook.com/senatorelizabethwarren
twitter: @senwarren

317 Hart Senate Office Building, Washington, DC 20510 .... (202) 224–4543
Chief of Staff.—Dan Geldon.
Deputy Chief of Staff.—Bruno Freitas.
Legislative Director.—Jon Donenberg.
2400 JFK Federal Building, 15 New Sudbury Street, Boston, MA 02203 .... (617) 565–3170
State Director.—Nikko Mendoza.
1550 Main Street, Suite 406, Springfield, MA 01103 .... (413) 788–2690

* * *

EDWARD J. MARKEY, Democrat, of Malden, MA; born in Malden, July 11, 1946; education: B.A., Boston College, Boston, MA, 1968; J.D., Boston College, Boston, 1972; U.S. Army Reserve, 1968–73; professional: member, Massachusetts House of Representatives, 1973–76; U.S. House of Representatives, 1976–2013; ranking member, Natural Resources Committee, 2011–13; chair, Select Committee on Energy Independence and Global Warming, 2007–11; chair, Subcommittee on Energy and the Environment, 2009–11; chair, subcommittee on Telecommunications and the Internet, 2007–09; married: Dr. Susan Blumenthal; committees: Commerce, Science, and Transportation; Environment and Public Works; Foreign Relations; Small Business and Entrepreneurship; elected to the U.S. Senate, by special election, on June 25, 2013, to fill the vacancy caused by the resignation of U.S. Senator John F. Kerry to become Secretary of State.

Office Listings

http://www.markey.senate.gov https://www.facebook.com/edjmarkey twitter: @senmarkey

255 Dirksen Senate Office Building, Washington, DC 20510 .... (202) 224–2742
Chief of Staff.—Paul Tencher.
Scheduler.—Sarah Butler.
Communications Director.—Giselle Barry.
JFK Federal Building, 15 New Sudbury Street, Suite 975, Boston, MA 02203 .... (617) 565–8519
222 Milliken Boulevard, Suite 312, Fall River, MA 02721 .... (508) 677–0523
1550 Main Street, 4th Floor, Springfield, MA 01101 .... (413) 785–4610

REPRESENTATIVES

FIRST DISTRICT

RICHARD E. NEAL, Democrat, of Springfield, MA; born in Springfield, February 14, 1949; education: graduated, Springfield Technical High School, 1968; B.A., American International College, Springfield, 1972; M.A., University of Hartford Barney School of Business and Public Administration, West Hartford, CT, 1976; professional: instructor and lecturer; assistant to Mayor of Springfield, 1973–78; Springfield City Council, 1978–84; Mayor, City of Springfield, 1983–89; member: Massachusetts Mayors Association; Adult Education Council; American International College Alumni Association; Boys Club Alumni Association; Emily Bill Athletic Association; Cancer Crusade; John Boyle O'Reilly Club; United States Conference of Mayors;

Valley Press Club; Solid Waste Advisory Committee for the State of Massachusetts; Committee on Leadership and Government; Mass Jobs Council; trustee: Springfield Libraries and Museums Association, Springfield Red Cross, Springfield YMCA; married: Maureen; children: Rory Christopher, Brendan Conway, Maura Katherine, and Sean Richard; committees: Ways and Means; Joint Committee on Taxation; elected on November 8, 1988 to the 101st Congress; reelected to each succeeding Congress.

Office Listings

http://www.neal.house.gov

341 Cannon House Office Building, Washington, DC 20515 .... (202) 225–5601
Administrative Assistant.—Tim Ranstrom. FAX: 225–8112
Executive Assistant.—Tim Ranstrom.
Press Secretary.—William Tranghese.
300 State Street, Suite 200, Springfield, MA 01105 .... (413) 785–0325
District Manager.—William Powers.
78 Center Street, Pittsfield, MA 01201 .... (508) 634–8198
Office Manager.—Cynthia Clark.

Counties: BERKSHIRE, FRANKLIN (part), HAMPDEN (part), HAMPSHIRE (part), and WORCESTER (part). Population (2010), 727,515.

ZIP Codes: 01001, 01008–13, 01020–22, 01026–30, 01032–34, 01036, 01039–40, 01050, 01056–57, 01069–71, 01073, 01075, 01077, 01079–81, 01083–86, 01089, 01092, 01095–98, 01103–09, 01118–19, 01128–29, 01151, 01199, 01201, 01220, 01222–26, 01229–30, 01235–38, 01240, 01242–45, 01247, 01253–60, 01262, 01264, 01266–67, 01270, 01301, 01330, 01337–41, 01343, 01346, 01350, 01367, 01370, 01506–07, 01515, 01518, 01521, 01550, 01566, 01571, 01585

* * *

SECOND DISTRICT

JAMES P. MCGOVERN, Democrat, of Worcester, MA; born in Worcester, November 20, 1959; education: B.A., M.P.A., American University; professional: legislative director and senior aide to Congressman Joe Moakley (D-South Boston); led the 1989 investigation into the murders of six Jesuit priests and two laywomen in El Salvador; interned for and managed Senator George McGovern's (D-SD) 1984 presidential campaign in Massachusetts and delivered his nomination speech at the Democratic National Convention; board of directors, Congressional Hunger Center; married: Lisa Murray McGovern; Democratic co-chair: Tom Lantos Human Rights Commission; caucuses: House Hunger Caucus; committees: Agriculture; Rules; elected to the 105th Congress; reelected to each succeeding Congress.

Office Listings

http://www.mcgovern.house.gov facebook: facebook.com/RepJimMcGovern twitter: @RepMcGovern

438 Cannon House Office Building, Washington, DC 20515 .... (202) 225–6101
Legislative Director.—Cindy Buhl. FAX: 225–5759
Press Secretary.—Abraham White.
12 East Worcester Street, Suite 1, Worcester, MA 01604 .... (508) 831–7356
District Director.—Kathleen Polanowicz.
24 Church Street, Suite 29, Leominster, MA 01543 .... (978) 466–3552
Regional Manager.—Eladia Romero.
94 Pleasant Street, Northampton, MA 01060 .... (413) 341–8700
Regional Manager.—Keith Barnicle.

Counties: FRANKLIN (part), HAMPDEN (part), HAMPSHIRE (part), NORFOLK (part), AND WORCESTER (part). CITIES AND TOWNSHIPS: Amherst, Athol, Auburn, Barre, Belchertown, Bellingham, Blackstone, Boylston, Deerfield, Douglas, Erving, Gill, Grafton, Greenfield, Hadley, Hardwick, Hatfield, Holden, Hubbardston, Leicester, Leominster, Leverett, Mendon, Millbury, Millville, Montague, New Braintree, New Salem, North Brookfield, Northampton, Northborough, Northbridge, Northfield, Oakham, Orange, Oxford, Palmer, Paxton, Pelham, Petersham, Phillipston, Princeton, Royalston, Rutland, Shrewsbury, Shutesbury, Spencer, Sterling, Sunderland, Sutton, Templeton, Upton, Uxbridge, Ware, Warwick, Webster, Wendell, West Boylston, West Brookfield, Westborough, Whately, Winchendon, and Worcester. Population (2010), 727,514.

ZIP Codes: 01002–03, 01005, 01007, 01031, 01035, 01037–39, 01053–54, 01060, 01062–63, 01066, 01068–69, 01072, 01074, 01082, 01088, 01093–94, 01301, 01331, 01342, 01344, 01347, 01349, 01351, 01354–55, 01360, 01364, 01366, 01368, 01370, 01373, 01375–76, 01378–79, 01420, 01436, 01438, 01440, 01452–53, 01468, 01475, 01501, 01504–05, 01516, 01519–20, 01522, 01524–25, 01527, 01529, 01531–32, 01534–37, 01540–43, 01545, 01560, 01562, 01564, 01568–70, 01581, 01583, 01585, 01588, 01590, 01602–12, 01756–57, 02019

* * *

THIRD DISTRICT

NIKI TSONGAS, Democrat, of Lowell, MA; born in Chico, CA, April 26, 1946; education: graduated from Narimasu American High School, Japan, 1964; B.A., Smith College, Northampton, MA, 1968; J.D., Boston University, Boston, MA, 1988; professional: social worker; lawyer; Middlesex Community College's Dean of External Affairs; widowed: Paul Tsongas; children: Ashley Tsongas, Katina Tsongas, and Molly Tsongas; committees: Armed Services; Natural Resources; elected to the 110th Congress, by special election, to fill the vacancy caused by the resignation of U.S. Representative Martin Meehan; elected to the 111th Congress on November 4, 2008; reelected to each succeeding Congress.

Office Listings

http://www.tsongas.house.gov facebook: facebook.com/RepTsongas
twitter: @Nikiinthehouse

1714 Longworth House Office Building, Washington, DC 20515 .... (202) 225–3411
Chief of Staff.—Katie Enos. FAX: 226–0771
Washington Director.—Sara Outterson.
Scheduler.—Bob Schneider.
126 John Street, Suite 12, Lowell, MA 01852 .... (978) 459–0101
District Director.—Ben Martello.

Counties: ESSEX, MIDDLESEX, AND WORCESTER. Population (2010), 732,090.

ZIP Codes: 01432, 01450–51, 01460, 01464, 01503, 01523, 01718–20, 01740–42, 01749, 01754, 01775–76, 01778, 01810, 01821, 01824, 01826–27, 01830, 01840–44, 01850–54, 01862–63, 01876, 01879, 01886

* * *

FOURTH DISTRICT

JOSEPH P. KENNEDY III, Democrat, of Brookline, MA; born in Brighton, MA, October 4, 1980; education: graduated, Buckingham, Browne & Nichols, 1999; B.S., Stanford College, 2003; J.D., Harvard University, 2009; professional: Peace Corps, 2004–06; Assistant District Attorney, Cape and Islands Office, 2009–11; Assistant District Attorney, Middlesex Office, 2011–12; committees: Energy and Commerce; elected to the 113th Congress on November 6, 2012; reelected to each succeeding Congress.

Office Listings

http://kennedy.house.gov

306 Cannon House Office Building, Washington, DC 20515 .... (202) 225–5931
Chief of Staff.—Greg Mecher. FAX: 225–0182
Deputy Chief of Staff/Legislative Director.—Sarah Curtis.
Scheduler.—Mariah Philips.
8 North Main Street, Suite 200, Attleboro, MA 02703 .... (508) 431–1110
29 Crafts Street, Suite 375, Newton, MA 02458 .... (617) 332–3333
District Director.—Nick Clemons.
Communications Director.—Emily Kaufman.

Counties: BRISTOL (part), MIDDLESEX (part), NORFOLK (part), PLYMOUTH (part), AND WORCESTER (part). CITIES AND TOWNSHIPS: Attleboro, Bellingham, Berkley, Brookline, Dighton, Dover, Easton, Fall River, Foxboro, Franklin, Freetown, Hopedale, Hopkinton, Lakeville, Mansfield, Medfield, Medway, Milford, Millis, Needham, Newton, Norfolk, North Attleborough, Norton, Plainville, Raynham, Rehoboth, Seekonk, Sharon, Somerset, Swansea, Taunton, Wellesley, and Wrentham. Population (2010), 727,514.

ZIP Codes: 01747–48, 01757, 02019, 02030–31, 02035, 02038, 02048, 02052–54, 02056, 02067, 02070, 02093, 02171, 02334, 02347–48, 02356–57, 02375, 02445–47, 02456–62, 02464–68, 02481–82, 02492, 02494–95, 02702–03, 02712, 02715, 02718, 02725–26, 02760–63, 02766–69, 02771, 02777, 02779–80

* * *

FIFTH DISTRICT

KATHERINE M. CLARK, Democrat, of Melrose, MA; born in New Haven, CT, July 17, 1963; education: B.A., Saint Lawrence University, 1985; J.D., Cornell School of Law, 1989; M.P.A., Harvard University, 1997; professional: admitted to the Massachusetts Bar, 1997;

served as general counsel for the Massachusetts Office of Child Care Services; Chief of the Policy Division for the Massachusetts Attorney General and prosecutor; elected in March 2008 to the Massachusetts House of Representatives; elected to the Massachusetts State Senate in November 2010; religion: Protestant; married: Rodney Dowell; children: Addison, Jared, and Nathaniel; Democratic Steering and Policy Committee; committees: Appropriations; elected to the 113th Congress, by special election, on December 10, 2013; reelected to each succeeding Congress.

Office Listings

http://www.katherineclark.house.gov facebook: @CongresswomanClark twitter: @RepKClark

1415 Longworth House Office Building, Washington, DC 20515 .... (202) 225–2836
Chief of Staff.—Brooke Scannell. FAX: 226–0092
Deputy Chief of Staff / Legislative Director.—David Bond.
District Director.—Christian Lobue.
701 Concord Avenue, Suite 101, Cambridge, MA 02138 .... (617) 354–0292
116 Concord Street, Suite 1, Framingham, MA 01702 .... (508) 319–9757

Counties: Middlesex (part), Suffolk (part), and Worcester (part). Cities and Townships: Arlington, Ashland, Belmont, Cambridge, Framingham, Holliston, Lexington, Lincoln, Malden, Medford, Melrose, Natick, Revere, Sherborn, Southborough, Stoneham, Sudbury, Waltham, Watertown, Wayland, Weston, Winchester, Winthrop, and Woburn. Population (2010), 727,515.

ZIP Codes: 01701–05, 01721, 01746, 01760, 01770, 01772–73, 01776, 01778, 01890, 02138–42, 02148, 02151–53, 02155, 02176, 02180, 02238, 02420–21, 02451–54, 02471–72, 02474, 02476–78, 02493

* * *

SIXTH DISTRICT

SETH MOULTON, Democrat, of Salem, MA; born in Salem, October 24, 1978; education: Phillips Academy Andover, 1997; A.B., Harvard College, 2001; M.B.A., Harvard Business School, 2011; M.P.A., Harvard Kennedy School of Government, 2011; professional: U.S. Marine Corps, 2002–08; business manager; committees: Armed Services; Budget; elected to the 114th Congress on November 4, 2014, elected to the 115th Congress on November 8, 2016.

Office Listings

http://moulton.house.gov facebook: RepMoulton twitter: @sethmoulton, @teammoulton

1408 Longworth House Office Building, Washington, DC 20515 .... (202) 225–8020
Chief of Staff.—Jeremy Joseph.
Deputy Chief of Staff.—Andy Flick.
Legislative Assistants: Peter Billerbeck, Eric Kanter.
Legislative Aide.—Margo Brown.
Staff Assistant.—Christine Raymond.
Scheduler.—Anna Stolitzka.
21 Front Street, Salem, MA 01970 .... (978) 531–1669
District Director.—Rick Jakious.
Communications Director.—Carrie Rankin.
Economic Development Director.—Jason Denoncourt.
Constituent Services Director.—Dylan O'Sullivan.
District Representatives: Morgan Bell, Dennis Magnasco, Lucas Santos.
District Aide and Caseworker.—Brendan Burke.
Caseworker.—Marven Hyppolite.

Counties: Essex and Middlesex. Cities and Townships: Amesbury, Andover, Bedford, Beverly, Billerica, Boxford, Burlington, Danvers, Essex, Georgetown, Gloucester, Groveland, Hamilton, Ipswich, Lynn, Lynnfield, Manchester-by-the-Sea, Marblehead, Merrimac, Middletown, Nahant, Newbury, Newburyport, North Andover, North Reading, Peabody, Reading, Rockport, Rowley, Salem, Salisbury, Saugus, Swampscott, Tewksbury, Topsfield, Wenham, West Newbury, Wakefield, and Wilmington. Population (2010), 731,681.

ZIP Codes: 01730–31, 01801, 01803, 01805, 01810, 01821–22, 01833–34, 01845, 01860, 01864, 01867, 01876, 01880, 01885, 01887, 01889, 01901–08, 01910, 01913, 01915, 01921–23, 01929–31, 01936–38, 01940, 01944–45, 01949–52, 01960–61, 01965–66, 01969–71, 01982–85

* * *

SEVENTH DISTRICT

MICHAEL E. CAPUANO, Democrat, of Somerville, MA; born in Somerville, January 9, 1952; education: graduated, Somerville High School, 1969; B.A., Dartmouth College, 1973;

J.D., Boston College Law School, 1977; professional: admitted to the Massachusetts Bar, 1977; Alderman in Somerville, MA, 1977–79; Alderman-at-Large, 1985–89; elected Mayor for five terms, 1990 to January, 1999, when he resigned to be sworn in as U.S. Representative; married: Barbara Teebagy of Somerville, MA, in 1974; children: Michael and Joseph; caucuses: Democratic Caucus; committees: Financial Services; Transportation and Infrastructure; elected to the 106th Congress; reelected to each succeeding Congress.

Office Listings

http://www.capuano.house.gov

1414 Longworth House Office Building, Washington, DC 20515 .... (202) 225–5111
Chief of Staff.—Robert Primus. FAX: 225–9322
Office Manager/Scheduler.—Mary Doherty.
Legislative Counsel.—Gira Bose.
110 First Street, Cambridge, MA 02141 .... (617) 621–6208
District Director.—Jon Lenicheck.

Counties: Middlesex (part), Norfolk (part), and Suffolk (part). Cities and townships: Boston (part), Cambridge (part), Chelsea, Everett, Milton (part), Randolph, and Somerville. Population (2010), 727,514.

ZIP Codes: 02111, 02115–26, 02128–32, 02134–36, 02138–45, 02149–50, 02163, 02186, 02199, 02368

* * *

EIGHTH DISTRICT

STEPHEN F. LYNCH, Democrat, of South Boston, MA; born in South Boston, March 31, 1955; education: South Boston High School, 1973; B.S., Wentworth Institute of Technology; J.D., Boston College Law School; master in public administration, JFK School of Government, Harvard University; professional: attorney; former president of Ironworkers Local #7; organizations: South Boston Boys and Girls Club; Colonel Daniel Marr Boys and Girls Club; public service: elected to the Massachusetts House of Representatives in 1994, and the State Senate in 1996; family: married to Margaret; one child: Victoria; committees: Financial Services; Oversight and Government Reform; elected to the 107th Congress, by special election, on October 16, 2001; reelected to each succeeding Congress.

Office Listings

http://lynch.house.gov

2268 Rayburn House Office Building, Washington, DC 20515 .... (202) 225–8273
Chief of Staff.—Kevin Ryan. FAX: 226–6513
Legislative Director.—Bruce Fernandez.
Scheduler.—Megan Hollingshead.
1 Harbor Place, Suite 304, Boston, MA 02210 .... (617) 428–2000
37 Belmont Street, Suite 3, Brockton, MA 02301 .... (508) 586–5555
1245 Hancock Street, Suite 41, Quincy, MA 02169 .... (617) 657–6305

Counties: Bristol (part), Norfolk (part), Plymouth (part), and Suffolk (part). Population (2010), 732,884.

ZIP Codes: 02021, 02025–26, 02032, 02043, 02045, 02047, 02050, 02062, 02066, 02071–72, 02081, 02090, 02108–10, 02113–14, 02118, 02122, 02124–25, 02127, 02130–32, 02136, 02169–71, 02184, 02186, 02188–91, 02203, 02210, 02301–02, 02322, 02324, 02333, 02343, 02351, 02368, 02379, 02382, 02467, 02767

* * *

NINTH DISTRICT

WILLIAM "BILL" KEATING, Democrat, of Bourne, MA; born in Norwood, MA, September 6, 1952; education: B.A., Boston College, MA, 1974; M.B.A., Boston College, 1982; J.D., Suffolk University Law School, MA, 1985; professional: admitted to the Massachusetts Bar in 1985 and began practice in Stoughton, MA; Massachusetts House of Representatives, 1977–84; vice chairman, Massachusetts State House Committee on Criminal Justice; Massachusetts State House Committee on Election Laws; Massachusetts State Senate, 1985–98; chairman, Joint Committee on the Judiciary; State Senate Committee on Taxation; Joint Committee on Public Safety; State Senate Steering and Policy Committee; Norfolk County District Attorney, 1999–2011; religion: Roman Catholic; family: wife, Tevis; two children, Kristen and Patrick; committees: Foreign Affairs; Homeland Security; elected to the 112th Congress on November 2, 2010; reelected to each succeeding Congress.

Office Listings

http://www.keating.house.gov

2351 Rayburn House Office Building, Washington, DC 20515	(202) 225–3111
Chief of Staff.—Garrett Donovan.	FAX: 225–5658
District Director.—Michael Jackman.	
170 Court Street, Plymouth, MA 02360	(508) 746–9000
297 Stevens Street, Suite E, Hyannis, MA 02601	(508) 771–6868
128 Union Street, Suite 103, New Bedford, MA 02740	(508) 999–6462

Counties: BARNSTABLE, BRISTOL (part), DUKES, NANTUCKET, AND PLYMOUTH. Population (2010), 727,514.

ZIP Codes: 02050, 02061, 02330, 02332, 02338–39, 02341, 02344–46, 02349, 02359–60, 02364, 02367, 02370, 02532, 02534–40, 02542–43, 02553–54, 02556–59, 02561–63, 02568, 02571, 02574–76, 02601, 02631, 02633, 02635–39, 02641–53, 02655, 02657, 02659–64, 02666–73, 02675, 02713–14, 02719–24, 02738–48, 02770, 02790

MICHIGAN

(Population 2010, 9,883,640)

SENATORS

DEBBIE STABENOW, Democrat, of Lansing, MI; born in Gladwin, MI, April 29, 1950; education: Clare High School; B.A., Michigan State University, 1972; M.SW., Michigan State University, 1975; public service: Ingham County, MI, Commissioner, 1975–78, chairperson for two years; Michigan State House of Representatives, 1979–90; Michigan State Senate, 1991–94; religion: Methodist; children: Todd and Michelle; committees: ranking member, Agriculture, Nutrition, and Forestry; Budget; Energy and Natural Resources; Finance; Joint Committee on Taxation; elected to the U.S. House of Representatives in 1996 and 1998; elected to the U.S. Senate on November 7, 2000; reelected to each succeeding Senate term.

Office Listings

http://stabenow.senate.gov twitter: @SenStabenow

731 Hart Senate Office Building, Washington, DC 20510 .... (202) 224–4822
Chief of Staff.—Matt VanKuiken. FAX: 228–0325
Legislative Director.—Emily Carwell.
Scheduler.—Anne Stanski.
221 West Lake Lansing Road, Suite 100, East Lansing, MI 48823 .... (517) 203–1760
719 Griswold Street, Suite 700, Detroit, MI 48226 .... (313) 961–4330
432 North Saginaw, Suite 301, Flint, MI 48502 .... (810) 720–4172
3335 South Airport Road West, Suite 6B, Traverse City, MI 49684 .... (231) 929–1031
3280 Beltline Court, Suite 400, Grand Rapids, MI 49525 .... (616) 975–0052
1901 West Ridge, Suite 7, Marquette, MI 49855 .... (906) 228–8756

* * *

GARY C. PETERS, Democrat, of Bloomfield Township, MI; born in Pontiac, MI, December 1, 1958; education: B.A., Alma College, Alma, MI, 1980; M.B.A. in finance, University of Detroit, Detroit, MI, 1984; J.D., Wayne State University Law School, Detroit, 1989; M.A. in philosophy, Michigan State University, East Lansing, MI, 2007; professional: assistant vice president, Merrill Lynch, 1980–89; vice president, UBS/Paine Webber, 1989–2003; former arbitrator, Financial Industry Regulatory Authority; At-Large City Councilman, Rochester Hills, MI, 1991–93; Lieutenant Commander, Seabee Combat Warfare Specialist, U.S. Navy Reserve, 1993–2000, 2001–05; Michigan State Senator, 1995–2002; Chief Administrative Officer for the Bureau of Investments, State of Michigan, 2003; Lottery Commissioner, State of Michigan, 2003–07; former instructor, Oakland University and Wayne State University; Griffin Endowed Chair in American Government, Central Michigan University, 2007–08; member, Michigan Bar Association; religion: Episcopalian; married: Colleen Ochoa Peters; three children: Gary, Jr., Madeleine, and Alana; committees: Armed Services; Commerce, Science, and Transportation; Homeland Security and Governmental Affairs; Joint Economic Committee; elected to the U.S. House of Representatives in 2008, 2010, and 2012; elected to the U.S. Senate on November 4, 2014.

Office Listings

http://www.peters.senate.gov https://www.facebook.com/senatorgarypeters
twitter: @sengarypeters instagram: @sengarypeters

724 Hart Senate Office Building, Washington, DC 20510 .... (202) 224–6221
Chief of Staff.—Eric Feldman. FAX: 224–7387
Legislative Director.—David Weinberg.
Communications Director.—Amber Moon.
Patrick V. McNamara Federal Building, 477 Michigan Avenue, Suite 1837, Detroit, MI 48226 .... (313) 226–6020
State Director.—Elise Lancaster.
124 West Allegan Street, Suite 1810, Lansing, MI 48933 .... (517) 377–1508
Gerald R. Ford Federal Building, 110 Michigan Street, NW., Suite 720, Grand Rapids, MI 49503 .... (616) 233–9150
407 6th Street, Suite C, Rochester, MI 48307 .... (248) 608–8040
515 North Washington Avenue, Suite 401, Saginaw, MI 48607 .... (989) 754–0112
818 Red Drive, Suite 40, Traverse City, MI 49684 .... (231) 947–7773
857 West Washington Street, Suite 308, Marquette, MI 49855 .... (906) 226–4554

REPRESENTATIVES

FIRST DISTRICT

JACK BERGMAN, Republican, of Watersmeet, MI; born in Savage, MN, on February 2, 1947; education: B.A., Gustavus Adolphus College, 1969; M.B.A., University of West Florida; military education: Naval Aviation Flight Training; Marine Corps Command and Staff College; Combined Forces Air Component Command; professional: commercial pilot for 22 years; Lieutenant General, USMC (Ret); former Commander of Marine Forces Reserve/Marine Forces North; awards: Air Medal; Defense Meritorious Service Medal; Joint Meritorious Service Medal; Navy Distinguished Service Medal; and numerous unit awards; religion: Lutheran; family: wife, Cindy; five children; eight grandchildren; caucuses: Freshman Caucus; Great Lakes Taskforce; Native American Caucus; Pro Life Caucus; Republican Study Committee; Sportsman's Caucus; Working Forests Caucus; committees: Budget; Natural Resources; Veterans' Affairs; elected to the 115th Congress on November 8, 2016.

Office Listings

http://www.bergman.house.gov

414 Cannon House Office Building, Washington, DC 20515 .... (202) 225–4735
Chief of Staff.—Tony Lis. FAX: 225–4710
Deputy Chief of Staff / Legislative Director.—Michelle Jelnicky.
Scheduler / Director of Operations.—Amelia Burns.
1396 Douglas Drive, Suite 22B, Traverse City, MI 49696 .... (231) 944–7633
Director of Michigan Operations.—Melanie Collinsworth.
Communications Director.—James Hogge.
1500 West Washington Street, Suite 2, Marquette, MI 49855 .... (906) 273–2227

Counties: ALCONA, ALGER, ALPENA, ANTRIM, BARAGA, BENZIE, CHARLEVOIX, CHEBOYGAN, CHIPPEWA, CRAWFORD, DELTA, DICKINSON, EMMET, GRAND TRAVERSE, HOUGHTON, IRON, KALKASKA, KEWEENAW, LEELANAU, LUCE, MACKINAC, MANISTEE, MARQUETTE, MASON (part), MENOMINEE, MONTMORENCY, ONTONAGON, OSCODA, OTSEGO, PRESQUE ISLE, AND SCHOOLCRAFT. Population (2010), 650,222.

ZIP Codes: 48621, 48636, 48705, 48721, 48740, 48742, 49402, 49405, 49410–11, 49431, 49610–11, 49614–15, 49617, 49619, 49621–22, 49626–29, 49634–37, 49645–46, 49648, 49650, 49653–54, 49660, 49664, 49666, 49670, 49673–75, 49680, 49682, 49685–86, 49696, 49705, 49709–11, 49715, 49717, 49719, 49722–26, 49728, 49734–37, 49739–40, 49743–45, 49748–49, 49752–53, 49757, 49759–62, 49764, 49766, 49768, 49775, 49779, 49781–86, 49788, 49791–93, 49796–97, 49799, 49802, 49805–06, 49808, 49812, 49814–16, 49819–21, 49826–27, 49829, 49833–35, 49837–41, 49845, 49847–49, 49852, 49858, 49862–66, 49868, 49870–72, 49874, 49876–77, 49881, 49886–87, 49891, 49893–94, 49896, 49901–03, 49905, 49908, 49910–12, 49915–19, 49921–22, 49925, 49927, 49929–31, 49934–35, 49938, 49942, 49946, 49948, 49950, 49952–53, 49955, 49959–64, 49968–71

* * *

SECOND DISTRICT

BILL HUIZENGA, Republican, of Zeeland, MI; born in Zeeland, January 31, 1969; education: graduated, Holland Christian High School; B.A., Calvin College, Grand Rapids, MI, 1987; professional: co-owner, Huizenga Gravel Company, Jenison, MI; formerly licensed realtor and developer; married: the former Natalie Tiesma; children: Garrett, Adrian, Alexandra, William, and Sieger; committees: Financial Services; elected to the 112th Congress on November 2, 2010; reelected to each succeeding Congress.

Office Listings

http://huizenga.house.gov facebook: https://www.facebook.com/rephuizenga
twitter: https://twitter.com/RepHuizenga

2232 Rayburn House Office Building, Washington, DC 20515 .... (202) 225–4401
Chief of Staff.—Jon DeWitte. FAX: 226–0779
Deputy Chief of Staff.—Marliss McManus.
Communications Director.—Brian Patrick.
Scheduler.—Sarah Lisman.
District Director of Policy.—Greg Van Woerkom.
4555 Wilson Avenue Southwest, Suite 3, Grandville, MI 49418 .... (616) 570–0917
1 South Harbor Avenue, Suite 6B, Grand Haven, MI 49417 .... (616) 414–5516

Counties: ALLEGAN (part), KENT (part), LAKE, MASON, MUSKEGON, NEWAYGO, OCEANA, OTTAWA. Population (2010), 705,975.

ZIP Codes: 49303–04, 49307, 49309, 49312, 49315–16, 49318, 49321, 49323, 49327, 49329–30, 49337–38, 49343, 49345, 49349, 49401–05, 49409–10, 49412–13, 49415, 49417–18, 49420–31, 49434–37, 49440–46, 49448–49, 49451–52, 49454–

61, 49463–64, 49504, 49508–09, 49512, 49519, 49534, 49544, 49546, 49548, 49601, 49623, 49642, 49644, 49655–56, 49677, 49688

* * *

THIRD DISTRICT

JUSTIN A. AMASH, Republican, of Cascade, MI; born in Grand Rapids, MI, April 18, 1980; education: attended Kelloggsville Christian School and Grand Rapids Christian High School; B.A., economics, *magna cum laude*, University of Michigan, Ann Arbor, MI, 2002; J.D., University of Michigan Law School, Ann Arbor, MI, 2005; professional: small business owner; attorney; member: State Bar of Michigan, Grand Rapids Bar Association; State Representative, Michigan's 72nd District, 2009–10; religion: member, St. Nicholas Antiochian Orthodox Christian Church; married: Kara; three children; committees: Oversight and Government Reform; elected to the 112th Congress on November 2, 2010; reelected to each succeeding Congress.

Office Listings

http://amash.house.gov twitter.com/amashoffice

114 Cannon House Office Building, Washington, DC 20515 .... (202) 225–3831
Chief of Staff.—Poppy Nelson. FAX: 225–5144
Legislative Director.—Carolyn Iodice.
Scheduler.—Jelena Matic.
110 Michigan Street, NW., Suite 460, Grand Rapids, MI 49503 .... (616) 451–8383
District Director.—Katherine Condon.
70 West Michigan Avenue, Suite 212, Battle Creek, MI 49017 .... (269) 205–3823

Counties: BARRY, CALHOUN, IONIA, KENT (part), MONTCALM (part). CITIES: Albion, Battle Creek, Belding, Cedar Springs, East Grand Rapids, Grand Rapids, Hastings, Ionia, Lowell, Marshall, Portland, Rockford, and Springfield. Population (2010), 707,973.

ZIP Codes: 48809, 48813, 48815, 48834, 48838, 48845–46, 48849, 48851, 48860–61, 48865, 48873, 48875, 48881, 48890, 48894, 48897, 49011–12, 49014–15, 49017, 49021, 49029, 49033–34, 49037, 49046, 49050–52, 49058, 49060, 49068, 49073, 49076, 49080, 49083, 49092, 49094, 49224, 49237, 49245, 49252, 49284, 49301–03, 49306, 49315–16, 49318–19, 49321, 49323, 49325–27, 49330–31, 49333, 49341, 49343–45, 49347–48, 49403, 49418, 49435, 49501, 49503–09, 49512, 49525, 49534, 49544, 49546, 49548, 49560

* * *

FOURTH DISTRICT

JOHN MOOLENAAR, Republican, of Midland, MI; born in Midland, May 8, 1961; education: graduated from Herbert Henry Dow High School, Midland; B.S., Hope College, Holland, MI, 1983; M.P.A., Harvard University, Cambridge, MA, 1989; professional: chemist; businessman; school administrator; member of the Midland, MI, City Council, 1997–2000; member of the Michigan House of Representatives, 2003–08; member of the Michigan State Senate, 2011–14; committees: Appropriations; elected to the 114th Congress on November 4, 2014; reelected to the 115th Congress on November 8, 2016.

Office Listings

http://www.moolenaar.house.gov facebook: facebook.com/repmoolenaar twitter: @repmoolenaar

117 Cannon House Office Building, Washington, DC 20515 .... (202) 225–3561
Chief of Staff.—Ryan Tarrant. FAX: 225–9679
Deputy Chief of Staff / Legislative Director.—Mike Telliga.
Communications Director.—David Russell.
Executive Assistant.—Eva Vrana.
200 East Main Street, Suite 230, Midland, MI 48640 .... (989) 631–2552
District Director.—Ashton Bortz.
201 North Mitchell Street, Suite 301, Cadillac, MI 49601 .... (231) 942–5070

Counties: CLARE COUNTY. CITIES: Clare, Farwell, Harrison, Lake, and Lake George. CLINTON COUNTY. CITIES: Dewitt, East Lansing (part), Grand Ledge (part), and St. Johns. GLADWIN COUNTY. CITIES: Beaverton and Gladwin. GRATIOT COUNTY. CITIES: Alma, Ashley, Bannister, Breckenridge, Elm Hall, Elwell, Ithaca, Middleton, North Star, Perrinton, Pompeii, Riverdale, Sumner, St. Louis, and Wheeler. ISABELLA COUNTY. CITIES: Blanchard, Millbrook, Mt. Pleasant, Rosebush, Shepherd, Weidman, and Winn. MECOSTA COUNTY. CITIES: Barryton, Big Rapids, Canadian Lakes, Chippewa Lakes, Mecosta, Morley, Paris, Remus, and Stanwood. MIDLAND COUNTY. CITIES: Coleman, Edenville, Hope, Laporte, Midland, North Bradley, Poseyville, and Sanford. MISSAUKEE COUNTY. CITIES: Falmouth, Lake City, McBain, Merritt, and Moorestown. MONTCALM COUNTY. CITIES: Alger, Butternut, Carson City, Cedar Lake, Coral, Crystal, Edmore, Entrican, Fenwick, Gowen, Greenville, Howard City, Lakeview, Langston, Maple Hill, McBride, Pierson, Sand Lake,

Sheridan, Sidney, Six Lakes, Stanton, Trufant, Vestaburg, and Vickeryville. OGEMAW COUNTY. CITIES: Rose City and West Branch. OSCEOLA COUNTY. CITIES: Evart, Hersey, LeRoy, Marion, Reed City, Sears, and Tustin. ROSCOMMON COUNTY. CITIES: Higgins Lake, Houghton Lake, Houghton Lake Heights, Prudenville, Roscommon, and St. Helen. SAGINAW COUNTY (part). CITIES: Birch Run, Brant, Burt, Carrollton, Chesaning, Frankenmuth, Freeland, Fremont, Hemlock, Merrill, Oakley, St. Charles, and University Center. SHIAWASSEE COUNTY. CITIES: Bancroft, Caledonia, Chapin, Corunna, Durand, Henderson, Laingsburg, Morrice, New Haven, New Lothrup, Owosso, Perry, Shaftsburg, Venice, and Vernon. WEXFORD COUNTY. CITIES: Cadillac and Manton. Population (2010), 705,974.

ZIP Codes: 48048, 48050, 48264, 48414–15, 48417–18, 48429, 48449, 48460, 48476, 48601, 48609–10, 48612, 48614–18, 48620, 48622–23, 48625–30, 48632–33, 48637, 48642, 48648–49, 48651, 48653–57, 48661–63, 48670, 48674, 48686, 48710, 48722, 48724, 48734, 48756, 48801, 48804, 48806–07, 48811–12, 48817–18, 48820, 48822, 48829–32, 48834–35, 48838, 48841, 48847–48, 48850, 48852, 48856–59, 48862, 48866–67, 48871–72, 48874, 48877–80, 48882–86, 48888–89, 48891, 48893–94, 48896, 49083, 49305, 49307, 49310, 49316, 49320, 49322, 49326, 49329, 49332, 49334, 49336, 49338–40, 49343, 49346–47, 49412–13, 49601, 49620, 49631–32, 49638–40, 49651, 49653, 49655, 49657, 49665, 49667–68, 49677, 49679, 49688, 49886

* * *

FIFTH DISTRICT

DANIEL T. KILDEE, Democrat, of Flint Township, MI; born in Flint, August 11, 1958; education: graduated, Northern High School, 1976; B.S., administration, Central Michigan University, 2011; married: Jennifer, 1988; children: Ryan, Kenneth, and Katy; two grandchildren, Caitlin and Colin; Senior Whip; Democratic Steering and Policy Committee; committees: vice ranking member, Financial Services; elected to the 113th Congress, November 6, 2012; reelected to each succeeding Congress.

Office Listings

http://www.dankildee.house.gov

227 Cannon House Office Building, Washington, DC 20515 .... (202) 225–3611
Chief of Staff.—Jennifer Cox. FAX: 225–6393
Legislative Director.—Alison Share.
Deputy Chief of Staff / Communications Director.—Mitchell Rivard.
Scheduler / Executive Assistant.—Tina Reyes.
111 East Court Street, #3B, Flint, MI 48502 .... (810) 238–8627
District Chief of Staff.—Andy Leavitt. FAX: 238–8658

Counties: ARENAC, BAY, GENESEE, IOSCO, SAGINAW (part), AND TUSCOLA (part). Population (2010), 705,975.

ZIP Codes: 48411, 48415, 48418, 48420–21, 48423, 48429–30, 48433, 48436–39, 48442, 48449, 48451, 48457–58, 48462–64, 48473, 48480, 48501–07, 48509, 48519, 48529, 48531–32, 48550–57, 48601–08, 48610–11, 48613, 48623, 48631, 48634, 48638, 48642, 48650, 48652, 48658–59, 48663, 48703, 48706–08, 48710, 48722, 48724, 48730, 48732–34, 48737–39, 48743, 48745–50

* * *

SIXTH DISTRICT

FRED UPTON, Republican, of St. Joseph, MI; born in St. Joseph, April 23, 1953; education: graduated, Shattuck School, Fairbault, MN, 1971; B.A., journalism, University of Michigan, Ann Arbor, 1975; professional: field manager, Dave Stockman Campaign, 1976; staff member, Congressman Dave Stockman, 1976–80; legislative assistant, Office of Management and Budget, 1981–83; deputy director of Legislative Affairs, 1983–84; director of Legislative Affairs, 1984–85; member: First Congregational Church, Emil Verbin Society; married: the former Amey Rulon-Miller; committees: Energy and Commerce; elected to the 100th Congress on November 4, 1986; reelected to each succeeding Congress.

Office Listings

http://www.upton.house.gov

2183 Rayburn House Office Building, Washington, DC 20515 .... (202) 225–3761
Chief of Staff.—Joan Hillebrands. FAX: 225–4986
Senior Advisor / Executive Assistant.—Bits Thomas.
720 Main Street, St. Joseph, MI 49085 .... (269) 982–1986
350 E. Michigan Avenue, Suite 130, Kalamazoo, MI 49007 .... (269) 385–0039

Counties: ALLEGAN (part), BERRIEN, CASS, KALAMAZOO, ST. JOSEPH, VAN BUREN. CITIES AND TOWNSHIPS: Allegan, Augusta, Bangor, Baroda, Benton Harbor, Berrien Springs, Berrien Center, Bloomingdale, Breedsville, Bridgman,

Buchanan, Burr Oak, Cassopolis, Centreville, Climax, Coloma, Colon, Comstock, Constantine, Covert, Decatur, Delton, Douglas, Dowagiac, Eau Claire, Edwardsburg, Fulton, Galesburg, Galien, Gobles, Grand Junction, Hagar Shores, Harbert, Hartford, Hickory Corners, Holland, Jones, Kalamazoo, Lakeside, Lawrence, Lawton, Leonidas, Marcellus, Mattawan, Mendon, Nazareth, New Troy, New Buffalo, Niles, Nottawa, Oshtemo, Otsego, Paw Paw, Plainwell, Portage, Pullman, Richland, Riverside, Saugatuck, Sawyer, Schoolcraft, Scotts, Sodus, South Haven, St. Joseph, Stevensville, Sturgis, Three Oaks, Three Rivers, Union Pier, Union, Vandalia, Vicksburg, Watervliet, and White Pigeon. Population (2010), 705,974.

ZIP Codes: 49001–13, 49015, 49019, 49022–24, 49026–27, 49030–32, 49034, 49038–43, 49045, 49047–48, 49052–53, 49055–57, 49060–67, 49070–72, 49074–75, 49077–81, 49083–85, 49087–88, 49090–91, 49093, 49095, 49097–99, 49101–04, 49106–07, 49111–13, 49115–17, 49119–20, 49125–30, 49311, 49314–16, 49323, 49328, 49333, 49335, 49344, 49348, 49406, 49408, 49416, 49419, 49423, 49426, 49450, 49453, 49464

* * *

SEVENTH DISTRICT

TIMOTHY L. WALBERG, Republican, of Tipton, MI; born in Chicago, IL, April 12, 1951; education: studied forestry at Western Illinois University, Macomb, IL; graduated from Moody Bible Institute, Chicago, IL; B.A., religious education, Fort Wayne Bible College, 1975; M.A., communications, Wheaton College Graduate School, Wheaton, IL, 1978; professional: minister, New Haven Baptist Church, 1973–77; minister, Union Gospel Church, 1978–82; member of the Michigan House of Representatives, 1983–98; president, Warren Reuther Center for Education and Community Impact; division manager, Moody Bible Institute; married: Susan; three adult children; committees: Education and the Workforce; Energy and Commerce; elected to the U.S. House of Representatives for the 110th Congress, 2007–09; elected to the 112th Congress on November 2, 2010; reelected to each succeeding Congress.

Office Listings

http://www.walberg.house.gov

2436 Rayburn House Office Building, Washington, DC 20515 .... (202) 225–6276
Chief of Staff.—R.J. Laukitis. FAX: 225–6281
Legislative Director.—Jonathan Hirte.
Communications Director.—Dan Kotman.
110 1st Street, Suite 2, Jackson, MI 49201 .... (517) 780–9075

Counties: BRANCH, EATON, HILLSDALE, JACKSON, LENAWEE, MONROE, AND WASHTENAW (part). Population (2010), 705,974.

ZIP Codes: 48103, 48105, 48108, 48111, 48117–18, 48130–31, 48133–34, 48137, 48140, 48144–45, 48157–62, 48164, 48166–70, 48176–79, 48182, 48189–91, 48197, 48813, 48821, 48827, 48837, 48849, 48861, 48876, 48890, 48897, 48906, 48911, 48917, 49011, 49021, 49028, 49030, 49036, 49040, 49073, 49076, 49082, 49089, 49092, 49094, 49096, 49201–03, 49220–21, 49224, 49227–30, 49232–38, 49240–42, 49245–56, 49259, 49261–72, 49274, 49276–77, 49279, 49282–89

* * *

EIGHTH DISTRICT

MIKE BISHOP, Republican, of Rochester, MI; born in Almont, MI, March 18, 1967; education: bachelor of arts, University of Michigan, Ann Arbor, MI, 1989; juris doctor, Michigan State University, East Lansing, MI, 1993; professional: private practice attorney; State Representative, 1999–2002; State Senator, 2003–10; State Senate Majority Leader, 2007–10; chief legal officer at International Bancard Corporation; religion: Protestant; family: wife, Cristina; children: ages 15, 13, 9; House Republican Steering Committee; committees: Ways and Means; elected to the 114th Congress on November 4, 2014; reelected to the 115th Congress on November 8, 2016.

Office Listings

http://www.mikebishop.house.gov

428 Cannon House Office Building, Washington, DC 20515 .... (202) 225–4872
Chief of Staff.—Allan Filip. FAX: 225–5820
Legislative Director.—Dan Harder.
Policy / Advisor Communications Director.—Kelli Ford.
Executive Assistant / Scheduler.—Susan Larson.
711 East Grand River Avenue, Suite A, Brighton, MI 48116 .... (810) 227–8600

Counties: INGHAM, LIVINGSTON, AND OAKLAND (part). CITIES AND TOWNSHIPS: Addison Township, Brandon Township, Brighton, Cohoctah, Dansville, East Lansing, Fenton, Fowlerville, Gregory, Groveland Township, Hamburg, Hartland,

Haslett, Hell, Holly Township, Holt, Howell, Independence Township, Lakeland, Lansing, Leslie, Mason, Meridian Township, Oak Grove, Oakland Township, Okemos, Onondaga, Orion Township, Oxford Township, Pinckney, Rochester, Rochester Hills (part), Rose Township, Springfield Township, Stockbridge, Unadilla, Village of Clarkston, Webberville, and Williamston. Population (2010), 705,974.

ZIP Codes: 48114, 48116, 48139, 48143, 48306–07, 48309, 48346, 48350, 48359–60, 48362–63, 48366–67, 48370–71, 48430, 48442, 48462, 48805, 48816, 48819, 48824–26, 48842–44, 48854–55, 48864, 48895, 48901, 48909–10, 48912–13, 48915–16, 48918–19, 48921–22, 48924, 48929–30, 48933, 48937, 48951, 48956, 48980, 49251

* * *

NINTH DISTRICT

SANDER M. LEVIN, Democrat, of Royal Oak, MI; born in Detroit, MI, September 6, 1931; education: graduated, Central High School, Detroit, 1949; B.A., University of Chicago, 1952; M.A., Columbia University, New York, NY, 1954; LL.B., Harvard University, Cambridge, MA, 1957; professional: attorney; admitted to the Michigan Bar in 1958 and commenced practice in Detroit, MI; member: Oakland Board of Supervisors, 1961–64; Michigan Senate, 1965–70; Democratic Floor Leader in State Senate; served on the Advisory Committee on the Education of Handicapped Children in the Department of Health, Education, and Welfare, 1965–68; chairman, Michigan Democratic Party, 1968–69; Democratic candidate for Governor, 1970 and 1974; fellow, Kennedy School of Government, Institute of Politics, Harvard University, 1975; assistant administrator, Agency for International Development, 1977–81; married: Dr. Pamela Cole; children (with the late Victoria Levin): Jennifer, Andrew, Madeleine, and Matthew; committees: Ways and Means; elected on November 2, 1982, to the 98th Congress; reelected to each succeeding Congress.

Office Listings

http://www.levin.house.gov https://www.facebook.com/repsandylevin
https://twitter.com/#!/repsandylevin

1236 Longworth Office House Building, Washington, DC 20515 .... (202) 225–4961
Chief of Staff.—Nick Gwyn. FAX: 226–1033
Scheduler.—Stephanie Mulka.
27085 Gratiot Avenue, Roseville, MI 48066 .... (586) 498–7122

Counties: MACOMB (part) AND OAKLAND (part). CITIES: Berkley, Beverly Hills, Bingham Farms, Bloomfield Township, Clawson (part), Center Line, Clinton Township, Eastpointe, Ferndale, Franklin, Fraser, Lake Township, Hazel Park, Huntington Woods, Madison Heights, Mount Clemens, Pleasant Ridge, Roseville, Royal Oak, Southfield Township, St. Clair Shores, Sterling Heights (part), and Warren. Population (2010), 705,975.

ZIP Codes: 48009 (part), 48015, 48017 (part), 48021, 48025 (part), 48026, 48030, 48034–36, 48038, 48043, 48045 (part), 48066–67, 48069–73, 48080–82, 48084 (part), 48088–89, 48091–93, 48220 (part), 48236–37 (part), 48301–02 (part), 48304 (part), 48310 (part), 48312–13 (part), 48320 (part), 48323 (part), 48341 (part)

* * *

TENTH DISTRICT

PAUL MITCHELL, Republican, of Dryden, MI; born in Boston, MA, November 14, 1956; education: attended James Madison College at Michigan State University, East Lansing, MI, 1978; professional: owned and operated Ross Medical Education Center; married: Sherry Mitchell; children: Brendan, Meghann, Luke, Claire, Emma, and Declan; committees: Armed Services; Oversight and Government Reform; Transportation and Infrastructure; elected to the 115th Congress on November 8, 2016.

Office Listings

http://mitchell.house.gov https://www.facebook.com/reppaulmitchell
https://twitter.com/RepPaulMitchell

211 Cannon House Office Building, Washington, DC 20515 .... (202) 225–2106
Chief of Staff.—Kyle Kizzier. FAX: 226–1169
Legislative Director.—Pat Pelletier.
Communications Director.—Ann Tumolo.
Scheduler.—Molly Harrington.
48701 Van Dyke Avenue, Shelby Township, MI 48317 .... (586) 997–5010

Counties: HURON, LAPEER, MACOMB (part), SAINT CLAIR, SANILAC, AND TUSCOLA (part). Population (2010), 719,712.

ZIP Codes: 48001–03, 48005–06, 48014, 48022–23, 48027–28, 48032, 48035, 48039–42, 48044–45, 48047–51, 48054, 48059–60, 48062–65, 48074, 48079, 48094–97, 48306, 48312–17, 48367, 48371, 48401, 48412–13, 48416, 48419, 48421–23, 48426–28, 48432, 48435, 48438, 48441, 48444–46, 48450, 48453–56, 48461–72, 48475, 48720, 48725–27, 48729, 48731, 48735, 48759–60, 48767

* * *

ELEVENTH DISTRICT

DAVID A. TROTT, Republican, of Birmingham, MI; born in Birmingham, October 16, 1960; education: B.A., University of Michigan, 1981; J.D., Duke University, 1985; professional: business owner; attorney; community service: teaching American government, served on University of Michigan Advisory Board; Detroit Country Day School Board of Trustees; Community House Board; Karmanos Cancer Center Board; Michigan State Building Authority Board of Trustees; Michigan Chamber of Commerce Board of Trustees; religion: Roman Catholic; married: Kappy; children: Duke, Taylor, and Courtney; committees: Financial Services; elected to the 114th Congress on November 4, 2014; reelected to the 115th Congress on November 8, 2016.

Office Listings

http://www.trott.house.gov

1722 Longworth House Office Building, Washington, DC 20515 .... (202) 225–8171
Chief of Staff.—Kyle Bonini.
Scheduler.—Marla Rondo.
Legislative Director.—Bridget Dobyan.
Communications Director.—Katie Vincentz.
625 East Big Beaver Road, Suite 204, Troy, MI 48083 .... (248) 528–0711

Counties: WAYNE COUNTY. CITIES: Caton Township, Livonia, Northville, Northville Township, Plymouth, and Plymouth Township. OAKLAND COUNTY. CITIES: Auburn Hills, Birmingham, Bloomfield Hills, Clawson, Commerce Township, Farmington, Highland, Lake Angelus, Lyon Township, Milford, Novi, Rochester Hills, South Lyon, Troy, Walled Lake, Waterford, West Bloomfield, White Lake, Wixom, and Wolverine Lake. Population (2010), 705,974.

ZIP Codes: 48009, 48017, 48073, 48083–85, 48098, 48150, 48152, 48154, 48165, 48167–68, 48170, 48178, 48187–88, 48304, 48309, 48320, 48323–24, 48326–29, 48335–36, 48341, 48346, 48356–57, 48359, 48374–75, 48377, 48380–83, 48386, 48390, 48393, 48442

* * *

TWELFTH DISTRICT

DEBBIE DINGELL, Democrat, of Dearborn, MI; born in Detroit, MI, November 23, 1953; education: B.S., Georgetown University, 1975; M.S., Georgetown University, 1998; professional: president, General Motors Foundation; executive director of Global Community Relations and Government Relations, GM; president, D2 Strategies; electoral: Wayne State University Board of Governors; married: former Congressman John D. Dingell; committees: Energy and Commerce; elected to the 114th Congress on November 4, 2014; reelected to 115th Congress on November 8, 2016.

Office Listings

http://www.debbiedingell.house.gov https://www.facebook.com/RepDebbieDingell
https://twitter.com/RepDebDingell

116 Cannon House Office Building, Washington, DC 20515 .... (202) 225–4071
Chief of Staff.—Peter Chandler.
Legislative Director.—Greg Sunstrum.
Scheduler.—Jennifer Holland.
Communications Director.—Hannah Smith.
19855 West Outer Drive, Suite 103–E, Dearborn, MI 48124 .... (313) 278–2936
District Administrator.—Callie Bruley.
301 West Michigan Avenue, Ypsilanti, MI 48197 .... (734) 481–1100
Office Manager.—Ryan Hunter.

Counties: WAYNE COUNTY (part). CITIES AND TOWNSHIPS: Allen Park, Belleville, Brownstown, Brownstone Township, Dearborn, Dearborn Heights (part), Flat Rock, Gibraltar, Grosse Ile Township, Huron Township, Lincoln Park, Riverview, Rockwood, Southgate, Sumpter Township, Taylor, Trenton, Van Buren Township, Woodhaven, and Wyandotte. WASHTENAW COUNTY (part). CITIES AND TOWNSHIPS: Ann Arbor, Ann Arbor Township, Pittsfield Township, Scio Township, Ypsilanti, Ypsilanti Township. Population (from Census.gov), 711,313.

ZIP Codes: 48101, 48103–05, 48108–09, 48111, 48114, 48120, 48122, 48124–28, 48130, 48134, 48139, 48146, 48164, 48173–74, 48176, 48180, 48183–84, 48188, 48192–93, 48195, 48197–98, 48127, 48229

* * *

THIRTEENTH DISTRICT

VACANT

Counties: WAYNE COUNTY (part). CITIES AND TOWNSHIPS: Detroit, Dearborn Heights, Ecorse, Garden City, Highland Park, Inkster, Melvindale, Redford, River Rouge, Romulus, Wayne, and Westland. Population (2010), 699,214.

ZIP Codes: 48122 (part), 48125–26 (part), 48127, 48135, 48141, 48174 (part), 48184 (part), 48185–86, 48201–02, 48203 (part), 48204, 48206, 48207 (part), 48208, 48209–17 (part), 48218–19, 48221 (part), 48223, 48226–27 (part), 48228, 48229 (part), 48235 (part), 48238 (part), 48239–40, 48242

* * *

FOURTEENTH DISTRICT

BRENDA L. LAWRENCE, Democrat, of Bloomfield, MI; born in Detroit, MI, October 18, 1954; education: attended University of Detroit; B.S., public administration, Central Michigan University; professional: U.S. Postal Service, letter carrier to human relations executive, 1978–2008; Mayor of Southfield, 2001–15; Southfield City Council, 1996–2000; South Field City Council President, 1999; Southfield Public School Board of Education President, Vice President, Secretary, 1992–96; religion: Christian, non-denominational; married: M. McArthur Lawrence; children: Michael and Michelle; granddaughter, Aysa; caucuses: Congressional Black Caucus; Congressional Progressive Caucus; Former Mayors Caucus; Skilled Workforce Caucus; committees: Oversight and Government Reform; Transportation and Infrastructure; elected to the 114th Congress on November 4, 2014; reelected to 115th Congress on November 8, 2016.

Office Listings

http://www.lawrence.house.gov https://facebook.com/Rep.BLawrence https://twitter.com/RepLawrence

1213 Longworth House Office Building, Washington, DC 20515 .... (202) 225–5802
Chief of Staff.—Duron Marshall. FAX: 226–2356
Legislative Director.—Varun Krovi.
Communications Director.—Nicole Julius.
26700 Lahser Road, Suite 330, Southfield, MI 48033 .... (248) 356–2052
District Office Director.—Jeremy Kaplan.

Counties: OAKLAND (part) AND WAYNE (part). CITIES AND TOWNSHIPS: Detroit, Farmington Hills, Grosse Pointe, Grosse Pointe Farms, Grosse Pointe Park, Grosse Pointe Woods, Hamtramck, Harper Woods, Keego Harbor, Lathrup Village, Oak Park, Orchard Lake, Pointe Shores, Pontiac, Royal Oak Township, Southfield, Sylvan Lake, Village of Grosse Pointe Shores, and West Bloomfield. Population (2010), 706, 429.

ZIP Codes: 48033–34, 48075–76, 48203, 48205, 48207, 48209, 48212, 48214, 48216, 48221, 48224–26, 48230, 48233–35, 48237, 48243, 48320–23, 48325, 48331, 48334, 48336, 48340–43

MINNESOTA

(Population 2010, 5,303,925)

SENATORS

AMY KLOBUCHAR, Democrat, of Minneapolis, MN; born in Plymouth, MN, May 25, 1960; education: B.A., *magna cum laude*, Yale University, 1982; J.D., *magna cum laude*, University of Chicago Law School, 1985; professional: attorney at law firm Dorsey & Whitney, 1985–93, partner in 1993; partner at law firm Gray, Plant, Mooty, Mooty & Bennett, 1993–98; public service: City of Minneapolis Prosecutor, 1988; elected Hennepin County Attorney, 1998, reelected, 2002; religion: Congregationalist; married: John; child: Abigail; committees: Agriculture, Nutrition, and Forestry; Commerce, Science, and Transportation; Joint Committee on Printing; Joint Committee on the Library; Joint Economic Committee; Judiciary; Rules and Administration; elected to the U.S. Senate on November 7, 2006; reelected to the U.S. Senate on November 6, 2012.

Office Listings

http://klobuchar.senate.gov

302 Hart Senate Office Building, Washington, DC 20510 .... (202) 224–3244
Chief of Staff.—Brigit Helgen.
Legislative Director.—Anne Knapke.
Deputy Chief of Staff.—Rosa Po.
Communications Director.—Caitlin Girouard.
Scheduler.—Blair Mallin.
Director of Operations.—Devan Cayea.
1200 Washington Avenue South, Suite 250, Minneapolis, MN 55415 .... (612) 727–5220
State Director.—Ben Hill.
1130½ 7th Street, Northwest, Suite 212, Rochester, MN 55901 .... (507) 288–5321
121 4th Street South, Moorhead, MN 56560 .... (218) 287–2219
Olcott Plaza, 820 9th Street North, Suite 105, Virginia, MN 55792 .... (218) 741–9690

* * *

TINA SMITH, Democrat, of Minneapolis, MN; born March 4, 1958; education: B.A., Stanford University, Stanford, CA, 1980; M.B.A., Tuck School of Business at Dartmouth College, Hanover, NH, 1984; professional: began working at Minnesota-based General Mills in 1984, later opened her own small business, and went on to serve as vice president for external affairs at Planned Parenthood Minnesota, North Dakota, South Dakota (PPMNS); served as chief of staff to both Minneapolis Mayor R.T. Rybak and Governor Mark Dayton. In 2014, Tina was elected to serve as Minnesota's 48th Lieutenant Governor; married: Archie Smith, for more than 30 years; two sons and two daughters-in-law; committees: Agriculture, Nutrition, and Forestry; Energy and Natural Resources; Health, Education, Labor, and Pensions; Indian Affairs; appointed to the U.S. Senate to fill the vacancy caused by the resignation of Senator Al Franken, for the term ending January 3, 2021, and took the oath of office on January 3, 2018.

Office Listings

www.smith.senate.gov

309 Hart Senate Office Building, Washington, DC 20510 .... (202) 224–5641
Chief of Staff.—Jeff Lomonaco. FAX: 224–0044
State Advisor / Deputy Chief of Staff.—Alana Petersen.
Legislative Director.—Gohar Sedighi.
Scheduler.—Brynna Schmidt.
Communications Director.—Ed Shelleby.
Press Secretary.—Molly Morrissey.
60 East Plato Boulevard, Suite 220, St. Paul, MN 55107 .... (651) 221–1016
FAX: 221–1078
1202½ Seventh Street, NW., Suite 213, Rochester, MN 55901 .... (507) 288–2003
FAX: 288–2217
515 West First Street, Suite 104, Duluth, MN 55802 .... (218) 722–2390
FAX: 722–4131
819 Center Avenue, Suite 2A, Moorhead, MN 56560 .... (218) 284–8721
FAX: 284–8722

REPRESENTATIVES

FIRST DISTRICT

TIMOTHY J. WALZ, Democrat, of Mankato, MN; born in West Point, NE, April 6, 1964; education: B.S., Chadron State College, Chadron, NE; M.S., Minnesota State University—Mankato; professional: high school teacher; military: Command Sergeant Major, Minnesota's 1st/34th Division of the Army National Guard, 1981–2005; awards: 2002 Minnesota Ethics in Education award winner; 2003 Mankato Teacher of the Year; and 2003 Minnesota Teacher of Excellence; married: Gwen Whipple Walz, 1994; children: Hope and Gus; committees: ranking member, Veterans' Affairs; Agriculture; elected to the 110th Congress on November 7, 2006; reelected to each succeeding Congress.

Office Listings

http://www.walz.house.gov twitter: @RepTimWalz

2313 Rayburn House Office Building, Washington, DC 20515 .... (202) 225–2472
Chief of Staff.—Josh Syrjamaki. FAX: 225–3433
Legislative Director.—Timothy Bertocci.
Scheduler.—Alyssa Berg.
527½ South Front Street, Mankato, MN 56001 .... (507) 388–2149
1202½ Seventh Street, NW., Suite 211, Rochester, MN 55901 .... (507) 388–2149

Counties: BLUE EARTH COUNTY. CITIES: Amboy, Eagle Lake, Garden City, Good Thunder, Lake Crystal, Madison Lake, Mankato, Mapleton, Pemberton, St. Clair, Vernon Center. BROWN COUNTY. CITIES: Comfrey (part), Hanska, New Ulm, Sleepy Eye, Springfield. COTTONWOOD COUNTY (part). CITIES: Mountain Lake. DODGE COUNTY. CITIES: Claremont, Dodge Center, Hayfield, Kasson, Mantorville, West Concord. FARIBAULT COUNTY. CITIES: Blue Earth, Bricelyn, Delavan, Easton, Elmore, Frost, Huntley, Kiester, Minnesota Lake, Walters, Wells, Winnebago. FILLMORE COUNTY. CITIES: Canton, Chatfield (part), Fountain, Harmony, Lanesboro, Mabel, Ostrander, Peterson, Preston, Rushford, Spring Valley, Whalan, Wykoff. FREEBORN COUNTY. CITIES: Albert Lea, Alden, Clarks Grove, Conger, Emmons, Freeborn, Geneva, Glenville, Hartland, Hayward, Hollandale, London, Manchester, Myrtle, Oakland, Twin Lakes. HOUSTON COUNTY. CITIES: Brownsville, Caledonia, Eitzen, Hokah, Houston, La Crescent (part), Spring Grove. JACKSON COUNTY. CITIES: Heron Lake, Jackson, Lakefield. LE SUEUR COUNTY. CITIES: Cleveland, Elysian, Heidelberg, Kasota, Kilkenny, Le Center, Le Sueur, Mankato, Montgomery, New Prague, Waterville. MARTIN COUNTY. CITY: Fairmount. MOWER COUNTY. CITIES: Adams, Austin, Brownsdale, Dexter, Elkton, Grand Meadow, Le Roy, Lyle, Rose Creek, Sargeant, Taopi, Waltham. NICOLLET COUNTY. CITIES: North Mankato, St. Peter. NOBLES COUNTY. CITIES: Adrian, Worthington. OLMSTED COUNTY. CITIES: Byron, Dover, Eyota, Oronoco, Rochester, Stewartville. RICE COUNTY (part). CITIES: Faribault, Morristown, Shieldsville, Walcott, Warsaw, Webster, Wheatland. ROCK COUNTY. CITIES: Lurverne. STEELE COUNTY. CITIES: Blooming Prairie, Ellendale, Medford, Owatonna. WASECA COUNTY. CITIES: Janesville, New Richland, Waldorf, Waseca. WATONWAN COUNTY. CITIES: Madelia, St. James. WINONA COUNTY. CITIES: Altura, Dakota, Goodview, Lewiston, Minnesota City, Rollingstone, St. Charles, Stockton, Utica, and Winona. Population (2010), 644,787.

ZIP Codes: 55019, 55021, 55046, 55049, 55052, 55057, 55060, 55087–88, 55332–35, 55901–02, 55904, 55906, 55909–10, 55912, 55917–27, 55929, 55931–36, 55939–41, 55943–44, 55947, 55949–56, 55959–65, 55967, 55969–77, 55979, 55982, 55985, 55987, 55990–01, 56001, 56003, 56007, 56009–11, 56013–14, 56016–17, 56019–29, 56031–37, 56039, 56041–48, 56050–52, 56054–58, 56060, 56062–63, 56065, 56068–69, 56071–75, 56078, 56080–83, 56085, 56087–91, 56093, 56096–98, 56101, 56110–11, 56116–22, 56127–29, 56131, 56134, 56137–38, 56141, 56143–47, 56150, 56153, 56155–56, 56158–62, 56165, 56167–68, 56171, 56173, 56176, 56181, 56185, 56187, 56266

* * *

SECOND DISTRICT

JASON LEWIS, Republican, of Burnsville, MN; born in Waterloo, IA, on September 23, 1955; education: B.A., education, University of Northern Iowa, Cedar Falls, IA; M.A., political science, University of Colorado at Denver, 1992; professional: nationally syndicated on the *Jason Lewis Show*; religion: Catholic; family: married to Leigh, with two daughters; committees: Budget; Education and the Workforce; Transportation and Infrastructure; elected to the 115th Congress on November 8, 2016.

Office Listings

http://www.jasonlewis.house.gov facebook.com/repjasonlewis twitter.com/repjasonlewis

418 Cannon House Office Building, Washington, DC 20515 .... (202) 225–2271
Chief of Staff.—Amy Smith.
Communications Director.—Stephen Bradford.
Scheduler.—Deborah Hansen.
2805 Cliff Road, Suite 200, Burnsville, MN 55337 .... (651) 808–1213
District Director.—Jack Dwyer.

Counties: DAKOTA COUNTY. CITIES: Apple Valley, Burnsville, Eagan, Farmington, Hastings, Inver Grove Heights, Lakeville, Rosemount, South St. Paul, and West St. Paul. GOODHUE COUNTY. CITIES: Cannon Falls, Pine Island, Red Wing, and Zumbrota. RICE COUNTY (part). CITIES: Northfield. SCOTT COUNTY. CITIES: Shakopee, Savage, Prior Lake, New Prague, Jordan, and Belle Plaine. WABASHA COUNTY. WASHINGTON COUNTY (part). CITIES: Cottage Grove and St. Paul Park. Population (2010), 668,891.

ZIP Codes: 55009, 55010 (part), 55016 (part), 55018, 55019–20 (part), 55024, 55026–27, 55031, 55033, 55041, 55044, 55053–54 (part), 55057 (part), 55065–66, 55068 (part), 55071 (part), 55075–76 (part), 55077, 55085, 55088–89 (part), 55118 (part), 55120–24, 55150 (part), 55306, 55337, 55352, 55372, 55378, 55379 (part), 55906, 55910 (part), 55932 (part), 55945, 55946 (part), 55956 (part), 55957, 55960 (part), 55963–64 (part), 55968, 55981, 55983 (part), 55985 (part), 55991, 55992 (part), 56071 (part), 56011 (part), 56044 (part), 56071 (part)

* * *

THIRD DISTRICT

ERIK PAULSEN, Republican, of Eden Prairie, MN; born in Bakersfield, CA, May 14, 1965; education: B.A., St. Olaf College, Northfield, MN, 1987; religion: Lutheran; married: Kelly; children: four daughters; caucuses: co-chair, Charter Schools Caucus; co-chair, Congressional Wellness Caucus; co-chair Digital Trade Caucus; co-chair, Friends of Norway Caucus; co-chair, Medical Technology Caucus; Bike Caucus; Civility Caucus; Diabetes Caucus; Financial Literacy Caucus; General Aviation Caucus; Hockey Caucus; India Caucus; Land Conservation Caucus; Law Enforcement Caucus; National Guard Caucus; National Parks Caucus; Nuclear Issues Working Group; Rare Disease Caucus; Renewable Energy Caucus; Sportsmen's Caucus; U.S.-China Working Group; Zoo Caucus; committees: chair, Joint Economic Committee; Ways and Means; elected to the 111th Congress on November 4, 2008; reelected to each succeeding Congress.

Office Listings

http://www.paulsen.house.gov facebook: congressmanerikpaulsen twitter: @reperikpaulsen
instagram: @reperikpaulsen

127 Cannon House Office Building, Washington, DC 20515 .... (202) 225–2871
Chief of Staff.—Laurie Esau. FAX: 225–6351
Legislative Director.—Andy Franke.
Press Secretary.—Andrew Johnson.
Scheduler.—Anna Fiedler.
250 Prairie Center Drive, Suite 230, Eden Prairie, MN 55344 .... (952) 405–8510
FAX: 405–8514

Counties: ANOKA (part), CARVER (part), AND HENNEPIN (part). CITIES AND TOWNSHIPS: Bloomington, Brooklyn Park, Champlin, Chanhassen, Chaska, Coon Rapids, Corcoran, Dayton, Deephaven, Eden Prairie, Edina (part), Excelsior, Greenfield, Greenwood, Independence, Long Lake, Loretto, Maple Grove, Maple Plain, Medina, Medicine Lake, Minnetonka, Minnetonka Beach, Minnetrista, Mound, Orono, Osseo, Plymouth, Rogers, Shorewood, Spring Park, St. Bonifacius, Tonka Bay, Victoria, Wayzata, and Woodland. Population (2010), 650,185.

ZIP Codes: 55305, 55311, 55316–18, 55327–28, 55331, 55340, 55343–47, 55356–57, 55359, 55364, 55369, 55373–75, 55384, 55386–88, 55391, 55420, 55423, 55425, 55428–31, 55433, 55435–39, 55441–48

* * *

FOURTH DISTRICT

BETTY MCCOLLUM, Democrat-Farmer-Labor, of St. Paul, MN; born in Minneapolis, MN, July 12, 1954; education: A.A., Inver Hills Community College; B.S., College of St. Catherine; professional: teacher and sales manager; public service: North St. Paul City Council, 1986–92; Minnesota House of Representatives, 1992–2000; organizations: Girl Scouts of America; VFW Ladies Auxiliary; American Legion Ladies Auxiliary; awards: Friend of the National Parks Award, National Parks Conservation Association, 2013; Congressional Leadership Award, National Council of Urban Indian Health, 2013; Groundwater Protector Award, National Ground Water Association, 2012; Bruce Vento Hope-Builder Award, Mesothelioma Applied Research Foundation, 2014; Champion of the Endangered Species Act, International Fund for Animal Welfare, 2016; Bruce Vento Public Service Award, National Park Trust, 2016; children: Sean and Katie; appointments: National Council on the Arts; caucuses: founder, Congressional Global Health Caucus; co-chair, Congressional Native American Caucus; committees: Appropriations; elected to the 107th Congress on November 7, 2000; reelected to each succeeding Congress.

Office Listings

http://www.mccollum.house.gov facebook.com/repbettymccollum twitter.com/BettyMcCollum04

2256 Rayburn House Office Building, Washington, DC 20515 .... (202) 225–6631

Office Listings—Continued

Chief of Staff.—Bill Harper. FAX: 225–1968
Legislative Director.—Jenn Holcomb.
Communications Director.—Evan Hollander.
Scheduler.—Ryan Houlihan.
661 LaSalle Street, Suite 110, St. Paul, MN 55114 .... (651) 224–9191
District Director.—Joshua Straka.

Counties: RAMSEY (part) AND WASHINGTON (part). Population (2010), 614,624.

ZIP Codes: 55001, 55003, 55038, 55042–43, 55055, 55071, 55082, 55090, 55101–10, 55112–19, 55125–30, 55418, 55432

* * *

FIFTH DISTRICT

KEITH ELLISON, Democrat-Farmer-Labor, of Minneapolis, MN; born in Detroit, MI, August 4, 1963; education: University of Detroit Jesuit High School and Academy, 1981; Wayne State University, 1987; University of Minnesota Law School, 1990; professional: Law Office of Lindquist & Vennum, 1990–93; executive director of the nonprofit Legal Rights Center in Minneapolis, 1993–98; Hassan & Reed Ltd., 1998–2001; Ellison Law Offices, 2003–06; served in Minnesota State Legislature District 58B, 2003–06; family: four children; commissions: Center for Strategic and International Studies; Commission on Global Health; House Democracy Assistance Commission; Tom Lantos Human Rights Commission; caucuses: founder, Consumer Justice Caucus; co-chair, Progressive Caucus; Bicameral Congressional Caucus on Parkinson's Disease; Children's Environmental Health Caucus; Congressional Adoption Caucus; Congressional Anti-Terrorism Caucus; Congressional Arts Caucus; Congressional Black Caucus; Congressional Caucus of India and Indian Americans; Congressional Caucus to Fight and Control Methamphetamine; Congressional Diabetes Caucus; Congressional E9–1–1 (Emergency Responders) Caucus; Congressional Human Rights Caucus; Congressional Labor and Working Families Caucus; Congressional Wildlife Caucus; Credit Caucus; Financial and Economic Literacy Caucus; Full Employment Caucus; Green Jobs Caucus; Hunger Caucus; Law Enforcement Caucus; Out of Iraq Caucus; Populist Caucus; Pro-Choice Caucus; committees: Financial Services; elected to the 110th Congress on November 7, 2006; reelected to each succeeding Congress.

Office Listings

http://ellison.house.gov

2263 Rayburn House Office Building, Washington, DC 20515 .... (202) 225–4755
Chief of Staff.—Kari Moe.
Legislative Director.—Carol Wayman.
Communications Director.—Brett Morrow.
2100 Plymouth Avenue, Minneapolis, MN 55411 .... (612) 522–1212
District Director.—Jamie Long.

Counties: ANOKA (part), HENNEPIN (part), AND RAMSEY (part). CITIES: Minneapolis and the surrounding suburbs of Brooklyn Center, Columbia Heights, Crystal, Edina (part), Fridley, Golden Valley, Hilltop, Hopkins, Richfield, Robbinsdale, St. Anthony, and St. Louis Park. Population (2010), 677,196.

ZIP Codes: 55305, 55343, 55401–19, 55421–24, 55426–30, 55432, 55436, 55444, 55450, 55454–55

* * *

SIXTH DISTRICT

TOM EMMER, Republican, of Delano, MN; born in South Bend, IN, March 3, 1961; education: B.A., political science, from the University of Alaska-Fairbanks, Fairbanks, AK, 1984; J.D. from William Mitchell College of Law, St. Paul, MN, 1988; professional: practiced insurance, banking, and equity law through his own practice; served in the Minnesota House of Representatives from 2004–08; was a radio host on Twin Cities News Talk AM 1130; married: Jacquie; children: Thomas Earl III ''Tripp,'' Jack, Bobby, Joey, Billy, and Johnny (sons), and Katie (daughter); House Republican Steering Committee; committees: Financial Services; elected to the 114th Congress on November 4, 2014; reelected to the 115th Congress on November 8, 2016.

Office Listings

http://www.emmer.house.gov facebook: https://www.facebook.com/reptomemmer
twitter: @RepTomEmmer

315 Cannon House Office Building, Washington, DC 20515 .... (202) 225–2331
Chief of Staff.—David FitzSimmons. FAX: 225–6475
Deputy Chief of Staff.—Robert Boland.
Legislative Director.—Christopher Maneval.
Communications Director.—Becky Alery.
9201 Quaday Avenue, NE., Otsego, MN 55330 .... (763) 241–6848

Counties: ANOKA (part), BENTON, CARVER (part), HENNEPIN (part), SHERBURNE, STEARNS (part), WASHINGTON (part), AND WRIGHT. Population (2010), 662,990.

ZIP Codes: 55005, 55011, 55014, 55025, 55038, 55047, 55070, 55073, 55079, 55082, 55092, 55110, 55126, 55301–04, 55308–09, 55313, 55315, 55318–22, 55327–30, 55339, 55341, 55349, 55353, 55357–58, 55360, 55362–63, 55367–68, 55371, 55373–76, 55382, 55387–90, 55395, 55397–98, 55434, 55449, 56011, 56301, 56303–04, 56307, 56310, 56314, 56320–21, 56329–30, 56340, 56357, 56362, 56367–69, 56373–75, 56377, 56379, 56387

* * *

SEVENTH DISTRICT

COLLIN C. PETERSON, Democrat, of Detroit Lakes, MN; born in Fargo, ND, June 29, 1944; education: graduated from Glyndon (MN) High School, 1962; B.A., business administration and accounting, Moorhead State University, 1966; professional: U.S. Army National Guard, 1963–69; CPA, owner and partner; Minnesota State Senator, 1976–86; member: AOPA, Safari Club, Ducks Unlimited, American Legion, Sea Plane Pilots Association, Pheasants Forever, Benevolent Protective Order of Elks, and Cormorant Lakes Sportsman's Club; three children: Sean, Jason, and Elliott; committees: ranking member, Agriculture; elected to the 102nd Congress on November 6, 1990; reelected to each succeeding Congress.

Office Listings

http://collinpeterson.house.gov

2204 Rayburn House Office Building, Washington, DC 20515 .... (202) 225–2165
Chief of Staff.—Allison Myhre. FAX: 225–1593
Deputy Chief of Staff / Legislative Director.—Adam Durand.
Assistants: Chelsea Cornett, Tamir Elnabraway, Chris Iacaruso, Richard Lee, Zach Martin, Rebekah Solem.
Lake Avenue Plaza Building, 714 Lake Avenue, Suite 107, Detroit Lakes, MN 56501 .... (218) 847–5056
324 3rd Street, SW., Suite 4, Willmar, MN 56201 .... (320) 235–1061

Counties: BECKER, BELTRAMI (part), BIG STONE, CHIPPEWA, CLAY, CLEARWATER, COTTONWOOD (part), DOUGLAS, GRANT, KANDIYOHI, KITTSON, LAC QUI PARLE, LAKE OF THE WOODS, LINCOLN, LYON, MAHNOMEN, MARSHALL, MCLEOD, MEEKER, MURRAY, NORMAN, OTTER TAIL, PENNINGTON, PIPESTONE, POLK, POPE, RED LAKE, REDWOOD, RENVILLE, ROSEAU, SIBLEY, STEARNS (part), STEVENS, SWIFT, TODD, TRAVERSE, WILKIN, AND YELLOW MEDICINE. Population (2010), 662,991.

ZIP Codes: 55307, 55310, 55312, 55314, 55324–25, 55329, 55332–36, 55338–39, 55342, 55350, 55353–55, 55366, 55370, 55381–82, 55385, 55389, 55395–97, 56011, 56044, 56054, 56058, 56083, 56085, 56087, 56101, 56113–14, 56122–23, 56128, 56131–32, 56136–37, 56139–42, 56144–45, 56149, 56151–52, 56157, 56164, 56166, 56169–70, 56172, 56174–75, 56177–78, 56180, 56183, 56186, 56201, 56207–12, 56214–16, 56218–32, 56235–37, 56239–41, 56243–45, 56248–49, 56251–53, 56255–58, 56260, 56262–67, 56270–71, 56273–74, 56276–85, 56287–89, 56291–97, 56307–12, 56315–16, 56318–19, 56323–27, 56331–32, 56334–36, 56339–40, 56343, 56349, 56352, 56354–55, 56360–62, 56368, 56371, 56376, 56378–79, 56381–82, 56385, 56389, 56434, 56437–38, 56440, 56443, 56446, 56453, 56464, 56466, 56470, 56477, 56479, 56481–82, 56501, 56510–11, 56514–25, 56527–29, 56531, 56533–37, 56540–54, 56556–57, 56560, 56565–81, 56583–94, 56601, 56621, 56623, 56634, 56644, 56646, 56650–52, 56666–67, 56670–71, 56673, 56676, 56678, 56684–87, 56701, 56710–11, 56713–16, 56720–29, 56731–38, 56741–42, 56744, 56748, 56750–51

* * *

EIGHTH DISTRICT

RICHARD M. NOLAN, Democrat-Farmer-Labor, of Crosby, MN; born in Brainerd, MN, December 17, 1943; education: attended St. John's University, Collegeville, MN, 1962; B.A., University of Minnesota, Minneapolis, MN, 1966; post-graduate work at the University of Maryland, College Park, MD; St. Cloud State, St. Cloud, MN; and Central Lakes Community College, Brainerd, MN; professional: high school social studies teacher; Head Start Program Director; curriculum coordinator; Fingerhut Corporation Assistant to the President; Minnesota State Representative; U.S. Congressman; U.S. Export Corporation President; Minnesota World Trade

Center President; international business consultant; Emily Forest Products CEO; religion: Roman Catholic; married: Mary Nolan; four children; ten grandchildren; committees: Agriculture; Transportation and Infrastructure; elected to the 94th Congress and did not seek reelection after serving three terms; elected to the 113th Congress on November 6, 2012; reelected to each succeeding Congress.

Office Listings

http://www.nolan.house.gov facebook: https://www.facebook.com/UsRepRickNolan
twitter: https://twitter.com/USRepRickNolan

2366 Rayburn House Office Building, Washington, DC 20515 .... (202) 225–6211
Chief of Staff.—Jodie Torkelson.
Legislative Director.—Will Mitchell.
Communications Director.—Steve Johnson.
Scheduler.—Taryn Brown.
Duluth Technology Village, 11 East Superior Street, Suite 125, Duluth, MN 55802 .... (218) 464–5095
District Director.—Jeff Anderson. FAX: 464–5098
Brainerd City Hall, 501 Laurel Street, Brainerd, MN 56401 .... (218) 454–4078
FAX: 454–4096
Chisago County Government Center, 313 North Main Street, Room 103, Center City, MN 55012 .... (218) 491–3131
Chisholm City Hall, 316 West Lake Street, Room 7, Chisholm, MN 55719 .... (218) 491–3114

Counties: AITKIN, BELTRAMI (part), CARLTON, CASS, CHISAGO, COOK, CROW WING, HUBBARD, ISANTI, ITASCA, KANABEC, KOOCHICHING, LAKE, MILLE LACS, MORRISON, PINE, ST. LOUIS, AND WADENA. CITIES: Baxter, Brainerd, Cambridge, Chisago City, Chisholm, Cloquet, Duluth, Ely, Eveleth, Grand Rapids, Hermantown, Hibbing, International Falls, Isanti, Lindstrom, Little Falls, Mora, North Branch, Park Rapids, Pine City, Princeton, Proctor, Rush City, Two Harbors, Virginia, Wadena, and Wyoming. Population (2010), 660,347.

ZIP Codes: 55006–08, 55012–13, 55017, 55025, 55029–30, 55032, 55036–37, 55040, 55045, 55051, 55056, 55063, 55069–70, 55072–74, 55079–80, 55084, 55092, 55371, 55398, 55601–07, 55609, 55612–16, 55702–13, 55716–26, 55731–36, 55738, 55741–42, 55744, 55746, 55748–53, 55756–58, 55760, 55763–69, 55771–72, 55775, 55779–87, 55790, 55792–93, 55795, 55797–98, 55802–08, 55810–12, 55814, 56313–14, 56318, 56328–30, 56338, 56340, 56342, 56345, 56350, 56353, 56357–59, 56363–64, 56373, 56382, 56384, 56386, 56401, 56425, 56431, 56433–36, 56441–44, 56447–50, 56452, 56455–56, 56458, 56461, 56464–70, 56472–75, 56477, 56479, 56481–82, 56484, 56601, 56623, 56626–30, 56633, 56636–37, 56639, 56641, 56647, 56649–50, 56653–55, 56657–63, 56667–69, 56672, 56678, 56680–81, 56683, 56688

MISSISSIPPI

(Population 2010, 2,967,297)

SENATORS

ROGER F. WICKER, Republican, of Tupelo, MS; born in Pontotoc, MS, July 5, 1951; education: graduated, Pontotoc High School; University of Mississippi: B.A., 1973; J.D., 1975; president, Associated Student Body, 1972–73; *Mississippi Law Journal*, 1973–75; Air Force ROTC; professional: U.S. Air Force, 1976–80; U.S. Air Force Reserve, 1980–2004 (retired with rank of Lieutenant Colonel); U.S. House of Representatives Rules Committee staff for Representative Trent Lott, 1980–82; private law practice, 1982–94; Lee County Public Defender, 1984–87; Tupelo City Judge Pro Tempore, 1986–87; Mississippi State Senate, 1988–94, chairman: Elections Committee (1992), Public Health and Welfare Committee (1993–94); member: Lions Club, University of Mississippi Hall of Fame, Sigma Nu Fraternity Hall of Fame, Omicron Delta Kappa, Phi Delta Phi; religion: Southern Baptist, deacon, adult choir of First Baptist Church, Tupelo, MS; married: Gayle Long Wicker; children: Margaret (Manning) McPhillips, Caroline (Kirk) Sims, and McDaniel (Kellee) Wicker; grandchildren: Caroline McPhillips, Henry McPhillips, Maury Beth McPhillips, and Evelyn Sims; chairman of the U.S. Helsinki Commission and chair of the Committee on Political Affairs and Security in the OSCE's Parliamentary Assembly; committees: Armed Services; Commerce, Science, and Transportation; Environment and Public Works; Joint Committee on Printing; Rules and Administration; elected to the 104th Congress, November 8, 1994; president, Republican freshman class, 1995; reelected to each succeeding Congress; appointed by the Governor, December 31, 2007, to fill the vacancy caused by the resignation of Senator Trent Lott; elected to the U.S. Senate on November 4, 2008; reelected to the U.S. Senate on November 6, 2012.

Office Listings

http://wicker.senate.gov http://facebook.com/senatorwicker twitter: @senatorwicker

555 Dirksen Senate Office Building, Washington, DC 20510 .... (202) 224–6253
Chief of Staff.—Michelle Barlow Richardson. FAX: 228–0378
Legislative Director.—Rob Murray.
Communications Director.—Rick VanMetter.
Scheduler.—Hall Carter.
U.S. Federal Courthouse, 501 East Court Street, Suite 3–500, Jackson, MS 39201 .... (601) 965–4644
FAX: 965–4007
2909 13th Street, Suite 303, Gulfport, MS 39501 .... (228) 871–7017
FAX: 871–7196
330 West Jefferson Street, Suite B, Tupelo, MS 33804 .... (662) 844–5010
321 Losher Street, Hernando, MS 38632 .... (662) 429–1002
FAX: 429–6002

* * *

CINDY HYDE-SMITH, Republican, of Brookhaven, MS; born in Brookhaven, May 10, 1959; education: graduated from Copiah-Lincoln Community College, Wesson, MS; B.A., University of Southern Mississippi, 1981; professional: cattle farmer; Mississippi State Senator, 2000–12; first woman elected as Commissioner of Agriculture and Commerce, State of Mississippi, 2012–18; awards: Agriculture Legislator of the Year Award from the Mississippi Association of Conservation Districts; Ambassador Award from the Mississippi Farm Bureau Federation; Achievement Award from the Delta Council; Outstanding Service to Small Farmers Award from Alcorn State University; religion: Baptist; family: husband, Michael; daughter, Anna-Michael; committees: Agriculture, Nutrition, and Forestry; Appropriations; Rules and Administration; appointed to the U.S. Senate to fill the vacancy caused by the resignation of U.S. Senator Thad Cochran; took the oath of office on April 9, 2018, to serve until a special election is held on November 6, 2018, for the remainder of the term ending January 3, 2021.

Office Listings

http://www.hydesmith.senate.gov twitter: @SenHydeSmith
instagram: @sencindyhydesmith youtube: U.S. Senator Cindy Hyde-Smith

113 Dirksen Senate Office Building, Washington, DC 20510 .... (202) 224–5054

Office Listings—Continued

Chief of Staff.—Brad White.
Deputy Chief of Staff for Administration.—John G. Campbell.
Deputy Chief of Staff for Policy.—Daniel Ulmer.
Legislative Director.—Tim Wolverton.
State Director.—Umesh Sanianwala.
190 East Capitol Street, Suite 550, Jackson, MS 39201 .... (601) 965–4459
911 East Jackson Avenue, Suite 249, Oxford, MS 38655 .... (662) 236–1018
2012 15th Street, Suite 451, Gulfport, MS 39501 .... (228) 867–9710

REPRESENTATIVES

FIRST DISTRICT

TRENT KELLY, Republican, of Saltillo, MS; born in Union, MS, March 1, 1966; education: Union High School, Union, MS, 1984; associate of arts, East Central Community College, Decatur, MS, 1986; bachelor of business administration, marketing, University of Mississippi, Oxford, MS, 1989; juris doctor, University of Mississippi, Oxford, MS, 1994; master's in strategic studies, United States Army War College, Carlisle, PA, 2010; professional: private law practice, Saltillo, MS, 1995–99; City Prosecutor, Tupelo, MS, 1999–2011; forfeiture attorney, North Mississippi Narcotics Unit, 2000–11; District Attorney for Lee, Pontotoc, Alcorn, Monroe, Itawamba, Prentiss, and Tishomingo Counties, 2012–June 2015; military: 31 years in the Mississippi Army National Guard as an engineer; currently a Colonel; mobilized for Desert Storm as an Engineer Second Lieutenant, 1990; deployed as a Major to Iraq with the 155th Brigade as the operations officer of the 150th Engineer Battalion, 2005; deployed as a Lieutenant Colonel to Iraq as the battalion commander of Task Force Knight of the 155th Brigade Combat Team and commanded over 670 troops from Mississippi, Ohio, and Kentucky, 2009–10; awards: two Bronze Stars; Combat Action Badge; DeFleury Medal, and numerous other federal and state awards; religion: Methodist; married: Sheila Stephens Kelly; children: John Forrest, Morgan, and Jackson; committees: Agriculture; Armed Services; Small Business; elected to the 114th Congress on June 2, 2015, by special election, to fill the vacancy caused by the death of U.S. Representative Alan S. Nunnelee; reelected to the 115th Congress on November 8, 2016.

Office Listings

http://trentkelly.house.gov www.facebook.com/reptrentkelly twitter: @reptrentkelly

1427 Longworth House Office Building, Washington, DC 20515 .... (202) 225–4306
Chief of Staff.—Ted Maness. FAX: 225–3549
Deputy Chief of Staff.—Elizabeth Parks.
Scheduler.—Whitney Porter.
431 West Main Street, Suite 450, Tupelo, MS 38804 .... (662) 841–8808
District Director.—Paul Howell. FAX: 841–8845
318 Seventh Street North, Suite D, Columbus, MS 39701 .... (662) 327–0748
Mailing: P.O. Box 1012, Columbus, MS 39703 .... FAX: 328–5982
2565 Caffey Street, #200, Hernando, MS 38632 .... (662) 449–3090
Mailing: P.O. Box 218, Hernando, MS 38632 .... FAX: 449–4836
855 South Dunn Street, Eupora, MS 39744 .... (662) 258–1545
FAX: 258–7240
4135 County Road 200, Corinth, MS 38844 .... (662) 687–1525

Counties: ALCORN, BENTON, CALHOUN, CHICKASAW, CHOCTAW, CLAY, DESOTO, ITAWAMBA, LAFAYETTE, LEE, LOWNDES, MARSHALL, MONROE, PONTOTOC, PRENTISS, TATE, TIPPAH, TISHOMINGO, UNION, WEBSTER, WINSTON, AND OKTIBBEHA (part). Population (2013), 756,459.

ZIP Codes: 38601, 38603, 38606 (part), 38610–11, 38618, 38619 (part), 38625, 38627, 38629, 38632–33, 38635, 38637, 38641–42, 38647, 38650–52, 38654–55, 38659, 38661, 38663, 38665, 38668, 38671–74, 38677, 38680, 38683, 38685, 38801, 38804, 38821, 38824, 38826–29, 38833–34, 38838, 38841, 38843–44, 38846–52, 38855–60, 38862–66, 38868–71, 38873, 38876, 38878–79, 38913–16, 38929 (part), 38949, 38951, 38965 (part), 39108 (part), 39339, 39346 (part), 39354 (part), 39701–02, 39705, 39730, 39735–37, 39740–41, 39743 (part), 39744, 39745 (part), 39746, 39750 (part), 39751–52, 39755 (part), 39756, 39766–67, 39769 (part), 39771, 39772 (part), 39773, 39776

* * *

SECOND DISTRICT

BENNIE G. THOMPSON, Democrat, of Bolton, MS; born in Bolton, January 28, 1948; education: graduated, Hinds County Agriculture High School; B.A., Tougaloo College, 1968; M.S.,

Jackson State University, 1972; professional: teacher; Bolton Board of Aldermen, 1969–73; Mayor of Bolton, 1973–79; Hinds County Board of Supervisors, 1980–93; Housing Assistance Council; NAACP 100 Black Men of Jackson, MS; Southern Regional Council; Kappa Alpha Psi Fraternity; married to the former London Johnson, Ph.D.; one daughter: BendaLonne; caucuses: Congressional Black Caucus; Congressional Gaming Caucus; Congressional Sportsmen's Caucus; House Education Caucus; Progressive Caucus; Rural Caucus; committees: ranking member, Homeland Security; elected to the 103rd Congress by special election; reelected to each succeeding Congress.

Office Listings

http://www.benniethompson.house.gov facebook: @CongressmanBennieGThompson
twitter: @BennieGThompson

2466 Rayburn House Office Building, Washington, DC 20515 .... (202) 225–5876
Chief of Staff.—Lanier Avant. FAX: 225–5898
Deputy Chief of Staff.—Cory Horton.
Legislative Assistant.—Shalonda Spencer.
Scheduler.—Andrea Lee.
Staff Assistant.—Meco Shoulders.
107 West Madison Street, P.O. Box 610, Bolton, MS 39041–0610 .... (601) 866–9003
District Director.—Fannie Ware.
3607 Medgar Evers Boulevard, Jackson, MS 39213 .... (601) 982–8582
263 East Main Street, Marks, MS 38646 .... (662) 326–9003
Mound Bayou City Hall, 106 West Green Street, Room 134, Mound Bayou, MS 38762 ..... (662) 741–9003
509 Highway 82 West, Greenwood, MS 38930 .... (662) 455–9003
910 Courthouse Lane, Greenville, MS 38701 .... (662) 335–9003

Counties: ATTALA, BOLIVAR, CARROLL, CLAIBORNE, COAHOMA, COPIAH, GRENADA, HINDS (part), HOLMES, HUMPHREYS, ISSAQUENA, JEFFERSON, LEAKE, LEFLORE, MADISON (part), MONTGOMERY, PANOLA, QUITMAN, SHARKEY, SUNFLOWER, TALLAHATCHIE, TUNICA, WARREN, WASHINGTON, YALOBUSHA, AND YAZOO. Population (2010), 741,862.

ZIP Codes: 38606, 38614, 38617, 38619–23, 38626, 38630–31, 38639, 38643–46, 38658, 38664–66, 38670, 38676, 38701–04, 38720–23, 38725–26, 38730–32, 38736–38, 38740, 38744–46, 38748–49, 38751, 38753–54, 38756, 38759–62, 38764–65, 38767–69, 38771–74, 38778, 38781, 38901, 38914, 38917, 38920–25, 38927–30, 38940–41, 38943–48, 38950, 38952–54, 38957–58, 38961–67, 39038–41, 39045–46, 39051, 39054, 39056, 39059, 39061, 39063, 39066–67, 39069, 39071, 39078–79, 39083, 39086, 39088, 39090, 39094–97, 39108, 39110, 39113, 39115, 39120, 39144, 39146, 39150, 39154, 39156–57, 39159–60, 39162, 39166, 39169–70, 39174–77, 39179–80, 39183, 39189, 39191–92, 39194, 39201–04, 39206, 39209, 39211–13, 39216–17, 39272, 39365, 39653, 39668, 39745, 39747, 39767

* * *

THIRD DISTRICT

GREGG HARPER, Republican, of Pearl, MS; born in Jackson, MS, June 1, 1956; education: graduated from Pearl High School, Pearl, 1974; B.S., Mississippi College, Clinton, MS, 1978; J.D., University of Mississippi, Oxford, MS, 1981; professional: private practice attorney and prosecuting attorney; member: Pearl Chamber of Commerce, Rankin County Chamber of Commerce; religion: Southern Baptist; married: the former Sidney Carol Hancock; children: Livingston and Maggie; committees: chair, House Administration; chair, Joint Committee on the Library; Energy and Commerce; Joint Committee on Printing; elected to the 111th Congress on November 4, 2008; reelected to each succeeding Congress.

Office Listings

http://www.harper.house.gov facebook: facebook.com/greggharper twitter: @greggharper

2227 Rayburn House Office Building, Washington, DC 20515 .... (202) 225–5031
Chief of Staff.—Michael Cravens. FAX: 225–5797
Policy Director.—Scot Malvaney.
Director of Communications.—Emerson George.
2507–A Old Brandon Road, Pearl, MS 39208 .... (601) 932–2410
District Director.—Chip Reynolds.
Scheduler.—Debra Boutwell.
1901 Front Street, Suite A, Meridian, MS 39301 .... (601) 693–6681
Special Assistant.—Frances White.
1 Research Boulevard, Suite 206, Starkville, MS 39759 .... (662) 324–0007
Senior Field Representative.—Kyle Jordan.

Counties: ADAMS, AMITE, CLARK (part), COVINGTON, FRANKLIN, HINDS (part), JASPER, JEFFERSON DAVIS, KEMPER, LAUDERDALE, LAWRENCE, LINCOLN, MADISON (part), NESHOBA, NEWTON, NOXUBEE, OKTIBBEHA (part), PIKE, RANKIN, SCOTT, SIMPSON, SMITH, WALTHALL, AND WILKINSON. Population (2014), 711,115.

ZIP Codes: 39042, 39044, 39046–47, 39501, 39057, 39062, 39071, 39073–74, 39082, 39092, 39094, 39110–11, 39114, 39116–17, 39119–20, 39410, 39145, 39149, 39152–53, 39157, 39167–68, 39189, 39191, 39193, 39201, 39203–04,

39206, 39208–09, 39211–13, 39216, 39218, 39232, 39269, 39301, 39305, 39307, 39309, 39320, 39323, 39325–28, 39330, 39332, 39335–38, 39341–42, 39345–48, 39350, 39352, 39354–56, 39358–61, 39363–66, 39401–02, 39421–22, 39428–29, 39439, 39443, 39474, 39478–83, 39601, 39629–31, 39633, 39635, 39638, 39641, 39643, 39645, 39647–48, 39652–54, 39657, 39661–63, 39666–69, 39743, 39750, 39759–60, 39762, 39769

* * *

FOURTH DISTRICT

STEVEN M. PALAZZO, Republican, of Biloxi, MS; born in Gulfport, MS, February 21, 1970; education: B.S., University of Southern Mississippi, Hattiesburg, MS, 1994; M.P.A., University of Southern Mississippi, Hattiesburg, 1996; professional: accountant; military: U.S. Marine Corps Reserve, 1988–96; Mississippi Army National Guard, 2007–present; member of Mississippi State House of Representatives, 2007–10; children: Barrett, Aubrey, and Bennett; caucuses: Aerospace Caucus; Congressional Sportsmen's Caucus; Gulf Coast Caucus; Home Protection Caucus; National Guard Caucus; Shipbuilding Caucus; committees: Appropriations; elected to the 112th Congress on November 2, 2010; reelected to each succeeding Congress.

Office Listings

http://www.palazzo.house.gov www.facebook.com/stevenpalazzo twitter.com/congpalazzo

2349 Rayburn House Office Building, Washington, DC 20515 .... (202) 225–5772
FAX: 225–7074
Chief of Staff.—Casey Street.
Legislative Director.—Patrick Large.
Scheduler.—Leslie Churchwell.
970 Tommy Munro Drive, Biloxi, MS 39532 .... (228) 864–7670
641 Main Street, Suite 215, Hattiesburg, MS 39401 .... (601) 582–3246
3118 Pascagoula Street, Suite 181, Pascagoula, MS 39567 .... (228) 202–8104
FAX: 202–8105
72 Technology Boulevard, Suite 216, Ellisville, MS 39437 .... (601) 428–9711

Counties: CLARKE (part), FORREST, GEORGE, GREENE, HANCOCK, HARRISON, JACKSON, JONES, LAMAR, MARION, PEARL RIVER, PERRY, STONE, AND WAYNE. CITIES AND TOWNSHIPS: Biloxi, Gulfport, Hattiesburg, Laurel, and Pascagoula. Population (2010), 741,776.

ZIP Codes: 39301, 39307, 39322, 39324, 39330, 39332, 39347–48, 39355–56, 39360, 39362–63, 39366–67, 39401–04, 39406, 39422–23, 39425–26, 39429, 39436–37, 39439–43, 39451–52, 39455–57, 39459, 39461–66, 39470, 39475–78, 39480–82, 39501–03, 39505–07, 39520–22, 39525, 39529–35, 39540, 39552–53, 39555–56, 39558, 39560–69, 39571–74, 39576–77, 39581, 39595

MISSOURI

(Population 2010, 5,988,927)

SENATORS

CLAIRE McCASKILL, Democrat, of Kirkwood, MO; born in Rolla, MO, July 24, 1953; raised in Lebanon, MO, and Columbia, MO; education: B.A., University of Missouri-Columbia, 1975; J.D., University of Missouri-Columbia School of Law, 1978; professional: clerk with the Missouri Court of Appeals, Western District in Kansas City, 1978; assistant prosecutor, Jackson County Prosecutor's Office, 1979–83; Missouri State Representative, 1983–88; practiced law in Kansas City, MO, 1983–92; Jackson County Legislator-at-Large, 1991–93; Jackson County Prosecutor, 1993–99; Missouri State Auditor, 1999–2006; married: Joseph Shephard, 2002; together, they have seven children: Benjamin, Carl, Marilyn, Michael, Austin, Maddie, and Lily; committees: ranking member, Homeland Security and Governmental Affairs; Armed Services; Finance; elected to the U.S. Senate on November 7, 2006; reelected to the U.S. Senate on November 6, 2012.

Office Listings

http://mccaskill.senate.gov https://www.facebook.com/senatormccaskill
https://twitter.com/mccaskilloffice

503 Hart Senate Office Building, Washington, DC 20510 .... (202) 224–6154
Chief of Staff.—Julie Dwyer. FAX: 228–6326
Deputy Chief of Staff.—Tod Martin.
Legislative Director.—Nichole Distefano.
Communications Director.—Sarah Feldman.
5850 Delmar Boulevard, Suite A, St. Louis, MO 63112 .... (314) 367–1364
Regional Director.—Joeana Middleton.
4141 Pennsylvania Avenue, Suite 101, Kansas City, MO 64111 .... (816) 421–1639
Regional Director.—Brooke Balentine.
555 Independence Avenue, Room 1600, Cape Girardeau, MO 63703 .... (573) 651–0964
District Director.—Christy Mercer.
28 North 8th Street, Suite 500, Columbia, MO 65201 .... (573) 442–7130
Regional Director.—Cindy Hall.
324 Park Central West, Suite 101, Springfield, MO 65806 .... (417) 868–8745
District Director.—David Stokely.

* * *

ROY BLUNT, Republican, of Springfield, MO; born in Niangua, MO, January 10, 1950; education: B.A., Southwest Baptist University, 1970; M.A., Missouri State University, 1972; professional: county clerk and chief election official of Greene County, MO, 1973–84; Secretary of State of Missouri, 1985–92; president of Southwest Baptist University, 1993–96; member, U.S. House of Representatives, for Missouri's 7th District, 1997–2010; married: Abigail Blunt; children: Governor Matthew Blunt, Amy Blunt, Andrew Blunt, and Alexander Charles Blunt; committees: chair; Joint Committee on Printing; chair, Rules and Administration; vice chair, Joint Committee on the Library; Appropriations; Commerce, Science, and Transportation; Select Committee on Intelligence; elected to the U.S. Senate on November 2, 2010; reelected to the U.S. Senate on November 7, 2016.

Office Listings

http://blunt.senate.gov

260 Russell Senate Office Building, Washington, DC 20510 .... (202) 224–5721
Chief of Staff.—Stacy McBride.
Deputy Chief of Staff.—Richard Eddings.
Legislative Director.—Tracy Henke.
Communications Director.—Katie Boyd.
Director of Scheduling.—Richard Eddings.
2740B East Sunshine, Springfield, MO 65804 .... (417) 877–7814
1000 Walnut Street, Suite 1560, Kansas City, MO 64106 .... (816) 471–7141
7700 Bonhomme, Suite 315, Clayton, MO 63105 .... (314) 725–4484
1123 Wilkes Boulevard, Suite 320, Columbia, MO 65201 .... (573) 442–8151
Deputy Chief of Staff, State.—Derek Coats.
338 Broadway, Suite 303, Cape Girardeau, MO 63701 .... (573) 334–7044

REPRESENTATIVES

FIRST DISTRICT

WM. LACY CLAY, Democrat, of St. Louis, MO; born in St. Louis, July 27, 1956; education: Springbrook High School, Silver Spring, MD, 1974; B.A., University of Maryland, College Park, MD, 1983; public service: Missouri House of Representatives, 1983–91; Missouri State Senate, 1991–2000; nonprofit organizations: St. Louis Gateway Classic Sports Foundation; Mary Ryder Homes; William L. Clay Scholarship and Research Fund; religion: Catholic; divorced; children: Carol and William III; committees: Financial Services; Natural Resources; Oversight and Government Reform; elected to the 107th Congress on November 7, 2000; reelected to each succeeding Congress.

Office Listings

http://www.lacyclay.house.gov https://www.facebook.com/CongressmanClayMO1

2428 Rayburn House Office Building, Washington, DC 20515 .... (202) 225–2406
Chief of Staff.—Yvette P. Cravins. FAX: 226–3717
Scheduler.—Karyn Long.
Legislative Assistants: Pauline Jamry, Perre Smalls.
Thomas F. Eagleton U.S. Courthouse, 111 South 10th Street, Suite 24–344, St. Louis, MO 63102 .... (314) 367–1970
FAX: 367–1341
6830 Gravois, St. Louis, MO 63116 .... (314) 669–9393
FAX: 669–9398
1281 Graham Road, Suite 202, Florissant, MO 63031 .... (314) 383–5240

Counties: CITY OF ST. LOUIS; AND ST. LOUIS COUNTY (part). Population (2010), 748,616.

ZIP Codes: 63031, 63033–34, 63042–45, 63074, 63101–25, 63130, 63132–41, 63143–44, 63146–47, 63155

* * *

SECOND DISTRICT

ANN L. WAGNER, Republican, of Ballwin, MO; born in St. Louis, MO, September 13, 1962; education: B.A.B.S., University of Missouri, Columbia, 1984; professional: businesswoman; Hallmark Cards; Ralston Purina; public service: Committeewoman for Lafayette Township; chair of Missouri Republican Party, 1999–2005; co-chair of the Republican National Committee, 2001–05; U.S. Ambassador to Luxembourg, 2005–09; family: married to Raymond, Jr.; children: Raymond III, Stephen, and Mary Ruth; committees: Financial Services; Foreign Affairs; elected to the 113th Congress on November 6, 2012; reelected to each succeeding Congress.

Office Listings

http://wagner.house.gov https://www.facebook.com/repannwagner
https://twitter.com/repannwagner

435 Cannon House Office Building, Washington, DC 20515 .... (202) 225–1621
Chief of Staff.—Christian Morgan.
Scheduler.—Molly Stevens.
301 Sovereign Court, Suite 201, St. Louis, MO 63011 .... (636) 779–5449
District Director.—Miriam Stonebraker.

Counties: JEFFERSON (part), CHARLES (part), AND ST. LOUIS (part). Population (2010), 706,622.

ZIP Codes: 63005, 63010–11, 63017, 63021, 63025–26, 63038, 63040, 63043–44, 63049, 63069, 63074, 63088, 63105, 63114, 63117, 63119, 63122–32, 63141, 63144, 63146, 63301, 63303–04, 63341, 63366, 63368, 63376

* * *

THIRD DISTRICT

BLAINE LUETKEMEYER, Republican, of St. Elizabeth, MO; born in Jefferson City, MO, May 7, 1952; education: graduate of Lincoln University, Jefferson City, MO, 1974, where he earned a degree with distinction in political science and a minor in business administration,

1999–2005; professional: served as Missouri State Representative, and after leaving office was appointed by the Governor to serve as director of the Missouri Division of Tourism; religion: lifelong member of St. Lawrence Catholic Church; married: Jackie, three children; committees: vice chair, Small Business; Financial Services; elected to the 111th Congress on November 4, 2008; reelected to each succeeding Congress.

Office Listings

http://luetkemeyer.house.gov facebook: https://www.facebook.com/BlaineLuetkemeyer
twitter: @RepBlainePress

2230 Rayburn House Office Building, Washington, DC 20515 .... (202) 225–2956
Chief of Staff.—Seth Appleton. FAX: 225–5712
Deputy Chief of Staff.—Chris Brown.
Legislative Director.—Lucas West.
Communications Director.—Kristina Weger.
Scheduler.—Ann Vogel.
Legislative Assistant.—Claire Trokey.
Legislative Aide.—Edward Rolwes.
Staff Assistant.—Josiah Boman.
2117 Missouri Boulevard, Jefferson City, MO 65109 .... (573) 635–7232
Deputy Chief of Staff.—Jeremy Ketterer. FAX: 635–8346
Director of Constituent Affairs.—Keri Stuart.
Congressional Liaison.—Lori Boyken.
Office Manager.—Laura Hardecke.
Special Assistant.—Matt Thompson.
516 Jefferson Street, Washington, MO 63090 .... (636) 239–2276
District Office Director.—Jim McNichols. FAX: 239–0478
113 East Pearce, Wentzville, MO 63385 .... (573) 327–7055
District Office Director.—Christa Montgomery.

Counties: CALLAWAY, CAMDEN (part), COLE, FRANKLIN, GASCONADE, JEFFERSON (part), LINCOLN, MARIES, MILLER, MONTGOMERY, OSAGE, ST. CHARLES (part), AND WARREN. Population (2010), 748,615.

ZIP Codes: 63005 (part), 63010 (part), 63012 (part), 63013–14, 63015–16 (part), 63019 (part), 63023 (part), 63025–26 (part), 63028 (part), 63037, 63039, 63041 (part), 63048, 63049–50 (part), 63051–53, 63055, 63057, 63060–61, 63068, 63069–70 (part), 63072 (part), 63073, 63077, 63079, 63080 (part), 63084, 63089–91, 63301 (part), 63302, 63303 (part), 63332–33, 63334 (part), 63341 (part), 63342, 63343–44 (part), 63346–51, 63352 (part), 63357, 63359 (part), 63361–63, 63365, 63366 (part), 63367, 63368 (part), 63369–70, 63373, 63376 (part), 63377–79, 63381, 63383, 63384 (part)

* * *

FOURTH DISTRICT

VICKY HARTZLER, Republican, of Harrisonville, MO; born in Archie, MO, October 13, 1960; education: B.S., in education, *summa cum laude*, University of Missouri-Columbia, Columbia, MO, 1983; M.S., in education, Central Missouri State University (now University of Central Missouri), Warrensburg, MO, 1992; professional: served as State spokesperson for the Coalition to Protect Marriage, 2004; member of the Missouri State House of Representatives, 124th District, 1995–2001; appointed chair, Missouri Women's Council, 2005; teacher of family and consumer sciences for 11 years in Lebanon and Belton, MO; religion: Evangelical Christian; family: married: Lowell Hartzler; one child: Tiffany; caucuses: Air Force Caucus; Army Caucus; China Caucus; Congressional Coalition on Adoption; EMP Caucus; General Aviation Caucus; Human Trafficking Caucus; International Religious Freedom Caucus; Israel Allies Caucus; Job Creators' Caucus; Long-Range Strike Caucus; Military Family Caucus; Missile Defense Caucus; Prayer Caucus; Pro-Life Caucus; Republican Study Committee; Rural Caucus; Small Business Caucus; Taiwan Caucus; committees: Agriculture; Armed Services; elected to the 112th Congress on November 2, 2010; reelected to each succeeding Congress.

Office Listings

http://www.hartzler.house.gov facebook: https://www.facebook.com/Congresswoman.Hartzler
twitter: https://twitter.com/rephartzler

2235 Rayburn House Office Building, Washington, DC 20515 .... (202) 225–2876
Chief of Staff.—Chris Connelly. FAX: 225–0148
Legislative Director.—Joe Tvrdy.
Communications Director.—Kyle Buckles.
Scheduler.—Mallory Fields.
2415 Carter Lane, Suite 4, Columbia, MO 65201 .... (573) 442–9311
1909 North Commercial Street, Harrisonville, MO 64701 .... (816) 884–3411
219 North Adams Street, Lebanon, MO 65536 .... (417) 532–5582

Counties: AUDRAIN (part), BARTON, BATES, BENTON, BOONE, CAMDEN, CASS, CEDAR, COOPER, DADE, DALLAS, HENRY, HICKORY, HOWARD, JOHNSON, LACLEDE, MONITIEAU, MORGAN, PULASKI, RANDOLPH, ST. CLAIR, VERNON, AND WEBSTER (part). Population (2010), 748,616.

ZIP Codes: 63352, 64011–12, 64019–20, 64030, 64034, 64037, 64040, 64061, 64070–71, 64076, 64078, 64080, 64082–83, 64090, 64093, 64147, 64149, 64701, 64720, 64722–26, 64728, 64730, 64733–35, 64738–48, 64750, 64752, 64755–56, 64759, 64761–63, 64765–67, 64769–72, 64776, 64778–81, 64783–84, 64788, 64790, 64832, 64855, 65010–11, 65018, 65020, 65023, 65025–26, 65034, 65037–39, 65042, 65046, 65050, 65055, 65064, 65068, 65072, 65074, 65078–79, 65081, 65084, 65201–03, 65205, 65211–12, 65215–18, 65230–33, 65237, 65239–40, 65243–44, 65247–48, 65250, 65254–57, 65259–60, 65264–65, 65270, 65274, 65276, 65278–80, 65284–85, 65287, 65299, 65301–02, 65305, 65322–26, 65329, 65332–38, 65340, 65345, 65347–48, 65350–51, 65354–55, 65360, 65452, 65457, 65459, 65461, 65463, 65470, 65473, 65534, 65536, 65543, 65550, 65552, 65556, 65567, 65583–84, 65590–91, 65603–04, 65607, 65622, 65632, 65634–36, 65644, 65646, 65648–50, 65652, 65661–62, 65668, 65674, 65682, 65685, 65706, 65713, 65722, 65724, 65732, 65735, 65742, 65746, 65752, 65757, 65764, 65767, 65770, 65774, 65779, 65783, 65785–87

* * *

FIFTH DISTRICT

EMANUEL CLEAVER II, Democrat, of Kansas City, MO; born in Waxahachie, TX, October 26, 1944; education: M.Div., Saint Paul School of Theology, MO, 1974; B.S., Prairie View A&M University, TX, 1972; professional: senior pastor, St. James United Methodist Church, 1973–2009; City Councilman, Kansas City, MO, 5th District, 1979–91; founder, Harmony in a World of Difference, 1991; founder, Southern Christian Leadership Conference, Kansas City Chapter; Mayor of Kansas City, MO, 1991–99; member, President-elect Bill Clinton's transitional team, 1992; host, Under the Clock, KCUR radio, 1999–2004; chairman of the Congressional Black Caucus, 2010–12; member, National Co-Chair of President Barack Obama Campaign Committee, 2012; married: Dianne; four children; four grandchildren; committees: Financial Services; elected to the 109th Congress on November 2, 2004; reelected to each succeeding Congress.

Office Listings

http://www.cleaver.house.gov https://www.facebook.com/emanuelcleaverii
https://twitter.com/repcleaver

2335 Rayburn House Office Building, Washington, DC 20515 .... (202) 225–4535
Chief of Staff.—John Jones. FAX: 225–4403
Legislative Director.—Christina Mahoney.
Scheduler.—Alex Ndikum.
101 West 31st Street, Kansas City, MO 64108 .... (816) 842–4545
Communications Director.—Heather Frierson.
211 Maple Avenue, Independence, MO 64050 .... (816) 833–4545
1923 Main Street, Higginsville, MO 64037 .... (660) 584–7373

Counties: CLAY COUNTY (part), JACKSON COUNTY (part), LAFAYETTE, RAY, AND SALINE COUNTIES. CITIES AND TOWNSHIPS: Blue Springs, Claycomo, Concordia, Gladstone, Grandview, Grain Valley, Higginsville, Independence, Kansas City, Lawson, Lee's Summit, Lexington, Marshall, North Kansas City, Oak Grove, Odessa, Raytown, Richmond, Slater Sugar Creek, and Sweet Springs. Population (2010), 747,573.

ZIP Codes: 64001, 64011, 64017, 64020–22, 64024, 64029, 64035–37, 64062, 64067, 64071, 64074–77, 64084–85, 64096–97, 64747–48, 65320, 65327, 65330, 65339–40, 65344, 65347, 65349, 65351

* * *

SIXTH DISTRICT

SAM GRAVES, Republican, of Tarkio, MO; born in Fairfax, MO, November 7, 1963; education: B.S., University of Missouri-Columbia, 1986; professional: farmer; organizations: Missouri Farm Bureau; Northwest Missouri State University Agriculture Advisory Committee; University Extension Council; Rotary Club; awards: Associated Industries Voice of Missouri Business Award; Tom Henderson Award; Tarkio Community Betterment Award; Missouri Physical Therapy Association Award; Outstanding Young Farmer Award, 1997; Hero of the Taxpayer Award; NFIB Guardian of Small Business Award; public service: elected to the Missouri House of Representatives, 1992; elected to the Missouri State Senate, 1994; religion: Baptist; committees: Armed Services; Transportation and Infrastructure; elected to the 107th Congress on November 7, 2000; reelected to each succeeding Congress.

Office Listings

http://www.graves.house.gov

1135 Longworth House Office Building, Washington, DC 20515 .... (202) 225–7041

Office Listings—Continued

Chief of Staff.—Paul J. Sass. FAX: 225–8221
Legislative Director.—Jack Ruddy.
Communications Director.—Wes Shaw.
Scheduler.—Amanda Sollazzo.
411 Jules Street, Suite 111, St. Joseph, MO 64501 .... (816) 233–9818
11724 Northwest Plaza Circle, Suite 900, Kansas City, MO 64153 .... (816) 792–3976
906 Broadway, P.O. Box 364, Hannibal, MO 63401 .... (573) 221–3400

Counties: ADAIR, ANDREW, ATCHISON, AUDRAIN (part), BUCHANAN, CALDWELL, CARROLL, CHARITON, CLARK, CLAY (part), CLINTON, DAVIESS, DEKALB, GENTRY, GRUNDY, HARRISON, HOLT, JACKSON (part), KNOX, LEWIS, LINN, LIVINGSTON, MACON, MARION, MERCER, MONROE, NODAWAY, PIKE, PLATTE, PUTNAM, RALLS, SCHUYLER, SCOTLAND, SHELBY, SULLIVAN, AND WORTH. Population (2010), 748,616.

ZIP Codes: 63119, 63330, 63334, 63336, 63339, 63343–45, 63352–53, 63359, 63382, 63384, 63401, 63430–43, 63445–48, 63450–54, 63456–69, 63471–74, 63501, 63530–41, 63543–49, 63551–52, 63555–61, 63563, 63565–67, 64013–16, 64018, 64024, 64028–30, 64048, 64051, 64055–58, 64060, 64062–64, 64066, 64068–69, 64072, 64074–75, 64077, 64079, 64085–86, 64088–89, 64092, 64098, 64106, 64112, 64116, 64118–19, 64134, 64150–58, 64163–68, 64188, 64190, 64195, 64401–02, 64420–24, 64426–34, 64436–46, 64448–49, 64451, 64453–59, 64461, 64463, 64465–71, 64473–77, 64479–87, 64489–94, 64496–99, 64501–08, 64601, 64620, 64622–25, 64628, 64630–33, 64635–61, 64664, 64667–68, 64670–74, 64676, 64679, 64681–83, 64686, 64688–89, 64701, 65065, 65202, 65205, 65230, 65232, 65236, 65240, 65243–44, 65246–47, 65254–55, 65258, 65260–61, 65263–65, 65270, 65275, 65280–83, 65286

* * *

SEVENTH DISTRICT

BILLY LONG, Republican, of Springfield, MO; born in Springfield, August 11, 1955; education: attended University of Missouri, Columbia, MO, 1973–74; Missouri Auction School, Kansas City, MO, 1979; Certified Auctioneer Institute designation, University of Indiana, Bloomington, IN, 1983; professional: owner, Billy Long Auctions, LLC; radio talk show host, KWTO AM 560, 1999–2006; former president, Missouri Professional Auctioneers Association; past board member, National Auctioneers Association; past member, Southeast Rotary Club, Springfield; awards: Missouri Professional Auctioneers' Hall of Fame; Outstanding Young Alumni Award, Greenwood Lab School; religion: Presbyterian; family: wife, Barbara Long; two daughters; caucuses: Republican Conference, 2011–present; committees: Energy and Commerce; elected to the 112th Congress on November 2, 2010; reelected to each succeeding Congress.

Office Listings

http://long.house.gov https://www.facebook.com/Rep.Billy.Long
https://twitter.com/USRepLong

2454 Rayburn House Office Building, Washington, DC 20515 .... (202) 225–6536
Chief of Staff.—Joe Lillis. FAX: 225–5604
Legislative Director.—Peter Stehouwer.
Scheduler.—Drew McDowell.
Communications Director.—Hannah Smith.
3232 East Ridgeview Street, Springfield, MO 65804 .... (417) 889–1899
FAX: 889–4915
2727 East 32nd Street, Suite 2, Joplin, MO 64804 .... (417) 781–1041
FAX: 781–2832

Counties: BARRY, CHRISTIAN, GREENE, JASPER, LAWRENCE, MCDONALD, NEWTON, POLK, STONE, TANEY, AND WEBSTER (part). Population (2010), 721,754.

ZIP Codes: 64748, 64755–56, 64766, 64769, 64801–04, 64830–36, 64840–44, 64847–50, 64853–59, 64861–70, 64873–74, 65603–05, 65608–20, 65622–27, 65629–31, 65633, 65635, 65637–38, 65640–41, 65645–50, 65652–58, 65661, 65663–64, 65666, 65669, 65672–76, 65679–82, 65686, 65702, 65705, 65707–08, 65710, 65712, 65714–15, 65720–21, 65723, 65725–30, 65733–34, 65737–42, 65744–45, 65747, 65752–57, 65759–62, 65765–73, 65781, 65784–85, 65801–10, 65814, 65817, 65890, 65898–99

* * *

EIGHTH DISTRICT

JASON T. SMITH, Republican, of Salem, MO; born in St. Louis, MO, June 16, 1980; education: graduate of Salem High School; received B.S. degrees, agricultural economics and business administration, with an emphasis in finance, University of Missouri, Columbia; earned law degree from Oklahoma City University School of Law; Trinity College, Cambridge, England; professional: attorney; real estate agent; small business owner and fourth generation owner of the family farm; NRA; Missouri Farm Bureau; former president, current member of the Salem FFA Alumni Association; holds an American FFA degree; elected to the Missouri State House of Representatives, 2005 (special election), 2006, and 2008; leadership: served as Majority Whip in the 96th General Assembly; youngest Speaker Pro Tem in the 97th General Assembly; religion: Assemblies of God; committees: Budget; Ways and Means; elected, by special election, to the 113th Congress on June 4, 2013, to fill the vacancy caused by the resignation of U.S. Representative Jo Ann Emerson; reelected to each succeeding Congress.

Office Listings

http://jasonsmith.house.gov https://www.facebook.com/repjasonsmith
https://twitter.com/repjasonsmith

1118 Longworth House Office Building, Washington, DC 20515 .... (202) 225–4404
Chief of Staff.—Eric Bohl. FAX: 226–0326
Executive Assistant / Scheduler.—Adrienne Schrodt.
2502 Tanner Drive, Suite 205, Cape Girardeau, MO 63703 .... (573) 335–0101
830A South Bishop, Rolla, MO 65401 .... (573) 364–2455
22 East Columbia, Farmington, MO 63640 .... (573) 756–9755
35 Court Square, Suite 300, West Plains, MO 65775 .... (417) 255–1515
2911 North Westwood Boulevard, Suite C, Poplar Bluff, MO 63907.

Counties: BOLLINGER, BUTLER, CAPE GIRARDEAU, CARTER, CRAWFORD, DENT, DOUGLAS, DUNKLIN, HOWELL, IRON, JEFFERSON (part), MADISON, MISSISSIPPI, NEW MADRID, OREGON, OZARK, PEMISCOT, PERRY, PHELPS, REYNOLDS, RIPLEY, SCOTT, SHANNON, ST. FRANCOIS, STE. GENEVIEVE, STODDARD, TEXAS, WASHINGTON, WAYNE, AND WRIGHT. Population (2010), 748,616.

ZIP Codes: 63036, 63071, 63601, 63620–26, 63628–33, 63636–38, 63640, 63648, 63650–51, 63653–56, 63660, 63662–66, 63674–75, 63701–03, 63730, 63732, 63735–40, 63742–48, 63750–52, 63755, 63758, 63760, 63763–64, 63766–67, 63769–72, 63774–76, 63779–85, 63787, 63801, 63820–30, 63833–34, 63837, 63839–41, 63845–53, 63855, 63857, 63860, 63862–63, 63866–70, 63873–82, 63901–02, 63931–45, 63950–57, 63960–67, 65401–02, 65409, 65436, 65438–41, 65444, 65446, 65449, 65453, 65456, 65459, 65461–62, 65464, 65466, 65468, 65479, 65483–84, 65501, 65529, 65532, 65541–42, 65546, 65548, 65550, 65552, 65555, 65557, 65564–66, 65570–71, 65586, 65588–89, 65606, 65608–09, 65614, 65616, 65618, 65620, 65626–27, 65629, 65637–38, 65652–53, 65655, 65660, 65662, 65666–67, 65676, 65679–80, 65688–90, 65692, 65701–02, 65704, 65711, 65713, 65715, 65717, 65720, 65729, 65731, 65733, 65740–41, 65744, 65746, 65753, 65755, 65759–62, 65766, 65768, 65773, 65775, 65777–78, 65784, 65788–91, 65793

MONTANA

(Population 2010, 989,415)

SENATORS

JON TESTER, Democrat, of Big Sandy, MT; born in Havre, MT, August 21, 1956; education: graduated, Big Sandy High School, 1974; B.S., music, University of Great Falls, 1978; professional: farmer, T-Bone Farms, Big Sandy, 1978–present; teacher, Big Sandy School District, 1978–80; member, Big Sandy Soil Conservation Service Committee, 1980–83; chairman, Big Sandy School Board of Trustees, 1983–92; past master, Treasure Lodge #95 of the Masons; member, Chouteau County Agricultural Stabilization and Conservation Service Committee, 1990–95; member, Organic Crop Improvement Association, 1996–97; served in Montana Senate, 1999–2007; Montana Senate Democratic Whip, 2001–03; Montana Senate Democratic Leader, 2003–05; Montana Senate President, 2005–07; vice chair, Congressional Sportsmen's Caucus; married: Sharla Tester; two children: Christine and Shon; committees: ranking member, Veterans' Affairs; Appropriations; Banking, Housing, and Urban Affairs; Commerce, Science, and Transportation; Indian Affairs; elected to the U.S. Senate on November 7, 2006; reelected to the U.S. Senate on November 6, 2012.

Office Listings

http://tester.senate.gov http://www.facebook.com/senatortester twitter: @senatortester

311 Hart Senate Office Building, Washington, DC 20510 .... (202) 224–2644
Chief of Staff.—Aaron Murphy. FAX: 224–8594
Legislative Director.—Dylan Laslovich.
Communications Director.—Marnee Banks.
Director of Scheduling.—Trecia McEvoy.
State Director.—Dayna Swanson.
222 North 32nd Street, Suite 101, Billings, MT 59101 .... (406) 252–0550
1 East Main Street, Suite 202, Bozeman, MT 59715 .... (406) 586–4450
125 West Granite, Suite 200, Butte, MT 59701 .... (406) 723–3277
122 West Towne, Glendive, MT 59330 .... (406) 452–9585
119 First Avenue North, Suite 102, Great Falls, MT 59401 .... (406) 452–9585
208 North Montana Avenue, Suite 202, Helena, MT 59601 .... (406) 449–5401
8 3rd Street East, Kalispell, MT 59901 .... (406) 257–3360
130 West Front Street, Missoula, MT 59801 .... (406) 728–3003

* * *

STEVE DAINES, Republican, of Bozeman, MT; born in Van Nuys, CA, August 20, 1962; education: B.S., Montana State University, Bozeman, MT, 1984; professional: businessman; public service: Republican National Convention delegate, 1984; U.S. Representative, 2013–15; married: Cindy; children: David, Annie, Michael, and Caroline; committees: Agriculture, Nutrition, and Forestry; Appropriations; Energy and Natural Resources; Homeland Security and Governmental Affairs; Indian Affairs; elected to the 113th Congress on November 6, 2012; elected to the U.S. Senate on November 4, 2014.

Office Listings

http://daines.senate.gov www.facebook.com/stevedainesmt
www.twitter.com/stevedaines

320 Hart Senate Office Building, Washington, DC 20510 .... (202) 224–2651
Chief of Staff.—Jason Thielman.
Deputy Chief of Staff.—Wally Hsueh.
Legislative Director.—Darin Thacker.
Communications Director.—Marcie Kinzel.
Scheduler.—Caitlin Dorman.
30 West 14th Street, Helena, MT 59601 .... (406) 443–3189
State Director.—Charles Robison.
222 North 32nd Street, Suite 100, Billings, MT 59101 .... (406) 245–6822
13 South Willson Avenue, Suite 8, Bozeman, MT 59718 .... (406) 587–3446
280 East Front Street, Suite 100, Missoula, MT 59802 .... (406) 549–8198
104 4th Street North, Suite 302, Great Falls, MT 59401 .... (406) 453–0148
609 South Central Avenue, Suite #4 (Central Plaza Building), Sidney, MT 59270 .... (406) 482–9010
40 2nd Street East, Suite 211 (KM Building), Kalispell, MT 59901 .... (406) 257–3765
310 North Center, Hardin, MT 59034 .... (406) 665–4126

REPRESENTATIVE

AT LARGE

GREG GIANFORTE, Republican, of Bozeman, MT; born April 17, 1961; education: M.S. and B.E., Stevens Institute of Technology, Hoboken, NJ, 1983; professional: co-founder, Brightwork Development Inc.; founder, RightNow Technologies; religion: nondenominational Christian, Grace Bible Church; married: Susan; children: Richard, David, Adam, and Rachel; committees: Natural Resources; Oversight and Government Reform; elected to the 115th Congress, by special election, on May 25, 2017, to fill the vacancy caused by the resignation of U.S. Representative Ryan Zinke.

Office Listings

https://gianforte.house.gov

1419 Longworth House Office Building, Washington, DC 20515 .... (202) 225–3211
Chief of Staff.—Charles Robison. FAX: 225–5687
Communications Director.—Travis Hall.
Legislative Director.—Will Carraco.
Scheduler.—Kendall Garraway.
222 North 32nd Street, Suite 900, Billings, MT 59101 .... (406) 969–1736
District Director.—Lesley Robinson.
7 West 6th Avenue, Suite 3B, Helena, MT 59601 .... (406) 502–1435
710 Central Avenue, Great Falls, MT 59401 .... (406) 952–1280

Counties: BEAVERHEAD, BIG HORN, BLAINE, BROADWATER, CARBON, CARTER, CASCADE, CHOUTEAU, CUSTER, DANIELS, DAWSON, DEER LODGE, FALLON, FERGUS, FLATHEAD, GALLATIN, GARFIELD, GLACIER, GOLDEN VALLEY, GRANITE, HILL, JEFFERSON, JUDITH BASIN, LAKE, LEWIS AND CLARK, LIBERTY, LINCOLN, MADISON, MCCONE, MEAGHER, MINERAL, MISSOULA, MUSSELLSHELL, PARK, PETROLEUM, PHILLIPS, PONDERA, POWDER RIVER, POWELL, PRAIRIE, RAVALLI, RICHLAND, ROOSEVELT, ROSEBUD, SANDERS, SHERIDAN, SILVER BOW, STILLWATER, SWEET GRASS, TETON, TOOLE, TREASURE, VALLEY, WHEATLAND, WIBAUX, AND YELLOWSTONE. Population (2010), 989,415.

ZIP Codes: 59001–04, 59006–08, 59010–16, 59018–20, 59022, 59024–39, 59041, 59043–44, 59046–47, 59050, 59052–55, 59057–59, 59061–72, 59074–79, 59081–89, 59101–08, 59201, 59211–15, 59217–19, 59221–23, 59225–26, 59230–31, 59240–44, 59247–48, 59250, 59252–63, 59270, 59273–76, 59301, 59311–19, 59322–24, 59326–27, 59330, 59332–33, 59336–39, 59341, 59343–45, 59347, 59349, 59351, 59353–54, 59401–06, 59410–12, 59414, 59416–22, 59424–25, 59427, 59430, 59432–36, 59440–48, 59450–54, 59456–57, 59460–69, 59471–72, 59474, 59477, 59479–80, 59482–87, 59489, 59501, 59520–32, 59535, 59537–38, 59540, 59542, 59544–47, 59601–02, 59604, 59620, 59623–24, 59626, 59631–36, 59638–45, 59647–48, 59701–03, 59710–11, 59713–22, 59724–25, 59727–33, 59735–36, 59739–41, 59743, 59745–52, 59754–56, 59758–62, 59771–73, 59801–04, 59806–08, 59812, 59820–21, 59823–35, 59837, 59840–48, 59851, 59853–56, 59858–60, 59863–68, 59870–75, 59901, 59903–04, 59910–23, 59925–37

NEBRASKA

(Population 2010, 1,826,341)

SENATORS

DEB FISCHER, Republican, of Valentine, NE; born in Lincoln, NE, March 1, 1951; education: B.S., University of Nebraska-Lincoln, Lincoln, NE, 1988; professional: rancher; Senator in the Nebraska Unicameral, 2005–13; president of the Nebraska Association of School Boards; commissioner on the Coordinating Commission for Post-Secondary Education; Valentine Rural High School Board of Education; awards: BILLD Fellow, Midwest Council of State Governments Bowhay Institute for Legislative Leadership, 2005; NRD Farm and Ranch Conservation Award, 1999; Nebraska Association of School Boards Lifetime Achievement Award, 1999; Nebraska Rural Community Schools Association Outstanding Board Member Award, 1998–99; Nebraska Cattlemen Environmental Stewardship Award, 1995; Rangeman's Award, Nebraska Section Society for Range Management, 1994; NRD State Grasslands Conservation Award, 1993; Kellogg Fellow, National Center for Food and Policy Research, Resources for the Future, Washington, DC, 1991; LEAD VIII Fellow, Nebraska Leadership Program, 1988–90; religion: Presbyterian; married: Bruce Fischer; three children; three grandchildren; caucuses: vice chair, Sportsmen's Caucus; General Aviation Caucus; National Guard Caucus; Republican High-Tech Task Force; Senate Rural Health Caucus; Senate Western Caucus; committees: Agriculture, Nutrition, and Forestry; Armed Services; Commerce, Science, and Transportation; Environment and Public Works; Rules and Administration; Special Committee on Aging; elected to the U.S. Senate on November 6, 2012.

Office Listings

http://fischer.senate.gov

454 Russell Senate Office Building, Washington, DC 20510 .... (202) 224–6551
Chief of Staff.—Joe Hack. FAX: 228–1325
Legislative Director.—Emily Leviner.
Communications Director.—Brianna Puccini.
Administrative Director.—Sherri Hupart.
11819 Miracle Hills Drive, Suite 205, Omaha, NE 68154 .... (402) 391–3411
State Director.—Dusty Vaughan. FAX: 391–4725
440 North 8th Street, Suite 120, Lincoln, NE 68508 .... (402) 441–4600
FAX: 476–8753
1110 Circle Drive, Suite 400, Scottsbluff, NE 69361 .... (308) 636–6344
20 West 23rd Street, Kearney, NE 68847 .... (308) 234–2361
FAX: 234–3684
P.O. Box 1021, Norfolk, NE 68702 .... (402) 200–8816

* * *

BEN SASSE, Republican, of Fremont, NE; born in Plainview, NE, February 22, 1972; education: B.A., Harvard University, Cambridge, MA, 1994; M.A., St. John's College, Annapolis, MD, 1998; M.A., M.Phil., and Ph.D., Yale University, New Haven, CT, 2004; professional: management strategist; policy strategist; historian; college president; religion: Evangelical; married: Melissa McLeod Sasse; three children: Elizabeth, Katherine, and Augustine; committees: Armed Services; Banking, Housing, and Urban Affairs; Joint Economic Committee; Judiciary; elected to the U.S. Senate on November 4, 2014.

Office Listings

http://sasse.senate.gov https://www.facebook.com/senatorsasse
https://twitter.com/sensasse

136 Russell Senate Office Building, Washington, DC 20510 .... (202) 224–4224
Chief of Staff.—Raymond Sass.
Deputy Chiefs of Staff: Shelly Blake, Tyler Grassmeyer.
Legislative Director.—Patrick Lehman.
1128 Lincoln Mall, Suite 305, Lincoln, NE 68508 .... (402) 476–1400
4111 Fourth Avenue, Suite 26, Kearney, NE 68845 .... (308) 233–3677
115 Railway Street, Suite C102, Scottsbluff, NE 69361 .... (308) 632–6032
304 North 168th Circle, Suite 213, Omaha, NE 68118 .... (402) 550–8040

REPRESENTATIVES

FIRST DISTRICT

JEFF FORTENBERRY, Republican, of Lincoln, NE; born in Baton Rouge, LA, December 27, 1960; education: B.A., Louisiana State University, 1982; M.P.P., Georgetown University, Washington, DC, 1986; M.Div., Franciscan University, Steubenville, Ohio, 1996; professional: Lincoln City Council, 1997–2001; publishing executive; worked as economist; managed a public relations firm; congressional aide for the Senate Subcommittee on Intergovernmental Relations; family: married to Celeste Gregory; children: five; committees: Appropriations; elected to the 109th Congress on November 2, 2004; reelected to each succeeding Congress.

Office Listings

http://www.fortenberry.house.gov https://www.facebook.com/jefffortenberry
twitter: @jefffortenberry

1514 Longworth House Office Building, Washington, DC 20515 .... (202) 225–4806
Chief of Staff.—Reyn Archer. FAX: 225–5686
Legislative Director.—Alan Feyerherm.
Communications Director.—James Crotty.
Executive Assistant.—Diana Shin.
301 South 13th Street, Suite 100, Lincoln, NE 68508 .... (402) 438–1598
641 North Broad Street, Fremont, NE 68026 .... (402) 727–0888
125 South 4th Street, Suite 101, Norfolk, NE 68701 .... (402) 379–2064

Counties: BURT, BUTLER, CASS, COLFAX, CUMING, DODGE, LANCASTER, MADISON, OTOE, PLATTE, POLK, SARPY, SAUNDERS, SEWARD, STANTON, THURSTON, AND WASHINGTON. Population (2015), 638,320.

ZIP Codes: 68001–05, 68007 (part), 68008–09, 68014–20, 68023 (part), 68025–26, 68029, 68031, 68033–34, 68036–42, 68044–45, 68047 (part), 68048, 68050, 68055–58, 68061–63, 68064 (part), 68065–67, 68068 (part), 68070–73, 68112 (part), 68113, 68122–23 (part), 68133 (part), 68142 (part), 68147 (part), 68152 (part), 68157 (part), 68301 (part), 68304, 68307, 68313 (part), 68314, 68316 (part), 68317, 68324 (part), 68329 (part), 68330, 68333 (part), 68336, 68339 (part), 68341 (part), 68343 (part), 68344, 68346–47, 68349, 68358–59 (part), 68360, 68364, 68366, 68367–68 (part), 68372, 68379 (part), 68382, 68402–03, 68404–05 (part), 68407, 68409–10, 68413, 68417–19, 68421 (part), 68423, 68428, 68430, 68431 (part), 68434, 68438–39, 68443 (part), 68446, 68448 (part), 68454–56, 68460 (part), 68461–63, 68465 (part), 68501–10, 68512, 68514, 68516–17, 68520–24, 68526–29, 68531–32, 68542, 68583, 68588, 68601 (part), 68602, 68621, 68624, 68626, 68628 (part), 68629, 68631–35, 68640 (part), 68641–44, 68647–49, 68651, 68653, 68654 (part), 68658–59, 68660 (part), 68661–62, 68663 (part), 68664, 68666 (part), 68667, 68669, 68701 (part), 68702, 68710 (part), 68714 (part), 68715–16, 68733 (part), 68738 (part), 68740 (part), 68748, 68752 (part), 68758 (part), 68761 (part), 68768 (part), 68778 (part), 68779, 68781 (part), 68784 (part), 68788, 68791 (part)

* * *

SECOND DISTRICT

DON BACON, Republican, of Papillion, NE; born in Momence, IL, August 16, 1963; education: B.A., political science, Northern Illinois University, 1984; M.A. management, University of Phoenix, 1995; M.A., national security strategy, National War College, 2004; professional: U.S. Air Force, 1985–2014; retired Brigadier General; Air Force Distinguished Service Medal, two Bronze Stars, two Legion of Merits, five Meritorious Service Medals, and Aerial Achievement Medal; military advisor to Congressman Jeff Fortenberry, 2014–15; candidate for Congress, 2015–16; religion: Christian; family: married to Angie Bacon; children: four; caucuses: Climate Solutions Caucus; committees: Agriculture; Armed Services; Homeland Security; elected to the 115th Congress on November 8, 2016.

Office Listings

http://bacon.house.gov facebook: @RepDonBacon twitter: @RepDonBacon

1516 Longworth House Office Building, Washington, DC 20515 .... (202) 225–4155
Chief of Staff.—Mark Dreiling.
Policy Director.—Jeff Kratz.
Executive Assistant.—Jason Tyler.
Communications Director.—Danielle Jensen.
13906 Gold Circle, Suite 101, Omaha, NE 68144 .... (402) 938–0300
Deputy Chief of Staff / District Director.—Ben Ungerman.

Counties: DOUGLAS AND SARPY (part). CITIES: Bennington, Boys Town, Elkhorn, Gretna, La Vista, Omaha, Papillion, Ralston, Springfield, Valley, and Waterloo. Population (2010), 608,781.

ZIP Codes: 68010, 68022, 68028, 68046, 68059, 68069, 68102, 68104–06, 68108, 68110–11, 68114, 68116–18, 68124, 68127–28, 68130–32, 68134–38, 68144, 68154, 68164, 68178

* * *

THIRD DISTRICT

ADRIAN SMITH, Republican, of Gering, NE; born in Scottsbluff, NE, December 19, 1970; education: graduated from Gering High School, Gering, 1989; B.S., University of Nebraska, 1993; professional: business owner; education coordinator; Gering, NE, City Council, 1994–98; member of the Nebraska State Legislature, 1999–2007; married: Andrea McDaniel Smith; committees: House Administration; Ways and Means; elected to the 110th Congress on November 7, 2006; reelected to each succeeding Congress.

Office Listings

http://adriansmith.house.gov twitter: @repadriansmith

320 Cannon House Office Building, Washington, DC 20515 .... (202) 225–6435
Chief of Staff.—Monica Didiuk. FAX: 225–0207
Legislative Director.—Josh Jackson.
Communications Director.—Emily Miller.
District Director.—Jena Hoehne.
Scheduler.—Jill Sims.
416 Valley View Drive, Suite 600, Scottsbluff, NE 69361 .... (308) 633–6333
1811 West Second Street, Suite 275, Grand Island, NE 68803 .... (308) 384–3900

Counties: ADAMS, ANTELOPE, ARTHUR, BANNER, BLAINE, BOONE, BOX BUTTE, BOYD, BROWN, BUFFALO, CEDAR, CHASE, CHERRY, CHEYENNE, CLAY, CUSTER, DAKOTA, DAWES, DAWSON, DEUEL, DIXON, DUNDY, FILLMORE, FRANKLIN, FRONTIER, FURNAS, GAGE, GARDEN, GARFIELD, GOSPER, GRANT, GREELEY, HALL, HAMILTON, HARLAN, HAYES, HITCHCOCK, HOLT, HOOKER, HOWARD, JEFFERSON, JOHNSON, KEARNEY, KEITH, KEYA PAHA, KIMBALL, KNOX, LINCOLN, LOGAN, LOUP, MCPHERSON, MERRICK, MORRILL, NANCE, NEMAHA, NUCKOLLS, PAWNEE, PERKINS, PHELPS, PIERCE, RED WILLOW, RICHARDSON, ROCK, SALINE, SCOTTSBLUFF, SHERIDAN, SHERMAN, SIOUX, THAYER, THOMAS, VALLEY, WAYNE, WEBSTER, WHEELER, AND YORK. Population (2010), 608,438.

ZIP Codes: 60902, 68030, 68305, 68309–10, 68315, 68318, 68320–21, 68326, 68328, 68330, 68337, 68340, 68350, 68352, 68355, 68361–62, 68375, 68377, 68380, 68401, 68406, 68414–15, 68422, 68429, 68431, 68433, 68440, 68444–45, 68450, 68457, 68467, 68620, 68622, 68710–11, 68713, 68717–18, 68720, 68722–24, 68727–28, 68731, 68736, 68738, 68741–43, 68749, 68751, 68753, 68756, 68760–61, 68763, 68765–66, 68774, 68776, 68778, 68780, 68783, 68787, 68789–90, 68802, 68810, 68812, 68814, 68816, 68818, 68820–22, 68824–27, 68837–38, 68841–44, 68846–50, 68852–54, 68861–62, 68865, 68870–71, 68873, 68879, 68881, 68901, 68920, 68923, 68925–26, 68929, 68932–33, 68939–40, 68946, 68950, 68952, 68954, 68956, 68959, 68961, 68966, 68969–71, 68973, 68975–76, 69020–21, 69023, 69032, 69034, 69036–37, 69041–42, 69046, 69103, 69121, 69123, 69125, 69131–33, 69140–44, 69150–52, 69154, 69160, 69162, 69170, 69171, 69190, 69211, 69218–21, 69331, 69339, 69345–46, 69354, 69361, 69363, 69366–67, 69855

NEVADA

(Population 2010, 2,700,551)

SENATORS

DEAN HELLER, Republican, of Carson City, NV; born in Castro Valley, CA, May 10, 1960; education: B.B.A., specializing in finance and securities analysis, University of Southern California, 1985; professional: institutional stockbroker and broker/trader on the Pacific Stock Exchange; Chief Deputy State Treasurer, Public Funds Representative; Nevada State Assemblyman, 1990–94; Secretary of State, 1994–2002; founding member of the Boys and Girls Club of Western Nevada Community College Foundation; married: Lynne Heller; children: Hillary, Harris, Drew, and Emmy; committees: Banking, Housing, and Urban Affairs; Commerce, Science, and Transportation; Finance; Veterans' Affairs; elected to the 110th Congress on November 7, 2006, reelected to two succeeding Congresses, when he resigned to become a U.S. Senator; appointed May 3, 2011, to the U.S. Senate for the term ending January 3, 2013, to fill the vacancy caused by the resignation of U.S. Senator John E. Ensign; took the oath of office on May 9, 2011; elected to the U.S. Senate on November 6, 2012.

Office Listings

http://heller.senate.gov https://www.facebook.com/SenDeanHeller
https://twitter.com/SenDeanHeller

324 Hart Senate Office Building, Washington, DC 20510 .... (202) 224–6244
Chief of Staff.—Mac Abrams. FAX: 228–6753
Legislative Director.—Sarah Timoney Paul.
Communications Director.—Megan Taylor.
Scheduler.—Meron Bayu.
8930 West Sunset Road, Suite 230, Las Vegas, NV 89148 .... (702) 388–6605
FAX: 388–6501
Bruce Thompson Federal Building, 400 South Virginia Street, Suite 738, Reno, NV 89501 (775) 686–5770
FAX: 686–5729

* * *

CATHERINE CORTEZ MASTO, Democrat, of Las Vegas, NV; born in Las Vegas, March 29, 1964; education: graduated Clark High School, Las Vegas; B.S., finance, University of Nevada, Reno, 1986; J.D., Gonzaga University, Spokane, WA, 1990; admitted to the Nevada State Bar in 1990; professional: Chief of Staff to Nevada Governor Bob Miller; Criminal Prosecutor, U.S. Attorney's Office, Washington, DC; elected Nevada Attorney General, 2007–2015; executive vice chancellor for the Nevada System of Higher Education; committees: Banking, Housing, and Urban Affairs; Commerce, Science, and Transportation; Energy and Natural Resources; Indian Affairs; Rules and Administration; Special Committee on Aging; elected to the U.S. Senate on November 8, 2016.

Office Listings

http://masto.senate.gov

B40A Dirksen Senate Office Building, Washington, DC 20510 .... (202) 224–3542
Chief of Staff.—Scott Fairchild. FAX: 224–7327
Senior Advisor.—Brynn Palmen.
Deputy Chief of Staff for Policy.—Laura Hatalsky.
Communications Director.—Rey Benitez.
Scheduler.—Anaisy Tolentino.
333 Las Vegas Boulevard South, Suite 8016, Las Vegas, NV 89101 .... (702) 388–5020
State Director.—Zach Zaragoza.
400 South Virginia Street, Suite 902, Reno, NV 89501 .... (775) 686–5750
State Director.—Zach Zaragoza.

REPRESENTATIVES

FIRST DISTRICT

DINA TITUS, Democrat, of Las Vegas, NV; born in Thomasville, Thomas County, GA, May 23, 1950; education: B.A., College of William and Mary, Williamsburg, VA, 1970; M.A., University of Georgia, Athens, GA, 1973; Ph.D., Florida State University, Tallahassee, FL, 1976; professional: professor, University of Nevada, Las Vegas, NV, 1977–2011; UNLV professor emeritus, 2011–present; member of Nevada State Senate, 1989–2008; Minority Leader of Nevada State Senate, 1993–2008; married: Thomas C. Wright, Ph.D.; committees: Foreign Affairs; Transportation and Infrastructure; elected to the 3rd District in the 111th Congress on November 4, 2008; elected to the 1st District on November 6, 2012 in the 113th Congress; reelected to each succeeding Congress.

Office Listings

http://www.titus.house.gov https://www.facebook.com/CongresswomanTitus
https://twitter.com/RepDinaTitus

2464 Rayburn House Office Building, Washington, DC 20515 .... (202) 225–5965
Chief of Staff.—Jay Gertsema. FAX: 225–3119
Legislative Director.—David Rosenbaum.
Communications Director.—Kyle Roerink.
Scheduler.—Eva Hicks.
550 East Charleston Boulevard, Las Vegas, NV 89104 .... (702) 220–9823
District Director.—Mike Naft. FAX: 220–9841

Counties: CLARK COUNTY (part). CITIES: Las Vegas and North Las Vegas. Population (2010), 659,962.

ZIP Codes: 89030, 89087, 89101–04, 89106–22, 89125–26, 89128, 89132, 89142, 89145–47, 89150–53, 89155–58, 89160, 89162, 89169–70, 89173, 89177, 89180, 89193

* * *

SECOND DISTRICT

MARK E. AMODEI, Republican, of Carson City, NV; born in Carson City, June 12, 1958; education: B.A., University of Nevada, Reno, NV, 1980; J.D., University of the Pacific, McGeorge School of Law, Sacramento, CA, 1983; professional: lawyer, Allison, MacKenzie et al., 1987–present; lawyer, U.S. Army Judge Advocate General Corps, 1983–87; Nevada State Assembly, 1996–98; Senator, Nevada State Senate, 1998–2010; President Pro Tempore, Nevada State Senate, 2003–08; member of Carson City Master Plan Advisory Committee; member of Education Commission of the States; vice chair of Governor's Task Force on Access to Public Health Care; member of Nevada Supreme Court's Committee on Court Funding; member of Tahoe Regional Planning Agency Legislative Oversight Committee; committees: Appropriations; elected, by special election, to the 112th Congress on September 13, 2011; reelected to each succeeding Congress.

Office Listings

http://www.amodei.house.gov https://www.facebook.com/markamodeinv2
twitter: @markamodeinv2

332 Cannon House Office Building, Washington, DC 20515 .... (202) 225–6155
Chief of Staff.—Bruce Miller. FAX: 225–5679
905 Railroad Street, Suite 104 D, Elko, NV 89801 .... (775) 777–7705
FAX: 753–9984
5310 Kietzke Lane, Suite 103, Reno, NV 89511..

Counties: CARSON CITY, CHURCHILL, DOUGLAS, ELKO, HUMBOLDT, LANDER, LYON (part), PERSHING, STOREY, AND WASHOE. Population (2010), 679,147.

ZIP Codes: 89310, 89316, 89402–06, 89408, 89410–14, 89418–19, 89421, 89423–26, 89428–29, 89431, 89433–34, 89436, 89438–42, 89444–51, 89460, 89501–03, 89506, 89508–12, 89519, 89521, 89523, 89701–06, 89801, 89815, 89820–23, 89825–26, 89828, 89830–35, 89883

* * *

THIRD DISTRICT

JACKY ROSEN, Democrat, of Henderson, NV; born in Chicago, IL, August 2, 1957; education: B.A., University of Minnesota, Twin Cities, Minneapolis, MN, 1979; professional: computer programmer, software developer, and designer for Summa Corporation, Citibank, and Southwest Gas Company; president of Congregation Ner Tamid; religion: Jewish; married: Larry Rosen; children: one daughter; caucuses: Congressional Caucus on Women's Issues; Congressional Cybersecurity Caucus; Democratic Israel Working Group; Problem Solvers Caucus; committees: Armed Services; Science, Space, and Technology; elected to the 115th Congress on November 8, 2016.

Office Listings

http://www.rosen.house.gov

413 Cannon House Office Building, Washington, DC 20515 .... (202) 225–3252
Chief of Staff.—David Furr. FAX: 225–2185
Scheduler.—Nicole Echeto.
Legislative Director.—Grant Dubler.
Communications Director.—Ivana Brancaccio.
8872 South Eastern Avenue, Suite 220, Las Vegas, NV 89123 .... (702) 963–9500
District Director.—Dane Hudson.

Counties: CLARK COUNTY (part). Population (2010), 675,138.

ZIP Codes: 89002, 89004–05 (part), 89011 (part), 89012, 89014 (part), 89015, 89019, 89026, 89029, 89039, 89044, 89046, 89052, 89054, 89074, 89113 (part), 89117–20 (part), 89122 (part), 89123, 89124 (part), 89134 (part), 89135, 89138–39, 89141, 89144–45 (part), 89147 (part), 89148, 89156 (part), 89161, 89178–79, 89183

* * *

FOURTH DISTRICT

RUBEN J. KIHUEN, Democrat, of Las Vegas, NV; born in Guadalajara, Jalisco, Mexico, April 25, 1980; education: College of Southern Nevada; B.S., education, University of Nevada; caucuses: Congressional Hispanic Caucus, Congressional LGBT Equality Caucus, Congressional Progressive Caucus, New Democrat Coalition; committees: Financial Services; elected to the 115th Congress on November 8, 2016, becoming the first Latino to represent the State of Nevada in the U.S. House of Representatives.

Office Listings

https://kihuen.house.gov

313 Cannon House Office Building, Washington, DC 20515 .... (202) 225–9894
Chief of Staff.—Dave Chase.
Legislative Director.—Mark Snyder.
Communications Director.—Miguel Salazar.
Scheduler.—Angie Toro.
2250 North Las Vegas Boulevard, Suite 500, North Las Vegas, NV 89030 .... (702) 963–9360
District Director.—Asha Jones.

Counties: CLARK COUNTY (most of the northern part), ESMERALDA, LINCOLN, LYON (part), MINERAL, NYE, AND WHITE PINE. Population (2010), 680,935.

ZIP Codes: 89001, 89003, 89007–08, 89010, 89013–14, 89017–18, 89020–23, 89025, 89027, 89030–32, 89034, 89040–43, 89045, 89047–49, 89060–61, 89081, 89084–86, 89101, 89103, 89106–10, 89115, 89124, 89128–31, 89134–35, 89142–43, 89149, 89156, 89158, 89161, 89166, 89191, 89301, 89310–11, 89314–19, 89409, 89415, 89420, 89422, 89427, 89430, 89444, 89447, 89833, 89883

NEW HAMPSHIRE

(Population 2010, 1,316,470)

SENATORS

JEANNE SHAHEEN, Democrat, of Madbury, NH; born in Saint Charles, MO, January 28, 1947; education: graduated, Selinsgrove Area High School, Selinsgrove, PA, 1965; B.A., Shippensburg University, Shippensburg, PA, 1969; M.S.S., University of Mississippi, 1973; professional: high school teacher; co-owner of a small retail business; consultant; New Hampshire State Senator; Governor of New Hampshire; director of Harvard's Institute of Politics; married: William Shaheen; three children: Stefany, Stacey, and Molly; Commission on Security and Cooperation in Europe; committees: Appropriations; Armed Services; Foreign Relations; Select Committee on Ethics; Small Business and Entrepreneurship; elected to the 111th U.S. Senate on November 4, 2008; reelected to the U.S. Senate on November 4, 2014.

Office Listings

http://shaheen.senate.gov https://www.facebook.com/senatorshaheen
https://twitter.com/senatorshaheen https://instagram.com/senatorshaheen

506 Hart Senate Office Building, Washington, DC 20510 .... (202) 224–2841
Chief of Staff.—Maura Keefe.
Deputy Chief of Staff.—Jennifer MacLellan.
Legislative Director.—Robert Diznoff.
Communications Director.—Ryan Nickel.
Press Secretary.—Sarah Weinstein.
Scheduler.—Meaghan D'Arcy.
2 Wall Street, Suite 220, Manchester, NH 03101 .... (603) 647–7500
60 Main Street, Nashua, NH 03060 .... (603) 883–0196
340 Central Avenue, Suite 205, Dover, NH 03820 .... (603) 750–3004
50 Opera House Square, Claremont, NH 03743 .... (603) 542–4872
961 Main Street, Berlin, NH 03570 .... (603) 752–6300
12 Gilbo Avenue, Suite C, Keene, NH 03431 .... (603) 358–6604

* * *

MARGARET WOOD HASSAN, Democrat, of Newfields, NH; born in Boston, MA, February 27, 1958; education: B.A., Brown University, Providence, RI, 1980; J.D., Northeastern University School of Law, Boston, MA, 1985; professional: attorney; New Hampshire State Senator, 2004–10, serving as Majority Leader, 2008–10; Governor of New Hampshire, 2013–16; married: Thomas Hassan; two children: Ben and Meg; committees: Commerce, Science, and Transportation; Health, Education, Labor, and Pensions; Homeland Security and Governmental Affairs; Joint Economic Committee; elected to the U.S. Senate on November 8, 2016.

Office Listings

http://hassan.senate.gov https://www.facebook.com/SenatorHassan
https://twitter.com/senatorhassan

330 Hart Senate Office Building, Washington, DC 20510 .... (202) 224–3324
Chief of Staff.—Marc Goldberg. FAX: 224–4952
Administrative Director.—Kelly Boyer.
Legislative Director.—Jude McCartin.
Communications Director.—Aaron Jacobs.
Scheduler.—Catherine George.
1200 Elm Street, Suite 2, Manchester, NH 03101 .... (603) 622–2204
FAX: 622–0422
14 Manchester Square, Suite 140, Portsmouth, NH 03801 .... (603) 436–7161

REPRESENTATIVES

FIRST DISTRICT

CAROL SHEA-PORTER, Democrat, of Rochester, NH; born in New York City, NY; December, 1952; education: graduated from Oyster River High School, Durham, NH, 1971; B.A., University of New Hampshire, Durham, 1975; M.P.A., University of New Hampshire, Durham, 1979; professional: social worker; professor; married: Gene; two children; committees: Armed

Services; Education and the Workforce; elected to the 110th Congress on November 7, 2006; reelected to the 111th Congress on November 4, 2008; elected to the 113th Congress on November 6, 2012; elected to the 115th Congress on November 8, 2016.

Office Listings

https://shea-porter.house.gov

1530 Longworth House Office Building, Washington, DC 20515 .... (202) 225–5456
Chief of Staff.—Naomi Andrews. FAX: 225–5822
Legislative Director.—Chris Hillesheim.
Communications Director.—Marjorie Connolly.
Scheduler.—Emily Mills.
660 Central Avenue, Unit 101, Dover, NH 03820 .... (603) 285–4300

Counties: BELKNAP (part), CARROLL, GRAFTON (part), HILLSBOROUGH (part), MERRIMACK (part), ROCKINGHAM (part), AND STRAFFORD. CITIES: Bedford, Campton, Goffstown, Hooksett, Manchester, and Merrimack. Population (2015), 671,640.

ZIP Codes: 03031–32, 03034, 03036, 03038, 03040–42, 03044–45, 03051, 03053–54, 03077, 03101–06, 03108–11, 03215, 03217–18, 03220, 03223, 03225–27, 03235, 03237, 03245–47, 03249, 03252–54, 03256, 03259, 03261, 03269, 03276, 03285, 03289–91, 03299, 03801–04, 03809–27, 03830, 03832–33, 03835–62, 03864–75, 03878, 03882–87, 03890, 03894, 03896–97

* * *

SECOND DISTRICT

ANN MCLANE KUSTER, Democrat, of Hopkinton, NH; born in Concord, NH, September 5, 1956; education: B.A., Dartmouth College, Hanover, NH, 1978; J.D., Georgetown University Law Center, Washington, DC, 1984; professional: consultant and owner, Newfound Strategies LLC; lawyer and partner, Rath, Young and Pignatelli; married: Brad Kuster; children: Zach and Travis; committees: Agriculture; Veterans' Affairs; elected to the 113th Congress on November 6, 2012; reelected to each succeeding Congress.

Office Listings

http://kuster.house.gov

137 Cannon House Office Building, Washington, DC 20515 .... (202) 225–5206
Chief of Staff.—Abby Curran Horrell. FAX: 225–2946
Legislative Director.—Blake Anderson.
Scheduler.—Corey Garry.
Press Secretary.—Rosie Hilmer.
18 North Main Street, Concord, NH 03301 .... (603) 226–1002
District Director.—Jake Berry. FAX: 226–1010
70 East Pearl Street, Nashua, NH 03060 .... (603) 595–2006
FAX: 595–2016
33 Main Street, Littleton, NH 03561 .... (603) 444–7700

Counties: BELKNAP (part), CHESHIRE, COOS, GRAFTON (part), HILLSBOROUGH (part), MERRIMACK (part), ROCKINGHAM (part), AND SULLIVAN. Population (2013), 658,237.

ZIP Codes: 03031, 03033–34, 03037–38, 03043, 03045–49, 03051–52, 03054–55, 03057, 03060–64, 03070–71, 03073, 03076, 03079, 03082, 03084, 03086–87, 03110, 03215–17, 03220–24, 03226, 03229–31, 03233–35, 03237–38, 03240–45, 03251, 03253, 03255–58, 03260–64, 03266, 03268, 03272–73, 03275–76, 03278–82, 03284–85, 03287, 03293, 03301–05, 03307, 03431, 03435, 03440–52, 03455–58, 03461–62, 03464–70, 03561, 03570, 03574–76, 03579–86, 03588–90, 03592–93, 03595, 03597–98, 03601–05, 03607–09, 03740–41, 03743, 03745–46, 03748–56, 03765–66, 03768–71, 03773–74, 03777, 03779–82, 03784–85, 03811, 03825, 03841

NEW JERSEY

(Population 2010 8,791,894)

SENATORS

ROBERT MENENDEZ, Democrat, of Paramus, NJ; born in New York City, NY, January 1, 1954; education: graduated, Union Hill High School, 1972; B.A., St. Peter's College, Jersey City, NJ, 1976; J.D., Rutgers Law School, Newark, NJ, 1979; professional: attorney; elected to the Union City Board of Education, 1974–78; admitted to the New Jersey Bar, 1980; Mayor of Union City, 1986–92; member: New Jersey Assembly, 1987–91; New Jersey State Senate, Alliance Civic Association; U.S. House of Representatives, 1993–2006; vice chair, Democratic Caucus, 1998–99; chair, Democratic Caucus, 2003–06; chair, Democratic Senatorial Campaign Committee, 2009–10; chairman, Senate Committee on Foreign Relations, 2013–15; children: Alicia and Robert; committees: ranking member, Foreign Relations; Banking, Housing, and Urban Affairs; Finance; elected on November 3, 1992, to the 103rd Congress; reelected to each succeeding Congress; appointed to the U.S. Senate on January 17, 2006, by Governor Jon S. Corzine; elected to the 110th Congress for a full Senate term on November 7, 2006; reelected to the 114th Congress on November 6, 2012.

Office Listings

http://menendez.senate.gov https://www.facebook.com/senatormenendez
https://twitter.com/SenatorMenendez

528 Hart Senate Office Building, Washington, DC 20510 .... (202) 224–4744
Chief of Staff.—Fred L. Turner. FAX: 228–2197
Administrative Director.—Robert Kelly.
Legislative Director.—Tim Del Monico.
One Gateway Center, 11th Floor, Newark, NJ 07102 .... (973) 645–3030
208 Whitehorse Pike, Suite 18, Barrington, NJ 08007 .... (856) 757–5353

* * *

CORY A. BOOKER, Democrat, of Newark, NJ; born in Washington, DC, April 27, 1969; education: graduated, Northern Valley Regional High School at Old Tappan, 1987; B.A., political science, Stanford University, 1991; M.A., sociology, Stanford University, 1992; Oxford University Rhodes Scholar, 1994; J.D., Yale Law School, 1997; professional: staff attorney, Urban Justice Center, New York, NY, 1997; member, Newark City Council, 1998–2002; partner, Booker, Rabinowitz, Trenk, Lubetkin, Tully, DiPasquale & Webster, P.C., 2002–06; Mayor, City of Newark, 2006–13; religion: Baptist; committees: Environment and Public Works; Foreign Relations; Judiciary, Small Business and Entrepreneurship; elected, by special election, to the U.S. Senate on October 16, 2013, to fill the vacancy caused by the death of U.S. Senator Frank R. Lautenberg; reelected to the U.S. Senate on November 4, 2014.

Office Listings

http://www.booker.senate.gov twitter: @senbookerofc

359 Dirksen Senate Office Building, Washington, DC 20510 .... (202) 224–3224
Chief of Staff.—Matt Klapper. FAX: 224–8378
Scheduler.—Unjin Lee.
Communications Director.—Jeff Giertz.
Scheduler.—Adam Topper.
One Gateway Center, 11–43 Raymond Plaza West, Suite 2300, Newark, NJ 07102 .... (973) 639–8700
One Port Center, 2 Riverside Drive, Suite 505, Camden, NJ 08101 .... (856) 338–8922

REPRESENTATIVES

FIRST DISTRICT

DONALD NORCROSS, Democrat, of Camden, NJ; born in Camden, December 13, 1958; education: graduated, Pennsauken High School, Pennsauken, NJ, 1977; associate's degree, criminal justice, Camden County College, Blackwood, NJ, 1979; professional: vice president of United Building Trades Council of Southern New Jersey, 2004–13; electrician at IBEW Local 351, 1979–93; United Way board member, 1992–2014; Union Organization for Social Service, president and CEO, 1993–98; business agent/assistant business manager of IBEW Local 351, 1998–2014; president of the Southern New Jersey AFL-CIO Central Labor Council, 1995–2011;

New Jersey General Assembly, 2010; New Jersey State Senate, 2010–14; married: Andrea Doran; children: Donald Jr., Corey, and Greg; committees: Armed Services; Education and the Workforce; elected simultaneously to the 113th and 114th Congress on November 4, 2014, by special election, to fill the vacancy caused by the resignation of U.S. Representative Robert Andrews; reelected to the 115th Congress on November 8, 2016.

Office Listings

http://www.norcross.house.gov https://www.facebook.com/DonaldNorcrossNJ
twitter: @DonaldNorcross

1531 Longworth House Office Building, Washington, DC 20515 .... (202) 225–6501
Chief of Staff.—Michael J. Maitland.
Legislative Director.—Morgan Jones.
Communications Director.—Allyson Kehoe.
10 Melrose Avenue, Suite 210, Cherry Hill, NJ 08003 .... (856) 427–7000
District Director.—Mary Campbell Cruz.

Counties: BURLINGTON COUNTY. CITIES AND TOWNSHIPS: Maple Shade Township, and Palmyra. CAMDEN COUNTY. CITIES AND TOWNSHIPS: Audubon, Audubon Park, Barrington, Bellmawr, Berlin, Berlin Township, Brooklawn, Camden, Cherry Hill, Chesilhurst, Clementon, Collingswood, Gibbsboro, Gloucester City, Gloucester Township, Haddon Heights, Haddon Township, Hi–Nella, Laurel Springs, Lawnside, Lindenwold, Magnolia, Merchantville, Mt. Ephraim, Oaklyn, Pennsauken Township, Pine Hill, Pine Valley, Runnemede, Somerdale, Stratford, Tavistock, Voorhees Township, Winslow Township, and Woodlynne. GLOUCESTER COUNTY. CITIES AND TOWNSHIPS: Deptford, East Greenwich, Greenwich, Logan Township, Monroe, National Park, Paulsboro, Washington Township, Wenonah, West Deptford Township, Westville, Woodbury Heights, and Woodbury. Population (2015), 727,496

ZIP Codes: 08002–04, 08007, 08009, 08012, 08014, 08020–21, 08026–33, 08037, 08043, 08045, 08049, 08051–52, 08056, 08059, 08061–63, 08065–66, 08077–78, 08080–81, 08083–86, 08089–91, 08093–94, 08096–97, 08099, 08101–05, 08107–10

* * *

SECOND DISTRICT

FRANK A. LOBIONDO, Republican, of Ventnor, NJ; born in Bridgeton, NJ, May 12, 1946; education: graduated, B.S., St. Joseph's University, Philadelphia, PA, 1968; professional: operations manager, LoBiondo Brothers Motor Express, 1968–94; Cumberland County Freeholder, 1985–87; New Jersey General Assembly, 1988–94; awards and honors: honorary Coast Guard Chief Petty Officer; Taxpayer Hero Award; Watchdog of the Treasury Award; Veterans of Foreign Wars, Outstanding Federal Legislator of the Year Award; Humane Society of the United States, Humane Champion Award; National Association of Community Health Centers, Distinguished Community Health Superhero; Super Friend of Seniors Award; two-time winner of the Friend of the National Parks Award; March of Dimes FDR Award for community service; 2001 President's Award, Literacy Volunteers of America, NJ, Inc.; committees: Armed Services; Permanent Select Committee on Intelligence; Transportation and Infrastructure; elected to the 104th Congress; reelected to each succeeding Congress.

Office Listings

http://www.lobiondo.house.gov facebook: https://www.facebook.com/FrankLoBiondo
twitter: @RepLoBiondo

2427 Rayburn House Office Building, Washington, DC 20515 .... (202) 225–6572
Chief of Staff.—Jason Galanes. FAX: 225–3318
Executive Assistant.—Mehgan Perez-Acosta.
5914 Main Street, Mays Landing, NJ 08330 .... (609) 625–5008
District Director.—Linda Hinckley.

Counties: BURLINGTON (part). CITIES AND TOWNSHIPS: Bass River and Washington. CAMDEN COUNTY (part) AND ATLANTIC COUNTY. CITIES AND TOWNSHIPS: Absecon, Atlantic City, Brigantine, Buena, Cardiff, Collings Lake, Cologne, Corbin City, Dorothy, Egg Harbor, Estell Manor, Galloway, Hammonton, Landisville, Leeds Point, Linwood, Longport, Margate, Mays Landing, Milmay, Minotola, Mizpah, Newtonville, Northfield, Oceanville, Pleasantville, Pomona, Port Republic, Richland, Somers Point, and Ventnor. CAPE MAY COUNTY. CITIES AND TOWNSHIPS: Avalon, Bargaintown, Beesley's, Belleplain, Burleigh, Cape May, Cape May C.H., Cape May Point, Cold Springs, Del Haven, Dennisville, Dias Creek, Eldora, Erma, Fishing Creek, Goshen, Green Creek, Marmora, Ocean City, Ocean View, Rio Grande, Sea Isle, South Dennis, South Seaville, Stone Harbor, Strathmere, Tuckahoe, Villas, Whitesboro, Wildwood, Woodbine. CUMBERLAND COUNTY. CITIES AND TOWNSHIPS: Bridgeton, Cedarville, Deerfield, Delmont, Dividing Creek, Dorchester, Fairton, Fortescue, Greenwich, Heislerville, Hopewell, Leesburg, Mauricetown, Millville, Newport, Port Elizabeth, Port Norris, Rosenhayn, Shiloh, and Vineland. GLOUCESTER COUNTY (part). CITIES AND TOWNSHIPS: Clayton, East Greenwich Ewan, Franklinville, Harrisonville, Malaga, Mantua, Mickleton, Mullica Hill, Newfield, Pitman, Richwood, Swedesboro, and Williamstown. OCEAN COUNTY (part). CITIES AND TOWNSHIPS: Barnegat Light, Harvey Cedars, Stafford Twp, Eagleswood, Tuckerton, Little Egg Harbor, Loveladies, Surf City, Ship Bottom, Long Beach Twp, and Beach Haven. SALEM COUNTY. CITIES AND TOWNSHIPS: Alloway, Carney's Point, Daretown, Deepwater, Elmer, Elsinboro, Hancocks Bridge, Monroeville, Norma, Pedricktown, Penns Grove, Pennsville, Quinton, Salem, and Woodstown. Population (2010), 736,397.

ZIP Codes: 08001, 08004–06, 08008–09, 08019–20, 08023, 08028, 08037–39, 08050–51, 08056, 08062, 08067, 08069–72, 08074, 08079–80, 08085, 08087, 08089, 08092, 08094, 08098, 08201–05, 08210, 08212, 08215, 08217, 08221, 08223–26, 08230, 08232, 08234, 08240–44, 08251, 08260, 08270, 08302, 08310–12, 08316–24, 08326–30, 08332, 08340–41, 08343–46, 08348–50, 08352–53, 08360–61, 08401–03, 08406

* * *

THIRD DISTRICT

THOMAS MACARTHUR, Republican, of Toms River, NJ; born in Hebron, CT, October 16, 1960; education: graduated from RHAM High School, Hebron; attended Hofstra University, Hempstead, NY, 1978–82; professional: insurance services industry chief executive officer; married: Debbie; committees: Financial Services; elected to the 114th Congress on November 4, 2014; reelected to 115th Congress on November 8, 2016.

Office Listings

http://macarthur.house.gov https://www.facebook.com/CongressmanTomMacArthur
https://twitter.com/RepTomMacArthur

506 Cannon House Office Building, Washington, DC 20515 .... (202) 225–4765
Chief of Staff.—Ryan Carney. FAX: 225–0778
Gibson House Community Center, 535 East Main Street, Marlton, NJ 08053 .... (856) 267–5182
New Jersey Chief of Staff.—Frank Luna. FAX: 574–4697
Township of Toms River Town Hall, 33 Washington Street, Toms River, NJ 08753 .... (732) 569–6495
FAX: 998–8137

Counties: BURLINGTON (part) AND OCEAN (part). Population (2010), 732,658.

ZIP Codes: 08005–06, 08008, 08010–11, 08015–16, 08019, 08022, 08036, 08041–42, 08046, 08048, 08050, 08052–55, 08057, 08060, 08064–65, 08068, 08073, 08075, 08077, 08087–88, 08092, 08501, 08505, 08511, 08515, 08518, 08554, 08562, 08610, 08620, 08640–41, 08701, 08721–24, 08731–32, 08734–35, 08738, 08740–42, 08751–53, 08755, 08757–59

* * *

FOURTH DISTRICT

CHRISTOPHER H. SMITH, Republican, of Robbinsville, NJ; born in Rahway, NJ, March 4, 1953; education: attended Worcester College, England, 1974; B.A., Trenton State College, 1975; professional: executive director, New Jersey Right to Life Committee, Inc.; businessman; religion: Catholic; married to the former Marie Hahn, 1977; four adult children; three grandchildren; caucuses and commissions: chair, Commission on Security and Cooperation in Europe; co-chair, Congressional-Executive Commission on China; co-chair, Congressional Pro-Life Caucus; former chair, House Veterans' Affairs Committee; Bicameral Congressional Task Force on Alzheimer's Disease; Bi-Partisan Coalition for Combating Anti-Semitism; Coalition on Autism Research and Education (CARE); Congressional Human Trafficking Caucus; Lyme Disease Caucus; U.S. Helsinki Commission; committees: Foreign Affairs; elected to the 97th Congress on November 4, 1980; reelected to each succeeding Congress.

Office Listings

http://www.chrissmith.house.gov https://twitter.com/repchrissmith
https://www.facebook.com/repchrissmith

2373 Rayburn House Office Building, Washington, DC 20515 .... (202) 225–3765
Chief of Staff.—Mary McDermott Noonan. FAX: 225–7768
112 Village Center Drive, 2nd Floor, Freehold, NJ 07728 .... (732) 780–3035
4573 South Broad Street, First Floor, Hamilton, NJ 08619 .... (609) 585–7878
405 Route 539, Plumsted, NJ 08514 .... (609) 286–2571

Counties: MERCER. MUNICIPALITIES: Hamilton and Robbinsville. MONMOUTH. MUNICIPALITIES: Allentown, Avon-by-the-Sea, Belmar, Bradley Beach, Brielle, Colts Neck, Eatontown, Englishtown, Fair Haven, Farmingdale, Freehold Borough, Freehold Township, Homdel, Howell, Lake Como, Little Silver, Manalapan, Manasquan, Middletown (part), Millstone, Neptune City, Neptune Township, Ocean Township, Red Bank, Roosevelt, Rumson, Sea Girt, Shrewsbury Township, Shrewsbury Borough, Spring Lake, Spring Lake Heights, Tinton Falls, Upper Freehold, and Wall. OCEAN. MUNICIPALITIES: Bay Head, Jackson, Lakehurst, Lakewood, Manchester, Plumsted, Point Pleasant (part), and Point Pleasant Beach. Population (2010), 732,657.

ZIP Codes: 07701 (part), 07702, 07703 (part), 07704, 07711–12 (part), 07717, 07719–20, 07722, 07723 (part), 07724, 07726 (part), 07727–28, 07730 (part), 07731, 07733 (part), 07738–39, 07740 (part), 07748 (part), 07753, 07755–

56, 07760 (part), 07762, 08501, 08510, 08514, 08520 (part), 08527, 08533, 08535, 08555, 08561, 08609 (part), 08610–11 (part), 08619, 08620 (part), 08629 (part), 08638 (part), 08690 (part), 08691, 08701 (part), 08720, 08724 (part), 08730, 08733, 08736, 08742 (part), 08750, 08757 (part), 08759

* * *

FIFTH DISTRICT

JOSH GOTTHEIMER, Democrat, of Wyckoff, NJ; born in Livingston, NJ, March 8, 1975; education: bachelor's in history, University of Pennsylvania, PA, 1997; J.D., Harvard Law School, Boston, MA, 2004; Thouron Fellow; professional: speechwriter to President Bill Clinton; senior advisor to the chair, U.S. Commission on Civil Rights; senior counselor to the chairman of the Federal Communications Commission; director of strategic communications at Ford Motor Company; general manager for corporate strategy at Microsoft; religion: Jewish; wife: Marla; two children: Ben and Ellie; caucuses: co-chair, Problem Solvers Caucus; committees: Financial Services; elected to the 115th Congress on November 8, 2016.

Office Listings

http://www.gottheimer.house.gov

213 Cannon House Office Building, Washington, DC 20515 .... (202) 225–4465
Chief of Staff.—Tricia Russell.
Legislative Director.—Michael Lukso.
Communications Director.—Vacant.
65 Harristown Road, Suite 104, Glen Rock, NJ 07452 .... (201) 389–1100
District Director.—Chris Tully.
93 Spring Street, Suite 408, Newton, NJ 07860 .... (973) 814–4078

Counties: BERGEN (part), PASSAIC (part), SUSSEX (part), AND WARREN (part). Population (2010), 731,055.

ZIP Codes: 07401, 07410, 07416–19, 07422–23, 07428, 07430, 07432, 07436, 07446, 07450–52, 07456, 07458, 07461–63, 07466, 07480–81, 07495, 07508, 07601–04, 07607, 07620–22, 07624, 07626–28, 07630–31, 07640–49, 07652–53, 07656, 07660–61, 07663, 07666, 07675–77, 07820–23, 07825–27, 07832–33, 07838–39, 07844, 07846, 07848, 07851, 07855, 07860, 07863, 07865, 07874–75, 07877, 07879–80, 07882, 07890

* * *

SIXTH DISTRICT

FRANK PALLONE, JR., Democrat, of Long Branch, NJ; born in Long Branch, October 30, 1951; education: B.A., Middlebury College, Middlebury, VT, 1973; M.A., Fletcher School of Law and Diplomacy, 1974; J.D., Rutgers University School of Law, 1978; professional: member of the bar: Florida, New York, Pennsylvania, and New Jersey; attorney, Marine Advisory Service; assistant professor, Cook College, Rutgers University Sea Grant Extension Program; counsel, Monmouth County, NJ, Protective Services for the Elderly; instructor, Monmouth College; Long Branch City Council, 1982–88; New Jersey State Senate, 1983–88; married the former Sarah Hospodor, 1992; committees: ranking member, Energy and Commerce; elected to the 100th Congress, by special election, on November 8, 1988, to fill the vacancy caused by the death of U.S. Representative James J. Howard; reelected to each succeeding Congress.

Office Listings

http://www.pallone.house.gov www.facebook.com/repfrankpallone twitter: @frankpallone

237 Cannon House Office Building, Washington, DC 20515 .... (202) 225–4671
Chief of Staff.—Janice Fuller. FAX: 225–9665
Legislative Director.—Brian Laughlin (Deputy COS).
Communications Director.—Anton Becker.
504 Broadway, Long Branch, NJ 07740 .... (732) 571–1140
67/69 Church Street, Kilmer Square, New Brunswick, NJ 08901–1242 .... (732) 249–8892

Counties: MIDDLESEX COUNTY. CITIES AND TOWNSHIPS: Avenel, Carteret, Colonia, Edison, Fords, Highland Park, Hopelawn, Iselin, Keasbey, Menlo Park Terrace, Metuchen, New Brunswick, Old Bridge, Perth Amboy, Piscataway, Port Reading, Sayreville, Sewaren, South Amboy, South Plainfield, and Woodbridge. MONMOUTH COUNTY. CITIES AND TOWNSHIPS: Aberdeen, Allenhurst, Asbury Park, Atlantic Highlands, Deal, Hazlet, Highlands, Interlaken, Keansburg, Keyport, Loch Arbor, Long Branch, Marlboro, Matawan, Middletown, Monmouth Beach, Oceanport, Sea Bright, Union Beach, and West Long Branch. Population (2010), 732,657.

ZIP Codes: 07001, 07008, 07060, 07064–65, 07067, 07077, 07080, 07095, 07701, 07703, 07711–12, 07716, 07718, 07721–23, 07726, 07728, 07730, 07732–35, 07737, 07740, 07746–48, 07750–53, 07755, 07757–58, 07760, 07764–65, 08812,

08817–18, 08820, 08830, 08832, 08837, 08840, 08846, 08854–55, 08857, 08859, 08861–63, 08871–73, 08879, 08899, 08901–04, 08906, 08933, 08989

* * *

SEVENTH DISTRICT

LEONARD LANCE, Republican, of Clinton Township, NJ; born in Easton, PA, June 25, 1952; education: B.A., Lehigh University, Bethlehem, PA, 1974; J.D., Vanderbilt University Law School, Memphis, TN, 1977; M.P.A., Woodrow Wilson School of Public and International Affairs, Princeton University, Princeton, NJ, 1982; professional: judicial clerk; lawyer, private practice; member, New Jersey State Assembly, 1991–2002; member, New Jersey State Senate, 2002–09; Minority Leader, New Jersey State Senate, 2004–08; caucuses: Congressional Arts Caucus; Congressional Caucus on the Deadliest Cancers; Congressional House Republican Israel Caucus; Congressional Humanities Caucus; Congressional Life Science Caucus; Congressional Pediatric and Adult Hydrocephalus Caucus; Congressional Rare Disease Caucus; religion: Roman Catholic; committees: Energy and Commerce; Select Committee on Ethics; elected to the 111th Congress on November 4, 2008; reelected to each succeeding Congress.

Office Listings

http://www.lance.house.gov https://www.facebook.com/CongressmanLance
https://twitter.com/replancenj7

2352 Rayburn House Office Building, Washington, DC 20515 .... (202) 225–5361
Chief of Staff.—Todd Mitchell. FAX: 225–9460
Deputy Chief of Staff / Communications Director.—John Byers.
Scheduler.—Anna Pellecchia.
425 North Avenue East, Westfield, NJ 07090 .... (908) 518–7733
361 Route 31, Unit 1400, Flemington, NJ 08822 .... (908) 789–6900
District Director.—Amanda Woloshen.

Counties: UNION COUNTY. MUNICIPALITIES: Berkeley Heights, Clark, Cranford, Garwood, Kenilworth, Linden, Mountainside, New Providence, Springfield, Summit, Union, Westfield, and Winfield. HUNTERDON COUNTY. MUNICIPALITIES: Alexandria, Bethlehem, Bloomsbury, Califon, Clinton Township, Clinton, Delaware Township, East Amwell, Flemington, Frenchtown, Glen Gardner, Hampton, High Bridge, Holland, Kingwood, Lambertville, Lebanon, Lebanon Township, Milford, Oldwick, Raritan, Readington, Whitehouse Station, Stockton, Tewksbury, Union, and West Amwell. SOMERSET COUNTY. MUNICIPALITIES: Bedminster, Bernards, Bernardsville, Branchburg, Bridgewater, Far Hills, Green Brook, Hillsborough, Montgomery Township, Millstone, North Plainfield, Peapack-Gladstone, Raritan, Rocky Hill, Somerville, Warren, and Watchung. MORRIS COUNTY. MUNICIPALITIES: Chester, Dover, Long Hill, Mine Hill, Mount Arlington, Mount Olive, Netcong, Roxbury, Washington, and Wharton. WARREN COUNTY. MUNICIPALITIES: Alpha, Franklin, Greenwich, Harmony, Lopatcong, and Phillipsburg. ESSEX COUNTY. MUNICIPALITIES: Millburn. Population (2010), 733,961.

ZIP Codes: 07016, 07027, 07033, 07036, 07041, 07059–60, 07066, 07069, 07081, 07083, 07090, 07092, 07416, 07676, 07801–03, 07806, 07828, 07830, 07836, 07856–57, 07869, 07885, 07901, 07920–22, 07930–31, 07933–34, 07974, 07977–78, 08323, 08502, 08504, 08530, 08540, 08551, 08553, 08557–59, 08801–04, 08807, 08809, 08812, 08821–22, 08825–27, 08829, 08833, 08836, 08844, 08848, 08853, 08858, 08865, 08867, 08869–70, 08876, 08889

* * *

EIGHTH DISTRICT

ALBIO SIRES, Democrat, of West New York, NJ; born in Bejucal, Provincia de la Habana, Cuba, January 26, 1951; education: graduated, Memorial High School; B.A., St. Peter's College, 1974; M.A., Middlebury College, Middlebury, VT, 1985; studied Spanish in Madrid, Spain; professional: businessman; teacher; part-owner, A.M. Title Agency, Union Township; Mayor, West New York, NJ, 1995–2006; member: New Jersey General Assembly, 1999–2006; Speaker, New Jersey General Assembly, 2002–05; family: wife, Adrienne; stepdaughter, Tara Kole; committees: Foreign Affairs; Transportation and Infrastructure; elected to the 109th Congress, by special election, to fill the vacancy caused by the resignation of U.S. Representative Robert Menendez; elected to the 110th Congress; reelected to each succeeding Congress.

Office Listings

http://www.sires.house.gov https://facebook.com/RepAlbioSires https://twitter.com/RepSires

2342 Rayburn House Office Building, Washington, DC 20515 .... (202) 225–7919
Chief of Staff.—Gene Martorony. FAX: 226–0792
Administrative Director / Scheduler.—Judi Wolford.
Legislative Director.—Kaylan Koszela.
257 Cornelison Avenue, Suite 4408, Jersey City, NJ 07302 .... (201) 309–0301
Communications Director.—Erica Daughtrey. FAX: 309–0384
5500 Palisades Avenue, Suite A, West New York, NJ 07093 .... (201) 558–0800

Office Listings—Continued

800 Anna Street, Elizabeth, NJ 07201 .... (908) 820–0692
FAX: 820–0694

Counties: BERGEN (part), ESSEX (part), HUDSON (part), and UNION (part). CITIES AND TOWNSHIPS: Bayonne, Belleville, East Newark, Elizabeth, Fairview, Guttenberg, Harrison, Hoboken, Jersey City, Kearny, Newark, North Bergen, Union City, Weehawken, and West New York. Population (2010), 732,658.

ZIP Codes: 07002–03 (part), 07017 (part), 07022, 07029–30, 07032 (part), 07047, 07083 (part), 07086–87, 07093, 07102, 07104–05 (part), 07107 (part), 07109 (part), 07114 (part), 07201–02, 07206, 07208 (part), 07302 (part), 07304–06 (part), 07307, 07310–11

* * *

NINTH DISTRICT

BILL PASCRELL, JR., Democrat, of Paterson, NJ; born in Paterson, January 25, 1937; education: B.A., journalism, and M.A., philosophy, Fordham University; veteran, U.S. Army and Army Reserve; professional: educator; elected Minority Leader Pro Tempore, New Jersey General Assembly, 1988–96; Mayor of Paterson, 1990–96; named Mayor of the Year by bipartisan NJ Conference of Mayors, 1996; started Paterson's first Economic Development Corporation; married the former Elsie Marie Botto; three children: William III, Glenn, and David; caucuses: co-chair, Congressional Fire Services Caucus; co-chair, Law Enforcement Caucus; co-chair, Italian-American Delegation; co-chair, Traumatic Brain Injury Task Force; committees: Ways and Means; elected to the 105th Congress; reelected to each succeeding Congress.

Office Listings

http://www.pascrell.house.gov https://www.facebook.com/pascrell
twitter: @billpascrell

2370 Rayburn House Office Building, Washington, DC 20515 .... (202) 225–5751
Chief of Staff.—Ben Rich. FAX: 225–5782
Legislative Director.—Alyssa Penna.
Economic Policy Advisor.—Elaina Houser.
200 Federal Plaza, Suite 500, Paterson, NJ 07505 .... (973) 523–5152
District Director.—Ritzy Morales.
Communications Director.—Timothy Carroll.
2–10 North Van Brunt Street, Englewood, NJ 07631 .... (201) 935–2248
367 Valley Brook Avenue, Lyndhurst, NJ 07071 .... (201) 935–2248
330 Passaic Street, Passaic, NJ 07055 .... (973) 472–4510

Counties: BERGEN COUNTY. CITIES: Carlstadt, Cliffside Park, Cresskill, East Rutherford, Edgewater, Elmwood Park, Englewood, Englewood Cliffs, Fort Lee, Garfield, Hasbrouck Heights, Leonia, Little Ferry, Lyndhurst, Moonachie, North Arlington, Palisades Park, Ridgefield, Ridgefield Park, Rutherford, Saddle Brook, South Hackensack, Teaneck (part), Tenafly, Teterboro, Wallington, and Wood-Ridge. HUDSON COUNTY. CITIES: Kearny (part) and Secaucus. PASSAIC COUNTY. CITIES: Clifton, Haledon, Hawthorne, Passaic, Paterson, and Prospect Park. Population (2010), 742,508.

ZIP Codes: 07010–15, 07020, 07024, 07026, 07031–32, 07055, 07057, 07070–75, 07094, 07096, 07099, 07407, 07501–14, 07522, 07524, 07533, 07538, 07543–44, 07604–06, 07608, 07626, 07631–32, 07643, 07650, 07657, 07660, 07663, 07666, 07670

* * *

TENTH DISTRICT

DONALD M. PAYNE, JR., Democrat, of Newark, NJ; born in Newark, December 17, 1958; education: graduated from Hillside High School; attended Kean College (now Kean University), Union, NJ; professional: elected to Newark Municipal Council, president, 2006–12; elected to Essex County Board of Chosen Freeholders, 2006–12; director of Student Transportation for the Essex County Educational Services Commission; married: wife, Beatrice; three children: Jack, Yvonne, and Donald III (triplets); caucuses: Addiction, Treatment, and Recovery Caucus; Congressional Animal Protection Caucus; Congressional Black Caucus; Congressional Caucus on Sudan and South Sudan; Congressional Diabetes Caucus; Congressional Down Syndrome Caucus; Congressional Full Employment Caucus; Congressional LGBT Equality Caucus; Congressional Library of Congress Caucus; Congressional Men's Health Caucus; Congressional Small Business Caucus; Congressional Taiwan Caucus; Congressional TRIO Caucus; Democratic Whip Task Force on Poverty, Income Equality, and Opportunity; Fire Services Caucus; Foster Care Youth Caucus; Homeland Security Task Force; House Medical Technology Caucus;

Indian and American Indian Caucus; Ports, Opportunity, Renewable, Trade, and Security (PORTS) Caucus; U.S. Senate International Conservation Caucus; U.S. Senate Oceans Caucus; committees: Homeland Security; Transportation and Infrastucture; elected simultaneously to the 112th and 113th Congresses, by special election, on November 6, 2012, to fill the vacancy caused by the death of U.S. Representative Donald Milford Payne; reelected to each succeeding Congress.

Office Listings

http://payne.house.gov twitter: @repdonaldpayne

132 Cannon House Office Building, Washington, DC 20515 .... (202) 225–3436
Chief of Staff.—LaVerne Alexander.
Communications Director.—Vacant.
60 Nelson Place, 14th Floor, Newark, NJ 07102 .... (973) 645–3213
253 Martin Luther King Drive, Jersey City, NJ 07305 .... (201) 369–0392
1455 Liberty Avenue, Hillside, NJ 07205 .... (862) 229–2994

Counties: ESSEX, HUDSON, AND UNION. CITIES AND TOWNSHIPS: Bayonne, East Orange, Hillside, Irvington, Jersey City, Linden, Maplewood, Montclair, Newark, Orange, Rahway, Roselle, Roselle Park, South Orange, Union, and West Orange. Population (2010), 732,658.

ZIP Codes: 07002–03 (part), 07017 (part), 07018, 07028, 07036 (part), 07040, 07041 (part), 07042, 07043–44 (part), 07050, 07052 (part), 07065, 07079, 07083 (part), 07088, 07102 (part), 07103, 07104–05 (part), 07106, 07107 (part), 07108, 07111–12, 07114 (part), 07203–05, 07208 (part), 07302 (part), 07304–06 (part)

* * *

ELEVENTH DISTRICT

RODNEY P. FRELINGHUYSEN, Republican, of Morristown, NJ; born in New York, NY, April 29, 1946; education: graduated, Hobart College, NY, 1969; attended graduate school in Connecticut; professional: served, U.S. Army, 93rd Engineer Construction Battalion; honorably discharged, 1971; Morris County State and Federal Aid Coordinator and Administrative Assistant, 1972; member, Morris County Board of Chosen Freeholders, 1974–83 (director, 1980); served on: Welfare and Mental Health Boards; Human Services and Private Industry Councils; New Jersey General Assembly, 1983–94; chairman, Assembly Appropriations Committee, 1988–89 and 1992–94; member: American Legion and Veterans of Foreign Wars; named Legislator of the Year by the Veterans of Foreign Wars, the New Jersey Association of Mental Health Agencies, and the New Jersey Association of Retarded Citizens; honored by numerous organizations; married: Virginia Frelinghuysen; children: two daughters; committees: chair, Appropriations; elected to the 104th Congress on November 8, 1994; reelected to each succeeding Congress.

Office Listings

http://www.frelinghuysen.house.gov

2306 Rayburn House Office Building, Washington, DC 20515 .... (202) 225–5034
Chief of Staff.—Kathleen Hazlett. FAX: 225–3186
Press Secretary.—Steve Wilson.
Legislative Director.—Austin Bone.
Scheduler.—Chris Hansell.
30 Schuyler Place, 2nd Floor, Morristown, NJ 07960 .... (973) 984–0711

Counties: ESSEX COUNTY. CITIES AND TOWNSHIPS: Bloomfield, Caldwell, Cedar Grove, Essex Fells, Fairfield Township, Livingston, Montclair, North Caldwell, Nutley, Roseland, Verona, West Caldwell, and West Orange. MORRIS COUNTY. CITIES AND TOWNSHIPS: Municipalities of Boonton Town, Boonton Township, Brookside, Budd Lake, Butler, Cedar Knolls, Chatham Borough, Chatham Township, Convent Station, Denville, East Hanover, Florham Park, Green Pond, Green Village, Hanover, Harding, Hibernia, Jefferson, Kinnelon, Lake Hiawatha, Lake Hopatcong, Lincoln Park, Madison, Mendham Borough, Mendham Township, Montville, Morris Plains, Morris Township, Morristown, Mountain Lakes, Mount Tabor, Newfoundland, New Vernon, Oak Ridge, Parsippany-Troy Hills, Pequannock, Picatinny, Pine Brook, Randolph, Riverdale, Rockaway Borough, Rockaway Township, Stanhope, Towaco, Victory Gardens, and Whippany. PASSAIC COUNTY. CITIES: Bloomingdale, Haskell, Little Falls, North Haledon, Pompton Lakes, Totowa, Wanaque, Wayne and Woodland Park. SUSSEX COUNTY. CITIES AND TOWNSHIPS: Byram, Hopatcong, Ogdensburg, Sparta, and Stanhope. Population (2010), 724,761.

ZIP Codes: 07003–07, 07009, 07021, 07028, 07034–39, 07042–46, 07052, 07054, 07058, 07068, 07082, 07110, 07403, 07405, 07420, 07424, 07435, 07438–40, 07442, 07444, 07457, 07465, 07470, 07474, 07508, 07512, 07806, 07821, 07828, 07834, 07837, 07842–43, 07845, 07848–49, 07866, 07869, 07871, 07874, 07878, 07920, 07926–28, 07932, 07935–36, 07930, 07940, 07945, 07950, 07960–63, 07976, 07980, 07999

* * *

TWELFTH DISTRICT

BONNIE WATSON COLEMAN, Democrat, of Ewing Township, NJ; born in Camden, NJ, February 6, 1945; first African American woman ever elected to Congress from New Jersey; education: B.A., Thomas Edison State College; professional: former Assistant Commissioner, New Jersey Department of Community Affairs; former Bureau Chief, New Jersey Division on Civil Rights; eight-term member of the New Jersey General Assembly; first African American woman to serve as Majority Leader of the New Jersey General Assembly; first African American woman to chair the New Jersey Democratic State Committee; religion: Baptist; married: Rev. William E. Coleman; children: William, Jared, and Troy; two grandchildren: Kamryn and William; committees: Homeland Security; Oversight and Government Reform; elected to the 114th Congress on November 4, 2014; reelected to the 115th Congress on November 8, 2016.

Office Listings

http://watsoncoleman.house.gov twitter: @repbonnie
facebook: https://www.facebook.com/RepBonnie

1535 Longworth House Office Building, Washington, DC 20515 .... (202) 225–5801
Chief of Staff.—James Gee. FAX: 225–6025
Legislative Director.—Michael Reed.
Communications Director.—Kirsten Allen.
Scheduler.—Jaimee Gilmartin.
850 Bear Tavern Road, Ewing, NJ 08628 .... (609) 883–0026
District Director.—Kari Osmond.

Counties: MERCER COUNTY. CITIES AND TOWNSHIPS: East Windsor, Ewing, Hightstown, Hopewell Borough, Hopewell Township, Lawrence, Pennington, Princeton, Trenton, and West Windsor. MIDDLESEX COUNTY. CITIES AND TOWNSHIPS: Cranbury, Dunellen, East Brunswick, Helmetta, Jamesburg, Middlesex, Milltown, Monroe, North Brunswick, Old Bridge, Plainsboro, South Brunswick, South River, and Spotswood. SOMERSET COUNTY. CITIES AND TOWNSHIPS: Bound Brook, Franklin, Manville, and South Bound Brook. UNION COUNTY. CITIES AND TOWNSHIPS: Fanwood, Plainfield, and Scotch Plains. Population (2010), 732,658.

ZIP Codes: 07023, 07060–63, 07076, 07747, 08512, 08520, 08525, 08528, 08530, 08534, 08536, 08540–44, 08550, 08560, 08608–11, 08618–19, 08628–29, 08638, 08648, 08691, 08805, 08810, 08812, 08816, 08823–24, 08828, 08831, 08835, 08846, 08850, 08852, 08857, 08859, 08873, 08875, 08880, 08882, 08884, 08890, 08902

NEW MEXICO

(Population 2010, 2,059,179)

SENATORS

TOM UDALL, Democrat, of Santa Fe, NM; born in Tucson, AZ, May 18, 1948; education: graduate of McLean High School, 1966; B.A., Prescott College, Prescott, AZ, 1970; LL.B., Cambridge University, Cambridge, England, 1975; J.D., University of New Mexico, Albuquerque, NM, 1977; professional: admitted to the New Mexico Bar, 1978; served as New Mexico Attorney General, 1990–98; served as U.S. Representative for New Mexico's 3rd Congressional District, 1998–2008; married: Jill Z. Cooper; children: Amanda; member of the Commission on Security and Cooperation in Europe; committees: Appropriations; Commerce, Science, and Transportation; Foreign Relations; Indian Affairs; Joint Committee on Printing; Rules and Administration; elected to the U.S. Senate on November 4, 2008; reelected to the U.S. Senate on November 4, 2014.

Office Listings

http://tomudall.senate.gov facebook: https://www.facebook.com/senatortomudall
twitter: https://twitter.com/SenatorTomUdall

531 Hart Senate Office Building, Washington, DC 20510 .... (202) 224–6621
Chief of Staff.—Bianca Ortiz Wertheim. FAX: 228–3261
Legislative Director.—Andrew Wallace.
Communications Director.—Ned Adriance.
Executive Assistant.—Devon Wohl.
400 Gold Avenue, SW., Suite 300, Albuquerque, NM 87102 .... (505) 346–6791
201 North Church Street, Suite 201B, Las Cruces, NM 88001 .... (575) 526–5475
120 South Federal Place, Suite 302, Santa Fe, NM 87501 .... (505) 988–6511
102 West Hagerman, Suite A, Carlsbad, NM 88220 .... (575) 234–0366
100 South Avenue A, Suite 113, Portales, NM 88130 .... (505) 356–6811

* * *

MARTIN HEINRICH, Democrat, of Albuquerque, NM; born in Fallon, NV, October 17, 1971; education: B.S., mechanical engineering, University of Missouri, Columbia, MO, 1995; professional: executive director of the Cottonwood Gulch Foundation, 1996–2001; Albuquerque City Council, 2003–07; State of New Mexico Natural Resources Trustee, 2006–07; served as U.S. Representative for New Mexico's First Congressional District, 2009–12; married: Julie Heinrich; children: Carter Heinrich and Micah Heinrich; caucuses: Congressional Dietary Supplement Caucus; Congressional Sportsmen's Caucus; National Service Congressional Caucus; Senate Climate Action Task Force; Senate Democratic Hispanic Task Force; committees: Armed Services; Energy and Natural Resources; Joint Economic Committee; Select Committee on Intelligence; elected to the U.S. Senate on November 6, 2012.

Office Listings

http://heinrich.senate.gov www.facebook.com/martinheinrich twitter: @martinheinrich

303 Hart Senate Office Building, Washington, DC 20510 .... (202) 224–5521
Chief of Staff.—Joe Britton. FAX: 228–2841
Deputy Chief of Staff.—Whitney Potter.
Legislative Director.—Virgilio Barrera.
Director of Scheduling.—Mike DeSpain.
400 Gold Avenue Southwest, Suite 1080, Albuquerque, NM 87102 .... (505) 346–6601
7450 East Main Street, Suite A, Farmington, NM 87402 .... (505) 325–5030
505 South Main Street, Suite 148, Las Cruces, NM 88001 .... (575) 523–6561
200 East 4th Street, Suite 300, Roswell, NM 88201 .... (575) 622–7113
123 East Marcy Street, Suite 103, Santa Fe, NM 87501 .... (505) 988–6647

REPRESENTATIVES

FIRST DISTRICT

MICHELLE LUJAN GRISHAM, Democrat, of Albuquerque, NM; born in Los Alamos, NM, October 24, 1959; education: B.U.S., University of New Mexico, 1981; J.D., University of New Mexico, 1987; professional: Director, New Mexico State Agency on Aging, 1991–2002; Secretary, New Mexico Department of Aging and Long-Term Services, 2002–04; Secretary, New Mexico Department of Health, 2004–07; Bernalillo County Commissioner, 2010–12; children: Taylor Stewart and Erin Grisham; chairwoman, Congressional Hispanic Caucus; committees: Agriculture; Budget; elected to the 113th Congress on November 6, 2012; reelected to each succeeding Congress.

Office Listings

http://www.lujangrisham.house.gov twitter: @replujangrisham
http://www.facebook.com/replujangrisham

214 Cannon House Office Building, Washington, DC 20515 .... (202) 225–6316
Chief of Staff.—Dominic Gabello.
Legislative Director.—Nathan Schelble.
Executive Assistant.—Natalie Armijo.
400 Gold Avenue, SW., Suite 680, Albuquerque, NM 87102 .... (505) 346–6781

Counties: BERNALILLO (part), SANDOVAL (part), SANTA FE (part), TORRANCE, AND VALENCIA (part). CITIES AND TOWNSHIPS: Albuquerque, Bernalillo, Edgewood, Estancia, Moriarty, Mountainair, Rio Rancho, and South Valley. Population (2010), 693,772.

ZIP Codes: 87004, 87008, 87015, 87026, 87035–36, 87047–48, 87059, 87063, 87067, 87102, 87104–14, 87116–17, 87120–24, 87131, 87144, 88321

* * *

SECOND DISTRICT

STEVAN PEARCE, Republican, of Hobbs, NM; born in Lamesa, TX, August 24, 1947; education: M.B.A., Eastern New Mexico University, Las Cruces, NM, 1991; B.B.A., New Mexico State University, Portales, NM, 1970; professional: owner, oil well services company; served in Vietnam as a pilot for the U.S. Air Force, Captain, 1970–76; member of the New Mexico State House of Representatives, 1997–2000; elected as a Republican to the 108th, 109th, 110th, 112th, and 113th Congresses; religion: Baptist; married: Cynthia; caucuses: chairman emeritus of Western Caucus; member of Sportsmen's Caucus; Prayer Caucus; Republican Study Committee; committees: Financial Services; Natural Resources; elected to the 112th Congress on November 2, 2010; reelected to each succeeding Congress.

Office Listings

http://www.pearce.house.gov twitter: @repstevepearce
facebook: repstevepearce instagram: repstevepearce

2432 Rayburn House Office Building, Washington, DC 20515 .... (202) 225–2365
Chief of Staff.—Todd Willens. FAX: 225–9599
Deputy Chief of Staff.—Patrick Cuff.
Press Secretary.—Keeley Christensen.
Scheduler.—Kristine Nichols.
Senior Legislative Assistants: Jacci Guy, Rob MacGregor.
Staff Assistant / Legislative Correspondent.—Ben Johnson.
570 North Telshor Boulevard, Las Cruces, NM 88011 .... (575) 522–0771
1717 West 2nd Street, Suite 110, Roswell, NM 88201 .... (575) 622–6200
111 School of Mines Road, Socorro, NM 87801 .... (575) 855–8979
200 East Broadway, Suite 200, Hobbs, NM 88240 .... (575) 393–6995

Counties: BERNALILLO (part), CATRON, CHAVES, CIBOLA, DEBACA, DONA ANA, EDDY, GRANT, GUADALUPE, HIDALGO, LEA, LINCOLN, LUNA, MCKINLEY (part), OTERO, ROOSEVELT (part), SIERRA, SOCORRO, AND VALENCIA (part). Population (2010), 702,936.

ZIP Codes: 79821, 79835, 79922, 79932, 79934, 85534, 87002, 87005–07, 87011, 87014, 87020–23, 87026, 87028, 87031, 87034, 87038, 87040, 87045, 87049, 87051, 87062, 87068, 87105, 87121, 88024–34, 88036, 88038–49, 88051–56, 88058, 88061–63, 88065, 88072, 88081, 88113–16, 88118–19, 88123–26, 88130, 88132, 88134, 88136, 88201–03, 88210–11, 88213 88220–21, 88230–32, 88240–42, 88250, 88252–56, 88260, 88262–65, 88267–68, 88301, 88310–12, 88314, 88316–18, 88323–25, 88330, 88336–55, 88417, 88431, 88435

* * *

THIRD DISTRICT

BEN RAY LUJÁN, Democrat, of Santa Fe, NM; born in Nambe, NM; June 7, 1972; education: New Mexico Highland University; business administration, Highlands University, Las

Vegas, NM; professional: elected to the New Mexico Public Regulation Commission, 2005–08; caucuses: co-chair, Nuclear Cleanup Caucus; co-chair, Science and National Labs Caucus; co-chair, Technology Transfer Caucus; Hispanic Caucus; Native American Caucus; committees: Energy and Commerce; elected to the 111th Congress on November 4, 2008; reelected to each succeeding Congress.

Office Listings

http://www.lujan.house.gov www.facebook.com/repbenraylujan www.twitter.com/repbenraylujan

2231 Rayburn House Office Building, Washington, DC 20515 .... (202) 225–6190
Chief of Staff.—Angela Ramirez. FAX: 226–1528
Deputy Chief of Staff / Communications Director.—Joe Shoemaker.
Legislative Director.—Graham Mason.
Executive Assistant / Scheduler.—Chris Garcia.
1611 Calle Lorca, Suite A, Santa Fe, NM 87505 .... (505) 984–8950
District Director.—Jennifer Catechis.
District Scheduler.—Julio Salazar.
800 Municipal Drive, Farmington, NM 87401 .... (505) 324–1005
Constituent Services Representative / Veterans Liaison.—Brian Lee.
110 West Aztec, Suite 102, Gallup, NM 87301 .... (505) 863–0582
Field Representative and Navajo Nation Liaison.—Brian Lee.
903 University Avenue, P.O. Box 1368, Las Vegas, NM 87701 .... (505) 454–3038
Constituent Liaison.—Stephen Salas.
404 West Route 66 Boulevard, Tucumcari, NM 88401 .... (575) 461–3029
Field Representative.—Ron Wilmot.
3200 Civic Center Circle, NE., Suite 330, Rio Rancho, NM 87144 .... (505) 994–0499
Constituent Liaison.—Joe Casados.

Counties: BERNALILLO (part), COLFAX, CURRY, HARDING, LOS ALAMOS, MCKINLEY (part), MORA, NAVAJO NATION, QUAY, RIO ARRIBA, ROOSEVELT (part), SANDOVAL (part), SAN JUAN, SAN MIGUEL, SANTA FE, TAOS, AND UNION. Population (2010), 686,393.

ZIP Codes: 87001, 87004, 87010, 87012–13, 87015, 87017–18, 87024–25, 87027, 87029, 87037, 87041, 87044–48, 87052–53, 87056, 87064, 87072, 87083, 87114, 87120, 87123–24, 87144, 87174, 87301–02, 87305, 87310–13, 87316–17, 87319–23, 87325–26, 87328, 87347, 87364–65, 87375, 87401–02, 87410, 87412–13, 87415–21, 87455, 87461, 87499, 87501–25, 87527–33, 87535, 87537–40, 87543–45, 87548–49, 87551–54, 87556–58, 87560, 87562, 87564–67, 87569, 87571, 87573–83, 87592, 87594, 87701, 87710, 87712–15, 87718, 87722–23, 87728–36, 87740, 87742–43, 87745–47, 87749–50, 87752–53, 88101–03, 88112–13, 88115–16, 88118, 88120–26, 88130, 88132–35, 88401, 88410–11, 88414–16, 88418–19, 88421–22, 88424, 88426–27, 88430, 88433–34, 88436–37, 88439

NEW YORK

(Population 2010, 19,378,102)

SENATORS

CHARLES E. SCHUMER, Democrat, of Brooklyn and Queens, NY; born in Brooklyn, November 23, 1950; education: graduated valedictorian, Madison High School; Harvard University, *magna cum laude*, 1971; J.D. with honors, Harvard Law School, 1974; professional: admitted to the New York State Bar in 1975; elected to the New York State Assembly, 1974; served on Judiciary, Health, Education, and Cities committees; chairman, subcommittee on City Management and Governance, 1977; chairman, Committee on Oversight and Investigation, 1979; reelected to each succeeding legislative session until December 1980; married: Iris Weinshall, 1980; children: Jessica Emily and Alison Emma; committees: Rules and Administration; Select Committee on Intelligence; elected to the 97th Congress on November 4, 1980; reelected to each succeeding Congress; elected to the U.S. Senate on November 3, 1998; reelected to each succeeding Senate term; Minority Leader, 2017 to present.

Office Listings

http://schumer.senate.gov

322 Hart Senate Office Building, Washington, DC 20510 .... (202) 224–6542
FAX: 228–3027
Chief of Staff.—Mike Lynch.
Deputy Chief of Staff.—Erin Sager Vaughn.
Communications Director.—Matt House.
Legislative Director.—Meghan Taira.
780 Third Avenue, Suite 2301, New York, NY 10017 .... (212) 486–4430
Leo O'Brien Building, Room 420, Albany, NY 12207 .... (518) 431–4070
130 South Elmwood Avenue, #660, Buffalo, NY 14202 .... (716) 846–4111
100 State Street, Room 3040, Rochester, NY 14614 .... (585) 263–5866
100 South Clinton, Room 841, Syracuse, NY 13261–7318 .... (315) 423–5471
Federal Office Building, 15 Henry Street, #100A–F, Binghamton, NY 13901 .... (607) 772–6792
145 Pine Lawn Road, #300N, Melville, NY 11747 .... (631) 753–0978
One Park Place, Suite 100, Peekskill, NY 10566 .... (914) 734–1532

* * *

KIRSTEN E. GILLIBRAND, Democrat, of Brunswick, NY; born in Albany, NY, December 9, 1966; education: B.A., Dartmouth College, Hanover, NH, 1988; J.D., UCLA, Los Angeles, CA, 1991; professional: attorney; Special Counsel to the U.S. Secretary of Housing and Urban Development Andrew Cuomo; private legal practice; religion: Catholic; married: Jonathan Gillibrand, 2001; two sons: Theodore, 2004, and Henry, 2008; committees: Agriculture, Nutrition, and Forestry; Armed Services; Environment and Public Works; Special Committee on Aging; appointed to the 111th Congress on January 23, 2009, to fill the vacancy caused by the resignation of U.S. Senator Hillary Clinton; subsequently elected on November 2, 2010, for the remaining two years of the unexpired term; reelected to the U.S. Senate on November 6, 2012.

Office Listings

http://gillibrand.senate.gov

478 Russell Senate Office Building, Washington, DC 20510 .... (202) 224–4451
FAX: 228–0282
Chief of Staff.—Jess Fassler.
Legislative Director.—Brooke Jamison.
Communications Director.—Whitney Brennan.
Scheduler.—Mary Sixbey.
780 Third Avenue, Suite 2601, New York, NY 10017 .... (212) 688–6262
Federal Office Building, 1 Clinton Square, Room 821, Albany, NY 12207 .... (518) 431–0120
Larkin at Exchange, 726 Exchange Street, Suite 511, Buffalo, NY 14210 .... (716) 854–9725
155 Pinelawn Road, Suite 250 North, Melville, NY 11747 .... (631) 249–2825
P.O. Box 273, Lowville, NY 13367 .... (315) 376–6118
Federal Office Building, 100 State Street, Room 4195, Rochester, NY 14614 .... (585) 263–6250
Federal Office Building, 100 South Clinton Street, Room 1470, P.O. Box 7378, Syracuse, NY 13261 .... (315) 448–0470
Lower Hudson Valley Office, P.O. Box 893, Mahopac, NY 10541 .... (845) 875–4585
Westchester County Office .... (914) 725–9294

REPRESENTATIVES

FIRST DISTRICT

LEE M. ZELDIN, Republican, of Shirley, NY; born in East Meadow, NY, January 30, 1980; education: William Floyd High School; University at Albany, SUNY; Albany Law School; religion: Jewish; married: Diana Zeldin; children: Mikayla and Arianna; committees: Financial Services; Foreign Affairs; elected to the 114th Congress on November 4, 2014; reelected to the 115th Congress on November 8, 2016.

Office Listings

https://zeldin.house.gov facebook.com/RepLeeZeldin twitter.com/RepLeeZeldin

1517 Longworth House Office Building, Washington, DC 20515 .... (202) 225–3826
Chief of Staff.—Eric Amidon.
Deputy Chief of Staff / Scheduler.—Nicole Paciello.
Legislative Director.—Kevin Dowling.
Communications Director.—Jennifer DiSiena.
31 Oak Street, Suite 20, Patchogue, NY 11772 .... (631) 289–1097
District Director.—Mark Woolley.
Director of Constituent Services.—William Doyle.
30 West Main Street, Suite 201, Riverhead, NY 11901 .... (631) 209–4235

Counties: SUFFOLK COUNTY (part). TOWNS: Brookhaven, Islip, East Hampton, Smithtown, Riverhead, Shelter Island, Southampton, and Southold. Population (2000), 654,360.

ZIP Codes: 00501, 00544, 11713, 11715, 11719–20, 11727, 11733, 11738, 11741–42, 11745, 11754–55, 11763–64, 11766–68, 11772, 11776–80, 11784, 11786–90, 11792, 11794, 11901, 11930–35, 11937, 11939–42, 11944, 11946–65, 11967–73, 11975–78, 11980

* * *

SECOND DISTRICT

PETER T. KING, Republican, of Seaford, NY; born in Manhattan, NY, April 5, 1944; education: B.A., St. Francis College, NY, 1965; J.D., University of Notre Dame Law School, IN, 1968; military service: served, U.S. Army Reserve National Guard, Specialist 5, 1968–73; admitted to New York Bar, 1968; professional: attorney; Deputy Nassau County Attorney, 1972–74; executive assistant to the Nassau County Executive, 1974–76; general counsel, Nassau Off-Track Betting Corporation, 1977; Hempstead Town Councilman, 1978–81; Nassau County Comptroller, 1981–92; member: Ancient Order of Hiberians; Long Island Committee for Soviet Jewry; Sons of Italy; Knights of Columbus; 69th Infantry Veterans Corps; American Legion; married: Rosemary Wiedl King, 1967; children: Sean and Erin; two grandchildren; committees: Financial Services; Homeland Security; Permanent Select Committee on Intelligence; elected on November 3, 1992 to the 103rd Congress; reelected to each succeeding Congress.

Office Listings

http://www.peteking.house.gov

339 Cannon House Office Building, Washington, DC 20515 .... (202) 225–7896
Chief of Staff / Press Secretary.—Kevin Fogarty. FAX: 226–2279
Legislative Director.—Jamie Matese.
1003 Park Boulevard, Massapequa Park, NY 11762 .... (516) 541–4225
District Director.—Anne Rosenfeld.
Suffolk County .... (631) 541–4225

Counties: NASSAU (part) AND SUFFOLK (part). CITIES AND TOWNSHIPS: Amityville, Babylon, Bayport, Bay Shore, Bethpage, Bohemia, Brentwood, Brightwaters, Copiague, Central Islip, Deer Park, East Islip, Farmingdale, Great River, Holbrook, Islip, Islip Terrace, Levittown, Lindenhurst, Massapequa, Massapequa Park, North Babylon, North Lindenhurst, Oakdale, Patemogue, Seaford, Wantagh, West Babylon, West Islip, and Wyandanch. Population (2010), 724,053.

ZIP Codes: 11701–06, 11714, 11716–18, 11722, 11726, 11730, 11735, 11739, 11741, 11751–53, 11756–58, 11762, 11769, 11772, 11779, 11782, 11793, 11795, 11798

* * *

THIRD DISTRICT

THOMAS R. SUOZZI, Democrat, of Glen Cove, NY; born in Glen Cove, August 31, 1962; education: B.S., accounting, Boston College 1984; J.D., Fordham Law School, 1989; professional: certified public accountant; attorney; Glen Cove Mayor, 1994–2002; Nassau County executive, 2002–10; religion: Catholic; family: married, wife: Helene; three children; caucuses: vice-chair, Problem Solvers Caucus; co-chair, Long Island Sound Caucus; co-chair, Quiet Skies Caucus; committees: Armed Services; Foreign Affairs; elected to the 115th Congress on November 8, 2016.

Office Listings

http://www.suozzi.house.gov

226 Cannon House Office Building, Washington, DC 20515 .... (202) 225–3335
Chief of Staff.—Mike Florio. FAX: 225–4669
Communications Director.—Lou Wasson.
Deputy COS / LD.—Diane Shust.
Scheduler.—Ellie Arbeit.
478A Park Avenue, Huntington, NY 11743 .... (631) 923–4100
250–02 Northern Boulevard, Little Neck, NY 11362 .... (718) 631–0400
District Director.—Cindy Rogers (631) 923–4100

Counties: NASSAU COUNTY (part), SUFFOLK COUNTY (part). CITIES: Asharoken, Bay Shore, Bayport, Bayside, Bayville, Centerport, Cold Springs Harbor, Commack, Deer Park, Dix Hills, Douglaston, East Hills, East Williston, East Northport, Eaton's Neck, Elwood, Farmingdale, Flushing, Fort Salonga, Glen Cove, Great Neck, Greenlawn, Greenvale, Halesite, Hauppauge, Herricks, Hicksville, Huntington, Huntington Station, Jericho, King's Park, Kings Point, Lake Success, Little Neck, Lloyd Harbor, Manhasset, Melville, Mill Neck, Mineola, Muttontown, North Hills, Northport, Old Bethpage, Old Brookville, Old Westbury, Oyster Bay, Plandome, Plainview, Port Washington, Queens Village, Roslyn, Roslyn Harbor, Roslyn Heights, Saddle Rock, Sands Point, Sea Cliff, Smithtown, South Huntington, Syosset, West Hills, Whitestone, Williston Park, Woodbury, and Wyandanch. Population (2013), 724,490.

ZIP Codes: 11101, 11004–05, 11020–21, 11023–24, 11030, 11040, 11042, 11050, 11357–63, 11426–28, 11507, 11542, 11545, 11547–48, 11560, 11577, 11579, 11590, 11596, 11709, 11714, 11721, 11724–25, 11729, 11731–32, 11739, 11743, 11746–47, 11753–54, 11756, 11765, 11768, 11771, 11787–88, 11791, 11797, 11801, 11803–04

* * *

FOURTH DISTRICT

KATHLEEN M. RICE, Democrat, of Garden City, NY; born in New York City, NY, February 15, 1965; education: graduated, Garden City High School, 1983; B.A., The Catholic University of America, Washington, DC, 1987; J.D., Touro Law Center, Long Island, NY, 1991; professional: Assistant District Attorney, Kings County, NY (Brooklyn), 1992–99; Assistant U.S. Attorney, U.S. Department of Justice, Philadelphia, PA, 1999–2005; elected District Attorney of Nassau County, NY, 2006–14; president, District Attorneys Association of the State of New York, 2013–14; awards: Mothers Against Drunk Driving (MADD) Lifetime Achievement Award; Governors Highway Safety Association (GHSA) James J. Howard Highway Safety Trailblazer Award; U.S. Inspector General's Integrity Award; U.S. Attorney General's Director's Award for Superior Performance as an Assistant U.S. Attorney; religion: Catholic; caucuses: Bipartisan Taskforce for Combating Anti-Semitism; Bipartisan Working Group; Congressional Caucus for Women's Issues; Congressional Coalition on Autism Research and Education; Congressional Diabetes Caucus; Congressional Fire Services Caucus; Congressional Long Island Sound Caucus; Congressional Pro-Choice Caucus; Congressional Stop DUI Caucus; Congressional Taiwan Caucus; Congressional Tourette Caucus; Democracy Task Force; Democratic Israel Working Group; New Democrat Coalition; NY Defense Working Group; Quiet Skies Caucus; U.S.-Philippines Friendship Caucus; committees: Homeland Security; Veterans' Affairs; elected to the 114th Congress on November 4, 2014; reelected to the 115th Congress on November 8, 2016.

Office Listings

http://kathleenrice.house.gov

1508 Longworth House Office Building, Washington, DC 20515 .... (202) 225–5516
Chief of Staff.—Nell Reilly. FAX: 225–5758
District Director.—Cheryl Rice.
Executive Assistant.—Amanda Walsh.
Communications Director.—Coleman Lamb.
229 7th Street, Suite 300, Garden City, NY 11530 .... (516) 739–3008

Counties: NASSAU (part). CITIES AND TOWNSHIPS: Atlantic Beach, Baldwin, Bellerose, Carle Place, Cedarhurst, East Meadow, East Rockaway, East Williston, Elmont, Floral Park, Franklin Square, Freeport, Garden City, Garden City Park, Hempstead, Hewlett, Inwood, Lakeview, Lawrence, Lynbrook, Malverne, Merrick, Mineola, New Cassel, New Hyde Park, North Bellmore, North New Hyde Park, Oceanside, Rockville Centre, Roosevelt, Salisbury, Stewart Manor, South Floral Park, South Valley Stream, Uniondale, Valley Stream, West Hempstead, Westbury, Williston Park, Woodmere, and Woodsburgh. Population (2010), 717,708.

ZIP Codes: 11003, 11010, 11040, 11096, 11501, 11509–10, 11514, 11516, 11518, 11520, 11530, 11549–50, 11552–54, 11556–59, 11561, 11563, 11565–66, 11569–70, 11572, 11575, 11580–81, 11590, 11596, 11598, 11710, 11793, 11801

* * *

FIFTH DISTRICT

GREGORY W. MEEKS, Democrat, of Southern Queens, NY; born in Harlem, NY, September 25, 1953; education: P.S. 183; Robert F. Wagner Junior High School; Julia Richman High School, New York, NY; B.A., Adelphi University, 1971–75; J.D., Howard University School of Law, 1975–78; professional: lawyer, admitted to bar, 1979; Queens District Attorney's Office, 1978–83, Assistant Specialist Narcotic Prosecutor, 1981–83; Assistant Counsel to State Investigation Commission, 1983–85; served as Assistant District Attorney; Supervising Judge, New York State Workers' Compensation Board; public service: New York State Assemblyman, 1992–97; organizations: Alpha Phi Alpha Fraternity; National Bar Association; caucuses: co-chair, Congressional Services Caucus; co-chair, European Union Caucus; co-chair, Malaria Caucus; co-chair, Organizations of American States; active member, Congressional Black Caucus; married: Simone-Marie Meeks, 1997; children: Aja, Ebony, and Nia-Ayana; committees: Financial Services; Foreign Affairs; elected to the 105th Congress on February 3, 1998; reelected to each succeeding Congress.

Office Listings

http://www.meeks.house.gov

2234 Rayburn House Office Building, Washington, DC 20515 .... (202) 225–3461
Chief of Staff.—Sophia Lafargue. FAX: 226–4169
Legislative Director.—Ernie Jolly.
Office Manager / Scheduler.—Kim Fuller.
153–01 Jamaica Avenue, Jamaica, NY 11432 .... (718) 725–6000
Chief of Staff.—Robert Simmons.
6712 Rockaway Beach Boulevard, Arverne, NY 11692 .... (347) 230–4032
Community Liaison.—Joseph Edwards.

Counties: QUEENS COUNTY (part). CITIES AND TOWNSHIPS: Belmont, Cambria Heights, Elmont, Floral Park, Glen Oaks, Hollis, Howard Beach, Jamaica, Jamaica Estates, Kew Gardens, Laurelton, New Hyde Park, Ozone Park, Queens Village, Richmond Hill, the Rockaway Peninsula, Rosedale, St. Albans, South Jamaica, South Ozone Park, Springfield Gardens, Valley Stream (North and South), and Woodhaven. Population (2015), 779,896.

ZIP Codes: 11001 (part), 11003 (part), 11010 (part), 11096 (part), 11366 (part), 11411–13, 11416–18 (part), 11419–20, 11422–23, 11426–28 (part), 11429–30, 11432 (part), 11433–34, 11435 (part), 11436, 11451, 11559 (part), 11580–81 (part), 11691–94, 11697

* * *

SIXTH DISTRICT

GRACE MENG, Democrat, of Queens, NY; born in Corona, NY, October 1, 1975; education: Stuyvesant High School; B.A., University of Michigan, 1997; J.D., Yeshiva University's Benjamin Cardozo School of Law, 2002; professional: practicing lawyer / pro bono attorney, 2003–08; New York State Assembly, 2008–12; religion: Christian; husband, Wayne Kye; children: Brandon and Tyler; caucuses: Congressional Asian Pacific American Caucus; Congressional Bangladesh Caucus; Congressional Caucus for Women's Issues; Congressional Caucus on India and Indian Americans; Congressional Caucus on Korea; Congressional Caucus on Sikh Americans; Congressional Creative Rights Caucus; Congressional Equality Caucus; Congressional Hellenic Caucus; Congressional Hellenic-Israel Caucus; Congressional Kids Safety Caucus; Congressional Oral Health Caucus; Congressional Pro-Choice Caucus; Congressional Quiet Skies Caucus; Congressional Taiwan Caucus; Gun Violence Prevention Task Force; United Solutions Caucus; U.S.-Philippines Friendship Caucus; Women's Working Group on Immigration Reform; committees: Appropriations; elected to the 113th Congress on November 6, 2012; reelected to each succeeding Congress.

Office Listings

http://meng.house.gov https://twitter.com/repgracemeng
https://www.facebook.com/repgracemeng

1317 Longworth House Office Building, Washington, DC 20515 .... (202) 225–2601
Chief of Staff.—Justin Oswald. FAX: 225–1589
Executive Assistant / Scheduler.—Brenda Connolly.
40–13 159 Street, Flushing, NY 11358 .... (718) 358–6364

Office Listings—Continued

FAX: 445–7868
118–15 Queens Boulevard, 17th Floor, Forest Hills, NY 11375 .... (718) 358–6364
District Director.—Anthony Lemma.
Communications Director.—Jordan Goldes.

Counties: QUEENS COUNTY (part). CITIES AND TOWNSHIPS: Auburndale, Bayside, Elmhurst, Electchester-Pomonok, Flushing, Forest Hills, Fresh Meadows, Glendale, Jamaica, Kew Gardens, Maspeth, Middle Village, Rego Park, Ridgewood, and Woodside. Population (2010), 724,352.

ZIP Codes: 11352, 11354–55, 11357–58, 11360–61, 11364–67, 11373–75, 11377–81, 11385, 11415, 11418, 11421, 11423–24, 11427, 11432, 11435

* * *

SEVENTH DISTRICT

NYDIA M. VELÁZQUEZ, Democrat, of New York, NY; born in Yabucoa, PR, March 28, 1953; education: B.A. in political science, University of Puerto Rico, 1974; M.A. in political science, New York University, 1976; professional: faculty member, University of Puerto Rico, 1976–81; adjunct professor, Hunter College of the City University of New York, 1981–83; special assistant to Congressman Ed Towns, 1983; member, City Council of New York, 1984–86; national director of Migration Division Office, Department of Labor and Human Resources of Puerto Rico, 1986–89; director, Department of Puerto Rican Community Affairs in the United States, 1989–92; committees: Financial Services; Natural Resources; Small Business; elected on November 3, 1992, to the 103rd Congress; reelected to each succeeding Congress.

Office Listings

http://www.velazquez.house.gov https://www.facebook.com/RepNydiaVelazquez
https://twitter.com/NydiaVelazquez

2302 Rayburn House Office Building, Washington, DC 20515 .... (202) 225–2361
Chief of Staff.—Adam Minehardt. FAX: 226–0327
Communications Director.—Alex Haurek.
Scheduler.—Tera Proby.
Legislative Director.—Justin Pelletier.
266 Broadway, Suite 201, Brooklyn, NY 11211 .... (718) 599–3658
16 Court Street, Suite 1006, Brooklyn, NY 11241 .... (718) 222–5819
500 Pearl Street, Suite 973, New York, NY 10007 .... (212) 619–2606

Counties: KINGS (part), NEW YORK (part), AND QUEENS (part). Population (2010), 717,708.

ZIP Codes: 10002, 10004, 10007, 10009, 10012–13, 10038, 11201, 11205–08, 11211, 11215, 11217–21, 11231–32, 11237, 11378–79, 11385, 11416–18, 11421

* * *

EIGHTH DISTRICT

HAKEEM S. JEFFRIES, Democrat, of New York, NY; born in Brooklyn, NY, August 4, 1970; education: graduated from Midwood High School, 1988; B.A., State University of New York at Binghamton, 1992; M.P.P., Georgetown University, 1994; J.D., New York University Law School, 1997; professional: member, New York State Assembly, 2007–13; religion: Baptist; married; two children; committees: Budget; Judiciary; elected to the 113th Congress on November 6, 2012; reelected to each succeeding Congress.

Office Listings

http://www.jeffries.house.gov facebook.com/rephakeemjeffries twitter: @repjeffries

1607 Longworth House Office Building, Washington, DC 20515 .... (202) 225–5936
Chief of Staff.—Cedric Grant. FAX: 225–1018
Scheduler.—Lauren Milnes.
Legislative Director.—Chris Randle.
Communications Director.—Michael Hardaway.
District Director.—Tasia Jackson.
55 Hanson Place, Suite 603, Brooklyn, NY 11217 .... (718) 237–2211

Office Listings—Continued

445 Neptune Avenue, 1st Floor, Brooklyn, NY 11224 .... (718) 373–0033

Counties: KINGS (part) AND QUEENS (part). Population (2010), 713,512.

ZIP Codes: 11201, 11205–08, 11210, 11212–13, 11216–17, 11221, 11224, 11229, 11233–36, 11238–39, 11243, 11245, 11247, 11256, 11414, 11416–17

* * *

NINTH DISTRICT

YVETTE D. CLARKE, Democrat, of Brooklyn, NY; born in Brooklyn, November 21, 1964; education: attended Edward R. Murrow High School; graduated from Oberlin College; professional: legislative aide to New York State Senator Velmanette Montgomery; executive assistant to New York Assemblywoman Barbara Clark; staff assistant, New York State Workers' Compensation Board Chair Barbara Patton; Director of Youth Programs, Hospital League / Local 1199 Training and Upgrading Fund; Director of Business Development for the Bronx Empowerment Zone (BOEDC); member of City Council of New York, 2001–06; committees: Energy and Commerce; Select Committee on Ethics; Small Business; elected to the 110th Congress on November 7, 2006; reelected to each succeeding Congress.

Office Listings

http://www.clarke.house.gov twitter: @repyvetteclarke
https://www.facebook.com/repyvettedclarke

2058 Rayburn House Office Building, Washington, DC 20515 .... (202) 225–6231
Chief of Staff.—LaDavia S. Drane. FAX: 226–0112
Legislative Director.—Asi Ofosu.
222 Lenox Road, Suite 1&2, Brooklyn, NY 11226 .... (718) 287–1142

Counties: KINGS (part). Population (2010), 717,708.

ZIP Codes: 11203, 11210, 11212–13, 11216–18, 11225–26, 11229–30, 11233–36, 11238

* * *

TENTH DISTRICT

JERROLD NADLER, Democrat, of New York, NY; born in Brooklyn, NY, June 13, 1947; education: graduated from Stuyvesant High School, 1965; B.A., Columbia University, 1970; J.D., Fordham University, 1978; professional: New York State Assembly, 1977–92; member: ACLU; NARAL Pro-Choice America; AIPAC; National Organization for Women; married: 1976; one child; Assistant Whip; committees: Judiciary; elected to the 102nd Congress on November 3, 1992, to fill the vacancy caused by the death of U.S. Representative Ted Weiss; at the same time elected to the 103rd Congress; reelected to each succeeding Congress.

Office Listings

http://www.nadler.house.gov

2109 Rayburn House Office Building, Washington, DC 20515 .... (202) 225–5635
Director.—John Doty. FAX: 225–6923
201 Varick Street, Suite 669, New York, NY 10014 .... (212) 367–7350
Chief of Staff.—Amy Rutkin.
6605 Fort Hamilton Parkway, NY 11229 .... (718) 373–3198

Counties: KINGS (part) AND NEW YORK (part). Population (2010), 716,172.

ZIP Codes: 10001, 10003 (part), 10004–06, 10007 (part), 10008, 10011–13 (part), 10014, 10018–19 (part), 10021–22 (part), 10023, 10024–25 (part), 10027–28 (part), 10032 (part), 10036 (part), 10038 (part), 10041, 10043, 10045, 10065 (part), 10069, 10080–81, 10087 (part), 10101, 10107 (part), 10108, 10115, 10116 (part), 10119 (part), 10121–22, 10123 (part), 10128 (part), 10129, 10185 (part), 10199, 10249, 10256, 10268–69, 10271–72, 10274–75, 10277, 10278 (part), 10279–82, 10285–86, 10204, 11214–15 (part), 11218–20 (part), 11223 (part), 11228 (part), 11230–32 (part)

* * *

ELEVENTH DISTRICT

DANIEL M. DONOVAN, Jr., Republican, of Staten Island, NY; born in Staten Island, November 6, 1956; education: B.S., St. John's University, Staten Island, NY; J.D., Fordham University School of Law, 1988; professional: Assistant District Attorney, Manhattan DA; Chief of Staff and Deputy Borough President, Office of the Staten Island Borough President; District Attorney, Richmond County, NY; religion: Roman Catholic; committees: Foreign Affairs; Homeland Security; elected to the 114th Congress on May 5, 2015, by special election, to fill the vacancy caused by the resignation of U.S. Representative Michael G. Grimm; reelected to the 115th Congress on November 8, 2016.

Office Listings

http://www.donovan.house.gov

1541 Longworth House Office Building, Washington, DC 20515 .... (202) 225–3371
FAX: 226–1272
Chief of Staff.—Ronald Carara.
Deputy Chief of Staff.—Blaire Bartlett.
Staff Assistant.—Joseph Kalmin.
265 New Dorp Lane, 2nd Floor, Staten Island, NY 10306 .... (718) 351–1062
Staten Island District Director.—Patrick Ryan.
7308 13th Avenue, Brooklyn, NY 11228 .... (718) 630–5277
Brooklyn District Director.—Fran Vella-Marrone.

Counties: Kings (part), Richmond. Population (2010), 717,707.

ZIP Codes: 10301–10, 10312–14, 11204, 11209, 11214, 11219–20, 11223, 11228, 11252

* * *

TWELFTH DISTRICT

CAROLYN B. MALONEY, Democrat, of New York City, NY; born in Greensboro, NC, February 19, 1946; education: B.A., Greensboro College, Greensboro, NC, 1968; professional: various positions, New York City Board of Education, 1970–77; legislative aide, New York State Assembly, senior program analyst, 1977–79; executive director of advisory council, 1979–82; director of special projects, New York State Senate Office of the Minority Leader; New York City Council member, 1982–93; chairperson, New York City Council Committee on Contracts; member: Council Committee on Aging, National Organization of Women, Common Cause, Sierra Club, Americans for Democratic Action, New York City Council Committee on Housing and Buildings, Citizens Union, Grand Central Business Improvement District, Harlem Urban Development Corporation (1982–91), Commission on Early Childhood Development Programs, Council of Senior Citizen Centers of New York City (1982–87); widowed (Clifton H.W. Maloney); children: Virginia Marshall Maloney and Christina Paul Maloney; committees: Financial Services; Oversight and Government Reform; Joint Economic Committee; elected on November 3, 1992, to the 103rd Congress; reelected to each succeeding Congress.

Office Listings

http://www.maloney.house.gov twitter: @repmaloney

2308 Rayburn House Office Building, Washington, DC 20515 .... (202) 225–7944
FAX: 225–4709
Chief of Staff.—Michael Iger.
Legislative Director.—Elizabeth Darnall.
Executive Assistant.—Rebecca Tulloch.
1651 Third Avenue, Suite 311, New York, NY 10128 .... (212) 860–0606
31–19 Newtown Avenue, Astoria, NY 11102 .... (718) 932–1804
619 Lorimer Street, Brooklyn, NY 11211 .... (718) 349–5972

Counties: Kings (part), New York (part), Queens (part). Cities and Neighborhoods: Astoria, Brooklyn, Greenpoint, Long Island City, Manhattan, Queens, Roosevelt Island, and Williamsburg. Population (2010), 712,053.

ZIP Codes: 10001–03, 10009, 10010–12, 10016–19, 10020–22, 10028–29, 10035–36, 10044, 10055, 10065, 10075, 10087, 10103–07, 10110–13, 10118–19, 10120–21, 10123–24, 10128, 10130–31, 10150–56, 10158–59, 10162–69, 10170–79, 10199, 10259, 10261, 10276, 11101–13, 11106, 11109, 11206, 11211, 11222, 11249, 11377–78

* * *

THIRTEENTH DISTRICT

ADRIANO ESPAILLAT, Democrat, of Manhattan, New York City, NY; born in Santiago, Dominican Republic, September 27, 1954; education: B.A., Queens College, 1979; professional: Manhattan Court Services coordinator for the NYC Criminal Justice Agency, 1980; director of the Washington Heights Victims Services Community Office, 1992; New York State Assembly, 1996; chair, New York State Black, Puerto Rican, Hispanic and Asian Legislative Caucus, 2002; New York State Assembly committees: Environmental Conservation; Economic Development; Codes; Insurance; Judiciary; New York State Senate, 2010; ranking member of the New York State Senate Housing, Construction, and Community Development Committee; chair of the Senate Puerto Rican / Latino Caucus; religion: Catholic; children: Adriano Espaillat, Jr., and Natalia Espaillat; caucuses: Congressional Hispanic Caucus (CHC); committees: Education and the Workforce; Foreign Affairs; Small Business; elected to the 115th Congress on November 8, 2016.

Office Listings

http://www.espaillat.house.gov http://www.facebook.com/RepEspaillat
http://www.twitter.com/RepEspaillat

1630 Longworth House Office Building, Washington, DC 20515 .... (202) 225–4365
Chief of Staff.—Aneiry Batista.
Harlem Office: 163 West 125th Street, Room 507, New York, NY 10027 .... (212) 663–3900
Deputy District Director.—David Baily.
Bronx Office: 2530 Grand Concourse, Ground Floor, Bronx, NY 10458 .... (718) 450–8241
Inwood Office: 5030 Broadway, Room 702, New York, NY 10034.

Counties: BRONX (part) AND NEW YORK (part). Population (2012), 738,943.

ZIP Codes: 10025 (part), 10026–27, 10029–35, 10037, 10039–40, 10453, 10458, 10463, 10467–68

* * *

FOURTEENTH DISTRICT

JOSEPH CROWLEY, Democrat, of Elmhurst, Queens, NY; born in Woodside, NY, March 16, 1962; education: graduated, Power Memorial High School, 1981; B.A., political science and communications, Queens College (City University of New York), Flushing, NY, 1985; professional: elected to the New York State Assembly, 1986–98; religion: Roman Catholic; married: Kasey Nilson; three children; caucuses: chair, House Democratic Caucus; previously vice chair, House Democratic Caucus; founder and co-chair, Bangladesh Caucus; three-time co-chair, Congressional Caucus on India and Indian Americans; co-chair, Ad Hoc Committee on Irish Affairs; committees: Ways and Means; elected to the 106th Congress; reelected to each succeeding Congress.

Office Listings

http://crowley.house.gov twitter: @repjoecrowley www.facebook.com/repjoecrowley

1035 Longworth House Office Building, Washington, DC 20515 .... (202) 225–3965
Chief of Staff.—Kate ''Winkler'' Keating.
Deputy Chief of Staff.—Jeremy Woodrum.
82–11 37th Avenue, Suite 402, Jackson Heights, NY 11372 .... (718) 779–1400
2800 Bruckner Boulevard, Suite 201, Bronx, NY 10465 .... (718) 931–1400

Counties: BRONX (part) AND QUEENS (part). Population (2010), 717,708.

ZIP Codes: 10458, 10460–62, 10464–67, 10469, 10475, 11101–05, 11354, 11356–57, 11368–73, 11375, 11377–78

* * *

FIFTEENTH DISTRICT

JOSÉ E. SERRANO, Democrat, of Bronx, NY; born in Mayagüez, PR, October 24, 1943; education: Dodge Vocational High School, Bronx, NY; attended Lehman College, City University of New York, NY; professional: served with the U.S. Army Medical Corps, 1964–66; employed by the Manufacturers Hanover Bank, 1961–69; Community School District 7, 1969–74; New York State Assemblyman, 1974–90; chairman, Consumer Affairs Committee, 1979–83; chairman, Education Committee, 1983–90; religion: Roman Catholic; five children: Lisa, José Marco, Justine, Jonathan, and Benjamin; committees: Appropriations; elected to the 101st Congress, by special election, March 28, 1990, to fill the vacancy caused by the resignation of U.S. Representative Robert Garcia; reelected to each succeeding Congress.

Office Listings

http://serrano.house.gov http://www.facebook.com/repjoseserrano
https://instagram.com/repjoseserrano http://www.youtube.com/user/congressmanserrano
http://twitter.com/repjoseserrano

2227 Rayburn House Office Building, Washington, DC 20515 .... (202) 225–4361
FAX: 225–6001
Chief Administrator.—Idalia Domínguez de Marty.
Chief of Staff.—Matthew Alpert.
Scheduler.—Frederick Vélez.
Communications Director.—Paola Amador.
Legislative Counsel.—Angel Nigaglioni.
Legislative Assistant.—Lukogho Kasomo.
1231 Lafayette Street, 4th Floor, Bronx, NY 10474 .... (718) 620–0084
District Director.—Anthony Jordan.

Counties: BRONX COUNTY (part). CITIES AND TOWNSHIPS: Bronx. Population (2013), 747,271.

ZIP Codes: 10451–60, 10462, 10468, 10472–74

* * *

SIXTEENTH DISTRICT

ELIOT L. ENGEL, Democrat, of Bronx, NY; born in Bronx, February 18, 1947; education: B.A., Hunter-Lehman College, 1969; M.A., City University of New York, 1973; J.D., New York Law School, 1987; professional: teacher and counselor in the New York City public school system, 1969–77; elected to the New York Legislature, 1977–88; chaired the Assembly Committee on Alcoholism and Substance Abuse and Subcommittee on Mitchell-Lama Housing (12 years prior to his election to Congress); married: Patricia Ennis, 1980; three children; caucuses: co-chairman, Albanian Issues Caucus; co-chair, Task Force on Anti-Semitism; board member, Congressional Ad Hoc Committee on Irish Affairs; Allergy and Asthma Caucus; Animal Protection Caucus; Arts Caucus; Congressional Human Rights Caucus; Diabetes Caucus; EU Caucus; Fragile X Caucus; HIV / AIDS Caucus; Long Island Sound Caucus; New Democrat Coalition; Oil and National Security Caucus; Pro-Choice Caucus; Renewable and Energy Efficiency Caucus; Tuberculosis Elimination Caucus; committees: ranking member, Energy and Commerce; Foreign Affairs; elected on November 8, 1988 to the 101st Congress; reelected to each succeeding Congress.

Office Listings

http://www.engel.house.gov

2462 Rayburn House Office Building, Washington, DC 20515 .... (202) 225–2464
FAX: 225–5513
Administrative Assistant.—E.H. "Ned" Michalek.
Office Manager.—Darlene Murray.
Legislative Director.—Brian Skretny.
3655 Johnson Avenue, Bronx, NY 10463 .... (718) 796–9700
FAX: 796–5134
Chief of Staff.—William F. Weitz.
6 Gramatan Avenue, Suite 205, Mt. Vernon, NY 10550 .... (914) 699–4100
FAX: 699–3646
177 Dreiser Loop, Room 3, Bronx, NY 10475 .... (718) 320–2314
FAX: 320–2047

Counties: BRONX (part) AND WESTCHESTER (part). CITIES AND TOWNSHIPS: Parts of Bronx, Eastchester, Greenburgh, Mamaroneck, Mount Vernon, New Rochelle, Pelham, Rye, Scarsdale, and Yonkers. Population (2010), 717,707.

ZIP Codes: 10463, 10466–67, 10469–71, 10475, 10502, 10528, 10530, 10538, 10543, 10550–53, 10557–58, 10580, 10583, 10701–05, 10707–10, 10801–02, 10804–05

* * *

SEVENTEENTH DISTRICT

NITA M. LOWEY, Democrat, of Harrison, NY; born in New York, NY, July 5, 1937; education: graduated, Bronx High School of Science, 1955; B.A., Mount Holyoke College, 1959; professional: assistant to the Secretary of State for Economic Development and Neighborhood Preservation, and deputy director, Division of Economic Opportunity, 1975–85; Assistant Secretary of State, 1985–87; member: boards of directors, Close-Up Foundation; Effective Parenting Information for Children; Windward School, Downstate (New York Region); Westchester Jewish Conference; Westchester Opportunity Program; National Committee of the Police Corps; Women's Network of the YWCA; Legal Awareness for Women; National Women's Political Caucus of Westchester; American Jewish Committee of Westchester; married: Stephen Lowey, 1961; children: Dana, Jacqueline, and Douglas; committees: Appropriations; elected on November 8, 1988 to the 101st Congress; reelected to each succeeding Congress.

Office Listings

http://www.lowey.house.gov twitter.com/nitalowey www.facebook.com/replowey

2365 Rayburn House Office Building, Washington, DC 20515 .... (202) 225–6506
Chief of Staff.—Elizabeth Stanley. FAX: 225–0546
Executive Assistant.—Kelly Healton.
Legislative Director.—Dana Acton.
Press Secretary.—Roy Loewenstein.
222 Mamaroneck Avenue, Suite 312, White Plains, NY 10605 .... (914) 428–1707
67 North Main Street, Suite 101, New City, NY 10956 .... (845) 639–3485
District Director.—Patricia Keegan.

Counties: ROCKLAND (all), WESTCHESTER (part). CITIES AND TOWNSHIPS: Briarcliff Manor; Buchanan; Chappaqua, Cortlandt, Cortlandt Manor, Crompond, Croton-on-Hudson, Dobbs Ferry, Elmsford, East Irvington, Fairview, Harrison, Hartsdale, Haverstraw, Hawthorne, Irvington, Jefferson Valley, Millwood, Mohegan Lake, Mount Kisco, Mount Pleasant, New City, North White Plains, Ossining, Peekskill, Pleasantville, Pocantico Hills, Port Chester, Purchase, Rye Brook, Scarborough, Sleepy Hollow, Tarrytown, Thornwood, Valhalla, Verplanck, West Harrison, West Haverstraw, White Plains, and Yorktown Heights. Population (2010), 717,708.

ZIP Codes: 10510–11, 10514, 10517, 10520, 10522–23, 10528, 10530, 10532–33, 10535, 10546–49, 10562, 10566–67, 10570, 10573, 10577, 10580, 10588, 10591, 10594–96, 10598, 10601, 10603–07, 10901, 10913, 10920, 10923, 10927, 10931, 10952, 10954, 10956, 10960, 10964–65, 10968, 10970, 10974, 10976–77, 10980, 10982–84, 10986, 10989, 10993–94

* * *

EIGHTEENTH DISTRICT

SEAN PATRICK MALONEY, Democrat, of Cold Spring, NY; born in Sherbrooke, Quebec, July 30, 1966; education: graduated, Hanover High School, Hanover, NH, 1984; B.A., University of Virginia, 1988; J.D., University of Virginia, 1992; professional: White House Deputy Staff Secretary, 1997–99; White House Staff Secretary and Assistant to the President of the United States, 1999–2000; chief operating officer, Kiodex, Inc., 2000–03; First Deputy Secretary to the Governor of New York, 2007–08; corporate partner, Kirkland & Ellis LLP, 2009–11; partner, Orrick, Herrington & Sutcliffe LLP; husband: Randy Florke, 1992–present; children: Jesus, Daley, and Essie; committees: Agriculture; Transportation and Infrastructure; elected to the 113th Congress on November 6, 2012; reelected to each succeeding Congress.

Office Listings

http://seanmaloney.house.gov https://facebook.com/repseanmaloney https://twitter.com/repseanmaloney

1027 Longworth House Office Building, Washington, DC 20515 .... (202) 225–5441
Chief of Staff.—Timothy Persico. FAX: 225–3289
Deputy Chief of Staff.—Ryan Lehman.
Communications Director/Deputy Chief of Staff.—Caitlin Girouard.
Legislative Director.—Tom Mintz.
Director of Scheduling.—Kevin Golden.
123 Grand Street, 2nd Floor, Newburgh, NY 12550 .... (845) 561–1259
District Director.—Joseph Donat. FAX: 561–2890

Counties: NORTHERN WESTCHESTER (part), ORANGE, PUTNAM, AND SOUTHERN DUTCHESS (part). CITIES AND TOWNSHIPS: Arlington, Balmville, Beacon, Beaver Dam Lake, Bedford, Bedford Hills, Brewster Hill, Brewster, Brinckerhoff, Carmel Hamlet, Chester, Cold Spring, Cornwall-on-Hudson, Crown Heights, Fairview, Firthcliffe, Fishkill, Florida, Fort Montgomery, Gardnertown, Golden's Bridge, Goshen, Greenwood Lake, Harriman, Heritage Hills, Highland Falls, Hillside

Lake, Hopewell Junction, Katonah, Kiryas Joel, Lake Carmel, Lincolndale, Mahopac, Maybrook, Mechanicstown, Merritt Park, Middletown, Monroe, Montgomery, Mountain Lodge Park, Myers Corner, Nelsonville, New Windsor, Newburgh, Orange Lake, Otisville, Peach Lake, Pine Bush, Port Jervis, Poughkeepsie, Putnam Lake, Red Oaks Mill, Salisbury Mills, Scotchtown, Scotts Corners, Shenorock, South Blooming Grove, Spackenkill, Titusville, Tuxedo Park, Vails Gate, Walden, Walton Park, Wappingers Falls, Warwick, Washington Heights, Washingtonville, West Point, and Woodbury. Population (2010), 717,707.

ZIP Codes: 10501, 10504–07, 10509, 10512, 10516, 10518–19, 10524, 10526–27, 10536–37, 10540–42, 10549, 10560, 10562, 10576, 10578–79, 10587, 10589–90, 10597–98, 10910, 10912, 10914–19, 10921–22, 10924–26, 10928, 10930, 10932–33, 10940–41, 10949–50, 10953, 10958–59, 10963, 10969, 10973–75, 10979, 10981, 10985, 10987–88, 12508, 12511–12, 12518, 12520, 12524, 12527, 12531, 12533, 12537–38, 12540, 12542–43, 12549–53, 12555, 12563–64, 12566, 12569, 12575, 12577, 12582, 12584, 12586, 12589–90, 12601–04, 12721, 12729, 12746, 12771, 12780, 12785

* * *

NINETEENTH DISTRICT

JOHN J. FASO, Republican, of Kinderhook, NY; born in Massapequa, Nassau County, NY, August 25, 1952; education: graduated from Archbishop Molloy High School, New York City, NY, 1970; B.S., State University of New York, Brockport, NY, 1974; J.D., Georgetown University, Washington, DC, 1979; professional: staff, U.S. House of Representatives Committee on Government Operations, 1979–81; commissioner, New York State Legislative Bill Drafting Commission, 1983–86; member of the New York State Assembly, 1986–2002; candidate for New York State Comptroller in 2002; member of the Buffalo Fiscal Stability Authority, NY, 2003–06; candidate for Governor of New York in 2006; lawyer, private practice; committees: Agriculture; Budget; Transportation and Infrastructure; elected to the 115th Congress on November 8, 2016.

Office Listings

http://www.faso.house.gov

1616 Longworth House Office Building, Washington, DC 20515 .... (202) 225–5614
Chief of Staff.—Dain Pascocello.
Deputy Chief of Staff.—Vacant.
District Director.—Ryan McAllister.
Legislative Director.—Patrick Rooney.
Scheduler / Executive Assistant.—Hope Costa.
2 Hudson Street, Kinderhook, NY 12106 .... (518) 610–8133
111 Main Street, Delhi, NY 13753 .... (607) 746–9537
721 Broadway, Kingston, NY 12401 .... (845) 514–2322

Counties: Columbia, Delaware, Greene, Otsego, Schoharie, Sullivan, Ulster, and parts of Broome, Dutchess, Montgomery, and Rensselaer counties.

ZIP Codes: 2015, 12017, 12022–24, 12029, 12031, 12033, 12035–37, 12042–43, 12050–53, 12057–58, 12060–63, 12110, 12115–16, 12118, 12121, 12153–57, 12160, 12165–68, 12172–76, 12180–82, 12184–85, 12187, 12189, 12192, 12194–98, 12401, 12404–05, 12407, 12409–21, 12435–36, 12438, 12451–61, 12463–75, 12481–82, 12485–87, 12489–96, 12498, 12501–04, 12506–07, 12561, 12563–65, 12592, 12594, 12601, 12603, 12701, 12719–27, 12732–34, 12736–38, 12740–45, 12747, 12749–52, 12754, 12758–60, 12762–64, 12766–67, 12776–79, 12781, 12783–92, 12816, 13315, 13317, 13459, 13468, 13475, 13482, 13485, 13755–57, 13774, 13786, 13788, 13796, 13804, 13806–10

* * *

TWENTIETH DISTRICT

PAUL D. TONKO, Democrat, of Amsterdam, NY; born in Amsterdam, June 18, 1949; education: graduated, Amsterdam High School, Amsterdam, NY, 1967; B.S. degree, mechanical and industrial engineering, Clarkson University, Potsdam, NY, 1971; professional: engineer, NYS Department of Transportation; engineer, NYS Department of Public Service; Montgomery County Board of Supervisors, 1976–83; chairman, Montgomery County Board of Supervisors, 1981–83; NYS Assembly, 1983–2007; chairman, NYS Assembly Standing Committee on Energy, 1992–2007; president and CEO, NYS Energy Research and Development Authority, 2007–08; caucuses: co-chair, Sustainable Energy and Environment Coalition; co-chair, Congressional Horse Caucus; committees: Energy and Commerce; Science, Space, and Technology; elected to the 111th Congress on November 4, 2008; reelected to each succeeding Congress.

Office Listings

http://www.tonko.house.gov https://www.facebook.com/reppaultonko
twitter: @reppaultonko

2463 Rayburn House Office Building, Washington, DC 20515 .... (202) 225–5076

Office Listings—Continued

Chief of Staff.—Clinton Britt. FAX: 225–5077
Communications Director.—Matt Sonneborn.
Legislative Director.—Jeff Morgan.
Director of Operations.—David Mastrangelo.
Legislative Assistants: Emily Duhovny, Brendan Larkin.
Legislative Correspondent.—Noor Teebi.
19 Dove Street, Suite 302, Albany, NY 12210 .... (518) 465–0700
105 Jay Street (Schenectady City Hall), Room 15, Schenectady, NY 12305 .... (518) 374–4547
61 Church Street (Amsterdam City Hall), Room 309, Amsterdam, NY 12010 .... (518) 843–3400

Counties: ALBANY, MONTGOMERY (part), RENSSELAER (part), SARATOGA (part), and SCHENECTADY. Population (2010), 720,133.

ZIP Codes: 12007–10, 12016, 12019–20, 12023, 12027, 12033, 12041, 12045–47, 12053–56, 12059, 12061, 12065–70, 12072, 12074, 12077, 12083–87, 12095, 12107, 12110, 12118, 12120, 12122–23, 12128, 12137, 12141, 12143–44, 12147–48, 12150–51, 12157–61, 12166, 12170, 12177, 12180–83, 12186, 12188–89, 12193, 12196, 12198, 12201–12, 12220, 12222–24, 12226–50, 12252, 12255–57, 12260–61, 12288, 12301–09, 12325, 12345, 12460, 12469, 12866

* * *

TWENTY-FIRST DISTRICT

ELISE M. STEFANIK, Republican, of Willsboro, NY; born in Albany, NY, July 2, 1984; education: graduated from Albany Academy for Girls, Albany, 2002; B.A., Harvard University, Cambridge, MA, 2006; professional: staff, President George W. Bush administration, 2006–09; campaign aide; businesswoman; committees: Armed Services; Education and the Workforce; Permanent Select Committee on Intelligence; elected to the 114th Congress on November 4, 2014; reelected to the 115th Congress on November 8, 2016.

Office Listings

https://stefanik.house.gov

318 Cannon House Office Building, Washington, DC 20515 .... (202) 225–4611
Chief of Staff.—Lindley Kratovil.
Communications Director.—Tom Flanagin.
Legislative Director.—Courtney Carrow.
136 Glen Street, Glens Falls, NY 12801 .... (518) 743–0964
District Director.—Anthony Pileggi.
23 Durkee Street, Suite C, Plattsburgh, NY 12901 .... (518) 561–2324
88 Public Square, Suite A, Watertown, NY 13601 .... (315) 782–3150

Counties: CLINTON, ESSEX, FRANKLIN, FULTON, HAMILTON, HERKIMER, JEFFERSON, LEWIS, SARATOGA, ST. LAWRENCE, WARREN, AND WASHINGTON. Population (2015), 716,340.

Zip Codes: 12010 (part), 12020 (part), 12025, 12028 (part), 12032, 12057 (part), 12068 (part), 12070 (part), 12074 (part), 12078, 12086 (part), 12094–95 (part), 12108, 12117, 12118 (part), 12134, 12139, 12154 (part), 12164, 12170 (part), 12185 (part), 12190, 12801, 12803–04, 12808–12, 12814–17, 12819, 12821–24, 12827–28, 12831–32, 12833 (part), 12834–39, 12841–47, 12849–53, 12855–65, 12866 (part), 12870–74, 12878, 12883–87, 12901, 12903, 12910–14, 12916–24, 12926–30, 12932–37, 12939, 12941–46, 12950, 12952–53, 12955–62, 12964–67, 12969–70, 12972–81, 12983, 12985–87, 12989, 12992–93, 12996–98, 13305, 13312, 13316 (part), 13324 (part), 13325, 13327, 13329, 13331, 13338–39 (part), 13343, 13345, 13353, 13360, 13367–68, 13404, 13420, 13431 (part), 13433, 13436–38, 13452 (part), 13454, 13470–73, 13489 (part), 13601–03, 13605–08, 13612–26, 13628, 13630, 13633–43, 13646–48, 13650–52, 13654–56, 13658–62, 13664–70, 13672–82, 13684–85, 13687, 13690–97

* * *

TWENTY-SECOND DISTRICT

CLAUDIA TENNEY, Republican, of New Hartford, NY; born in New Hartford, February 4, 1961; education: B.A, Colgate University, Hamilton, NY, 1983; J.D., Taft College of Law, University of Cincinnati, 1987; professional: lawyer and business owner; family: one son, serving in the U.S. Marine Corps; committees: Financial Services; elected to the 115th Congress on November 8, 2016.

Office Listings

http://www.tenney.house.gov

512 Cannon House Office Building, Washington, DC 20515 .... (202) 225–3665

Office Listings—Continued

Chief of Staff.—Nick Stewart. FAX: 225–1891
Communications Director / Deputy Chief.—Hannah Andrews.
Legislative Director.—Ryan Rusbuldt.
Scheduler / Legislative Aide.—Joan Stanton.
555 French Road, Suite 101, New Hartford, NY 13413 .... (315) 732–0713
49 Court Street, Metro Center, Suite 210, Binghamton, NY 13901 .... (607) 376–6002

Counties: BROOME (part), CHENANGO, CORTLAND, HERKIMER, MADISON, ONEIDA, OSWEGO (part), TIOGA (part), AND TOMPKINS (part). CITIES, TOWNS, AND VILLAGES: Binghamton, Camden, Cortland, Cortlandville, Forestport, Little Falls, Mexico, New Berlin, Norwich, Oneida, Sandy Creek, Sherrill, Sullivan, Utica, Vestal, and Windsor. Population (2010), 717,708.

ZIP Codes: 13028, 13030, 13032, 13035–37, 13040, 13042, 13044–45, 13052–54, 13061, 13072, 13076–77, 13082–83, 13087, 13101, 13103–04, 13114, 13122–24, 13126, 13131–32, 13134, 13136, 13141–42, 13144–45, 13155, 13157–59, 13162–63, 13167, 13301–04, 13308–10, 13313–14, 13316, 13318–19, 13321–24, 13328, 13332, 13334, 13338–41, 13346, 13350, 13352, 13354–55, 13357, 13361–65, 13402–03, 13406–09, 13411, 13413, 13416–18, 13421, 13424–25, 13431, 13435, 13437–41, 13456, 13460–61, 13464, 13469, 13471, 13475–78, 13480, 13483–86, 13489–95, 13501–02, 13661, 13730, 13732–33, 13736, 13744, 13746, 13748, 13760, 13777–78, 13780, 13784, 13787, 13790, 13794–95, 13797, 13801–03, 13809, 13811–13, 13815, 13826–27, 13830, 13832–33, 13835, 13841, 13843–44, 13850, 13862–63, 13865, 13901–05

* * *

TWENTY-THIRD DISTRICT

TOM REED, Republican, of Corning, NY; born in Joliet, IL, November 18, 1971; education: graduated, B.A., Alfred University, Alfred, NY, 1993; J.D., Ohio Northern University College of Law, Ada, OH, 1996; professional: lawyer, private practice, Law Office of Thomas W. Reed II; business owner; Mayor of Corning, NY, 2008–09; religion: Catholic; family: wife, Jean, and two children; committees: Ways and Means; elected to the 111th Congress, by special election, on November 2, 2010, to fill the vacancy caused by the resignation of U.S. Representative Eric J.J. Massa; subsequently elected to a full term in the 112th Congress on November 2, 2010; reelected to each succeeding Congress.

Office Listings

http://www.reed.house.gov https://www.facebook.com/RepTomReed
https://twitter.com/RepTomReed https://www.instagram.com/rep.tomreed

2437 Rayburn House Office Building, Washington, DC 20515 .... (202) 225–3161
Chief of Staff.—Tim Kolpien. FAX: 226–6599
Legislative Director.—Drew Wayne.
Communications Director.—Samantha Cotten.
District Director.—Alison Hunt.
89 West Market Street, Corning, NY 14830 .... (607) 654–7566
433 Exchange Street, Geneva, NY 14456 .... (315) 759–5229
401 East State Street, Suite 304–1, Ithaca, NY 14850 .... (607) 222–2027
2 East 2nd Street, Suite 208, Jamestown, NY 14701 .... (716) 708–6369
One Bluebird Square, Olean, NY 14760 .... (716) 379–8434

Counties: ALLEGANY, CATTARAUGUS, CHAUTAUQUA, CHEMUNG, ONTARIO (part), SCHUYLER, SENECA, STEUBEN, TIOGA (part), TOMPKINS, AND YATES. Population (2010), 717,707.

ZIP Codes: 13053, 13062, 13068, 13073, 13102, 13734, 13736, 13743, 13811–12, 13827, 13835, 13840, 13845, 13864, 14029, 14041–42, 14048, 14060, 14062–63, 14065, 14070, 14081, 14101, 14129, 14133, 14135–36, 14168, 14171, 14173, 14415, 14418, 14424, 14432, 14441, 14453, 14456, 14461, 14463, 14478, 14504, 14507, 14512, 14518, 14527, 14529, 14532, 14537, 14544, 14547–48, 14561, 14572, 14701–02, 14706–24, 14726–45, 14747–48, 14750–58, 14760, 14766–67, 14769–70, 14772, 14774–75, 14777–79, 14781–88, 14801–10, 14812–27, 14830, 14837–43, 14845, 14850, 14854–59, 14861, 14863–65, 14867, 14869–74, 14876–87, 14889, 14891–95, 14897–98, 14901–05, 14925

* * *

TWENTY-FOURTH DISTRICT

JOHN KATKO, Republican, of Camillus, NY; education: graduated from Bishop Ludden High School; B.A., Niagara University, *cum laude*; J.D., Syracuse University College of Law, *cum laude*; professional: Federal Prosecutor (most recently as Assistant U.S. Attorney with the Northern District of New York) for over 20 years; married: wife of over 27 years, Robin; three sons; committees: Homeland Security; Transportation and Infrastructure; elected to the 114th Congress on November 4, 2014; reelected to the 115th Congress on November 8, 2016.

Office Listings

http://katko.house.gov

1620 Longworth House Office Building, Washington, DC 20515 .... (202) 225–3701
Chief of Staff.—Zach Howell.
Executive Assistant.—Emily Bazydlo.
440 South Warren Street, 7th Floor, Suite 711, Syracuse, NY 13202 .... (315) 423–5657
FAX: 423–5604
71 Genesee Street, Auburn, NY 13021 .... (315) 253–4068
FAX: 253–2435
7376 State Route 31, Lyons, NY 14489 (open Wednesdays, 10 a.m. until 4 p.m.).
13 West Oneida Street, 2nd Floor, Oswego, NY 13126 (open Wednesdays, 10 a.m. until 3 p.m.).

Counties: CAYUGA, ONONDAGA, OSWEGO (part), AND WAYNE. Population (2010), 717,707.

ZIP Codes: 13020–21, 13024, 13026–31, 13033–37, 13039, 13041, 13045, 13051–52, 13057, 13060, 13063–64, 13066, 13069, 113071, 13073–74, 13077–78, 13080–84, 13088, 13090, 13092, 13102, 13104, 13108, 13110–18, 13120, 13122, 13126, 13131–32, 13135, 13138, 13140–41, 13143, 13146–47, 13152–53, 13156, 13158–60, 13164, 13166, 13202–12, 13214–15, 13219, 13224, 13290, 14433, 14450, 14489, 14502, 14505, 14551, 14555, 14568, 14580, 14589, 14590

* * *

TWENTY-FIFTH DISTRICT

VACANT

Counties: MONROE (majority). CITIES AND TOWNSHIPS: Brighton, Brockport, Chili, Churchville, Clarkson, East Rochester, Fairport, Gates, Greece, Hamlin, Henrietta, Hilton, Irondequoit, Ogden, Parma, Penfield, Perinton, Pittsford, Riga, Rochester, Rush, Scottsville, Spencerport, Sweden, and Webster. Population (2013), 724,587.

ZIP Codes: 14416, 14420, 14428, 14445, 14450, 14464, 14467–68, 14502, 14514, 14519, 14526, 14534, 14543, 14546, 14559, 14564, 14580, 14586, 14604–10, 14612–13, 14615–18, 14620–26

* * *

TWENTY-SIXTH DISTRICT

BRIAN HIGGINS, Democrat, of Buffalo, NY; born in Buffalo, October 6, 1959; education: B.A., Buffalo State College, NY, 1984; M.P.A., Harvard University, Cambridge, MA, 1996; professional: lecturer, Buffalo State College; member of the Buffalo Common Council, 1988–93; member of the New York State Assembly, 1999–2004; married: Mary Jane Hannon; two children: John and Maeve; committees: Budget; Ways and Means; elected to the 109th Congress on November 2, 2004; reelected to each succeeding Congress.

Office Listings

http://www.higgins.house.gov twitter: @repbrianhiggins
www.facebook.com/repbrianhiggins

2459 Rayburn House Office Building, Washington, DC 20515 .... (202) 225–3306
FAX: 226–0347
Chief of Staff.—Chuck Eaton.
Chief of Staff/DC and Legislative Director.—Matthew Fery.
Communications Director.—Theresa Kennedy.
Larkin at Exchange, 726 Exchange Street, Suite 601, Buffalo, NY 14210 .... (716) 852–3501
800 Main Street, Suite 3C, Niagara Falls, NY 14301 .... (716) 282–1274

Counties: ERIE (part) AND NIAGARA (part). CITIES AND TOWNSHIPS: Amherst (part), Buffalo, Cheektowaga, Grand Island, Lackawanna, Niagara Falls (part), North Tonawanda, Tonawanda (city), Tonawanda (township), and West Seneca. Population (2010), 717,707.

ZIP Codes: 14043, 14051, 14068, 14072, 14120, 14150, 14201–28, 14261, 14301–05

* * *

TWENTY-SEVENTH DISTRICT

CHRIS COLLINS, Republican, of Clarence, NY; born in Schenectady, NY, May 20, 1950; education: graduated, Hendersonville High School, Hendersonville, NC, 1968; B.S.M.E., mechanical engineering, NC State University, Raleigh, NC, 1972; M.B.A., University of Alabama at Birmingham, Birmingham, AL, 1975; professional: businessman; elected as Erie County Executive, NY, 2007; married to Mary Collins; children: Caitlin and Cameron; caucuses: co-chairman, Congressional Scouting Caucus; co-chairman, Energy Storage Caucus; co-chairman, New York Defense Working Group; co-chairman, Specialty Crop Caucus; Air Force Caucus; Auto Industry Pension Task Force; Automotive Caucus; Canada-U.S. Caucus; Congressional Cigar Caucus; Congressional Internet of Things Caucus; Congressional Native American Caucus; Dairy Farmers Caucus; Diabetes Caucus; Fire Services Caucus; Friends of the Job Corps Caucus; General Aviation Caucus; Great Lakes Task Force; International Conservation Caucus; Internet Caucus; Job Creators Caucus; Law Enforcement Caucus; Manufacturing Caucus; Medicaid Task Force; Mitochondrial Disease Caucus; Morocco Caucus; National Guard and Reserve Components Caucus; Natural Gas Caucus; Northeast-Midwest (NEMW) Congressional Coalition; Northern Border Caucus; Pilot Caucus; Propane Caucus; Republican Israel Caucus; Republican Study Committee; Rural Telecommunications Working Group; Small Brewers Caucus; Small Business Caucus; Small Business Information Technology Caucus; Sportsmen's Caucus; STEM Education Caucus; Taiwan Caucus; Technology Transfer Caucus; Toy Caucus; Upstate New York Caucus; committees: Energy and Commerce; elected to the 113th Congress on November 6, 2012; reelected to each succeeding Congress.

Office Listings

http://www.chriscollins.house.gov

1117 Longworth House Office Building, Washington, DC 20515 .... (202) 225–5265
Chief of Staff.—Michael Hook.
Staff Assistant.—Elizabeth Murphy.
Legislative Director.—Erynn Hook.
Communications Director.—Sarah Minkel.
2813 Wehrle Drive, Suite 13, Williamsville, NY 14221 .... (716) 634–2324
District Director.—Michael Kracker.
75 Main Street, Suite C, Geneseo, NY 14454 .... (585) 519–4002

Counties: ERIE (part), GENESEE, LIVINGSTON, MONROE (part) NIAGARA (part), ONTARIO (part), ORLEANS, AND WYOMING. Population (2010), 717,707.

ZIP Codes: 14001, 14004–06, 14008–13, 14020–21, 14024–28, 14030–40, 14043, 14047, 14051–52, 14054–59, 14061, 14066–67, 14069–70, 14075, 14080–83, 14085–86, 14091–92, 14094–95, 14098, 14102–03, 14105, 14107–13, 14120, 14125–27, 14130–32, 14134, 14139–41, 14143–45, 14167, 14169–70, 14172, 14174, 14218–19, 14221, 14224, 14228, 14304–05, 14411, 14414, 14416, 14420, 14422–25, 14427–29, 14435, 14437, 14443, 14452–54, 14462, 14464, 14466–72, 14475–77, 14479–82, 14485–88, 14506, 14508, 14510–12, 14517, 14522, 14525, 14530, 14533–34, 14536, 14539, 14543, 14545–46, 14548–50, 14556–58, 14560, 14564, 14569, 14571–72, 14585–86, 14591–92, 14735, 14822, 14836, 14846, 14884

NORTH CAROLINA

(Population 2010, 9,535,483)

SENATORS

RICHARD BURR, Republican, of Winston-Salem, NC; born in Charlottesville, VA, November 30, 1955; education: R.J. Reynolds High School, Winston-Salem, NC, 1974; B.A., communications, Wake Forest University, Winston-Salem, NC, 1978; professional: sales manager, Carswell Distributing; member: Reynolds Rotary Club; board member, Brenner Children's Hospital; public service: U.S. House of Representatives, 1995–2005; served as vice-chairman of the Energy and Commerce Committee; married: Brooke Fauth, 1984; children: two sons; committees: chair, Select Committee on Intelligence; Finance; Health, Education, Labor, and Pensions; Special Committee on Aging; elected to the U.S. Senate on November 2, 2004; reelected to each succeeding Senate term.

Office Listings

http://burr.senate.gov

217 Russell Senate Office Building, Washington, DC 20510 .... (202) 224–3154
Office Manager.—Polly Walker. FAX: 228–2981
Chief of Staff.—Natasha Hickman.
Legislative Director.—Christopher Toppings..
Scheduler and Executive Assistant.—Molly Harper.
2000 West First Street, Suite 508, Winston-Salem, NC 27104 .... (336) 631–5125
State Director and Deputy Chief of Staff.—Dean Myers.
100 Coast Line Street, Room 210, Rocky Mount, NC 27804 .... (252) 977–9522
201 North Front Street, Suite 809, Wilmington, NC 28401 .... (910) 251–1058
151 Patton Avenue, Suite 204, Asheville, NC 28801 .... (828) 350–2437

* * *

THOM TILLIS, Republican, of Huntersville, NC; born in Jacksonville, FL, August 30, 1960; education: B.S., University of Maryland University College, 1997; professional: partner, IBM Global Business Services, 2002–09; partner, PricewaterhouseCoopers, 1990–2002; public service: North Carolina State House Speaker, 2011–15, North Carolina State House, 2009–15; religion: Catholic; married: Susan Tillis; children: one daughter, one son; committees: Armed Services; Banking, Housing, and Urban Affairs; Judiciary; Veterans' Affairs; Special Committee on Aging; elected to the U.S. Senate on November 4, 2014.

Office Listings

http://tillis.senate.gov facebook: senatorthomtillis
twitter: @senthomtillis

185 Dirksen Senate Office Building, Washington, DC 20510 .... (202) 224–6342
Chief of Staff.—Ted Lehman.
Communications Director.—Daniel Keylin.
State Director.—Kim Canady Barnes.
1694 East Arlington Boulevard, Suite B, Greenville, NC 27858 .... (252) 329–0371
310 New Bern Avenue, Suite 122, Raleigh, NC 27601 .... (919) 856–4630
9300 Harris Corners Parkway, Suite 170, Charlotte, NC 28269 .... (704) 509–9087
1840 Eastchester Drive, Suite 200, High Point, NC 27265 .... (336) 885–0685

REPRESENTATIVES

FIRST DISTRICT

G. K. BUTTERFIELD, Democrat, of Wilson County, NC; born, April 27, 1947; education: North Carolina Central University, graduated in 1971, with degrees in sociology and political science; North Carolina Central University School of Law, graduated in 1974, with a juris doctor degree; military service: U.S. Army, 1968–70; served as a Personnel Specialist; discharged with the rank of Specialist E–4; professional: attorney; private practice, 1974–88; public service: elected to the North Carolina Superior Court bench in November, 1988; appointed on February 8, 2001, by Governor Michael F. Easley to the North Carolina Supreme Court; after leaving the Supreme Court, following the 2002 election, Governor Easley appointed Justice Butterfield as a Special Superior Court Judge; served until his retirement on May 7, 2004; organizations: North Carolina Bar Association; North Carolina Association of Black Lawyers; Wilson Opportunities Industrialization Center; religion: Baptist; appointed Chief Deputy Whip, 110th Congress; chair, Congressional Black Caucus; committees: Energy and Commerce; elected to the 108th Congress, by special election, on July 20, 2004; elected to the 109th Congress on November 2, 2004; reelected to each succeeding Congress.

Office Listings

http://www.butterfield.house.gov facebook: https://www.facebook.com/congressmangkbutterfield
twitter: https://twitter.com/GKButterfield

2080 Rayburn House Office Building, Washington, DC 20515 .... (202) 225–3101
Chief of Staff.—Troy Clair.
Communications Director.—Meaghan Lynch.
Scheduler.—Lindsey Bowen.
216 Northeast Nash Street, Suite B, Wilson, NC 27893 .... (252) 237–9816
411 West Chapel Hill Street, Suite 905, Durham, NC 27701.

Counties: BERTIE, DURHAM (part), EDGECOMBE, GATES, GRANVILLE, HALIFAX, HERTFORD, MARTIN, NORTHAMPTON, PITT (part), VANCE, WARREN, WASHINGTON, AND WILSON (part). Population (2014) 724,668.

ZIP Codes: 27509, 27522, 27536, 27544, 27551, 27556, 27563, 27565, 27581–82, 27589, 27701, 27801, 27805, 27812, 27818–20, 27822–23, 27825, 27831–32, 27834, 27839–41, 27843, 27845–47, 27849–50, 27852, 27855, 27857, 27861, 27864, 27869–74, 27876–78, 27881, 27883, 27886, 27890–93, 27897, 27910, 27922, 27924, 27928, 27938, 27942, 27962, 27967, 27970, 27983, 27986

* * *

SECOND DISTRICT

GEORGE HOLDING, Republican, of Raleigh, NC; born in Raleigh, April 17, 1968; education: B.A., classics, Wake Forest University, Winston-Salem, NC, 1991; J.D., Wake Forest University Law School, Winston-Salem, NC, 1996; professional: law clerk for U.S. District Judge Terrence Boyle; practiced law in Raleigh with Kilpatrick Stockton; served as legislative counsel to U.S. Senator Jessie Helms, 1998–2002; joined the U.S. Attorney's office for the Eastern District of North Carolina, 2002–06; confirmed by U.S. Senate as the U.S. Attorney for Eastern North Carolina, 2006–11; religion: Baptist; committees: Ways and Means; elected to the 113th Congress on November 6, 2012; reelected to each succeeding Congress.

Office Listings

http://www.holding.house.gov

1110 Longworth House Office Building, Washington, DC 20515 .... (202) 225–3032
FAX: 225–0181
Chief of Staff.—Tucker Knott.
Legislative Director.—Kris Denzel.
Communications Director.—William Glenn.
Scheduler.—Katie Lawrence.
6404 Falls of Neuse Road, Suite 103, Raleigh, NC 27615.

Counties: FRANKLIN, HARNETT, JOHNSTON (part), NASH, WAKE (part), AND WILSON (part).

ZIP Codes: 27203, 27205, 27207–09, 27215, 27233, 27242, 27248, 27252, 27260, 27263, 27281, 27283, 27298, 27312–13, 27316–17, 27325, 27330, 27332, 27341, 27344, 27349–50, 27355–56, 27360, 27370–71, 27376, 27501–02, 27504–05, 27511, 27513, 27517, 27519, 27521, 27523, 27526, 27539–40, 27546, 27559–60, 27562, 27592, 27607, 27713, 28301, 28303–08, 28310–12, 28314–15, 28323, 28326–27, 28334, 28339, 28342, 28344, 28347–48, 28350, 28356–57, 28371, 28373–74, 28376, 28386–87, 28390–91, 28394–95

* * *

THIRD DISTRICT

WALTER B. JONES, Republican, of Farmville, NC; born in Farmville, February 10, 1943; education: graduated, Hargrave Military Academy, Chatham, VA, 1961; B.A., Atlantic Christian College, Wilson, NC, 1966; professional: served in North Carolina National Guard; self-employed, sales; member: North Carolina House of Representatives, 1983–92; married: Joe Anne Whitehurst Jones; one child, Ashley Elizabeth Jones; committees: Armed Services; elected to the 104th Congress; reelected to each succeeding Congress.

Office Listings

http://www.jones.house.gov twitter: @repwalterjones
https://www.facebook.com/pages/walter-jones/15083070102

2333 Rayburn House Office Building, Washington, DC 20515 .... (202) 225–3415
Chief of Staff.—Joshua Bowlen.
Director.—Allison Tucker.
1105–C Corporate Drive, Greenville, NC 27858 .... (252) 931–1003
District Constituent Outreach Director.—Catherine Jordan.

Counties: BEAUFORT, CAMDEN, CARTERET, CHOWAN, CRAVEN, CURRITUCK, DARE, GREENE, HYDE, JONES, LENOIR, ONSLOW, PAMLICO, PASQUOTANK, PERQUIMANS, PITT (part), AND TYRRELL. CITIES: Atlantic Beach, Ayden, Beaufort, Belhaven, Camp Lejeune, Cape Carteret, Cherry Point, Chocowinity, Columbia, Corolla, Currituck, Edenton, Elizabeth City, Emerald Isle, Farmville, Greenville, Harkers Island, Hatteras, Havelock, Hertford, Holly Ridge, Hubert, Jacksonville, Kill Devil Hills, Kinston, Kitty Hawk, Manteo, Maysville, Morehead City, Moyock, Nags Head, New Bern, Newport, North Topsail Beach, Ocracoke, Oriental, Pantego, Pine Knoll Shores, Richlands, Sneads Ferry, Surf City, Swansboro, Vanceboro, Washington, and Winterville. Population (2010), 749,823.

ZIP Codes: 27530, 27806, 27808, 27810–11, 27814, 27817, 27821, 27824, 27826–29, 27834–35, 27837, 27852, 27858, 27860, 27863, 27865, 27871, 27875, 27879, 27883, 27885, 27888–89, 27892, 27906–07, 27909, 27915–17, 27919–21, 27923, 27925, 27927–29, 27932, 27936, 27939, 27941, 27943–44, 27946–50, 27953–54, 27956, 27958–59, 27960, 27962, 27964–66, 27968, 27972–74, 27976, 27978, 27980–82, 27985, 28445, 28454, 28460, 28501, 28504, 28509–13, 28515–16, 28518–21, 28523–33, 28537–40, 28542–44, 28546–47, 28550–53, 28555–57, 28560, 28562, 28570–75, 28577–87, 28589–90, 28594

* * *

FOURTH DISTRICT

DAVID E. PRICE, Democrat, of Chapel Hill, NC; born in Erwin, TN, August 17, 1940; education: B.A., Morehead Scholar, University of North Carolina; bachelor of divinity, 1964, and Ph.D., political science, 1969, Yale University; professional: professor of political science and public policy, Duke University; past chairman and executive director, North Carolina Democratic Party; author of four books and numerous book chapters, essays, and scholarly articles on Congress and the American political system; leadership roles: ranking member, House Democracy Partnership; co-chair, Democratic Budget Group; Assistant Democratic Whip; legislative accomplishments: Home Equity Loan Consumer Protection Act (100th Congress); Scientific and Technical Education Act (102nd Congress); Education Affordability Act (105th Congress); Stand By Your Ad Act (107th Congress); Teaching Fellows Act (110th Congress); Credit Card Minimum Payment Warning Act (111th Congress); selected awards: Hubert Humphrey Public Service Award, American Political Science Association, 1990; Champion of Science Award, The Science Coalition, 2002; Charles Dick Medal of Merit, North Carolina National Guard, 2002; William Sloane Coffin Award for Peace and Justice, Yale Divinity School, 2006; Legislator of the Year, Biotechnology Industry Association, 2011; John Tyler Caldwell Award for the Humanities, North Carolina Humanities Council, 2011; past chairman of the board and Sunday School teacher, Binkley Memorial Baptist Church; married: Lisa Price; children: Karen and Michael; committees: Appropriations; elected to the 100th–103rd Congresses; elected to the 105th Congress; reelected to each succeeding Congress.

Office Listings

http://www.price.house.gov facebook: https://www.facebook.com/RepDavidEPrice
twitter: @repdavideprice

2108 Rayburn House Office Building, Washington, DC 20515 .... (202) 225–1784
Deputy Chief of Staff.—Justin Wein. FAX: 225–2014
Legislative Director.—James Hunter.
Executive Assistant.—Bayly Hassell.
Systems Manager.—Neel Mandavilli.
436 North Harrington Street, Suite 100, Raleigh, NC 27603 .... (919) 859–5999
Chief of Staff.—Asher Hildebrand.
Communications Director.—Lawrence Kluttz.
1777 Fordham Boulevard, Suite 204, Chapel Hill, NC 27514 .... (919) 967–7924

Counties: DURHAM (part), ORANGE (all), AND WAKE (part). CITIES: Apex, Bahama, Carrboro, Cary, Cedar Grove, Chapel Hill, Durham, Efland, Fuquay Varina, Garner, Hillsborough, Holly Springs, Knightdale, Morrisville, New Hill, Raleigh, Research Triangle Park, Rolesville, Rougemont, Wake Forest, Wendell, Willow Spring, Zebulon. Population (2010), 835,589.

ZIP Codes: 27231, 27243, 27278, 27502–03, 27510–19, 27523, 27526, 27529, 27539–40, 27545, 27560, 27562, 27571–72, 27587–88, 27591–92, 27597, 27599, 27701–13, 27715, 27717, 27722

* * *

FIFTH DISTRICT

VIRGINIA FOXX, Republican, of Banner Elk, NC; born in New York, NY, June 29, 1943; education: A.B., University of North Carolina, Chapel Hill, NC, 1968; M.A.C.T., University of North Carolina, Chapel Hill, 1972; Ed.D., University of North Carolina, Greensboro, NC, 1985; professional: instructor, Caldwell Community College, Hudson, NC; instructor, Appalachian State University, Boone, NC; assistant dean, Appalachian State University, Boone, NC; president, Mayland Community College, Spruce Pine, NC, 1987–94; nursery operator; deputy secretary for management, North Carolina Department of Administration; organizations: member, Watauga County Board of Education, 1967–88; member, North Carolina State Senate, 1994–2004; Executive Committee of North Carolina Citizens for Business and Industry; Z. Smith Reynolds Foundation Advisory Panel; National Advisory Council for Women's Educational Programs; Board of Directors of the NC Center for Public Research; UNC-Chapel Hill Board of Visitors; National Conference of State Legislatures' Blue Ribbon Advisory Panel on Child Care; Foscoe-Grandfather Community Center Board; family: married to Tom Foxx; one daughter; elected House GOP Conference Secretary in the 113th and 114th Congresses; committees: chair, Education and the Workforce; Oversight and Government Reform; elected to the 109th Congress on November 2, 2004; reelected to each succeeding Congress.

Office Listings

http://www.foxx.house.gov

2262 Rayburn House Office Building, Washington, DC 20515 .... (202) 225–2071
FAX: 225–2995
Chief of Staff.—Cyrus Artz.
Legislative Director.—Carson Middleton.
Communications Director.—Sheridan Watson.
400 Shadowline Drive, Suite 205, Boone, NC 28607 .... (828) 265–0240
FAX: 265–0390
3540 Clemmons Road, Suite 125, Clemmons, NC 27012 .... (336) 778–0211
FAX: 778–2290

Counties: ALEXANDER, ALLEGHANY, ASHE, AVERY, CATAWBA, DAVIDSON, FORSYTH, STOKES, SURRY, WATAUGA, WILKES, AND YADKIN. CITIES: Ararat, Banner Elk, Belews Creek, Blowing Rock, Boomer, Boone, Boonville, Clemmons, Cleveland, Creston, Crumpler, Danbury, Deep Gap, Dobson, East Bend, Elk Park, Elkin, Ennice, Ferguson, Fleetwood, Germanton, Glade Valley, Glendale Springs, Granite Falls, Grassy Creek, Hamptonville, Hays, Hickory, Hiddenite, High Point, Jefferson, Jonesville, Kernersville, King, Lansing, Laurel Springs, Lenoir, Lewisville, Lowgap, McGrady, Millers Creek, Mooresville, Moravian Falls, North Wilkesboro, Pfafftown, Pilot Mountain, Piney Creek, Purlear, Roaring Gap, Roaring River, Ronda, Rural Hall, Sandy Ridge, Siloam, Sparta, State Road, Stokesdale, Stony Point, Sugar Grove, Taylorsville, Thurmond, Toast, Tobaccoville, Todd, Traphill, Troutman, Union Grove, Vilas, Walkertown, Walnut Cove, Warrensville, West Jefferson, Westfield, White Plains, Wilkesboro, Winston Salem, Yadkinville, and Zionville. Population (2010), 741,095.

ZIP Codes: 27007, 27009–13, 27016–19, 27021–25, 27030, 27284, 28604–08, 28615–18, 28621–24, 28626–27, 28629–30, 28634–36, 28640, 28642–44, 28646, 28649, 28652–53, 28657, 28731, 28734

* * *

SIXTH DISTRICT

MARK WALKER, Republican, of Greensboro, NC; born in Dothan, Houston County, AL, May 20, 1969; education: attended Trinity Baptist College, Jacksonville, FL, 1987–88; B.A., Piedmont International University, Winston-Salem, NC, 1999; professional: businessman; minister; caucuses: chair, Republican Study Committee; committees: House Administration; Oversight and Government Reform; Joint Committee on Printing; elected to the 114th Congress on November 4, 2014; reelected to the 115th Congress.

Office Listings

https://walker.house.gov facebook.com/repmarkwalker
twitter: @repmarkwalker instagram.com/repmarkwalker

1305 Longworth House Office Building, Washington, DC 20515 .... (202) 225–3065
FAX: 225–8611
Chief of Staff.—Scott Luginbill.
Scheduler.—Katie Abrames.
Legislative Director.—Ryan Walker.
Communications Director.—Jack Minor.
809 Green Valley Road, Suite 104, Greensboro, NC 27408 .... (336) 333–5005
219 B. West Elm Street, P.O. Box 812, Graham, NC 27253 .... (336) 229–0159
FAX: 350–9514
District Director.—Julie Scott Emmons.
Director of Constituent Services.—Janine Osborne.
222 Sunset Avenue, Suite 101, Asheboro, NC 27203 .... (336) 626–3060

Office Listings—Continued

FAX: 629–7819

Counties: ALAMANCE, CASWELL, CHATHAM, GUILFORD (part), LEE, PERSON, RANDOLPH, AND ROCKINGHAM. Population (2010), 762,758.

ZIP Codes: 27025, 27027, 27048, 27201–05, 27207–08, 27212–17, 27220, 27228, 27230, 27235, 27237, 27244, 27248–49, 27252–53, 27256, 27258, 27283–84, 27288–89, 27291, 27298, 27301–02, 27305, 27310–12, 27314–17, 27320–23, 27326, 27330–32, 27340–41, 27343–44, 27349–50, 27355, 27357–59, 27370, 27375, 27377, 27379, 27395, 27409–10, 27455, 27505, 27541, 27559, 27573–74, 27583, 28355

* * *

SEVENTH DISTRICT

DAVID ROUZER, Republican, of McGee's Crossroads, NC; born at Landstuhl Army Medical Center in Landstuhl, Germany, February 16, 1972; education: B.S. in agriculture business management, agricultural economics; B.A. in chemistry; professional: legislative assistant, Office of U.S. Senator Jesse Helms; senior policy advisor, U.S. Senator Jesse Helms; assistant to the Dean and Director of Commodity Relations, College of Agriculture and Life Sciences, NC State University; senior advisor, U.S. Senator Elizabeth Dole; Associate Administrator, Rural Business-Cooperative Programs/Director, Legislative and Public Affairs, U.S. Department of Agriculture; principal, The Rouzer Company; committees: Agriculture; Transportation and Infrastructure; elected to the 114th Congress on November 4, 2014; reelected to the 115th Congress on November 8, 2016.

Office Listings

https://rouzer.house.gov www.facebook.com/reprouzer

424 Cannon House Office Building, Washington, DC 20515 .... (202) 225–2731
Chief of Staff.—Melissa Murphy. FAX: 225–5773
Communications Director.—Danielle Adams Smotkin.
Legislative Director.—Jason Cooke.
District Director.—Dwight Williams.
230 Government Center Drive, Suite 113, Wilmington, NC 28403 .... (910) 395–0202
310 Government Center Drive, Unit 1, Bolivia, NC 28422 .... (910) 253–6111
2736 North Carolina Highway 210, Smithfield, NC 27577 .... (919) 938–3040

Counties: BLADEN, BRUNSWICK, COLUMBUS, DUPLIN, JOHNSTON, NEW HANOVER, PENDER, SAMPSON, AND WAYNE. Population (2013), 762,540.

ZIP Codes: 27501, 27504, 27524, 27530–31, 27534, 27542, 27568–69, 27576–77, 27592, 27603, 27830, 27863, 27883, 28318, 28320, 28325, 28328, 28333–34, 28337, 28341, 28344, 28349, 28365–66, 28382, 28385, 28393, 28398, 28401, 28403, 28405, 28409, 28411, 28412, 28420–25, 28428–36, 28438–39, 28441–45, 28447–58, 28461–70, 28472, 28478–80, 28508, 28518, 28521, 28525, 28551, 28572, 28574, 28578

* * *

EIGHTH DISTRICT

RICHARD HUDSON, Republican, of Concord, NC; born in Franklin, VA, November 4, 1971; education: B.A. in history and political science, University of North Carolina at Charlotte, 1996; professional: served as District Director for 8th District Congressman Robin Hayes; served as Chief of Staff for Congresswoman Virginia Foxx, Congressman John Carter, and Congressman Mike Conaway; religion: Christian; married: Renee; caucuses: Atlantic Offshore Energy Caucus; Agriculture and Rural America Task Force; Agriculture Policy Group; Carbonated and Non-alcoholic (CAN) Caucus; Congressional Army Aviation Caucus; Congressional Chicken Caucus; Congressional General Aviation Caucus; Congressional Peanut Caucus; Congressional Prayer Caucus; Congressional Sportsmen's Caucus; Congressional Textile Caucus; House National Guard and Reserve Components Caucus; House Republican Israel Caucus; House Special Operations Forces Caucus; Pediatric Trauma Caucus; Republican Policy Committee; Republican Study Committee; committees: Energy and Commerce; elected to the 113th Congress on November 6, 2012; reelected to each succeeding Congress.

Office Listings

http://www.hudson.house.gov

429 Cannon House Office Building, Washington, DC 20515 .... (202) 225–3715

Office Listings—Continued

Chief of Staff.—Chris Carter. FAX: 225–4036
Press Secretary.—Tatum Gibson.
Deputy Chief of Staff / Legislative Director.—Aaron Ringel.
Scheduler.—Summer Fields.
325 McGill Avenue, Suite 500, Concord, NC 28027 .... (704) 786–1612
225 Green Street, Suite 202, Fayetteville, NC 28301 .... (910) 997–2070

Counties: CABARRUS, CUMBERLAND (part), HOKE, MONTGOMERY, MOORE, ROWAN (part), AND STANLY. Population (2010), 701,000.

ZIP Codes: 27205, 27208–09, 27229, 27239, 27281, 27292, 27306, 27325, 27330, 27341, 27356, 27360, 27370–71, 27376, 28001–02, 28009, 28023, 28025–27, 28036, 28039, 28041, 28071–72, 28075, 28078–79, 28081–83, 28088, 28097, 28103, 28107, 28109–10, 28112, 28115, 28124–25, 28127–29, 28137–38, 28144, 28146–47, 28159, 28170, 28174, 28213, 28215, 28227, 28262, 28269, 28301–11, 28314–15, 28326–27, 28331, 28334, 28338, 28342, 28344, 28347–48, 28350–52, 28356–58, 28360, 28364, 28370–74, 28376–77, 28379, 28383–84, 28386–88, 28390, 28394–96

* * *

NINTH DISTRICT

ROBERT M. PITTENGER, Republican, of Charlotte, NC; born in Dallas, TX, August 15, 1948; education: psychology and political science, University of Texas, Austin, TX, 1970; professional: former assistant to the president of Campus Crusade for Christ; founder of Pittenger Land Investments; North Carolina State Senate, 2002–08; former board member of the Presbyterian Hospital Foundation, Jesse Helms Educational Foundation, and Central Piedmont Community College Foundation; religion: Christian; family: wife, Suzanne Pittenger; four children and seven grandchildren; commissions: Congressional-Executive Commission on China; caucuses: co-chairman of the United Solutions Caucus; committees: Financial Services; elected to the 113th Congress on November 6, 2012; reelected to each Succeeding Congress.

Office Listings

http://pittenger.house.gov www.facebook.com/congressmanpittenger
twitter: @reppittenger

224 Cannon House Office Building, Washington, DC 20515 .... (202) 225–1976
Chief of Staff.—Stephen Billy. FAX: 225–3389
Deputy Chief of Staff and Legislative Director.—Clark Fonda.
Senior Legislative Assistant.—Charles Thomas.
Legislative Assistant.—John Caison.
Legislative Correspondent.—Hamilton Lovett.
Executive Assistant.—Hayden Bumgardner.
Staff Assistant.—Marco Sylvester.
5970 Fairview Road, Suite 430, Charlotte, NC 28211 .... (704) 362–1060
District Director and Veterans Specialist.—Robert Becker. FAX: 365–6384
Communications Director.—Jamie Bowers.
Constituent Services Director.—Linda Ferseter.
Constituent Liaisons: Anna Cashwell, Chris Sullivan.
100 West Jefferson Street, Suite 1A, Monroe, NC 28112 .... (704) 917–9573
Regional District Director.—Graham Long.
301 Green Street, Suite 315, Fayetteville, NC .... (910) 303–0669

Counties: ANSON, BLADEN (part), CUMBERLAND (part), MECKLENBURG (part), RICHMOND, ROBESON, SCOTLAND, AND UNION. Population (2010), 733,498.

ZIP Codes: 27229, 27281, 27306, 28007, 28079, 28091, 28102–05, 28107, 28110, 28112, 28119, 28133, 28135, 28170, 28173–74, 28204, 28207, 28209–11, 28226–27, 28270, 28274, 28277, 28301, 28305–06, 28312, 28318, 28320, 28330, 28332, 28337–38, 28340, 28343, 28345, 28347–48, 28351–52, 28357–58, 28360, 28362–64, 28367, 28369, 28371–72, 28375, 28377–79, 28382–84, 28386, 28391–92, 28395–96, 28399, 28433, 28438, 28441, 28444, 28448

* * *

TENTH DISTRICT

PATRICK T. MCHENRY, Republican, of Denver, NC; born in Gastonia, NC, October 22, 1975; education: graduated Ashbrook High School, Gastonia, NC; attended North Carolina State University, Raleigh, NC; B.A., Belmont Abbey College, Belmont, NC, 1999; professional: realtor; media executive; appointed special assistant to the U.S. Secretary of Labor by President George W. Bush in 2001; member, North Carolina House of Representatives, 2002–04; organizations: Gaston Chamber of Commerce, Gastonia Rotary Club, the National Rifle Association, Saint Michael Church; board of directors, United Way's Success by Six Youth Program; married: Giulia, 2010; daughter Cecelia born in 2014; selected Chief Deputy Whip on June 26, 2014; committees: vice chair, Financial Services; elected to the 109th Congress on November 2, 2004; reelected to each succeeding Congress.

Office Listings

http://mchenry.house.gov www.facebook.com/congressmanmchenry
twitter: @patrickmchenry

2334 Rayburn House Office Building, Washington, DC 20515 .... (202) 225–2576
Chief of Staff/Communications Director.—Jeff Butler. FAX: 225–0316
Legislative Director.—Matt Mulder.
Scheduler.—Lindsey Shackelford.
1990 Main Avenue, SE., 28602, P.O. Box 1830, Hickory, NC 28603 .... (828) 327–6100
Constituent Services Director.—David McCrary. FAX: 327–8311
128 West Main Avenue, Suite 115, Gastonia, NC 28053 704–833–0096
District Director.—Brett Keeter. FAX: 833–0887
160 Midland Avenue, Black Mountain, NC 28711 828–669–0600
Regional Representative.—Roger Kumpf.

Counties: BUNCOMBE (part), CATAWBA (part), CLEVELAND, GASTON, IREDELL (part), LINCOLN, POLK, AND RUTHERFORD. CITIES AND TOWNSHIPS: Hickory, Lincolnton, Asheville, Shelby, and Gastonia. Population (2010), 733,499.

ZIP Codes: 28006, 28012, 28016–21, 28032–34, 28037, 28040, 28043, 28052, 28054, 28056, 28073, 28076–77, 28080, 28086, 28089–90, 28092, 28098, 28101, 28114, 28117, 28120, 28139, 28150, 28152, 28160, 28164, 28167–69, 28601–02, 28609–10, 28612–13, 28650, 28658, 28673, 28682, 28704, 28709, 28711, 28720, 28722, 28730, 28732, 28746, 28756–57, 28773, 28778, 28782, 28787, 28792, 28801, 28803–06

* * *

ELEVENTH DISTRICT

MARK R. MEADOWS, Republican, of Cashiers, NC; born in Maginot Barracks (Army), Verdun, France, July 28, 1959; education: graduated from the University of South Florida, Tampa, FL, 1980; professional: real estate developer; restaurateur; energy company customer relations director; Macon County Republican Party chairman, 2001–02; serves as a congressional liaison to the United Nations; religion: Christian; married: Debbie Meadows; two children; caucuses: appointed to the Congressional-Executive Commission on China; committees: Foreign Affairs; Oversight and Government Reform; Transportation and Infrastructure; elected to the 113th Congress on November 6, 2012; reelected to each succeeding Congress.

Office Listings

http://www.meadows.house.gov

1024 Longworth House Office Building, Washington, DC 20515 .... (202) 225–6401
Chief of Staff.—Paul Fitzpatrick. FAX: 226–6422
Legislative Director.—Graham Haile.
Communications Director.—Alyssa Farah.
Scheduler.—Megan Compton.
Legislative Assistants: Martha Van Lieshout, Chad Yelinski.
Press Secretary.—Ben Williamson.
Legislative Correspondent.—Josh Wentzel.
200 North Grove Street, Suite 90, Hendersonville, NC 28792 .... (828) 693–5660

Counties: BUNCOMBE (part), BURKE, CALDWELL, CHEROKEE, CLAY, GRAHAM, HAYWOOD, HENDERSON, JACKSON, MACON, MADISON, MCDOWELL, MITCHELL, SWAIN, TRANSYLVANIA, AND YANCEY. CITIES AND TOWNSHIPS: Hayesville, Hendersonville, Lenoir, Morganton, and Waynesville. Population (2010), 619,178.

ZIP Codes: 28604, 28645, 28655, 28657, 28701–02, 28704–05, 28707–08, 28712–13, 28715, 28717–19, 28721, 28723, 28730, 28734, 28736, 28739–43, 28747, 28751–54, 28759, 28763, 28765, 28771, 28774–75, 28779, 28781, 28783, 28786–87, 28789–91, 28901–02, 28904–06, 28909

* * *

TWELFTH DISTRICT

ALMA S. ADAMS, Democrat, of Greensboro, NC; born in High Point, NC, May 27, 1946; education: art education, North Carolina A&T State University, Greensboro, NC, 1968; master's degree in art education, North Carolina A&T State University, Greensboro, 1972; Ph.D. in art education and multicultural education from The Ohio State University in Columbus, Ohio, 1981; professional: Greensboro City School Board, 1984–86; Greensboro City Council, 1987–94; Bennett College art professor, curator, and administrator; North Carolina State House, 1994–2014; family: two children, Linda Jeanelle Lindsay and Billy Eugene Adams II; four grandchildren; caucuses: founder of the Congressional Bipartisan HBCU Caucus; AIDS / HIV Caucus; Art Caucus; Congressional Black Caucus; Congressional Progress Caucus; Diabetes Caucus; Historic Preservation Caucus; Hunger Caucus; Women's Caucus; committees: Agriculture; Education and the Workforce; Small Business; Joint Economic Committee; elected, by special election, in 2014 to fill the vacancy caused by the resignation of U.S. Representative Mel Watt, while simultaneously elected to the 114th Congress on November 4, 2014, to serve a full two-year term; reelected to the 115th Congress on November 8, 2016.

Office Listings

http://www.adams.house.gov facebook: https://www.facebook.com/CongresswomanAdams
twitter: @RepAdams

222 Cannon House Office Building, Washington, DC 20515 .... (202) 225–1510
Chief of Staff.—Rhonda Foxx. FAX: 225–1512
Press Secretary.—Hailey Barringer.
801 East Morehead Street, Suite 150, Charlotte, NC 28202 .... (704) 344–9950
District Director.—Phanalphie Rhue.
Director of Operations.—Sandra Brown.

Counties: MECKLENBURG (part). Population (2015), 830,225.

ZIP Codes: 28031, 28036 (part), 28078 (part), 28105 (part), 28134 (part), 28202–03, 28204 (part), 28205–06, 28207 (part), 28208, 28209–11 (part), 28212, 28213 (part), 28214, 28215 (part), 28216–17, 28226–27 (part), 28244, 28262 (part), 28269–70 (part), 28273, 28277 (part), 28278, 28280, 28282

* * *

THIRTEENTH DISTRICT

TED BUDD, Republican, of Advance, NC; born in Winston-Salem, NC, October 21, 1971; education: B.S.B.A., business management, Appalachian State University; M.B.A., Wake Forest University; masters, educational leadership and family life, Dallas Theological Seminary; professional: executive vice president, The Budd Group; owner, ProShots Indoor Range & Training; religion: Christian; family: spouse, Amy Kate Budd; three children; committees: Financial Services; elected to the 115th Congress on November 8, 2016.

Office Listings

http://www.budd.house.gov

118 Cannon House Office Building, Washington, DC 20515 .... (202) 225–4531
Chief of Staff.—Andrew Bell.
Legislative Director.—Alex Vargo.
Press Secretary.—Melissa Brown.
Scheduler.—Elizabeth Dews.
128 Peachtree Lane, Suite A, Advance, NC 27006 .... (336) 998–1313
4000 Piedmont Parkway, Suite 313, High Point, NC 27265 .... (336) 858–5013

Counties: DAVIDSON, DAVIE, GUILFORD (part), IREDELL, AND ROWAN (part). Population (2010), 732,434.

ZIP Codes: 27006, 27012 (part), 27013–14, 27020 (part), 27028, 27054, 27055 (part), 27104 (part), 27107 (part), 27114–16 (part), 27127 (part), 27202 (part), 27233 (part), 27235 (part), 27239 (part), 27260 (part), 27261, 27262–65 (part), 27268 (part), 27284 (part), 27292 (part), 27293–94, 27295 (part), 27299, 27310 (part), 27313 (part), 27317 (part), 27351, 27360 (part), 27261, 27373–74, 27401 (part), 27402–04, 27405–06 (part), 27407, 27408–10 (part), 27412, 27413 (part), 27415 (part), 27416–17, 27419–20, 27425 (part), 27427 (part), 27429, 27435, 27438, 27455 (part), 27495, 27497 (part), 27498–99, 28010, 28036 (part), 28115 (part), 28117 (part), 28123, 28125 (part), 28127 (part), 28144–47 (part), 28159 (part), 28166 (part), 28625 (part), 28634 (part), 28636 (part), 28660, 28677–78 (part), 28687–88, 28689 (part), 28699

NORTH DAKOTA

(Population 2010, 675,591)

SENATORS

JOHN HOEVEN, Republican, of Bismarck, ND; born in Bismarck, March 13, 1957; education: B.A., Dartmouth College, Hanover, NH, 1979; M.B.A., Northwestern University, Chicago, IL, 1981; professional: executive vice president, First Western Bank, Minot, 1986–93; president and CEO, Bank of North Dakota, 1993–2000; Governor of North Dakota, 2000–10; religion: Catholic; family: married to Mikey; two children; caucuses: Air Force Caucus; Congressional Sportsmen's Caucus; Senate Western Caucus; Norway Caucus; Rural Education Caucus; National Guard Caucus; E–911 Caucus; Rural Health Caucus; General Aviation Caucus; Impact Aid Coalition; Senate Republican High-Tech Task Force; Senate Veterans Jobs Caucus; Unmanned Aerial Systems Caucus; Hydrogen Fuel Cell Caucus; ICBM Coalition; Port-to-Plains Caucus; UAS Integration Working Group; committees: chair, Indian Affairs; Agriculture, Nutrition, and Forestry; Appropriations; Energy and Natural Resources; Homeland Security and Governmental Affairs; elected to the U.S. Senate on November 2, 2010; reelected to the U.S. Senate on November 8, 2016.

Office Listings

http://hoeven.senate.gov www.facebook.com/senatorjohnhoeven
https://twitter.com/senjohnhoeven

338 Russell Senate Office Building, Washington, DC 20510 .... (202) 224–2551
Chief of Staff.—Cassie Bladow. FAX: 224–7999
Legislative Director.—Daniel Auger.
Communications Director.—Kami Capener.
U.S. Federal Building, 220 East Rosser Avenue, Room 312, Bismarck, ND 58501 .... (701) 250–4618
State Director.—Jessica Lee. FAX: 239–5112
1802 32nd Avenue South, Suite B, Fargo, ND 58103 .... (701) 239–5389
Federal Building, 102 North Fourth Street, Room 108, Grand Forks, ND 58203 .... (701) 746–8972
100 1st Street SouthWest, Suite 107, Minot, ND 58701 .... (701) 838–1361
Williston, ND .... (701) 580–4535

* * *

HEIDI HEITKAMP, Democrat, of Mandan, ND; born in Breckenridge, MN, October 30, 1955; education: B.A., University of North Dakota, ND, 1977; J.D., Lewis and Clark Law School, 1980; professional: attorney, United States Environmental Protection Agency, 1980–81; attorney, Office of the North Dakota State Tax Commissioner, 1981–86; Tax Commissioner, State of North Dakota, 1986–92; Attorney General, State of North Dakota, 1992–2000; director, Dakota Gasification Company, 2001–12; religion: Catholic; family: married to Dr. Darwin Lange; two children; caucuses: Afterschool Caucus; Bicameral Congressional Arthritis Caucus; Bipartisan Task Force on Tribal Colleges and Universities; Career and Technical Education Caucus; Congressional Caucus on Foster Youth; Congressional Coalition on Adoption; Congressional Diabetes Caucus; Congressional ICBM Coalition; Congressional Next Generation 9-1-1 Caucus; Congressional Sportsmen's Caucus; Congressional Veterans Jobs Caucus; Deadly Cancers Caucus; Defense Communities Caucus; General Aviation Caucus; Impact Aid Coalition; Law Enforcement Caucus; National Guard Caucus; Nursing Caucus; Ports to Plains Caucus; Rural Health Caucus; Senate Cultural Caucus; Social Work Caucus; committees: Agriculture, Nutrition, and Forestry; Banking, Housing, and Urban Affairs; Homeland Security and Governmental Affairs; Indian Affairs; Small Business and Entrepreneurship; elected to the U.S. Senate on November 6, 2012.

Office Listings

http://heitkamp.senate.gov https://twitter.com/senatorheitkamp
www.facebook.com/senatorheidiheitkamp

516 Hart Senate Office Building, Washington, DC 20510 .... (202) 224–2043
Chief of Staff.—Tessa Gould. FAX: 224–7776
Legislative Director.—Tracee Sutton.
220 East Rosser Avenue, Room 228, Bismarck, ND 58501 .... (701) 258–4648
State Director.—Ross Keys.
657 Second Avenue North, Room 306, Fargo, ND 58102 .... (701) 232–8030
33 South 3rd Street, Suite B, Grand Forks, ND 58201 .... (701) 775–9601
100 First Street, SW., Room 105, Minot, ND 58701 .... (701) 852–0703
40 First Avenue West, Suite 202, Dickinson, ND 58601 .... (701) 225–0974

REPRESENTATIVE

AT LARGE

KEVIN CRAMER, Republican, of Bismarck, ND; born in Rolette, ND, January 21, 1961; education: B.A., social work, Concordia College, Moorhead, MN, 1983; M.A., management, University of Mary, Bismarck, ND, 2003; professional: chairman, North Dakota Republican Party, 1991–93; North Dakota Tourism Director, 1993–97; State Economic Development and Finance Director, 1997–2000; Executive Director, Harold Schafer Leadership Foundation, 2000–03; North Dakota Public Service Commissioner, 2003–12; married: Kris Cramer; children: Ian, Isaac, Rachel ''Cale'' Wegner, Annie ''Nick'' Senne, and Abel; grandchildren: Lila, Beau, Nico, and Chet; committees: Energy and Commerce; elected to the 113th Congress on November 6, 2012 and reelected to each succeeding Congress.

Office Listings

http://cramer.house.gov facebook.com/congressmankevincramer twitter.com/repkevincramer

1717 Longworth House Office Building, Washington, DC 20515 .... (202) 225–2611
Chief of Staff.—Mark Gruman.
Legislative Director.—Chris Marohl.
Communications Director.—Adam Jorde.
Federal Building, 220 East Rosser Avenue, Room 328, Bismarck, ND 58501 .... (701) 224–0355
3217 Fiechtner Drive South, Suite D, Fargo, ND 58103 .... (701) 356–2216
315 Main Street South, Suite 203, Minot, ND 58701 .... (701) 839–0255
4200 James Ray Drive, Office 600, Grand Forks, ND 58202 .... (701) 738–4880
State Director.—Lisa Gibbens.

Population (2010), 672,591.

ZIP Codes: 58001–02, 58004–09, 58011–13, 58015–18, 58021, 58027, 58029, 58030–33, 58035–36, 58038, 58040–43, 58045–49, 58051–54, 58056–65, 58067–69, 58071–72, 58074–79, 58081, 58102–09, 58121–22, 58124–26, 58201–06, 58208, 58210, 58212, 58214, 58216, 58218–20, 58222–25, 58227–31, 58233, 58235–41, 58243–44, 58249–51, 58254–62, 58265–67, 58269–78, 58281–82, 58301, 58310–11, 58313, 58316–19, 58321, 58323–25, 58327, 58329–32, 58335, 58338–39, 58341, 58343–46, 58348, 58351–53, 58355–57, 58359, 58361–63, 58365–70, 58372, 58374, 58377, 58379–82, 58384–86, 58401–02, 58405, 58413, 58415–16, 58418, 58420–26, 58428–31, 58433, 58436, 58438–45, 58448, 58451–52, 58454–56, 58458, 58460–61, 58463–64, 58466–67, 58472, 58474–84, 58486–88, 58490, 58492, 58494–97, 58501–07, 58520–21, 58523–24, 58528–33, 58535, 58538, 58540–42, 58544–45, 58549, 58552, 58554, 58558–66, 58568–73, 58575–77, 58579–81, 58601–02, 58620–23, 58625–27, 58630–32, 58634, 58636, 58638–47, 58649–56, 58701–05, 58707, 58710–13, 58716, 58718, 58721–23, 58725, 58727, 58730–31, 58733–37, 58740–41, 58744, 58746–48, 58750, 58752, 58755–63, 58765, 58768–73, 58775–76, 58778–79, 58781–85, 58787–90, 58792–95, 58801–02, 58830–31, 58833, 58835, 58838, 58843–45, 58847, 58849, 58852–54, 58856

OHIO

(Population 2010, 11,536,504)

SENATORS

SHERROD BROWN, Democrat, of Cleveland, OH; born in Mansfield, OH, November 9, 1952; education: B.A., Yale University, New Haven, CT, 1974; M.A., education, Ohio State University, Columbus, OH, 1979; M.A., public administration, Ohio State University, Columbus, 1981; professional: Ohio House of Representatives, 1975–82; Ohio Secretary of State, 1983–91; U.S. House of Representatives, 1992–2006; member: Eagle Scouts of America; married: Connie Schultz; children: Emily, Elizabeth, Andrew, and Caitlin; committees: ranking member, Banking, Housing, and Urban Affairs; Agriculture, Nutrition, and Forestry; Finance; Veterans' Affairs; elected to the 103rd Congress on November 3, 1992; reelected to each succeeding Congress; elected to the U.S. Senate on November 7, 2006; reelected to the U.S. Senate on November 6, 2012.

Office Listings

http://brown.senate.gov

713 Hart Senate Office Building, Washington, DC 20510 .... (202) 224–2315
Chief of Staff.—Sarah Benzing. FAX: 228–6321
Legislative Director.—Jeremy Hekhuis.
Communications Director.—Jennifer Donohue.
Press Secretary.—Rachael Hartford.
801 West Superior Avenue, Suite 1400, Cleveland, OH 44113 .... (216) 522–7272
State Director.—John Ryan.
Deputy State Director.—Beth Thames.
425 Walnut Street, Suite 2310, Cincinnati, OH 45202 .... (513) 684–1021
200 North High Street, Room 614, Columbus, OH 43215 .... (614) 469–2083
200 West Erie Avenue, Suite 312, Lorain, OH 44052 .... (440) 242–4100

* * *

ROBERT J. PORTMAN, Republican, of Terrace Park, OH; born in Cincinnati, OH, December 19, 1955; education: B.A., Dartmouth College, Hanover, NH, 1979; J.D., University of Michigan Law School, Ann Arbor, MI, 1984; professional: associate counsel to George H.W. Bush, 1989; Deputy Assistant and Director, White House Office of Legislative Affairs, 1989–91; member of the U.S. House of Representatives, 1993–2005; U.S. Trade Representative, 2005–06; Director of the Office of Management and Budget, 2006–07; religion: Methodist; married: Jane Portman; three children: Jed, Will, and Sally; committees: Energy and Natural Resources; Finance; Foreign Relations; Homeland Security and Governmental Affairs; Joint Economic Committee; elected to the U.S. Senate on November 2, 2010; reelected to the U.S. Senate on November 8, 2016.

Office Listings

http://portman.senate.gov

448 Russell Senate Office Building, Washington, DC 20510 .... (202) 224–3353
Chief of Staff.—Mark Isakowitz.
Communications Director.—Kevin Smith.
Legislative Director.—Pam Thiessen.
Scheduler.—Angie Youngen.
37 West Broad Street, Suite 300, Columbus, OH 43215 .... (614) 469–6774
State Director.—Teri Geiger.
District Director.—Steve White.
District Representative.—Vacant.
312 Walnut Street, Suite 3425, Cincinnati, OH 45202 .... (513) 684–3265
District Director.—Connie Laug.
District Representative.—Vacant.
1240 East 9th Street, Room 3061, Cleveland, OH 44199 .... (216) 522–7095
District Director.—Caryn Candisky.
District Representative.—Josh Prest.
420 Madison Avenue, Room 1210, Toledo, OH 43604 .... (419) 259–3895
District Representative.—Kelsey Krull.

REPRESENTATIVES

FIRST DISTRICT

STEVE CHABOT, Republican, of Cincinnati, OH; born in Cincinnati, January 22, 1953; education: graduated from LaSalle High School in Cincinnati; B.A., College of William and Mary, Williamsburg, VA, 1975; J.D., Salmon P. Chase College of Law, Highland Heights, KY, 1978; professional: teacher, 1975–76; member of the City Council, Cincinnati, OH, 1985–90; commissioner, Hamilton County, OH, 1990–94; family: wife, Donna; two children: Erica and Randy; elected as a Republican to the 104th–110th Congresses, January 3, 1995–January 3, 2009; served as ranking member on the Committee on Small Business, 110th Congress; committees: chair, Small Business; Foreign Affairs; Judiciary; elected to the 112th Congress on November 2, 2010; reelected to each succeeding Congress.

Office Listings

http://chabot.house.gov facebook: repstevechabot twitter: @repstevechabot

2371 Rayburn House Office Building, Washington, DC 20515 .... (202) 225–2216
FAX: 225–3012
Chief of Staff.—Stacy Palmer Barton.
Legislative Director.—Jonathan Lowe.
Scheduler.—Lisa McGhie.
Carew Tower, 441 Vine Street, Room 3003, Cincinnati, OH 45202 .... (513) 684–2723
FAX: 421–8722
District Director.—Mike Cantwell.
Communications Director.—Brian Griffith.
11 South Broadway Street, Third Floor, Lebanon, OH 45036 .... (513) 421–8704

Counties: HAMILTON (part), WARREN. Population (2010), 721,032.

ZIP Codes: 45001–02, 45005, 45030, 45033–34, 45036, 45039–40, 45052, 45054, 45065–66, 45068, 45111, 45140, 45152, 45162, 45202–07, 45210–11, 45214–17, 45219–21, 45223–25, 45229, 45232–33, 45237–43, 45246–49, 45251–52

* * *

SECOND DISTRICT

BRAD WENSTRUP, Republican, of Cincinnati, OH; born in Cincinnati, June 17, 1958; education: B.A., University of Cincinnati, 1980; B.S. and D.P.M., William M. Scholl College of Podiatric Medicine, Chicago, IL, 1985; professional: private practice physician/surgeon, 1986–2012; U.S. Army Reserve, 1998–present; religion: Catholic; married: Monica; children: Brad R. Wenstrup, Jr.; committees: Ways and Means; Permanent Select Committee on Intelligence; elected to the 113th Congress on November 6, 2012; reelected to each succeeding Congress.

Office Listings

http://wenstrup.house.gov https://www.facebook.com/repbradwenstrup twitter: @repbradwenstrup

2419 Rayburn House Office Building, Washington, DC 20515 .... (202) 225–3164
FAX: 225–1992
Chief of Staff.—Derek Harley.
Legislative Director.—Lisa Langenderfer.
Communications Director.—Hailey Sadler.
Scheduler.—April Lyman.
7954 Beechmont Avenue, Suite 200, Cincinnati, OH 45255 .... (513) 474–7777
District Director.—Jeff Groenke.
170 North Main Street, Peebles, OH 45660 .... (513) 605–1380
4350 Aicholtz Road, Cincinnati, OH 45245 .... (513) 605–1389

Counties: ADAMS, BROWN, CLERMONT, HAMILTON (part), HIGHLAND, PIKE, SCIOTO (part), AND ROSS (part). CITIES AND TOWNSHIPS: Anderson Township, Batavia, Blue Ash, Cincinnati (part), Chillicothe, Georgetown, Hillsboro, Loveland, Manchester, Milford, Mount Orab, New Richmond, Norwood, Peebles, Piketon, Portsmouth, Ripley, Sardinia, and Union TWP. Population (2010), 721,031.

ZIP Codes: 45101–03, 45106–07, 45112, 45115, 45118, 45120–22, 45130–31, 45133, 45140, 45142, 45144, 45150, 45153–54, 45156–57, 45160, 45162, 45167–68, 45171, 45174, 45176, 45202, 45206, 45208–09, 45212–13, 45226–27, 45230, 45236, 45241–46, 45255, 45601, 45612–13, 45616, 45624, 45642, 45646, 45648, 45650, 45652, 45657, 45660–63, 45671, 45679, 45684, 45690, 45693, 45697

* * *

THIRD DISTRICT

JOYCE BEATTY, Democrat, of Blacklick, OH; born in Dayton, OH, March 12, 1950; education: B.A., Central State University, Wilberforce, OH, 1972; M.S., Wright State University, Fairborn, OH, 1974; attended University of Cincinnati, Cincinnati, OH; professional: executive director, Montgomery County, OH; human services, professor; businesswoman; member, Ohio State House of Representatives, 1999–2008, Minority Leader, 2006–08; senior vice-president, The Ohio State University, 2008–12; Delta Sigma Theta Sorority, Inc. (life member) and The Links, Inc.; House Region 10 Whip; named one of the 150 most powerful African Americans, *Ebony Magazine*, 2008; recipient, YWCA Women of Achievement Award, 2002; NAACP Freedom Award; United Way Key Club Community Leadership Award, 2014; married: Otto; stepchildren: Laurel and Otto; Tom Lantos Human Rights Commission; caucuses: Brain Injury Taskforce; CBC Taskforce on Economic Development and Wealth Creation; Financial Literacy Caucus; Heart and Stroke Coalition; House Human Trafficking Caucus; Women's Caucus; committees: Financial Services; elected to the 113th Congress on November 6, 2012; reelected to each succeeding Congress.

Office Listings

http://www.beatty.house.gov facebook: @RepJoyceBeatty twitter: @RepBeatty

133 Cannon House Office Building, Washington, DC 20515 .... (202) 225–4324
Chief of Staff.—Kimberly Ross. FAX: 225–1984
Legislative Director.—Jennifer Storipan.
Scheduler/Executive Assistant.—Juan Negron.
Communications Director.—Dominic Manecke.
471 East Broad Street, Suite 1100, Columbus, OH 43215 .... (614) 220–0003
District Director.—Geoffrey Collver. FAX: 220–5640

Counties: FRANKLIN (part). Population (2010), 732,258.

ZIP Codes: 43004, 43026, 43054, 43068, 43081, 43085, 43109–10, 43119, 43123, 43125, 43137, 43201–07, 43209–15, 43217, 43219, 43221–24, 43227–32

* * *

FOURTH DISTRICT

JAMES D. "JIM" JORDAN, Republican, of Urbana, OH; born in Troy, OH, February 17, 1964; education: graduated, Graham High School, St. Paris, OH, 1982; B.S. in economics, University of Wisconsin, Madison, WI, 1986; M.A. in education, The Ohio State University, Columbus, OH, 1991; J.D., Capital University School of Law, Columbus, 2001; professional: assistant wrestling coach, The Ohio State University, 1987–95; State Representative, Ohio House of Representatives, 85th District, 1995–2001; State Senator, Ohio State Senate, 12th District, 2001–06; awards: four-time high school wrestling champion (Ohio), 1979–82; two-time NCAA Division I National Wrestling Champion, 1985–86; three-time All American, 1984–86; Wisconsin Badgers Hall of Fame; third place, Olympic Trials in Wrestling, 1988; Friend of the Taxpayer, Americans for Tax Reform, 1997; Leadership in Government Award from the Ohio Roundtable and Freedom Forum, 2001; awards from the United Conservatives of Ohio: Outstanding Freshman Legislator Award, 1996; Watchdog of the Treasury, 1996, 2000, 2004; Pro-Life Legislator of the Year, 1998; Outstanding Legislator Award, 2004; Hero of the Taxpayer, Americans for Tax Reform, 2007; National Legislator of the Year, Coalitions for America, 2012; Freedom Fighter Award, Freedom Works, 2012; activities: Grace Bible Church, Springfield; Local and National Right to Life organizations; Champaign County Republican Executive Committee; married: Polly (Stickley) Jordan; parents: John and Shirley Jordan; children: Rachel, Benjamin, Jessie, and Issac; committees: Judiciary; Oversight and Government Reform; elected to the 110th Congress on November 7, 2006; reelected to each succeeding Congress.

Office Listings

http://www.jordan.house.gov https://www.facebook.com/repjimjordan
twitter.com/jim_jordan

2056 Rayburn House Office Building, Washington, DC 20515 .... (202) 225–2676
Chief of Staff.—Ray Yonkura. FAX: 226–0577
Legislative Director.—Jared Dilley.
Executive Assistant/Scheduler.—Melissa Wade.
3121 West Elm Plaza, Lima, OH 45805–2516 .... (419) 999–6455

Office Listings—Continued

13B East Main Street, Norwalk, OH 44857 .... (419) 663–1426
District Director.—Cameron Warner.

Counties: ALLEN, AUGLAIZE, CHAMPAIGN, CRAWFORD, ERIE (part), HURON (part), LOGAN (part), MARION (part), MERCER (part), SANDUSKY, SENECA, SHELBY, AND UNION. Population (2010), 721,032.

ZIP Codes: 43009, 43036, 43044–45, 43047, 43060, 43067, 43070, 43072, 43077, 43084, 43310–11, 43314–26, 43330–38, 43340–51, 43356–60, 43407, 43410, 43420, 43431, 43435, 43442, 44049, 44802, 44809, 44814–16, 44818, 44820, 44828, 44836, 44841, 44846, 44849, 44853–54, 44856, 44861, 44864–65, 44867, 44875, 44881, 44883, 44887, 45302, 45306, 45312, 45317, 45326, 45333–34, 45336, 45340, 45344, 45353, 45356, 45360, 45363, 45365, 45380, 45388–89, 45502, 45801–02, 45804–10, 45812, 45819–20, 45822, 45830, 45833, 45845, 45850, 45854, 45865–66, 45969–71, 45877, 45884–85, 45887–88, 45894–96

* * *

FIFTH DISTRICT

ROBERT E. ''BOB'' LATTA, Republican, of Bowling Green, OH; born in Bluffton, OH, April 18, 1956; education: graduated, Bowling Green High School, Bowling Green, OH, 1974; B.A., history, Bowling Green State University, Bowling Green, 1978; J.D., University of Toledo School of Law, Toledo, OH, 1981; professional: legislator, lawyer; elected Wood County Commissioner, 1990, reelected 1994; elected to the Ohio Senate, 1996; elected to the Ohio House of Representatives in 2000, reelected to successive terms in 2002, 2004, and 2006; awards: Ohio Farm Bureau, Friend of Farm Bureau Award; U.S. Chamber of Commerce, Spirit of Enterprise Award; American Conservative Union, ACU Conservative Award; United Conservatives of Ohio, Watchdog of the Treasury; U.S. Sportsmen's Alliance, Patriot Award; Ohio National Guard, Major General Charles Dick Award for Legislative Excellence; President's Award; National Federation of Independent Business's (NFIB) Guardian of Small Business Award; National Association of Manufacturer's Manufacturing Legislative Excellence Award; Prism Propane Award; National Grocer's Association, Spirit of America Award; Family Research Council's True Blue Award; National Retail Federation's Hero of Main Street Award; Healthcare Distribution Management Association's (HDMA) Rx Safety and Leadership Award (Rx Award); Safari Club International's Federal Legislator of the Year; the National Shooting Sports Foundation's Legislator of the Year; member, Bowling Green Noon Kiwanis; Bowling Green Chamber of Commerce; Wood County Farm Bureau; caucuses: co-chair of the Congressional French Caucus; co-chair of the Propane Caucus; co-chair of the Rural Broadband Caucus; former co-chair of the Congressional Sportsmen Caucus; committees: Energy and Commerce; elected to the 110th Congress, by special election, on December 11, 2007 to fill the vacancy caused by the death of U.S. Representative Paul Eugene Gillmor; reelected to each succeeding Congress.

Office Listings

http://latta.house.gov facebook: facebook.com/boblatta twitter: @boblatta

2448 Rayburn House Office Building, Washington, DC 20515 .... (202) 225–6405
FAX: 225–1985
Chief of Staff.—Allison Poulios.
Legislative Director.—Jason Isakovic.
Scheduler.—Erin Partee.
1045 North Main Street, Suite 6, Bowling Green, OH 43402 .... (419) 354–8700
101 Clinton Street, Suite 1200, Defiance, OH 43512 .... (419) 782–1996
318 Dorney Plaza, Room 302, Findlay, OH 45840 .... (419) 422–7791

Counties: DEFIANCE, FULTON, HANCOCK, HARDIN, HENRY, LUCAS (part), MERCER (part), OTTAWA, PAULDING, PUTNAM, VAN WERT, WILLIAMS, WOOD, AND WYANDOT. Population (2010), 726,090.

ZIP Codes: 43310, 43316, 43323, 43326, 43330–32, 43337, 43340, 43345, 43347, 43351, 43359, 43402–03, 43406, 43408, 43412–13, 43416, 43430, 43432, 43437, 43443, 43445, 43447, 43449–52, 43457–58, 43460, 43462–63, 43465–69, 43501–02, 43504–06, 43511–12, 43515–19, 43521–29, 43531–37, 43540–43, 43545, 43547–49, 43551, 43553–58, 43560, 43565–67, 43569–71, 43605–06, 43613–15, 43617, 43619, 43623, 44802, 44804, 44817, 44830, 44844, 44849, 44882, 45810, 45812–14, 45816–17, 45821–22, 45827–28, 45830, 45831–33, 45835–36, 45838, 45840–41, 45843–44, 45846, 45849–51, 45853, 45855–56, 45858–59, 45861–64, 45867–68, 45872–77, 45879–82, 45886–87, 45889–91, 45894, 45896–99

* * *

SIXTH DISTRICT

WILLIAM L. ''BILL'' JOHNSON, Republican, of Marietta, OH; born in Roseboro, NC, November 10, 1954; raised in Roseboro, NC; education: B.A., graduated *summa cum laude* at Troy

University, Troy, AL, 1979; M.A., computer sciences, Georgia Tech, Atlanta, GA, 1984; professional: co-founder of Johnson-Schley Management Group, Inc.; founder of J2 Business Solutions, Inc.; chief information officer of a global manufacturer of highly electronic components for the transportation industry; military: retired as Lieutenant Colonel; distinguished graduate from the Air Force Reserve Officer Training Corps, Squadron Officers School, and Air Command and Staff College; religion: Protestant; family: married to LeeAnn Johnson; children: Nathan, Joshua, Julie, and Jessica; awards: recipient of Air Force Meritorious Service Medal; Air Force Commendation Medal; National Defense Service Medal; caucuses: Air Force Caucus; Aluminum Caucus; Army Aviation Caucus; Automotive Caucus; Baseball Caucus; China Caucus; Cybersecurity Caucus; Diabetes Caucus; Dyslexia Caucus; E-Learning Caucus; Ethnic and Religious Freedom in Sri Lanka Caucus; Fire Services Caucus; General Aviation Caucus; Hellenic Issues Caucus; House Law Enforcement Caucus; Invisible Wounds Caucus; Israel Allies Caucus; Joint Strike Fighter Caucus; Military Sexual Assault Prevention Caucus; Military Veterans Caucus; Mobility Air Forces Caucus; Natural Gas Caucus; Ohio River Basin Congressional Caucus; Prayer Caucus; Problem Solvers Caucus; Pro-Israel Caucus; Republican Israel Caucus; Rock and Roll Caucus; Sportsmen's Caucus; Steel Caucus; U.S.-Turkish Relations and Turkish Americans Caucus; USO Congressional Caucus; Veterans Jobs Caucus; Congressional Vision Caucus; committees: Budget; Energy and Commerce; elected to the 112th Congress on November 2, 2010; reelected to each succeeding Congress.

Office Listings

http://billjohnson.house.gov

1710 Longworth House Office Building, Washington, DC 20515 .... (202) 225–5705
Chief of Staff.—Mike Smullen.
Legislative Director.—David Rardin.
Communications Director.—Ben Keeler.
Scheduler / Office Manager.—Taryn Vieweger.
246 Front Street, Marietta, OH 45750 .... (740) 376–0868
192 East State Street, Salem, OH 44460 .... (330) 337–6951
202 Park Avenue, Suite C, Ironton, OH 45638 .... (740) 534–9431
116 Southgate Parkway, Cambridge, OH 43725 .... (740) 432–2366

Counties: ATHENS (part), BELMONT, CARROLL, COLUMBIANA, GALLIA, GUERNSEY, HARRISON, JACKSON, JEFFERSON, LAWRENCE, MAHONING (part), MEIGS, MONROE, MUSKINGUM (part), NOBLE, SCIOTO (part), TUSCARAWAS (part), AND WASHINGTON. Population (2010), 721,032.

ZIP Codes: 43701, 43711, 43713, 43716–19, 43722–25, 43732–33, 43736, 43747, 43749–50, 43754–55, 43759, 43762, 43767–68, 43772–73, 43778–80, 43786–88, 43793, 43802, 43812, 43821–22, 43830, 43832, 43837, 43842, 43901–08, 43910, 43912–15, 43917, 43920, 43925–28, 43930–35, 43938–40, 43942–48, 43950–53, 43961–64, 43967–68, 43970–74, 43976–77, 43983, 43985–86, 43988, 44401, 44406, 44408, 44413, 44423, 44427, 44431–32, 44441–45, 44449, 44451–52, 44454–55, 44460, 44493, 44514, 44601, 44607, 44609, 44615, 44620–21, 44625, 44629, 44634, 44643–44, 44651, 44653, 44656–57, 44663, 44672, 44675, 44682–83, 44688, 44693, 44695, 44699, 44730, 45601, 45613–14, 45619–21, 45623, 45629, 45631, 45634, 45636, 45638, 45640, 45645, 45648, 45650, 45652, 45653, 45656, 45658–59, 45662–63, 45669, 45672, 45674, 45678, 45680, 45682, 45685–86, 45688, 45692, 45694, 45696, 45701, 45710–11, 45714–15, 45721, 45723–24, 45727, 45729, 45734–35, 45741–46, 45750, 45760, 45767–73, 45775–76, 45779, 45784, 45786–89

* * *

SEVENTH DISTRICT

ROBERT B. GIBBS, Republican, of Lakeville, OH; born in Peru, IN, June 14, 1954; education: graduated from Bay Village Senior High School, Bay Village, OH; A.A.S., Ohio State University Agricultural Technical Institute, Wooster, OH, 1974; professional: technician; farmer; business owner; president, Ohio Farm Bureau Federation; member of the Ohio State House of Representatives, 2003–09; member of the Ohio State Senate, 2009–10; married: Jody Gibbs; children: Adam, Amy, and Andrew; grandchildren: Luke; committees: Agriculture; Transportation and Infrastructure; elected to the 112th Congress on November 2, 2010; reelected to each succeeding Congress.

Office Listings

http://www.gibbs.house.gov facebook: https://www.facebook.com/RepBobGibbs
twitter: @RepBobGibbs

2446 Rayburn House Office Building, Washington, DC 20515 .... (202) 225–6265
Chief of Staff.—Meredith Dolan. FAX: 225–3394
Scheduler.—Rachael Van Mersbergen.
Legislative Director.—Hillary Gross.
Legislative Aides: Alex Briggs, Addison Miller.
Communications Director.—Dallas Gerber.
110 Cottage Street, Ashland, OH 44805 .... (419) 207–0650

Office Listings—Continued

District Director.—Tim Ross. FAX: 207–0655

Counties: ASHLAND, COSHOCTON (part), HOLMES, HURON (part), KNOX, LORAIN (part), MEDINA (part), RICHLAND (part), STARK (part), AND TUSCARAWAS (part). Population (2010), 726,076.

ZIP Codes: 43005–06, 43011, 43014, 43019, 43022, 43028, 43037, 43050, 43080, 43749, 43804, 43811–12, 43821–22, 43824, 43832, 43836, 43843–45, 44011, 44028, 44035, 44039, 44044, 44050, 44090, 44149, 44212, 44214–15, 44235, 44253–54, 44256, 44273, 44275, 44280, 44287, 44601, 44608, 44610–13, 44618, 44624, 44626–28, 44632–34, 44637–38, 44641, 44643, 44646–47, 44652, 44654, 44657, 44661–62, 44666, 44669–70, 44676, 44681, 44685, 44687–90, 44702–10, 44714, 44718, 44720–21, 44805, 44807, 44811, 44813, 44822, 44826–27, 44833, 44837–38, 44840, 44842–43, 44847–48, 44850–51, 44855, 44857, 44859, 44864–66, 44874–75, 44878, 44880–90, 44903, 44905–07

* * *

EIGHTH DISTRICT

WARREN DAVIDSON, Republican, of Troy, OH; born in Sidney, OH, March 1, 1970; education: B.S., American history, United States Military Academy, West Point, NY, 1995; M.B.A., University of Notre Dame, South Bend, Indiana, 2005; professional: managing director, West Troy, 2000–15; president, Global Source Manufacturing, 2002–15; founder, Factory Techs, 2008–15; managing director, RK Metals, 2014–15; managing director, Integral Manufacturing, 2015–16; religion: Christian; family: married, two children; committees: Financial Services; elected to the 114th Congress, by special election, on June 7, 2016, to fill the vacancy caused by the resignation of U.S. Representative John Andrew Boehner; sworn in on June 9, 2016; reelected to the 115th Congress on November 8, 2016.

Office Listings

https://davidson.house.gov

1004 Longworth House Office Building, Washington, DC 20515 .... (202) 225–6205
Chief of Staff.—Jason Yaworske.
Press Secretary.—Alexei Woltornist.
8857 Cincinnati-Dayton Road, Suite 102, West Chester, OH 45069 .... (513) 779–5400
12 South Plum Street, Troy, Ohio 45373 .... (937) 339–1524
76 East High Street, 3rd Floor, Springfield, OH 45502 .... (937) 322–1120

Counties: BUTLER, CLARK, DARKE, MERCER (part), MIAMI, AND PREBLE. Population (2010), 721,032.

ZIP Codes: 43010, 43044, 43153, 45003–04, 45011–15, 45018, 45042, 45044, 45050, 45053, 45055–56, 45061–64, 45067, 45069–71, 45241, 45246, 45303–04, 45308, 45310–12, 45317–26, 45328, 45330–32, 45337–39, 45341, 45344, 45346–49, 45361–62, 45368–69, 45371–74, 45378, 45380–83, 45387–88, 45390, 45501–06, 45822, 45826, 45828, 45846, 45860, 45862, 45866, 45869, 45882–83, 45894, 45898

* * *

NINTH DISTRICT

MARCY KAPTUR, Democrat, of Toledo, OH; born in Toledo, June 17, 1946; education: graduated, St. Ursula Academy, Toledo, 1964; B.A., University of Wisconsin, Madison, 1968; master of urban planning, University of Michigan, Ann Arbor, 1974; attended University of Manchester, England, 1974; professional: urban planner; Assistant Director for Urban Affairs, Domestic Policy Staff, White House, 1977–79; American Planning Association and American Institute of Certified Planners Fellow; member: National Center for Urban Ethnic Affairs Advisory Committee; University of Michigan Urban Planning Alumni Association; NAACP Urban League; Polish Museum; Polish American Historical Association; Lucas County Democratic Party Executive Committee; Democratic Women's Campaign Association; Little Flower Parish Church; religion: Roman Catholic; caucuses: co-chair, Congressional Great Lakes Caucus; co-chair, House Auto Caucus; co-chair, House Auto Parts Task Force; co-chair and co-founder, House Ukrainian Caucus; co-chair House Hungarian, Polish, and 4–H Caucuses; committees: Appropriations; elected on November 2, 1982, to the 98th Congress; reelected to each succeeding Congress.

Office Listings

http://www.kaptur.house.gov

2186 Rayburn House Office Building, Washington, DC 20515 .... (202) 225–4146

Office Listings—Continued

Chief of Staff.—Steve Katich.
Office Manager / Scheduler.—Courtney Hruska.
Legislative Director.—Jenny Perrino.
One Maritime Plaza, Suite 600, Toledo, OH 43604 .... (419) 259–7500
17021 Lorain Avenue, Cleveland, OH 44114 .... (216) 767–5933
200 West Erie Avenue, Room 300, Lorain, OH 44052 .... (440) 799 8499
FAX: (419) 225 9623

Counties: CUYAHOGA COUNTY (part). CITIES AND TOWNSHIPS: Bay Village, Berea, Brooklyn, Brooklyn Heights, Brook Park, Cleveland, Lakewood, Linndale, Parma, and Rocky River. ERIE COUNTY (part). CITIES AND TOWNSHIPS: Castalia, Huron, and Sandusky. LORAIN COUNTY (part). CITIES AND TOWNSHIPS: Amherst, Avon Lake, Elyria, Grafton, Lorain, North Eaton, Oberlin, Ridgeville, Rochester, Sheffield Lake, South Amherst, and Vermilion. LUCAS COUNTY (part). CITIES AND TOWNSHIPS: Curtice, Gypsum, Harbor View, Oregon, Reno Beach, Washington, Toledo. OTTAWA COUNTY. CITIES AND TOWNSHIPS: Bay Shore, Bono, Catawba Island, Danbury, Eagle Beach, Gem Beach, Graytown, Hessville, Isle St. George, Kelleys Island, Lacarne, Lakeside, Lindsey, Marblehead, Martin, Middle Bass, Oak Harbor, Port Clinton, Portage, Put-in-Bay, Rocky Ridge, Vickery, Whites Landing, and Williston. Population (2010), 721,032.

ZIP Codes: 43412, 43433–34, 43436, 43438–40, 43445–46, 43449, 43452, 43456, 43464, 43601–16, 43620, 43635, 43697, 43699, 44001, 44012, 44017, 44052–55, 44089, 44102, 44107, 44109, 44111, 44116, 44129–30, 44134–35, 44140, 44142, 44144, 44181, 44824, 44839, 44870–71

* * *

TENTH DISTRICT

MICHAEL R. TURNER, Republican, of Dayton, OH; born in Dayton, January 11, 1960; education: B.A., Ohio Northern University, 1982; J.D., Case Western Reserve University Law School, 1985; M.B.A., University of Dayton, 1992; professional: attorney; Ohio Bar Association; California Bar Association; Bar of the Supreme Court of the United States; public service: Mayor of Dayton, 1994–2002; wife: Majida; children: Jessica and Carolyn; committees: Armed Services; Permanent Select Committee on Intelligence; elected to the 108th Congress on November 5, 2002; reelected to each succeeding Congress.

Office Listings

http://www.turner.house.gov

2368 Rayburn House Office Building, Washington, DC 20515 .... (202) 225–6465
Chief of Staff.—Adam Howard. FAX: 225–6754
Legislative Director.—Jeffrey Wilson.
Scheduler.—Emily Ziegler.
120 West Third Street, Suite 305, Dayton, OH 45402 .... (937) 225–2843
District Director.—Frank DeBrosse.

Counties: MONTGOMERY, GREENE, AND FAYETTE (northern part). Population (2010), 721,032.

ZIP Codes: 43106, 43128, 43142–43, 43145, 43153, 43160, 45005, 45066, 45068–69, 45301, 45305, 45307, 45309, 45314–16, 45322, 45324, 45327, 45335, 45342, 45344–45, 45354, 45368, 45370–71, 45381, 45384–85, 45387, 45402–06, 45409–10, 45414–20, 45424, 45426, 45428–34, 45439–40, 45449, 45458–59

* * *

ELEVENTH DISTRICT

MARCIA L. FUDGE, Democrat, of Warrensville Heights, OH; born in Cleveland, OH, October 29, 1952; education: B.S., Ohio State University, 1975; J.D., Cleveland Marshall College of Law, 1983; professional: Director of Budget and Finance, Cuyahoga County Prosecutor's Office; chief administrator for Cuyahoga County Prosecutor; Mayor of Warrensville Heights, OH; committees: Agriculture; Education and the Workforce; elected to the 110th Congress, by special election, to fill the vacancy caused by the death of U.S. Representative Stephanie Tubbs Jones; elected to the 111th Congress on November 4, 2008; reelected to each succeeding Congress.

Office Listings

http://www.fudge.house.gov

2344 Rayburn House Office Building, Washington, DC 20515 .... (202) 225–7032

Office Listings—Continued

Chief of Staff.—Veleter Mazyck.
Senior Policy Advisor.—Clifton Williams.
Communications Director.—Lauren Williams.
Scheduler/Office Manager.—Lewis Myers.
4834 Richmond Road, Suite 150, Warrensville Heights, OH 44128 .... (216) 522–4900
District Director.—Jasmine Rowan.
Scheduler/Office Manager.—Linda Matthews.
1225 Lawton Street, Akron, OH 44320 .... (330) 835–4758
Outreach Coordinator.—Ginger Baylor.

Counties: CUYAHOGA COUNTY (part) AND SUMMIT COUNTY (part). CITIES: Akron, Bath Township, Beachwood, Bedford, Bedford Heights, Bratenahl, Broadview Heights, Brooklyn Heights, Cleveland, Cleveland Heights, Cuyahoga Heights, East Cleveland, Euclid, Fairlawn, Garfield Heights, Glenwillow, Highland Hills, Maple Heights, Newburg Heights, North Randall, Oakwood Village, Orange, Pepper Pike, Richfield Township, Richfield Village, Richmond Heights, Seven Hills, Shaker Heights, South Euclid, University Heights, Warrensville Heights, and Woodmere. Population (2010), 705,659.

ZIP Codes: 44022, 44101–15, 44117–25, 44127–28, 44131–33, 44137, 44139, 44141, 44143, 44146–47, 44256, 44264, 44286, 44301–08, 44310–14, 44319–21, 44333

* * *

TWELFTH DISTRICT

VACANT

Counties: DELAWARE, FRANKLIN (part), LICKING, MARION (part), MORROW, MUSKINGUM (part), AND RICHLAND (part). Population (2010), 728,420.

ZIP Codes: 43001–04, 43008, 43011, 43013, 43015–19, 43021, 43023, 43025–27, 43030–33, 43035, 43040, 43046, 43050, 43054–56, 43058, 43061–62, 43065–66, 43068–69, 43071, 43073–74, 43076, 43080–82, 43085–86, 43093, 43105, 43147, 43201–02, 43214, 43217–21, 43226, 43229–30, 43235–36, 43240, 43302, 43314–15, 43317, 43320–21, 43334, 43338, 43342, 43344, 43356, 43701–02, 43720–21, 43727, 43731–32, 43734–35, 43738–40, 43746, 43756, 43760, 43762, 43767, 43771, 43777, 43791, 43822, 43830, 44813, 44822, 44833, 44862, 44864, 44901–07

* * *

THIRTEENTH DISTRICT

TIM RYAN, Democrat, of Howland, OH; born in Niles, July 16, 1973; education: B.S., Bowling Green University, 1995; J.D., University of New Hampshire School of Law (formerly Franklin Pierce Law Center), 2000; professional: legislative aide, Washington, DC; married: Andrea Ryan; committees: Appropriations; elected to the 108th Congress on November 5, 2002; reelected to each succeeding Congress.

Office Listings

http://timryan.house.gov facebook: congressmantimryan twitter: @reptimryan

1126 Longworth House Office Building, Washington, DC 20515 .... (202) 225–5261
Chief of Staff.—Ron Grimes. FAX: 225–3719
Scheduler.—Erin Isenberg.
Legislative Director.—Anne Sokolov.
197 West Market Street, Warren, OH 44481 .... (330) 373–0074
241 Federal Plaza West, Youngstown, OH 44503 .... (330) 740–0193
1030 East Tallmadge Avenue, Akron, OH 44310 .... (330) 630–7311

Counties: MAHONING (part), PORTAGE (part), STARK, SUMMIT (part), AND TRUMBULL (part). Population (2010), 723,713.

ZIP Codes: 44141, 44201, 44203, 44221, 44223–24, 44231, 44236, 44240, 44241, 44243, 44255, 44260, 44262, 44264, 44266, 44272, 44278, 44285, 44288, 44301–08, 44310–14, 44319–20, 44333, 44401–06, 44410–12, 44418, 44420, 44425, 44429–30, 44436–38, 44440, 44444, 44446, 44449, 44451, 44470–71, 44473, 44481, 44483–85, 44491, 44502–07, 44509–12, 44514–15, 44601, 44640

* * *

FOURTEENTH DISTRICT

DAVID JOYCE, Republican, of Geauga, OH; born in Cleveland, OH, March 17, 1957; education: B.S., University of Dayton, Dayton, OH, 1979; J.D., University of Dayton, 1982; professional: prosecuting attorney, Geauga County, 1988–2012; married: Kelly Joyce; children: Trenton, Keighle, and Bridey; committees: Appropriations; elected to the 113th Congress on November 6, 2012; reelected to each succeeding Congress.

Office Listings

http://joyce.house.gov

1124 Longworth House Office Building, Washington, DC 20515 .... (202) 225–5731
Chief of Staff.—Dino DiSanto. FAX: 225–3307
Scheduler.—Anna Alburger.
Legislative Director.—Chris Cooper.
Communications Director.—Tim Lolli.
1 Victoria Place, Suite 320, Painesville, OH 44077 .... (440) 352–3939
FAX: 352–3622
10075 Ravenna Road, Twinsburg, OH 44087 .... (330) 425–9291
FAX: 425–7071

Counties: ASHTABULA, CUYAHOGA (part), GEAUGA, LAKE, PORTAGE (part), SUMMIT (part), AND TRUMBULL (part). Population (2010), 721,032.

ZIP Codes: 44003–04, 44010, 44021–24, 44026, 44030, 44032, 44040–41, 44045–48, 44056–57, 44060, 44062, 44064–65, 44067, 44072, 44076–77, 44080–82, 44084–87, 44092–95, 44099, 44122, 44124–25, 44131, 44139, 44141, 44143, 44146–47, 44202, 44221, 44223–24, 44231, 44234, 44236, 44240–41, 44255, 44262, 44264, 44266, 44278, 44313, 44402, 44404, 44410, 44417–18, 44428, 44439, 44450, 44473, 44481, 44491

* * *

FIFTEENTH DISTRICT

STEVE STIVERS, Republican, of Columbus, OH; born in Cincinnati, OH, March 24, 1965; education: B.A., Ohio State University, Columbus, OH, 1989; M.B.A., Ohio State University, 1996; M.A., United States Army War College; professional: military; colonel, Ohio Army National Guard, 1988–present; Ohio Company and Bank One; member of the Ohio State Senate, 2003–08; married: Karen Stivers; children: Sarah and Samuel; committees: Financial Services; elected to the 112th Congress on November 2, 2010; reelected to each succeeding Congress.

Office Listings

http://www.stivers.house.gov

1022 Longworth House Office Building, Washington, DC 20515 .... (202) 225–2015
Chief of Staff.—Courtney Whetstone. FAX: 225–3529
Scheduler.—Sara Donlon.
Legislative Director.—Nick Bush.
Communications Director.—Tim Alford.
3790 Municipal Way, Hilliard, OH 43026 .... (614) 771–4968
FAX: 771–3990
Fairfield County District Office, 104 East Main Street, Lancaster, OH 43130 .... (740) 654–2654
FAX: 654–2482
Clinton County District Office, 69 North South Street, Wilmington, OH 45177 .... (937) 283–7049
FAX: 283–7052

Counties: ATHENS (part), CLINTON, FAIRFIELD, FAYETTE (part), FRANKLIN (part), HOCKING, MADISON, MORGAN, PERRY, PICKAWAY, ROSS (part), AND VINTON. Population (2010), 721,031.

ZIP Codes: 43002, 43016–17, 43026, 43029, 43044, 43046, 43062, 43064, 43068, 43076, 43101–03, 43105, 43107, 43110–13, 43115–17, 43119, 43123, 43125–27, 43130, 43135–38, 43140, 43143–58, 43160, 43162, 43164, 43201, 43204, 43206–07, 43210, 43212, 43215, 43217, 43220–23, 43228, 43235, 43724, 43728, 43730–31, 43739, 43748, 43756, 43758, 43760–61, 43764, 43766, 43777, 43782–83, 43787, 45068, 45107, 45113, 45123, 45135, 45142, 45146, 45148, 45159, 45164, 45166, 45169, 45177, 45335, 45369, 45601, 45622, 45628, 45634, 45644, 45647, 45651, 45654, 45672, 45681, 45686, 45695, 45698, 45701, 45710–11, 45715–16, 45719, 45723, 45732, 45735, 45740, 45761, 45764, 45766, 45776, 45778, 45780, 45782

* * *

SIXTEENTH DISTRICT

JIM RENACCI, Republican, of Wadsworth, OH; born in Monongahela, PA, December 3, 1958; education: B.S., Indiana University of Pennsylvania, 1980; professional: certified public accountant (CPA); owner, nursing home facility; executive, professional arena football team; Wadsworth Board of Zoning Appeals, 1994–95; president, Wadsworth City Council, 1999–

2003; Mayor of Wadsworth, 2004–08; business management consultant; religion: Roman Catholic; married: Tina Renacci; 3 children; caucuses: Congressional Coal; Congressional CPA; Congressional Steel; General Aviation; Hydrogen and Fuel Cell; Northeast-Midwest Coalition; committees: Budget; Ways and Means; elected to the 112th Congress on November 2, 2010; re-elected to each succeeding Congress.

Office Listings

http://www.renacci.house.gov

328 Cannon House Office Building, Washington, DC 20515 .... (202) 225–3876
Chief of Staff.—Surya Gunasekara. FAX: 225–3059
Communications Director.—Kelsey Knight.
Director of Operations.—Michelle Runk.
Legislative Director.—Stephen Hostelley.
1 Park Center Drive, Suite 302, Wadsworth, OH 44281 .... (330) 334–0040
Constituent Service Director.—Heidi Matthews. FAX: 493–9265

Counties: CUYAHOGA (part), MEDINA (part), PORTAGE (part), STARK (part), SUMMIT (part), AND WAYNE. Population (2010), 724,108.

ZIP Codes: 44017, 44070, 44116, 44126, 44129–30, 44133–34, 44136, 44138, 44145, 44149, 44201, 44203, 44212, 44214–17, 44230, 44233, 44235, 44240, 44250–51, 44254, 44256, 44260, 44265–66, 44270, 44272–74, 44276, 44278, 44280–81, 44287, 44306, 44312, 44319–21, 44333, 44601, 44606, 44611, 44614, 44618, 44624, 44627, 44632, 44636, 44638, 44645–47, 44659, 44662, 44666–67, 44676–77, 44685, 44691, 44703, 44706, 44708–10, 44718, 44720–21, 44840

OKLAHOMA

(Population 2010, 3,751,351)

SENATORS

JAMES M. INHOFE, Republican, of Tulsa, OK; born in Des Moines, IA, November 17, 1934; education: graduated, Central High School, Tulsa, OK, 1953; B.A., University of Tulsa, OK, 1959; military service: served in the U.S. Army, private first class, 1957–58; professional: businessman; active pilot; president, Quaker Life Insurance Company; Oklahoma House of Representatives, 1967–69; Oklahoma State Senate, 1969–77; Mayor of Tulsa, OK, 1978–84; religion: member, First Presbyterian Church of Tulsa; married: Kay Kirkpatrick; children: Jim, Perry, Molly, and Katy; twelve grandchildren; committees: Armed Services; Commerce, Science, and Transportation; Environment and Public Works; Small Business and Entrepreneurship; elected to the 100th Congress on November 4, 1986; reelected to each succeeding Congress; elected to the U.S. Senate on November 8, 1994, finishing the unexpired term of Senator David Boren; reelected to each succeeding Senate term.

Office Listings

http://inhofe.senate.gov

205 Russell Senate Office Building, Washington, DC 20510 .... (202) 224–4721
FAX: 228–0380
Chief of Staff.—Luke Holland.
Legislative Director.—Andrew Forbes.
Communications Director.—Leacey Burke.
Scheduler.—Wendi Price.
1924 South Utica, Suite 530, Tulsa, OK 74104–6511 .... (918) 748–5111
1900 Northwest Expressway, Suite 1210, Oklahoma City, OK 73118 .... (405) 608–4381
302 North Independence, Suite 104, Enid, OK 73701 .... (580) 234–5105
215 East Choctaw, Suite 106, McAlester, OK 74501 .... (918) 426–0933

* * *

JAMES LANKFORD, Republican, of Oklahoma City, OK; born in Dallas, TX, March 4, 1968; education: B.S. Secondary Education, University of Texas, 1990; master of divinity, Southwestern Baptist Theological Seminary, 1994; professional: Baptist General Convention of Oklahoma, youth ministry specialist and director of the Falls Creek Youth Camp, 1995–2009; public service: U.S. House of Representatives, 2011–14; elected House Republican Policy Committee Chair, 2012–14; married: Cindy, 1992; children: Hannah and Jordan; religion: Christian; committees: Appropriations; Homeland Security and Governmental Affairs; Indian Affairs; Select Committee on Intelligence; elected to the U.S. Senate on November 4, 2014 to complete the unexpired term of U.S. Senator Tom Coburn; reelected to the U.S. Senate on November 8, 2016.

Office Listings

http://lankford.senate.gov https://www.facebook.com/senatorlankford
https://www.flickr.com/photos/senatorlankford https://instagram.com/senatorlankford
https://twitter.com/SenatorLankford

316 Hart Senate Office Building, Washington, DC 20510 .... (202) 225–5754
Chief of Staff.—Michelle Altman.
Legislative Director.—Sarah Seitz.
Scheduler.—Jaclyn O'Neil.
Communications Director.—Darrell ''DJ'' Jordan.
State Director.—Mona Taylor.
1015 North Broadway Avenue, Suite 310, Oklahoma City, OK 73102 .... (405) 231–4941
5810 East Skelly Drive (Remington Tower), Tulsa, OK 74135 .... (918) 581–7651

REPRESENTATIVES

FIRST DISTRICT

VACANT

Counties: CREEK (part), ROGERS (part), TULSA, WAGONER, AND WASHINGTON. Population (2010), 750,270.

ZIP Codes: 74003–06, 74008, 74011–12, 74014–15, 74021–22, 74029, 74033, 74036–37, 74041, 74047, 74050–51, 74055, 74061, 74063, 74066, 74070, 74073, 74080, 74082–83, 74103–08, 74110, 74112, 74114–17, 74119–20, 74126–37, 74145–46, 74337, 74352, 74403, 74429, 74434, 74436, 74446, 74454, 74458, 74467, 74477

* * *

SECOND DISTRICT

MARKWAYNE MULLIN, Republican, of Westville, OK; born in Tulsa, OK, July 26, 1977; education: attended Missouri Valley College, Marshall, MO, 1996; A.A.S., Oklahoma State University Institute of Technology, Okmulgee, OK, 2010; professional: business owner; plumber; rancher; married on June 14, 1997; children: father of five; committees: Energy and Commerce; elected to the 113th Congress on November 6, 2012; reelected to each succeeding Congress.

Office Listings

http://mullin.house.gov

1113 Longworth House Office Building, Washington, DC 20515 .... (202) 225–2701
Chief of Staff.—Mike Stopp.
Deputy Chief of Staff.—Kayla Priehs.
Legislative Director.—Jonathan Gray.
Communications Director.—Amy Lawrence.
Executive Assistant / Scheduler.—Madison Thames.
3109 Azalea Park Drive, Muskogee, OK 74401 .... (918) 687–2533
1 East Choctaw, Suite 175, McAlester, OK 74501 .... (918) 423–5951

Counties: ADAIR, ATOKA, BRYAN, CHEROKEE, CHOCTAW, COAL, CRAIG, DELAWARE, HASKELL, HUGHES, JOHNSTON, LATIMER, LEFLORE, MARSHALL, MAYES, MCCURTAIN, MCINTOSH, MUSKOGEE, NOWATA, OKFUSKEE, OKMULGEE, OTTAWA, PITTSBURGH, PUSHMATAHA, ROGERS, AND SEQUOYAH. Population (2010), 750,270.

ZIP Codes: 73432, 73439–40, 73446–47, 73449–50, 73455, 73460–61, 74016–19, 74027, 74042, 74048, 74053, 74072, 74301, 74330–33, 74338–40, 74342–44, 74346–47, 74349–50, 74354, 74358–70, 74401, 74421–23, 74425–28, 74430–32, 74435, 74437–38, 74441–42, 74445, 74447, 74450–52, 74455–57, 74459–60, 74462–64, 74468–72, 74501, 74521–23, 74525, 74528, 74530–31, 74533–36, 74538, 74540, 74543, 74546–47, 74549, 74552–53, 74556, 74560–63, 74565, 74569–72, 74576, 74578, 74701, 74720, 74723, 74726–30, 74733, 74735–36, 74740–41, 74743, 74745, 74747–48, 74750, 74756, 74759, 74764, 74766, 74829, 74833, 74839, 74845, 74848, 74850, 74856, 74859–60, 74880, 74883, 74885, 74901–02, 74930, 74932, 74935–37, 74940–42, 74944–46, 74948, 74951, 74953–56, 74959–60, 74962, 74964–66

* * *

THIRD DISTRICT

FRANK D. LUCAS, Republican, of Cheyenne, OK; born in Cheyenne, January 6, 1960; education: B.S., agricultural economics, Oklahoma State University, 1982; professional: rancher and farmer; served in Oklahoma State House of Representatives, 1989–94; secretary, Oklahoma House Republican Caucus, 1991–94; member: Oklahoma Farm Bureau, Oklahoma Cattlemen's Association, and Oklahoma Shorthorn Association; married: Lynda Bradshaw Lucas; children: Jessica, Ashlea, and Grant; committees: Agriculture; Financial Services; Science, Space, and Technology; elected to the 103rd Congress, by special election, in May 1994; reelected to each succeeding Congress.

Office Listings

http://www.lucas.house.gov facebook: https://www.facebook.com/RepFrankLucas
twitter: https://twitter.com/repfranklucas

2405 Rayburn House Office Building, Washington, DC 20515 .... (202) 225–5565
FAX: 225–8698
Senior Advisor.—Josh Mathis.
Communications Director.—Andrew Witmer.
Scheduler / Office Manager.—Meg Wagner.
Legislative Assistants: Conner Carroll, Christian Dibblee, Alison Slagell.
10952 Northwest Expressway, Suite B, Yukon, OK 73099 .... (405) 373–1958
Chief of Staff.—Stacey Glasscock.

Counties: ALFALFA, BEAVER, BECKHAM, BLAINE, CADDO, CANADIAN (part), CIMARRON, CREEK (part), CUSTER, DEWEY, ELLIS, GARFIELD, GRANT, GREER, HARMON, HARPER, JACKSON, KAY, KINGFISHER, KIOWA, LINCOLN, LOGAN, MAJOR, NOBLE, OSAGE, PAWNEE, PAYNE, ROGER MILLS, TEXAS, WASHITA, WOODS, AND WOODWARD. CITIES: Altus, Clinton, El Reno, Elk City, Enid, Guthrie, Guymon, Oklahoma City, Perry, Ponce City, Sapulpa, Stillwater, Tulsa, Weatherford, Woodward, and Yukon. Population (2010), 745,941.

ZIP Codes: 73001, 73005–07, 73009, 73014–17, 73021–22, 73024, 73027–29, 73033–34, 73036, 73038, 73040–45, 73047–48, 73050, 73053–54, 73056, 73058–59, 73061–64, 73073, 73077–79, 73085, 73090, 73096–97, 73099, 73127, 73521–

23, 73526, 73532, 73537, 73539, 73544, 73547, 73549–50, 73554, 73556, 73559–60, 73564, 73566, 73571, 73601, 73620, 73622, 73624–28, 73632, 73638–39, 73641–42, 73644–48, 73650–51, 73654–55, 73658–64, 73666–69, 73673, 73701–03, 73705–06, 73716–20, 73722, 73724, 73726–31, 73733–39, 73741–44, 73746–47, 73749–50, 73753–64, 73766, 73768, 73770–73, 73801–02, 73832, 73834–35, 73838, 73840–44, 73848, 73851–53, 73855, 73857–60, 73901, 73931–33, 73937–39, 73942, 73944–47, 73949–51, 74001–03, 74010, 74020, 74023, 74026, 74028, 74030, 74032, 74034–35, 74038–39, 74044–47, 74051–52, 74054, 74056, 74058–60, 74062–63, 74066–68, 74070–71, 74073–79, 74081, 74084–85, 74106, 74126–27, 74131–32, 74601–02, 74604, 74630–33, 74636–37, 74640–41, 74643–44, 74646–47, 74650–53, 74824, 74832, 74834, 74851, 74855, 74864, 74869, 74875, 74881

* * *

FOURTH DISTRICT

TOM COLE, Republican, of Moore, OK; born in Shreveport, LA, April 28, 1949; education: B.A., Grinnell College, 1971; M.A., Yale University, 1974; Ph.D., University of Oklahoma, 1984; Watson Fellow, 1971–72; Fulbright Fellow, 1977–78; professional: former college professor of history and politics; president, Cole Hargrave Snodgrass & Associates (political consulting firm); public service: Oklahoma State Senate, 1988–91; Oklahoma Secretary of State, 1995–99; has served as chairman, and executive director, of the Oklahoma Republican Party; former chairman of the National Republican Congressional Committee; and chief of staff of the Republican National Committee; family: married to Ellen; one child: Mason; religion: United Methodist; committees: Appropriations; Budget; Rules; elected to the 108th Congress on November 5, 2002; reelected to each succeeding Congress.

Office Listings

http://www.cole.house.gov facebook: @TomColeOK04 twitter: @TomColeOK04

2467 Rayburn House Office Building, Washington, DC 20515 .... (202) 225–6165
Chief of Staff.—Vacant. FAX: 225–3512
Deputy Chief of Staff / Legislative Director.—Maria Bowie.
Communications Director.—Teresa Davis.
Scheduler.—Sabrina Parker.
2424 Springer Drive, Suite 201, Norman, OK 73069 .... (405) 329–6500
711 Southwest, D Avenue, Suite 201, Lawton, OK 73501 .... (580) 357–2131
Sugg Clinic Office Building, 100 East 13th Street, Suite 213, Ada, OK 74820 .... (580) 436–5375

Counties: CANADIAN (part), CARTER, CLEVELAND, COMANCHE, COTTON, GARVIN, GRADY, JEFFERSON, LOVE, MCCLAIN, MURRAY, OKLAHOMA (part), PONTOTOC, STEPHENS, AND TILLMAN. Population (2010), 750,270.

ZIP Codes: 73002, 73004, 73006, 73010–11, 73017–20, 73026, 73030, 73032, 73051–52, 73055, 73057, 73059, 73064–69, 73071–72, 73074–75, 73079–80, 73082, 73086, 73089, 73092–93, 73095, 73098, 73110, 73130, 73135, 73139, 73141, 73145, 73149–50, 73159–60, 73165, 73169–70, 73173, 73401, 73425, 73430, 73433–34, 73437–38, 73441–44, 73448, 73453, 73456, 73458–59, 73463, 73481, 73487, 73491, 73501, 73503, 73505, 73507, 73520, 73527–31, 73533, 73538, 73540–43, 73546, 73548, 73551–53, 73555, 73557, 73559, 73562, 73564–70, 73572–73, 74572, 74820, 74825, 74831, 74842–44, 74852, 74856–57, 74865, 74871–72, 74878

* * *

FIFTH DISTRICT

STEVE RUSSELL, Republican, of Choctaw, OK; born in Oklahoma City, OK; May 25, 1963; education: graduated from Del City High School, 1981; B.A., in public speaking, Ouachita Baptist University; M.M.A.S., Fort Leavenworth, KS, 1998; professional: owner and founder of Two Rivers Arms; U.S. Army, 1985–2006; author; member of the Oklahoma State Senate, 2008–12; awards: Meritorious Service Medal, 6 x awards; Joint Forces Commendation Medal; Army Commendation Medal, 3 x awards; Army Achievement Medal, 4 x awards; National Defense Service Medal, 2 x awards; National Defense Service Medal, 2 x awards; Armed Forces Expeditionary Medal; Kosovo Campaign Medal; Afghanistan Campaign Medal; Iraq Campaign Medal; Global War on Terrorism Expeditionary Medal; Global War on Terrorism Service Medal; Outstanding Volunteer Service Medal; NATO Medal; member of the Military Order of the Loyal Legion of the United States; Ranger Tab; Combat Infantryman Badge; U.S. Army and Korean Parachutists Badge; married: Cindy; member of the House Steering Committee; committees: Armed Services; Oversight and Government Reform; elected to the 114th Congress on November 4, 2014; reelected to the 115th Congress on November 8, 2016.

Office Listings

http://www.russell.house.gov https://facebook.com/reprussell https://twitter.com/RepRussell

128 Cannon House Office Building, Washington, DC 20515 .... (202) 225–2132

Office Listings—Continued

Chief of Staff.—Steve Moffitt. FAX: 226–1463
Deputy Chief of Staff / Legislative Director.—Alex Hutkin.
Scheduler.—Hannah Dirks.
Communications Director.—Gabriel Bastomski.

4600 Southeast 29th, Suite 400, Del City, OK 73115 .... (405) 602–3074

Counties: OKLAHOMA (part), POTTAWATOMIE, AND SEMINOLE. CITIES: Arcadia, Asher, Aydelotte, Bethany, Bethel Acres, Bowlegs, Brooksville, Choctaw, Cromwell, Del City, Earlsboro, Edmond, Forest Park, Harrah, Johnson, Jones, Konawa, Lake Aluma, Lima, Luther, Macomb, Maud, McLoud, Midwest City, Newalla, Nichols Hills, Nicoma Park, Oklahoma City, Pink, Prague, Sasakwa, Seminole, Shawnee, Smith Village, Spencer, St. Louis, Tecumesh, The Village, Tribbey, Valley Brook, Wanette, Warr Acres, Wewoka, and Woodlawn Park. Population (2010), 750,271.

ZIP Codes: 73003, 73007–08, 73013, 73020, 73034, 73045, 73049, 73054, 73066, 73083–84, 73101–32, 73134–37, 73139, 73141–49, 73151–52, 73154–57, 73159–60, 73162, 73164, 73169, 73172–73, 73178–79, 73184–85, 73190, 73194–96, 73198, 74587, 74801–02, 74804, 74818, 74826, 74830, 74837, 74840, 74849, 74851–52, 74854, 74857, 74866–68, 74873, 74878, 74884

OREGON

(Population 2010, 3,831,074)

SENATORS

RON WYDEN, Democrat, of Portland, OR; born in Wichita, KS, May 3, 1949; education: graduated from Palo Alto High School, 1967; B.A. in political science, with distinction, Stanford University, 1971; J.D., University of Oregon Law School, 1974; professional: attorney; member, American Bar Association; former director, Oregon Legal Services for the Elderly; former public member, Oregon State Board of Examiners of Nursing Home Administrators; cofounder and codirector, Oregon Gray Panthers, 1974–80; married: Nancy Bass Wyden; children: Adam David, Lilly Anne, Ava Rose, William Peter, and Scarlett Willa; committees: ranking member, Finance; Budget; Energy and Natural Resources; Joint Committee on Taxation; Select Committee on Intelligence; elected to the 97th Congress, November 4, 1980; reelected to each succeeding Congress; elected to the U.S. Senate on February 6, 1996, to fill the unexpired term of Senator Bob Packwood; reelected to each succeeding Senate term.

Office Listings

http://wyden.senate.gov https://twitter.com/ronwyden

221 Dirksen Senate Office Building, Washington, DC 20510 .... (202) 224–5244
Chief of Staff.—Jeff Michels. FAX: 228–2717
Legislative Director.—Isaiah Akin.
Director of Scheduling.—Montana Judd.
911 Northeast 11th Avenue, Suite 630, Portland, OR 97232 .... (503) 326–7525
405 East Eighth Avenue, Suite 2020, Eugene, OR 97401 .... (541) 431–0229
The Federal Courthouse, 310 West Sixth Street, Room 118, Medford, OR 97501 .... (541) 858–5122
The Jamison Building, 131 Northwest Hawthorne Avenue, Suite 107, Bend, OR 97701 .... (541) 330–9142
SAC Annex Building, 105 Fir Street, Suite 201, LaGrande, OR 97850 .... (541) 962–7691
707 Thirteenth Street, SE., Suite 285, Salem, OR 97310 .... (503) 589–4555

* * *

JEFF MERKLEY, Democrat, of Portland, OR; born in Myrtle Creek, OR; October 24, 1956; education: graduated from David Douglas High School; B.A., international relations, Stanford University, 1979; M.P.P., Woodrow Wilson School, Princeton University, 1982; professional: Presidential Fellow at the Office of the Secretary of Defense, 1982–85; Policy Analyst at the Congressional Budget Office, 1985–89; Executive Director of Portland Habitat for Humanity, 1991–94; Director of Housing Development at Human Solutions, 1995–96; President of World Affairs Council of Oregon, 1996–2003; elected to Oregon House of Representatives, 1999; Democratic Leader of the Oregon House of Representatives, 2003; elected Speaker of the Oregon House of Representatives, 2007; married: Mary Sorteberg; children: Brynne and Jonathan; committees: Appropriations; Budget; Environment and Public Works; Foreign Relations; elected to the U.S. Senate on November 4, 2008; reelected to the U.S. Senate on November 4, 2014.

Office Listings

http://merkley.senate.gov https://facebook.com/jeffmerkley twitter: @SenJeffMerkley

313 Hart Senate Office Building, Washington, DC 20510 .... (202) 224–3753
Chief of Staff.—Michael Zamore. FAX: 228–3997
Legislative Director.—Adrian Deveny.
Deputy Chief of Staff of Operations.—Jennifer Piorkowski.
Communications Director.—Ray Zaccaro.
1400 One World Trade Center, 121 Southwest Salmon, Portland, OR 97204 .... (503) 326–3386
Jamison Building, 131 Northwest Hawthorne, Suite 208, Bend, OR 97701 .... (541) 318–1298
Wayne Morse Federal Courthouse, 405 East 8th, Suite 2010, Eugene, OR 97401 .... (541) 465–6750
10 South Bartlett Street, Suite 201, Medford, OR 97501 .... (541) 608–9102
495 State Street, Suite 330, Salem, OR 97301 .... (503) 362–8102
310 Southeast Second Street, Suite 105, Pendleton, OR 97801 .... (541) 278–1129

REPRESENTATIVES

FIRST DISTRICT

SUZANNE MARIE BONAMICI, Democrat, of Beaverton, OR; born in Michigan, October 14, 1954; education: J.D., University of Oregon, Eugene, OR, 1983; B.A., journalism, University of Oregon, Eugene, 1980; A.A., Lane Community College, Eugene, 1978; professional: lawyer, Federal Trade Commission, Washington, DC; lawyer, private practice; staff, Oregon State House, 2001–06; served in the Oregon State House from 2007–08; served in the Oregon State Senate from 2008–11; married: husband, Michael Simon; children: son, Andrew Simon; daughter, Sara Simon; caucuses: co-founder and co-chair of the STEAM Caucus; co-chair of the Oceans Caucus; committees: vice ranking member, Education and the Workforce; Science, Space, and Technology; elected to the 112th Congress, by special election, on January 31, 2012; reelected to each succeeding Congress.

Office Listings

http://www.bonamici.house.gov facebook: https://facebook.com/CongresswomanBonamici
twitter: https://twitter.com/RepBonamici instagram: https://www.instagram.com/repbonamici

439 Cannon House Office Building, Washington, DC 20515 .... (202) 225–0855
Chief of Staff.—Rachael Bornstein. FAX: 225–9497
Legislative Director.—Allison Smith.
Scheduler.—James Puerini.
Press Secretary.—Maggie Rousseau.
12725 SW. Millikan Way, Suite 220, Beaverton, OR 97005 .... (503) 469–6010
District Director.—Sarah Baessler. FAX: 469–6018
District Scheduler.—Barbara Allen.

Counties: CLATSOP, COLUMBIA, MULTNOMAH (part), WASHINGTON, AND YAMHILL. Population (2010), 766,216.

ZIP Codes: 97005–08, 97016, 97018, 97048, 97051, 97053–54, 97056, 97064, 97103, 97106, 97109–11, 97113–17, 97119, 97121, 97123–25, 97127–28, 97133, 97138, 97144–46, 97148, 97208, 97223–24, 97229, 97231

* * *

SECOND DISTRICT

GREG WALDEN, Republican, of Hood River, OR; born in The Dalles, OR, January 10, 1957; education: B.S., journalism, University of Oregon, 1981; member: Associated Oregon Industries; Oregon Health Sciences Foundation; Hood River Rotary Club; Hood River Elk's Club; National Federation of Independent Business; Hood River Chamber of Commerce; Hood River Memorial Hospital; Columbia Bancorp; Oregon State House of Representatives, 1989–95, and Majority Leader, 1991–93; Assistant Majority Leader, Oregon State Senate, 1995–97; awards: Oregon Jaycees Outstanding Young Oregonian, 1991; National Republican Legislators Association Legislator of the Year, 1993; married: Mylene Walden; one child: Anthony David Walden; committees: chair, Energy and Commerce; elected to the 106th Congress on November 3, 1998; reelected to each succeeding Congress.

Office Listings

http://www.walden.house.gov

2185 Rayburn House Office Building, Washington, DC 20515 .... (202) 225–6730
Chief of Staff.—Lorissa Bounds. FAX: 225–5774
Scheduler.—Jenny Forrest.
Communications Director.—Justin Discigil.
14 North Central Avenue, Suite 112, Medford, OR 97504 .... (541) 776–4646
1211 Washington Avenue, LaGrande, OR 97850 .... (541) 624–2400
FAX: 624–2402
1051 Northwest Bond Street, Suite 400, Bend, OR 97701 .... (541) 389–4408
FAX: 389–4452

Counties: BAKER, CROOK, DESCHUTES, GILLIAM, GRANT, HARNEY, HOOD RIVER, JACKSON, JEFFERSON, JOSEPHINE (part), KLAMATH, LAKE, MALHEUR, MORROW, SHERMAN, UMATILLA, UNION, WALLOWA, WASCO, AND WHEELER. Population (2010), 766,215.

ZIP Codes: 89421, 97001, 97014, 97021, 97029, 97031, 97033, 97037, 97039–41, 97050, 97057–58, 97063, 97065, 97497, 97501–04, 97520, 97522, 97524–27, 97530, 97535–37, 97539–41, 97601, 97603–04, 97620–27, 97630, 97632–41, 97701–02, 97707, 97710–12, 97720–22, 97730–39, 97741, 97750–56, 97758–61, 97801, 97810, 97812–14, 97817–20, 97823–28, 97830, 97833–46, 97848, 97850, 97856–57, 97859, 97862, 97864–65, 97867–70, 97873–77, 97880, 97882–86, 97901, 97903–11, 97913–14, 97918, 97920, 99362

* * *

THIRD DISTRICT

EARL BLUMENAUER, Democrat, of Portland, OR; born in Portland, August 16, 1948; education: graduated from Centennial High School; B.A., Lewis and Clark College; J.D., Northwestern School of Law; professional: assistant to the president, Portland State University; served in Oregon State Legislature, 1973–78; chaired Revenue and School Finance Committee; Multnomah County Commissioner, 1978–85; Portland City Commissioner, 1986–96; served on Governor's Commission on Higher Education; National League of Cities Transportation Committee; National Civic League Board of Directors; Portland Community College; married: Margaret Kirkpatrick; children: Jon and Anne; committees: Ways and Means; elected to the U.S. House of Representatives, by special election, on May 21, 1996, to fill the vacancy caused by Representative Ron Wyden's election to the U.S. Senate; reelected to each succeeding Congress.

Office Listings

http://blumenauer.house.gov

1111 Longworth House Office Building, Washington, DC 20515 .... (202) 225–4811
Chief of Staff.—Willie Smith. FAX: 225–8941
Deputy Chief of Staff.—David Skillman.
Scheduler.—Lena Spilman.
Communications Director.—Nicole L'Esperance.
Legislative Director.—Laura Thrift.
911 Northeast 11th Avenue, Suite 200, Portland, OR 97232 .... (503) 231–2300
District Director.—Willie Smith.

Counties: CLACKAMUS (part) and MULTNOMAH (part). Population (2010), 766,215.

ZIP Codes: 97004, 97009, 97011, 97014–15, 97017, 97019, 97022–24, 97028, 97030, 97035, 97045, 97049, 97055, 97060, 97067, 97080, 97124, 97133, 97202–03, 97206, 97210–18, 97220, 97222, 97227, 97229–33, 97236, 97238, 97242, 97256, 97266–67, 97269, 97282–83, 97286, 97290, 97292–94, 97299

* * *

FOURTH DISTRICT

PETER A. DEFAZIO, Democrat, of Springfield, OR; born in Needham, MA, May 27, 1947; education: B.A., Tufts University, 1969; M.S., University of Oregon, 1977; professional: aide to Representative Jim Weaver, 1977–82; commissioner, Lane County, 1983–86; married: Myrnie Daut; committees: ranking member, Transportation and Infrastructure; elected to the 100th Congress, November 4, 1986; reelected to each succeeding Congress.

Office Listings

http://www.defazio.house.gov

2134 Rayburn House Office Building, Washington, DC 20515 .... (202) 225–6416
Chief of Staff.—Kristie Greco.
Legislative Director.—Kris Pratt.
Scheduler.—Matt Leasure.
405 East Eighth Avenue, Suite 2030, Eugene, OR 97401 .... (541) 465–6732
District Director.—Dan Whelan.
125 Central Avenue, Room 350, Coos Bay, OR 97420 .... (541) 269–2609
612 Southeast Jackson Street, Room 9, Roseburg, OR 97470 .... (541) 440–3523

Counties: BENTON (part), COOS, CURRY, DOUGLAS, JOSEPHINE (part), LANE, AND LINN. CITIES: Eugene, Roseburg, and Coos Bay. Population (2010), 766,214.

ZIP Codes: 97321–22, 97324, 97326–27, 97329–31, 97333, 97345–46, 97348, 97350, 97352, 97355, 97358, 97360–61, 97370, 97374, 97377, 97383, 97386, 97389–90, 97401–06, 97408, 97410–17, 97419–20, 97423–24, 97426, 97429–31, 97434–39, 97446–59, 97461–63, 97465–67, 97469–71, 97476–81, 97484, 97486–90, 97492–99, 97523, 97526–27, 97531–32, 97534, 97538, 97543–44, 97731, 97759

* * *

FIFTH DISTRICT

KURT SCHRADER, Democrat, of Canby, OR; born in Bridgeport, CT, October 19, 1951; education; B.A., Cornell University, 1973; D.V.M., University of Illinois, 1977; professional:

small business owner; veterinarian; farmer; past member: Oregon State Senate; Oregon House of Representatives; Canby Planning Commission; religion: Episcopalian; spouse: Susan Mora; children: Clare, Maren, Steven, Travis, R.J., Michael, Marie, and Renee; committees: Energy and Commerce; elected to the 111th Congress on November 4, 2008; reelected to each succeeding Congress.

Office Listings

http://schrader.house.gov www.facebook.com/repschrader twitter: @repschrader

2431 Rayburn House Office Building, Washington, DC 20515 .... (202) 225–5711
Chief of Staff.—Paul Gage. FAX: 225–5699
Deputy Chief of Staff.—Chris Huckleberry.
Executive Assistant/Scheduler.—Whitlee Preim-Siddon.
530 Center Street, NE., Suite 415, Salem, OR 97301 .... (503) 588–9100
621 High Street, Oregon City, OR 97045 .... (503) 557–1324
District Director.—Suzanne Kunse.

Counties: BENTON (part), CLACKAMAS (part), LINCOLN, MARION, MULTNOMAH (part), POLK, AND TILLAMOOK. CITIES: Lincoln City, Lake Oswego, Oregon City, Salem, and Tillamook. Population (2010), 766,214.

ZIP Codes: 97002, 97013, 97015, 97017, 97020, 97023, 97026–27, 97032, 97034–36, 97038, 97042, 97045, 97062, 97068, 97070–71, 97086, 97101, 97107–08, 97112, 97118, 97122, 97130–32, 97135–37, 97140–41, 97143, 97147, 97149, 97201–02, 97206, 97219, 97222, 97236, 97239, 97266–69, 97301–12, 97314, 97317, 97321, 97324–26, 97338, 97341–44, 97346–47, 97350–52, 97357–58, 97360–62, 97364–71, 97373, 97375–76, 97378, 97380–81, 97383–85, 97388, 97390–92, 97394, 97396, 97498

PENNSYLVANIA

(Population 2010, 12,702,379)

SENATORS

ROBERT P. CASEY, JR., Democrat, of Scranton, PA; born in Scranton, April 13, 1960; education: A.B., English, College of the Holy Cross, 1982; J.D., Catholic University of America, 1988; professional: lawyer; Pennsylvania State Auditor General, 1997–2005; Pennsylvania State Treasurer, 2005–07; married: Terese; four daughters: Elyse, Caroline, Julia, and Marena; committees: Agriculture, Nutrition, and Forestry; Finance; Health, Education, Labor, and Pensions; Special Committee on Aging; elected to the U.S. Senate on November 7, 2006; reelected to the U.S. Senate on November 6, 2012.

Office Listings

http://casey.senate.gov http://www.facebook.com/senatorbobcasey
http://twitter.com/senbobcasey http://youtube.com/senatorbobcasey

393 Russell Senate Office Building, Washington, DC 20510 .... (202) 224–6324
Chief of Staff.—Kristen Gentile. (866) 802–2833
Legislative Director.—Derek Miller. FAX: 228–0604
Communications Director.—John Rizzo.
22 South Third Street, Suite 6A, Harrisburg, PA 17101 .... (717) 231–7540
(866) 461–9159
FAX: 231–7542
2000 Market Street, Suite 1870, Philadelphia, PA 19103 .... (215) 405–9660
FAX: 405–9669
Grant Building, 310 Grant Street, Suite 2415, Pittsburgh, PA 15219 .... (412) 803–7370
FAX: 803–7379
409 Lackawanna Avenue, Suite 301, Scranton, PA 18503 .... (570) 941–0930
FAX: 941–0937
817 East Bishop Street, Suite C, Bellefonte, PA 16823 .... (814) 357–0314
FAX: 375–0318
17 South Park Row, Suite B–150, Erie, PA 16501 .... (814) 874–5080
FAX: 874–5084
840 Hamilton Street, Suite 301, Allentown, PA 18101 .... (610) 782–9470
FAX: 782–9474

* * *

PAT TOOMEY, Republican, of Zionsville, PA; born in East Providence, RI, November 17, 1961; education: graduated as valedictorian from La Salle Academy in 1980; B.A., political science, *cum laude*, Harvard University, Cambridge, MA, 1984; professional: worked for Chemical Bank and Morgan Grenfell in New York City; has deep experience in the financial services sector, culminating with building a community bank from the ground up; founded several restaurants in Allentown, PA, with his two brothers, Steve and Michael Toomey, 1990–97; member of the Allentown Government Study Commission, 1994; elected to the U.S. House of Representatives in 1998, winning two reelections, 2000–02; president, Club for Growth, 2005; co-chairman of the Board of Directors of Team Capital Bank, 2005–09; married: Kris Duncan, 1997; children: Bridget, Patrick, and Duncan; committees: Banking, Housing, and Urban Affairs; Budget; Finance; elected to the U.S. Senate on November 2, 2010; reelected to the U.S. Senate on November 8, 2016.

Office Listings

http://toomey.senate.gov https://www.facebook.com/senatortoomey
https://twitter.com/SenToomey https://www.youtube.com/user/sentoomey

248 Russell Senate Office Building, Washington, DC 20510 .... (202) 224–4254
Chief of Staff.—Daniel Brandt. FAX: 228–0284
Legislative Director.—Brad Grantz.
Director of Operations.—Laurel Edmondson.
Communications Director.—Kasia Mulligan.
1150 South Cedar Crest Boulevard, Suite 101, Allentown, PA 18103 .... (610) 434–1444
(855) 552–1831
FAX: 228–2727
Federal Building, 17 South Park Row, Suite B–120, Erie, PA 16501 .... (814) 453–3010
FAX: 455–9925
Federal Building, 228 Walnut Street, Room 1104, Harrisburg, PA 17101 .... (717) 782–3951
FAX: 782–4920
Richland Square III, Suite 302, 1397 Eisenhower Boulevard, Johnstown, PA 15904 .... (814) 266–5970

Office Listings—Continued

	FAX: 266–5973
U.S. Custom House, 200 Chestnut Street, Suite 600, Philadelphia, PA 19106	(215) 241–1090
	FAX: 241–1095
310 Grant Street, Suite 1440, Pittsburgh, PA 15219	(412) 803–3501
	FAX: 803–3504
7 North Wilkes-Barre Boulevard, Suite 406, Wilkes-Barre, PA 18702	(570) 820–4088
	FAX: 820–6442

REPRESENTATIVES

FIRST DISTRICT

ROBERT A. BRADY, Democrat, of Philadelphia, PA; born in Philadelphia, April 7, 1945; education: graduated from St. Thomas More High School; professional: carpenter; union official; assistant Sergeant-at-Arms, Philadelphia City Council, 1975–83; Deputy Mayor for Labor, W. Wilson Goode Administration; consultant to Pennsylvania State Senate; Pennsylvania Turnpike Commissioner; board of directors, Philadelphia Redevelopment Authority; Democratic Party executive; ward leader; chairman, Philadelphia Democratic Party; member of Pennsylvania Democratic State Committee, and Democratic National Committee; religion: Catholic; married: Debra Brady; children: Robert and Kimberly; committees: ranking member, House Administration; Armed Services; Joint Committee on the Library; Joint Committee on Printing; elected to the 105th Congress on May 21, 1998, to fill the unexpired term of Representative Tom Foglietta; reelected to each succeeding Congress.

Office Listings

http://brady.house.gov

2004 Rayburn House Office Building, Washington, DC 20515	(202) 225–4731
Chief of Staff.—Stan White.	FAX: 225–0088
Appointments.—Zach Rosen.	
Press Secretary.—Karen Warrington.	
1909 South Broad Street, Philadelphia, PA 19148	(215) 389–4627
1350 Edgemont Avenue, Suite 2575, Chester, PA 19103	(610) 874–7094
2637 East Clearfield Street, Philadelphia, PA 19134	(267) 519–2252
2630 Memphis Street, Philadelphia, PA 19121	(215) 426–4616

Counties: PHILADELPHIA (part), DELAWARE (part). CITIES AND TOWNSHIPS: Chester City, Chester Township, Collingdale Borough, Colwyn Borough, Darby Township, East Lansdowne Borough, Eddystone Borough, Folcroft Borough, Glenolden Borough, Lansdowne Borough, Millbourne Borough, Nether Providence Township, Philadelphia City, Ridley Township, Rose Valley Borough, Sharon Hill Borough, Swarthmore Borough, Tinicum Township, Upland Borough, Upper Darby Township, and Yeadon Borough. Population (2010), 705,688.

ZIP Codes: 19013–16, 19018, 19020, 19022–23, 19026, 19029, 19032, 19036, 19050, 19063–64, 19066, 19074, 19078–79, 19081–82, 19086, 19094, 19096, 19102, 19105–09, 19112–14, 19121–25, 19130–31, 19133–37, 19139–40, 19142–43, 19145–49, 19151, 19153, 19171–72, 19175–76, 19181–82, 19188

* * *

SECOND DISTRICT

DWIGHT EVANS, Democrat, of Philadelphia, PA; born in Philadelphia, May 16, 1954; education: graduate of the Community College of Philadelphia; La Salle University, Philadelphia, PA; professional: Pennsylvania House of Representatives, representing 203rd District, Philadelphia County; elected Democratic chair of House Appropriations Committee in 1990 and served in this role until November 2010; caucuses: Congressional Black Caucus; Congressional Progressive Caucus; LGBT Equality Caucus; committees: Agriculture; Small Business; elected simultaneously to the 114th and the 115th Congresses, by special election, on November 8, 2016, to fill the vacancy caused by the resignation of U.S. Representative Chaka Fattah.

Office Listings

http://www.evans.house.gov

1105 Longworth House Office Building, Washington, DC 20515	(202) 225–4001
Chief of Staff.—Kimberly Turner.	FAX: 225–5392
Legislative Director and Deputy Chief of Staff.—Kendra Brown.	
Communications Director.—Becca Brukman.	
7174 Ogontz Avenue, Philadelphia, PA 19138	(215) 276–0340

Counties: MONTGOMERY (part), PHILADELPHIA. Population (2010), 705,688.

ZIP Codes: 19003–04, 19010, 19035, 19038, 19041, 19066, 19072, 19083, 19085, 19087, 19092–93, 19095–96, 19101–04, 19110, 19118–22, 19126–33, 19138–41, 19143–46, 19150–51, 19161–62, 19170–72, 19175, 19178, 19182, 19187–88, 19190–92, 19195–97, 19428, 19444

* * *

THIRD DISTRICT

MIKE KELLY, Republican, of Butler, PA; born in Pittsburgh, PA, May 10, 1948; education: B.A., sociology, with a minor in philosophy and theology, University of Notre Dame, South Bend, IN, 1970; professional: owner and operator of Kelly Automotive Cadillac, Chevrolet, Hyundai, and Kia car dealership; married 42 years: Vicki Kelly; four children; committees: Ways and Means; elected to the 112th Congress on November 2, 2010; reelected to each succeeding Congress.

Office Listings

http://www.kelly.house.gov

1519 Longworth House Office Building, Washington, DC 20515 .... (202) 225–5406
FAX: 225–3103
Chief of Staff.—Matthew Stroia.
Policy Director / Tax Counsel.—Lori Prater.
Director of Communications.—Tom Qualtere.
Director of Administration.—Tim Butler.
Senior Legislative Assistant.—Sam Breene.
Legislative Assistant.—Brendan Fulmer.
Legislative Correspondent.—James Marsh.
Staff Assistant.—Kevin Dawson.

208 East Bayfront Parkway, Suite 102, Erie, PA 16507 .... (814) 456–8190
District Director.—Brad Moore.

101 East Diamond Street, Suite 218, Butler, PA 16001 .... (724) 282–2557
FAX: 282–3682

33 Chestnut Avenue, Sharon, PA 16146 .... (724) 885–1113
FAX: 885–1114

430 Court Street, New Castle, PA 16101.
Office Hours: Friday from 9 a.m. to 4 p.m.

Counties: ARMSTRONG, BUTLER, CLARION (part), CRAWFORD (part), ERIE (part), LAWRENCE (part), and MERCER. Population (2010), 705,688.

ZIP Codes: 16001–03, 16016–18, 16020, 16022–23, 16025, 16027–30, 16033–35, 16037–41, 16045–46, 16048–53, 16055–57, 16059, 16061, 16110–11, 16113–14, 16124–25, 16127, 16130–31, 16133–34, 16137, 16142–43, 16145–46, 16148, 16150–51, 16153–54, 16156, 16159, 16201, 16210, 16218, 16222–24, 16226, 16229, 16232, 16242, 16244–45, 16249–50, 16253, 16259, 16261–63, 16311–12, 16314, 16316–17, 16327, 16335, 16342, 16354, 16360, 16362, 16388, 16401–07, 16410–12, 16415, 16417, 16420–23, 16430, 16433–35, 16438, 16440–43, 16475, 16501–12, 16514–15, 16522, 16530–34, 16538, 16541, 16544, 16546, 16550, 16553–54

* * *

FOURTH DISTRICT

SCOTT PERRY, Republican, of York County, PA; born in San Diego, CA, May 27, 1962; education: Northern York High School, 1980; B.S in business administration management, Pennsylvania State University, 1991; M.S. in strategic studies, United States Army War College, 2012; professional: small business owner at Hydrotech Mechanical Services; military: active Colonel (Promotable), Pennsylvania Army National Guard; organizations: former president of Pennsylvania Young Republicans; former regional director for Pennsylvania Chapter of Jaycees; Dillsburg Legion Post #2; Dillsburg VFW Post #6771; public service: Pennsylvania House of Representatives, 2006–12; married: Christy; children: Ryenn and Mattea; committees: Foreign Affairs; Homeland Security; Transportation and Infrastructure; elected to the 113th Congress on November 6, 2012; reelected to each succeeding Congress.

Office Listings

http://perry.house.gov twitter: @repscottperry

1207 Longworth House Office Building, Washington, DC 20515 .... (202) 225–5836

Office Listings—Continued

Chief of Staff.—Lauren Muglia. FAX: 226–1000
Legislative Director.—John Drzewicki.
Communications Director.—Brandy Brown.
Legislative Assistants: Laura Detter, Patrick Schilling.
Legislative Correspondent.—Allison Turk.
Staff Assistant.—Milly Lothian.
22 Chambersburg Street, Gettysburg, PA 17325 .... (717) 338–1919
Field Representative.—Holly Sutphin.
2209 East Market Street, York, PA 17402 .... (717) 600–1919
Deputy Chief of Staff.—Bob Reilly.
Scheduler.—Carol Wiest.
Legislative Assistants: Donna Austin, Yatzi Garcia, Jamie Hopkins.
Staff Assistant.—Jefferson Odom.
730 North Front Street, Wormleysburg, PA 17043 .... (717) 635–9504
Director of Constituent Services.—Tyra Wallace.

Counties: ADAMS, CUMBERLAND, DAUPHIN, AND YORK. CITIES AND TOWNSHIPS: Abbottstown, Arendtsville, Bendersville, Berwick, Biglerville, Bonneauville, Butler, Camp Hill, Carroll Valley, Carroll, Chanceford, Codorus, Conewago, Cross Roads, Cumberland, Dallastown, Delta, Dillsburg, Dover, East Berlin, East Hopewell, East Manchester, East Pennsboro, East Prospect, Fairfield, Fairview, Fawn Grove, Fawn, Felton, Franklin, Franklintown, Freedom, Germany, Gettysburg, Glen Rock, Goldsboro, Hallam, Hamilton, Hamiltonban, Hampden, Hanover, Harrisburg, Heidelberg, Hellam, Highland, Hopewell, Huntington, Jackson, Jacobus, Jefferson, Latimore, Lemoyne, Lewisberry, Liberty, Littlestown, Loganville, Lower Allen, Lower Chanceford, Lower Windsor, Manchester, Manheim, McSherrystown, Mechanicsburg, Menallen, Monaghan, Mount Joy, Mount Pleasant, Mount Wolf, New Cumberland, New Freedom, New Oxford, New Salem, Newberry, North Codorus, North Hopewell, North York, Oxford, Paradise, Peach Bottom, Penn, Railroad, Reading, Red Lion, Seven Valleys, Shiremanstown, Shrewsbury, Silver Spring, Spring Garden, Spring Grove, Springettsbury, Springfield, Stewartstown, Straban, Susquehanna, Tyrone, Union, Upper Allen, Warrington, Washington, Wellsville, West Manchester, West Manheim, West York, Windsor, Winterstown, Wormleysburg, Wrightsville, Yoe, York Haven, York Springs, York, and Yorkana. Population (2010), 705,687.

ZIP Codes: 17070, 17072, 17093, 17101–04, 17109–11, 17120, 17301–02, 17304, 17306–07, 17309, 17311, 17313–22, 17324–25, 17327, 17329, 17331, 17339–40, 17343–45, 17347, 17349–50, 17352–53, 17355–56, 17360–66, 17368, 17370–72, 17401–04, 17406–08

* * *

FIFTH DISTRICT

GLENN "GT" THOMPSON, Republican, of Howard Township, PA; born in Bellefonte, PA, July 27, 1959; education: B.S., therapeutic recreation, Pennsylvania State University, 1981; M.Ed., health science / therapeutic recreation, Temple University, 1998; NHA / L, nursing home administrator, Marywood University, 2006; professional: rehabilitation services manager for Susquehanna Health Services, adjunct faculty for Cambria County Community College; chief recreational therapist for the Williamsport Hospital; residential services aid for Hope Enterprises; orderly for Centre Crest Nursing Home; organization / awards: past president / fire fighter / EMT / rescue technician for Howard VFD; former, Howard Boy Scout Master; former, president and senior VP for Juniata Valley Boy Scout Council; International Advisory Council member for the Accreditation of Rehabilitation Facilities Commission; board member / vice chair of the Private Industry Council of Central Corridors; political career: Centre County Republican chair, Pennsylvania Republican State Committee, alternate delegate for the Republican National Convention; candidate for the Pennsylvania House of Representatives, 1998 and 2000; member, Bald Eagle Area School District Board of Education; religion: Protestant; married to Penny Ammerman-Thompson; three sons, Parker, Logan, and Kale; committees: Agriculture; Education and the Workforce; Natural Resources; elected to the 111th Congress on November 4, 2008; reelected to each succeeding Congress.

Office Listings

http://thompson.house.gov

124 Cannon House Office Building, Washington, DC 20515 .... (202) 225–5121
FAX: 225–5796
Chief of Staff.—Matthew Brennan.
Legislative Director.—John Busovsky.
Scheduler.—Lindsay Reusser.
Communications Director.—Renée Gamela.
127 West Spring Street, Suite C, Titusville, PA 16354 .... (814) 827–3985
District Director.—Peter Winkler.
3555 Benner Pike, Suite 101, Bellefonte, PA 16823 .... (814) 353–0215

Counties: CAMERON, CENTRE, CLARION (part), CLEARFIELD, CLINTON, CRAWFORD (part), ELK, ERIE (part), FOREST, HUNTINGDON (part), JEFFERSON, MCKEAN, POTTER, TIOGA (part), VENANGO, AND WARREN. Population (2010), 705,688.

ZIP Codes: 15711, 15715, 15721, 15724, 15730, 15733, 15742, 15744, 15753, 15757, 15764, 15767, 15770, 15776, 15778, 15780–81, 15784, 15801, 15821, 15823–25, 15827–29, 15832, 15834, 15840–41, 15845–49, 15851, 15853,

15856–57, 15860–61, 15863–66, 15868, 15870, 16036, 16038, 16054, 16127, 16153, 16214, 16217, 16222, 16224, 16232–33, 16235, 16239–40, 16242, 16254–55, 16258, 16260, 16301, 16311–14, 16317, 16319, 16321–23, 16326, 16329, 16331–34, 16340–47, 16350–54, 16361–62, 16364–65, 16370–74, 16402–03, 16405, 16407, 16410, 16412, 16415–17, 16420–21, 16426–28, 16434, 16436, 16438, 16441–42, 16444, 16504, 16506, 16509–11, 16563, 16611, 16616, 16620, 16622, 16627, 16639, 16645–47, 16651–52, 16656–57, 16661, 16666, 16669, 16671, 16677, 16680, 16683, 16686, 16692, 16701, 16720, 16724–35, 16738, 16740, 16743–46, 16748–50, 16801–03, 16820–23, 16825–30, 16832–41, 16843–45, 16847–49, 16851–55, 16858–61, 16863, 16865–66, 16868, 16870–72, 16874–79, 16881–82, 16901, 16915, 16921–23, 16927–28, 16935, 16937–38, 16941, 16943, 16948, 16950, 17002, 17052, 17060, 17066, 17243, 17260, 17721, 17729, 17740, 17745, 17747–48, 17750–51, 17760, 17764, 17767, 17778–79

* * *

SIXTH DISTRICT

RYAN A. COSTELLO, Republican, of West Chester, PA; born in Phoenixville, PA, September 7, 1976; education: B.A., Ursinus College, 1999; J.D., Villanova School of Law, 2002; professional: attorney in the law firm of O'Donnell, Weiss & Mattei, P.C.; public service: chairman, East Vincent Township Board of Supervisors, 2002–08; Chester County Recorder of Deeds, 2008–11; chairman, Chester County Board of Commissioners, 2011–14; children: Ryan Jr.; committees: Energy and Commerce; elected to the 114th Congress on November 4, 2014; reelected to the 115th Congress on November 8, 2016.

Office Listings

http://www.costello.house.gov www.facebook.com/congressmanryancostello
twitter: www.twitter.com/repryancostello

326 Cannon House Office Building, Washington, DC 20515 .... (202) 225–4315
Chief of Staff.—Lauryn Bernier Schothorst. FAX: 225–8440
Legislative Director.—Dante Cutrona.
Communications Director.—Natalie Gillam.
21 West Market Street, Suite 105, West Chester, PA 19382 .... (610) 696–2982
840 North Park Road, Wyomissing, PA 19610 .... (610) 376–7630

Counties: Berks (part), Chester (part), Lebanon (part), and Montgomery (part). Population (2010), 720,487.

ZIP Codes: 17016, 17039, 17042, 17046, 17064, 17067, 17073, 17083, 17087–88, 17545, 17569, 18011, 18041, 18054, 18056, 18062, 18070, 18073–74, 18076, 18092, 19073, 19087, 19301, 19312, 19319, 19333, 19335, 19341–43, 19345, 19355, 19372, 19380, 19382–83, 19403, 19425–26, 19435, 19442, 19453, 19456–57, 19460, 19464–65, 19468, 19472–73, 19475, 19503–06, 19508, 19510, 19512, 19518, 19520, 19522, 19525–26, 19530, 19533, 19535, 19539, 19541, 19545, 19547, 19551, 19555, 19560, 19564–65, 19567, 19601–02, 19604–10

* * *

SEVENTH DISTRICT

VACANT

Counties: Berks (part), Chester (part), Delaware (part), Lancaster (part), and Montgomery (part). Population (2010), 692,866.

ZIP Codes: 17503, 17505, 17509, 17527, 17529, 17534–36, 17555, 17557, 17562, 17566, 17569, 17572, 17579, 18964, 19002–04, 19008, 19010, 19013–15, 19017–18, 19022, 19025–26, 19028–29, 19031, 19033–34, 19036–39, 19041, 19043–44, 19050, 19052, 19060–61, 19063–64, 19070, 19073–76, 19078, 19081–83, 19085, 19087, 19094, 19096, 19310–11, 19316–17, 19319–20, 19330–31, 19333, 19335, 19342–44, 19346–48, 19350–54, 19357, 19363, 19365–67, 19369, 19371–76, 19380–83, 19390, 19395, 19401, 19403–04, 19406, 19409, 19422–23, 19426, 19428, 19430, 19436–38, 19440, 19444, 19446, 19454, 19462, 19465, 19470, 19473–74, 19477, 19484, 19486, 19490, 19501, 19508, 19512, 19518–20, 19523, 19535, 19540, 19542–43, 19547–48, 19606–09

* * *

EIGHTH DISTRICT

BRIAN K. FITZPATRICK, Republican, of Middletown Township, PA; born in Philadelphia, December 17, 1973; education: B.S., LaSalle University, Philadelphia, PA, 1996; J.D., Pennsylvania State University Dickenson School of Law, 2001; M.B.A., Pennsylvania State University, 2001; professional: FBI Supervisory Special Agent; Special Assistant U.S. Attorney; Certified Public Accountant; Emergency Medical Technician; religion: Roman Catholic; caucuses: Problem Solvers Caucus; Bipartisan Heroin Task Force; Animal Protection Caucus; Climate Solutions Caucus; Congressional Citizen Legislature Caucus; committees: Foreign Affairs; Homeland Security; Small Business; elected to the 115th Congress on November 8, 2016.

Office Listings

http://brianfitzpatrick.house.gov www.facebook.com/repbrianfitzpatrick twitter: @repbrianfitz

514 Cannon House Office Building, Washington, DC 20515 .... (202) 225–4276
Chief of Staff.—Justin Rusk. FAX: 225–9511
Legislative Counsel.—Joseph Knowles.
1717 Langhorne Newtown Road, Suite 400, Langhorne, PA 19047 .... (215) 579–8102
District Director.—Meghan Schroeder. FAX: 579–8109

Counties: BUCKS AND MONTGOMERY (part). Population (2010), 705,688.

ZIP Codes: 18036, 18042, 18054–55, 18073–74, 18076–77, 18081, 18902, 18907, 18912–15, 18917, 18920, 18923, 18925, 18929–30, 18932, 18935, 18938, 18940, 18942, 18944, 18947, 18950–51, 18954–55, 18960, 18962, 18964, 18966, 18969–70, 18972, 18974, 18976–77, 18980, 19006–07, 19021, 19030, 19040, 19047, 19053–57, 19067, 19438, 19440, 19446, 19473, 19492, 19504

* * *

NINTH DISTRICT

BILL SHUSTER, Republican, of Hollidaysburg, PA; born in McKeesport, PA, January 10, 1961; education: Everett High School, Bedford County, PA; B.A., Dickinson College; M.B.A., American University; professional: businessman; Goodyear Tire & Rubber Corp.; Bandag, Inc.; president and general manager, Shuster Chrysler; organizations: National Federation of Independent Business; National Rifle Association; YMCA; Precious Life, Inc.; Rotary Club; board of directors, Pennsylvania Automotive Association; board of trustees, Homewood Home Retirement Community; Sigma Chi Fraternity; religion: member, Zion Lutheran Church; committees: chair, Transportation and Infrastructure; Armed Services; elected to the 107th Congress, by special election, on May 15, 2001; reelected to each succeeding Congress.

Office Listings

http://www.shuster.house.gov

2079 Rayburn House Office Building, Washington, DC 20515 .... (202) 225–2431
Chief of Staff.—Eric Burgeson. FAX: 225–2486
Legislative Director.—Denny Wirtz.
Executive Assistant.—Brittany Smith.
310 Penn Street, Suite 200, Hollidaysburg, PA 16648 .... (814) 696–6318
100 Lincoln Way East, Suite B, Chambersburg, PA 17201 .... (717) 264–8308
827 Water Street, Suite 3, Indiana, PA 15701 .... (724) 463–0516
Western Representative, Fayette County, PA (724) 994–6220

Counties: BEDFORD, BLAIR, CAMBRIA (part), FAYETTE, FRANKLIN, FULTON, GREENE (part), HUNTINGDON (part), INDIANA, SOMERSET (part), WASHINGTON (part), and WESTMORELAND (part). Population (2010), 664,701.

ZIP Codes: 15012, 15022, 15033, 15062, 15067, 15314–15, 15320, 15322, 15325, 15327, 15332–34, 15338, 15344, 15346, 15348–49, 15351, 15357–58, 15366, 15368, 15370, 15401, 15410–13, 15415–17, 15419–25, 15427–40, 15442–47, 15449–51, 15454–56, 15458–70, 15472–78, 15480, 15482–86, 15488–92, 15501, 15510, 15521–22, 15530, 15532–42, 15545, 15550, 15552–54, 15557–60, 15562–65, 15610, 15618, 15622, 15631, 15666, 15681, 15683, 15701, 15705, 15710, 15712–14, 15716–17, 15720, 15722–25, 15727–29, 15731–31, 15734, 15737–39, 15741–43, 15745–48, 15750, 15752, 15754, 15756–59, 15761–63, 15765, 15767, 15771–75, 15777, 15783, 15920, 15924, 15926, 15929, 15931, 15938, 15940, 15944, 15946, 15949, 15954, 15957, 15961, 16211, 16222, 16246, 16256, 16601–03, 16611, 16613, 16617, 16619, 16621–25, 16627, 16629–31, 16633–41, 16644, 16646–48, 16650, 16655, 16657, 16659, 16662, 16664–65, 16667–68, 16670, 16672–75, 16678–79, 16682, 16684–86, 16689, 16691, 16693–95, 17002, 17013, 18015, 17024, 17040, 17052–53, 17060, 17066, 17068, 17201–02, 17210–15, 17217, 17219–25, 17228–29, 17231–33, 17235–41, 17243–44, 17246–47, 17249–57, 17261–65, 17267–72, 17324

* * *

TENTH DISTRICT

TOM A. MARINO, Republican, of Cogan Station, PA; born in Williamsport, PA, August 13, 1952; education: American Institute of Baking, 1982; A.A., general studies, Williamsport Area Community College, 1983; B.A., political science/education, Lycoming College, 1985; J.D., Dickinson School of Law, 1987; United States Army War College, 2005; professional: manufacturing manager; lawyer, private practice; served as a Lycoming County District Attorney, PA, 1992–2002; U.S. Attorney for the Middle District of Pennsylvania, 1992–2002; married: Edith, 1974; two children: Chloe and Victor; committees: Foreign Affairs; Judiciary; elected to the 112th Congress on November 2, 2010; reelected to each succeeding Congress.

Office Listings

http://www.marino.house.gov https://twitter.com/reptommarino
https://www.facebook.com/congressmanmarino

2242 Rayburn House Office Building, Washington, DC 20515 .... (202) 225–3731
Chief of Staff.—Sara Rogers. FAX: 225–9594
Legislative Director / Counsel.—Jeff Wieand.
Counsel.—Judd Smith.
Scheduler.—Elizabeth Hyers.
Press Secretary.—N/A.
Legislative Assistant.—Matthew Powell.
Communication Assistant.—Mark Hancock.
Staff Assistant.—Michael Perry.
1020 Commerce Park Drive, Suite 1A, Williamsport, PA 17701 .... (570) 322–3961
Constituent Services Manager.—Jacqueline Bell.
District Representative.—Matt Hutchinson.
Senior Advisor.—Ryan Barton.
543 Easton Turnpike, Suite 101, Lake Ariel, PA 18436 .... (570) 689–6024
Deputy Chief of Staff / District Director.—Dave Weber.
District Representatives: Tom Cahill, Cathy Romaniello.
713 Bridge Street, Room 29, Selinsgrove, PA 17870 .... (570) 374–9469
District Representatives: Mike Knouse, Amiee Snyder.

Counties: BRADFORD, JUNIATA, LACKAWANNA (part), LYCOMING, MIFFLIN, MONROE (part), NORTHUMBERLAND (part), PERRY, PIKE, SNYDER, SULLIVAN, SUSQUEHANNA, TIOGA, UNION, AND WAYNE. Population (2010), 669,257.

ZIP Codes: 16911–12, 16914, 16917, 16920, 16925–26, 16929–30, 16932–33, 16936, 16939–40, 16942, 16946–47, 17004, 17006, 17009, 17029, 17035, 17037, 17044–45, 17047, 17049, 17051, 17056, 17058–59, 17062–63, 17069, 17071, 17075–76, 17082, 17084, 17086, 17094, 17099, 17701–02, 17723–24, 17727–28, 17730–31, 17737, 17739, 17742, 17744, 17749, 17752, 17754, 17758, 17762–63, 17765, 17768, 17771, 17776, 17810, 17812–13, 17827, 17829, 17835, 17837, 17841–42, 17844–45, 17850, 17853, 17855–57, 17861–62, 17864–65, 17870, 17876, 17880, 17885–87, 17889, 18323, 18325, 18328, 18332, 18336–37, 18340, 18342, 18349, 18352, 18357, 18370–72, 18405, 18413, 18415, 18417, 18420–21, 18425–28, 18430–31, 18435–39, 18441, 18443, 18445, 18451, 18453–65, 18469–73, 18616, 18619, 18626, 18628, 18632, 18653, 18801, 18810, 18812, 18814, 18816–18, 18821–26, 18828–34, 18837, 18840, 18842–43, 18848, 18850–51, 18853–54

* * *

ELEVENTH DISTRICT

LOU BARLETTA, Republican, of Hazleton, PA; born in Hazleton, January 28, 1956; education: attended Bloomsburg University, Bloomsburg, PA; professional: business owner; member of City Council of Hazleton, PA, 1998–2000; Mayor of Hazleton, PA, 2000–10; married: Mary Grace; four daughters; committees: Education and the Workforce; Homeland Security; Transportation and Infrastructure; elected to the 112th Congress on November 2, 2010; reelected to each succeeding Congress.

Office Listings

http://www.barletta.house.gov

2049 Rayburn House Office Building, Washington, DC 20515 .... (202) 225–6511
Chief of Staff.—Andrea Niethold Waldock. FAX: 226–6250
Deputy Chief of Staff / Legislative Director.—Mira Lezell.
Executive Assistant.—Cherie Homa.
Communications Director.—Jon Anzur.
1 South Church Street, Hazleton, PA 18201–5283 .... (570) 751–0050
126 North Hanover Street, Carlisle, PA 17013 .... (717) 249–0190
4813 Jonestown Road, Suite 101, Harrisburg, PA 17109 .... (717) 525–7002
106 Arch Street, Sunbury, PA 17801 .... (570) 988–7801

Counties: CARBON (part), COLUMBIA, CUMBERLAND (part), DAUPHIN (part), LUZERNE (part), MONTOUR, NORTHUMBERLAND (part), PERRY (part), and WYOMING. Population (2010), 702,158.

ZIP Codes: 17005, 17007, 17013, 17015, 17017–20, 17023–24, 17030, 17032, 17034, 17036, 17040, 17048, 17050, 17053, 17055, 17057, 17061, 17065, 17068, 17074, 17080–81, 17090, 17094, 17097, 17103–04, 17109–13, 17240–41, 17257, 17266, 17307, 17324, 17756, 17772, 17774, 17777, 17801, 17814–15, 17822–24, 17829–30, 17832, 17834, 17836, 17840, 17846–47, 17851, 17859–60, 17866–68, 17872, 17878, 17881, 17884, 17888, 17920–21, 17941, 17945, 17964, 17980, 17985, 18201–02, 18210, 18221–25, 18229–30, 18234–35, 18237, 18239, 18241, 18244, 18246, 18249, 18251, 18254–56, 18414, 18417, 18424, 18446, 18602–03, 18610, 18612, 18614–15, 18617–18, 18621–25, 18629–31, 18634–36, 18643–44, 18651, 18655–57, 18660–61, 18702, 18704, 18706–09, 18844

* * *

TWELFTH DISTRICT

KEITH J. ROTHFUS, Republican, of Sewickley, PA; born in Endicott, NY, April 25, 1962; education: B.S., information systems, State University of New York College at Buffalo, Buffalo, NY, 1984; J.D., University of Notre Dame Law School, Notre Dame, IN, 1990; profession: lawyer; religion: Roman Catholic; family: wife, Elsie; six children; caucuses: Congressional Coal Caucus; Congressional Cybersecurity Caucus; Congressional Diabetes Caucus; Congressional Down Syndrome Caucus; Congressional Multiple Sclerosis Caucus; Congressional Pro-Life Caucus; Congressional Steel Caucus; Congressional Wire and Wire Producers Caucus; National Guard and Reserve Components Caucus; Ohio River Basin Congressional Caucus; Republican Policy Committee; committees: Financial Services; Judiciary; elected to the 113th Congress on November 6, 2012; reelected to each succeeding Congress.

Office Listings

http://www.rothfus.house.gov https://www.facebook.com/keithrothfus
https://twitter.com/keithrothfus

1205 Longworth House Office Building, Washington, DC 20515 .... (202) 225–2065
FAX: (202) 225–5709
Chief of Staff.—Alex Shively.
Office Manager / Schedule Coordinator.—Kirsten Hasler.
Legislative Director.—David Goldfarb.
Communications Director.—Kate Rosario.
Armed Services Staff.—Craig Kemper.
Small Business Staff.—David Goldfarb.

6000 Babcock Boulevard, Suite 104, Pittsburgh, PA 15237 .... (412) 837–1361
FAX: (412) 593–2022
District Director.—Jose Otero.

650 Corporation Street, Suite 304, Beaver, PA 15009 .... (724) 359–1626
FAX: (412) 593–2022
Field Representative.—Patty Hoover.
Constituent Advocate.—Shannon Smith.

110 Franklin Street, Suite 239, Johnstown, PA 15901 .... (814) 619–3659
FAX: (412) 593–2022
Constituent Advocate.—Brian Subich.

Counties: ALLEGHENY COUNTY (part). CITIES AND TOWNSHIPS: Allison Park, Aspinwall, Bairdford, Bakerstown, Bell Acres, Bradford Woods, Curtisville, Fawn Harrison, Fox Chapel, Franklin Park, Frazer, Hampton, Haysville, Gibsonia, Glen Osborne, Glenshaw, Indiana, Kilbuck, Marshall, McCandless, O'Hara, Ohio, Pine, Richland, Ross, Russellton, Sewickley, Sewickley Heights, Sewickley Hills, Shaler, West Deer, and West View. BEAVER. CITIES AND TOWNSHIPS: Aliquippa, Ambridge, Baden, Beaver, Big Beaver, Beaver Falls, Bridgewater, Brighton Township, Center, Chippewa, Conway, Darlington, Daugherty, East Rochester, Eastvale, Economy, Fallston, Frankfort Springs, Franklin, Freedom, Georgetown, Glasgow, Greene Township, Hanover, Harmony, Homewood, Hookstown, Hopewell, Independence, Industry, Koppel, Marion, Midland, Monaca, New Brighton, New Galilee, New Sewickley, North Sewickley, Ohioville, Patterson, Patterson Heights, Potter, Pulaski, Raccoon, Rochester, Shippingport, South Beaver, South Heights, Vanport, West Mayfield, and White Township. CAMBRIA (part). CITIES AND TOWNSHIPS: Barr, Beaverdale, Belmont, Blacklick, Brownstown, Cambria, Carrolltown, Cassandra, Colver, Conemaugh, Croyle, Daisytown, Dale, Dunlo, East Carroll, East Conemaugh, East Taylor, Ehrenfeld, Geistown, Ebensburg, Elim, Ferndale, Johnstown, Jackson, Lilly, Lorain, Lower Yoder, Middle Taylor, Mundy's Corner, Nanty-Glo, Portagem, Revloc, Riverside, Salix, Scalp Level, Sidman, South Fork, Spring Hill, St. Michael, Stonycreek, Summerhill, Upper Yoder, Vinco, Vintonsale, Washington, West Taylor, Westmont, and Wilmore. LAWRENCE (part). CITIES AND TOWNSHIPS: Ellport, Ellwood City, Enon Valley, Little Beaver, Perry, Wampum, and Wayne. SOMERSET (part). CITIES AND TOWNSHIPS: Benson, Black, Boswell, Cairnbrook, Casselman, Central City, Conemaugh, Davidsville, Edie, Friedens, Hooversville, Jefferson, Jenner, Jennersown, Jerome, Lincoln, Middle Creek, New Centerville, Ogle, Paint, Quemahoning, Rockwood, Somerset, Shade, Stoystown, Upper Turkeyfoot, and Windber. WESTMORELAND (part). CITIES AND TOWNSHIPS: Allegheny, Avonmore, Bell, Bolivar, Bradenville, Delmont, Derry, East Vandergrift, Fairfield, Hyde Park, Lower Burrell, Loyalhanna, Millwood, Monroeville, Murrysville, New Alexandria, New Florence, Oklahoma, Plum, Salem, Seward, Slickville, St. Clair, Upper Burrell, Vandergrift, Washington, and West Leechburg. Population (2010), 700,573.

ZIP Codes: 15001, 15003, 15005–07, 15009–10, 15015, 15024, 15026–27, 15030, 15042–44, 15050–52, 15059, 15061, 15065–66, 15068, 15074–77, 15081, 15084, 15086, 15090, 15101, 15116, 15139, 15143, 15146–47, 15202, 15209, 15212, 15214–15, 15223, 15229, 15235, 15237–39, 15424–25, 15501–02, 15510, 15520, 15530–31, 15540–42, 15544, 15546–47, 15551, 15555, 15557, 15561, 15563, 15601, 15613, 15618, 15620, 15622, 15624, 15626–27, 15629, 15632–33, 15641, 15644, 15650, 15656, 15658, 15661, 15668, 15670–71, 15680–81, 15684, 15690, 15714, 15717, 15722, 15760, 15762, 15775, 15779, 15901–02, 15904–06, 15909, 15921–28, 15930–31, 15934–38, 15940, 15942–46, 15948, 15951–58, 15960–63, 16037, 16046, 16051, 16055, 16059, 16063, 16101, 16115, 16117, 16120, 16123, 16136, 16141, 16157, 16229

* * *

THIRTEENTH DISTRICT

BRENDAN F. BOYLE, Democrat, of Philadelphia, PA; born in the Olney section of Philadelphia, PA, February 6, 1977; education: graduated from the Cardinal Dougherty High School in Philadelphia, PA, 1995; B.A., University of Notre Dame, South Bend, IN, 1999; M.P.P., John F. Kennedy School of Government, Harvard University, Cambridge, MA, 2005; professional:

Representative, Pennsylvania House of Representatives, 170th District, 2009–15; U.S. House of Representatives, 2015–present; married: Jennifer Boyle; children: Abigail; committees: Budget; Foreign Affairs; elected to the 114th Congress on November 4, 2014; reelected to the 115th Congress on November 8, 2016.

Office Listings

http://www.boyle.house.gov facebook: https://www.facebook.com/CongressmanBoyle
twitter: @congboyle

1133 Longworth House Office Building, Washington, DC 20515 .... (202) 225–6111
Chief of Staff.—John McCarthy. FAX: 226–0611
Legislative Director.—Helena Mastrogianis.
Communications Director.—Sean Tobin.
115 East Glenside Avenue, Suite 1, Glenside, PA 19038 .... (215) 517–6572
District Director.—Scott Heppard.
2375 Woodward Street, Philadelphia, PA 19115 .... (215) 335–3355
5675 North Front Street, Suite 180, Philadelphia, PA 19120 .... (267) 335–5643
District Office Director.—Nicholas Himebaugh.
101 East Main Street, Norristown, PA 19401 .... (610) 270–8081

County: PHILADELPHIA COUNTY. CITY OF: Philadelphia. MONTGOMERY COUNTIES. CITIES AND TOWNSHIPS: Abington, Ambler, Blue Bell, Bridgeport, Bryn Athyn, Cheltenham, Conshohocken, Dresher, Elkins Park, Fort Washington, Glenside, Gwynedd, Hatboro, Horsham, Huntingdon Valley, Jenkintown, King of Prussia, Lansdale, Meadowbrook, Montgomeryville, Norristown, North Wales, Philadelphia, Plymouth Meeting, Rockledge, Roslyn, Rydal, and Willow Grove. Population (2017), 735,867.

ZIP Codes: 18915 (part), 18936, 19001, 19002 (part), 19006 (part), 19009, 19012, 19025 (part), 19027, 19031 (part), 19034–35 (part), 19038 (part), 19040 (part), 19044 (part), 19046, 19075 (part), 19087 (part), 19090, 19095, 19111, 19114 (part), 19115–16, 19118 (part), 19120 (part), 19124 (part), 19126 (part), 19136–37 (part), 19140 (part), 19149–50 (part), 19152, 19154, 19401 (part), 19403 (part), 19405, 19406 (part), 19422 (part), 19428 (part), 19436, 19437 (part), 19444 (part), 19446 (part), 19454 (part), 19462 (part)

* * *

FOURTEENTH DISTRICT

MIKE DOYLE, Democrat, of Forest Hills, PA; born in Swissvale, PA, August 5, 1953; education: graduated, Swissvale Area High School, 1971; B.S., Pennsylvania State University, 1975; professional: co-owner, Eastgate Insurance Agency, Inc., 1983; elected and served as finance and recreation chairman, Swissvale Borough Council, 1977–81; member: Ancient Order of the Hibernians, Italian Sons and Daughters of America, Leadership Pittsburgh Alumni Association, Lions Club, National Italian-American Foundation, Penn State Alumni Association, Pennsylvania Democratic Delegation; caucuses: co-chair, Autism Caucus; co-chair, Robotics Caucus; Ad Hoc Committee on Irish Affairs; Congressional Steel Caucus; Democratic Caucus; Democratic Study Group; married: Susan Beth Doyle, 1975; children: Michael, David, Kevin, and Alexandra; committees: Energy and Commerce; elected to the 104th Congress on November 8, 1994; reelected to each succeeding Congress.

Office Listings

http://doyle.house.gov facebook: https://www.facebook.com/usrepmikedoyle
twitter: https://twitter.com/usrepmikedoyle

239 Cannon House Office Building, Washington, DC 20515 .... (202) 225–2135
Chief of Staff.—David Lucas. FAX: 225–3084
Legislative Director.—Phil Murphy.
Office Manager / Scheduler.—Ellen Young.
2637 East Carson Street, Pittsburgh, PA 15203 .... (412) 390–1499
District Director.—Paul D'Alesandro.
11 Duff Road, Penn Hills, PA 15235 .... (412) 241–6055
627 Lysle Boulevard, McKeesport, PA 15132 .... (412) 664–4049

Counties: ALLEGHENY AND WESTMORELAND. CITIES AND TOWNSHIPS: Arnold (Westmoreland), Avalon, Baldwin Borough, Baldwin Township, Bellevue, Ben Avon, Ben Avon Heights, Blawnox, Brackenridge, Braddock, Braddock Hills, Brentwood, Chalfant, Cheswick, Churchill, Clairton, Coraopolis, Crafton, Dormont, Duquesne, Dravosburg, East Deer, East McKeesport, East Pittsburgh, Edgewood, Emsworth, Etna, Forest Hills, Glassport, Glenfield, Greentree, Harmar, Harrison (Ward 1, District 1; Ward 2; Ward 5–District 1), Homestead, Ingram, Kennedy, Liberty, Lincoln, McKees Rocks, McKeesport, Millvale, Monroeville (Ward 1; Ward 2, District 2; Ward 3, District 3; Ward 5, District 1, 2, 4; Ward 6; Ward 7), Mt. Oliver, Munhall, Neville, New Kensington (Westmoreland), North Braddock, North Versailles, Oakmont, Penn Hills, Pitcairn, Pittsburgh, Port Vue, Rankin, Robinson (Districts 3 and 5), Sharpsburg, Springdale Borough, Springdale Township, Stowe, Swissvale, Tarentum, Trafford (Allegheny), Turtle Creek, Verona, Versailles, Wall, West Homestead, West Mifflin, Whitaker, Whitehall (Part District 1; Districts 2–16), White Oak, Wilkins, Wilkinsburg, and Wilmerding. Population (2010), 705,688.

ZIP Codes: 15014, 15024–25, 15030, 15034–35, 15037, 15045, 15049, 15065, 15068, 15084–85, 15104, 15106, 15108, 15110, 15112, 15120, 15122, 15131–33, 15135–37, 15139–40, 15143–48, 15201–28, 15232–36, 15238, 15260, 15290, 15642

* * *

FIFTEENTH DISTRICT

VACANT

Counties: BERKS (part), DAUPHIN (part), LEBANON (part), LEHIGH, AND NORTHAMPTON (part). Population (2010), 705,687.

ZIP Codes: 17003, 17010, 17022, 17026, 17028, 17033, 17036, 17038, 17041–42, 17046, 17057, 17064, 17067, 17077–78, 17087, 1711–12, 17545, 17963, 18011, 18014–18, 18020, 18031–32, 18034–38, 18040–42, 18045–46, 18049, 18051–53, 18055, 18059, 18062, 18064, 18066–69, 18072, 18077–80, 18086–88, 18091–92, 18101–06, 18109, 18195, 18951, 19504–07, 19511, 19526, 19529–30, 19533–34, 19536, 19538–39, 19541, 19544, 19550, 19554–55, 19559, 19562, 19567

* * *

SIXTEENTH DISTRICT

LLOYD SMUCKER, Republican, of West Lampeter Township, PA; born in Lancaster, PA, January 23, 1964; education: Lancaster Mennonite High School, Lancaster, PA, 1981; attended Franklin & Marshall College, Lancaster, PA; professional: small business owner, Smucker Company; religion: Lutheran; family: wife, Cindy; children: Paige, Regan, and Nicholas; caucuses: Republican Main Street Partnership; Republican Study Committee; committees: Budget; Education, and the Workforce; Transportation and Infrastructure; elected to the 115th Congress on November 8, 2016.

Office Listings

http://www.smucker.house.gov https://www.facebook.com/RepSmucker
https://twitter.com/RepSmucker

420 Cannon House Office Building, Washington, DC 20515 .... (202) 225–2411
Chief of Staff.—Greg Facchiano. FAX: 225–2013
Legislative Director.—Andrew Robreno.
Communications Director.—Bill Jaffee.
51 South Duke Street, Suite 201, Lancaster, PA 17602 .... (717) 393–0667

Counties: LANCASTER COUNTY. CITY: Lancaster. TOWNSHIPS: Brecknock, Caernarvon, Clay, Conestoga, Conoy, Drumore, Earl, East Cocalico, East Donegal, East Drumore, East Earl, East Hempfield, East Lampeter, Eden, Elizabeth, Ephrata, Fulton, Lancaster, Little Britain, Manheim, Manor, Martic, Mount Joy, Penn, Pequea, Providence, Rapho, Strasburg, Upper Leacock, Warwick, West Cocalico, West Donegal, West Earl, West Hempfield, and West Lampeter. BOROUGHS: Adamstown, Akron, Columbia, Denver, East Petersburg, Elizabethtown, Ephrata, Lititz, Manheim, Marietta, Millersville, Mount Joy, Mountville, New Holland, Quarryville, Strasburg, and Terre Hill. BERKS COUNTY. CITY: Reading. TOWNSHIPS: Cumru (District 1 only), Lower Alsace (District 1 only), Muhlenberg (Districts 1 and 4), Spring (Districts 2, 3, 4, 9, 10, 12). BOROUGHS: Laureldale (Districts 1 and 2), Mount Penn, Sinking Spring, West Reading, Wyomissing (District 3). CHESTER COUNTY. CITY: Coatesville. TOWNSHIPS: Caln (District 2), East Fallowfield, East Marlborough, East Nottingham, Elk, Franklin, Kennett (District 2 and 3), London Grove, Lower Oxford, New London, Pennsbury (North District), Sadsbury (South District), Valley, West Marlborough, West Nottingham. BOROUGHS: Avondale, Kennett, Square, Modena, Oxford, Parkesburg, South Coatesville, and West Grove. Population (2010), 705,688.

ZIP Codes: 17022, 17073, 17501–02, 17505, 17507–08, 17512, 17516–20, 17522, 17529, 17532, 17536, 17538, 17540, 17543, 17545, 17547, 17550–52, 17554–55, 17557, 17560, 17562–63, 17565–66, 17569–70, 17572, 17576, 17578–79, 17581–82, 17584, 17601–03, 17606, 19311, 19317, 19320, 19330, 19344, 19348, 19350, 19352, 19358, 19362–63, 19365, 19367, 19375, 19382, 19390, 19501, 19540, 19543, 19551, 19560–02, 19604–11

* * *

SEVENTEENTH DISTRICT

MATT CARTWRIGHT, Democrat, of Moosic, PA; born in Erie, PA, May 1, 1961; education: B.A., history, Hamilton College, Clinton, NY, 1983; J.D., University of Pennsylvania, Philadelphia, PA, 1986; professional: attorney, Munley, Munley and Cartwright, 1987–2012; religion: Roman Catholic; family: wife, Marion; two sons, Jack and Matt; caucuses: Academic Medicine Caucus; Ad-Hoc Committee for Irish Affairs; Admadiyya Muslim Caucus; Adult Literacy Caucus; Aluminum Caucus; Animal Protection Caucus; Autism Caucus; Battlefield Caucus; Baseball Caucus; Bike Caucus; Bipartisan Congressional Watchdog Caucus; Bipartisan Disaster Relief Caucus; Bipartisan Peace Corps Caucus; Bipartisan Taskforce for Combating Anti-Semitism; Blue-Collar Caucus; Brain Injury Task Force; Caucus on Parkinson's Disease; Caucus on Travel and Tourism; Cement Caucus; Childhood Cancer Caucus; Clean Water Caucus; Coal Caucus; Cybersecurity Caucus; Cystic Fibrosis Caucus; Defense Communities Caucus; Democratic Caucus; Diabetes Caucus; Energy Savings Performance Caucus; Financial and Economic Literacy Caucus; Fire Services Caucus; Foster Youth Caucus; Friends of Ireland Caucus; Friends of Thailand Caucus; Full Employment Caucus; Free File Caucus; General Aviation Caucus; German-American Caucus; Hazards Caucus; Hearing Health Caucus; Historic Preservation Caucus; History Caucus; House Manufacturing Caucus; House Renewable Energy and Energy Efficiency Caucus; International Conservation Caucus; Iran Human Rights and Democracy Caucus; Kidney Caucus; LGBT Equality Caucus; Maker Caucus; Men's Health Caucus; Military Depot Caucus; Military Families Caucus; Military Mental Health Caucus; Military Sexual Assault Prevention Caucus; Military Veterans, Motorsports Caucus; National Parks Caucus; Nursing Caucus; Organ and Tissue Donation Awareness Caucus; P3 Caucus; Philanthropy Caucus; Poland Caucus; Pollinator Protection Caucus; Prescription Drug Abuse Caucus; Progressive Caucus; Public Broadcasting Caucus; Public Service Caucus; Public Transportation Caucus; Recycling Caucus; Safe Climate Caucus; Savings and Ownership Caucus; School Health & Safety Caucus; Scouting Caucus; Seniors Task Force; Ski and Snowboard Caucus; Skin Cancer Caucus; Small Brewers Caucus; Small Business Caucus; Soils Caucus; STEAM Caucus; Steel Caucus; Structured Settlements Caucus; Submarine Caucus; Sustainable Energy and Environment Coalition (SEEC); Taiwan Caucus; Tourette Syndrome Caucus; Ukrainian Caucus; USO Caucus; Veterans Job Caucus; Wildlife Refuge Caucus; Whip's Task Force on Poverty and Opportunity; Writers Caucus; committees: Appropriations; Oversight and Government Reform; elected to the 113th Congress; reelected to each succeeding Congress.

Office Listings

http://cartwright.house.gov www.facebook.com/repmattcartwright
www.twitter.com/repcartwright

1034 Longworth House Office Building, Washington, DC 20515 .... 202) 225–5546
Chief of Staff.—Hunter Ridgway. FAX: 226–0996
Deputy Chief of Staff / Legislative Director.—Jeremy Marcus.
Scheduler.—Emily Sweda.
226 Wyoming Avenue, Scranton, PA 18503 .... (570) 341–1050
20 North Pennsylvania Avenue, Suite 201, Wilkes-Barre, PA 18711 .... (570) 371–0317
400 Northampton Street, Suite 307, Easton, PA 18042 .... (484) 546–0776
121 Progress Avenue, Suite 310, Pottsville, PA 17901 .... (570) 624–0140

Counties: CARBON (part), LACKAWANNA (part), LUZERNE (part), MONROE (part), NORTHAMPTON (part), and SCHUYLKILL. Population (2010), 705,687.

ZIP Codes: 17830, 17901, 17921–23, 17925, 17929–36, 17938, 17941, 17943–46, 17948–49, 17951–54, 17957, 17959–61, 17963–68, 17970, 17972, 17974, 17976, 17978–83, 18012–13, 18015, 18017, 18020, 18030, 18040, 18042–45, 18053, 18058, 18063–64, 18071–72, 18083, 18085, 18091, 18202, 18210–12, 18214, 18218, 18220, 18229, 18231–32, 18235, 18237, 18240–42, 18244–45, 18248–50, 18252, 18301–02, 18320–22, 18327, 18330–31, 18333–34, 18343–44, 18346–48, 18350–51, 18353–56, 18360, 18403, 18407, 18421, 18424, 18433–34, 18444, 18447–48, 18452, 18466, 18501–05, 18507–10, 18512, 18515, 18517–19, 18610, 18640–44, 18701–06, 18710–11, 18762, 18764, 18766–67, 18769, 18773, 19549

* * *

EIGHTEENTH DISTRICT

CONOR LAMB, Democrat, of Mt. Lebanon, PA; born in Washington, DC, June 27, 1984; education: graduated from Pittsburgh Central Catholic High School, 2002; University of Pennsylvania, Philadelphia, PA, 2006; J.D., University of Pennsylvania Law School, 2009; Captain, active duty U.S. Marine Corps, 2009–13; continues to serve as a Major in the U.S. Marine Corps Reserves; Assistant U.S. Attorney, Pittsburgh, PA, 2014–17; committees: Science, Space, and Technology; Veterans' Affairs; elected to the 115th Congress, by special election, on March 13, 2018, to fill the vacancy caused by the resignation of U.S. Representative Timothy Murphy.

Office Listings

https://lamb.house.gov

504 Washington Road, Pittsburgh, PA 15228 .... (412) 344–5583
2040 Frederickson Place, Greensburg, PA 15601 .... (724) 850–7312

Counties: ALLEGHENY (part), GREENE (part), WASHINGTON (part), AND WESTMORELAND (part). CITIES AND TOWNSHIPS: Greensburg, Upper St. Clair, and Washington. Population (2010), 705,688.

ZIP Codes: 15003–04, 15012, 15017–21, 15025–26, 15028, 15031, 15037–38, 15046–47, 15053–57, 15060, 15062–64, 15067, 15071–72, 15078, 15082–83, 15085, 15087–89, 15102, 15108, 15122, 15126, 15129, 15131, 15135–37, 15143, 15146, 15205, 15216, 15220, 15226–28, 15234, 15236, 15241, 15243, 15301, 15310–14, 15316–17, 15321–24, 15329–33, 15337, 15340–42, 15344–45, 15347, 15349–50, 15352–53, 15359–64, 15367, 15370, 15376–80, 15417, 15423, 15427, 15448, 15479, 15501, 15531, 15601, 15610–12, 15615–17, 15621–25, 15628, 15632–40, 15642, 15644, 15646–47, 15650, 15655, 15658, 15660, 15662–63, 15665–66, 15670, 15672, 15675–80, 15683, 15687–89, 15691–93, 15695–98

RHODE ISLAND

(Population 2010, 1,052,567)

SENATORS

JACK REED, Democrat, of Jamestown, RI; born in Providence, RI, November 12, 1949; graduated, La Salle Academy, Providence, RI, 1967; B.S., U.S. Military Academy, West Point, NY, 1971; M.P.P., Kennedy School of Government, Harvard University, 1973; J.D., Harvard Law School, 1982; professional: served in the U.S. Army, 1967–79; platoon leader, company commander, battalion staff officer, 1973–77; associate professor, Department of Social Sciences, U.S. Military Academy, West Point, NY, 1978–79; 2nd BN (Abn) 504th Infantry, 82nd Airborne Division, Fort Bragg, NC; lawyer, admitted to the Washington, DC Bar, 1983; military awards: Army commendation medal with Oak Leaf Cluster, ranger, senior parachutist, jumpmaster, expert infantryman's badge; elected to the Rhode Island State Senate, 1985–90; ex-officio member of the Select Committee on Intelligence; committees: ranking member, Armed Services; Appropriations; Banking, Housing, and Urban Affairs; elected to the 102nd Congress on November 6, 1990; served three terms in the U.S. House of Representatives; elected to the U.S. Senate, November 5, 1996; reelected to each succeeding Senate term.

Office Listings

http://reed.senate.gov facebook.com/SenJackReed twitter.com/SenJackReed

728 Hart Senate Office Building, Washington, DC 20510 .... (202) 224–4642
Chief of Staff.—Neil Campbell. FAX: 224–4680
Deputy Chief of Staff.—Cathy Nagle.
Press Secretary.—Chip Unruh.
1000 Chapel View Boulevard, Suite 290, Cranston, RI 02920 .... (401) 943–3100
Chief of Staff.—Raymond Simone.
U.S. District Courthouse, One Exchange Terrace, Suite 408, Providence, RI 02903 .... (401) 528–5200

* * *

SHELDON WHITEHOUSE, Democrat, of Newport, RI; born in New York City, NY, October 20, 1955; education: B.A., Yale University, New Haven, CT, 1978; J.D., University of Virginia, Charlottesville, VA, 1982; professional: director, Rhode Island Department of Business Regulation, 1992–94; United States Attorney, 1994–98; Attorney General, Rhode Island State, 1999–2003; committees: Budget; Environment and Public Works; Finance; Judiciary; elected to the U.S. Senate on November 7, 2006; reelected to the U.S. Senate on November 6, 2012.

Office Listings

http://whitehouse.senate.gov

530 Hart Senate Office Building, Washington, DC 20510 .... (202) 224–2921
Chief of Staff.—Sam Goodstein. FAX: 228–6362
Legislative Director.—Josh Karetny.
Communications Director.—Caleb Gibson.
170 Westminster Street, Suite 1100, Providence, RI 02903 .... (401) 453–5294
State Director.—George Carvalho.

REPRESENTATIVES

FIRST DISTRICT

DAVID N. CICILLINE, Democrat, of Providence, RI; born in Providence, July 15, 1961; education: graduated, Narragansett High School, Narragansett, RI; B.A., Brown University, Providence, 1983; J.D., Georgetown University Law Center, Washington, DC, 1986; professional: public defender, Washington, DC, 1986–87; lawyer, private practice; lawyer, American Civil Liberties Union; faculty, Roger Williams Law School, Bristol, RI; member of the Rhode Island State House of Representatives, 1995–2003; Mayor of Providence, RI, 2002–10; committees: Foreign Affairs; Judiciary; elected to the 112th Congress on November 2, 2010; reelected to each succeeding Congress.

Office Listings

http://www.cicilline.house.gov https://twitter.com/repcicilline
https://www.facebook.com/congressmandavidcicilline

2244 Rayburn House Office Building, Washington, DC 20515 .... (202) 225–4911
Chief of Staff.—Peter Karafotas. FAX: 225–3290
Legislative Director.—Sarah Trister.
Legislative Assistant / Scheduler.—Katie Spoerer.
Communications Director.—Richard Luchette.
1070 Main Street, Suite 300, Pawtucket, RI 02860 .... (401) 729–5600

Counties: Bristol, Newport, and Providence (part). Cities and Townships: Barrington, Bristol, Burrillville, Central Falls, Cumberland, East Providence, Jamestown, Lincoln, Little Compton, Middleton, Newport, North Providence, North Smithfield, Providence, Pawtucket, Portsmouth, Smithfield, Tiverton, Warren, and Woonsocket. Population (2010), 526,283.

ZIP Codes: 02802, 02806, 02809, 02828, 02835, 02837, 02838, 02840–42, 02860–61, 02863–65, 02871–72, 02876, 02878, 02885, 02895–96, 02903–12, 02914–17, 02919

* * *

SECOND DISTRICT

JAMES R. LANGEVIN, Democrat, of Warwick, RI; born in Providence, RI, April 22, 1964; education: B.A., political science / public administration, Rhode Island College, 1990; M.P.A., Harvard University, 1994; community service: American Red Cross; March of Dimes; Lions Club of Warwick; PARI Independent Living Center; Knights of Columbus; public service: secretary, Rhode Island Constitutional Convention, 1986; Rhode Island State Representative, 1989–95; Rhode Island Secretary of State, 1995–2000; committees: Armed Services; Homeland Security; elected to the 107th Congress; reelected to each succeeding Congress.

Office Listings

http://www.langevin.house.gov twitter: @jimlangevin
https://www.facebook.com/congressmanjimlangevin

2077 Rayburn House Office Building, Washington, DC 20515 .... (202) 225–2735
Chief of Staff.—Todd Adams. FAX: 225–5976
Legislative Director.—Nick Leiserson.
Office Manager.—Stu Rose.
The Summit South, 300 Centerville Road, Suite 200, Warwick, RI 02886 .... (401) 732–9400
District Director.—Seth Klaiman.

Counties: Kent, Providence (part), and Washington. Cities and Townships: Charleston, Coventry, Cranston, Exeter, Foster, Glocester, Greenwich (East and West), Hopkinton, Johnston, Kingstown (North and South), Narragansett, New Shoreham, Providence, Richmond, Scituate, Warwick, West Warwick, and Westerly. Population (2010), 516,587.

ZIP Codes: 02804, 02807–08, 02812–18, 02822–23, 02825, 02827–29, 02831–33, 02836, 02852, 02857, 02873–75, 02877, 02879–83, 02886–89, 02891–94, 02898, 02901–05, 02907–11, 02917, 02919–21

SOUTH CAROLINA

(Population 2010, 4,625,364)

SENATORS

LINDSEY GRAHAM, Republican, of Seneca, SC; born in Seneca, July 9, 1955; education: graduated, Daniel High School, Central, SC; B.A., University of South Carolina, 1977; awarded J.D., 1981; military service: joined the U.S. Air Force, 1982; Base Legal Office and Area Defense Counsel, Rhein Main Air Force Base, Germany, 1984; circuit trial counsel, U.S. Air Force; Base Staff Judge Advocate, McEntire Air National Guard Base, SC, 1989–94; 2015, Retired as a Colonel in the US Air Force Reserves; award: Meritorious Service Medal for Outstanding Service; Meritorious Service Medal for Active Duty Tour in Europe; professional: established private law practice, 1988; former member, South Carolina House of Representatives; Assistant County Attorney for Oconee County, 1988–92; City Attorney for Central, SC, 1990–94; member: Walhalla Rotary; American Legion Post 120; appointed to the Judicial Arbitration Commission by the Chief Justice of the Supreme Court; religion: attends Corinth Baptist Church; committees: Appropriations; Armed Services; Budget; Judiciary; elected to the 104th Congress on November 8, 1994; reelected to each succeeding Congress; elected to the U.S. Senate on November 5, 2002, reelected to each succeeding Senate term.

Office Listings

http://lgraham.senate.gov

290 Russell Senate Office Building, Washington, DC 20510 .... (202) 224–5972
Chief of Staff.—Richard Perry. FAX: 224–3808
Legislative Director.—Mathew Rimkunas.
Scheduler / Press Secretary.—Alice James.
Deputy Communications Director.—Taylor Reidy.
130 South Main Street, Suite 700, Greenville, SC 29601 .... (864) 250–1417
State Director.—Van Cato.
Communications Director.—Kevin Bishop.
Upstate Regional Director.—Angela Omer.
State Scheduler.—Edward Mercer.
530 Johnnie Dodds Boulevard, Suite 202, Mt. Pleasant, SC 29464 .... (843) 849–3887
Low Country Regional Director.—Dan Head.
508 Hampton Street, Suite 202, Columbia, SC 29201 .... (803) 933–0112
Midlands Regional Director.—Yvette Rowland.
John L. McMillan Federal Building, 401 West Evans Street, Suite 111, Florence, SC 29501 (843) 669–1505
Pee Dee Regional Director.—Celia Urquhart.
235 East Main Street, Suite 100, Rock Hill, SC 29730 .... (803) 366–2828
Piedmont Regional Outreach Director.—Theresa Thomas.
124 Exchange Street, Suite A, Pendleton, SC 29670 .... (864) 646–4090
Senior Advisor.—Denise Bauld.

* * *

TIM SCOTT, Republican, of North Charleston, SC; born in North Charleston, September 19, 1965; education: R.B. Stall High School; B.S., Charleston Southern University, Charleston, SC, 1988; professional: former owner of Tim Scott Allstate and partner of Pathway Real Estate Group; served on Charleston County Council, 1995–2008; four terms as chair of the Charleston County Council; member of the South Carolina State House of Representatives, 2009–10; member of the U.S. House of Representatives 2010–12; committees: Armed Services; Banking, Housing, and Urban Affairs; Finance; Health, Education, Labor, and Pensions; Small Business and Entrepreneurship; Special Committee on Aging; appointed by the Governor, January 2, 2013, to fill the vacancy caused by the resignation of Senator James DeMint; appointment took effect upon his resignation from the House of Representatives on January 2, 2013; took the oath of office on January 3, 2013; elected, by special election, on November 4, 2014, for the final two years of Senator DeMint's second term; reelected to the U.S. Senate on November 8, 2016.

Office Listings

http://scott.senate.gov

717 Hart Senate Office Building, Washington, DC 20510 .... (202) 224–6121
Chief of Staff.—Jennifer DeCasper. FAX: 228–5143
Legislative Director.—Chuck Cogar.
Communications Director.—Sean Smith.
Scheduler.—Brie Kelly.
2500 City Hall Lane, 3rd Floor Suite, North Charleston, SC 29406 .... (843) 727–4525

Office Listings—Continued

State Director.—Joe McKeown. FAX: (855) 802–9355
104 South Main Street, Suite 803, Greenville, SC 29601 .... (861) 233–5366
1301 Gervais Street, Suite 825, Columbia, SC 29201 .... (803) 771–6112

REPRESENTATIVES

FIRST DISTRICT

MARK SANFORD, Republican, of Mount Pleasant, SC; born in Ft. Lauderdale, FL, May 28, 1960; education: B.A., Furman University, Greenville, SC, 1983; M.B.A., Darden School of Business, University of Virginia, Charlottesville, VA, 1988; prior congressional service, 104th–106th Congresses; Governor of South Carolina: 2003–11; religion: Episcopalian; family: son of Margaret (Peg) Sanford and the late Dr. Marshall Sanford, Sr.; children: Marshall III, Landon, Bolton, and Blake; committees: Budget; Oversight and Government Reform; Transportation and Infrastructure; elected to the 113th Congress, by special election, on May 7, 2013, to fill the vacancy caused by the appointment of U.S. Representative Tim Scott to the U.S. Senate; reelected to each succeeding Congress.

Office Listings

http://www.sanford.house.gov fb.com/repsanfordsc youtube.com/repsanfordsc
twitter: @repsanfordsc

2211 Rayburn House Office Building, Washington, DC 20515–4001 .... (202) 225–3176
Chief of Staff.—Matthew Taylor.
530 Johnnie Dodds Bouvelard, Suite 201, Mount Pleasant, SC 29464–3083 .... (843) 352–7572
District Director.—April Paris Derr.
710 Boundary Street, Suite 1D, P.O. Box 1538, Beaufort, SC 29902 .... (843) 521–2530
FAX: 521–2535

Counties: BEAUFORT (part), BERKELEY (part), CHARLESTON (part), COLLETON (part), AND DORCHESTER (part). Population (2010), 660,766.

ZIP Codes: 29401–03, 29405–07, 29410, 29412, 29414, 29417–18, 29420, 29422, 29424–25, 29429, 29430–31, 29438–39, 29445, 29450, 29453, 29455–58, 29461, 29464–66, 29469–70, 29472, 29479, 29482–85, 29487, 29492, 29901–07, 29909–10, 29915, 29920, 29925–26, 29928, 29935–36, 29938

* * *

SECOND DISTRICT

JOE WILSON, Republican, of Springdale, SC; born in Charleston, SC, July 31, 1947; education: graduated, B.A., Washington & Lee University, Lexington, VA; J.D., University of South Carolina School of Law; professional: attorney; Kirkland, Wilson, Moore, Taylor; former Deputy General Counsel, U.S. Department of Energy; former Judge of the town of Springdale, SC; military service: U.S. Army Reserves, 1972–75; retired Colonel in the South Carolina Army National Guard as a Staff Judge Advocate for the 218th Mechanized Infantry Brigade, 1975–2003; organizations: Cayce-West Columbia Rotary Club; Sheriff's Department Law Enforcement Advisory Council; Reserve Officers Association; Lexington County Historical Society; Columbia Home Builders Association; County Community and Resource Development Committee; American Heart Association; Mid-Carolina Mental Health Association; Cayce-West Columbia Jaycees; Kidney Foundation; South Carolina Lung Association; Alston-Wilkes Society; Cayce-West Metro Chamber of Commerce; Columbia World Affairs Council; Fellowship of Christian Athletes, Sinclair Lodge 154; Jamil Temple; Woodmen of the World; Sons of Confederate Veterans; Military Order of the World Wars; Lexington, Greater Irmo, Chapin, Columbia, West Metro, and Batesburg-Leesville Chambers of Commerce; West Metro and Dutch Fork Women's Republican Clubs; Executive Council of the Indian Waters Council, Boy Scouts of America; awards: U.S. Chamber of Commerce, Spirit of Enterprise Award; Americans for Tax Reform, Friend of the Taxpayer Award; National Taxpayers' Union, Taxpayers' Friend Award; Americans for Prosperity, Friend of the American Motorist Award; public service: South Carolina State Senate, 1984–2001; family: married to Roxanne Dusenbury McCrory; four sons; Assistant GOP Whip; member, Republican Policy Committee; committees: Armed Services; Education and the Workforce; Foreign Affairs; elected to the 107th Congress, by special election, on December 18, 2001; reelected to each succeeding Congress.

Office Listings

http://joewilson.house.gov https://www.facebook.com/joewilson
twitter: @repjoewilson

1436 Longworth House Office Building, Washington, DC 20515 .... (202) 225–2452
Chief of Staff.—Jonathan Day. FAX: 225–2455
Communications Director.—Leacy Burke.
Legislative Director.—Taylor Andreae.
1930 University Parkway, Suite 1600, Aiken, SC 29801 .... (803) 642–6416
1700 Sunset Boulevard (U.S. 378), Suite 1, West Columbia, SC 29169 .... (803) 939–0041

Counties: AIKEN, BARNWELL, LEXINGTON, ORANGEBURG (part), AND RICHLAND (part). CITIES AND TOWNSHIPS: Aiken, Arcadia Lakes, Ballentine, Barnwell, Batesburg-Leesville (part), Bath, Beech Island, Belvedere, Blackville, Blythewood, Bowman, Boyden Arbor, Branchville, Burnettown, Capitol View, Cayce, Chapin, Clearwater, Columbia (part), Cope, Cordova, Dentsville, Eastover, Eau Claire, Elko, Fairwood Acres, Gadsden, Gaston, Gilbert, Gloverville, Graniteville, Harbison, Hilda, Hilton, Hopkins, Horrell Hill, Irmo (part), Jackson, Killian, Kingville, Kline, Lake Murray, Langley, Lexington (county seat), Livingston, Lykes, Monetta, Montmorenci, Mountain Brook, Neeses, New Ellenton, North, North Augusta, Norway, Oak Grove, Pelion, Perry, Pine Ridge, Pontiac, Red Bank, Ridge Spring, Rowesville, Salley, Santee, Seven Oaks, Snelling, South Congaree, Springdale, Springfield, St. Andrews, State Park, Summit, Swansea, Vance, Vaucluse, Wagener, Warrenville, Wateree, West Columbia, Williston, Windsor, Windsor Estates, White Rock, and Woodford. Population (2010), 670,436.

ZIP Codes: 29002, 29006, 29016, 29033, 29036, 29038–39, 29044–45, 29053–54, 29061, 29063, 29070–73, 29075, 29078, 29105, 29107, 29112–13, 29115, 29123, 29129–30, 29137, 29146, 29160, 29164, 29169–72, 29177, 29180, 29203–07, 29209–10, 29212, 29219, 29223, 29229, 29260, 29801–05, 29808–09, 29812–13, 29816–17, 29822, 29826, 29898, 29829, 29831–32, 29834, 29836, 29839, 29841–43, 29847, 29849–51, 29853, 29856, 29860–61

* * *

THIRD DISTRICT

JEFF DUNCAN, Republican, of Laurens, SC; born in Greenville, SC, January 7, 1966; education: B.A., political science, Clemson University, 1988; professional: small business owner; public service: South Carolina House of Representatives, 2002–10; religion: Southern Baptist, attends Clinton First Baptist Church; married: Melody; children: Graham, John Philip, and Parker; committees: Energy and Commerce; elected to the 112th Congress on November 2, 2010; reelected to each succeeding Congress.

Office Listings

http://jeffduncan.house.gov facebook: facebook.com/RepJeffDuncan

2229 Rayburn House Office Building, Washington, DC 20515 .... (202) 225–5301
Chief of Staff.—Lance Williams. FAX: 225–3216
Deputy Chief of Staff.—Allen Klump.
Legislative Director.—Joshua Gross.
303 West Beltline Boulevard, Anderson, SC 29625 .... (864) 224–7401
Deputy Chief of Staff.—Rick Adkins.
200 Courthouse Public Square, P.O. Box 471, Laurens, SC 29360 .... (864) 681–1028

Counties: ABBEVILLE, ANDERSON, EDGEFIELD, GREENWOOD, LAURENS, MCCORMICK, OCONEE, PICKENS, SALUDA, NEWBERRY (part), GREENVILLE (part). Population (2010), 660,767.

ZIP Codes: 29006, 29037, 29070, 29105, 29108, 29127, 29129, 29138, 29145, 29166, 29178, 29325, 29332, 29335, 29351, 29355, 29360, 29370, 29384, 29388, 29605, 29611, 29620–21, 29624–28, 29630–35, 29638–46, 29649, 29653–59, 29661, 29664–67, 29669–73, 29675–78, 29680, 29682, 29684–86, 29689, 29691–93, 29695–97, 29801, 29803, 29805, 29808, 29819, 29821–22, 29824, 29832, 29835, 29838, 29840, 29844–45, 29847–48, 29853, 29860, 29899

* * *

FOURTH DISTRICT

TREY GOWDY, Republican, of Spartanburg, SC; born in Greenville, SC, August 22, 1964; native of Spartanburg, SC; education: Spartanburg High School, Spartanburg, 1982; B.A., Baylor University, Waco, TX, 1986; J.D., University of South Carolina Law School, Columbia, SC, 1989; professional: Nelson, Mullins, Riley & Scarborough (law firm), 1992–94; United States Attorney, 1994–2000; South Carolina Solicitor, 7th Circuit, 2001–10; religion: Baptist; member, First Baptist Church of Spartanburg; married: the former Terri Dillard, 1989; two children; committees: chair, Oversight and Government Reform; Judiciary; Permanent Select Committee on Intelligence; elected to the 112th Congress on November 2, 2010; reelected to each succeeding Congress.

Office Listings

http://www.gowdy.house.gov

1404 Longworth House Office Building, Washington, DC 20515 .... (202) 225–6030
Chief of Staff.—Cindy Crick. FAX: 226–1177
Legislative Director.—Anna Bartlett.
Legislative Assistants: Mike Moran, Clayton Tufts.
Scheduler.—Mary-Langston Willis.
Communications Director.—Amanda Duvall.

104 South Main Street, Greenville, SC 29601 .... (864) 241–0175
Chief of Staff.—Cindy Crick.
Constituent Liaisons: Belle Mercado, Suzette Jordan.
Grants Coordinator.—Kam Turner.

101 West St. John Street, Spartanburg, SC 29306 .... (864) 583–3264
Field Representative.—Missy House.
Constituent Liaison Coordinator.—Emily Davis.

Counties: GREENVILLE (part), SPARTANBURG (part). Population (2010), 660,766.

ZIP Codes: 29301–07, 29316, 29329–31, 29333–36, 29346, 29356, 29372–79, 29385–86, 29388, 29601–17, 29635–36, 29650–52, 29661–62, 29673, 29680–81, 29683, 29687–88, 29690

* * *

FIFTH DISTRICT

RALPH NORMAN, Republican, of Rock Hill, SC; born in Rock Hill, June 20, 1953; education: graduated from Rock Hill High School in 1971; B.S., business, Presbyterian College, Clinton, SC, 1975; professional: real estate developer; member of South Carolina State House of Representatives, 2005–06 and 2009–17; family: married to Elaine Rice Norman; 4 children: Ralph Warren, Anne, Mary Catherine, and Caroline; 15 grandchildren; committees: Science, Space, and Technology; Small Business; elected to the 115th Congress, by special election, on June 20, 2017, to fill the vacancy caused by the resignation of U.S. Representative Mick Mulvaney.

Office Listings

http://www.norman.house.gov facebook: RepRalphNorman twitter: @RepRalphNorman

2350 Rayburn House Office Building, Washington, DC 20515 .... (202) 225–5501
Chief of Staff.—Walter Whetsell.
Communications Director.—Jessica T. Cahill.

454 South Anderson Road, Suite 302 B, Rock Hill, SC 29730 .... (803) 327–1114
District Director.—David O'Neal.

Counties: CHEROKEE, CHESTER, FAIRFIELD, KERSHAW, LANCASTER, LEE, NEWBERRY (part), SPARTANBURG (part), SUMTER (part), UNION, AND YORK. Population (2013), 675,124.

ZIP Codes: 29009 (part), 29010, 29014–15, 29016 (part), 29020, 29031–32, 29036 (part), 29040, 29045 (part), 29046, 29055, 29058, 29062, 29065, 29067, 29069 (part), 29074, 29075 (part), 29078 (part), 29080 (part), 29104 (part), 29108 (part), 29122, 29125 (part), 29126, 29127 (part), 29128, 29130 (part), 29150 (part), 29152, 29153 (part), 29154, 29168, 29175, 29178 (part), 29180 (part), 29303 (part), 29307 (part), 29316 (part), 29321, 29322 (part), 29323, 29330 (part), 29335 (part), 29338, 29340–41, 29349 (part), 29353, 29355 (part), 29364, 29368, 29372 (part), 29374 (part), 29379, 29550 (part), 29702, 20704, 29706–08, 29710, 29712, 29714–15, 29717, 29718 (part), 29720, 29724, 29726, 29729, 29730, 29732–33, 29742–43, 29745

* * *

SIXTH DISTRICT

JAMES E. CLYBURN, Democrat, of Columbia, SC; born in Sumter, SC, July 21, 1940; education: graduated, Mather Academy, Camden, SC, 1957; B.S., South Carolina State University, Orangeburg, 1962; attended University of South Carolina Law School, Columbia, 1972–74; professional: South Carolina State Human Affairs Commissioner; assistant to the Governor for Human Resource Development; executive director, South Carolina Commission for Farm Workers, Inc.; director, Neighborhood Youth Corps and New Careers; counselor, South Carolina Employment Security Commission; member: lifetime member, NAACP; Southern Regional Council; Omega Psi Phi Fraternity, Inc.; Arabian Temple, No. 139; Nemiah Lodge No. 51 F&AM; married: the former Emily England; children: Mignon, Jennifer, and Angela; elected vice chair, Democratic Caucus, 2002; chair, Democratic Caucus, 2006; Majority Whip; Assistant

Democratic Leader, 2010 and 2012; elected on November 3, 1992, to the 103rd Congress; reelected to each succeeding Congress.

Office Listings

http://www.clyburn.house.gov

242 Cannon House Office Building, Washington, DC 20515 .... (202) 225–3315
Chief of Staff.—Yelberton Watkins. FAX: 225–2313
Deputy Chief of Staff.—Lindy Birch Kelly, Washington Office.
Scheduler.—Lindy Birch Kelly.
1225 Lady Street, Suite 200, Columbia, SC 29201 .... (803) 799–1100
District Director.—Robert Nance.
District Scheduler.—Melissa Lindler.
130 West Main Street, Kingstree, SC 29556 .... (843) 355–1211

Counties: ALLENDALE COUNTY. CITIES AND TOWNS: Allendale, Appleton, Barton, CAvenue, Fairfax, Martin, Millett, Ulmer, and Sycamore. BAMBERG COUNTY. CITIES AND TOWNSHIPS: Bamberg, Denmark, Erhardt, and Olar. BEAUFORT COUNTY. CITIES AND TOWNS: Corner, Dale, Gardens, Lobeco, Sheldon, and Yemasee. BERKELEY COUNTY (part). CITIES AND TOWNSHIPS: Bethera, Cross, Daniel Island, Huger, Jamestown, Pineville, Russellville, Saint Stephen, and Wando. CALHOUN COUNTY (part). CITY: Cameron, Creston, Fort Motte, and St. Matthews. CHARLESTON COUNTY (part). CITIES AND TOWNSHIPS: Adams Run, Charleston, Edisto Island, Hollywood, Johns Island, Ravenel, and Wadmalaw Island. CLARENDON COUNTY. CITIES AND TOWNSHIPS: Alcolu, Davis Station, Gable, Manning, New Zion, Rimini, Summerton, and Turbeville. COLLETON COUNTY. CITIES AND TOWNSHIPS: Ashton, Cottageville, Green Pond, Hendersonville, Islandton, Jacksonboro, Lodge, Ritter, Round O, Smoaks, Walterboro, and Williams. DORCHESTER COUNTY (part). CITIES AND TOWNSHIPS: Dorchester, Harleyville, Reevesville, Ridgeville, Rosinville, and Saint George. HAMPTON COUNTY. CITIES AND TOWNS: Brunson, Crockettvillle, Cummings, Early Branch, Estill, Furman, Garnett, Gifford, Hampton, Luray, Miley, Scotia, Varnville, and Yemasee. JASPER COUNTY. CITIES AND TOWNS: Coosawhatchie, Gillisonville, Grays, Hardeeville, Pineland, Pocotaligo, Ridgeland, Robertville, Switzerland, Tarboro, and Tillman. ORANGEBURG COUNTY (part). CITIES AND TOWNSHIPS: Bowman, Branchville, Elloree, Eutawville, Holly Hill, Norway, Orangeburg, Rowesville, Santee, and Vance. RICHLAND COUNTY (part). CITIES AND TOWNSHIPS: Blythewood, Columbia, Eastover, Gadsden, and Hopkins. SUMTER COUNTY (part). CITIES AND TOWNSHIPS: Mayesville and Sumter. WILLIAMSBURG COUNTY. CITIES AND TOWNSHIPS: Cades, Greeleyville, Hemingway, Kingstree, Lane, Nesmith, Salters, and Trio. Population (2010), 660,766.

ZIP Codes: 29001, 29003, 29016, 29018, 29030, 29039, 29042, 29044, 29047–48, 29051–53, 29056, 29059, 29061, 29078, 29080–82, 29102, 29104, 29107, 29111–12, 29114–15, 29117–18, 29125, 29133, 29135, 29142, 29147–148, 29150, 29153, 29160, 9162–63, 29201–06, 29208–10, 29212, 29223, 29225, 29229, 29401, 29403–06, 29409–10, 29418, 29420, 29426, 29431–32, 29434–37, 29445–46, 29448–50, 29452–53, 29456, 29461, 29464, 29468–72, 29474–75, 29477, 29479, 29481, 29483, 29487–88, 29492–93, 29510, 29518, 29530, 29554–56, 29560, 29564, 29580, 29583, 29590–91, 29810, 29812, 29817, 29827, 29836, 29843, 29849, 29906–07, 29909, 29911–12, 29916, 29918, 29921–24, 29927, 29929, 29932, 29934, 29936, 29939, 29940–41, 29943–45

* * *

SEVENTH DISTRICT

TOM RICE, Republican, of South Carolina; born in Charleston County, SC, August 4, 1957; education: attended high school in Myrtle Beach, SC; B.S., University of South Carolina, Columbia, SC, 1979; M.A., University of South Carolina, Columbia, 1982; J.D., University of South Carolina, Columbia, 1982; professional: lawyer, private practice; accountant; chairman of the Horry County Council, 2010–12; committees: Ways and Means; elected to the 113th Congress on November 6, 2012; reelected to each succeeding Congress.

Office Listings

http://rice.house.gov

223 Cannon House Office Building, Washington, DC .... (202) 225–9895
Chief of Staff.—Jennifer Watson. FAX: 225–9690
Legislative Director.—Walker Barrett.
2411 North Oak Street, Suite 405, Myrtle Beach, SC 29577 .... (843) 445–6459
1831 West Evans Street, Suite 300, Florence, SC 29501 .... (843) 679–9781

Counties: CHESTERFIELD, DARLINGTON, DILLON, FLORENCE (part), GEORGETOWN, HORRY, MARION, AND MARLBORO. Population (2010), 660,767.

ZIP Codes: 28112, 29009, 29069, 29101, 29114, 29161, 29440, 29442, 29501, 29505–06, 29510–12, 29516, 29519–20, 29525–27, 29530, 29532, 29536, 29540–41, 29543–47, 29550, 29554–55, 29560, 29563, 29565–72, 29574–77, 29579, 29581–85, 29588–89, 29591–94, 29596, 29709, 29718, 29727–28, 29741

SOUTH DAKOTA

(Population 2010, 814,180)

SENATORS

JOHN THUNE, Republican, of Murdo, SD; born in Pierre, SD, January 7, 1961; education: Jones County High School, 1979; B.S., business administration, Biola University, CA; M.B.A., University of South Dakota, 1984; professional: executive director, South Dakota Municipal League; board of directors, National League of Cities; executive director, South Dakota Republican Party, 1989–91; appointed, State Railroad Director, 1991; former congressional legislative assistant, and deputy staff director; elected, U.S. House of Representatives, 1997–2003; married: Kimberly Weems, 1984; children: Brittany (married to Luke Lindberg) and Larissa (married to Scott Hargens); grandchildren: Henley Joy Hargens; committees: chair, Commerce, Science, and Transportation; Agriculture, Nutrition, and Forestry; Finance; chairman, Senate Republican Conference; elected to the U.S. Senate on November 2, 2004; reelected to each succeeding Senate term.

Office Listings

http://thune.senate.gov twitter: @SenJohnThune

511 Dirksen Senate Office Building, Washington, DC 20510 .... (202) 224–2321
Chief of Staff.—Ryan Nelson. FAX: 228–5429
Deputy Chief of Staff.—Brendon Plack.
Legislative Director.—Jessica McBride.
Communications Director.—Ryan Wrasse.
5015 South Bur Oak, Sioux Falls, SD 57108 .... (605) 334–9596
246 Founders Park Drive, Suite 102, Rapid City, SD 57701 .... (605) 348–7551
320 South First Street, Suite 101, Aberdeen, SD 57401 .... (605) 225–8823

* * *

MIKE ROUNDS, Republican, of Fort Pierre, SD; born in Huron, SD, October 24, 1954; education: South Dakota State University, B.S., political science, 1977. Elected to South Dakota Senate in 1990 and reelected in 1992, 1994, 1996, and 1998; committees: Commerce, Education, Legislative Procedure, Local Government, Retirement, State Affairs, and Taxation; became Senate Minority Whip in 1993. Selected as Senate Majority Leader in 1995; elected as Governor of South Dakota in 2002; reelected in 2006; religion: Roman Catholic; married: Jean Vedvei, 1978; children: Christopher, Brian, Carrie, and John; committees: Armed Services; Banking, Housing, and Urban Affairs; Environment and Public Works; Small Business and Entrepreneurship; Veterans' Affairs; elected to the U.S. Senate in 2014.

Office Listings

http://rounds.senate.gov https://www.facebook.com/senatormikerounds
https://twitter.com/senatorrounds

502 Hart Senate Office Building, Washington, DC 20510 .... (202) 224–5842
Chief of Staff.—Rob Skjonsberg.
Deputy Chief of Staff.—Mark Johnson.
Legislative Director.—Gregg Rickman.
Communications Director.—Natalie Krings.
320 North, Main Street, Suite A, Sioux Falls, SD 57104 .... (605) 336–0486
1312 West, Main Street, Rapid City, SD 57701 .... (605) 343–5035
111 West, Capitol Avenue, Suite 210, P.O. Box 309, Pierre, SD 57501 .... (605) 244–1450
514 South Main Street, Suite 100, Aberdeen, SD 57401 .... (605) 936–0992

REPRESENTATIVE

AT LARGE

KRISTI NOEM, Republican, of Castlewood, SD; born in Watertown, SD, November 30, 1971; professional: farmer; rancher; member of South Dakota State House of Representatives, 2007–10; committees: Ways and Means; elected to the 112th Congress on November 2, 2010; reelected to each succeeding Congress.

Office Listings

http://www.noem.house.gov

2457 Rayburn House Office Building, Washington, DC 20515 .... (202) 225–2801
FAX: 225–5823
Chief of Staff.—Andrew Christianson.
Legislative Director.—Matthew Hittle.
Communications Director.—Brittany Comins.
Scheduler.—Christiana Frazee.

300 North Dakota Avenue, Suite 314, Sioux Falls, SD 57104 .... (605) 275–2868
Southeast Director.—Andrew Curley.

2525 West Main Street, Suite 310, Rapid City, SD 57702 .... (605) 791–4673
West River Director.—Brad Otten.

415 South Main Street, Suite 203, Aberdeen, SD 57401 .... (605) 262–2862
Rep. Noem has a regular staff presence in Aberdeen, although not a physical office location. For assistance or to schedule an appointment, please call (605) 878-2868.

818 South Broadway, Suite 113, Watertown, SD 57201 .... (605) 878–2868
State Director.—Beth Hollatz.

Population (2010), 814,180.

ZIP Codes: 57001–07, 57010, 57012–18, 57020–22, 57024–59, 57061–73, 57075–79, 57101, 57103–10, 57117–18, 57186, 57188–89, 57192–98, 57201, 57212–14, 57216–21, 57223–27, 57231–39, 57241–43, 57245–49, 57251–53, 57255–66, 57268–74, 57276, 57278–79, 57301, 57311–15, 57317, 57319, 57321–26, 57328–32, 57334–35, 57337, 57339–42, 57344–46, 57348–50, 57353–56, 57358–59, 57361–71, 57373–76, 57379–86, 57399, 57401–02, 57420–22, 57424, 57426–30, 57432–42, 57445–46, 57448–52, 57454–57, 57460–61, 57465–77, 57479, 57481, 57501, 57520–23, 57528–29, 57531–34, 57536–38, 57540–44, 57547–48, 57551–53, 57555, 57559–60, 57562–64, 57566–72, 57574, 57576–77, 57579–80, 57584–85, 57601, 57620–23, 57625–26, 57630–34, 57636, 57638–42, 57644–46, 57648–52, 57656–61, 57701–03, 57706, 57709, 57714, 57716–20, 57722, 57724–25, 57730, 57732, 57735, 57737–38, 57741, 57744–45, 57747–48, 57750–52, 57754–56, 57758–64, 57766–67, 57769–70, 57772–73, 57775–77, 57779–80, 57782–83, 57785, 57787–88, 57790–94, 57799

TENNESSEE

(Population 2010, 6,346,105)

SENATORS

LAMAR ALEXANDER, Republican, of Maryville, TN; born in Maryville, July 3, 1940; education: graduated with honors in Latin American history, *Phi Beta Kappa*, Vanderbilt University; New York University Law School; served as *Law Review* editor; professional: clerk to Judge John Minor Wisdom, U.S. Court of Appeals in New Orleans; legislative assistant to Senator Howard Baker (R–TN), 1967; executive assistant to Bryce Harlow, counselor to President Nixon, 1969; president, University of Tennessee, 1988–91; co-director, Empower America, 1994–95; helped found a company that is now the nation's largest provider of worksite day care, Bright Horizons; public service: Republican nominee for Governor of Tennessee, 1974; Governor of Tennessee, 1979–87; U.S. Secretary of Education, 1991–93; community service: chairman, Salvation Army Red Shield Family Initiative; Museum of Appalachia in Norris, TN; received Tennessee Conservation League Conservationist of the Year Award; family: married to Honey Alexander; four children; eight grandchildren; chair, Senate Republican Conference, 2007–12; committees: chair, Health, Education, Labor, and Pensions; Appropriations; Energy and Natural Resources; Rules and Administration; elected to the U.S. Senate on November 5, 2002; reelected to each succeeding Senate term.

Office Listings

http://alexander.senate.gov https://twitter.com/senalexander handle: @senalexander
www.facebook.com/senatorlamaralexander

455 Dirksen Senate Office Building, Washington, DC 20510 .... (202) 224–4944
Chief of Staff.—David Cleary. FAX: 228–3398
Legislative Director/Counsel.—Allison Martin.
Communications Director.—Liz Wolgemuth.
Executive Assistant/Scheduler.—Sarah Fairchild.
3322 West End Avenue, Suite 120, Nashville, TN 37203 .... (615) 736–5129
Howard H. Baker, Jr., U.S. Courthouse, 800 Market Street, Suite 112, Knoxville, TN 37902 .... (865) 545–4253
Federal Building, 167 North Main Street, Suite 1068, Memphis, TN 38103 .... (901) 544–4224
111 Murray Guard Drive, Suite D, Jackson, TN 38305 .... (731) 664–0289
Joel E. Solomon Federal Building, 900 Georgia Avenue, Suite 260, Chattanooga, TN 37402 .... (423) 752–5337
Tri-Cities Regional Airport, Terminal Building, P.O. Box 1113, 2525 Highway 75, Suite 101, Blountville, TN 37617 .... (423) 325–6240

* * *

BOB CORKER, Republican, of Chattanooga, TN; born in Orangeburg, SC, August 24, 1952; education: B.S., Industrial Management, University of Tennessee, Knoxville, TN, 1974; professional: founder of Bencor Corporation, a construction company specializing in retail properties which operated in 18 states, 1978–90; founder of the Corker Group: acquisition, development, and operation of commercial real estate, 1982–2006; honors: named to the University of Tennessee at Chattanooga's ''Entrepreneurial Hall of Fame,'' 2005; community service: founding chair, Chattanooga Neighborhood Enterprise, Inc., a non-profit organization that has helped over 10,000 families secure decent, fit, and affordable housing, 1986–92; public service: Commissioner, State of Tennessee Department of Finance and Administration, 1995–96; Mayor, City of Chattanooga, 2001–05; married: Elizabeth Corker, 1987; two children: Julia and Emily; committees: chair, Foreign Relations; Banking, Housing, and Urban Affairs; Budget; Special Committee on Aging; elected to the U.S. Senate on November 7, 2006; reelected to the U.S. Senate on November 6, 2012.

Office Listings

http://corker.senate.gov https://www.facebook.com/bobcorker https://twitter.com/SenBobCorker

425 Dirksen Senate Office Building, Washington, DC 20510 .... (202) 224–3344
Chief of Staff.—Todd Womack. FAX: 228–0566
Legislative Director.—David Kinzler.
Executive Assistant/Scheduler.—Hallie Williams.
Communications Director.—Micah Johnson.
3322 West End Avenue, Suite 610, Nashville, TN 37203 .... (615) 279–8125
100 Peabody Place, Suite 1125, Memphis, TN 38103 .... (901) 683–1910
Howard Baker Federal Building, 800 Market Street, Suite 121, Knoxville, TN 37902 .... (865) 637–4180

Office Listings—Continued

1105 East Jackson Boulevard, Suite 4, Jonesborough, TN 37659 .... (423) 753–2263
10 West Martin Luther King Boulevard, Sixth Floor, Chattanooga, TN 37402 .... (423) 756–2757
91 Stonebridge Boulevard, Suite 103, Jackson, TN 38305 .... (731) 664–2294

REPRESENTATIVES

FIRST DISTRICT

DAVID ''PHIL'' ROE, Republican, of Johnson City, TN; born in Clarksville, TN; July 21, 1945; education: B.S., Austin Peay State University, Clarksville, TN, 1967; M.D., University of Tennessee, Knoxville, TN, 1970; professional: U.S. Army Medical Corps, 1970–72; Vice Mayor of Johnson City, 2003–07; Mayor of Johnson City, 2007–09; religion: member of Munsey United Methodist Church; spouse: Clarinda; children: David C. Roe, John Roe, and Whitney Larkin; caucuses: Academic Medicine Caucus; Doctors Caucus; committees: chair, Veterans' Affairs; Education and the Workforce; elected to the 111th Congress; reelected to each succeeding Congress.

Office Listings

http://www.roe.house.gov https://www.facebook.com/drphilroe https://twitter.com/drphilroe

336 Cannon House Office Building, Washington, DC 20515 .... (202) 225–6356
Chief of Staff.—Matt Meyer. FAX: 225–5714
Press Secretary.—Lani Short.
Scheduler.—Catherine Bartley.
Legislative Director.—Aaron Bill.
Legislative Staff: Catherine Bartley, Kyle Jacobs, Otto Katt, John Witherspoon.
Legislative Correspondent.—Caroline Tarwid.
Staff Assistant.—Nicole Neilson.
205 Revere Street, Kingsport, TN 37660 .... (423) 247–8161
FAX: 247–0119
Higher Education Building, 205 Revere Street, Kingsport, TN 37662.
District Director.—John Abe Teague.
Administrative Assistant.—Sheila Houser.
Caseworkers: Carolyn Ferguson, Tracie O'Hara, Fran Woods.
1609 Walters State CC Drive, Suite 4, Morristown, TN 37813 .... (423) 254–1400
District Representative.—Bill Darden. FAX: 254–1403
Caseworkers: Cheryl Bennett, Angie Jarnagin.

Counties: CARTER, COCKE, GREENE, HAMBLEN, HANCOCK, HAWKINS, JEFFERSON, JOHNSON, SEVIER, SULLIVAN, UNICOI, AND WASHINGTON. Population (2010), 705,123.

ZIP Codes: 37601, 37604, 37614–18, 37620, 37640–43, 37645, 37650, 37656–60, 37663–65, 37681–83, 37686–88, 37690–92, 37694, 37711, 37713, 37722, 37725, 37727, 37731, 37738, 37743, 37745, 37748, 37753, 37760, 37764–65, 37809–11, 37813–14, 37818, 37821, 37843, 37857, 37860, 37862–63, 37865, 37869, 37871, 37873, 37876–77, 37879, 37881, 37890, 37891

* * *

SECOND DISTRICT

JOHN J. DUNCAN, JR., Republican, of Knoxville, TN; born in Lebanon, TN, July 21, 1947; education: B.S., journalism, University of Tennessee, 1969; J.D., National Law Center, George Washington University, 1973; professional: served in both the Army National Guard and the U.S. Army Reserves, retiring with the rank of Captain; private law practice, Knoxville, 1973–81; appointed State Trial Judge by Governor Lamar Alexander in 1981 and elected to a full 8-year term in 1982, without opposition, receiving the highest number of votes of any candidate on the ballot that year; member: American Legion 40 and 8; Elks; Sertoma Club; Masons; Scottish Rite and Shrine; present or past board member: Red Cross; Girl's Club; YWCA; Sunshine Center for the Mentally Retarded; Beck Black Heritage Center; Knoxville Union Rescue Mission; Senior Citizens Home Aid Service; religion: active elder at Eastminster Presbyterian Church; married: the former Lynn Hawkins; children: Tara, Whitney, John J. III, and Zane; committees: Oversight and Government Reform; Transportation and Infrastructure; elected to both the 100th Congress, by special election, and the 101st Congress in separate elections held on November 8, 1988; reelected to each succeeding Congress.

Office Listings

http://www.duncan.house.gov

2207 Rayburn House Office Building, Washington, DC 20515 .... (202) 225–5435
FAX: 225–6440
Chief of Staff.—Bob Griffitts.
Deputy Chief of Staff.—Don Walker.
Press Secretary.—Patrick Newton.
800 Market Street, Suite 100, Knoxville, TN 37902 .... (865) 523–3772
District Director.—Bob Griffitts.
331 Court Street, Blount County Courthouse, Maryville, TN 37804 .... (865) 984–5464

Counties: BLOUNT, CAMPBELL, CLAIBORNE, GRAINGER, JEFFERSON, KNOX, AND LOUDON. CITIES AND TOWNSHIPS: Alcoa, Farragut, Halls (Knox Co.), Harrogate, Jefferson City, Jellico, Knoxville, Lenoir City, Loudon, Maryville, Powell, and Seymour. Population (2010), 714,622.

ZIP Codes: 37701, 37709, 37721 (part), 37725 (part), 37737, 37742 (part), 37754 (part), 37764 (part), 37771 (part), 37772, 37774 (part), 37777, 37779 (part), 37801 (part), 37802–04, 37806, 37807 (part), 37820 (part), 37830 (part), 37846 (part), 37849 (part), 37853, 37865 (part), 37871 (part), 37874 (part), 37876 (part), 37878, 37882, 37884, 37885 (part), 37886, 37901–02, 37909, 37912, 37914–19, 37920 (part), 37921–24, 37927–30, 37931 (part), 37932–33, 37938 (part), 37939–40, 37950, 37995–98

* * *

THIRD DISTRICT

CHUCK FLEISCHMANN, Republican, of Ooltewah, TN; born in New York City, NY, October 11, 1962; education: graduated from Elk Grove High School, Elk Grove Village, IL, 1980; B.A., political science, University of Illinois, Urbana-Champaign, IL, 1983; J.D., University of Tennessee College of Law, Knoxville, TN, 1986; professional: attorney; small business owner; former president of the Chattanooga Bar Association, 1996; former chairman of the Chattanooga Lawyers Pro Bono Committee; religion: Catholic; married: Brenda Fleischmann; three children; committees: Appropriations; elected to the 112th Congress on November 2, 2010; reelected to each succeeding Congress.

Office Listings

http://www.fleischmann.house.gov https://www.facebook.com/repchuck
https://twitter.com/repchuck

2410 Rayburn House Office Building, Washington, DC 20515 .... (202) 225–3271
Chief of Staff.—Jim Hippe.
Legislative Director.—Daniel Tidwell.
Communications Director.—Conner Ingram.
Scheduler.—Holly Hendrix.
900 Georgia Avenue, Suite 126, Chattanooga, TN 37402 .... (423) 756–2342
District Director.—Bob White.
200 Administration Road, Suite 100, Oak Ridge, TN 37830 .... (865) 576–1976
6 East Madison Avenue, Athens, TN 37303 .... (423) 745–4671

Counties: ANDERSON, BRADLEY (part), CAMPBELL (part), HAMILTON, MCMINN, MONROE, MORGAN, POLK, ROANE, SCOTT, AND UNION. Population (2010), 711,391.

ZIP Codes: 37302–03, 37307–11, 37315, 37317, 37322–23, 37325–26, 37329, 37331, 37333, 37336, 37338, 37341, 37343, 37350–51, 37353–54, 37361–63, 37369–70, 37373, 37377, 37379, 37385, 37391, 37402–12, 37415, 37419, 37421, 37705, 37710, 37714, 37716, 37719, 37721, 37729, 37732–33, 37754–57, 37763, 37766, 37769, 37770–71, 37774, 37779, 37801, 37807, 37825–26, 37828–30, 37840–41, 37845–49, 37852, 37854, 37866, 37870, 37872, 37874, 37880, 37885, 37887–88, 37892, 37931, 38504

* * *

FOURTH DISTRICT

SCOTT DESJARLAIS, Republican, of South Pittsburg, TN; born in Sturgis, SD, February 21, 1964; education: B.S., chemistry and psychology, University of South Dakota, 1987; M.D., University of South Dakota School of Medicine, Vermillion, 1991; professional: general practitioner, Grand View Medical Center, Jasper, TN; religion: member, Epiphany Episcopalian Church, Sherwood, TN; married: Amy; children: Tyler, Ryan, and Maggie; committees: Agriculture; Armed Services; Oversight and Government Reform; elected to the 112th Congress on November 2, 2010; reelected to each succeeding Congress.

Office Listings

http://www.desjarlais.house.gov

2301 Rayburn House Office Building, Washington, DC 20515 .... (202) 225–6831
Chief of Staff.—Richard Vaughn. FAX: 226–5172
Legislative Director.—Richard Wilkins.
Communications Director.—Brendan Thomas.
301 Keith Street, Suite 212, Cleveland, TN 37311 .... (423) 472–7500
711 North Garden Street, Columbia, TN 38401 .... (931) 381–9920
200 South Jefferson Street, Federal Building, Winchester, TN 37398 .... (931) 962–3180
305 West Main Street, Murfreesboro, TN 37130 .... (931) 962–3180

Counties: BEDFORD, BLEDSOE, BRADLEY (part), FRANKLIN, GRUNDY, LINCOLN, MARION, MARSHALL, MAURY (part), MOORE, RHEA, RUTHERFORD, SEQUATCHIE, VAN BUREN (part), AND WARREN. Population (2010), 705,123.

ZIP Codes: 37014, 37018–20, 37025, 37034, 37037, 37046–47, 37060, 37063–64, 37085–86, 37090–91, 37110–11, 37118, 37122, 37127–30, 37132, 37135, 37144, 37149, 37153, 37160, 37166–67, 37174, 37180, 37183, 37190, 37301, 37305–06, 37308–13, 37318, 37321–24, 37327–28, 37330, 37332, 37334–40, 37345, 37347–49, 37352–53, 37356–57, 37359–60, 37365–67, 37373–83, 37387–89, 37394, 37396–98, 37405, 37419, 37773, 37778, 37826, 37880, 38402, 38449, 38451, 38453, 38459, 38472, 38474, 38483, 38488, 38550, 38555, 38557, 38559, 38572, 38581, 38583, 38585, 39401

* * *

FIFTH DISTRICT

JIM COOPER, Democrat, of Nashville, TN; born in Nashville, June 19, 1954; education: B.A., history and economics, University of North Carolina at Chapel Hill, 1975; Rhodes Scholar, Oxford University, 1977; J.D., Harvard Law School, 1980; admitted to Tennessee Bar, 1980; professional: attorney; Waller, Lansden, Dortch, and Davis (law firm), 1980–82; managing director, Equitable Securities, 1995–99; adjunct professor, Vanderbilt University Owen School of Management, 1995–2002 and 2006–present; partner, Brentwood Capital Advisors LLC, 1999–2002; married: Martha Hays; three children; caucuses: Blue Dog Coalition; New Democrat Coalition; committees: Armed Services; Oversight and Government Reform; elected to the U.S. House of Representatives, 1982–95; elected to the 108th Congress on November 5, 2002; reelected to each succeeding Congress.

Office Listings

http://www.cooper.house.gov https://www.facebook.com/jimcooper
https://twitter.com/repjimcooper

1536 Longworth House Office Building, Washington, DC 20515 .... (202) 225–4311
Chief of Staff.—Lisa Quigley. FAX: 226–1035
Legislative Director/Deputy Chief of Staff.—Jason Lumia.
605 Church Street, Nashville, TN 37219 .... (615) 736–5295

Counties: CHEATHAM (part), DAVIDSON, AND DICKSON. Population (2010), 713,990.

ZIP Codes: 37011, 37013, 37015, 37024–25, 37027, 37029, 37032, 37035–36, 37043, 37051–52, 37055–56, 37062, 37064, 37070, 37072–73, 37076, 37080, 37082, 37086, 37101, 37115–16, 37122, 37135, 37138, 37143, 37146, 37165, 37171, 37181, 37187, 37189, 37201–22, 37224, 37227–30, 37232, 37234–36, 37238, 37240–44, 37246, 37250

* * *

SIXTH DISTRICT

DIANE BLACK, Republican, of Gallatin, TN; born in Baltimore, MD, January 16, 1951; education: A.S.N., Arundel Community College, Baltimore, MD, 1971; B.S.N., Belmont University, Nashville, TN, 1991; professional: nurse; nonprofit community organization fundraiser; member of the Tennessee State House of Representatives, 1999–2005; member of the Tennessee State Senate, 2005–10; religion: attends Community Church of Hendersonville; married: Dr. David Black; three children; six grandchildren; caucuses: co-chair of the Congressional Caucus on Foster Youth; co-chair of the Congressional Range and Testing Center Caucus; vice chair of the GOP Doctors Caucus; member of the Congressional Military Families Caucus; Pro Life Caucus; Republican Study Committee; committees: Budget; Ways and Means; elected to the 112th Congress on November 2, 2010; reelected to each succeeding Congress.

Office Listings

http://www.black.house.gov facebook: facebook.com/DianeBlackTN06 twitter: @RepDianeBlack

1131 Longworth House Office Building, Washington, DC 20515 .... (202) 225–4231

Office Listings—Continued

Chief of Staff.—Teresa Koeberlein. FAX: 225–6887
Scheduler.—Greg Dowell.
321 East Spring Street, Suite 301, Cookeville, TN 38501 .... (931) 854–0069
355 North Belvedere Drive, Suite 308, Gallatin, TN 37066 .... (615) 206–8204
District Director.—Josh Helton.

Counties: CANNON, CLAY, COFFEE, CUMBERLAND, DEKALB, FENTRESS, JACKSON, MACON, OVERTON, PICKETT, PUTNAM, ROBERTSON, SMITH, SUMNER, TROUSDALE, WHITE, WILSON, CHEATHAM (part), and VAN BUREN. CITIES AND TOWNSHIPS: Byrdstown, Carthage, Celina, Cookeville, Crossville, Gainesboro, Gallatin, Grimsley, Hartsville, Hillsboro, Lafayette, Lebanon, Livingston, Mt. Juliet, Pleasant Hill, Sparta, Smithville, Springfield, Watertown, and Woodbury. Population (2010), 705,123.

ZIP Codes: 37010, 37012, 37015–16, 37018, 37022, 37030–32, 37034–36, 37048–49, 37059, 37066, 37072–75, 37077, 37080, 37082–83, 37085, 37087, 37090, 37095, 37143, 37155, 37118–19, 37122, 37141, 37146, 37150, 37152, 37166, 37172, 37183–84, 37186–88, 37190, 37337, 37342, 37355, 37357, 37360, 37388, 37723, 37726, 37854, 38501–06, 38543–44, 38547–49, 38551, 38553, 38555–56, 38558–59, 38562, 38565, 38570–74, 38577, 38579, 38581, 38583, 38585, 38587, 38589

* * *

SEVENTH DISTRICT

MARSHA BLACKBURN, Republican, of Franklin, TN; born in Laurel, MS, June 6, 1952; education: B.S., Mississippi State University, 1973; professional: retail marketing; public service: American Council of Young Political Leaders; executive director, Tennessee Film, Entertainment, and Music Commission; chairman, Governor's Prayer Breakfast; Tennessee State Senate, 1998–2002; Minority Whip; community service: Rotary Club; Chamber of Commerce; Arthritis Foundation; Nashville Symphony Guild Board; Tennessee Biotechnology Association; March of Dimes; American Lung Association; awards: Chi Omega Alumnae Greek Woman of the Year, 1999; Middle Tennessee 100 Most Powerful People, 1999–2002; *More* magazine, ''Women Run The World'' honoree, April 2013; married: Chuck; children: Mary Morgan Ketchel and Chad; founding member of the Republican Women's Policy Committee; committees: Energy and Commerce; elected to the 108th Congress on November 5, 2002; reelected to each succeeding Congress.

Office Listings

http://blackburn.house.gov www.facebook.com/marshablackburn
twitter: @marshablackburn

2266 Rayburn House Office Building, Washington, DC 20515 .... (202) 225–2811
Chief of Staff.—Mike Platt. FAX: 225–3004
Legislative Director.—Chuck Flint.
Executive Assistant.—Grace Burch.
305 Public Square, Suite 212, Franklin, TN 37064 .... (615) 591–5161
128 North 2nd Street, Suite 202, Clarksville, TN 37040 .... (931) 503–0391

Counties: BENTON (part), CHESTER, DECATUR, GILES, HARDEMAN, HARDIN, HENDERSON, HICKMAN, HOUSTON, HUMPHREYS, LAWRENCE, LEWIS, MAURY (part), MCNAIRY, MONTGOMERY, PERRY, STEWART, WAYNE, AND WILLIAMSON. Population (2010), 705,192.

ZIP Codes: 37010, 37014–15, 37023, 37025, 37027–28, 37032, 37037, 37040, 37042–43, 37046–47, 37050–52, 37055, 37059–62, 37067, 37078–79, 37096–98, 37101, 37134–35, 37137, 37140, 37142, 37144, 37171, 37174–79, 37181, 37185, 37191, 37214–15, 37220, 38008, 38039, 38042, 38044, 38052, 38061, 38067, 38075, 38221, 38310, 38463–64, 38468–69, 38471–78, 38481–83, 38485–87, 42223

* * *

EIGHTH DISTRICT

DAVID KUSTOFF, Republican, of Germantown, TN; born in Memphis, TN, October 8, 1966; education: undergraduate degree, University of Memphis, Memphis, TN; law degree, University of Memphis Cecil C. Humphreys School of Law, 1992; professional: opened a law firm in Memphis, in 1998; chairman, Shelby County GOP, 1995–99; Tennessee chairman of both Bush/Cheney presidential campaigns in 2000 and 2004; appointed U.S. Attorney for the Western District of Tennessee by President Bush in 2006; served on the board of BankTennessee, 2010–16; appointed to the Tennessee Higher Education Commission by Tennessee Governor Bill Haslam in 2015; religion: Jewish; married: Roberta Kustoff; children: two; caucuses: Pro-

Israel Caucus, Sportsmens Caucus; committees: Financial Services; elected to the 115th Congress on November 8, 2016.

Office Listings

http://www.kustoff.house.gov

508 Cannon House Office Building, Washington, DC 20515 .... (202) 225–4714
Chief of Staff.—Tyler Threadgill.
Press Secretary.—Casey Black.
Legislative Director.—Justin Melvin.
Scheduler.—Anderson Briggs.
Staff Assistant.—Al David Saab.
Legislative Assistants: Olivia Dickey, Andrew Hogin.
Legislative Correspondent.—Eliana Goodman.
100 South Main Street, Suite 1, Dyersburg, TN 38024 .... (731) 412–1037
117 North Liberty Street, Jackson, TN 38301 .... (731) 423–4848
406 Lindell Street South, Suite C, Martin, TN 38237 .... (731) 412–1043
5900 Poplar Avenue, Suite 202, Memphis, TN 38119 .... (901) 682–4422

Counties: BENTON (part), CARROLL, CROCKETT, DYER, FAYETTE, GIBSON, HAYWOOD, HENRY, LAKE, LAUDERDALE, MADISON, OBION, SHELBY (part), TIPTON, AND WEAKLEY. Population (2010), 705,122.

ZIP Codes: 38001–02, 38004, 38006–07, 38011–12, 38015–19, 38021, 38023–24, 38028–30, 38034, 38036–37, 38039–42, 38046–47, 38049–50, 38053–54, 38057–60, 38063, 38066, 38068–70, 38075–77, 38079–80, 38111, 38117, 38119–20, 38125, 38128, 38133–35, 38138–39, 38141, 38152, 38201, 38220–22, 38224–26, 38229–33, 38235, 38237, 38240–42, 38251, 38253–61, 38301, 38305, 38313, 38316–18, 38326, 38330, 38337, 38341–44, 38348, 38351, 38355–56, 38358, 38362, 38366, 38369, 38382, 38387, 38390–92, 38401

* * *

NINTH DISTRICT

STEPHEN IRA "STEVE" COHEN, Democrat, of Memphis, TN; born in Memphis, May 24, 1949 to Dr. Morris D. Cohen and Genevieve Cohen; education: B.A., Vanderbilt University in Nashville, TN, 1971; J.D., Cecil C. Humphreys School of Law of Memphis State University (renamed University of Memphis), 1973; professional: legal advisor for the Memphis Police Department, 1974–77; delegate to and vice president of the Tennessee Constitutional Convention, 1977; Commissioner on the Shelby County Commission, 1978–80; Tennessee State Senator for District 30, 1982–2006; delegate to the 1980, 1992, 2004, 2008, 2012, and 2016 Democratic National Conventions; Commission on Security and Cooperation in Europe; House Democratic Steering and Policy; committees: Judiciary; Select Committee on Ethics; Transportation and Infrastructure; elected to the 110th Congress on November 7, 2006; reelected to each succeeding Congress.

Office Listings

http://www.cohen.house.gov https://twitter.com/repcohen
https://www.facebook.com/congressmanstevecohen

2404 Rayburn House Office Building, Washington, DC 20515 .... (202) 225–3265
Chief of Staff.—Marilyn Dillihay. FAX: 225–5663
Scheduler.—Patrick Cassidy.
Legislative Director.—Matt Weisman.
Communications Director.—Michael Eisenstatt.
167 North Main Street, Suite 369, Memphis, TN 38103 .... (901) 544–4131
FAX: 544–4329

County: SHELBY COUNTY (part). CITY: Memphis. Population (2010), 705,123.

ZIP Codes: 37501, 38016, 38018, 38053, 38101, 38103–109, 38111–20, 38122–28, 38130–36, 38138, 38141, 38146, 38148, 38151–52, 38159, 38167–68, 38173–75, 38181–82, 38186, 38188, 38190, 38193–94

TEXAS

(Population 2010, 25,145,561)

SENATORS

JOHN CORNYN, Republican, of Austin, TX; born in Houston, TX, February 2, 1952; education: graduated, Trinity University, and St. Mary's School of Law, San Antonio, TX; master of laws, University of Virginia, Charlottesville, VA; professional: attorney; Bexar County District Court Judge; Presiding Judge, Fourth Administrative Judicial Region; Texas Supreme Court, 1990–97; Texas Attorney General, 1999–2002; community service: Salvation Army Adult Rehabilitation Council; World Affairs Council of San Antonio; Lutheran General Hospital Board; chair, National Republican Senatorial Committee, 2009–13; committees: Finance; Judiciary; Select Committee on Intelligence; elected to the U.S. Senate on November 5, 2002, for the term beginning January 3, 2003; appointed to the Senate on December 2, 2002, to fill the vacancy caused by the resignation of Senator Phil Gramm; reelected to each succeeding Senate term.

Office Listings

http://cornyn.senate.gov https://www.facebook.com/sen.johncornyn

517 Hart Senate Office Building, Washington, DC 20510 .... (202) 224–2934
Republican Whip Office, S–208 Capitol Building, Washington, DC 20510 .... (202) 224–2708
Chief of Staff.—Beth Jafari. FAX: 224–5220
Legislative Director.—Stephen Tausend.
5300 Memorial Drive, Suite 980, Houston, TX 77007 .... (713) 572–3337
Providence Tower, 5001 Spring Valley Road, #1125E, Dallas, TX 75244 .... (972) 239–1310
100 East Ferguson Street, Suite 1004, Tyler, TX 75702 .... (903) 593–0902
221 West Sixth Street, Suite 1530, Austin, TX 78701 .... (512) 469–6034
Wells Fargo Center, 1500 Broadway, #1230, Lubbock, TX 79401 .... (806) 472–7533
222 East Van Buren, Suite 404, Harlingen, TX 78550 .... (956) 423–0162
600 Navarro Street, Suite 210, San Antonio, TX 78205 .... (210) 224–7485

* * *

TED CRUZ, Republican, of Houston, TX; born December 22, 1970; raised in Houston, TX; education: graduated *cum laude* from Princeton University with a B.A. from the Woodrow Wilson School of Public and International Affairs in 1992 and *magna cum laude* from Harvard Law School with a J.D. in 1995; professional: domestic policy advisor of the 2000 Bush-Cheney campaign; director of the Office of Policy Planning at the Federal Trade Commission; Associate Deputy Attorney General at the U.S. Department of Justice; adjunct professor of law at the University of Texas School of Law; Solicitor General of the State of Texas; partner at Morgan, Lewis & Bockius LLP; religion: Southern Baptist; married: Heidi Cruz; committees: Armed Services; Commerce, Science, and Transportation; Joint Economic Committee; Judiciary; Rules and Administration; elected to the U.S. Senate on November 6, 2012.

Office Listings

http://cruz.senate.gov https://www.facebook.com/senatortedcruz
https://twitter.com/sentedcruz

404 Russell Senate Office Building, Washington, DC 20510 .... (202) 224–5922
Chief of Staff.—Pre Shah. FAX: 228–0755
Deputy Chief of Staff/Legislative Director.—Steve Chartan.
State Director.—Carl Mica.
300 East 8th Street, Suite 961, Austin, TX 78701 .... (512) 916–5834
808 Travis Street, Suite 1420, Houston, TX 77002 .... (713) 718–3057
Lee Park Tower II, 3626 North Hall Street, Suite 410, Dallas, TX 75219 .... (214) 599–8749
9901 IH–10 West, Suite 950, San Antonio, TX 78230 .... (210) 340–2885
305 South Broadway Avenue, Suite 501, Tyler, TX 75702 .... (903) 593–5130
200 South 10th Street, Suite 1603, McAllen, TX 78501 .... (956) 686–7339

REPRESENTATIVES

FIRST DISTRICT

LOUIE GOHMERT, Republican, of Tyler, TX; born in Pittsburg, TX, August 18, 1953; education: B.A., Texas A&M University, 1975; J.D., Baylor University, Waco, TX, 1977; professional: U.S. Army, 1978–82; District Judge, Smith County, 1992–2002; appointed by Governor Rick Perry to complete an unexpired term as Chief Justice of the 12th Court of Appeals, 2002–03; Brigade Commander of the Corps of Cadets, Texas A&M; organizations: president of the South Tyler Rotary Club; Boy Scout District Board of Directors; religion: deacon of Green Acres Baptist Church; director of Leadership Tyler; director of Centrepoint Ministries; married: Kathy; children: Katy, Caroline, and Sarah; committees: Judiciary; Natural Resources; elected to the 109th Congress on November 2, 2004; reelected to each succeeding Congress.

Office Listings

http://www.gohmert.house.gov twitter: @replouiegohmert

2243 Rayburn House Office Building, Washington, DC 20515 .... (202) 225–3035
Chief of Staff.—Connie Hair. FAX: 226–1230
Legislative Director.—Austin Smithson.
Communications Director.—Kimberly Willingham.
1121 East Southeast Loop 323, Suite 206, Tyler, TX 75701 .... (903) 561–6349

Counties: ANGELINA, GREGG, HARRISON, NACOGDOCHES, PANOLA, RUSK, SABINE, SAN AUGUSTINE, SHELBY, SMITH, UPSHUR (part), AND WOOD (part). Population (2010), 710,704.

ZIP Codes: 75140, 75451, 75480, 75494, 75601–08, 75615, 75631, 75633, 75637, 75639–47, 75650–54, 75657–63, 75666–67, 75669–72, 75680–85, 75687–89, 75691–94, 75701–13, 75750, 75755, 75757, 75760, 75762, 75765, 75771, 75773, 75783–84, 75788–89, 75790–92, 75798–99, 75901–04, 75915, 75925–26, 75929–31, 75934–39, 75941–44, 75946, 75948–49, 75954, 75958–65, 75968–69, 75972–76, 75978, 75980

* * *

SECOND DISTRICT

TED POE, Republican, of Humble, TX; born in Temple, TX, September 10, 1948; education: B.A., political science, Abilene Christian University, Abilene, TX, 1970; J.D., University of Houston, TX, 1973; professional: U.S. Air Force, 1970–1976; Felony Court Judge, 1981–2003; trainer, Federal Bureau of Investigation National Academy; Chief Felony Prosecutor, District Attorney, Harris County, TX; U.S. Air Force Reserves Instructor, University of Houston; caucuses: Congressional PORTS Caucus; Congressional Victim's Rights Caucus; committees: Foreign Affairs; Judiciary; elected to the 109th Congress on November 2, 2004; reelected to each succeeding Congress.

Office Listings

http://www.poe.house.gov

2412 Rayburn House Office Building, Washington, DC 20515 .... (202) 225–6565
Chief of Staff.—Gina Foote. FAX: 225–5547
Press Secretary.—Shaylyn Hynes.
Scheduler.—Maddie Hoburg.
1801 Kingwood Drive, Suite 240, Kingwood, TX 77339 .... (866) 447–0242

Counties: HARRIS. Population (2010), 698,488.

ZIP Codes: 77002, 77004–08, 77018–19, 77024–25, 77030, 77040–41, 77043–44, 77055, 77064–66, 77069–70, 77079–80, 77084, 77086, 77088, 77092, 77095, 77098, 77336, 77338–39, 77345–46, 77357, 77365, 77373, 77375, 77377, 77379, 77388, 77396, 77429, 77532

* * *

THIRD DISTRICT

SAM JOHNSON, Republican, of Dallas, TX; born in San Antonio, TX, October 11, 1930; education: B.S., business administration, Southern Methodist University, Dallas, TX, 1951; M.A., international affairs, George Washington University, Washington, DC, 1974; military service: served in the U.S. Air Force, 29 years; Korea and Vietnam (POW in Vietnam, 6 years, 10 months); director, Air Force Fighter Weapons School; flew with Air Force Thunderbirds Precision Flying Demonstration Team; graduate of Armed Services Staff College and National War College; military awards: two Silver Stars, two Legions of Merit, Distinguished Flying Cross, one Bronze Star with Valor, two Purple Hearts, four Air Medals, and three Outstanding Unit awards; ended military career with rank of Colonel and Air Division Commander; retired, 1979; professional: opened homebuilding company, 1979; served 7 years in Texas House of Representatives; Smithsonian Board of Regents; U.S./Russian Joint Commission on POW/MIA;

Texas State Society; Congressional Medal of Honor Society; National Patriot Award Recipient, 2009; awards: Living Legends of Aviation ''Freedom of Flight'' Award recipient, 2011; Rotary International, Paul Harris Fellow; chairman of the Board of Directors, Institute of Basic Life Principles; married the former Shirley L. Melton, 1950; three children: Dr. James Robert Johnson, Shirley Virginia (Gini) Mulligan, and Beverly Briney; caucuses: co-chair, Air Force Caucus; founder, Republican Study Committee (formerly Conservative Action Team); Deputy Whip; committees: Joint Committee on Taxation; Ways and Means; elected to the 102nd Congress, by special election, on May 18, 1991, to fill the vacancy caused by the resignation of U.S. Representative Steve Bartlett; reelected to each succeeding Congress.

Office Listings

http://www.samjohnson.house.gov https://www.facebook.com/repsamjohnson
https://twitter.com/samspressshop

2304 Rayburn House Office Building, Washington, DC 20515 .... (202) 225–4201
Chief of Staff.—David Eiselsberg.
Legislative Director.—Jett Thompson.
Executive Assistant.—Amanda Hamilton.
1255 West 15th Street, Suite 170, Plano, TX 75075 .... (469) 304–0382

Counties: The 3rd District of Texas encompasses the majority of COLLIN COUNTY, including all or part of the CITIES of Allen, Anna, Blue Ridge, Dallas, Fairview, Frisco, Lavon, Lowry Crossing, Lucas, McKinney, Melissa, Murphy, New Hope, Parker, Plano, Princeton, Prosper, Richardson, St. Paul, Wylie, and portions of unincorporated land in COLLIN COUNTY. Population (2010), 747,284.

ZIP Codes: 75002 (part), 75009 (part), 75013, 75023, 75024 (part), 75025, 75035, 75044 (part), 75048 (part), 75069–70, 75071 (part), 75074–75, 75078 (part), 75080 (part), 75082 (part), 75093–94 (part), 75098 (part), 75166 (part), 75173 (part), 75248 (part), 75252 (part), 75287 (part), 75407, 75409 (part), 75424 (part), 75442 (part), 75454

* * *

FOURTH DISTRICT

JOHN RATCLIFFE, Republican, of Heath, TX; born in Mt. Prospect, IL, October 20, 1965; education: attended the University of Notre Dame, 1987; J.D., Southern Methodist University Law School, 1989; professional: Chief of Anti-Terrorism and National Security for the Eastern District of Texas, 2004–07; U.S. Attorney for the Eastern District of Texas, 2007–08; Mayor of Heath, TX, 2004–12; lawyer, the Ashcroft Law Firm, TX, 2008–14; religion: member, Our Lady of the Lake Catholic Church; wife: Michele Ratcliffe; children: Darby and Riley; committees: Ethics; Homeland Security; Judiciary; elected to the 114th Congress on November 4, 2014; reelected to the 115th Congress on November 8, 2016.

Office Listings

https://ratcliffe.house.gov https://www.facebook.com/repratcliffe
https://twitter.com/repratcliffe https://www.youtube.com/channel/uco37ersrga4fuyijda6j6oa

325 Cannon House Office Building, Washington, DC 20515 .... (202) 225–6673
Chief of Staff.—Daniel Kroese. FAX: 225–3332
Legislative Director and Counsel.—Emily Leviner.
Communications Director.—Shayne Martin.
6531 Horizon Road, Suite A, Rockwall, TX 75032 .... (972) 771–0100
District Director.—Jason Ross. FAX: 771–1222
2600 North Robison Road, Texarkana, TX 75505 .... (903) 823–3173
FAX: 823–3232
100 West Houston Street, 1st Floor, Sherman, TX 75090 .... (903) 813–5270
FAX: 868–8613

Counties: BOWIE COUNTY. CITIES AND TOWNSHIPS: DeKalb, Hooks, Leary, Maud, Nash, New Boston, Red Lick, Redwater, Texarkana, and Wake Village. CAMP COUNTY. CITIES AND TOWNSHIPS: Pittsburg and Rocky Mound. CASS COUNTY. CITIES AND TOWNSHIPS: Atlanta, Avinger, Bloomburg, Domino, Douglassville, Hughes Springs, Linden, Marietta, and Queen City. COLLIN COUNTY. CITIES AND TOWNSHIPS: Anna, Blue Ridge, Celina, Farmersville, Josephine, Lavon, Nevada, Royse City, Van Alstyne, Westminster, Weston, and Wylie. DELTA COUNTY. CITIES AND TOWNSHIPS: Cooper and Pecan Gap. FANNIN COUNTY. CITIES AND TOWNSHIPS: Bailey, Bonham, Dodd City, Ector, Honey Grove, Ladonia, Leonard, Pecan Gap, Ravenna, Savoy, Trenton, Whitewright, and Windom. FRANKLIN COUNTY. CITIES AND TOWNSHIPS: Mount Vernon and Winnsboro. GRAYSON COUNTY. CITIES AND TOWNSHIPS: Bells, Collinsville, Denison, Dorchester, Gunter, Howe, Knollwood, Pottsboro, Sadler, Sherman, Southmayd, Tioga, Tom Bean, Van Alstyne, Whitesboro, and Whitewright. HOPKINS COUNTY. CITIES AND TOWNSHIPS: Como, Cumby, Sulphur Springs, and Tira. HUNT COUNTY. CITIES AND TOWNSHIPS: Caddo Mills, Campbell, Celeste, Commerce, Greenville, Hawk Cove, Josephine, Lone Oak, Neylandville, Quinlan, West Tawakoni, and Wolfe City. LAMAR COUNTY. CITIES AND TOWNSHIPS: Blossom, Deport, Paris, Reno, Roxton, Sun Valley, and Toco. MARION COUNTY. CITIES AND TOWNSHIPS: Jefferson City and Pine Harbor. MORRIS COUNTY. CITIES AND TOWNSHIPS: Daingerfield, Hughes Springs, Lone Star, Naples, and Omaha. RAINS COUNTY. CITIES AND TOWNSHIPS: Alba, East Tawakoni, Emory, and Point. RED RIVER COUNTY. CITIES AND TOWNSHIPS: Annona, Avery, Bogata, Clarksville, Deport, and Detroit. ROCKWALL COUNTY. CITIES AND TOWNSHIPS: Fate, Garland, Heath,

Mclendon-Chisholm, Mobile City, Rockwall, Rowlett, Royse City, and Wylie. TITUS COUNTY. CITIES AND TOWNSHIPS: Miller's Cove, Mount Pleasant, and Talco. UPSHUR COUNTY. CITIES AND TOWNSHIPS: Clarksville City, East Mountain, Gilmer, Gladewater, Ore City, Union Grove, and Warren City. Population (2010), 705,523.

ZIP Codes: 75002, 75009, 75013, 75019, 75030, 75032, 75034–35, 75040–41, 75058, 75069, 75071, 75074, 75076, 75078, 75087–88, 75090, 75094, 75097–98, 75132, 75135, 75164, 75166, 75173, 75189, 75407, 75409, 75413–14, 75416–18, 75422–24, 75426, 75428–29, 75431–33, 75435–36, 75438–40, 75442, 75446, 75449, 75452–55, 75457, 75459, 75460, 75462, 75469, 75472–74, 75476–77, 75479, 75482, 75486–87, 75489, 75490–95, 75501, 75550–51, 75554, 75556, 75559–61, 75563, 75566–73, 75572, 75630, 75638, 75644–47, 75656, 75657, 75668, 75683, 75686, 75855, 76233, 76264, 76268, 76271, 76273

* * *

FIFTH DISTRICT

JEB HENSARLING, Republican, of Dallas, TX; born in Stephenville, TX, May 29, 1957; education: B.A., economics, Texas A&M University, 1979; J.D., University of Texas School of Law, 1982; professional: businessman; vice president, Maverick Capital, 1993–96; owner, San Jacinto Ventures, 1996–2002; vice president, Green Mountain Energy Co., 1999–2001; community service: American Cancer Society for the Dallas Metro Area; Children's Education Fund; Habitat for Humanity; religion: Christian; married: Melissa; children: Claire and Travis; committees: chair, Financial Services; elected to the 108th Congress on November 5, 2002; reelected to each succeeding Congress.

Office Listings

http://www.hensarling.house.gov twitter: @rephensarling
https://www.facebook.com/rephensarling

2228 Rayburn House Office Building, Washington, DC 20515 .... (202) 225–3484
Chief of Staff.—Andrew Duke. FAX: 226–4888
Legislative Director.—Kyle Jackson.
Press Secretary.—Liz Hill.
6510 Abrams Road, Suite 243, Dallas, TX 75238 .... (214) 349–9996
810 East Corsicana Street, Suite C, Athens, TX 77571 .... (903) 675–8288

Counties: ANDERSON, CHEROKEE, DALLAS (part), HENDERSON, KAUFMAN, VAN ZANDT, AND WOOD. Population (2010), 698,498.

ZIP Codes: 75041–43, 75103, 75114, 75117–18, 75124, 75126–27, 75140, 75142–43, 75147–50, 75156–61, 75163, 75169, 75180–82, 75185, 75187, 75214, 75217–18, 75227–28, 75231, 75238, 75243, 75253, 75336, 75355, 75382, 75389, 75410, 75431, 75440, 75444, 75474, 75494, 75497, 75751–52, 75754, 75756–59, 75763–64, 75766, 75770, 75772–73, 75778–80, 75782–85, 75789–90, 75801–03, 75832, 75839, 75844, 75853, 75861, 75880, 75882, 75884, 75886, 75925, 75976

* * *

SIXTH DISTRICT

JOE BARTON, Republican, of Ennis, TX; born in Waco, TX, September 15, 1949; education: graduated, Waco High School, 1968; B.S., industrial engineering, Texas A&M University, College Station, 1972; M.S., industrial administration, Purdue University, West Lafayette, IN, 1973; professional: plant manager, and assistant to the vice president, Ennis Business Forms, Inc., 1973–81; awarded White House Fellowship, 1981–82; served as aide to James B. Edwards, Secretary, Department of Energy; member, Natural Gas Decontrol Task Force in the Office of Planning, Policy and Analysis; worked with the Department of Energy task force in support of the President's Private Sector Survey on Cost Control; natural gas decontrol and project cost control consultant, Atlantic Richfield Company; cofounder, Houston County Volunteer Ambulance Service, 1976; vice president, Houston County Industrial Development Authority, 1980; chairman, Crockett Parks and Recreation Board, 1979–80; vice president, Houston County Chamber of Commerce, 1977–80; member, Dallas Energy Forum; religion: Methodist; children: Brad, Alison, Kristin, Jack; committees: vice chair, Energy and Commerce; elected to the 99th Congress on November 6, 1984; reelected to each succeeding Congress.

Office Listings

http://www.joebarton.house.gov https://www.facebook.com/repjoebarton
twitter: @RepJoeBarton

2107 Rayburn House Office Building, Washington, DC 20515 .... (202) 225–2002

Office Listings—Continued

Chief of Staff.—Ryan Thompson. FAX: 225–3052
Communications Director.—Daniel Rhea.
Legislative Director.—Krista Rosenthall.
Senior Legislative Assistant.—Amy Murphy.
Legislative Assistants: Gable Brady, Nick Grimes.
Staff Assistant.—Levi Gibson.

6001 West Ronald Reagan Memorial Highway, Suite 200, Arlington, TX 76017 .... (817) 543–1000
Casework Director.—Deborah Rollins. FAX: 548–7029
Special Projects Director.—Jodi Saegesser.
District Staff Assistant.—Rhonda Taylor.

2106A West Ennis Avenue, Ennis, TX 75119 (direct phone) .... (972) 875–8488
Deputy Chief of Staff.—Linda Gillespie. FAX: 875–1907
Outreach Coordinator.—Hunter Thedford.

Counties: Ellis, Navarro, and Tarrant. Cities and Townships: Alma, Angus, Arlington, Bardwell, Barry, Blooming Grove, Burleson, Cedar Hill, Corsicana, Crowley, Dawson, Emhouse, Ennis, Eureka, Ferris, Fort Worth, Frost, Garrett, Glenn Heights, Goodlow, Grand Prairie, Italy, Kennedale, Kerens, Mansfield, Maypearl, Midlothian, Milford, Mustang, Navarro, Oak Leaf, Oak Valley, Ovilla, Palmer, Pecan Hill, Powell, Red Oak, Rendon, Retreat, Rice, Richland, Venus, and Waxahachie. Population (2010), 720,861.

ZIP Codes: 75050, 75052, 75054, 75101–02, 75104–06, 75109–10, 75119–20, 75125, 75144, 75146, 75151–55, 75165, 75167–68, 75859, 76001–04, 76006, 76010–19, 76028, 76036, 76041, 76050, 76060, 76094, 76096, 76119–20, 76123, 76133–34, 76140, 76623, 76626, 76639, 76641, 76651, 76670, 76679, 76681

* * *

SEVENTH DISTRICT

JOHN ABNEY CULBERSON, Republican, of Harris County, TX; born in Houston, TX, August 24, 1956; education: B.A., Southern Methodist University; J.D., South Texas College of Law; professional: attorney; awards: Citizens for a Sound Economy, Friend of the Taxpayer Award; Texas Eagle Forum Freedom and Family Award; Houston Jaycees, Outstanding Young Houstonian Award; Champion of Border Security; Ancient Coin Collectors Guild; Friend of Numismatics; Club for Growth's Defender of Economic Freedom; Congressional Management Foundation's Silver Mouse Award; Family Research Council True Blue Award; Water Advocate, ''Friend of the Shareholder'' Recognition; U.S. Chamber of Commerce; Spirit of Enterprise Guardian of Small Business by NFIB; Recognition from the 60 Plus Association; NumbersUSA ''A'' for Consistently Voting for American Workers and the Environment through Immigration Reduction; public service: Texas House of Representatives, 1987–2000; married: Belinda Burney, 1989; child: Caroline; committees: Appropriations; elected to the 107th Congress on November 7, 2000; reelected to each succeeding Congress.

Office Listings

http://www.culberson.house.gov

2161 Rayburn House Office Building, Washington, DC 20515 .... (202) 225–2571
Chief of Staff.—Jamie Gahun. FAX: 225–4381
Legislative Director.—Corey Inglee.

10000 Memorial Drive, Suite 620, Houston, TX 77024–3490 .... (713) 682–8828
District Director.—Mary Schneider.

County: Harris (part). Population (2010), 717,354.

ZIP Codes: 77005, 77019, 77024–25, 77027, 77035–36, 77040–42, 77046, 77055–57, 77063–65, 77074, 77077, 77079, 77080–82, 77084, 77094–96, 77098, 77401–02, 77429, 77433, 77449–50

* * *

EIGHTH DISTRICT

KEVIN BRADY, Republican, of The Woodlands, TX; born in Vermillion, SD, April 11, 1955; education: B.S., business, University of South Dakota; professional: served in Texas House of Representatives, 1991–96, the second Republican to capture the 8th District seat since the district's creation; chair, Council of Chambers of Greater Houston; president, East Texas Chamber Executive Association; president, South Montgomery County Woodlands Chamber of Commerce, 1985–present; director, Texas Chamber of Commerce Executives; Rotarian; awards: Achievement Award, Texas Conservative Coalition; Outstanding Young Texan (one of five),

Texas Jaycees; Ten Best Legislators for Families and Children, State Bar of Texas; Legislative Standout, Dallas Morning News; Scholars Achievement Award for Excellence in Public Service, North Harris Montgomery Community College District; Victims Rights Equalizer Award, Texans for Equal Justice Center; Support for Family Issues Award, Texas Extension Homemakers Association; religion: attends Saints Simon and Jude Catholic Church; married: Cathy Brady; committees: chair, Ways and Means; vice chair, Joint Committee on Taxation; elected to the 105th Congress; reelected to each succeeding Congress.

Office Listings

http://www.kevinbrady.house.gov https://www.facebook.com/kevinbrady
https://twitter.com/repkevinbrady

1011 Longworth House Office Building, Washington, DC 20515 .... (202) 225–4901
Chief of Staff.—David Davis.
Legislative Director.—Sahra Su.
Director of Scheduling.—Jen Jett.
Press Secretary / Washington.—Allyson Manley.
Press Secretary / Texas.—Tracee Evans.
200 River Pointe Drive, Suite 304, Conroe, TX 77304 .... (936) 441–5700
District Director.—Todd Stephens.
1300 11th Street, Suite 400, Huntsville, TX 77340 .... (936) 439–9532

Counties: Grimes, Harris (part), Houston, Leon, Madison, Montgomery, San Jacinto, Trinity, and Walker. Cities and Townships: Anderson, Augusta, Bedias, Centerville, Conroe, Crockett, Decker Prairie, Grapeland, Groveton, Huntsville, Madisonville, Magnolia, Maynard, Midway, Montgomery, Navasota, New Caney, Normangee, Pinehurst, Plantersville, Point Blank, Porter Springs, Roans Prairie, Shepherd, Splendora, Spring, The Woodlands, Todd Mission, Tomball, Trinity, Weches, Willis, and Woodlake. Population (2010), 743,782.

ZIP Codes: 75833, 75835, 75844–45, 75847, 75852, 75856, 75858, 75862, 75849–51, 75926, 77070, 77301–06, 77316, 77318, 77320, 77328, 77331, 77333–34, 77340–42, 77353–59, 77365, 77367, 77371–73, 77375, 77377–89, 77393, 77447, 77830–31, 77855, 77861, 77864, 77868, 77876

* * *

NINTH DISTRICT

AL GREEN, Democrat, of Houston, TX; born in New Orleans, LA, September 1, 1947; raised in Florida; education: Florida A&M University, Tallahassee, FL, 1966–71; attended Tuskegee University, Tuskegee, AL; J.D., Texas Southern University, Houston, TX, 1974; professional: co-founded and co-managed the law firm of Green, Wilson, Dewberry and Fitch; Justice of the Peace, Precinct 7, Position 2, 1977–2004; organizations: former president of the Houston NAACP; Houston Citizens Chamber of Commerce; awards: Memorial Foundation's Leader of Democracy Award, 2014; VetsFirst Congressional Bronze Star; Texas Association of Realtors' Legacy Award, 2011; Texas Black Democrats' Profiles of Courage Award, 2007; AFL-CIO MLK Drum Major Award for Service, 2007; *Ebony* magazine's 100 Most Influential Black People, 2006; NAACP Mickey Leland Humanitarian Award, from the Houston branch, as well as the Fort Bend branch of the NAACP; committees: Financial Services; elected to the 109th Congress on November 2, 2004; reelected to each succeeding Congress.

Office Listings

http://www.algreen.house.gov twitter: @RepAlGreen

2347 Rayburn House Office Building, Washington, DC 20515 .... (202) 225–7508
Chief of Staff.—Amena Ross. FAX: 225–2947
Legislative Director.—Amena Ross.
Communications Director.—Kamau Marshall.
3003 South Loop West, Suite 460, Houston, TX 77054 .... (713) 383–9234
District Director.—Rachael Rodriguez. FAX: 383–9202
District Manger of Administration.—Crystal Webster.

Counties: Fort Bend (part) and Harris (part). Population (2010), 698,488.

ZIP Codes: 77004, 77025, 77030–31, 77033, 77035–36, 77042, 77045, 77047–48, 77051, 77053–54, 77061, 77063, 77071–72, 77074, 77077, 77082–83, 77085, 77087, 77096, 77099, 77407, 77459, 77477, 77489, 77498, 77545

* * *

TENTH DISTRICT

MICHAEL T. McCAUL, Republican, of Austin, TX; born in Dallas, TX, January 14, 1962; education: B.S., Trinity University, San Antonio, TX, 1984; J.D., St. Mary's University, San Antonio, TX, 1987; professional: lawyer, private practice; Deputy Attorney General, Office of Texas State Attorney General; committees: chair, Homeland Security; Foreign Affairs; elected to the 109th Congress on November 2, 2004; reelected to each succeeding Congress.

Office Listings

http://www.mccaul.house.gov

2001 Rayburn House Office Building, Washington, DC 20515 .... (202) 225–2401
Chief of Staff.—Jessica Nalepa. FAX: 225–5955
Legislative Director.—Thomas Hester.
Communications Director.—Elizabeth Litzow.
Scheduler / Office Manager.—Kelly Cotner.
9009 Mountain Ridge Drive, Suite 230, Austin, TX 78731 .... (512) 473–2357
Rosewood Professional Building, 990 Village Square, Suite B, Tomball, TX 77375 .... (281) 255–8372
1773 Westborough Drive, Suite 223, Katy, TX 77084 .... (281) 398–1247
2000 South Market Street, Suite 303, Brenham, TX 77833 .... (979) 830–8497

Counties: Austin, Bastrop, Colorado, Fayette, Harris, Lee, Travis, Waller, and Washington. Population (2010), 698,487.

ZIP Codes: 77070, 77355, 77363, 77375, 77377, 77389, 77412, 77418, 77423, 77426, 77428–29, 77433–35, 77442, 77445–47, 77449–50, 77460, 77466, 77470, 77473–75, 77484–85, 77493–94, 77833, 77835, 77868, 77880, 77964, 78602, 78612–13, 78621, 78641, 78645, 78650, 78653, 78703, 78705, 78723–24, 78726, 78730–32, 78746, 78751–54, 78756–59, 78931–35, 78938, 78940–51, 78954, 78956–57, 78959, 78962–63

* * *

ELEVENTH DISTRICT

K. MICHAEL CONAWAY, Republican, of Midland, TX; born in Borger, TX, June 11, 1948; education: B.B.A., Texas A&M-Commerce, 1970; professional: Spec 5, U.S. Army, 1970–72; tax manager, Price Waterhouse & Company, 1972–80; chief financial officer, Keith D. Graham & Lantern Petroleum Company, 1980–81; chief financial officer, Bush Exploration Company, 1982–84; chief financial officer, Spectrum 7 Energy Corporation, 1984–86; senior vice president / chief financial officer, United Bank, 1987–90; senior vice president, Texas Commerce Bank, 1990–92; owner, K. Conaway CPA, 1993–present; religion: Baptist; married: Suzanne; children: Brian, Erin, Kara, and Stephanie; Deputy Republican Whip; committees: chair, Agriculture; Armed Services; Permanent Select Committee on Intelligence; elected to the 109th Congress on November 2, 2004; reelected to each succeeding Congress.

Office Listings

http://www.conaway.house.gov https://www.facebook.com/mikeconaway twitter: @ConawayTX11

2430 Rayburn House Office Building, Washington, DC 20515 .... (202) 225–3605
Chief of Staff.—Mark Williams. FAX: 225–1783
Legislative Director.—Matthew Russell.
Scheduler.—Emily Keener.
6 Desta Drive, Suite 2000, Midland, TX 79705 .... (432) 687–2390
Regional Director.—Evan Thomas.

Counties: Andrews, Brown, Callahan, Coke, Coleman, Comanche, Concho, Dawson, Eastland, Ector, Erath, Glasscock, Hood, Irion, Kimble, Llano, Martin, Mason, McCulloch, Menard, Midland, Mills, Mitchell, Palo Pinto, Runnels, San Saba, Stephens, Sterling, and Tom Green. Population (2010), 698,488.

ZIP Codes: 76033, 76035, 76048–49, 76066–67, 76087, 76401, 76424, 76429, 76432–33, 76435–37, 76442–46, 76448–50, 76452–55, 76462–64, 76466, 76469–72, 76474–76, 76484, 76486, 76531, 76801–02, 76820–21, 76823, 76825, 76827–28, 76831–32, 76834, 76836–37, 76841–42, 76844–45, 76848–49, 76852–54, 76856–59, 76861–62, 76864–66, 76869–75, 76877–78, 76882, 76884–85, 76887–88, 76890, 76901, 76903–05, 76908, 76930, 76933–35, 76937, 76939–41, 76945, 76949, 76951, 76953, 76955, 76957–58, 78607, 78609, 78618, 78631, 78639, 78643, 78657, 78672, 79331, 79351, 79377, 79504, 79506, 79510, 79512, 79519, 79532, 79538, 79541, 79565–67, 79601–02, 79701, 79703, 79705–07, 79713–14, 79720, 79739, 79741, 79748, 79749, 79758–59, 79761–66, 79782–83

* * *

TWELFTH DISTRICT

KAY GRANGER, Republican, of Fort Worth, TX; born in Greenville, TX, January 18, 1943; education: B.S., *magna cum laude*, 1965, and honorary doctorate of humane letters, 1992, Texas Wesleyan University; professional: owner, Kay Granger Insurance Agency, Inc.; former public school teacher; elected Mayor of Fort Worth, 1991, serving three terms; during her tenure, Fort Worth received All-America City Award from the National Civic League; former Fort Worth Councilwoman; past chair, Fort Worth Zoning Commission; past board member: Dallas- Fort Worth International Airport; North Texas Commission; Fort Worth Convention and Visitors Bureau; U.S. Conference of Mayors Advisory Board; Business and Professional Women's Woman of the Year, 1989; three grown children: J.D., Brandon, and Chelsea; first woman Republican to represent Texas in the U.S. House of Representatives; Republican Whip; committees: Appropriations; elected to the 105th Congress; reelected to each succeeding Congress.

Office Listings

http://www.granger.house.gov

1026 Longworth House Office Building, Washington, DC 20515 .... (202) 225–5071
Chief of Staff.—Eric Wiese. FAX: 225–5683
Legislative Director.—Ben Kochman.
Staff Assistant.—John Muscolini.
Scheduler.—Brenan Tjelmeland.
1701 River Run Road, Suite 407, Fort Worth, TX 76107 .... (817) 338–0909
District Director.—Kristin Vandergiff. FAX: 335–5852

Counties: PARKER, TARRANT (part), AND WISE. Population (2010), 728,142.

ZIP Codes: 76008, 76020, 76023 (part), 76035 (part), 76049 (part), 76052 (part), 76066 (part), 76071, 76078 (part), 76082 (part), 76085, 76098, 76101, 76104 (part), 76106 (part), 76113, 76121, 76126, 76129, 76147, 76161, 76177 (part), 76179, 76185, 76191, 76195, 76234 (part), 76244 (part), 76246 (part), 76439, 76462 (part), 76485, 76490

* * *

THIRTEENTH DISTRICT

MAC THORNBERRY, Republican, of Clarendon, TX; born in Clarendon, July 15, 1958; education: graduate, Clarendon High School; B.A., Texas Tech University; law degree, University of Texas; professional: rancher; attorney; admitted to the Texas Bar, 1983; member: Joint Forces Command Transformation; Republican Study Committee; married: Sally Adams, 1986; children: Will and Mary Kemp; committees: chair, Armed Services; elected to the 104th Congress; reelected to each succeeding Congress.

Office Listings

http://www.thornberry.house.gov https://www.facebook.com/repmacthornberry
https://twitter.com/mactxpress http://www.youtube.com/repmacthornberry

2208 Rayburn House Office Building, Washington, DC 20515 .... (202) 225–3706
Administrative Assistant.—Ariel McCord. FAX: 225–3486
Office Managers: Ariel McCord, Jordan Hunter.
620 South Taylor Street, Suite 200, Amarillo, TX 79101 .... (806) 371–8844
Chief of Staff.—Josh Martin.
2525 Kell Boulevard, Suite 406, Wichita Falls, TX 76308 .... (940) 692–1700

Counties: ARCHER, ARMSTRONG, BAYLOR, BRISCOE, CARSON, CHILDRESS, CLAY, COLLINGSWORTH, COOKE, COTTLE, DALLAM, DEAF SMITH, DICKENS, DONLEY, FLOYD, FOARD, GRAY, HALL, HANSFORD, HARDEMAN, HARTLEY, HEMPHILL, HUTCHINSON, JACK, KING, KNOX, LIPSCOMB, MONTAGUE, MOORE, MOTLEY, OCHILTREE, OLDHAM, POTTER, RANDALL, ROBERTS, SHERMAN, SWISHER, WHEELER, WICHITA, WILBARGER, AND WISE (part). Population (2010), 703,835.

ZIP Codes: 73448, 73539, 73562, 73848–49, 76023, 76073, 76078, 76082, 76225, 76228, 76230, 76233–34, 76238–40, 76250–52, 76255, 76259, 76261, 76263, 76265–66, 76270–73, 76301–02, 76305–06, 76308–11, 76351, 76354, 76357, 76360, 76363–67, 76371, 76373–74, 76377, 76379–80, 76384, 76389, 76426–27, 76431, 76458–59, 76486–87, 79001, 79005, 79007, 79011, 79014–16, 79018–19, 79022, 79029, 79034, 79036, 79039–40, 79042, 79044–46, 79052, 79056–59, 79061–62, 79065, 79068, 79070, 79079–81, 79083–84, 79086–88, 79092, 79094–98, 79101–04, 79106–11, 79118–19, 79121, 79124, 79178, 79201, 79220, 79225–27, 79229–30, 79234–35, 79237, 79239–41, 79243–45, 79247–48, 79251–52, 79255–57, 79259, 79261, 79370, 79529

* * *

FOURTEENTH DISTRICT

RANDY WEBER, Republican, of Friendswood, TX; born in Pearland, TX, July 2, 1953; education: B.S., University of Houston, Clear Lake, 1977; professional: owner, Weber's Air and Heat, 1981–present; married: 1976; children: Kristin, Keith, and Kyle; grandchildren: seven; committees: Science, Space, and Technology; Transportation and Infrastructure; elected to the 113th Congress on November 6, 2012; reelected to each succeeding Congress.

Office Listings

http://weber.house.gov https://www.facebook.com/txrandy14
https://twitter.com/txrandy14

1708 Longworth House Office Building, Washington, DC 20515 .... (202) 225–2831
Chief of Staff.—Chara McMichael. FAX: 225–0271
Legislative Director.—Sarah Noack.
Communications Director.—Emma Polefko.
505 Orleans Street, Suite 103, Beaumont, TX 77701 .... (409) 835–0108
122 West Way Street, Suite 301, Lake Jackson, TX 77566 .... (979) 285–0231
174 Calder Road, Suite 150, League City, TX 77573 .... (281) 316–0231

Counties: BRAZORIA (part), GALVESTON, AND JEFFERSON. Population (2010), 705,051.

ZIP Codes: 77510, 77517–18, 77539, 77546, 77549–55, 77563, 77565, 77568, 77573–74, 77590–92, 77617, 77623, 77650

* * *

FIFTEENTH DISTRICT

VICENTE GONZALEZ, Democrat, of McAllen, TX; born in Corpus Christi, TX, September 4, 1967; education: G.E.D., 1985; associate degree in banking and finance, Del Mar College, 1990; bachelor's degree in aviation business administration, Embry Riddle University, 1992; J.D., Texas Wesleyan University School of Law (now Texas A&M School of Law), 1996; professional: lawyer; private practice, V. Gonzalez & Associates, PC, 1997–present; religion: Roman Catholic; married: Lorena Gonzalez; committees: Financial Services; elected to the 115th Congress on November 8, 2016.

Office Listings

http://www.gonzalez.house.gov https://www.facebook.com/USCongressmanVicenteGonzalez

113 Cannon House Office Building, Washington, DC 20515 .... (202) 225–2531
Chief of Staff.—Jose Borjon. FAX: 225–5688
2864 West Trenton Road, Edinburg, TX 78539 .... (956) 682–5545
District Director.—Robert Villarreal. FAX: 682–0141
North District .... (956) 682–5545
North District Director.—Robert Villarreal.

Counties: BROOKS, DUVALL, GUADALUPE, HIDALGO, JIM HOGG, KARNES, LIVE OAK (part), AND WILSON. CITIES AND TOWNSHIPS: Alamo, Alton, Cibolo, Edinburg, Hidalgo, McAllen, Mercedes, Mission, New Braunfels, Pharr, San Juan, Schertz, Seguin, Taft, Three Rivers, Weslaco, and Whitsett. Population (2011), 722,529.

ZIP Codes: 78008, 78022, 78060, 78071, 78108, 78111, 78113–19, 78121, 78123–24, 78130, 78132, 78140–41, 78143–44, 78151, 78154–56, 78160, 78164, 78332, 78341, 78349–50, 78353, 78355, 78357, 78360–61, 78368, 78372, 78376, 78383–84, 78501–05, 78516, 78537–43, 78549, 78557–59, 78562–63, 78569–70, 78572–74, 78577, 78589, 78596, 78599, 78638, 78648, 78655, 78666, 78670

* * *

SIXTEENTH DISTRICT

BETO O'ROURKE, Democrat, of TX; born in El Paso, El Paso County, TX, September 26, 1972; education: B.A., Columbia University, New York, NY, 1995; professional: business owner; member of the El Paso, Texas City Council, 2005–11; committees: Armed Services; Veterans' Affairs; elected to the 113th Congress on November 6, 2012; reelected to each succeeding Congress.

Office Listings

http://www.orourke.house.gov

1330 Longworth House Office Building, Washington, DC 20515 .... (202) 225–4831
Chief of Staff.—David Wysong.
Scheduler / Office Manager.—Samantha Stiles.
Legislative Director.—Aaron Woolf.
303 North Oregon Street, Suite 210, El Paso, TX 79901 .... (915) 541–1400

Counties: El Paso (part). Population (2010), 698,488.

ZIP Codes: 79901–06, 79908, 79911–12, 79915–16, 79920, 79922, 79924–25, 79930, 79932, 79934–36

* * *

SEVENTEENTH DISTRICT

WILLIAM H. ''BILL'' FLORES, Republican, of Bryan, TX; born at Warren Air Force Base, Cheyenne, WY, February 25, 1954; education: graduated, Stratford High School, Stratford, TX, 1972; B.B.A., *cum laude*, Texas A&M University, College Station, TX, 1976; M.B.A., Houston Baptist University, Houston, TX, 1985; Texas Certified Public Accountant (CPA), 1978–present; commissioner, Texas Real Estate Commission (appointed by Governor Perry), 2004–09; CEO and president, Phoenix Exploration Company, 2006–09; Texas A&M University Distinguished Alumnus, 2010; Houston Baptist University Distinguished Alumnus, 2013; married: the former Gina Bass; children: Will and John; daughter-in-law, Aimee; granddaughters, Britain and Charlie; committees: Energy and Commerce; elected to the 112th Congress on November 2, 2010; reelected to each succeeding Congress.

Office Listings

http://flores.house.gov

2440 Rayburn House Office Building, Washington, DC 20515 .... (202) 225–6105
Chief of Staff.—Jon Oehmen. FAX: 225–0350
Communications Director.—Andre Castro.
400 Austin Avenue, Suite 302, Waco, TX 76701 .... (254) 732–0748
District Director.—Jana Hixson.
14205 Burnet Road, Suite 230, Austin, TX 78728 .... (512) 373–3378
3000 Briarcrest Drive, Suite 406, Bryan, TX 77802 .... (979) 703–4037
FAX: 691–8939

Counties: Brazos, Burleson, Falls, Freestone, Lee, Leon, Limestone, McLennan, Milam, Robertson, and Travis (part). Population (2010), 710,793.

ZIP Codes: 75833, 75840, 75848, 75850, 75860, 76518, 76520, 76523, 76632, 76635, 76638, 76640, 76643, 76654, 76656, 76661, 76678, 76680, 76684, 76686, 76701–05, 76707–08, 76710–12, 76714–16, 76797–99, 77801–03, 77805–06, 77837–38, 77840–45, 77850, 77852–53, 77855–57, 77862–63, 77865–67, 77870, 77878–79, 77881–82, 78660, 78691, 78727–28, 78753, 78948

* * *

EIGHTEENTH DISTRICT

SHEILA JACKSON LEE, Democrat, of Houston, TX; born in Queens, NY, January 12, 1950; education: graduated, Jamaica High School; B.A., Yale University, New Haven, CT, 1972; J.D., University of Virginia Law School, 1975; professional: practicing attorney for 12 years; AKA Sorority; Houston Area Urban League; American Bar Association; staff counsel, U.S. House Select Committee on Assassinations, 1977–78; admitted to the Texas Bar, 1975; City Council (at large), Houston, 1990–94; Houston Municipal Judge, 1987–90; married: Dr. Elwyn Cornelius Lee, 1973; two children: Erica Shelwyn and Jason Cornelius Bennett; two grandchildren; U.S. Helsinki Commission; committees: Budget; Homeland Security; Judiciary; elected to the 104th Congress; reelected to each succeeding Congress.

Office Listings

http://www.jacksonlee.house.gov

twitter: @JacksonLeeTX18 instagram: http://instagram.com/sjltx18

2187 Rayburn House Office Building, Washington, DC 20515 .... (202) 225–3816

Office Listings—Continued

Chief of Staff.—Glenn Rushing. FAX: 225–3317
Chief Counsel.—Gregory Berry.
Policy Director.—Lillie Coney.
Legislative Counsel.—Karis Johnson.
Communications Director.—Rucks Russell.
Scheduler.—LaDedra Drummond.
Executive / Staff Assistant.—Remmington Belford.
Staff Assistant.—Richard Bruno.

1919 Smith Street, Suite 1180, Houston, TX 77002 .... (713) 655–0050
District Director.—Clint Diamond.
District Counsel.—Booker Morris.
Executive Assistant.—Martha Hernandez.
Field Representatives and Caseworkers: James Doggette, Daniel Espinoza, Alma Sanchez, Ivan Sanchez, Tonya Williams.
Account and Finance.—Michelle Donches.

420 West 19th Street, Houston, TX 77008 .... (713) 861–4070
6719 West Montgomery, Suite 204, Houston, TX 77091 .... (713) 691–4882

Counties: HARRIS COUNTY (part). CITY: Houston. Population (2010), 698,488.

ZIP Codes: 77001–10, 77013, 77016, 77018–24, 77026, 77028–30, 77033, 77035, 77038, 77040–41, 77045, 77047–48, 77051–52, 77054–55, 77064, 77066–67, 77076, 77078, 77080, 77086–88, 77091–93, 77097–98, 77201–06, 77208, 77210, 77212, 77216, 77219, 77221, 77226, 77230, 77233, 77238, 77240–41, 77251–53, 77255, 77265–66, 77277, 77288, 77291–93, 77297–99

* * *

NINETEENTH DISTRICT

JODEY C. ARRINGTON, Republican, of Lubbock, TX; born in Kansas City, MO, March 9, 1972; education: B.A. in political science, Texas Tech University, Lubbock, 1994; master of public administration, Texas Tech University, 1997; Certificate of International Business Management, McDonough School of Business at Georgetown University, Washington, DC, 2004; professional: appointments manager for Governor George W. Bush, Austin, TX, 1996–2000; Special Assistant to the President and Associate Director of Presidential Personnel during the George W. Bush administration, Washington, DC, 2000–01; Chief of Staff to the Chairman of the FDIC, Washington, DC, 2001–05; Deputy Federal Coordinator and Chief Operating Officer at the Office of the Federal Coordinator for Gulf Coast Rebuilding, Washington, DC, 2005–06; chief of staff to the chancellor of the Texas Tech University System, Lubbock, TX, 2006–11; vice chancellor for research and commercialization at Texas Tech University System, Lubbock, TX, 2011–14; president, Scott Laboratories, Lubbock, TX, 2014–16; awards: 2003 Distinguished Public Service Award as part of the 22nd annual Center for Public Service Symposium in Lubbock, TX; religion: Presbyterian; married: Anne; three children; committees: Agriculture; Budget; Veterans' Affairs; elected to the 115th Congress on November 7, 2016.

Office Listings

http://www.arrington.house.gov

1029 Longworth House Office Building, Washington, DC 20515 .... (202) 225–4005
Chief of Staff.—Russell Thomasson. FAX: 225–9615
Deputy Chief of Staff.—Emily Shaw.
Communications Director.—Kate McBrayer.
Legislative Director.—Davis Pace.
Legislative Assistant.—Dominique Spadavecchia.
Legislative Assistant / Legislative Correspondent.—Elissa McLerran.
Executive Assistant.—Kayla Nation.
Staff Assistant.—Laura Carr.

1312 Texas Avenue, Suite 219, Lubbock, TX 79401 .... (806) 763–1611
District Director.—Jay Hardaway.
Constituent Services Representative.—Lauren Heinrich.
Constituent Services Representative.—Joel Riedel.

500 Chestnut Street, #819, Abilene, TX 79602 .... (325) 675–9779
Constituent Services Representative.—Bobbi Hanson.
Constituent Services Representative.—Lauren Decker.

Counties: BAILEY, BORDEN, CASTRO, COCHRAN, CROSBY, FISHER, FLOYD (part), GAINES, GARZA, HALE, HASKELL, HOCKLEY, HOWARD, JONES, KENT, LAMB, LUBBOCK, LYNN, NOLAN, PARMER, SCURRY, SHACKELFORD, STEPHENS (part), STONEWALL, TAYLOR, TERRY, THROCKMORTON, YOAKUM, AND YOUNG. Population (2010), 707,772.

ZIP Codes: 76372, 76374 (part), 76388, 76424 (part), 76429 (part), 76430, 76450 (part), 76460, 76464 (part), 76481, 76483, 76491, 79009, 79021, 79027, 79031–32, 79035 (part), 79041, 79042 (part), 79043, 79045 (part), 79052 (part),

79053, 79063–64, 79072 (part), 79082, 79085, 79088 (part), 79231, 79235 (part), 79241 (part), 79250, 79311–14, 79316, 79322–26, 79329, 79330, 79331 (part), 79336, 79339, 79342–47, 79350, 79351 (part), 79353, 79355–60, 79363–64, 79366–67, 79369, 79370 (part), 79371–73, 79376, 79378–82, 79401, 79403–04, 79406–07, 79410–16, 79423–24, 79501–03, 79504 (part), 79506 (part), 79508, 79511, 79512 (part), 79517–18, 79520–21, 79525–28, 79529 (part), 79530, 79532 (part), 79533–37, 79539, 79540, 79541 (part), 79543–49, 79553, 79556, 79560–63, 79566 (part), 79567 (part), 79601 (part), 79602 (part), 79603, 79605–07, 79699, 79713 (part), 79720 (part), 79733, 79738, 79748 (part)

* * *

TWENTIETH DISTRICT

JOAQUIN CASTRO, Democrat, of San Antonio, TX; born in San Antonio, September 16, 1974; education: Thomas Jefferson High School, 1992; B.A., Stanford University, CA, 1996; J.D., Harvard University, Cambridge, MA, 2000; professional: attorney; law instructor; religion: Catholic; family: wife, Anna Flores; caucuses: Congressional Caucus on ASEAN; Congressional Hispanic Caucus; Congressional Pre-K Caucus; New Democrat Coalition; U.S.-Japan Caucus; committees: Foreign Affairs; Permanent Select Committee on Intelligence; elected to the 113th Congress on November 6, 2012; reelected to each succeeding Congress.

Office Listings

http://castro.house.gov https://www.facebook.com/joaquincastrotx
twitter: @joaquincastrotx

1221 Longworth House Office Building, Washington, DC 20515 .... (202) 225–3236
Scheduler.—Danielle Moon.
Legislative Director.—Ben Thomas.
Legislative Assistant.—Jacqueline Sanchez.
Chief of Staff.—Danny Meza.
Legislative Correspondent.—Emily Richardson.
Press Secretary.—Erin Hatch.

Counties: BEXAR (part). CITIES: Alamo Heights, Balcones Heights, Lackland AFB, Helotes, Leon Valley, and San Antonio. Population (2010), 716,759.

ZIP Codes: 78023, 78073, 78201, 78204, 78207, 78209, 78211–14, 78216, 78221, 78224–31, 78236–38, 78240, 78242, 78245, 78249–57

* * *

TWENTY-FIRST DISTRICT

LAMAR S. SMITH, Republican, of San Antonio, TX; born in San Antonio, November 19, 1947; education: graduated, Texas Military Institute, San Antonio, 1965; B.A., Yale University, New Haven, CT, 1969; intern, Small Business Administration, Washington, DC, 1969–70; business and financial writer, *The Christian Science Monitor*, Boston, MA, 1970–72; J.D., Southern Methodist University School of Law, Dallas, TX, 1975; professional: admitted to the State Bar of Texas, 1975, and commenced practice in San Antonio with the firm of Maebius and Duncan, Inc.; elected chairman of the Republican Party of Bexar County, TX, 1978 and 1980; elected District 57-F State Representative, 1981; elected Precinct 3 Commissioner of Bexar County, 1982 and 1984; partner, Lamar Seeligson Ranch, Jim Wells County, TX; married: Beth Schaefer; children: Nell and Tobin; committees: chair, Science, Space, and Technology; Homeland Security; Judiciary; elected to the 100th Congress on November 4, 1986; reelected to each succeeding Congress.

Office Listings

http://lamarsmith.house.gov

2409 Rayburn House Office Building, Washington, DC 20515 .... (202) 225–4236
Chief of Staff.—Ashlee Vinyard. FAX: 225–8628
Legislative Director.—Abby Gunderson-Schwarz
Scheduler.—Christa Danford.
The Tetco Center, 1100 North East Loop 410, Suite 640, San Antonio, TX 78207 .... (210) 821–5024
District Director.—Mike Asmus.
2211 IH 35 South, Suite 106, Austin, TX 78741 .... (512) 912–7508
301 Junction Highway, Suite 346C, Kerrville, TX 78028 .... (830) 896–0154

Counties: BANDERA, BEXAR (part), BLANCO, COMAL (part), KENDALL, KERR, REAL, TRAVIS (part), GILLESPIE, AND HAYS (part). Population (2010), 698,488.

ZIP Codes: 78003, 78006, 78010, 78013, 78015, 78024–25, 78027–29, 78055, 78058, 78063, 78070, 78130–33, 78135, 78148, 78163, 78209, 78212–13, 78216–18, 78230–33, 78239, 78241, 78247, 78258–59, 78261, 78265–66, 78270,

78606, 78610, 78618–20, 78623–24, 78631, 78635–36, 78641, 78645, 78652, 78663, 78666, 78669, 78675–76, 78726, 78730–39, 78741, 78746, 78748–50, 78759, 78883, 78885

* * *

TWENTY-SECOND DISTRICT

PETE OLSON, Republican, of Sugar Land, TX; born in Fort Lewis, WA, December 9, 1962; education: B.A., Rice University, Houston, TX, 1985; law degree, University of Texas, Austin, TX, 1988; professional: U.S. Navy, 1988–98; U.S. Senate, 1998–2007; Naval Aviator wings, 1991; Naval Liaison, U.S. Senate; religion: United Methodist; married: Nancy Olson; children: Kate and Grant; committees: Energy and Commerce; elected to the 111th Congress on November 4, 2008; reelected to each succeeding Congress.

Office Listings

http://olson.house.gov

2133 Rayburn House Office Building, Washington, DC 20515 .... (202) 225–5951
Chief of Staff.—Bill Zito.
Legislative Director.—Rich England.
Deputy Chief of Staff/Communications Director.—Melissa Kelly.
Scheduler.—Victoria Blackwell.
1650 Highway 6, Suite 150, Sugar Land, TX 77478 .... (281) 494–2690
District Director.—Ty Petty.
1920 Country Place Parkway, Suite 140, Pearland, TX 77584 .... (281) 485–4855

Counties: BRAZORIA, FORT BEND, AND HARRIS (part). CITIES: Alvin, Arcola, Beasley, Brookside Village, Friendswood, Fulshear, Katy, Meadows Place, Missouri City, Manvel, Needville, Orchard, Pleak, Pearland, Richmond, Rosenberg, Sugar Land, Simonton, Stafford, Villages of Fairchild, Webster, and Weston Lakes. Population (2010), 698,504.

ZIP Codes: 77406–07, 77417, 77441, 77450, 77461, 77464, 77469, 77471, 77476, 77477–79, 77487, 77489, 77493–94, 77511–12, 77545–46, 77578, 77581, 77583–84, 77588, 77598

* * *

TWENTY-THIRD DISTRICT

WILL HURD, Republican, of San Antonio, TX; born in San Antonio, August 19, 1977; education: attended public schools in San Antonio, TX; B.S., computer science, Texas A&M University, College Station, TX, 1999; professional: cybersecurity consultant; CIA officer; religion: Christian; committees: Homeland Security; Oversight and Government Reform; Permanent Select Committee on Intelligence; elected to the 114th Congress on November 4, 2014; reelected to 115th Congress on November 8, 2016.

Office Listings

https://hurd.house.gov https://www.facebook.com/hurdonthehill
https://twitter.com/hurdonthehill

317 Cannon House Office Building, Washington, DC 20515 .... (202) 225–4511
Chief of Staff.—Stoney Burke. FAX: 225–2237
Legislative Director.—Matthew Haskins.
Executive Assistant.—Nancy Pack.
Communications Director.—Rachel Holland.
Press Secretary.—Camlin Moore.
Legislative Assistant.—Austin Agrella.
Legislative Aide.—Salim Alameddin.
Legislative Correspondent.—Chris Malen.
Press Assistants: Eliezer Flores, Callie Strock.
Staff Assistant.—Jazmin Perez.
17721 Rogers Ranch Parkway, Suite 120, San Antonio, TX 78258 .... (210) 921–3130
FAX: 927–4903
One University Drive, Patriot's Casa, Suite 202A, San Antonio, TX 78224 .... (210) 784–5023
124 South Horizon Boulevard, Socorro, TX 79927 .... (915) 235–6421
1104 West 10th, Del Rio, TX 78840 .... (210) 238–4296
100 Monroe Street, Eagle Pass, TX 78852 .... (210) 238–4296
103 West Callaghan, Second Floor, Fort Stockton, TX 79735 .... (210) 245–1548

Counties: Bexar (part), BREWSTER, CRANE, CROCKETT, CULBERSON, DIMMIT, EDWARDS, EL PASO (part), FRIO, HUDSPETH, JEFF DAVIS, KINNEY, LA SALLE (part), LOVING, MAVERICK, MEDINA, PECOS, PRESIDIO, REAGAN, REEVES, SCHLEICHER, SUTTON, TERRELL, UPTON, UVALDE, VAL VERDE, WARD, WINKLER, AND ZAVALA. Population (2014), 725,874.

ZIP Codes: 76841, 76932, 76935–36, 76943, 76950, 78001–03, 78005–06, 78009, 78014–17, 78019, 78021, 78023, 78039, 78052, 78056–57, 78059, 78061, 78066, 78069, 78073, 78112, 78211, 78214, 78220–24, 78227, 78230–32, 78236, 78245, 78248–49, 78251–58, 78260, 78264, 78801–02, 78827–30, 78832–34, 78836–40, 78843, 78850–52, 78860–61, 78870–73, 78877, 78879–81, 78884, 78886, 79718–19, 79730–31, 79734–35, 79739, 79742–45, 79752, 79754–56, 79766, 79770, 79772, 79777–78, 79780–81, 79785, 79788–89, 79830–31, 79834, 79836–39, 79842–43, 79845–49, 79851–55, 79907, 79927–28, 79938, 79942, 88220

* * *

TWENTY-FOURTH DISTRICT

KENNY MARCHANT, Republican, of Coppell, TX; born in Bonham, TX, February 23, 1951; education: B.A., Southern Nazarene University, Bethany, OK, 1974; attended Nazarene Theological Seminary, Kansas City, MO, 1975–76; professional: real estate developer; member of the Carrollton, TX, City Council, 1980–84; Mayor of Carrollton, TX, 1984–87; member of the Texas State House of Representatives, 1987–2004; member, Advisory Board of Children's Medical Center; married: Donna; four children; committees: Ethics; Ways and Means; elected to the 109th Congress on November 2, 2004; reelected to each succeeding Congress.

Office Listings

http://www.marchant.house.gov https://www.facebook.com/repkennymarchant
https://twitter.com/repkenmarchant

2313 Rayburn House Office Building, Washington, DC 20515 .... (202) 225–6605
Chief of Staff.—Brian Thomas. FAX: 225–0074
Deputy Chief of Staff, Washington.—Scott Cunningham.
Legislative Director.—John Deoudes.
Communications Director.—Rob Damschen.
Tax Counsel.—Robert Vega.
Deputy Communications Director and Scheduler.—Nicholas Smith.
Legislative Correspondent.—Nicholas Smith.
Staff Assistant.—Ryan Hamilton.
9901 East Valley Ranch Parkway, Suite 2060, Irving, TX 75063 .... (972) 556–0162
Deputy Chief of Staff, District.—Susie Miller.
Military and Veterans Liaison.—John Hayes.
Director of District Affairs.—Todd Martin.
Communications and Outreach Representative.—Rhett Gum.
Constituent Services Representative.—Chelsey Payne.

Counties: DALLAS (part), DENTON (part), AND TARRANT (part). CITIES AND TOWNSHIPS: Addison, Bedford, Carrollton, Colleyville, Coppell, Dallas (part), Euless, Farmer's Branch, Fort Worth (part), Grapevine, Hurst, Irving (part), Lewisville (part), Plano (part), Southlake, and The Colony. Population (2010), 698,488.

ZIP Codes: 75001, 75006–07, 75010–11, 75014, 75016, 75019, 75022, 75024, 75028, 75038–39, 75056, 75061–63, 75067, 75093, 75099, 75209, 75220, 75229–30, 75234, 75240, 75244, 75248, 75252, 75254, 75261, 75287, 75354, 75368, 75379–81, 75391, 76021–22, 76034, 76039–40, 76051, 76053–54, 76092, 76095, 76099, 76118, 76120, 76155, 76180, 76182, 76248, 76262

* * *

TWENTY-FIFTH DISTRICT

ROGER WILLIAMS, Republican, of Austin, TX; born in Evanston, IL, September 13, 1949; education: graduated, Arlington Heights High School; B.S., Texas Christian University, Fort Worth, TX, 1972; professional: drafted by the Atlanta Braves Organization; owner Roger Williams Car Dealerships; 105th Secretary of State of Texas, 2004–07; regional finance chair for Governor Bush, 1994, 1998; North Texas chairman for the Bush/Cheney 2000 campaign; North Texas finance chairman and national grassroots fundraising chairman for Bush/Cheney 2004, Inc.; appointed chairman of the Republican National Finance Committee's Eagles Program by President George W. Bush, 2001; state finance chair for John Cornyn for U.S. Senate, Inc., 2002; chief liaison for Texas Border and Mexican Affairs, 2005; chair of the Texas Base Realignment and Closure Response Strike Force; boards: Texas Christian University Board of Trustees; National Football Foundation; College Football Hall of Fame; religion: member, University Christian Church; married: Patty Williams; children: Sabrina and Jaclyn; committees: Financial Services; elected to the 113th Congress on November 6, 2012; reelected to each succeeding Congress.

Office Listings

http://www.williams.house.gov

1323 Longworth House Office Building, Washington, DC 20515 .... (202) 225–9896

Office Listings—Continued

Chief of Staff.—Colby Hale. FAX: 225–9692
Deputy Chief.—Spencer Freebairn.
Legislative Director.—Sean Dillon.
Legislative Aide.—Nicole Lansford.
Legislative Correspondent.—Zack Barth.
Staff Assistant.—Kathryn Dalke.
Press Secretary.—Vince Zito.
Scheduler.—Hanna Allred.
1005 Congress Avenue, Suite 925, Austin, TX 78701 .... (512) 473–8910
District Director.—John Etue. FAX: 473–8946
115 South Main Street, Suite 206, Cleburne, TX 76033 .... (817) 774–2575
Case Worker.—Robert Camacho. FAX: 774–2577

Counties: BELL (part), BOSQUE, BURNET, CORYELL, ERATH (part), HAMILTON, HAYS (part), HILL, JOHNSON, LAMPASAS, SOMERVELL, TARRANT (part), AND TRAVIS (part). Population (2010), 698,478.

ZIP Codes: 76009, 76028, 76031, 76033, 76035–36, 76043–44, 76048–49, 76050, 76055, 76058–59, 76063, 76070, 76077, 76084, 76093, 76401–02, 76433, 76436, 76446, 76457, 76522, 76525, 76526–28, 76531, 76538–39, 76544, 76549–50, 76557, 76561, 76565–66, 76621–22, 76627, 76631, 76633–34, 76636–38, 76645, 76648–49, 76652, 76657, 76660, 76665–66, 76671, 76673, 76676, 76689–90, 76692, 76853, 76877, 76880, 78605, 78608, 78610–11, 78613, 78619–20, 78623, 78639, 78641–42, 78645, 78652, 78654, 78657, 78666, 78669, 78676, 78701–03, 78705, 78712, 78721–25, 78730–34, 78736–39, 78745–46, 78749–50

* * *

TWENTY-SIXTH DISTRICT

MICHAEL C. BURGESS, Republican, of Denton County, TX; born, December 23, 1950; education: B.A., biology, North Texas State University; M.S., physiology, North Texas State University; M.D., University of Texas Medical School, Houston; M.S., medical management, University of Texas, Dallas; completed medical residency programs, Parkland Hospital in Dallas; professional: founder, Private Practice Specialty Group for Obstetrics and Gynecology; former Chief of Staff and Chief of Obstetrics, Lewisville Medical Center; organizations: former president, Denton County Medical Society; Denton County delegate, Texas Medical Association; alternate delegate, American Medical Association; married: Laura; three children; committees: Energy and Commerce; Rules; elected to the 108th Congress on November 5, 2002; reelected to each succeeding Congress.

Office Listings

http://www.burgess.house.gov https://www.facebook.com/michaelcburgess
twitter: @michaelcburgess

2336 Rayburn House Office Building, Washington, DC 20515 .... (202) 225–7772
Chief of Staff.—Kelle Strickland. FAX: 225–2919
Legislative Director.—James Decker.
Press Secretary.—Lesley Fulop.
Scheduler.—Amanda Stevens.
2000 South Stemmons Freeway, Suite 200, Lake Dallas, TX 75065 .... (940) 497–5031

Counties: DALLAS (part), DENTON (part), AND TARRANT (part). Population (2010), 698,488.

ZIP Codes: 75009, 75019, 75022, 75027–29, 75033–34, 75056–57, 75065, 75067–68, 75077–78, 76034, 76052, 76065, 76078, 76092, 76117, 76137, 76148, 76177, 76180, 76182, 76201–10, 76226–27, 76234, 76244, 76247–49, 76258–59, 76262

* * *

TWENTY-SEVENTH DISTRICT

MICHAEL CLOUD, Republican, of Victoria, TX; born in Baton Rouge, LA, May 13, 1975; education: graduated from Miamisburg High School, Miamisburg, OH, 1993; B.S., Oral Roberts University, Tulsa, OK, 1997; professional: communications director; business owner; committees: Oversight and Government Reform; Science, Space, and Technology; elected to the 115th Congress, by special election, on June 30, 2018, to fill the vacancy caused by the resignation of U.S. Representative Blake Farenthold.

Office Listings

http://www.cloud.house.gov

2331 Rayburn House Office Building, Washington, DC 20515 .... (202) 225–7742

Office Listings—Continued

Chief of Staff.—Bob Haueter. FAX: 226–1134
Executive Assistant / Scheduler.—Thad Brock.
Deputy Chief of Staff / Legislative Director.—Blake Adami.
101 North Shoreline Boulevard, Suite 300, Corpus Christi, TX 78401 .... (361) 884–2222
5606 North Navarro Street, Suite 203, Victoria, TX 77904 .... (361) 894–6446

Counties: ARANSAS, BASTROP, CALDWELL, CALHOUN, GONZALES, JACKSON, LAVACA, MATAGORDA, NUECES, REFUGIO, SAN PATRICIO, VICTORIA, AND WHARTON. Population (2010), 702,804.

ZIP Codes: 77404, 77414–15, 77419–20, 77428, 77432, 77435–37, 77440, 77443, 77448, 77453–58, 77465, 77467–68, 77482–83, 77488, 77901–05, 77950–51, 77957, 77961–62, 77964, 77968–71, 77973, 77975–79, 77982–84, 77986–88, 77990–91, 77995, 78330, 78335–36, 78339–40, 78343, 78347, 78351–52, 78358–59, 78362, 78368, 78370, 78373–74, 78377, 78380–82, 78387, 78390, 78393, 78401–19, 78426–27, 78460, 78463, 78465–69, 78472, 78480, 78602, 78612, 78614, 78616, 78629, 78632, 78648, 78655–56, 78658, 78661–62, 78953, 78957

* * *

TWENTY-EIGHTH DISTRICT

HENRY CUELLAR, Democrat, of Laredo, TX; born in Laredo, September 19, 1955; education: associate's degree from Laredo Community College, Laredo, TX, 1976 (then known as Laredo Junior College); B.S., *cum laude*, foreign service, from the Edmund A. Walsh School of Foreign Service at Georgetown University, Washington, DC, 1978; J.D., University of Texas, Austin, TX, 1981; M.B.A., international trade, Texas A&M University, Laredo, TX, 1982; Ph.D., government, University of Texas, Austin, 1998; with a total of five advanced degrees, Congressman Cuellar is the most degreed member of Congress; professional: lawyer, private practice; attorney, Law Office of Henry Cuellar, 1981–present; instructor, Department of Government, Laredo Community College, Laredo, TX, 1982–86; licensed U.S. Customs broker, 1983–present; adjunct professor, international commercial law, Texas A&M International, 1984–86; Representative, Texas State House of Representatives, 1986–2001; Secretary of State, State of Texas, 2001; public and civic organizations: board of directors, Kiwanis Club of Laredo, TX, 1982–83; co-founder / president, Laredo Volunteers Lawyers Program, Inc., 1982–83; board of directors, United Way, 1982–83; co-founder / treasurer, Stop Child Abuse and Neglect, 1982–83, and advisory board member, 1984; president, board of directors, Laredo Legal Aid Society, Inc., 1982–84; president, board of directors, Laredo Young Lawyers Association, 1983–84; sustaining member, Texas Democratic Party, 1984; legal advisor, American GI, local chapter, 1986–87; International Trade Association, Laredo State University, 1988; Texas Delegate, National Democratic Convention, 1992; president, board of directors, International Good Neighbor Council; member, the College of the State Bar of Texas, 1994; Texas Lyceum, 1997; policy board of advisors, *Texas Hispanic Journal of Law*, University of Texas Law School, 2002; member: American Bar Association; Inter-American Bar Association; Texas Bar Association; Webb / Laredo Bar Association; recipient of various awards; religion: Catholic; married: wife, Imelda; two daughters, Christina Alexandra and Catherine Ann; Senior Whip; vice chairman of the Steering and Policy Committee; caucuses: co-chair of the Blue Dog Coalition; Congressional Unmanned Systems Caucus; committees: Appropriations; elected to the 109th Congress on November 2, 2004; reelected to each succeeding Congress.

Office Listings

http://www.cuellar.house.gov https://www.facebook.com/repcuellar
twitter: @repcuellar

2209 Rayburn House Office Building, Washington, DC 20515 .... (202) 225–1640
Chief of Staff.—Cynthia Gaona. FAX: 225–1641
Legislative Director.—Ryan Ehly.
Scheduler.—Andrea Trevino.
615 East Houston Street, Suite 451, San Antonio, TX 78205 .... (210) 271–2851
602 East Calton Road, Suite 2, Laredo, TX 78041 .... (956) 725–0639
FAX: 725–2647
117 East Tom Landry, Mission, TX 78572 .... (956) 424–3942
FAX: 424–3936
100 North F.M. 3167, Rio Grande City, Texas 78582 .... (956) 487–5603
FAX: 488–0952
615 East Houston Street, Suite 563, San Antonio, TX 78205 .... (210) 271–2851
FAX: 277–6671

Counties: ATASCOSA, BEXAR (part), HIDALGO (part), LA SALLE (part), MCMULLEN, STARR, WEBB, WILSON (part), AND ZAPATA. Population (2010), 698,488.

ZIP Codes: 78005, 78007–08, 78011–12, 78014, 78019, 78021, 78026, 78040–41, 78043–46, 78050, 78052, 78064–65, 78067, 78069, 78071–73, 78075–76, 78101, 78108–09, 78112–14, 78121, 78124, 78147–48, 78150, 78152, 78154,

78160–61, 78218–20, 78222–23, 78233, 78239, 78244, 78263–64, 78344, 78361, 78369, 78371, 78536, 78541, 78545, 78548, 78560, 78564–65, 78572–74, 78576, 78582, 78584–85, 78588, 78591, 78595

* * *

TWENTY-NINTH DISTRICT

GENE GREEN, Democrat, of Houston, TX; born in Houston, October 17, 1947; education: B.A., University of Houston, 1971; J.D., University of Houston Bates College of Law, 1977; admitted, Texas Bar, 1977; professional: business manager; attorney; Texas State Representative, 1973–85; Texas State Senator, 1985–92; member: Houston Bar Association; Texas Bar Association; American Bar Association; Communications Workers of America; Aldine Optimist Club; Gulf Coast Conservation Association; Lindale Lions Club; Texas Historical Society; Texas State Society; married: Helen Albers, January 23, 1970; children: Angela and Christopher; caucuses: co-chair, Democratic Israel Working Group; co-chair, Natural Gas Caucus; co-chair, Sportsmen's Caucus; co-chair, Tuberculosis Elimination Caucus; co-chair, Vision Caucus; Aerospace Caucus; Autism Caucus; Azerbaijani Caucus; Caucus to Cure Blood Cancers and Other Blood Disorders; Congressional Steel Caucus; Diabetes Caucus; Financial and Economic Literacy Caucus; Friends of Job Corps Caucus; Grid Reliability Caucus; Guard and Reserve Caucus; House Cancer Caucus; India Caucus; Israel Allies Caucus; Manufacturing Caucus; National Marine Sanctuary Caucus; Nursing Caucus; PORTS Caucus; Pro-Choice Caucus; Public Health Caucus; Rare Disease Congressional Caucus; Seniors Task Force; State Medicaid Expansion Caucus; Traumatic Brain Injury Task Force; Unmanned Systems Caucus; Urban Caucus; Victim's Rights Caucus; Wire and Wire Product Caucus; Democratic Senior Whip; committees: Energy and Commerce; elected on November 3, 1992 to the 103rd Congress; reelected to each succeeding Congress.

Office Listings

http://www.green.house.gov https://www.facebook.com/repgenegreen twitter: @repgenegreen

2470 Rayburn House Office Building, Washington, DC 20515 .... (202) 225–1688
Legislative Director.—Sergio Espinosa. FAX: 225–9903
Press Secretary.—Joseph Puente.
Legislative Assistants: Ben Jackson, Kristen O'Neill, Susannah Ross.
Scheduler.—Joseph Puente.
256 North Sam Houston Parkway East, Suite 29, Houston, TX 77060 .... (281) 999–5879
Chief of Staff / Administrative Assistant.—Rhonda Jackson.
11811 I–10 East, Suite 430, Houston, TX 77029 .... (713) 330–0761

Counties: HARRIS (part). CITIES AND TOWNSHIPS: Channelview, Galena Park, Houston, Humble, Jacinto City, Pasadena, and South Houston. Population (2013), 729,827.

ZIP Codes: 77003, 77009, 77011–13, 77015–17, 77020, 77022–23, 77026, 77029, 77032, 77034, 77037, 77039, 77044, 77049–50, 77060–61, 77075–76, 77087, 77089, 77091, 77093, 77396, 77502–06, 77530, 77536, 77547, 77587

* * *

THIRTIETH DISTRICT

EDDIE BERNICE JOHNSON, Democrat, of Dallas, TX; born in Waco, TX, December 3, 1935; education: nursing diploma, St. Mary's at Notre Dame, 1955; B.S., nursing, Texas Christian, 1967; M.P.A., Southern Methodist, 1976; professional: proprietor, Eddie Bernice Johnson and Associates, consulting and airport concession management; Texas House of Representatives, 1972–77; Carter Administration appointee, 1977–81; Texas State Senate, 1986–92; awards: NABTP Mickey Leland Award for Excellence in Diversity, 2000; National Association of School Nurses, Inc., Legislative Award, 2000; the State of Texas Honorary Texan issued by the Governor of Texas, 2000; Links, Inc., Co-Founders Award, 2000; 100 Black Men of America, Inc., Woman of the Year, 2001; National Black Caucus of State Legislators Image Award, 2001; National Conference of Black Mayors, Inc. President's Award, 2001; Alpha Kappa Alpha Trailblazer, 2002; Thurgood Marshall Scholarship Community Leader, 2002; Phi Beta Sigma Fraternity Woman of the Year, 2002; CBCF Outstanding Leadership, 2002; congressional caucuses: Asian-Pacific; Airpower; Army; Arts; Biomedical Research; chair (107th Congress), Congressional Black Caucus; Children's Working Group; co-chair, Task Force on International HIV / AIDS; Fire Services; Human Rights Caucus; Korean Caucus; Livable Communities Task Force; Medical Technology; Oil and Gas Educational Forum; Singapore Caucus; Study Group on Japan; TX–21 Transportation Caucus; Urban; Womens' Caucus; Women's Issues; member: St. John Baptist Church, Dallas; children: Dawrence Kirk; grandchildren: Kirk, Jr., David, and

James; committees: ranking member, Science, Space, and Technology; Transportation and Infrastructure; elected on November 3, 1992 to the 103rd Congress; reelected to each succeeding Congress.

Office Listings

http://www.ebjohnson.house.gov https://facebook.com/CongresswomanEBJtx30
twitter: https://twitter.com/RepEBJ

2468 Rayburn House Office Building, Washington, DC 20515 .... (202) 225–8885
Chief of Staff / Legislative Director.—Murat Gokcigdem. FAX: 226–1477
Communications Director.—TreShonda Sheffey.
Legislative Assistants: Don Andres, Justin Clayton, Carrie Palmer.
Staff Assistant.—Nawaid Ladak.
1825 Market Center Boulevard, Suite 440, Dallas, TX 75207 .... (214) 922–8885
District Director.—Germaine White.

Counties: DALLAS (part). CITIES AND TOWNSHIPS: Downtown Dallas, Fair Park, Kessler Park, Old East Dallas, Pleasant Grove, South Dallas, and South Oak Cliff; all of Cedar Hill, DeSoto, Duncanville, Hutchins, Lancaster, and Wilmer and parts of Ferris, Glenn Heights, South Grand Prairie, Oak Lawn, Ovilla, Uptown/Victory Park, and West Dallas. Population (2010), 698,487.

ZIP Codes: 75051–52, 75054, 75115–16, 75125, 75134, 75137, 75141, 75146, 75149–50, 75154, 75159, 75172, 75180, 75201–04, 75207–12, 75214–20, 75223–28, 75232–33, 75235–37, 75241, 75246–47, 75249, 75253, 75270

* * *

THIRTY-FIRST DISTRICT

JOHN R. CARTER, Republican, of Round Rock, TX; born in Houston, TX, November 6, 1941; education: Texas Tech University, 1964; University of Texas Law School, 1969; professional: attorney; private law practice; public service: appointed and elected a Texas District Court Judge, 1981–2001; awards: recipient and namesake of the Williamson County ''John R. Carter Lifetime Achievement Award''; family: married to Erika Carter; children: Gilianne, John, Theodore, and Danielle; committees: Appropriations; elected to the 108th Congress on November 5, 2002; reelected to each succeeding Congress.

Office Listings

http://www.carter.house.gov

2110 Rayburn House Office Building, Washington, DC 20515 .... (202) 225–3864
Chief of Staff.—Jonas Miller. FAX: 225–5886
Communications Director.—Corry Schiemeyer.
Scheduler.—Carol Richmond.
1717 North IH 35, Suite 303, Round Rock, TX 78664 .... (512) 246–1600
6544B South General Bruce Drive, Temple, TX 76502 .... (254) 933–1392

Counties: BELL AND WILLIAMSON. Population (2010), 739,975.

ZIP Codes: 76501, 76504, 76511, 76513, 76527, 76530, 76534, 76537, 76542–43, 76548–49, 76557, 76559, 76569, 76571, 76574, 76578, 78613, 78615, 78621, 78628, 78633–34, 78641–42, 78664–65, 78681, 78717, 78728–29

* * *

THIRTY-SECOND DISTRICT

PETE SESSIONS, Republican, of Dallas, TX; born in Waco, TX, March 22, 1955; education: B.S., in social sciences, political science, Southwestern University, Georgetown, TX, 1978; professional: worked for Southwestern Bell, and Bell Communications Research (formerly Bell Labs), 1978–94; vice president for public policy, National Center for Policy Analysis, 1994–95; board member, White Rock YMCA; trustee, Southwestern University; member, National Eagle Scout Association's national committee; advisor to president, Special Olympics Texas; past chairman, East Dallas Chamber of Commerce; awards: Honorary Doctorate, Dallas Baptist University; National Distinguished Eagle Scout Award; Boy Scouts of America; Leadership Award, American College of Emergency Physicians; Spirit of Enterprise Award, U.S. Chamber of Commerce; Best and Brightest, American Conservative Union; Guardian of Small Business Award, National Federation of Independent Business; Taxpayers' Friend Award, National Taxpayers Union; National Leadership Award, National Down Syndrome Society; Champion of

Healthcare Innovation Award, Healthcare Leadership Council; Wireless Industry Achievement Award, Cellular Telecommunications and Internet Association; religion: Methodist; married: Karen Sessions; two sons: Bill and Alex; three stepsons: Conor, Liam, and Nicholas; caucuses: co-chair, Congressional Down Syndrome Caucus; co-chair, Congressional Missile Defense Caucus; former chairman, National Republican Congressional Committee; committees: chair, Rules; elected to the 105th Congress on November 5, 1996; reelected to each succeeding Congress.

Office Listings

http://sessions.house.gov https://www.facebook.com/petesessions
https://twitter.com/petesessions http://www.flickr.com/photos/petesessions
https://instagram.com/congressmanpetesessions

2233 Rayburn House Office Building, Washington, DC 20515 .... (202) 225–2231
Chief of Staff.—Kyle Matous. FAX: 225–5878
Communications Director.—Caroline Boothe.
Legislative Director.—Ryan Ethington.
Lakeside Square, 12377 Merit Drive, Suite 750, Dallas, TX 75251–2224 .... (972) 392–0505
Chief of Staff.—Matt Garcia.

County: DALLAS (part) AND COLLIN (part). CITIES AND TOWNSHIPS: Dallas, Richardson, University Park, Highland Park, Mesquite, Garland, Sachse, Rowlett and Wylie. Population (2010), 698,488.

ZIP Codes: 75002, 75040–44, 75048, 75080–82, 75088–89, 75094, 75098, 75150, 75166, 75182, 75201, 75204–06, 75209, 75214, 75218–19, 75223, 75225–26, 75229–31, 75235, 75238, 75243–46, 75248, 75251–52

* * *

THIRTY-THIRD DISTRICT

MARC VEASEY, Democrat, of Fort Worth, TX; born in Fort Worth, January 3, 1971; education: B.S., Texas Wesleyan University, Fort Worth, 1995; professional: journalist; staff, U.S. Representative J. Martin Frost of Texas; real estate; Texas State Representative, 2004–12; religion: Christian; married: Tonya Veasey; children: Adam Veasey; caucuses: Blue Collar Caucus; Congressional Black Caucus; Congressional Voting Rights Caucus; committees: Armed Services; Science, Space, and Technology; elected to the 113th Congress on November 6, 2012; reelected to each succeeding Congress.

Office Listings

http://www.veasey.house.gov www.facebook.com/congressmanmarcveasey
twitter: @repveasey instagram: @repveasey

1519 Longworth House Office Building, Washington, DC 20515 .... (202) 225–9897
Chief of Staff.—Askia Suruma. FAX: 225–9702
Communications Director.—Nelly Decker.
Executive Assistant / Scheduler.—Jane Phipps.
Legislative Director.—Ashley Baker.
Legislative Assistant.—Thaddeus Woody.
Deputy Communications Director / Legislative Aide.—Paloma Perez.
Legislative Aide.—Nicole Varner.
Legislative Correspondent / Aide.—Palak Gosar.
6707 Brentwood Stair Road, Suite 200, Fort Worth, TX 76112 .... (817) 920–9086
District Director.—Anne Hagan.
1881 Sylvan Avenue, Suite 108, Dallas, TX 75208 .... (214) 741–1387

Counties: DALLAS (part) AND TARRANT (part). CITIES AND TOWNSHIPS: Arlington, Cockrell Hill, parts of Dallas, Everman, Forest Hill, Fort Worth, Grand Prairie, Haltom City, Irving, Saginaw, and Sansom Park. Population (2010), 698,488.

ZIP Codes: 75050–52, 75060–62, 75203, 75208, 75211–12, 75216, 75220, 75224, 75229, 75233–36, 75247, 76006, 76010–12, 76014, 76040, 76053, 76103–06, 76109–12, 76114–15, 76117–20, 76133–34, 76137, 76140, 76155, 76164, 76179

* * *

THIRTY-FOURTH DISTRICT

FILEMON VELA, Democrat, of Brownsville, TX; born in Harlingen, TX, February 13, 1963; education: B.A., Georgetown University, 1985; J.D., University of Texas at Austin School of Law, 1987; professional: attorney; admitted, Texas Bar and U.S. District Court, Western and Southern Districts of Texas, 1988; married: Rose Rivera, February 3, 1990; caucuses: co-chair,

Border Caucus; co-chair, Citrus Caucus; co-chair, Zika Caucus; Career and Technical Education Caucus; Coastal Communities Caucus; Community College Caucus; Community Health Center Caucus; Congressional Friends of the National Park Service; Congressional Hispanic Caucus; Diabetes Caucus; Disaster Relief Caucus; Friends of Job Corps Congressional Caucus; General Aviation Caucus; I-69 Caucus; Ports Caucus; Pre-K Caucus; Texas Caucus on Shale Oil and Gas; Texas Maritime Caucus; TX-21 Transportation Congressional Caucus; U.S.-Mexico Friendship Caucus; committees: Agriculture; Homeland Security; elected to the 113th Congress on November 6, 2012; reelected to each succeeding Congress.

Office Listings

http://www.vela.house.gov

437 Cannon House Office Building, Washington, DC 20515 .... (202) 225–9901
Chief of Staff.—Perry Brody.
Scheduler.—Liza Lynch.
Deputy Chief of Staff.—Karen De Los Santos.
Senior Policy Advisor.—Julie Merberg.
Senior Policy Advisor.—Luke Theriot.
Press Director.—Mickeala Carter.
Press Secretary.—Clarissa Robles.
Staff.—Mariana Adame.
333 Ebony Avenue, Brownsville, TX 78520 .... (956) 544–8352
District Director.—Marisela Cortez.
Senior Caseworker.—Maria Barrera Jaross.
District Press Secretary / Caseworker.—Brenda Lopez.
500 East Main Street, Alice, TX 78332 .... (361) 230–9776
District Director.—Jose Pereida.
1390 West Expressway 83, San Benito, TX 78586 .... (956) 276–4497
Office Manager / Caseworker.—Sally Lara.
301 West Railroad Avenue, Weslaco, TX 78596 .... (956) 520–8273
Caseworker.—Anissa Guajardo.

Counties: Bee, Cameron, DeWitt, Goliad, Gonzales, Hidalgo, Jim Wells, Kenedy, Kleberg, San Patricio, and Willacy. Population (2010), 716,416.

ZIP Codes: 77954, 77960, 77963, 77993–94, 78104, 78107, 78122, 78125, 78142, 78145–46, 78159, 78162, 78164, 78338, 78342, 78363, 78375, 78379, 78385, 78389, 78391, 78520–21, 78526, 78535, 78550, 78552, 78559, 78561, 78566–67, 78575, 78578–80, 78583, 78586, 78590, 78592–94, 78597–98, 78614, 78677

* * *

THIRTY-FIFTH DISTRICT

LLOYD DOGGETT, Democrat, of Austin, TX; born in Austin, October 6, 1946; education: graduated, Austin High School; B.B.A., University of Texas, Austin, 1967; J.D., University of Texas, 1970; president, University of Texas student body; associate editor, *Texas Law Review*; professional: Outstanding Young Lawyer, Austin Association of Young Lawyers; president, Texas Consumer Association; admitted to the Texas State Bar, 1971; Texas State Senate, 1973–85, elected at age 26; Senate author of 124 state laws and Senate sponsor of 63 House bills enacted into law; elected President Pro Tempore of Texas Senate; served as acting governor; named Outstanding Young Texan by Texas Jaycees; Arthur B. DeWitty Award for outstanding achievement in human rights, Austin NAACP; honored for work by Austin Rape Crisis Center, Planned Parenthood of Austin; Austin chapter, American Institute of Architects; Austin Council on Alcoholism; Disabled American Veterans; Save the Children Congressional Champion for Real and Lasting Change; AARP Legislative Achievement Award; Justice on Texas Supreme Court, 1989–94; chairman, Supreme Court Task Force on Judicial Ethics, 1992–94; Outstanding Judge (Mexican-American Bar of Texas), 1993; adjunct professor, University of Texas School of Law, 1989–94; James Madison Award, Texas Freedom of Information Foundation, 1990; First Amendment Award, National Society of Professional Journalists, 1990; religion: member, First United Methodist Church; married: Libby Belk Doggett, 1969; children: Lisa and Cathy; caucuses: Congressional Task Force on Tobacco and Health; Democratic Caucus Task Force on Child Care; committees: Ways and Means; elected to the 104th Congress; reelected to each succeeding Congress.

Office Listings

http://www.doggett.house.gov https://twitter.com/repllloyddoggett
https://www.facebook.com/lloyddoggett

2307 Rayburn House Office Building, Washington, DC 20515 .... (202) 225–4865

Office Listings—Continued

Chief of Staff.—Michael J. Mucchetti. FAX: 225–3073
Communications Director.—Jaimie Woo.
Staff Assistant / Scheduler.—Christina Nunez.
217 West Travis, San Antonio, TX 78205 .... (210) 704–1080
District Director.—MaryEllen Veliz.
300 East 8th Street, Suite 763, Austin, TX 78701 .... (512) 916–5921
District Director.—Lee Ann Calaway.

Counties: BEXAR, CALDWELL, COMAL, GUADALUPE, HAYS, AND TRAVIS. Population (2010), 698,488.

ZIP Codes: 78108, 78130, 78132, 78154, 78201–05, 78207–08, 78210, 78212, 78214–15, 78217–20, 78222–23, 78228, 78233–35, 78239, 78244, 78247, 78266, 78610, 78612, 78617, 78622, 78640, 78644, 78653, 78655–56, 78666, 78702, 78704, 78719, 78721, 78725, 78741–42, 78744–45, 78747–48, 78753–54, 78758

* * *

THIRTY-SIXTH DISTRICT

BRIAN BABIN, Republican, of Woodville, TX; born in Port Arthur, TX, March 23, 1948; education: B.S., Lamar University; D.D.S., University of Texas; professional: dentist; Mayor of Woodville, 1982–84; Woodville City Councilman, 1984–1989; Woodville Independent School Board, 1992–95; director of Tyler County Chamber of Commerce; president of Texas State Board of Dental Examiners, 1981–87; Deep East Texas Council of Governments member, 1982–84; Texas Historical Commission, 1989–1995; Appointee to Lower Neches Valley Authority, 1999–2014; caucuses: Air Force Caucus; Autism Caucus; Boating Caucus; Border Security Caucus; Congressional Aerospace Caucus; Congressional Sportsmen's Caucus; Diabetes Caucus; Foster Youth Caucus; GOP Doctors Caucus; House Republican Israel Caucus; Israel Allies Caucus; Military Veterans Caucus; Oral Health Caucus; Ports Caucus; Pro Life Caucus; Refinery Caucus; Republican Study Committee; committees: Science, Space, and Technology; Transportation and Infrastructure; elected to the 114th Congress on November 4, 2014; reelected to the 115th Congress on November 8, 2016.

Office Listings

http://babin.house.gov https://twitter.com/repbrianbabin https://facebook.com/repbrianbabin

316 Cannon House Office Building, Washington, DC 20515 .... (202) 225–1555
Chief of Staff.—Stuart Burns. FAX: 226–0396
Legislative Director.—Ben Couhig.
Press Secretary.—Jimmy Milstead.
Legislative Staff: Steve Janushkowsky, Mary Moody.
Staff Assistant.—Sarah Reese.
Scheduler.—Beth Barber.
203 Ivy Avenue, Suite 600, Deer Park, TX 77536 .... (832) 780–0966
420 Green Avenue, Orange, TX 77630 .... (409) 883–8075
100 West Bluff Drive, Woodville, TX 75979 .... (844) 303–8934

Counties: CHAMBERS, HARDIN, HARRIS (part), JASPER, LIBERTY, NEWTON, ORANGE, POLK, AND TYLER. Population (2010), 712,433.

ZIP Codes: 75326–27, 75335, 75350, 75360, 75368, 75928, 75932–39, 75942, 75951, 75956, 75960, 75966, 75977, 75979, 77369, 77374, 77376, 77505, 77507, 77514, 77519, 77520–21, 77523, 77533, 77535, 77538, 77560–62, 77564, 77571, 77575, 77580, 77585–86, 77597, 77611–12, 77614–16, 77624–25, 77630, 77632, 77656–57, 77659–64

UTAH

(Population 2010, 2,763,885)

SENATORS

ORRIN G. HATCH, Republican, of Salt Lake City, UT; born in Pittsburgh, PA, March 22, 1934; education: B.S., Brigham Young University, Provo, UT, 1959; J.D., University of Pittsburgh, 1962; practiced law in Salt Lake City, UT, and Pittsburgh, PA; senior partner, Hatch and Plumb law firm, Salt Lake City; worked his way through high school, college, and law school at the metal lathing building trade; holds ''AV'' rating in Martindale-Hubbell Law Directory; member: AFL–CIO; Salt Lake County Bar Association; Utah Bar Association; American Bar Association; Pennsylvania Bar Association; Allegheny County Bar Association and numerous other professional and fraternal organizations; honorary doctorate, University of Maryland; honorary doctor of laws: Pepperdine University; Southern Utah University; Widener University; University of Pittsburgh; honorary national ski patroller and other honorary degrees; Senate Republican High-Tech Task Force; Congressional International Anti-Privacy Caucus; author of numerous national publications; member, Church of Jesus Christ of Latter-Day Saints; married: Elaine Hansen of Newton, UT; children: Brent, Marcia, Scott, Kimberly, Alysa, and Jess; President Pro Tempore; committees: chair, Finance; Health, Education, Labor, and Pensions; chair, Joint Committee on Taxation; Judiciary; Special Committee on Aging; elected to the U.S. Senate on November 2, 1976; reelected to each succeeding Senate term.

Office Listings

http://hatch.senate.gov https://www.facebook.com/senatororrinhatch
https://twitter.com/senorrinhatch

104 Hart Senate Office Building, Washington, DC 20510 .... (202) 224–5251
Chief of Staff.—Matt Sandgren. FAX: 224–6331
Legislative Director.—Matt Jensen.
Communications Director.—Matt Whitlock.
Scheduler.—Ruth Montoya.
Federal Building, Suite 8402, 125 South State Street, Salt Lake City, UT 84138 .... (801) 524–4380
State Director.—Melanie Bowen.
Federal Building, 324 25th Street, Suite 1006, Ogden, UT 84401 .... (801) 625–5672
51 South University Avenue, Suite 320, Provo, UT 84601 .... (801) 375–7881
196 East Tabernacle, Suite 14, St. George, UT 84770 .... (435) 634–1795
77 North Main Street, Suite 112, Cedar City, UT 84720 .... (435) 586–8435

* * *

MICHAEL S. LEE, Republican, of Alpine, UT; born in Mesa, AZ, June 4, 1971; education: B.S., Brigham Young University, Provo, UT, 1994; J.D., Brigham Young University, 1997; professional: law clerk to Judge Dee Benson of the U.S. District Court for the District of Utah; law clerk to Judge Samuel A. Alito, Jr. on the U.S. Court of Appeals for the Third Circuit Court; attorney with the law firm Sidley & Austin; Assistant U.S. Attorney in Salt Lake City; general counsel to the Governor of Utah; law clerk to Supreme Court Justice Samuel A. Alito; partner at Howrey law firm; religion: Church of Jesus Christ of Latter-Day Saints; married: Sharon Burr of Provo, UT; children: James, John, and Eliza; committees: vice chair, Joint Economic Committee; Commerce, Science, and Transportation; Energy and Natural Resources; Judiciary; elected to the U.S. Senate on November 2, 2010; reelected to the U.S. Senate on November 8, 2016.

Office Listings

http://lee.senate.gov http://youtube.com/senatormikelee
http://facebook.com/senatormikelee http://twitter.com/senmikelee

361A Russell Senate Office Building, Washington, DC 20510 .... (202) 224–5444
Chief of Staff.—Allyson Bell. FAX: 228–1168
Legislative Director.—Christy Woodruff.
Communications Director.—Conn Carroll.
Press Secretary.—Jillian Wheeler.
Administrative Director.—Alyssa Burleson.
State Director.—Robert Axson.
Federal Building, 125 South State, Suite 4425, Salt Lake City, UT 84138 .... (801) 524–5933
Federal Building, 324 25th Street, Suite 1410, Ogden, UT 84401 .... (801) 392–9633
285 West Tabernacle Street, Suite 200, St. George, UT 84770 .... (435) 628–5514

REPRESENTATIVES

FIRST DISTRICT

ROB BISHOP, Republican, of Brigham City, UT; born in Kaysville, UT, July 13, 1951; education: B.A., political science, *magna cum laude*, University of Utah, 1974; professional: high school teacher; public service: Utah House of Representatives, 1979–94, Speaker of the House during his last two years; elected, chair, Utah Republican Party, 1997 (served two terms); religion: Church of Jesus Christ of Latter-Day Saints; family: married to Jeralynn Hansen; children: Shule, Jarom, Zenock, Maren, and Jashon; committees: chair, Natural Resources; Armed Services; elected to the 108th Congress on November 5, 2002; reelected to each succeeding Congress.

Office Listings

http://www.robbishop.house.gov

123 Cannon House Office Building, Washington, DC 20515 .... (202) 225–0453
Chief of Staff.—Devin Wiser. FAX: 225–5857
Legislative Assistants: Lee Lonsberry, Steve Petersen, Adam Stewart.
Scheduler.—Carolyn Turner.
6 North Main Street, Brigham City, UT 84302 .... (435) 734–2270
FAX: 734–2290
324 25th Street, 1017 Federal Building, Ogden, UT 94401 .... (801) 625–0107

Counties: Box Elder, Cache, Davis (part), Daggett, Duchesne, Morgan, Rich, Summit, Uintah, and Weber. Population (2010), 690,971.

ZIP Codes: 82930, 83312, 83342, 84001–02, 84007, 84015, 84017–18, 84021, 84023–28, 84031, 84033, 84035–41, 84046, 84050–53, 84055–56, 84060–61, 84063–64, 84066–67, 84072–73, 84075–76, 84078, 84083, 84085–86, 84098, 84301–02, 84304–21, 84324–41, 84401, 84403–05, 84414, 84526, 84540

* * *

SECOND DISTRICT

CHRIS STEWART, Republican, of Farmington, UT; born in Logan, UT, July 15, 1960; education: B.S., economics, Utah State University; professional: president and CEO, Shipley Group; independent author; military: pilot, U.S. Air Force; religion: Church of Jesus Christ of Latter-Day Saints; married: Evie; children: Sean, Dane, Lance, Kayla, Bryce, and Megan; committees: Appropriations; Permanent Select Committee on Intelligence; elected to the 113th Congress on November 6, 2012; reelected to each succeeding Congress.

Office Listings

http://stewart.house.gov facebook.com/repchrisstewart
twitter.com/repchrisstewart instagram.com/repchrisstewart youtube.com/repchrisstewart

323 Cannon House Office Building, Washington, DC 20515 .... (202) 225–9730
Chief of Staff.—Brian Steed. FAX: 225–9627
Executive Assistant.—Mark Coffield.
Press Secretary.—Daryn Frischknecht.
420 East South Temple, #390, Salt Lake City, UT 84111 .... (801) 364–5550
District Director.—Gary Webster. FAX: 364–5551
253 West S. George Boulevard, Suite 100, St. George, UT 84770 .... (435) 627–1500
Southern Utah Director.—Gary Webster. FAX: 627–1911

Counties: Beaver, Davis (part), Garfield, Iron, Juab (part), Kane, Millard, Piute, Salt Lake (part), Sanpete (part), Sevier, Tooele, Washington, and Wayne. Cities: Alton Town, Annabella Town, Antimony Town, Apple Valley Town, Aurora City, Beaver City, Beryl Junction, Bicknell Town, Big Water Town, Boulder Town, Bountiful City, Brian Head Town, Bryce Canyon, Cannonville Town, Cedar City, Centerfield Town, Centerville City, Central, Central Valley Town, Circleville Town, Dammeron Valley, Delta City, Deseret, Dugway, Elsinore Town, Emigration Canyon, Enoch City, Enterprise City, Ephraim City, Erda, Escalante City, Eureka City, Farmington City (part), Fayette Town, Fillmore City, Fremont, Fruit Heights City (part), Glendale Town, Glenwood Town, Grantsville City, Gunnison City, Hanksville Town, Hatch Town, Henrieville Town, Hildale City, Hinckley Town, Holden Town, Hurricane City, Ivins City, Joseph Town, Junction Town, Kanab City, Kanarraville Town, Kanosh Town, Kaysville City (part), Kearns (part), Kingston Town, Koosharem Town, La Verkin City, Leamington Town, Leeds Town, Loa Town, Lyman Town, Lynndyl Town, Magna, Manti City, Marysvale Town, Mayfield Town, Meadow Town, Milford City, Minersville Town, Monroe City, New Harmony Town, Newcastle, North Salt Lake City, Oak City Town, Oasis, Ophir Town, Orderville Town, Panguitch City, Paragonah Town, Parowan City, Pine Valley, Redmond Town, Richfield City, Rockville Town, Rush Valley Town, Salina City, Salt Lake City (part), Santa Clara City, Scipio Town, Sigurd Town, Springdale Town, St. George City, Stansbury Park, Sterling Town, Stockton Town, Summit, Sutherland, Teasdale, Tooele City, Toquerville Town, Torrey Town, Tropic Town, Vernon Town, Veyo, Virgin Town, Washington City, Wendover City, West Bountiful City, West Valley City (part), and Woods Cross City. Population (2010), 690,971.

ZIP Codes: 84010, 84014, 84022, 84025, 84029, 84034, 84037, 84044, 84054, 84069, 84071, 84074–75, 84080–81, 84083, 84087, 84101–06, 84108–09, 84111–13, 84115–16, 84118–20, 84128, 84144, 84180, 84533, 84620–24, 84627–28, 84630–31, 84634–38, 84640, 84642–43, 84648–49, 84652, 84654, 84656–57, 84662, 84665, 84701, 84710–16, 84718–26, 84728–47, 84749–67, 84770, 84772–76, 84779–84, 84790

* * *

THIRD DISTRICT

JOHN CURTIS, Republican, of Provo, UT; born in Salt Lake City, UT, May 10, 1980; education: B.S., business management, Brigham Young University, Provo, UT, 1985; professional: Mayor, Provo City, 2010–17; COO and part-owner, Action Target, 1999–2010; manager, O.C. Tanner Co., 1989–99; overseas lead buyer, Brazil International, 1987–88; territory representative, Citizen Watch Co., 1984–86; missionary, Church of Jesus Christ of Latter-Day Saints, Taiwan, 1979–81; religion: Church of Jesus Christ of Latter-Day Saints; married: Sue; children: Kirsten, Zane, Jacob, Sarah Jane, Emily, and Nicole; grandchildren: Jet, Jane, Clare, Sage, Hazel, and Genevieve; caucuses: Dietary Supplement Caucus; Friends of Wales Caucus; Republican Main Street Partnership; Western Caucus; committees: Foreign Affairs; Natural Resources; Small Business; elected to the 115th Congress on November 17, 2017.

Office Listings

http://curtis.house.gov

2236 Rayburn House Office Building, Washington, DC 20515 .... (202) 225–7751
Chief of Staff.—Corey Norman.
Deputy Chief of Staff / Legislative Director.—Ryan Leavitt.
Scheduler.—Kate Cannon.
Press Secretary.—Katie Thompson.
Legislative Assistant.—Jake Bornstein.
Counsel.—Liz Mann.
Senior Advisor.—Danny Laub.
Staff Assistant / Legislative Correspondent: Austin Fulton, Dillon Redd.
3549 North University Avenue, Suite 275, Provo, UT 84604 .... (801) 922–5400
District Director.—Lorie Fowlke.

Counties: CARBON, EMERY, GRAND, SALT LAKE (part), SAN JUAN, UTAH (part), WASATCH. Population (2010), 708,809.

ZIP Codes: 84003–04, 84020, 84032, 84036 (part), 84042, 84043 (part), 84047 (part), 84049, 84057–59, 84060 (part), 84062, 84070 (part), 84082, 84090–94, 84097, 84109, 84117 (part), 84121 (part), 84124 (part), 84171, 84501, 84510–13, 84515–16, 84518, 84520–23, 84525–26, 84528–37, 84539–40, 84542, 84601–06, 84651 (part), 84653, 84655 (part), 84660 (part), 84663 (part), 84664

* * *

FOURTH DISTRICT

MIA B. LOVE, Republican, of Saratoga Springs, UT; born in Brooklyn, NY, December 6, 1975; education: B.A., University of Hartford; professional / politician: Mayor of Saratoga Springs, UT; Saratoga Springs, Utah City Council member; flight attendant; religion: Church of Jesus Christ of Latter-Day Saints; married: Jason; children: Alessa, Abigail, and Peyton; committees: Financial Services; elected to the 114th Congress on November 4, 2014; reelected to the 115th Congress on November 8, 2016.

Office Listings

http://love.house.gov facebook: https://facebook.com/repmialove
twitter: https://twitter.com/RepMiaLove

217 Cannon House Office Building, Washington, DC 20515 .... (202) 225–3011
Chief of Staff.—Muffy Day. FAX: 225–5638
Scheduler.—Kayla Herron.
9067 South 1300 West, Suite 101, West Jordan, UT 84115 .... (801) 996–8729
District Director.—Laurel Price.

Counties: SALT LAKE (part), UTAH (part), JUAB (part), AND SAN PETE (part). Population (2010), 690,971.

ZIP Codes: 84003 (part), 84005–06, 84013, 84020 (part), 84043 (part), 84045, 84047 (part), 84065, 84070 (part), 84081 (part), 84084, 84088, 84095–96, 84106 (part), 84107, 84109 (part), 84115 (part), 84117–21 (part), 84123, 84124 (part), 84129, 84141, 84157, 84165, 84170, 84184, 84623, 84626, 84629, 84632–33, 84639, 84645–48, 84651 (part), 84655 (part), 84660 (part), 84662, 84663 (part), 84667

VERMONT

(Population 2010, 625,741)

SENATORS

PATRICK LEAHY, President Pro Tempore Emeritus; Democrat, of Middlesex, VT; born in Montpelier, VT, March 31, 1940, son of Howard and Alba Leahy; education: graduate of St. Michael's High School, Montpelier, 1957; B.A., St. Michael's College, 1961; J.D., Georgetown University, 1964; professional: attorney, admitted to the Vermont Bar, 1964; admitted to the District of Columbia Bar, 1979; admitted to practice before: the Vermont Supreme Court, 1964; the Federal District Court of Vermont, 1965; the Second Circuit Court of Appeals in New York, 1966; and the U.S. Supreme Court, 1968; State's Attorney, Chittenden County, 1966–74; vice president, National District Attorneys Association, 1971–74; member, Smithsonian Board of Regents; married: the former Marcelle Pomerleau, 1962; children: Kevin, Alicia, and Mark; first Democrat and youngest person in Vermont to be elected to the U.S. Senate; committees: Agriculture, Nutrition, and Forestry; Appropriations; Joint Committee on the Library; Judiciary; Rules and Administration; elected to the Senate on November 5, 1974; reelected to each succeeding Senate term.

Office Listings

http://leahy.senate.gov facebook: senatorparticklеahy
twitter: @senatorleahy instagram: @senatorleahy

437 Russell Senate Office Building, Washington, DC 20510 .... (202) 224–4242
Chief of Staff.—John P. Dowd. FAX: 224–3479
Deputy Chief of Staff.—Ann Berry.
Legislative Director.—Erica Chabot.
Communications Director.—David Carle.
87 State Street, Room 338, Montpelier, VT 05602 .... (802) 229–0569
199 Main Street, Courthouse Plaza, Burlington, VT 05401 .... (802) 863–2525

* * *

BERNARD SANDERS, Independent, of Burlington, VT; born in Brooklyn, NY, September 8, 1941; education: graduated, Madison High School, Brooklyn; B.S., political science, University of Chicago, 1964; professional: carpenter; writer; college professor; Mayor of Burlington, VT, 1981–89; married: the former Jane O'Meara, 1988; children: Levi, Heather, Carina, and David; committees: ranking member, Budget; Energy and Natural Resources; Environment and Public Works; Health, Education, Labor, and Pensions; Veterans' Affairs; elected to the 102nd Congress on November 6, 1990; reelected to each succeeding Congress; elected to the U.S. Senate on November 7, 2006; reelected to the U.S. Senate on November 6, 2012.

Office Listings

http://sanders.senate.gov facebook.com/senatorsanders twitter.com/sensanders

332 Dirksen Senate Office Building, Washington, DC 20510 .... (202) 224–5141
Chief of Staff.—Michaeleen Crowell. FAX: 228–0776
Legislative Director.—Caryn Compton.
Communications Director.—Josh Miller-Lewis.
1 Church Street, Second Floor, Burlington, VT 05401 .... (800) 339–9834

REPRESENTATIVE

AT LARGE

PETER WELCH, Democrat, of Hartland, VT; born in Springfield, MA, May 2, 1947; education: Cathedral High School, Springfield, MA, 1969; B.A., *magna cum laude*, College of the Holy Cross, 1969; J.D., University of California at Berkeley, 1973; professional: attorney, admitted to Vermont Bar, 1974; founding partner, Welch, Graham & Manby; served in Vermont State Senate, 1981–89, 2001–07; Minority Leader, 1983–85; President Pro Tempore, 1985–89, 2003–07; family: wife, Joan Smith (deceased), currently married to Margaret Cheney; five children: Beth, Mary, Bill, John, and Michael; three stepchildren; committees: Energy and Commerce; Oversight and Government Reform; elected to the 110th Congress on November 7, 2006; reelected to each succeeding Congress.

Office Listings

http://www.welch.house.gov twitter: @PeterWelch facebook: @PeterWelch
instagram: @RepPeterWelch

2303 Rayburn House Office Building, Washington, DC 20515 .... (202) 225–4115
Chief of Staff.—Bob Rogan.
Scheduler / Executive Assistant.—Patrick Etka.
Legislative Director.—Patrick Satalin.
Communications Director.—Kristen Hartman.
128 Lakeside Avenue, Suite 235, Burlington, VT 05401 .... (802) 652–2450
State Director.—George Twigg.

Population (2014), 626,562.

ZIP Codes: 05001, 05009, 05030–43, 05045–56, 05058–62, 05065, 05067–77, 05079, 05081, 05083–86, 05088–89, 05091, 05101, 05141–43, 05146, 05148–56, 05158–59, 05161, 05201, 05250–55, 05257, 05260–62, 05301–04, 05340–46, 05350–63, 05401–07, 05439–66, 05468–74, 05476–79, 05481–83, 05485–92, 05494–95, 05601–04, 05609, 05620, 05633, 05640–41, 05647–58, 05660–67, 05669–82, 05701–02, 05730–48, 05750–51, 05753, 05757–70, 05772–78, 05819–30, 05832–33, 05836–43, 05845–51, 05853, 05855, 05857–63, 05866–68, 05871–75, 05901–07

VIRGINIA

(Population 2010, 8,001,024)

SENATORS

MARK R. WARNER, Democrat, of Alexandria, VA; born in Indianapolis, IN, December 15, 1954; son of Robert and Marge Warner of Vernon, CT; education: B.A., political science, George Washington University, 1977; J.D., Harvard Law School, 1980; professional: Governor, Commonwealth of Virginia, 2002–06; chairman of the National Governor's Association, 2004–05; religion: Presbyterian; wife: Lisa Collis; children: Madison, Gillian, and Eliza; committees: Banking, Housing, and Urban Affairs; Budget; Finance; Rules and Administration; Select Committee on Intelligence; elected to the U.S. Senate on November 4, 2008; reelected to the U.S. Senate on November 4, 2014.

Office Listings

http://warner.senate.gov

475 Russell Senate Office Building, Washington, DC 20510 .... (202) 224–2023
Chief of Staff.—Mike Harney.
Legislative Director.—Elizabeth Falcone.
Communications Director.—Rachel Cohen.
Press Secretary.—Nelly Decker.
Scheduler.—Andrea Friedhoff.
8000 Towers Crescent Drive, Suite 200, Vienna, VA 22182 .... (703) 442–0670
FAX: 442–0408
180 West Main Street, Abingdon, VA 24210 .... (276) 628–8158
FAX: 628–1036
101 West Main Street, Suite 7771, Norfolk, VA 23510 .... (757) 441–3079
FAX: 441–6250
919 East Main Street, Richmond, VA 23219 .... (804) 775–2314
FAX: 775–2319
110 Kirk Avenue, Southwest, Roanoke, VA 24011 .... (540) 857–2676
FAX: 857–2800

* * *

TIM KAINE, Democrat, of Richmond, VA; born in St. Paul, MN, February 26, 1958; education: B.A., University of Missouri, 1979; J.D., Harvard University, 1983; professional: worked with the Jesuit order as a Catholic missionary in Honduras, 1980–81; civil rights lawyer; professor, University of Richmond, 1987–2013; Richmond City Council, 1994–98; Mayor of Richmond, VA, 1998–2001; Lieutenant Governor of Virginia, 2002–06; Governor of Virginia, 2006–10; married: Anne Holton, who serves on the Virginia Board of Education; one of the Senate's few members who speak fluent Spanish; 51st chair of the Democratic National Committee, 2009–11; caucuses: chair, Senate Career and Technical Education (CTE) Caucus; Military Families Caucus; committees: Armed Services; Budget; Foreign Relations; Health, Education, Labor, and Pensions; elected to the U.S. Senate on November 6, 2012.

Office Listings

http://kaine.senate.gov https://twitter.com/@senkaineoffice
https://www.facebook.com/senatorkaine

231 Russell Senate Office Building, Washington, DC 20510 .... (202) 224–4024
Chief of Staff.—Mike Henry. FAX: 228–6363
Communications Director.—Sarah Peck.
Legislative Director.—Mary Naylor.
Scheduler.—Kate McCarroll.
State Director.—John Knapp.
222 Central Park Avenue, Suite 120, Virginia Beach, VA 23462 .... (757) 518–1674
919 East Main Street, Suite 970, Richmond, VA 23219 .... (804) 771–2221
611 South Jefferson, Suite 5B, Roanoke, VA 24011 .... (540) 682–5693
121 Russell Road, Suite 2, Abingdon, VA 24210 .... (276) 525–4790
9408 Grant Avenue, Suite 202, Manassas, VA 20110 .... (703) 361–3192
308 Craghead Street, Suite 102A, Danville, VA 24541 .... (434) 792–0976

REPRESENTATIVES

FIRST DISTRICT

ROBERT J. WITTMAN, Republican, of Montross, VA; born in Washington, DC, February 2, 1959; education: B.S., biology, Virginia Polytechnic Institute and State University, 1981; M.P.H., health policy and administration, University of North Carolina at Chapel Hill, 1989; Ph.D., Virginia Commonwealth University, Richmond, VA, 2002; professional: field director for the Virginia Health Department's Division of Shellfish Sanitation; public service: Montross Town Council, 1986–96; public policy and administration, 1992; Mayor of Montross, 1992–96; Westmoreland County Board of Supervisors, 1995–2003, and chairman, 2003–05; Virginia House of Delegates, 2005–07; religion: Episcopalian; married: Kathryn Wittman; children: Devon and Joshua; committees: Armed Services; Natural Resources; elected to the 110th Congress, by special election, on December 11, 2007; elected to the 111th Congress; reelected to each succeeding Congress.

Office Listings

http://www.wittman.house.gov

2454 Rayburn House Office Building, Washington, DC 20515 .... (202) 225–4261
Chief of Staff.—Jamie Miller. FAX: 225–4382
Legislative Director.—Brent Robinson.
Communications Director.—Greg Lemon.
Scheduler/Office Manager.—Carolyn King.
6501 Mechanicsville Turnpike, Suite 102, Mechanicsville, VA 23111 .... (804) 730–6595
District Director.—Joe Schumacher.
95 Dunn Drive, Suite 201, Stafford, VA 22554 .... (540) 659–2734
508 Church Lane, Tappahannock, VA 22560 .... (804) 443–0668

Counties: ALL OF CAROLINE, ESSEX, GLOUCESTER, HANOVER, KING AND QUEEN, KING GEORGE, KING WILLIAM, LANCASTER, MATHEWS, MIDDLESEX, NEW KENT, NORTHUMBERLAND, RICHMOND, STAFFORD, AND WESTMORELAND COUNTIES; all of the City of Fredericksburg; part of FAUQUIER COUNTY comprised of the Bealeton (303), Catlett (102), Lois (104), and Morrisville (301) Precincts and part of the Remington (302) Precinct; part of JAMES CITY COUNTY comprised of the Berkeley A Part 1 (101), Berkeley B Part 1 (1012), Berkeley B Part 2 (1022), Berkeley C (103), Powhatan A (301), Powhatan B (302), Powhatan C (303), Powhatan D (304), Stonehouse A (401), Stonehouse B (402), and Stonehouse C (403) Precincts and part of the Jamestown A (201), Jamestown B (202) Precincts; part of PRINCE WILLIAM COUNTY comprised of the Ashland (309), Bennett (102), Benton (203), Brentsville (101), Bristow Run (111), Cedar Point (112), Ellis (106), Forest Park (310), Glenkirk (408), Henderson (307), Lake Ridge (501), Limestone (113), Lodge (207), Marshall (202), Marsteller (107), McCoart (204), Montclair (308), Mullen (411), Nokesville (104), Park (109), Pattie (305), Penn (210), Powell (211), Quantico (304), Sinclair (404), Stonewall (405), Sudley North (409), Victory (108), Washington-Reid (306), Westgate (407), Westridge (208), and Woodbine (209) Precincts and part of the Buckland Mills (110) Precinct; part of SPOTSYLVANIA COUNTY comprised of The Battlefield (701), Lee Hill (403), Massaponax (104), and Summit (401) Precincts and part of the Brent's Mill (702), Fairview (703), and Travelers Rest (103) Precincts. Population (2010), 727,366.

ZIP Codes: 20109–12 (part), 20119 (part), 20136, 20181 (part), 22025, 22026 (part), 22134 (part), 22172 (part), 22401, 22405–06, 22407–08 (part), 22427, 22432, 22435–38, 22443, 22448, 22454, 22460, 22469, 22473, 22476, 22480, 22482, 22485, 22488, 22503–04, 22509, 22511, 22514, 22520, 22529–30, 22535, 22538–39, 22546, 22548, 22551 (part), 22554, 22556, 22560, 22572, 22576, 22578–79, 22580 (part), 22712 (part), 22720, 22728 (part), 22734 (part), 22742, 23005, 23009, 23011, 23015 (part), 23021, 23023, 23024 (part), 23025, 23032, 23035, 23043, 23045, 23047, 23050, 23056, 23059 (part), 23061–62, 23064, 23066, 23068–72, 23076, 23079, 23085–86, 23089, 23091–92, 23102 (part), 23106, 23108–11, 23115–16, 23119, 23124–26, 23128, 23130, 23138, 23140 (part), 23141, 23146 (part), 23148–49, 23156, 23161, 23163, 23168–69, 23175–77, 23180–81, 23185 (part), 23188 (part), 23192 (part)

* * *

SECOND DISTRICT

SCOTT TAYLOR, Republican, of Virginia Beach, VA; born in Hebron, MD, June 27, 1979; education: B.A., Harvard University Extension School; military: former Navy Seal, 1997–2005; religion: Christian; committees: Appropriations; elected to the 115th Congress on November 8, 2016.

Office Listings

http://www.taylor.house.gov https://www.facebook.com/repscotttaylor
twitter: @RepScottTaylor

418 Cannon House Office Building, Washington, DC 20515 .... (202) 225–4215
Chief of Staff.—John Thomas. FAX: 225–4218
Communications Director.—Scott Weldon.
Legislative Director.—Reginald Darby.
4772 Euclid Road, Suite E, Virginia Beach, VA 23462 .... (757) 687–8290

Office Listings—Continued

District Director.—Brenda Roberts.
36312 Lankford Highway, Suite 5, Belle Haven, VA 23306 .... (757) 442–4790

Counties: ACCOMACK, NORTHAMPTON, JAMES CITY (part), AND YORK. CITIES: Hampton (part), Norfolk (part), Northampton, Poquoson City, Virginia Beach, Williamsburg, and York. Population (2010), 721,969.

ZIP Codes: 23185 (part), 23187, 23188 (part), 23301–03, 23306–08, 23310, 23313, 23316, 23336–37, 23347, 23350, 23354, 23356–59, 23389, 23395, 23398, 23401, 23405, 23407–10, 23413–18, 23420–23, 23440–42, 23451–57, 23459–62, 23464, 23480, 23486, 23488, 23502 (part), 23503, 23505 (part), 23509 (part), 23511 (part), 23513 (part), 23518 (part), 23551, 23602 (part), 23603 (part), 23651, 23662, 23663–64 (part), 23665, 23666 (part), 23669 (part), 23690–93, 23696

* * *

THIRD DISTRICT

ROBERT C. ''BOBBY'' SCOTT, Democrat, of Newport News, VA; born in Washington, DC, April 30, 1947; education: graduated, Groton High School; B.A., Harvard University; J.D., Boston College Law School; professional: served in the Massachusetts National Guard; attorney; admitted to the Virginia Bar; Virginia House of Delegates, 1978–83; Senate of Virginia, 1983–92; member: Alpha Phi Alpha Fraternity; NAACP; Sigma Pi Phi Fraternity; committees: ranking member, Education and the Workforce; elected on November 3, 1992 to the 103rd Congress; reelected to each succeeding Congress.

Office Listings

http://www.bobbyscott.house.gov www.facebook.com/repbobbyscott
twitter.com/bobbyscott

1201 Longworth House Office Building, Washington, DC 20515 .... (202) 225–8351
Chief of Staff.—Vacant. FAX: 225–8354
Senior Advisor.—Randi Petty.
Legislative Director.—David Dailey.
2600 Washington Avenue, Suite 1010, Newport News, VA 23607 .... (757) 380–1000
District Director.—Vacant.

Counties: ISLE OF WIGHT. CITIES: Chesapeake (part), Franklin, Hampton (part), Newport News, Norfolk (part), Portsmouth, and Suffolk (part). Population (2015), 737,635.

ZIP Codes: 23011 (part), 23030 (part), 23075 (part), 23089 (part), 23111 (part), 23124 (part), 23140–41 (part), 23150 (part), 23168 (part), 23181 (part), 23185 (part), 23219–25 (part), 23227 (part), 23230–31 (part), 23234–35 (part), 23250 (part), 23284 (part), 23298 (part), 23304, 23314–15, 23320–21 (part), 23323–25 (part), 23397 (part), 23424 (part), 23430, 23432–33, 23434 (part), 23435–36, 23487, 23502 (part), 23504, 23505 (part), 23507–08, 23509 (part), 23510, 23511 (part), 23513 (part), 23517, 23518 (part), 23523, 23601, 23602–03 (part), 23604–08, 23661, 23663–64 (part), 23666 (part), 23667–68, 23669 (part), 23693 (part), 23701–04, 23707–09, 23801 (part), 23803 (part), 23805 (part), 23839 (part), 23842 (part), 23846 (part), 23851 (part), 23860 (part), 23866 (part), 23875 (part), 23881 (part), 23883 (part), 23888 (part), 23890 (part), 23898–99 (part)

* * *

FOURTH DISTRICT

A. DONALD MCEACHIN, Democrat, of Henrico County, VA; born in Nuremberg, Germany, October 10, 1961; education: B.S., political history, American University, Washington, DC, 1982; J.D., University of Virginia, Charlottesville, VA; M.Div., Virginia Union University, Richmond, VA, 2008; leadership: co-president of Freshman Class; Democratic Leadership's Environmental Messaging Team; Regional Whip; religion: Episcopal; married: Collette McEachin; three adult children; commissions: Franking Commission; caucuses: Chesapeake Bay Watershed Caucus; Congressional Black Caucus; Congressional PORTS Caucus; Congressional Ship-Building Caucus; House Democratic Caucus; House Pro-Choice Caucus; LGBT Equality Caucus; Sustainable Energy and Environment Coalition; taskforces: United for Climate Environmental Justice Congressional Taskforce; Community Based Special Needs Taskforce; committees: Armed Services; Natural Resources; elected to the 115th Congress on November 8, 2016.

Office Listings

http://mceachin.house.gov

314 Cannon House Office Building, Washington, DC 20515 .... (202) 225–6365

Office Listings—Continued

Chief of Staff.—Abbi Easter. FAX: 226–1170
DC Chief of Staff.—Keenan Austin Reed.
Legislative Direction.—Cody McClelland.
Communications Director.—Jamitress Bowden.
District Director.—Eldon Burton.
Director of Scheduling.—Tara Rountree.
110 North Robinson Street, Suite 401, Richmond, VA 23220 .... (804) 486–1840
131 North Saratoga Street, Suite B, Suffolk, VA 23434.

Counties: CHARLES CITY, CHESAPEAKE (part), CHESTERFIELD (part), COLONIAL HEIGHTS, DINWIDDIE, EMPORIA, GREENSVILLE, HENRICO (part), HOPEWELL, PETERSBURG, PRINCE GEORGE, RICHMOND, SOUTHAMPTON, SUFFOLK (part), SURRY, AND SUSSEX. Population (2010), 881,217.

ZIP Codes: 22402–04 (part), 22555 (part), 22901 (part), 23030, 23058 (part), 23075, 23113 (part), 23140 (part), 23147, 23150, 23173, 23185 (part), 23187 (part), 23218–21, 23222 (part), 23223, 23224–27 (part), 23229–32, 23234–35 (part), 23237, 23241, 23242 (part), 23249–50, 23255 (part), 23260–61, 23269, 23273 (part), 23274, 23276, 23278, 23282, 23284–86, 23290–93, 23294 (part), 23298, 23315, 23320–23 (part), 23327–28 (part), 23430 (part), 23434 23437–38, 23439 (part), 23450 (part), 23454 (part), 23457 (part), 23464 (part), 23466–67 (part), 23471 (part), 23487 (part), 23612 (part), 23801, 23803–05, 23822, 23824 (part), 23827–31, 23832–33 (part), 23834, 23836–37, 23838 (part), 23839–42 (part), 23844, 23846, 23847 (part), 23850–51 (part), 23856 (part), 23860, 23866 (part), 23867, 23870, 23872, 23874–75, 23878–79, 23881–85, 23887 (part), 23888, 23890–91, 23894 (part), 23897, 23898 (part), 23899

* * *

FIFTH DISTRICT

THOMAS A. GARRETT, JR., Republican, of Scottsville, VA; born in Atlanta, GA, March 27, 1972; undergraduate (1994) and juris doctor (2002) degrees, University of Richmond; military: Field Artillery Officer, U.S. Army, 1995–2000; professional: deputy director, Virginia Republican Convention, 2004; Assistant Attorney General under then Virginia State Attorney General Bob McDonnell, 2006–07; elected as Louisa County Commonwealth's Attorney in 2007; awards: 2015 American Conservative Union's Defender of Liberty; 2014 Champion of Justice by the Virginia Association of Commonwealth's Attorneys; 2014 Legislator of the Year by the Virginia Chamber of Commerce; 2013 Defender of Liberty by the American Conservative Union; and the 2012 Freshman Legislator of the Year by the Virginia Chamber of Commerce; family: married Flanna Garrett in 2016; two daughters: Carolyn and Laura; caucuses: House Freedom Caucus; committees: Education and the Workforce; Foreign Affairs; Homeland Security; elected to the 115th Congress on November 8, 2016.

Office Listings

http://www.tomgarrett.house.gov https://www.facebook.com/RepGarrett
twitter: @RepTomGarrett

415 Cannon House Office Building, Washington, DC 20515 .... (202) 225–4711
Chief of Staff.—Kevin Reynolds. FAX: 225–5681
Deputy Chief of Staff/Communications Director.—Andrew Griffin.
Scheduler.—Denzel Jones.
Legislative Director.—Elliott Harding.
308 Craghead Street, Suite 102–D, Danville, VA 24541 .... (434) 791–2596
District Director.—Denise Van Valkenburg.
686 Berkmar Circle, Charlottesville, VA 22901 .... (434) 973–9631

Counties: ALBEMARLE (all). CITIES AND TOWNSHIPS: Barboursville, Batesville, Charlotteville, Covesville, Crozet, Earlysville, Esmont, Free Union, Greenwood, Hatton, Ivy, Keene, Keswick, North Garden, and Scottsville. APPOMATTOX (all). CITIES AND TOWNSHIPS: Appomattox, Evergreen, Pamplin, and Spout Spring. BEDFORD (part). CITIES AND TOWNSHIPS: Bedford, Big Island, Coleman Falls, Forest, Goode, Goodview, Hardy, Huddleston, Lowry, Moneta, and Thaxton. BRUNSWICK (all). CITIES AND TOWNSHIPS: Alberta, Brodnax, Gasburg, Lawrenceville, and White Plains. BUCKINGHAM. CITIES AND TOWNSHIPS: Andersonville, Arvonia, Buckingham, Dillwyn, and New Canton. CAMPBELL (all). CITIES AND TOWNSHIPS: Altavista, Brookneal, Concord, Evington, Gladys, Long Island, Lynch Station, Naruna, and Rustburg. CHARLOTTE (all). CITIES AND TOWNSHIPS: Barnesville, Charlotte Court House, Cullen, Drakes Branch, Keysville, Phenix, Randolph, Red House, Red Oak, Saxe, and Wylliesburg. CHARLOTTESVILLE CITY: Charlottesville. CUMBERLAND (all). CITIES AND TOWNSHIPS: Cartersville, Cumberland, and Tamworth. DANVILLE CITY: Danville. FAUQUIER (part). CITIES AND TOWNSHIPS: Airlie, Bealeton, Belle Meade, Belvoir, Broad Run, Calverton, Casanova, Delaplane, Germantown, Halfway, Hume, Linden (part), Markham, Marshall, Midland (part), Morrisville, New Baltimore, Old Tavern, Opal (part), Orlean, Paris, Rectortown, Remington, The Plains, Upperville, and Warrenton. FLUVANNA (all). CITIES AND TOWNSHIPS: Bremo Bluff, Bybee, Carysbrook, Columbia, Fork Union, Kents Store, Palmyra, and Troy. FRANKLIN (all). CITIES AND TOWNSHIPS: Boones Mill, Callaway, Ferrum, Gladehill, Henry, Redwood, Penhook, Rocky Mount, Union Hall, Waidsboro, and Wirtz. GREENE (all). CITIES AND TOWNSHIPS: Amicus, Barnes, Burtonville, Dawsonville, Dyke, Geer, Haneytown, Lydia, McMullen, Midway, Newton, Pirkey, Quinque, Ruckersville, Stanardsville, St. George, Shady Grove, Simmons Gap, Twin Lakes, Upper Pocosin, and Williams Fork. HALIFAX (all). CITIES AND TOWNSHIPS: Alton, Clover, Cluster Springs, Crystal Hill, Denniston, Halifax, Ingram, Lennig, Mayo, Nathalie, Republican Grove, Scottsburg, Turbeville, Vernon Hill, and Virgilina. HENRY (part). CITIES AND TOWNSHIPS: Axton, Chatmoss, and Ridgeway. LUNENBURG (all). CITIES AND TOWNSHIPS: Dundas, Fort Mitchell, Kenbridge, Lunenburg, Rehoboth, and Victoria. MADISON (all).

CITIES AND TOWNSHIPS: Achash, Aroda, Aylor, Banco, Beaver Park, Big Meadows, Burnt Tree, Criglersville, Decapolis, Duet, Elly, Etlan, Five Forks, Fletcher, Fordsville, Graves Mill, Haywood, Hood, Kinderhook, Leon, Locust Dale, Madison, Madison Mills, Nethers, Novum, O'Neal, Oakpark, Oldrag, Pratts, Radiant, Repton Mills, Rochelle, Ruth, Shelby, Shifflet Corner, Syria, Tanners, Tryme, Twymans Mill, Uno, Wolftown, and Zeus. MECKLENBURG (all). CITIES AND TOWNSHIPS: Baskerville, Blackridge, Boydton, Bracey, Buffalo Junction, Chase City, Clarksville, Forksville, LaCrosse, Nelson, Palmer Springs, Skipwith, South Hill, and Union Level. NELSON (all). CITIES AND TOWNSHIPS: Afton, Arrington, Faber, Gladstone, Lovingston, Massies Mill, Montebello, Nellysford, Norwood, Piney River, Roseland, Schuyler, Shipman, Tye River, Tyro, and Wingina. PITTSYLVANIA (all). CITIES AND TOWNSHIPS: Blairs, Callands, Cascade, Chatham, Dry Fork, Gretna, Hurt, Java, Keeling, Pittsville, Ringgold, Sandy Level, and Sutherlin. PRINCE EDWARD (all). CITIES AND TOWNSHIPS: Darlington Heights, Farmville, Green Bay, Hampden-Sydney, Meherrin, Prospect, and Rice. RAPPAHANNOCK (all). CITIES AND TOWNSHIPS: Amissville, Castleton, Chester Gap, Flint Hill, Huntly, Laurel Mills, Massies Corner, Peola Mills, Revercombs Corner, Sperryville, Wakefield Manor, Washington, and Woodville. Population (2010), 727,365.

ZIP Codes: 20106 (part), 20115, 20117 (part), 20119 (part), 20130 (part), 20137 (part), 20139, 20144, 20181 (part), 20184 (part), 20186 (part), 20187, 20198, 22623 (part), 22627, 22630 (part), 22639–40, 22642 (part), 22643, 22701 (part), 22709, 22711, 22712–13 (part), 22715–16, 22719, 22722–23, 22727, 22728 (part), 22730–32, 22733–35 (part), 22738, 22740 (part), 22743, 22747, 22749, 22835 (part), 22901–04, 22911, 22920 (part), 22922–23 (part), 22931–32, 22935–38, 22940, 22942 (part), 22943, 22946, 22947 (part), 22948–49, 22958 (part), 22959, 22960 (part), 22963–64, 22967 (part), 22968–69, 22971, 22973, 22974 (part), 22976, 22989, 23004, 23022, 23027, 23038 (part), 23040, 23055, 23084 (part), 23093 (part), 23123, 23139 (part), 23821, 23824 (part), 23843, 23845, 23847 (part), 23856 (part), 23857, 23868, 23876, 23887, 23889, 23893, 23901, 23909, 23915, 23917, 23919–21, 23922 (part), 23923–24, 23927, 23934, 23936–38, 23942–44, 23947, 23950, 23952, 23954, 23958–60, 23962–64, 23966 (part), 23967–68, 23970, 23974, 23976, 24054–55 (part), 24059 (part), 24064–65 (part), 24067, 24069, 24079 (part), 24088 (part), 24091 (part), 24092, 24095, 24101, 24102 (part), 24104, 24112 (part), 24121, 24122 (part), 24137, 24139, 24148 (part), 24151, 24161, 24174 (part), 24176, 24179 (part), 24184, 24464, 24501–02 (part), 24504 (part), 24517, 24520, 24521 (part), 24522, 24523 (part), 24527–31, 24534, 24538–41, 24549, 24550–51 (part), 24553 (part), 24554, 24557–58, 24562–63, 24565–66, 24569–71, 24577, 24580–81, 24586, 24588–90, 24592–94, 24597–99

* * *

SIXTH DISTRICT

BOB GOODLATTE, Republican, of Roanoke, VA; born in Holyoke, MA, September 22, 1952; education: B.A., Bates College, Lewiston, ME, 1974; J.D., Washington and Lee University, 1977; Massachusetts Bar, 1977; Virginia Bar, 1978; professional: began practice in Roanoke, VA, 1979; district director for Congressman M. Caldwell Butler, 1977–79; attorney, sole practitioner, 1979–81; partner, 1981–92; chairman of the 6th District Virginia Republican Committee, 1983–88; member: Civitan Club of Roanoke (president, 1989–90); former member, Building Better Boards Advisory Council; married: Maryellen Flaherty, 1974; children: Jennifer and Robert; Deputy Republican Whip; committees: chair, Judiciary; Agriculture; elected on November 3, 1992, to the 103rd Congress; reelected to each succeeding Congress.

Office Listings

http://www.goodlatte.house.gov twitter: @repgoodlatte
facebook.com/bobgoodlatte

2309 Rayburn House Office Building, Washington, DC 20515 .... (202) 225–5431
DC Chief of Staff.—Charlie Keller. FAX: 225–9681
Legislative Director.—Lindsay Black.
Communications Director.—Beth Breeding.
10 Franklin Road, SE., Suite 540, Roanoke, VA 24011 .... (540) 857–2672
Chief of Staff.—Pete Larkin.
916 Main Street, Suite 300, Lynchburg, VA 24504 .... (434) 845–8306
117 South Lewis Street, Suite 215, Staunton, VA 24401 .... (540) 885–3861
District Director.—Debbie Garrett.
70 North Mason Street, Harrisonburg, VA 22802 .... (540) 432–2391

Counties: AMHERST, AUGUSTA, BATH, BEDFORD (part), BOTETOURT, HIGHLAND, PAGE, ROANOKE (part), ROCKBRIDGE, ROCKINGHAM, SHENANDOAH, AND WARREN. CITIES: Buena Vista, Harrisonburg, Lexington, Lynchburg, Roanoke, Staunton, and Waynesboro. Population (2010), 737,755.

ZIP Codes: 22610, 22623, 22630, 22641–42, 22644–45, 22650, 22652, 22654–55, 22657, 22660, 22664, 22801–02, 22807, 22810–12, 22815, 22820–21, 22824, 22827, 22830–32, 22834–35, 22840–47, 22849–51, 22853, 22920, 22922, 22939, 22952, 22958, 22967, 22980, 24011–20, 24064–66, 24077, 24083, 24085, 24090, 24122, 24130, 24153, 24174–75, 24179, 24401, 24411–13, 24415–16, 24421–22, 24430–33, 24435, 24437, 24439–42, 24445, 24450, 24458–60, 24465, 24467, 24471–73, 24476–77, 24479, 24482–87, 24501–04, 24521, 24523, 24526, 24536, 24550–51, 24553, 24555–56, 24572, 24574, 24578–79, 24595

* * *

SEVENTH DISTRICT

DAVE BRAT, Republican, of Glen Allen, VA; born in Detroit, MI, June 6, 1963; education: B.A., Hope College, Holland, MI, 1986; M.Div., Princeton Theological Seminary, Princeton,

NJ, 1990; Ph.D., in economics, American University, Washington, DC, 1995; family: wife, Laura; children: Jonathan and Sophia; committees: Budget; Education and the Workforce; Small Business; elected to the 114th Congress on November 4, 2014; reelected to the 115th Congress on November 8, 2016.

Office Listings

http://www.brat.house.gov facebook: representativedavebrat twitter: @repdavebrat

1628 Longworth House Office Building, Washington, DC 20515 .... (202) 225–2815
Chief of Staff.—Mark Kelly. FAX: 225–0011
Scheduler.—Grace Walt.
Legislative Director.—Zoë O'Herin.
Press Secretary.—Julianna Heerschap.
4201 Dominion Boulevard, Suite 110, Glen Allen, VA 23060 .... (804) 747–4073
9104 Courthouse Road, Room 249, Spotsylvania, VA 22553 .... (540) 507–7216

Counties: AMELIA, CHESTERFIELD (part), CULPEPER, GOOCHLAND, HENRICO (part), LOUISA, NOTTOWAY, ORANGE, POWHATAN, AND SPOTSYLVANIA (part). Population (2010), 727,366.

ZIP Codes: 20106, 20186, 22407–08, 22433, 22508, 22534, 22542, 22551, 22553, 22565, 22567, 22580, 22701, 22713–14, 22718, 22724, 22726, 22729, 22733–37, 22740–41, 22923, 22942, 22947, 22957, 22960, 22972, 22974, 23002, 23015, 23024, 23038–39, 23058–60, 23063, 23065, 23067, 23083–84, 23093, 23102–03, 23112–14, 23117, 23120, 23129, 23139, 23146, 23153, 23160, 23222, 23224–30, 23233–38, 23294, 23297, 23824, 23832–33, 23838, 23850, 23922, 23930, 23955, 23966

* * *

EIGHTH DISTRICT

DONALD S. BEYER, JR., Democrat, of Alexandria, VA; born in the Free Territory of Trieste, June 20, 1950; education: B.A., Williams College, MA, 1972; professional: Ambassador to Switzerland and Liechtenstein 2009–13; 36th Lieutenant Governor of Virginia, 1990–98; co-founder of the Northern Virginia Technology Council; former chair of Jobs for Virginia Graduates; served on Board of the D.C. Campaign to Prevent Teen Pregnancy; former chair of the Virginia Economic Recovery Commission; spouse: Megan; children: Don, Stephanie, Clara, and Grace; caucuses: New Democrat Coalition, Congressional Progressive Caucus; committees: Natural Resources; Science, Space, and Technology; Joint Economic Committee; elected to the 114th Congress on November 4, 2014; reelected to the 115th Congress.

Office Listings

http://beyer.house.gov https://www.facebook.com/repdonbeyer https://twitter.com/repdonbeyer

1119 Longworth House Office Building, Washington, DC 20515 .... (202) 225–4376
Chief of Staff.—Ann O'Hanlon. FAX: 225–0017
Legislative Director.—Zach Cafritz.
5285 Shawnee Road, Alexandria, VA 22312 .... (703) 971–4700
District Director.—Noah Simon.

Counties: ARLINGTON, FAIRFAX (part). CITIES: Alexandria and Falls Church. Population (2010), 767,596.

ZIP Codes: : 22003 (part), 22041–44 (part), 22046, 22060, 22079 (part), 22101–02 (part), 22150–51 (part), 22153 (part), 22201–07, 22209, 22211, 22213–14, 22301–12, 22314–15

* * *

NINTH DISTRICT

H. MORGAN GRIFFITH, Republican, of Salem, VA; born March 15, 1958; education: graduated, Andrew Lewis High School, 1976; B.A., Emory and Henry College, 1980; J.D., Washington and Lee University School of Law, 1983; professional: attorney, private practice, 1983–2011; partner, Albo & Oblon, LLP, 2008–11; Virginia House of Delegates, 1994–2011; Majority Leader, Virginia House of Delegates, 2001–11; married: Hilary; children: Abby, Davis, and Starke; committees: Energy and Commerce; elected to the 112th Congress on November 2, 2010; reelected to each succeeding Congress.

Office Listings

http://www.morgangriffith.house.gov twitter: @repmgriffith
https://www.facebook.com/repmorgangriffith

2202 Rayburn House Office Building, Washington, DC 20515 .... (202) 225–3861

Office Listings—Continued

Chief of Staff.—Kelly Lungren McCollum. FAX: 225–0076
Legislative Director.—Bobby Hamill.
Communications Director.—Kevin Baird.
323 West Main Street, Abingdon, VA 24210 .... (276) 525–1405
District Director.—Michelle Jenkins.
17 West Main Street, Christiansburg, VA 24073 .... (540) 381–5671

Counties: ALLEGHANY, BLAND, BUCHANAN, CARROLL, CRAIG, DICKENSON, FLOYD, GILES, GRAYSON, HENRY (part), LEE, MONTGOMERY, PATRICK, PULASKI, ROANOKE (part), RUSSELL, SCOTT, SMYTH, TAZEWELL, WASHINGTON, WISE, AND WYTHE. CITIES: Bristol, Covington, Galax, Martinsville, Norton, Radford, and Salem. Population (2010), 727,366.

ZIP Codes: 24019 (part), 24053, 24055 (part), 24058, 24059 (part), 24060, 24070, 24072–73, 24076, 24078, 24079 (part), 24082, 24084, 24085 (part), 24086–87, 24088 (part), 24089, 24091 (part), 24093, 24102 (part), 24105, 24112 (part), 24120, 24124, 24127–28, 24131–34, 24136, 24138, 24141–42, 24147, 24148 (part), 24149–50, 24153 (part), 24162, 24165, 24167–68, 24171, 24175 (part), 24185, 24201–02, 24210–11, 24216–17, 24219–21, 24224–26, 24228, 24230, 24236–37, 24239, 24243–46, 24248, 24250–51, 24256, 24258, 24260, 24263, 24265–66, 24269–73, 24277, 24279–83, 24290, 24292–93, 24301, 24311–19, 24322–26, 24328, 24330, 24333, 24340, 24343, 24347–48, 24350–52, 24360–61, 24363, 24366, 24368, 24370, 24374–75, 24377–78, 24380–82, 24422 (part), 24426, 24445 (part), 24448, 24457, 24474, 24601–07, 24609, 24612–14, 24620, 24622, 24628, 24630–31, 24634–35, 24637, 24639, 24641, 24646, 24649, 24651, 24656–57

* * *

TENTH DISTRICT

BARBARA COMSTOCK, Republican, of McLean, VA; born in Springfield, Hampden County, MA, June 30, 1959; B.A., Middlebury College, Middlebury, VT, 1981; J.D., Georgetown University, Washington, DC, 1986; intern, U.S. Senator Edward Kennedy of Massachusetts, 1979; senior staff, U.S. Representative Frank Wolf of Virginia, 1991–95; chief counsel, U.S. House of Representatives Committee on Oversight and Government Reform, 1995–99; Republican National Committee, director of strategic planning, 1999–2001; director of public affairs, United States Justice Department, 2002–03; senior partner, Blank Rome LLC + LLP 2003–06; partner, Corallo Comstock and Comstock Strategies, 2006–14; member of the Virginia House of Delegates, 2009–15; committees: Joint Economic Committee; House Administration; Science, Space, and Technology; Transportation and Infrastructure; Joint Economic Committee; elected to the 114th Congress; reelected to the 115th Congress on November 8, 2016.

Office Listings

https://comstock.house.gov

229 Cannon House Office Building, Washington, DC 20515 .... (202) 225–5136
Chief of Staff.—Susan Falconer. FAX: 225–0437
Legislative Director.—Michael Mansour.
21430 Cedar Drive, Suite 218, Sterling, VA 20164 .... (703) 404–6903
District Director.—Lucy Norment.
117 East Piccadilly Street, Suite 100–D, Winchester, VA 22601 .... (540) 773–3600

Counties: CLARKE, FAIRFAX (part), FREDERICK, LOUDOUN, AND PRINCE WILLIAM (part). CITIES: Manassas, Manassas Park, and Winchester. Population (2010), 758,321.

ZIP Codes: 20105, 20109–12 (part), 20117 (part), 20118, 20120–21 (part), 20124 (part), 20129, 20130 (part), 20132, 20135, 20137 (part), 20141, 20143, 20147–48, 20151 (part), 20152, 20155, 20158, 20164–66, 20169, 20170–71 (part), 20175–76, 20180, 20184 (part), 20190–91 (part), 20194 (part), 20197, 22015 (part), 22030 (part), 22033 (part), 22039 (part), 22066, 22079 (part), 22101–02 (part), 22124 (part), 22153 (part), 22182 (part), 22601–03, 22611, 22620, 22624–25, 22630 (part), 22637, 22645–46, 22654–55 (part), 22656, 22663

* * *

ELEVENTH DISTRICT

GERALD E. CONNOLLY, Democrat, of Fairfax, VA; born in Boston, MA, March 30, 1950; education: B.A., Maryknoll College; M.A., public administration, Harvard University, 1979; professional: member, Fairfax County Board of Supervisors, 1995–2003, chairman, 2003–08; religion: Roman Catholic; married: Cathy; children: Caitlin; committees: Foreign Affairs; Oversight and Government Reform; elected to the 111th Congress on November 4, 2008; reelected to each succeeding Congress.

Office Listings

http://www.connolly.house.gov

2238 Rayburn House Office Building, Washington, DC 20515 .... (202) 225–1492

Office Listings—Continued

Chief of Staff.—James Walkinshaw.
Legislative Director.—Collin Davenport.
Communications Director.—Jamie Smith.

4115 Annandale Road, Suite 103, Annandale, VA 22003 .... (703) 256–3071
District Director.—Sharon Stark.

2241–D Tackett's Mill Drive, Woodbridge, VA 22192 .... (571) 408–4407
Prince William Director.—Briana Sewell.

Counties: FAIRFAX (part) AND PRINCE WILLIAM (part). CITIES: Annandale, Burke, Centreville, Dale City, Fairfax, Fairfax Station, Herndon, Lorton, Manassas, Oakton, Occoquan, Reston, Springfield, Vienna, and Woodbridge. Population (2010), 770,944.

ZIP Codes: 20112, 20120–21, 20124, 20151, 20170–71, 20190–91, 20194, 22003, 22015, 22026–27, 22030–33, 22035, 22039, 22041–44, 22079, 22102, 22124–25, 22134, 22150–53, 22172, 22180–82, 22185, 22191–93

WASHINGTON

(Population 2010, 6,724,540)

SENATORS

PATTY MURRAY, Democrat, of Seattle, WA; born in Seattle, October 11, 1950; education: B.A., Washington State University, 1972; professional: teacher; Shoreline Community College; citizen lobbyist for environmental and educational issues, 1983–88; parent education instructor for Crystal Springs, 1984–87; school board member, 1985–89; elected board of directors, Shoreline School District, 1985–89; Washington State Senate, 1988–92; Democratic Whip, 1990–92; State Senate committees: chair, School Transportation Safety Task Force; Commerce and Labor; Domestic Timber Processing Select Committee; Education; Open Government Select Committee; Ways and Means; award: Washington State Legislator of the Year, 1990; married: Rob Murray; children: Randy and Sara; committees: ranking member, Health, Education, Labor, and Pensions; Appropriations; Budget; Veterans' Affairs; elected to the U.S. Senate on November 3, 1992; reelected to each succeeding Senate term.

Office Listings

http://murray.senate.gov

154 Russell Senate Office Building, Washington, DC 20510 .... (202) 224–2621
Chief of Staff.—Mike Spahn. FAX: 224–0238
Legislative Director.—Livia Lam. TDD: 224–4430
Communications Director.—Eli Zupnick.
2988 Jackson Federal Building, 915 Second Avenue, Seattle, WA 98174 .... (206) 553–5545
State Director.—Shawn Bills.
The Marshall House, 1323 Officer's Row, Vancouver, WA 98661 .... (360) 696–7797
District Director.—David Hodges.
10 North Post Road, Suite 600, Spokane, WA 99201 .... (509) 624–9515
District Director.—John Culton.
2930 Wetmore Avenue, Suite 903, Everett, WA 98201 .... (425) 259–6515
District Director.—Ann Seabott.
402 East Yakima Avenue, Suite 390, Yakima, WA 98901 .... (509) 453–7462
District Director.—Raquel Crowley.
950 Pacific Avenue, Room 650, Tacoma, WA 98402 .... (253) 572–3636
District Director.—Kierra Phifer.

* * *

MARIA CANTWELL, Democrat, of Edmonds, WA; born in Indianapolis, IN, October 13, 1958; education: B.A., Miami University, Miami, OH, 1980; professional: businesswoman; RealNetworks, Inc.; organizations: South Snohomish County Chamber of Commerce; Alderwood Rotary; Mountlake Terrace Friends of the Library; public service: Washington State House of Representatives, 1987–92; U.S. House of Representatives, 1992–94; religion: Roman Catholic; committees: ranking member, Energy and Natural Resources; Commerce, Science, and Transportation; Finance; Indian Affairs; Small Business and Entrepreneurship; elected to the U.S. Senate on November 7, 2000; reelected to each succeeding Senate term.

Office Listings

http://cantwell.senate.gov twitter: @senatorcantwell

511 Hart Senate Office Building, Washington, DC 20510 .... (202) 224–3441
Chief of Staff.—Travis Lumpkin.
Legislative Director/Deputy Chief of Staff.—Rosemary Gutierrez.
Administrative Director.—Nancy Hadley.
915 Second Avenue, Suite 3206, Seattle, WA 98174 .... (206) 220–6400
The Marshall House, 1313 Officers Row, Vancouver, WA 98661 .... (360) 696–7838
950 Pacific Avenue, Suite 615, Tacoma, WA 98402 .... (253) 572–2281
U.S. Federal Courthouse, West 920 Riverside, Suite 697, Spokane, WA 99201 .... (509) 353–2507
825 Jadwin Avenue, 204/204A, Richland, WA 99352 .... (509) 946–8106
2930 Wetmore Avenue, Suite 9B, Everett, WA 98201 .... (425) 303–0114

REPRESENTATIVES

FIRST DISTRICT

SUZAN K. DELBENE, Democrat, of Medina, WA; born in Selma, Dallas County, AL, February 17, 1962; education: B.A., Reed College, Portland, OR, 1983; M.B.A., University of

Washington, Seattle, WA, 1990; professional: business executive; director, Washington State Department of Revenue, 2010–12; married: Kurt; two children: Becca and Zach; committees: Budget; Ways and Means; elected simultaneously as a Democrat to the 112th Congress and 113th Congress, by special election, to fill the vacancy caused by the resignation of U.S. Representative Jay Inslee; reelected to each succeeding Congress.

Office Listings

http://delbene.house.gov facebook: facebook.com/RepDelBene twitter: @RepDelBene

2442 Rayburn House Office Building, Washington, DC 20515 .... (202) 225–6311
Chief of Staff.—Aaron Schmidt. FAX: 226–1606
Legislative Director.—Lauren Soltani.
Communications Director.—Ramsey Cox.
Scheduler.—Melissa Plummer.
Canyon Park Business Center, 22121 17th Avenue Southeast, Suite 220, Bothell, WA 98021 .... (425) 485–0085
204 West Montgomery Street, Mount Vernon, WA 98273 .... (360) 417–7879
District Director.—Molly Keenan.

Counties: KING (part), SKAGIT (part), SNOHOMISH (part), WHATCOM (part). CITIES AND TOWNSHIPS: Blaine, Bothell, Carnation, Concrete, Darrington, Duvall, Everson, Ferndale, Gold Bar, Granite Falls, Hamilton, Hunts Point, Index, Kenmore, Kirkland, Lake Stevens, Lyman, Lynden, Medina, Mill Creek, Monroe, Mount Vernon, Nooksack, Point Roberts, Redmond, Skykomish, Snohomish, Sultan, Sumas, Woodinville, and Yarrow Point. Population (2010), 691,738.

ZIP Codes: 98004 (part), 98007–08 (part), 98011, 98012 (part), 98014, 98019, 98021 (part), 98024 (part), 98028, 98033–34, 98036 (part), 98039, 98041, 98045 (part), 98052 (part), 98053, 98065 (part), 98072–73, 98074 (part), 98077, 98082–83, 98155 (part), 98201 (part), 98208 (part), 98220, 98223 (part), 98224, 98225–26 (part), 98230–31, 98233 (part), 98235, 98237, 98240–41, 98244, 98247–48, 98251–52, 98255–56, 98258 (part), 98262–64, 98266–67, 98270 (part), 98272, 98273–74 (part), 98276, 98281, 98283, 98284 (part), 98288, 98290–91, 98293–96

* * *

SECOND DISTRICT

RICK LARSEN, Democrat, of Everett, WA; born in Arlington, WA, June 15, 1965; education: B.A., Pacific Lutheran University; M.P.A., University of Minnesota; professional: economic development official at the Port of Everett; director of public affairs for a health provider association; public service: Snohomish County Council; religion: Methodist; married: Tiia Karlen; children: Robert and Per; committees: Armed Services; Transportation and Infrastructure; elected to the 107th Congress on November 7, 2000; reelected to each succeeding Congress.

Office Listings

http://www.larsen.house.gov

2113 Rayburn House Office Building, Washington, DC 20515 .... (202) 225–2605
Chief of Staff.—Kimberly Johnston. FAX: 225–4420
Legislative Director.—Terra Sabag.
Communications Director.—Douglas Wagoner.
2930 Wetmore Avenue, Suite 9F, Everett, WA 98201 .... (425) 252–3188
119 North Commercial Street, Suite 1350, Bellingham, WA 98225 .... (360) 733–5144

Counties: ISLAND, SAN JUAN, SKAGIT (part), SNOHOMISH (part), AND WHATCOM (part). CITIES AND TOWNSHIPS: Anacortes, Arlington, Bellingham, Blakely Island, Bow, Burlington, Clinton, Conway, Coupeville, Deer Harbor, East Sound, Everett, Freeland, Friday Harbor, Greenbank, Langley, Lopez Island, Lynnwood, Marysville, Mountlake Terrace, Mukilteo, Oak Harbor, Olga, Orcas, Shaw Island, Silvana, Stanwood, Tulalip, and Waldron. Population (2015), 726,951.

ZIP Codes: 98012, 98021, 98026, 98036–37, 98043, 98087, 98201, 98203–05, 98207–08, 98220–23, 98225–26, 98229

* * *

THIRD DISTRICT

JAIME HERRERA BEUTLER, Republican, of Battle Ground, WA; born in Glendale, CA, November 3, 1978; education: communications, University of Washington, Seattle, WA, 2004; religion: Christian; family: married to Daniel Beutler; committees: Appropriations; elected to the 112th Congress on November 2, 2010; reelected to each succeeding Congress.

Office Listings

http://www.jhb.house.gov facebook: @herrerabeutler twitter: @herrerabeutler

1107 Longworth House Office Building, Washington, DC 20515 .... (202) 225–3536
Chief of Staff.—Casey Bowman.
Deputy Chief of Staff / Legislative Director.—Jordan Evich.
Legislative Assistants: Anna Schartner, Jessica Wixson.
Press Secretary.—Amy Pennington.
Executive Assistant / Scheduler.—Angela Riesterer.
Legislative Correspondent.—Courtney Webb.
Staff Assistant.—Rebecca Sikora.
750 Anderson Street, Suite B, Vancouver, WA 98661 .... (360) 695–6292
District Director.—Shari Hildreth.
Deputy District Director.—Pam Peiper.
District Issues Director.—Dale Lewis.
Caseworkers: Ashley Lara, Jordan Meade.
District Staff Assistant.—Parker Truax.

Counties: CLARK, COWLITZ, KLICKITAT, LEWIS, PACIFIC, SKAMANIA, THURSTON (part), and WAHKIAKUM. Population (2010), 672,448.

ZIP Codes: 98304 (part), 98330 (part), 98336, 98355–56, 98361, 98377, 98522, 98527, 98530–33, 98537 (part), 98538–39, 98542, 98544, 98547 (part), 98554, 98561, 98564–65, 98568 (part), 98570, 98572, 98576 (part), 98577, 98579 (part), 98581–82, 98585–86, 98589 (part), 98590–91, 98593, 98596, 98597 (part), 98601–07, 98609–14, 98616–17, 98619–26, 98628–29, 98631–32, 98635, 98637–45, 98647–51, 98660–66, 98668, 98670–75, 98682–87, 98935 (part), 99322 (part), 99350 (part), 99356

* * *

FOURTH DISTRICT

DAN NEWHOUSE, Republican, of Sunnyside, WA; born in Sunnyside, July 10, 1955; education: graduated, Sunnyside High School, 1973; B.S., Washington State University, 1977; graduated, Washington Agriculture and Forestry Leadership Program, 1981; member: Washington State House of Representatives, 2003–09; Assistant Whip; Assistant Floor Leader; Floor Leader; Water Caucus; Drought Committee Chairman; CSG Leadership Academy; director, Washington State Department of Agriculture, 2009–13; married: Carol Hammond, 1982; children: Jensena and Devon; committees: Appropriations; Rules; elected to 114th Congress on November 4, 2014; reelected to the 115th Congress on November 8, 2016.

Office Listings

http://www.newhouse.house.gov twitter: @repnewhouse
https://www.facebook.com/repnewhouse

1318 Longworth House Office Building, Washington, DC 20515 .... (202) 225–5816
Chief of Staff.—Carrie Meadows.
Scheduler / Office Manager.—Hailey Ghee.
Communications Director.—Will Boyington.
3100 George Washington Way, #135, Richland, WA 99354 .... (509) 713–7374
402 East Yakima Avenue, Suite 445, WA 98901 .... (509) 452–3243

Counties: ADAMS COUNTY. CITIES: Othello, Ritzville. BENTON COUNTY. CITIES AND TOWNSHIPS: Benton City, Kennewick, Paterson, Plymouth, Prosser, Richland, West Richland. DOUGLAS COUNTY. CITIES AND TOWNSHIPS: Bridgeport, East Wenatchee, Leahy, Mansfield, Orondo, Palisades, Rock Island, Waterville. FRANKLIN COUNTY. CITIES AND TOWNSHIPS: Basin City, Connell, Eltopia, Kahlotus, Mesa, Pasco, Windust. GRANT COUNTY. CITIES AND TOWNSHIPS: Beverly, Coulee City, Desert Aire, Electric City, Ephrata, George, Grand Coulee, Hartline, Marlin, Mattawa, Moses Lake, Quincy, Royal City, Soap Lake, Stratford, Warden, Wilson Creek. OKANOGAN COUNTY. CITIES: Brewster, Nespelem, Okanogan, Omak, Oroville, Tonasket, and Twisp. WALLA WALLA COUNTY (part). CITIES: BURBANK. YAKIMA COUNTY. CITIES AND TOWNSHIPS: Brownstown, Buena, Carson, Cowiche, Grandview, Granger, Harrah, Mabton, Moxee, Naches, Outlook, Parker, Selah, Sunnyside, Tieton, Toppenish, Underwood, Wapato, White Swan, Yakima, and Zillah. Population (2010), 695,040.

ZIP Codes: 98068, 98602, 98605, 98610, 98613, 98617, 98619–20, 98623, 98628, 98635, 98648, 98650–51, 98670, 98672–73, 98801–02, 98807, 98811–13, 98815–17, 98819, 98821–24, 98826, 98828–32, 98834, 98836–37, 98840–44, 98843, 98845, 98847–48, 98850–53, 98855–56, 98857–58, 98860, 98901–04, 98907–09, 98920–23, 98925–26, 98929–30, 98932–44, 98946–48, 98950–53, 99103, 99115–16, 99123–24, 99133, 99135, 99155, 99169, 99301–02, 99320–22, 99323, 99326, 99330, 99335–38, 99343–46, 99349–50, 99352–54, 99356–57

* * *

FIFTH DISTRICT

CATHY MCMORRIS RODGERS, Republican, of Spokane, WA; born in Salem, OR, May 22, 1969; education: graduated from Kettle Falls High School, Kettle Falls, WA, 1986; B.A.,

Pensacola Christian College, Pensacola, FL, 1990; M.B.A., University of Washington, Seattle, WA, 2002; professional: family orchard business; member, Washington State House of Representatives, 1994–2004; Minority Leader, 2002–03; chair, House Republican Conference; committees: Energy and Commerce; elected to the 109th Congress on November 2, 2004; reelected to each succeeding Congress.

Office Listings

http://www.mcmorris.house.gov https://twitter.com/cathymcmorris
https://www.facebook.com/mcmorrisrodgers

1314 Longworth House Office Building, Washington, DC 20515 .... (202) 225–2006
Chief of Staff.—Ian Field. FAX: 225–3392
Scheduler.—Emily King.
Policy Director.—Jerry White.
Legislative Director.—Megan Perez.
Press Secretary.—Jared Powell.
Legislative Correspondent.—Andrew Neill.
10 North Post Street, Suite 625, Spokane, WA 99201 .... (509) 353–2374
District Director.—Traci Couture.
Manager, Constituent and Community Relations.—Jessica Laughery.
AG and Natural Resources.—Mike Poulson.
Veterans Outreach Liaison.—John Davis.
Staff Assistant.—Collin Tracy.
555 South Main Street, Colville, WA 99114 .... (509) 684–3481
District Representative.—Andrew Engall.
26 East Main Street, Suite 2, Walla Walla, WA 99362 .... (509) 529–9358
Deputy District Director.—Cathy Schaeffer.

Counties: ASOTIN, COLUMBIA, FERRY, GARFIELD, LINCOLN, PEND OREILLE, SPOKANE, STEVENS, WALLA WALLA, AND WHITMAN. Population (2015), 696,416.

ZIP Codes: 98832, 99001, 99003–06, 99008–09, 99011–13, 99016–23, 99025–27, 99029–34, 99036–37, 99039–40, 99101–03, 99109–11, 99113–14, 99117–19, 99121–22, 99125–26, 99128–31, 99133–34, 99136–41, 99143–44, 99146–61, 99163–64, 99166–67, 99169–71, 99173–74, 99176, 99179–81, 99185, 99201–08, 99212, 99216–18, 99223–24, 99324, 99328–29, 99333, 99347–48, 99359–62, 99401–03

* * *

SIXTH DISTRICT

DEREK KILMER, Democrat, of Gig Harbor, WA; born in Port Angeles, January 1, 1974; education: graduated, Port Angeles High School, 1992; B.A., public affairs, Princeton University, 1996; Ph.D., University of Oxford, 1999; professional: worked as a consultant with McKinsey & Company from 1999–2002; worked for the Economic Development Board for Tacoma-Pierce County; elected to be a Washington State Representative in 2004; served in the Washington State Senate from 2007–12; Rotary; married: the former Jennifer Saunders; children: Sophie and Tess; caucuses: co-chair of the Puget Sound Recovery Caucus; member, Democratic Caucus; New Democrats; committees: Appropriations; elected to the 113th Congress on November 6, 2012; reelected to each succeeding Congress.

Office Listings

http://kilmer.house.gov https://www.facebook.com/derek.kilmer https://twitter: @repderekkilmer

1520 Longworth House Office Building, Washington, DC 20515 .... (202) 225–5916
Chief of Staff.—Jonathan Smith. FAX: 226–3575
Press Secretary.—Jason Phelps.
Legislative Director.—Aaron Wasserman.
Scheduler.—Julia O'Connor.
950 Pacific Avenue, Suite 1320, Tacoma, WA 98402 .... (253) 272–3515
District Director.—Andrea Roper.
345 Sixth Street, Suite 500, Bremerton, WA 98337 .... (360) 373–9725
322 East Fifth Street, Port Angeles, WA 98362 .... (360) 797–3623

Counties: CLALLAM. CITIES AND TOWNSHIPS: Blyn, Forks, Joyce, LaPush, Neah Bay, Port Angeles, Sequim, and Sieku. GRAYS HARBOR. CITIES AND TOWNSHIPS: Aberdeen, Amanda Park, Cosmopolis, Elma, Hoquiam, McCleary, MoClips, Montesano, Oakville, Ocean City, Ocean Shores, Quinault, Seabrook, Taholah, and Westport. JEFFERSON. CITIES AND TOWNSHIPS: Chimicum, Nordland, Port Hadlock, Port Ludlow, Port Townsend, and Quilcene. KITSAP. CITIES AND TOWNSHIPS: Bainbridge Island, Bremerton, Hansville, Indianola, Kingston, Manchester, Olalla, Port Orchard, Poulsbo, Seabeck, Silverdale, and Southworth. MASON (part). CITIES AND TOWNSHIPS: Allyn, Belfair, Grapeview, Harstine Island, Shelton, Skokomish, and Union. PIERCE (part). CITIES AND TOWNSHIPS: Fox Island, Gig Harbor, Key Center, Lakebay, Longbranch, Purdy, Tacoma, Vaughn, and Wauna. Population (2010), 687,387.

ZIP Codes: 98061, 98110, 98305, 98310–12, 98315, 98320, 98322, 98324–26, 98329, 98331–33, 98335, 98337, 98339–40, 98342–43, 98345–46, 98349–51, 98353, 98357–59, 98362–68, 98370, 98376, 98378, 98380–84, 98386, 98392–95, 98401–03, 98405–09, 98411–13, 98415, 98417–19, 98421, 98444, 98465–67, 98471, 98499, 98502, 98520, 98524, 98526, 98528, 98535–37, 98541, 98546–48, 98550, 98552, 98555, 98557, 98559–60, 98562–63, 98566, 98568–69, 98571, 98575, 98583–84, 98587–88, 98592, 98595

* * *

SEVENTH DISTRICT

PRAMILA JAYAPAL, Democrat, of Seattle, WA; born in Chennai, Tamil Nadu, India, September, 21, 1965; education: B.A., Georgetown University, Washington, DC; M.B.A, Northwestern University, Evanston, IL; professional: director of technology transfer, Program for Appropriate Technology in Health (PATH); founder, Hate Free Zone, 2004–08; founder, OneAmerica 2008–12; White House Champion of Change, 2013; married: Steven Williamson; mother to son and stepson: Janak and Michael; dog owner: Otis the Labradoodle; Senior Whip; Democratic Caucus; caucuses: first vice chair, Congressional Progressive Caucus; co-chair, Women's Working Group on Immigration; Congressional Asian Pacific American Caucus; LGBT Equality Caucus; committees: vice ranking member, Budget; Judiciary; elected to the 115th Congress on November 8, 2016.

Office Listings

http://www.jayapal.house.gov

319 Cannon House Office Building, Washington, DC 20515 .... (202) 225–3106
Chief of Staff.—Carmen Frias. FAX: 225–6197
Scheduler.—Wendy Hamilton.
Communications Director.—Omer Farooque.
1904 Third Avenue, Suite 510, Seattle, WA 98101–1313 .... (206) 674–0040

Counties: KING COUNTY. CITIES AND TOWNSHIPS: Included in the district (in whole or in part): Burien, Des Moines, Edmonds, Lake Forest Park, Normandy Park, Seattle, Shoreline, Vashon, and Woodway. Population (2010), 672,455.

ZIP Codes: 98013, 98020, 98026, 98037, 98043, 98070, 98101–09, 98111–13, 98115–17, 98119, 98121–22, 98125–27, 98129, 98133–34, 98136, 98139, 98141, 98146, 98148, 98154–55, 98161, 98164–66, 98168, 98174–75, 98177, 98181, 98185, 98191, 98194–95, 98198–99

* * *

EIGHTH DISTRICT

DAVID G. REICHERT, Republican, of Auburn, WA; born in Detroit Lakes, MI, August 29, 1950; education: graduated, Kent Meridian High School, Renton, WA, 1968; A.A., Concordia Lutheran College, Portland, OR, 1970; professional: U.S. Air Force Reserve, 1971–76; U.S. Air Force, 1976; police officer, King County, WA, 1972–97; sheriff, King County, WA, 1997–2004; member: president, Washington State Sheriff's Association; executive board member, Washington Association of Sheriffs and Police Chiefs; co-chair, Washington State Partners in Crisis; awards: recipient of the 2004 National Sheriff's Association's ''Sheriff of the Year'' award; two-time Medal of Valor Award recipient from the King County Sheriff's Office; Washington Policy Center's Champion of Freedom Award; Families Northwest Public Policy Award; married: Julie; children: Angela, Tabitha, and Daniel; committees: Ways and Means; elected to the 109th Congress on November 2, 2004; reelected to each succeeding Congress.

Office Listings

http://www.reichert.house.gov https://www.facebook.com/repdavereichert
twitter: @davereichert

1127 Longworth House Office Building, Washington, DC 20515 .... (202) 225–7761
Deputy Chief of Staff.—Lindsay Manson. FAX: 225–4282
Legislative Director.—Natalie Kamphaus.
Executive Assistant / Scheduler.—Jill Sims.
22605 Southeast 56th Street, Suite 130, Issaquah, WA 98029 .... (425) 677–7414
Chief of Staff / District Director.—Sue Foy.
5 South Wenatchee Avenue, Suite 315, Wenatchee, WA 98801 .... (509) 885–6615

Counties: KING COUNTY (part). CITIES AND TOWNSHIPS: Auburn, Black Diamond, Bonney Lake, Covington, Enumclaw, Federal Way, Issaquah, North Bend, Sammamish, and Snoqualmie. CHELAN COUNTY. CITIES AND TOWNSHIPS: Cashmere, Chelan, Leavenworth, and Wenatchee. KITTITAS. CITIES AND TOWNSHIPS: Cle Elum, Easton, Ellensburg, Kittitas, Roslyn, Snoqualmie Pass, and Thorp. DOUGLAS. CITIES AND TOWNSHIPS: East Wenatchee. PIERCE COUNTY (part). CITIES AND TOWNSHIPS: Ashfort, Bonney Lake, Buckley, Eatonville, Graham, Orting, and Sumner. Population (2010), 690,250.

ZIP Codes: 98001–03, 98010, 98022, 98024, 98027, 98029–32, 98038, 98042, 98045, 98047, 98050–51, 98058–59, 98065, 98068, 98074–75, 98092, 98304, 98321, 98323, 98328, 98330, 98338, 98354, 98360, 98372, 98374–75, 98385, 98387, 98390–91, 98396, 98424, 98558, 98580, 98801–02, 98811, 98815–17, 98821–22, 98826, 98828, 98831, 98836, 98847, 98852, 98901, 98922, 98925–26, 98934, 98937, 98940–41, 98943, 98946, 98950

* * *

NINTH DISTRICT

ADAM SMITH, Democrat, of Tacoma, WA; born in Washington, DC, June 15, 1965; education: graduated, Tyee High School, 1983; graduated, Fordham University, NY, 1987; law degree, University of Washington, 1990; admitted to the Washington Bar in 1991; professional: Prosecutor for the city of Seattle; Washington State Senate, 1990–96; member: Kent Drinking Driver Task Force; board member, Judson Park Retirement Home; married: Sara Smith, 1993; committees: ranking member, Armed Services; elected to the 105th Congress; reelected to each succeeding Congress.

Office Listings

http://www.adamsmith.house.gov

2264 Rayburn House Office Building, Washington, DC 20515 .... (202) 225–8901
Chief of Staff.—Shana Chandler. FAX: 225–5893
Communications Director.—Rebecca Bryant.
101 Evergreen Building, 15 South Grady Way, Renton, WA 98057 .... (425) 793–5180
District Director.—Debra Entenman.
Office Manager.—Kristen Johnsen.

Counties: KING (part) AND PIERCE (part). CITIES: Bellevue, Burien, Des Moines, Federal Way, Kent, Mercer Island, Newcastle, Renton, SeaTac, Seattle, Tacoma, and Tukwila. Population (2010), 672,460.

ZIP Codes: 98001 (part), 98003–04 (part), 98005–06, 98007–08 (part), 98009, 98015, 90823, 98027 (part), 98030–33 (part), 98035 (part), 98040, 98042 (part), 98055–57, 98058–59 (part), 98063, 98089 (part), 98093, 98102 (part), 98104 (part), 98108–09 (part), 98112 (part), 98114, 98118, 98122 (part), 98124 (part), 98131, 98134 (part), 98138, 98141 (part), 98144, 98148 (part), 98155 (part), 98158, 98168 (part), 98178, 98188 (part), 98190, 98198 (part), 98354 (part), 98402 (part), 98421 (part), 98422, 98424 (part)

* * *

TENTH DISTRICT

DENNY HECK, Democrat, of Olympia, WA; born in Vancouver, WA, July 29, 1952; education: graduated, Columbia River High School, WA, 1970; graduated, The Evergreen State College, WA, 1973; professional: small business owner; president and co-founder of TVW, Washington's statewide public affairs cable channel, 1993–2003; Chief of Staff to Governor Booth Gardner, 1989–93; elected to five consecutive terms in the Washington State House of Representatives, starting in 1976; religion: member, The Lutheran Church of The Good Shepherd; former trustee, Washington State Historical Society; former trustee, The Evergreen State College; married: Paula Heck, 1976; committees: Financial Services; Permanent Select Committee on Intelligence; elected to the 113th Congress on November 6, 2012; reelected to each succeeding Congress.

Office Listings

http://www.dennyheck.house.gov www.facebook.com/congressmandennyheck
twitter: www.twitter.com/repdennyheck

425 Cannon House Office Building, Washington, DC 20515 .... (202) 225–9740
Chief of Staff.—Jami Burgess. FAX: 225–0129
Legislative Director.—Brendan Woodbury.
Communications Director.—Kati Rutherford.
420 College Street Southeast, Suite 3000, Lacey, WA 98503 .... (360) 459–8514
6000 Main Street, SW., Suite 3B, Lakewood, WA 98499 .... (253) 533–8332
District Director.—Phil Gardner.

Counties: MASON (part), PIERCE (part), AND THURSTON (part). CITIES: Chehalis Indian Reservation (part), DuPont, Edgewood, Fife, Fircrest, Joint Base Lewis-McChord, Lacey, Lakewood, Nisqually Indian Reservation, Olympia, Puyallup, Puyallup Indian Reservation (part), Rainier, Roy, Shelton, Squaxin Island Indian Reservation (part), Steilacoom, Sumner, Tacoma (part), Tenino, Tumwater, University Place, and Yelm. Population (2010), 672,455.

ZIP Codes: 98047, 98303, 98327, 98338, 98354, 98371–75, 98387–88, 98390–91, 98404, 98408, 98418, 98421, 98424, 98430, 98433, 98438–39, 98443–47, 98466–67, 98498–99, 98501–03, 98506, 98512–13, 98516, 98558, 98576, 98579–80, 98584, 98589, 98597

WEST VIRGINIA

(Population 2010, 1,852,994)

SENATORS

JOE MANCHIN III, Democrat, of Fairmont, WV; born in Farmington, WV, August 24, 1947; education: graduated, Farmington High School, Farmington, 1965; B.A., West Virginia University, WV, 1970; professional: businessman; member of the West Virginia House of Delegates, 1982–86; member of the West Virginia State Senate, 1986–96; Secretary of State, West Virginia, 2000–04; elected Governor of West Virginia in 2004 and reelected in 2008; chairman of the National Governors Association, 2010; religion: Catholic; married: Gayle Conelly; three children: Heather, Joseph IV, and Brooke; seven grandchildren; committees: Appropriations; Energy and Natural Resources; Select Committee on Intelligence; Veterans' Affairs; elected to the 111th U.S. Senate, by special election, on November 2, 2010, to the term ending January 3, 2013, to fill the seat previously held by Senator Carte Goodwin, and took the oath of office on November 15, 2010; reelected to the U.S. Senate on November 6, 2012.

Office Listings

http://manchin.senate.gov https://www.facebook.com/joemanchinIII
https://twitter.com/sen_joemanchin

306 Hart Senate Office Building, Washington, DC 20510 .... (202) 224–3954
Chief of Staff.—Pat Hayes. FAX: 228–0002
Legislative Director.—Wes Kungel.
Communications Director.—Jonathan Kott.
900 Pennsylvania Avenue, Suite 629, Charleston, WV 25302 .... (304) 342–5855
State Director.—Mara Boggs.
261 Aikens Center, Suite 305, Martinsburg, WV 25404 .... (304) 264–4626
48 Donley Street, Suite 504, Morgantown, WV 26501 .... (304) 284–8663
FAX: 284–8681

* * *

SHELLEY MOORE CAPITO, Republican, of Charleston, WV; born in Glen Dale, WV, November 26, 1953; education: B.S., Duke University; M.Ed., University of Virginia; professional: career counselor, West Virginia State College; West Virginia Board of Regents; organizations: Community Council of Kanawha Valley; YWCA; West Virginia Interagency Council for Early Intervention; Habitat for Humanity; public service: elected to the West Virginia House of Delegates, 1996; reelected in 1998; awards: Coalition for a Tobacco-Free West Virginia Legislator of the Year; elected to the 107th Congress on November 7, 2000; served in the U.S. House of Representatives from 2001–14; religion: Presbyterian; married: Charles L. Capito, Jr.; three children; four grandchildren; first woman elected to the U.S. Senate from West Virginia; committees: Appropriations; Commerce, Science, and Transportation; Energy and Natural Resources; Environment and Public Works; Rules and Administration; elected to the U.S. Senate on November 4, 2014.

Office Listings

http://www.capito.senate.gov https://www.facebook.com/senshelley
https://twitter.com/sencapito

172 Russell Senate Office Building, Washington, DC 20510 .... (202) 224–6472
Chief of Staff.—Joel Brubaker. FAX: 224–7665
Legislative Director.—Adam Tomlinson.
Communications Director.—Tyler Hernandez.
Office Manager.—Shay Kelly.
State Director.—Mary Elisabeth Eckerson.
500 Virginia Street East, Suite 950, Charleston, WV 25301 .... (304) 347–5372
300 Foxcroft Avenue, Suite 202A, Martinsburg, WV 25401 .... (304) 262–9285
48 Donley Street, Suite 504, Morgantown, WV 26501 .... (304) 292–2310
220 North Kanawha Street, Suite 1, Beckley, WV 25801 .... (304) 347–5372

REPRESENTATIVES

FIRST DISTRICT

DAVID B. McKINLEY, Republican, of Wheeling, WV; born in Wheeling, March 28, 1947; education: B.S.C.E., civil engineering, Purdue University, West Lafayette, IN, 1969; professional: engineer (started McKinley and Associates with offices in Wheeling and Charleston, WV and Washington, PA); member of West Virginia State House of Representatives, 1981–94; chairman, West Virginia Republican Party, 1990–94; religion: Episcopalian; married: Mary McKinley; children: David, Amy, Elizabeth, and Bennett; committees: Energy and Commerce; elected to the 112th Congress on November 2, 2010; reelected to each succeeding Congress.

Office Listings

http://mckinley.house.gov

412 Cannon House Office Building, Washington, DC 20515 .... (202) 225–4172
Chief of Staff.—Mike Hamilton. FAX: 225–7564
Executive Assistant.—Lou Hrkman.
Legislative Director.—Margie Almanza.
Communications Director.—John Stapleton.
709 Beechurst Avenue, Suite 29, Morgantown, WV 26505 .... (304) 284–8506
Horne Building, 1100 Main Street, Suite 101, Wheeling, WV 26003 .... (304) 232–3801
408 Market Street, Parkersburg, WV 26101 .... (304) 422–5972

Counties: BARBOUR, BROOKE, DODDRIDGE, GILMER, GRANT, HANCOCK, HARRISON, MARION, MARSHALL, MINERAL, MONONGALIA, OHIO, PLEASANTS, PRESTON, RITCHIE, TAYLOR, TUCKER, TYLER, WETZEL, AND WOOD. CITIES AND TOWNSHIPS: Albright, Alma, Alvy, Anmoore, Arthur, Arthurdale, Auburn, Aurora, Baldwin, Barrackville, Baxter, Bayard, Beech Bottom, Belington, Belleville, Bellview, Belmont, Bens Run, Benwood, Berea, Bethany, Big Run, Blacksville, Blandville, Booth, Brandonville, Bretz, Bridgeport, Bristol, Brownton, Bruceton Mills, Burlington, Burnt House, Burton, Cabins, Cairo, Cameron, Carolina, Cassville, Cedarville, Center Point, Central Station, Century, Chester, Clarksburg, Coburn, Colfax, Colliers, Core, Corinth, Cove, Coxs Mills, Cuzzart, Dallas, Davis, Davisville, Dawmont, Dellslow, Dorcas, Eglon, Elk Garden, Ellenboro, Elm Grove, Enterprise, Eureka, Everettville, Fairmont, Fairview, Farmington, Flemington, Flower, Follansbee, Folsom, Fort Ashby, Fort Neal, Four States, Friendly, Galloway, Gilmer, Glen Dale, Glen Easton, Glenville, Goffs, Gormania, Grafton, Grant Town, Granville, Greenwood, Gypsy, Hambleton, Harrisville, Hastings, Haywood, Hazelton, Hebron, Hendricks, Hepzibah, Highland, Hundred, Idamay, Independence, Industrial, Jacksonburg, Jere, Jordan, Junior, Keyser, Kingmont, Kingwood, Knob Fork, Lahmansville, Letter Gap, Lima, Linn, Littleton, Lockney, Lost Creek, Lumberport, MacFarlan, Mahone, Maidsville, Mannington, Masontown, Maysville, McMechen, McWhorter, Meadowbrook, Medley, Metz, Middlebourne, Mineral Wells, Moatsville, Monongah, Montana Mines, Morgantown, Moundsville, Mount Clare, Mount Storm, Mountain, New Creek, New Cumberland, New England, New Manchester, New Martinsville, New Milton, Newberne, Newburg, Newell, Normantown, North Parkersburg, Nutter Fort, Osage, Owings, Paden City, Parkersburg, Parsons, Pennsboro, Pentress, Perkins, Petersburg, Petroleum, Philippi, Piedmont, Pine Grove, Porters Falls, Proctor, Pullman, Pursglove, Rachel, Reader, Red Creek, Reedsville, Reynoldsville, Ridgeley, Rivesville, Rocket Center, Rockport, Rosedale, Rosemont, Rowlesburg, Saint George, Saint Marys, Salem, Sand Fork, Shinnston, Shirley, Shocks, Short Creek, Simpson, Sistersville, Smithburg, Smithfield, Smithville, Spelter, Stonewood, Stouts Mill, Stumptown, Tanner, Terra Alta, Thomas, Thornton, Toll Gate, Troy, Triadelphia, Tunnelton, Valley Grove, Vienna, Volga, Wadestown, Walker, Wallace, Wana, Warwood, Washington, Watson, Waverly, Weirton, Wellsburg, Wendel, West Liberty, West Milford, West Union, Westover, Wheeling, Wick, Wilbur, Wiley Ford, Wileyville, Williamstown, Wilson, Wilsonburg, Windsor Heights, Wolf Summit, Worthington, and Wyatt. Population (2010), 615,991.

ZIP Codes: 25267, 26003, 26030–41, 26047, 26050, 26055–56, 26059–60, 26062, 26070, 26074–75, 26101, 26104–05, 26133–34, 26136–37, 26142–43, 26146, 26148–50, 26155, 26159, 26161, 26164, 26167, 26169–70, 26175, 26178, 26180–81, 26184, 26187, 26201, 26238, 26250, 26260, 26263, 26267, 26269, 26271, 26275–76, 26283, 26287, 26292, 26301, 26320, 26323, 26325, 26327, 26330, 26335, 26337, 26339, 26342, 26346–49, 26351, 26354, 26361–62, 26366, 26369, 26374, 26377–78, 26384–86, 26404–05, 26408, 26410–12, 26415–16, 26419, 26421–22, 26424–26, 26430–31, 26435–38, 26440, 26443–44, 26448, 26451, 26456, 26501, 26505, 26508, 26519–21, 26525, 26534, 26537, 26541–43, 26547, 26554, 26559–60, 26562–63, 26568, 26570–72, 26574–76, 26581–82, 26585–88, 26590–91, 26611, 26636, 26638, 26705, 26707, 26710, 26716–17, 26719–20, 26726, 26731, 26739, 26743, 26750, 26753, 26763–64, 26767, 26833, 26847, 26855

* * *

SECOND DISTRICT

ALEXANDER X. MOONEY, Republican, of Charles Town, WV; born in Washington, DC, June 7, 1971; education: B.A., philosophy, Dartmouth College, 1993; professional: owner, AXM Consulting, LLC; executive director, The National Journalism Center (a program of Young America's Foundation), 2005–12; State Senator, Maryland State Senate, 1999–2010; religion: Roman Catholic; married: Dr. Grace Gonzalez Mooney, Ph.D., M.D.; three children; committees: Financial Services; elected to the 114th Congress on November 4, 2014; reelected to the 115th Congress on November 8, 2016.

Office Listings

http://www.mooney.house.gov facebook: @CongressmanAlexMooney twitter: @repalexmooney

1232 Longworth House Office Building, Washington, DC 20515 .... (202) 225–2711
Chief of Staff.—Michael Hough. FAX: 225–7856
Executive Assistant.—Anita Itnyre.
Legislative Director.—Scott Rausch.
Communications Director.—Ted Dacey.
405 Capitol Street, Suite 514, Charleston, WV 25301 .... (304) 925–5964
300 Foxcroft Avenue, Suite 102, Martinsburg, WV 25401 .... (304) 264–8810

Counties: BERKELEY, BRAXTON, CALHOUN, CLAY, HAMPSHIRE, HARDY, JACKSON, JEFFERSON, KANAWHA, LEWIS, MORGAN, PENDLETON, PUTNAM, RANDOLPH, ROANE, UPSHUR, AND WIRT. Population (2010), 654,275.

ZIP Codes: 25002–03, 25005, 25011, 25015, 25019, 25025–26, 25030, 25033, 25035, 25039, 25043, 25045–46, 25054, 25059, 25061, 25063–64, 25067, 25070–71, 25075, 25079, 25081–83, 25085–86, 25088, 25102–03, 25106–07, 25109–13, 25123–26, 25132–34, 25136, 25139, 25141, 25143, 25147, 25150, 25156, 25159–60, 25162, 25164, 25168, 25177, 25187, 25201–02, 25211, 25213–14, 25231, 25234–35, 25239, 25241, 25243–45, 25247–48, 25251–53, 25259–62, 25264–68, 25270–71, 25275–76, 25279, 25281, 25285–87, 25301–06, 25309, 25311–15, 25317, 25320–39, 25350, 25356–58, 25360–62, 25364–65, 25375, 25392, 25396, 25401–02, 25410–11, 25413–14, 25419–23, 25425, 25427–32, 25434, 25437–38, 25440–44, 25446, 25502–03, 25510, 25515, 25520, 25523, 25526, 25541, 25550, 25560, 25569, 26133, 26136–38, 26141, 26143, 26147, 26151–52, 26160–61, 26164, 26173, 26180, 26201–02, 26205, 26210, 26215, 26218, 26224, 26228–30, 26234, 26236–38, 26241, 26253–54, 26257, 26259, 26261, 26263, 26267–68, 26270, 26273, 26276, 26278, 26280, 26282–83, 26285, 26293–94, 26296, 26321, 26335, 26338, 26342–43, 26351, 26372, 26376, 26378, 26384–85, 26412, 26430, 26443, 26447, 26452, 26546, 26590, 26601, 26610–11, 26615, 26617, 26619, 26621, 26623–24, 26627, 26629, 26631, 26636, 26638–39, 26641, 26651, 26656, 26660, 26662, 26667, 26671, 26675–76, 26678–79, 26681, 26684, 26690–91, 26704–05, 26707, 26710–11, 26714, 26717, 26722, 26731, 26739, 26743, 26750, 26755, 26757, 26761, 26763–64, 26801–02, 26804, 26807–08, 26810, 26812, 26814–15, 26817–18, 26823–24, 26836, 26838, 26845, 26847, 26851–52, 26865–66, 26884, 26886

* * *

THIRD DISTRICT

EVAN H. JENKINS, Republican, of Huntington, WV; born in Huntington, September 12, 1960; education: graduated from Virginia Episcopal School in 1979; Bachelor of Science in business administration, University of Florida, Gainesville, FL, 1983; J.D., Cumberland School of Law at Samford University, Birmingham, AL, 1987; professional: associate attorney, Jenkins Fenstermaker, P.L.L.C, 1987–92; general counsel, West Virginia State Chamber of Commerce, 1992–99; executive director, West Virginia State Medical Association, 1999–2014; member, West Virginia House of Delegates, 1995–2001; member, West Virginia Senate, 2003–2015; religion: First Presbyterian Church in Huntington; married: Elizabeth; children: Evan Jr. ''Hollin'', Charles, and Olivia; caucuses: Congressional Arts Caucus; Congressional Career and Technical Education Caucus; Congressional Caucus on Prescription Drug Abuse; Congressional Historic Preservation Caucus; Congressional Humanities Caucus; Congressional Steel Caucus; Congressional TRiO Caucus; House General Aviation Caucus; Ohio River Basin Congressional Caucus; committees: Appropriations; elected to the 114th Congress on November 4, 2014; reelected to the 115th Congress on November 8, 2016.

Office Listings

http://www.evanjenkins.house.gov facebook: www.facebook.com/repevanjenkins
twitter: @repevanjenkins

1609 Longworth House Office Building, Washington, DC 20515 .... (202) 225–3452
Chief of Staff.—Patrick Howell. FAX: 225–9061
Legislative Director.—Brian Barnard.
Scheduler.—Brittany Fortier.
Communications Director.—Rebecca Neal.
845 Fifth Avenue, Room 314, Huntington, WV 25701 .... (304) 522–2201
223 Prince Street, Beckley, WV 25801 .... (304) 250–6177
601 Federal Street, Room 1003, Bluefield, WV 24701 .... (304) 325–6800

Counties: BOONE, CABELL, FAYETTE, GREENBRIER, LINCOLN, LOGAN, MASON, MCDOWELL, MERCER, MINGO, MONROE, NICHOLAS, POCAHONTAS, RALEIGH, SUMMERS, WAYNE, WEBSTER, AND WYOMING. Population (2010), 613,376.

ZIP Codes: 24701, 24712, 24714–16, 24719, 24724, 24726, 24729, 24731–33, 24736–40, 24747, 24751, 24801, 24808, 24811, 24813, 24815–18, 24820–31, 24834, 24836, 24839, 24842–57, 24859–62, 24866–74, 24878–82, 24884, 24887–88, 24892, 24894–99, 24901–02, 24910, 24915–18, 24920, 24924–25, 24927, 24931, 24934–36, 24938, 24941, 24943–46, 24950–51, 24954, 24957, 24961–63, 24966, 24970, 24974, 24976–77, 24981, 24983–86, 24991, 24993, 25002–04, 25007–10, 25021–22, 25024, 25028, 25031, 25036, 25040, 25043–44, 25047–49, 25051, 25053, 25057, 25059–60, 25062, 25076, 25081, 25083, 25085, 25090, 25093, 25108, 25114–15, 25118–19, 25121, 25130, 25136, 25139–40, 25142, 25148–49, 25152, 25154, 25161, 25165, 25169, 25173–74, 25180–81, 25183, 25185–86, 25193, 25202–06, 25208–09, 25213, 25247, 25265, 25082, 25106, 25123, 25239, 25241, 25253, 25260, 25264, 25287, 25502–03, 25525, 25520, 25541, 25550–01, 25504–08, 25510–12, 25514, 25517, 25520–21, 25523–24, 25526, 25529–30, 25534–35, 25537, 25540–41, 25544–45, 25547, 25555, 25557, 25559, 25562, 25564–65, 25567, 25570–73, 25601, 25606–08, 25611–12, 25614, 25617, 25621, 25624–25, 25628, 25630, 25632, 25634–39, 25644, 25646–47, 25649–54, 25661, 25665–67, 25669–72, 25674, 25676, 25678, 25682, 25685–88, 25690–92, 25694, 25696, 25699, 25701–29, 25755, 25770–79, 25801–02, 25810–13, 25816–18, 25820, 25823, 25825–27, 25831–33, 25836–37, 25839–41, 25843–49, 25851, 25853–57, 25859–60, 25862, 25864–66, 25868, 25870–71, 25873, 25875–76, 25878–80, 25882, 25901–02, 25904, 25906–09, 25911, 25913–22, 25927–28, 25931–32, 25934, 25936, 25938, 25942–43, 25951, 25958, 25961–62, 25965–67, 25969, 25971–72, 25976–79, 25981, 25984–86, 25989, 26202–03, 26205–06, 26208–09, 26217, 26222, 26230, 26234, 26261, 26264, 26266, 26288, 26291, 26294, 26298, 26610, 26617, 26639, 26651, 26656, 26660, 26662, 26674, 26676, 26678–81, 26684, 26690–91

WISCONSIN

(Population 2010, 5,686,986)

SENATORS

RONALD H. JOHNSON, Republican, of Oshkosh, WI; born in Mankato, MN, April 18, 1955; education: B.A., business administration, University of Minnesota, Twin Cities, MN, 1977; professional: CEO Pacur, LLC.; married: wife, Jane; three children: daughters, Carey and Jenna; son, Ben; committees: chair, Homeland Security and Governmental Affairs; Budget; Commerce, Science, and Transportation; Foreign Relations; elected to the U.S. Senate on November 2, 2010; reelected to the U.S. Senate on November 8, 2016.

Office Listings

http://ronjohnson.senate.gov facebook: facebook.com/SenRonJohnson twitter: @SenRonJohnson

328 Hart Senate Office Building, Washington, DC 20510 .... (202) 224–5323
Chief of Staff.—Tony Blando. FAX: 228–6965
Deputy Chief of Staff.—Marlo Meuli.
Legislative Director.—Sean Riley.
Communications Director.—Ben Voelkel.
517 East Wisconsin Avenue, Room 408, Milwaukee, WI 53202 .... (414) 276–7282
219 Washington Avenue, Suite 100, Oshkosh, WI 54901 .... (920) 230–7250
Deputy Chief of Staff.—Julie Leschke.

* * *

TAMMY BALDWIN, Democrat, of Madison, WI; born in Madison, February 11, 1962; education: graduated, Madison West High School, Madison, 1980; A.B., Smith College, Northampton, MA, 1984; J.D., University of Wisconsin Law School, Madison, 1989; appointed to Madison Common Council, Madison, 1986; elected to Dane County Board of Supervisors, Madison, served 1986–94; elected to the Wisconsin State Assembly, Madison, served 1992–98; elected to the U.S. House of Representatives, served 1998–2012; committees: Appropriations; Commerce, Science, and Transportation; Health, Education, Labor, and Pensions; elected to the U.S. Senate on November 6, 2012.

Office Listings

http://baldwin.senate.gov facebook.com/senatortammybaldwin twitter: @senatorbaldwin

709 Hart Senate Office Building, Washington, DC 20510 .... (202) 224–5653
Chief of Staff.—Bill Murat.
Legislative Director.—Dan McCarthy.
Communications Director.—John Kraus.
Executive Assistant.—Carolyn Walser.
30 West Mifflin Street, Suite 700, Madison, WI 53703 .... (608) 264–5338
State Director.—Janet Piraino.
633 West Wisconsin Avenue, Suite 1920, Milwaukee, WI 53203 .... (414) 297–4451
From Wisconsin Only (800) 247–5645
205 5th Avenue South, Room 216, La Crosse, WI 54601 .... (608) 796–0045
2100 Stewart Avenue, Suite 250B, Wausau, WI 54401 .... (715) 261–2611
1039 West Mason Street, Suite 119, Green Bay, WI 54303 .... (920) 498–2668
402 Gorham Avenue, Eau Claire, WI 54701 .... (715) 832–8424

REPRESENTATIVES

FIRST DISTRICT

PAUL D. RYAN, Republican, of Janesville, WI; born in Janesville, January 29, 1970; education: Joseph A. Craig High School; economic and political science degrees, Miami University, Ohio; professional: marketing consultant, Ryan Inc., Central (construction firm); aide to former U.S. Senator Bob Kasten (R–WI); advisor to former vice presidential candidate Jack Kemp, and U.S. Drug Czar Bill Bennett; legislative director, U.S. Senate; Republican vice presidential candidate, 2012; organizations: Janesville Bowmen, Inc.; Ducks Unlimited; married: Janna Ryan; three children: daughter, Liza; sons, Charlie and Sam; elected to the 106th Congress; reelected to each succeeding Congress; elected Speaker of the U.S. House of Representatives on October 29, 2015.

Office Listings

http://paulryan.house.gov

1233 Longworth House Office Building, Washington, DC 20515 .... (202) 225–3031
Chief of Staff.—Danyell Tremmel. FAX: 225–3393
Deputy Chief of Staff.—Allison Steil.
Legislative Director.—Katie Donnell.
Director of Scheduling.—Tricia Stoneking.
20 South Main Street, Suite 10, Janesville, WI 53545 .... (608) 752–4050
5031 Seventh Avenue, Kenosha, WI 53140 .... (262) 654–1901
216 Sixth Street, Racine, WI 53403 .... (262) 637–0510

Counties: KENOSHA, MILWAUKEE (part), RACINE, ROCK (part), WALWORTH, AND WAUKESHA (part). Population (2010), 728,042.

ZIP Codes: 53018 (part), 53066 (part), 53101–05, 53108–09, 53114–15, 53118–19 (part), 53120–21, 53125–30, 53132, 53138–44, 53146 (part), 53147–49, 53150–51 (part), 53152–53, 53154 (part), 53157–59, 53167–68, 53170–71, 53176–77, 53179, 53181–82, 53183 (part), 53184–85, 53188–90 (part), 53191–92, 53194–95, 53220 (part), 53121, 53228 (part), 53401–08, 53505, 53511 (part), 53525, 53538 (part), 53545–46 (part), 53547, 53548 (part), 53563 (part), 53585

* * *

SECOND DISTRICT

MARK POCAN, Democrat, of the Town of Vermont, WI; born in Kenosha, WI, August 14, 1964; education: graduated from Bradford High School, 1982; journalism, University of Wisconsin, 1986; professional: small business owner, 1986–present; elected to the Dane County Board of Supervisors, 1991–96; elected to the State Assembly from the 78th District, 1999–2013; married: Philip Frank in 2006; committees: Appropriations; elected to the 113th Congress on November 6, 2012; reelected to each succeeding Congress.

Office Listings

http://pocan.house.gov facebook: https://www.facebook.com/repmarkpocan
twitter: https://twitter.com/repmarkpocan

1421 Longworth House Office Building, Washington, DC 20515 .... (202) 225–2906
Chief of Staff.—Glenn Wavrunek. FAX: 225–6942
Legislative Director.—Alicia Molt.
Scheduler.—Nick Greene.
Communications Director.—David Kolovson.
10 East Doty Street, Suite 405, Madison, WI 53703 .... (608) 258–9800
District Director.—Dane Varese.
100 State Street, 3rd Floor, Beloit, WI 53511 .... (608) 365–8001

Counties: DANE, GREEN, IOWA, LAFAYETTE, RICHLAND (part), ROCK (part), and SAUK. Population (2010), 729,417.

ZIP Codes: 53501–04, 53506–08, 53510–11, 53515–17, 53520–23, 53526–37, 53540–46, 53548, 53553–56, 53558–63, 53565–66, 53569–78, 53580–83, 53586–90, 53593–94, 53597–99, 53703–06, 53711, 53713–19, 53726, 53792, 53803, 53807, 53811, 53818, 53911, 53913, 53924–25, 53937, 53941, 53943–44, 53951, 53959, 53961, 53965, 53968

* * *

THIRD DISTRICT

RON KIND, Democrat, of La Crosse, WI; born in La Crosse, March 16, 1963; education: B.A., Harvard University, 1985; M.A., London School of Economics, 1986; J.D., University of Minnesota Law School, 1990; professional: admitted to the Wisconsin Bar, 1990; State Prosecutor, La Crosse County District Attorney's Office; board of directors, La Crosse Boys and Girls Club; Coulee Council on Alcohol and Drug Abuse; Wisconsin Harvard Club; Wisconsin Bar Association; La Crosse County Bar Association; married: Tawni Zappa in 1994; two sons: Jonathan and Matthew; committees: Ways and Means; elected to the 105th Congress; reelected to each succeeding Congress.

Office Listings

http://www.kind.house.gov

1502 Longworth House Office Building, Washington, DC 20515 .... (202) 225–5506

Office Listings—Continued

Chief of Staff.—Mike Goodman. FAX: 225–5739
Press Secretary.—Amanda Sherman.
Legislative Director.—Elizabeth Stower.
Scheduler.—Aaron White.
205 Fifth Avenue South, Suite 400, La Crosse, WI 54601 .... (608) 782–2558
District Director.—Loren Kannenberg.
131 South Barstow Street, Suite 301, Eau Claire, WI 54701 .... (715) 831–9214
Congressional Aide.—Mark Aumann.

Counties: ADAMS, BUFFALO, CHIPPEWA, CRAWFORD, DUNN, EAU CLAIRE, GRANT, JACKSON, JUNEAU, LA CROSSE, MONROE, PEPIN, PIERCE, PORTAGE, RICHLAND, TREMPEALEAU, VERNON, AND WOOD. Population (2010), 710,873.

ZIP Codes: 53518, 53543, 53554, 53556, 53569, 53573, 53581, 53801–02, 53804, 53805–11, 53813, 53816–18, 53820–21, 53825–27, 53910, 53920, 53924, 53929, 53934, 53936–37, 53941, 53944, 53948, 53950, 53952, 53964–65, 53968, 54003, 54005, 54010–11, 54013–14, 54021–22, 54406–07, 54410, 54412–13, 54423, 54443, 54454–55, 54457–58, 54466–67, 54469, 54473, 54475, 54481–82, 54489, 54494–95, 54499, 54601, 54603, 54610–16, 54618–19, 54621–32, 54634–39, 54642–45, 54648, 54650–61, 54664–67, 54669–70, 54701, 54703, 54720–27, 54729–30, 54734, 54736–42, 54747, 54749–51, 54754–63, 54765, 54767–70, 54772–73, 54909, 54921, 54930, 54943, 54945, 54966, 54977, 54981, 54984

* * *

FOURTH DISTRICT

GWENDOLYNNE S. ''GWEN'' MOORE, Democrat, of Milwaukee, WI; born in Racine, WI, April 18, 1951; education: graduated, Northern Division High School, Milwaukee, WI, 1969; B.A., Marquette University, Milwaukee, WI, 1978; professional: housing officer, Wisconsin Housing and Development Authority; member: Wisconsin State Assembly, 1989–92; Wisconsin State Senate, 1993–2004; president pro tempore, 1997–98; three children; committees: Financial Services; elected to the 109th Congress on November 2, 2004; reelected to each succeeding Congress.

Office Listings

http://gwenmoore.house.gov facebook: https://www.facebook.com/GwenSMoore
twitter: https://twitter.com/RepGwenMoore

2252 Rayburn House Office Building, Washington, DC 20515 .... (202) 225–4572
Chief of Staff.—Sean Gard.
316 North Milwaukee Street, Suite 406, Milwaukee, WI 53202 .... (414) 297–1140
District Administrator.—Shirley Ellis. FAX: 297–1086

Counties: MILWAUKEE (part). CITIES AND TOWNSHIPS: Bayside, Brown Deer, Fox Point, Glendale, Milwaukee, Shorewood, South Milwaukee, St. Francis, West Milwaukee, Whitefish Bay. Population (2016), 715,895.

ZIP Codes: 53051, 53110, 53154, 53172, 53201–28, 53233, 53235, 53295

* * *

FIFTH DISTRICT

F. JAMES SENSENBRENNER, JR., Republican, of Menomonee Falls, WI; born in Chicago, IL, June 14, 1943; education: graduated, Milwaukee Country Day School, 1961; A.B., Stanford University, 1965; J.D., University of Wisconsin Law School, 1968; admitted to the Wisconsin Bar, 1968; commenced practice in Cedarburg, WI; admitted to practice before the U.S. Supreme Court in 1972; professional: attorney; staff member of former U.S. Congressman J. Arthur Younger of California, 1965; elected to the Wisconsin Assembly, 1968, reelected in 1970, 1972, and 1974; elected to Wisconsin Senate in a special election, 1975, reelected in 1976 (Assistant Minority Leader); member: Waukesha County Republican Party; Wisconsin Bar Association; American Philatelic Society; awards: Schuman Medal; Order of the Rising Sun; married: the former Cheryl Warren, 1977; children: Frank James III and Robert Alan; grandchild: Kevin Vartan; committees: Foreign Affairs; Judiciary; elected to the 96th Congress on November 7, 1978; reelected to each succeeding Congress.

Office Listings

http://www.sensenbrenner.house.gov

2449 Rayburn House Office Building, Washington, DC 20515–4905 .... (202) 225–5101

Office Listings—Continued

Chief of Staff.—Bart Forsyth.
Legislative Director.—Amy Bos.
Communications Director.—Nicole Tieman.
Scheduler / Office Manager.—Jacob Peterson.
120 Bishops Way, Room 154, Brookfield, WI 53005–6294 .... (262) 784–1111
Deputy Chief of Staff.—Loni Hagerup.

Counties: JEFFERSON, MILWAUKEE (part), DODGE (part), WASHINGTON, WAUKESHA (part). Population (2010), 716,218.

ZIP Codes: 53005, 53007, 53018, 53022, 53029, 53032, 53035–40, 53045–46, 53051–52, 53056, 53058, 53066, 53072, 53076, 53078, 53089, 53090, 53094–95, 53098, 53122, 53137, 53146, 53151, 53156, 53178, 53186, 53188–90, 53210, 53213–14, 53219, 53220–21, 53226–28, 53538, 53549, 53551, 53579, 53594

* * *

SIXTH DISTRICT

GLENN GROTHMAN, Republican, of Glenbeulah, WI; Born in Milwaukee, WI, July 3, 1955; education: graduated, Homestead High School, 1973; B.B.A., University of Wisconsin, 1978; J.D., University of Wisconsin, 1983; professional: admitted to the Wisconsin State Bar Association; lawyer, Schloemer Law Firm; elected to the Wisconsin State Assembly, 1993; elected to the Wisconsin State Senate, 2004, served until 2015; committees: Budget; Education and the Workforce; Oversight and Government Reform; elected to the 114th Congress on November 4, 2014; reelected to 115th Congress on November 8, 2016.

Office Listings

http://www.grothman.house.gov

1217 Longworth House Office Building, Washington, DC 20515 .... (202) 225–2476
Chief of Staff.—Rachel Ver Velde.
Legislative Director.—Ryan Croft.
Communications Director.—Bernadette Green.
Executive Assistant.—Samantha Baker.
District Director.—Alan Ott.
24 West Pioneer Road, Fond du Lac, WI 54935 .... (920) 907–0624

Counties: COLUMBIA, DODGE (part), FOND DU LAC, GREEN LAKE, MANITOWOC, MILWAUKEE (part), OZAUKEE, SHEBOYGAN, WAUSHARA, AND WINNEBAGO (part). Population (2010), 709,482.

ZIP Codes: 53001, 53004, 53006, 53010–11, 53012–15, 53019–21, 53023–24, 53031–32, 53035, 53040, 53042, 53044, 53048–50, 53057, 53061–63, 53065, 53070, 53073–75, 53079–85, 53090–93, 53095, 53097, 53217, 53532, 53555, 53561, 53578, 53583, 53901, 53911–23, 53925–28, 53930–33, 53935, 53939, 53946–47, 53949, 53952–56, 53960, 53963–65, 53969, 54110, 54126, 54207–08, 54214, 54220–28, 54230–32, 54241–47, 54901–09, 54914–15, 54923, 54930, 54932, 54934–41, 54943, 54947, 54952–60, 54963–74, 54979–86

* * *

SEVENTH DISTRICT

SEAN P. DUFFY, Republican, of Wausau, WI; born in Hayward, WI, October 3, 1971; education: B.A., marketing, St. Mary's University, Winona, MN, 1994; J.D., William Mitchell College of Law, St. Paul, MN, 1999; professional: lawyer, private practice; prosecutor, Ashland County, WI; district attorney, Ashland County, WI, 2002–10; religion: Roman Catholic; married: wife, Rachel Campos-Duffy; eight children; committees: Financial Services; elected to the 112th Congress on November 2, 2010; reelected to each succeeding Congress.

Office Listings

http://duffy.house.gov

2330 Rayburn House Office Building, Washington, DC 20515 .... (202) 225–3365
Chief of Staff.—Pete Meachum.
Communications Director.—Mark Bednar.
Scheduler.—Eleanor Traynham.
208 Grand Avenue, Wausau, WI 54403 .... (715) 298–9344
District Director.—Jesse Garza. FAX: 298–9348
District Scheduler.—Maggie Cronin.
Director of Constituent Services.—Johnathan Lanctin.
15954 Rivers Edge Drive, Suite 2016, Hayward, WI 54843 .... (715) 392–3984

Office Listings—Continued

502 Second Street, Suite 202, Hudson, WI 54016 .... (715) 808–8160

Counties: ASHLAND, BARRON, BAYFIELD, BURNETT, CHIPPEWA (part), CLARK, DOUGLAS, FLORENCE, FOREST, IRON, JACKSON (part), JUNEAU (part), LANGLADE, LINCOLN, MARATHON, MONROE (part), ONEIDA, POLK, PRICE, RUSK, SAWYER, ST. CROIX, TAYLOR, VILAS, WASHBURN, AND WOOD (part). Population (2010), 710,873.

ZIP Codes: 53950, 54001–02, 54004–07, 54009, 54013, 54015–17, 54020, 54022–28, 54082, 54103–04, 54120–21, 54125, 54151, 54175, 54401, 54403, 54405, 54408–14, 54417–18, 54420–22, 54424–28, 54430, 54433, 54435–37, 54440–43, 54446–49, 54451–52, 54454–57, 54459–60, 54462–63, 54465–66, 54470–71, 54473–74, 54476, 54479–80, 54484–85, 54487–91, 54493, 54495, 54498–99, 54501, 54511–15, 54517, 54519–21, 54524–27, 54529–31, 54534, 54536–42, 54545–48, 54550, 54552, 54554–66, 54568, 54611, 54615–16, 54618, 54635, 54641, 54646, 54660, 54666, 54724, 54726–34, 54741, 54745–46, 54748–49, 54754, 54757, 54762–63, 54765–68, 54771, 54801, 54805–06, 54810, 54812–14, 54817, 54819–22, 54824, 54826–30, 54832, 54835–50, 54853–59, 54861–62, 54864–65, 54867–68, 54870–76, 54880, 54888–89, 54891, 54893, 54895–96

* * *

EIGHTH DISTRICT

MIKE GALLAGHER, Republican, of Green Bay, WI; born in Green Bay, March 3, 1984; education: A.B., Princeton University, Princeton, NJ, 2006; M.S., National Intelligence University, Washington, DC, 2010; M.A., Georgetown University, Washington, DC, 2012, 2013; Ph.D., Georgetown University, Washington, DC, 2015; professional: U.S. Marine Corps, 2006–13; staff, U.S. Senate Foreign Relations Committee, 2013–15; Scott Walker presidential campaign staff, 2015; businessman; religion: Catholic; committees: Armed Services; Homeland Security; Transportation and Infrastructure; elected to the 115th Congress on November 8, 2016.

Office Listings

http://www.gallagher.house.gov

1513 Longworth House Office Building, Washington, DC 20515 .... (202) 225–5665
Chief of Staff.—McKay Daniels.
Scheduler.—Nicole Tardif.
Communications Director.—Madison Wiberg.
333 West College Avenue, Appleton, WI 54911 .... (920) 380–0061
District Director.—Rick Sense.
550 North Military Avenue, Suite 4B, Green Bay, WI 54303 .... (920) 471–1950

Counties: BROWN, CALUMET, DOOR, KEWAUNEE, MARINETTE, MENOMINEE, OCONTO, OUTAGAMIE (part), SHAWANO, WAUPACA, AND WINNEBAGO (part). Population (2010), 706,840.

ZIP Codes: 53014 (part), 53020 (part), 53042 (part), 53049 (part), 53061 (part), 53088, 54101–02, 54103–04 (part), 54106–07, 54110 (part), 54111–15, 54119, 54120 (part), 54123–24, 54125–26 (part), 54127–30, 54135–41, 54143, 54149–50, 54151 (part), 54153–57, 54159–62, 54165–66, 54169–71, 54173–74, 54175 (part), 54177, 54180, 54201–02, 54204–05, 54208 (part), 54209–13, 54216–17, 54229, 54234–35, 54246, 54301–04, 54307, 54311, 54313, 54408–09 (part), 54414 (part), 54416, 54427 (part), 54450, 54486, 54491 (part), 54499 (part), 54904 (part), 54911, 54913, 54914–15 (part), 54922, 54927–29, 54931, 54933, 54940 (part), 54942, 54944, 54945 (part), 54946, 54947 (part), 54948–50, 54952 (part), 54956 (part), 54961–62, 54963 (part), 54965 (part), 54977 (part), 54981 (part), 54983 (part), 54986 (part)

WYOMING

(Population 2010, 563,626)

SENATORS

MICHAEL B. ENZI, Republican, of Gillette, WY; born in Bremerton, WA, February 1, 1944; education: B.A., accounting, George Washington University, 1966; M.B.A., Denver University, 1968; professional: served in Wyoming National Guard, 1967–73; accounting manager and computer programmer, Dunbar Well Service, 1985–97; director, Black Hills Corporation, a New York Stock Exchange company, 1992–96; member, founding board of directors, First Wyoming Bank of Gillette, 1978–88; owner, with wife, of NZ Shoes; served in Wyoming House of Representatives, 1987–91, and in Wyoming State Senate, 1991–96; Mayor of Gillette, 1975–82; commissioner, Western Interstate Commission for Higher Education, 1995–96; served on the Education Commission of the States, 1989–93; president, Wyoming Association of Municipalities, 1980–82; president, Wyoming Jaycees, 1973–74; member: Lions Club; Eagle Scout; elder, Presbyterian Church; married: Diana Buckley, 1969; children: Amy, Brad, and Emily; committees: chair, Budget; Finance; Health, Education, Labor, and Pensions; Homeland Security and Governmental Affairs; Small Business and Entrepreneurship; elected to the U.S. Senate in November, 1996; reelected to each succeeding Senate term.

Office Listings

http://enzi.senate.gov https://www.facebook.com/mikeenzi
https://twitter.com/senatorenzi

379–A Russell Senate Office Building, Washington, DC 20510 .... (202) 224–3424
FAX: 228–0359
Chief of Staff.—Tara Shaw.
Legislative Director.—Doug Dziak.
Press Secretary.—Max D'Onofrio.
Office Manager.—Christen Thompson.
Federal Center, Suite 2007, 2120 Capitol Avenue, Cheyenne, WY 82001 .... (307) 772–2477
223 South Gillette Avenue, Suite 503, Gillette, WY 82716 .... (307) 682–6268
100 East B Street, Room 3201, P.O. Box 33201, Casper, WY 82602 .... (307) 261–6572
1110 Maple Way, Suite G, P.O. Box 12470, Jackson, WY 83002 .... (307) 739–9507
1285 Sheridan Avenue, Suite 210, Cody, WY 82414 .... (307) 527–9444

* * *

JOHN BARRASSO, Republican, of Casper, WY; born in Reading, PA, July 21, 1952; education: B.S., Georgetown University, Washington, DC, 1974; M.D., Georgetown University, Washington, DC, 1978; professional: Casper Orthopaedic Associates, 1983–2007; chief of staff, Wyoming Medical Center, 2003–05; president, Wyoming Medical Society; president, National Association of Physician Broadcasters, 1988–89; member, Wyoming State Senate, 2002–06; wife: Bobbi; children: Peter, Emma, and Hadley; committees: chair, Environment and Public Works; chair, Senate Republican Policy Committee; Energy and Natural Resources; Foreign Relations; Indian Affairs; appointed to the U.S. Senate on June 22, 2007; sworn in by Vice President Cheney on June 25, 2007 to the 110th Congress to fill the vacancy caused by the death of Senator Craig Thomas; elected to the U.S. Senate on November 4, 2008; reelected to the 113th Congress for a full Senate term on November 6, 2012.

Office Listings

http://barrasso.senate.gov www.facebook.com/johnbarrasso www.twitter.com/senjohnbarrasso

307 Dirksen Senate Office Building, Washington, DC 20510 .... (202) 224–6441
FAX: 224–1724
Chief of Staff.—Dan Kunsman.
Legislative Director.—Bryn Stewart.
Communications Director.—Bronwyn Lance Chester.
Office Manager.—Amber Moyerman.
100 East B Street, Suite 2201, Casper, WY 82602 .... (307) 261–6413
FAX: 265–6706
2120 Capitol Avenue, Suite 2013, Cheyenne, WY 82001 .... (307) 772–2451
FAX: 638–3512
324 East Washington Avenue, Riverton, WY 82501 .... (307) 856–6642
FAX: 856–5901
1575 Dewar Drive, Suite 218, Rock Springs, WY 82901 .... (307) 362–5012
FAX: 362–5129
2 North Main Street, Suite 206, Sheridan, WY 82801 .... (307) 672–6456
FAX: 672–8227

REPRESENTATIVE

AT LARGE

LIZ CHENEY, Republican, of Wilson, WY; born in Madison, WI, July 28, 1966; education: B.A., Colorado College, 1988; J.D., University of Chicago Law School, 1996; religion: Methodist; married: Philip Perry; children: five; Whip team; caucuses: Congressional Air Force Caucus; Congressional Army Caucus; Congressional Coal Caucus; Congressional Navy and Marine Corps Caucus; Republican Study Committee; Congressional Western Caucus; committees: Armed Services; Natural Resources; Rules; elected to the 115th Congress on November 8, 2016.

Office Listings

http://cheney.house.gov

416 Cannon House Office Building, Washington, DC 20515	(202) 225–2311
Chief of Staff.—Kara Ahern.	FAX: 225–3057
Legislative Director.—Scott Hughes.	
Press Secretary.—Joseph Jackson.	
Scheduler.—Robert Edelman.	
100 East B Street, Suite 4003, Casper, WY 82602	(307) 261–6595
	FAX: 261–6597
2120 Capitol Avenue, Suite 8005, Cheyenne, WY 82001	(307) 772–2595
	FAX: 772–2597
45 East Loucks, Suite 300F, Sheridan, WY 82801	(307) 673–4608
	FAX: 261–6597
300 South Gillette Avenue, Suite 2000, Gillette, WY 82716	(307) 414–1677
	FAX: 414–1711

Population (2010), 563,626.

ZIP Codes: 82001, 82003, 82005–10, 82050–55, 82058–61, 82063, 82070–73, 82081–84, 82190, 82201, 82210, 82212–15, 82217–19, 82221–25, 82227, 82229, 82240, 82242–44, 82301, 82310, 82321–25, 82327, 82329, 82331–32, 82334–36, 82401, 82410–12, 82414, 82420–23, 82426, 82428, 82430–35, 82440–43, 82450, 82501, 82510, 82512–16, 82520, 82523–24, 82601–02, 82604–05, 82609, 82615, 82620, 82630, 82633, 82635–40, 82642–44, 82646, 82648–49, 82701, 82710–12, 82714–18, 82720–21, 82723, 82725, 82727, 82729–32, 82801, 82831–40, 82842, 82844–45, 82901–02, 82922–23, 82925, 82929–39, 82941–45, 83001–02, 83011–14, 83025, 83101, 83110–16, 83118–24, 83126–28

AMERICAN SAMOA

(Population 2010, 67,380)

DELEGATE

AUMUA AMATA COLEMAN RADEWAGEN, Republican, of Pago Pago, AS; born in Washington, DC, December 29, 1947; holds the orator (talking chief) title of Aumua from the village of Pago Pago, AS; education: graduate of Sacred Hearts High School in Hawaii; B.A. from University of Guam; professional: executive assistant to the first Delegate-at-Large to Washington from American Samoa; scheduling director for U.S. House of Representatives Majority Leadership for eight years; scheduling director for U.S. Representative Philip Crane of Illinois; appointed by President George W. Bush in 2001 as a White House Commissioner for Asian Americans and Pacific Islanders (AAPI), chairman of the Community Security Committee; member: American Council of Young Political Leaders, 1986; ACYPL Alumni Council in 1987; Business and Professional Women and board member of Goodwill Industries; Field House 100 American Samoa, a non-profit organization devoted to finding athletic scholarships for high school athletes in American Samoa; spokesperson for the Samoan Women's Health Project; liaison to the National Breast Cancer Coalition since 1993; married: Fred Radewagen; three children and two grandchildren; committees: Natural Resources; Small Business; Veterans' Affairs; elected to the 114th Congress on November 4, 2014; reelected to the 115th Congress on November 8, 2016.

Office Listings

http://radewagen.house.gov https://twitter.com/repamata
https://www.facebook.com/congresswomanaumuaamata

1339 Longworth House Office Building, Washington, DC 20515 .... (202) 225–8577
Chief of Staff.—Leafaina O. Yahn. FAX: 225–8757
Scheduler / Office Manager.—Nancy Dehlinger.
Legislative Director.—Casey Brinck.
P.O. Box 5859, Pago Pago, AS 96799 .... (684) 633–3601

ZIP Codes: 96799

* * *

DISTRICT OF COLUMBIA

(Population 2010, 601,723)

DELEGATE

ELEANOR HOLMES NORTON, Democrat, of Washington, DC; born in Washington, DC, June 13, 1937; education: graduated, Dunbar High School, 1955; B.A., Antioch College, 1960; M.A., Yale Graduate School, 1963; J.D., Yale Law School, 1964; honorary degrees: Cedar Crest College, 1969; Bard College, 1971; Princeton University, 1973; Marymount College, 1974; City College of New York, 1975; Georgetown University, 1977; New York University, 1978; Howard University, 1978; Brown University, 1978; Wilberforce University, 1978; Wayne State University, 1980; Gallaudet College, 1980; Denison University, 1980; Syracuse University, 1981; Yeshiva University, 1981; Lawrence University, 1981; Emanuel College, 1981; Spelman College, 1982; University of Massachusetts, 1983; Smith College, 1983; Medical College of Pennsylvania, 1983; Tufts University, 1984; Bowdoin College, 1985; Antioch College, 1985; Haverford College, 1986; Lesley College, 1986; New Haven University, 1986; University of San Diego, 1986; Sojourner-Douglas College, 1987; Salem State College, 1987; Rutgers University, 1988; St. Joseph's College, 1988; University of Lowell, 1988; Colgate University, 1989; Drury College, 1989; Florida International University, 1989; St. Lawrence University, 1989; University of Wisconsin, 1989; University of Hartford, 1990; Ohio Wesleyan University, 1990; Wake Forest University, 1990; Fisk University, 1991; Tougalvo University, 1992; University of Southern Connecticut, 1992; professional: professor of law, Georgetown University, 1982–90; past / present member: chair, New York Commission on Human Rights, 1970–76; chair, Equal Employment Opportunity Commission, 1977–81; Community Foundation of Greater Washington, board; Yale Corporation, 1982–88; trustee, Rockefeller Foundation, 1982–90; Executive Assistant to the Mayor of New York City (concurrent appointment); law clerk, Judge A. Leon Higginbotham, Federal District Court, 3rd Circuit; attorney, admitted to practice by examination in the District of Columbia, Pennsylvania, and in the U.S. Supreme Court; Council on Foreign Relations; Overseas Development Council; U.S. Committee to Monitor the Helsinki Accords; Carter Center, Atlanta, Georgia; boards of Martin Luther King, Jr. Center for Social Change and Environmental Law Institute; Workplace Health Fund; honors awards: Harper Fellow, Yale Law School, 1976, (for "a person . . . who has made a distinguished contribution to the public life of the nation . . ."); Yale Law School Association Citation of Merit Medal to the Outstanding Alumnus of the Law School, 1980; Chancellor's Distinguished Lecturer, University of California Law School (Boalt Hall), Berkeley, 1981; visiting fellow, Harvard University, John F. Kennedy School of Government, spring 1984; visiting Phi Beta Kappa scholar, 1985; Distinguished Public Service Award, Center for National Policy, 1985; Ralph E. Shikes Bicentennial Fellow, Harvard Law School, 1987; One Hundred Most Important Women (*Ladies Home Journal*, 1988); One Hundred Most Powerful Women in Washington (The *Washingtonian* magazine, September 1989); divorced; two children: John and Katherine; committees: Oversight and Government Reform; Transportation and Infrastructure; elected to the 102nd Congress on November 6, 1990; reelected to each succeeding Congress.

Office Listings

http://www.norton.house.gov https://twitter.com/eleanornorton
https://www.facebook.com/congresswomannorton

2136 Rayburn House Office Building, Washington, DC 20515 .... (202) 225–8050
Chief of Staff.—Raven Reeder. FAX: 225–3002
Legislative Director.—Bradley Truding.
Communications Director.—Benjamin Fritsch.

ZIP Codes: 20001–13, 20015–20, 20024, 20026–27, 20029–30, 20032–33, 20035–45, 20047, 20049–53, 20055–71, 20073–77, 20080, 20088, 20090–91, 20099, 20201–04, 20206–08, 20210–13, 20215–24, 20226–33, 20235, 20237, 20239–42, 20244–45, 20250, 20254, 20260, 20268, 20270, 20277, 20289, 20301, 20303, 20306–07, 20310, 20314–15, 20317–19, 20330, 20340, 20350, 20370, 20372–76, 20380, 20388–95, 20398, 20401–16, 20418–29, 20431, 20433–37, 20439–42, 20444, 20447, 20451, 20453, 20456, 20460, 20463, 20469, 20472, 20500, 20503–10, 20515, 20520–27, 20530–36, 20538–44, 20546–49, 20551–55, 20557, 20559–60, 20565–66, 20570–73, 20575–77, 20579–81, 20585–86, 20590–91, 20593–94, 20597, 20599

* * *

GUAM

(Population 2010, 159,358)

DELEGATE

MADELEINE Z. BORDALLO, Democrat, of Tamuning, Guam; born on May 31, 1933; professional: First Lady of Guam, 1975–78 and 1983–86; Guam Senator, 1981–82 and 1987–94 (five terms); Lt. Governor of Guam, 1995–2002 (two terms); National Committeewoman for the Democratic Party of Guam, 1964–2004; family: Ricardo J. Bordallo (deceased); daughter, Deborah; granddaughter, Nicole; committees: Armed Services; Natural Resources; elected to the 108th Congress on November 5, 2002; reelected to each succeeding Congress.

Office Listings

http://www.bordallo.house.gov https://www.facebook.com/madeleine.bordallo

2441 Rayburn House Office Building, Washington, DC 20515 .... (202) 225–1188
Chief of Staff.—Matthew Herrmann. FAX: 226–0341
Legislative Director.—Matthew Herrmann.
Communications Director.—Adam Carbullido.
Scheduler.—Rosanne Meno.
120 Father Duenas Avenue, Suite 107, Hagåtña, GU 96910 .... (671) 477–4272

ZIP Codes: 96910, 96912–13, 96915–17, 96919, 96921, 96923, 96926, 96928–29, 96931–32

NORTHERN MARIANA ISLANDS

(Population 2010, 53,883)

DELEGATE

GREGORIO KILILI CAMACHO SABLAN, Independent, of Saipan, MP; born in Saipan, January 19, 1955; education: University of Hawaii, Manoa Honolulu, HI; 1989–90; professional: member, Northern Mariana Islands Commonwealth Legislature, 1982–86 (two terms); special assistant to Senator Daniel Inouye; special assistant to Northern Mariana Islands Governor Pedro P. Tenorio; executive director of the Commonwealth Election Commission; family: married to Andrea C. Sablan; son: Jesse; daughters: Sharlene, Barbara Jean, Diane, Patricia, and Madonna; caucuses: American Citizens Abroad Caucus; Bipartisan Disabilities Caucus; Community College Caucus; Congressional Asian Pacific American Caucus; Congressional Hispanic Caucus; Democratic Caucus; Friends of New Zealand Caucus; International Conservation Caucus; National Marine Sanctuary Caucus; committees: Education and the Workforce; Natural Resources; elected to the 111th Congress on November 4, 2008; reelected to each succeeding Congress.

Office Listings

http://www.sablan.house.gov
https://www.facebook.com/pages/gregorio-kilili-camacho-sablan/153423912663

423 Cannon House Office Building, Washington, DC 20515 .... (202) 225–2646
Chief of Staff.—Robert J. Schwalbach. FAX: 226–4249
Scheduler.—Agnes Cornibert.
JCT II Building, Susupe, P.O. Box 504879, Saipan, MP 96950 .... (670) 323–2647
Dolores Plaza Building, Songsong, P.O. Box 1361, Rota, MP 96951 .... (670) 532–2647
Villagomez Ent. Building, San Jose, P.O. Box 520394, Tinian, MP 96952 .... (670) 433–2647
District Officer Director.—Mike Tenorio. FAX: 323–2649

ZIP Codes: 96950–52

* * *

PUERTO RICO

(Population 2010, 3,725,789)

RESIDENT COMMISSIONER

JENNIFFER GONZÁLEZ-COLÓN, Republican, of Carolina, PR; born in San Juan, PR, August 5, 1976; education: B.A., political science, University of Puerto Rico, Rio Piedras, PR, 2001; J.D., Inter American University of Puerto Rico, San Juan, PR, 2010; LL.M., Inter American University of Puerto Rico, San Juan, PR, 2014; professional: member of the Puerto Rico House of Representatives, 2002–16; Speaker of the Puerto Rico House of Representatives, 2009–12; Minority Leader of the Puerto Rico House of Representatives, 2013–16; vice president of the New Progressive Party of Puerto Rico, 2008–present; chair of the Puerto Rico Republican Party, 2015–present; religion: Catholic; committees: Natural Resources; Small Business; Veterans' Affairs; elected to the 115th Congress on November 8, 2016.

Office Listings

http://www.gonzalez-colon.house.gov

1529 Longworth House Office Building, Washington, DC 20515 .... (202) 225–2615
Chief of Staff.—Luis Bacó. FAX: 225–2154
Deputy Chief of Staff and Legal Counsel.—Janille Rodriguez.
Communications Director.—Marieli Padró-Raldiris.
Scheduler.—Gabriel Bravo.
Legislative Director.—Greg Tosi.
Legislative Assistants: Natalia Gandía, Estefanía Rodriguez.
157 Avenida de la Constitución Antiguo Edificio de Medicina Tropical, Ala de la Enfermería 2ndo Piso, San Juan, PR 00901 .... (787) 723–6333

Office Listings—Continued

District Office Director.—Lilmarie Ferrer. FAX: 729–7738
Senior Policy Advisor.—José Díaz Marrero.
Communications Specialists: Ednel Cartagena, Nydia Tossas.
Field Representative and District Scheduler.—Michael Ayala.
Office Manager.—Allison Rodriguez-Arroyo.
Immigration Case Worker.—Luis Ortiz.
Social Security Case Worker.—Cristina Sierra.
Veterans' Case Workers: Segundo Ferro, Norma Miranda.
Congressional Aide.—Narel Colón Torres.

ZIP Codes: 00601–06, 00610–14, 00616–17, 00622–24, 00627, 00631, 00636–38, 00641, 00646–47, 00650, 00652–53, 00656, 00659–60, 00662, 00664, 00667, 00669–70, 00674, 00676–78, 00680–83, 00685, 00687–88, 00690, 00692–94, 00698, 00703–05, 00707, 00714–21, 00723, 00725–42, 00744–45, 00751, 00754, 00757, 00765–67, 00769, 00771–73, 00775, 00777–78, 00780, 00782–86, 00791–92, 00794–95, 00901–02, 00906–31, 00933–37, 00939–40, 00949–63, 00965–66, 00968–71, 00975–79, 00981–88

* * *

VIRGIN ISLANDS

(Population 2010, 106,405)

DELEGATE

STACEY PLASKETT, Democrat, of St. Croix, VI; born in New York, NY, May 13, 1966; education: B.S.F.S, Georgetown University, Washington, DC, 1988; J.D., American University School of Law, Washington, DC, 1994; professional: Bronx Assistant District Attorney; Counsel on U.S. House of Representatives' Committee on Ethics; Senior Counsel to the Deputy Attorney General at U.S. Justice Department; Deputy General Counsel at United Health Group; General Counsel, Virgin Islands Economic Development Authority; family: spouse, Jonathan Buckney-Small; children: Jeremiah, Christian, Ariel, Israel Duffy, and Taliah Buckney-Small; caucuses: Congressional Black Caucus; Congressional Caribbean Caucus; Congressional Caucus on Public-Private Partnerships; Congressional Coastal Communities Caucus; Congressional Historically Black Colleges and Universities (HBCU) Caucus; Congressional Liquefied Natural Gas (LNG) Export Caucus; Congressional Women's Caucus; House National Guard and Reserve Components Caucus; committees: Agriculture; Oversight and Government Reform; Transportation and Infrastructure; elected to the 114th Congress on November 4, 2014; reelected to the 115th Congress on November 8, 2016.

Office Listings

https://plaskett.house.gov

331 Cannon House Office Building, Washington, DC 20515 .... (202) 225–1790
Chief of Staff.—Jerome Murray. FAX: 225–5517
Executive Assistant / Scheduler.—Samantha Roberts.
District Director.—Elizabeth Centeno.
60 King Street, Frederiksted, St. Croix, VI 00840 .... (340) 778–5900
9100 Port of Sale, St. Thomas, VI 00803 .... (340) 774–4408
Case Worker / Field Representative.—Cletis Clendenin.

ZIP Codes: 00801–05, 00820–24, 00830–31, 00840–41, 00850–51

STATE DELEGATIONS

Number before names designates Congressional district. Senate and House Republicans in roman; Senate and House Democrats in *italic*; Independents in SMALL CAPS; Resident Commissioner and Delegates in **boldface**.

ALABAMA

SENATORS
Richard C. Shelby
Doug Jones [1]

REPRESENTATIVES
[Republicans 6, Democrat 1]

1. Bradley Byrne
2. Martha Roby
3. Mike Rogers
4. Robert B. Aderholt
5. Mo Brooks
6. Gary J. Palmer
7. *Terri A. Sewell*

ALASKA

SENATORS
Lisa Murkowski
Dan Sullivan

REPRESENTATIVE
[Republican 1]
At Large – Don Young

ARIZONA

SENATORS
John McCain
Jeff Flake

REPRESENTATIVES
[Republicans 5, Democrats 4]

1. *Tom O'Halleran*
2. Martha McSally
3. *Raúl M. Grijalva*
4. Paul A. Gosar
5. Andy Biggs
6. David Schweikert
7. *Ruben Gallego*
8. Debbie Lesko [2]
9. *Kyrsten Sinema*

ARKANSAS

SENATORS
John Boozman
Tom Cotton

REPRESENTATIVES
[Republicans 4]

1. Eric A. "Rick" Crawford
2. J. French Hill
3. Steve Womack
4. Bruce Westerman

CALIFORNIA

SENATORS
Dianne Feinstein
Kamala D. Harris

REPRESENTATIVES
[Republicans 14, Democrats 39]

1. Doug LaMalfa
2. *Jared Huffman*
3. *John Garamendi*
4. Tom McClintock
5. *Mike Thompson*
6. *Doris O. Matsui*
7. *Ami Bera*
8. Paul Cook

9. *Jerry McNerney*
10. Jeff Denham
11. *Mark DeSaulnier*
12. *Nancy Pelosi*
13. *Barbara Lee*
14. *Jackie Speier*
15. *Eric Swalwell*
16. *Jim Costa*
17. *Ro Khanna*
18. *Anna G. Eshoo*
19. *Zoe Lofgren*
20. *Jimmy Panetta*
21. David G. Valadao
22. Devin Nunes
23. Kevin McCarthy
24. *Salud O. Carbajal*
25. Stephen Knight
26. *Julia Brownley*
27. *Judy Chu*
28. *Adam B. Schiff*
29. *Tony Cárdenas*
30. *Brad Sherman*
31. *Pete Aguilar*
32. *Grace F. Napolitano*
33. *Ted Lieu*
34. *Jimmy Gomez*[3]
35. *Norma J. Torres*
36. *Raul Ruiz*
37. *Karen Bass*
38. *Linda T. Sánchez*
39. Edward R. Royce
40. *Lucille Roybal-Allard*
41. *Mark Takano*
42. Ken Calvert
43. *Maxine Waters*
44. *Nanette Diaz Barragán*
45. Mimi Walters
46. *J. Luis Correa*
47. *Alan S. Lowenthal*
48. Dana Rohrabacher
49. Darrell E. Issa
50. Duncan Hunter
51. *Juan Vargas*
52. *Scott H. Peters*
53. *Susan A. Davis*

COLORADO

SENATORS
Michael F. Bennet
Cory Gardner

REPRESENTATIVES
[Republicans 4, Democrats 3]

1. *Diana DeGette*
2. *Jared Polis*
3. Scott R. Tipton
4. Ken Buck
5. Doug Lamborn
6. Mike Coffman
7. *Ed Perlmutter*

CONNECTICUT

SENATORS
Richard Blumenthal
Christopher Murphy

REPRESENTATIVES
[Democrats 5]

1. *John B. Larson*
2. *Joe Courtney*
3. *Rosa L. DeLauro*
4. *James A. Himes*
5. *Elizabeth H. Esty*

DELAWARE

SENATORS
Thomas R. Carper
Christopher A. Coons

REPRESENTATIVE
[Democrat 1]

At Large – *Lisa Blunt Rochester*

FLORIDA

SENATORS
Bill Nelson
Marco Rubio

REPRESENTATIVES
[Republicans 16, Democrats 11]

1. Matt Gaetz
2. Neal P. Dunn
3. Ted S. Yoho
4. John H. Rutherford
5. *Al Lawson, Jr.*
6. Ron DeSantis
7. *Stephanie N. Murphy*
8. Bill Posey
9. *Darren Soto*
10. *Val Butler Demings*
11. Daniel Webster
12. Gus M. Bilirakis
13. *Charlie Crist*
14. *Kathy Castor*

15. Dennis A. Ross
16. Vern Buchanan
17. Thomas J. Rooney
18. Brian J. Mast
19. Francis Rooney
20. *Alcee L. Hastings*
21. *Lois Frankel*
22. *Theodore E. Deutch*
23. *Debbie Wasserman Schultz*
24. *Frederica S. Wilson*
25. Mario Diaz-Balart
26. Carlos Curbelo
27. Ileana Ros-Lehtinen

GEORGIA

SENATORS
Johnny Isakson
David Perdue

REPRESENTATIVES
[Republicans 10, Democrats 4]

1. Earl L. ''Buddy'' Carter
2. *Sanford D. Bishop, Jr.*
3. A. Drew Ferguson, IV
4. *Henry C. ''Hank'' Johnson, Jr.*
5. *John Lewis*
6. Karen C. Handel [4]
7. Rob Woodall
8. Austin Scott
9. Doug Collins
10. Jody B. Hice
11. Barry Loudermilk
12. Rick W. Allen
13. *David Scott*
14. Tom Graves

HAWAII

SENATORS
Brian Schatz
Mazie K. Hirono

REPRESENTATIVES
[Democrats 2]

1. *Colleen Hanabusa*
2. *Tulsi Gabbard*

IDAHO

SENATORS
Mike Crapo
James E. Risch

REPRESENTATIVES
[Republicans 2]

1. Raúl R. Labrador
2. Michael K. Simpson

ILLINOIS

SENATORS
Richard J. Durbin
Tammy Duckworth

REPRESENTATIVES
[Republicans 7, Democrats 11]

1. *Bobby L. Rush*
2. *Robin L. Kelly*
3. *Daniel Lipinski*
4. *Luis V. Gutiérrez*
5. *Mike Quigley*
6. Peter J. Roskam
7. *Danny K. Davis*
8. *Raja Krishnamoorthi*
9. *Janice D. Schakowsky*
10. *Bradley Scott Schneider*
11. *Bill Foster*
12. Mike Bost
13. Rodney Davis
14. Randy Hultgren
15. John Shimkus
16. Adam Kinzinger
17. *Cheri Bustos*
18. Darin LaHood

INDIANA

SENATORS
Joe Donnelly
Todd Young

REPRESENTATIVES
[Republicans 7, Democrats 2]

1. *Peter J. Visclosky*
2. Jackie Walorski
3. Jim Banks
4. Todd Rokita
5. Susan W. Brooks
6. Luke Messer
7. *André Carson*
8. Larry Bucshon
9. Trey Hollingsworth

IOWA

SENATORS
Chuck Grassley
Joni Ernst

REPRESENTATIVES
[Republicans 3, Democrat 1]
1. Rod Blum
2. *David Loebsack*
3. David Young
4. Steve King

KANSAS

SENATORS
Pat Roberts
Jerry Moran

REPRESENTATIVES
[Republicans 4]
1. Roger W. Marshall
2. Lynn Jenkins
3. Kevin Yoder
4. Ron Estes [5]

KENTUCKY

SENATORS
Mitch McConnell
Rand Paul

REPRESENTATIVES
[Republicans 5, Democrat 1]
1. James Comer
2. Brett Guthrie
3. *John A. Yarmuth*
4. Thomas Massie
5. Harold Rogers
6. Andy Barr

LOUISIANA

SENATORS
Bill Cassidy
John Kennedy

REPRESENTATIVES
[Republicans 5, Democrat 1]
1. Steve Scalise
2. *Cedric L. Richmond*
3. Clay Higgins
4. Mike Johnson
5. Ralph Lee Abraham
6. Garret Graves

MAINE

SENATORS
Susan M. Collins
ANGUS S. KING, JR.

REPRESENTATIVES
[Republican 1, Democrat 1]
1. *Chellie Pingree*
2. Bruce Poliquin

MARYLAND

SENATORS
Benjamin L. Cardin
Chris Van Hollen

REPRESENTATIVES
[Republican 1, Democrats 7]
1. Andy Harris
2. *C. A. Dutch Ruppersberger*
3. *John P. Sarbanes*
4. *Anthony G. Brown*
5. *Steny H. Hoyer*
6. *John K. Delaney*
7. *Elijah E. Cummings*
8. *Jamie Raskin*

MASSACHUSETTS

SENATORS
Elizabeth Warren
Edward J. Markey

REPRESENTATIVES
[Democrats 9]

1. *Richard E. Neal*
2. *James P. McGovern*
3. *Niki Tsongas*
4. *Joseph P. Kennedy III*
5. *Katherine M. Clark*
6. *Seth Moulton*
7. *Michael E. Capuano*
8. *Stephen F. Lynch*
9. *William R. Keating*

MICHIGAN

SENATORS
Debbie Stabenow
Gary C. Peters

REPRESENTATIVES
[Republicans 9, Democrats 4, Vacant 1]

1. Jack Bergman
2. Bill Huizenga
3. Justin Amash
4. John R. Moolenaar
5. *Daniel T. Kildee*
6. Fred Upton
7. Tim Walberg
8. Mike Bishop
9. *Sander M. Levin*
10. Paul Mitchell
11. David A. Trott
12. *Debbie Dingell*
13. ——[6]
14. *Brenda L. Lawrence*

MINNESOTA

SENATORS
Amy Klobuchar
Tina Smith

REPRESENTATIVES
[Republicans 3, Democrats 5]

1. *Timothy J. Walz*
2. Jason Lewis
3. Erik Paulsen
4. *Betty McCollum*
5. *Keith Ellison*
6. Tom Emmer
7. *Collin C. Peterson*
8. *Richard M. Nolan*

MISSISSIPPI

SENATORS
Roger F. Wicker
Cindy Hyde-Smith[7]

REPRESENTATIVES
[Republicans 3, Democrat 1]

1. Trent Kelly
2. *Bennie G. Thompson*
3. Gregg Harper
4. Steven M. Palazzo

MISSOURI

SENATORS
Claire McCaskill
Roy Blunt

REPRESENTATIVES
[Republicans 6, Democrats 2]

1. *Wm. Lacy Clay*
2. Ann Wagner
3. Blaine Luetkemeyer
4. Vicky Hartzler
5. *Emanuel Cleaver*
6. Sam Graves
7. Billy Long
8. Jason Smith

MONTANA

SENATORS
Jon Tester
Steve Daines

REPRESENTATIVE
[Republican 1]

At Large – Greg Gianforte[8]

NEBRASKA

SENATORS
Deb Fischer
Ben Sasse

REPRESENTATIVES
[Republicans 3]
1. Jeff Fortenberry
2. Don Bacon
3. Adrian Smith

NEVADA

SENATORS
Dean Heller
Catherine Cortez Masto

REPRESENTATIVES
[Republican 1, Democrats 3]
1. *Dina Titus*
2. Mark E. Amodei
3. *Jacky Rosen*
4. *Ruben J. Kihuen*

NEW HAMPSHIRE

SENATORS
Jeanne Shaheen
Margaret Wood Hassan

REPRESENTATIVES
[Democrats 2]
1. *Carol Shea-Porter*
2. *Ann M. Kuster*

NEW JERSEY

SENATORS
Robert Menendez
Cory A. Booker

REPRESENTATIVES
[Republicans 5, Democrats 7]
1. *Donald Norcross*
2. Frank A. LoBiondo
3. Thomas MacArthur
4. Christopher H. Smith
5. *Josh Gottheimer*
6. *Frank Pallone, Jr.*
7. Leonard Lance
8. *Albio Sires*
9. *Bill Pascrell, Jr.*
10. *Donald M. Payne, Jr.*
11. Rodney P. Frelinghuysen
12. *Bonnie Watson Coleman*

NEW MEXICO

SENATORS
Tom Udall
Martin Heinrich

REPRESENTATIVES
[Republican 1, Democrats 2]
1. *Michelle Lujan Grisham*
2. Stevan Pearce
3. *Ben Ray Luján*

NEW YORK

SENATORS
Charles E. Schumer
Kirsten E. Gillibrand

REPRESENTATIVES
[Republicans 9, Democrats 17, Vacant 1]
1. Lee M. Zeldin
2. Peter T. King
3. *Thomas R. Suozzi*
4. *Kathleen M. Rice*
5. *Gregory W. Meeks*
6. *Grace Meng*
7. *Nydia M. Velázquez*
8. *Hakeem S. Jeffries*
9. *Yvette D. Clarke*
10. *Jerrold Nadler*

11. Daniel M. Donovan, Jr.
12. *Carolyn B. Maloney*
13. *Adriano Espaillat*
14. *Joseph Crowley*
15. *José E. Serrano*
16. *Eliot L. Engel*
17. *Nita M. Lowey*
18. *Sean Patrick Maloney*
19. John J. Faso
20. *Paul Tonko*
21. Elise M. Stefanik
22. Claudia Tenney
23. Tom Reed
24. John Katko
25. ——[9]
26. *Brian Higgins*
27. Chris Collins

NORTH CAROLINA

SENATORS
Richard Burr
Thom Tillis

REPRESENTATIVES
[Republicans 10, Democrats 3]

1. *G. K. Butterfield*
2. George Holding
3. Walter B. Jones
4. *David E. Price*
5. Virginia Foxx
6. Mark Walker
7. David Rouzer
8. Richard Hudson
9. Robert Pittenger
10. Patrick T. McHenry
11. Mark Meadows
12. *Alma S. Adams*
13. Ted Budd

NORTH DAKOTA

SENATORS
John Hoeven
Heidi Heitkamp

REPRESENTATIVE
[Republican 1]

At Large – Kevin Cramer

OHIO

SENATORS
Sherrod Brown
Rob Portman

REPRESENTATIVES
[Republicans 11, Democrats 4, Vacant 1]

1. Steve Chabot
2. Brad R. Wenstrup
3. *Joyce Beatty*
4. Jim Jordan
5. Robert E. Latta
6. Bill Johnson
7. Bob Gibbs
8. Warren Davidson
9. *Marcy Kaptur*
10. Michael R. Turner
11. *Marcia L. Fudge*
12. ——[10]
13. *Tim Ryan*
14. David P. Joyce
15. Steve Stivers
16. James B. Renacci

OKLAHOMA

SENATORS
James M. Inhofe
James Lankford

REPRESENTATIVES
[Republicans 4, Vacant 1]

1. ——[11]
2. Markwayne Mullin
3. Frank D. Lucas
4. Tom Cole
5. Steve Russell

OREGON

SENATORS
Ron Wyden
Jeff Merkley

REPRESENTATIVES
[Republican 1, Democrats 4]

1. *Suzanne Bonamici*

2. Greg Walden
3. *Earl Blumenauer*
4. *Peter A. DeFazio*
5. *Kurt Schrader*

PENNSYLVANIA

SENATORS
Robert P. Casey, Jr.
Patrick J. Toomey

REPRESENTATIVES
[Republicans 11, Democrats 6, Vacant 1]

1. *Robert A. Brady*
2. *Dwight Evans*
3. Mike Kelly
4. Scott Perry
5. Glenn Thompson
6. Ryan A. Costello
7. ——[12]
8. Brian K. Fitzpatrick
9. Bill Shuster
10. Tom Marino
11. Lou Barletta
12. Keith J. Rothfus
13. *Brendan F. Boyle*
14. *Michael F. Doyle*
15. ——[13]
16. Lloyd Smucker
17. *Matt Cartwright*
18. *Conor Lamb*[14]

RHODE ISLAND

SENATORS
Jack Reed
Sheldon Whitehouse

REPRESENTATIVES
[Democrats 2]

1. *David N. Cicilline*
2. *James R. Langevin*

SOUTH CAROLINA

SENATORS
Lindsey Graham
Tim Scott

REPRESENTATIVES
[Republicans 6, Democrat 1]

1. Mark Sanford
2. Joe Wilson
3. Jeff Duncan
4. Trey Gowdy
5. Ralph Norman[15]
6. *James E. Clyburn*
7. Tom Rice

SOUTH DAKOTA

SENATORS
John Thune
Mike Rounds

REPRESENTATIVE
[Republican 1]

At Large – Kristi L. Noem

TENNESSEE

SENATORS
Lamar Alexander
Bob Corker

REPRESENTATIVES
[Republicans 7, Democrats 2]

1. David P. Roe
2. John J. Duncan, Jr.
3. Charles J. ''Chuck'' Fleischmann
4. Scott DesJarlais
5. *Jim Cooper*
6. Diane Black
7. Marsha Blackburn
8. David Kustoff
9. *Steve Cohen*

TEXAS

SENATORS
John Cornyn
Ted Cruz

REPRESENTATIVES
[Republicans 25, Democrats 11]

1. Louie Gohmert
2. Ted Poe
3. Sam Johnson
4. John Ratcliffe

5. Jeb Hensarling
6. Joe Barton
7. John Abney Culberson
8. Kevin Brady
9. *Al Green*
10. Michael T. McCaul
11. K. Michael Conaway
12. Kay Granger
13. Mac Thornberry
14. Randy K. Weber, Sr.
15. *Vicente Gonzalez*
16. *Beto O'Rourke*
17. Bill Flores
18. *Sheila Jackson Lee*
19. Jodey C. Arrington
20. *Joaquin Castro*
21. Lamar Smith
22. Pete Olson
23. Will Hurd
24. Kenny Marchant
25. Roger Williams
26. Michael C. Burgess
27. Michael Cloud [16]
28. *Henry Cuellar*
29. *Gene Green*
30. *Eddie Bernice Johnson*
31. John R. Carter
32. Pete Sessions
33. *Marc A. Veasey*
34. *Filemon Vela*
35. *Lloyd Doggett*
36. Brian Babin

UTAH

SENATORS
Orrin G. Hatch
Mike Lee

REPRESENTATIVES
[Republicans 4]

1. Rob Bishop
2. Chris Stewart
3. John R. Curtis [17]
4. Mia B. Love

VERMONT

SENATORS
Patrick J. Leahy
BERNARD SANDERS

REPRESENTATIVE
[Democrat 1]

At Large – *Peter Welch*

VIRGINIA

SENATORS
Mark R. Warner
Tim Kaine

REPRESENTATIVES
[Republicans 7, Democrats 4]

1. Robert J. Wittman
2. Scott Taylor
3. *Robert C. "Bobby" Scott*
4. *A. Donald McEachin*
5. Thomas A. Garrett, Jr.
6. Bob Goodlatte
7. Dave Brat
8. *Donald S. Beyer, Jr.*
9. H. Morgan Griffith
10. Barbara Comstock
11. *Gerald E. Connolly*

WASHINGTON

SENATORS
Patty Murray
Maria Cantwell

REPRESENTATIVES
[Republicans 4, Democrats 6]

1. *Suzan K. DelBene*
2. *Rick Larsen*
3. Jaime Herrera Beutler
4. Dan Newhouse
5. Cathy McMorris Rodgers
6. *Derek Kilmer*
7. *Pramila Jayapal*
8. David G. Reichert
9. *Adam Smith*
10. *Denny Heck*

WEST VIRGINIA

SENATORS
Joe Manchin III
Shelley Moore Capito

REPRESENTATIVES
[Republicans 3]

1. David B. McKinley
2. Alexander X. Mooney
3. Evan H. Jenkins

WISCONSIN

SENATORS
Ron Johnson
Tammy Baldwin

REPRESENTATIVES
[Republicans 5, Democrats 3]

1. Paul D. Ryan
2. *Mark Pocan*
3. *Ron Kind*
4. *Gwen Moore*
5. F. James Sensenbrenner, Jr.
6. Glenn Grothman
7. Sean P. Duffy
8. Mike Gallagher

WYOMING

SENATORS
Michael B. Enzi
John Barrasso

REPRESENTATIVE
[Republican 1]

At Large – Liz Cheney

AMERICAN SAMOA

DELEGATE
[Republican 1]

Aumua Amata Coleman Radewagen

DISTRICT OF COLUMBIA

DELEGATE
[Democrat 1]

Eleanor Holmes Norton

GUAM

DELEGATE
[Democrat 1]

Madeleine Z. Bordallo

NORTHERN MARIANA ISLANDS

DELEGATE
[Democrat 1]

Gregorio Kilili Camacho Sablan

PUERTO RICO

RESIDENT COMMISSIONER
[Republican 1]

Jenniffer González-Colón

VIRGIN ISLANDS

DELEGATE
[Democrat 1]

Stacey E. Plaskett

[1] Elected December 12, 2017, to fill the vacancy caused by the resignation of Jeff Sessions, a seat subsequently held by appointed Senator Luther Strange.
[2] Elected April 24, 2018, to fill the vacancy due to the resignation of Trent Franks, December 8, 2017.
[3] Elected June 6, 2017, to fill the vacancy due to the resignation of Xavier Becerra, January 24, 2017.
[4] Elected June 20, 2017, to fill the vacancy due to the resignation of Tom Price, February 10, 2017.
[5] Elected April 11, 2017, to fill the vacancy due to the resignation of Mike Pompeo, January 23, 2017.
[6] Vacancy due to the resignation of John Conyers, Jr., December 5, 2017.
[7] Appointed to the U.S. Senate to fill the vacancy caused by the resignation of Thad Cochran; took the oath of office on April 9, 2018, to serve until a special election is held on November 6, 2018, for the remainder of the term ending January 3, 2021.
[8] Elected May 25, 2017, to fill the vacancy due to the resignation of Ryan K. Zinke, March 1, 2017.

[9] Vacancy due to the death of Louise McIntosh Slaughter, March 16, 2018.
[10] Vacancy due to the resignation of Patrick J. Tiberi, January 15, 2018.
[11] Vacancy due to the resignation of Jim Bridenstine, April 23, 2018.
[12] Vacancy due to the resignation of Patrick Meehan, April 27, 2018.
[13] Vacancy due to the resignation of Charles W. Dent, May 12, 2018.
[14] Elected March 13, 2018, to fill the vacancy due to the resignation of Timothy Murphy, October 21, 2017.
[15] Elected June 20, 2017, to fill the vacancy due to the resignation of Mick Mulvaney, February 16, 2017.
[16] Elected June 30, 2018, to fill the vacancy due to the resignation of Blake Farenthold, April 6, 2018.
[17] Elected November 7, 2017, to fill the vacancy due to the resignation of Jason Chaffetz, June 30, 2017.

ALPHABETICAL LIST

SENATORS

Alphabetical list of Senators, Representatives, Delegates, and Resident Commissioner. Republicans in roman (51); Democrats in *italic* (47); Independents in SMALL CAPS (2).

Alexander, Lamar, TN
Baldwin, Tammy, WI
Barrasso, John, WY
Bennet, Michael F., CO
Blumenthal, Richard, CT
Blunt, Roy, MO
Booker, Cory A., NJ
Boozman, John, AR
Brown, Sherrod, OH
Burr, Richard, NC
Cantwell, Maria, WA
Capito, Shelley Moore, WV
Cardin, Benjamin L., MD
Carper, Thomas R., DE
Casey, Robert P., Jr., PA
Cassidy, Bill, LA
Collins, Susan M., ME
Coons, Christopher A., DE
Corker, Bob, TN
Cornyn, John, TX
Cortez Masto, Catherine, NV
Cotton, Tom, AR
Crapo, Mike, ID
Cruz, Ted, TX
Daines, Steve, MT
Donnelly, Joe, IN
Duckworth, Tammy, IL
Durbin, Richard J., IL
Enzi, Michael B., WY
Ernst, Joni, IA
Feinstein, Dianne, CA
Fischer, Deb, NE
Flake, Jeff, AR
Gardner, Cory, CO
Gillibrand, Kirsten E., NY
Graham, Lindsey, SC
Grassley, Chuck, IA
Harris, Kamala D., CA
Hassan, Margaret Wood, NH
Hatch, Orrin G., UT
Heinrich, Martin, NM
Heitkamp, Heidi, ND
Heller, Dean, NV
Hirono, Mazie K., HI
Hoeven, John, ND
Hyde-Smith, Cindy, MS
Inhofe, James M., OK
Isakson, Johnny, GA
Johnson, Ron, WI
Jones, Doug, AL
Kaine, Tim, VA
Kennedy, John, LA
KING, ANGUS S., JR., ME
Klobuchar, Amy, MN
Lankford, James, OK
Leahy, Patrick J., VT
Lee, Mike, UT
McCain, John, AZ
McCaskill, Claire, MO
McConnell, Mitch, KY
Manchin, Joe, III, WV
Markey, Edward J., MA
Menendez, Robert, NJ
Merkley, Jeff, OR
Moran, Jerry, KS
Murkowski, Lisa, AK
Murphy, Christopher, CT
Murray, Patty, WA
Nelson, Bill, FL
Paul, Rand, KY
Perdue, David, GA
Peters, Gary C., MI
Portman, Rob, OH
Reed, Jack, RI
Risch, James E., ID
Roberts, Pat, KS
Rounds, Mike, SD
Rubio, Marco, FL
SANDERS, BERNARD, VT
Sasse, Ben, NE
Schatz, Brian, HI
Schumer, Charles E., NY
Scott, Tim, SC
Shaheen, Jeanne, NH
Shelby, Richard C., AL
Smith, Tina, MN
Stabenow, Debbie, MI
Sullivan, Dan, AK
Tester, Jon, MT
Thune, John, SD
Tillis, Thom, NC
Toomey, Patrick J., PA
Udall, Tom, NM
Van Hollen, Chris, MD
Warner, Mark R., VA
Warren, Elizabeth, MA
Whitehouse, Sheldon, RI
Wicker, Roger F., MS
Wyden, Ron, OR
Young, Todd, IN

REPRESENTATIVES, RESIDENT COMMISSIONER, AND DELEGATES

Republicans in roman (236); Democrats in *italic* (193); Vacancies (6); Resident Commissioner and Delegates in **boldface** (6); total, 441.

Abraham, Ralph Lee, LA (5th)
Adams, Alma S., NC (12th)
Aderholt, Robert B., AL (4th)
Aguilar, Pete, CA (31st)
Allen, Rick W., GA (12th)
Amash, Justin, MI (3d)
Amodei, Mark E., NV (2d)
Arrington, Jodey C., TX (19th)
Babin, Brian, TX (36th)
Bacon, Don, NE (2d)
Banks, Jim, IN (3d)
Barletta, Lou, PA (11th)
Barr, Andy, KY (6th)
Barragán, Nanette Diaz, CA (44th)
Barton, Joe, TX (6th)
Bass, Karen, CA (37th)
Beatty, Joyce, OH (3d)
Bera, Ami, CA (7th)
Bergman, Jack, MI (1st)
Beyer, Donald S., Jr., VA (8th)
Biggs, Andy, AZ (5th)
Bilirakis, Gus M., FL (12th)
Bishop, Mike, MI (8th)
Bishop, Rob, UT (1st)
Bishop, Sanford D., Jr., GA (2d)
Black, Diane, TN (6th)
Blackburn, Marsha, TN (7th)
Blum, Rod, IA (1st)
Blumenauer, Earl, OR (3d)
Blunt Rochester, Lisa, DE (At Large)
Bonamici, Suzanne, OR (1st)
Bost, Mike, IL (12th)
Boyle, Brendan F., PA (13th)
Brady, Kevin, TX (8th)
Brady, Robert A., PA (1st)
Brat, Dave, VA (7th)
Brooks, Mo, AL (5th)
Brooks, Susan W., IN (5th)
Brown, Anthony G., MD (4th)
Brownley, Julia, CA (26th)
Buchanan, Vern, FL (16th)
Buck, Ken, CO (4th)
Bucshon, Larry, IN (8th)
Budd, Ted, NC (13th)
Burgess, Michael C., TX (26th)
Bustos, Cheri, IL (17th)
Butterfield, G. K., NC (1st)
Byrne, Bradley, AL (1st)
Calvert, Ken, CA (42d)
Capuano, Michael E., MA (7th)
Carbajal, Salud O., CA (24th)
Cárdenas, Tony, CA (29th)
Carson, André, IN (7th)
Carter, Earl L. "Buddy", GA (1st)
Carter, John R., TX (31st)
Cartwright, Matt, PA (17th)
Castor, Kathy, FL (14th)
Castro, Joaquin, TX (20th)
Chabot, Steve, OH (1st)
Cheney, Liz, WY (At Large)
Chu, Judy, CA (27th)
Cicilline, David N., RI (1st)
Clark, Katherine M., MA (5th)
Clarke, Yvette D., NY (9th)
Clay, Wm. Lacy, MO (1st)
Cleaver, Emanuel, MO (5th)
Cloud, Michael, TX (27th)
Clyburn, James E., SC (6th)
Coffman, Mike, CO (6th)
Cohen, Steve, TN (9th)
Cole, Tom, OK (4th)
Collins, Chris, NY (27th)
Collins, Doug, GA (9th)
Comer, James, KY (1st)
Comstock, Barbara, VA (10th)
Conaway, K. Michael, TX (11th)
Connolly, Gerald E., VA (11th)
Cook, Paul, CA (8th)
Cooper, Jim, TN (5th)
Correa, J. Luis, CA (46th)
Costa, Jim, CA (16th)
Costello, Ryan A., PA (6th)
Courtney, Joe, CT (2d)
Cramer, Kevin, ND (At Large)
Crawford, Eric A. "Rick", AR (1st)
Crist, Charlie, FL (13th)
Crowley, Joseph, NY (14th)
Cuellar, Henry, TX (28th)
Culberson, John Abney, TX (7th)
Cummings, Elijah E., MD (7th)
Curbelo, Carlos, FL (26th)
Curtis, John R., UT (3d)
Davidson, Warren, OH (8th)
Davis, Danny K., IL (7th)
Davis, Rodney, IL (13th)
Davis, Susan A., CA (53d)
DeFazio, Peter A., OR (4th)
DeGette, Diana, CO (1st)
Delaney, John K., MD (6th)
DeLauro, Rosa L., CT (3d)
DelBene, Suzan K., WA (1st)
Demings, Val Butler, FL (10th)
Denham, Jeff, CA (10th)
DeSantis, Ron, FL (6th)
DeSaulnier, Mark, CA (11th)
DesJarlais, Scott, TN (4th)
Deutch, Theodore E., FL (22d)
Diaz-Balart, Mario, FL (25th)
Dingell, Debbie, MI (12th)
Doggett, Lloyd, TX (35th)
Donovan, Daniel M., Jr., NY (11th)
Doyle, Michael F., PA (14th)
Duffy, Sean P., WI (7th)
Duncan, Jeff, SC (3d)
Duncan, John J., Jr., TN (2d)
Dunn, Neal P., FL (2d)
Ellison, Keith, MN (5th)
Emmer, Tom, MN (6th)

Engel, Eliot L., NY (16th)
Eshoo, Anna G., CA (18th)
Espaillat, Adriano, NY (13th)
Estes, Ron, KS (4th)
Esty, Elizabeth H., CT (5th)
Evans, Dwight, PA (2d)
Faso, John J., NY (19th)
Ferguson, A. Drew IV, GA (3d)
Fitzpatrick, Brian K., PA (8th)
Fleischmann, Charles J. "Chuck", TN (3d)
Flores, Bill, TX (17th)
Fortenberry, Jeff, NE (1st)
Foster, Bill, IL (11th)
Foxx, Virginia, NC (5th)
Frankel, Lois, FL (21st)
Frelinghuysen, Rodney P., NJ (11th)
Fudge, Marcia L., OH (11th)
Gabbard, Tulsi, HI (2d)
Gaetz, Matt, FL (1st)
Gallagher, Mike, WI (8th)
Gallego, Ruben, AZ (7th)
Garamendi, John, CA (3d)
Garrett, Thomas A., Jr., VA (5th)
Gianforte, Greg, MT (At Large)
Gibbs, Bob, OH (7th)
Gohmert, Louie, TX (1st)
Gomez, Jimmy, CA (34th)
Gonzalez, Vicente, TX (15th)
Goodlatte, Bob, VA (6th)
Gosar, Paul A., AZ (4th)
Gottheimer, Josh, NJ (5th)
Gowdy, Trey, SC (4th)
Granger, Kay, TX (12th)
Graves, Garret, LA (6th)
Graves, Sam, MO (6th)
Graves, Tom, GA (14th)
Green, Al, TX (9th)
Green, Gene, TX (29th)
Griffith, H. Morgan, VA (9th)
Grijalva, Raúl M., AZ (3d)
Grothman, Glenn, WI (6th)
Guthrie, Brett, KY (2d)
Gutiérrez, Luis V., IL (4th)
Hanabusa, Colleen, HI (1st)
Handel, Karen C., GA (6th)
Harper, Gregg, MS (3d)
Harris, Andy, MD (1st)
Hartzler, Vicky, MO (4th)
Hastings, Alcee L., FL (20th)
Heck, Denny, WA (10th)
Hensarling, Jeb, TX (5th)
Herrera Beutler, Jaime, WA (3d)
Hice, Jody B., GA (10th)
Higgins, Brian, NY (26th)
Higgins, Clay, LA (3d)
Hill, J. French, AR (2d)
Himes, James A., CT (4th)
Holding, George, NC (2d)
Hollingsworth, Trey, IN (9th)
Hoyer, Steny H., MD (5th)
Hudson, Richard, NC (8th)
Huffman, Jared, CA (2d)
Huizenga, Bill, MI (2d)
Hultgren, Randy, IL (14th)
Hunter, Duncan, CA (50th)
Hurd, Will, TX (23d)
Issa, Darrell E., CA (49th)
Jackson Lee, Sheila, TX (18th)
Jayapal, Pramila, WA (7th)
Jeffries, Hakeem S., NY (8th)
Jenkins, Evan H., WV (3d)
Jenkins, Lynn, KS (2d)
Johnson, Bill, OH (6th)
Johnson, Eddie Bernice, TX (30th)
Johnson, Henry C. "Hank", Jr., GA (4th)
Johnson, Mike, LA (4th)
Johnson, Sam, TX (3d)
Jones, Walter B., NC (3d)
Jordan, Jim, OH (4th)
Joyce, David P., OH (14th)
Kaptur, Marcy, OH (9th)
Katko, John, NY (24th)
Keating, William R., MA (9th)
Kelly, Mike, PA (3d)
Kelly, Robin L., IL (2d)
Kelly, Trent, MS (1st)
Kennedy, Joseph P., III, MA (4th)
Khanna, Ro, CA (17th)
Kihuen, Ruben J., NV (4th)
Kildee, Daniel T., MI (5th)
Kilmer, Derek, WA (6th)
Kind, Ron, WI (3d)
King, Peter T., NY (2d)
King, Steve, IA (4th)
Kinzinger, Adam, IL (16th)
Knight, Stephen, CA (25th)
Krishnamoorthi, Raja, IL (8th)
Kuster, Ann M., NH (2d)
Kustoff, David, TN (8th)
Labrador, Raúl R., ID (1st)
LaHood, Darin, IL (18th)
LaMalfa, Doug, CA (1st)
Lamb, Conor, PA (18th)
Lamborn, Doug, CO (5th)
Lance, Leonard, NJ (7th)
Langevin, James R., (RI) (2d)
Larsen, Rick, WA (2d)
Larson, John B., CT (1st)
Latta, Robert E., OH (5th)
Lawrence, Brenda L., MI (14th)
Lawson, Al, Jr., FL (5th)
Lee, Barbara, CA (13th)
Lesko, Debbie, AZ (8th)
Levin, Sander M., MI (9th)
Lewis, Jason, MN (2d)
Lewis, John, GA (5th)
Lieu, Ted, CA (33d)
Lipinski, Daniel, IL (3d)
LoBiondo, Frank A., NJ (2d)
Loebsack, David, IA (2d)
Lofgren, Zoe, CA (19th)
Long, Billy, MO (7th)
Loudermilk, Barry, GA (11th)
Love, Mia B., UT (4th)
Lowenthal, Alan S., CA (47th)
Lowey, Nita M., NY (17th)
Lucas, Frank D., OK (3d)
Luetkemeyer, Blaine, MO (3d)
Luján, Ben Ray, NM (3d)
Lujan Grisham, Michelle, NM (1st)
Lynch, Stephen F., MA (8th)
MacArthur, Thomas, NJ (3d)

Maloney, Carolyn B., NY (12th)
Maloney, Sean Patrick, NY (18th)
Marchant, Kenny, TX (24th)
Marino, Tom, PA (10th)
Marshall, Roger W., KS (1st)
Massie, Thomas, KY (4th)
Mast, Brian J., FL (18th)
Matsui, Doris O., CA (6th)
McCarthy, Kevin, CA (23d)
McCaul, Michael T., TX (10th)
McClintock, Tom, CA (4th)
McCollum, Betty, MN (4th)
McEachin, A. Donald, VA (4th)
McGovern, James P., MA (2d)
McHenry, Patrick T., NC (10th)
McKinley, David B., WV (1st)
McMorris Rodgers, Cathy, WA (5th)
McNerney, Jerry, CA (9th)
McSally, Martha, AZ (2d)
Meadows, Mark, NC (11th)
Meeks, Gregory W., NY (5th)
Meng, Grace, NY (6th)
Messer, Luke, IN (6th)
Mitchell, Paul, MI (10th)
Moolenaar, John R., MI (4th)
Mooney, Alexander X., WV (2d)
Moore, Gwen, WI (4th)
Moulton, Seth, MA (6th)
Mullin, Markwayne, OK (2d)
Murphy, Stephanie N., FL (7th)
Nadler, Jerrold, NY (10th)
Napolitano, Grace F., CA (32d)
Neal, Richard E., MA (1st)
Newhouse, Dan, WA (4th)
Noem, Kristi L., SD (At Large)
Nolan, Richard M., MN (8th)
Norcross, Donald, NJ (1st)
Norman, Ralph, SC (5th)
Nunes, Devin, CA (22d)
O'Halleran, Tom, AZ (1st)
Olson, Pete, TX (22d)
O'Rourke, Beto, TX (16th)
Palazzo, Steven M., MS (4th)
Pallone, Frank, Jr., NJ (6th)
Palmer, Gary J., AL (6th)
Panetta, Jimmy, CA (20th)
Pascrell, Bill, Jr., NJ (9th)
Paulsen, Erik, MN (3d)
Payne, Donald M., Jr., NJ (10th)
Pearce, Stevan, NM (2d)
Pelosi, Nancy, CA (12th)
Perlmutter, Ed, CO (7th)
Perry, Scott, PA (4th)
Peters, Scott H., CA (52d)
Peterson, Collin C., MN (7th)
Pingree, Chellie, ME (1st)
Pittenger, Robert, NC (9th)
Pocan, Mark, WI (2d)
Poe, Ted, TX (2d)
Poliquin, Bruce, ME (2d)
Polis, Jared, CO (2d)
Posey, Bill, FL (8th)
Price, David E., NC (4th)
Quigley, Mike, IL (5th)
Raskin, Jamie, MD (8th)
Ratcliffe, John, TX (4th)
Reed, Tom, NY (23d)
Reichert, David G., WA (8th)
Renacci, James B., OH (16th)
Rice, Kathleen M., NY (4th)
Rice, Tom, SC (7th)
Richmond, Cedric L., LA (2d)
Roby, Martha, AL (2d)
Roe, David P., TN (1st)
Rogers, Harold, KY (5th)
Rogers, Mike, AL (3d)
Rohrabacher, Dana, CA (48th)
Rokita, Todd, IN (4th)
Rooney, Francis, FL (19th)
Rooney, Thomas J., FL (17th)
Rosen, Jacky, NV (3d)
Roskam, Peter J., IL (6th)
Ros-Lehtinen, Ileana, FL (27th)
Ross, Dennis A., FL (15th)
Rothfus, Keith J., PA (12th)
Rouzer, David, NC (7th)
Roybal-Allard, Lucille, CA (40th)
Royce, Edward R., CA (39th)
Ruiz, Raul, CA (36th)
Ruppersberger, C. A. Dutch, MD (2d)
Rush, Bobby L., IL (1st)
Russell, Steve, OK (5th)
Rutherford, John H., FL (4th)
Ryan, Paul D., WI (1st)
Ryan, Tim, OH (13th)
Sánchez, Linda T., CA (38th)
Sanford, Mark, SC (1st)
Sarbanes, John P., MD (3d)
Scalise, Steve, LA (1st)
Schakowsky, Janice D., IL (9th)
Schiff, Adam B., CA (28th)
Schneider, Bradley Scott, IL (10th)
Schrader, Kurt, OR (5th)
Schweikert, David, AZ (6th)
Scott, Austin, GA (8th)
Scott, David, GA (13th)
Scott, Robert C. "Bobby", VA (3d)
Sensenbrenner, F. James, Jr., WI (5th)
Serrano, José E., NY (15th)
Sessions, Pete, TX (32d)
Sewell, Terri A., AL (7th)
Shea-Porter, Carol, NH (1st)
Sherman, Brad, CA (30th)
Shimkus, John, IL (15th)
Shuster, Bill, PA (9th)
Simpson, Michael K., ID (2d)
Sinema, Kyrsten, AZ (9th)
Sires, Albio, NJ (8th)
Smith, Adam, WA (9th)
Smith, Adrian, NE (3d)
Smith, Christopher H., NJ (4th)
Smith, Jason, MO (8th)
Smith, Lamar, TX (21st)
Smucker, Lloyd, PA (16th)
Soto, Darren, FL (9th)
Speier, Jackie, CA (14th)
Stefanik, Elise M., NY (21st)
Stewart, Chris, UT (2d)
Stivers, Steve, OH (15th)
Suozzi, Thomas R., NY (3d)
Swalwell, Eric, CA (15th)
Takano, Mark, CA (41st)

Taylor, Scott, VA (2d)
Tenney, Claudia, NY (22d)
Thompson, Bennie G., MS (2d)
Thompson, Glenn, PA (5th)
Thompson, Mike, CA (5th)
Thornberry, Mac, TX (13th)
Tipton, Scott R., CO (3d)
Titus, Dina, NV (1st)
Tonko, Paul, NY (20th)
Torres, Norma J., CA (35th)
Trott, David A., MI (11th)
Tsongas, Niki, MA (3d)
Turner, Michael R., OH (10th)
Upton, Fred, MI (6th)
Valadao, David G., CA (21st)
Vargas, Juan, CA (51st)
Veasey, Marc A., TX (33d)
Vela, Filemon, TX (34th)
Velázquez, Nydia M., NY (7th)
Visclosky, Peter J., IN (1st)
Wagner, Ann, MO (2d)
Walberg, Tim, MI (7th)
Walden, Greg, OR (2d)
Walker, Mark, NC (6th)
Walorski, Jackie, IN (2d)
Walters, Mimi, CA (45th)
Walz, Timothy J., MN (1st)
Wasserman Schultz, Debbie, FL (23d)
Waters, Maxine, CA (43d)
Watson Coleman, Bonnie, NJ (12th)
Weber, Randy K., Sr., TX (14th)
Webster, Daniel, FL (11th)
Welch, Peter, VT (At Large)
Wenstrup, Brad R., OH (2d)
Westerman, Bruce, AR (4th)
Williams, Roger, TX (25th)
Wilson, Frederica S., FL (24th)
Wilson, Joe, SC (2d)
Wittman, Robert J., VA (1st)
Womack, Steve, AR (3d)
Woodall, Rob, GA (7th)
Yarmuth, John A., KY (3d)
Yoder, Kevin, KS (3d)
Yoho, Ted S., FL (3d)
Young, David, IA (3d)
Young, Don, AK (At Large)
Zeldin, Lee M., NY (1st)

RESIDENT COMMISSIONER
González-Colón, Jenniffer, PR

DELEGATES
Radewagen, Aumua Amata Coleman, AS
Norton, Eleanor Holmes, DC
Bordallo, Madeleine Z., GU
Sablan, Gregorio Kilili Camacho, MP
Plaskett, Stacey E., VI

115th Congress
Nine-Digit Postal ZIP Codes

Senate Post Office (20510): The four-digit numbers in these tables were assigned by the Senate Committee on Rules and Administration. Mail to all Senate offices is delivered by the main Post Office in the Dirksen Senate Office Building.

Senate Committees

Committee on Agriculture, Nutrition, and Forestry	–6000
Committee on Appropriations	–6025
Committee on Armed Services	–6050
Committee on Banking, Housing, and Urban Affairs	–6075
Committee on the Budget	–6100
Committee on Commerce, Science, and Transportation	–6125
Committee on Energy and Natural Resources	–6150
Committee on Environment and Public Works	–6175
Committee on Finance	–6200
Committee on Foreign Relations	–6225
Committee on Health, Education, Labor and Pensions	–6300
Committee on Homeland Security and Governmental Affairs	–6250
Committee on Indian Affairs	–6450
Committee on the Judiciary	–6275
Committee on Rules and Administration	–6325
Committee on Small Business and Entrepreneurship	–6350
Committee on Veterans' Affairs	–6375
Committee on Aging (Special)	–6400
Committee on Ethics (Select)	–6425
Committee on Intelligence (Select)	–6475

Joint Committee Offices, Senate Side

Joint Economic Committee	–6602
Joint Committee on the Library	–6625
Joint Committee on Printing	–6650
Joint Committee on Taxation	–6675

Senate Leadership Offices

President Pro Tempore	–7000
Chaplain	–7002
Majority Leader	–7010
Assistant Majority Leader	–7012
Secretary for the Majority	–7014
Minority Leader	–7020
Assistant Minority Leader	–7022
Secretary for the Minority	–7024
Democratic Policy Committee	–7050
Republican Conference	–7060
Secretary to the Republican Conference	–7062
Republican Policy Committee	–7064
Republican Steering Committee	–7066
National Security Working Group	–7070

Senate Officers

Secretary of the Senate	–7100
Curator	–7102
Disbursing Office	–7104
Printing and Document Service	–7106
Historical Office	–7108
Human Resources	–7109
Interparliamentary Services	–7110
Senate Library	–7112
Office of Senate Security	–7114
Office of Public Records	–7116
Office of Official Reporters of Debates	–7117
Stationery Room	–7118
U.S. Capitol Preservation Commission	–7122
Office of Conservation and Preservation	–7124
Information Systems	–7125
Web Technology Office	–7126
Legislative Systems	–7127
Senate Gift Shop	–7128
Senate Legal Counsel	–7130
Emergency Terror Response (COOP)	–7131
Chief Counsel for Employment	–7132
Senate Sergeant at Arms	–7200
General Counsel	–7201
Finance Division	–7205
Budget	–7205
Accounting	–7205
Hair Care Services	–7206
Procurement	–7207
Capitol Guide Service	–7209
Employee Assistance Program Office	–7211
Human Resources	–7212
Safety Program	–7212
Health Promotion/Seminars	–7213
Placement Office	–7214
Workman's Compensation	–7214
Joint Office of Education and Training	–7215
Capitol Police	–7218
Congressional Special Services Office	–7228
Office Support Services	–7230
Customer Support	–7231
IT Request Processing	–7232
Chief Information Officer	–7233
State Liaison	–7285
Periodical Press Gallery	–7234
Press Gallery	–7238
Press Photo Gallery	–7242
Radio and TV Gallery	–7246
Webster Hall	–7248
Office of Protective Services and Continuity (OPSAC)	–7249
Law Enforcement Support Office	–7249
Intelligence & Protective Services	–7249
State Office Readiness Program	–7249
Police Operations Security Emergency Preparedness (POSEP)	–7249
Office of Continuity & Emergency Preparedness (CEPO)	–7249

Other Offices on the Senate Side

Senate Legal Counsel	–7250
Central Operations—Administration	–7260
Parking/ID	–7262
Printing Graphics and Direct Mail—PSQ	–7264
Printing Graphics and Direct Mail—Capitol Hill	–7266
Facilities	–7204
Furniture Shop	–7204
Framing Shop	–7204

Cabinet Shop .... –7204
Photo Studio .... –7216
Post Office .... –7220
Recording Studio .... –7222
Senate Legislative Counsel .... –7275
Program Management .... –7276
IT Support Services—Administration .... –7280
Telecom Support .... –7281
Equipment Services .... –7282
Desktop/Lan Support .... –7284
IT Research/Deployment .... –7292
Technology Development—Administration .... –7290
Systems Architecture .... –7277
Information Security .... –7278
Applications Development .... –7291
Network Engineering and Management .... –7293
Enterprise IT Systems .... –7294
Inter/Intranet Services .... –7296
Architect of the Capitol .... –8000
Superintendent of Senate Buildings .... –8002
Restaurant .... –8050
Amtrak Ticket Office .... –9010
Airlines Ticket Office (CATO) .... –9014
Child Care Center .... –9022
Credit Union .... –9026
Veterans' Liaison .... –9054
Social Security Liaison .... –9064
Caucus of International Narcotics Control .... –9070
Army Liaison .... –9082
Air Force Liaison .... –9083
Coast Guard Liaison .... –9084
Navy Liaison .... –9085
Marine Liaison .... –9087

House Post Office (20515): Mail to all House offices is delivered by the House Postal Operations.

House Committees Leadership

U.S. House of Representatives .... –0001
Cannon House Office Building .... –0002
Rayburn House Office Building .... –0003
Longworth House Office Building .... –0004
Ford House Office Building .... –0006
The Capitol .... –0007
Committee on Agriculture .... –6001
Committee on Appropriations .... –6015
Committee on Armed Services .... –6035
Committee on the Budget .... –6065
Committee on Education and the Workforce .... –6100
Committee on Energy and Commerce .... –6115
Committee on Ethics .... –6328
Committee on Financial Services .... –6050
Committee on Foreign Affairs .... –6128
Committee on Homeland Security .... –6480
Committee on House Administration .... –6157
Committee on the Judiciary .... –6216
Committee on Natural Resources .... –6201
Committee on Oversight and Government Reform –6143
Committee on Rules .... –6269
Committee on Science, Space, and Technology .... –6301
Committee on Small Business .... –6315
Committee on Transportation and Infrastructure .... –6256
Committee on Veterans' Affairs .... –6335
Committee on Ways and Means .... –6348
Permanent Select Committee on Intelligence .... –6415

Joint Committee Offices, House Side

Joint Economic Committee .... –6432
Joint Committee on the Library .... –6157
Joint Committee on Printing .... –6157
Joint Committee on Taxation .... –6453

House Leadership Offices

Office of the Speaker .... –6501
Office of the Majority Leader .... –6502
Office of the Majority Whip .... –6503
Democratic Caucus .... –6524
Democratic Congressional Campaign Committee .... –6525
Democratic Steering and Policy Committee .... –6527
Democratic Cloakroom .... –6528
Office of the Democratic Leader .... –6537
Office of the Democratic Whip .... –6538
House Republican Conference .... –6544
Republican Congressional Committee, National .... –6547
Republican Policy Committee .... –6549
Republican Cloakroom .... –6650

House Officers

Office of the Clerk .... –6601
Office of Art and Archives .... –6612
Office of Employment and Counsel .... –6622
Legislative Computer Systems .... –6618
Office of Legislative Operations .... –6602
Legislative Resource Center .... –6612
Official Reporters .... –6615
Office of Communications .... –6611
Office of Interparliamentary Affairs .... –6579
Office of the Chaplain .... –6655
Office of the House Historian .... –6701
Office of the Parliamentarian .... –6731
Chief Administrative Officer .... –6860
First Call .... –6660
Administrative Counsel .... –6660
Periodical Press Gallery .... –6624
Press Gallery .... –6625
Radio/TV Correspondents' Gallery .... –6627
HIR Call Center .... –6165
HIR Information Systems Security .... –6165
Outplacement Services .... –9920
Office of Employee Assistance .... –6619
ADA Services .... –6860
Personnel and Benefits .... –9980
Child Care Center .... –0001
Payroll and Benefits .... –6604
Financial Counseling .... –6604
Members' Services .... –9970
Office Supply Service .... –6860
House Gift Shop .... –6860
Mail List/Processing .... –6860
Mailing Services .... –6860
Contractor Management .... –6860
Photography .... –6623
House Recording Studio .... –6613
Furniture Support Services .... –6610
House Office Service Center .... –6860
Budget .... –6604
Financial Counseling .... –6604
Procurement Management .... –9940
Office of the Sergeant at Arms .... –6634

House Commissions and Offices

Congressional Executive Commission on China	–6481
Commission on Security and Cooperation in Europe	–6460
Commission on Congressional Mailing Standards	–6461
Office of the Law Revision Counsel	–6711
Office of Emergency Management	–6462
Office of the Legislative Counsel	–6721
General Counsel	–6532
Architect of the Capitol	–6906
Attending Physician	–6907
Congressional Budget Office	–6925

Liaison Offices

Air Force	–6854
Army	–6855
Coast Guard	–6856
Navy	–6857
Office of Personnel Management	–6858
Veterans' Administration	–6859

TERMS OF SERVICE

EXPIRATION OF THE TERMS OF SENATORS

CLASS I.—SENATORS WHOSE TERMS OF SERVICE EXPIRE IN 2019

[33 Senators in this group: Republicans, 8; Democrats, 23; Independents, 2]

Name	Party	Residence
Baldwin, Tammy	D.	Madison, WI.
Barrasso, John [1]	R.	Casper, WY.
Brown, Sherrod	D.	Cleveland, OH.
Cantwell, Maria	D.	Edmonds, WA.
Cardin, Benjamin L.	D.	Baltimore, MD.
Carper, Thomas R.	D.	Wilmington, DE.
Casey, Robert P., Jr.	D.	Scranton, PA.
Corker, Bob	R.	Chattanooga, TN.
Cruz, Ted	R.	Houston, TX.
Donnelly, Joe	D.	Granger, IN.
Feinstein, Dianne [2]	D.	San Francisco, CA.
Fischer, Deb	R.	Valentine, NE.
Flake, Jeff	R.	Mesa, AZ.
Gillibrand, Kirsten E. [3]	D.	Brunswick, NY.
Hatch, Orrin G.	R.	Salt Lake City, UT.
Heinrich, Martin	D.	Albuquerque, NM.
Heitkamp, Heidi	D.	Mandan, ND.
Heller, Dean [4]	R.	Carson City, NV.
Hirono, Mazie K.	D.	Honolulu, HI.
Kaine, Tim	D.	Richmond, VA.
King, Angus S., Jr.	I.	Brunswick, ME.
Klobuchar, Amy	D.	Minneapolis, MN.
Manchin, Joe III [5]	D.	Fairmont, WV.
McCaskill, Claire	D.	Kirkwood, MO.
Menendez, Robert [6]	D.	Paramus, NJ.
Murphy, Christopher	D.	Cheshire, CT.
Nelson, Bill	D.	Orlando, FL.
Sanders, Bernard	I.	Burlington, VT.
Stabenow, Debbie	D.	Lansing, MI.
Tester, Jon	D.	Big Sandy, MT.
Warren, Elizabeth	D.	Cambridge, MA.
Whitehouse, Sheldon	D.	Newport, RI.
Wicker, Roger F. [7]	R.	Tupelo, MS.

[1] Senator Barrasso was appointed on June 22, 2007, to fill the vacancy caused by the death of Senator Craig Thomas and took the oath of office on June 25, 2007; won the special election on November 4, 2008, for the term ending January 3, 2013; elected to a full term on November 6, 2012.

[2] Senator Feinstein won the special election on November 3, 1992, for the term ending January 3, 1995, to fill the vacancy caused by the resignation of Senator Pete Wilson and took the oath of office on November 10, 1992, replacing appointed Senator John Seymour; elected to a full term on November 8, 1994.

[3] Senator Gillibrand was appointed on January 23, 2009, to fill the vacancy caused by the resignation of Senator Hillary Rodham Clinton and took the oath of office on January 27, 2009; won the special election on November 2, 2010, for the term ending January 3, 2013; elected to a full term on November 6, 2012.

[4] Senator Heller was appointed on May 3, 2011, to fill the vacancy caused by the resignation of Senator John Ensign and took the oath of office on May 9, 2011; elected to a full term on November 6, 2012.

[5] Senator Manchin won the special election on November 2, 2010, for the term ending January 3, 2013, to fill the vacancy caused by the death of Senator Robert C. Byrd and took the oath of office on November 15, 2010, replacing appointed Senator Carte P. Goodwin; elected to a full term on November 6, 2012.

[6] Senator Menendez was appointed on January 17, 2006, to fill the vacancy caused by the resignation of Senator Jon S. Corzine and took the oath of office on January 18, 2006; elected to a full term on November 7, 2006.

[7] Senator Wicker was appointed on December 31, 2007, to fill the vacancy caused by the resignation of Senator Trent Lott and took the oath of office on December 31, 2007; won the special election on November 4, 2008, for the term ending January 3, 2013; elected to a full term on November 6, 2012.

CLASS II.—SENATORS WHOSE TERMS OF SERVICE EXPIRE IN 2021

[33 Senators in this group: Republicans, 21; Democrats, 12]

Name	Party	Residence
Alexander, Lamar	R.	Maryville, TN.
Booker, Cory A.[1]	D.	Newark, NJ.
Capito, Shelley Moore	R.	Charleston, WV.
Cassidy, Bill	R.	Baton Rouge, LA.
Collins, Susan M.	R.	Bangor, ME.
Coons, Christopher A.[2]	D.	Wilmington, DE.
Cornyn, John	R.	Austin, TX.
Cotton, Tom	R.	Dardanelle, AR.
Daines, Steve	R.	Bozeman, MT.
Durbin, Richard J.	D.	Springfield, IL.
Enzi, Michael B.	R.	Gillette, WY.
Ernst, Joni	R.	Red Oak, IA.
Gardner, Cory	R.	Yuma, CO.
Graham, Lindsey	R.	Seneca, SC.
Hyde-Smith, Cindy[3]	R.	Brookhaven, MS.
Inhofe, James M.[4]	R.	Tulsa, OK.
Jones, Doug[5]	D.	Birmingham, AL.
McConnell, Mitch	R.	Louisville, KY.
Markey, Edward J.[6]	D.	Malden, MA.
Merkley, Jeff	D.	Portland, OR.
Perdue, David	R.	Glynn County, GA.
Peters, Gary C.	D.	Bloomfield Township, MI.
Reed, Jack	D.	Jamestown, RI.
Risch, James E.	R.	Boise, ID.
Roberts, Pat	R.	Dodge City, KS.
Rounds, Mike	R.	Fort Pierre, SD.
Sasse, Ben	R.	Fremont, NE.
Shaheen, Jeanne	D.	Madbury, NH.
Smith, Tina[7]	D.	Minneapolis, MN.
Sullivan, Dan	R.	Anchorage, AK.
Tillis, Thom	R.	Huntersville, NC.
Udall, Tom	D.	Santa Fe, NM.
Warner, Mark R.	D.	Alexandria, VA.

[1] Senator Booker won the special election on October 16, 2013, for the term ending January 3, 2015, to fill the vacancy caused by the death of Senator Frank Lautenberg and took the oath of office on October 31, 2013, replacing appointed Senator Jeffrey Chiesa; elected to a full term on November 4, 2014.

[2] Senator Coons won the special election on November 2, 2010, for the term ending January 3, 2015, to fill the vacancy caused by the resignation of Senator Joseph R. Biden, Jr., and took the oath of office on November 15, 2010, replacing appointed Senator Ted Kaufman; elected to a full term on November 4, 2014.

[3] Senator Hyde-Smith was appointed on April 2, 2018, to fill the vacancy caused by the resignation of Senator Thad Cochran and took the oath of office on April 9, 2018.

[4] Senator Inhofe won the special election on November 8, 1994, for the term ending January 3, 1997, to fill the vacancy caused by the resignation of Senator David Boren and took the oath of office on November 17, 1994; elected to a full term on November 5, 1996.

[5] Senator Jones won the special election on December 12, 2017, for the term ending January 3, 2021, to fill the vacancy caused by the resignation of Senator Jeff Sessions, and took the oath of office on January 3, 2018, replacing appointed Senator Luther Strange.

[6] Senator Markey won the special election on June 25, 2013, for the term ending January 3, 2015, to fill the vacancy caused by the resignation of Senator John F. Kerry, and took the oath of office on July 16, 2013, replacing appointed Senator William Cowan; elected to a full term on November 4, 2014.

[7] Senator Smith was appointed on January 3, 2018, to fill the vacancy caused by the resignation of Senator Al Franken.

CLASS III.—SENATORS WHOSE TERMS OF SERVICE EXPIRE IN 2023

[34 Senators in this group: Republicans, 22; Democrats, 12]

Name	Party	Residence
Bennet, Michael F.[1]	D.	Denver, CO.
Blumenthal, Richard	D.	Greenwich, CT.
Blunt, Roy	R.	Springfield, MO.
Boozman, John	R.	Rogers, AR.
Burr, Richard	R.	Winston-Salem, NC.
Cortez Masto, Catherine	D.	Las Vegas, NV.
Crapo, Mike	R.	Idaho Falls, ID.
Duckworth, Tammy	D.	Hoffman Estates, IL.
Grassley, Chuck	R.	New Hartford, IA.
Harris, Kamala D.	D.	Los Angeles, CA.
Hassan, Margaret Wood	D.	Newfields, NH.
Hoeven, John	R.	Bismarck, ND.
Isakson, Johnny	R.	Marietta, GA.
Johnson, Ron	R.	Oshkosh, WI.
Kennedy, John	R.	Madisonville, LA.
Lankford, James[2]	R.	Oklahoma City, OK.
Leahy, Patrick J.	D.	Middlesex, VT.
Lee, Mike	R.	Alpine, UT.
McCain, John	R.	Phoenix, AZ.
Moran, Jerry	R.	Manhattan, KS.
Murkowski, Lisa[3]	R.	Anchorage, AK.
Murray, Patty	D.	Seattle, WA.
Paul, Rand	R.	Bowling Green, KY.
Portman, Rob	R.	Terrace Park, OH.
Rubio, Marco	R.	West Miami, FL.
Schatz, Brian[4]	D.	Honolulu, HI.
Schumer, Charles E.	D.	Brooklyn, NY.
Scott, Tim[5]	R.	North Charleston, SC.
Shelby, Richard C.[6]	R.	Tuscaloosa, AL.
Thune, John	R.	Murdo, SD.
Toomey, Patrick J.	R.	Zionsville, PA.
Van Hollen, Chris	D.	Kensington, MD.
Wyden, Ron[7]	D.	Portland, OR.
Young, Todd	R.	Bloomington, IN.

[1] Senator Bennet was appointed on January 21, 2009, to fill the vacancy caused by the resignation of Senator Kenneth L. Salazar and took the oath of office on January 22, 2009; elected to a full term on November 2, 2010.

[2] Senator Lankford won the special election on November 4, 2014, for the term ending January 3, 2017, to fill the vacancy caused by the resignation of Senator Tom Coburn and took the oath of office on January 3, 2015; elected to a full term on November 8, 2016.

[3] Senator Murkowski was appointed on December 20, 2002, to fill the vacancy caused by the resignation of her father, Senator Frank Murkowski; elected to a full term on November 2, 2004.

[4] Senator Schatz was appointed on December 26, 2012, to fill the vacancy caused by the death of Senator Daniel Inouye and took the oath of office on December 27, 2012; won the special election on November 4, 2014, for the term ending January 3, 2017; elected to a full term on November 8, 2016.

[5] Senator Scott was appointed on January 2, 2013, to fill the vacancy caused by the resignation of Senator James DeMint and took the oath of office on January 3, 2013; won the special election on November 4, 2014, for the term ending January 3, 2017; elected to a full term on November 8, 2016.

[6] Senator Shelby changed party affiliation from Democrat to Republican on November 5, 1994.

[7] Senator Wyden won the special election on January 30, 1996, for the term ending January 3, 1999, to fill the vacancy caused by the resignation of Senator Robert Packwood and began service on February 6, 1996; elected to a full term on November 3, 1998.

CONTINUOUS SERVICE OF SENATORS

[Republicans in roman (51); Democrats in *italic* (47); Independents in SMALL CAPS (2); total, 100]

Rank	Name	State	Beginning of present service
1	*Leahy, Patrick J.*	Vermont	Jan. 3, 1975.
2	Hatch, Orrin G.	Utah	Jan. 3, 1977.
4	Grassley, Chuck †	Iowa	Jan. 3, 1981.
5	McConnell, Mitch	Kentucky	Jan. 3, 1985.
6	McCain, John †	Arizona	Jan. 3, 1987.
	Shelby, Richard C.†	Alabama	
7	*Feinstein, Dianne* [1]	California	Nov. 10, 1992.‡
8	*Murray, Patty*	Washington	
9	Inhofe, James M. † [2]	Oklahoma	Nov. 17, 1994. ‡
10	*Wyden, Ron* † [3]	Oregon	Feb. 6, 1996. ‡
11	Collins, Susan M.	Maine	Jan. 3, 1997.
	Durbin, Richard J. †	Illinois	
	Enzi, Michael B.	Wyoming	
	Reed, Jack †	Rhode Island	
	Roberts, Pat †	Kansas	
12	Crapo, Mike †	Idaho	Jan. 3, 1999.
	Schumer, Charles E. †	New York	
13	*Cantwell, Maria* †	Washington	Jan. 3, 2001.
	Carper, Thomas R.†	Delaware	
	Nelson, Bill †	Florida	
	Stabenow, Debbie †	Michigan	
14	Cornyn, John [4]	Texas	Dec. 2, 2002.
15	Murkowski, Lisa [5]	Alaska	Dec. 20, 2002.
16	Alexander, Lamar	Tennessee	Jan. 3, 2003.
	Graham, Lindsey †	South Carolina	
17	Burr, Richard †	North Carolina	Jan. 3, 2005.
	Isakson, Johnny †	Georgia	
	Thune, John †	South Dakota	
18	*Menendez, Robert* † [6]	New Jersey	Jan. 17, 2006.
19	*Brown, Sherrod* †	Ohio	Jan. 3, 2007.
	Cardin, Benjamin L. †	Maryland	
	Casey, Robert P., Jr.	Pennsylvania	
	Corker, Bob	Tennessee	
	Klobuchar, Amy	Minnesota	
	McCaskill, Claire	Missouri	
	SANDERS, BERNARD †	Vermont	
	Tester, Jon	Montana	
	Whitehouse, Sheldon	Rhode Island	
20	Barrasso, John [7]	Wyoming	June 22, 2007.
21	Wicker, Roger F. † [8]	Mississippi	Dec. 31, 2007.
22	*Merkley, Jeff*	Oregon	Jan. 3, 2009.
	Risch, James E.	Idaho	
	Shaheen, Jeanne	New Hampshire	
	Udall, Tom †	New Mexico	
	Warner, Mark R.	Virginia	
23	*Bennet, Michael F.* [9]	Colorado	Jan. 21, 2009.
24	*Gillibrand, Kirsten E.*† [10]	New York	Jan. 26, 2009.
26	*Coons, Christopher A.* [11]	Delaware	Nov. 15, 2010.
	Manchin, Joe III [12]	West Virginia	
27	*Blumenthal, Richard*	Connecticut	Jan. 3, 2011.
	Blunt, Roy	Missouri	
	Boozman, John †	Arkansas	
	Hoeven, John	North Dakota	
	Johnson, Ron	Wisconsin	

CONTINUOUS SERVICE OF SENATORS—CONTINUED

[Republicans in roman (51); Democrats in *italic* (47); Independents in SMALL CAPS (2); total, 100]

Rank	Name	State	Beginning of present service
	Lee, Mike	Utah	
	Moran, Jerry	Kansas	
	Paul, Rand	Kentucky	
	Portman, Rob	Ohio	
	Rubio, Marco	Florida	
	Toomey, Patrick J.	Pennsylvania	
28	Heller, Dean † [13]	Nevada	May 9, 2011.
29	*Schatz, Brian*[14]	Hawaii	Dec. 26, 2012.
30	Scott, Tim † [15]	South Carolina	Jan. 2, 2013.
31	*Baldwin, Tammy*	Wisconsin	Jan. 3, 2013.
	Cruz, Ted	Texas	
	Donnelly, Joe	Indiana	
	Fischer, Deb	Nebraska	
	Flake, Jeff	Arizona	
	Heinrich, Martin	New Mexico	
	Heitkamp, Heidi	North Dakota	
	Hirono, Mazie K.	Hawaii	
	Kaine, Tim	Virginia	
	KING, ANGUS S., JR.	Maine	
	Murphy, Christopher	Connecticut	
	Warren, Elizabeth	Massachusetts	
32	*Markey, Edward J.* † [16]	Massachusetts	July 16, 2013. ‡
33	*Booker, Cory A.* [17]	New Jersey	Oct. 31, 2013. ‡
34	Capito, Shelley Moore †	West Virginia	Jan. 3, 2015.
	Cassidy, Bill †	Louisiana	
	Cotton, Tom †	Arkansas	
	Daines, Steve †	Montana	
	Ernst, Joni	Iowa	
	Gardner, Cory †	Colorado	
	Lankford, James †	Oklahoma	
	Perdue, David	Georgia	
	Peters, Gary C. †	Michigan	
	Rounds, Mike	South Dakota	
	Sasse, Ben	Nebraska	
	Sulivan, Dan	Alaska	
	Tillis, Thom	North Carolina	
	Cortez Masto, Catherine	Nevada	Jan. 3, 2017.
	Duckworth, Tammy †	Illinois	
	Harris, Kamala	California	
	Hassan, Maggie	New Hampshire	
	Kennedy, John †	Louisiana	
	Van Hollen, Chris †	Maryland	
	Young, Todd †	Indiana	
	Jones, Doug [18]	Alabama	Jan. 3, 2018.‡
	Smith, Tina [19]	Minnesota	Jan. 3, 2018.
	Hyde-Smith, Cindy [20]	Mississippi	April 9, 2018.

† Served in the House of Representatives previous to service in the Senate.

‡ Senators elected to complete unexpired terms typically begin their terms on the day following the election, but individual cases may vary.

[1] Senator Feinstein won the special election on November 3, 1992, for the term ending January 3, 1995, to fill the vacancy caused by the resignation of Senator Pete Wilson and took the oath of office on November 10, 1992, replacing appointed Senator John Seymour; elected to a full term on November 8, 1994.

[2] Senator Inhofe won the special election on November 8, 1994, for the term ending January 3, 1997, to fill the vacancy caused by the resignation of Senator David Boren and took the oath of office on November 17, 1994; elected to a full term on November 5, 1996.

[3] Senator Wyden won the special election on January 30, 1996, for the term ending January 3, 1999, to fill the vacancy caused by the resignation of Senator Robert Packwood and began service on February 6, 1996; elected to a full term on November 3, 1998.

[4] Senator Cornyn was elected on November 5, 2002, for the 6-year term commencing January 3, 2003; subsequently appointed on December 2, 2002, to fill the vacancy caused by the resignation of Senator Phil Gramm.

[5] Senator Murkowski was appointed on December 20, 2002, to fill the vacancy caused by the resignation of her father, Senator Frank Murkowski; elected to a full term on November 2, 2004.

[6] Senator Menendez was appointed on January 17, 2006, to fill the vacancy caused by the resignation of Senator Jon S. Corzine and took the oath of office on January 18, 2006; elected to a full term on November 7, 2006.

[7] Senator Barrasso was appointed on June 22, 2007, to fill the vacancy caused by the death of Senator Craig Thomas and took the oath of office on June 25, 2007; won the special election on November 4, 2008, for the term ending January 3, 2013; elected to a full term on November 6, 2012.

[8] Senator Wicker was appointed on December 31, 2007, to fill the vacancy caused by the resignation of Senator Trent Lott and took the oath of office on December 31, 2007; won the special election on November 4, 2008, for the term ending January 3, 2013; elected to a full term on November 6, 2012.

[9] Senator Bennet was appointed on January 21, 2009, to fill the vacancy caused by the resignation of Senator Kenneth L. Salazar and took the oath of office on January 22, 2009; elected to a full term on November 2, 2010.

[10] Senator Gillibrand was appointed on January 23, 2009, to fill the vacancy caused by the resignation of Senator Hillary Rodham Clinton and took the oath of office on January 27, 2009; won the special election on November 2, 2010, for the term ending January 3, 2013; elected to a full term on November 6, 2012.

[11] Senator Coons won the special election on November 2, 2010, for the term ending January 3, 2015, to fill the vacancy caused by the resignation of Senator Joseph R. Biden, Jr., and took the oath of office on November 15, 2010, replacing appointed Senator Ted Kaufman; elected to a full term on November 4, 2014.

[12] Senator Manchin won the special election on November 2, 2010, for the term ending January 3, 2013, to fill the vacancy caused by the death of Senator Robert C. Byrd and took the oath of office on November 15, 2010, replacing appointed Senator Carte P. Goodwin; elected to a full term on November 6, 2012.

[13] Senator Heller was appointed on May 3, 2011, to fill the vacancy caused by the resignation of Senator John Ensign and took the oath of office on May 9, 2011; elected to a full term on November 6, 2012.

[14] Senator Schatz was appointed on December 26, 2012, to fill the vacancy caused by the death of Senator Daniel Inouye and took the oath of office on December 27, 2012; won the special election on November 4, 2014, for the term ending January 3, 2017; elected to a full term on November 8, 2016.

[15] Senator Scott was appointed on January 2, 2013, to fill the vacancy caused by the resignation of Senator James DeMint and took the oath of office on January 3, 2013; won the special election on November 4, 2014, for the term ending January 3, 2017; elected to a full term on November 8, 2016.

[16] Senator Markey won the special election on June 25, 2013, for the term ending January 3, 2015, to fill the vacancy caused by the resignation of Senator John F. Kerry, and took the oath of office on July 16, 2013, replacing appointed Senator William Cowan; elected to a full term on November 4, 2014.

[17] Senator Booker won the special election on October 16, 2013, for the term ending January 3, 2015, to fill the vacancy caused by the death of Senator Frank Lautenberg and took the oath of office on October 31, 2013, replacing appointed Senator Jeffrey Chiesa; elected to a full term on November 4, 2014.

[18] Senator Jones won the special election on December 12, 2017, for the term ending January 3, 2021, to fill the vacancy caused by the resignation of Senator Jeff Sessions, and took the oath of office on January 3, 2018, replacing appointed Senator Luther Strange.

[19] Senator Tina Smith was appointed on January 3, 2018, to fill the vacancy caused by the resignation of Senator Al Franken, to serve until a special election is held on November 6, 2018, for the remainder of the term ending January 3, 2021.

[20] Senator Cindy Hyde-Smith was appointed on April 2, 2018, to fill the vacancy caused by the resignation of Senator Thad Cochran, to serve until a special election is held on November 6, 2018, for the remainder of the term ending January 3, 2021.

CONGRESSES IN WHICH REPRESENTATIVES, RESIDENT COMMISSIONER, AND DELEGATES HAVE SERVED WITH BEGINNING OF PRESENT SERVICE

[*Elected to fill a vacancy; Republicans in roman (236); Democrats in *italic* (193); Vacancies (6); Resident Commissioner and Delegates in **boldface** (6); total, 441]

Name	State	Congresses (inclusive)	Beginning of present service
23 terms, consecutive			
Young, Don	AK	*93d to 115th	Mar. 6, 1973
20 terms, consecutive			
Sensenbrenner, F. James, Jr.	WI	96th to 115th	Jan. 3, 1979
19 terms, consecutive			
Hoyer, Steny H.	MD	*97th to 115th	May 19, 1981
Rogers, Harold	KY	97th to 115th	Jan. 3, 1981
Smith, Christopher H.	NJ	97th to 115th	Jan. 3, 1981
18 terms, consecutive			
Kaptur, Marcy	OH	98th to 115th	Jan. 3, 1983
Levin, Sander M.	MI	98th to 115th	Jan. 3, 1983
17 terms, consecutive			
Barton, Joe	TX	99th to 115th	Jan. 3, 1985
Visclosky, Peter J.	IN	99th to 115th	Jan. 3, 1985
16 terms, consecutive			
DeFazio, Peter A.	OR	100th to 115th	Jan. 3, 1987
Duncan, John J., Jr.	TN	*100th to 115th	Nov. 8, 1988
Lewis, John	GA	100th to 115th	Jan. 3, 1987
Pallone, Frank, Jr.	NJ	*100th to 115th	Nov. 8, 1988
Pelosi, Nancy	CA	*100th to 115th	June 2, 1987
Smith, Lamar	TX	100th to 115th	Jan. 3, 1987
Upton, Fred	MI	100th to 115th	Jan. 3, 1987
15 terms, consecutive			
Engel, Eliot L.	NY	101st to 115th	Jan. 3, 1989
Lowey, Nita M.	NY	101st to 115th	Jan. 3, 1989
Neal, Richard E.	MA	101st to 115th	Jan. 3, 1989
Rohrabacher, Dana	CA	101st to 115th	Jan. 3, 1989
Ros-Lehtinen, Ileana	FL	*101st to 115th	Aug. 29, 1989
Serrano, José E.	NY	*101st to 115th	Mar. 20, 1990
15 terms, not consecutive			
Price, David E.	NC	100th to 103d, 105th to 115th.	Jan 3. 1997
14 terms, consecutive			
DeLauro, Rosa L.	CT	102d to 115th	Jan. 3, 1991
Johnson, Sam	TX	*102d to 115th	May 8, 1991
Nadler, Jerrold	NY	*102d to 115th	Nov. 3, 1992
Peterson, Collin C.	MN	102d to 115th	Jan. 3, 1991
Waters, Maxine	CA	102d to 115th	Jan. 3, 1991

CONGRESSES IN WHICH REPRESENTATIVES, RESIDENT COMMISSIONER, AND DELEGATES HAVE SERVED WITH BEGINNING OF PRESENT SERVICE—CONTINUED

[* Elected to fill a vacancy; Republicans in roman (236); Democrats in *italic* (193); Vacancies (6); Resident Commissioner and Delegates in **boldface** (6); total, 441]

Name	State	Congresses (inclusive)	Beginning of present service
14 terms, not consecutive			
Cooper, Jim	TN	98th to 103d and 108th to 115th.	Jan. 3, 2003
13 terms, consecutive			
Bishop, Sanford D., Jr.	GA	103d to 115th	Jan. 3, 1993
Calvert, Ken	CA	103d to 115th	Jan. 3, 1993
Clyburn, James E.	SC	103d to 115th	Jan. 3, 1993
Eshoo, Anna G.	CA	103d to 115th	Jan. 3, 1993
Goodlatte, Bob	VA	103d to 115th	Jan. 3, 1993
Green, Gene	TX	103d to 115th	Jan. 3, 1993
Gutiérrez, Luis V.	IL	103d to 115th	Jan. 3, 1993
Hastings, Alcee L.	FL	103d to 115th	Jan. 3, 1993
Johnson, Eddie Bernice	TX	103d to 115th	Jan. 3, 1993
King, Peter T.	NY	103d to 115th	Jan. 3, 1993
Lucas, Frank D.	OK	*103d to 115th	May 10, 1994
Maloney, Carolyn B.	NY	103d to 115th	Jan. 3, 1993
Roybal-Allard, Lucille	CA	103d to 115th	Jan. 3, 1993
Royce, Edward R.	CA	103d to 115th	Jan. 3, 1993
Rush, Bobby L.	IL	103d to 115th	Jan. 3, 1993
Scott, Robert C. ''Bobby''	VA	103d to 115th	Jan. 3, 1993
Thompson, Bennie G.	MS	*103d to 115th	Apr. 13, 1993
Velázquez, Nydia M.	NY	103d to 115th	Jan. 3, 1993
12 terms, consecutive			
Blumenauer, Earl	OR	*104th to 115th	May 21, 1996
Cummings, Elijah E.	MD	*104th to 115th	Apr. 16, 1996
Doggett, Lloyd	TX	104th to 115th	Jan. 3, 1995
Doyle, Michael F.	PA	104th to 115th	Jan. 3, 1995
Frelinghuysen, Rodney P.	NJ	104th to 115th	Jan. 3, 1995
Jackson Lee, Sheila	TX	104th to 115th	Jan. 3, 1995
Jones, Walter B.	NC	104th to 115th	Jan. 3, 1995
LoBiondo, Frank A.	NJ	104th to 115th	Jan. 3, 1995
Lofgren, Zoe	CA	104th to 115th	Jan. 3, 1995
Thornberry, Mac	TX	104th to 115th	Jan. 3, 1995
11 terms, consecutive			
Aderholt, Robert B.	AL	105th to 115th	Jan. 3, 1997
Brady, Kevin	TX	105th to 115th	Jan. 3, 1997
Brady, Robert A.	PA	*105th to 115th	May 19, 1998
Davis, Danny K.	IL	105th to 115th	Jan. 3, 1997
DeGette, Diana	CO	105th to 115th	Jan. 3, 1997
Granger, Kay	TX	105th to 115th	Jan. 3, 1997
Kind, Ron	WI	105th to 115th	Jan. 3, 1997
Lee, Barbara	CA	*105th to 115th	Apr. 7, 1998
McGovern, James P.	MA	105th to 115th	Jan. 3, 1997
Meeks, Gregory W.	NY	*105th to 115th	Feb. 3, 1998
Pascrell, Bill, Jr.	NJ	105th to 115th	Jan. 3, 1997
Sessions, Pete	TX	105th to 115th	Jan. 3, 1997
Sherman, Brad	CA	105th to 115th	Jan. 3, 1997
Shimkus, John	IL	105th to 115th	Jan. 3, 1997

CONGRESSES IN WHICH REPRESENTATIVES, RESIDENT COMMISSIONER, AND DELEGATES HAVE SERVED WITH BEGINNING OF PRESENT SERVICE—CONTINUED

[*Elected to fill a vacancy; Republicans in roman (236); Democrats in *italic* (193); Vacancies (6); Resident Commissioner and Delegates in **boldface** (6); total, 441]

Name	State	Congresses (inclusive)	Beginning of present service
Smith, Adam	WA	105th to 115th	Jan. 3, 1997
11 terms, not consecutive			
Chabot, Steve	OH	104th to 110th and 113th to 115th.	Jan. 3, 2011
10 terms, consecutive			
Capuano, Michael E.	MA	106th to 115th	Jan. 3, 1999
Crowley, Joseph	NY	106th to 115th	Jan. 3, 1999
Larson, John B.	CT	106th to 115th	Jan. 3, 1999
Napolitano, Grace F.	CA	106th to 115th	Jan. 3, 1999
Ryan, Paul D.	WI	106th to 115th	Jan. 3, 1999
Schakowsky, Janice D.	IL	106th to 115th	Jan. 3, 1999
Simpson, Michael K.	ID	106th to 115th	Jan. 3, 1999
Thompson, Mike	CA	106th to 115th	Jan. 3, 1999
Walden, Greg	OR	106th to 115th	Jan. 3, 1999
9 terms, consecutive			
Clay, Wm. Lacy	MO	107th to 115th	Jan. 3, 2001
Culberson, John Abney	TX	107th to 115th	Jan. 3, 2001
Davis, Susan A.	CA	107th to 115th	Jan. 3, 2001
Graves, Sam	MO	107th to 115th	Jan. 3, 2001
Issa, Darrell E.	CA	107th to 115th	Jan. 3, 2001
Langevin, James R.	RI	107th to 115th	Jan. 3, 2001
Larsen, Rick	WA	107th to 115th	Jan. 3, 2001
Lynch, Stephen F.	MA	*107th to 115th	Oct. 16, 2001
McCollum, Betty	MN	107th to 115th	Jan. 3, 2001
Schiff, Adam B.	CA	107th to 115th	Jan. 3, 2001
Shuster, Bill	PA	*107th to 115th	May 15, 2001
Wilson, Joe	SC	*107th to 115th	Dec. 18, 2001
8 terms, consecutive			
Bishop, Rob	UT	108th to 115th	Jan. 3, 2003
Blackburn, Marsha	TN	108th to 115th	Jan. 3, 2003
Burgess, Michael C.	TX	108th to 115th	Jan. 3, 2003
Butterfield, G. K.	NC	*108th to 115th	July 20, 2004
Carter, John R.	TX	108th to 115th	Jan. 3, 2003
Cole, Tom	OK	108th to 115th	Jan. 3, 2003
Diaz-Balart, Mario	FL	108th to 115th	Jan. 3, 2003
Grijalva, Raúl M.	AZ	108th to 115th	Jan. 3, 2003
Hensarling, Jeb	TX	108th to 115th	Jan. 3, 2003
King, Steve	IA	108th to 115th	Jan. 3, 2003
Nunes, Devin	CA	108th to 115th	Jan. 3, 2003
Rogers, Mike	AL	108th to 115th	Jan. 3, 2003
Ruppersberger, C. A. Dutch	MD	108th to 115th	Jan. 3, 2003
Ryan, Tim	OH	108th to 115th	Jan. 3, 2003
Sánchez, Linda T.	CA	108th to 115th	Jan. 3, 2003
Scott, David	GA	108th to 115th	Jan. 3, 2003
Turner, Michael R.	OH	108th to 115th	Jan. 3, 2003

CONGRESSES IN WHICH REPRESENTATIVES, RESIDENT COMMISSIONER, AND DELEGATES HAVE SERVED WITH BEGINNING OF PRESENT SERVICE—CONTINUED

[* Elected to fill a vacancy; Republicans in roman (236); Democrats in *italic* (193); Vacancies (6); Resident Commissioner and Delegates in **boldface** (6); total, 441]

Name	State	Congresses (inclusive)	Beginning of present service
7 terms, consecutive			
Cleaver, Emanuel	MO	109th to 115th	Jan. 3, 2005
Conaway, K. Michael	TX	109th to 115th	Jan. 3, 2005
Costa, Jim	CA	109th to 115th	Jan. 3, 2005
Cuellar, Henry	TX	109th to 115th	Jan. 3, 2005
Fortenberry, Jeff	NE	109th to 115th	Jan. 3, 2005
Foxx, Virginia	NC	109th to 115th	Jan. 3, 2005
Gohmert, Louie	TX	109th to 115th	Jan. 3, 2005
Green, Al	TX	109th to 115th	Jan. 3, 2005
Higgins, Brian	NY	109th to 115th	Jan. 3, 2005
Lipinski, Daniel	IL	109th to 115th	Jan. 3, 2005
Marchant, Kenny	TX	109th to 115th	Jan. 3, 2005
Matsui, Doris O.	CA	*109th to 115th	Mar. 8, 2005
McCaul, Michael T.	TX	109th to 115th	Jan. 3, 2005
McHenry, Patrick T.	NC	109th to 115th	Jan. 3, 2005
McMorris Rodgers, Cathy	WA	109th to 115th	Jan. 3, 2005
Moore, Gwen	WI	109th to 115th	Jan. 3, 2005
Poe, Ted	TX	109th to 115th	Jan. 3, 2005
Reichert, David G.	WA	109th to 115th	Jan. 3, 2005
Sires, Albio	NJ	*109th to 115th	Nov. 7, 2006
Wasserman Schultz, Debbie	FL	109th to 115th	Jan. 3, 2005
7 terms, not consecutive			
Pearce, Stevan	NM	108th to 110th and 112th to 115th.	Jan. 3. 2011
6 terms, consecutive			
Bilirakis, Gus M.	FL	110th to 115th	Jan. 3, 2007
Buchanan, Vern	FL	110th to 115th	Jan. 3, 2007
Carson, André	IN	*110th to 115th	Mar. 11, 2008
Castor, Kathy	FL	110th to 115th	Jan. 3, 2007
Clarke, Yvette D.	NY	110th to 115th	Jan. 3, 2007
Cohen, Steve	TN	110th to 115th	Jan. 3, 2007
Courtney, Joe	CT	110th to 115th	Jan. 3, 2007
Ellison, Keith	MN	110th to 115th	Jan. 3, 2007
Fudge, Marcia L.	OH	*110th to 115th	Nov. 18, 2008
Johnson, Henry C. "Hank", Jr.	GA	110th to 115th	Jan. 3, 2007
Jordan, Jim	OH	110th to 115th	Jan. 3, 2007
Lamborn, Doug	CO	110th to 115th	Jan. 3, 2007
Latta, Robert E.	OH	*110th to 115th	Dec. 11, 2007
Loebsack, David	IA	110th to 115th	Jan. 3, 2007
McCarthy, Kevin	CA	110th to 115th	Jan. 3, 2007
McNerney, Jerry	CA	110th to 115th	Jan. 3, 2007
Perlmutter, Ed	CO	110th to 115th	Jan. 3, 2007
Roskam, Peter J.	IL	110th to 115th	Jan. 3, 2007
Sarbanes, John P.	MD	110th to 115th	Jan. 3, 2007
Scalise, Steve	LA	*110th to 115th	May 3, 2008
Smith, Adrian	NE	110th to 115th	Jan. 3, 2007
Speier, Jackie	CA	*110th to 115th	Apr. 8, 2008
Tsongas, Niki	MA	*110th to 115th	Oct. 16, 2007

CONGRESSES IN WHICH REPRESENTATIVES, RESIDENT COMMISSIONER, AND DELEGATES HAVE SERVED WITH BEGINNING OF PRESENT SERVICE—CONTINUED

[* Elected to fill a vacancy; Republicans in roman (236); Democrats in *italic* (193); Vacancies (6); Resident Commissioner and Delegates in **boldface** (6); total, 441]

Name	State	Congresses (inclusive)	Beginning of present service
Walz, Timothy J.	MN	110th to 115th	Jan. 3, 2007
Welch, Peter	VT	110th to 115th	Jan. 3, 2007
Wittman, Robert J.	VA	*110th to 115th	Dec. 11, 2007
Yarmuth, John A.	KY	110th to 115th	Jan. 3, 2007
6 terms, not consecutive			
Nolan, Richard M.	MN	94th to 96th and 113th to 115th.	Jan. 3, 2013
Sanford, Mark	SC	*104th to 106th and 113th to 115th.	May 7, 2013
5 terms, consecutive			
Chu, Judy	CA	*111th to 115th	July 14, 2009
Coffman, Mike	CO	111th to 115th	Jan. 3, 2009
Connolly, Gerald E.	VA	111th to 115th	Jan. 3, 2009
Deutch, Theodore E.	FL	*111th to 115th	Apr. 13, 2010
Garamendi, John	CA	*111th to 115th	Nov. 3, 2009
Graves, Tom	GA	*111th to 115th	June 8, 2010
Guthrie, Brett	KY	111th to 115th	Jan. 3, 2009
Harper, Gregg	MS	111th to 115th	Jan. 3, 2009
Himes, James A.	CT	111th to 115th	Jan. 3, 2009
Hunter, Duncan	CA	111th to 115th	Jan. 3, 2009
Jenkins, Lynn	KS	111th to 115th	Jan. 3, 2009
Lance, Leonard	NJ	111th to 115th	Jan. 3, 2009
Luetkemeyer, Blaine	MO	111th to 115th	Jan. 3, 2009
Luján, Ben Ray	NM	111th to 115th	Jan. 3, 2009
McClintock, Tom	CA	111th to 115th	Jan. 3, 2009
Olson, Pete	TX	111th to 115th	Jan. 3, 2009
Paulsen, Erik	MN	111th to 115th	Jan. 3, 2009
Pingree, Chellie	ME	111th to 115th	Jan. 3, 2009
Polis, Jared	CO	111th to 115th	Jan. 3, 2009
Posey, Bill	FL	111th to 115th	Jan. 3, 2009
Quigley, Mike	IL	*111th to 115th	Apr. 7, 2009
Reed, Tom	NY	*111th to 115th	Nov. 2, 2010
Roe, David P.	TN	111th to 115th	Jan. 3, 2009
Rooney, Thomas J.	FL	111th to 115th	Jan. 3, 2009
Schrader, Kurt	OR	111th to 115th	Jan. 3, 2009
Thompson, Glenn	PA	111th to 115th	Jan. 3, 2009
Tonko, Paul	NY	111th to 115th	Jan. 3, 2009
5 terms, not consecutive			
Foster, Bill [1]	IL	*110th to 111th and 113th to 115th.	Jan. 3, 2013
Walberg, Tim	MI	110th and 112th to 115th.	Jan. 3, 2011
4 terms, consecutive			
Amash, Justin	MI	112th to 115th	Jan. 3, 2011
Amodei, Mark E.	NV	*112th to 115th	Sept. 13, 2011
Barletta, Lou	PA	112th to 115th	Jan. 3, 2011

CONGRESSES IN WHICH REPRESENTATIVES, RESIDENT COMMISSIONER, AND DELEGATES HAVE SERVED WITH BEGINNING OF PRESENT SERVICE—CONTINUED

[*Elected to fill a vacancy; Republicans in roman (236); Democrats in *italic* (193); Vacancies (6); Resident Commissioner and Delegates in **boldface** (6); total, 441]

Name	State	Congresses (inclusive)	Beginning of present service
Bass, Karen	CA	112th to 115th	Jan. 3, 2011
Benishek, Dan	MI	112th to 115th	Jan. 3, 2011
Black, Diane	TN	112th to 115th	Jan. 3, 2011
Bonamici, Suzanne	OR	*112th to 115th	Jan. 31, 2012
Brooks, Mo	AL	112th to 115th	Jan. 3, 2011
Bucshon, Larry	IN	112th to 115th	Jan. 3, 2011
Cicilline, David N.	RI	112th to 115th	Jan. 3, 2011
Crawford, Eric A. ''Rick''	AR	112th to 115th	Jan. 3, 2011
DelBene, Suzan K.	WA	*112th to 115th	Nov. 6, 2012
Denham, Jeff	CA	112th to 115th	Jan. 3, 2011
DesJarlais, Scott	TN	112th to 115th	Jan. 3, 2011
Duffy, Sean P.	WI	112th to 115th	Jan. 3, 2011
Duncan, Jeff	SC	112th to 115th	Jan. 3, 2011
Fleischmann, Charles J. ''Chuck''	TN	112th to 115th	Jan. 3, 2011
Flores, Bill	TX	112th to 115th	Jan. 3, 2011
Gibbs, Bob	OH	112th to 115th	Jan. 3, 2011
Gosar, Paul A.	AZ	112th to 115th	Jan. 3, 2011
Gowdy, Trey	SC	112th to 115th	Jan. 3, 2011
Griffith, H. Morgan	VA	112th to 115th	Jan. 3, 2011
Harris, Andy	MD	112th to 115th	Jan. 3, 2011
Hartzler, Vicky	MO	112th to 115th	Jan. 3, 2011
Herrera Beutler, Jaime	WA	112th to 115th	Jan. 3, 2011
Huizenga, Bill	MI	112th to 115th	Jan. 3, 2011
Hultgren, Randy	IL	112th to 115th	Jan. 3, 2011
Johnson, Bill	OH	112th to 115th	Jan. 3, 2011
Keating, William R.	MA	112th to 115th	Jan. 3, 2011
Kelly, Mike	PA	112th to 115th	Jan. 3, 2011
Kinzinger, Adam	IL	112th to 115th	Jan. 3, 2011
Labrador, Raúl R.	ID	112th to 115th	Jan. 3, 2011
Long, Billy	MO	112th to 115th	Jan. 3, 2011
Marino, Tom	PA	112th to 115th	Jan. 3, 2011
Massie, Thomas	KY	*112th to 115th	Nov. 6, 2012
McKinley, David B.	WV	112th to 115th	Jan. 3, 2011
Noem, Kristi L.	SD	112th to 115th	Jan. 3, 2011
Palazzo, Steven M.	MS	112th to 115th	Jan. 3, 2011
Payne, Donald M., Jr.	NJ	*112th to 115th	Nov. 6, 2012
Renacci, James B.	OH	112th to 115th	Jan. 3, 2011
Richmond, Cedric L.	LA	112th to 115th	Jan. 3, 2011
Roby, Martha	AL	112th to 115th	Jan. 3, 2011
Rokita, Todd	IN	112th to 115th	Jan. 3, 2011
Ross, Dennis A.	FL	112th to 115th	Jan. 3, 2011
Schweikert, David	AZ	112th to 115th	Jan. 3, 2011
Scott, Austin	GA	112th to 115th	Jan. 3, 2011
Sewell, Terri A.	AL	112th to 115th	Jan. 3, 2011
Stivers, Steve	OH	112th to 115th	Jan. 3, 2011
Tipton, Scott R.	CO	112th to 115th	Jan. 3, 2011
Webster, Daniel	FL	112th to 115th	Jan. 3, 2011
Wilson, Frederica S.	FL	112th to 115th	Jan. 3, 2011
Womack, Steve	AR	112th to 115th	Jan. 3, 2011
Woodall, Rob	GA	112th to 115th	Jan. 3, 2011
Yoder, Kevin	KS	112th to 115th	Jan. 3, 2011

CONGRESSES IN WHICH REPRESENTATIVES, RESIDENT COMMISSIONER, AND DELEGATES HAVE SERVED WITH BEGINNING OF PRESENT SERVICE—CONTINUED

[* Elected to fill a vacancy; Republicans in roman (236); Democrats in *italic* (193); Vacancies (6); Resident Commissioner and Delegates in **boldface** (6); total, 441]

Name	State	Congresses (inclusive)	Beginning of present service
4 terms, not consecutive			
Hanabusa, Colleen	HI	*112th to 113th and 114th to 115th.	Nov. 8, 2016
Shea-Porter, Carol	NH	110th to 111th and 113th; 115th.	Jan. 3, 2017
Titus, Dina	NV	111th and 113th to 115th.	Jan. 3, 2013
3 terms, consecutive			
Adams, Alma S.	NC	*113th to 115th	Nov. 4, 2014
Barr, Andy	KY	113th to 115th	Jan. 3, 2013
Beatty, Joyce	OH	113th to 115th	Jan. 3, 2013
Bera, Ami	CA	113th to 115th	Jan. 3, 2013
Brat, Dave	VA	*113th to 115th	Nov. 4, 2014
Brooks, Susan W.	IN	113th to 115th	Jan. 3, 2013
Brownley, Julia	CA	113th to 115th	Jan. 3, 2013
Bustos, Cheri	IL	113th to 115th	Jan. 3, 2013
Byrne, Bradley	AL	*113th to 115th	Dec. 17, 2013
Cárdenas, Tony	CA	113th to 115th	Jan. 3, 2013
Cartwright, Matt	PA	113th to 115th	Jan. 3, 2013
Castro, Joaquin	TX	113th to 115th	Jan. 3, 2013
Clark, Katherine M.	MA	*113th to 115th	Dec. 10, 2013
Collins, Chris	NY	113th to 115th	Jan. 3, 2013
Collins, Doug	GA	113th to 115th	Jan. 3, 2013
Cook, Paul	CA	113th to 115th	Jan. 3, 2013
Cramer, Kevin	ND	113th to 115th	Jan. 3, 2013
Davis, Rodney	IL	113th to 115th	Jan. 3, 2013
Delaney, John K.	MD	113th to 115th	Jan. 3, 2013
DeSantis, Ron	FL	113th to 115th	Jan. 3, 2013
Esty, Elizabeth H.	CT	113th to 115th	Jan. 3, 2013
Frankel, Lois	FL	113th to 115th	Jan. 3, 2013
Gabbard, Tulsi	HI	113th to 115th	Jan. 3, 2013
Heck, Denny	WA	113th to 115th	Jan. 3, 2013
Holding, George	NC	113th to 115th	Jan. 3, 2013
Hudson, Richard	NC	113th to 115th	Jan. 3, 2013
Huffman, Jared	CA	113th to 115th	Jan. 3, 2013
Jeffries, Hakeem S.	NY	113th to 115th	Jan. 3, 2013
Joyce, David P.	OH	113th to 115th	Jan. 3, 2013
Kelly, Robin L.	IL	*113th to 115th	Apr. 9, 2013
Kennedy, Joseph P. III	MA	113th to 115th	Jan. 3, 2013
Kildee, Daniel T.	MI	113th to 115th	Jan. 3, 2013
Kilmer, Derek	WA	113th to 115th	Jan. 3, 2013
Kuster, Ann M.	NH	113th to 115th	Jan. 3, 2013
LaMalfa, Doug	CA	113th to 115th	Jan. 3, 2013
Lowenthal, Alan S.	CA	113th to 115th	Jan. 3, 2013
Lujan Grisham, Michelle	NM	113th to 115th	Jan. 3, 2013
Maloney, Sean Patrick	NY	113th to 115th	Jan. 3, 2013
Meadows, Mark	NC	113th to 115th	Jan. 3, 2013
Meng, Grace	NY	113th to 115th	Jan. 3, 2013
Messer, Luke	IN	113th to 115th	Jan. 3, 2013

CONGRESSES IN WHICH REPRESENTATIVES, RESIDENT COMMISSIONER, AND DELEGATES HAVE SERVED WITH BEGINNING OF PRESENT SERVICE—CONTINUED

[* Elected to fill a vacancy; Republicans in roman (236); Democrats in *italic* (193); Vacancies (6); Resident Commissioner and Delegates in **boldface** (6); total, 441]

Name	State	Congresses (inclusive)	Beginning of present service
Mullin, Markwayne	OK	113th to 115th	Jan. 3, 2013
Norcross, Donald	NJ	*113th to 115th	Nov. 4, 2014
O'Rourke, Beto	TX	113th to 115th	Jan. 3, 2013
Perry, Scott	PA	113th to 115th	Jan. 3, 2013
Peters, Scott H.	CA	113th to 115th	Jan. 3, 2013
Pittenger, Robert	NC	113th to 115th	Jan. 3, 2013
Pocan, Mark	WI	113th to 115th	Jan. 3, 2013
Rice, Tom	SC	113th to 115th	Jan. 3, 2013
Rothfus, Keith J.	PA	113th to 115th	Jan. 3, 2013
Ruiz, Raul	CA	113th to 115th	Jan. 3, 2013
Sinema, Kyrsten	AZ	113th to 115th	Jan. 3, 2013
Smith, Jason	MO	*113th to 115th	June 4, 2013
Stewart, Chris	UT	113th to 115th	Jan. 3, 2013
Swalwell, Eric	CA	113th to 115th	Jan. 3, 2013
Takano, Mark	CA	113th to 115th	Jan. 3, 2013
Valadao, David G.	CA	113th to 115th	Jan. 3, 2013
Vargas, Juan	CA	113th to 115th	Jan. 3, 2013
Veasey, Marc A.	TX	113th to 115th	Jan. 3, 2013
Vela, Filemon	TX	113th to 115th	Jan. 3, 2013
Wagner, Ann	MO	113th to 115th	Jan. 3, 2013
Walorski, Jackie	IN	113th to 115th	Jan. 3, 2013
Weber, Randy K., Sr.	TX	113th to 115th	Jan. 3, 2013
Wenstrup, Brad R.	OH	113th to 115th	Jan. 3, 2013
Williams, Roger	TX	113th to 115th	Jan. 3, 2013
Yoho, Ted S.	FL	113th to 115th	Jan. 3, 2013
2 terms, consecutive			
Abraham, Ralph Lee	LA	114th to 115th	Jan. 3, 2015
Aguilar, Pete	CA	114th to 115th	Jan. 3, 2015
Allen, Rick W.	GA	114th to 115th	Jan. 3, 2015
Babin, Brian	TX	114th to 115th	Jan. 3, 2015
Beyer, Donald S., Jr.	VA	114th to 115th	Jan. 3, 2015
Bishop, Mike	MI	114th to 115th	Jan. 3, 2015
Blum, Rod	IA	114th to 115th	Jan. 3, 2015
Bost, Mike	IL	114th to 115th	Jan. 3, 2015
Boyle, Brendan F.	PA	114th to 115th	Jan. 3, 2015
Buck, Ken	CO	114th to 115th	Jan. 3, 2015
Carter, Earl L. "Buddy"	GA	114th to 115th	Jan. 3, 2015
Comer, James	KY	*114th to 115th	Nov. 8, 2016
Comstock, Barbara	VA	114th to 115th	Jan. 3, 2015
Costello, Ryan A.	PA	114th to 115th	Jan. 3, 2015
Curbelo, Carlos	FL	114th to 115th	Jan. 3, 2015
Davidson, Warren	OH	*114th to 115th	June 7, 2016
DeSaulnier, Mark	CA	114th to 115th	Jan. 3, 2015
Dingell, Debbie	MI	114th to 115th	Jan. 3, 2015
Donovan, Daniel M., Jr.	NY	*114th to 115th	May 5, 2015
Emmer, Tom	MN	114th to 115th	Jan. 3, 2015
Evans, Dwight	PA	*114th to 115th	Nov. 8, 2016
Gallego, Ruben	AZ	114th to 115th	Jan. 3, 2015
Graves, Garret	LA	114th to 115th	Jan. 3, 2015
Grothman, Glenn	WI	114th to 115th	Jan. 3, 2015

CONGRESSES IN WHICH REPRESENTATIVES, RESIDENT COMMISSIONER, AND DELEGATES HAVE SERVED WITH BEGINNING OF PRESENT SERVICE—CONTINUED

[*Elected to fill a vacancy; Republicans in roman (236); Democrats in *italic* (193); Vacancies (6); Resident Commissioner and Delegates in **boldface** (6); total, 441]

Name	State	Congresses (inclusive)	Beginning of present service
Hice, Jody B.	GA	114th to 115th	Jan. 3, 2015
Hill, J. French	AR	114th to 115th	Jan. 3, 2015
Hurd, Will	TX	114th to 115th	Jan. 3, 2015
Jenkins, Evan H.	WV	114th to 115th	Jan. 3, 2015
Katko, John	NY	114th to 115th	Jan. 3, 2015
Kelly, Trent	MS	*114th to 115th	June 2, 2015
Knight, Stephen	CA	114th to 115th	Jan. 3, 2015
LaHood, Darin	IL	*114th to 115th	Sept. 10, 2015
Lawrence, Brenda L.	MI	114th to 115th	Jan. 3, 2015
Lieu, Ted	CA	114th to 115th	Jan. 3, 2015
Loudermilk, Barry	GA	114th to 115th	Jan. 3, 2015
Love, Mia B.	UT	114th to 115th	Jan. 3, 2015
MacArthur, Thomas	NJ	114th to 115th	Jan. 3, 2015
McSally, Martha	AZ	114th to 115th	Jan. 3, 2015
Moolenaar, John R.	MI	114th to 115th	Jan. 3, 2015
Mooney, Alexander X.	WV	114th to 115th	Jan. 3, 2015
Moulton, Seth	MA	114th to 115th	Jan. 3, 2015
Newhouse, Dan	WA	114th to 115th	Jan. 3, 2015
Palmer, Gary J.	AL	114th to 115th	Jan. 3, 2015
Poliquin, Bruce	ME	114th to 115th	Jan. 3, 2015
Ratcliffe, John	TX	114th to 115th	Jan. 3, 2015
Rice, Kathleen M.	NY	114th to 115th	Jan. 3, 2015
Rouzer, David	NC	114th to 115th	Jan. 3, 2015
Russell, Steve	OK	114th to 115th	Jan. 3, 2015
Stefanik, Elise M.	NY	114th to 115th	Jan. 3, 2015
Torres, Norma J.	CA	114th to 115th	Jan. 3, 2015
Trott, David A.	MI	114th to 115th	Jan. 3, 2015
Walker, Mark	NC	114th to 115th	Jan. 3, 2015
Walters, Mimi	CA	114th to 115th	Jan. 3, 2015
Watson Coleman, Bonnie	NJ	114th to 115th	Jan. 3, 2015
Westerman, Bruce	AR	114th to 115th	Jan. 3, 2015
Young, David	IA	114th to 115th	Jan. 3, 2015
Zeldin, Lee M.	NY	114th to 115th	Jan. 3, 2015
2 terms, not consecutive			
Schneider, Bradley Scott	IL	113th and 115th	Jan. 3, 2017
1 term			
Arrington, Jodey C.	TX	115th	Jan. 3, 2017
Bacon, Don	NE	115th	Jan. 3, 2017
Banks, Jim	IN	115th	Jan. 3, 2017
Barragán, Nanette Diaz	CA	115th	Jan. 3, 2017
Bergman, Jack	MI	115th	Jan. 3, 2017
Biggs, Andy	AZ	115th	Jan. 3, 2017
Blunt Rochester, Lisa	DE	115th	Jan. 3, 2017
Brown, Anthony G.	MD	115th	Jan. 3, 2017
Budd, Ted	NC	115th	Jan. 3, 2017
Carbajal, Salud O.	CA	115th	Jan. 3, 2017
Cheney, Liz	WY	115th	Jan. 3, 2017
Cloud, Michael	TX	115th	June 30, 2018
Correa, J. Luis	CA	115th	Jan. 3, 2017

CONGRESSES IN WHICH REPRESENTATIVES, RESIDENT COMMISSIONER, AND DELEGATES HAVE SERVED WITH BEGINNING OF PRESENT SERVICE—CONTINUED

[* Elected to fill a vacancy; Republicans in roman (236); Democrats in *italic* (193); Vacancies (6); Resident Commissioner and Delegates in **boldface** (6); total, 441]

Name	State	Congresses (inclusive)	Beginning of present service
Crist, Charlie	FL	115th	Jan. 3, 2017
Curtis, John R.	UT	115th	Nov. 13, 2017
Demings, Val Butler	FL	115th	Jan. 3, 2017
Dunn, Neal P.	FL	115th	Jan. 3, 2017
Espaillat, Adriano	NY	115th	Jan. 3, 2017
Estes, Ron	KS	115th	Apr. 11, 2017
Faso, John J.	NY	115th	Jan. 3, 2017
Ferguson, A. Drew IV	GA	115th	Jan. 3, 2017
Fitzpatrick, Brian K.	PA	115th	Jan. 3, 2017
Gaetz, Matt	FL	115th	Jan. 3, 2017
Gallagher, Mike	WI	115th	Jan. 3, 2017
Garrett, Thomas A., Jr.	VA	115th	Jan. 3, 2017
Gianforte, Greg	MT	115th	May 25, 2017
Gomez, Jimmy	CA	115th	June 6, 2017
Gonzalez, Vicente	TX	115th	Jan. 3, 2017
Gottheimer, Josh	NJ	115th	Jan. 3, 2017
Handel, Karen C.	GA	115th	June 20, 2017
Higgins, Clay	LA	115th	Jan. 3, 2017
Hollingsworth, Trey	IN	115th	Jan. 3, 2017
Jayapal, Pramila	WA	115th	Jan. 3, 2017
Johnson, Mike	LA	115th	Jan. 3, 2017
Khanna, Ro	CA	115th	Jan. 3, 2017
Kihuen, Ruben J.	NV	115th	Jan. 3, 2017
Krishnamoorthi, Raja	IL	115th	Jan. 3, 2017
Kustoff, David	TN	115th	Jan. 3, 2017
Lamb, Conor	PA	115th	Mar. 13, 2018
Lawson, Al, Jr.	FL	115th	Jan. 3, 2017
Lesko, Debbie	AZ	115th	May 7, 2018
Lewis, Jason	MN	115th	Jan. 3, 2017
Marshall, Roger W.	KS	115th	Jan. 3, 2017
Mast, Brian J.	FL	115th	Jan. 3, 2017
McEachin, A. Donald	VA	115th	Jan. 3, 2017
Mitchell, Paul	MI	115th	Jan. 3, 2017
Murphy, Stephanie N.	FL	115th	Jan. 3, 2017
Norman, Ralph	SC	115th	June 20, 2017
O'Halleran, Tom	AZ	115th	Jan. 3, 2017
Panetta, Jimmy	CA	115th	Jan. 3, 2017
Raskin, Jamie	MD	115th	Jan. 3, 2017
Rooney, Francis	FL	115th	Jan. 3, 2017
Rosen, Jacky	NV	115th	Jan. 3, 2017
Rutherford, John H.	FL	115th	Jan. 3, 2017
Smucker, Lloyd	PA	115th	Jan. 3, 2017
Soto, Darren	FL	115th	Jan. 3, 2017
Suozzi, Thomas R.	NY	115th	Jan. 3, 2017
Taylor, Scott	VA	115th	Jan. 3, 2017
Tenney, Claudia	NY	115th	Jan. 3, 2017
RESIDENT COMMISSIONER			
González-Colón, Jenniffer	PR	115th	Jan. 3, 2017

CONGRESSES IN WHICH REPRESENTATIVES, RESIDENT COMMISSIONER, AND DELEGATES HAVE SERVED WITH BEGINNING OF PRESENT SERVICE—CONTINUED

[* Elected to fill a vacancy; Republicans in roman (236); Democrats in *italic* (193); Vacancies (6); Resident Commissioner and Delegates in **boldface** (6); total, 441]

Name	State	Congresses (inclusive)	Beginning of present service
DELEGATES			
Norton, Eleanor Holmes	DC	102d to 115th	Jan. 3, 1991
Bordallo, Madeleine Z.	GU	108th to 115th	Jan. 3, 2003
Sablan, Gregorio Kilili Camacho ...	MP	111th to 115th	Jan. 3, 2009
Plaskett, Stacey E.	VI	114th to 115th	Jan. 3, 2015
Radewagen, Aumua Amata	AS	114th to 115th	Jan. 3, 2015

[1] Special Election, March 8, 2008.

NOTE: Members elected by special election are considered to begin service on the date that they were sworn in, except for those elected after a sine die adjournment. If elected after the Congress has adjourned for the session, Members are considered to begin their service on the day after the election.

STANDING COMMITTEES OF THE SENATE

[Republicans in roman; Democrats in *italic*; Independents in SMALL CAPS]

[Room numbers beginning with SD are in the Dirksen Building, SH in the Hart Building, SR in the Russell Building, and S in The Capitol]

Agriculture, Nutrition, and Forestry

328A Russell Senate Office Building 20510–6000

phone 224–2035, fax 228–2125, TTY / TDD 224–2587

http://agriculture.senate.gov

meets first and third Wednesdays of each month

Pat Roberts, of Kansas, *Chair*

Mitch McConnell, of Kentucky.
John Boozman, of Arkansas.
John Hoeven, of North Dakota.
Joni Ernst, of Iowa.
Chuck Grassley, of Iowa.
John Thune, of South Dakota.
Steve Daines, of Montana.
David Perdue, of Georgia.
Deb Fischer, of Nebraska.
Cindy Hyde-Smith, of Mississippi.

Debbie Stabenow, of Michigan.
Patrick J. Leahy, of Vermont.
Sherrod Brown, of Ohio.
Amy Klobuchar, of Minnesota.
Michael F. Bennet, of Colorado.
Kirsten E. Gillibrand, of New York.
Joe Donnelly, of Indiana.
Heidi Heitkamp, of North Dakota.
Robert P. Casey, Jr., of Pennsylvania.
Tina Smith, of Minnesota.

SUBCOMMITTEES

[The chair and ranking minority member are ex officio (non-voting) members of all subcommittees on which they do not serve.]

Commodities, Risk Management, and Trade

John Boozman, of Arkansas, *Chair*

John Hoeven, of North Dakota.
Chuck Grassley, of Iowa.
John Thune, of South Dakota.
Steve Daines, of Montana.
David Perdue, of Georgia.
Cindy Hyde-Smith, of Mississippi.

Heidi Heitkamp, of North Dakota.
Sherrod Brown, of Ohio.
Michael F. Bennet, of Colorado.
Kirsten E. Gillibrand, of New York.
Joe Donnelly, of Indiana.
Tina Smith, of Minnesota.

Conservation, Forestry, and Natural Resources

Steve Daines, of Montana, *Chair*

Mitch McConnell, of Kentucky.
John Boozman, of Arkansas.
Chuck Grassley, of Iowa.
David Perdue, of Georgia.
Cindy Hyde-Smith, of Mississippi.

Michael F. Bennet, of Colorado.
Patrick J. Leahy, of Vermont.
Amy Klobuchar, of Minnesota.
Joe Donnelly, of Indiana.
Robert P. Casey, Jr., of Pennsylvania.

Livestock, Marketing, and Agriculture Security

Deb Fischer, of Nebraska, *Chair*

Mitch McConnell, of Kentucky.
Joni Ernst, of Iowa.
Chuck Grassley, of Iowa.
John Thune, of South Dakota.
Steve Daines, of Montana.

Kirsten E. Gillibrand, of New York.
Patrick J. Leahy, of Vermont.
Amy Klobuchar, of Minnesota.
Heidi Heitkamp, of North Dakota.
Robert P. Casey, Jr., of Pennsylvania.

Nutrition, Agricultural Research, and Specialty Crops

David Perdue, of Georgia, *Chair*

Mitch McConnell, of Kentucky.
John Boozman, of Arkansas.
John Hoeven, of North Dakota.
Joni Ernst, of Iowa.
Deb Fischer, of Nebraska.

Robert P. Casey, Jr., of Pennsylvania.
Patrick J. Leahy, of Vermont.
Sherrod Brown, of Ohio.
Kirsten E. Gillibrand, of New York.
Tina Smith, of Minnesota.

Rural Development and Energy

Joni Ernst, of Iowa, *Chair*

John Boozman, of Arkansas.
John Hoeven, of North Dakota.
John Thune, of South Dakota.
Steve Daines, of Montana.
Deb Fischer, of Nebraksa.
Cindy Hyde-Smith, of Mississippi.

Tina Smith, of Minnesota.
Sherrod Brown, of Ohio.
Amy Klobuchar, of Minnesota.
Michael F. Bennet, of Colorado.
Joe Donnelly, of Indiana.
Heidi Heitkamp, of North Dakota.

STAFF

Committee on Agriculture, Nutrition, and Forestry (SR–328A), 224–2035, fax 228–2125.
Majority Staff:
Staff Director.—James Glueck.
Chief Counsel and Policy Director.—DaNita Murray.
Chief Counsel and Senior Advisor.—Anne Hazlett.
Senior Counsel.—Fred Clark.
Chief Economist.—Matthew Erickson.
Investigative Counsel.—Andrew Rezendes.
Press Secretary.—Meghan Cline.
Special Advisor.—CJ Mann.
Senior Professional Staff: Janae Brady, Darin Guries, Chelsie Keys, Robert Rosado, Andrew Vlasaty.
Professional Staff.—Wayne Stoskopf.
Legislative Assistant.—Katherine Thomas.
Staff Assistants/Legislative Correspondents: Haley Donohue, Chance Hunley, Alexandra Swee.
Minority Staff:
Staff Director.—Joe Shultz.
Deputy Staff Director/Policy Director.—Jacqlyn Schneider.
Chief Counsel.—Mary Beth Schultz.
Senior Professional Staff: Sean Babington, Ashley McKeon, Mike Schmidt.
Professional Staff: Kevin Bailey, Katie Naessens.
Special Counsel.—Susan Keith.
CFTC.—Ward Griffin.
Press Secretary.—Jess McCarron.
Policy Analysts: Katie Bergh, Kyle Varner.
Staff Assistant.—Rosalyn Brummette.
Non-Designated:
Chief Clerk.—Jessie Williams.
Deputy Chief Clerk.—Amanda Kelly.
Director of Printing and Binding.—Micah Wortham.
System Administrator.—Bobby Mehta.

Appropriations

S–128 The Capitol 20510–6025, phone 224–7257

http://appropriations.senate.gov

meets upon call of the chair

Richard C. Shelby, of Alabama, *Chair*

Mitch McConnell, of Kentucky.
Lamar Alexander, of Tennessee.
Susan M. Collins, of Maine.
Lisa Murkowski, of Alaska.
Lindsey Graham, of South Carolina.
Roy Blunt, of Missouri.
Jerry Moran, of Kansas.
John Hoeven, of North Dakota.
John Boozman, of Arkansas.
Shelley Moore Capito, of West Virginia.
James Lankford, of Oklahoma.
Steve Daines, of Montana.
John Kennedy, of Louisiana.
Marco Rubio, of Florida.
Cindy Hyde-Smith, of Mississippi.

Patrick J. Leahy, of Vermont.
Patty Murray, of Washington.
Dianne Feinstein, of California.
Richard J. Durbin, of Illinois.
Jack Reed, of Rhode Island.
Jon Tester, of Montana.
Tom Udall, of New Mexico.
Jeanne Shaheen, of New Hampshire.
Jeff Merkley, of Oregon.
Christopher A. Coons, of Delaware.
Brian Schatz, of Hawaii.
Tammy Baldwin, of Wisconsin.
Christopher Murphy, of Connecticut.
Joe Manchin III, of West Virginia.
Chris Van Hollen, of Maryland.

SUBCOMMITTEES

[The chair and ranking minority member are ex officio members of all subcommittees on which they do not serve.]

Agriculture, Rural Development, Food and Drug Administration, and Related Agencies

John Hoeven, of North Dakota, *Chair*

Mitch McConnell, of Kentucky.
Susan M. Collins, of Maine.
Roy Blunt, of Missouri.
Jerry Moran, of Kansas.
Marco Rubio, of Florida.
Cindy Hyde-Smith, of Mississippi.

Jeff Merkley, of Oregon.
Dianne Feinstein, of California.
Jon Tester, of Montana.
Tom Udall, of New Mexico.
Patrick J. Leahy, of Vermont.
Tammy Baldwin, of Wisconsin.

Commerce, Justice, Science, and Related Agencies

Jerry Moran, of Kansas, *Chair*

Lamar Alexander, of Tennessee.
Lisa Murkowski, of Alaska.
Susan M. Collins, of Maine.
Lindsey Graham, of South Carolina.
John Boozman, of Arkansas.
Shelley Moore Capito, of West Virginia.
James Lankford, of Oklahoma.
John Kennedy, of Louisiana.

Jeanne Shaheen, of New Hampshire.
Patrick J. Leahy, of Vermont.
Dianne Feinstein, of California.
Jack Reed, of Rhode Island.
Christopher A. Coons, of Delaware.
Brian Schatz, of Hawaii.
Joe Manchin III, of West Virginia.
Chris Van Hollen, of Maryland.

Defense

Richard C. Shelby, of Alabama, *Chair*

Mitch McConnell, of Kentucky.
Lamar Alexander, of Tennessee.
Susan M. Collins, of Maine.
Lisa Murkowski, of Alaska.
Lindsey Graham, of South Carolina.
Roy Blunt, of Missouri.
Steve Daines, of Montana.
Jerry Moran, of Kansas.
John Hoeven, of North Dakota.

Richard J. Durbin, of Illinois.
Patrick J. Leahy, of Vermont.
Dianne Feinstein, of California.
Patty Murray, of Washington.
Jack Reed, of Rhode Island.
Jon Tester, of Montana.
Tom Udall, of New Mexico.
Brian Schatz, of Hawaii.
Tammy Baldwin, of Wisconsin.

Energy and Water Development

Lamar Alexander, of Tennessee, *Chair*

Mitch McConnell, of Kentucky.
Richard C. Shelby, of Alabama.
Susan M. Collins, of Maine.
Lisa Murkowski, of Alaska.
Lindsey Graham, of South Carolina.
John Hoeven, of North Dakota.
John Kennedy, of Louisiana.
James Lankford, of Oklahoma.

Dianne Feinstein, of California.
Patty Murray, of Washington.
Jon Tester, of Montana.
Richard J. Durbin, of Illinois.
Tom Udall, of New Mexico.
Jeanne Shaheen, of New Hampshire.
Jeff Merkley, of Oregon.
Christopher A. Coons, of Delaware.

Financial Services and General Government

James Lankford, of Oklahoma, *Chair*

Jerry Moran, of Kansas.
John Boozman, of Arkansas.
Steve Daines, of Montana.
John Kennedy, of Louisiana.

Christopher A. Coons, of Delaware.
Richard J. Durbin, of Illinois.
Joe Manchin III, of West Virginia.
Chris Van Hollen, of Maryland.

Homeland Security

Shelley Moore Capito, of West Virginia, *Chair*

Richard C. Shelby, of Alabama.
Lisa Murkowski, of Alaska.
John Boozman, of Arkansas.
John Hoeven, of North Dakota.
James Lankford, of Oklahoma.
John Kennedy, of Louisiana.

Jon Tester, of Montana.
Jeanne Shaheen, of New Hampshire.
Patrick J. Leahy, of Vermont.
Patty Murray, of Washington.
Tammy Baldwin, of Wisconsin.
Joe Manchin III, of West Virginia.

Interior, Environment, and Related Agencies

Lisa Murkowski, of Alaska, *Chair*

Lamar Alexander, of Tennessee.
Roy Blunt, of Missouri.
Mitch McConnell, of Kentucky.
Steve Daines, of Montana.
Shelley Moore Capito, of West Virginia.
Marco Rubio, of Florida.
Cindy Hyde-Smith, of Mississippi.

Tom Udall, of New Mexico.
Dianne Feinstein, of California.
Patrick J. Leahy, of Vermont.
Jack Reed, of Rhode Island.
Jon Tester, of Montana.
Jeff Merkley, of Oregon.
Chris Van Hollen, of Maryland.

Labor, Health and Human Services, Education, and Related Agencies

Roy Blunt, of Missouri, *Chair*

Richard C. Shelby, of Alabama.
Lamar Alexander, of Tennessee.
Lindsey Graham, of South Carolina.
Jerry Moran, of Kansas.
Shelley Moore Capito, of West Virginia.
James Lankford, of Oklahoma.
John Kennedy, of Louisiana.
Marco Rubio, of Florida.
Cindy Hyde-Smith, of Mississippi.

Patty Murray, of Washington.
Richard J. Durbin, of Illinois.
Jack Reed, of Rhode Island.
Jeanne Shaheen, of New Hampshire.
Jeff Merkley, of Oregon.
Brian Schatz, of Hawaii.
Tammy Baldwin, of Wisconsin.
Christopher Murphy, of Connecticut.
Joe Manchin III, of West Virginia.

Legislative Branch

Steve Daines, of Montana, *Chair*

Cindy Hyde-Smith, of Mississippi.
Richard C. Shelby, of Alabama.

Christopher Murphy, of Connecticut.
Chris Van Hollen, of Maryland.

Military Construction, Veterans Affairs, and Related Agencies

John Boozman, of Arkansas, *Chair*

Mitch McConnell, of Kentucky.
Lisa Murkowski, of Alaska.
John Hoeven, of North Dakota.
Susan M. Collins, of Maine.
Shelley Moore Capito, of West Virginia.
Jerry Moran, of Kansas.
Marco Rubio, of Florida.

Brian Schatz, of Hawaii.
Jon Tester, of Montana.
Patty Murray, of Washington.
Jack Reed, of Rhode Island.
Tom Udall, of New Mexico.
Tammy Baldwin, of Wisconsin.
Christopher Murphy, of Connecticut.

State, Foreign Operations, and Related Programs

Lindsey Graham, of South Carolina, *Chair*

Mitch McConnell, of Kentucky.
Roy Blunt, of Missouri.
John Boozman, of Arkansas.
James Lankford, of Oklahoma.
Steve Daines, of Montana.
Marco Rubio, of Florida.
Cindy Hyde-Smith, of Mississippi.

Patrick J. Leahy, of Vermont.
Richard J. Durbin, of Illinois.
Jeanne Shaheen, of New Hampshire.
Christopher A. Coons, of Delaware.
Jeff Merkley, of Oregon.
Christopher Murphy, of Connecticut.
Chris Van Hollen, of Maryland.

Transportation, Housing and Urban Development, and Related Agencies

Susan M. Collins, of Maine, *Chair*

Richard C. Shelby, of Alabama.
Lamar Alexander, of Tennessee.
Roy Blunt, of Missouri.
John Boozman, of Arkansas.
Shelley Moore Capito, of West Virginia.
Steve Daines, of Montana.
Lindsey Graham, of South Carolina.
John Hoeven, of North Dakota.

Jack Reed, of Rhode Island.
Patty Murray, of Washington.
Richard J. Durbin, of Illinois.
Dianne Feinstein, of California.
Christopher A. Coons, of Delaware.
Brian Schatz, of Hawaii.
Christopher Murphy, of Connecticut.
Joe Manchin III, of West Virginia.

STAFF

Committee on Appropriations (S–128), 224–7257.
Staff Director.—Shannon Hines (S–128).
Chief Clerk.—Robert W. Putnam (SD–114).
Deputy Staff Director.—Jonathan Graffeo.

Chief Counsel.—David Adkins.
Communications Director.—Blair Taylor (S–128).
Professional Staff: (S–128); Lucas Agnew, Jenny Winkler (SD–114).
Technical Systems Manager.—Hong Nguyen (SD–114).
Security Manager.—Clint Trocchio (SD–118).
Executive Assistant.—Mary Collins Atkinson.
Clerical Assistant.—George Castro (SD–120), 4–5433.
Minority Staff Director.—Charles E. Kieffer (S–146A), 4–7363.
Minority Deputy Staff Director.—Chanda Betourney (S–146A).
Press Secretary.—Jay Tilton (S–146A).
Senior Advisor.—Jessica Berry (S–146A).
Executive Assistant.—Teri Curtin (SH–125).
Staff Assistant.—Jean Kwon (S–146A).
Subcommittee on Agriculture, Rural Development, Food and Drug Administration, and Related Agencies (SD–127), 4–5270.
Majority Clerk.—Carlisle Clarke (SD–127).
Professional Staff: Patrick Carroll (SD–127); Elizabeth Dent (SD–127).
Staff Assistant.—Carlos Elias (SD–122).
Minority Clerk.—Jessica Arden Schulken (SD–190), 4–8090.
Professional Staff: Dianne Nellor (SD–190); Bob Ross (SD–190).
Staff Assistant.—Teri Curtin (SH–125).
Subcommittee on Commerce, Justice, Science, and Related Agencies (SD–142), 4–7277.
Majority Clerk.—Jeremy Weirich (SD–142).
Professional Staff: Amber Busby Beck (SD–142); Allen Cutler (SD–142); Matt Womble (SD–142).
Minority Clerk.—Jean Toal Eisen (SH–125), 4–5202.
Professional Staff: Jennifer Eskra (SH–125); Blaise Sheridan (SH–125).
Staff Assistant.—Jordan Stone (SH–125).
Subcommittee on Defense (SD–122), 4–7255.
Majority Clerk.—Brian Potts (SD–122).
Professional Staff: Mike Clementi (SD–122); Colleen Gaydos (SD–122); Katy Hagan (SD–122); Chris Hall (SD–122); Kate Kaufer (SD–122), Jacqui Russell (SD–122); Jennifer S. Santos (SD–122); Will Todd (SD–122).
Staff Assistant.—Carlos Elias (SD–122).
Minority Clerk.—Erik Raven (SD–117), 4–6688.
Professional Staff: David C. Gillies (SD–115); Brigid Houton (SD–115); John Lucio; Andy Vanlandingham (SD–115).
Subcommittee on Energy and Water Development (SD–142), 4–7260.
Majority Clerk.—Tyler Owens (SD–142).
Professional Staff: Jen Armstrong (SD–142); Adam DeMella (SD–142); Molly Marsh (SD–142); Meyer Seligman (SD–142).
Staff Assistant.—Rachel Littleton
Minority Clerk.—Doug Clapp (SD–188), 4–8119.
Professional Staff: Chris Hanson (SD–188); Samantha Nelson (SD–188).
Subcommittee on Financial Services and General Government (SD–133), 4–2104.
Majority Clerk.—Andrew Newton (SD–133).
Professional Staff: Lauren Comeau; Brian Daner; LaShawnda Smith (SD–131).
Minority Clerk.—Ellen Murray (SH–125), 4–1133.
Professional Staff.—Diana Gourlay Hamilton (SH–125).
Staff Assistant.—Reeve Hart (SD–128).
Subcommittee on Homeland Security (SD–131), 4–4319.
Majority Clerk.—Adam Telle (SD–131).
Professional Staff: Peter Babb (SD–131); Chris Cook (SD–131); Reeve Hart; Christian Lee (SD–131); LaShawnda Smith (SD–131).
Minority Clerk.—Scott Nance (SD–128), 4–8244.
Professional Staff: Drenan A. Dudley (SD–128); Chip Walgren (SD–128).
Staff Assistant.—Irina Bajic (SD–128).
Subcommittee on Interior, Environment, and Related Agencies (SD–131), 4–7233.
Majority Clerk.—Leif Fonnesbeck (SD–131).
Professional Staff: Emy Lesofski (SD–131); Nona McCoy (SD–131); LaShawnda Smith (SD–131); Chris Tomassi (SD–131).
Minority Clerk.—Rachael Taylor (SH–125), 8–0774.
Professional Staff: Ryan Hunt (SH–125); Melissa Zimmerman (SH–125).
Staff Assistant.—Teri Curtin (SH–125).
Subcommittee on Labor, Health and Human Services, Education, and Related Agencies (SD–135), 4–7230.
Majority Clerk.—Laura A. Friedel (SD–135).

Professional Staff: Michael Gentile (SD–135); Ashley Palmer; Jeff Reczek (SD–135); Adam Sullivan (SD–135).
Staff Assistant.—Courtney Bradford.
Professional Staff: Lisa Bernhardt (SD–156); Kelly Brown (SD–156); Catie Finley (SD–156); Mark Laisch (SD–156).
Staff Assistant.—Teri Curtin (SD–156).

Subcommittee on Legislative Branch (S–128), 4–9747.
Majority Clerk.—Sarah Boliek (S–128).
Professional Staff.—Lucas Agnew (S–135).
Minority Clerk.—Melissa Zimmerman (SH–125).
Staff Assistant.—Jean Kwon (S–146A).

Subcommittee on Military Construction, Veterans Affairs, and Related Agencies (SD–125), 4–5245.
Majority Clerk.—Patrick Magnuson (SD–125).
Professional Staff: Jennifer Bastin, Joane Hoff.
Staff Assistant.—Carlos Elias (SD–122).
Minority Clerk.—Chad Schulken (SH–125), 4–8224.
Professional Staff.—Jason McMahon (SH–125).

Subcommittee on State, Foreign Operations, and Related Programs (SD–127), 4–2104.
Majority Clerk.—Paul Grove (SD–127).
Professional Staff: Kali Matalon; LaShawnda Smith (SD–131); Jason Wheelock (SD–127); Adam Yezerski (SD–127).
Minority Clerk.—Tim Rieser (SH–125), 4–7284.
Professional Staff.—Alex Carnes (SH–125).

Subcommittee on Transportation, Housing and Urban Development, and Related Agencies (SD–184), 4–5310.
Majority Clerk.—Clare Dogerty (SD–184).
Professional Staff: Gus Maples (SD–184); Rajat Mathur (SD–184); Jacob Press; Jason Woolwine (SD–184).
Minority Clerk.—Dabney Hegg (SH–125), 4–7281.
Professional Staff: Christina Monroe (SH–125); Nathan Robinson (SH–125); Jordan Stone (SH–125).
Editorial and Printing (SD–126): Elmer Barnes (GPO), 4–7266; Valerie A. Hutton, 4–7267; Penny Miles; Karin Thames (GPO), 4–7217.

Armed Services

228 Russell Senate Office Building 20510–6050

phone 224–3871, http://www.armed-services.senate.gov

meets every Tuesday and Thursday

John McCain, of Arizona, *Chair*

James M. Inhofe, of Oklahoma.
Roger F. Wicker, of Mississippi.
Deb Fischer, of Nebraska.
Tom Cotton, of Arkansas.
Mike Rounds, of South Dakota.
Joni Ernst, of Iowa.
Thom Tillis, of North Carolina.
Dan Sullivan, of Alaska.
David Perdue, of Georgia.
Ted Cruz, of Texas.
Lindsey Graham, of South Carolina.
Ben Sasse, of Nebraska.
Tim Scott, of South Carolina.

Jack Reed, of Rhode Island.
Bill Nelson, of Florida.
Claire McCaskill, of Missouri.
Jeanne Shaheen, of New Hampshire.
Kirsten E. Gillibrand, of New York.
Richard Blumenthal, of Connecticut.
Joe Donnelly, of Indiana.
Mazie K. Hirono, of Hawaii.
Tim Kaine, of Virginia.
ANGUS S. KING, JR., of Maine.
Martin Heinrich, of New Mexico.
Elizabeth Warren, of Massachusetts.
Gary C. Peters, of Michigan.

SUBCOMMITTEES

[The chair and the ranking minority member are ex officio (non-voting) members of all subcommittees on which they do not serve.]

Airland

Tom Cotton, of Arkansas, *Chair*

James M. Inhofe, of Oklahoma.
Roger F. Wicker, of Mississippi.
Thom Tillis, of North Carolina.
Dan Sullivan, of Alaska.
Ted Cruz, of Texas.
Ben Sasse, of Nebraska.

ANGUS S. KING, JR., of Maine.
Claire McCaskill, of Missouri.
Richard Blumenthal, of Connecticut.
Joe Donnelly, of Indiana.
Elizabeth Warren, of Massachusetts.
Gary C. Peters, of Michigan.

Cybersecurity

Mike Rounds, of South Dakota, *Chair*

Deb Fischer, of Nebraska.
David Perdue, of Georgia.
Lindsey Graham, of South Carolina.
Ben Sasse, of Nebraska.

Bill Nelson, of Florida.
Claire McCaskill, of Missouri.
Kirsten E. Gillibrand, of New York.
Richard Blumenthal, of Connecticut.

Emerging Threats and Capabilities

Joni Ernst, of Iowa, *Chair*

Roger F. Wicker, of Mississippi.
Deb Fischer, of Nebraska.
David Perdue, of Georgia.
Ted Cruz, of Texas.

Martin Heinrich, of New Mexico.
Bill Nelson, of Florida.
Jeanne Shaheen, of New Hampshire.
Gary C. Peters, of Michigan.

Personnel

Thom Tillis, of North Carolina, *Chair*

Joni Ernst, of Iowa.
Lindsey Graham, of South Carolina.
Ben Sasse, of Nebraska.
Kirsten E. Gillibrand, of New York.
Claire McCaskill, of Missouri.
Elizabeth Warren, of Massachusetts.

Readiness and Management Support

James M. Inhofe, of Oklahoma, *Chair*

Mike Rounds, of South Dakota.
Joni Ernst, of Iowa.
David Perdue, of Georgia.
Tim Scott, of South Carolina.
Tim Kaine, of Virginia.
Jeanne Shaheen, of New Hampshire.
Mazie K. Hirono, of Hawaii.

Seapower

Roger F. Wicker, of Mississippi, *Chair*

Tom Cotton, of Arkansas.
Mike Rounds, of South Dakota.
Thom Tillis, of North Carolina.
Dan Sullivan, of Alaska.
Tim Scott, of South Carolina.
Mazie K. Hirono, of Hawaii.
Jeanne Shaheen, of New Hampshire.
Richard Blumenthal, of Connecticut.
Tim Kaine, of Virginia.
ANGUS S. KING, JR., of Maine.

Strategic Forces

Deb Fischer, of Nebraska, *Chair*

James M. Inhofe, of Oklahoma.
Tom Cotton, of Arkansas.
Dan Sullivan, of Alaska.
Ted Cruz, of Texas.
Lindsey Graham, of South Carolina.
Joe Donnelly, of Indiana.
Martin Heinrich, of New Mexico.
Elizabeth Warren, of Massachusetts.
Gary C. Peters, of Michigan.

STAFF

Committee on Armed Services (SR–228), 224–3871.
Majority and Non-Designated Staff:
Staff Director.—Chris Brose.
Deputy Staff Director.—Samantha Clark.
Policy Director.—Mark Montgomery.
General Counsel.—Samantha Clark.
Senior Military Advisor.—James Hickey.
Budget and Deputy Policy Director.—Diem Salmon.
Chief Clerk.—Greg Lilly.
Communications Director and Policy Advisor.—Rachel Hoff.
Professional Staff Members: Adam Barker, Augusta Binns-Berkey, Lauren Davis, Allen Edwards, Jackie Kerber, Matt Lampert, Allison Lazarus, John Lehman, Sean O'Keefe, Brad Patout, Jason Potter, Will Quinn, Dustin Walker, Gwyneth Woolwine.
Nominations and Hearings Clerk.—Leah Brewer.
Security Manager.—Debbie Chiarello.
Systems Administrator.—Gary Howard.
Special Assistant.—Gabriel Noronha.
Staff Assistants: Nick Hatcher, Katie Magnus, Lindsay Markle, Cara Mumford, Madison Sparber, Arthur Tellis.
Subcommittee on Airland
Lead.—James Hickey.
Staff Assistant.—Nick Hatcher.
Subcommittee on Cybersecurity
Lead.—Mark Montgomery.
Staff Assistant.—Arthur Tellis.

Subcommittee on Emerging Threats and Capabilities
Lead.—Adam Barker.
Staff Assistant.—Lindsay Markle.
Subcommittee on Personnel
Lead.—Allen Edwards.
Staff Assistant.—Katie Magnus.
Subcommittee on Readiness and Management Support
Lead.—Brad Patout.
Staff Assistant.—Cara Mumford.
Subcommittee on Seapower
Lead.—Jason Potter.
Staff Assistant.—Nick Hatcher.
Subcommittee on Strategic Forces
Lead.—Augusta Binns-Berkey.
Staff Assistant.—Arthur Tellis.
Majority Staff Subject Areas
Acquisition Issues
AbilityOne Program.—Gwyneth Woolwine.
Acquisition Policy.—Gwyneth Woolwine.
Acquisition Workforce.—Samantha Clark.
Competition and Competitive Sourcing.—Samantha Clark.
Contracting.—Gwyneth Woolwine.
Industrial Base Policy.—Gwyneth Woolwine.
Industrial Base Workforce.—Samantha Clark.
Information Technology and Software-Intensive Systems.—Gwyneth Woolwine.
Ammunition.—Jackie Kerber.
Arms Control.—Augusta Binns-Berkey.
Arsenals.—Jackie Kerber.
Authorized Use of Military Force.—Samantha Clark.
Aviation Systems (Except Rotary).—John Lehman.
Base Realignment and Closure (BRAC).—Brad Patout.
Budget.—Diem Salmon.
Chemical-Biological Defense.—Jackie Kerber.
Chemical Demilitarization.—Jackie Kerber.
Civilian Nominations.—Allen Edwards.
Civilian Personnel Policy.—Sean O'Keefe.
Combatant Commands / Regions
AFRICOM.—Adam Barker.
CENTCOM (except Central Asia).—Will Quinn.
EUCOM (plus Central Asia).—Dustin Walker.
NORTHCOM.—Will Quinn.
PACOM.—Dustin Walker.
SOCOM.—Adam Barker.
SOUTHCOM.—Will Quinn.
STRATCOM.—Augusta Binns-Berkey.
TRANSCOM.—Allison Lazarus.
CYBERCOM.—Mark Montgomery.
Combating Terrorism.—Adam Barker.
Competition Policy.—Samantha Clark.
Competitive Sourcing / A–76.—Samantha Clark.
Cooperative Threat Reduction Programs.—Lauren Davis.
Counter-Narcotics Programs.—Will Quinn.
Cross-Functional Teaming.—Allison Lazarus.
Cybersecurity.—Mark Montgomery.
Defense Business Operations.—Allison Lazarus.
Defense Laboratory Management.—Allison Lazarus.
Defense Security Assistance.—Adam Barker.
Department of Energy Issues
Nuclear Weapons Activities.—Augusta Binns-Berkey.
Non-Proliferation Programs.—Lauren Davis.
Nuclear Cleanup.—Jackie Kerber.
Depot Maintenance Policy.—Brad Patout.
Detainee Policy.—Samantha Clark.
Domestic Preparedness.—Will Quinn.
Electronic Warfare.—Mark Montgomery.
Environmental Issues.—Jackie Kerber.
Facilities, Sustainment, Restoration and Modernization.—Brad Patout.

Financial Management.—Allison Lazarus.
Foreign Policy
Afghanistan/Pakistan.—Matt Lampert.
Africa.—Adam Barker.
Asia, Pacific.—Dustin Walker.
Central Asia.—Dustin Walker.
Europe, Russia.—Dustin Walker.
Iraq.—Will Quinn.
Middle East.—Will Quinn.
South and Central Americas.—Will Quinn.
Global Force Posture and Basing.—Mark Montgomery.
Ground Systems: James Hickey, Matt Lampert.
Industrial Operations (Military).—Brad Patout.
Information Assurance.—Gwyneth Woolwine.
Information Management.—Gwyneth Woolwine.
Information Operations.—Mark Montgomery.
Intelligence Issues.—Adam Barker.
Interagency Reform.—Allison Lazarus.
International Defense Cooperation.—Adam Barker.
Inventory Management.—Jackie Kerber.
Investigations: Brad Patout, Gwyneth Woolwine.
Joint Improvised-Threat Defeat Organization.—Matt Lampert.
Land Use.—Brad Patout.
Logistics Policy.—Allison Lazarus.
Marine Corps Programs.—Matt Lampert.
Maritime Issues.—Jason Potter.
Mergers and Acquisitions.—Gwyneth Woolwine.
Military Construction.—Brad Patout.
Military Personnel Issues
Cemeteries and Memorials.—Allen Edwards.
Commissaries and Exchanges.—Allen Edwards.
Defense Officer Personnel Management.—Sean O'Keefe.
DOD Schools.—Allen Edwards.
End Strength.—Sean O'Keefe.
Military Family Policy.—Allen Edwards.
Health Care.—Allen Edwards.
Military Justice.—Samantha Clark.
Military Nominations.—Allen Edwards.
Morale, Welfare, and Recreation.—Allen Edwards.
National Defense Strategy Review.—Mark Montgomery, Diem Salmon.
POW/MIA Issues.—Allen Edwards.
Pay, Benefits, and Retirement: Samantha Clark, Sean O'Keefe.
Military Personnel Policy.—Sean O'Keefe.
National Guard and Reserves.—Sean O'Keefe.
Sexual Harassment/Assault Policy: Samantha Clark, Sean O'Keefe.
Suicide Prevention.—Allen Edwards.
Wounded Warrior Issues.—Allen Edwards.
Military Space.—Augusta Binns-Berkey.
Military Strategy: James Hickey, Mark Montgomery.
Missile Defense.—Lauren Davis.
Munitions.—Diem Salmon.
National Defense Stockpile.—Jackie Kerber.
Nuclear Weapons Stockpile
Nuclear Weapons Activities.—Augusta Binns-Berkey.
Non-Proliferation Programs.—Lauren Davis.
Nuclear Cleanup.—Jackie Kerber.
Operational and Installation Energy.—Jackie Kerber.
Operations and Maintenance
Army.—Jackie Kerber.
Navy.—Brad Patout.
Marine Corps.—Matt Lampert.
Air Force.—Brad Patout.
Readiness.—Brad Patout.
Reprogramming.—Diem Salmon.
Rotary Systems: James Hickey, Matt Lampert.
Science and Technology.—Allison Lazarus.
Shipbuilding Programs.—Jason Potter.

Small Business Programs.—Gwyneth Woolwine.
Special Operations Forces.—Adam Barker.
Test and Evaluation.—Gwyneth Woolwine.
Training
Army.—Jim Hickey.
Navy.—Jason Potter.
Marine Corps.—Matt Lampert.
Air Force.—John Lehman.
Transportation Policy.—Allison Lazarus.
Unmanned Aircraft Systems: James Hickey, John Lehman.
War Powers.—Samantha Clark.
Working Capital Fund.—Allison Lazarus.
Minority Staff:
Staff Director.—Elizabeth L. King.
Clerk.—Mariah K. McNamara.
Minority General Counsel.—Gerald J. Leeling.
Counsel: Jonathan D. Clark, Jonathan S. Epstein, Ozge Guzelsu, William G.P. Monahan.
Professional Staff Members: Jody L. Bennett, Carolyn A. Chuhta, Creighton Greene, Thomas K. McConnell, Mariah K. McNamara, Michael J. Noblet, John H. Quirk V, Arun A. Seraphin.
Special Assistant.—Jonathan D. Green.
Subcommittee on Airland
Minority Staff Members: Jody L. Bennett (lead), Creighton Greene.
Subcommittee on Cyber
Minority Staff Members: Thomas K. McConnell (lead), William G.P. Monahan.
Subcommittee on Emerging Threats and Capabilities
Minority Staff Members: Michael J. Noblet (lead), Jonathan S. Epstein, Ozge Guzelsu, Thomas K. McConnell, Mariah K. McNamara, William G.P. Monahan, Arun A. Seraphin.
Subcommittee on Personnel
Minority Staff Members: Jonathan D. Clark (lead), Gerald J. Leeling.
Subcommittee on Readiness and Management Support
Minority Staff Members: John H. Quirk V (lead), Arun A. Seraphin.
Subcommittee on Seapower
Minority Staff Members: Creighton Greene (lead), Jody L. Bennett.
Subcommittee on Strategic Forces
Minority Staff Members: Jonathan S. Epstein (lead), Carolyn A. Chuhta, Creighton Greene, Thomas K. McConnell, Mariah K. McNamara.
Minority Staff Subject Areas
Acquisition Policy.—Arun A. Seraphin.
Acquisition Workforce.—Arun A. Seraphin.
Alternative Energy: John H. Quirk V, Arun A. Seraphin.
Ammunition.—John H. Quirk V.
Arms Control.—Jonathan S. Epstein.
Aviation Systems: Jonathan S. Epstein, Creighton Greene.
Base Realignment and Closure (BRAC).—John H. Quirk V.
Border Security.—Carolyn A. Chuhta.
Budget.—Carolyn A. Chuhta.
Buy America.—Arun A. Seraphin.
Chemical-Biological Defense.—Jonathan S. Epstein.
Chemical Demilitarization.—Jonathan S. Epstein.
Combatant Commands / Foreign Policy
AFRICOM.—Mariah K. McNamara.
CENTCOM: Mariah K. McNamara, Michael J. Noblet.
Central Asia.—Mariah K. McNamara.
Iraq.—Michael J. Noblet.
Middle East.—Michael J. Noblet.
CYBERCOM.—Thomas K. McConnell.
EUCOM/NATO.—William G.P. Monahan.
Israel.—Carolyn A. Chuhta.
NORTHCOM.—Carolyn A. Chuhta.
PACOM.—Ozge Guzelsu.
SOCOM.—Michael J. Noblet.
SOUTHCOM.—Ozge Guzelsu.
STRATCOM.—Jonathan S. Epstein.
TRANSCOM.—Creighton Greene.
Counterterrorism Partnership Fund.—Michael J. Noblet.

Counterterrorism Policy: Ozge Guzelsu, Thomas K. McConnell, Mariah K. McNamara, Michael J. Noblet.
Housing Construction.—John H. Quirk V.
Overseas Humanitarian, Disaster, and Civic Aid (OHDACA) Account.—Mariah K. McNamara.
Information Assurance: Creighton Greene, Thomas K. McConnell.
Information Management: Creighton Greene, Arun A. Seraphin.
Information Operations: Mariah K. McNamara, Michael J. Noblet.
Information Technology Systems
IT Acquisition Policy: Thomas K. McConnell, Arun A. Seraphin.
Business Systems.—Arun A. Seraphin.
Tactical Systems.—Creighton Greene.
Intelligence Issues: Creighton Greene, Thomas K. McConnell, Michael J. Noblet.
Interagency Reform: Thomas K. McConnell, Michael J. Noblet.
Inventory Management.—Arun A. Seraphin.
Investigations.—Ozge Guzelsu.
Insider Threat.—Thomas K. McConnell.
Joint IED Defeat Fund (JIEDDF).—Jody L. Bennett.
Joint Improvised-Threat Defense Organization (JIDO).—Jonathan D. Green.
Land Use.—John H. Quirk V.
Laboratory Management.—Arun A. Seraphin.
Logistics Policy.—Creighton Greene.
Mergers and Acquisitions.—Arun A. Seraphin.
Military Construction.—John H. Quirk V.
Military Space.—Jonathan S. Epstein.
Military Strategy.—Jody L. Bennett.
Missile Defense.—Carolyn A. Chuhta.
National Defense Stockpile.—John H. Quirk V.
Nominations
Civilian.—Gerald J. Leeling.
Military.—Jonathan D. Clark.
Non-Proliferation.—Jonathan S. Epstein.
Nuclear Weapons Stockpile.—Jonathan S. Epstein.
Operation and Maintenance.—John H. Quirk V.
Peacekeeping.—Mariah K. McNamara.
Personnel Policy
Civilian Personnel Policy.—Jonathan D. Clark.
Commissaries and Exchanges.—Jonathan D. Clark.
Education.—Jonathan D. Clark.
End Strength.—Jonathan D. Clark.
Health Care.—Gerald J. Leeling.
Military Family Policy.—Gerald J. Leeling.
Military Justice.—Gerald J. Leeling.
Military Nominations.—Jonathan D. Clark.
Military Personnel Policy.—Gerald J. Leeling.
Morale, Welfare, and Recreation.—Jonathan D. Clark.
National Guard and Reserves: Jonathan D. Clark, Gerald J. Leeling.
Pay, Benefits, and Retirement.—Jonathan D. Clark.
POW/MIA Issues.—Jonathan D. Clark.
Religious Accommodation.—Jonathan D. Clark.
Sexual Conduct Policy.—Gerald J. Leeling.
Suicide Prevention and Response.—Gerald J. Leeling.
Women in Service.—Jonathan D. Clark.
Wounded Warrior Issues.—Gerald J. Leeling.
Personnel Security.—Thomas K. McConnell.
Personnel Protective Items.—John H. Quirk V.
Readiness.—John H. Quirk V.
Reprogramming.—Carolyn A. Chuhta.
Science and Technology.—Arun A. Seraphin.
Security Assistance Programs: Ozge Guzelsu, William G.P. Monahan, Mariah K. McNamara, Michael J. Noblet.
Shipbuilding Programs.—Creighton Greene.
Small Business.—Arun A. Seraphin.
Southeast Asia Maritime Initiative.—Ozge Guzelsu.
Special Operations Forces.—Michael J. Noblet.
Strategic Programs.—Jonathan S. Epstein.
Test and Evaluation.—Arun A. Seraphin.

Training.—John H. Quirk V.
Transportation Policy.—Creighton Greene.
Unified Command Plan.—Jody L. Bennett.
Unmanned Aircraft Systems: Creighton Greene, Thomas K. McConnell.
Working Capital Fund.—John H. Quirk V.

Banking, Housing, and Urban Affairs

534 Dirksen Senate Office Building 20510
phone 224–7391, http://banking.senate.gov

Mike Crapo, of Idaho, *Chair*

Richard C. Shelby, of Alabama.
Bob Corker, of Tennessee.
Patrick J. Toomey, of Pennsylvania.
Dean Heller, of Nevada.
Tim Scott, of South Carolina.
Ben Sasse, of Nebraska.
Tom Cotton, of Arkansas.
Mike Rounds, of South Dakota.
David Perdue, of Georgia.
Thom Tillis, of North Carolina.
John Kennedy, of Louisiana.
Jerry Moran, of Kansas.

Sherrod Brown, of Ohio.
Jack Reed, of Rhode Island.
Robert Menendez, of New Jersey.
Jon Tester, of Montana.
Mark R. Warner, of Virginia.
Elizabeth Warren, of Massachusetts.
Heidi Heitkamp, of North Dakota.
Joe Donnelly, of Indiana.
Brian Schatz, of Hawaii.
Chris Van Hollen, of Maryland.
Catherine Cortez Masto, of Nevada.
Doug Jones, of Alabama.

SUBCOMMITTEES

[The chair and ranking minority member are ex officio members of all subcommittees.]

Economic Policy

Tom Cotton, of Arkansas, *Chair*

Patrick J. Toomey, of Pennsylvania.
David Perdue, of Georgia.
Thom Tillis, of North Carolina.
John Kennedy, of Louisiana.
Jerry Moran, of Kansas.

Heidi Heitkamp, of North Dakota.
Robert Menendez, of New Jersey.
Elizabeth Warren, of Massachusetts.
Joe Donnelly, of Indiana.
Doug Jones, of Alabama.

Financial Institutions and Consumer Protection

Patrick J. Toomey, of Pennsylvania, *Chair*

Richard C. Shelby, of Alabama.
Bob Corker, of Tennessee.
Dean Heller, of Nevada.
Tim Scott, of South Carolina.
Ben Sasse, of Nebraska.
Tom Cotton, of Arkansas.
David Perdue, of Georgia.
John Kennedy, of Louisiana.

Elizabeth Warren, of Massachusetts.
Jack Reed, of Rhode Island.
Jon Tester, of Montana.
Mark R. Warner, of Virginia.
Joe Donnelly, of Indiana.
Brian Schatz, of Hawaii.
Chris Van Hollen, of Maryland.
Catherine Cortez Masto, of Nevada.

Housing, Transportation, and Community Development

Tim Scott, of South Carolina, *Chair*

Richard C. Shelby, of Alabama.
Dean Heller, of Nevada.
Mike Rounds, of South Dakota.
Thom Tillis, of North Carolina.
John Kennedy, of Louisiana.
Jerry Moran, of Kansas.

Robert Menendez, of New Jersey.
Jack Reed, of Rhode Island.
Heidi Heitkamp, of North Dakota.
Brian Schatz, of Hawaii.
Chris Van Hollen, of Maryland.
Doug Jones, of Alabama.

National Security and International Trade and Finance

Ben Sasse, of Nebraska, *Chair*

Bob Corker, of Tennessee.
Tom Cotton, of Arkansas.
Mike Rounds, of South Dakota.
David Perdue, of Georgia.

Joe Donnelly, of Indiana.
Mark R. Warner, of Virginia.
Heidi Heitkamp, of North Dakota.
Brian Schatz, of Hawaii.

Securities, Insurance, and Investment

Dean Heller, of Nevada, *Chair*

Richard C. Shelby, of Alabama.
Bob Corker, of Tennessee.
Patrick J. Toomey, of Pennsylvania.
Tim Scott, of South Carolina.
Ben Sasse, of Nebraska.
Mike Rounds, of South Dakota.
Thom Tillis, of North Carolina.
Jerry Moran, of Kansas.
Mark R. Warner, of Virginia.
Jack Reed, of Rhode Island.
Robert Menendez, of New Jersey.
Jon Tester, of Montana.
Elizabeth Warren, of Massachusetts.
Chris Van Hollen, of Maryland.
Catherine Cortez Masto, of Nevada.
Doug Jones, of Alabama.

STAFF

Committee on Banking, Housing, and Urban Affairs (SD–534), 224–7391, fax 224–5137.
Majority Staff Director.—Gregg Richard.
Communications Director.—Amanda Critchfield.
Chief Counsel.—Elad Roisman.
Chief Counsel, National Security Policy.—John O'Hara.
Policy Director.—Mike Quickel.
Deputy Chief Counsel: Joseph Carapiet, Jonathan Gould.
Counsel.—Matt Jones.
Economist.—Kristine Johnson.
Professional Staff Members: Brandon Beall, Jen Deci.
Minority Staff Director.—Mark Powden.
Chief Counsel.—Elisha Tuku.
Policy Director.—Colin McGinnis.
Press Secretary.—Ashley Lewis.
Counsel and Chief Investigator.—Bob Roach.
Professional Staff Members: Homer Carlisle, Megan Cheney, Beth Cooper, Amanda Fischer, Corey Frayer.
Legislative Assistant.—Phil Rudd.
Non-Designated Staff:
Chief Clerk.—Dawn Ratliff.
IT Director.—Shelvin Simmons.
Editor.—Jim Crowell.
GPO Detailees.—Sheryl Arrington, Jason Parker.
Deputy Clerk.—Cameron Ricker.
Hearing Clerk/Staff Assistant.—James Guiliamo.
Staff Assistant.—Pamela Streeter.
Subcommittee on Economic Policy
Majority Staff Director.—Kyle Hauttman.
Minority Staff Director.—Craig Radcliffe.
Subcommittee on Financial Institutions and Consumer Protection
Majority Staff Director.—John Crews.
Minority Staff Director.—Bharat Ramamurti.
Subcommittee on Housing, Transportation, and Community Development
Majority Staff Director.—Saathvik Alety.
Minority Staff Director.—Rebecca Schatz.
Subcommittee on National Security and International Trade and Finance
Majority Staff Director.—Ammon Simon.
Minority Staff Director.—Nick Catino.
Subcommittee on Securities, Insurance, and Investment
Majority Staff Director.—Scott Riplinger.
Minority Staff Director.—Jared Roscoe.

Budget

624 Dirksen Senate Office Building 20510–6100

phone 224–0642, http://budget.senate.gov

meets first Thursday of each month

Michael B. Enzi, of Wyoming, *Chair*

Chuck Grassley, of Iowa.
Mike Crapo, of Idaho.
Lindsey Graham, of South Carolina.
Patrick J. Toomey, of Pennsylvania.
Ron Johnson, of Wisconsin.
Bob Corker, of Tennessee.
David Perdue, of Georgia.
Cory Gardner, of Colorado.
John Kennedy, of Louisiana.
John Boozman, of Arkansas.
Tom Cotton, of Arkansas.

BERNARD SANDERS, of Vermont.
Patty Murray, of Washington.
Ron Wyden, of Oregon.
Debbie Stabenow, of Michigan.
Sheldon Whitehouse, of Rhode Island.
Mark R. Warner, of Virginia.
Jeff Merkley, of Oregon.
Tim Kaine, of Virginia.
ANGUS S. KING, JR., of Maine.
Chris Van Hollen, of Maryland.
Kamala Harris, of California.

(No Subcommittees)

STAFF

Committee on the Budget (SD–624), 224–0642.
Majority Staff Director.—Eric Ueland.
Deputy Staff Director.—Matthew Giroux.
Chief Counsel.—George Everly.
Counsel.—Thomas Fuller.
Professional Staff Member.—David Ditch.
Policy Director.—Thomas Borck.
Assistant Staff Director.—Grace Bruno.
Editor.—Elizabeth Keys.
Minority Staff Director.—Warren Gunnels.
Deputy Staff Director.—Mike Jones.
Chief Counsel.—Robert Etter.
Budget Policy Director.—Josh Smith.
Counsel and Analyst for Transportation and Revenue.—Jill Harrelson.
Senior Analyst for Social Security and Income Security.—Jeff Cruz.
Budget Analyst.—Josh Caplan.
Health Policy Analyst.—Marissa Barrera.
Senior Budget Analyst for National Defense.—Ethan Rosenkranz.
Budget Review Professional.—Bobby Kogan.
Policy Adviser.—Bill Gendell.
Staff Non-Designated:
Chief Clerk.—Kim Proctor.
Deputy Chief Clerk.—Katie Smith.
Computer Systems Administrator.—George Woodall.
Archivist.—Katie Smith.
Staff Assistant.—Kevin Walsh.

Commerce, Science, and Transportation

512 Dirksen Senate Office Building 20510–6125

phone 224–1251, TTY / TDD 224–8418, http://commerce.senate.gov

meets Wednesday of each month

John Thune, of South Dakota, *Chair*

Roger F. Wicker, of Mississippi.
Roy Blunt, of Missouri.
Ted Cruz, of Texas.
Deb Fischer, of Nebraska.
Jerry Moran, of Kansas.
Dan Sullivan, of Alaska.
Dean Heller, of Nevada.
James M. Inhofe, of Oklahoma.
Mike Lee, of Utah.
Ron Johnson, of Wisconsin.
Shelley Moore Capito, of West Virginia.
Cory Gardner, of Colorado.
Todd Young, of Indiana.

Bill Nelson, of Florida.
Maria Cantwell, of Washington.
Amy Klobuchar, of Minnesota.
Richard Blumenthal, of Connecticut.
Brian Schatz, of Hawaii.
Edward J. Markey, of Massachusetts.
Tom Udall, of New Mexico.
Gary C. Peters, of Michigan.
Tammy Baldwin, of Wisconsin.
Tammy Duckworth, of Illinois.
Margaret Wood Hassan, of New Hampshire.
Catherine Cortez Masto, of Nevada.
Jon Tester, of Montana.

SUBCOMMITTEES

[The chair and the ranking minority member are ex officio members of all subcommittees.]

Aviation Operations, Safety, and Security

Roy Blunt, of Missouri, *Chair*

Roger F. Wicker, of Mississippi.
Ted Cruz, of Texas.
Deb Fischer, of Nebraska.
Jerry Moran, of Kansas.
Dan Sullivan, of Alaska.
Dean Heller, of Nevada.
James M. Inhofe, of Oklahoma.
Mike Lee, of Utah.
Shelley Moore Capito, of West Virginia.
Cory Gardner, of Colorado.
Todd Young, of Indiana.

Maria Cantwell, of Washington.
Amy Klobuchar, of Minnesota.
Richard Blumenthal, of Connecticut.
Brian Schatz, of Hawaii.
Edward J. Markey, of Massachusetts.
Tom Udall, of New Mexico.
Gary C. Peters, of Michigan.
Tammy Baldwin, of Wisconsin.
Tammy Duckworth, of Illinois.
Margaret Wood Hassan, of New Hampshire.
Jon Tester, of Montana.

Communications, Technology, Innovation, and the Internet

Roger F. Wicker, of Mississippi, *Chair*

Roy Blunt, of Missouri.
Ted Cruz, of Texas.
Deb Fischer, of Nebraska.
Jerry Moran, of Kansas.
Dan Sullivan, of Alaska.
Dean Heller, of Nevada.
James M. Inhofe, of Oklahoma.
Mike Lee, of Utah.
Ron Johnson, of Wisconsin.
Shelley Moore Capito, of West Virginia.
Cory Gardner, of Colorado.
Todd Young, of Indiana.

Brian Schatz, of Hawaii.
Maria Cantwell, of Washington.
Amy Klobuchar, of Minnesota.
Richard Blumenthal, of Connecticut.
Edward J. Markey, of Massachusetts.
Tom Udall, of New Mexico.
Gary C. Peters, of Michigan.
Tammy Baldwin, Wisconsin.
Tammy Duckworth, Illinois.
Margaret Wood Hassan, of New Hampshire.
Catherine Cortez Masto, of Nevada.
Jon Tester, of Montana.

Consumer Protection, Product Safety, Insurance, and Data Security

Jerry Moran, of Kansas, *Chair*

Roy Blunt, of Missouri.
Ted Cruz, of Texas.
Deb Fischer, of Nebraska.
Dean Heller, of Nevada.
James M. Inhofe, of Oklahoma.
Mike Lee, of Utah.
Shelley Moore Capito, of West Virginia.
Todd Young, of Indiana.

Richard Blumenthal, of Connecticut.
Amy Klobuchar, of Minnesota.
Edward J. Markey, of Massachusetts.
Tom Udall, of New Mexico.
Tammy Duckworth, of Illinois.
Margaret Wood Hassan, of New Hampshire.
Catherine Cortez Masto, of Nevada.

Oceans, Atmosphere, Fisheries, and Coast Guard

Dan Sullivan, of Alaska, *Chair*

Roger F. Wicker, of Mississippi.
Deb Fischer, of Nebraska.
James M. Inhofe, of Oklahoma.
Mike Lee, of Utah.
Ron Johnson, of Wisconsin.
Cory Gardner, of Colorado.
Todd Young, of Indiana.

Tammy Baldwin, of Wisconsin.
Maria Cantwell, of Washington.
Richard Blumenthal, of Connecticut.
Brian Schatz, of Hawaii.
Edward J. Markey, of Massachusetts.
Gary C. Peters, of Michigan.

Space, Science, and Competitiveness

Ted Cruz, of Texas, *Chair*

Jerry Moran, of Kansas.
Dan Sullivan, of Alaska.
Mike Lee, of Utah.
Ron Johnson, of Wisconsin.
Shelley Moore Capito, of West Virginia.
Cory Gardner, of Colorado.

Edward J. Markey, of Massachusetts.
Brian Schatz, of Hawaii.
Tom Udall, of New Mexico.
Gary C. Peters, of Michigan.
Tammy Baldwin, of Wisconsin.
Margaret Wood Hassan, of New Hampshire.

Surface Transportation and Merchant Marine Infrastructure, Safety and Security

Deb Fischer, of Nebraska, *Chair*

Roger F. Wicker, of Mississippi.
Roy Blunt, of Missouri.
Dean Heller, of Nevada.
James M. Inhofe, of Oklahoma.
Ron Johnson, of Wisconsin.
Shelley Moore Capito, of West Virginia.
Cory Gardner, of Colorado.
Todd Young, of Indiana.

Gary C. Peters, of Michigan.
Maria Cantwell, of Washington.
Amy Klobuchar, of Minnesota.
Richard Blumenthal, of Connecticut.
Tom Udall, of New Mexico.
Tammy Baldwin, of Wisconsin.
Tammy Duckworth, of Illinois.
Margaret Wood Hassan, of New Hampshire.

STAFF

Committee on Commerce, Science, and Transportation (SD–512), 224–1251.
Majority Staff Director.—Nick Rossi.
Deputy Staff Director.—Adrian Arnakis.
General Counsel.—Jason Van Beek.
Communications Director.—Frederick Hill.
Digital Director/Press Secretary.—Brianna Manzelli.
Director of Operations.—Theresa Eugene.
Staff Assistant.—Paul Bertram.
Minority Staff Director.—Kim Lipsky.
Deputy Staff Director.—Chris Day.
General Counsel.—Hazeen Ashby.
Communications Director.—Bryan Gulley.
Press Assistant.—Maria Stratienko.
Counsel.—Renae Black.
Special Assistant.—Mary Guenther.

Oversight and Investigations Staff:
General Counsel.—Jason Van Beek.
Investigative Counsel.—Chapin Gregor.
Senior Professional Staff Member/Investigator.—Cheri Pascoe.
Legislative Aide.—Andrew Timm.
Minority Oversight Counsel.—Brad Torppey.
Counsel.—Meeran Ahn.
Aviation Operations, Safety, and Security Staff:
Majority Policy Director.—Mike Reynolds.
Professional Staff Member.—Simon Perez.
Counsel.—Mike Reynolds.
Senior Professional Staff Members: Missye Brickell, Jaclyn Keshian.
Minority Staff Director.—Mohsin Syed.
Counsel.—Tom Chapman.
Research Assistant.—Isaiah Wonnenberg.
FAA Detailee.—Daniel Blum.
Communications, Technology, Innovation and the Internet Staff:
Majority Policy Director.—Crystal Tully.
General Counsel.—Jason Van Beek.
Research Assistant.—Alex Sachtjen.
Professional Staff Members: Cort Bush, Matthew Plaster.
Counsel/FCC Detailee.—Daniel Ball.
Minority Staff Director.—John Branscome.
Counsel.—Shawn Bone.
FCC Detailee.—Randy Clarke.
Consumer Protection, Product Safety, Insurance, and Data Security Staff:
Majority Senior Counsel.—Peter Feldman.
Professional Staff Member/Investigator.—Cheri Pascoe.
Legislative Aide.—Andrew Timm.
Research Assistant.—Reed Cook.
Minority Staff Director.—Christian Tamotsu Fjeld.
Detailee.—Kathleen Benway.
Oceans, Atmosphere, Fisheries, and Coast Guard Staff:
Majority Policy Director.—Fern Gibbons.
Research Assistant.—Chance Costello.
Professional Staff Member.—Alexis Rudd.
Legislative Aide.—Ross Dietrich.
NOAA Detailee.—Zach Cress.
Coast Guard Fellow.—Jason Smith.
Fisheries Fellow.—Janan Evans-Vilent.
Minority Counsel.—Jeff Lewis.
Senior Consel.—Sara Gonzalez-Rothi.
Coast Guard Fellow.—Katherine Carabine.
Sea Grant Fellow.—Lauren Linsmayer.
Space, Science, and Competitiveness Staff:
Majority Senior Counsel.—Mike Reynolds.
Professional Staff Members: Missye Brickell, Jaclyn Keshian.
Minority Staff Director.—Nick Cummings.
Professional Staff Member.—Alicia Brown.
Legislative Assistant.—Maria Stratienko.
NASA Detailee.—Joy Burkey.
Surface Transportation and Merchant Marine Infrastructure, Safety and Security Staff:
Majority Policy Director.—Fern Gibbons.
Senior Professional Staff Member.—Patrick Fuchs.
Professional Staff Member.—Andrew Neely.
Research Assistant.—Chance Costello.
Minority Staff Director.—Devon Barnhart.
Legislative Assistant.—Stephen Stadius.
Bipartisan Staff:
Deputy Chief Clerk.—Stephanie Gamache.
Director, Information Technology.—Jonathan Bowen.
Archivist.—Sarah Schmitz.
GPO Detailee.—Jacqueline Washington.
Staff Assistant.—Stephanie Lieu.
Bipartisan Staff, Legislative Counsel's Office:
Legislative Counsel.—Jennifer Dorrer.
Legislative Clerk.—Celina Inman.

Energy and Natural Resources

304 Dirksen Senate Office Building 20510

phone 224–4971, fax 224–6163, http://energy.senate.gov

meets upon call of the chair

Lisa Murkowski, of Alaska, *Chair*

John Barrasso, of Wyoming.	*Maria Cantwell,* of Washington.
James E. Risch, of Idaho.	*Ron Wyden,* of Oregon.
Mike Lee, of Utah.	BERNARD SANDERS, of Vermont.
Jeff Flake, of Arizona.	*Debbie Stabenow,* of Michigan.
Steve Daines, of Montana.	*Joe Manchin III,* of West Virginia.
Cory Gardner, of Colorado.	*Martin Heinrich,* of New Mexico.
Lamar Alexander, of Tennessee.	*Mazie K. Hirono,* of Hawaii.
John Hoeven, of North Dakota.	ANGUS S. KING, JR., of Maine.
Bill Cassidy, of Louisiana.	*Tammy Duckworth,* of Illinois.
Rob Portman, of Ohio.	*Catherine Cortez Masto,* of Nevada.
Shelley Moore Capito, of West Virginia.	*Tina Smith,* of Minnesota.

SUBCOMMITTEES

[The chair and the ranking minority member are ex officio members of all subcommittees.]

Energy

Cory Gardner, of Colorado, *Chair*

James E. Risch, of Idaho.	*Joe Manchin III,* of West Virginia.
Jeff Flake, of Arizona.	*Ron Wyden,* of Oregon.
Steve Daines, of Montana.	BERNARD SANDERS, of Vermont.
Lamar Alexander, of Tennessee.	*Martin Heinrich,* of New Mexico.
John Hoeven, of North Dakota.	ANGUS S. KING, JR., of Maine.
Bill Cassidy, of Louisiana.	*Tammy Duckworth,* of Illinois.
Rob Portman, of Ohio.	*Catherine Cortez Masto,* of Nevada.
Shelley Moore Capito, of West Virginia.	*Tina Smith,* of Minnesota.

National Parks

Steve Daines, of Montana, *Chair*

John Barrasso, of Wyoming.	ANGUS S. KING, JR., of Maine.
Mike Lee, of Utah.	BERNARD SANDERS, of Vermont.
Cory Gardner, of Colorado.	*Debbie Stabenow,* of Michigan.
Lamar Alexander, of Tennessee.	*Martin Heinrich,* of New Mexico.
John Hoeven, of North Dakota.	*Mazie K. Hirono,* of Hawaii.
Rob Portman, of Ohio.	*Tammy Duckworth,* of Illinois.

Public Lands, Forests, and Mining

Mike Lee, of Utah, *Chair*

John Barrasso, of Wyoming.	*Ron Wyden,* of Oregon.
James E. Risch, of Idaho.	*Debbie Stabenow,* of Michigan.
Jeff Flake, of Arizona.	*Joe Manchin III,* of West Virginia.
Steve Daines, of Montana.	*Martin Heinrich,* of New Mexico.
Cory Gardner, of Colorado.	*Mazie K. Hirono,* of Hawaii.
Lamar Alexander, of Tennessee.	*Catherine Cortez Masto,* of Nevada.
John Hoeven, of North Dakota.	*Tina Smith,* of Minnesota.
Bill Cassidy, of Louisiana.	
Shelley Moore Capito, of West Virginia.	

Water and Power

Jeff Flake, of Arizona, *Chair*

John Barrasso, of Wyoming.
James E. Risch, of Idaho.
Mike Lee, of Utah.
Bill Cassidy, of Louisiana.
Rob Portman, of Ohio.
Shelley Moore Capito, of West Virginia.

Catherine Cortez Masto, of Nevada.
Ron Wyden, of Oregon.
BERNARD SANDERS, of Vermont.
Joe Manchin III, of West Virginia.
Tammy Duckworth, of Illinois.
Tina Smith, of Minnesota.

STAFF

Committee on Energy and Natural Resources (SD–304), 224–4971, fax 224–6163.
Majority Staff Director.—Brian Hughes.
Chief Counsel.—Patrick McCormick.
Deputy Chief Counsel.—Kellie Donnelly.
Senior Counsel.—Isaac Edwards.
Senior Counsel and Public Lands and Natural Resources Policy Director.—Lucy Murfitt.
Senior Professional Staff Member and Energy Policy Advisor.—Brianne Miller.
Communications Director.—Nicole Daigle.
Professional Staff Members: Chester Carson, Lane Dickson, Michelle Lane, Annie Hoefler, Benjamin Reinke, Ph.D.
Congressional Detailee.—Robert Ivanauskas.
Executive Assistant.—Melissa Enriquez.
Staff Assistants: Sean Solie, John Starkey.
Non-Designated Staff:
Chief Clerk.—Darla Ripchensky.
Staff Assistant.—Gabriel Prout.
Systems Administrator.—Dominic Taylor.
Minority Staff Director.—Mary Louise Wagner.
Chief Counsel.—Sam Fowler.
General Counsel.—David Brooks.
Senior Counsel.—David Gillers.
Press Secretary.—Peter True.
Senior Professional Staff Member.—Bryan Petit.
Professional Staff Members: Rebecca Bonner, Spencer Gray, Scott McKee, Rory Stanley, Brie Van Cleve.
Congressional Fellows: Tom Schaff, Zach Valder.
Research Analyst.—Ada Waelder.
Staff Assistant.—Davide Poyer.

Environment and Public Works

410 Dirksen Senate Office Building 20510–6175

phone 224–6176, www.epw.senate.gov

meets first and third Thursdays of each month

John Barrasso, of Wyoming, *Chair*

James M. Inhofe, of Oklahoma.
Shelley Moore Capito, of West Virginia.
John Boozman, of Arkansas.
Roger F. Wicker, of Mississippi.
Deb Fischer, of Nebraska.
Jerry Moran, of Kansas.
Mike Rounds, of South Dakota.
Joni Ernst, of Iowa.
Dan Sullivan, of Alaska.
Richard C. Shelby, of Alabama.

Thomas R. Carper, of Delaware.
Benjamin L. Cardin, of Maryland.
BERNARD SANDERS, of Vermont.
Sheldon Whitehouse, of Rhode Island.
Jeff Merkley, of Oregon.
Kirsten E. Gillibrand, of New York.
Cory A. Booker, of New Jersey.
Edward J. Markey, of Massachusetts.
Tammy Duckworth, of Illinois.
Chris Van Hollen, of Maryland.

SUBCOMMITTEES

[The chair and the ranking minority member are ex officio (non-voting) members of all subcommittees on which they do not serve.]

Clean Air and Nuclear Safety

Shelley Moore Capito, of West Virginia, *Chair*

James M. Inhofe, of Oklahoma.
John Boozman, of Arkansas.
Roger F. Wicker, of Mississippi.
Deb Fischer, of Nebraska.
Jerry Moran, of Kansas.
Joni Ernst, of Iowa.
Richard C. Shelby, of Alabama.

Sheldon Whitehouse, of Rhode Island.
Benjamin L. Cardin, of Maryland.
BERNARD SANDERS, of Vermont.
Jeff Merkley, of Oregon.
Kirsten E. Gillibrand, of New York.
Edward J. Markey, of Massachusetts.
Tammy Duckworth, of Illinois.

Fisheries, Water, and Wildlife

John Boozman, of Arkansas, *Chair*

James M. Inhofe, of Oklahoma.
Shelley Moore Capito, of West Virginia.
Roger F. Wicker, of Mississippi.
Deb Fischer, of Nebraska.
Mike Rounds, of South Dakota.
Dan Sullivan, of Alaska.
Richard C. Shelby, of Alabama.

Tammy Duckworth, of Illinois.
Benjamin L. Cardin, of Maryland.
Sheldon Whitehouse, of Rhode Island.
Jeff Merkley, of Oregon.
Kirsten E. Gillibrand, of New York.
Edward J. Markey, of Massachusetts.
Chris Van Hollen, of Maryland.

Superfund, Waste Management, and Regulatory Oversight

Mike Rounds, of South Dakota, *Chair*

Jerry Moran, of Kansas.
Joni Ernst, of Iowa.
Dan Sullivan, of Alaska.

Cory A. Booker, of New Jersey.
BERNARD SANDERS, of Vermont.
Chris Van Hollen, of Maryland.

Transportation and Infrastructure

James M. Inhofe, of Oklahoma, *Chair*

Shelley Moore Capito, of West Virginia.
John Boozman, of Arkansas.
Roger F. Wicker, of Mississippi.
Deb Fischer, of Nebraska.
Jerry Moran, of Kansas.
Joni Ernst, of Iowa.
Dan Sullivan, of Alaska.
Richard C. Shelby, of Alabama.

Benjamin L. Cardin, of Maryland.
BERNARD SANDERS, of Vermont.
Sheldon Whitehouse, of Rhode Island.
Jeff Merkley, of Oregon.
Kirsten E. Gillibrand, of New York.
Edward J. Markey, of Massachusetts.
Tammy Duckworth, of Illinois.
Cory A. Booker, of New Jersey.

STAFF

Committee on Environment and Public Works (SD–410), phone 224–6176; Majority fax (SD–410), 224–5167; (SH–415), 22–2322.
Majority Staff Director.—Richard Russell.
Deputy Staff Director.—Brian Clifford.
Majority Chief Counsel.—Matt Leggett.
Majority Senior Counsels: Elizabeth Horner, Justin Memmott.
Counsels: Andrew Harding, James Wilson.
Editorial Director.—Stephen Chapman.
Chief Clerk.—Alicia Hawkins.
Director of Information Technology.—Rae Ann Phipps.
GPO Detailees: LaVern Finks, Sonya Kunkle.
Majority Communications Director.—Mike Danylak.
Majority Counsel and Director of Operations.—Elizabeth Olsen.
Majority New Media Director.—Elise Mullen.
Majority Research Assistants: Thomas Craig, Sean Heaslip, Abigale Tardif.
Majority Staff Assistant.—Sam French.
Majority Deputy Director of Operations.—Beth Trenti.

Committee on Environment and Public Works (SD–456), phone 224–8832; Minority fax (SD–456), 224–1273; (SH–508), 228–0574.
Minority Staff Director.—Mary Frances Repko.
Minority Chief Counsel.—Andrew Rogers.
Minority Chief Counsel, Environment.—Christophe Tulou.
Minority Director of Oversight.—Michal Freedhoff.
Minority Senior Policy Advisor for Clean Air and Climate.—Laura Haynes Gillam.
Office Manager.—Carolyn Mack.
Director of Information Technology.—Rae Ann Phipps.
Minority Press Secretary.—Kelly Scully.
Senior Professional Staff Members: John Kane, Kusai Merchant.
DOT Detailee.—Andrew Wishnia.
Brookings Fellow.—Zach Pilchen.
Professional Staff Members: Rebecca Higgins, Elizabeth Mabry.
Senior Policy Advisor for Infrastructure.—Kenneth Martin.
Oversight Counsel.—Rachit Choksi.
Minority Legislative Correspondent.—Avery Mulligan.
Press Assistant.—Campbell Wallace.
Minority Staff Assistants: Madeline Canning, Ashley Morgan.
Army Corps Detailee.—Christina Basinger.

Finance

219 Dirksen Senate Office Building 20510

phone 224–4515, fax 224–0554, http://finance.senate.gov

meets second and fourth Tuesdays of each month

Orrin G. Hatch, of Utah, *Chair*

Chuck Grassley, of Iowa.
Mike Crapo, of Idaho.
Pat Roberts, of Kansas.
Michael B. Enzi, of Wyoming.
John Cornyn, of Texas.
John Thune, of South Dakota.
Richard Burr, of North Carolina.
Johnny Isakson, of Georgia.
Rob Portman, of Ohio.
Patrick J. Toomey, of Pennsylvania.
Dean Heller, of Nevada.
Tim Scott, of South Carolina.
Bill Cassidy, of Louisiana.

Ron Wyden, of Oregon.
Debbie Stabenow, of Michigan.
Maria Cantwell, of Washington.
Bill Nelson, of Florida.
Robert Menendez, of New Jersey.
Thomas R. Carper, of Delaware.
Benjamin L. Cardin, of Maryland.
Sherrod Brown, of Ohio.
Michael F. Bennet, of Colorado.
Robert P. Casey, Jr., of Pennsylvania.
Mark R. Warner, of Virginia.
Claire McCaskill, of Missouri.
Sheldon Whitehouse, of Rhode Island.

SUBCOMMITTEES

[The chair and ranking minority member are ex officio (non-voting) members of all subcommittees on which they do not serve.]

Energy, Natural Resources, and Infrastructure

Dean Heller, of Nevada, *Chair*

Chuck Grassley, of Iowa.
Mike Crapo, of Idaho.
Michael B. Enzi, of Wyoming.
John Cornyn, of Texas.
Richard Burr, of North Carolina.
Tim Scott, of South Carolina.
Bill Cassidy, of Louisiana.

Michael F. Bennet, of Colorado.
Maria Cantwell, of Washington.
Bill Nelson, of Florida.
Robert Menendez, of New Jersey.
Thomas R. Carper, of Delaware.
Mark R. Warner, of Virginia.
Sheldon Whitehouse, of Rhode Island.

Fiscal Responsibility and Economic Growth

Tim Scott, of South Carolina, *Chair*

Orrin G. Hatch, of Utah.

Ron Wyden, of Oregon.

Health Care

Patrick J. Toomey, of Pennsylvania, *Chair*

Chuck Grassley, of Iowa.
Pat Roberts, of Kansas.
Michael B. Enzi, of Wyoming.
John Thune, of South Dakota.
Richard Burr, of North Carolina.
Johnny Isakson, of Georgia.
Rob Portman, of Ohio.
Dean Heller, of Nevada.
Bill Cassidy, of Louisiana.

Debbie Stabenow, of Michigan.
Robert Menendez, of New Jersey.
Maria Cantwell, of Washington.
Thomas R. Carper, of Delaware.
Benjamin L. Cardin, of Maryland.
Sherrod Brown, of Ohio.
Mark R. Warner, of Virginia.
Ron Wyden, of Oregon.
Sheldon Whitehouse, of Rhode Island.

International Trade, Customs, and Global Competitiveness

John Cornyn, of Texas, *Chair*

Chuck Grassley, of Iowa.
Pat Roberts, of Kansas.
Johnny Isakson, of Georgia.
John Thune, of South Dakota.
Dean Heller, of Nevada.

Robert P. Casey, Jr., of Pennsylvania.
Debbie Stabenow, of Michigan.
Bill Nelson, of Florida.
Claire McCaskill, of Missouri.
Benajmin L. Cardin, of Maryland.

Social Security, Pensions, and Family Policy

Bill Cassidy, of Louisiana, *Chair*

Rob Portman, of Ohio.
Mike Crapo, of Idaho.
Patrick J. Toomey, of Pennsylvania.

Sherrod Brown, of Ohio.
Robert P. Casey, Jr, of Pennsylvania.

Taxation and IRS Oversight

Rob Portman, of Ohio, *Chair*

Mike Crapo, of Idaho.
Pat Roberts, of Kansas.
Michael B. Enzi, of Wyoming.
John Cornyn, of Texas.
John Thune, of South Dakota.
Richard Burr, of North Carolina.
Johnny Isakson, of Georgia.
Patrick J. Toomey, of Pennsylvania.
Tim Scott, of South Carolina.

Mark R. Warner, of Virginia.
Thomas R. Carper, of Delaware.
Benjamin L. Cardin, of Maryland.
Claire McCaskill, of Missouri.
Robert Menendez, of New Jersey.
Michael F. Bennet, of Colorado.
Robert P. Casey, Jr., of Pennsylvania.
Maria Cantwell, of Washington.
Sheldon Whitehouse, of Rhode Island.

STAFF

Committee on Finance (SD–219), 224–4515, fax 228–0554.
Majority Staff Director.—Jeff Wrase.
Tax Counsels: Jennifer Acuna, Tony Coughlan.
Senior Tax Policy Advisor.—Christopher Hanna.
Tax and Nomination Professional Staff.—Nick Wyatt.
Senior Policy Advisor for Tax and Accounting.—Eric Oman.
Professional Staff Members: Joshua Blume, Alex Monie.
Chief Healthcare Investigative Counsel.—Kim Brandt.
Deputy Chief Oversight Counsel.—Christopher Armstrong.
Professional Staff Member.—Maddie Davidson.
Hispanic Outreach Director.—Jeyben Castro.
Health Policy Advisors: Brett Baker, Erin Dempsey.
Senior Health Policy Advisor.—Jennifer Kuskowski.
Health Policy Advisor and Human Services Director.—Ryan Martin.
Office Manager.—Tim Corley.
Chief International Trade Counsel.—Shane Warren.
International Trade Counsels: Bryan Bombassaro, Nasim Sussell.
Policy Analyst.—Rory Heslington.
Communications Director.—Julia Lawless.
Press Secretary.—Katie Niederee.
Detailees: Dan Burd, Queena Fan.
Democratic Staff Director.—Joshua Sheinkman.
Assistant to the Democratic Staff Director.—Sam Conchuratt.
Democratic Chief Counsel.—Mike Evans.
Senior Advisor.—Isaiah Akin.
Chief Tax Counsel.—Tiffany Smith.
Senior Tax Counsel, Business and International.—Ryan Abraham.
Senior Tax and ERISA Counsel.—Drew Crouch.
Senior Tax and Economic Advisor.—Adam Carasso.
Tax Policy Advisor.—Christopher Arneson.
Tax and Economic Advisor.—Bobby Andres.
Tax Policy Analyst.—Jay Weismuller.

Chief Health Policy Advisor.—Elizabeth Jurinka.
Senior Health Advisor.—Matt Kazan.
Senior Health Counsels: Dr. Beth Vrabel, Arielle Woronoff.
Health Counsel.—Anne Dwyer.
Health Policy Analyst.—Vacant.
Chief Advisor for International Competitiveness and Innovation.—Jayme White.
International Trade Counsels: Elissa Alben, Greta Peisch.
Senior Advisor for Technology and Trade.—Andy Heiman.
Chief Human Services Director.—Laura Berntsen.
Chief Investigator.—Dave Berick.
Investigations Counsel.—Dan Goshorn.
Investigator, Lead Nominations Staff.—Ian Nicholson.
Investigators: Peter Gartrell, Josh Heath.
Senior Domestic Policy Advisor—Social Security.—Tom Klouda.
Senior Communications Advisor for Natural Resources, Trade, Intelligence, Defense, Foreign Policy, Technology, and Digital Trade.—Keith Chu.
Chief Communications Advisor, Tax, Oversight, and Investigations.—Rachel McCleery.
Senior Advisor for Policy Communications, Speechwriter.—Ryan Carey.
Deputy Press Secretary for Health and Human Services.—Taylor Harvey.
Press Secretary for Child Welfare, Higher Education, Domestic Policy, Agriculture, and Energy.—Vacant.
Digital Director.—Lucy Vernasco.
NON Desk Clerk.—Susanna Segal.
Staff Assistants: Tim Corley, Eliza Smith.
NON Staff Assistants: Samine Mirfakhrai, Michael Pinkerton.
IT Director.—Joe Carnucci.
Assistant to the Systems Administrator.—Mark Blair.
Chief Clerk and Historian.—Josh LeVasseur.
Deputy Clerk.—Jewel Harper.
Hearing Clerk.—Athena Schritz.
Archivist.—Dina Mazina.
Editor.—Tim Danowski.
Detailee.—Mark Moore.

Foreign Relations

423 Dirksen Senate Office Building 20510–6225

phone 224–4651, http://foreign.senate.gov

meets each Tuesday

Bob Corker, of Tennessee, *Chair*

James E. Risch, of Idaho.
Marco Rubio, of Florida.
Ron Johnson, of Wisconsin.
Jeff Flake, of Arizona.
Cory Gardner, of Colorado.
Todd Young, of Indiana.
John Barrasso, of Wyoming.
Johnny Isakson, of Georgia.
Rob Portman, of Ohio.
Rand Paul, of Kentucky.

Benjamin L. Cardin, of Maryland.
Robert Menendez, of New Jersey.
Jeanne Shaheen, of New Hampshire.
Christopher A. Coons, of Delaware.
Tom Udall, of New Mexico.
Christopher Murphy, of Connecticut.
Tim Kaine, of Virginia.
Edward J. Markey, of Massachusetts.
Jeff Merkley, of Oregon.
Cory A. Booker, of New Jersey.

SUBCOMMITTEES

[The chair and ranking minority member are ex officio (non-voting) members of all subcommittees on which they do not serve.]

Africa and Global Health Policy

Jeff Flake, of Arizona, *Chair*

Todd Young, of Indiana.
John Barrasso, of Wyoming.
Johnny Isakson, of Georgia.
Rand Paul, of Kentucky.

Cory A. Booker, of New Jersey.
Christopher A. Coons, of Delaware.
Tom Udall, of New Mexico.
Jeff Merkley, of Oregon.

East Asia, the Pacific, and International Cybersecurity Policy

Cory Gardner, of Colorado, *Chair*

James E. Risch, of Idaho.
Marco Rubio, of Florida.
John Barrasso, of Wyoming.
Johnny Isakson, of Georgia.

Edward J. Markey, of Massachusetts.
Jeff Merkley, of Oregon.
Christopher Murphy, of Connecticut.
Tim Kaine, of Virginia.

Europe and Regional Security Cooperation

Ron Johnson, of Wisconsin, *Chair*

James E. Risch, of Idaho.
John Barrasso, of Wyoming.
Rob Portman, of Ohio.
Rand Paul, of Kentucky.

Christopher Murphy, of Connecticut.
Edward J. Markey, of Massachusetts.
Robert Menendez, of New Jersey.
Jeanne Shaheen, of New Hampshire.

Multilateral International Development, Multilateral Institutions, and International Economic, Energy, and Environmental Policy

Todd Young, of Indiana, *Chair*

Jeff Flake, of Arizona.
Cory Gardner, of Colorado.
John Barrasso, of Wyoming.
Rob Portman, of Ohio.

Jeff Merkley, of Oregon.
Tom Udall, of New Mexico.
Christopher A. Coons, of Delaware.
Edward J. Markey, of Massachusetts.

Near East, South Asia, Central Asia, and Counterterrorism

James E. Risch, of Idaho, *Chair*

Marco Rubio, of Florida.
Ron Johnson, of Wisconsin.
Todd Young, of Indiana.
Rob Portman, of Ohio.
Tim Kaine, of Virginia.
Robert Menendez, of New Jersey.
Christopher Murphy, of Connecticut.
Cory A. Booker, of New Jersey.

State Department and USAID Management, International Operations, and Bilateral International Development

Johnny Isakson, of Georgia, *Chair*

James E. Risch, of Idaho.
Marco Rubio, of Florida.
Rob Portman, of Ohio.
Rand Paul, of Kentucky.
Jeanne Shaheen, of New Hampshire.
Christopher A. Coons, of Delaware.
Cory A. Booker, of New Jersey.
Tom Udall, of New Mexico.

Western Hemisphere, Transnational Crime, Civilian Security, Democracy, Human Rights, and Global Women's Issues

Marco Rubio, of Florida, *Chair*

Ron Johnson, of Wisconsin.
Jeff Flake, of Arizona.
Cory Gardner, of Colorado.
Johnny Isakson, of Georgia.
Robert Menendez, of New Jersey.
Tom Udall, of New Mexico.
Jeanne Shaheen, of New Hampshire.
Tim Kaine, of Virginia.

STAFF

Committee on Foreign Relations (SD–423), 224–4651.
Majority Staff:
Chief of Staff.—Todd Womack.
Policy Director.—Christopher Tuttle.
Communications Director.—Micah Johnson.
Press Secretary.—Chuck Harper.
Senior Professional Staff Members: Thomas Callahan, Trey Hicks, Carolyn Leddy, Caleb McCarry, Stacie Oliver, Michael Phelan.
Senior Advisor and Treaty Counsel.—Andy Olson.
Professional Staff Members: Brooke Eisele, Eric Trager.
Counsels: Grant Mullins, Scott Richardson, Sarah Stone.
Policy Analysts / Assistants: Joe Curtsinger, Emily Manning.
Legislative Correspondent.—Alex Eblen.
Director of Operations.—Caroline Hodge.
Minority Staff:
Staff Director.—Jessica Lewis.
Director of Operations.—Leslie Bull.
Chief Counsel.—Margaret Taylor.
Deputy Chief Counsel.—John Ryan.
Policy Director.—Sarah Arkin.
Press Secretary.—Juan Pachon.
Senior Advisor / Counselor.—Michael Schiffer.
Research / Legislative Assistants: Chris Barr, Joel Cohen, Nury Gambarrotti, Daniel Ricchetti, Jonathan Tsentas.
Senior Professional Staff Members: David Fite, Heather Flynn, Jim Greene, Josh Klein, Charlotte Oldham-Moore, Lowell Schwartz, Dana Stroul, Brandon Yoder.
Senior Professional Staff Member on Europe.—Damian Murphy.
Legislative Fellow.—Laura Carey.
Non-Designated Staff:
Chief Clerk.—John Dutton.
Deputy Chief Clerk.—Samantha Hamilton.
Hearing Clerk.—Bertie Bowman.
Executive Clerk.—Lexie Simpson.
Chief of Protocol / Foreign Travel.—Meg Murphy.
Protocol Assistant.—Rebecca Rile.
Staff Assistants: Kateri Dahl, Anna Knight.
Printing Clerks: Michael Bennett, Justin West.

Health, Education, Labor, and Pensions

428 Dirksen Senate Office Building 20510–6300

phone 224–5375, http://help.senate.gov

Lamar Alexander, of Tennessee, *Chair*

Michael B. Enzi, of Wyoming.
Richard Burr, of North Carolina.
Johnny Isakson, of Georgia.
Rand Paul, of Kentucky.
Susan M. Collins, of Maine.
Bill Cassidy, of Louisiana.
Todd Young, of Indiana.
Orrin G. Hatch, of Utah.
Pat Roberts, of Kansas.
Lisa Murkowski, of Alaska.
Tim Scott, of South Carolina.

Patty Murray, of Washington.
BERNARD SANDERS, of Vermont.
Robert P. Casey, Jr., of Pennsylvania.
Michael F. Bennet, of Colorado.
Tammy Baldwin, of Wisconsin.
Christopher Murphy, of Connecticut.
Elizabeth Warren, of Massachusetts.
Tim Kaine, of Virginia.
Margaret Wood Hassan, of New Hampshire.
Tina Smith, of Minnesota.
Doug Jones, of Alabama.

SUBCOMMITTEES

[The chair and ranking minority member are ex officio members of all subcommittees on which they do not serve.]

Children and Families

Rand Paul, of Kentucky, *Chair*

Lisa Murkowski, of Alaska.
Richard Burr, of North Carolina.
Bill Cassidy, of Louisiana.
Todd Young, of Indiana.
Orrin G. Hatch, of Utah.
Pat Roberts, of Kansas.

Robert P. Casey, Jr., of Pennsylvania.
BERNARD SANDERS, of Vermont.
Michael F. Bennet, of Colorado.
Tim Kaine, of Virginia.
Margaret Wood Hassan, of New Hampshire.
Tina Smith, of Minnesota.

Employment and Workplace Safety

Johnny Isakson, of Georgia, *Chair*

Pat Roberts, of Kansas.
Tim Scott, of South Carolina.
Richard Burr, of North Carolina.
Rand Paul, of Kentucky.
Bill Cassidy, of Louisiana.
Todd Young, of Indiana.

Tammy Baldwin, of Wisconsin.
Robert P. Casey, Jr., of Pennsylvania.
Christopher Murphy, of Connecticut.
Elizabeth Warren, of Massachusetts.
Tina Smith, of Minnesota.
Doug Jones, of Alabama.

Primary Health and Retirement Security

Michael B. Enzi, of Wyoming, *Chair*

Richard Burr, of North Carolina.
Susan M. Collins, of Maine.
Bill Cassidy, of Louisiana.
Todd Young, of Indiana.
Orrin G. Hatch, of Utah.
Pat Roberts, of Kansas.
Tim Scott, of South Carolina.
Lisa Murkowski, of Alaska.

BERNARD SANDERS, of Vermont.
Michael F. Bennet, of Colorado.
Tammy Baldwin, of Wisconsin.
Christopher Murphy, of Connecticut.
Elizabeth Warren, of Massachusetts.
Tim Kaine, of Virginia.
Margaret Wood Hassan, of New Hampshire.
Doug Jones, of Alabama.

STAFF

Committee on Health, Education, Labor, and Pensions (SH–835), 224–6770, fax 224–6510.

Staff Director.—David P. Cleary, SH–835, 4–6770.
Deputy Staff Director.—Lindsey Seidman, SH–835, 4–6770.
Operations Director.—Misty Marshall, SH–835, 4–6770.
General Counsel.—Bobby McMillin, SH–835, 4–6770.
HELP Staff Assistant.—Grant English, SH–835, 8–6770.
Health Policy Office, SH–725, 4–0623.
Health Policy Director.—Grace Stuntz, SH–404, 4–0623.
Chief Counsel for Outreach and Coalitions.—Elizabeth Wroe, SH–725, 4–0623.
Sr. Health Policy Advisor.—Jennifer Boyer, SH–725, 4–0623.
Health Counsel.—Brett Meeks, SH–725, 4–0623.
Health Policy Advisors: Margaret Coulter, Virginia Heppner, SH–725, 4–0623.
Professional Staff Members: Virginia Heppner, Kristi Thompson, Curtis Vann, Andy Vogt, SH–725, 4–0623.
Health Research Assistants: Andrew Burnett, Meredith Good-Cohn, SH–725, 4–0623.
Health Staff Assistant.—Tyler Shrive, SH–404, 4–0623.
Education Office, SH–632, 4–8484.
Education Policy Director and Counsel.—Robert Moran, SH–632, 4–8484.
Education Policy Advisors: Lauren Davies, Andrew LaCasse, SH–828, 4–8484.
Education Professional Staff: Jake Baker, Jordan Hynes, Matt Stern, SH–632, 8–8484.
Staff Assistant.—Mary Catherine Cook.
Education Research Assistant.—Jenn Hatfield.
Labor Policy Office, SH–835, 8–6770.
Labor and Pensions Policy Director.—Andy Banducci, SH–835, 8–6770.
Labor and Pensions Counsel.—Greg Proseus, SH–833, 4–6770.
Labor Research Assistant.—Will Campbell, SH–835, 8–6770.
Chief Counsel for Oversight.—Kristin Nelson Spiridon, SD–424, 4–6770.
Oversight and Investigations Counsel.—Elizabeth Gorman, SD–424, 4–6770.
Oversight Research Assistant.—Charles Snodgrass, SD–424, 4–6770.
Communications Office, SH–132, 4–6770.
Press Secretary and Speechwriter.—Elizabeth Gibson, SH–132, 4–6770.
Deputy Press Secretary and Digital Media.—Evan Dixon, SH–132, 4–6770.
Subcommittee on Children and Families, SH–440, 4–0121.
No Staff.
Subcommittee on Employment and Workplace Safety, SH–607, 4–5800.
Staff Director.—Tommy Nguyen, SH–607, 4–5800.
Subcommittee on Primary Health and Retirement Security, SH–828, 4–5406.
Professional Staff Members: Garnett Decosi, Amanda Lincoln.
Minority Staff:
Staff Director.—Evan Schatz, SD–644, 4–0767.
Deputy Staff Director.—John Righter, SD–644, 4–0767.
Special Assistant.—Sara Zaheer, SD–644, 4–0767.
Deputy Communications Director.—Helen Hare, SD–644, 4–0767.
Press Secretary.—Mairead Lynn, SD–644, 4–0767.
Deputy Press Secretary.—Ryan Myers SD–644, 4–0767.
Health Policy Office, 4–7675.
Health Policy Director.—Nick Bath, SH–527, 4–7675.
Deputy Director, Health Policy.—Andi Fristedt, SH–527, 4–7675.
Senior Health Policy Advisor.—Colin Goldfinch, SH–527, 4–7675.
Health Policy Advisor.—Madeleine Pannel, SH–527, 4–7675.
Senior FDA Counsel.—Vacant, SH–527, 4–7675.
Senior Counsel.—Laurel Sakai, SH–527, 4–7675.
Health Policy Fellow.—Sherie Lou Santos, SH–527, 4–7675.
Staff Assistant.—Osaremen Okolo.
Labor Policy Office, 4–5441.
Labor Policy Director.—Nikki McKinney, SH–622B, 4–5441.
Senior Advisor.—Jake Cornett, SH–622B, 4–5441.
Disability Fellow.—Jacqueline Hubbard, SH–622B, 4–5441.
Labor Counsel.—John D'Elia, SH–622B, 4–5441.
Labor Counsel.—Joseph Shantz, SH–622B, 4–5441.
Senior Pensions Counsel.—Kendra Issaacson, SH–440, 4–5441.
Education Policy Office, 4–5501.
Senior Policy Advisor.—Allie Kimmel, SH–632, 4–5501.
Education Policy Director.—Kara Marchione, SH–632, 4–5501.

Deputy Education Policy Director.—Amanda Beaumont, SH–632, 4–5501.
Senior Policy Advisor.—Bryce McKibben, SH–632, 4–5501.
Legislative Aide.—Manuel Contreras, SH–632, 4–5501.
Policy Advisors: Mary Nguyen Barry, Katherine McClelland.
Oversight and Investigation Office, 4–6403.
General Counsel and Chief Oversight Counsel.—Beth Stein, SH–833, 4–6403.
Deputy General Counsel and Deputy Chief Oversight Counsel.—Carly Rush, SH–833, 4–6403.
Counsel.—Lizzy Letter, SH–833, 4–6403.
Policy Advisor.—Laura Aguilar, SH–833, 4–6403.
Subcommittee on Children and Families, 8–1455.
Subcommittee Staff Director.—Larry Smar, SH–143, 8–1455.
Subcommittee on Employment and Workplace Safety, 4–9243.
Senior Policy Advisor.—Michael Waske, SH–143, 4–2570.
Subcommittee on Primary Health and Retirement Security, 4–5480.
Subcommittee Staff Director.—Britt Weinstock, SH–622A, 4–5480.
Legislative Aide.—Michaela Yarnell, SH–622A, 4–5480.

Homeland Security and Governmental Affairs

340 Dirksen Senate Office Building 20510

phone 224–4751, fax 224–9603, http://hsgac.senate.gov

Hearing Room—SD–342 Dirksen Senate Office Building

meets first Wednesday of each month

Ron Johnson, of Wisconsin, *Chair*

John McCain, of Arizona.
Rob Portman, of Ohio.
Rand Paul, of Kentucky.
James Lankford, of Oklahoma.
Michael B. Enzi, of Wyoming.
John Hoeven, of North Dakota.
Steve Daines, of Montana.

Claire McCaskill, of Missouri.
Thomas R. Carper, of Delaware.
Heidi Heitkamp, of North Dakota.
Gary C. Peters, of Michigan.
Margaret Wood Hassan, of New Hampshire.
Kamala D. Harris, of California.
Doug Jones, of Alabama.

SUBCOMMITTEES

[The chair and the ranking minority member are ex officio members of all subcommittees.]

Federal Spending Oversight and Emergency Management

Rand Paul, of Kentucky, *Chair*

James Lankford, of Oklahoma.
Michael B. Enzi, of Wyoming.
John Hoeven, of North Dakota.

Gary C. Peters, of Michigan.
Kamala D. Harris, of California.
Doug Jones, of Alabama.

Permanent Subcommittee on Investigations

Rob Portman, of Ohio, *Chair*

James Lankford, of Oklahoma.
John McCain, of Arizona.
Rand Paul, of Kentucky.
Steve Daines, of Montana.

Thomas R. Carper, of Delaware.
Heidi Heitkamp, of North Dakota.
Gary C. Peters, of Michigan.
Margaret Wood Hassan, of New Hampshire.

Regulatory Affairs and Federal Management

James Lankford, of Oklahoma, *Chair*

John McCain, of Arizona.
Rob Portman, of Ohio.
Michael B. Enzi, of Wyoming.
Steve Daines, of Montana.

Heidi Heitkamp, of North Dakota.
Thomas R. Carper, of Delaware.
Margaret Wood Hassan, of New Hampshire.
Kamala D. Harris, of California.

STAFF

Committee on Homeland Security and Governmental Affairs (SD–340), 224–4751.
Majority Staff Director.—Chris Hixon.
Chief Counsel.—Gabrielle D'Adamo Singer.
Chief Clerk.—Laura W. Kilbride.
Policy Director.—Dan Lips.
Chief Counsel for Governmental Affairs.—Patrick Bailey.
Chief Investigative Counsel.—David Brewer.
Senior Policy Advisor.—Jerry Markon.
Chief Economist.—Satya Thallam.
Senior Investigator.—Brian Downey.
Counsels: Courtney Allen, Kyle Brosnan.

Investigative Counsel.—Michael Lueptow.
Senior Professional Staff: Joske Bautista, Elizabeth McWhorter, Scott Wittmann.
Professional Staff: Colleen Berny, Christopher Boness, Josh McLeod, Rebecca Nuzzi, Jennifer Selde, Daniel Spino, Elliott Walden.
Research Assistants: Melissa Egred, Barrett Percival.
Staff Assistants: Morgan McCord, Maria Pereyra-Vera.
GAO Detailee.—Michelle Woods.
Fellow.—Maurice Turner.
Publications Clerk.—Joyce Ward.
Financial Clerk.—Rachel Mairella.
Systems Administrator.—Dan Muchow.
Minority Staff Director.—Margaret Daum (SH–442), 224–2627.
Senior Legislative Counsel.—Charlie Moskowitz.
Communications Director and Senior Advisor.—Drew Pusateri.
Senior Counsels: Jackson Eaton, Sarah Garcia.
Counsels: Claudine Brenner, Michael Broome, Courtney Cardin, Sue Ramanathan, Brandon Reavis, Charles Shaw, Kata Sybenga, Caitlin Warner.
Professional Staff Members: Hannah Berner, Julie Klein, Thomas Richards, Joel Walsh.
Press Assistant.—Jordan Wong.
Advisor.—Michelle Benecke.
Staff Assistants: Scarlett Ho, Rina Patel.
GAO Detailee.—Chris Mulkins.
NIST Detailee.—Tim Brennan.
USPS OIG Detailee.—Kirk Kaneer.
Fellow.—Elena Love.

Permanent Subcommittee on Investigations (PSI), (SR–199), 224–3721.
Majority Staff Director/General Counsel.—Matt Owen.
Subcommittee Clerk.—Kate Kielceski.
Senior Policy Advisor.—Brent Bombach.
Chief Investigator and Counsel.—Andrew Dockham.
Deputy Chief Counsel.—Amanda Neely.
Senior Counsel: Stephanie Hall, Andrew Polesovsky.
Investigator.—Will Dagusch.
Professional Staff Member.—Adam Henderson.
Minority Staff Director.—John Kilvington (SR–199), 224–9505.
Chief Counsel.—Portia Bamiduro.
Deputy Chief Counsel.—Peter Kenny.
Counsel: Roberto Berrios, Lauren Dudley.
OMB OIG Detailee.—Shanon Richter.
USPS OIG Detailee.—Felicia Hawkins.

Subcommittee on Federal Spending Oversight and Emergency Management (FSO), (SH–439), 224–2254.
Majority Staff Director.—Greg McNeill.
Subcommittee Clerk.—Kate Kielceski.
Research Assistants: Aaron Gottesman, Adam Salmon.
Legislative Assistant.—Jim Webb.
Minority Staff Director and Chief Counsel.—Zachary Schram (SH–432), 224–7155.
Professional Staff Members: Joseph Lindblad, Alexa Noruk.

Subcommittee on Regulatory Affairs and Federal Management (RAFM), (SH–601), 224–4551.
Majority Staff Director.—John Cuaderes.
Subcommittee Clerk.—Mallory Nersesian.
Deputy Staff Director.—Amanda Hill.
Counsel.—Jake Windhause.
Minority Staff Director.—Eric Bursch (SH–605), 224–3682.
Counsel.—Ashley Poling.
Professional Staff Members: Jared Lennon, Anthony Papian.
CBP Detailee.—Dean Williams.

Judiciary

224 Dirksen Senate Office Building 20510–6275

phone 224–5225, fax 224–9102, http://www.judiciary.senate.gov

meets upon call of the chair

Chuck Grassley, of Iowa, *Chair*

Orrin G. Hatch, of Utah.
Lindsey Graham, of South Carolina.
John Cornyn, of Texas.
Mike Lee, of Utah.
Ted Cruz, of Texas.
Ben Sasse, of Nebraska.
Jeff Flake, of Arizona.
Mike Crapo, of Idaho.
Thom Tillis, of North Carolina.
John Kennedy, of Louisiana.

Dianne Feinstein, of California.
Patrick J. Leahy, of Vermont.
Richard J. Durbin, of Illinois.
Sheldon Whitehouse, of Rhode Island.
Amy Klobuchar, of Minnesota.
Christopher A. Coons, of Delaware.
Richard Blumenthal, of Connecticut.
Mazie K. Hirono, of Hawaii.
Cory A. Booker, of New Jersey.
Kamala D. Harris, of California.

SUBCOMMITTEES

Antitrust, Competition Policy and Consumer Rights

Mike Lee, of Utah, *Chair*

Chuck Grassley, of Iowa.
Orrin G. Hatch, of Utah.
Lindsey Graham, of South Carolina.
Thom Tillis, of North Carolina.

Amy Klobuchar, of Minnesota.
Patrick J. Leahy, of Vermont.
Richard Blumenthal, of Connecticut.
Cory A. Booker, of New Jersey.

Border Security and Immigration

John Cornyn, of Texas, *Chair*

Thom Tillis, of North Carolina.
John Kennedy, of Louisiana.
Chuck Grassley, of Iowa.
Ted Cruz, of Texas.
Jeff Flake, of Arizona.
Mike Crapo, of Idaho.
Mike Lee, of Utah.

Richard J. Durbin, of Illinois.
Dianne Feinstein, of California.
Patrick J. Leahy, of Vermont.
Amy Klobuchar, of Minnesota.
Richard Blumenthal, of Connecticut.
Mazie K. Hirono, of Hawaii.
Cory A. Booker, of New Jersey.

Constitution

Ted Cruz, of Texas, *Chair*

John Cornyn, of Texas.
Mike Crapo, of Idaho.
Ben Sasse, of Nebraska.
Lindsey Graham, of South Carolina.
John Kennedy, of Louisiana.

Mazie K. Hirono, of Hawaii.
Richard J. Durbin, of Illinois.
Sheldon Whitehouse, of Rhode Island.
Christopher A. Coons, of Delaware.
Kamala D. Harris, of California.

Crime and Terrorism

Lindsey Graham, of South Carolina, *Chair*

Chuck Grassley, of Iowa.
Orrin G. Hatch, of Utah.
John Cornyn, of Texas.
Ted Cruz, of Texas.
Ben Sasse, of Nebraska.
John Kennedy, of Louisiana.

Sheldon Whitehouse, of Rhode Island.
Dianne Feinstein, of California.
Richard J. Durbin, of Illinois.
Amy Klobuchar, of Minnesota.
Christopher A. Coons, of Delaware.
Cory A. Booker, of New Jersey.

Oversight, Agency Action, Federal Rights and Federal Courts

Ben Sasse, of Nebraska, *Chair*

Chuck Grassley, of Iowa.
Mike Crapo, of Idaho.
John Kennedy, of Louisiana.
Orrin G. Hatch, of Utah.
Mike Lee, of Utah.
Jeff Flake, of Arizona.
Thom Tillis, of North Carolina.

Richard Blumenthal, of Connecticut.
Patrick J. Leahy, of Vermont.
Sheldon Whitehouse, of Rhode Island.
Amy Klobuchar, of Minnesota.
Christopher A. Coons, of Delaware.
Mazie K. Hirono, of Hawaii.
Kamala D. Harris, of California.

Privacy, Technology and the Law

Jeff Flake, of Arizona, *Chair*

Orrin G. Hatch, of Utah.
Mike Lee, of Utah.
Thom Tills, of North Carolina.
Mike Crapo, of Idaho.
Ben Sasse, of Nebraska.
John Kennedy, of Louisiana.

Christopher A. Coons, of Delaware.
Patrick J. Leahy, of Vermont.
Sheldon Whitehouse, of Rhode Island.
Richard Blumenthal, of Connecticut.
Mazie K. Hirono, of Hawaii.
Kamala D. Harris, of California.

STAFF

Committee on the Judiciary (SD–224), 224–5225.
Chief Clerk.—Roslyne Turner.
Law Librarian.—Charles Papirmeister.
Legislative Calendar Clerk.—Alberta Easter.
Deputy Clerk.—Michelle Heller.
Hearings Clerk.—Jason Covey.
Majority Office (SD–224), 224–5225, fax 224–9102.
Majority Staff Director and Chief Counsel.—Kolan Davis.
Deputy Staff Director and Chief Civil Counsel.—Rita Lari Jochum.
Chief Constitution Counsel and Crime Counsel.—Aaron Cummings.
Chief Counsel for Nominations.—Mike Davis.
Chief Investigative Counsel.—Jason Foster.
Chief Counsel for Justice Programs, Juvenile Justice and Violence Against Women.—Evelyn Fortier.
Chief National Security Counsel and Crime Counsel.—Richard DiZinno.
Deputy Chief Investigative Counsel.—Patrick Davis.
Senior Investigative Counsel, Oversight Whistleblower Policy.—DeLisa Lay.
Investigative Counsels: Josh Flynn-Brown, Katherine Nikas.
Counsels: Ryan Dattilo, Steve Kenny, Kyle McCollum, Lauren Mehler, Jessica Vu, Katharine Willey.
Associate Counsel.—Brian Simonsen.
Professional Staff Member.—Barbara Ledeen.
Investigative Assistant.—Daniel Parker.
Communications Director.—Taylor Foy.
Press Secretary.—George Hartmann.
Staff Assistants: Theresa Baumann, Jordan Kuchta, Michael Perkins.
Archivist.—Stuart Paine.
Director of Information Systems.—Steve Kirkland.
Minority Office (SD–152), 224–7703, fax 224–9516.
Minority Staff Director and Chief Counsel.—Jennifer Duck.
General Counsel.—Heather Sawyer.
Chief Counsel for Crime.—Peter Hyun.
Senior Counsels: Marc Hearron, Annie Owens, Jenn Piatt.
Counsels: Rachel Appleton, Phil Brest, Christina Calce, Patrick Day, Sarah Griswold, Alex Haskell, Gabe Kader, Anant Raut, Nick Xenakis.
Professional Staff Member.—Caitlin Meyer.
Legislative Aides: Alexandria Deitz, Matthew Halek.
Legislative Staff Assistants: Elizabeth Bernal, John Lowry, Oliver Mittelstaedt.
Staff Assistants: Madeline Alasia, Kelly McCormick.
Archivist.—Jennifer Wiley.
Systems Administrator.—Lane Giardina.

Subcommittee on Antitrust, Competition Policy and Consumer Rights.
Majority Chief Counsel.—Phil Alito.
Minority Chief Counsel.—Elizabeth Farrar.
Subcommittee on the Constitution.
Majority Chief Counsel.—Judd Stone.
Minority Chief Counsel.—Helaine Greenfeld.
Subcommittee on Crime and Terrorism.
Majority Chief Counsel.—Lee Holmes.
Minority Chief Counsel.—Lara Quint.
Subcommittee on Border Security and Immigration.
Majority Chief Counsel.—Carter Burwell.
Minority Chief Counsel.—Joseph Zogby.
Subcommittee on Oversight, Agency Action, Federal Rights and Federal Courts.
Majority Chief Counsel.—William Payne.
Minority Chief Counsel.—Sam Simon.
Subcommittee on Privacy, Technology and the Law.
Majority Chief Counsel.—Kateland Jackson.
Minority Chief Counsel.—Erica Songer.
Senator Hatch Judiciary Staff:
Chief Counsel.—Christopher Bates.
Senator Crapo Judiciary Staff:
Professional Staff Member.—Ken Flanz.
Senator Kennedy Judiciary Staff:
Legislative Counsel.—Nick Hawatmeh.
Senator Tillis Judiciary Staff:
Counsel.—Brad Watts.
Senator Leahy Judiciary Staff:
Chief Counsel.—David Pendle.
Senator Booker Judiciary Staff:
Chief Counsel.—Tona Boyd.
Senator Harris Judiciary Staff:
General Counsel.—Josh Hsu.

Rules and Administration

305 Russell Senate Office Building 20510–6325

phone 224–6352, http://rules.senate.gov

[Legislative Reorganization Act of 1946]

meets second and fourth Wednesday of each month

Roy Blunt, of Missouri, *Chair*

Mitch McConnell, of Kentucky.
Lamar Alexander, of Tennessee.
Pat Roberts, of Kansas.
Richard C. Shelby, of Alabama.
Ted Cruz, of Texas.
Shelley Moore Capito, of West Virginia.
Roger F. Wicker, of Mississippi.
Deb Fischer, of Nebraska.
Cindy Hyde-Smith, of Mississippi.

Amy Klobuchar, of Minnesota.
Dianne Feinstein, of California.
Charles E. Schumer, of New York.
Richard J. Durbin, of Illinois.
Tom Udall, of New Mexico.
Mark R. Warner, of Virginia.
Patrick J. Leahy, of Vermont.
ANGUS S. KING, JR., of Maine.
Catherine Cortez Masto, of Nevada.

(No Subcommittees)

STAFF

Committee on Rules and Administration (SR–305), 224–6352.
Majority Staff Director.—Fitzhugh Elder IV.
Deputy Staff Director.—Rachelle Schroeder.
Chief Counsel.—Jackie Barber.
Senior Professional Staff.—Nichole Kotschwar.
Professional Staff: —Elizabeth Brennan, Kasey Shelly.
Minority Staff Director.—Elizabeth Peluso.
Deputy Staff Director.—Travis Talvitie.
Chief Counsels: Lindsey Kerr, Benjamin Hovland (acting).
Senior Policy Professional Staff.—Abbie Sorrendino.
Professional Staff.—Denise Flemming.
Non-Designated Staff:
Chief Clerk.—Cindy Qualley.
Auditors: Lesya Eppes, Kacie Jones, Alex Stoddard.
Staff Assistants: Garrison Holmberg, Robert Krebs.

Small Business and Entrepreneurship

428A Russell Senate Office Building 20510

phone 224–5175, fax 224–5619, http://sbc.senate.gov

[Created pursuant to S. Res. 58, 81st Congress]

meets first Thursday of each month

James E. Risch, of Idaho, *Chair*

Marco Rubio, of Florida.
Rand Paul, of Kentucky.
Tim Scott, of South Carolina.
Joni Ernst, of Iowa.
James M. Inhofe, of Oklahoma.
Todd Young, of Indiana.
Michael B. Enzi, of Wyoming.
Mike Rounds, of South Dakota.
John Kennedy, of Louisiana.

Benjamin L. Cardin, of Maryland.
Maria Cantwell, of Washington.
Jeanne Shaheen, of New Hampshire.
Heidi Heitkamp, of North Dakota.
Edward J. Markey, of Massachusetts.
Cory A. Booker, of New Jersey.
Christopher A. Coons, of Delaware.
Mazie K. Hirono, of Hawaii.
Tammy Duckworth, of Illinois.

(No Subcommittees)

STAFF

Committee on Small Business and Entrepreneurship (SR–428A), 224–5175, fax 224–5619.
Majority Staff Director.—Skiffington Holderness.
Deputy Staff Director.—Meredith West.
Professional Staff Members: Renee Bender, Zach Forster.
Outreach and Policy Director.—Suzanne Wrasse.
Counsel.—Tara Schonhoff.
Research Assistants: Jim Robertson, J.R. Walker III.
Chief Clerk.—Kathryn Eden.
Systems Administrator.—Steve Gingerich.
Staff Assistant.—Stephanie Villalobos.
Minority Committee Main Office (SR–471), 224–2809, fax 228–1128.
Democratic Staff Director.—Sean Moore.
Deputy Staff Director.—Kevin Wheeler.
Policy Director and Tax Counsel.—Beth Bell.
Senior Press and Policy Advisor.—Sean Bartlett.
Communications Director.—Brian Weiss.
Counsel.—Becky McNaught.
Professional Staff Member.—Ellen Harrington.
Staff Assistant.—Olivia Nutter.

Veterans' Affairs

SR–412 Russell Senate Office Building

phone 224–9126, http://veterans.senate.gov

meets first Wednesday of each month

Johnny Isakson, of Georgia, *Chair*

Jerry Moran, of Kansas.
John Boozman, of Arkansas.
Dean Heller, of Nevada.
Bill Cassidy, of Louisiana.
Mike Rounds, of South Dakota.
Thom Tillis, of North Carolina.
Dan Sullivan, of Alaska.

Jon Tester, of Montana.
Patty Murray, of Washington.
BERNARD SANDERS, of Vermont.
Sherrod Brown, of Ohio.
Richard Blumenthal, of Connecticut.
Mazie K. Hirono, of Hawaii.
Joe Manchin III, of West Virginia.

(No Subcommittees)

STAFF

Committee on Veterans' Affairs Majority Staff (SR–412), 224–9126, fax 224–9575.
Majority Staff Director.—Robert Henke.
Deputy Staff Director.—Adam Reece.
Senior Policy Advisor.—Leslie Campbell.
Professional Staff: Patrick McGuigan, David Shearman, Jillian Workman.
Press Assistant.—Camline Moore.
Senior Staff Assistant.—Thomas Coleman.
Legislative Aide.—John Ashley.
Committee on Veterans' Affairs Minority Staff (825A Hart), 224–2074, fax 228–1852.
Minority Staff Director.—Tony McClain.
General Counsel.—Dahlia Melendrez.
Counsel.—Jon Coen.
Director of Oversight.—Michelle Dominguez.
Professional Staff Members: Steve Colley, Simon Coon, Amy Smith.
Press/Research Assistant.—Cassie Byerly.
Staff Assistant.—Sophie Friedl.
Non-Designated (SR–412), 224–9126.
Chief Clerk.—Heather Vachon.

SELECT AND SPECIAL COMMITTEES OF THE SENATE

Committee on Indian Affairs

838 Hart Senate Office Building 20510–6450
phone 224–2251, http://indian.senate.gov

[Created pursuant to S. Res. 4, 95th Congress; amended by S. Res. 71, 103d Congress]

meets every Wednesday of each month

John Hoeven, of North Dakota, *Chair*

Tom Udall, of New Mexico, *Vice Chair*

John Barrasso, of Wyoming.
John McCain, of Arizona.
Lisa Murkowski, of Alaska.
James Lankford, of Oklahoma.
Steve Daines, of Montana.
Mike Crapo, of Idaho.
Jerry Moran, of Kansas.

Maria Cantwell, of Washington.
Jon Tester, of Montana.
Brian Schatz, of Hawaii.
Heidi Heitkamp, of North Dakota.
Catherine Cortez Masto, of Nevada.
Tina Smith, of Minnesota.

(No Subcommittees)

STAFF

Majority Staff Director/Chief Counsel.—Mike Andrews..
Deputy Chief Counsel.—Rhonda Harjo.
Senior Policy Advisor.—Brandon Ashley.
Counsel.—Holmes Whelan.
Policy Advisors: Jacqueline Bisille, John Simermeyer.
Legal Fellow.—Chase Goodnight.
Staff Assistant.—Reid Dagul.
Minority Staff Director/Chief Counsel.—Jennifer Romero.
Senior Counsel.—Ken Rooney.
Counsel.—Ray Martin.
Senior Policy Advisor.—Anthony Sedillo.
Policy Advisor.—Kim Moxley.
Administrative Director.—Jim Eismeier.
Clerk.—Avis Dubose.
Systems Administrator.—Dasan Fish.
GPO Detailee.—Jack Fulmer.
Legal Fellow.—Connie Tsofie de Harro.
Staff Assistant.—Elise Planchet.
GPO Detailee.—Josh Bertalotto.

Select Committee on Ethics

220 Hart Senate Office Building 20510, phone 224–2981, fax 224–7416

[Created pursuant to S. Res. 338, 88th Congress; amended by S. Res. 110, 95th Congress]

Johnny Isakson, of Georgia, *Chair*

Christopher A. Coons, of Delaware, *Vice Chair*

Pat Roberts, of Kansas.
James E. Risch, of Idaho.

Brian Schatz, of Hawaii.
Jeanne Shaheen, of New Hampshire.

STAFF

Staff Director and Chief Counsel.—Deborah Sue Mayer.
Chief Clerk.—Emily Gershon.
Counsel: Brian Harris, Lindsay Reimschussel, Kelly Selesnick, Geoff Turley, Charlotte Underwood.
Director of Information Technology.—Danny Remington.
Financial Disclosure Specialist.—Sarah Bartlett.
Special Assistant.—Brittany Prager.
Staff Assistants: Joseph Lenz, Graham Pough, Gabrielle Quintana, Mary Yuengert.

Select Committee on Intelligence

211 Hart Senate Office Building 20510–6475, phone 224–1700

http://www.senate.gov/~intelligence

[Created pursuant to S. Res. 400, 94th Congress]

Richard Burr, of North Carolina, *Chair*

Mark R. Warner, of Virginia, *Vice Chair*

James E. Risch, of Idaho.
Marco Rubio, of Florida.
Susan M. Collins, of Maine.
Roy Blunt, of Missouri.
James Lankford, of Oklahoma.
Tom Cotton, of Arkansas.
John Cornyn, of Texas.

Dianne Feinstein, of California.
Ron Wyden, of Oregon.
Martin Heinrich, of New Mexico.
ANGUS S. KING, JR., of Maine.
Joe Manchin III, of West Virginia.
Kamala D. Harris, of California.

Ex Officio

Mitch McConnell, of Kentucky.
John McCain, of Arizona.

Charles E. Schumer, of New York.
Jack Reed, of Rhode Island.

STAFF

Majority Staff Director.—Christopher A. Joyner.
Minority Staff Director.—Michael Casey.
Chief Clerk.—Kelsey Stroud Bailey.

Special Committee on Aging

G–31 Dirksen Senate Office Building 20510, phone 224–5364

http://aging.senate.gov

[Reauthorized pursuant to S. Res. 4, 95th Congress]

Susan M. Collins, of Maine, *Chair*

Orrin G. Hatch, of Utah.
Jeff Flake, of Arizona.
Tim Scott, of South Carolina.
Thom Tillis, of North Carolina.
Bob Corker, of Tennessee.
Richard Burr, of North Carolina.
Marco Rubio, of Florida.
Deb Fischer, of Nebraska.

Robert P. Casey, Jr., of Pennsylvania.
Bill Nelson, of Florida.
Kirsten E. Gillibrand, of New York.
Richard Blumenthal, of Connecticut.
Joe Donnelly, of Indiana.
Elizabeth Warren, of Massachusetts.
Catherine Cortez Masto, of Nevada.
Doug Jones, of Alabama.

STAFF

Majority Staff Director.—Kevin Kelley.
Chief Counsel.—Mark LeDuc.
Senior Counsel / Chief Investigator.—Amber Talley.
Health Policy Director.—Amy Pellegrino.
Professional Staff.—Sarah Khasawinah.
Assistant Investigator.—Tim Stretton.
Legislative Aides: Katelynn Boynton, Owen Mahan, Maria Olson.
Staff Assistant.—Jacob Towle.
Non-Designated:
Chief Clerk / System Administrator.—Matt Lawrence.
GPO Detailee.—Ruby Ahmed.
Minority Staff (SH–628), 224–8710, Fax 224–9926.
Staff Director.—Kate Mevis.
Deputy Staff Director.—Stacy Sanders.
Disability Policy Director.—Michael Gamel-McCormick.
Chief Counsel.—Kevin Barstow.
Deputy Chief Counsel.—Rashage Green.
Senior Policy Advisor.—Keith Miller.
Press Secretary / Outreach Coordinator.—Aisha Johnson.
Policy Aide.—Samantha Koehler.
Research Assistant.—Joshua Dubensky.
Fellow.—Liz Weintrab.
Staff Assistant.—Madison West.

Democratic Senatorial Campaign Committee

120 Maryland Avenue, NE., 20002, phone 224–2447

Chris Van Hollen, of Maryland, *Chair*

Charles E. Schumer, of New York, *Democratic Leader*

STAFF

Executive Director.—Mindy Myers.
Deputy Executive Director.—Tracey Lewis.
Communications Director.—Lauren Passalacqua.
Political Director.—Dan McNally.
Finance Director.—Eben Duross.
Legal Counsel.—Mark Elias.

Democratic Policy and Communications Center

419 Hart Senate Office Building, phone 224–3232

Charles E. Schumer, of New York, *Democratic Leader*

Debbie Stabenow, of Michigan, *Chair*

Joe Manchin III, of West Virginia, *Vice Chair*

STAFF

Staff Director.—Bill Sweeney.
Communications Director.—Miranda Margowsky.
Policy Director.—Amanda Perez.
Counsel and Policy Advisor.—Alvaro Zarco.
Policy Advisors: Alex Jacquez, Katie Rubinger.
Senior Vote Analyst.—Douglas Connolly.
Votes Director.—Mike Mozden.
Investigators: Patricio Gonzalez, Jim Secreto.
Junior Investigator.—John B. Donnelly.

Democratic Steering and Outreach Committee

712 Hart Senate Office Building, phone 224–9048

Amy Klobuchar, of Minnesota, *Chair*

Jeanne Shaheen, of New Hampshire, *Vice Chair*

Charles E. Schumer, of New York, *Democratic Leader*

Richard J. Durbin, of Illinois, *Democratic Whip*

Christopher A. Coons, of Delaware, *Chair of Business Outreach*

Robert Menendez, of New Jersey, *Chair of the Hispanic Task Force*

Cory A. Booker, of New Jersey, *Chair of Metropolitan Area Outreach*

Patrick J. Leahy, of Vermont.
Kirsten E. Gillibrand, of New York.
Christopher A. Coons, of Delaware.
Bill Nelson, of Florida.
Robert P. Casey, Jr., of Pennsylvania.
Jon Tester, of Montana.
Brian Schatz, of Hawaii.
Tammy Baldwin, of Wisconsin.
Christopher Murphy, of Connecticut.

STAFF

Staff Director.—Laura Schiller.
Director of Outreach.—Eduardo Lerma.
Associate Directors: Amira Hassan, Rayshon Payton.

Senate Democratic Conference

154 Russell Senate Office Building, phone 224–2621, fax 224–0238

Secretary.—*Tammy Baldwin,* of Wisconsin.
Chief of Staff.—Bill Murat.

Senate Democratic Media Center

619 Hart Senate Office Building, phone 224–1430

Charles E. Schumer, of New York, *Chair*

STAFF

Director of Digital Media.—Lindsay Kryzak.
Creative Director.—Quinn Bowman.
Production Manager.—Basmah Nada.
Digital Producer.—Abele Tuwafie.
Digital Strategists: Iesha Daboya, Anthony Juarez, Sarah Walters.
Engineer.—Tushar Dayal.
Video Editors: Ezra Deutsch-Feldman, Chris Northcross.
Videographers: Dave Cooke, Nora Younkin.

National Republican Senatorial Committee

425 Second Street, NE., 20002, phone 675–6000, fax 675–6058

Cory Gardner, of Colorado, *Chair*

Thom Tillis, of North Carolina, *Vice Chair*

STAFF

Executive Director.—Chris Hansen.
Director of:
Communications.—Katie Martin.
Finance.—Katie Behnke.
Legal Counsel.—Jessica Furst Johnson.
Political Director.—Sarah Morgan.
Research.—Jeff Snow.
Digital.—Jon Adams.
Data & Analytics.—Logan Dobson.

Senate Republican Policy Committee

347 Russell Senate Office Building, phone 224–2946
fax 224–1235, http://rpc.senate.gov

John Barrasso, of Wyoming, *Chair*

STAFF

Staff Director.—Dan Kunsman.
Policy Director.—Chris Barkley.
Communications Director.—Bronwyn Lance Chester.
Administrative Director.—Craig Cheney.
Analysts:
Agriculture, Energy, and Environment.—Jack Thorlin.
Budget, Tax, Appropriations.—Spencer Wayne.
Health Care.—Whitney Jones.
Commerce, Judiciary/Immigration, Transportation, Trade.—Brendan Parets.
Education, Labor, Banking, Housing.—Emily Goff.
Defense, Foreign Affairs, Intelligence, Veterans Affairs.—Jeremy Hayes.
Professional Staff:
Editorial Director.—John Mitchell.
System Administrator/RVA Analyst.—Thomas Pulju.
Station Manager/Special Projects.—Carolyn Laird.
Station Operator/Project Assistant.—Erich Schultz.
Digital Director.—Christy Lewis.
Deputy Digital Director.—Jesica Randolph.

Senate Republican Conference

405 Hart Senate Office Building, phone 224–2764
http://src.senate.gov

John Thune, of South Dakota, *Chair*

Roy Blunt, of Missouri, *Vice Chair*

STAFF

Conference of the Majority (SH–405), 224–2764.
Staff Director.—Brendon Plack.
Deputy Staff Director.—Ann Marie Hauser.
Media Services Director.—Dave Hodgdon.
Administrative Director.—Becky Marr.
Communications Director.—Chandler Smith.
Senior Writer.—Mary Katherine Ascik.
Internal Communications Advisor.—Dominique McKay.
Production Manager.—Cyrus Pearson.
Videographer / Editor.—Lane Marshall.
Digital Director.—Dianna Colasurdo.
Senior Graphics Designers: Chris Angrisani, Laura Allen.
Systems Engineer.—Nic Budde.
Floor Monitor.—Alex Charow.
Creative Director.—Adam Scheidler.

OFFICERS AND OFFICIALS OF THE SENATE

Capitol Telephone Directory, 224–3121

Senate room prefixes:
Capitol—S, Russell Senate Office Building—SR
Dirksen Senate Office Building—SD, Hart Senate Office Building—SH

PRESIDENT OF THE SENATE

Vice President of the United States and President of the Senate.—Mike Pence.

The Ceremonial Office of the Vice President is S–212 in the Capitol. The Vice President has offices in the Dirksen Senate Office Building, the Eisenhower Executive Office Building (EEOB), and the White House (West Wing).

Phone (202) 456–1414

Assistant to the President and Chief of Staff to the Vice President.—Nick Ayers.
Assistant to the President and National Security Advisor to the Vice President.—Keith Kellogg.
Deputy Assistants to the President and Deputy Chiefs of Staff to the Vice President: Jarrod Agen, John Horne.
Deputy Assistant to the President and Chief of Staff to Mrs. Karen Pence.—Jana Toner.
Deputy Assistant to the President and Domestic Policy Director to the Vice President.—Steve Pinkos.
Deputy Assistant to the President and Director of Public Liaison and Intergovernmental Affairs for the Vice President.—Sarah Makin.
Special Assistant to the President and Deputy Director of Public Liaison and Intergovernmental Affairs.—Andeliz Castillo.
Special Assistant to the President and Director of External Affairs.—Billy Kirkland.
Special Assistant to the President and Director of Media Affairs.—Rebeccah Propp.
Special Assistant to the President and Press Secretary to the Vice President.—Alyssa Farah.
Assistant to the Vice President and Counsel.—Matt Morgan.
Assistant to the Vice President and Director of Legislative Affairs.—Jonathan Hiler.
Deputy Director of House Legislative Affairs.—Chris Hodgson.
Deputy Assistant to the Vice President and Director of Administration.—Katherine Purucker.
Director of Advance.—Saibatu Mansaray.
Deputy Assistant to the Vice President and Director of Scheduling.—Meghan Patenaude.
Special Assistant to the Vice President.—Zach Bauer.
Executive Assistant to the Vice President.—Heather Whitaker.

PRESIDENT PRO TEMPORE

S–125 The Capitol, phone 224–9400

President Pro Tempore of the Senate.—Orrin G. Hatch.
Chief of Staff.—Matt Sandgren.
Administrative Director and Diplomatic Liaison.—Celeste Gold.
Legislative Correspondent.—Jordan Roberts.

MAJORITY LEADER

S–230 The Capitol, phone 224–3135, fax 228–1264

Majority Leader.—Mitch McConnell.
Chief of Staff.—Sharon Soderstrom.

Deputy Chief of Staff.—Don Stewart.
Director of Operations.—Stefanie Muchow.
Scheduler.—Laura Vincent.
Office Manager.—Alexandra Jenkins.
Policy Director.—Hazen Marshall.
Chief Legal Counsel.—John Abegg.
National Security Advisor.—Tom Hawkins.
Communications Director.—David Popp.
Chief Economic Policy Counsel.—Jay Khosla.
Policy Advisors: Steve Donaldson, Jane Lee, Jim Neill, Scott Raab, Erica Suares, Terry Van Doren, Kathy Wright.
Speechwriter.—Andrew Quinn.
Deputy Speechwriter.—Dylan Vorbach.
Deputy Press Secretary.—Georgeanna Sullivan.
Systems Administrator.—Elmamoun Sulfab.
Scheduling Assistant and Special Assistant to the Chief of Staff.—Hannah Wardell.
Staff and Protocol Assistant.—Cassie Gerhardstein.
Staff Assistants: Josh Peaster, Leslie Rolfe.

REPUBLICAN COMMUNICATIONS CENTER

S–230 The Capitol, phone 228–6397

Communications Staff Director.—Antonia Ferrier.
Research Advisor.—David Hauptmann.
Broadcast Communications Advisor.—Kathryn McQuade.
Creative Director.—Anang Mittal.

OFFICE OF THE MAJORITY WHIP

S–208 The Capitol, phone 224–2708, fax 228–1507

Majority Whip.—John Cornyn.
Chief of Staff.—Monica Popp.
Deputy Chief.—Jonathan Chapuis.
Policy Advisers: Sam Beaver, Jody Wright.
Policy Assistant.—Noah McCullough.
Staff Assistant.—John Paul Watson.

DEMOCRATIC LEADER

S–221 The Capitol, phone 224–2158, fax 224–7362

Democratic Leader.—Charles E. Schumer.
Chief of Staff.—Mike Lynch.
Deputy Chief of Staff.—Erin Sager Vaughn.
Special Assistant.—Ruth Carnegie.
Director of Scheduling.—Michelle Mittler.
Scheduling Assistant.—Emily Sweda.
Policy Director.—Gerry Petrella.
Legislative Director.—Meghan Taira.
Communications Director.—Matt House.
Director of Engagement.—Cietta Kiandoli.
Chief Speechwriter.—Josh Molofsky.
General Counsel.—Mark Patterson.
Director of Operations.—Amy Mannering.
Director of Information Technology.—Scott Rodman.
Capitol Staff Assistant.—Juan Negrete.
Capitol Staff Assistant/Room Coordinator.—Kara Pitts.

DEMOCRATIC WHIP

S–321 The Capitol, phone 224–9447

Democratic Whip.—Richard J. Durbin.

Chief of Staff.—Pat Souders.
Director of Operations.—Sally Brown-Shaklee.
Director of Scheduling.—Claire Reuschel.
Special Assistant.—Katie O'Leary.
Communications Director.—Emily Hampsten.
Floor Director.—Reema Dodin.
Deputy Floor Director.—MJ Kenny.
Staff Assistant.—Andrew Posegay.

ASSISTANT DEMOCRATIC LEADER
SR–154, phone 224–2621

Assistant Democratic Leader.—Patty Murray.
Chief of Staff.—Mike Spahn.
Leadership Staff Director.—Stacy Rich.
Communications Director.—Eli Zupnick.
Leadership Advisor.—Emma Rodriguez.

OFFICE OF THE SECRETARY
S–312 The Capitol, phone 224–3622

JULIE E. ADAMS, Secretary of the Senate; elected and sworn in as the 33rd Secretary of the Senate on January 6, 2015; native of Iowa; bachelor's degree in political science from Luther College, Decorah, IA; master's degree in education from the University of Iowa; Director of Administration, Majority Leader Mitch McConnell; spokesperson, First Lady Laura Bush; Deputy Communications Director, then-Senate Majority Whip Mitch McConnell.

Secretary of the Senate.—Julie E. Adams (S–312), 224–3622.
Assistant Secretary of the Senate.—Mary Suit Jones (S–333), 224–3622.
Chief of Staff.—Rachel Creviston (S–414C), 224–3895.
Deputy Chief of Staff.—Sydney G. Butler (S–333), 224–9461.
General Counsel.—Dan Schwager (S–414D), 224–0634.
Executive Accounts Administrator.—Zoraida Torres (S–414B), 224–7099.
Executive Assistant.—McKinley Mason (S–312), 224–9278.
Capitol Offices Liaison.—Gerald Thompson (SB–36C), 224–1483.

ADMINISTRATIVE SERVICES

Chief Counsel for Employment.—Claudia A. Kostel (SH–103), 224–5424.
Conservation and Preservation.—Beverly Adams (S–416), 224–4550.
Curator.—Melinda K. Smith (S–411), 224–2955.
Gift Shop.—Neil Schwartz (SD–G42), 224–7308.
Historian.—Betty K. Koed (SH–201), 224–6900.
Human Resources.—John McIlveen (SH–231B), 224–3625.
Information Systems.—Dan Kulnis (S–422), 224–4883.
Interparliamentary Services.—Sally Walsh (SH–808), 224–3047.
Joint Office of Education and Training.—Megan Daly (SD–180), 224–7628.
Legislative Info Systems (LIS) Project.—John Pollock (SD–B44A), 224–9419.
Library.—Leona Faust (SR–B15), 224–7106.
Page School.—Kathryn S. Weeden (Webster Hall), 224–3927.
Printing and Document Services.—Karen Moore (SH–B04), 224–0205.
Public Records.—Dana McCallum (SH–232), 224–0322.
Senate Security.—Michael P. DiSilvestro (SVC–217), 224–5632.
Stationery Room.—Terri Keller (SD–B42), 224–4771.
Web Technology.—Arin Shapiro (PSQ 6960), 224–2020.

FINANCIAL SERVICES

Disbursing Office.—Ileana M. Garcia (SH–127), 224–3205.

LEGISLATIVE SERVICES

Bill Clerk.—Sara Schwartzman (S–123), 224–2120.

Captioning Services.—Sandra Schumm (SVC–111), 224–4321.
Daily Digest, Editor.—Elizabeth Tratos (S–421), 224–2658.
Enrolling Clerk.—Margarida Curtis (S–139), 224–8427.
Executive Clerk.—Jennifer Gorham (S–138), 224–4341.
Journal Clerk.—Scott M. Sanborn (S–135), 224–4650.
Legislative Clerk.—John J. Merlino (S–134), 224–4350.
Official Reporters of Debates.—Patrick Renzi (S–410A), 224–3152.
Parliamentarian.—Elizabeth C. MacDonough (S–133), 224–6128.

OFFICE OF THE CHAPLAIN

S–332 The Capitol, phone 224–2510, fax 224–9686

BARRY C. BLACK, Chaplain, U.S. Senate; born in Baltimore, MD, on November 1, 1948; education: bachelor of arts, theology, Oakwood College, 1970; master of divinity, Andrews Theological Seminary, 1973; master of arts, counseling, North Carolina Central University, 1978; doctor of ministry, theology, Eastern Baptist Seminary, 1982; master of arts, management, Salve Regina University, 1989; doctor of philosophy, psychology, United States International University, 1996; military service: U.S. Navy, 1976–2003; rising to the rank of Rear Admiral; Chief of Navy Chaplains, 2000–03; awards: Navy Distinguished Service Medal; Legion of Merit Medal; Defense Meritorious Service Medal; Meritorious Service Medals (two awards); Navy and Marine Corps Commendation Medals (two awards); 1995 NAACP Renowned Service Award; family: married to Brenda; three children: Barry II, Brendan, and Bradford.

Chaplain of the Senate.—Barry C. Black.
Chief of Staff.—Lisa Schultz, 224–3849.
Communications Director.—Jody Spraggins-Scott, 224–2048.
Staff Scheduler/Executive Assistant.—Suzanne Chapuis, 224–7456.

OFFICE OF THE SERGEANT AT ARMS

S–151 The Capitol, phone 224–2341, fax 224–7690

MICHAEL C. STENGER was nominated as the 41st Sergeant at Arms under Senate Resolution 465, on April 16, 2018. Michael C. Stenger has served as the Chief of Staff for the U.S. Senate Sergeant as Arms since January 2015. He began working for the Senate Sergeant at Arms in 2011, serving as Assistant Sergeant at Arms for the Office of Protective Services and Continuity until his appointment as Deputy Sergeant at Arms in May 2014.

As Assistant Sergeant at Arms, Mr. Stenger was charged with overseeing security and continuity of operations policies and programs, and providing strategic and analytical assistance. Mr. Stenger is a 35-year veteran of the United States Secret Service (USSS), appointed in 2008 as Assistant Director for the USSS Office of Government and Public Affairs, where he administered USSS liaison activities with the United States Congress, Department of Homeland Security, other federal agencies, and members of the media and general public.

During his career with the USSS, he served in Newark, New York City, and Washington, D.C., in protective, investigative, and staff assignments. Mr. Stenger served as the senior official overseeing the agency's investigations as Assistant Director for the Office of Investigations. In this capacity, he developed and implemented investigative policies for cyber- and fraud-related crimes. He also served as Assistant Director of the Office of Protective Research, Special Agent in Charge of the Washington Field Office, Deputy Assistant Director of the Office of Investigations, and Special Agent in Charge of the Financial Crimes Division.

Mr. Stenger was selected in 2004 as a Presidential Meritorious Rank Award recipient. He has also received the Vice President's Award for Excellence in Financial Crimes Management and the Department of the Treasury Secretary's Annual Award for Outstanding Performance in the Area of Financial Crimes.

Mr. Stenger received his Bachelor of Arts degree from Farleigh Dickinson University in New Jersey and attained the rank of Captain in the United States Marine Corps.

Sergeant at Arms.—Michael C. Stenger, S–151, 224–2341.
Deputy Sergeant at Arms.—James W. Morhard, S–151, 224–2341.
Education and Training Director.—Megan Daly, SD–180, 224–7588.
Employee Assistance Program Director.—Kristin Welsh-Simpson, SH–627B, 224–3902.
Executive Advisor.—Kelly Fado, S–151, 224–6031.
General Counsel.—Terence Liley, S–151, 224–2341.
Page Progam Director.—Elizabeth Roach, Page School, 228–1291.

Protocol Officer.—Becky Daugherty, S–147, 224–2341.

HUMAN RESOURCES

Director.—Tammy Buckingham, SH–142, 4–8199.
Placement Office Manager.—Brian Bean, SH–142, 4–9167.
Human Resources Managers: Anne Lyles, SH–142, 4–4909; Nicole Wojahn, SH–142, 4–9442.
Safety Program.—Taurus Moore, SH–142, 4–5717.

CAPITOL OPERATIONS

Assistant Sergeant at Arms.—Krista Beal, SVC–131, 4–6067.
Capitol Operations Special Assistant.—Bryan Huus, 4–3372.
Senate Recording Studio Manager.—Bob Swanner, SVC–160, 4–5080.
Appointment Desk Manager.—Mele Williams, 4–6302.
Director of Doorkeepers.—Cindy Hasiak, S–213, 4–6067.

MEDIA GALLERIES

Director of the Daily Press Gallery.—Laura Lytle, S–316, 4–0241.
Director of the Periodical Press Gallery.—Justin Wilson, S–320, 4–0265.
Director of the Press Photographers Gallery.—Jeff Kent, S–317, 4–6548.
Director of the Radio and Television Gallery.—Michael Mastrian, S–325, 4–6421.

CHIEF INFORMATION OFFICER

Assistant Sergeant at Arms and Chief Information Officer.—John Jewell, PSB 6245, 4–5463.
Deputy Sergeant at Arms and Chief Information Officer.—Lynden Armstrong, PSB 6614, 4–7078.
Economic and Technical Analysis Manager.—Megan Dockery, PSB 6613, 4–9514.

COMMUNICATION AND TECHNOLOGY INTEGRATION

Director of Communication and Technology Integration.—Charles Marshall (acting), SH–121, 4–3543.

CYBERSECURITY

Director of Cybersecurity.—Linus Barloon, PSB 6215, 4–6454.
Information Assurance Manager.—Tim Craig, PSB 6405, 8–0472.

IT SUPPORT SERVICES

Director of IT Support Services.—Robert Harris, PSB 6735, 8–3499.
Desktop/LAN Support Manager.—Tim Dean, PSB 6280, 4–3564.
Equipment and Capitol Exchange Services Manager.—Win Grayson, SR–B59, 4–8065.
Contingency and IT Operations Manager.—Lynette Anderson, PSB 6985, 4–1609.
Telecom Assistance Center Supervisor.—Katie Miller, SH–121, 8–6365.
Capitol Telephone Exchange Manager.—Mary Anne Williams, PSB 6115, 4–3431.

PROCESS MANAGEMENT AND INNOVATION

Director of Process Management and Innovation.—Ed Jankus, PSB 6608, 4–7780.
Identity Management Manager.—Christopher Carpenter, PSB 6950, 8–2586.
IT Research and Deployment Manager.—John Pino, PSB 6220, 4–6685.
Systems Design, Development and Implementation Manager.—Joe Eckert, PSB 6240, 4–2982.

TECHNOLOGY DEVELOPMENT

Director of Technology Development.—Jay Moore, PSB 6730, 4–0092.
Network Engineering and Management Manager.—Bill Hill, PSB 6610, 4–9380.
Enterprise IT Operations Manager.—Joe LaPalme, PSB 6375, 8–4451.

Systems Development Manager.—Laura Robertson, PSB 6612, 4–1831.
Enterprise Infrastructure Services Manager.—Bryan Steward, PSB 6611, 4–9703.
LAN Administration Supervisor.—Tony Skarlatos, PSB 6370, 4–6338.

FINANCIAL MANAGEMENT

Chief Financial Officer.—Robin Gallant, PSB 6607, 4–6292.
Accounts Payable Manager.—David Salem, PSB 6604, 4–8844.
Controller.—Mary Ann Sifford, PSB 6605, 4–1035.
Budget Manager.—Morgan Peters, PSB 6606, 4–8759.
Procurement Manager.—David Baker, PSB 6603, 4–2547.

OFFICE OF SECURITY AND EMERGENCY PREPAREDNESS

Assistant Sergeant at Arms.—Richard M. Attridge, SVC–305, 4–3691.
Deputy Assistant Sergeant at Arms.—Brian McGinty, SVC–305, 8–9788.
Director for Security Policy and Planning.—Ronda Stewart, SVC–305, 4–7173.
Director for Emergency Preparedness.—David Kayea, PSB 6015, 8–0637.
Director for Intelligence and Protective Services.—Stephen Klopp, SVC–305, 8–3618.

CENTRAL OPERATIONS

Director.—Mike Brown, SD–150, 4–4035.
ID Office Manager.—Luke Hendrixson, SD–G58, 4–8938.
Parking Office Manager.—Robert Brindle, SD–G84, 4–7054.

OPERATIONS

Assistant Sergeant at Arms.—Michael L. Chandler, SD–G61, 8–0635.
Deputy Assistant Sergeant at Arms.—Doug White, SD–G61, 8–4877.

CAPITOL FACILITIES

Director of Capitol Facilities.—Grace Ridgeway, SC–5, 4–5524.
Facilities Systems Manager.—Pam Weddle, SC–5, 4–4656.
Events Coordinator.—Delice Tavernier, SC–5, 4–2563.
Furnishings and Design Coordinator.—Monique Beckford, SC–5, 4–1457.

CONTINGENCY PROGRAMS

Director.—John Haverstock, SVC–305, 4–8646.
Plans Division Chief.—Jillian Lerda, SVC–305, 4–6894.

PRINTING, GRAPHICS, AND DIRECT MAIL

Director.—Brian Trott, SD–G82, 4–9443.
Capitol Hill Operations Manager.—George Thompson, SD–G82, 4–6664.
Landover Operations Manager.—Mike Peterson, Printing and Mailing Facility, 4–9568.
Senate Support Facility Supervisor.—Mike Wilson, Senate Support Facility, 4–1970.

SENATE POST OFFICE

Postmaster.—Donnie Cook, SD–B23, 4–3731.
Retail Services Superintendent.—Lisa Cain, SD–B17, 4–5330.
Mail and Packages Superintendent.—Lee Reynolds, SD–B28, 4–9096.
Senate Mail Facility Superintendent.—Anthony Simmons, Senate Mail Facility, 4–0078.

STATE OFFICE OPERATIONS

State Office Liaison.—Kate Summers, PSB 6225, 4–9576.
Project Management.—Lauren Suranno, PSB 6295, 4–7723.
State Office Readiness.—Mark Peterson, PSB 6310–B2, 4–3725.

SUPPORT SERVICES

Director.—Sam Jacobs, PSB 6455, 4–9927.
Administrative Services Manager.—Kelli Ashton, PSB 6230, 4–0850.
Facilities Supervisor.—Amy York, PSB 6235, 4–1507.
Fleet and Transportation Manager.—Shawn Fretz, SR–G06, 8–0346.
Hair Care Manager.—Cindi Brown, SR–B70, 4–4560.
Office of Communications Manager.—Kristan Trugman, PSB 6010, 4–8997.
Photo Studio Manager.—Bill Allen, SD–G85 4–7084.
Photo Studio Supervisor.—Jeff McEvoy, SD–G85, 4–8570.
Lab Manager.—Lynn Dunigan, PSB 6820, 4–6634.

OFFICE OF THE SECRETARY FOR THE MAJORITY

S–337 The Capitol, phone 224–3835, fax 224–2860

Secretary for the Majority.—Laura C. Dove (S–337).
Assistant Secretary for the Majority.—Robert Duncan (S–335).
Administrative Assistant.—Noelle Busk Ringel (S–337).
Senior Floor Assistant.—Chris Tuck (S–335), 224–6191
Floor Assistant.—Megan Mercer (S–335), 224–6191.

S–226 Majority Cloakroom, phone 224–6191

Senior Cloakroom Assistant.—Tony Hanagan.
Cloakroom Assistants: Chloe Barz, Katherine Kilroy, Mike Smith.

OFFICE OF THE SECRETARY FOR THE MINORITY

S–309 The Capitol, phone 224–3735

Secretary for the Minority.—Gary Myrick.
Assistant Secretary for the Minority.—Ryan McConaghy (S–118), 224–5551.
Administrative Assistant to the Secretary.—Amber Huus.

S–118 The Capitol, phone 224–5551

Senior Floor Assistant.—Tricia Engle.
Floor Assistant.—Daniel Tinsley.
Executive Assistant to the Floor Staff.—Terri Taylor.

S–225 Minority Cloakroom, phone 224–4691

Cloakroom Assistants: Stephanie Paone, Danica Rodman, Maalik Simmons, Brad Watt.

OFFICE OF THE LEGISLATIVE COUNSEL

668 Dirksen Senate Office Building, phone 224–6461, fax 224–0567

Legislative Counsel.—Gary L. Endicott.
Deputy Legislative Counsel.—William R. Baird.
Senior Counsels: Charles E. Armstrong, Ruth Ann Ernst, John A. Goetcheus, Elizabeth Aldridge King.
Assistant Counsels: Kimberly D. Albrecht-Taylor, John W. Baggaley, Margaret A. Bomba, Kathryne M. Bonander, Heather L. Burnham, Maureen C. Contreni, Kevin M. Davis, Stephanie Easley, Deanna E. Edwards, Evan H. Frank, Vincent J. Gaiani, Amy E. Gaynor, John A. Henderson, Thomas B. Heywood, Christina N. Jacquet, Heather A. Lowell, Philip B. Lynch, Matthew D. McGhie, Mark M. McGunagle, Christine E. Miranda, James L. Ollen-Smith, Allison M. Otto, Kristin K. Romero, Margaret A. Rose, Patrick N. Ryan, Robert F. Silver, Kimberly A. Tamber, Kelly M. Thornburg.
Staff Attorneys: Larissa Eltsefon, Carol L. Lewis, Mark L. Mazzone.
Systems Integrator.—Thomas E. Cole.
Office Manager.—Donna L. Pasqualino.
Senior Staff Assistants: Kimberly R. Bourne-Goldring, Rebekah J. Musgrove, Daniela A. Navia, Diane E. Nesmeyer, Patricia H. Olsavsky.

OFFICE OF SENATE LEGAL COUNSEL

642 Hart Senate Office Building, phone 224–4435, fax 224–3391

Senate Legal Counsel.—Patricia Mack Bryan.
Deputy Senate Legal Counsel.—Morgan J. Frankel.
Assistant Senate Legal Counsels: Thomas E. Caballero, Grant R. Vinik.
Systems Administrator/Legal Assistant.—Jenny H. Smith.
Administrative Assistant.—Kathleen M. Parker.

STANDING COMMITTEES OF THE HOUSE

[Republicans in roman; Democrats in *italic*; Resident Commissioner and Delegates in **boldface**]

[Room numbers beginning with H are in the Capitol, with CHOB in the Cannon House Office Building, with LHOB in the Longworth House Office Building, with RHOB in the Rayburn House Office Building, with H1 in O'Neill House Office Building, and with H2 in the Ford House Office Building]

Agriculture

1301 Longworth House Office Building, phone 225–2171

http://agriculture.house.gov

K. Michael Conaway, of Texas, *Chair*

Bob Goodlatte, of Virginia.
Frank D. Lucas, of Oklahoma.
Steve King, of Iowa.
Mike Rogers, of Alabama.
Glenn Thompson, of Pennsylvania.
Bob Gibbs, of Ohio.
Austin Scott, of Georgia.
Eric A. ''Rick'' Crawford, of Arkansas.
Scott DesJarlais, of Tennessee.
Vicky Hartzler, of Missouri.
Jeff Denham, of California.
Doug LaMalfa, of California.
Rodney Davis, of Illinois.
Ted S. Yoho, of Florida.
Rick W. Allen, of Georgia.
Mike Bost, of Illinois.
David Rouzer, of North Carolina.
Ralph Lee Abraham, of Louisiana.
Trent Kelly, of Mississippi.
James Comer, of Kentucky.
Roger W. Marshall, of Kansas.
Don Bacon, of Nebraska.
John J. Faso, of New York.
Neal P. Dunn, of Florida.
Jodey C. Arrington, of Texas.

Collin C. Peterson, of Minnesota.
David Scott, of Georgia.
Jim Costa, of California.
Timothy J. Walz, of Minnesota.
Marcia L. Fudge, of Ohio.
James P. McGovern, of Massachusetts.
Filemon Vela, of Texas.
Michelle Lujan Grisham, of New Mexico.
Ann M. Kuster, of New Hampshire.
Richard M. Nolan, of Minnesota.
Cheri Bustos, of Illinois.
Sean Patrick Maloney, of New York.
Stacey E. Plaskett, of Virgin Islands.
Alma S. Adams, of North Carolina.
Dwight Evans, of Pennsylvania.
Al Lawson, Jr., of Florida.
Tom O'Halleran, of Arizona.
Jimmy Panetta, of California.
Darren Soto, of Florida.
Lisa Blunt Rochester, of Delaware.

SUBCOMMITTEES

[The chair and ranking minority member are ex officio (voting) members of all subcommittees on which they do not serve.]

Biotechnology, Horticulture, and Research

Rodney Davis, of Illinois, *Chair*

Bob Gibbs, of Ohio.
Jeff Denham, of California.
Ted S. Yoho, of Florida.
David Rouzer, of North Carolina.
Don Bacon, of Nebraska.
Neal P. Dunn, of Florida.
Jodey C. Arrington, of Texas.

Michelle Lujan Grisham, of New Mexico.
Al Lawson, Jr., of Florida.
Jimmy Panetta, of California.
Jim Costa, of California.
James P. McGovern, of Massachusetts.
Lisa Blunt Rochester, of Delaware.

Commodity Exchanges, Energy, and Credit

Austin Scott, of Georgia, *Chair*

Bob Goodlatte, of Virginia.
Mike Rogers, of Alabama.
Doug LaMalfa, of California.
Rodney Davis, of Illinois.
James Comer, of Kentucky.
Roger W. Marshall, of Kansas.
John J. Faso, of New York.

David Scott, of Georgia.
Sean Patrick Maloney, of New York.
Ann M. Kuster, of New Hampshire.
Stacey E. Plaskett, of Virgin Islands.
Tom O'Halleran, of Arizona.
Darren Soto, of Florida.

Conservation and Forestry

Frank D. Lucas, of Oklahoma, *Chair*

Glenn Thompson, of Pennsylvania.
Jeff Denham, of California.
Doug LaMalfa, of California.
Rick W. Allen, of Georgia.
Mike Bost, of Illinois.
Ralph Lee Abraham, of Louisiana.
Trent Kelly, of Mississippi.

Marcia L. Fudge, of Ohio.
Timothy J. Walz, of Minnesota.
Ann M. Kuster, of New Hampshire.
Richard M. Nolan, of Minnesota.
Tom O'Halleran, of Arizona.
Filemon Vela, of Texas.

General Farm Commodities and Risk Management

Eric A. ''Rick'' Crawford, of Arkansas, *Chair*

Frank D. Lucas, of Oklahoma.
Mike Rogers, of Alabama.
Bob Gibbs, of Ohio.
Austin Scott, of Georgia.
Scott DesJarlais, of Tennessee.
Rick W. Allen, of Georgia.
Mike Bost, of Illinois.
Ralph Lee Abraham, of Louisiana.
Don Bacon, of Nebraska.
Neal P. Dunn, of Florida.
Jodey C. Arrington, of Texas.

Richard M. Nolan, of Minnesota.
Timothy J. Walz, of Minnesota.
Cheri Bustos, of Illinois.
Lisa Blunt Rochester, of Delaware.
David Scott, of Georgia.
Sean Patrick Maloney, of New York.
Stacey E. Plaskett, of Virgin Islands.
Al Lawson, Jr., of Florida.
Tom O'Halleran, of Arizona.

Livestock and Foreign Agriculture

David Rouzer, of North Carolina, *Chair*

Bob Goodlatte, of Virginia.
Steve King, of Iowa.
Scott DesJarlais, of Tennessee.
Vicky Hartzler, of Missouri.
Ted S. Yoho, of Florida.
Trent Kelly, of Mississippi.
Roger W. Marshall, of Kansas.

Jim Costa, of California.
Filemon Vela, of Texas.
Cheri Bustos, of Illinois.
Stacey E. Plaskett, of Virgin Islands.
Dwight Evans, of Pennsylvania.
Vacant.

Nutrition

Glenn Thompson, of Pennsylvania, *Chair*

Steve King, of Iowa.
Eric A. ''Rick'' Crawford, of Arkansas.
Scott DesJarlais, of Tennessee.
Vicky Hartzler, of Missouri.
Rodney Davis, of Illinois.
Ted S. Yoho, of Florida.
David Rouzer, of North Carolina.
James Comer, of Kentucky.
Roger W. Marshall, of Kansas.
John J. Faso, of New York.
Jodey C. Arrington, of Texas.

James P. McGovern, of Massachusetts.
Alma S. Adams, of North Carolina.
Dwight Evans, of Pennsylvania.
Marcia L. Fudge, of Ohio.
Michelle Lujan Grisham, of New Mexico.
Al Lawson, Jr., of Florida.
Jimmy Panetta, of California.
Darren Soto, of Florida.
Sean Patrick Maloney, of New York.

STAFF

Committee on Agriculture (1301 LHOB), 225–2171.
Majority Staff:
Staff Director.—Matt Schertz.
Deputy Staff Director and Chief Economist.—Bart Fischer.
Chief Counsel.—Jackie Barber.
Deputy Chief Counsel.—Patricia Straughn.
Counsel and Professional Staff.—Caleb Crosswhite.
Oversight Counsel.—Emily Wong.
Chief Clerk.—Nicole Scott.
Director of Coalitions and Outreach.—Christine Heggem.
Financial Administrator.—Dean Lester.
Communications Director.—Rachel Millard.
Press Secretary.—Mollie Wilken.
Deputy Press Secretary.—Stephanie Addison.
Information Technology Director.—John Konya.
Information Technology Assistant.—Faisal Siddiqui.
Senior Professional Staff.—Josh Maxwell.
Professional Staff: Paul Balzano, Stacy Revels, Jennifer Tiller, Trevor White.
Deputy Economist.—Callie McAdams.
Legislative Assistants: Darryl Blakey, Ashton Johnston, Mykel Wedig, John Weber.
Deputy Clerk.—Carly Reedholm.
Staff Assistant.—Yasmin Rey.
Minority Staff (1305 LHOB), 225–0317.
Staff Director.—Anne Simmons.
Deputy Staff Director.—Troy Phillips.
Senior Counsel.—Kellie Adesina.
Professional Staff: Keith Jones, Evan Jurkovich, Mary Knigge, Lisa Shelton, Mike Stranz.
Senior Counsel.—Matthew MacKenzie.
Communications Director.—Liz Friedlander.
Office Manager.—Faye Smith.

Appropriations

H–305 The Capitol, phone 225–2771

http://www.house.gov/appropriations

Rodney P. Frelinghuysen, of New Jersey, *Chair*

Harold Rogers, of Kentucky.
Robert B. Aderholt, of Alabama.
Kay Granger, of Texas.
Michael K. Simpson, of Idaho.
John Abney Culberson, of Texas.
John R. Carter, of Texas.
Ken Calvert, of California.
Tom Cole, of Oklahoma.
Mario Diaz-Balart, of Florida.
Tom Graves, of Georgia.
Kevin Yoder, of Kansas.
Steve Womack, of Arkansas.
Jeff Fortenberry, of Nebraska.
Thomas J. Rooney, of Florida.
Charles J. ''Chuck'' Fleischmann, of Tennessee.
Jaime Herrera Beutler, of Washington.
David P. Joyce, of Ohio.
David G. Valadao, of California.
Andy Harris, of Maryland.
Martha Roby, of Alabama.
Mark E. Amodei, of Nevada.
Chris Stewart, of Utah.
David Young, of Iowa.
Evan H. Jenkins, of West Virginia.
Steven M. Palazzo, of Mississippi.
Dan Newhouse, of Washington.
John R. Moolenaar, of Michigan.
Scott Taylor, of Virginia.
John H. Rutherford, of Florida.

Nita M. Lowey, of New York.
Marcy Kaptur, of Ohio.
Peter J. Visclosky, of Indiana.
José E. Serrano, of New York.
Rosa L. DeLauro, of Connecticut.
David E. Price, of North Carolina.
Lucille Roybal-Allard, of California.
Sanford D. Bishop, Jr., of Georgia.
Barbara Lee, of California.
Betty McCollum, of Minnesota.
Tim Ryan, of Ohio.
C. A. Dutch Ruppersberger, of Maryland.
Debbie Wasserman Schultz, of Florida.
Henry Cuellar, of Texas.
Chellie Pingree, of Maine.
Mike Quigley, of Illinois.
Derek Kilmer, of Washington.
Matt Cartwright, of Pennsylvania.
Grace Meng, of New York.
Mark Pocan, of Wisconsin.
Katherine M. Clark, of Massachusetts.
Pete Aguilar, of California.

SUBCOMMITTEES

[The chair and ranking minority member are ex officio (voting) members of all subcommittees on which they do not serve.]

Agriculture, Rural Development, Food and Drug Administration, and Related Agencies

Robert B. Aderholt, of Alabama, *Chair*

David G. Valadao, of California, *Vice Chair*

Kevin Yoder, of Kansas.
Thomas J. Rooney, of Florida.
Andy Harris, of Maryland.
David Young, of Iowa.
Steven M. Palazzo, of Mississippi.

Sanford D. Bishop, Jr., of Georgia.
Rosa L. DeLauro, of Connecticut.
Chellie Pingree, of Maine.
Mark Pocan, of Wisconsin.

Commerce, Justice, Science, and Related Agencies

John Abney Culberson, of Texas, *Chair*

Evan H. Jenkins, of West Virginia, *Vice Chair*

Harold Rogers, of Kentucky.
Robert B. Aderholt, of Alabama.
John R. Carter, of Texas.
Martha Roby, of Alabama.
Steven M. Palazzo, of Mississippi.

José E. Serrano, of New York.
Derek Kilmer, of Washington.
Matt Cartwright, of Pennsylvania.
Grace Meng, of New York.

Defense

Kay Granger, of Texas, *Chair*

Ken Calvert, of California, *Vice Chair*

Harold Rogers, of Kentucky.
Tom Cole, of Oklahoma.
Steve Womack, of Arkansas.
Robert B. Aderholt, of Alabama.
John R. Carter, of Texas.
Mario Diaz-Balart, of Florida.
Tom Graves, of Georgia.
Martha Roby, of Alabama.

Peter J. Visclosky, of Indiana.
Betty McCollum, of Minnesota.
Tim Ryan, of Ohio.
C. A. Dutch Ruppersberger, of Maryland.
Marcy Kaptur, of Ohio.
Henry Cuellar, of Texas.

Energy and Water Development, and Related Agencies

Michael K. Simpson, of Idaho, *Chair*

Charles J. ''Chuck'' Fleischmann, of Tennessee, *Vice Chair*

Ken Calvert, of California.
Jeff Fortenberry, of Nebraska.
Kay Granger, of Texas.
Jaime Herrera Beutler, of Washington.
David P. Joyce, of Ohio.
Dan Newhouse, of Washington.

Marcy Kaptur, of Ohio.
Peter J. Visclosky, of Indiana.
Debbie Wasserman Schultz, of Florida.
Pete Aguilar, of California.
José E. Serrano, of New York.

Financial Services and General Government

Tom Graves, of Georgia, *Chair*

Jaime Herrera Beutler, of Washington, *Vice Chair*

Kevin Yoder, of Kansas.
Mark E. Amodei, of Nevada.
Chris Stewart, of Utah.
David Young, of Iowa.
John R. Moolenaar, of Michigan.

Mike Quigley, of Illinois.
José E. Serrano, of New York.
Matt Cartwright, of Pennsylvania.
Sanford D. Bishop, Jr., of Georgia.

Homeland Security

Kevin Yoder, of Kansas, *Chair*

Steven M. Palazzo, of Mississippi, *Vice Chair*

John Abney Culberson, of Texas.
Charles J. ''Chuck'' Fleischmann, of Tennessee.
Andy Harris, of Maryland.
Dan Newhouse, of Washington.
Scott Taylor, of Virginia.

Lucille Roybal-Allard, of California.
Henry Cuellar, of Texas.
David E. Price, of North Carolina.
C. A. Dutch Ruppersberger, of Maryland.

Interior, Environment, and Related Agencies

Ken Calvert, of California, *Chair*

Chris Stewart, of Utah, *Vice Chair*

Michael K. Simpson, of Idaho.
Tom Cole, of Oklahoma.
David P. Joyce, of Ohio.
Mark E. Amodei, of Nevada.
Evan H. Jenkins, of West Virginia.

Betty McCollum, of Minnesota.
Chellie Pingree, of Maine.
Derek Kilmer, of Washington.
Marcy Kaptur, of Ohio.

Labor, Health and Human Services, Education, and Related Agencies

Tom Cole, of Oklahoma, *Chair*

Steve Womack, of Arkansas, *Vice Chair*

Michael K. Simpson, of Idaho.
Charles J. "Chuck" Fleischmann, of Tennessee.
Andy Harris, of Maryland.
Martha Roby, of Alabama.
Jaime Herrera Beutler, of Washington.
John R. Moolenaar, of Michigan.
Rosa L. DeLauro, of Connecticut.
Lucille Roybal-Allard, of California.
Barbara Lee, of California.
Mark Pocan, of Wisconsin.
Katherine M. Clark, of Massachusetts.

Legislative Branch

Rodney P. Frelinghuysen, of New Jersey, *Acting Chair*

Mark E. Amodei, of Nevada, *Vice Chair*

Dan Newhouse, of Washington.
John R. Moolenaar, of Michigan.
Scott Taylor, of Virginia.
John H. Rutherford, of Florida.
Tim Ryan, of Ohio.
Betty McCollum, of Minnesota.
Debbie Wasserman Schultz, of Florida.

Military Construction, Veterans Affairs, and Related Agencies

John R. Carter, of Texas, *Chair*

Jeff Fortenberry, of Nebraska, *Vice Chair*

Thomas J. Rooney, of Florida.
David G. Valadao, of California.
Steve Womack, of Arkansas.
Evan H. Jenkins, of West Virginia.
Scott Taylor, of Virginia.
Debbie Wasserman Schultz, of Florida.
Sanford D. Bishop, Jr., of Georgia.
Barbara Lee, of California.
Tim Ryan, of Ohio.

State, Foreign Operations, and Related Programs

Harold Rogers, of Kentucky, *Chair*

Thomas J. Rooney, of Florida, *Vice Chair*

Kay Granger, of Texas.
Mario Diaz-Balart, of Florida.
Jeff Fortenberry, of Nebraska.
Chris Stewart, of Utah.
John H. Rutherford, of Florida.
Nita M. Lowey, of New York.
Barbara Lee, of California.
C. A. Dutch Ruppersberger, of Maryland.
Grace Meng, of New York.
David E. Price, of North Carolina.

Transportation, Housing and Urban Development, and Related Agencies

Mario Diaz-Balart, of Florida, *Chair*

David P. Joyce, of Ohio, *Vice Chair*

John Abney Culberson, of Texas.
David Young, of Iowa.
David G. Valadao, of California.
Tom Graves, of Georgia.
John H. Rutherford, of Florida.
David E. Price, of North Carolina.
Mike Quigley, of Illinois.
Katherine M. Clark, of Massachusetts.
Pete Aguilar, of California.

STAFF

Committee on Appropriations (H–305), 225–2771.
Majority Clerk and Staff Director.—Nancy Fox.
Deputy Clerk and Staff Director.—Jim Kulikowski.
Staff Assistants: Carol Murphy, Stephen Sepp.
Member Services Director.—Shannon O'Keefe.
Communications Director.—Jennifer Hing.
Press Assistant.—Marta Dehmlow.

Administrative Assistant.—Tammy Hughes.
Special Assistant.—Rachel Kahler.
Administrative Assistant.—David Roth.
Administrative Aide.—Brad Allen.
Editors: Jim Cahill, Cathy Edwards (B–301A RHOB), 5–2851.
Computer Operations: Eric Jackson, Lonnie Johnson, Cathy Little, Don McKinnon, Linda Muir, Jay Sivulich, Jennifer Wheelock (B–305 RHOB), 5–2718.
Minority Staff Director.—Shalanda Young (1016 LHOB), 5–3481.
Minority Deputy Staff Director.—Chris Bigelow.
Minority Press Secretary.—Matt Dennis.
Administrative Aide.—Deborah Spriggs.
Subcommittee on Agriculture, Rural Development, Food and Drug Administration, and Related Agencies (2362–A RHOB), 5–2638.
Staff Assistants: Andrew Cooper, Pam Miller, Tom O'Brien.
Administrative Aide.—Elizabeth King.
Minority Staff Assistant.—Martha Foley (1016 LHOB), 5–3481.
Subcommittee on Commerce, Justice, Science, and Related Agencies (H–310), 5–3351.
Staff Assistants: Leslie Albright, Jeff Ashford, John Martens, Colin Samples, Aschley Schiller.
Administrative Aide.—Taylor Kelly.
Minority Staff Assistants: Bob Bonner, Matt Smith (1016 LHOB), 5–3481.
Subcommittee on Defense (H–405), 5–2847.
Staff Assistants: Matthew Bower, Brooke Boyer, Allison Deters, Walter Hearne, Collin Lee, Megan Milam, Jennifer Miller, Adrienne Ramsay, Cornell Teague, Paul Terry, B.G. Wright.
Administrative Aide.—Sherry Young.
Minority Staff Assistants: Taunja Berquam, Rebecca Leggieri (1016 LHOB), 5–3481.
Subcommittee on Energy and Water Development, and Related Agencies (2362–B RHOB), 5–3421.
Staff Assistants: Angie Giancarlo, Loraine Heckenberg, Donna Shahbaz, Perry Yates.
Administrative Aide.—Matthew Anderson.
Minority Staff Assistant.—Taunja Berquam (1016 LHOB), 5–3481.
Subcommittee on Financial Services (B–300 RHOB), 5–7245.
Staff Assistants: Dena Baron, Kelly Hitchcock, Marybeth Nassif, Ariana Sarar.
Administrative Aide.—Amy Cushing.
Minority Staff Assistant.—Angela Ohm (1016 LHOB), 5–3481.
Subcommittee on Homeland Security (B–307 RHOB), 5–5834.
Staff Assistants: Valerie Baldwin, Laura Cylke, Kris Mallard, Christopher Romig.
Administrative Aide.—Vacant.
Minority Staff Assistant.—Darek Newby (1016 LHOB), 5–3481.
Subcommittee on Interior, Environment, and Related Agencies (B–308 RHOB), 5–3081.
Staff Assistants: Darren Benjamin, Betsy Bina, Jason Gray, Jaclyn Kilroy, Dave LesStrang.
Administrative Aide.—Kristin Richmond.
Minority Staff Assistants: Joe Carlile, Rita Culp (1016 LHOB), 5–3481.
Subcommittee on Labor, Health and Human Services, Education, and Related Agencies (2358 RHOB), 5–3508.
Staff Assistants: Jennifer Cama, Justin Gibbons, Susan Ross, Kathryn Salmon.
Administrative Aide.—Lori Bias.
Minority Staff Assistants: Siobhan Hulihan, Robin Juliano, Stephen Steigleder (1016 LHOB), 5–3481.
Subcommittee on Legislative Branch (HT–2), 6–7252.
Staff Assistants: Liz Dawson, Tim Monahan, Jennifer Panone.
Minority Staff Assistant.—Shalanda Young.
Subcommittee on Military Construction, Veterans Affairs, and Related Agencies (HVC–227), 5–3047.
Staff Assistants: Maureen Holohan, Sue Quantius, Sarah Young.
Administrative Aide.—Tracey Russell.
Minority Staff Assistant.—Matt Washington (1016 LHOB), 5–3481.
Subcommittee on State and Foreign Operations (HT–2), 5–2401.
Staff Assistants: Susan Adams, David Bortnick, Winnie Chang, Craig Higgins.
Administrative Aide.—Clelia Alvarado.
Minority Staff Assistants: Erin Kolodjeski, Steve Marchese (1016 LHOB), 5–3481.
Subcommittee on Transportation, HUD, and Independent Agencies (2358A RHOB), 5–2141.
Staff Assistants: Carl Barrick, Doug Disrud, Jennifer Hollrah, Cheryle Tucker.
Administrative Aide.—Vacant.
Minority Staff Assistant.—Joe Carlile (1016 LHOB), 5–3481.

Armed Services

2216 Rayburn House Office Building, phone 225–4151, fax 225–9077

http://www.armedservices.house.gov

Mac Thornberry, of Texas, *Chair*

Walter B. Jones, of North Carolina.
Joe Wilson, of South Carolina.
Frank A. LoBiondo, of New Jersey.
Rob Bishop, of Utah.
Michael R. Turner, of Ohio.
Mike Rogers, of Alabama.
Bill Shuster, of Pennsylvania.
K. Michael Conaway, of Texas.
Doug Lamborn, of Colorado.
Robert J. Wittman, of Virginia.
Duncan Hunter, of California.
Mike Coffman, of Colorado.
Vicky Hartzler, of Missouri.
Austin Scott, of Georgia.
Mo Brooks, of Alabama.
Paul Cook, of California.
Bradley Byrne, of Alabama.
Sam Graves, of Missouri.
Elise M. Stefanik, of New York.
Martha McSally, of Arizona.
Stephen Knight, of California.
Steve Russell, of Oklahoma.
Scott DesJarlais, of Tennessee.
Ralph Lee Abraham, of Louisiana.
Trent Kelly, of Mississippi.
Mike Gallagher, of Wisconsin.
Matt Gaetz, of Florida.
Don Bacon, of Nebraska.
Jim Banks, of Indiana.
Liz Cheney, of Wyoming.
Jody B. Hice, of Georgia.
Paul Mitchell, of Michigan.
Vacant.

Adam Smith, of Washington.
Robert A. Brady, of Pennsylvania.
Susan A. Davis, of California.
James R. Langevin, of Rhode Island.
Rick Larsen, of Washington.
Jim Cooper, of Tennessee.
Madeleine Z. Bordallo, of Guam.
Joe Courtney, of Connecticut.
Niki Tsongas, of Massachusetts.
John Garamendi, of California.
Jackie Speier, of California.
Marc A. Veasey, of Texas.
Tulsi Gabbard, of Hawaii.
Beto O'Rourke, of Texas.
Donald Norcross, of New Jersey.
Ruben Gallego, of Arizona.
Seth Moulton, of Massachusetts.
Colleen Hanabusa, of Hawaii.
Carol Shea-Porter, of New Hampshire.
Jacky Rosen, of Nevada.
A. Donald McEachin, of Virginia.
Salud O. Carbajal, of California.
Anthony G. Brown, of Maryland.
Stephanie N. Murphy, of Florida.
Ro Khanna, of California.
Tom O'Halleran, of Arizona.
Thomas R. Suozzi, of New York.
Jimmy Panetta, of California.

SUBCOMMITTEES

Emerging Threats and Capabilities

Elise M. Stefanik, of New York, *Chair*

Liz Cheney, of Wyoming, *Vice Chair*

Bill Shuster, of Pennsylvania.
Ralph Lee Abraham, of Louisiana.
Joe Wilson, of South Carolina.
Frank A. LoBiondo, of New Jersey.
Doug Lamborn, of Colorado.
Austin Scott, of Georgia.
Jody B. Hice, of Georgia.
Vacant.

James R. Langevin, of Rhode Island.
Rick Larsen, of Washington.
Jim Cooper, of Tennessee.
Jackie Speier, of California.
Marc A. Veasey, of Texas.
Tulsi Gabbard, of Hawaii.
Beto O'Rourke, of Texas.
Stephanie N. Murphy, of Florida.

Military Personnel

Mike Coffman, of Colorado, *Chair*

Walter B. Jones, of North Carolina.
Steve Russell, of Oklahoma.
Don Bacon, of Nebraska.
Martha McSally, of Arizona.
Ralph Lee Abraham, of Louisiana.
Trent Kelly, of Mississippi.
Vacant.

Jackie Speier, of California.
Robert A. Brady, of Pennsylvania.
Niki Tsongas, of Massachusetts.
Ruben Gallego, of Arizona.
Carol Shea-Porter, of New Hampshire.
Jacky Rosen, of Nevada.

Oversight and Investigations

Vicky Hartzler, of Missouri, *Chair*

K. Michael Conaway, of Texas.
Matt Gaetz, of Florida.
Jim Banks, of Indiana.
Liz Cheney, of Wyoming.
Austin Scott, of Georgia.

Seth Moulton, of Massachusetts.
Tom O'Halleran, of Arizona.
Thomas R. Suozzi, of New York.
Jimmy Panetta, of California.

Readiness

Joe Wilson, of South Carolina, *Chair*
Martha McSally, of Arizona, *Vice Chair*

Rob Bishop, of Utah.
Austin Scott, of Georgia.
Steve Russell, of Oklahoma.
Mike Rogers, of Alabama.
Vicky Hartzler, of Missouri.
Elise M. Stefanik, of New York.
Scott DesJarlais, of Tennessee.
Trent Kelly, of Mississippi.
Mike Gallagher, of Wisconsin.

Madeleine Z. Bordallo, of Guam.
Joe Courtney, of Connecticut.
Tulsi Gabbard, of Hawaii.
Carol Shea-Porter, of New Hampshire.
A. Donald McEachin, of Virginia.
Salud O. Carbajal, of California.
Anthony G. Brown, of Maryland.
Stephanie N. Murphy, of Florida.
Ro Khanna, of California.

Seapower and Projection Forces

Robert J. Wittman, of Virginia, *Chair*
Bradley Byrne, of Alabama, *Vice Chair*

K. Michael Conaway, of Texas.
Vicky Hartzler, of Missouri.
Scott DesJarlais, of Tennessee.
Mike Gallagher, of Wisconsin.
Duncan Hunter, of California.
Paul Cook, of California.
Stephen Knight, of California.
Ralph Lee Abraham, of Louisiana.
Paul Mitchell, of Michigan.

Joe Courtney, of Connecticut.
Susan A. Davis, of California.
James R. Langevin, of Rhode Island.
Madeleine Z. Bordallo, of Guam.
John Garamendi, of California.
Donald Norcross, of New Jersey.
Seth Moulton, of Massachusetts.
Colleen Hanabusa, of Hawaii.
A. Donald McEachin, of Virginia.

Strategic Forces

Mike Rogers, of Alabama, *Chair*

Doug Lamborn, of Colorado.
Duncan Hunter, of California.
Mo Brooks, of Alabama.
Michael R. Turner, of Ohio.
Mike Coffman, of Colorado.
Bradley Byrne, of Alabama.
Sam Graves, of Missouri.
Jody B. Hice, of Georgia.
Paul Mitchell, of Michigan.

Jim Cooper, of Tennessee.
Susan A. Davis, of California.
Rick Larsen, of Washington.
John Garamendi, of California.
Beto O'Rourke, of Texas.
Donald Norcross, of New Jersey.
Colleen Hanabusa, of Hawaii.
Ro Khanna, of California.

Tactical Air and Land Forces

Michael R. Turner, of Ohio, *Chair*

Paul Cook, of California, *Vice Chair*

Frank A. LoBiondo, of New Jersey.
Sam Graves, of Missouri.
Martha McSally, of Arizona.
Stephen Knight, of California.
Trent Kelly, of Mississippi.
Matt Gaetz, of Florida.
Don Bacon, of Nebraska.
Jim Banks, of Indiana.
Walter B. Jones, of North Carolina.
Rob Bishop, of Utah.
Robert J. Wittman, of Virginia.
Mo Brooks, of Alabama.

Niki Tsongas, of Massachusetts.
James R. Langevin, of Rhode Island.
Jim Cooper, of Tennessee.
Marc A. Veasey, of Texas.
Ruben Gallego, of Arizona.
Jacky Rosen, of Nevada.
Salud O. Carbajal, of California.
Anthony G. Brown, of Maryland.
Tom O'Halleran, of Arizona.
Thomas R. Suozzi, of New York.
Jimmy Panetta, of California.

STAFF

Committee on Armed Services (2216 RHOB), 225–4151, fax 225–9077.
Staff Director.—Jenness Simler.
Minority Staff Director.—Paul Arcangeli.
General Counsel.—Andrew Peterson.
Counsels: William S. Johnson, Timothy Morrison, Matthew Sullivan, Leonor Tomero, Barron YoungSmith.
Director, Legislative Operations.—Zach Steacy.
Professional Staff: Kari Bingen, Jennifer Bird, Heath R. Bope, Christopher J. Bright, Douglas Bush, Everett Coleman, Craig Collier, Elizabeth Conrad, Robert Daigle, Margaret Dean, Brian Garrett, Kevin Gates, David Giachetti, Craig Greene, Brian Greer, Thomas Hawley, Bruce Johnson, Lindsay Kavanaugh, Steve Kitay, Phil MacNaughton, Mark Morehouse, Vickie Plunkett, Katy Quinn, Alexis Lasselle Ross, Rebecca A. Ross, Jason Schmid, Jack Schuler, Andrew Schulman, Catherine Sendak, Daniel Sennott, David Sienicki, John F. Sullivan, Jesse D. Tolleson, Jr., Peter Villano, Andrew T. Walter, Andrew Warren, John Wason, Ari Zimmerman.
Communications Director.—Claude Chafin.
Spokesman and Director of Member Initiatives.—Alison Lynn.
Press Secretary.—Nick Mikula.
Security Manager.—Kathryn Thompson.
Executive Assistants: Betty B. Gray, Candace Wagner.
Research Assistant.—Anna Waterfield.
Clerks: Jodi Brignola, Britton Burkett, Michael Gancio, Megan Handal, Nevada Schadler, Danielle Steitz.
Staff Assistant.—John N. Johnson.

Budget

B234 Longworth House Office Building 20515–6065, phone 226–7270, fax 226–7174

http://www.budget.house.gov

Steve Womack, of Arkansas, *Chair*

Todd Rokita, of Indiana, *Vice Chair*

Diane Black, of Tennessee.
Mario Diaz-Balart, of Florida.
Tom Cole, of Oklahoma.
Tom McClintock, of California.
Rob Woodall, of Georgia.
Mark Sanford, of South Carolina.
Dave Brat, of Virginia.
Glenn Grothman, of Wisconsin.
Gary J. Palmer, of Alabama.
Bruce Westerman, of Arkansas.
James B. Renacci, of Ohio.
Bill Johnson, of Ohio.
Jason Smith, of Missouri.
Jason Lewis, of Minnesota.
Jack Bergman, of Michigan.
John J. Faso, of New York.
Lloyd Smucker, of Pennsylvania.
Matt Gaetz, of Florida.
Jodey C. Arrington, of Texas.
A. Drew Ferguson IV, of Georgia.

John A. Yarmuth, of Kentucky.
Barbara Lee, of California.
Michelle Lujan Grisham, of New Mexico.
Seth Moulton, of Massachusetts.
Hakeem S. Jeffries, of New York.
Brian Higgins, of New York.
Suzan K. DelBene, of Washington.
Debbie Wasserman Schultz, of Florida.
Brendan F. Boyle, of Pennsylvania.
Ro Khanna, of California.
Pramila Jayapal, of Washington.
Salud O. Carbajal, of California.
Sheila Jackson Lee, of Texas.
Janice D. Schakowsky, of Illinois.

(No Subcommittees)

STAFF

Committee on Budget (B234 LHOB), 226–7270, fax 226–7174.
Majority Staff Director.—Dan Keniry.
Policy Director.—Jenna Spealman.
Chief Economist.—Andy Morton.
Senior Economist.—Timothy Flynn.
Chief Counsel.—Jim Bates.
Counsels: Elise Anderson, Mary Popadiuk, Jonathan Romito.
Senior Tax Advisor.—Robert Cogan.
Senior Advisor to the Chair.—Patrick Louis Knudsen.
Policy Advisors: Eric Davis, Emily Goff, Steven Gonzalez, Ellen Johnson, Brittany Madni, Steve Waskiewicz, Brad Watson, Robert Yeakel.
Communications Director.—Will Allison.
Press Secretary.—Chris Hartline.
Digital and Social Media Coordinator.—Maeve Gallivan.
Coalitions and Member Services: Gary Beck, Sage Peterson.
Chief Administrator.—Alex Stoddard.
Systems Administrator.—Jose Guillen.
Executive Assistant and Intern Coordinator.—Benjamin Gardenhour.
Staff Assistant.—Gary Haglund.
Minority Staff Director.—Ellen J. Balis (134 Cannon), 226–7200, fax 225–9905.
Deputy Staff Director.—Diana Meredith.
Counsel.—Jocelyn Harris.
Budget Review Director.—Kimberly Overbeek.
Senior Tax Counsel.—Jon Goldman.
Budget Analysts: Jonathan Antista, Erika Appel, Farouk Ophaso, Scott R. Russell, Beth Stephenson, Ted E. Zegers.
Tax Counsel.—Jonathan Goldman.
Communications Director.—Sam Lau.
Digital Director.—Najy Kamal.
Office Manager.—Sheila A. McDowell.
Minority Staff Assistant.—Hayden Flanery.

Education and the Workforce

2176 Rayburn House Office Building, phone 225–4527, fax 225–9571

http://edworkforce.house.gov

Virginia Foxx, of North Carolina, *Chair*

Joe Wilson, of South Carolina, *Vice Chair*

Duncan Hunter, of California.
David P. Roe, of Tennessee.
Glenn Thompson, of Pennsylvania.
Tim Walberg, of Michigan.
Brett Guthrie, of Kentucky.
Todd Rokita, of Indiana.
Lou Barletta, of Pennsylvania.
Luke Messer, of Indiana.
Bradley Byrne, of Alabama.
Dave Brat, of Virginia.
Glenn Grothman, of Wisconsin.
Elise M. Stefanik, of New York.
Rick W. Allen, of Georgia.
Jason Lewis, of Minnesota.
Francis Rooney, of Florida.
Thomas A. Garrett, Jr., of Virginia.
Lloyd Smucker, of Pennsylvania.
A. Drew Ferguson IV, of Georgia.
Ron Estes, of Kansas.
Karen C. Handel, of Georgia.
Jim Banks, of Indiana.

Robert C. ''Bobby'' Scott, of Virginia.
Susan A. Davis, of California.
Raúl M. Grijalva, of Arizona.
Joe Courtney, of Connecticut.
Marcia L. Fudge, of Ohio.
Jared Polis, of Colorado.
Gregorio Kilili Camacho Sablan, of Northern Mariana Islands.
Frederica S. Wilson, of Florida.
Suzanne Bonamici, of Oregon.
Mark Takano, of California.
Alma S. Adams, of North Carolina.
Mark DeSaulnier, of California.
Donald Norcross, of New Jersey.
Lisa Blunt Rochester, of Delaware.
Raja Krishnamoorthi, of Illinois.
Carol Shea-Porter, of New Hampshire.
Adriano Espaillat, of New York.

SUBCOMMITTEES

[The chair and ranking minority member are ex officio (non-voting) members of all subcommittees on which they do not serve.]

Early Childhood, Elementary, and Secondary Education

Todd Rokita, of Indiana, *Chair*

Duncan Hunter, of California.
David P. Roe, of Tennessee.
Glenn Thompson, of Pennsylvania.
Luke Messer, of Indiana.
Dave Brat, of Virginia.
Thomas A. Garrett, Jr., of Virginia.
Karen C. Handel, of Georgia.

Jared Polis, of Colorado.
Raúl M. Grijalva, of Arizona.
Marcia L. Fudge, of Ohio.
Suzanne Bonamici, of Oregon.
Susan A. Davis, of California.
Frederica S. Wilson, of Florida.

Health, Employment, Labor, and Pensions

Tim Walberg, of Michigan, *Chair*

Joe Wilson, of South Carolina.
David P. Roe, of Tennessee.
Todd Rokita, of Indiana.
Lou Barletta, of Pennsylvania.
Rick W. Allen, of Georgia.
Jason Lewis, of Minnesota.
Francis Rooney, of Florida.
Lloyd Smucker, of Pennsylvania.
A. Drew Ferguson IV, of Georgia.
Ron Estes, of Kansas.
Jim Banks, of Indiana.

Gregorio Kilili Camacho Sablan, of Northern Mariana Islands.
Frederica S. Wilson, of Florida.
Donald Norcross, of New Jersey.
Lisa Blunt Rochester, of Delaware.
Carol Shea-Porter, of New Hampshire.
Adriano Espaillat, of New York.
Joe Courtney, of Connecticut.
Marcia L. Fudge, of Ohio.
Suzanne Bonamici, of Oregon.

Higher Education and Workforce Development

Brett Guthrie, of Kentucky, *Chair*

Glenn Thompson, of Pennsylvania.
Lou Barletta, of Pennsylvania.
Luke Messer, of Indiana.
Bradley Byrne, of Alabama.
Glenn Grothman, of Wisconsin.
Elise M. Stefanik, of New York.
Rick W. Allen, of Georgia.
Jason Lewis, of Minnesota.
Thomas A. Garrett, Jr., of Virginia.
Lloyd Smucker, of Pennsylvania.
Ron Estes, of Kansas.
Jim Banks, of Indiana.

Susan A. Davis, of California.
Joe Courtney, of Connecticut.
Alma S. Adams, of North Carolina.
Mark DeSaulnier, of California.
Raja Krishnamoorthi, of Illinois.
Jared Polis, of Colorado.
Gregorio Kilili Camacho Sablan, of Northern Mariana Islands.
Mark Takano, of California.
Lisa Blunt Rochester, of Delaware.
Adriano Espaillat, of New York.

Workforce Protections

Bradley Byrne, of Alabama, *Chair*

Joe Wilson, of South Carolina.
Duncan Hunter, of California.
Dave Brat, of Virginia.
Glenn Grothman, of Wisconsin.
Elise M. Stefanik, of New York.
Francis Rooney, of Florida.
A. Drew Ferguson IV, of Georgia.
Karen C. Handel, of Georgia.

Mark Takano, of California.
Raúl M. Grijalva, of Arizona.
Alma S. Adams, of North Carolina.
Mark DeSaulnier, of California.
Donald Norcross, of New Jersey.
Raja Krishnamoorthi, of Illinois.
Carol Shea-Porter, of New Hampshire.

STAFF

Committee on Education and the Workforce (2176 RHOB), 225–4527.
Majority Staff Director.—Brandon Renz.
General Counsel.—Krisann Pearce.
Director of Education and Human Services Policy.—Amy Jones.
Director of Workforce Policy.—Rob Green.
Communications Director.—Kelley McNabb.
Press Secretaries: Bethany Aronhalt, Michael Woeste.
Deputy Press Secretaries: Marty Boughton, Michael Comer.
Director of Coalitions and Member Services.—Courtney Butcher.
Education Deputy Director and Senior Counsel.—Amanda Schaumburg.
Senior Education Policy Advisor.—Brad Thomas.
Professional Staff Members—Education: Kathlyn Ehl, James Forester, Emmanual Guillory, Jonas Linde, James Redstone, Alex Ricci, Emily Slack, Leslie Tatum.
Legislative Assistants—Education: Caitlin Burke, Jake Middlebrooks.
Deputy Director of Workforce Policy.—Molly Salmi.
Workforce Policy Counsel.—Andrew Banducci.
Professional Staff Members—Workforce: Callie Harman, Geoffrey MacLeay, Alexis Murray, Joe Wheeler, Lauren Williams.
Professional Staff Member and Counsel.—Rachel Mondl.
Legislative Assistant—Workforce.—Olivia Voslow.
Chief Clerk.—Nancy Locke.
Finance and Personnel Advisor.—Dianna Ruskowsky.
Administrative Director.—Elizabeth Podgorski.
Staff Assistants: Madison Hardimon, Blake Johnson.
Staff Assistant—Education.—Andrew Morley.
Staff Assistant—Workforce.—Vacant.
Minority Staff (2101 RHOB), 5–3725.
Staff Director.—Veronique Pluviose.
General Counsel.—Vacant.
Special Assistant to the Staff Director.—Liz Hollis.
Clerk/Intern and Fellow Coordinator.—Tylease Alli.
Staff Assistant.—Mishawn Freeman.
Communications Director.—Kiara Pesante.
Deputy Communications Director.—Arika Trim.

Digital Press Secretary.—Stephanie Lalle.
Director of Labor Policy.—Richard Miller.
Director of Health Policy/Senior Labor Policy Advisor—Carrie Hughes.
Labor Policy Counsels: Kyle DeCant, Udochi Onwubiko.
Senior Labor Policy Advisor.—Kevin McDermott.
Labor Policy Advisor.—Eunice Ikene.
Policy Associate.—Christine Godinez.
Director of Education Policy.—Jacque Chevalier.
Senior Education Policy Counsel.—Christian Haines.
Senior Education Policy Advisor.—Katherine Valle.
Disability Policy Advisor.—Kimberly Knackstedt.
Education Policy Advisor.—Alexander Payne.
Senior Counsel.—Ilana Brunner.
Systems Administrator.—Sheila Havenner.

Energy and Commerce

2125 Rayburn House Office Building, phone 225–2927

http://www.energycommerce.house.gov

Greg Walden, of Oregon, *Chair*

Joe Barton, of Texas, *Vice Chair*

Fred Upton, of Michigan.
John Shimkus, of Illinois.
Michael C. Burgess, of Texas.
Marsha Blackburn, of Tennessee.
Steve Scalise, of Louisiana.
Robert E. Latta, of Ohio.
Cathy McMorris Rodgers, of Washington.
Gregg Harper, of Mississippi.
Leonard Lance, of New Jersey.
Brett Guthrie, of Kentucky.
Pete Olson, of Texas.
David B. McKinley, of West Virginia.
Adam Kinzinger, of Illinois.
H. Morgan Griffith, of Virginia.
Gus M. Bilirakis, of Florida.
Bill Johnson, of Ohio.
Billy Long, of Missouri.
Larry Bucshon, of Indiana.
Bill Flores, of Texas.
Susan W. Brooks, of Indiana.
Markwayne Mullin, of Oklahoma.
Richard Hudson, of North Carolina.
Chris Collins, of New York.
Kevin Cramer, of North Dakota.
Tim Walberg, of Michigan.
Mimi Walters, of California.
Ryan A. Costello, of Pennsylvania.
Earl L. ''Buddy'' Carter, of Georgia.
Jeff Duncan, of South Carolina.

Frank Pallone, Jr., of New Jersey.
Bobby L. Rush, of Illinois.
Anna G. Eshoo, of California.
Eliot L. Engel, of New York.
Gene Green, of Texas.
Diana DeGette, of Colorado.
Michael F. Doyle, of Pennsylvania.
Janice D. Schakowsky, of Illinois.
G. K. Butterfield, of North Carolina.
Doris O. Matsui, of California.
Kathy Castor, of Florida.
John P. Sarbanes, of Maryland.
Jerry McNerney, of California.
Peter Welch, of Vermont.
Ben Ray Luján, of New Mexico.
Paul Tonko, of New York.
Yvette D. Clarke, of New York.
David Loebsack, of Iowa.
Kurt Schrader, of Oregon.
Joseph P. Kennedy III, of Massachusetts.
Tony Cárdenas, of California.
Raul Ruiz, of California.
Scott H. Peters, of California.
Debbie Dingell, of Michigan.

SUBCOMMITTEES

[The chair and ranking minority member are ex officio (voting) members of all subcommittees on which they do not serve.]

Communications and Technology

Marsha Blackburn, of Tennessee, *Chair*

Leonard Lance, of New Jersey, *Vice Chair*

John Shimkus, of Illinois.
Steve Scalise, of Louisiana.
Robert E. Latta, of Ohio.
Brett Guthrie, of Kentucky.
Pete Olson, of Texas.
Adam Kinzinger, of Illinois.
Gus M. Bilirakis, of Florida.
Bill Johnson, of Ohio.
Billy Long, of Missouri.
Bill Flores, of Texas.
Susan W. Brooks, of Indiana.
Chris Collins, of New York.
Kevin Cramer, of North Dakota.
Mimi Walters, of California.
Ryan A. Costello, of Pennsylvania.

Michael F. Doyle, of Pennsylvania.
Peter Welch, of Vermont.
Yvette D. Clarke, of New York.
David Loebsack, of Iowa.
Raul Ruiz, of California.
Debbie Dingell, of Michigan.
Bobby L. Rush, of Illinois.
Anna G. Eshoo, of California.
Eliot L. Engel, of New York.
G. K. Butterfield, of North Carolina.
Doris O. Matsui, of California.
Jerry McNerney, of California.

Digital Commerce and Consumer Protection

Robert E. Latta, of Ohio, *Chair*

Adam Kinzinger, of Illinois, *Vice Chair*

Fred Upton, of Michigan.
Michael C. Burgess, of Texas.
Leonard Lance, of New Jersey.
Brett Guthrie, of Kentucky.
David B. McKinley, of West Virginia.
Gus M. Bilirakis, of Florida.
Larry Bucshon, of Indiana.
Markwayne Mullin, of Oklahoma.
Mimi Walters, of California.
Ryan A. Costello, of Pennsylvania.
Jeff Duncan, of South Carolina.

Janice D. Schakowsky, of Illinois.
Ben Ray Luján, of New Mexico.
Yvette D. Clarke, of New York.
Tony Cárdenas, of California.
Debbie Dingell, of Michigan.
Doris O. Matsui, of California.
Peter Welch, of Vermont.
Joseph P. Kennedy III, of Massachusetts.
Gene Green, of Texas.

Energy

Fred Upton, of Michigan, *Chair*

Pete Olson, of Texas, *Vice Chair*

Joe Barton, of Texas.
John Shimkus, of Illinois.
Robert E. Latta, of Ohio.
Gregg Harper, of Mississippi.
David B. McKinley, of West Virginia.
Adam Kinzinger, of Illinois.
H. Morgan Griffith, of Virginia.
Bill Johnson, of Ohio.
Billy Long, of Missouri.
Larry Bucshon, of Indiana.
Bill Flores, of Texas.
Markwayne Mullin, of Oklahoma.
Richard Hudson, of North Carolina.
Kevin Cramer, of North Dakota.
Tim Walberg, of Michigan.
Jeff Duncan, of South Carolina.

Bobby L. Rush, of Illinois.
Jerry McNerney, of California.
Scott H. Peters, of California.
Gene Green, of Texas.
Michael F. Doyle, of Pennsylvania.
Kathy Castor, of Florida.
John P. Sarbanes, of Maryland.
Peter Welch, of Vermont.
Paul Tonko, of New York.
David Loebsack, of Iowa.
Kurt Schrader, of Oregon.
Joseph P. Kennedy III, of Massachusetts.
G. K. Butterfield, of North Carolina.

Environment

John Shimkus, of Illinois, *Chair*

David B. McKinley, of West Virginia, *Vice Chair*

Joe Barton, of Texas.
Marsha Blackburn, of Tennessee.
Gregg Harper, of Mississippi.
Pete Olson, of Texas.
Bill Johnson, of Ohio.
Bill Flores, of Texas.
Richard Hudson, of North Carolina.
Kevin Cramer, of North Dakota.
Tim Walberg, of Michigan.
Earl L. ''Buddy'' Carter, of Georgia.
Jeff Duncan, of South Carolina.

Paul Tonko, of New York.
Raul Ruiz, of California.
Scott H. Peters, of California.
Gene Green, of Texas.
Diana DeGette, of Colorado.
Jerry McNerney, of California.
Tony Cárdenas, of California.
Debbie Dingell, of Michigan.
Doris O. Matsui, of California.

Health

Michael C. Burgess, of Texas, *Chair*

Brett Guthrie, of Kentucky, *Vice Chair*

Joe Barton, of Texas.
Fred Upton, of Michigan.
John Shimkus, of Illinois.
Marsha Blackburn, of Tennessee.
Robert E. Latta, of Ohio.
Cathy McMorris Rodgers, of Washington.
Leonard Lance, of New Jersey.
H. Morgan Griffith, of Virginia.
Gus M. Bilirakis, of Florida.
Billy Long, of Missouri.
Larry Bucshon, of Indiana.
Susan W. Brooks, of Indiana.
Markwayne Mullin, of Oklahoma.
Richard Hudson, of North Carolina.
Chris Collins, of New York.
Earl L. ''Buddy'' Carter, of Georgia.

Gene Green, of Texas.
Eliot L. Engel, of New York.
Janice D. Schakowsky, of Illinois.
G. K. Butterfield, of North Carolina.
Doris O. Matsui, of California.
Kathy Castor, of Florida.
John P. Sarbanes, of Maryland.
Ben Ray Luján, of New Mexico.
Kurt Schrader, of Oregon.
Joseph P. Kennedy III, of Massachusetts.
Tony Cárdenas, of California.
Anna G. Eshoo, of California.
Diana DeGette, of Colorado.

Oversight and Investigations

Gregg Harper, of Mississippi, *Chair*

H. Morgan Griffith, of Virginia, *Vice Chair*

Joe Barton, of Texas.
Michael C. Burgess, of Texas.
Susan W. Brooks, of Indiana.
Chris Collins, of New York.
Tim Walberg, of Michigan.
Mimi Walters, of California.
Ryan A. Costello, of Pennsylvania.
Earl L. ''Buddy'' Carter, of Georgia.

Diana DeGette, of Colorado.
Janice D. Schakowsky, of Illinois.
Kathy Castor, of Florida.
Paul Tonko, of New York.
Yvette D. Clarke, of New York.
Raul Ruiz, of California.
Scott H. Peters, of California.

STAFF

Committee on Energy and Commerce (2125 RHOB), 225–2927, fax 225–1919.
Majority Staff Director.—Michael Bloomquist.
General Counsel.—Karen Christian.
Deputy General Counsel.—Peter Kielty.
Director of Policy and External Affairs.—Jordan Davis.
Director, Communications.—Zachary Hunter.
Director, Coalitions and Outreach.—Adam Fromm.
Chief Counsel, Communications and Technology.—David Redl.
Chief Counsel, Digital Commerce and Consumer Protection.—Paul Nagle.
Chief Counsel, Energy and Power/Environment.—Thomas Hassenboehler.
Chief Counsel, Health.—Paul Edattel.
Chief Counsel, Oversight and Investigations.—Jennifer Barblan.
Chief Investigative Counsel, Oversight.—Alan Slobodin.
Chief Environmental Advisor.—Gerald Couri.
Deputy Chief Energy Counsel.—Brandon Mooney.
Deputy Chief Health Counsel.—Josh Trent.
Senior Counsels: Ben Lieberman, Jason Stanek, John Stone.
Senior Policy Advisor.—Ann Johnston.
Senior Professional Staff: Timothy Kurth, Andy Zach.
Special Advisor for External Affairs.—Hamlin Wade.
Counsels: Lamar Echols, Melissa Froelich, Kelsey Guyselman, Brighton Haslett, Bijan Koohmaraie, Lauren McCarty, Tina Richards, Annelise Rickert.
Professional Staff: Adam Buckalew, Caleb Graff, Brittany Havens, John Ohly, JP Paluskiewicz, Kristen Shatynski, Peter Spencer, Joshua Trent, Jessica Wilkerson.
Press Secretaries: Blair Ellis, Dan Schneider, Jennifer Sherman.
Press Assistant.—Katie McKeogh.
Video Production Aide and Press Assistant.—Alex Miller.
Policy Coordinator.—Lorissa Bounds.

Policy Coordinator, Communications and Technology.—Charles Flint.
Policy Coordinator, Digital Commerce and Consumer Protection.—Madeline Vey.
Policy Coordinator, Energy and Power.—Mark Ratner.
Policy Coordinator, Environment.—Jordan Haverly.
Policy Coordinator, Health.—Danielle Steele.
Policy Coordinator, Oversight and Investigations.—Samuel Spector.
Research Associate.—Wyatt Ellertson.
Legislative Clerks: Elena Brennan, Giulia Giannangeli, Jay Gulshen.
Director, Information Technology.—Everett Winnick.
Financial and Administrative Coordinator.—Sean Corcoran.
Human Resources and Office Administrator.—Theresa Gambo.
Executive Assistant.—Drew McDowell.
Staff Assistants: Kelly Collins, Zachary Dareshori, Evan Viau.

Minority Staff Director.—Jeff Carroll.
Deputy Committee Staff Director/Chief Health Advisor.—Tiffany Guarascio.
Chief Counsel.—Timothy Robinson.
Chief Counsel, Communications and Technology.—David Goldman.
Chief Counsel, Digital Commerce and Consumer Protection.—Michelle Ash.
Staff Director for Energy and Environment.—Rick Kessler.
Oversight Staff Director.—Chris Knauer.
Senior Health Counsel.—Una Lee.
Senior Counsel.—Jacqueline Cohen.
Counsels: Julie Babayan, Waverly Gordon, Lisa Goldman, Gerald Leverich, Jon Monger.
Senior Health Policy Advisors: Rachel Pryor, Kimberlee Trzeciak.
Energy and Environment Policy Advisors: Jean Fruci, Tuley Wright.
Office Manager.—Elizabeth Ertel.
Professional Staff: Jacquelyn Bolen, Caitlin Haberman, Kevin McAloon.
Director of Communications, Member Services and Outreach.—Andrew Souvall.
Outreach and Member Services Coordinator.—Jessica Martinez.
Policy Analysts: Miles Lichtman, Dan Miller, Caroline Paris-Behr, Alexander Ratner, Samantha Satchell.
Policy Coordinator.—John Marshall.
Staff Assistant.—Jourdan Lewis.
Director of Technology.—Edward Walker.
Press Secretary.—CJ Young.
Press Assistant.—Evan Gilbert.
Deputy Press Secretary.—Matt Schumacher.

Ethics

1015 Longworth House Office Building, phone 225–7103, fax 225–7392

Susan W. Brooks, of Indiana, *Chairwoman*

Kenny Marchant, of Texas.
Leonard Lance, of New Jersey.
Mimi Walters, of California.
John Ratcliffe, of Texas.

Theodore E. Deutch, of Florida.
Yvette D. Clarke, of New York.
Jared Polis, of Colorado.
Anthony G. Brown, of Maryland.
Steve Cohen, of Tennessee.

(No Subcommittees)

STAFF

Chief Counsel / Staff Director.—Tom Rust.
Chief of Staff and Counsel to the Chairwoman.—Megan Savage.
Counsel to the Ranking Member.—Dan Taylor.
Director of Administration.—Donna Herbert.
Director of Advice and Education.—Tonia Smith.
Director of Investigations.—Patrick McMullen.
Senior Counsel.—Tamar Nedzar.
Counsels: David Arrojo, Katy Daly, Kathryn Donahue, Robert Eskridge, Sarah Myers-Mutschall, Zeke Ross, Tonya Sloans, Wendy Smith.
Professional Staff.—Adam Wambold.
Investigator.—Molly McCarty.
Senior Financial Disclosure Advisor.—Deborah Bethea.
Systems Administrator.—Craig Barber.
Investigative Clerk.—Michael Koren.
Advice and Education Clerk.—Christian Hollowell.
Financial Disclosure Clerk.—Destinae Demery.
Staff Assistants: Olivia Gardner, Andrew Kleiman.

Financial Services

2129 Rayburn House Office Building, phone 225–7502

http://www.house.gov/financialservices

Jeb Hensarling, of Texas, *Chair*

Patrick T. McHenry, of North Carolina, *Vice Chair*

Peter T. King, of New York.
Edward R. Royce, of California.
Frank D. Lucas, of Oklahoma.
Stevan Pearce, of New Mexico.
Bill Posey, of Florida.
Blaine Luetkemeyer, of Missouri.
Bill Huizenga, of Michigan.
Sean P. Duffy, of Wisconsin.
Steve Stivers, of Ohio.
Randy Hultgren, of Illinois.
Dennis A. Ross, of Florida.
Robert Pittenger, of North Carolina.
Ann Wagner, of Missouri.
Andy Barr, of Kentucky.
Keith J. Rothfus, of Pennsylvania.
Luke Messer, of Indiana.
Scott R. Tipton, of Colorado.
Roger Williams, of Texas.
Bruce Poliquin, of Maine.
Mia B. Love, of Utah.
J. French Hill, of Arkansas.
Tom Emmer, of Minnesota.
Lee M. Zeldin, of New York.
David A. Trott, of Michigan.
Barry Loudermilk, of Georgia.
Alexander X. Mooney, of West Virginia.
Thomas MacArthur, of New Jersey.
Warren Davidson, of Ohio.
Ted Budd, of North Carolina.
David Kustoff, of Tennessee.
Claudia Tenney, of New York.
Trey Hollingsworth, of Indiana.

Maxine Waters, of California.
Carolyn B. Maloney, of New York.
Nydia M. Velázquez, of New York.
Brad Sherman, of California.
Gregory W. Meeks, of New York.
Michael E. Capuano, of Massachusetts.
Wm. Lacy Clay, of Missouri.
Stephen F. Lynch, of Massachusetts.
David Scott, of Georgia.
Al Green, of Texas.
Emanuel Cleaver, of Missouri.
Gwen Moore, of Wisconsin.
Keith Ellison, of Minnesota.
Ed Perlmutter, of Colorado.
James A. Himes, of Connecticut.
Bill Foster, of Illinois.
Daniel T. Kildee, of Michigan.
John K. Delaney, of Maryland.
Kyrsten Sinema, of Arizona.
Joyce Beatty, of Ohio.
Denny Heck, of Washington.
Juan Vargas, of California.
Josh Gottheimer, of New Jersey.
Vicente Gonzalez, of Texas.
Charlie Crist, of Florida.
Ruben J. Kihuen, of Nevada.

SUBCOMMITTEES

[The chair and ranking minority member are ex officio (voting) members of all subcommittees on which they do not serve.]

Capital Markets, Securities, and Investments

Bill Huizenga, of Michigan, *Chair*

Randy Hultgren, of Illinois, *Vice Chair*

Peter T. King, of New York.
Patrick T. McHenry, of North Carolina.
Sean P. Duffy, of Wisconsin.
Steve Stivers, of Ohio.
Ann Wagner, of Missouri.
Luke Messer, of Indiana.
Bruce Poliquin, of Maine.
J. French Hill, of Arkansas.
Tom Emmer, of Minnesota.
Alexander X. Mooney, of West Virginia.
Thomas MacArthur, of New Jersey.
Warren Davidson, of Ohio.
Ted Budd, of North Carolina.
Trey Hollingsworth, of Indiana.

Carolyn B. Maloney, of New York.
Brad Sherman, of California.
Stephen F. Lynch, of Massachusetts.
David Scott, of Georgia.
James A. Himes, of Connecticut.
Keith Ellison, of Minnesota.
Bill Foster, of Illinois.
Gregory W. Meeks, of New York.
Kyrsten Sinema, of Arizona.
Juan Vargas, of California.
Josh Gottheimer, of New Jersey.
Vicente Gonzalez, of Texas.

Financial Institutions and Consumer Credit

Blaine Luetkemeyer, of Missouri, *Chair*

Keith J. Rothfus, of Pennsylvania, *Vice Chair*

Edward R. Royce, of California.
Frank D. Lucas, of Oklahoma.
Bill Posey, of Florida.
Dennis A. Ross, of Florida.
Robert Pittenger, of North Carolina.
Andy Barr, of Kentucky.
Scott R. Tipton, of Colorado.
Roger Williams, of Texas.
Mia B. Love, of Utah.
David A. Trott, of Michigan.
Barry Loudermilk, of Georgia.
David Kustoff, of Tennessee.
Claudia Tenney, of New York.

Wm. Lacy Clay, of Missouri.
Carolyn B. Maloney, of New York.
Gregory W. Meeks, of New York.
David Scott, of Georgia.
Nydia M. Velázquez, of New York.
Al Green, of Texas.
Keith Ellison, of Minnesota.
Michael E. Capuano, of Massachusetts.
Denny Heck, of Washington.
Gwen Moore, of Wisconsin.
Charlie Crist, of Florida.

Housing and Insurance

Sean P. Duffy, of Wisconsin, *Chair*

Dennis A. Ross, of Florida, *Vice Chair*

Edward R. Royce, of California.
Stevan Pearce, of New Mexico.
Bill Posey, of Florida.
Blaine Luetkemeyer, of Missouri.
Steve Stivers, of Ohio.
Randy Hultgren, of Illinois.
Keith J. Rothfus, of Pennsylvania.
Lee M. Zeldin, of New York.
David A. Trott, of Michigan.
Thomas MacArthur, of New Jersey.
Ted Budd, of North Carolina.

Emanuel Cleaver, of Missouri.
Nydia M. Velázquez, of New York.
Michael E. Capuano, of Massachusetts.
Wm. Lacy Clay, of Missouri.
Brad Sherman, of California.
Joyce Beatty, of Ohio.
Daniel T. Kildee, of Michigan.
John K. Delaney, of Maryland.
Ruben J. Kihuen, of Nevada.
Vicente Gonzalez, of Texas.

Monetary Policy and Trade

Andy Barr, of Kentucky, *Chair*

Roger Williams, of Texas, *Vice Chair*

Frank D. Lucas, of Oklahoma.
Bill Huizenga, of Michigan.
Robert Pittenger, of North Carolina.
Mia B. Love, of Utah.
J. French Hill, of Arkansas.
Tom Emmer, of Minnesota.
Alexander X. Mooney, of West Virginia.
Warren Davidson, of Ohio.
Claudia Tenney, of New York.
Trey Hollingsworth, of Indiana.

Gwen Moore, of Wisconsin.
Gregory W. Meeks, of New York.
Bill Foster, of Illinois.
Brad Sherman, of California.
Al Green, of Texas.
Denny Heck, of Washington.
Daniel T. Kildee, of Michigan.
Juan Vargas, of California.
Charlie Crist, of Florida.

Oversight and Investigations

Ann Wagner, of Missouri, *Chair*

Scott R. Tipton, of Colorado, *Vice Chair*

Peter T. King, of New York.
Patrick T. McHenry, of North Carolina.
Dennis A. Ross, of Florida.
Luke Messer, of Indiana.
Lee M. Zeldin, of New York.
David A. Trott, of Michigan.
Barry Loudermilk, of Georgia.
David Kustoff, of Tennessee.
Claudia Tenney, of New York.
Trey Hollingsworth, of Indiana.

Al Green, of Texas.
Keith Ellison, of Minnesota.
Emanuel Cleaver, of Missouri.
Joyce Beatty, of Ohio.
Michael E. Capuano, of Massachusetts.
Gwen Moore, of Wisconsin.
Josh Gottheimer, of New Jersey.
Vicente Gonzalez, of Texas.
Charlie Crist, of Florida.

Terrorism and Illicit Finance

Stevan Pearce, of New Mexico, *Chair*

Robert Pittenger, of North Carolina, *Vice Chair*

Keith J. Rothfus, of Pennsylvania.
Luke Messer, of Indiana.
Scott R. Tipton, of Colorado.
Roger Williams, of Texas.
Bruce Poliquin, of Maine.
Mia B. Love, of Utah.
J. French Hill, of Arkansas.
Tom Emmer, of Minnesota.
Lee M. Zeldin, of New York.
Warren Davidson, of Ohio.
Ted Budd, of North Carolina.
David Kustoff, of Tennessee.

Ed Perlmutter, of Colorado.
Carolyn B. Maloney, of New York.
James A. Himes, of Connecticut.
Bill Foster, of Illinois.
Daniel T. Kildee, of Michigan.
John K. Delaney, of Maryland.
Kyrsten Sinema, of Arizona.
Juan Vargas, of California.
Josh Gottheimer, of New Jersey.
Ruben J. Kihuen, of Nevada.
Stephen F. Lynch, of Massachusetts.

STAFF

Committee on Financial Services (2129 RHOB), 225–7502.
Majority Staff:
Staff Director.—Kirsten J. Mork.
Chief Counsel.—Kevin R. Edgar.
Deputy Staff Director/Communications.—Jeffrey Wade Emerson.
Policy Director.—Edward G. Skala.
General Counsel and Parliamentarian.—Joseph R. Clark.
Chief Economist.—Dino D. Falaschetti.
Communications Director.—Sarah Rozier.
Chief Financial Institutions Counsel.—Brian Johnson.
Chief Housing and Insurance Counsel.—Clinton Columbus Jones III.
Senior Counsels: Samuel Everett Dewey, Rebekah E. Goshorn, Francisco Medina.
Senior Policy Advisor.—Andrew Quinn Eck.
Director of International Affairs.—Anthony E. Chang.
Senior Professional Staff: Jonathan M. Blum, Katelyn E. Christ, Tallman Johnson, Joe Pinder.
Counsels: Brian R. Anderson, Joseph A. Gammello, Elie S. Greenbaum, Holli N. Heiles, Hallee Katherine Morgan, Brett A. Sisto, Bryan Alexander Wood.
Professional Staff: Thomas Christian Brown, Edward Chase Burgess, Patrick Cuff, John Hair, Marliss A. McManus, Matthew Kinley Mulder, Erik R. Rust, Kevin D. Wysocki.
Administrative Assistant.—Angela S. Gambo.
Chief Clerk.—Rosemary E. Keech.
Systems Administrator.—Kim Trimble.
Editor.—Terisa L. Allison.
Digital Director.—Adam J. Scheidler.
Legislative Assistants: Taylor R. Hewes, Kelly E. McGrath, James Redfield.
Director of Member Services and Coalitions.—Isaac Borden Hoskins.
Member Services and Coalitions Assistant.—Monica L. Zagame.
Scheduler.—Jennifer Renee Stalzer.
Staff Assistant.—Francesco Antonio Castella.
Minority Staff:
Staff Director.—Charla Ouertatani.
Deputy Staff Director.—Kristofor Erickson.
General Counsel/Legislative Director.—Lisa Peto.
Chief Oversight Counsel.—Kevin Burris.
Senior Counsels: Katelynn Bradley, Bruce Johnson II, Courtney Robinson.
Counsels: Esther Kahng, Jason Powell, Jennifer Read.
Senior Policy Director.—Erika Jeffers.
Senior Policy Advisor.—Glen Sears.
Systems Administrator.—Alfred J. Forman, Jr.
Director of Housing Policy.—Theresa Dumais.
Chief Administrative Officer.—Anita L. Johnson.
Financial and Administrative Officer.—Denise Scott.
Communications Director.—Eric Hersey.
Press Assistant.—Marcos F. Manosalvas.
Press Secretary.—Lina Francis.
Senior Professional Staff: Daniel P. McGlinchey, Kirk Schwarzbach.
Research and Special Assistant.—Paniz Rezaee-Rod.

Foreign Affairs

2170 Rayburn House Office Building, phone 225–5021

http://www.foreignaffairs.house.gov

Edward R. Royce, of California, *Chair*

Christopher H. Smith, of New Jersey.
Ileana Ros-Lehtinen, of Florida.
Dana Rohrabacher, of California.
Steve Chabot, of Ohio.
Joe Wilson, of South Carolina.
Michael T. McCaul, of Texas.
Ted Poe, of Texas.
Darrell E. Issa, of California.
Tom Marino, of Pennsylvania.
Mo Brooks, of Alabama.
Paul Cook, of California.
Scott Perry, of Pennsylvania.
Ron DeSantis, of Florida.
Mark Meadows, of North Carolina.
Ted S. Yoho, of Florida.
Adam Kinzinger, of Illinois.
Lee M. Zeldin, of New York.
Daniel M. Donovan, Jr., of New York.
F. James Sensenbrenner, Jr., of Wisconsin.
Ann Wagner, of Missouri.
Brian J. Mast, of Florida.
Francis Rooney, of Florida.
Brian K. Fitzpatrick, of Pennsylvania.
Thomas A. Garrett, Jr., of Virginia.
John R. Curtis, of Utah.

Eliot L. Engel, of New York.
Brad Sherman, of California.
Gregory W. Meeks, of New York.
Albio Sires, of New Jersey.
Gerald E. Connolly, of Virginia.
Theodore E. Deutch, of Florida.
Karen Bass, of California.
William R. Keating, of Massachusetts.
David N. Cicilline, of Rhode Island.
Ami Bera, of California.
Lois Frankel, of Florida.
Tulsi Gabbard, of Hawaii.
Joaquin Castro, of Texas.
Robin L. Kelly, of Illinois.
Brendan F. Boyle, of Pennsylvania.
Dina Titus, of Nevada.
Norma J. Torres, of California.
Bradley Scott Schneider, of Illinois.
Thomas R. Suozzi, of New York.
Adriano Espaillat, of New York.
Ted Lieu, of California.

SUBCOMMITTEES

[The chair and ranking minority member are ex officio (non-voting) members of all subcommittees on which they do not serve.]

Africa, Global Health, Global Human Rights, and International Organizations

Christopher H. Smith, of New Jersey, *Chair*

Mark Meadows, of North Carolina.
Daniel M. Donovan, Jr., of New York.
F. James Sensenbrenner, Jr., of Wisconsin.
Thomas A. Garrett, Jr., of Virginia.

Karen Bass, of California.
Ami Bera, of California.
Joaquin Castro, of Texas.
Thomas R. Suozzi, of New York.

Asia and the Pacific

Ted S. Yoho, of Florida, *Chair*

Dana Rohrabacher, of California.
Steve Chabot, of Ohio.
Tom Marino, of Pennsylvania.
Mo Brooks, of Alabama.
Scott Perry, of Pennsylvania.
Adam Kinzinger, of Illinois.
Ann Wagner, of Missouri.

Brad Sherman, of California.
Ami Bera, of California.
Dina Titus, of Nevada.
Gerald E. Connolly, of Virginia.
Theodore E. Deutch, of Florida.
Tulsi Gabbard, of Hawaii.

Europe, Eurasia, and Emerging Threats

Dana Rohrabacher, of California, *Chair*

Joe Wilson, of South Carolina.
Ted Poe, of Texas.
Tom Marino, of Pennsylvania.
F. James Sensenbrenner, Jr., of Wisconsin.
Francis Rooney, of Florida.
Brian K. Fitzpatrick, of Pennsylvania.
John R. Curtis, of Utah.

Gregory W. Meeks, of New York.
Brad Sherman, of California.
Albio Sires, of New Jersey.
William R. Keating, of Massachusetts.
David N. Cicilline, of Rhode Island.
Robin L. Kelly, of Illinois.

The Middle East and North Africa

Ileana Ros-Lehtinen, of Florida, *Chair*

Steve Chabot, of Ohio.
Darrell E. Issa, of California.
Ron DeSantis, of Florida.
Mark Meadows, of North Carolina.
Adam Kinzinger, of Illinois.
Lee M. Zeldin, of New York.
Daniel M. Donovan, Jr., of New York.
Ann Wagner, of Missouri.
Brian J. Mast, of Florida.
Brian K. Fitzpatrick, of Pennsylvania.
John R. Curtis, of Utah.

Theodore E. Deutch, of Florida.
Gerald E. Connolly, of Virginia.
David N. Cicilline, of Rhode Island.
Lois Frankel, of Florida.
Brendan F. Boyle, of Pennsylvania.
Tulsi Gabbard, of Hawaii.
Bradley Scott Schneider, of Illinois.
Thomas R. Suozzi, of New York.
Ted Lieu, of California.

Terrorism, Nonproliferation, and Trade

Ted Poe, of Texas, *Chair*

Joe Wilson, of South Carolina.
Darrell E. Issa, of California.
Paul Cook, of California.
Scott Perry, of Pennsylvania.
Lee M. Zeldin, of New York.
Brian J. Mast, of Florida.
Thomas A. Garrett, Jr., of Virginia.

William R. Keating, of Massachusetts.
Lois Frankel, of Florida.
Brendan F. Boyle, of Pennsylvania.
Dina Titus, of Nevada.
Norma J. Torres, of California.
Bradley Scott Schneider, of Illinois.

The Western Hemisphere

Paul Cook, of California, *Chair*

Christopher H. Smith, of New Jersey.
Ileana Ros-Lehtinen, of Florida.
Michael T. McCaul, of Texas.
Mo Brooks, of Alabama.
Ron DeSantis, of Florida.
Ted S. Yoho, of Florida.
Francis Rooney, of Florida.

Albio Sires, of New Jersey.
Joaquin Castro, of Texas.
Robin L. Kelly, of Illinois.
Norma J. Torres, of California.
Adriano Espaillat, of New York.
Gregory W. Meeks, of New York.

STAFF

Committee on Foreign Affairs (2170 RHOB), 225–5021, fax 225–5394.
Majority Staff:
Chief of Staff.—Amy Porter.
Majority Staff Director.—Thomas P. Sheehy.
Deputy Staff Director.—Edward A. Burrier.
Deputy Staff Director for Communications.—Cory Fritz.
General Counsel and Parliamentarian.—Doug Anderson.
Chief Counsel for Oversight and Investigations.—Thomas Alexander.
Professional Staff Member, Oversight and Investigations.—Shellie Bressler.
Communications Director.—Audra McGeorge.
Digital Director.—Russell Solomon.
Senior Professional Staff Members: Sarah Blocher, Joan Condon, Jamie McCormick, Doug Seay, Matthew Zweig.

Senior Advisors: Leah Campos, Kristen Marquardt.
Professional Staff Members: Thomas Hill, Gabriella Ra'anan, Shelley Su, Andrew Taylor.
Chief Economic Advisor.—Nien Su.
Security Officer/Professional Staff Member.—George Ritchey.
Chief of Outreach and Protocol.—Elizabeth Heng.
Director of Committee Operations.—Jean Marter.
Policy Analysts.—Meghan Gallagher.
Counsel and Policy Coordinator.—Jessica Kelch.
Policy Analyst.—Brady Howell.
Hearing Coordinator.—Marie Spear.
Staff Associates: Taylor Clausen, Elizabeth Cunningham.
Finance Administrator.—John Gleason.
Information Resource Manager.—Vlad Cerga.
Assistant Systems Administrator.—Danny Marca.
Printing Manager/Web Assistant.—Shirley Alexander.
Minority Staff (B–360 RHOB), 226–8467.
Minority Staff Director.—Jason Steinbaum.
Minority Deputy Staff Director.—Doug Campbell.
Minority Chief Counsel.—Janice Kaguyutan.
Communications Director/Senior Professional Staff Member.—Tim Mulvey.
Senior Professional Staff Members: Sajit Gandhi, Kyle Parker, Mira Resnick, Edmund Rice, Brian Skretny.
Democratic Senior Policy Advisor.—Eric Jacobstein.
Professional Staff Members: Catherine Barnao, Jennifer Hendrixson-White, Mark Iozzi, Lesley Warner.
Professional Staff Member and Deputy Communications Director.—Jamie Geller.
Subcommittee on Africa, Global Health, Global Human Rights, and International Organizations (5210 O'Neill FOB), 226–7812.
Subcommittee Staff Director.—Gregory Simpkins.
Subcommittee Counsel.—Piero Tozzi.
Staff Associate.—Mark Kearney.
Minority Professional Staff.—Vacant.
Subcommittee on Asia and the Pacific (5190 O'Neill FOB), 226–7825.
Subcommittee Staff Director.—Hunter Strupp.
Professional Staff Member.—Bryan Burack.
Staff Associate.—Joshua Young.
Minority Professional Staff.—Don MacDonald.
Subcommittee on Europe, Eurasia, and Emerging Threats (5210 O'Neill FOB), 226–6434.
Subcommittee Staff Director.—Paul Behrends.
Professional Staff Member.—Scott Cullinane.
Staff Associate.—Steve Smolinsky.
Minority Professional Staff.—Philip Bednarczyk.
Subcommittee on the Middle East and North Africa (5220 O'Neill FOB), 225–3345.
Subcommittee Staff Director.—Eddy Acevedo.
Professional Staff Members: Nathan Gately, Golan Rodgers.
Staff Associate.—Antonella Davalos.
Minority Professional Staff.—Casey Kustin.
Subcommittee on Terrorism, Nonproliferation, and Trade (5100 O'Neill FOB), 226–1500.
Subcommittee Staff Director.—Oren Adaki.
Professional Staff Member.—Patrick Megahan.
Staff Associate.—Miranda Lutz.
Minority Professional Staff.—Garrett Donovan.
Subcommittee on the Western Hemisphere (5100 O'Neill FOB), 226–9980.
Subcommittee Staff Director.—Rebecca Ulrich.
Professional Staff Member.—Carlos Monje.
Staff Associate.—Claire Figel.
Minority Professional Staff.—Sadaf Khan.

Homeland Security

176 Ford House Office Building, phone 226–8417, fax 226–3399

Michael T. McCaul, of Texas, *Chair*

Lamar Smith, of Texas.
Peter T. King, of New York.
Mike Rogers, of Alabama.
Lou Barletta, of Pennsylvania.
Scott Perry, of Pennsylvania.
John Katko, of New York.
Will Hurd, of Texas.
Martha McSally, of Arizona.
John Ratcliffe, of Texas.
Daniel M. Donovan, Jr., of New York.
Mike Gallagher, of Wisconsin.
Clay Higgins, of Louisiana.
Thomas A. Garrett, Jr., of Virginia.
Brian K. Fitzpatrick, of Pennsylvania.
Ron Estes, of Kansas.
Don Bacon, of Nebraska.
Debbie Lesko, of Arizona.

Bennie G. Thompson, of Mississippi.
Sheila Jackson Lee, of Texas.
James R. Langevin, of Rhode Island.
Cedric L. Richmond, of Louisiana.
William R. Keating, of Massachusetts.
Donald M. Payne, Jr., of New Jersey.
Filemon Vela, of Texas.
Bonnie Watson Coleman, of New Jersey.
Kathleen M. Rice, of New York.
J. Luis Correa, of California.
Val Butler Demings, of Florida.
Nanette Diaz Barragán, of California.

SUBCOMMITTEES

[The chair and ranking minority member are ex officio members of all subcommittees on which they do not serve.]

Border and Maritime Security

Martha McSally, of Arizona, *Chair*

Lamar Smith, of Texas.
Mike Rogers, of Alabama.
Lou Barletta, of Pennsylvania.
Will Hurd, of Texas.
Clay Higgins, of Louisiana.
Don Bacon, of Nebraska.

Filemon Vela, of Texas.
Cedric L. Richmond, of Louisiana.
J. Luis Correa, of California.
Val Butler Demings, of Florida.
Nanette Diaz Barragán, of California.

Counterterrorism and Intelligence

Peter T. King, of New York, *Chair*

Lou Barletta, of Pennsylvania.
Scott Perry, of Pennsylvania.
Will Hurd, of Texas.
Mike Gallagher, of Wisconsin.

Kathleen M. Rice, of New York.
Sheila Jackson Lee, of Texas.
William R. Keating, of Massachusetts.

Cybersecurity and Infrastructure Protection

John Ratcliffe, of Texas, *Chair*

John Katko, of New York.
Daniel M. Donovan, Jr., of New York.
Mike Gallagher, of Wisconsin.
Brian K. Fitzpatrick, of Pennsylvania.
Don Bacon, of Nebraska.

Cedric L. Richmond, of Louisiana.
Sheila Jackson Lee, of Texas.
James R. Langevin, of Rhode Island.
Val Butler Demings, of Florida.

Emergency Preparedness, Response, and Communications

Daniel M. Donovan, Jr., of New York, *Chair*

Peter T. King, of New York.
Martha McSally, of Arizona.
Thomas A. Garrett, Jr., of Virginia.
Debbie Lesko, of Arizona.

Donald M. Payne, Jr., of New Jersey.
James R. Langevin, of Rhode Island.
Bonnie Watson Coleman, of New Jersey.

Oversight and Management Efficiency

Scott Perry, of Pennsylvania, *Chair*

John Ratcliffe, of Texas.
Clay Higgins, of Louisiana.
Thomas A. Garrett, Jr., of Virginia.
Ron Estes, of Kansas.
J. Luis Correa, of California.
Kathleen M. Rice, of New York.
Nanette Diaz Barragán, of California.

Transportation and Protective Security

John Katko, of New York, *Chair*

Mike Rogers, of Alabama.
Brian K. Fitzpatrick, of Pennsylvania.
Ron Estes, of Kansas.
Debbie Lesko, of Arizona.
Bonnie Watson Coleman, of New Jersey.
William R. Keating, of Massachusetts.
Donald M. Payne, Jr., of New Jersey.

STAFF

Committee on Homeland Security (H2–176 Ford House Office Building) phone 226–8417, fax 226–3399.

Majority Staff Director.—Brendan P. Shields.
Deputy Staff Director.—Laura Fullerton.
General Counsel.—Steven Giaier.
Staff Directors:
Subcommittee on Border and Maritime Security.—Paul Anstine.
Subcommittee on Counterterrorism and Intelligence.—Mandy Bowers.
Subcommittee on Cybersecurity and Infrastructure Protection.—Brett DeWitt.
Subcommittee on Emergency Preparedness, Response, and Communications.—Kerry Kinirons.
Subcommittee on Oversight and Management Efficiency.—Ryan Consaul.
Subcommittee on Transportation and Protective Security.—Krista P. Harvey.
Deputy General Counsel.—Katy Crooks Flynn.
National Security Senior Advisor.—Jamal Ware.
Director of Member Services and Coalitions.—Claire Duval.
Counsels: Dena Kozanas, Tyler Lowe, Ryan Propis.
Parliamentarian.—Jenny Gorski.
Chief Clerk.—Michael S. Twinchek.
Communications Director.—Susan Phalen.
Press Secretary.—Tess Glancey.
Deputy Press Secretary.—Renn Osborne.
Digital Manager.—Sarah Matthews.
Press Assistant.—Caroline Campbell.
Security Director.—Kyle McFarland.
Senior Professional Staff / Investigator.—Luke Burke.
Senior Professional Staff: Diana Bergwin, Kate Bonvechio, Alan Carroll, Kirsten Duncan, Elizabeth Hoffman, Kyle Klein.
Professional Staff: Samia Brahimi, Kris Carlson, Natalie Matson, Madeline Matthews, Jason Olin, Erik Peterson, Alyssa Schroeder, Martha Simms.
Administrative Director.—Ann Pierce.
Staff Assistants: Alex Rosen, John Sullivan.
Special Assistant to the Chief of Staff.—Albert Kammler.
GPO Detailee, Printer.—Heather Crowell.

Minority Staff Director.—Hope Goins, FHOB / H2–117, 226–2616.
Chief Counsel for Legislation.—Rosaline Cohen, FHOB / H2–117, 226–2616.
Subcommittee on Border and Maritime Security Director and Counsel for Oversight.—Alison B. Northrop, FHOB / H2–117, 226–2616.
Subcommittee on Oversight and Management Efficiency Director.—Erica Woods, FHOB / H2–117, 226–2616.
Subcommittee on Counterterrorism and Intelligence Director and Counsel.—Nichole Tisdale, FHOB / H2–117, 226–2616.
Subcommittee on Emergency Preparedness, Response, and Communications.—Moira Bergin, FHOB / H2–117, 226–2616.
Senior Professional Staff Member / Counsel.—Alicia Smith, FHOB / H2–117, 226–2616.
Press Secretary.—Adam M. Comis, FHOB / H2–117, 226–2616.
Professional Staff Members: Christian Bolden, Frank Bradford, Alexandra Carnes, Cory Horton, Nzinga Hutchinson, Lauren McClain, Rene Munoz, FHOB / H2–117, 226–2616.

Office Manager.—Elise Phillips, FHOB / H2–117, 226–2616.
Executive Assistant.—Kimaya Davis, FHOB / H2–117, 226–2616.
Legislative Assistants: Imani Gunn, Brittany Lynch, FHOB / H2–117, 226–2616.
Research Assistant.—Shalonda Spencer, FHOB/ H2–117, 226–2616.

House Administration

1309 Longworth House Office Building, phone 225–8281, fax 225–9957

http://cha.house.gov

Gregg Harper, of Mississippi, *Chair*

Rodney Davis, of Illinois, *Vice-Chair*

Barbara Comstock, of Virginia.
Mark Walker, of North Carolina.
Adrian Smith, of Nebraska.
Barry Loudermilk, of Georgia.

Robert A. Brady, of Pennsylvania.
Zoe Lofgren, of California.
Jamie Raskin, of Maryland.

(No Subcommittees)

STAFF

Committee on House Administration (1309 LHOB), 5–8281.
Staff Director.—Sean Moran.
Deputy Staff Director, Policy and Oversight.—Kimberly Betz.
Deputy Staff Director, Member Services, Outreach, and Communications.—Katie Patru.
General Counsel.—Bob Sensenbrenner.
Director of:
Administration and Operations.—Mary Sue Englund.
Member and Committee Services.—Katie Ryan.
Technology Policy.—Reynold Schweickhardt.
Senior Advisor.—George Hadijski.
Communications Director.—Erin McCracken.
Deputy General Counsel.—Cole Felder.
Franking and Member Services Counsel.—Nick Hawatmeh.
Legislative Clerk / Finance Administrator.—C. Maggie Moore.
Outreach Coordinator.—Alyssa Hinman.
Professional Staff: Amanda Anger, Alex Hammond, Jeff Orzechowski, Courtney Parella, Ed Puccerella, Tim Sullivan.
Deputy Clerk / Oversight.—Rob Taggart.
Staff Assistants: Ashley Hebert, Dan Jarrell.
Administrative Assistant.—Austin Cho.
Minority Staff:
Staff Director.—Jamie Fleet (1307 LHOB), 5–2061.
Deputy Staff Director / Deputy Chief Counsel.—Teri Morgan.
Deputy Staff Director / Director of Legislative Operations.—Khalil Abboud.
Chief Clerk.—Eddie Flaherty.
Director of Member and Committee Services.—Robert Henline.
Finance Director.—Kim Stevens.
Elections Counsel.—Tanya Sehgal.
Professional Staff: Aislan Sims, Kristie Small.
Staff Assistant.—Meredith Conner.
Shared Employees: ZJ Hull, Richard Subbio, Julie Tagen, Stanley White.
Commission on Congressional Mailing Standards (1216 LHOB), 6–0647.
Staff Director.—Max Engling.
Minority Staff:
Staff Director.—Matthew DeFreitas.

Judiciary

2138 Rayburn House Office Building, phone 225–3951

http://www.judiciary.house.gov

Bob Goodlatte, of Virginia, *Chair*

F. James Sensenbrenner, Jr., of Wisconsin.
Lamar Smith, of Texas.
Steve Chabot, of Ohio.
Darrell E. Issa, of California.
Steve King, of Iowa.
Louie Gohmert, of Texas.
Jim Jordan, of Ohio.
Ted Poe, of Texas.
Tom Marino, of Pennsylvania.
Trey Gowdy, of South Carolina.
Raúl R. Labrador, of Idaho.
Doug Collins, of Georgia.
Ron DeSantis, of Florida.
Ken Buck, of Colorado.
John Ratcliffe, of Texas.
Martha Roby, of Alabama.
Matt Gaetz, of Florida.
Mike Johnson, of Louisiana.
Andy Biggs, of Arizona.
John H. Rutherford, of Florida.
Karen C. Handel, of Georgia.
Keith J. Rothfus, of Pennsylvania.
Vacant.

Jerrold Nadler, of New York.
Zoe Lofgren, of California.
Sheila Jackson Lee, of Texas.
Steve Cohen, of Tennessee.
Henry C. "Hank" Johnson, Jr., of Georgia.
Theodore E. Deutch, of Florida.
Luis V. Gutiérrez, of Illinois.
Karen Bass, of California.
Cedric L. Richmond, of Louisiana.
Hakeem S. Jeffries, of New York.
David N. Cicilline, of Rhode Island.
Eric Swalwell, of California.
Ted Lieu, of California.
Jamie Raskin, of Maryland.
Pramila Jayapal, of Washington.
Bradley Scott Schneider, of Illinois.
Val Butler Demings, of Florida.

SUBCOMMITTEES

[The chair and the ranking minority member are ex officio (non-voting) members of all subcommittees on which they do not serve.]

The Constitution and Civil Justice

Steve King, of Iowa, *Chair*

Ron DeSantis, of Florida, *Vice Chair*

Louie Gohmert, of Texas.
Karen C. Handel, of Georgia.
Vacant.

Steve Cohen, of Tennessee.
Jamie Raskin, of Maryland.
Theodore E. Deutch, of Florida.

Courts, Intellectual Property, and the Internet

Darrell E. Issa, of California, *Chair*

Doug Collins, of Georgia, *Vice Chair*

Lamar Smith, of Texas.
Steve Chabot, of Ohio.
Jim Jordan, of Ohio.
Ted Poe, of Texas.
Tom Marino, of Pennsylvania.
Trey Gowdy, of South Carolina.
Raúl R. Labrador, of Idaho.
Ron DeSantis, of Florida.
Matt Gaetz, of Florida.
Andy Biggs, of Arizona.
John H. Rutherford, of Florida.
Keith J. Rothfus, of Pennsylvania.

Henry C. "Hank" Johnson, Jr., of Georgia.
Theodore E. Deutch, of Florida.
Karen Bass, of California.
Cedric L. Richmond, of Louisiana.
Hakeem S. Jeffries, of New York.
Eric Swalwell, of California.
Ted Lieu, of California.
Bradley Scott Schneider, of Illinois.
Zoe Lofgren, of California.
Steve Cohen, of Tennessee.
David N. Cicilline, of Rhode Island.
Pramila Jayapal, of Washington.

Crime, Terrorism, Homeland Security, and Investigations

F. James Sensenbrenner, Jr., of Wisconsin, *Chair*

Louie Gohmert, of Texas, *Vice Chair*

Steve Chabot, of Ohio.
Ted Poe, of Texas.
Trey Gowdy, of South Carolina.
John Ratcliffe, of Texas.
Martha Roby, of Alabama.
Mike Johnson, of Louisiana.
John H. Rutherford, of Florida.
Keith J. Rothfus, of Pennsylvania.

Sheila Jackson Lee, of Texas.
Val Butler Demings, of Florida.
Karen Bass, of California.
Cedric L. Richmond, of Louisiana.
Hakeem S. Jeffries, of New York.
Ted Lieu, of California.
Jamie Raskin, of Maryland.

Immigration and Border Security

Raúl R. Labrador, of Idaho, *Chair*

Ken Buck, of Colorado, *Vice Chair*

F. James Sensenbrenner, Jr., of Wisconsin.
Lamar Smith, of Texas.
Steve King, of Iowa.
Jim Jordan, of Ohio.
Mike Johnson, of Louisiana.
Andy Biggs, of Arizona.

Zoe Lofgren, of California.
Luis V. Gutiérrez, of Illinois.
Pramila Jayapal, of Washington.
Sheila Jackson Lee, of Texas.
Jamie Raskin, of Maryland.

Regulatory Reform, Commercial and Antitrust Law

Tom Marino, of Pennsylvania, *Chair*

John Ratcliffe, of Texas, *Vice Chair*

Darrell E. Issa, of California.
Doug Collins, of Georgia.
Ken Buck, of Colorado.
Matt Gaetz, of Florida.
Karen C. Handel, of Georgia.
Vacant.

David N. Cicilline, of Rhode Island.
Henry C. ''Hank'' Johnson, Jr., of Georgia.
Eric Swalwell, of California.
Bradley Scott Schneider, of Illinois.
Val Butler Demings, of Florida.

STAFF

Committee on the Judiciary (2138 RHOB), 225–3951, fax 5–7680.
Chief of Staff and General Counsel.—Shelley Husband.
Deputy Chief of Staff and Chief Counsel.—Branden Ritchie.
Professional Staff: Natasha Eby, John Manning.
Parliamentarian and General Counsel.—Zachary Somers.
Senior Legislative Clerk.—Eric Bagwell.
Legislative Clerk.—Alley Adcock.
Senior Counsel.—Stephanie Gadbois.
Communications Director.—Kathryn Rexrode.
Deputy Communications Director.—Jessica Collins.
Deputy Press Secretary.—Vacant.
Digital Director.—Jonathan McKinstry.
Public Affairs Liaison.—Bryan Alphin.
Coalitions Director.—Joe Russo.
Staff Assistant.—Carlee Tousman.
Financial Administrator.—Patrick Baugh.
Publications Specialist.—Tim Pearson.
Constitution and Civil Justice Subcommittee, H2–362 Ford, phone: 5–2825, fax: 5–4299.
Chief Counsel.—Paul Taylor.
Counsel.—John Coleman.
Clerk.—Jake Glancy.
Courts, Intellectual Property, and the Internet Subcommittee, 6310 O'Neill, phone: 5–5741, fax: 5–3673.
Chief Counsel.—Joe Keeley.

Counsel.—Vishal Amin.
Clerk.—Vacant.

Crime, Terrorism, Homeland Security, and Investigations Subcommittee, 6340 O'Neill, phone: 5–5727, fax: 5–3672.
Chief Counsel.—Bobby Parmiter.
Counsels: Tony Angeli, Meg Barr, Ryan Breitenbach, Jason Cervenak.
Clerk.—Scott Johnson.

Immigration and Border Security Subcommittee, 6320 O'Neill, phone: 5–3926, fax: 5–3737.
Chief Counsel.—George Fishman.
Counsels: Joseph Edlow, Andrea Loving.
Clerk.—Tanner Black.

Regulatory Reform, Commercial and Antitrust Law Subcommittee, 6240 O'Neill, phone: 6–7680, fax: 5–3746.
Chief Counsel.—Daniel Flores.
Counsels: Anthony Grossi, Dan Huff.
Clerk.—Andrea Woodard.
IT Office, 2451 Rayburn, fax: 5–1842.
Director of Information Technology.—Tom Ullrich.
Deputy Director of Information Technology.—Banyon Vassar.

Minority Staff Members:
Minority Chief Counsel and Staff Director.—Perry Apelbaum, 2142 Rayburn, phone: 5–6504, fax: 5–7686.
Professional Staff: Joe Ehrenkrantz, Elizabeth McElvein.

Minority Offices, B–2035 Rayburn, H2–252 Ford, and H2–189 Ford, phone: 5–6906, fax: 5–7682.
Chief Legislative Counsel.—Danielle Brown.
Minority Counsels: Jason Everett, Joe Graupensperger, David Greengrass, Aaron Hiller, Susan Jensen, Keenan Keller, Matt Morgan, James Park, Maunica Sthanki, David Shahoulian.
Press Secretary.—Shadawn Reddick-Smith.
Professional Staff: Veronica Eligan, Rosalind Jackson.

Natural Resources

1324 Longworth House Office Building, phone 225–2761

http://naturalresources.house.gov

Rob Bishop, of Utah, *Chair*

Don Young, of Alaska.
Louie Gohmert, of Texas.
Doug Lamborn, of Colorado.
Robert J. Wittman, of Virginia.
Tom McClintock, of California.
Stevan Pearce, of New Mexico.
Glenn Thompson, of Pennsylvania.
Paul A. Gosar, of Arizona.
Raúl R. Labrador, of Idaho.
Scott R. Tipton, of Colorado.
Doug LaMalfa, of California.
Jeff Denham, of California.
Paul Cook, of California.
Bruce Westerman, of Arkansas.
Garret Graves, of Louisiana.
Jody B. Hice, of Georgia.
Aumua Amata Coleman Radewagen, of American Samoa.
Daniel Webster, of Florida.
Jack Bergman, of Michigan.
Liz Cheney, of Wyoming.
Mike Johnson, of Louisiana.
Jenniffer González-Colón, of Puerto Rico.
Greg Gianforte, of Montana.
John R. Curtis, of Utah.

Raúl M. Grijalva, of Arizona.
Grace F. Napolitano, of California.
Madeleine Z. Bordallo, of Guam.
Jim Costa, of California.
Gregorio Kilili Camacho Sablan, of Northern Mariana Islands.
Niki Tsongas, of Massachusetts.
Jared Huffman, of California.
Alan S. Lowenthal, of California.
Donald S. Beyer, Jr., of Virginia.
Ruben Gallego, of Arizona.
Colleen Hanabusa, of Hawaii.
Nanette Diaz Barragán, of California.
Darren Soto, of Florida.
A. Donald McEachin, of Virginia.
Anthony G. Brown, of Maryland.
Wm. Lacy Clay, of Missouri.
Jimmy Gomez, of California.
Nydia M. Velázquez, of New York.

SUBCOMMITTEES

[The chair and ranking minority member are ex officio (non-voting) members of all subcommittees on which they do not serve.]

Energy and Mineral Resources

Paul A. Gosar, of Arizona, *Chair*

Louie Gohmert, of Texas.
Doug Lamborn, of Colorado.
Robert J. Wittman, of Virginia.
Stevan Pearce, of New Mexico.
Glenn Thompson, of Pennsylvania.
Scott R. Tipton, of Colorado.
Paul Cook, of California.
Garret Graves, of Louisiana.
Jody B. Hice, of Georgia.
Jack Bergman, of Michigan.
Liz Cheney, of Wyoming.
John R. Curtis, of Utah.

Alan S. Lowenthal, of California.
Anthony G. Brown, of Maryland.
Jim Costa, of California.
Niki Tsongas, of Massachusetts.
Jared Huffman, of California.
Donald S. Beyer, Jr., of Virginia.
Darren Soto, of Florida.
Nanette Diaz Barragán, of California.
Nydia M. Velázquez, of New York.
Vacant.

Federal Lands

Tom McClintock, of California, *Chair*

Don Young, of Alaska.
Stevan Pearce, of New Mexico.
Glenn Thompson, of Pennsylvania.
Raúl R. Labrador, of Idaho.
Scott R. Tipton, of Colorado.
Bruce Westerman, of Arkansas.
Daniel Webster, of Florida.
Jack Bergman, of Michigan.
Liz Cheney, of Wyoming.
Greg Gianforte, of Montana.
John R. Curtis, of Utah.

Colleen Hanabusa, of Hawaii.
Niki Tsongas, of Massachusetts.
Alan S. Lowenthal, of California.
Ruben Gallego, of Arizona.
A. Donald McEachin, of Virginia.
Anthony G. Brown, of Maryland.
Jimmy Gomez, of California.
Vacant.
Vacant.

Indian, Insular and Alaska Native Affairs

Doug LaMalfa, of California, *Chair*

Don Young, of Alaska.
Jeff Denham, of California.
Paul Cook, of California.
Aumua Amata Coleman Radewagen, of American Samoa.
Jack Bergman, of Michigan.
Jenniffer González-Colón, of Puerto Rico.
Vacant.

Ruben Gallego, of Arizona.
Madeleine Z. Bordallo, of Guam.
Gregorio Kilili Camacho Sablan, of Northern Mariana Islands.
Darren Soto, of Florida.
Colleen Hanabusa, of Hawaii.
Nydia M. Velázquez, of New York.

Oversight and Investigations

Bruce Westerman, of Arkansas, *Chair*

Louie Gohmert, of Texas.
Raúl R. Labrador, of Idaho.
Aumua Amata Coleman Radewagen, of American Samoa.
Mike Johnson, of Louisiana.
Jenniffer González-Colón, of Puerto Rico.

A. Donald McEachin, of Virginia.
Ruben Gallego, of Arizona.
Jared Huffman, of California.
Darren Soto, of Florida.
Wm. Lacy Clay, of Missouri.

Water, Power and Oceans

Doug Lamborn, of Colorado, *Chair*

Robert J. Wittman, of Virginia.
Tom McClintock, of California.
Paul A. Gosar, of Arizona.
Doug LaMalfa, of California.
Jeff Denham, of California.
Garret Graves, of Louisiana.
Jody B. Hice, of Georgia.
Daniel Webster, of Florida.
Mike Johnson, of Louisiana.
Greg Gianforte, of Montana.

Jared Huffman, of California.
Grace F. Napolitano, of California.
Jim Costa, of California.
Donald S. Beyer, Jr., of Virginia.
Nanette Diaz Barragán, of California.
Madeleine Z. Bordallo, of Guam.
Gregorio Kilili Camacho Sablan, of Northern Mariana Islands.
Jimmy Gomez, of California.

STAFF

Committee on Natural Resources (1324 LHOB), 5–2761.
Majority Staff Director.—Jason Knox.
Deputy Staff Director.—Todd Ungerecht.
Director of Operations.—Ilene Clauson.
Deputy Director of Operations.—Sophia Varnasidis.
Chief Counsel.—Lisa Pittman.
Deputy Chief Counsel.—Charles Park.
Director of Coalitions.—Matt Schafle.
Staff Assistant.—Steven Parr.

Calendar Clerk.—Joycelyn Coleman.
Director, Information Technology.—Jean Woodrow.
IT Staff.—David DeMarco.
GPO Detailee.—Darlene Davis.
Democratic Staff Director.—David Watkins (1329 LHOB), 5–6065.
Democratic Chief Counsel.—Sarah Parker (1329 LHOB), 5-6065.
Democratic Deputy Chief Counsel.—Emily Lande.
Democratic Senior Policy Advisor.—Matt Strickler.
Democratic Professional Staff Member.—Emily Lande.
Chief Democratic Clerk.—Peter Gallagher.
Democratic Staff Assistant.—Daniel Torrez.
Manager of Operations.—Cristina Villa.
Communications (1328 LHOB), ext. 6–9109.
Director of Communications.—Parish Braden.
Press Secretary.—Molly Block.
Digital Media Coordinator.—Sara Roberts.
Communications Assistant.—Katie Schoettler.
Press Assistant.—Heather Douglass.
Democratic Communications Director.—Adam Sarvana (H2–186), 5–6065.
Democratic Director of Public Engagement.—Bertha Guerrero.
Democratic Press Secretary.—Diane Padilla.
Subcommittee on Energy and Mineral Resources (1522 LHOB), ext. 5–9297.
Majority Staff Director.—Andrew Vecera.
Professional Staff: Josh Hoffman, Ashley Nichols.
Counsel.—Kate Juelis.
Clerk.—Rebecca Konolige.
Democratic Senior Energy Policy Advisor.—Steve Feldgus (H2–186), 5–6065.
AAAS Fellow.—Emily Lewis.
Subcommittee on Federal Lands (1332 LHOB), ext. 6–7736.
Majority Staff Director.—Erica Rhoad.
Professional Staff: Aniela Butler, Terry Camp, Chris Marklund, Brandon Miller.
Clerk.—Will Layden.
Democratic Professional Staff Member.—Brandon Bragato (H2–269), 5–6065.
NPS Bevinetto Fellow.—Maggie Tyler.
Subcommittee on Indian, Insular and Alaska Native Affairs (4450 OFOB), ext. 6–9725.
Majority Staff Director.—Chris Fluhr.
Professional Staff: Marc Alberts, Ken Degenfelder.
Research Assistant.—Alex Perez.
Democratic Professional Staff Member.—Chris Kaumo (H2–269), 5–6065.
Democratic Counsel, Insular Affairs.—Brian Modeste (H2–186), 5–6065.
Subcommittee on Oversight and Investigations (4170 OFOB), ext. 5–7107.
Majority Staff Director.—Sang Yi.
Counsels: Christen Harsha, Megan Olmstead, Chris Santini.
Democratic Director of Investigations.—Vic Edgerton (H2–186), 5–6065.
Subcommittee on Water, Power and Oceans (4120 OFOB), ext. 5–8331.
Majority Staff Director.—William Ball.
Professional Staff.—Bryson Wong.
Research Assistant.—Richie O'Connell.
Democratic Professional Staff Members: Matthew Muirragui-Villagomez, Matt Strickler.
Sea Grant Knauss Fellow.—Christine Sur.
American Political Science Association Fellow.—Michael Parrott.

Oversight and Government Reform

2157 Rayburn House Office Building, phone 225–5074, fax 225–3974, TTY 225–6852

http://oversight.house.gov

Trey Gowdy, of South Carolina, *Chair*

John J. Duncan, Jr., of Tennessee.
Darrell E. Issa, of California.
Jim Jordan, of Ohio.
Mark Sanford, of South Carolina.
Justin Amash, of Michigan.
Paul A. Gosar, of Arizona.
Scott DesJarlais, of Tennessee.
Virginia Foxx, of North Carolina.
Thomas Massie, of Kentucky.
Mark Meadows, of North Carolina.
Ron DeSantis, of Florida.
Dennis A. Ross, of Florida.
Mark Walker, of North Carolina.
Rod Blum, of Iowa.
Jody B. Hice, of Georgia.
Steve Russell, of Oklahoma.
Glenn Grothman, of Wisconsin.
Will Hurd, of Texas.
Gary J. Palmer, of Alabama.
James Comer, of Kentucky.
Paul Mitchell, of Michigan.
Greg Gianforte, of Montana.
Michael Cloud, of Texas.

Elijah E. Cummings, of Maryland.
Carolyn B. Maloney, of New York.
Eleanor Holmes Norton, of District of Columbia.
Wm. Lacy Clay, of Missouri.
Stephen F. Lynch, of Massachusetts.
Jim Cooper, of Tennessee.
Gerald E. Connolly, of Virginia.
Robin L. Kelly, of Illinois.
Brenda L. Lawrence, of Michigan.
Bonnie Watson Coleman, of New Jersey.
Raja Krishnamoorthi, of Illinois.
Jamie Raskin, of Maryland.
Jimmy Gomez, of California.
Peter Welch, of Vermont.
Matt Cartwright, of Pennsylvania.
Mark DeSaulnier, of California.
Stacey E. Plaskett, of Virgin Islands.
John P. Sarbanes, of Maryland.

SUBCOMMITTEES

[The chair and ranking minority member are ex officio (voting) members of all subcommittees.]

Government Operations

Mark Meadows, of North Carolina, *Chair*

Jody B. Hice, of Georgia, *Vice Chair*

Jim Jordan, of Ohio.
Mark Sanford, of South Carolina.
Thomas Massie, of Kentucky.
Ron DeSantis, of Florida.
Dennis A. Ross, of Florida.
Rod Blum, of Iowa.

Gerald E. Connolly, of Virginia.
Carolyn B. Maloney, of New York.
Eleanor Holmes Norton, of District of Columbia.
Wm. Lacy Clay, of Missouri.
Brenda L. Lawrence, of Michigan.
Bonnie Watson Coleman, of New Jersey.

Health Care, Benefits, and Administrative Rules

Jim Jordan, of Ohio, *Chair*

Mark Walker, of North Carolina, *Vice Chair*

Darrell E. Issa, of California.
Mark Sanford, of South Carolina.
Scott DesJarlais, of Tennessee.
Mark Meadows, of North Carolina.
Glenn Grothman, of Wisconsin.
Paul Mitchell, of Michigan.

Raja Krishnamoorthi, of Illinois.
Jim Cooper, of Tennessee.
Eleanor Holmes Norton, of District of Columbia.
Robin L. Kelly, of Illinois.
Bonnie Watson Coleman, of New Jersey.
Stacey E. Plaskett, of Virgin Islands.

Information Technology

Will Hurd, of Texas, *Chair*

Paul Mitchell, of Michigan, *Vice Chair*

Darrell E. Issa, of California.
Justin Amash, of Michigan.
Steve Russell, of Oklahoma.
Greg Gianforte, of Montana.
Michael Cloud, of Texas.

Robin L. Kelly, of Illinois.
Jamie Raskin, of Maryland.
Stephen F. Lynch, of Massachusetts.
Gerald E. Connolly, of Virginia.
Raja Krishnamoorthi, of Illinois.

Intergovernmental Affairs

Gary J. Palmer, of Alabama, *Chair*

Glenn Grothman, of Wisconsin, *Vice Chair*

John J. Duncan, Jr., of Tennessee.
Virginia Foxx, of North Carolina.
Thomas Massie, of Kentucky.
Mark Walker, of North Carolina.
Mark Sanford, of South Carolina.

Jamie Raskin, of Maryland.
Mark DeSaulnier, of California.
Matt Cartwright, of Pennsylvania.
Wm. Lacy Clay, of Missouri.

Interior, Energy, and Environment

Greg Gianforte, of Montana, *Chair*

Paul A. Gosar, of Arizona, *Vice Chair*

Dennis A. Ross, of Florida.
Gary J. Palmer, of Alabama.
James Comer, of Kentucky.
Michael Cloud, of Texas.

Stacey E. Plaskett, of Virgin Islands.
Jamie Raskin, of Maryland.
Jimmy Gomez, of California.
Vacant.

National Security

Ron DeSantis, of Florida, *Chair*

Steve Russell, of Oklahoma, *Vice Chair*

John J. Duncan, Jr., of Tennessee.
Justin Amash, of Michigan.
Paul A. Gosar, of Arizona.
Virginia Foxx, of North Carolina.
Jody B. Hice, of Georgia.
James Comer, of Kentucky.

Stephen F. Lynch, of Massachusetts.
Peter Welch, of Vermont.
Mark DeSaulnier, of California.
Jimmy Gomez, of California.
Vacant.
Vacant.
Vacant.

STAFF

Oversight and Government Reform (2157 RHOB), (202) 225–5074.
Majority Staff Director.—Sheria Clarke.
Deputy Staff Director.—Rob Borden.
General Counsel.—Liam McKenna.
Deputy General Counsel.—Steve Castor.
Chief Policy Counsel.—Jonathan Skladany.
Senior Counsel.—Carlton Davis.
Senior Advisor.—Rachel Weaver.
Legislative Director.—Alexa Armstrong.
Member Services Director.—William Marx.
Director of Information Technology.—Stacy Baker.
Communications Director and Press Secretary.—Marijane Henshaw.
Digital Director.—Matthew Flunker.
Press Assistant.—Charli Huddelston.
Chief Clerk.—Laura Rush.
Deputy Chief Clerk.—Sharon Casey.
Clerk.—Kiley Bidelman.

Finance and Administrative Manager.—Robin Butler.
Staff Assistants: Cameron Connor, Michael Watson.
Senior Professional Staff Member.—Donna Harkins.
Government Operations Subcommittee Staff Director.—Julie Dunne.
Government Operations Subcommittee Deputy Staff Director.—John Thorlin.
Counsels: Mary Doocy, Patrick Hartobey.
Professional Staff Members: Drew Baney, Kevin Ortiz.
Health Care, Benefits, and Administrative Rules Subcommittee Staff Director.—Kevin Eichinger.
Counsel.—Michael Koren.
Senior Professional Staff Member.—Sarah Vance.
Information Technology Subcommittee Staff Director.—Troy Stock.
Senior Counsel.—Sean Brebbia.
Senior Professional Staff Member.—Sarah Moxley.
Professional Staff Member.—Meghan Green.
Intergovernmental Affairs Subcommittee Staff Director.—Christina Aizcorbe.
Senior Counsel.—Mary Catherine Rother.
Counsel.—Jessica Conrad.
Professional Staff Member.—Kelsey Wall.
Interior, Energy, and Environment Subcommittee Staff Director.—Ryan Hambleton.
Counsels: Rebecca Brown, Christen Harsha.
National Security Subcommittee Staff Director.—Sharon Eshelman.
Senior Counsel.—Cordell Hull.
Senior Military Advisor.—Brick Christensen.
Professional Staff Member.—Samuel Wisch.

2471 Rayburn House Office Building (2471 RHOB) phone 225–5051, fax 225–4784,

TTY 225–6852, http://democrats.oversight.house.gov

Minority Staff Director.—Dave Rapallo.
Deputy Staff Director/Chief Counsel.—Susanne Sachsman Grooms.
Director of Legislation.—Mark Stephenson.
Policy Director.—Lucinda Lessley.
Administrative Director.—Jaron Bourke.
General Counsel.—Krista Boyd.
Deputy General Counsel.—Tim Lynch.
Communications Director.—Jennifer Werner.
Director of Operations.—Elisa LaNier.
Deputy Communications Director.—Aryele Bradford.
Digital Director.—Jessica Presley.
Legislative Director.—Suzanne Owen.
Senior Counsel.—Kapil Longani.
Chief Health Counsel.—Alexandra Golden.
Counsels: Aaron Blacksberg, Marc Broady, Lena Chang, William Cunningham, Courtney French, Janet Kim, Sean Perryman, Todd Phillips, Valerie Shen.
Press Secretary.—Fabion Seaton.
Professional Staff Members: Francesca McCrary, Katie Teleky.
Deputy Clerk.—Nicholas McCulloch.
Technology Director.—Eddie Walker.
Minority GAO Detailee.—Marietta Revesz.
CFPB Detailee.—Chris Davis.
USPS OIG Detailee.—Jennifer Daehn.

Rules

H–312 The Capitol, phone 225–9191

http://www.rules.house.gov

Pete Sessions, of Texas, *Chair*

Tom Cole, of Oklahoma.
Rob Woodall, of Georgia.
Michael C. Burgess, of Texas.
Doug Collins, of Georgia.
Bradley Byrne, of Alabama.
Dan Newhouse, of Washington.
Ken Buck, of Colorado.
Liz Cheney, of Wyoming.

James P. McGovern, of Massachusetts.
Alcee L. Hastings, of Florida.
Jared Polis, of Colorado.
Norma J. Torres, of California.

SUBCOMMITTEES

Legislative and Budget Process

Rob Woodall, of Georgia, *Chair*

Michael C. Burgess, of Texas.
Bradley Byrne, of Alabama.
Dan Newhouse, of Washington.
Ken Buck, of Colorado.

Alcee L. Hastings, of Florida.
Jared Polis, of Colorado.

Rules and Organization of the House

Doug Collins, of Georgia, *Chair*

Bradley Byrne, of Alabama.
Dan Newhouse, of Washington.
Liz Cheney, of Wyoming.
Pete Sessions, of Texas.

James P. McGovern, of Massachusetts.
Vacant.

STAFF

Committee on Rules (H–312 The Capitol), 225–9191.
Majority Staff Director.—Stephen Cote.
Deputy Staff Director.—Karas Gross.
Policy Director.—Kevin Hubbard.
Communications Director.—Caroline Boothe.
Senior Professional Staff.—Nathan Blake.
Professional Staff: Alec Davis, Annie Minkler.
Director of Information Technology.—Chris Erb.
Legislative Clerk.—James Fitzella.
Assistant Clerk.—Hannah Gill.
Staff Assistants: Parker Fleming, Eric Shepard.
Associate Staff: Garret Bess (1130 LHOB); James Decker (2336 RHOB); Matt Diller (2467 RHOB); Jason Herbert (1641 LHOB); Jennifer Lackey (2233 RHOB); Sarah Meier (416 CHOB); Mitch Relfe (119 CHOB); Sally Rose Larson (1504 LHOB); Janet Rossi (1724 LHOB).
Minority Staff Director.—Don Sisson.
Deputy Staff Director and Counsel.—Liz Pardue.
Senior Professional Staff and Policy Advisor: George Agurkis, David Vince.
Professional Staff: Lori Ismail, Rose Laughlin.
Director of Legislative Operations.—Natalie Nixon.
Communications Director.—Jeff Gohringer.
Press Assistant.—Cara Koontz.
Associate.—Cindy Buhl (McGovern).
Subcommittee on Legislative and Budget Process.
Minority Staff Director.—Lale Mamaux (Hastings).
Subcommittee on Rules and Organization of the House.
Minority Staff Director.—Liz Pardue.

Science, Space, and Technology

2321 Rayburn House Office Building, phone 225–6371, fax 226–0113

http://www.science.house.gov

Lamar Smith, of Texas, *Chair*

Frank D. Lucas, of Oklahoma, *Vice Chair*

Dana Rohrabacher, of California.
Mo Brooks, of Alabama.
Randy Hultgren, of Illinois.
Bill Posey, of Florida.
Thomas Massie, of Kentucky.
Randy K. Weber, Sr., of Texas.
Stephen Knight, of California.
Brian Babin, of Texas.
Barbara Comstock, of Virginia.
Barry Loudermilk, of Georgia.
Ralph Lee Abraham, of Louisiana.
Gary J. Palmer, of Alabama.
Daniel Webster, of Florida.
Andy Biggs, of Arizona.
Roger W. Marshall, of Kansas.
Neal P. Dunn, of Florida.
Clay Higgins, of Louisiana.
Ralph Norman, of South Carolina.
Debbie Lesko, of Arizona.
Michael Cloud, of Texas.

Eddie Bernice Johnson, of Texas.
Zoe Lofgren, of California.
Daniel Lipinski, of Illinois.
Suzanne Bonamici, of Oregon.
Ami Bera, of California.
Elizabeth H. Esty, of Connecticut.
Marc A. Veasey, of Texas.
Donald S. Beyer, Jr., of Virginia.
Jacky Rosen, of Nevada.
Conor Lamb, of Pennsylvania.
Jerry McNerney, of California.
Ed Perlmutter, of Colorado.
Paul Tonko, of New York.
Bill Foster, of Illinois.
Mark Takano, of California.
Colleen Hanabusa, of Hawaii.
Charlie Crist, of Florida.

SUBCOMMITTEES

[The chair and ranking minority member are ex officio (voting) members of all subcommittees on which they do not serve.]

Energy

Randy K. Weber, Sr., of Texas, *Chair*

Stephen Knight, of California, *Vice Chair*

Dana Rohrabacher, of California.
Frank D. Lucas, of Oklahoma.
Mo Brooks, of Alabama.
Randy Hultgren, of Illinois.
Gary J. Palmer, of Alabama.
Daniel Webster, of Florida.
Neal P. Dunn, of Florida.
Ralph Norman, of South Carolina.
Michael Cloud, of Texas.

Marc A. Veasey, of Texas.
Zoe Lofgren, of California.
Daniel Lipinski, of Illinois.
Jacky Rosen, of Nevada.
Jerry McNerney, of California.
Paul Tonko, of New York.
Bill Foster, of Illinois.
Mark Takano, of California.

Environment

Andy Biggs, of Arizona, *Chair*

Dana Rohrabacher, of California.
Bill Posey, of Florida.
Mo Brooks, of Alabama.
Randy K. Weber, Sr., of Texas.
Brian Babin, of Texas.
Gary J. Palmer, of Alabama.
Clay Higgins, of Louisiana.
Ralph Norman, of South Carolina.
Debbie Lesko, of Arizona.

Suzanne Bonamici, of Oregon.
Colleen Hanabusa, of Hawaii.
Charlie Crist, of Florida.
Conor Lamb, of Pennsylvania.
Vacant.
Vacant.
Vacant.

Oversight

Ralph Lee Abraham, of Louisiana, *Chair*

Clay Higgins, of Louisiana, *Vice Chair*

Bill Posey, of Florida.
Thomas Massie, of Kentucky.
Barry Loudermilk, of Georgia.
Roger W. Marshall, of Kansas.
Ralph Norman, of South Carolina.

Donald S. Beyer, Jr., of Virginia.
Jerry McNerney, of California.
Ed Perlmutter, of Colorado.
Vacant.
Vacant.

Research and Technology

Barbara Comstock, of Virginia, *Chair*

Roger W. Marshall, of Kansas, *Vice Chair*

Frank D. Lucas, of Oklahoma.
Randy Hultgren, of Illinois.
Stephen Knight, of California.
Barry Loudermilk, of Georgia.
Daniel Webster, of Florida.
Debbie Lesko, of Arizona.
Michael Cloud, of Texas.

Daniel Lipinski, of Illinois.
Elizabeth H. Esty, of Connecticut.
Jacky Rosen, of Nevada.
Suzanne Bonamici, of Oregon.
Ami Bera, of California.
Donald S. Beyer, Jr., of Virginia.

Space

Brian Babin, of Texas, *Chair*

Mo Brooks, of Alabama, *Vice Chair*

Dana Rohrabacher, of California.
Frank D. Lucas, of Oklahoma.
Randy Hultgren, of Illinois.
Thomas Massie, of Kentucky.
Bill Posey, of Florida.
Stephen Knight, of California.
Barbara Comstock, of Virginia.
Ralph Lee Abraham, of Louisiana.
Daniel Webster, of Florida.
Andy Biggs, of Arizona.
Neal P. Dunn, of Florida.
Clay Higgins, of Louisiana.

Ami Bera, of California.
Zoe Lofgren, of California.
Donald S. Beyer, Jr., of Virginia.
Marc A. Veasey, of Texas.
Daniel Lipinski, of Illinois.
Ed Perlmutter, of Colorado.
Charlie Crist, of Florida.
Bill Foster, of Illinois.
Conor Lamb, of Pennsylvania.
Vacant.

STAFF

Committee on Science, Space, and Technology (2321 RHOB), 225–6371, fax 226–0113.
Majority Staff:
Chief of Staff.—Jennifer Brown.
Deputy Chief of Staff.—Mark Marin.
Legislative Director and Senior Advisor to the Chair.—Chris Wydler.
Administrative Director and Senior Counsel to the Chair.—Ashley Smith.
Administration:
Chief Clerk.—Ashley Smith.
Financial Administrator.—John Ross.
Policy Assistant.—Bess Larson.
Printer.—Sangina Wright.
Communications:
Communications Director.—Kristina Baum.
Press Secretary.—Thea McDonald.
Editor/Speechwriter.—James Danford.
Press Assistant.—Alicia Criscuolo.
Counsel:
General Counsel.—Molly Boyl.
Legal Assistant.—James Danford.
Energy Subcommittee
Staff Director.—Emily Domenech.

Professional Staff.—Richard Yamada.
Policy Assistant.—Bess Larson.
Environment Subcommittee
Staff Director.—Joe Brazauskas.
Professional Staff: Juliya Grigoryan, Taylor Jordan.
Policy Assistant.—Bess Larson.
Oversight Subcommittee
Staff Director.—Ashley Callen.
Professional Staff.—Drew Colliatie.
Counsel.—Caroline Ingram.
Policy Assistant.—Bess Larson.
Research and Technology Subcommittee
Staff Director.—Cliff Shannon.
Deputy Staff Director.—Raj Bharwani.
Professional Staff: Sarah Jorgenson, Jenn Wickre.
Policy Assistant.—Sara Ratliff.
Space Subcommittee
Staff Director.—Tom Hammond.
Professional Staff.—Ryan Faith.
Counsel.—Mike Mineiro.
Policy Assistants: Jonathan Charlton, Sara Ratliff.
Minority Staff:
Chief of Staff.—Richard Obermann.
Chief Counsel.—John Piazza.
Deputy Chief Counsel.—Russell Norman.
Administrative and Communications Director.—Kristin Kopshever.
Press Secretary.—Rebekah Eskandani.
Research Assistant.—Sara Palasits.
Energy Subcommittee
Staff Director.—Adam Rosenberg.
Professional Staff.—Joe Flarida.
Environment Subcommittee
Professional Staff: Priyanka Hooghan, Pamitha Weerasinghe.
Oversight Subcommittee
Staff Director.—Doug Pasternak.
Professional Staff.—Stanton Johnson.
Research and Technology Subcommittee
Staff Director.—Dahlia Sokolov.
Professional Staff: Sara Barber, Brystol English.
Space Subcommittee
Professional Staff: Sara Barber, Allen Li, Pam Whitney.

Small Business

2361 Rayburn House Office Building, phone 225–5821, fax 226–5276

http://www.smallbusiness.house.gov

Steve Chabot, of Ohio, *Chair*

Blaine Luetkemeyer, of Missouri, *Vice Chair.*

Steve King, of Iowa.
Dave Brat, of Virginia.
Aumua Amata Coleman Radewagen, of American Samoa.
Stephen Knight, of California.
Trent Kelly, of Mississippi.
Rod Blum, of Iowa.
James Comer, of Kentucky.
Jenniffer González-Colón, of Puerto Rico.
Brian K. Fitzpatrick, of Pennsylvania.
Roger W. Marshall, of Kansas.
Ralph Norman, of South Carolina.
John R. Curtis, of Utah.

Nydia M. Velázquez, of New York.
Dwight Evans, of Pennsylvania.
Stephanie N. Murphy, of Florida.
Al Lawson, Jr., of Florida.
Yvette D. Clarke, of New York.
Judy Chu, of California.
Alma S. Adams, of North Carolina.
Adriano Espaillat, of New York.
Bradley Scott Schneider, of Illinois.
Vacant.

SUBCOMMITTEES

[The chair and ranking minority member are ex officio (non-voting) members of all subcommittees for purposes of any meeting or hearing.]

Agriculture, Energy, and Trade

Rod Blum, of Iowa, *Chair*

Steve King, of Iowa.
Blaine Luetkemeyer, of Missouri.
Aumua Amata Coleman Radewagen, of American Samoa.
James Comer, of Kentucky.
John R. Curtis, of Utah.

Bradley Scott Schneider, of Illinois.
Al Lawson, Jr., of Florida.
Vacant.
Vacant.

Contracting and Workforce

Stephen Knight, of California, *Chair*

Steve King, of Iowa.
James Comer, of Kentucky.
Ralph Norman, of South Carolina.
Vacant.
Vacant.

Stephanie N. Murphy, of Florida.
Yvette D. Clarke, of New York.
Dwight Evans, of Pennsylvania.
Al Lawson, Jr., of Florida.

Economic Growth, Tax, and Capital Access

Dave Brat, of Virginia, *Chair*

Stephen Knight, of California.
Trent Kelly, of Mississippi.
Jenniffer González-Colón, of Puerto Rico.
Brian K. Fitzpatrick, of Pennsylvania.
Vacant.

Dwight Evans, of Pennsylvania.
Judy Chu, of California.
Stephanie N. Murphy, of Florida.
Yvette D. Clarke, of New York.

Health and Technology

Aumua Amata Coleman Radewagen, of American Samoa, *Chair*

Blaine Luetkemeyer, of Missouri.
Dave Brat, of Virginia.
Jenniffer González-Colón, of Puerto Rico.
Brian K. Fitzpatrick, of Pennsylvania.
Roger W. Marshall, of Kansas.

Al Lawson, Jr., of Florida.
Adriano Espaillat, of New York.
Vacant.
Vacant.

Investigations, Oversight, and Regulations

Trent Kelly, of Mississippi, *Chair*

Rod Blum, of Iowa.
Roger W. Marshall, of Kansas.
Ralph Norman, of South Carolina.
John R. Curtis, of Utah.
Vacant.

Alma S. Adams, of North Carolina.
Vacant.
Vacant.
Vacant.

STAFF

Committee on Small Business (2361 RHOB).
Staff Director.—Kevin Fitzpatrick.
Deputy Staff Director and Chief Counsel.—Jan Oliver.
Policy Director.—Joe Hartz.
Senior Investigative Counsel.—Jessica Donlon.
Counsels: Stephanie Fekete, Vivian Ling.
Senior Professional Staff.—Sharon Utz.
Professional Staff: James Burchfield, Maggie Moore, Robert Yavor.
Clerk.—Delia Barr.
Policy Assistant.—Dan Brown.
Staff Assistant.—Hannah Schmidt.
Democratic Staff:
Staff Director.—Adam Minehardt.
Deputy Staff Director.—Melissa Jung.
Office Manager.—Mory García.
Communications Director.—Alex Haurek.
Counsels: Meredith Graves, Julia Sferlazzo.
Professional Staff: Halimah Najieb-Locke, Rosanna Torres.

Transportation and Infrastructure

2165 Rayburn House Office Building, phone 225–9446

http://www.transportation.house.gov

Majority (202) 225–9446, Room 2165 RHOB

Minority (202) 225–4472, Room 2163 RHOB

Bill Shuster, of Pennsylvania, *Chair*

John J. Duncan, Jr., of Tennessee, *Vice Chair*

Don Young, of Alaska.
Frank A. LoBiondo, of New Jersey.
Sam Graves, of Missouri.
Duncan Hunter, of California.
Eric A. ''Rick'' Crawford, of Arkansas.
Lou Barletta, of Pennsylvania.
Bob Gibbs, of Ohio.
Daniel Webster, of Florida.
Jeff Denham, of California.
Thomas Massie, of Kentucky.
Mark Meadows, of North Carolina.
Scott Perry, of Pennsylvania.
Rodney Davis, of Illinois.
Mark Sanford, of South Carolina.
Rob Woodall, of Georgia.
Todd Rokita, of Indiana.
John Katko, of New York.
Brian Babin, of Texas.
Garret Graves, of Louisiana.
Barbara Comstock, of Virginia.
David Rouzer, of North Carolina.
Mike Bost, of Illinois.
Randy K. Weber, Sr., of Texas.
Doug LaMalfa, of California.
Bruce Westerman, of Arkansas.
Lloyd Smucker, of Pennsylvania.
Paul Mitchell, of Michigan.
John J. Faso, of New York.
A. Drew Ferguson IV, of Georgia.
Brian J. Mast, of Florida.
Jason Lewis, of Minnesota.
Mike Gallagher, of Wisconsin.

Peter A. DeFazio, of Oregon.
Eleanor Holmes Norton, of District of Columbia.
Eddie Bernice Johnson, of Texas.
Elijah E. Cummings, of Maryland.
Rick Larsen, of Washington.
Michael E. Capuano, of Massachusetts.
Grace F. Napolitano, of California.
Daniel Lipinski, of Illinois.
Steve Cohen, of Tennessee.
Albio Sires, of New Jersey.
John Garamendi, of California.
Henry C. ''Hank'' Johnson, Jr., of Georgia.
André Carson, of Indiana.
Richard M. Nolan, of Minnesota.
Dina Titus, of Nevada.
Sean Patrick Maloney, of New York.
Elizabeth H. Esty, of Connecticut.
Lois Frankel, of Florida.
Cheri Bustos, of Illinois.
Jared Huffman, of California.
Julia Brownley, of California.
Frederica S. Wilson, of Florida.
Donald M. Payne, Jr., of New Jersey.
Alan S. Lowenthal, of California.
Brenda L. Lawrence, of Michigan.
Mark DeSaulnier, of California.
Stacey E. Plaskett, of Virgin Islands.

SUBCOMMITTEES

[The chair and ranking minority member are ex officio (voting) members of all subcommittees on which they do not serve.]

Aviation

Frank A. LoBiondo, of New Jersey, *Chair*

Don Young, of Alaska.
John J. Duncan, Jr., of Tennessee.
Sam Graves, of Missouri.
Duncan Hunter, of California.
Bob Gibbs, of Ohio.
Daniel Webster, of Florida.
Jeff Denham, of California.
Thomas Massie, of Kentucky.
Mark Meadows, of North Carolina.
Scott Perry, of Pennsylvania.
Rodney Davis, of Illinois.
Mark Sanford, of South Carolina.
Rob Woodall, of Georgia.
Todd Rokita, of Indiana.
Barbara Comstock, of Virginia.
Doug LaMalfa, of California.
Bruce Westerman, of Arkansas.
Lloyd Smucker, of Pennsylvania.
Paul Mitchell, of Michigan.
Jason Lewis, of Minnesota.

Rick Larsen, of Washington.
Eddie Bernice Johnson, of Texas.
Daniel Lipinski, of Illinois.
André Carson, of Indiana.
Cheri Bustos, of Illinois.
Eleanor Holmes Norton, of District of Columbia.
Dina Titus, of Nevada.
Sean Patrick Maloney, of New York.
Julia Brownley, of California.
Donald M. Payne, Jr., of New Jersey.
Brenda L. Lawrence, of Michigan.
Michael E. Capuano, of Massachusetts.
Grace F. Napolitano, of California.
Steve Cohen, of Tennessee.
Henry C. ''Hank'' Johnson, Jr., of Georgia.
Richard M. Nolan, of Minnesota.

Coast Guard and Maritime Transportation

Duncan Hunter, of California, *Chair*

Don Young, of Alaska.
Frank A. LoBiondo, of New Jersey.
Garret Graves, of Louisiana.
David Rouzer, of North Carolina.
Randy K. Weber, Sr., of Texas.
Brian J. Mast, of Florida.
Jason Lewis, of Minnesota.

John Garamendi, of California.
Elijah E. Cummings, of Maryland.
Rick Larsen, of Washington.
Jared Huffman, of California.
Alan S. Lowenthal, of California.
Stacey E. Plaskett, of Virgin Islands.

Economic Development, Public Buildings, and Emergency Management

Lou Barletta, of Pennsylvania, *Chair*

Eric A. ''Rick'' Crawford, of Arkansas.
Barbara Comstock, of Virginia.
Mike Bost, of Illinois.
John J. Faso, of New York.
A. Drew Ferguson IV, of Georgia.
Brian J. Mast, of Florida.
Mike Gallagher, of Wisconsin.

Dina Titus, of Nevada.
Henry C. ''Hank'' Johnson, Jr., of Georgia.
Eleanor Holmes Norton, of District of Columbia.
Albio Sires, of New Jersey.
Stacey E. Plaskett, of Virgin Islands.

Highways and Transit

Sam Graves, of Missouri, *Chair*

Don Young, of Alaska.
John J. Duncan, Jr., of Tennessee.
Frank A. LoBiondo, of New Jersey.
Duncan Hunter, of California.
Eric A. "Rick" Crawford, of Arkansas.
Lou Barletta, of Pennsylvania.
Bob Gibbs, of Ohio.
Jeff Denham, of California.
Thomas Massie, of Kentucky.
Mark Meadows, of North Carolina.
Scott Perry, of Pennsylvania.
Rodney Davis, of Illinois.
Rob Woodall, of Georgia.
John Katko, of New York.
Brian Babin, of Texas.
Garret Graves, of Louisiana.
Barbara Comstock, of Virginia.
David Rouzer, of North Carolina.
Mike Bost, of Illinois.
Doug LaMalfa, of California.
Bruce Westerman, of Arkansas.
Lloyd Smucker, of Pennsylvania.
Paul Mitchell, of Michigan.
John J. Faso, of New York.
A. Drew Ferguson IV, of Georgia.
Mike Gallagher, of Wisconsin.

Eleanor Holmes Norton, of District of Columbia.
Steve Cohen, of Tennessee.
Albio Sires, of New Jersey.
Richard M. Nolan, of Minnesota.
Dina Titus, of Nevada.
Sean Patrick Maloney, of New York.
Elizabeth H. Esty, of Connecticut.
Jared Huffman, of California.
Julia Brownley, of California.
Alan S. Lowenthal, of California.
Brenda L. Lawrence, of Michigan.
Mark DeSaulnier, of California.
Eddie Bernice Johnson, of Texas.
Michael E. Capuano, of Massachusetts.
Grace F. Napolitano, of California.
Daniel Lipinski, of Illinois.
Henry C. "Hank" Johnson, Jr., of Georgia.
Lois Frankel, of Florida.
Cheri Bustos, of Illinois.
Frederica S. Wilson, of Florida.
Donald M. Payne, Jr., of New Jersey.

Railroads, Pipelines, and Hazardous Materials

Jeff Denham, of California, *Chair*

John J. Duncan, Jr., of Tennessee.
Sam Graves, of Missouri.
Lou Barletta, of Pennsylvania.
Daniel Webster, of Florida.
Mark Meadows, of North Carolina.
Scott Perry, of Pennsylvania.
Mark Sanford, of South Carolina.
Todd Rokita, of Indiana.
John Katko, of New York.
Brian Babin, of Texas.
Randy K. Weber, Sr., of Texas.
Bruce Westerman, of Arkansas.
Lloyd Smucker, of Pennsylvania.
Paul Mitchell, of Michigan.
John J. Faso, of New York.
Jason Lewis, of Minnesota.
Mike Gallagher, of Wisconsin.

Michael E. Capuano, of Massachusetts.
Donald M. Payne, Jr., of New Jersey.
Elijah E. Cummings, of Maryland.
Steve Cohen, of Tennessee.
Albio Sires, of New Jersey.
John Garamendi, of California.
André Carson, of Indiana.
Richard M. Nolan, of Minnesota.
Elizabeth H. Esty, of Connecticut.
Cheri Bustos, of Illinois.
Frederica S. Wilson, of Florida.
Mark DeSaulnier, of California.
Daniel Lipinski, of Illinois.
Grace F. Napolitano, of California.

Water Resources and Environment

Garret Graves, of Louisiana, *Chair*

Eric A. ''Rick'' Crawford, of Arkansas.
Bob Gibbs, of Ohio.
Daniel Webster, of Florida.
Thomas Massie, of Kentucky.
Rodney Davis, of Illinois.
Mark Sanford, of South Carolina.
Rob Woodall, of Georgia.
Todd Rokita, of Indiana.
John Katko, of New York.
Brian Babin, of Texas.
David Rouzer, of North Carolina.
Mike Bost, of Illinois.
Randy K. Weber, Sr., of Texas.
Doug LaMalfa, of California.
A. Drew Ferguson IV, of Georgia.
Brian J. Mast, of Florida.

Grace F. Napolitano, of California.
Lois Frankel, of Florida.
Frederica S. Wilson, of Florida.
Jared Huffman, of California.
Alan S. Lowenthal, of California.
Eddie Bernice Johnson, of Texas.
John Garamendi, of California.
Dina Titus, of Nevada.
Sean Patrick Maloney, of New York.
Elizabeth H. Esty, of Connecticut.
Cheri Bustos, of Illinois.
Julia Brownley, of California.
Brenda L. Lawrence, of Michigan.

STAFF

Committee on Transportation and Infrastructure (2165 RHOB) 225–9446, fax 225–6782.
Majority Full Committee Staff:
Staff Director.—Mathew M. Sturges.
Deputy Staff Director.—Chris Vieson.
General Counsel.—Fred Miller.
Deputy General Counsel.—Holly E. Woodruff Lyons.
Senior Advisor to the Chair.—Geoff Gosselin.
Director of Budget and Program Analysis.—Clare C. Doherty.
Director of Member Services.—Collin McCune.
Director of Outreach and Coalitions.—Misty McGowen.
Financial Administrator.—April Blankenship.
Legislative Operations Assistant.—Hannah Matesic.
Director of Community Facilities.—Mike Legg.
Staff Assistant.—Jack Meehan.
Minority Full Committee Staff:
Staff Director.—Katherine W. Dedrick.
Chief Counsel.—Ward McCarragher.
Counsel.—Russ Kelley.
Director of Administration and Member Services.—Jamie Harrell.
Director of Pacific Northwest Policy.—Liz Hill.
Legislative Assistant.—Alexa Old Crowe.
Information Systems
Systems Administrator.—Larry Whittaker.
Assistant Systems Administrator.—Scott Putz.
Majority Communications
Communications Director.—Justin Harclerode.
Deputy Communication Director.—Jeff Urbanchuk.
Digital Coordinator.—Keith Hall.
Minority Communications
Communications Director.—Jen Gilbreath.
Digital Director.—Bayley Sandy.
Clerk's Office
Clerk.—Tracy G. Mosebey.
Printer.—Jean Paffenback.
Oversight and Investigations
Majority Staff:
Director of Oversight and Investigations.—Wiley Deck.
Subcommittee on Aviation
Majority Staff:
Staff Director.—Holly E. Woodruff Lyons.
Counsel.—Naveen Rao.
Professional Staff: Simone Perez, Thomas Hunter Presti.
Staff Assistant.—Max Rosen.

Minority Staff:
Counsels: Alex Burkett, Michael Tien.
Legislative Assistant.—Luke Strimer.
Subcommittee on Coast Guard and Maritime Transportation
Majority Staff:
Staff Director.—John C. Rayfield.
Professional Staff.—Bonnie Bruce.
Research Assistant.—Kevin Rieg.
Staff Assistant.—Cameron Humphrey.
Minority Staff:
Staff Director.—Dave Jansen.
Legislative Assistant.—Alexa Old Crow.
Subcommittee on Economic Development, Public Buildings, and Emergency Management
Majority Staff:
Staff Director.—Daniel W. Mathews.
Counsels: Johanna Hardy, Pamela S. Williams.
Research Assistant.—Tyler Menzler.
Minority Staff:
Counsels: Elliot Doomes, Janet Erickson.
Legislative Assistant.—Alexa Old Crow.
Subcommittee on Highways and Transit
Majority Staff:
Staff Director.—Murphie Barrett Koonce.
Senior Professional Staff.—Geoff Gosselin.
Professional Staff: Nicole Christus, Alex Etchen, Caryn Moore.
Minority Staff:
Staff Director.—Helena Zyblikewycz.
Professional Staff: Auke Merrill Mahar-Piersma, Andrew Okuyiga.
Legislative Assistant.—Luke Strimer.
Subcommittee on Railroads, Pipelines, and Hazardous Materials
Majority Staff:
Staff Director.—Mary B. Phillips.
Counsel.—Arielle Giordano.
Staff Assistant.—Tom Supinka.
Minority Staff:
Staff Director.—Jennifer Homendy.
Professional Staff.—Liz Hill.
Legislative Assistant.—Alexa Old Crow.
Subcommittee on Water Resources and Environment
Majority Staff:
Senior Counsel.—Jonathan R. Pawlow.
Professional Staff.—Elizabeth Fox.
Staff Assistant.—Victor Sarmiento.
Minority Staff:
Staff Director and Counsel.—Ryan Seiger.
Counsel.—Michael Brain.
Legislative Assistant.—Alexa Old Crow.

Veterans' Affairs

335 Cannon House Office Building, phone 225–3527, fax 225–5486

http://www.veterans.house.gov

David P. Roe, of Tennessee, *Chair*

Gus M. Bilirakis, of Florida, *Vice Chair*

Mike Coffman, of Colorado.
Aumua Amata Coleman Radewagen, of American Samoa.
Mike Bost, of Illinois.
Bruce Poliquin, of Maine.
Neal P. Dunn, of Florida.
Jodey C. Arrington, of Texas.
Clay Higgins, of Louisiana.
Jack Bergman, of Michigan.
Jim Banks, of Indiana.
Jenniffer González-Colón, of Puerto Rico.
Brian J. Mast, of Florida.
Vacant.

Timothy J. Walz, of Minnesota.
Mark Takano, of California.
Julia Brownley, of California.
Ann M. Kuster, of New Hampshire.
Beto O'Rourke, of Texas.
Kathleen M. Rice, of New York.
J. Luis Correa, of California.
Conor Lamb, of Pennsylvania.
Elizabeth H. Esty, of Connecticut.
Scott H. Peters, of California.

SUBCOMMITTEES

Disability Assistance and Memorial Affairs

Mike Bost, of Illinois, *Chair*

Mike Coffman, of Colorado.
Aumua Amata Coleman Radewagen, of American Samoa.
Jack Bergman, of Michigan.
Jim Banks, of Indiana.

Elizabeth H. Esty, of Connecticut.
Julia Brownley, of California.
Conor Lamb, of Pennsylvania.

Economic Opportunity

Jodey C. Arrington, of Texas, *Chair*

Gus M. Bilirakis, of Florida.
Jim Banks, of Indiana.
Brian J. Mast, of Florida.

Beto O'Rourke, of Texas.
Mark Takano, of California.
J. Luis Correa, of California.
Kathleen M. Rice, of New York.

Health

Neal P. Dunn, of Florida, *Chair*

Gus M. Bilirakis, of Florida.
Aumua Amata Coleman Radewagen, of American Samoa.
Clay Higgins, of Louisiana.
Jenniffer González-Colón, of Puerto Rico.
Brian J. Mast, of Florida.

Julia Brownley, of California.
Mark Takano, of California.
Ann M. Kuster, of New Hampshire.
Beto O'Rourke, of Texas.
J. Luis Correa, of California.

Oversight and Investigations

Jack Bergman, of Michigan, *Chair*

Mike Bost, of Illinois.
Bruce Poliquin, of Maine.
Neal P. Dunn, of Florida.
Jodey C. Arrington, of Texas.
Jenniffer González-Colón, of Puerto Rico.

Ann M. Kuster, of New Hampshire.
Kathleen M. Rice, of New York.
Scott H. Peters, of California.
Conor Lamb, of Pennsylvania.

STAFF

Committee on Veterans' Affairs (335 CHOB), 225–3527, fax 225–5486.
Majority Staff Director.—Jon Towers.
Deputy Staff Director.—Chris McNamee.
Director of Member Services and Strategic Oversight.—Matt Meyer.
Communications Director.—Tiffany Haverly.
Financial Administrator and Office Manager.—Bernadine Dotson.
Legislative Assistant.—Grayson Westmoreland.
Chief Clerk.—Alissa Strawcutter.
Press Secretary.—Caroline Ponseti.
Staff Assistant.—Matt Kessler.
Minority Staff Director.—Ray Kelley (333 CHOB), 225–9756, fax 225–2034.
Deputy Staff Director.—Matt Reel.
Chief Counsel.—Grace Rodden.
Communications Director.—Sara Severs (acting).
Press Secretary.—Griffin Anderson.
Executive Assistant.—Rasheedah Hasan.
Legislative Coordinator and Office Manager.—Carol Murray.
Subcommittee on Disability Assistance and Memorial Affairs (337 CHOB), 225–9164, fax 226–4691.
Majority Subcommittee Staff Director and Counsel.—Maria Tripplaar.
Legislative Aide.—Vacant.
Professional Staff Member and Counsel.—Cecilia Daly.
Minority Staff Director.—Carolyn Blaydes.
Professional Staff Member.—Chris Bennett.
Subcommittee on Economic Opportunity (335 CHOB), 226–5491, fax 225–5486.
Majority Staff Director.—Jon Clark.
Professional Staff Member.—Kelsey Baron.
Minority Staff Director and Counsel.—Vacant.
Professional Staff Member.—Chris Bennett.
Subcommittee on Health (338 CHOB), 225–9154, fax 226–4536.
Majority Staff Director.—Christine Hill.
Professional Staff Member.—Samantha Gonzalez.
Legislative Aide.—Hillary Dickinson.
Professional Staff Member and Coalitions Director.—Alex Large.
Healthcare Investigator.—Tamara Bonzanto.
Minority Staff Director.—Vacant.
Professional Staff Member.—Megan Bland.
Subcommittee on Oversight and Investigations (337A CHOB), 225–3569, fax 225–6392.
Majority Staff Director and Counsel.—Jon Hodnette.
Investigative Counsels.—Amy Centanni.
Contract Investigator.—Bill Mallison.
Minority Staff Director and Investigative Counsel.—Grace Rodden.
Professional Staff Member.—Megan Bland.

Ways and Means

1102 Longworth House Office Building, phone 225–3625

http://waysandmeans.house.gov

Kevin Brady, of Texas, *Chair*

Sam Johnson, of Texas.
Devin Nunes, of California.
David G. Reichert, of Washington.
Peter J. Roskam, of Illinois.
Vern Buchanan, of Florida.
Adrian Smith, of Nebraska.
Lynn Jenkins, of Kansas.
Erik Paulsen, of Minnesota.
Kenny Marchant, of Texas.
Diane Black, of Tennessee.
Tom Reed, of New York.
Mike Kelly, of Pennsylvania.
James B. Renacci, of Ohio.
Kristi L. Noem, of South Dakota.
George Holding, of North Carolina.
Jason Smith, of Missouri.
Tom Rice, of South Carolina.
David Schweikert, of Arizona.
Jackie Walorski, of Indiana.
Carlos Curbelo, of Florida.
Mike Bishop, of Michigan.
Darin LaHood, of Illinois.
Brad R. Wenstrup, of Ohio.

Richard E. Neal, of Massachusetts.
Sander M. Levin, of Michigan.
John Lewis, of Georgia.
Lloyd Doggett, of Texas.
Mike Thompson, of California.
John B. Larson, of Connecticut.
Earl Blumenauer, of Oregon.
Ron Kind, of Wisconsin.
Bill Pascrell, Jr., of New Jersey.
Joseph Crowley, of New York.
Danny K. Davis, of Illinois.
Linda T. Sánchez, of California.
Brian Higgins, of New York.
Terri A. Sewell, of Alabama.
Suzan K. DelBene, of Washington.
Judy Chu, of California.

SUBCOMMITTEES

[The chair and ranking minority member are ex officio (non-voting) members of all subcommittees.]

Health

Peter J. Roskam, of Illinois, *Chair*

Sam Johnson, of Texas.
Devin Nunes, of California.
Vern Buchanan, of Florida.
Adrian Smith, of Nebraska.
Lynn Jenkins, of Kansas.
Kenny Marchant, of Texas.
Diane Black, of Tennessee.
Erik Paulsen, of Minnesota.
Tom Reed, of New York.
Mike Kelly, of Pennsylvania.

Sander M. Levin, of Michigan.
Mike Thompson, of California.
Ron Kind, of Wisconsin.
Earl Blumenauer, of Oregon.
Brian Higgins, of New York.
Terri A. Sewell, of Alabama.
Judy Chu, of California.

Human Resources

Adrian Smith, of Nebraska, *Chair*

Jackie Walorski, of Indiana.
Carlos Curbelo, of Florida.
David Schweikert, of Arizona.
Darin LaHood, of Illinois.
Brad R. Wenstrup, of Ohio.
David G. Reichert, of Washington.

Danny K. Davis, of Illinois.
Lloyd Doggett, of Texas.
Terri A. Sewell, of Alabama.
Judy Chu, of California.

Oversight

Lynn Jenkins, of Kansas, *Chair*

Jackie Walorski, of Indiana.
Carlos Curbelo, of Florida.
Mike Bishop, of Michigan.
Darin LaHood, of Illinois.
Brad R. Wenstrup, of Ohio.
Kenny Marchant, of Texas.

John Lewis, of Georgia.
Joseph Crowley, of New York.
Suzan K. DelBene, of Washington.
Earl Blumenauer, of Oregon.

Social Security

Sam Johnson, of Texas, *Chair*

Mike Bishop, of Michigan.
Vern Buchanan, of Florida.
Mike Kelly, of Pennsylvania.
Tom Rice, of South Carolina.
David Schweikert, of Arizona.
Darin LaHood, of Illinois.

John B. Larson, of Connecticut.
Bill Pascrell, Jr., of New Jersey.
Joseph Crowley, of New York.
Linda T. Sánchez, of California.

Tax Policy

Vern Buchanan, of Florida, *Chair*

Peter J. Roskam, of Illinois.
David G. Reichert, of Washington.
James B. Renacci, of Ohio.
Kristi L. Noem, of South Dakota.
George Holding, of North Carolina.
Jason Smith, of Missouri.
Tom Rice, of South Carolina.
David Schweikert, of Arizona.

Lloyd Doggett, of Texas.
John B. Larson, of Connecticut.
Linda T. Sánchez, of California.
Mike Thompson, of California.
Suzan K. DelBene, of Washington.
Earl Blumenauer, of Oregon.

Trade

David G. Reichert, of Washington, *Chair*

Devin Nunes, of California.
Erik Paulsen, of Minnesota.
Mike Kelly, of Pennsylvania.
Tom Reed, of New York.
Kristi L. Noem, of South Dakota.
George Holding, of North Carolina.
Tom Rice, of South Carolina.
Kenny Marchant, of Texas.
Jason Smith, of Missouri.

Bill Pascrell, Jr., of New Jersey.
Ron Kind, of Wisconsin.
Lloyd Doggett, of Texas.
Sander M. Levin, of Michigan.
Danny K. Davis, of Illinois.
Brian Higgins, of New York.

STAFF

Committee on Ways and Means (1102 LHOB), 225–3625, fax 225–2610.
Staff Director.—David Stewart.
Deputy Staff Director.—Matt Weidinger.
General Counsel.—Allison Halataei.
Chief Economist.—Robert O'Quinn.
Senior Economist.—Donald Schneider.
Financial Administrator.—April Blankenship.
Senior Clerk.—Michael K. Baker.
Systems Administrators: Edward Baird, Rene Macias.
Committee Administrator.—Chris Stottmann.
Special Assistant to the Staff Director.—Kathryn Chakmak.
Staff Assistants: Dylan Bosserman, Thomas Kutz.
Chief Tax Counsel.—Barbara Angus.
Senior Tax Counsel.—Aharon Friedman.
Tax Counsels: Randy Gartin, Aaron Junge, Loren Ponds, John Sandell, John Schoenecker.
Tax Advisor.—Victoria Glover.

Legislative Assistant, Tax Policy.—Danielle DuBose.
Oversight Staff Director.—Machalagh Carr.
Oversight Counsel.—Rachel Kaldahl.
Professional Staff, Oversight: Meinan Goto, Lindsay Steward.
Legislative Assistant, Oversight.—Brighton Haslett.
Staff Director/Chief Trade Counsel.—Angela Ellard.
Trade Counsels: Blake Harden, Kelly Ann Shaw, Josh Snead.
Legislative Assistant, Trade.—Lila Nieves-Lee.
Staff Director, Health.—Emily Murry.
Professional Staff, Health: Lisa Grabert, Alyssa Palisi, Stephanie Parks, Nick Uehlecke.
Legislative Assistant, Health.—Taylor Trott.
Staff Director, Social Security.—Amy Shuart.
Social Security Counsel.—Shaun Freiman.
Professional Staff, Social Security.—Lara Rosner.
Legislative Assistant, Social Security.—Matt Russell.
Staff Director, Human Resources.—Anne DeCesaro.
Professional Staff, Human Resources: Rosemary Lahasky, Ryan Martin.
Legislative Assistant, Human Resources.—Andrew Rocca.
Press Secretary.—Lauren Aronson.
Deputy Press Secretary.—Katharine Cooksey.
Speechwriter.—Shane McDonald.
Digital Director.—Roman Burleson.
Coalitions Director.—Rick Limardo.
Coalitions Coordinator.—Paul Guaglianone.

Minority Chief of Staff.—Brandon Casey.
Communications Director.—Dan Rubin.
Office/Finance Manager.—Jennifer O'Connor.
Director of Outreach/Member Services.—Lee Slater.
Staff Assistant/Intern Coordinator.—Carrie Breidenbach.
Staff/Research Assistant.—Moyer McCoy.
IT Director.—Antoine Walker.
Press Secretary.—Kevin Parker.
General Counsel/Oversight Staff Director.—Karen McAfee.
Chief Tax Counsel.—Kara Getz.
Tax Policy Staff Director.—Aruna Kalyanam.
Tax Counsel.—Ji Prichard.
Staff Director, Health.—Amy Hall.
Professional Staff, Health: Melanie Egorin, Sarah Levin.
Fellow (Health): Jonathan Moore, Daniel Ochylski.
Staff Director, Human Resources.—Morna Miller.
Staff Director, Social Security.—Kathryn Olson.
Staff Director, Trade.—Jason Kearns.
Trade Counsels: Keigan Mull, Katherine Tai.

SELECT AND SPECIAL COMMITTEES OF THE HOUSE

Permanent Select Committee on Intelligence

HVC–304 The Capitol, phone 225–4121

[Created pursuant to H. Res. 658, 95th Congress]

Devin Nunes, of California, *Chair*

K. Michael Conaway, of Texas.
Peter T. King, of New York.
Frank A. LoBiondo, of New Jersey.
Thomas J. Rooney, of Florida.
Ileana Ros-Lehtinen, of Florida.
Michael R. Turner, of Ohio.
Brad R. Wenstrup, of Ohio.
Chris Stewart, of Utah.
Eric A. ''Rick'' Crawford, of Arkansas.
Trey Gowdy, of South Carolina.
Elise M. Stefanik, of New York.
Will Hurd, of Texas.

Adam B. Schiff, of California.
James A. Himes, of Connecticut.
Terri A. Sewell, of Alabama.
André Carson, of Indiana.
Jackie Speier, of California.
Mike Quigley, of Illinois.
Eric Swalwell, of California.
Joaquin Castro, of Texas.
Denny Heck, of Washington.

SUBCOMMITTEES

[The Speaker and Minority Leader are ex officio (non-voting) members of the committee.]

Central Intelligence Agency

Frank A. LoBiondo, of New Jersey, *Chair*

K. Michael Conaway, of Texas.
Peter T. King, of New York.
Thomas J. Rooney, of Florida.
Ileana Ros-Lehtinen, of Florida.
Chris Stewart, of Utah.

Eric Swalwell, of California.
James A. Himes, of Connecticut.
Joaquin Castro, of Texas.
Denny Heck, of Washington.

Department of Defense Intelligence and Overhead Architecture

Chris Stewart, of Utah, *Chair*

Michael R. Turner, of Ohio.
Brad R. Wenstrup, of Ohio.
Eric A. ''Rick'' Crawford, of Arkansas.
Elise M. Stefanik, of New York.
Will Hurd, of Texas.

Terri A. Sewell, of Alabama.
André Carson, of Indiana.
Joaquin Castro, of Texas.
Denny Heck, of Washington.

Emerging Threats

Peter T. King, of New York, *Chair*

Frank A. LoBiondo, of New Jersey.
Brad R. Wenstrup, of Ohio.
Eric A. ''Rick'' Crawford, of Arkansas.
Trey Gowdy, of South Carolina.
Will Hurd, of Texas.

André Carson, of Indiana.
Jackie Speier, of California.
Mike Quigley, of Illinois.
Eric Swalwell, of California.

National Security Agency and Cybersecurity

Thomas J. Rooney, of Florida, *Chair*

K. Michael Conaway, of Texas.
Ileana Ros-Lehtinen, of Florida.
Michael R. Turner, of Ohio.
Trey Gowdy, of South Carolina.
Elise M. Stefanik, of New York.
James A. Himes, of Connecticut.
Terri A. Sewell, of Alabama.
Jackie Speier, of California.
Mike Quigley, of Illinois.

STAFF

Majority Staff Director.—Damon Nelson.
Senior Advisor.—George Pappas.
General Counsel.—Mark Stewart.
Deputy General Counsel and Policy Director.—Scott Glabe.
Senior Counsel for Counterterrorism.—Kash Patel.
Counsel.—Allen Souza.
Chief Clerk.—Nick Ciarlante.
Director of Program Evaluation and Budget.—Shannon Stuart.
Communications Director.—Jack Langer.
Professional Staff: Chelsey Campbell, William Flanigan, Andrew House, Steve Keith, Lisa Major, Doug Presley, Angel Smith, Jacqueline Tame.
Research Assistant.—Marissa Skaggs.
Minority Staff Director.—Michael Bahar.
Deputy Minority Staff Director.—Timothy Bergreen.
Policy Advisor.—Robert Minehart.
General Counsel.—Maher Bitar.
Deputy General Counsel.—Wells Bennett.
Minority Budget Director.—Carly Blake.
Communications Director.—Patrick Boland.
Professional Staff: Linda Cohen, Amanda Rogers Thorpe, Rheanne Wirkkala.
Associate Professional Staff Member.—Thomas Eager.
Director of Information Technology.—Brandon Smith.
Security Director.—Kristin Jepson.
Director of Information Management.—Kim Kerr.

National Republican Congressional Committee

320 First Street, SE., 20003, phone 479–7000

Steve Stivers, of Ohio, *Chair*

Deputy Chairs:
Mimi Walters, of California.
Tom Emmer, of Minnesota.
Vice Chair of:
Finance.—Lee M. Zeldin, of New York.
Recruitment.—Elise M. Stefanik, of New York.
Patriots.—Ryan A. Costello, of Pennsylvania.
Digital.—Matt Gaetz, of Florida.
Coalitions.—Ken Buck, of Colorado.
Regional.—Bill Johnson, of Ohio.
Candidate Development.—Will Hurd, of Texas.
Mentorship.—John Katko, of New York.
Primary Patriot.—Rodney Davis, of Illinois.
Data.—David Schweikert, of Arizona.
Member Services.—Kevin Yoder, of Kansas.
Redistricting.—Francis Rooney, of Florida.
Audit.—K. Michael Conaway, of Texas.
Transformation.—Keith J. Rothfus, of Pennsylvania.

STAFF

Executive Director.—John Rogers.
General Counsel.—Chris Winkelman.

Political Director.—Joe Pileggi.
Communications Director.—Matt Gorman.
Finance Director.—Emma Nelson.
Digital Director.—Ted Peterson.
Member Services Director.—Jesse Walls.

House Republican Policy Committee

1230 Longworth House Office Building, phone 222–1374

http://policy.house.gov

meets at the call of the Chair or the Speaker

Luke Messer, of Indiana, *Chair*

House Leadership:
Speaker of the House.—Paul D. Ryan, of Wisconsin.
Majority Leader.—Kevin McCarthy, of California.
Conference Chair.—Cathy McMorris Rodgers, of Washington.
Conference Vice Chair.—Doug Collins, of Georgia.
Conference Secretary.—Jason Smith, of Missouri.
NRCC Chair.—Steve Stivers, of Ohio.

Policy Committee Staff.—1230 Longworth HOB, 222–1374.
Director.—Jake Vreeburg.
Legislative Director.—John Huston.
Communications Director.—Molly Gillaspie.
Legislative Assistant.—Dominique Yantko.
Internship Coordinator.—Katie Murphy.

House Republican Conference

202A Cannon House Office Building, phone 225–5107, fax 226–0154

Cathy McMorris Rodgers, of Washington, *Chair*
Doug Collins, of Georgia, *Vice Chair*
Jason Smith, of Missouri, *Secretary*

STAFF

Chief of Staff.—Jeremy Deutsch.
Deputy Chief of Staff.—Nate Hodson.
Director of Member Services.—Sarah Rogers.
Deputy Member Services Director.—Nick Crocker.
Policy Director.—Jerry White.
Policy Advisor.—David Smentek.
Director of Coalitions.—Rachel Barkley.
Director of Digital Media.—Maurice Lewis.
Communications Director.—Kara Hauck.
Director of Media Affairs.—Katherine McQuade.
Press Secretary.—Molly Drenkard.
Speechwriter.—Mikayla Hall.
Scheduler.—Emily King.

Democratic Congressional Campaign Committee

430 South Capitol Street, SE., 20003, phone (202) 863–1500

Executive Committee:
Nancy Pelosi, of California, *Democratic Leader.*
Ben Ray Luján, of New Mexico, *Chair.*

STAFF

Executive Director.—Dan Sena, 485–3434.
Deputy Executive Director.—Nicole Eynard, 485–3436.
Chief Operating Officer.—Jacqui Newman, 741–1853.
Chief Financial Officer.—Jackie Forte-Mackay, 485–3401.
Chief of Staff.—Aaron Trujillo, 485–3530.
Political Director.—Jason Bresler, 485–3442.
Candidate Fundraising Director.—Emily Crerand, 485–3535.
Communications Director.—Meredith Kelly, 741–1858.
Managing Director of Member Services.—Charles Benton, 485–3516.
Director of Member Engagement and Relations.—Hans Goff, 478–9485.
Director of Research and Strategic Communications.—Matt Fuehrmeyer, 485–3523.
Digital Director.—Julia Ager, 741–1353.
Director of Digital Strategy.—Brian Krebs, 485–3521.
Director of Campaigns and Voter Contact.—Steve Sisneros, 485–3517.
National Finance Director.—Mike Smith, 485–3529.
National Press Secretary.—Tyler Law, 741–1870.
National Field Director.—Kurt Bagley, 485–3506.
Policy Director.—Lyron Blum-Evitts, 485–3526.
Polling and Modeling Director.—Amber Carrier, 485–3432.
Data and Reporting Director.—John Faas, 485–3510.
Targeting Director.—Claire Low, 741–1351.
National Strategic Analytics Director.—Rosa Mendoza, 485–3407.

Democratic Steering and Policy Committee

H–204 The Capitol, phone 225–0100

Steering and Policy Chair.—Nancy Pelosi, of California, *Democratic Leader.*
Steering Co-Chair.—Rosa L. DeLauro, of Connecticut.
Policy Co-Chair.—Eric Swalwell,of California.
Vice Chair and Parliamentarian.—Jared Polis, of Colorado.

DEMOCRATIC STEERING AND POLICY COMMITTEE STAFF

Steering: George Kundanis, Michael Long.
Policy: George Kundanis, Richard Meltzer.

Democratic Caucus

1420 Longworth House Office Building, phone 225–1400, fax 226–4412

www.dems.gov

Joseph Crowley, of New York, *Chair*
Linda T. Sánchez, of California, *Vice Chair*

STAFF

Chief of Staff.—Kate Winkler Keating.
Executive Director.—Carlos Sanchez.
Director of Policy.—Kevin Casey.
Director for Strategic Communications.—Courtney Gidner.
Director of Operations.—Manuel Joe Carrillo.
Communications Director.—Lauren French.
Senior Caucus Policy Advisor.—Nicole Cohen.
Digital Director.—Anthony Martinez.
Press Secretary and Director for Hispanic Media.—Elizabeth Lopez-Sandoval.
Outreach and Member Services Coordinator.—Andrew Sachse.
Legislative Correspondent.—Shane T. Smith.
Press Assistant.—Alaina Berner.
Staff Assistants: Anisah Assim, Christofer Horta.

Chief of Staff to the Vice Chair.—Lea Sulkala.
Legislative Director to the Vice Chair.—Melissa Kiedrowicz.
Communications Director to the Vice Chair.—Alex Nguyen.

OFFICERS AND OFFICIALS OF THE HOUSE

OFFICE OF THE SPEAKER

H–232 The Capitol, phone 225–0600, fax 225–5117

Speaker of the House of Representatives.—Paul D. Ryan.
Chief of Staff.—Jonathan Burks.
Deputy Chief of Staff.—Andy Speth.
Counselor.—Brendan Buck.
Policy Director.—Austin Smythe.
Director of Administration.—Kristene Blake.
Director of Scheduling.—Maureen Mitchell.
Deputy Directory of Scheduling.—Tory Wickiser.
Special Assistant to the Speaker.—Will Miller.
Director of House Operations.—Jennifer Hemingway.
Press Secretaries: Doug Andres, AshLee Strong.
Deputy Press Secretary.—Molly Edwards.
Director of Media Affairs.—Jenna Sakwa.
Communications Director.—Mike Ricci.
Deputy Communications Director.—Julia Slingsby.
Communications Advisor.—Michael Shapiro.
Digital Communications Director.—Caleb Smith.
Director of Special Events and Protocol.—Seton Easby-Smith.
Special Events Staff Assistant.—Carah Goldoust.
Member Services Director.—Tom Andrews.
Directors, Information Technology: Billy Benjamin, Merrick Munday.
General Counsel.—Mark Epley.
Floor Director.—Hugh Halpern.
Deputy Floor Director.—Nicole Foltz.
Floor Assistants: Sarah Coyle, Jamie Gillespie, Ryan O'Toole, Katie Pointer.
Cloakroom Director.—Jared Eichhorn.
Assistants to the Speaker for Policy: Geoff Antell, George Callas, Jeff Dressler, Cindy Herrle, Casey Higgins, Matt Hoffman, Ted McCann, Kiel Weaver.
Coalitions Coordinators: Derrick Dockery, Joshua Althouse.
Staff Assistants: Peter Castine, Andrew Letsch, Vanessa VandeHey.

OFFICE OF THE MAJORITY LEADER

H–107 The Capitol, phone 225–4000, fax 225–0781

Majority Leader.—Kevin McCarthy.
Chief of Staff.—Barrett Karr.
Deputy Chief of Staff and Counsel.—James Min.
Director of Communications.—Matt Sparks.
Director of Floor Operations.—John Leganski.
Director of Legislative Operations.—Kelly Dixon.
Director of Member Services.—Natalie Buchanan.
Policy Director.—Will Dunham.
Senior Policy Advisors: Brandon Consolvo, Roger Mahan, Katie Meyer, Luke Murry.
Executive Assistant.—Kristin Stipicevic.
Scheduler.—Alexandra Gourdikian.
Press Secretary.—Erin Perrine.
Floor Assistant.—Chris Bien.
Speechwriter and Conservative Coalitions Advisor.—Alec Torres.
Deputy Press Secretary.—Drew Florio.

Special Assistant.—Preston Hill.
Staff Assistants: Devin Gerzof, Joe Picozzi.

OFFICE OF THE MAJORITY WHIP

H–329 The Capitol, phone 225–0197

Majority Whip.—Steve Scalise.
Chief of Staff.—Brett Horton.
Chief Deputy Whip.—Patrick T. McHenry.
Chief of Staff to the Chief Deputy Whip.—Parker Poling.
Floor Director.—Matt Bravo.
Coalitions Coordinator.—Kelley Hudak.
Policy Director.—Bill Hughes.
Legislative Counsel.—Marty Reiser.
Communications Director.—Chris Bond.
Member Services Director.—Bart Reising.
Policy Advisors: Andrew Cavazos, Dan Sadlosky, Jeff Wieand.
Scheduler.—Ellen Gosnell.
Press Secretary.—Lauren Fine.
Deputy Floor Director.—Chris Hodgson.
Assistant to the Chief of Staff.—Andrew Cavazos.
Director of Operations.—Bart Reising.
Staff Assistants: Miller Lewis, Dennis Nalls.
Special Assistant.—David Planning.
Floor Assistant.—Ben Napier.

OFFICE OF THE DEMOCRATIC LEADER

H–204 The Capitol, phone 225–0100, fax 225–4188

www.democraticleader.gov

Office of the Democratic Leader.—Hon. Nancy Pelosi.
Chief of Staff.—Nadeam Elshami.
Chief of Staff (CA08 Office).—Robert Edmonson, 235 CHOB, 225–4965.
Deputy Chiefs of Staff: Diane Dewhirst, George Kundanis.
Counsel to the Democratic Leader.—Bernie Raimo, 225–0100.
Special Assistants to the Democratic Leader: Emily Berret, Bina Surgeon.
Assistant to the Executive Office.—Savannah Polzin.
Co-Directors of Correspondence: Robyn Lea, David Silverman, 421 Cannon, 225–0100.
Director of Scheduling and Advance.—Kelsey Smith.
Deputy Director of Scheduling.—Nathaniel Holmes.
Policy Director.—Dick Meltzer.
Policy Advisor.—Michael Tecklenburg.
Senior Policy Advisors: Kenneth DeGraff, Katherine Monge, Wyndee Parker, Wendell Primus.
Senior Advance Policy and Communications.—Margaret Capron.
Director of Member Services.—Jaime Lizarraga.
Director of Floor Operations.—Keith Stern.
Senior Advisor for Member Services and Floor.—Michael Long.
Member Services Advisor.—Julius West.
Director of Protocol and Special Events.—Kate Knudson.
IT Director.—Wil Haynes, HB–13, The Capitol, 225–0100.
Deputy IT Director.—Kamilah Keita, HB–13, The Capitol, 225–0100.
Director of Outreach.—Reva Price.

DEMOCRATIC LEADER'S PRESS OFFICE

H–204 The Capitol, phone 225–0100

Deputy Chief of Staff.—Drew Hammill.
Communications Director.—Ashley Etienne.
Senior Communications Advisor.—Caroline Behringer.

Press Secretary.—Taylor Griffin.
Deputy Press Secretary.—Joy Lee.
Director of Media Affairs.—Stephanie Cherry.
Director of Research.—April Greener.
Director of Speechwriting.—Henry Connelly.
Deputy Director of Speechwriting.—Shana Mansbach.
Digital Director.—Dylan Gibson.
Digital Manager and Director of Hispanic Media.—Julio Obscura.
Senior Press Assistant.—Elena Kuhn.
Press Assistant.—Christina Wilkes.

DEMOCRATIC LEADER'S FLOOR OFFICE

H–204 The Capitol, phone 225–0100

Director of Floor Operations.—Jerry Hartz.

OFFICE OF THE DEMOCRATIC WHIP

H–148 The Capitol, phone 225–3130, fax 226–0663

Democratic Whip.—Steny H. Hoyer.
Chief of Staff.—Alexis Covey-Brandt.
Deputy Chief of Staff.—Brian Romick.
Director of Legislative Operations.—Shuwanza Goff.
Deputy Floor Director.—Danielle Aviles.
Floor Assistant.—Ray Salazar.
Director of Member Services.—Courtney Fry.
Deputy Director of Member Services and Outreach Advisor.—Claudia Urrabazo.
Communications Director.—Katie Grant.
Press Secretary.—Mariel Saez.
Press and Research Assistant.—Margaret Mulkerrin.
Speechwriter.—Adam Weissmann.
Policy Director.—Tom Mahr.
Senior Policy Advisors: Keith Abouchar, Trent Bauserman, James Leuschen, Char MacDonald, Daniel Silverberg.
Office Manager/Executive Assistant.—Deborah Rowe.
Director of Scheduling and Special Events.—Jordan Sugar-Carlsgaard.
Special Assistant.—Joseph Cortina.
Digital Director and Policy Advisor.—Steve Dwyer.
Staff Assistants: Jake Bayer, Sara Margolis.

OFFICE OF THE ASSISTANT DEMOCRATIC LEADER

132 The Capitol, phone 226–3210

http://assistantdemocraticleader.house.gov

Assistant Democratic Leader.—James E. Clyburn.
Chief of Staff.—Yelberton R. Watkins.
Director of Policy.—Ashli Palmer.
Communications Director.—Patrick Devlin.
Senior Advisor.—Amy Miller Pfeiffer.
Legislative Director and Counsel.—Craig Link.
Special Assistant to the Assistant Democratic Leader.—Tamika Day.

OFFICE OF THE CLERK

H–154 The Capitol, phone 225–7000

KAREN L. HAAS, Clerk of the House of Representatives; Karen Lehman Haas, a native of Catonsville, MD, was sworn in as Clerk of the House of Representatives on January 5, 2011. She is the 34th individual to serve as Clerk. This is Ms. Haas' second occupancy of this position—in 2005, Speaker J. Dennis Hastert appointed Ms. Haas as Clerk of the U.S. House of Representatives. As Clerk, Ms. Haas plays a central role in the daily operations and legislative activities of the House. Ms. Haas began her service on Capitol Hill in 1984, when she worked for then-Minority Leader Robert H. Michel. For nearly 11 years, she served as his Executive Legislative Assistant. Following a brief leave to work in the private sector, Ms. Haas returned to Capitol Hill in June 1999 to serve as Floor Assistant to Speaker Hastert. Following her first term as Clerk, she served as Executive Director of the House Republican Conference and Minority Staff Director for the House Small Business Committee. Ms. Haas attended public schools in Maryland and received a bachelor's degree from the University of Maryland, College Park, with a major in political science and a minor in economics.

Clerk.—Karen L. Haas.
Deputy Clerk.—Robert F. Reeves.
Senior Advisor.—Marjorie ''Gigi'' Kelaher.
Chief of:
Legislative Computer Systems.—Scott Kim, 2401 RHOB, 225–1182.
Legislative Operations.—Frances Chiappardi, HT–13, 225–7925.
Legislative Resource Center.—Ronald Dale Thomas, 135 CHOB, 226–5200.
Art and Archives.—Farar Elliott, 5140 OFOB, 226–1300.
Communications.—Catherine Cooke, 5120 OFOB, 225–1908.
House Employment Counsel.—Gloria Lett, 4300 OFOB, 225–7075.
Official Reporter.—Melinda Walker, HT–59, The Capitol, 225–5621.

CHIEF ADMINISTRATIVE OFFICER

HB–28 The Capitol, phone 225–5555

PHILIP G. KIKO, Chief Administrative Officer of the House of Representatives, is a native of Canton, Ohio, was nominated by Speaker Paul Ryan, and elected to serve as the Chief Administrative Officer effective August 1, 2016. As CAO, Mr. Kiko is responsible for the information technology, financial, logistical, human resources, and procurement services provided to Members of the U.S. House and their staff. Mr. Kiko began his service on Capitol Hill with Representative Jim Sensenbrenner (WI-5) as Legislative Director and later served as his Chief of Staff. Mr. Kiko has also worked in the Executive Branch at the Department of Education's Office for Civil Rights and at the Department of Interior's Office of Legislative Affairs, Office of Budget and Program Resources Management, and Office of Hearings and Appeals. In 1995, he returned to Capitol Hill as Associate Administrator of Procurement and Purchasing at the newly formed CAO. Mr. Kiko was called again to serve then-Chairman Jim Sensenbrenner as Deputy Staff Director for the House Committee on Science and then as General Counsel and Chief of Staff for the House Committee on the Judiciary. He has also served as Staff Director and General Counsel of the Committee on House Administration and the House Select Committee on Benghazi.

In addition to his extensive Capitol Hill experience, Mr. Kiko served as ''Of Counsel'' at the Washington, DC law firm Foley & Lardner, LLC and Vice Chairman of the Smith-Free Group. He is a graduate of Mount Union College in Alliance, Ohio and George Mason University School of Law. Mr. Kiko is a Member of the D.C. Bar, the Virginia State Bar, and the United States Court of Appeals for both the Federal Circuit and the D.C. circuit.

Chief Administrative Officer.—Philip Kiko.
Deputy Chief Administrative Officer.—John Clocker, HB-28, The Capitol.
Chief of Staff.—Anne Binsted, HB-28, The Capitol.
Chief Financial Officer.—Traci Beaubian, 3140, OHOB.
Chief Human Resources Officer.—John Salamone, H2–102, FHOB.
Chief Information Officer.—Catherine Szpindor, H2–631, FHOB.
Chief Logistics Officer.—Tom Coyne, WA–34, RHOB.
Chief Procurement Officer.—Lisa Grant, 5110, OHOB.
Administrative Counsel.—Christopher Brewster, H2–217, FHOB.

CHAPLAIN

HB–25 The Capitol, phone 225–2509, fax 226–4928

PATRICK J. CONROY, S.J., Chaplain, House of Representatives, residence, Portland, OR; a Jesuit of the Oregon Province of the Society of Jesus, graduated from Claremont McKenna College in CA in 1972, attended Gonzaga University Law School for one year before entering the Jesuit Order in 1973. Earned an M.A. in philosophy from Gonzaga University, a J.D. from St. Louis University, an M.Div. from the Jesuit School of Theology at Berkeley (CA), and an STM from Regis College of the University of Toronto in missiology. Practiced law for the Colville Confederated Tribes in Omak, WA, and the U.S. Conference of Catholic Bishops, representing Salvadoran refugees in San Francisco. Ordained a priest in 1983. From 1984 to 1989, pastored four villages on the Colville and Spokane Indian Reservations. Worked for the national Jesuit Office of Social Ministries in Washington, DC, then began a career of university chaplaincy at Georgetown University and Seattle University. In 2003 transferred to Jesuit High School in Portland, OR, to teach freshman theology and coach the mighty JV II girls' softball team. Also served as the Oregon Province's Provincial Assistant for Formation and as superior of the Jesuit community at Jesuit High School in Portland. Sworn in as 60th House Chaplain on May 25, 2011.

Chaplain of the House.—Patrick J. Conroy, S.J.
  Assistant to the Chaplain/Liaison to Staff.—Karen Bronson.

OFFICE OF THE HOUSE HISTORIAN

5150 O'Neill Office Building, phone 226–1300

http://history.house.gov; history@mail.house.gov; @UShousehistory

House Historian.—Matthew Wasniewski.
  Associate Historian.—Ken Kato.
  Director—Office of House Historian Staff.—Erin M. Hromada.
  Manager of Oral History.—Kathleen Johnson.

OFFICE OF INTERPARLIAMENTARY AFFAIRS

HC–4 Capitol, phone 226–1766

Director.—Janice Robinson.
  Assistant Director.—Vacant.

OFFICE OF ATTENDING PHYSICIAN

H–166 The Capitol, phone 225–5421

(After office hours, call Capitol Operator 224–2145)

Attending Physician.—Dr. Brian P. Monahan.
  Chief of Staff.—Keith Pray.

OFFICE OF INSPECTOR GENERAL

H2–386 Ford House Office Building, phone 226–1250

Inspector General.—Michael T. Ptasienski.
  Deputy Inspector General, Advisory and Administrative Services.—Vacant.
  Deputy Inspector General, Audit and Investigative Services.—Debbie B. Hunter.
  Director of Support Services.—R. Terry Upshur.
  Assistant Director, Finance and Administration.—Susan Kozubski.
  Assistant Director, Technology and Quality Assurance.—Steven Johnson.
  Administrative Assistant.—Deborah E. Jones.
  Director, Performance and Financial Audits, and Investigative Services.—Susan Simpson.
  Assistant Director, Performance Audits and Investigative Services.—Julie Poole.
  Assistant Director, Performance and Financial Audits.—Christen Stevenson.

Auditors: Ronnette Bailey, Nicole Loutsenhizer, Alexander Stewart.
Director, Information Systems Audits.—Gregory Roberts.
Assistant Directors, Information Systems Audits: Michael Howard, Clifton Persaud.
Auditors: Emmanuel Akowuah, Keith Sullenberger.
Director, Management and Advisory Services.—Joseph C. Picolla.
Assistant Directors: Saad Patel, Donna Wolfgang.
Management Analysts: Kevin Cornell, Terry Leahy, David DeMarco.

OFFICE OF THE LAW REVISION COUNSEL

H2–308 Ford House Office Building, 20515–6711, phone 226–2411, fax 225–0010

Law Revision Counsel.—Ralph V. Seep.
Deputy Counsel.—Robert M. Sukol.
Senior Counsels: Brian Lindsey, Kenneth I. Paretzky, John F. Wagner, Jr.
Assistant Counsels: Joseph Cohen, Michelle Evans, Katrina M. Hall, Katherine L. Lane, Deborah Letz, Edward T. Mulligan, Michele K. Skarvelis, Lindsey Skouras.
Staff Assistants: Sylvia Tahirkheli, Monica Thompson.
Printing Editor.—Robert E. Belcher.
Senior Systems Engineer.—Eric Loach.
Systems Engineer.—Kenneth Thomas.

OFFICE OF THE LEGISLATIVE COUNSEL

H2–337 Ford House Office Building, phone 225–6060

Legislative Counsel.—Ernest Wade Ballou, Jr.
Deputy Legislative Counsel.—Sherry L. Chriss.
Senior Counsels: Douglass Bellis, Paul Callen, Lisa Daly, Susan Fleishman, Rosemary Gallagher, Edward Grossman, James Grossman, Curt Haensel, Jean Harmann, Gregory M. Kostka, Hank Savage, Mark Synnes, Robert Weinhagen, Noah Wofsy.
Counsels: Marshall Barksdale, Hallet Brazelton, Warren Burke, Thomas Cassidy, Megan Chasnoff, Henry Christrup, Jesse Cross, Thomas Dillon, Mathew Eckstein, Justin Gross, Alison Hartwich, Kakuti Lin, Christopher Osborne, Scott Probst, Hadley Ross, Anthony Sciascia, Jessica Shapiro, Anna Shpak, Michelle Vanek, Sally Walker, Brady Young.
Assistant Counsels: Karen Anderson, Lisa Castillo, Kenneth Cox, Kimberly Faith, Brendan Gallagher, Lucy Wolfe Goss, Stephen Hagenbuch, Karl Hagnauer, Fiona Heckscher, Kalyani Parthasarathy, Veena Srinivasa, Kathryn Swiss.
Office Administrator.—Nancy McNeillie.
Assistant Office Administrator.—Debra Birch.
Director, Information Systems.—Willie Blount.
Senior Systems Analyst.—Peter Szwec.
Systems Administrator.—David Topper.
Publications Coordinator.—Craig Sterkx.
Office Managerial Assistant.—Ashley Anderson.
Staff Assistants/Paralegals: Elonda Blount, Kelly Meryweather, Tom Meryweather.
Staff Assistants: Joseph Birch, Tomas Contreras, Miekl Joyner, Matthew Loggie, Angelina Plater.

OFFICE OF THE PARLIAMENTARIAN

H–209 The Capitol, phone 225–7373

Parliamentarian.—Thomas J. Wickham, Jr.
Deputy Parliamentarian.—Ethan B. Lauer.
Assistant Parliamentarians: Julia C. Cook, Anne D. Gooch, Kyle T. Jones, Jason A. Smith.
Clerk to the Parliamentarian.—Lloyd A. Jenkins.
Assistant Clerk to the Parliamentarian.—Kristen B. Donahue.
Precedent Consultant.—Charles W. Johnson III.
Precedent Editors: Catherine A. Moran, Andrew S. Neal, Max A. Spitzer.
Information Technology Manager.—Bryan J. Feldblum.

OFFICE OF THE SERGEANT AT ARMS

H–124 The Capitol, phone 225–2456

PAUL D. IRVING, was sworn in as the 36th Sergeant at Arms of the U.S. House of Representatives on January 17, 2012, during the 2nd session of the 112th Congress. Prior to serving as Sergeant at Arms, Mr. Irving was an Assistant Director of the U.S. Secret Service from 2001 to 2008. Paul Irving was born August 21, 1957, in Tampa, Florida. He received a Bachelor of Science degree in Justice from American University in Washington, DC, and a Juris Doctorate from Whittier Law School in Los Angeles, California. He began his law enforcement career in 1980 as a clerk for the Federal Bureau of Investigation in Los Angeles, California; was appointed a Special Agent at the Secret Service's Los Angeles Field Office; was transferred to Washington, DC, where he served as the head legal instructor for constitutional law, statutory authority, and criminal procedure at the Secret Service Training Academy; and was assigned to the Presidential Protective Division at the White House during the administrations of George H.W. Bush and William Jefferson Clinton, where he rose to a supervisory position. Subsequent to his White House duty, Mr. Irving served as Deputy Assistant Director for Congressional Affairs, Assistant Director for Government and Public Affairs, Assistant Director for Homeland Security, and Assistant Director for Administration.

Mr. Irving is the recipient of numerous awards and commendations during his distinguished law enforcement career, among them the Senior Executive Service Presidential Rank Award for Meritorious Service, and the Presidential Rank Award for Distinguished Service in the Senior Executive Service; he has been a member of the California State Bar since 1982, the U.S. District Court for the Central District of California, the U.S. Court of Appeals for the Ninth Circuit, the District of Columbia Bar, and the Supreme Court Bar; Irving resides in Washington, DC.

Sergeant at Arms.—Paul D. Irving.
Deputy Sergeant at Arms.—Tim Blodgett.
Assistant Sergeant at Arms, Administration.—Kathleen Joyce.
Assistant Sergeant at Arms, Protocol and Chamber Operations.—Ted Daniel.
Assistants to the Sergeant at Arms, Floor Security: Joyce Hamlett, Rick Villa.
Assistant Sergeant at Arms, Emergency Management.—Bob Dohr.
Deputy Assistant Sergeant at Arms, Police Services.—Robert Fitzpatrick.
Chief Information Officer.—Jim Kaelin.
Directors:
Division of Garage and Parking Security.—Jim Abbott.
Division of House Security.—William McFarland.
Division of Identification Services.—Jack Looney.
Managers:
Appointments Desk.—Teresa Johnson.
Chamber Support Services.—Andrew Burns.
Assistants: LaKeisha Commodore, Lorraine Foreman, KaSandra Greenhow, Melissa Moffitt.

JOINT COMMITTEES

Joint Economic Committee

G01 Dirksen Senate Office Building, 20510–6432, phone 224–5171

[Created pursuant to sec. 5(a) of Public Law 304, 79th Congress]

Erik Paulsen, Representative from Minnesota, *Chair*
Mike Lee, Senator from Utah, *Vice Chair*

HOUSE

David Schweikert, of Arizona.
Barbara Comstock, of Virginia.
Darin LaHood, of Illinois.
Francis Rooney, of Florida.
Karen C. Handel, of Georgia.

Carolyn B. Maloney, of New York.
John K. Delaney, of Maryland.
Alma S. Adams, of North Carolina.
Donald S. Beyer, Jr., of Virginia.

SENATE

Tom Cotton, of Arkansas.
Ben Sasse, of Nebraska.
Rob Portman, of Ohio.
Ted Cruz, of Texas.
Bill Cassidy, of Louisiana.

Martin Heinrich, of New Mexico.
Amy Klobuchar, of Minnesota.
Gary C. Peters, of Michigan.
Margaret Wood Hassan, of New Hampshire.

STAFF

Joint Economic Committee (G–01), 224–5171, fax 224–0240.
Republican Staff:
Executive Director.—Colin Brainard.
Chief Economist.—Theodore Boll.
Senior Economists: Gavin Ekins, Russell Rhine, Alexander Schibuola.
Economist.—Beila Laboueuf, A. J. McKeown.
Senior Advisor.—Doug Branch.
Policy Advisor.—Brooks Keefer.
Policy Analyst.—Matt Kaido.
Chief Counsel.—Karin Hope.
Communications Director.—J.P. Freire.
Financial Director.—Colleen Healy.
System Administrator.—Barry Dexter.
Executive Assistant.—Connie Foster.
Office of the Vice Chair, Republican Staff:
Project Director.—Scott Winship.
Deputy Project Director.—Justus Myers.
Senior Economist.—Christina King.
Senior Policy Advisor.—Rachel Sheffield.
Digital Media Specialist.—Matthew Nolan.
Digital Director.—Ruben Verastigui.
Democratic Staff:
Staff Director.—Kim Corbin.
Senior Policy Advisors: Ryan Ehly, Paul Lapointe, Jim Whitney.
Senior Policy Analyst.—Gerardo Bonilla.
Economists: Ricky Gandhi, Owen Haaga.
Policy Advisor.—Gabrielle Elul.

Policy Analysts: Alice Lin, Rohan Shetty.
Senior Counsel.—Ernesto Rodriguez.
Research Assistant.—Natalie George.
Communications Director.—Latoya Veal.
Deputy Press Secretary.—Victoria Park.
Digital Press Secretary.—Morgan Butler.

Joint Committee on the Library of Congress

1309 Longworth House Office Building, 20510, phone 225–8281

Gregg Harper, Representative from Mississippi, *Chair*

Roy Blunt, Senator from Missouri, *Vice Chair*

HOUSE

Kevin Yoder, of Kansas.
Barry Loudermilk, of Georgia.
Robert A. Brady, of Pennsylvania.
Zoe Lofgren, of California.

SENATE

Pat Roberts, of Kansas.
Richard C. Shelby, of Alabama.
Amy Klobuchar, of Minnesota.
Patrick J. Leahy, of Vermont.

STAFF

Staff Director.—Sean Moran.
Deputy Clerk.—Rob Taggart.
Counsel.—Khalil Abboud.
Professional Staff.—Matt McGowan.

Joint Committee on Printing

305 Russell Senate Office Building, 20510, phone 224–6352

[Created by act of August 3, 1846 (9 Stat. 114); U.S. Code 44, Section 101]

Roy Blunt, Senator from Missouri, *Chair*

Rodney Davis, Representative from Illinois, *Vice Chair*

SENATE

Pat Roberts, of Kansas.
Roger F. Wicker, of Mississippi.
Amy Klobuchar, of Minnesota.
Tom Udall, of New Mexico.

HOUSE

Gregg Harper, of Mississippi.
Mark Walker, of North Carolina.
Robert A. Brady, of Pennsylvania.
Jamie Raskin, of Maryland.

Joint Committee on Taxation

H2–502 Ford House Office Building, 20515, phone 225–3621
fax 225–0832, http://www.jct.gov

SD–G18, Senate Dirksen Office Building, 20510, phone 224–5561
fax 224–1785, http://www.jct.gov

[Created by Public Law 20, 69th Congress]

Orrin G. Hatch, Senator from Utah, *Chair*
Kevin Brady, Representative from Texas, *Vice Chair*

SENATE

Chuck Grassley, of Iowa.
Mike Crapo, of Idaho.
Ron Wyden, of Oregon.
Debbie Stabenow, of Michigan.

HOUSE

Sam Johnson, of Texas.
Devin Nunes, of California.
Richard E. Neal, of Massachusetts.
John Lewis, of Georgia.

NON-DESIGNATED STAFF

Joint Committee on Taxation (H2–502 FHOB), 225–3621.

Chief of Staff.—Thomas Barthold, H2–502 FHOB, 225–3621.

Deputy Chiefs of Staff: Robert Harvey, 596 FHOB, 226–7575; David Lenter, H2–502 FHOB, 225–3621.

Office Administrator.—Pamela Williams, H2–502 FHOB, 225–3621.

Administrative Specialist.—Frank Shima, H2–502 FHOB, 225–3621.

Senior Legislation Counsels: Gordon Clay, SD G–18, 224–5561; Harold Hirsch, H2–502 FHOB, 225–7377; Deirdre James, H2–502 FHOB, 225–7377; Patricia McDermott, H2–502 FHOB, 225–7377; Cecily Rock, H2–502 FHOB, 225–7377; Kashi Way, SD G–18, 224–5561.

Legislation Counsels: Jeffrey Arbeit, H2–502 FHOB, 225–7377; Nita Asher, H2–502 FHOB, 225–7377; Adam Gropper, SD G–18, 224–5561; Andrew Grossman, H2–502 FHOB, 225–7377; Viva Hammer, H2–502 FHOB, 225–7377; Paul McLaughlin, H2–502 FHOB, 225–7377; Veena Murthy, H2–502 FHOB, 225–7377; Kristine Roth, SD G–18, 224–5561.

Senior Refund Counsel.—Norman Brand, 1111 (IRS), 317–4463.

Refund Counsels: Chase Gibson, 1111 (IRS), 317–4463; Robert Gotwald, 1111 (IRS), 317–4463.

Senior Economist.—Nicholas Bull, 596 FHOB, 226–7575; James Cilke, 596 FHOB, 226–7575; Tim Dowd, 596 FHOB, 226–7575; Chris Giosa, 596 FHOB, 226–7575; Thomas Holtmann, 596 FHOB, 226–7575; Pamela Moomau, 596 FHOB, 226–7575; Christopher Overend, 596 FHOB, 226–7575; Brent Trigg, 596 FHOB, 226–7575.

Economist.—Paul Chen, H2–502 FHOB, 225–7377; Sally Kwak, SD G–18, 224–5561; Paul Landefeld, 596 FHOB, 226–7575; Joseph LeCates, 596 FHOB, 226–7575; Bert Lue, H2–502 FHOB, 226–7377; Kathleen T. Mackie, 596 FHOB, 226–7575; James McGuire, 596 FHOB, 226–7575; Rachel Moore, 596 FHOB, 226–7575; Brandon Pecoraro, 596 FHOB, 226–7575; Zachary Richards, 596 FHOB, 226–7575; Karl Russo, H2–502 FHOB, 225–7377; Heidi Schramm, 596 FHOB, 226–7575; David Splinter, 596 FHOB, 226–7575; Lori Stuntz, 596 FHOB, 226–7575.

Chief Statistical Analyst.—Melani Houser, 596 FHOB, 226–7575.

Statistical Analyst.—Tanya Butler, 596 FHOB, 226–7575.

Legislation Tax Accountants: Heather Harman, H2–502 FHOB, 225–7377; Natalie Tucker, H2–502 FHOB, 225–7377.

Director of Information Technology.—Damion Jedlicka, 596 FHOB, 226–7575.

Information Technology Specialists: Mark High, 596 FHOB, 226–7575; Merrick Munday, 596 FHOB, 226–7575; Jonathan Newton, 596 FHOB, 226–7575; Dennis Ortega, 596 FHOB, 226–7575.

Executive Assistants: Jean Best, H2–502 FHOB, 225–7377; Jayne Northern, SD G–18, 224–5561; Lucia Rogers, 596 FHOB, 226–7575; Sharon Watts, 1111 (IRS), 317–4463.
Document Production Specialist.—Chris Simmons, H2–502 FHOB, 225–7377.
Economic Research Assistants: Lucas Goodman, H2–502 FHOB, 225–7377; Nicholas Guttmann, H2–FHOB, 225–7377.
Senior Staff Assistant.—Debra McMullen, H2–502 FHOB, 225–7377.
Staff Assistants: Neval McMullen, H2–502 FHOB, 225–7377; Kristine Means, H2–502 FHOB, 225–7377.
Tax Resource Specialist.—Melissa O'Brien, SD G–18, 224–0494.

Joint Select Committee on Budget and Appropriations Process Reform

Longworth House Office Building, 20515, phone 226–7270 (Majority), 225–3481 (Minority)

https://budgetappropriationsprocessreform.house.gov

Steve Womack, Representative from Arkansas, *Co-Chair*

Nita M. Lowey, Representative from New York, *Co-Chair*

HOUSE

Pete Sessions, of Texas.
Rob Woodall, of Georgia.
Jodey C. Arrington, of Texas.
John A. Yarmuth, of Kentucky.
Lucille Roybal-Allard, of California.
Derek Kilmer, of Washington.

SENATE

Roy Blunt, of Missouri.
David Perdue, of Georgia.
James Lankford, of Oklahoma.
Joni Ernst, of Iowa.
Sheldon Whitehouse, of Rhode Island.
Michael F. Bennet, of Colorado.
Brian Schatz, of Hawaii.
Mazie K. Hirono, of Hawaii.

STAFF

Joint Select Committee on Budget and Appropriations Process Reform (B–234 LHOB), 226–7270.
Republican Staff:
Staff Director.—Dan Keniry.
Democratic Staff (1016 LHOB), 225–3481:
Counsel to Co-Chair Lowey.—David Reich.

Joint Select Committee on Solvency of Multiemployer Pension Plans

219 Dirksen Senate Office Building, 20510, phone 224–4515

Orrin G. Hatch, Senator from Utah, *Co-Chair*

Sherrod Brown, Senator from Ohio, *Co-Chair*

SENATE

Lamar Alexander, of Tennessee.
Rob Portman, of Ohio.
Mike Crapo, of Idaho.
Joe Manchin III, of West Virginia.
Heidi Heitkamp, of North Dakota.
Tina Smith, of Minnesota.

HOUSE

Virginia Foxx, of North Carolina.
David P. Roe, of Tennessee.
Vern Buchanan, of Florida.
David Schweikert, of Arizona.

Richard E. Neal, of Massachusetts.
Robert C. ''Bobby'' Scott, of Virginia.
Donald Norcross, of New Jersey.
Debbie Dingell, of Michigan.

ASSIGNMENTS OF SENATORS TO COMMITTEES

[Republicans in roman (51); Democrats in *italic* (47); Independents in SMALL CAPS (2); total, 100]

Senator	Committees (Standing, Joint, Select, and Special)
Alexander	Health, Education, Labor, and Pensions, *chair*. Appropriations. Energy and Natural Resources. Rules and Administration.
Baldwin	Appropriations. Commerce, Science, and Transportation. Health, Education, Labor, and Pensions.
Barrasso	Environment and Public Works, *chair*. Energy and Natural Resources. Foreign Relations. Indian Affairs.
Bennet	Agriculture, Nutrition, and Forestry. Finance. Health, Education, Labor, and Pensions.
Blumenthal	Armed Services. Commerce, Science, and Transportation. Judiciary. Veterans' Affairs. Special Committee on Aging.
Blunt	Rules and Administration, *chair*. Joint Committee on Printing, *chair*. Joint Committee on the Library, *vice chair*. Appropriations. Commerce, Science, and Transportation. Select Committee on Intelligence.
Booker	Environment and Public Works. Foreign Relations. Judiciary. Small Business and Entrepreneurship.
Boozman	Agriculture, Nutrition, and Forestry. Appropriations. Budget. Environment and Public Works. Veterans' Affairs.
Brown	Agriculture, Nutrition, and Forestry. Banking, Housing, and Urban Affairs. Finance. Veterans' Affairs.
Burr	Select Committee on Intelligence, *chair*. Finance. Health, Education, Labor, and Pensions. Special Committee on Aging.
Cantwell	Commerce, Science, and Transportation. Energy and Natural Resources. Finance. Indian Affairs. Small Business and Entrepreneurship.

Senator	Committees (Standing, Joint, Select, and Special)
Capito	Appropriations. Commerce, Science, and Transportation. Energy and Natural Resources. Environment and Public Works. Rules and Administration.
Cardin	Environment and Public Works. Finance. Foreign Relations. Small Business and Entrepreneurship.
Carper	Environment and Public Works. Finance. Homeland Security and Governmental Affairs.
Casey	Agriculture, Nutrition, and Forestry. Finance. Health, Education, Labor, and Pensions. Special Committee on Aging.
Cassidy	Energy and Natural Resources. Finance. Health, Education, Labor, and Pensions. Veterans' Affairs. Joint Economic Committee.
Collins	Special Committee on Aging, *chair.* Appropriations. Health, Education, Labor, and Pensions. Select Committee on Intelligence.
Coons	Select Committee on Ethics, *vice chair.* Appropriations. Foreign Relations. Judiciary. Small Business and Entrepreneurship.
Corker	Foreign Relations, *chair.* Banking, Housing, and Urban Affairs. Budget. Special Committee on Aging.
Cornyn	Finance. Judiciary. Select Committee on Intelligence.
Cortez Masto	Banking, Housing, and Urban Affairs. Commerce, Science, and Transportation. Energy and Natural Resources. Indian Affairs. Rules and Administration. Special Committee on Aging.
Cotton	Armed Services. Banking, Housing, and Urban Affairs. Budget. Joint Economic Committee. Select Committee on Intelligence.
Crapo	Banking, Housing, and Urban Affairs, *chair.* Budget. Finance. Indian Affairs. Judiciary. Joint Committee on Taxation.

Senator	Committees (Standing, Joint, Select, and Special)
Cruz	Armed Services. Commerce, Science, and Transportation. Judiciary. Rules and Administration. Joint Economic Committee.
Daines	Agriculture, Nutrition, and Forestry. Appropriations. Energy and Natural Resources. Homeland Security and Governmental Affairs. Indian Affairs.
Donnelly	Agriculture, Nutrition, and Forestry. Armed Services. Banking, Housing, and Urban Affairs. Special Committee on Aging.
Duckworth	Commerce, Science, and Transportation. Energy and Natural Resources. Environment and Public Works. Small Business and Entrepreneurship.
Durbin	Appropriations. Judiciary. Rules and Administration.
Enzi	Budget, *chair*. Finance. Health, Education, Labor, and Pensions. Homeland Security and Governmental Affairs. Small Business and Entrepreneurship.
Ernst	Agriculture, Nutrition, and Forestry. Armed Services. Environment and Public Works. Small Business and Entrepreneurship.
Feinstein	Appropriations. Judiciary. Rules and Administration. Select Committee on Intelligence.
Fischer	Agriculture, Nutrition, and Forestry. Armed Services. Commerce, Science, and Transportation. Environment and Public Works. Rules and Administration. Special Committee on Aging.
Flake	Energy and Natural Resources. Foreign Relations. Judiciary. Special Committee on Aging.
Gardner	Budget. Commerce, Science, and Transportation. Energy and Natural Resources. Foreign Relations.
Gillibrand	Agriculture, Nutrition, and Forestry. Armed Services. Environment and Public Works. Special Committee on Aging.
Graham	Appropriations. Armed Services. Budget. Judiciary.

Senator	Committees (Standing, Joint, Select, and Special)
Grassley	Judiciary, *chair.* Agriculture, Nutrition, and Forestry. Budget. Finance. Joint Committee on Taxation.
Harris	Budget. Homeland Security and Governmental Affairs. Judiciary. Select Committee on Intelligence.
Hassan	Commerce, Science, and Transportation. Health, Education, Labor, and Pensions. Homeland Security and Governmental Affairs. Joint Economic Committee.
Hatch	Finance, *chair.* Joint Committee on Taxation, *chair.* Health, Education, Labor, and Pensions. Judiciary. Special Committee on Aging.
Heinrich	Armed Services. Energy and Natural Resources. Joint Economic Committee. Select Committee on Intelligence.
Heitkamp	Agriculture, Nutrition, and Forestry. Banking, Housing, and Urban Affairs. Homeland Security and Governmental Affairs. Indian Affairs. Small Business and Entrepreneurship.
Heller	Banking, Housing, and Urban Affairs. Commerce, Science, and Transportation. Finance. Veterans' Affairs.
Hirono	Armed Services. Energy and Natural Resources. Judiciary. Small Business and Entrepreneurship. Veterans' Affairs.
Hoeven	Indian Affairs, *chair.* Agriculture, Nutrition, and Forestry. Appropriations. Energy and Natural Resources. Homeland Security and Governmental Affairs.
Hyde-Smith	Agriculture, Nutrition, and Forestry. Appropriations. Rules and Administration.
Inhofe	Armed Services. Commerce, Science, and Transportation. Environment and Public Works. Small Business and Entrepreneurship.
Isakson	Veterans' Affairs, *chair.* Select Committee on Ethics, *chair.* Finance. Foreign Relations. Health, Education, Labor, and Pensions.
Johnson	Homeland Security and Governmental Affairs, *chair.* Budget. Commerce, Science, and Transportation. Foreign Relations.

Senator	Committees (Standing, Joint, Select, and Special)
Jones	Banking, Housing, and Urban Affairs. Health, Education, Labor, and Pensions. Homeland Security and Governmental Affairs. Special Committee on Aging.
Kaine	Armed Services. Budget. Foreign Relations. Health, Education, Labor, and Pensions.
Kennedy	Appropriations. Banking, Housing, and Urban Affairs. Budget. Judiciary. Small Business and Entrepreneurship.
KING	Armed Services. Budget. Energy and Natural Resources. Rules and Administration. Select Committee on Intelligence.
Klobuchar	Agriculture, Nutrition, and Forestry. Commerce, Science, and Transportation. Judiciary. Rules and Administration. Joint Committee on the Library. Joint Committee on Printing. Joint Economic Committee.
Lankford	Appropriations. Homeland Security and Governmental Affairs. Indian Affairs. Select Committee on Intelligence.
Leahy	Agriculture, Nutrition, and Forestry. Appropriations. Judiciary. Rules and Administration. Joint Committee on the Library.
Lee	Joint Economic Committee, *vice chair.* Commerce, Science, and Transportation. Energy and Natural Resources. Judiciary.
Manchin	Appropriations. Energy and Natural Resources. Veterans' Affairs. Select Committee on Intelligence.
Markey	Commerce, Science, and Transportation. Environment and Public Works. Foreign Relations. Small Business and Entrepreneurship.
McCain	Armed Services, *chair.* Homeland Security and Governmental Affairs. Indian Affairs. Select Committee on Intelligence.
McCaskill	Armed Services. Finance. Homeland Security and Governmental Affairs.
McConnell	Agriculture, Nutrition, and Forestry. Appropriations. Rules and Administration.

Senator	Committees (Standing, Joint, Select, and Special)
	Select Committee on Intelligence.
Menendez	Banking, Housing, and Urban Affairs. Finance. Foreign Relations.
Merkley	Appropriations. Budget. Environment and Public Works. Foreign Relations.
Moran	Appropriations. Banking, Housing, and Urban Affairs. Commerce, Science, and Transportation. Environment and Public Works. Indian Affairs. Veterans' Affairs.
Murkowski	Energy and Natural Resources, *chair.* Appropriations. Health, Education, Labor, and Pensions. Indian Affairs.
Murphy	Appropriations. Foreign Relations. Health, Education, Labor, and Pensions.
Murray	Appropriations. Budget. Health, Education, Labor, and Pensions. Veterans' Affairs.
Nelson	Armed Services. Commerce, Science, and Transportation. Finance. Special Committee on Aging.
Paul	Foreign Relations. Health, Education, Labor, and Pensions. Homeland Security and Governmental Affairs. Small Business and Entrepreneurship.
Perdue	Agriculture, Nutrition, and Forestry. Armed Services. Banking, Housing, and Urban Affairs. Budget.
Peters	Armed Services. Commerce, Science, and Transportation. Homeland Security and Governmental Affairs. Joint Economic Committee.
Portman	Energy and Natural Resources. Finance. Foreign Relations. Homeland Security and Governmental Affairs. Joint Economic Committee.
Reed	Appropriations. Armed Services. Banking, Housing, and Urban Affairs. Select Committee on Intelligence.
Risch	Small Business and Entrepreneurship, *chair.* Energy and Natural Resources. Foreign Relations. Select Committee on Ethics. Select Committee on Intelligence.
Roberts	Agriculture, Nutrition, and Forestry, *chair.*

Senator	Committees (Standing, Joint, Select, and Special)
	Finance. Health, Education, Labor, and Pensions. Rules and Administration. Joint Committee on the Library. Joint Committee on Printing. Select Committee on Ethics.
Rounds	Armed Services. Banking, Housing, and Urban Affairs. Environment and Public Works. Small Business and Entrepreneurship. Veterans' Affairs.
Rubio	Appropriations. Foreign Relations. Small Business and Entrepreneurship. Select Committee on Intelligence. Special Committee on Aging.
SANDERS	Budget. Energy and Natural Resources. Environment and Public Works. Health, Education, Labor, and Pensions. Veterans' Affairs.
Sasse	Armed Services. Banking, Housing, and Urban Affairs. Judiciary. Joint Economic Committee.
Schatz	Appropriations. Banking, Housing, and Urban Affairs. Commerce, Science, and Transportation. Indian Affairs. Select Committee on Ethics.
Schumer	Rules and Administration. Select Committee on Intelligence.
Scott	Armed Services. Banking, Housing, and Urban Affairs. Finance. Health, Education, Labor, and Pensions. Small Business and Entrepreneurship. Special Committee on Aging.
Shaheen	Appropriations. Armed Services. Foreign Relations. Small Business and Entrepreneurship. Select Committee on Ethics.
Shelby	Appropriations, *chair*. Banking, Housing, and Urban Affairs. Environment and Public Works. Rules and Administration. Joint Committee on the Library.
Smith	Agriculture, Nutrition, and Forestry. Energy and Natural Resources. Health, Education, Labor, and Pensions. Indian Affairs.
Stabenow	Agriculture, Nutrition, and Forestry. Budget. Energy and Natural Resources.

Senator	Committees (Standing, Joint, Select, and Special)
	Finance. Joint Committee on Taxation.
Sullivan	Armed Services. Commerce, Science, and Transportation. Environment and Public Works. Veterans' Affairs.
Tester	Appropriations. Banking, Housing, and Urban Affairs. Commerce, Science, and Transportation. Indian Affairs. Veterans' Affairs.
Thune	Commerce, Science, and Transportation, *chair.* Agriculture, Nutrition, and Forestry. Finance.
Tillis	Armed Services. Banking, Housing, and Urban Affairs. Judiciary. Veterans' Affairs. Special Committee on Aging.
Toomey	Banking, Housing, and Urban Affairs. Budget. Finance.
Udall	Appropriations. Commerce, Science, and Transportation. Foreign Relations. Indian Affairs. Rules and Administration. Joint Committee on Printing.
Van Hollen	Appropriations. Banking, Housing, and Urban Affairs. Budget. Environment and Public Works.
Warner	Banking, Housing, and Urban Affairs. Budget. Finance. Rules and Administration. Select Committee on Intelligence.
Warren	Armed Services. Banking, Housing, and Urban Affairs. Health, Education, Labor, and Pensions. Special Committee on Aging.
Whitehouse	Budget. Environment and Public Works. Finance. Judiciary.
Wicker	Armed Services. Commerce, Science, and Transportation. Environment and Public Works. Rules and Administration. Joint Committee on Printing.
Wyden	Budget. Energy and Natural Resources. Finance.

Senator	Committees (Standing, Joint, Select, and Special)
	Joint Committee on Taxation. Select Committee on Intelligence.
Young	Commerce, Science, and Transportation. Foreign Relations. Health, Education, Labor, and Pensions. Small Business and Entrepreneurship.

ASSIGNMENTS OF REPRESENTATIVES, RESIDENT COMMISSIONER, AND DELEGATES TO COMMITTEES

[Republicans in roman (236); Democrats in *italic* (193); Vacancies (6); Resident Commissioner and Delegates in **boldface** (6); total, 441]

Representative	Committees (Standing, Joint, and Select)
Abraham	Agriculture. Armed Services. Science, Space, and Technology.
Adams	Agriculture. Education and the Workforce. Small Business. Joint Economic Committee.
Aderholt	Appropriations.
Aguilar	Appropriations.
Allen	Agriculture. Education and the Workforce.
Amash	Oversight and Government Reform.
Amodei	Appropriations.
Arrington	Agriculture. Budget. Veterans' Affairs.
Babin	Science, Space, and Technology. Transportation and Infrastructure.
Bacon	Agriculture. Armed Services. Homeland Security.
Banks, Jim, of Indiana	Armed Services. Education and the Workforce Veterans' Affairs.
Barletta	Education and the Workforce. Homeland Security. Transportation and Infrastructure.
Barr	Financial Services.
Barragán	Homeland Security. Natural Resources.
Barton	Energy and Commerce, *vice chair.*
Bass	Foreign Affairs. Judiciary.
Beatty	Financial Services.
Bera	Foreign Affairs. Science, Space, and Technology.
Bergman	Budget. Natural Resources. Veterans' Affairs.
Beyer	Natural Resources. Science, Space, and Technology. Joint Economic Committee.

Representative	Committees (Standing, Joint, and Select)
Biggs	Judiciary. Science, Space, and Technology.
Bilirakis	Veterans' Affairs, *vice chair.* Energy and Commerce.
Bishop, Mike, of Michigan	Ways and Means.
Bishop, Rob, of Utah	Natural Resources, *chair.* Armed Services.
Bishop, Sanford D., Jr., of Georgia	Appropriations.
Black	Budget. Ways and Means.
Blackburn	Energy and Commerce.
Blum	Oversight and Government Reform. Small Business.
Blumenauer	Ways and Means.
Blunt Rochester	Agriculture. Education and the Workforce.
Bonamici	Education and the Workforce. Science, Space, and Technology.
Bordallo	Armed Services. Natural Resources.
Bost	Agriculture. Transportation and Infrastructure. Veterans' Affairs.
Boyle, Brendan F., of Pennsylvania	Budget. Foreign Affairs.
Brady, Kevin, of Texas	Ways and Means, *chair.* Joint Committee on Taxation, *vice chair.*
Brady, Robert A., of Pennsylvania	Armed Services. House Administration. Joint Committee on the Library. Joint Committee on Printing.
Brat	Budget. Education and the Workforce. Small Business.
Brooks, Mo, of Alabama	Armed Services. Foreign Affairs. Science, Space, and Technology.
Brooks, Susan W., of Indiana	Ethics, *chair.* Energy and Commerce.
Brown, Anthony G., of Maryland	Armed Services. Ethics. Natural Resources.
Brownley, Julia, of California	Transportation and Infrastructure. Veterans' Affairs.
Buchanan	Ways and Means.
Buck	Judiciary. Rules.
Bucshon	Energy and Commerce.

Representative	Committees (Standing, Joint, and Select)
Budd	Financial Services.
Burgess	Energy and Commerce. Rules.
Bustos	Agriculture. Transportation and Infrastructure.
Butterfield	Energy and Commerce.
Byrne	Armed Services. Education and the Workforce. Rules.
Calvert	Appropriations.
Capuano	Financial Services. Transportation and Infrastructure.
Carbajal	Armed Services. Budget.
Cárdenas	Energy and Commerce.
Carson, André, of Indiana	Transportation and Infrastructure. Permanent Select Committee on Intelligence.
Carter, Earl L. ''Buddy'', of Georgia	Energy and Commerce.
Carter, John R., of Texas	Appropriations.
Cartwright	Appropriations. Oversight and Government Reform.
Castor, Kathy, of Florida	Energy and Commerce.
Castro, Joaquin, of Texas	Foreign Affairs. Permanent Select Committee on Intelligence.
Chabot	Small Business, *chair*. Foreign Affairs. Judiciary.
Cheney	Armed Services. Natural Resources. Rules.
Chu, Judy, of California	Small Business. Ways and Means.
Cicilline	Foreign Affairs. Judiciary.
Clark, Katherine M., of Massachusetts	Appropriations.
Clarke, Yvette D., of New York	Energy and Commerce. Ethics. Small Business.
Clay	Financial Services. Natural Resources. Oversight and Government Reform.
Cloud	Oversight and Government Reform. Science, Space, and Technology.
Cleaver	Financial Services.
Clyburn	Assistant Democratic Leader.
Coffman	Armed Services. Veterans' Affairs.
Cohen	Ethics. Judiciary. Transportation and Infrastructure.
Cole	Appropriations. Budget. Rules.

Representative	Committees (Standing, Joint, and Select)
Collins, Chris, of New York	Energy and Commerce.
Collins, Doug, of Georgia	Judiciary. Rules.
Comer	Agriculture. Oversight and Government Reform. Small Business.
Comstock	House Administration. Science, Space, and Technology. Transportation and Infrastructure. Joint Economic Committee
Conaway	Agriculture, *chair.* Armed Services. Permanent Select Committee on Intelligence.
Connolly	Foreign Affairs. Oversight and Government Reform.
Cook	Armed Services. Foreign Affairs. Natural Resources.
Cooper	Armed Services. Oversight and Government Reform.
Correa	Homeland Security. Veterans' Affairs.
Costa	Agriculture. Natural Resources.
Costello, Ryan A., of Pennsylvania	Energy and Commerce.
Courtney	Armed Services. Education and the Workforce.
Cramer	Energy and Commerce.
Crawford	Agriculture. Transportation and Infrastructure. Permanent Select Committee on Intelligence.
Crist	Financial Services. Science, Space, and Technology.
Crowley	Ways and Means.
Cuellar	Appropriations.
Culberson	Appropriations.
Cummings	Oversight and Government Reform. Transportation and Infrastructure.
Curbelo, Carlos, of Florida	Ways and Means.
Curtis	Foreign Affairs. Natural Resources. Small Business.
Davidson	Financial Services.
Davis, Danny K., of Illinois	Ways and Means.
Davis, Rodney, of Illinois	Agriculture. House Administration. Transportation and Infrastructure. Joint Committee on Printing, *vice chair.*
Davis, Susan A., of California	Armed Services. Education and the Workforce.
DeFazio	Transportation and Infrastructure.

Representative	Committees (Standing, Joint, and Select)
DeGette	Energy and Commerce.
Delaney	Financial Services. Joint Economic Committee.
DeLauro	Appropriations.
DelBene	Budget. Ways and Means.
Demings	Homeland Security. Judiciary.
Denham	Agriculture. Natural Resources. Transportation and Infrastructure.
DeSantis	Foreign Affairs. Judiciary. Oversight and Government Reform.
DeSaulnier	Education and the Workforce. Oversight and Government Reform. Transportation and Infrastructure.
DesJarlais	Agriculture. Armed Services. Oversight and Government Reform.
Deutch	Ethics. Foreign Affairs. Judiciary.
Diaz-Balart	Appropriations. Budget.
Dingell	Energy and Commerce.
Doggett	Ways and Means.
Donovan	Foreign Affairs. Homeland Security.
Doyle, Michael F., of Pennsylvania	Energy and Commerce.
Duffy	Financial Services.
Duncan, Jeff, of South Carolina	Energy and Commerce.
Duncan, John J., Jr., of Tennessee	Oversight and Government Reform. Transportation and Infrastructure.
Dunn	Agriculture. Science, Space, and Technology. Veterans' Affairs.
Ellison	Financial Services.
Emmer	Financial Services.
Engel	Energy and Commerce. Foreign Affairs.
Eshoo	Energy and Commerce.
Espaillat	Education and the Workforce. Foreign Affairs. Small Business.
Estes, Ron, of Kansas	Education and the Workforce. Homeland Security.

Representative	Committees (Standing, Joint, and Select)
Esty, Elizabeth H., of Connecticut	Science, Space, and Technology. Transportation and Infrastructure. Veterans' Affairs.
Evans	Agriculture. Small Business.
Faso	Agriculture. Budget. Transportation and Infrastructure.
Ferguson	Budget. Education and the Workforce. Transportation and Infrastructure.
Fitzpatrick	Foreign Affairs. Homeland Security. Small Business.
Fleischmann	Appropriations.
Flores	Energy and Commerce.
Fortenberry	Appropriations.
Foster	Financial Services. Science, Space, and Technology.
Foxx	Education and the Workforce, *chair.* Oversight and Government Reform.
Frankel, Lois, of Florida	Foreign Affairs. Transportation and Infrastructure.
Frelinghuysen	Appropriations, *chair.*
Fudge	Agriculture. Education and the Workforce.
Gabbard	Armed Services. Foreign Affairs.
Gaetz	Armed Services. Budget. Judiciary.
Gallagher	Armed Services. Homeland Security. Transportation and Infrastructure.
Gallego	Armed Services. Natural Resources.
Garamendi	Armed Services. Transportation and Infrastructure.
Garrett	Education and the Workforce. Foreign Affairs. Homeland Security.
Gianforte	Natural Resources. Oversight and Government Reform.
Gibbs	Agriculture. Transportation and Infrastructure.
Gohmert	Judiciary. Natural Resources.
Gomez	Natural Resources. Oversight and Government Reform.
Gonzalez, Vicente, of Texas	Financial Services.
González-Colón, Jenniffer, of Puerto Rico	Natural Resources. Small Business. Veterans' Affairs.

Representative	Committees (Standing, Joint, and Select)
Goodlatte	Judiciary, *chair.* Agriculture.
Gosar	Natural Resources. Oversight and Government Reform.
Gottheimer	Financial Services.
Gowdy	Oversight and Government Reform, *chair.* Judiciary. Permanent Select Committee on Intelligence.
Granger	Appropriations.
Graves, Garret, of Louisiana	Natural Resources. Transportation and Infrastructure.
Graves, Sam, of Missouri	Armed Services. Transportation and Infrastructure.
Graves, Tom, of Georgia	Appropriations.
Green, Al, of Texas	Financial Services.
Green, Gene, of Texas	Energy and Commerce.
Griffith	Energy and Commerce.
Grijalva	Education and the Workforce. Natural Resources.
Grothman	Budget. Education and the Workforce. Oversight and Government Reform.
Guthrie	Education and the Workforce. Energy and Commerce.
Gutiérrez	Judiciary.
Hanabusa	Armed Services. Natural Resources. Science, Space, and Technology.
Handel	Education and the Workforce. Judiciary. Joint Economic Committee.
Harper	House Administration, *chair.* Joint Committee on the Library, *chair.* Energy and Commerce. Joint Committee on Printing.
Harris	Appropriations.
Hartzler	Agriculture. Armed Services.
Hastings	Rules.
Heck	Financial Services. Permanent Select Committee on Intelligence.
Hensarling	Financial Services, *chair.*
Herrera Beutler	Appropriations.
Hice, Jody B., of Georgia	Armed Services. Natural Resources. Oversight and Government Reform.
Higgins, Brian, of New York	Budget. Ways and Means.
Higgins, Clay, of Louisiana	Homeland Security.

Representative	Committees (Standing, Joint, and Select)
	Science, Space, and Technology. Veterans' Affairs.
Hill	Financial Services.
Himes	Financial Services. Permanent Select Committee on Intelligence.
Holding	Ways and Means.
Hollingsworth	Financial Services.
Hoyer	Democratic Whip.
Hudson	Energy and Commerce.
Huffman	Natural Resources. Transportation and Infrastructure.
Huizenga	Financial Services.
Hultgren	Financial Services. Science, Space, and Technology.
Hunter	Armed Services. Education and the Workforce. Transportation and Infrastructure.
Hurd	Homeland Security. Oversight and Government Reform. Permanent Select Committee on Intelligence.
Issa	Foreign Affairs. Judiciary. Oversight and Government Reform.
Jackson Lee	Budget. Homeland Security. Judiciary.
Jayapal	Budget. Judiciary.
Jeffries	Budget. Judiciary.
Jenkins, Evan H., of West Virginia.	Appropriations.
Jenkins, Lynn, of Kansas	Ways and Means.
Johnson, Bill, of Ohio	Budget. Energy and Commerce.
Johnson, Eddie Bernice, of Texas	Science, Space, and Technology. Transportation and Infrastructure.
Johnson, Henry C. "Hank", Jr., of Georgia	Judiciary. Transportation and Infrastructure.
Johnson, Mike, of Louisiana	Judiciary. Natural Resources.
Johnson, Sam, of Texas	Ways and Means. Joint Committee on Taxation.
Jones	Armed Services.
Jordan	Judiciary. Oversight and Government Reform.
Joyce, David P., of Ohio	Appropriations.

Representative	Committees (Standing, Joint, and Select)
Kaptur	Appropriations.
Katko	Homeland Security. Transportation and Infrastructure.
Keating	Foreign Affairs. Homeland Security.
Kelly, Mike, of Pennsylvania	Ways and Means.
Kelly, Robin L., of Illinois	Foreign Affairs. Oversight and Government Reform.
Kelly, Trent, of Mississippi	Agriculture. Armed Services. Small Business.
Kennedy	Energy and Commerce.
Khanna	Armed Services. Budget.
Kihuen	Financial Services.
Kildee	Financial Services.
Kilmer	Appropriations.
Kind	Ways and Means.
King, Peter T., of New York	Financial Services. Homeland Security. Permanent Select Committee on Intelligence.
King, Steve, of Iowa	Agriculture. Judiciary. Small Business.
Kinzinger	Energy and Commerce. Foreign Affairs.
Knight	Armed Services. Science, Space, and Technology. Small Business.
Krishnamoorthi	Education and the Workforce. Oversight and Government Reform.
Kuster	Agriculture. Veterans' Affairs.
Kustoff	Financial Services.
Labrador	Judiciary. Natural Resources.
LaHood	Ways and Means. Joint Economic Committee.
LaMalfa	Agriculture. Natural Resources. Transportation and Infrastructure.
Lamb	Science, Space, and Technology. Veterans' Affairs.
Lamborn	Armed Services. Natural Resources.
Lance	Energy and Commerce. Ethics.
Langevin	Armed Services. Homeland Security.

Representative	Committees (Standing, Joint, and Select)
Larsen, Rick, of Washington	Armed Services. Transportation and Infrastructure.
Larson, John B., of Connecticut	Ways and Means.
Latta	Energy and Commerce.
Lawrence	Oversight and Government Reform. Transportation and Infrastructure.
Lawson, Al, Jr., of Florida	Agriculture. Small Business.
Lee	Appropriations. Budget.
Lesko	Homeland Security. Science, Space, and Technology.
Levin	Ways and Means.
Lewis, Jason, of Minnesota	Budget. Education and the Workforce. Transportation and Infrastructure.
Lewis, John, of Georgia	Ways and Means. Joint Committee on the Taxation.
Lieu, Ted, of California	Foreign Affairs. Judiciary.
Lipinski	Science, Space, and Technology. Transportation and Infrastructure.
LoBiondo	Armed Services. Transportation and Infrastructure. Permanent Select Committee on Intelligence.
Loebsack	Energy and Commerce.
Lofgren	House Administration. Judiciary. Science, Space, and Technology. Joint Committee on the Library.
Long	Energy and Commerce.
Loudermilk	Financial Services. House Administration. Science, Space, and Technology. Joint Committee on the Library.
Love	Financial Services.
Lowenthal	Natural Resources. Transportation and Infrastructure.
Lowey	Appropriations.
Lucas	Agriculture. Financial Services. Science, Space, and Technology.
Luetkemeyer	Small Business, *vice chair.* Financial Services.
Luján, Ben Ray, of New Mexico	Energy and Commerce.
Lujan Grisham, Michelle, of New Mexico	Agriculture. Budget.
Lynch	Financial Services. Oversight and Government Reform.
MacArthur	Financial Services.

Representative	Committees (Standing, Joint, and Select)
Maloney, Carolyn B., of New York	Financial Services. Oversight and Government Reform. Joint Economic Committee.
Maloney, Sean Patrick, of New York	Agriculture. Transportation and Infrastructure.
Marchant	Ethics. Ways and Means.
Marino	Foreign Affairs. Judiciary.
Marshall	Agriculture. Science, Space, and Technology. Small Business.
Massie	Oversight and Government Reform. Science, Space, and Technology. Transportation and Infrastructure.
Mast	Foreign Affairs. Transportation and Infrastructure. Veterans' Affairs
Matsui	Energy and Commerce.
McCarthy	Majority Leader.
McCaul	Homeland Security, *chair*. Foreign Affairs.
McClintock	Budget. Natural Resources.
McCollum	Appropriations.
McEachin	Armed Services. Natural Resources.
McGovern	Agriculture. Rules.
McHenry	Financial Services, *vice chair*.
McKinley	Energy and Commerce.
McMorris Rodgers	Energy and Commerce.
McNerney	Energy and Commerce. Science, Space, and Technology.
McSally	Armed Services. Homeland Security.
Meadows	Foreign Affairs. Oversight and Government Reform. Transportation and Infrastructure.
Meeks	Financial Services. Foreign Affairs.
Meng	Appropriations.
Messer	Education and the Workforce. Financial Services.
Mitchell	Armed Services. Oversight and Government Reform. Transportation and Infrastructure.
Moolenaar	Appropriations.

Representative	Committees (Standing, Joint, and Select)
Mooney, Alexander X., of West Virginia	Financial Services.
Moore	Financial Services.
Moulton	Armed Services. Budget.
Mullin	Energy and Commerce.
Murphy	Armed Services. Small Business.
Nadler	Judiciary.
Napolitano	Natural Resources. Transportation and Infrastructure.
Neal	Ways and Means. Joint Committee on Taxation.
Newhouse	Appropriations. Rules.
Noem	Ways and Means.
Nolan	Agriculture. Transportation and Infrastructure.
Norcross	Armed Services. Education and the Workforce.
Norman	Science, Space, and Technology. Small Business.
Norton	Oversight and Government Reform. Transportation and Infrastructure.
Nunes	Permanent Select Committee on Intelligence, *chair*. Ways and Means. Joint Committee on Taxation.
O'Halleran	Agriculture. Armed Services.
Olson	Energy and Commerce.
O'Rourke	Armed Services. Veterans' Affairs.
Palazzo	Appropriations.
Pallone	Energy and Commerce.
Palmer	Budget. Oversight and Government Reform. Science, Space, and Technology.
Panetta	Agriculture. Armed Services.
Pascrell	Ways and Means.
Paulsen	Joint Economic Committee, *chair*. Ways and Means.
Payne	Homeland Security. Transportation and Infrastructure.
Pearce	Financial Services. Natural Resources.
Pelosi	Democratic Leader.
Perlmutter	Financial Services. Science, Space, and Technology.

Representative	Committees (Standing, Joint, and Select)
Perry	Foreign Affairs. Homeland Security. Transportation and Infrastructure.
Peters	Energy and Commerce. Veterans' Affairs.
Peterson	Agriculture.
Pingree	Appropriations.
Pittenger	Financial Services.
Plaskett	Agriculture. Oversight and Government Reform. Transportation and Infrastructure.
Pocan	Appropriations.
Poe, Ted, of Texas	Foreign Affairs. Judiciary.
Poliquin	Financial Services. Veterans' Affairs.
Polis	Education and the Workforce. Ethics. Rules.
Posey	Financial Services. Science, Space, and Technology.
Price, David E., of North Carolina	Appropriations.
Quigley	Appropriations. Permanent Select Committee on Intelligence.
Radewagen	Natural Resources. Small Business. Veterans' Affairs.
Raskin	House Administration. Judiciary. Oversight and Government Reform. Joint Committee on Printing.
Ratcliffe	Ethics. Homeland Security. Judiciary.
Reed	Ways and Means.
Reichert	Ways and Means.
Renacci	Budget. Ways and Means.
Rice, Kathleen M., of New York	Homeland Security. Veterans' Affairs.
Rice, Tom, of South Carolina	Ways and Means.
Richmond	Homeland Security. Judiciary.
Roby	Appropriations. Judiciary.
Roe, David P., of Tennessee	Veterans' Affairs, *chair*. Education and the Workforce.
Rogers, Harold, of Kentucky	Appropriations.
Rogers, Mike, of Alabama	Agriculture. Armed Services. Homeland Security.

Representative	Committees (Standing, Joint, and Select)
Rohrabacher	Foreign Affairs. Science, Space, and Technology.
Rokita	Budget, *vice chiar*. Education and the Workforce. Transportation and Infrastructure.
Rooney, Francis, of Florida	Education and the Workforce. Foreign Affairs. Joint Economic Committee.
Rooney, Thomas J., of Florida	Appropriations. Permanent Select Committee on Intelligence.
Rosen	Armed Services. Science, Space, and Technology.
Roskam	Ways and Means.
Ros-Lehtinen	Foreign Affairs. Permanent Select Committee on Intelligence.
Ross	Financial Services. Oversight and Government Reform.
Rothfus	Financial Services. Judiciary.
Rouzer	Agriculture. Transportation and Infrastructure.
Roybal-Allard	Appropriations.
Royce, Edward R., of California	Foreign Affairs, *chair*. Financial Services.
Ruiz	Energy and Commerce.
Ruppersberger	Appropriations.
Rush	Energy and Commerce.
Russell	Armed Services. Oversight and Government Reform.
Rutherford	Appropriations. Judiciary.
Ryan, Paul D., of Wisconsin	The Speaker.
Ryan, Tim, of Ohio	Appropriations.
Sablan	Education and the Workforce. Natural Resources.
Sánchez	Ways and Means.
Sanford	Budget. Oversight and Government Reform. Transportation and Infrastructure.
Sarbanes	Energy and Commerce. Oversight and Government Reform.
Scalise	Majority Whip. Energy and Commerce.
Schakowsky	Budget. Energy and Commerce.
Schiff	Permanent Select Committee on Intelligence.
Schneider	Foreign Affairs. Judiciary. Small Business.

Representative	Committees (Standing, Joint, and Select)
Schrader	Energy and Commerce.
Schweikert	Ways and Means. Joint Economic Committee.
Scott, Austin, of Georgia	Agriculture. Armed Services.
Scott, David, of Georgia	Agriculture. Financial Services.
Scott, Robert C. ''Bobby'', of Virginia	Education and the Workforce.
Sensenbrenner	Foreign Affairs. Judiciary.
Serrano	Appropriations.
Sessions	Rules, *chair.*
Sewell, Terri A., of Alabama	Ways and Means. Permanent Select Committee on Intelligence.
Shea-Porter	Armed Services. Education and the Workforce.
Sherman	Financial Services. Foreign Affairs.
Shimkus	Energy and Commerce.
Shuster	Transportation and Infrastructure, *chair.* Armed Services.
Simpson	Appropriations.
Sinema	Financial Services.
Sires	Foreign Affairs. Transportation and Infrastructure.
Smith, Adam, of Washington	Armed Services.
Smith, Adrian, of Nebraska	House Administration. Ways and Means.
Smith, Christopher H., of New Jersey	Foreign Affairs.
Smith, Jason, of Missouri	Budget. Ways and Means.
Smith, Lamar, of Texas	Science, Space, and Technology, *chair.* Homeland Security. Judiciary.
Smucker	Budget. Education and the Workforce. Transportation and Infrastructure.
Soto	Agriculture. Natural Resources.
Speier	Armed Services. Permanent Select Committee on Intelligence.
Stefanik	Armed Services. Education and the Workforce. Permanent Select Committee on Intelligence.
Stewart	Appropriations. Permanent Select Committee on Intelligence.
Stivers	Financial Services.

Representative	Committees (Standing, Joint, and Select)
Suozzi	Armed Services. Foreign Affairs.
Swalwell, Eric, of California	Judiciary. Permanent Select Committee on Intelligence.
Takano	Education and the Workforce. Science, Space, and Technology. Veterans' Affairs.
Taylor	Appropriations.
Tenney	Financial Services.
Thompson, Bennie G., of Mississippi	Homeland Security.
Thompson, Glenn, of Pennsylvania	Agriculture. Education and the Workforce. Natural Resources.
Thompson, Mike, of California	Ways and Means.
Thornberry	Armed Services, *chair.*
Tipton	Financial Services. Natural Resources.
Titus	Foreign Affairs. Transportation and Infrastructure.
Tonko	Energy and Commerce. Science, Space, and Technology.
Torres	Foreign Affairs. Rules.
Trott	Financial Services.
Tsongas	Armed Services. Natural Resources.
Turner	Armed Services. Permanent Select Committee on Intelligence.
Upton	Energy and Commerce.
Valadao	Appropriations.
Vargas	Financial Services.
Veasey	Armed Services. Science, Space, and Technology.
Vela	Agriculture. Homeland Security.
Velázquez	Financial Services. Natural Resources. Small Business.
Visclosky	Appropriations.
Wagner	Financial Services. Foreign Affairs.
Walberg	Education and the Workforce. Energy and Commerce.
Walden	Energy and Commerce, *chair.*
Walker	House Administration. Oversight and Government Reform. Joint Committee on Printing.

Representative	Committees (Standing, Joint, and Select)
Walorski	Ways and Means.
Walters, Mimi, of California	Energy and Commerce. Ethics.
Walz	Agriculture. Veterans' Affairs.
Wasserman Schultz	Appropriations. Budget.
Waters, Maxine, of California	Financial Services.
Watson Coleman	Homeland Security. Oversight and Government Reform.
Weber, Randy K., Sr., of Texas	Science, Space, and Technology. Transportation and Infrastructure.
Webster, Daniel, of Florida	Natural Resources. Science, Space, and Technology. Transportation and Infrastructure.
Welch	Energy and Commerce. Oversight and Government Reform.
Wenstrup	Ways and Means. Permanent Select Committee on Intelligence.
Westerman	Budget. Natural Resources. Transportation and Infrastructure.
Williams	Financial Services.
Wilson, Frederica S., of Florida	Education and the Workforce. Transportation and Infrastructure.
Wilson, Joe, of South Carolina	Armed Services. Education and the Workforce. Foreign Affairs.
Wittman	Armed Services. Natural Resources.
Womack	Budget, *chair.* Appropriations.
Woodall	Budget. Rules. Transportation and Infrastructure.
Yarmuth	Budget.
Yoder	Appropriations. Joint Committee on the Library.
Yoho	Agriculture. Foreign Affairs.
Young, David, of Iowa	Appropriations.
Young, Don, of Alaska	Natural Resources. Transportation and Infrastructure.
Zeldin	Financial Services. Foreign Affairs.

CONGRESSIONAL ADVISORY BOARDS, COMMISSIONS, AND GROUPS

UNITED STATES AIR FORCE ACADEMY BOARD OF VISITORS

[Title 10, U.S.C., Section 9355(a)]

Board Member	**Year Appointed**
Appointed by the President:	
Roel Campos	2016
Linda Cubero	2016
Benjamin Drew	2016
Judith Fedder	2016
Soudarak Hoppin	2016
Edward Rice (Chair)	2016
Appointed by the Vice President or the Senate President Pro Tempore:	
Senator *Mazie K. Hirono,* of Hawaii	2015
Senator Jerry Moran, of Kansas	2015
Senator *Tom Udall,* of New Mexico	2015
Appointed by the Speaker of the House of Representatives:	
Representative *Jared Polis,* of Colorado	2010
Representative Doug Lamborn, of Colorado	2009
Representative Martha McSally, of Arizona	2015
Bruce Swezey	2017
Appointed by the Chairman, Senate Armed Services Committee:	
Senator Cory Gardner, of Colorado	2015
Appointed by the Chairman, House Armed Services Committee:	
Vacant.	

UNITED STATES MILITARY ACADEMY BOARD OF VISITORS

[Title 10, U.S.C., Section 4355(a)]

Members of Congress

Senate

Richard Burr, of North Carolina.
Jerry Moran, of Kansas.
Kirsten E. Gillibrand, of New York.
Christopher Murphy, of Connecticut.

House

Steve Womack, Representative of Arkansas, Chair.
K. Michael Conaway, Representative of Texas.
Thomas J. Rooney, Representative of Florida.
Sean Patrick Maloney, Representative of New York.
Stephanie N. Murphy, Representative of Florida.

Presidential Appointees:

Brenda Sue Fulton, of New Jersey, Vice Chair.

Elizabeth McNally, of New York.
Frederick H. Black, Sr., of North Carolina.
Bridget Altenburg, of Illinois.
Hon. Gerald McGowan, of Washington, DC.
Jane Holl Lute, of Virginia.

UNITED STATES NAVAL ACADEMY BOARD OF VISITORS

[Title 10, U.S.C., Section 6968(a)]

Appointed by the President:

Judge Evan Wallach, U.S. Court of Appeals (Vice Chairman).
CAPT E. Elliott Barker, USN (Ret.).
LCDR Dan Cnossen, USN (Ret.).
Christine Fox.
ADM James Winnefeld, USN (Ret.), former Vice Chairman of the Joint Chiefs of Staff.
Matice J. Wright.

Appointed by the Vice President:

Senator *Benjamin L. Cardin,* of Maryland.
Senator James Lankford, of Oklahoma.
Senator *Jeanne Shaheen,* of New Hampshire.

Designees of the Chairmen, SASC/HASC:

Senator Dan Sullivan, of Alaska.
Representative Robert J. Wittman, of Virginia (Chairman).

Appointed by the Speaker of the House:

Representative *Elijah E. Cummings,* of Maryland.
Representative Ron DeSantis, of Florida.
Representative Mike Gallagher, of Wisconsin.
Representative *C. A. Dutch Ruppersberger,* of Maryland.

UNITED STATES COAST GUARD ACADEMY BOARD OF VISITORS *

[Title 14 U.S.C., Section 194(a)]

Roger F. Wicker, of Mississippi.
Dan Sullivan, of Alaska.
Bill Shuster, of Pennsylvania.
Adrian Smith, of Nebraska.
Richard Blumenthal, of Connecticut.
Maria Cantwell, of Washington.

BRITISH-AMERICAN PARLIAMENTARY GROUP

Senate Hart Building, Room 808, phone 224–3047

[Created by Public Law 98–164]

Senate Delegation:
Chair.—Vacant.
Vice Chair.—*Patrick J. Leahy,* Senator from Vermont.

CANADA-UNITED STATES INTERPARLIAMENTARY GROUP

Senate Hart Building, Room 808, phone 224–3047

[Created by Public Law 86–42, 22 U.S.C., 1928a–1928d, 276d–276g]

Senate Delegation:
Chair.—Vacant.

* This list is incomplete; three Congressional seats remain vacant at time of press.

Vice Chair.—Vacant.

House Delegation:
Chair.—Bill Huizenga, Representative of Michigan.
Vice Chair.—Vacant.

CHINA-UNITED STATES INTERPARLIAMENTARY GROUP

Senate Hart Building, Room 808, phone 224–3047

[Created by Public Law 108–199, Section 153]

Senate Delegation:
Chair.—Vacant.
Vice Chair.—Vacant.

KOREA-UNITED STATES INTERPARLIAMENTARY GROUP

House Delegation:
Chair.—Edward R. Royce, Representative of California.

MEXICO-UNITED STATES INTERPARLIAMENTARY GROUP

Senate Hart Building, Room 808, phone 224–3047

[Created by Public Law 82–420, 22 U.S.C. 276h–276k]

Senate Delegation:
Chair.—Vacant.
Vice Chair.—Vacant.

House Delegation:
Chair.—Michael T. McCaul, Representative of Texas.
Vice Chair.—Sean P. Duffy, Representative of Wisconsin.

NATO PARLIAMENTARY ASSEMBLY

Headquarters: Place du Petit Sablon 3, B–1000 Brussels, Belgium

[Created by Public Law 84–689, 22 U.S.C., 1928z]

Senate Delegation:
Chair.—Vacant.
Vice Chair.—Vacant.

House Delegation:
Chair.—Michael R. Turner, Representative of Ohio.
Vice Chair.—Ted Poe, Representative of Texas.

STAFF

Secretary, Senate Delegation.—Julia Hart Reed, Interparliamentary Services, SH–808, 224–3047.
Secretary, House Delegation.—Jeff Dressler.

COMMISSION ON CONGRESSIONAL MAILING STANDARDS

1216 Longworth House Office Building, phone 226–0647

[Created by Public Law 93–191]

Chair.—Rodney Davis, of Illinois.
Robert E. Latta, of Ohio.
Barbara Comstock, of Virginia.
Susan A. Davis, of California.
Brad Sherman, of California.
A. Donald McEachin, of Virginia.

STAFF

Majority Staff Director.—Max Engling, 226–0647.

Professional Staff.—Tim Sullivan.
Staff Assistants: Austin Cho, Ashley Herbert.
Counsel.—Nick Hawatmeh.
Democratic Staff Director.—Matthew DeFreitas.
Democratic Professional Staff: Aislan Sims, 225–9337; Kimberly Stevens.
Democratic Counsel.—Khalil Abboud.
Democratic Staff Assistant.—Meredith Conner.

COMMISSION ON SECURITY AND COOPERATION IN EUROPE

234 Ford House Office Building, phone 225–1901, fax 226–4199

http://www.csce.gov

Roger F. Wicker, Senator from Mississippi, *Chair*

Christopher H. Smith, Representative from New Jersey, *Co-Chair*

LEGISLATIVE BRANCH COMMISSIONERS

House

Robert B. Aderholt, of Alabama.
Michael C. Burgess, of Texas.
Randy Hultgren, of Illinois.
Richard Hudson, of North Carolina.
Alcee L. Hastings, of Florida.
Steve Cohen, of Tennessee.
Sheila Jackson Lee, of Texas.
Gwen Moore, of Wisconsin.

Senate

John Boozman, of Arkansas.
Cory Gardner, of Colorado.
Marco Rubio, of Florida.
Thom Tillis, of North Carolina.
Benjamin L. Cardin, of Maryland.
Jeanne Shaheen, of New Hampshire.
Tom Udall, of New Mexico.
Sheldon Whitehouse, of Rhode Island.

EXECUTIVE BRANCH COMMISSIONERS

Department of State.—Vacant.
Department of Commerce.—Vacant.
Department of Defense.—Vacant.

COMMISSION STAFF

Chief of Staff.—Ambassador David T. Killion.
House Senior Staff Person.—Mark Milosch.
Senior State Department Advisor.—Scott Rauland.
Policy Advisor; Secretary of the U.S. Delegation to the OSCE Parliamentary Assembly.—Bob Hand.
Representative of the Helsinki Commission to the USOSCE.—Janice Helwig.
Policy Advisors: Everett Price, Mischa Thompson, Alex Tiersky.
Counsel; General Counsel.—Allison B. Hollabaugh (acting).
Policy Advisor; CSCE Liaison to the Chairman's Office; Chief Administration Officer.—A. Paul Massaro III, (acting).
Counsel for International Law.—Erika B. Schlager.
Staff Associate.—Jordan Warlick.

CONGRESSIONAL AWARD FOUNDATION

379 Ford House Office Building, phone (202) 226–0130, fax 226–0131

[Created by Public Law 96–114]

Chair.—Paxton K. Baker, Washington Nationals Baseball.
Vice Chairs:
Linda Mitchell, Mississippi State University Extension Service.
Hon. Rodney E. Slater, Squire Patton Boggs, LLP.
Secretary.—Cheryl Maddox, Humana, Inc.
Treasurer.—Lee Klumpp, BDO.

Members:

Cliff Akiyama, Philadelphia College of Osteopathic Medicine.
Simeon Banister, Greater Rochester Martin Luther King Jr. Commission.
Ed Blansitt, Montgomery County Inspector General Office.
Romero Brown, Georgia.
Anne Oswalt Bruce, Johnson & Johnson.
Nick Cannon, New York.
Edward Cohen, Lerner Enterprises.
Kathy Didawick, BlueCross BlueShield Association.
Hon. Debbie Dingell, U.S. House of Representatives.
Mitch Draizin, Longview Capital Advisors, Inc.
MaryAnne Dunlap, Sanofi, US.
David Falk, FAME.
Beverly Gilyard, AARP.
George B. Gould, Washington, DC.
Dr. Lawrence Green, Maryland.
J. Steven Hart, Esq., Williams and Jensen, P.C.
Erica Wheelan Heyse, National Director.
Jesse Hill, Edward Jones.
Hon. Richard Hudson, U.S. House of Representatives.
David W. Hunt, Esq., Nexant.
Hon. Johnny Isakson, U.S. Senate.
Hon. Sheila Jackson Lee, U.S. House of Representatives.
Karlos LaSane, Caesars Entertainment.
Lynn Lyons, Florida.
Raul Magdaleno, Magdaleno Consulting Group.
Hon. Joe Manchin III, U.S. Senate.
Lance Mangum, FedEx Corporation.
Kim Norman, G2 Secure Staff, LLC.
Steven Roberts, The Roberts Companies.
Beth Ann Ruoff, Washington, DC.
David Schiappa, The Duberstein Group.
Chris Spear, American Trucking Associations.
Will Stute, McDermott, Will & Emery, LLP.
Chiling Tong, National Ace.
Jason Van Pelt, Crossroads Strategies.
Rita Vaswani, Nevada State Bank.
Kathryn Weeden, United States Senate Page School.
Shawn Whitman, FMC Corporation.

CONGRESSIONAL CLUB

2001 New Hampshire Avenue, NW., 20009, phone (202) 332–1155, fax 797–0698

Executive Board
President.—Vera G. Davis.
Vice Presidents:
(1st) Jennifer Messer.
(2d) Helen Green.
(3d) Judy Benishek.
(4th) Patricia Garamendi.
(5th) Billie Gingrey.
(6th) April McClain Delaney.

Treasurer.—Martha Brooks.
Recording Secretary.—Sonya Horsford.
Corresponding Secretary.—Simone Marie Meeks.
Executive Director.—Lydia de La Vina de Foley.

CONGRESSIONAL EXECUTIVE COMMISSION ON CHINA

243 Ford House Office Building, phone 226–3766, fax 226–3804

[Created by Public Law 106–286]

Marco Rubio, Senator from Florida, *Chair*

Christopher H. Smith, Representative of New Jersey, *Co-Chair*

LEGISLATIVE BRANCH COMMISSIONERS

House

Robert Pittenger, of North Carolina.
Randy Hultgren, of Illinois.
Vacant.

Timothy J. Walz, of Minnesota.
Marcy Kaptur, of Ohio.
Ted Lieu, of California.
Vacant.

Senate

James Lankford, of Oklahoma.
Tom Cotton, of Arkansas.
Steve Daines, of Montana.
Todd Young, of Indiana.

Dianne Feinstein, of California.
Jeff Merkley, of Oregon.
Gary C. Peters, of Michigan.
ANGUS S. KING, JR., of Maine.

EXECUTIVE BRANCH COMMISSIONERS

Vacant, U.S. Department of Labor.
Vacant, U.S. Department of State.
Vacant, U.S. Department of Commerce.
Vacant, U.S. Department of State.
Vacant, U.S. Department of State.

COMMISSION STAFF

Staff Director.—Paul B. Protic.
Deputy Staff Director.—Elyse Anderson.
Director of Administration, Budget, and Contracts.—Judy Wright.
Senior Advisor and Prisoner Database Program Director.—Jen Salen.
Counsels: Steve Andrews, Andy Wong.
Research Associates: Mingzhi Chen, Sophie Jen, David Petrick, Amy Reger, Sabrina Tsai.
Research Associate and Manager of Annual Report Production.—Megan Fluker.
Director of Communications and Policy.—Scott Flipse.

HOUSE DEMOCRACY PARTNERSHIP

227 Cannon House Office Building, phone 225–4561, fax 225–1166

democracy@mail.house.gov, http://democracy.house.gov

[Created by H. Res. 5, 112th Congress]

Chair.—Peter J. Roskam, of Illinois.
Ranking Member.—David E. Price, of North Carolina.

COMMISSIONERS

Jeff Fortenberry, of Nebraska.
Adrian Smith, of Nebraska.
Vern Buchanan, of Florida.
Jackie Walorski, of Indiana.
Stephen Knight, of California.
Tom Rice, of South Carolina.
Steve Womack, of Arkansas.
Rob Woodall, of Georgia.
Bill Flores, of Texas.
Lucille Roybal-Allard, of California.
Ted Lieu, of California.
Norma J. Torres, of California.
Keith Ellison, of Minnesota.
Gwen Moore, of Wisconsin.
Susan A. Davis, of California.
Dina Titus, of Nevada.
Gerald E. Connolly, of Virginia.

Deputy Chief for Representative (Roskam).—Jeff Billman.
Deputy Chief for Representative (Price).—Justin Wein.

HOUSE OFFICE BUILDING COMMISSION

H–232 The Capitol, phone 225–0600

[Title 40, U.S.C. 175–176]

Chair.—Paul D. Ryan, Speaker of the House of Representatives.
Kevin McCarthy, House Majority Leader.
Nancy Pelosi, House Minority Leader.

JAPAN-UNITED STATES FRIENDSHIP COMMISSION

1201 15th Street, NW., Suite 330, phone (202) 653–9800, fax 653–9802

[Created by Public Law 94–118]

Chair.—Harry A. Hill, President and CEO, Oaklawn Marketing, Inc.
Vice-Chair.—Dr. Sheila Smith, Senior Fellow for Japan Studies, Council on Foreign Relations (CFR).
Executive Director.—Paige Cottingham-Streater.
Assistant Executive Director.—Niharika C. Joe.
Assistant Executive Director, CULCON.—Pamela L. Fields.
Executive Assistant.—Sylvia L. Dandridge.
Members:
Assistant Secretary of State for East Asian and Pacific Affairs, U.S. Department of State.
Assistant Secretary of State for Educational and Cultural Affairs, U.S. Department of State.
Dr. Deanna Marcum, Managing Director, Ithaka.
Dr. Patricia Maclachlan, Associate Professor of Government and Asian Studies, University of Texas.
Dr. Edward Lincoln, Professorial Lecturer, George Washington University.
David Sneider, Simpson Thacher & Bartlett, LLP.
Hon. Jane Chu, Chair, National Endowment for the Arts.
National Endowment for the Humanities.
Hon. Mark Takano, U.S. House of Representatives.
Dr. Anne Nishimura Morse, Curator of Japanese Art, Museum of Fine Arts, Boston.
Hon. Lisa Murkowski, U.S. Senate.
U.S. Department of Education.
Dr. T.J. Pempel, Professor of Political Science, University of California, Berkeley.
Vacant, U.S. House of Representatives.
Dr. Leonard J. Schoppa, Jr., Director, Woodrow Wilson Department of Politics, The University of Virginia.
Vacant, U.S. Senate.

MIGRATORY BIRD CONSERVATION COMMISSION

5275 Leesburg Pike, Falls Church, 22041
phone (703) 358–1716, fax (703) 358–2234

[Created by act of February 18, 1929, 16 U.S.C. 715a]

Chair.—Ryan Zinke, Secretary of the Interior.

John Boozman, Senator from Arkansas.
Martin Heinrich, Senator from New Mexico.
Robert J. Wittman, Representative from Virginia.
Mike Thompson, Representative from California.
Sonny Perdue, Secretary of Agriculture.
Andrew Wheeler, Acting Administrator of Environmental Protection Agency.
Secretary.—A. Eric Alvarez.

PERMANENT COMMITTEE FOR THE OLIVER WENDELL HOLMES DEVISE FUND

Library of Congress, 20540, phone 707–1082

[Created by act of Congress approved August 5, 1955 (Public Law 246, 84th Congress), to administer Oliver Wendell Holmes Devise Fund, established by same act]

Chairman ex officio.—Carla Hayden.
Administrative Officer for the Devise.—James H. Hutson.

UNITED STATES-CHINA ECONOMIC AND SECURITY REVIEW COMMISSION

444 North Capitol Street, NW., Suite 602, phone 624–1407, fax 624–1406

[Created by Public Law 106–398, 114 STAT]

COMMISSIONERS

Chair.—Carolyn Bartholomew.
Vice Chair.—Hon. Dennis C. Shea.

Members:
Robin Cleveland.
Hon. Byron L. Dorgan.
Hon. Carte P. Goodwin.
Glenn Hubbard.
Daniel M. Slane.
Hon. Jonathan N. Stivers.
Hon. James M. Talent.
Hon. Katherine C. Tobin, Ph.D.
Michael R. Wessel.
Larry M. Wortzel, Ph.D.

COMMISSION STAFF

Executive Director.—Michael R. Danis.
Congressional Liaison and Communications Coordinator.—Leslie A. Tisdale.
Management Analyst.—Christopher P. Fioravante.
Research Director and Policy Analyst, Economics and Trade.—Katherine E. Koleski.
Security and Foreign Affairs Analysts: Ethan S. Meick, Matthew O. Southerland, Jordan Wilson.
Economics and Trade Analysts: Michelle Ker, Sean O'Connor, Matthew Snyder.
Senior Policy Analyst, Security and Foreign Affairs.—Kristien T. Bergerson.
Supervisory Senior Policy Analyst, Economics and Trade.—Nargiza Salidjanova.
Supervisory Senior Policy Analyst, Security and Foreign Affairs.—Caitlin E. Campbell.
Finance and Operations Director.—Kathleen Wilson.

SENATE NATIONAL SECURITY WORKING GROUP

311 Hart Senate Office Building, 20510, phone 228–6425

Administrative Co-Chair.—James E. Risch, Senator from Idaho.
Administrative Co-Chair.—*Dianne Feinstein,* Senator from California.
Republican Leader.—Mitch McConnell, Senator from Kentucky.
Democratic Leader.—*Charles E. Schumer,* Senator from New York.
Co-Chair.—*Jack Reed,* Senator from Rhode Island.
Co-Chair.—Vacant.

Co-Chair.—Robert Menendez, Senator from New Jersey.
Co-Chair.—Marco Rubio, Senator from Florida.
Co-Chair.—Lindsey Graham, Senator from South Carolina.

Members:

James M. Inhofe, Senator from Oklahoma.
Bob Corker, Senator from Tennessee.
Roy Blunt, Senator from Missouri.
John McCain, Senator from Arizona.
Ben Sasse, Senator from Nebraska.
Richard J. Durbin, Senator from Illinois.
Robert P. Casey, Jr., Senator from Pennsylvania.
Bill Nelson, Senator from Florida.
Heidi Heitkamp, Senator from North Dakota.
Benjamin L. Cardin, Senator from Maryland.
Tammy Duckworth, Senator from Illinois.

STAFF

Democratic Staff Director.—Chris Gaspar, 224–3841.
Republican Staff Director.—Chris Socha, 224–2752.

UNITED STATES ASSOCIATION OF FORMER MEMBERS OF CONGRESS

1401 K Street, NW., Suite 503, 20005

phone (202) 222–0972, www.usafmc.org

The bipartisan United States Association of Former Members of Congress (FMC) was founded in 1970 as a nonprofit, educational, research, and social organization. It has been chartered by the U.S. Congress and has approximately 600 members who represented American citizens in both the U.S. Senate and House of Representatives. FMC works to strengthen the Congress in the conduct of its Constitutional responsibility through promoting a collaborative approach to policymaking. FMC seeks to deepen the understanding of our democratic system, domestically and internationally, and to engage the citizenry through civic education about Congress and public service.

President.—Cliff Stearns, of Florida.
Vice President.—Martin Frost, of Texas.
Treasurer.—Tim Petri, of Wisconsin.
Secretary.—Karen Thurman, of Florida.
Immediate Past President.—Barbara Kennelly, of Connecticut.
Honorary Co-Chair.—Norm Mineta, of California.
Chief Executive Officer.—Peter M. Weichlein.
Presidents Emeritus Council: Jack Buechner, of Missouri; Lou Frey, of Florida; Dennis Hertel, of Michigan; Larry LaRocco, of Idaho; Connie Morella, of Maryland; Matt McHugh, of New York; Jim Slattery, of Kansas.

U.S. CAPITOL HISTORICAL SOCIETY

200 Maryland Avenue, NE., 20002, phone (202) 543–8919, fax (202) 525–2790

[Congressional Charter, October 20, 1978, Public Law 95–493, 95th Congress, 92 Stat. 1643]

Chair of the Board.—Donald G. Carlson.
Vice Chair of the Board.—Connie Tipton.
President.—Hon. Ron Sarasin.

BOARD OF TRUSTEES

Mitch Bainwol
Hon. Kenneth E. Bentsen, Jr.
Hon. Roy Blunt
Jean P. Bordewich
Kenneth Bowling, Ph.D.
Marc Cadin
Nicholas E. Calio
Sean Callinicos
Donald G. Carlson
Hon. Bob Casey
Jeanne deCervens
Joseph W. Dooley
Andrew Durant
Hon. Virginia Fox
Mary Moore Hamrick
Mark Hopkins
Hon. John B. Larson
Brett Loper
Lorraine Miller
Hon. Edward A. Pease
Craig Purser
Cokie Roberts
Hon. Ron Sarasin
Anna Schneider
Jan Schoonmaker
Matthew Shay
Dontai Smalls
William G. Sutton, CAE
James A. Thurber, Ph.D.
Connie Tipton
Brigadier General Tim White
Mike Zarrelli

STAFF

Vice President of:
Membership and Development.—Laura McCulty Stepp.
Merchandising.—Diana E. Wailes.
Finance and Administration.—Peter McGuire.
Chief Historian.—William G. diGiacomantonio.
Director of:
Corporate Giving.—Marilyn Green.
Historical Programs.—Lauren Borchard.
Public Programs and Chief Guide.—Steve Livengood.
Manager of:
Accounting.—Sheri Williams.
Development and Outreach.—Jennifer Romberg.
Membership and Development.—Bee Barnett.
Public Programs.—Brandi Gasser.
Operations.—Vince Scott.
Receiving.—Mike Lawson.
Receptionist, Merchandise Clerk.—Shannice Moore.

U.S. CAPITOL PRESERVATION COMMISSION

[Created pursuant to Public Law 100–696]

Co-Chairs:
Paul D. Ryan, Speaker of the House.
Orrin G. Hatch, Senate President Pro Tempore.

MEMBERS

Senate
Mitch McConnell, Majority Leader.
Charles E. Schumer, Democratic Leader.
Richard C. Shelby.
Amy Klobuchar.
John Hoeven.
Richard J. Durbin.
Vacant.

House
Kevin McCarthy, Majority Leader.
Nancy Pelosi, Democratic Leader.
Gregg Harper.
Robert A. Brady.
Barbara Comstock.
Marcy Kaptur.
Vacant.

Ex-Officio Member-Architect of the Capitol.—Stephen T. Ayers, AIA, LEED AP.

U.S. HOUSE OF REPRESENTATIVES FINE ARTS BOARD

1309 Longworth House Office Building, phone 225–8281

[Created by Public Law 101–696]

Chair.—Gregg Harper, of Mississippi.

Members:
Barry Loudermilk, of Georgia.
Kevin Yoder, of Kansas.
Robert A. Brady, of Pennsylvania.
Zoe Lofgren, of California.

U.S. SENATE COMMISSION ON ART

S–411 The Capitol, phone 224–2955

[Created by Public Law 100–696]

Chair.—Mitch McConnell, of Kentucky.
Vice Chair.—*Charles E. Schumer,* of New York.

Members:
Orrin G. Hatch, of Utah.
Richard C. Shelby, of Alabama.
Amy Klobuchar, of Minnesota.

STAFF

Executive Secretary.—Julie E. Adams.
Curator.—Melinda K. Smith.
Associate Curator.—Alexander ''Sasha'' Lourie.
Administrator.—Scott M. Strong.
Historic Preservation Officer.—Kelly Steele.
Collections Manager.—Josephine Shea.
Assistant Curator.—Amy Elizabeth Burton.
Registrar.—Theresa Malanum.
Collections Specialist.—Megan Hipsley.
Museum Specialist.—Richard L. Doerner.
Executive Assistant.—Anum Mirza.

OTHER CONGRESSIONAL OFFICIALS AND SERVICES

ARCHITECT OF THE CAPITOL

ARCHITECT'S OFFICE

SB–16, U.S. Capitol, phone 228–1793, fax 228–1893, http://www.aoc.gov

Architect of the Capitol.—Stephen T. Ayers.
Assistant Architect of the Capitol.—Michael G. Turnbull.
Chief Operating Officer.—Christine Merdon.
Inspector General.—Christopher Failla.
Director of:
Communications and Congressional Relations.—Mamie Bittner.
Safety, Fire and Environmental Programs.—Patricia Williams.
Chief Administrative Officer.—Dan Cassil.
Chief Financial Officer.—Tom Carroll.
Communications Officer.—Laura Condeluci.
General Counsel.—Jason Baltimore.
Executive Officer, U.S. Botanic Garden.—Sahara Moon Chapotin.
Curator.—Michele Cohen.

U.S. CAPITOL

HT–42, Capitol Superintendent's Service Center, phone 228–8800, fax 225–1957

[The Capitol Superintendent's Service Center provides Facility Services for the Capitol and CVC.]

Superintendent.—Mark Reed.
Deputy Superintendent.—Kristy Long.
Assistant Superintendents: Luis Rosaro, John Deubler.

U.S. CAPITOL VISITOR CENTER

U.S. Capitol Visitor Center, Room SVC–101, 20515, phone 593–1816

Recorded Information 226–8000, Special Services 224–4048, TTY 224–4049

CEO for Visitor Services.—Beth Plemmons.
Deputy CEO for Visitor Services.—Nik Apostolides.
Director of Communications and Marketing.—Tome Casey.
Exhibits and Education.—Carol Beebe.
Gift Shops.—Susan Sisk.
Visitor Services.—Tina Pearson.
Volunteer Coordinator.—Wayne Kehoe.
Special Events.—Sharita Holt.
Director of Retail.—Susan Sisk.

SENATE OFFICE BUILDINGS

G–45 Dirksen Senate Office Building, phone 224–3141, fax 224–0652

Superintendent.—Takis Tzamaras.
Deputy Superintendent.—Lawrence Barr.

Assistant Superintendents: Jean Gilles, Paul Kirkpatrick, Michael Shirven, Eric Swanson.

HOUSE OFFICE BUILDINGS

B–341 Rayburn House Office Building, phone 225–4141, fax 225–3003

Superintendent.—William M. Weidemeyer, P.E., CFM.
Deputy Superintendent.—Michelle Kayon.
Assistant Superintendents: Barron Dill, Jason McIntyre, Daniel Murphy, William Wood.

CAPITOL TELEPHONE EXCHANGE

6110 Postal Square Building, phone 224–3121

Supervisors: Debra Morgan, Joan Sartori.

CHILD CARE CENTERS

HOUSE OF REPRESENTATIVES CHILD CARE CENTER

147 Ford House Office Building
Virginia Avenue and 3rd Street, SW., 20515
phone 226–9320, fax 225–6908

Director.—Monica Barnabae.
Program Director.—Paige Beatty.

SENATE EMPLOYEES' CHILD CARE CENTER

United States Senate, 20510
phone 224–1461, fax 228–3686

Director.—Shannon Mara.
Assistant Director.—Bridgette Waters.

COMBINED AIRLINES TICKET OFFICES (CATO)

344 Maple West, Suite 224, Vienna, VA 22180

phone (703) 522–8664, 1 (888) 205–4482

General Manager.—Susan Willis.

SENATE AND HOUSE

B–222 Longworth House Office Building

phone (703) 522–2286, fax (202) 226–5992

Manager.—Misty Conner.

CONGRESSIONAL RECORD DAILY DIGEST

HOUSE SECTION

HT–13 The Capitol, phone 225–2868 (committees), 225–1501 (chamber)

Editors for—
Committee Meetings.—Jessica M. Rager.
Chamber Action.—Glennis Webb.

SENATE SECTION

S–421 The Capitol, phone 224–2658, fax 224–1220

Editor.—Elizabeth Tratos.
Assistant Editor.—Joseph Johnston.

CONGRESSIONAL RECORD INDEX OFFICE

U.S. Government Publishing Office, Room C–738
North Capitol and H Streets, NW., 20401, phone 512–0275

Chief.—Marcia Thompson, 512–2010, ext. 3–1975.
Manager.—Philip C. Hart, 512–2010, ext. 3–1973.
Historian of Bills.—Barbre A. Brunson, 512–2010, ext. 3–1957.
Editors: Grafton J. Daniels, Jason Parsons.
Indexers: Ytta B. Carr, Joel K. Church, Jennifer E. Jones, Jane M. Wallace.

OFFICE OF CONGRESSIONAL ACCESSIBILITY SERVICES

S–156 Crypt of the Capitol, 20510, phone 224–4048, TTY 224–4049

Director.—David Hauck.

LIAISON OFFICES

AIR FORCE

2021 Rayburn House Office Building
phone 225–6656, 685–4530, DSN 325–4530, fax 685–2592

Chief.—Col. Thomas Kunkel.
Deputy Chief.—Lt. Col. Paul Babiarz.
Liaison Officers: Lt. Col. Paul Delanio, Maj. Terri Prosperie, Maj. Ryan Rose.
Budget and Appropriations Liaison Officer.—Lt. Col. Laurie Lanpher.
Legislative Assistant.—MSgt Miguel Rosario.
Civilian.—Ms. Kathy Reece.

182 Russell Senate Office Building, phone 224–2481, 685–2573, fax (703) 571–3233

Chief.—Col. John Allen, Jr.
Deputy Chief.—Lt. Col. Anthony McCarty.
Liaison Officers: Lt. Col. Elizabeth Brienza, Maj. Marjorie Molloy, Maj. Omar Perea.
Appropriations Liaison Officer.—CMSgt Tom Temple.
Office Manager/Scheduler.—Charlotte ''Charli'' Kiley.

ARMY

2024 Rayburn House Office Building, phone (202) 685–2676, fax 685–2674

Chief.—COL Tim Holman.
Deputy Chief.—Jodi Mitchell.
Liaison Officers: LTC Jenn Tyler; MAJ Sindi Connell; MAJ Sean Donohue; MAJ Dan Krueger; CPT Mike Calcagni; CPT Ryan Goulet; CPT Andrea Kaman; CPT Miles Miller; SGM Robert Hawkins.

183 Russell Senate Office Building, phone 224–2881, fax (703) 693–4574

Chief.—COL Michael J. Lawson.
Deputy Chief.—Kenneth Davis.
Liaison Officers: LTC Ned Ash, Donna Buono, MAJ David Hawkins, MAJ J. Kevin McKittrick, MAJ Lee Small III.

COAST GUARD

2019 Rayburn House Office Building, phone 225–4775

Director, House Liaison Officer.—CDR JoAnn Burdian.

Deputy, House Liaison Officer.—LCDR Kent Reinhold.
Assistant House Liaison.—LT Mike Johnson.

183 Russell Senate Office Building, phone 224–2913, fax 755–1695

Liaison Officer.—CDR Brian LeFebvre.

NAVY / MARINE CORPS

2022 Rayburn House Office Building, phone: Navy 225–7126, Marine Corps 225–7124

Director USN.—CAPT Todd Flannery, USN.
Deputy Director USN.—CDR Justin Goss, USN.
USN Liaison Officers: LCDR Ryan Chamberlain, USN; LT Victoria Marum, USN; LT Shannon Yingling, USN; LT Lara Bzik, USN; LNC Ronnie Ratliff, USN.
Director USMC.—Col. John Ostrowski, USMC.
Deputy Director USMC.—Maj. Rocky Checca, USMC.
USMC Liaison Officers: Maj. Eric Skoczenski, USMC; Maj. Kelly Repair, USMC; Capt. Mia Hencinski, USMC; Capt. Lucas Helms, USMC.
Office Manager/Administrative Clerk: MSgt. Lacorie Delaney, USMC; SSgt. Katherinne Mendez-Sanchez, USMC; Sgt. Gabriela Torian, USMC.

182 Russell Senate Office Building, phone: Navy 685–6003, Marine Corps 685–6010

Director.—CAPT Scott Sciretta, USN.
Deputy Director.—CDR Ed Murray, USN.
USN Liaison Officers: LT Jacques ''Don'' Archer, USN; LT Kaitlyn Bower, USN; LT Joseph Buckley, USN; LT Mary Sly, USN.
Director, USMC.—COL Kyle Ellison, USMC.
Deputy Director.—MAJ Rachel Matthes, USMC.
USMC Liaison Officers: Maj. Jim Purekal, USMC; Capt. Amber Schroeder, USMC.
Liaison Staff Non-Commissioned Officers: GySgt. Efren Casas, USMC; Sgt. Jovanka Jaimefranco, USMC; Sgt. Alex Ruiz, USMC.

GOVERNMENT ACCOUNTABILITY OFFICE

Room 7125, 441 G Street, 20548, phone 512–4400, fax 512–7919 or 512–4641

Managing Director, Congressional Relations.—Katherine Siggerud, 512–4400.
Executive Assistant.—Jane Lusby, 512–4378.
Legislative Advisers: Patrick Dibattista, 512–6787; Carlos Diz, 512–8256; Rosa Harris, 512–9492; Carolyn Kirby, 512–9843; David Lewis, 512–7176; Tim Minelli, 512–8443; Paul Thompson, 512–9867; Mary Frances Widner, 512–3804.
Associate Legislative Adviser.—Martene Rhed, 512–5414.
Congressional Information Systems Specialist.—Ellen Wedge, 512–6817.
Engagement and Administrative Operations Assistant.—Theodora Guardado-Gallegos, 512–6224.

OFFICE OF PERSONNEL MANAGEMENT

B–332 Rayburn House Office Building, phone 225–4955

Chief.—Kristen Soper.
Constituent Services Officers: Sean McKew, Carlos Tingle, Melony Witherspoon.

SOCIAL SECURITY ADMINISTRATION

G3, L1, Rayburn House Office Building, phone 225–3133, fax 225–3144

Director.—Robert Forrester.

Congressional Relations Liaisons: Sylvia Taylor-Mackey, Latrice Wingo.

STATE DEPARTMENT LIAISON OFFICES

2028 Rayburn House Office Building

For all Consular issues email: ConsularOnTheHill@state.gov
For all other issues email: House@state.gov
Phone: (202) 226–4642

Director.—Kem Anderson (acting), 228–1603.
Consular Officer.—Stacy Mactaggart, 226–4641.

189 Russell Senate Office Building

For all Consular issues email: ConsularOnTheHill@state.gov
For all other issues email: Senate@state.gov
Phone: (202) 228–1602

Director.—Daniel McCartney, 228–1602.

VETERANS' AFFAIRS

2026 Rayburn House Office Building, phone 225–2280, fax 273–9988

Assistant Director.—Annmarie Amaral.
Representatives: Tasha Adams, Richard Armstrong, Jr., Jeremy Dillard, Elena Joa, Alma Bourne.
Outreach.—Ca Asia Lane.

189 Russell Senate Office Building, phone 224–5351, fax 273–9988

Assistant Director.—Annmarie Amaral.
Representative.—Geisela Wimberly.
Outreach: Tim Embree, Nikki Brown.

UNITED STATES SENATE PAGE SCHOOL

United States Senate, Washington, DC 20510–7248, fax 224–1838

Principal.—Kathryn S. Weeden, 224–3926.
Executive Assistant.—Nikita Thompson, 224–3927.
English.—Frances Owens, 228–1024.
Mathematics.—Joshua Dorsey, 228–1018.
Science.—John Malek, 228–1025.
Social Studies.—Mark Fiorill, 228–1012.

U.S. CAPITOL POLICE

119 D Street, NE., 20510–7218

Office of the Chief 224–9806, Command Center 224–0908
Communications 224–5151, Emergency 224–0911

U.S. CAPITOL POLICE BOARD

Sergeant at Arms, U.S. House of Representatives.—Paul D. Irving.
Sergeant at Arms, U.S. Senate.—Michael C. Stenger.

Architect of the Capitol.—Stephen T. Ayers, FAIA, LEED AP.

OFFICE OF THE CHIEF

Chief of Police.—Matthew Verderosa.
Chief of Staff.—Dominic A. Storelli.
Office of:
General Counsel.—Gretchen DeMar.
Professional Responsibility.—Insp. Patrick Herrle.
Public Information.—Eva Malecki.
Task Force (Discipline Process Review).—Insp. Yogananda Pittman.

CHIEF OF OPERATIONS

Assistant Chief of Police.—Steven Sund.
Executive Officer.—Vacant.

MISSION ASSURANCE BUREAU

Bureau Commander.—Insp. Wesley Mahr (acting).
Command Center: Insp. Wesley Mahr, Capt. Michael Spochart.
Communications.—Capt. Darrin Bloxson.
Emergency Management Division.—Capt. Sean Patton.
Special Events.—Lt. Darrell Staton.

OPERATIONAL SERVICES BUREAU

Bureau Commander.—Deputy Chief Fredinal Rogers.
Hazardous Incident Response Division.—Capt. Kathleen McBride.
Patrol/Mobile Response Division.—Insp. Eric Belknap.

PROTECTIVE SERVICES BUREAU

Bureau Commander.—Deputy Chief Chad Thomas.
Dignitary Protection Division.—Insp. Kimberlie Bolinger.
Investigations Division.—Capt. Timothy Bowen.

SECURITY SERVICES BUREAU

Bureau Commander.—Robert Ford.

UNIFORMED SERVICES BUREAU

Bureau Commander.—Deputy Chief Richard Rudd.
Capitol Division Commander.—Insp. Eric Waldow.
House Division Commander.—Insp. Thomas Loyd.
Library Division Commander.—Insp. Donald Rouiller.
Senate Division Commander.—Insp. Jeffrey Pickett.

CHIEF ADMINISTRATIVE OFFICER

Chief Administrative Officer.—Richard Braddock.
Deputy Chief Administrative Officer.—Jay Miller.

Director, Office of:
Employment Counsel.—Frederick Herrera.
Inclusion, Diversity, Equity, and Action.—Natalie Holder.
Facilities and Logistics.—Cathleen English.
Financial Management.—Cherry Clipper.
Human Resources.—Jacqueline Whitaker.
Information Systems.—Heath Anderson.
Policy and Management Systems.—Jerome Boerste.
Training Services Bureau.—Thomas J. Madigan.

STATISTICAL INFORMATION

VOTES CAST FOR SENATORS IN 2012, 2014, and 2016

[Compiled from official statistics obtained by the Clerk of the House. Figures in the last column, for the 2016 election, may include totals for more candidates than the ones shown.]

State	Vote						Total vote cast in 2016
	2012		2014		2016		
	Democrat	Republican	Republican	Democrat	Republican	Democrat	
Alabama	...	...	795,606	...	1,335,104	748,709	2,087,444
Alaska	...	...	135,445	129,431	138,149	36,200	311,441
Arizona	1,036,542	1,104,457	...	...	1,359,267	1,031,245	2,530,730
Arkansas	...	...	478,819	334,174	661,984	400,602	1,107,522
California	7,864,624	4,713,887	...	...	...	12,244,170	12,244,170
Colorado	...	...	983,891	944,203	1,215,318	1,370,710	2,743,023
Connecticut	792,983	604,569	...	...	552,621	920,766	1,596,276
Delaware	265,415	115,700	98,823	130,655	...	...	234,038
Florida	4,523,451	3,458,267	...	...	4,835,191	4,122,088	9,301,820
Georgia	...	...	1,358,088	1,160,811	2,135,806	1,599,726	3,898,605
Hawaii	269,489	160,994	98,006	246,827	92,653	306,604	437,664
Idaho	...	...	285,596	151,574	449,017	188,249	678,943
Illinois	...	...	1,538,522	1,929,637	2,184,692	3,012,940	5,491,878
Indiana	1,281,181	1,133,621	...	...	1,423,991	1,158,947	2,732,546
Iowa	...	...	588,575	494,370	926,007	549,460	1,541,036
Kansas	...	...	460,350	...	732,376	379,740	1,177,922
Kentucky	...	...	806,787	584,698	1,090,177	813,246	1,903,465
Louisiana	...	...	929,108 (1)	581,041	1,239,489	705,271	1,997,218
Maine	92,900 (2)	215,399	413,505	190,254	...	...	616,996
Maryland	1,474,028	693,291	...	...	972,557	1,659,907	2,726,170
Massachusetts	1,696,346	1,458,048	791,950	1,289,944	...	...	2,186,789
Michigan	2,735,826	1,767,386	1,290,199	1,704,936	...	...	3,121,771
Minnesota	1,854,595	867,974	850,227	1,053,205	...	...	1,981,528
Mississippi	503,467	709,626	378,481	239,439	...	...	631,858
Missouri	1,494,125	1,066,159	...	...	1,378,458	1,300,200	2,802,641
Montana	236,123	218,051	213,709	148,184	...	...	369,826
Nebraska	332,979	455,593	347,636	170,127	...	...	540,337
Nevada	446,080	457,656	...	...	495,079	521,994	1,108,294
New Hampshire	...	...	235,347	251,184	353,632	354,649	739,140
New Jersey	1,987,680	1,329,534	791,297	1,043,866	...	...	1,869,535
New Mexico	395,717	351,260	229,097	286,409	...	...	515,506
New York	4,420,043	1,514,647	...	...	1,723,927	4,784,220	7,800,725
North Carolina	...	...	1,423,259	1,377,651	2,395,376	2,128,165	4,691,133
North Dakota	161,337	158,401	...	...	268,788	58,116	342,501
Ohio	2,762,690	2,435,712	...	...	3,118,567	1,996,908	5,374,164
Oklahoma	...	...	1,115,168	472,230	980,892	355,911	1,448,047
Oregon	...	...	538,847	814,537	651,106	1,105,119	1,952,478
Pennsylvania	3,021,364	2,509,132	...	...	2,951,702	2,865,012	6,051,856
Rhode Island	271,034	146,222	92,684	223,675	...	...	316,898
South Carolina	...	...	1,430,156	916,309	1,241,609	704,540	2,049,893
South Dakota	...	...	140,741	82,456	265,516	104,140	369,656
Tennessee	705,882	1,506,443	850,087	437,848	...	...	1,374,065
Texas	3,194,927	4,440,137	2,861,531	1,597,387	...	...	4,648,358
Utah	301,873	657,608	...	...	760,220	301,858	1,115,583
Vermont	(3)	72,898	...	...	103,637	192,243	320,467
Virginia	2,010,067	1,785,542	1,055,940	1,073,667	...	...	2,184,473
Washington	1,855,493	1,213,924	...	...	1,329,338	1,913,979	3,243,317
West Virginia	399,898	240,787	281,820	156,360	...	...	453,689
Wisconsin	1,547,104	1,380,126	...	...	1,479,471	1,380,335	2,948,741
Wyoming	53,019	185,250	121,554	29,377	...	...	171,153

[1] This vote count is from Louisiana's December 6, 2014, general (runoff) election, which was held because neither candidate received a majority of the vote in Louisiana's open (nonpartisan) primary on November 4, 2014. Bill Cassidy received 603,048 votes in the primary, and Mary L. Landrieu received 619,402.

[2] Independent Angus S. King, Jr., was elected on November 6, 2012 with 370,580 votes.

[3] Independent Bernard Sanders was elected on November 6, 2012 with 207,848 votes.

VOTES CAST FOR REPRESENTATIVES, RESIDENT COMMISSIONER, AND DELEGATES IN 2012, 2014, and 2016

[The figures, compiled from official statistics obtained by the Clerk of the House, show the votes for the Republican and Democratic nominees, except as otherwise indicated. Figures in the last column, for the 2016 election, may include totals for more candidates than the ones shown.]

State and district	Vote cast in 2012		Vote cast in 2014		Vote cast in 2016		Total vote cast in 2016
	Repub- lican	Demo- crat	Repub- lican	Demo- crat	Repub- lican	Demo- crat	
AL:							
1st	196,374	....	103,758	48,278	208,083	....	215,893
2d	180,591	103,092	113,103	54,692	134,886	112,089	276, 584
3d	175,306	98,141	103,558	52,816	192,164	94,549	287,104
4th	199,071	69,706	132,831	....	235,925	....	239,444
5th	189,185	101,772	115,338	....	205,647	102,234	308,326
6th	219,262	88,267	135,945	42,291	245,313	83,709	329,306
7th	73,835	232,520	....	133,687	....	229,330	233,028
AK:							
At large	185,296	82,927	142,572	114,602	155,088	111,019	308,198
AZ:							
1st	113,594	122,774	87,723	97,391	121,745	142,219	280,710
2d	144,884	147,338	109,704	109,543	179,806	135,873	315,679
3d	62,663	98,468	46,185	58,192	....	148,973	151,035
4th	162,907	69,154	122,560	45,179	203,487	81,296	284,783
5th	183,470	89,589	124,867	54,596	205,184	114,940	320,124
6th	179,706	97,666	129,578	70,198	201,578	122,866	324,444
7th	....	104,489	....	54,235	39,286	119,465	158,811
8th	172,809	95,635	128,710	....	204,942	....	298,971
9th	111,630	121,881	67,841	88,609	108,350	169,055	277,507
AR:							
1st	138,800	96,601	124,139	63,555	183,866	....	241,047
2d	158,175	113,156	123,073	103,477	176,472	111,347	302,464
3d	186,467	....	151,630	....	217,192	....	280,907
4th	154,149	95,013	110,789	87,742	182,885	....	244,159
CA:							
1st	168,827	125,386	132,052	84,320	185,448	128,588	314,036
2d	91,310	226,216	54,400	163,124	76,572	254,194	330,766
3d	107,086	126,882	71,036	79,224	104,453	152,513	256,966
4th	197,803	125,885	211,134	....	220,133	130,845	350,978
5th	69,545	202,872	....	129,613	67,565	224,526	292,091
6th	53,406	160,667	36,448	97,008	57,848	177,565	235,413
7th	132,050	141,241	91,066	92,521	145,168	152,133	297,301
8th	179,644	....	77,480	37,056	136,972	83,035	220,007
9th	94,704	118,373	57,729	63,475	98,992	133,163	232,155
10th	110,265	98,934	70,582	55,123	124,671	116,470	241,141
11th	87,136	200,743	57,160	117,502	83,341	214,868	298,209
12th	44,478	253,709	32,197	160,067	....	274,035	338,845
13th	....	250,436	21,940	168,491	29,754	293,117	322,871
14th	54,455	203,828	34,757	114,389	54,817	231,630	286,447
15th	....	231,034	43,150	99,756	70,619	198,578	269,197
16th	62,801	84,649	44,943	46,277	70,483	97,473	167,956
17th	57,336	159,392	....	134,408	....	233,192	233,192
18th	89,103	212,831	63,326	133,060	93,470	230,460	323,930
19th	59,313	162,300	....	127,788	64,061	181,802	245,863
20th	60,566	172,996	....	106,034	74,811	180,980	255,791
21st	67,164	49,119	45,907	33,470	75,126	57,282	132,408
22d	132,386	81,555	96,053	37,289	158,755	76,211	234,966
23d	158,161	....	100,317	33,726	167,116	74,468	241,584
24th	127,746	156,749	95,566	103,228	144,780	166,034	310,814
25th	129,593	106,982	114,072	....	138,755	122,406	261,161
26th	124,863	139,072	82,653	87,176	111,059	169,248	280,307
27th	86,817	154,191	51,852	75,728	81,655	168,977	250,632
28th	58,008	188,703	....	91,996	59,526	210,883	270,409
29th	....	111,287	17,045	50,096	....	171,824	171,824
30th	....	247,851	45,315	86,568	77,325	205,279	282,604
31st	161,219	....	48,162	51,622	94,866	121,070	215,936
32d	65,208	124,903	34,053	50,353	....	186,646	186,646
33d	....	171,860	74,700	108,331	110,822	219,397	330,219
34th	20,223	120,367	....	61,621	....	159,156	159,156
35th	....	142,680	....	62,255	47,309	124,044	171,353
36th	97,953	110,189	61,457	72,682	88,269	144,348	232,617
37th	32,541	207,039	18,051	96,787	....	237,272	237,272
38th	69,807	145,280	40,288	58,192	68,524	163,590	232,114
39th	145,607	106,360	91,319	41,906	150,777	112,679	263,456
40th	....	125,553	....	49,379	....	106,554	149,297
41st	72,074	103,578	35,936	46,948	69,159	128,164	197,323
42d	130,245	84,702	74,540	38,850	149,547	104,689	254,236
43d	....	200,894	28,521	69,681	52,499	167,017	219,516
44th	....	165,898	....	59,670	....	178,413	178,413
45th	171,417	121,814	106,083	56,819	182,618	129,231	311,849
46th	54,121	95,694	33,577	49,738	....	164,593	164,593
47th	99,919	130,093	54,309	69,091	88,109	154,759	242,868
48th	177,144	113,358	112,082	62,713	178,701	127,715	306,416
49th	159,725	114,893	98,161	64,981	155,888	154,267	310,155
50th	174,838	83,455	111,997	45,302	179,937	103,646	283,583

VOTES CAST FOR REPRESENTATIVES, RESIDENT COMMISSIONER, AND DELEGATES IN 2012, 2014, and 2016—CONTINUED

[The figures, compiled from official statistics obtained by the Clerk of the House, show the votes for the Republican and Democratic nominees, except as otherwise indicated. Figures in the last column, for the 2016 election, may include totals for more candidates than the ones shown.]

State and district	Vote cast in 2012		State and district	Vote cast in 2014		State and district	Vote cast in 2016		Total vote cast in 2016
	Repub-lican	Demo-crat		Repub-lican	Demo-crat		Repub-lican	Demo-crat	
51st	45,464	113,934	51st	25,577	56,373	51st	54,362	145,162	199,524
52d	144,459	151,451	52d	92,746	98,826	52d	139,403	181,253	320,656
53d	103,482	164,825	53d	60,940	87,104	53d	97,968	198,988	296,956
CO:			CO:			CO:			
1st	93,217	237,579	1st	80,682	183,281	1st	105,030	257,254	379,036
2d	162,639	234,758	2d	149,645	196,300	2d	170,001	260,175	457,312
3d	185,291	142,619	3d	163,011	100,364	3d	204,220	150,914	374,037
4th	200,006	125,800	4th	185,292	83,727	4th	248,230	123,642	390,633
5th	199,639	....	5th	157,182	105,673	5th	225,445	111,676	361,993
6th	163,938	156,937	6th	143,467	118,847	6th	191,626	160,372	376,417
7th	139,066	182,460	7th	120,918	148,225	7th	144,066	199,758	362,010
CT:			CT:			CT:			
1st	82,321	192,840	1st	78,609	127,430	1st	105,674	187,021	312,925
2d	88,103	189,444	2d	80,837	131,294	2d	111,149	186,210	330,257
3d	73,726	197,163	3d	69,454	130,009	3d	95,786	192,274	309,379
4th	117,503	167,320	4th	88,209	101,401	4th	120,653	187,811	313,540
5th	128,927	137,631	5th	92,404	106,256	5th	124,900	163,499	309,082
DE:			DE:			DE:			
At large	129,757	249,933	At large	85,146	137,251	At large	172,301	233,554	420,617
FL:			FL:			FL:			
1st	238,440	92,961	1st	165,086	54,976	1st	255,107	114,079	369,186
2d	175,856	157,634	2d	123,262	126,096	2d	231,163	102,811	343,362
3d	204,331	102,468	3d	148,691	73,910	3d	193,843	136,338	342,700
4th	239,988	....	4th	177,887	....	4th	287,509	113,088	409,662
5th	70,700	190,472	5th	59,237	112,340	5th	108,325	194,549	302,874
6th	195,962	146,489	6th	166,254	99,563	6th	213,519	151,051	364,570
7th	185,518	130,479	7th	144,474	73,011	7th	171,583	182,039	353,655
8th	205,432	130,870	8th	180,728	93,724	8th	246,483	127,127	390,561
9th	98,856	164,891	9th	74,963	93,850	9th	144,450	195,311	339,761
10th	164,649	153,574	10th	143,128	89,426	10th	107,498	198,491	305,989
11th	218,360	120,303	11th	181,508	90,786	11th	258,016	124,713	394,719
12th	209,604	108,770	12th	(1)	....	12th	253,559	116,110	369,669
13th	189,605	139,742	13th	168,172	....	13th	171,149	184,693	355,842
14th	83,480	197,121	14th	....	(1)	14th	121,088	195,789	316,877
15th	(1)	....	15th	128,750	84,832	15th	182,999	135,475	318,474
16th	187,147	161,929	16th	169,126	105,483	16th	230,654	155,262	385,916
17th	165,488	116,766	17th	141,493	82,263	17th	209,348	115,974	338,675
18th	164,353	166,257	18th	101,896	151,478	18th	201,488	161,918	375,918
19th	189,833	109,746	19th	159,354	80,824	19th	239,225	123,812	363,166
20th	....	214,727	20th	28,968	128,498	20th	54,646	222,914	277,560
21st	....	221,263	21st	....	153,395	21st	118,038	210,606	335,861
22d	142,050	171,021	22d	90,685	125,404	22d	138,737	199,113	337,850
23d	98,096	174,205	23d	61,519	103,269	23d	130,818	183,225	323,120
24th	....	(1)	24th	15,239	129,192	24th	....	(1)	(1)
25th	151,466	....	25th	(1)	....	25th	157,921	95,319	253,240
26th	108,820	135,694	26th	83,031	78,306	26th	148,547	115,493	280,542
27th	138,488	85,020	27th	(1)	....	27th	157,917	129,760	287,677
GA:			GA:			GA:			
1st	157,181	92,399	1st	95,337	61,175	1st	210,243	....	211,112
2d	92,410	162,751	2d	66,537	96,363	2d	94,056	148,543	242,599
3d	232,380	....	3d	156,277	....	3d	207,218	95,969	303,187
4th	75,041	208,861	4th	....	161,211	4th	70,593	220,146	290,739
5th	43,335	234,330	5th	....	170,326	5th	46,768	253,781	300,549
6th	189,669	104,365	6th	139,018	71,486	6th	201,088	124,917	326,005
7th	156,689	95,377	7th	113,557	60,112	7th	174,081	114,220	288,301
8th	197,789	....	8th	129,938	....	8th	173,983	83,225	257,208
9th	192,101	60,052	9th	146,059	34,988	9th	256,535	....	256,535
10th	211,065	....	10th	130,703	65,777	10th	243,725	....	244,821
11th	196,968	90,353	11th	161,532	....	11th	217,935	105,383	323,318
12th	119,973	139,148	12th	91,336	75,478	12th	159,492	99,420	258,912
13th	79,550	201,988	13th	....	159,445	13th	....	252,833	252,833
14th	159,947	59,245	14th	118,782	....	14th	216,743	....	216,743
HI:			HI:			HI:			
1st	96,824	116,505	1st	86,454	93,390	1st	45,958	145,417	213,531
2d	40,707	168,503	2d	33,630	142,010	2d	39,668	170,848	224,133
ID:			ID:			ID:			
1st	199,402	97,450	1st	143,580	77,277	1st	242,252	113,052	355,357
2d	207,412	110,847	2d	131,492	82,801	2d	205,292	95,940	326,237
IL:			IL:			IL:			
1st	83,989	236,854	1st	59,749	162,268	1st	81,817	234,037	315,862
2d	69,115	188,303	2d	43,799	160,337	2d	59,471	235,051	294,522
3d	77,653	168,738	3d	64,091	116,764	3d	....	225,320	225,411
4th	27,279	133,226	4th	22,278	79,666	4th	....	171,297	171,297
5th	77,289	177,729	5th	56,350	116,364	5th	86,222	212,842	313,724
6th	193,138	132,991	6th	160,287	78,465	6th	208,555	143,591	352,146

VOTES CAST FOR REPRESENTATIVES, RESIDENT COMMISSIONER, AND DELEGATES IN 2012, 2014, and 2016—CONTINUED

[The figures, compiled from official statistics obtained by the Clerk of the House, show the votes for the Republican and Democratic nominees, except as otherwise indicated. Figures in the last column, for the 2016 election, may include totals for more candidates than the ones shown.]

State and district	Vote cast in 2012		State and district	Vote cast in 2014		State and district	Vote cast in 2016		Total vote cast in 2016
	Republican	Democrat		Republican	Democrat		Republican	Democrat	
7th	31,466	242,439	7th	27,168	155,110	7th	46,882	250,584	297,466
8th	101,860	123,206	8th	66,878	84,178	8th	103,617	144,954	248,571
9th	98,924	194,869	9th	72,384	141,000	9th	109,550	217,306	326,948
10th	130,564	133,890	10th	95,992	91,136	10th	135,535	150,435	285,996
11th	105,348	148,928	11th	81,335	93,436	11th	108,995	166,578	275,573
12th	129,902	157,000	12th	110,038	87,860	12th	169,976	124,246	313,002
13th	137,034	136,032	13th	123,337	86,935	13th	187,583	126,811	314,394
14th	177,603	124,351	14th	145,369	76,861	14th	200,508	137,589	338,097
15th	205,775	94,162	15th	166,274	55,652	15th	274,554	....	274,554
16th	181,789	112,301	16th	153,388	63,810	16th	259,722	....	259,853
17th	134,623	153,519	17th	88,785	110,560	17th	113,943	173,125	287,068
18th	244,467	85,164	18th	184,363	62,377	18th	250,506	96,770	347,283
IN:			IN:			IN:			
1st	91,291	187,743	1st	51,000	86,579	1st	....	207,515	254,583
2d	134,033	130,113	2d	85,583	55,590	2d	164,355	102,401	277,357
3d	187,872	92,363	3d	97,892	39,771	3d	201,396	66,023	287,247
4th	168,688	93,015	4th	94,998	47,056	4th	193,412	91,256	299,434
5th	194,570	125,347	5th	105,277	49,756	5th	221,957	123,849	361,135
6th	162,613	96,678	6th	102,187	45,509	6th	204,920	79,135	296,385
7th	95,828	162,122	7th	46,887	61,443	7th	94,456	158,739	264,670
8th	151,533	122,325	8th	103,344	61,384	8th	187,702	93,356	294,713
9th	165,332	132,848	9th	101,594	55,016	9th	174,791	130,627	322,843
IA:			IA:			IA:			
1st	162,465	222,422	1st	147,762	141,145	1st	206,903	177,403	384,977
2d	161,977	211,863	2d	129,455	143,431	2d	170,933	198,571	370,032
3d	202,000	168,632	3d	148,814	119,109	3d	208,598	155,002	390,287
4th	200,063	169,470	4th	169,834	105,504	4th	226,719	142,993	370,259
5th									
KS:			KS:			KS:			
1st	211,337	....	1st	138,764	65,397	1st	169,992	....	257,971
2d	167,463	113,735	2d	128,742	87,153	2d	181,228	96,840	297,401
3d	201,087	....	3d	134,493	89,584	3d	176,022	139,300	343,113
4th	161,094	81,770	4th	138,757	69,396	4th	166,998	81,495	275,251
KY:			KY:			KY:			
1st	199,956	87,199	1st	173,022	63,596	1st	216,959	81,710	299,001
2d	181,508	89,541	2d	156,936	69,898	2d	251,825	....	251,825
3d	111,452	206,385	3d	87,981	157,056	3d	122,093	212,401	334,494
4th	186,036	104,734	4th	150,464	71,694	4th	233,922	94,065	327,987
5th	195,408	55,447	5th	171,350	47,617	5th	221,242	....	221,242
6th	153,222	141,438	6th	147,404	98,290	6th	202,099	128,728	330,827
LA:			LA:			LA:			
1st	218,340	61,703	1st	189,250	46,047	1st	243,645	63,785	326,788
2d	50,146	230,417	2d	....	190,006	2d	....	284,269	284,269
3d	240,558	67,070	3d	207,926	....	3d	220,621	56,215	282,443
4th	187,894	....	4th	152,683	....	4th	216,540	46,579	268,761
5th	202,536	....	5th	247,211	75,006	5th	255,662	....	255,662
6th	243,553	....	6th	234,200	95,127	6th	241,075	79,202	331,098
ME:			ME:			ME:			
1st	128,440	236,363	1st	94,751	186,674	1st	164,569	227,546	406,942
2d	137,542	191,456	2d	133,320	118,568	2d	192,878	159,081	364,886
MD:			MD:			MD:			
1st	214,204	92,812	1st	176,342	73,843	1st	242,574	103,622	362,097
2d	92,071	194,088	2d	70,411	120,412	2d	102,577	192,183	309,480
3d	94,549	213,747	3d	87,029	128,594	3d	115,048	214,640	339,675
4th	64,560	240,385	4th	54,217	134,628	4th	68,670	237,501	320,650
5th	95,271	238,618	5th	80,752	144,725	5th	105,931	242,989	360,634
6th	117,313	181,921	6th	91,930	94,704	6th	133,081	185,770	331,973
7th	67,405	247,770	7th	55,860	144,639	7th	69,556	238,838	318,912
8th	113,033	217,531	8th	87,859	136,722	8th	124,651	220,657	364,324
MA:			MA:			MA:			
1st	....	261,936	1st	....	167,612	1st	....	235,803	349,676
2d	....	259,257	2d	....	169,640	2d	....	275,487	363,197
3d	109,372	212,119	3d	81,638	139,104	3d	107,519	236,713	360,124
4th	129,936	221,303	4th	....	184,158	4th	113,055	265,823	395,304
5th	82,944	257,490	5th	....	182,100	5th	....	285,606	385,455
6th	176,612	180,942	6th	111,989	149,638	6th	....	308,923	415,749
7th	....	210,794	7th	....	142,133	7th	....	253,354	309,645
8th	82,242	263,999	8th	....	200,644	8th	102,744	271,019	396,009
9th	116,531	212,754	9th	114,971	140,413	9th	127,803	211,790	403,642
MI:			MI:			MI:			
1st	167,060	165,179	1st	130,414	113,263	1st	197,777	144,334	360,271
2d	194,653	108,973	2d	135,568	70,851	2d	212,508	110,391	339,328
3d	171,675	144,108	3d	125,754	84,720	3d	203,545	128,400	342,365
4th	197,386	104,996	4th	123,962	85,777	4th	194,572	101,277	315,751
5th	103,931	214,531	5th	69,222	148,182	5th	112,102	195,279	319,291

VOTES CAST FOR REPRESENTATIVES, RESIDENT COMMISSIONER, AND DELEGATES IN 2012, 2014, and 2016—CONTINUED

[The figures, compiled from official statistics obtained by the Clerk of the House, show the votes for the Republican and Democratic nominees, except as otherwise indicated. Figures in the last column, for the 2016 election, may include totals for more candidates than the ones shown.]

State and district	Vote cast in 2012		State and district	Vote cast in 2014		State and district	Vote cast in 2016		Total vote cast in 2016
	Repub-lican	Demo-crat		Repub-lican	Demo-crat		Repub-lican	Demo-crat	
6th	174,955	136,563	6th	116,801	84,391	6th	193,259	119,980	329,565
7th	169,668	136,849	7th	119,564	92,083	7th	184,321	134,010	334,807
8th	202,217	128,657	8th	132,739	102,269	8th	205,629	143,791	366,968
9th	114,760	208,846	9th	81,470	136,342	9th	128,937	199,661	344,775
10th	226,075	97,734	10th	157,069	67,143	10th	215,132	110,112	340,983
11th	181,788	158,879	11th	140,435	101,681	11th	200,872	152,461	379,488
12th	92,472	216,884	12th	64,716	134,346	12th	96,104	211,378	328,542
13th	38,769	235,336	13th	27,234	132,710	13th	40,541	198,771	257,797
14th	51,395	270,450	14th	41,801	165,272	14th	58,103	244,135	310,974
MN:			MN:			MN:			
1st	142,164	193,211	1st	103,536	122,851	1st	166,524	169,071	335,873
2d	193,587	164,338	2d	137,778	95,565	2d	173,970	....	370,515
3d	222,335	159,937	3d	167,515	101,846	3d	223,075	....	393,457
4th	109,659	216,685	4th	79,492	147,857	4th	121,033	203,299	351,945
5th	88,753	262,102	5th	56,577	167,079	5th	80,660	249,957	361,875
6th	179,240	174,944	6th	133,328	90,926	6th	235,385	....	358,930
7th	114,151	197,791	7th	109,955	130,546	7th	156,944	173,572	330,823
8th	160,520	191,976	8th	125,358	129,090	8th	177,088	179,097	356,971
MS:			MS:			MS:			
1st	186,760	114,076	1st	102,622	43,713	1st	206,455	83,947	300,423
2d	99,160	214,978	2d	....	100,688	2d	83,542	192,343	286,626
3d	234,717	....	3d	117,771	47,744	3d	209,490	96,101	316,445
4th	182,998	82,344	4th	108,776	37,869	4th	181,323	77,505	278,779
MO:			MO:			MO:			
1st	60,832	267,927	1st	35,273	119,315	1st	62,714	236,993	314,024
2d	236,971	146,272	2d	148,191	75,384	2d	241,954	155,689	413,296
3d	214,843	111,189	3d	130,940	52,021	3d	249,865	102,891	368,333
4th	192,237	113,120	4th	120,014	46,464	4th	225,348	92,510	332,234
5th	122,149	200,290	5th	69,071	79,256	5th	123,771	190,766	324,270
6th	216,906	108,503	6th	124,616	55,157	6th	238,388	99,692	350,444
7th	203,565	98,498	7th	104,054	47,282	7th	228,692	92,756	338,607
8th	216,083	73,755	8th	106,124	38,721	8th	229,792	70,009	308,871
MT:			MT:			MT:			
At large	255,468	204,939	At large	203,871	148,690	At large	285,358	205,919	507,831
NE:			NE:			NE:			
1st	174,889	81,206	1st	123,219	55,838	1st	189,771	83,467	273,238
2d	133,964	129,767	2d	78,157	83,872	2d	141,066	137,602	288,308
3d	187,423	65,266	3d	139,440	45,524	3d	226,720	....	226,720
NV:			NV:			NV:			
1st	56,521	113,967	1st	30,413	45,643	1st	54,174	116,537	188,352
2d	162,213	102,019	2d	122,402	52,016	2d	182,676	115,722	313,336
3d	137,244	116,823	3d	88,528	52,644	3d	142,926	146,869	310,963
4th	101,261	120,501	4th	63,466	59,844	4th	118,328	128,985	265,846
NH:			NH:			NH:			
1st	158,659	171,650	1st	125,508	116,769	1st	157,176	162,080	365,984
2d	152,977	169,275	2d	106,871	130,700	2d	158,825	174,371	350,509
NJ:			NJ:			NJ:			
1st	92,459	210,470	1st	64,073	93,315	1st	112,388	183,231	305,473
2d	166,677	116,462	2d	108,875	66,026	2d	176,338	110,838	297,795
3d	174,253	145,506	3d	100,471	82,537	3d	194,596	127,526	328,060
4th	195,145	107,991	4th	118,826	54,415	4th	211,992	111,532	332,684
5th	167,501	130,100	5th	104,678	81,808	5th	157,690	172,587	337,701
6th	84,360	151,782	6th	46,891	72,190	6th	91,908	167,895	263,435
7th	175,662	123,057	7th	104,287	68,232	7th	185,850	148,188	343,635
8th	31,763	130,853	8th	15,141	61,510	8th	32,337	134,733	174,889
9th	55,091	162,822	9th	36,246	82,498	9th	65,376	162,642	233,242
10th	24,271	201,435	10th	14,154	95,734	10th	26,450	190,856	222,771
11th	182,237	123,897	11th	109,455	65,477	11th	194,299	130,162	334,992
12th	80,906	189,926	12th	54,168	90,430	12th	92,407	181,430	288,634
NM:			NM:			NM:			
1st	112,473	162,924	1st	74,558	105,474	1st	96,879	181,088	277,967
2d	133,180	92,162	2d	95,209	52,499	2d	143,515	85,232	228,817
3d	97,616	167,103	3d	70,775	113,249	3d	102,730	170,612	273,342
NY:			NY:			NY:			
1st	106,678	134,205	1st	77,062	68,387	1st	158,409	126,635	341,554
2d	....	93,375	2d	....	41,814	2d	....	102,270	317,552
3d	....	146,016	3d	63,219	80,393	3d	133,954	171,775	350,966
4th	84,982	152,590	4th	67,811	83,772	4th	111,246	181,861	343,179
5th	17,875	167,835	5th	....	75,712	5th	26,791	197,852	249,236
6th	45,992	107,505	6th	....	49,227	6th	43,770	131,463	210,378
7th	....	132,456	7th	5,713	47,142	7th	14,941	165,819	206,983
8th	15,841	178,687	8th	....	70,469	8th	....	203,235	257,602
9th	20,899	178,168	9th	....	70,997	9th	....	198,886	256,853
10th	35,440	155,908	10th	....	73,945	10th	46,275	180,117	266,516
11th	91,030	87,718	11th	48,291	41,429	11th	122,606	85,257	251,718

VOTES CAST FOR REPRESENTATIVES, RESIDENT COMMISSIONER, AND DELEGATES IN 2012, 2014, and 2016—CONTINUED

[The figures, compiled from official statistics obtained by the Clerk of the House, show the votes for the Republican and Democratic nominees, except as otherwise indicated. Figures in the last column, for the 2016 election, may include totals for more candidates than the ones shown.]

State and district	Vote cast in 2012		State and district	Vote cast in 2014		State and district	Vote cast in 2016		Total vote cast in 2016
	Repub-lican	Demo-crat		Repub-lican	Demo-crat		Repub-lican	Demo-crat	
12th	41,969	184,864	12th	19,564	78,440	12th	49,398	230,153	312,289
13th	12,132	170,470	13th	....	63,437	13th	13,129	207,194	255,239
14th	19,191	116,117	14th	....	45,370	14th	26,891	138,367	197,301
15th	3,487	150,243	15th	....	53,128	15th	6,129	165,688	193,703
16th	53,935	173,885	16th	....	90,088	16th	....	198,811	287,556
17th	91,899	161,624	17th	63,549	89,295	17th	....	193,819	325,571
18th	113,386	132,456	18th	66,523	76,235	18th	111,117	140,951	319,123
19th	122,654	120,302	19th	102,118	60,533	19th	135,905	125,956	326,588
20th	79,102	181,092	20th	61,820	103,437	20th	83,328	188,428	332,499
21st	104,368	117,856	21st	79,615	53,140	21st	152,597	75,965	288,611
22d	145,042	102,080	22d	113,574	....	22d	113,287	102,734	296,086
23d	117,641	114,590	23d	94,375	60,233	23d	136,964	106,600	269,198
24th	105,584	133,908	24th	93,881	72,631	24th	150,330	110,550	315,429
25th	109,292	168,761	25th	75,990	87,264	25th	113,840	168,660	336,386
26th	57,368	195,234	26th	38,477	100,648	26th	56,930	195,322	310,819
27th	137,250	140,008	27th	109,171	50,939	27th	175,509	107,832	354,426
NC:			NC:			NC:			
1st	77,288	254,644	1st	55,990	154,333	1st	101,567	240,661	350,699
2d	174,066	128,973	2d	122,128	85,479	2d	221,485	169,082	390,567
3d	195,571	114,314	3d	139,415	66,182	3d	217,531	106,170	323,701
4th	88,951	259,534	4th	57,416	169,946	4th	130,161	279,380	409,541
5th	200,945	148,252	5th	139,279	88,973	5th	207,625	147,887	355,512
6th	222,116	142,467	6th	147,312	103,758	6th	207,983	143,167	351,150
7th	168,041	168,695	7th	134,431	84,054	7th	211,801	135,905	347,706
8th	160,695	137,139	8th	121,568	65,854	8th	189,863	133,182	323,045
9th	194,537	171,503	9th	163,080	....	9th	193,452	139,041	332,493
10th	190,826	144,023	10th	133,504	85,292	10th	220,825	128,919	349,744
11th	190,319	141,107	11th	144,682	85,342	11th	230,405	129,103	359,508
12th	63,317	247,591	12th	42,568	130,096	12th	115,185	234,115	349,300
13th	210,495	160,115	13th	153,991	114,718	13th	199,443	156,049	355,492
ND:			ND:			ND:			
At large ..	173,585	131,870	At large ..	138,100	95,678	At large ..	233,980	80,377	338,459
OH:			OH:			OH:			
1st	201,907	131,490	1st	124,779	72,604	1st	210,014	144,644	354,788
2d	194,296	137,077	2d	132,658	68,453	2d	221,193	111,694	340,279
3d	77,901	201,897	3d	51,475	91,769	3d	91,560	199,791	291,351
4th	182,643	114,214	4th	125,907	60,165	4th	210,227	98,981	309,208
5th	201,514	137,806	5th	134,449	58,507	5th	244,599	100,392	344,991
6th	164,536	144,444	6th	111,026	73,561	6th	231,975	88,780	302,755
7th	178,104	137,708	7th	143,959	....	7th	198,221	89,638	309,553
8th	246,378	....	8th	126,539	51,534	8th	223,833	87,794	325,506
9th	68,668	217,771	9th	51,704	108,870	9th	88,427	193,966	282,398
10th	208,201	131,097	10th	130,752	63,249	10th	215,724	109,981	336,602
11th	....	258,359	11th	35,461	137,105	11th	59,769	242,917	302,686
12th	233,869	134,605	12th	150,573	61,360	12th	251,266	112,638	377,534
13th	88,120	235,492	13th	55,233	120,230	13th	99,377	208,610	308,004
14th	183,657	131,637	14th	135,736	70,856	14th	219,191	130,907	350,269
15th	205,274	128,188	15th	128,496	66,125	15th	222,847	113,960	336,807
16th	185,165	170,600	16th	132,176	75,199	16th	225,794	119,830	345,624
OK:			OK:			OK:			
1st	181,084	91,421	1st	[3]	....	1st	[3]	....	[3]
2d	143,701	96,081	2d	110,925	38,964	2d	189,839	62,387	268,870
3d	201,744	53,472	3d	133,335	36,270	3d	227,525	63,090	290,615
4th	176,740	71,846	4th	117,721	40,998	4th	204,143	76,472	293,189
5th	153,603	97,504	5th	95,632	57,790	5th	160,184	103,273	280,570
OR:			OR:			OR:			
1st	109,699	197,845	1st	96,245	160,038	1st	139,756	225,391	378,095
2d	228,043	....	2d	202,374	73,785	2d	272,952	106,640	380,739
3d	70,325	264,979	3d	57,424	211,748	3d	....	274,687	382,355
4th	....	212,866	4th	116,534	181,624	4th	157,743	220,628	397,568
5th	139,223	177,229	5th	110,332	150,944	5th	160,443	199,505	373,108
PA:			PA:			PA:			
1st	41,708	235,394	1st	27,193	131,248	1st	53,219	245,791	299,010
2d	33,381	318,176	2d	25,397	181,141	2d	35,131	322,514	357,645
3d	165,826	123,933	3d	113,859	73,931	3d	244,893	....	244,893
4th	181,603	104,643	4th	147,090	50,250	4th	220,628	113,372	334,000
5th	177,740	104,725	5th	115,018	65,839	5th	206,761	101,082	307,843
6th	191,725	143,803	6th	119,643	92,901	6th	207,469	155,000	362,469
7th	209,942	143,509	7th	145,869	89,256	7th	225,678	153,824	379,502
8th	199,379	152,859	8th	137,731	84,767	8th	207,263	173,555	380,818
9th	169,177	105,128	9th	110,094	63,223	9th	186,580	107,985	294,565
10th	179,563	94,227	10th	112,851	44,737	10th	211,282	89,823	301,105
11th	166,967	118,231	11th	122,464	62,228	11th	199,421	113,800	313,221
12th	175,352	163,589	12th	127,993	87,928	12th	221,851	137,353	359,204
13th	93,918	209,901	13th	60,549	123,601	13th	....	239,316	239,316

VOTES CAST FOR REPRESENTATIVES, RESIDENT COMMISSIONER, AND DELEGATES IN 2012, 2014, and 2016—CONTINUED

[The figures, compiled from official statistics obtained by the Clerk of the House, show the votes for the Republican and Democratic nominees, except as otherwise indicated. Figures in the last column, for the 2016 election, may include totals for more candidates than the ones shown.]

State and district	Vote cast in 2012		State and district	Vote cast in 2014		State and district	Vote cast in 2016		Total vote cast in 2016
	Repub-lican	Demo-crat		Repub-lican	Demo-crat		Repub-lican	Demo-crat	
14th	75,702	251,932	14th	....	148,351	14th	87,999	255,293	343,292
15th	168,960	128,764	15th	128,285	....	15th	190,618	124,129	326,474
16th	156,192	111,185	16th	101,722	74,513	16th	168,669	134,586	313,773
17th	106,208	161,393	17th	71,371	93,680	17th	135,430	157,734	293,164
18th	216,727	122,146	18th	166,076	....	18th	293,684	....	293,684
RI:			RI:			RI:			
1st	83,737	108,612	1st	58,877	87,060	1st	71,023	130,534	202,371
2d	78,189	124,067	2d	63,844	105,716	2d	70,301	133,108	229,148
SC:			SC:			SC:			
1st	179,908	98,154	1st	119,392	....	1st	190,410	110,539	325,170
2d	196,116	....	2d	121,649	68,719	2d	183,746	105,306	304,996
3d	169,512	84,735	3d	116,741	47,181	3d	196,325	72,933	269,540
4th	173,201	84,087	4th	126,452	....	4th	198,648	91,676	295,670
5th	154,324	113,904	5th	103,078	66,802	5th	161,669	105,772	273,006
6th	....	218,717	6th	44,311	125,747	6th	70,099	177,947	253,901
7th	153,068	114,594	7th	102,833	68,576	7th	176,468	103,454	289,463
SD:			SD:			SD:			
At large ..	207,640	153,789	At large ..	183,834	92,485	At large ..	237,163	132,810	369,973
TN:			TN:			TN:			
1st	182,252	47,663	1st	115,533	....	1st	198,293	39,024	253,025
2d	196,894	54,522	2d	120,883	37,612	2d	212,455	68,401	280,856
3d	157,830	91,094	3d	97,344	53,983	3d	176,613	76,727	266,006
4th	128,568	102,022	4th	84,815	51,357	4th	165,796	89,141	254,937
5th	86,240	171,621	5th	55,078	96,148	5th	102,433	171,111	273,544
6th	184,383	....	6th	115,231	37,232	6th	202,234	61,995	284,490
7th	182,730	61,679	7th	110,534	42,280	7th	200,407	65,226	277,513
8th	190,923	79,490	8th	122,255	42,433	8th	194,386	70,925	282,733
9th	59,742	188,422	9th	27,173	87,376	9th	41,123	171,631	217,957
TX:			TX:			TX:			
1st	178,322	67,222	1st	115,084	33,476	1st	192,434	62,847	260,409
2d	159,664	80,512	2d	101,936	44,462	2d	168,692	100,231	278,236
3d	187,180	....	3d	113,404	....	3d	193,684	109,420	316,467
4th	182,679	60,214	4th	115,085	....	4th	216,643	....	246,220
5th	134,091	69,178	5th	88,998	....	5th	155,469	....	192,875
6th	145,019	98,053	6th	92,334	55,027	6th	159,444	106,667	273,296
7th	142,793	85,553	7th	90,606	49,478	7th	143,542	111,991	255,533
8th	194,043	51,051	8th	125,066	....	8th	236,379	....	236,379
9th	36,139	144,075	9th	....	78,109	9th	36,491	152,032	188,523
10th	159,783	95,710	10th	109,726	60,243	10th	179,221	120,170	312,600
11th	177,742	41,970	11th	107,939	....	11th	201,871	....	225,548
12th	175,649	66,080	12th	113,186	41,757	12th	196,482	76,029	283,115
13th	187,775	....	13th	110,842	16,822	13th	199,050	....	221,242
14th	131,460	109,697	14th	90,116	52,545	14th	160,631	99,054	259,685
15th	54,056	89,296	15th	39,016	48,708	15th	66,877	101,712	177,479
16th	51,043	101,403	16th	21,324	49,338	16th	....	150,228	175,229
17th	143,284	....	17th	85,807	43,049	17th	149,417	86,603	245,728
18th	44,015	146,223	18th	26,249	76,097	18th	48,306	150,157	204,308
19th	163,239	....	19th	90,160	21,458	19th	176,314	....	203,475
20th	62,376	119,032	20th	....	66,554	20th	....	149,640	187,669
21st	187,015	109,326	21st	135,660	....	21st	202,967	129,765	356,031
22d	160,668	80,203	22d	100,861	47,844	22d	181,864	123,679	305,543
23d	87,547	96,676	23d	57,459	55,037	23d	110,577	107,526	228,965
24th	148,586	87,645	24th	93,712	46,548	24th	154,845	108,389	275,635
25th	154,245	98,827	25th	107,120	64,463	25th	180,988	117,073	310,196
26th	176,642	74,237	26th	116,944	....	26th	211,730	94,507	319,080
27th	120,684	83,395	27th	83,342	44,152	27th	142,251	88,329	230,580
28th	49,309	112,456	28th	....	62,508	28th	57,740	122,086	184,442
29th	....	86,053	29th	....	41,321	29th	31,646	95,649	131,982
30th	41,222	171,059	30th	....	93,041	30th	41,518	170,502	218,826
31st	145,348	82,977	31st	91,607	45,715	31st	166,060	103,852	284,588
32d	146,653	99,288	32d	96,495	55,325	32d	162,868	....	229,171
33d	30,252	85,114	33d	....	43,769	33d	33,222	93,147	126,369
34th	52,448	89,606	34th	30,811	47,503	34th	62,323	104,638	166,961
35th	52,894	105,626	35th	32,040	60,124	35th	62,384	124,612	197,579
36th	165,405	62,143	36th	101,663	29,543	36th	193,675	....	218,565
UT:			UT:			UT:			
1st	175,487	60,611	1st	84,231	36,422	1st	182,925	73,380	277,451
2d	154,523	83,176	2d	88,915	47,585	2d	170,534	93,778	276,819
3d	198,828	60,719	3d	102,952	32,059	3d	209,589	75,716	285,305
4th	119,035	119,803	4th	74,936	67,425	4th	147,597	113,413	274,569
VT:			VT:			VT:			
At large ..	67,543	208,600	At large ..	59,432	123,349	At large ..	....	264,414	320,467
VA:			VA:			VA:			
1st	200,845	147,036	1st	131,861	72,059	1st	230,213	140,785	384,601
2d	166,231	142,548	2d	101,558	71,178	2d	190,475	119,440	310,567

VOTES CAST FOR REPRESENTATIVES, RESIDENT COMMISSIONER, AND DELEGATES IN 2012, 2014, and 2016—CONTINUED

[The figures, compiled from official statistics obtained by the Clerk of the House, show the votes for the Republican and Democratic nominees, except as otherwise indicated. Figures in the last column, for the 2016 election, may include totals for more candidates than the ones shown.]

State and district	Vote cast in 2012		State and district	Vote cast in 2014		State and district	Vote cast in 2016		Total vote cast in 2016
	Republican	Democrat		Republican	Democrat		Republican	Democrat	
3d	58,931	259,199	3d	....	139,197	3d	103,289	208,337	312,340
4th	199,292	150,190	4th	120,684	75,270	4th	145,731	200,136	346,656
5th	193,009	149,214	5th	124,735	73,482	5th	207,758	148,339	356,756
6th	211,278	111,949	6th	133,898	....	6th	225,471	112,170	338,409
7th	222,983	158,012	7th	148,026	89,914	7th	218,057	160,159	379,163
8th	107,370	226,847	8th	63,810	128,102	8th	98,387	246,653	360,676
9th	184,882	116,400	9th	117,465	....	9th	212,838	87,877	310,314
10th	214,038	142,024	10th	125,914	89,957	10th	210,791	187,712	400,083
11th	117,902	202,606	11th	75,796	106,780	11th	....	247,818	282,003
WA:			WA:			WA:			
1st	151,187	177,025	1st	101,428	124,151	1st	155,779	193,619	349,398
2d	117,465	184,826	2d	79,518	122,173	2d	117,094	208,314	325,408
3d	177,446	116,438	3d	124,796	78,018	3d	193,457	119,820	313,277
4th	154,749	78,940	4th	153,079	....	4th	229,919	....	229,919
5th	191,066	117,512	5th	135,470	87,772	5th	192,959	130,575	323,534
6th	129,725	186,661	6th	83,025	141,265	6th	126,116	201,718	327,834
7th	76,212	298,368	7th	47,921	203,954	7th	....	378,754	378,754
8th	180,204	121,886	8th	125,741	73,003	8th	193,145	127,720	320,865
9th	76,105	192,034	9th	48,662	118,132	9th	76,317	205,165	281,482
10th	115,381	163,036	10th	82,213	99,279	10th	120,104	170,460	290,564
WV:			WV:			WV:			
1st	133,809	80,342	1st	92,491	52,109	1st	163,469	73,534	237,003
2d	158,206	68,560	2d	72,619	67,687	2d	140,807	101,207	242,014
3d	92,238	108,199	3d	77,713	62,688	3d	140,741	49,708	207,332
WI:			WI:			WI:			
1st	200,423	158,414	1st	182,316	105,552	1st	230,072	107,003	354,245
2d	124,683	265,422	2d	103,619	224,920	2d	124,044	273,537	398,060
3d	121,713	217,712	3d	119,540	155,368	3d	....	257,401	260,370
4th	80,787	235,257	4th	68,490	179,045	4th	....	220,181	286,909
5th	250,335	118,478	5th	231,160	101,190	5th	260,706	114,477	390,844
6th	223,460	135,921	6th	169,767	122,212	6th	204,147	133,072	357,183
7th	201,720	157,524	7th	169,891	112,949	7th	223,418	138,649	362,271
8th	198,874	156,287	8th	188,553	101,345	8th	227,892	135,682	363,780
WY:			WY:			WY:			
At large	166,452	57,573	At large	113,038	37,803	At large	156,176	75,466	258,788

[Table continues on next page]

VOTES CAST FOR REPRESENTATIVES, RESIDENT COMMISSIONER, AND DELEGATES IN 2012, 2014, and 2016—CONTINUED

[The figures, compiled from official statistics obtained by the Clerk of the House, show the votes for the Republican and Democratic nominees, except as otherwise indicated. Figures in the last column, for the 2016 election, may include totals for more candidates than the ones shown.]

Commonwealth of Puerto Rico	Vote						Total vote cast in 2016
	2012		2014		2016		
	Popular Democrat	Democrat	Popular Democrat	Democrat	New Progressive	Popular Democrat	
Resident Commissioner (4-year term)	881,181	905,066	....	....	718,591	695,073	1,472,401

District of Columbia	Vote						Total vote cast in 2016
	2012		2014		2016		
	Libertarian	Democrat	Republican	Democrat	Democrat	Libertarian	
Delegate	16,524	246,664	11,673	14,923	265,178	18,713	312,575

Guam	Vote						Total vote cast in 2016
	2012		2014		2016		
	Republican	Democrat	Republican	Democrat	Republican	Democrat	
Delegate	12,995	19,765	14,956	20,693	15,617	18,345	35,854

Virgin Islands	Vote						Total vote cast in 2016
	2012		2014		2016		
	Republican	Democrat	Republican	Democrat	Democrat	Write-in	
Delegate	2,131	11,512	1,964	21,224	14,531	371	14,902

American Samoa	Vote						Total vote cast in 2016
	2012		2014		2016		
	Conservative	Democrat	Republican	Democrat	Republican	No Party	
Delegate	4,420	7,221	4,306	3,157	8,924	2,911	11,835

Northern Mariana Islands	Vote					Total vote cast in 2016
	2012		2014		2016	
	Republican	Democrat	Democrat	Democrat	Democrat	
Delegate	2,503	9,829	8,549	4,547	10,605	10,605

[1] According to Florida law, the names of those with no opposition are not printed on the ballot.
[2] According to Louisiana law, the names of those with no opposition are not printed on the ballot.
[3] According to Oklahoma law, the names of those with no opposition are not printed on the ballot.

SESSIONS OF CONGRESS, 1st–115th CONGRESSES, 1789–2018

[Closing date for this table was July 27, 2018.]

MEETING DATES OF CONGRESS: Pursuant to a resolution of the Confederation Congress in 1788, the Constitution went into effect on March 4, 1789. From then until the 20th amendment took effect in January 1934, the term of each Congress began on March 4th of each odd-numbered year; however, Article I, section 4, of the Constitution provided that ''The Congress shall assemble at least once in every Year, and such Meeting shall be on the first Monday in December, unless they shall by law appoint a different day.'' The Congress therefore convened regularly on the first Monday in December until the 20th amendment became effective, which changed the beginning of Congress's term as well as its convening date to January 3rd. So prior to 1934, a new Congress typically would not convene for regular business until 13 months after being elected. One effect of this was that the last session of each Congress was a ''lame duck'' session. After the 20th amendment, the time from the election to the beginning of Congress's term as well as when it convened was reduced to two months. Recognizing that the need might exist for Congress to meet at times other than the regularly scheduled convening date, Article II, section 3 of the Constitution provides that the President ''may, on extraordinary occasions, convene both Houses, or either of them''; hence these sessions occur only if convened by Presidential proclamation. Except as noted, these are separately numbered sessions of a Congress, and are marked by an E in the session column of the table. Until the 20th amendment was adopted, there were also times when special sessions of the Senate were convened, principally for confirming Cabinet and other executive nominations, and occasionally for the ratification of treaties or other executive business. These Senate sessions were also called by Presidential proclamation (typically by the outgoing President, although on occasion by incumbents as well) and are marked by an S in the session column. MEETING PLACES OF CONGRESS: Congress met for the first and second sessions of the First Congress (1789 and 1790) in New York City. From the third session of the First Congress through the first session of the Sixth Congress (1790 to 1800), Philadelphia was the meeting place. Congress has convened in Washington since the second session of the Sixth Congress (1800).

Congress	Session	Convening Date	Adjournment Date	Length in days[1]	Recesses[2]		President pro tempore of the Senate[3]	Speaker of the House of Representatives
					Senate	House of Representatives		
1st	1	Mar. 4, 1789	Sept. 29, 1789	210			John Langdon, of New Hampshire	Frederick A.C. Muhlenberg, of Pennsylvania.
	2	Jan. 4, 1790	Aug. 12, 1790	221			...do.	
	3	Dec. 6, 1790	Mar. 3, 1791	88			...do.	
2d	S	Mar. 4, 1791	Mar. 4, 1791	1			...do.	
	1	Oct. 24, 1791	May 8, 1792	197			Richard Henry Lee, of Virginia	Jonathan Trumbull, of Connecticut.
	2	Nov. 5, 1792	Mar. 2, 1793	119			John Langdon, of New Hampshire.	
3d	S	Mar. 4, 1793	Mar. 4, 1793	1			...do.	
	1	Dec. 2, 1793	June 9, 1794	190			John Langdon, of New Hampshire; Ralph Izard, of South Carolina.	Frederick A.C. Muhlenberg, of Pennsylvania.
	2	Nov. 3, 1794	Mar. 3, 1795	121			Henry Tazewell, of Virginia.	
4th	S	June 8, 1795	June 26, 1795	19			...do.	
	1	Dec. 7, 1795	June 1, 1796	177			Henry Tazewell, of Virginia; Samuel Livermore, of New Hampshire.	Jonathan Dayton, of New Jersey.
	2	Dec. 5, 1796	Mar. 3, 1797	89			William Bingham, of Pennsylvania.	
5th	S	Mar. 4, 1797	Mar. 4, 1797	1				
	1–E	May 15, 1797	July 10, 1797	57			William Bradford, of Rhode Island	Do.
	S	July 17, 1798	July 19, 1798	3				
	2	Nov. 13, 1797	July 16, 1798	246			Jacob Read, of South Carolina; Theodore Sedgwick, of Massachusetts.	
	3	Dec. 3, 1798	Mar. 3, 1799	91			John Laurance, of New York; James Ross, of Pennsylvania.	
6th	1	Dec. 2, 1799	May 14, 1800	164			Samuel Livermore, of New Hampshire; Uriah Tracy, of Connecticut.	Theodore Sedgwick, of Massachusetts.
	2	Nov. 17, 1800	Mar. 3, 1801	107	Dec. 23–Dec. 30, 1800	Dec. 24–Dec. 29, 1800	John E. Howard, of Maryland; James Hillhouse, of Connecticut.	
7th	S	Mar. 4, 1801	Mar. 5, 1801	2				
	1	Dec. 7, 1801	May 3, 1802	148			Abraham Baldwin, of Georgia	Nathaniel Macon, of North Carolina.

	2	Dec. 6, 1802	Mar. 3, 1803	88			Stephen R. Bradley, of Vermont.	
8th	1–E	Oct. 17, 1803	Mar. 27, 1804	163			John Brown, of Kentucky; Jesse Franklin, of North Carolina.	Do.
	2	Nov. 5, 1804	Mar. 3, 1805	119			Joseph Anderson, of Tennessee.	
9th	1	Dec. 2, 1805	Apr. 21, 1806	141			Samuel Smith, of Maryland	Do.
	2	Dec. 1, 1806	Mar. 3, 1807	93			...do.	
10th	1–E	Oct. 26, 1807	Apr. 25, 1808	182			...do	Joseph B. Varnum, of Massachusetts.
	2	Nov. 7, 1808	Mar. 3, 1809	117			Stephen R. Bradley, of Vermont; John Milledge, of Georgia.	
11th	S	Mar. 4, 1809	Mar. 7, 1809	4				
	1–E	May 22, 1809	June 28, 1809	38			Andrew Gregg, of Pennsylvania	Do.
	2	Nov. 27, 1809	May 1, 1810	156			John Gaillard, of South Carolina.	
	3	Dec. 3, 1810	Mar. 3, 1811	91			John Pope, of Kentucky.	
12th	1–E	Nov. 4, 1811	July 6, 1812	245			William H. Crawford, of Georgia	Henry Clay, of Kentucky.
	2	Nov. 2, 1812	Mar. 3, 1813	122			...do.	
13th	1	May 24, 1813	Aug. 2, 1813	71			...do	Do.[4]
	2	Dec. 6, 1813	Apr. 18, 1814	134			Joseph B. Varnum, of Massachusetts; John Gaillard, of South Carolina.	Langdon Cheves, of South Carolina.[4]
	3–E	Sept. 19, 1814	Mar. 3, 1815	166			John Gaillard, of South Carolina.	
14th	1	Dec. 4, 1815	Apr. 30, 1816	148			...do	Henry Clay, of Kentucky.
	2	Dec. 2, 1816	Mar. 3, 1817	92			...do.	
15th	S	Mar. 4, 1817	Mar. 6, 1817	3			...do.	
	1	Dec. 1, 1817	Apr. 20, 1818	141	Dec. 24–Dec. 29, 1817	Dec. 25–Dec. 28, 1817	...do	Do.
	2	Nov. 16, 1818	Mar. 3, 1819	108			James Barbour, of Virginia.	
16th	1	Dec. 6, 1819	May 15, 1820	162			James Barbour, of Virginia; John Gaillard, of South Carolina.	Do.[5]
	2	Nov. 13, 1820	Mar. 3, 1821	111			John Gaillard, of South Carolina	John W. Taylor, of New York.[5]
17th	1	Dec. 3, 1821	May 8, 1822	157			...do	Philip P. Barbour, of Virginia.
	2	Dec. 2, 1822	Mar. 3, 1823	92			...do.	
18th	1	Dec. 1, 1823	May 27, 1824	178			...do	Henry Clay, of Kentucky.
	2	Dec. 6, 1824	Mar. 3, 1825	88			...do.	
19th	S	Mar. 4, 1825	Mar. 9, 1825	6			...do.	
	1	Dec. 5, 1825	May 22, 1826	169			Nathaniel Macon, of North Carolina	John W. Taylor, of New York.
	2	Dec. 4, 1826	Mar. 3, 1827	90			...do.	
20th	1	Dec. 3, 1827	May 26, 1828	175			Samuel Smith, of Maryland	Andrew Stevenson, of Virginia.
	2	Dec. 1, 1828	Mar. 3, 1829	93	Dec. 24–Dec. 29, 1828	Dec. 25–Dec. 28, 1828	...do.	
21st	S	Mar. 4, 1829	Mar. 17, 1829	14			...do.	
	1	Dec. 7, 1829	May 31, 1830	176			...do	Do.
	2	Dec. 6, 1830	Mar. 3, 1831	88			...do.	
22d	1	Dec. 5, 1831	July 16, 1832	225			Littleton Waller Tazewell, of Virginia	Do.
	2	Dec. 3, 1832	Mar. 2, 1833	91			Hugh Lawson White, of Tennessee.	
23d	1	Dec. 2, 1833	June 30, 1834	211			Hugh Lawson White, of Tennessee; George Poindexter, of Mississippi.	Do.[6]
	2	Dec. 1, 1834	Mar. 3, 1835	93			John Tyler, of Virginia	John Bell, of Tennessee.[6]
24th	1	Dec. 7, 1835	July 4, 1836	211			William R. King, of Alabama	James K. Polk, of Tennessee.
	2	Dec. 5, 1836	Mar. 3, 1837	89			...do.	
25th	S	Mar. 4, 1837	Mar. 10, 1837	7			...do.	
	1–E	Sept. 4, 1837	Oct. 16, 1837	43			...do	Do.
	2	Dec. 4, 1837	July 9, 1838	218			...do.	
	3	Dec. 3, 1838	Mar. 3, 1839	91			...do.	
26th	1	Dec. 2, 1839	July 21, 1840	233			...do	Robert M.T. Hunter, of Virginia.
	2	Dec. 7, 1840	Mar. 3, 1841	87			...do.	
27th	S	Mar. 4, 1841	Mar. 15, 1841	12			William R. King, of Alabama; Samuel L. Southard, of New Jersey.	

SESSIONS OF CONGRESS, 1st–115th CONGRESSES, 1789–2018—CONTINUED

[Closing date for this table was July 27, 2018.]

MEETING DATES OF CONGRESS: Pursuant to a resolution of the Confederation Congress in 1788, the Constitution went into effect on March 4, 1789. From then until the 20th amendment took effect in January 1934, the term of each Congress began on March 4th of each odd-numbered year; however, Article I, section 4, of the Constitution provided that "The Congress shall assemble at least once in every Year, and such Meeting shall be on the first Monday in December, unless they shall by law appoint a different day." The Congress therefore convened regularly on the first Monday in December until the 20th amendment became effective, which changed the beginning of Congress's term as well as its convening date to January 3rd. So prior to 1934, a new Congress typically would not convene for regular business until 13 months after being elected. One effect of this was that the last session of each Congress was a "lame duck" session. After the 20th amendment, the time from the election to the beginning of Congress's term as well as when it convened was reduced to two months. Recognizing that the need might exist for Congress to meet at times other than the regularly scheduled convening date, Article II, section 3 of the Constitution provides that the President "may, on extraordinary occasions, convene both Houses, or either of them"; hence these sessions occur only if convened by Presidential proclamation. Except as noted, these are separately numbered sessions of a Congress, and are marked by an E in the session column of the table. Until the 20th amendment was adopted, there were also times when special sessions of the Senate were convened, principally for confirming Cabinet and other executive nominations, and occasionally for the ratification of treaties or other executive business. These Senate sessions were also called by Presidential proclamation (typically by the outgoing President, although on occasion by incumbents as well) and are marked by an S in the session column. MEETING PLACES OF CONGRESS: Congress met for the first and second sessions of the First Congress (1789 and 1790) in New York City. From the third session of the First Congress through the first session of the Sixth Congress (1790 to 1800), Philadelphia was the meeting place. Congress has convened in Washington since the second session of the Sixth Congress (1800).

Congress	Session	Convening Date	Adjournment Date	Length in days[1]	Recesses[2]		President pro tempore of the Senate[3]	Speaker of the House of Representatives
					Senate	House of Representatives		
	1–E	May 31, 1841	Sept. 13, 1841	106			Samuel L. Southard, of New Jersey	John White, of Kentucky.
	2	Dec. 6, 1841	Aug. 31, 1842	269			Willie P. Mangum, of North Carolina.	
	3	Dec. 5, 1842	Mar. 3, 1843	89			...do.	
28th	1	Dec. 4, 1843	June 17, 1844	196			...do	John W. Jones, of Virginia.
	2	Dec. 2, 1844	Mar. 3, 1845	92			...do.	
29th	S	Mar. 4, 1845	Mar. 20, 1845	17				
	1	Dec. 1, 1845	Aug. 10, 1846	253			Ambrose H. Sevier; David R. Atchison, of Missouri.	John W. Davis, of Indiana.
	2	Dec. 7, 1846	Mar. 3, 1847	87			David R. Atchison, of Missouri.	
30th	1	Dec. 6, 1847	Aug. 14, 1848	254			...do	Robert C. Winthrop, of Massachusetts.
	2	Dec. 4, 1848	Mar. 3, 1849	90			...do.	
31st	S	Mar. 5, 1849	Mar. 23, 1849	19			...do.	
	1	Dec. 3, 1849	Sept. 30, 1850	302			William R. King, of Alabama	Howell Cobb, of Georgia.
	2	Dec. 2, 1850	Mar. 3, 1851	92			...do.	
32d	S	Mar. 4, 1851	Mar. 13, 1851	10				
	1	Dec. 1, 1851	Aug. 31, 1852	275			...do	Linn Boyd, of Kentucky.
	2	Dec. 6, 1852	Mar. 3, 1853	88			David R. Atchison, of Missouri.	
33d	S	Mar. 4, 1853	Apr. 11, 1853	39			...do.	
	1	Dec. 5, 1853	Aug. 7, 1854	246			...do	Do.
	2	Dec. 4, 1854	Mar. 3, 1855	90			Lewis Cass, of Michigan; Jesse D. Bright, of Indiana.	
34th	1	Dec. 3, 1855	Aug. 18, 1856	260			Charles E. Stuart, of Michigan; Jesse D. Bright, of Indiana.	Nathaniel P. Banks, of Massachusetts.
	2–E	Aug. 21, 1856	Aug. 30, 1856	10			Jesse D. Bright, of Indiana.	
	3	Dec. 1, 1856	Mar. 3, 1857	93			James M. Mason, of Virginia.	
35th	S	Mar. 4, 1857	Mar. 14, 1857	11			James M. Mason, of Virginia; Thomas J. Rusk, of Texas.	
	1	Dec. 7, 1857	June 14, 1858	189	Dec. 23, 1857–Jan. 4, 1858	Dec. 24, 1857–Jan. 3, 1858	Benjamin Fitzpatrick, of Alabama	James L. Orr, of South Carolina.

	S	June 15, 1858	June 16, 1858	2				
	2	Dec. 6, 1858	Mar. 3, 1859	88	Dec. 23, 1858–Jan. 4, 1859	Dec. 24, 1858–Jan. 3, 1859	...do.	
36th	S	Mar. 4, 1859	Mar. 10, 1859	7			...do.	
	1	Dec. 5, 1859	June 25, 1860	202			Benjamin Fitzpatrick, of Alabama; Jesse D. Bright, of Indiana.	William Pennington, of New Jersey.
	S	June 26, 1860	June 28, 1860	3			Benjamin Fitzpatrick, of Alabama.	
	2	Dec. 3, 1860	Mar. 3, 1861	93			Solomon Foot, of Vermont.	
37th	S	Mar. 4, 1861	Mar. 28, 1861	25			...do.	
	1–E	July 4, 1861	Aug. 6, 1861	34			...do	Galusha A. Grow, of Pennsylvania.
	2	Dec. 2, 1861	July 17, 1862	228			...do.	
	3	Dec. 1, 1862	Mar. 3, 1863	93	Dec. 23, 1862–Jan. 5, 1863	Dec. 24, 1862–Jan. 4, 1863	...do.	
38th	S	Mar. 4, 1863	Mar. 14, 1863	11			...do.	
	1	Dec. 7, 1863	July 4, 1864	209	Dec. 23, 1863–Jan. 5, 1864	Dec. 24, 1863–Jan. 4, 1864	Solomon Foot, of Vermont; Daniel Clark, of New Hampshire.	Schuyler Colfax, of Indiana.
	2	Dec. 5, 1864	Mar. 4, 1865	89	Dec. 22, 1864–Jan. 5, 1865	Dec. 22, 1864–Jan. 4, 1865	Daniel Clark, of New Hampshire.	
39th	S	Mar. 4, 1865	Mar. 11, 1865	8			Lafayette S. Foster, of Connecticut.	
	1	Dec. 4, 1865	July 28, 1866	237	Dec. 6–Dec. 11, 1865 Dec. 21, 1865–Jan. 5, 1866	Dec. 7–Dec. 10, 1865 Dec. 23, 1865–Jan. 4, 1866	...do	Do.
	2	Dec. 3, 1866	Mar. 3, 1867	91	Dec. 20, 1866–Jan. 3, 1867	Dec. 20, 1866–Jan. 3, 1867	Benjamin F. Wade, of Ohio.	
40th	1–E	Mar. 4, 1867	Dec. 1, 1867	273	Mar. 30–July 3, 1867 July 20–Nov. 21, 1867	Mar. 31–July 2, 1867 July 21–Nov. 20, 1867	...do	Do.[7]
	S	Apr. 1, 1867	Apr. 20, 1867	20				
	2	Dec. 2, 1867	Nov. 10, 1868	345	Dec. 20, 1867–Jan. 6, 1868 July 27–Sept. 21, 1868 Sept. 21–Oct. 16, 1868 Oct. 16–Nov. 10, 1868	Dec. 21, 1867–Jan. 5, 1868 July 26–Sept. 20, 1868 Sept. 22–Oct. 15, 1868 Oct. 17–Nov. 9, 1868		
	3	Dec. 7, 1868	Mar. 3, 1869	87	Dec. 21, 1868–Jan. 5, 1869	Dec. 22, 1868–Jan. 4, 1869	...do	Theodore M. Pomeroy, of New York.[7]
41st	1	Mar. 4, 1869	Apr. 10, 1869	38			Henry B. Anthony, of Rhode Island	James G. Blaine, of Maine.
	S	Apr. 12, 1869	Apr. 22, 1869	11				
	2	Dec. 6, 1869	July 15, 1870	222	Dec. 22, 1869–Jan. 10, 1870	Dec. 23, 1869–Jan. 9, 1870	...do.	
	3	Dec. 5, 1870	Mar. 3, 1871	89	Dec. 23, 1870–Jan. 4, 1871	Dec. 23, 1870–Jan. 3, 1871	...do.	
42d	1–E	Mar. 4, 1871	Apr. 20, 1871	48			...do	Do.
	S	May 10, 1871	May 27, 1871	18			...do.	
	2	Dec. 4, 1871	June 8, 1872	190	Dec. 21, 1871–Jan. 8, 1872	Dec. 22, 1871–Jan. 7, 1872	...do.	
	3	Dec. 2, 1872	Mar. 3, 1873	92	Dec. 20, 1872–Jan. 6, 1873	Dec. 21, 1872–Jan. 5, 1873	...do.	
43d	S	Mar. 4, 1873	Mar. 26, 1873	23			Matthew H. Carpenter, of Wisconsin.	
	1	Dec. 1, 1873	June 23, 1874	204	Dec. 19, 1873–Jan. 5, 1874	Dec. 20, 1873–Jan. 4, 1874	...do	Do.
	2	Dec. 7, 1874	Mar. 3, 1875	87	Dec. 23, 1874–Jan. 5, 1875	Dec. 24, 1874–Jan. 4, 1875	Matthew H. Carpenter, of Wisconsin; Henry B. Anthony, of Rhode Island.	
44th	S	Mar. 5, 1875	Mar. 24, 1875	20			Thomas W. Ferry, of Michigan.	
	1	Dec. 6, 1875	Aug. 15, 1876	254	Dec. 20, 1875–Jan. 5, 1876	Dec. 21, 1875–Jan. 4, 1876	...do	Michael C. Kerr, of Indiana.[8]
	2	Dec. 4, 1876	Mar. 3, 1877	90			...do	Samuel J. Randall, of Pennsylvania.[8]
45th	S	Mar. 5, 1877	Mar. 17, 1877	13			...do.	
	1–E	Oct. 15, 1877	Dec. 3, 1877	50			...do	Do.
	2	Dec. 3, 1877	June 20, 1878	200	Dec. 15, 1877–Jan. 10, 1878	Dec. 16, 1877–Jan. 10, 1878	...do.	
	3	Dec. 2, 1878	Mar. 3, 1879	92	Dec. 20, 1878–Jan. 7, 1879	Dec. 21, 1878–Jan. 6, 1879	...do.	
46th	1–E	Mar. 18, 1879	July 1, 1879	106			Allen G. Thurman, of Ohio	Do.
	2	Dec. 1, 1879	June 16, 1880	199	Dec. 19, 1879–Jan. 6, 1880	Dec. 20, 1879–Jan. 5, 1880	...do.	
	3	Dec. 6, 1880	Mar. 3, 1881	88	Dec. 23, 1880–Jan. 5, 1881	Dec. 23, 1880–Jan. 4, 1881	...do.	
47th	S	Mar. 4, 1881	May. 20, 1881	78				
	S	Oct. 10, 1881	Oct. 29, 1881	20			Thomas F. Bayard, of Delaware; David Davis, of Illinois.	
	1	Dec. 5, 1881	Aug. 8, 1882	247	Dec. 22, 1881–Jan. 5, 1882	Dec. 22, 1881–Jan. 4, 1882	David Davis, of Illinois	J. Warren Keifer, of Ohio.

SESSIONS OF CONGRESS, 1st–115th CONGRESSES, 1789–2018—CONTINUED

[Closing date for this table was July 27, 2018.]

MEETING DATES OF CONGRESS: Pursuant to a resolution of the Confederation Congress in 1788, the Constitution went into effect on March 4, 1789. From then until the 20th amendment took effect in January 1934, the term of each Congress began on March 4th of each odd-numbered year; however, Article I, section 4, of the Constitution provided that ''The Congress shall assemble at least once in every Year, and such Meeting shall be on the first Monday in December, unless they shall by law appoint a different day.'' The Congress therefore convened regularly on the first Monday in December until the 20th amendment became effective, which changed the beginning of Congress's term as well as its convening date to January 3rd. So prior to 1934, a new Congress typically would not convene for regular business until 13 months after being elected. One effect of this was that the last session of each Congress was a ''lame duck'' session. After the 20th amendment, the time from the election to the beginning of Congress's term as well as when it convened was reduced to two months. Recognizing that the need might exist for Congress to meet at times other than the regularly scheduled convening date, Article II, section 3 of the Constitution provides that the President ''may, on extraordinary occasions, convene both Houses, or either of them''; hence these sessions occur only if convened by Presidential proclamation. Except as noted, these are separately numbered sessions of a Congress, and are marked by an E in the session column of the table. Until the 20th amendment was adopted, there were also times when special sessions of the Senate were convened, principally for confirming Cabinet and other executive nominations, and occasionally for the ratification of treaties or other executive business. These Senate sessions were also called by Presidential proclamation (typically by the outgoing President, although on occasion by incumbents as well) and are marked by an S in the session column. MEETING PLACES OF CONGRESS: Congress met for the first and second sessions of the First Congress (1789 and 1790) in New York City. From the third session of the First Congress through the first session of the Sixth Congress (1790 to 1800), Philadelphia was the meeting place. Congress has convened in Washington since the second session of the Sixth Congress (1800).

Congress	Session	Convening Date	Adjournment Date	Length in days[1]	Recesses[2] Senate	Recesses[2] House of Representatives	President pro tempore of the Senate[3]	Speaker of the House of Representatives
	2	Dec. 4, 1882	Mar. 3, 1883	90			George F. Edmunds, of Vermont.	J. Warren Keifer, of Ohio.
48th	1	Dec. 3, 1883	July 7, 1884	218	Dec. 24, 1883–Jan. 7, 1884	Dec. 25, 1883–Jan. 6, 1884	...do	John G. Carlisle, of Kentucky.
	2	Dec. 1, 1884	Mar. 3, 1885	93	Dec. 24, 1884–Jan. 5, 1885	Dec. 25, 1884–Jan. 4, 1885	...do.	
49th	S	Mar. 4, 1885	Apr. 2, 1885	30				
	1	Dec. 7, 1885	Aug. 5, 1886	242	Dec. 21, 1885–Jan. 5, 1886	Dec. 22, 1885–Jan. 4, 1886	John Sherman, of Ohio	Do.
	2	Dec. 6, 1886	Mar. 3, 1887	88	Dec. 22, 1886–Jan. 4, 1887	Dec. 23, 1886–Jan. 3, 1887	John J. Ingalls, of Kansas.	
50th	1	Dec. 5, 1887	Oct. 20, 1888	321	Dec. 22, 1887–Jan. 4, 1888	Dec. 23, 1887–Jan. 3, 1888	...do	Do.
	2	Dec. 3, 1888	Mar. 3, 1889	91	Dec. 21, 1888–Jan. 2, 1889	Dec. 22, 1888–Jan. 1, 1889	...do.	
51st	S	Mar. 4, 1889	Apr. 2, 1889	30			...do.	
	1	Dec. 2, 1889	Oct. 1, 1890	304	Dec. 21, 1889–Jan. 6, 1890	Dec. 22, 1889–Jan. 5, 1890	...do	Thomas B. Reed, of Maine.
	2	Dec. 1, 1890	Mar. 3, 1891	93			Charles F. Manderson, of Nebraska.	
52d	1	Dec. 7, 1891	Aug. 5, 1892	251			...do	Charles F. Crisp, of Georgia.
	2	Dec. 5, 1892	Mar. 3, 1893	89	Dec. 22, 1892–Jan. 4, 1893	Dec. 23, 1892–Jan. 3, 1893	...do.	
53d	S	Mar. 4, 1893	Apr. 15, 1893	43			Charles F. Manderson, of Nebraska; Isham G. Harris, of Tennessee.	
	1–E	Aug. 7, 1893	Nov. 3, 1893	89			Isham G. Harris, of Tennessee	Do.
	2	Dec. 4, 1893	Aug. 28, 1894	268		Dec. 22, 1893–Jan. 2, 1894	...do.	
	3	Dec. 3, 1894	Mar. 4, 1895	97		Dec. 23, 1894–Jan. 2, 1895	Matt W. Ransom, of North Carolina; Isham G. Harris, of Tennessee.	
54th	1	Dec. 2, 1895	June 11, 1896	193			William P. Frye, of Maine	Thomas B. Reed, of Maine.
	2	Dec. 7, 1896	Mar. 3, 1897	87	Dec. 22, 1896–Jan. 5, 1897	Dec. 23, 1896–Jan. 4, 1897	...do.	
55th	S	Mar. 4, 1897	Mar. 10, 1897	11			...do.	
	1–E	Mar. 15, 1897	July 24, 1897	131			...do	Do.
	2	Dec. 6, 1897	July 8, 1898	215	Dec. 18, 1897–Jan. 5, 1898	Dec. 19, 1897–Jan. 4, 1898	...do.	
	3	Dec. 5, 1898	Mar. 4, 1899	89	Dec. 21, 1898–Jan. 4, 1899	Dec. 20, 1898–Jan. 3, 1899	...do.	
56th	1	Dec. 4, 1899	June 7, 1900	186	Dec. 20, 1899–Jan. 3, 1900	Dec. 21, 1899–Jan. 2, 1900	...do	David B. Henderson, of Iowa.
	2	Dec. 3, 1900	Mar. 3, 1901	91	Dec. 20, 1900–Jan. 3, 1901	Dec. 22, 1900–Jan. 2, 1901	...do.	
57th	S	Mar. 4, 1901	Mar. 9, 1901	6			...do.	

	1	Dec. 2, 1901	July 1, 1902	212	Dec. 19, 1901–Jan. 6, 1902	Dec. 20, 1901–Jan. 5, 1902	...do	Do.
	2	Dec. 1, 1902	Mar. 3, 1903	93	Dec. 20, 1902–Jan. 5, 1903	Dec. 21, 1902–Jan. 4, 1903	...do.	
58th	S	Mar. 5, 1903	Mar. 19, 1903	15			...do.	
	1–E	Nov. 9, 1903	Dec. 7, 1903	29			...do	Joseph G. Cannon, of Illinois.
	2	Dec. 7, 1903	Apr. 28, 1904	144	Dec. 19, 1903–Jan. 4, 1904	Dec. 19, 1903–Jan. 4, 1904	...do.	
	3	Dec. 5, 1904	Mar. 3, 1905	89	Dec. 21, 1904–Jan. 4, 1905	Dec. 22, 1904–Jan. 3, 1905	...do.	
59th	S	Mar. 4, 1905	Mar. 18, 1905	15			...do.	
	1	Dec. 4, 1905	June 30, 1906	209	Dec. 21, 1905–Jan. 4, 1906	Dec. 22, 1905–Jan. 3, 1906	...do	Do.
	2	Dec. 3, 1906	Mar. 3, 1907	91	Dec. 20, 1906–Jan. 3, 1907	Dec. 21, 1906–Jan. 2, 1907	...do.	
60th	1	Dec. 2, 1907	May 30, 1908	181	Dec. 21, 1907–Jan. 6, 1908	Dec. 22, 1907–Jan. 5, 1908	...do	Do.
	2	Dec. 7, 1908	Mar. 3, 1909	87	Dec. 19, 1908–Jan. 4, 1909	Dec. 20, 1908–Jan. 3, 1909	...do.	
61st	S	Mar. 4, 1909	Mar. 6, 1909	3			...do.	
	1–E	Mar. 15, 1909	Aug. 5, 1909	144			...do	Do.
	2	Dec. 6, 1909	June 23, 1910	202	Dec. 21, 1909–Jan. 4, 1910	Dec. 22, 1909–Jan. 3, 1910	...do.	
	3	Dec. 5, 1910	Mar. 3, 1911	89	Dec. 21, 1910–Jan. 5, 1911	Dec. 22, 1910–Jan. 4, 1911	...do.	
62d	1–E	Apr. 4, 1911	Aug. 22, 1911	141			...do.[9]	Champ Clark, of Missouri.
	2	Dec. 4, 1911	Aug. 26, 1912	267	Dec. 21, 1911–Jan. 3, 1912	Dec. 22, 1911–Jan. 2, 1912	Charles Curtis, of Kansas; Augustus O. Bacon, of Georgia; Jacob H. Gallinger, of New Hampshire; Henry Cabot Lodge, of Massachusetts; Frank B. Brandegee, of Connecticut.	
	3	Dec. 2, 1912	Mar. 3, 1913	92	Dec. 19, 1912–Jan. 2, 1913	Dec. 20, 1912–Jan. 1, 1913	Augustus O. Bacon, of Georgia; Jacob H. Gallinger, of New Hampshire.	
63d	S	Mar. 4, 1913	Mar. 17, 1913	14			James P. Clarke, of Arkansas.	
	1–E	Apr. 7, 1913	Nov. 29, 1913	239			...do	Do.
	2	Dec. 1, 1913	Oct. 24, 1914	328	Dec. 23, 1913–Jan. 12, 1914	Dec. 24, 1913–Jan. 11, 1914	...do.	
	3	Dec. 7, 1914	Mar. 3, 1915	87	Dec. 23–Dec. 28, 1914	Dec. 24–Dec. 28, 1914	...do.	
64th	1	Dec. 6, 1915	Sept. 8, 1916	278	Dec. 17, 1915–Jan. 4, 1916	Dec. 18, 1915–Jan. 3, 1916	...do[10]	Do.
	2	Dec. 4, 1916	Mar. 3, 1917	90	Dec. 22, 1916–Jan. 2, 1917	Dec. 23, 1916–Jan. 1, 1917	Willard Saulsbury, of Delaware[10]	
65th	S	Mar. 5, 1917	Mar. 16, 1917	12			...do.	
	1–E	Apr. 2, 1917	Oct. 6, 1917	188			...do	Do.
	2	Dec. 3, 1917	Nov. 21, 1918	354	Dec. 18, 1917–Jan. 3, 1918	Dec. 19, 1917–Jan. 2, 1918	...do.	
	3	Dec. 2, 1918	Mar. 3, 1919	92			...do.	
66th	1–E	May 19, 1919	Nov. 19, 1919	185	July 1–July 8, 1919	July 2–July 7, 1919	Albert B. Cummins, of Iowa	Frederick H. Gillett, of Massachusetts.
	2	Dec. 1, 1919	June 5, 1920	188	Dec. 20, 1919–Jan. 5, 1920	Dec. 21, 1919–Jan. 4, 1920	...do.	
	3	Dec. 6, 1920	Mar. 3, 1921	88			...do.	
67th	S	Mar. 4, 1921	Mar. 15, 1921	12			...do.	
	1–E	Apr. 11, 1921	Nov. 23, 1921	227	Aug. 24–Sept. 21, 1921	Aug. 25–Sept. 20, 1921	...do	Do.
	2	Dec. 5, 1921	Sept. 22, 1922	292	Dec. 22, 1921–Jan. 3, 1922	Dec. 23, 1921–Jan. 2, 1922 July 1–Aug. 14, 1922	...do.	
	3–E	Nov. 20, 1922	Dec. 4, 1922	15			...do.	
	4	Dec. 4, 1922	Mar. 3, 1923	90			...do.	
68th	1	Dec. 3, 1923	June 7, 1924	188	Dec. 20, 1923–Jan. 3, 1924	Dec. 21, 1923–Jan. 2, 1924	...do	Do.
	2	Dec. 1, 1924	Mar. 3, 1925	93	Dec. 20–Dec. 29, 1924	Dec. 21–Dec. 28, 1924	...do.	
69th	S	Mar. 4, 1925	Mar. 18, 1925	15			Albert B. Cummins, of Iowa; George H. Moses, of New Hampshire.	
	1	Dec. 7, 1925	July 3, 1926	209	Dec. 22, 1925–Jan. 4, 1926	Dec. 23, 1925–Jan. 3, 1926	...do	Nicholas Longworth, of Ohio.
	2	Dec. 6, 1926	Mar. 4, 1927	88	Dec. 22, 1926–Jan. 3, 1927	Dec. 23, 1926–Jan. 2, 1927	...do.	
70th	1	Dec. 5, 1927	May 29, 1928	177	Dec. 21, 1927–Jan. 4, 1928	Dec. 22, 1927–Jan. 3, 1928	...do	Do.
	2	Dec. 3, 1928	Mar. 3, 1929	91	Dec. 22, 1928–Jan. 3, 1929	Dec. 23, 1928–Jan. 2, 1929	...do.	
71st	S	Mar. 4, 1929	Mar. 5, 1929	2			...do.	
	1–E	Apr. 15, 1929	Nov. 22, 1929	222	June 19–Aug. 19, 1929	June 20–Sept. 22, 1929	...do	Do.
	2	Dec. 2, 1929	July 3, 1930	214	Dec. 21, 1929–Jan. 6, 1930	Dec. 22, 1929–Jan. 5, 1930	...do.	

SESSIONS OF CONGRESS, 1st–115th CONGRESSES, 1789–2018—CONTINUED

[Closing date for this table was July 27, 2018.]

Meeting Dates of Congress: Pursuant to a resolution of the Confederation Congress in 1788, the Constitution went into effect on March 4, 1789. From then until the 20th amendment took effect in January 1934, the term of each Congress began on March 4th of each odd-numbered year; however, Article I, section 4, of the Constitution provided that ''The Congress shall assemble at least once in every Year, and such Meeting shall be on the first Monday in December, unless they shall by law appoint a different day.'' The Congress therefore convened regularly on the first Monday in December until the 20th amendment became effective, which changed the beginning of Congress's term as well as its convening date to January 3rd. So prior to 1934, a new Congress typically would not convene for regular business until 13 months after being elected. One effect of this was that the last session of each Congress was a ''lame duck'' session. After the 20th amendment, the time from the election to the beginning of Congress's term as well as when it convened was reduced to two months. Recognizing that the need might exist for Congress to meet at times other than the regularly scheduled convening date, Article II, section 3 of the Constitution provides that the President ''may, on extraordinary occasions, convene both Houses, or either of them''; hence these sessions occur only if convened by Presidential proclamation. Except as noted, these are separately numbered sessions of a Congress, and are marked by an E in the session column of the table. Until the 20th amendment was adopted, there were also times when special sessions of the Senate were convened, principally for confirming Cabinet and other executive nominations, and occasionally for the ratification of treaties or other executive business. These Senate sessions were also called by Presidential proclamation (typically by the outgoing President, although on occasion by incumbents as well) and are marked by an S in the session column. Meeting Places of Congress: Congress met for the first and second sessions of the First Congress (1789 and 1790) in New York City. From the third session of the First Congress through the first session of the Sixth Congress (1790 to 1800), Philadelphia was the meeting place. Congress has convened in Washington since the second session of the Sixth Congress (1800).

Congress	Session	Convening Date	Adjournment Date	Length in days[1]	Recesses[2]		President pro tempore of the Senate[3]	Speaker of the House of Representatives
					Senate	House of Representatives		
	S	July 7, 1930	July 21, 1930	15			...do.	
	3	Dec. 1, 1930	Mar. 4, 1931	93	Dec. 20, 1930–Jan. 5, 1931	Dec. 21, 1930–Jan. 4, 1931	George H. Moses, of New Hampshire	Nicholas Longworth, of Ohio.
72d	1	Dec. 7, 1931	July 16, 1932	223	Dec. 22, 1931–Jan. 4, 1932	Dec. 23, 1931–Jan. 3, 1932	...do	John N. Garner, of Texas.
	2	Dec. 5, 1932	Mar. 4, 1933	89			...do.	
73d	S	Mar. 4, 1933	Mar. 6, 1933	3			...do.	
	1–E	Mar. 9, 1933	June 16, 1933	99			Key Pittman, of Nevada	Henry T. Rainey, of Illinois.
	2	Jan. 3, 1934	June 18, 1934	167			...do.	
74th	1	Jan. 3, 1935	Aug. 26, 1935	236			...do	Joseph W. Byrns, of Tennessee.[11]
	2	Jan. 3, 1936	June 20, 1936	170	June 8–June 15, 1936	June 9–June 14, 1936	...do	William B. Bankhead, of Alabama.[11]
75th	1	Jan. 5, 1937	Aug. 21, 1937	229			...do	Do.
	2–E	Nov. 15, 1937	Dec. 21, 1937	37			...do.	
	3	Jan. 3, 1938	June 16, 1938	165			...do.	
76th	1	Jan. 3, 1939	Aug. 5, 1939	215			...do	Do.[12]
	2–E	Sept. 21, 1939	Nov. 3, 1939	44			...do.	
	3	Jan. 3, 1940	Jan. 2, 1941	366	July 11–July 22, 1940	June 23–June 30, 1940 July 12–July 21, 1940	Key Pittman, of Nevada;[13] William H. King, of Utah.[13]	Sam Rayburn, of Texas.[12]
77th	1	Jan. 3, 1941	Jan. 2, 1942	365			Pat Harrison, of Mississippi;[14] Carter Glass, of Virginia.[14]	Do.
	2	Jan. 5, 1942	Dec. 16, 1942	346			Carter Glass, of Virginia.	
78th	1	Jan. 6, 1943	Dec. 21, 1943	350	July 8–Sept. 14, 1943	Apr. 23–May 2, 1943 July 8–Sept. 13, 1943	...do	Do.
	2	Jan. 10, 1944	Dec. 19, 1944	345	Apr. 1–Apr. 12, 1944 June 23–Aug. 1, 1944 Sept. 21–Nov. 14, 1944	Apr. 2–Apr. 11, 1944 June 24–June 31, 1944 Sept. 22–Nov. 13, 1944	...do.	
79th	1	Jan. 3, 1945	Dec. 21, 1945	353	Aug. 1–Sept. 5, 1945	July 22–Sept. 4, 1945	Kenneth McKellar, of Tennessee	Do.
	2	Jan. 14, 1946	Aug. 2, 1946	201		Apr. 19–Apr. 29, 1946	...do.	
80th	[15] 1	Jan. 3, 1947	Dec. 19, 1947	351	July 27–Nov. 17, 1947	July 28–Nov. 16, 1947	Arthur H. Vandenberg, of Michigan	Joseph W. Martin, Jr., of Massachusetts.

	[15] 2	Jan. 6, 1948	Dec. 31, 1948	361	June 20–July 26, 1948 Aug. 7–Dec. 31, 1948	June 21–July 25, 1948 Aug. 8–Dec. 30, 1948	...do.	
81st	1	Jan. 3, 1949	Oct. 19, 1949	290	Apr. 15–May 2, 1949		Kenneth McKellar, of Tennessee	Sam Rayburn, of Texas.
	2	Jan. 3, 1950	Jan. 2, 1951	365		Apr. 6–Apr. 18, 1950 Sept. 23–Nov. 27, 1950	...do.	
82d	1	Jan. 3, 1951	Oct. 20, 1951	291		Mar. 23–Apr. 1, 1951 Aug. 24–Sept. 11, 1951	...do	Do.
	2	Jan. 8, 1952	July 7, 1952	182		Apr. 11–Apr. 21, 1952	...do.	
83d	1	Jan. 3, 1953	Aug. 3, 1953	213		Apr. 3–Apr. 12, 1953	Styles Bridges, of New Hampshire	Joseph W. Martin, Jr., of Massachusetts.
	2	Jan. 6, 1954	Dec. 2, 1954	331	Aug. 20–Nov. 8, 1954 Nov. 18–Nov. 29, 1954	Apr. 16–Apr. 25, 1954 Adjourned sine die Aug. 20, 1954	...do.	
84th	1	Jan. 5, 1955	Aug. 2, 1955	210	Apr. 4–Apr. 13, 1955	Apr. 5–Apr. 12, 1955	Walter F. George, of Georgia	Sam Rayburn, of Texas.
	2	Jan. 3, 1956	July 27, 1956	207	Mar. 29–Apr. 9, 1956	Mar. 30–Apr. 8, 1956	...do.	
85th	1	Jan. 3, 1957	Aug. 30, 1957	239	Apr. 18–Apr. 29, 1957	Apr. 19–Apr. 28, 1957	Carl Hayden, of Arizona	Do.
	2	Jan. 7, 1958	Aug. 24, 1958	230	Apr. 3–Apr. 14, 1958	Apr. 4–Apr. 13, 1958	...do.	
86th	1	Jan. 7, 1959	Sept. 15, 1959	252	Mar. 26–Apr. 7, 1959	Mar. 27–Apr. 6, 1959	...do	Do.
	2	Jan. 6, 1960	Sept. 1, 1960	240	Apr. 14–Apr. 18, 1960 May 27–May 31, 1960 July 3–Aug. 8, 1960	July 4–Aug. 14, 1960	...do.	
87th	1	Jan. 3, 1961	Sept. 27, 1961	268		Mar. 31–Apr. 9, 1961	...do	Do.[16]
	2	Jan. 10, 1962	Oct. 13, 1962	277		Apr. 20–Apr. 29, 1962	...do	John W. McCormack, of Massachusetts.[16]
88th	1	Jan. 9, 1963	Dec. 30, 1963	356		Apr. 11–Apr. 21, 1963	...do	Do.
	2	Jan. 7, 1964	Oct. 3, 1964	270	July 10–July 20, 1964 Aug. 21–Aug. 31, 1964	Mar. 27–Apr. 5, 1964 July 3–July 19, 1964 Aug. 22–Aug. 30, 1964	...do.	
89th	1	Jan. 4, 1965	Oct. 23, 1965	293			...do	Do.
	2	Jan. 10, 1966	Oct. 22, 1966	286	Apr. 7–Apr. 13, 1966 June 30–July 11, 1966	Apr. 8–Apr. 17, 1966 June 1–June 10, 1966	...do.	
90th	1	Jan. 10, 1967	Dec. 15, 1967	340	Mar. 23–Apr. 3, 1967 June 29–July 10, 1967 Aug. 31–Sept. 11, 1967 Nov. 22–Nov. 27, 1967	Mar. 24–Apr. 2, 1967 June 30–July 9, 1967 Sept. 1–Sept. 10, 1967 Nov. 23–Nov. 26, 1967	...do	Do.
	2	Jan. 15, 1968	Oct. 14, 1968	274	Apr. 11–Apr. 17, 1968 May 29–June 3, 1968 July 3–July 8, 1968 Aug. 2–Sept. 4, 1968	Apr. 12–Apr. 21, 1968 May 30–June 2, 1968 July 4–July 7, 1968 Aug. 3–Sept. 3, 1968	...do.	
91st	1	Jan. 3, 1969	Dec. 23, 1969	355	Feb. 7–Feb. 17, 1969 Apr. 3–Apr. 14, 1969 July 2–July 7, 1969 Aug. 13–Sept. 3, 1969 Nov. 26–Dec. 1, 1969	Feb. 8–Feb. 16, 1969 Apr. 4–Apr. 13, 1969 May 29–June 1, 1969 July 3–July 6, 1969 Aug. 14–Sept. 2, 1969 Nov. 7–Nov. 11, 1969 Nov. 27–Nov. 30, 1969	Richard B. Russell, of Georgia	Do.

SESSIONS OF CONGRESS, 1st–115th CONGRESSES, 1789–2018—CONTINUED

[Closing date for this table was July 27, 2018.]

MEETING DATES OF CONGRESS: Pursuant to a resolution of the Confederation Congress in 1788, the Constitution went into effect on March 4, 1789. From then until the 20th amendment took effect in January 1934, the term of each Congress began on March 4th of each odd-numbered year; however, Article I, section 4, of the Constitution provided that ''The Congress shall assemble at least once in every Year, and such Meeting shall be on the first Monday in December, unless they shall by law appoint a different day.'' The Congress therefore convened regularly on the first Monday in December until the 20th amendment became effective, which changed the beginning of Congress's term as well as its convening date to January 3rd. So prior to 1934, a new Congress typically would not convene for regular business until 13 months after being elected. One effect of this was that the last session of each Congress was a ''lame duck'' session. After the 20th amendment, the time from the election to the beginning of Congress's term as well as when it convened was reduced to two months. Recognizing that the need might exist for Congress to meet at times other than the regularly scheduled convening date, Article II, section 3 of the Constitution provides that the President ''may, on extraordinary occasions, convene both Houses, or either of them''; hence these sessions occur only if convened by Presidential proclamation. Except as noted, these are separately numbered sessions of a Congress, and are marked by an E in the session column of the table. Until the 20th amendment was adopted, there were also times when special sessions of the Senate were convened, principally for confirming Cabinet and other executive nominations, and occasionally for the ratification of treaties or other executive business. These Senate sessions were also called by Presidential proclamation (typically by the outgoing President, although on occasion by incumbents as well) and are marked by an S in the session column. MEETING PLACES OF CONGRESS: Congress met for the first and second sessions of the First Congress (1789 and 1790) in New York City. From the third session of the First Congress through the first session of the Sixth Congress (1790 to 1800), Philadelphia was the meeting place. Congress has convened in Washington since the second session of the Sixth Congress (1800).

Congress	Session	Convening Date	Adjournment Date	Length in days[1]	Recesses[2]		President pro tempore of the Senate[3]	Speaker of the House of Representatives
					Senate	House of Representatives		
	2	Jan. 19, 1970	Jan. 2, 1971	349	Feb. 10–Feb. 16, 1970 Mar. 26–Mar. 31, 1970 Sept. 2–Sept. 8, 1970 Oct. 14–Nov. 16, 1970 Nov. 25–Nov. 30, 1970 Dec. 22–Dec. 28, 1970	Feb. 11–Feb. 15, 1970 Mar. 27–Mar. 30, 1970 May 28–May 31, 1970 July 2–July 5, 1970 Aug. 15–Sept. 8, 1970 Oct. 15–Nov. 15, 1970 Nov. 26–Nov. 29, 1970 Dec. 23–Dec. 28, 1970	...do.	
92d	1	Jan. 21, 1971	Dec. 17, 1971	331	Feb. 11–Feb. 17, 1971 Apr. 7–Apr. 14, 1971 May 26–June 1, 1971 June 30–July 6, 1971 Aug. 6–Sept. 8, 1971 Oct. 21–Oct. 26, 1971 Nov. 24–Nov. 29, 1971	Feb. 11–Feb. 16, 1971 Apr. 8–Apr. 18, 1971 May 28–May 31, 1971 July 2–July 5, 1971 Aug. 7–Sept. 7, 1971 Oct. 8–Oct. 11, 1971 Oct. 22–Oct. 25, 1971 Nov. 20–Nov. 28, 1971	Richard B. Russell, of Georgia;[17] Allen J. Ellender, of Louisiana.[17]	Carl B. Albert, of Oklahoma.
	2	Jan. 18, 1972	Oct. 18, 1972	275	Feb. 9–Feb. 14, 1972 Mar. 30–Apr. 4, 1972 May 25–May 30, 1972 June 30–July 17, 1972 Aug. 18–Sept. 5, 1972	Feb. 10–Feb. 15, 1972 Mar. 30–Apr. 9, 1972 May 25–May 29, 1972 June 1–July 16, 1972 Aug. 19–Sept. 4, 1972	Allen J. Ellender, of Louisiana;[18] James O. Eastland, of Mississippi.[18]	

93d	1	Jan. 3, 1973	Dec. 22, 1973 ...	354	Feb. 8–Feb. 15, 1973 .... Apr. 18–Apr. 30, 1973 May 23–May 29, 1973 June 30–July 9, 1973 Aug. 3–Sept. 5, 1973 Oct. 18–Oct. 23, 1973 Nov. 21–Nov. 26, 1973	Feb. 9–Feb. 18, 1973 .... Apr. 20–Apr. 29, 1973 May 25–May 28, 1973 July 1–July 9, 1973 Aug. 4–Sept. 4, 1973 Oct. 5–Oct. 8, 1973 Oct. 19–Oct. 22, 1973 Nov. 16–Nov. 25, 1973	James O. Eastland, of Mississippi	Do.
	2	Jan. 21, 1974	Dec. 20, 1974 ...	334	Feb. 8–Feb. 18, 1974 .... Mar. 13–Mar. 19, 1974 Apr. 11–Apr. 22, 1974 May 23–May 28, 1974 Aug. 22–Sept. 4, 1974 Oct. 17–Nov. 18, 1974 Nov. 26–Dec. 2, 1974	Feb. 8–Feb. 12, 1974 .... Apr. 12–Apr. 21, 1974 May 24–May 27, 1974 July 4–July 8, 1974 Aug. 23–Sept. 10, 1974 Oct. 18–Nov. 17, 1974 Nov. 27–Dec. 2, 1974	...do.	
94th ...	1	Jan. 14, 1975	Dec. 19, 1975 ...	340	Mar. 26–Apr. 7, 1975 .... May 22–June 2, 1975 June 27–July 7, 1975 Aug. 1–Sept. 3, 1975 Oct. 9–Oct. 20, 1975 Oct. 23–Oct. 28, 1975 Nov. 20–Dec. 1, 1975	Mar. 27–Apr. 6, 1975 .... May 23–June 1, 1975 June 27–July 7, 1975 Aug. 2–Sept. 2, 1975 Oct. 10–Oct. 19, 1975 Oct. 24–Oct. 27, 1975 Nov. 21–Nov. 30, 1975	...do	Do.
	2	Jan. 19, 1976	Oct. 1, 1976	257	Feb. 6–Feb. 16, 1976 .... Apr. 14–Apr. 26, 1976 May 28–June 2, 1976 July 2–July 19, 1976 Aug. 10–Aug. 23, 1976 Sept. 1–Sept. 7, 1976	Feb. 12–Feb. 15, 1976 .... Apr. 15–Apr. 25, 1976 May 28–May 31, 1976 July 3–July 18, 1976 Aug. 11–Aug. 22, 1976 Sept. 3–Sept. 7, 1976	...do.	
95th ...	1	Jan. 4, 1977	Dec. 15, 1977 ...	346	Feb. 11–Feb. 21, 1977 .... Apr. 7–Apr. 18, 1977 May 27–June 6, 1977 July 1–July 11, 1977 Aug. 6–Sept. 7, 1977	Feb. 10–Feb. 15, 1977 .... Apr. 7–Apr. 17, 1977 May 27–May 31, 1977 July 1–July 10, 1977 Aug. 6–Sept. 6, 1977 Oct. 7–Oct. 10, 1977	...do	Thomas P. O'Neill, Jr., of Massachusetts.
	2	Jan. 19, 1978	Oct. 15, 1978 ...	270	Feb. 10–Feb. 20, 1978 .... Mar. 23–Apr. 3, 1978 May 26–June 5, 1978 June 29–July 10, 1978 Aug. 25–Sept. 6, 1978	Feb. 10–Feb. 13, 1978 .... Mar. 23–Apr. 2, 1978 May 26–May 30, 1978 June 30–July 9, 1978 Aug. 18–Sept. 5, 1978	...do.	
96th ...	1	Jan. 15, 1979	Jan. 3, 1980	354	Feb. 9–Feb. 19, 1979 .... Apr. 10–Apr. 23, 1979 May 24–June 4, 1979 June 27–July 9, 1979 Aug. 3–Sept. 5, 1979 Nov. 20–Nov. 26, 1979 Adjourned sine die, Dec. 20, 1979	Feb. 9–Feb. 12, 1979 .... Apr. 11–Apr. 22, 1979 May 25–May 29, 1979 June 30–July 8, 1979 Aug. 3–Sept. 4, 1979 Nov. 21–Nov. 25, 1979	Warren G. Magnuson, of Washington ...	Do.

SESSIONS OF CONGRESS, 1st–115th CONGRESSES, 1789–2018—CONTINUED

[Closing date for this table was July 27, 2018.]

MEETING DATES OF CONGRESS: Pursuant to a resolution of the Confederation Congress in 1788, the Constitution went into effect on March 4, 1789. From then until the 20th amendment took effect in January 1934, the term of each Congress began on March 4th of each odd-numbered year; however, Article I, section 4, of the Constitution provided that "The Congress shall assemble at least once in every Year, and such Meeting shall be on the first Monday in December, unless they shall by law appoint a different day." The Congress therefore convened regularly on the first Monday in December until the 20th amendment became effective, which changed the beginning of Congress's term as well as its convening date to January 3rd. So prior to 1934, a new Congress typically would not convene for regular business until 13 months after being elected. One effect of this was that the last session of each Congress was a "lame duck" session. After the 20th amendment, the time from the election to the beginning of Congress's term as well as when it convened was reduced to two months. Recognizing that the need might exist for Congress to meet at times other than the regularly scheduled convening date, Article II, section 3 of the Constitution provides that the President "may, on extraordinary occasions, convene both Houses, or either of them"; hence these sessions occur only if convened by Presidential proclamation. Except as noted, these are separately numbered sessions of a Congress, and are marked by an E in the session column of the table. Until the 20th amendment was adopted, there were also times when special sessions of the Senate were convened, principally for confirming Cabinet and other executive nominations, and occasionally for the ratification of treaties or other executive business. These Senate sessions were also called by Presidential proclamation (typically by the outgoing President, although on occasion by incumbents as well) and are marked by an S in the session column. MEETING PLACES OF CONGRESS: Congress met for the first and second sessions of the First Congress (1789 and 1790) in New York City. From the third session of the First Congress through the first session of the Sixth Congress (1790 to 1800), Philadelphia was the meeting place. Congress has convened in Washington since the second session of the Sixth Congress (1800).

Congress	Session	Convening Date	Adjournment Date	Length in days[1]	Recesses[2]		President pro tempore of the Senate[3]	Speaker of the House of Representatives
					Senate	House of Representatives		
	2	Jan. 3, 1980	Dec. 16, 1980	349	Apr. 3–Apr. 15, 1980 May 22–May 28, 1980 July 2–July 21, 1980 Aug. 6–Aug. 18, 1980 Aug. 27–Sept. 3, 1980 Oct. 1–Nov. 12, 1980 Nov. 25–Dec. 1, 1980	Jan. 18–21, 1980 Feb. 14–Feb. 18, 1980 Apr. 3–Apr. 14, 1980 May 23–May 27, 1980 July 3–July 20, 1980 Aug. 2–Aug. 17, 1980 Aug. 29–Sept. 2, 1980 Oct. 3–Nov. 11, 1980 Nov. 22–Nov. 30, 1980	Warren G. Magnuson, of Washington; Milton Young, of North Dakota;[19] Warren G. Magnuson, of Washington.[19]	
97th	1	Jan. 5, 1981	Dec. 16, 1981	347	Feb. 6–Feb. 16, 1981 Apr. 10–Apr. 27, 1981 June 25–July 8, 1981 Aug. 3–Sept. 9, 1981 Oct. 7–Oct. 14, 1981 Nov. 24–Nov. 30, 1981	Feb. 7–Feb. 16, 1981 Apr. 11–Apr. 26, 1981 June 27–July 7, 1981 Aug. 5–Sept. 8, 1981 Oct. 8–Oct. 12, 1981 Nov. 24–Nov. 29, 1981	Strom Thurmond, of South Carolina	Do.
	2	Jan. 25, 1982	Dec. 21, 1982	333	Feb. 11–Feb. 22, 1982 Apr. 1–Apr. 13, 1982 May 27–June 8, 1982 July 1–July 12, 1982 Aug. 20–Sept. 8, 1982 Oct. 1–Nov. 29, 1982	Feb. 11–Feb. 21, 1982 Apr. 7–Apr. 19, 1982 May 29–June 1, 1982 July 2–July 11, 1982 Aug. 21–Sept. 7, 1982 Oct. 3–Nov. 28, 1982	...do	
98th	1	Jan. 3, 1983	Nov. 18, 1983	320	Jan. 3–Jan. 25, 1983 Feb. 3–Feb. 14, 1983 Mar. 24–Apr. 5, 1983 May 26–June 6, 1983 June 29–July 11, 1983 Aug. 4–Sept. 12, 1983 Oct. 7–Oct. 17, 1983	Jan. 7–Jan. 24, 1983 Feb. 18–Feb. 21, 1983 Mar. 25–Apr. 4, 1983 May 27–May 31, 1983 July 1–July 10, 1983 Aug. 5–Sept. 11, 1983 Oct. 7–Oct. 16, 1983	Strom Thurmond, of South Carolina	Thomas P. O'Neill, Jr., of Massachusetts.

	2	Jan. 23, 1984	Oct. 12, 1984	264	Feb. 9–Feb. 20, 1984 Apr. 12–Apr. 24, 1984 May 24–May 31, 1984 June 29–July 23, 1984 Aug. 10–Sept. 5, 1984	Feb. 10–Feb. 20, 1984 Apr. 13–Apr. 23, 1984 May 25–May 29, 1984 June 30–July 22, 1984 Aug. 11–Sept. 4, 1984	...do.	
99th	1	Jan. 3, 1985	Dec. 20, 1985	352	Jan. 7–Jan. 21, 1985 Feb. 7–Feb. 18, 1985 Apr. 4–Apr. 15, 1985 May 9–May 14, 1985 May 24–June 3, 1985 June 27–July 8, 1985 Aug. 1–Sept. 9, 1985 Nov. 23–Dec. 2, 1985	Jan. 8–Jan. 20, 1985 Feb. 8–Feb. 18, 1985 Mar. 8–Mar. 18, 1985 Apr. 5–Apr. 14, 1985 May 24–June 2, 1985 June 28–July 7, 1985 Aug. 2–Sept. 3, 1985 Nov. 22–Dec. 1, 1985	...do	Do.
	2	Jan. 21, 1986	Oct. 18, 1986	278	Feb. 7–Feb. 17, 1986 Mar. 27–Apr. 8, 1986 May 21–June 2, 1986 June 26–July 7, 1986 Aug. 15–Sept. 8, 1986	Feb. 7–Feb. 17, 1986 Mar. 25–Apr. 7, 1986 May 23–June 2, 1986 June 27–July 13, 1986 Aug. 17–Sept. 7, 1986	...do.	
100th	1	Jan. 6, 1987	Dec. 22, 1987	351	Jan. 6–Jan. 12, 1987 Feb. 5–Feb. 16, 1987 Apr. 10–Apr. 21, 1987 May 21–May 27, 1987 July 1–July 7, 1987 Aug. 7–Sept. 9, 1987 Nov. 20–Nov. 30, 1987	Jan. 9–Jan. 19, 1987 Feb. 12–Feb. 17, 1987 Apr. 10–Apr. 20, 1987 May 22–May 26, 1987 July 2–July 6, 1987 July 16–July 19, 1987 Aug. 8–Sept. 9, 1987 Nov. 11–Nov. 15, 1987 Nov. 21–Nov. 29, 1987	John C. Stennis, of Mississippi	James C. Wright, Jr., of Texas.
	2	Jan. 25, 1988	Oct. 22, 1988	272	Feb. 4–Feb. 15, 1988 Mar. 4– Mar. 14, 1988 Mar. 31–Apr. 11, 1988 Apr. 29–May 9, 1988 May 27–June 6, 1988 June 29–July 6, 1988 July 14–July 25, 1988 Aug. 11–Sept. 7, 1988	Feb. 10–Feb. 15, 1988 Apr. 1–Apr. 10, 1988 May 27–May 31, 1988 July 1–July 5, 1988 July 15–July 25, 1988 Aug. 12–Sept. 6, 1988	...do.	
101st	1	Jan. 3, 1989	Nov. 22, 1989	324	Jan. 4–Jan. 20, 1989 Jan. 20–Jan. 25, 1989 Feb. 9–Feb. 21, 1989 Mar. 17–Apr. 4, 1989 Apr. 19–May 1, 1989 May 18–May 31, 1989 June 23–July 11, 1989 Aug. 4–Sept. 6, 1989	Jan. 5–Jan. 18, 1989 Feb. 10–Feb. 20, 1989 Mar. 24–Apr. 2, 1989 Apr. 19–Apr. 24, 1989 May 26–May 30, 1989 June 30–July 9, 1989 Aug. 6–Sept. 5, 1989	Robert C. Byrd, of West Virginia	James C. Wright, Jr., of Texas;[20] Thomas S. Foley, of Washington.[20]
	2	Jan. 23, 1990	Oct. 28, 1990	260	Feb. 8–Feb. 20, 1990 Mar. 9–Mar. 20, 1990 Apr. 5–Apr. 18, 1990 May 24–June 5, 1990 June 28–July 10, 1990 Aug. 4–Sept. 10, 1990	Feb. 8–Feb. 19, 1990 Apr. 5–Apr. 17, 1990 May 26–June 4, 1990 June 29–July 9, 1990 Aug. 5–Sept. 4, 1990	...do.	

SESSIONS OF CONGRESS, 1st–115th CONGRESSES, 1789–2018—CONTINUED

[Closing date for this table was July 27, 2018.]

MEETING DATES OF CONGRESS: Pursuant to a resolution of the Confederation Congress in 1788, the Constitution went into effect on March 4, 1789. From then until the 20th amendment took effect in January 1934, the term of each Congress began on March 4th of each odd-numbered year; however, Article I, section 4, of the Constitution provided that ''The Congress shall assemble at least once in every Year, and such Meeting shall be on the first Monday in December, unless they shall by law appoint a different day.'' The Congress therefore convened regularly on the first Monday in December until the 20th amendment became effective, which changed the beginning of Congress's term as well as its convening date to January 3rd. So prior to 1934, a new Congress typically would not convene for regular business until 13 months after being elected. One effect of this was that the last session of each Congress was a ''lame duck'' session. After the 20th amendment, the time from the election to the beginning of Congress's term as well as when it convened was reduced to two months. Recognizing that the need might exist for Congress to meet at times other than the regularly scheduled convening date, Article II, section 3 of the Constitution provides that the President ''may, on extraordinary occasions, convene both Houses, or either of them''; hence these sessions occur only if convened by Presidential proclamation. Except as noted, these are separately numbered sessions of a Congress, and are marked by an E in the session column of the table. Until the 20th amendment was adopted, there were also times when special sessions of the Senate were convened, principally for confirming Cabinet and other executive nominations, and occasionally for the ratification of treaties or other executive business. These Senate sessions were also called by Presidential proclamation (typically by the outgoing President, although on occasion by incumbents as well) and are marked by an S in the session column. MEETING PLACES OF CONGRESS: Congress met for the first and second sessions of the First Congress (1789 and 1790) in New York City. From the third session of the First Congress through the first session of the Sixth Congress (1790 to 1800), Philadelphia was the meeting place. Congress has convened in Washington since the second session of the Sixth Congress (1800).

Congress	Session	Convening Date	Adjournment Date	Length in days[1]	Recesses[2]		President pro tempore of the Senate[3]	Speaker of the House of Representatives
					Senate	House of Representatives		
102d ...	1	Jan. 3, 1991	Jan. 3, 1992	366	Feb. 7–Feb. 19, 1991 .... Mar. 22–Apr. 9, 1991 Apr. 25–May 6, 1991 May 24–June 3, 1991 June 28–July 8, 1991 Aug. 2–Sept. 10, 1991 Nov. 27, 1991–Jan. 3, 1992	Feb. 7–Feb. 18, 1991 .... Mar. 23–Apr. 8, 1991 May 24–May 28, 1991 June 28–July 8, 1991 Aug. 3–Sept. 10, 1991 Nov. 28, 1991–Jan. 2, 1992	...do	Thomas S. Foley, of Washington.
	2	Jan. 3, 1992	Oct. 9, 1992	281	Jan. 3–Jan. 21, 1992 .... Apr. 10–Apr. 28, 1992 May 21–June 1, 1992 July 2–July 20, 1992 Aug. 12–Sept. 8, 1992	Jan. 4–Jan. 21, 1992 .... Apr. 11–Apr. 27, 1992 May 22–May 25, 1992 July 3–July 6, 1992 July 10–July 20, 1992 Aug. 13–Sept. 8, 1992	...do.	
103d ...	1	Jan. 5, 1993	Nov. 26, 1993 ..	326	Jan. 7–Jan. 20, 1993 .... Feb. 4–Feb. 16, 1993 Apr. 7–Apr. 19, 1993 May 28–June 7, 1993 July 1–July 13, 1993 Aug. 7–Sept. 7, 1993 Oct. 7–Oct. 13, 1993 Nov. 11–Nov. 16, 1993	Jan. 7–Jan. 19, 1993 .... Jan. 28–Feb. 1, 1993 Feb. 5–Feb. 15, 1993 Apr. 8–Apr. 18, 1993 May 28–June 7, 1993 July 2–July 12, 1993 Aug. 7–Sept. 7, 1993 Sept. 16–Sept. 20, 1993 Oct. 8–Oct. 11, 1993 Nov. 11–Nov. 14, 1993	Robert C. Byrd, of West Virginia	Thomas S. Foley, of Washington.

	2	Jan. 25, 1994	Nov. 29, 1994	311	Feb. 11–Feb. 22, 1994 Mar. 26–Apr. 11, 1994 May 25–June 7, 1994 July 1–July 11, 1994 Aug. 25–Sept. 12, 1994 Oct. 8–Nov. 30, 1994	Jan. 27–Jan. 31, 1994 Feb. 12–Feb. 21, 1994 Mar. 25–Apr. 11, 1994 May 27–June 7, 1994 July 1–July 11, 1994 Aug. 27–Sept. 11, 1994 Oct. 8–Nov. 28, 1994	...do.	
104th	1	Jan. 4, 1995	Jan. 3, 1996	365	Feb. 16–Feb. 22, 1995 Apr. 7–Apr. 24, 1995 May 26–June 5, 1995 June 30–July 10, 1995 Aug. 11–Sept. 5, 1995 Sept. 29–Oct. 10, 1995 Nov. 20–Nov. 27, 1995	Feb. 17–Feb. 20, 1995 Mar. 17–Mar. 20, 1995 Apr. 8–Apr. 30, 1995 May 4–May 8, 1995 May 26–June 5, 1995 July 1–July 9, 1995 Aug. 5–Sept. 5, 1995 Sept. 30–Oct. 5, 1995 Nov. 21–Nov. 27, 1995	Strom Thurmond, of South Carolina	Newt Gingrich, of Georgia.
	2	Jan. 3, 1996	Oct. 4, 1996	276	Jan. 10–Jan. 22, 1996 Mar. 29–Apr. 15, 1996 May 24–June 3, 1996 June 28–July 8, 1996 Aug. 2–Sept. 3, 1996	Jan. 10–Jan. 21, 1996 Mar. 30–Apr. 14, 1996 May 24–May 28, 1996 June 29–July 7, 1996 Aug. 3–Sept. 3, 1996	...do.	
105th	1	Jan. 7, 1997	Nov. 13, 1997	311	Jan. 9–Jan. 21, 1997 Feb. 13–Feb. 24, 1997 Mar. 21–Apr. 7, 1997 June 27–July 7, 1997 July 31–Sept. 2, 1997 Oct. 9–Oct. 20, 1997	Jan. 10–Jan. 19, 1997 Jan. 22–Feb. 3, 1997 Feb. 14–Feb. 24, 1997 Mar. 22–Apr. 7, 1997 June 27–July 7, 1997 Aug. 2–Sept. 2, 1997 Oct. 10–Oct. 20, 1997	...do	Do.
	2	Jan. 27, 1998	Dec. 19, 1998	327	Feb. 13–Feb. 23, 1998 Apr. 3–Apr. 20, 1998 May 22–June 1, 1998 June 26–July 6, 1998 July 31–Aug. 31, 1998 Adjourned sine die, Oct. 21, 1998.	Jan. 29–Feb. 2, 1998 Feb. 6–Feb. 10, 1998 Feb. 13–Feb. 23, 1998 Apr. 2–Apr. 20, 1998 May 23–June 2, 1998 June 25–July 13, 1998 Aug. 8–Sept. 8, 1998 Oct. 22–Dec. 16, 1998	...do.	
106th	1	Jan. 6, 1999	Nov. 22, 1999	321	Feb. 12–Feb. 22, 1999 Mar. 25–Apr. 12, 1999 May 27–June 7, 1999 July 1–July 12, 1999 Aug. 5–Sept. 8, 1999	Jan. 7–Jan. 18, 1999 Jan. 20–Feb. 1, 1999 Feb. 13–Feb. 22, 1999 Mar. 26–Apr. 11, 1999 May 28–June 6, 1999 July 2–July 11, 1999 Aug. 7–Sept. 7, 1999	...do	J. Dennis Hastert, of Illinois.
	2	Jan. 24, 2000	Dec. 15, 2000	326	Feb. 10–Feb. 22, 2000 Mar. 9–Mar. 20, 2000 Apr. 13–Apr. 25, 2000 May 25–June 6, 2000 June 30–July 10, 2000 July 27–Sept. 5, 2000 Nov. 2–Nov. 14, 2000 Nov. 14–Dec. 5, 2000	Feb. 17–Feb. 28, 2000 Apr. 14–May 1, 2000 May 26–June 5, 2000 July 1–July 9, 2000 July 28–Sept. 5, 2000 Nov. 4–Nov. 12, 2000 Nov. 15–Dec. 3, 2000	...do.	

SESSIONS OF CONGRESS, 1st–115th CONGRESSES, 1789–2018—CONTINUED

[Closing date for this table was July 27, 2018.]

MEETING DATES OF CONGRESS: Pursuant to a resolution of the Confederation Congress in 1788, the Constitution went into effect on March 4, 1789. From then until the 20th amendment took effect in January 1934, the term of each Congress began on March 4th of each odd-numbered year; however, Article I, section 4, of the Constitution provided that ''The Congress shall assemble at least once in every Year, and such Meeting shall be on the first Monday in December, unless they shall by law appoint a different day.'' The Congress therefore convened regularly on the first Monday in December until the 20th amendment became effective, which changed the beginning of Congress's term as well as its convening date to January 3rd. So prior to 1934, a new Congress typically would not convene for regular business until 13 months after being elected. One effect of this was that the last session of each Congress was a ''lame duck'' session. After the 20th amendment, the time from the election to the beginning of Congress's term as well as when it convened was reduced to two months. Recognizing that the need might exist for Congress to meet at times other than the regularly scheduled convening date, Article II, section 3 of the Constitution provides that the President ''may, on extraordinary occasions, convene both Houses, or either of them''; hence these sessions occur only if convened by Presidential proclamation. Except as noted, these are separately numbered sessions of a Congress, and are marked by an E in the session column of the table. Until the 20th amendment was adopted, there were also times when special sessions of the Senate were convened, principally for confirming Cabinet and other executive nominations, and occasionally for the ratification of treaties or other executive business. These Senate sessions were also called by Presidential proclamation (typically by the outgoing President, although on occasion by incumbents as well) and are marked by an S in the session column. MEETING PLACES OF CONGRESS: Congress met for the first and second sessions of the First Congress (1789 and 1790) in New York City. From the third session of the First Congress through the first session of the Sixth Congress (1790 to 1800), Philadelphia was the meeting place. Congress has convened in Washington since the second session of the Sixth Congress (1800).

Congress	Session	Convening Date	Adjournment Date	Length in days[1]	Recesses[2]		President pro tempore of the Senate[3]	Speaker of the House of Representatives
					Senate	House of Representatives		
107th	1	Jan. 3, 2001	Dec. 20, 2001	352	Jan. 8–Jan. 20, 2001 Feb. 15–Feb. 26, 2001 Apr. 6–Apr. 23, 2001 May 26–June 5, 2001 June 29–July 9, 2001 Aug. 3–Sept. 4, 2001 Oct. 18–Oct. 23, 2001 Nov. 16–Nov. 27, 2001	Jan. 7–Jan. 19, 2001 Jan. 21–Jan 29, 2001 Feb. 1–Feb. 5, 2001 Feb. 15–Feb. 25, 2001 Apr. 5–Apr. 23, 2001 May 27–June 4, 2001 June 29–July 9, 2001 Aug. 3–Sept. 4, 2001 Oct. 18–Oct. 22, 2001 Nov. 20–Nov. 26, 2001	Robert C. Byrd, of West Virginia;[21] Strom Thurmond, of South Carolina;[21] Robert C. Byrd, of West Virginia.[21]	Do.
	2	Jan. 23, 2002	Nov. 22, 2002	304	Jan. 29–Feb. 4, 2002 Feb. 15–Feb. 25, 2002 Mar. 22–Apr. 8, 2002 May 23–June 3, 2002 June 28–July 8, 2002 Aug. 1–Sept. 3, 2002	Jan. 30–Feb. 3, 2002 Feb. 15–Feb. 25, 2002 Mar. 21–Apr. 8, 2002 May 25–June 3, 2002 June 29–July 7, 2002 July 28–Sept. 3, 2002	Robert C. Byrd, of West Virginia.	
108th	1	Jan. 7, 2003	Dec. 8, 2003	337	Feb. 14–Feb. 24, 2003 Apr. 11–Apr. 28, 2003 May 23–June 2, 2003 June 27–July 7, 2003 Aug. 1–Sept 2, 2003 Oct. 3–Oct. 14, 2003 Nov. 25–Dec. 9, 2003	Jan. 9–Jan. 26, 2003 Feb. 14–Feb. 24, 2003 Apr. 13–Apr. 28, 2003 May 24–June 1, 2003 June 28–July 6, 2003 July 30–Sept. 2, 2003 Nov. 26–Dec. 7, 2003	Ted Stevens, of Alaska	J. Dennis Hastert, of Illinois.

	2	Jan. 20, 2004	Dec. 7, 2004	324	Feb. 12–Feb. 23, 2004 .... Mar. 12–Mar. 22, 2004 Apr. 8–Apr. 19, 2004 May 21–June 1, 2004 June 9–June 14, 2004 June 25–July 6, 2004 July 22–Sept. 7, 2004 Oct. 11–Nov. 16, 2004 Nov. 24–Dec. 7, 2004	Feb. 12–Feb. 23, 2004 .... Apr. 3–Apr. 19, 2004 May 21–May 31, 2004 June 10–June 13, 2004 June 26–July 5, 2004 July 23–Sept. 6, 2004 Oct. 10–Nov. 15, 2004 Nov. 25–Dec. 5, 2004	...do.	
109th.	1	Jan. 4, 2005	Dec. 22, 2005 ...	353	Jan. 6–Jan. 20, 2005 .... Jan. 26–Jan. 31, 2005 Feb. 18–Feb. 28, 2005 Mar. 20–Apr. 4, 2005 Apr. 29–May 9, 2005 May 26–June 6, 2005 July 1–July 11, 2005 July 29–Sept. 1, 2005 Sept. 1–Sept. 6, 2005 Oct. 7–Oct. 17, 2005 Nov. 18–Dec. 12, 2005	Jan. 7–Jan. 19, 2005 .... Jan. 21–Jan. 24, 2005 Jan. 27–Jan. 31, 2005 Feb. 3–Feb. 7, 2005 Feb. 18–Feb. 28, 2005 Mar. 22–Apr. 4, 2005 May 27–June 6, 2005 July 1–July 8, 2005 July 30–Sept. 1, 2005 Oct. 8–Oct. 16, 2005 Nov. 19–Dec. 5, 2005	...do	Do.
	2	Jan. 3, 2006	Dec. 9, 2006	341	Jan. 3–Jan. 18, 2006 .... Feb. 17–Feb. 27, 2006 Mar. 16–Mar. 27, 2006 Apr. 7–Apr. 24, 2006 May 26–June 5, 2006 June 29–July 10, 2006 Aug. 4–Sept. 5, 2006 Sept. 30–Nov. 9, 2006 Nov. 16–Dec. 4, 2006	Jan. 4–Jan. 30, 2006 .... Feb. 2–Feb. 6, 2006 Feb. 9–Feb. 13, 2006 Feb. 17–Feb. 27, 2006 Mar. 17–Mar. 27, 2006 Apr. 7–Apr. 24, 2006 May 26–June 5, 2006 June 30–July 9, 2006 Aug. 3–Sept. 5, 2006 Oct. 1–Nov. 8, 2006 Nov. 16–Dec. 3, 2006	...do.	
110th.	1	Jan. 4, 2007	Dec. 19, 2007 ...	362	Feb. 17–Feb. 26, 2007 .... Mar. 29–Apr. 10, 2007 May 25–June 4, 2007 June 29–July 9, 2007 Aug. 3–Sept. 4, 2007 Oct. 5–Oct. 15, 2007	Jan. 25–Jan. 28, 2007 .... Feb. 1–Feb. 4, 2007 Feb. 17–Feb. 26, 2007 Mar. 31–Apr. 15, 2007 May 25–June 4, 2007 June 29–July 9, 2007 Aug. 6–Sept. 3, 2007 Nov. 16–Dec. 3, 2007	Robert C. Byrd, of West Virginia	Nancy Pelosi, of California.
	2	Jan. 3, 2008	Jan. 3, 2009	367	June 27–July 7, 2008	Jan. 4–Jan. 14, 2008 .... Jan. 24–Jan. 27, 2008 Jan. 30–Feb. 5, 2008 Mar. 15–Mar. 30, 2008 May 23–June 2, 2008 June 27–July 7, 2008 Aug. 2–Sept. 7, 2008 Oct. 4–Nov. 18, 2008 Nov. 21–Dec. 8, 2008 Dec. 11, 2008–Jan. 3, 2009	...do.	

SESSIONS OF CONGRESS, 1st–115th CONGRESSES, 1789–2018—CONTINUED

[Closing date for this table was July 27, 2018.]

MEETING DATES OF CONGRESS: Pursuant to a resolution of the Confederation Congress in 1788, the Constitution went into effect on March 4, 1789. From then until the 20th amendment took effect in January 1934, the term of each Congress began on March 4th of each odd-numbered year; however, Article I, section 4, of the Constitution provided that ''The Congress shall assemble at least once in every Year, and such Meeting shall be on the first Monday in December, unless they shall by law appoint a different day.'' The Congress therefore convened regularly on the first Monday in December until the 20th amendment became effective, which changed the beginning of Congress's term as well as its convening date to January 3rd. So prior to 1934, a new Congress typically would not convene for regular business until 13 months after being elected. One effect of this was that the last session of each Congress was a ''lame duck'' session. After the 20th amendment, the time from the election to the beginning of Congress's term as well as when it convened was reduced to two months. Recognizing that the need might exist for Congress to meet at times other than the regularly scheduled convening date, Article II, section 3 of the Constitution provides that the President ''may, on extraordinary occasions, convene both Houses, or either of them''; hence these sessions occur only if convened by Presidential proclamation. Except as noted, these are separately numbered sessions of a Congress, and are marked by an E in the session column of the table. Until the 20th amendment was adopted, there were also times when special sessions of the Senate were convened, principally for confirming Cabinet and other executive nominations, and occasionally for the ratification of treaties or other executive business. These Senate sessions were also called by Presidential proclamation (typically by the outgoing President, although on occasion by incumbents as well) and are marked by an S in the session column. MEETING PLACES OF CONGRESS: Congress met for the first and second sessions of the First Congress (1789 and 1790) in New York City. From the third session of the First Congress through the first session of the Sixth Congress (1790 to 1800), Philadelphia was the meeting place. Congress has convened in Washington since the second session of the Sixth Congress (1800).

Congress	Session	Convening Date	Adjournment Date	Length in days[1]	Recesses[2] Senate	Recesses[2] House of Representatives	President pro tempore of the Senate[3]	Speaker of the House of Representatives
111th	1	Jan. 6, 2009	Dec. 23, 2009	353	Apr. 2–Apr. 20, 2009 May 21–June 1, 2009 June 25–July 6, 2009 Nov. 10–Nov. 16, 2009 Nov. 21–Nov. 30, 2009	Jan. 29–Feb. 1, 2009 Feb. 5–Feb. 8, 2009 Feb. 14–Feb. 22, 2009 Apr. 3–Apr. 20, 2009 May 22–June 1, 2009 June 27–July 6, 2009 Aug. 1–Sept. 7, 2009 Nov. 8–Nov. 15, 2009 Nov. 20–Nov. 30, 2009	...do	Do.
	2	Jan. 5, 2010	Dec. 22, 2010	352	Feb. 11–Feb. 23, 2010 Mar. 26–Apr. 12, 2010 May 28–June 7, 2010 June 30–July 12, 2010 Aug. 5–Aug. 12, 2010 Aug. 12–Sept. 13, 2010 Nov. 19–Nov. 29, 2010	Jan. 6–Jan. 11, 2010 Feb. 10–Feb. 21, 2010 Mar. 26–Apr. 12, 2010 May 29–June 7, 2010 July 2–July 12, 2010 July 31–Aug. 8, 2010 Aug. 11–Sept. 13, 2010 Oct. 1–Nov. 14, 2010 Nov. 19–Nov. 28, 2010	Robert C. Byrd, of West Virginia;[22] Daniel K. Inouye, of Hawaii.[22]	
112th	1	Jan. 5, 2011	Jan. 3, 2012	360	Jan. 5 –Jan. 25, 2011 Feb. 17–Feb. 28, 2011 Mar. 17–Mar. 28, 2011 Apr. 14–May 2, 2011	Jan. 13–Jan. 17, 2011 Jan. 27–Feb. 7, 2011 Feb. 20–Feb. 27, 2011 Mar. 18–Mar. 28, 2011 Apr. 16–May 1, 2011 May 14–May 22, 2011	Daniel K. Inouye, of Hawaii	John A. Boehner, of Ohio.

	2	Jan. 3, 2012	Jan. 3, 2013	367	Aug. 3–Sept. 10, 2012	Mar. 31–Apr. 15, 2012 Apr. 28–May 6, 2012 June 30–July 8, 2012 Aug. 8–Sept. 9, 2012 Nov. 17–Nov. 26, 2012	Daniel K. Inouye, of Hawaii;[23] Patrick J. Leahy, of Vermont.[23]	
113th.	1	Jan. 3, 2013	Jan. 3, 2014	356	Jan. 4–Jan. 22, 2013 Feb. 15–Feb. 25, 2013 Mar. 22–Apr. 8, 2013 May 23–June 3, 2013 June 28–July 8, 2013 Aug. 2–Aug. 12, 2013 Aug. 12–Sept. 6, 2013	Jan. 5–Jan. 13, 2013 Feb. 16–Feb. 24, 2013 Mar. 26–Apr. 8, 2013 May 25–June 2, 2013 June 29–July 7, 2013 Aug. 3–Sept. 5, 2013 Oct. 31–Nov. 11, 2013 Nov. 23–Dec. 1, 2013 Dec. 27, 2013–Jan. 2, 2014	Patrick J. Leahy, of Vermont	Do.
	2	Jan. 3, 2014	Jan. 2, 2015	365	Apr. 11–Apr. 28, 2014 Aug. 8–Sept. 8, 2014 Sept. 18–Oct. 15, 2014 Oct. 15–Nov. 12, 2014	Apr. 11–Apr. 27, 2014 Aug. 5–Sept. 7, 2014 Sept. 20–Nov. 11, 2014 Nov. 21–Nov. 30, 2014 Dec. 17–Jan. 1, 2015	...do	Do.
114th.	1	Jan. 6, 2015	Dec. 18, 2015	347	Mar. 26–Apr. 13, 2015 June 25–July 7, 2015 Aug. 6–Sept. 8, 2015 Nov. 19–Nov. 30, 2015	Mar. 27–Apr. 12, 2015 June 26–July 6, 2015 Aug. 5–Sept. 7, 2015 Nov. 6–Nov. 15, 2015 Nov. 20–Nov. 29, 2015	Orrin Hatch, of Utah	John A. Boehner, of Ohio[24] Paul D. Ryan, of Wisconsin[24]
	2	Jan. 4, 2016	Jan. 3, 2017	366	Feb. 12–Feb. 22, 2016	Jan. 14–Jan 24, 2016 Feb. 13–Feb. 22, 2016 Mar. 24–April 10, 2016 July 26–Sep. 5, 2016 Sep. 29–Nov. 13, 2016	...do	...Do.
115th.	1	Jan. 3, 2017	Jan. 2, 2018	365			Orrin Hatch, of Utah	...Do.
	2	Jan. 3, 2018					...do	...Do.

[1] For the purposes of this table, a session's "length in days" is defined as the total number of calendar days from the convening date to the adjournment date, inclusive. It does not mean the actual number of days that Congress met during that session.

[2] For the purposes of this table, a "recess" is defined as a break in House or Senate proceedings of three or more days, excluding Sundays. According to Article I, section 5 of the U.S. Constitution, neither house may adjourn for more than three days without the consent of the other.

[3] The election and role of the President pro tempore has evolved considerably over the Senate's history. "*Pro tempore* is Latin for 'for the time being'; thus, the post was conceived as a temporary presiding officer. In the eighteenth and nineteenth centuries, the Senate frequently elected several Presidents pro tempore during a single session. Since Vice Presidents presided routinely, the Senate thought it necessary to choose a President pro tempore only for the limited periods when the Vice President might be ill or otherwise absent." Since no provision was in place (until the 25th amendment was adopted in 1967) for replacing the Vice President if he died or resigned from office, or if he assumed the Presidency, the President pro tempore would continue under such circumstances to fill the duties of the chair until the next Vice President was elected. Since Mar. 12, 1890, however, Presidents pro tempore have served until "the Senate otherwise ordered." Since 1949, while still elected, the position has gone to the most senior member of the majority party (see footnote 19 for a minority party exception). To gain a more complete understanding of this position, see Robert C. Byrd's *The Senate 1789–1989: Addresses on the History of the United States Senate*, vol. 2, ch. 6 "The President Pro Tempore," pp. 167–183, from which the quotes in this footnote are taken. Also, a complete listing of the dates of election of the Presidents pro tempore is in vol. 4 of the Byrd series (*The Senate 1789–1989: Historical Statistics, 1789–1992*), table 6–2, pp. 647–653.

[4] Henry Clay resigned as Speaker on Jan. 19, 1814. He was succeeded by Langdon Cheves who was elected on that same day.

[5] Henry Clay resigned as Speaker on Oct. 28, 1820, after the sine die adjournment of the first session of the 16th Congress. He was succeeded by John W. Taylor who was elected at the beginning of the second session.

[6] Andrew Stevenson resigned as Speaker on June 2, 1834. He was succeeded by John Bell who was elected on that same day.

[7] Speaker Schuyler Colfax resigned as Speaker on the last day of the 40th Congress, Mar. 3, 1869, in preparation for becoming Vice President of the United States on the following day. Theodore M. Pomeroy was elected Speaker on Mar. 3, and served for only that one day.

[8] Speaker Michael C. Kerr died on Aug. 19, 1876, after the sine die adjournment of the first session of the 44th Congress. Samuel J. Randall was elected Speaker at the beginning of the second session.

[9] William P. Frye resigned as President pro tempore on Apr. 27, 1911.

[10] President pro tempore James P. Clarke died on Oct. 1, 1916, after the sine die adjournment of the first session of the 64th Congress. Willard Saulsbury was elected President pro tempore during the second session.

[11] Speaker Joseph W. Byrns died on June 4, 1936. He was succeeded by William B. Bankhead who was elected Speaker on that same day.

[12] Speaker William B. Bankhead died on Sept. 15, 1940. He was succeeded by Sam Rayburn who was elected Speaker on that same day.

[13] President pro tempore Key Pittman died on Nov. 10, 1940. He was succeeded by William H. King who was elected President pro tempore on Nov. 19, 1940.

[14] President pro tempore Pat Harrison died on June 22, 1941. He was succeeded by Carter Glass who was elected President pro tempore on July 10, 1941.

[15] President Harry S. Truman called the Congress into extraordinary session twice, both times during the 80th Congress. Each time Congress had essentially wrapped up its business for the year, but for technical reasons had not adjourned sine die, so in each case the extraordinary session is considered an extension of the regularly numbered session rather than a separately numbered one. The dates of these extraordinary sessions were Nov. 17 to Dec. 19, 1947, and July 26 to Aug. 7, 1948.

[16] Speaker Sam Rayburn died on Nov. 16, 1961, after the sine die adjournment of the first session of the 87th Congress. John W. McCormack was elected Speaker at the beginning of the second session.

[17] President pro tempore Richard B. Russell died on Jan. 21, 1971. He was succeeded by Allen J. Ellender who was elected to that position on Jan. 22, 1971.

[18] President pro tempore Allen J. Ellender died on July 27, 1972. He was succeeded by James O. Eastland who was elected President pro tempore on July 28, 1972.

[19] Milton Young was elected President pro tempore for one day, Dec. 5, 1980, which was at the end of his 36-year career in the Senate. He was a Republican, which was the minority party at that time. Warren G. Magnuson resumed the position of President pro tempore on Dec. 6, 1980.

[20] James C. Wright, Jr., resigned as Speaker on June 6, 1989. He was succeeded by Thomas S. Foley who was elected on that same day.

[21] The 2000 election resulted in an even split in the Senate between Republicans and Democrats. From the date the 107th Congress convened on Jan. 3, 2001, until Inauguration Day on Jan. 20, 2001, Vice President Albert Gore's tie breaking vote resulted in a Democratic majority, hence Robert C. Byrd served as President pro tempore during this brief period. When Vice President Richard B. Cheney took office on Jan. 20, the Republicans became the majority party, and Strom Thurmond was elected President pro tempore. On June 6, 2001, Republican Senator James Jeffords became an Independent, creating a Democratic majority, and Robert C. Byrd was elected President pro tempore on that day.

[22] President pro tempore Robert C. Byrd died on June 28, 2010. He was succeeded by Daniel K. Inouye who was elected President pro tempore on that same day.

[23] President pro tempore Daniel K. Inouye died on December 17, 2012. He was succeeded by Patrick J. Leahy who was elected President pro tempore on that same day.

[24] John A. Boehner, resigned as Speaker on Oct. 29, 2015. He was succeeded by Paul D. Ryan who was elected on that same day.

CEREMONIAL MEETINGS OF CONGRESS

The following ceremonial meetings of Congress occurred on the following dates, at the designated locations, and for the reasons indicated. Please note that Congress was not in session on these occasions.

-July 16, 1987, 100th Congress, Philadelphia, Pennsylvania, Independence Hall and Congress Hall—In honor of the bicentennial of the Constitution, and in commemoration of the Great Compromise of the Constitutional Convention which was agreed to on July 16, 1787.

-September 6, 2002, 107th Congress, New York City, New York, Federal Hall—In remembrance of the victims and heroes of September 11, 2001, and in recognition of the courage and spirit of the City of New York.

JOINT SESSIONS AND MEETINGS, ADDRESSES TO THE SENATE OR THE HOUSE, AND INAUGURATIONS

1st–115th CONGRESSES, 1789–2018 [1]

The parliamentary difference between a joint session and a joint meeting has evolved over time. In recent years the distinctions have become clearer: a joint session is more formal, and occurs upon the adoption of a concurrent resolution; a joint meeting occurs when each body adopts a unanimous consent agreement to recess to meet with the other legislative body. Joint sessions typically are held to hear an address from the President of the United States or to count electoral votes. Joint meetings typically are held to hear an address from a foreign dignitary or visitors other than the President.

The Speaker of the House of Representatives usually presides over joint sessions and joint meetings; however, the President of the Senate does preside over joint sessions where the electoral votes are counted, as required by the Constitution.

In the earliest years of the Republic, 1789 and 1790, when the national legislature met in New York City, joint gatherings were held in the Senate Chamber in Federal Hall. In Philadelphia, when the legislature met in Congress Hall, such meetings were held in the Senate Chamber, 1790–1793, and in the Hall of the House of Representatives, 1794–1799. Once the Congress moved to the Capitol in Washington in 1800, the Senate Chamber again was used for joint gatherings through 1805. Since 1809, with few exceptions, joint sessions and joint meetings have occurred in the Hall of the House.

Presidential messages on the state of the Union were originally known as the "Annual Message," but since the 80th Congress, in 1947, have been called the "State of the Union Address." After President John Adams's Annual Message on November 22, 1800, these addresses were read by clerks to the individual bodies until President Woodrow Wilson resumed the practice of delivering them to joint sessions on December 2, 1913.

In some instances more than one joint gathering has occurred on the same day. For example, on January 6, 1941, Congress met in joint session to count electoral votes for President and Vice President, and then met again in joint session to receive President Franklin Delano Roosevelt's Annual Message.

Whereas in more recent decades, foreign dignitaries invited to speak before Congress have typically done so at joint meetings, in earlier times (and with several notable exceptions), such visitors were received by the Senate and the House separately, or by one or the other singly, a tradition begun with the visit of General Lafayette of France in 1824. At that time a joint committee decided that each body would honor Lafayette separately, establishing the precedent. (See footnote 7 for more details.) Not all such occasions included formal addresses by such dignitaries (e.g., Lafayette's reception by the Senate in their chamber, at which he did not speak before they adjourned to greet him), hence the "occasions" listed in the third column of the table include not only addresses, but also remarks (defined as brief greetings or off-the-cuff comments often requested of the visitor at the last minute) and receptions. Relatively few foreign dignitaries were received by Congress before World War I.

Congress has hosted inaugurations since the first occasion in 1789. They always have been formal joint gatherings, and sometimes they also were joint sessions. Inaugurations were joint sessions when both houses of Congress were in session, and they processed to the ceremony as part of the business of the day. In many cases, however, one or both houses were not in session or were in recess at the time of the ceremony. In this table, inaugurations that were not joint sessions are listed in the second column. Those that were joint sessions are so identified and described in the third column.

JOINT SESSIONS AND MEETINGS, ADDRESSES TO THE SENATE OR THE HOUSE, AND INAUGURATIONS

[See notes at end of table]

Congress and Date	Type	Occasion, topic, or inaugural location	Name and position of dignitary (where applicable)
		NEW YORK CITY	
1st CONGRESS			
Apr. 6, 1789	Joint session	Counting electoral votes	N.A.
Apr. 30, 1789	...do	Inauguration and church service [2]	President George Washington; Right Reverend Samuel Provoost, Senate-appointed Chaplain.
Jan. 8, 1790	...do	Annual Message	President George Washington.
		PHILADELPHIA	
Dec. 8, 1790	...do	...do	Do.
2d CONGRESS			
Oct. 25, 1791	...do	...do	Do.
Nov. 6, 1792	...do	...do	Do.
Feb. 13, 1793	...do	Counting electoral votes	N.A.
3d CONGRESS			
Mar. 4, 1793	Inauguration	Senate Chamber	President George Washington.
Dec. 3, 1793	Joint session	Annual Message	Do.
Nov. 19, 1794	...do	...do	Do.
4th CONGRESS			
Dec. 8, 1795	...do	...do	Do.
Dec. 7, 1796	...do	...do	Do.
Feb. 8, 1797	...do	Counting electoral votes	N.A.
5th CONGRESS			
Mar. 4, 1797	Inauguration	Hall of the House	President John Adams.
May 16, 1797	Joint session	Relations with France	Do.
Nov. 23, 1797	...do	Annual Message	Do.
Dec. 8, 1798	...do	...do	Do.
6th CONGRESS			
Dec. 3, 1799	...do	...do	Do.
Dec. 26, 1799	...do	Funeral procession and oration in memory of George Washington.[3]	Representative Henry Lee.
		WASHINGTON	
Nov. 22, 1800	...do	Annual Message	President John Adams.
Feb. 11, 1801	...do	Counting electoral votes [4]	N.A.
7th CONGRESS			
Mar. 4, 1801	Inauguration	Senate Chamber	President Thomas Jefferson.
8th CONGRESS			
Feb. 13, 1805	Joint session	Counting electoral votes	N.A.
9th CONGRESS			
Mar. 4, 1805	Inauguration	Senate Chamber	President Thomas Jefferson.
10th CONGRESS			
Feb. 8, 1809	Joint session	Counting electoral votes	N.A.
11th CONGRESS			
Mar. 4, 1809	Inauguration	Hall of the House	President James Madison.
12th CONGRESS			
Feb. 10, 1813	Joint session	Counting electoral votes	N.A.
13th CONGRESS			
Mar. 4, 1813	Inauguration	Hall of the House	President James Madison.
14th CONGRESS			
Feb. 12, 1817	Joint session	Counting electoral votes [5]	N.A.
15th CONGRESS			
Mar. 4, 1817	Inauguration	In front of Brick Capitol	President James Monroe.
16th CONGRESS			
Feb. 14, 1821	Joint session	Counting electoral votes [6]	N.A.
17th CONGRESS			
Mar. 5, 1821	Inauguration	Hall of the House	President James Monroe.
18th CONGRESS			
Dec. 9, 1824	Senate	Reception	General Gilbert du Motier, Marquis de Lafayette, of France.

JOINT SESSIONS AND MEETINGS, ADDRESSES TO THE SENATE OR THE HOUSE, AND INAUGURATIONS—CONTINUED

[See notes at end of table]

Congress and Date	Type	Occasion, topic, or inaugural location	Name and position of dignitary (where applicable)
Dec. 10, 1824	House[7]	Address	Speaker Henry Clay; General Gilbert du Motier, Marquis de Lafayette, of France.
Feb. 9, 1825	Joint session	Counting electoral votes[8]	N.A.
19th CONGRESS			
Mar. 4, 1825	Inauguration	Hall of the House	President John Quincy Adams.
20th CONGRESS			
Feb. 11, 1829	Joint session	Counting electoral votes	N.A.
21st CONGRESS			
Mar. 4, 1829	Inauguration	East Portico[9]	President Andrew Jackson.
22d CONGRESS			
Feb. 13, 1833	Joint session	Counting electoral votes	N.A.
23d CONGRESS			
Mar. 4, 1833	Inauguration	Hall of the House[10]	President Andrew Jackson.
Dec. 31, 1834	Joint session	Lafayette eulogy	Representative and former President John Quincy Adams; ceremony attended by President Andrew Jackson.
24th CONGRESS			
Feb. 8, 1837	...do	Counting electoral votes	N.A.
25th CONGRESS			
Mar. 4, 1837	Inauguration	East Portico	President Martin Van Buren.
26th CONGRESS			
Feb. 10, 1841	Joint session	Counting electoral votes	N.A.
27th CONGRESS			
Mar. 4, 1841	Inauguration	East Portico	President William Henry Harrison.
28th CONGRESS			
Feb. 12, 1845	Joint session	Counting electoral votes	N.A.
29th CONGRESS			
Mar. 4, 1845	Inauguration	East Portico	President James Knox Polk.
30th CONGRESS			
Feb. 14, 1849	Joint session	Counting electoral votes	N.A.
31st CONGRESS			
Mar. 5, 1849	Inauguration	East Portico	President Zachary Taylor.
July 10, 1850	Joint session	Oath of office to President Millard Fillmore.[11]	N.A.
32d CONGRESS			
Jan. 5, 1852	Senate	Reception	Louis Kossuth, exiled Governor of Hungary.
Jan. 7, 1852	House	Remarks and Reception	Do.
Feb. 9, 1853	Joint session	Counting electoral votes	N.A.
33d CONGRESS			
Mar. 4, 1853	Inauguration	East Portico	President Franklin Pierce.
34th CONGRESS			
Feb. 11, 1857	Joint session	Counting electoral votes	N.A.
35th CONGRESS			
Mar. 4, 1857	Inauguration	East Portico	President James Buchanan.
36th CONGRESS			
Feb. 13, 1861	Joint session	Counting electoral votes	N.A.
37th CONGRESS			
Mar. 4, 1861	Inauguration	East Portico	President Abraham Lincoln.
Feb. 22, 1862	Joint session	Reading of Washington's farewell address.	John W. Forney, Secretary of the Senate.
38th CONGRESS			
Feb. 8, 1865	...do	Counting electoral votes	N.A.
39th CONGRESS			
Mar. 4, 1865	Inauguration	East Portico	President Abraham Lincoln.
Feb. 12, 1866	Joint session	Memorial to Abraham Lincoln	George Bancroft, historian; ceremony attended by President Andrew Johnson.

JOINT SESSIONS AND MEETINGS, ADDRESSES TO THE SENATE OR THE HOUSE, AND INAUGURATIONS—CONTINUED

[See notes at end of table]

Congress and Date	Type	Occasion, topic, or inaugural location	Name and position of dignitary (where applicable)
40th CONGRESS			
June 9, 1868	House	Address	Anson Burlingame, Envoy to the U.S. from China, and former Representative.
Feb. 10, 1869	Joint session	Counting electoral votes	N.A.
41st CONGRESS			
Mar. 4, 1869	Inauguration	East Portico	President Ulysses S. Grant.
42d CONGRESS			
Mar. 6, 1872	House	Address	Tomomi Iwakura, Ambassador from Japan.
Feb. 12, 1873	Joint session	Counting electoral votes [12]	N.A.
43d CONGRESS			
Mar. 4, 1873	Inauguration	East Portico	President Ulysses S. Grant.
Dec. 18, 1874	Joint meeting	Reception and Remarks	Speaker James G. Blaine; David Kalakaua, King of the Hawaiian Islands.[13]
44th CONGRESS			
Feb. 1, 1877 Feb. 10, 1877 Feb. 12, 1877 Feb. 19, 1877 Feb. 20, 1877 Feb. 21, 1877 Feb. 24, 1877 Feb. 26, 1877 Feb. 28, 1877 Mar. 1, 1877 Mar. 2, 1877	Joint session	Counting electoral votes [14]	N.A.
45th CONGRESS			
Mar. 5, 1877	Inauguration	East Portico	President Rutherford B. Hayes.
46th CONGRESS			
Feb. 2, 1880	House	Address	Charles Stewart Parnell, member of Parliament from Ireland.
Feb. 9, 1881	Joint session	Counting electoral votes	N.A.
47th CONGRESS			
Mar. 4, 1881	Inauguration	East Portico	President James A. Garfield.
Feb. 27, 1882	Joint session	Memorial to James A. Garfield	James G. Blaine, former Speaker, Senator, and Secretary of State; ceremony attended by President Chester A. Arthur.
48th CONGRESS			
Feb. 11, 1885	...do	Counting electoral votes	N.A.
Feb. 21, 1885	...do	Completion of Washington Monument	Representative John D. Long; Representative-elect John W. Daniel,[15] ceremony attended by President Chester A. Arthur.
49th CONGRESS			
Mar. 4, 1885	Inauguration	East Portico	President Grover Cleveland.
50th CONGRESS			
Feb. 13, 1889	Joint session	Counting electoral votes	N.A.
51st CONGRESS			
Mar. 4, 1889	Inauguration	East Portico	President Benjamin Harrison.
Dec. 11, 1889	Joint session	Centennial of George Washington's first inauguration.	Melville W. Fuller, Chief Justice of the United States; ceremony attended by President Benjamin Harrison.
52d CONGRESS			
Feb. 8, 1893	...do	Counting electoral votes	N.A.
53d CONGRESS			
Mar. 4, 1893	Inauguration	East Portico	President Grover Cleveland.
54th CONGRESS			
Feb. 10, 1897	Joint session	Counting electoral votes	N.A.
55th CONGRESS			
Mar. 4, 1897	Inauguration	In front of original Senate Wing of Capitol.	President William McKinley.

JOINT SESSIONS AND MEETINGS, ADDRESSES TO THE SENATE OR THE HOUSE, AND INAUGURATIONS—CONTINUED

[See notes at end of table]

Congress and Date	Type	Occasion, topic, or inaugural location	Name and position of dignitary (where applicable)
56th CONGRESS			
Dec. 12, 1900	Joint meeting	Centennial of the Capital City	Representatives James D. Richardson and Sereno E. Payne, and Senator George F. Hoar; ceremony attended by President William McKinley.
Feb. 13, 1901	Joint session	Counting electoral votes	N.A.
57th CONGRESS			
Mar. 4, 1901	Inauguration	East Portico	President William McKinley.
Feb. 27, 1902	Joint session	Memorial to William McKinley	John Hay, Secretary of State; ceremony attended by President Theodore Roosevelt and Prince Henry of Prussia.
58th CONGRESS			
Feb. 8, 1905	...do	Counting electoral votes	N.A.
59th CONGRESS			
Mar. 4, 1905	Inauguration	East Portico	President Theodore Roosevelt.
60th CONGRESS			
Feb. 10, 1909	Joint session	Counting electoral votes	N.A.
61st CONGRESS			
Mar. 4, 1909	Inauguration	Senate Chamber [16]	President William Howard Taft.
Feb. 9, 1911	House	Address	Count Albert Apponyi, Minister of Education from Hungary.
62d CONGRESS			
Feb. 12, 1913	Joint session	Counting electoral votes	N.A.
Feb. 15, 1913	...do	Memorial for Vice President James S. Sherman.[17]	Senators Elihu Root, Thomas S. Martin, Jacob H. Gallinger, John R. Thornton, Henry Cabot Lodge, John W. Kern, Robert M. LaFollette, John Sharp Williams, Charles Curtis, Albert B. Cummins, George T. Oliver, James A. O'Gorman; Speaker Champ Clark; President William Howard Taft.
63d CONGRESS			
Mar. 4, 1913	Inauguration	East Portico	President Woodrow Wilson.
Apr. 8, 1913	Joint session	Tariff message	Do.
June 23, 1913	...do	Currency and bank reform message	Do.
Aug. 27, 1913	...do	Mexican affairs message	Do.
Dec. 2, 1913	...do	Annual Message	Do.
Jan. 20, 1914	...do	Trusts message	Do.
Mar. 5, 1914	...do	Panama Canal tolls	Do.
Apr. 20, 1914	...do	Mexico message	Do.
Sept. 4, 1914	...do	War tax message	Do.
Dec. 8, 1914	...do	Annual Message	Do.
64th CONGRESS			
Dec. 7, 1915	...do	...do	Do.
Aug. 29, 1916	...do	Railroad message (labor-management dispute).	Do.
Dec. 5, 1916	...do	Annual Message	Do.
Jan. 22, 1917	Senate	Planning ahead for peace	Do.
Feb. 3, 1917	Joint session	Severing diplomatic relations with Germany.	Do.
Feb. 14, 1917	...do	Counting electoral votes	N.A.
Feb. 26, 1917	...do	Arming of merchant ships	President Woodrow Wilson.
65th CONGRESS			
Mar. 5, 1917	Inauguration	East Portico	Do.
Apr. 2, 1917	Joint session	War with Germany	Do.
May 1, 1917	Senate	Address	René Raphaël Viviani, Minister of Justice from France; Jules Jusserand, Ambassador from France; address attended by Marshal Joseph Jacques Césaire Joffre, member of French Commission to U.S.
May 3, 1917	House	...do	Do.
May 5, 1917	...do	...do	Arthur James Balfour, British Secretary of State for Foreign Affairs.
May 8, 1917	Senate	...do	Do.
May 31, 1917	...do	...do	Ferdinando di'Savoia, Prince of Udine, Head of Italian Mission to U.S.
June 2, 1917	House	...do	Ferdinando di'Savoia, Prince of Udine, Head of Italian Mission to U.S.; Guglielmo Marconi, member of Italian Mission to U.S.

JOINT SESSIONS AND MEETINGS, ADDRESSES TO THE SENATE OR THE HOUSE, AND INAUGURATIONS—CONTINUED

[See notes at end of table]

Congress and Date	Type	Occasion, topic, or inaugural location	Name and position of dignitary (where applicable)
June 22, 1917	Senate	Address	Baron Moncheur, Chief of Political Bureau of Belgian Foreign Office at Havre.
June 23, 1917	House	...do	Boris Bakhmetieff, Ambassador from Russia.[18]
June 26, 1917	Senate	...do	Do.
June 27, 1917	House	...do	Baron Moncheur, Chief of Political Bureau of Belgian Foreign Office at Havre.
Aug. 30, 1917	Senate	...do	Kikujirō Ishii, Ambassador from Japan.
Sept. 5, 1917	House	...do	Do.
Dec. 4, 1917	Joint session	Annual Message/War with Austria-Hungary.	President Woodrow Wilson.
Jan. 4, 1918	...do	Federal operation of transportation systems.	Do.
Jan. 5, 1918	Senate	Address	Milenko Vesnic, Head of Serbian War Mission.
Jan. 8, 1918	House	...do	Do.
Do	Joint session	Program for world's peace	President Woodrow Wilson.
Feb. 11, 1918	...do	Peace message	Do.
May 27, 1918	...do	War finance message	Do.
Sept. 24, 1918	Senate	Address and Reception[19]	Jules Jusserand, Ambassador from France; Vice President Thomas R. Marshall.
Sept. 30, 1918	...do	Support of woman suffrage	President Woodrow Wilson.
Nov. 11, 1918	Joint session	Terms of armistice signed by Germany	Do.
Dec. 2, 1918	...do	Annual Message	Do.
Feb. 9, 1919	...do	Memorial to Theodore Roosevelt	Senator Henry Cabot Lodge, Sr.; ceremony attended by former President William Howard Taft.
66th CONGRESS			
June 23, 1919	Senate	Address	Epitácio da Silva Pessoa, President-elect of Brazil.
July 10, 1919	...do	Versailles Treaty	President Woodrow Wilson.
Aug. 8, 1919	Joint session	Cost of living message	Do.
Sept. 18, 1919	...do	Address	President pro tempore Albert B. Cummins; Speaker Frederick H. Gillett; Representative and former Speaker Champ Clark; General John J. Pershing.
Oct. 28, 1919	Senate	...do	Albert I, King of the Belgians.
Do	House	...do	Do.
Feb. 9, 1921	Joint session	Counting electoral votes	N.A.
67th CONGRESS			
Mar. 4, 1921	Inauguration	East Portico	President Warren G. Harding.
Apr. 12, 1921	Joint session	Federal problem message	Do.
July 12, 1921	Senate	Adjusted compensation for veterans of the World War[20].	Do.
Dec. 6, 1921	Joint session	Annual Message	Do.
Feb. 28, 1922	...do	Maintenance of the merchant marine	Do.
Aug. 18, 1922	...do	Coal and railroad message	Do.
Nov. 21, 1922	...do	Promotion of the American merchant marine.	Do.
Dec. 8, 1922	...do	Annual Message[21]	Do.
Feb. 7, 1923	...do	British debt due to the United States	Do.
68th CONGRESS			
Dec. 6, 1923	...do	Annual Message	President Calvin Coolidge.
Feb. 27, 1924	...do	Memorial to Warren G. Harding	Charles Evans Hughes, Secretary of State; ceremony attended by President Calvin Coolidge.
Dec. 15, 1924	...do	Memorial to Woodrow Wilson	Dr. Edwin Anderson Alderman, President of the University of Virginia; ceremony attended by President Calvin Coolidge.
Feb. 11, 1925	...do	Counting electoral votes	N.A.
69th CONGRESS			
Mar. 4, 1925	Inauguration	East Portico	President Calvin Coolidge.
Feb. 22, 1927	Joint session	George Washington birthday message	Do.
70th CONGRESS			
Jan. 25, 1928	House	Reception and Address	William Thomas Cosgrave, President of Executive Council of Ireland.
Feb. 13, 1929	Joint session	Counting electoral votes	N.A.
71st CONGRESS			
Mar. 4, 1929	Inauguration	East Portico	President Herbert Hoover.

JOINT SESSIONS AND MEETINGS, ADDRESSES TO THE SENATE OR THE HOUSE, AND INAUGURATIONS—CONTINUED

[See notes at end of table]

Congress and Date	Type	Occasion, topic, or inaugural location	Name and position of dignitary (where applicable)
Oct. 7, 1929	Senate	Address	James Ramsay MacDonald, Prime Minister of the United Kingdom.
Jan. 13, 1930	...do	Reception	Jan Christiaan Smuts, former Prime Minister of South Africa.
72d CONGRESS			
Feb. 22, 1932	Joint session	Bicentennial of George Washington's birth.	President Herbert Hoover.
May 31, 1932	Senate	Emergency character of economic situation in U.S..	Do.
Feb. 6, 1933	Joint meeting	Memorial to Calvin Coolidge	Arthur Prentice Rugg, Chief Justice of the Supreme Judicial Court of Massachusetts; ceremony attended by President Herbert Hoover.
Feb. 8, 1933	Joint session	Counting electoral votes	N.A.
73d CONGRESS			
Mar. 4, 1933	Inauguration	East Portico	President Franklin Delano Roosevelt.
Jan. 3, 1934	Joint session	Annual Message	Do.
May 20, 1934	...do	100th anniversary, death of Lafayette	André de Laboulaye, Ambassador of France; President Franklin Delano Roosevelt; ceremony attended by Count de Chambrun, great-grandson of Lafayette.
74th CONGRESS			
Jan. 4, 1935	...do	Annual Message	President Franklin Delano Roosevelt.
May 22, 1935	...do	Veto message	Do.
Jan. 3, 1936	...do	Annual Message	Do.
75th CONGRESS			
Jan. 6, 1937	...do	Counting electoral votes	N.A.
Do	...do	Annual Message	President Franklin Delano Roosevelt.
Jan. 20, 1937	Inauguration	East Portico	President Franklin Delano Roosevelt; Vice President John Nance Garner.[22]
Apr. 1, 1937	Senate	Address	John Buchan, Lord Tweedsmuir, Governor General of Canada.
Do	House	...do	Do.
Jan. 3, 1938	Joint session	Annual Message	President Franklin Delano Roosevelt.
76th CONGRESS			
Jan. 4, 1939	...do	...do	Do.
Mar. 4, 1939	...do	Sesquicentennial of the 1st Congress	Do.
May 8, 1939	Senate	Address	Anastasio Somoza Garcia, President of Nicaragua.
Do	House	...do	Do.
June 9, 1939	Joint meeting	Reception[23]	George VI and Elizabeth, King and Queen of the United Kingdom.
Sept. 21, 1939	Joint session	Neutrality address	President Franklin Delano Roosevelt.
Jan. 3, 1940	...do	Annual Message	Do.
May 16, 1940	...do	National defense message	Do.
77th CONGRESS			
Jan. 6, 1941	...do	Counting electoral votes	N.A.
Do	...do	Annual Message	President Franklin Delano Roosevelt.
Jan. 20, 1941	...do	Inauguration, East Portico	President Franklin Delano Roosevelt; Vice President Henry A. Wallace.
Dec. 8, 1941	...do	War with Japan	President Franklin Delano Roosevelt.
Dec. 26, 1941	Joint meeting[24]	Address	Winston Churchill, Prime Minister of the United Kingdom.
Jan. 6, 1942	Joint session	Annual Message	President Franklin Delano Roosevelt.
May 11, 1942	Senate	Address	Manuel Prado, President of Peru.
Do	House	...do	Do.
June 2, 1942	...do	...do	Manuel Luis Quezon, President of the Philippines.[25]
June 4, 1942	Senate	...do	Do.
June 15, 1942	...do	...do	George II, King of Greece.[26]
Do	House	...do	Do.
June 25, 1942	Senate	...do	Peter II, King of Yugoslavia.[26]
Do	House	...do	Do.
Aug. 6, 1942	Senate[27]	...do	Wilhelmina, Queen of the Netherlands.[26]
Nov. 24, 1942	House	...do	Carlos Arroyo del Río, President of Ecuador.
Nov. 25, 1942	Senate	...do	Do.
Dec. 10, 1942	House	...do	Fulgencio Batista, President of Cuba.
78th CONGRESS			
Jan. 7, 1943	Joint session	Annual Message	President Franklin Delano Roosevelt.
Feb. 18, 1943	Senate	Remarks	Madame Chiang Kai-shek, of China.
Do	House	Address	Do.

JOINT SESSIONS AND MEETINGS, ADDRESSES TO THE SENATE OR THE HOUSE, AND INAUGURATIONS—CONTINUED

[See notes at end of table]

Congress and Date	Type	Occasion, topic, or inaugural location	Name and position of dignitary (where applicable)
May 6, 1943	Senate	Address	Enrique Peñaranda, President of Bolivia.
Do	House	...do	Do.
May 13, 1943	Senate	...do	Edvard Beneš, President of Czechoslovakia.[26]
Do	House	...do	Do.
May 19, 1943	Joint meeting	...do	Winston Churchill, Prime Minister of the United Kingdom.
May 27, 1943	Senate	Remarks	Edwin Barclay, President of Liberia.
Do	House	Address	Do.
June 10, 1943	Senate	...do	President Hininio Moríñigo M., President of Paraguay.
Do	House	...do	Do.
Oct. 15, 1943	Senate	...do	Elie Lescot, President of Haiti.
Nov. 18, 1943	Joint meeting	Moscow Conference	Cordell Hull, Secretary of State.
Jan. 20, 1944	Senate	Address	Isaías Medina Angarita, President of Venezuela.
Do	House	...do	Do.
79th CONGRESS			
Jan. 6, 1945	Joint session	Counting electoral votes	N.A.
Do	...do	Annual Message	President Roosevelt was not present. His message was read before the Joint Session of Congress.
Jan. 20, 1945	Inauguration	South Portico, The White House[28]	President Franklin Delano Roosevelt; Vice President Harry S. Truman.
Mar. 1, 1945	Joint session	Yalta Conference	President Franklin Delano Roosevelt.
Apr. 16, 1945	...do	Prosecution of the War	President Harry S. Truman.
May 21, 1945	...do	Bestowal of Congressional Medal of Honor on Tech. Sgt. Jake William Lindsey.	General George C. Marshall, Chief of Staff, U.S. Army; President Harry S. Truman.
June 18, 1945	Joint meeting	Address	General Dwight D. Eisenhower, Supreme Commander, Allied Expeditionary Force.
July 2, 1945	Senate	United Nations Charter	President Harry S. Truman.
Oct. 5, 1945	Joint meeting	Address	Admiral Chester W. Nimitz, Commander-in-Chief, Pacific Fleet.
Oct. 23, 1945	Joint session	Universal military training message	President Harry S. Truman.
Nov. 13, 1945	Joint meeting	Address	Clement R. Attlee, Prime Minister of the United Kingdom.
May 25, 1946	Joint session	Railroad strike message	President Harry S. Truman.
July 1, 1946	...do	Memorial to Franklin Delano Roosevelt	John Winant, U.S. Representative on the Economic and Social Council of the United Nations; ceremony attended by President Harry S. Truman and Mrs. Franklin Delano Roosevelt.
80th CONGRESS			
Jan. 6, 1947	...do	State of the Union Address[29]	President Harry S. Truman.
Mar. 12, 1947	...do	Greek-Turkish aid policy	Do.
May 1, 1947	Joint meeting	Address	Miguel Alemán, President of Mexico.
Nov. 17, 1947	Joint session	Aid to Europe message	President Harry S. Truman.
Jan. 7, 1948	...do	State of the Union Address	Do.
Mar. 17, 1948	...do	National security and conditions in Europe.	Do.
Apr. 19, 1948	...do	50th anniversary, liberation of Cuba	President Harry S. Truman; Guillermo Belt, Ambassador of Cuba.
July 27, 1948	...do	Inflation, housing, and civil rights	President Harry S. Truman.
81st CONGRESS			
Jan. 5, 1949	...do	State of the Union Address	Do.
Jan. 6, 1949	...do	Counting electoral votes	N.A.
Jan. 20, 1949	...do	Inauguration, East Portico	President Harry S. Truman; Vice President Alben W. Barkley.
May 17, 1949	House	Reception	General Lucius D. Clay.
Do	Senate	Address	Do.
May 19, 1949	Joint meeting	...do	Eurico Gaspar Dutra, President of Brazil.
Aug. 9, 1949	House	...do	Elpidio Quirino, President of the Philippines.
Do	Senate	...do	Do.
Oct. 13, 1949	...do	...do	Jawaharlal Nehru, Prime Minister of India.
Do	House	...do	Do.
Jan. 4, 1950	Joint session	State of the Union Address	President Harry S. Truman.
Apr. 13, 1950	Senate	Address	Gabriel González-Videla, President of Chile.
May 4, 1950	...do	...do	Liaquat Ali Khan, Prime Minister of Pakistan.
Do	House	...do	Do.
May 31, 1950	Joint meeting	...do	Dean Acheson, Secretary of State.

JOINT SESSIONS AND MEETINGS, ADDRESSES TO THE SENATE OR THE HOUSE, AND INAUGURATIONS—CONTINUED

[See notes at end of table]

Congress and Date	Type	Occasion, topic, or inaugural location	Name and position of dignitary (where applicable)
July 28, 1950	Senate	Address	Chōjirō Kuriyama, member of Japanese Diet.
July 31, 1950	House	...do	Tokutarō Kitamura, member of Japanese Diet.
Aug. 1, 1950	...do	...do	Robert Gordon Menzies, Prime Minister of Australia.
Do	Senate	...do	Do.
82d CONGRESS			
Jan. 8, 1951	Joint session	State of the Union Address	President Harry S. Truman.
Feb. 1, 1951	Joint meeting [30]	North Atlantic Treaty Organization	General Dwight D. Eisenhower.
Apr. 2, 1951	...do	Address	Vincent Auriol, President of France.
Apr. 19, 1951	...do	Return from Pacific Command	General Douglas MacArthur.
June 21, 1951	...do	Address	Galo Plaza, President of Ecuador.
July 2, 1951	Senate	Addresses	Tadao Kuraishi, and Aisuke Okamoto, members of Japanese Diet.
Aug. 23, 1951	...do	Address	Zentarō Kosaka, member of Japanese Diet.
Sept. 24, 1951	Joint meeting	...do	Alcide de Gasperi, Prime Minister of Italy.
Jan. 9, 1952	Joint session	State of the Union Address	President Harry S. Truman.
Jan. 17, 1952	Joint meeting	Address	Winston Churchill, Prime Minister of the United Kingdom.
Apr. 3, 1952	...do	...do	Juliana, Queen of the Netherlands.
May 22, 1952	...do	Korea	General Matthew B. Ridgway.
June 10, 1952	Joint session	Steel industry dispute	President Harry S. Truman.
83d CONGRESS			
Jan. 6, 1953	...do	Counting electoral votes	N.A.
Jan. 20, 1953	...do	Inauguration, East Portico	President Dwight D. Eisenhower; Vice President Richard M. Nixon.
Feb. 2, 1953	...do	State of the Union Address	President Dwight D. Eisenhower.
Jan. 7, 1954	...do	...do	Do.
Jan. 29, 1954	Joint meeting	Address	Celal Bayar, President of Turkey.
May 4, 1954	...do	...do	Vincent Massey, Governor General of Canada.
May 28, 1954	...do	...do	Haile Selassie I, Emperor of Ethiopia.
July 28, 1954	...do	...do	Syngman Rhee, President of South Korea.
Nov. 12, 1954	Senate	Remarks	Shigeru Yoshida, Prime Minister of Japan.
Nov. 17, 1954	...do	Address [31]	Sarvepalli Radhakrishnan, Vice President of India.
Nov. 18, 1954	...do	Remarks	Pierre Mendès-France, Premier of France.
84th CONGRESS			
Jan. 6, 1955	Joint session	State of the Union Address	President Dwight D. Eisenhower.
Jan. 27, 1955	Joint meeting	Address	Paul E. Magliore, President of Haiti.
Mar. 16, 1955	Senate	...do	Robert Gordon Menzies, Prime Minister of Australia.
Do	House	...do	Do.
Mar. 30, 1955	Senate	...do	Mario Scelba, Prime Minister of Italy.
Do	House	...do	Do.
May 4, 1955	Senate	...do	P. Phibunsongkhram, Prime Minister of Thailand.
Do	House	...do	Do.
June 30, 1955	Senate	...do	U Nu, Prime Minister of Burma.
Do	House	...do	Do.
Jan. 5, 1956	Senate	...do	Juscelino Kubitschek de Oliverira, President-elect of Brazil.
Feb. 2, 1956	...do	...do	Anthony Eden, Prime Minister of the United Kingdom.
Do	House	...do	Do.
Feb. 29, 1956	Joint meeting	...do	Giovanni Gronchi, President of Italy.
Mar. 15, 1956	Senate	...do	John Aloysius Costello, Prime Minister of Ireland.
Do	House	...do	Do.
Apr. 30, 1956	Senate	...do	João Goulart, Vice President of Brazil.
May 17, 1956	Joint meeting	...do	Sukarno, President of Indonesia.
85th CONGRESS			
Jan. 5, 1957	Joint session	Middle East message	President Dwight D. Eisenhower.
Jan. 7, 1957	...do	Counting electoral votes	N.A.
Jan. 10, 1957	...do	State of the Union Address	President Dwight D. Eisenhower.
Jan. 21, 1957	...do	Inauguration, East Portico	President Dwight D. Eisenhower; Vice President Richard M. Nixon.
Feb. 27, 1957	House	Address	Guy Mollet, Premier of France.
Do	Senate	...do	Do.
May 9, 1957	Joint meeting	...do	Ngo Dinh Diem, President of Vietnam.

JOINT SESSIONS AND MEETINGS, ADDRESSES TO THE SENATE OR THE HOUSE, AND INAUGURATIONS—CONTINUED

[See notes at end of table]

Congress and Date	Type	Occasion, topic, or inaugural location	Name and position of dignitary (where applicable)
May 28, 1957	House	Address	Konrad Adenauer, Chancellor of West Germany.
Do	Senate	...do	Do.
June 20, 1957	...do	...do	Nobusuke Kishi, Prime Minister of Japan.
Do	House	...do	Do.
July 11, 1957	Senate	...do	Husseyn Shaheed Suhrawardy, Prime Minister of Pakistan.
Jan. 9, 1958	Joint session	State of the Union Address	President Dwight D. Eisenhower.
June 5, 1958	Joint meeting	Address	Theodor Heuss, President of West Germany.
June 10, 1958	Senate	...do	Harold Macmillan, Prime Minister of the United Kingdom.
June 18, 1958	Joint meeting	...do	Carlos F. Garcia, President of the Philippines.
June 25, 1958	House	...do	Muhammad Daoud Khan, Prime Minister of Afghanistan.
Do	Senate	...do	Do.
July 24, 1958	...do	...do	Kwame Nkrumah, Prime Minister of Ghana.
July 25, 1958	House	...do	Do.
July 29, 1958	Senate	...do	Amintore Fanfani, Prime Minister of Italy.
Do	House	...do	Do.
86th CONGRESS			
Jan. 9, 1959	Joint session	State of the Union Address	President Dwight D. Eisenhower.
Jan. 21, 1959	Joint meeting	Address	Arturo Frondizi, President of Argentina.
Feb. 12, 1959	Joint session	Sesquicentennial of Abraham Lincoln's birth.	Fredric March, actor; Carl Sandburg, poet.
Mar. 11, 1959	Joint meeting	Address	Jose Maria Lemus, President of El Salvador.
Mar. 18, 1959	...do	...do	Sean T. O'Kelly, President of Ireland.
May 12, 1959	...do	...do	Baudouin, King of the Belgians.
Jan. 7, 1960	Joint session	State of the Union Address	President Dwight D. Eisenhower.
Mar. 30, 1960	Senate	Address	Harold Macmillan, Prime Minister of the United Kingdom.
Apr. 6, 1960	Joint meeting	...do	Alberto Lleras-Camargo, President of Colombia.
Apr. 25, 1960	...do	...do	Charles de Gaulle, President of France.
Apr. 28, 1960	...do	...do	Mahendra, King of Nepal.
June 29, 1960	...do	...do	Bhumibol Adulyadej, King of Thailand.
87th CONGRESS			
Jan. 6, 1961	Joint session	Counting electoral votes	N.A.
Jan. 20, 1961	...do	Inauguration, East Portico	President John F. Kennedy; Vice President Lyndon B. Johnson.
Jan. 30, 1961	...do	State of the Union Address	President John F. Kennedy.
Apr. 13, 1961	Senate	Remarks	Konrad Adenauer, Chancellor of West Germany.
Apr. 18, 1961	House	Address	Constantine Karamanlis, Prime Minister of Greece.
May 4, 1961	Joint meeting	...do	Habib Bourguiba, President of Tunisia.
May 25, 1961	Joint session	Urgent national needs: foreign aid, defense, civil defense, and outer space.	President John F. Kennedy.
June 22, 1961	Senate	Remarks	Hayato Ikeda, Prime Minister of Japan.
Do	House	Address	Do.
July 12, 1961	Joint meeting	...do	Mohammad Ayub Khan, President of Pakistan.
July 26, 1961	House	...do	Abubakar Tafawa Balewa, Prime Minister of Nigeria.
Sept. 21, 1961	Joint meeting	...do	Manuel Prado, President of Peru.
Jan. 11, 1962	Joint session	State of the Union Address	President John F. Kennedy.
Feb. 26, 1962	Joint meeting	Friendship 7: 1st United States orbital space flight.	Lt. Col. John H. Glenn, Jr., USMC; Friendship 7 astronaut.
Apr. 4, 1962	...do	Address	João Goulart, President of Brazil.
Apr. 12, 1962	...do	...do	Mohammad Reza Shah Pahlavi, Shahanshah of Iran.
88th CONGRESS			
Jan. 14, 1963	Joint session	State of the Union Address	President John F. Kennedy.
May 21, 1963	Joint meeting	Flight of Faith 7 Spacecraft	Maj. Gordon L. Cooper, Jr., USAF, Faith 7 astronaut.
Oct. 2, 1963	Senate	Address	Haile Selassie I, Emperor of Ethiopia.
Nov. 27, 1963	Joint session	Assumption of office	President Lyndon B. Johnson.
Jan. 8, 1964	...do	State of the Union Address	Do.
Jan. 15, 1964	Joint meeting	Address	Antonio Segni, President of Italy.
May 28, 1964	...do	...do	Eamon de Valera, President of Ireland.
89th CONGRESS			
Jan. 4, 1965	Joint session	State of the Union Address	President Lyndon B. Johnson.

JOINT SESSIONS AND MEETINGS, ADDRESSES TO THE SENATE OR THE HOUSE, AND INAUGURATIONS—CONTINUED

[See notes at end of table]

Congress and Date	Type	Occasion, topic, or inaugural location	Name and position of dignitary (where applicable)
Jan. 6, 1965	Joint session	Counting electoral votes	N.A.
Jan. 20, 1965	...do[32]	Inauguration, East Portico	President Lyndon B. Johnson; Vice President Hubert H. Humphrey.
Mar. 15, 1965	...do	Voting rights	President Lyndon B. Johnson.
Sept. 14, 1965	Joint meeting	Flight of Gemini 5 Spacecraft	Lt. Col. Gordon L. Cooper, Jr., USAF; and Charles Conrad, Jr., USN; Gemini 5 astronauts.
Jan. 12, 1966	Joint session	State of the Union Address	President Lyndon B. Johnson.
Sept. 15, 1966	Joint meeting	Address	Ferdinand E. Marcos, President of the Philippines.
90th CONGRESS			
Jan. 10, 1967	Joint session	State of the Union Address	President Lyndon B. Johnson.
Apr. 28, 1967	Joint meeting	Vietnam policy	General William C. Westmoreland.
Aug. 16, 1967	Senate	Address	Kurt George Kiesinger, Chancellor of West Germany.
Oct. 27, 1967	Joint meeting	...do	Gustavo Diaz Ordaz, President of Mexico.
Jan. 17, 1968	Joint session	State of the Union Address	President Lyndon B. Johnson.
91st CONGRESS			
Jan. 6, 1969	...do	Counting electoral votes[33]	N.A.
Jan. 9, 1969	Joint meeting	Apollo 8: 1st flight around the moon	Col. Frank Borman, USAF; Capt. James A. Lowell, Jr., USN; Lt. Col. William A. Anders, USAF; Apollo 8 astronauts.
Jan. 14, 1969	Joint session	State of the Union Address	President Lyndon B. Johnson.
Jan. 20, 1969	...do[32]	Inauguration, East Portico	President Richard M. Nixon; Vice President Spiro T. Agnew.
Sept. 16, 1969	Joint meeting	Apollo 11: 1st lunar landing	Neil A. Armstrong; Col. Edwin E. Aldrin, Jr., USAF; and Lt. Col. Michael Collins, USAF; Apollo 11 astronauts.
Nov. 13, 1969	House	Executive-Legislative branch relations and Vietnam policy.	President Richard M. Nixon.
Do	Senate	...do	Do.
Jan. 22, 1970	Joint session	State of the Union Address	Do.
Feb. 25, 1970	Joint meeting	Address	Georges Pompidou, President of France.
June 3, 1970	...do	...do	Rafael Caldera, President of Venezuela.
Sept. 22, 1970	...do	Report on prisoners of war	Col. Frank Borman, Representative to the President on Prisoners of War.
92d CONGRESS			
Jan. 22, 1971	Joint session	State of the Union Address	President Richard M. Nixon.
Sept. 9, 1971	...do	Economic policy	Do.
Do	Joint meeting	Apollo 15: lunar mission	Col. David R. Scott, USAF; Col. James B. Irwin, USAF; and Lt. Col. Alfred M. Worden, USAF; Apollo 15 astronauts.
Jan. 20, 1972	Joint session	State of the Union Address	President Richard M. Nixon.
June 1, 1972	...do	European trip report	Do.
June 15, 1972	Joint meeting	Address	Luis Echeverria Alvarez, President of Mexico.
93d CONGRESS			
Jan. 6, 1973	Joint session	Counting electoral votes	N.A.
Jan. 20, 1973	Inauguration	East Portico	President Richard M. Nixon; Vice President Spiro T. Agnew.
Dec. 6, 1973	Joint meeting	Oath of office to, and Address by Vice President Gerald R. Ford.	Vice President Gerald R. Ford; ceremony attended by President Richard M. Nixon.
Do	Senate	Remarks and Reception	Vice President Gerald R. Ford.
Jan. 30, 1974	Joint session	State of the Union Address	President Richard M. Nixon.
Aug. 12, 1974	...do	Assumption of office	President Gerald R. Ford.
Oct. 8, 1974	...do	Economy	Do.
Dec. 19, 1974	Senate	Address[34]	Vice President Nelson A. Rockefeller.
94th CONGRESS			
Jan. 15, 1975	Joint session	State of the Union Address	President Gerald R. Ford.
Apr. 10, 1975	...do	State of the World message	Do.
June 17, 1975	Joint meeting	Address	Walter Scheel, President of West Germany.
Nov. 5, 1975	...do	...do	Anwar El Sadat, President of Egypt.
Jan. 19, 1976	Joint session	State of the Union Address	President Gerald R. Ford.
Jan. 28, 1976	Joint meeting	Address	Yitzhak Rabin, Prime Minister of Israel.
Mar. 17, 1976	...do	...do	Liam CosgrAvenue, Prime Minister of Ireland.
May 18, 1976	...do	...do	Valery Giscard d'Estaing, President of France.
June 2, 1976	...do	...do	Juan Carlos I, King of Spain.

JOINT SESSIONS AND MEETINGS, ADDRESSES TO THE SENATE OR THE HOUSE, AND INAUGURATIONS—CONTINUED

[See notes at end of table]

Congress and Date	Type	Occasion, topic, or inaugural location	Name and position of dignitary (where applicable)
Sept. 23, 1976	Joint meeting	Address	William R. Tolbert, Jr., President of Liberia.
95th CONGRESS			
Jan. 6, 1977	Joint session	Counting electoral votes	N.A.
Jan. 12, 1977	...do	State of the Union Address	President Gerald R. Ford.
Jan. 20, 1977	Inauguration	East Portico	President Jimmy Carter; Vice President Walter F. Mondale.
Feb. 17, 1977	House	Address	José López Portillo, President of Mexico.
Feb. 22, 1977	Joint meeting	...do	Pierre Elliot Trudeau, Prime Minister of Canada.
Apr. 20, 1977	Joint session	Energy	President Jimmy Carter.
Jan. 19, 1978	...do	State of the Union Address	Do.
Sept. 18, 1978	...do	Middle East Peace agreements	President Jimmy Carter; joint session attended by Anwar El Sadat, President of Egypt, and by Menachem Begin, Prime Minister of Israel.
96th CONGRESS			
Jan. 23, 1979	...do	State of the Union Address	Do.
June 18, 1979	...do	Salt II agreements	Do.
Jan. 23, 1980	...do	State of the Union Address	Do.
97th CONGRESS			
Jan. 6, 1981	...do	Counting electoral votes	N.A.
Jan. 20, 1981	...do [32]	Inauguration, West Front	President Ronald Reagan; Vice President George Bush.
Feb. 18, 1981	...do	Economic recovery	President Ronald Reagan.
Apr. 28, 1981	...do	Economic recovery—inflation	Do.
Jan. 26, 1982	...do	State of the Union Address	Do.
Jan. 28, 1982	Joint meeting	Centennial of birth of Franklin Delano Roosevelt.	Dr. Arthur Schlesinger, historian; Senator Jennings Randolph; Representative Claude Pepper; Averell Harriman, former Governor of New York [35]; former Representative James Roosevelt, son of President Roosevelt.
Apr. 21, 1982	...do	Address	Beatrix, Queen of the Netherlands.
98th CONGRESS			
Jan. 25, 1983	Joint session	State of the Union Address	President Ronald Reagan.
Apr. 27, 1983	...do	Central America	Do.
Oct. 5, 1983	Joint meeting	Address	Karl Carstens, President of West Germany.
Jan. 25, 1984	Joint session	State of the Union Address	President Ronald Reagan.
Mar. 15, 1984	Joint meeting	Address	Dr. Garett FitzGerald, Prime Minister of Ireland.
Mar. 22, 1984	...do	...do	François Mitterand, President of France.
May 8, 1984	...do	Centennial of birth of Harry S. Truman	Representatives Ike Skelton and Alan Wheat; former Senator Stuart Symington; Margaret Truman Daniel, daughter of President Truman; and Senator Mark Hatfield.
May 16, 1984	...do	Address	Miguel de la Madrid, President of Mexico.
99th CONGRESS			
Jan. 7, 1985	Joint session	Counting electoral votes	N.A.
Jan. 21, 1985	Inauguration	Rotunda [36]	President Ronald Reagan; Vice President George Bush.
Feb. 6, 1985	Joint session	State of the Union Address	President Ronald Reagan.
Feb. 20, 1985	Joint meeting	Address	Margaret Thatcher, Prime Minister of the United Kingdom.
Mar. 6, 1985	...do	...do	Bettino Craxi, President of the Council of Ministers of Italy.
Mar. 20, 1985	...do	...do	Raul Alfonsin, President of Argentina.
June 13, 1985	...do	...do	Rajiv Gandhi, Prime Minister of India.
Oct. 9, 1985	...do	...do	Lee Kuan Yew, Prime Minister of Singapore.
Nov. 21, 1985	Joint session	Geneva Summit	President Ronald Reagan.
Feb. 4, 1986	...do	State of the Union Address	Do.
Sept. 11, 1986	Joint meeting	Address	Jose Sarney, President of Brazil.
Sept. 18, 1986	...do	...do	Corazon C. Aquino, President of the Philippines.
100th CONGRESS			
Jan. 27, 1987	Joint session	State of the Union Address	President Ronald Reagan.
Nov. 10, 1987	Joint meeting	Address	Chaim Herzog, President of Israel.
Jan. 25, 1988	Joint session	State of the Union Address	President Ronald Reagan.
Apr. 27, 1988	Joint meeting	Address	Brian Mulroney, Prime Minister of Canada.

JOINT SESSIONS AND MEETINGS, ADDRESSES TO THE SENATE OR THE HOUSE, AND INAUGURATIONS—CONTINUED

[See notes at end of table]

Congress and Date	Type	Occasion, topic, or inaugural location	Name and position of dignitary (where applicable)
June 23, 1988	Joint meeting	Address	Robert Hawke, Prime Minister of Australia.
101st CONGRESS			
Jan. 4, 1989	Joint session	Counting electoral votes	N.A.
Jan. 20, 1989	Inauguration	West Front	President George Bush; Vice President Dan Quayle.
Feb. 9, 1989	Joint session	Building a Better America	President George Bush.
Mar. 2, 1989	Joint meeting	Bicentennial of the 1st Congress	President Pro Tempore Robert C. Byrd; Speaker James C. Wright, Jr.; Representatives Lindy Boggs, Thomas S. Foley, and Robert H. Michel; Senators George Mitchell and Robert Dole; Howard Nemerov, Poet Laureate of the United States; David McCullough, historian; Anthony M. Frank, Postmaster General; former Senator Nicholas Brady, Secretary of the Treasury.
Apr. 6, 1989	Senate [37]	Addresses on the 200th anniversary commemoration of Senate's first legislative session.	Former Senators Thomas F. Eagleton and Howard H. Baker, Jr.
June 7, 1989	Joint meeting	Address	Benazir Bhutto, Prime Minister of Pakistan.
Oct. 4, 1989	...do	...do	Carlos Salinas de Gortari, President of Mexico.
Oct. 18, 1989	...do	...do	Roh Tae Woo, President of South Korea.
Nov. 15, 1989	...do	...do	Lech Walesa, chairman of Solidarnosć labor union, Poland.
Jan. 31, 1990	Joint session	State of the Union Address	President George Bush.
Feb. 21, 1990	Joint meeting	Address	Vaclav Hável, President of Czechoslovakia.
Mar. 7, 1990	...do	...do	Giulio Andreotti, President of the Council of Ministers of Italy.
Mar. 27, 1990	...do	Centennial of birth of Dwight D. Eisenhower.	Senator Robert Dole; Walter Cronkite, television journalist; Winston S. Churchill, member of British Parliament and grandson of Prime Minister Churchill; Clark M. Clifford, former Secretary of Defense; James D. Robinson III, chairman of Eisenhower Centennial Foundation; Arnold Palmer, professional golfer; John S.D. Eisenhower, former Ambassador to Belgium and son of President Eisenhower; Representatives Beverly Byron, William F. Goodling, and Pat Roberts.
June 26, 1990	...do	Address	Nelson Mandela, Deputy President of the African National Congress, South Africa.
Sept. 11, 1990	Joint session	Invasion of Kuwait by Iraq	President George Bush.
102d CONGRESS			
Jan. 29, 1991	...do	State of the Union Address	Do.
Mar. 6, 1991	...do	Conclusion of Persian Gulf War	Do.
Apr. 16, 1991	Joint meeting	Address	Violeta B. de Chamorro, President of Nicaragua.
May 8, 1991	House [38]	...do	General H. Norman Schwarzkopf.
May 16, 1991	Joint meeting	...do	Elizabeth II, Queen of the United Kingdom; joint meeting also attended by Prince Philip.
Nov. 14, 1991	...do	...do	Carlos Saul Menem, President of Argentina.
Jan. 28, 1992	Joint session	State of the Union Address	President George Bush.
Apr. 30, 1992	Joint meeting	Address	Richard von Weizsäcker, President of Germany.
June 17, 1992	...do	...do	Boris Yeltsin, President of Russia.
103d CONGRESS			
Jan. 6, 1993	Joint session	Counting electoral votes	N.A.
Jan. 20, 1993	Inauguration	West Front	President William J. Clinton; Vice President Albert Gore.
Feb. 17, 1993	Joint session	Economic Address [39]	President William J. Clinton.
Sept. 22, 1993	...do	Health care reform	Do.
Jan. 25, 1994	...do	State of the Union Address	Do.
May 18, 1994	Joint meeting	Address	Narasimha Rao, Prime Minister of India.
July 26, 1994	...do	Addresses	Hussein I, King of Jordan; Yitzhak Rabin, Prime Minister of Israel.
Oct. 6, 1994	...do	Address	Nelson Mandela, President of South Africa.

JOINT SESSIONS AND MEETINGS, ADDRESSES TO THE SENATE OR THE HOUSE, AND INAUGURATIONS—CONTINUED

[See notes at end of table]

Congress and Date	Type	Occasion, topic, or inaugural location	Name and position of dignitary (where applicable)
104th CONGRESS			
Jan. 24, 1995	Joint session	State of the Union Address	President William J. Clinton.
July 26, 1995	Joint meeting	Address	Kim Yong-sam, President of South Korea.[40]
Oct. 11, 1995	...do	Close of the Commemoration of the 50th Anniversary of World War II.	Speaker Newt Gingrich; Vice President Albert Gore; President Pro Tempore Strom Thurmond; Representatives Henry J. Hyde and G.V. "Sonny" Montgomery; Senators Daniel K. Inouye and Robert Dole; former Representative Robert H. Michel; General Louis H. Wilson (ret.), former Commandant of the Marine Corps.
Dec. 12, 1995	...do	Address	Shimon Peres, Prime Minister of Israel.
Jan. 30, 1996	Joint session	State of the Union Address	President William J. Clinton.
Feb. 1, 1996	Joint meeting	Address	Jacques Chirac, President of France.
July 10, 1996	...do	...do	Binyamin Netanyahu, Prime Minister of Israel.
Sept. 11, 1996	...do	...do	John Bruton, Prime Minister of Ireland.
105th CONGRESS			
Jan. 9, 1997	Joint session	Counting electoral votes	N.A.
Jan. 20, 1997	Inauguration	West Front	President William J. Clinton; Vice President Albert Gore.
Feb. 4, 1997	Joint session	State of the Union Address[41]	President William J. Clinton.
Feb. 27, 1997	Joint meeting	Address	Eduardo Frei, President of Chile.
Jan. 27, 1998	Joint session	State of the Union Address	President William J. Clinton.
June 10, 1998	Joint meeting	Address	Kim Dae-jung, President of South Korea.
July 15, 1998	...do	...do	Emil Constantinescu, President of Romania.
106th CONGRESS			
Jan. 19, 1999	Joint session	State of the Union Address	President William J. Clinton.
Jan. 27, 2000	...do	...do	Do.
Sept. 14, 2000	Joint meeting	Address	Atal Bihari Vajpayee, Prime Minister of India.
107th CONGRESS			
Jan. 6, 2001	Joint session	Counting electoral votes	N.A.
Jan. 20, 2001	Inauguration	West Front	President George W. Bush; Vice President Richard B. Cheney.
Feb. 27, 2001	Joint session	Budget message[39]	President George W. Bush.
Sept. 6, 2001	Joint meeting	Address	Vicente Fox, President of Mexico.
Sept. 20, 2001	Joint session	War on terrorism	President George W. Bush; joint session attended by Tony Blair, Prime Minister of the United Kingdom, by Tom Ridge, Governor of Pennsylvania, by George Pataki, Governor of New York, and by Rudolph Giuliani, Mayor of New York City.
Jan. 29, 2002	...do	State of the Union Address	President George W. Bush; joint session attended by Hamid Karzai, Chairman of the Interim Authority of Afghanistan.
June 12, 2002	Joint meeting	Address[42]	John Howard, Prime Minister of Australia.
108th CONGRESS			
Jan. 28, 2003	Joint session	State of the Union Address	President George W. Bush.
July 17, 2003	Joint meeting	Address	Tony Blair, Prime Minister of the United Kingdom; joint meeting attended by Mrs. George W. Bush.
Jan. 20, 2004	Joint session	State of the Union Address	President George W. Bush.
Feb. 4, 2004	Joint meeting	Address	Jose Maria Aznar, President of the Government of Spain.
June 15, 2004	...do	...do	Hamid Karzai, President of Afghanistan.
Sept. 23, 2004	...do	...do	Ayad Allawi, Interim Prime Minister of Iraq.
109th CONGRESS			
Jan. 6, 2005	Joint session	Counting electoral votes[43]	N.A.
Jan. 20, 2005	Inauguration	West Front	President George W. Bush; Vice President Richard B. Cheney.
Feb. 2, 2005	Joint session	State of the Union Address	President George W. Bush.
Apr. 6, 2005	Joint meeting	Address	Viktor Yushchenko, President of Ukraine.
July 19, 2005	...do	...do	Dr. Manmohan Singh, Prime Minister of India.
Jan. 31, 2006	Joint session	State of the Union Address	President George W. Bush.
Mar. 1, 2006	Joint meeting	Address	Silvio Berlusconi, Prime Minister of Italy.

JOINT SESSIONS AND MEETINGS, ADDRESSES TO THE SENATE OR THE HOUSE, AND INAUGURATIONS—CONTINUED

[See notes at end of table]

Congress and Date	Type	Occasion, topic, or inaugural location	Name and position of dignitary (where applicable)
Mar. 15, 2006	Joint meeting	Address	Ellen Johnson Sirleaf, President of Liberia.
May 24, 2006	...do	...do	Ehud Olmert, Prime Minister of Israel.
June 7, 2006	...do	...do	Dr. Vaira Vike-Freiberga, President of Latvia.
July 26, 2006	...do	...do	Nouri Al-Maliki, Prime Minister of Iraq.
110th CONGRESS			
Jan. 23, 2007	Joint session	State of the Union Address	President George W. Bush.
Mar. 7, 2007	Joint meeting	Address	Abdullah II Ibn Al Hussein, King of Jordan.
Nov. 7, 2007	...do	...do	Nicolas Sarkozy, President of France.
Jan. 28, 2008	Joint session	State of the Union Address	President George W. Bush.
Apr. 30, 2008	Joint meeting	Address	Bertie Ahern, Prime Minister of Ireland.
111th CONGRESS			
Jan. 8, 2009	Joint session	Counting electoral votes	N.A.
Jan. 20, 2009	Inauguration	West Front	President Barack H. Obama; Vice President Joseph R. Biden, Jr.
Feb. 24, 2009	Joint session	Economic Address	President Barack H. Obama.
Mar. 4, 2009	Joint meeting	...do	Gordon Brown, Prime Minister of the United Kingdom.
Sept. 9, 2009	Joint session	Health care reform	President Barack H. Obama.
Nov. 2, 2009	Joint meeting	Address	Angela Merkel, Chancellor of Germany.
Jan. 27, 2010	Joint session	State of the Union Address	President Barack H. Obama.
May 20, 2010	Joint meeting	Address	Felipe Calderon Hinojosa, President of Mexico.
112th CONGRESS			
Jan. 25, 2011	Joint session	State of the Union Address	President Barack H. Obama.
Mar. 9, 2011	Joint meeting	Address	Julia Gillard, Prime Minister of Australia.
May 24, 2011	...do	...do	Binyamin Netanyahu, Prime Minister of Israel.
Sept. 8, 2011	Joint session	American Jobs Act	President Barack H. Obama.
Oct. 13, 2011	Joint meeting	Address	Lee Myung-bak, President of the Republic of Korea.
Jan. 24, 2012	Joint session	State of the Union Address	President Barack H. Obama.
113th CONGRESS			
Jan. 4, 2013	...do	Counting electoral votes	N.A.
Jan. 21, 2013	Inauguration	West Front	President Barack H. Obama; Vice President Joseph R. Biden, Jr.
Feb. 12, 2013	Joint session	State of the Union Address	President Barack H. Obama.
May 8, 2013	Joint meeting	Address	Park Geun-hye, President of the Republic of Korea.
Jan. 28, 2014	Joint session	State of the Union Address	President Barack H. Obama.
Sept. 18, 2014	Joint meeting	Address	Petro Poroshenko, President of Ukraine.
114th CONGRESS			
Jan. 20, 2015	Joint session	State of the Union Address	President Barack H. Obama.
Mar. 3, 2015	Joint meeting	Address	Binyamin Netanyahu, Prime Minister of Israel.
Mar. 25, 2015	...do	...do	Mohammad Ashraf Ghani, President of the Islamic Republic of Afghanistan.
Apr. 29, 2015	...do	...do	Shinzo Abe, Prime Minister of Japan.
Sept. 24, 2015	...do	...do	Pope Francis of the Holy See.
Jan. 12, 2016	Joint session	State of the Union Address	President Barack H. Obama.
June 12, 2016	Joint meeting	Address	Narendra Modi, Prime Minister of the Republic of India.
115th CONGRESS			
Jan. 6, 2017	Joint session	Counting electoral votes	N.A.
Jan. 20, 2017	Inauguration	West Front	President Donald J. Trump; Vice President Mike Pence.
Feb. 28, 2017	Joint meeting	Address	President Donald J. Trump.
Jan. 6, 2017	Joint Session	Counting electoral votes	N.A.
Jan. 20, 2017	Inauguration	West Front	President Donald J. Trump; Vice President Mike Pence.
Feb. 28, 2017	Joint Session	Address (http://houselive.gov/MediaPlayer.php?view_id=2&clip_id=11726)	President Donald J. Trump.
Jan. 30, 2018	Joint Session	State of the Union Address	President Donald J. Trump.
April 25, 2018	Joint Meeting	Address	Emmanuel Macron, President of France.

[1] Closing date for this table was July 27, 2018.

[2] The oath of office was administered to George Washington outside on the gallery in front of the Senate Chamber, after which the Congress and the President returned to the chamber to hear the inaugural address. They then proceeded to St. Paul's Chapel for the "divine service" performed by the Chaplain of the Congress. Adjournment of the ceremony did not occur until the Congress returned to Federal Hall.

[3] Funeral oration was delivered at the German Lutheran Church in Philadelphia.

[4] Because of a tie in the electoral vote between Thomas Jefferson and Aaron Burr, the House of Representatives had to decide the election. Thirty-six ballots were required to break the deadlock, with Jefferson's election as President and Burr's as Vice President on February 17. The Twelfth Amendment was added to the Constitution to prevent the 1800 problem from recurring.

[5] During most of the period while the Capitol was being reconstructed following the fire of 1814, the Congress met in the "Brick Capitol," constructed on the site of the present Supreme Court building. This joint session took place in the Representatives' chamber on the 2d floor of the building.

[6] The joint session to count electoral votes was dissolved because the House and Senate disagreed on Missouri's status regarding statehood. The joint session was reconvened the same day and Missouri's votes were counted.

[7] While this occasion has historically been referred to as the first joint meeting of Congress, the Journals of the House and Senate indicate that Lafayette actually addressed the House of Representatives, with some of the Senators present as guests of the House (having been invited at the last minute to attend). Similar occasions, when members of the one body were invited as guests of the other, include the Senate address by Queen Wilhelmina of the Netherlands on Aug. 6, 1942, and the House address by General H. Norman Schwarzkopf on May 8, 1991.

[8] Although Andrew Jackson won the popular vote by a substantial amount and had the highest number of electoral votes from among the several candidates, he did not receive the required majority of the electoral votes. The responsibility for choosing the new President therefore devolved upon the House of Representatives. As soon as the Senators left the chamber, the balloting proceeded, and John Quincy Adams was elected on the first ballot.

[9] The ceremony was moved outside to accommodate the extraordinarily large crowd of people who had come to Washington to see the inauguration.

[10] The ceremony was moved inside because of cold weather.

[11] Following the death of President Zachary Taylor, Vice President Millard Fillmore took the Presidential oath of office in a special joint session in the Hall of the House.

[12] The joint session to count electoral votes was dissolved three times so that the House and Senate could resolve several electoral disputes.

[13] Because of a severe cold and hoarseness, the King could not deliver his speech, which was read by former Representative Elisha Hunt Allen, then serving as Chancellor and Chief Justice of the Hawaiian Islands.

[14] The contested election between Rutherford B. Hayes and Samuel J. Tilden created a constitutional crisis. Tilden won the popular vote by a close margin, but disputes concerning the electoral vote returns from four states deadlocked the proceedings of the joint session. Anticipating this development, the Congress had created a special commission of five Senators, five Representatives, and five Supreme Court Justices to resolve such disputes. The Commission met in the Supreme Court Chamber (the present Old Senate Chamber) as each problem arose. In each case, the Commission accepted the Hayes electors, securing his election by one electoral vote. The joint session was convened on 15 occasions, with the last on March 2, just three days before the inauguration.

[15] The speech was written by former Speaker and Senator Robert C. Winthrop, who could not attend the ceremony because of ill health.

[16] Because of a blizzard, the ceremony was moved inside, where it was held as part of the Senate's special session. President William Howard Taft took the oath of office and gave his inaugural address after Vice President James S. Sherman's inaugural address and the swearing-in of the new senators.

[17] Held in the Senate Chamber.

[18] Bakhmetieff represented the provisional government of Russia set up after the overthrow of the monarchy in March 1917 and recognized by the United States. The Bolsheviks took over in November 1917.

[19] The address and reception were in conjunction with the presentation to the Senate by France of two Sèvres vases in appreciation of the United States' involvement in World War I. The vases are today in the Senate lobby, just off the Senate floor. Two additional Sèvres vases were given without ceremony to the House of Representatives, which today are in the Rayburn Room, not far from the floor of the House.

[20] Senators later objected to President Harding's speech (given with no advance notice to most of the Senators) as an unconstitutional effort to interfere with the deliberations of the Senate, and Harding did not repeat visits of this kind.

[21] This was the first Annual Message broadcast live on radio.

[22] This was the first inauguration held pursuant to the Twentieth Amendment, which changed the date from March 4 to January 20. The Vice Presidential oath, which previously had been given earlier on the same day in the Senate Chamber, was added to the inaugural ceremony as well, but the Vice Presidential inaugural address was discontinued.

[23] A joint reception for the King and Queen of the United Kingdom was held in the Rotunda, authorized by Senate Concurrent Resolution 17, 76th Congress. Although the concurrent resolution was structured to establish a joint meeting, the Senate, in fact, adjourned rather than recessed as called for by the resolution.

[24] Held in the Senate Chamber.

[25] At this time, the Philippines was still a possession of the United States, although it had been made a self-governing commonwealth in 1935, in preparation for full independence in 1946. From 1909 to 1916, Quezon had served in the U.S. House of Representatives as the resident commissioner from the Philippines.

[26] In exile.

[27] For this Senate Address by Queen Wilhelmina, the members of the House of Representatives were invited as guests. This occasion has sometimes been mistakenly referred to as a joint meeting.

[28] The oaths of office were taken in simple ceremonies at the White House because the expense and festivity of a Capitol ceremony were thought inappropriate because of the war. The Joint Committee on Arrangements of the Congress was in charge, however, and both the Senate and the House of Representatives were present.

[29] This was the first time the term "State of the Union Address" was used for the President's Annual Message. Also, it was the first time the address was shown live on television.

[30] This was an informal meeting in the Coolidge Auditorium of the Library of Congress.

[31] Presentation of new ivory gavel to the Senate.

[32] According to the Congressional Record, the Senate adjourned prior to the inaugural ceremonies, even though the previously adopted resolution had stated the adjournment would come immediately following the inauguration. The Senate Journal records the adjournment as called for in the resolution, hence this listing as a joint session.

[33] The joint session to count electoral votes was dissolved so that the House and Senate could each resolve the dispute regarding a ballot from North Carolina. The joint session was reconvened the same day and the North Carolina vote was counted.

[34] Rockefeller was sworn in as Vice President by Chief Justice Warren E. Burger, after which, by unanimous consent, he was allowed to address the Senate.

[35] Because the Governor had laryngitis, his speech was read by his wife, Pamela.

[36] The ceremony was moved inside because of extremely cold weather.

[37] These commemorative addresses were given in the Old Senate Chamber during a regular legislative session.

[38] For this House Address by General Schwarzkopf, the members of the Senate were invited as guests.

[39] This speech was mislabeled in many sources as a State of the Union Address.

[40] President Kim Yong-sam was in Washington for the dedication of the Korean Veterans' Memorial, held the day after this joint meeting.

[41] This was the first State of the Union Address carried live on the Internet.

[42] Prime Minister Howard was originally scheduled to address a joint meeting on September 12, 2001, but because of the attack on the United States on September 11, 2001, the event was postponed until this occasion.

[43] The joint session to count electoral votes was dissolved so that the House and Senate could each discuss the dispute regarding the ballots from Ohio. The joint session was reconvened the same day and the Ohio votes were counted.

REPRESENTATIVES UNDER EACH APPORTIONMENT

The original apportionment of Representatives was assigned in 1787 in the Constitution and remained in effect for the 1st and 2d Congresses. Subsequent apportionments based on the censuses over the years have been figured using several different methods approved by Congress, all with the goal of dividing representation among the states as equally as possible. After each census up to and including the thirteenth in 1910, Congress would enact a law designating the specific changes in the actual number of Representatives as well as the increase in the ratio of persons-per-Representative. After having made no apportionment after the Fourteenth census in 1920, Congress by statute in 1929 fixed the total number of Representatives at 435 (the number attained with the apportionment after the 1910 census), and since that time, only the ratio of persons-per-Representative has continued to increase, in fact, significantly so. Since the total is now fixed, the specific number of Representatives per state is adjusted after each census to reflect its percentage of the entire population. Since the Sixteenth Census in 1940, the "equal proportions" method of apportioning Representatives within the 435 total has been employed. A detailed explanation of the entire apportionment process can be found in *The Historical Atlas of United States Congressional Districts, 1789–1983*. Kenneth C. Martis, The Free Press, New York, 1982.

State	Constitutional apportionment	First Census, 1790	Second Census, 1800	Third Census, 1810	Fourth Census, 1820	Fifth Census, 1830	Sixth Census, 1840	Seventh Census, 1850	Eighth Census, 1860	Ninth Census, 1870	Tenth Census, 1880	Eleventh Census, 1890	Twelfth Census, 1900	Thirteenth Census, 1910	Fifteenth Census, 1930 [1]	Sixteenth Census, 1940	Seventeenth Census, 1950	Eighteenth Census, 1960	Nineteenth Census, 1970	Twentieth Census, 1980	Twenty-First Census, 1990	Twenty-Second Census, 2000	Twenty-Third Census, 2010
AL	......	......	......	[2]	3	5	7	7	6	8	8	9	9	10	9	9	9	8	7	7	7	7	7
AK	......	......	......	......	......	......	......	......	......	......	......	......	......	......	......	......	[2,3]	1	1	1	1	1	1
AZ	......	......	......	......	......	......	......	......	......	......	......	......	[2]	[4]1	1	2	2	3	4	5	6	8	9
AR	......	......	......	......	......	[2]	1	2	3	4	5	6	7	7	7	7	6	4	4	4	4	4	4
CA	......	......	......	......	......	......	[2]	[4]2	3	4	6	7	8	11	20	23	30	38	43	45	52	53	53
CO	......	......	......	......	......	......	......	......	......	[2]	1	2	3	4	4	4	4	4	5	6	6	7	7
CT	5	7	7	7	6	6	4	4	4	4	4	4	5	5	6	6	6	6	6	6	6	5	5
DE	1	1	1	2	1	1	1	1	1	1	1	1	1	1	1	1	1	1	1	1	1	1	1
FL	......	......	......	......	......	......	[2]	1	1	2	2	2	3	4	5	6	8	12	15	19	23	25	27
GA	3	2	4	6	7	9	8	8	7	9	10	11	11	12	10	10	10	10	10	10	11	13	14
HI	......	......	......	......	......	......	......	......	......	......	......	......	......	......	......	......	[2,3]	2	2	2	2	2	2
ID	......	......	......	......	......	......	......	......	......	......	[2]	1	1	2	2	2	2	2	2	2	2	2	2
IL	......	......	......	[2]	1	3	7	9	14	19	20	22	25	27	27	26	25	24	24	22	20	19	18
IN	......	......	......	[2]	3	7	10	11	11	13	13	13	13	13	12	11	11	11	11	10	10	9	9
IA	......	......	......	......	......	......	[2]	2	6	9	11	11	11	11	9	8	8	7	6	6	5	5	4
KS	......	......	......	......	......	......	......	[2]	[4]1	3	7	8	8	8	7	6	6	5	5	5	4	4	4
KY	[2]	[4]2	6	10	12	13	10	10	9	10	11	11	11	11	9	9	8	7	7	7	6	6	6
LA	......	......	......	[2]	3	3	4	4	5	6	6	6	7	8	8	8	8	8	8	8	7	7	6
ME	......	......	......	[5]	7	8	7	6	5	5	4	4	4	4	3	3	3	2	2	2	2	2	2
MD	6	8	9	9	9	8	6	6	5	6	6	6	6	6	6	6	7	8	8	8	8	8	8
MA	8	14	17	[5]20	13	12	10	11	10	11	12	13	14	16	15	14	14	12	12	11	10	10	9
MI	......	......	......	......	......	[2]	3	4	6	9	11	12	12	13	17	17	18	19	19	18	16	15	14
MN	......	......	......	......	......	......	......	[2]	2	3	5	7	9	10	9	9	9	8	8	8	8	8	8
MS	......	......	......	[2]	1	2	4	5	5	6	7	7	8	8	7	7	6	5	5	5	5	4	4
MO	......	......	......	[2]	[4]1	2	5	7	9	13	14	15	16	16	13	13	11	10	10	9	9	9	8
MT	......	......	......	......	......	......	......	......	......	......	[2]	1	1	2	2	2	2	2	2	2	1	1	1
NE	......	......	......	......	......	......	......	......	[2]	1	3	6	6	6	5	4	4	3	3	3	3	3	3
NV	......	......	......	......	......	......	......	......	[2]	1	1	1	1	1	1	1	1	1	1	2	2	3	4
NH	3	4	5	6	6	5	4	3	3	3	2	2	2	2	2	2	2	2	2	2	2	2	2
NJ	4	5	6	6	6	6	5	5	5	7	7	8	10	12	14	14	14	15	15	14	13	13	12
NM	......	......	......	......	......	......	......	......	......	......	......	......	[2]	[4]1	1	2	2	2	2	3	3	3	3
NY	6	10	17	27	34	40	34	33	31	33	34	34	37	43	45	45	43	41	39	34	31	29	27
NC	5	10	12	13	13	13	9	8	7	8	9	9	10	10	11	12	12	11	11	11	12	13	13
ND	......	......	......	......	......	......	......	......	......	......	[2]	1	2	3	2	2	2	2	1	1	1	1	1
OH	......	......	[2]	6	14	19	21	21	19	20	21	21	21	22	24	23	23	24	23	21	19	18	16
OK	......	......	......	......	......	......	......	......	......	......	......	......	[2]	8	9	8	6	6	6	6	6	5	5
OR	......	......	......	......	......	......	......	[2]	1	1	1	2	2	3	3	4	4	4	4	5	5	5	5
PA	8	13	18	23	26	28	24	25	24	27	28	30	32	36	34	33	30	27	25	23	21	19	18
RI	1	2	2	2	2	2	2	2	2	2	2	2	2	3	2	2	2	2	2	2	2	2	2
SC	5	6	8	9	9	9	7	6	4	5	7	7	7	7	6	6	6	6	6	6	6	6	7
SD	......	......	......	......	......	......	......	......	......	......	[2]	2	2	3	2	2	2	2	2	1	1	1	1
TN	......	[2]	3	6	9	13	11	10	8	10	10	10	10	10	9	10	9	9	8	9	9	9	9
TX	......	......	......	......	......	......	[2]	2	4	6	11	13	16	18	21	21	22	23	24	27	30	32	36
UT	......	......	......	......	......	......	......	......	......	......	......	[2]	1	2	2	2	2	2	2	3	3	3	4
VT	[2]	[4]2	4	6	5	5	4	3	3	3	2	2	2	2	1	1	1	1	1	1	1	1	1
VA	10	19	22	23	22	21	15	13	[6]11	9	10	10	10	10	9	9	10	10	10	10	11	11	11
WA	......	......	......	......	......	......	......	......	......	......	[2]	2	3	5	6	6	7	7	7	8	9	9	10
WV	......	......	......	......	......	......	......	......	[6]	3	4	4	5	6	6	6	6	5	4	4	3	3	3
WI	......	......	......	......	......	......	[2]	3	6	8	9	10	11	11	10	10	10	10	9	9	9	8	8
WY	......	......	......	......	......	......	......	......	......	......	[2]	1	1	1	1	1	1	1	1	1	1	1	1
Total ..	65	105	141	181	213	240	223	234	241	292	325	356	386	435	435	435	435	435	435	435	435	435	435

NOTE: Information for table obtained from the U.S. Census Bureau.

[1] No apportionment was made after the 1920 census.

[2] The following Representatives were added after the indicated apportionments when these states were admitted in the years listed. The number of these additional Representatives for each state remained in effect until the next census's apportionment (with the exceptions of California and New Mexico, as explained in footnote 4). They are not included in the total for each column. In reading this table, please remember that the apportionments made after each census took effect with the election two years after the census date. As a result, in the table footnote 2 is placed for several states under the decade preceding the one in which it entered the Union, since the previous decade's apportionment was still in effect at the time of statehood. *Constitutional:* Vermont (1791), 2; Kentucky (1792), 2; *First:* Tennessee (1796), 1; *Second:* Ohio (1803), 1; *Third:* Louisiana (1812), 1; Indiana (1816), 1; Mississippi (1817), 1; Illinois (1818), 1; Alabama (1819), 1; Missouri (1821), 1; *Fifth:* Arkansas (1836), 1; Michigan (1837), 1; *Sixth:* Florida (1845), 1; Texas (1845), 2; Iowa (1846), 2; Wisconsin (1848), 2; California (1850), 2; *Seventh:* Minnesota (1858), 2; Oregon (1859), 1; Kansas (1861), 1; *Eighth:* Nevada (1864), 1; Nebraska (1867), 1; *Ninth:* Colorado (1876), 1; *Tenth:* North Dakota (1889), 1; South Dakota (1889), 2; Montana (1889), 1; Washington (1889), 1; Idaho (1890), 1; Wyoming (1890), 1; *Eleventh:* Utah (1896), 1; *Twelth:* Oklahoma (1907), 5; New Mexico (1912), 2; Arizona (1912), 1; *Seventeenth:* Alaska (1959), 1; Hawaii (1959), 1.

[3] When Alaska and then Hawaii joined the Union in 1959, the law was changed to allow the total membership of the House of Representatives to increase to 436 and then to 437, apportioning one new Representative for each of those states. The total returned to 435 in 1963, when the 1960 census apportionment took effect.

[4] Even though the respective censuses were taken before the following states joined the Union, Representatives for them were apportioned either because of anticipation of statehood or because they had become states in the period between the census and the apportionment, hence they are included in the totals of the respective columns. *First:* Vermont (1791); Kentucky (1792); *Fourth:* Missouri (1821); *Seventh:* California (1850); *Eighth:* Kansas (1861); *Thirteenth:* New Mexico (1912); Arizona (1912). (Please note: These seven states are also included in footnote 2 because they became states while the previous decade's apportionment was still in effect for the House of Representatives.) California's situation was unusual. It was scheduled for inclusion in the figures for the 1850 census apportionment; however, when the apportionment law was passed in 1852, California's census returns were still incomplete so Congress made special provision that the state would retain "the number of Representatives [two] prescribed by the act of admission * * * into the Union until a new apportionment [i.e., after the 1860 census]" would be made. The number of Representatives from California actually increased before the next apportionment to three when Congress gave the state an extra Representative during part of the 37th Congress, from 1862 to 1863. Regarding New Mexico, the 1911 apportionment law, passed by the 62d Congress in response to the 1910 census and effective with the 63d Congress in 1913, stated that "if the Territor[y] of * * * New Mexico shall become [a State] in the Union before the apportionment of Representatives under the next decennial census [it] shall have one Representative * * *." When New Mexico became a state in 1912 during the 62d Congress, it was given two Representatives. The number was decreased to one beginning the next year in the 63d.

[5] The "Maine District" of Massachusetts became a separate state during the term of the 16th Congress, in 1820. For the remainder of that Congress, Maine was assigned one "at large" Representative while Massachusetts continued to have 20 Representatives, the number apportioned to it after the 1810 census. For the 17th Congress (the last before the 1820 census apportionment took effect), seven of Massachusetts's Representatives were reassigned to Maine, leaving Massachusetts with 13.

[6] Of the 11 Representatives apportioned to Virginia after the 1860 census, three were reassigned to West Virginia when that part of Virginia became a separate state in 1863. Since the Virginia seats in the House were vacant at that time because of the Civil War, all of the new Representatives from West Virginia were able to take their seats at once. When Representatives from Virginia reentered the House in 1870, only eight members represented it.

IMPEACHMENT PROCEEDINGS

The provisions of the United States Constitution which apply specifically to impeachments are as follows: Article I, section 2, clause 5; Article I, section 3, clauses 6 and 7; Article II, section 2, clause 1; Article II, section 4; and Article III, section 2, clause 3.

For the officials listed below, the date of impeachment by the House of Representatives is followed by the dates of the Senate trial, with the result of each listed at the end of the entry.

WILLIAM BLOUNT, a Senator of the United States from Tennessee; impeached July 7, 1797; tried Monday, December 17, 1798, to Monday, January 14, 1799; charges dismissed for want of jurisdiction.

JOHN PICKERING, judge of the United States District Court for the District of New Hampshire; impeached March 2, 1803; tried Thursday, March 3, 1803, to Monday, March 12, 1804; removed from office.

SAMUEL CHASE, Associate Justice of the Supreme Court of the United States; impeached March 12, 1804; tried Friday, November 30, 1804, to Friday, March 1, 1805; acquitted.

JAMES H. PECK, judge of the United States District Court for the District of Missouri; impeached April 24, 1830; tried Monday, April 26, 1830, to Monday, January 31, 1831; acquitted.

WEST H. HUMPHREYS, judge of the United States District Court for the Middle, Eastern, and Western Districts of Tennessee; impeached May 6, 1862; tried Wednesday, May 7, 1862, to Thursday, June 26, 1862; removed from office and disqualified from future office.

ANDREW JOHNSON, President of the United States; impeached February 24, 1868; tried Tuesday, February 25, 1868, to Tuesday, May 26, 1868; acquitted.

MARK DELAHAY, judge of the United States District Court of Kansas; impeached February 28, 1873; resigned office Friday, December 12, 1873, before the Senate trial was held, with no further action taken by the Senate.

WILLIAM W. BELKNAP, Secretary of War; impeached March 2, 1876; tried Friday, March 3, 1876, to Tuesday, August 1, 1876; acquitted.

CHARLES SWAYNE, judge of the United States District Court for the Northern District of Florida; impeached December 13, 1904; tried Wednesday, December 14, 1904, to Monday, February 27, 1905; acquitted.

ROBERT W. ARCHBALD, associate judge, United States Commerce Court; impeached July 11, 1912; tried Saturday, July 13, 1912, to Monday, January 13, 1913; removed from office and disqualified from future office.

GEORGE W. ENGLISH, judge of the United States District Court for the Eastern District of Illinois; impeached April 1, 1926; tried Friday, April 23, 1926, to Monday, December 13, 1926; resigned office Thursday, November 4, 1926; Court of Impeachment adjourned to December 13, 1926, when, on request of House managers, the proceedings were dismissed.

HAROLD LOUDERBACK, judge of the United States District Court for the Northern District of California; impeached February 24, 1933; tried Monday, May 15, 1933, to Wednesday, May 24, 1933; acquitted.

HALSTED L. RITTER, judge of the United States District Court for the Southern District of Florida; impeached March 2, 1936; tried Monday, April 6, 1936, to Friday, April 17, 1936; removed from office.

HARRY E. CLAIBORNE, judge of the United States District Court of Nevada; impeached July 22, 1986; tried Tuesday, October 7, 1986, to Thursday, October 9, 1986; removed from office.

ALCEE L. HASTINGS, judge of the United States District Court for the Southern District of Florida; impeached August 3, 1988; tried Wednesday, October 18, 1989, to Friday, October 20, 1989; removed from office.

WALTER L. NIXON, judge of the United States District Court for the Southern District of Mississippi; impeached May 10, 1989; tried Wednesday, November 1, 1989, to Friday, November 3, 1989; removed from office.

WILLIAM JEFFERSON CLINTON, President of the United States; impeached December 19, 1998; tried Thursday, January 7, 1999, to Friday, February 12, 1999; acquitted.

SAMUEL B. KENT, judge of the United States District Court for the Southern District of Texas; impeached June 19, 2009; resigned office effective Tuesday, June 30, 2009; Court of Impeachment convened on Wednesday, July 22, 2009, when, on request of House managers, proceedings were dismissed.

G. THOMAS PORTEOUS, Jr., judge of the United States District Court for the Eastern District of Louisiana; impeached March 11, 2010; tried Tuesday, December 7, 2010, to Wednesday, December 8, 2010; removed from office and disqualified from future office.

REPRESENTATIVES, SENATORS, DELEGATES, AND RESIDENT COMMISSIONERS SERVING IN THE 1st–115th CONGRESSES*

Since the U.S. Congress convened on March 4, 1789, 12,249 individuals have served as Representatives, Senators, or in both capacities. There have been 10,275 Members who served only as Representatives, 1,302 Members who served only in the Senate, and 672 Members with service in both chambers. The total number of Representatives (including individuals serving in both bodies) is 10,947. The total number of Senators (including individuals serving in both bodies) is 1,974.

These numbers do not include statutory representatives: Resident Commissioners and Delegates. An additional 144 people have served only as Territorial Delegates in the House and 33 people have served only as Resident Commissioners from Puerto Rico or the Philippines.

State/Territory	Date Became a U.S. Territory	Date Entered the Union	Delegates (Only)	Resident Commissioners [1]	Representatives (Only) [2]	Representatives and Delegates	Senators (Only) [3]	Senators and Representatives [4]	Senators and Delegates	Senators, Representatives, and Delegates	Total House Members
Alabama	Mar. 3, 1817	Dec. 14, 1819 (22d)	0	0	169	1	29	13	0	0	183
Alaska	Aug. 24, 1912	Jan. 3, 1959 (49th)	7	0	4	0	7	0	1	0	12
American Samoa	Apr. 17, 1900		3	0	0	0	0	0	0	0	3
Arizona	Feb. 24, 1863	Feb. 14, 1912 (48th)	10	0	37	0	5	4	2	0	53
Arkansas	Mar. 2, 1819	June 15, 1836 (25th)	2	0	87	0	22	12	1	0	102
California		Sept. 9, 1850 (31st)	0	0	361	0	35	9	0	0	370
Colorado	Feb. 28, 1861	Aug. 1, 1876 (38th)	2	0	59	0	23	10	2	1	74
Connecticut		Jan. 9, 1788 (5th)	0	0	209	0	29	26	0	0	235
Delaware		Dec. 7, 1787 (1st)	0	0	63	0	37	14	0	0	77
District of Columbia	July 16, 1790		3	0	0	0	0	0	0	0	3
Florida	Mar. 20, 1822	Mar. 3, 1845 (27th)	4	0	140	0	27	6	1	0	151
Georgia		Jan. 2, 1788 (4th)	0	0	286	0	39	22	0	0	308
Guam	Apr. 11, 1899		4	0	0	0	0	0	0	0	4
Hawaii	June 14, 1900	Aug. 21, 1959 (50th)	10	0	10	0	3	4	0	0	24
Idaho	Mar. 3, 1863	July 3, 1890 (43d)	8	0	27	0	19	6	1	0	42
Illinois	Feb. 3, 1809	Dec. 3, 1818 (21st)	3	0	453	0	31	20	0	0	476
Indiana	May 7, 1800	Dec. 11, 1816 (19th)	2	0	302	1	27	19	0	0	324
Iowa	June 12, 1838	Dec. 28, 1846 (29th)	1	0	171	0	22	11	1	0	184
Kansas	May 30, 1854	Jan. 29, 1861 (34th)	2	0	110	0	24	9	0	0	121
Kentucky		June 1, 1792 (15th)	0	0	313	0	38	28	0	0	341
Louisiana [5]	Mar. 4, 1804	Apr. 30, 1812 (18th)	2	0	151	0	36	14	0	0	167
Maine		Mar. 15, 1820 (23d)	0	0	135	0	22	15	0	0	150
Mariana Islands	Apr. 11, 1899		1	0	0	0	0	0	0	0	1
Maryland		Apr. 28, 1788 (7th)	0	0	281	0	29	28	0	0	309
Massachusetts		Feb. 6, 1788 (6th)	0	0	404	0	24	29	0	0	433
Michigan	Jan. 11, 1805	Jan. 26, 1837 (26th)	5	0	262	0	23	14	1	1	283
Minnesota	Mar. 3, 1849	May 11, 1858 (32d)	2	0	123	0	29	10	1	0	136
Mississippi	Apr. 17, 1798	Dec. 10, 1817 (20th)	3	0	111	0	30	14	0	1	129
Missouri	June 4, 1812	Aug. 10, 1821 (24th)	2	0	293	1	35	10	0	0	306
Montana	May 26, 1864	Nov. 8, 1889 (41st)	5	0	27	0	15	6	0	1	39

Nebraska	May 30, 1854	Mar. 1, 1867 (37th)	5	0	88	0	31	6	1	0	100
Nevada	Mar. 2, 1861	Oct. 31, 1864 (36th)	2	0	33	0	20	6	0	0	41
New Hampshire	....	June 21, 1788 (9th)	0	0	137	0	38	26	0	0	163
New Jersey	....	Dec. 18, 1787 (3d)	0	0	325	0	51	15	0	0	340
New Mexico	Sept. 9, 1850	Jan. 6, 1912 (47th)	16	0	23	1	11	5	1	0	46
New York	....	July 26, 1788 (11th)	0	0	1,448	0	36	23	0	0	1,471
North Carolina	....	Nov. 21, 1789 (12th)	0	0	334	0	37	18	0	0	352
North Dakota[6]	Mar. 2, 1861	Nov. 2, 1889 (39th)	9	0	14	0	17	6	0	0	29
Ohio	....	Mar. 1, 1803 (17th)	2	0	633	0	36	19	0	1	655
Oklahoma	May 2, 1890	Nov. 16, 1907 (46th)	3	0	75	1	11	6	0	0	85
Oregon	Aug. 14, 1848	Feb. 14, 1859 (33d)	1	0	57	0	32	4	1	0	63
Pennsylvania	....	Dec. 12, 1787 (2d)	0	0	1,057	0	33	21	0	0	1,078
Philippines[7]	Apr. 11, 1899	....	0	13	0	0	0	0	0	0	13
Puerto Rico[7]	Apr. 11, 1899	....	0	20	0	0	0	0	0	0	20
Rhode Island	....	May 29, 1790 (13th)	0	0	78	0	38	10	0	0	88
South Carolina	....	May 23, 1788 (8th)	0	0	226	0	39	17	0	0	243
South Dakota[6]	Mar. 2, 1861	Nov. 2, 1889 (40th)	9	0	14	1	15	10	1	0	35
Tennessee	....	June 1, 1796 (16th)	1	0	247	0	40	18	0	0	266
Texas	....	Dec. 29, 1845 (28th)	0	0	252	0	23	9	0	0	261
Utah	Sept. 9, 1850	Jan. 4, 1896 (45th)	5	0	35	0	11	3	2	0	45
Vermont	....	Mar. 4, 1791 (14th)	0	0	80	0	24	16	0	0	96
Virgin Islands	Mar. 31, 1917	....	5	0	0	0	0	0	0	0	5
Virginia	....	June 25, 1788 (10th)	0	0	419	0	27	27	0	0	446
Washington	Mar. 2, 1853	Nov. 11, 1889 (42d)	12	0	74	0	12	10	1	0	97
West Virginia	....	June 20, 1863 (35th)	0	0	87	0	24	9	0	0	96
Wisconsin	Apr. 20, 1836	May 29, 1848 (30th)	4	0	173	1	19	8	1	0	187
Wyoming	July 25, 1868	July 10, 1890 (44th)	6	0	16	0	17	3	1	0	26

* State Representation March 4, 1789 to July 27, 2018.

[1] Includes 3 members who served as Representatives and 2 members who served as Senators from a different state.

[2] Includes 3 members who served as Delegates and 18 members who served as Senators from a different state.

[3] Includes 18 members who served as Representatives from a different state. One Senator served from two states and one Senator served from three states.

[4] Includes only those members who served as both a Representative and a Senator from the same state. Eighteen members served as a Senator from one state and a Representative from a different state.

[5] Designated Orleans Territory before attaining statehood in 1812.

[6] Dakota Territory became North and South Dakota in 1889. The nine Delegates from this territory are included in counts for both states. The two Delegates who became Representatives from South Dakota are included only in that state's count.

[7] Resident Commissioners served the Philippines (1902–1946) and continue to serve Puerto Rico (1900 to present). Floor and committee privileges granted to statutory representatives (Territorial Delegates and Resident Commissioners) have changed over time; however, they have never been permitted to vote on the final passage of a bill. The Resident Commissioner's duties vary from that of a Delegate in that he has diplomatic privileges as well as most of those of a Member of Congress. The Puerto Rican Resident Commissioner has served a four-year term since 1917. For more information, see "Status of Delegates and Resident Commissioner," Deschler's Precedents, H.Doc. 94–661, Volume 2, Chapter 7, Section 3.

Source: Biographical Directory of the United States Congress.

POLITICAL DIVISIONS OF THE SENATE AND HOUSE FROM 1855 TO 2017

[All Figures Reflect Immediate Results of Elections. Figures Supplied by the Clerk of the House]

Congress	Years	SENATE					HOUSE OF REPRESENTATIVES				
		No. of Senators	Democrats	Republicans	Other parties	Vacancies	No. of Representatives	Democrats	Republicans	Other parties	Vacancies
34th	1855–1857	62	42	15	5	....	234	83	108	43	....
35th	1857–1859	64	39	20	5	....	237	131	92	14	....
36th	1859–1861	66	38	26	2	....	237	101	113	23	....
37th	1861–1863	50	11	31	7	1	178	42	106	28	2
38th	1863–1865	51	12	39	....	....	183	80	103	....	....
39th	1865–1867	52	10	42	....	....	191	46	145	....	....
40th	1867–1869	53	11	42	....	....	193	49	143	....	1
41st	1869–1871	74	11	61	....	2	243	73	170	....	....
42d	1871–1873	74	17	57	....	....	243	104	139	....	....
43d	1873–1875	74	19	54	....	1	293	88	203	....	2
44th	1875–1877	76	29	46	....	1	293	181	107	3	2
45th	1877–1879	76	36	39	1	....	293	156	137	....	....
46th	1879–1881	76	43	33	....	....	293	150	128	14	1
47th	1881–1883	76	37	37	2	....	293	130	152	11	....
48th	1883–1885	76	36	40	....	....	325	200	119	6	....
49th	1885–1887	76	34	41	....	1	325	182	140	2	1
50th	1887–1889	76	37	39	....	....	325	170	151	4	....
51st	1889–1891	84	37	47	....	....	330	156	173	1	....
52d	1891–1893	88	39	47	2	....	333	231	88	14	....
53d	1893–1895	88	44	38	3	3	356	220	126	10	....
54th	1895–1897	88	39	44	5	....	357	104	246	7	....
55th	1897–1899	90	34	46	10	....	357	134	206	16	1
56th	1899–1901	90	26	53	11	....	357	163	185	9	....
57th	1901–1903	90	29	56	3	2	357	153	198	5	1
58th	1903–1905	90	32	58	....	....	386	178	207	....	1
59th	1905–1907	90	32	58	....	....	386	136	250	....	....
60th	1907–1909	92	29	61	....	2	386	164	222	....	....
61st	1909–1911	92	32	59	....	1	391	172	219	....	....
62d	1911–1913	92	42	49	....	1	391	228	162	1	....
63d	1913–1915	96	51	44	1	....	435	290	127	18	....
64th	1915–1917	96	56	39	1	....	435	231	193	8	3
65th	1917–1919	96	53	42	1	....	435	[1] 210	216	9	....
66th	1919–1921	96	47	48	1	....	435	191	237	7	....
67th	1921–1923	96	37	59	....	....	435	132	300	1	2
68th	1923–1925	96	43	51	2	....	435	207	225	3	....
69th	1925–1927	96	40	54	1	1	435	183	247	5	....
70th	1927–1929	96	47	48	1	....	435	195	237	3	....
71st	1929–1931	96	39	56	1	....	435	163	267	1	4
72d	1931–1933	96	47	48	1	....	435	[2] 216	218	1	....
73d	1933–1935	96	59	36	1	....	435	313	117	5	....
74th	1935–1937	96	69	25	2	....	435	322	103	10	....
75th	1937–1939	96	75	17	4	....	435	333	89	13	....
76th	1939–1941	96	69	23	4	....	435	262	169	4	....
77th	1941–1943	96	66	28	2	....	435	267	162	6	....
78th	1943–1945	96	57	38	1	....	435	222	209	4	....
79th	1945–1947	96	57	38	1	....	435	243	190	2	....
80th	1947–1949	96	45	51	....	....	435	188	246	1	....
81st	1949–1951	96	54	42	....	....	435	263	171	1	....
82d	1951–1953	96	48	47	1	....	435	234	199	2	....
83d	1953–1955	96	46	48	2	....	435	213	221	1	....
84th	1955–1957	96	48	47	1	....	435	232	203	....	....
85th	1957–1959	96	49	47	....	....	435	234	201	....	....
86th	1959–1961	98	64	34	....	....	[3] 436	283	153	....	....
87th	1961–1963	100	64	36	....	....	[4] 437	262	175	....	....
88th	1963–1965	100	67	33	....	....	435	258	176	....	1
89th	1965–1967	100	68	32	....	....	435	295	140	....	....
90th	1967–1969	100	64	36	....	....	435	248	187	....	....
91st	1969–1971	100	58	42	....	....	435	243	192	....	....
92d	1971–1973	100	54	44	2	....	435	255	180	....	....
93d	1973–1975	100	56	42	2	....	435	242	192	1	....
94th	1975–1977	100	61	37	2	....	435	291	144	....	....
95th	1977–1979	100	61	38	1	....	435	292	143	....	....
96th	1979–1981	100	58	41	1	....	435	277	158	....	....
97th	1981–1983	100	46	53	1	....	435	242	192	1	....
98th	1983–1985	100	46	54	....	....	435	269	166	....	....
99th	1985–1987	100	47	53	....	....	435	253	182	....	....
100th	1987–1989	100	55	45	....	....	435	258	177	....	....
101st	1989–1991	100	55	45	....	....	435	260	175	....	....
102d	1991–1993	100	56	44	....	....	435	267	167	1	....
103d	1993–1995	100	57	43	....	....	435	258	176	1	....
104th	1995–1997	100	48	52	....	....	435	204	230	1	....
105th	1997–1999	100	45	55	....	....	435	207	226	2	....
106th	1999–2001	100	45	55	....	....	435	211	223	1	....
107th	2001–2003	100	50	50	....	....	435	212	221	2	....
108th	2003–2005	100	48	51	1	....	435	204	229	1	1
109th	2005–2007	100	44	55	1	....	435	202	232	1	....
110th	2007–2009	100	49	49	2	....	435	233	202	....	....
111th	2009–2011	100	55	41	2	2	435	256	178	....	1
112th	2011–2013	100	51	47	2	....	435	193	242	....	....
113th	2013–2015	100	53	45	2	....	435	200	234	....	1
114th	2015–2017	100	44	54	2	....	435	188	246	....	1
115th	2017–2019	100	47	51	2	....	435	193	236	....	6

[1] Democrats organized House with help of other parties.
[2] Democrats organized House due to Republican deaths.
[3] Proclamation declaring Alaska a State issued January 3, 1959.
[4] Proclamation declaring Hawaii a State issued August 21, 1959.

GOVERNORS OF THE STATES, COMMONWEALTH, AND TERRITORIES—2017

State, Commonwealth, or Territory	Capital	Governor	Party	Term of service	Expiration of term
STATE				*Years*	
Alabama	Montgomery	Kay Ivey	Republican	[c] 4	Jan. 2019
Alaska	Juneau	Bill Walker	Independent	[f] 4	Dec. 2018
Arizona	Phoenix	Doug Ducey	Republican	[f] 4	Jan. 2019
Arkansas	Little Rock	Asa Hutchinson	Republican	[c] 4	Jan. 2019
California	Sacramento	Jerry Brown	Democrat	[c] 4	Jan. 2019
Colorado	Denver	John Hickenlooper	Democrat	[c] 4	Jan. 2019
Connecticut	Hartford	Dan Malloy	Democrat	[b] 4	Jan. 2019
Delaware	Dover	John Carney	Democrat	[c] 4	Jan. 2021
Florida	Tallahassee	Rick Scott	Republican	[f] 4	Jan. 2019
Georgia	Atlanta	Nathan Deal	Republican	[f] 4	Jan. 2019
Hawaii	Honolulu	David Ige	Democrat	[c] 4	Dec. 2018
Idaho	Boise	C.L. "Butch" Otter	Republican	[b] 4	Jan. 2019
Illinois	Springfield	Bruce Rauner	Republican	[b] 4	Jan. 2019
Indiana	Indianapolis	Eric Holcomb	Republican	[f] 4	Jan. 2021
Iowa	Des Moines	Kim Reynolds	Republican	[b] 4	Jan. 2019
Kansas	Topeka	Sam Brownback	Republican	[c] 4	Jan. 2019
Kentucky	Frankfort	Matt Bevin	Republican	[c] 4	Dec. 2019
Louisiana	Baton Rouge	John Bel Edwards	Democrat	[f] 4	Jan. 2020
Maine	Augusta	Paul LePage	Republican	[f] 4	Jan. 2019
Maryland	Annapolis	Larry Hogan	Republican	[f] 4	Jan. 2019
Massachusetts	Boston	Charlie Baker	Republican	[b] 4	Jan. 2019
Michigan	Lansing	Rick Snyder	Republican	[b] 4	Jan. 2019
Minnesota	St. Paul	Mark Dayton	Democrat	[b] 4	Jan. 2019
Mississippi	Jackson	Phil Bryant	Republican	[c] 4	Jan. 2020
Missouri	Jefferson City	Mike Parson	Republican	[c] 4	Jan. 2021
Montana	Helena	Steve Bullock	Democrat	[g] 4	Jan. 2021
Nebraska	Lincoln	Pete Ricketts	Republican	[c] 4	Jan. 2019
Nevada	Carson City	Brian Sandoval	Republican	[c] 4	Jan. 2019
New Hampshire	Concord	Chris Sununu	Republican	[b] 2	Jan. 2019
New Jersey	Trenton	Phil Murphy	Democrat	[c] 4	Jan. 2022
New Mexico	Santa Fe	Susana Martinez	Republican	[c] 4	Jan. 2019
New York	Albany	Andrew Cuomo	Democrat	[b] 4	Jan. 2019
North Carolina	Raleigh	Roy Cooper	Democrat	[c] 4	Jan. 2021
North Dakota	Bismarck	Doug Burgum	Republican	[b] 4	Dec. 2020
Ohio	Columbus	John Kasich	Republican	[c] 4	Jan. 2019
Oklahoma	Oklahoma City	Mary Fallin	Republican	[c] 4	Jan. 2019
Oregon	Salem	Kate Brown	Democrat	[f] 4	Jan. 2019
Pennsylvania	Harrisburg	Tom Wolf	Democrat	[c] 4	Jan. 2019
Rhode Island	Providence	Gina Raimondo	Democrat	[c] 4	Jan. 2019
South Carolina	Columbia	Henry McMaster	Republican	[c] 4	Jan. 2019
South Dakota	Pierre	Dennis Daugaard	Republican	[c] 4	Jan. 2019
Tennessee	Nashville	Bill Haslam	Republican	[c] 4	Jan. 2019
Texas	Austin	Greg Abbott	Republican	[b] 4	Jan. 2019
Utah	Salt Lake City	Gary R. Herbert	Republican	[b] 4	Jan. 2021
Vermont	Montpelier	Phil Scott	Republican	[b] 2	Jan. 2019
Virginia	Richmond	Ralph Northam	Democrat	[a] 4	Jan. 2022
Washington	Olympia	Jay Inslee	Democrat	[d] 4	Jan. 2021
West Virginia	Charleston	Jim Justice	Republican	[c] 4	Jan. 2021
Wisconsin	Madison	Scott Walker	Republican	[b] 4	Jan. 2019
Wyoming	Cheyenne	Matthew Mead	Republican	[c] 4	Jan. 2019
COMMONWEALTH OF					
Puerto Rico	San Juan	Ricardo Rosselló	PNP[h]	[b] 4	Jan. 2021
TERRITORIES					
Guam	Agana	Eddie Calvo	Republican	[c] 4	Jan. 2019
Virgin Islands	Charlotte Amalie	Kenneth Mapp	Independent	[c] 4	Jan. 2019
American Samoa	Pago Pago	Lolo Matalasi Moliga	Independent	[c] 4	Jan. 2017
Northern Mariana Islands.	Saipan	Ralph Deleon Guerrero Torres	Republican	[i] 5	Jan. 2019

[a] Cannot succeed himself. [b] No limit. [c] Can serve 2 consecutive terms. [d] Can serve 3 consecutive terms. [e] Can serve 4 consecutive terms. [f] Can serve no more than 8 years in a 12-year period. [g] Can serve no more than 8 years in a 16-year period. [h] New Progressive Party of Puerto Rico/Democrat. [i] Absolute two-term limitation.

NOTE: Information for table obtained from the National Governors Association.

PRESIDENTS AND VICE PRESIDENTS AND THE CONGRESSES COINCIDENT WITH THEIR TERMS [1]

President	Vice President	Service	Congresses
George Washington	John Adams	Apr. 30, 1789–Mar. 3, 1797	1, 2, 3, 4.
John Adams	Thomas Jefferson	Mar. 4, 1797–Mar. 3, 1801	5, 6.
Thomas Jefferson	Aaron Burr	Mar. 4, 1801–Mar. 3, 1805	7, 8.
Do	George Clinton	Mar. 4, 1805–Mar. 3, 1809	9, 10.
James Madison	...do. [2]	Mar. 4, 1809–Mar. 3, 1813	11, 12.
Do	Elbridge Gerry [3]	Mar. 4, 1813–Mar. 3, 1817	13, 14.
James Monroe	Daniel D. Tompkins	Mar. 4, 1817–Mar. 3, 1825	15, 16, 17, 18, 19.
John Quincy Adams	John C. Calhoun	Mar. 4, 1825–Mar. 3, 1829	19, 20.
Andrew Jackson	...do. [4]	Mar. 4, 1829–Mar. 3, 1833	21, 22.
Do	Martin Van Buren	Mar. 4, 1833–Mar. 3, 1837	23, 24.
Martin Van Buren	Richard M. Johnson	Mar. 4, 1837–Mar. 3, 1841	25, 26.
William Henry Harrison [5]	John Tyler	Mar. 4, 1841–Apr. 4, 1841	27.
John Tyler		Apr. 6, 1841 –Mar. 3, 1845	27, 28.
James K. Polk	George M. Dallas	Mar. 4, 1845–Mar. 3, 1849	29, 30.
Zachary Taylor [5]	Millard Fillmore	Mar. 5, 1849–July 9, 1850	31.
Millard Fillmore		July 10, 1850–Mar. 3, 1853	31, 32.
Franklin Pierce	William R. King [6]	Mar. 4, 1853–Mar. 3, 1857	33, 34.
James Buchanan	John C. Breckinridge	Mar. 4, 1857–Mar. 3, 1861	35, 36.
Abraham Lincoln	Hannibal Hamlin	Mar. 4, 1861–Mar. 3, 1865	37, 38.
Do. [5]	Andrew Johnson	Mar. 4, 1865–Apr. 15, 1865	39.
Andrew Johnson		Apr. 15, 1865–Mar. 3, 1869	39, 40.
Ulysses S. Grant	Schuyler Colfax	Mar. 4, 1869–Mar. 3, 1873	41, 42.
Do	Henry Wilson [7]	Mar. 4, 1873–Mar. 3, 1877	43, 44.
Rutherford B. Hayes	William A. Wheeler	Mar. 4, 1877–Mar. 3, 1881	45, 46.
James A. Garfield [5]	Chester A. Arthur	Mar. 4, 1881–Sept. 19, 1881	47.
Chester A. Arthur		Sept. 20, 1881–Mar. 3, 1885	47, 48.
Grover Cleveland	Thomas A. Hendricks [8]	Mar. 4, 1885–Mar. 3, 1889	49, 50.
Benjamin Harrison	Levi P. Morton	Mar. 4, 1889–Mar. 3, 1893	51, 52.
Grover Cleveland	Adlai E. Stevenson	Mar. 4, 1893–Mar. 3, 1897	53, 54.
William McKinley	Garret A. Hobart [9]	Mar. 4, 1897–Mar. 3, 1901	55, 56.
Do. [5]	Theodore Roosevelt	Mar. 4, 1901–Sept. 14, 1901	57.
Theodore Roosevelt		Sept. 14, 1901–Mar. 3, 1905	57, 58.
Do	Charles W. Fairbanks	Mar. 4, 1905–Mar. 3, 1909	59, 60.
William H. Taft	James S. Sherman [10]	Mar. 4, 1909–Mar. 3, 1913	61, 62.
Woodrow Wilson	Thomas R. Marshall	Mar. 4, 1913–Mar. 3, 1921	63, 64, 65, 66, 67.
Warren G. Harding [5]	Calvin Coolidge	Mar. 4, 1921–Aug. 2, 1923	67.
Calvin Coolidge		Aug. 3, 1923–Mar. 3, 1925	68.
Do	Charles G. Dawes	Mar. 4, 1925–Mar. 3, 1929	69, 70.
Herbert C. Hoover	Charles Curtis	Mar. 4, 1929–Mar. 3, 1933	71, 72.
Franklin D. Roosevelt	John N. Garner	Mar. 4, 1933–Jan. 20, 1941	73, 74, 75, 76, 77.
Do	Henry A. Wallace	Jan. 20, 1941–Jan. 20, 1945	77, 78, 79.
Do. [5]	Harry S. Truman	Jan. 20, 1945–Apr. 12, 1945	79.
Harry S. Truman		Apr. 12, 1945–Jan. 20, 1949	79, 80, 81.
Do	Alben W. Barkley	Jan. 20, 1949–Jan. 20, 1953	81, 82, 83.
Dwight D. Eisenhower	Richard M. Nixon	Jan. 20, 1953–Jan. 20, 1961	83, 84, 85, 86, 87.
John F. Kennedy [5]	Lyndon B. Johnson	Jan. 20, 1961–Nov. 22, 1963	87, 88, 89.
Lyndon B. Johnson		Nov. 22, 1963–Jan. 20, 1965	88, 89.
Do	Hubert H. Humphrey	Jan. 20, 1965–Jan. 20, 1969	89, 90, 91.
Richard M. Nixon	Spiro T. Agnew [11]	Jan. 20, 1969–Dec. 6, 1973	91, 92, 93.
Do. [13]	Gerald R. Ford [12]	Dec. 6, 1973–Aug. 9, 1974	93.
Gerald R. Ford		Aug. 9, 1974–Dec. 19, 1974	93.
Do	Nelson A. Rockefeller [14]	Dec. 19, 1974–Jan. 20, 1977	93, 94, 95.
James Earl "Jimmy" Carter	Walter F. Mondale	Jan. 20, 1977–Jan. 20, 1981	95, 96, 97.
Ronald Reagan	George Bush	Jan. 20, 1981–Jan. 20, 1989	97, 98, 99, 100, 101.
George Bush	Dan Quayle	Jan. 20, 1989–Jan. 20, 1993	101, 102, 103.
William J. Clinton	Albert Gore	Jan. 20, 1993–Jan. 20, 2001	103, 104, 105, 106, 107.
George W. Bush	Richard B. Cheney	Jan. 20, 2001–Jan. 20, 2009	107, 108, 109, 110, 111.
Barack H. Obama	Joseph R. Biden, Jr.	Jan. 20, 2009–Jan. 20, 2017	111, 112, 113, 114.
Donald J. Trump	Mike Pence	Jan. 20, 2017	115.

[1] From 1789 until 1933, the terms of the President and Vice President and the term of the Congress coincided, beginning on March 4 and ending on March 3. This changed when the 20th amendment to the Constitution was adopted in 1933. Beginning in 1934 the convening date for Congress became January 3, and beginning in 1937 the starting date for the Presidential term became January 20. Because of this change, the number of Congresses overlapping with a Presidential term increased from two to three, although the third only overlaps by a few weeks.

[2] Died Apr. 20, 1812.

[3] Died Nov. 23, 1814.

[4] Resigned Dec. 28, 1832, to become a United States Senator from South Carolina.

[5] Died in office.

[6] Died Apr. 18, 1853.

[7] Died Nov. 22, 1875.

[8] Died Nov. 25, 1885.

[9] Died Nov. 21, 1899.

[10] Died Oct. 30, 1912.

[11] Resigned Oct. 10, 1973.

[12] Nominated to be Vice President by President Richard M. Nixon on Oct. 12, 1973; confirmed by the Senate on Nov. 27, 1973; confirmed by the House of Representatives on Dec. 6, 1973; took the oath of office on Dec. 6, 1973 in the Hall of the House of Representatives. This was the first time a Vice President was nominated by the President and confirmed by the Congress pursuant to the 25th amendment to the Constitution.

[13] Resigned from office.

[14] Nominated to be Vice President by President Gerald R. Ford on Aug. 20, 1974; confirmed by the Senate on Dec. 10, 1974; confirmed by the House of Representatives on Dec. 19, 1974; took the oath of office on Dec. 19, 1974, in the Senate Chamber.

CAPITOL BUILDINGS AND GROUNDS

UNITED STATES CAPITOL

Overview of the Building and its Function

The United States Capitol is among the most architecturally impressive and symbolically important buildings in the world. It has housed the chambers of the Senate and the House of Representatives for more than two centuries. Begun in 1793, the Capitol has been built, burnt, rebuilt, extended, and restored; today, it stands as a monument not only to its builders but also to the American people and their government.

As the focal point of the government's legislative branch, the Capitol is the centerpiece of the Capitol complex, which includes the six principal congressional office buildings and three Library of Congress buildings constructed on Capitol Hill in the 19th and 20th centuries.

In addition to its active use by Congress, the Capitol is a museum of American art and history. Each year, it is visited by millions of people from around the world.

A fine example of 19th-century neoclassical architecture, the Capitol combines function with aesthetics. Its design was derived from ancient Greece and Rome and evokes the ideals that guided the nation's founders as they framed their new republic. As the building was expanded from its original design, harmony with the existing portions was carefully maintained.

Today, the Capitol covers a ground area of 175,170 square feet, or about 4 acres, and has a floor area of approximately 16½ acres. Its length, from north to south, is 751 feet 4 inches; its greatest width, including approaches, is 350 feet. Its height above the base line on the east front to the top of the Statue of Freedom is 288 feet; from the basement floor to the top of the dome is an ascent of 365 steps.

The building is divided into five levels. The first, or ground, floor is occupied chiefly by committee rooms and the spaces allocated to various congressional officers. The areas accessible to visitors on this level include the Hall of Columns, the restored Old Supreme Court Chamber, and the Crypt beneath the Rotunda.

The second floor holds the chambers of the House of Representatives (in the south wing) and the Senate (in the north wing). This floor also contains three major public areas. In the center under the dome is the Rotunda, a circular ceremonial space that also serves as a gallery of paintings and sculpture depicting significant people and events in the nation's history. The Rotunda is 96 feet in diameter and rises 180 feet 3 inches to the canopy. The semicircular chamber south of the Rotunda served as the Hall of the House until 1857; now designated National Statuary Hall, it houses part of the Capitol's collection of statues donated by the states in commemoration of notable citizens. The Old Senate Chamber northeast of the Rotunda, which was used by the Senate until 1859, has been returned to its mid-19th-century appearance.

The third floor allows access to the galleries from which visitors to the Capitol may watch the proceedings of the House and the Senate when Congress is in session. The rest of this floor is occupied by offices, committee rooms, and press galleries.

The fourth floor and the basement/terrace level of the Capitol are occupied by offices, machinery rooms, workshops, and other support areas.

Located beneath the East Front plaza, the newest addition to the Capitol is the Capitol Visitor Center (CVC). Preparatory construction activities began in 2002, and the CVC was opened to the public on December 2, 2008. This date was chosen for its significance in the Capitol's history: it was on December 2, 1863, that the Statue of Freedom was placed atop the Capitol. The CVC occupies 580,000 square feet of space on three levels and includes an Exhibition Hall, a restaurant, orientation theaters, gift shops, and other visitor amenities as well as meeting space for the House and Senate.

Location of the Capitol

The Capitol is located at the eastern end of the Mall on a plateau 88 feet above the level of the Potomac River, commanding a westward view across the Capitol Reflecting

Pool to the Washington Monument 1.4 miles away and the Lincoln Memorial 2.2 miles away.

Before 1791, the Federal Government had no permanent site. The early Congresses met in eight different cities: Philadelphia, Baltimore, Lancaster, York, Princeton, Annapolis, Trenton, and New York City. The subject of a permanent capital for the Government of the United States was first raised by Congress in 1783; it was ultimately addressed in Article I, Section 8 of the Constitution (1787), which gave the Congress legislative authority over "such District (not exceeding ten Miles square) as may, by Cession of Particular States, and the Acceptance of Congress, become the Seat of the Government of the United States. . . ."

In 1788, the State of Maryland ceded to Congress "any district in this State, not exceeding ten miles square," and in 1789 the State of Virginia ceded an equivalent amount of land. In accordance with the "Residence Act" passed by Congress in 1790, President Washington in 1791 selected the area that is now the District of Columbia from the land ceded by Maryland (private landowners whose property fell within this area were compensated by a payment of £25 per acre); that ceded by Virginia was not used for the capital and was returned to Virginia in 1846. Also under the provisions of that Act, he selected three commissioners to survey the site and oversee the design and construction of the capital city and its government buildings. The commissioners, in turn, selected the French-American engineer Pierre Charles L'Enfant to plan the new city of Washington. L'Enfant's plan, which was influenced by the gardens at Versailles, arranged the city's streets and avenues in a grid overlaid with baroque diagonals; the result is a functional and aesthetic whole in which government buildings are balanced against public lawns, gardens, squares, and paths. The Capitol itself was located at the elevated east end of the Mall, on the brow of what was then called Jenkins' Hill. The site was, in L'Enfant's words, "a pedestal waiting for a monument."

Selection of a Plan

L'Enfant was expected to design the Capitol and to supervise its construction. However, he refused to produce any drawings for the building, claiming that he carried the design "in his head"; this fact and his refusal to consider himself subject to the commissioners' authority led to his dismissal in 1792. In March of that year, the commissioners announced a competition, suggested by Secretary of State Thomas Jefferson, that would award $500 and a city lot to whoever produced "the most approved plan" for the Capitol by mid-July. None of the 17 plans submitted, however, was wholly satisfactory. In October, a letter arrived from Dr. William Thornton, a Scottish-trained physician living in Tortola, British West Indies, requesting an opportunity to present a plan even though the competition had closed. The commissioners granted this request.

Thornton's plan depicted a building composed of three sections. The central section, which was topped by a low dome, was to be flanked on the north and south by two rectangular wings (one for the Senate and one for the House of Representatives). President Washington commended the plan for its "grandeur, simplicity and convenience," and on April 5, 1793, it was accepted by the commissioners; Washington gave his formal approval on July 25.

Brief Construction History

1793–1829

The cornerstone was laid by President Washington in the building's southeast corner on September 18, 1793, with Masonic ceremonies. Work progressed under the direction of three architects in succession. Stephen H. Hallet (an entrant in the earlier competition) and George Hadfield were eventually dismissed by the commissioners because of inappropriate design changes that they tried to impose; James Hoban, the architect of the White House, saw the first phase of the project through to completion.

Construction was a laborious and time-consuming process: the sandstone used for the building had to be ferried on boats from the quarries at Aquia, Virginia; workers had to be induced to leave their homes to come to the relative wilderness of Capitol Hill; and funding was inadequate. By August 1796, the commissioners were forced to focus the entire work effort on the building's north wing so that it at least could be ready for government occupancy as scheduled. Even so, some third-floor rooms were still unfinished when the Congress, the Supreme Court, the Library of Congress, and the courts of the District of Columbia occupied the Capitol in late 1800.

In 1803, Congress allocated funds to resume construction. A year earlier, the office of the Commissioners had been abolished and replaced by a superintendent of the city of Washington. To oversee the renewed construction effort, Benjamin Henry Latrobe was appointed surveyor of public buildings. The first professional architect and engineer to work in America, Latrobe modified Thornton's plan for the south wing to include space for offices and committee rooms; he also introduced alterations to simplify the construction work. Latrobe began work by removing a squat, oval, temporary building known as "the Oven," which had been erected in 1801 as a meeting place for the House of Representatives. By 1807, construction on the south wing was sufficiently advanced that the House was able to occupy its new legislative chamber, and the wing was completed in 1811.

In 1808, as work on the south wing progressed, Latrobe began the rebuilding of the north wing, which had fallen into disrepair. Rather than simply repair the wing, he redesigned the interior of the building to increase its usefulness and durability; among his changes was the addition of a chamber for the Supreme Court. By 1811, he had completed the eastern half of this wing, but funding was being increasingly diverted to preparations for a second war with Great Britain. By 1813, Latrobe had no further work in Washington and so he departed, leaving the north and south wings of the Capitol connected only by a temporary wooden passageway.

The War of 1812 left the Capitol, in Latrobe's later words, "a most magnificent ruin": on August 24, 1814, British troops set fire to the building, and only a sudden rainstorm prevented its complete destruction. Immediately after the fire, Congress met for one session in Blodget's Hotel, which was at Seventh and E Streets, NW. From 1815 to 1819, Congress occupied a building erected for it on First Street, NE., on part of the site now occupied by the Supreme Court Building. This building later came to be known as the Old Brick Capitol.

Latrobe returned to Washington in 1815, when he was rehired to restore the Capitol. In addition to making repairs, he took advantage of this opportunity to make further changes in the building's interior design (for example, an enlargement of the Senate Chamber) and introduce new materials (for example, marble discovered along the upper Potomac). However, he came under increasing pressure because of construction delays (most of which were beyond his control) and cost overruns; finally, he resigned his post in November 1817.

On January 8, 1818, Charles Bulfinch, a prominent Boston architect, was hired to succeed Latrobe. Continuing the restoration of the north and south wings, he was able to make the chambers for the Supreme Court, the House, and the Senate ready for use by 1819. Bulfinch also redesigned and supervised the construction of the Capitol's central section. The copper-covered wooden dome that topped this section was made higher than Bulfinch considered appropriate to the building's size (at the direction of President James Monroe and Secretary of State John Quincy Adams). After completing the last part of the building in 1826, Bulfinch spent the next few years on the Capitol's decoration and landscaping. In 1829, his work was done and his position with the government was terminated. In the 38 years following Bulfinch's tenure, the Capitol was entrusted to the care of the commissioner of public buildings.

1830–1868

The Capitol was by this point already an impressive structure. At ground level, its length was 351 feet 7½ inches and its width was 282 feet 10½ inches. Up to the year 1827—records from later years being incomplete—the project cost was $2,432,851.34. Improvements to the building continued in the years to come (running water in 1832, gas lighting in the 1840s), but by 1850 its size could no longer accommodate the increasing numbers of Senators and Representatives from newly admitted states. The Senate therefore voted to hold another competition, offering a prize of $500 for the best plan to extend the Capitol. Several suitable plans were submitted, some proposing an eastward extension of the building and others proposing the addition of large north and south wings. However, Congress was unable to decide between these two approaches, and the prize money was divided among five architects. Thus, the tasks of selecting a plan and appointing an architect fell to President Millard Fillmore.

Fillmore's choice was Thomas U. Walter, a Philadelphia architect who had entered the competition. On July 4, 1851, in a ceremony whose principal oration was delivered by Secretary of State Daniel Webster, the president laid the cornerstone in the northeast corner of the House wing. Over the next 14 years, Walter supervised the construction of the extension, ensuring their compatibility with the architectural style of the existing building. However, because the Aquia Creek sandstone used earlier had deteriorated noticeably, he chose to use marble for the exterior. For the veneer, Walter selected marble quarried at Lee, Massachusetts, and for the columns he used marble from Cockeysville, Maryland.

Walter faced several significant challenges during the course of construction. Chief among these was the steady imposition by the government of additional tasks without additional pay. Aside from his work on the Capitol extension, Walter designed the wings of the Patent

Office building, extensions to the Treasury and Post Office buildings, and the Marine barracks in Pensacola and Brooklyn. When the Library of Congress in the Capitol's west central section was gutted by a fire in 1851, Walter was commissioned to restore it. He also encountered obstacles in his work on the Capitol extensions. His location of the legislative chambers was changed in 1853 at the direction of President Franklin Pierce, based on the suggestions of the newly appointed supervising engineer, Captain Montgomery C. Meigs. In general, however, the project progressed rapidly: the House of Representatives was able to meet in its new chamber on December 16, 1857, and the Senate first met in its present chamber on January 4, 1859. The old House chamber was later designated National Statuary Hall. In 1861 most construction was suspended because of the Civil War, and the Capitol was used briefly as a military barracks, hospital, and bakery. In 1862 work on the entire building was resumed.

As the new wings were constructed, more than doubling the length of the Capitol, it became apparent that the dome erected by Bulfinch no longer suited the building's proportions. In 1855, Congress voted for its replacement based on Walter's design for a new, fireproof cast-iron dome. The old dome was removed in 1856, and 5,000,000 pounds of new masonry was placed on the existing rotunda walls. Iron used in the dome construction had an aggregate weight of 8,909,200 pounds and was lifted into place by steam-powered derricks.

In 1859, Thomas Crawford's plaster model for the Statue of Freedom, designed for the top of the dome, arrived from the sculptor's studio in Rome. With a height of 19 feet 6 inches, the statue was almost 3 feet taller than specified, and Walter was compelled to make revisions to his design for the dome. When cast in bronze by Clark Mills at his foundry on the outskirts of Washington, it weighed 14,985 pounds. The statue was lifted into place atop the dome in 1863, its final section being installed on December 2 to the accompaniment of gun salutes from the forts around the city.

The work on the dome and the extension was completed under the direction of Edward Clark, who had served as Walter's assistant and was appointed Architect of the Capitol in 1865 after Walter's resignation. In 1866, the Italian-born artist Constantino Brumidi finished the canopy fresco, a monumental painting entitled *The Apotheosis of George Washington*. The Capitol extension was completed in 1868.

1869–1902

Clark continued to hold the post of Architect of the Capitol until his death in 1902. During his tenure, the Capitol underwent considerable modernization. Steam heat was gradually installed in the old Capitol. In 1874, the first elevator was installed, and in the 1880s electric lighting began to replace gas lights.

Between 1884 and 1891, the marble terraces on the north, west, and south sides of the Capitol were constructed. As part of the landscape plan devised by Frederick Law Olmsted, these terraces not only added over 100 rooms to the Capitol but also provided a broader, more substantial visual base for the building.

On November 6, 1898, a gas explosion and fire in the original north wing dramatically illustrated the need for fireproofing. The roofs over the Statuary Hall wing and the original north wing were reconstructed and fireproofed, the work being completed in 1902 by Clark's successor, Elliott Woods. In 1901, the space in the west central front vacated by the Library of Congress was converted to committee rooms.

1903–1970

During the remainder of Woods's service, which ended with his death in 1923, no major structural work was required on the Capitol. The activities performed in the building were limited chiefly to cleaning and refurbishing the interior. David Lynn, the Architect of the Capitol from 1923 until his retirement in 1954, continued these tasks. Between July 1949 and January 1951, the corroded roofs and skylights of both wings and the connecting corridors were replaced with new roofs of concrete and steel, covered with copper. The cast-iron and glass ceilings of the House and Senate chambers were replaced with ceilings of stainless steel and plaster, with a laylight of carved glass and bronze in the middle of each. The House and Senate chambers were completely redecorated, modern lighting was added, and acoustical problems were solved. During this renovation program, the House and Senate vacated their chambers on several occasions so that the work could progress.

The next significant modification made to the Capitol was the east front extension. This project was carried out under the supervision of Architect of the Capitol J. George Stewart, who served from 1954 until his death in 1970. Begun in 1958, it involved the construction of a new east front 32 feet 6 inches east of the old front, faithfully reproducing the sandstone structure in marble. The old sandstone walls were not destroyed; rather, they were left in place to become a part of the interior wall and are now buttressed by the addition. The marble columns of the connecting corridors were also moved and reused. Other elements of this project included repairing the dome, constructing a subway terminal under the Senate steps, reconstructing those steps, cleaning both wings, birdproofing the building, providing furniture and furnishings for 90 new rooms created by the extension, and improving the lighting throughout the building. The project was completed in 1962.

1971–Present

During the nearly 25-year tenure (1971–1995) of Architect of the Capitol George M. White, FAIA, the building was both modernized and restored. Electronic voting equipment was installed in the House chamber in 1973; facilities were added to allow television coverage of the House and Senate debates in 1979 and 1986, respectively; and improved climate control, electronic surveillance systems, and new computer and communications facilities have been added to bring the Capitol up-to-date. The Old Senate Chamber, National Statuary Hall, and the Old Supreme Court Chamber, on the other hand, were restored to their mid-19th-century appearance in the 1970s.

In 1983, work began on the strengthening, renovation, and preservation of the west front of the Capitol. Structural problems had developed over the years because of defects in the original foundations, deterioration of the sandstone facing material, alterations to the basic building fabric (a fourth-floor addition and channeling of the walls to install interior utilities), and damage from the fires of 1814 and 1851 and the 1898 gas explosion.

To strengthen the structure, over 1,000 stainless steel tie rods were set into the building's masonry. More than 30 layers of paint were removed, and damaged stonework was repaired or replicated. Ultimately, 40 percent of the sandstone blocks were replaced with limestone. The walls were treated with a special consolidant and then painted to match the marble wings. The entire project was completed in 1987.

A related project, completed in January 1993, effected the repair of the Olmsted terraces, which had been subject to damage from settling, and converted the terrace courtyards into several thousand square feet of meeting space.

As the Capitol enters its third century, restoration and modernization work continues. Alan M. Hantman, FAIA, was appointed in February 1997 to a 10-year term as Architect of the Capitol. Projects under his direction included rehabilitation of the Capitol dome; conservation of murals; improvement of speech-reinforcement, electrical, and fire-protection systems in the Capitol and the Congressional office buildings; work on security improvements within the Capitol complex; restoration of the U.S. Botanic Garden Conservatory; the design and construction of the National Garden adjacent to the Botanic Garden Conservatory; renovation of the building systems in the Dirksen Senate Office Building; publication of the first comprehensive history of the Capitol to appear in a century; and construction of the Capitol Visitor Center. At the end of Mr. Hantman's term in February 2007, Mr. Stephen T. Ayers, FAIA, LEED AP, assumed the position of Acting Architect of the Capitol. On February 24, 2010, President Barack Obama nominated Mr. Ayers to serve as the 11th Architect of the Capitol. On May 12, 2010, the United States Senate, by unanimous consent, confirmed Mr. Ayers, and on May 13, 2010, the President officially appointed Mr. Ayers to a 10-year term as Architect of the Capitol.

HOUSE OFFICE BUILDINGS

Cannon House Office Building

An increased membership of the Senate and House resulted in a demand for additional rooms for the accommodations of the Senators and Representatives. On March 3, 1903, the Congress authorized the erection of a fireproofed office building for the use of the House. It was designed by the firm of Carrere & Hastings of New York City in the Beaux Arts style. The first brick was laid July 5, 1905, in square No. 690, and formal exercises were held at the laying of the cornerstone on April 14, 1906, in which President Theodore Roosevelt participated. The building was completed and occupied January 10, 1908. A subsequent change in the basis of congressional representation made necessary the building of an additional story in 1913–1914. The total cost of the building, including site, furnishings, equipment, and the subway connecting it with the U.S. Capitol, amounted to $4,860,155.

This office building contains about 500 rooms, and was considered at the time of its completion fully equipped for all the needs of a modern building for office purposes. A garage was added in the building's courtyard in the 1960s.

Pursuant to authority in the Second Supplemental Appropriations Act, 1955, and subsequent action of the House Office Building Commission, remodeling of the Cannon Building began in 1966. The estimated cost of this work was $5,200,000. Pursuant to the provisions of Public Law 87–453, approved May 21, 1962, the building was named in honor of Joseph G. Cannon of Illinois, who was Speaker at the time the building was constructed.

LONGWORTH HOUSE OFFICE BUILDING

Under legislation contained in the Authorization Act of January 10, 1929, and in the urgent deficiency bill of March 4, 1929, provisions were made for an additional House office building, to be located on the west side of New Jersey Avenue (opposite the first House office building). The building was designed by the Allied Architects of Washington in the Neoclassical Revival style.

The cornerstone was laid June 24, 1932, and the building was completed on April 20, 1933. It contains 251 two-room suites and 16 committee rooms. Each suite and committee room is provided with a storeroom. Eight floors are occupied by members. The basement and subbasement contain shops and mechanical areas needed for the maintenance of the building. A cafeteria was added in the building's courtyard in the 1960s. The cost of this building, including site, furnishings, and equipment, was $7,805,705. Pursuant to the provisions of Public Law 87–453, approved May 21, 1962, the building was named in honor of Nicholas Longworth of Ohio, who was Speaker when the second House office building was constructed.

RAYBURN HOUSE OFFICE BUILDING AND OTHER RELATED CHANGES AND IMPROVEMENTS

Under legislation contained in the Second Supplemental Appropriations Act, 1955, provision was made for construction of a fireproof office building for the House of Representatives.

All work was carried forward by the Architect of the Capitol under the direction of the House Office Building Commission at a cost totaling $135,279,000.

The Rayburn Building is connected to the Capitol by a subway. Designs for the building were prepared by the firm of Harbeson, Hough, Livingston & Larson of Philadelphia, Associate Architects. The building contains 169 congressional suites; full-committee hearing rooms for 9 standing committees, 16 subcommittee hearing rooms, committee staff rooms, and other committee facilities; a large cafeteria and other restaurant facilities; an underground garage; and a variety of liaison offices, press and television facilities, maintenance and equipment shops or rooms, and storage areas. This building has nine stories and a penthouse for machinery.

The cornerstone was laid May 24, 1962, by John W. McCormack, Speaker of the House of Representatives. President John F. Kennedy participated in the cornerstone laying and delivered the address.

A portion of the basement floor was occupied beginning March 12, 1964, by House of Representatives personnel moved from the George Washington Inn property. Full occupancy of the Rayburn Building, under the room-filing regulations, was begun February 23, 1965, and completed April 2, 1965. Pursuant to the provisions of Public Law 87–453, approved May 21, 1962, the building was named in honor of Sam Rayburn of Texas.

House Office Building Annex No. 2, named the ''Gerald R. Ford House of Representatives Office Building,'' was acquired in 1975 from the General Services Administration. The structure, located at Second and D Streets, SW., was built in 1939 for the Federal Bureau of Investigation as a fingerprint file archives. This building has approximately 432,000 square feet of space.

SENATE OFFICE BUILDINGS

RICHARD BREVARD RUSSELL SENATE OFFICE BUILDING

In 1891, the Senate provided itself with office space by the purchase of the Maltby Building, then located on the northwest corner of B Street (now Constitution Avenue) and

New Jersey Avenue, NW. When it was condemned as an unsafe structure, Senators needed safer and more commodious office space. Under authorization of the Act of April 28, 1904, square 686 on the northeast corner of Delaware Avenue and B Street, NE., was purchased as a site for the Senate Office Building. The plans for the House Office Building were adapted for the Senate Office Building by the firm of Carrere & Hastings, with the exception that the side of the building fronting on First Street, NE., was temporarily omitted. The cornerstone was laid without special exercises on July 31, 1906, and the building was occupied March 5, 1909. In 1931, the completion of the fourth side of the building was commenced. In 1933, it was completed, together with alterations to the C Street facade and the construction of terraces, balustrades, and approaches. The cost of the completed building, including the site, furnishings, equipment, and the subway connecting it with the United States Capitol, was $8,390,892.

The building was named the "Richard Brevard Russell Senate Office Building" by Senate Resolution 296, 92nd Congress, agreed to October 11, 1972, as amended by Senate Resolution 295, 96th Congress, agreed to December 3, 1979.

Everett McKinley Dirksen Senate Office Building

Under legislation contained in the Second Deficiency Appropriations Act, 1948, Public Law 80–785, provision was made for an additional office building for the United States Senate with limits of cost of $1,100,000 for acquisition of the site and $20,600,000 for constructing and equipping the building.

The construction cost limit was subsequently increased to $24,196,000. All work was carried forward by the Architect of the Capitol under the direction of the Senate Office Building Commission. The New York firm of Eggers & Higgins served as the consulting architect.

The site was acquired and cleared in 1948–1949 at a total cost of $1,011,492.

A contract for excavation, concrete footings, and mats for the new building was awarded in January 1955, in the amount of $747,200. Groundbreaking ceremonies were held January 26, 1955.

A contract for the superstructure of the new building was awarded September 9, 1955, in the amount of $17,200,000. The cornerstone was laid July 13, 1956.

As a part of this project, a new underground subway system was installed from the Capitol to both the Old and New Senate Office Buildings.

An appropriation of $1,000,000 for furniture and furnishings for the new building was provided in 1958. The building was accepted for beneficial occupancy on October 15, 1958.

The building was named the "Everett McKinley Dirksen Senate Office Building" by Senate Resolution 296, 92nd Congress, agreed to October 11, 1972, and Senate Resolution 295, 96th Congress, agreed to December 3, 1979.

Philip A. Hart Senate Office Building

Construction as an extension to the Dirksen Senate Office Building was authorized on October 31, 1972; legislation enacted in subsequent years increased the scope of the project and established a total cost ceiling of $137,700,400. The firm of John Carl Warnecke & Associates served as Associate Architect for the project.

Senate Resolution 525, passed August 30, 1976, amended by Senate Resolution 295, 96th Congress, agreed to December 3, 1979, provided that upon completion of the extension it would be named the "Philip A. Hart Senate Office Building" to honor the Senator from Michigan.

The contract for clearing of the site, piping for utilities, excavation, and construction of foundation was awarded in December 1975. Groundbreaking took place January 5, 1976. The contract for furnishing and delivery of the exterior stone was awarded in February 1977, and the contract for the superstructure, which included wall and roof systems and the erection of all exterior stonework, was awarded in October 1977. The contract for the first portion of the interior and related work was awarded in December 1978. A contract for interior finishing was awarded in July 1980. The first suite was occupied on November 22, 1982. Alexander Calder's mobile/stabile *Mountains and Clouds* was installed in the building's atrium in November 1986.

CAPITOL POWER PLANT

During the development of the plans for the Cannon and Russell Buildings, the question of heat, light, and power was considered. The Senate and House wings of the Capitol were heated by separate heating plants. The Library of Congress also had a heating plant for that building. It was determined that needs for heating and lighting and electrical power could be met by a central power plant.

A site was selected in Garfield Park. Since this park was a Government reservation, an appropriation was not required to secure title. The determining factors leading to the selection of this site were its proximity to the tracks of what is now the Penn Central Railroad and to the buildings to be served.

The dimensions of the Capitol Power Plant, which was authorized on April 28, 1904, and completed in 1910, were 244 feet 8 inches by 117 feet.

The buildings originally served by the Capitol Power Plant were connected to it by a reinforced-concrete steam tunnel.

In September 1951, when the demand for electrical energy was reaching the maximum capacity of the Capitol Power Plant, arrangements were made to purchase electrical service from the local public utility company and to discontinue electrical generation. The heating and cooling functions of the Capitol Power Plant were expanded in 1935, 1939, 1958, 1973, and 1980. A new refrigeration plant modernization and expansion project was completed in 2007.

U.S. CAPITOL GROUNDS

A Description of the Grounds

Originally a wooded wilderness, the U.S. Capitol Grounds today provide a park-like setting for the Nation's Capitol, offering a picturesque counterpoint to the building's formal architecture. The grounds immediately surrounding the Capitol are bordered by a stone wall and cover an area of 58.8 acres. Their boundaries are Independence Avenue on the south, Constitution Avenue on the north, First Street, NE./SE., on the east, and First Street, NW./SW., on the west. Over 100 varieties of trees and bushes are planted around the Capitol, and thousands of flowers are used in seasonal displays. In contrast to the building's straight, neoclassical lines, most of the walkways in the grounds are curved. Benches along the paths offer pleasant spots for visitors to appreciate the building, its landscape, and the surrounding areas, most notably the Mall to the west.

The grounds were designed by Frederick Law Olmsted (1822–1903), who planned the landscaping of the area that was performed from 1874 to 1892. Olmsted, who also designed New York's Central Park, is considered the greatest American landscape architect of his day. He was a pioneer in the development of public parks in America, and many of his designs were influenced by his studies of European parks, gardens, and estates. In describing his plan for the Capitol Grounds, Olmsted noted that, "The ground is in design part of the Capitol, but in all respects subsidiary to the central structure." Therefore, he was careful not to group trees or other landscape features in any way that would distract the viewer from the Capitol. The use of sculpture and other ornamentation has also been kept to a minimum.

Many of the trees on the Capitol Grounds have historic or memorial associations. Over 30 states have made symbolic gifts of their state trees to the Capitol Grounds. Many of the trees on the grounds bear plaques that identify their species and their historic significance.

At the East Capitol Street entrance to the Capitol plaza are two large rectangular stone fountains. Six massive red granite lamp piers topped with light fixtures in wrought-iron cages, and 16 smaller bronze light fixtures, line the paved plaza. Three sets of benches are enclosed with wrought-iron railings and grilles; the roofed bench was originally a shelter for streetcar passengers.

The northern part of the grounds offers a shaded walk among trees, flowers, and shrubbery. A small, hexagonal brick structure, named the Summer House, may be found in the northwest corner of the grounds. This structure contains shaded benches, a central ornamental fountain, and three public drinking fountains. In a small grotto on the eastern side of the Summer House, a stream of water flows and splashes over rocks to create a pleasing sound and cool the summer breezes.

A Brief History of the Grounds Before Olmsted

The land on which the Capitol stands was first occupied by the Manahoacs and the Monacans, who were subtribes of the Algonquin Indians. Early settlers reported that these tribes occasionally held councils not far from the foot of the hill. This land eventually became a part of Cerne Abbey Manor, and at the time of its acquisition by the Federal Government it was owned by Daniel Carroll of Duddington.

The "Residence Act" of 1790 provided that the Federal Government should be established in a permanent location by the year 1800. In early March 1791, the commissioners of the city of Washington, who had been appointed by President George Washington, selected the French engineer Pierre Charles L'Enfant to plan the new federal city. L'Enfant decided to locate the Capitol at the elevated east end of the Mall (on what was then called Jenkins' Hill); he described the site as "a pedestal waiting for a monument."

At this time, the site of the Capitol was a relative wilderness partly overgrown with scrub oak. Oliver Wolcott, a signer of the Declaration of Independence, described the soil as an "*exceedingly stiff* clay, becoming dust in dry and mortar in rainy weather."

In 1825, a plan was devised for imposing order on the Capitol Grounds, and it was carried out for almost 15 years. The plan divided the area into flat, rectangular grassy areas bordered by trees, flower beds, and gravel walks. The growth of the trees, however, soon deprived the other plantings of nourishment, and the design became increasingly difficult to maintain in light of sporadic and small appropriations. John Foy, who had charge of the grounds during most of this period, was "superseded for political reasons," and the area was then maintained with little care or forethought. Many rapidly growing but short-lived trees were introduced and soon depleted the soil; a lack of proper pruning and thinning left the majority of the area's vegetation ill-grown, feeble, or dead. Virtually all was removed by the early 1870s, either to make way for building operations during Thomas U. Walter's enlargement of the Capitol or as required by changes in grading to accommodate the new work on the building or the alterations to surrounding streets.

The Olmsted Plan

The mid-19th-century extension of the Capitol, in which the House and Senate wings and the new dome were added, also required that the Capitol Grounds be enlarged, and in 1874 Frederick Law Olmsted was commissioned to plan and oversee the project. As noted above, Olmsted was determined that the grounds should complement the building. In addition, he addressed an architectural problem that had persisted for some years: from the west (the growth of the city had nothing to do with the terraces)—the earthen terraces at the building's base made it seem inadequately supported at the top of the hill. The solution, Olmsted believed, was to construct marble terraces on the north, west, and south sides of the building, thereby causing it to "gain greatly in the supreme qualities of stability, endurance, and repose." He submitted his design for these features in 1875, and after extensive study, it was approved.

Work on the grounds began in 1874, concentrating first on the east side and then progressing to the west, north, and south sides. First, the ground was reduced in elevation. Almost 300,000 cubic yards of earth and other material were eventually removed, and over 200 trees were removed. New sewer, gas, and water lines were installed. The soil was then enriched with fertilizers to provide a suitable growth medium for new plantings. Paths and roadways were graded and laid.

By 1876, gas and water service was completed for the entire grounds, and electrical lamp-lighting apparatuses had been installed. Stables and workshops had been removed from the northwest and southwest corners. A streetcar system north and south of the west grounds had been relocated farther from the Capitol, and ornamental shelters were in place at the north and south car-track termini. The granite and bronze lamp piers and ornamental bronze lamps for the east plaza area were completed.

Work accelerated in 1877. By this time, according to Olmsted's report, "altogether 7,837 plants and trees [had] been set out." However, not all had survived: hundreds were stolen or destroyed by vandals, and, as Olmsted explained, "a large number of cattle [had] been caught trespassing." Other work met with less difficulty. Foot-walks were laid with artificial stone, a mixture of cement and sand, and approaches were paved with concrete. An ornamental iron trellis had been installed on the northern east-side walk, and another was under way on the southern walk.

The 1878 appointment of watchmen to patrol the grounds was quite effective in preventing further vandalism, allowing the lawns to be completed and much shrubbery to be added. Also in that year, the roads throughout the grounds were paved.

Most of the work required on the east side of the grounds was completed by 1879, and effort thus shifted largely to the west side. The Pennsylvania Avenue approach was virtually finished, and work on the Maryland Avenue approach had begun. The stone walls on the west side of the grounds were almost finished, and the red granite lamp piers were placed at the eastward entrance from Pennsylvania Avenue.

In the years 1880–1882, many features of the grounds were completed. These included the walls and coping around the entire perimeter, the approaches and entrances, and the Summer House. Work on the terraces began in 1882, and most work from this point until 1892 was concentrated on these structures.

In 1885, Olmsted retired from superintendency of the terrace project; he continued to direct the work on the grounds until 1889. Landscaping work was performed to adapt the surrounding areas to the new construction, grading the ground and planting shrubs at the bases of the walls, as the progress of the masonry work allowed. Some trees and other types of vegetation were removed, either because they had decayed or as part of a careful thinning-out process.

In 1888, the wrought-iron lamp frames and railings were placed at the Maryland Avenue entrance, making it the last to be completed. In 1892, the streetcar track that had extended into grounds from Independence Avenue was removed.

The Grounds After Olmsted

In the last years of the 19th century, work on the grounds consisted chiefly of maintenance and repairs as needed. Trees, lawns, and plantings were tended, pruned, and thinned to allow their best growth. This work was quite successful: by 1894, the grounds were so deeply shaded by trees and shrubs that Architect of the Capitol Edward Clark recommended an all-night patrol by watchmen to ensure public safety. A hurricane in September 1896 damaged or destroyed a number of trees, requiring extensive removals in the following year. Also in 1897, electric lighting replaced gas lighting in the grounds.

Between 1910 and 1935, 61.4 acres north of Constitution Avenue were added to the grounds. Approximately 100 acres was added in subsequent years, bringing the total area to 274 acres. Late in 2011, care for the Grant Memorial and the reflecting pool at the eastern end of the National Mall was transferred from the National Park Service to the Architect of the Capitol.

Since 1983, increased security measures have been put into effect; however, the area still functions in many ways as a public park, and visitors are welcome to use the walks to tour the grounds. Demonstrations and ceremonies are often held on the grounds. In the summer, a series of evening concerts by the bands of the Armed Forces is offered free of charge on the west front plaza. On various holidays, concerts by the National Symphony Orchestra are held on the west front lawn.

LEGISLATIVE BRANCH

CONGRESSIONAL BUDGET OFFICE

H2–405 Ford House Office Building, Second and D Streets, SW., 20515
phone (202) 226–2600, http://www.cbo.gov

[Created by Public Law 93–344]

Director.—Keith Hall, 6–2700.
Deputy Director.—Mark P. Hadley, 6–2700.
Associate Director for—
Communications.—Deborah Kilroe, 6–2602.
Legislative Affairs.—Leigh Angres, 6–2701.
Economic Analysis.—Jeffrey Kling, 6–2700.
Economic Analysis.—Wendy Edelberg, 6–2700.
General Counsel.—T.J. McGrath, 6–2700.
Assistant Director for—
Budget Analysis.—Theresa Gullo, 6–2800.
Financial Analysis.—Sebastian Gay, 6–3579.
Health, Retirement, and Long-Term Analysis.—David Weaver, 6–2666.
Macroeconomic Analysis.—Jeffrey Werling, 6–2750.
Management, Business and Information Services.—Joseph E. Evans Jr., 6–2600.
Microeconomic Studies.—Joseph Kile, 6–2940.
National Security.—David E. Mosher, 6–2900.
Tax Analysis.—John McClelland, 6–2680.

GOVERNMENT ACCOUNTABILITY OFFICE

441 G Street, NW., 20548, phone (202) 512–3000

http://www.gao.gov

Comptroller General of the United States.—Gene L. Dodaro, 512–5500, fax 512–5507.
Chief Operating Officer.—Patricia Dalton, 512–5600.
Chief Administrative Officer/Chief Financial Officer.—Karl Maschino, 512–5800.
General Counsel.—Susan A. Poling, 512–5400.
Deputy General Counsel and Ethics Counselor.—Thomas A. Armstrong, 512–5207.
Deputy Ethics Counselor.—James Lager, 512–8170.

TEAMS

Acquisition and Sourcing Management.—Michele Mackin, 512–4841.
Applied Research and Methods.—Nancy Kingsbury, 512–2700.
Defense Capabilities and Management.—Cathleen A. Berrick, 512–4300.
Education Workforce and Income Security.—Barbara D. Bovbjerg, 512–7215.
Financial Management and Assurance.—Gary Engel, 512–2600.
Financial Markets and Community Investments.—Orice Williams Brown, 512–8678.
Forensic Audits and Investigative Services.—Johana Ayers, 512–6722.
Health Care.—Angela (Nikki) Clowers, 512–7114.
Homeland Security and Justice.—George A. Scott, 512–8777.
Information Technology.—Valerie Melvin, 512–7351.
International Affairs and Trade.—Charles Johnson, 512–4128.
Natural Resources and Environment.—Mark Gaffigan, 512–3841.
Physical Infrastructure.—Dan Bertoni, 512–2834.
Strategic Issues.—J. Christopher Mihm, 512–6806.

SUPPORT FUNCTIONS

Congressional Relations.—Katherine Siggerud, 512–4400.
Legislative Advisers: Carlos Diz, 512–8256; Rosa Harris, 512–9492; Carolyn Kirby, 512–9843; David Lewis, 512–7176; Tim Minelli, 512–8443; Paul Thompson, 512–9867; Mary Frances Widner, 512–3804; Dibattista Patrick, 512–6576.
Associate Legislative Adviser.—Martene Rhed, 512–5414.
Field Operations.—Linda Calbom (206) 287–4809.
Inspector General.—Adam Trzeciak, 512–8110.
Opportunity and Inclusiveness.—Reginald E. Jones, 512–8401.
Personnel Appeals Board.—Robert Hermann, 512–7507.
Public Affairs.—Charles ''Chuck'' Young, 512–3823.
Audit Policy and Quality Assurance.—Tim Bowling, 512–6100.
Strategic Planning and External Liaison.—James-Christian Blockwood, 512–2639.

MISSION SUPPORT OFFICES

Chief Information Officer.—Howard Williams, Jr., 512–5589.
Controller/Deputy Chief Financial Officer.—William Anderson, 512–2908.
Chief Human Capital Officer.—William (Bill) White, 512–5811.
Infrastructure Operations.—Terry Dorn, 512–6923.
Professional Development Program.—Terri Russell, 512–5649.

U.S. GOVERNMENT PUBLISHING OFFICE

732 North Capitol Street, NW., 20401

Phone (202) 512–0000, http://www.gpo.gov

Director.—Vacant.
Deputy Director.—Herbert H. Jackson, Jr., (acting), 512–1100, hjackson@gpo.gov.
Chief of Staff.—Richard G. Davis (acting), 512–1100, rdavis@gpo.gov.
General Counsel.—Kerry L. Miller (acting), 512–0033, kmiller@gpo.gov.
Managing Director, Equal Employment Opportunity.—Mark A. ''Tony'' Paras (acting), 512–2331, mparas@gpo.gov.
Chief Financial Officer.—Steven T. Shedd, 512–2073, sshedd@gpo.gov.
Chief Administrative Officer.—Herbert H. Jackson, Jr., 512–0952, hjackson@gpo.gov.
Superintendent of Documents.—Laurie Beyer Hall, 512–1313, lhall@gpo.gov.
Inspector General.—Melinda M. Miguel, 512–0039, mmiguel@gpo.gov.

CHIEF OF STAFF

Chief of Staff.—Richard G. Davis (acting), 512–1622, rdavis@gpo.gov.

COMMUNICATIONS

Congressional Relations Officer.—Yalanda Johnson (acting), 512–1991, yjohnson@gpo.gov.
Chief Public Relations Officer.—Gary G. Somerset, 512–1957, gsomerset@gpo.gov.
Manager, Branding and Web Design.—Dean A. Gardei, 512–0245, dgardei@gpo.gov.

PROGRAMS, STRATEGY, AND TECHNOLOGY

Chief Technology Officer.—Richard G. Davis, 512–1622, rdavis@gpo.gov.

GENERAL COUNSEL

General Counsel.—Kerry L. Miller (acting), 512–0033, kmiller@gpo.gov.
Deputy General Counsel.—Kerry L. Miller, 512–0033, kmiller@gpo.gov.
Associate General Counsel, Labor Relations.—Melissa S. Hatfield, 512–0064, mhatfield@gpo.gov.

EQUAL EMPLOYMENT OPPORTUNITY

Managing Director, Equal Employment Opportunity.—Mark A. "Tony" Paras (acting), 512–2331, mparas@gpo.gov.
Assistant Managing Director, Equal Employment Opportunity Program.—Mark A. "Tony" Paras, 512–2331, mparas@gpo.gov.

FINANCE

Chief Financial Officer.—Steven T. Shedd, 512–2073, sshedd@gpo.gov.
Deputy Chief Financial Officer.—William L. Boesch, Jr., 512–2073, wboesch@gpo.gov.

CHIEF ADMINISTRATIVE OFFICER

Chief Administrative Officer.—Herbert H. Jackson, Jr., 512–1100, hjackson@gpo.gov.

HUMAN CAPITAL

Chief Human Capital Officer.—Dan M. Mielke, 512–1182, dmielke@gpo.gov.
Chief of:
Human Capital Operations.—Lyvette Wallace, 512–1182, lwallace@gpo.gov.
Workforce Development, Education and Training.—Stewart Lane, 512–1144, slane@gpo.gov.
Employee Relations and Policy.—Jose Conejo, 512–0097, jconejo@gpo.gov.
Medical Officer.—Telisha D. Anthony, FNP–BC, 512–2061, tanthony@gpo.gov.

INFORMATION TECHNOLOGY

Chief Information Officer.—Vacant, 512–1040.
Deputy Chief Information Officer.—Vacant, 512–1394.
Chief of:
Applications Development and Management Division.—Layton F. Clay, 512–2001, lclay@gpo.gov.
Information Technology Security Division.—John L. Hannan, 512–1021, jhannan@gpo.gov.
Information Technology Operations Division.—Nadeem Sahibzada, 512–1406, nsahibzada@gpo.gov.

SECURITY SERVICES

Chief Security Officer.—LaMont R. Vernon, 512–1103, lvernon@gpo.gov.
Commander, Uniformed Police Branch.—Paul D. Epley, 512–0872, pepley@gpo.gov.
Chief of:
Physical Security.—Gresham Harkless, 512–0988, gharkless@gpo.gov.
Product Security.—Aaron P. Williams, 512–2041, apwilliams@gpo.gov.
Safety Branch.—Lonny Beal, 512–0537, lbeal@gpo.gov.

ACQUISITION SERVICES

Managing Director, Chief Acquisition Officer.—Lorna Baptiste-Jones, 512–0351, lbaptiste-jones@gpo.gov.
Supervisor, Post-Award Team.—Beverly J. Williams, 512–2010, ext. 31200, bwilliams@gpo.gov.
Supervisor, Pre-Award Team.—Ronald Ortega, 512–0803, rortega@gpo.gov.
Supervisor, Acquisition Planning and Support Team.—Reginald Walker, 512–2010, ext. 31500, rwalker@gpo.gov.

DEPUTY DIRECTOR OF THE GOVERNMENT PUBLISHING OFFICE

Deputy Director.—Herbert H. Jackson, Jr., (acting), 512–1100, hjackson@gpo.gov.

OFFICIAL JOURNALS OF GOVERNMENT

Managing Director.—Lyle L. Green, 512–0224, llgreen@gpo.gov.

Chief of:

Congressional Publishing Services.—Vacant, 512–0224.

Congressional Record Index Office.—Marcia Thompson, 512–0275, mthompson2@gpo.gov.

Office of Federal Register Publishing Services Manager.—Jeffrey D. MacAfee, 512–2100, jmacafee@gpo.gov.

PLANT OPERATIONS

Managing Director.—John W. Crawford, 512–0707, jcrawford@gpo.gov.

Deputy Managing Director.—Gregory E. Estep, 512–0707, gestep@gpo.gov.

Chief, Engineering Services.—Michael Dietz, 512–1976, mdietz@gpo.gov.

Production Manager (shift 1).—Vacant, 512–1407.

Assistant Production Manager.—Ibrahim N. ''Abe'' Sussan, 512–0589, isussan@gpo.gov.

Production Manager (shift 3).—Vacant, 512–0625.

Manager of:

Bindery Operations.—Gary W. Evans, 512–0673, gevans@gpo.gov.

Prepress Operations.—Francine R. ''Renee'' Rosa, 512–1651, frosa@gpo.gov.

Production Engineering.—David J. Robare, 512–1370, drobare@gpo.gov.

Press Operations.—Vacant, 512–0593.

Production Planning and Control.—Robert M. Martein, 512–1470, rmartein@gpo.gov.

Quality Control and Inventory Management.—Michael P. Mooney, 512–0766, mmooney@gpo.gov.

SECURITY AND INTELLIGENT DOCUMENTS

Managing Director.—Stephen G. LeBlanc, 512–2285, sleblanc@gpo.gov.

Operations Manager.—David H. Ford, 512–1194, dford@gpo.gov.

Manager of:

Business Development.—Gerald Egan, 512–2010, gegan@gpo.gov.

New Product and Program Development.—Scott Stole, 512–0697, sstole@gpo.gov.

Secure Production (DC).—Melinda Ford, 512–1485, mford@gpo.gov.

Secure Production (Stennis).—David Spiers (228) 813–1716, dspiers@gpo.gov.

CUSTOMER SERVICES

Managing Director.—Sandra K. MacAfee, 512–0320, smacafee@gpo.gov.

Deputy Managing Director.—Vacant, 512–2213.

Chief of:

DC Agency Procurement Services.—Julie A. Hasenfus, 512–0655, jhasenfus@gpo.gov.

Regional Agency Procurement Services.—Teddy J. Priebe, 512–2015, tpriebe@gpo.gov.

Sales and Publishing Support.—Kirk D. Knoll, 512–1147, kknoll@gpo.gov.

Manager, Creative and Digital Media Services.—Ronald J. Keeney, 512–2012, rkeeney@gpo.gov.

GPO REGIONAL PRINTING PROCUREMENT OFFICES

Atlanta.—Elizabeth A. Rich, Manager, 3715 Northside Parkway, Suite 4–305, Atlanta, GA 30327 (404) 605–9160, fax 605–9185, infoatlanta@gpo.gov.

Boston.—Debra L. Rozdzielski, Manager, John F. Kennedy Federal Building, 15 New Sudbury Street, E270, Boston, MA 02203–0002 (617) 565–1370, fax 565–1385, infoboston@gpo.gov.

Charleston Office.—Richard W. Gilbert, Manager, 2825 Noisette Boulevard, Charleston, SC 29405–1819 (843) 743–2036, fax 743–2068, infocharleston@gpo.gov.

Chicago.—Clint J. Mixon, Manager, 200 North LaSalle Street, Suite 810, Chicago, IL 60601–1055 (312) 353–3916, fax 886–3163, infochicago@gpo.gov.

Columbus.—Michael J. Sommer, Manager, 1335 Dublin Road, Suite 112–B, Columbus, OH 43215–7034 (614) 488–4616, fax 488–4577, infocolumbus@gpo.gov.

Dallas.—Vacant, Manager, Federal Office Building, 1100 Commerce Street, Room 731, Dallas, TX 75242–1027 (214) 767–0451, fax 767–4101, infodallas@gpo.gov.

Denver.—Diane L. Abeyta, Manager, 12345 West Alameda Parkway, Suite 208, Lakewood, CO 80228–2824 (303) 236–5292, fax 236–5304, infodenver@gpo.gov.

Philadelphia.—Debra L. Rozdzielski, Manager, 928 Jaymore Road, Suite A190, Southampton, PA 18966–3820 (215) 364–6465, fax 364–6479, infophiladelphia@gpo.gov.

San Antonio Office.—Vacant, Manager, 1531 Connally Street, Suite 2, Lackland AFB, TX 78236–5515 (210) 675–1480, fax 675–2429, infosanantonio@gpo.gov.

San Diego Office.—Michael A. Barnes, Manager, 8880 Rio San Diego Drive, 8th Floor, San Diego, CA 92108–3609 (619) 209–6178, fax 209–6179, infosandiego@gpo.gov.

San Francisco.—Michael A. Barnes, Manager, 536 Stone Road, Suite 1, Benicia, CA 94510–1170 (707) 748–1970, fax 748–1980, infosanfran@gpo.gov.

Seattle.—Roland Whitehurst, Manager, Federal Center South, 4735 East Marginal Way South, Seattle, WA 98134–2397 (206) 764–3726, fax 764–3301, infoseattle@gpo.gov.

Virginia Beach, VA.—Richard W. Gilbert, Manager, 291 Independence Boulevard, Suite 401, Virginia Beach, VA 23462 (757) 490–7940, fax 490–7950, infovirginiabeach@gpo.gov.

SUPERINTENDENT OF DOCUMENTS

Superintendent of Documents.—Laurie Beyer Hall, 512–1313, lhall@gpo.gov.

LIBRARY SERVICES AND CONTENT MANAGEMENT

Managing Director.—Laurie Beyer Hall, 512–0185, lhall@gpo.gov.
Chief of:
LSCM Outreach and Support.—Robin L. Haun-Mohamed, 512–0052, rhaun-mohamed @gpo.gov.
Projects and Systems.—Anthony Donovan Smith, 512–1431, adsmith@gpo.gov.
Library Technical Services.—Fang H. Gao, 512–1966, fgao@gpo.gov.

PUBLICATION AND INFORMATION SALES

Managing Director.—Vacant.
Chief, Publication Sales and Marketing.—Jeffrey Turner, 512–1055, jturner@gpo.gov.
Content Acquisitions and Contact Center.

GPO BOOKSTORE

Metropolitan Area: GPO Bookstore, 710 North Capitol Street, NW., Washington, DC 20401, 512–0132.

TO ORDER PUBLICATIONS

Phone toll free (866) 512–1800 for Subscriptions and Publications [DC area: (202) 512–1800, fax: (202) 512–2104; bookstore walk-in: (202) 512–1032]. Mail orders to the Superintendent of Documents, P.O. Box 371954, Pittsburgh, PA 15250–7954, or order online from the U.S. Government Bookstore at *http://bookstore.gpo.gov.* GPO customer support: ContactCenter@gpo.gov.

DISTRIBUTION SERVICES AND OUTREACH

Chief, Publication and Information Sales.—Lisa L. Williams, 512–1065, llwilliams@gpo.gov.

LAUREL FACILITY

Operations Manager.—Robert E. Mitchell, 8660 Cherry Lane, Mail Stop: SSR, Laurel, MD 20707–4982 (202) 512–2317, remitchell@gpo.gov.

CONGRESSMAN FRANK EVANS GOVERNMENT PUBLISHING OFFICE DISTRIBUTION CENTER

Operations Manager.—Thomas Hunt, P.O. Box 4007, Pueblo, CO 81003 (719) 295–2678, fax 948–3315, thunt@gpo.gov.

LIBRARY OF CONGRESS

101 Independence Avenue, SE., 20540, phone (202) 707–5000

http://www.loc.gov

OFFICE OF THE LIBRARIAN, LM 608, 707–5205

The Librarian of Congress.—Carla Hayden, 707–5205.
Deputy Librarian of Congress.—Mark Sweeney (acting), 707–0351.
Assistant to the Deputy Librarian.—Terri Humphries, LM 608, 707–0351.
Chief of Staff.—Liz Morrison, LM 608, 707–5205.
Chief Communications Officer.—Roswell Encina, LM 608, 707–5205.
Senior Advisor to the Librarian.—Ryan Ramsey, LM 608, 707–5205.
Director, Office of:
Communications.—Gayle Osterberg, LM 106, 707–2905.
Congressional Relations.—Kathleen G. Ott, LM 611, 707–6577.
Development.—Susan Siegel, LM 605, 707–1447.
General Counsel.—Elizabeth Pugh, LM 601, 707–6316.
EEO and DP.—Vicki Magnus, LM 612, 707–3343.
Strategic Planning and Performance Management.—Dianne Houghton, LM 608, 707–3096.
Special Events and Public Programs.—Mary Eno, LM 623, 707–5218.
Multimedia.—Jim Cannady, LM G51, 707–4595.

OFFICE OF THE CHIEF OPERATING OFFICER, LM 643

Chief Operating Officer.—Edward R. Jablonski, LM 643, 707–8397.
Chief Financial Officer.—Mary Klutts, LM 613, 707–2418.
Director, Office of:
Contracts and Grants Management.—Ronald Backes, 707–0833.
Human Resources Services.—Rachel Bouman, LM 645, 707–7364.
Integrated Support Services.—Elizabeth Scheffler, LM 327, 707–6042.
Security and Emergency Preparedness.—Kenneth Lopez, LM G03, 707–9410.

CONGRESSIONAL RESEARCH SERVICE, LM 203, 707–5700

Director.—Mary B. Mazanec, LM 203, 707–5775.
Deputy Director.—TJ Halstead, LM 203, 707–7981.
Counselor to the Director.—Lizanne D. Kelley, LM 203, 707–8833.
Associate Director, Office of:
Administrative Operations.—Francois A. DiFolco, LM 203, 707–2877.
Congressional Information and Publishing.—Clifford T. Cohen, LM 223, 707–1858.
Information Management and Technology.—John E. Rutledge, LM 413, 707–0442.
Assistant Director, Division of:
American Law.—Karen J. Lewis, LM 227, 707–7460.
Domestic Social Policy.—Laura B. Shrestha, LM 323, 707–7046.
Foreign Affairs, Defense, and Trade.—Michael L. Moodie, LM 315, 707–8470.
Government and Finance.—Jeffrey W. Seifert, LM 303, 707–0781.
Knowledge Services Group.—Lillian W. Gassie, LM 215, 707–7573.
Resources, Science, and Industry.—Dana A. Shea, LM 423, 707–6844.

U.S. COPYRIGHT OFFICE, LM 403, 707–8350

Register of Copyrights and Director.—Karyn Temple Claggett (acting), LM 403, 707–8128.
Special Assistant.—Terri Vincent, LM 403, 707–8128.
Chief Financial Officer.—Jody A. Harry, LM 403, 707–8772.
Chief of Operations.—David J. Christopher, LM 403, 707–8825.
Chief Information Officer.—Douglas P. Ament, LM 403, 707–5440.
Associate Register of Copyrights and Director:
General Counsel.—Sarang (Sy) Damle, LM 403, 707–3572.
Policy and International Affairs.—Karyn Temple Claggett, LM 403, 707–7845.
Public Information and Education.—William J. Roberts, LM 453, 707–8391.
Registration Policy and Practice.—Robert J. Kasunic, LM 443, 707–0229.
Director of:
Copyright Technology Office.—Ricardo Farraj-Feijoo, LM 560, 707–0110.
Public Records and Repositories.—Denise Wofford, LM 433, 707–2638.

Chief of:

Acquisitions Division.—Stephen D. Want, LM 526, 707–6781.

Administrative Services Office.—Bruce J. McCubbin, LM 458, 707–8395.

Licensing Division.—James B. Enzinna, LM 504, 707–6801.

Literary Division.—Vacant.

Performing Arts Division.—Laura Lee Fischer, LM 443, 707–5751.

Receipt Analysis and Control Division.—Craig R. Taylor, LM 424, 707–2830.

Visual Arts Division.—John H. Ashley, LM 433, 707–8223.

Head of:

Copyright Information Section.—Denise Garrett, LM 401, 707–6665.

Publications Section.—Vacant.

Recordation Section.—Zarifa Madyun, LM 433, 707–1643.

Records Management Section.—Paul Capel, LM 438, 707–7923.

Records Research and Certification Section.—McKenna Rain, LM 453, 707–5516.

LAW LIBRARY, OFFICE OF THE LAW LIBRARIAN, LM 240, 707–5065

Law Librarian.—Jane Sánchez, LM 240, 707–9825.

Administrative Operations.—Roberto Salazar, LM 240, 707–0947.

Director of:

Global Legal Collection.—Janice Hyde, LM 240, 707–9836.

Global Legal Research.—Peter Roudik, LM 240, 707–9861.

Chief of:

Collections Services.—Kurt Carroll, LM 232, 707–1494.

Foreign, Comparative and International Law Division I.—Kelly Buchanan, LM 240, 707–1166.

Foreign, Comparative and International Law Division II.—Luis Acosta, LM 240, 707–9131.

Public Services.—Debbie Keysor, LM 201, 707–3164.

LIBRARY SERVICES, LM 642, 707–5325

Associate Librarian.—Joseph Puccio (acting), LM 642, 707–1413.

Deputy Associate Librarian/Administrative Services and Operations.—Alvert ''Al'' Banks (acting), LM 642, 707–9562.

Director for:

Acquisitions and Bibliographic Access.—Beacher Wiggins, LM 642, 707–5137.

American Folklife Center.—Elizabeth Peterson, LJ G49, 707–1745.

Collection Development Office.—Joseph Puccio, LA 5181, 707–1413.

Veterans History Project.—Karen Lloyd, LM 603, 707–6074.

Chief of:

Acquisitions, Fiscal, and Support Office.—Richard Yarnall (acting), LM B42/B46, 707–9474.

African, Latin American, and Western European Division.—Angela Kinney, LM 542, 707–5572.

Asian and Middle Eastern Division.—Randall Barry, LM 523, 707–5118.

Cooperative and Instructional Programs Division.—Judith Cannan, LA 140, 707–2031.

Germanic and Slavic Division.—Zbigniew Kantorosinski, LM 527, 707–3093.

Network Development and MARC Standards Office.—Sally H. McCallum, LA 309, 707–5119.

Policy and Standards Division.—Beacher Wiggins (acting), LM 642, 707–5137.

U.S./Anglo Division.—Linda Geisler, LM G35, 707–0116.

U.S. and Arts, Sciences, and Humanities Division.—Vera Clyburn, LM 515, 707–3943.

U.S. Programs, Law, and Literature Division.—Karl Debus-Lopez, LM 501, 707–6641.

Director, Collections and Services.—Helena Zinkham, LM 642, 707–2922.

Chief of:

African and Middle Eastern Division.—Mary Jane Deeb, LJ 220, 707–1221.

Asian Division.—Dongfang Shao, LJ 149, 707–5919.

Children's Literature Center.—Sybille A. Jagusch, LJ 100, 707–5535.

Collections Access, Loan and Management.—Steven J. Herman, LJ G02, 707–7400.

Digital Conversion Team.—Michael Neubert, LA 516, 707–3706.

European Division.—Grant Harris, LJ 250, 707–5859.

Geography and Map Division.—Paulette Hasier, LM B02, 707–3400.

Hispanic Division.—Georgette M. Dorn, LJ 240, 707–5400.

Humanities and Social Sciences Division.—Kimberley Bugg, LJ 139A, 707–5530.

Manuscript Division.—James H. Hutson, LM 102, 707–5383.

Music Division.—Susan H. Vita, LM 113, 707–5503.
Packard Campus for Audio-Visual Conservation/Motion Picture, Broadcasting, and Recorded Sound Division.—Gregory Lukow, PC 2013, 707–5709.
Prints and Photographs Division.—Helena Zinkham, LM 339, 707–2922.
Rare Book and Special Collections Division.—Mark G. Dimunation, LJ 230, 707–2025.
Science, Technology, and Business Division.—Ronald S. Bluestone, LA 5203, 707–0948.
Serial and Government Publications Division.—Teresa V. Sierra, LM 133, 707–5277.
Director, Preservation.—Jacob Nadal, LM 642, 707–2068.
Chief of:
Binding and Collections Care Division.—Jeanne Drewes, LM G21, 707–5330.
Conservation Division.—Elmer Eusman, LM G38, 707–5838.
Preservation Reformatting Division.—Adrija Henley, LM G05, 707–0788.
Preservation Research and Testing Division.—Fenella France, LM G38, 707–5525.
Director, Technology Policy.—Alvert ''Al'' Banks, LM 642, 707–9562.
Chief of:
Automation Planning and Liaison Office.—Robert Palian, LM 532, 707–1576.
Digital Collections Management and Services..—Beth Dulabahn, LA G04, 707–2369.
Integrated Library System Program Office.—Ann Della Porta, LA 301, 707–4761.

NATIONAL AND INTERNATIONAL OUTREACH, LM 637, 707–3100

Director.—Jane McAuliffe, LM 637, 707–3100.
Deputy Director.—Colleen Shogan (acting), LM 637, 707–8231.
Chief Operating Officer.—Joe Cappello, LM 637, 707–3411.
Chief Communications Officer.—Ellis Brachman, LM 637, 707–7816.
Director of National Programs.—Eugene Flanagan, LM 637, 707–8203.
Center for the Book.—Rebecca Brasington Clark (acting), LM 604, 707–1520.
Head, Poetry and Literature Center.—Rob Casper, LJ A02, 707–1308.
Head, Young Readers Center.—Vacant, LJ G29, 707–1950.
National Digital Initiatives.—Katherine Zwaard, LA 209, 707–5242.
National Library Service for the Blind and Physically Handicapped.—Karen Keninger, 707–5104.
Director of National Enterprises.—Joe Cappello (acting), LM 637, 707–3411.
Office of Business Enterprises.—Deirdre Scott, LA 130, 707–1421.
Federal Research Division.—Mukta Ohri, LA 5282, 707–3919.
FEDLINK.—Vacant, LA 217, 707–4800.
Publishing.—Rebecca Brasington Clark, LM 604, 707–1520.
Director of Scholarly and Educational Programs.—Jason Yasner (acting), LM 637, 707–2255.
Educational Outreach.—Lee Ann Potter, LM 629, 707–8735.
Interpretive Programs.—David Mandel, LA 230, 707–3689.
Internships and Fellowships Programs.—Vacant, LA 209, 707–9855.
Kluge Center.—John Haskell, LJ 120, 707–3302.
Visitor Services.—Giulia Adelfio, LJ G59, 707–2153.
World Digital Library.—John Van Oudenaren, LA 300, 707–4543.

OFFICE OF THE INSPECTOR GENERAL, LM 630, 707–6314

Inspector General.—Kurt Hyde, LM 630, 707–6314.

UNITED STATES BOTANIC GARDEN

245 First Street, SW., Washington, DC 20515

(202) 225–8333 (information); (202) 226–8333 (administration)

http://www.usbg.gov

Director.—Stephen T. Ayers (acting), Architect of the Capitol, 228–1793.
Executive Director.—Ari E. Novy, Ph.D., 225–6670.
Administrative Officer.—Tonda S. Cave, 225–5002.
Science and Public Programs Manager.—Susan K. Pell, Ph.D., 225–1269.
Horticulture Division Manager.—Frank E. Brooks (acting), 438–9526.
Facility Manager.—Ian M. Donegan, 225–6646.

THE CABINET

Vice President of the United States	MICHAEL R. PENCE.
Secretary of State	MIKE POMPEO.
Secretary of the Treasury	STEVEN T. MNUCHIN.
Secretary of Defense	JAMES MATTIS.
Attorney General	JEFF SESSIONS.
Secretary of the Interior	RYAN ZINKE.
Secretary of Agriculture	SONNY PERDUE.
Secretary of Commerce	WILBUR L. ROSS, JR.
Secretary of Labor	ALEXANDER R. ACOSTA.
Secretary of Health and Human Services	ALEX AZAR.
Secretary of Housing and Urban Development	BENJAMIN S. CARSON, SR.
Secretary of Transportation	ELAINE L. CHAO.
Secretary of Energy	JAMES RICHARD PERRY.
Secretary of Education	ELISABETH PRINCE DEVOS.
Secretary of Veterans Affairs	ROBERT WILKIE.
Secretary of Homeland Security	KIRSTJEN M. NIELSEN.
White House Chief of Staff	JOHN F. KELLY.
U.S. Trade Representative	ROBERT LIGHTHIZER.
Director of National Intelligence	DANIEL COATS.
Representative of the United States to the United Nations	NIKKI R. HALEY.
Director of the Office of Management and Budget	MICK MULVANEY.
Administrator of the Small Business Administration	LINDA E. MCMAHON.

EXECUTIVE BRANCH

THE PRESIDENT

DONALD J. TRUMP, 45th President of the United States; born in Queens, NY, June 14, 1946; graduated from New York Military Academy in Cornwall, NY, in 1964; received a bachelor of science degree in economics in 1968 from the Wharton School of the University of Pennsylvania in Philadelphia, PA; joined Trump Management Company in 1968; became president of the Trump Organization in 1971 until 2016, when elected President of the United States; family: married to Melania; five children: Donald Jr., Ivanka, Eric, Tiffany, and Barron; nine grandchildren; elected as President of the United States on November 8, 2016, and took the oath of office on January 20, 2017.

EXECUTIVE OFFICE OF THE PRESIDENT

1600 Pennsylvania Avenue, NW., 20500
Eisenhower Executive Office Building (EEOB), 17th Street and Pennsylvania Avenue, NW., 20500, phone (202) 456–1414, http://www.whitehouse.gov

The President of the United States.—Donald J. Trump.
Deputy Assistant to the President and Director of Oval Office Operations.—Jordan Karem.
Executive Assistant to the President.—Madeleine Westerhout.

OFFICE OF THE VICE PRESIDENT

phone (202) 456–1414

The Vice President.—Mike Pence.
Assistant to the President and Chief of Staff to the Vice President.—Nick Ayers.
Assistant to the President and National Security Advisor to the Vice President.—Keith Kellogg.
Deputy Assistants to the President and Deputy Chiefs of Staff to the Vice President: Jarrod Agen, John Horne.
Deputy Assistant to the President and Chief of Staff to Mrs. Karen Pence.—Jana Toner.
Deputy Assistant to the President and Domestic Policy Director to the Vice President.—Steve Pinkos.
Deputy Assistant to the President and Director of Public Liaison and Intergovernmental Affairs for the Vice President.—Sarah Makin.
Special Assistant to the President and Deputy Director of Public Liaison and Intergovernmental Affairs.—Andeliz Castillo.
Special Assistant to the President and Director of External Affairs.—Billy Kirkland.
Special Assistant to the President and Director of Media Affairs.—Rebeccah Propp.
Special Assistant to the President and Press Secretary to the Vice President.—Alyssa Farah.
Assistant to the Vice President and Counsel.—Matt Morgan.
Assistant to the Vice President and Director of Legislative Affairs.—Jonathan Hiler.
Deputy Director of House Legislative Affairs.—Chris Hodgson.
Deputy Assistant to the Vice President and Director of Administration.—Katherine Purucker.
Director of Advance.—Saibatu Mansaray.
Deputy Assistant to the Vice President and Director of Scheduling.—Meghan Patenaude.
Special Assistant to the Vice President.—Zach Bauer.
Executive Assistant to the Vice President.—Heather Whitaker.

COUNCIL OF ECONOMIC ADVISERS

1650 Pennsylvania Avenue, Room 360, Washington, DC 20006, phone (202) 456–4779, http://www.whitehouse.gov/cea/staff

Chair.—Kevin Hassett.
Chief of Staff.—DJ Nordquist.
Members: Richard Burkhauser, Tomas Philipson.

COUNCIL ON ENVIRONMENTAL QUALITY

730 Jackson Place, NW., 20503, phone (202) 456–6224
http://www.whitehouse.gov/ceq

Chair.—Vacant.
Chief of Staff.—Mary Neumayr.
Special Assistant.—Katherine Smith.
Speechwriter.—David Sorensen.
General Counsel.—Vacant.
Deputy General Counsel.—Viktoria Seale.
Attorney Advisors: Michael Jensen, Howard Sun.
Director of Finance and Administration.—Angela Matos.
Administrative Officer.—Essence Tillett.
Administrative Assistants: Mary Green, Juschelle McLaurin.
Associate Director for NEPA.—Edward ''Ted'' Boling.
Deputy Associate Directors for NEPA: Michael Drummond, Karen Hanley, Sarah Shattuck, Sara Upchurch.
Associate Director for Infrastructure.—Alexander ''Alex'' Herrgott.
Senior Advisors on Infrastructure: Michael Harkins, April Marchese, Michael Patella.
Deputy Advisors on Infrastructure: Allison Rusnak, Mark Wingate.
Associate Director for Natural Resources.—Christopher ''Chris'' Prandoni.
Deputy Associate Director for Ecosystems.—Tabitha Cale.
Associate Director for Regulatory Reform.— Mario Loyola.
Deputy Chief Sustainability Officer.—Bernice ''Dee'' Siegel.
Senior Sustainability Officers: Mark Ackiewicz, Caroline D'Angelo.

PRESIDENT'S INTELLIGENCE ADVISORY BOARD

phone (202) 456–2352

Executive Director.—Stefanie Osburn.

NATIONAL SECURITY COUNCIL

Eisenhower Executive Office Building, 20504

phone (202) 456–1414, http://www.whitehouse.gov/nsc

MEMBERS

The President.—Donald J. Trump.
The Vice President.—Mike Pence.
The Secretary of State.—Mike Pompeo.
The Secretary of Defense.—James Mattis.

STATUTORY ADVISERS

Director of National Intelligence.—Daniel Coats.
Chair, Joint Chiefs of Staff.—Gen. Joseph F. Dunford, Jr.

STANDING PARTICIPANTS

The Secretary of the Treasury.—Steven T. Mnuchin.
Chief of Staff to the President.—John F. Kelly.
Counsel to the President.—Donald F. McGahn.
National Security Adviser.—John R. Bolton.
Assistant to the President for Economic Policy.—Larry Kudlow.

OFFICIALS

Assistant to the President for National Security Affairs.—John R. Bolton.
Assistant to the President for National Security Affairs and Deputy National Security Adviser.—Rick Waddell.

OFFICE OF ADMINISTRATION

Eisenhower Executive Office Building, phone (202) 395–5555

(Director of White House Management and Administration and) Director of the Office of Administration.—Marcia Lee Kelly.
Deputy Director, Office of Administration.—William C. Hughes.
Equal Employment Opportunity Office.—Clara Patterson.
Office of the Chief Financial Officer.—Y. David Feit.
Office of the Chief Operations Officer.—Samuel T. Price II.
Office of the Chief Administrative Officer.—Cecilia M. Trujillo.
Office of the Chief of Security and Emergency Preparedness.—Samuel T. Price II.
Office of the Chief Information Officer.—Charles C. Herndon.
General Counsel.—Gineen M. Bresso.

OFFICE OF MANAGEMENT AND BUDGET

Eisenhower Executive Office Building, phone (202) 395–4840

Director.—Mick Mulvaney.
Deputy Director.—Tom Reilly (acting).
Deputy Director for Management.—Dustin Brown (acting).
General Counsel.—Jim Carroll.
Administrator, Office of:
Federal Chief Information Officer.—Margaret Graves (acting).
Federal Financial Management/Controller.—Mark Reger (acting).
Federal Procurement Policy.—Lesley Field (acting).
Information and Regulatory Affairs.—Neomi Rao.
Assistant Director for—
Budget.—Kelly Kinneen.
Legislative Reference.—Matthew Vaeth.
Associate Director for—
Communications.—John ''CZ'' Czwartacki.
Economic Policy.—Jeff Schlagenhauf.
Education, Income Maintenance, and Labor Programs.—John Gray.
General Government Programs.—Kathy Kraninger.
Health Programs.—Joe Grogan.
Intergovernmental Affairs and Strategic Initiatives.—Jessica Anderson.
Legislative Affairs.—Jonny Slemrod.
National Security Programs.—Rob Blair.
Natural Resources, Energy, and Science Programs.—Jim Herz.
Performance and Personnel Management.—Dustin Brown (acting).

OFFICE OF NATIONAL DRUG CONTROL POLICY

750 17th Street, NW., phone (202) 395–6700, fax 395–6711

Director.—James Carroll (acting), Room 810, 395–6700.
Chief of Staff.—Lawrence L. Muir (acting), Room 518, 395–6601.
Deputy Chief of Staff.—Taylor P. Weyeneth, Room 805, 395–7336.
Deputy Director.—James Carroll, Room 810, 395–6700.
Assistant Deputy Director, Office of:
Supply Reduction.—James C. Olson, Room 825, 395–5535.
Policy, Research, and Budget.—Terry W. Zobeck, Room 609, 395–5503.
General Counsel.—Lawrence L. Muir, Room 518, 395–6601.
Associate Director, Office of:
Intelligence.—Gerard Burns, room 755, 395–6764.
Legislative Affairs.—Kayla Tonnessen, Room 825, 395–4693.
Management and Administration.—Michele C. Marx, Room 326, 395–6883.
Public Affairs.—Vacant.
Programs.—Michael Gottlieb, Room 836, 395–4868.
Policy, Research, and Budget.—Jon E. Rice, Room 661, 395–6791.
Heroin Task Force.—Kemp Chester, Room 731, 395–5615.
Cocaine Task Force.—Eric Talbot, Room 756, 395–6885.

OFFICE OF SCIENCE AND TECHNOLOGY POLICY

Eisenhower Executive Office Building, phone (202) 456–4444, fax 456–6021
https://www.whitehouse.gov/ostp

Director.—Vacant.
Deputy Chief of Staff and Assistant Director.—Ted Wackler.
Deputy Assistant to the President for Technology Policy.—Michael Kratsios.
Principal Assistant Director for—
National Security and Senior Policy Advisor.—Jack Wilmer.
Oceans and Environment.—Deerin Babb-Brott.
Physical Sciences and Engineering.—Lloyd Whitman.
General Counsel.—Rachael Leonard.
Assistant Director for Legislative Affairs.—Sean Bonyun.
Director of Strategic Communications.—Ross Gillfillan.
Executive Director, National Science and Technology Council.—Chloe Kontos.

OFFICE OF THE UNITED STATES TRADE REPRESENTATIVE

600 17th Street, NW., 20508, phone (202) 395–6890
http://www.ustr.gov

United States Trade Representative.—Robert E. Lighthizer.
Deputy United States Trade Representatives: Jeff Gerrish, C.J. Mahoney.
Deputy United States Trade Representative and Chief of Mission, Geneva.—Dennis Shea.
Chief Agricultural Negotiator.—Gregg Doud.
Chief Innovation and Intellectual Property Negotiator.—Vacant.
Chief of Staff.—Jamieson L. Greer.
General Counsel.—Stephen Vaughn.
Assistant United States Trade Representatives (AUSTR) for—
Administration.—Fred Ames.
Agricultural Affairs.—Sharon Bomer Lauritsen.
China Affairs.—Terrence J. McCartin (acting).
Congressional Affairs.—Christopher Jackson.
Environment and Natural Resources.—Jennifer Y. Prescott.
Europe and the Middle East.—L. Daniel Mullaney.
Intergovernmental Affairs and Public Engagement.—Gregory Martin Walters.
Japan, Korea, and APEC.—Michael Beeman.
Labor Affairs.—Lewis Karesh.
Monitoring and Enforcement.—Juan A. Millan.
Post-Conflict Countries.—Michael J. Delaney (Special Trade Representative).
Public and Media Affairs.—Jeff Emerson.
Services and Investment.—Daniel Bahar.
Small Business, Market Access, and Industrial Competitiveness.—Jim Sanford.
South and Central Asian Affairs.—Mark Linscott.
Textiles.—Bill Jackson.
Trade Policy and Economics.—Edward Gresser.
Western Hemisphere.—John M. Melle.
WTO (World Trade Organization) and Multilateral Affairs.—Dawn Shackleford.
Director.—Interagency Trade Enforcement Center.—Bradford Ward.

THE WHITE HOUSE OFFICE

CABINET AFFAIRS

Deputy Assistant to the President and Cabinet Secretary.—William McGinley.

CHIEF OF STAFF

Assistant to the President and Chief of Staff.—John Kelly.
Assistant to the President and Deputy Chief of Staff for Operations.—Joseph Hagin.
Assistant to the President and Deputy Chief of Staff for Legislative, Cabinet, Intergovernmental Affairs, and Implementation.—Rick Dearborn.

COMMUNICATIONS AND PRESS

Assistant to the President and Director of Communications.—Hope Hicks.

Assistant to the President and Senior Advisor for Strategic Communications.—Mercedes Schlapp.

Assistant to the President and Press Secretary.—Sarah Huckabee Sanders.

Assistant to the President and Director of Social Media.—Daniel Scavino.

Deputy Assistant to the President and Principal Deputy Press Secretary.—Raj Shah.

Deputy Assistant to the President and Deputy Director for Communications.—Jessica Ditto.

Deputy Assistant to the President and Communications Advisor.—Joshua Raffel.

OFFICE OF DIGITAL STRATEGY

Deputy Assistant to the President and Chief Digital Officer.—Ory Rinat.

OFFICE OF AMERICAN INNOVATION

Assistant to the President and Senior Advisor.—Jared Kushner.

Assistant to the President for Strategic Initiatives.—Chris Liddell.

Assistant to the President for Intergovernmental and Technology Initiatives.—Reed Cordish.

Assistant to the President and Special Representative for International Negotiations.—Jason Greenblatt.

Deputy Assistant to the President and Strategist.—Ira Greenstein.

DOMESTIC POLICY COUNCIL

Assistant to the President and Director of the Domestic Policy Council.—Andrew Bremberg.

OFFICE OF THE SENIOR ADVISOR FOR POLICY

Assistant to the President and Senior Advisor for Policy.—Stephen Miller.

Deputy Assistant to the President and Director of Policy and Interagency Coordination.—Carlos Diaz-Rosillo.

Deputy Assistant to the President and Advisor for Policy, Strategy, and Speechwriting.—Vincent Haley.

OFFICE OF ECONOMIC INITIATIVES AND ENTREPRENEURSHIP

Assistant to the President and Advisor to the President.—Ivanka Trump.

Deputy Assistant to the President and Chief of Staff to the Advisor.—Julie Radford.

OFFICE OF THE FIRST LADY

Assistant to the President and Chief of Staff to the First Lady.—Lindsay Reynolds.

Special Assistant to the President and Social Secretary.—Rickie Niceta.

OFFICE OF LEGISLATIVE AFFAIRS

Assistant to the President for Legislative Affairs.—Shahira Knight.

Deputy Assistants to the President for Legislative Affairs: Joyce Meyer, Amy Swonger.

Special Assistants to the President for Legislative Affairs: Alexander Angelson, Virginia Boney, Andy Koenig, Joseph Lai, Timothy Pataki, Bethany Scully, Cynthia Simms, Mary Taylor, Paul Teller.

OFFICE OF MANAGEMENT AND ADMINISTRATION

Deputy Assistant to the President and Director of White House Management and Administration (and Director of the Office of Administration).—Marcia Lee Kelly.

NATIONAL ECONOMIC COUNCIL

Assistant to the President for Economic Policy.—Larry Kudlow.

Deputy Assistant to the President for International Economic Affairs and Deputy Director of the National Economic Council.—Everett Eissenstat.

Deputy Assistant to the President for Economic Policy and Deputy Director of the National Economic Council.—Jeremy Katz.

Deputy Assistant to the President for Trade and Manufacturing Policy.—Peter Navarro.

Special Assistant to the President for Economic Policy and Chief of Staff of the National Economic Council.—Ashley Marquis.

PRESIDENTIAL PERSONNEL OFFICE

Assistant to the President and Director of Presidential Personnel.—John DeStefano.

Special Assistant to the President and Deputy Director of Presidential Personnel.—Sean Doocey.

OFFICE OF INTERGOVERNMENTAL AFFAIRS

Deputy Assistant to the President and Director of Intergovernmental Affairs.—Douglas Lynn Hoelscher.

OFFICE OF POLITICAL AFFAIRS

Deputy Assistant to the President and Director of Political Affairs.—William Stepien.

OFFICE OF PUBLIC LIASION

Deputy Assistant to the President and Principal Deputy Director of the Office of Public Liaison.—Stephen Munisteri.

OFFICE OF PRESIDENTIAL APPOINTMENTS AND SCHEDULING

Special Assistant to the President and Director for Appointments and Scheduling.—Michael Haidet.

OFFICE OF PRESIDENTIAL ADVANCE

Deputy Assistant to the President and Director of Presidential Advance.—Robert Peede.

OFFICE OF THE SENIOR COUNSELOR

Assistant to the President and Senior Counselor.—Kellyanne Conway.

Deputy Assistant to the President and Chief of Staff to the Senior Counselor.—Hope Renee Hudson.

OFFICE OF THE STAFF SECRETARY

Assistant to the President and Staff Secretary.—Derek Lyons.

Deputy Assistant to the President and Deputy Staff Secretary.—Catherine Bellah Keller.

WHITE HOUSE COUNSEL

Assistant to the President and Counsel to the President.—Donald McGahn.

Deputy Assistant to the President and Special Counsel to the President and Chief of Staff for the Office of the White House Counsel.—Ann Donaldson.

Deputy Assistant to the President and Deputy Counsel to the President for National Security Affairs and Legal Advisor to the NSC.—John Eisenberg.

Deputy Assistants to the President and Deputy Counsel to the President: Uttam Dhillon, Stefan Passantino.

SPECIAL COUNSEL

Assistant to the President and Special Counsel.—Ty Cobb.

DEPARTMENT OF STATE

2201 C Street, NW., 20520, phone (202) 647–4000

MIKE POMPEO, Secretary of State; born in Orange, CA, December 30, 1963; education: B.S., mechanical engineering, United States Military Academy at West Point, NY, 1986, graduated first in his class; J.D., Harvard Law School, Cambridge, MA, 1994; editor of *Harvard Law Review*; professional: owner/founder, Thayer Aerospace; president, Sentry International; religion: Presbyterian; married: Susan Pompeo of Wichita, KS; children: Nick; elected to the 112th Congress, from the 4th District of Kansas, on November 2, 2010, and reelected to the three succeeding Congresses; Director, Central Intelligence Agency (CIA), January, 2017 to April, 2018; nominated by President Donald Trump to become the 70th Secretary of State on March 13, 2018, and was sworn in on April 26, 2018.

OFFICE OF THE SECRETARY

Secretary of State.—Mike Pompeo, Room 7226 (202) 647–9572.
Deputy Secretary.—John Sullivan, Room 7220, 647–8636.

DEPUTY SECRETARY FOR MANAGEMENT AND RESOURCES

Deputy Secretary.—John Sullivan, Room 7220, 647–8636.

AMBASSADOR-AT-LARGE FOR GLOBAL CRIMINAL JUSTICE

Ambassador-at-Large.—Vacant, Room 7419A, 647–6051.
Deputy.—Bertram Braun, 647–8172.

OFFICE OF THE CHIEF OF PROTOCOL

Chief of Protocol.—Sean P. Lawler, Room 1238, 647–4543.
Deputy Chief of Protocol.—Katherine C. Henderson, 647–1144.

OFFICE OF CIVIL RIGHTS

Director.—Gregory B. Smith, Room 7428, 647–9294.
Deputy Director.—Audrey Huon-Dumentat.

BUREAU OF COUNTERTERRORISM

Coordinator.—Nathan Sales, Room 2509, 647–9892.
Principal Deputy Coordinator.—Alina Romanowski, 647–9892.

BUREAU OF CONFLICT AND STABILIZATION OPERATIONS

Assistant Secretary.—Thomas Hushek (acting), Room 7100 SA–3 (202) 663–0807.

EXECUTIVE SECRETARIAT

Special Assistant and Executive Secretary.—Lisa Kenna, Room 7224, 647–8448.
Deputy Executive Secretaries: Elizabeth Fitzsimmons, 647–5528; Derek Hogan, 647–5287; Eva Weigold Schultz, 647–8449.

OFFICE OF THE INSPECTOR GENERAL
2121 Virginia Avenue, NW., 20037

Inspector General.—Steve Linick, Room 8100, 663–0361.
Deputy Inspector General.—Emilia DiSanto, 663–0365.

BUREAU OF INTELLIGENCE AND RESEARCH

Assistant Secretary.—Daniel B. Smith, Room 6468, 647–9177.
Principal Deputy Assistant Secretary.—Kathleen Fitzpatrick, 647–7826.
Deputy Assistant Secretaries: Catherine Brown, 647–7754; Victor Raphael, 647–9633.

OFFICE OF THE LEGAL ADVISER

Legal Adviser.—Jennifer Gillian Newstead, Room 6421, 647–5036.
Principal Deputy Legal Adviser.—Vacant, 647–5036.
Deputy Legal Advisers: Joshua Dorosin, 647–7942; Kathleen Hooke, 647–2187; Katherine McManus, 647–7976.

BUREAU OF LEGISLATIVE AFFAIRS

Assistant Secretary.—Mary K. Waters, Room 7531, 647–4204.
Deputy Assistant Secretary (Global, Regional, and Functional).—Charles Faulkner, 647–1656.
Deputy Assistant Secretary (Senate).—Vacant, 647–8733.
Deputy Assistant Secretary (House).—Vacant, 647–1656.

POLICY PLANNING STAFF

Director.—Brian Hook, Room 7311, 647–2972.
Principal Deputy Director.—Vacant.

OFFICE OF THE U.S. GLOBAL AIDS COORDINATOR

Coordinator.—Dr. Deborah Birx, Room SA–22, 663–2579.
Principal Deputy U.S. Global AIDS Coordinator.—Mark Brown, 663–2464.

UNDER SECRETARY FOR POLITICAL AFFAIRS

Under Secretary.—Thomas Shannon, Room 7250, 647–2471.
Executive Assistant.—Samantha Carl-Yoder, 647–1598.

AFRICAN AFFAIRS

Assistant Secretary.—Vacant, Room 6234A, 647–2530.
Principal Deputy Assistant Secretary.—Vacant, 647–4485.

EAST ASIAN AND PACIFIC AFFAIRS

Assistant Secretary.—Susan Thornton (acting), 647–9596.
Principal Deputy Assistant Secretary.—Vacant, 647–6600.
Deputy Assistant Secretaries: Walter Douglas, 647–7341; Matt Matthews, 647–6904; Patrick Murphy, 647–6910; Laura Stone (acting), 647–8929; Joseph Yun, 736–4393.

EUROPEAN AND EURASIAN AFFAIRS

Assistant Secretary.—A. Wess Mitchell, Room 6226, 647–9626.
Principal Deputy Assistant Secretary.—John Heffern, 647–6233.
Deputy Assistant Secretaries: Bridget Brink, 647–5447; Jonathan Cohen, 647–5174; Kathleen Kavalec, 647–5146; Conrad Tribble, 647–9373; Hoyt Yee, 647–6415; Benjamin Ziff, 647–6402.

NEAR EASTERN AFFAIRS

Assistant Secretary.—Vacant, Room 6242, 647–7209.

Principal Deputy Assistant Secretary.—Vacant, 647–7207.

Deputy Assistant Secretaries: Richard Albright, 647–4042; Yael Lempert, 647–7170; Timothy Lenderking, 647–0554; Michael Ratney, 647–7168; Larry Schwartz, 647–9547.

SOUTH AND CENTRAL ASIAN AFFAIRS

Assistant Secretary.—Alice Wells (acting), Room 6254, 736–4325.

Executive Director.—Howard VanVranken, 647–9505.

Deputy Assistant Secretaries: Nini Forino (acting), 736–4325; David Ranz (acting), 736–4325; Daniel Rosenblum (acting), 736–4325; Thomas Vajda (acting), 736–4325.

WESTERN HEMISPHERE AFFAIRS

Assistant Secretary.—Vacant, Room 6262, 647–5780.

Principal Deputy Assistant Secretary.—Francisco Palmieri, 647–5750.

Deputy Assistant Secretaries: John Creamer, 647–6755; Michael Fitzpatrick, 647–8563; Kenneth Merten, 647–3903; Mara Tekach, 647–9921.

INTERNATIONAL NARCOTICS AND LAW ENFORCEMENT AFFAIRS

Assistant Secretary.—Kirsten Dawn Madison, Room 7826, 647–8464.

Principal Deputy Assistant Secretary.—Vacant, 647–6642.

Deputy Assistant Secretaries: Brooke Darby (acting); Richard Glenn (acting); Heather Merritt (acting); James A. Walsh, 647–9822.

INTERNATIONAL ORGANIZATION AFFAIRS

Assistant Secretary.—Kevin Edward Moley, Room 6323, 647–9600.

Principal Deputy Assistant Secretary.—Molly Phee, 647–9602.

Deputy Assistant Secretaries: Eric M. Barclay, 647–9431; Nerissa J. Cook, 647–5798; Eric Gaudiosi (acting), 647–9604.

UNDER SECRETARY FOR ECONOMIC GROWTH, ENERGY, AND THE ENVIRONMENT

Under Secretary.—Vacant, Room 7256, 647–7575.

Executive Assistant.—Michael Dodman, 647–7674.

ECONOMIC AND BUSINESS AFFAIRS

Assistant Secretary.—Manisha Singh, Room 4932/4934, 647–9496.

Principal Deputy Assistant Secretary.—Brian McFeeters, 647–9496.

Deputy Assistant Secretaries: Robert L. Strayer, 647–5968; Roland de Marcelus (acting); David Meale (acting); Peter Haas (acting); Hugo Yon (acting).

UNDER SECRETARY FOR ARMS CONTROL AND INTERNATIONAL SECURITY

Under Secretary.—Andrea L. Thompson, Room 7208, 647–1049.

Chief of Staff.—Maureen Tucker, 647–0302.

INTERNATIONAL SECURITY AND NONPROLIFERATION

Assistant Secretary.—Dr. Christopher A. Ford, Room 3932, 647–5999.

Principal Deputy Assistant Secretary.—Eliott Kang, Room 3932, 647–5999.

Deputy Assistant Secretary for Non-Nuclear Encounter for Proliferation.—Ann Ganzer (acting), Room 3932, 647–5122.

Deputy Assistant Secretary for Nonproliferation Programs.—Phillip Dolliff (acting), 647–5999.

POLITICAL-MILITARY AFFAIRS

Assistant Secretary.—Tina Kaidanow, Room 6212, 647–9022.
Principal Deputy Assistant Secretary.—Vacant, 647–9023.
Deputy Assistant Secretaries: Brian Nilsson (acting), 663–3704; Kevin O'Keefe, 663–3450; Vacant, 647–9023.

ARMS CONTROL, VERIFICATION AND COMPLIANCE

Assistant Secretary.—Yleem D.S. Poblete, Room 5950, 647–5315.
Principal Deputy Assistant Secretary.—Anita Friedt, 647–6830.
Deputy Assistant Secretaries: Bruce Turner, 647–9399; Vacant, 647–5315.

UNDER SECRETARY FOR PUBLIC DIPLOMACY AND PUBLIC AFFAIRS

Under Secretary.—Heather Nauert (acting), Room 5932, 647–9199.
Executive Assistant/Chief of Staff.—J. Jeff Daigle, 647–7017.

EDUCATIONAL AND CULTURAL AFFAIRS

Assistant Secretary.—Marie Thérèse Royce, 632–9940.
Principal Deputy Assistant Secretary.—Jennifer Zimdahl Galt, 632–9444.
Deputy Assistant Secretary.—Alyson L. Grunder.
Assistant Secretaries/Managing Directors: Mariane Craven, 632–9331; Chris Miner, 632–6446; Kevin Saba, 632–6193.

INTERNATIONAL INFORMATION PROGRAMS

Coordinator.—Jonathan Henick (acting), 632–9931.

PUBLIC AFFAIRS

Assistant Secretary.—Michelle S. Giuda, Room 6634, 647–6608.
Assistant Secretary/Principal Deputy Assistant Secretary.—Susan Stevenson (acting), 647–6088.
Spokesperson.—Heather Nauert, 647–6608.
Deputy Assistant Secretaries: Vacant.

UNDER SECRETARY FOR MANAGEMENT

Under Secretary.—Vacant, Room 7207, 647–1500.
Executive Assistant.—Gregory Stanford, 647–1501.

ADMINISTRATION

Assistant Secretary.—Harry Mahar (acting), Room 6529, 647–1492.
Deputy Assistant Secretaries: Harry Mahar, 647–2082; Jennifer McIntyre (703) 875–6956; Vacant (202) 261–8300.

CONSULAR AFFAIRS

Assistant Secretary.—Carl Risch, Room 6826, 647–9576.
Principal Deputy Assistant Secretary.—Karen Christensen (acting), 647–7736.
Deputy Assistant Secretaries: Karen Christensen, 647–9003; Edward Ramotowski, 647–6947; Brenda Sprague, 647–7149.

DIPLOMATIC SECURITY

Assistant Secretary.—Michael T. Evanoff, Room 6316, 647–6290.
Principal Deputy Assistant Secretary.—Vacant (571) 345–3815.

Deputy Assistant Secretaries: Wayne Ashbery (571) 345–3836; Scott Moretti (571) 226–9760; Tim Riley (571) 345–3492; Christian Schurman (571) 345–3815; Vacant (571) 345–3785; Vacant (571) 345–3809.

DIRECTOR GENERAL OF THE FOREIGN SERVICE AND DIRECTOR OF HUMAN RESOURCES

Director General.—William Todd (acting), Room 6218, 647–5942.
Principal Deputy Assistant Secretary.—William Todd, 647–5942.
Deputy Assistant Secretaries: Constance Dierman, 647–9442; Philippe Lussier, 647–5152; Bruce Williamson, 647–5188.

FOREIGN SERVICE INSTITUTE

Director.—Marc Oestfield (acting), Room F2101 (703) 302–6703.
Deputy Director.—Amb. Wanda Nesbitt (acting), 302–6707.

INFORMATION RESOURCE MANAGEMENT

Chief Information Officer.—Frontis Wiggins, 647–2889.
Deputy CIO for Operations.—Glen Johnson, 634–3683.
Deputy CIO for Business Management and Planning.—Karen Mummaw, 634–3083.
Chief Information Security Officer of Information Assurance.—Alford Bowden, 634–3690.

MEDICAL SERVICES

Medical Director.—Dr. Charles Rosenfarb, 663–1649.
Principal Deputy Medical Director.—Mark Cohen, 663–1641.

OVERSEAS BUILDINGS OPERATIONS

Director.—William Moser (acting), (703) 875–6361.
Principal Deputy Directors: Marjorie Phillips (acting), (571) 345–0215; Nicole Varnes (703) 875–5036.

UNDER SECRETARY OF STATE FOR CIVILIAN SECURITY, DEMOCRACY, AND HUMAN RIGHTS

Under Secretary.—Vacant, Room 7261, 647–1189.
Executive Assistant.—Vacant, 647–7818.

DEMOCRACY, HUMAN RIGHTS, AND LABOR

Assistant Secretary.—Virginia Bennett (acting), Room 7827, 647–3273.
Principal Deputy Assistant Secretary.—Virginia Bennett, 647–3273.

OCEANS AND INTERNATIONAL ENVIRONMENTAL AND SCIENTIFIC AFFAIRS

Assistant Secretary.—Amb. Judith Garber (acting), Room 3880, 647–6950.
Principal Deputy Assistant Secretary.—Vacant, 647–1554.
Deputy Assistant Secretaries: David A. Balton, 647–2396; Jonathan Margolis, 647–3584; Daniel Reifsnyder, 647–2232.

POPULATION, REFUGEES, AND MIGRATION

Assistant Secretary.—Simon Henshaw (acting), Room 6825, 647–7360.
Principal Deputy Assistant Secretary.—Simon Henshaw, 647–5982.
Deputy Assistant Secretaries: Nancy I. Jackson, 647–7360; Mark Storella, 647–5822.

U.S. MISSION TO THE UNITED NATIONS

U.S. Permanent Representative.—Amb. Nikki Haley, Room 633 (212) 415–4404.
Deputy to the Ambassador.—Jon Lerner (202) 736–7578.

OFFICE OF U.S. FOREIGN ASSISTANCE RESOURCES

Director.—Hari Sastry, Room 5923, 647–2608.
Chief of Staff.—Lisa Greene, 647–3690.

UNITED STATES DIPLOMATIC OFFICES—FOREIGN SERVICE

(C = Consular Office, N = No Embassy or Consular Office)

http://usembassy.state.gov

LIST OF CHIEFS OF MISSION

AFGHANISTAN, ISLAMIC REPUBLIC OF (Kabul).
Hon. John R. Bass.
ALBANIA, REPUBLIC OF (Tirana).
Hon. Donald Lu.
ALGERIA, DEMOCRATIC AND POPULAR REPUBLIC OF (Algiers).
Hon. John Desrocher.
ANDORRA (Andorra La Vella) (N).
Richard Duke Buchan III (Also U.S. Ambassador to Spain).
ANGOLA, REPUBLIC OF (Luanda).
Hon. Nina Maria Fite.
ARGENTINA (Buenos Aires).
Hon. Edward C. Prado.
ARMENIA, REPUBLIC OF (Yerevan).
Hon. Richard M. Mills, Jr.
ASSOCIATION OF SOUTHEAST ASIAN NATIONS (ASEAN).
Vacant.
AUSTRALIA (Canberra).
Vacant.
AUSTRIA, REPUBLIC OF (Vienna).
Trevor D. Traina.
AZERBAIJAN, REPUBLIC OF (Baku).
Hon. Robert F. Cekuta.
BAHAMAS, THE COMMONWEALTH OF THE (Nassau).
Vacant.
BAHRAIN, STATE OF (Manama).
Hon. Justin Siberell.
BANGLADESH, PEOPLE'S REPUBLIC OF (Dhaka).
Hon. Marcia Stephens Bloom Bernicat.
BARBADOS (Bridgetown).
Hon. Linda Taglialatela.
BELARUS, REPUBLIC OF (Minsk).
Robert J. Riley (Charge d'Affaires).
BELGIUM (Brussels).
Hon. Matthew Lussenhop (Deputy Chief of Mission).
BELIZE (Belmopan).
Vacant.
BENIN, REPUBLIC OF (Cotonou).
Hon. Lucy Tamlyn.
BOLIVIA, REPUBLIC OF (La Paz).
Vacant.
BOSNIA—HERZEGOVINA (Sarajevo).
Hon. Maureen Cormack.
BOTSWANA, REPUBLIC OF (Gaborone).
Hon. Earl Miller.
BRAZIL, FEDERATIVE REPUBLIC OF (Brasilia).
Hon. Michael McKinley.
BRUNEI DARUSSALAM (Bandar Seri Begawan).
Hon. Craig Allen.
BULGARIA, REPUBLIC OF (Sofia).
Hon. Eric Rubin.
BURKINA FASO (Ouagadougou).
Hon. Andrew Young.
BURMA, UNION OF (Rangoon).
Hon. Scot Marciel.
BURUNDI, REPUBLIC OF (Bujumbura).
Hon. Anne Casper.
CABO VERDE.
Hon. Donald L. Heflin.
CAMBODIA, KINGDOM OF (Phnom Penh).
Hon. William A. Heidt.
CAMEROON, REPUBLIC OF (Yaounde).
Hon. Peter Barlerin.
CANADA (Ottawa).
Hon. Kelly Craft.
CENTRAL AFRICAN REPUBLIC (Bangui).
Vacant.
CHAD, REPUBLIC OF (N'Djamena).
Hon. Geeta Pasi.
CHILE, REPUBLIC OF (Santiago).
Hon. Carol Perez.
CHINA, PEOPLE'S REPUBLIC OF (Beijing).
Hon. Terry Branstad.
COLOMBIA, REPUBLIC OF (Bogota).
Hon. Kevin Whitaker.
COMOROS, UNION OF (Moroni) (N).
Hon. Robert T. Yamate (Also Ambassador to the Republic of Madagascar).
CONGO, DEMOCRATIC REPUBLIC OF THE (Kinshasa).

Vacant.
CONGO, REPUBLIC OF THE (Brazzaville).
Hon. Todd Haskell.
COSTA RICA, REPUBLIC OF (San Jose).
Hon. Sharon Day.
COTE D'IVOIRE, REPUBLIC OF (Abidjan).
Vacant.
CROATIA, REPUBLIC OF (Zagreb).
Hon. W. Robert Kohorst.
CUBA (Havana).
Hon. Philip S. Goldberg (Charge d'Affaires).
CURACAO and ARUBA (Consul General).
Hon. Margaret Hawthorne (Charge d'Affaires).
CYPRUS, REPUBLIC OF (Nicosia).
Hon. Kathleen A. Doherty.
CZECH REPUBLIC (Prague).
Stephen B. King.
DENMARK (Copenhagen).
Carla Sands.
DJIBOUTI, REPUBLIC OF (Djibouti).
Hon. Larry André.
DOMINICAN REPUBLIC (Santo Domingo).
Hon. Robert Copley (Charge d'Affaires).
ECUADOR, REPUBLIC OF (Quito).
Hon. Todd Chapman.
EGYPT, ARAB REPUBLIC OF (Cairo).
Hon. Thomas Goldberger (Charge d'Affaires).
EL SALVADOR, REPUBLIC OF (San Salvador).
Hon. Jean Manes.
EQUATORIAL GUINEA, REPUBLIC OF (Malabo) (N).
Hon. Julie Furuta-Toy.
ERITREA, STATE OF (Asmara).
Hon. Natalie Brown (Charge d'Affaires).
ESTONIA.
Hon. James Melville.
ETHIOPIA, FEDERAL DEMOCRATIC REPUBLIC OF (Addis Ababa).
Hon. Michael Arthur Raynor.
EUROPEAN UNION.
Hon. Adam Shub (Charge d'Affaires).
FIJI ISLANDS, REPUBLIC OF THE (Suva).
Hon. Judith Beth Cefkin.
FINLAND, REPUBLIC OF (Helsinki).
Robert F. Pence.
FRANCE (Paris).
Jamie D. McCourt.
GABONESE REPUBLIC (Libreville).
Hon. Joel Danies (Also Ambassador to the Democratic Republic of Sao Tome and Principe).
GAMBIA, REPUBLIC OF THE (Banjul).
Hon. Carolyn Alsup.
GEORGIA (Tbilisi).
Hon. Ian C. Kelly.
GERMANY, FEDERAL REPUBLIC OF (Berlin).
Richard A. Grenell.
GHANA, REPUBLIC OF (Accra).
Hon. Robert P. Jackson.
GREECE (Athens).
Hon. Geoffrey Pyatt.
GUATEMALA, REPUBLIC OF (Guatemala).
Hon. Luis E. Arreaga.
GUINEA, REPUBLIC OF (Conakry).
Hon. Dennis Hankins.
GUINEA-BISSAU, REPUBLIC OF (Bissau) (N).
Hon. Tuli Salama Mushingi (Also Ambassador to the Republic of Senegal).
GUYANA, CO-OPERATIVE REPUBLIC OF (Georgetown).
Hon. Perry Holloway.
HAITI, REPUBLIC OF (Port-au-Prince).
Michele Jeanne Sison.
HOLY SEE (Vatican City).
Callista L. Gingrich.
HONDURAS, REPUBLIC OF (Tegucigalpa).
Hon. Heide Fulton (Charge d'Affaires).
HONG KONG (Hong Kong) (C).
Hon. Kurt W. Tong (Consul General).
HUNGARY, REPUBLIC OF (Budapest).
Vacant.
ICELAND, REPUBLIC OF (Reykjavik).
Vacant.
INDIA (New Delhi).
Hon. Kenneth I. Juster.
INDONESIA, REPUBLIC OF (Jakarta).
Hon. Joseph Donovan, Jr.
IRAN.
No Diplomatic Relations.
IRAQ, REPUBLIC OF (Baghdad).
Hon. Douglas Silliman.
IRELAND (Dublin).
Hon. Reece Smyth (Charge d'Affaires).
ISRAEL, STATE OF (Tel Aviv).
Hon. David Friedman.
ITALY (Rome).
Hon. Lewis Eisenberg.
JAMAICA (Kingston).
Vacant.
JAPAN (Tokyo).
Hon. William Hagerty.
JERUSALEM (Consul General).
Hon. Donald Blome.
JORDAN, HASHEMITE KINGDOM OF (Amman).
Vacant.
KAZAKHSTAN, REPUBLIC OF (Almaty).
Hon. George A. Krol.
KENYA, REPUBLIC OF (Nairobi).
Hon. Robert F. Godec.
KOSOVO (Pristina).
Hon. Greg Delawie.
KUWAIT, STATE OF (Kuwait City).
Hon. Lawrence Silverman.

KYRGYZ REPUBLIC (Bishkek).
Hon. Alan Meltzer (Charge d' Affaires).
LAO PEOPLE'S DEMOCRATIC REPUBLIC (Vientiane).
Hon. Rena Bitter.
LATVIA, REPUBLIC OF (Riga).
Hon. Nancy Bikoff Pettit.
LEBANON, REPUBLIC OF (Beirut).
Hon. Elizabeth Richard.
LESOTHO, KINGDOM OF (Maseru).
Hon. Rebecca E. Gonzales.
LIBERIA, REPUBLIC OF (Monrovia).
Hon. Christine Elder.
LIBYA (Tripoli).
Vacant.
LIECHTENSTEIN, PRINCIPALITY OF (Vaduz) (N).
Hon. Edward McMullen, Jr. (Also Ambassador to the Swiss Confederation).
LITHUANIA, REPUBLIC OF (Vilnius).
Hon. Anne Hall.
LUXEMBOURG, GRAND DUCHY OF (Luxembourg).
Vacant.
MACEDONIA, REPUBLIC OF (Skopje).
Hon. Jess L. Baily.
MADAGASCAR, REPUBLIC OF (Antananarivo).
Hon. Robert T. Yamate (Also Ambassador to Union of Comoros).
MALAWI, REPUBLIC OF (Lilongwe).
Hon. Virginia E. Palmer.
MALAYSIA (Kuala Lumpur).
Hon. Kamala Lakhdhir.
MALI, REPUBLIC OF (Bamako).
Hon. Paul A. Folmsbee.
MALTA, REPUBLIC OF (Valletta).
Hon. G. Kathleen Hill.
MARSHALL ISLANDS, REPUBLIC OF THE (Majuro).
Hon. Karen Stewart.
MAURITANIA, ISLAMIC REPUBLIC OF (Nouakchott).
Hon. Michael J. Dodman.
MAURITIUS, REPUBLIC OF (Port Louis).
David Reimer (Also Ambassador to the Republic of the Seychelles).
MEXICO (Mexico City).
Hon. Roberta Jacobson.
MICRONESIA, FEDERATED STATES OF (Kolonia).
Hon. Robert A. Riley.
MOLDOVA, REPUBLIC OF (Chisinau).
Hon. James D. Pettit.
MONACO (Monaco).
Jamie D. McCourt (Also Ambassador to the French Republic).
MONGOLIA (Ulaanbaatar).
Vacant.
MONTENEGRO, REPUBLIC OF (Podgorica).
Hon. Margaret Ann Uyehara.
MOROCCO, KINGDOM OF (Rabat).
Vacant.
MOZAMBIQUE, REPUBLIC OF (Maputo).
Hon. Dean Pittman.
NAMIBIA, REPUBLIC OF (Windhoek).
Hon. Lisa Johnson.
NEPAL, KINGDOM OF (Kathmandu).
Hon. Alaina Teplitz.
NETHERLANDS, KINGDOM OF THE (The Hague).
Peter Hoekstra.
NEW ZEALAND (Wellington).
Hon. Scott P. Brown (Also Ambassador to the State of Samoa).
NICARAGUA, REPUBLIC OF (Managua).
Hon. Laura F. Dogu.
NIGER, REPUBLIC OF (Niamey).
Hon. Eric Whitaker.
NIGERIA, FEDERAL REPUBLIC OF (Abuja).
Hon. Stuart Symington.
NORTH ATLANTIC TREATY ORGANIZATION (NATO).
Hon. Kay Bailey Hutchison.
NORTH KOREA.
No Diplomatic Relations.
NORWAY (Oslo).
Kenneth J. Braithwaite.
OMAN, SULTANATE OF (Muscat).
Hon. Marc J. Sievers.
ORGANIZATION FOR SECURITY AND COOPERATION IN EUROPE (OSCE)
Vacant.
ORGANIZATION OF AMERICAN STATES (OAS)
Hon. Carlos Trujillo (Permanent Representative).
PAKISTAN, ISLAMIC REPUBLIC OF (Islamabad).
Hon. David Hale.
PALAU, REPUBLIC OF (Koror).
Hon. Amy J. Hyatt.
PANAMA, REPUBLIC OF (Panama).
Vacant.
PAPUA NEW GUINEA (Port Moresby).
Hon. Catherine Ebert-Gray.
PARAGUAY, REPUBLIC OF (Asuncion)
Lee McClenny.
PERU, REPUBLIC OF (Lima).
Hon. Krishna R. Urs.
PHILIPPINES, REPUBLIC OF THE (Manila).
Hon. Sung Kim.
POLAND, REPUBLIC OF (Warsaw).
Hon. Paul W. Jones.
PORTUGAL, REPUBLIC OF (Lisbon).
Hon. George Glass.
QATAR, STATE OF (Doha).
Vacant.
ROMANIA (Bucharest).
Hon. Hans Klemm.
RUSSIAN FEDERATION (Moscow).
Hon. Jon M. Hunstman, Jr.

RWANDA, REPUBLIC OF (Kigali).
Hon. Peter Vrooman.
SAN MARINO, REPUBLIC OF (San Marino) (N).
Hon. Lewis Eisenberg (Also Ambassador to the Italian Republic).
SAO TOME AND PRINCIPE, DEMOCRATIC REPUBLIC OF (Sao Tome) (N).
Hon. Joel Danies (Also Ambassador to Gabonese Republic).
SAUDI ARABIA, KINGDOM OF (Riyadh).
Vacant.
SENEGAL, REPUBLIC OF (Dakar).
Hon. Tulinabo Salama Mushingi (Also Ambassador to the Republic of Guinea-Bissau).
SERBIA (Belgrade).
Hon. Kyle R. Scott.
SEYCHELLES, REPUBLIC OF (Victoria) (N).
David Reimer (Also Ambassador to the Republic of Mauritius).
SIERRA LEONE, REPUBLIC OF (Freetown).
Hon. Maria Brewer.
SINGAPORE, REPUBLIC OF (Singapore).
Hon. Stephanie Syptak-Ramnath (Deputy Chief of Mission).
SLOVAK REPUBLIC (Bratislava).
Hon. Adam Sterling.
SLOVENIA, REPUBLIC OF (Ljubljana).
Hon. Brent Hartley.
SOLOMON ISLANDS (Honiara) (N).
Hon. Catherine Ebert-Gray (Also Ambassador to Papua New Guinea and Republic of Vanuatu).
SOMALIA.
Vacant.
SOUTH AFRICA, REPUBLIC OF (Pretoria).
Hon. Jessica Lapenn (Deputy Chief of Mission).
SOUTH KOREA.
Hon. Marc Knapper (Deputy Chief of Mission).
SOUTH SUDAN, REPUBLIC OF (Juba).
Thomas J. Hushek.
SPAIN (Madrid).
Richard Duke Buchan III (Also Ambassador to the Principality of Andorra).
SRI LANKA, DEMOCRATIC SOCIALIST REPUBLIC OF (Colombo).
Hon. Atul Keshap (Also Ambassador to the Republic of Maldives).
SUDAN, REPUBLIC OF THE (Khartoum).
Hon. Steven Koutsis (Charge d'Affaires).
SURINAME, REPUBLIC OF (Paramaribo).
Hon. Edwin Nolan.
SWAZILAND, KINGDOM OF (Mbabane).
Hon. Lisa Peterson.
SWEDEN (Stockholm).
Hon. David Lindwall (Charge d'Affaires).
SWITZERLAND (Bern).
Hon. Edward McMullen, Jr. (Also Ambassador to the Principality of Liechtenstein).
SYRIAN ARAB REPUBLIC (Damascus).
(No relations with U.S.)
TAJIKISTAN, REPUBLIC OF (Dushanbe).
Hon. Kevin Covert (Charge d'Affaires).
TANZANIA, UNITED REPUBLIC OF (Dar es Salaam).
Hon. Inmi Patterson (Charge d'Affaires).
THAILAND, KINGDOM OF (Bangkok).
Hon. Glyn T. Davies.
TIMOR-LESTE.
Hon. Kathleen M. Fitzpatrick.
TOGO.
Hon. David Gilmour.
TRINIDAD AND TOBAGO, REPUBLIC OF (Port-of-Spain).
Hon. John McIntyre (Charge d'Affaires).
TUNISIA, REPUBLIC OF (Tunis).
Hon. Daniel Rubinstein.
TURKEY, REPUBLIC OF (Ankara).
Hon. Philip Kosnett (Charge d'Affaires).
TURKMENISTAN (Ashgabat).
Hon. Allan Phillip Mustard.
U.S. MISSION TO UNESCO.
Vacant.
U.S. MISSION TO THE AFRICAN UNION (AU).
Hon. Mary Beth Leonard.
UGANDA, REPUBLIC OF (Kampala).
Hon. Deborah Malac.
UKRAINE (Kyiv).
Hon. Marie Yovanovitch.
UNITED ARAB EMIRATES (Abu Dhabi).
Vacant.
UNITED KINGDOM OF GREAT BRITAIN AND NORTHERN IRELAND (London).
Hon. Robert Wood Johnson IV.
UNITED NATIONS HUMAN RIGHTS COUNCIL.
Hon. Theodore Allegra (Deputy Chief of Mission).
UNITED NATIONS IN GENEVA.
Hon. Theodore Allegra (Deputy Chief of Mission).
UNITED NATIONS IN ROME.
Hon. Thomas Duffy (Charge d' Affaires).
UNITED NATIONS IN VIENNA.
Nicole Shampaine (Charge d'Affaires) (Also International Atomic Energy Agency (IAEA)).

UNITED NATIONS.
Hon. Nikki Haley.
URUGUAY, ORIENTAL REPUBLIC OF (Montevideo).
Hon. Kelly Keiderling.
UZBEKISTAN, REPUBLIC OF (Tashkent).
Hon. Pamela L. Spratlen.
VANUATU, REPUBLIC OF (Port Vila) (N).
Hon. Catherine Ebert-Gray (Also Ambassasdor to Solomon Islands and Papua New Guinea).
VENEZUELA, BOLIVARIAN REPUBLIC OF (Caracas).
Vacant.
VIETNAM, SOCIALIST REPUBLIC OF (Hanoi).
Hon. Daniel J. Kritenbrink.
YEMEN, REPUBLIC OF (Sanaa).
Hon. Matthew H. Tueller.
ZAMBIA, REPUBLIC OF (Lusaka).
Hon. Daniel L. Foote.
ZIMBABWE, REPUBLIC OF (Harare).
Hon. Harry K. Thomas, Jr. (Chief of Mission).

UNITED STATES PERMANENT DIPLOMATIC MISSIONS TO INTERNATIONAL ORGANIZATIONS

ASSOCIATION OF SOUTHEAST ASIAN NATIONS (Jakarta).
Hon. Daniel Shields (Charge d'Affaires).
AFRICAN UNION (Addis Ababa).
Hon. Mary Beth Leonard.
NORTH ATLANTIC TREATY ORGANIZATION (Brussels).
Hon. Kay Bailey Hutchison.
ORGANIZATION FOR ECONOMIC COOPERATION AND DEVELOPMENT (Paris).
Vacant.
ORGANIZATION FOR SECURITY AND COOPERATION IN EUROPE (Vienna).
Vacant.
ORGANIZATION OF AMERICAN STATES (Washington, DC).
Carlos Trujillo.

DEPARTMENT OF THE TREASURY

1500 Pennsylvania Avenue, NW., 20220, phone (202) 622–2000, http://www.ustreas.gov

STEVEN T. MNUCHIN, Secretary of the Treasury; nominated by President Donald J. Trump January 20, 2017, to become the 77th Secretary of the Treasury and confirmed by the U.S. Senate on February 13, 2017.

OFFICE OF THE SECRETARY

Secretary of the Treasury.—Steven T. Mnuchin, Room 3330, 622–1100.
Executive Assistant.—Shirley E. Gathers, 622–1100.
Confidential Assistant.—Vacant.

OFFICE OF THE DEPUTY SECRETARY

Deputy Secretary.—Vacant, Room 3326, 622–1080.
Executive Assistant.— Pat Griffin, Room 3326, 622–7588.

OFFICE OF THE CHIEF OF STAFF

Chief of Staff.—Eli Miller, Room 3408, 622–1135.
Deputy Chief of Staff.—Alden Wood, Room 3410, 622–5501.
White House Liaison.—Baylor Myers, Room 3420, 622–0987.
Special Assistant to the Chief of Staff.—Tricia McLaughlin, Room 3408, 622–0502.

OFFICE OF THE GENERAL COUNSEL

General Counsel.—Brent McIntosh, Room 3000 (202) 622–0283.
Deputy General Counsel.—Brian Callanan, 622–0283.
Staff Assistant.—Kim Wilson, 622–0283.
Senior Advisor to the General Counsel.—Joseph R. Clark, Room 3006, 622–4931.
Counselor to the General Counsel.—Himamauli ''Him'' Das, Room 3014, 622–1147.
Assistant General Counsel for Banking and Finance.—Steven Laughton, Room 2304, 622–8413.
Principal Deputy Assistant General Counsel for Banking and Finance.—Eric Froman, Room 3023, 622–1942.
Deputy Assistant General Counsel for Banking and Finance.—Joel Pulliam, Room 2202, 622–5949.
Assistant General Counsel for Enforcement and Intelligence.—Paul Ahern, Room 2000, 622–3108.
Deputy Assistant General Counsel for Enforcement and Intelligence.—Heather Trew, Room 2000, 622–0348.
Assistant General Counsel for General Law, Ethics, and Regulation.—Vacant, Room 2312, 622–6052.
Deputy Assistant General Counsel for General Law, Ethics, and Regulation.—Brian Sonfield, Room 2020, 622–9804.
Deputy Assistant General Counsel for General Law, Ethics, and Regulation (Ethics).—Elizabeth ''Beth'' Horton, Room 2221, 622–9794.
Assistant General Counsel for International Affairs.—David Sullivan, Room 2308, 622–7148.
Deputy Assistant General Counsel for International Affairs.—Jeffrey Klein, Room 2306, 622–2122.
Chief Counsel, Foreign Assets Control.—Bradley Smith, Annex 3123, 622–6922.
Deputy Chief Counsel.—Matthew Tuchband, Annex 3121, 622–1654.

OFFICE OF THE INSPECTOR GENERAL

Inspector General.—Eric Thorson, Room 4436 (202) 622–1090.
Deputy Inspector General.—Vacant.
Counsel to the Inspector General.—Richard Delmar, Suite 400 (202) 927–0650.
Assistant Inspector General for—
Audit.—Deborah Harker, Suite 300, 927–5400.
Investigations.—John L. Phillips, Suite 400, 927–5260.
Management Services.—Patricia Hollis, Suite 200, 927–5200.
Deputy Assistant Inspector General for—
Audits: Pauletta Battle, Suite 300, 927–5400; Lisa Carter, Suite 300, 927–5400; Donna Joseph, Suite 300, 927–5400.
Investigation.—Jerome Marshall, Suite 400, 927–5260.
Management.—Jeffrey Lawrence, Suite 200, 927–5200.

OFFICE OF THE UNDER SECRETARY FOR DOMESTIC FINANCE

Under Secretary.—Vacant (202) 622–1703.

OFFICE OF THE ASSISTANT SECRETARY FOR FINANCIAL INSTITUTIONS

Assistant Secretary.—Christopher Campbell.
Deputy Assistant Secretary, Office of:
Consumer Policy.—Vacant.
Financial Institutions Policy.—Vacant.
Small Business, Community Development, and Housing Policy.—Vacant.
Director, Office of:
Community Development Financial Institutions Fund.—Annie Donovan.
Consumer Policy.—Susan Weinstock.
Critical Infrastructure Protection and Compliance Policy.—Brian Peretti.
Federal Insurance Office.—Vacant.
Financial Institutions Policy.—Sarah Hammer.
Financial Security (and Financial Education).—Louisa Quittman.
Small Business, Community Development, and Housing Policy.—Jodie Harris.
Small Business Lending Fund.—Sally Phillips.
State Small Business Credit Initiative.—Jeffrey Stout.
Terrorism Risk Insurance Program.—Vacant.
Deputy Director, Office of:
Financial Institutions Policy.—Moses Kim.
Consumer Policy.—Christopher Weaver.

OFFICE OF THE ASSISTANT SECRETARY FOR FINANCIAL MARKETS

Assistant Secretary.—Monique Rollins (acting), (202) 622–0481.
Deputy Assistant Secretary, Office of:
Capital Markets.—Monique Rollins.
Federal Finance.—Vacant.
Public Finance.—Gary Grippo.
Director, Office of:
Capital Markets.—Brian Smith.
Debt Management.—Fred Pietrangeli.
Federal Lending.—Gary Burner.
Federal Program Finance.—Vacant.
State and Local Finance.—Kent Hiteshew.

OFFICE OF THE FISCAL ASSISTANT SECRETARY

Assistant Secretary.—Dave A. Lebryk (202) 622–0560.
Deputy Assistant Secretary, Office of:
Accounting Policy and Financial Transparency.—Christina Ho.
Fiscal Operations and Policy.—Kristine Conrath.
Director, Office of:
Fiscal Projections.—David Monroe.
Grants and Asset Management.—Theodore Kowalsky.
Program Manager, Office of:

Gulf Coast Restoration.—Laurie McGilvray.
Housing and Energy.—Ellen Neubauer.
Supervisory Financial Analyst, Office of Financial Agents.—Alex Abawi.

OFFICE OF THE ASSISTANT SECRETARY FOR FINANCIAL STABILITY

Assistant Secretary.—Vacant (202) 622–0897.
Deputy Assistant Secretary.—Vacant.
Chief of Staff.—Vacant.
Chief:
Finance and Operations Officer.—Lorenzo Rasetti.
Investment Officer.—Trevor Montano.
Director of Programs.—Danielle Johnson-Kutch.

FINANCIAL STABILITY OVERSIGHT COUNCIL

Deputy Assistant Secretary.—Vacant.
Independent Member with Insurance Expertise.—Roy Woodall.

FINANCIAL MANAGEMENT SERVICE

401 14th Street, SW., 20227, phone (202) 874–6740, fax 874–7016

Commissioner.—David A. Lebryk.
Deputy Commissioner.—Wanda Rogers.
Assistant Commissioner for—
Debt Management Services.—Jeffrey Schramek.
Enterprise Business Information Security and Services (EBISS).—Kim McCoy.
Federal Finance.—Kristine Conrath.
Government-wide Accounting.—Christina Ho.
Management (Chief Financial Officer).—Marty Greiner.
Payments Management.—John Hill.
Chief Counsel.—Margaret Marquette.
Director for Legislative and Public Affairs.—Joyce Harris.

BUREAU OF THE FISCAL SERVICE

401 14th Street, SW., 20227, phone (202) 504–3535, fax (202) 874–7016

Commissioner.—Kimberly A. McCoy.
Chief Counsel.—Paul Wolfteich.
Deputy Commissioner—
Finance and Administration.—Steve Manning.
Financial Services and Operations.—Jeff Schramek (acting).
Fiscal Accounting and Shared Services.—Matt Miller (acting).
Assistant Commissioner for—
Debt Management Services.—Daniel Vavasour.
Financial Innovation and Transformation.—John Hill.
Fiscal Accounting Operations.—Matt Miller.
Information and Security Services (Chief Information Officer).—Laura Buschor.
Office of Legislative and Public Affairs.—Joyce Harris (Director).
Office of Management (Chief Financial Officer).—Mike Linder (acting).
Office of Shared Services.—Doug Anderson.
Payments Management (Chief Disbursing Officer).—Ronda Kent.
Retail Securities Services.—David Copenhaver.
Revenue Collections Management.—Corvelli McDaniel.
Wholesale Securities Services.—Dara Seaman (acting).
Executive Director, Government Securities Regulations.—Lori Santamorena.

OFFICE OF THE UNDER SECRETARY FOR INTERNATIONAL AFFAIRS

Under Secretary.—David Malpass, Room 3436 MT (202) 622–1270.
Staff Assistants: Trinda Boyne, Room 3234A MT, 622–1624; Karen DeLaBarre Chase, Room 3430A MT, 622–0060.
Special Assistant.—Cooper Godfrey, Room 3432B MT, 622–2345.

Senior Advisors: Mauricio Claver Carone, Room 3224 MT, 622–8125; Alex Grohovsky, Room 3203 MT, 622–6145.
Deputy Assistant Secretary for International Economics Analysis.—Robert Dohner, Room 3218 MT, 622–7222.
Director, IA Business and Programs Operations.—Diane Klopack, Room 3041B MT, 662–6405.
China Affairs and the Comprehensive Economic Dialogue (CED).—Christopher Adams, Room 3209 MT, 622–6883.

OFFICE OF THE ASSISTANT SECRETARY FOR INTERNATIONAL AFFAIRS

Assistant Secretary for International Finance.—Andy Baukol (acting), Room 3216 MT, 622–2159.
Senior Advisor.—Vacant.
Staff Assistant.—Loretta Fogle, Room 5313B MT, 622–0139.
Deputy Assistant Secretary for—
Africa and the Middle East.—Eric Meyer, Room 3036 MT, 622–2156.
Asian Nations.—Robert Kaproth, Room 3217 MT, 622–0132.
Europe and Eurasia.—Andy Baukol (acting), Room 3216 MT, 622–2159.
International Monetary and Financial Policy.—Andy Baukol, Principal, Room 3216 MT, 622–2159.
Western Hemisphere.—Michael Kaplan, Room 3221 MT, 622–4262.
Assistant Secretary for International Markets and Developments.—Heath P. Tarbert, Room 3428 MT, 622–0020.
Senior Advisor.—Susan Friedman, Room 3024 MT, 622–4620.
Special Assistant.—Meghan Herwig, Room 3430B MT, 622–0766.
Deputy Assistant Secretary for—
Afghanistan and Technical Assistance Policy.—W. Larry McDonald, Room 3208 MT, 622–5504.
Environment and Energy.—Mitchell (Mitch) Silk, Room 3216 MT, 622–5504.
International Development Policy.—Geoffrey ''Geoff'' Okamoto, Room 3202 MT, 622–3890.
International Financial Stability and Regulation.—Rebekah Goshorn, Room 3037 MT, 622–1309.
Investment Security.—Aimen Mir, Room 3203 MT, 622–0478.
Trade and Investment Policy.—Douglas Bell, Room 3213 MT, 622–0832.
Director for International Affairs:
Africa (INN).—Susan Driano, Room 1064D, 622–6565.
Development Results and Accountability (IDR).—C. Alex Severens, Room 5406A MT, 622–0763.
East Asia (ISA).—Leslie Hull, Room 4462A MT, 622–4644.
Energy, Infrastructure and Environment (ILE).—Peter Wisner, Room 1024B, 622–2956.
Europe and Eurasia (ICN).—Evangelia ''Lea'' Bouzis, Room 4138D MT, 622–9190.
Global Economics Group (IMG).—John Weeks, Room 5428 MT, 622–9885.
International Banking and Securities Markets (IPS).—Sharon Yang, Room 3016 MT, 622–9066.
International Debt Policy (IDD).—Joanne Veltri, Room 5417B MT, 622–0159.
International Monetary Policy (IMP).—Elizabeth Shortino, Room 5326 MT, 622–6407.
International Trade (ITT).—Lailee Moghtader, Room 5204A MT, 622–1819.
Investment Security (IFI).—Stephen Hanson, Room 5211A MT, 622–0184.
Markets Room (IMR).—John Fagan, Room 1328G MT, 622–1746.
Middle East and North Africa (INM).—Anthony Marcus, Room 5008 MT, 622–6565.
Multilateral Development Banks (IDB).—Charles Moravec, Room 5313M MT, 622–3831.
South and Southeast Asia (ISS).—Seth Bleiweis, Room 4440M MT, 622–4262.
Technical Assistance.—Jason Orlando, 1750 Pennsylvania Avenue, NW., Room 8026, 622–5792.
Trade Finance and Investment Negotiations (ITF).—Anthony Ieronimo, Room 5419J MT, 622–1747.
Western Hemisphere (IWH).—Matthew Malloy, Room 1446A MT, 622–5795.

U.S. BANKS

U.S. Executive Director of:
Inter-American Development Bank.—Mark Lopez (202) 623–3959.
International Monetary Fund.—Sunil Sabharwal, Alternate, 623–7719.
World Bank.—Karen Mathiasen (acting), 458–5333.

OVERSEAS

U.S. Executive Director of:

African Development Bank and Fund (Cote d'Ivoire).—Matthew Turner, Alternate USED, 011–225–75–75–0139.

Asian Development Bank (Manila, Philippines).—Michael Strauss, Alternate USED, 011–63–2–632–6051.

European Bank for Reconstruction and Development (London, England).—Brian McCauley, Alternate USED, 011–44–20–7338–6459.

UNDER SECRETARY FOR TERRORISM AND FINANCIAL INTELLIGENCE

Under Secretary.—Sigal P. Mandelker, MT Room 4326 (202) 622–8260.

ASSISTANT SECRETARY FOR TERRORIST FINANCING AND FINANCIAL CRIMES

Assistant Secretary.—Marshall S. Billingslea, MT Room 4316, 622–1943.

Deputy Assistant Secretary for Terrorist Financing and Financial Crimes.—Jennifer Fowler (acting), MT Room 4000, 622–1634.

Director, Office of:

Global Affairs.—Daniel Moger, MT Room 4001, 622–6464.

Strategic Policy.—Sarah Runge, MT Room 4308, 622–8667.

ASSISTANT SECRETARY FOR INTELLIGENCE AND ANALYSIS

Assistant Secretary.—A. Daniel McGlynn (acting), Room 4332 (202) 622–1835.

Deputy Assistant Secretary.—Michael Neufeld (acting), Room 2441, 622–1841.

Deputy Assistant Secretary for Security.—Michael Mason, Room 2441, 622–6583.

Deputy Assistant Secretary for Intelligence Community Integration.—Everette Jordan, Room 2441, 622–9049.

OFFICE OF FOREIGN ASSETS CONTROL

Director.—John Smith, Room 2240 (202) 622–2510.

EXECUTIVE OFFICE FOR ASSET FORFEITURE

1341 G Street, NW., Suite 900, 20005, phone (202) 622–9600

Director.—John M. Farley.

FINANCIAL CRIMES ENFORCEMENT NETWORK (FINCEN)

P.O. Box 39, Vienna, VA 22183

Director.—Kenneth A. Blanco (202) 354–6393.

Deputy Director.—Jamal El-Hindi, 354–6392.

OFFICE OF THE ASSISTANT SECRETARY FOR ECONOMIC POLICY

Assistant Secretary.—Karen Dynan, Room 3454 (202) 622–2200.

Senior Advisor to the Assistant Secretary.—Gauri Subramani, Room 3127, 622–2020.

Deputy Assistant Secretary for Policy Coordination.—Elaine Buckberg, Room 3449, 622–2220.

Deputy Assistant Secretary for Macroeconomic Analysis.—Gerald Cohen, Room 3450, 622–2734.

Director, Office of Macroeconomic Analysis.—Rachel Cononi, Room 2454, 622–0156.

Deputy Assistant Secretary for Microeconomic Analysis.—Jennifer Hunt, Room 3445, 622–1513.

Director, Office of Microeconomic Analysis.—Jason Brown, Room 4426, 622–1757.

OFFICE OF THE ASSISTANT SECRETARY FOR LEGISLATIVE AFFAIRS

Assistant Secretary for Legislative Affairs.—Andrew K. Maloney.

Senior Advisor.—J. Brady Howell, Room 3464, 622–1900.
Special Advisor to the Assistant Secretary.—Brittany Carey, Room 3134, 622–1900.
Executive Assistant.—Linda L. Powell, Room 3453–D, 622–1900.
Deputy Assistant Secretary, Banking and Finance.—Matthew Kellogg, Room 3132, 622–1900.
Deputy Assistant Secretary, Appropriations and Management.—Andrew Newton, Room 3122, 622–1900.
Special Advisor.—Francisco Riojas, Room 3453–A, 622–1900.
Deputy Assistant Secretary, Tax and Budget.—Bradley Bailey, Room 3108, 622–1900.
Deputy Assistant Secretary, International Affairs.—Stephen Pavlick, Room 3124–B, 622–1900.
Deputy Assistant Secretary, TFI.—Luke Ballman, Room 3124–C, 622–1900.

OFFICE OF THE ASSISTANT SECRETARY FOR MANAGEMENT

Assistant Secretary for Management.—Kody Kinsley, Room 2438, Main Treasury (202) 927–5639.
Special Assistant.—Samantha Upwright, 622–1149.
Senior Advisors: Daniel Brandt, 622–6240; Karen Burkes, 927–7198; Mike Lewis, 622–3068.
Deputy Assistant Secretary for Management and Budget.—Beverly Babers, 622–0323.
Departmental Budget Director.—Robert Mahaffie, 622–1497.
Conference Events and Meeting Services.—Lucinda Gooch, 622–2071.
Strategic Planning and Performance Improvement.—Katie Malague, 622–5515.
Director, Office of Budget and Travel.—Saesha Carlile, 622–8841.
Deputy Assistant Secretary for Treasury Operations.—Michael Thomas, 622–2195.
Environmental Safety and Health.—Jonathan Weeda, 662–6771.
Facilities Management.—Polly Dietz, 622–7067.
Deputy Assistant Secretary for Information Systems and Chief Information Officer.—Eric Olson (acting), 622–2015.
Deputy Assistant Secretary for Human Resources and Chief Human Capital Officer.—Trevor Norris, 622–1282.
Equal Opportunity and Diversity.—Mariam Harvey, 622–0316.
Deputy Assistant Secretary for Privacy, Transparency, and Records.—Ryan Law, 622–0494.
Deputy Chief Financial Officer.—Carole Banks, 622–0818.
Director, Financial Reporting and Policy.—Kawan Taylor, 622–7899.
Senior Procurement Executive.—Iris Cooper, 622–1039.
Director, General and Special Entity Accounting.—Stephen Cotter, 622–4279.
Director, Office of:
Emergency Programs.—J. Michael Thomas, 927–9213.
Minority and Women Inclusion.—Lorraine Cole, 927–8181.

OFFICE OF THE ASSISTANT SECRETARY FOR PUBLIC AFFAIRS

Assistant Secretary.—Tony Sayegh, Jr., Room 3438 MT (202) 622–2910.
Principal Deputy Assistant Secretary, Public Affairs.—Molly Meiners, Room 3439 MT, 622–2920.
Deputy Assistant Secretary, Public Affairs for International Affairs.—Jason Chung, Room 3111 MT.
Deputy Assistant Secretary for TFI.—Seth Unger, Room 3111 MT.
Senior Advisor, Public Affairs.—Vacant.
Deputy Assistant Secretary/Public Liaison.—Vacant.
Review Analyst and Scheduling Coordinator.—Carmen Alvarado, Room 3442 MT, 622–7483.
Spokesperson for Domestic Finance.—Vacant.
Enforcement Specialist.—Vacant.
International Affairs.—Vacant.
MHA & HHF.—Vacant.
OFS.—Vacant.
Tax, Budget, Economic Policy.—Vacant.
Speechwriter.—Max Raskin, Room 3111 MT, 622–0054.
Media Coordinator.—Vacant.
Media Affairs Specialists: Vacant.
Senior Advisor (Public Liaison).—Vacant.
Special Assistant.—Vacant.

Press Assistant.—Vacant.

OFFICE OF THE ASSISTANT SECRETARY FOR TAX POLICY

Assistant Secretary.—David J. Kautter, Room 3120 MT (202) 622–0050.
Deputy Assistant Secretary, International Tax Affairs.—L. ''Chip'' Harter, Room 3045 MT, 622–1317.
Tax Analysis.—Vacant, Room 3064 MT, 622–0992.
Tax Policy.—Dana L. Trier, Room 3112 MT, 622–0140.
Tax, Trade and Tariff Policy.—Timothy Skud, Room 3104 MT, 622–0220.
Retirement and Health Policy and Senior Advisor to the Secretary.—Vacant, Room 3063 MT, 622–7827.
Senior Advisor.—Austin Bramwell, Room 3064, 622–7827.
Tax Legislative Counsel.—Thomas West, Room 3040 MT, 622–6707.
Deputy Tax Legislative Counsel.—Krishna Vallabhaneni, Room 4202 MT, 622–0835.
International Tax Counsel.—Vacant, Room 3045 MT, 622–0843.
Deputy International Tax Counsels: Henry Louis, Room 5064 MT, 622–1791; Douglas Poms, Room 5104C MT, 622–1754.
Benefits Tax Counsel.—Robert Neis, Room 3050 MT, 622–5293.
Deputy Benefits Tax Counsel.—Carol Weiser, Room 4203 MT, 622–0869.
Director, Office of Tax Analysis.—James Mackie, Room 4116 MT, 622–1326.
Director, Division of:
Business and International Taxation.—Edith Brashares, Room 4221 MT, 622–0463.
Economic Modeling and Computer Applications.—Robert Gillette, Room 4039 MT, 622–0852.
Individual Taxation.—Janet McCubbin, Room 4043 MT, 622–0589.
Revenue and Receipts Forecasting/Business Revenue Division.—Curtis Carlson, Room 4112 MT, 622–0130.
Revenue and Receipts Forecasting/Individual Revenue Division.—Scott Jaquette, Room 4064 MT, 622–1319.

BUREAU OF ENGRAVING AND PRINTING

14th and C Streets, SW., 20228, phone (202) 874–2000

[Created by act of July 11, 1862; codified under U.S.C. 31, section 303]

Director.—Leonard R. Olijar (817) 874–2016.
Deputy Director (Chief Operating Officer).—Charlene Williams, 874–3880.
Deputy Director (Chief Administrative Officer).—Vacant.
Chief Counsel.—Sidney Rocke, 874–2306.
Associate Directors:
Chief Financial Officer.—Debra Richardson, 874–2020.
Chief Technology Officer.—Justin Draheim (acting), 874–1239.
Chief Information Officer.—Harry Singh, 874–3000.
Management.—Will Levy III, 874-2040.
Manufacturing.—Ron Voelker (acting), 847–3979.
Quality.—Brian Lawler, 874–2436.

OFFICE OF THE COMPTROLLER OF THE CURRENCY

400 7th Street, SW., 20219, phone (202) 649–6800

Comptroller.—Joseph M. Otting, 649–6400.
Public Affairs Operations.—Joseph Adamoli, 649–6480.
Senior Deputy Comptroller and Chief Counsel.—Karen Solomon, 649–5276.
Senior Deputy Comptrollers for—
Bank Supervision Policy and Chief National Bank Examiner.—Grace Dailey, 649–6770.
Economics.—Michael Sullivan, 649–5472.
Large Bank Supervision.—Morris Morgan, 649–6395.
Management and Chief Financial Officer.—Kathy Murphy, 649–6993.
Midsize and Community Bank Supervision.—Toney Bland, 649–5420.
Director for Congressional Liaison.—Carrie Moore, 649–6737.
Senior Deputy Comptroller EG and Ombudsman.—Larry Hattix, 649–6857.
Chief Information Officer.—Stephen W. Warren, 649–8661.

INTERNAL REVENUE SERVICE

1111 Constitution Avenue, NW., 20224, phone (202) 622–5000

[Created by act of July 1, 1862; codified under U.S.C. 26, section 7802]

Commissioner.—John Koskinen, 317–7070.
Chief of Staff.—Crystal Philcox, 317–7070.
Deputy Commissioner, Services and Enforcement.—Kirsten Wielobob, 317–4263.
Commissioner of:
Large Business and International Division.—Douglas O'Donnell, 515–4400.
Small Business / Self-Employed.—Mary Beth Murphy, 317–6500.
Tax Exempt and Government Entities.—Sunita Lough, 317–8400.
Wage and Investment.—Kenneth Corbin, 317–7060.
Chief, Criminal Investigation.—Richard Weber, 317–3200.
Directors:
Office of Professional Responsibility.—Steven Whitlock, 317–4676.
Whistleblower Office.—Lee Martin, 317–3500.
Deputy Commissioner, Operations Support.—Jeffrey Tribiano, 317–3950.
Chief:
Agency-Wide Shared Services.—Kevin McIver, 317–7500.
Appeals.—Donna Hansberry, 317–8975.
Communications and Liaison.—Terry Lemons, 317–6849.
Equity, Diversity and Inclusion.—Elita Christiansen, 317–5400.
Financial Officer.—Ursula Gillis, 317–6400.
IRS Human Capital Officer.—Daniel Riordan, 317–7600.
Office of Privacy, Information Protection and Data Security.—Edward Killen, 317–6449.
Technology Officer.—Gina Garza, 317–5000.
Chief Counsel.—William Paul, 317–3300.
National Taxpayer Advocate.—Nina E. Olson, 317–6100.
Director, Office of Research, Analysis and Statistics.—Benjamin Herndon, 803–9700.
Office of Legislative Affairs.—Leonard Oursler, 317–4316.

INSPECTOR GENERAL FOR TAX ADMINISTRATION (TIGTA)

1401 H Street, NW., Suite 469, 20005

phone (202) 622–6500, fax 927–0001

Inspector General.—J. Russell George.
Principal Deputy Inspector General.—Vacant.
Congressional Liaison.—David Barnes, 622–3062.
Chief Counsel.—Gladys M. Hernandez, 622–3103.
Deputy Inspector General for Audit.—Michael E. McKenney, 622–5916.
Assistant Inspector General for Compliance and Enforcement Operations.—Matthew A. Weir, 622–3837.
Assistant Inspector General for Management Planning and Workforce Development.—Nancy A. LaManna, 927–7076.
Assistant Inspector General for Management Services and Organizations—Greg D. Kutz, 622–5089.
Assistant Inspector General for Returns Processing and Accounts Services.—Russell Martin (978) 809–0296.
Assistant Inspector General for Security and Information Technology Services.—Danny Verneuille (acting), (901) 546–3111.
Deputy Inspector General for Investigations.—Timothy P. Camus, 927–7234.
Assistant Inspectors General for Investigations: Michael A. Delgado, 927–7183; James S. Jackson, 927–0029; Randy M. Silvis, 927–0150.
Deputy Assistant Inspector General for Investigations.—Gayle A. Hatheway, 927–7178.
Deputy Inspector General for Inspections and Evaluations.—Greg D. Kutz (acting), 622–5089.
Deputy Inspector General for Mission Support.—Mervin Hyndman (acting), 622–7586.

OFFICE OF THE TREASURER OF THE UNITED STATES

Treasurer.—Jovita Carranza (202) 622–0100.
Senior Advisor.—Vacant.
Executive Assistant.—Gail Harris-Berry (detail).
Director, Advanced Counterfeit Deterrence.—Vacant.

UNITED STATES MINT

801 9th Street, NW., 20220, phone (202) 354–7200, fax 756–6160

Director.—David J. Ryder (202) 354–7200.
Executive Assistant to the Director.—Arnetta Cain, 354–7200.
Deputy Director.—David Motl (acting), 354–7200.
Executive Assistant to the Deputy Director.—Sabrina Littlejohn, 354–7200.
Chief Counsel.—Jean A. Gentry, 354–7200.
Director, Legislative and Intergovernmental Affairs.—Vacant, 354–6700.
Deputy Director, Legislative and Intergovernmental Affairs.—Betty Birdsong, 354–7770.
Chief, Corporate Communications.—Thomas Johnson, 354–7720.
Chief, Office of Protection.—Dennis O'Connor, 354–7300.
Deputy Chief, Office of Protection.—Bill R. Bailey, 354–7300.
Associate Director/Chief Information Officer.—DeAnna Wynn (acting), 354–7700.
Deputy Associate Director.—Joseph Gioeli (acting), 354–7700.
Associate Director/Chief Financial Officer.—Kristie McNally (acting), 354–7800.
Deputy Associate Director.—Kenyatta Fletcher (acting), 354–7800.
Associate Director, Sales and Marketing.—Jon Cameron, 354–7500.
Deputy Associate Director.—Greg Dawson (acting), 354–7800.
Associate Director, Manufacturing.—David Croft, 354–7400.
Deputy Associate Director.—Frank Goulart, 354–7400.

DEPARTMENT OF DEFENSE

The Pentagon, 20301–1155, phone (703) 545–6700

JAMES N. ''JIM'' MATTIS, Secretary of Defense; born in Pullman, WA, September 8, 1950; education: B.A., history, Central Washington University, Ellensburg, WA, 1971; M.A., international security affairs, National War College, Washington, DC, 1994; military/professional: after college in 1971, commissioned as Second Lieutenant in the U.S. Marine Corps. During his more than four decades in uniform, Secretary Mattis commanded Marines at all levels—from an infantry rifle platoon to a Marine Expeditionary Force. He led an infantry battalion in Iraq in 1991, an expeditionary brigade in Afghanistan after the 9/11 terror attack in 2001, a Marine Division in the initial attack and subsequent stability operations in Iraq in 2003, and led all U.S. Marine Forces in the Middle East as Commander, I Marine Expeditionary Force and U.S. Marine Forces Central Command. During his non-combat assignments, Secretary Mattis served as Senior Military Assistant to the Deputy Secretary of Defense; as Director, Marine Corps Manpower Plans and Policy; as Commanding General, Marine Corps Combat Development Command; and as Executive Secretary to the Secretary of Defense. As a joint force commander, Secretary Mattis commanded U.S. Joint Forces Command, NATO's Supreme Allied Command for Transformation, and U.S. Central Command. At U.S. Central Command, he directed military operations of more than 200,000 soldiers, sailors, airmen, Coast Guardsmen, Marines, and allied forces across the Middle East. Following his retirement from the U.S. Marine Corps in 2013, Secretary Mattis served as the Davies Family Distinguished Visiting Fellow at the Hoover Institution, Stanford University, specializing in the study of leadership, national security, strategy, innovation, and the effective use of military force. In 2016, he co-edited the book *Warriors & Citizens: American Views of Our Military*; nominated by President Donald J. Trump as the 26th Secretary of Defense, and was confirmed by the U.S. Senate on January 20, 2017.

OFFICE OF THE SECRETARY

1000 Defense Pentagon, Room 3E880, 20301–1000
phone (703) 692–7100, fax (703) 571–8951

Secretary of Defense.—James N. Mattis.

OFFICE OF THE DEPUTY SECRETARY

1010 Defense Pentagon, Room 3E944, 20301–1010, phone (703) 692–7150

Deputy Secretary of Defense.—Patrick M. Shanahan.

EXECUTIVE SECRETARIAT

Pentagon, Room 3E880, 20301–1000, phone (703) 692–7120, fax 571–8951

Executive Secretary.—Hallock N. Mohler, Jr.

GENERAL COUNSEL

Pentagon, Room 3E788, 20301–1600, phone (703) 695–3341, fax 693–7278

General Counsel.—William S. Castle (acting).
Principal Deputy.—Vacant.

OPERATIONAL TEST AND EVALUATION

Pentagon, Room 3E1088, 20301–1700, phone (703) 697–3655, fax 614–9103

Director.—Mr. David W. Duma (acting).

INSPECTOR GENERAL

4800 Mark Center Drive, Suite 15G27, Alexandria, VA 22350–1500

phone (703) 604–8300, fax 604–8310

hotline 1–800–424–9098, hotline fax (703) 604–8567

Inspector General.—Jon T. Rymer.
Principal Deputy Inspector General.—Vacant.

UNDER SECRETARY OF DEFENSE FOR ACQUISITION, TECHNOLOGY, AND LOGISTICS

Pentagon, Room 3E1010, phone (703) 697–7021

Under Secretary.—Ellen M. Lord.
Principal Deputy Under Secretary.—Vacant.
Assistant Secretary for—
Acquisition.—Kevin Fahey.
Logistics and Materiel Readiness.—Robert H. McMahon.
Energy, Installations, and Environment.—Lucian Niemeyer.
Research and Engineering.—Mary Miller (acting).
Nuclear, Chemical, and Biological Defense Programs.—Guy B. Roberts.
Deputy Assistant Secretary for Manufacturing and Industrial Base Policy.—John McGinn (acting).
Director, Office of Small Business Programs.—James Galvin (acting).

JOINT STRIKE FIGHTER PROGRAM OFFICE

200 12th Street South, Suite 600, Arlington, VA 22202–5402, phone (703) 602–7640

Program Executive Officer.—VADM Mathias W. Winter, USN.

UNDER SECRETARY OF DEFENSE (COMPTROLLER) AND CHIEF FINANCIAL OFFICER

Pentagon, Room 3E770, 20301–1100, phone (703) 695–3237

Under Secretary/Chief Financial Officer.—David Norquist.
Principal Deputy Under Secretary.—Elaine A. McCusker.

UNDER SECRETARY OF DEFENSE FOR PERSONNEL AND READINESS

Pentagon, Room 3E986, 20301–4000, phone (703) 697–2121

Under Secretary.—Robert Wilkie.
Principal Deputy Under Secretary.—Vacant.
Military Deputy.—Lt. Gen. Herman S. Clardy.
Assistant Secretary of Defense for—
Health Affairs.—Thomas McCaffery, 697–2111.
Performing the Duites of Readiness.—Veronica B. Daigle (703) 693–0466.
Reserve Affairs.—Stephanie A. Barna (703) 614–3240.

UNDER SECRETARY OF DEFENSE FOR POLICY

Pentagon, Room 3E806, 20301–2000, phone (703) 697–7200

Under Secretary.—John C. Rood.
Principal Deputy Under Secretary.—David Trachtenberg.
Assistant Secretary of Defense for—
Asian and Pacific Security Affairs.—Randall Schriver.
Homeland Defense and Global Security.—Kenneth Rapuano.
International Security Affairs.—Robert Karem.
Special Operations/Low-Intensity Conflict.—Owen West.
Strategy, Plans, and Capabilities.—Todd Harvey.

DEPARTMENT OF DEFENSE CHIEF INFORMATION OFFICER (DoD CIO)

Pentagon, Room 3E1030, 20301–6000, phone (703) 695–0348

DoD CIO.—Dana Deasy.
Principal Deputy DoD CIO.—Essye B. Miller (acting).

ASSISTANT SECRETARY FOR LEGISLATIVE AFFAIRS

Pentagon, Room 3E970, 20301–1300, phone (703) 697–6210, fax 695–5860

Assistant Secretary.—Robert R. Hood.
Principal Deputy.—E. Peter Giambastiani III.
Deputy Assistant (Senate Affairs).—Laura P. McAleer.

ASSISTANT TO THE SECRETARY FOR PUBLIC AFFAIRS

Pentagon, Room 2E964, 20301–1400, phone (703) 697–9312, fax 695–4299
public inquiries, 571–3343

Assistant to the Secretary.—Dana W. White.
Principal Deputy.—Vacant.

OFFICE OF THE CHIEF MANAGEMENT OFFICER

Pentagon, Room 3E146, 20301–9010, phone (703) 614–8888, fax 695–5395

Chief Management Officer.—John H. Gibson II.
Assistant Deputy Chief Management Officer.—David Tillotson III.

DEPARTMENT OF DEFENSE FIELD ACTIVITIES

DEFENSE MEDIA ACTIVITY

6700 Taylor Avenue, Fort George G. Meade, MD 20755

phone (301) 222–6700, http://www.dma.mil/

Director.—Ray B. Shepherd.
Deputy Director.—COL Andrew Mutter, USA.

DEPARTMENT OF DEFENSE EDUCATION ACTIVITY

4800 Mark Center Drive, Arlington, VA 22350–1400

School Information (571) 372–0610

Director.—Thomas M. Brady, 372–1885.
Principal Deputy Director and Associate Director for Education.—Linda Curtis, 372–1893.
Associate Director for Finance and Business Operations.—Robert Brady, 372–1901.
General Counsel.—Edwin Daniel, 372–0976.

DEPARTMENT OF DEFENSE HUMAN RESOURCES ACTIVITY

4800 Mark Center Drive, Suite 06J25–01, Alexandria, VA 22350–4000

Director.—William Booth.
Deputy Director.—Jeffrey Register.
Executive Assistant.—Katherine Roddy.

OFFICE OF ECONOMIC ADJUSTMENT

2231 Crystal Drive, Suite 520, Arlington, VA 22202, phone (703) 697–2130

Director.—Patrick J. O'Brien.
Interim Deputy Director for Programs.—COL Douglas E. Brown, USA, 697–2015.
Deputy Director for Compliance and Integration.—Nia A. Hope, 697–2088.

Sacramento Western Regional Office Director.—Gary Kuwabara (916) 557–7365.

WASHINGTON HEADQUARTERS SERVICES

Pentagon, phone (703) 693–7906

Director.—Patricia M. Young.
Deputy Director.—Marcia Case.
Director for—
Acquisition Directorate.—Tim Applegate (acting), (703) 545–0423.
Enterprise Information Technology Services Directorate.—Lytwaive Hutchinson (703) 695–2865.
Enterprise Management.—Sajeel Ahmed, 693–7995.
Executive Services.—Darren Irvine (acting), 693–7965.
Financial Management.—William Relyea, 545–0019.
Human Resources Directorate.—Susan Yarwood (571) 256–4504.
OSD Chief Information Office.—Lytwaive Hutchinson, 695–2865.
Raven Rock Mountain Complex.—Col. Ramona Plemmons (717) 878–3343.
WHS General Counsel.—John Albanese (acting), 693–7374.

JOINT CHIEFS OF STAFF

OFFICE OF THE CHAIR

Pentagon, Room 2E872, 20318–0001, phone (703) 697–9121

Chair.—Gen. Joseph F. Dunford, Jr., USMC.
Vice Chair.—Gen. Paul J. Selva, USAF, Room 2E868, 614–8949.
Assistant to the Chair, Joint Chiefs of Staff.—VADM Frank C. Pandolfe, USN, Room 2E858, 695–4605.

JOINT STAFF

Director.—Lt. Gen. Kenneth F. McKenzie, USMC, Room 2E936, 614–5221.
Vice Director.—RADM Michael J. Dumont, USN, Room 2E936, 614–5223.
Director for—
Manpower and Personnel, J–1.—Brig. Gen. Kyle J. Kremer, USAF, Room 2D857, 697–9644.
Intelligence, J–2.—Maj. Gen. James R. Marrs, USAF, Room 2D877, 697–9773.
Operations, J–3.—Lt. Gen. John L. Dolan, USAF, Room 2D874, 697–3702.
Logistics, J–4.—LTG Stephen R. Lyons, USA, Room 2D867, 697–7000.
Strategic Plans and Policy, J–5.—LTG Richard D. Clarke, USA, Room 2E800, 697–9716.
Command, Control, Communications, and Computer/Cyber, J–6.—VADM Marshall B. Lytle III, USCG, Room 1E1044, 695–4420.
Joint Force Development, J–7.—VADM Kevin D. Scott, USN, Room 2D864, 697–9031.
Force Structure, Resources, and Assessment, J–8.—LTG Anthony R. Ierardi, USA, Room 2E838, 697–6605.

DEFENSE AGENCIES

MISSILE DEFENSE AGENCY

5700 18th Street, Fort Belvoir, VA 22060–5573

Director.—Lt. Gen. Samuel A. Greaves, USAF (571) 231–8006.
Deputy Director.—RADM Jon A. Hill, USN, 231–8022.
Director, Public Affairs.—Mark Wright, 231–8212.
Director, Legislative Affairs.—Kimo Hollingsworth, 231–8105.

DEFENSE ADVANCED RESEARCH PROJECTS AGENCY

675 North Randolph Street, Arlington, VA 22203

Director.—Dr. Steven Walker (acting), 696–2402.
Deputy Director.—Dr. Stefanie Tompkins (acting), 248–1540.

DEFENSE COMMISSARY AGENCY

1300 E Avenue, Fort Lee, VA 23801–1800, phone (804) 734–8720/8330

Director.—Michael J. Dowling (acting), 734–8720.
Chief Operating Officer.—Michael J. Dowling, 734–8330.

WASHINGTON OFFICE

4100 Defense Pentagon, Room 5D636, 20301–4100, phone (703) 571–7186/7184

Chief.—Robin Schmidt.

DEFENSE CONTRACT AUDIT AGENCY

8725 John J. Kingman Road, Suite 2135, Fort Belvoir, VA 22060
phone (703) 767–3200

Director.—Anita F. Bales, 767–3200.
Deputy Director.—Kenneth J. Saccoccia, 767–3272.

DEFENSE FINANCE AND ACCOUNTING SERVICE

8899 East 56th Street, Indianapolis, IN 46249–0100
phone (317) 212–0714

Director.—Teresa A. McKay.
Principal Deputy Director.—Audrey Y. Davis.

DEFENSE HEALTH AGENCY

7700 Arlington Boulevard, Falls Church, VA 22042–5101, phone (703) 681–8707

Director.—VADM Raquel C. Bono, MC, USN.
Deputy Director.—Guy T. Kiyokawa, SES.

DEFENSE INFORMATION SYSTEMS AGENCY

P.O. Box 549, Command Building, Fort Meade, MD 20755

Director.—VADM. Nancy Norton, USN (301) 225–6007.
Executive Deputy Director.—Anthony Montemarano, 225–6010.
Chief of Staff.—COL Joel Lindeman, USA, 225–6020.

DEFENSE INTELLIGENCE AGENCY

200 MacDill Boulevard, Washington, DC 20340, phone (202) 231–0800

Director.—Lt. Gen. Vincent R. Stewart, USMC.
Deputy Director.—Melissa A. Drisko.

DEFENSE LEGAL SERVICES AGENCY

Pentagon, Room 3E788, 20301–1600, phone (703) 695–3341, fax 693–7278

Director/General Counsel.—Paul S. Koffsky (Performing the Duties of the DoD General Counsel/Director, DLSA).
Principal Deputy Director.—Charles A. Allen (acting), 695–2604.

DEFENSE LOGISTICS AGENCY

8725 John J. Kingman Road, Suite 2533, Ft. Belvoir, VA 22060
phone (703) 767–5264

Director.—Edward J. Case (acting).

Vice Director.—Edward J. Case.

DEFENSE POW/MIA ACCOUNTING AGENCY
2300 Defense Pentagon, Washington, DC 20301–2300
phone (703) 699–1102, fax 602–1890

Director.—Kelly K. McKeague.

DEFENSE SECURITY COOPERATION AGENCY
201 12th Street South, Suite 203, Arlington, VA 22202–5408, phone (703) 604–6605

Director.—VADM Joseph W. Rixey, 604–6604.
Deputy Director.—Jennifer N. Zakriski, 604–6606.

DEFENSE SECURITY SERVICE
27130 Telegraph Road, Quantico, VA 22134, phone (703) 617–2352

Director.—Stanley L. Sims.

DEFENSE THREAT REDUCTION AGENCY
8725 John J. Kingman Road, Stop 6201, Ft. Belvoir, VA 22060–6201
phone (703) 767–7594

Director.—Kenneth A. Myers III.
Deputy Director.—Maj. Gen. John P. Horner, USAF.
Chief, Governmental and Public Affairs.—Chris Geeslin.

NATIONAL GEOSPATIAL-INTELLIGENCE AGENCY
7500 GEOINT Drive, Springfield, VA 22150, phone (571) 557–7300

Director.—Robert Cardillo.
Deputy Director.—Susan Gordon.

NATIONAL SECURITY AGENCY/CENTRAL SECURITY SERVICE
Ft. George G. Meade, MD 20755, phone (301) 688–6524

Director, NSA/Chief, CSS.—ADM Michael S. Rogers, USN.
Deputy Director, NSA.—Richard H. Ledgett, Jr.
Deputy Chief, CSS.—Brig. Gen. John Bansemer, USAF.

JOINT SERVICE SCHOOLS
9820 Belvoir Road, Ft. Belvoir, VA 22060, phone (800) 845–7606

DEFENSE ACQUISITION UNIVERSITY

President.—James P. Woolsey (703) 805–3360.
Vice President.—Roy L. Wood (acting), 805–2828.
Chief of Staff.—Joseph E. Johnson, 805–2828.

NATIONAL INTELLIGENCE UNIVERSITY

President.—David R. Ellison (202) 231–3344.

NATIONAL DEFENSE UNIVERSITY
Fort McNair, Building 62, 300 Fifth Avenue, 20319
phone (202) 685–3912

President.—Maj. Gen. Frederick Padilla, USMC, Building 62, Room 307, 685–3936.

Senior Vice President.—Amb. Wanda Nesbitt, Building 62, Room 307A, 685–3923.

Provost and Vice President for Academic Affairs.—Dr. John Yaeger, Building 62, Room 309C, 685–0080.

CAPSTONE / PINNACLE / KEYSTONE

Director.—Dr. Ricky L. Waddell, Building 64, Room 3510, 685–2330.

COLLEGE OF INTERNATIONAL SECURITY AFFAIRS

Chancellor.—Dr. Michael Bell, Building 64, Room 2102 (202) 685–7209.

COLLEGE OF INFORMATION AND CYBERSPACE

Chancellor.—RADM Janice M. Hamby (Ret.), USN, Building 62, Room 201G (202) 685–3886.

JOINT FORCES STAFF COLLEGE

7800 Hampton Boulevard, Norfolk, VA 23511–1702, phone (757) 443–6200

Commandant.—RADM John Smith, USN, Room A202.

NATIONAL WAR COLLEGE

Commandant.—BG Tom Cosentino, USA, Building 61, Room 124 (202) 685–4341.

DWIGHT D. EISENHOWER SCHOOL FOR NATIONAL SECURITY AND RESOURCE STRATEGY

Commandant.—Brig. Gen. Thomas A. Gorry, USMC, Room 200 (202) 685–4337.

UNIFORMED SERVICES UNIVERSITY OF THE HEALTH SCIENCES

4301 Jones Bridge Road, Bethesda, MD 20814

President.—Charles L. Rice, M.D., Room A1019 (301) 295–3013.

DEPARTMENT OF THE AIR FORCE

Pentagon, 1670 Air Force, Washington, DC 20330–1670
phone (703) 697–7376, fax 695–8809

SECRETARY OF THE AIR FORCE

Secretary of the Air Force.—Hon. Heather Wilson, Room 4E878.
Confidential Assistant.—Rudy Sheffer.
Senior Military Assistant.—Brig. Gen. David Iverson.
Deputy Military Assistant.—Lt. Col. Tyler Lewis.
Military Aid.—Lt. Col. Nicci Rucker.
Executive Assistants: MSgt. Charles Allen, MSgt. Ashlie Chacon.

SECAF/CSAF EXECUTIVE ACTION GROUP

Director.—Col. Rodney Lewis (703) 697–5540.
Deputy Chief.—Catherine Perro.

UNDER SECRETARY OF THE AIR FORCE

Pentagon, 1670 Air Force, Room 4E858, 20330–1670, phone (703) 697–1361

Under Secretary.—Hon. Matthew Donovan.
Confidential Assistant.—Rosa Ramirez.
Senior Military Assistant.—Col. Doug Schiess.
Military Assistant.—Maj. Scott Korell.
Executive Assistant.—MSgt Taisha Ross.

CHIEF OF STAFF

Pentagon, 1670 Air Force, Room 4E924, 20330
phone (703) 697–9225

Chief of Staff.—Gen. David Goldfein.
Confidential Assistant.—Terri Stern.
Special Assistant.—Samuel Neill, Room 4E929, 697–1930.
Executive Officer.—Col. Matthew Davidson.
Vice Chief of Staff.—Gen. Stephen Wilson, Room 4E938, 695–7911.
Director of Staff.—Lt. Gen. Jacqueline Van Ovost, Room 4E944, 695–7913.
Chief Master Sergeant of the Air Force.—CMSAF Kaleth Wright, Room 4E941, 695–0498.

DEPUTY UNDER SECRETARY FOR INTERNATIONAL AFFAIRS

Pentagon, 1080 Air Force Pentagon, Room 4E192, 20330–1080

Deputy Under Secretary.—Heidi H. Grant (703) 695–7263.
Assistant Deputy.—Maj. Gen. Stephen "Steve" Oliver, 695–7261.
Executive Officers: Maj. Robert Radesky, 693–1941; Georgia Smothers, 695–7263.

Pentagon, 1080 Air Force Pentagon, Room 4C253, 20330–1080

Director of Policy.—Anthony P. Reardon (571) 256–7491.
Executive Officer.—Lt. Col. John Smith, 256–7494.
Executive Assistant.—Michelle Polk, 256–7495.

Pentagon, 1080 Air Force Pentagon, Room 4C947, 20330–1080

Director of Regional Affairs.—Brig. Gen. David Nahom (703) 695–2022.

Executive Officer.—Maj. Linda Thierauf, 695–2077.
Executive Assistant.—Sanura Wade, 695–2080.

Pentagon, 1080 Air Force Pentagon, Room 4C253, 20330–1080

Director of Strategy, Resources, and Integration.—Maj. Gen. Brian Neal (ANG), (571) 256–9492.
Executive Assistant.—Patricia Green, 256–9491.

ASSISTANT SECRETARY FOR ACQUISITION, TECHNOLOGY AND LOGISTICS

Pentagon, 1060 Air Force, 20330

110 Luke Avenue, Suite 200, Bolling AFB, DC 20032–6400

Assistant Secretary.—Dr. Will Roper (703) 697–6361.
Senior Military Assistant.—Col. Amy McCain, 697–6990.
Military Assistant.—Lt. Col. Sean Halen, 697–6362.
Principal Deputy.—Darlene Costello, 697–9373.
Military Deputy.—Lt. Gen. Arnold Bunch, 697–6363.
Executive Officer.—Maj. Travis Gomez, 695–7311.

DEPUTY ASSISTANT SECRETARY FOR ACQUISITION INTEGRATION

Deputy Assistant Secretary.—John Miller (571) 256–0355.
Associate Deputy Assistant Secretary.—Vacant, 256–0351.
Executive Officer.—Maj. Todd Dawson, 256–0356.

DEPUTY ASSISTANT SECRETARY FOR CONTRACTING

Deputy Assistant Secretary.—Brig. Gen. Casey Blake (571) 256–2397.
Associate Deputy Assistant Secretary.—Scott Kiser, 256–2397.
Executive Officer.—Maj. Brian Sheehan, 256–2397.

DEPUTY ASSISTANT SECRETARY FOR SCIENCE, TECHNOLOGY AND ENGINEERING

Deputy Assistant Secretary.—Jeff Stanley (571) 256–0303.
Associate Deputy Assistant Secretary.—Dennis Miller, 256–0303.
Executive Officer.—Julianne Vilca, 256–0294.

CAPABILITY DIRECTORATE FOR GLOBAL POWER PROGRAMS

Director.—Maj. Gen. Michael Fantini (571) 256–0191.
Deputy Director.—Vacant, 256–0192.
Executive Officer.—Maj. Derick Wolf, 256–0196.

CAPABILITY DIRECTORATE FOR GLOBAL REACH PROGRAMS

Director.—Brig. Gen. Ryan Britton (571) 256–0489.
Deputy Director.—Col. Amanda Myers, 256–0497.
Executive Officer.—Maj. Dalbert Shaw, 256–0522.

CAPABILITY DIRECTORATE FOR INFORMATION DOMINANCE

Director.—Susan Thornton (571) 256–0081.
Deputy Director.—Col. Christopher Lohr, 256–0082.
Executive Officer.—Maj. Todd Watson, 256–0083.

CAPABILITY DIRECTORATE FOR SPACE PROGRAMS

Director.—Brig. Gen. Mark Baird (571) 695–3423.
Deputy Director.—Col. Greg Barnhart, 695–3499.
Executive Officer.—Maj. Craig Hackbarth, 695–3435.

DIRECTORATE FOR SPECIAL PROGRAMS

Director.—Col. Darin Hoenle (202) 767–3890.
Deputy Director.—Chris DiNenna (571) 256–0005.
Executive Assistant.—Alesia Clark, 767–3890.

DIRECTORATE FOR AIR FORCE RAPID CAPABILITIES

Director.—Randall Walden (202) 767–1800.
Deputy Director.—William Bailey, 767–1800.
Executive Officer.—Maj. Andrew MacDonald, 767–3203.

ASSISTANT SECRETARY FOR FINANCIAL MANAGEMENT AND COMPTROLLER OF THE AIR FORCE (SAF/FM)

Pentagon, 1130 Air Force Pentagon, 20330–1130

Air Force Cost Analysis Agency, Jones Building

1500 West Perimeter Road, Joint Base Andrews-Naval Air Facility Washington MD 20762

Assistant Secretary.—John P. Roth, Room 4E978 (703) 695–0829.
Senior Military Assistant.—Lt. Col. Phelemon T. Williams, 695–0829.
Chief, Enlisted Matters.—CMSgt John A. Writer, 614–5429.

PRINCIPAL DEPUTY ASSISTANT SECRETARY FOR FINANCIAL MANAGEMENT

Principal Deputy Assistant Secretary.—Marilyn M. Thomas (703) 695–0837.
Military Assistant.—Maj. Ashley A. Housley, 695–0837.

DEPUTY ASSISTANT SECRETARY FOR BUDGET (SAF/FMB)

Deputy Assistant Secretary.—Maj. Gen. James F. Martin, Room 5D912 (703) 695–1876.
Executive Officer.—Lt. Col. Scott J. Thompson, 695–1876.
Deputy.—Carolyn M. Gleason, 697–1876.
Director of:
Budget and Appropriations Liaison.—Col. Kerry D. Britt, Room 5C949, 614–8114.
Budget Investment.—Carlos Rodgers, Room 5D912, 697–1220.
Budget Operations and Personnel.—Brig. Gen. James D. Peccia, Room 5D912, 697–0627.
Budget Programs.—Col. James R. Culpepper, Room 5C950, 614–7883.

DEPUTY ASSISTANT SECRETARY FOR COST AND ECONOMICS (SAF/FMC)

Deputy Assistant Secretary.—Pamela C. Schwenke, Room 5E975 (703) 697–5311.
Associate Deputy Assistant Secretary.—Grant McVicker, Room 5E975, 697–5313.
Executive Officer.—Lt. Col. David E. Stephens, Room 5E975, 697–5312.
Technical Director for Cost and Economics.—Ranae P. Woods, Suite 3500 (240) 612–5615.
Director, Economics and Business Management.—Dr. Anne L. Gorney, Room 4C843 (703) 693–9347.
Director, Cost Analysis Division.—Col. Davis H. Maulding, Room 4C943, 697–0288.

DEPUTY ASSISTANT SECRETARY FOR FINANCIAL OPERATIONS (SAF/FMF)

Deputy Assistant Secretary.—Thomas J. Murphy, Room 5D739 (703) 614–4180.
Associate Deputy Assistant Secretary.—Fredrick E. Carr, 5D739, 614–4180.
Chief Information Officer and Technology.—Shirley L. Reed, 5D739, 614–5437.
Military Assistant.—Lt. Col. Nyree D. Lensch, 614–4180.
Director for—
Accounting Policy and Reporting.—Omolola A. Fawole, Andrews AFB, MD (240) 612–5212.

AF Financial Systems Organization.—Glena G. Gibson, Wright-Patterson AFB, OH (937) 257–2262.
AFAFO.—Eric Cuebas, JB Andrews, MD (240) 612–5600.
AF–IPPS.—Deborah Kennedy, San Antonio, TX (210) 565–4329.
DEAMS.—Todd M. Baker, Wright-Patterson AFB, OH (937) 656–8554.
FIAR.—Katrina M. Rawls, Andrews AFB, MD (240) 612–5281.
Financial Services.—Gregory Wilson, Ellsworth AFB, SD (605) 385–8682.
Information Systems and Technology.—John Koski, Andrews AFB, MD (240) 612–5283.

DEPUTY ASSISTANT SECRETARY FOR PROGRAMS (SAF/FMP)

Deputy Assistant Secretary.—Brig. Gen. Edward A. Fienga, Room 5E857 (703) 695–3695.
Executive Officer.—Maj. Clarence F. McRae, 695–3695.
Deputy.—Judith B. Oliva, 695–3695.
Director of:
Program Integration.—Col. James Jacobson, Room 5C950, 614–7977.
Program Panel.—Gregory Parker, Room 5C950, 614–7970.

ASSISTANT SECRETARY FOR INSTALLATIONS, ENVIRONMENT AND ENERGY
1665 Air Force Pentagon, 20330–1665

Assistant Secretary.—Hon. John W. Henderson.
Principal Deputy Assistant Secretary.—Richard K. Hartley.
Executive Officers: Col. Davy B. Novy; Lt. Col. Aaron N. Wilt, 697–5023.
Executive Secretary.—Heather Pittman, 697–4936.

DEPUTY ASSISTANT SECRETARY FOR INSTALLATIONS (SAF/IEI)

Deputy Assistant Secretary.—Jennifer Miller, 695–3592.
Executive Officer.—Maj. Ferdinand Maldonado.
Executive Secretary/Administrative Support.—Sheenia T. Williams, 695–3592.
Deputy, Installation Planning.—Steve Arenson (571) 256–2471.
Director, Installation Planning (IEIP).—Col. Terry Walter, 693–7003.
Director, Real Estate Policy.—Mark Pohlmeier.
Manager, Legislative/Public Affairs.—Frank Smolinsky, 697–1980.
Cooperative, Installation Policy.—James Sample, 693–3349.
Program Managers: Tim P. Brennan, 695–5730; Ed McCarthy, 693–9339; John Smith, 693–8309; Terry Tallent, 693–7244.
AFCEC Liaison.—Robert McCann, 692–9515.

DEPUTY ASSISTANT SECRETARY FOR ENVIRONMENT, SAFETY AND INFRASTRUCTURE (SAF/IEE)

Deputy Assistant Secretary.—Mark A. Correll, 697–9297.
Principal Director, E/S/I Policy.—Lee Conesa, 697–2066.
Executive Officer.—Maj. Marc Graessle.
Executive Secretary/Administrative Support.—Sheenia T. Williams, 695–3592.
Cooperative, Environment Policy.—Michelle Brown, 697–0989.
Director:
Environment Policy.—Andrea Lehn.
Environmental Policy and Programs.—Otis Hicks, 693–9328.
Infrastructure Policy.—Lt. Col. Walt Gibbins, 693–2047.
Installation Energy Policy and Programs.—Douglas Tucker.
Occupational Health Plans and Programs.—Col. Joseph Costantino.
Occupational Health Policy.—Lt. Col. Freeman Holifield.
Safety Policy.—William Walkowiak.
Manager:
Facilities Energy.—John Hayes, 571–5771.
Process Energy and Vehicles.—Andrea L. Hodges, 693–3254.
Contract Support, ESOH Policy.—Daniel Kowalczyk, 697–1198.
Facilities Energy Analyst.—Richard Brill, 697–1018.

DEPUTY ASSISTANT SECRETARY FOR OPERATIONAL ENERGY (SAF/IEN)

Deputy Assistant Secretary.—Roberto I. Guerrero (571) 256–4711.
Principal Director, Operational Energy Policy and Chief of Staff.—Michael Penland (571) 256–3944.
Executive Officer.—Capt. Charles McDaniel (703) 697–6032.
Executive Secretary.—Ann Belfield (571) 256–4711.
Director, Energy Analysis Task Force.—Col. Chip Bulger (703) 614–8279.
Chief of:
Aviation Energy Logistics Policy.—Mike Lynch.
Aviation Energy Operations Policy.—William Spacy.
Education and Training and Strategic Communication Policy.—Lt. Col. Breanna Lankford (703) 697–1207.
Future Operations and Acquisitions Policy.—Fred Parker.

DEPUTY ASSISTANT SECRETARY FOR RESERVE AFFAIRS

Deputy Assistant Secretary, Reserve Affairs and Airman Readiness.—John A. Fedrigo, Room 5D742 (703) 697–6376.
Executive Secretary.—Stephanie Parry, 697–6375.
Assistant Deputy, Auxiliary, Education and Development Programs—Thomas Shubert (571) 256–4044.
Air Force Reserve Matters.—Col. Michael Phan, 697–6431.
ANG Matters.—Col. Mark Sheehan (571) 256–4043.
Assistant Deputy, Force Support and Family Programs.—Kimberly Yates (703) 693–9511.
Assistant Deputy for Health Policy.—Martha Soper, 693–9512.
Senior Enlisted Advisor.—CMSgt. Jennifer Koenig, 693–9505.
Executive Director for Air Reserve Forces Policy Committee.—Vacant, 697–6430.
Assistant Force Support and Family Programs.—Lt. Col. Steven C. Combs, 693–9504.

DEPUTY ASSISTANT SECRETARY FOR STRATEGIC DIVERSITY INTEGRATION

Deputy Assistant Secretary.—Vacant, Room 5E1083 (703) 697–6586.
Assistant Deputy.—Vacant, 697–6583.
Executive Secretary.—Karen Sauls, 697–6586.

AIR FORCE REVIEW BOARDS AGENCY (SAF/MRB)

1500 West Perimeter Road, Suite 3700, Joint Base Andrews NAF–Washington, MD 20762

Director.—Mark S. Teskey (240) 612–5400.
Deputy Director.—Dixie Morrow, 612–5403.
Agency Senior Legal Advisor.—Ralph "Brian" Arnold, 612–5404.
Agency Senior Medical Advisor.—Dr. Horace Carson, 612–5405.
Senior Enlisted Advisor.—CMSgt Jasper C. Howard, 612–5408.
Confidential Assistant.—Marilyn Redmond, 612–5400.

AIR FORCE CIVILIAN APPELLATE REVIEW OFFICE (AFCARO), SAF/MRBA (Suite 4350)

Director.—Rita S. Looney (240) 612–5330.
Assistant Director.—Kenneth Sibley, 612–5331.

AIR FORCE SECURITY PROTECTION DIRECTORATE, SAF/MRBB

President.—Bruce Brown (240) 612–5364.
Deputy.—Joseph Schott, 612–5350.
Executive Secretary/Attorney Advisor on Clemency/Parole Board.—Bruce Brown, 612–5364.
Executive Secretary, DoD Civilian/Military Service Review Board.—Bruce Brown, 612–5364.
President Remissions Board.—Bruce Brown, 612–5364.

AIR FORCE BOARD FOR CORRECTION OF MILITARY RECORDS (AFBCMR) SAF / MRBC

Executive Director.—John Vallario (240) 612–5392.

Associate Directors: Nicole Jackson, 612–5385; Daryl Lawrence, 612–5381; Kenneth Sibley, 612–5331.

Lead Examiners: Deborah Davidson, 612–5383; Christopher Honeycutt, 612–4865; Janet Hutson, 612–5373.

DoD PHYSICAL DISABILITY BOARD OF REVIEW (PDBR), SAF / MRBD (Suite 4350)

President.—Troy D. McIntosh (240) 612–4390.

Deputy.—Gregory E. Johnson, 612–4392.

AIR FORCE REVIEW BOARDS AGENCY LEGAL DIRECTORATE, SAF / MRBL

Director.—Col. Mynda Ohman (240) 612–4529.

AIR FORCE REVIEW BOARDS AGENCY MEDICAL SUPPORT DIRECTORATE, SAF / MRBM

Director.—Col. Brian Pinkston (240) 612–5407.

SECRETARY OF THE AIR FORCE PERSONNEL COUNCIL (SAFPC), SAF / MRBP

Director.—Col. Andrew Weaver (240) 612–5369.

Deputy Director.—Algie Walker, Jr., 612–5380.

Chief, Air Force Discharge Review Board.—Col. Lisa Craig, 612–5355.

Chief, Awards / Decorations / Air Force Reserve Advisor.—Col. Amy Storm, 612–5365.

MISSION SUPPORT DIRECTORATE, SAF / MRBX

Director.—Clifford R. Tompkins (240) 612–5408.

Resource Manager.—Timothy Nolte, 612–6269.

Human Resources.—Jameill Barksdale, 612–5357.

Chief, Case Management Office.—Sean Spriggs, 612–5387.

Information Technology Manager.—Michael Cusick, 612–5359.

CHIEF, INFORMATION DOMINANCE AND CHIEF INFORMATION OFFICER

1800 Air Force Pentagon, Room 4E1050, 20330

Chief, Information Dominance and Chief Information Officer.—Lt. Gen. William J. ''Bill'' Bender (703) 695–6829.

Deputy Chief, Information Dominance and Chief Information Officer.—William E. ''Bill'' Marion, 695–6829.

Director of:

Cyberspace Operations and Warfighting Integration.—Col. Don Fielden (acting), Room 5D1068, 695–1835.

Cyberspace Strategy and Policy.—Brig. Gen. Patrick Higby, Room 5D1068, 614–2997.

Cyberspace Capabilities and Compliance.—Mr. Arthur ''AG'' Hatcher Jr., Room 5D1067, 695–1839.

DEPUTY CHIEF OF STAFF FOR INTELLIGENCE, SURVEILLANCE AND RECONNAISSANCE (ISR)

Deputy Chief of Staff.—Lt. Gen. Robert Otto (703) 695–5613.

Assistant Deputy Chief of Staff.—Maj. Gen. Linda Urrutia-Varhall.

Executive Officer.—Lt. Col. Tracy Ward.

Director of:

ISR Capabilities.—Brig. Gen. John Rauch, 697–5818.

ISR Innovations.—James Clark, 693–3377.

ISR Resources.—Keith Holt, 697–4925.

ISR Strategy, Plans, Doctrine, and Force Development.—Kenneth Dumm, 614–3478.
Special Programs.—Dean Yount, 693–5201.

DEPUTY CHIEF OF STAFF FOR LOGISTICS, ENGINEERING AND FORCE PROTECTION

Pentagon, 1030 Air Force, 20330

Deputy Chief of Staff.—Lt. Gen. John B. Cooper, Room 4E154 (703) 695–5590.
Assistant Deputy.—Tim Bridges, Pentagon, Room 4E154, 695–2664.
Director of:
Civil Engineer.—Brig. Gen. Tim Green, Pentagon, Room 4C1057, 693–4308.
Logistics.—Maj. Gen. Donald Kirkland, Pentagon, Room 4C1065, 695–4900.
Resources Integration.—Lorna Estep, Pentagon, Room 4B1088, 697–2822.
Security Forces.—Brig. Gen. Andrea Tullos, Pentagon, Room 5E1040, 693–5401.

DEPUTY CHIEF OF STAFF FOR MANPOWER, PERSONNEL AND SERVICES

Pentagon, 1040 Air Force, Room 4E168, 20330

Deputy Chief of Staff.—Lt. Gen. Samuel D. Cox (703) 697–6088.
Assistant Deputy Chief of Staff.—Robert E. Corsi, Jr.
Chief, AF/A1 Action Group.—Lt. Col. Catherine Logan, Room 4E169, 695–4212.
Director of:
Air Force General Officer Management.—Col. Christopher Craige, Room 4D1066, 697–1181.
Services.—Brig. Gen. Patrick Doherty, Room 4D1054 (571) 256–8598.
Force Development.—Russell Frasz, Room 4D950, 695–2144.
Force Management Policy.—Brig. Gen. Brian Kelly, Room 4D950A, 695–6770.
Manpower, Organization, and Resources.—Brig. Gen. Richard Murphy, Room 5B349, 692–1601.
Plans and Integration.—Michelle LoweSolis, Room 4D1054A, 697–5222.

DEPUTY CHIEF OF STAFF FOR OPERATIONS

Pentagon, 1630 Air Force, Room 4E1024, 20330

Deputy Chief of Staff.—Lt. Gen. Mark Nowland (703) 697–9991.
Assistant Deputy.—Maj. Gen. Brian Robinson, 697–9881.
Mobility Assistant.—Brig. Gen. Robert Polumbo, 697–3087.
Director of:
Cyberspace Operations and Warfighting Integration.—Brig. Gen. David Gaedecke, Room 5D1068, 697–1835.
Training and Readiness.—Maj. Gen. Scott Smith, Room 5D756, 697–9996.
Current Operations.—Brig. Gen. Bradley Saltzman, Room 5D756, 697–6745.
Resource Integration.—Robert Graves, Room 5E873, 697–7823.

DEPUTY CHIEF OF STAFF FOR STRATEGIC PLANS AND REQUIREMENTS

Pentagon, 1070 Air Force, Room 4E1082, 20330–1070

Deputy Chief of Staff.—Lt. Gen. James M. Holmes (703) 697–4469.
Assistant Deputy Chief of Staff.—Richard Hartley (703) 692–9944.
Directorate of:
Operational Capability Requirements.—Maj. Gen. Paul Johnson, Room 5C889 (703) 695–3018.
Plans.—Maj. Gen. Jerry Harris, Room 5D1088 (703) 614–2863.
Strategy, Concepts, and Assessments.—Maj. Gen. David Alvin, Room 5D1050 (703) 697–3117.

DIRECTORATE OF STUDIES AND ANALYSIS AND ASSESSMENTS

Pentagon, 1570 Air Force, Room 4E214, 20330–1570

Director.—Kevin E. Williams, SES (571) 256–2015.
Principal Deputy Director.—Michael D. Payne, SES.

Military Deputy Director.—Col. Jay Sabia.
Technical Director.—Dr. Mark A. Gallagher, Ph.D., SL.
Chief Analyst.—Col. Johnathan T. Hamill.

STRATEGIC DETERRENCE AND NUCLEAR INTEGRATION (A10)

Pentagon, 1488 Air Force, Suite 4E240, 20330

Assistant Chief of Staff.—Maj. Gen. Garrett Harencak (703) 693–9747.
Deputy Assistant Chief of Staff.—Michael Shoults, SES, 693–9747.
Associate Assistant Chief of Staff.—Dr. Billy Mullins, Ph.D., SES, 693–9747.
HQE.—Dr. Jim Blackwell, Ph.D. (703) 695–1365.
MA.—Brig. Gen. Thomas Clark (703) 697–1545.
Director of Staff.—Darphaus Mitchell, 693–9747.
Senior Executive.—Maj. Chris Maroney, 693–9747.
Junior Executive.—Maj. Nate Osborne, 693–9747.
Administrative Assistant.—Rhonda Gill, 693–9747.
Division Chiefs:
Assessments.—David O'Donnell (202) 767–7420.
Capabilities.—Col. Carl Jones (202) 404–7938.
Executive Services.—Wilbert Smith, 695–7810.
Functional Authority.—Zannis Pappas, 697–6056.
NC3.—Col. Eric Beene (202) 767–4259.
Strategic Stability and CWMD Policy.—Col. Thomas Summers (703) 614–6009.
Planning, Policy and Strategy.—Col. Frank Link, 697–4098.

ADMINISTRATIVE ASSISTANT TO THE SECRETARY

Pentagon, 1720 Air Force, 20330

Administrative Assistant.—Patricia J. Zarodkiewicz, Room 4E824 (703) 695–9492.
Deputy Administrative Assistant.—Jeffery R. Shelton, 695–9492.
Director of Staff.—Mary Morfitt, 697–2717.
Executive Officer.—Lt. Col. Eugene Moore, 695–9492.
Confidential Assistant.—Ruby Hill, 695–9492.
Executive Administrator.—MSgt. Tracy Jackson, 695–3151.
Director of:
Executive Dining Facility.—Shad Glover, Room 4D869, 697–1112.
Information Management.—Kent Chadrick, 5E915, 697–6529.
Operations.—Ralph F. Davis, Room 5D855, 697–8225.
Resources—Personnel.—Heather Meyer, Room 4D846, 693–9503.
Resources—Finance.—Holly Mehringer, Room 4D846, 695–3148.
Security, Counterintelligence and Special Programs Oversight Division.—Wendy Kay, Room MD779, 693–2013.
Concepts, Development and Management: Waples Mills, John Salvatori (571) 256–7081 and 697–7509.
Sensitive Activities Office.—Russell Wyler (202) 404–1500.

AUDITOR GENERAL

Pentagon, 1120 Air Force, 20330

4170 Hebble Creek Road, Building 280, Door 1

Wright-Patterson AFB, OH 45433–5643 (WPAFB)

1500 West Perimeter Road, Suite 4700

Joint Base Andrews, MD 20762

470 I Street East, Randolph AFB, TX 78150–4332

Auditor General.—Douglas M. Bennett, Room 4E204 (703) 614–5626.

AIR FORCE AUDIT AGENCY

Director of Operations.—Nicole L. Neal, JBA Andrews (240) 612–5114.
Assistant Auditor General for—

Acquisition, Logistics, and Financial Audits.—Michael D. Petersen, WPAFB (937) 257–6355.
Deputy Auditor General/Field Activities Directorate.—Laura N. Jankovich, Pentagon (703) 614–5626.
Operations and Support Audits.—Terri L. Dilly, Randolph AFB (210) 652–0035.

CHIEF OF CHAPLAINS

1380 AF Pentagon, Room 4E260, Washington, DC 20330

Chief.—Chaplain (Maj. Gen.) Dondi E. Costin (571) 256–7729.
Deputy Chief.—Chaplain (Brig. Gen.) Steven A. Schaick, 256–7729.

AIR FORCE CHIEF OF SAFETY

Pentagon, 1400 Air Force Pentagon, Room 4E252, 20330–1400

Chief of Air Force Safety/Commander, Air Force Safety Center.—Maj. Gen. Kurt Neubauer (703) 693–7281.
Deputy Chief of Air Force Safety/Executive Director, Air Force Safety Center.—James Rubeor (505) 846–2372.
Executive Officer.—Maj. Patrick Schuldt (703) 614–3389.
Director, Safety Issues Division.—Col. Jason Edelblute, 693–3333.

AIR FORCE GENERAL COUNSEL

Pentagon, 1740 Air Force Pentagon, Suite 4E836, 20330

General Counsel.—Thomas E. Ayres (703) 697–0941.
Principal Deputy.—Joseph M. McDade, 697–4406.
Senior Military Assistant.—Col. Gail E. Crawford, 693–7304.
Military Assistant.—Maj. Karl J. Vogel, 697–4406.
Executive Assistant.—Debra R. Swanson, 697–8418.
Deputy General Counsel for—
Acquisition.—Richard B. Clifford, Jr., Room 5B914, 693–7284.
Contractor Responsibility and Conflict Resolution.—Vacant, Crystal City, 604–0423; Derek Santos (acting), 604–1626.
Fiscal, Ethics and Administrative Law.—Douglas D. Sanders, Room 4C934, 693–9291.
Intelligence, International and Military Affairs.—Craig A. Smith, Room 4C756, 695–5663.
Installations, Energy and Environment.—Vacant, Room 5E773 (571) 256–4809; Carolyn White (acting), 256–4808.

AIR FORCE HISTORIAN

1190 Air Force Pentagon, Room 4E1062, Washington, DC 20330–1190

Director.—Walter Grudzinskas (703) 697–5603.
Executive Officer.—David Bragg, 697–9119.
Director, Air Force Historical Research Agency, Maxwell AFB, AL.—Dr. Charles O'Connell (334) 953–5342.

INSPECTOR GENERAL

Pentagon, 1140 Air Force, Room 4E1040, 20330–1140

Inspector General.—Lt. Gen. Gregory A. Biscone (703) 697–6733.
Deputy Inspector General.—Maj. Gen. Craig N. Gourley, 697–4351.
Executive Officer.—Lt. Col. Zachary L. Smith, 697–4787.
Advisor for—
Air National Guard Matters.—Col. Suzanne B. Lipcaman, Room 4E1037, 697–0339.
Reserve Matters.—Col. Kathleen R. Mikkelson, Room 4E1037, 614–3863.
Director of:
Complaints Resolution Directorate.—Col. John Payne, JBAB-Building 5863, Room 150 (202) 404–5262.
Inspections.—Col. William Reese, JBAB-Building 5863, Room 350, 404–3263.
Senior Officials Inquiries.—Col. Matthew Bartlett, Room 5B937 (703) 693–3579.

Special Investigations.—Col. Jeffrey Hurlbert, Room 5B919, 697–0411.

JUDGE ADVOCATE GENERAL

Pentagon, 1420 Air Force, 20330

1501 West Perimeter Road, Joint Base Andrews Naval Air Facility Washington, MD 20762

The Judge Advocate General.—Lt. Gen. Christopher F. Burne, Room 4E180 (703) 614–5732.

Deputy Judge Advocate General.—Maj. Gen. Jeffrey A. Rockwell, Room 4E180, 614–5732.

Senior Paralegal Manager to TJAG.—CMSgt Bo Stout, Room 5D116, 614–9004.

Director for—

Administrative Law.—Conrad Von Wald, Room 5D116, 614–4075.

Civil Law and Litigation.—Col. Any Momber, JBANAFW, Suite 1530 (240) 612–4610.

Strategic, Plans and Programs.—Col. Lance E. Mathews, Room 5D116, 692–2828.

Acquisition Law and Litigation.—Col. James H. Kennedy, JBANAFW, Suite 1780, 612–6620.

Operations and International Law.—Edward J. Monahan, Room 5D116 (703) 695–9631.

Professional Development.—Col. Robert J. Preston, Room 5D116, 614–3021.

USAF Court of Criminal Appeals.—Col. Karen E. Mayberry, JBANAFW, Suite 1900, 612–5070.

USAF Judiciary.—Col. Douglas P. Cordova, JBANAFW, Suite 1310, 612–4760.

USAF Trial Judiciary.—Col. Vance H. Spath, JBANAFW, Suite 1150, 612–4570.

LEGAL OPERATIONS

Commander, Air Force Legal Operations Agency.—Brig. Gen. Charles L. Plummer, JB Andrews, Suite 1320 (240) 612–4590.

Command Paralegal Manager, Air Force Legal Operations Agency.—CMSgt Richard S. Rusk, Suite 1320, 612–4594.

DIRECTORATE OF LEGISLATIVE LIAISON

Pentagon, 1160 Air Force, 20330

Rayburn House Office Building, Room B–322, 20515 (RHOB)

Russell Senate Office Building, Room SR–182, 20510 (RSOB)

Director.—Maj. Gen. Thomas W. Bergeson, Room 4E812 (703) 697–4142.

Deputy Director.—Christy Nolta (703) 697–4142.

Director of Staff.—Col. Daniel A. Blake, 4B852, 693–0315.

Mobilization Assistant to the Director.—Col. Farris ''Carlos'' Hill, 697–4142.

Executive Officer to the Director.—Lt. Col. Heather C.D. Marshall, 697–4142.

Congressional Actions.—Stephen Frye, Room 4B852, 695–0182.

Congressional Inquiry and Travel.—Col. Matthew H. Yetishefsky, Room 4B852, 697–3786.

House Liaison Office.—Col. Wesley Hallman, RHOB (202) 685–4531.

Programs and Legislation.—Matt Ernest, Room 4B852 (703) 693–9111.

Senate Liaison Office.—Brig. Gen. Billy D. Thompson, RSOB (202) 685–2573.

Weapons Systems.—Col. David Slaydon, Room 4B852 (703) 697–3376.

NATIONAL GUARD BUREAU

1636 Defense Pentagon (1E169), Washington, DC 20301

Chief.—GEN Frank G. Grass, Pentagon, Room 1E169 (703) 614–3087.

Vice Chief.—Lt. Gen. Joseph L. Lengyel, Pentagon, Room 1E169, 614–3038.

Legislative Liaison.—Brig. Gen. James K. Vogel, Pentagon, Room 1D157 (571) 256–7339.

Director for—

Air National Guard.—Lt. Gen. Stanley Clarke, Pentagon, Room 4E126, 614–8033.

Army National Guard.—LTG Timothy J. Kadavy, Arlington Hall Readiness Center, 111 South George Mason Drive, Arlington, VA 22204 (703) 607–7005.

OFFICE OF PUBLIC AFFAIRS

Director.—Brig. Gen. Kathleen Cook (703) 697–6061.

Executive Officer.—Maj. Christina Sukach.
Chief of:
Current Operations.—Lt. Col. Brett Ashworth, 695–0640.
Engagement.—Wendy Varhegyi, 695–9664.
Requirements and Development.—Sherry Medders, 697–6701.
Strategy and Assessment.—Col. Sean Monogue, 697–6715.

AIR FORCE RESERVE

Pentagon, 1150 Air Force, Room 4E138, 20330

Chief, Air Force Reserve/Commander, Air Force Reserve Command.—Lt. Gen. James F. Jackson (703) 695–9225.
Deputy to Chief of Air Force Reserve.—Maj. Gen. Maryanne Miller, 695–5528.
Executive Officer.—Col. Melissa A. Coburn, 695–5528.
Assistant Executive Officer.—Lt. Col. Angela Gundersen, 695–5528.
Executive SNCO.—SMSgt Adele Ruiz, 614–7307.

SCIENTIFIC ADVISORY BOARD

1500 West Perimeter Road, Suite 3300, Joint Base Andrews, MD 20762

Chair.—Dr. James Chow (240) 612–5513.
Vice Chair.—Dr. Melissa Choi, 612–5513.
Military Director.—Lt. Gen. Arnold Bunch, Pentagon, Room 4E962 (703) 697–6363.
Executive Director.—Lt. Col. Domenic Smeraglia, Pentagon, Room 5E815, 697–1109.
Administration.—MSgt Michael Salopek, 612–5500.

AIR FORCE SCIENTIST

Pentagon, 1075 Air Force, Room 4E130, 20330

Chief Scientist.—Dr. Richard J. Joseph (703) 697–7842.
Military Assistant.—Col. Michelle Ewy.

AIR FORCE OFFICE OF SMALL BUSINESS PROGRAMS

1060 Air Force Pentagon, Room 4E268, Washington, DC 20330–1060

Director.—Mark S. Teskey.
Deputy Director.—Carol E. White.
Executive Assistant.—Nina M. Payne.

SURGEON GENERAL

Pentagon, 1780 Air Force, Room 4E114, 20330–1780

7700 Arlington Boulevard, Suite 5152, Falls Church, VA 22042–5152

Surgeon General.—Lt. Gen. Thomas Travis (703) 692–6800.
Executive Officer.—Lt. Col. Terence Cunningham, 692–6990.
Deputy Surgeon General.—Maj. Gen. Mark Ediger, 681–6994.
Executive Officer.—Maj. Vanessa Wong, 681–6994.
Director for—
Congressional and Public Affairs.—Tony Joyner, 681–7921.
Financial Management.—Col. Billy Cecil, 681–6933.
Force Development.—Maj. Gen. Charles Potter, 681–8157.
Medical Operations.—Brig. Gen. Dorothy Hogg, 681–7113.
Modernization.—Brig. Gen. James Carroll, 681–8137.
Strategic Plans and Programs.—Farah Sharshar, 681–5639.
Corps Director for—
Biomedical Sciences.—Col. Richard Mooney, 681–7616.
Dental Corps.—Col. Michael Cunningham, 681–6993.
Medical.—Col. Dominic Hootsman, 681–6993.
Medical Services.—Col. Patrick Dawson, 681–6993.
Nursing.—Col. Stephen Donaldson, 681–8157.

DIRECTORATE OF TEST AND EVALUATION

Pentagon, 1650 Air Force, Room 4E276, 20330

Director.—Devin L. Cate (703) 697–4774.
Deputy Director.—Tanya M. Skeen.
Executive Assistant.—Dawniel C. Conner.

ARMY AND AIR FORCE EXCHANGE SERVICE

3911 S. Walton Walker Boulevard, Dallas, TX 75236, phone 1–800–527–6790

Director/Chief Executive Officer.—Thomas C. Shull.
Deputy Director.—Michael E. Immler.
Chief Operating Officer.—Samuel David Nelson.

WASHINGTON OFFICE/OFFICE OF THE BOARD OF DIRECTORS

2530 Crystal Drive, Suite 4158, 4th Floor

Arlington, VA 22202, phone (703) 602–3439

Director.—Gregg Cox.

DEPARTMENT OF THE ARMY

The Pentagon, Washington, DC 20310

phone (703) 695–2442

SECRETARY OF THE ARMY

101 Army Pentagon, Room 3E700, Washington, DC 20310–0101

phone (703) 695–1717, fax (703) 697–8036

Secretary of the Army.—Dr. Mark T. Esper.
Executive Officer.—COL Joel Bryant ''JB'' Vowell.

UNDER SECRETARY OF THE ARMY

102 Army Pentagon, Room 3E700, Washington, DC 20310–0102

phone (703) 695–4311, fax (703) 697–8036

Under Secretary of the Army.—Ryan D. McCarthy.
Executive Officer.—COL Patrick R. Michaelis.

CHIEF OF STAFF OF THE ARMY (CSA)

200 Army Pentagon, Room 3E672, Washington, DC 20310–0200

phone (703) 697–0900, fax (703) 614–5268

Chief of Staff of the Army.—GEN Mark A. Milley.
Vice Chief of Staff of the Army.—GEN James C. McConville (703) 695–4371.
Executive Officers: COL Milford H. Beagle, Jr., 695–4371; COL Joseph A. Ryan.
Director of the CSA Staff Group.—COL Peter N. Benchoff, Room 3D654 (703) 693–8371.
Director of the Army Staff.—LTG Gary H. Cheek, Room 3E663, 693–7707.
Sergeant Major of the Army.—SMA Daniel A. Dailey, Room 3E677, 695–2150.
Directors:
Army Protocol.—Michele K. Fry, Room 3A532, 692–6701.
Executive Communications and Control.—Thea Harvell III, Room 3D664, 695–7552.
Joint and Defense Affairs.—COL Anthony W. Rush, Room 3D644 (703) 614–8217.

Direct Reporting Units
Commanding General, U.S. Army Test and Evaluation Command.—MG John W. Charlton (443) 861–9954/861–9989.
Superintendent, U.S. Military Academy.—LTG Robert L. Caslen, Jr. (845) 938–2610.
Commanding General, U.S. Army Military District of Washington.—MG Michael L. Howard (202) 685–2807.
Commandant, U.S. Army War College.—MG John S. Kem (717) 245–4400.

DEPUTY UNDER SECRETARY OF THE ARMY (DUSA)

101 Army Pentagon, Room 3E650, Washington, DC 20310–0001

phone (703) 697–5075, fax (703) 697–3145

Deputy Under Secretary of the Army.—Thomas E. Kelly III.
Executive Officer.—COL Eric P. Shwedo (703) 695–4392.
Executive Assistant.—Natalie S. Bosse, 697–8150.

ASSISTANT SECRETARY OF THE ARMY

(ACQUISITION, LOGISTICS, AND TECHNOLOGY) (ASA(ALT))

103 Army Pentagon, Room 2E532, Washington, DC 20310–0103

phone (703) 693–6153, fax (703) 693–9728

Assistant Secretary.—Dr. Bruce D. Jette.
Principal Deputy.—Jeffrey S. White, Room 2E516 (703) 614–4372.
Principal Military Deputy.—LTG Paul A. Ostrowski, Room 2E532 (703) 697–4278.
Chief of Staff.—COL Gordon T. Wallace (703) 695–5749.
Executive Officer.—COL Timothy R. Fuller, 695–6742.
Confidential Assistant.—Anita J. Odom, 695–6153.
Executive Assistant to the Military Deputy.—Patty Shotwell, 693–3927.
Deputy Assistant Secretary of the Army (DASA):
Acquisition and Systems Management.—MG Robert L. Marion, 695–3115.
Acquisition, Policy, and Logistics.—Timothy G. Goddette (acting), 697–5050.
Defense Exports and Cooperation.—Ann Castiglione-Cataldo (703) 614–3434.
Plans, Programs, and Resources.—John J. Daniels, 697–0387.
Procurement.—Stuart A. Hazlett, 695–2488.
Research and Technology.—Dr. Thomas P. Russell, 692–1830.
Strategy, Acquisition and Reform.—Dr. Alexis L. Ross, 695–2549.

Direct Reporting Units
Director, U.S. Army Acquisition Support Center.—Craig Spisak (703) 664–5606.

ASSISTANT SECRETARY OF THE ARMY (CIVIL WORKS) (ASA(CW))

108 Army Pentagon, Room 3E446, Washington, DC 20310–0108

phone (703) 697–4672, fax (703) 697–7401

Senior Official Performing the Duties of the Assistant Secretary.—R.D. James.
Principal Deputy.—Ryan A. Fisher (703) 695–1370.
Executive Officer.—COL Anthony ''Tony'' Mitchell, 697–9809.
Military Assistant.—LTC Joseph C. Goetz II, 695–0482.
Executive Assistant.—Regena L. Townsend-Treleaven, 697–4672.
Deputy Assistant Secretary of the Army (DASA):
Management and Budget.—Joseph P. Bentz, Room 3E441, 695–1376.
Project Planning and Review.—David J. Leach, GAO–6S91 (202) 761–0033 / 761–0016.

ASSISTANT SECRETARY OF THE ARMY

(FINANCIAL MANAGEMENT AND COMPTROLLER) (ASA(FM&C))

109 Army Pentagon, Room 3E320, Washington, DC 20310–0109

phone (703) 614–4356, fax (703) 693–7584

Assistant Secretary.—Michael T. Powers (acting).
Principal Deputy.—Michael T. Powers, 614–4337.
Military Deputy for Budget.—LTG Thomas A. Horlander, 614–4104.
Executive Officer.—COL Bob Agans, 614–5548.
Military Assistant.—LTC Patrice N. Johnson, 614–4240.
Administrative Officer.—Judy A. Gupton, 614–4034.
Deputy Assistant Secretary of the Army:
Cost and Economics.—Stephen G. Barth, Room 3E352, 614–7550.
Financial Information Management.—Andrew S. Morgan, Room 3A320 (703) 692–8529.
Financial Operations.—Wesley C. Miller, Room 3A320A (703) 693–2758.
Director, Army Budget.—MG Paul A. Chamberlain, Room 3E336, 614–1573.
Director, U.S. Army Financial Management Command.—MG David C. Coburn (317) 212–4449.

ASSISTANT SECRETARY OF THE ARMY (INSTALLATIONS, ENERGY, AND ENVIRONMENT) (ASA(IE&E))

110 Army Pentagon, Room 3E464, Washington, DC 20310–0110

phone (703) 692–9800, fax (703) 692–9808

Assistant Secretary.—Jordan Gillis (acting).
Senior Official Performing the Duties of the Principal Deputy.—J. Randall Robinson, 692–9802.
Executive Officer.—COL G. Shawn Wells, 692–9804.
Military Assistant.—LTC Joshua L. Campbell, 692–9805.
Executive Assistant.—Maria A. Margary, 692–9800.
Deputy Assistant Secretary of the Army:
Energy and Sustainability.—John E. Surash (acting), Room 3D453, 692–9890.
Environment, Safety, and Occupational Health.—Eugene Collins, Room 3D453 (703) 697–1913.
Installations, Housing, and Partnerships.—Paul D. Cramer, Room 3E475, 697–0867.
Strategic Integration.—Richard E. Kidd, Room 3D453, 692–9817.

ASSISTANT SECRETARY OF THE ARMY (MANPOWER AND RESERVE AFFAIRS) (ASA(M&RA))

111 Army Pentagon, Room 2E460, Washington, DC 20310–0111

phone (703) 697–9253, fax (703) 692–9000

Senior Official Performing the Duties of the Assistant Secretary.—Marshall M. Williams.
Senior Official Performing the Duties of the Principal Deputy.—Diane M. Randon (703) 692–1292.
Executive Officer.—COL Lori A. Golya (703) 614–2850.
Executive Assistant.—Wanda L. Artis, 697–9253.
Deputy Assistant Secretary of the Army:
Army Review Boards/Director, Army Review Boards Agency.—Francine C. Blackmon (703) 545–5639.
Deputy Director.—COL J.R. Tillery, Crystal City (703) 571–0542.
Military Personnel Policy and Quality of Life.—Donald G. Salo, Room 2D484 (703) 614–1648.
Civilian Personnel/Director, Civilian Senior Leader Management Office.—Sue A. Engelhardt, Room 2E485, 614–8143.
Diversity and Leadership.—COL Joanne Moore (acting), 614–5284.
Marketing/Director, Army Marketing and Research Group.—Elizabeth F. Wilson (703) 545–3439.
Training, Readiness, and Mobilization.—Raymond F. ''Fred'' Rees, Room 2E482, 697–2631.

Direct Reporting Unit
U.S. Army Marketing and Engagement Brigade.—COL Oscar H. Pintado (502) 626–1751.

ARMY GENERAL COUNSEL (GC)

104 Army Pentagon, Room 2E724, Washington, DC 20310–0104

phone (703) 697–9235, fax (703) 693–9254

General Counsel of the Army.—James E. McPherson.
Principal Deputy General Counsel.—Earl G. Matthews, 697–9235.
Executive Officer/Special Counsel.—Michael Lacey (703) 692–8252.
Executive Assistant.—CW4 Amy M. Reeves, 692–9141.
Deputy General Counsels:
Acquisition.—Levator Norsworthy, Jr., Room 3C546, 697–5120.
Ethics and Fiscal Law.—John C. Kent (acting), Room 3C546 (703) 695–4296.
Installations, Environment, and Civil Works.—Craig R. Schmauder, Room 3C546, 695–3024.
Operations and Personnel.—Daniel F. McCallum, Room 3C546, 695–0562.

ADMINISTRATIVE ASSISTANT TO THE SECRETARY OF THE ARMY (AASA)

105 Army Pentagon, Room 3E733, Washington, DC 20310–0105

phone (703) 695–2442, fax (703) 697–6194

Administrative Assistant to the Secretary of the Army.—Gerald B. O'Keefe.
Deputy Administrative Assistant.—Mark F. Averill (703) 697–7741.
Executive Officer.—COL Jonathan C. Larsen, 695–7444.
Executive Assistant.—Sheila M. Kensinger-Clark, 695–2442.
Director, Civilian Aides to the Secretary of the Army (CASA).—Angela K. Ritz, Room 3D742 (703) 545–0525.
Executive Directors:
U.S. Army Center of Military History.—Charles R. Bowery, Jr., Fort McNair, Building 35, Room 147 (202) 685–2705.
U.S. Army Headquarters Services.—Susan D. Tigner, Fort Belvoir, Building 1458 (703) 545–4870.

ARMY AUDITOR GENERAL

6000 6th Street, Building 1464, Fort Belvoir, VA 22060–5609

phone (703) 545–5907, fax (703) 806–1199

Auditor General of the Army.—Anne L. Richards.
Principal Deputy Auditor General.—Elizabeth L. Casciaro (acting), 545–5910.
Executive Officer.—COL Eric A. Martinez, 545–5909.
Executive Assistant.—Lotus Leal, 545–5907.
General Counsel.—Michael Hoadley, 545–5879.
Deputy Auditors General:
Acquisition, Logistics, and Technology Audits.—Kathleen A. Nelson, 545–5903.
Financial Management and Comptroller Audits.—Elizabeth Catiaro, 545–5851.
Installations, Energy, and Environment Audits.—William Jenkins, 545–5853.
Manpower, Reserve Affairs, and Training Audits.—Felix Strelsky, 545–5874.

ARMY NATIONAL MILITARY CEMETERIES (ANMC)

phone (703) 614–0615, fax (571) 256–3366

Executive Director.—Karen L. Durham-Aguilera.
Chief of Staff.—COL Jerry Farnsworth, 614–1062.
Executive Officer.—LTC Mark O'Brien, 614–0615.

Direct Reporting Unit
Executive Director, Arlington National Cemetery.—Karen L. Durham-Aguilera.
Superintendent, Arlington National Cemetery.—Katharine ''Kate'' Kelley.

ASSISTANT CHIEF OF STAFF FOR INSTALLATION MANAGEMENT (ACSIM)

600 Army Pentagon, Room 3E484, Washington, DC 20310–0600

phone (703) 693–3233, fax (703) 693–3507

Assistant Chief of Staff.—LTG Kenneth R. Dahl.
Deputy Assistant Chief of Staff.—Carla K. Coulson (acting).
Executive Officer.—COL Brian P. Foley (571) 256–1435.
Executive Assistant.—Colleen V. Smith.

CHIEF ARMY RESERVE (CAR)

2400 Army Pentagon, Room 3E562, Washington, DC 20310–2400

phone (703) 695–0031, fax (703) 697–1891

Chief of Army Reserve.—LTG Charles D. Luckey.
Assistant Chief.—Stephen D. Austin, 695–0047.
Executive Officer.—COL John Manning, 695–0042.

Executive Assistant.—Brandy DiMarco, 695–0031.
Congressional Affairs Communication Officer.—COL Gregory Scheidhauer (703) 835–3357.

CHIEF INFORMATION OFFICER, G–6 (CIO, G–6)

107 Army Pentagon, Room 3E608, Washington, DC 20310–0107

phone (703) 695–4366, fax (703) 695–3091

Chief Information Officer.—Gary Wang (acting).
Deputy Chief.—Gary Wang, 695–6604.
Executive Officer.—COL Jeth B. Rey (703) 697–5503.

CHIEF LEGISLATIVE LIAISON (CLL)

1600 Army Pentagon, Room 1E416, Washington, DC 20310–1600

phone (703) 697–6767, fax (703) 614–7599

Chief Legislative Liaison.—MG Brian E. Winski.
Principal Deputy.—Bernard P. Ingold, 697–0278.
Deputy.—COL Thomas Dorame (703) 695–1235.
Executive Officer.—COL Michael L. Davidson, 695–1235.
Enlisted Aide.—SFC Natasha S. Williams, 695–1353.
Executive Assistant.—Keirsten Davis, 697–6767.
Chief:
Congressional Inquiry.—Harry B. Williams, Room 1E423, 697–2583.
House Liaison Division.—COL Timothy Holman, Room 2024, Rayburn House Office Building, Washington, DC (202) 685–2675.
Investigations and Legislative Division.—COL Olga M. ''Marie'' Anderson, Room 1E433, 697–8218.
Programs Division.—COL Trevor Bredenkamp, Room 1E385 (703) 693–8766.
Senate Liaison Division.—COL Michael J. Lawson, Room SR183, Senate Russell Office Building, Washington, DC (202) 685–3633.
ACoS Operations.—CPT Jessica Armstrong, Room 1E416, 695–1351.
Congressional Operations Division.—LTC Thomas Galli, Room 1D437 (703) 692–2235.
Management and Support Operations Division.—Kyle McClelland, Room 1E423, 692–4159.

CHIEF NATIONAL GUARD BUREAU (CNGB)

Pentagon, Room 1E169, Washington, DC 20301–1636

phone (703) 614–3087, fax (703) 614–0274

Chief.—GEN Joseph L. Lengyel.
Vice Chief.—Lt. Gen. Daniel R. Hokanson, 614–3038.
Executive Officer.—COL Phillip F. Johnson, 614–3087.
Executive Assistant.—Carol Lagasse, 614–3117.
Directors:
Air National Guard.—Lt. Gen. L. Scott Rice, 614–8033.
Army National Guard.—LTG Timothy J. Kadavy, Room 2A514B (703) 693–8464.

CHIEF OF CHAPLAINS (CCH)

2700 Army Pentagon, Room 3E524, Washington, DC 20310–2700

phone (703) 695–1133, fax (703) 695–9834

Chief of Chaplains.—Chaplain (MG) Paul K. Hurley.
Deputy Chief of Chaplains.—Chaplain (BG) Thomas L. Solhjem, 695–1133.
Executive Officer.—Chaplain (COL) Bryan J. Walker, 695–1133.
Executive Assistant.—Caridad ''Carie'' Gelineau, 695–1135.

CHIEF OF ENGINEERS (CoE)

GAO Building, 441 G Street, NW., 20314–0001

phone (202) 761–0000, fax (202) 761–4463

Chief of Engineers.—LTG Todd T. Semonite.
Deputy Chief of Engineers.—MG Richard L. Stevens, 761–0002.
Director.—COL Mark Quander (703) 693–4407.

Direct Reporting Unit
Commanding General, U.S. Army Corps of Engineers.—LTG Todd T. Semonite.
Deputy.—MG Richard L. Stevens, 761–0002.
Chief of Staff.—COL Richard Hansen, 761–0761.
Executive Officer.—LTC Karl Jansen, 761–0468.
Executive Assistant.—Christina Hiatt, 761–0001.

CHIEF OF PUBLIC AFFAIRS (CPA)

1500 Army Pentagon, Room 1E484, Washington, DC 20310–1500

phone (703) 695–5135, fax (703) 693–8362

Chief of Public Affairs.—BG Omar J. Jones IV.
Principal Deputy.—Michael P. Brady (703) 697–1747.
Chief of Staff.—COL Jeffrey McCoy (703) 693–8605
Executive Officer.—MAJ Meghan Ederle, 697–4200.
Executive Assistant.—M. Delores Mitchell, 695–5135.
Chief, Media Relations Division.—LTC Jason Brown, 693–4723.
Director:
U.S. Army Public Affairs Center.—COL Eric Bloom (301) 677–7270.
U.S. Army Field Band.—COL Jim R. Keene, 677–5763.

DEPUTY CHIEF OF STAFF, G–1 (DCS, G–1) (PERSONNEL)

300 Army Pentagon, Room 2E446, Washington, DC 20310–0300

phone (703) 697–8060

Deputy Chief of Staff.—LTG James C. McConville.
Assistant Deputy Chief of Staff.—Roy A. Wallace (703) 692–1585.
Executive Officer.—COL Allan G. Kellogg, 697–2893.
Military Assistant.—MAJ April Wharton (703) 614–1862.
Executive Assistant.—Lacresha D. Snow, 697–8060.
Director:
Assistant G–1 for Civilian Personnel.—Michael Reheuser (acting), 614–8143.
Army Resiliency.—Sharyn Saunders (703) 571–7357.
Human Systems Integration.—Dr. Beverly Knapp (acting), (703) 695–6761.
Military Personnel Management.—MG Joseph Calloway, 695–5871.
Plans and Resources.—Dr. Robert Steinrauf, 697–5263.
Sexual Harassment/Assault Response and Prevention.—Monique Ferrell, 695–5568.
Technology and Business Architecture Integration.—Terry Watson, 614–5138.

Field Operating Agencies
Commanding General, U.S. Army Human Resources Command.—MG Jason T. Evans (502) 613–8844.
Director, U.S. Army Civilian Human Resources Agency.—Larry D. Gottardi (410) 306–1701.

DEPUTY CHIEF OF STAFF, G–2 (DCS, G–2) (INTELLIGENCE)

1000 Army Pentagon, Room 2E408, Washington, DC 20310–1000

phone (703) 695–3033, fax (703) 697–7605

Deputy Chief of Staff.—LTG Robert P. Ashley, Jr.
Assistant Deputy Chief of Staff.—Jeffrey N. Rapp.

Military Deputy.—BG Kevin C. Wulfhorst.
Executive Officer.—COL Pierre Gervais, 695–3033.
Executive Assistant.—Anne H. Fesmire, 695–3033.

Direct Reporting Unit

Commanding General, U.S. Army Intelligence and Security Command.—MG Christopher S. Ballard (703) 706–1603.

DEPUTY CHIEF OF STAFF, G–3 (DCS, G–3) (OPERATIONS)

400 Army Pentagon, Room 2E670, Washington, DC 20310–0400

phone (703) 695–2904, fax (703) 697–4660

Deputy Chief of Staff.—LTG Joseph Anderson.
Assistant Deputy Chief.—Kathleen S. Miller, 695–0728.
Executive Officer.—COL John D. Kline (703) 697–4521.
Executive Assistant.—Maureen Marshall, 695–3447.
Director:
Operations, Readiness, and Mobilization.—BG Douglas A. Simms, 695–0526.
Strategy, Plans, and Policy.—MG Christopher McPadden (703) 692–8805.
Training.—MG Patrick E. Matlock, 692–7332.
Cyber.—MG Patricia A. Frost, 692–2224.
Aviation.—MG Frank W. Tate, 692–1628.

Field Operating and Staff Support Agencies

Director, U.S. Army Force Management Support Agency.—MG Brian J. Mennes (703) 693–3227.
Director, U.S. Army Command and Control Support Agency.—COL Chad Campfield (703) 697–1245.
Director, U.S. Army Nuclear and Combating WMD Agency.—Daniel M. Klippstein (703) 614–2670.

DEPUTY CHIEF OF STAFF, G–4 (DCS, G–4) (LOGISTICS)

500 Army Pentagon, Room 1E394, Washington, DC 20310–0500

phone (703) 695–4104, fax (703) 692–0759

Deputy Chief of Staff.—LTG Aundre F. Piggee.
Assistant Deputy Chief.—William F. Moore (703) 697–9138.
Assistant Deputy Chief/Operations.—MG John P. Sullivan, 697–5032.
Executive Officer.—COL Gavin A. Lawrence, 697–9039.
Executive Assistant.—Torwanna D. Herbert, 695–4102.
Director:
Logistics Information Management.—Dr. Edward M. Siomacco, Room 1E360, 695–6160.
Maintenance Policy, Programs, and Processes.—Michael B. Cervone, Room 1E360 (703) 693–1624.
Resource Management.—John A. "Art" Hagler, Room 1E380, 693–1900.
Plans and Integration.—BG Darren Werner, Room 1E369 (703) 692–5127.
Supply Policy, Programs, and Processes.—Peter B. Bechtel, Room 1E380, 692–2282.

Field Operating Agency

Director, U.S. Army Logistics Innovation Agency.—Dr. Barbara Sotirin (703) 805–5440.

DEPUTY CHIEF OF STAFF, G–8 (DCS, G–8) (PROGRAMS)

700 Army Pentagon, Room 3E406, Washington, DC 20310–0700

phone (703) 697–8232, fax (703) 697–8242

Deputy Chief of Staff.—LTG John M. Murray.
Assistant Deputy Chief.—Dr. David Markowitz (703) 692–9099.
Executive Officer.—COL John W. Reynolds, 697–8232.
Executive Assistant.—Jessica M. Collins, 697–8236.
Director:

Force Development.—MG John A. George, 692–7707.
Program Analysis and Evaluation.—MG John G. Ferrari, 697–1475.
Director, Quadrennial Defense Review.—Tim Muchmoore (703) 695–8997.

Field Operating Agency

Director, U.S. Army Center for Army Analysis.—Dr. William F. Crain (703) 806–5510.

DIRECTOR OF THE ARMY STAFF (DAS)

202 Army Pentagon, Room 3E663, Washington, DC 20310–0202

phone (703) 693–7710, fax (703) 695–6117

Director of the Army Staff.—LTG Gary H. Cheek.
Vice Director.—Steven J. Redmann, Room 3D644 (703) 695–0294.
Executive Officer.—COL John L. Rafferty, Jr., 693–7710.
Executive Assistant.—Samantha Johnson, 695–6117.

Field Operating Agency

Commanding General, U.S. Army Combat Readiness/Safety Center.—BG David Francis (334) 255–9360.

PROVOST MARSHAL GENERAL (PMG)

2800 Army Pentagon, Room 1E596, Washington, DC 203103–2800

phone (703) 692–6966, fax (703) 614–5628

Provost Marshal General.—MG David P. Glaser.
Deputy Provost Marshal General.—COL Christopher Burns, 692–7290.
Executive Officer.—COL Geoff Stewart, 692–6970.
Chief of Staff.—Herman ''Tracy'' Williams III, 692–6829.
Executive Assistant.—Deborah L. Van Heest (703) 695–4036.

Direct Reporting Unit

Commanding General, U.S. Army Criminal Investigation Command.—MG David P. Glaser.

Field Operating Agencies

Commanding General, U.S. Army Corrections Command.—BG Brian R. Bisacre.
Director, Defense Forensics and Biometrics Agency.—Glen Krizay (acting), (703) 571–0507.

OFFICE OF SMALL BUSINESS PROGRAMS (OSBP)

106 Army Pentagon, Room 3B514, Washington, DC 20310–0106

phone (703) 697–2868, fax (703) 693–3898

Director.—Tommy L. Marks.
Deputy/Executive Officer.—Pamela D. Callicutt (703) 695–5588.
Executive Assistant.—Jasmine Barrett (703) 806–8659.

THE INSPECTOR GENERAL (TIG)

1700 Army Pentagon, Room 3E588, Washington, DC 20310–1700

phone (703) 695–1500, fax (703) 614–5628

The Inspector General.—LTG Leslie C. Smith.
Deputy Inspector General.—MG Donald E. Jackson, 695–1501.
Executive Officer.—COL Mark Holler, 695–1502.
Executive Assistant.—LTC Jacqueline Escobar, 695–1500.

Field Operating Agency

Commanding General, U.S. Army Inspector General Agency.—LTG Leslie C. Smith, 695–1500.

THE JUDGE ADVOCATE GENERAL (TJAG)

2200 Army Pentagon, Room 3E542, Washington, DC 20310–2200

phone (703) 697–5151, fax (703) 697–1059

The Judge Advocate General.—LTG Charles N. Pede.
Deputy Judge Advocate General.—MG Stewart W. Risch (703) 693–5112.
Executive Officer.—COL David E. Mendelson (703) 695–3786.
Executive Assistant.—Cindy G. Mitchell, 697–5151.

Field Operating Agencies
Commander, U.S. Army Legal Services Agency.—BG Joseph Berger (703) 693–1100.
Commander/Commandant, U.S. Army Judge Advocate General's Legal Center and School.—BG Partrick R. Huston (434) 971–3301.

THE SURGEON GENERAL (TSG)

7700 Arlington Boulevard, Defense Health Headquarters (DHHQ)

Falls Church, VA 22042, phone (703) 681–3000, fax (703) 681–3167

The Surgeon General.—LTG Nadja Y. West.
Deputy Surgeon General.—MG Robert D. Tenhet, 681–3002.
Chief of Staff.—Mark S. Davis, 681–9514.
Executive Officer.—COL Roger S. Giraud, 681–3010.
Executive Assistant.—LTC Robert Montz (703) 695–1647.
Command Sergeant Major.—CSM Michael L. Gragg, 681–8046.
Operations Center.—Duty Officer-in-Charge, 681–8052.

Direct Reporting Unit
Commanding General, U.S. Army Medical Command.—LTG Nadja Y. West.

ARMY COMMANDS

U.S. ARMY FORCES COMMAND (FORSCOM)

4700 Knox Street, Fort Bragg, NC 28310–5000

phone (910) 570–5052, fax (910) 570–1971

Commanding General.—GEN Robert B. Abrams.
Deputy Commanding General.—LTG Laura Richardson, 570–5001.
Chief of Staff.—MG Jody Daniels, 570–5002.
Executive Officer.—COL Larry Burris, 570–5051.
Command Sergeant Major.—CSM Michael Grinston, 570–5045.
Secretary of the General Staff.—COL Thomas B. Ham, 570–5066.
Operations Center.—COL Andrew Herbst, 570–6533.
Staff Action Control Officer.—Jennifer Bhartiya (703) 697–2552.
Liaison Office (Washington, DC).—LTC Kevin Baird, 697–2591.

U.S. ARMY TRAINING AND DOCTRINE COMMAND (TRADOC)

950 Jefferson Avenue, Fort Eustis, VA 23604–5700

phone (757) 501–6469, fax (757) 501–6476

Commanding General.—GEN Stephen J. Townshend.
Deputy Commanding General/Chief of Staff.—LTG Theodore D. Martin, 501–6478.
Executive Officers: COL John F. Dunleavy, 501–6466; LTC Kevin L. Gilliard, 501–6485; COL Randy E. White, 501–6472.
Deputy Chief of Staff.—MG Paul M. Benenati, 501–6495.
Command Sergeant Major.—CSM David S. Davenport, Sr., 501–6464.
Secretary of the General Staff.—Victor Holman, 501–5199.
Director, G–33/Operations Center.—James G. Lynch, 501–5094.

U.S. ARMY MATERIEL COMMAND (AMC)

4400 Martin Road, Redstone Arsenal, AL 35898–5000

phone (256) 450–6000, fax (256) 450–8833

Commanding General.—GEN Gustave ''Gus'' Perna.
Deputy Commanding General.—LTG Edward M. Daly, 450–6100.
Executive Deputy Commanding General.—Lisha H. Adams, 450–6200.
Chief of Staff.—MG Allan W. Elliot, 450–7867.
Executive Officer.—COL Christopher L. Day, 450–6005.
Command Sergeant Major.—CSM Rodger W. Mansker, 450–6300.
Secretary of the General Staff.—LTC Julian Dominguez, 450–6440.
Operations Center.—Duty Officer-in-Charge, 450–9496.

ARMY SERVICE COMPONENT COMMANDS LIAISON OFFICES

Pentagon, Washington, DC 20310

U.S. Army Africa/Southern European Task Force (USARAF/SETAF).—COL Gregory S. Harkins, Room 3D513 (571) 256–1803.
U.S. Army Central (USARCENT): Hank Foresman, Room 2B475A4 (703) 693–4033; Mark R. Seeger, Room 2B485 (703) 693–4035.
U.S. Army Europe (USAREUR).—Timothy C. Touzinsky, Room 1E1074 (703) 692–6886.
U.S. Army North (USARNORTH).—John D. Nelson, Room 2B485, 692–6893.
U.S. Army Pacific (USARPAC).—Robert Ralston, Room 2B485 (703) 697–6952.
U.S. Army South (USARSO).—Marcello Salles, Room 2A474 (703) 692–8221.
U.S. Army Space and Missile Defense Command/Army Strategic Command (SMCD/ARSTRAT): Christine Kral, Room 2D831, (703) 614–9592; COL Jared Galazin, 614–9593.
Military Surface Deployment and Distribution Command (SDDC): COL Gary Cregan (703) 571–9708; Todd Wolf, Room 2B858, 571–9710.

JOINT FORCE HEADQUARTERS–NATIONAL CAPITAL REGION AND MILITARY DISTRICT OF WASHINGTON (JFHQ–NCR/MDW)

102 3rd Avenue, Building 39, Fort Lesley J. McNair, 20319
phone (202) 685–2807, fax (202) 685–3481

Commanding General.—MG Michael L. Howard.
Executive Officer.—LTC Luconda Wilson, 685–2817.
Aide de Camp.—CPT Scott Harra, 685–2807.
Deputy Commander.—Egon F. Hawrylak, 685–1949.
JTF Deputy.—RDML Charles Rock (202) 433–2777.
Command Sergeant Major.—CSM Paul Biggs, 685–2812.
Chief of Staff.—COL Matthew Zimmerman, 685–2812.
Secretary of the General Staff.—Corey R. Langenwalter, 685–0640.

U.S. ARMY SPECIAL OPERATIONS COMMAND

Fort Bragg, NC 28310–5200
phone (910) 432–3000, fax (910) 432–4243

Commanding General.—LTG Kenneth E. Tovo.
Deputy Commanding General.—Vacant, 432–6622.
Chief of Staff.—COL Richard E. Angle, 432–9861.
Command Sergeant Major.—CSM Robert V. Abernathy, 432–0946.
Secretary of the General Staff.—Russ Vona, 432–0946.

DEPARTMENT OF THE NAVY

Pentagon 20350–1000, phone (703) 695–3131

OFFICE OF THE SECRETARY OF THE NAVY

Pentagon, Room 4E686, phone (703) 695–3131

Secretary of the Navy.—Richard Spencer.
Chief of Staff.—J. Odegaard.
Deputy Chief of Staff.—E. Mate.
Administrative Aide.—CDR A. Cheatham, USN, 695–5410.
Marine Personal Aide.—MAJ J. Matzelle, USMC, 614–3100.
Navy Personal Aide.—LT K. Calhoun, USN, 614–6473.
Special Assistant for Public Affairs.—CAPT P. McNally, 697–7491.
Senior Military Assistant.—COL S. Liszewski, USMC.

OFFICE OF THE UNDER SECRETARY OF THE NAVY

Pentagon, Room 4E720, phone (703) 695–3141

Under Secretary of the Navy.—Thomas B. Modly.
Chief of Staff.—Andrew Haeuptle.
Military Aide (Navy).—CDR Andria L. Slough.
Military Aide (Marine).—Vacant.
Executive Assistant.—Johnny J. Jaramillo.
Administrative Assistants: Sgt Ronald Hughes, YN1 Sheldon Serrano.

GENERAL COUNSEL

Pentagon, Room 4E782, phone (703) 614–1994

General Counsel.—Anne M. Brennan (acting).
Principal Deputy General Counsel.—Anne Brennan, 614–8733.
Executive Assistant and Special Counsel.—CAPT Gordon Modari, JAGC, USN.
Associate General Counsel for—
Litigation.—R. Borro, Washington Navy Yard, Building 36 (202) 685–6989.
Deputy General Counsel.—Thomas Ledvina, Room 4E791, 614–6870.
Assistant General Counsel for—
Ethics.—Sara Thompson, Room 4D641, 614–7433.
Manpower and Reserve Affairs.—R. Woods, Room 4D548, 614–1377.
Research, Development and Acquisition.—Tom Frankfurt, Room 4C682, 614–6985.
Military Assistant.—Lt. Col. Stephen Stewart, USMC, Room 4E782, 692–6164.
Administrative Assistant.—LT John Erickson, USN, Room 4E782, 693–7813.

NAVAL INSPECTOR GENERAL

Washington Navy Yard, 1254 9th Street, SE., Building 172, 20374, phone (202) 433–2000

Inspector General.—VADM James P. Wisecup.
Deputy Naval Inspector General.—Andrea Brotherton.

U.S. NAVY OFFICE OF INFORMATION

1200 Navy Pentagon, Room 4B463, Phone (703) 697–7391

Duty (703) 850–1047

Chief of Information (CI).—CAPT Gregory L. Hicks.
Vice Chief of Information (VCI).—RDML Vic M. Beck.
Deputy, Chief of Information (DCI).—CAPT Dawn E. Cutler.
Executive Assistant to Chief of Information (EA).—CDR Tamara D. Lawrence.
Flag Aide to Chief of Information.—LT Rebecca Rebarich.

Senior Enlisted Advisor (SEA).—MCPO Jon McMillan.
Staff Senior Enlisted Leader (SEL).—CPO Cody Harmon.
Flag Writer-PO1.—Juan P. Cisneros.
Assistant Chief for—
Administration and Resource Management (OI–1).—William Mason, 692–4747.
Afloat Media Systems (OI–7).—Janet Quigley (202) 781–3313.
Communication Integration and Strategy (OI–9).—CDR Elissa Smith, 692–4728.
Community Outreach (OI–6).—Rob Newell, 614–1879.
Defense Media Activity (DMA) Liaison (OI–4).—LCDR David Luckett (301) 222–6401.
Media Operations (OI–3).—CDR Ryan Perry, 697–5342.
Navy Media Content Services (OI–2).—Chris Madden, 614–9154.
Requirements and Policy (OI–8).—Bruce Cole, 695–0911.

JUDGE ADVOCATE GENERAL

Pentagon, Room 4C 642
Washington Navy Yard, 1322 Patterson Avenue, Suite 3000, 20374–5066
phone (703) 614–7420, fax (703) 697–4610

Judge Advocate General.—VADM James W. Crawford III.
Executive Assistant.—CAPT Florencio Yuzon.
Deputy Judge Advocate General.—RADM John Hannink.
Executive Assistant to the Deputy Judge Advocate General.—CDR Matt Sklerov.
Assistant Judge Advocate General for Civil Law.—CAPT Paul C. Kiamos, Pentagon, Room 4D640 (703) 614–7415, fax (703) 614–9400.
Deputy Assistant Judge Advocate General for—
Administrative Law.—CAPT Eva Loser (703) 614–0925.
Admiralty.—CAPT Al Janin (202) 685–5075.
Claims, Investigations and Tort Litigation.—Hal Dronberger (202) 685–4627, fax (202) 685–5484.
General Litigation.—Grant Lattin (202) 685–5492, fax (202) 685–5472.
International and Operational Law.—CAPT Joe Hoelz (703) 697–5406.
Legal Assistance.—CDR David Gonzalez (202) 685–4642, fax 685–5393.
National Security Litigation and Intelligence Law.—LCDR Urula Smith (202) 685–5464/5481, fax 685–5467.
Assistant Judge Advocate General for Military Justice.—COL Dan Lecce, USMC, Building 58, 3rd Floor, Washington Navy Yard, 20374–1111 (202) 685–7051.
Deputy Assistant Judge Advocate General for Criminal Law.—CAPT Art Record, USN (202) 685–7057.
Assistant Judge Advocate General for Operations and Management.—CAPT Gary Sharp (202) 685–5190.
Deputy Assistant Judge Advocate General for—
Military Personnel.—CAPT Mark F. Klein (202) 685–7254, fax (202) 685–5489.
Technology, Operations and Plans.—CDR Matthew Beran (202) 685–5230, fax (202) 685–5479.
Special Assistants to the Judge Advocate General—
Command Master Chief.—LNCM Jondell Ritchie (202) 685–5194, fax (202) 685–8510.
Comptroller.—Dawn C. Rooney (202) 685–5274, fax 685–5455.
Inspector General.—CAPT Jeffrey Casler USN (202) 685–5192, fax (202) 685–5461.

LEGISLATIVE AFFAIRS

Room 4C549, phone (703) 697–7146, fax (703) 697–1009

Chief.—RADM Jim Loeblein.
Deputy Chief.—CAPT Jon Rodgers.
Deputy Chief, Strategy and Assessment.—Sandra Latta.
Executive Assistant.—LCDR Kristina Stoner.
Congressional Information and Public Affairs.—CDR William Clinton, 695–0395.
Congressional Operations.—Dee Wingfield, 693–5764.
Director for—
House Liaison.—CAPT Scott Farr (202) 225–7808.
Assistant House Liaison.—CDR Justin Goss (202) 225–3075.
Legislation.—CAPT Joseph Eldred, 697–2851.
Naval Programs.—Geno Autrey, 693–2919.

Senate Liaison.—CAPT Scott Sciretta (202) 685–6006.
Assistant Senate Liaison.—CDR Edward Murray (202) 685–6007.

ASSISTANT SECRETARY FOR FINANCIAL MANAGEMENT AND COMPTROLLER
Pentagon, Room 4E618, phone (703) 697–2325

Assistant Secretary.—Thomas W. Harker.
Executive Assistant and Naval Aide.—CAPT James Aiken, USN.
Military Assistant and Marine Aide.—CAPT Luis Martinez, USMC.
Deputy Assistant Secretary for—
Budget.—RADM Randy Crites, USN, Room 4E348, 697–7105.
Financial Operations.—Karen Fenstermacher, WNY (202) 685–6701.

ASSISTANT SECRETARY FOR ENERGY, INSTALLATIONS AND ENVIRONMENT
Pentagon, Room 4E739, phone (703) 693–4530

Assistant Secretary.—Steven R. Iselin (acting).
Executive Assistant and Naval Aide.—CAPT Yancy Lindsey.
Confidential Assistant.—Sgt Karl Strong.
Military Aide.—LCDR Ben Wainwright.
Principal Deputy for Energy, Installations and Environment.—Roger Natsuhara, Room 4E739, 693–4530.
Assistant General Counsel.—Craig Jensen, 614–1098.
Deputy of:
Energy.—Tom Hicks (571) 256–7879.
Environment.—D. Schregardus, 614–5493.
Safety.—Paul Hanley, 614–5516.

ASSISTANT SECRETARY FOR MANPOWER AND RESERVE AFFAIRS
Pentagon, Room 4E598, phone (703) 695–4333

Assistant Secretary.—Robert L. Woods (acting), Room 4E598, 695–4333.
Principal Deputy.—Robert L. Woods, Room 4E598, 692–6162.
Executive Assistant and Naval Aide.—CAPT Ralita Hildebrand, Room 4E598, 695–4537.
Military Assistant and Marine Aide.—Col Gary Reidenbach, Room 4E598, 697–0975.
Secretary.—Antonio Sturgis, Room 4E598, 695–4333.
Administrative Officer.—Michael Stokes, Room 4E590, 697–2179.
Administrative Chief.—SSgt Mary Atuatasi, Room 4E590, 695–6472.
Administrative Assistant.—Sgt Peter Barko, Room 4E590, 614–4439.
Deputy Assistant Secretary of:
Civilian Human Resources.—Paige Hinkle-Bowles, Room 4D548, 695–2633.
Manpower Personnel Policy.—Juliet Beyler, Room 4D548, 693–1213.
Reserve Affairs.—Dennis Biddick, Room 4D548, 614–1327.

SECRETARY OF THE NAVY COUNCIL OF REVIEW BOARDS
Washington Navy Yard, 720 Kennon Street, SE., Room 309, 20374–5023
phone (202) 685–6408, fax 685–6610

Director.—Jeffrey Riehl.
Counsel.—Roger R. Claussen.
Office Administrator.—Christopher Philson.
Physical Evaluation Board.—Robert Powers.
Naval Clemency and Parole Board.—Randall Lamoureux.
Naval Discharge Review Board.—John D. Reeser.
Combat-Related Special Compensation Board.—Leif Larsen.
Board of Decorations and Medals.—James Nierle.

ASSISTANT SECRETARY FOR RESEARCH, DEVELOPMENT AND ACQUISITION
Pentagon, Room 4E665, phone (703) 695–6315

Assistant Secretary.—James F. Geurts.

Special Assistant.—Candy R. Hearn.
Executive Assistant and Naval Aide.—CAPT John Lowery, USN.
Military Assistant and Marine Aide.—COL Richard Marigliano, USMC.
Principal Military Deputy.—VADM David Johnson, USN.
Executive Assistant and Naval Aide.—CAPT Thomas Heck.
Principal Civilian Deputy.—Allison Stiller, 614–6430.
Executive Assistant and Naval Aide.—Ed Foster.
Deputy Assistant Secretary of the Navy for—
Acquisition and Procurement.—Elliott Branch, Room BF992A, 614–9595.
Air Programs.—Daniel L. Nega.
C4I and Space Programs.—Victor Gavin, Room BF963, 614–6619.
Logistics Management.—Jimmy Smith, Room 4C746, 614–4794.
International Programs.—RDML Frank D. Morley, WNY (202) 433–5900.
Management and Budget.—B.J. White-Olson, Room 4C681, 695–6370.
Ship Programs.—Frederick J. Stefany.
Unmanned Systems.—Frank Kelley.

DEPARTMENT OF THE NAVY CHIEF INFORMATION OFFICER

Chief Information Officer.—Thomas B. Modly, Pentagon, Room 4E720 (703) 695–3141.

CHIEF OF NAVAL OPERATIONS

Pentagon, Room 4E662, phone (703) 695–5664, fax 693–9408

Chief of Naval Operations.—ADM John Richardson.
Vice Chief of Naval Operations.—ADM Bill Moran.
Judge Advocate General of the Navy.—VADM James Crawford III.
Directors:
Naval Criminal Investigative Service.—Andrew Traver.
Naval Intelligence.—VADM Jan Tighe.
Naval Nuclear Propulsion Program.—ADM James Caldwell.
Navy Staff.—VADM Kevin Donegan.
Chief of:
Chaplains.—RADM Margaret Kibben.
Information.—CAPT Greg Hicks (acting).
Legislative Affairs.—RADM Jim Loeblein.
Navy Reserve.—VADM Luke McCollum.
Surgeon General of the Navy.—VADM Clinton Faison III.
Oceanographer of the Navy.—RADM Tim Gallaudent.
Master Chief Petty Officer of the Navy.—MCPON Steven Giordano.
President, Board of Inspection and Survey.—RDML Jon Kreitz.
Commander, Naval Education and Training.—RADM Kyle Cozad.
Commander, Naval Safety Center.—RDML Christopher Murray.
Deputy Chief of Naval Operations for—
Fleet Readiness and Logistics.—VADM Dixon Smith.
Integration of Capabilities and Resources.—VADM Bill Lescher.
Manpower, Personnel, Training, and Education.—VADM Robert Burke.
Operations, Plans, and Strategy.—RADM Andrew Lewis.
Warfare Systems.—VADM Bill Merz.
Information Warfare.—Jan Tighe.

BUREAU OF MEDICINE AND SURGERY

7700 Arlington Boulevard, Suite 5113, Arlington, VA 22042–5113
phone (703) 681–5200, fax 681–9527

Chief.—VADM C. Forrest Faison, MC, USN.

MILITARY SEALIFT COMMAND

914 Charles Morris Court, SE., Washington Navy Yard, 20398–5540
phone (202) 685–5001, fax 685–5020

Commander.—RADM Dee L. Mewbourne.

WALTER REED NATIONAL MILITARY MEDICAL CENTER

8901 Wisconsin Avenue, Bethesda, MD 20889–5600

phone (301) 295–5800 / 5802, fax 295–5336

Director.—CAPT Mark A. Kobelja.

NAVAL AIR SYSTEMS COMMAND

47123 Buse Road, Building 2272, Suite 540, Patuxent River, MD 20670

phone (301) 757–7825

Commander.—VADM Paul Grosklags.

NAVAL CRIMINAL INVESTIGATIVE SERVICE HEADQUARTERS

27130 Telegraph Road, Quantico, VA 22134, phone (571) 305–9000

Director.—Andrew Traver.

NAVAL DISTRICT OF WASHINGTON

1343 Dahlgren Avenue, SE., Building 1, 20374–5001, phone (202) 433–2777, fax 433–2207

Commandant.—RDML Charles ''Chip'' Rock.
Chief of Staff.—CAPT Roy Undersander.

NAVAL FACILITIES ENGINEERING COMMAND

1322 Patterson Avenue, SE., Washington Navy Yard, 20374–5065

phone (202) 685–9499, fax 685–1463

Commander.—RADM Bret Muilenburg, CEC, USN.

OFFICE OF NAVAL INTELLIGENCE

4251 Suitland Road, SE., Washington, DC 20020, phone (301) 669–3001, fax 669–3509

Commander.—RADM Robert D. Sharp.

NAVAL SEA SYSTEMS COMMAND

1333 Isaac Hull Avenue, SE., Stop 1010, Washington Navy Yard, 20376–1010

phone (202) 781–0100

Commander.—RADM William Galinas.

NAVAL SUPPLY SYSTEMS COMMAND

5450 Carlisle Pike, Mechanicsburg, PA 17050, phone (717) 605–3433

Commander.—RADM Jon Yuen.

SPACE AND NAVAL WARFARE SYSTEMS COMMAND SPACE FIELD ACTIVITY

14675 Lee Road, Chantilly, VA 20151, phone (703) 808–6104, fax 808–8504

Commander.—CAPT Eric Hendrickson.

U.S. NAVAL ACADEMY

121 Blake Road, Annapolis, MD 21402, phone (410) 293–1000

Superintendent.—VADM Walter E. ''Ted'' Carter, Jr.

U.S. MARINE CORPS HEADQUARTERS

Pentagon, Room 4E734, phone (703) 614–2500

Commandant.—Gen. R.B. Neller.
Assistant Commandant.—Gen. G.M. Walters, 614–1201.
Aide-de-Camp.—Lt. Col. D.W. Sampson.
Chaplain.—RDML B.W. Scott, 614–4627.
Dental Officer.—CAPT W.R. Davidson.
Fiscal Director of the Marine Corps.—SES C.E. Spangler.
Inspector General of the Marine Corps.—Brig. Gen. D.A. Ottignon, 614–1533.
Judge Advocate.—Maj. Gen. J.A. Ewers, 614–8661.
Legislative Assistant.—Brig. Gen. N.L. Cooling, 614–1686.
Medical Officer.—RDML D.A. Lane.
Military Secretary.—Col. T.J. Gordon.
Sergeant Major of the Marine Corps.—Sgt. Maj. R.L. Green, 614–8762.
Deputy Commandant of Marine Corps for—
Aviation.—Lt. Gen. S. Rudder, 614–1010.
Installations and Logistics.—Lt. Gen. M.G. Dana, 695–8572.
Manpower and Reserve Affairs.—Lt. Gen. M.A. Rocco, 695–1929.
Plans, Policies, and Operations.—Lt. Gen. B.D. Beaudreault, 614–8521.
Programs and Resources.—Lt. Gen. G.L. Thomas, 614–3435.
Public Affairs.—Brig. Gen. W.H. Seely III, 614–8010.
Director of:
Intelligence.—Brig. Gen. D. Henry.
Marine Corps History and Museums.—Vacant.

MARINE BARRACKS

Eighth and I Streets, SE., 20390, phone (202) 433–4094

Commanding Officer.—Col. T.J. Zagurski.

TRAINING AND EDUCATION COMMAND

3300 Russell Road, Quantico, VA 22134, phone (703) 784–3730, fax 784–3724

Commanding General.—Maj. Gen. K.M. Iiams.

DEPARTMENT OF JUSTICE

Robert F. Kennedy Department of Justice Building

950 Pennsylvania Avenue, NW., 20530, phone (202) 514–2000

http://www.usdoj.gov

JEFFERSON B. SESSIONS III, Attorney General; born in Selma, AL; education: Huntingdon College, 1969; University of Alabama Law School, 1973; professional: Assistant U.S. Attorney, Southern District of Alabama, 1975–79; U.S. Attorney for the Southern District of Alabama, 1981–93, Attorney General of Alabama, 1995–97; U.S. Senator from Alabama, 1997–2017; sworn in as the 84th Attorney General of the United States on February 9, 2017 by Michael R. Pence. President Donald J. Trump announced his intention to nominate Mr. Sessions on November 18, 2016.

OFFICE OF THE ATTORNEY GENERAL

RFK Main Justice Building, Room 5111, phone (202) 514–2001

Attorney General.—Jefferson B. Sessions III.

Chief of Staff and Counselor to the Attorney General.—Joseph H. Hunt, Room 5115, 514–3893.

Counselors to the Attorney General: Danielle Cutrona, Room 5110, 514–9665; Gustav Eyler, Room 5224, 514–4969; Alice LaCour, Room 5230, 514–9797; Brian Morrissey, Room 5214, 305–8674; Rachael Tucker, Room 5134, 616–7740.

White House Liaison.—Mary Blanche Hankey, Room 5116, 353–4435.

Director of Advance.—Vacant, Room 5127, 514–7281.

Director of Scheduling.—Errical Bryant, Room 5133, 514–4195.

Confidential Assistant.—Peggi Hanrahan, Room 5111, 514–2001.

OFFICE OF THE DEPUTY ATTORNEY GENERAL

RFK Main Justice Building, Room 4111, phone (202) 514–2101

Deputy Attorney General.—Rod J. Rosenstein, Room 4111.

Principal Associate Deputy Attorney General.—Robert K. Hur, Room 4208, 514–2105.

Chief of Staff and Associate Deputy Attorney General.—James A. Crowell IV, Room 4210, 514–8699.

Deputy Chief of Staff and Associate Deputy Attorney General.—G. Zachary Terwilliger, Room 4210, 307–1045.

Chief, Professional Misconduct Review Unit.—John Geise, Room 4131, 514–0049.

Associate Deputy Attorneys General: Antoinette Bacon, Room 4110, 616–1621; Steven Cook, Room 4415, 305–0180; Tashina Gauhar, Room 4218, 514–3712; Iris Lan, Room 4311, 514–6907; Sujit Raman, Room 4222, 307–0697; Scott Schools, Room 4113, 305–7848; James Swanson, Room 4135, 305–8657; Robert Troester, Room 4224, 514–3853.

Associate Deputy Attorney General and National Criminal Discovery Coordinator.—Andrew D. Goldsmith, Room 4214, 514–5705.

Associate Deputy Attorney General and Director, OCDETF.—Bruce G. Ohr, Room 4115, 307–2510.

Counsels to the Deputy Attorney General: Zachary Bolitho, Room 4114, 514–7473; Leah Bressack, Room 4129, 514–6753; Patrick Bumatay, Room 4226, 305–0071; Brendan Groves, Room 4304, 305–4127; John Hill, Room 4214, 353–3030; Daniel Loveland, Room 4315, 305–0620; Amelia Medina, Room 4121, 616–0663; Chad Mizelle, Room 4116, 305–3481; Michael Murray, Room 4220, 307–2090; Matthew Sheehan, Room 4119, 514–4995.

Emergency Preparedness and Crisis Response Coordinator.—Mark E. Michalic, Room 4112, 514–0438.

Senior Advisor on Forensics.—Ted Hunt, Room 4303, 514–4995.

Confidential Assistant to the Deputy Attorney General.—Marcia Murphy, Room 4111, 514–2101.

National Coordinator for Child Exploitation Prevention and Interdiction.—Michael Frank, Room 4217, 305–0273.

OFFICE OF THE ASSOCIATE ATTORNEY GENERAL

RFK Main Justice Building, Room 5706, phone (202) 514–9500

Associate Attorney General.—Jesse M. Panuccio (acting).
Principal Deputy Associate Attorney General.—Jesse M. Panuccio.
Deputy Associate Attorneys General: Jeremy Bylund, Stephen Cox, Patrick Hovakiman, Eric McArthur.
Counsel to the Associate Attorney General.—James Percival.
Senior Counsel to the Associate Attorney General.—Jeffrey Hall.
Chief of Staff and Counselor to the Associate Attorney General.—Rachel K. Parker.
Confidential Assistant/Office Manager.—Mollie Timmons, Room 5706, 514–9500.
Staff Assistant.—Vacant, Room 5706, 616–0565.

Note: * Indicates detailed from other component within DOJ.
All telephone numbers should be (202) 514–9500.

OFFICE OF THE SOLICITOR GENERAL

RFK Main Justice Building, Room 5143, phone (202) 514–2201

http://www.usdoj.gov/osg

Solicitor General.—Noel Francisco, Room 5143, 514–2201.
Principal Deputy Solicitor General.—Jeffrey Wall, Room 5143, 514–2206.
Executive Officer.—Valerie Hall Yancey, Room 5142, 514–3957.
Supervisory Case Management Specialist.—Charlene Goodwin, Room 5608, 514–2218.
Research and Publications Section Manager.—Vacant, Room 6634, 514–4459.

ANTITRUST DIVISION

RFK Main Justice Building, 950 Pennsylvania Avenue, NW., 20530

Liberty Square Building, 450 5th Street, NW., 20530 (LSB)

Assistant Attorney General.—Makan Delrahim, Room 3109 (202) 514–2401.
Principal Deputy Assistant Attorney General.—Andrew C. Finch, Room 3208, 307–1342.
Deputy Assistant Attorneys General: Roger Alford, Room 3115, 514–2408; Luke Froeb, Room 3214, 353–0232; Donald Kempf, Room 3114, 532–4698; Bernard Nigro, Room 3212, 353–4656.
Deputy Assistant Attorney General.—Marvin N. Price, Jr. (acting), Room 3214, 307–0719.
Director of:
Civil Enforcement.—Patricia A. Brink, Room 3213, 514–2562.
Criminal Enforcement.—Michelle Rindone (acting), Room 3336, 532–4877.
Economics Enforcement.—W. Robert Majure, Room 3416.
Freedom of Information Act Officer.—SueAnn Slates (LSB), Room 1040, 307–1398.
Executive Officer.—Scott Cohen (LSB), Room 10150, 514–4005.
Section Chiefs:
Appellate.—Kristen Limarzi, Room 3222, 514–2413.
Competition Policy.—W. Robert Majure, Room 3416, 9400, 307–6341.
Economic Litigation.—Norman Familant (LSB), Room 9912, 307–6323.
Economic Regulatory.—Beth Armington (LSB), Room 3700, 307–6332.
Foreign Commerce.—Lynda Marshall (LSB), Room 11000, 514–2264.
Legal Policy.—Robert A. Potter (LSB), Room 11700, 514–2512.
Litigation I.—Peter J. Mucchetti (LSB), Room 4700, 307–0001.
Litigation II.—Maribeth Petrizzi (LSB), Room 8700, 307–0924.
Litigation III.—Owen Kendler (LSB), Room 4000, 305–8376.
National Criminal Enforcement.—Lisa M. Phelan (LSB), Room 11400, 307–6694.
Networks and Technology.—Aaron Hoag (LSB), Room 7700, 307–6153.
Telecommunications and Media.—Scott A. Scheele (LSB), Room 7000, 307–6132.
Transportation, Energy, and Agriculture.—Kathleen S. O'Neil (LSB), Room 8000, 307–2931.

FIELD OFFICES

California: Elieka Kate Patchen, 450 Golden Gate Avenue, Room 10–0101, Box 36046, San Francisco, CA 94102 (415) 934–5309.
Illinois: Frank J. Vondrak (acting), Rookery Building, 209 South LaSalle Street, Suite 600, Chicago, IL 60604 (312) 353–7530.

New York: Jeffrey Martino, 26 Federal Plaza, Room 3630, New York, NY 10278–1040 (212) 385–8019.

BUREAU OF ALCOHOL, TOBACCO, FIREARMS, AND EXPLOSIVES (ATF)

99 New York Avenue, NE., Suite 5S–100, 20226

OFFICE OF THE DIRECTOR

Deputy Director.—Thomas E. Brandon (202) 648–8700.
Associate Deputy Director.—Ronald B. Turk, 648–8710.
Chief of Staff.—Joseph J. Allen (acting), 648–7113.
Deputy Chief of Staff.—Cherie Knoblock, 648–9211.
Special Assistant to the Deputy Director.—Betty L. Coleman, 648–8710.
Confidential Project Manager to the Acting Director.—Michelle A. Back, 648–8700.

OFFICE OF STRATEGIC MANAGEMENT

Chief.—Christopher A. Pellettiere, 648–7425.

OFFICE OF DIVERSITY AND INCLUSION (ODI)

Chief, Diversity Officer.—Vacant, Suite 2S–125, 648–8770.

OFFICE OF CHIEF COUNSEL

Chief Counsel.—Charles R. Gross, 648–7836.
Deputy Chief Counsel.—Joel J. Roessner, 648–7058.

OFFICE OF ENFORCEMENT PROGRAMS AND SERVICES

Assistant Director.—Marvin G. Richardson, 648–7080.
Deputy Assistant Director.—Curtis W. Gilbert, 648–7080.

OFFICE OF EQUAL OPPORTUNITY

Chief.—Snider Page, 648–8760.
Deputy Chief.—Robynn Ferguson-Russ, 684–8760.

OFFICE OF FIELD OPERATIONS

Assistant Director.—Michael Gleysteen, 648–8324.
Deputy Assistant Director for—
Central.—Regina Lombardo, 648–7201.
East.—Kenneth Croke, 648–7205.
West.—William McMullan, 648–8122.
Programs.—Carlos Canino, 648–7203.
Industry Operations.—Andrew R. Graham, 648–7254.

OFFICE OF MANAGEMENT

Assistant Director/CFO.—Vivian B. Michalic, 648–7800.
Deputy Assistant Director.—Francis H. Frandé, 648–7800.

OFFICE OF OMBUDSPERSON

Ombudsperson.—Grace M. Reisling, 648–7351.

OFFICE OF PROFESSIONAL RESPONSIBILITY AND SECURITY OPERATIONS

Assistant Director.—Melvin D. King, Jr., 648–7500.
Deputy Assistant Director.—Daryl R. McCrary, 648–7500.

OFFICE OF PUBLIC AND GOVERNMENTAL AFFAIRS

Assistant Director.—Christopher C. Shaefer, 648–8520.
Deputy Assistant Director.—Megan Bennett, 648–8344.
Chief, Division of:
Intergovernmental Affairs.—Dean Kueter, 648–7213.
Legislative Affairs.—Ross Arends, 648–7722.
Public Affairs.—Vacant.

OFFICE OF SCIENCE AND TECHNOLOGY / CIO

Assistant Director / Chief Information Officer.—Roger Beasley, 648–8390.
Deputy Assistant Director for IT Services / Deputy CIO.—Victoria Gold, 648–8390.
Deputy Assistant Director for Forensic Services.—Greg Czarnopys, 648–6001.

OFFICE OF STRATEGIC INTELLIGENCE AND INFORMATION

Assistant Director.—James E. McDermond, 648–7600.
Deputy Assistant Director.—James Modzelewski, 648–7600.

OFFICE OF HUMAN RESOURCES AND PROFESSIONAL DEVELOPMENT

Assistant Director.—Marino F. Vidoli, 648–7979.
Deputy Assistant Director, Professional Development.—Lisa T. Boykin, 648–7489.
Deputy Assistant Director, Human Resources.—Kelly D. Brady, 648–8415.

CIVIL DIVISION

RFK Main Justice Building, 950 Pennsylvania Avenue, NW., 20530

20 Massachusetts Avenue, NW., 20530 (20MASS)

1100 L Street, NW., 20530 (L ST)

National Place Building, 1331 Pennsylvania Avenue, NW., 20530 (NPB)

1425 New York Avenue, NW., 20530 (NYA)

Patrick Henry Building, 601 D Street, NW., 20530 (PHB)

Liberty Square Building, 450 5th Street, NW., 20530

Assistant Attorney General.—Chad A. Readler (acting), Room 3601 (202) 514–3301.
Chief of Staff.—Vacant, Room 3605 (202) 353–2793.

APPELLATE STAFF

Deputy Assistant Attorney General.—Hashim Mooppan, Room 3135, 353–8679.
Director.—Douglas Letter, Room 7519, 514–3602.
Deputy Director.—Dana Martin, Room 7517, 514–2541.

COMMERCIAL LITIGATION BRANCH

Deputy Assistant Attorney General.—Vacant, Room 3607, 307–0231.
Directors: David M. Cohen (L ST), Room 12124, 514–7300; John N. Fargo (L ST), Room 11116, 514–7223; Vacant (L ST), Room 10036, 514–7450.
Office of Foreign Litigation.—Vacant (L ST), Room 11006, 514–7455.
Deputy Directors: Jeanne Davidson (L ST), Room 12132, 307–0290; Michael Granston (PHB), Room 9902, 305–0632.
Legal Officer.—Donna C. Maizel, Esq., U.S. Department of Justice, Civil Division European Office, The American Embassy, London, England, PSC 801, Box 42, FPO AE, 09498–4042, 9+011–44–20–7894–0840.
Attorney-in-Charge.—Barbara Williams, Suite 359, 26 Federal Plaza, New York, NY 10278, (212) 264–9240.

CONSUMER LITIGATION

Deputy Assistant Attorney General.—Ethan Davis, Room 3611, 307–6482.
Director.—Vacant (LSB), Room 6254, 307–3009.

FEDERAL PROGRAMS BRANCH

Deputy Assistant Attorney General.—Brett A. Schumate, Room 3137, 514–2331.
Directors: John Griffiths (20MASS), Room 7100, 514–4651; Joseph H. Hunt, Room 7348, 514–1259; Jennifer D. Richetts (20MASS), Room 6100, 514–3671.
Deputy Directors: Tony Coppolino (20MASS), Room 6102, 514–4782; Sheila M. Lieber (20MASS), Room 7102, 514–3786.

IMMIGRATION LITIGATION

Deputy Assistant Attorney General.—August Flentje (acting), Room 3613, 514–3309.
Director.—Thomas W. Hussey (NPB), Room 7026S, 616–4852.
Deputy Directors: Donald E. Keener (NPB), Room 7022S, 616–4878; David M. McConnell (NPB), Room 7260N, 616–4881; Vacant (NPB), Room 7006N, 616–4856.

MANAGEMENT PROGRAMS

Executive Officer of Management Programs.—Catherine E. Emerson, Room 3140, 514–4552.
Director, Office of:
Administration.—Vacant (L ST), Room 9018, 307–0261.
Litigation Support.—Vacant (L ST), Room 9126, 616–5014.
Management Information.—Dorothy Bahr (L ST), Room 8044, 616–8026.
Planning, Budget, and Evaluation.—Vacant (L ST), Room 9040, 307–0842.
Policy and Management Operations.—Vacant (L ST), Room 9040, 307–0842.

TORTS BRANCH

Deputy Assistant Attorney General.—Vacant, Room 3131, 353–9328.
Directors: Rupa Bhattacharyya (NYA), Room 8122, 305–0008; J. Patrick Glynn (NPB), Room 8028S, 616–4200; James Touhey (NPB), Room 8064N, 616–4292.
Deputy Directors: JoAnn J. Bordeaux (NPB), Room 8024S, 616–4204; Paul F. Figley (NPB), Room 8096N, 616–4248.
Attorneys-in-Charge: Robert Underhill, 450 Golden Gate Avenue, 10/6610, Box 36028, San Francisco, CA 94102–3463, FTS: (415) 436–6630; Vacant, Suite 320, 26 Federal Plaza, New York, NY 10278–0140, FTS: (212) 264–0480.

CIVIL RIGHTS DIVISION

RFK Main Justice Building, 950 Pennsylvania Avenue, NW., 20530

1425 New York Avenue, NW., 20035 (NYAV)

601 D Street, NW., 20004 (PHB)

100 Indiana Avenue, NW., 20004 (NALC)

1800 G Street, NW., 20004 (NWB)

http://www.usdoj.gov/crt

Assistant Attorney General.—Thomas E. Wheeler II (acting), Room 5748A, (202) 514–2151.
Principal Deputy Assistant Attorney General.—Vacant.
Deputy Assistant Attorneys General: Greg Friel, Room 5744, 353–9418; John Gore, Room 5529, 353–9430; Rebecca Bond (acting), Room 5535, 514–2151; Robert Moossy, Room 5541, 514–0621.
(Acting) Counsels to the Assistant Attorney General: Eric Treene, Room 5531, 353–8622; Beth Kelley, Room 5642, 616–2179; Alberto Ruisanchez, Room 5533, 353–1994; Sean Keveney, Room 5537, 514–2151, Maureen Riordan, Room 5644, 616–2354.
Chief of Staff.—Vacant.
Director of Operational Management.—Kathleen Toomey, Room 5646, 323–0283.
Section Chiefs:

Appellate.—Diana K. Flynn, Room 3704, 514–2195.
Criminal.—Tamara Kessler (PHB), Room 5102, 305–3963.
Disability Rights.—Anne Raish (acting) (NYAV), Room 4053, 305–1321.
Educational Opportunities.—Shaheena Simons (PHB), Room 4002, 305–3360.
Employment Litigation.—Delora Kenebrew (PHB), Room 4040, 514–3831.
Housing and Civil Enforcement.—Sameena Shina Majeed (NWB), Room 7108, 305–1311.
Policy and Strategy Section.—Shelia Foran (PHB), Room 5006, 305–0160.
Special Litigation.—Steven Rosenbaum (PHB), Room 5034, 616–3244.
Voting.—Chris Herren (NWB), Room 7254, 307–2767.
Immigrant and Employee Rights.—Jody Danis, Room 9030, 307–5768.

OFFICE OF COMMUNITY ORIENTED POLICING SERVICES

145 N Street, NE., 20530

DIRECTOR'S OFFICE

Director.—Russell Washington (acting), 11th Floor, 616–2888.
Chief of Staff.—Katherine McQuay (acting).
Deputy Director for Management.—Wayne Henry.

COMMUNICATIONS DIVISION

Assistant Director.—Shannon Long, 11th Floor, 514–9079.

COMMUNITY RELATIONS SERVICE

600 E Street, NW., Suite 6000, 20530, phone (202) 305–2935

fax 353–2164 (BICN)

Director.—Vacant.
Deputy Director (SES).—Gerri Ratliff.
General Counsel.—Antoinette Barksdale.
Media Affairs Officer.—Vacant.

REGIONAL DIRECTORS

New England.—Theresa Segovia (Associate Director), 408 Atlantic Avenue, Suite 222, Boston, MA 02110–1032 (617) 424–5715.
Northeast Region.—Theresa Segovia (Associate Director), 26 Federal Plaza, Suite 36–118, New York, NY 10278 (212) 264–0700.
Mid-Atlantic Region.—Ben Lieu, 200 2nd and Chestnut Streets, Suite 208, Philadelphia, PA 19106 (215) 597–2344.
Southeast Region.—Thomas Battles, 61 Forsyth Street, SW., Suite 7B65, Atlanta, GA 30303 (404) 331–6883.
Midwest Region.—Mary Gorecki, 230 South Dearborn Street, Suite 2130, Chicago, IL 60604 (312) 353–4391.
Southwest Region.—Synthia Taylor, Hardwood Center Building, 1999 Bryan Street, Suite 2050, Dallas, TX 75201 (214) 655–8175.
Central Region.—Christian Van Alstyne, 601 East 12th Street, Suite 0802, Kansas City, MO 64106 (816) 426–7434.
Rocky Mountain Region.—Theresa Segovia (Associate Director), 1244 Speer Boulevard, Suite 650, Denver, CO 80204–3584 (303) 844–2973.
Western Region.—Ronald Wakabayashi, 888 South Figueroa Street, Suite 2010, Los Angeles, CA 90017 (213) 894–2941.
Northwest Region.—Carol Russo, 915 Second Avenue, Suite 1808, Seattle, WA 98174 (206) 220–6700.

CRIMINAL DIVISION

RFK Main Justice Building, 950 Pennsylvania Avenue, NW., 20530

Mainline Telephone (202) 514–7200

Bond Building, 1400 New York Avenue, NW., 20530 (Bond)

1331 F Street, NW., 20530 (F Street)

John C. Keeney Building, 1301 New York Avenue, NW., 20530 (1301 NYA)

2CON Building, 2 Constitution Square, 145 N Street, NE., 20530 (2CON)

Assistant Attorney General.—Kenneth A. Blanco (acting), Room 2107, 514–7200.

Principal Deputy Assistant Attorney General.—Trevor N. McFadden (acting), Room 2121, 353–3165.

Deputy Assistant Attorneys General: Kenneth A. Blanco, Room 2107, 514–7200; Bruce C. Swartz, Room 2212, 514–2333; Trevor N. McFadden, Room 2121, 353–3165; Richard W. Downing (acting), Room 2119, 353–7849; M. Kendall Day (acting), Room 2118, 353–2248; Raymond N. Hulser (acting), Room 2115, 616–0387.

Chief of Staff and Counselor to the Assistant Attorney General.—James C. Mann (acting), Room 2208, 305–4763.

Counsels to the Assistant Attorney General: David Dalton, Room 2114, 616–1579; Michael Lang, Room 2222, 616–0381; Samer Korkor, Room 2224, 598–2772; Anitha Ibrahim, Room 2116, 616–3181.

Executive Officer.—Tracy Melton (Bond), Room 5100, 305–0534.

Section Chiefs/Office Directors:

Appellate.—Patty M. Stemler (RFK), Room 1521, 514–2611.

Capital Case.—P. Kevin Carwile (F Street), Suite 600, 514–3705.

Child Exploitation and Obscenity.—Steve Grocki (Bond), Suite 6000, 616–8900.

Computer Crime and Intellectual Property.—John Lynch (1301 NYA), Suite 600, 305–8732.

Enforcement Operations.—Jennifer Hodge (1301 NYA), Suite 1200, 305–9291.

Fraud.—Andrew Weissman (Bond), Room 4100, 353–8855.

Human Rights and Special Prosecution.—Teresa McHenry (1301 NYA), Room 215, 616–8385.

International Affairs.—Vaughn Ary (1301 NYA), Suite 900, 616–1503.

International Criminal Investigative Training Assistant Program.—Gary Barr (F Street), Suite 500, 616–7418.

Money Laundering & Asset Recovery.—Deborah Connor (acting) (Bond), Suite 10100, 616–2886.

Narcotics and Dangerous Drugs.—Arthur Wyatt (2CON), Room 2E.200, 307–2382.

Organized Crime and Gangs.—David Jaffe (acting) (1301 NYA), Suite 700, 514–0865.

Overseas Prosecutorial Development, Assistance and Training.—Faye Ehrenstamm (F Street), Suite 700, 514–1437.

Policy and Legislation.—Jonathan Wroblewski, Room 1744, 514–4730.

Public Integrity.—AnnaLou Tirol (acting) (Bond), Suite 12100, 307–2125.

OFFICE OF DISPUTE RESOLUTION

RFK Main Justice Building, Room 4531, phone (202) 616–9471/616–9472

http://www.usdoj.gov/odr

Director and Senior Counsel.—Joanna M. Jacobs, Room 4529, 305–4439.

DRUG ENFORCEMENT ADMINISTRATION

Lincoln Place-1 (East), 600 Army-Navy Drive, Arlington, VA 22202 (LP–1)

Lincoln Place-2 (West), 700 Army-Navy Drive, Arlington, VA 22202 (LP–2)

Administrator.—Robert W. Patterson (acting), Room W–12060 (202) 307–8000.

Chief of Staff.—Michael P. Ben'Ary, Room 12060, 307–8246.

Deputy Administrator.—Preston L. Grubbs (acting), Room W–12058–F, 307–7345.

Equal Employment Opportunity Officer.—Elizabeth ''Kelly'' Goode, Room E–9371, 307–8900.

Executive Assistants: Vacant.

Chief, Congressional and Public Affairs.—Gary Owen, Room W–12228, 307–7363.
Section Chiefs:
Electronic and Internal Communications.—Michael Shavers, Room E–9049–E, 307–2402.
Congressional Affairs.—Sean Mitchell, Room W–12104, 307–4307.
Community Outreach and Prevention Support.—Sean Fearns, Room W–12222, 307–3479.
National Media Affairs.—Mary Brandenberger, Room W–12200, 307–1650.
Chief Counsel.—Wendy H. Goggin, Room W–12142–C, 307–7322.
Deputy Chief Counsel.—Robert C. Gleason, Room E–12375, 307–8083.
Chief, Office of Administrative Law Judges.—John Mulrooney, 307–8188.

FINANCIAL MANAGEMENT DIVISION

Chief Financial Officer.—Jeffrey Sutton, Room W–12138, 307–7330.
Deputy Assistant Administrator for—
Acquisition Management.—Christinia K. Sisk, Room W–5100, 307–7888.
Finance.—Daniel Gillette, Room E–7397, 307–7001.
Resource Management.—Brian Horn, Room E–5102, 307–4800.
Section Chiefs:
Acquisition Management.—Jeffrey Saylor, Room E–8281, 307–7812.
Controls and Coordination.—Bryan Parks, Room E–5384, 307–5276.
Financial Integrity.—Angela Ivy, Room E–7331, 307–5459.
Financial Operations.—Daanish Ahmed, Room E–7165, 307–7270.
Financial Reports.—Sherri Woodle, Room E–7297, 307–7040.
Financial Systems.—Andrew Kenny, Room E–8001, 307–7215.
Organization and Staffing Management.—Amanda R. Voight, Room E–5284, 307–5052.
Policy and Transportation.—Carol S. Burger, Room E–8161, 307–4732.
Program Liaison and Analysis.—Kenneshia D. Ruto, Room E–5102 (202) 598–8083.
Statistical Services.—Gamaliel Rose, Room E–5332, 307–8276.

HUMAN RESOURCES DIVISION

Assistant Administrator.—Diane E. Filler, Room W–12020, 307–4195.
Section Chiefs:
Budget and Workforce Planning.—Glenda A. Rollins, Room W–6108, 307–4701.
Recruitment, Staffing, and Placement.—Jill Colburn, Room W–3262, 307–4027.
Career Board Executive Secretary.—Jonathan Schleffer, Room W–2270 (202) 353–1165.
Chair, Board of Professional Conduct.—Christopher Quaglino, Room E–9359, 307–7382.
Special Agent-in-Charge, Office of Training.—Gregory J. Cherundolo, 2500 Investigation Parkway, DEA Academy, Quantico, VA 22135 (703) 632–5010.
Assistant Special Agents-in-Charge:
Domestic Training Section 1.—Wendy Woolcock (703) 632–5110.
Specialized Training Section.—Brian Townsend (703) 632–5310.
International Training Section.—Thurman Peterson (703) 632–5330.

INSPECTIONS DIVISION

Chief Inspector.—Brian McKnight, Room W–12042A, 307–7358.
Deputy Chief Inspector, Office of:
Inspections.—Michael Stanfill, Room W–4348, 307–1584.
Professional Responsibility.—William ''Tim'' McDermott, Room W–4176, 307–6035.
Security Programs.—Mark Mazzei, Room W–2340 (202) 353–1577.

INTELLIGENCE DIVISION

Assistant Administrator.—Douglas W. Poole, Room W–12036, 307–3607.
Director/Special Agent-in-Charge, El Paso Intelligence Center.—Kevin ''Scott'' McRory, Building11339, SSG Sims Street, El Paso, TX 79908–8098 (915) 760–2011.
Deputy Assistant Administrator, Office of Intelligence.—Durell Hope, Room W–12020C, 307–3607.
Executive Assistant.—Cheryl Hooper, 307–3607.
Deputy Assistant Administrator, Office of:
OCDETF Fusion Center.—Phillip Jacobs (703) 561–7607.
National Security Intelligence.—Joseph Donovan (acting), 307–7923.

Special Intelligence.—Willard B. "Bond" Wells, Jr., Merrifield, VA (703) 561–7100.
Section Chiefs:
Data Management.—Dawn Marseilles (703) 561–7671.
Intelligence Policy and Strategic Planning Section.—Carrie Thompson, 307–8168.
Intelligence Programs Section.—Benjamin C. Sanborn, 307–4358.
Investigative Support.—Art Doty (703) 561–7320.
Operation Support Section.—Elaine Fontana (703) 561–7623.
Program Management and Budget Section.—Demetrice Crumley, 307–7534.
Requirements and Collection Section.—Joseph Donovan, 307–7923.
Strategic Intelligence Section.—Kirsten Walters, 307–6845.
Technical Support Section.—Kurt Lund, 307–3651.

OPERATIONS DIVISION

Chief of Operations.—Anthony D. Williams, Room W–12050, 307–7340.
Chief of:
Foreign/Administrative Support.—Lawyer Wilson, Jr., Room W–6350 (202) 353–1552.
Global Enforcement.—Paul Knierim, Room W–11166, 307–4446.
Operations Management.—Michael T. DellaCorte, Room W–11148 (202) 353–1164.
Special Agent-in-Charge, Aviation Division.—Gary W. Hill, Fort Worth, TX (817) 837–2000.
Special Agent-in-Charge, Special Operations Division.—Raymond P. Donovan, Chantilly, VA (703) 488–4205.

DIVERSION CONTROL DIVISION

Deputy Assistant Administrator, Office of Diversion Control.—Demetra Ashley (acting), Room E–6295, 307–7165.

OPERATIONAL SUPPORT DIVISION

Assistant Administrator.—Preston Grubbs, Room W–12142, 307–4730.
Deputy Assistant Administrator, Office of:
Administration.—Renaldo Prillman, Room W–9088, 307–7703.
Forensic Sciences.—Nelson Santos, Room W–7342, 307–8866.
Information Systems.—Maura Quinn, Room E–3105, 307–3653.
Investigative Technology.—Fred Smith, Lorton, VA (703) 495–6500.
Section Chiefs:
Administrative Operations.—Vacant, Room W–5104–A, 307–7866.
Business Program Management.—Millie Tyler, Room E–3007, 307–9895.
Facilities and Finance.—Mike Barbour, Room W–5244, 307–7792.
Hazardous Waste Disposal.—Stephen Wasem, Room W–7310, 307–7206.
Integration and Management.—Anna Pacula, Room E–4063 (703) 285–7302.
Laboratory Operations.—Lance Kvetko, Room W–7312, 307–8880.
Software Operations.—Deborah Roberts (acting), Room E–3101, 307–8673.
Surveillance Support.—Richard Rosa, Lorton, VA (703) 495–6574.
Technology Officer.—Mark Shafernich (703) 285–4456.
Telecommunications/Intercept Support.—Brian Rob, Lorton, VA (703) 495–6676.
Associate Deputy Assistant Administrator, Office of:
Forensic Sciences.—Scott Oulton, Room W–7344, 307–8866.
Information Systems.—Michelle Bower, Room E–3005, 307–5269.

FIELD OFFICES

Special Agents-in-Charge:
Atlanta Division.—Daniel R. Salter, 75 Spring Street, SW., Room 800, Atlanta, GA 30303 (404) 893–7100.
Caribbean Division.—Apolonio J. Collazo, Jr., Metro Office Park, Millennium Park Plaza #15, 2nd Street, Suite 710, Guaynabo, PR 00968 (787) 277–4700.
Chicago Division.—Dennis A. Wichern, John C. Kluczynski Federal Building, 230 South Dearborn Street, Suite 1200, Chicago, IL 60604 (312) 353–7875.
Dallas Division.—Clyde E. Shelley, Jr., 10160 Technology Boulevard East, Dallas, TX 75220 (214) 366–6900.
Denver Division.—Barbra M. Roach, 12154 East Easter Avenue, Centennial, CO 80112–6740 (720) 895–4040.

Detroit Division.—Timothy J. Plancon, 431 Howard Street, Detroit, MI 48226 (313) 234–4000.

El Paso Division.—Karen I. Flowers, 660 Mesa Hills Drive, Suite 2000, El Paso, TX 79912 (915) 832–6000.

Houston Division.—William R. Glaspy, 1433 West Loop South, Suite 600, Houston, TX 77027–9506 (713) 693–3000.

Los Angeles Division.—David J. Downing, 255 East Temple Street, 17th Floor, Los Angeles, CA 90012 (213) 621–6700.

Miami Division.—Adolphus P. Wright, 2100 North Commerce Parkway, Weston, FL 33326 (954) 660–4500.

New England Division.—Michael J. Ferguson, JFK Federal Building, 15 New Sudbury Street, Room E–400, Boston, MA 02203 (617) 557–2100.

New Jersey Division.—Valerie A. Nickerson, 80 Mulberry Street, 2nd Floor, Newark, NJ 07102–4206 (973) 776–1200.

New Orleans Division.—Stephen G. Azzam, 3 Lakeway Center, 3838 North Causeway Boulevard, Suite 1800, Metaire, LA 70002 (504) 840–1100.

New York Division.—James J. Hunt, 99 10th Avenue, New York, NY 10011 (212) 337–3900.

Philadelphia Division.—Gary Tuggle, William J. Green Federal Building, 600 Arch Street, Room 10224, Philadelphia, PA 19106 (215) 861–3474.

Phoenix Division.—Douglas W. Coleman, 3010 North Second Street, Suite 100, Phoenix, AZ 85012 (602) 664–5600.

San Diego Division.—William R. Sherman, 4560 Viewridge Avenue, San Diego, CA 92123–1672 (858) 616–4100.

San Francisco Division.—John J. Martin, 450 Golden Gate Avenue, 14th Floor, San Francisco, CA 94102 (415) 436–7900.

Seattle Division.—Keith R. Weis, 300 Fifth Avenue, Suite 1300, Seattle, WA 98104–2398 (206) 553–5443.

St. Louis Division.—James P. Shroba, 317 South 16th Street, St. Louis, MO 63103 (314) 538–4600.

Washington, DC, Division.—Karl C. Colder, 800 K Street, NW., Suite 500, Washington, DC 20001 (202) 305–8500.

OTHER DEA OFFICES

Special Agents-in-Charge:

Kevin ''Scott'' McRory, El Paso Intelligence Center, Building 11339, SSG Sims Street, El Paso, TX 79908 (915) 760–2000.

Gary W. Hill, Aviation Operations Division, 2300 Horizon Drive, Fort Worth, TX 76177 (817) 837–2000.

Raymond P. Donovan, Special Operations Division, 14560 Avion Parkway, Chantilly, VA 20151 (703) 488–4200.

Gregory J. Cherundolo, Office of Training, P.O. Box 1475, Quantico, VA 22134 (703) 632–5000.

FOREIGN OFFICES

Ankara, Turkey: American Embassy Ankara, DEA / Justice, PSC 93, Box 5000, APO AE 09823–5000, 9–011–90–312–468–6136.

Asuncion, Paraguay: DEA / Justice, American Embassy Asuncion, Unit 4740, APO AA 34036, 9–011–595–21–210–738.

Athens, Greece: American Embassy Athens, DEA / Justice, PSC 108, Box 14, APO AE 09842, 9–011–30–210–643–4328.

Bangkok, Thailand: American Embassy, DEA / Justice, Box 49, APO AP 96546–0001, 9–011–662–205–4984.

Beijing, China: American Embassy Beijing, DEA / Justice, PSC 461, Box 50, FPO AP 96521–0002, 9–011–8610–8529–6880.

Belmopan, Belize: American Embassy Belmopan, DEA / Justice, PSC 120, Unit 7405, APO AA 34025, 301–985–9387.

Bern, Switzerland: Department of State, DEA / Justice, 5110 Bern Place, Washington, DC 20521–5110, 9–011–41–31–357–7367.

Bogota, Colombia: American Embassy Bogota, DEA / Justice, Unit 5116, APO AA 34038, 9–011–571–315–2121.

Brasilia, Brazil: DEA / Justice, American Embassy Brasilia, Unit 3500, APO AA 34030, 9–011–55–61–3312–7122.

Bridgetown, Barbados: American Embassy Bridgetown, CMR 1014, DEA / Justice, FPO AA 34055, 9–1–246–227–4171.

Brussels, Belgium: American Embassy Brussels, DEA / Justice, PSC 82, Box 137, APO AE 09710, 9–011–32–2–508–2420.

Buenos Aires, Argentina: DEA / Justice, American Embassy Buenos Aires, Unit 4309, APO AA 34034, 9–011–5411–5777–4696.

Cairo, Egypt: American Embassy Cairo, DEA / Justice, Unit 64900, Box 25, APO AE 09839–4900, 9–011–20–2–2797–2461.

Canberra, Australia: American Embassy Canberra, DEA / Justice, APO AP 96549, 9–011–61–2–6214–5903.

Caracas, Venezuela: American Embassy Caracas, DEA / Justice, Unit 4962, APO AA 34037, 9–011–582–212–975–8380 / 8443 / 8407.

Cartagena, Resident Office: American Embassy, DEA Cartagena, Unit 5141, APO AA 34038, 9–011–575–664–9369.

Chiang-Mai, Resident Office: American Embassy Chiang-Mai, Box C, APO AP 96546, 9–011–66–53–217–285.

Ciudad, Resident Office: U.S. Consulate / Ciudad Juarez Resident Office, P.O. Box 10545, El Paso, TX 79925, 9–011–52–656–611–1179.

Cochabamba, Resident Office: Unit 3220, Box 211, APO AA 34032, 9–011–591–4–429–3320.

Copenhagen, Denmark: American Embassy Copenhagen, DEA / Justice, PSC 73, APO AE 09716, 9–011–45–35–42–2680.

Curacao, Netherlands Antilles: American Consulate Curacao, DEA / Justice, Washington, DC 20521, 9–011–5999–461–6985.

Dubai, United Arab Emirates: U.S. Consulate General, DEA / Justice, 6020 Dubai Place, Dulles, VA 20189–6020, 9–011–971–4–311–6220.

Dushanbe, Tajikistan: American Embassy Dushanbe, DEA / Justice, Drug Enforcement Administration, 7090 Dushanbe Place, Dulles, VA 20189–7090, 9–011–992–37–229–2807.

Frankfurt, Resident Office: American Consulate General Frankfurt, DEA / Justice, PSC 115, Box 1017, APO AE 09213–0115, 9–011–49–69–7535–3770.

Freeport, Bahamas Resident Office: GPS, c/o U.S. Embassy, DEA, 5115 Northwest 17th Terrace, Hanger #39A, Ft. Lauderdale, FL 33309, 9–1–242–352–5353 / 5354.

Guadalajara, Resident Office: DEA, Guadalajara Resident Office, P.O. Box 9001, Brownsville, TX 78520, 9–011–52–33–3268–2191.

Guatemala City, Guatemala: American Embassy Guatemala City, DEA / Justice, Unit 3311, APO AA 34024, 9–011–502–331–4389.

Guayaquil, Resident Office: DEA / Justice, American Embassy Guayaquil, Unit 5350, APO AA, 34039, 9–011–593–42–32–3715.

The Hague, Netherlands: American Embassy The Hague, DEA / Justice, Unit 6707, Box 8, APO AE 09715, 9–011–31–70–310–2327.

Hanoi, Vietnam: American Embassy Hanoi, DEA / Justice, PSC 461, Box 400, FPO AP 96521–0002, 9–011–844–850–5011.

Hermosillo, Resident Office: U.S. Consulate-Hermosillo, P.O. Box 1689, Nogales, AZ 85628–1689, 9–011–52–662–289–3550.

Hong Kong, Resident Office: U.S. Consulate General Hong Kong, DEA / Justice, PSC 461, Box 16, FPO AP 96521–0006, 9–011–852–2521–4536.

Islamabad, Pakistan Country Office: DEA / Justice, American Embassy Islamabad, DEA / Justice, Unit 62215, APO AE 09812–2215, 9–011–92–51–208–2918.

Istanbul, Turkey Resident Office: American Consulate General, DEA / Justice, PSC 97, Box 0002, APO AE 09827, 9–011–90–212–335–9179.

Kabul, Afghanistan Country Office: DEA / Justice, American Embassy Kabul, 8160 Kabul Place, Washington, DC 20521–6180, 301–490–1042.

Kingston, Jamaica Country Office: U.S. Embassy Kingston, 142 Old Hope Road, Kingston 6, Jamaica, 9–1–876–702–6004.

Kuala Lumpur, Malaysia Country Office: American Embassy Kuala Lumpur, DEA / Justice, APO AP 96535–8152, 9–011–603–2142–1779.

Lagos, Nigeria: Department of State, DEA / Justice, 8300 Lagos Place, Washington, DC 20521–8300, 9–011–234–1–261–9837.

La Paz, Bolivia: American Embassy La Paz, DEA / Justice, Unit 3220, DPO AA 34032, 9–011–591–2–216–8313.

Lima, Peru: American Embassy Lima, DEA / Justice, Unit 3810, APO AA 34031, 9–011–511–618–2475.

London, England: American Embassy London, DEA / Justice, Unit 8400, Box 0008, FPO AE 09498–4008, 9–011–44–207–894–0826.

Madrid, Spain: American Embassy Madrid, DEA / Justice, PSC 61, Box 0014, APO AE 09642, 9–011–34–91–587–2280.

Managua, Nicaragua: DEA, American Embassy Nicaragua, Unit 2700, Box 21, APO AA 34021, 9–011–505–252–7738.

Manila, Philippines: American Embassy Manila, DEA / Justice, PSC 500, Box 11, FPO AP 96515, 9–011–632–301–2084.

Matamoros, Mexico Resident Office: Matamoros DEA, P.O. Box 9004, Brownsville, TX 78501, 9–011–52–868–149–1285.

Mazatlan, Resident Office: DEA, Mazatlan Resident Office, P.O. Box 9006, Brownsville, TX 78520–0906, 9–011–669–982–1775.

Merida, Mexico: U.S. Consulate-Merida, P.O. Box 9003, Brownsville, TX 78520–0903, 9–011–52–999–942–5738.

Mexico City, Mexico: DEA / Justice, U.S. Embassy Mexico City, P.O. Box 9000, Brownsville, TX 78520, 9–011–52–55–5080–2600.

Milan, Resident Office: American Consulate Milan, DEA / Justice, PSC 833, Box 60–M, FPO AE 09624, 9–011–39–02–2903–5422.

Monterrey, Resident Office: U.S. Consulate General, Monterrey Resident Office, P.O. Box 9002, Brownsville, TX 78520–0902, 9–011–5281–8340–1299.

Moscow, Russia: American Embassy Moscow, DEA / Justice, PSC 77, APO AE 09721, 9–011–7–495–728–5218.

Nassau: Nassau Country Office, DEA / Justice, American Embassy Nassau, 3370 Nassau Place, Washington, DC 20520, 9–1–242–322–1700.

New Delhi, India: American Embassy New Delhi, Department of State, 9000 New Delhi Place, Washington, DC 20521, 9–011–91–11–2419–8495.

Nicosia, Cyprus: American Embassy Nicosia, DEA / Justice, PSC 815, Box 1, FPO AE 09836–0001, 9–011–357–22–393–302.

Nuevo Laredo, Mexico: DEA, Nuevo Laredo Resident Office, P.O. Box 3089, Laredo, TX 78044–3089, 9–011–52–867–714–0512.

Ottawa, Canada: American Embassy Ottawa, DEA / Justice, P.O. Box 35, Ogdensburg, New York 13669, 9–1–613–238–5633.

Panama City, Panama: American Embassy Panama, DEA / Justice, Unit 0945, APO AA 34002, 9–011–507–317–5541.

Paramaribo, Suriname: American Embassy Paramaribo, DEA / Justice, 3390 Paramaribo Place, Dulles, VA 20189–3390, 301–985–8693.

Paris, France: American Embassy Paris, DEA / Justice, PSC 116, Box A–224, APO AE 09777, 9–011–33–1–4312–2732.

Peshawar, Pakistan: American Consulate Peshawar, DEA / Justice, Unit 62217, APO AE 09812–2217, 9–011–92–91–584–0424 / 0425.

Port-au-Prince, Haiti: U.S. Department of State, 3400 Port-au-Prince, DEA, Washington, DC 20521, 9–011–509–2–229–8413.

Port of Spain, Trinidad and Tobago: Department of State, DEA / Justice, Port of Spain Country Office, 3410 Port of Spain Place, Washington, DC 20537, 9–1–868–628–8136.

Pretoria, South Africa: American Embassy Pretoria, Department of State, DEA / Justice, Washington, DC 20521–9300, 9–011–2712–362–5008.

Quito, Ecuador: DEA / Justice, American Embassy Quito, Unit 5338, APO AA 34039, 9–011–593–22–231–547.

Rangoon, Burma: American Embassy Rangoon, DEA / Justice, Box B, APO AP 96546, 9–011–95–1–536–509.

Rome, Italy: American Embassy Rome, DEA / Justice, PSC 833, Box 22, FPO AE 09624, 9–011–39–06–4674–2319.

San Jose, Costa Rica: American Embassy San Jose, DEA / Justice, Unit 3440, Box 376, APO AA 34020–0376, 9–011–506–22–20–2433.

San Salvador, El Salvador: American Embassy San Salvador, DEA / Justice, Unit 3130, APO AA 34023, 9–011–503–2278–6005.

Santa Cruz, Resident Office: DEA / Justice, American Embassy, Unit 3913 (Santa Cruz), APO AA 34032, 9–011–591–332–7153.

Santiago, Chile: DEA / Justice, American Embassy Santiago, Unit 3460, Box 136, APO AA34033–0136, 9–011–56–2–330–3401.

Santo Domingo, Dominican Republic: American Embassy Santo Domingo, DEA / Justice, Unit 3470, APO AA 34041, 9–1–809–687–3754.

Sao Paulo, Resident Office: DEA / Justice, American Embassy Sao Paulo, Unit 3502, APO AA 34030, 301–985–9364.

Seoul, Korea: American Embassy Seoul, DEA / Justice, Unit 15550, APO AP 96205–0001, 9–011–82–2–397–4260.

Singapore: American Embassy Singapore, Unit 4280, Box #30, FPO AP 96507–90030, 9–011–65–6476–9021.

Tashkent: Uzbekistan Country Office, DEA / Justice, 7110 Tashkent Place, Washington, DC 20521, 9–011–998–371–120–8924.

Tegucigalpa, Honduras: American Embassy Tegucigalpa, Tegucigalpa Country Office, Unit 3480, Box 212, APO AA 34022, 301–985–9321.

Tijuana, Resident Office: DEA, Tijuana Resident Office, P.O. 439039, San Diego, CA 92143–9039, 9–011–526–646–22–7452.

Tokyo, Japan: American Embassy Tokyo, DEA / Justice, Unit 45004, Box 224, APO AP 96337–5004, 9–011–81–3–3224–5452.

Trinidad, Bolivia Resident Office: American Embassy La Paz, DEA / Justice, Unit 3220 TRO, DPO AA 34032, 301–985–9398.

Udorn, Thailand Resident Office: American Embassy (Udorn), Box UD, APO AP 96546, 9–011–66–42–247–636.

Vancouver Resident Office: DEA Vancouver, 1574 Gulf Road, #1509, Point Roberts, WA 98281, 9–1–604–694–7710.

Vienna, Austria: Vienna Country Office, DEA / Justice, American Embassy, 9900 Vienna Place, Dulles, VA 20189–9900, 9–011–43–1–31339–7551.

Vientiane, Laos: American Embassy Vientiane, DEA / Justice, Unit 8165, Box V, APO AP 96546, 9–011–856–21–219–565.

Warsaw, Poland Country Office: DEA / Justice, American Embassy Warsaw, Unit 5010, Box 27, DPO AE 09730–5010, 9–011–48–22–504–2000.

ENVIRONMENT AND NATURAL RESOURCES DIVISION

RFK Main Justice Building, 950 Pennsylvania Avenue, NW., 20530

601 D Street, NW., 20004 (PHB)

Assistant Attorney General.—Vacant, Room 2143 (202) 514–2701.

Assistant Attorney General.—Jeffrey H. Wood (acting), Room 2603, 514–3370.

Deputy Assistant Attorneys General: Bruce Gelber, Room 2609, 514–4624; Jean Williams, Room 2135, 305–0228; Vacant, Room 2611, 514–0943; Brandon M. Middleton, Special Assistant and Counsel, Room 2607, 305–0312.

Executive Officer.—Andrew Collier (PHB), Room 2038, 616–3147.

Section Chiefs:

Appellate.—James C. Kilbourne (PHB), Room 2339, 514–2748.

Environmental Crimes.—Deborah Harris (PHB), Room 2102, 305–0347.

Environmental Defense.—Letitia J. Grishaw (PHB), Room 8002, 514–2219.

Environmental Enforcement.—Tom Mariani (PHB), Room 6002, 514–4620.

Indian Resources.—Craig Alexander (PHB), Room 3016, 514–9080.

Land Acquisition.—Andrew Goldfrank (PHB), Room 3638, 305–0316.

Law and Policy.—Karen Wardzinski (RFK), Room 2617, 514–0474.

Natural Resources.—Lisa Russell (PHB), Room 3102, 305–0438.

Wildlife and Marine Resources.—Seth Barsky (PHB), Room 3902, 305–0210.

EXECUTIVE OFFICE FOR IMMIGRATION REVIEW (EOIR)

5107 Leesburg Pike, Suite 2600, Falls Church, VA 22041

Director.—Juan P. Osuna, 2600 SKYT (703) 305–0169.

Deputy Director.—Ana M. Kocur.

Counsel to the Director.—Rena E. Cutlip-Mason.

Executive Secretariat.—Rhonda L. Caldwell.

General Counsel.—Jean C. King, 2600 SKYT, 305–0470.

Deputy General Counsel.—Helaine Perlman.

Assistant Director of Administration.—Lisa Ward (acting), 2300 SKYT, 605–1730.

Deputy Assistant Directors of Administration: James McDaniel, Kathryn D. Sheehey (acting).

Assistant Director of Planning, Analysis, and Statistics.—Vacant, 2638 SKYT, 605–0445.

Deputy Assistant Director of Planning, Analysis, and Statistics.—Vacant.

Program Director, Planning, Analysis, and Statistics.—Mike Tennyson.

Chair, Board of Immigration Appeals.—David L. Neal, 2400 SKYT, 305–1194.

Vice Chair, Board of Immigration Appeals.—Charles Adkins-Blanch.

Chief Judge, Office of the Chief Immigration Judge.—MaryBeth Keller (acting), 2500 SKYT, 305–1247.

Deputy Chief Immigration Judges: Michael C. McGoings, Mary Cheng, R. Print Maggard.

Chief, Office of the Chief Administrative Hearing Officer.—Robin M. Stutman, 2519 SKYT, 305–0864.

Counsel to the Chief Administrative Hearing Officer.—Elizabeth Vayo.

Chief Information Officer, Information Technology.—Kekoa LumHo (acting), 2300 SKYT, 605–6933.

Deputy Chief Information Officer, Information Technology.—Christopher G. Thornton.

Telephone Directory Coordinator.—Annette Thomas, 2300 SKYT, 605–1336.

EXECUTIVE OFFICE FOR UNITED STATES ATTORNEYS (EOUSA)

RFK Main Justice Building, Room 2245, phone (202) 252–1300

Director.—Monty Wilkinson, Room 2243.
Deputy Director and Counsel to the Director.—Norman Wong, Room 2246.
Deputy Director for Legal Management.—Suzanne L. Bell, Room 2242.
Administrative Officer.—Joy Smith, Room 2006, BICN, 252–5553.
Executive Assistant/Attorney General's Advisory Committee Liaison.—Karen Winzenberg, Room 2261, RFK, 252–1374.
Victims Rights Ombudsman.—Marie O'Rourke, Room 2245, RFK Main Justice Building, 252–1317.
Director, Office of Legal Education.—Chammy Chandler, National Advocacy Center, 1620 Pendleton Street, Columbia, SC 29201 (803) 705–5100.
General Counsel.—Jay Macklin, Room 5000, BICN (202) 252–1600.
Assistant Directors:
Communication and Law Enforcement Coordinator Staff.—David Ausiello, Room 2523, RFK, 252–5985.
Data Analysis Staff.—Michelle Slusher, Room 2000, BICN, 252–5571.
Equal Employment Opportunity Staff.—Jason Osborne, Room 5100, BICN, 252–1460.
Evaluation and Review Staff.—Dayle Elieson, Room 6800, BICN, 252–5917.
FOIA and Privacy Act Staff.—Susan Gerson, Room 7300, BICN, 252–6020.
Counsels for—
Asset Recovery Staff.—Mark Redmiles, Room 7600, 252–5877.
Crisis Management and Resource.—Vacant.
Indian Violent and Cyber Crimes Staff.—Gretchen C. Shappert, Room 7622, BICN, 252–5841.
Legal and Victim Programs.—Dan Villegas, Room 7600, BICN, 252–5888.
Legal Initiatives.—David Smith, Room 2256, RFK, 252–1326.
Legislative Counsel.—Scott Laragy, Room 2509, 252–1435.
Victim Witness Staff.—Kristina Neal, Room 7600, BICN, 252–5833.
White Collar and Civil Litigation Staff.—Tammy Reno, Room 7600, 252–5493.
Chief Financial Officer.—Paul Suddes, Room 2200, BICN, 252–5605.
Assistant Director of:
Audit and Review.—Louisa McCarter Dadzie, Room 2200, BICN, 252–5624.
Budget Execution.—Tracy Hall, Room 2200, BICN, 252–5627.
Budget Formulation.—Vacant.
Financial Systems Staff.—Jonathan Pelletier, Room 2200, BICN, 252–5628.
Acquisitions Staff.—Stephanie Girard, Room 5200, BICN, 252–5407.
Facilities/Support Services Staff.—Ana Indovina, Room 5200, BICN, 252–5964.
Chief Information Officer.—Mark Fleshman, Room 9078, BICN, 252–6246.
Assistant Director of:
Case Management Staff.—Siobhan Sperin, Room 9125, BICN, 252–6120.
EVOIP Program Staff.—Joe Pfeifer, Room 9012, BICN, 252–4468.
Information Security Staff.—Gregory Hall, Room 9074, BICN, 252–6090.
Office Automation Staff.—Glenn Shrieves, Room 9039, BICN, 252–6281.
Records and Information Management Staff (RIM).—Bonnie Curtin, Room 9080, BICN, 252–6488.
Telecommunications and Technology Development Staff.—Denny Ko, Room 9136, BICN, 252–6430.
Litigation Technology Service Center.—Marc Fulkert, ITEC, Columbia, SC (803) 705–5432.
Chief Human Resources Officer, Human Resources Staff.—Shawn Flinn, Room 8509, BICN, 252–5310.
Assistant Director of:
District Management and Assistance Program.—Mary Lapitino (919) 264–3618.
Employee Assistance Staff.—Ed Neunlist, Room 2400, BICN, 252–5455.
HR Operations Staff.—Valerie Mulcahy, Room 8430, BICN, 252–5357.
HR Policy Staff.—Vacant.
Pre-Employment Security.—Wayne Engram, Room 2400, BICN, 252–5719.
Security Programs Staff.—Tim George, Room 2600, BICN, 252–5694.

EXECUTIVE OFFICE FOR UNITED STATES TRUSTEES

441 G Street, NW., 20530, phone (202) 307–1391

http://www.usdoj.gov/ust

Director.—Clifford J. White III, Suite 6150.
Deputy Directors:
Field Operations.—William T. Neary (acting), Suite 6150.
General Counsel.—Ramona D. Elliott, Suite 6150, 307–1399.
Management.—Patricia Dugan Fahey (acting), Suite 6150.
Chief Information Officer.—Barbara A. Brown, 353–8754.
Assistant Director, Office of:
Administration.—Carrie B. Weinfeld (acting), Suite 6150, 305–0550.
Oversight.—Doreen Solomon, Suite 6150, 305–0222.
Planning and Evaluation.—Christopher Haverstock (acting), Suite 6150, 305–7827.

U.S. TRUSTEES

Region I:
Suite 1000, 5 Post Office Square, Boston, MA 02109 (617) 788–0400.
Suite 300, 537 Congress Street, Portland, ME 04101 (207) 780–3564.
14th Floor, Sovereign Tower Building, 446 Main, Worcester, MA 01608 (508) 793–0555.
Suite 605, 1000 Elm Street, Manchester, NH 03101 (603) 666–7908.
Suite 431, One Exchange Terrace, Providence, RI 02903 (401) 528–5551.

Region II:
Suite 1006, U.S. Federal Building, 201 Varick Street, New York, NY 10014 (212) 510–0500.
Suite 200, 74 Chapel Street, Albany, NY 12207 (518) 434–4553.
Suite 401, 300 Pearl Street, Buffalo, NY 14202 (716) 551–5541.
Suite 560, Long Island Federal Courthouse, 560 Federal Plaza, Central Islip, NY 11722–4456 (631) 715–7800.
Suite 302, 150 Court Street, New Haven, CT 06510 (203) 773–2210.
Room 609, 100 State Street, Rochester, NY 14614 (585) 263–5812.
Room 105, 10 Broad Street, Utica, NY 13501 (315) 793–8191.

Region III:
Suite 500, 833 Chestnut Street, Philadelphia, PA 19107 (215) 597–4411.
Suite 2100, One Newark Center, Newark, NJ 07102 (973) 645–3014.
Suite 970, 1001 Liberty Avenue, Pittsburgh, PA 15222 (412) 644–4756.
Suite 1190, 228 Walnut Street, Harrisburg, PA 17101 or P.O. Box 969, Harrisburg, PA 17108 (717) 221–4515.
Suite 2207, 844 King Street, Wilmington, DE 19801 (302) 573–6491.

Region IV:
Suite 953, 1835 Assembly Street, Columbia, SC 29201 (803) 765–5250.
Room 210, 115 South Union Street, Alexandria, VA 22314 (703) 557–7176.
Room 625, 200 Granby Street, Norfolk, VA 23510 (757) 441–6012.
Room 2025, 300 Virginia Street East, Charleston, WV 25301 (304) 347–3400.
First Campbell Square Building, 210 First Street, SW., Suite 505, Roanoke, VA 24011 (540) 857–2806.
Suite 4304, U.S. Courthouse, 701 East Broad Street, Richmond, VA 23219 (804) 771–2310.
Suite 600, 6305 Ivy Lane, Greenbelt, MD 20770 (301) 344–6216.
Suite 2625, 101 West Lombard Street, Baltimore, MD 21201 (410) 962–4300.

Region V:
Suite 2110, 400 Poydras Street, New Orleans, LA 70130 (504) 589–4018.
Suite 3196, 300 Fannin Street, Shreveport, LA 71101-3099 (318) 676–3456.
Suite 6–430, 501 East Court Street, Jackson, MS 39201 (601) 965–5241.

Region VI:
Room 976, 1100 Commerce Street, Dallas, TX 75242 (214) 767–8967.
Room 300, 110 North College Avenue, Tyler, TX 75702 (903) 590–1450.

Region VII:
Suite 3516, 515 Rusk Street, Houston, TX 77002 (713) 718–4650.
Room 230, 903 San Jacinto, Austin, TX 78701 (512) 916–5328.
Suite 533, 615 East Houston Street, San Antonio, TX 78205 (210) 472–4640.
Suite 1107, 606 North Carancahua Street, Corpus Christi, TX 78401 (361) 888–3261.

Region VIII:

Suite 400, 200 Jefferson Avenue, Memphis, TN 38103 (901) 544–3251.
Suite 512, 601 West Broadway, Louisville, KY 40202 (502) 582–6000.
Fourth Floor, 31 East 11th Street, Chattanooga, TN 37402 (423) 752–5153.
Suite 318, 701 Broadway, Nashville, TN 37203 (615) 736–2254.
Suite 500, 100 East Vine Street, Lexington, KY 40507 (859) 233–2822.

Region IX:
Suite 441, BP Building, 201 Superior Avenue East, Cleveland, OH 44114 (216) 522–7800.
Suite 200, Schaff Building, 170 North High Street, Columbus, OH 43215–2403 (614) 469–7411.
Suite 2030, 36 East Seventh Street, Cincinnati, OH 45202 (513) 684–6988.
Suite 700, 211 West Fort Street, Detroit, MI 48226 (313) 226–7999.
Suite 200R, 125 Ottawa Street, Grand Rapids, MI 49503 (616) 456–2002.

Region X:
Room 1000, 101 West Ohio Street, Indianapolis, IN 46204 (317) 226–6101.
Suite 1100, 401 Main Street, Peoria, IL 61602 (309) 671–7854.
Suite 555, 100 East Wayne Street, South Bend, IN 46601 (574) 236–8105.

Region XI:
Suite 873, 219 South Dearborn Street, Chicago, IL 60604 (312) 886–5785.
Suite 430, 517 East Wisconsin Avenue, Milwaukee, WI 53202 (414) 297–4499.
Suite 304, 780 Regent Street, Madison, WI 53715 (608) 264–5522.

Region XII:
Suite 2800, 111 Seventh Avenue, SE., Cedar Rapids, IA 52401 (319) 364–2211.
Suite 1015, U.S. Courthouse, 300 S. Fourth Street, Minneapolis, MN 55415 (612) 334–1350.
Room 793, 210 Walnut Street, Des Moines, IA 50309–2108 (515) 284–4982.
Suite 303, 314 South Main Avenue, Sioux Falls, SD 57104 (605) 330–4450.

Region XIII:
Suite 3440, 400 East 9th Street, Kansas City, MO 64106–1910 (816) 512–1940.
Suite 6353, 111 South 10th Street, St. Louis, MO 63102 (314) 539–2976.
Suite 1200, 200 West Capitol Avenue, Little Rock, AR 72201–3344 (501) 324–7357.
Suite 1148, 111 South 18th Plaza, Omaha, NE 68102 (402) 221–4300.

Region XIV:
Suite 204, 230 North First Avenue, Phoenix, AZ 85003 (602) 682–2600.

Region XV:
Suite 3230, 800 Front Street Third Floor, San Diego, CA 92101–8511 (619) 557–5013.
Suite 602, 1132 Bishop Street, Honolulu, HI 96813–2836 (808) 522–8150.

Region XVI:
Suite 1850, 915 Wilshire Boulevard, Los Angeles, CA 90017 (213) 894–6811.
Suite 7160, 411 West Fourth Street, Santa Ana, CA 92701–8000 (714) 338–3400.
Suite 720, 3801 University Avenue, Riverside, CA 92501 (951) 276–6990.

Region XVII:
Suite #05–0153, 450 Golden Gate Avenue, 5th Floor, San Francisco, CA 94102 (415) 705–3300.
Suite 7–500, U.S. Courthouse, 501 I Street, Sacramento, CA 95814–2322 (916) 930–2100.
Suite 1401, 2500 Tulare Street, Fresno, CA 93721 (559) 487–5002.
Oakland Office—Suite #05–0153, 450 Golden Gate Avenue, 5th Floor, San Francisco, CA 94102 (415) 252–2080.
Room 4300, 300 Las Vegas Boulevard South, Las Vegas, NV 89101 (702) 388–6600.
Suite 3009, 300 Booth Street, Reno, NV 89509 (775) 784–5335.
Room 268, 280 South First Street, San Jose, CA 95113 (408) 535–5525.

Region XVIII:
Suite 5103, 700 Stewart Street, Seattle, WA 98101 (206) 553–2000.
Suite 213, 620 Southwest Main Street, Portland, OR 97205 (503) 326–4000.
Suite 220, 720 Park Boulevard, Boise, ID 83712 (208) 334–1300.
Room 593, 920 West Riverside, Spokane, WA 99201 (509) 353–2999.
Suite 204, 301 Central Avenue, Great Falls, MT 59401 (406) 761–8777.
Anchorage Office—Suite 5103, 700 Stewart Street, Seattle, WA 98101 (206) 553–2000.
Suite 1100, 405 East Eighth Avenue, Eugene, OR 97401 (541) 465–6330.

Region XIX:
Suite 12–200, Byron G. Rogers Federal Building, 1961 Stout Street, Denver, CO 80294 (303) 312–7230.
Suite 203, 308 West 21st Street, Cheyenne, WY 82001 (307) 772–2790.
Suite 300, 405 South Main Street, Salt Lake City, UT 84111 (801) 524–5734.

Region XX:

Suite 1150, Epic Center, 301 North Main Street, Wichita, KS 67202 (316) 269–6637.
Suite 112, 421 Gold Street, SW., Albuquerque, NM 87102 (505) 248–6544.
Suite 408, 215 Northwest Dean A. McGee Avenue, Oklahoma City, OK 73102 (405) 231–5950.
Suite 225, 224 South Boulder Avenue, Tulsa, OK 74103 (918) 581–6670.

Region XXI:

Suite 362, 75 Ted Turner Drive, SW., Atlanta, GA 30303 (404) 331–4437.
Suite 301, Edificio Ochoa, 500 Tanca Street, San Juan, PR 00901 (787) 729–7444.
Suite 1204, 51 Southwest First Avenue, Miami, FL 33130 (305) 536–7285.
Suite 725, Johnson Square Business Center, 2 East Bryan Street, Savannah, GA 31401 (912) 652–4112.
Suite 1200, 501 East Polk Street, Tampa, FL 33602 (813) 228–2000.
Suite 302, 440 Martin Luther King Boulevard, Macon, GA 31201 (478) 752–3544.
Suite 128, 110 East Park Avenue, Tallahassee, FL 32301 (850) 942–1660.
Suite 1101, George C. Young Federal Building and Courthouse, 400 West Washington Street, Orlando, FL 32801 (407) 648–6301.

FEDERAL BUREAU OF INVESTIGATION

J. Edgar Hoover Building, 935 Pennsylvania Avenue, NW., 20535–0001

phone (202) 324–3000, http://www.fbi.gov

Director.—Christopher A. Wray, 324–6500.
Deputy Director.—Andrew McCabe, 324–3316.
Associate Deputy Director.—David Bowdich, 324–0308.
Chief of Staff.—James Rybicki, 324–5212.

OFFICE OF THE DIRECTOR / DEPUTY DIRECTOR / ASSOCIATE DEPUTY DIRECTOR

Office of the General Counsel.—James A. Baker, 324–6810.
Office of Congressional Affairs.—Gregory A. Brower, 324–5051.
Office of Equal Employment Opportunity Affairs.—Arlene Gaylor, 324–4128.
Office of the Ombudsman.—Monique Bookstein, 324–2156.
Office of Partner Engagement.—Kerry Sleeper, 324–7126.
Office of Professional Responsibility.—Candice M. Will (202) 436–7470.
Office of Public Affairs.—Michael Kortan, 324–5352.
Inspection Division.—Nancy McNamara, 324–2901.
Facilities and Logistics Services Division.—Richard Haley II, 324–1345.
Finance Division.—Richard Haley II, 324–1345.
Records Management Division.—Stephen P. Rees (540) 868–4400.

INFORMATION AND TECHNOLOGY BRANCH

Executive Assistant Director / Chief Information Officer.—James L. Turgal, Jr., 324–6165.
Associate EAD and Deputy Chief Information Officer.—Vacant.
Assistant Director of:
Information Technology and Customer Relationship Division.—Jeremy M. Wiltz 324–7209.
IT Applications and Data Division.—Tracey A. North, 323–5180.
IT Infrastructure Division.—W.L. Scott Bean III, 324–4507.

CRIMINAL, CYBER, RESPONSE, AND SERVICES BRANCH

Executive Assistant Director.—Paul D. Abbate, 324–4180.
Assistant Director of:
Criminal Investigative Division.—Stephen E. Richardson, 324–4260.
Critical Incident Response Group.—Gregory D. Cox (703) 632–4100.
Cyber Division.—Scott S. Smith, 324–7770.
International Operations Division.—George Piro, 324–5904.
Office of Victim Assistance.—Kathryn M. Turman, 324–1339.

HUMAN RESOURCES BRANCH

Executive Assistant Director.—Valerie Parlave, 324–3000.
Assistant Director of:
Human Resources Division.—David W. Schlendorf, 324–3514.
Training and Development Division.—David T. Resch (703) 632–1100.
Security Division.—Gerald Roberts, 203–1700.

NATIONAL SECURITY BRANCH

Executive Assistant Director.—Carl Ghattas, 324–7045.
Assistant Director of:
Counterintelligence Division.—E.W. Priestap, 324–4614.
Counterterrorism Division.—Bradley ''Grant'' Mendenhall, 324–2770.
Weapons of Mass Destruction Directorate.—Robert Allen Jones, 324–4965.

SCIENCE AND TECHNOLOGY BRANCH

Executive Assistant Director.—Christopher M. Piehota, 324–0805.
Assistant Director of:
Criminal Justice Information Services Division.—Douglas E. Lindquist (304) 625–2700.
Laboratory Division.—Christopher Todd Doss (703) 632–7001.
Operational Technology Division.—Brian K. Brooks (703) 632–6100.

INTELLIGENCE BRANCH

Executive Assistant Director.—Joshua Skule, 324–7705.
Assistant Director of Directorate of Intelligence.—John S. Adams, 324–7605.

FIELD DIVISIONS

Albany: 200 McCarty Avenue, Albany, NY 12209 (518) 465–7551.
Albuquerque: 4200 Luecking Park Avenue, NE., Albuquerque, NM 87107 (505) 224–2000.
Anchorage: 101 East 6th Avenue, Anchorage, AK 99501 (907) 258–5322.
Atlanta: 2635 Century Center Parkway, NE., Suite 400, Atlanta, GA 30345 (404) 679–9000.
Baltimore: 2600 Lord Baltimore Avenue, Baltimore, MD 21244 (410) 265–8080.
Birmingham: 1000 18th Street North, Birmingham, AL 35203 (205) 326–6166.
Boston: 201 Maple Street, Chelsea, MA 02150 (617) 742–5533.
Buffalo: 68–94 South Elwood Avenue, Buffalo, NY 14202 (716) 856–7800.
Charlotte: 7915 Microsoft Way, Charlotte, NC 28273 (704) 377–9200.
Chicago: 2111 West Roosevelt Road, Chicago, IL 60608–1128 (312) 431–1333.
Cincinnati: 2012 Ronald Reagan Drive, Cincinnati, OH 45236 (513) 421–4310.
Cleveland: 1501 Lakeside Avenue, Cleveland, OH 44114 (216) 522–1400.
Columbia: 151 Westpark Boulevard, Columbia, SC 29210 (803) 551–4200.
Dallas: J. Gordon Shanklin Building, One Justice Way, Dallas, TX 75220 (972) 559–5000.
Denver: Federal Office Building, 8000 East 36th Avenue, Denver, CO 80238 (303) 629–7171.
Detroit: P.V. McNamara Federal Office Building, 477 Michigan Avenue, 26th Floor, Detroit, MI 48226 (313) 965–2323.
El Paso: 660 South Mesa Hills Drive, Suite 3000, El Paso, TX 79912 (915) 832–5000.
Honolulu: Kalanianaole Federal Office Building, 91 Enterprise Avenue, Honolulu, HI 96850 (808) 566–4300.
Houston: 1 Justice Park Drive, Houston, TX 77092 (713) 693–5000.
Indianapolis: Federal Office Building, 8825 Nelson B Klein Parkway, Indianapolis, IN 46250 (371) 639–3301.
Jackson: Federal Office Building, 1220 Echelon Parkway, Jackson, MS 39213 (601) 948–5000.
Jacksonville: 6061 Gate Parkway, Jacksonville, FL 32256 (904) 721–1211.
Kansas City: 1300 Summit, Kansas City, MO 64105 (816) 512–8200.
Knoxville: John J. Duncan Federal Office Building, 1501 Dowell Springs Boulevard, Knoxville, TN 37909 (423) 544–0751.
Las Vegas: John Lawrence Bailey Building, 1787 West Lake Mead Boulevard, Las Vegas, NV 89106–2135 (702) 385–1281.

Little Rock: 24 Shackleford West Boulevard, Little Rock, AR 72211 (501) 221–9100.
Los Angeles: Federal Office Building, 11000 Wilshire Boulevard, Suite 1700, Los Angeles, CA 90024 (310) 477–6565.
Louisville: 12401 Sycamore Station Place, Louisville, KY 40299 (502) 583–2941.
Memphis: Eagle Crest Building, 225 North Humphreys Boulevard, Suite 3000, Memphis, TN 38120 (901) 747–4300.
Miami: 2030 Southwest 145th Avenue, Miami, FL 33027 (305) 944–9101.
Milwaukee: 3600 South Lake Drive, Milwaukee, WI 53235 (414) 276–4684.
Minneapolis: 1501 Freeway Boulevard, Brooklyn Center, MN 55430 (612) 376–3200.
Mobile: 200 North Royal Street, Mobile, AL 36602 (334) 438–3674.
New Haven: 600 State Street, New Haven, CT 06511 (203) 777–6311.
New Orleans: 2901 Leon C. Simon Boulevard, New Orleans, LA 70126 (504) 816–3122.
New York: 26 Federal Plaza, 23rd Floor, New York, NY 10278 (212) 384–1000.
Newark: Claremont Tower Building, 11 Centre Street, Newark, NJ 07102 (973) 792–3000.
Norfolk: 509 Resource Road, Chesapeake Beach, VA 23320 (757) 455–0100.
Oklahoma City: 3301 West Memorial, Oklahoma City, OK 73134 (405) 290–7770.
Omaha: 4411 South 121st Court, Omaha, NE 68137 (402) 493–8688.
Philadelphia: William J. Green, Jr. Federal Office Building, 600 Arch Street, 9th Floor, Philadelphia, PA 19106 (215) 418–4000.
Phoenix: 21711 North 7th Street, Phoenix, AZ 85024 (602) 279–5511.
Pittsburgh: Martha Dixon Building, 3311 East Carson Street, Pittsburgh, PA 15203 (412) 432–4000.
Portland: 9109 Northeast Cascades Parkway, Portland, OR 97220 (503) 224–4181.
Richmond: 1970 East Parham Road, Richmond, VA 23228 (804) 261–1044.
Sacramento: 2001 Freedom Way, Roseville, CA 95678 (916) 481–9110.
Salt Lake City: 5425 West Amelia Earhart Drive, Salt Lake City, UT 84116 (801) 579–1400.
San Antonio: 5740 University Heights Boulevard, San Antonio, TX 78249 (210) 225–6741.
San Diego: Federal Office Building, 10385 Vista Sorrento Parkway, San Diego, CA 92121 (858) 565–1255.
San Francisco: 450 Golden Gate Avenue, 13th Floor, San Francisco, CA 64102 (415) 553–7400.
San Juan: U.S. Federal Office Building, 150 Carlos East Chardon Avenue, Room 526, Hato Rey, PR 00918 (787) 754–6000.
Seattle: 1110 3rd Avenue, Seattle, WA 98101 (206) 622–0460.
Springfield: 900 East Linton Avenue, Springfield, IL 62703 (217) 522–9675.
St. Louis: 2222 Market Street, St. Louis, MO 63103 (314) 241–5357.
Tampa: 5525 West Gray Street, Tampa, FL 33609 (813) 273–4566.
Washington, DC: 601 4th Street, NW., Washington, DC 20535 (202) 278–3400.

FEDERAL BUREAU OF PRISONS (BOP)

320 First Street, NW., 20534

General Information Number (202) 307–3198

Director.—Mark S. Inch, Room 654, HOLC, 307–3250.
Deputy Director.—Vacant, Room 654, HOLC, 307–3250.
Director, National Institute of Corrections.—Vacant, 2nd Floor, 500 First Street, 514–4202.
Assistant Director of:
Administration.—Bradley T. Gross, 9th Floor, 500 FRST, 307–3230.
Correctional Programs.—Frank Lara, Room 554, HOLC, 307–3226.
General Counsel.—Ken Hyde, Room 958C, HOLC, 307–3062.
Health Services.—Deborah G. Schult, Ph.D., Room 454, HOLC, 307–3055.
Human Resources Management.—L. Christina Griffith, Room 754, HOLC, 307–3082.
Federal Prison Industries.—Gary Simpson, 8th Floor, 400 FRST, 305–3501.
Information, Policy, and Public Affairs.—Judi Simon Garrett, Room 670, HOLC, 514–6537.
Program Review.—Steve Mora, Room 1054, HOLC, 307–1076.
Regional Director for—
Mid-Atlantic.—Angela Dunbar (301) 317–3101.
North Central.—Sara Revell (913) 551–1000.
Northeast.—Michael Carvajal (215) 521–7300.
South Central.—John F. Caraway (972) 730–8800.
Southeast.—Jeff Keller (678) 686–1200.
Western.—Mary Mitchell (209) 956–9700.
Telephone Directory Coordinator.—Marla Clayton, 307–3250.

FOREIGN CLAIMS SETTLEMENT COMMISSION

Bicentennial Building (BICN), 600 E Street, NW., Suite 6002, 20579

phone (202) 616–6975

Chair.—Vacant.
Commissioners: Sylvia M. Becker, Anuj C. Desai.
Chief Counsel.—Brian M. Simkin.
Chief Administrative Counsel.—Jeremy R. LaFrancois.

OFFICE OF INFORMATION POLICY

1425 New York Avenue, NW., Suite 11050

Washington, DC 20530, phone (202) 514–3642

Director.—Melanie Ann Pustay.
Chief of Staff.—Carmen L. Mallon.

OFFICE OF THE INSPECTOR GENERAL

RFK Main Justice Building, Room 4706, phone (202) 514–3435

950 Pennsylvania Avenue, NW., 20530

Inspector General.—Michael E. Horowith.
Deputy Inspector General.—Robert P. Storch.
Senior Counsel to the Inspector General: John S. Lavinsky, Rene R. Lee.
Counsel to the Inspector General: Yvonne Garcia, Adam Miles.
General Counsel.—William Blier (RFK), Suite 4726 (202) 616–0646.
Assistant Inspectors General:
Audit.—Jason R. Malmstrom (NYAV), Suite 13000, 616–1697.
Evaluations and Inspections.—Nina Pelletier (NYAV), Suite 6100, 616–4620.
Investigations.—Eric Johnson (NYAV), Suite 7100, 616–4760.
Management and Planning.—Gregory T. Peters (NYAV), Suite 7000, 616–4550.
Oversight and Review.—Dan C. Beckhard (NYAV), Suite 13000, 616–0645.

REGIONAL AUDIT OFFICES

Atlanta: Ferris B. Polk, Suite 1130, 75 Spring Street, Atlanta, GA 30303 (404) 331–5928.
Chicago: Carol S. Taraszka, Suite 3510, Citicorp Center, 500 West Madison Street, Chicago, IL 60661 (312) 353–1203.
Dallas: Fletcher Couglas, Suite 410, Box 21, 2505 State Highway 360, Grand Prairie, TX 75050 (214) 655–5000.
Denver: David M. Sheeren, Suite 1500, Chancery Building, 1120 Lincoln Street, Denver, CO 80203 (303) 864–2000.
Philadelphia: Thomas O. Puerzer, Suite 201, 701 Market Street, Philadelphia, PA 19106 (215) 580–2111.
San Francisco: David J. Gaschke, Suite 201, 1200 Bayhill Drive, San Bruno, CA 94066 (650) 876–9220.
Washington: John Manning, 1300 North 17th Street, Suite 3400, Arlington, VA 22209 (202) 616–4688.
Computer Security and Information Technology Audit Office: Reginald Allen, Room 5000 (202) 616–3801.
Financial Statement Audit Office: Mark L. Hayes, 1425 New York Avenue, NW., #13000, Washington, DC 20530 (202) 616–4660.

REGIONAL INVESTIGATIONS OFFICES

Atlanta: Eddie D. Davis, 60 Forsyth Street, SW., Room 8M45, Atlanta, GA 30303 (404) 562–1980.
Boston: Daniel Benedict, U.S. Courthouse, 1 Courthouse Way, Room 9200, Boston, MA 02210 (617) 748–3218.
Chicago: John F. Oleskowicz, P.O. Box 1802, Chicago, IL 60690 (312) 886–7050.
Denver: Sandra D. Barnes, Suite 1501, 1120 Lincoln Street, Denver, CO 80203 (303) 335–4201.

Dallas: Monte A. Cason, 2505 State Highway 360, Room 410, Grand Prairie, TX 75050 (817) 385–5200.

Detroit: Nicholas V. Candela, Suite 1402, 211 West Fort Street, Detroit, MI 48226 (313) 226–4005.

El Paso: Eric Benn, Suite 135, 4050 Rio Bravo, El Paso, TX 79902 (915) 577–0102.

Houston: Douglas B. Bruce, P.O. Box 53509, Houston, TX 77052 (713) 718–4888.

Los Angeles: James K. Cheng, Suite 655, 330 North Brand Street, Glendale, CA 91203 (818) 543–1172.

Miami: Robert Allen Bourbon, Suite 200, 510 Shotgun Road, Sunrise, FL 33326 (954) 370–8300.

New York: Ronald Gardella, One Battery Park Plaza, 29th Floor, New York, NY 10004 (212) 824–3650.

New Jersey: Kenneth R. Connaughton, Jr., 361 Scotch Road, West Trenton, NJ 08628 (609) 883–5423.

San Francisco: Michael Barranti, Suite 220, 1200 Bayhill Drive, San Bruno, CA 94066 (650) 876–9058.

Seattle: Wayne Hawney, Suite 104, 620 Kirkland Way, Kirkland, WA 98033 (253) 852–0194.

Tucson: James Greer, 405 West Congress, Room 3600, Tucson, AZ 85701 (520) 620–7389.

Washington: Michael P. Tompkins, 1425 New York Avenue, NW., Suite 7100, Washington, DC 20530 (202) 616–4760.

Fraud Detection Office.—Lewe F. Sessions, Room 7100 (202) 353–2975.

INTERPOL WASHINGTON (U.S. NATIONAL CENTRAL BUREAU)

phone (202) 616–9000

Director.—Wayne H. Salzgaber (acting), 532–4239.

Deputy Director.—Vacant, 532–4239.

General Counsel.—Kevin Smith, 616–4103.

Public and Congressional Affairs Officer.—LaTonya Turner, 616–8006.

JUSTICE MANAGEMENT DIVISION

RFK Main Justice Building, 950 Pennsylvania Avenue, NW., 20530

2CON—145 N Street, NE., 20530

LSB—Liberty Square Building, 450 5th Street, NW., 20530

Assistant Attorney General for Administration.—Lee J. Lofthus, Room 1111 (202) 514–3101.

Deputy Assistant Attorney General, Policy, Management and Planning.—Michael H. Allen, Room 1113, 514–3101.

Staff Directors:

Department Ethics Office.—Cindy Shaw (2CON), Room 8E310, 514–8196.

Facilities and Administrative Services Staff.—Scott Snell (2CON), Room 9E.204, 616–2995.

General Counsel Office.—Arthur Gary, General Counsel (2CON), Room 8E528, 514–3452.

Internal Review and Evaluation Office.—Neil Ryder (2CON), Room 8W1419, 616–5499.

Senior Procurement Executive.—Michael H. Allen, Room 1113, 514–3101.

Office of Small and Disadvantaged Business Utilization.—Robert Connolly (2CON), Room 8E1009, 616–0521.

Procurement Services Staff.—Mark Selweski, Room 8E202, 307–2000.

Records Management Policy Office.—Jeanette Plante (2CON), Room 8W1401, 514–3528.

Deputy Assistant Attorney General/Controller.—Jolene Lauria, Room 1117, 514–1843.

Staff Directors:

Asset Forfeiture Management.—Kenneth Arnold (2CON), Room 5W725, 616–8000.

Budget Staff.—Robin Funston, Room 7601, 514–4082.

Debt Collection Management.—Dennis Dauphin (2CON), Room 5E103, 514–5343.

Finance.—Chris Alvarez (2CON), Room 7E202, 616–5800.

Deputy Assistant Attorney General, Human Resources and Administration.—Mari Santangelo, Room 1112, 514–5501.

Staff Directors:

Attorney Recruitment and Management Office.—Jamilia Frone, Suite 10200, 450 5th Street, NW. (Liberty Square), 514–3905.

Consolidated Executive Office.—Cyntoria Carter, Room 7113, 514–5537.
DOJ Executive Secretariat.—Dana Paige, Room 4412, 514–2063.
Equal Employment Opportunity.—Richard Toscano (2CON), Room 1W102, 616–4800.
Library.—Dennis Feldt, Room 7535, 514–2133.
Human Resources Staff.—Mary Lamary (2CON), Room 9W102, 514–6788.
Security and Emergency Planning Staff.—James Dunlap, Room 6217, 514–2094.
Deputy Assistant Attorney General, Information Resources Management/CIO.—Joseph Klimavicz, Room 1310–A, 514–0507.
Staff Directors:
Cyber Security and Service Staff.—Melinda Rogers (2CON), Room 4E1407, 353–2421.
Services Engineering Staff (SES).—Melinda Rogers (acting), (RDC), Room 203, 307–6944.
Policy and Planning.—John Raymond, (2CON), Room 4E202, 616–2420.
Service Delivery Staff.—Daniel McCrea (2CON), Room 3W701, 305–9635.

OFFICE OF JUSTICE PROGRAMS (OJP)

810 7th Street, NW., 20531

OFFICE OF THE ASSISTANT ATTORNEY GENERAL

Assistant Attorney General.—Vacant (202) 307–5933.
Principal Deputy Assistant General.—Alan R. Hanson, 307–5933.
Deputy Assistant Attorney General.—Maureen Henneberg, 307–5933.
Manager, Equal Employment Opportunity.—Laura Colón-Marrero (202) 616–1998.

BUREAU OF JUSTICE ASSISTANCE

Director.—Denise E. O'Donnell, 616–6500.
Deputy Director of:
Planning.—Eileen Garry, 616–6500.
Policy.—Kristen Mahoney, 616–6500.
Programs.—Tracey Trautman, 616–6500.

BUREAU OF JUSTICE STATISTICS

Director.—Jeri M. Mulrow (acting), (202) 307–0765.
Principal Deputy Director, Statistical Operations.—Vacant, 307–0765.
Deputy Director of:
Statistical Collections Division.—Vacant, 307–0765.
Statistical Programs Division.—Howard Snyder, 307–0765.
Planning, Policy, and Operations Division.—Gerard Ramker, 307–0765.

NATIONAL INSTITUTE OF JUSTICE

Director.—Howard Spivak (acting), 307–2942.
Deputy Directors: Jennifer Scherer, 307–2942; Howard Spivak, 307–2942.
Investigative and Forensic Sciences.—Gerald LaPorte, 307–2942.
Research and Evaluation.—Seri Irazola, 307–2942.
Science and Technology.—George Tillery, 307–2942.

OFFICE OF JUVENILE JUSTICE AND DELINQUENCY PREVENTION

Administrator.—Eileen Garry (acting), 307–6226.
Deputy Administrator.—Chyrl Y. Jones, 353–0798.
Deputy Administrator.—Vacant.

OFFICE FOR VICTIMS OF CRIME

Director.—Darlene L. Hutchinson, 307–5983.
Deputy Directors: Marilyn Robert, 307–5983; Allison Turkel, 307–5983; Susan Williams (acting), 307–5983.

OFFICE OF ADMINISTRATION

Director.—Phillip K. Merkle, 307–0087.
Deputy Director, Division of:
Acquisition Management.—Phillip K. Merkle (acting), 307–0087.
Human Resources.—Jennifer McCarthy, 307–0730.
Business Resources.—Angela Noel Gantt, 305–8006.

OFFICE OF THE CHIEF FINANCIAL OFFICER

Chief Financial Officer.—Leigh Benda, 307–0623.
Deputy Chief Financial Officer.—Mikki Atsatt, 307–0623.

OFFICE OF THE CHIEF INFORMATION OFFICER

Chief Information Officer.—Brian McGrath, 305–9071.
Chief Technology Officer.—Ira Baron, 305–9071.

OFFICE FOR CIVIL RIGHTS

Director.—Michael Alston, 307–0690.

OFFICE OF COMMUNICATIONS

Director.—Silas V. Darden III, 307–0703.
Deputy Director.—Robert Davis, 307–0703.
Associate Director for Congressional and Intergovernmental Affairs.—Adam Spector, 307–0703.
Associate Director of Public Affairs.—Charles Wagner, 307–0703.
Senior Program Manager.—Sharon J. Williams, 307–0703.

OFFICE OF THE GENERAL COUNSEL

General Counsel.—Rafael A. Madan (202) 307–6235.
Deputy General Counsels: Rosemary Carradini (202) 616–3257; Carolyn Kennedy, 616–7056; Charles T. Moses III (202) 305–2536; Matthew Scodellaro, 305–8219.

OFFICE OF SEX OFFENDER SENTENCING, MONITORING, APPREHENDING, REGISTERING, AND TRACKING

Director.—Vacant.
Director/Deputy Director.—Dawn Doran (acting), 514–4689.

OFFICE OF LEGAL COUNSEL

RFK Main Justice Building, Room 5218, phone (202) 514–2051

Assistant Attorney General.—Steven A. Engel, Room 5218, 514–2051.
Principal Deputy Assistant Attorney General.—Curtis Gannon, Room 5218, 514–4132.
Deputy Assistant Attorneys General: Liam Hardy, Room 5235; Sarah Harris, Room 5229; Daniel Koffsky, Room 5238, 514–2030; Henry Whitaker, Room 5231 (202) 305–8521.
Special Counsels: Paul P. Colborn, Room 5240, 514–2048; Rosemary Hart, Room 5242, 514–2027.
Senior Counsel.—Jeffrey Singdahlsen, Room 5262, 514–4174.

OFFICE OF LEGAL POLICY

RFK Main Justice Building, Room 4234, phone (202) 514–4601

Assistant Attorney General.—Beth A. Williams, Room 4230, 514–0624.
Principal Deputy Assistant Attorney General.—Mark Champoux, Room 4238, 514–6131.
Deputy Assistant Attorneys General: Michael Fragoso, Room 4511, 514–2456; Kevin Jones, Room 4248, 514–4604; Brett Talley, Room 4240, 305–4870; Robyn Thiemann, Room 4237, 514–8356.

Chief of Staff.—Katherine Crytzer, Room 4228, 353–3069.
Executive Officer.—Matrina Matthews, Room 4517, 616–0040.

OFFICE OF LEGISLATIVE AFFAIRS (OLA)

RFK Main Justice Building, Room 1145, phone (202) 514–2141

Assistant Attorney General.—Stephen E. Boyd.
Principal Deputy Assistant Attorney General.—Prim Escalona.
Deputy Assistant Attorneys General: David Lasseter, Jill C. Tyson.
Chief of Staff and Counsel.—Mary Blanche Hankey.

NATIONAL SECURITY DIVISION

RFK Main Justice Building, Room 7339, phone (202) 514–1057

Assistant Attorney General.—John C. Demers.
Principal Deputy Assistant Attorney General.—Vacant.
Deputy Assistant Attorneys General: Stuart Evans, Adam Hickey, George Toscas, Brad Wiegmann.
Chief of Staff.—Bradley Weinsheimer (acting).
Executive Officer.—Mark A. Jenkins.

COUNTERINTELLIGENCE AND EXPORT CONTROL SECTION

RFK Main Justice Building, 7th Floor, phone (202) 233–0986

Chief.—Vacant.
Principal Deputy Chief.—Jay Bratt.

COUNTERTERRORISM SECTION

RFK Main Justice Building, 7th Floor, phone (202) 514–0849

Chief.—Michael J. Mullaney.
Principal Deputy Chief.—Jennifer Smith.
International Terrorism Unit I.—Anthony Asuncion.
International Terrorism Unit II.—Matthew Blue.
International Terrorism Unit III.—Kelli Andrews.
International Terrorism Unit IV.—Clement McGovern.

FOREIGN INVESTMENT REVIEW STAFF

600 E Street, NW., Room 10000, phone (202) 622–1860

Chief.—Sanchitha Jayaram.

OFFICE OF INTELLIGENCE

RFK Main Justice Building, Room 6150, phone (202) 514–5600

Chief, Litigation.—John Scully.
Chief, Operations.—Gabrielle Sanz-Rexach.
Chief, Oversight.—Kevin O'Connor.

OFFICE OF JUSTICE FOR VICTIMS OF OVERSEAS TERRORISM

600 E Street, NW., Room 10102, phone (202) 233–0701

Director.—Heather Cartwright.

OFFICE OF THE PARDON ATTORNEY

2CON Building, 145 N Street, NE., 20530, phone (202) 616–6070

Pardon Attorney.—Vacant.

Deputy Pardon Attorney.—Larry Kupers.
Executive Officer.—William Taylor II.

OFFICE OF PROFESSIONAL RESPONSIBILITY

RFK Main Justice Building, Room 3266, phone (202) 514–3365

Counsel.—Robin C. Ashton.
Deputy Counsel.—G. Bradley Weinsheimer.
Senior Associate Counsel.—William J. Birney.
Associate Counsels: Raymond C. ''Neil'' Hurley, Margaret McCarty.
Senior Counsel.—Lyn Hardy.
Senior Assistant Counsels: Suzanne Drouet, Frederick Leiner, Mark Masling.
Assistant Counsels: Allison Barlotta, Sarah Cable, Paul Colby, Leonard Evans, Mark G. Fraase, John ''Jack'' Geise, Gregory Gonzalez, Albert Herring, John Sciortino, James Vargason, Barbara Ward.

PROFESSIONAL RESPONSIBILITY ADVISORY OFFICE

1425 New York Avenue, NW., 20530, phone (202) 514–0458

Director.—Stacy M. Ludwig.
Deputy Director.—Benjamin K. Grimes.

OFFICE OF PUBLIC AFFAIRS

RFK Main Justice Building, Room 1220, phone (202) 514–2007

Director.—Sarah Isgur Flores.
Deputy Directors: Wyn Hornbuckle, Ian Prior.

TAX DIVISION

RFK Main Justice Building, 950 Pennsylvania Avenue, NW., 20530

Judiciary Center Building, 555 Fourth Street, NW., 20001 (JCB)

Maxus Energy Tower, 7717 North Harwood Street, Suite 400, Dallas, TX 75242 (MAX)

Patrick Henry Building, 601 D Street, NW., 20004 (PHB)

Assistant Attorney General.—David A. Hubbert (acting/appellate and review), (Main), Room 4137 (202) 514–2901.
Deputy Assistant Attorneys General: Stuart M. Goldberg (acting) (Main), Room 4603, 514–2915 (Criminal Matters); Travis A. Greaves (Main), Room 4607, 514–5109 (Policy and Planning); David A. Hubbert (Main), Room 4137, 514–1958 (Civil Trial Matters).
Senior Legislative Counsel.—Eileen M. Shatz (Main), Room 4134, 307–6419.
Civil Trial Section Chiefs:
Central Region.—R. Scott Clarke (JCB), Room 8921–B, 514–6502.
Eastern Region.—Deborah S. Meland (JCB), Room 6126, 307–6426.
Northern Region.—D. Patrick Mullarkey (JCB), Room 7804–A, 307–6533.
Southern Region.—Michael Kearns (JCB), Room 6243–A, 514–5905.
Southwestern Region.—Cynthia Messersmith (MAX), Suite 400 (214) 880–9721.
Western Region.—Richard R. Ward (JCB), Room 7907–B, 307–6413.
Criminal Enforcement Section Chiefs:
Northern Region.—Rosemary E. Paguni (PHB), Room 7802, 514–5150.
Southern Region.—Bruce Salad (PHB), Room 7640, 514–5145.
Western Region.—Larry J. Wszalek (PHB), Room 7034, 514–5762.
Section Chiefs:
Appellate.—Gilbert S. Rothenberg (Main), Room 4326, 514–3361.
Court of Federal Claims.—David I. Pincus (JCB), Room 8804–A, 307–6440.
Criminal Appeals and Tax Enforcement Policy.—S. Robert ''Bob'' Lyons (PHB), Room 7002 (202) 514–2839.
Office of Review.—Ann Carroll Reid (JCB), Room 6846–D, 514–6567.
Executive Officer.—Robert Bruffy (PHB), Room 10002 (202) 616–8412.

UNITED STATES MARSHALS SERVICE (USMS)

Washington, DC 20530–1000

Communications Center (202) 307–9100

Director.—David L. Harlow (acting), 307–9100.
Deputy Director.—Vacant, 307–9100.
Chief of Staff.—John Kilgallon (acting), 307–9100.
Chief of District Affairs.—James Cunfer, 307–9100.
Associate Director for Administration.—David Musel, 307–9100.
Associate Director for Operations.—William Snelson, 307–9100.
Chief, Office of Congressional and Public Affairs.—William Delaney (703) 740–1603.

OFFICE OF EQUAL EMPLOYMENT OPPORTUNITY

Equal Employment Opportunity Officer.—Marcus Williams.

OFFICE OF THE GENERAL COUNSEL

General Counsel.—Gerald M. Auerbach.
Deputy General Counsel.—Lisa Dickinson.

OFFICE OF PROFESSIONAL RESPONSIBILITY

Assistant Director.—Donald P. O'Hearn.
Deputy Assistant Director.—Stanley Griscavage.

JUDICIAL SECURITY DIVISION

Assistant Director.—John O. Bolen.
Deputy Assistant Directors: Charlotta Allen-Brown, Darrell White.

INVESTIGATIVE OPERATIONS DIVISION

Assistant Director.—Derrick Driscoll.
Deputy Assistant Directors: Scott Samuels, Jeff Tyler.

PRISONER OPERATIONS DIVISION

Assistant Director.—Nelson Hackmaster.
Deputy Assistant Director.—John ''Jack'' Sheehan.

JUSTICE PRISONER AND ALIEN TRANSPORTATION SYSTEM (JPATS)

1251 Northwest Briar Cliff Parkway, Suite 300, Kansas City, MO 64116

Assistant Director.—Shannon Brown.
Deputy Assistant Director.—Scott Flood.

ASSET FORFEITURE DIVISION

Assistant Director.—Timothy Virtue.
Deputy Assistant Director.—Pam Bass.

WITNESS SECURITY DIVISION

Assistant Director.—Marcus Walker (acting).
Deputy Assistant Director.—Michael Stout (acting).

TACTICAL OPERATIONS DIVISION

Assistant Director.—Roberto Robinson (acting).
Deputy Assistant Director.—Craig Babcock (acting).

FINANCIAL SERVICES DIVISION

Chief Financial Officer.—Holley O'Brien.
Deputy CFO.—Mary Ellen Kline.

HUMAN RESOURCES DIVISION

Assistant Director.—Katherine Mohan.
Deputy Assistant Director.—Beth Brown-Ghee.

INFORMATION TECHNOLOGY DIVISION

Assistant Director.—Karl Mathias.
Deputy Assistant Directors: Christine Finnelle (acting), Gwendolyn Miller.

MANAGEMENT SUPPORT DIVISION

Assistant Director.—Kate Hickman.
Deputy Assistant Director.—Jim Murphy.

TRAINING DIVISION

Federal Law Enforcement Training Center, Building 20, Glynco, GA 31524

Assistant Director.—David Anderson.
Deputy Assistant Director.—Stephanie Creasy.

U.S. PAROLE COMMISSION

90 K Street, NE., 3rd Floor, 20530, phone (202) 346–7000, fax (202) 357–1085

Chair.—J. Patricia Wilson Smoot.
Vice Chair.—Patricia K. Cushwa.
Commissioners: Patricia K. Cushwa, Charles T. Massarone, J. Patricia Wilson Smoot.
Chief of Staff.—James E. Bacchus.
Case Operations Administrator.—Stephen J. Husk.
Case Services Administrator.—Deirdre M. McDaniel.
General Counsel.—Helen H. Krapels.
Executive Officer.—Zelia M. Carter.
Staff Assistant to the Chair.—Jacquelyn E. Graham.

OFFICE ON VIOLENCE AGAINST WOMEN (OVW)

145 N Street, NE., Suites 10W.121, 20530

Director.—Nadine M. Neufville (acting), (202) 307–6026.
Principal Deputy Director.—Vacant.
Chief of Staff.—Allison Randal, 532–4548.
General Counsel.—Jennifer E. Kaplan, 514–0052
Deputy Director, Tribal Affairs.—Sherriann C. Moore, 514–8804.
Deputy Director, Grant Development and Management.—Nadine M. Neufville, 307–6026
Executive Officer.—Sybil N. Barksdale, 353–7378.
Chief Financial Officer.—Angela Wood, 353–3982.

DEPARTMENT OF THE INTERIOR

Interior Building, 1849 C Street, NW., 20240, phone (202) 208–3100, http://www.doi.gov

RYAN ZINKE, Secretary of the Interior; born in Bozeman, MT, 1961; education: B.S., University of Oregon; M.B.A., National University; M.S., University of San Diego; professional: served in the United States Navy as a Navy SEAL officer from 1985–2008; business executive; member of the Montana State Senate, 2009–12; elected as a Republican to serve as the At-Large Representative from Montana in the 114th and 115th Congress, where he was a member of the House Natural Resources and House Armed Services Committees until his resignation on March 1, 2017; nominated by President Donald Trump to become the 52nd Secretary of the Interior, and was confirmed by the U.S. Senate on March 1, 2017.

OFFICE OF THE SECRETARY

Secretary of the Interior.—Ryan Zinke, Room 6154.
Special Assistants to the Secretary: Caroline Boulton, Room 6154; Elinor Renner, Room 6154.
Chief of Staff.—Scott Hommel, Room 6152.
Deputy Chief of Staff for Policy.—Downey Magallanes, Room 6140.
Deputy Chief of Staff for Operations.—Mike Argo, Room 6126.
Counselor to the Secretary for Energy.—Vincent DeVito, Room 5149.
Senior Advisors to the Secretary: Rick May, Room 6142; Dave Mihalic, Room 6124.
Director for Scheduling and Advance.—Rusty Roddy, Room 6245.
Director of External and Intergovernmental Affairs.—Todd Wynn, Room 6211.
Senior Advisor for Alaska Affairs.—Steve Wackowski, Anchorage, AK.

EXECUTIVE SECRETARIAT

Director.—Juliette Lillie, Room 7314.

CONGRESSIONAL AND LEGISLATIVE AFFAIRS

Director.—John Tanner, Room 6258, 208–7693.
Deputy Director.—Micah Chambers, Room 6254.
Legislative Counsel.—Chris Salotti, Room 6259.

OFFICE OF COMMUNICATIONS

Director.—Laura Rigas.
Deputy Director.—Russell Newell.
Press Secretary.—Heather Swift.

OFFICE OF THE DEPUTY SECRETARY

Deputy Secretary.—David Bernhardt, Room 6114.
Associate Deputy Secretary.—Jim Cason, Room 6113.
Assistant Deputy Secretary.—Todd Willens, Room 6116.
Counselor to the Deputy Secretary.—Gary Lawkowski, Room 6118.
Executive Assistant to the Deputy Secretary.—Gareth Rees, Room 6117.

ASSISTANT SECRETARY FOR FISH AND WILDLIFE AND PARKS

Assistant Secretary.—Vacant, Room 7256 (202) 208–5347.

Principal Deputy Assistant Secretary.—Michael J. Bean, Room 7257, 208–4416.
Deputy Assistant Secretary.—Vacant.
Chief of Staff.—Israporn Pananon, Room 7246, 208–5914.

U.S. FISH AND WILDLIFE SERVICE

Director.—Vacant.
Principal Deputy Director.—Gregory Sheehan, Room 3358 (202) 208–4717.
Deputy Directors: Steve Guertin, Jim Kurth, 208–4545.
Associate Director.—Vacant.
Senior Advisor for Energy.—Bud Cribley, 208–4331.
Chief, Office of Law Enforcement.—Ed Grace (acting), 208–7361.
Assistant Director for External Affairs.—Barbara Wainman, 208–5256.
Chief of Staff.—Charisa Morris, 208–3843.
Chief, Division of:
Congressional and Legislative Affairs.—Marty Kodis (703) 358–2241.
Public Affairs.—Gavin Shire (703) 358–2649.
Assistant Director for—
Migratory Birds.—Jerome Ford, 208–1050.
Science Applications.—Benjamin Tuggle, 208–7168.
Budget, Planning, and Human Capital.—Denise Sheehan (703) 358–2400.
Business Management and Operations.—Paul Rauch (703) 358–1822.
Ecological Services.—Gary Frazer, 208–4646.
Fisheries and Habitat Conservation.—David Hoskins, 208–6394.
Information Resources and Technology Management.—Kenneth Taylor (703) 358–1729.
International Affairs.—Gloria Bell (acting), 208–4266.
Wildlife and Sport Fish Restoration.—Paul Rauch, 208–5078.
Chief, National Wildlife Refuge System.—Cynthia Martinez, 208–4889.
Regional Directors:
Region 1.—Robyn Thorson, Eastside Federal Complex, 911 Northeast 11th Avenue, Portland, OR 97232 (503) 231–6118, fax 872–2716.
Region 2.—Amy Leuders, 500 Gold Avenue, SW., Room 1306, Albuquerque, NM 87103 (505) 248–6282, fax (503) 872–2716.
Region 3.—Thomas Melius, Federal Building, Fort Snelling, Twin Cities, MN 55111 (612) 713–5301, fax 713–5284.
Region 4.—Mike Oetker, 1875 Century Boulevard, Atlanta, GA 30345 (404) 679–4000, fax 679–4006.
Region 5.—Wendi Weber, 300 Westgate Center Drive, Hadley, MA 01035 (413) 253–8300, fax 253–8308.
Region 6.—Noreen Walsh, 134 Union Boulevard, #400, Lakewood, CO 80228 (303) 236–7920, fax 236–8295.
Region 7.—Greg Siekaniec, 1011 East Tudor Road, Anchorage, AK 99503 (907) 786–3542, fax 786–3306.
Region 8.—Paul Souza, 2800 Cottage Way, #W2606, Sacramento, CA 95825 (916) 414–6464, fax 414–6484.

NATIONAL PARK SERVICE

Director.—Michael T. Reynolds (acting), Room 3110 (202) 208–4621.
Deputy Director, Operations.—Bob Vogel (acting), Room 3111, 208–3818.
Deputy Director, Management and Administration.—Lena McDowall, Room 2711, 513–7240.
Deputy Director, Congressional and External Relations.—Vacant.
Chief of Staff.—Lisa Mendelson (acting), Room 3116, 208–3818.
Associate Director for—
Business Services.—Teresa Austin, Room 2717, 513–7280.
Cultural Resources, Partnerships, and Science.—Joy Beasley (acting), Room 3118, 354–6991.
Information Resources.—Shane Compton, Room 2212, 354–1820.
Interpretation, Education, and Volunteers.—Tom Medema (acting), Room 3124, 354–6998.
Natural Resource Stewardship and Science.—Ray Sauvajot, Room 3122, 354–6992.
Park Planning, Facilities, and Lands.—Shawn Benge, Room 3132, 354–6996.
Visitor and Resource Protection.—Charles Cuvelier (acting), Room 3128, 354–6995.
Workforce and Inclusion.—Tony Nguyen, Room 2216, 354–1990.

Comptroller.—Jessica Bowron, Room 2721, 513–7280.
Assistant Director for—
Communications.—April Slayton, Room 3121, 208–6843.
Legislative and Congressional Affairs.—Melissa Kuckro (acting), Room 3125, 208–5656.
Partnerships and Civic Engagement.—Jeffrey Reinbold, Room 3138, 354–6997.
Regional Directors:
Alaska.—Bert Frost, 240 West Fifth Avenue, Room 114, Anchorage, AK 99501 (907) 644–3510, fax 644–3816.
Intermountain.—Sue Masica, 12795 West Alameda Parkway, P.O. Box 25287, Denver, CO 80225 (303) 969–2503, fax 969–2785.
Midwest.—Cam Sholly, 601 Riverfront Drive, Omaha, NE 68102 (402) 661–1520, fax 661–1737.
National Capital.—Rick Obernesser (acting), 1100 Ohio Drive, SW., Washington, DC 20242 (202) 619–7020, fax 619–7220.
Northeast.—Gay Vietzke, U.S. Custom House, 200 Chestnut Street, Suite 502, Philadelphia, PA 19106 (215) 597–3503, fax 597–0815.
Southeast.—Stan Austin, 100 Alabama Street, NW., 1924 Building, Atlanta, GA 30303 (404) 507–5604, fax 562–3216.
Pacific West.—Laura Joss, 333 Bush Street, Suite 500, San Francisco, CA 94104, (415) 623–2102, fax 623–2380.

ASSISTANT SECRETARY FOR INDIAN AFFAIRS

Assistant Secretary.—Michael Black (acting), Room 4158 (202) 208–7163.
Principal Deputy Assistant Secretary.—Vacant.
Deputy Assistant Secretary for—
Management.—James Burckman (acting), Room 4659, 219–0440.
Policy and Economic Development.—Vacant.
Chief of Staff.—Sarah Walters, Room 4154, 513–0784.
Director of:
Congressional Affairs.—Darren Pete, Room 4012, 208–6160.
Public Affairs.—Nedra Darling, Room 4140, 208–3710.

BUREAU OF INDIAN AFFAIRS

Director.—Weldon Loudermilk, Room 4606, 208–5116.
Deputy Director of:
Field Operations.—Hankie Ortiz (acting), Room 4606, 208–5116.
Justice Services.—Jason Thompson (acting), Room 2603, 208–5787.
Tribal Services.—Spike Bighorn (acting), Room 3644, 513–7640.
Trust Services.—Helen Riggs (acting), 208–5831.

BUREAU OF INDIAN EDUCATION

Director.—Tony Dearman, Room 3609, 208–6123.
Deputy Bureau Director:
School Operations.—Bart Stephens, Room 3615, 208–6123.
Chief of Staff.—Juanita Mendoza, 208–5504.
Special Assistant.—Jacquelyn Cheek, 208–6983.
Associate Deputy Director of:
BIE Operated Schools.—Jimmy Hastings (acting), (602) 265–1592.
Division of Performance and Accountability.—Jeffrey Hamley (202) 208–6666.
Navajo Schools.—Emily Arviso (acting), (928) 871–5961.
Tribally Controlled Schools.—Rose Marie Davis (acting), (952) 851–5424.

ASSISTANT SECRETARY FOR LAND AND MINERALS MANAGEMENT

Assistant Secretary.—Joseph Balash, Room 6614 (202) 208–6734.
Deputy Assistant Secretary.—Katharine MacGregor, Room 6614.

BUREAU OF LAND MANAGEMENT

Director.—Vacant, 1849 C Street, NW., Room 5665, Washington DC 20240 (202) 208–3801, fax 208–5242.

Deputy Director of:

Operations.—Mike Nedd (acting), 208–3801, fax 208–5242.

Programs and Policy.—Brian Steed, 208–3801, fax 208–5242.

Division Chief, Legislative Affairs.—Patrick Wilkerson (202) 912–7429, fax 245–0050.

Deputy Division Chief.—Jill Ralston, 912–7173, fax 245–0050.

State Directors:

Alaska.—Karen Mouritsen (acting), 222 West Seventh Avenue, No. 13, Anchorage, AK 99513 (907) 271–5080, fax 271–4596.

Arizona.—Raymond Suazo, One North Central Avenue, Suite 800, Phoenix, AZ 85004 (602) 417–9500, fax 417–9398.

California.—Jerome Perez, 2800 Cottage Way, Suite W1623, Sacramento, CA 95825 (916) 978–4600, fax 978–4699.

Colorado.—Gregory Shoop (acting), 2850 Youngfield Street, Lakewood, CO 80215 (303) 239–3700, fax 239–3933.

Eastern States.—Mitch Leverette (acting), 20th M Street, SE., Suite 950, Washington, DC 20003 (202) 912–7701, fax 912–7186.

Idaho.—Peter Ditton (acting), 1387 South Vinnell Way, Boise, ID 83709 (208) 373–4001, fax 373–4005.

Montana/Dakotas.—Jon Raby (acting), 5001 Southgate Drive, Billings, MT 59101 (406) 896–5000, fax 896–5298.

Nevada.—Mike Courtney (acting), 1340 Financial Boulevard, Reno, NV 89502 (775) 861–6400, fax 861–6606.

New Mexico.—Aden Seidlitz (acting), 301 Dinosaur Trail, Santa Fe, NM 87508 (505) 954–2222, fax 954–2010.

Oregon/Washington.—Jamie Connell, 1220 SW., 3rd Avenue, Portland, OR 97204 (503) 808–6026, fax 808–6390.

Utah.—Ed Roberson, 440 West 200 South, Suite 500, Salt Lake City, UT 84101 (801) 539–4010, fax 539–4013.

Wyoming.—Mary Jo Rudwell, 5353 Yellowstone Road, Cheyenne, WY 82009 (307) 775–6001, fax 775–6003.

BUREAU OF OCEAN ENERGY MANAGEMENT

Director.—Walter D. Cruickshank (acting), (202) 208–6300.

Deputy Director/Chief Financial Officer.—Walter D. Cruickshank, 208–6300.

Budget and Program Coordination.—James G. Anderson, 208–6264.

Congressional Affairs.—Lee Tilton, 208–3502.

Policy, Regulation and Analysis.—Deanna P. Meyer-Pietruszka, 208–6352.

Public Affairs.—Connie Gillette, 208–5387.

Environmental Programs.—William Y. Brown, 208–6249.

Outer Continental Shelf Regional Directors:

Alaska.—James J. Kendall, Jr., 3801 Centerpoint Drive, Anchorage, AK 99503 (907) 334–5200.

Gulf of Mexico.—John Celata, 1201 Elmwood Park Boulevard, New Orleans, LA 70123 (504) 736–2592.

Pacific.—Joan Barminski, 760 Paseo, Camarillo, CA 93010–6002 (805) 389–7502.

Renewable Energy.—James F. Bennett (703) 787–1300.

Strategic Resources Programs.—L. Renee Orr, 208–3515.

BUREAU OF SAFETY AND ENVIRONMENTAL ENFORCEMENT

Director.—Scott A. Angelle (202) 208–3500.

Deputy Director.—Margaret N. Schneider.

Chief of Administration.—Scott Mabry, 208–3220.

Budget.—Eric Modrow (703) 787–1694.

Offshore Regulatory Programs.—Doug Morris, 208–3974.

Policy and Analysis.—Molly Madden (202) 219–7271.

Congressional Affairs.—Julie Fleming, 208–3827.

Outer Continental Shelf Regional Directors:

Alaska.—Mark Fesmire, 3801 Centerpoint Drive, Suite 500, Anchorage, AK 99503 (907) 334–5300.

Gulf of Mexico.—Lars T. Herbst, 1201 Elmwood Park Boulevard, New Orleans, LA 70123 (504) 736–2589.

Pacific.—Mark Fesmire (acting), 770 Paseo Camarillo, Camarillo, CA 93010 (805) 389–7514.

OFFICE OF SURFACE MINING RECLAMATION AND ENFORCEMENT

Director.—Vacant, Room 4511 (202) 208–4006.
Deputy Director.—Glenda H. Owens, 208–4006.
Assistant Director for Finance and Administration.—Ted Woronka, 208–2546.
Congressional Contact.—Tristan Weis, 208–2838.
Regional Director for—
Appalachian Region.—Thomas D. Shope, Three Parkway Center, Pittsburgh, PA 15220 (412) 937–2828, fax 937–2903.
Mid-Continent Region.—Alfred Clayborne, 501 Belle Street, Room 216, Alton, IL 62002 (618) 463–6460, fax 463–6470.
Western Region.—David Berry, 1999 Broadway, Suite 3320, Denver, CO 80202 (303) 293–5001, fax 293–5006.

ASSISTANT SECRETARY FOR POLICY, MANAGEMENT, AND BUDGET

Assistant Secretary.—Scott J. Cameron (acting), Room 5113 (202) 208–1927.
Principal Deputy Assistant Secretary.—Scott J. Cameron, Room 5113, 208–1927.
Deputy Assistant Secretary for—
Budget, Finance, Performance, and Acquisition.—Olivia Ferriter, 208–4775.
Human Capital and Diversity.—Mary Pletcher, 208–1738.
Natural Resources Revenue Management.—Greg Gould (acting), (303) 231–3429.
Policy and International Affairs.—Steve Glomb (acting), 208–1927.
Public Safety, Resource Protection, and Emergency Services.—Harry Humbert, 208–5773.
Technology, Information, and Business Services.—Elena Gonzales, 208–7966.

ASSISTANT SECRETARY FOR WATER AND SCIENCE

Assistant Secretary.—Timothy R. Petty, Room 6654 (202) 208–0969.
Deputy Assistant Secretaries: Austin Ewell, Room 6650, 208–3186; Andrea Travnicek, Room 6657, 208–3136.
Chief of Staff.—Kerry Rae, Room 6651 (202) 513–0535.

U.S. GEOLOGICAL SURVEY

The National Center, 12201 Sunrise Valley Drive, Reston, VA 20192
phone (703) 648–7411, fax 648–4454

Director.—William H. Werkheiser (acting), 648–7411.
Deputy Director.—David Applegate (acting), 648–7412.
Chief of Staff.—Judy Nowakowski, 648–4411.
Office of:
Administration (Administrative Policy and Services/Budget and Performance).—Roseann Gonzales-Schreiner, 648–7200.
Communications and Outreach.—Betsy Hildebrandt, 648–5750.
Congressional Liaison Officer.—Timothy J. West, 648–4300.
Human Capital.—Roseann Gonzales-Schreiner, 648–7200.
Public Affairs Officer.—Anne-Berry Wade, 648–4483.
Associate Director for—
Climate and Land Use Change.—Douglas Beard (acting), 648–4212.
Core Science Systems.—Kevin Gallagher, 648–5747.
Ecosystems.—Anne Kinsinger, 648–4050.
Energy and Minerals, and Environmental Health.—Daniel Hayba (acting), 648–6403.
Natural Hazards.—William Leith (acting), 648–6600.
Water Resources.—Donald Cline, 648–4557.
Regional Director for—
Northeast Area.—Michael Tupper, 12201 Sunrise Valley Drive, Reston, VA 20192 (703) 648–6600.
Southeast Area.—Holly Weyers, 1770 Corporate Drive, Suite 500, Norcross, GA 30093 (678) 924–6614.
Midwest Area.—Leon Carl, 1451 Green Road, Anne Arbor, MI 48105 (734) 214–7201.
Southwest Area.—Max Ethridge, P.O. Box 25046, Denver Federal Center, Building 810, Denver, CO 80225 (303) 236–5438.
Northwest Area.—Rich Ferrero, Federal Office Building, 909 First Avenue, 8th Floor, Seattle, WA 98104 (206) 220–4600.

Pacific Area.—Mark Sogge, Modoc Hall, 3020 State University Drive East, Sacramento, CA 95819 (206) 795–4527.
Alaska.—Aimee Devaris, 4230 University Drive, Suite 201, Anchorage, AK 99508 (907) 786–7055.

BUREAU OF RECLAMATION

Commissioner.—Brenda Burman, Room 7657 (202) 513–0501.
Deputy Commissioner.—Alan Mikkelsen, Room 7653, 513–0501.
Deputy Commissioner for Operations.—David Palumbo, Room 7645, 513–0616.
Deputy Commissioner for Policy, Administration, and Budget.—Grayford Payne, Room 7650, 513–0509.
Chief of Staff.—James Hess, Room 7646.
Chief of:
Congressional and Legislative Affairs.—Vacant, Room 7643, 513–0570.
Public Affairs.—Daniel J. DuBray, Room 7644, 513–0574.
Regional Directors:
Great Plains.—Michael J. Ryan, P.O. Box 36900, Billings, MT 59107 (406) 247–7795, fax 247–7793.
Lower Colorado.—Terrance Fulp, P.O. Box 61470, Boulder City, NV 89006 (702) 293–8000, fax 293–8333.
Mid-Pacific.—David Murillo, 2800 Cottage Way, Sacramento, CA 95825 (916) 978–5000, fax 978–5005.
Pacific Northwest.—Lorri Gray, 1150 North Curtis Road, Suite 100, Boise, ID 83706 (208) 378–5012, fax 378–5019.
Upper Colorado.—Brent Rhees, 125 South State Street, Room 6107, Salt Lake City, UT 84138 (801) 524–3600, fax 524–3855.

OFFICE OF INSPECTOR GENERAL

Inspector General.—Vacant, Room 4411 (202) 208–5745.
Deputy Inspector General.—Mary Kendall, Room 4411, 208–5745.
Chief of Staff.—Stephen Hardgrove, Room 4410, 208–5745.
Associate Inspector General for Whistleblower Protection.—Jennifer French, Room 4456.
Associate Inspector General for External Affairs.—Nancy DiPaolo, Room 4416.

OFFICE OF THE SOLICITOR

Solicitor.—Vacant, Room 6352 (202) 208–4423.
Principal Deputy Solicitor.—Daniel H. Jorjani.
Deputy Solicitor for—
General Law.—Ed Keable.
Indian Affairs.—Vacant.
Land Resources.—Vacant.
Energy and Mineral Resources.—K. Jack Haugrud.
Parks and Wildlife.—Vacant.
Water Resources.—Vacant.
Associate Solicitor for—
General Law.—Kaprice Tucker.
Indian Affairs.—Eric Shepard.
Land and Water.—Laura Brown.
Mineral Resources.—Karen Hawbecker.
Parks and Wildlife.—Ann Navaro (acting).
Administration.—Marc Smith.
Designated Agency Ethics Official.—Melinda Loftin, 208–5295.

OFFICE OF THE SPECIAL TRUSTEE FOR AMERICAN INDIANS

Principal Deputy Special Trustee.—Jerold Gidner (202) 208–3946.

DEPARTMENT OF AGRICULTURE

Jamie L. Whitten Building, 1400 Independence Avenue, SW., 20250

phone (202) 720–3631, http://www.usda.gov

SONNY PERDUE, Secretary of Agriculture; education: D.V.M, University of Georgia; professional: State Senator, 1991–2001; Governor, Georgia, 2002–10; nominated by President Donald J. Trump to become the 31st Secretary of Agriculture, and was confirmed by the U.S. Senate on April 25, 2017.

OFFICE OF THE SECRETARY

Secretary of Agriculture.—Sonny Perdue, Room 200–A (202) 720–3631.
Deputy Secretary.—Stephen Censky.
Chief of Staff.—Heidi Green.
Deputy Chief of Staff.—Vacant.

OFFICE OF THE ASSISTANT SECRETARY FOR ADMINISTRATION

Jamie L. Whitten Building, Room 240–W, phone (202) 720–3291

Assistant Secretary.—Vacant, 720–3291.
Deputy Assistant Secretary.—Malcom A. Shorter, 720–3291.
Chief of Staff.—Dr. Johanna Briscoe (acting), (202) 260–8260.
Administrative Specialist.—Vandetta Mack (202) 720–3291.
Program Assistant.—Marcia Waldstreicher (202) 690–3899.

OFFICE OF ADMINISTRATIVE LAW JUDGES

South Agriculture Building, Room 1049–S, phone (202) 720–6383

Chief Administrative Law Judge.—Bobbie J. McCartney.
Executive Assistant to the Chief Administrative Law Judge.—Marilyn Kennedy (acting).
Administrative Law Judges: Jill S. Clifton, Channing D. Strother, 720–8423.
Hearing Clerk.—Renee Leach-Carlos, 720–4443.

OFFICE OF HUMAN RESOURCES MANAGEMENT

Jamie L. Whitten Building, Room 318–W, phone (202) 720–3585

Chief Human Capital Officer.—Marsha A. Wiggins (acting).
Executive Assistant.—Sharntay Harry.
Deputy Director.—Patricia Moore (acting).
Chief of Staff.—Lynne Short, 690–3973.
Management Analyst.—Darcelle Walker, 692–0263.
Directors:
Employee and Labor Relations Division.—Bryan Knowles, 720–6784.
HR Enterprise Systems Management Division.—Marquette Defillo, 302–6137.
HR Policy Division.—John Decato (acting), 720–6706.
Recruitment, Diversity, and Work/Life Division.—Dr. Karlease Kelly (acting), 720–0185.
Strategic HR, Planning and Accountability Division.—Allen Hatcher, 720–0941.
Virtual University.—Dr. Karlease Kelly, Provost, 720–0185.
Executive Resources Management Division.—Patricia Moore, 720–8629.

OFFICE OF THE JUDICIAL OFFICER

South Agriculture Building, Room 1633–S, phone (202) 720–4764

Judicial Officer.—William G. Jenson.

Attorney.—Kathleen Bright.
Legal Technician.—Sherida Hardy.

OFFICE OF OPERATIONS

South Agriculture Building, Room 1456–S, phone (202) 720–3937

Director of Operations.—Duane Williams.
Deputy Director of Operations.—James Brent.
Director, Office of:
Executive Services.—Camelnita Fossum, 720–3199.
Facilities Management.—Thomas Hoffman, 720–8290.
Mail and Reproduction Management.—Dennis Banks (acting), 720–8393.
Materiel Management Service Center.—Roselyn Roebuck (acting), (301) 394–0415.
Program, Policy and Support Staff.—Carlos Casaus, 720–4134.
Protective Operations.—Gilbert Stokes, 720–6270.
Safety, Sustainability and Emergency Operations.—Edward Hogberg, 205–8923.

OFFICE OF PROCUREMENT AND PROPERTY MANAGEMENT

Whitten Building, Room 335W, phone (202) 720–9448

Director.—Richard Jiron (acting), (970) 295–5487.
Division Director for—
Procurement Operations.—Richard Jiron (970) 295–5487.
Procurement Policy.—Crandall Watson, 720–7529.
Procurement Systems.—Loretta Smith-Hawkins, 401–1023.
Property Management.—Paul Walden, 720–7283.
Safety and Health Management.—Theresa Ferguson, 690–0653.

OFFICE OF HOMELAND SECURITY

Director.—Todd Repass, Room 1457 (202) 720–2582.
Division Chief for—
Continuity and Planning.—John Aucott, 205–3587.
Personnel and Document Security.—Brodrick Wilcox, 720–7373.
Physical Security.—Richard Holman, 720–3901.
Director, Office of:
Emergency Programs.—Todd Barrett, 690–3191.
Protective Operations.—Chad Carroll, 720–6270.

OFFICE OF SMALL AND DISADVANTAGED BUSINESS UTILIZATION

South Agriculture Building, Room 1085–S, phone (202) 720–7117

Director.—Vacant.

ASSISTANT SECRETARY FOR CIVIL RIGHTS

Jamie L. Whitten Building, Room 507–A, phone (202) 720–3808

Assistant Secretary.—Vacant.
Deputy Assistant Secretary.—Vacant.

OFFICE OF BUDGET AND PROGRAM ANALYSIS

Jamie L. Whitten Building, Room 101–A, phone (202) 720–3323

Director.—Diem-Linh Jones (acting).
Associate Director.—Christopher Zehren (acting), 720–5303.
Deputy Director for—
Budget, Legislative and Regulatory Systems.—Diem-Linh Jones, Room 102–E, 720–6667.
Program Analysis.—Christopher Zehren, Room 126–W, 720–3396.

OFFICE OF THE CHIEF ECONOMIST

Jamie L. Whitten Building, Room 112A, phone (202) 720–4164

Chief Economist.—Robert Johansson, Room 112A, 720–4164.
Deputy Chief Economist.—Warren Preston, Room 112A, 720–5955.
Chair, World Agricultural Outlook Board.—Seth Meyer, Room 4419–S, 720–6030.
Chief Meteorologist.—Vacant, Room 4441–S, 720–8651.
Supervisory Meteorologist, National Weather Service.—Mark Brusberg, Room 4443–S, 720–6030.
Director, Climate Change Program Office.—William Hohenstein, Room 4407–S, 720–6698.
Director, Office of Environmental Markets.—William Hohenstein, Room 4407–S, 720–6698.
Director, Office of Energy Policy and New Uses.—Harry Baumes, Room 4059–S, 401–0461.
Director, Risk Assessment and Cost Benefit Analysis.—Linda C. Abbott, Room 4032–S, 720–8022.
Director, Sustainable Development.—Elise Golan, Room 112A, 720–2456.

OFFICE OF THE CHIEF FINANCIAL OFFICER

Jamie L. Whitten Building, Room 143–W, phone (202) 720–5539

Chief Financial Officer.—Lynn Moaney (acting), 720–5539.
Deputy Chief Financial Officer.—Vacant.
Associate Chief Financial Officers for—
Financial Operations.—Stanley McMichael, Room 3414–S, 720–0564.
Financial Policy and Planning.—Lynn Moaney, Room 3054–S, 720–0065.
Shared Services.—Michael Clanton, Room 3057–S, 690–3068.
Director, National Finance Center.—Calvin Turner, P.O. Box 60000, New Orleans, LA 70160 (504) 426–0120.

OFFICE OF THE CHIEF INFORMATION OFFICER

Jamie L. Whitten Building, Room 420–W, phone (202) 720–8833

Chief Information Officer.—Jonathan Alboum.
Deputy Chief Information Officers for—
Operations.—Douglas Nash, 260–8551 or 720–8833.
Associate Chief Information Officers for—
Agriculture Security Operations Center (ASOC).—Christopher Lowe, 720–8281.
Data Center Operations (National Information Technology Center).—Victoria Turley (acting), (816) 823–1468.
Enterprise Network Services.—John Donovan (202) 205–4394.
Resource Management.—Lisa Keeter, 720–4109.
Director, Distance Learning Program.—Jerome Davin (970) 291–1564.

OFFICE OF COMMUNICATIONS

Jamie L. Whitten Building, Room 412–A, phone (202) 720–4623

Director.—Tim Murtaugh.
Deputy Director.—Michawn Rich.
Deputy Director for—
Creative Development.—Brian Mabry.
Press Operations.—David Blair.
Press Secretary.—Meghan Rodgers.
Director, Center for—
Brand Review.—Carolyn O'Connor.
Broadcast Media and Technology.—Garth Clark.
Constituent Affairs: Kathryn Hill, Mocile Trotter.
Information Technology.—Wayne Moore.
Web Communication.—Peter Rhee.

OFFICE OF CONGRESSIONAL RELATIONS

Jamie L. Whitten Building, Room 212–A, phone (202) 720–7095

Assistant Secretary.—Kenneth Steven Barbic.

Chief of Staff.—Joby Young.
Director of Congressional Relations.—Abbey Fretz.
Congressional Liaisons:
TFAA.—Peter Bachmann.
FPAC.—Peter Bachmann.
FNCS.—Kailee Tkacz.
Food Safety.—Misty Giles.
MRP.—Misty Giles.
NRE.—Robyn Whitney.
REE.—Brock Densel.
RD.—Brock Densel.

EXTERNAL AND INTERGOVERNMENTAL AFFAIRS

Jamie L. Whitten Building, Room 211–A, phone (202) 720–6643

Director.—Blake Rollins.
Deputy Director.—Henry Turner Bridgforth.

OFFICE OF TRIBAL RELATIONS

Room 501–A, phone (202) 205–2249

Director.—Linda Cronin (acting).

OFFICE OF THE EXECUTIVE SECRETARIAT

Jamie L. Whitten Building, Room 116–A, phone (202) 720–7100

Director.—Jean Daniel.
Branch Chiefs: Loureatha Gibson, Adrian Lindsey.

OFFICE OF THE GENERAL COUNSEL

Jamie L. Whitten Building, Room 107–W, phone (202) 720–3351

General Counsel.—Stephen Alexander Vaden (acting).
Principal Deputy General Counsel.—Stephen Alexander Vaden.
Deputy General Counsel.—Inga Bumbary-Langston.
Associate General Counsel for—
Civil Rights, Labor, and Employment Law.—Arlean Leland, 720–1760.
International Affairs, Food Assistance, and Farm and Rural Programs.—David P. Grahn, 720–8063.
General Law and Research.—Benjamin Young, 720–4814.
Marketing, Regulatory, and Food Safety Programs.—Carrie Ricci, 720–3155.
Natural Resources and Environment.—Ralph Linden, 720–6883.
Assistant General Counsel, Division of:
Civil Rights Litigation.—Steven Brammer, 720–4375.
Civil Rights Policy, Compliance, and Counsel.—Tami Trost, 690–3993.
General Law and Research.—Shawn McGruder, 720–5565.
International Affairs, Food Assistance, and Farm and Rural Programs: Peter Bonner, 720–3569; Janet Safian, 720–2923.
Marketing, Regulatory, and Food Safety: Mai Dinh, 720–5935; Sheila Novak, 720–2670.
Natural Resources and Environment.—Ronald Mulach, 720–2063.
Director, Administration and Resource Management.—Charlene Buckner, 720–6324.
Resource Management Specialist.—Robyn Davis, 720–4861.

OFFICE OF INSPECTOR GENERAL

Jamie L. Whitten Building, Room 117–W, phone (202) 720–8001, fax 690–1278

Inspector General.—Phyllis K. Fong.
Deputy Inspector General.—David Gray.
Assistant Inspector General for—
Audit.—Gil Harden, Room 403–E, 720–6945.

Offfice of Investigations.—Ann Coffey (acting), Room 146–W, 720–3965.
Office of Management.—Lane Timm, Room 5–E, 720–6979.

NATIONAL APPEALS DIVISION

3101 Park Center Drive, Suite 1100, Alexandria, VA 22302

Director.—Steven C. Silverman (703) 305–2708.

UNDER SECRETARY FOR NATURAL RESOURCES AND ENVIRONMENT

Jamie L. Whitten Building, Room 240–E, phone (202) 720–7173

Under Secretary.—Vacant.
Deputy Under Secretaries: Dan Jiron (acting); Vacant.

FOREST SERVICE

Sydney R. Yates Building, 201 14th Street, SW., 20024, phone (202) 205–1661

Chief.—Vicki Christiansen (interim), 205–8439.
Associate Chief.—Dan Jiron, 205–1779.
Director for—
International Programs.—Valdis E. Mezainis, 644–4621.
Law Enforcement and Investigations.—Tracy Perry (703) 605–4690.
Legislative Affairs.—Douglas Crandall, 205–1637.
Office of Communications.—Erin O'Connor, 205–1470.

BUSINESS OPERATIONS

Sydney R. Yates Building, 4th Floor, phone (202) 205–1707

Deputy Chief.—Robert Velasco (acting), (703) 605–4726.
Associate Deputy Chiefs: Malcom Shorter (703) 605–4167; Tina Terrell (acting), (703) 605–4167.
Chiefs of Staff: Anna Briatico, 205–1707; Andria Weeks (acting), 205–5102.
Senior Staff Assistants: Donna Drelick, 205–0914; Vacant, 205–1545.
Deputy Area Budget Coordinator.—Tracey Hanson (202) 403–8975.
Director for—
Acquisition Management.—George Sears (703) 605–4744.
Enterprise.—Laura Nance (acting), (909) 382–2613.
Homeland Security.—Arthur Bryant, 205–0942.
Human Resources Management.—Mary Beth Lepore (703) 605–4604.
Information Resources Management.—Don Modder (acting), (703) 605–4811.
Job Corps.—Vacant.
Regulatory and Management Services.—Meg Scofield (acting), (202) 401–4410.
Safety and Occupational Health.—Steven Schlientz (703) 605–4482.
Strategic Program and Budget Analysis.—John Rapp (acting), 205–1282.

NATIONAL FOREST SYSTEM

Sydney R. Yates Building, Fifth Floor, phone (202) 205–1523

Deputy Chief.—Leslie A.C. Weldon.
Associate Deputy Chiefs: Glenn Casamassa, 205–3171; Jeanne Higgins (acting), 205–0824.
Staff Director of:
Ecosystem Management Coordination.—Chris French, 205–0830.
Engineering Technology and Geo-Spatial Service.—Emilee Blount (703) 605–4616.
Forest Management.—Allen Rowley, 644–4715.
Lands and Realty.—Greg Smith, 205–1769.
Minerals and Geology Management.—Nicholas Douglas (703) 605–4785.
National Partnership Office.—Jacqueline Emanuel, 205–1072.
Rangeland Management Vegetation Ecology.—Allen Rowley, 644–4715.
Recreation Heritage and Volunteer Resources.—Joe Meade, 205–1240.
Watershed, Fish, Wildlife, Air, and Rare Plants.—Robert Harper, 205–1671.

Wilderness, Wild and Scenic Rivers.—Susan Spear, 644–4862.

RESEARCH AND DEVELOPMENT

Sydney R. Yates Building, Second Floor, Fax (202) 205–1530

Deputy Chief.—Dr. Carlos Rodriguez-Franco, 205–1665.
Associate Deputy Chiefs: George Chris Iverson (acting), Monica M. Lear, 205–1702.
Senior Staff Assistants: Deborah Bush-Butler (703) 605–4979; Linda Jones, 205–1200.
Deputy Budget Coordinator.—Felipe Sanchez, 205–0833.
Staff Directors:
Inventory, Monitoring, and Assessment Research.—Linda Heath (703) 605–4177.
Knowledge Management and Communications.—Tracy Hancock, 205–1724.
Landscape Restoration and Ecosystem Services Research.—Carl Lucero, 405–3823.
Policy Analysis.—Bill Lange (202) 207–8306.
Sustainable Forest Management Research.—Toral Patel-Weynand, 205–0878.

STATE AND PRIVATE FORESTRY

Sydney R. Yates Building, Third Floor, phone (202) 205–1657

Deputy Chief.—Vicki Christiansen, 205–1606.
Associate Deputy Chiefs: Jaelith Hall-Rivera, Becki Heath, Patti Hirami.
Chief of Staff.—Debbie Pressman.
Director of:
Conservation Education.—Michiko Martin, 205–1241.
Cooperative Forestry.—Steve Koehn, 205–1389.
Fire and Aviation Management.—Shawna Legarza, 205–1483.
Forest Health Protection.—Rick Cooksey (703) 605–5332.
Office of Tribal Relations.—Fred Clark, 205–1514.

NATURAL RESOURCES CONSERVATION SERVICE

South Building, Room 5105–A, phone (202) 720–4525

Chief.—Leonard Jordan (acting).
Associate Chiefs: Thomas Christensen 720–5811; James E. Tillman, Sr. (acting), 720–4531.
Director, Division of:
Civil Rights.—Garry Lee (acting), (301) 504–2181.
Legislative.—Leslie Deavers (acting), 720–2771.
Public Affairs.—Kaveh Sadeghzadeh, 720–3210.

OFFICE OF THE CHIEF FINANCIAL OFFICER

Chief Financial Officer.—Jeffrey S. Machelski (202) 720–5904, 720–4251.
Directors:
Corporate Accounting Division.—Selma Cowan (202) 690–0037.
Quality Assurance Division.—Ravenna Bohan, 690–0432.
Program and Information Management.—Brenda Rodriguez (202) 205–6143.
Financial Management Service Delivery.—Kristin Salzer (acting), 720–3857.
Strategic Budget Division.—Jeffrey S. Machelski (acting), 205–5904.

DEPUTY CHIEF FOR PROGRAMS

Deputy Chief.—Jimmy Bramblett (202) 720–4630.
Director, Division of:
Conservation Technical Assistance.—Katrina Thompson (acting), 205–9689.
Easement.—Kim M. Berns, 720–4927.
Financial Assistance Programs.—Juan Hernandez, 720–1844.
Outreach and Advocacy.—Ron Harris, 720–6646.

Chief Human Resources Officer

Chief Human Resources Officer.—Melissa Drummond (202) 720–7847.
National Employee Development Center.—Jeffrey Dziedzic (817) 509–3241.
Supervisory Agency Representative.—Lauren Ruby (301) 504–2197.
Director, Workforce Strategy.—Sherry Dixon, 720–8676.
Director, Workforce Services Division.—Richard Nelson (202) 260–9203.
Director, Workforce Management Division.—Melissa Drummond (acting), 720–7847.
Quality Assurance and Policy Division Director.—Leslie Violette, 720–3042.

DEPUTY CHIEF OF SCIENCE AND TECHNOLOGY

Deputy Chief.—Roylene Rides at the Door, (acting), (202) 720–4528.
Director, Division of:
Conservation Engineering.—Noller Herbert, 720–2520.
Ecological Sciences.—Terrell Erickson, 720–4716.
Soil Health Division.—Bianca Moebius-Clune (202) 205–7712.

DEPUTY CHIEF OF SOIL SURVEY AND RESOURCE ASSESSMENT

Deputy Chief.—David Smith (301) 504–2302.
Director, Division of:
International Programs.—Lillian Woods, 504–2271.
National Geospatial Center of Excellence.—Darren Hickman (817) 509–3420.
Resources Assessment.—Daniel Mullarkey, 504–2311.
Resources Inventory and Assessment.—Patrick Flanagan, 504–2222.
Soil Survey.—David Lindbo (202) 260–9233.

DEPUTY CHIEF OF STRATEGIC PLANNING AND ACCOUNTABILITY

Deputy Chief.—Mark Xu (acting), (301) 504–0056.
Director, Division of:
Compliance.—Leon Brooks, 504–2190.
Resource Economics, Analysis and Policy.—Mark Xu, 504–0303.
Strategic and Performance Planning.—Machelle Simmons, 504–0023.

UNDER SECRETARY FOR FARM PRODUCTION AND CONSERVATION

Under Secretary.—William Northey.

DEPUTY UNDER SECRETARY FOR FARM PRODUCTION AND CONSERVATION

Deputy Under Secretary.—Robert Johansson (acting).
Deputy Under Secretaries: Vacant.
Chief of Staff.—Vacant.
Special Assistants: Galon Hall (acting), Kimberly Graham (acting), Robert Stephenson (acting).
Executive Assistant.—Brandi Greenleaf.

UNDER SECRETARY FOR TRADE AND FOREIGN AGRICULTURAL AFFAIRS

Under Secretary.—Ted McKinney.
Chief of Staff.—Vacant.
Special Assistant.—Zhulieta Willbrand (acting).
Executive Assistant.—Robert Perry.

FARM SERVICE AGENCY

South Building, Room 3086–S, phone (202) 720–3467

Administrator.—Steven J. Peterson (acting).
Civil Rights.—Brian Garner.
Economic and Policy Analysis Staff.—Joy Harwood, Room 3741–S (202) 720–3451.
Deputy Administrator for Farm Programs.—Brad Karmen, Room 3612–S, 720–3175.

Assistant Deputy Administrator.—Vacant, 720–2070.
Conservation and Environmental Programs Division.—Martin Bomar, Room 4714–S, 720–6221.
Price Support Division.—Raellen Ericson (acting), Room 4095–S, 720–7901.
Production, Emergencies and Compliance Division.—Lisa Berry (acting), Room 4754, 720–7641.
Deputy Administrator for Farm Loan Programs.—Jim Radintz (acting), 720–4671.
Program Development and Economic Enhancement Division.—Nancy New, Room 4919–S, 720–3647.
Loan Making Division.—Vacant, Room 5438–S, 720–1632.
Loan Servicing and Property Management Division.—Michael Hinton, Room 5449–S, 720–4572.
Deputy Administrator for Field Operations.—Linda Treese (acting), Room 3092, 690–2807.
Assistant Deputy Administrator.—Vacant, Room 8092, 690–2807.
Operations Review and Analysis Staff.—Phillip Sharp, Room 2720–S, 690–2532.
Deputy Administrator for Commodity Operations.—Sandra Wood, Room 3080–S, 720–3217.
Kansas City Commodity Office.—Vacant (816) 926–6301.
Deputy Administrator for Management.—Mark A. Rucker, Room 3095–S, 720–3438.
Budget Division.—Margo Erny, Room 4720–S.
Human Resources Division.—Vacant, Room 5200 (L–St), 418–8950.
Information Technology Services Division.—Darren Ash, Room 5768–S, 720–5320.
Management Services Division.—Robert Haughton, Room 520–PRTL, 720–3438.

FOREIGN AGRICULTURAL SERVICE

South Building, Room 5071, phone (202) 720–3935, fax (202) 690–2159

Administrator.—Holly Higgins (acting).
Associate Administrator.—Daniel Whitley (acting), 720–6301.
Associate Administrator/COO.—Bryce Quick, 720–2706.
General Sales Manager.—Bryce Quick (acting), 720–2706.
Chief of Staff.—Ryan Brewster (acting), 690–8064.
Deputy Chief of Staff.—Chase McGrath (acting), 720–7458.
Director of:
Civil Rights Staff.—Adriano Vasquez, 720–8907.
Legislative and Public Affairs.—Christopher Church, 720–6830.
Public Affairs and Executive Correspondence.—Ellen Dougherty, 720–0328.

OFFICE OF THE CHIEF OPERATING OFFICER

Associate Administrator and Chief Operating Officer.—Bryce Quick (202) 720–2706.
Associate Chief Operating Officers: Ronald Croushorn, 720–3038; Robert McGary, 720–1738.
Budget.—Dennis Martin, 378–1067.
Information Technology.—Richard Young, 720–7741.
International Travel.—Ted Goldammer, 690–1800.

OFFICE OF CAPACITY BUILDING AND DEVELOPMENT

Deputy Administrator.—Jocelyn Brown (202) 690–1779.
Assistant Deputy Administrators: Michelle Calhoun (202) 720–9513, Brian Guse, 690–2870.
Policy Coordination and Planning Staff.—Jarrod Jones, 690–4058.
Director, Division of:
Development Resources and Disaster Assistance.—Laura Scandurra, 720–0823.
Food Assistance.—Benjamin Muskovitz, 720–0886.
Trade and Scientific Capacity Building.—Betsy Baysinger, 720–1667.
Trade and Scientific Exchanges.—Avis Watts-Massenburg, 690–0032.

OFFICE OF COUNTRY AND REGIONAL AFFAIRS

Deputy Administrator.—Mark Dries (202) 690–4062.
Assistant Deputy Administrator.—Sharynne Nenon, 690–3412.
Director, Division of:
Europe, Africa, and Middle East.—Catherine Fulton (202) 720–2461.

Asia.—Maria Pool, 720–8371.
Western Hemisphere.—John Passino, 720–5219.

OFFICE OF FOREIGN SERVICE OPERATIONS

Deputy Administrator.—Cynthia Guven (acting), (202) 720–0303.
Assistant Deputy Administrators: Cynthia Guven, 720–0303; Sarah Hanson, 720–3065.
Director for—
Africa and Middle East Area.—Hoa Huynh (acting), 791–8472.
Europe Area.—James Butterworth, 720–6968.
North Asia Area.—Valerie Brown, 720–1340.
South Asia Area.—Erik Hansen, 720–1340.
Western Hemisphere Area.—Michael Riedel, 690–4851.
International Services.—Hedy Armstrong, 720–1346.
Planning and Global Resources Staff.—Karen Darden, 720–1346.
Protocol and Representation.—Yvette Bomersheim-Wedderburn, 720–1980.

OFFICE OF GLOBAL ANALYSIS

Deputy Administrator.—Daniel Whitley (202) 720–6301.
Assistant Deputy Administrator.—Patrick Packnett, 720–1590.
Director, Division of:
Global Commodities Analysis Division.—Aileen Mannix, 720–6791.
Global Policy Analysis Division.—Paul Trupo, 720–1335.
International Production Assessment Division.—Ronald Frantz, 720–4056.

OFFICE OF AGREEMENTS AND SCIENTIFIC AFFAIRS

Deputy Administrator.—Robert Macke, 720–4434.
Assistant Deputy Administrators: Charles Bertsch, 720–6278; Katherine Nishiura, 720–7457.
Policy Formulation Staff:
Senior Policy Advisors: Phil Jarrell, 720–2043; Bob Spitzer, 720–4825; Andrew Stephens, 720–0663.
Chief, Planning and Operations Group.—JonAnn Flemings, 720–1277.
Division Director of:
Animal Division.—Laura Anderson, 720–6064.
Multilateral Affairs.—Michelle Moore, 720–1341.
Bilateral Agreements and Enforcement Division.—Emel Lyons, 720–1818.
International Regulations and Standards Division.—Cathy McKinnell, 690–0929.
New Technologies and Production Methods Division.—Paul Spencer, 690–2868.
Plant Division.—Mark Rasmussen (acting), 720–0765.
Processed Products and Technical Regulations Division.—David Cottrell, 720–5764.

OFFICE OF TRADE PROGRAMS

Deputy Administrator.—Mark Slupek (202) 720–9516.
Assistant Deputy Administrators: William Bomersheim, 720–9516; Marianne McElroy, 720–9516.
Director, Division of:
Cooperator Programs Division.—Corey Pickelsimer (202) 690–6888.
Credit Programs.—Mark Rowse, 720–0624.
Import Policies and Export Reporting Division.—Ronald Lord, 720–0638.
Program Operations Division.—Curt Alt, 720–4327.
Trade Services Staff.—Shane Danielson, 720–1230.

RISK MANAGEMENT AGENCY

South Building, Room 6092–S, phone (202) 690–2803

Administrator.—Heather Manzano (acting).
Associate Administrator and Deputy Manager, FCIC, Board of Directors.—Michael A. Alston.
Associate Administrator.—Robert Ibarra (acting).
Deputy Administrator for—
Compliance.—Heather Manzano, Room 6603–S, 720–0642.

Insurance Services.—Robert Ibarra, Room 6709–S, 690–4494.
Product Management.—Richard Flournoy, Kansas City (816) 926–7394.

UNDER SECRETARY FOR RURAL DEVELOPMENT

Jamie L. Whitten Building, phone (202) 720–4581

Under Secretary.—Lisa Mensah.
Deputy Under Secretary.—Vernita Dore (acting).
Chief of Staff.—Andrews Given (acting).
Deputy Chief of Staff.—Irene Lin.
Director, Legislative and Public Affairs.—David Sandretti, 720–1019.

BUSINESS AND COOPERATIVE PROGRAMS

South Building, Room 5801–S, phone (202) 690–4730

Administrator.—Lillian Salerno.
Chief of Staff.—Justin Hatmaker, 720–6165.
Deputy Administrator.—Sam Rikkers, 720–6165.
Oversight/Resource Coordination Staff (OCS).—Vacant, 690–4100.
Deputy Administrator for Business Programs.—Tom Hannah, 720–0813.
Assistant Deputy Administrator.—William ''Bill'' Smith, 720–0813.
Director of:
Business and Industry Division.—John Broussard, 690–4103.
Specialty Lenders Division.—Kristi Kubista-Hovis (acting), 720–1400.
Deputy Administrator for Cooperative Programs.—Chad Parker, 720–7558.
Assistant Deputy Administrator.—Andy Jermolowizc, 720–8460.
Director of:
Cooperative Marketing Division.—David Sears, 690–0368.
Cooperative Resources Management Division.—Bruce Reynolds (acting), 690–1374.
Education and Research.—Claudette Fernandez (acting), 720–3350.
Grants and Agreements.—Amy Cavanaugh, 690–1376.

RURAL HOUSING SERVICE

South Building, Room 5014–S, phone (202) 692–0268

Administrator.—Richard A. Davis (acting), 720–1500.
Director, Program Support Staff.—Ed Duval, 720–9619.
Deputy Administrator for Single Family.—Joyce Allen, 205–4996.
Assistant Deputy Administrator for Single Family.—Cathy Glover, 720–0343.
Deputy Administrator for Multi-Family Housing.—Bryan Hooper, 720–9739.
Deputy Administrator for Community Facilities.—Joseph Ben-Israel (acting), 720–1505.
Director of:
Direct Loan and Grant Processing Division (CF).—Martha Torrez, 720–4072.
Guaranteed Loan Processing and Servicing Division (CF).—Deb Jackson, 720–8454.
Family Housing Direct Loan Division (SFH).—Barry Ramsey, 720–5378.
Family Housing Guaranteed Loan Division (SFH).—Joaquin Tremols, 720–1465.
Multi-Family Housing Portfolio Management Division, Direct Housing.—Janice Stouder, 720–9728.
Guaranteed Loan Division (MFH).—Michael Steininger, 720–1610.
Preservation and Direct Loan Division (MFH).—C.B. Alonso, 720–1624.

RURAL UTILITIES SERVICE

South Building, Room 5135, phone (202) 720–9540

Administrator.—Christopher McLean (acting), Room 5135–S, 720–9540.
Deputy Administrator.—Vacant.
Chief of Staff.—Alan Krapf (acting), Room 5135–S, 720–9540.
Assistant Administrator for Electric Division.—Christopher McLean, Room 5165, 720–9505.
Deputy Assistant Administrator, Office of Loan Origination and Approval.—Joseph Badin, Room 0221–S, 720–0409.
Deputy Assistant Administrator, Office of Operations.—James Elliott, Room 5165–S, 720–9545.

Deputy Assistant Administrator, Office of Policy, Outreach and Standards.—Gerard Moore, Room 0243–S, 720–1900.

Deputy Assistant Administrator, Office of Portfolio Management and Risk Assessment.—Victor T. Vu, Room 0270–S, 720–6436.

Policy Advisor.—Jon Claffey, Room 5165–S, 720–9545.

Assistant Administrator for Telecommunications.—Chad Parker, Room 5151, 720–9556.

Deputy Assistant Administrator.—Laurel Leverrier, Room 5151, 720–3416.

Deputy Assistant Administrator, Loan Origination and Approval.—Shawn Arner, Room 2808–S, 720–0800.

Deputy Assistant Administrator, Policy and Outreach Division.—Ken Kuchno, Room 2868–S, 690–4673.

Deputy Assistant Administrator, Portfolio Management and Risk Assessment.—Peter Aimable, Room 2839–S, 720–1025.

Assistant Administrator, Water and Environmental Programs (WEP).—Claudette Fernandez, Room 5145–S, 690–2670.

Deputy Assistant Administrator, WEP.—Scott Barringer, Room 5145–S, 690–2670.

Director, Engineering and Environmental Staff.—Kellie McGuiness Kubena, Room 2237–S, 720–1649.

Director, Water Programs Division.—Kent Evans, Room 2232–S, 720–2567.

Chief, Program Operations Branch.—Cheryl Francis, 2236–S, 720–1937.

Chief, Portfolio Management Branch.—Steve Saulnier, Room 2231–S, 720–2526.

Assistant Administrator, Program Accounting and Regulatory Analysis.—James Murray, Room 5159–S, 720–9450.

Legislative and Public Affairs Staff.—Anne Mayberry, Room 5144–S, 690–1756.

Senior Level Program and Policy Advisor, Policy Analysis and Regulatory Management.—Gary A. Bojes, Room 5150–S, 720–1256.

FOOD, NUTRITION, AND CONSUMER SERVICES

1400 Independence Avenue, SW., Room 216–E, Whitten Building, 20250

Under Secretary.—Vacant (202) 720–7711.

Deputy Under Secretary.—Brandon Lipps (acting).

Chief of Staff/Policy Advisor.—Maggie Lyons.

FOOD AND NUTRITION SERVICE

3101 Park Center Drive, Room 906, Alexandria, VA 22302 (703) 305–2060

OFFICE OF THE ADMINISTRATOR

Administrator.—Audrey Rowe (703) 305–2060.

Executive Assistant.—Angela Torres, 305–2060.

Chief, Governmental Affairs.—Scott A. Carter, 305–2313.

OFFICE OF POLICY SUPPORT

Deputy Administrator.—Rich Lucas, Room 1014 (703) 305–2017.

Assistant Deputy Administrator.—Melissa Abelev, Room 1010, 305–2209.

Director, Division of:

SNAP Research and Analysis.—Kathryn Law, Room 1025, 305–2138.

Special Nutrition Research and Analysis.—Kelley Scanlon, Room 1007, 457–7767.

OFFICE OF THE CHIEF COMMUNICATIONS OFFICER (OCCO)

Communications Division:

Director.—Bruce C. Alexander, Room 926–A (703) 305–1615.

Branch Chief:

Media.—Johnathan Monroe, Room 941, 605–3236.

Social Media.—Carol Johnson, Room 941, 605–4009.

External and Government Affairs Division:

Director.—Katherine Fink, Room 926B, 305–4372.

Branch Chief:

Stakeholder Relations.—Pam Phillip, Room 941, 305–2298.

Governmental Affairs.—Scott A. Carter, Room 941, 305–2313.
Special Assistant.—Jessica Milteer, Room 941, 305–2707.
Controlled Correspondence Officer.—Twanda Rodgers, Room 941, 305–2066.

OFFICE OF MANAGEMENT TECHNOLOGY AND FINANCE

Associate Administrator and Chief Operating Officer.—Telora Dean, Room 906 (703) 305–2064.
Director of Civil Rights.—Robert Contreras, Room 1200, 305–2195. (Reports to the Administrator)

Office of Management:
Deputy Administrator for Management.—Cristina Chiappe, Room 1441, 303–2030.
Contracts.—Shawn O'Donnell.
HR.—Vilma Alejandro.
Facilities.—Patrick Bush.

MANAGEMENT

Deputy Administrator.—Telora Dean, Room 1400 (703) 305–2030.
Director, Division of:
Contracts Management.—Lance Petteway, Room 220, 305–2251.
Human Resources.—Cristina Chiappe (acting), Room 404, 305–2326.
Logistics and Facility Management.—Javier Inclan, Room 222, 305–2220.

FINANCIAL MANAGEMENT

Deputy Administrator (Chief Financial Officer).—David Burr, Room 712C (703) 305–2191.
Director, Division of:
Accounting (Chief Accounting Officer).—Larry Blim, Room 716, 305–1548.
Budget (Chief Budget Officer).—Lisa Greenwood, Room 708, 305–2172.
Grants and Fiscal Policy.—Lael Lubing, Room 732, 305–2161.
Funds Management and Planning.—Lisha Dorman, Room 442, 305–2754.
Director, Office of Internal Controls, Audits, and Investigations.—Mark Porter, Room 733, 305–0901.

INFORMATION TECHNOLOGY

Deputy Administrator.—Kimberly R. Jackson, Room 314 A (703) 305–4370.
Chief, Information Security Office.—Joseph Binns, Room 316, 605–1181.
Director, Division of:
Portfolio Management.—Kristin Ruiz, Room 310, 305–1437.
Technology.—Sonja Farrell, Room 314 C, 305–2275.

REGIONAL OPERATIONS AND SUPPORT

Associate Administrator.—Yvette Jackson, Room 906 (703) 305–2060.
Director, Division of:
Emergency Management.—Steve Hortin, Room 1134, 305–4375.
Retailer Operations.—Neva Terry, Room 1138 (703) 605–4315.
State Systems.—Karen Painter-Jacquess, Room 1146 (303) 844–6533.

OFFICE OF SUPPLEMENTAL NUTRITION ASSISTANCE PROGRAM

SNAP Associate Administrator.—Jessica Shahin, Suite 808 (703) 305–2026.
Retailer Policy and Management Division Director.—Andrea Gold, Room 424, 305–2434.
Program Accountability and Administration Division Director.—Ron Ward, Room 816, 305–2523.
Program Development Division Director.—Lizbeth Silbermann, Room 814, 305–2494.
Office of Employment and Training Director.—Moira Johnston, Room 806, 305–2515.

OFFICE OF SPECIAL NUTRITION PROGRAMS

Deputy Administrator.—Diane M. Kriviski, Room 628 (703) 305–2052.
Director, Division of:
Child Nutrition.—Cindy Long, Room 640, 305–2590.
Food Distribution.—Laura Castro, Room 500, 305–2680.
Supplemental Food Program.—Sarah Widor, Room 520, 305–2746.

CENTER FOR NUTRITION POLICY AND PROMOTION

Executive Director.—Vacant.
Deputy Director.—Jackie Haven, Suite 1034, 305–7600.
Director, Office of Nutrition Guidance and Analysis.—Colette Rihane, Suite 1034, 305–2403.
Director, Office of Marketing and Communication Division.—Brooke Hardison, Suite 1034 (703) 605–0220.
Senior Policy Advisor.—Stephenie Fu, Suite 1034, 305–2217.

UNDER SECRETARY FOR FOOD SAFETY

Deputy Under Secretary.—Carmen Rottenberg (acting), (202) 720–7025.

FOOD SAFETY AND INSPECTION SERVICE
Jamie L. Whitten Building, Room 331–E, phone (202) 720–7025, fax 690–0550

Administrator.—Paul Kiecker (acting).

OFFICE OF FIELD OPERATIONS (OFO)

Assistant Administrator.—William C. Smith, Room 344–E (202) 720–8803.
Deputy Assistant Administrator.—Jessica Pulz (acting), 720–8804.
Executive Associates, Regulatory Operations: Dr. Keith Gilmore, Lawrence, Kansas (785) 766–9830; Hany Sidrak, Room 3171–S (202) 205–4208; Dr. Armia Tawadrous, Room 3161–S, 720–5714.
Director, Recall Management Staff.—Atyia Khan, Room 0006–S, 720–1640.

OFFICE OF DATA INTEGRATION AND FOOD PROTECTION (ODIFP)

Assistant Administrator.—Terri Nintemann, Room 3130–S (202) 720–5643.
Deputy Assistant Administrator.—Soumaya Tohamy, Ph.D., Room 3130–S, 720–5643.
Director of:
Data Analysis Integration Staff.—Christopher Alvares, Room 3126–S (202) 690–6418.
Emergency Coordination Staff.—Mary K. Cutshall, PPIII, 9–140, 690–6523.
Director, Food Defense Assessment Staff.—Greg Grover (acting), PPIII, 9–148 (202) 772–9115.
Director, Inspection Data Analysis Staff.—Julie Smith, PPIII, 9–142, 690–3976.

OFFICE OF INTERNATIONAL COORDINATION (OIC)

International Coordination Executive.—Jane H. Doherty, Room 3143–S (202) 708–8769.
Senior Advisor.—Mary Stanley, Room 3151–S, 720–0287.
International Program Specialist.—Shannon McMurtrey, Room 3149–S, 720–9966.

OFFICE OF MANAGEMENT (OM)

Assistant Administrator.—Jacqueline Myers, Room 347–E (202) 720–4432.
Deputy Assistant Administrator.—Gabrielle James, Room 347–E, 720–4745.
Program Evaluation and Improvement Staff.—Matthew Michael.

OFFICE OF POLICY AND PROGRAM DEVELOPMENT (OPPD)

Assistant Administrator.—Roberta Wagner, Room 350–E, JLW Building (202) 205–0495.

Deputy Assistant Administrator.—Rachel Edelstein, Room 350–E, JLW Building, 205–0495.

OFFICE OF INVESTIGATION, ENFORCEMENT AND AUDIT (OIEA)

Assistant Administrator.—Carl A. Mayes, Room 3133–S (202) 720–8609.
Deputy Assistant Administrator.—Peter E. Bridgeman, Room 3133–S, 720–8609.
Director of:
Compliance and Investigations Division.—Jerry Elliott, Room 2149–S, 720–3781.
Management Controls and Audit.—Vincent Fayne, Room 2175–S (202) 690–5662.
Resource Management Staff (Budget).—Michelle Long, Room 2175–S (202) 708–8177.

OFFICE OF PUBLIC AFFAIRS AND CONSUMER EDUCATION (OPACE)

Assistant Administrator.—Carol Blake, Room 339–E (202) 720–3884.
Deputy Assistant Administrator.—Aaron Lavallee, Room 3137–S, 720–0460.
Director of:
Congressional and Public Affairs Staff.—Michelle Catlin (acting), Room 1175–S, 720–9113.
Executive Correspondence and Issues Management Staff.—Karen Hunter, Room 1167–S, 690–3882.

OFFICE OF PUBLIC HEALTH SCIENCE (OPHS)

Assistant Administrator.—Dr. David Goldman, Room 341–E (202) 720–2644.
Deputy Assistant Administrator.—Vacant, Room 341–E, 720–1281.

OFFICE OF OUTREACH, EMPLOYEE EDUCATION AND TRAINING (OOEET)

Assistant Administrator.—Michael G. Watts, Room 4862–S, 205–0194.

UNDER SECRETARY FOR RESEARCH, EDUCATION, AND ECONOMICS

Deputy Under Secretary.—Dr. Chavonda Jacobs-Young (acting), (202) 720–1542.
Chief of Staff.—Michele Esch (acting), 720–1542.
Communications Director.—Damon Thompson, 720–1375.
Executive Assistant.—Michele Simmons, 720–1542.
Program Assistant.—Tiffany Jones (202) 690–1254.

AGRICULTURAL RESEARCH SERVICE

Administration Building, Room 302–A, phone (202) 720–3656, fax 720–5427

Administrator.— Dr. Chavonda Jacobs-Young.
Associate Administrator for—
Research Operations.—Dr. Simon Liu, 720–3658.
Research Programs.—Dr. Steven Kappes (301) 504–5084.
Director of:
Budget and Program Management Staff.—Michael Arnold, Room 358–A, 720–4421.
Legislative Affairs.—Gary Mayo (202) 260–9494.
Office of Communications.—Chris Bentley (301) 504–1638.
Assistant Administrator, Research Operations and Management, Office of Technology Transfer.—Mojdeh Bahar, 504–6905.
Deputy Administrator, Administrative and Financial Management.—Joon Park (202) 690–2575.
Director, National Agricultural Library.—Paul Wester (301) 504–5248.

AREA OFFICES

Director of:
Midwest Area.—J.L. Willett (acting), 1815 North University Street, Room 2004, Peoria, IL 61604–0000 (309) 681–6602.

Northeast Area.—Dariusz Swietlik, Building 003, Room 223, BARC-West, Beltsville, MD 20705 (301) 504–6078.
Pacific West Area.—Robert Matteri, 800 Buchanan Street, Room 2030, Albany, CA 94710 (510) 559–6060.
Plains Area.—Larry Chandler, 2150 Centre Avenue, Building D, Suite 300, Ft. Collins, CO 80525–8119, (970) 492–7057.
Southeast Area.—Deborah Brennan, 141 Experiment Station Road, Stoneville, MS 38776 (662) 686–5265.

NATIONAL INSTITUTE OF FOOD AND AGRICULTURE

Jamie L. Whitten Building, Room 305–A, phone (202) 720–4423, fax 720–8987

Director.—Dr. Sonny Ramaswamy.
Associate Director of Programs.—Meryl Broussard, 720–7441.
Associate Director of Operation.—Dr. Robert Holland.
Assistant Administrators/Legislative Liaisons: Betty Lou Gilliland, Room 305–A, 720–8187; Kimberly Whittet, Room 305–A, 720–8291.
Director, Office of:
Budget.—Paula Geiger, Room 332–A, 720–2675.
Communications.—Virgina Bueno, Room 4231, 720–2677.
Equal Opportunity Staff.—Curt DeVille, Room 1230, 720–2700.
Planning and Accountability.—Bart Hewitt, Room 1315, 720–5623.
Deputy Administrator for—
Bioenergy, Climate, Environment/Science and Education Resources Development.—Luis Tupas, Room 4343, 720–7947.
Grants and Financial Management.—Cynthia Montgomery, Room 2256, 401–6021.
Information Systems and Technology Management.—Michel Desbois, Room 4122, 401–0117.
Institute of Food/Production and Sustainability.—Parag Chitnis, Room 2334, 401–5024.
Youth Families Community.—Muquarrab Qureshi, Room 3231, 401–4555.

ECONOMIC RESEARCH SERVICE

355 E Street, SW., 20024–3221, phone (202) 694–5000

Administrator.—Mary Bohman, Room 6–201.
Associate Administrator.—Greg Pompelli, Room 6–197.
Assistant Administrator.—Ephraim Leibtag, Room 6–222.
Civil Rights Director.—Henry Norcom, Room 5–268, 694–5162.
Director, Division of:
Food Economics.—Jay Variyam, Room 5–203, 694–5457.
Information Services.—Tony Williams, Room 4–197, 694–5101.
Market Trade and Economics.—Gopinath "Gopi" Munisamy, Room 5–197, 694–5201.
Resource and Rural Economics.—Marca Weinberg, Room 6–131, 694–5478.

NATIONAL AGRICULTURAL STATISTICS SERVICE

South Agriculture Building, Room 5041A–S, phone (202) 720–2707

Administrator.—Hubert Hamer, Room 5041A, 720–4333.
Associate Administrator.—Renee Picanso, Room 5041A, 720–2707.
Director for—
Census and Survey.—Barbara Rater, Room 6306, 720–4557.
Eastern Field Operations.—Jay Johnson, Room 5053, 720–3638.
Information Technology.—Ron Thompson, Room 5847, 720–2984.
Methodology.—Joe Parsons, Room 5305 (202) 690–8141.
National Operations.—Joseph Prusacki (314) 595–9501 ext. 57501.
Research and Development.—Dr. Linda Young, Room 6035, 690–1401.
Statistics.—Daniel Kerestes, Room 5431, 720–3896.
Western Field Operations.—Kevin Barnes, Room 5053, 720–8220.

UNDER SECRETARY FOR MARKETING AND REGULATORY PROGRAMS

Jamie L. Whitten Building, Room 228–W, phone (202) 720–4256, fax 720–5775

Under Secretary.—Greg Ibach.

Deputy Under Secretary.—Vacant.
Special Assistant to the Under Secretary.—Vacant.
Chief of Staff.—Beth Gaston (acting).

AGRICULTURAL MARKETING SERVICE

South Agriculture Building, Room 3069–S, phone (202) 720–5115, fax 692–0313

Administrator.—Bruce Summers (acting).
Associate Administrator.—Erin Morris, 690–4024.
Deputy Associate Administrators: Karen Comfort, 690–0187; Charles Parrott, 690–9144.
Deputy Administrator for—
Management and Analysis Programs.—Sonia Jimenez, Room 2095–S, 720–6766.
Cotton and Tobacco Programs.—Darryl Earnest (901) 384–3060.
Dairy Programs.—Dana Coale, Room 2968–S, 720–4392.
Specialty Crops Program.—Melissa Bailey (acting), Room 2077–S, 720–4722.
National Organic Program.—Miles McEvoy, Room 2646, 720–3252.
Livestock, Poultry and Seed Poultry Program.—Craig Morris, Room 2092–S, 720–3215.
Science and Technology.—Ruihong Guo, Room 3543–S, 720–8556.
Transportation and Marketing.—Arthur Neal, Room 4543, 690–1300.
Director, Legislative and Regulatory Review Staff.—Bill Allen, Room 3943–S, 720–2468.

ANIMAL AND PLANT HEALTH INSPECTION SERVICE (APHIS)

Jamie L. Whitten Building, Room 312–E, phone (202) 720–3668, fax 720–3054

OFFICE OF THE ADMINISTRATOR

Administrator.—Kevin Shea.
Associate Administrators: Michael Gregoire, Dr. Michael Watson.
Director:
Office of Civil Rights, Diversity, and Inclusion.—Michon Oubichon, Room 1137–S, 720–7012, fax 720–2365.

ANIMAL CARE

4700 River Road, Riverdale, MD 20737, phone (301) 851–3751, fax 734–4328

Deputy Administrator.—Bernadette Juarez.
Associate Deputy Administrator.—Elizabeth Goldentyer.

BIOTECHNOLOGY REGULATORY SERVICES

4700 River Road, Riverdale, MD 20737, phone (301) 851–3877, fax (301) 734–6352

Deputy Administrator.—Michael J. Firko, 851–3941.
Associate Deputy Administrator.—Ibrahim M. Shaqir, 851–3938.
Assistant Deputy Administrator.—Sidney W. Abel, 851–3896.

INTERNATIONAL SERVICES

Jamie L. Whitten Building, Room 324–E, phone (202) 799–7132, fax 690–1484

Deputy Administrator.—Cheryle Blakely, 799–7132.
Associate Deputy Administrators: Vacant, 799–7132; Rebecca Bech, 799–7131.
Assistant Deputy Administrator.—Jessica Mahalingappa, 799–7121.
Chief of Staff.—Robin White, 799–7130.

LEGISLATIVE AND PUBLIC AFFAIRS

South Building, Room 1147–S, phone (202) 799–7031, fax 720–3982

Deputy Administrator.—Bethany Jones.
Associate Deputy Administrator.—James Ivy.

Director of:
Executive Correspondence.—Christina Myers (301) 851–4111.
Freedom of Information.—Tonya Woods, 851–4102.
Public Affairs.—Ed Curlett, 851–4100.

MARKETING AND REGULATORY PROGRAMS BUSINESS SERVICES

Jamie L. Whitten Building, Room 308–E, phone (202) 799–7065, fax 690–0686

Deputy Administrator.—Robert J. Huttenlocker, 799–7064.
Associate Deputy Administrator.—Michael T. Watson, 799–7066.

PLANT PROTECTION AND QUARANTINE

Jamie L. Whitten Building, Room 302–E, phone (202) 799–7163, fax 690–0472

Deputy Administrator.—Osama El-Lissy.
Associate Deputy Administrator for—
Field Operations.—Matthew Royer (919) 855–7300.
Policy Management.—Alan Dowdy (202) 799–7163.
Science and Technology.—Ronald Sequeira (301) 851–2244.

POLICY AND PROGRAM DEVELOPMENT

4700 River Road, Riverdale, MD 20737, phone (301) 851–3098, fax (301) 734–6357

Deputy Administrator.—Christine Zakarka.
Associate Deputy Administrator.—Shannon Hamm.
Unit Chiefs:
Budget and Program Analysis.—Michelle Wenberg, 851–3143.
Environmental and Risk Analysis Service.—Elizabeth Nelson, 851–3089.
Program Assessment and Accountability.—Erik Anderson (612) 336–3393.
Planning, Evaluation, and Decision Support.—Connie Williams, 851–3087.
Policy Analysis and Development.—Parveen Setia, 851–3126.
Regulatory Analysis and Development.—Stephen O'Neill, 851–3072.

VETERINARY SERVICES

Jamie L. Whitten Building, Room 317–E, phone (202) 799–7146, fax 690–4171

Deputy Administrator.—Jack Shere, 799–7147.
Administrative Assistant.—Paula Lee, 799–7146.
Associate Deputy Administrator.—Burke Healey, 799–7145.
Deputy Chief of Staff.—Ashley Levesque, 799–7151.
Associate Deputy Administrator for—
Export Services.—Mark Davidson (301) 851–3547.
Surveillance, Preparedness, and Response Services.—Brian McCluskey (970) 494–7395.
Science, Technology, and Analysis Services.—Beth Lautner (515) 337–6161.
Program Support Services.—Kevin Richardson (301) 851–3603.

WILDLIFE SERVICES

South Building, Room 1624, phone (202) 799–7095, fax 690–0053

Deputy Administrator.—Vacant.
Associate Deputy Administrator.—Martin Mendoza, Jr.
Director for Operational Support.—David S. Reinhold (301) 851–4009.

GRAIN INSPECTION, PACKERS AND STOCKYARDS ADMINISTRATION

South Building, Room 2055, phone (202) 720–0219, fax 205–9237

Administrator.—Randall Jones (acting), Room 2055–S (202) 720–0219.
Director of:

Management and Budget Services.—Marianne Plaus, Room 2049–S (202) 690–3460.
Civil Rights.—Kevin Smith, Room 2508–S, 690–3640.
Deputy Administrator for Federal Grain Inspection Service.—Randall Jones, Room 2043–S, 720–9170.
Director of:
Compliance.—Karen Guagliardo, Room 2420–S, 720–7312.
Departmental and International Affairs.—Byron Reilly, Room 2410–S, 690–3206.
Field Management Division.—Samantha Simon, Room 2409–S, 720–0228.
Technical Services Division.—Vacant.
Deputy Administrator for Packers and Stockyards Programs.—Vacant.
Director, Litigation and Economic Analysis Division.—Brett Offutt, Room 2505–S, 690–4355.
Regional Directors:
Atlanta, GA.—Elkin Parker (404) 562–5840.
Aurora, CO.—Kraig J. Roesch (303) 375–4240.
Des Moines, IA.—Stuart Frank (515) 323–2579.

DEPARTMENT OF COMMERCE

Herbert C. Hoover Building

14th Street between Pennsylvania and Constitution Avenues, NW., 20230

phone (202) 482–2000, http://www.doc.gov

WILBUR ROSS, Secretary of Commerce; born in Weehawken, NJ, November 28, 1937; education: B.A., Yale University, New Haven, CT, 1959; M.B.A., Harvard University, Cambridge, MA, 1961; professional: U.S. Army Adjutant General Corps, 1961–63; president, Faulkner Dawkins and Sullivan Securities Corp., New York, NY, 1964–76; executive managing director, Rothschild, Inc. (and its predecessor, New Court Securities Corp.), New York, 1976–2000; chairman and chief strategy officer, WL Ross & Co. LLC, New York, 2000–17; named by Bloomberg Markets as one of the 50 most influential people in global finance; only person elected to both Private Equity Hall of Fame and Turnaround Management Hall of Fame; married: Hilary Geary Ross; children: Jessica Ross, Amanda Ross, Ted Geary, and Jack Geary; nominated by President Donald J. Trump to become the 39th Secretary of Commerce, and was sworn in by Vice President Mike Pence on February 28, 2017.

OFFICE OF THE SECRETARY

Secretary of Commerce.—Wilbur Ross, Room 5854 (202) 482–2112.
Deputy Secretary.—Bruce H. Andrews, Room 5838, 482–8376.
Chief of Staff.—Jim Hock, Room 5854, 482–4246.
Senior Advisor.—Kate McAdams, Room 5862, 482–4246.
Deputy Chiefs of Staff: Theodore LeCompte, 482–3028; Stephanie Valencia, 482–2771.
Director, Office of:
Business Liaison.—Theodore Johnston, Room 5062, 482–1360.
Executive Secretariat.—Madhura Valverde, Room 5516, 482–3934.
Policy and Strategic Planning.—John Ratliff, Room 5865, 482–4127.
Public Affairs.—Erin Weinstein (acting), Room 5413, 482–4883.
Scheduling and Advance.—Sally Cluthe, Room 5883, 482–5129.
White House Liaison.—Lauren Leonard (acting), Room 5835, 482–4147.

GENERAL COUNSEL

General Counsel.—Peter B. Davidson, Room 5870 (202) 482–4772.
Deputy General Counsel.—Michael J. Walsh.

ASSISTANT SECRETARY FOR LEGISLATIVE AND INTERGOVERNMENTAL AFFAIRS

Assistant Secretary.—Michael Platt, Jr., Room 5421 (202) 482–3663, fax 482–4420.
Deputy Assistant Secretary.—Jim Stowers, Room 5421, 482–3663, fax 482–4420.
Director for—
Intergovernmental Affairs.—William Ramos, Room 5422, 482–3663, fax 482–4420.
Associate Director for—
EDA, MBDA and Senior Advisor for Native American Affairs.—Cisco Minthorn, Room 5422, 482–4602.
NOAA, ESA, Census, BEA.—Jen Costanza, Room 5422, 482–1286.
NTIA, NIST, NTIS, USPTO, BIS.—Jenilee Keefe Singer, Room 5422, 482–7473.
Oversight.—Vacant.
Director of Legislative Outreach.—Emma Poorman, Room 5421, 482–4030.

CHIEF FINANCIAL OFFICER (CFO) AND ASSISTANT SECRETARY FOR ADMINISTRATION

Chief Financial Officer and Assistant Secretary.—Ellen Herbst, Room 5830 (202) 482–6269, fax 482–3592.

Deputy Assistant Secretary for Administration.—Fred Stephens, Room 5830.
Deputy Chief Financial Officer/Director for Financial Management.—Lisa Casias, Room 6827, 482–1207, fax 482–5070.
Director for—
Acquisition Management.—Barry Berkowitz, Room 6422, 482–4248, fax 482–1711.
Administrative Services.—Mary Pleffner, Room 6316, 482–1200, fax 482–8890.
Budget.—Michael Phelps, Room 7313, 482–4648, fax 482–3361.
Civil Rights.—Tinisha Agramonte, Room 6058, 482–4535, fax 482–3364.
Human Resources Management.—Kevin Mahoney, Room 5003, 482–4807, fax 482–0249.
Program Evaluation and Risk Management.—Vacant, Room 5327, 482–3707, fax 482–1423.
Security.—Tom Predmore, Room 1069, 482–4371, fax 501–6355.

CHIEF INFORMATION OFFICER

Chief Information Officer.—Steve Cooper, Room 5029B (202) 482–4797.
Deputy Chief Information Officer.—Izella Dornell, Room 5027.
Office of:
IT Policy and Planning, Deputy Chief Information Officer and Chief Technology Officer.—Kirit Amin, Room 6612, 482–4444.
IT Security, Infrastructure and Technology, Chief Information Security Officer.—Rod Turk, Room 6895, 482–4708.
Networking and Telecommunications Operations.—Ricardo Farraj-Feijoo, Room 6625, 482–4444.

INSPECTOR GENERAL

Inspector General.—Peggy E. Gustafson, Room 7898C (202) 482–4661.
Deputy Inspector General.—Allen R. Crawley, Jr., Room 7898C, 482–4661.
Counsel to the Inspector General.—Wade Green, Room 7896, 482–5992.
Principal Assistant Inspector General for Audit.—Mark Zabarsky, Room 7099C, 482–3884.
Assistant Inspector General, Office of Investigations.—Mark Greenblatt, Room 7886B, 482–0300.

ECONOMICS AND STATISTICS ADMINISTRATION

1401 Constitution Avenue, NW., 20230, phone (202) 482–6607

Under Secretary for Economic Affairs.—Karen Dunn Kelley, Room 4848 (202) 482–3727.
Deputy Under Secretary for Economic Affairs.—Brad Burke, Room 4850, 482–3038.
Chief Counsel.—Barry Robinson, Room 4877, 482–5394.
Chief Economist.—Vacant, Room 4860, 482–3523.
Deputy Chief Economist.—Robert Rubinovitz, Room 4861, 482–4871.
Chief Financial Officer.—Jeremy Pelter, Room 4843, 482–6117.
Director of External Affairs.—Raul Cisneros, Room 4838, 482–3331.

BUREAU OF ECONOMIC ANALYSIS

4600 Silver Hill Road, Washington, DC 20230, phone (301) 278–9004

Director.—Brian Moyer, Room 8K405A, 278–9600.
Deputy Director.—Sally Thompson, Room 8K403, 278–9602.
Chief Economist.—Dennis Fixler, Room 8K417, 278–9607.
Chief Information Officer.—Brian Callahan, Room 8K126, 278–9332.
Associate Director for—
Industry Economics.—Erich Strassner, Room 6K406, 278–9612.
International Economics.—Paul Farello, Room 7K102, 278–9561.
National Economic Accounts.—Sally Thompson (acting), Room 8K403, 278–9602.
Regional Economics.—Joel Platt, Room 7K408, 278–9605.
Chief Administrative Officer.—Kathleen James, Room 8K102, 278–9014.
Division Chiefs:
Administrative Services.—Spence Burton, Room 8K104, 278–9043.
Balance of Payments.—Paul Farello (acting), Room 7K102, 278–9561.
Communications.—H. Lucas Hitt, Room 8K122, 278–9223.

Direct Investment Division.—Patricia Abaroa, Room 7K136, 278–9591.
Government.—Pamela Kelly, Room K136, 278–9781.
Industry Applications Division.—Tom Howells, Room 6K411, 278–9586.
Industry Sector Division.—Ted Morgan, Room 6K403B, 278–9541.
National Income and Wealth.—David Wasshausen, Room 6K108, 278–9752.
Regional Income Division.—Mauricio Ortiz, Room 7K411, 278–9269.
Regional Product Division.—Ledia Guci, Room 7K207, 278–9788.

THE BUREAU OF THE CENSUS

4600 Silver Hill Road, Suitland, MD 20746

Director.—John H. Thompson, Room 8H002 (301) 763–2135.
Deputy Director and Chief Operating Officer.—Vacant, Room 8H006, 763–2138.
Associate Director for—
Chief Administrative Officer.—David R. Ziaya, Room 8H140, 763–7924.
Chief Financial Officer.—Joanne Buenzli Crane, Room 8H128, 763–3652.
Performance Improvement.—Ted A. Johnson, Room 8H144, 763–3464.
Communications.—Stephen L. Buckner (acting), Room 8H140, 763–4644.
Decennial Census Programs.—Lisa M. Blumerman, Room 8H122, 763–8050.
Demographic Programs.—Enrique Lamas, Room 8H134, 763–2160.
Economic Programs.—Ron S. Jarmin, Room 8K132, 763–1858.
Field Operations.—Timothy P. Olson, Room 8H126, 763–2072.
Information Technology and CIO.—Kevin B. Smith, Room 8H138, 763–2117.
Office of Strategic Planning, Innovation and Collaboration.—Laura K. Furgione, Room 8H116C, 763–0264.
Research and Methodology.—John M. Abowd, Room 8H120, 763–5880.
Assistant Director for—
Communications.—Stephen L. Buckner, Room 8H062, 763–3586.
Decennial Census Programs.—Vacant, Room 2K276, 763–8050.
Demographic Programs.—Eloise K. Parker, Room 8H182, 763–1679.
Information Technology and Deputy Chief Information.—Vacant, Room 4K030, 763–4037.
Economic Programs.—Nick Orsini, Room 7K154, 763–6959.
Field Division.—Albert E. Fontenote, Room 5H128, 763–4668.
Research and Methodology.—John L. Eltinge, Room 5K156, 763–9604.
Division and Office Chief for—
Acquisition.—Michael L. Palensky, Room 3J438, 763–1818.
Administrative and Customer Services.—Vincent R. Gordon, Room 3J436, 763–4691.
American Community Survey Office.—Victoria A. Velkoff, Room 4K276, 763–1372.
Applications Development and Services Division.—David J. Peters, Room 3H174, 763–9359.
Budget.—Everett G. Whiteley, Room 2K122, 763–3861.
Center for Adaptive Design.—Michael T. Thieme, Room 5K030, 763–9062.
Center for Administrative Records Research and Applications.—Amy O'Hara, Room 6H103, 763–5757.
Center for Disclosure Avoidance Research.—Dr. Simson Garfinkel, Room 5K141, 763–5361.
Center for Economic Studies.—Lucia S. Foster, Room 2K0324, 763–6444.
Customer Liaison and Marketing Services Office.—Jeffrey Meisel (acting), Room 8H173 (512) 299–3139.
Center for New Media and Promotions.—Raul Cisneros, Room 8H484, 763–5204.
Center for Statistical Research and Methodology.—Tommy Wright, Room 5K108, 763–1702.
Center for Survey Measurement.—Paul C. Beatty, Room 5K418, 763–5001.
Computer Services Division.—Kenneth R. Boyd, Bowie, 763–4341.
Chief Technology Office.—Dr. Nitin S. Naik, Room 3H162, 763–2398.
Decennial Census Management Division.—Deborah M. Stempowski, Room 2H174, 763–1417.
Decennial Contracts Execution Office.—Luis J. Cano, Greenbelt, 763–3968.
Decennial Information Technology Division.—Atri Kalluri, Room 4H128, 763–9007.
Decennial Statistical Studies Division.—Patrick Cantwell, Room 4K276, 763–4982.
Demographic Surveys Division.—Berry F. Sessamen, Room 7H128, 763–3773.
Demographic Statistical Methods Division.—James B. Treat, Room 7H162, 763–3609.
Equal Employment Opportunity Office.—Joseph E. Hairston, Room 3K221, 763–9002.
Economic Applications Division.—Samuel C. Jones, Room 6K062, 763–2265.
Economic Indicators Division.—Stephanie I. Studds, Room 7K154, 763–2633.
Economic Management Division.—Lisa Endy Donaldson, Room 6K064, 763–7296.

Economic Reimbursable Surveys Division.—Kevin E. Deardorff, Room 6H128, 763–6033.
Economic Statistical Methods Division.—Carol V. Caldwell, Room 5H174,763–390.
Economy Wide Statistics Division.—Kimberly P. Moore, Room 8K154, 763–7643.
Field Division.—Albert E. Fontenote, Room 5H128, 763–4668.
Finance Division.—Sandi Walters (acting), Room 2K106, 763–9398.
Geography Division.—Deirdre Dalpiaz Bishop, Room 4H174, 763–1696.
Human Resources Division.—Vonda K. Bell, Room 2J436, 763–3721.
Information Systems Support and Review Office.—Teresa S. Sabol, Room 3K138, 763–6846.
International Trade Management Division.—Dale Kelly, Room 5K158, 763–6937.
LAN Technology Support Office.—Patricia T. Musselman, Room 4K108, 763–5632.
National Processing Center.—David E. Hackbarth (812) 218–3344.
Office of Congressional and Intergovernmental Affairs.—Vacant, Room 8H166, 763–6100.
Office of Cost Estimation, Analysis and Assessment.—Kevin G. Metcalf, Room 8H151, 763–6318.
Office of Information Security.—Jeffrey W. Jackson, Room 5K124, 763–5032.
Office of Risk Management and Program Evaluation.—Douglas Clift, Room 2K124, 763–5499.
Policy Coordination Office.—Robin J. Bachman, Room 8H028, 763–1302.
Public Information Office.—Michael C. Cook, Room 8H065, 763–4083.
Population Division.—Karen Battle, Room 6H174, 763–2071.
Security Office.—Harold L. Washington, Jr., Room 3J438, 763–1716.
Social, Economic, and Housing Statistics.—David G. Waddington, Room 7H174, 763–3195.
Telecommunications Office.—Kenneth R. Harrison, Room 4K032, 763–1793.

BUREAU OF INDUSTRY AND SECURITY

Under Secretary.—Mira Radielovic Ricardel, Room 3898B (202) 482–1455.
Deputy Under Secretary.—Daniel O. Hill, Room 3894, 482–1427.
Chief Counsel.—John Masterson, Room 3839, 482–2315.
Office of Congressional and Public Affairs.—Vacant, Room 3895, 482–0097.
Director, Office of Administration.—Carol Rose, Room 6622, 482–1900.
Chief Information Officer.—Roger Clark, Room 6092, 482–4296.
Assistant Secretary for Export Administration.—Vacant, Room 3886C, 482–5491.
Deputy Assistant Secretary.—Matthew Borman, Room 3886C, 482–5711.
Operating Committee Chair.—MiYong Kim, Room 3889, 482–5863 / 5864.
End-User Review Committee Chair.—Joseph Cristofaro, Room 2625, 482–5991.
Office of:
Exporter Services.—Karen Nies-Vogel, Room 1093, 482–0436.
National Security and Technology Transfer Controls.—Eileen M. Albanese, Room 2616, 482–0092.
Nonproliferation and Treaty Compliance.—Alexander Lopes, Room 2627, 482–3825.
Strategic Industries and Economic Security.—Michael Vaccaro, Room 3878, 482–4506.
Technology Evaluation.—Gerard Horner, Room 1093, 482–2078.
Assistant Secretary for Export Enforcement.—Vacant, Room 3723, 482–3618.
Deputy Assistant Secretary.—Richard Majauskas, Room 3723, 482–3618.
Office of:
Antiboycott Compliance.—Cathleen Ryan, Room 6098, 482–2381.
Enforcement Analysis.—Kevin Kurland, Room 4065, 482–4255.
Export Enforcement.—Douglas Hassebrock, Room 4508, 482–5079.

ECONOMIC DEVELOPMENT ADMINISTRATION

Assistant Secretary.—Vacant, Room 78006 (202) 482–5081.
Deputy Assistant Secretary for—
EDA and Chief Operating Officer.—Vacant, Room 78006, 482–5081.
Regional Affairs.—Dennis Alvord, Room 71030, 482–5081.
Chief Counsel.—Stephen Kong, Room 72023, 482–4687.
Chief Financial Officer and Chief Administrative Officer.—Gregory Brown, Room 70025, 482–5892.
Director, Office of:
Budget and Finance Division.—Robert White, Room 70023, 482–0547.
External Affairs.—Vacant, Room 71004, 482–2900.
Innovation and Entrepreneurship.—Vacant, Room 78018, 482–8001.

Legislative Affairs.—Angela Ewell-Madison, Room 71019, 482–2900.
Public Affairs.—Vacant, Room 71004, 482–4085.
Performance and National Programs.—Bryan Borlik, Room 71030, 482–4122.

INTERNATIONAL TRADE ADMINISTRATION

Under Secretary.—Gilbert B. Kaplan, Room 3850 (202) 482–2867.
Deputy Under Secretary.—Ken Hyatt, Room 3842, 482–3917.
Chief of Staff.—Jannine Versi, Room 3850, 482–2867.
Legislative and Intergovernmental Affairs.—Arun V, Room 3424, 482–3015.
Public Affairs.—Mary Trupo, Room 3416, 482–3809.
Chief Counsel for International Commerce.—John Cobau, Room 5624, 482–0937.

ADMINISTRATION

Director and Chief Financial Officer.—Tim Rosado, Room 3827 (202) 482–5855.
Deputy Chief Administrative Officer.—Kurt Bersani, Room 41012, 482–8026.
Office of Financial Management and Administrative Oversight.—Anne McDonagh, Room 41018, 482–2136.
Chief Information Officer.—Joe Paiva, Room 4800, 482–3801.
Management and Operations.—Victor E. Powers, Suite 40001R, 482–5436.
Strategic Resources.—Blanche Ziv, Room 41017, 482–3302.
Office of Budget.—Michael House, Room 41028, 482–5739.

GLOBAL MARKETS AND U.S. AND FOREIGN COMMERCIAL SERVICE

Assistant Secretary for Global Markets and Director General of the U.S. and Foreign Commercial Service.—Elizabeth Erin Walsh, Room 38006 (202) 482–5777.
Deputy Director General.—Judy Reinke, HCH 38006, 482–5777.
Deputy Assistant Secretary for Domestic Operations.—Antwaun Griffin, RRB STE 800–M, 482–4767.
Regional Director, Office of:
Africa, Near East and South Asia.—Janice Corbett, HCH 200–A, 482–1209.
East Asia and Pacific.—Dan Harris, HCH 31018, 482–0423.
Europe.—Danny Devito, HCH 200–A, 482–5402.
National Field.—Dan O'Brien, RRB STE 800–M, 482–2732.
Western Hemisphere.—John Andersen, RMC 300, 482–3484.
Director, Office of:
Advocacy Center.—Jennifer Pilat, HCH 3814–A, 482–3896.
Budget.—Barbara Gilchrist, HCH 21010, 482–0823.
Business Information Technology.—Stanley Ed Howard, 482–3861.
Foreign Service Human Capital.—Joseph Jackson, HCH 1842, 482–4939.
Office of Administrative Services.—Jerome Holloway, 482–1594.
Global Knowledge Center.—Anand Basu, RRB STE 800–M, 482–1489.
Trade Promotion Coordinating Committee.—Pat Kirwan, HCH 31027, 482–5455.
SelectUSA.—Vinay Thummalapally, HCHB 1235, 482–1889.
Strategic Planning and Resource Management.—Debra Delay, HCH 21022, 482–8003.

ASSISTANT SECRETARY FOR ENFORCEMENT AND COMPLIANCE

Assistant Secretary.—Paul Piquado, Room 3099B (202) 482–1780.
Deputy Assistant Secretary.—Ronald Lorentzen, Room 3705, 482–2104.
Chief Counsel.—John D. McInerney, Room 3622, 482–5589.
Director for—
Office of Accounting.—Neal Halper, Room 3087B, 482–2210.
Office of Policy.—Carole Showers, Room 3713, 482–4412.
Executive Secretary for Foreign Trade Zones Board.—Andrew McGilvray, Room 21013, 482–2862.
Deputy Assistant Secretary for—
Antidumping Countervailing Duty Operations.—Christian Marsh, Room 3095, 482–5497.
Antidumping Countervailing Duty Policy and Negotiations.—Lynn Fischer Fox, Room 3089, 482–6199.
Textiles and Apparel.—Josh Teitelbaum, Room 30003, 482–3737.

ASSISTANT SECRETARY FOR INDUSTRY AND ANALYSIS

Assistant Secretary.—Marcus Jadotte, Room 3832 (202) 482–1461.
Deputy Assistant Secretary.—Maureen Smith, Room 3832.
Deputy Assistant Secretary for Industry Analysis.—Praveen Dixit, Room 21028, 482–3177.
Director, Office of:
Advisory Committees.—Shannon Roche, Room 4043 (202) 482–4501.
Energy and Environmental Industries.—Adam O'Malley, Room 4055, 482–4850.
Manufacturing.—Chandra Brown, Room 28004, 482–1872.
Planning, Coordination and Management.—J. Slade Broom, Room 4324 (202) 482–4921.
Technology and Electronic Commerce.—Robin Roark (acting), Room 28008R, 482–3090.
Trade and Economic Analysis.—Joseph Flynn, Room 7025R, 482–1606.
Trade Industry Information.—Wassel Mashagbeh, Room A211, 482–4691.
Trade Policy Analysis.—Jean Janicke, Room C126, 482–5947.
Trade Programs and Strategic Partnerships.—Anne Grey (acting), 482–5927.
Director, National Travel and Tourism Office.—Kelly Craigshead, 482–4931.
Deputy Assistant Secretary for Services.—Ted Dean, Room 1128, 482–5261.

PRESIDENT'S EXPORT COUNCIL

[Authorized by Executive Orders 12131, 12534, 12551, 12610, 12692, 12774, 12869, and 12974 (May through September 1995)]

Executive Director, Under Secretary of International Trade.—Francisco Sanchez, Room 3850 (202) 482–1124.
Executive Secretary and Staff Director.—Tricia Van Orden, Room 4043.

MINORITY BUSINESS DEVELOPMENT AGENCY

National Director.—Christopher Garcia (acting), Room 5053 (202) 482–2332.
National Deputy Director.—Christopher Garcia, Room 5053, 482–2332.
Chief Counsel.—Josephine Arnold, Room 5093, 482–5461.
Associate Director for Business Development.—Efrain Gonzalez, Room 5079, 482–1940.
Chief for Business Development.—Joann Hill, Room 5079, 482–1940.
Associate Director for Legislative, Education and Intergovernmental Affairs.—Vacant.
Chief of Legislative, Education and Intergovernmental Affairs.—Bridget Gonzales, Room 5089, 482–6272.
Public Affairs Supervisor.—Velicia Woods, Room 5089, 482–6272.
Associate Director for Management.—Edith McCloud, Room 5082, 482–2332.
Chief Financial Officer.—Tania White (acting), Room 5606, 482–1631.

NATIONAL OCEANIC AND ATMOSPHERIC ADMINISTRATION

Under Secretary of Commerce for Oceans and Atmosphere.—RDML Timothy Gallaudet, Ph.D., USN (Ret.), (acting), Room 51030 (202) 482–3436.
Assistant Secretary for Conservation and Management/Deputy Administrator.—Dr. Paul Doremus (acting), Room 51027, 482–6255.
Assistant Secretary for Environmental Observation and Prediction/Deputy Administrator.—Dr. Stephen M. Volz (acting).
Chief Scientist.—Craig McLean (acting), Room 51207, 482–5688.
Deputy Under Secretary for Operations.—Benjamin Friedman, Room 58014, 482–4569.
Chief of Staff.—Ellen Clark, Room 58014, 482–4569.
Deputy Assistant Secretary for International Fisheries.—Sam Rauch (acting), Room 61013, 482–5682.
Senior Advisor for International Affairs.—Elizabeth McLanahan, Room 68029, 482–6196.
Director, Office of:
Communications and External Affairs.—Julie Roberts, 482–6090.
Education.—Louisa Koch, Room 6869, 482–3384.
Federal Coordinator for Meteorology.—William Schulz, SSMC2, Room 7130 (301) 628–0112.
General Counsels: Jeff Dillen (acting); Kristen Gustafson (acting), Room 78032, 482–4080.
Legislative and Intergovernmental Affairs.—Robert Moller (acting), Room 62008, 482–4981.

Marine and Aviation Operations.—RADM David Score, 8403 Colesville Road, Suite 500, Silver Spring, MD 20910 (301) 713–7600.
Chief Financial Officer.—Mark Seller, Room D200, 482–0917.
Chief Administrative Officer.—Edward Horton, SSMC4, Room 8431 (301) 713–0836, ext. 105.
Chief Information Officer/High Performance Computing and Communications.—Zachary Goldstein, SSMC3, Room 9651 (301) 713–9600.
Acquisition and Grants.—Jeffrey Thomas (acting), SSMC1, Room 6300 (301) 713–0325.
Decision Coordination and Executive Secretariat.—Kelly Quickle, Room 48026, 482–2985.
Workforce Management.—Kimberlyn Bauhs, SSMC4, Room 12520 (301) 713–6300.

NATIONAL MARINE FISHERIES SERVICE

1315 East-West Highway, Silver Spring, MD 20910

Assistant Administrator.—Chris Oliver, Room 14636 (301) 427–8000.
Deputy Assistant Administrator for—
Operations.—Brian Pawlak (acting), Room 14743, 427–8000.
Regulatory Programs.—Samuel Rauch, Room 14657, 427–8000.
Director, Office of:
Habitat Conservation.—Pat Montanio, Room 14828, 427–8600.
International Affairs and Seafood Inspection.—John Henderschedt, Room 12659, 427–8350.
Law Enforcement.—Jim Landon, Room 415, 427–2300.
Management and Budget.—Stuart Merrill, Room 14450, 427–8720.
Protected Resources.—Donna Wieting, Room 13821, 427–8400.
Science and Technology.—Ned Cyr, Ph.D., Room 12450, 427–8100.
Scientific Programs and Chief Science Advisor.—Francisco Werner, Ph.D, Room 14659, 427–8000.
Sustainable Fisheries.—Alan Risenhoover, Room 13362, 427–8500.
Chief Information Officer.—Nancy Majower (acting), Room 3657, 427–8800.
Aquaculture Program.—Michael Rubino, Room 13117, 427–8325.
Policy.—Jennifer Lukens, Room 14451, 427–8004.

NATIONAL OCEAN SERVICE

Assistant Administrator.—Russell Callender, Room 13632 (301) 713–3074.
Deputy Assistant Administrator.—Nicole LeBoeuf, Room 13635, 713–3074.
Director, Center for Operational Oceanographic Products and Services.—Richard Edwing, Room 6650, 713–2981.
Deputy Director.—Marian Westley, Room 6633, 713–2981.
Management and Budget.—Donna Rivelli (acting), Room 13442, 713–3056.
Director, Office of:
Coast Survey.—RADM Shep Smith, Room 6147, 713–2770.
Coastal Management.—Jeff Payne, Room 10413, 713–3155.
National Centers for Coastal Ocean Science.—Steve Thur, Room 8211, 713–3020.
National Geodetic Survey.—Juliana Blackwell, Room 8657, 713–3222.
National Marine Sanctuaries.—John Armor, Room 11523, 713–7235.
Response and Restoration.—Dave Westerholm, Room 10102, 713–2989.

NATIONAL ENVIRONMENTAL SATELLITE, DATA, AND INFORMATION SERVICE

1335 East-West Highway, Silver Spring, MD 20910

Assistant Administrator.—Stephen M. Volz, Room 8268 (301) 713–3578.
Deputy Assistant Administrator.—Mark Paese, Room 8300, 713–2010.
Deputy Assistant Administrator, Systems.—Vacant.
Chief Information Officer.—Irene Parker, Room 7103, 713–9220.
Chief Financial Officer.—Cherish Johnson, Room 8338, 713–9476.
Deputy Chief Financial Officer.—James Donnellon, Room 8340, 713–9228.
International and Interagency Affairs Chief.—Charles Wooldridge, Room 7315, 713–2024.
Office of System Architecture and Advanced Planning.—Karen St German, Room 5410, 713–7342.
Director, Office of:
Commercial Remote Sensing Regulatory Affairs.—Tahara Dawkins, Room 8260, 713–3385.

GOES–R Program.—Mark Stringer (acting), NASA GSFC, Room C100D, 286–1355.
Joint Polar Satellite System.—Greg Mandt, Room 3301, 713–4782.
National Center for Environmental Information.—Mary Wohlgemuth, Room 557–C (828) 271–4476.
Satellite and Product Operations.—Vanessa Griffin, NSOF, Room 1605, 817–4000.
Satellite Applications and Research.—Harry Cikanek, Room 701, 763–8127.
Satellite Ground Services.—Steven Petersen, SS3 Room 4117, 713–7111.
Space Commercialization.—Mark Paese (acting), Room 8300, 713–2010.
Systems Development.—Dr. Karen St German, Room 6234, 713–0100.

NATIONAL WEATHER SERVICE

1325 East-West Highway, Silver Spring, MD 20910

Assistant Administrator.—Louis W. Uccellini, Room 18150 (301) 713–9095.
Deputy Assistant Administrator.—Mary C. Erickson, Room 18130, 713–0711.
Chief Financial Officer.—John Potts, Room 18176 (301) 427–6911.
Deputy Chief Financial Officer.—Marie Lovern, Room 18212, 427–6914.
Assistant Chief Information Officer for Weather.—Richard Varn, Room 17424, 427–9018.
Director, Office of:
Climate, Water, and Weather Services.—Andrew Stern, Room 14348, 427–9120.
Hydrologic Development.—Thomas Graziano, Room 8176, 427–9522.
National Centers for Environmental Prediction.—William Lapenta, Room 101 (301) 683–1315.
Operational Systems.—Joseph Pica, Room 16212, 427–9183.
Science and Technology.—Ming Ji, Room 15146, 427–9119.

OCEANIC AND ATMOSPHERIC RESEARCH

1315 East-West Highway, Silver Spring, MD 20910

Assistant Administrator.—Craig McLean (301) 713–2458.
Deputy Assistant Administrator for—
Labs and Cooperative Institutes.—Vacant.
Programs and Administration.—Ko Barrett, 734–1167.
Chief Science Advisor.—Dr. Cynthia Decker, 734–1156.
Director of:
Air Resources Laboratory.—Vacant.
Atlantic Oceanographic and Meteorological Laboratory.—Dr. Robert Atlas (305) 361–4300.
Earth System Research Laboratory.—Alexander MacDonald, Ph.D. (303) 497–6005.
Division of:
Chemical Sciences.—David Fahey, Ph.D. (303) 497–5277.
Global Monitoring.—James Butler, Ph.D. (303) 497–6898.
Global Systems.—Kevin Kelleher (303) 497–4104.
Physical Science.—Robert Webb, Ph.D. (303) 497–5942.
Geophysical Fluid Dynamics Laboratory.—Venkatachalam Ramaswamy, Ph.D. (609) 452–6510.
Great Lakes Environmental Research Laboratory.—Deborah H. Lee (734) 741–2245.
National Severe Storms Laboratory.—Steve Koch, Ph.D. (405) 325–6800.
Pacific Marine Environmental Laboratory.—Chris Sabine, Ph.D. (206) 526–6810.
Director, Office of:
Climate Program.—Wayne Higgins, Ph.D. (301) 427–1263.
Ocean Acidification.—Libby Jewett, Ph.D. (301) 734–1075.
Oceanic Exploration and Research.—Alan Leonardi, Ph.D. (301) 734–1016.
National Sea Grant College Program.—Jonathan Pennock, Ph.D. (301) 734–1089.
Weather and Air Quality.—John Cortinas, Ph.D. (301) 734–1198.

PROGRAM PLANNING AND INTEGRATION

Director.—Patricia Montanio, Room 15628 (240) 533–9012.
Deputy Director.—Paul Hirschberg, Room 15629, 533–9017.

UNITED STATES PATENT AND TRADEMARK OFFICE

P.O. Box 1450, 600 Dulany Street, Arlington, VA 22313–1450

Phone (571) 272–8600

Under Secretary of Commerce for Intellectual Property and Director of the U.S. Patent and Trademark Office.—Andrei Iancu.

Deputy Under Secretary of Commerce for Intellectual Property and Deputy Director of the U.S. Patent and Trademark Office.—Russell Slifer.

Chief of Staff.—Andrew Byrnes (571) 272–8600.

Deputy Chief of Staff.—Vikrum Aiyer, 272–8600

Chief Communications Officer.—Todd Elmer, 272–3500.

Chief Administrative Patent Judge, Board of Patent Appeals and Interferences.—James Donald Smith, 272–9797.

Deputy Chief Administrative Patent Judge.—Nate Kelly, 272–9797.

Chief Administrative Trademark Judge, Trademark Trial and Appeal Board.—Gerard Rogers, 272–8500.

Director, Office of Enrollment and Discipline.—William Covey, 272–4097.

COMMISSIONER FOR PATENTS

Commissioner.—Andrew Faile (acting), (571) 272–8800.

Deputy Commissioner for—

International Patent Cooperation.—Mark Powell.

Patent Administration.—Bruce Kisliuk.

Patent Examination Policy.—Andrew Hirshfeld.

Patent Operations.—Robert Oberleitner (acting).

Patent Quality.—Valencia Martin Wallace.

Associate Commissioner for—

Innovation Development.—Anthony Knight (acting).

Patent Examination Policy.—Janet Gongola.

Patent Information Management.—Deborah Stephens.

Patent Resources and Planning.—Vacant.

Director, Office of:

Patent Cooperation Treaty Legal Administration.—Charles A. Pearson, 272–3224.

Patent Legal Administration.—Brian Hanlon, 272–7735.

Assistant Deputy Commissioner for Patent Operations:

Chemical and Design Discipline.—Jacqueline Stone (TC 1600, 1700, and 2900).

Electrical and Mechanical Discipline.—Remy Yucel (TC 2100 and 3700).

Electrical Discipline and Patent Examination Support Services (OPESS).—Don Hajec (TC 2800 and Patent Examination Support Services (OPESS)).

Electrical Discipline and Central Re-Exam Unit (CRU).—Robert Oberleitner (TC 2400 and Central Re-Exam Unit).

Electrical and Mechanical Discipline.—Richard Seidel (TC 2600 and TC 3600).

Patent Examining Group Directors:

Technology Center 1600 (biotechnology and organic chemistry): Jerry Lorengo, 272–0600; Wanda Walker, 272–0500, 272–7600.

Technology Center 1700 (chemical and materials engineering): Yvonne Eyler, 272–1200; Karen Young, 272–1100; Gladys Corcoran, 272–1300.

Technology Center 2100 (computer architecture and software): Wendy Garber, 272–1400; Seema Rao, 272–0800; David Talbott, 272–4150.

Technology Center 2400 (networking, multiplexing, cable, and security): Timothy Callahan, 272–4066; Nancy Le, 272–4056; Nestor Ramirez, 272–3174.

Technology Center 2600 (communications): Derris Banks, 272–4750; Tariq Hafiz, 272–4550; John LeGuyader, 272–4650; David Wiley, 272–4750.

Technology Center 2800 (semiconductor, electrical, mechanical and physics/optical systems and components): James Kramer, 272–1850; Jack Harvey, 272–1850; Joseph Thomas, 272–1550; Robyn Evans, 272–1850.

Technology Center 2900 (Designs).—Robert Olszewski, 272–2200.

Technology Center 3600 (transportation, construction, electronic commerce, agriculture, national security, and license and review): Greg Vidovich, 272–5350; Katherine Matecki, 272–5250; Edward Lefkowitz, 272–5150; Rada Rinaldi, 272–5050.

Technology Center 3700 (mechanical engineering, manufacturing, and products): Dmitry Suhol (acting), 272–2975; Angela Sykes, 272–4390; Andrew Wang, 272–3750; Diego Gutierrez, 272–3680.

Technology Center 3900 (Central Reexamination Unit).—Steve Stein (acting), 272–1544.

Technology Center 4100 (Patent Training).—Gary Jones, 272–8320.
Director, Office of:
Central Reexamination Unit.—Steve Stein (acting), 272–1544.
Classification Quality and International Solutions.—Chris Kim, 272–7980.
Classification Standards and Development.—John Salotto (acting),
Data Management (PUBS).—Thomas Koontz (703) 756–1492.
International Patent Business Solutions.—Don Levin, 272–3785(703) 756–1850.
International Patent Legal Administration.—Charles Pearson, 272–3224.
Patent Application Processing.—Kevin Little (703) 756–1489.
Patent Financial Management.—John Buie, 272–6283.
Patent Information Resources (OPIR).—Sandra Bigsby (703) 756–1489.
Patent Legal Administration.—Brian Hanlon, 272–7735.
Patent Quality Assurance.—Anthony Caputa, 272–5021.
Patent Training Academy.—Gary Jones, 272–8320.
Petitions.—John Cottingham (acting), 272–3282.
Work Sharing Planning and Implementation.—Dan Hunter (acting), 272–8050.
Director, Satellite Offices:
Denver.—Robin Evans (acting), (303) 297–2026.
Detroit.—Christal Sheppard, (313) 446–4886.
Silicon Valley.—John Cabeca (571) 272–3100.

COMMISSIONER FOR TRADEMARKS

Commissioner.—Mary Boney Denison (571) 272–8901.
Deputy Commissioner for Trademark Operations.—Meryl Hershkowitz, 272–8901.
Group Director, Trademark Law Offices:
Tomas Vleek (571) 272–8901
Dan Vanonese (acting), 272–9288.
Chris Doninger (acting), 272–9297.
Trademark Examination Law Office Managing Attorneys:
Law Office 101.—Ron Sussman, 272–9696.
Law Office 102.—Mitchell Front, 272–9382.
Law Office 103.—Michael Hamilton, 272–9278.
Law Office 104.—Dayna Brown (acting), 272–836.
Law Office 105.—Susan Hayash, 272–9692.
Law Office 106.—Mary Sparrow, 272–9332.
Law Office 107.—Leslie Bishop, 272–9445.
Law Office 108.—Andrew Lawrence, 272–9342.
Law Office 109.—Michael Kazazian (acting), 272–9434.
Law Office 110.—Chris Pedersen, 272–9371.
Law Office 111.—Robert Lorenzo, 272–9387.
Law Office 112.—Angela Wilson, 272–9443.
Law Office 113.—Odette Bonnet, 272–9426.
Law Office 114.—Margaret Le, 272–9456.
Law Office 115.—John Lincoski, 272–9436.
Law Office 116.—Christine Cooper, 272–9844.
Law Office 117.—Hellen Bryan-Johnson, 272–9446.
Virtual Law Office—Pilot Sometime in January 2014:
Law Office 118.—Tomas Howell, 272–9302.
Law Office 119.—Brett Golden, 272–9257.
Law Office 120.—Michael Baird, 272–9487.
Director, Office of Trademark Program Control.—Betty Andrews, 272–9666.
Deputy Commissioner for Trademark Examination Policy.—Sharon Marsh, 272–8901.
Director, Office of Trademark Quality Review.—Kevin Peska, 272–9658.

POLICY AND EXTERNAL AFFAIRS

Chief Policy Officer and Director for International Affairs.—Shira Perlmutter.
Deputy Chief Policy Officer for Operations.—George Elliott, 272–9300.
Director, Office of:
Copyright.—Michael Shapiro, 272–9300.
Enforcement.—Michael Smith, 272–9300.
Governmental Affairs.—Dana Colarulli, 272–7300.
International Trade.—Paul Salmon, 272–9300.
Patents.—Chuck Eloshway, 272–9300.

Trademarks.—Amy Cotton, 272–9300.
Director of Global Intellectual Property Academy.—Rachel Wallace, 272–1500.

CHIEF FINANCIAL OFFICER

Chief Financial Officer.—Anthony Scardino (571) 272–9200.
Deputy Chief Financial Officer.—Frank Murphy, 272–9200.
Senior Financial Manager.—Michelle Picard, 272–6354.
Director, Office of Planning and Budget.—Brendan Hourigan, 272–8966.
Finance.—Mark Krieger, 272–6339.
Financial Management Systems.—Gita Zoks, 272–6363.
Procurement.—Scott Palmer, 270–7149.

CHIEF PERFORMANCE IMPROVEMENT OFFICER

Chief Performance Improvement Officer.—Vacant (571) 272–9200.

CHIEF ADMINISTRATIVE OFFICER

Chief Administrative Officer.—Frederick Steckler (571) 272–9600.
Deputy Chief Administrative Officer.—Wynn Coggins, 272–9600.
Director of Administrative Services.—Lisle Hannah (acting), 272–6541.
Human Resources.—Karen Karlinchak, 272–6200.

DIRECTOR OF THE OFFICE OF EQUAL EMPLOYMENT OPPORTUNITY AND DIVERSITY

Director.—Bismarck Myrick (571) 272–6315.

OFFICE OF GENERAL COUNSEL

General Counsel.—Sarah Harris (571) 272–7000.
Deputy General Counsels for—
General Law.—James O. Payne Jr., 272–3000.
Intellectual Property Law and Solicitor.—Nathan Kelley, 272–9035.

CHIEF INFORMATION OFFICER

Chief Information Officer.—John B. Owens II (571) 272–9400.
Deputy Chief Information Officer.—Anthony ''Tony'' Chiles, 272–9410.
Chief of Staff.—John S. Williams, 272–5664.
Director of:
Application Engineering and Development.—Pamela Isom, 272–0341.
Budget and Finance.—Keith M. VanderBrink (571) 272–5662.
Customer Information Services.—Vacant.
Information Management Services.—Rhonda Foltz, 272–6147.
Infrastructure Engineering and Operations.—Robert Cobert, 272–5481.
Organizational Policy and Governance.—Kevin Smith, 272–3200.
Program Administration Organization.—Toby Bennett, 272–6205.
Quality Management.—Brian R. Jones, 272–1659.
Systems Development and Maintenance.—Patsy Riley, 272–3925.
Manager, Office of:
Customer Support Services.—Vacant.
Electronic Information Products.—James Thompson (571) 756–1422.
Enterprise Systems Services.—Carol R. Eakins, 272–5426.
Network and Telecommunications.—Vacant.
Public Information Services.—Ted L. Parr (703) 756–1267.
Public Records Division.—Donna Cooper, 756–1893.

NATIONAL INSTITUTE OF STANDARDS AND TECHNOLOGY

100 Bureau Drive, Gaithersburg, MD 20899 (301) 975–NIST (6478)

Under Secretary for Standards and Technology and NIST Director.—Walter G. Kopan (301) 975–2300.

Associate Director for Laboratory Programs.—Kent Rochford, 975–2300.
Associate Director for Industry and Innovation Services.—Phillip Singerman, 975–2340.
Associate Director for Management Resources.—Del Brockett (acting), 975–5000.
Chief of Staff.—Kevin Kimball, 975–3070.
Congressional and Legislative Affairs Office.—Jim Schufreider, 975–5675.
International and Academic Affairs Office.—Claire M. Saundry, 975–2386.
Program Coordination Office.—Kevin Kimball, 975–3070.
Public Affairs Office.—Gail J. Porter, 975–3392.
Management and Organization Office.—Catherine Fletcher, 975–4054.
Human Subjects Protection Office.—Anne Andrews, 975–5445.
Baldrige Performance Excellence Program.—Robert Fangmeyer, 975–4781.
Hollings Manufacturing Extension Partnership Program.—Carroll Thomas, 975–4676.
Office of Advanced Manufacturing.—Mike Molnar, 975–3673.
NIST Center for Neutron Research.—Robert Dimeo, 975–6210.
Center for Nanoscale Science and Technology.—James Kushmerick (acting), 975–5697.
Material Measurement Laboratory.—Mike Fasolka (acting), 975–8301.
Communications Technology Laboratory.—Derek Orr (acting), (303) 497–5400.
Physical Measurement Laboratory.—Jim Olthoff, 975–2220.
Engineering Laboratory.—Howard Harary, 975-5900.
Information Technology Laboratory.—Charles Romine, 975–2900.
Acquisition and Agreements Management.—Cecelia Royster, 975–6336.
Safety, Health, and Environment.—Richard Kayser, 975–4502.
Financial Resource Management.—George Jenkins, 975–5080.
Human Resources Management.—Susanne Porch, 975–2487.
Information Systems Management.—Susannah Schiller (acting), 975–6500.
Facilities and Property Management.—Skip Vaughn, 975–8832.
Special Programs Office.—Richard Cavanagh, 975–4447.
Standards Coordination Office.—Gordon Gillerman, 975–8406.
Technology Partnerships Office.—Paul Zielinski, 975–4980.
Civil Rights and Diversity Office.—Mirta-Marie M. Keys, 975–2042.
Emergency Services Office.—Mark Spurrier, 975–2660.
Information Services Office.—Mary-Deirdre Coraggio, 975–5158.
Fabrication Technology Office.—Mark Luce, 975–2159.

NATIONAL TECHNICAL INFORMATION SERVICE

5301 Shawnee Road, Alexandria, VA 22312

Director.—Avi Bender (703) 605–6401.

NATIONAL TELECOMMUNICATIONS AND INFORMATION ADMINISTRATION

1401 Constitution Avenue, NW., 20230

Assistant Secretary and Administrator.—David Redl, Room 4898 (202) 482–1840.
Deputy Assistant Secretary.—Vacant, 482–1830.
Chief of Staff.—Glenn Reynolds, 482–1840.
Deputy Chief of Staff and Congressional Affairs Director.—James Wasilewski, 482–1830.
Chief Counsel.—Kathy Smith.
Director, Office of:
Institute for Telecommunication Sciences.—Keith Gremban (303) 497–3500.
International Affairs.—Fiona Alexander.
Policy Analysis and Development.—John B. Morris, Jr.
Public Affairs.—Vacant.
Public Safety Communications.—Marsha MacBride.
Spectrum Management.—Paige R. Atkins.
Telecommunications and Information Applications.—Douglas Kinkoph.

DEPARTMENT OF LABOR

Frances Perkins Building, Third Street and Constitution Avenue, NW., 20210
phone (202) 693–5000, http://www.dol.gov

R. ALEXANDER ACOSTA, Secretary of Labor; education: A.B., Harvard University, 1990; J.D., Harvard Law School, 1994; professional: Law Clerk, U.S. Court of Appeals for the Third Circuit, 1994–95; professor, George Mason University School of Law, 1995–2000; Senior Fellow, Ethics and Public Policy Center, 1998–2000; attorney, Kirkland & Ellis, 1995–2000; Principal Deputy Assistant Attorney General, Civil Rights Division, U.S. Department of Justice, 2001–02; member, National Labor Relations Board, 2002–03; Assistant Attorney General, Civil Rights Division, U.S. Department of Justice, 2003–05; U.S. Attorney for the Southern District of Florida, 2005–09; dean, Florida International University College of Law, 2009–17; chairman, U.S. Century Bank, 2013–17; married: Jan Elizabeth Acosta; nominated by President Donald J. Trump to become the 27th Secretary of Labor, and was confirmed by the U.S. Senate on April 27, 2017.

OFFICE OF THE SECRETARY

phone (202) 693–6000

Secretary of Labor.—R. Alexander Acosta.
Deputy Secretary.—Vacant.
Associate Deputy Secretary.—Nancy Rooney.
Executive Secretariat Director.—Elizabeth Way (acting).
Chief of Staff.—Vacant.
Director of Advance and Scheduling.—Vacant.

OFFICE OF PUBLIC ENGAGEMENT

Director.—Allison Zelman (202) 693–6459.

ADMINISTRATIVE LAW JUDGES

Techworld, 800 K Street, NW., Suite 400, 20001–8002

Chief Administrative Law Judge.—Stephen R. Henley (202) 693–7424.
Associate Chief Judges: Paul Almanza, 693–7344; William S. Colwell, 693–7355.

ADMINISTRATIVE REVIEW BOARD

Chief and Chair.—Paul M. Igasaki, Room N–5404, 693–6200.
Vice Chair.—E. Cooper Brown, Room N–5404, 693–6200.

OFFICE OF THE ASSISTANT SECRETARY FOR ADMINISTRATION AND MANAGEMENT (OASAM)

Assistant Secretary.—Bryan Slater, Room S–2203 (202) 693–4040.
Deputy Assistant Secretary for—
Operations.—Edward C. Hugler, Room S–2203, 693–4040.
Policy.—Vacant, Room S–2203, 693–4040.
Special Assistants: Braye Cloud, Douglas Robins, Traci Smith, 693–4040.
Administrative Officer.—Christopher Yerxa, 693–4040.

BUSINESS OPERATIONS CENTER

Director.—Al Stewart, Room S–1524 (202) 693–4028.

Deputy Director.—Vacant.
Office of:
Acquisition Management Services.—Carl V. Campbell, Room S–1510–C, 693–7246.
Administrative Services.—Phil Puckett, Room S–1521, 693–6650.
Asset and Resource Management.—Tanisha Bynum-Frazier, Room S–1519B, 693–4546.
Procurement Services.—Vacant, Room S–4307, 693–4570.
Small and Disadvantaged Business Utilization.—Gladys Bailey, Room N–6402, 693–7262.
Worker Safety and Health Services.—Stephanie Semmer, Room S–1321, 693–6678.

PERFORMANCE MANAGEMENT CENTER

Director.—Vacant, Room S–3317 (202) 693–7125.
Deputy Director.—Dennis Johnson, Room S–3317, 693–7123.

CIVIL RIGHTS CENTER

Director.—Naomi Barry-Perez, Room N–4123 (202) 693–6500.
Chief of Staff.—Dennis Fish, Room N–4123, 693–6532.
Administrative Officer.—Aquila Branch-James, Room N–4123, 693–6519.
Office of:
Compliance Assistance and Planning.—Roger Ocampo, 693–6562.
Enforcement/External.—Lee Perselay (acting), 693–6519.
Enforcement/Internal.—Samuel Rhames, 693–6500.
Reasonable Accommodation Hotline.—Kim Borowicz, Room N–4123, 693–6527.

EMERGENCY MANAGEMENT CENTER

800 K Street, NW., Suite 450 North, 20001–8002

Director.—Greg Rize (202) 693–7514.
Deputy Director.—Robert Butler, 693–7504.

BENEFITS.GOV

Program Manager.—Al Sloane, Room N–4309 (202) 693–8067.

HUMAN RESOURCES CENTER

Director.—Sydney Rose, Room C–5526 (202) 693–7600.
Deputy Director.—Kim Sasajima, Room C–5526, 693–7600.
Office of:
Administration and Management Services.—Donna Childs Speight, Room C–5517, 693–7773.
Diversity and Inclusion.—Paul Plasencia, Room S–4015, 693–5840.
Employee and Labor Management Relations.—Shawn Hooper, Room N–5476, 693–7612.
Executive Resources.—Lucy Cunningham, Room N–2453, 693–7800.
HRWorks.—Vacant, Room S3314, 693–4324.
Human Resources Consulting and Operations.—Kristin Siegfried, Room C–5516, 693–7690.
Human Resources Policy and Accountability.—Vacant.
Human Resources Systems.—Vacant, Room S–3314, 693–4324.
Training and Development.—Vacant.
Worklife, Leave, Benefits Policy, and Programs.—Maria Jordan, Room N–5454, 693–7610.

OFFICE OF THE CHIEF INFORMATION OFFICER

Chief Information Officer.—Gundeep Ahluwalia, Room N–1301 (202) 693–4200.
Associate Deputy CIO.—Vacant.
Office of:
Advanced Technology.—Vacant.
Applications and Platform as a Service: Vacant, N–1301, 693–4179; Tim Erskine (acting), N–1301, 693–8128.

Customer Advocacy.—Duane Eldridge, Room N–1301, 693–0326.
Information Assurance.—Tonya Manning, Room N–1301, 693–4431.
Infrastructure Services.—Lou Charlier, Room N–1301, 693–4147.
IT Administration.—Cheryle Greenaugh (acting), Room N–1301, 693–4158.
IT Acquisitions.—Jeff Johnson, Room N–1301, 693–4556.
IT Governance.—Vacant, Room N–1301, 693–4211.
IT Policies and Procedures.—Cheryle Greenaugh, Room N–1301, 693–4158.
Systems Engineering: Vacant, Room N–1301, 693–4179; Fred Whiteside (acting), Room N–4416, 693–0440.
Enterprise Service Desk.—24/7, Room N–1505 (855) 522–6748, or EnterpriseServiceDesk @dol.gov.

SECURITY CENTER

Director.—Vacant, Room S–1229G (202) 693–7994.
Deputy Director.—Stacey Thompson, 693–7210.
Staff Assistant.—Dianna Cornish, 693–7991.

ASSISTANT SECRETARY FOR POLICY

Assistant Secretary.—Vacant, Room S–2312 (202) 693–5959.
Deputy Assistant Secretary.—Nathan Mehrens.
Career Deputy Assistant Secretary.—Stephanie Swirsky.
Chief of Staff.—Vacant.
Regulatory and Programmatic Policy.—Laura Dawkins, 693–5072.
Chief Evaluation Officer.—Molly Irwin, Room S–2312, 693–5959.

BENEFITS REVIEW BOARD

Chair.—Betty Jean Hall, Room N5101 (202) 693–6300.

BUREAU OF LABOR STATISTICS

Postal Square Building, Suite 4040, 2 Massachusetts Avenue, NE., 20212

phone (202) 691–7800

Commissioner.—William Wiatrowski (acting), 691–7802.
Deputy Commissioner.—William Wiatrowski.
Associate Commissioner, Office of:
Administration.—Nancy Ruiz de Gamboa, Suite 4060, 691–7777.
Compensation and Working Conditions.—Kristen Monaco, Suite 4130, 691–7527.
Employment and Unemployment Statistics.—Michael Horrigan, Suite 4945, 691–6400.
Field Operations.—Jay Mousa, Suite 2935, 691–5800.
Prices and Living Conditions.—David Friedman, Suite 3120, 691–6960.
Productivity and Technology.—Lucy Eldridge, Suite 2150, 691–6598.
Publications and Special Studies.—Michael Levi, Suite 2850, 691–5100.
Survey Methods Research.—Jennifer Edgar, Suite 5930, 691–7528.
Technology and Survey Processing.—Carol Mullins, Suite 5025, 691–7604.
Assistant Commissioner, Office of:
Compensation Levels and Trends.—Hilery Simpson, Suite 4130, 691–5184.
Current Employment Analysis.—Julie Hatch Maxfield, Suite 4675, 691–5473.
Industrial Prices and Price Indexes.—Jeffrey Hill, Suite 3840, 691–7156.
Industry Employment Statistics.—Kenneth Robertson, Suite 4860, 691–5440.
Occupational Statistics and Employment Projections.—Rebecca Rust, Suite 2135, 691–5701.
Consumer Prices and Price Indexes.—John Layng, Suite 3130, 691–6955.
Director of:
Survey Processing.—Rick Kryger, Suite 5025, 691–7562.
Technology and Computing Services.—Wesley Chou, Suite 5025, 691–7203.

BUREAU OF INTERNATIONAL LABOR AFFAIRS

Deputy Under Secretary.—Vacant, Room S–2235 (202) 693–4770.

Associate Deputy Under Secretaries: Mark Mittelhauser, Room S–2235, 693–4770; Vacant, Room S–2235, 693–4770.
Chief of Staff.—Vacant, Room S–2235, 693–4770.
Administrative Officer.—Deborah Becker, Room S–2235, 693–4845.
Budget and Procurement Analyst.—Bruce Yoon, Room S–2235, 693–4876.
Executive Assistant.—Diane Ward, Room S–2235, 693–4770.
Program and Management Analyst.—Alfreda Johnson, Room S–2235, 693–4773.
Special Assistant.—Kia Gaskins, Room S–2235, 693–4903.

OFFICE OF CHILD LABOR, FORCED LABOR, AND HUMAN TRAFFICKING

Director.—Marcia Eugenio, Room S–5315 (202) 693–4849.
Deputy Director.—Kevin Willcutts, Room S–5317, 693–4832.
Senior Advisor.—Brandie Sasser, Room S–5315, 693–4807.

OFFICE OF TRADE AND LABOR AFFAIRS

Director.—Matthew Levin, Room S–5315 (202) 693–5745.
Deputy Directors: Joshua Kagan, Room S–5315, 693–4883; Katy Mastman, Room S–5315, 693–4800.

OFFICE OF INTERNATIONAL RELATIONS

Director.—Robert B. Shepard, Room S–5315 (202) 693–4808.
Deputy Director.—Zhao Li, Room S–5315, 693–4803.
Chief, Division of Multilateral Issues.—Joan Barrett, Room S–5315, 693–4857.

OFFICE OF ECONOMIC AND LABOR RESEARCH

Director.—Vacant, Room S–5315 (202) 693–4887.
Deputy Director.—Kenneth Swinnerton, Room S–5315, 693–4916.

OFFICE OF THE CHIEF FINANCIAL OFFICER

Principal Deputy Chief Financial Officer.—Geoffrey Kenyon, Room S4020 (202) 693–6800.
Deputy Chief Financial Officer.—Karen Tekleberhan, Room S4030, 693–6800.
Administrative Officer.—Marella Turner, Room S4030.
Operations Support.—Andrew Allen, Room N2719.
E–Travel.—Sheila Alexander, Room N2719.
Financial Reporting.—Jennifer DiGiantommaso, Room S4502.
Central Accounting Operations.—Westley Everette, Room S5526.
Accounts Payable (Vendor Payment).—Natasha Brown, Room S5526.
Associate Deputy CFO.—Kevin Brown, Room N2719.
Security and Technology.—Robert Springfield, Room N2719.
Customer Support.—Sharnell Montgomery, Room N2719.
Audit Liaison.—Neil Starzynski, Room S4030.
Financial Performance and Payment Integrity (A–123 Compliance).—Chris Polen, Room S4030.
Travel/Conference Policy and A–123 Compliance.—Dylan Sacchetti, Room S4030.
Deputy Chief Financial Officer for Budget.—Mark Wichlin (acting), Room S4020.
Deputy Director Budget Officer.—James Martin (acting), Room S4020.
Office of Agency Budget Programs.—Chris Calogero (acting), Room S4020.
Office of Budget Policy and Systems.—Andrew Rider, Room S4020.

OFFICE OF CONGRESSIONAL AND INTERGOVERNMENTAL AFFAIRS

Assistant Secretary.—Katherine McGuire, Room S–2006 (202) 693–4601.
Chief of Staff.—David M Thomas, Room S–2220, 693–4600.
Staff Assistants: Glenda Manning, Room S–2006, 693–4601; Jaunae Young, Room S–2220, 693–4600.
Deputy Assistant Secretary for Congressional and Intergovernmental Affairs.—John Mashburn, Room S–2220, 693–4601.
Director, Intergovernmental Affairs.—Vacant, S–2220, 693–6400.

Deputy Director, Intergovernmental Affairs.—Vacant, S–2220, 693–4600.
Associate Director, Intergovernmental Affairs.—Vacant, Room S–2220, 693–4600.
Administrative Officer.—Tracey Schaeffer (acting), Room S–2220, 693–4600.
Deputy Assistant Secretary, Appropriations/Budget.—Vacant, Room S–2220, 693–4600.
Senior Legislative Assistant, Employee Benefits/COBRA.—Kristin Chapman, Room S–2220, 693–4600.
Senior Legislative Officer, Foreign Labor Certification/Employment and Training.—Byron Anderson, Room S–2220, 693–4600.
Senior Legislative Officer, Wage and Hour Division ILAB/Trade and Labor Affairs/Child Labor.—Kristin Chapman, Room S–2220, 693–4600.
Legislative Officer, International Affairs/Child Labor.—Kristin Chapman, Room S–2220, 693–4600.
Legislative Officer, Mine Safety and Health/Occupational Safety and Health.—Aaron Krejci, Room S–2220, 693–4600.
Legislative Assistant, Labor Management Standards.—Robert Burkett, Room S–2220, 693–4600.
Legislative Officer, Women's Bureau/Veterans' Affairs.—Margarita Almanza, Room S–2220, 693–4600.

SECRETARY'S REPRESENTATIVES IN THE REGIONAL OFFICES

Region II, New York.—Vacant: Connecticut, Delaware, District of Columbia, Georgia, Florida, Maine, Massachusetts, New Hampshire, New Jersey, New York, North Carolina, Pennsylvania, South Carolina, Vermont, Virginia, West Virginia.
Region V, Chicago.—Vacant: Illinois, Indiana, Iowa, Kentucky, Michigan, Minnesota, Missouri, Ohio, Tennessee, Wisconsin.
Region VIII, Denver.—Vacant: Colorado, Kansas, Louisiana, Mississippi, Oklahoma, Texas.
Region IX, San Francisco.—Vacant: Arizona, California, Hawaii, New Mexico, Utah.
Region X, Seattle.—Vacant: Alaska, Idaho, Kansas, Montana, Nebraska, North Dakota, Oregon, South Dakota, Washington, Wyoming.

OFFICE OF DISABILITY EMPLOYMENT POLICY

Assistant Secretary.—Vacant, Room S–1303 (202) 693–7880.
Deputy Assistant Secretary.—Jennifer Sheehy.
Chief of Staff.—Vacant.
Special Assistant.—Elena Brown.
Director of Policy Development.—Vacant.

EMPLOYEE BENEFITS SECURITY ADMINISTRATION

Assistant Secretary.—Preston Rutledge, Room S–2524 (202) 693–8300.
Deputy Assistant Secretary.—Jeanne Klinefelter Wilson, 693–8300.
Special Assistant.—Valerie Gatesman, 693–8312.
Senior Advisor.—Mark Dundee, 693–8305.
Confidential Assistant.—Monique Love.
Deputy Assistant Secretary for Program Operations.—Timothy Hauser, Room N–5677, 693–8315.
Executive Assistant.—Becki Marchand, 693–8315.
Director of:
Enforcement.—Mabel Capolongo, 122 C Street, Suite 600, 693–8440.
Exemption Determinations.—Lyssa Hall, Room N–5649, 693–8540.
Health Plan Standards and Compliance Assistance.—Amy Turner, Room 5653, 693–8335.
Participant Assistance.—Mark Connor, Room N–5625, 693–8630.
Policy and Research.—Joseph Piacentini, Room N–5718, 693–8410.
Program, Planning, Evaluation, and Management.—Joel Lovelace, Room N–5668, 693–8480.
Regulations and Interpretations.—Joseph Canary, Room N–5669, 693–8500.
Technology and Information Services.—Diane Schweizer, Room N–5459, 693–8600.
Chief Accountant.—Ian Dingwall, 122 C Street, Suite 400, 693–8360.

EMPLOYEES' COMPENSATION APPEALS BOARD

Chair.—Christopher James Godfrey, Room N–5416 (202) 693–6374.

EMPLOYMENT AND TRAINING ADMINISTRATION

Assistant Secretary.—Vacant, Room S–2307.
Deputy Assistant Secretaries: Thomas Dowd, Rosemary Lahasky, Nancy Rooney, Room S–2307, 693–2772.
Administrator, Office of—
Apprenticeship.—John Ladd, Room N–5311, 693–3799.
Grants and Management.—Laura P. Watson, Room N–4673, 693–3333.
Contracts Management.—Sandra Foster, Room N–4643, 693–2899.
Financial Administration.—Adrienne E. Young, Room N–4702, 693–3132.
Foreign Labor Certification.—William W. Thompson II, Patriots Plaza II, 513–7350.
Job Corps.—Lenita Jacobs-Simmons, Room N–4463, 693–3000.
Policy Development and Research.—Adele Gagliardi, Room N–5637, 693–3700.
Trade Adjustment Assistance.—Norris Tyler, Room C–5428, 693–3560.
Unemployment Insurance.—Gay Gilbert, Room S–4524, 693–3029.
Workforce Investment.—Amanda Ahlstrand, Room S–4510, 693–3980.
Management and Administrative Services.—Nalini Close, Deputy Administrator, Room N–4653, 693–3001.

DOL CENTER FOR FAITH-BASED AND NEIGHBORHOOD PARTNERSHIPS

Director.—Benjamin Seigel (acting), (202) 693–6032.

OFFICE OF THE INSPECTOR GENERAL

Inspector General.—Scott S. Dahl, Room S–5502 (202) 693–5100.
Deputy Inspector General.—Larry D. Turner, Room S–5502, 693–5100.
Assistant Inspector General for—
Audit.—Elliot P. Lewis, Room S–5512, 693–5170.
Labor Racketeering and Fraud Investigations.—Cheryl Garcia, Room S–5014, 693–7034.
Legal Services.—Delores Thompson, Room S–5506, 693–5116.
Management and Policy.—Thomas Williams, Room S–5028, 693–5191.

MINE SAFETY AND HEALTH ADMINISTRATION

201 12th Street South, Arlington, VA 22202–5452, phone (202) 693–9414

fax 693–9401, http://www.msha.gov

Assistant Secretary.—David G. Zatezalo, Room 5C330, 693–9402.
Deputy Assistant Secretary for Policy.—Wayne Palmer, Room 5C329, 693–9407.
Deputy Assistant Secretary for Operations.—Patricia W. Silvey, Room 5C328, 693–9642.
Director, Office of:
Assessments, Accountability, Special Enforcement, and Investigations.—Thomas Charboneau, Room 2518, 693–9700.
Program Education and Outreach Services.—David Wycinsky, Room 5C314, 693–9422.
Program Evaluation and Information Resources.—Syed Hafeez, Room 5W130, 693–9765.
Standards, Regulations, and Variances (OSRV).—Sheila McConnell, Room 5W208, 693–9440.
Technical Support.—William Francart, Room 4W210, 693–9470.

COAL MINE SAFETY AND HEALTH

Administrator.—Kevin Stricklin, Room 4W255 (202) 693–9500.
Deputy Administrator.—Timothy Watkins, Room 4C312, 693–9503.

METAL AND NONMETAL MINE SAFETY AND HEALTH

Administrator.—Kevin Stricklin (acting), Room 4W255 (202) 693–9600.
Deputy Administrator for Metal and Nonmetal.—Marvin Lichtenfels, Room 4C316, 693–9645.

EDUCATIONAL POLICY AND DEVELOPMENT

Director.—Jeffrey A. Duncan, Room 5W204 (202) 693–9570.

Administration and Management (A&M).—Eugene F. Hubbard, Room 4E462, 693–9802.

OCCUPATIONAL SAFETY AND HEALTH ADMINISTRATION

Assistant Secretary.—Vacant, Room S–2315 (202) 693–2000.
Deputy Assistant Secretary.—Dorothy Dougherty, 693–2000.
Chief of Staff.—Vacant, 693–2000.
Senior Policy Advisor.—Vacant, 693–2000.
Director of:
Administrative Programs.—Kimberly A. Locey, 693–1600.
Communications.—Frank Meilinger, 693–1999.
Construction.—Dean McKenzie, 693–2100.
Cooperative and State Programs.—Doug Kalinowski, 693–2200.
Enforcement Programs.—Thomas Galassi, 693–2100.
Technology Support and Emergency Management.—Amanda Edens, 693–2300.
Standards and Guidance.—Bill Perry, 693–1950.
Whistleblower Protection Programs.—MaryAnn Garrahan, 693–2199.

OFFICE OF PUBLIC AFFAIRS

Assistant Secretary.—Vacant, Room S–2514 (202) 693–4676.
Deputy Assistant Secretaries: G. Stephen Barr, Vacant.

REGIONAL OFFICES

Region I.—Boston.
Regional Director.—Ted Fitzgerald, JFK Federal Building, Government Center, 25 New Sudbury Street, Room 525–A, Boston, MA 02203 (617) 565–2075.
Region III.—Philadelphia.
Regional Director.—Leni Uddyback-Fortson, Curtis Center, 170 South Independence Mall West, Suite 633 East, Philadelphia, PA 19106–3306 (215) 861–5102.
Region IV.—Atlanta.
Regional Director.—Michael D'Aquino, Atlanta Federal Center, 61 Forsyth, SW., Suite 6B75, Atlanta, GA 30303 (678) 237–0630.
Region V.—Chicago.
Regional Director.—Scott Allen, 230 South Dearborn Street, Room 3194, Chicago, IL 60604 (312) 353–4727.
Region VI.—Dallas.
Regional Director.—Chauntra Rideaux, 525 Griffin Street, Room 734, Dallas, TX 75202 (972) 850–4710.
Region IX.—California.
Regional Director.—Leo Kay, 90 7th Street, Suite 2–650, San Francisco, CA 94103–1516 (415) 625–2630.

OFFICE OF SMALL AND DISADVANTAGED BUSINESS UTILIZATION

Director.—Gladys Bailey, N–6432 (202) 693–7244.

OFFICE OF THE SOLICITOR

Solicitor.—Kate O'Scannlain, Room S–2002 (202) 693–5260.
Deputy Solicitor.—Nicholas Geale.
Deputy Solicitor for National Operations.—Susan Harthill, 693–5260.
Deputy Solicitor for Regional Enforcement.—Katherine Bissell, 693–5260.
Senior Advisors: Jamila Gleason, Arthur Rosenfeld, Edward Sieger.
Attorney Advisor.—Shawn Packer.
Counsel.—David Dorey.

DIVISION OF BLACK LUNG AND LONGSHORE LEGAL SERVICES

Associate Solicitor.—Maia Fisher, Room N–2117 (202) 693–5660.
Deputy Associate Solicitor.—Kevin Lyskowski.
Counsel for Administrative Litigation and Legal Advice.—Michael J. Rutledge.

Appellate Litigation.—Gary K. Stearman.
Enforcement and Appellate Litigation.—Sean G. Bajkowski.
Longshore.—Mark A. Reinhalter.
Regulations and Legislation.—Vacant.

DIVISION OF CIVIL RIGHTS AND LABOR-MANAGEMENT

Associate Solicitor.—Beverly Dankowitz, Room N–2474 (202) 693–5740.
Deputy Associate Solicitor.—Consuela Pinto.
Counsel for Civil Rights and Appellate Litigation.—Eleanor Simms.
Interpretation and Advice.—Kier Bickerstaff.
Litigation and Regional Coordination.—Consuela Pinto.
LMRDA Advice.—Clinton Wolcott.
LMRDA Programs.—Radine Legum.

DIVISION OF EMPLOYMENT AND TRAINING LEGAL SERVICES

Associate Solicitor.—Jeffrey L. Nesvet, Room N–2101 (202) 693–5710.
Deputy Associate Solicitor.—Jessica Lyn.
Counsel for Employment and Training Advice.—Heather Vitale.
Immigration Programs.—Nora Carroll.
International Affairs and USERRA.—Derek Baxter.

DIVISION OF FAIR LABOR STANDARDS

Associate Solicitor.—Jennifer S. Brand, Room N–2716 (202) 693–5555.
Deputy Associate Solicitor.—William C. Lesser.
Counsel for Appellate Litigation.—Paul L. Frieden.
Contract Labor Standards.—Jonathan T. Rees.
Legal Advice.—Lynn McIntosh.
Trial Litigation.—Jonathan M. Kronheim.
Whistleblower Programs.—Megan E. Guenther.

DIVISION OF FEDERAL EMPLOYEE AND ENERGY WORKERS COMPENSATION

Associate Solicitor.—Thomas G. Giblin (acting), Room S–4325 (202) 693–5320.
Deputy Associate Solicitor.—Alexandra Tsiros (acting).
Counsel for Claims and Compensation.—Catherine P. Carter.
Energy Employees Compensation.—Sheldon O. Turley, Jr.
FECA Subrogation.—Jim Gordon.

DIVISION OF MANAGEMENT AND ADMINISTRATIVE LEGAL SERVICES

Associate Solicitor.—Rose Marie L. Audette, Room N–2420 (202) 693–5405.
Deputy Associate Solicitors: Allen K. Goshi, David Koeppel.
Counsel for Appropriations.—Omyra Ramsingh.
Employment Law.—Elizabeth L. Beason.
FOIA and Information Law.—Joseph J. Plick.
FOIA Appeals, Paperwork Reduction Act and Federal Records Act.—Ray Mitten, Jr.
Procurement and Contracts.—Peter Dickson.
Chief, Human Resources Office.—Michael Parrish.
Chief, Financial Management Office.—Michelle Fox.
Chief, Legal Technology Unit.—Denise Hoffman.
Director, Office of Information Services.—Ramona Oliver.

DIVISION OF MINE SAFETY AND HEALTH

201 12th Street South, Suite 401, Arlington, VA 22202–5414

Associate Solicitor.—April Nelson, Suite 401 (202) 693–9333.
Deputy Associate Solicitor.—Thomas A. Paige.
Counsel for Appellate Litigation.—Ali Beydoun.
Standards and Legal Advice.—Brad J. Mantel.

Trial Litigation.—Jason Grover.

DIVISION OF OCCUPATIONAL SAFETY AND HEALTH

Associate Solicitor.—Ann S. Rosenthal, Room S–4004 (202) 693–5452.
Deputy Associate Solicitor.—Edmund Baird.
Counsel for Appellate Litigation: Charles F. James, Heather Phillips.
Health Standards.—Ian Moar.
Regional Litigation and Legal Advice: Orlando J. Pannocchia, Robert W. Swain.
Safety Standards.—Ian Moar.
Special Litigation.—Vacant.

DIVISION OF PLAN BENEFITS SECURITY

Associate Solicitor.—William Scott, Room N–4611 (202) 693–5600.
Deputy Associate Solicitor.—Joanne Roskey.
Counsel for Appellate and Special Litigation.—Thomas Tso.
Fiduciary Litigation.—Risa D. Sandler.
Financial Litigation.—Robert Furst.
General Litigation.—Glenn M Loos.
Regulations.—James Craig.

OFFICE OF LEGAL COUNSEL

Associate Solicitor.—Vacant, Room N–2700 (202) 693–5500.
Counsel for Ethics.—Robert M. Sadler.
Legislative Affairs.—Jill M. Otte.
Honors Program Director.—Susan Hutton.

VETERANS' EMPLOYMENT AND TRAINING SERVICE

Assistant Secretary.—Vacant, Room S–1325 (202) 693–4700.
Deputy Assistant Secretary for Policy.—Matthew M. Miller, 693–4700.
Deputy Assistant Secretary for Operations and Management.—J.S. Shellenberger, 693–4700.
Chief of Staff.—Vacant, 693–4700.
Executive Assistant.—Ann Dubois, 693–4759.
Agency Management and Budget.—Maurice "Buck" Buchanan, 693–4724.
National Programs.—Ivan Denton, 693–4750.
Field Operations.—Bill Metheny, 693–4739.
Strategic Outreach.—Tim Green, 693–4723.

REGIONAL OFFICES

Administrators:
Atlanta: John Savage (404) 665–4335.
Boston: Mike Colman (617) 565–2086.
Chicago: Heather Higgins (312) 353–4932.
Dallas: Robert Creel (972) 850–4718.
Philadelphia: Timothy Crowley (215) 861–5385.
San Francisco: Alfred Kwok (415) 625–7670.

WOMEN'S BUREAU

Director.—Latifa Lyles, Room S–3002 (202) 693–6719.
Deputy Directors: Joan Harrigan-Farrelly, Room S–3002, 693–6712; Pronita Gupta, Room S–3002, 693–6762.
Chief, Office of:
Information and Support Services.—Paris M. Mack, Room S–3002, 693–6754.
Policy and Programs.—Tiffany Boiman, Room S–3002, 693–6753.

OFFICE OF WORKERS' COMPENSATION PROGRAMS

Director.—Leonard Howie, Room S–3524 (202) 343–5580.

Chief of Staff.—Donna Kramer, Room S–3229, 343–5580.
Deputy Director.—Gary Steinberg, Room S–3524, 343–5580.
Director, Division of Financial Administration.—Sam Shellenberger, Room 3524, 343–5580.
Deputy Director.—Zoya Kaplan, Room S–3524, 343–5580.
Director, Division of Administration and Operations.—Vincent Alvarez (acting), Room S–3201 (202) 354–5580.
Deputy Director.—Vincent Alvarez, Room S–3201, 354–5580.
Director, Division of Federal Employees' Compensation.—Douglas Fitzgerald, Room S–3229 (202) 693–0040.
Director, Division of Longshore and Harbor Workers' Compensation.—Douglas C. Fitzgerald, Room C–4319 (202) 354–9620.
Director, Division of Coal Mine Workers' Compensation.—Michael Chance, Room C–3520 (202) 693–0046.
Director, Division of Energy Employees Occupational Illness Compensation.—Rachel Leiton, Room C–3317, 693–0081.
Regional Directors:
Mid-Atlantic Region.—John McKenna (267) 687–4160.
Midwest Region.—Robert Sullivan (312) 789–2800.
Pacific Region.—Sharon Tyler (415) 241–3300.
Northeast Region.—Zev Sapir (212) 863–0800.
Southeast Region.—Magdalena Fernandez (904) 366–0100.
Southwest Region.—Dean Woodard (214) 749–2320.

OFFICE OF LABOR-MANAGEMENT STANDARDS

Director.—Andrew Auerbach (acting), Room N–5603 (202) 693–0123.
Deputy Director.—Andrew Auerbach, Room N–5603, 693–0123.
Director of Field Operations.—Stephen Willertz, Room N–5119, 693–1182.
Director of Programs Operations.—Lorenzo Harrison, Room N–5609, 693–1299.
Regional Directors:
Northeastern Region.—Andriana Vamvakas (643) 264–3190.
Central Region.—Daniel LaFond (414) 297–1504.
Southern Region.—Daniel Cherry (504) 589–6174.
Western Region.—Jena de Mers Raney (720) 264–3232.
Division of:
Planning, Management, and Technology.—Teresa Thomas, Room N–5613, 693–0506.
Enforcement.—Sharon Hanley, Room N–5119, 693–1204.
Interpretations and Standards.—Andrew Davis, Room N–5609, 693–1254.
Reports, Disclosure and Audits.—Larry King, Room N–5603, 693–1259.
Statutory Programs.—Karen Torre, Room N–5119, 693–1209.

WAGE AND HOUR DIVISION

Administrator.—Vacant, Room S–3502 (202) 693–0051.
Deputy Administrator.—Bryan Jarrett, Room S–3502, 693–0051.
Chief of Staff.—Vacant, Room S–3502, 693–0686.
Senior Policy Advisor.—Keith Sonderling, Room S–3502, 693–0051.
Deputy Administrator for Program Operations.—Patricia Davidson, Room S–3502, 693–0663.
Assistant Administrator, Office of:
Government Contracts.—Michael Lazzeri, Room S–3502, 693–1283.
Planning, Performance, Evaluation, and Communications.—Ann Lichter, Room S–3502, 693–0621.
Administrative Operations.—Rachel Torres, Room S–3502, 693–1252.
Policy.—Mary Ziegler, Room S–3502, 693–0597.

OFFICE OF FEDERAL CONTRACT COMPLIANCE PROGRAMS

Director.—Ondray T. Harris, Room C–3325 (202) 693–0101.
Deputy Director.—Thomas M. Dowd, Room C–3325, 693–0101.
Chief of Staff.—Kelley J. Smith, Room C–3325, 693–0101.
Senior Advisor.—Craig Leen, Room C–3325, 693–0101.
Special Assistant.—Lissette Geán, Room C–3325, 693–0101.

Director, Division of:

Enforcement.—Marika Litras, Room C–3325, 693–0101.

Management and Administrative Programs.—Javaid Kaiser (acting), Room C–3315, 693–0119.

Policy and Program Development.—Debra A. Carr, Room N–3422, 693–0105.

Program Operations.—Marika Litras (acting), Room C–3325, 693–0101.

DEPARTMENT OF HEALTH AND HUMAN SERVICES

200 Independence Avenue, SW., 20201, http://www.hhs.gov

ALEX M. AZAR II, Secretary of Health and Human Services; born in Johnstown, PA; education: B.A., *summa cum laude*, economics and government, Dartmouth College, Hanover, NH; J.D., Yale University, New Haven, CT; professional: attorney; General Counsel, 2001–05, and Deputy Secretary, 2005–07, Health and Human Services Department, Washington, DC; vice president for corporate affairs and communications, 2007–12, and president, 2012–17, Eli Lilly and Co., Indianapolis, IN; appointed by President Donald Trump to become the Secretary of Health and Human Services on November 13, 2017, confirmed by the Senate on January 24, 2018, and sworn into office on January 29, 2018.

OFFICE OF THE SECRETARY

Secretary of Health and Human Services.—Alex M. Azar II.
Chief of Staff.—Peter Urbanowicz (202) 690–3905.
Executive Assistant to the Secretary.—Rose Lusi, 690–7000.
Deputy Chief of Staff for Operations.—Brian Harrison (202) 260–9660.
Deputy Secretary.—Eric D. Hargan.
Executive Secretary.—Ann Agnew (202) 868–9642.
Director, Intergovernmental and External Affairs.—Jack Kalavritinos (acting), (202) 690–6060.
Chair, Departmental Appeals Board.—Constance B. Tobias (202) 565–0220.

ASSISTANT SECRETARY FOR ADMINISTRATION AND MANAGEMENT

Assistant Secretary for Administration.—John Bardis (260) 609–7431.
Chief Information Officer.—Beth Anne Killoran (202) 570–1296.
Deputy Assistant Secretary for Human Resources and Chief Human Capital Officer.—Christine Major (202) 205–9538.
Security and Strategic Information.—Michael Schmoyer (202) 690–6162.
Director, Office of Equal Employment Opportunity Compliance and Operations.—Cynthia Richardson-Crooks (301) 796–0115.

PROGRAM SUPPORT CENTER

5600 Fishers Lane, Rockville, MD 20857, 7700 Wisconsin Avenue, Bethesda, MD 20852

Deputy Assistant Secretary for Program Support.—Allen Sample (301) 492–4630.
Occupational Health Portfolio.—CDR Tomas Bonome, 492–5410.
Financial Management and Procurement Portfolio.—William McCabe, 492–4950.
Real Estate, Logistics, and Operations Portfolio.—Michael Saunders (202) 401–1437.

ASSISTANT SECRETARY FOR LEGISLATION

Assistant Secretary.—Matthew Bassett (202) 690–7627.
Principal Deputy Assistant Secretary.—Sarah Arbes, 690–7627.
Deputy Assistant Secretary for—
Congressional Liaison.—Sara Morse, 690–6786.
Mandatory Health.—Alec Aramanda, 690–7450.
Discretionary Health.—Laura Kemper, 690–7450.
Health Reform.—Ashley Palmer, 690–7450.
Human Services.—Courtney Lawrence, 690–6311.
Director of Oversight and Investigations.—Sean Hayes, 690–7627.

ASSISTANT SECRETARY FOR PLANNING AND EVALUATION

Assistant Secretary for Planning and Evaluation.—John R. Graham (acting), (202) 690–7858.
Principal Deputy Assistant Secretary.—John R. Graham, 690–7858.
Deputy Assistant Secretary for—
Disability and Long Term Care.—Ruth Katz (acting), 690–6443.
Health Policy.—John O'Brien, 690–6870.
Human Services Policy.—Jennifer Burnszynski (acting), 690–7409.
Science and Data Policy.—Laina Bush (acting), 690–7100.

ASSISTANT SECRETARY FOR PUBLIC AFFAIRS

Assistant Secretary.—Vacant.
Assistant Secretary.—Bill Hall (acting), (202) 690–6344, fax 690–6247.
Principal Deputy Assistant Secretary.—Vacant.
Deputy Assistant Secretary for—
Health Care.—Vacant.
Human Services.—Mark Weber (202) 260–6412, fax 690–6247.
Public Health.—Bill Hall, 690–6344, fax 690–6247.
Executive Officer/Deputy Agency Chief FOIA Officer.—Catherine Teti (202) 205–3592.
Director, Freedom of Information/Privacy Act Division.—Michael Marquis, 260–7100.

ASSISTANT SECRETARY FOR PREPAREDNESS AND RESPONSE

Assistant Secretary.—Robert Kadlec, M.D. (202) 205–2882.
Principal Deputy Assistant Secretary.—Edward Gabriel, 205–2882.
Deputy Assistant Secretary and Director, Office of:
Biomedical Advanced Research and Development Authority.—Rick Bright, Ph.D., 260–1200.
Emergency Management.—Don Boyce, J.D., 205–8387.
Policy and Planning.—Sally Phillips, Ph.D., 260–1202.

ASSISTANT SECRETARY FOR FINANCIAL RESOURCES

Assistant Secretary.—Jen Moughalian (acting), (202) 690–6396.
Principal Deputy Assistant Secretary.—Jen Moughalian, 690-6061.
Senior Advisor of Operations.—John Gentile, 690–7512.
Deputy Assistant Secretary for—
Budget.—Norris Cochran, 690–7393.
Finance.—Sheila Conley, 690–7084.
Grants.—Andrea Brandon, 690–6377.

OFFICE FOR CIVIL RIGHTS

Director.—Roger Severino (202) 619–0403.
Chief of Staff.—March Bell, 619–0403.
Principal Deputy Director.—Robinsue Frohboese, 619–0403.
Deputy Director for—
Civil Rights Division.—Sunu Chandy, 619–0403.
Operations and Resources Division.—Steve Novy, 619–0403.
Health Information Privacy.—Deven McGraw, 619–0403.
Toll Free Voice Number (Nationwide).—1–800–368–1019.
Toll Free TDD Number (Nationwide).—1–800–527–7697.

OFFICE OF THE GENERAL COUNSEL

fax [Immediate Office] 690–7998

General Counsel.—Robert P. Charrow, 690–7741.
Deputy General Counsels: Matthew S. Bowman, Kelly M. Cleary, Jeffrey S. Davis, Heather Flick, Brian R. Stimson (202) 690–7741.
Senior Advisor to the General Counsel.—Elizabeth Jordan Gianturco, 690–7741.
Associate General Counsels for—
Centers for Medicare and Medicaid Division.—Janice L. Hoffman (202) 619–0300.

Children, Family, and Aging Division.—Robert Keith (202) 690–8005.
Civil Rights Division.—Aaron Schuham (202) 619–0900.
Ethics Division/Special Counsel for Ethics.—Elizabeth J. Fischmann (202) 690–7258.
Food and Drug Division.—Rebecca K. Wood (301) 796–3978.
General Law Division.—Dan Barry (202) 619–0150.
Legislation Division.—Edith R. Blackwell (202) 690–7773.
Public Health Division.—David E. Benor (301) 443–2644.

OFFICE OF GLOBAL AFFAIRS

Assistant Secretary.—Dr. Mitchell Wolfe (acting), (202) 690–6174.

OFFICE OF THE INSPECTOR GENERAL

330 Independence Avenue, SW., 20201

Principal Deputy Inspector General.—Joanne M. Chiedi (202) 619–3148.
Chief Counsel to the Inspector General.—Gregory E. Demske, 619–2078.
Director, External Affairs.—Christopher Seagle, 260–7006.
Deputy Inspectors for—
Audit Services.—Gloria L. Jarmon, 619–3157.
Evaluation and Inspections.—Suzanne Murrin, 619–0480.
Investigations.—Gary L. Cantrell, 205–4081.
Management and Policy.—Robert Owens, 205–9117.

OFFICE OF MEDICARE HEARINGS AND APPEALS

Chief Administrative Law Judge.—Nancy J. Griswold (703) 235–0635.
Deputy Chief Administrative Law Judge.—Vacant.
Director of Programs.—Eileen McDaniel, 235–0635.

OFFICE OF THE NATIONAL COORDINATOR FOR HEALTH INFORMATION TECHNOLOGY

National Coordinator for Health Information Technology.—Donald W. Rucker, M.D. (202) 969–3374.

OFFICE OF THE ASSISTANT SECRETARY FOR HEALTH

Assistant Secretary for Health.—ADM Brett P. Giroir, M.D. (202) 690–7694.
Senior Executive Assistant to the Assistant Secretary for Health.—Dinah Bembo, 690–7694.
Principal Deputy Assistant Secretary for Health.—Vacant, 690–7694.
The Surgeon General.—VADM Jerome M. Adams, M.D., M.P.H., (202) 205–0143.
Deputy Assistant Secretary, Office of:
Science and Medicine.—Vacant (202) 260–2873.
Disease Prevention and Health Promotion.—Don Wright, M.D., M.P.H. (240) 453–8280.
HIV/AIDS and Infectious Disease Policy.—Richard Wolitski, Ph.D. (202) 795–7697.
Minority Health.—Matthew Y.C. Lin, M.D. (240) 453–6179.
National Vaccine Program.—Melinda Wharton, M.D., M.P.H. (202) 205–5294.
Population Affairs.—Valerie Huber, M.Ed., (acting), (240) 453–2805.
Women's Health.—Nicole Greene (202) 690–7650.
Director, Office of:
Adolescent Health.—Evelyn Kappeler (240) 453–2846.
Communications.—Mark Vasiades (202) 205–1842.
Human Research Protections.—Jerry Menikoff, M.D., J.D. (240) 453–6900.
Research Integrity.—Wanda Jones, DrPH (interim), (240) 453–8200.
Executive Director of:
President's Council on Sports, Fitness, and Nutrition.—Don Wright, M.D., M.P.H. (acting), 276–9567.
Presidential Commission for the Study of Bioethical Issues.—Lisa Lee, Ph.D., M.S. (202) 233–3960.
Regional Health Administrator for—
Region I: CT, ME, MA, NH, RI, VT.—Betsy Rosenfeld, JD–C (617) 565–1505.
Region II: NJ, NY, PR, VI.—April Smith-Hirak (acting), (212) 264–2560.

Region III: DE, DC, MD, PA, VA, WV.—Dalton G. Paxman, Ph.D. (215) 861–4631.
Region IV: AL, FL, GA, KY, MS, NC, SC, TN.—Sharon Ricks (404) 562–7906.
Region V: IL, IN, MI, MN, OH, WI.—CAPT Anna Gonzales, M.P.H. (acting), (312) 353–1385.
Region VI: AR, LA, NM, OK, TX.—CAPT Mehran S. Massoudi, Ph.D., M.P.H. (214) 767–3879.
Region VII: IA, KS, MO, NE.—CAPT Shary Jones, Pharm.D., M.P.H., BCPS (acting), (816) 426–3330.
Region VIII: CO, MT, ND, SD, UT, WY.—Laurie Konsella, M.P.A. (acting), (303) 844–7860.
Region IX: AZ, CA, HI, NV, Guam, American Samoa, CNMI, FSMI, RMI, Republic of Palau.—CAPT Brad Austin, M.P.H., FACHE (415) 437–8096.
Region X: AK, ID, OR, WA.—Renée Bouvion, M.P.H. (acting), (206) 615–2469.

ADMINISTRATION FOR COMMUNITY LIVING

330 C Street, SW., 20201

Assistant Secretary for Aging and Administrator, Administration for Community Living.—Lance Allen Robertson (202) 795–7354.
Principal Deputy Administrator, Administration for Community Living.—Mary Lazare, 795–7385.
Chief of Staff and Executive Secretary.—Richard Nicholls, 795–7415.
Commissioner, Administration on Disabilities.—Melissa Ortiz, 795–7309.
Deputy Assistant Secretary for Aging.—Edwin L. Walker, 795–7463.
Legislative Affairs.—Vacant.
Deputy Administrator, Center for Management and Budget.—Daniel Berger, 795–7307.
Director, National Institute on Disability, Independent Living, and Rehabilitation Research.—Kristi Hill (acting), 795–7363.
Deputy Administrator, Center for Integrated Programs.—Josh Hodges (acting), 795–7364.
Director, Center for Policy and Evaluation.—Vicki Gottlich, 795–7352.
Director, Office of Regional Operations.—Robert Logan, 795–7388.

ADMINISTRATION FOR CHILDREN AND FAMILIES

330 C Street, SW., 20201, (202) 401–9215

Assistant Secretary.—Amanda Barlow (acting), (202) 401–5383.
Chief of Staff.—Vacant, 401–5180.
Deputy Assistant Secretary and Inter-Departmental Liaison for Early Childhood Development.—Collen Rathgeb (acting), 401–9204.
Deputy Assistant Secretary for External Affairs.—Anna Pilato, 401–4657.
Deputy Assistant Secretary for Administration.—Ben Goldhaber, 401–3438.
Deputy Assistant Secretary for Planning, Research, and Evaluation.—Naomi Goldstein, 401–9220.
Commissioner for Administration on Children, Youth, and Families.—Naomi Goldstein (acting), 401–9220.
Commissioner, Administration for Native Americans.—Stacey Ecoffey (acting), 690–5780.
Commissioner, Office of Child Support Enforcement.—Donna Bonar (acting), 401–9369.
Associate Commissioner, Children's Bureau.—Joe Bock (acting), 205–8594.
Associate Commissioner, Family and Youth Services Bureau.—Debbie Powell (acting), 205–2360.
Senior Advisor to the Assistant Secretary.—Vacant, 401–6947.
Chief Information Officer.—Sebrina Blake, 818–8450.
Director, Office of:
Refugee Resettlement.—Scott Lloyd, 401–9246.
Trafficking in Persons.—Katherine Chon, 401–9200.
Child Care.—Ellen C. Wheatley, Ph.D. (acting), 401–4558.
Community Services.—Janelle George (acting), 401–4830.
Family Assistance.—Susan Golonka (acting), 401–9275.
Head Start.—Ann Linehan (acting), 205–8767.
Human Services Emergency Preparedness and Response.—CDR Cole Weeks (acting), 401–5458.
Legislative Affairs and Budget.—Amanda Barlow, 401–9223.
Regional Operations.—Mishaela Duran, 401–4605.
Communications.—Johnathan Monroe, 401–4777.

AGENCY FOR HEALTHCARE RESEARCH AND QUALITY (AHRQ)

Director.—Sharon B. Arnold, Ph.D. (acting), (301) 427–1200.
Deputy Director.—Boyce Ginieczki, Ph.D., (acting), 427–1200.

AGENCY FOR TOXIC SUBSTANCES AND DISEASE REGISTRY

1600 Clifton Road, NE., Atlanta, GA 30333

Administrator.—Anne Schuchat, M.D. (RADM, USPHS) (acting), (404) 639–7000.
Principal Deputy Administrator.—Stephen C. Redd, M.D. (RADM, USPHS), (acting).

CENTERS FOR DISEASE CONTROL AND PREVENTION

1600 Clifton Road, NE., Atlanta, GA 30329–4027, phone (404) 639–7000

Director.—Vacant.
Principal Deputy Director.—Anne Schuchat, M.D. (RADM, USPHS).
Chief Operating Officer.—Sherri A. Berger, M.S.P.H.
Chief of Staff.—Vacant.
Chief Medical Officer.—Mitchell Wolfe, M.D., M.P.H. (RADM, USPHS).
CDC Washington Director.—Vacant (202) 245–0600.
Director, Office of:
Equal Employment Opportunity.—Reginald R. Mebane, M.S.
Minority Health and Health Equity.—Leandris Liburd, Ph.D., M.P.H., M.A.
Program Performance and Evaluation.—Vacant.
Associate Director for—
Communication.—Katherine Lyon Daniel, Ph.D.
Science.—Vacant.
Policy.—Vacant.
Directors:
Center for Global Health.—Rebecca Martin, Ph.D. (404) 639–6232.
National Institute for Occupational Safety and Health.—John Howard, M.D., M.P.H., J.D. (202) 245–0625.
Office of Public Health Preparedness and Response.—Stephen C. Redd, M.D. (RADM, USPHS), (404) 639–7405.
Deputy Director, Office of:
Infectious Diseases.—Sonja Rasmussen, M.D., M.S. (404) 498–1829.
Non-Communicable Diseases, Injury and Environmental Health.—Robin Ikeda, M.D., M.P.H. (RADM, USPHS), (770) 488–0608.
Directors:
Center for Surveillance, Epidemiology and Laboratory Services.—Michael F. Iademarco, M.D. M.P.H. (CAPT, USPHS).
National Center on Birth Defects and Developmental Disabilities.—Coleen Boyle, Ph.D., M.S. (404) 498–3800.
Director, National Center for—
Chronic Disease Prevention and Health Promotion.—Ursula Bauer, Ph.D., M.P.H. (770) 488–5401.
Emerging and Zoonotic Infectious Diseases.—Rima Khabbaz, M.D. (404) 639–3967.
Environmental Health/Agency for Toxic Substances and Disease Registry.—Patrick Breysse, Ph.D. (770) 488–0604.
Health Statistics.—Charles J. Rothwell, M.B.A., M.S.
HIV/AIDS, Viral Hepatitis, STD, and TB Prevention.—Jonathan Mermin, M.D., M.P.H., (404) 639–8000.
Immunization and Respiratory Diseases.—Nancy Messonnier, M.D. (CAPT, USPHS, Ret.).
Injury Prevention and Control.—Debra Houry, M.D., M.P.H. (770) 488–4696.
Deputy Director, Office of Public Health Scientific Services.—Chelsey Richards, M.D., M.P.H., FACP (404) 498–6001.
Deputy Director, Office for State, Tribal, Local, and Territorial Support.—Jose T. Montero, M.D., M.H.C.D.S. (404) 498–1668.

CENTER FOR FAITH-BASED AND NEIGHBORHOOD PARTNERSHIPS

Director.—Shannon O. Royce, Esq. (202) 358–3595.

CENTERS FOR MEDICARE & MEDICAID SERVICES

200 Independence Avenue, SW., 20201, phone (202) 690–6726

Headquarters: https://www.cms.gov/About-CMS/Agency-Information/CMSLeadership/index.html

Regional Offices: https://www.cms.gov/About-CMS/Agency-Information/Consortia/index.html

Administrator.—Seema Verma.
Principal Deputy Administrator for Medicare.—Demetrios Kouzoukas.
Chief Operating Officer.—Vacant.
Deputy Chief Operating Officer.—Karen Jackson (410) 786–3151.
Chief Actuary, Office of the Actuary.—Paul Spitalnic, 786–6374.
Deputy Administrator and Director, Center for—
Consumer Information and Insurance Oversight.—Randolph Pate (202) 690–6360.
Medicaid and CHIP Services.—Brian Neale, 690–7428.
Medicare.—Vacant (410) 690–6301.
Program Integrity.—Vacant (410) 786–1892.
Director, Center for Medicare and Medicaid Innovation.—Patrick Conway, M.D., 786–3151.
Director and CMS Chief Medical Officer, Center for Clinical Standards and Quality.—Kate Goodrich, M.D., 786–5878.
Director and Chief Information Officer, Office of Information Technology.—Vacant.
Director, Office of Support and Operations.—James Weber, 786–1051.
Director, Office of:
Acquisition and Grants Management.—Melissa Starinsky, 786–1391.
Communications.—Jane Norris (202) 205–9450.
Enterprise Data and Analytics.—Vacant (202) 690–6627.
Equal Opportunity and Civil Rights.—Anita Pinder (410) 786–5493.
Federal Coordinated Health Care.—Tim Engelhardt (202) 260–1291.
CMS Chief Financial Officer and Director, Office of Financial Management.—Jennifer Main (410) 786–5448.
Director, Office of:
Legislation.—Emily Felder (202) 690–5960.
Minority Health.—Cara James (410) 786–6842.
Hearings and Inquiries.—Randy Brauer, 786–1618.
Strategic Operations and Regulatory Affairs.—Kathleen Cantwell (202) 690–8390.
Consortium Administrator for—
Financial Management and FFS Operations.—Nanette Foster Reilly (816) 426–5233.
Medicaid and Children's Health Operations.—Jackie Garner (312) 886–6432.
Medicare Health Plans Operations.—James T. Kerr (917) 647–9652.
Quality Improvement and Survey and Certification Operations.—Renard Murray (404) 562–7150.

FOOD AND DRUG ADMINISTRATION

10903 New Hampshire Avenue, Silver Spring, MD 20993

Commissioner.—Scott Gottlieb, M.D. (301) 796–5000.
Chief of Staff.—Lauren Silvis (acting), 796–8583.
The Executive Secretariat.—Martina Varnado, 796–8331.
Counselor to the Commissioner.—Vacant.
Deputy Commissioner for—
Foods and Veterinary Medicine.—Erik P. Mettler, M.P.A., M.P.H. (acting), 796–4500.
Global Regulatory Operations and Policy.—Dara Corrigan, J.D., 796–7460.
Medical Products and Tobacco.—Rachel Sherman, M.D., M.P.H., 796–5017.
Policy, Planning, and Legislation.—Anna Abram, 796–8770.
Chiefs:
Counsel.—Liz Dickinson, J.D., 796–8540.
Information Officer.—Todd Simpson, 796–6700.
Scientist (Informatics).—Elaine Johanson (acting), 796–4583.
Operating Officer.—James Sigg, 796–4700.
Scientist.—Luciana Borio (acting), 796–4880.
Financial.—James Tyler, 796–4770.
Associate Commissioner for—
External Affairs.—Jack Kalavritinos, 796–3347.

Foods and Veterinary Medicine.—Erik Mettler, 796–9254.
International Programs.—Mary Lou Valdez, 796–8400.
Legislation.—Dayle Cristinzio, 796–8900.
Planning.—Malcolm Bertoni, 796–4850.
Policy.—Leslie Kux, J.D., 796–4830.
Public Health Strategy and Analysis.—Peter Lurie, M.D., M.P.H. (240) 402–4431.
Regulatory Affairs.—Melinda Plaisier, M.SW., 796–8800.
Special Medical Programs.—Janice M. Soreth, M.D., 796–4810.
Director, Center for—
Biologics Evaluation and Research.—Peter Marks, M.D., Ph.D. (240) 402–8000.
Center for Drug Evaluation and Research.—Janet Woodcock, M.D., 796–5400.
Devices and Radiological Health.—Jeffrey Shuren, M.D., J.D., 796–5900.
Food Safety and Applied Nutrition.—Susan Mayne, Ph.D. (240) 402–1600.
Office of Crisis Management.—Mark Russo (acting), 796–8250.
Office of Minority Health.—Jonca Bull, M.D., 796–4649.
Tobacco Products.—Mitch Zeller, J.D., 796–9200.
Veterinary Medicine.—Steven Solomon, D.V.M. (240) 276–9000.
Director, National Center for Toxicological Research.—William Slikker, Jr., Ph.D. (870) 543–7517.
Senior Advisor for Science, Innovation, and Policy.—Vacant, 847–3530.
Senior Advisor to the Commissioner.—Vacant, 796–7064.

HEALTH RESOURCES AND SERVICES ADMINISTRATION

5600 Fishers Lane, Rockville, MD 20857

Administrator.—James Macrae (acting), (301) 443–2216.
Deputy Administrator.—Diana Espinosa, 443–2216.
Senior Advisor.—Joanne Hoff (acting), 443–2216.
Senior Health Advisor.—Deborah Parham-Hopson, Ph.D., MSPH, RN, RADM, USPHS, 443–2216.
Chief Operating Officer.—Wendy Ponton, 443–4244.
Associate Administrator for:
Federal Assistance Management.—Rick Goodman, 443–5877.
Health Workforce.—Luis Padilla, M.D., 443–5794.
Healthcare Systems.—Cheryl Dammons, 443–3300.
HIV/AIDS.—Laura Cheever, M.D., 443–1993.
Maternal and Child Health.—Michael Lu, M.D., 443–2170.
Primary Health Care.—Tonya Bowers (acting), 594–4110.
Regional Operations.—Dennis Malcomson, 443–7070.
Rural Health Policy.—Tom Morris, 443–0835.
Director, Office of:
Communications.—Martin Kramer, 443–3376.
Legislation.—Leslie Atkinson, 443–1890.
Planning, Analysis and Evaluation.—Carrie Cochran, 443–3983.
Civil Rights, Diversity and Inclusion.—Anthony Archeval, J.D., 443–5636.
Global Health.—Kerry Nesseler, M.S., RN, FAAN, RADM, USPHS, 443–2741.
Health Equity.—Michelle Allender-Smith, RN, 443–2964.
Women's Health.—Sabrina Matoff-Stepp, Ph.D., 443–8664.

INDIAN HEALTH SERVICE

5600 Fishers Lane, Rockville, MD 20857

Director.—RADM Michael D. Weahkee (acting), (301) 443–1083.
Deputy Director.—RADM Chris Buchanan, 443–1083.
Deputy Director for—
Field Operations.—RADM Kevin Meeks.
Quality Health Care.—Jonathan Merrell (acting).
Intergovernmental Affairs.—Benjamin Smith, 443–1083.
Management Operations.—Elizabeth Fowler, 443–1083.
Chief Medical Officer.—CAPT Michael Toedt, M.D., 443–1083.
Chief of Staff.—RADM Kelly Taylor (acting), 443–1083.
Senior Advisor.—Emily Newman, 443–1083.
Director of:
Clinical and Preventative Services.—RADM Sarah Linde, M.D. (acting), 443–4644.

Direct Service and Contracting Tribes.—Roselyn Tso (acting), 443–1104.
Environmental Health and Engineering.—Gary Hartz, 443–1247.
Equal Employment Opportunity.—Sarah Nelson, 443–1108.
Executive Secretariat.—Julie Czajkowski, 443–1011.
Finance and Accounting.—Ann Church (acting), 443–1270.
Human Resources.—Lisa Gyorda, 443–6520.
Information Technology.—CAPT Mark Rives, 443–2019.
Legislative and Congressional Affairs.—June Tracy, 443–7261.
Management Services.—Robert McSwain, 443–6290.
Public Affairs.—Jennifer Buschick, 443–1865.
Public Health Support.—CAPT Francis Frazier, 443–0222.
Resource Access and Partnerships.—Terri Schmidt (acting), 443–2694.
Tribal Self-Governance.—Jennifer Cooper (acting), 443–7821.
Urban Indian Health Programs.—Raho Ortiz (acting), 443–4680.

NATIONAL INSTITUTES OF HEALTH

9000 Rockville Pike, Bethesda, MD 20892

Director.—Francis S. Collins, M.D., Ph.D. (301) 496–2433.
Principal Deputy Director.—Lawrence A. Tabak, D.D.S., Ph.D., 496–2433.
Chief of Staff and Associate Director for Science Policy.—Carrie Wolinetz, Ph.D. (acting), 496–2122.
Director, Executive Secretariat.—Patrice Allen-Gifford, 496–1461.
Director, Office of Federal Advisory Committee Policy.—Claire Harris (acting), 496–2123.
Director, NIH Office of Ethics.—Holli Beckerman Jaffe, J.D. (301) 402–6628.
Executive Officer, Office of the Director.—LaVerne Y. Stringfield (301) 594–8231.
Chief Information Officer and Director, Center for Information Technology.—Andrea T. Norris (301) 496–5703.
Legal Advisor, Office of the General Counsel.—David Lankford (acting), 496–6043.
Deputy Director for—
Intramural Research.—Michael M. Gottesman, M.D., 496–1921.
Extramural Research.—Michael S. Lauer, M.D., 496–1096.
Management.—Alfred C. Johnson, Ph.D., 496–3271.
Deputy Director, Division of Program Coordination, Planning, and Strategic Initiatives.—James Anderson, M.D., Ph.D. (301) 402–9852.
Associate Director for—
Budget.—Neil Shapiro, J.D. (301) 496–4477.
Communications and Public Liaison.—John T. Burklow, 496–4461.
Legislative Policy and Analysis.—Adrienne Hallett, 496–3471.
Science Policy.—Carrie Wolinetz, Ph.D., 496–2122.
Clinical Research.—John I. Gallin, M.D. (301) 827–5428.
Director, Office of—
AIDS Research.—Maureen M. Goodenow, Ph.D. (301) 496–0357.
Behavioral and Social Sciences Research.—William T. Riley, Ph.D. (301) 402–1146.
Disease Prevention.—David Murray, Ph.D. (301) 827–5561.
Research on Women's Health.—Janine Clayton, M.D. (301) 402–1770.
Research Services.—Timothy Tosten (301) 496–2215.
Acquisition and Logistics Management.—Diane Frasier, 496–4422.
Equal Opportunity and Diversity Management.—Debra Chew, Esq., 496–6301.
Financial Management.—Glenda Conroy (301) 435–7995.
Human Resources.—Julie Berko (acting), (301) 496–3592.
Management Assessment.—Michael D. Shannon, 496–1873.
Research Facilities Development and Operations.—Daniel Wheeland (301) 594–0999.
Technology Transfer.—Karen L. Rogers (acting), (301) 435–4359.
Institute and Center Directors:
National Cancer Institute.—Norman E. ''Ned'' Sharpless, M.D. (240) 781–3300.
National Eye Institute.—Paul A. Sieving, M.D., Ph.D. (301) 496–2234.
National Heart, Lung, and Blood Institute.—Gary Gibbons, M.D., 496–5166.
National Human Genome Research Institute.—Eric Green, M.D., Ph.D., 496–0844.
Eunice Kennedy Shriver National Institute of Child Health and Human Development.—Diana W. Bianchi, M.D., 496–3454.
National Institute on Aging.—Richard J. Hodes, M.D., 496–9265.
National Institute on Alcohol Abuse and Alcoholism.—George Koob, Ph.D. (301) 443–3885.
National Institute of Allergy and Infectious Diseases.—Anthony S. Fauci, M.D. (301) 496–2263.

National Institute of Arthritis and Musculoskeletal and Skin Diseases.—Stephen I. Katz, M.D., Ph.D., 496–4353.
National Institute of Biomedical Imaging and Bioengineering.—Jill Heemskerk, Ph.D. (acting), 496–8859.
National Institute on Deafness and Other Communication Disorders.—Judith Cooper, Ph.D. (acting), 496–5061.
National Institute of Dental and Craniofacial Research.—Martha Somerman, D.D.S., Ph.D., 496–3571.
National Institute of Diabetes and Digestive and Kidney Diseases.—Griffin P. Rodgers, M.D., M.A.C.P., 496–5877.
National Institute on Drug Abuse.—Nora D. Volkow, M.D. (301) 443–6480.
National Institute of Environmental Health Sciences.—Linda S. Birnbaum, Ph.D., D.A.B.T., A.T.S. (919) 541–3201.
National Institute of General Medical Sciences.—Jon Lorsch, Ph.D. (301) 594–2172.
National Institute of Mental Health.—Joshua Gordon, M.D., Ph.D. (301) 443–3673.
National Institute on Minority Health and Health Disparities.—Eliseo J. Pérez-Stable, M.D. (301) 402–1366.
National Institute of Neurological Disorders and Stroke.—Walter Koroshetz, M.D. (301) 496–3167.
National Institute of Nursing Research.—Patricia A. Grady, Ph.D., R.N., F.A.A.N., 496–8230.

Chief Executive Officer, NIH Clinical Center.—James Gilman, M.D., 496–4114.

Director:

National Library of Medicine.—Patricia F. Brennan, R.N., Ph.D., 496–6221.
Fogarty International Center.—Roger I. Glass, M.D., Ph.D., 496–1415.
National Center for Advancing Translational Sciences.—Christopher Austin, M.D. (301) 435–0736.
National Center for Complementary and Integrative Health.—David Shurtleff, Ph.D. (acting), 435–6826.
Center for Information Technology.—Andrea T. Norris (301) 496–5703.
Center for Scientific Review.—Noni Byrnes, Ph.D. (acting), (301) 435–1114.

SUBSTANCE ABUSE AND MENTAL HEALTH SERVICES ADMINISTRATION (SAMHSA)

5600 Fishers Lane, Rockville, MD 20857

www.samhsa.gov

Assistant Secretary for Mental Health and Substance Use.—Elinore F. McCance-Katz, M.D., Ph.D., Room 18E41 (240) 276–2000.

Deputy Assistant Secretary for Mental Health and Substance Use.—Kana Enomoto, Room 18E51, 276–2000.

Director, Office of:

Behavioral Health Equity.—Larke Huang, Ph.D., Room 18E59, 276–2014.
Communications.—Marla Hendriksson, Room 18E31, 276–2130.
Financial Resources.—Deepa Avula, Room 17E51, 276–2200.
Management, Technology, and Operations.—Michael E. Etzinger, Room 12E41, 276–1110.
Policy, Planning, and Innovation.—Mirtha R. Beadle (acting), Room 18E16, 276–2307.

Director, Center for—

Behavioral Health Statistics and Quality.—Daryl Kade, Room 15E41, 276–1660.
Mental Health Services.—Paolo del Vecchio, Room 14E41, 276–1310.
Substance Abuse Prevention.—Frances M. Harding, Room 16E41, 276–2420.
Substance Abuse Treatment.—Kimberly Johnson, Ph.D., Room 13E41, 276–1660.

DEPARTMENT OF HOUSING AND URBAN DEVELOPMENT

Robert C. Weaver Federal Building, 451 Seventh Street, SW., 20410

phone (202) 708–1112, http://www.hud.gov

BENJAMIN CARSON, Secretary of Housing and Urban Development, born in Detroit, MI, September 18, 1951; education: B.A., psychology, Yale University, New Haven, CT, 1973; M.D., University of Michigan Medical School, Ann Arbor, MI, 1977; professional: in 1984, at age 33, became youngest physician to head a major division (pediatric neurosurgery) at Johns Hopkins Hospital in Baltimore, MD, where he remained until his retirement in 2013; in 1994, started Carson Scholars Fund with his wife to help fund college education and install reading rooms around the country; served on President's Council on Bioethics, 2004–08; awarded Spingarn Medal, highest honor given by NAACP (National Association for the Advancement of Colored People), 2006; awarded the Presidential Medal of Freedom, nation's highest civilian honor, 2008; married to Candy; three adult sons and three grandchildren; nominated by President Donald J. Trump to become the 17th Secretary of Housing and Urban Development on December 5, 2016; confirmed by the U.S. Senate, and was sworn in on March 2, 2017.

OFFICE OF THE SECRETARY

Secretary of Housing and Urban Development.—Dr. Benjamin Carson, Room 10000 (202) 708–0417.
Chief of Staff.—Andrew Hughes, 402–2713.
Deputy Chiefs of Staff: Deana Bass, 402–2713; Drew McCall, 708–2713.
Executive Secretariat Senior Advisor.—John Bravacos (acting), 708–3750.
Chief Operations Officer.—Ralph Gaines.

OFFICE OF THE DEPUTY SECRETARY

Deputy Secretary.—Pamela Hughes Patenaude, Room 10100 (202) 402–5430.
Deputy Chief of Staff.—Victoria Barton, Room 10100, 708–0123.

ASSISTANT SECRETARY FOR ADMINISTRATION

Assistant Secretary for Administration.—Suzanne Israel Tufts, Room 6100 (202) 402–5298.

ASSISTANT SECRETARY FOR COMMUNITY PLANNING AND DEVELOPMENT

Assistant Secretary.—Neal J. Rackleff, Room 7100 (202) 708–2690.
General Deputy Assistant Secretary.—Lori Michalski (acting), 402–3921.
Deputy Assistant Secretary for—
Grant Programs.—Stanley Gimont, Room 7204, 402–4559.
Special Needs.—Jemine Bryon, Room 7244, 708–2404.

ASSISTANT SECRETARY FOR CONGRESSIONAL AND INTERGOVERNMENTAL RELATIONS

Assistant Secretary.—Len Wolfson, Room 10120 (202) 708–0980.
General Deputy Assistant Secretary.—Seth Appleton, Room 10120, 708–0005.
Deputy Assistant Secretary for—
Congressional Relations.—Michael Kelley, Room 10120, 708–0005.
Intergovernmental Relations.—Stephanie Fila, Room 10148, 708–0005.

ASSISTANT SECRETARY FOR FAIR HOUSING AND EQUAL OPPORTUNITY

Assistant Secretary.—Anna María Farías, Room 5100.
General Deputy Assistant Secretary.—Bryan Greene, 708–4211.
Deputy Assistant Secretary for—
Enforcement and Programs.—Timothy Smyth, 402–2439.
Operations and Management.—Jason E. Stayanovich, 402–5525.
Policy, Legislative Initiatives, and Outreach.—Krista Mills, 402–6577.

ASSISTANT SECRETARY FOR HOUSING

Assistant Secretary/Federal Housing Commissioner.—Vacant, Room 9100 (202) 708–2601.
General Deputy Assistant Secretary.—Dana Wade, Room 9100, 708–2601.
Associate General Deputy Assistant Secretary.—Vacant, Room 9100, 708–2601.
Deputy Assistant Secretary for—
Finance and Budget.—Susan Betts, 708–2004.
Healthcare Programs.—Roger Lukoff, Room 6264, 708–0599.
Housing Counseling.—Sarah Gerecke, Room 9224, 402–3453.
Housing Operations.—Jeffrey Little, Room 9136, 402–5649.
Multifamily Housing Programs.—C. Lamar Seats, Room 6106, 708–2495.
Risk Management and Regulatory Affairs.—Shawn Jones (acting), Room 9162, 402–2398.
Single Family Housing.—Gisele Roget, Room 9282, 708–3175.

ASSISTANT SECRETARY FOR POLICY DEVELOPMENT AND RESEARCH

Assistant Secretary.—Vacant, Room 8100 (202) 708–1600.
General Deputy Assistant Secretary.—Todd M. Richardson (acting), Room 8100, 708–1600.
Deputy Assistant Secretary for the Office of:
Economic Affairs.—Kurt G. Usowski, Room 8204, 708–3080.
International and Philanthropic Innovation.—Vacant, Room 8138, 708–0770.
Research, Evaluation, and Monitoring.—Calvin C. Johnson, Room 8124, 708–4230.
Deputy Assistant Secretary, Policy Development.—Todd M. Richardson, Room 8106, 708–1537.

ASSISTANT SECRETARY FOR PUBLIC AFFAIRS

Assistant Secretary for Public Affairs.—Amy Thompson, Room 10130 (202) 708–0980.
General Deputy Assistant Secretary.—Jereon M. Brown.
Deputy Assistant Secretary.—Raphael Williams.
Communications Director.—Vacant.
Press Secretary.—Caitlin Thompson.

ASSISTANT SECRETARY FOR PUBLIC AND INDIAN HOUSING

Assistant Secretary.—Vacant.
General Deputy Assistant Secretary.—Dominique G. Blom (202) 708–0950.
Deputy Assistant Secretary for—
Field Operations.—Unabyrd Wadhams, Room 3180, 708–4016.
Native American Programs.—Heidi Frechette, Room 4126, 401–7914.
Policy, Planning, and Legislative Initiatives.—Danielle Bastarache, Room 3178, 402–5264.
Public Housing and Voucher Programs.—Milan Ozdinec, Room 4130, 708–1380.
Public Housing Investments.—Susan Wilson (acting), Room 4130, 401–8500.
Real Estate Assessment Center.—Donald J. Lavoy, Potomac Center (202) 475–7949.

OFFICE OF FIELD POLICY AND MANAGEMENT

Assistant Deputy Secretary.—Mathew F. Hunter, Room 7108 (202) 402–6512.
Associate Assistant Deputy Secretary.—Nelson Bregón, Room 7108, 402–3498.
Director, Office of Davis Bacon and Labor Standards.—Pamela Glekas, Room 7122, 708–2426.

GOVERNMENT NATIONAL MORTGAGE ASSOCIATION

President, Executive Vice President, and COO.—Michael Bright (202) 708–0926.

Executive Vice President.—Maren Kasper, 708–0926.
Senior Vice Presidents, Office of:
Capital Markets.—John F. Getchis, 401–8970.
Enterprise Data and Technology Solutions.—Barbara Cooper-Jones, 708–0926.
Issuer and Portfolio Management.—Michael R. Drayne, 708–4141.
Securities Operations.—John T. Daugherty, 708–2884.
Enterprise Risk.—Gregory A. Keith (also Chief Risk Office), 708–0926.
Management Operations.—Tawanna Preston.
Chief Financial Officer.—Keith Donzell.

CHIEF FINANCIAL OFFICER

Chief Financial Officer.—Irving L. Dennis (202) 708–1946.
Deputy Chief Financial Officer.—George J. Tomchick, 402–5911.
Assistant Chief Financial Officer for—
Accounting.—Nita Nigam, 402–6850.
Budget.—Emily Kornegay, 402–6824.
Financial Management.—MelaJo Kubacki (acting), 402–6549.
Systems.—Joseph Hungate, 402–2801.

CHIEF INFORMATION OFFICER

Chief Information Officer.—Chad Cowan (acting), Room 4160 (202) 402–6453.
Principal Deputy Chief Information Officer.—Kevin R. Cooke, Jr., Room 4160, 708–0306.
Chief Information Security Officer.—Tracey Bigesby (acting), Room 4282, 402–3616.
Deputy Chief Information Officer for—
Officer Business and IT Resource Management Office.—Janice Ausby, Room 4278 HQ, 402–7605.
Infrastructure and Operations.—James Bresnahan (acting), Room 4180 HQ, 402–6383.

CHIEF PROCUREMENT OFFICER

Chief Procurement Officer.—Keith Surber, Room 5280 (202) 708–0600.
Deputy Chief Procurement Officer.—Jimmy Scott, Room 5256, 708–1290.

GENERAL COUNSEL

General Counsel.—J. Paul Compton, Jr., Room 10110 (202) 708–2240.
Principal Deputy General Counsel.—Vacant, Room 10110, 708–2244.
Deputy General Counsel for—
Enforcement and Fair Housing.—David Woll, Jr., Room 10110 (202) 402–7040.
Housing Programs.—Millicent B. Potts (acting), Room 9226, 402–5255.
Operations.—Linda M. Cruciani, Room 10240, 402–5108.
Associate General Counsel for—
Assisted Housing and Community Development.—Althea Forrester, Room 8166, 402–5268.
Ethics, Appeals, and Personnel Law.—Anthony Cummings, Room 2134, 402–2024.
Fair Housing.—Jeanine Worden, Room 10272, 402–5188.
Finance, Procurement, and Administrative Law.—Kevin M. Simpson, Room 8150, 402–2036.
Insured Housing.—Amy Brown (acting), Room 9240, 402–3826.
Legislation and Regulations.—Ariel Pereira, Room 10282, 402–5138.
Litigation.—Nancy Christopher, Room 10258, 402–2364.
Program Enforcement.—Dane M. Narode, Portals Building (202) 245–4141.
Director, Departmental Enforcement Center.—Craig Clemmensen, Portals Building, 245–4195.

INSPECTOR GENERAL

Inspector General.—Helen Albert (acting), Room 8256 (202) 708–0430.
Counsel to the Inspector General.—Jeremy Kirkland, 708–1613.
Assistant Inspector General for—
Audit.—Vacant.
Investigation.—Nicolas Padilla.
Management and Technology.—Vacant.

Evaluation.—Brian Pattison.

OFFICE OF DEPARTMENTAL EQUAL EMPLOYMENT OPPORTUNITY

Director.—John P. Benison, Room 2102 (202) 708–3362.
Deputy Director.—Aisa K. McCullough, Room 2102, 708–5582.

OFFICE OF THE CHIEF HUMAN CAPITAL OFFICER

Chief Human Capital Officer.—Towanda Brooks, Room 2254 (202) 708–0940.
Deputy Chief Human Capital Officer.—Peter Constantine, 402–2377.
Office of Performance Management:
Chief Performance Officer.—Charles Butler (acting), Room 2174A, 402–6310.
Office of Human Capital Services:
Director.—Felicia Purifoy, Room 2272A, 402–2356.
HUD LEARN:
Chief Learning Officer.—Sheila Wright, Room 2250, 708–3368.
Management and Administration:
Chief Management Officer.—Nancy Corsiglia, Room 2172B, 402–4025.

OFFICE OF LEAD HAZARD CONTROL AND HEALTHY HOMES

Director.—Matthew Ammon, Room 8236 (202) 402–4337.
Deputy Director.—Michelle Miller, Room 8236, 402–5769.

OFFICE OF SMALL AND DISADVANTAGED BUSINESS UTILIZATION

Director.—Jean Lin Pao, Room 2200 (202) 402–5713.

HUD REGIONAL ADMINISTRATORS

Region I.—Connecticut, Maine, Massachusetts, New Hampshire, Rhode Island, Vermont.
Regional Administrator.—David E. Tille, Thomas P. O'Neill, Jr. Federal Building, 10 Causeway Street, 3rd Floor, Boston, MA 02222–1092 (617) 994–8223.

Region II.—New Jersey, New York.
Regional Administrator.—Lynne M. Patton, 26 Federal Plaza, Suite 3541, New York, NY 10278–0068 (212) 542–7109.

Region III.—Delaware, District of Columbia, Maryland, Pennsylvania, Virginia, West Virginia.
Regional Administrator.—Joseph J. DeFelice, The Wanamaker Building, 100 Penn Square East, Philadelphia, PA 19107–3380 (215) 656–0600.

Region IV.—Alabama, Florida, Georgia, Kentucky, Mississippi, North Carolina, Puerto Rico, South Carolina, Tennessee.
Regional Administrator.—Denise Cleveland-Leggett, Five Points Plaza, 40 Marietta Street, NW., 2nd Floor, Atlanta, GA 30303–2806 (687) 732–2009.

Region V.—Illinois, Indiana, Michigan, Minnesota, Ohio, Wisconsin.
Regional Administrator.—Joseph P. Galvan, Ralph Metcalfe Federal Building, 77 West Jackson Boulevard, Chicago, IL 60604–3507 (312) 353–5680.

Region VI.—Arkansas, Louisiana, New Mexico, Oklahoma, Texas.
Regional Administrator.—Beth A. Van Duyne, 801 Cherry Street, Fort Worth, TX 76113–2905 (817) 978–5965.

Region VII.—Iowa, Kansas, Missouri, Nebraska.
Regional Administrator.—Jason Mohr, Gateway Tower II, 400 State Avenue, Room 507, Kansas City, KS 66101–2406 (913) 551–5462.

Region VIII.—Colorado, Montana, North Dakota, South Dakota, Utah, Wyoming.
Regional Administrator.—Vacant, 1670 Broadway, Denver, CO 80202–4801 (303) 672–5440.

Region IX.—Arizona, California, Hawaii, Nevada, Guam, Northern Mariana Islands, American Samoa.
Regional Administrator.—Jimmy Stracner, One Sansome Street, Suite 1200, San Francisco, CA 94104–1300 (415) 489–6400.

Region X.—Alaska, Idaho, Oregon, Washington.
Regional Administrator.—Jeffrey McMorris, Seattle Federal Office Building, 909 First Avenue, Suite 200, Seattle, WA 98104–1000 (206) 220–5101.

DEPARTMENT OF TRANSPORTATION

1200 New Jersey Avenue, SE., Washington, DC 20590

phone (202) 366–4000, http://www.dot.gov

ELAINE L. CHAO, Secretary of Transportation; born in Taipei, Taiwan, March 26; education: MBA, Harvard Business School; B.A., Mount Holyoke College, South Hadley, MA; professional: Distinguished Fellow at The Heritage Foundation, 2009–17 and 1996–2001; U.S. Secretary of Labor, 2001–09; president and CEO of the United Way of America, 1992–96; director of the Peace Corps, 1991–92; Deputy Secretary of Transportation, 1989–91; chair of the Federal Maritime Commission, 1988–89; Deputy Administrator, Maritime Administration, 1986–88; family: married to Mitch McConnell, U.S. Senator (KY); nominated by President Donald J. Trump to become the 18th Secretary of Transportation, and was confirmed by the U.S. Senate on January 31, 2017.

OFFICE OF THE SECRETARY

[Created by the act of October 15, 1966; codified under U.S.C. 49]

Secretary of Transportation.—Elaine L. Chao, Room W91–320 (202) 366–1111.
Deputy Secretary.—Jeff Rosen, Room W91–308, 366–2222.
Chief of Staff.—Geoffrey Burr, Room W90–314, 366–2165.
Director of Operations.—J. Todd Inman, Room W90–321, 366–2276.
Under Secretary of Transportation for Policy.—Derek Kan, Room W80–308, 366–9570.
Director, Office of:
Civil Rights.—Charles James, Room W78–320, 366–8825.
Executive Secretariat.—Ruth Knouse, Room W93–324, 366–9747.
Intelligence and Security.—Michael Lowder, Room W56–308, 366–6525.
Small and Disadvantaged Business Utilization.—Willis Morris, Room W56–310, 366–1084.

ASSISTANT SECRETARY FOR ADMINISTRATION

Assistant Secretary.—Keith Nelson, Room W80–322 (202) 366–2332.
Deputy Assistant Secretary.—Keith Washington, W80–320, 366–2332.
Director, Office of:
Facilities, Information and Asset Management.—Yvonne Medina, Room W58–334, 366–9756.
Financial Management.—Marie Petrosino-Wolverton, Room W81–306, 366–3967.
Hearings, Chief Administrative Law Judge.—Judge Ronnie A. Yoder, 55 M Street, 366–2137.
Human Resource Management.—Lisa Williams, Room W81–302, 366–4088.
Security.—Keith Szakal (acting), Room W54–328, 366–9422.
Senior Procurement Executive.—Willie Smith, Room W83–306, 366–4212.

ASSISTANT SECRETARY FOR AVIATION AND INTERNATIONAL AFFAIRS

Assistant Secretary.—Vacant, Room W88–314 (202) 366–8822.
Deputy Assistant Secretaries: Vacant, Room W88–324; Susan McDermott, Room W88–326, 366–4551.
Director, Office of:
Aviation Analysis.—Todd Homan, Room W86–481, 366–5903.
International Aviation.—Brian Hedberg, Room W86–406, 366–2423.
International Transportation and Trade.—Julie Abraham, Room W88–306, 366–4398.

ASSISTANT SECRETARY FOR BUDGET AND PROGRAMS

Chief Financial Officer/Assistant Secretary.—Lana Hurdle (acting), Room W95–316 (202) 366–9192.

Deputy Assistant Secretary.—Lana Hurdle, Room W95–316, 366–9192.

Special Advisor to the Secretary, Office of Budget and Programs.—Keith Nelson, Room W95–320, 366–9191.

Deputy Chief Financial Officer.—Vacant, Room W95–320, 366–9192.

Director, Office of:

Budget and Program Performance.—Laura Ziff, Room W93–308, 366–4594.

Financial Management.—Jennifer Funk, Room W93–322, 366–5628.

ASSISTANT SECRETARY FOR GOVERNMENTAL AFFAIRS

Assistant Secretary.—Adam Sullivan, Room W85–326 (202) 366–4573.

Deputy Assistant Secretaries: Anthony Bedell, Sean McMaster.

Governmental Affairs Officers: Bobby Fraser, Chris Mitton, Phillip Newman.

OFFICE OF THE UNDER SECRETARY OF TRANSPORTATION FOR POLICY

Under Secretary of Transportation for Policy.—Derek Kan, Room W80–308 (202) 366–4540.

Assistant Secretary for Policy.—Vacant.

Deputy Assistant Secretaries for Policy: Grover Burthey, Room W82–308, 366–7265; Finch Fulton, Room W82–312.

GENERAL COUNSEL

General Counsel.—Steven G. Bradbury, Room W92–300, 366–4702.

Deputy General Counsels: Judith S. Kaleta, Room W92–312, 366–4713; James C. Owens, Jr., Room W92–318, 366–4702.

Legal Advisor to the General Counsel.—Andrew R. Kloster, Room W94–320, 366–4702.

Assistant General Counsel for—

Aviation Enforcement and Proceedings.—Blane A. Workie, Room W96–322, 366–9345.

General Law.—Terence W. Carlson, Room W94–306, 366–9152.

International Law.—Donald H. Horn, Room W98–324, 366–2972.

Legislation.—Thomas W. Herlihy, Room W96–326, 366–4687.

Litigation and Enforcement.—Paul M. Geier, Room W94–310, 366–4731.

Operations.—Ronald A. Jackson, Room W96–304, 366–4710.

Regulation.—Jonathan P. Moss, Room W94–302, 366–9314.

INSPECTOR GENERAL

Inspector General.—Calvin L. Scovel III, Room W70–300 (202) 366–1959.

Deputy Inspector General.—Mitch Behm, 366–6767.

Chief of Staff.—Amanda Seese, 366–5583.

Principal Assistant Inspector General for—

Auditing and Evaluation.—Joseph Comé, 366–8751.

Investigations.—Michelle McVicker, 366–1967.

Assistant Inspector General for—

Acquisition and Procurement Audits.—Mary Kay Langan Feirson, 366–5225.

Administration.—Eileen Ennis, 366–2704.

Aviation Audits.—Matthew Hampton, 366–0500.

Financial and Information Technology Audits.—Louis King, 366–1407.

Legal, Legislative and External Affairs.—Brian A. Dettelbach, 366–1967.

Surface Transportation Audits.—Barry DeWeese, 366–5630.

Deputy Assistant Inspector General for—

Aviation Audits.—Anthony Zakel, 366–0500.

Investigations.—Max Smith, 366–1967.

Surface Transportation Audits.—David Pouliott, 366–5630.

REGIONAL AUDIT OFFICES

Regional Program Directors:

Tina Nysted, 61 Forsyth Street, SW., Suite 17T60, Atlanta, GA 30303 (404) 562–3770.
Robin Koch, 61 Forsyth Street, SW., Suite 17T60, Atlanta, GA 30303 (404) 562–3770.
Darren Murphy, 915 Second Avenue, Room 644, Seattle, WA 98174 (206) 220–7754.
George Banks, 10 South Howard Street, Suite 4500, Baltimore, MD 21201 (410) 962–3612.
Kerry Barras, 819 Taylor Street, Room 13A42, Fort Worth, TX 76102 (817) 978–3545.

REGIONAL INVESTIGATIONS OFFICES

Special Agents-In-Charge:
Region I.—Todd Damiani, 55 Broadway, Room 1055, Cambridge, MA 02142 (617) 494–2240.
Region II.—Douglas Shoemaker, 201 Varick Street, Room 1161, New York, NY 10014 (212) 337–1280.
Region III.—Floyd Sherman, 1200 New Jersey Avenue, SE., 7th Floor, Washington, DC 20590 (202) 366–4189.
Region IV.—Marlies Gonzalez, 510 Shotgun Road, Suite 220, Sunrise, FL 33326 (954) 382–6645.
Region V.—Tom Ullom, 200 West Adams Street, Suite 300, Chicago, IL 60606 (312) 353–0106.
Region VI.—Joe Zschiesche, 819 Taylor Street, Room 13A42, Fort Worth, TX 76102 (817) 978–3545.
Region IX.—Bill Swallow, 17785 Center Court Drive, Suite 350, Cerritos, CA 90703 (562) 467–5360.

OFFICE OF PUBLIC AFFAIRS

Assistant to the Secretary and Director of Public Affairs.—Marianne McInerney (202) 366–0305.
Deputy Director.—Allison Moore, 366–5037.
Associate Director of Media Relations.—Vacant, 366–4570.

FEDERAL AVIATION ADMINISTRATION

800 Independence Avenue, SW., 20591 (202) 267–3111

Administrator.—Vacant, 267–3111.
Deputy Administrator.—Daniel Elwell, 267–8111.
Chief of Staff.—Vacant, 267–7416.
Senior Technical Advisor to the Deputy Administrator.—Colleen Donovan, 267–3173
Senior Advisor to the Deputy Administrator.—Elisabeth Smeda, 267–6541.
Executive Assistant to the Administrator.—Megan Bailey, 267–3111.
Executive Assistant to the Deputy Administrator.—Michelle Guynn, 267–8111.
Executive Secretariat.—Vacant, 267–3518.
Director of Audit and Evaluation.—H. Clayton Foushee, 267–9000.
Assistant Administrator for Finance and Management.—Victoria Wassmer, 267–8627.
Deputy Associate Administrator for:
Acquisitions and Business Services.—Nathan Tash, 267–7222.
Financial Services/CFO.—Allison Ritman (acting), 267–9105.
Information Services/CIO.—Tina Amereihn, 267–9692.
Regions and Property Operations.—Vacant, 267–9011.
Director of:
Budget and Programs.—Carl Burrus, 267–8010.
Financial Analysis.—David Rickard, 267–7940.
Financial Operations.—Peter Basso, 267–8242.
Financial Reporting and Accountability.—Allison Ritman, 267–5657.
Investment Planning and Analysis.—Katrina Hall, 267–3422.
Labor Analysis.—Rich McCormick, 267–5943.
Regional Administrators:
Alaskan.—Kerry Long (907) 271–5645.
Central.—Joseph N. Miniace (816) 329–3050.
Eastern.—Jennifer Solomon (718) 553–3000.
Great Lakes.—Rebecca MacPherson (847) 294–7294.
New England.—Vacant (781) 238–7020.
Northwest Mountain.—David Suomi (425) 227–2001.

Southern.—Michael O'Harra (404) 305–5000.
Southwest.—Terry Biggio (817) 222–5001.
Western-Pacific.—Dennis Roberts (310) 725–3550.
Director, Aviation Logistics Organization.—Donald Drummer, 267–7369.
Director, Mike Monroney Aeronautical Center.—Michelle Coppedge (405) 954–4521.
Assistant Administrator for Civil Rights.—Vacant, 267–3254.
Deputy Assistant Administrator for Civil Rights.—Courtney Wilkerson, 267–3254.
Assistant Administrator for Policy, International Affairs and Environment.—Vacant, 267–3927.
Deputy Assistant Administrator for Policy, International Affairs and Environment.—Carl Burleson, 267–7954.
Executive Director of:
Aviation Policy and Plans.—Nan Shellabarger, 267–3274.
Environment and Energy.—Kevin Welsh, 267–3576.
International Affairs.—Chris Rocheleau, 267–1000.
Director of:
Asia-Pacific.—Carey Fagan, 011–65–6575–9475.
Europe, Africa, and Middle East.—Kate Lang, 011–322–811–5159.
Western Hemisphere.—Christopher Banks, 011–507–317–5370.
Chief Counsel.—Charlie Trippe, 267–3222.
Deputy Chief Counsel.—Patricia McNall, 267–3773.
Assistant Administrator for Government and Industry Affairs.—Chris Brown, 267–3277.
Deputy Assistant Administrator for Government and Industry Affairs.—Kate Howard, 267–3277.
Assistant Administrator for Human Resource Management.—Annie Andrews, 267–3456.
Deputy Assistant Administrator.—Gwendolyn DeFillippi, 267–3850.
Director of:
Accountability Board.—Tammy Van Keuren, 267–3065.
Employee and Labor Relations.—Laura Glading, 267–6268.
Talent Development and Chief Learning Officer.—Melissa King, 267–9041.
Regional Human Resource Services.—Renee Coates, 267–2990.
Compensation, Benefits and Work-Life.—Elizabeth Dayan, 267–4028.
Assistant Administrator for Communications.—Greg Martin, 267–3883.
Deputy Assistant Administrator for Public Affairs.—Laura Brown, 267–3883.
Deputy Assistant Administrator for Corporate Communications.—Jeannie Shiffer, 267–3883.
Assistant Administrator for Security and Hazardous Material Safety.—Claudio Manno, 267–7211.
Deputy Assistant Administrator for Security and Hazardous Material Safety.—Angela Stubblefield, 267–7211.
Director, Office of:
National Security and Incident Response.—Joshua Holtzman, 267–7980.
Hazardous Materials Safety.—Janet McLaughlin, 267–9419.
Infrastructure Protection.—Patricia Pausch (847) 294–7411.
Office of Investigations.—Michelle Root, 267–2480.
Business and Mission Services.—Don Faulkner, 267–8005.
Personnel Security.—Gerald Moore (310) 725–3730.
Chief Operating Officer for Air Traffic Organization.—Teri Bristol, 267–1240.
Deputy Chief Operating Officer.—Tim Arel, 267–7224.
Vice President for—
En Route and Oceanic Services.—Gregory Burke, 385–8501.
Management Services.—Lizbeth Mack, 267–5724.
Mission Support.—Vacant, 267–8261.
Program Management.—Kristen Burnham, 267–8626.
Safety and Technical Training.—Vacant, 267–3341.
System Operations.—Mike Artist, 267–0753.
Technical Operations.—Vaughn Turner, 267–3366.
Air Traffic Services.—Glen Martin, 267–0634.
Assistant Administrator for NextGen.—Vacant, 267–7111.
Deputy Assistant Administrator.—Pamela Whitley, 267–7111.
William J. Hughes Technical Center.—Shelley Yak (609) 485–6085.
Director of:
Chief Scientist.—Steve Bradford, 267–1218.
Management Services.—Geofrey Frazier, 267–7255.
NAS Systems Engineering and Integration.—Vacant, 267–2708.
Portfolio Management and Technology Development.—Paul Fontaine, 267–9250.
NextGen Performance and Outreach.—Mark Allen, 267–4544.
Director of Interagency Planning.—Ted Mercer, Jr., 267–4693.

Associate Administrator for Airports.—Vacant, 267–9471.
Deputy Associate Administrator.—Winsome Lenfert, 267–9590.
Director of:
Airport Safety and Standards.—John Dermody, 267–3053.
Airport Planning and Programming.—Elliott Black, 267–8775.
Airport Compliance and Management Analysis.—Kevin Willis, 267–3085.
Associate Administrator for Commercial Space Transportation.—George C. Nield, 267–7793.
Deputy Associate Administrator, Commercial Space Transportation.—Kelvin Coleman, 267–7972.
Director of:
Space Integration.—Michael Romanowski, 267–5417.
Strategic Operations.—Dorothy Reimold, 267–4743.
Chief Engineer.—Michael Kelly, 267–8737.
Associate Administrator for Aviation Safety.—Ali Bahrami, 267–3131.
Deputy Associate Administrator.—John Hickey, 267–7804.
Director of:
Federal Air Surgeon.—Michael Berry, 267–3535.
Flight Standards Service.—John Duncan, 267–8237.
Aircraft Certification Service.—Dorenda Baker, 267–8235.
Office of Air Traffic Oversight.—Vacant, 267–5202.
Quality, Integration and Executive Service.—Sunny Lee Fanning, 267–9664.
Rulemaking.—Lirio Liu, 267–9677.
Accident Investigation and Prevention.—Michael O'Donnell, 267–9612.

FEDERAL HIGHWAY ADMINISTRATION

Washington Headquarters, 1200 New Jersey Avenue, SE., 20590–9898
Turner-Fairbank Highway Research Center (TFHRC)
6300 Georgetown Pike, McLean, VA 22201

Administrator.—Vacant.
Deputy Administrator.—Walter ''Butch'' Waidelich (acting), 366–2242.
Associate Administrator/Director of TFHRC.—Michael F. Trentacoste, 493–3259.
Associate Administrator for Administration.—Sarah J. Shores, 366–0604.
Executive Director.—Gloria Shepherd (acting), 366–8169.
Deputy Chief Counsel.—Nicolle Fleury, 366–1379.
Chief Financial Officer.—Brian Bezio, 366–0622.
Associate Administrator for—
Civil Rights.—Irene Rico, 366–0752.
Federal Lands.—Tim Hess, 366–9472.
Infrastructure.—Tom Everett, 366–0370.
Operations.—Martin Knopp, 366–9210.
Planning, Environment, and Realty.—Hari Kalla (acting), 366–5915.
Policy.—Cheryl Walker (acting), 366–0690.
Public Affairs.—Doug Hecox (acting), 366–6035.
Safety.—Beth Alicandri, 366–8568.

FIELD SERVICES

Organizationally report to Executive Director (HOA–3), Washington, DC

Director of Technical Services.—Amy Lucero, 12300 West Dakota Avenue, Suite 340, Lakewood, CO 80228 (720) 963–3246.
Director of:
Field Services-North.—Bob Arnold (acting), 10 South Howard Street, Baltimore, MD 21201–2819 (410) 962–0739.
Field Services-South.—Derrell Turner, 61 Forsyth Street, SW., Suite 17T26, Atlanta, GA 30303–3104 (404) 562–3571.
Field Services-West.—Janice Brown, 2520 West 4700 South, Suite 9C, Salt Lake City, UT 84118–1847 (720) 963–3730.
Field Services-Mid America.—John Rohlf, 4749 Lincoln Mall Drive, Suite 600, Matteson, IL 60443 (605) 776–1000.

FEDERAL MOTOR CARRIER SAFETY ADMINISTRATION

Administrator.—Raymond P. Martinez, Room W60–308 (202) 366–1927.

Deputy Administrator.—Cathy F. Gautreaux, 366–1927.
Chief Safety Officer.—John Van Steenburg, 366–1927.
Chief Counsel.—Vacant, 366–2866.
Associate Administrator for Field Operations.—Anne L. Collins, 493–0013.
Director, Office of:
External Affairs.—Sharon Worthy, 366–2309.
Governmental Affairs.—Wiley Deck, 366–8729.

FIELD OFFICES

Eastern Service Center (CT, DC, DE, MA, MD, ME, NJ, NH, NY, PA, PR, RI, VA, VT, WV).—Fallon Federal Building, 31 Hopkins Plaza, Suite 800, Baltimore, MD 21201 (443) 703–2240.
Midwestern Service Center (IA, IL, IN, KS, MI, MO, MN, NE, OH, WI).—4749 Lincoln Mall Drive, Suite 300A, Matteson, IL 60443 (708) 283–3577.
Southern Service Center (AL, AR, FL, GA, KY, LA, MS, NC, OK, SC, TN).—1800 Century Boulevard, NE., Suite 1700, Atlanta, GA 30345 (404) 327–7400.
Western Service Center (American Samoa, AK, AZ, CA, CO, Guam, HI, ID, Northern Mariana Islands, MT, ND, NV, NM, OR, SD, TX, UT, WA, WY).—Golden Hills Office Centre, 12600 West Colfax Avenue, Suite B–300, Lakewood, CO 80215 (303) 407–2350.

FEDERAL RAILROAD ADMINISTRATION

1200 New Jersey Avenue, SE., Washington, DC 20590

http://www.fra.dot.gov

Administrator.—Ronald Batory, Room W30–308, 493–6014.
Deputy Administrator.—Mathew Sturges, Room W30–311, 493–6015.
Executive Director.—Vacant, Room W30–310, 493–6194.
Associate Administrator for—
Administration.—Tami Riggs, Room W34–332, 493–6301.
Chief Financial Officer.—Rebecca Pennington, Room W36–306, 440–2870.
Railroad Policy and Development.—Paul Nissenbaum, Room W38–328, 493–6312.
Safety.—Robert Lauby, Room W35–306, 493–6474.
Chief Counsel.—Juan Reyes III, Room W31–320, 493–6022.
Deputy Chief Counsel.—Brett Jortland (acting), Room W31–318, 493–6035.
Communications and Legislative Affairs.—Christopher Hess, Room W32–204, 366–4285.
Director of:
Budget.—Scott Keene, Room W36–306, 493–0786.
Civil Rights.—Calvin Gibson, Room W33–316, 493–6010.
Financial Management.—Tiwalade Bello, Room W36–304, 493–6163.
Public Engagement.—Timothy Barkley, Room W33–320, 493–1305.

REGIONAL OFFICES (RAILROAD SAFETY)

Region 1 (Northeastern).—Connecticut, Maine, Massachusetts, New Hampshire, New Jersey, New York, Rhode Island, Vermont.
Regional Administrator.—Les Fiorenzo, Room 1077, 55 Broadway, Cambridge, MA 02142 (617) 494–3484.
Region 2 (Eastern).—Delaware, District of Columbia, Maryland, Pennsylvania, Virginia, West Virginia, Ohio.
Regional Administrator.—Dave Kannenberg, 1510 Chester Pike, Baldwin Tower, Suite 660, Crum Lynne, PA 19022 (610) 521–8200.
Region 3 (Southern).—Kentucky, Tennessee, Mississippi, North Carolina, South Carolina, Georgia, Alabama, Florida.
Regional Administrator.—Carmen Patriarca, 61 Forsyth Street, NW., Suite 16T20, Atlanta, GA 30303 (404) 562–3809.
Region 4 (Central).—Minnesota, Illinois, Indiana, Michigan, Wisconsin.
Regional Administrator.—Mike Turnbull, 200 West Adams Street, Chicago, IL 60606 (312) 353–6203.
Region 5 (Southwestern).—Arkansas, Louisiana, New Mexico, Oklahoma, Texas.
Regional Administrator.—Vence Haggard, 4100 International Plaza, Suite 450, Ft. Worth, TX 96109 (817) 862–2220.
Region 6 (Midwestern).—Iowa, Missouri, Kansas, Nebraska, Colorado.

Regional Administrator.—Steven Fender, DOT Building, 901 Locust Street, Suite 464, Kansas City, MO 64106 (816) 329–3840.

Region 7 (Western).—Arizona, California, Nevada, Utah.

Regional Administrator.—James Jordan, 801 I Street, Suite 466, Sacramento, CA 95814 (916) 498–6547.

Region 8 (Northwestern).—Idaho, Oregon, Wyoming, Montana, North Dakota, South Dakota, Washington, Alaska.

Regional Administrator.—Mark Daniels, 500 Broadway, Murdock Executive Plaza, Suite 240, Vancouver, WA 98660 (360) 696–7536.

FEDERAL TRANSIT ADMINISTRATION

Administrator.—Vacant.

Deputy Administrator.—K. Jane Williams (202) 366–4040.

Chief Counsel.—Dana Nifosi (acting), 366–1643.

Director, Office of Civil Rights.—Selene Dalton-Kumins (acting), 366–5401.

Planning and Environment.—Lucy Garliauskas, 366–4033.

Associate Administrator for—

Administration.—Matt Crouch, 366–4007.

Budget and Policy.—Robert Tuccillo, 366–4050.

Communications and Congressional Affairs.—David Longo (acting), 366–0608.

Program Management.—Henrika Buchanan-Smith, 366–4020.

Research, Demonstration, and Innovation.—Vincent Valdes, 366–3052.

Safety and Oversight.—Thomas Littleton, 366–9239.

MARITIME ADMINISTRATION

Administrator and Chair, Maritime Subsidy Board.—RADM Mark H. Buzby, USN (Ret.), Room W22–318 (202) 366–1719.

Deputy Administrator.—Richard A. Balzano, Room W22–314, 366–5823.

Secretary, Maritime Administration and Maritime Subsidy Board.—Vacant, 366–5746.

Chief Counsel and Member, Maritime Subsidy Board.—Douglas Burnett, Room W24–310, 366–0709.

Director, Office of Congressional and Public Affairs.—Vacant, Room W22–324, 366–9407.

Public Affairs Officer.—Kim Strong, Room W22–324, 366–5067.

Executive Director.—Vacant, Room W28–316, 366–3907.

Director of:

International Activities.—Lonnie T. Kishiyama, Room W28–312, 366–5493.

Policy and Plans.—Douglas McDonald, Room W26–326, 366–2145.

Associate Administrator for Budget and Programs/Chief Financial Officer.—Lydia Moschkin, Room W21–334, 366–3071.

Director, Office of:

Accounting.—Inga Maik, Room W25–333, 366–1947.

Budget.—Alex J. Caine, Room W26–310, 493–0362.

National Security Program/Funds Control.—Inga Maik, Room W25–333, 366–1947.

Resources.—Vacant, Room W26–309, 366–5110.

Associate Administrator for Administration.—Delia P. Davis, Room W26–312, 366–2181.

Director, Office of:

Acquisition.—Wayne Leong, Room W26–324, 366–5620.

Information Technology.—Robert Ellington, Room W26–320, 366–2531.

Management and Information Services.—Steve Snipes, Room W26–302, 366–2811.

Personnel.—Sandra Ambrose, Room W26–319, 366–0619.

Associate Administrator for Environment and Compliance.—John Quinn, Room W21–326, 366–1931.

Director, Office of:

Environment.—Michael C. Carter, Room W25–302, 366–9431.

Safety.—Kevin Kohlman, Room W25–302, 366–5126.

Security.—Cameron Naron, Room W28–340, 366–1883.

Associate Administrator for Intermodal System Development.—Lauren K. Brand, Room W21–320, 366–7057.

Deputy.—Scott Davies (acting), Room W21–324, 366–0720.

Director, Office of:

Deepwater Ports and Offshore Activities.—Yvette Fields, Room W21–309, 366–0926.

Gateway Offices.—William Paape, Room W21–307, 366–5005.

Infrastructure Development and Congestion Mitigation.—Robert Bouchard, Room W21–308, 366–5076.

Marine Highways and Passenger Services.—Scott Davies, Room W21–312, 366–0951.
Shipper and Carrier Outreach.—Vacant, Room W21–310, 366–0704.
Associate Administrator for National Security.—Kevin M. Tokarski, Room W25–330, 366–5400.
Director, Office of:
Emergency Preparedness.—Thomas M.P. Christensen, Room W23–304, 366–5909.
Sealift Support.—Bill Kurfehs, Room W25–318, 366–2318.
Ship Disposal.—Vacant, Room W25–334, 366–6467.
Ship Operations.—William H. Cahill, Room W25–336, 366–1875.
Associate Administrator for Business and Finance Development.—Owen Doherty, Room W21–318, 366–9595.
Director, Office of:
Cargo Preference and Domestic Trade.—Dennis Brennan, Room W23–316, 366–1029.
Financial Approvals and Marine Insurance.—Michael Yarrington, Room W23–312, 366–1915.
Chief, Division of Business Finance.—Vacant, Room W23–321, 366–1908.
Director, Office of:
Maritime Workforce Development.—Anne Wehde, Room W23–314, 366–5469.
Shipyards and Marine Finance.—David Heller, Room W23–324, 366–1850.

FIELD ACTIVITIES

Director for:
Great Lakes and Upper Inland Waterways Region.—Floyd Miras, Suite 185, 2860 South River Road, Des Plaines, IL 60018 (847) 905–0122.
North Atlantic Region.—Jeffrey Flumignan, 1 Bowling Green, Room 418, New York, NY 10004 (212) 668–2064.
Northern California/Hawaii Region.—John Hummer, Suite 2200, 201 Mission Street, San Francisco, CA 94105 (415) 744–3125.
South Atlantic Region.—Frances Bohnsack, Building 4D, Room 211, 7737 Hampton Boulevard, Norfolk, VA 23505 (757) 441–6393.

U.S. MERCHANT MARINE ACADEMY

Superintendent.—RADM James Helis, Kings Point, NY 11024 (516) 773–5000.
Deputy Superintendent for Academic Affairs (Academic Dean).—RDML Susan Dunlap.

NATIONAL HIGHWAY TRAFFIC SAFETY ADMINISTRATION

Administrator.—Heidi R. King (acting), Room W42–302 (202) 366–1836.
Deputy Administrator.—Heidi R. King, 366–1836.
Director, Communications.—Vacant, 366–1836.
Director, Governmental Affairs, Policy and Strategic Planning.—Vacant, 366–1836.
Chief Counsel.—Jonathan Morrison, 366–9511.
Executive Director.—Jack Danielson, 366–1836.
Associate Administrator for—
Communications and Consumer Information.—Susan Gorcowski, 366–9550.
Enforcement.—Jeffrey Giuseppe, 366–5756.
National Center for Statistics and Analysis.—Terry Sheldon, 366–1503.
Administrative Management.—Vanester Williams (acting), 366–4773.
Regional Operations and Program Delivery.—Maggi Gunnels, 366–2121.
Research and Program Development.—Jeff Michael, 366–4299.
Rulemaking.—Ryan Posten, 366–1810.
Vehicle Safety Research Program.—Nathaniel Beuse, 366–4862.
Chief Information Officer.—Colleen Coggins, 366–4878.
Director, Office of Civil Rights.—Regina Morgan, 366–8046.
Chief Financial Officer.—Cynthia Parker, 366–2255.
Supervisor, Executive Correspondence.—Julie Korkor, 366–5470.

REGIONAL OFFICES

Region 1.—Maine, Massachusetts, New Hampshire, Rhode Island, Vermont.
Regional Administrator.—Art Kinsman, Volpe National Transportation Center, 55 Broadway, Kendall Square, Code RTV–8E, Cambridge, MA 02142 (617) 494–3427.

Region 2.—Connecticut, New York, New Jersey, Pennsylvania, Puerto Rico, Virgin Islands.
Regional Administrator.—Michael N. Geraci, 245 Main Street, Suite 210, White Plains, NY 10601 (914) 682–6162.

Region 3.—Delaware, District of Columbia, Maryland, Kentucky, North Carolina, Virginia, West Virginia.
Regional Administrator.—Elizabeth Baker, George H. Fallon Federal Building, 31 Hopkins Plaza, Room 902, Baltimore, MD 21201 (410) 962–0090.

Region 4.—Alabama, Florida, Georgia, South Carolina, Tennessee.
Regional Administrator.—Carmen Hayes, Atlanta Federal Center, 61 Forsyth Street, SW., Suite 17T30, Atlanta, GA 30303–3106 (404) 562–3739.

Region 5.—Illinois, Indiana, Michigan, Minnesota, Ohio, Wisconsin.
Regional Administrator.—Michael N. Geraci (acting), 19900 Governors Drive, Suite 201, Olympia Fields, IL 60461 (708) 503–8892.

Region 6.—Louisiana, Mississippi, New Mexico, Oklahoma, Texas, Indian Nations.
Regional Administrator.—Susan DeCourcy (acting), 819 Taylor Street, Room 8A38, Fort Worth, TX 76102–6177 (817) 978–3653.

Region 7.—Arkansas, Iowa, Kansas, Missouri, Nebraska.
Regional Administrator.—Susan DeCourcy, 901 Locust Street, Room 466, Kansas City, MO 64106 (816) 329–3900.

Region 8.—Colorado, North Dakota, Nevada, South Dakota, Utah, Wyoming.
Regional Administrator.—Gina Espinosa-Salcedo, 12300 West Dakota Avenue, Suite 140, Lakewood, CO 80228–2583 (720) 963–3100.

Region 9.—American Samoa, Arizona, California, Guam, Mariana Islands, Hawaii.
Regional Administrator.—Chris Murphy, John E. Moss Federal Building, 650 Capitol Mall, Suite 5–400, Sacramento, CA 95814 (916) 498–5058.

Region 10.—Alaska, Idaho, Montana, Oregon, Washington.
Regional Administrator.—Greg T. Fredericksen, Federal Building, 915 Second Avenue, Suite 3140, Seattle, WA 98174 (206) 220–7645.

PIPELINE AND HAZARDOUS MATERIALS SAFETY ADMINISTRATION

Administrator.—Howard ''Skip'' Elliott, Room E27–300 (202) 366–4433.
Deputy Administrator.—Drue Pearce, Room E27–300, 366–4433.
Executive Director.—Howard ''Mac'' McMillan, Room E27–325, 366–4433.
Chief Counsel.—Vasiliki Tsaganos (acting), Room E26–320, 366–4400.
Director, Office of Civil Rights.—Rosanne Goodwill, Room E27–334, 366–9638.
Chief Financial Officer.—Tami Perriello, Room E22–312, 366–4433.
Associate Administrator for—
Management and Administration.—Everett Lott, Room E32–330, 366–4831.
Hazardous Materials Safety.—William Schoonover, Room E21–316, 366–4488.
Pipeline Safety.—Alan Mayberry, Room E22–321, 366–4595.
Planning and Analytics.—Kim Curry, Room E25–336, 366–4433.
Governmental, International, and Public Affairs.—Patricia Klinger (acting), Director, Room E27–300, 366–4831.

HAZARDOUS MATERIALS SAFETY OFFICES

Chief of:
Eastern Region.—Vincent Mercandante, 820 Bear Tavern Road, Suite 306, West Trenton, NJ 08628 (609) 989–2256.
Central Region.—Vacant, Suite 478, 2350 East Devon Avenue, Des Plaines, IL 60018 (847) 294–8580.
Western Region.—Marc Nichols, 3401 Centre Lake Drive, Suite 550–B, Ontario, CA 91761 (909) 937–3279.
Southern Region.—John Heneghan, 233 Peachtree Street, NE., Suite 602, Atlanta, GA 30303 (404) 832–1140.
Southwest Region.—Vacant, 8701 South Gessner Road, Suite 1110, Houston, TX 77004 (713) 272–2820.

PIPELINE SAFETY OFFICES

Director of:
Eastern Region.—Vacant, 820 Bear Tavern Road, Suite 103, West Trenton, NJ 08628 (609) 989–2171.

Central Region.—Alan Beshore, 901 Locust Street, Room 462, Kansas City, MO 64106 (816) 329–3800.
Western Region.—Vacant, 12300 West Dakota Avenue, Suite 110, Lakewood, CO 80228 (720) 963–3160.
Southwest Region.—Vacant, 8701 South Gessner, Suite 1110, Houston, TX 77074 (713) 272–2859.
Southern Region.—James Urisko, 233 Peachtree Street, NE., Suite 600, Atlanta, GA 30303 (404) 832–1140.

OFFICE OF THE ASSISTANT SECRETARY FOR RESEARCH AND TECHNOLOGY (OST–R)

https://www.transportation.gov/administrations/research-and-technology

Assistant Secretary.—Vacant.
Deputy Assistant Secretary.—Vacant.
Executive Director.—Audrey Farley, Room E33–302 (202) 366–4112.
Public Affairs Contact, Bureau of Transportation Statistics.—David Smallen, Room E36–328, 366–5568; OST–R.—Nancy Wilochka, Room E36–331, 366–5128.
Director for—
Intelligent Transportation Systems.—Kenneth M. Leonard, Room E31–301, 366–9536.
Office of Technology Policy and Outreach.—Timothy Klein, Room E36–332, 366–0075.
Transportation Safety Institute.—Kevin Womack, 6500 South MacArthur Boulevard, MPB–343, Oklahoma City, OK 73169 (405) 954–7312.
Volpe National Transportation Systems Center.—Anne Aylward, Room 1240, 55 Broadway, Kendall Square, Cambridge, MA 02142 (617) 494–2191.

SAINT LAWRENCE SEAWAY DEVELOPMENT CORPORATION–U.S. DOT

www.greatlakes-seaway.com/en

Administrator.—Vacant (202) 366–0091, fax 366–7147.
Deputy Administrator.—Craig H. Middlebrook, 366–0105.
Chief of Staff.—Wayne A. Williams, 366–0107.
Director, Office of:
Budget and Economic Development.—Kevin P. O'Malley, 366–8982.
Congressional and Public Relations.—Nancy T. Alcalde, 366–6114.

SEAWAY OPERATIONS

180 Andrews Street, Massena, NY 13662–0520

phone (315) 764–3200, fax 764–3235

Associate Administrator.—Thomas A. Lavigne.
Deputy Associate Administrator.—Vacant.
Chief Counsel.—Carrie Mann Lavigne.
Director, Office of:
Engineering and Maintenance.—Jeffrey W. Scharf.
Financial Management and Administration and CFO.—Nancy C. Scott.
Lock Operations and Marine Services.—Christopher L. Guimond.

SURFACE TRANSPORTATION BOARD

395 E Street, SW., 20423–0001, phone (202) 245–0238

http://www.stb.dot.gov

Chair.—Ann Begeman, 245–0203.
Vice Chair.—Deb Miller, 245–0210.
Office of the Managing Director.—Rachel Campbell (acting), 245–0357.
General Counsel.—Craig Keats, 245–0264.
Director, Office of:

Economics.—William Brennan (acting), 245–0321.
Environmental Analysis.—Victoria Rutson, 245–0295.
Proceedings.—Scott Zimmerman (acting), 245–0386.
Public Assistance, Governmental Affairs, and Compliance.—Lucille Marvin, 245–0238.

DEPARTMENT OF ENERGY

James Forrestal Building, 1000 Independence Avenue, SW., 20585

phone (202) 586–5000, http://www.energy.gov

RICK PERRY, Secretary of Energy; born on March 4, 1950, in Haskell, TX; education: B.S., animal science, Texas A&M University, 1972; professional: served, U.S. Air Force, 1972–77, discharged as captain; Texas State Representative, District 64, 1985–90; Texas State Commissioner of Agriculture, 1991–98; Texas Lieutenant Governor, 1999–December 2000; longest serving Governor of Texas, December 2000–15; married: Anita Thigpen; two children, two granddaughters; nominated by President Donald J. Trump to become the 14th Secretary of Energy, and was confirmed by the U.S. Senate on March 2, 2017.

OFFICE OF THE SECRETARY

Secretary of Energy.—James Richard ''Rick'' Perry (202) 586–6210.
Deputy Secretary.—Dan Brouillette, 586–5500.
Associate Deputy Secretary.—Vacant, 586–6210.
Chief of Staff.—Brian McCormack, 586–6210.
Inspector General.—April Stephenson (acting), 586–6462.
Assistant Secretary for—
Congressional and Intergovernmental Affairs.—Shari Davenport (acting), 586–5450.
Policy and International Affairs.—Andrea Lockwood (acting), 586–5800.
General Counsel.—John Lucas (acting), 586–5281.
Chief Information Officer.—Robert Green (acting), 586–0166.
Chief Human Capital Officer.—Bob Gibbs, 586–1234.
Chief Financial Officer.—Alison Doone (acting), 586–4171.
Chief Health Safety and Security Officer.—Glenn Podonsky, 586–9275.
Executive Director of the Loan Programs Office.—Peter Davidson (acting), 287–5854.
Director, Office of:
Economic Impact and Diversity.—Andre Sayles (acting), 586–8383.
Hearings and Appeals.—Poli Marmolejos, 287–1566.
Intelligence and Counterintelligence.—Steve Black, 586–1352.
Management.—Ingrid Kolb, 586–2550.
Public Affairs.—Michelle Laver (acting), 586–4940.
Director for Advanced Research Projects Agency—Energy.—Eric A. Rohlfing (acting), 287–5865.
Administrator for Energy Information Administration.—Howard Gruenspecht (acting), 586–6351.

UNDER SECRETARY FOR MANAGEMENT AND PERFORMANCE

Under Secretary for Management and Performance.—Mark Menezes.
Deputy Under Secretary for Management and Performance.—Vacant.
Assistant Secretary for Environmental Management.—James Owendoff (acting), (202) 586–7709.
Chiefs:
Health Safety and Security Officer.—Matthew Moury, 586–1285.
Human Capital Officer.—Tonya Mackey (acting), 586–1234.
Information Officer.—Max Everett, 586–0166.
Director, Office of:
Economic Impact and Diversity.—Andre Sayles (acting), 586–8383.
Hearings and Appeals.—Poli Marmolejos, 287–1566.
Management.—Ingrid Kolb, 586–2550.
Legacy Management.—Carmelo Melendez, 586–3559.
Project Management Oversight and Assessments.—Paul Bosco, 586–1784.

UNDER SECRETARY FOR SCIENCE

Under Secretary for Science.—Paul M. Dabbar (202) 586–0505.
Assistant Secretary for—
Electricity Delivery and Energy Reliability.—Patricia Hoffman (acting), 586–1411.
Energy Efficiency and Renewable Energy.—Steven Chalk (acting), 586–9220.
Fossil Energy.—Douglas Hollett (acting), 586–6660.
Nuclear Energy.—Raymond Furstenau (acting), 586–6630.
Director, Office of:
Indian Energy Policy and Programs.—Christopher Deschene, 596–1272.
Science.—Steve Binkley (acting), 586–5430.

NATIONAL NUCLEAR SECURITY ADMINISTRATION

Administrator for National Nuclear Security Administration/Under Secretary for Nuclear Security.—Lisa E. Gordon-Hagerty (202) 586–5555.
Principal Deputy Administrator.—Vacant.
Deputy Administrator for—
Defense Programs.—Philip T. Calbos (acting), 586–2179.
Defense Nuclear Nonproliferation.—David Huizenga (acting), 586–0645.
Naval Reactors.—Admiral James Caldwell, USN, 781–6174.
Deputy Under Secretary for Counterterrorism.—Jay A. Tilden, 586–1734.
Associate Administrator for—
Defense Nuclear Security.—Jeffrey Johnson, 586–8900.
Emergency Operations.—Eric Smith (acting), 586–9892.
Safety, Infrastructure and Operations.—James J. McConnell, 586–0131.

MAJOR FIELD ORGANIZATIONS

OPERATIONS OFFICES

Managers:
Idaho.—Richard Provencher (866) 495–7440, fax (208) 526–5406.
Oak Ridge.—Ken Tarcza (865) 576–4444, fax 576–0006.
Richland.—Doug Shoop (509) 376–7395, fax 376–4789.
Savannah River.—Jack Craig, Jr. (803) 952–7697, fax 725–1910.

INTEGRATED SUPPORT/BUSINESS CENTERS

Managers:
Chicago Office.—Roxanne E. Purucker (630) 252–2110.
EM Consolidated Business Center.—Ralph Holland (513) 246–0500.
NNSA Service Center.—Geoffrey Beausoleil (505) 845–4392.

POWER MARKETING ADMINISTRATIONS

Administrator, Power Administration:
Bonneville.—Elliott Mainzer (503) 230–5101, fax 230–4018.
Southeastern Area.—Kenneth Legg (706) 213–3800, fax 213–3884.
Southwestern Area.—Scott Carpenter (918) 595–6601, fax 595–6755.
Western Area.—Mark Gabriel (720) 962–7077, fax 962–7083.

PETROLEUM RESERVES

Deputy Assistant Secretary for Petroleum Reserves.—Robert Corbin (202) 586–9460.

FEDERAL ENERGY REGULATORY COMMISSION

888 First Street, NE., 20426

Chair.—Kevin McIntyre (202) 502–8000.

Commissioners: Neil Chatterjee, 502–6477; Richard Glick, 502–6530; Cheryl A. LaFleur, 502–8961; Robert F. Powelson, 502–6481.
Chief Administrative Law Judge.—Carmen A. Cintron, 502–8500.
Executive Director.—Anton C. Porter, 502–8300.
General Counsel.—James Danly, 502–6000.
Secretary, Office of the Secretary.—Kimberly Bose, 502–8400.
Director, Office of:
Administrative Litigation.—Nils Nichols, 502–6100.
Electric Reliability.—Vacant.
Energy Infrastructure Security.—Joseph McClelland, 502–8867.
Energy Market Regulation.—Anna V. Cochrane, 502–6700.
Energy Policy and Innovation.—J. Arnold Quinn, 502–8693.
Energy Projects.—Terry Turpin, 502–8700.
Enforcement.—Larry R. Parkinson, 502–8100.
External Affairs.—Leonard Tao, 502–8004.

DEPARTMENT OF EDUCATION

400 Maryland Avenue, SW., 20202

phone (202) 401–3000, fax 260–7867, http://www.ed.gov

BETSY DEVOS, Secretary of Education, born in Holland, MI, January 8, 1958; education: B.A., business economics, Calvin College, Grand Rapids, MI, 1979; professional: chairwoman, The Windquest Group; organizations: the Kennedy Center for the Performing Arts; Kids Hope USA; ArtPrize; Mars Hill Bible Church; and the Kendall College of Art and Design; married: Dick DeVos; four children; six grandchildren; nominated by President Donald Trump to become the 11th Secretary of Education on November 23, 2016; confirmed by the U.S. Senate on February 7, 2017.

OFFICE OF THE SECRETARY

Room 7W301, phone (202) 401–3000, fax 260–7867

Secretary of Education.—Betsy DeVos.
Chief of Staff.—Joshua Venable.
Deputy Chief of Staff, Operations.—Dougie Simmons.
Deputy Chief of Staff, Policy.—Ebony Lee.

OFFICE OF THE DEPUTY SECRETARY

Room 7W308, phone (202) 401–1000

Deputy Secretary.—Joe Canty (acting).
Chief of Staff.—Vacant.

OFFICE OF THE UNDER SECRETARY

Room 7E307, phone (202) 401–0429

Under Secretary.—James Manning (acting).
Deputy Under Secretaries: Vacant.
Chief of Staff.—Vacant.

OFFICE OF THE CHIEF FINANCIAL OFFICER

PCP 550 12th Street, SW., phone (202) 245–8144, fax 485–0160

Chief Financial Officer.—Douglas Webster, PCP, 550 12th Street, SW., Room 6124, 245–8144.
Deputy Chief Financial Officer.—Tim Soltis, PCP, Room 6124, 245–6555.
Executive Officer.—Jennifer Sheriff-Parker, PCP, Room 6096, 245–8257.
Director of:
Contracts and Acquisitions Management.—James Hairfield, PCP, Room 7153, 245–6219.
Financial Improvement Operations.—Phillip Juengst, PCP, Room 6057, 245–8030.
Financial Management Operations.—Gary Wood, PCP, Room 6089, 245–8118.

OFFICE OF THE CHIEF INFORMATION OFFICER

PCP 550 12th Street, SW., phone (202) 245–6400, fax 245–6621

Chief Information Officer.—Jason K. Gray, PCP, Room 9112, 245–6252.
Deputy Chief Information Officer.—Ann Kim, PCP, Room 9149, 245–7076.

Executive Officer.—Jennifer Sheriff-Parker, PCP, Room 6096, 245–8257.
Director of:
Financial Systems Services.—Greg Robison, PCP, Room 9150, 245–7187.
Information Assurance Services.—Daniel Galik, PCP, Room 10057, 245–6406.
Information Technology Program Services.—Walter McDonald, PCP, Room 9109, 245–6794.
Information Technology Services.—Vacant, PCP, Room 9151, 245–6400.

OFFICE OF MANAGEMENT

400 Maryland Avenue, SW., phone (202) 401–5848, fax 401–0520

Assistant Secretary.—Vacant, Room 212–20, 401–5848, fax 401–0520.
Principal Deputy Assistant Secretary.—Denise L. Carter, Room 212–30, 401–5848, fax 401–0520.
Chief of Staff.—Richard Smith, Room 210–24, 260–8987, fax 401–0520.
Executive Officer.—Wanda Davis, Room 210–40, 401–5931, fax 401–3513.
Director, Alternative Dispute Resolution Center.—Frank J. Furey, PCP–10089, 245–7185, fax 245–6929.
Service Director of:
Equal Employment Opportunity Services.—Michael Chew, Room 226–10, 401–0691, fax 205–5760.
Facilities Services.—Vacant, Room 238–60, 401–9496, fax 453–5579.
Office of Human Resources.—Cassandra Cuffee-Graves, Room 220–30, 453–5588, fax 401–0520.
Management Services.—David Cogdill, Room 226–70, 401–0695, fax 205–1866.
Office of Hearings and Appeals.—Frank J. Furey, PCP–10089, 245–7185, fax 245–6931.
Office of the Chief Privacy Officer.—Kathleen Styles, Room 218–70, 453–5587, fax 401–0920.
Security Services.—Ronald Luczak, Room 226–20, 260–7727, fax 205–7940.

OFFICE FOR CIVIL RIGHTS

400 Maryland Avenue, SW., Room 4E340, 20202–1100, phone (202) 423–5900

fax 423–6010

Assistant Secretary for Civil Rights/Deputy Assistant Secretary for Strategic Operations and Outreach.—Candice Jackson (acting), Room 4E329, 453–6761.
Confidential Assistant to the Acting Assistant Secretary for Civil Rights.—Chelsea Henderson, Room 4E340, 453–5799.
Attorney Advisors: Brittany Bull, Room 4E311, 453–5548; Brandon Sherman, Room 4E311, 260–1115.
Deputy Assistant Secretary for Policy and Development.—William E. Trachman, Room 4E348, 453–7424.
Deputy Assistant Secretary for Strategic Management and Operations/Executive Officer.—Earl Morgan, Room 4E329, 453–7115.
Special Assistant to the Deputy Assistant Secretary for Management and Operations.—Anna Kasior, Room 4E317, 453–6613.
Deputy Assistant Secretary for Enforcement.—Sandra Battle, Room 4E314, 453–5749.
Enforcement Directors: Carol Ashley, Room 4E312, 453–6790; Lisa Chang, Room 4E330, 453–6849; Mia Karvonides, Room 4E310, 453–7070; Randolph Wills, Room 4E332, 453–5956.
Executive Assistant to the Deputy Assistant Secretary for Enforcement.—Marvida Scarbrough, Room 4E328, 453–5749.
Director, Program Legal Group.—Alejandro Reyes, Room 4E308, 453–6639.
Deputy Director, Program Legal Group.—Matt Faiella, Room 4E306, 453–6027.
Senior Counsel/FOIA.—Kristine Minami, Room 4E303, 453–6626.
Special Assistant for Diversity and Inclusion.—Olegario ''Ollie'' Cantos, Room 4E327, 453–6543.
Human Resources Team Supervisor.—Nichelle Boone, Room 4C144, 401–3710.
Budget and Planning Support Team Lead.—Crystal Foster (acting), Room 4E109, 453–6454.
Customer Service and Technology Team Supervisor.—Carla Reed, Room 4C153, 453–5686.

OFFICE OF CAREER, TECHNICAL, AND ADULT EDUCATION

550 12th Street, SW., 11th Floor, 20202, phone (202) 245–7700, fax 245–7171

Assistant Secretary.—Vacant.
Chief of Staff.—George Smith, george.smith@ed.gov.
Deputy Assistant Secretaries: Mark Mitsui, mark.mitsui@ed.gov; Johan Uvin, johan.uvin@ed.gov.
Staff Assistants: Francine Sinclair, francine.sinclair@ed.gov; Isabel Soto, isabel.soto@ed.gov.

OFFICE OF COMMUNICATIONS AND OUTREACH

Information Resource Center

Room 5E233, phone (202) 453–7000, (202) 401–2000

Assistant Secretary.—Jonathan Schorr (acting), Room 7W101, LBJ, 401–6359.
Press Secretary.—Dorie Nolt, Room 7C115, 453–6544, LBJ, press@ed.gov.
Deputy Assistant Secretaries:
Communication Development.—Vacant.
National Engagement.—Karen Stratman-Krusemark (acting), Room 316, LBJ, 401–2559.
Operations.—Cynthia Dorfman, Room 5E231, LBJ, 205–2604.

OFFICE OF ELEMENTARY AND SECONDARY EDUCATION

Room 3W300, phone (202) 401–0113, fax 205–0303

Assistant Secretary.—Deb Delisle, Room 3W315, 401–0113.
Deputy Assistant Secretary for—
Early Learning.—Libby Doggett, Room 3W311, 205–2828.
Management.—Alex Goniprow, Room 3W314, 401–9090.
Policy and Strategic Initiatives.—Scott Sargrad, Room 3W307, 453–7254.
Chief of Staff.—Heather Rieman, Room 3W313, 260–1700.
Program Director, Office of:
Academic Improvement.—Sylvia Lyles, Room 3E314, 260–8228, fax 260–8969.
Impact Aid Programs.—Alfred Lott, Room 3E105, 260–3858, fax 205–0088.
Indian Education.—Joyce Silverthorne, Room 3W203, 401–0767.
Migrant Education/School Support and Rural Programs.—Lisa Ramirez, Room 3E317, 260–1127, fax 205–0089.
School Support Programs.—Monique Chism, Room 3W224, 260–0826.
Safe and Healthy Students Programs.—David Esquith, Room 3E328, 453–6722.

OFFICE OF ENGLISH LANGUAGE ACQUISITION

400 Maryland Avenue, SW., 5C–132, 20202, phone (202) 401–4300, fax 401–8452

Assistant Deputy Secretary and Director.—Jose Viana.
Deputy Director.—Supreet Anand.

OFFICE OF FEDERAL STUDENT AID

830 First Street, NE., 20202, phone (202) 377–3000, fax 275–5000

Chief Operating Officer.—Dr. A Wayne Johnson.
Deputy Chief Operating Officer.—Matthew Sessa.
Chief of Staff.—Colleen McGinnis, Room 112C1, 377–4330.
Ombudsman.—Joyce DeMoss, Room 41I1, 377–3992.
Chiefs:
Administration Officer.—Quasette Crowner, Room 21A5, 377–3064.
Business Operations Officer.—William Leith, Room 111I1, 377–3676.
Compliance Officer.—Robin Minor, Room 81J3, 377–3717.
Customer Experience Officer.—Christopher Greene, Room 114F11, 377–4141.
Enterprise Risk Officer.—Dr. Michael Dean, Room 112J1, 377–4132.
Financial Officer.—Jay Hurt, Room 54E1, 377–3453.
Information Officer.—Keith Wilson, Room 101G3, 377–3591.
Performance Management Officer.—John Fare, Room 92B2, 377–3707.

Directors:
Director, Communications.—Christopher Green (acting), Room 22C7, 377–4003.
Director, Enforcement.—Dr. Julian Schmoke, Room 111/4, 377–3083.
Head of Contracting Activity.—Patrick Bradfield, Room 93G1, 377–3105.
Director, Policy Liaison and Implementation Staff.—Vacant.

OFFICE OF THE GENERAL COUNSEL

Room 6E313, phone (202) 401–6000, fax 205–2689

General Counsel.—Vacant.
Delegated the authority to perform the functions and duties of the General Counsel.— Steven J. Menashi.
Confidential Assistant.—Patrick Shaheen (202) 453–6339.
Chief of Staff.—Vacant.
Senior Counsels: Ron Petracca, Robert Wexler.
Senior Counsel for Information and Technology.—''Bucky'' Methfessel.
Executive Officer.—Paula Shipp (202) 205–5203.
Deputy General Counsel for Postsecondary Education.—Steven Menashi.
Assistant General Counsel (Postsecondary Education).—Vacant.
Assistant General Counsel (Business and Administrative Law).—Tracey Sasser.
Deputy General Counsel for Ethics, Legislative Counsel, and Regulatory Service.—Elizabeth McFadden.
Assistant General Counsel (Ethics).—Marcella Keller-Goodridge.
Assistant General Counsel (Legislative Counsel).—Paul Riddle.
Assistant General Counsel (Regulatory Services).—Hilary Malawer.
Deputy General Counsel for Program Service.—Philip H. Rosenfelt.
Assistant General Counsel (Educational, Equity, and Research).—Kathryn Ellis.
Assistant General Counsel (Education Program Services).—Dennis Koeppel.

OFFICE OF INNOVATION AND IMPROVEMENT

phone (202) 205–4500

Assistant Deputy Secretary.—Margo Anderson (acting).
Associate Assistant Deputy Secretary for—
Innovation and Reform.—Margo Anderson.
Special Projects.—Vacant.
Chief of Staff.—Vacant.

OFFICE OF INSPECTOR GENERAL

Potomac Center Plaza (PCP), 8th Floor, 20024, phone (202) 245–6900, fax 245–6993

Inspector General.—Kathleen Tighe.
Deputy Inspector General.—Sandra D. Bruce.
Counsel to the Inspector General.—Vacant, 245–7015.
Assistant Inspector General for—
Audit Services.—Patrick Howard, 245–6949.
Investigations.—Aaron Jordan, 245–7829.
IT Audit and Computer Crimes Investigations.—Charles Coe, 245–7033.
Management Services.—David Morris, 245–6369.

INTERNATIONAL AFFAIRS OFFICE

Room 6W108, phone (202) 453–6699

Senior Advisor to the Secretary and Director.—Maureen McLaughlin.
International Affairs Specialists: JoAnne Livingston, Jadon Marianetti, Rebecca Miller, Rafael Nevarez, Sambia Shivers-Barclay.
Staff Assistant.—Veronica Tahir.

INSTITUTE OF EDUCATION SCIENCES

550 12th Street, SW., 4th Floor, Washington DC 20004, phone (202) 245–7095, fax 245–6752

Director.—Thomas Brock (acting), 245–8123.
Deputy Director for—
Administration and Policy.—Sue Betka, 245–6605.
Science.—Anne Riccuiti, 245–8455.
National Center for—
Education Evaluation and Regional Assistance.—Ricky Takai, 245–6279.
Education Research.—Thomas W. Brock, 245–8123.
Education Statistics.—Peggy Carr (acting), 245–6168.
Special Education Research.—Joan McLaughlin (acting), 245–8201.

OFFICE OF LEGISLATION AND CONGRESSIONAL AFFAIRS

Room 6W301, phone (202) 401–0020, email: OLCAinquiries@ed.gov

Assistant Secretary.—Peter Oppenheim, 401–0020.
Deputy Assistant Secretary.—Nicholas Abramczyk (202) 453–7774.
Confidential Assistant.—Madeleine Huizinga (202) 543–6966.
Chief of Staff.—Vacant.
Director of Legislative Affairs.—Molly Petersen, 453–5707.

OFFICE OF PLANNING, EVALUATION, AND POLICY DEVELOPMENT

Room 5E301, phone (202) 401–0831, fax (202) 260–7741

Assistant Secretary.—Frank Brogan, Deputy Assistant Secretary, delegated the authority to perform the functions and duties of Assistant Secretary of OPEPD, Room 5E311.
Executive Officer.—William Doyle, Room 7E205.
Director of:
Budget Service.—Erica Navarro, Room 5W313.
Policy and Program Studies Service.—Vacant.

OFFICE OF POSTSECONDARY EDUCATION

400 Maryland Avenue, SW., 20202, phone (202) 453–6914

Assistant Secretary.—Kathleen Smith (Delegated Authority of Assistant Secretary).
Chief of Staff.—Vacant.
Deputy Assistant Secretary for—
Higher Education Programs.—Adam Kissel, 453–7337.
International and Foreign Language Education.—Vacant.
Policy, Planning, and Innovation.—Lynn Mahaffie, 453–7862.

OFFICE OF SPECIAL EDUCATION AND REHABILITATIVE SERVICES

Potomac Center Plaza (PCP), 550 12th Street, SW., 5th Floor, 20202

phone (202) 245–7468, fax 245–7638

Assistant Secretary.—Johnny W. Collett.
Deputy Assistant Secretary.—Kimberly M. Richey, Room 5138, 245–8357.
Directory of Office of Special Education Programs.—Ruth Ryder (acting), Room 5139, 245–7513.
Commissioner of the Rehabilitation Services Administration.—Vacant.
Deputy Commissioner of the Rehabilitation Services Administration.—Carol L. Dobak (acting), (delegated the authority to perform the functions and duties of the Commissioner), Room 5153, 245–7325.
Executive Administrator.—Andrew J. Pepin, Room 5106, 245–7632.
Executive Officer.—Melanie Winston, Room 5148–1, 245–7419.

DEPARTMENT OF VETERANS AFFAIRS

Mail should be addressed to 810 Vermont Avenue, NW., Washington, DC 20420

http://www.va.gov

ROBERT WILKIE, Secretary of Veterans Affairs; born August 6, 1962, Frankfurt, Germany; education: B.A., Wake Forest University, Winston-Salem, NC, 1985; J.D., Loyola University School of Law, New Orleans, LA, 1988; LLM, Georgetown University Law School, Washington, DC, 1992; M.S.S., U.S. Army War College, Carlisle Barracks, PA, 2002; professional: Counsel, Office of Senate Majority Leader Trent Lott, 1997–2003; Special Assistant to the President, National Security Council, 2003–05; Principal Deputy Assistant Secretary of Defense (Legislative Affairs), Department of Defense, 2005–06; Assistant Secretary of Defense (Legislative Affairs), 2006–09; Under Secretary of Defense for Personnel and Readiness, 2017–18; Acting Secretary of Veterans Affairs Department, March-May, 2018; military: U.S. Air Force Reserve, U.S. Navy Reserve; nominated by President Donald J. Trump to serve as the tenth Secretary of the Department of Veterans Affairs on May 18, 2018, confirmed on July 23, 2018 and sworn in on July 30, 2018.

OFFICE OF THE SECRETARY

Secretary of Veterans Affairs.—Robert Wilkie, (202) 461–4800.
  Deputy Secretary of Veterans Affairs.—Thomas G. Bowman, 461–4817.
  Chief of Staff.—Peter M. O'Rourke, 461–4808.
  Deputy Chief of Staff.—Jacquelyn Hayes-Byrd, 461–4808.
  Veterans Service Organization Liaison.—Jacob B. Gadd, M.B.A. (acting), 461–6781.
  Executive Secretary.—Tonia Bock, 461–4869.
  Director, Center for—
    Faith-Based Community Initiative.—Stephen Dillard (acting), 461–7689.
    Minority Veterans.—Barbara Ward, 461–6191.
    Women Veterans.—Kayla M. Williams, 461–6193.
  Director—
    Strategic Partnerships.—Deborah Scher, 461–0325.
    Strategic Communications.—Ashleigh Barry, 461–7173.
    Employment Discrimination and Complaint Adjudication.—Maxanne R. Witkin, 1575 I Street, NW., 461–4050.
    Office of Survivors Assistance.—Moira Flanders, 1717 H Street, NW., 461–1077.
    Regulation Policy and Management.—Michael Shores, 461–4921.
  Committee Management Officer.—Jeffrey Moragne, 1717 H Street, NW., 461–4660.
  Executive Director, Small and Veterans Business Programs.—Tom Leney, 801 I Street, NW., 461–4600.

BOARD OF VETERANS' APPEALS

Chairman.—Cheryl L. Mason, 425 I Street, NW. (202) 632–5710.
  Vice Chairman.—David C. Spickler, 632–5591.

OFFICE OF GENERAL COUNSEL

General Counsel.—Jim Byrne (202) 461–4995.
  Deputy General Counsel for—
    Legal Policy.—Richard Hipolit, 461–4995.
    Legal Operations.—Catherine Mitrano, 461–7661.
  Executive Director, Management, Planning, and Analysis.—Michael R. Hogan, 461–7685.

OFFICE OF INSPECTOR GENERAL

Inspector General.—Michael Missal, 801 I Street, NW. (202) 461–4720.
  Deputy Inspector General.—David T. Case, 461–4720.

OFFICE OF ACQUISITIONS, LOGISTICS, AND CONSTRUCTION

Principal Executive Director.—Phillip ''Phil'' Christy (acting), 425 I Street, NW. (202) 632–4607.
Chief of Staff.—Robert Madden (acting), 425 I Street, NW., 632–6470.
Executive Director for—
Acquisition and Logistics.—Jan Frye, 461–6920.
Procurement, Acquisition, and Logistics.—Michele Foster (acting), (732) 795–1134.
Construction and Facilities Management.—Stella S. Fiotes, 425 I Street, NW., 632–4607.

ASSISTANT SECRETARY FOR CONGRESSIONAL AND LEGISLATIVE AFFAIRS

Assistant Secretary.—Brooks D. Tucker (202) 461–6490.
Principal Deputy Assistant Secretary.—Christopher E. O'Connor, 461–6456.
Deputy Assistant Secretary for Congressional Affairs.—David Balland, 461–4690.
Director of—
Operations.—Regina Mack-Abney (acting), 461–7856.
Legislative Affairs Service.—David Ballenger, 461–6464.
Health Team.—Glenn Johnson, 461–5707.
Benefits Team.—Glenn Johnson, 461–5707.
Outreach Team.—Annmarie Amaral (202) 224–2250.
Corporate Enterprise Legislative Affairs Service.—Lesia Mandzia, 461–6177.

ASSISTANT SECRETARY FOR PUBLIC AND INTERGOVERNMENTAL AFFAIRS

Assistant Secretary.—John Ullyot (202) 461–7500.
Principal Deputy Assistant Secretary.—John ''Wolf'' Wagner, 461–5722.
Executive Director, Strategic Planning and Veterans Outreach.—Gary C. Tallman, 461–7430.
Chief of Staff.—Lyndon Johnson, 461–6448.
Press Secretary.—Curt Cashour, 461–7388.
Deputy Press Secretary.—Lydia Blaha, 461–7458.
Deputy Assistant Secretary for Public Affairs.—James Hutton, 461–7558.
Executive Director for Intergovernmental Affairs.—Thayer Verschoor, 461–7385.
Director—
State of Local Government Affairs.—Christopher Syrek, 461–7486.
Tribal Government Relations.—Stephanie Birdwell, 461–4851.

ASSISTANT SECRETARY FOR ENTERPRISE INTEGRATION

Assistant Secretary.—Melissa S. Glynn, Ph.D. (202) 461–5800.
Principal Deputy Assistant Secretary.—Dat P. Tran, 461–5800.
Chief of Staff.—Shana Love-Holmon, 632–5285.
Deputy Assistant Secretary for—
Planning and Performance Management.—John Basso, 461–7073.
Data Governance and Analysis.—Susan Sullivan, 461–5831.
Executive Director for—
Policy and Interagency Collaboration.—John Medve, 461–5626.
VA Center for Innovation.—Amber Schleuning (acting), (562) 912–0095.
Office of Modernization.—Surafeal Asgedom, 461–5817.

ASSISTANT SECRETARY FOR OPERATIONS, SECURITY, AND PREPAREDNESS

Assistant Secretary.—Donald P. Loren (202) 461–4980.
Principal Deputy Assistant Secretary.—Kevin T. Hanretta, 461–4980.
Director, Operations, Security, and Preparedness Resource Management.—Sylvia B. Dunn, DM, 461–4984.
Deputy Assistant Secretary for Emergency Management and Resilience.—Lewis Ratchford, Jr., 461–5930.
Executive Director—
Security and Law Enforcement.—Frederick R. Jackson, 461–5544.
Personnel Security and Identity Management.—Rodney Emery, 461–4460.

ASSISTANT SECRETARY FOR MANAGEMENT

Assistant Secretary/Chief Financial Officer.—Jon J. Rychalski (202) 461–6703.
Principal Deputy Assistant Secretary for Management/Deputy Chief Financial Officer.—Edward Murray, 461–6703.
Executive Director of Financial Planning and Analysis.—Amy L. Parker, 461–5369.
Chief of Staff.—Latriece Prince-Wheeler, 461–6703.
Deputy Assistant Secretary for—
Budget.—Laura Duke, 461–7790.
Finance.—Joanne Choi (acting), 461–6180.
Director—
Office of Asset Enterprise Management.—Jim Sullivan, 461–6771.
Office of Programming Analysis and Evaluation.—Vacant.
Executive Director, Financial Management Business Transformation Initiative.—Laurie Park (acting), 461–6154.

ASSISTANT SECRETARY FOR INFORMATION AND TECHNOLOGY

Executive in Charge.—Camilo J. Sandoval (202) 461–6910.
Principal Deputy Assistant Secretary for Information Technology.—Bill James (acting), (202) 632–7390.
Deputy Assistant Secretary for—
Enterprise Program Management Office.—Bill James, 632–7390.
IT Operations and Services.—Susan McHugh-Polley (727) 502–1379.
Deputy Chief Information Officer, Quality, Privacy, and Risk.—Martha Orr (202) 461–5139.
Chief of Staff.—Eric Huweart (202) 815–9424.

ASSISTANT SECRETARY FOR HUMAN RESOURCES AND ADMINISTRATION

Assistant Secretary.—Peter J. Shelby (202) 461–7750.
Principal Deputy Assistant Secretary.—Nathan Maenle, 461–7750.
Principal Deputy Assistant Secretary for Human Resources Administration.—Nathan Maenle, 461–7750.
Deputy Assistant Secretary for—
Administration.—Roy Hurndon, 461–5000.
Diversity and Inclusion.—Carolyn Wong (acting), 461–4131.
Human Resources Management.—Carin Otero, 461–7765.
Resolution Management.—Harvey Johnson, 1575 I Street, NW., 461–4064.
Executive Director—
Labor-Management Relations.—Kimberly P. McLeod, 461–4122.
Corporate Senior Executive Management Office.—Tracy Therit, 461–0235.

NATIONAL CEMETERY ADMINISTRATION

Under Secretary for Memorial Affairs.—Randy C. Reeves (202) 461–6112.
Principal Deputy Under Secretary.—Ronald E. Walters, 461–6013.
Chief of Staff.—Tom Howard, 461–6013.
Deputy Under Secretary for—
Field Programs and Cemetery Operations.—Glenn Powers, 461–6071.
Finance and Planning/CFO.—Matthew Sullivan, 461–7334.
Management.—Anita Hanson, 461–6234.
Director of:
Budget Service.—Kathleen McManaman (202) 632–8841.
Design and Construction Service.—Michael Roth, 632–4691.
Information Management and Business Support Service.—Timothy Godlove, 632–7209.
Strategic Communications.—Patricia "Tish" Tyson (202) 461–6307.
Veterans Cemetery Grants Program.—George Eisenbach, 632–7369.
Deputy Director, Memorial Programs Service.—Eric Powell, 632–8670.
Executive Director—
Field Programs.—Kimberly Wright, 461–6748.
Engagement and Memorial Innovations.—Tom Howard (acting), 461–6013.

VETERANS BENEFITS ADMINISTRATION

Executive in Charge.—Thomas J. Murphy, 1800 G Street, NW. (202) 461–9300.
Principal Deputy Under Secretary.—James E. Manker, Jr. (acting), 461–9300.
Chief of Staff.—Michael J. Frueh, 461–9300.
Deputy Chief of Staff.—Brandye Terrell, 461–9300.
Chief Management Officer.—Teri McClelland, 632–8472.
Deputy Under Secretary for—
Disability Assistance.—Robert Reynolds, 461–9320.
Economic Opportunity.—Vacant (202) 443–6080.
Field Operations.—Willie Clark, 461–9340.
Chief Financial Officer.—Ervin Pearson (acting), 461–9900.
Director of:
Administration and Facilities.—Vacant.
Appeals Management Office.—David McLenachen (202) 530–9455.
Benefits Assistance Service.—Margarita Devlin, 530–9111.
Business Process Integration.—Brad Houston, 461–9797.
Chief Human Capitol Office.—David Fitchitt, 461–9450.
Compensation.—Beth Murphy, 461–9700.
Education.—Robert Worley, 461–9800.
Employee Development and Training.—Dr. George Tanner, 461–9860.
Insurance.—Vincent Markey (215) 381–3029.
Loan Guaranty.—Jeffrey London (202) 632–8862.
Management.—Robert Waltemeyer, 461–9412.
Pension and Fiduciary.—Cheryl Rawls, 632–8863.
Performance Analysis and Integrity.—Mark Seastrom, 461–9040.
Strategic Planning.—Michael McNeal, 461–9003.
Vocational Rehabilitation and Employment.—Jack Kammerer, 461–9600.

VETERANS HEALTH ADMINISTRATION

Executive in Charge.—Carolyn Clancy, M.D. (202) 461–7000.
Principal Deputy Under Secretary for Health.—Christopher Vojta, M.D., 461–7008.
Deputy Principal Deputy Under Secretary for Health.—Vacant.
Chief of Staff.—Lisa Pape (acting), 461–1635.
Deputy Chief of Staff.—Barbara Hyduke (202) 632–8283.
Senior Advisor to the Under Secretary for Health.—Patricia Wallace (202) 407–1521.
Deputy Under Secretary for Health for—
Community Care.—Amy Fahrenkopf, M.D. (acting), 461–5672; Kameron Matthews, M.D. (acting), 461–4240.
Organizational Excellence.—Gerard Cox, M.D. (acting), 461–7571.
Operations and Management.—Steve W. Young, 461–7026.
Policy and Services.—Lucille Beck, Ph.D. (acting), 461–7590.
Principal Deputy Under Secretary for Health.—Miguel LaPuz, M.D. (acting), 461–7008.
Chief—
Nursing Officer.—Linda McConnell, M.S., 461–7260.
Readjustment Counseling Officer.—Michael Fisher, M.S.W., 461–6525.
Finance Officer.—Mark Yow, M.B.A., 461–6666.
Employee Education System.—Elizabeth James (acting), 461–4089.
Procurement and Logistics.—Rick Lemmon (acting), (615) 225–6480.
Director of Member Services.—Garth Miller (678) 924–6480.
Chief Officer for Research and Development.—Rachel Ramoni, D.M.D., 461–1700.
Medical Inspector.—Erica Scavalla, M.D. (acting), 461–1075.
Assistant Deputy Under Secretary for Health for—
Workforce Services.—Jessica Bonjorni (acting), 461–6720.
Clinical Operations and Management.—Theresa Boyd, M.D. (acting), 461–0474.
Administrative Operations.—Tammy Czarnecki, M.S.O.L., 461–7026.
Access to Care.—Steve Lieberman, M.D., 461–7107.
Informatics and Information Governance.—Chuck Hume, FACHE (acting), 461–5834.
Policy and Planning.—Regan Crump, M.S.N., Dr.PH., 461–7100.
Patient Care Services.—Harold Kudler, M.D. (acting), 461–7590.
Community Care.—Amy Fahrenkopf, M.D. (acting), 461–5672.
Quality, Safety, and Value.—Saurabha Bhatnagar, M.D. (acting), (617) 483–0645.

Executive Director—

Office of Research Oversight.—Doug Bannerman, Ph.D., 632–6122.

Veterans Health Administrations Communications.—Gina Screen (acting), 461–7221.

Patient Centered Care and Cultural Transformation.—Tracy Gaudet, M.D. (202) 266–4670.

National Center for Patient Safety.—Douglas Paull, M.D. (acting), (734) 930–5897.

National Center for Ethics.—Toby Schonfeld, Ph.D. (acting), 632–7229.

DEPARTMENT OF HOMELAND SECURITY

U.S. Naval Security Station,

3801 Nebraska Avenue, NW., 20016

Phone (202) 282–8000

KIRSTJEN MICHELE NIELSEN, Secretary of Homeland Security, born in Clearwater, FL, May 14, 1972; education: B.S., Georgetown School of Foreign Service, Washington, DC, 1994; J.D., University of Virginia School of Law, Charlottesville, VA, 1999; professional: associate, Haynes and Boone, LLP, Washington, DC, 1999–2002; special assistant for homeland security to President George W. Bush and senior director for prevention, preparedness, and response, White House Homeland Security Council, 2004–07; president, Homeland Security and Preparedness Practice, Civitas Group, Washington, DC, 2007–12; president, Sunesis Consulting, LLC, Alexandria, VA, 2012–17; assistant to President Donald J. Trump and White House principal deputy chief of staff, Washington, DC, 2017; nominated by President Donald J. Trump on October 16, 2017, to become the 6th Secretary of Homeland Security, was confirmed by the U.S. Senate on December 5, 2017, and sworn in on December 6, 2017, becoming the first former Department of Homeland Security employee to become the secretary.

OFFICE OF THE SECRETARY

Secretary of Homeland Security.—Kirstjen M. Nielsen.
Deputy Secretary of Homeland Security.—Elaine C. Duke.
Chief of Staff.—Chad F. Wolf (acting).

CITIZENSHIP AND IMMIGRATION SERVICES OMBUDSMAN

Phone (202) 357–8100

Ombudsman.—Julie Kirchner.

CIVIL RIGHTS AND CIVIL LIBERTIES

Phone (202) 401–1474, Toll Free: 1–866–644–8360

Officer for Civil Rights and Civil Liberties.—Cameron Quinn.

EXECUTIVE SECRETARIAT

Phone (202) 282–8221

Executive Secretary.—Scott Krause.
Deputy Executive Secretary.—Donald Swain.

OFFICE OF THE GENERAL COUNSEL

Phone (202) 282–8137

General Counsel.—John Mitnick.

OFFICE OF INSPECTOR GENERAL

Phone (202) 254–4100

Inspector General.—John V. Kelly (acting).

OFFICE OF INTELLIGENCE AND ANALYSIS

Phone (202) 282–8353

Under Secretary and Chief Intelligence Officer.—David J. Glawe.
Principal Deputy Under Secretary.—David A. Grannis.
Chief of Staff.—Caroline Gregg (acting).
Deputy Under Secretary for Intelligence Operations.—Robin Taylor (acting).
Associate Deputy Under Secretary for Analysis.—Vacant.
Executive Director for Plans, Integration, and Evaluation.—Robert Vehe.

OFFICE OF PARTNERSHIP AND ENGAGEMENT

Phone (202) 282–9310

Assistant Secretary.—John Barsa (acting).
Chief of Staff.—Karinda L. Washington.

OFFICE OF LEGISLATIVE AFFAIRS

Phone (202) 447–5890

Assistant Secretary.—Benjamin Cassidy.
Deputy Assistant Secretaries: Uyen Dinh (House), David Wonnenberg (Senate).

MILITARY ADVISOR'S OFFICE

Phone (202) 282–8245

Military Advisor to the Secretary.—Rear Admiral (Lower Half), Eric C. Jones.

PRIVACY OFFICE

Phone (202) 343–1717

Chief Privacy Officer.—Sam Kaplan.

OFFICE OF PUBLIC AFFAIRS

Phone (202) 282–8069

Assistant Secretary.—Jonathan Rath Hoffman.

NATIONAL PROTECTION AND PROGRAMS DIRECTORATE

Phone (202) 282–8400

Under Secretary.—Christopher C. Krebs.
Deputy Under Secretary.—Robert Kolasky (acting).
Chief of Staff.—David Hess.
Assistant Secretary for Cybersecurity and Communications.—Jeanette Manfra.
Assistant Secretary for Infrastructure Protection.—Christopher C. Krebs.
Director of:
Federal Protective Service.—L. Eric Patterson.
Office of Biometric Identity Management.—Shonnie Lyon.
Office of Cyber and Infrastructure Analysis.—Steven Harris.

SCIENCE AND TECHNOLOGY DIRECTORATE

Phone (202) 254–6033

Under Secretary.—William Bryan (Senior Official Performing the Duties of the Under Secretary).
Deputy Under Secretary.—Andre Hentz (acting).
Chief of Staff.—Kathryn Coulter.
Deputy Chief of Staff.—Gail Miller.
Director of:

Capability Development Support (CDS).—Dr. Steven Hutchison.
Finance and Budget.—Carol Cribbs.
Homeland Security Advanced Research Projects Agency.—William Bryan.
Research and Development Partnerships.—Joseph Martin.
Support to the Homeland Security Enterprise and First Responders.—Daniel Cotter.

MANAGEMENT DIRECTORATE

Phone (202) 447–3400

Under Secretary.—Claire M. Grady.
Deputy Under Secretary.—Chip Fulghum.
Chief of Staff.—Laurie Boulden (acting).
Chief Readiness Support Officer.—Jeffery Orner.
Chief Human Capital Officer.—Angela Bailey.
Chief Information Officer.—Dr. John A. Zangardi.
Chief Procurement Officer.—Soraya Correa.
Chief Security Officer.—Rich McComb.
Deputy Chief Financial Officer.—Stacy Marcott.
Executive Director, Office of Program Accountability and Risk Management.—Debra Cox.

OFFICE OF POLICY

Phone (202) 282–9708

Under Secretary.—Vacant.
Assistant Secretary.—Vacant.
Assistant Secretary/Office of International Affairs.—James D. Nealon.
Principal Deputy Assistant Secretary.—Vacant.
Chief of Staff.—Vacant.
Deputy Chief of Staff.—Briana Petyo.
Assistant Secretary, Office of Border, Immigration and Trade Policy.—Michael Dougherty.
Deputy Assistant Secretary for—
Americas.—Vacant.
Trade and Transportation Security.—Christa Brzozowski.
Immigration Policy.—Vacant.
Immigration Statistics.—Marc Rosenblum.
Office of Cyber Policy.—Thomas McDermott.
Office of International Engagement.—Matthew King.
Assistant Secretary, Office of Strategy, Planning, Analysis, and Risk.—Nathaniel Jensen.
Director, Immigration Statistics.—Vacant.
Deputy Assistant Secretary for—
Plans.—Vacant.
Strategy and Analysis.—Susan Coller-Monarez.
Unity of Effort.—Andrew Kuepper.
Assistant Secretary, Office of Threat Prevention and Security Policy.—Vacant.
Deputy Assistant Secretary for—
Information Sharing Policy.—Vacant.
Law Enforcement Policy.—Vacant.
Screening Coordination.—Vacant.

FEDERAL EMERGENCY MANAGEMENT AGENCY (FEMA)

500 C Street, SW., 20472, phone (202) 646–2500

Administrator.—Brock Long.
Deputy Administrator.—Dan Kaniewski (acting).
Chief of Staff.—Eric Heighberger.
Senior Law Enforcement Advisor to the Administrator.—Roberto L. Hylton.
Director, Office of:
Center of Faith-Based and Neighborhood Partnerships.—Vacant.
Director, Office of Executive Operations.—Marcia Hodges.
Executive Secretariat.—Alyson Vert.
National Advisory Council.—Deana Platt.
National Capital Region Coordination.—Kim Kadesch.
Regional Operations.—Elizabeth Edge.

Office of Chief Counsel.—Adrian Sevier.
Chief Financial Officer.—Mary Comans (acting).
Director, Office of:
Disability Integration and Coordination.—Linda Mastrandea.
External Affairs.—Susan Phalen.
Congressional Affairs.—Jessica Nalepa.
Equal Rights.—Regis Phelan (acting).
Associate Administrator for Policy, Program Analysis and International Affairs.—David Bibo (acting).
Deputy Administrator, Protection and National Preparedness.—Kathleen Fox (acting).
Assistant Administrators:
Grant Programs.—Thomas diNanno.
National Continuity Programs.—John E. Veatch.
National Preparedness.—Kathleen Fox.
Administrator, U.S. Fire Administration.—G. Keith Bryant.
Associate Administrator, Mission Support.—David Grant.
Chiefs:
Administrative Officer, Mission Support.—Tracey Showman.
Component Human Capital Officer, Mission Support.—Corey Coleman.
Information Officer, Mission Support.—Adrian R. Gardner.
Procurement Officer, Mission Support.—Bobby McCane.
Security Officer, Mission Support.—Dwight Williams.
Associate Administrator, Response and Recovery.—Jeff Byard.
Deputy Associate Administrator, Response and Recovery.—Corey Gruber.
Assistant Administrators:
Logistics.—Jeffrey Dorko.
Response.—Damon Penn.
Recovery.—Alex Amparo.
Field Operations.—Michael Byrne.
Deputy Associate Administrator for Insurance and Mitigation, Federal Insurance and Mitigation Administration.—Roy E. Wright.

COUNTERING WEAPONS OF MASS DESTRUCTION (CWMD)

phone (202) 254–7300

Assistant Secretary.—James F. McDonnell (acting).
Chief of Staff.—Mary Kruger.

TRANSPORTATION SECURITY ADMINISTRATION (TSA)

601 South 12th Street, Arlington, VA 20598–6001

Administrator/Assistant Secretary.—David P. Pekoske.
Deputy Administrator.—Roderick Allison (acting).
Chief of Staff.—Ha Nguyen McNeill.

UNITED STATES CUSTOMS AND BORDER PROTECTION (CBP)

1300 Pennsylvania Avenue, NW., 20229

Commissioner.—Kevin McAleenan (202) 344–1010/344–2001.
Deputy Commissioner.—Ronald D. Vitiello (acting), 344–1010/2001.
Chief of Staff.—Patrick Flanagan (acting), 344–1080/1001.
Deputy Chief of Staff.—Stephen Schorr, 344–1080/1001.
Deputy Chief of Staff (Policy).—Shannon McCully, 344–2819.
Chief Counsel.—Scott Falk, 344–2955.
Assistant Commissioner, Office of:
Operations Support.—Robert Perez (acting), 344–2230.
Air and Marine.—Edward Young (acting), 344–3950.
Congressional Affairs.—John P. Ladowicz, 344–1760.
Field Operations.—Todd Owen, 344–1620.
Human Resources Management.—Linda Jacksta, 863–6100.
Information and Technology.—Phillip A. Landfried (571) 468–8200.
Intelligence.—Jennifer Ley (acting), 344–1150.
Finance.—Sean Mildrew, 325–2163.

Facilities and Asset Management.—Karl Calvo, 344–3101.
Professional Responsibility.—Matthew Klein, 344–1800.
International Affairs.—Ian Saunders (acting), 344–3000.
International Trade.—Brenda Smith, 863–6098.
Public Affairs.—Michael Friel (acting), 344–1700.
Acquisition.—Mark Borkowski (571) 468–7479.
Training and Development.—Christopher Hall, 325–7100.
Enterprise Services.—Kathryn Kolbe, 325–1925.
Chief, United States Border Patrol.—Carla Provost (acting), 344–1366.
Executive Director, Office of:
Privacy and Diversity.—Anselm Beach (acting), 344–1610.
Policy and Planning.—Harold Hanson (acting), 344–2700.
Director, Intergovernmental Public Liaison.—Timothy Quinn, 325–0759.
Director, Executive Secretariat.—Joseph E. Tezak, 344–1040.
Senior Advisor, Trade Relations.—Bradley Hayes, 325–1285.

UNITED STATES IMMIGRATION AND CUSTOMS ENFORCEMENT (ICE)

Director.—Thomas Homan (acting), (202) 732–3000.
Deputy Director.—Peter Edge (acting), 732–3000.
Chief of Staff.—Thomas Blank, 732–3000.
Assistant Director of:
Professional Responsibility.—Timothy Moynihan, 732–8300.
Principal Legal Advisor.—Tracy Short, 732–5001.
Assistant Director of:
Congressional Relations.—Sean Hackbarth (acting), 732–6171.
Public Affairs.—Barbara Gonzalez, 732–4250.
Executive Secretariat.—Patricia Baldovich (acting), 732–6159.
Executive Associate Director, Enforcement and Removal Operations.—Matthew T. Albence, 732–3100.
Deputy Executive Associate Director, Enforcement and Removal Operations.—Philip T. Miller, 732–3100.
Assistant Director of:
Custody Management.—Tae D. Johnson, 732–3100.
Enforcement.—Thomas E. Feeley, 732–3100.
Field Operations.—Nathalie R. Asher (acting), 732–3100.
ICE Health Service Corps.—CAPT Luzviminda Peredo Berger, MD, 732–3100.
Operational Support.—Jacki B. Klopp (acting), 732–3100.
Repatriation.—Marlen Piñeiro, 732–3100.
Deputy Assistant Director, Law Enforcement Systems and Analysis.—Tadgh Smith, 732–3100.
Deputy Executive Associate Director, Homeland Security Investigations.—Derek N. Benner, 732–5100.
Assistant Director for—
Domestic Operations.—Tatum King, 732–3907.
Information Management.—Alysa Erichs, 732–5808.
Intelligence.—Patricia Cogswell, 732–3101.
International Affairs.—Raymond Villanueva, 732–3932.
Mission Support.—Staci Barrera, 732–5702.
National Intellectual Property Rights Coordination Center.—Matthew Allen (acting), (703) 603–3900.
National Security Investigations Division.—Clark Settles, 287–6870.
Programs.—Matthew Allen (202) 732–5852.
Executive Associate Director, Management and Administration.—Tracey Bardorf, 732–3000.
Director, Acquisition Management.—Bill Weinberg, 732–2481.
Assistant Director, Diversity Officer and Civil Rights.—Scott F. Lanum, 732–0125.
Director, Chief Financial Officer.—Stephen Roncone (acting), 732–6208.
Chief Information Officer.—Michael C. Brown, 732–2000.
Freedom of Information Act Officer.—Catrina Pavlik Keenan, 732–6259.
Human Capital Officer.—Karen W. Pane, 732–3713.
Assistant Director, Office of Training and Tactical Programs.—Jose M. Jeronimo, 732–4716.
Assistant Director, Office of Policy.—Debbie Seguin, 732–5323.
Assistant Director, Information Governance and Privacy Officer.—Lyn Rahilly, 732–3300.

FEDERAL LAW ENFORCEMENT TRAINING CENTERS

1131 Chapel Crossing Road, Glynco, GA 31524

Director.—Thomas J. Walters (912) 267–2070.
Deputy Director.—William Fallon, 267–2070.
Chief of Staff.—Daniel W. Auer (acting), 267–2070.
Assistant Director for—
Mission Readiness and Support Directorate.—Marcus L. Hill, 267–2231.
Office of Washington Operations.—George E. Kovatch (202) 233–0260.
Assistant Director/Chief Financial Officer.—Donald R. Lewis, 267–2999.
Assistant Director/Chief Information Officer.—Michael L.Vesta, 267–2014.
Assistant Director for—
Centralized Training Management Directorate.—Valerie J. Atkins, 267–2451.
Assistant Director/Chief Counsel.—David H. Brunjes, 267–2851.
Glynco Training Directorate.—Michael S. Milner, 267–3373.
Regional and International Training Directorate.—Dominic D. Braccio, 267–2040.
Training Research and Innovation Directorate.—James R. Gregorius, 554–4284.
Chief for—
Office of Organizational Health.—Brenda M. Lloyd, 267–2280.
Office of Security and Professional Responsibility.—Kaizad Munshi, 267–3027.
Protocol and Communications Office.—Susan Thornton (acting), 267–2447.

UNITED STATES CITIZENSHIP AND IMMIGRATION SERVICES

20 Massachusetts Avenue, NW., Washington, DC 20529, phone (202) 272–1000

Director.—L. Francis Cissna.
Deputy Director.—James W. McCament.
Chief of Staff.—Lora Ries.
Chief Information Officer.—Mark Schwartz.
Associate Director for—
Fraud Detection and National Security Directorate.—Matthew Emrich.
Refugee, Asylum and International Operations Directorate.—Jennifer Higgins.
Service Center Operations Directorate.—Donald Neufeld.
Chief, Office of:
Administration.—Michael Gibbs.
Administrative Appeals.—Ron Rosenberg.
Chief Counsel.—Craig Symons.
Chief Financial Officer.—Joseph Moore.
External Affairs Directorate.—Angelica Alfonso-Royals. (Communications, Citizenship, and Legislative Affairs are now under this directorate.)
Policy and Strategy.—Kathy Nuebel-Kovarik.

UNITED STATES COAST GUARD

2703 Martin Luther King Jr. Avenue, SE., 20593, phone (202) 372–4400

Commandant.—ADM Karl Schultz.
Vice Commandant.—ADM Charles D. Michel.
Deputy Commandant for—
Mission Support.—VADM Sandra L. Stosz.
Operations.—VADM Charles W. Ray.
Chief Administrative Law Judge.—Hon. Walter Brudzinski.
Judge Advocate General/Chief Counsel.—RDML Steven J. Anderson.
Deputy Judge Advocate General/Deputy Chief Counsel.—Calvin Lederer.
Director of Governmental and Public Affairs.—RDML Anthony J. Vogt.
Senior Military Advisor to the Secretary of Homeland Security.—RDML Joanna M. Nunan.

UNITED STATES SECRET SERVICE

245 Murray Drive, SW., Building T–5, 20223

Director.—Randolph D. Alles.
Deputy Director.—William J. Callahan.
Deputy Assistant Director, Congressional Affairs Program.—R. Christopher Stanley (202) 406–5676, fax 406–5740.

INDEPENDENT AGENCIES, COMMISSIONS, BOARDS

ADVISORY COUNCIL ON HISTORIC PRESERVATION

401 F Street, NW., Suite 308, 20001

phone (202) 517–0200, http://www.achp.gov

[Created by Public Law 89–665, as amended]

Chair.—Milford Wayne Donaldson, Sacramento, California.
Vice Chair.—Leonard A. Forsman, Suquamish, Washington.
Expert Members:
Terry Guen-Murray, Chicago, Illinois.
Dorothy Lippert, Washington, District of Columbia.
Robert G. Stanton, Fairfax Station, Virginia.
Luis G. Hoyos, Los Angeles County, California.
Citizen Members:
Bradford J. White, Evanston, Illinois.
Jordan E. Tannenbaum, Fairfax, Virginia.
Native American Member.—Chair Reno Keoni Franklin, Santa Rosa, California.
Governor.—Vacant.
Mayor.—Vacant.
Architect of the Capitol.—Hon. Stephen T. Ayers, FAIA.
Secretary, Department of:
Agriculture.—Hon. Sonny Purdue.
Defense.—Hon. James Mattis.
Education.—Hon. Elisabeth DeVos.
Homeland Security.—Hon. Kirstjen Nielsen.
Housing and Urban Development.—Hon. Benjamin Carson, M.D.
Interior.—Hon. Ryan Zinke.
Transportation.—Hon. Elaine L. Chao.
Veterans Affairs.—Robert Wilkie.
Administrator of General Services Administration.—Emily W. Murphy.
National Conference of State Historic Preservation Officer.—Mark Wolfe, Austin, Texas.
National Association of Tribal Historic Preservation Officers.—Janine Ledford, Neah Bay, Washington.
National Trust for Historic Preservation.—Marita Rivero, Washington, DC.
ACHP Staff:
Executive Director.—John M. Fowler.
Manager for:
Office of Administration.—Ismail Ahmed.
Office of Communications, Education, and Outreach.—Susan A. Glimcher.
Office of Federal Agency Programs.—Reid J. Nelson.
Office of General Counsel.—Javier Marqués.
Office of Information Technology.—Rezaur Rahman.
Office of Native American Affairs.—Valerie Hauser.
Office of Preservation Initiatives.—Ronald D. Anzalone.

AMERICAN BATTLE MONUMENTS COMMISSION

2300 Clarendon Boulevard, Suite 500, Arlington, VA 22201–3367

phone (703) 696–6902

[Created by Public Law 105–225]

Chair.—Merrill A. ''Tony'' McPeak appointed as of 6/3/11.
Commissioners:

Hon. Cindy Campbell.
Hon. Barbaralee Diamonstein-Spielvogel.
Hon. Darrell Dorgan.
Hon. Larry R. Ellis.
Hon. Lisa Hallett.
Hon. Jerry Hultin.
Hon. Rolland Kidder.
Hon. Richard L. Klass.
Hon. Thomas R. Lamont.
Hon. Constance Morella.

Secretary.—Robert J. Dalessandro (acting).
Deputy Secretary.—John Wessels.
Executive Officer.—Mike Conley.
Chief Engineer.—Tom Sole.
Chief Financial Officer.—Christine Philpot.
Chief of:
Administration.—W.A. ''Bud'' Shatzer.
External Affairs.—Tim Nosal.
Human Resources.—Tom Clark.
Knowledge Management.—Monique Ceruti.
Strategy, Plans, and Policy.—Gerald Torrence.

(Note: Public law changed to 105–225, August 1998; H.R. 1085.)

AMERICAN NATIONAL RED CROSS

National Headquarters, 430 17th Street, NW., 20006, phone (202) 303–5000

Government Relations, phone (202) 303–4371

HONORARY OFFICERS

Honorary Chair.—Donald J. Trump, President of the United States.

CORPORATE OFFICERS

Chair.—Bonnie McElveen-Hunter.
President/CEO.—Gail J. McGovern.
General Counsel/Chief International Officer.—David B. Meltzer.
Chief Financial Officer.—Brian J. Rhoa.
Corporate Secretary.—Jennifer L. Hawkins.

BOARD OF GOVERNORS

Jennifer Bailey
Ajay Banga
Afsaneh M. Beschloss
Herman E. Bulls
Enrique A. Conterno
Richard K. Davis
Joseph E. Madison
Bonnie McElveen-Hunter
Gail J. McGovern
David A. Thomas, Ph.D.
Tina M. Tyler
Kirt A. Walker
Dennis M. Woodside

EXECUTIVE LEADERSHIP

Chief Diversity Officer.—Floyd Pitts.
Chief Human Resources Officer.—Melissa Hurst.
Chief Marketing Officer.—Neal Litvack.
Chief Public Affairs Officer.—Suzanne DeFrancis.
Corporate Ombudsman.—Jacqueline Villafañe.
President Biomedical Services.—Shaun P. Gilmore.
President Humanitarian Services.—Cliff Holtz.
President Preparedness and Health and Safety Services.—Jack McMaster.

GOVERNMENTAL RELATIONS

Senior Vice President for Government Relations.—Cherae L. Bishop.
Manager, Government Relations.—Jacqueline G. Bassermann.

Senior Director, Government Relations.—Dawn P. Latham.
Director, Government Relations.—Marvin Steele.

APPALACHIAN REGIONAL COMMISSION

1666 Connecticut Avenue, NW., 20009, phone (202) 884–7660, fax 884–7693

Federal Co-Chair.—Tim Thomas.
Alternate Federal Co-Chair.—Vacant.
States' Washington Representative.—James Hyland.
Executive Director.—Scott T. Hamilton.
Chief of Staff.—Guy Land.

ARMED FORCES RETIREMENT HOME

3700 North Capitol Street, NW., Box 1303, Washington, DC 20011–8400

phone (202) 541–7532, fax 541–7506

Chief Operating Officer.—Lt. Col. (Ret.) James M. Branham, U.S. Army.
Chief Financial Officer.—Vicki Marrs.
Chief Information Officer.—Maurice Swinton.

ARMED FORCES RETIREMENT HOME—WASHINGTON

phone (202) 541–7536, fax 541–7588 or 7615

Administrator.—Shaun Servais.

ARMED FORCES RETIREMENT HOME—GULFPORT

1800 Beach Drive, Gulfport, MS 39507

phone (202) 897–4408, fax 897–4488

Administrator.—Jeff Eads.

BOARD OF GOVERNORS OF THE FEDERAL RESERVE SYSTEM

Constitution Avenue and 20th Street, NW., 20551, phone (202) 452–3000

Chair.—Jerome H. Powell.
Vice Chair.—Randal K. Quarles.
Member.—Lael Brainard.

OFFICE OF BOARD MEMBERS

Assistant to the Board and Division Director.—Michelle A. Smith.
Assistants to the Board: Lucretia M. Boyer, Linda L. Robertson, David W. Skidmore.
Special Assistant to the Board.—Jennifer C. Gallagher.
Senior Special Adviser to the Chair.—Trevor A. Reeve.

DIVISION OF BANKING SUPERVISION AND REGULATION

Director.—Michael S. Gibson.
Deputy Directors: Jennifer Burns, Maryann F. Hunter.
Senior Associate Directors: Mary Aiken, Barbara J. Bouchard, Arthur W. Lindo, Steve Merriett, Todd Vermilyea.
Associate Directors: Kevin M. Bertsch, Sean Campbell, Nida Davis, Christopher Finger, Jeffery W. Gunther, Anna L. Hewko, Mike Hsu, Richard A. Naylor, Lisa H. Ryu, Michael Solomon, Thomas Sullivan.
Deputy Associate Directors: John Beebe, Constance M. Horsley, Ryan Lordos, David Lynch, Molly Mahar, Kirk Odegard, Catherine Piche, Laurie Priest, Suzanne L. Williams.
Assistant Directors: Robert Ashman, James Diggs, Kathleen Johnson, Keith Ligon, Susan Motyka, Steve Spurry, Catherine Tilford, Joanne Wakim, Donna Webb.

Senior Adviser.—Norah M. Barger.
Advisers: Ann McKeehan, William F. Treacy, Sarkis D. Yoghourtdjian.

DIVISION OF CONSUMER AND COMMUNITY AFFAIRS

Director.—Eric S. Belsky.
Deputy Director.—V. Nicole Bynum.
Senior Associate Directors: Anna Alvarez Boyd, Suzanne G. Killian.
Associate Directors: Carol A. Evans, Allen J. Fishbein, Phyllis L. Harwell, James A. Michaels.
Deputy Associate Directors: David E. Buchholz, Joseph Firschein, Marisa A. Reid.

DIVISION OF FEDERAL RESERVE BANK OPERATIONS AND PAYMENT SYSTEMS

Director.—Matthew J. Eichner.
Deputy Directors: Jeffrey C. Marquardt, David P. Sidari.
Senior Associate Directors: Marta Chaffee, Gregory L. Evans, Susan V. Foley.
Associate Directors: Michael J. Lambert, Lawrence Mize.
Deputy Associate Directors: Jennifer Chang, Jennifer A. Lucier, David C. Mills, Stuart E. Sperry.
Assistant Directors: Timothy W. Maas, Travis Nesmith, Mark Olechowski, Rebecca Royer, Jeffrey D. Walker.
Assistant Director.—Amy Burr (acting).

DIVISION OF INFORMATION TECHNOLOGY

Director.—Sharon L. Mowry.
Deputy Directors: Lisa Bell, Raymond Romero, Kofi Sapong.
Associate Directors: Glenn S. Eskow, Sheryl L. Warren, Rajasekhar R. Yelisetty.
Deputy Associate Directors: William K. Dennison, Marietta Murphy, Theresa C. Palya, Charles B. Young.
Assistant Directors: Tom Nguyen, Deborah Prespare, Jonathan Shrier, Eric Turner, Virginia M. Wall, Edgar Wang, Ivan Wun.
Adviser.—Tillena G. Clark.

DIVISION OF INTERNATIONAL FINANCE

Director.—Steve B. Kamin.
Deputy Directors: Thomas A. Connors, Beth Anne Wilson.
Senior Associate Director.—Christopher J. Erceg.
Associate Directors: Shaghil Ahmed, David H. Bowman, Mark S. Carey, Brian M. Doyle, Joseph W. Gruber, Charles P. Thomas.
Deputy Associate Directors: James A. Dahl, Sally M. Davies.
Assistant Directors: Carol Bertaut, Stephanie Curcuru, Matteo Iacoviello, Paul Wood.
Senior Adviser.—John H. Rogers.

DIVISION OF MONETARY AFFAIRS

Director.—Thomas Laubach.
Deputy Directors: James A. Clouse, Brian Madigan, Stephen A. Meyer.
Senior Associate Director.—Gretchen C. Weinbach.
Associate Directors: Margaret DeBoer, Jane E. Ihrig, David Lopez-Salido.
Deputy Associate Directors: Mary T. Hoffman, Matthew M. Luecke, Min Wei.
Assistant Directors: Christopher Gust, Elizabeth Klee, Laura Lipscomb, Jason Wu.
Senior Advisers: Antulio Bomfim, Ellen Meade, Edward Nelson, Robert Tetlow, Egon Zakrajsek, Joyce K. Zickler.
Advisers: Eric C. Engstron, Don Kim.

DIVISION OF RESEARCH AND STATISTICS

Director.—David Wilcox.

Deputy Directors: Jeff Campione, Daniel Covitz, William L. Wascher III.
Senior Associate Directors: Eric M. Engen, Joshua H. Gallin, Diana Hancock, David E. Lebow, Michael G. Palumbo.
Associate Directors: Elizabeth K. Kiser, John J. Stevens, Stacey M. Tevlin.
Deputy Associate Directors: Timothy Mullen, Steven A. Sharpe.
Assistant Directors: Stephanie Aaronson, Burcu Duygan-Bump, J. Andrew Figura, Glenn Follette, Erik Heitfield, Normin Morin, Karen M. Pence, John Sabelhaus, Shane M. Sherlund, Lillian Sewmaker, Paul Smith.
Senior Advisers: S. Wayne Passmore, Robin Prager, Jeremy Rudd.
Advisers: Eric Engstrom, Patrick McCabe, John M. Roberts.

INSPECTOR GENERAL

Inspector General.—Mark Bialek.
Deputy Inspector General.—J. Anthony Ogden.
Associate Inspectors General: Jacqueline M. Becker, Melissa Heist, Alberto Rivera-Journier, Lawrence Valett.
Assistant Inspectors General: Gerald Maye, Peter Sheridan.

LEGAL DIVISION

General Counsel.—Mark Van Der Weide.
Deputy General Counsels.—Richard M. Ashton.
Associate General Counsels: Stephanie Martin, Laurie S. Schaffer, Katherine H. Wheatley.
Assistant General Counsels: Jean C. Anderson, Patrick M. Bryan, Alye S. Foster, Benjamin McDonough, Alison M. Thro, Cary K. Williams.

MANAGEMENT DIVISION

Director.—Michell C. Clark.
Deputy Directors: Steven Miranda, Winona Varnon.
Senior Associate Directors: Tameika Pope, Marie S. Savoy.
Deputy Associate Director.—Reginald V. Roach.
Associate Directors: Curtis Eldridge, Catherine Jack, Tara Tinsley Pelitere.
Assistant Directors: Keith F. Bates, Ann Buckingham, Timothy E. Markey, Jeffrey Martin, Stephen Pearson, Katherine Perez-Grines, Theresa A. Trimble.

OFFICE OF THE SECRETARY

Secretary.—Ann E. Misback.
Deputy Secretary.—Margaret M. Shanks.
Associate Secretaries: Yao-Chin Chao, Michele T. Fennell.

DIVISION OF FINANCIAL STABILITY POLICY AND RESEARCH

Director.—Andreas W. Lehnert.
Deputy Director.—Michael T. Kiley.
Assistant Directors: William Bassett, Rochelle M. Edge, John Schindler.
Deputy Associate Director.—Luca Guerrieri.
Assistant Directors: Andrew Cohen, Jennifer Roush, Skander Van den Heuvel.

OFFICE OF THE CHIEF OPERATING OFFICER

Chief Operating Officer.—Donald V. Hammond.
Chief Data Officer.—Michael J. Kraemer.
ODI Program Director.—Sheila Clark.
Assistant Directors: Philip Daher, Todd A. Glissman, Jeff Monica.

DIVISION OF FINANCIAL MANAGEMENT

Director.—Ricardo A. Aguliera.

Deputy Director.—Stephen J. Bernard.
Associate Director.—Christine M. Fields.
Deputy Associate Directors: Jeffret R. Peirce, Karen Vassallo.
Senior Adviser.—Andrew Leonard.

BROADCASTING BOARD OF GOVERNORS

330 Independence Avenue, SW., Suite 3300, 20237

phone (202) 203–4545, fax 203–4568

The Broadcasting Board of Governors oversees the operation of the IBB and provides yearly funding grants approved by Congress to three non-profit grantee corporations, Radio Free Europe / Radio Liberty, Radio Free Asia, and the Middle East Broadcasting Networks.

Chair.—Kenneth Weinstein (acting).

INTERNATIONAL BROADCASTING BUREAU

[Created by Public Law 103–236]

The International Broadcasting Bureau (IBB) is composed of the Voice of America and, Office of Cuba Broadcasting, Radio and TV Marti.

Chief Executive Officer and Director of Broadcasting Board of Governors.—John F. Lansing (202) 203–4545, fax 203–4568.
Director of:
Office of Cuba Broadcasting.—María ''Malule'' González (305) 437–7012, fax 437–7016.
Voice of America.—Amanda Bennett (202) 203–4500, fax 203–4513.
President, Radio Free Asia.—Libby Liu (202) 530–4900, fax 530–7795.
President, Radio Free Europe.—Tom Kent (202) 457–6900, fax 457–6933.
President, Middle East Broadcasting Networks.—Brian Conniff (703) 852–9000, fax 991–1250.

GOVERNORS

Leon Aron
Ryan Crocker
Michael Kempner
Karen Kornbluh
Jeffrey Shell
Mike Pompeo (ex officio)

CENTRAL INTELLIGENCE AGENCY

phone (703) 482–1100

Director.—Gina C. Haspel.
Deputy Director.—Vacant.
Chief Operating Officer.—Brian Bulatao.
General Counsel.—Courtney S. Elwood.
Director of:
Analysis.—Richard W. Hoch.
Public Affairs.—R. Dean Boyd.
Science and Technology.—Dawn C. Meyerriecks.
Support.—Christopher D. Murray.
Congressional Affairs.—Jaime Cheshire.

COMMISSION OF FINE ARTS

National Building Museum, 401 F Street, NW., Suite 312, 20001–2728

phone (202) 504–2200, fax 504–2195, http://www.cfa.gov

Commissioners:

Earl A. Powell III, Washington, DC, *Chair.*
Elizabeth K. Meyer, Charlottesville, VA.
Alex Krieger, Boston, MA.
Mia Lehrer, Los Angeles, CA.
Liza Gilbert, Washington, DC.
Edward D. Dunson, Jr., Washington, DC.
Toni L. Griffin, New York, NY.

Secretary.—Thomas Luebke, FAIA.
Assistant Secretary.—Frederick J. Lindstrom.

BOARD OF ARCHITECTURAL CONSULTANTS
FOR THE OLD GEORGETOWN ACT

H. Alan Brangman, AIA, *Chair.*
Richard Williams, FAIA.
Mary Katherine Lanzillotta, FAIA.

COMMITTEE FOR PURCHASE FROM PEOPLE WHO ARE BLIND OR SEVERELY DISABLED

1401 S. Clark Street, Suite 715, Arlington, VA 22202–3259

phone (703) 603–7740, fax 603–0655

[Operating as U.S. AbilityOne Commission]

Chair.—James M. Kesteloot.
Vice Chair.—Thomas D. Robinson.
Executive Director.—Tina Ballard.
Members:
Perry Edward ''Ed'' Anthony, Department of Education.
Jan R. Frye, Department of Veterans Affairs.
Vacant, Department of Army.
Vacant, Department of Defense.
Thomas D. Robinson, Department of the Air Force.
William Sisk, General Services Administration.
Vacant, Department of Agriculture.
Virna L. Winters, Department of Commerce.
Rear Adm. Jonathan A. Yuen, Department of the Navy.
James M. Kesteloot, Private Citizen (Obstacles to Employment of People Who Are Blind).
Anil Lewis, Private Citizen (Nonprofit Agency Employees Who Are Blind).
Vacant, (Nonprofit Agency Employees with Other Severe Disabilities).
Robert T. Kelly, Jr., Private Citizen (Obstacles to Employment of People with Other Severe Disabilities).
Vacant, Department of Justice.
Jennifer Sheehy, Department of Labor.

COMMODITY FUTURES TRADING COMMISSION

Three Lafayette Centre, 1155 21st Street, NW., 20581, phone (202) 418–5000

fax 418–5521, http://www.cftc.gov

Chair.—J. Christopher Giancarlo, 418–5030, fax 418–5533.
Chief of Staff.—Michael Gill, 418–5713.
Senior Counsel.—Marcia Blasé, 418–5138.
Special Advisor.—Richard Danker, 418–5609.
Market Intelligence Advisor.—Andrew Busch (312) 596–0598.
Executive Assistant.—Shonneice Jones (202) 418–5770.
Commissioner.—Rostin Behnam, 418–5575, fax 418–5067.
Special Counsels: John Dunfee, 418–5575; Laura Gardy, 418–5575.
Executive Assistant.—Kyndra Burke, 418–5575.
Commissioner.—Brian D. Quintenz, 418–5010, fax 418–5072.
Chief of Staff.—Kevin Webb, 418–5010.
Executive Assistant.—Andrea Owens, 418–5010.
Director, Division of:
Clearing and Intermediary Oversight.—Eileen Flaherty (312) 596–0600.
Enforcement.—Jamie McDonald (202) 418–5637, fax 418–5523.

Market Oversight.—Amir Zaidi, 418–6770, fax 418–5527.
Executive Director.—Anthony C. Thompson, 418–5697, fax 418–5541.
Chief Economist.—Sayee Srinivasan, 418–5309, fax 418–5660.
General Counsel.—Daniel Davis, 418–5649, fax 418–5524.
Inspector General.—A. Roy Lavik, 418–5110, fax 418–5522.
Data and Technology Chief Information Officer.—John Rogers, 418–5240.
Director, Office of:
Diversity and Inclusion.—Lorena McElwain, 418–5935, fax 418–5546.
International Affairs.—Eric Pan, 418–5559, fax 418–5548.
Legislative Affairs.—Charlie Thornton, 418–5145, fax 418–5525.
Public Affairs.—Erica Elliott Richardson, 418–5382, fax 418–5525.
Office of the Secretariat, Secretary of the Commission.—Chris Kirkpatrick, 418–5100, fax 418–5521.

REGIONAL OFFICES

Central Region: 525 West Monroe Street, Suite 1100, Chicago, IL 60601 (312) 596–0700, fax 596–0716, TTY 596–0565.
Southwestern Region: 4900 Main Street, Suite 500, Kansas City, MO 64112 (816) 960–7700, fax 960–7750, TTY 960–7704.
Eastern Region: 140 Broadway, Nineteenth Floor, New York, NY 10005 (646) 746–9700, fax 746–9938, TTY 746–9820.

CONSUMER PRODUCT SAFETY COMMISSION

4330 East West Highway, Bethesda, MD 20814, phone (301) 504–7923
fax 504–0124, http://www.cpsc.gov

[Created by Public Law 92–573]

Chair.—Ann Marie Buerkle (acting), (301) 504–7878.
Commissioners:
Robert ''Bob'' Adler, 504–7731.
Marietta Robinson, 504–7253.
Elliot Kaye, 504–7900.
Joseph Mohorovic, 504–7738.
Executive Director.—Patricia Adkins, 504–7582.
Deputy Executive Director for—
Operations Support.—Monica Summit, 504–7691.
Safety Operations.—DeWane Ray, 504–7547.
Director, Office of:
The Secretary.—Todd A. Stevenson, 504–7923.
Legislative Affairs.—Aaron Hernandez (acting), 504–7853.
General Counsel.—Mary Boyle, 504–7859.

CORPORATION FOR NATIONAL AND COMMUNITY SERVICE

250 E Street, SW., 20525, phone (202) 606–5000
http://www.cns.gov

[Executive Order 11603, June 30, 1971; codified in 42 U.S.C., section 4951]

Chief Executive Officer.—Barbara Stewart.
Chief of Staff.—Desiree Tucker-Sorini.
Chief Financial Officer.—Robert McCarty, 606–6652.
Director of:
Office of Government Relations.—J.P. Fish, 606–6707.
AmeriCorps State and National.—Chester Spellman, 606–6991.
AmeriCorps National Civilian Community Corps.—Gina Cross (acting), 606–3233.
AmeriCorps VISTA.—Eileen Conoboy (acting), 606–6871.
Senior Corps.—Deborah Cox-Roush, 606–6634.
General Counsel.—Tim Noelker, 606–6985.

DEFENSE NUCLEAR FACILITIES SAFETY BOARD

625 Indiana Avenue, NW., Suite 700, 20004, phone (202) 694–7000
fax 208–6518, http://www.dnfsb.gov

Chair.—Sean Sullivan.

Vice Chair.—Bruce Hamilton.
Members: Joyce Connery, Jessie Roberson, Daniel Santos.
General Counsel.—James Biggins.
General Manager.—Glenn Sklar.
Technical Director.—Steven Stokes.

DELAWARE RIVER BASIN COMMISSION

25 Cosey Road, P.O. Box 7360, West Trenton, NJ 08628–0360

phone (609) 883–9500, fax 883–9522, http://www.drbc.net

[Created by Public Law 87–328]

FEDERAL REPRESENTATIVES

Federal Commissioner.—BG William H. Graham, Commander, Division Engineer, U.S. Army Corps of Engineers, North Atlantic Division (347) 370–4500.
First Alternate.—LTC Kristen N. Dahle, Philadelphia District Commander, U.S. Army Corps of Engineers, Philadelphia (215) 656–6501.
Second Alternate.—Alternate Pending, Regional Director of Programs, U.S. Army Corps of Engineers, North Atlantic Division, 370–4629.
Third Alternate.—Henry W. Gruber, Program Manager, U.S. Army Corps of Engineers, North Atlantic Division, 370–4566.

STAFF

Executive Director.—Steven J. Tambini, P.E., ext. 200.
Commission Secretary/Assistant General Counsel.—Pamela M. Bush, J.D., M.R.P., ext. 203.
Communications Manager.—Clarke D. Rupert, ext. 260.

DELAWARE REPRESENTATIVES

State Commissioner.—John C. Carney, Governor (302) 577–3210.
First Alternate.—Shawn M. Garvin, Secretary, Delaware Department of Natural Resources and Environmental Control (DNREC), 739–9000.
Second Alternate.—Alternate Pending, Deputy Secretary, Division of Water Resources (DNREC), 739–9949.
Third Alternate.—Virgil R. Holmes, Director, Division of Water Management Section (DNREC), 739–9949.
Fourth Alternate.—Bryan A. Ashby, Program Manager, Surface Water Section (DNREC), 739–9946.

NEW JERSEY REPRESENTATIVES

State Commissioner.—Philip D. Murphy, Governor (609) 292–6000.
First Alternate.—Catherine R. McCabe, Commissioner, New Jersey Department of Environmental Protection (NJDEP), 292–2885.
Second Alternate.—Alternate Pending, Assistant Commissioner, Water Resource Management (NJDEP), 292–4543.
Third Alternate.—Jeffrey L. Hoffman, P.G., State Geologist, New Jersey Geological and Water Survey, Division of Water Supply and Geoscience (NJDEP), 292–1185.

NEW YORK REPRESENTATIVES

State Commissioner.—Andrew M. Cuomo, Governor (518) 474–8390.
First Alternate.—Basil Seggos, Commissioner, New York State Department of Environmental Conservation (NYSDEC), (518) 402–8545.
Second Alternate.—Mark Klotz, P.E., Director, Division of Water (NYSDEC), 402–8233.
Third Alternate.—Vacant.
Fourth Alternate.—Kenneth Kosinski, P.E., Chief, Watershed Implementation Section (NYSDEC), 402–8110.

PENNSYLVANIA REPRESENTATIVES

State Commissioner.—Tom Wolf, Governor (717) 787–2500.

First Alternate.—Patrick McDonnell, Secretary, Pennsylvania Department of Environmental Protection (PADEP), 787–2814.
Second Alternate.—Timothy D. Schaeffer (acting), Deputy Secretary, Office of Water Programs (PADEP), 783–4693.
Third Alternate.—Jennifer Orr, Director, Office of Compacts and Commissions (PADEP), (717) 772–5633.

ENVIRONMENTAL PROTECTION AGENCY

1200 Pennsylvania Avenue, NW., 20460, phone (202) 564–4700, http://www.epa.gov

Administrator.—Andrew Wheeler (acting), 564–4700.
Deputy Administrator.—Vacant, 564–4700.
Chief of Staff.—Ryan Jackson, 564–6999.
Deputy Chief of Staff.—Helena Wooden-Aguilar (acting), 564–0792.
Agriculture Counsel.—Jeffrey Sands, 564–2263.
White House Liaison.—Charles Munoz, 564–7960.
Environmental Appeals Board: Mary Kay Lynch, Mary Beth Ward, 233–0122.
Associate Administrator for—
Congressional and Intergovernmental Relations.—Troy Lyons, 564–5200.
Homeland Security.—Vacant.
Policy, Economics, and Innovation.—Samantha Dravis, 564–4332.
Public Affairs.—Liz Bowman, 564–8368.
Public Engagement and Environmental Education.—Tate Bennett, 564–1460.
Director, Office of:
Children's Health Protection.—Ruth Etzel, 564–2188.
Civil Rights.—Tanya Lawrence (acting), 564–7272.
Cooperative Environmental Management.—Vacant.
Executive Secretariat.—Elizabeth White, 564–7311.
Executive Services.—Reginald E. Allen, 564–1029.
Science Advisory Board.—Christopher Zarba, 564–2221.
Small and Disadvantaged Business Utilization.—Denise Benjamin-Sirmons, 564–2075.
Director of Management, Office of Administrative Law Judges.—Susan Biro, 564–6255.

ADMINISTRATION AND RESOURCES MANAGEMENT

Assistant Administrator.—Donna Vizian (acting), 564–4600.
Principal Deputy Assistant Administrator.—John Showman (acting), 564–4600.

AIR AND RADIATION

Assistant Administrator.—Bill Wehrum, 564–7404.
Deputy Assistant Administrator.—Betsy Shaw, 564–7400.

ENFORCEMENT AND COMPLIANCE ASSURANCE

Assistant Administrator.—Susan Bodine, 564–2440.
Deputy Assistant Administrator.—Patrick Traylor, 564–2440

OFFICE OF ENVIRONMENTAL INFORMATION

Assistant Administrator.—Steven Fine (acting), 564–6665.
Principal Deputy Assistant Administrator.—Harvey Simon (acting), 564–6665.

CHIEF FINANCIAL OFFICER

Chief Financial Officer.—Holly Greaves, 564–3028.
Deputy Chief Financial Officer.—David Bloom, 564–1151.

GENERAL COUNSEL

General Counsel.—Matthew Z. Leopold, 564–8040.
Principal Deputy General Counsel.—Kevin Minoli, 564–8064.
Deputy General Counsel.—Justin Schwab, 564–3135.

INSPECTOR GENERAL

Inspector General.—Arthur Elkins, Jr., 566–0847.
Deputy Inspector General.—Charles Sheehan, 566–0847.

INTERNATIONAL AFFAIRS

Assistant Administrator.—Jane Nishida (acting), 564–6600.
Deputy Assistant Administrator.—Katrina Cherry (acting), 564–2478.

CHEMICAL SAFETY AND POLLUTION PREVENTION

Principal Deputy Assistant Administrator.—Charlotte Bertrand (acting), 564–0539.
Deputy Assistant Administrator.—Louise Wise, 564–2910.

RESEARCH AND DEVELOPMENT

Assistant Administrator.—Jennifer Orme-Zavaleta (acting), (919) 541–2283.
Deputy Assistant Administrator of:
Research and Development.—Richard (Yujiro) Yamada, 564–6620.
Associate Director of Science.—Bruce Rodan, 564–6620.

LAND AND EMERGENCY RESPONSE

Assistant Administrator.—Barry Breen (acting), 566–0200.
Principal Deputy Assistant Administrator.—Nigel Simon (acting), 566–0200.

WATER

Assistant Administrator.—Dave Ross, 564–5700.
Deputy Assistant Administrator.—Lee Forsgren, 564–5700.

REGIONAL ADMINISTRATION

Region I, Boston.—Connecticut, Maine, New Hampshire, Rhode Island, Vermont.
Regional Administrator.—Deb Szaro (acting), One Congress Street, Suite 1100, Boston, MA 02114 (617) 918–1011.
Public Affairs.—Doug Gutro.

Region II, New York City.—New Jersey, New York, Puerto Rico, Virgin Islands.
Regional Administrator.—Pete Lopez, 290 Broadway, New York, NY 10007 (212) 637–5000.
Public Affairs.—Mary Mears (212) 637–3660.

Region III, Philadelphia.—Delaware, Washington DC, Maryland, Pennsylvania, Virginia, West Virginia.
Regional Administrator.—Cosmo Servidio, 1650 Arch Street, Philadelphia, PA 19103–2029 (215) 814–2900.
Public Affairs.—Michael D'Andrea (215) 814–5615.

Region IV, Atlanta.—Alabama, Florida, Georgia, Kentucky, Mississippi, North Carolina, South Carolina, Tennessee.
Regional Administrator.—Trey Glenn, 61 Forsyth Street, SW., Atlanta, GA 30303–8960 (404) 562–8357.
Public Affairs.—Larry Lincoln (404) 562–8327.

Region V, Chicago.—Illinois, Indiana, Michigan, Minnesota, Ohio, Wisconsin.
Regional Administrator.—Robert Kaplan (acting), 77 West Jackson Boulevard, Chicago, IL 60604–3507 (312) 886–3000.
Public Affairs.—Anne Rowan (312) 886–3000.

Region VI, Dallas.—Arkansas, Louisiana, New Mexico, Oklahoma, Texas.
Regional Administrator.—Sam Coleman (acting), Fountain Place, 1445 Ross Avenue, 12th Floor, Suite 1200, Dallas, TX 75202–2733 (214) 665–2100.
Public Affairs.—David W. Gray (214) 665–2200.

Region VII, Kansas City.—Iowa, Kansas, Missouri, Nebraska.
Regional Administrator.—Jim Gulliford, 901 North 5th Street, Kansas City, MO 66101 (913) 551–7006.

Public Affairs.—Curtis Carey (913) 551–7003.

Region VIII, Denver.—Colorado, Montana, North Dakota, South Dakota, Utah, Wyoming.
Regional Administrator.—Doug Benevento, 999 18th Street, Suite 300, Denver, CO 80202–2466 (303) 312–6532.
Public Affairs.—Andrew Mutter (303) 312–6448.

Region IX, San Francisco.—Arizona, California, Hawaii, Nevada, American Samoa, Guam.
Regional Administrator.—Alexis Strauss (acting), 75 Hawthorne Street, San Francisco, CA 94105 (415) 947–8702.
Public Affairs.—Kelly Zito (415) 947–8702.

Region X, Seattle.—Alaska, Idaho, Oregon, Washington.
Regional Administrator.—Michelle Pirzadeh (acting), 1200 Sixth Avenue, Seattle, WA 98101 (206) 553–1234.
Public Affairs.—Marianne Holsman (206) 553–1234.

EQUAL EMPLOYMENT OPPORTUNITY COMMISSION

131 M Street, NE., 20507, phone (202) 663–4900

Chair.—Victoria Lipnic (acting), Suite 6NW08F, 663–4001, fax 663–4110.
Chief Operating Officer.—Cynthia Pierre, Suite 6NW08F.
Deputy Chief Operating Officer.—Vacant.
Confidential Assistant.—Shawanda Hardy, Suite 6NW08F, 663–4002.
Commissioners: Charlotte A. Burrows, Suite 6NE37F, 663–4052, fax 663–4108; Chai Feldblum, Suite 6NE07F, 663–4090, fax 663–7101; Jenny Yang, Suite 6NE25F, 663–4027, fax 663–7086.
Deputy General Counsel.—James Lee, 5th Floor, 663–7034, fax 663–4196.
Legal Counsel.—Chris Kuczynski, 5th Floor, 663–4655, fax 663–4639.
Director, Office of:
Chief Financial Officer.—Germaine Roseboro, 4th Floor, 663–4200, fax 663–7068.
Communications and Legislative Affairs.—Brett Brenner (acting), 6th Floor, 663–4191, fax 663–4912.
Equal Opportunity.—Erica White-Dunston, 6th Floor, 663–7081, fax 663–7003.
Executive Secretariat/Executive Secretary.—Bernadette Wilson (acting), 6th Floor, 663–4070, fax 663–4114.
Field Operations.—Carlton Hadden, 5th Floor, 663–4599, fax 663–7022.
Field Programs.—Nicholas Inzeo, 5th Floor, 663–4801, fax 663–7190.
Human Resources.—Traci DiMartini, 4th Floor, 663–4306, fax 663–4324.
Information Technology.—Bryan Burnett, 4th Floor, 663–4447, fax 663–4451.
Inspector General.—Milton Mayo, 6th Floor, 663–4327, fax 663–7204.
Research, Information, and Planning.—Ron Edwards, 4th Floor, 663–4853, fax 663–4093.

EXPORT-IMPORT BANK OF THE UNITED STATES

811 Vermont Avenue, NW., 20571, phone (800) 565–EXIM, fax 565–3380

President and Chairman of Board.—Charles J. Hall (acting), 565–3500.
First Vice President and Vice Chair of Board.—Scott P. Schloegel (acting), 565–3502.
Board of Directors Member: Vacant.
Board of Directors Member: Vacant.
Board of Directors Member: Vacant.
Executive Vice President and Chief Operating Officer.—Charles J. Hall, 565–3500.
Senior Vice President and Chief of Staff.—Scott P. Schloegel, 565–3502.
Senior Vice President and Chief Financial Officer.—David M. Sena, 565–3272.
Senior Vice President and General Counsel.—Angela M. Freyre, 565–3430.
Senior Vice President of:
Business and Product Development.—Robert A. Morin, 565–3453.
Communications.—Caroline L. Scullin, 565–3201.
Congressional and Intergovernmental Affairs.—Kevin R. Warnke (acting), 565–3230.
Ethics and Chief Ethics Officer.—Lisa V. Terry, 565–3195.
Export Finance and Chief Banking Officer.—Madolyn C. Phillips (acting), 565–3701.
Information Management and Technology and Chief Information Officer.—Howard Spira, 565–3844.
Innovation and Performance.—Michele A. Kuester, 565–3221.
Policy Analysis and International Relations.—James C. Cruse, 565–3761.
Resource Management.—Michael Cushing, 565–3561.

Risk Management and Chief Risk Officer.—Kenneth M. Tinsley, 565–3668.
Small Business.—James G. Burrows, 565–3801.
Deputy:
Chief Banking Officer.—Madolyn C. Phillips, 565–3701.
Chief Financial Officer.—Inci Tonguch-Murray, 565–3356.
Chief of Staff.—Carolyn Schopp, 565–3396.
General Counsel.—Doug Adler, 565–3435.
Vice President of:
Acquisition and Business Services.—Maria A. Fleetwood, 565–3349.
Asset Management.—Walter F. Keating, 565–3623.
Business Credit.—Pamela S. Bowers, 565–3792.
Communications.—Rebecca M. Rose, 565–3209.
Congressional and Intergovernmental Affairs.—Kevin R. Warnke, 565–3230.
Controller.—Patricia A. Wolf, 565–3268.
Country Risk and Economic Analysis.—William A. Marsteller, 565–3739.
Credit Policy.—David W. Carter, 565–3667.
Credit Review and Compliance.—Walter B. Hill, Jr., 565–3672.
Customer and Business Solutions.—Rochele A. Barham, 565–3603.
Engineering and Environment.—James A. Mahoney, 565–3573.
Global Business Development.—Madolyn C. Phillips, 565–3701.
Human Capital and Chief Human Capital Officer.—George H. Garcia, 565–3321.
International Relations.—Isabel Galdiz, 565–3763.
Operations and Management Reporting.—Nicole M. Valtos, 565–3411.
Policy Analysis.—Helene S. Walsh, 565–3768.
Public Affairs.—Catrell Brown, 565–3203.
Sales and Marketing.—Sean Luke, 565–3472.
Structured and Project Finance.—Michael Whelan, 565–3880.
Trade Finance and Insurance.—Annette B. Maresh, 565–3665.
Transportation.—Robert F.X. Roy, Jr., 565–3557.
Transportation Portfolio Management.—Andrew E. Falk, 565–3447.
Treasurer.—Nathalie S. Herman, 565–3881.

OFFICE OF INSPECTOR GENERAL

Inspector General.—Michael T. McCarthy (acting), 565–3908.
Deputy Inspector General.—Michael T. McCarthy, 565–3908.

FARM CREDIT ADMINISTRATION

1501 Farm Credit Drive, McLean, VA 22102–5090

phone (703) 883–4000, fax 734–5784

[Reorganization pursuant to Public Law 99–205, December 23, 1985]

Board Chair and Chief Executive Officer.—Dallas P. Tonsager.
Board Members:
Jeffery S. Hall.
Glen R. Smith.
Secretary to the Board.—Dale L. Aultman, 883–4009, fax 883–4181.
Chief Operating Officer.—William J. Hoffman, 883–4340, fax 883–4181.
Director, Office of:
Congressional and Public Affairs.—Michael A. Stokke, 883–4056, fax 790–3260.
Examination.—S. Robert Coleman, 883–4160, fax 893–2978.
General Counsel.—Charles R. Rawls, 883–4020, fax 790–0052.
Inspector General.—Wendy LaGuarda, 883–4030, fax 883–4059.
Agency Services.—A. Jerome Fowlkes, 883–4200, fax 883–4151.
Regulatory Policy.—Gary K. Van Meter, 883–4414, fax 883–4477.
Secondary Market Oversight.—Laurie Rea, 883–4280, fax 883–4056.
Chief Financial Officer.—Stephen G. Smith, 883–4275, fax 883–4151.
Chief Human Capital Officer.—A. Jerome Fowlkes, 883–4200, fax 883–4151.
Chief Information Officer.—Jerald Golley, 883–4444, fax 734–1950.
Director, Equal Employment Opportunity and Inclusion.—Thais Burlew, 883–4290, fax 883–4352.

FEDERAL COMMUNICATIONS COMMISSION

445 12th Street, SW., 20554, phone (202) 418–0200, http: //www.fcc.gov

FCC National Consumer Center: 1–888–225–5322 / 1–888–835–5322 (TTY)

Chair.—Ajit Pai.
Chief of Staff.—Matthew Berry.
Senior Counselor to the Chair.—Nicholas Degani.
Special Counsel.—Michael Carowitz.
Policy Advisor.—Nathan Leamer.
Legal Advisors: Rachael Bender, Zenji Nakazawa, Alison Nemeth, Jay Schwarz.
Confidential Assistants: Lori Alexiou, Deanne Erwin, Kim Mattos, Carlos Minnix.
Commissioner.—Michael P. O'Rielly.
Chief of Staff, Media Legal Advisor.—Brooke Ericson.
Wireline Legal Advisors: Amy Bender, Erin McGrath.
Confidential Assistant.—Susan Fisenne.
Staff Assistant.—Ovonda Walker.
Commissioner.—Mignon Clyburn.
Chief of Staff.—David Grossman.
Senior Legal Advisor.—Louis Peraertz.
Legal Advisor.—Claude Aiken.
Staff Assistant.—DeeAnn Smith.
Commissioner.—Jessica Rosenworcel.
Chief of Staff.—Travis Litman.
Legal Advisor.—Umair Javed.
Policy Advisor.—Kate Black.
Staff Assistant.—Lashion Pratt.
Commissioner.—Brendan Carr.
Chief of Staff.—Jamie Susskind.
Legal Advisors: Kevin Holmes, Nirali Patel.
Confidential Assistant.—Drema Johnson.

OFFICE OF ADMINISTRATIVE LAW JUDGES

Administrative Law Judge.—Richard L. Sippel, Room 1–C768, 418–2280.

OFFICE OF COMMUNICATIONS BUSINESS OPPORTUNITIES

Director.—Sanford Williams, Room 4–A760, 418–1508.

CONSUMER AND GOVERNMENTAL AFFAIRS BUREAU

Chief.—Patrick Webre (acting), Room 5–C758, 418–0952.
Deputy Bureau Chiefs: Karen Peltz-Strauss, Room 5–C755; Mark Stone, Room 5–C754, 418–0816.
Associate Bureau Chief.—Roger Goldblatt, Room 5–A848, 418–1035.
Assistant Bureau Chief for Management.—Tamika Jackson, Room 5–A847, 418–0159.
Chief, Division of:
Consumer Affairs and Outreach.—Anita Dey (acting), Room 1–A822, 418–0743.
Consumer Inquiries and Complaints.—Vacant.
Deputy Chief.—Sharon Wright (acting), Room 5–C818, 418–2898.
Consumer Policy.—Kurt Schroeder, Room 5–A812, 418–0966.
Web and Print Publishing.—Howard Parnell, Room 4–C456, 418–7280.
Chief, Office of:
Disability Rights.—Suzanne Singleton, Room 3–B431 (202) 510–9446.
Intergovernmental Affairs.—Elizabeth Mumaw, Room 5–A630, 418–1381.
Office of Native Affairs and Policy.—Matthew Duchesne, Room 4–C763, 418–3629.
Reference Information Center.—Melissa Askew, Room CY–C203D, 418–0292.

ENFORCEMENT BUREAU

Chief.—Rosemary Harold, Room 3–C252, 418–7450.
Deputy Bureau Chiefs: Lisa Gelb, Room 3–C254, 418–7450; Keith Morgan, Room 3–C255, 418–7450; Phillip Rosario, Room 3–C250, 418–7450.

Assistant Bureau Chiefs: Hilary Burchuk, Room 3–C410, 418–1719; Jennifer Epperson, Room 3–C217, 418–1890; Jeremy Marcus, Room 3–C163, 418–0059; Geoffrey Starks, Room 3–C300, 418–1365.
Chief, Division of:
Investigations and Hearings.—Jeffrey Gee, Room 4–C322, 418–7479.
Market Disputes Resolutions.—Rosemary McEnery, Room 4–C324, 418–7336.
Spectrum Enforcement.—Aspasia Paroutsas, Room 3–C366, 418–7285.
Telecommunications.—Kristi Thompson, Room 4–C220, 418–1318.
Field Director.—Charles Cooper, Room 4–A433, 418–7590.
Deputy Field Director.—Janet Moran, Room 4–A336, 418–7923.

OFFICE OF ENGINEERING AND TECHNOLOGY

Chief.—Julius P. Knapp, Room 7–C155, 418–2470.

OFFICE OF GENERAL COUNSEL

General Counsel.—Thomas Johnson, Jr., Room 8–C750, 418–1744.
Deputy General Counsels: Ashley Boizelle, Room 8–C755, 418–1736; Michele Ellison, Room 8–C712, 418–1718; David Gossett, Room 8–C758, 418–0980.
Associate General Counsel.—Karen Onyeije, Room 8–C758, 418–1757.

OFFICE OF INSPECTOR GENERAL

Inspector General.—David L. Hunt, Room 2–C347, 418–0470.

INTERNATIONAL BUREAU

Chief.—Thomas P. Sullivan, Room 6–C750, 418–0437.
Deputy Chiefs: Jim Schlichting, Room 6–C752, 418–1547; Troy Tanner, Room 6–C475, 418–1475.
Chief, Division of:
Telecommunications and Analysis Division.—Denise Coca, Room 7–A760, 418–0574.
Satellite Division.—Jose Albuquerque, Room 6–A665, 418–2288.
Strategic Analysis and Negotiations Division.—Olga Madruga Forti, Room 6–A763, 418–2489.

OFFICE OF LEGISLATIVE AFFAIRS

Director.—Timothy Strachan, Room 8–C453, 418–2242.
Deputy Director.—James "Jim" Balaguer, Room 8–C464, 418–1915.

OFFICE OF MANAGING DIRECTOR

Managing Director.—Mark Stephens, Room 1–C152, 418–1919.
Deputy Managing Director.—Mindy Ginsburg, Room 1–C154, 418–0983.
Secretary.—Marlene Dortch, Room TW–B204, 418–0300.
Chief, Human Capital Office.—Tom Green, Room 1–A100, 418–0293, TTY 481–0150 (employment verification).
Associate Managing Directors:
Administrative Operations.—MaryKay Mitchell, Room 1–C402, 418–2173.
Financial Operations.—Kathleen Heuer, 418–4560.
Information Technology.—Christine Calvosa, Room 1–C264, 418–7455.
Performance Evaluations and Records Management.—Vanessa Lamb, Room 1–C804, 418–7044.

MEDIA BUREAU

Chief.—Michelle Carey, Room 3–C486, 418–7200.
Deputy Bureau Chief.—Mary Beth Murphy, Room 3–C742, 418–7200.
Chief of Staff.—Thomas Horan, Room 3–C478, 418–7200.
Assistant Bureau Chief for Management.—India Malcolm, Room 3–C838, 418–7200.

Chief, Division of:
Audio Division.—Peter Doyle, Room 2–A360, 418–2700.
Engineering Division.—John Wong, Room 4–C838, 418–7012.
Industry Analysis Division.—Brendan Holland, Room 2–C360, 418–2330.
Policy Division.—Martha Heller, Room 4–A766, 418–2120.
Video Division.—Barbara A. Kreisman, Room 2–A666, 418–1600.

OFFICE OF MEDIA RELATIONS

Director.—Brian Hart, Room CY–C314B, 418–0505.
Deputy Director.—Mark Wigfield, Room CY–C314C, 418–0253.

OFFICE OF STRATEGIC PLANNING AND POLICY ANALYSIS

Chief.—Wayne Leighton, Room 7–C450, 418–0950.
Deputy Chief.—Vacant.
Chief Economist.—Jerry Ellig, Room 7–C452, 418–1699.
Chief Technology Officer.—Eric Burger, Room 7–C252, 418–0267.
Chief of Incentive Auctions/Senior Advisor to the Chair.—Jean Kiddoo, Room 7–C357, 418–7757.

PUBLIC SAFETY AND HOMELAND SECURITY BUREAU

Chief.—Lisa M. Fowlkes, Room 7–C485, 418–7452.
Deputy Chiefs: David Furth, Room 7–C753, 418–0632; Debra Jordan, Room 7–C751, 418–0676; Nicole McGinnis, Room 7–C745, 418–2877.
Chief of Staff.—Lauren Kravetz, Room 7–C737, 418–7944.
Associate Chiefs: Jeffery Goldthorp, Room 7–A325, 418–1096; Anita Patankar-Stoll, Room 7–C749, 418–7121.
Chief Economist.—Emily Talaga, Room 7–C738, 418–7396.
Chief Technologist.—Kenneth Carlberg, Room 7–C841, 418–0214.
Senior Counsel.—Erika Olsen, Room 7–B443, 418–2868.
Special Counsel.—Renee Roland, Room 3–A232, 418–2357.
Media Director.—Rochelle Cohen, Room 7–C747, 418–1162.

WIRELESS TELECOMMUNICATIONS BUREAU

Bureau Chief.—Donald Stockdale, Room 6–C160, 418–0600.
Deputy Bureau Chief and Chief of Staff.—Dana Shaffer, Room 6–C140, 418–0832.
Senior Deputy Bureau Chief.—Nese Guendelsberger, Room 6–C162; 418–0634.
Deputy Bureau Chiefs: Jean Kiddoo, Room 7–C357, 418–7757; Joel Taubenblatt, Room 6–C260, 418–1513; Suzanne Tetreault, Room 6–C164, 418–1769.
Associate Bureau Chiefs: Charles Mathias, Room 6–C110, 418–7147; Michael Janson, Room 6–C120, 418–0627.
Assistant Bureau Chief for Management.—Johnny Drake, Room 6–A223, 418–7328.
Chief, Division of:
Auctions and Spectrum Access.—Margaret Wiener, Room 6–C217, 418–0660.
Broadband.—Blaise Scinto, Room 3–C124, 418–2487.
Competition and Infrastructure Policy.—Garnet Hanly, Room 6–C241, 418–1310.
Mobility.—Roger Noel, Room 2–B554, 418–0620.
Technology, Systems, and Innovation.—Diane Dupert, Gettysburg, PA (717) 338–2512.

WIRELINE COMPETITION BUREAU

Chief.—Kris Monteith, Room 5–C450, 418–1500.
Deputy Bureau Chief.—Madeleine Findley, Room 5–C356, 418–1500.
Associate Bureau Chiefs: Trent Harkrader, Room 5–C352, 418–1500; Lisa Hone, Room 5–C315, 418–1500; Sue McNeil, Room 5–C441, 418–1500; D'wana Terry, Room 5–C330, 418–0643.
Chief of Staff.—Kirk Burgee, Room 5–C354, 418–1500.
Chief Economist.—Eric Ralph, Room 5–C408, 418–0771.
Chief Data Officer.—Steven Rosenberg, Room 5–C455, 418–3614.

Legal Advisors: Joseph Calascione (acting), Room 5–B414, 418–2085; Christian Hoefly (acting), Room 5–C453, 418–3607; Thomas Parisi, Room 5–C434, 418–1356; Arielle Roth, Room 5–C413, 418–1015.

Program Manager for USF.—Rachael Kazan, Room 5–C360, 418–0651.

OFFICE OF WORKPLACE DIVERSITY

Director.—Larry Hudson, Room 5–C750, 418–0591.

REGIONAL AND FIELD OFFICES

Region 1: David Dombrowski, Columbia Office, Columbia, MD; Boston Office, Quincy, MA; Chicago Office, Park Ridge, IL; New York Office, New York, NY.

Region 2: Ronald Ramage, Powder Springs, GA; Atlanta Office, Duluth, GA; Dallas Office, Dallas, TX; Miami Office, Sunrise, FL; New Orleans Office, Metairie, LA.

Region 3: Lark Hadley, Los Angeles Offices, Cerritos, CA; Denver Office, Lakewood, CO.

FEDERAL DEPOSIT INSURANCE CORPORATION

550 17th Street, NW., 20429

phone (877) 275–3342, http://www.fdic.gov

Chair.—Martin J. Gruenberg, 898–3888.
Deputy to the Chair, Chief of Staff, and Chief Operating Officer.—Barbara Ryan, 898–3841.
Deputy to the Chair and Chief Financial Officer.—Steve App, 898–8732.
Vice Chair.—Thomas M. Hoenig, 898–6616.
Deputy to the Vice Chair.—Michael Spencer (acting), 898–7041.
Director.—Vacant.
Deputy to the Director.—Vacant.
Director (OCC).—Keith Noreika, 874–4900.
Deputy.—William Rowe, 898–6960.
Director (CFPB).—Richard Cordray, 435–9637.
Deputy.—Stephanie Richo, 435–9307.
Director, Office of Legislative Affairs.—M. Andy Jiminez, 898–6761, fax 898–3745.

FEDERAL ELECTION COMMISSION

999 E Street, NW., 20463

phone (202) 694–1000, Toll Free (800) 424–9530, fax 219–3880, http://www.fec.gov

Chair.—Steven T. Walther, 694–1055.
Vice Chair.—Caroline C. Hunter, 694–1045.
Commissioners:
Lee E. Goodman, 694–1050.
Matthew S. Petersen, 694–1011.
Ellen L. Weintraub, 694–1035.
Staff Director.—D. Alec Palmer, 694–1007, fax 219–2338.
Deputy Staff Director for—
Compliance/Chief Compliance Officer.—Patricia C. Orrock, 694–1150.
Information Technology/Chief Information Officer.—D. Alec Palmer, 694–1250.
Management and Administration.—Edward W. Holder (acting), 694–1365.
Communications.—Vacant.
Assistant Staff Director for—
Public Disclosure and Media Relations.—Judith Ingram, 694–1220.
Information Division.—Greg J. Scott, 694–1100.
Director for Congressional, Legislative, and Intergovernmental Affairs.—J. Duane Pugh, 694–1006.
Director Human Resources.—Derrick Allen, 694–1080.
Administrative Officer.—India K. Robinson, 694–1240.
EEO Director.—Kevin Salley, 694–1229.
General Counsel.—Lisa J. Stevenson (acting), 694–1650.

Deputy General Counsel for—
Administration.—Gregory R. Baker, 694–1650.
Law.—Lisa J. Stevenson, 694–1650.
Associate General Counsel for—
Enforcement.—Kathleen M. Guith, 694–1650.
Litigation.—Kevin Deeley, 694–1650.
Policy.—Vacant.
Library Director (Law).—Leta L. Holley, 694–1516.
Chief Financial Officer.—Gilbert Ford (acting), 694–1216.
Deputy Chief Financial Officer/Budget Director.—Gilbert Ford, 694–1216.
Director of Accounting.—Vacant.
Inspector General.—Vacant.
Deputy Inspector General.—James C. Thurber, 694–1015.

FEDERAL HOUSING FINANCE AGENCY

400 7th Street, NW., 20024

phone (202) 649–3800, fax 649–1017, http://www.fhfa.gov

[Created by Housing and Economic Recovery Act of 2008, 122 Stat. 2654, Public Law 110–289—July 30, 2008]

Director.—Melvin L. Watt, 649–3001.
Deputy Director, Division of:
Bank Regulation.—Fred Graham, 649–3500.
Enterprise Regulation.—Nina Nichols, 649–3265.
Housing, Mission and Goals.—Sandra Thompson, 649–3384.
General Counsel.—Alfred Pollard, 649–3050.
Senior Deputy General Counsel.—Christopher Curtis, 649–3051.
Senior Associate Director, Conservatorship.—Robert Fishman, 649–3527.

OFFICE OF CONGRESSIONAL AFFAIRS AND COMMUNICATIONS

Senior Associate Director.—Megan Moore (acting), 649–3018.
Associate Director for Congressional Affairs.—Peter Brereton, 649–3022.
Congressional Affairs Staff: Gabriel Bitol, 649–3506; Julian Colbert, 649–3318; Jeannine Schroeder, 649–3029; Dion Spencer, 649–3207.
Director of Communications.—Vacant, 649–3700.
Public Affairs Staff: Stefanie Johnson, 649–3030; Corinne Russell, 649–3032.
Executive Advisor for Consumer Communications.—Dion Spencer (acting), 649–3207.
Ombudsman.—Janell Byrd-Chichester (acting), (888) 665–1474.
Associate Director for the Office of Minority and Women Inclusion.—Sharron Levine, 649–3496.
Chief Operating Officer.—Lawrence Stauffer (acting), 649–3402.
Chief Information Officer.—Kevin Winkler, 649–3600.
Inspector General.—Laura S. Wertheimer (800) 793–7724.

FEDERAL LABOR RELATIONS AUTHORITY

1400 K Street, NW., 20424–0001, phone (202) 218–7770, fax 482–6635

FLRA Agency Head.—Colleen Kiko, 218–7930.
Executive Director.—William Tosick, 218–7982.
Counsel for Regulatory and External Affairs.—Gina K. Grippando, 218–7776.
Solicitor.—Fred B. Jacob, 218–7906.
Inspector General.—Dana Rooney, 218–7744.
Collaboration and Alternative Dispute Resolution Program.—Michael Wolf, 218–7933.
Foreign Service Impasse Disputes Panel.—Kimberly Moseley (FSIP Executive Director), 218–7790.
Foreign Service Labor Relations Board Chair.—Colleen Kiko, 218–7900.

AUTHORITY

Chair.—Colleen Kiko, 218–7930.

Chief Counsel.—James T. Abbott, 218–7930.
Member.—Ernest DuBester, 218–7920.
Chief Counsel.—William R. Tobey, 218–7920.
Member.—Vacant, 218–7900.
Chief Counsel.—David S. Eddy III, 218–7900.
Chief, Case Intake and Publication.—Anna Molpus (acting), 218–7740.

GENERAL COUNSEL OF THE FLRA

General Counsel.—Peter A. Sutton (acting), 218–7910.
Deputy General Counsel.—Peter A. Sutton, 218–7910.
Assistant General Counsel for—
Advice and Legal Policy.—Kurt Rumsfeld, 218–7910.
Appeals.—Cabrina S. Smith, 218–7910.

OFFICE OF ADMINISTRATIVE LAW JUDGES

Chief Judge.—Charles Center, 218–7950.

FEDERAL SERVICE IMPASSES PANEL (FSIP)

FSIP Chair.—Mark A. Carter, 218–7790.
Executive Director.—Kimberly Moseley, 218–7790.

REGIONAL OFFICES

Regional Directors:
Atlanta.—Richard S. Jones, Marquis Two Tower, 285 Peachtree Center Avenue, Suite 701, Atlanta, GA 30303 (404) 331–5300, fax 331–5280.
Boston.—Philip T. Roberts, 10 Causeway Street, Suite 472, Boston, MA 02222 (617) 565–5100, fax 565–6262.
Chicago.—Sandra LeBold, 224 South Michigan Avenue, Suite 445, Chicago, IL 60604 (312) 886–3465, fax 886–5977.
Dallas.—Charlotte A. Dye, 525 Griffin Street, Suite 926, LB 107, Dallas, TX 75202 (214) 767–6266, fax 767–0156.
Denver.—Tim Sullivan, 1244 Speer Boulevard, Suite 446, Denver, CO 80204 (303) 844–5224, fax 844–2774.
San Francisco.—John R. Pannozzo, Jr., 901 Market Street, Suite 470, San Francisco, CA 94103 (415) 356–5000, fax 356–5017.
Washington, DC.—Jessica Bartlett, 1400 K Street, NW., Suite 200, Washington, DC 20005 (202) 357–6029, fax 482–6724.

FEDERAL MARITIME COMMISSION

800 North Capitol Street, NW., 20573

phone (202) 523–5725, fax 523–0014

OFFICE OF THE CHAIR

Chair.—Michael A. Khouri (acting), Room 1000, 523–5911.
Chief of Staff.—Mary T. Hoang.
Counsel.—John A. Moran.
Commissioner.—Rebecca F. Dye, Room 1038, 523–5715.
Counsel.—Robert M. Blair.
Commissioner.—Daniel B. Maffei, Room 1032, 523–5721.
Counsel.—Carrol P. Hand.

OFFICE OF THE SECRETARY

Assistant Secretary.—Rachel E. Dickon, Room 1046, 523–5725.

OFFICE OF EQUAL EMPLOYMENT OPPORTUNITY

Director.—Ebony Jarrett, Room 1052, 523–5859.

OFFICE OF THE GENERAL COUNSEL

General Counsel.—Tyler J. Wood, Room 1018, 523–5740.

OFFICE OF CONSUMER AFFAIRS AND DISPUTE RESOLUTION

Director.—Rebecca A. Fenneman, Room 932, 523–5807.
Deputy Director.—Jennifer M. Gartlan.

OFFICE OF ADMINISTRATIVE LAW JUDGES

Chief Judge.—Clay G. Guthridge, Room 1088, 523–5750.
Administrative Law Judge.—Erin M. Wirth, Room 1088, 523–5750.

OFFICE OF THE INSPECTOR GENERAL

Inspector General.—Jonathan Hatfield, Room 1054, 523–5863.

OFFICE OF THE MANAGING DIRECTOR

Director.—Karen V. Gregory, Room 1082, 523–5800.
Assistant Director.—Peter J. King.
Assistant Managing Director for Administration.—James A. Nussbaumer.
Area Representatives:
Houston.—Adam Sinko (281) 386–8211.
Los Angeles.—Nash D. Asandas (310) 514–8618; Karl Hansen (310) 514–4905.
New York.—Matthew D. Forst (732) 283–2497; Erin Tasova (732) 283–2496.
Seattle.—Diane Rebollo (732) 731–7319; Shadrack Scheirman (253) 922–7622.
South Florida.—Andrew Margolis (954) 963–5362; Eric O. Mintz (954) 963–5284.
Director, Office of:
Budget and Finance.—Leonard L. Ballard, Room 916, 523–5770.
Human Resources.—William T. Cole, Room 924, 523–5773.
Information Technology.—Edward D. Anthony, Room 904, 523–5835.
Management Services.—Katona Bryan-Wade, Room 926, 523–5900.

BUREAU OF CERTIFICATION AND LICENSING

Director.—Sandra K. Kusumoto, Room 970, 523–5787.
Deputy Director.—Clifford R. Johnson.
Director, Office of:
Passenger Vessels and Information Processing.—Tajuanda L. Singletary, 523–5818.
Transportation Intermediaries.—Aline A. Hull, 523–5843.

BUREAU OF ENFORCEMENT

Deputy Director.—Brian L. Troiano, Room 900, 523–5783 or 523–5860.

BUREAU OF TRADE ANALYSIS

Director.—Florence A. Carr, Room 940, 523–5796.
Deputy Director.—Tanga S. FitzGibbon.
Director, Office of:
Agreements.—Jason W. Guthrie, 523–5793.
Economics and Competition Analysis.—Anthony Homan, 523–5845.
Service Contracts and Tariffs.—Gary G. Kardian, Room 940, 523–5856.

FEDERAL MEDIATION AND CONCILIATION SERVICE

250 E Street, SW., 20427, phone (202) 606–8100, fax 606–4251

[Codified under 29 U.S.C. 172]

Director.—John Pinto (acting).
Deputy Director.—Scot L. Beckenbaugh.
Chief of Staff.—Fran L. Leonard, 606–8100.
General Counsel.—Dawn Starr, 606–8090.
Director for—
ADR/International.—Eileen Hoffman, 606–5447.
Arbitration Services.—Arthur Pearlstein, 606–5111.
Budget and Finance.—Will Shield, 606–3660.
Finance.—Prasad Kotiswaran, 606–3660.
Grants.—Linda Gray-Broughton, 606–8181.
Human Resources.—Traci Coddington, 606–5460.
Information Systems.—Doug Jones, 606–5483.
Administrative Services.—Cynthia Washington, 606–5477.
Regional Director (Eastern/Western).—Vacant.

FEDERAL MINE SAFETY AND HEALTH REVIEW COMMISSION

1331 Pennsylvania Avenue, NW., Suite 520N, 20004
phone (202) 434–9900, fax 434–9944

[Created by Public Law 95–164]

Chair.—William I. Althen (acting), Room 545, 434–9951.
Commissioners: Robert Cohen, Room 547, 434–9912; Mary Jordan, Room 548, 434–9925; Michael Young, Room 543, 434–9914.
Executive Director.—Lisa M. Boyd, Room 553, 434–9905.
Chief Administrative Law Judge.—Robert J. Lesnick, Room 1414, 434–9958.
General Counsel.—Michael McCord, Room 554, 434–9920.

FEDERAL RETIREMENT THRIFT INVESTMENT BOARD

77 K Street, NE., 20002, phone (202) 942–1600, fax 942–1676

[Authorized by 5 U.S.C. 8472]

Executive Director.—Ravindra Deo, 942–1601.
Office of Chief Operating Officer, Deputy Executive Director.—Suzanne Tosini, 942–1440.
General Counsel.—Megan Grumbine, 942–1670.
Director, Office of:
Communications and Education.—Jim Courtney, 942–1450.
Enterprise Planning.—Renee Wilder, 942–1630.
Enterprise Risk Management.—Jay Ahuja, 942–1630.
External Affairs.—Kimberly Weaver, 942–1640.
Financial Management.—Susan Crowder, 942–1620.
Investments.—Ravindra Deo (acting), 942–1601.
Participant Operations.—Tee Ramos, 942–1460.
Resource Management.—Gisile Goethe, 942–1630.
Technology Services.—Suzanne Tosini (acting), 942–1440.
Chair.—Michael Kennedy, 942–1660.
Board Members:
Dana K. Bilyeu.
Ronald D. McCray.
David A. Jones.
William Jasien.

FEDERAL TRADE COMMISSION

600 Pennsylvania Avenue, NW., 20580
phone (202) 326–2222, http://www.ftc.gov

Chair.—Maureen K. Ohlhausen (acting), Room 338, 326–2150.

Staff Assistant.—Bridget Borrelli, Room 340, 326–2122.
Chief of Staff.—Svetlana Gans, Room 342, 326–3708.
Commissioner.—Terrell McSweeny, Room 326, 326–2606.
Director, Office of:
Competition.—Abbott ''Tad'' Lipsky, Jr. (acting), Room 370, 326–3238.
Congressional Relations.—Jeanne Bumpus, Room 408, 326–2195.
Consumer Protection.—Thomas B. Pahl (acting), Room 470, 326–3240.
Economics.—Ginger Z. Jin, Room 270, 326–3419.
Policy Planning.—Tara Isa Koslov (acting), Room 382, 326–2386.
Public Affairs.—Peter Kaplan (acting), Room 456, 326–2180.
International Affairs.—Randolph W. Tritell, Room 492, 326–3051.
Executive Director.—David B. Robbins, Room 426, 326–3146.
General Counsel.—David Shonka (acting), Room 584, 326–2436.
Secretary.—Donald S. Clark, Room 172, 326–2514.
Inspector General.—Roslyn A. Mazer, Room CC–5216A, 326–3527.
Chief Administrative Law Judge.—D. Michael Chappell, Room 111, 326–3637.

REGIONAL DIRECTORS

East Central Region: Jon M. Steiger, 1111 Superior Avenue, Suite 200, Cleveland, OH 44114 (216) 263–3455.
Midwest Region: Todd Kossow, 55 East Monroe Street, Suite 1825, Chicago, IL 60603 (312) 960–5634.
Northeast Region: William Efron, One Bowling Green, Suite 318, New York, NY 10004 (212) 607–2829.
Northwest Region: Charles Harwood, 915 Second Avenue, Suite 2896, Seattle, WA 98174 (206) 220–6350.
Southeast Region: Cindy A. Liebes, 225 Peachtree Street, NE., Suite 1500, Atlanta, GA 30303 (404) 656–1390.
Southwest Region: Dama J. Brown, 1999 Bryan Street, Suite 2150, Dallas, TX 75201 (214) 979–9350.
Western Region—Los Angeles: Tom Dahdouh, 18077 Wilshire Boulevard, Suite 700, Los Angeles, CA 90024–3679 (310) 824–4343.
Western Region—San Francisco: Tom Dahdouh, 901 Market Street, Suite 570, San Francisco, CA 94103 (415) 848–5100.

FOREIGN-TRADE ZONES BOARD

1401 Constitution Avenue, NW., Room 21013, 20230

phone (202) 482–2862, fax 482–0002

Chair.—Wilbur L. Ross, Jr., Secretary of Commerce.
Member.—Steven T. Mnuchin, Secretary of the Treasury.
Executive Secretary.—Andrew McGilvray.

GENERAL SERVICES ADMINISTRATION

1800 F Street, NW., 20405 phone (202) 501–0800, http://www.gsa.gov

OFFICE OF THE ADMINISTRATOR

Administrator.—Emily W. Murphy.
Deputy Administrator.—Allison F. Brigati.
Chief of Staff.—Robert Borden.
Deputy Chief of Staff.—Vacant.

NATIONAL SERVICES

PUBLIC BUILDING SERVICE

Commissioner.—Dan Matthews (202) 501–1100.
Deputy Commissioner.—Michael Gelber.
Chief of Staff.—LaFondra Lynch.
Assistant Commissioner, Office of:
Acquisition Management.—Chaun Benjamin (acting).
Design and Construction.—Laura Stagner.

Facilities Management.—Aimee Whiteman (acting).
Leasing.—Allison Azevedo.
Portfolio Management and Customer Engagement.—Stuart Burns.
Real Property Utilization and Disposal.—Flavio Peres.
Chief Architect.—David Insinga.

FEDERAL ACQUISITION SERVICE

Commissioner.—Alan Thomas.
Deputy Commissioner.—Mary Davie.
Deputy Commissioner (Director, Technology Transformation Services).—Rob Cook.
Chief of Staff.—Judith Zawatsky.
Assistant Commissioner, Office of:
Strategy Management.—Laura Stanton.
Acquisition Management.—Mark Lee.
Assisted Acquisition Services.—Tom Howder.
General Supplies and Services.—Bob Noonan (acting).
Systems Management.—Dave Zvenyach (acting).
Information Technology Category.—Kay Ely.
Travel, Transportation, and Logistics.—William Toth (acting).
Customer and Stakeholder Engagement.—Erv Koehler.
Professional Services and Human Capital Categories.—Tiffany T. Hixson.

STAFF OFFICES

OFFICE OF THE CHIEF FINANCIAL OFFICER

Chief Financial Officer.—Gerard Badorrek (202) 501–1721.
Deputy Chief Financial Officer.—Evan Farley.
Chief of Staff.—Matthew Watt.
Director of:
Budget.—Andrew Fisher-Colwill (acting).
Financial Operations.—Lisa Ziehmann.
Regional Financial Operations.—Steven Varnum (acting).
Analytics, Performance and Improvement.—Stephen Brockelman (acting).

OFFICE OF CONGRESSIONAL AND INTERGOVERNMENTAL AFFAIRS

Associate Administrator.—Saul Japson (acting), (202) 501–0563.
Deputy Associate Administrator.—Vacant.
Senior Policy Advisor.—Saul Japson.
Director of:
Congressional Operations.—Erin Mewhirter.
Congressional Support Services.—Michael Gurgo.

OFFICE OF STRATEGIC COMMUNICATIONS

Associate Administrator.—Mark McHale.
Press Secretary.—Pam Dixon.
Senior Communications Advisor.—Jeff Leieritz.
Deputy Associate Administrator of:
Communications and Marketing.—Donna Garland.
Operations.—Justin Ward.

OFFICE OF GOVERNMENTWIDE POLICY

Associate Administrator.—Jessica Salmoiraghi (202) 501–8880.
Deputy Associate Administrator.—Giancarlo Brizzi.
Chief Acquisition Officer.—Allison F. Brigati.
Senior Procurement Executive.—Jeff Koses.
Chief of Staff.—Jonathan Clinton.
Deputy Associate Administrator, Office of:
Asset and Transportation.—Alexander Kurien.
Acquisition Policy.—Jeff Koses.
High Performance Green Buildings.—Kevin Kampschroer.
Information, Integrity, and Access.—Dominic Sale.

OFFICE OF THE GENERAL COUNSEL

General Counsel.—Jack St. John (acting), (202) 501–2200.
Deputy General Counsel.—Lennard S. Loewentritt.
Associate General Counsel for:
General Law.—Eugenia D. Ellison.
Personal Property.—Janet Harney.
Real Property.—Berry Segal.

OFFICE OF THE CHIEF INFORMATION OFFICER

Chief Information Officer.—David Shive (202) 501–1000.
Deputy Chief Information Officer.—Steve Grewal.
Chief of Staff.—Vanessa Ros.
Chief Data Officer.—Kris Rowley.
Chief Technology Officer.—Navin Vembar.
Chief Information Security Officer.—Kurt Garbars.
Associate CIO:
Office of Enterprise Infrastructure Operations.—David Harrity.
Office of Corporate IT Services.—Elizabeth DelNegro.
Office of Public Building IT Services.—Philip Klokis.
Office of Acquisition IT Services.—Sagar Samant.
Office of Enterprise Planning and Governance.—Lesley Briante.
Deputy Associate CIO, Office of Corporate IT Services.—Daryle "Mike" Seckar.
Director, Management Services Division.—Erika Dinnie.

OFFICE OF SMALL BUSINESS UTILIZATION

Associate Administrator.—Charles Manger (202) 501–1021.
Chief of Staff.—Stephanie Wilson-Coleman.

OFFICE OF HUMAN RESOURCES MANAGEMENT

Chief Human Capital Officer.—Antonia T. Harris (202) 501–0398.
Deputy Chief Human Capital Officer.—Daria Ingram (acting).
Chief of Staff.—Autumn Jones.

OFFICE OF CIVIL RIGHTS

Associate Administrator.—Mary Gilbert (202) 501–0767.
Chief of Staff.—Aaron Scurlock.

OFFICE OF MISSION ASSURANCE

Associate Administrator.—Robert Carter (202) 219–0291.

OFFICE OF ADMINISTRATIVE SERVICES

Chief Administrative Services Officer.—Bob Stafford (acting), (202) 357–9697.
Deputy Chief Administrative Services Officer.—Bob Stafford.
Chief of Staff.—Thomas Mueller.

REGIONAL OFFICES

National Capital Region (NCR 11): 17th and D Street, SW., Washington, DC 20407 (202) 708–9100.
Regional Administrator.—Scott Anderson.
Regional Commissioner for Federal Acquisition Service.—Houston Taylor.
Regional Commissioner for Public Buildings Service.—Darren Blue.
New England Region I: Thomas P. O'Neill Federal Building, 10 Causeway Street, Boston, MA 02222 (617) 565–5860.
Regional Administrator.—Glenn Rotondo (acting).
Regional Commissioner for Federal Acquisition Service.—Joe Nickerson.
Regional Commissioner for Public Buildings Service.—Glenn Rotondo (acting).
Northeast and Caribbean Region 2: 26 Federal Plaza, New York, NY 10278 (212) 264–2600.

Regional Administrator.—John A. Sarcone III (acting).
Regional Commissioner for Federal Acquisition Service.—Jeff Lau (acting).
Regional Commissioner for Public Building Service.—Darren Gomez (acting).

Mid-Atlantic Region 3: The Strawbridge's Building, 20 North Eight Street, Philadelphia, PA 19107 (215) 446–4900.
Regional Administrator.—Joyce C. Haas.
Regional Commissioner for Federal Acquisition Service.—Dena McLaughlin.
Regional Commissioner for Public Buildings Service.—Joanna Rosato.

Southeast Sunbelt Region 4: 77 Forsyth Street, Suite 600, Atlanta, GA 30303 (404) 331–3200.
Regional Administrator.—Brian Stern.
Regional Commissioner for Federal Acquisition Service.—Joel Rogero (acting).
Regional Commissioner for Public Buildings Service.—Mike Goodwin.

Great Lakes Region 5: 230 South Dearborn, Chicago, IL 60604 (312) 353–5395.
Regional Administrator.—John Cooke (acting).
Regional Commissioner for Federal Acquisition Service.—Anne Mesch.
Regional Commissioner for Public Buildings Service.—John Cooke.

Heartland Region 6: 1500 East Bannister Road, Kansas City, MO 64131 (816) 926–7201.
Regional Administrator.—Michael Copeland.
Regional Commissioner for Federal Acquisition Service.—Mary Ruwwe.
Regional Commissioner for Public Buildings Service.—Kevin Rothmier (acting).

Great Southwest Region 7: 819 Taylor Street, Fort Worth, TX 76102 (817) 978–2321.
Regional Administrator.—Robert Babcock.
Regional Commissioner for Federal Acquisition Service.—George Prochaska.
Regional Commissioner for Public Buildings Service.—James Ferracci (acting).

Rocky Mountain Region 8: Building 41, Denver Federal Center, Denver, CO 80225 (303) 236–7329.
Regional Administrator.—Timothy Horne (acting).
Regional Commissioner for Federal Acquisition Service.—Penny Grout (acting).
Regional Commissioner for Public Buildings Service.—Timothy Horne.

Pacific Mountain Region 9: 450 Golden Gate Avenue, Room 5–2690, San Francisco, CA 94102 (415) 522–3001.
Regional Administrator.—Daniel Brown (acting).
Regional Commissioner for Federal Acquisition Service.—Les Yamagata (acting).
Regional Commissioner for Public Buildings Service.—Daniel Brown (acting).

Northwest / Arctic Region 10: GSA Center, 400 15th Street, SW., Auburn, WA 98001 (253) 931–7000.
Regional Administrator.—Corey Cooke (acting).
Regional Commissioner for Federal Acquisition Service.—Tiffany Hixson.
Regional Commissioner for Public Buildings Service.—Lisa Pearson (acting).

INDEPENDENT OFFICES

OFFICE OF THE INSPECTOR GENERAL

Inspector General.—Carol F. Ochoa (202) 501–0450.
Deputy Inspector General.—Robert C. Erickson.
Congressional Relations Officer.—Robert Preiss.
General Counsel.—Vacant.
Assistant Inspector General for:
Inspections.—Patricia Sheenan.
Administration.—Larry Gregg.
Auditing.—Vacant.
Investigations.—Vacant.

CIVILIAN BOARD OF CONTRACT APPEALS

Chair.—Jeri K. Somers (202) 606–8820.
Vice Chair.—Erica S. Beardsley.
Chief Counsel.—J. Gregory Parks, 606–8787.
Clerk.—Cheryl L. Hilton, 606–8800.

Board Judges:
Jeri K. Somers, Chair
Erica S. Beardsley, Vice Chair
Kyle E. Chadwick
Jerome M. Drummond
Allan H. Goodman

Catherine B. Hyatt
Harold C. Kullberg
Harold D. ''Harv'' Lester, Jr.
Kathleen J. O'Rourke
Beverly M. Russell
Patricia J. Sheridan
Marian E. Sullivan
Joseph A. Vergilio
Jonathan D. Zischkau

HARRY S. TRUMAN SCHOLARSHIP FOUNDATION

712 Jackson Place, NW., 20006

phone (202) 395–4831, fax 395–6995

[Created by Public Law 93–642]

BOARD OF TRUSTEES

President.—Madeleine K. Albright.
Vice President.—Max Sherman.
Treasurer.—Frederick Slabach.
General Counsel.—Westbrook Murphy.
Members:
Hon. Roy Blunt, Senator from Missouri.
Steven H. Cohen, Attorney, Cohen Law Group.
Hon. Laura Cordero, Associate Judge, D.C. Superior Court.
Hon. Theodore E. Deutch, Representative of Florida.
Hon. Betsy DeVos, U.S. Secretary of Education.
Ingrid Gregg, President, the Philadelphia Society.
Michael W. Hail, Professor of Government, Morehead State University.
Hon. James Henderson, Judge / County Executive, Simpson County, Kentucky.
Hon. Claire McCaskill, Senator from Missouri.
Westbrook Murphy, General Counsel, Harry S. Truman Scholarship Foundation.
Andrew Rich, Executive Secretary, Harry S. Truman Scholarship Foundation.
Hon. Max Sherman, Professor and Dean Emeritus, Lyndon B. Johnson School of Public Affairs, University of Texas.
Hon. Frederick Slabach, President, Texas Wesleyan University.
Chief Information Officer.—Tonji Wade.
Deputy Executive Secretary.—Tara Yglesias.
Education Officer.—Ruth Keen.
Executive Secretary.—Andrew Rich.
Program Manager.—Andrew Kirk.

INTER-AMERICAN FOUNDATION

1331 Pennsylvania Avenue, NW., 1200 North, Washington, DC, phone (202) 360–4530

Chair, Board of Directors.—Eddy Arriola.
Vice Chair, Board of Directors.—Juan Carlos Iturregui.
President and Chief Executive Officer.—Paloma Adams-Allen.
Chief Operating Officer.—Lesley Duncan.
General Counsel.—Paul Zimmerman.
Managing Director of:
External and Government Affairs.—Manuel Nuñez.
Grant-Making and Portfolio Management.—Marcy Kelley.
Networks and Strategic Initiatives.—Stephen Cox.

JAMES MADISON MEMORIAL FELLOWSHIP FOUNDATION

1613 Duke Street, Alexandria, VA 22314

phone (571) 858–4200, fax (703) 838–2180

[Created by Public Law 99–591]

BOARD OF TRUSTEES

Members Appointed by the President of the United States:

John Cornyn, Senator from Texas, Chair.
Benjamin L. Cardin, Senator from Maryland.
Betsy DeVos, U.S. Secretary of Education (ex officio).

Foundation Staff:

President Emeritus.—Admiral Paul A. Yost, Jr.
President.—Lewis F. Larsen.
Director of Academics.—Dr. Jeffry Morrison.
Director of Special Programs.—Claire Griffin.
Support Services Specialist.—Jason McCray.
Director of Development.—Kimberly A. Alldredge.
Academic Advisor.—Sheila Osbourne.
Management and Program Analysis Officer.—Elizabeth G. Ray.

THE JOHN F. KENNEDY CENTER FOR THE PERFORMING ARTS

2700 F Street, NW., 20566, phone (202) 416–8000, fax 416–8205

BOARD OF TRUSTEES

Honorary Chairs:

Mrs. Melania Trump
Mrs. Michelle Obama
Mrs. Laura Bush
Hon. Hillary Rodham Clinton
Mrs. George Bush†
Mrs. Ronald Reagan†
Mrs. Jimmy Carter

Officers:

Chair.—David M. Rubenstein.
President.—Deborah F. Rutter.
Secretary.—Jacqueline Badger Mars.
Treasurer.—Michael F. Neidorff.
General Counsel.—Maria C. Kersten.

Members Appointed by the President of the United States:

Adrienne Arsht
David C. Bohnett
Fred Eychaner
Giselle Fernandez
Sakurako Fisher
Norma Lee Funger
John Goldman
Janet Hill
Frank F. Islam
Valerie Jarrett
Victoria Reggie Kennedy
Michael Lombardo
Andrés W. López
Bryan Lourd
Amalia Perea Mahoney
Barbara Goodman Manilow
Alyssa Mastromonaco
W. James McNerney, Jr.
Charles B. Ortner
Rebecca Pohlad
Shonda L. Rhimes
Susan Rice
Laura Ricketts
David M. Rubenstein
Margaret Russell
Rose Kennedy Schlossberg
Susan S. Sher
Alexandra C. Stanton
Bryan Traubert
Ranvir Trehan
Walter F. Ulloa
Reginald Van Lee
Romesh Wadhwani
Anthony Welters
Ann Marie Wilkins
Elaine Wynn

Members Ex Officio Designated by Act of Congress

Alex Azar II, Secretary of Health and Human Services.
Dr. Carla Hayden, Librarian of Congress.
Mike Pompeo, Secretary of State.
Earl A. Powell III, Chair of the Commission of Fine Arts.
Muriel E. Bowser, Mayor, District of Columbia.
Amanda Alexander, Interim Chancellor, D.C. Public Schools.
Dan Smith, Acting Director, National Park Service.
Betsy DeVos, Secretary of Education.
David J. Skorton, Secretary, Smithsonian Institution.
Paul D. Ryan, Speaker of the House of Representatives from Wisconsin.
Nancy Pelosi, Democratic Leader of the House of Representatives from California.
Bill Shuster, Representative from Connecticut.

Peter A. DeFazio, Representative from Oregon.
Joseph P. Kennedy, Representative from Massachusetts.
Barbara Comstock, Representative from Virginia.
Tom MacArthur, Representative from New Jersey.
Mitch McConnell, Senate Majority Leader from Kentucky.
Charles E. Schumer, Senate Democratic Leader from New York.
John Barrasso, Senator from Wyoming.
Thomas R. Carper, Senator from Delaware.
Mark Warner, Senator from Virginia.
Roy Blunt, Senator from Missouri.

Senior Counsel.—Robert Barnett.
Founding Chair.—Roger L. Stevens.†
Chair Emeriti: James A. Johnson, Stephen A. Schwarzman, James D. Wolfensohn.
President Emeritus.—Michael M. Kaiser.

Honorary Trustees:

Buffy Cafritz	Alma Gildenhorn	Leonard L. Silverstein †
Kenneth M. Duberstein	Melvin R. Laird †	Jean Kennedy Smith

†*Deceased*

LEGAL SERVICES CORPORATION

3333 K Street, NW., 3rd Floor, 20007–3522

phone (202) 295–1500, fax 337–6797

BOARD OF DIRECTORS

John G. Levi, Board *Chair*	Victor B. Maddox
Martha L. Minow, Board *Vice Chair*	Laurie I. Mikva
Robert J. Grey, Jr.	Rev. Joseph Pius Pietrzyk
Charles N.W. Keckler	Julie A. Reiskin
Harry Korrell	Gloria Valencia-Weber

President.—James J. Sandman.
Vice President, Legal Affairs, General Counsel and Corporate Secretary.—Ronald Flagg.
Vice President for Grants Management.—Lynn Jennnings.
Vice President, Government Relations and Public Affairs.—Carol Bergman.
Comptroller and Treasurer.—David L. Richardson.
Inspector General.—Jeffrey E. Schanz.
Director of Communications and Media Relations.—Carl Rauscher.

NATIONAL AERONAUTICS AND SPACE ADMINISTRATION

300 E Street, SW., 20546, phone (202) 358–0000, http://www.nasa.gov

OFFICE OF THE ADMINISTRATOR

Suite 9F44, phone 358–1010

Administrator.—Jim Bridenstine.
Executive Assistant.—Rise Williams, 358–1808.
Deputy Administrator.—Vacant.
Associate Administrator.—Steve Jurczyk.
Chief of Staff.—Thomas E. Cremins (acting).
Deputy Associate Administrator.—Krista Paquin, 358–1405.
Associate Administrator for Strategy and Plans.—Thomas E. Cremins, 358–1747.
White House Liaison.—Jonathan Dimock, 358–2198.
Chiefs:
Financial Officer.—Andrew Hunter (acting), 358–2514.
Information Officer.—Renee Wynn, 358–5125.
Engineer.—Ralph Roe (757) 864–2400.
Health and Medical Officer.—Dr. James Polk, 358–1959.
Safety and Mission Assurance.—Terrence Wilcutt (281) 244–8715.
Scientist.—Jim Green, 358–4580.
Technologist.—Dr. Douglas Terrier (acting), (281) 483–0903.

OFFICE OF THE GENERAL COUNSEL

Suite 9V39, phone 358–2450

General Counsel.—Sumara Thompson-King.
Deputy General Counsel.—Tom McMurray.

OFFICE OF INSPECTOR GENERAL

Suite 8U79, phone 358–1220

Inspector General.—Paul K. Martin.
Deputy Inspector General.—Vacant.

OFFICE OF COMMUNICATIONS

Suite 5S87, phone 358–1898

Associate Administrator.—Robert Jacobs (acting), 358–1600.
Deputy Associate Administrator.—Robert Jacobs, 358–1600.

OFFICE OF DIVERSITY AND EQUAL OPPORTUNITY PROGRAMS

Suite 6J81, phone 358–2167

Associate Administrator.—Stephen T. Shih.

OFFICE OF EDUCATION

Suite 4V76, phone 358–0100

Associate Administrator.—Mike Kincaid (acting).

OFFICE OF INTERNATIONAL AND INTERAGENCY RELATIONS

Suite 5V16, phone 358–0450

Associate Administrator.—Al Condes.
Deputy Associate Administrator.—Karen Feldstein.

OFFICE OF LEGISLATIVE AND INTERGOVERNMENTAL AFFAIRS

Code VA000, Room 9K24, phone 358–1948

Associate Administrator.—Rebecca L. Lee (acting).
Deputy Associate Administrator.—Rebecca L. Lee.

OFFICE OF SMALL BUSINESS PROGRAMS

Suite 4F22, phone 358–2088

Associate Administrator.—Glenn A. Delgado.

AERONAUTICS RESEARCH MISSION DIRECTORATE

Suite 6J39–A, phone 358–4700

Associate Administrator.—Jaiwon Shin.
Deputy Associate Administrator.—Thomas B. Irvine.

HUMAN EXPLORATION AND OPERATIONS MISSION DIRECTORATE

Suite 7K22, phone 358–2015

Associate Administrator.—William H. Gerstenmaier.
Deputy Associate Administrator for Technical.—Mark Geyer.

SCIENCE MISSION DIRECTORATE

Suite 3K20, phone 358–3889

Associate Administrator.—Dr. Thomas H. Zurbuchen.

Deputy Associate Administrator.—Dennis Andrucyk, 358–1389.

SPACE TECHNOLOGY MISSION DIRECTORATE

Associate Administrator.—James Reuter (acting), 358–1405.

MISSION SUPPORT DIRECTORATE

Suite 4J19, phone 358–2789

Associate Administrator.—Daniel J. Tenney.
Executive Director, Headquarters Operations.—Jay Henn, 358–4741.

OFFICE OF HUMAN CAPITAL MANAGEMENT

Suite 4V85, phone 358–0100

Assistant Administrator.—Robert Gibbs.

OFFICE OF PROCUREMENT

Suite 5O16, phone 358–2090

Assistant Administrator.—Monica Manning.
Deputy Assistant Administrator.—Vacant.

OFFICE OF PROTECTIVE SERVICES

Suite 6T26, phone 358–3752

Assistant Administrator.—Joseph Mahaley.
Deputy Associate Administrator.—Charles Lombard.

OFFICE OF STRATEGIC INFRASTRUCTURE

Suite 2Z88, phone 358–2800

Assistant Administrator.—Calvin F. Williams.
Deputy Assistant Administrator.—Richard L. Marrs.

NASA MANAGEMENT OFFICE

Phone (818) 354–5359

Director.—Marcus Watkins.

NASA NATIONAL OFFICES

Air Force Space Command / XPX (NASA): Peterson Air Force Base, CO 80914.
NASA Senior Representative.—Thomas Plumb (719) 554–4900.
Ames Research Center: Moffett Field, CA 94035.
Director.—Dr. Eugene Tu (650) 604–5062.
Deputy Center Director.—Carol Carroll.
Armstrong Flight Research Center: P.O. Box 273, Edwards, CA 93523.
Director.—David McBride (661) 276–3101.
Deputy Center Director.—Patrick Stoliker.
Glenn Research Center at Lewisfield: 21000 Brookpark Road, Cleveland, OH 44135.
Director.—Dr. Janet L. Kavandi (216) 433–2734.
Deputy Director.—Marla E. Perez-Davis, Ph.D.
Goddard Institute for Space Studies: Goddard Space Flight Center, 2880 Broadway, New York, NY 10025.
Chief.—Dr. Gavin A. Schmidt (212) 678–5500.
Goddard Space Flight Center: 8800 Greenbelt Road, Greenbelt, MD 20771.
Director.—Christopher J. Scolese (301) 286–6727.
Deputy Director.—George W. Morrow.
Jet Propulsion Laboratory: 4800 Oak Grove Drive, Pasadena, CA 91109.
Director.—Dr. Michael M. Watkins (818) 354–4321.

Lyndon B. Johnson Space Center: 2101 NASA Parkway Houston, TX 77058–3696.
Director.—Dr. Ellen Ochoa (281) 483–5000.
John F. Kennedy Space Center: Kennedy Space Center, FL 32899.
Director.—Robert Cabana (321) 867–5000.
Langley Research Center: Hampton, VA 23681.
Director.—David Bowles (757) 864–1000.
George C. Marshall Space Flight Center: Marshall Space Flight Center, AL 35812.
Director.—Todd A. May (256) 544–1910.
Michoud Assembly Facility: P.O. Box 29300, New Orleans, LA 70189.
Manager.—Keith Hefner (504) 257–3311.
NASA IV and V Facility: NASA Independent Verification and Validation Facility, 100 University Drive, Fairmont, WV 26554.
Director.—Gregory D. Blaney (304) 367–8200.
NASA Management Office: Jet Propulsion Laboratory, 4800 Oak Grove Drive, Pasadena, CA 91109.
Director.—Marcus Watkins (818) 354–5359.
John C. Stennis Space Center: Stennis Space Center, MS 39529.
Director.—Dr. Richard Gilbrech (228) 688–2121.
Deputy.—Randy Galloway (228) 688–2123.
Vandenberg AFB: P.O. Box 425, Lompoc, CA 93438.
Manager.—Ted L. Oglesby (805) 866–5859.
Wallops Flight Facility: Goddard Space Flight Center, Wallops Island, VA 23337.
Director.—William Wrobel (757) 824–1000.
White Sands Test Facility: Johnson Space Center, P.O. Drawer MM, Las Cruces, NM 88004.
Manager.—Frank J. Benz (505) 524–5771.

NASA OVERSEAS REPRESENTATIVES

Europe: U.S. Embassy, Paris, Unit 9200, Box 1653, DPO, AE 09777, 011–33–1–4312–7070.
NASA Representative.—Timothy Tawney.
Japan: U.S. Embassy, Tokyo, 1–10–5 Akasaka, Minato-ku, Tokyo, Japan 107–8420 81–3–3224–5000.
NASA Representative.—Garvey McIntosh.
Russia: U.S. Embassy, 5433 Moscow Place, Apt 35, Dulles, VA 20189 (256) 961–6333.
NASA Representative.—Justin Tilman.

NATIONAL ARCHIVES AND RECORDS ADMINISTRATION

700 Pennsylvania Avenue, NW., 20408–0001

8601 Adelphi Road, College Park, MD 20740–6001

http://www.archives.gov

[Created by Public Law 98–497]

Archivist of the United States.—David Ferriero (202) 357–5900, (301) 837–1600, fax (202) 357–5901.
Deputy Archivist of the United States.—Debra S. Wall (202) 357–5900, (301) 837–1600, fax (202) 357–5901.
Chief Officers:
Chief of Staff.—Maria Stanwich (202) 357–5900, fax 357–5901.
Operating.—William J. Bosanko (301) 837–3604, fax 837–3217.
Management and Administration.—Micah Cheatham (301) 837–2992, fax 837–3224.
Human Capital.—Sean Clayton (301) 837–3710, fax 837–3195.
Innovation.—Pamela Wright (301) 837–2029, fax 837–0312.
Records.—Lawrence Brewer (301) 837–1539, fax 837–3697.
Information Services.—Swarnali Haldar (301) 837–1583.
Financial.—Colleen Murphy (acting), (301) 837–1723, fax 837–0312.
Executive for—
Agency Services.—Jay Trainer (301) 837–3064.
Research Services.—Ann Cummings (301) 837–3110, fax 837–3633.
Business Support Services.—Donna Forbes (301) 837–1719, fax 837–3657.
Legislative Archives, Presidential Libraries, and Museum Services.—Susan Donius (acting), (202) 357–5472, fax 357–5939.

Director for—

Federal Register.—Oliver A. Potts (202) 741–6100, fax 741–6012.

Congressional Affairs.—John O. Hamilton (202) 357–5100, fax 357–5959.

National Historical Publications and Records Commission.—Kathleen Williams (202) 357–5263, fax 357–5914.

Equal Employment Opportunity and Diversity Office.—Ismael Martinez (301) 837–1849, fax 837–0869.

Information Security Oversight Office.—Mark Bradley (202) 357–5250, fax 357–5907.

Government Information Services.—Alina Semo (202) 741–5770, fax 741–5769.

General Counsel.—Gary M. Stern (301) 837–3025, fax 837–0293.

Communications and Marketing.—John Valceanu (202) 357–5300, fax 357–6809.

External Affairs.—Meg Phillips (202) 837–3111.

Inspector General.—James Springs (301) 837–3000, fax 837–3197.

Presidential Libraries.—Susan K. Donius (301) 837–3250, fax 837–3199.

Director for—

Herbert Hoover Library.—Thomas Schwartz, West Branch, IA 52358–0488 (319) 643–5301.

Franklin D. Roosevelt Library.—Robert Clark (acting), Hyde Park, NY 12538–1999 (845) 486–7770.

Harry S. Truman Library.—Amy Williams (acting), Independence, MO 64050–1798 (816) 268–8200.

Dwight D. Eisenhower Library.—Karl Weissenbach, Abilene, KS 67410–2900 (785) 263–6700.

John F. Kennedy Library.—Thomas Putnam, Boston, MA 02125–3398 (617) 514–1600.

Lyndon Baines Johnson Library.—Mark Updegrove, Austin, TX 78705–5737 (512) 721–0200.

Richard Nixon Library.—Michael Ellzey, Yorba Linda, CA 92886 (714) 983–9120.

Gerald R. Ford Library.—Elaine K. Didier, Ann Arbor, MI 48109–2114 (734) 205–0555.

Gerald R. Ford Museum.—Elaine K. Didier, Grand Rapids, MI 49504–5353 (616) 254–0400.

Jimmy Carter Library.—Sam McClure (acting), Atlanta, GA 30307–1498 (404) 865–7100.

Ronald Reagan Library.—R. Duke Blackwood, Simi Valley, CA 93065–0699 (800) 410–8354.

George Bush Library.—Warren Finch, College Station, TX 77845 (979) 691–4000.

William J. Clinton Library.—Terri Garner, Little Rock, AR 72201 (501) 374–4242.

George W. Bush Library.—Alan Lowe, Dallas, TX 75205–2300 (214) 346–1650.

ADMINISTRATIVE COMMITTEE OF THE FEDERAL REGISTER

7 G Street, NW., Suite A–734, 20401, phone (202) 741–6000

Mailing Address: 8601 Adelphi Road, College Park, MD 20740

Members:

David Ferriero, Archivist of the United States, *Chair.*

Herbert H. Jackson, Jr., (acting), Deputy Director of the U.S. Government Publishing Office.

Rosemary Hart, Senior Counsel, Department of Justice.

Secretary.—Oliver A. Potts, Director of the Federal Register, National Archives and Records Administration.

NATIONAL ARCHIVES TRUST FUND BOARD

phone (301) 837–3550, fax 837–3191

Members:

David Ferriero, Archivist of the United States, *Chair.*

Dr. William Adams, Chair, National Endowment for the Humanities.

David Lebryk, Fiscal Assistant Secretary, Department of the Treasury.

Secretary.—Lawrence Post.

NATIONAL HISTORICAL PUBLICATIONS AND RECORDS COMMISSION

700 Pennsylvania Avenue, NW., 20408

phone (202) 357–5010, fax 357–5914

http://www.archives.gov/nhprc

Members:

David S. Ferriero, Archivist of the United States, National Archives and Records Administration, *Chair.*

Judge Jeremy D. Fogel, Director, Federal Judicial Center, Judicial Branch.

Daniel Sullivan, member of the U.S. Senate, Alaska.

Mark Meadows, member of the U.S. House of Representatives, 11th District, North Carolina.

Naomi Nelson, Associate University Librarian, Duke University, Presidential Appointee.

Rebecca Hankins, Associate Professor, Curator, and Librarian for Africana Studies, Women's and Gender Studies, and Arabic Language, Texas A&M University, Presidential Appointee.

Erin Mahan, Chief Historian, Office of the Secretary, Department of Defense.

Nicole Saylor, Head, American Folklife Center Archive, Library of Congress.

Stephen P. Randolph, Chief Historian, Office of the Historian, Department of State.

Michael Stevens, State Historian of Wisconsin Emeritus, Association for Documentary Editing.

W. Eric Emerson, Director, South Carolina Department of Archives and History, American Association for State and Local History.

William G. Thomas III, Chair, Department of History, University of Nebraska-Lincoln, American Historical Association.

Kaye Lanning Minchew, former Director, Troup County Archives (GA), National Association of Government Archives and Records Administrators.

George A. Miles, Curator, Western Americana Collection at the Bienecke Rare Book and Manuscript Library, Yale University, Organization of American Historians.

Dennis Meissner, former Deputy Director, Minnesota Historical Society and past President of the Society of American Archivists.

Executive Director.—Kathleen Williams (202) 357–5010.

NATIONAL CAPITAL PLANNING COMMISSION

401 9th Street, NW., North Lobby, Suite 500, 20004, phone (202) 482–7200

fax 482–7272, info@ncpc.gov, http://www.ncpc.gov

APPOINTIVE MEMBERS

Presidential Appointees:

L. Preston Bryant, Jr., Chair.

Beth White.

Thomas Gallas.

Mayoral Appointees:

Arrington Dixon.

Geoffrey Griffis.

Ex Officio Members:

Jim Mattis, Secretary of Defense.

First Alternate.—Michael L. Rhodes.

Second Alternate.—Sajeel S. Ahmed.

Third Alternate.—Bradley Provancha.

Ryan Zinke, Secretary of the Interior.

First Alternate.—Michael Reynolds.

Second Alternate.—Robert ''Bob'' Vogel.

Third Alternate.—Peter May.

Emily W. Murphy, Administrator of General Services.

First Alternate.—Anthony E. Costa.

Second Alternate.—Mary D. Gibert.

Third Alternate.—Mina Wright.

Fourth Alternate.—Scott MacRae.

Ron Johnson, Chair, Senate Committee on Homeland Security and Governmental Affairs.

Alternate.—Patrick Bailey.

Alternate.—Josh McLeod.

Trey Gowdy, Chair, House Committee on Oversight and Government Reform.

First Alternate.—Katie Bailey.
Second Alternate.—Jeffrey Post.
Third Alternate.—Patrick Hartobey.
Muriel E. Bowser, Mayor of the District of Columbia.
First Alternate.—Eric Shaw.
Second Alternate.—Jennifer Steingasser.
Phil Mendelson, Chair, Council of the District of Columbia.
First Alternate.—Evan Cash.

EXECUTIVE STAFF

Executive Director.—Marcel C. Acosta, 482–7221.
Chief Operating Officer.—Barry S. Socks, 482–7209.
Secretariat.—Julia A. Koster, 482–7211.
General Counsel.—Anne R. Schuyler, 482–7223.
Director, Office of:
Administration.—Deborah B. Young, 482–7228.
Physical Planning.—Elizabeth Miller, 482–7246.
Policy and Research.—Michael A. Sherman, 482–7254.
Public Engagement.—Julia A. Koster, 482–7211.
Urban Design and Plan Review.—Diane Sullivan, 482–7244.

NATIONAL COUNCIL ON DISABILITY

1331 F Street, NW., Suite 850, 20004, phone (202) 272–2004
TTY 272–2074, fax 272–2022

Chair.—Neil Romano, New York, NY.
Vice Chair.—Benro Ogunyipe Chicago, IL.
Members:
Billy Altom, Little Rock, AR.
Rabia Belt, Stanford, CA.
James Brett, Boston, MA.
Lt. Col. Daniel Gade, New Windsor, NY.
Andres Gallegos, Chicago, IL.
Wendy Harbour, Minneapolis, MN.
Clyde Terry, Concord, NH.

NATIONAL CREDIT UNION ADMINISTRATION

1775 Duke Street, Alexandria, VA 22314–3428, phone (703) 518–6300, fax 518–6319

Chair.—J. Mark McWatters (acting).
Board Member.—Rick Metsger.
Secretary to the Board.—Gerard Poliquin.
Executive Director.—Mark Treichel, 518–6320, fax 518–6661.
Deputy Executive Director.—John Kutchey, 518–6320.
Inspector General.—Jim Hagen, 518–6350.
Chief Financial Officer.—Rendell Jones, 518–6570, fax 518–6664.
Chief Information Officer.—Edward Dorris, 518–6440, fax 518–6669.
National Examinations and Supervision.—Scott Hunt, 518–6640, fax 518–6665.
Minority and Women Inclusion.—Monica Davy, 518–1650.
Examination and Insurance.—Larry Fazio, 518–6360, fax 518–6666.
General Counsel.—Michael McKenna, 518–6540, fax 518–6667.
Deputy General Counsel.—Lara Rodriguez.
Human Resources.—Cheryl Eyre, 518–6510, fax 518–6668.
Public and Congressional Affairs.—Robert U. Foster, 518–6330.
Small Credit Union Initiatives.—Martha Ninichuk, 518–6610.

REGIONAL OFFICES

Director, Office of:
Region I (Albany).—L.J. Blankenberger, 9 Washington Square, Washington Avenue Extension, Albany, NY 12205 (518) 862–7400, fax 862–7420.

Region II (National Capital Region).—Jane A. Walters, 1900 Duke Street, Suite 300, Alexandria, VA 22314 (703) 519–4600, fax 519–4620.
Region III (Atlanta).—Myra Toeppe, 7000 Central Parkway, Suite 1600, Atlanta, GA 30328 (678) 443–3000, fax 443–3020.
Region IV (Austin).—Keith Morton, 4807 Spicewood Springs Road, Suite 5200, Austin, TX 78759–8490 (512) 342–5600, fax 342–5620.
Region V (Tempe).—Elizabeth Whitehead, 1230 West Washington Street, Suite 301, Tempe, AZ 85281 (602) 302–6000, fax 302–6024.

President, Asset Management and Assistance Center (Austin).—Mike Barton, 4807 Spicewood Springs Road, Suite 5100, Austin, TX 78759–8490 (512) 231–7900, fax 231–7920.

NATIONAL FOUNDATION ON THE ARTS AND THE HUMANITIES

400 7th Street, SW., Washington, DC 20506

NATIONAL ENDOWMENT FOR THE ARTS

http://www.arts.gov

Chair.—Jane Chu.
Senior Deputy Chair.—Mary Anne Carter, 682–5099.
Deputy Chair for Management and Budget.—Vacant.
Chief of Staff.—Mike Griffin, 682–5773.
Congressional Liaison.—David M. Tucker, 682–5477.
Senior Adviser to the Chair.—Bill O'Brien, 682–5550.
Director of Research and Analysis.—Sunil Iyengar, 682–5654.
General Counsel.—India Pinkney, 682–5418.
Inspector General.—Ronald Stith, 682–5774.

THE NATIONAL COUNCIL ON THE ARTS

Chair.—Jane Chu.

Members:

Bruce Carter, Ph.D.
Aaron Dworkin
Lee Greenwood
Deepa Gupta
Paul Hodes
Maria Rosario Jackson, Ph.D.
Emil J. Kang
Charlotte Kessler
María López De León
Rick Lowe
David ''Mas'' Masumoto
Barbara Ernst Prey
Ranee Ramaswamy
Diane Rodriguez
Tim Rothman
Olga Viso

Ex Officio Members:

Tammy Baldwin, Senator
Chellie Pingree, Representative

NATIONAL ENDOWMENT FOR THE HUMANITIES

phone 1–800–NEH–1121, or (202) 606–8446, questions@neh.gov, http://www.neh.gov

Chair.—Jon Parrish Peede (acting), 606–8310.
Deputy Chair.—Vacant, 606–8310.
Director, Communications.—Carmen Covelli-Ingwell, 606–8255.
Director, White House and Congressional Affairs.—Timothy Robison, 606–8273.
General Counsel.—Michael McDonald, 606–8322.
Inspector General.—Laura M.H. Davis, 606–8574.
Public Information Officer.—Christopher Flynn, 606–8440.
Director, Planning and Budget.—David Dohanic (acting), 606–8444.

NATIONAL COUNCIL ON THE HUMANITIES

Members:

Rolena K. Adorno
Camila A. Alire
Francine Berman
Albert J. Beveridge III
Allison Blakely
Constance M. Carroll
Jamsheed K. Choksy
Dawn H. Delbanco
Paula B. Duffy

Gerald L. Early
David M. Hertz
Dorothy M. Kosinski
Marvin Krislov
Patricia Nelson Limerick
Shelly C. Lowe
Christopher Merrill
Ramón Saldívar
Bruce R. Sievers
Katherine H. Tachau
John M. Unsworth
Martha W. Weinberg

FEDERAL COUNCIL ON THE ARTS AND THE HUMANITIES

Federal Council Members:

Jane Chu, Chair, National Endowment for the Arts.
Jon Parrish Peede (acting), Chair, National Endowment for the Humanities.
Betsy DeVos, Secretary, Department of Education.
David J. Skorton, Secretary, Smithsonian Institution.
France A. Córdova, Director, National Science Foundation.
Carla Hayden, Librarian of Congress, Library of Congress.
Earl A. Powell III, Director, National Gallery of Art; Chair, Commission of Fine Arts.
David Ferriero, Archivist of the United States, National Archives and Records Administration.
Daniel Matthews, Commissioner, Public Buildings Service, General Services Administration.
Jennifer Zimdahl Galt, Assistant Secretary of State, Bureau of Educational and Cultural Affairs, Department of State.
Julie E. Adams, Secretary, United States Senate.
Wilbur Ross, Secretary, Department of Commerce.
Elaine L. Chao, Secretary, Department of Transportation.
Kathryn K. Matthew, Chair, National Museum and Library Services Board; Director, Institute of Museum and Library Services.
Ben Carson, Secretary, Department of Housing and Urban Development.
Emily W. Murphy, Administrator, General Services Administration.
R. Alexander Acosta, Secretary, Department of Labor.
Robert Wilkie, Secretary, Department of Veterans Affairs.
Lance Allen Robertson, Assistant Secretary for Aging, Department of Health and Human Services.

INSTITUTE OF MUSEUM AND LIBRARY SERVICES

phone (202) 653–4657, fax 653–4625, http://www.imls.gov

[The Institute of Museum and Library Services was created by the Museum and Library Services Act of 1996, Public Law 104–208]

Director.—Dr. Kathryn K. Matthew, 653–4644.
Deputy Director for Library Services.—Robin Dale, 653–4650.
Deputy Director for Museum Services.—Paula Gangopadhyay, 653–4717.
Deputy Director of Digital and Information Strategy.—Benjamin Sweezy, 653–4690.
Chief Operating Officer.—Michael Jerger, 653–4721.
General Counsel.—Nancy Weiss, 653–4640.
Communications Manager.—Elizabeth Holtan, 653–4630.

NATIONAL MUSEUM AND LIBRARY SERVICES BOARD

Chair.—Dr. Kathryn K. Matthew, IMLS *

Members:

Sayeed Choudhury
Lisa Funderburke Hoffman
Paula Gangopadhyay, IMLS *
Luis Herrera
Lynne M. Ireland
Tammie Kahn
George Kerscher
Robin Dale, IMLS *
Mary Minow
Homa Naficy
Tey Marianna Nunn
Sylvia Orozco
Jane Pickering
Mort Sajadian
Kenneth J. Schutz
Annette Evans Smith
Jacquelyn K. Sundstrand
Beth Takekawa
Deborah Taylor
Suzanne Thorin
Robert Wedgeworth
Jonathan L. Zittrain

* Nonvoting member

NATIONAL GALLERY OF ART

6th Street and Constitution Avenue, NW., Washington, DC 20565

phone (202) 737–4215, http://www.nga.gov

Mailing Address: 2000B South Club Drive, Landover, Maryland 20785

[Under the direction of the Board of Trustees of the National Gallery of Art]

The National Gallery of Art is governed by a nine-member board of trustees, composed of five general trustees, who are appointed to staggered ten-year terms, and four *ex officio* trustees.

BOARD OF TRUSTEES

General Trustees:
Sharon Percy Rockefeller, Chair.
Frederick W. Beinecke, President.
Mitchell P. Rales.
Andrew M. Saul.
David M. Rubenstein.
Trustees Emeriti:
Julian Ganz, Jr.
Alexander M. Laughlin.
David O. Maxwell.
Victoria P. Sant.
John Wilmerding.
Ex Officio Trustees:
John G. Roberts, Jr., Chief Justice of the United States.
Mike Pompeo, Secretary of State.
Steven T. Mnuchin, Secretary of the Treasury.
David J. Skorton, Secretary of the Smithsonian Institution.

The board of trustees appoints the National Gallery of Art director and five executive officers, who manage the day-to-day operations of the museum.

Executive Officers:
Director.—Earl A. Powell III.
Deputy Director and Chief Curator.—Franklin Kelly.
Administrator.—Darrell R. Willson.
Treasurer.—William W. McClure.
Secretary and General Counsel.—Nancy Robinson Breuer.
Dean, Center for Advanced Study in the Visual Arts.—Elizabeth Cropper.

NATIONAL LABOR RELATIONS BOARD

1099 14th Street, NW., 20570–0001

Personnel Locator (202) 273–1000

Chair.—Philip A. Miscimarra, 273–1070, fax 273–4270. (Term expires December 16, 2018.)
Chief Counsel.—Peter J. Carlton.
Deputy Chief Counsel.—Robert F. Kane.
Members:
Board Member.—William J. Emanuel, 273–1740.
Chief Counsel.—Vacant.
Deputy Chief Counsel.—Lara Zick.
Board Member.—Marvin E. Kaplan, 273–1770.
Chief Counsel.—James R. Murphy.
Deputy Chief Counsel.—Rachel G. Lennie.
Board Member.—Lauren McGarity McFerran, 273–1700.
Chief Counsel.—John F. Colwell.
Deputy Chief Counsel.—Andrew J. Krafts.
Board Member.—Mark Gaston Pearce, 273–1790.
Chief Counsel.—Ellen Dichner.
Deputy Chief Counsel.—Kathleen Nixon.
Executive Secretary.—Gary W. Shinners, 273–1940, fax 273–4270.
Deputy Executive Secretary.—Roxanne Rothchild, 273–2917.

Associate Executive Secretaries: Farah Qureshi, 273–1949; Leigh Reardon, 273–1736.

Associate Solicitor.—Susan Leverone, 273–2914, fax 273–1962.

Inspector General.—David P. Berry, 273–1960, fax 273–2344.

Director, Representation Appeals; Assistant Chief Counsel.—Terence Schoone-Jongen, 273–1971, fax 273–1962.

Director, Office of Congressional and Public Affairs.—Carmen F. Spell, 273–1991, fax 273–1789.

Chief Information Officer, Office of the Chief Information Officer.—Prem Aburvasamy, 273–3925, fax 273–2850.

DIVISION OF JUDGES

Chief Administrative Law Judge.—Robert A. Giannasi, 501–8800, fax 501–8686.

Deputy Chief Administrative Law Judge.—Arthur Amchan, 501–8800.

Associate Chief Administrative Law Judges: Vacant; Gerald Etchingham, 901 Market Street, Suite 300, San Francisco, CA 94103–1779 (415) 356–5255, fax 356–5254; Mindy Landow, 120 West 45th Street, 11th Floor, New York, NY 10036–5503 (212) 944–2941, fax 944–4904.

General Counsel.—Peter B. Robb, 273–3700, fax 273–4483.

Deputy General Counsel.—Jennifer A. Abruzzo, 273–3700.

Associate General Counsel, Ethics.—Lori Ketcham, 273–2939.

Special Counsel and Labor Relations; Senior Special Counsel.—Barry F. Smith, 273–2998.

Director, Division of Administration.—Lasharn Hamilton, 273–3936, fax 273–2928.

Chief Financial Officer, Office of the Chief Financial Officer.—Mehul Parekh, 273–3884, fax 273–2928.

DIVISION OF OPERATIONS MANAGEMENT

Associate General Counsel.—Beth Tursell, 273–2900, fax 273–4274.

Deputy Associate General Counsel.—Richard Wainstein.

Assistant General Counsels: Yvette Hatfield, 273–3798; Aaron Karsh, 273–3828; David A. Kelly, 273–2878; Elizabeth Kilpatrick, 273–0058; Joan A. Sullivan, 273–3742.

DIVISION OF ADVICE

Associate General Counsel.—Jayme Sophir, 273–3800, fax 273–4275.

Deputy Associate General Counsel.—Vacant.

Assistant General Counsels:

Injunction Litigation Branch.—Elinor Merberg, 273–3833.

Regional Advice Branch.—Miriam Szapiro, 273–0998.

DIVISION OF ENFORCEMENT LITIGATION

Associate General Counsel.—John H. Ferguson, 273–2950, fax 273–4244.

Deputy Associate General Counsel.—Vacant.

Appellate and Supreme Court Litigation Branch:

Deputy Associate General Counsel.—Linda J. Dreeben, 273–2960.

Assistant General Counsel.—David Habenstreit, 273–0979.

Deputy Assistant General Counsels: Ruth E. Burdick, 273–7958; Meredith Jason, 273–2945.

DIVISION OF LEGAL COUNSEL

Associate General Counsel.—Barbara O'Neill, 273–2958.

Deputy Associate General Counsel.—Nancy Platt, 273–2937.

Contempt Litigation and Compliance Branch:

Assistant General Counsel.—William Mascioli, 273–3746.

Deputy Assistant General Counsel.—Dawn Goldstein, 273–2936.

Freedom of Information Act Branch:

FOIA Officer/Assistant General Counsel.—Synta Keeling, 273–2995.

NATIONAL MEDIATION BOARD

1301 K Street, NW., Suite 250 East, 20005, phone (202) 692–5000, fax 692–5081

Chair.—Gerald W. Fauth III, 692–5022.
Board Members: Kyle Fortson, 692–5000; Linda Puchala, 692–5019.
Assistant Chief of Staff, Office of Administration.—Samantha T. Jones, 692–5010.
Chief of Staff, Office of the Chief of Staff.—Vacant.
Director, Office of Arbitration Services.—Roland Watkins, 692–5055.
General Counsel, Office of Legal Affairs.—Mary L. Johnson, 692–5040.
Deputy Chief of Staff, Office of Mediation Services and ADR Services.—Michael Kelliher, 692–5040.

THE NATIONAL ACADEMIES OF SCIENCES, ENGINEERING, AND MEDICINE

2101 Constitution Avenue, NW., 20418, phone (202) 334–2000

(Mailing address: 500 Fifth Street, NW., 20001)

The National Academies of Sciences, Engineering, and Medicine serve as an independent adviser to the Federal Government on scientific and technical questions of national importance. Although operating under a congressional charter granted to the National Academy of Sciences in 1863, the three organizations are private organizations, not agencies of the Federal Government, and receive no appropriations from Congress.

NATIONAL ACADEMY OF SCIENCES

President.—Marcia McNutt, 334–2101.
Vice President.—Diane E. Griffin, Johns Hopkins Bloomberg School of Public Health.
Home Secretary.—Susan R. Wessler, University of California, Riverside.
Foreign Secretary.—John Hildebrand, University of Arizona.
Treasurer.—William H. Press, The University of Texas.
Executive Officer.—Bruce B. Darling, 334–3000.
Executive Director, Office of Congressional Affairs, National Academies of Sciences, Engineering, and Medicine.—Christopher J. King, 334–1601.

NATIONAL ACADEMY OF ENGINEERING

President.—C.D. ''Dan'' Mote, Jr., 334–3200.
Chair.—Gordon R. England, Chair, PFP Cybersecurity.
Vice President.—Corale L. Brierley, Principal, Brierley Consultancy LLC.
Home Secretary.—Julia M. Phillips, retired Vice President and CTO, Sandia National Laboratories.
Foreign Secretary.—Ruth A. David, retired President and CEO, Analytic Services, Inc.
Executive Officer.—Alton D. Romig, Jr., 334–3677.
Treasurer.—Martin B. Sherwin (Ret.), W.R. Grace.

NATIONAL ACADEMY OF MEDICINE

President.—Victor J. Dzau, M.D., 334–3300.
The Leonard D. Schaeffer Executive Officer.—J. Michael McGinnis, M.D.
Chair.—Victor J. Dzau, M.D.
Home Secretary.—Jane E. Henney, M.D.
Foreign Secretary.—Margaret Hamburg, M.D.

NATIONAL SCIENCE FOUNDATION

2415 Eisenhower Avenue, Alexandria, VA 22314

phone (703) 292–8000, http://www.nsf.gov

Director.—France A. Córdova (703) 292–8000.
Deputy Director.—Vacant.
Chief Operating Officer.—Joan Ferrini-Mundy, 292–8400.
Director, Office of:
General Counsel.—Lawrence Rudolph, 292–8060.

Inspector General.—Allison C. Lerner, 292–7100.
Assistant Director for—
Biological Sciences.—Dr. James L. Olds, 292–8400.
Computer and Information Science and Engineering.—Dr. James F. Kurose, 292–8900.
Education and Human Resources.—William ''Jim'' Lewis (acting), 292–8600.
Engineering.—Dawn Tillbury, 292–8300.
Geosciences.—William E. Easterling, 292–8500.
Mathematical and Physical Sciences.—James S. Ulvestad (acting), 292–8800.
Social, Behavioral, and Economic Sciences.—Fay L. Cook, 292–8700.
Director, Office of:
Budget, Finance, and Award Management/Chief Financial Officer.—Teresa Grancorvitz (acting), 292–8200.
Diversity and Inclusion.—Rhonda J. Davis, 292–8020.
Information and Resource Management/Chief Human Capital Officer.—Joanne S. Tornow, 292–8100.
Integrative Activities.—Suzanne Iacono, 292–8040.
International Science and Engineering.—Rebecca L. Keiser, 292–8710.
Legislative and Public Affairs.—Amanda Hallberg Greenwell, 292–8070.

NATIONAL SCIENCE BOARD

Chair.—Maria T. Zuber, 292–7000.
Vice Chair.—Diane L. Souvaine.

MEMBERS

John L. Anderson
Deborah L. Ball
Roger Beachy
Arthur Bienenstock
Vinton G. Cerf
Vicki Chandler
Ruth David
W. Kent Fuchs
Inez Fung
Robert M. Groves
James S. Jackson
G. Peter LePage
Alan I. Leshner
W. Carl Lineberger
Steven L. Mayo
Victor R. McCrary
Emilio F. Moran
Ellen Ochoa
Sethuraman Panchanathan
G.P. ''Bud'' Peterson
Julia M. Phillips
Geraldine Richmond
Annelia Sargent
Diane L. Souvaine
Maria T. Zuber

NATIONAL TRANSPORTATION SAFETY BOARD

490 L'Enfant Plaza, SW., 20594, phone (202) 314–6000

Chair.—Robert L. Sumwalt III (acting), 314–6145.
Vice Chair.—Robert L. Sumwalt III, 314–6145.
Members: T. Bella Dinh-Zarr, 314–6495; Christopher Hart, 314–6145; Earl Weener, 314–6072.
Managing Director.—Dennis Jones (acting), 314–6320.
Deputy Managing Director.—Sharon Bryson (acting), 314–6188.
General Counsel.—David Tochen, 314–6616.
Chief Administrative Law Judge.—Alfonso Montano, Jr., 314–6150.
Chief Financial Officer.—Edward Benthall, 314–6241.
Director, Office of:
Aviation Safety.—John Delisi, 314–6302.
Highway Safety.—Robert Molloy, 314–6471.
Marine Safety.—Brian Curtis, 314–6456.
Railroad, Pipeline and Hazardous Materials Investigations.—Robert Hall, 314–6463.
Research and Engineering.—James Ritter, 314–6502.
Safety Recommendations and Communications.—Paul Sledzik (acting), 314–6134.
Government and Industry Affairs.—Christopher Wallace, 314–6007.
Media Relations.—Christopher O'Neil, 314–6100.
Safety Advocacy.—Nicholas Worrell, 314–6608.
Transportation Disaster Assistance.—Elias Kontanis, 314–6187.

NEIGHBORHOOD REINVESTMENT CORPORATION

(Doing business as NeighborWorks America)

999 North Capitol Street, NE., Suite 900, 20002, phone (202) 760–4000, fax 376–2600

BOARD OF DIRECTORS

Chair.—Hon. Grovetta Gardineer, Senior Deputy Comptroller for Compliance and Community Affairs, Office of the Comptroller.

Members:

Hon. Lael Brainard, Member, Board of Governors, Federal Reserve System.
Hon. Thomas Hoenig, Vice Chair, Federal Deposit Insurance Corporation.
Pamela Hughes Patenaude, Deputy Secretary, Department of Housing and Urban Development.
J. Mark McWatters, Chairman, National Credit Union Administration.

President and Chief Executive Officer.—Paul Weech, 760–4020.
General Counsel / Secretary.—Jeffrey T. Bryson, 760–4101.
EVP and Chief Operating Officer.—Tom Chabolla, 760–4070.
Chief Financial Officer.—Rebecca Bond (acting), 760–4088.
Senior Vice President for—

Resource Development.—Rose McManus Coleman, 760–4038.
Public Relations.—Christina McHenry, 760–4058.
Field Operations.—Kathryn Watts, 683–6659.
Controller.—Yonas Tessema (acting), 760–4092.
Internal Audit.—Frederick Udochi, 524–9937.
Public Policy and Legislative Affairs.—Kirsten Johnson-Obey, 760–4139.
Training.—John McCloskey (acting), 760–4205.

NUCLEAR REGULATORY COMMISSION

Washington, DC 20555–0001, phone (301) 415–7000, http://www.nrc.gov

[Authorized by 42 U.S.C. 5801 and U.S.C. 1201]

OFFICE OF THE CHAIR

Chair.—Kristine L. Svinicki, 415–1855.
Chief of Staff.—Patrick Castleman, 415–1855.
Administrative Assistant.—Janet L. Lepre, 415–1855.

COMMISSIONERS

Jeff Baran, 415–1839.
Chief of Staff.—Amy Powell, 415–1839.
Administrative Assistant.—Stacy Schumann, 415–1839.
Stephen G. Burns, 415–8420.
Chief of Staff.—Jason Zorn, 415–8420.
Administrative Assistant.—Kathleen Blake, 415–8420.

STAFF OFFICES OF THE COMMISSION

Secretary.—Annette L. Vietti-Cook, 415–1969, fax 415–1672.
Chief Financial Officer.—Maureen Wylie, 415–7322, fax 415–4236.
Commission Appellate Adjudication.—Brooke P. Clark, 415–2653, fax 415–3200.
Congressional Affairs.—Eugene Dacus, 415–1776, fax 415–2162.
General Counsel.—Margaret M. Doane, 415–1743, fax 415–3086.
Inspector General.—Hubert T. Bell, 415–5930, fax 415–5091.
International Programs.—Nader L. Mamish (301) 287–9056.
Public Affairs.—David Castelveter, 415–8200, fax 415–2234.

ADVISORY COMMITTEE ON MEDICAL USES OF ISOTOPES

Chair.—Philip O. Anderson.

ADVISORY COMMITTEE ON REACTOR SAFEGUARDS

Executive Director.—Andrea Veil, 415–7360, fax 415–5589.

ATOMIC SAFETY AND LICENSING BOARD PANEL

Chief Administrative Judge.—E. Roy Hawkens, 415–7454, fax 415–5599.

OFFICE OF THE EXECUTIVE DIRECTOR FOR OPERATIONS

Executive Director for Operations.—Victor M. McCree, 415–1700, fax 415–2700.
Deputy Executive Director for—
Materials, Waste, Research, State, Tribal, Compliance, Administration, and Human Capital Programs.—Frederick D. Brown, 415–1705, fax 415–2700.
Reactor and Preparedness Programs.—Michael R. Johnson, 415–1713, fax 415–2700.
Director, Office of:
Administration.—Cynthia A. Carpenter, 415–8747, fax 415–5352.
Enforcement.—Patricia Holahan (301) 287–9527, fax (301) 287–3325.
Human Resources.—Miriam L. Cohen (301) 287–0747, fax (301) 287–9343.
Information Services.—David J. Nelson, 415–8700, fax 415–4246.
Investigations.—Kimberly A. Howell, 415–2373, fax 415–2370.
New Reactors.—Vonna Ordaz (acting), 415–1897, fax 415–2700.
Nuclear Material Safety and Safeguards.—Marc L. Dapas, 415–0595, fax 492–3360.
Nuclear Reactor Regulation.—Brian Holian (acting), 415–1270, fax 415–8333.
Nuclear Regulatory Research.—Michael F. Weber, 415–1914, fax 415–6671.
Nuclear Security and Incident Response.—K. Steven West (acting), (301) 287–3734, fax (301) 287–9351.
Small Business and Civil Rights.—Pamela R. Baker, 415–7380, fax 415–5953.

REGIONAL OFFICES

Region I: Daniel Dorman, 2100 Renaissance Boulevard, Suite 100, King of Prussia, PA 19406 (610) 337–5299, fax (610) 337–5241.
Region II: Catherine Haney, 245 Peachtree Center Avenue, NE., Suite 1200, Atlanta, GA 30303 (404) 997–4411, fax (404) 997–4901.
Region III: Cynthia Pederson, 2443 Warrenville Road, Suite 210, Lisle, IL 60532 (630) 829–9657, fax (630) 515–1096.
Region IV: Kriss M. Kennedy, 1600 East Lamar Boulevard, Arlington, TX 76011 (817) 200–1225, fax (817) 200–1122.

OCCUPATIONAL SAFETY AND HEALTH REVIEW COMMISSION

1120 20th Street, NW., 9th Floor, 20036–3457, phone (202) 606–5100

[Created by Public Law 91–596]

Chair.—Heather L. MacDougall, 606–5375.
Chief Counsel to the Chair.—Donald G. Shalhoub, 606–5711.
Confidential Assistant to the Chair (Public Affairs Officer).—Sienna Goering, 606–5723.
Commissioner.—James J. Sullivan, 606–5373.
Chief Counsel to the Commissioner.—Amanda Wood Laihow, 606–5373.
Commissioner.—Cynthia L. Attwood, 606–5370.
Chief Counsel to the Commissioner.—Nathan K. Kupka, 606–5370.
Confidential Assistant to the Commissioner.—Madeleine C. Pope, 606–5370.
Administrative Law Judges:
Patrick B. Augustine, U.S. Customs House, 721 19th Street, Room 407, Denver, CO 80202–2517.
Peggy S. Ball, U.S. Customs House, 721 19th Street, Room 407, Denver, CO 80202–2517.
Carol A. Baumerich, 1120 20th Street, NW., 9th Floor, Washington, DC 20036–3457.
Keith E. Bell, 1120 20th Street, NW., 9th Floor, Washington, DC 20036–3457.
Sharon D. Calhoun, 100 Alabama Street, SW., Building 1924, Room 2R90, Atlanta, GA 30303–3104.
William S. Coleman, 1120 20th Street, NW., 9th Floor, Washington, DC 20036–3457.
Brian A. Duncan, U.S. Customs House, 721 19th Street, Room 407, Denver, CO 80202–2517.

John B. Gatto, 100 Alabama Street, SW., Building 1924, Room 2R90, Atlanta, GA 30303–3104.
Heather A. Joys, 100 Alabama Street, SW., Building 1924, Room 2R90, Atlanta, GA 30303–3104.
Dennis L. Phillips, 1120 20th Street, NW., 9th Floor, Washington, DC 20036–3457.
Covette Rooney, 1120 20th Street, NW., 9th Floor, Washington, DC 20036–3457.
John H. Schumacher, U.S. Customs House, 721 19th Street, Room 407, Denver, CO 80202–2517.

General Counsel.—Nadine N. Mancini.
Executive Secretary.—John X. Cerveny.
Executive Director.—Debra A. Hall.

OFFICE OF GOVERNMENT ETHICS

1201 New York Avenue, NW., Suite 500, 20005, phone (202) 482–9300, fax 482–9238

[Created by Act of October 1, 1989; codified in 5 U.S.C. app., section 401]

Director.—David J. Apol (acting).
Confidential Assistant.—Matthew A. Marinec.
Chief of Staff and Program Counsel.—Shelley K. Finlayson.
General Counsel.—David J. Apol.
Deputy Director for—
Compliance.—Dale A. Christopher.
Financial Disclosure.—Barbara A. Mullen-Roth.
Chief for Internal Operations.—Emory A. Rounds (acting).

OFFICE OF PERSONNEL MANAGEMENT

Theodore Roosevelt Building, 1900 E Street, NW., 20415

phone (202) 606–1800, http://www.opm.gov

OFFICE OF THE DIRECTOR

Director.—Jeff T.H. Pon, 606–1000.
Special Assistant.—Mary E. Anderson.
Deputy Director.—Michael J. Rigas.
Senior Advisor to the Director.—Vacant.
Chief of Staff.—Michael D. Dovilla.
Executive Assistant.—Vacant.
Deputy Chief of Staff.—Stephen Billy.
Counselor to the Director.—Vacant.
White House Liaison.—Kathleen M. Bullock, 606–1000.
Executive Assistant.—Torlanda Young, 606–1467.
Chief Management Officer.—Kathleen McGettigan, 606–2938.
Executive Assistant.—Delicia T. Harrell, 606–2732.
Senior Advisor.—Basil Parker.
Chief Privacy Officer.—Kelly C. Riley.
Executive Director, Chief Human Capital Officers (CHCO) Council.—Sara B. Ratcliff.

OFFICE OF THE EXECUTIVE SECRETARIAT

Director.—Jozetta Robinson, 606–1000.
Deputy Director.—Stephen Hickman, 606–1973.
International Affairs.—Jill Feldman, 606–5099.
Regulatory Affairs.—Keira Jones, 606–1183.

CHIEF FINANCIAL OFFICER

Chief Financial Officer.—Dennis D. Coleman, 606–2938.
Deputy Chief Financial Officer.—Daniel K. Marella, 606–2638.
Executive Officer/Resource Management.—Katina P. Cotton, 606–4725.
OPM Projects and Initiatives.—Teresa F. Williams, 606–1414.
Associate Chief Financial Officer:
Policy and Internal Control.—Thomas Moschetto, 418–3149.

Budget and Performance.—Margaret P. Pearson, 606–0087.
Financial Services.—Tonya R. Johnson, 606–1531.
Financial Operations Management.—Rochelle S. Bayard, 606–4366.

OFFICE OF COMMUNICATIONS

Director.—Dean Hunter (acting), 606–2402.
Deputy Director.—LaShonne Williams, 606–2402.
Administrative Assistant.—Jean Smith, 606–2402.
Speechwriter.—Lauren R. Westcott, 606–2402.
Press Secretary.—Vacant.
Digital Director.—Briana Kaya, 606–2402.

CONGRESSIONAL, LEGISLATIVE, AND INTERGOVERNMENTAL AFFAIRS (CLIA)

Director.—Janel Fitzhugh (acting), 606–1300.
Executive Assistant.—Justin Jeffress.
Deputy Director.—Vacant.
Congressional Relations Officer.—Kevin Franklin, 606–5197.
Chief, Legislative Analysis Group.—Janel Fitzhugh.
Legislative Analysts: John Barone, 606–1224, Steven J. Driscoll, 606–5089.
Correspondence Analyst.—Jerson Matias, 418–4360
Chief, Constituent Services, Capitol Hill.—Kristen Soper, B332 Rayburn House Office Building, 225–4955, FAX: 225–4974.
Constituent Services Representatives: Sean McKew, Carlos E. Tingle.

NATIONAL BACKGROUND INVESTIGATIONS BUREAU (NBIB)

Director.—Charles S. Phalen, Jr., 606–5206.
Chief of Staff.—Christy K. Wilder, 606–5206.
Deputy Director.—Vacant.
Deputy Associate Directors:
Customer Service, Communications, and Engagements.—Mark R. Pekrul, 606–5206.
Contracting and Business Solutions.—Nicole K. Evans, 606–5206.
Information Technology Management Office.—N. Roy Parkinson (acting), (724) 794–5612.
Deputy Assistant Directors:
Federal Investigative Records Enterprise.—James C. Onusko, 606–5206.
Field Operations.—Mark P. Sherwin (724) 794–5612.
Quality Oversight.—Jeffrey C. Flora (443) 698–9400.
Policy, Strategy, and Business Transformation.—Jorge M. Shimabukuro, 606–2712.

MERIT SYSTEM ACCOUNTABILITY AND COMPLIANCE

Associate Director.—Mark W. Lambert, 606–2980.
Deputy Associate Director.—Ana Mazzi, 606–2980.
Directors:
Combined Federal Campaign (CFC) Operations.—Keith Willingham, 606–2564.
Internal Oversight and Compliance.—Janet L. Barnes, 606–3207.
Program Manager, Voting Rights and Resource Management.—Jeremy J. Leahy (acting), 606–5290.
Administrative Assistant.—Kimberlin C. Chaney, 606–3207.

CHIEF INFORMATION OFFICER

Chief Information Officer.—David A. Garcia, 606–2150.
Deputy Chief Information Officer.—Robert M. Leahy, 606–2150.
Resource Management.—Vacant.
Chief Information Security Officer.—Cord Chase, 606–6210.
IT Security/Security Operations Center.—Jeffrey Wagner, 606–2571.
Chief Technology Officer.—Vacant.
IT Strategy and Policy:
Associate Chief Information Officer.—Dovarius L. Peoples, 606–2150.
Strategic Planning.—Vacant.

IT Enterprise Architect.—Vacant.
IT Investment Management.—Stephen L. Schultz, 606–8089.
Information Management.—Vacant.
Quality Assurance.—Huy Le, 606–1384.
Freedom of Information and Privacy Act.—Vacant.
Federal Data Solutions:
Associate CIO.—Dovarius L. Peoples, 606–2150.
Data Management.—Vacant.
Data Warehouse.—Victor A. Karcher, Jr. (724) 794–2005, ext. 3209.
Enterprise Infrastructure Solutions (EIS):
Associate Chief Information Officer.—Jeffrey Wagner (acting), 606–2571.
Web Services.—Linzie T. Oliver (acting), 606–2445.
Network Management.—Vacant.
Data Center.—Heather Kowalski, 606–1893.
Program Office Support IT PMO.—Oliver Linzie, 606–2445.
Federal IT Business Solutions:
Associate Chief Information Officer.—Lawrence L. Anderson, 606–2150.
Retirement Services IT PMO.—May T. Cheng, 606–7009.
Federal Investigative Services IT PMO.—Vacant.
Human Resources Solutions IT PMO.—MC Price (478) 744–2051.
Employee Services IT PMO.—Michelle Gilder Early, 606–2641.
Healthcare and Insurance and *Merit System Accountability and Compliance IT PMO.*—Juan C. García Rolón, 418–4362.
Federal Applications IT PMO.—MC Price (acting), (478) 744–2051.

HUMAN RESOURCES SOLUTIONS (HRS)

Associate Director.—Joseph S. Kennedy, 606–0900.
Principal Deputy Associate Director.—Reginald M. Brown (acting), 606–1332.
Executive Assistant.—Shirl Sibley, 606–1304.
Deputy Associate Directors:
Center for Leadership Development, and Director, Federal Executive Institute.—Susan G. Logann (434) 980–6220.
Center for Leadership Development, and Innovation Lab.—Sydney Smith-Heimborck, 606–2762.
Center for Management Services.—Reginald M. Brown, 606–1332.
Federal Staffing Group.—Dianna M. Saxman (215) 362–3154.
HR Strategy and Evaluation Solutions.—Leslie Pollack, 606–1426.
Training and Management Assistance Program.—James McPherson, 606–4667.

RETIREMENT SERVICES

Associate Director.—Kenneth J. Zawodny, Jr. (724) 794–7759.
Deputy Associate Director (Boyers).—Nicholas Ashenden, 794–2005 ext. 3214.
Executive Assistant.—Christy Bernhart, 794–7760.
Deputy Associate Director (DC).—Tia N. Butler (202) 606–4168.
Executive Assistant.—Arminta Thompson-Smith, 606–3803.

OFFICE OF THE GENERAL COUNSEL

General Counsel.—Ted M. Cooperstein, 606–1700.
Deputy General Counsels: Steven D. Dillingham, 606–1700; Kathie Ann Whipple, 606–1700.
Special Counsel and Senior Advisor.—Vacant.
Special Counsel.—Amy W. Apostol, 606–5206.
Associate General Counsel (Compensation, Benefits, Products and Services).—Jason C. Foster, 606–1700.
Assistant General Counsel (Merit Systems and Accountability).—Steven E. Abow.
Chief, Administrative Operations.—Paul J. Carr, 606–4018.

OFFICE OF THE INSPECTOR GENERAL

Inspector General.—Norbert E. Vint (acting), 606–1200.
Deputy Inspector General.—Norbet E. Vint, 606–1200.

Executive Assistant.—A. Paulette Berry, 606–3807.
Counsel to the Inspector General.—Robin M. Richardson, 606–2037.
Assistant Inspector General for Audits.—Michael R. Esser, 606–1200.
Deputy Assistant Inspectors General for Audits: Melissa D. Brown, 606–4714; Lewis F. Parker, 606–4738.
Assistant Inspector General for Investigations.—Drew M. Grimm, 606–1200.
Deputy Assistant Inspector General for Investigations.—Thomas Sourth, 606–4730.
Assistant Inspector General for Legal Affairs.—Vacant.
Assistant Inspector General for Management.—James L. Ropelewski, 606–0846.
Deputy Assistant Inspector General for Management.—Nicholas E. Hoyle, 606–2156.
Chief Information Technology Officer.—Gopala Seelamneni.

OFFICE OF SMALL AND DISADVANTAGED BUSINESS UTILIZATION (OSDBU)

Director.—Desmond Brown, 606–2862.

OFFICE OF PROCUREMENT OPERATIONS (OPO)

Senior Procurement Executive.—Juan Arratia, 606–1984.
Executive Assistant.—Eva X. Lopez, 606–7933.
Director, Contracting.—Elijah Anderson (acting), 606–6429.
Division Director, Procurement Policy and Innovation.—Gregory F. Blaszko (215) 861–3112.

FACILITIES, SECURITY, AND EMERGENCY MANAGEMENT (FSEM)

Director.—Dean Hunter, 606–3130.
Executive Assistant.—Eva X. Lopez, 606–7933.
Administrative Operations:
Director.—Mark A. Anderson, 418–3214.
Facilities Management:
Director.—Mariano Aquino, 606–4590.
Facility Services and Logistics.—Marla Neustadt, 606–2502.
Building Operations.—Timothy J. Allman, 606–1457.
Safety and Occupational Health.—Victoria Pearson, 606–2220.
Security Services:
Director.—Kevin McCombs, 418–0201.
Physical Security.—Elvis Chase, 606–2872.
Security Assessment.—Dairel L. Rawson (724) 794–7137.
Personnel Security.—Melinda M. Davis (724) 794–7112.
Adjudication and Compliance.—Patricia Neiderhiser (724) 794–7171.
Adjudication and Clearance Processing.—Michael Price (724) 794–7110.
Special Agreements and Identity Processing.—Scott Kaminski (724) 794–7128.
Emergency Management:
Director.—Sandra L. Hawthorne, 606–5068.
SitRoom Operations.—Dwayne Butler, 606–7016.
Emergency Actions.—Brien Gibney, 418–9920.

EQUAL EMPLOYMENT OPPORTUNITY

Director.—LaShonn M. Woodland, 606–2460.
Lead EEO Specialist.—Yasmin A. Rosa, 606–2460.

HUMAN RESOURCES

Director, OPM Human Resources and Chief Human Capital Officer.—Andrea J. Bright, 606–3590.
Deputy Director, Human Resources and OPM Learning.—Tyshawn J. Thomas, 606–2646.

DIVERSITY AND INCLUSION

Director.—Zina B. Sutch, 606–0020.

Deputy Director.—Nicole Lassiter (acting), 606–2267.

HEALTHCARE AND INSURANCE

Director.—Alan P. Spielman, 606–4995.
Deputy Director.—Laurie Bodenheimer, 606–1572.
Staff Assistant.—Lorraine Waller, 606–4017.
Chief Medical Officer.—Christine Hunter, 606–4653.
Federal Employee Insurance Operations:
Assistant Director.—Edward DeHarde, 606–0522.
Deputy Assistant Director.—Cindy Butler, 606–7019.
Program Development Support:
Assistant Director.—Lori H. Amos, 606–0277.
Deputy Assistant Director.—Holly Schumann, 606–7112.

PLANNING AND POLICY ANALYSIS

Director.—Anne Easton (acting), 606–2213.
Deputy Director.—Vacant.
Senior Advisor, Research and Evaluation.—Kimya Lee, 606–6428.
Program Management Office.—Dennis Hardy, 606–4182.
Office of Actuaries.—Steve Niu, 606–1578.
Data Analysis.—Lance Harris, 606–1449.
Survey Analysis.—Kim Wells, 606–9088.
Policy Analysis.—Jodi Miller, 418–3398.
Human Resources Line of Business.—David Vargas, 418–3236.

EMPLOYEE SERVICES

Associate Director.—Mark Reinhold, 606–2520.
Principal Deputy Associate Director.—Veronica Villalobos, 606–7992.
Deputy Associate Directors:
Outreach, Diversity, and Inclusion.—Zina B. Sutch, 606–2433.
Partnership and Labor Relations.—Tim F. Curry, 606–2402.
Pay and Leave.—Brenda Roberts, 606–2858.
Recruitment and Hiring.—Kimberly Holden, 418–3218.
Senior Executive Service and Performance Management.—Vacant.
Strategic Workforce Planning.—Veronica Villalobos (acting), 606–7992.
Veterans Services.—Hakeem Basheerud-Deen, 606–3602.

OFFICE OF THE SPECIAL COUNSEL

1730 M Street, NW., Suite 300, 20036–4505, phone (202) 804–7000

[Authorized by 5 U.S.C. 1101 and 5 U.S.C. 1211]

Special Counsel.—Henry Kerner.
Principal Deputy Special Counsel.—Tristan Leavitt.

PEACE CORPS

1111 20th Street, NW., 20526, phone (202) 692–2000

Toll-Free Number (855) 855–1961, http://www.peacecorps.gov

[Created by Public Law 97–113]

OFFICE OF THE DIRECTOR

phone (202) 962–2100, fax 692–2101

Director.—Jody Olsen.
Deputy Director.—Kathy Stroker (acting).
Chief of Staff.—Carl Sosebee (acting).
White House Liaison.—Matthew McKinney.
Senior Advisors: Sheila Crowley, Maryann Minutillo, Heather Schwenk.

Executive Secretary.—Melanie Wilhelm.
Chief Administrative Officer.—Lisset Castro.
Chief Compliance Officer.—Angela Kissel (acting).

OFFICE OF VICTIM ADVOCACY

Director.—Da Shawnna Townsend.

OFFICE OF CIVIL RIGHTS AND DIVERSITY

Director.—Alicia Crain.

OFFICE OF COMMUNICATIONS

Director of Press Relations.—Matthew Sheehey.

OFFICE OF CONGRESSIONAL RELATIONS

Director.—Nancy Herbolsheimer.
Deputy Director.—Joske Bautista.

OFFICE OF THE GENERAL COUNSEL

General Counsel.—Robert Shanks.

OFFICE OF STRATEGIC PARTNERSHIPS AND INTERGOVERNMENTAL AFFAIRS

Director.—Shannon Kendrick.

OFFICE OF EXTERNAL AFFAIRS

Associate Director.—Joel Frushone.

OFFICE OF GIFTS AND GRANTS MANAGEMENT

Director.—Karen Roberts.
Deputy Director.—Charlotte Kea.

OFFICE OF STRATEGIC INFORMATION, RESEARCH, AND PLANNING

Director.—Steven Dillingham.
Deputy Director.—Jeff Kwiecinski.

OFFICE OF THIRD GOAL AND RETURNED VOLUNTEER SERVICES

Director.—Keith Honda.

OFFICE OF GLOBAL OPERATIONS

Associate Director.—Patrick Young.
Senior Advisors: Peter Redmond, Diana Schmidt.

Africa Region:

Regional Director.—Tim Hartman (acting).
Chiefs of Operations: Julie Burns, Tim Hartman.

Europe/Mediterranean/Asia Region:

Regional Director.—Jean Seigle (acting).
Chief of Operations.—Jean Seigle.

Inter-America and Pacific Region:

Regional Director.—Emily Untermeyer (acting).

Chief of Operations.—George Like.

OFFICE OF OVERSEAS PROGRAMMING AND TRAINING SUPPORT

Director.—Stephanie Rust.

PEACE CORPS RESPONSE

Director.—Vacant.
Chief of Operations.—Thomas Ross.

OFFICE OF GLOBAL HEALTH AND HIV

Director—Marie McLeod.

OFFICE OF MANAGEMENT

Associate Director.—Jeffrey Harrington.
Chief Administrative Officer.—Kathy Perdue.
FOIA/Privacy Act Officer.—Virginia Burke.

OFFICE OF HUMAN RESOURCE MANAGEMENT

Director.—Tina Williams (acting).

OFFICE OF THE INSPECTOR GENERAL

Inspector General.—Kathy Buller.
Deputy Inspector General.—Joaquin Ferrao.

OFFICE OF THE CHIEF FINANCIAL OFFICER

Chief Financial Officer.—Richard Swarttz.
Deputy Chief Financial Officer.—Vacant.

OFFICE OF THE CHIEF INFORMATION OFFICER

Chief Information Officer.—Vacant.
Deputy Chief Information Officer.—Scott Knell.

OFFICE OF VOLUNTEER RECRUITMENT AND SELECTION

Associate Director.—Erin Gibbs (acting).
Chief of Operations.—Erin Gibbs.
Chief Administrative Officer—Lauren Engel.
Director of:
Placement.—Stephanie Galeota.
Recruitment and Diversity.—Tina Williams.
University Programs.—Clayton Kennedy.
Analysis and Evaluations.—Andrew Hokenson.

REGIONAL OFFICES

Central Region (Alabama, Arkansas, Illinois, Indiana, Iowa, Kansas, Kentucky, Louisiana, Michigan, Minnesota, Mississippi, Missouri, Nebraska, North Dakota, Ohio, Oklahoma, South Dakota, Tennessee, Texas, West Virginia, Wisconsin): 230 South Dearborn Street, Suite 2020, Chicago, IL 60604 (312) 353–4990.
Regional Manager.—Brad Merryman.
East Region (Connecticut, Delaware, District of Columbia, Florida, Georgia, Maine, Maryland, Massachusetts, New Hampshire, New Jersey, New York, North Carolina, Pennsylvania,

Rhode Island, South Carolina, Vermont, Virginia, Puerto Rico, U.S. Virgin Islands): 201 Varick Street, Suite 1025, New York, NY 10014 (212) 352–5440.

Regional Manager.—Katrina Bowser (acting).

West Region (Alaska, Arizona, California, Colorado, Hawaii, Idaho, Montana, Nevada, New Mexico, Oregon, Utah, Washington, Wyoming): 1301 Clay Street, Suite 620N, Oakland, CA 94612 (510) 452–8444.

Regional Manager.—Michael McKay.

OFFICE OF SAFETY AND SECURITY

Associate Director.—Shawn Bardwell.

Physical Security Specialist.—John McIntire.

OFFICE OF HEALTH SERVICES

Associate Director.—Jill Carty (acting).

Director of:

Counseling and Outreach.—Brynn Huyssen (acting).

Medical Services.—Alison Colantino.

PENSION BENEFIT GUARANTY CORPORATION

1200 K Street, 20005–4026, (202) 326–4000

BOARD OF DIRECTORS

Chair.—R. Alexander Acosta, Secretary of Labor.

Members:

Steven T. Mnuchin, Secretary of the Treasury.

Wilbur Ross, Secretary of Commerce.

OFFICIALS

Director.—Tom Reeder, 326–4010.

Deputy Chief Policy Officer.—Michael Rae, 326–4010.

Chief Officers for—

Benefits Administration.—Cathy Kronopolus, 326–4000.

Finance.—Patricia Kelly, 326–4170.

General Counsel.—Judith Starr, 326–4020.

Information Technology.—Robert Scherer, 326–4000.

Management.—Alice Maroni, 326–4000.

Negotiations and Restructuring.—Karen Morris, 326–4000.

Department Director for—

Budget.—Edgar Bennett, 326–4000.

Communications Outreach and Public Affairs.—Martha Threatt, 326–3727.

Contracts and Controls Review.—Martin Boehm, 326–4161.

Corporate Finance and Restructuring.—Adi Berger, 326–4000.

Financial Operations.—Theodore Winter, 326–4060.

Human Resources.—Arrie Etheridge, 326–4110.

Information Technology Infrastructure Operations.—Joshua Kossoy, 326–4130.

Business Innovation Services.—Srividhya Shyamsunder, 326–4130.

Policy, Research and Analysis.—Jensen Chan (acting), 326–4000.

Workplace Solutions.—Alisa Cottone, 326–4150.

POSTAL REGULATORY COMMISSION

901 New York Avenue, NW., Suite 200, 20268–0001

phone (202) 789–6800, fax 789–6891

Chair.—Robert Taub, 789–6897.

Vice Chair.—Mark Acton, 789–6866.

Commissioners:

Tony Hammond, 789–6805.

Nanci Langley, 789–6887.

Vacant, 789–6810.
Chief Administrative Officer and Secretary.—Stacy Ruble, 789–6842.
Director, Public Affairs and Government Relations.—Ann Fisher, 789–6803.
General Counsel.—David Trissell, 789–6818.
Director, Office of Accountability and Compliance.—Margaret Cigno, 789–6855.

SECURITIES AND EXCHANGE COMMISSION

100 F Street, NE., 20549, phone (202) 551–7500

TTY Relay Service 1–800–877–8339 http://www.sec.gov

THE COMMISSION

Chair.—Jay Clayton, 551–2100, fax 772–9200.
Chief of Staff.—Lucas Moskowitz.
Deputy Chief of Staff.—Sean Memon.
Chief Counsel.—Jaime Klima.
Senior Advisors to the Chairman: John Cook, Jeffrey Dinwoodie, Raquel Fox, Kristina Littman, Mark Uyeda.
Commissioners:
Robert J. Jackson, Jr., 551–2500, fax 772–9335.
Hester M. Peirce.
Counsel to the Commissioner.—Adam Glazer.
Michael S. Piwowar, 551–2700, fax 772–9330.
Kara M. Stein, 551–2800, fax 772–9340.

OFFICE OF THE SECRETARY

Secretary.—Brent J. Fields, 551–5400.
Deputy Secretaries: Lynn Powalski, 551–5400; Vacant.
Assistant Secretary.—Jill Peterson, 551–5400.

OFFICE OF LEGISLATIVE AND INTERGOVERNMENTAL AFFAIRS

Director.—Timothy Henseler, 551–2010, fax 772–9250.
Deputy Directors: Keith Cassidy, 551–2010; Anne-Marie Kelley, 551–2010.

OFFICE OF THE CHIEF OPERATING OFFICER

Chief Operating Officer.—Jeff Heslop, 551–2200.

OFFICE OF INVESTOR EDUCATION AND ADVOCACY

Director.—Lori J. Schock, 551–6500, fax 772–9295.
Deputy Director.—Mary S. Head, 551–6500.

OFFICE OF SUPPORT OPERATIONS

Director/Chief FOIA Officer.—Barry Walters, 551–8400.
FOIA Officer.—John Livornese, 551–8300, fax 772–9336/9337.

OFFICE OF EQUAL EMPLOYMENT OPPORTUNITY

Director.—Alta Rodriguez, 551–6040, fax 772–9316.

OFFICE OF MINORITY AND WOMEN INCLUSION

Director.—Pamela Gibbs, 551–6046.
Deputy Director.—Laura Stomski, 551–6046.

OFFICE OF THE CHIEF ACCOUNTANT

Chief Accountant.—Wesley R. Bricker, 551–5300, fax 772–9253.

Chief Counsel.—Jeff Minton, 551–5300.

OFFICE OF COMPLIANCE INSPECTIONS AND EXAMINATIONS

Director.—Andrew Bowden, 551–6200, fax 772–9184.
Deputy Director.—Marc Wyatt, 551–6200.
Associate Director/Chief Counsel.—Robert Fisher, 551–6460
Associate Directors: Kevin Goodman (Broker/Dealer); Barbara Lorenzen (Clearance and Settlement); John Polise (Market Oversight); Jane Jarcho (Investment Adviser/Investment Company).

DIVISION OF RISK, STRATEGY, AND FINANCIAL INNOVATION

Director and Chief Economist.—Mark J. Flannery, 551–6600, fax 772–9290.
Deputy Directors.—Scott Bauguess, 551–6600; Jennifer Marietta-Westberg, 551–6600.

OFFICE OF THE GENERAL COUNSEL

General Counsel.—Ann K. Small, 551–5100, fax 772–9260.
Deputy General Counsels: Michael Conley, 551–5100; Meredith Mitchell, 551–5100; Jeffrey Rosenblum, 551–5100.
Associate General Counsel for Litigation and Adjudication.—Laura Jarsulic, 551–5150.
Solicitor, Appellate Litigation and Bankruptcy.—Jacob Stillman, 551–5100.
Deputy Solicitor.—John Avery, 551–5100.
Associate General Counsel for Legal Policy 1.—Vacant, 551–5120.
Associate General Counsel for Legal Policy 2.—Vacant, 551–5120.
Associate General Counsel for Litigation and Administrative Practice: Richard M. Humes, 551–5140; Samuel Forstein; Melinda Hardy.

OFFICE OF ETHICS COUNSEL

Ethics Counsel and Designated Ethics Officer.—Shira Minton, 551–5170.

DIVISION OF INVESTMENT MANAGEMENT

Director.—David Grim 551–6720, fax 772–9234.
Deputy Director.—David Grim, 551–6720.
Associate Director, Chief Counsel.—Douglas J. Scheidt, 551–6720.
Enforcement Liaison.—Janet Grossnickle, 551–6785.
Chief Counsel.—Vacant, 551–6825.
Associate Director, Office of:
Exemptive Application.—Vacant, 551–6821.
Disclosure Review and Accounting.—Vacant, 551–6921.
Insured Investments.—Vacant, 551–6795.
Regulatory Policy and Investment Adviser Regulation.—Vacant.
Rulemaking.—Vacant, 551–6702.
Chief Accountant.—Vacant, 551–6918.
EDGAR Filer Support.—Vacant, 551–6989.
Investment Advisor Regulation Office.—Vacant, 551–6999.
Risk and Examinations Office.—Vacant, 551–6972.
Investment Company Regulation Office.—Vacant, 551–6792.

DIVISION OF CORPORATION FINANCE

Director.—Keith Higgins, 551–3110.
Managing Executive.—Peter Uhlmann, 551–3130.
Deputy Director of Disclosure Operations.—Shelley E. Parratt, 551–3130.
Associate Director Legal.—Elizabeth Murphy, 551–3180.
Policy and Capital Markets.—Vacant.
Associate Director, Regulatory Policy.—Vacant.
Chief Accountant.—Mark Kronforst, 551–3400.
Disclosure Operations: James Daly, 551–3140; Karen Garnett, 551–3032; Cicely LaMothe, 551–3411; Kyle Moffatt, 551–3031; Barry Summer, 551–3160.
Chief Counsel.—David Fredrickson, 551–3500.

DIVISION OF ENFORCEMENT

Director.—Andrew Ceresney, 551–4500, fax 772–9279.
Deputy Director.—Stephanie Avakian, 551–4500.
Managing Executive.—Victor Valdez, 551–4500.
Associate Directors: Antonia Chion, Stephen Cohen, Scott Friestad, Gerald Hodgkins.
Chief, Market Surveillance.—Vincente Martinez, 551–4500.
Chief Counsel.—Joseph Brenner, 551–4500.
Deputy Chiefs Litigation Counsel: Charlotte Buford, 551–4500; Samuel Waldon, 551–4500.
Chief Accountant.—Michael Maloney, 551–4610.
Senior Associate Chief Accountants: Dwayne Brown, Kristen Dieter, David Estabrook, Peter Rosario, 551–4647.
Office of Collections: Gordon Brumback, 551–4500; Marsha Massey, 551–4500.
Office of Whistleblower, Chief.—Sean McKessey, 551–4790.
Trial Unit.—Vacant, 551–4900.

DIVISION OF TRADING AND MARKETS

Director.—Stephen Luparello, 551–5500.
Deputy Directors: Gary Barnett, Gary Goldsholle, 551–5500.
Associate Director, Chief Counsel.—Heather Seidel, 551–5554.
Associate Directors:
Broker Dealer Finances.—Michael Macchiaroli, 551–5889.
Clearance and Settlement.—Peter Curley, 551–5696.
Trading Practices.—Brian Bussey, 551–5799.
Market Supervision.—David Shillman, 551–5600.

OFFICE OF CREDIT RATINGS

Director.—Tom Butler (212) 336–9080.

OFFICE OF MUNICIPAL SECURITIES

Director.—Vacant, 551–5680.

OFFICE OF ADMINISTRATIVE LAW JUDGES

Chief Administrative Law Judge.—Brenda Murray, 551–6030, fax 777–1031.
Administrative Law Judges: Cameron Elliot, Carol Fox Foelak, James Grimes, Jason S. Patil.

OFFICE OF INTERNATIONAL AFFAIRS

Director.—Paul A. Leder, 551–6690.
Deputy Director.—Elizabeth Jacobs, 551–6690.

OFFICE OF THE INVESTOR ADVOCATE

Investor Advocate.—Rick Fleming, 551–3302.

OFFICE OF THE INSPECTOR GENERAL

Inspector General.—Carl Hoecker, 551–6061, fax 772–9265.
Deputy Inspector General for Audits, Evaluations, and Special Projects.—Rebecca Sharek, 551–6061.
Deputy Inspector General for Management Support.—Mary Beth Harrell, 551–6061.
Assistant Inspector General in Investigations.—Vacant, 551–6069.

OFFICE OF PUBLIC AFFAIRS

Director.—John Nester, 551–4120, fax 777–1026.

Deputy Director.—Florence Harmon, 551–4120.

OFFICE OF FINANCIAL MANAGEMENT

Chief Financial Officer.—Kenneth Johnson, 551–7840, fax 756–0473.
Chief Accounting Officer.—Caryn Kauffman, 551–7840.

OFFICE OF INFORMATION TECHNOLOGY

Director/Chief Information Officer.—Pamela Dyson, 551–8800.
Deputy Director/Deputy Chief Information Officer.—Vacant.

OFFICE OF ADMINISTRATIVE SERVICES

Associate Executive Director.—Vance Cathrell, 551–8385, fax (703) 914–4459.

OFFICE OF HUMAN RESOURCES

Director/Chief Human Capital Officer.—Lacey Dingman, 551–7500, fax 777–1028.
Disability Office.—Vacant, 551–7500.
Employee and Labor Relations.—Vacant, 551–7770.
Recruitment, Retention, and Worklife.—Vacant, 551–4100.
SEC University.—Vacant, 551–7328.

REGIONAL OFFICES

Atlanta Regional Office: 950 East Paces Ferry Road, NE., Suite 900, Atlanta, GA 30326 (404) 842–7600, fax 842–7633.
Regional Director.—Walter Jospin.
Associate Regional Director, Enforcement.—William P. Hicks.
Boston Regional Office: 33 Arch Street, 23rd Floor, Boston, MA 02110 (617) 573–8900, fax 573–4590.
Regional Director.—Paul Levenson.
Associate District Director, Enforcement.—John Dugan.
Associate Regional Director, Examinations.—Michael Garrity.
Chicago Regional Office: 175 West Jackson Boulevard, Suite 900, Chicago, IL 60604 (312) 353–7390, fax 353–7398.
Regional Director.—David Glockner.
Associate Regional Director, Enforcement.—Timothy L. Warren.
Associate Regional Directors, Examinations: Steven Levine, Daniel Gregus.
Denver Regional Office: Byron G. Rogers Federal Building, 1961 Stout St., Suite 1700, Denver, CO 80294 (303) 844–1000, fax 844–1010.
Regional Director.—Julie K. Lutz.
Assistant Regional Director.—Christopher Friedman.
Associate Regional Director, Enforcement.—Thomas J. Krysa.
Fort Worth Regional Office: 801 Cherry Street, Unit #18, Fort Worth, TX 76102 (817) 978–3821, fax 978–4096.
Regional Director.—David Woodcock.
Associate Regional Director, Enforcement.—David Peavler.
Regional Trial Counsel.—David Reece.
Associate Regional Director, Examinations.—Marshall Gandy.
Los Angeles Regional Office: 444 South Flower Street, Suite 900, Los Angeles, CA 90071 (323) 965–3998, fax 443–1902.
Regional Director.—Michele Layne.
Associate Regional Directors:
Enforcement: Lorraine Echavarria.
Examinations.—Karol Pollock.
Supervisory Regional Trial Counsel.—John W. Berry.
Miami Regional Office: 801 Brickell Avenue, Suite 1800, Miami, FL 33131 (305) 982–6300, fax 536–4120.
Regional Director.—Eric Bustillo.
Associate Regional Directors:
Enforcement.—Glenn S. Gordon.

Examination.—John C. Mattimore.

New York Regional Office: 200 Vesey Street, Suite 400, New York, NY 10281–1022, (212) 336–1100, fax 336–1323.

Regional Director.—Andrew Calamari.

Associate Regional Directors, Enforcement: Amelia A. Cottrell, David Rosenfeld, Sanjay Wadhwa.

Associate Regional Directors:

Broker/Dealer.—Robert A. Sollazzo.

Investment Management.—Ken Joseph.

Philadelphia Regional Office: One Penn Center, 1617 John F. Kennedy Boulevard, Suite 520, Philadelphia, PA 19103 (215) 597–3100, fax 597–1036.

Regional Director.—Sharon B. Binger.

Associate Regional Directors:

Enforcement.—G. Jeffrey Boujoukos.

Examinations.—Joy G. Thompson.

Salt Lake Regional Office: 351 South West Temple, Suite 6.100, Salt Lake City, UT 84101 (801) 524–5796, fax 524–3558.

Regional Director.—Karen L. Martinez.

San Francisco Regional Office: 44 Montgomery Street, Suite 2800, San Francisco, CA 94104 (415) 705–2500, fax 705–2501.

Regional Director.—Jina L. Choi.

Associate Regional Directors:

Enforcement.—Erin Schneider.

Examinations.—Kristin A. Snyder.

SELECTIVE SERVICE SYSTEM

1515 Wilson Boulevard, 5th Floor, Arlington, VA 22209–2425

phone (703) 605–4100, fax 605–4106, http://www.sss.gov

Director.—Donald M. Benton, 605–4111.

Director for—

Operations.—Adam J. Coop, 605–4111.

Public and Intergovernmental Affairs.—Vacant, 605–4100, fax 605–4106.

Financial Management.—Roderick R. Hubbard, 605–4022.

Registration Information Office, P.O. Box 94638, Palatine, IL 60094–4638, phone (847) 688–6888, fax 688–2860.

SMITHSONIAN INSTITUTION

Smithsonian Institution Building—The Castle (SIB), 1000 Jefferson Drive, SW., 20560

phone (202) 633–1000, http://www.si.edu

The Smithsonian Institution is an independent trust instrumentality created in accordance with the terms of the will of James Smithson of England who in 1826 bequeathed his property to the United States of America "to found at Washington under the name of the Smithsonian Institution an establishment for the increase and diffusion of knowledge among men." Congress pledged the faith of the United States to carry out the trust in 1836 (Act of July 1, 1836, C. 252, 5 Stat. 64), and established the Institution in its present form in 1846 (August 10, 1846, C. 178, 9 Stat. 102), entrusting the management of the institution to its independent Board of Regents.

THE BOARD OF REGENTS

ex officio

Chief Justice of the United States.—John G. Roberts, Jr., Chancellor.

Vice President of the United States.—Mike Pence.

Appointed by the President of the Senate

Hon. Patrick J. Leahy

Hon. David Perdue

Hon. John Boozman

Appointed by the Speaker of the House

Hon. Sam Johnson

Hon. Tom Cole

Hon. Doris Matsui

Appointed by Joint Resolution of Congress

John W. McCarter, Jr.
Shirley Ann Jackson
Robert P. Kogod
David M. Rubenstein
Steve Case
Barbara M. Barrett
John Fahey
Risa J. Lavizzo-Mourey
Michael M. Lynton

Chief of Staff to the Regents.—Porter Wilkinson, 633–8899.

OFFICE OF THE SECRETARY

Secretary.—David J. Skorton, 633–1846.
Chief of Staff.—Greg Bettwy, 633–1869.
Inspector General.—Cathy Helm, 633–7095.
General Counsel.—Judith Leonard, 633–5099.
Director of:
Communications and Public Affairs.—John Lapiana (acting), 633–5190.
External Affairs.—Virginia Clark, 633–5021.
Government Relations.—Maura Reidy (acting), 633–5125.
Assistant Secretary for Education and Access.—Patricia Bartlett, 633–0077.
Smithsonian Affiliations Program.—Harold Closter, 633–5321.
Smithsonian Associates Program.—Frederica Adelman, 633–8628.
Smithsonian Center for Learning and Digital Access.—Stephanie L. Norby, 633–5297.
Smithsonian Institution Traveling Exhibition Service.—Director Myriam Springuel, 633–3136.
Smithsonian Science Education Center.—Carol O'Donnell, 633–2972.

OFFICE OF THE UNDER SECRETARY FOR FINANCE AND ADMINISTRATION

Under Secretary and CFO.—Albert G. Horvath, 633–5240.
Director of:
Accessibility Program.—Elizabeth Ziebarth, 633–2946.
Special Events and Protocol.—Karen Keller, 633–2020.
Director, Office of:
Equal Employment and Minority Affairs.—Era Marshall, 633–6414.
Facilities Engineering and Operations.—Nancy Bechtol, 633–1873.
Human Resources.—James Douglas, 633–6301.
Information Technology and CIO.—Deron Burba, 633–4901.
Ombudsman.—Chandra Heilman, 633–2010.

OFFICE OF THE PROVOST

Provost.—Richard Kurin (acting), 633–5240.
Director of:
Anacostia Community Museum.—Lori Yarrish (acting), 633–4839.
Archives of American Art.—Kate Haw, 633–7969.
Asian Pacific American Program.—Lisa Sasaki, 786–2963.
Center for Folklife and Cultural Heritage.—Michael Mason, 633–6440.
Cooper Hewitt, Smithsonian Design Museum.—Caroline Baumann (212) 849–8320.
Freer and Sackler Galleries.—Julian Raby, 633–0456.
Hirshhorn Museum and Sculpture Garden.—Melissa Chiu, 633–2824.
National Museum of African American History and Culture.—Lonnie Bunch, 633–4751.
National Museum of African Art.—Christine Kreamer (acting), 633–4610.
National Museum of American History.—John L. Gray, 633–3435.
National Museum of the American Indian.—Kevin Gover, 633–6700.
National Portrait Gallery.—Kim Sajet, 275–1740.
National Postal Museum.—Marshall Emery (acting), 633–5500.
Smithsonian American Art Museum.—Stephanie Stebich, 275–1515.
Smithsonian Latino Center.—Eduardo Diaz, 633–1240.
Smithsonian Institution Archives.—Anne Van Camp, 633–5908.
Smithsonian Institution Libraries.—Nancy Gwinn, 633–2240.
Director of:
International Relations.—Molly Fannon, 633–4795.
National Air and Space Museum.—Jack Dailey, 633–2350.
National Museum of Natural History.—Kirk Johnson, 633–2664.
National Zoological Park.—Dennis Kelly, 633–4442.

Office of Sponsored Projects.—Tracey Fraser, 633–3763.
Smithsonian Astrophysical Observatory.—Charles Alcock (617) 495–7100.
Smithsonian Environmental Research Center.—Anson Hines (443) 482–2208.
Smithsonian Museum Conservation Institute.—Robert Koestler (301) 238–1205.
Smithsonian Tropical Research Institute.—Matt Larsen, 011–507–212–8110.

SMITHSONIAN ENTERPRISES

President.—Chris Liedel, 633–5169.
Publisher, Smithsonian Magazine.—Lori Erdos (212) 916–1337.
Editor, Smithsonian Magazine.—Michael Caruso, 633–6072.

SOCIAL SECURITY ADMINISTRATION

Altmeyer Building, 6401 Security Boulevard, Baltimore, MD 21235 (ALTMB)

Annex Building, 6401 Security Boulevard, Baltimore, MD 21235 (ANXB)

East High Rise Building, 6401 Security Boulevard, Baltimore, MD 21235 (EHRB)

International Trade Commission Building, 500 E Street, SW., Washington, DC 20024 (ITCB)

Joseph P. Addabbo Federal Building, 155–10 Jamaica Avenue, Jamaica, NY 11432 (JAFB)

Meadows East Building, 6300 Security Boulevard, Baltimore, MD 21235 (MEB)

National Computer Center, 6201 Security Boulevard, Baltimore, MD 21235 (NCC)

Oak Meadows Building, 6340 Security Boulevard, Baltimore, MD 21235 (OMB)

One Skyline Tower, 5107 Leesburg Pike, Falls Church, VA 22041 (SKY)

Robert M. Ball Building, 6401 Security Boulevard, Baltimore, MD 21235 (RMBB)

Rolling Road Commerce Center, 2709 Rolling Road, Baltimore, MD 21244 (RRCC)

Security West Tower, 1500 Woodlawn Drive, Baltimore, MD 21241 (SWTB)

West High Rise Building, 6401 Security Boulevard, Baltimore, MD 21235 (WHRB)

West Low Rise Building, 6401 Security Boulevard, Baltimore, MD 21235 (WLRB)

http://www.socialsecurity.gov

OFFICE OF THE COMMISSIONER

Commissioner.—Vacant, ALTMB, Suite 900 (410) 965–3995 or ITCB, Room 850 (202) 358–6000.
Deputy Commissioner.—Vacant.
Chief of Staff.—Beatrice Disman (acting), ALTMB, Suite 900 (410) 965–0386 or ITCB, Room 858 (202) 358–6000.
Deputy Chief of Staff.—Stephanie Hall (acting), ALTMB, Suite 900 (410) 965–9704 or ITCB, Room 861 (202) 358–6000.
Executive Counselor to the Commissioner.—Frank Cristaudo, ALTMB, Suite 960 (410) 965–4991.
Executive Secretary.—Darlyanda K. Bogle, ALTMB, Suite 960 (410) 966–3609.

OFFICE OF THE CHIEF ACTUARY

Chief Actuary.—Stephen C. Goss, ALTMB, Room 700 (410) 965–3000.
Deputy Chief Actuary for—
Long Range.—Karen P. Glenn, ALTMB, Room 700 (410) 965–3002.
Short Range.—Eli N. Donkar, ALTMB, Room 760 (410) 965–3004.

OFFICE OF THE CHIEF STRATEGIC OFFICER

Chief Strategic Officer/Performance Improvement Officer.—Joe Lopez (acting), ALTMB, Suite 860 (410) 965–5075.

Deputy Chief Strategic Officer/Performance Improvement Officer.—Alan Lane (acting), ALTMB, Suite 860 (410) 965–4331.

Director, Office of:

Performance Management and Business Analytics.—Avis Payne, ALTMB, Suite 571 (410) 965–2518.

Strategic Planning and Innovation.—Steven Knight, Jr., ALTMB, Suite 571 (410) 965–5522.

Executive Director, Office of Open Government.—Alan Lane, WHRB, Suite 1126 (410) 965–4331.

OFFICE OF COMMUNICATIONS

Deputy Commissioner.—Jim Borland (acting), ALTMB, Room 460 (410) 966–2030.

Assistant Deputy Commissioner.—Jim Borland, ALTMB, Room 460 (410) 966–2030.

Associate Commissioner, Office of:

Communications Planning and Technology.—Jeffrey Buckner (acting), ANXB, Room 3165 (410) 965–5865.

External Affairs.—Maria Artista-Cuchna (acting), ANXB, Room 3505 (410) 965–1804.

Public Inquiries.—Steven L. Patrick, WHRB, Room 1100 (410) 965–0709.

Press Officer.—Mark Hinkle (acting), ALTMB, Room 446 (410) 965–8904.

OFFICE OF DISABILITY ADJUDICATION AND REVIEW

Deputy Commissioner.—Theresa Gruber, ALTMB, Suite 560 (410) 965–6006, or SKY, Suite 1600 (709) 605–8200.

Assistant Deputy Commissioner.—Donna Calvert, ALTMB, Suite 560 (410) 965–6006, or SKY, Suite 1600 (703) 605–8200.

Executive Director, Office of Appellate Operations.—Kelly Salzmann (acting), SKY, Suite 1400 (703) 605–7100.

Chief Administrative Law Judge.—Patrick Nagle, SKY, Suite 1608 (703) 605–8500.

Associate Commissioner, Office of:

Budget, Facilities and Security.—Dean Landis, ALTMB, Room 560 (410) 965–6006.

Electronic Services and Strategic Information.—Nancy Webb, ALTMB, Room 540 (410) 965–6006 or SKY, Suite 1509 (703) 605–8970.

Executive Operations and Human Resources.—Robert Jandrlich, ALTMB, Room 528 (410) 965–6006 or SKY, Suite 1700 (703) 605–8700.

Regional Chief Administrative Law Judges:

Atlanta.—Joan Parks Saunders (acting), 61 Forsyth Street, SW., Suite 20T10, Atlanta, GA 30303 (404) 562–1182.

Boston.—Aaron Morgan, 10 Causeway Street, Suite 565, Boston, MA 02222 (888) 870–7578.

Chicago.—Sherry Thompson, 200 West Adams Street, Suite 2901, Chicago, IL 60606 (877) 800–7576.

Dallas.—Joan Parks Saunders, 1301 Young Street, Suite 460, Dallas, TX 75202 (214) 767–9401.

Denver.—Nicholas J. LoBurgio, 1244 North Speer Boulevard, Suite 600, Denver, CO 80204 (888) 397–9803.

Kansas City.—Sherianne Laba, 1100 Main Street, Suite 1700, Kansas City, MO 64105 (888) 238–7975.

New York.—Aaron Morgan, 26 Federal Plaza, Room 34–102, New York, NY 10278 (212) 264–4036.

Philadelphia.—Tamara Turner-Jones, 300 Spring Garden Street, 4th Floor, Philadelphia, PA 19123 (215) 597–9980.

San Francisco.—Jennifer Horne, 555 Battery Street, 5th Floor, San Francisco, CA 94111 (866) 964–7584.

Seattle.—John Rolph (acting), 701 5th Avenue, Suite 2900 M/S 904, Seattle, WA 98104 (206) 615–2236.

OFFICE OF RETIREMENT AND DISABILITY POLICY

Deputy Commissioner.—Marianna LaCanfora (acting), ALTMB, Room 100 (410) 965–5514.

Assistant Deputy Commissioner.—Marianna LaCanfora, ALTMB, Room 100 (410) 965–5514.

Associate Commissioner, Office of:

Data Exchange and Policy Publications.—Stephen Evangelista, ANXB, Room 4701 (410) 965–6522.
Disability Programs.—Gina Clemmons, ANXB, Room 4555 (410) 966–9897.
Income Security Programs.—Samara Richardson, RMBB, Room 2607 (410) 966–5856.
International Programs.—Vance N. Teel, RMBB, Room 3718 (410) 965–9800.
Research, Demonstration, and Employment Support.—Susan Wilschke, ALTMB, Room 128 (410) 966–8906.
Research, Evaluation, and Statistics.—John Phillips, MEB, Room 4700–C (410) 965–2841 or ITCB, Room 828 (202) 358–6020.
Retirement Policy.—Natalie Lu, ALTMB, Room 118 (410) 965–3327.

OFFICE OF BUDGET, FINANCE, QUALITY, AND MANAGEMENT

Deputy Commissioner.—Michelle A. King, ALTMB, Room 800 (410) 965–7748.
Assistant Deputy Commissioners.—Kate Hickman, ALTMB, Room 800 (410) 966–5325; Sean Brune, ALTMB, Room 800 (410) 966–2762.
Associate Commissioner, Office of:
Acquisition and Grants.—Seth P. Binstock, RMBB, Room 1540, (410) 965–9538.
Anti-Fraud Programs.—Rafael Moya, RMBB, Room 1513 (410) 965–4857.
Budget.—Bonnie Kind, WHRB, Room 2126 (410) 965–3501.
Facilities and Supply Management.—Chris Molander, RMBB, Room 2710 (410) 965–7401.
Financial Policy and Operations.—Carla A. Krabbe, EHRB, Room 2154 (410) 965–0759.
Quality Improvement.—Daryl Wise, EHRB, Room 4138 (410) 965–4557.
Quality Review.—Vera Bostick Borden, JAFB (718) 557–5346.
Security and Emergency Preparedness.—Jonas M. Garland, ALTMB, Room G–25 (410) 965–6660.
Senior Advisors, Audit Liaison Staff.—Gary Hatcher, ALTMB, Room 814 (410) 965–0680; Regina B. Smith, ALTMB, Room 820 (410) 966–9423.
Director, Systems Support Staff.—Jim Guidry, EHRB, Room 5139 (410) 965–9794.

OFFICE OF THE GENERAL COUNSEL

General Counsel.—Patricia Jonas (acting), ALTMB, Suite 600 (410) 965–0600.
Deputy General Counsel.—Daniel F. Callahan, ALTMB, Suite 600 (410) 965–0644.
Associate General Counsel for—
General Law.—Mitchell Chitwood, WHRB, Room G300 (410) 965–4660.
Program Law.—Jeffrey C. Blair, ALTMB, Room 624 (410) 965–3157.
Executive Director, Office of Privacy and Disclosure.—Glenn Sklar (acting), WHRB, Room G400–F (410) 965–6247.
Regional Chief Counsels for—
Atlanta.—Mary Ann Sloan, Atlanta Federal Center, 61 Forsyth Street, SW., Suite 20T45, Atlanta, GA 30303 (404) 562–1010.
Boston.—Michael Pelgro, JFK Federal Building, 15 New Sudbury Street, Room 625, Boston, MA 02203 (617) 565–1844.
Chicago.—Kathryn Caldwell, 200 West Adams Street, 30th Floor, Chicago, IL 60606 (877) 800–7578, ext. 19110.
Dallas.—Traci Davis (acting), 1301 Young Street, Room A–702, Dallas, TX 75202–5433 (214) 767–3462.
Denver.—John J. Lee, 1961 Stout Street, Suite 4169, Denver, CO 80294 (303) 844–0013.
Kansas City.—Lisa Thomas (acting), Richard Bolling Federal Building, 601 East 12th Street, Room 965, Federal Office Building, Kansas City, MO 64106 (816) 936–5754.
New York.—Stephen P. Conte, 26 Federal Plaza, Suite 3904, New York, NY 12078 (212) 264–2216.
Philadelphia.—Nora Koch, 300 Spring Garden Street, 6th Floor, Philadelphia, PA 19123 (215) 597–4642.
San Francisco.—Deborah Stachel (acting), 160 Spear Street, Suite 800, San Francisco, CA 94105 (415) 977–8968.
Seattle.—Mathew Pile (acting), 701 Fifth Avenue, Columbia Tower, Suite 2900, M/S 221A, Seattle, WA 98104 (206) 615–3760.

OFFICE OF HUMAN RESOURCES

Deputy Commissioner.—Dr. Reginald F. Wells, ALTMB, Suite 200 (410) 965–1900.

Assistant Deputy Commissioner.—Tina Waddell, ALTMB, Suite 200 (410) 965–5215.
Associate Commissioner, Office of:
Civil Rights and Equal Opportunity.—Kojuan L. Almond, WHRB, Room 3350 (410) 965–4531.
Labor Management and Employee Relations.—Ralph Patinella, ANXB, Room 2170 (410) 966–7860.
Learning.—Laura Train, EHRB, Room 100 (410) 966–9223.
Personnel.—Lydia Marshall, ANXB, Room 2570 (410) 966–9916.
Director for—
Diversity and Inclusion.—Sean Boston, ANXB, Room 2249 (410) 965–0217.
Executive and Special Services.—Bonnie L. Doyle, ANXB, Room 2510 (410) 965–4463.
Human Capital Management.—Kecia S. Rome (acting), ANXB, Room 2242 (410) 965–3390.
Information Technology for Human Resources.—David R. Bacon, EHRB, Room G–140 (410) 594–2099.

OFFICE OF THE INSPECTOR GENERAL

Inspector General.—Gale Stallworth Stone (acting), ALTMB, Suite 300 (410) 966–8385.
Deputy Inspector General.—Gale Stallworth Stone, ALTMB, Suite 300 (410) 966–8385.
Chief of Staff.—Steve Schaeffer, ALTMB, Suite 300 (410) 966–8385.
Counsel to the Inspector General.—Joe Gangloff, MEB, Room 3–ME–1 (410) 965–6263.
Assistant Inspector General for—
Audit.—Rona Lawson, MEB, Room 3–ME–2 (410) 965–8701.
Investigations.—Michael D. Robinson, MEB, Room 3–ME–3 (410) 966–8523.
Office of Communications and Resource Management.—Kelly Bloyer, MEB, Room 2–ME–4 (410) 965–4866.

OFFICE OF LEGISLATION AND CONGRESSIONAL AFFAIRS

Deputy Commissioner.—Royce Min (acting), ITCB, Room 819 (202) 358–6030, or ALTMB, Room 500–C (410) 965–4511.
Assistant Deputy Commissioner.—Royce Min, ITCB, Room 819 (202) 358–6030 or ALTMB, Room 500–C (410) 965–4511.
Associate Commissioner, Office of:
Congressional Affairs.—Suzanne Payne, ITCB, Room 818 (202) 358–6046.
Legislative Development and Operations.—Erik Hansen, WHRB, Room 3103–A (410) 965–3112.
Director for—
Disability Insurance.—Nitin Jagdish (acting), WHRB, Room 3109 (410) 965–2649.
Immigration, Data Exchange and Enumeration.—Elizabeth Tino, WHRB, Room 3104 (410) 965–2871.
Legislative and Constituent Services Staff.—Robert J. Forrester, WHRB, Room 3105 (410) 966–6706.
Program Administration and Financing Staff.—Perry Cocke (acting), WHRB, Room 3107 (410) 965–4725.
Regulations and Reports Clearance.—Faye Lipsky, ALTMB, Room 152 (410) 965–8783.
Retirement and Survivors Insurance Benefits.—Susan Bussman, WHRB, Room 3102 (410) 965–3313.

OFFICE OF OPERATIONS

Deputy Commissioner.—Mary Horne (acting), WHRB, Room 1204 (410) 965–3145.
Assistant Deputy Commissioner.—Erik Jones, WHRB, Room 1204 (410) 965–0130.
Associate Commissioner, Office of:
Central Operations.—Jan Foushee, SWTB, Room 7000 (410) 966–7000.
Customer Service.—Cynthia Bennett, ANXB, Room 4845 (410) 965–7507.
Disability Determinations.—John Owen, ANXB, Room 3570 (410) 966–6111.
Electronic Services and Technology.—Robin Sabatino, ANXB, Room 4705 (410) 965–9885.
Public Service and Operations Support.—Janet Walker, ANXB, Room 1540 (410) 965–4599.
Regional Commissioner for—
Atlanta.—Rose Mary Buehler, 61 Forsyth Street, Suite 23T30, Atlanta, GA 30303 (404) 562–5600.

Boston.—Linda M. Dorn, JFK Federal Building, 15 New Sudbury Street, Room 1900, Boston, MA 02203 (617) 565–2870.

Chicago.—Phyllis Smith (acting), Harold Washington Social Security Center, 600 West Madison Street, Chicago, IL 60661 (312) 575–5914.

Dallas.—Sheila Everett, 1301 Young Street, Suite 130, Dallas, TX 75202–5433 (214) 767–4207.

Denver.—Stanley C. Friendship, Federal Office Building, 1961 Stout Street, Suite 07–115, Denver, CO 80294 (206) 615–2100.

Kansas City.—Mike Kramer, Federal Office Building, 601 East 12th Street, Room 1016, Kansas City, MO 64106 (816) 936–5700.

New York.—Fred Maurin, 26 Federal Plaza, Room 40–102, New York, NY 10278 (212) 264–3915.

Philadelphia.—Terry M. Stradtman, 300 Spring Garden Street, Philadelphia, PA 19123 (215) 597–5157.

San Francisco.—Grace Kim, 1221 Nevin Avenue, Richmond, CA 94801 (510) 970–8400.

Seattle.—Stanley C. Friendship, 701 5th Avenue, Seattle, Suite 2900, M/S 301, WA 98104–7075 (206) 615–2100.

OFFICE OF SYSTEMS / OFFICE OF THE CHIEF INFORMATION OFFICER

Deputy Commissioner and Chief Information Officer.—Robert Klopp, ALTMB, Room 400 (410) 965–8399.

Assistant Deputy Commissioner and Deputy Chief Information Officer.—Herb Strauss, ALTMB, Room 400 (410) 965–0710.

Assistant Deputy Commissioner for IT Business Support.—Sylviane Haldiman, ALTMB, Room 400 (410) 966–8040.

Assistant Deputy Commissioner for Software Engineering.—Diana Andrews, ALTMB, Room 420 (410) 965–7641.

Assistant Deputy Commissioner for Systems Operations and Hardware Engineering.—Tom Grzymski, ALTMB, Room 400 (410) 965–7626.

Chief Technology Officer.—John Morenz, ALTMB, Room 405 (410) 966–4205.

Associate Commissioner, Office of:

Benefit Information Systems.—John Simermeyer, RMBB, Room 4700 (410) 965–5789.

Disability Information Systems.—Rachel Dumser, RMBB, Room 3606 (410) 965–6398.

Enterprise Information Systems.—Frank Sotaski, RMBB, Room 2100 (410) 965–6546.

Hardware Engineering.—Dave Thomas, NCC, Room 550 (410) 965–1500.

Information Security.—Marti Eckert, ANXB, Room 3100 (410) 965–0445.

IT Enterprise Business Support.—Ann Amrhein, RMBB, Room 3100 (410) 965–9019.

IT Financial Management and Support.—Christopher Barrett, RMBB, Room 3111 (410) 965–2815.

IT Programmatic Business Support.—William Martinez, RMBB, Room 3003 (410) 965–5122.

Systems Architecture.—Dan Parry, RMBB, Room 4100 (410) 966–0778.

Systems Operations.—Tom Fellona, NCC, Room 440 (410) 965–4090.

STATE JUSTICE INSTITUTE

11951 Freedom Drive, Suite 1020, Reston, VA 20190, phone (571) 313–8843

http://www.sji.gov

BOARD OF DIRECTORS

Chair.—Chase T. Rogers.
Vice Chair.—Daniel J. Becker.
Secretary.—Gayle A. Nachtigal.
Treasurer.—John B. Nalbandian.

Members:

Jonathan Lippman.
David V. Brewer.
Wilfredo Martinez.
Marsha J. Rabiteau.
Hernan D. Vera.
Isabel Framer.

Officer:

Executive Director.—Jonathan D. Mattiello.

SUSQUEHANNA RIVER BASIN COMMISSION

COMMISSIONERS AND ALTERNATES

Federal Government:
Commissioner.—BG William H. Graham.
Alternate.—COL Edward P. Chamberlayne.
2nd Alternate.—Amy M. Guise.

New York:
Commissioner.—Basil Seggos.
Alternate.—James M. Tierney.
2nd Alternate.—Paul D'Amato.
3rd Alternate.—Scott Foti.

Pennsylvania:
Commissioner.—Patrick McDonnell.
Alternate.—Lisa Daniels.
2nd Alternate.—Jen Orr.

Maryland:
Commissioner.—Ben Grumbles.
Alternate.—Saeid Kasraei.
2nd Alternate.—Virginia Kearney.

STAFF

4423 North Front Street, Harrisburg, PA 17110, phone (717) 238–0423

srbc@srbc.net, http://www.srbc.net

Executive Director.—Andrew D. Dehoff.
Deputy Executive Director.—Andrew G. Gavin.
Director of Administration and Finance.—Marcia E. Rynearson.
Secretary to the Commission.—Stephanie L. Richardson.

TENNESSEE VALLEY AUTHORITY

500 North Capitol Street, NW., Suite 220, Washington, DC 20001 (202) 898–2999

400 West Summit Hill Drive, Knoxville, TN 37902 (865) 632–2101

1101 Market Street, Chattanooga, TN 37402 (423) 751–0011

BOARD OF DIRECTORS

Chair.—Richard C. Howorth.
Directors: Kenneth E. Allen, A. D. Frazier, Virginia S. Lodge, Eric M. Satz, Jeff W. Smith, James R. Thompson III, Ronald A. Walter.

EXECUTIVE OFFICERS

President and Chief Executive Officer.—William D. Johnson (865) 632–2366.
Executive Vice Presidents:
Chief External Relations Officer.—Van M. Wardlaw (423) 751–2555.
Chief Financial Officer.—John M. Thomas III, 751–8919.
Generation.—Joe Patrick Grimes, 751–8682.
Operations.—Michael D. Skaggs (865) 632–6503.
General Counsel.—Sherry A. Quirk (865) 632–4131.
Senior Vice Presidents:
Chief Communications and Marketing Officer.—Janet J. Brewer (865) 632–7435.
Chief Human Resources Officer.—Susan E. Collins (423) 751–8584.

WASHINGTON OFFICE

Director, Federal Government Relations.—Nick Pearson (202) 898–2999, fax: 898–2998.

U.S. ADVISORY COMMISSION ON PUBLIC DIPLOMACY

301 4th Street, SW., SA–44, M–04, 20547

phone (202) 203–7386, fax 203–7886

[Created by Executive Order 12048 and Public Law 96–60]

Chair.—William J. Hybl.
Members: Vice-Chair, Sim Farar; Vice-Chair, Amb. Lyndon Olson, Jr.; Amb. Penne K. Peacock; Anne Terman Wedner; Lezlee Westine.
Executive Director.—Katherine Brown.

U.S. AGENCY FOR INTERNATIONAL DEVELOPMENT

1300 Pennsylvania Avenue, NW., 20523, phone (202) 712–0000

http://www.usaid.gov

Administrator.—Mark A. Green, Room 6.09, 712–4040, fax 216–3445.
Deputy Administrator.—Vacant, Room 6.09, 712–4040, fax 216–3445.
Counselor.—Tom Staal, Room 6.08, 712–5010.
Executive Secretary.—Neilesh Shelat, Room 6.08–032, 712–0700.
Assistant Administrator for—
Africa.—Cheryl Anderson (acting), Room 4.08–031, 712–0500.
Asia.—Gloria Steele, Senior Deputy Assistant Administrator, Room 4.09, 712–1573.
Democracy, Conflict and Humanitarian Assistance.—Karen Freeman, Senior Deputy Assistant Administrator, Room 8.06–084, 712–0100.
Economic Growth, Education and Environment.—Michelle Bekkering, Senior Deputy Assistant Administrator, Room 3.09–008, 712–0670.
Europe and Eurasia.—Brock Bierman, Room 5.06, 567–4001.
Global Health.—Irene Koek, Senior Deputy Assistant Administrator, Room 3.06, 712–4120.
Latin America and the Caribbean.—Sarah-Ann Lynch, Senior Deputy Assistant Administrator, Room 5.09–012, 712–4800.
Legislative and Public Affairs.—Brynn Barnett, Senior Deputy Assistant Administrator, Room 6.10–107, 712–4300.
Management.—Angelique Crumbly (acting), Room 6.08, 712–1200.
Middle East.—Maria Longi, Senior Deputy Assistant Administrator, Room 4.09–005 (202) 567–4020.
Director, Office of:
Security.—John Voorhees, Room 2.06, 712–0990.
Small and Disadvantaged Business Utilization.—Mauricio Vera, Room 848–E, 567–4735, SA–44.
General Counsel.—David H. Moore, Room 6.06–125, 712–0900.
Inspector General.—Ann Calvaresi Barr, Room 6.06D, 712–1150.

U.S. COMMISSION ON CIVIL RIGHTS

1331 Pennsylvania Avenue, NW., Suite 1150, 20425

phone (202) 376–8591, fax 376–7672

(Codified in 42 U.S.C., section 1975)

Chair.—Catherine E. Lhamon.
Vice Chair.—Patricia Timmons-Goodson.
Commissioners: Roberta Achtenberg, Gail Heriot, Peter N. Kirsanow, David Kladney, Karen Narasaki, Michael Yaki.
Staff Director.—Mauro A. Morales.

U.S. ELECTION ASSISTANCE COMMISSION

1335 East-West Highway, Suite 4300, Silver Spring, MD 20910

phone (301) 563–3919, (866) 747–1471, fax (301) 734–3108, http://www.eac.gov

[Created by Public Law 107–252]

Commissioners:

Thomas Hicks.
Matthew Masterson.
Christy McCormick.
Vacant.

OFFICE OF THE EXECUTIVE DIRECTOR

Executive Director.—Brian Newby (301) 563–3919.
Chief Financial Officer.—Annette Lafferty.

OFFICE OF THE GENERAL COUNSEL

General Counsel.—Cliff Tatum, 563–3919.

OFFICE OF NATIONAL CLEARINGHOUSE ON ELECTIONS

Director of National Clearinghouse on Elections.—Bryan Whitener, 563–3919.

OFFICE OF THE INSPECTOR GENERAL

Inspector General.—Patricia Layfield (301) 734–3104.

U.S. HOLOCAUST MEMORIAL COUNCIL

The United States Holocaust Memorial Museum

100 Raoul Wallenberg Place, SW., 20024, phone (202) 488–0400

fax (202) 314–7881

Officials:
Chair.—Howard M. Lorber, New York, NY.
Vice Chair.—Allan M. Holt, Washington, DC.
Director.—Sara J. Bloomfield, Washington, DC.

Members:
Walter Ray Allen, Jr., Coral Gables, FL.
Lawrence M. Baer, San Francisco, CA.
Daniel Benjamin, Hanover, NH.
Tom A. Bernstein, New York, NY.
Elisa Spungen Bildner, Montclair, NJ.
Joshua B. Bolten, Washington, DC.
Michael S. Bosworth, New York, NY.
Ethel C. Brooks, Metuchen, NJ.
Lee T. Bycel, Kensington, CA.
Sara Darehshori, New York, NY.
Shefali Razdan Duggal, San Francisco, CA.
Norman L. Eisen, Washington, DC.
Lee A. Feinstein, Bloomington, IN.
Raffi M. Freedman-Gurspan, Washington, DC.
Jordan T. Goodman, Chicago, IL.
Samuel N. Gordon, Wilmette, IL.
Grant T. Harris, Davis, CA.
Sarah K. Hurwitz, Washington, DC.
Pricilla Levine Kersten, Chicago, IL.
Howard Konar, West Henrietta, NY.
Jonathan S. Lavine, Boston, MA.
Edward P. Lazarus, Bethesda, MD.
Alan B. Lazowski, Hartford, CT.
Stuart A. Levey, London, England.
Eric A. LeVine, Seattle, WA.
Susan G. Levine, Paradise Valley, AZ.
Susan E. Lowenberg, San Francisco, CA.
David M. Marchick, Washington, DC.
Leslie Meyers, Tel Aviv, Israel.
Tamar Newberger, Chicago, IL.
Deborah A. Oppenheimer, Los Angeles, CA.
Eric P. Ortner, Los Angeles, CA.
Dana M. Perlman, Beverly Hills, CA.
Michael P. Polsky, Chicago, IL.
Michael H. Posner, New York, NY.
Richard S. Price, Chicago, IL.
Ronald Ratner, Cleveland, OH.
Benjamin J. Rhodes, Washington, DC.
Melissa Rogers, Falls Church, VA.
Daniel J. Rosen, New York, NY.
Menachem Z. Rosensaft, New York, NY.
Michael P. Ross, Boston, MA.
Elliot J. Schrage, Menlo Park, CA.
Maureen Schulman, Chicago, IL.
Irvin N. Shapell, Wheeling, WV.
Cindy Simon Skjodt, Carmel, IN.
Scott Straus, Madison, WI.
Michéle Taylor, Atlanta, GA.
Howard D. Unger, Briarcliff Manor, NY.
Clemantine Wamariya, San Francisco,

CA.Andrew J. Weinstein, Coral Springs, FL.
Jeremy M. Weinstein, Stanford, CA.
Daniel G. Weiss, Los Angeles, CA.

Congressional Members:

U.S. House of Representatives:
Theodore E. Deutch, of Florida.
David Kustoff, of Tennessee.
Ileana Ros-Lehtinen, of Florida.
Bradley Scott Schneider, of Illinois.
Lee M. Zeldin, of New York.

U.S. Senate:
Orrin G. Hatch, of Utah.
Marco Rubio, of Florida.
BERNARD SANDERS, of Vermont.
Tim Scott, of South Carolina.

Ex Officio Members:
U.S. Department of:
Education.—Philip H. Rosenfelt.
Interior.—Vacant.
State.—Thomas K. Yazdgerdi.

Council Staff:
General Counsel.—Gerard Leval.
Secretary of the Council.—Jessica Viggiano.

Former Chairs:
Tom A. Bernstein, 2010–2017.
Fred S. Zeidman, 2002–2010.
Irving Greenberg, 2000–2002.
*Miles Lerman, 1993–2000.
Harvey M. Meyerhoff, 1987–1993.
*Elie Wiesel, 1980–1986.

Fomer Vice Chairs:
Joshua B. Bolten, 2010–2015.
Joel M. Geiderman, 2005–2010.
Ruth B. Mandel, 1993–2005.
*William J. Lowenberg, 1986–1993.
Mark E. Talisman, 1980–1986.

**Deceased*

U.S. INSTITUTE OF PEACE

2301 Constitution Avenue, NW., 20037

phone (202) 457–1700, fax 429–6063

BOARD OF DIRECTORS

Public Members:
Chair.—Stephen J. Hadley.
Vice Chair.—George E. Moose.
Members:
Judith A. Ansley
Eric E. Edelman
Joseph T. Eldridge
Kerry Kennedy
Ikram U. Khan
Stephen D. Krasner
John A. Lancaster
Jeremy A. Rabkin
J. Robinson West
Nancy M. Zirkin
Ex Officio:
Department of Defense.—Secretary Jim Mattis (or his Senate-confirmed designee).
Department of State.—Deputy Secretary John J. Sullivan.
National Defense University.—Vice Admiral Fritz Roegge, USN.
United States Institute of Peace.—President Nancy Lindborg (non-voting).
Officials:
President.—Nancy Lindborg.
Executive Vice President.—William B. Taylor.
Vice President for External Relations.—Diane Zeleny.
Congressional Relations.—Anne Hingeley.
Communications—Shai Korman.

U.S. INTERNATIONAL TRADE COMMISSION

500 E Street, SW., 20436

phone (202) 205–2000, fax 205–2798, http://www.usitc.gov

COMMISSIONERS

Chair.—Rhonda K. Schmidtlein.
Vice Chair.—David S. Johanson.
Commissioners:
Jason Kearns.

Vacant.
Vacant.
Director, Office of External Relations/Executive Liaison.—Martha Lawless (acting), 205–3141.
Congressional Relations Officer.—Laura Bloodgood (acting), 205–3151.
Public Affairs Officer.—Margaret O'Laughlin.
General Counsel.—Dominic Bianchi.
Secretary to the Commission.—Lisa Barton.
Inspector General.—Philip M. Heneghan.
Director, Office of:
Operations.—Catherine DeFilippo.
Economics.—William Powers.
Industries.—Jonathan Coleman.
Tariff Affairs and Trade Agreements.—James Holbein.

U.S. MERIT SYSTEMS PROTECTION BOARD

1615 M Street, NW., 20419

phone (202) 653–7200, toll-free (800) 209–8960, fax 653–7130

[Created by Public Law 95–454]

Chair.—Mark A. Robbins (acting).
Vice Chair.—Mark A. Robbins.
Member.—Vacant.
Executive Director.—James M. Eisenmann.
General Counsel.—Vacant.
Deputy General Counsel.—Katherine Smith.
Appeals Counsel.—Susan Swafford.
Legislative Counsel.—Rosalyn L. Coates, 653–7171.
Clerk of the Board.—Jennifer Everling (acting), 653–7200.

REGIONAL OFFICES

Regional Directors:

Atlanta Regional Office: Covering Alabama, Florida, Georgia, Mississippi, South Carolina, Tennessee.—Thomas J. Lanphear, 401 West Peachtree Street, NW., 10th Floor, Atlanta, GA 30308–3519 (404) 730–2751, fax 730–2767.

Central Regional Office: Covering Illinois, Iowa, Kansas City, Kansas, Kentucky, Indiana, Michigan, Minnesota, Missouri, Ohio, Wisconsin.—Michele Schroeder, 230 South Dearborn Street, 31st Floor, Chicago, IL 60604–1669 (312) 353–2923, fax 886–4231.

Dallas Regional Office: Covering Arkansas, Louisiana, Oklahoma, Texas.—Laura Albornoz, 1100 Commerce Street, Room 620, Dallas, TX 75242–9979 (214) 767–0555, fax 767–0102.

Northeastern Regional Office: Covering Connecticut, Delaware, Maine, Maryland (except Montgomery and Prince Georges counties), Massachusetts, New Hampshire, New Jersey (except the counties of Bergen, Essex, Hudson, and Union), Pennsylvania, Rhode Island, Vermont, West Virginia.—William L. Boulden, 1601 Market Street, Suite 1700, Philadelphia, PA 19103–2310 (215) 597–9960, fax 597–3456.

Western Regional Office: Covering Alaska, California, Hawaii, Idaho, Nevada, Oregon, Washington, and Pacific Overseas.—Sara Snyder, 1301 Clay Street, Suite 1380N, Oakland, CA 94612–5217 (510) 273–7022, fax 273–7136.

Washington Regional Office: Covering Washington, DC, Maryland (counties of Montgomery and Prince Georges), North Carolina, Virginia, all overseas areas not otherwise covered.—Jeremiah Cassidy, 1811 Diagonal Road, Suite 205, Alexandria, VA 22314–2840 (703) 756–6250, fax 756–7112.

New York Field Office: Covering New York, Puerto Rico, Virgin Islands, the following counties in New Jersey: Bergen, Essex, Hudson, Union.—Arthur Joseph, Chief Administrative Judge, 26 Federal Plaza, Room 3137–A, New York, NY 10278–0022 (212) 264–9372, fax 264–1417.

Denver Field Office: Covering Arizona, Colorado, Kansas (except Kansas City), Montana, Nebraska, New Mexico, North Dakota, South Dakota, Utah, Wyoming.—Stephen Mish, Chief Administrative Judge, 165 South Union Boulevard, Suite 318, Lakewood, CO 80228–2211 (303) 969–5101, fax 969–5109.

U.S. OVERSEAS PRIVATE INVESTMENT CORPORATION

1100 New York Avenue, NW., 20527, phone (202) 336–8400

President and CEO.—Ray W. Washburne.
Executive Vice President.—David Bohigian.
Chief of Staff.—Douglas Sellers (acting).
Vice President and General Counsel.—William Doffermyre.
Vice President, Investment Funds.—Lynn Nguyen (acting).
Vice President, Office of Investment Policy.—Ryan Brennan.
Managing Director for Global Women's Initiatives.—Kathryn C. Kaufman.
Vice President, Office of External Affairs.—Edward A. Burrier.
Vice Presidents:
Small and Medium Enterprise Finance.—James Polan.
Structured Finance and Insurance.—Tracey Webb.
Human Resources Management.—Dr. Paula Molloy.
Financial and Portfolio Management.—Mildred Callear.
Department of Management and Administration.—Michele Perez.
Special Assistant for Congressional and Intergovernmental Affairs.—James W. Morrison.

BOARD OF DIRECTORS

Government Directors:
R. Alexander Acosta, Secretary, U.S. Department of Labor.
Ambassador Mark Green, Administrator, U.S. Agency for International Development.
Ambassador Robert E. Lighthizer, U.S. Trade Representative.
David R. Malpass, Under Secretary for International Affairs, U.S. Department of the Treasury.
Wilbur L. Ross, Jr., Secretary, U.S. Department of Commerce.
John J. Sullivan, Deputy Secretary, U.S. Department of State.
Ray W. Washburne, President and Chief Executive Officer, OPIC.
Private Sector Directors:
James Demers, President, Demers and Blaisdell, Inc.
Todd Fisher, CAO, Kohlberg Kravis Roberts & Co.
Roberto Herencia, President and CEO, BXM Holdings, Inc.
Matthew Maxwell Taylor Kennedy, Director, Kennedy Enterprises.
Terry Lewis, Principal, LIA Advisors, LLC.
Deven Parekh, Managing Director, Insight Venture Partners.
Michael J. Warren, Principal, Albright Stonebridge Group, LLC.

U.S. POSTAL SERVICE

475 L'Enfant Plaza, SW., 20260–0010, phone (202) 268–2000

BOARD OF GOVERNORS

Postmaster General and Chief Executive Officer.—Megan J. Brennan.
Deputy Postmaster General and Chief Government Relations Officer.—Ronald A. Stroman.

OFFICERS OF THE BOARD OF GOVERNORS

Secretary to the Board of Governors.—Julie S. Moore.

OFFICERS OF THE POSTAL SERVICE

Postmaster General and Chief Executive Officer.—Megan J. Brennan, 268–2550.
Deputy Postmaster General and Chief Government Relations Officer.—Ronald A. Stroman, 268–2519.
Congressional Contact:
Government Relations and Public Policy.—Roderick Sallay, 268–2505.
Judicial Officer.—Hon. Gary E. Shapiro (703) 812–1904, 2101 Wilson Boulevard, Suite 600, Arlington, VA 22201–3078.
Chief Operating Officer and Executive Vice President.—David Williams, 268–4841.

Vice President of:
Delivery Operations.—Kevin McAdams, 268–4359.
Facilities.—Tom A. Samra, 268–2729.
Network Operations.—Robert Cintron, 268–3250.
Retail and Customer Service Operations.—Kelly Sigmon, 268–2871.
Chief Information Officer and Executive Vice President.—Kristin Seaver, 268–5710.
Chief Information Security Officer and Digital Solutions Vice President.—Gregory Crabb (acting), 268–6164.
Vice President of:
Engineering Systems.—Michael J. Amato (703) 280–7002, 8403 Lee Highway, 4th Floor, Merrifield, VA 22082–8101.
Enterprise Analytics.—Isaac Cronkhite, 268–7458.
Information Technology.—Jeff Johnson, 268–4851.
Mail Entry and Payment Technology.—Pritha Mehra, 268–6406.
Chief Financial Officer and Executive Vice President.—Joseph Corbett, 268–2447.
Vice President of:
Controller.—Maura McNerney, 268–4229.
Finance and Planning.—Luke Grossman, 268–5285.
Pricing and Costing.—Sharon Owens, 268–4982.
Supply Management.—Susan M. Brownell, 268–4041.
Chief Human Resources Officer and Executive Vice President.—Jeffrey Williamson, 268–4010.
Vice President of:
Employee Resource Management.—Simon Storey (acting), 268–3784.
Labor Relations.—Douglas A. Tulino, 268–6202.
Chief Customer and Marketing Officer and Executive Vice President.—Jim Cochrane, 268–5710.
Vice President of:
Sales and Customer Relations.—Cliff Rucker, 268–5301.
Marketing.—Steve Monteith, 268–7261.
Production Innovation.—Gary C. Reblin, 268–3177.
General Counsel and Executive Vice President.—Thomas Marshall, 268–2951.
Chief Postal Inspector.—Guy J. Cottrell, 268–4264.
Vice President of:
Corporate Communications.—Janice Walker, 268–2145.

U.S. RAILROAD RETIREMENT BOARD

844 North Rush Street, Chicago, IL 60611, phone (312) 751–4777, fax 751–7154
Office of Legislative Affairs, 1310 G Street, NW., Suite 500, 20005
phone (202) 272–7742, fax 272–7728, e-mail: ola@rrb.gov
http://www.rrb.gov

Chair.—Vacant.
Labor Member.—Walter A. Barrows, 751–4905, fax 751–7194.
Assistants to the Labor Member: Geraldine L. Clark, Brigitte A. Munoz, Michele L. Neuendorf, Mark L. Thomson.
Counsel to the Labor Member.—Nancy V. Russell.
Management Member.—Steven J. Anthony, 751–4910, fax 751–7189.
Assistants to the Management Member: Natasha L. Marx, Joseph M. Waechter.
Counsel to the Management Member.—Robert M. Perbohner.
Inspector General.—Martin J. Dickman, 751–4690, fax 751–4342.
General Counsel.—Ana M. Kocur, 751–4984, fax 751–7102.
Secretary to the Board.—Martha P. ''Pat'' Rico, 751–4920, fax 751–4923.
Director of:
Administration.—Keith B. Earley, 751–4990, fax 751–7197.
Disability Benefits.—Sherita Boots, 751–4740, fax 751–7167.
Equal Opportunity.—Lynn E. Cousins, 751–4942, fax 751–7179.
Hearings and Appeals.—Rachel L. Simmons, 751–4946, fax 751–7159.
Human Resources.—Marguerite V. Daniels, 751–4384, fax 751–7164.
Legislative Affairs.—Beverly Britton Fraser (202) 272–7742, fax 272–7728.
Policy and Systems.—Kimberly A. Price-Butler.
Program Evaluation and Management Services.—Janet M. Hallman, 751–4543, fax 751–7190.
Programs.—Michael A. Tyllas, 751–4515, fax 751–4333.
Public Affairs.—Michael P. Freeman, 751–4777, fax 751–7154.

Retirement and Survivor Benefits.—Valerie F. Allen, 751–3323, fax 751–7104.
Unemployment and Programs Support.—Micheal T. Pawlak, 751–4708, fax 751–7157.
Supervisor of:
Congressional Inquiry.—Carl D. Mende, 751–4970, fax 751–7154.
Chief of:
Acquisition Management.—Paul T. Ahern, 751–7130, fax 751–4923.
Actuary.—Frank J. Buzzi, 751–4915, fax 751–7129.
Benefit and Employment Analysis.—Michael J. Rizzo, 751–4771, fax 751–7129.
Finance.—Vacant.
Information.—Ram Murthy, 751–4851, fax 751–7169.
Librarian.—Anne C. Mentkowski, 751–4926, fax 751–4924.
SEO/Director of Field Service.—Daniel J. Fadden, 751–4627, fax 751–3360.

U.S. SENTENCING COMMISSION

One Columbus Circle, NE., Suite 2–500, South Lobby, 20002–8002

phone (202) 502–4500, fax 502–4699

Chair.—Judge William H. Pryor, Jr. (acting).
Commissioners: Rachel E. Barkow, Judge Charles R. Breyer, Judge Danny C. Reeves.
Commissioners ex officio: Zachary C. Bolitho, J. Patricia Wilson Smoot.
Staff Director.—Kenneth P. Cohen, 502–4523.
General Counsel.—Kathleen C. Grilli, 502–4563.
Director of Legislative and Public Affairs.—Christine M. Leonard, 502–4519.
Director of:
Administration.—Susan M. Brazel, 502–4587.
Research and Data.—Glenn R. Schmitt, 502–4531.
Education and Sentencing Practice.—Raquel K. Wilson, 502–4526.
Senior Publishing and Public Affairs Specialist.—Jennifer Dukes Jordan 502–4593.

U.S. SMALL BUSINESS ADMINISTRATION

409 Third Street, SW., 20416

phone (202) 205–6600, fax 205–7064, http://www.sba.gov

Administrator.—Linda McMahon, 205–6605.
Deputy Administrator.—Althea Coetzee Leslie, 205–6605.
Chief of Staff.—Pradeep Belur, 205–6605.
Director of Executive Secretariat.—Kim Bradley, 205–2410.
General Counsel.—Chris Pilkerton, 619–1848.
Chief Counsel for Advocacy.—Major L. Clark III (acting), 205–6804.
Inspector General.—Hannibal ''Mike'' Ware, 205–6586.
Chief Financial Officer.—Tim Gribben, 205–7420.
Associate Administrator, Office of:
Disaster Assistance.—James Rivera, 205–6734.
Field Operations.—Jason Simmons, 205–6411.
Assistant Administrator, Office of:
Communications and Public Liaison.—Patricia Gibson, 205–6948.
Associate Administrator, Office of:
Congressional and Legislative Affairs.—Michael Hershey, 205–6634.
Diversity, Inclusion and Civil Rights.—Larry Stubblefield, 205–6750.
Assistant Administrator, Office of:
Hearings and Appeals.—Delorice Price Ford (202) 401–8200.
Chief Operating Officer.—Joseph P. Loddo, 205–6340.
Chief Information Officer.—Maria Roat, 205–6708.
Chief Human Capital Officer.—Elias Hernandez, 205–6749.
Associate Administrator, Office of:
Capital Access.—William Manger, 205–6663.
Director of:
Entrepreneurship Education.—Donald Malcolm Smith, 205–6665.
Financial Assistance.—Dianna Seaborn (acting), 205–3645.
Associate Administrator, Office of:
Investment and Innovation.—Joseph Shepard, 205–6513.
Assistant Administrator, Office of:
Technology.—Edsel Brown, 205–7343.
Director of:

Credit Risk Management.—Linda Rusche, 205–6538.
Associate Administrator, Office of:
Small Business Development Centers.—Adriana Menchaca-Gendron, 205–6439.
Director of:
Surety Guarantees.—Frank Lalumiere, 205–6540.
Associate Administrator, Office of:
International Trade.—Peter J. Cazamias, 205–6720.
Veterans Business Development.—Barbara E. Carson, 205–6773.
Assistant Administrator, Office of:
Women's Business Ownership.—Kathleen McShane, 205–6774.
Associate Administrator, Office of:
Government Contracting and Business Development.—Robb Wong, 205–6459.
Business Development.—Jackie Robinson-Burnette, 205–7026.
Director of Government Contracting.—Sean Crean, 205–6933.
Office of Size Standards.—Khem Sharma, 205–7189.

U.S. TRADE AND DEVELOPMENT AGENCY

1000 Wilson Boulevard, Suite 1600, Arlington, VA 22209, phone (703) 875–4357

Director.—Vacant.
Deputy Director.—Enoh T. Ebong.
General Counsel.—Susan Richardson (acting).
Chief of Staff.—Vacant.
Director for Congressional and Public Affairs.—Thomas R. Hardy.
Chief of Acquisitions Management.—Garth Hibbert.
Director of Finance.—Michelle Bivins (acting).
Senior Advisor for Policy and Operations.—Kendra Link.
Chief Information Officer.—Benjamin Bergersen.
Program Director for—
East Asia.—Carl B. Kress.
Latin America and the Caribbean.—Nathan Younge.
Middle East, North Africa, Europe and Eurasia.—Carl B. Kress.
South and Southeast Asia.—Henry Steingass.
Sub-Saharan Africa.—Lida Fitts.
Global Programs.—Andrea Lupo.
Program Monitoring and Evaluations.—Diana Harbison.
Partnerships and Innovation.—Paul A. Marin.

WASHINGTON METROPOLITAN AREA TRANSIT AUTHORITY

600 Fifth Street, NW., 20001, phone (202) 637–1234

General Manager and Chief Executive Officer.—Paul J. Wiedefeld.
General Counsel.—Patricia Lee.
Chief Financial Officer.—Dennis Anosike.
Assistant General Managers for—
Bus Service.—Robert Potts.
Customer Service, Communications and Marketing.—Lynn Bowersox.
Chief Operating Officer.—Joe Leader.
Chief Safety Officer.—Pat Lavin.
Managing Director, Office of Government Relations.—Regina Sullivan.
Managing Director, Public Relations.—Dan Stessel.
Chief, Metro Transit Police Department.—Ronald Pavlik.

WASHINGTON NATIONAL MONUMENT SOCIETY

[Organized 1833; chartered 1859; amended by Acts of August 2, 1876, October, 1888]

President Ex Officio.—Donald J. Trump, President of the United States.
First Vice President.—Outerbridge Horsey, AIA, 1632 32nd Street, NW., Washington, DC 20007 (202) 714–4826.
Treasurer.—Henry Ravenel, Jr.
Secretary.—Karen Cucurullo, Acting Superintendent, National Mall and Memorial Parks, 900 Ohio Drive, SW., Washington, DC 20024–2000 (202) 485–9875.
Members:

Christopher Addison
Neil C. Folger
James M. Goode
Gilbert M. Grosvenor
Outerbridge Horsey, AIA
Henry Ravenel, Jr.
Hon. James W. Symington
John A. Washington
Robert Vogel, Regional Director of the National Capital Region, National Park Service.

Member Emeritus:
Harry F. Byrd, Jr.†

† *Deceased*

WOODROW WILSON INTERNATIONAL CENTER FOR SCHOLARS
One Woodrow Wilson Plaza, 1300 Pennsylvania Avenue, NW., 20004–3027
phone (202) 691–4000, fax 691–4001
[Under the direction of the Board of Trustees of Woodrow Wilson International Center for Scholars]

Director/President/CEO.—Hon. Jane Harman, 691–4202.
Senior Vice President/Scholar and Academic Relations/Programs/External Relations.—Robert S. Litwak, 691–4179.
Senior Vice President/Chief Financial Officer.—Michael Forster, 691–4366.
Vice President for—
External Relations.—Linda Roth, 691–4122.
Development.—Christine Emery, 691–4162.

Board of Trustees:
Chair.—Frederic V. Malek, Founder and Chairman, Thayer Lodging Group, a Brookfield Property.

Private Members:
Peter J. Beshar, Vice President and General Counsel, Marsh & McLennan Companies, Inc.
Thelma Duggin, President, The AnBryce Foundation.
Barry S. Jackson, Managing Director, The Lindsey Group, and Strategic Advisor, Brownstein Hyatt Farber Schreck.
David C. Jacobson, Vice Chair, BMO Financial Group.
Nathalie Rayes, Vice President of Public Affairs, Grupo Salinas.
Earl W. Stafford, Chief Executive Officer, The Wentworth Group, LLC.
Jane Watson Stetson, Philanthropist.
Louis Susman, Manager, CBI Holdings, L.P.

Public Members:
Betsy DeVos, Secretary, U.S. Department of Education.
David Ferriero, Archivist of the United States.
Carla D. Hayden, Librarian of Congress.
Jon Parrish Peede, Acting Chair, National Endowment for the Humanities.
David J. Skorton, Secretary, Smithsonian Institution.
John Sullivan, Deputy Secretary, U.S. Department of State.
Alex M. Azar II, Secretary, U.S. Department of Health and Human Services.

Designated Appointee of the President from within the Federal Government:
Vacant.

JUDICIAL BRANCH

SUPREME COURT OF THE UNITED STATES

One First Street, NE., 20543, phone (202) 479–3000

JOHN G. ROBERTS, JR., Chief Justice of the United States, was born in Buffalo, NY, January 27, 1955. He married Jane Marie Sullivan in 1996 and they have two children, Josephine and Jack. He received an A.B. from Harvard College in 1976 and a J.D. from Harvard Law School in 1979. He served as a law clerk for Judge Henry J. Friendly of the United States Court of Appeals for the Second Circuit from 1979–80 and as a law clerk for then Associate Justice William H. Rehnquist of the Supreme Court of the United States during the 1980 term. He was Special Assistant to the Attorney General, U.S. Department of Justice from 1981–82, Associate Counsel to President Ronald Reagan, White House Counsel's Office from 1982–86, and Principal Deputy Solicitor General, U.S. Department of Justice from 1989–93. From 1986–89 and 1993–2003, he practiced law in Washington, DC. He was appointed to the United States Court of Appeals for the District of Columbia Circuit in 2003. President George W. Bush nominated him as Chief Justice of the United States, and he took his seat September 29, 2005.

ANTHONY M. KENNEDY, Associate Justice, was born in Sacramento, CA, July 23, 1936. He married Mary Davis and has three children. He received his B.A. from Stanford University and the London School of Economics, and his LL.B. from Harvard Law School. He was in private practice in San Francisco, CA, from 1961–63, as well as in Sacramento, CA, from 1963–75. From 1965 to 1988, he was a Professor of Constitutional Law at the McGeorge School of Law, University of the Pacific. He has served in numerous positions during his career, including a member of the California Army National Guard in 1961, the board of the Federal Judicial Center from 1987–88, and two committees of the Judicial Conference of the United States: the Advisory Panel on Financial Disclosure Reports and Judicial Activities, subsequently renamed the Advisory Committee on Codes of Conduct, from 1979–87, and the Committee on Pacific Territories from 1979–90, which he chaired from 1982–90. He was appointed to the United States Court of Appeals for the Ninth Circuit in 1975. President Reagan nominated him as an Associate Justice of the Supreme Court, and he took his seat February 18, 1988.

CLARENCE THOMAS, Associate Justice, was born in the Pin Point community near Savannah, Georgia on June 23, 1948. He attended Conception Seminary from 1967–68 and received an A.B., *cum laude*, from Holy Cross College in 1971 and a J.D. from Yale Law School in 1974. He was admitted to law practice in Missouri in 1974, and served as an Assistant Attorney General of Missouri, 1974–77; an attorney with the Monsanto Company, 1977–79; and Legislative Assistant to Senator John Danforth, 1979–81. From 1981–82, he served as Assistant Secretary for Civil Rights, U.S. Department of Education, and as Chairman of the U.S. Equal Employment Opportunity Commission, 1982–90. From 1990–91, he served as a Judge on the United States Court of Appeals for the District of Columbia Circuit. President Bush nominated him as an Associate Justice of the Supreme Court and he took his seat October 23, 1991. He married Virginia Lamp on May 30, 1987 and has one child, Jamal Adeen by a previous marriage.

RUTH BADER GINSBURG, Associate Justice, was born in Brooklyn, NY, March 15, 1933. She married Martin D. Ginsburg in 1954, and has a daughter, Jane, and a son, James. She received her B.A. from Cornell University, attended Harvard Law School, and received her LL.B. from Columbia Law School. She served as a law clerk to the Honorable Edmund L. Palmieri, Judge of the United States District Court for the Southern District of New York, from 1959–61. From 1961–63, she was a research associate and then Associate Director of the Columbia Law School Project on International Procedure. She was a Professor of Law at Rutgers University School of Law from 1963–72, and Columbia Law School from

1972–80, and a fellow at the Center for Advanced Study in the Behavioral Sciences in Stanford, CA, from 1977–78. In 1971, she was instrumental in launching the Women's Rights Project of the American Civil Liberties Union, and served as the ACLU's General Counsel from 1973–80, and on the National Board of Directors from 1974–80. She was appointed a Judge of the United States Court of Appeals for the District of Columbia Circuit in 1980. President Clinton nominated her as an Associate Justice of the Supreme Court, and she took her seat August 10, 1993.

STEPHEN G. BREYER, Associate Justice, was born in San Francisco, CA, August 15, 1938. He married Joanna Hare in 1967, and has three children, Chloe, Nell, and Michael. He received an A.B. from Stanford University, a B.A. from Magdalen College, Oxford, and an LL.B. from Harvard Law School. He served as a law clerk to Justice Arthur Goldberg of the Supreme Court of the United States during the 1964 term, as a Special Assistant to the Assistant U.S. Attorney General for Antitrust, 1965–67, as an Assistant Special Prosecutor of the Watergate Special Prosecution Force, 1973, as Special Counsel of the U.S. Senate Judiciary Committee, 1974–75, and as Chief Counsel of the committee, 1979–80. He was an Assistant Professor, Professor of Law, and Lecturer at Harvard Law School, 1967–94, a Professor at the Harvard University Kennedy School of Government, 1977–80, and a Visiting Professor at the College of Law, Sydney, Australia, and at the University of Rome. From 1980–90, he served as a Judge of the United States Court of Appeals for the First Circuit, and as its Chief Judge, 1990–94. He also served as a member of the Judicial Conference of the United States, 1990–94, and of the United States Sentencing Commission, 1985–89. President Clinton nominated him as an Associate Justice of the Supreme Court, and he took his seat August 3, 1994.

SAMUEL ANTHONY ALITO, Jr., Associate Justice, was born in Trenton, NJ, April 1, 1950. He married Martha-Ann Bomgardner in 1985, and has two children, Philip and Laura. He served as a law clerk for Leonard I. Garth of the United States Court of Appeals for the Third Circuit from 1976–77. He was Assistant U.S. Attorney, District of New Jersey, 1977–81, Assistant to the Solicitor General, U.S. Department of Justice, 1981–85, Deputy Assistant Attorney General, U.S. Department of Justice, 1985–87, and U.S. Attorney, District of New Jersey, 1987–90. He was appointed to the United States Court of Appeals for the Third Circuit in 1990. President George W. Bush nominated him as an Associate Justice of the Supreme Court, and he took his seat January 31, 2006.

SONIA SOTOMAYOR, Associate Justice, was born in Bronx, NY, June 25, 1954. She earned a B.A. in 1976 from Princeton University, graduating *summa cum laude* and receiving the university's highest academic honor. In 1979, she earned a J.D. from Yale Law School where she served as an editor of the *Yale Law Journal.* She served as Assistant District Attorney in the New York County District Attorney's Office from 1979–84. She then litigated international commercial matters in New York City at Pavia & Harcourt, where she served as an associate and then partner from 1984–92. In 1991, President George H.W. Bush nominated her to the U.S. District Court Southern District of New York, and she served in that role from 1992–98. She served as a judge on the United States Court of Appeals for the Second Circuit from 1998–2009. President Barack Obama nominated her as an Associate Justice of the Supreme Court on May 26, 2009, and she assumed this role August 8, 2009.

ELENA KAGAN, Associate Justice, was born in New York, New York, on April 28, 1960. She received an A.B. from Princeton in 1981, an M.Phil. from Oxford in 1983, and a J.D. from Harvard Law School in 1986. She clerked for Judge Abner Mikva of the U.S. Court of Appeals for the D.C. Circuit from 1986–87 and for Justice Thurgood Marshall of the U.S. Supreme Court during the 1987 Term. After briefly practicing law at a Washington, DC, law firm, she became a law professor, first at the University of Chicago Law School and later at Harvard Law School. She also served for four years in the Clinton Administration, as Associate Counsel to the President and then as Deputy Assistant to the President for Domestic Policy. Between 2003 and 2009, she served as the Dean of Harvard Law School. In 2009, President Obama nominated her as the Solicitor General of the United States. A year later, the President nominated her as an Associate Justice of the Supreme Court on May 10, 2010. She took her seat on August 7, 2010.

NEIL M. GORSUCH, Associate Justice, was born in Denver, CO, August 29, 1967. He and his wife Louise have two daughters. He received a B.A. from Columbia University, a J.D. from Harvard Law School, and a D.Phil. from Oxford University. He served as a law clerk to Judge David B. Sentelle of the United States Court of Appeals for the District of Columbia Circuit, and as a law clerk to Justice Byron White and Justice Anthony M. Kennedy of the Supreme Court of the United States. From 1995–2005, he was in private practice, and from 2005–06 he was Principal Deputy Associate Attorney General at the

U.S. Department of Justice. He was appointed to the United States Court of Appeals for the Tenth Circuit in 2006. He served on the Standing Committee on Rules for Practice and Procedure of the U.S. Judicial Conference, and as chairman of the Advisory Committee on Rules of Appellate Procedure. He taught at the University of Colorado Law School. President Donald J. Trump nominated him as an Associate Justice of the Supreme Court, and he took his seat on April 10, 2017.

RETIRED ASSOCIATE JUSTICES

SANDRA DAY O'CONNOR (Retired), Associate Justice, was born in El Paso, TX, March 26, 1930. She married John Jay O'Connor III in 1952 and has three sons, Scott, Brian, and Jay. She received her B.A. and LL.B. from Stanford University. She served as Deputy County Attorney of San Mateo County, CA, from 1952–53 and as a civilian attorney for Quartermaster Market Center, Frankfurt, Germany, from 1954–57. From 1958–60, she practiced law in Maryvale, AZ, and served as Assistant Attorney General of Arizona from 1965–69. She was appointed to the Arizona State Senate in 1969 and was subsequently reelected to two two-year terms. In 1975, she was elected Judge of the Maricopa County Superior Court and served until 1979, when she was appointed to the Arizona Court of Appeals. President Reagan nominated her as an Associate Justice of the Supreme Court, and she took her seat September 25, 1981. Justice O'Connor retired from the Supreme Court on January 31, 2006.

DAVID H. SOUTER (Retired), Associate Justice, was born in Melrose, MA, September 17, 1939. He graduated from Harvard College, from which he received his A.B. After two years as a Rhodes Scholar at Magdalen College, Oxford, he received an A.B. in Jurisprudence from Oxford University and an M.A. in 1989. After receiving an LL.B. from Harvard Law School, he was an associate at Orr and Reno in Concord, NH, from 1966 to 1968, when he became an Assistant Attorney General of New Hampshire. In 1971, he became Deputy Attorney General and in 1976, Attorney General of New Hampshire. In 1978, he was named an Associate Justice of the Superior Court of New Hampshire, and was appointed to the Supreme Court of New Hampshire as an Associate Justice in 1983. He became a Judge of the United States Court of Appeals for the First Circuit on May 25, 1990. President Bush nominated him as an Associate Justice of the Supreme Court, and he took his seat October 9, 1990. Justice Souter retired from the Supreme Court on June 29, 2009.

JOHN PAUL STEVENS (Retired), Associate Justice, was born in Chicago, IL, April 20, 1920. He married Maryan Mulholland, and has four children, John Joseph (deceased), Kathryn, Elizabeth Jane, and Susan Roberta. He received an A.B. from the University of Chicago, and a J.D. from Northwestern University School of Law. He served in the United States Navy from 1942–45, and was a law clerk to Justice Wiley Rutledge of the Supreme Court of the United States during the 1947 term. He was admitted to law practice in Illinois in 1949. He was Associate Counsel to the Subcommittee on the Study of Monopoly Power of the Judiciary Committee of the U.S. House of Representatives, 1951–52, and a member of the Attorney General's National Committee to Study Antitrust Law, 1953–55. He was Second Vice President of the Chicago Bar Association in 1970. From 1970–75, he served as a Judge of the United States Court of Appeals for the Seventh Circuit. President Ford nominated him as an Associate Justice of the Supreme Court, and he took his seat December 19, 1975. Justice Stevens retired from the Supreme Court on June 29, 2010.

Officers of the Supreme Court

Counselor to the Chief Justice.—Jeffrey P. Minear.
Clerk.—Scott S. Harris.
Librarian.—Linda Maslow.
Marshal.—Pamela Talkin.
Reporter of Decisions.—Christine L. Fallon.
Court Counsel.—Ethan V. Torrey.
Curator.—Catherine E. Fitts.
Director of Information Technology.—Robert J. Hawkins.
Public Information Officer.—Kathleen L. Arberg.

UNITED STATES COURTS OF APPEALS

First Judicial Circuit (Districts of Maine, Massachusetts, New Hampshire, Puerto Rico, and Rhode Island).—*Chief Judge:* Jeffrey R. Howard. *Circuit Judges:* Juan R. Torruella; Sandra L. Lynch; O. Rogeriee Thompson; William J. Kayatta, Jr.; David J. Barron. *Senior Circuit Judges:* Bruce M. Selya; Michael Boudin; Norman H. Stahl; Kermit V. Lipez. *Circuit Executive:* Susan J. Goldberg (617) 748–9614. *Clerk:* Margaret Carter (617) 748–9057, John Joseph Moakley U.S. Courthouse, One Courthouse Way, Suite 2500, Boston, MA 02210.

Second Judicial Circuit (Districts of Connecticut, New York [Eastern, Northern, Southern, and Western], and Vermont).—*Chief Judge:* Robert A. Katzmann. *Circuit Judges:* José A. Cabranes; Susan L. Carney; Denny Chin; Christopher F. Droney; Peter W. Hall; Dennis Jacobs; Robert A. Katzmann; Debra A. Livingston; Raymond J. Lohier, Jr.; Rosemary S. Pooler; Reena Raggi. *Senior Judges:* Giudo Calabresi; Amalya L. Kearse; Pierre N. Leval; Gerard E. Lynch; Jon O. Newman; Barrington D. Parker, Jr.; Robert D. Sack; Chester J. Straub; John M. Walker, Jr.; Richard C. Wesley; Ralph K. Winter. *Circuit Executive:* Karen Greve Milton. *Clerk:* Catherine O'Hagan Wolfe (212) 857–8700, Thurgood Marshall United States Courthouse, 40 Foley Square, New York, NY 10007–1581.

Third Judicial Circuit (Districts of Delaware, New Jersey, Pennsylvania, and Virgin Islands).—*Chief Judge:* D. Brooks Smith. *Circuit Judges:* Theodore A. McKee; Thomas L. Ambro; Michael A. Chagares; Kent A. Jordan; Thomas M. Hardiman; Joseph A. Greenaway, Jr.; Thomas I. Vanaskie; Patty Shwartz; Cheryl Ann Krause; L. Felipe Restrepo; Stephanos Bibas. *Senior Judges:* Walter K. Stapleton; Morton I. Greenberg; Anthony J. Scirica; Robert E. Cowen; Richard L. Nygaard; Jane R. Roth; Marjorie O. Rendell; Maryanne Trump Barry; Julio M. Fuentes; D. Michael Fisher. *Circuit Executive:* Margaret A. Wiegand (215) 597–0718. *Clerk:* Patricia S. Dodszuweit (215) 597–2995, U.S. Courthouse, 601 Market Street, Philadelphia, PA 19106.

Fourth Judicial Circuit (Districts of Maryland, North Carolina, South Carolina, Virginia, and West Virginia).—*Chief Judge:* Roger L. Gregory. *Circuit Judges:* J. Harvie Wilkinson III; Paul V. Niemeyer; Diana Gribbon Motz; William B. Traxler, Jr.; Robert B. King; Dennis W. Shedd; Allyson K. Duncan; G. Steven Agee; Barbara Milano Keenan; James A. Wynn, Jr.; Albert Diaz; Henry F. Floyd; Stephanie D. Thacker; Pamela A. Harris. *Senior Circuit Judge:* Clyde H. Hamilton. *Circuit Executive:* James N. Ishida (804) 916–2184. *Clerk:* Patricia S. Connor (804) 916–2700, Lewis F. Powell, Jr., U.S. Courthouse Annex, 1100 E. Main Street, Richmond, VA 23219.

Fifth Judicial Circuit (Districts of Louisiana, Mississippi, and Texas).—*Chief Judge:* Carl E. Stewart. *Circuit Judges:* E. Grady Jolly; Edith H. Jones; Jerry E. Smith; James L. Dennis; Edith Brown Clement; Edward C. Prado; Priscilla R. Owen; Jennifer Walker Elrod; Leslie H. Southwick; Catharina Haynes; James E. Graves, Jr.; Stephen A. Higginson; Gregg J. Costa; Don R. Willett; James C. Ho. *Senior Circuit Judges:* W. Eugene Davis; Thomas M. Reavley; Carolyn Dineen King; Patrick E. Higginbotham; John M. Duhé, Jr.; Jacques L. Wiener, Jr.; Rhesa H. Barksdale; Fortunato P. Benavides. *Circuit Executive:* Paul Benjamin Anderson, Jr. (504) 310–7777. *Clerk:* Lyle W. Cayce (504) 310–7700, John Minor Wisdom U.S. Court of Appeals Building, 600 Camp Street, New Orleans, LA 70130–3425.

Sixth Judicial Circuit (Districts of Kentucky, Michigan, Ohio, and Tennessee).—*Chief Judge:* R. Guy Cole, Jr. *Circuit Judges:* Alice M. Batchelder; Karen Nelson Moore; Eric Lee Clay; Julia Smith Gibbons; John M. Rogers; Jeffrey S. Sutton; Deborah L. Cook; David W. McKeague; Richard Allen Griffin; Raymond M. Kethledge; Helene N. White; Jane B. Stranch; Bernice Bouie Donald; John Kenneth Bush; Joan Louise Larsen. *Senior Circuit Judges:* Damon J. Keith; Gilbert S. Merritt; Ralph B. Guy; Alan E. Norris; Richard F. Suhrheinrich; Eugene E. Siler, Jr.; Martha Craig Daughtrey; Ronald Lee Gilman; David W. McKeague. *Circuit Executive:* Clarence Maddox (513) 564–7200. *Clerk:* Deborah Hunt (513) 564–7000, Potter Stewart U.S. Courthouse, 100 E. Fifth Street, Cincinnati, OH 45202.

Seventh Judicial Circuit (Districts of Illinois, Indiana, and Wisconsin).—*Chief Judge:* Diane P. Wood. *Circuit Judges:* Joel M. Flaum; Frank H. Easterbrook; Michael S. Kanne; Ilana Diamond Rovner; Diane S. Sykes; David F. Hamilton; Amy Coney Barrett. *Senior Circuit Judges:* William J. Bauer; Kenneth F. Ripple; Daniel A. Manion. *Circuit Executive:* Collins T. Fitzpatrick (312) 435–5803. *Clerk:* Gino J. Agnello (312) 435–5850, 2722 U.S. Courthouse, 219 S. Dearborn Street, Chicago, IL 60604.

Eighth Judicial Circuit (Districts of Arkansas, Iowa, Minnesota, Missouri, Nebraska, North Dakota, and South Dakota).—*Chief Judge:* Lavenski R. Smith. *Circuit Judges:* Roger L. Wollman; James B. Loken; Diana E. Murphy; Steven M. Colloton; Raymond W. Gruender; Duane Benton; Bobby E. Shepherd; Jane L. Kelly; Ralph R. Erickson. *Senior Circuit Judges:* Pasco M. Bowman II; C. Arlen Beam; Morris S. Arnold; Michael J. Melloy. *Circuit Executive:* Millie Adams (314) 244–2600. *Clerk:* Michael E. Gans (314) 244–2400, 111 S. Tenth Street, Suite 24.329, St. Louis, MO 63102.

Ninth Judicial Circuit (Districts of Alaska, Arizona, Central California, Eastern California, Northern California, Southern California, Guam, Hawaii, Idaho, Montana, Nevada, Northern Mariana Islands, Oregon, Eastern Washington, Western Washington).—*Chief Judge:* Sidney R. Thomas. *Circuit Judges:* Diarmuid F. O'Scannlain; Barry G. Silverman; Susan P. Graber; M. Margaret McKeown; Kim McLane Wardlaw; William A. Fletcher; Ronald M. Gould; Richard A. Paez; Marsha L. Berzon; Richard C. Tallman; Johnnie B. Rawlinson; Richard R. Clifton; Jay S. Bybee; Consuelo M. Callahan; Carlos T. Bea; Milan D. Smith, Jr.; Sandra S. Ikuta; N. Randy Smith; Mary H. Murguia; Morgan Christen; Jacqueline H. Nguyen; Paul J. Watford; Andrew D. Hurwitz; John B. Owens; Michelle T. Friedland. *Senior Circuit Judges:* Alfred T. Goodwin; J. Clifford Wallace; Mary M. Schroeder; J. Jerome Farris; Dorothy W. Nelson; William C. Canby, Jr.; Edward Leavy; Stephen S. Trott; Ferdinand F. Fernandez; Andrew J. Kleinfeld; Michael D. Hawkins; A. Wallace Tashima; Raymond C. Fisher. *Circuit Executive:* Elizabeth A. Smith (415) 355–8800. *Clerk:* Molly C. Dwyer (415) 355–8000, P.O. Box 193939, San Francisco, CA 94119–3939.

Tenth Judicial Circuit (Districts of Colorado, Kansas, New Mexico, Oklahoma, Utah, and Wyoming).—*Chief Judge:* Timothy M. Tymkovich. *Circuit Judges:* Mary Beck Briscoe; Carlos F. Lucero; Harris L. Hartz; Jerome A. Holmes; Scott M. Matheson, Jr.; Robert E. Bacharach; Gregory A. Phillips, Carolyn B. McHugh, Nancy L. Moritz; Allison H. Eid. *Senior Circuit Judges:* Monroe G. McKay; Stephanie K. Seymour; John C. Porfilio; Bobby R. Baldock; David M. Ebel; Michael R. Murphy; Terrence L. O'Brien; Paul J. Kelly, Jr. *Circuit Executive:* David Tighe (303) 844–2067. *Clerk:* Betsy Shumaker (303) 844–3157, Byron White United States Courthouse, 1823 Stout Street, Denver, CO 80257.

Eleventh Judicial Circuit (Districts of Alabama, Florida, and Georgia).—*Chief Judge:* Ed Carnes. *Circuit Judges:* Gerald Bard Tjoflat; Frank M. Hull; Stanley Marcus; Charles R. Wilson; William H. Pryor, Jr.; Beverly B. Martin; Adalberto Jordán; Robin S. Rosenbaum; Julie E. Carnes; Jill A. Pryor. *Senior Circuit Judges:* James C. Hill; Peter T. Fay; Phyllis A. Kravitch; R. Lanier Anderson III; J. L. Edmondson; Emmett R. Cox; Joel F. Dubina; Susan H. Black. *Circuit Executive:* James P. Gerstenlauer (404) 335–6535. *Clerk:* David J. Smith (404) 335–6100, 56 Forsyth Street, NW., Atlanta, GA 30303.

UNITED STATES COURT OF APPEALS FOR THE DISTRICT OF COLUMBIA CIRCUIT

333 Constitution Avenue, NW., 20001, phone (202) 216–7300

MERRICK BRIAN GARLAND, chief circuit judge; born in Chicago, IL, 1952; A.B., Harvard University, 1974, *summa cum laude*, Phi Beta Kappa, Paul Revere Frothingham Award and Richard Perkins Parker Award; J.D., Harvard Law School, 1977, *magna cum laude*, articles editor, *Harvard Law Review*; law clerk to Judge Henry J. Friendly, U.S. Court of Appeals for the 2d Circuit, 1977–78; law clerk to Justice William J. Brennan, Jr., U.S. Supreme Court, 1978–79; Special Assistant to the Attorney General, 1979–81; associate then partner, Arnold and Porter, Washington, DC, 1981–89; Assistant U.S. Attorney, Washington, DC, 1989–92; partner, Arnold and Porter, 1992–93; Deputy Assistant Attorney General, Criminal Division, U.S. Department of Justice, 1993–94; Principal Associate Deputy Attorney General, 1994–97; Lecturer on Law, Harvard Law School, 1985–86. Edmund J. Randolph Award, U.S. Department of Justice, 1997. Admitted to the bars of the District of Columbia; U.S. District Court; Court of Appeals, District of Columbia Circuit; U.S. Courts of Appeals for the 4th, 9th, and 10th Circuits; and U.S. Supreme Court. Author: Antitrust and State Action, 96 Yale Law Journal 486 (1987); Antitrust and Federalism, 96 Yale Law Journal 1291 (1987); *Deregulation and Judicial Review*, 98 Harvard Law Review 505 (1985); co-chair, Administrative Law Section, District of Columbia Bar, 1991–94; President, Board of Overseers, Harvard University, 2009–10, member, 2003–09; American Law Institute; U.S. Judicial Conference Executive Committee, 2013–present, Committee on Judicial Security, 2008–13, Committee on the Judicial Branch, 2001–05; appointed to the U.S. Court of Appeals for the District of Columbia Circuit on April 9, 1997.

KAREN LECRAFT HENDERSON, circuit judge. [Biographical information not supplied, per Judge Henderson's request.]

JUDITH W. ROGERS, circuit judge; born in New York, NY; A.B. (with honors), Radcliffe College, 1961; Phi Beta Kappa honors member; LL.B., Harvard Law School, 1964; LL.M., University of Virginia School of Law, 1988; law clerk, D.C. Juvenile Court, 1964–65; assistant U.S. Attorney for the District of Columbia, 1965–68; trial attorney, San Francisco Neighborhood Legal Assistance Foundation, 1968–69; Attorney, U.S. Department of Justice, Office of the Associate Deputy Attorney General and Criminal Division, 1969–71; General Counsel, Congressional Commission on the Organization of the D.C. Government, 1971–72; legislative assistant to D.C. Mayor Walter E. Washington, 1972–79; Corporation Counsel for the District of Columbia, 1979–83; trustee, Radcliffe College, 1982–90; member of Visiting Committee to Harvard Law School, 1984–90 and 2006–11; appointed by President Reagan to the District of Columbia Court of Appeals as an Associate Judge on September 15, 1983; served as Chief Judge, November 1, 1988 to March 17, 1994; appointed by President Clinton to the U.S. Court of Appeals for the District of Columbia Circuit on March 18, 1994, and entered on duty March 21, 1994; member of Executive Committee, Conference of Chief Justices, 1993–94; member, U.S. Judicial Conference Committee on the Codes of Conduct, 1998–2004.

DAVID S. TATEL, circuit judge; born in Washington, DC, March 16, 1942; son of Molly and Dr. Howard Tatel (both deceased); married to the former Edith Bassichis, 1965; children: Rebecca, Stephanie, Joshua, and Emily; grandchildren: Olivia, Maya, Olin, Reuben, Rae, Cameron, Ozzie, and Daria; B.A., University of Michigan, 1963; J.D., University of Chicago Law School, 1966; instructor, University of Michigan Law School, 1966–67; associate, Sidley and Austin, 1967–69, 1970–72; director, Chicago Lawyers' Committee for Civil Rights Under Law, 1969–70; director, National Lawyers' Committee for Civil Rights Under Law, 1972–74; director, Office for Civil Rights, U.S. Department of Health, Education and Welfare, 1977–79; associate and partner, Hogan and Hartson, 1974–77, 1979–94; lecturer, Stanford University Law School, 1991–92; board of directors, Spencer Foundation, 1987–97 (chair, 1990–97); board of directors, National Board for Professional Teaching Standards, 1997–

2000; National Lawyers' Committee for Civil Rights Under Law, co-chair, 1989–91; board of directors, Carnegie Foundation for the Advancement of Teaching, (chair, 2005–09); member of the American Academy of Arts and Sciences, member of the American Philosophical Society, the National Academy of Education, and the National Academy of Sciences Committee on Science, Technology and Law; admitted to practice law in Illinois in 1966 and the District Columbia in 1970; appointed to the U.S. Court of Appeals for the District of Columbia Circuit by President Clinton on October 7, 1994, and entered on duty October 11, 1994.

JANICE ROGERS BROWN, circuit judge; born in Greenville, AL; B.A., California State University, 1974; J.D., UCLA School of Law, 1977; LL.M., University of Virginia School of Law, 2004; Deputy Legislative Counsel, Legislative Counsel Bureau, 1977–79; Deputy Attorney General, California Department of Justice, 1979–87; Deputy Secretary and General Counsel, California Business, Transportation, and Housing Agency, 1987–90; Senior Associate, Nielsen, Merksamer, Parinello, Mueller and Naylor, 1990–91; Legal Affairs Secretary for Governor Pete Wilson, 1991–94; Associate Justice, California Court of Appeals for the Third District, 1994–96; Associate Justice, California Supreme Court, 1996–2005; appointed to the U.S. Court of Appeals for the District of Columbia Circuit by President George W. Bush on June 10, 2005 and sworn in on July 1, 2005.

THOMAS B. GRIFFITH, circuit judge; born in Yokohama, Japan, July 5, 1954; B.A., Brigham Young University, 1978; J.D., University of Virginia School of Law, 1985; editor, *Virginia Law Review*; associate, Robinson, Bradshaw and Hinson, Charlotte, NC, 1985–89; associate and then a partner, Wiley, Rein and Fielding, Washington, DC, 1989–95 and 1999–2000; Senate Legal Counsel of the United States, 1995–99; Assistant to the President and General Counsel, Brigham Young University, Provo, UT, 2000–05; appointed to the United States Court of Appeals for the District of Columbia Circuit on June 14, 2005 and sworn in on July 1, 2005.

BRETT M. KAVANAUGH, circuit judge; born in Washington, DC, February 12, 1965; son of Edward and Martha Kavanaugh; married to Ashley Estes; two daughters; B.A., *cum laude*, Yale College, 1987; J.D., Yale Law School, 1990; law clerk to Judge Walter Stapleton of the U.S. Court of Appeals for the Third Circuit, 1990–91; law clerk for Judge Alex Kozinski of the U.S. Court of Appeals for the Ninth Circuit, 1991–92; attorney, Office of the Solicitor General of the United States, 1992–93; law clerk to Associate Justice Anthony Kennedy of the U.S. Supreme Court, 1993–94; Associate Counsel, Office of Independent Counsel, 1994–97; partner, Kirkland & Ellis LLP, 1997–98, 1999–2001; Associate Counsel and then Senior Associate Counsel to President George W. Bush, 2001–03; Assistant to the President and Staff Secretary to President Bush, 2003–06; Adjunct Professor of Law, Georgetown University Law Center, 2007; Lecturer on Law, Harvard Law School, 2008–14; appointed to the U.S. Court of Appeals for the District of Columbia Circuit on May 30, 2006.

SRI SRINIVASAN, circuit judge; born in Chandigarh, India, February 23, 1967; son of Saroja and T.P. Srinivasan; two children; B.A. Stanford University, 1989; J.D. Stanford Law School, 1995; M.B.A. Stanford Graduate School of Business, 1995; law clerk to Judge J. Harvie Wilkinson III of the U.S. Court of Appeals for the Fourth Circuit, 1995–96; Bristow Fellow, Office of the Solicitor General of the United States, 1996–97; law clerk to Associate Justice Sandra Day O'Connor of the U.S. Supreme Court, 1997–98; associate, O'Melveny & Myers LLP, 1998–2002; Assistant to the Solicitor General, 2002–07; partner, O'Melveny & Myers LLP, 2007–11; Lecturer on Law, Harvard Law School, 2009–10; Principal Deputy Solicitor General, 2011–13; appointed to the U.S. Court of Appeals for the District of Columbia Circuit on May 24, 2013.

PATRICIA A. MILLETT, circuit judge; born in Dexter, MA, 1963; B.A., *summa cum laude*, University of Illinois at Urbana-Champaign, 1985; Harvard Law School, 1988, *magna cum laude*; litigation associate, Miller and Chevalier, 1988–90; law clerk, Judge Thomas Tang, U.S. Court of Appeals for the 9th Circuit, 1990–92; appellate staff, U.S. Department of Justice Civil Division, 1992–96; Assistant U.S. Solicitor General, 1996–2007; partner, Akin Gump Strauss Hauer and Feld, 2007–13; appointed by President Obama to the United States Court of Appeals for the District of Columbia Circuit on December 10, 2013.

CORNELIA T.L. PILLARD, circuit judge; born in Cambridge, MA, 1961; B.A. Yale College, *magna cum laude*, with distinction in History; J.D., Harvard Law School, *magna cum laude*, Editor, *Harvard Women's Law Journal*, 1984–85; Book Review and Commentary Editor, *Harvard Law Review*; law clerk to Judge Louis H. Pollak, U.S. District Court for the Eastern District of Pennsylvania, 1987–88; Marvin M. Karpatkin Fellowship, American Civil Liberties Union, 1988–89; member of the Bars of New York (1989), Massachusetts

(1989), D.C. (1990); Assistant Counsel, NAACP Legal Defense and Education Fund, Inc., 1989–94; Assistant to the Solicitor General of the United States, 1994–97; Assistant Professor, then Professor, Georgetown University Law Center, 1997–2013; Deputy Assistant Attorney General, Office of Legal Counsel, 1998–2000; Chair, American Bar Association Scholars' Reading Group, Standing Committee on the Federal Judiciary, 2005–06; Visiting Scholar, Institute for Advanced Legal Studies (London, U.K.), 2006; Academic Co-Director and Professor, Center for Transnational Legal Studies (London, U.K.), 2008–09; Advisory Board (2003–11) and Faculty Co-Director (2011–13) Georgetown Law Supreme Court Institute; member, Board of Directors, American Arbitration Association, 2005–13; Fellow, Woodrow Wilson International Center for Scholars, 2012–13; member, American Law Institute; appointed to the United States Court of Appeals for the District of Columbia Circuit on December 2013.

ROBERT L. WILKINS, circuit judge; born in Muncie, IN, 1963, B.S., Rose-Hulman Institute of Technology, 1986, *cum laude*, Herman A. Moench Distinguished Senior Commendation; J.D., Harvard Law School, 1989, executive editor and comments editor of the *Civil Rights-Civil Liberties Law Review*; law clerk to Judge Earl B. Gilliam of the U.S. District Court for the Southern District of California, 1989–90; staff attorney, Public Defender Service for the District of Columbia, 1990–95; chief, Special Litigation and Programs Division of Public Defender Service for the District of Columbia, 1995–2000; president, National African American Museum and Cultural Complex, Inc., 2000–02; partner, Venable LLP, 2002–11; selected one of the "90 Greatest Washington Lawyers of the Last 30 Years" by the *Legal Times* in 2008; selected one of the "40 under 40 most successful young litigators in America" by the *National Law Journal* in 2002; named one of "Washington's Top Lawyers: Criminal Defense," 2004, *Washingtonian* magazine; named one of "Washington's Top Lawyers: Education," 2007, *Washingtonian* magazine; Honor Alumni Award, 2005, Rose-Hulman Institute of Technology; Henry W. Edgerton Civil Liberties Award, 2001, American Civil Liberties Union Fund of the National Capital Area; Pro Bono Attorney of the Year, 2001, American Civil Liberties Union of Maryland; "Practitioner of the Year" Award, 1999, University of Maryland Black Law Students Association; Nominee, "Roger Baldwin Medal of Liberty" Award, 1999, American Civil Liberties Union of Maryland; District of Columbia Access to Justice Commission (2005–08); Board of Trustees, Public Defender Service for the District of Columbia (2002–08); National Museum of African American History and Culture Plan for Action Presidential Commission (chairman of the Site and Building Committee) (2002–03); member, District of Columbia Advisory Commission on Sentencing (1998–2000); member, District of Columbia Truth-In-Sentencing Commission (1997–98); District of Columbia Juvenile Justice Advisory Group (1998–2000); *Federal Influence on Sentencing Policy in the District of Columbia: An Oppressive and Dangerous Experiment*, 11 Fed. Sent. Rptr. 143–148 (Nov./Dec. 1998); *The South African Legal System: Black Lawyer's Views*, 7 TransAfrica Forum 9 (Fall 1990); *Black Neighborhoods Becoming Black Cities: Group Empowerment, Local Control and the Implications of Being Darker than Brown*, 23 Harv. C.R.—C.L. L. Rev. 415 (1988) (co-author); admitted to the bars of the District of Columbia; Massachusetts; U.S. Supreme Court, U.S. Court of Appeals for the D.C. Circuit, U.S. Court of Appeals for the Federal Circuit, U.S. District Court for the District of Columbia, U.S. District Court for the District of Maryland, and U.S. District Court for the Eastern District of Wisconsin; member, Judicial Conference of the United States, Committee on Judicial Security, 2013–present; appointed to the U.S. District Court for the District of Columbia on December 27, 2010; appointed to the U.S. Court of Appeals for the District of Columbia Circuit on January 13, 2014.

SENIOR CIRCUIT JUDGES

HARRY T. EDWARDS, senior circuit judge; born in New York, NY, November 3, 1940; son of George H. Edwards and Arline (Ross) Lyle; married to Pamela Carrington-Edwards; children: Brent and Michelle; B.S., Cornell University, 1962; J.D. (with distinction), University of Michigan Law School, 1965; associate with Seyfarth, Shaw, Fairweather and Geraldson, 1965–70; professor of law, University of Michigan, 1970–75 and 1977–80; professor of law, Harvard University, 1975–77; visiting professor of law, Free University of Brussels, 1974; arbitrator of labor/management disputes, 1970–80; vice president, National Academy of Arbitrators, 1978–80; member (1977–79) and chairman (1979–80), National Railroad Passenger Corporation (Amtrak); Executive Committee of the Association of American Law Schools, 1979–80; public member of the Administrative Conference of the United States, 1976–80; International Women's Year Commission, 1976–77; American Bar Association Commission of Law and the Economy; co-author of five books: *Labor Relations Law in the Public Sector, The Lawyer as a Negotiator, Higher Education and the Law*, and *Collective Bargaining and Labor Arbitration*; and, most recently, Edwards, Ellliot, and Levy, *Federal Standards of Review* (2d ed. 2013), recipient of the Judge William B. Groat Alumni Award, 1978, given by Cornell University; the Society of American Law Teachers Award (for ''distinguished contributions to teaching and public service''); the Whitney North Seymour Medal presented by the American Arbitration Association for outstanding contributions to the use of arbitration; Recipient of the 2004 Robert J. Kutak Award, presented by the American Bar Association Selection of Legal Education and Admission to the Bar ''to a person who meets the highest standards of professional responsibility and demonstrates substantial achievement toward increased understanding between legal education and the active practice of law'', and several Honorary Doctor of Laws degrees; Professor of Law at NYU School of Law (member of faculty since 1990); has also taught part-time at Duke, Georgetown, Michigan, Harvard Law, Pennsylvania, and University of California Irvine Schools of Law; co-chair of the Forensics Science Committee established by the National Academy of Sciences, 2006–09; member of the Committee on Science, Technology, and Law at the National Academy of Sciences; appointed to the U.S. Court of Appeals, February 20, 1980; served as chief judge September 15, 1994 to July 16, 2001.

LAURENCE HIRSCH SILBERMAN, senior circuit judge; recipient of the Presidential Medal of Freedom, June 19, 2008; born in York, PA, October 12, 1935; son of William Silberman and Anna (Hirsch); married to Rosalie G. Gaull on April 28, 1957 (deceased), married Patricia Winn on January 5, 2008; children: Robert Stephen Silberman, Katherine DeBoer Balaban, and Anne Gaull Otis; B.A., Dartmouth College, 1957; LL.B., Harvard Law School, 1961; admitted to Hawaii Bar, 1962; District of Columbia Bar, 1973; associate, Moore, Torkildson and Rice, 1961–64; partner (Moore, Silberman and Schulze), Honolulu, 1964–67; attorney, National Labor Relations Board, Office of General Counsel, Appellate Division, 1967–69; Solicitor, Department of Labor, 1969–70; Under Secretary of Labor, 1970–73; partner, Steptoe and Johnson, 1973–74; Deputy Attorney General of the United States, 1974–75; Ambassador to Yugoslavia, 1975–77; President's Special Envoy on ILO Affairs, 1976; senior fellow, American Enterprise Institute, 1977–78; visiting fellow, 1978–85; managing partner, Morrison and Foerster, 1978–79 and 1983–85; executive vice president, Crocker National Bank, 1979–83; lecturer, University of Hawaii, 1962–63; board of directors, Commission on Present Danger, 1978–85, Institute for Educational Affairs, New York, NY, 1981–85, member: General Advisory Committee on Arms Control and Disarmament, 1981–85; Defense Policy Board, 1981–85; vice chairman, State Department's Commission on Security and Economic Assistance, 1983–84; American Bar Association (Labor Law Committee, 1965–72, Corporations and Banking Committee, 1973, Law and National Security Advisory Committee, 1981–85); Hawaii Bar Association Ethics Committee, 1965–67; Council on Foreign Relations, 1977–present; Judicial Conference Committee on Court Administration and Case Management, 1994; member, U.S. Foreign Intelligence Surveillance Act Court of Review, 1996–2003; Adjunct Professor of Law (Administrative Law and Labor Law) Georgetown Law Center, 1987–94; 1997; Adjunct Professor of Law, New York University Law School, 1995–96; Distinguished Visitor from the Judiciary, Georgetown Law Center, 2003–present; co-chairman of the President's Commission on The Intelligence Capabilities of the United States Regarding Weapons of Mass Destruction, 2004–05; appointed to the U.S. Court of Appeals for the District of Columbia Circuit by President Reagan on October 28, 1985.

STEPHEN F. WILLIAMS, senior circuit judge; born in New York, NY, September 23, 1936; son of Charles Dickerman Williams and Virginia (Fain); married to Faith Morrow, 1966; children: Susan, Geoffrey, Sarah, Timothy, and Nicholas; B.A., Yale, 1958, J.D., Harvard Law School, 1961; U.S. Army Reserves, 1961–62; associate, Debevoise, Plimpton, Lyons and Gates, 1962–66; Assistant U.S. Attorney, Southern District of New York, 1966–69; associate professor and professor of law, University of Colorado School of Law, 1969–86; visiting professor of law, UCLA, 1975–76; visiting professor of law and fellow in law and economics, University Chicago Law School, 1979–80; visiting George W. Hutchison Professor of Energy Law, SMU, 1983–84; consultant to: Administrative Conference of the United States, 1974–76; Federal Trade Commission on energy-related issues, 1983–85; member, American Law Institute; appointed to the U.S. Court of Appeals for the District of Columbia Circuit by President Reagan, June 16, 1986.

DOUGLAS HOWARD GINSBURG, circuit judge; born in Chicago, IL, May 25, 1946; diploma, Latin School of Chicago, 1963; B.S., Cornell University, 1970 (Phi Kappa Phi, Ives Award); J.D., University of Chicago, 1973 (Mecham Prize Scholarship 1970–73, Casper Platt Award, 1973, Order of Coif, Articles and Book Rev. Ed., 40 U. Chi. L. Rev.); bar admissions: Illinois (1973), Massachusetts (1982), U.S. Supreme Court (1984), U.S. Court of Appeals for the Ninth Circuit (1986); member: Mont Pelerin Society, American Economic Association, American Law and Economics Association, Honor Society of Phi Kappa Phi, American Bar Association, Antitrust Section, Council, 1985–86 (ex officio), judicial liaison (2000–03 and 2009–12); advisory boards: Competition Policy International; Harvard Journal of Law and Public Policy; *Journal of Competition Law and Economics*; Law and Economics Center, George Mason University School of Law; *Supreme Court Economic Review; University of Chicago Law Review*; Board of Directors: Foundation for Research in Economics and the Environment, 1991–2004; Rappahannock County Conservation Alliance, 1998–2004; Rappahannock Association for Arts and Community, 1997–99; Committees: Judicial Conference of the United States, 2002–08, Budget Committee, 1997–2001, Committee on Judicial Resources, 1987–96; Boston University Law School, Visiting Committee, 1994–97; University of Chicago Law School, Visiting Committee, 1985–88; law clerk to: Judge Carl McGowan, U.S. Court of Appeals for the District of Columbia Circuit, 1973–74; Associate Justice Thurgood Marshall, U.S. Supreme Court, 1974–75; previous positions: assistant professor, Harvard University Law School, 1975–81; Professor 1981–83; Deputy Assistant Attorney General, Antitrust Division, U.S. Department of Justice, 1983–84; Administrator for Information and Regulatory Affairs, Executive Office of the President, Office of Management and Budget, 1984–85; Assistant Attorney General, Antitrust Division, U.S. Department of Justice, 1985–86; lecturer in law, Columbia University, New York City, 1987–88, 2009–11; lecturer in law, Harvard University, Cambridge, MA, 1988–89; distinguished professor of law, George Mason University, Arlington, VA, 1988–present; senior lecturer, University of Chicago Law School, 1990–present; lecturer on law, New York Law School, 2005–09; Visiting Professor, Faculty of Laws, University College, London, 2010–15; appointed to U.S. Court of Appeals for the District of Columbia Circuit by President Reagan on October 14, 1986, taking the oath of office on November 10, 1986, Chief Judge, 2001–08.

DAVID BRYAN SENTELLE, circuit judge, born in Canton, NC, February 12, 1943; son of Horace and Maude Sentelle; married to Jane LaRue Oldham; three daughters and four granddaughters; B.A., University of North Carolina at Chapel Hill, 1965; J.D. with honors, University of North Carolina School of Law, 1968; associate, Uzzell and Dumont, Asheville, 1968–70; Assistant U.S. Attorney, Charlotte, 1970–74; North Carolina State District Judge, 1974–77; partner, Tucker, Hicks, Sentelle, Moon and Hodge, Charlotte, 1977–85; U.S. District Judge for the Western District of North Carolina, 1985–87. Adjunct professor, University of North Carolina, Florida State, George Mason University, and University of Georgia. Appointed to the U.S. Court of Appeals by President Reagan in October 1987; Chief Judge, 2008–13; assumed senior status February 12, 2013. Member, U.S. Judicial Conference Committee on Court Administration and Case Management, 1992; Presiding Judge, Special Division of the Court for the Appointment of Independent Counsels, 1992–2006; Member, Judicial Conference Committee on Code of Conduct, 2004–05; Chair, Judicial Conference Committee on Judicial Security, 2005–08; Member, Judicial Conference Executive Committee, 2008–13 (Chair 2010–13); past President, Edward Bennett Williams Inn of the American Inns of Court. Recipient, 2008 American Inns of Court Professionalism Award in the DC Circuit.

A. RAYMOND RANDOLPH, senior circuit judge; born in Riverside, NJ, November 1, 1943; son of Arthur Raymond Randolph, Sr. and Marile (Kelly); two children: John Trevor and Cynthia Lee Randolph; married to Eileen Janette O'Connor, May 18, 1984. B.S., Drexel University, 1966; J.D., University of Pennsylvania Law School, 1969, *summa cum laude;* managing editor, *University of Pennsylvania Law Review*; Order of the Coif. Admitted to Supreme Court of the United States; Supreme Court of California; District of Columbia Court of Appeals; U.S. Courts of Appeals for the First, Second, Fourth, Fifth, Sixth, Seventh, Ninth, Eleventh, and District of Columbia Circuits. Memberships: American Law Institute. Law clerk to Judge Henry J. Friendly, U.S. Court of Appeals for the Second Circuit, 1969–70; Assistant to the Solicitor General, 1970–73; adjunct professor of law, Georgetown University Law Center, 1974–78; George Mason School of Law, 1992; Deputy Solicitor General, 1975–77; Special Counsel, Committee on Standards of Official Conduct, House of Representatives, 1979–80; special assistant attorney general, State of Montana (honorary), 1983–July 1990; special assistant attorney general, State of New Mexico, 1985–July 1990; special assistant attorney general, State of Utah, 1986–July 1990; advisory panel, Federal Courts Study Committee, 1989–July 1990; partner, Pepper, Hamilton and Scheetz, 1987–July 1990; chairman, Committee on Codes of Conduct, U.S. Judicial Conference, 1995–98; distinguished professor of law, George Mason Law School, 1999–present; recipient, Distinguished Alumnus Award, University of Pennsylvania Law School, 2002; appointed to the U.S. Court of Appeals for the District of Columbia Circuit by President George H.W. Bush on July 16, 1990, and took oath of office on July 20, 1990.

OFFICERS OF THE UNITED STATES COURT OF APPEALS
FOR THE DISTRICT OF COLUMBIA CIRCUIT

Circuit Executive.—Betsy Paret (202) 216–7340.
Clerk.—Mark J. Langer, 216–7300.
Chief Deputy Clerk.—Marilyn R. Sargent, 216–7300.
Director, Legal Division.—Melissa McKenney Ryan, 216–7500.

UNITED STATES COURT OF APPEALS FOR THE FEDERAL CIRCUIT

717 Madison Place, NW., 20439, phone (202) 275–8000

SHARON PROST, chief judge; was appointed by President George W. Bush in 2001. Prior to her appointment, Judge Prost served as Minority Chief Counsel, Deputy Chief Counsel, and Chief Counsel of the Committee on the Judiciary, United States Senate from 1993 to 2001. She also served as Chief Labor Counsel (Minority), Senate Committee on Labor and Human Resources from 1989 to 1993. She was Assistant Solicitor, Associate Solicitor, and Acting Solicitor of the National Labor Relations Board from 1984 to 1989. She was an Attorney at the Internal Revenue Service from 1983 to 1984, and Field Attorney at the Federal Labor Relations Authority from 1980 to 1983. Judge Prost also served as Labor Relations Specialist/Auditor at the United States General Accounting Office from 1976 to 1980 and Labor Relations Specialist at the United States Civil Service Commission from 1973 to 1976. Judge Prost received a B.S. from Cornell University in 1973, an M.B.A. from George Washington University in 1975, a J.D. from the Washington College of Law, American University in 1979, and an LL.M. from George Washington University School of Law in 1984.

PAULINE NEWMAN, circuit judge; was appointed by President Ronald Reagan in 1984. From 1982 to 1984, Judge Newman was Special Adviser to the United States Delegation to the Diplomatic Conference on the Revision of the Paris Convention for the Protection of Industrial Property. She served on the advisory committee to the Domestic Policy Review of Industrial Innovation from 1978 to 1979 and on the State Department Advisory Committee on International Intellectual Property from 1974 to 1984. From 1969 to 1984, Judge Newman served as director, Patent, Trademark and Licensing Department, FMC Corp. From 1961 to 1962 she worked for the United Nations Educational, Scientific and Cultural Organization as a science policy specialist in the Department of Natural Sciences. She served as patent attorney and house counsel of FMC Corp. from 1954 to 1969 and as research scientist, American Cyanamid Co. from 1951 to 1954. Judge Newman received a B.A. from Vassar College in 1947, an M.A. from Columbia University in 1948, a Ph.D. from Yale University in 1952 and an LL.B. from New York University School of Law in 1958.

ALAN D. LOURIE, circuit judge; was appointed to the United States Court of Appeals for the Federal Circuit on April 6, 1990, by President George H.W. Bush. He was formerly Vice President, Corporate Patents and Trademarks, and Associate General Counsel of SmithKline Beecham Corporation. Born in Boston, Massachusetts, on January 13, 1935, Judge Lourie received his Bachelor's degree from Harvard University (1956), his Master's degree in organic chemistry from the University of Wisconsin (1958), and his Ph.D. in chemistry from the University of Pennsylvania (1965). He received his J.D. degree from Temple University in 1970. Before being appointed to the court, Judge Lourie had been President of the Philadelphia Patent Law Association, a member of the Board of Directors of the American Intellectual Property Law Association (formerly American Patent Law Association), treasurer of the Association of Corporate Patent Counsel, and a member of the board of directors of the Intellectual Property Owners Association. He was also Vice Chairman of the Industry Functional Advisory Committee on Intellectual Property Rights for Trade Policy Matters (IFAC 3) for the Department of Commerce and the Office of the U.S. Trade Representative. He was a member of the U.S. delegation to the Diplomatic Conference on the Revision of the Paris Convention for the Protection of Industrial Property, held in Geneva in October and November 1982, and in March 1984. He was chairman of the Patent Committee of the Law Section of the Pharmaceutical Manufacturers Association from 1980 to 1985. Judge Lourie was awarded the Jefferson Medal of the New Jersey Intellectual Property Law Association for extraordinary contributions to the field of intellectual property law in 1998; was a recipient of the Intellectual Property Owners Education Foundation Distinguished Intellectual Property Professional Award for extraordinary leadership in the intellectual property community and a lifetime commitment to invention and innovation in 2008; was a recipient of the Philadelphia Intellectual Property Law Association's Award for outstanding IP achievement in 2010; was a recipient of the Boston Patent Law Association's Distinguished Public Service Award in 2011; was a recipient of a ''lifetime achievement'' award from The Sedona Conference in 2011; and recently was a recipient of NYIPLA's 10th Annual Outstanding Public Service Award in 2012. He was a member of the Judicial Conference Committee on Financial Disclosure from 1990 to 1998 and has been a member of the Committee on Codes of Conduct since 2005. He is a member of the American Intellectual Property Law Association, the American Chemical Society, the Cosmos Club, and the Harvard Club of Washington. Judge Lourie is married and has two daughters and four grandchildren.

TIMOTHY B. DYK, circuit judge; was appointed by President William J. Clinton in 2000. Prior to his appointment, Judge Dyk was Partner and Chair, Issues and Appeals Practice Area, at Jones, Day, Reavis and Pogue from 1990 to 2000. He was Adjunct Professor at Yale Law School from 1986 to 1987 and 1989, at the University of Virginia Law School in 1984 and 1985, and from 1987 to 1988, and at the Georgetown University Law Center in 1983, 1986, 1989 and 1991. Judge Dyk was Associate and Partner, Wilmer Cutler and Pickering from 1964 to 1990. From 1963 to 1964, Judge Dyk served as Special Assistant to Assistant Attorney General Louis F. Oberdorfer. He also served as Law Clerk to Chief Justice Warren from 1962 to 1963, and to Justices Reed and Burton (retired) from 1961 to 1962. Judge Dyk received an A.B. from Harvard College in 1958 and an LL.B. from Harvard Law School in 1961. He was First President of the Edward Coke Appellate Inn of Court from 2000 to 2001 and President of the Giles Sutherland Rich Inn of Court from 2006 to 2007. He was the recipient of the 2012 American Inns of Court Professionalism Award for the Federal Circuit. Judge Dyk is the co-author of the Chapter on Patents in the Third Edition of the treatise, Business and Commercial Litigation in Federal Courts.

KIMBERLY A. MOORE, circuit judge; was appointed by President George W. Bush in 2006. Prior to her appointment, Judge Moore was a Professor of Law from 2004–06 and Associate Professor of Law from 2000 to 2004 at the George Mason University School of Law. She was an Assistant Professor of Law at the University of Maryland School of Law from 1999 to 2000. She served both as an Assistant Professor of Law from 1997 to 1999 and the Associate Director of the Intellectual Property Law Program from 1998 to 1999 at the Chicago-Kent College of Law. Judge Moore clerked from 1995 to 1997 for the Honorable Glenn L. Archer, Jr., Chief Judge of the United States Court of Appeals for the Federal Circuit, and was an Associate at Kirkland and Ellis from 1994 to 1995. From 1988 to 1992, Judge Moore was employed in electrical engineering with the Naval Surface Warfare Center. Judge Moore received her B.S.E.E. in 1990, M.S. in 1991, both from the Massachusetts Institute of Technology, and her J.D., *cum laude* from the Georgetown University Law Center in 1994. Judge Moore has written and presented widely on patent litigation. She co-authored a legal casebook entitled Patent Litigation and Strategy and served as the Editor of The Federal Circuit Bar Journal from 1998 to 2006.

KATHLEEN M. O'MALLEY, circuit judge; was appointed to the United States Court of Appeals for the Federal Circuit by President Barack Obama in 2010. Prior to her elevation to the Federal Circuit, Judge O'Malley was appointed to the United States District Court for the Northern District of Ohio by President William J. Clinton on October 12, 1994. Judge O'Malley served as First Assistant Attorney General and Chief of Staff for Ohio Attorney General Lee Fisher from 1992–94, and Chief Counsel to Attorney General Fisher from 1991–92. From 1985–91, she worked for Porter, Wright, Morris and Arthur, where she became a partner. From 1983–84, she was an associate at Jones, Day, Reavis and Pogue. During her sixteen years on the district court bench, Judge O'Malley presided over in excess of 100 patent and trademark cases and sat by designation on the United States Circuit Court for the Federal Circuit. As an educator, Judge O'Malley has regularly taught a course on Patent Litigation at Case Western Reserve University Law School; she is a member of the faculty of the Berkeley Center for Law and Technology's program designed to educate Federal Judges regarding the handling of intellectual property cases. Judge O'Malley serves as a board member of the Sedona Conference; as the judicial liaison to the Local Patent Rules Committee for the Northern District of Ohio; and as an advisor to national organizations publishing treatises on patent litigation (Anatomy of a Patent Case, Complex Litigation Committee of the American College of Trial Lawyers; Patent Case Management Judicial Guide, Berkeley Center for Law and Technology). Judge O'Malley began her legal career as a law clerk to the Honorable Nathaniel R. Jones, Sixth Circuit Court of Appeals in 1982–83. She received her J.D. degree from Case Western Reserve University School of Law, Order of the Coif, in 1982, where she served on Law Review and was a member of the National Mock Trial Team. Judge O'Malley attended Kenyon College in Gambier, Ohio where she graduated *magna cum laude* and Phi Beta Kappa in 1979.

JIMMIE V. REYNA, circuit judge; was appointed to the United States Court of Appeals for the Federal Circuit by President Barack Obama in 2011. Prior to his appointment, Judge Reyna was an international trade attorney and shareholder at Williams Mullen, where, from 1998 to 2011, he directed the firm's Trade and Customs Practice Group and its Latin America Task Force, and served on its board of directors (2006–08, 2009–11). He was an associate and partner at the law firm of Stewart and Stewart (1986–98). From 1981 to 1986, Judge Reyna was a solo practitioner in Albuquerque, New Mexico and, prior to that, an associate at Shaffer, Butt, Thornton and Baehr, also in Albuquerque, New Mexico. Judge Reyna served on the U.S. roster of dispute settlement panelists for trade disputes under Chapter 19 of the North American Free Trade Agreement, and the U.S. Indicative List of Non-Governmental Panelists for the World Trade Organization, Dispute Settlement Mechanism, for both trade in goods and trade in services. Judge Reyna is the author of two books, Passport to North American Trade: Rules of Origin and Customs Procedures Under the NAFTA (Shepards 1995), and The GATT Uruguay Round, A Negotiating History: Services, 1986–92 (Kluwer 1993) and numerous articles on international trade and customs issues. He was the founder and Senior Co-Editor of the Hispanic National Bar Association *Journal of Law and Policy*. Judge Reyna is a recipient of the Ohtli Award (the highest honor bestowed by the Mexican Government for non-Mexican citizens). Other awards include: 100 Influentials, *Hispanic Business Magazine*, 2011; 101 Latino Leaders in America, *Latino Leaders Magazine*, 2011 and 2012; Minority Business Leader, *Washington Business Journal*; Extraordinary Leadership, Hispanic National Bar Association (HNBA); Lifetime Honorary Membership, Society of Hispanic Professional Engineers; Distinguished Citizen Award, Military Airlift Command, U.S. Air Force; Spirit of Excellence Award, Albuquerque Hispano Chamber of Commerce. Judge Reyna served over a decade of leadership in the HNBA, including as National President (2006–07). He served in various leadership positions in the ABA Sections on International Law and Dispute Settlement. He was a founder and member of the board of directors of the U.S. Mexico Law Institute, and the Community Services for Autistic Adults and Children Foundation. He currently serves on the Nationwide Hispanic Advisory Council of Big Brothers Big Sisters of America. He received a B.A. from the University of Rochester in 1975 and a J.D. from the University of New Mexico School of Law in 1978.

EVAN J. WALLACH, circuit judge; was appointed to the United States Court of Appeals for the Federal Circuit by President Barack Obama in 2011, confirmed by the Senate on November 9, 2011, and assumed the duties of his office on November 18, 2011. Prior to his appointment, he served for sixteen years as a judge of the United States Court of International Trade, having been appointed to that court by President William J. Clinton in 1995. Judge Wallach worked as a general litigation partner with an emphasis on media representation at the law firm of Lionel Sawyer and Collins in Las Vegas, Nevada from 1982 to 1995. He was an associate at the same firm from 1976 to 1982. While working with the firm, Judge Wallach took a leave of absence to serve as General Counsel and Public Policy Advisor to Senator Harry Reid from 1987 to 1988. From 1989 to 1995, he served in the Nevada National Guard as a Judge Advocate. In 1991, while on leave from his firm, he served as an Attorney/Advisor in the International Affairs Division of the Judge Advocate of the Army at the Pentagon. Judge Wallach, a recognized expert in the law of war, has taught at a number of law schools, including Brooklyn Law School, New York Law School, George Mason University School of Law, and the University of Müenster in Münster, Germany. Judge Wallach has received a number of awards, including: the ABA Liberty Bell Award in 1993; the Nevada Press Association President's Award in 1994; and the Clark County School Librarians Intellectual Freedom Award in 1995. Judge Wallach served on active duty in the Army of the United States from 1969 to 1971. During his military career, he was awarded the Bronze Star, the Air Medal, the Good Conduct Medal, the Meritorious Service Medal, the Nevada Medal of Merit, the Valorous Unit Citation, a Vietnam Campaign Medal, and the RVN Cross of Gallantry with Palm. Judge Wallach received his B.A. in Journalism from the University of Arizona in 1973, his J.D. from the University of California, Berkeley in 1976, and an LLB with honors in International Law from Cambridge University in 1981.

RICHARD G. TARANTO, circuit judge; was appointed to the United States Court of Appeals for the Federal Circuit by President Barack H. Obama, in 2013, confirmed by the Senate on March 11, 2013 and assumed the duties of his office on March 15, 2013. Judge Taranto practiced law with the firm of Farr and Taranto from 1989 to 2013, where he specialized in appellate litigation. From 1986 to 1989, he served as an Assistant to the Solicitor General, representing the United States in the Supreme Court. He was in private practice from 1984 to 1986 with the law firm of Onek, Klein and Farr. Judge Taranto served as a law clerk at all three levels of the federal court system. He clerked for Justice Sandra Day O'Connor of the Supreme Court of the United States from 1983 to 1984; for Judge Robert Bork of the United States Court of Appeals for the District of Columbia Circuit from 1982 to 1983; and for Judge Abraham Sofaer of the United States District Court for the Southern District of New York from 1981 to 1982. Judge Taranto received a J.D. from Yale Law School in 1981 and a B.A. from Pomona College in 1977.

RAYMOND T. CHEN, circuit judge; was appointed to the United States Court of Appeals for the Federal Circuit by President Barack H. Obama in 2013, confirmed by the Senate on August 1, 2013 and assumed his office on August 5, 2013. Judge Chen served as Deputy General Counsel for Intellectual Property Law and Solicitor at the United States Patent and Trademark Office from 2008 to 2013. He was an Associate Solicitor in that office from 1998 to 2008. From 1996 to 1998, Judge Chen served as a Technical Assistant at the United States Court of Appeals for the Federal Circuit. Before joining the court staff, Judge Chen was an associate with Knobbe, Martens, Olson and Bear from 1994 to 1996. Before entering law school, Judge Chen worked as a scientist at the law firm of Hecker and Harriman from 1989 to 1991. Judge Chen received his J.D. from the New York University School of Law in 1994 and his B.S. in Electrical Engineering from the University of California, Los Angeles in 1990.

TODD M. HUGHES, circuit judge; was appointed to the United States Court of Appeals for the Federal Circuit by President Barack H. Obama in 2013, confirmed by the Senate on September 24, 2013 and assumed the duties of his office on September 30, 2013. Judge Hughes served as Deputy Director of the Commercial Litigation Branch of the Civil Division of the United States Department of Justice from 2007 to 2013. He was the Assistant Director in that office from 1999 to 2007 and a Trial Attorney from 1994 to 1999. From 1992 to 1994, Judge Hughes served as a Law Clerk to Circuit Judge Robert Krupansky of the United States Court of Appeals for the Sixth Circuit. He was an Adjunct Lecturer in Law at Cleveland-Marshall College of Law during the Spring, 1994 semester. Judge Hughes received a J.D. from Duke Law School in 1992, an M.A. from Duke University in 1992, and an A.B. from Harvard College in 1989.

KARA FARNANDEZ STOLL, circuit judge; was appointed to the United States Court of Appeals for the Federal Circuit by President Barack H. Obama on November 12, 2014, was confirmed unanimously by the United States Senate on July 7, 2015, and assumed her duties on July 17, 2015. Judge Stoll practiced law with the firm of Finnegan, Henderson, Farabow, Garrett and Dunner from 1998 to 2015, and became a partner at the firm in 2006. While in private practice, Judge Stoll specialized in patent litigation with an emphasis on appeals. Judge Stoll was an adjunct professor at George Mason University Law School from 2008 to 2015 and at the Howard University School of Law from 2004 to 2008. From 1997 to 1998, Judge Stoll served as a law clerk to The Honorable Alvin A. Schall of the United States Court of Appeals for the Federal Circuit. Judge Stoll worked as a patent examiner at the United States Patent and Trademark Office from 1991 to 1997. Judge Stoll received a J.D. from the Georgetown University School of Law in 1997, where she received the Leon Robin Patent Award, and a B.S.E.E. from Michigan State University in 1991.

SENIOR CIRCUIT JUDGES

HALDANE ROBERT MAYER, circuit judge; has been a member of the court since 1987. He served as Chief Judge from 1997 to 2004. Born in Buffalo, Judge Mayer was educated in the public schools of Lockport, New York, before attending the United States Military Academy at West Point, from which he graduated with a Bachelor of Science degree in 1963. He earned a law degree in 1971 at the Marshall-Wythe School of Law of The College of William and Mary, where he was editor-in-chief of the *William and Mary Law Review* as well as a member of Omicron Delta Kappa National Leadership Society. He has served as a director of the William and Mary Law School Association. Judge Mayer served on active duty in the Army of the United States from 1963 until 1975 in the Infantry and the Judge Advocate General's Corps. He was awarded the Bronze Star Medal, the Meritorious Service Medal, the Army Commendation Medal with Oak Leaf Cluster, the Combat Infantryman Badge, Parachutist Badge, Ranger Tab, RVN Ranger Combat Badge, and several campaign and service ribbons. He resigned his Regular Army commission to take an Army Reserve commission, retiring in 1985 as a lieutenant colonel. In 1971, Judge Mayer served as a law clerk for Judge John D. Butzner, Jr., of the United States Court of Appeals for the Fourth Circuit in Richmond, VA. He practiced law in Charlottesville, VA, in the mid-1970's, simultaneously serving as an adjunct at the University of Virginia School of Law, as he did again in the 1990's. He has also been an adjunct at George Washington University National Law Center. From 1977 through 1980, Judge Mayer was the Special Assistant to the Chief Justice of the United States, Warren E. Burger, after which he returned to private law practice in Washington, DC, until he became Deputy and Acting Special Counsel (by designation of the President). President Ronald Reagan appointed Judge Mayer to what is now the United States Court of Federal Claims in 1982, and to the United States Court of Appeals for the Federal Circuit in 1987. He assumed senior status on June 30, 2010.

S. JAY PLAGER, circuit judge; was appointed Circuit Judge by President George H.W. Bush in 1989. Prior to his appointment, Judge Plager served in the Executive Office of the President from 1987 to 1989, as Associate Director of OMB and as Administrator, OIRA. He served as Counselor to the Under Secretary, Department of Health and Human Services from 1986 to 1987. Judge Plager was Dean and Professor, Indiana University School of Law from 1977 to 1984. He was Professor, Faculty of Law, University of Illinois from 1964 to 1977, and from 1958 to 1964 was Professor, Faculty of Law, University of Florida. Judge Plager was Visiting Scholar, Stanford University Law School from 1984 to 1985, Visiting Fellow, Trinity College, and Visiting Professor, Cambridge University in 1980, and Visiting Research Professor of Law, University of Wisconsin from 1967 to 1968. Judge Plager served on active duty in the United States Navy during the Korean Conflict. Judge Plager grew up in New Jersey, where he attended public schools. In 1952, he received an A.B. degree from the University of North Carolina, a J.D. in 1958 from the University of Florida, with high honors, where he was editor-in-chief of the *Florida Law Review*, and in 1961 an LL.M. from Columbia University. He has three children. Judge Plager assumed senior status in 2000.

RAYMOND C. CLEVENGER III, circuit judge; was appointed by President George H.W. Bush in 1990. Judge Clevenger received a B.A. from Yale University in 1959. As a Carnegie Teaching Fellow, he taught European History at Yale College in the 1959–60 academic year. From 1960 to 1963, he was employed by the Morgan Guaranty Trust Company in New York City. He received an LL.B. from Yale University in 1966. Judge Clevenger served as a law clerk to Mr. Justice White in October Term 1966. Judge Clevenger joined Wilmer, Cutler and Pickering in 1967, serving as a partner in the firm from 1974 until his appointment to the bench. Judge Clevenger assumed senior status on February 1, 2006.

ALVIN A. SCHALL, circuit judge; was appointed by President George H.W. Bush in 1992. Prior to his appointment, Judge Schall served as Assistant to the Attorney General of the United States from 1988 to 1992. He was a member of the Washington, DC law firm of Perlman and Partners from 1987 to 1988. He served as Trial Attorney and Senior Trial Counsel, Civil Division, United States Department of Justice, from 1978 to 1987. Judge Schall was an Assistant United States Attorney, Office of the United States Attorney for the Eastern District of New York, from 1973 to 1978, and served as Chief of the Appeals Division from 1977 to 1978. From 1969 to 1973, Judge Schall was in private practice with the New York City law firm of Shearman and Sterling. Judge Schall received a B.A. degree from Princeton University in 1966 and a J.D. degree from Tulane Law School in 1969. Judge Schall assumed senior status on October 5, 2009.

WILLIAM C. BRYSON, circuit judge; was appointed by President William J. Clinton in 1994. Prior to his appointment, Judge Bryson was with the United States Department of Justice from 1978 to 1994. During that period, he served as an Assistant to the Solicitor General [1978–79], Chief of the Appellate Section of the Criminal Division [1979–83], Counsel to the Organized Crime and Racketeering Section [1983–86], Deputy Solicitor General [1986–94], Acting Solicitor General [1989 and 1993], and Acting Associate Attorney General [1994]. He was an Associate at the Washington, DC law firm of Miller, Cassidy, Larroca and Lewin from 1975 to 1978. Judge Bryson served as Law Clerk to the Honorable Henry J. Friendly, United States Court of Appeals for the Second Circuit from 1973 to 1974, and as Law Clerk to the Honorable Thurgood Marshall, Supreme Court of the United States, from 1974 to 1975. Judge Bryson received an A.B. from Harvard College in 1969 and a J.D. from the University of Texas School of Law in 1973.

RICHARD LINN, circuit judge; was appointed by President William J. Clinton in 1999. Prior to his appointment, Judge Linn was a Partner and Practice Group Leader at the Washington, DC law firm of Foley and Lardner from 1997 to 1999. He was a Partner and head of the intellectual property department at Marks and Murase, LLP from 1977 to 1997.

Judge Linn served as Patent Advisor, United States Naval Air Systems Command from 1971 to 1972, was a Patent Agent at the United States Naval Research Laboratory from 1968 to 1969, and served as a Patent Examiner at the United States Patent Office from 1965 to 1968. He was a member of the founding Board of Governors of the Virginia Bar Section on Patent, Trademark, and Copyright Law and served as Chairman in 1975. In 2000, Judge Linn received the Rensselaer Alumni Association Fellows Award. He was honored in 2006 for dedication, service, and devotion to justice by the Austin Intellectual Property Law Association. Judge Linn was awarded the 2009 New York Intellectual Property Law Association Leadership Award. He also received the 2009 Jefferson Medal from the New Jersey Intellectual Property Law Association ''in recognition of meritorious and outstanding contributions in support of the Constitution of the United States of America and furtherance of a fundamental principle thereof—'to promote the progress of Science and useful Arts.' '' In 2010, Judge Linn received the Outstanding Public Service Award from the New York Intellectual Property Law Association. In 2011, he was awarded the inaugural Mark Banner Award by the American Bar Association for his contributions to intellectual property law and the A. Sherman Christensen Award by the American Inns of Court Foundation for distinguished, exceptional and significant leadership to the American Inns of Court movement. He served as an Adjunct Professor and Professorial Lecturer in Law at George Washington University Law School from 2001 to 2003, and currently serves on the Law School's Intellectual Property Advisory Board. Judge Linn is a past president of the Giles Sutherland Rich American Inn of Court, a member of the Richard Linn American Inn of Court, a visiting member of the Hon. William C. Conner American Inn of Court, and an honorary lifetime member of the Benjamin Franklin American Inn of Court. He received a B.E.E. from Rensselaer Polytechnic Institute in 1965, and a J.D. from Georgetown University Law Center in 1969.

OFFICERS OF THE UNITED STATES COURT OF APPEALS FOR THE FEDERAL CIRCUIT

Circuit Executive and Clerk of Court.—Peter R. Marksteiner (202) 275–8020.
General Counsel.—J. Douglas Steere, 275–8080.
Circuit Librarian.—John D. Moore, 275–8403.
Chief Deputy Clerk.—Jarrett B. Perlow, 275–8021.
Director of Information Technology.—Mona Harrington, 275–8420.
Deputy Circuit Executive and Operations Officer.—Dale Bosley, 275–8141.

UNITED STATES DISTRICT COURT FOR THE DISTRICT OF COLUMBIA

E. Barrett Prettyman U.S. Courthouse, 333 Constitution Avenue, NW., 20001
Room 2002, phone (202) 354–3320, fax 354–3412

BERYL A. HOWELL, chief judge; born in Fort Benning, GA; daughter of Col. (Ret.) Leamon and Ruth Howell; Killeen High School, Killeen, TX, 1974; B.A. with honors in philosophy, Bryn Mawr College (President and Member, Honor Board, 1976–78); J.D., Columbia University School of Law, 1983 (Harlan Fiske Stone Scholar, 1981–82; International Fellows Program, 1982–83, *Transnational Law Journal*, Notes Editor); law clerk to Hon. Dickinson R. Debevoise, District of New Jersey, 1983–84; litigation associate, Schulte, Roth and Zabel, 1985–87; Assistant United States Attorney, United States District Court for the Eastern District of New York, 1987–93; Deputy Chief, Narcotics Section, 1990–93; Senior Counsel, U.S. Senate Committee on the Judiciary Subcommittee on Technology and the Law, 1993–94; Senior Counsel, U.S. Senate Committee on the Judiciary Subcommittee on Antitrust, Business Rights and Competition, 1995–96; General Counsel, U.S. Senate Committee on the Judiciary, 1997–2003; Executive Managing Director and General Counsel, Stroz Friedberg, 2003–09; Commissioner, United States Sentencing Commission, 2004–11; Member, Commission on Cyber Security for the 44th Presidency, 2008; Adjunct Professor of Law, American University's Washington College of Law, 2010; appointed judge, U.S. District Court for the District of Columbia by President Obama on December 27, 2010, took oath of office on January 21, 2011; appointed by Chief Justice Roberts to serve on the Judicial Conference of the U.S. Committee on Information Technology, 2013–16, and to the Judicial Conference, 2016–present. Awards include U.S. Attorney's Special Achievement Award for Sustained Superior Performance, 1990, 1991; Drug Enforcement Administration Commendations, 1990, 1992, 1993; Attorney General's Director's Award for Superior Performance, 1991; Federal Bureau of Investigation Award and New York City Department of Investigation Award for public corruption investigation and prosecution, 1992; Freedom of Information Hall of Fame, 2001; First Amendment Award, Society of Professional Journalists, 2004; Federal Bureau of Investigation Director's Award, 2006; Book chapters and law review article publications include Seven Weeks: The Making of the USA PATRIOT Act, *The George Washington Law Review*, 2004; FISA's Fruits in Criminal Cases: An Opportunity for Improved Accountability, UCLA Journal of International Law and Foreign Affairs, 2007; Book Chapters include: Real World Problems of Virtual Crime, in Cybercrime: Digital Cops in a Networked Environment, 2007; Foreign Intelligence Surveillance Act: Has the Solution Become the Problem, in Protecting What Matters: Technology, Security, and Liberty Since 9/11, 2006; and articles in the *New York Law Journal, Journal of Internet Law, Vermont Bar Journal*, and *Yale Journal of Law and Technology*.

EMMET G. SULLIVAN, judge; son of Emmet A. Sullivan and Eileen G. Sullivan; born in Washington, DC; graduated McKinley High School, 1964; B.A., Howard University, 1968; J.D., Howard University Law School, 1971; recipient of Reginald Heber Smith Fellowship, assigned to the Neighborhood Legal Services Program in Washington, DC, 1971–72; law clerk to Judge James A. Washington, Jr., 1972–73; joined the law firm of Houston and Gardner, 1973–80, became a partner; thereafter, was a partner with Houston, Sullivan and Gardner; board of directors of the DC Law Students in Court Program; DC Judicial Conference Voluntary Arbitration Committee; Nominating Committee of the Bar Association of the District of Columbia; U.S. District Court Committee on Grievances; adjunct professor at Howard University School of Law; adjunct professor at American University, Washington College of Law; member: National Bar Association, Washington Bar Association, Bar Association of the District of Columbia; appointed by President Reagan to the Superior Court of the District of Columbia as an associate judge, 1984; deputy presiding judge and presiding judge of the probate and tax division; chairperson of the rules committees for the probate and tax divisions; member: Court Rules Committee and the Jury Plan Committee; appointed by President George H.W. Bush to serve as an associate judge of the District of Columbia Court of Appeals, 1991; chairperson for the nineteenth annual judicial conference of the

District of Columbia, 1994 (the Conference theme was "Rejuvenating Juvenile Justice—Responses to the Problems of Juvenile Violence in the District of Columbia"); appointed by chief judge Wagner to chair the "Task Force on Families and Violence for the District of Columbia Courts"; nominated to the U.S. District Court by President Clinton on March 22, 1994; and confirmed by the U.S. Senate on June 15, 1994; appointed by Chief Justice Rehnquist to serve on the Judicial Conference of the U.S. Committee on Criminal Law 1998–2005; District of Columbia Judicial Disabilities and Tenure Commission, 1996–2001; chair of the District of Columbia Judicial Nomination Commission since 2005; appointed by Chief Justice Roberts to serve on the Judicial Conference of the U.S. Committee on Space and Facilities, 2012, re-appointed by the Chief Justice in 2015; only person in the District of Columbia to have been appointed to three judicial positions by three different U.S. Presidents; recipient of the Ollie May Cooper Award, awarded by the Washington Bar Association; the Thurgood Marshall Award of Excellence, awarded by the Howard University Alumni Association; the Howard University Distinguished Alumni Award, awarded by the President and Board of Trustees of Howard University; American Inns of Court Professionalism Award for the District of Columbia Circuit for 2015; the National Bar Association's Gertrude E. Rush Award; the Charles Hamilton Houston Medallion of Merit, awarded by the Washington Bar Association; named Judge of the Year for 2017 by the Bar Association of the District of Columbia; founder and current director of the Frederick B. Abramson Scholarship Foundation.

COLLEEN KOLLAR-KOTELLY, judge; born in New York, NY; daughter of Konstantine and Irene Kollar; attended bilingual schools in Mexico, Ecuador, and Venezuela and Georgetown Visitation Preparatory School in Washington, DC; received B.A. degree in English at Catholic University (Delta Epsilon Honor Society); received J.D. at Catholic University's Columbus School of Law (Moot Court Board of Governors); law clerk to Hon. Catherine B. Kelly, District of Columbia Court of Appeals, 1968–69; attorney, United States Department of Justice, Criminal Division, Appellate Section, 1969–72; chief legal counsel, Saint Elizabeths Hospital, Department of Health and Human Services, 1972–84; received Saint Elizabeths Hospital Certificate of Appreciation, 1981; Meritorious Achievement Award from Alcohol, Drug Abuse and Mental Health Administration (ADAMHA), Department of Health and Human Services, 1981; appointed judge, Superior Court of the District of Columbia by President Reagan, October 3, 1984, took oath of office October 21, 1984; served as Deputy Presiding Judge, Criminal Division, January 1996–April 1997; received Achievement Recognition Award, Hispanic Heritage CORO Awards Celebration, 1996; appointed judge, U.S. District Court for the District of Columbia by President Clinton on March 26, 1997, took oath of office May 12, 1997; appointed by Chief Justice Rehnquist to serve on the Financial Disclosure Committee, 2000–02; presiding judge of the United States Foreign Intelligence Surveillance Court, 2002–09; appointed by Chief Justice John Roberts to the Judicial Resources Committee of the Judicial Conference, 2009–16; appointed by Chief Judge Beryl A. Howell to the District of Columbia Commission on Judicial Disabilities and Tenure, 2017.

JAMES E. BOASBERG, judge; born in San Francisco, CA, 1963; son of Emanuel Boasberg III and Sarah Szold Boasberg; graduated St. Albans School, Washington, DC, 1981; B.A., *magna cum laude*, in history from Yale College, 1985; M.St. in modern European history from Oxford University, 1986; J.D. from Yale Law School, 1990; law clerk to Judge Dorothy W. Nelson on the U.S. Court of Appeals for the Ninth Circuit, 1990–91; associate, Keker and Van Nest in San Francisco, CA, 1991–94; associate, Kellogg, Huber, Hansen, Todd and Evans in Washington, DC, 1995–96; Assistant United States Attorney for the District of Columbia, 1996–2002; visiting lecturer, George Washington Law School, 2003; Associate Judge, District of Columbia Superior Court, 2002–11; United States District Judge for the District of Columbia, 2011–present; appointed to the U.S. Foreign Intelligence Surveillance Court, May 2014.

AMY BERMAN JACKSON, judge; appointed March of 2011; prior to joining the Court, engaged in private practice in Washington, DC, as a member of Trout Cacheris, specializing in complex criminal and civil trials and appeals; earlier, partner at Venable, Baetjer, Howard, and Civiletti; Assistant United States Attorney for the District of Columbia, 1980–86; received Department of Justice Special Achievement Awards for work on murder and sexual assault cases; J.D., *cum laude*, Harvard Law School, 1979; A.B. *cum laude*, Harvard College, 1976; law clerk to the Honorable Harrison L. Winter of the United States Court of Appeals for the Fourth Circuit; lectured on corporate criminal investigations and has been a regular teacher at the National Institute of Trial Advocacy, the Georgetown University Law Center CLE Intensive Session in Trial Advocacy Skills, and the Harvard Law School Trial Advocacy workshop; while in private practice, was elected to serve as a DC Bar delegate to the ABA House of Delegates; active in the ABA Litigation Section, the ABA Criminal Justice Section White Collar Crime Committee, and DC Bar and Women's Bar Association committee activities; member of the Parent Steering Committee of the Interdisciplinary Council on Developmental and Learning Disorders; served on the Board of the DC Rape Crisis Center and other educational and community organizations.

RUDOLPH CONTRERAS, judge, appointed to the District Court in March 2012. In April 2016, Chief Justice John Roberts appointed Contreras to the United States Foreign Intelligence Surveillance Court for a term starting May 19, 2016. Prior to joining the District Court, Judge Contreras served from 2006 to 2012 as the Chief of the Civil Division of the United States Attorney's Office of the District of Columbia. In that capacity, he supervised 39 Assistant United States Attorneys who defend and bring civil cases on behalf of the United States. Judge Contreras was awarded his Bachelor of Science degree from Florida State University in 1984 and his Juris Doctor degree, *cum laude*, from the University of Pennsylvania Law School in 1991, where he was a member of the Order of the Coif and Editor of the *University of Pennsylvania Law Review*. Following law school, Judge Contreras joined the law firm of Jones, Day, Reavis and Pogue, where he was an Associate in the General Litigation Group. In 1994, Judge Contreras joined the United States Attorney's Office for the District of Columbia as an Assistant United States Attorney in the Civil Division, where he was responsible for a wide array of cases, including employment, Federal Tort Claims Act, Administrative Procedure Act, Bivens and Affirmative Civil Enforcement matters. In 2003, Judge Contreras left the DC Office to become the Chief of the Civil Division for the United States Attorney's Office in Delaware, where he oversaw that civil program and personally handled a wide variety of matters, including environmental and health care fraud cases.

KETANJI BROWN JACKSON, judge, received her commission as a United States District Judge in March 2013. Until December 2014, she also served as a Vice Chair and Commissioner on the United States Sentencing Commission, and she taught a seminar on Sentencing Policy at the George Washington University Law School as an adjunct professor. Prior to her service on the Commission, Judge Jackson was Of Counsel at Morrison and Foerster LLP for three years, with a practice that focused on criminal and civil appellate litigation in both state and federal courts, as well as cases in the Supreme Court of the United States. From 2005 until 2007, prior to joining Morrison and Foerster LLP, Judge Jackson served as an assistant federal public defender in the Appeals Division of the Office of the Federal Public Defender in the District of Columbia. Before that appointment, Judge Jackson worked as an assistant special counsel at the United States Sentencing Commission and as an associate with two law firms: one, specializing in white collar criminal defense; the other, focusing on the negotiated settlement of mass-tort claims. Judge Jackson also served as a law clerk to three federal judges: Associate Justice Stephen G. Breyer of the Supreme Court of the United States (October Term 1999), Judge Bruce M. Selya of the U.S. Court of Appeals for the First Circuit (1997–98), and Judge Patti B. Saris of the U.S. District Court for the District of Massachusetts (1996–97). In 2017, Chief Justice Roberts appointed Judge Jackson to serve a three-year term on the Judicial Conference of the U.S. Committee on Defender Services. Judge Jackson is currently a member of the Board of Overseers of Harvard University and of the Council of the American Law Institute and also serves on the board of the DC Circuit Historical Society. She received an A.B., *magna cum laude*, in Government from Harvard-Radcliffe College in 1992, and, in 1996, a J.D., *cum laude*, from Harvard Law School, where she served as a supervising editor of the *Harvard Law Review*.

CHRISTOPHER R. COOPER, judge; born in Mobile, Alabama, 1966; son of Paulette Reid Cooper and William Madison Cooper; graduated Trinity Preparatory School, Winter Park, Florida, 1984; B.A., *summa cum laude*, in economics and political science, Yale University, 1988, and member of Phi Beta Kappa; Research Analyst, Strategic Planning Associates, Washington, DC, 1988–90; J.D., with distinction, Stanford Law School, 1993; President, Volume 45, *Stanford Law Review*, 1992–93; Board Member, East Palo Alto Community Law Project, 1992–93; law clerk to then-Chief Judge Abner J. Mikva, United States Court of Appeals for the D.C. Circuit, 1993–94; United States Department of Justice, Special Assistant to the Deputy Attorney General, Washington, DC, 1994–96; Associate (1996–2000) and Partner (2000), Miller, Cassidy, Larroca and Lewin LLC, Washington, DC; Partner, Baker Botts LLP, Washington, DC (2000–10) and London (2010–12); Partner, Covington and Burling LLP, London (2012–13) and Washington, DC (2013–14); appointed to the United States District Court for the District of Columbia on March 28, 2014.

TANYA S. CHUTKAN, judge; born in Kingston, Jamaica; daughter of Dr. Winston Chutkan and Noelle Chutkan, Esq.; B.A., George Washington University, 1983; J.D., University of Pennsylvania Law School, 1987 (Associate Editor, *Law Review*; Arthur Littleton Legal Writing Fellow); Associate, Hogan and Hartson LLP, 1987–90; Associate, Donovan, Leisure, Rogovin, Huge and Schiller, 1990–91; Staff Attorney and Supervisor, Public Defender Service for the District of Columbia, 1991–2002; Counsel and Partner, Boies, Schiller and Flexner LLP, 2002–14; Steering Committee, Criminal Law and Individual Rights Section of the District of Columbia Bar, 2000–03; member of Visiting Faculty, Harvard Law School Trial Advocacy Workshop; nominated judge, U.S. District Court for the District of Columbia by President Obama; confirmed by the Senate on June 4, 2014; took the oath of office on July 25, 2014.

RANDOLPH D. MOSS, judge, born in Springfield, Ohio 1961; son of Dr. Howard A. Moss and Adrienne Moss. A.B., *summa cum laude*, phi beta kappa, philosophy, from Hamilton College in 1983; J.D., Yale Law School, 1986. Law clerk to Judge Pierre Leval, United States District Court for the Southern District of New York, 1986–87. Law clerk to Justice John Paul Stevens, United States Supreme Court, 1988–89. Private practice at Wilmer, Cutler and Pickering, first as associate then as partner, 1989–96. Department of Justice Office of Legal Counsel, 1996–2001; Deputy Assistant Attorney General, 1996–98; Acting Assistant Attorney General, 1998–2000; Assistant Attorney General, 2000–01. Partner, Wilmer, Cutler, Pickering Hale and Dorr, 2001–14; chair of the firm's Regulatory and Government Affairs Department. Confirmed to the bench November 2014.

AMIT MEHTA, judge; born in Patan, India; son of Priyavadan and Ragini Mehta. B.A., *magna cum laude* and Phi Beta Kappa in political science and economics from Georgetown University, 1993; J.D., Order of the Coif, University of Virginia, 1997; Law Clerk to Judge Susan P. Graber, United States Court of Appeals for the Ninth Circuit, 1998–1999; Associate, Counsel and Partner, Zuckerman Spaeder, LLP, 1999–2002, 2007–14; Staff Attorney, Public Defender Service for the District of Columbia, 2002–07; Judge, U.S. District Court for the District of Columbia, 2014–present.

TIMOTHY J. KELLY, judge; born in Glen Cove, NY, 1969; son of Timothy Noel Kelly and Helen Ann Kelly (Stevens); graduated Delbarton School, Morristown, NJ, 1987; A.B., *cum laude*, Duke University, 1991; J.D., Georgetown University, 1997; Senior Associate Editor, *American Criminal Law Review*, 1996–97; Associate, Arnold & Porter, Washington, DC, 1997–2001, 2002–03; Loaned Associate to the Legal Aid Society of the District of Columbia, 1999–2000; Law Clerk to the Honorable Ronald L. Buckwalter, United States District Court for the Eastern District of Pennsylvania, 2001–02; Assistant United States Attorney for the District of Columbia, 2003–07; Trial Attorney, Public Integrity Section, Criminal Division, United States Department of Justice, 2007–13; Recipient of the Assistant Attorney General's Award for Distinguished Service, 2012; Treasurer, District of Columbia Bar's Criminal Law and Individual Rights Section Steering Committee, 2013–16; Chief Counsel for National Security and Senior Crime Counsel to Ranking Member (2013–14) and Chairman (2015–17) of the Senate Judiciary Committee Charles E. Grassley; Staff Director to Co-Chairman of the Senate Caucus on International Narcotics Control, Charles E. Grassley, 2013–17; appointed to the United States District Court for the District of Columbia on September 8, 2017.

TREVOR N. MCFADDEN, judge; born in Alexandria, VA, 1978; son of William J. and Carol (Prester) McFadden. Attended the American School in London and Robinson Secondary School, Fairfax, VA. B.A., *magna cum laude*, in English and political science, from Wheaton College, IL, 2001; J.D., Order of the Coif and *Virginia Law Review*, University of Virginia, 2006; Law Clerk to Judge Steven M. Colloton, United States Court of Appeals for the Eighth Circuit, 2006–07; Counsel to the Deputy Attorney General, United States Department of Justice, 2007–09; Assistant United States Attorney, District of Columbia, 2009–13; Associate and Partner, Baker & McKenzie, LLP, Washington, DC, 2013–17; Acting Principal Deputy Assistant Attorney General and Deputy Assistant Attorney General, United States Department of Justice Criminal Division, 2017. Confirmed to the bench October 2017.

DABNEY L. FRIEDRICH, judge; B.A., *magna cum laude*, Phi Beta Kappa, economics, from Trinity University, 1988; Diploma in Legal Studies from University College, Oxford University, 1989; J.D. from Yale Law School, 1992; law clerk to Judge Thomas F. Hogan of the United States District Court for the District of Columbia, 1992–94; associate, Latham & Watkins in San Diego, CA, 1994–95; Assistant United States Attorney for the Southern District of California, 1995–98; Assistant United States Attorney for the Eastern District of Virginia, 1998–2002; counsel to Ranking Member and Chairman Orrin G. Hatch of the United States Senate Committee on the Judiciary, 2002–03; associate counsel to President George W. Bush, 2003–06; member, United States Sentencing Commission, 2006–17; adjunct law professor, George Washington Law School, 2014; United States District Judge for the District of Columbia, December 2017–present.

SENIOR JUDGES

THOMAS F. HOGAN, senior judge; born in Washington, DC, 1938; son of Adm. Bartholomew W. (MC) (USN) Surgeon Gen., USN, 1956–62, and Grace (Gloninger) Hogan; Georgetown Preparatory School, 1956; A.B., Georgetown University (classical), 1960; master's program, American and English literature, George Washington University, 1960–62; J.D., Georgetown University, 1965–66; Honorary Degree, Doctor of Laws, Georgetown University Law Center, May 1999; St. Thomas More Fellow, Georgetown University Law Center, 1965–66; American Jurisprudence Award: Corporation Law; member, bars of the District of Columbia and Maryland; law clerk to Hon. William B. Jones, U.S. District Court for the District of Columbia, 1966–67; counsel, Federal Commission on Reform of Federal Criminal Laws, 1967–68; private practice of law in the District of Columbia and Maryland, 1968–82; adjunct professor of law, Potomac School of Law, 1977–79; adjunct professor of law, Georgetown University Law Center, 1986–88; public member, officer evaluation board, U.S. Foreign Service, 1973; member: American Bar Association, State Chairman, Maryland Drug Abuse Education Program, Young Lawyers Section (1970–73), District of Columbia Bar Association, Bar Association of the District of Columbia, Maryland State Bar Association, Montgomery County Bar Association, National Institute for Trial Advocacy, Defense Research Institute, The Barristers, The Lawyers Club; chairman, board of directors, Christ Child Institute for Emotionally Ill Children, 1971–74; served on many committees; USDC Executive Committee; Conference Committee on Administration of Federal Magistrates System, 1988–91; chairman, Inter-Circuit Assignment Committee, 1990–96; appointed judge of the U.S. District Court for the District of Columbia by President Reagan on October 4, 1982; chief judge, June 19, 2001; member: Judicial Conference of the United States, 2001–08; Executive Committee, U.S. District Court for the District of Columbia 873 of the Judicial Conference, July 2001–08, Chair 2005–08; Edward J. Devitt Distinguished Service to Justice Award, 2011; Director of the Administrative Office of the United States Courts, 2011–13; member, Foreign Intelligence Surveillance Court, 2009–16, Presiding Judge, 2014–16.

ROYCE C. LAMBERTH, senior judge; born in San Antonio, TX, 1943; son of Nell Elizabeth Synder and Larimore S. Lamberth, Sr.; South San Antonio High School, 1961; B.A., University of Texas at Austin, 1966; LL.B., University of Texas School of Law, 1967; permanent president, class of 1967, University of Texas School of Law; U.S. Army (Captain, Judge Advocate General's Corps, 1968–74; Vietnam Service Medal, Air Medal, Bronze Star with Oak Leaf Cluster, Meritorious Service Medal with Oak Leaf Cluster); Assistant U.S. Attorney, District of Columbia, 1974–87 (chief, Civil Division, 1978–87); President's Reorganization Project, Federal Legal Representation Study, 1978–79; honorary faculty, Army Judge Advocate General's School, 1976; Attorney General's Special Commendation Award; Attorney General's John Marshall Award, 1982; vice chairman, Armed Services and Veterans Affairs Committee, Section on Administrative Law, American Bar Association, 1979–82, chairman, 1983–84; chairman, Professional Ethics Committee, 1989–91; co-chairman, Committee of Article III Judges, Judiciary Section 1989–present; chairman, Federal Litigation Section, 1986–87; chairman, Federal Rules Committee, 1985–86; deputy chairman, Council of the Federal Lawyer, 1980–83; chairman, Career Service Committee, Federal Bar Association, 1978–80; appointed judge, U.S. District Court for the District of Columbia by President Reagan, November 16, 1987; appointed by Chief Justice Rehnquist to be presiding judge of the United States Foreign Intelligence Surveillance Court, 1995–2002.

PAUL L. FRIEDMAN, senior judge; born in Buffalo, NY, 1944; son of Cecil A. and Charlotte Wagner Friedman; B.A., political science, Cornell University, 1965; J.D., *cum laude*, School of Law, State University of New York at Buffalo, 1968; admitted to the bars of the District of Columbia, New York, U.S. Supreme Court, and U.S. Courts of Appeals for the D.C., Federal, Fourth, Fifth, Sixth, Seventh, Ninth and Eleventh Circuits; Law Clerk to Judge Aubrey E. Robinson, Jr., U.S. District Court for the District of Columbia, 1968–69; Law Clerk to Judge Roger Robb, U.S. Court of Appeals for the District of Columbia Circuit, 1969–70; Assistant U.S. Attorney for the District of Columbia, 1970–74; assistant to the Solicitor General of the United States, 1974–76; associate independent counsel, Iran-Contra investigation, 1987–88, private law practice, White and Case, partner, 1979–94; associate, 1976–79; member: American Bar Association, Commission on Multidisciplinary Practice 1998–2000, District of Columbia Bar (president, 1986–87), American Law Institute (1984) and ALI Council, 1998–present (member of Executive Committee as Secretary, 2013–present), American Academy of Appellate Lawyers, Bar Association of the District of Columbia, Women's Bar Association of the District of Columbia, Washington Bar Association, Hispanic Bar Association, Assistant United States Attorneys Association of the District of Columbia (president, 1976–77), Civil Justice Reform Act Advisory Group (chair, 1991–94), District of Columbia Judicial Nomination Commission (member, 1990–94; chair, 1992–94), Advisory

Committee on Procedures, U.S. Court of Appeals for the D.C. Circuit (1982–88), Grievance Committee; U.S. District Court for the District of Columbia (member, 1981–87; chair, 1983–85); fellow, American College of Trial Lawyers; fellow, American Bar Foundation; board of directors: Frederick B. Abramson Memorial Foundation (president, 1991–94), Washington Area Lawyers for the Arts (1988–92), Washington Legal Clinic for the Homeless (member, 1987–92; vice-president, 1988–91), Stuart Stiller Memorial Foundation (1980–94), American Judicature Society (1990–94), District of Columbia Public Defender Service (1989–92); member: Cosmos Club, Lawyers Club of Washington; recipient of Distinguished Alumnus Award, the University at Buffalo Law Alumni Association (1998); Civil Justice Award, Academy of Court Appointed Masters (2007); Judicial Honoree, the 138th Annual Banquet of the Bar Association of the District of Columbia (2009); Buffalo Law Review Award, the University at Buffalo Law Review (2016); Judge Charles R. Richey Equal Justice Award, the George Washington University Law School (2016); appointed 874 *Congressional Directory judge, U.S. District Court for the District of Columbia by President Clinton, June 16, 1994, and took oath of office August 1, 1994; U.S. Judicial Conference Advisory Committee on Federal Criminal Rules.*

ELLEN SEGAL HUVELLE, senior judge; born in Boston, MA, 1948; daughter of Robert M. Segal, Esq., and Sharlee Segal; B.A., Wellesley College, 1970; Masters in City Planning, Yale University, 1972; J.D., *magna cum laude*, Boston College Law School, 1975 (Order of the Coif; Articles Editor of the *Law Review*); law clerk to Chief Justice Edward F. Hennessey, Massachusetts Supreme Judicial Court, 1975–76; associate, Williams and Connolly, 1976–84; partner, Williams and Connolly, 1984–90; associate judge, Superior Court of the District of Columbia, 1990–99; appointed judge, U.S. District Court for the District of Columbia by President Clinton in October 1999, and took oath of office on February 25, 2000. Member: American Bar Association, District of Columbia Bar, Women's Bar Association; Fellow of the American Bar Foundation; Master in the Edward Bennett Williams Inn of Court and member of the Inn's Executive Committee; instructor of Trial Advocacy at the University of Virginia Law School; member of Visiting Faculty at Harvard Law School's Trial Advocacy Workshop; Boston College Law School Board of Overseers; seminar instructor at the Peking University School of Transnational Law in Shenzhen, 2010; faculty, CEELI Institute for training Tunisian judges, 2012; appointed by the Chief Justice of the United States to Judicial Conference Committee on Judicial Resources, 2002–09, Judicial Conference Committee on Criminal Law, 2011–17, Judicial Panel on Multidistrict Litigation, 2013–present; American Inns of Court Professionalism Award for the District of Columbia Circuit for 2017; Board Member for the Frederick B. Abramson Scholarship Foundation.

REGGIE B. WALTON, judge; born in Donora, PA, 1949; son of the late Theodore and Ruth (Garard) Walton; B.A., West Virginia State College, 1971; J.D., American University, Washington College of Law, 1974; admitted to the bars of the Supreme Court of Pennsylvania, 1974; United States District Court for the Eastern District of Pennsylvania, 1975; District of Columbia Court of Appeals, 1976; United States Court of Appeals for the District of Columbia Circuit, 1977; Supreme Court of the United States, 1980; United States District Court for the District of Columbia; Staff Attorney, Defender Association of Philadelphia, 1974–76; Assistant United States Attorney for the District of Columbia, 1976–80; Chief, Career Criminal Unit, Assistant United States Attorney for the District of Columbia, 1979–80; Executive Assistant United States Attorney for the District of Columbia, 1980–81; Associate Judge, Superior Court of the District of Columbia, 1981–89; deputy presiding judge of the Criminal Division, Superior Court of the District of Columbia, 1986–89; Associate Director, Office of National Drug Control Policy, Executive Office of the President, 1989–91; Senior White House Advisor for Crime, The White House, 1991; Associate Judge, Superior Court of the District of Columbia, 1991–2001; Presiding Judge of the Domestic Violence Unit, Superior Court of the District of Columbia, 2000; Presiding Judge of the Family Division, Superior Court of the District of Columbia, 2001; Instructor: National Judicial College, Reno, Nevada, 1999–present; Harvard University Law School, Trial Advocacy Workshop, 1994–present; National Institute of Trial Advocacy, Georgetown University Law School, 1983–present; co-author, Pretrial Drug Testing—An Essential Component of the National Drug Control Strategy, *Brigham Young University Journal of Public Law* (1991); Distinguished Alumnus Award, American University, Washington College of Law (1991); The William H. Hastie Award, The Judicial Council of the National Bar Association (1993); Commissioned as a Kentucky Colonel by the Governor (1990, 1991); Governor's Proclamation declaring April 9, 1991, Judge Reggie B. Walton Day in the State of Louisiana; The West Virginia State College National Alumni Association James R. Waddy Meritorious Service Award (1990); Secretary's Award, United States Department of Veterans Affairs (1990); Outstanding Alumnus Award, Ringgold High School (1987); Director's Award for Superior Performance as an Assistant United States Attorney (1980); Profiled in book entitled *Black Judges on Justice: Perspectives From The Bench* by Linn Washington (1995); appointed district judge, United

States District Court for the District of Columbia by President George W. Bush, September 24, 2001, and took oath of office October 29, 2001; appointed by President Bush in 2004 to serve as the Chairperson of the National Prison Rape Reduction Commission, a two-year commission created by the United States Congress tasked with the mission of identifying methods to curb the incidents of prison rape; appointed by former Chief Justice Rehnquist to serve on Judicial Conference Criminal Law Committee, 2005–11; member, United States Foreign Intelligence Surveillance Court, 2007–14; Presiding Judge, 2013–14; appointed by Chief Justice Roberts to serve on Judicial Conference Committee on Court Administration and Management, 2014–present; sitting by designation, United States District Court for the Western District of Pennsylvania, 2016–present; established and assists in operation of reentry court in United States District Court for the District of Columbia, 2016–present; serves on American Law Institute Committee on the Model Penal Code for Sexual Assault and Related Offenses, 2013–present; active youth mentor and participant in Big Brother program.

JOHN D. BATES, senior judge; born in Elizabeth, NJ, 1946; son of Richard D. and Sarah (Deacon) Bates; B.A., Wesleyan University, 1968; J.D., University of Maryland School of Law, 1976; U.S. Army (1968–71, 1st Lt., Vietnam Service Medal, Bronze Star); law clerk to Hon. Roszel Thomsen, U.S. District Court for the District of Maryland, 1976–77; Assistant U.S. Attorney, District of Columbia, 1980–97 (Chief, Civil Division, 1987–97); Director's Award for Superior Performance (1983); Attorney General's Special commendation Award (1986); Deputy Independent Counsel, Whitewater Investigation, 1995–97; private practice of law, Miller and Chevalier (partner, 1998–2001), Chair of Government Contracts Litigation Department and member of Executive Committee), Steptoe and Johnson (associate, 1977–80); District of Columbia Circuit Advisory Committee for Procedures, 1989–93; Civil Justice Reform Committee of the U.S. District Court for the District of Columbia, 1996–2001; Treasurer, D.C. Bar, 1992–93; Publications Committee, D.C. Bar (1991–97, Chair 1994–97); D.C. Bar Special Committee on Government Lawyers, 1990–91; D.C. Bar Task Force on Civility in the Profession, 1994–96; D.C. Bar Committee on Examination of Rule 49, 1995–96; Chair, Litigation Section, Federal Bar Association, 1986–89; Board of Directors, Washington Lawyers Committee for Civil Rights and Urban Affairs, 1999–2001; appointed to the U.S. District Court for the District of Columbia in December, 2001; member, Court Administration and Case Management Committee of the Judicial Conference, 2003–09; member, United States Foreign Intelligence Surveillance Court, 2006–13, presiding judge, 2009–13; Director, Administrative Office of United States Courts, 2013–14; Chairman, Advisory Committee on Federal Rules of Civil Procedure, 2015–present.

RICHARD J. LEON, judge; born in South Natick, MA, 1949; son of Silvano B. Leon and Rita (O'Rorke) Leon; A.B., Holy Cross College, 1971, J.D., *cum laude*, Suffolk Law School, 1974; LL.M., Harvard Law School, 1981; Law Clerk to Chief Justice McLaughlin and the Associate Justices, Superior Court of Massachusetts, 1974–75; Law Clerk to Hon. Thomas F. Kelleher, Supreme Court of Rhode Island, 1975–76; admitted to the bar, Rhode Island, 1975, and District of Columbia, 1991; Special Assistant U.S. Attorney, Southern District of New York, 1977–78; Assistant Professor of Law, St. John's Law School, New York, 1979–83; Senior Trial Attorney, Criminal Section, Tax Division, U.S. Department of Justice, 1983–87; Deputy Chief Minority Counsel, U.S. House Select ''Iran-Contra'' Committee, 1987–88; Deputy Assistant U.S. Attorney General, Environment Division, 1988–89; Partner, Baker and Hostetler, Washington, DC, 1989–99; Commissioner, The White House Fellows Commission, 1990–92; Chief Minority Counsel, U.S. House Foreign Affairs Committee ''October Suprise'' Task Force, 1992–93; Special Counsel, U.S. House Banking Committee ''Whitewater'' Investigation, 1994; Special Counsel, U.S. House Ethics Reform Task Force, 1997; Adjunct Professor, Georgetown University Law Center, 1997–present; Partner, Vorys, Sater, Seymour and Pease, Washington, DC, 1999–2002; Commissioner, Judicial Review Commission on Foreign Asset Control, 2000–01; Master, Edward Bennett Williams Inn of Court; appointed U.S. District Judge for the District of Columbia by President George W. Bush on February 19, 2002; took oath of office on March 20, 2002.

ROSEMARY M. COLLYER, judge; born in White Plains, NY, 1945; daughter of Thomas C. and Alice Henry Mayers; educated in parochial and public schools in Stamford, Connecticut; B.A., Trinity College, Washington, DC, 1968; J.D., University of Denver College of Law, 1977; practiced with Sherman and Howard, Denver, Colorado, 1977–81; Chairman, Federal Mine Safety and Health Review Commission, 1981–84, by appointment of President Ronald Reagan with Senate confirmation; General Counsel, National Labor Relations Board, 1984–89, by appointment of President Reagan with Senate confirmation; private practice with Crowell and Moring LLP, Washington, DC, 1989–2003; member and chairman of the firm's Management Committee; appointed U.S. District Judge for the District of Columbia by President George W. Bush and took oath of office on January 2, 2003. Member, Foreign Intelligence

Surveillance Court, 2013–present. Presiding Judge, Foreign Intelligence Surveillance Court, 2016–present. Chief Judge, Alien Terrorist Removal Court, 2016–present.

OFFICERS OF THE UNITED STATES DISTRICT COURT FOR THE DISTRICT OF COLUMBIA

Bankruptcy Judge.—S. Martin Teel, Jr.
United States Magistrate Judges: G. Michael Harvey, Robin M. Meriweather, Deborah A. Robinson.
Clerk of Court.—Angela D. Caesar.
Administrative Assistant to the Chief Judge.—Lisa J. Klem.

UNITED STATES COURT OF INTERNATIONAL TRADE

One Federal Plaza, New York, NY 10278–0001, phone (212) 264–2800

TIMOTHY C. STANCEU, chief judge; born in Canton, OH; A.B., Colgate University, 1973; J.D., Georgetown University Law Center, 1979; appointed to the U.S. Court of International Trade by President George W. Bush and began serving on April 15, 2003; prior to appointment, private practice for 13 years in Washington, DC, with the law firm Hogan and Hartson, LLP, during which he represented clients in a variety of matters involving customs and international trade law; Deputy Director, Office of Trade and Tariff Affairs, U.S. Department of the Treasury; where his responsibilities involved the regulatory and enforcement matters of the U.S. Customs Service and other agencies; Special Assistant to the Assistant Secretary of the Office of Enforcement, U.S. Department of the Treasury; Program Analyst and Environmental Protection Specialist, U.S. Environmental Protection Agency, where he concentrated on the development and review of regulations on various environmental subjects.

DELISSA A. RIDGWAY, judge; born in Kirksville, MO, June 28, 1955; B.A. (honors), University of Missouri-Columbia, 1975; graduate work, University of Missouri-Columbia, 1975–76; J.D., Northeastern University School of Law, 1979; Duke University School of Law, LL.M. in Judicial Studies–2014; Shaw Pittman Potts and Trowbridge (Washington, DC), 1979–94; Chair, Foreign Claims Settlement Commission of the U.S., 1994–98; Adjunct Professor of Law, Cornell Law School, 1999–present; Adjunct Professor of Law / Lecturer, Washington College of Law / The American University, 1992–94; District of Columbia Bar, Secretary, 1991–92; Board of Governors, 1992–98; President, Women's Bar Association, 1992–93; American Bar Association, Standing Committee on Federal Judicial Improvements (2008–11); Co-Chair, Section of Litigation Task Force on Implicit Bias (2010–13); Commission on Women in the Profession, 2002–05; Federal Bar Association, National Council, 1993–2002, 2003–present; Government Relations Committee, 1996–2008, Public Relations Committee Chair, 1998–99; Board of Directors, Federal Bar Building Corporation; Executive Committee, National Conference of Federal Trial Judges, 2004–11; Chair, National Conference of Federal Trial Judges, 2009–10; Board of Directors, American Judicature Society (2010–present); Founding Member of Board, D.C. Conference on Opportunities for Minorities in the Legal Profession, 1992–93; Chair, D.C. Bar Summit on Women in the Legal Profession, 1995–98; Fellow, American Bar Foundation; Member, American Law Institute; Fellow, Federal Bar Foundation; Earl W. Kintner Award of the Federal Bar Association (2000); Woman Lawyer of the Year, Washington, DC (2001); Distinguished Visiting Scholar-in-Residence, University of Missouri-Columbia (2003); sworn in as a judge to the U.S. Court of International Trade in May 1998.

LEO M. GORDON, judge; graduate of Newark Academy in Livingston, NJ; University of North Carolina-Chapel Hill, Phi Beta Kappa, 1973; J.D., Emory University School of Law, 1977; member of the Bars of New Jersey, Georgia and the District of Columbia; Assistant Counsel at the Subcommittee on Monopolies and Commercial Law, Committee on the Judiciary, U.S. House of Representatives, 1977–81; in that capacity, Judge Gordon was the principal attorney responsible for the Customs Courts Act of 1980 that created the U.S. Court of International Trade; for 25 years, Judge Gordon was on the staff at the Court, serving first as Assistant Clerk from 1981–99, and then Clerk of the Court from 1999–2006; appointed to the U.S. Court of International Trade in March 2006.

MARK A. BARNETT, judge; graduated *magna cum laude*, Phi Beta Kappa from Dickinson College; studied at the Dickinson Center for European Studies; J.D., *cum laude* from the University of Michigan Law School; member of the Bars of Pennsylvania and the District of Columbia and admitted to practice before the U.S. Court of International Trade and the U.S. Court of Appeals for the Federal Circuit; practiced in the international trade group at Steptoe and Johnson; joined the Office of Chief Counsel for Import Administration at the U.S. Department of Commerce as a staff attorney, served as a senior counsel, and subsequently served as the Deputy Chief Counsel for Import Administration; member of the U.S. negotiating teams for the U.S.-Morocco Free Trade Agreement, the World Trade Organization's Doha Round Rules Negotiating Group, and the Trans-Pacific Partnership; represented the United States before dispute settlement panels and the Appellate Body of the World Trade Organization and binational panels composed under the North American Free Trade Agreement; detailed to the U.S. House of Representatives, Committee on Ways and Means, Subcommittee on Trade as a Trade Counsel; served two terms as a member of the board of directors of the International Model United Nations Association, Inc., including Vice-Chairman and Chairman; nominated to the U.S. Court of International Trade by President Obama on July 12, 2012, and confirmed by the U.S. Senate on May 23, 2013.

CLAIRE R. KELLY, judge; born in New York, NY. Married to Joseph A DiBartolo. Child: Joseph J. DiBartolo. Attended Sacred Heart Academy, Hempstead, NY; Barnard College, B.A. 1987, *cum laude*; and Brooklyn Law School, J.D., 1993, *magna cum laude*. Professional experience: Coudert Brothers (1993–97) associated; Brooklyn Law School (1997–2013), Legal Writing Instructor, Associate Professor of Law and Professor of Law and Co-Director of the Dennis J. Block Center for the Study of International Business Law. Elected Member of the American Law Institute, 2011; nominated to the U.S. Court of International Trade by President Obama on November 14, 2012, and confirmed by the U.S. Senate on May 23, 2013.

SENIOR JUDGES

GREGORY W. CARMAN, senior judge; born in Farmingdale, Long Island, NY; son of Nassau County District Court Judge Willis B. and Marjorie Sosa Carman; B.A., St. Lawrence University, Canton, NY, 1958; J.D., St. John's University School of Law (honors program), 1961; University of Virginia Law School, JAG (with honors), 1962; admitted to New York Bar, 1961; practiced law with firm of Carman, Callahan and Sabino, Farmingdale, NY; admitted to practice: U.S. Court of Military Appeals, 1962, U.S. District Courts, Eastern and Southern Districts of New York, 1965, Second Circuit Court of Appeals, 1966, Supreme Court of the United States, 1967, U.S. Court of Appeals, District of Columbia, 1982; Councilman Town of Oyster Bay, 1972–80; member, U.S. House of Representatives, 97th Congress; member, Banking, Finance and Urban Affairs Committee and Select Committee on Aging; member, International Trade, Investment, and Monetary Policy Subcommittee; U.S. Congressional Delegate to International I.M.F. Conference; nominated by President Reagan, confirmed and appointed Judge of the U.S. Court of International Trade, March 2, 1983; Acting Chief Judge, 1991; Chief Judge, 1996–2003; Statutory Member, Judicial Conference of United States; member, Executive Committee, Judicial Branch Committee, and Subcommittees on Long Range Planning, Benefits, Civic Education, and Seminars; Captain, U.S. Army, 1958–64; awarded Army Commendation Medal for Meritorious Service, 1964; member, Rotary International, 1964–present; named Paul Harris Fellow of the Rotary Foundation of Rotary International; member, Holland Society, and recipient of its 1999 Gold Medal for Distinguished Achievement in Jurisprudence; member, Federal Bar Association, American Bar Association, Fellow of American Bar Foundation, New York State Bar Association; member, and former Chair, New York State Bar Association's Committee on Courts and the Community, and recipient of its 1996 Special Recognition Award; Doctor of Laws, *honoris causa*, Nova Southeastern University, 1999; Distinguished Jurist in Residence, Touro College Law Center, 2000; Doctor of Laws, *honoris causa*, St. John's University, 2002; Inaugural Lecturer, DiCarlo U.S. Court of International Trade Lecture, John Marshall Law School, 2003; Distinguished Alumni Citation, St. Lawrence University, 2003; Italian Board of Guardians Public Service Award, 2003; director and member, Respect for Law Alliance, Inc.; Recipient of Respect for Law Alliance, 2010, Judiciary Leader Award; Executive Committee member and past president, Theodore Roosevelt American Inn of Court; past president, Protestant Lawyers Association of Long Island; member, Vestry, St. Thomas's Episcopal Church, Farmingdale, NY; married to Nancy Endruschat (deceased); children: Gregory Wright, Jr., John Frederick, James Matthew, and Mira Catherine; married to Judith L. Dennehy.

JANE A. RESTANI, senior judge; born in San Francisco, CA, 1948; parents: Emilia C. and Roy J. Restani; husband: Ira Bloom; B.A., University of California at Berkeley, 1969; J.D., University of California at Davis, 1973; law review staff writer, 1971–72; articles editor, 1972–73; member, Order of the Coif; elected to Phi Kappa Phi Honor Society; admitted to the bar of the Supreme Court of the State of California, 1973; joined the civil division of the Department of Justice under the Attorney General's Honor Program in 1973 as a trial attorney; assistant chief commercial litigation section, civil division, 1976–80; director, commercial litigation branch, civil division, 1980–83; recipient of the John Marshall Award of outstanding legal achievement in 1983; Judicial Improvements Committee (now Committee on Court Administration and Case Management) of the Judicial Conference of the United States, 1987–94; Judicial Conference Advisory Committee on the Federal Rules of Bankruptcy Procedure, and liaison to the Advisory Committee on the Federal Rules of Civil Procedure, 1994–96; member, Judicial Conference of the United States, 2003–10; Executive Committee of the Judicial Conference, 2010; ABA Standing Committee on Customs Laws, 1990–93;

and the Board of Directors, New York State Association of Women Judges, 1992–present; nominated to the United States Court of International Trade on November 2, 1983 by President Reagan; entered upon the duties of that office on November 25, 1983; Chief Judge, 2003–10.

THOMAS J. AQUILINO, JR., senior judge; born in Mount Kisco, NY, December 7, 1939; son of Thomas J. and Virginia B. (Doughty) Aquilino; married to Edith Berndt Aquilino; children: Christopher Thomas, Philip Andrew, Alexander Berndt; attended Cornell University, 1957–59; B.A., Drew University, 1959–60, 1961–62; University of Munich, Germany, 1960–61; Free University of Berlin, Germany, 1965–66; J.D., Rutgers University School of Law, 1966–69; research assistant, Prof. L.F.E. Goldie (Resources for the Future-Ford Foundation), 1967–69; administrator, Northern Region, 1969 Jessup International Law Moot Court Competition; served in the U.S. Army, 1962–65; law clerk, Hon. John M. Cannella, U.S. District Court for the Southern District of New York, 1969–71; attorney with Davis Polk and Wardwell, New York, NY, 1971–85; admitted to practice New York, U.S. Supreme Court, U.S. Court of Appeals for Second and Third Circuits, U.S. Court of International Trade, U.S. Court of Claims, U.S. District Courts for Eastern, Southern and Northern Districts of New York, Interstate Commerce Commission; adjunct professor of law, Benjamin N. Cardozo School of Law, 1984–95; Mem., Drew University Board of Visitors, 1997–present; appointed to the U.S. Court of International Trade by President Reagan on February 22, 1985; confirmed by U.S. Senate, April 3, 1985.

NICHOLAS TSOUCALAS, senior judge; born in New York, NY, August 24, 1926; one of five children of George M. and Maria (Monogenis) Tsoucalas; married to Catherine Aravantinos; two daughters: Stephanie and Georgia; five grandchildren; B.S., Kent State University, 1949; LL.B., New York Law School, 1951; attended New York University Law School; entered U.S. Navy, 1944–46; served in the American and European Theaters of War on board the *USS Oden*, the *USS Monticello* and *USS Europa*; reentered Navy, 1951–52 and served on the carrier, *USS Wasp*; admitted to New York Bar, 1953; appointed Assistant U.S. Attorney for the Southern District of New York, 1955–59; appointed in 1959 as supervisor of 1960 census for the 17th and 18th Congressional Districts; appointed chairman, Board of Commissioners of Appraisal; appointed judge of Criminal Court of the City of New York, 1968; designated acting Supreme Court Justice, Kings and Queens Counties, 1975–82; resumed service as judge of the Criminal Court of the City of New York until June 1986; former chairman: Committee on Juvenile Delinquency, Federal Bar Association, and the Subcommittee on Public Order and Responsibility of the American Citizenship Committee of the New York County Lawyers' Association; member of the American Bar Association, New York State Bar Association; founder of Eastern Orthodox Lawyers' Association; former president: Greek-American Lawyers' Association, and Board of Directors of Greek Orthodox Church of "Evangelismos", St. John's Theologos Society, and Parthenon Foundation; member, Order of Ahepa, Parthenon Lodge, F.A.M.; appointed judge of the U.S. Court of International Trade by President Reagan on September 9, 1985, and confirmed by U.S. Senate on June 6, 1986; assumed senior status on September 30, 1996.

R. KENTON MUSGRAVE, senior judge; born in Clearwater, FL, September 7, 1927; married May 7, 1949 to former Ruth Shippen Hoppe, of Atlanta, GA; three children: Laura Marie Musgrave (deceased), Ruth Shippen Musgrave, Esq., and Forest Kenton Musgrave; attended Augusta Academy (Virginia); B.A., University of Washington, 1948; editorial staff, *Journal of International Law*, Emory University; J.D., with distinction, Emory University, 1953; assistant general counsel, Lockheed Aircraft and Lockheed International, 1953–62; vice president and general counsel, Mattel, Inc., 1963–71; director, Ringling Bros. and Barnum and Bailey Combined Shows, Inc., 1968–72; commissioner, BSA (Atlanta), 1952–55; partner, Musgrave, Welbourn and Fertman, 1972–75; assistant general counsel, Pacific Enterprises, 1975–81; vice president, general counsel and secretary, Vivitar Corporation, 1981–85; vice president and director, Santa Barbara Applied Research Corp., 1982–87; trustee, Morris Animal Foundation, 1981–94; director Emeritus, Pet Protection Society, 1981–present; director, Dolphins of Shark Bay (Australia) Foundation, 1985–present; trustee, The Dian Fossey Gorilla Fund, 1987–present; trustee, The Ocean Conservancy, 2000–present; vice president and director, South Bay Social Services Group, 1963–70; director, Palos Verdes Community Arts Association, 1973–79; member, Governor of Florida's Council of 100, 1970–73; director, Orlando Bank and Trust, 1970–73; counsel, League of Women Voters, 1964–66; member, State Bar of Georgia, 1953–present; State Bar of California, 1962–present; Los Angeles County Bar Association, 1962–87 and chairman, Corporate Law Departments Section, 1965–66; admitted to practice before the U.S. Supreme Court, 1962; Supreme Court of Georgia, 1953; California Supreme Court, 1962; U.S. Customs Court, 1967; U.S. Court of International Trade, 1980; nominated to the U.S. Court of International Trade by President Reagan on July 1, 1987; confirmed by the Senate on November 9, and took oath of office on November 13, 1987.

RICHARD W. GOLDBERG, senior judge; born in Fargo, ND, September 23, 1927; married; two children, a daughter and a son; J.D., University of Miami, 1952; served on active duty as an Air Force Judge Advocate, 1953–56; admitted to Washington, DC Bar, Florida Bar and North Dakota Bar; from 1959 to 1983, owned and operated a regional grain processing firm in North Dakota; served as State Senator from North Dakota for eight years; taught military law for the Army and Air Force ROTC at North Dakota State University; was vice-chairman of the board of Minneapolis Grain Exchange; joined the Reagan Administration in 1983 in Washington at the U.S. Department of Agriculture; served as Deputy Under Secretary for International Affairs and Commodity Programs and later as Acting Under Secretary; in 1990 joined the Washington, DC law firm of Anderson, Hibey and Blair; appointed judge of the U.S. Court of International Trade in 1991; assumed senior status in 2001.

DONALD C. POGUE, senior judge; graduated *magna cum laude*, Phi Beta Kappa from Dartmouth College; did graduate work at the University of Essex, England; J.D., Yale Law School and a Masters of Philosophy, Yale University; married 1971; served as judge in Connecticut's Superior Court; appointed to the bench in 1994; served as chairman of Connecticut's Commission on Hospitals and Health Care; practiced law in Hartford for 15 years; lectured on labor law at the University of Connecticut School of Law; assisted in teaching the Harvard Law School's program on negotiations and dispute resolution for lawyers; chaired the Connecticut Bar Association's Labor and Employment Law Section; appointed a judge of the United States Court of International Trade in 1995; Chief Judge, 2010–14; prior to becoming judge, he chaired the Court's Long Range Planning Committee and Budget Committee; he also chaired the Judicial Conference's Committee on the Administrative Office; service by designation in the 2d, 3d, 5th, 9th, 11th and Federal Circuits and in the D.C. and New York Southern district courts. Judge Pogue also serves as a member of the Judicial Conference.

JUDITH M. BARZILAY, senior judge; born in Russell, KS, January 3, 1944; husband, Sal (Doron) Barzilay; children, Ilan and Michael; parents, Arthur and Hilda Morgenstern; B.A., Wichita State University, 1965; M.L.S., Rutgers University School of Library and Information Science, 1971; J.D., Rutgers University School of Law, 1981, Moot Court Board, 1980–81; trial attorney, U.S. Department of Justice (International Trade Field Office), 1983–86; litigation associate, Siegel, Mandell and Davidson, New York, NY, 1986–88; Sony Corporation of America, 1988–98; customs and international trade counsel, 1988–89; vice-president for import and export operations, 1989–96; vice-president for government affairs, 1996–98; executive board of the American Association of Exporters and Importers, 1993–98; appointed by Treasury Secretary Robert Rubin to the Advisory Committee on Commercial Operations of the United States Customs Service, 1995–98; nominated for appointment on January 27, 1998 by President Clinton; sworn in as judge June 3, 1998.

RICHARD K. EATON, senior judge; born in Walton, NY; married to Susan Henshaw Jones; two children: Alice and Elizabeth; attended Walton public schools; B.A., Ithaca College, J.D., Union University Albany Law School, 1974; professional experience: Eaton and Eaton, partner; Mudge Rose Guthrie Alexander and Ferdon, New York, NY, associate and partner; Stroock and Stroock and Lavan, partner; served on the staff of Senator Daniel Patrick Moynihan; confirmed by the United States Senate to the U.S. Court of International Trade on October 22, 1999.

OFFICERS OF THE UNITED STATES COURT OF INTERNATIONAL TRADE

Clerk.—Tina Potuto Kimble (212) 264–2814.

UNITED STATES COURT OF FEDERAL CLAIMS

Lafayette Square, 717 Madison Place, NW., 20439, phone (202) 357–6406

SUSAN G. BRADEN, chief judge, born in Youngstown, OH, November 8, 1948; married to Thomas M. Susman; daughter (Daily); B.A., Case Western Reserve University, 1970; J.D., Case Western Reserve University School of Law, 1973; post graduate study Harvard Law School, Summer, 1979; private practice, 1985–2003 (1997–2003 Baker and McKenzie); Federal Trade Commission: special counsel to Chairman, 1984–85, senior attorney advisor to Commissioner and Acting Chairman, 1980–83; U.S. Department of Justice, Antitrust Division, Senior Trial Attorney, Energy Section, 1978–80; Cleveland Field Office, 1973–78; Special Assistant Attorney General for the State of Alabama, 1990; Consultant to the Administrative Conference of the United States, 1984–85; 2000 co-chair, Lawyers for Bush-Cheney; General Counsel Presidential Debate for Dole-Kemp Campaign, 1996; counsel to RNC Platform, 1996; coordinator for Regulatory Reform and Antitrust Policy, Dole Presidential Campaign, 1995–96; National Steering Committee, Lawyers for Bush-Quayle, 1992; Assistant General Counsel, Republican National Convention, 1988, 1992, 1996, 2000; elected At-Large Member, D.C. Republican National Committee, 2000–02; member of the American Bar Association (Council Member, Section on Administrative Law and Regulatory Practice, 1996–99), Federal Circuit Bar Association, District of Columbia Bar Association, Computer Law Bar Association; admitted to the Supreme Court of Ohio, 1973, U.S. District Court for the District of Columbia, 1980, U.S. Supreme Court, 1980; U.S. Court of Appeals for the District of Columbia, 1992; U.S. Court of Appeals for the Second Circuit, 1993, U.S. Court of Appeals for the Federal Circuit, 2001; appointed to the U.S. Court of Federal Claims by President George W. Bush on July 14, 2003. Appointed chief judge by President Donald Trump on March 13, 2017.

MARIAN BLANK HORN, judge; born in New York, NY, 1943; daughter of Werner P. and Mady R. Blank; married to Robert Jack Horn; three daughters; attended Fieldston School, New York, NY, Barnard College, Columbia University, and Fordham University School of Law; admitted to practice U.S. Supreme Court, 1973, Federal and State courts in New York, 1970, and Washington, DC, 1973; assistant district attorney, Deputy Chief Appeals Bureau, Bronx County, NY, 1969–72; attorney, Arent, Fox, Kintner, Plotkin and Kahn, 1972–73; adjunct professor of law, Washington College of Law, American University, 1973–76; litigation attorney, Federal Energy Administration, 1975–76; senior attorney, Office of General Counsel, Strategic Petroleum Reserve Branch, Department of Energy, 1976–79; deputy assistant general counsel for procurement and financial incentives, Department of Energy, 1979–81; deputy associate solicitor, Division of Surface Mining, Department of the Interior, 1981–83; associate solicitor, Division of General Law, Department of the Interior, 1983–85; principal deputy solicitor and acting solicitor, Department of Interior, 1985–86; adjunct professor of law, George Washington University National Law Center, 1991–present; Woodrow Wilson Visiting Fellow, 1994; assumed duties of judge, U.S. Court of Federal Claims in 1986 and confirmed for a second term in 2003.

CHARLES F. LETTOW, judge, born in Iowa Falls, IA, 1941; son of Carl F. and Catherine Lettow; B.S.Ch.E., Iowa State University, 1962; LL.B., Stanford University, 1968, Order of the Coif; M.A., Brown University, 2001; Note Editor, Stanford Law Review; married to B. Sue Lettow; children: Renee Burnett, Carl Frederick II, John Stangland, and Paul Vorbeck; served U.S. Army, 1963–65; law clerk to Judge Ben C. Duniway, U.S. Court of Appeals for the Ninth Circuit, 1968–69, and Chief Justice Warren E. Burger, Supreme Court of the United States, 1969–70; counsel, Council on Environmental Quality, Executive Office of the President, 1970–73; associate (1973–76) and partner (1976–2003), Cleary, Gottlieb, Steen and Hamilton, Washington, DC; admitted to practice before the U.S. Supreme Court, the U.S. Courts of Appeals for the D.C., Second, Third, Fourth, Fifth, Sixth, Eighth, Ninth, Tenth, and Federal Circuits, the U.S. District Courts for the District of Columbia, the Northern District of California, and the District of Maryland, and the U.S. Court of Federal Claims; member: American Law Institute, the American Bar Association, the D.C. Bar, the California State Bar, the Iowa State Bar Association, and the Maryland State Bar;

nominated by President George W. Bush to the U.S. Court of Federal Claims in 2001 and confirmed and took office in 2003.

MARY ELLEN COSTER WILLIAMS, judge; born in Flushing, NY, April 3, 1953; married with two children; B.A. *summa cum laude* (Greek and Latin) and M.A. (Latin), The Catholic University of America, 1974; J.D., Duke University, 1977; Editorial Board, Duke Law Journal, 1976–77; admitted to the District of Columbia Bar; associate, Fulbright and Jaworski, 1977–79; associate, Schnader, Harrison, Segal and Lewis, 1979–83; Assistant U.S. Attorney, Civil Division, District of Columbia, 1983–87; partner, Janis, Schuelke and Wechsler, 1987–89; administrative judge, General Services Board of Contract Appeals, March 1989–July 2003; secretary, District of Columbia Bar, 1988–89; Fellow, American Bar Foundation, elected 1985; Board of Directors, Bar Association of the District of Columbia, 1985–88; Chairman, Young Lawyers Section, Bar Association of the District of Columbia, 1985–86; Chair, Public Contract Law Section of the American Bar Association, 2002–03; Chair-Elect, Vice-Chair, Secretary, Council, 1995–2002; Delegate, Section of Public Contract Law, ABA House of Delegates, 2003–08 and 2014–present; ABA Board of Governors, 2010–13; Adjunct Professor, Johns Hopkins University, 2006–present; Adjunct Professor, The Catholic University of America Columbus School of Law, 2004–06; appointed to the U.S. Court of Federal Claims on July 21, 2003.

VICTOR JOHN WOLSKI, judge; born in New Brunswick, NJ, November 14, 1962; son of Vito and Eugenia Wolski; B.A., B.S., University of Pennsylvania, 1984; J.D., University of Virginia School of Law, 1991; married to Lisa Wolski; admitted to Supreme Court of the United States, 1995; California Supreme Court, 1992; Washington Supreme Court, 1994; Oregon Supreme Court, 1996; District of Columbia Court of Appeals, 2001; U.S. Court of Appeals for the Ninth Circuit, 1993; U.S. Court of Appeals for the Federal Circuit, 2001; U.S. District Court for the Eastern District of California, 1993; U.S. District Court for the Northern District of California, 1995; U.S. Court of Federal Claims, 2001; U.S. District Court for the District of Columbia, 2002; research assistant, Center for Strategic and International Studies, 1984–85; research associate, Institute for Political Economy, 1985–88; confidential assistant and speechwriter to the Secretary, U.S. Department of Agriculture, 1988; paralegal specialist, Office of the general counsel, U.S. Department of Energy, 1989; law clerk to Judge Vaughn R. Walker, U.S. District Court for the Northern District of California, 1991–92; attorney, Pacific Legal Foundation, 1992–97; general counsel, Sacramento County Republican Central Committee, 1995–97; counsel Senator Connie Mack, Vice-Chairman of the Joint Economic Committee, U.S. Congress, 1997–98; general counsel and chief tax adviser, Joint Economic Committee, U.S. Congress, 1999–2000; associate, Cooper, Carvin and Rosenthal, 2000–01; associate, Cooper and Kirk, 2001–03; associate editor, *Public Contract Law Journal*, 2006–present; appointed by President George W. Bush to the U.S. Court of Federal Claims on July 14, 2003.

THOMAS C. WHEELER, judge; born in Chicago, IL, March 18, 1948; married; two grown children; B.A., Gettysburg College, 1970; J.D., Georgetown University Law School, 1973; private practice in Washington, DC, 1973–2005; associate and partner, Pettit and Martin until 1995; partner, Piper and Marbury (later Piper Marbury Rudnick and Wolfe, and then DLA Piper Rudnick Gray Cary); member of the District of Columbia Bar; American Bar Association's Public Contracts and Litigation Sections; appointed to the U.S. Court of Federal Claims on October 24, 2005.

MARGARET M. SWEENEY, judge; born in Baltimore, MD; B.A. in history, Notre Dame of Maryland, 1977; J.D., Delaware Law School, 1981; Delaware Family Court Master, 1981–83; litigation associate, Fedorko, Gilbert, and Lanctot, Morrisville, PA, 1983–85; law clerk to Hon. Loren A. Smith, Chief Judge of the U.S. Court of Federal Claims, 1985–87; trial attorney in the General Litigation Section of the Environment and Natural Resources Division of the United States Department of Justice, 1987–99; president, U.S. Court of Federal Claims Bar Association, 1999; attorney advisor, United States Department of Justice Office of Intelligence Policy and Review, 1999–2003; special master, U.S. Court of Federal Claims, 2003–05; member of the Bars of the Supreme Court of Pennsylvania and the District of Columbia Court of Appeals; appointed to the U.S. Court of Federal Claims by President George W. Bush on October 24, 2005, and entered duty on December 14, 2005.

PATRICIA E. CAMPBELL-SMITH, judge; born in Baltimore, MD, 1966; B.S.E.E., Duke University, 1987; J.D., Tulane Law School, 1992; admitted to the Bar of Louisiana; judicial extern to Hon. John Minor Wisdom, U.S. Court of Appeals for the Fifth Circuit, 1991; law clerk to Hon. Martin L. C. Feldman, U.S. District Court for Eastern District of Louisiana, 1992–93; associate, Liskow and Lewis, 1993–96, 1997–98; law clerk to Hon. Sarah S. Vance

(Chief Judge), U.S. District Court for Eastern District of Louisiana, 1996–97; senior law clerk to Hon. Emily C. Hewitt (Chief Judge), U.S. Court of Federal Claims, 1998–2005; special master, U.S. Court of Federal Claims, 2005–11; chief special master, U.S. Court of Federal Claims, 2011–13; appointed to the U.S. Court of Federal Claims by President Obama on September 19, 2013; chief judge from October 21, 2013–March 13, 2017.

ELAINE D. KAPLAN, judge; born in Brooklyn, New York, December 18, 1955; B.A., State University of New York at Binghamton, 1976; J.D., Georgetown University, 1979; Office of the Solicitor General, Department of Labor, 1979–83; Attorney, State and Local Legal Center, 1983–84; Attorney and Deputy General Counsel, National Treasury Employees Union, 1984–98; Special Counsel, Office of Special Counsel, 1998–03; Of Counsel, Bernabei and Katz, 2003–04; Senior Deputy General Counsel, National Treasury Employees Union, 2004–09; General Counsel, U.S. Office of Personnel Management, 2009–13; Acting Director, U.S. Office of Personnel Management, 2013; appointed to the U.S. Court of Federal Claims by President Barack Obama on September 17, 2013.

LYDIA KAY GRIGGSBY, judge; born in Baltimore, MD, January 16, 1968; educated at the Park School, Brooklandville, MD, 1980–86; B.A., University of Pennsylvania, 1990; J.D., Georgetown University Law Center, 1993; member, Bar of Maryland and Bar of the District of Columbia; private practice of law, DLA Piper, 1993–95; Trial Attorney, United States Department of Justice, Civil Division, Commercial Litigation Branch, 1995–98; Assistant United States Attorney, United States Attorney's Office for the District of Columbia, 1998–2004; Counsel, United States Senate Select Committee on Ethics, 2004–06; Privacy Counsel, United States Senate Committee on the Judiciary, 2006–08; Chief Counsel for Privacy and Information Policy, United States Senate Committee on the Judiciary 2008–14; appointed by President Obama to the U.S. Court of Federal Claims on December 5, 2014; entered duty on December 15, 2014.

SENIOR JUDGES

JOHN PAUL WIESE, senior judge; born in Brooklyn, NY, April 19, 1934; son of Gustav and Margaret Wiese; B.A., *cum laude*, Hobart College, 1962, Phi Beta Kappa; LL.B., University of Virginia School of Law, 1965; married to Alice Mary Donoghue, June, 1961; one son, John Patrick; served U.S. Army, 1957–59; law clerk: U.S. Court of Claims, trial division, 1965–66, and Judge Linton M. Collins, U.S. Court of Claims, appellate division, 1966–67; private practice in District of Columbia, 1967–74 (specializing in government contract litigation); trial judge, U.S. Court of Claims, 1974–82; admitted to the Bar of the District of Columbia, 1966; admitted to practice in the U.S. Supreme Court, the U.S. Court of Appeals for the Federal Circuit, the U.S. Court of Federal Claims; member: District of Columbia Bar Association and American Bar Association; designated in Federal Courts Improvement Act of 1982 as judge, U.S. Court of Federal Claims and reappointed by President Reagan to 15-year term on October 14, 1986.

ERIC G. BRUGGINK, senior judge; born in Kalidjati, Indonesia, September 11, 1949; naturalized U.S. citizen, 1961; married to Melinda Harris Bruggink; sons: John and David; B.A., *cum laude* (sociology), Auburn University, AL, 1971; M.A. (speech), 1972; J.D., University of Alabama, 1975; Hugo Black Scholar and Note and Comments Editor of *Alabama Law Review*; member, Alabama State Bar and District of Columbia Bar; served as law clerk to chief judge Frank H. McFadden, Northern District of Alabama, 1975–76; associate, Hardwick, Hause and Segrest, Dothan, AL, 1976–77; assistant director, Alabama Law Institute, 1977–79; director, Office of Energy and Environmental Law, 1977–79; associate, Steiner, Crum and Baker, Montgomery, AL, 1979–82; Director, Office of Appeals Counsel, Merit Systems Protection Board, 1982–86; appointed to the U.S. Court of Federal Claims on April 15, 1986.

LYNN J. BUSH, senior judge; born in Little Rock, AR, December 30, 1948; daughter of John E. Bush III and Alice (Saville) Bush; one son, Brian Bush Ferguson; B.A., Antioch College, 1970, Thomas J. Watson Fellow; J.D., Georgetown University Law Center, 1976; admitted to the Arkansas Bar in 1976 and to the District of Columbia Bar in 1977; trial attorney, Commercial Litigation Branch, Civil Division, U.S. Department of Justice, 1976–87; senior trial attorney, Naval Facilities Engineering Command, Department of the Navy, 1987–89; counsel, Engineering Field Activity Chesapeake, Naval Facilities Engineering Command, Department of the Navy, 1989–96; administrative judge, U.S. Department of Housing and Urban Development Board of Contract Appeals, 1996–98; nominated by President Clinton to the U.S. Court of Federal Claims, June 22, 1998; and assumed duties of the office on October 26, 1998.

EDWARD J. DAMICH, senior judge; born in Pittsburgh, PA, June 19, 1948; son of John and Josephine (Lovrencic) Damich; A.B., St. Stephen's College, 1970; J.D., Catholic University, 1976; professor of law at Delaware School of Law of Widener University, 1976–84; served as a Law and Economics Fellow at Columbia University School of Law, where he earned his L.L.M. in 1983 and his J.S.D. in 1991; professor of law at George Mason University, 1984–98; appointed by President George H.W. Bush to be a Commissioner of the Copyright Royalty Tribunal, 1992–93; Chief Intellectual Property Counsel for the Senate Judiciary Committee, 1995–98; admitted to the Bar of the District of Columbia; member of the District of Columbia Bar Association, American Bar Association, Supreme Court of the United States, the Federal Circuit and *Association litteraire et artistique internationale*; president of the National Federation of Croatian Americans, 1994–95; appointed by President Clinton as judge, U.S. Court of Federal Claims, October 22, 1998; served as chief judge May 13, 2002–March 11, 2009.

NANCY B. FIRESTONE, senior judge; born in Manchester, NH, October 17, 1951; B.A., Washington University, 1973; J.D., University of Missouri, Kansas City, 1977; one child; attorney, Appellate Section and Environmental Enforcement Section, U.S. Department of Justice, Washington, DC, 1977–84; assistant chief, Policy Legislation and Special Litigation, Environment and Natural Resources Division, Department of Justice, Washington, DC, 1984–85; Deputy Chief, Environmental Enforcement Section, Department of Justice, Washington, DC, 1985–89; associate deputy administrator, Environmental Protection Agency, Washington, DC, 1989–92; judge, Environmental Appeals Board, Environmental Protection Agency, Washington, DC, 1992–95; Deputy Assistant Attorney General, Environment and Natural Resources Division, Department of Justice, Washington, DC, 1995–98; adjunct professor, Georgetown University Law Center, 1985–present; appointed to the U.S. Court of Federal Claims by President Clinton on October 22, 1998.

UNITED STATES TAX COURT

400 Second Street, NW., 20217, phone (202) 521–0700

L. PAIGE MARVEL, chief judge; born in Maryland; B.A., *magna cum laude*, College of Notre Dame, 1971; J.D. with honors, University of Maryland School of Law, Baltimore, MD, 1974; Order of the Coif; member, Maryland Law Review and Moot Court Board; Garbis and Schwait, P.A., associate (1974–76) and shareholder (1976–85); shareholder, Garbis, Marvel and Junghans, P.A., 1985–86; shareholder, Melnicove, Kaufman, Weiner, Smouse and Garbis, P.A., 1986–88; partner, Venabel, Baetjer and Howard LLP, 1988–98; member, American Bar Association, Section of Taxation, Vice-Chair, Committee Operations, 1993–95; Council Director 1989–92; Chair, Court Procedure Committee, 1985–87; Maryland State Bar Association, Board of Governors, 1988–90, and 1996–98; Chair, Taxation Section 1982–83; Federal Bar Association, Section of Taxation, Section Council, 1984–90; Fellow, American Bar Foundation; Fellow, Maryland Bar Foundation; fellow and former Regent, American College of Tax Counsel, 1996–98; member, American Law Institute; advisor, ALI *Restatement of Law, Third, The Law Governing Lawyers* 1988–98; University of Maryland Law School Board of Visitors, 1995–2001; Loyola/Notre Dame Library, Inc. Board of Trustees, 1996–2003; Advisory Committee, University of Baltimore Graduate Tax Program, 1986–present; Co-editor, Procedure Department, The Journal of Taxation, 1990–98; member, Commissioner's Review Panel on IRS Integrity, 1989–91; member and Chair, Procedure Subcommittee, Commission to Revise the Annotated Code of Maryland (Tax Provisions), 1981–87; member, Advisory Commission to the Maryland State Department of Economic and Community Development, 1978–81; recipient, President's Medal, College of Notre Dame, 2006; Jules Ritholz award, ABA Tax Section's Civil and Criminal Tax Penalties Comm., 2004; First Annual Tax Excellence Award, Maryland State Bar Association Tax Section, 2002; named one of Maryland's Top 100 Women, 1998; recipient, ABA Tax Section's Distinguished Service Award, 1995; MSBA Distinguished Service Award, 1982–83; listed in *Best Lawyers in America*, 1991–98, *Who's Who in America, Who's Who in American Law, Who's Who in the East*; author of various articles and book chapters on tax and tax litigation topics; appointed by President William J. Clinton as Judge, United States Tax Court, on April 6, 1998, for a term ending April 5, 2013; reappointed by President Barack H. Obama on December 3, 2014, for a term ending December 2, 2029. Elected as Chief Judge for a two-year term effective June 1, 2016.

MAURICE B. FOLEY, judge; born in Illinois; B.A., Swarthmore College; J.D., Boalt Hall School of Law at the University of California at Berkeley; LL.M., Georgetown University Law Center; attorney for the Legislation and Regulations Division of the Internal Revenue Service, Tax Counsel for the United States Senate Committee on Finance; Deputy Tax Legislative Counsel in the U.S. Treasury's Office of Tax Policy; appointed by President William J. Clinton as Judge, United States Tax Court, on April 9, 1995, for a term ending April 8, 2010; reappointed on November 25, 2011, for a term ending November 24, 2026.

JUAN F. VASQUEZ, judge; born in San Antonio, Texas; attended Fox Tech High School; A.D. (Data Processing), San Antonio Junior College; B.B.A. (Accounting), University of Texas, Austin, 1972; attended State University of New York, Buffalo in 1st year law school, 1975; J.D., University of Houston Law Center, 1977; LL.M., Taxation, New York University Law School of Law, 1978; Certified Public Accountant, Certificate from Texas, 1976; admitted to State Bar of Texas, 1977; admitted to the United States Tax Court, 1978; certified in tax law by Texas Board of Legal Specialization, 1984; admitted to the United States District Court, Southern District of Texas, 1982, Western District of Texas, 1985 and United States Court of Appeals for the Fifth Circuit, 1982; and the Supreme Court of the United States of America, 1996; private practice of tax law, in San Antonio, TX, 1987–April 1995; partner, Leighton, Hood and Vasquez, in San Antonio, TX, 1982–87; Trial Attorney, Office of Chief Counsel, Internal Revenue Service, Houston, TX, 1978–82; accountant, Coopers and Lybrand, Los Angeles, CA, 1972–74; member of American Bar Association, Tax Section; Texas State Bar, Tax Section; Fellow of Texas and San Antonio Bar Foundations; College of State

Bar of Texas; National Hispanic Bar Association and Hispanic Bar Association of the District of Columbia; Mexican American Bar Association (MABA) of San Antonio 1982–95; Houston MABA 1978–82; Texas MABA 1986–88; National Association of Hispanic CPA's San Antonio Chapter (founding member) 1983–88; member of Greater Austin Tax Litigation Association 1989–95; served on Austin Internal Revenue Service District Director's Practitioner Liaison Committee, 1990–91 (chairman, 1991); appointed by President William J. Clinton as Judge, United States Tax Court, on May 1, 1995, for a term ending April 30, 2010; reappointed by President Barack H. Obama on October 13, 2011, for a term ending October 12, 2026.

JOSEPH H. GALE, judge; born in Virginia; A.B., Philosophy, Princeton University, 1976; J.D., University of Virginia School of Law, Dillard Fellow, 1980; practiced law as an Associate Attorney, Dewey Ballantine, Washington, DC, and New York, 1980–83; Dickstein, Shapiro and Morin, Washington, DC, 1983–85; served as Tax Legislative Counsel for Senator Daniel Patrick Moynihan (D-NY), 1985–88; Administrative Assistant and Tax Legislative Counsel, 1989; Chief Counsel, 1990–93; Chief Tax Counsel, Committee on Finance, U.S. Senate, 1993–95; minority Chief Tax Counsel, Senate Finance Committee, January 1995–July 1995; minority Staff Director and Chief Counsel, Senate Finance Committee, July 1995–January 1996; admitted to District of Columbia Bar; member of American Bar Association, Section of Taxation; appointed by President William J. Clinton as Judge, United States Tax Court, February 6, 1996, for a term ending February 5, 2011; reappointed on October 18, 2011, for a term ending October 17, 2026.

MICHAEL B. THORNTON, judge; born in Mississippi; B.S. in Accounting, *summa cum laude*, University of Southern Mississippi, 1976; M.S. in Accounting, 1997; M.A. in English Literature, University of Tennessee, 1979; J.D. (with distinction), Duke University School of Law, 1982; Order of the Coif, Duke Law Journal Editorial Board; admitted to District of Columbia Bar, 1982; served as Law Clerk to the Honorable Charles Clark, Chief Judge, U.S. Court of Appeals for the Fifth Circuit, 1983–84; practiced law as an Associate Attorney, Sutherland, Asbill and Brennan, Washington, DC, 1982–83 and summer 1981; Miller and Chevalier, Chartered, Washington, DC, 1985–88; served as Tax Counsel, U.S. House Committee on Ways and Means, 1988–93; Chief Minority Tax Counsel, U.S. House Committee on Ways and Means, January 1995; Attorney-Adviser, U.S. Treasury Department, February–April 1995; Deputy Tax Legislative Counsel in the Office of Tax Policy, United States Treasury Department, April 1995–February 1998; recipient of Treasury Secretary's Annual Award, U.S. Department of the Treasury, 1997; Meritorious Service Award, U.S. Department of the Treasury, 1998; appointed by President William J. Clinton as Judge, United States Tax Court, on March 8, 1998, for a term ending March 7, 2013; served as Chief Judge from June 1, 2012, to March 7, 2013; reappointed by President Barack H. Obama on August 7, 2013, for a term ending August 6, 2028, and at that time resumed the position of Chief Judge; served as Chief Judge for a second two-year term from June 1, 2014, to May 31, 2016.

JOSEPH ROBERT GOEKE, judge; born in Kentucky; B.S., *cum laude*, Xavier University, 1972; J.D., University of Kentucky College of Law, 1975 (Order of the Coif); admitted to Illinois and Kentucky Bar, U.S. District Court for the Northern District of Illinois (Trial Bar), U.S. Court of Federal Claims; Trial Attorney, Chief Counsel's Office, Internal Revenue Service, New Orleans, LA, 1975–80; Senior Trial Attorney, Chief Counsel's Office, Internal Revenue Service, Cincinnati, OH, 1980–85; Special International Trial Attorney, Chief Counsel's Office, Internal Revenue Service, Cincinnati, OH, 1985–88; partner, Law Firm of Mayer, Brown, Rowe and Maw, Chicago, IL, 1988–2003; appointed by President George W. Bush as Judge, United States Tax Court, on April 22, 2003, for a term ending April 21, 2018.

MARK V. HOLMES, judge; born in New York; B.A., Harvard College, 1979; J.D., University of Chicago Law School, 1983; admitted to New York and District of Columbia Bars; U.S. Supreme Court; DC, Second, Fifth and Ninth Circuits; Southern and Eastern Districts of New York, Court of Federal Claims; practiced in New York as an Associate, Cahill Gordon and Reindel, 1983–85; Sullivan and Cromwell, 1987–91; served as clerk to the Hon. Alex Kozinski, Ninth Circuit, 1985–87; and in Washington, DC as Counsel to Commissioners, United States International Trade Commission, 1991–96; Counsel, Miller and Chevalier, 1996–2001; Deputy Assistant Attorney General, Tax Division, 2001–03; member, American Bar Association (Litigation and Tax Sections); appointed by President George W. Bush as Judge, United States Tax Court, on June 30, 2003, for a term ending June 29, 2018.

DAVID GUSTAFSON, judge; born in Greenville, South Carolina; Bob Jones University, B.A. *summa cum laude*, 1978. Duke University School of Law, J.D. with distinction, 1981. Order of the Coif (1981). Executive Editor of the Duke Law Journal (1980–81). Admitted to the District of Columbia Bar, 1981. Associate at the law firm of Sutherland, Asbill and Brennan, in Washington, DC, 1981–83. Trial Attorney (1983–89), Assistant Chief (1989–2005), and Chief (2005–08) in the Court of Federal Claims Section of the Tax Division in the U.S. Department of Justice; and Coordinator of Tax Shelter Litigation for the entire Tax Division (2002–06). Tax Division Outstanding Attorney Awards, 1985, 1989, 1997, 2001–05. Federal Bar Association's Younger Attorney Award, 1991. President of the Court of Federal Claims Bar Association (2001). Appointed by President George W. Bush as Judge, United States Tax Court, on July 29, 2008, for a term ending July 29, 2023.

ELIZABETH CREWSON PARIS, judge; born in Oklahoma; B.S., University of Tulsa, 1980; J.D., University of Tulsa School of Law, 1987; LL.M., Taxation, University of Denver College of Law, 1993. Admitted to the Supreme Court of Oklahoma and U.S. District Court for the District of Oklahoma, 1988; U.S. Tax Court, U.S. Court of Federal Claims, U.S. Court of Appeals for the Tenth Circuit, 1993; Supreme Court of Colorado, 1994. Former partner, Brumley Bishop and Paris, 1992; Senior Associate, McKenna and Cueno, 1994; Tax Partner, Reinhart, Boerner, Van Deuren, Norris and Rieselbach, 1998. Tax Counsel to the United States Senate Finance Committee, 2000–08. Member of the American Bar Association, Section of Taxation and Real Property and Probate Sections, formerly served as Vice Chair to both Agriculture and Entity Selection Committees. Member of Colorado and Oklahoma Bar Associations. Recognized as Distinguished Alumnus by the University of Tulsa School of law. Author of numerous tax, estate planning, real property, agriculture articles and chapters. Former adjunct professor, Georgetown University Law Center, LL.M. Taxation Program, and University of Tulsa College of Law. Appointed by President George W. Bush as Judge, United States Tax Court, on July 30, 2008, for a term ending July 29, 2023.

RICHARD T. MORRISON, judge; born in Hutchinson, Kansas; B.A., B.S., University of Kansas, 1989; visiting student at Mansfield College, Oxford University, 1987–88; J.D., University of Chicago Law School, 1993; M.A., University of Chicago, 1994. Clerk to Judge Jerry E. Smith, United States Court of Appeals for the Fifth Circuit, 1993–94. Associate, Baker and McKenzie, Chicago, Illinois, 1994–96. Associate, Mayer Brown and Platt, Chicago, Illinois 1996–2001. Deputy Assistant Attorney General for Review and Appellate Matters, Tax Division, United States Department of Justice, from 2001 to 2008 (except for term as Acting Assistant Attorney General, from July 2007 to January 2008). Appointed by President George W. Bush as Judge, United States Tax Court, on August 28, 2008, for a term ending August 27, 2023.

KATHLEEN KERRIGAN, judge; born in Springfield, Massachusetts; B.S., Boston College 1985; J.D., University of Notre Dame Law School, 1990; admitted to Massachusetts Bar, 1991 and District of Columbia Bar, 1992; Legislative Director for Congressman Richard E. Neal, Member of the Ways and Means Committee, 1990 to 1998; associate and partner at Baker and Hostetler LLP, Washington, DC, 1998–2005; tax counsel for Senator John F. Kerry, Member of Senate Finance Committee, 2005–12; appointed by President Barack H. Obama as Judge, United States, Tax Court, on May 4, 2012, for a term ending on May 3, 2027.

RONALD L. BUCH, judge; born in Flint, Michigan; B.B.A., Northwood Institute, 1987; J.D. with Taxation Concentration, Detroit College of Law, 1993; LL.M. in Taxation, Capital University Law School, 1994; Research Editor of the *Detroit College of Law Review*, 1992–93; Ohio Tax Review Fellow, 1993–94; admitted to the bars of Michigan, inactive (1993), Ohio, inactive (1994), Florida (1994), and the District of Columbia (1995); consultant at KPMG Washington National Tax (1995–97); Attorney-Advisor (1997–2000) and Senior Legal Counsel (2000–01) at the IRS Office of Chief Counsel; associate (2001–05) and partner (2005–09) at McKee Nelson LLP; partner at Bingham McCutchen LLP (2009–13); James E. Markham Attorney of the Year Award, 1999; Chair of the DC Bar Tax Audits and Litigation Committee, 2006–08; Chair of the ABA Tax Section's Administrative Practice Committee, 2008–09; appointed by President Barack H. Obama as Judge, United States Tax Court, on January 14, 2013, for a term ending January 13, 2028.

ALBERT G. LAUBER, judge; born in Bronxville, New York; Yale College (B.A., *summa cum laude*, 1971); Clare College, Cambridge University (M.A., Classics, 1974); Yale Law School (J.D., 1977). Phi Beta Kappa; Woodrow Wilson Fellow; Mellon Fellow; Note Editor,

Yale Law Journal; Moot Court Prize Argument; Cardozo Prize, Best Moot Court Brief. Law Clerk to Malcolm R. Wilkey, U.S. Court of Appeals for the DC Circuit (1977–78); Law Clerk to Justice Harry A. Blackmun, U.S. Supreme Court (1978–79). Associate Attorney, Caplin and Drysdale, Chtd., Washington, DC (1979–83); Tax Assistant to the Solicitor General, U.S. Department of Justice (1983–86); Deputy Solicitor General, U.S. Department of Justice (1986–87); Partner, Caplin and Drysdale, Chtd., Washington, DC (1988–2005); Visiting Professor and Director, Graduate Tax and Securities Programs, Georgetown University Law Center (2006–13). Professorial Lecturer, George Washington University Law School (1983–84); Lecturer, University of Virginia Law School (1988–90); Adjunct Professor, Georgetown University Law Center (2013–present); Board of Trustees, the Studio Theatre (1993–present); Member, District of Columbia Alcoholic Beverage Control Board (2004–08). Admitted to the Bars of the District of Columbia (1978); U.S. Supreme Court (1983); U.S. Court of Appeals, DC Circuit (1983); U.S. Court of Appeals, Federal Circuit (1994); Connecticut (inactive); Member, American Bar Association, Section of Taxation; appointed by President Barack H. Obama as Judge, United States Tax Court, on January 31, 2013, for a term ending January 30, 2028.

JOSEPH W. NEGA, judge; born in Illinois; DePaul University, B.S.C. in Accounting, 1981; DePaul University School of Law, J.D., 1984; Georgetown University School of Law, M.L.T., 1986. Admitted to the Illinois Bar, 1984. On staff of the Joint Committee on Taxation of the United States Congress: Legislation Attorney, 1985–1989; Legislation Counsel, 1989–2009; and Senior Legislation Counsel, 2009–2013; appointed by President Barack H. Obama as Judge, United States Tax Court, on September 4, 2013, for a term ending September 3, 2028.

CARY DOUGLAS PUGH, judge; born in Virginia; B.A., in Political Science and Russian, *magna cum laude*, Duke University, 1987; M.A., in Russian and East European Studies, Stanford University, 1988; J.D., University of Virginia School of Law, 1994; Order of the Coif, *Virginia Law Review*, Executive Editor. Admitted to Virginia State Bar, 1994, District of Columbia Bar, 1995, United States Supreme Court Bar, 1997. Served as Law Clerk to the Honorable Jackson L. Kiser, Chief Judge, U.S. District Court, Western District of Virginia, 1994–1995. Practiced law as an Associate, Vinson and Elkins LLP, Washington, DC, 1995–1999. Served as Minority Tax Counsel and Majority Tax Counsel, Committee on Finance, United States Senate, 1999–2002. Served as Special Counsel to the Chief Counsel, 2002–2005. Recipient of the Chief Counsel's Award 2003. Practiced law as Counsel, Skadden, Arps, Slate, Meagher and Flom LLP, 2005–2014. Member of American Bar Association, Section of Taxation; named John S. Nolan Tax Law Fellow, 2001–2002; served as Chair, Tax Shelter Committee and Government Relations Committee and as Council Director. Fellow, American College of Tax Counsel. Former Adjunct Professor, Georgetown University Law Center, LL.M. Taxation Program; appointed by President Barack H. Obama as Judge, United States Tax Court, on December 16, 2014, for a term ending December 15, 2029.

TAMARA W. ASHFORD, judge; born in Boston, Massachusetts; B.A., in public policy studies, Duke University (1991); J.D., Vanderbilt University Law School (1994); LL.M., Master of Laws in Taxation, with an honors certificate of specialization in international tax, University of Miami School of Law (1997). Admitted to the Bars of North Carolina; District of Columbia; United States Tax Court; United States Courts of Appeals for the District of Columbia, First, Second, Fourth, Fifth, Sixth, Ninth and Tenth Circuits; United States Supreme Court. Served as Law Clerk to the Honorable John C. Martin, North Carolina Court of Appeals (1994–1996). Practiced law as a Trial Attorney in the Appellate Section, Tax Division, United States Department of Justice (1997–2001). Practiced law as a Senior Associate, Miller and Chevalier, Chartered (2001–04). Served as Assistant to the Commissioner (2004–07) and U.S. Director for the Joint International Tax Shelter Information Centre / Senior Advisor to the Commissioner, Large and Mid-Size Business Division (2007–08) in the Internal Revenue Service. Recipient of the Sheldon S. Cohen National Outstanding Support to the Office of Chief Counsel Award (2006). Practiced law as Counsel, Dewey and LeBoeuf, LLP (2008–11). Recognized for Tax Controversy by the 2010 edition of The Legal 500. Served as Deputy Assistant Attorney General for Appellate and Review (2011–14), Principal Deputy Assistant Attorney General and Acting Deputy Assistant Attorney General for Policy and Planning (2013–14), and Acting Assistant Attorney General (June 2014–December 2014) in the Tax Division, United States Department of Justice. Named a 2012 Person of the Year by Tax Analysts. Appointed by President Barack H. Obama as Judge, United States Tax Court, on December 19, 2014, for a term ending December 18, 2029.

SENIOR JUDGES

MARY ANN COHEN, senior judge; born in New Mexico, 1943; attended public schools in Los Angeles, CA; B.S., University of California, at Los Angeles, 1964; J.D., University of Southern California School of Law, 1967; practiced law in Los Angeles, member in law firm of Abbott and Cohen; American Bar Association, Section of Taxation, and Continuing Legal Education activities; received Dana Latham Memorial Award from Los Angeles County Bar Association Taxation Section, 1997; Jules Ritholz Memorial Merit Award from ABA Tax Section Committee on Civil and Criminal Tax Penalties, 1999; Bruce I. Hochman Award from the UCLA Tax Controversy Program, 2007; and Joanne M. Garvey Award from California Bar Taxation Section, 2008; appointed by President Ronald W. Reagan as Judge, United States Tax Court, on September 24, 1982, for a term ending September 23, 1997; served as Chief Judge from June 1, 1996 to September 23, 1997; reappointed on November 7, 1997, for a term ending November 6, 2012, and served again as Chief Judge from November 7, 1997 to May 31, 2000. Assumed senior status on October 1, 2012.

JULIAN I. JACOBS, senior judge; born in Maryland, 1937; B.A., University of Maryland, 1958; LL.B., University of Maryland Law School, 1960; LL.M., Taxation, Georgetown Law Center, 1965; admitted to Maryland Bar, 1960; attorney, Internal Revenue Service, Washington, DC, 1961–65, and Buffalo, NY, in Regional Counsel's Office, 1965–67; entered private practice of law in Baltimore, MD, 1967; associate (1972–74) and partner (1974–84) in the Law Firm of Gordon, Feinblatt, Rothman, Hoffberger and Hollander; Chairman, study commission to improve the quality of the Maryland Tax Court, 1978; member, study groups to consider changes in the Maryland tax laws; Commissioner on a commission to reorganize and recodify article of Maryland law dealing with taxation, 1980; Lecturer, tax seminars and professional programs; Chairman, Section of Taxation, Maryland State Bar Association; adjunct professor of Law, Graduate Tax Program, University of Baltimore School of Law, 1991–93; Adjunct Professor of Law, Graduate Tax Program, University of San Diego School of Law, 2001; Adjunct Professor of Law, Graduate Tax Program, University of Denver School of Law, 2001–04; appointed by President Ronald W. Reagan as Judge, United States Tax Court, on March 30, 1984, for a term ending March 29, 1999; recalled on March 30, 1999, as Senior Judge to perform judicial duties from that date to the present.

JOEL GERBER, senior judge; born in Illinois, 1940; B.S., business administration, Roosevelt University, 1962; J.D., DePaul University, 1965; LL.M., Taxation, Boston University Law School, 1968; admitted to the Illinois Bar, 1965; Georgia Bar, 1974; Tennessee Bar, 1978; served with U.S. Treasury Department, Internal Revenue Service, as trial attorney, Boston, MA, 1965–72; senior trial attorney, Atlanta, GA, 1972–76; District Counsel, Nashville, TN, 1976–80; Deputy Chief Counsel, Washington, DC, 1980–84; Acting Chief Counsel, May 1983–March 1984; recipient of a Presidential Meritorious Rank Award, 1983; Secretary of the Treasury's Exceptional Service Award, 1984; Lecturer in Law, Vanderbilt University, 1976–80; appointed by President Ronald W. Reagan as Judge, United States Tax Court, on June 18, 1984, for a term ending June 17, 1999; served as Senior Judge on recall performing judicial duties until reappointed on December 15, 2000, for a term ending December 14, 2015; served as Chief Judge from June 1, 2004, to May 31, 2006; assumed senior status on June 1, 2006.

THOMAS B. WELLS, senior judge; born in Ohio, 1945; B.S., Miami University, Oxford, OH, 1967; J.D., Emory University Law School, Atlanta, GA, 1973; LL.M., Taxation, New York University Law School, New York, 1978; Supply Corps Officer, U.S. Naval Reserve, active duty 1967–70, Morocco and Vietnam, received Joint Service Commendation Medal; admitted to practice law in Georgia; member of law firm of Graham and Wells, P.C.; County Attorney for Toombs County, GA; City Attorney, Vidalia, GA, until 1977; law firm of Hurt, Richardson, Garner, Todd and Cadenhead, Atlanta, until 1981; law firm of Shearer and Wells, P.C. until 1986; member of American Bar Association, Section of Taxation; State Bar of Georgia, member of Board of Governors; Board of Editors, Georgia State Bar Journal; member, Atlanta Bar Association; Editor of the *Atlanta Lawyer*; active in various tax organizations, such as Atlanta Tax Forum (presently, Honorary Member); Director, Atlanta Estate Planning Council; Director, North Atlanta Tax Council; American College of Tax Counsel, Honorary Fellow; Emory Law Alumni Association's Distinguished Alumnus Award, 2001; Life Member, National Eagle Scout Association, Eagle Scout, 1960; member: Vidalia Kiwanis Club (President); recipient, Distinguished President Award; appointed by President Ronald W. Reagan as Judge, United States Tax Court, on October 13, 1986, for a term ending October 12, 2001; reappointed by President George W. Bush on October 10, 2001, for a term ending October 9, 2016; served as Chief Judge from September 24, 1997 to

November 6, 1997, and from June 1, 2000 to May 31, 2004. Assumed senior status on January 1, 2011.

ROBERT PAUL RUWE, senior judge; born in Ohio, 1941; Roger Bacon High School, St. Bernard, OH, 1959; Xavier University, Cincinnati, OH, 1963; J.D., Salmon P. Chase College of Law (graduated first in class), 1970; admitted to Ohio Bar, 1970; Special Agent, Intelligence Division, Internal Revenue Service, 1963–70; joined Office of Chief Counsel, Internal Revenue Service in 1970, and held the following positions: Trial Attorney (Indianapolis), Director, Criminal Tax Division, Deputy Associate Chief Counsel (Litigation), and Director, Tax Litigation Division. Appointed by President Ronald W. Reagan as Judge, United States Tax Court, on November 20, 1987, for a term ending November 19, 2002; recalled on November 20, 2002, as Senior Judge to perform judicial duties from that date to the present.

LAURENCE J. WHALEN, senior judge; born in Pennsylvania, 1944; A.B., Georgetown University, 1967; J.D., Georgetown University Law Center, 1970; LL.M., 1971; admitted to District of Columbia and Oklahoma Bars; Special Assistant to the Assistant Attorney General, Tax Division, Department of Justice, 1971–72; trial attorney, Tax Division, 1971–75; private law practice in Washington, DC, with Hamel and Park (now Hopkins, Sutter, Hamel and Park), 1977–84; also in Oklahoma City, OK, with Crowe and Dunlevy, 1984–87; member of Oklahoma Bar Association, District of Columbia Bar Association, and American Bar Association, appointed by President Ronald W. Reagan as Judge, United States Tax Court, on November 23, 1987, for a term ending November 22, 2002; recalled on November 23, 2002, as Senior Judge to perform judicial duties from that date to the present.

JOHN O. COLVIN, senior judge; born in Ohio; A.B., University of Missouri, 1968; J.D., 1971; LL.M., Taxation, Georgetown University Law Center, 1978; admitted to practice law in Missouri (1971) and District of Columbia (1974); Office of the Chief Counsel, U.S. Coast Guard, Washington, DC, 1971–75; served as Tax Counsel, Senator Bob Packwood, 1975–84; Chief Counsel (1985–87), and Chief Minority Counsel (1987–88), U.S. Senate Finance Committee; past Chair, Tax Section, Federal Bar Association and recipient of the FBA Tax Section's Liles Award; Adjunct Professor of Law, Georgetown University Law Center and recipient of Charles Fahy Distinguished Adjunct Professor Award; appointed by President Ronald W. Reagan as Judge, United States Tax Court, on September 1, 1988, for a term ending August 31, 2003; reappointed on August 12, 2004, for a term ending August 11, 2019; served as Chief Judge for two-year terms beginning June 1, 2006, June 1, 2008, and June 1, 2010; served as Chief Judge for an interim period effective March 8, 2013, to August 7, 2013. Assumed senior status on November 17, 2016.

JAMES S. HALPERN, senior judge; born in New York; Hackley School, Terrytown, NY, 1963; B.S., Wharton School, University of Pennsylvania, 1967; J.D., University of Pennsylvania Law School, 1972; LL.M., Taxation, New York University Law School, 1975; Associate Attorney, Mudge, Rose, Guthrie and Alexander, New York City, 1972–74; assistant professor of law, Washington and Lee University, 1975–76; assistant professor of law, St. John's University, New York City, 1976–78; visiting professor, Law School, New York University, 1978–79; associate attorney, Roberts and Holland, New York City, 1979–80; Principal Technical Advisor, Assistant Commissioner (Technical) and Associate Chief Counsel (Technical), Internal Revenue Service, Washington, DC, 1980–83; partner, Baker and Hostetler, Washington, DC, 1983–90; Adjunct Professor, George Washington University Law School, Washington, DC, 1984–present; Colonel, U.S. Army Reserve (retired); appointed by President George H.W. Bush as Judge, United States Tax Court, on July 3, 1990, for a term ending July 2, 2005; reappointed on November 2, 2005, for a term ending November 1, 2020. Assumed senior status on October 16, 2015.

CAROLYN P. CHIECHI, senior judge; born in New Jersey, 1943; B.S. (*magna cum laude*, Class Rank: 1), Georgetown University, 1965; J.D., 1969 (Class Rank: 9); LL.M., Taxation, 1971; Doctor of Laws, Honoris Causa, 2000; practiced with law firm of Sutherland, Asbill and Brennan, Washington, DC and Atlanta, GA (partner, 1976–92; associate, 1971–76); served as attorney-adviser to Judge Leo H. Irwin, United States Tax Court, 1969–71; member, District of Columbia Bar, 1969–present (member, Taxation Section, 1973–99; member, Taxation Section Steering Committee, 1980–82, Chairperson, 1981–82; member, Tax Audits and Litigation Committee, 1986–92, Chairperson, 1987–88); member, American Bar Association, 1969–present (member, Section of Taxation, 1969–present; member, Committee on Court Procedure, 1991–present; member, Litigation Section, 1995–2000; member, Judicial

Division, 1997–2000); Federal Bar Association, 1969–present (member, Section of Taxation, 1969–present; member, Judiciary Division, 1992–present); Fellow, American College of Tax Counsel; Fellow, American Bar Foundation; member, Women's Bar Association of the District of Columbia, 1992–present; Board of Governors, Georgetown University Alumni Association, 1994–97, 1997–2000; Board of Regents, Georgetown University, 1988–94, 1995–2001; National Law Alumni Board, Georgetown University, 1986–93; Board of Directors, Stuart Stiller Memorial Foundation, 1986–99; American Judicature Society, 1994–present; one of several recipients of the first Georgetown University Law Alumni Awards (1994); one of several recipients of the first Georgetown University Law Center Alumnae Achievement Awards (1998); admitted to *Who's Who in American Law, Who's Who of American Women, Who's Who in America,* and *Who's Who in the East*; appointed by President George H.W. Bush as Judge, United States Tax Court, on October 1, 1992, for a term ending September 30, 2007; recalled October 1, 2007, as senior judge to perform judicial duties from that date to the present.

DAVID LARO, senior judge; born in Michigan, 1942; Graduate of New York University Law School (LL.M. in Taxation, 1970), the University of Illinois Law School (J.D. 1967) and the University of Michigan (B.A. 1964). Formerly practiced tax law in Flint and Ann Arbor Michigan for 24 years. Regent of the University of Michigan, a member of the State Board of Education in Michigan, and Chairman of the State Tenure Commission in Michigan. Teaches corporate tax and business planning at Georgetown Law School, and the University of San Diego Law School. Co-Author of *Business Valuation and Taxes: Procedure, Law and Perspective* (Second edition, 2011), a 500 page text on tax valuation. At the request of the American Bar Association (CEELI), contributed written comments on the Draft Laws of Ukraine and Uzbekistan. As a consultant for Harvard University (Harvard Institute for International Development) and Georgia State University, lectured in Moscow on the subjects of tax reform and litigation. Consultant on Russian Tax Reform under a project through USAID. At the invitation of the Supreme Court of Kazakhstan in 2007, lectured to members of the Kazakhstan Judiciary, and lectured to members of the Russian Judiciary in Moscow in 2007–10. In May 2006, and June 2007, at the invitation of the State Tax Administration and other government officials, lectured in Beijing, China on economic substance. Appointed by President George H.W. Bush as Judge, United States Tax Court, on November 2, 1992, for a term ending November 1, 2007; recalled as senior judge to perform judicial duties to the present date.

ROBERT A. WHERRY, Jr., senior judge; born in Virginia, 1944; B.S. and J.D., University of Colorado; LL.M., Taxation, New York University Law School; fellow and former Regent of the American College of Tax Counsel and former chairman of the Taxation Section of the Colorado Bar Association; served as chairman of the Small-Business Tax Committee of the Colorado Association of Commerce and Industry, as president of the Greater Denver Tax Counsel Association, is a past chairman of the Administrative Practice Committee of the American Bar Association Tax Section, a member of the Council, and a member of the Advisory Committee of the American Bar Association Section of Dispute Resolution; listed in *The Best Lawyers in America* (in tax litigation); his articles have appeared in ALI–ABA publications, *The Colorado Lawyer, Tax Notes*, and *State Tax Notes*; former Colorado correspondent for *State Tax Notes* and has spoken at numerous tax institutes, including the University of Denver Tax Institute, Tulane University Tax Institute, and American Bar Association Tax Section programs; was an instructor in Tax Court litigation for the National Institute for Trial Advocacy; appointed by President George W. Bush as Judge, United States Tax Court, on April 23, 2003, for a term ending April 22, 2018. Assumed senior status on April 8, 2014.

SPECIAL TRIAL JUDGES OF THE COURT

Peter J. Panuthos (Chief Special Trial Judge); Robert N. Armen, Jr.; Lewis R. Carluzzo; Daniel A. Guy; Diana L. Leyden.

Court Staff

Clerk.—Stephanie A. Servoss.
Deputy Clerk.—Jennifer E. Siegel.
General Counsel.—Douglas W. Snoeyenbos.
Court Administrator.—Fig Ruggieri.
Case Services Director.—Tina Buckler.

Facilities Management Director.—Joyce Russell Dyck.
Financial Management Director.—Joseph L. Hardy, Jr.
Human Resources Director.—Janet L. Boyer.
Information Systems Director.—Gordon S. Goodrick.
Librarian.—Nancy A. Ciliberti.
Reporter of Decisions.—Sheila A. Murphy.

UNITED STATES COURT OF APPEALS FOR THE ARMED FORCES[1]

450 E Street, NW., 20442–0001, phone 761–1448, fax 761–4672

SCOTT W. STUCKY, chief judge; born in Hutchinson, KS; B.A. *summa cum laude*, Wichita State University, 1970; J.D., Harvard Law School, 1973; M.A., Trinity University, 1980; LL.M. with highest honors, George Washington University, 1983; Federal Executive Institute, 1988; Harvard Program for Senior Officials in National Security, 1990; National War College, 1993; admitted to bar, Kansas and District of Columbia; U.S. Air Force, judge advocate, 1973–78; U.S. Air Force Reserve, 1982–2003 (retired as colonel); married to Jean Elsie Seibert of Oxon Hill, MD, August 18, 1973; children: Mary-Clare and Joseph; private law practice, Washington, DC, 1978–82; branch chief, U.S. Nuclear Regulatory Commission, 1982–83; legislative counsel and principal legislative counsel, U.S. Air Force, 1983–96; General Counsel, Committee on Armed Services, U.S. Senate, 1996–2001 and 2003–06; Minority Counsel, 2001–03; National Commander-in-Chief, Military Order of the Loyal Legion of the United States, 1993–95; Board of Directors, Adoption Service Information Agency, 1998–2002 and 2004–07; Board of Directors, Omicron Delta Kappa Society, 2006–10; member, Federal Bar Association (Pentagon Chapter), Judge Advocates Association, the District of Columbia Bar; OPM LEGIS Fellow, office of Senator John Warner (R–VA), 1986–87; member and panel chairman, Air Force Board for Correction of Military Records, 1989–96; nominated by President George W. Bush to serve on the U.S. Court of Appeals for the Armed Forces on November 15, 2006; confirmed by the Senate, December 9, 2006; began service on December 20, 2006, and became Chief Judge on August 1, 2017.

MARGARET A. RYAN, judge; born in Chicago, IL; B.A. cum laude, Knox College; J.D., *summa cum laude*, University of Notre Dame Law School; recipient of the William T. Kirby Legal Writing Award and the Colonel William J. Hoynes Award for Outstanding Scholarship; active duty in the U.S. Marine Corps, 1986–99, serving as a communications officer, staff officer, company commander, platoon commander, and operations officer in units within the II and III Marine Expeditionary Forces and as a judge advocate in Okinawa, Japan, and Quantico, VA; also served as Aide de Camp to General Charles C. Krulak, the 31st Commandant of the Marine Corps; law clerk to the Honorable J. Michael Luttig, U.S. Court of Appeals for the Fourth Circuit, and law clerk to the Honorable Clarence Thomas, Associate Justice of the Supreme Court of the United States; litigation partner at the law firm of Bartlik Beck Herman Palenchar and Scott LLP and partner in litigation and appellate practices at the law firm Wiley Rein Fielding LLP; nominated by President George W. Bush to serve on the U.S. Court of Appeals for the Armed Forces on November 15, 2006; confirmed by the Senate on December 9, 2006; began service on December 20, 2006.

KEVIN A. OHLSON, judge; born in Sterling, MA; B.A., Washington and Jefferson College, 1982; four-year Army R.O.T.C. scholarship; Phi Beta Kappa; Air Assault training with the 101st Airborne Division at Fort Campbell, Kentucky, 1980; J.D., University of Virginia School of Law, 1985; Airborne training at Fort Benning, GA, 1986; administrative law officer and trial counsel at Fort Bragg, NC, 1986–89; federal prosecutor in Washington, D.C., 1989–97; volunteered to return to active duty and served as a legal advisor to the XVIII Airborne Corps Command Staff during Operation Desert Storm, 1990–91; awarded the Bronze Star; returned to the United States Attorney's Office for the District of Columbia and resumed duties as a federal prosecutor; Chief of Staff to the Deputy Attorney General, 1997–2001; member of the Board of Immigration Appeals, 2001–03; deputy director, and then the director, of the Executive Office for Immigration Review, 2003–09; Chief of Staff and Counselor to the Attorney General of the United States, 2009–2011; chief of the Professional Misconduct Review Unit at the Department of Justice, 2011–13; nominated by the President and confirmed

[1] Prior to October 5, 1994, United States Court of Military Appeals.

by the Senate to serve on the U.S. Court of Appeals for the Armed Forces; began service on November 1, 2013.

JOHN E. SPARKS, Jr., judge; born in Mount Holly, NJ; B.S., U.S. Naval Academy, 1976; J.D., University of Connecticut School of Law, 1986; Military Service, U.S. Navy 1971; U.S. Marine Corps 1976–98, as an Infantry Officer, and a variety of legal positions including military prosecutor, defense counsel, legal adviser to a naval hospital, military judge, Military Assistant and Special Counsel to the General Counsel of the Navy, and in the White House as a Deputy Legal Adviser to the National Security Council; Special Assistant for Civil Rights to the Secretary of Agriculture, 1998; Principal Deputy General Counsel of the Navy, 1999–2000; senior legal advisor to then Judge and later Chief Judge James E. Baker, United States Court of Appeals for the Armed Forces, 2000–15; nominated by President Barack Obama and confirmed by the Senate to serve on the United States Court of Appeals for the Armed Forces; began service on April 8, 2016.

SENIOR JUDGES

WALTER THOMPSON COX III, senior judge; born in Anderson, SC; son of Walter T. Cox and Mary Johnson Cox; married to Vicki Grubbs of Anderson, SC, February 8, 1963; children: Lisa and Walter; B.S., Clemson University, 1964; J.D., *cum laude*, University of South Carolina School of Law, 1967; graduated Defense Language Institute (German), 1969; graduated basic course, the Judge Advocate General's School, Charlottesville, VA, 1967; studied procurement law at that same school, 1968; active duty, U.S. Army judge advocate general's corps, 1964–72 (1964–67, excess leave to U.S.C. Law School); private law practice, 1973–78; elected resident judge, 10th Judicial Circuit, South Carolina, 1978–84; also served as acting associate justice of South Carolina supreme court, on the judicial council, on the circuit court advisory committee, and as a hearing officer of the judicial standards commission; member: bar of the Supreme Court of the United States; bar of the U.S. Court of Military Appeals; South Carolina Bar Association; Anderson County Bar Association; the American Bar Association; the South Carolina Trial Lawyers Association; the Federal Bar Association; and the Bar Association of the District of Columbia; has served as a member of the House of Delegates of the South Carolina Bar, and the Board of Commissioners on Grievances and Discipline; nominated by President Reagan, as judge of U.S. Court of Military Appeals, June 28, 1984, for a term of 15 years; confirmed by the Senate, July 26, 1984; sworn-in and officially assumed his duties on September 6, 1984; retired on September 30, 1999 and immediately assumed status of Senior Judge on October 1, 1999 and returned to full active service until September 19, 2000.

EUGENE R. SULLIVAN, senior judge; born in St. Louis, MO; son of Raymond V. and Rosemary K. Sullivan; married to Lis U. Johansen of Ribe, Denmark, June 18, 1966; children: Kim A. and Eugene R. II; B.S., U.S. Military Academy, West Point, 1964; J.D., Georgetown Law Center, Washington, DC, 1971; active duty with the U.S. Army, 1964–69; service included duty with the 3rd Armored Division in Germany, and the 4th Infantry Division in Vietnam; R&D assignments with the Army Aviation Systems Command; one year as an instructor at the Army Ranger School, Ft. Benning, GA; decorations include: Bronze Star, Air Medal, Army Commendation Medal, Ranger and Parachutist Badges, Air Force Exceptional Civilian Service Medal; following graduation from law school, clerked with U.S. Court of Appeals (8th Circuit), St. Louis, 1971–72; private law practice, Washington, DC, 1972–74; assistant special counsel, White House, 1974; trial attorney, U.S. Department of Justice, 1974–82; deputy general counsel, Department of the Air Force, 1982–84; general counsel of the Department of Air Force, 1984–86; Governor of Wake Island, 1984–86; presently serves on the Board of Governors for the West Point Society of the District of Columbia; the American Cancer Society (Montgomery County Chapter); nominated by President Reagan, as judge, U.S. Court of Military Appeals on February 25, 1986, and confirmed by the Senate on May 20, 1986, and assumed his office on May 27, 1986; President George H.W. Bush named him the chief judge of the U.S. Court of Military Appeals, effective October 1, 1990, a position he held for five years; he retired on September 30, 2001 and immediately assumed status of Senior Judge and returned to full active service until Sept. 30, 2002.

SUSAN J. CRAWFORD, senior judge; born in Pittsburgh, PA; daughter of William E. and Joan B. Crawford; married to Roger W. Higgins of Geneva, NY, September 8, 1979; one child, Kelley S. Higgins; B.A., Bucknell University, Pennsylvania, 1969; J.D., *cum laude*, Dean's Award, Arthur McClean Founder's Award, New England School of Law, Boston, MA, 1977; history teacher and coach of women's athletics, Radnor High School, Pennsylvania, 1969–74; associate, Burnett and Eiswert, Oakland, MD, 1977–79; Assistant State's Attorney,

Garrett County, Maryland, 1978–80; partner, Burnett, Eiswert and Crawford, 1979–81; instructor, Garrett County Community College, 1979–81; deputy general counsel, 1981–83, and general counsel, Department of the Army, 1983–89; special counsel to Secretary of Defense, 1989; inspector general, Department of Defense, 1989–91; member: bar of the Supreme Court of the United States; bar of the U.S. Court of Military Appeals, Maryland Bar Association, District of Columbia Bar Association, American Bar Association, Federal Bar Association, and the Edward Bennett Williams American Inn of Court; member: board of trustees, 1989–present, and Corporation, 1992–present, of New England School of Law; board of trustees, 1988–present, Bucknell University; nominated by President Bush as judge, U.S. Court of Military Appeals, February 19, 1991, for a term of 15 years; confirmed by the Senate on November 14, 1991, sworn in and officially assumed her duties on November 19, 1991; on October 1, 1999, she became the Chief Judge for a term of five years; retired on September 30, 2006 and assumed the status of Senior Judge on October 1, 2006.

ANDREW S. EFFRON, senior judge; born in Stamford, CT; A.B., Harvard College, 1970; J.D., Harvard Law School, 1975; The Judge Advocate General's School, U.S. Army, 1976, 1983; legislative aide to the late Representative William A. Steiger, 1970–76 (two years full-time, the balance between school semesters); judge advocate, Office of the Staff Judge Advocate, Fort McClellan, Alabama, 1976–77; attorney-adviser, Office of the General Counsel, Department of Defense, 1977–87; Counsel, General Counsel, and Minority Counsel, Committee on Armed Services, U.S. Senate, 1987–96; nominated by President Clinton to serve on the U.S. Court of Appeals for the Armed Forces, June 21, 1996; confirmed by the Senate, July 12, 1996; took office on August 1, 1996; assumed his duties on August 1, 1996. On October 1, 2006, he became Chief Judge for a five year term, and immediately assumed status as Senior Judge on October 1, 2011.

JAMES E. BAKER, senior judge; born in New Haven, CT; education: BA., Yale University, 1982; J.D., Yale Law School, 1990; Attorney, Department of State, 1990–93; Counsel, President's Foreign Intelligence Advisory Board/Intelligence Oversight Board, 1993–94; Deputy Legal Advisor, National Security Council, 1994–97; Special Assistant to the President and Legal Advisor, National Security Council, 1997–2000; military service: U.S. Marine Corps and U.S. Marine Corp Reserve; nominated by President Clinton to serve on the U.S. Court of Appeals for the Armed Forces; began service on September 19, 2000, and became Chief Judge on October 1, 2011; became a Senior Judge on August 1, 2015.

CHARLES E. ERDMANN, senior judge; born in Great Falls, MT; B.A., Montana State University, 1972; J.D., University of Montana Law School, 1975; Air Force Judge Advocate Staff Officers Course, 1981; Air Command and Staff College, 1992; Air War College, 1994; Military Service: U.S. Marine Corps, 1967–70; Air National Guard, 1981–2002 (retired as a Colonel); Assistant Montana Attorney General, 1975–76; Chief Counsel, Montana State Auditor's Office, 1976–78; Chief Staff Attorney, Montana Attorney General's Office, Antitrust Bureau; Bureau Chief, Montana Medicaid Fraud Bureau, 1980–82; General Counsel, Montana School Boards Association, 1982–86; private practice of law, 1986–95; Associate Justice, Montana Supreme Court, 1995–97; Office of High Representative of Bosnia and Herzegovina, Judicial Reform Coordinator, 1998–99; Office of High Representative of Bosnia and Herzegovina, Head of Human Rights and Rule of Law Department, 1999; Chairman and Chief Judge, Bosnian Election Court, 2000–01; Judicial Reform and International Law Consultant, 2001–02; appointed by President George W. Bush to serve on the U.S. Court of Appeals for the Armed Forces on October 9, 2002, commenced service on October 15, 2002 and became Chief Judge on August 1, 2015; became a Senior Judge on August 1, 2017.

Officers of the U.S. Court of Appeals for the Armed Forces

Clerk of the Court.—Joseph R. Perlak.
Chief Deputy Clerk of the Court.—David A. Anderson.
Deputy Clerk for Opinions.—Patricia Mariani.
Court Executive.—Keith Roberts.
Librarian.—Agnes Kiang.

UNITED STATES COURT OF APPEALS FOR VETERANS CLAIMS

625 Indiana Avenue, NW., Suite 900, 20004, phone (202) 501–5970

ROBERT N. DAVIS, chief judge; born in Kewanee, IL, September 20, 1953; graduated from Davenport Central High School, Davenport, IA, 1971; B.A., University of Hartford, 1975; J.D., Georgetown University Law Center, 1978; admitted to the bars of the U.S. Supreme Court, the Ninth Circuit Court of Appeals; the State of Virginia; and the State of Iowa; career record 1978–83 appellate attorney with the Commodity Futures Trading Commission; 1983–88 attorney with the United States Department of Education, Business and Administrative Law Division of the Office of General Counsel; 1983 Governmental exchange program with the United States Attorneys office, District of Columbia; Special Assistant United States Attorney; 1988–2001 Professor of Law, University of Mississippi School of Law; 2001–05 Professor of Law, Stetson University College of Law; Published extensively in the areas of constitutional law, administrative law, national security law, and sports law. Founder and Faculty Editor-in-Chief, *Journal of National Security Law*, arbitrator/mediator with the American Arbitration Association and the United States Postal Service. Gubernatorial appointment to the National Conference of Commissioners on Uniform State Laws 1993–2000. Joined the United States Navy Reserve Intelligence Program in 1988. Presidential recall to active duty in 1999, Bosnia and 2001 for the Global War on Terrorism. Military decorations include Joint Service Commendation Medal, Joint Service Achievement Medal, Navy Achievement Medal, NATO Medal, Armed Forces Expeditionary Medal, Armed Forces Reserve Medal with ''M'' device, Overseas Service Ribbon, National Defense Ribbon, Joint Meritorious Unit Award, and Global War on Terrorism Medal. Nominated for appointment by President George W. Bush on March 23, 2003; confirmed by the United States Senate on November 21, 2004; commissioned on December 4, 2004 as a Judge, United States Court of Appeals for Veterans Claims. He became the Chief Judge on October 9, 2016.

MARY J. SCHOELEN, judge; born in Rota, Spain; B.A., political science, University of California at Irvine, 1990; J.D., George Washington University Law School, 1993; admitted to the State Bar of California; law clerk for the National Veterans Legal Services Project, 1992–93; legal intern to the U.S. Senate Committee on Veterans' Affairs, 1994; staff attorney for Vietnam Veterans of America's Veterans Benefits Program, 1994–97; Minority Counsel, U.S. Senate Committee on Veterans' Affairs, 1997–2001; Minority General Counsel, March 2001–June 2001; Deputy Staff Director, Benefits Programs/General Counsel, June 2001–03; Minority Deputy Staff Director, Benefits Programs/General Counsel, 2003–04; nominated by President George W. Bush; appointed a Judge of the United States Court of Appeals for Veterans Claims; confirmed by the U.S. Senate to the United States Court of Appeals for Veterans Claims on November 20, 2004; sworn in December 20, 2004.

CORAL WONG–PIETSCH, judge; born in Waterloo, IA, Judge Pietsch has a distinguished career in public service, both in the military and as a civilian. She was commissioned in the U.S. Army Judge Advocate General's Corps and served six years on active duty. Judge Pietsch continued her service in the U.S. Army Reserve and rose to the rank of Brigadier General. She became the first woman to be promoted to the rank of Brigadier General in the U.S. Army Judge Advocate General's Corps and the first woman of Asian ancestry to be promoted to Brigadier General in the Army. Until her appointment to the bench, Judge Pietsch held the position of Senior Attorney and Special Assistant at Headquarters, U.S. Army Pacific located in Honolulu, Hawaii. In this position, she provided and managed legal services in support of the U.S. Army Pacific's mission to train Army Forces for military operations and peacetime engagements aimed at promoting regional stability. As part of the 2007 ''surge'' in Iraq, Judge Pietsch volunteered as a Department of Defense civilian to deploy to Iraq for a year, where she was seconded to the U.S. Department of State to serve as the Deputy Rule of Law Coordinator for the Baghdad Provincial Reconstruction Team. During her deployment to Iraq, Judge Pietsch assisted with numerous civil society projects involving a variety of Rule of Law partners, including the Iraqi Jurist Union, Iraqi Bar Association, law schools, and international rights, women's rights, and human rights organizations. She evaluated and sought funding for numerous projects aimed at building capacity within the Iraqi legal community to include the establishment, in close collaboration with the Iraqi Bar Association, of a Legal Aid Clinic at one of Iraq's largest detention facilities. In 2006 Judge Pietsch was appointed by the Governor of Hawaii to the Hawaii Civil Rights Commission where she served for seven years. Shortly after the appointment, the Governor selected Judge Pietsch as its Chair. Earlier in her civilian legal career, Judge Pietsch had been appointed a Deputy Attorney General for the State of Hawaii, advising the State Department of Health, State Department of Agriculture, and the State Criminal History Records Division. Judge Pietsch's academic degrees include a bachelor of arts, master of arts, and a juris doctor degree. She was also a Senior Executive Fellow at the Harvard University Kennedy School of Government, is a graduate of the Defense Leadership and Management Program, and a graduate of the Army War College. Her awards and decorations include the Distinguished Service Medal, Legion of Merit, Meritorious Service Medal, Joint Service Commendation Medal, Decoration for Exceptional Civilian Service, the Meritorious Civilian Service Medal, Superior Civilian Performance Medal, and the Global War on Terrorism Medal. She has been the recipient of the Organization of Chinese Americans Pioneer Award, the Hawaii Women Lawyers Attorney of the Year Award, the Honolulu YWCA Achievement in Leadership Award, the Catholic University Alumni Achievement Award, the Federal Executive Board Award for Excellence, the U.S. Army Pacific Community Service Award and recognized for lifetime accomplishments by the Women Veterans Igniting the Spirit of Entrepreneurship. Judge Pietsch is admitted to the bars of the United States Supreme Court, the Ninth Circuit Court of Appeals, U.S. District Court of the District of Hawaii, State Bar of Hawaii, State Bar of Iowa, and the United States Court of Appeals for the Armed Forces; nominated by President Barack Obama and subsequently appointed a Judge of the U.S. Court of Appeals for Veterans Claims on May 24, 2012 and sworn in June 2012.

MARGARET BARTLEY, judge; born in Pittsburgh, PA, 1959; B.S., *cum laude*, Pennsylvania State University, 1981; J.D., *cum laude*, American University Washington College of Law, 1993; admitted to the bars of the State of Maryland and the United States Court of Appeals for the Federal Circuit; law clerk to now-retired Judge Jonathan R. Steinberg of the United States Court of Appeals for Veterans Claims, 1993–94; staff attorney for National Veterans Legal Services Program, 1994–2005; senior staff attorney for National Veterans Legal Services Program, 2005–12; editor of the NVLSP veterans' law quarterly, *The Veterans Advocate*, 2004–12; Director of Outreach and Education for the Veterans Consortium Pro Bono Program, 2005–12; nominated as a Judge of the United States Court of Appeals for Veterans Claims on June 21, 2011, by President Barack Obama; confirmed by the U.S. Senate May 21, 2012 and sworn in June 28, 2012.

WILLIAM S. GREENBERG, judge; Judge Greenberg was a partner of McCarter and English, LLP. He initially joined the firm as an associate following a judicial clerkship in 1968, then returned as a partner in 1993. The majority of his career has involved litigation in Federal and state courts. Judge Greenberg had been a Certified Civil Trial Attorney by the Supreme Court of New Jersey since 1983. He served as Chairman of the Judicial and Prosecutorial Appointments Committee of the New Jersey State Bar Association, which considers all candidates to be a judge or prosecutor submitted by the Governor of New Jersey. He was President of the Association of Trial Lawyers of America, New Jersey, (The New Jersey Association for Justice) and has served as Trustee of the New Jersey State Bar Association and of the New Jersey State Bar Foundation. He also served as a member of the New Jersey Supreme Court Committee on the Admission of Foreign Attorneys. He established and chaired the New Jersey State Bar Association (public service/pro bono) program of military legal assistance for members of the Reserve Components called to active duty after September 11, 2001. He was a member of the New Jersey Supreme Court Civil Practice Committee. With the approval of the Secretary of Defense, on the recommendation of the White House, Judge Greenberg became Chairman of the Reserve Forces Policy Board in 2009, a Board established by the Secretary of Defense in 1951 and by Act of Congress in 1952. On July 26, 2011, Judge Greenberg was awarded the Secretary of Defense Medal for Outstanding Public Service, the second highest civilian award in the Defense Department, at a public ceremony in the Pentagon, and completed his term in August 2011. In 2006 his *Civil Trial Handbook*, Volume 47 of the *New Jersey Practice Series*, was published by Thomson/West. A special 20th anniversary issue was published in 2009, to commemorate the 1989 publication of its predecessor, *Trial Handbook for New Jersey Lawyers*. A retired Brigadier General, he served as a member of the New Jersey World War II Memorial Commission. In June 2009 he received the highest honor granted by the New Jersey State Bar Foundation, its medal of honor for his work in establishing the military legal assistance program, and especially in his public service representation of soldiers at Walter Reed Army Medical Center during their Physician Disability Hearings. His article in the June 2007 issue of *New Jersey Lawyer Magazine* describes the program in detail. He has served as special litigation counsel to the Adjutants General Association of the United States and was special litigation counsel *pro bono* to the National Guard Association of the United States. Judge Greenberg was a Commissioner of the New Jersey State Commission of Investigation. He also served as Assistant Counsel to the Governor of New Jersey and as Commissioner of the New Jersey State Scholarship Commission. Professor Greenberg served as the first Adjunct Professor of Military Law at the Seton Hall University School of Law. He was chosen the New Jersey Lawyer of the Year for 2009 by the *New Jersey Law Journal.* He received the Distinguished Alumnus Award from the Johns Hopkins University in 2010, and the Rutgers Law School Public Service Award in 2010 for his work in developing and leading the efforts to represent wounded and injured soldiers at Walter Reed. Judge Greenberg is admitted in New Jersey, New York, and the District of Columbia. He is a member of the bar of the Supreme Court of the United States, and of the Third, Fourth, and Federal Circuits, the Southern District of New York, and the United States Court of Appeals for the Armed Forces. Judge Greenberg is a graduate of the Johns Hopkins University (A.B., 1964) and Rutgers University Law School (J.D., 1967). He is married to the former Betty Kaufmann Wolf of Pittsburgh. They have three children, Katherine of New York, Anthony of Baltimore, and Elizabeth of New York; nominated to the United States Court of Appeals for Veterans Claims by President Barack Obama on November 15, 2012, confirmed by the United States Senate on December 21, 2012, appointed by the President on December 27, 2012, and took the judicial oath on December 28, 2012, for a term of fifteen years.

OFFICERS OF THE U.S. COURT OF APPEALS FOR VETERANS CLAIMS

Clerk of the Court.—Gregory O. Block, 501–5970.
Chief Deputy Clerk Operations Manager.—Anne P. Stygles.
Counsel to the Clerk.—Cary P. Sklar.
Senior Staff Attorney (Central Legal Staff).—Cynthia Brandon-Arnold.
Deputy Executive Officer.—Patrick H. Barnwell.
Librarian.—Allison Fentress.

UNITED STATES JUDICIAL PANEL ON MULTIDISTRICT LITIGATION

Thurgood Marshall Federal Judiciary Building, Room G–255, North Lobby, One Columbus Circle, NE., 20002, phone (202) 502–2800, fax 502–2888

(National jurisdiction to centralize related cases pending in multiple circuits and districts under 28 U.S.C. §§ 1407 & 2112)

Chairman.—Sarah S. Vance, U.S. District Judge, Eastern District of Louisiana.
Judges:
Marjorie O. Rendell, U.S. Court of Appeals Judge, Third Circuit.
Charles R. Breyer, Senior U.S. District Judge, Northern District of California.
Lewis A. Kaplan, Senior U.S. District Judge, Southern District of New York.
Ellen Segal Huvelle, U.S. District Judge, District of Columbia.
R. David Proctor, U.S. District Judge, Northern District of Alabama.
Catherine D. Perry, U.S. District Judge, Eastern District of Missouri.
Panel Executive.—Thomasenia P. Duncan.
Clerk.—Jeffery N. Lüthi.

ADMINISTRATIVE OFFICE OF THE UNITED STATES COURTS

Thurgood Marshall Federal Judiciary Building

One Columbus Circle, NE., 20544, phone (202) 502–2600

Director.—James C. Duff, 502–3000.
Deputy Director.—Lee Ann Bennett, 502–3015.
Chief of Staff.—Gary A. Bowden, 502–1300.
Audit Officer, Office of Audit.—Veleda T. Henderson, 502–1000.
Fair Employment Practices Officer, Office of Fair Employment Practices.—Nancy J. Dunham, 502–3080.
General Counsel, Office of the General Counsel.—Sheryl L. Walter, 502–1100.
Deputy General Counsel.—William E. Meyers, 502–1100.
Ethics Staff.—Sheryl L. Walter, 502–1100.
Chief, Rules Committee Support Staff.—Rebecca Womeldorf, 502–1820.
Judicial Conference Secretariat Officer, Judicial Conference Secretariat.—Katherine Hord Simon, 502–2400.
Public Affairs Officer, Office of Public Affairs.—David A. Sellers, 502–2600.
Legislative Affairs Officer, Office of Legislative Affairs.—Cordia A. Strom, 502–1700.
Deputy Legislative Affairs Officer.—Daniel A. Cunningham, 502–1700.
Associate Director, Department of Administrative Services.—James R. Baugher, 502–2000.
Chief of Staff.—Michael Milby, 502–2000.
Chief, Administrative Systems Office.—Joseph W. Bossi, 502–2200.
Chief Financial Officer, Budget, Accounting and Procurement Office.—Karin O'Leary, 502–2100.
Chief, Financial Liaison and Analysis Staff.—Edward O'Kane, 502–2000.
Judiciary Budget Officer, Budget Division.—Elena J. Simms, 502–2100.
Judiciary Procurement Executive, Procurement Division.—Francis Sullivan, 502–1330.
Chief, Facilities and Security Office.—Melanie F. Gilbert, 502–1200.
Human Resources Officer, Human Resources Office.—Patricia J. Fitzgibbons, 502–1170.
Associate Director, Department of Program Services.—Laura C. Minor, 502–3500.
Chief of Staff.—Michel M. Ishakian, 502–3500.
Chief, Judicial Services Office.—Michele E. Reed, 502–1800.
Chief, Court Services Office.—Mary Louise Mitterhoff, 502–1500.
Chief, Defender Services Office.—Cait T. Clarke, 502–3030.
Chief, Probation and Pretrial Services Office.—Matthew Rowland, 502–1600.
Chief, Case Management Systems Office.—Andrew M. Zaso, 502–2500.
Chief, Judiciary Data and Analysis Office.—Gary Yakimov, 502–1400.
Associate Director, Department of Technology Services.—Joseph R. Peters, Jr., 502–2300.
Chief of Staff.—Terry A. Cain, 502–2300.
Chief, Cloud Technology and Hosting Office.—Robert D. Morse, 502–2730.
Chief, IT Security Office.—Bethany De Lude, 502–2350.
Chief, Systems Deployment and Support Office.—Ronald E. Blankenship, 502–2700.
Chief, Technology Solutions Office.—Farhad K. Safaie, 502–2730.
Chief, Infrastructure Management Office.—Tim Hanlon, 502–2640.
Chief, AO Technology Office.—John C. Chang, 502–2830.

FEDERAL JUDICIAL CENTER

One Columbus Circle, NE., 20002–8003, phone (202) 502–4160

Director.—Judge Jeremy D. Fogel, 502–4160, fax 502–4099.
Deputy Director.—John S. Cooke, 502–4060, fax 502–4099.

Director of:
Editorial and Information Services Office.—Sylvan A. Sobel, 502–4250, fax 502–4077.
Education Division.—John S. Cooke (acting), 502–4060, fax 502–4099.
Federal Judicial History Office.—Clara Altman, 502–4181, fax 502–4099.
International Judicial Relations Office.—Mira Gur-Arie, 502–4191, fax 502–4099.
Research Division.—James B. Eaglin, 502–4070, fax 502–4199.
Information Technology Office.—Esther DeVries, 502–4223, fax 502–4288.

DISTRICT OF COLUMBIA COURTS

500 Indiana Avenue, NW., 20001

phone (202) 879–1010

Executive Officer.—Anne B. Wicks, 879–1700.
Deputy Executive Officer.—Cheryl R. Bailey, 879–1700; fax 879–4829.
Director, Media and Public Relations.—Leah Gurowitz, 879–1700.
Manager, Government Relations.—Callie Coffman, 879–1700.

DISTRICT OF COLUMBIA COURT OF APPEALS

Historic Courthouse, 430 E Street, NW., 20001

phone (202) 879–1010

Chief Judge.—Anna Blackburne-Rigsby.
Associate Judges:
Stephen H. Glickman.
John R. Fisher.
Phyllis D. Thompson.
Corinne Beckwith.
Catharine F. Easterly.
Roy W. McLeese.

Senior Judges:
Theodore R. Newman, Jr.
William C. Pryor.
James A. Belson.
Frank Q. Nebeker.
John M. Steadman.
John A. Terry.
John M. Ferren.
Inez Smith Reid.
Michael W. Farrell.
Vanessa Ruiz.
Eric T. Washington.

Clerk.—Julio Castillo, 879–2725.
Chief Deputy Clerk.—Herb Rouson, 879–2722.
Administration Director.—Reginald Turner, 879–2755.
Admissions, Interim Director.—Marie Robertson, 879–2714.
Public Office Operations Director.—Terry Lambert, 879–2702.
Staff Counsel.—Rosanna Mason, 879–2718.

SUPERIOR COURT OF THE DISTRICT OF COLUMBIA

Moultrie Courthouse, 500 Indiana Avenue, NW., 20001

phone (202) 879–1010

Chief Judge.—Robert E. Morin.
Associate Judges:
Jennifer M. Anderson.
Judith Bartnoff.
Ronna L. Beck.
Julie Becker.
Steven Berk.
Patricia A. Broderick.
Zoe Bush.
John M. Campbell.
Russell F. Canan.
Erik P. Christian.
Jeanette Clark.
Laura A. Cordero.
Carol Dalton.
Danya A. Dayson.

Marisa Demeo.
Jennifer A. DiToro.
Todd E. Edelson.
Anthony Epstein.
Gerald I. Fisher.
Wendell P. Gardner, Jr.
Brian Holeman.
Alfred S. Irving.
Craig Iscoe.
Gregory Jackson.
William M. Jackson.
J. Ramsey Johnson.
Anita Josey-Herring.
Kimberley S. Knowles.
Peter Krauthamer.
Neal E. Kravitz.
Milton C. Lee
Lynn Leibowitz.
José M. López.
John McCabe.
Juliet J. McKenna.
Thomas J. Motley.
John M. Mott.
William Nooter.
Michael R. O'Keefe.
Robert D. Okun.
Florence Y. Pan.
Heidi Pasichow.
Hiram E. Puig-Lugo.
Maribeth Raffinan.
Michael L. Rankin.
Robert Rigsby.
Maurice Ross.
Michael J. Ryan.
Fern Flanagan Saddler.
Robert Salerno.
Judith Smith.
Darlene M. Soltys.
Frederick H. Weisberg.
Steven Wellner.
Yvonne Williams.
Elizabeth Wingo.

Magistrate Judges:
Janet Albert.
Errol Arthur.
Joseph E. Beshouri.
Tanya Jones Bosier.
Rahkel Bouchet.
Rainey R. Brandt.
Diane M. Brenneman.
Julie Breslow.
Tyrona DeWitt.
Tara Fentress.
Heide Herrmann.
Noel Johnson.
Diane Lepley.
Kenia Seoane Lopez.
Shana Frost Matini.
Aida Melendez.
Shelly A. Mulkey.
Lloyd U. Nolan.
Adrienne Noti.
Renee Raymond.
Mary Grace Rook.
Sean Staples.
Frederick J. Sullivan.
Sherry Trafford.

Senior Judges:
Geoffrey M. Alprin.
John H. Bayly.
A. Franklin Burgess, Jr.
Kaye R. Christian.
Natalia Combs-Greene.
Harold Cushenberry, Jr.
Linda Kay Davis.
Herbert B. Dixon, Jr.
Stephanie Duncan-Peters.
Stephen F. Eilperin.
Henry F. Greene.
Brook Hedge.
Ann O'Regan Keary.
Rufus G. King III.
Richard A. Levie.
Cheryl M. Long.
Judith N. Macaluso.
Bruce S. Mencher.
Zinora Mitchell-Rankin.
Gregory E. Mize.
Truman A. Morrison III.
Judith E. Retchin.
Robert I. Richter.
Lee F. Satterfield.
Nan R. Shuker.
Robert S. Tignor.
Linda D. Turner.
Curtis Von Kann.
Ronald P. Wertheim.
Susan R. Winfield.
Rhonda Reid Winston.
Peter H. Wolf.
Melvin R. Wright.
Patricia A. Wynn.
Joan Zeldon.

Clerk of the Court.—James McGinley, 879–1400.

GOVERNMENT OF THE DISTRICT OF COLUMBIA

John A. Wilson Building, 1350 Pennsylvania Avenue, NW., 20004

phone (202) 724–8000

[All area codes within this section are (202)]

COUNCIL OF THE DISTRICT OF COLUMBIA

Council Chairman.—Phil Mendelson, Suite 504, 724–8032.
Council Members (at-Large):
Anita Bonds, Suite 404, 724–8064.
David Grosso, Suite 402, 724–8105.
Elissa Silverman, Suite 408, 724–7772.
Robert J. White, Jr., Suite 107, 724–8174.
Council Members:
Brianne Nadeau, Ward 1, Suite 102, 724–8181.
Jack Evans, Ward 2, Suite 106, 724–8058.
Mary M. Cheh, Ward 3, Suite 108, 724–8062.
Brandon T. Todd, Ward 4, Suite 105, 724–8052.
Kenyan McDuffie, Ward 5, Suite 506, 724–8028.
Charles Allen, Ward 6, Suite 110, 724–8072.
Vincent C. Gray, Ward 7, Suite 406, 724–8068.
Trayvon White, Sr., Ward 8, Suite 400, 724–8045.
Council Officers:
Secretary to the Council.—Nyasha Smith, Suite 5, 724–8080.
Budget Director.—Jennifer Budoff, Suite 508, 724–8139.
General Counsel.—Ellen Efros, Suite 4, 724–8026.
Chief Technology Officer.—Christopher Warren, Suite 13, 724–8018.

EXECUTIVE OFFICE OF THE MAYOR

Suite 300, phone (202) 727–6263, fax 727–6561

Mayor of the District of Columbia.—Hon. Muriel E. Bowser.
Assistant to the Mayor.—Tonya Poindexter, Suite 300, 727–2643, fax 727–7743.
Chief of Staff.—John Falcicchio.
Deputy Chief of Staff.—Lindsey Parker.
City Administrator.—Rashad Young, Suite 513, 478–9200, fax 727–9878.
Senior Advisor.—Beverly Perry, Suite 324, 724–7173.
Legal Counsel.—Mark Tuohey, Suite 407, 727–8812.
Deputy Mayor for—
Education.—Jennifer Niles, Suite 307, 727–3636, fax 727–8198.
Greater Economic Opportunity.—Courtney Snowden, 2235 Shannon Place, SE., Suite 3040, 545–3071.
Health and Human Services.—HyeSook Chung, Suite 223, 727–7973, fax 442–5066.
Planning and Economic Development.—Brian Kenner, Suite 317, 727–6365, fax 727–6703.
Public Safety and Justice.—Kevin Donahue, Suite 533, 724–5400.
Inspector General.—Daniel Lucas, 717 14th Street, NW., 5th Floor, 727–2540, fax 727–9846.
General Counsel.—Betsy Cavendish, Suite 300, 727–7681, fax 724–7743.
Secretary of Washington, DC.—Lauren Vaughn, Suite 419, 727–6306, fax 727–3582.
Director of:
Budget and Finance.—Matthew Brown, Suite 211, 727–3380, fax 727–5931.
Communications.—Kevin Harris, Suite 311, 727–5011, fax 727–8527.
Community Affairs.—Charon Hines, Suite 327, 442–8150, fax 727–2357.
Policy and Legislative Affairs.—Alana Intrieri, Suite 531, 727–6979, fax 727–3765.

OFFICE OF THE CITY ADMINISTRATOR

Suite 513, phone (202) 478–9200, fax (202) 727–9878

City Administrator.—Rashad Young.
Executive Assistant to City Administrator.—Timothy Banner.

COMMISSIONS

Arts and Humanities, 200 I (Eye) Street, SE., Suite 1400, Washington, DC 20003, 724–5613, fax 727–4135, e-mail: lionell.thomas@dc.gov, website: http://dcarts.dc.gov/DC/DCARTS.
Executive Director.—Lisa Richards Toney.
Chairperson.—Judith F. Terra.

Judicial Disabilities and Tenure, 515 5th Street, NW., Building A, Room 246, Washington, DC 20001, 727–1363, fax 727–9718, e-mail: cathaee.hudgins@dc.gov, website: http://cjdt.dc.gov/DC/CJDT.
Executive Director.—Cathaee Hudgins.
Chairperson.—Hon. Gladys Kessler.

Judicial Nominations, 515 5th Street, NW., Suite 235, Washington, DC 20001, 879–0478, fax 879–0755, e-mail: kim.whatley@dc.gov, website: http://jnc.dc.gov/DC/JNC.
Executive Director.—Kim M. Whatley.
Chairperson.—Hon. Emmet G. Sullivan.

Serve DC, Frank D. Reeves Municipal Center, 2000 14th Street, NW., Suite 101, Washington, DC 20009, 727–7200, fax 727–9942, e-mail: jeffrey.richardson@dc.gov, website: http://serve.dc.gov/page/about-serve-dc.
Executive Director.—Kristal Knight.
Chairperson.—Peter Brusoe.

Washington Metropolitan Area Transit, 8701 Georgia Avenue, Suite 808, Silver Spring, MD 20910–3700 (301) 427–0140, fax 588–5262, e-mail: wmorrow@wmatc.gov, website: http://www.wmatc.gov.
Executive Director/General Counsel.—William S. Morrow, Jr.
Chairperson.—Lawrence Brenner.

DEPARTMENTS

Child and Family Services Agency, 400 6th Street, SW., 5th Floor, 20024, 442–6100, fax 727–6505.
Director.—Raymond Davidson.

Consumer and Regulatory Affairs, 941 North Capitol Street, NE., 20002, 442–4400, fax 442–9445.
Director.—Melinda Boling.

Corrections, 1923 Vermont Avenue, NW., Room 207 North, 20001, 673–7316, fax 671–2043.
Director.—Thomas Faust.

Environment, 1200 First Street, NE., 5th Floor, 20002, 535–2600, fax 673–6993.
Director.—Tommy Wells.

Employment Services, 4058 Minnesota Avenue, NE., 20019, 724–7000, fax 673–6993.
Director.—Deborah Carroll.

Fire and Emergency Medical Services, 1923 Vermont Avenue, NW., Suite 201, 20001, 673–3320, fax 462–0807.
Fire Chief.—Gregory Dean.

Health, 899 North Capitol Street, NE., 5th Floor, 20002, 442–5955, fax 442–4795.
Director.—LaQuandra Nesbitt.

Housing and Community Development, 1800 Martin Luther King Jr. Avenue, SE., 20020, 442–7200, fax 645–6730.
Director.—Polly Donaldson.

Human Services, 64 New York Avenue, NE., 6th Floor, 20002, 671–4200, fax 671–4325.
Director.—Laura Zeilinger.

Insurance, Securities and Banking, 810 1st Street, NE., Suite 701, 20002, 727–8000, fax 535–1196.
Commissioner.—Stephen Taylor.

Behavioral Health, 64 New York Avenue, NE., 4th Floor, 20002, 673–7440, fax 673–3433.
Director.—Dr. Tanya Royster.

Metropolitan Police, 300 Indiana Avenue, NW., 20001, phone 311 or (202) 737–4404 if calling from outside DC, fax 727–9524.
Police Chief.—Peter Newsham.

Motor Vehicles, 301 C Street, NW., 20001, 727–5000, fax 727–4653.
Director.—Lucinda M. Babers.

Parks and Recreation, 3149 16th Street, NW., 20010, 673–7647, fax 673–2087.
Director.—Keith Anderson.

Public Works, 2000 14th Street, NW., 6th Floor, 20009, 673–6833, fax 671–0642.
Director.—Chris Shorter (interim).

Small and Local Business Development, 441 4th Street, NW., Suite 970 North, 20001, 727–3900, fax 724–3786.
Director.—Ana Harvey.

Transportation, 55 M Street, SE., Suite 400, 20003, 673–6813, fax 671–0650.
Director.—Leif Dormsjo.

Youth Rehabilitation Services, 450 H Street, NW., 10th Floor, 20001, 576–8175, fax 727–4434.
Director.—Clinton Lacey.

OFFICES

Administrative Hearings, One Judiciary Square, 441 4th Street, NW., 20001, 442–9091, fax 442–9451.
Chief Judge.—Eugene Adams.

Aging, 441 4th Street, NW., Suite 900 South, 20001, 724–5622, fax 724–4979.
Director.—Brenda Donald (interim).

Asian and Pacific Islander Affairs, 441 4th Street, NW., Suite 721 North, 20001, 727–3120, fax 727–9655.
Executive Director.—David Do.

Attorney General, 441 4th Street, NW., Suite 400 South, 20001, 727–3400, fax 347–8922.
Attorney General.—Karl Racine.

Talent and Appointments, 1350 Pennsylvania Avenue, NW., Suite 600, 20004, 727–1372, fax 727–2359.
Director.—Steven Walker.

Cable Television and Telecommunications, 3007 Tilden Street, NW., Pod P, 20008, 671–0066, fax 332–7020.
Director.—Angie Gates.

Chief Financial Officer, 1350 Pennsylvania Avenue, NW., Suite 203, 20004, 727–2476, fax 727–1643.
Chief Financial Officer.—Jeffrey DeWitt.

Chief Medical Examiner, 1910 Massachusetts Avenue, SE., Building 27, 20003, 698–9000, fax 698–9100.
Chief Medical Examiner.—Dr. Roger Mitchell.

Chief Technology Officer, 441 4th Street, NW., Suite 930 South, 20001, 727–2277, fax 727–6857.
Chief Technology Officer.—Tegene Baharu.

Communications Office, 1350 Pennsylvania Avenue, NW., Suite 310, 20004, 727–5011, fax 727–8527.
Director.—Michael Czin.

Office of Community Affairs, 1350 Pennsylvania Avenue, NW., Suite 327, 20004, 442–8150, fax 727–5931.
Director.—Charon Hines.

Contracting and Procurement, 441 4th Street, NW., Suite 700 South, 20001, 727–0252, fax 727–0245.
Chief Procurement Officer.—George Schutter.

Emergency Management Agency, 2720 Martin Luther King Jr. Avenue, SE., 20032, 727–6161, fax 715–7288.
Director.—Chris Geldart.

Employee Appeals, 1100 4th Street, SW., Suite 620 East, 20024, 727–0004, fax 727–5631.
Executive Director.—Sheila Barfield, Esq.

Finance and Resource Management, 441 4th Street, NW., Suite 890 North, 20001, 727–0333, fax 727–0659.
Director of Finance Operations.—Mohamed Mohamed.

Human Resources, 441 4th Street, NW., Suite 330 South, 20001, 442–9600, fax 727–6827.
Director.—Ventris Gibson.

Human Rights, 441 4th Street, NW., Suite 570 North, 20001, 727–4559, fax 727–9589.
Director.—Monica Palacio.

Labor Relations and Collective Bargaining, 441 4th Street, NW., Suite 820 North, 20001, 724–4953, fax 727–6887.
Director.—Lionel Sims.

Latino Affairs, 2000 14th Street, NW., 2nd Floor, 20009, 671–2825, fax 673–4557.
Director.—Jackie Reyes-Yanes.

Lesbian, Gay, Bisexual and Transgender Affairs, 1350 Pennsylvania Avenue, NW., Suite 327, 20004, 727–9493, fax 727–5931.
Director.—Sheila Alexander-Reid.

Motion Picture and Television Development, 3007 Tilden Street, NW., 4th Floor, 20008, 727–6608, fax 727–3246.
Director.—Angie Gates.

Office of Planning, 1100 4th Street, SW., Suite E650, 20024, 442–7600, fax 442–7638.
Director.—Eric Shaw.

Policy and Legislative Affairs, 1350 Pennsylvania Avenue, NW., Suite 533, 20004, 727–6979, fax 727–3765.
Director.—Maia Estes.

Department of General Services, 2000 14th Street, NW., 8th Floor, 20009, 724–4400, fax 727–9877.
Director.—Jonathan Kayne.

Risk Management, 441 4th Street, NW., Suite 800 South, 20001, 727–8600, fax 727–8319.
Director.—Jed Ross.

Office of the State Superintendent of Education, 810 First Street, NE., 9th Floor, 20002, 727–6436, fax 727–2019.
Superintendent.—Hanseul Kang.

Unified Communications, 2720 Martin Luther King Jr. Avenue, SE., 20032, 730–0524, fax 730–1425.
Director.—Chris Geldart (interim).

Veterans Affairs, 441 4th Street, NW., Suite 570 South, 20001, 724–5454, fax 727–7117.
Director.—Tammi Lambert (interim).

Victim Services, 441 4th Street, NW., Suite 700, 20004, 727–3934, fax 727–1617.
Director.—Edward Smith.
Zoning, 441 4th Street, NW., Suite 200 South, 20001, 727–6311, fax 727–6072.
Director.—Sara Benjamin Bardin.

INDEPENDENT AGENCIES

Advisory Neighborhood Commissions, 1350 Pennsylvania Avenue, NW., Room 8, 20004, 727–9945, fax 727–0289.
Executive Director.—Gottlieb Simon.

Alcoholic Beverage Regulation Administration, 2000 14th Street, NW., Suite 400 South, 20009, 442–4423, fax 442–9563.
Director.—Fred Moosally.

Board of Elections and Ethics, 441 4th Street, NW., Suite 250 North, 20001, 727–2525, fax 347–2648.
Chairperson of the Board.—Cliff Tatum.

Criminal Justice Coordinating Council, 441 4th Street, NW., Suite 727 North, 20001, 442–9283, fax 724–3691.
Executive Director.—Mannone Butler.

District of Columbia Court of Appeals, 430 E Street, Room 115, 20001, 879–2701, fax 626–8840.
Chief Judge.—Eric T. Washington.

District of Columbia Housing Authority, 1133 North Capitol Street, NE., 20001, 535–1500, fax 535–1740.
Executive Director.—Adrianne Todman.

District of Columbia Public Defender Service, 633 Indiana Avenue, NW., 20001, 628–1200, fax 824–2784.
Director.—Avis Buchanan.

District of Columbia Public Library, 901 G Street, NW., Suite 400, 20001, 727–1101, fax 727–1129.
Director.—Richard Reyes-Gavilan.

District of Columbia Public Schools, 825 North Capitol Street, NW., Suite 9026, 20002, 442–4226, fax 442–5026.
Chancellor.—Kaya Henderson.

District of Columbia Retirement Board, 900 7th Street, NW., 2nd Floor, 20001, 343–3200, fax 566–5000.
Executive Director.—Eric Stanchfield.

District of Columbia Sentencing and Criminal Code Revision Commission, 441 4th Street, NW., Suite 830 South, 20001, 727–8822, fax 727–7929.
Executive Director.—Barbara Tombs-Souvey.

District Lottery and Charitable Games Control Board, 2101 Martin Luther King Jr. Avenue, SE., 20020, 645–8000, fax 645–7914.
Executive Director.—Tracey Cohen.

Housing Finance Agency, 815 Florida Avenue, NW., 20001, 777–1600, fax 986–6705.
Executive Director.—Maria Day Marshall.

Metropolitan Washington Council of Governments, 777 North Capitol Street, NE., 20002, 962–3200, fax 962–3201.
Executive Director.—Dave Robertson.

People's Counsel, 1133 15th Street, NW., Suite 500, 20005, 727–3071, fax 727–1014.
People's Counsel.—Sandra Mattavous-Frye, Esq.

Police Complaints, 1400 I Street, NW., Suite 700, 20005, 727–3838, fax 727–9182.
Executive Director.—Philip K. Eure.

Public Charter School Board, 3333 14th Street, NW., Suite 210, 20010, 328–2660, fax 328–2661.
Executive Director.—Scott Pearson (interim).

Public Employee Relations Board, 1100 4th Street, SW., Suite E630, 20024, 727–1822, fax 727–9116.
Executive Director.—Clarene Phyllis Martin.

Public Service Commission, 1333 H Street, NW., Suite 200, West Tower, 20005, 626–5100, fax 393–1389.
Chairperson.—Betty Ann Kane.

Superior Court of the District of Columbia, H. Carl Moultrie I Courthouse, 500 Indiana Avenue, NW., 20001, 879–1010.
Chief Judge.—Lee F. Satterfield.

Taxicab Commission, 2041 Martin Luther King Jr. Avenue, SE., Suite 204, 20020, 645–6018, fax 889–3604.
Chairperson.—Ernest Chrappah.

Washington Convention Center Authority, 801 Mount Vernon Place, NW., 20001, 249–3012, fax 249–3133.
President and CEO.—Greg O'Dell.

Destination DC, 1212 New York Avenue, NW., Suite 600, 20005, 904–0616 or 249–3012, fax 789–7037.
President and CEO.—Elliot Ferguson.

Water and Sewer Authority, 5000 Overlook Avenue, SW., 20032, 787–2000, fax 787–2210.
Chairman.—William M. Walker.
General Manager.—George S. Hawkins.

Workforce Investment Council, 4058 Minnesota Avenue, NE., 20009, 671–1900, fax 673–6993.
Chairperson.—Vacant.

OTHER

Board of Real Property Assessments and Appeals, 441 4th Street, NW., Suite 430, 20001, 727–6860, fax 727–0392.
Chairperson.—Towanda Paul-Bryant.

Contract Appeals Board, 441 4th Street, NW., Suite N350, 727–6597, fax 727–3993.
Chief Administrative Judge.—Marc D. Loud, Sr.

Justice Grants Administration, 1350 Pennsylvania Avenue, NW., Suite 327A, 20004, 727–6239, fax 727–1617.
Director.—Josh Weber.

Rehabilitation Services Administration, 1125 15th Street, NW., 20005, 730–1700, fax 730–1516.
Administrator.—Vacant.

DISTRICT OF COLUMBIA POST OFFICE LOCATIONS

900 Brentwood Road, NE., 20066–9998, General Information (202) 636–1200

Postmaster.—Gerald A. Roane.

CLASSIFIED STATIONS

Station	Phone	Location / Zip Code
Anacostia	(301) 423–9091/9092	3719 Branch Ave., Temple Hills, MD 20748
Ben Franklin	523–2386	1200 Pennsylvania Ave., NW., 20044
B.F. Carriers	636–2289	900 Brentwood Rd., NE., 20004
Benning	523–2391	3937½ Minnesota Ave., NE., 20029
Bolling AFB	767–4419	Bldg. 10, Brookley Ave., 20332
Brightwood	726–8119	6323 Georgia Ave., NW., 20011
Brookland	523–2126	3401 12th St., NE., 20017
Calvert	523–2908	2336 Wisconsin Ave., NW., 20007
Cleveland Park	523–2396	3430 Connecticut Ave., NW., 20008
Columbia Heights	523–2192	6510 Chillum Place, NW., 20010
Congress Heights	523–2112	400 Southern Ave., SE., 20032
Customs House	523–2195	3178 Bladensburg Rd., NE., 20018
Dulles	(703) 471–9497	Dulles International Airport, 20041
Farragut	523–2507	1145 19th St., NW., 20033
Fort Davis	842–4964	3843 Pennsylvania Ave., SE., 20020
Fort McNair	523–2144	300 A St., SW., 20319
Frederick Douglass	842–4959	Alabama Ave., SE., 20020
Friendship	523–2130	4005 Wisconsin Ave., NW., 20016
Georgetown	523–2406	1215 31st St., NW., 20007
Government Mail	523–2138 / 2139	3300 V Street, NE., 20018–9998
Headsville	357–3029	Smithsonian Institute, 20560
Kalorama	523–2906	2300 18th St., NW., 20009
Lamond Riggs	523–2041	6200 North Capitol St., NW., 20011
LeDroit Park	483–0973	416 Florida Ave., NW., 20001
L'Enfant Plaza	268–4970	458 L'Enfant Plaza, SW., 20026

CLASSIFIED STATIONS—CONTINUED

Station	Phone	Location / Zip Code
Main Office Window	636–2130	Curseen / Morris P&DC, 900 Brentwood Rd., NE., 20066–9998
Martin L. King Jr.	523–2001	1400 L St., NW., 20043
McPherson	842–1229	1750 Pennsylvania Ave., NW., 20038
Mid City	....	Temporarily Closed
NASA	358–0235	600 Independence Ave., SW., 20546
National Capitol	523–2368	2 Massachusetts Ave., NE., 20002
Naval Research Lab	767–3426	4565 Overlook Ave., 20390
Navy Annex	(703) 920–0815	1668 D Street, 20335
Northeast	388–5216	1563 Maryland Ave., NE., 20002
Northwest	523–2570	5632 Connecticut Ave., NW., 20015
Palisades	842–2291	5136 MacArthur Blvd., NW., 20016
Pavilion Postique	523–2571	1100 Pennsylvania Ave., NW., 20004
Pentagon	(703) 695–6835	Concourse Pentagon (Army-20301 / 20310; Air Force-20330; Navy-20350)
Petworth	523–2681	4211 9th St., NW., 20011
Postal Mus	523–2022	2 Massachusetts Ave., NW., 20002
Randle	584–6807	2341 Pennsylvania Ave., SE., 20023
River Terrace	523–2988	3621 Benning Rd., NE., 20019
Section 2	636–2272 / 2273	Section 2, Curseen / Morris P&DC, 900 Brentwood Rd., NE., 20002–9998
Southeast	523–2174	327 7th St., SE., 20003
Southwest	523–2597	45 L St., SW., 20024
State Department	523–2574	2201 C St., NW., 20520
14th/T Street	232–6301	2000 14th St., NW., 20009
Tech World	523–2019	800 K St., NW., 20001
Temple Heights	523–2563	1921 Florida Ave., NW., 20009
22nd Street	523–2411	1255 22nd St., NW., 20037
U.S. Naval	433–2216	940 M St., SE., 20374
V Street	523–2138/2139	3300 V St., NE., 20018
Walter Reed	....	6800 Georgia Ave., NW., 20012
Ward Place	523–2109	2121 Ward Place, NW., 20037
Washington Square	523–3632	1050 Connecticut Ave., NW., 20035
Watergate	965–6278	2512 Virginia Ave., NW., 20037
Woodridge	523–2195	2211 Rhode Island Ave., NE., 20018

INTERNATIONAL ORGANIZATIONS

EUROPEAN SPACE AGENCY (E.S.A.)

Headquarters: 8–10 Rue Mario Nikis, 75738 Paris Cedex 15, France
phone 011–33–1–5369–7654, fax 011–33–1–5369–7560

Director General.—Johann-Dietrich Woerner.

Member Countries:

Austria	Hungary	Romania
Belgium	Ireland	Spain
Denmark	Italy	Sweden
Estonia	Luxembourg	Switzerland
Finland	Netherlands	United Kingdom
France	Norway	Czech Republic
Germany	Poland	
Greece	Portugal	

Associate Member Countries.—Slovenia.

Cooperative Agreement.—Canada.

European Space Operations Center (ESOC), Robert-Bosch-Str. 5, D–64293 Darmstadt, Germany, phone 011–49–6151–900, fax 011–49–6151–90495.

European Space Research and Technology Center (ESTEC), Keplerlaan 1, NL–2201, AZ Noordwijk, ZH, The Netherlands, phone 011–31–71–565–6565, Telex: 844–39098, fax 011–31–71–565–6040.

European Space Research Institute (ESRIN), Via Galileo Galilei, Casella Postale 64, 00044 Frascati, Italy, phone 011–39–6–94–18–01, fax 011–39–6–9418–0280.

European Space Astronomy Centre (ESAC), P.O. Box, E–28691 Villanueva de la Cañada, Madrid, Spain, phone 011–34 91 813 11 00, fax: 011–34 91 813 11 39.

European Astronaut Centre (EAC), Linder Hoehe, 51147 Cologne, Germany, phone 011–49–220360–010, fax 011–49–2203–60–1103.

European Centre for Space Applications and Telecommunications (ECSAT), Atlas Building, Harwell Science & Innovation Campus, Didcot, Oxfordshire, OX11 0QX, United Kingdom, phone 011–44 1235 567900.

European Space Agency Washington Office (EWO), 1201 F Street, NW., Suite 470, Washington, DC 20004.

Head of Office.—Micheline Tabache (202) 488–4158, micheline.tabache@esa.int.

INTER-AMERICAN DEFENSE BOARD

2600 16th Street, NW., 20441, phone (202) 939–6041, fax 319–2791

Chairman.—General de Brigada DEM Luis Rodríguez Bucio, México.

Vice Chairman.—Mayor General Gabriel Hermano Pinilla Franco, Colombia.

Chairman's Chefe de Cabinet.—Coronel José Cabrejos, Peru.

Director General.—General Brigadier Stephen Michel Lacroix, Canada.

Deputy Secretary for Administration.—Coronel José Polanco, United States.

Director Conferences.—Coronel Fernando Bartholomeu Fernandes, Brazil.

CHIEFS OF DELEGATION

Antigua and Barbuda.—Consejera Guilliam Ingrid Joseph.

Argentina.—Gral Brig Gustavo Javier Vidal.

Barbados.—Ministra Consejera Jane Bratahwaite.
Belize.—Embajador Patrick Andrews.
Brazil.—General Jorge Cardoso Martins.
Canada.—Contralmirante William S. Truelove.
Chile.—GD Sergio Ahumada.
Colombia.—COL Mario Fernando Jaramillo.
Dominican Republic.—GB Julio Ernesto Florian Pérez.
El Salvador.—COL Edwin Oswaldo Vides Padilla.
Guatemala.—General Herbert Alexandre Lopez Rodríguez.
Guyana.—COL Nazrul Hussain.
Haiti.—Minister Counselor Charles Leon.
Honduras.—COL Lenin Dario Gonzalez Cruz.
Jamaica.—Oral Pascoe.
Mexico.—GB Andrés Fernando Aguirre O. Sunga.
Nicaragua.—Coronel Lenin Serrano.
Panama.—Commisionado Gilberto Rene Glen Quiroz.
Paraguay.—General de Brigada Gualberto Ramon Mariño Galván.
Peru.—General de División Leonardo José Longa Lopez.
Suriname.—Vacant.
Trinidad and Tobago.—COL Darnley Eddison Wyke.
United States.—MG Richard D. Clarke.
Uruguay.—General Alejandro Salaberry Cóccaro.
Grenada.—Comisionado Michael Francois.
Saint Kitts y Nevis.—Everson Hull.
Venezuela.—Vacant.

INTER-AMERICAN DEFENSE COLLEGE

Director.—RADM (Contralmirante) Martha Herb, U.S.A.
Vice Director.—Mayor General Rolemberg Ferreira da Cunha, Brazil.
Chief of Studies.—General Brigadier Arturo Javier González Jiménez, México.

INTER-AMERICAN DEVELOPMENT BANK

1300 New York Avenue, NW., 20577, phone (202) 623–1000

http://www.iadb.org

OFFICERS

President.—Luis Alberto Moreno.
Chief, Office of the President.—Luis Giorgio.
Executive Vice President.—Julie T. Katzman (United States).
Chief Advisor.—Jose Jorge Seligmann-Silva.
Director, Office of Evaluation and Oversight.—Cheryl Gray.
Manager of the Research Department and Chief Economist.—Jose Juan Ruiz Gomez.
Executive Auditor.—Jorge Da Silva.
Manager, Office of External Relations—Federico Basañes.
Ombudsperson.—Marta Abello.
Secretary.—German Quintana.
Manager, Office of Outreach and Partnerships.—Bernardo Guillamón.
Advisor, Office of Risk Management.—Federico Galizia.
Manager, Office of Strategic Planning and Development Effectiveness.—Luis Miguel Castilla Rubio.
Chief, Office of Institutional Integrity.—Laura Profeta, ai.
Vice-President for Countries.—Alexandre Meira da Rosa.
Country Manager, Office of:
Department Andean Group.—Rafael de la Cruz.
Department Caribbean Group.—Therese Turner-Jones.
Department Central America, Haiti, Mexico, Panama, and Dominican Republic.—Gina Montiel.
Department Southern Cone.—José Luis Lupo.
Vice President for Sectors and Knowledge.—Santiago Levy.
Manager of:

Climate Change and Sustainable Development.—Juan Pablo Bonilla.
Knowledge and Learning.—Federico Basañes.
Infrastructure and Energy.—Jose Agustin Aguerre.
Institutions for Development.—Ana María Rodríguez-Ortiz.
Integration and Trade.—Antoni Estevadeorval.
Social Sector.—Marcelo Cabrol.

Vice President for Finance and Administration.—Jaime Sujoy.
Manager of:
Budget and Administrative Services.—Yeshvanth Edwin.
Finance Department.—Gustavo De Rosa.
Human Resources.—Claudia Bock-Valotta.
Information Technology.—Nuria Simo Vila.
Legal Department.—John Scott.

IDB INVEST

Chief Executive Officer.—James P. Scriven.
Chief Investment Officer.—Gema Sacristán.
Chief Strategy Officer.—Orlando Ferreira.
General Counsel.—H. Rosemary Jeronimides.
Chief Risk Officer.—Christian Novak.
Chief Finance and Administration Officer.—Rocío Palafox.

MULTILATERAL INVESTMENT FUND

General Manager.—Keisuke Nakamura, ai.

BOARD OF EXECUTIVE DIRECTORS

Argentina and Haiti.—Raúl Novoa.
Austria, Denmark, Finland, France, Norway, Spain, and Sweden.—Alicia Montalvo Santamaría.
Alternate.—Patrick Jean Hervé.
Bahamas, Barbados, Guyana, Jamaica, and Trinidad and Tobago.—Jerry Christopher Butler.
Alternate.—Cheryl Anita Morris-Skeete.
Belgium, China, Germany, Israel, Italy, The Netherlands, and Switzerland.—Stefania Antonella Bazzoni.
Alternate.—Marlene Olivia L. Beco.
Belize, Costa Rica, El Salvador, Guatemala, Honduras, and Nicaragua.—José Mauricio Silva.
Alternate.—Francisco José Mayorga Balladares.
Bolivia, Paraguay, and Uruguay.—Marcelo Bisogno.
Alternate.—Marko Marcelo Machicao Bankovic.
Brazil and Suriname.—Antonio Hernique Pinheiro Silveira.
Alternate.—Frederico Gonzaga Jayme, Jr.
Canada.—Guillermo Enrique Rishchynski.
Alternate.—Ian Christopher MacDonald.
Chile and Peru.—Guillermo Enrique Rishchynski.
Alternate.—Maria Soledad Barrera.
Colombia and Ecuador.—Patricia María Miloslavich Hart.
Alternate.—Sergio Díaz Granados.
Croatia, Japan, Korea, Portugal, Slovenia, and United Kingdom.—Toshiyuki Yasui.
Alternate.—Tom Matthew Crowards.
Dominican Republic and Mexico.—Juan Bosco Marti Ascencio.
Alternate.—Carlos Augusto Pared Vidal.
Panama and Venezuela.—Armando José León Rojas.
Alternate.—Fernando Ernesto de León.
United States of America.—Mark Edward Lopes.

INTER-AMERICAN TROPICAL TUNA COMMISSION

8901 La Jolla, Shores Drive, La Jolla, CA 92037–1508
phone (858) 546–7100, fax (858) 546–7133, http://www.iattc.org

Director.—Guillermo A. Compeán.

Commissioners:

Belize:

Valerie Lanza, Ministry of Finance / Belize High Seas Fisheries Unit, Marina Towers, Suite 204, Newtown Barracks, Belize City, Belize, phone (501) 223–4918, fax (501) 223–5087; e-mail: director@bhsfu.gov.bz.

Delice Pinkard, Ministry of Finance / Belize High Seas Fisheries Unit, Marina Towers, Suite 204, Newtown Barracks, Belize City, Belize, phone (501) 223–4918, fax (501) 223–5087; e-mail: sr.fishofficer@bhsfu.gov.bz.

Robert Robinson, Ministry of Finance / Belize High Seas Fisheries Unit, Marine Towers, Suite 204, Newtown Barracks, Belize City, Belize, phone (501) 223–4918, fax (501) 223–5048; e-mail: deputydirector@bhsfu.gov.bz.

Canada:

Robert Day, Fisheries and Oceans Canada, 200 Kent Street, Station 8E240, Ottawa, ONT K1A 0E6, Canada, phone (613) 991–6135, fax (613) 993–5995; e-mail: robert.day@dfo-mpo.gc.ca.

Larry Teague, British Columbia Tuna Fishermen's Association (BCTFA), Box 372, Shawnigan Lake, British Columbia V0R 2W0, Canada, phone (250) 743–5002; e-mail: bctfa@shaw.ca.

China: (Focal Points)

Sun Haiwen, Ministry of Agriculture / Bureau of Fisheries, No. 11 Nongzhanguan Nanli, Beijing 100125, People's Republic of China, phone (86–10) 5919–2928, fax (86–10) 5919–2951; e-mail: fishcngov@126.com.

Zhao Liling, Ministry of Agriculture / Bureau of Fisheries, No. 11 Nongzhanguan Nanli, Beijing, 100125, People's Republic of China, phone (86–10) 5919–2928, fax (86–10) 5919–2951; e-mail: liling.zhao@hotmail.com.

Colombia:

Maria Paula Arenas, Ministerio de Comercio, Industria y Turismo, Calle 28 n 13A–15, Bogotá, DC, Colombia, phone (57–1) 606–7676; e-mail: marenas@mincit.gov.co.

Luis Humberto Guzmán Vergara, Ministerio de Agricultura y Desarrollo Rural, Avenida Jiménez 7–65, Bogotá, DC 001, Colombia, phone (57–1) 334–1199 ext. 310 (57–1) 283–3977, fax (57–1) 334–1199; e-mail: luis.guzman@minagricultura.gov.co.

Andrea Ramirez Martinez, Ministerio de Ambiente y Desarrollo Sostenible, Calle 35 No. 24–48, Bogota, Colombia, phone (57–1) 288–2132, (57–1) 332–3400; e-mail: ARamirez@minambiente.gov.co.

Maria Claudia Vásquez Marazzani, Ministerio de Relaciones Exteriores, Calle 10 No. 5–51 Palacio de San Carlos, Bogotá, DC, Colombia, phone (57–1) 381–4265, fax (57–1) 381–4747; e-mail: Claudia.Vasquez@cancilleria.gov.co.

Costa Rica:

Luis Felipe Arauz Cavallini, Ministerio de Agricultura y Ganadería, Sabana Sur, antiguo Colegio La Salle, San José, Costa Rica, phone (506) 2231–2344, fax: (506) 2232–2103; e-mail: despachoministro@mag.go.cr.

Gustavo Meneses, INCOPESCA, Frente a las Instalaciones del Instituto Nacional de Aprendizaje, El Cocal, Puntarenas 5400, Costa Rica, phone (506) 8726–0876, fax (506) 2630–0636; e-mail: gmeneses@incopesca.go.cr.

Germán Pochet, Ministerio de Agricultura y Ganadería, San José, Sabana Sur, antiguo Colegio La Salle, San José, 113–2010, Costa Rica, phone (506) 2223–2461, fax (506) 2258–6678; e-mail: gpochet@legalambiental.com.

Ecuador:

Javier Cardoso, Ministerio de Acuacultura y Pesca, Puerto Pesquero Artesanal de San Mateo, Manta, Ecuador, phone (593–5) 266–6109; e-mail: javier.cardoso@acuaculturaypesca.gob.ec.

Jorge Costain, Ministerio de Acuacultura y Pesca, Puerto Pesquero Artesanal de San Mateo, Manta, Ecuador, phone (593–5) 262–7930, fax (593–5) 262–7911; e-mail: jorge.costain@acuaculturaypesca.gob.ec.

Katuska Drouet, Ministerio de Acuacultura y Pesca, Puerto Pesquero Artesanal de San Mateo, Manta, Ecuador, phone (593–5) 262–7930, e-mail: katuska.drouet@acuaculturaypesca.gob.ec.

Guillermo Morán, Ministerio de Acuacultura y Pesca, Puerto Pesquero Artesanal de San Mateo, Manta, Ecuador, phone (593–9) 8488–1516; e-mail: gamv6731@gmail.com.

El Salvador:

Diana Elizabeth Barahona Hernández, CENDEPESCA, Final 1a. Ave. Norte y Ave. Manuel Gallardo, Santa Tecla, La Libertad, El Salvador, phone (503) 2210–1913 fax (503) 2534–9885; e-mail: diana.barahona@mag.gob.sv.

Manuel Calvo, Calvopesca/Grupo Calvo, Via de Los Poblados No. 1 Edificio B, Planta 5, Madrid, Spain, phone (34–91) 782–3300, fax (34–91) 782–3312; e-mail: mane.calvo@calvo.es.

Hugo Alexander Flores, Ministerio de Agricultura y Ganadería, Final 1a. Av. Norte y Av. Manuel Gallardo, Santa Tecla, El Salvador, phone (503) 2534–9882; e-mail: hugo.flores@mag.gob.sv.

Gustavo Antonio Portillo, CENDEPESCA, Final 1a. Avenida Norte y Avenida Manuel Gallardo, Santa Tecla, La Libertad, El Salvador, phone (503) 2210–1700 fax (503) 2534–9885; e-mail: gustavo.portillo@mag.gob.sv.

European Union:

Angela Martini, European Commission, Rue Joseph II, 99, Brussels, 1049, Belgium, phone (32–2) 299–4276, fax (32–2) 299–5570; e-mail: Angela.MARTINI@ec.europa.eu.

Luis Molledo, European Commission, Rue Joseph II, 99, Brussels, 1049, Belgium, phone (32–2) 299–3765, fax (32–2) 299–5570; e-mail: Luis.MOLLEDO@ec.europa.eu.

France:

Marie-Sophie Dufau-Richet, Secrétariat d'Etat à la Mer, 16 Boulevard Raspail, Paris, 75700, France, phone (33–1) 5363–4153, fax (33–1) 5363–4178; e-mail: marie.sophie.dufau-richet@pm.gouv.fr.

Christiane Laurent-Monpetit, Ministère de l'Intérieur, de l'Outre-Mer et des Collectivités T., 27, rue Oudinot, Paris, 75358 F SPO7, France, phone (33–1) 5369–2466, fax (33–1) 5369–2065; e-mail: christiane.laurent-monpetit@outre-mer.gouv.fr.

Anne-France Mattlet, Ministère de l'Écologie, du Développement durable et de l'Énergie, Direction des pêches maritimes et de l'aquaculture, 1 Place Carpeaux, Paris, 92055, France, phone (33–1) 6313–4235; e-mail: anne-france.mattlet@developpement-durable.gouv.fr.

Michel Sallenave, Haut Commissariat de la République Française en Polynésie, 43 Avenue Bruat. BP 115, Papeete, 98713, French Polynesia, phone (689) 549–525, fax (689) 434–390; e-mail: affmar@affaires-maritimes.pf.

Guatemala:

Byron Omar Acevedo Cordón, Ministerio de Agricultura, Ganadería y Alimentación, 7ma. Avenida 12–90 Zona 13, Guatemala, Guatemala, phone (502) 2413–7035, fax (502) 2413–7036; e-mail: bacevedo@maga.gob.gt.

Carlos Francisco Marín Arriola, Ministerio de Agricultura, Ganadería y Alimentación, Km. 22 Carretera al Pacífico, Edif. La Ceiba, 3er. Nivel, Villa Nueva, Guatemala, phone (502) 6640–9334, fax (502) 6640–9324; e-mail: dipescaguatemala@gmail.com.

Carlos Alejandro Tejeda Velásquez, Ministerio de Agricultura, Ganadería y Alimentación, 7a. Ave. 12–90 zona 13, Guatemala, Guatemala, phone (502) 3102–0125 e-mail: platelmito69@gmail.com.

Japan:

Tatsuo Hirayama, Ministry of Foreign Affairs, 2–2–1 Kasumigaseki 2–2–1, Chiyoda-ku, Tokyo, Japan, phone (81–3) 5501–8338, fax (81–3) 5501–8332; e-mail: tatsuo.hirayama@mofa.go.jp.

Kengo Tanaka, Fisheries Agency of Japan, 1–2–1 Kasumigaseki, Chiyoda-ku, Tokyo, 100–8907, Japan, phone (81–3) 3502–8459; e-mail: kengo—tanaka880@maff.go.jp.

Jun Yamashita, Japan Tuna Fisheries Cooperative Association, 2–3–22 Kudankita, Tokyo, 102, Japan, phone (81–3) 5646–2380, fax (81–3) 5646–2651; e-mail: gyojyo@japantuna.or.jp.

Kiribati: (Contacts, not appointed Commissioners)

Naomi Biribo, Ministry of Fisheries and Marine Resources Development, P.O. Box 64 Bairiki, Tarawa, Kiribati, phone (686) 21099, fax: (686) 21120; e-mail: naomib@mfmrd.gov.ki.

Aketa Tanga, Ministry of Fisheries and Marine Resources Development, P.O. Box 64 Bairiki, Tarawa, Kiribati, phone (686) 21099, fax: (686) 21120; e-mail: aketat@mfmrd.gov.ki.

Korea:

Kim Hongwon, Ministry of Oceans and Fisheries, Government Complex Bldg. #5, Room 508, Dasom2-ro, Sejong-City, Sejong, 339–012 Republic of Korea, phone (82–44) 2005368, fax (82–44) 2005379; e-mail: hiro9900@korea.kr.

Il Jeong Jeong, Ministry of Food, Agriculture, Forestry and Fisheries, 88, Gwanmundo, Gwacheon-si, Gyeonggi-do, 427–719, Republic of Korea, phone (82–2) 500–2422, fax (82–2) 503–9174; e-mail: ijeong@korea.kr, icdmomaf@chol.com.

Jeongseok Park, Ministry of Oceans and Fisheries, Government Complex, Sejong 94, Damason2-ro, Sejong-City, Republic of Korea, phone (82–2) 500–2426, fax (82–2) 503–9174; e-mail: jspark2@mifaff.go.kr.

Mexico:

Mario Aguilar Sánchez, Comisión Nacional de Pesca y Acuacultura, Av. Camarón Sábalo S/N, Mazatlán, Sin 82100, Mexico, phone (52–669) 915–6900, fax (52–669) 915–6904; e-mail: mario.aguilar@conapesca.gob.mx.

Pablo Roberto Arenas Fuentes, Instituto Nacional de la Pesca, Pitágoras #1320, Piso 8vo. Col. Sta Cruz Atoyac, Mexico, D.F. 03310 Mexico, phone (52–55) 3781–9501 (52–55) 3871–9502, fax (52–55) 3626–8421; e-mail: pablo.arenas@inapesca.gob.mx.

Michel Dreyfus León, Instituto Nacional de la Pesca, Km 97.5 Carretera Tijuana-Ensenada Ensenada, B.C. 22760, Mexico, phone (52–646) 174–6140, fax (52–646) 174–6135; e-mail: dreyfus@cicese.mx.

Luis Fleischer, Centro Regional de Investigaciones Pesqueras de La Paz, Km 1 carretera Pichilingue s/n Col. Esterito, La Paz 23020, Baja California Sur, Mexico, phone (612) 122–1367; e-mail: lfleischer21@hotmail.com.

Nicaragua:

Julio César Guevara, Industrial Atunera de Nicaragua, Balboa Ancón, Panama City, 0843–02264, Panama, phone (507) 6997–5100, fax (507) 204–4651; e-mail: juliocgq@hotmail.com.

Edward Jackson, Instituto Nicaraguense de la Pesca y Acuicultura, Km. 3.5 Carretera Norte, Managua, Nicaragua, phone (505) 2244–2460, fax (505) 2244–2552; e-mail: ejackson@inpesca.gob.ni.

Miguel Marenco Urcuyo, Nicaraguense de Atun S.A, ip Top Los Robles 1 1/2 C al Oeste, Edificio Lendinero. Oficina #1 al Oeste, Edf. INMSA, ARGO, Managua, Nicaragua; phone (505) 8850–7220, fax (505) 2270–4992; e-mail: seawolf@turbonett.com.ni.

Armando Segura Espinoza, Cámara de la Pesca de Nicaragua, Av. 27 de Mayo, Managua, Nicaragua, phone (505) 2266–6704, fax (505) 2222–5818; e-mail: capenic@ibw.com.ni.

Panama:

Raúl Delgado, Autoridad de los Recursos Acuáticos de Panamá Edificio La Riviera, Avenida Justo Arosemena y Calle 46 Bella Vista, diagonal a Estación el Árbol, Panama City, Panama, phone (507) 511–6057, fax (507); e-mail: rdelgado@arap.gob.pa.

Arnulfo Franco, FIPESCA, Corozal, Zona Libre de Proceso, Edif. 319, Panama, phone (507) 317–3644, fax (507) 317–3862; e-mail: arnulfofranco@fipesca.com.

Lucas Pacheco, Autoridad de los Recursos Acuáticos de Panamá Edificio La Riviera, Avenida Justo Arosemena y Calle 45 Bella Vista, diagonal a Estación el Arbol, Panama City, Panama, phone (507) 511–6000; e-mail: lpacheco@arap.gob.pa.

Zuleika Pinzón, Autoridad de los Recursos Acuáticos de Panamá, Edificio La Riviera, Avenida Justo Arosemena y Calle 45 Bella Vista, diagonal a Estación el Arbol, Panama City, 0819–05850, Panama, phone (507) 511–6000, fax (507) 511–6071; e-mail: administraciongeneral@arap.gob.pa.

Peru:

Gladys Cárdenas, Instituto del Mar del Perú, Esquina de Gamarra y General Valle s/n Chucuito-Callao Lima, Peru, phone (51–1) 208–8650, fax (51–1) 420–0144; e-mail: gcardenas@imarpe.gob.pe.

Rossy Yesenia Chumbe Cedeño, Ministerio de Producción, Calle 1 Oeste #066, San Isidro, Lima 27, Peru, phone (51–1) 988004419; e-mail: rchumbe@produce.gob.pe.

Jesús Ponce Bravo, Ministerio de Relaciones Exteriores, Jirón Lampa 545, Cercado de Lima, Peru, phone (51–1) 204–3244; e-mail: jponce@rree.gob.pe.

Omar Ricardo Ríos Bravo de Rueda, Ministerio de Producción, Calle 1 Oeste #066, San Isidro, Lima 27, Peru, phone (51–1) 616–2222; e-mail: orios@produce.gob.pe.

Chinese Taipei:

Hong-Yen Huang, Fisheries Agency, No. 2 Chaozhou St. Zhongzheng Dist., Taipei City, Taiwan, 100, phone (886–7) 823–9828, fax (886–7) 815–8278; e-mail: hangyen@ms1.fa.gov.tw.

Chi-Chao Liu, Fisheries Agency, Council of Agriculture, 6F No. 100, Sec. 2 Heping W. Rd Zhongzheng Dist., Taipei, 100, Taiwan, phone (886–2) 2383–5882; e-mail: chichao@ms1.fa.gov.tw.

Ted Tien-Hsiang Tsai, Fisheries Agency, No. 2, Chaozhou St. Zhongzheng Dist., Taipei City, Taiwan, phone (886–2) 3343–6045, fax (886–2) 3343–6128, e-mail: ted@ms1.fa.gov.tw.

USA:

William Fox, U.S. Commissioner-IATTC, P.O. Box 60633, San Diego, CA 92166, USA, phone (202) 495–4397, fax (619) 222–2489; e-mail: bill.fox@wwfus.org.

Donald Hansen, Pacific Fishery Management Council, 34675 Golden Lantern, Dana Point, CA 92629, USA, phone (949) 496–5794; e-mail: don.hansen@noaa.gov.

Barry Thom, NOAA / National Marine Fisheries Service, 1201, NE., Lloyd Blvd., Suite 1100, Portland, OR 97232, USA, phone (503) 231–6266, fax (503) 230–5441; email: barry.thom@noaa.gov.

Edward Weissman, U.S. Commissioner-IATTC, 1857 Spindrift Dr., La Jolla, CA 92037, USA, phone (858) 454–1558; e-mail: eweissman@aol.com.

Vanuatu:

Christophe Emelee, Vanuatu Government, P.O. Box 1640, Port Vila, Vanuatu, phone (678) 774–0219; e-mail: tunafishing@vanuatu.com.vu, c.emelee@yahoo.co.nz.

Roy M. Joy, Embassy of Vanuatu, Avenue de Tervueren 380 Chemin de Ronde, Brussels 1150, Belgium, phone (32–2) 771–7494, fax (32–2) 771–7494; e-mail: rjoy@vanuatuembassy.net, joyroymickey@gmail.com.

Dimitri Malvirlani, Vanuatu IATTC Commissioner, Marine Quay, P.O. Box 320, Port-Vila, Vanuatu, phone (678) 23128, fax (678) 22949; e-mail: vma@vanuatu.com.vn.

Laurent Parente, Vanuatu IATTC Commissioner, P.O. Box 1435, Port Vila Vanuatu, phone (447–55) 438–0005; e-mail: laurentparente-vanuatu-imo@hotmail.com.

Venezuela:

Alvin Delgado Martínez, FUNDATUN–PNOV, Urb. La Floresta Calle B I22, Cumaná, Sucre, 6101, Venezuela, phone (58–293) 433–0431, fax (58–293) 433–0431; e-mail: fundatunpnov@gmail.com.

Orlando Maneiro Gaspar, Ministerio del Poder Popular de Pesca y Acuicultura, Avenida Lecuna, Parque Central, Torre Este, Piso 17, Caracas, Venezuela, phone (58–212) 573–1055; e-mail: ori@insopesca.gob.ve.

Nancy Tablante, Instituto Socialista de la Pesca y Acuicultura, Centro Simón Bolívar, Avenida Lecuna Parque Central, Torre Este, Piso 12 al 14, Caracas, Venezuela, phone (58–212) 461–9225, fax (58–212) 953–9972; e-mail: ntablante@hotmail.com, orinsopesca@gmail.com.

INTERNATIONAL BOUNDARY AND WATER COMMISSION, UNITED STATES AND MEXICO

UNITED STATES SECTION

The Commons, Building C, Suite 100, 4171 North Mesa, El Paso, TX 79902–1441

phone (915) 832–4100, http://www.ibwc.gov

Commissioner.—Edward Drusina, 832–4101.
Foreign Affairs Secretary.—Sally Spencer, 832–4175.
Principal Engineer.—Jose Nuñez, 832–4749.
Human Resources Director.—Fred Graf, 832–4114.
General Counsel/Legal Advisor.—Matt Myers, 832–4728.

MEXICAN SECTION

Avenida Universidad, No. 2180, Zona de El Chamizal, A.P. 1612–D, C.P. 32310

Ciudad Juarez, Chihuahua, Mexico

P.O. Box 10525, El Paso, TX 79995

phone 011–52–16–13–7311 or 011–52–16–13–7363 (Mexico)

Commissioner.—Roberto F. Salmon Castello.
Foreign Affairs Secretary.—Jose de Jesus Luevano Grano.
Principal Engineers: Gilberto Elizalde Hernandez, L. Antonio Rascon Mendoza.

INTERNATIONAL BOUNDARY COMMISSION, UNITED STATES AND CANADA

UNITED STATES SECTION

1717 H Street, NW., Suite 845, Washington, DC 20006, phone (202) 736–9100

Commissioner.—Kyle K. Hipsley.
Deputy Commissioner.—John T. Moore, Jr.
Administrative Officer.—Tracy Morris.

CANADIAN SECTION

588 Booth Street, Suite 210, Ottawa, ON, Canada K1A 0Y7, phone (613) 944–4515

Commissioner.—Jean Gagnon.
Deputy Commissioner.—Vacant.

INTERNATIONAL COTTON ADVISORY COMMITTEE

Headquarters: 1629 K Street, NW., Suite 702, 20006, secretariat@icac.org
phone (202) 463–6660, fax 463–6950, www.icac.org

(Permanent Secretariat of the Organization)

MEMBER COUNTRIES

Argentina
Australia
Brazil
Burkina Faso
Cameroon
Chad
China (Taiwan)
Côte d'Ivoire
Egypt
European Union
India
Kazakhstan
Kenya
Korea, Republic of
Mali
Mozambique
Pakistan
Russia
South Africa
Sudan
Switzerland
Tanzania
Togo
Turkey
Uganda
United States
Uzbekistan
Zimbabwe

Executive Director.—Kai Hughes.
Statistician.—Vacant.
Director of Trade Analysis.—Andrei Guitchounts.
Economist.—Lorena Ruíz.
Head of Technical Information Section.—Keshava Raj Kranthi.

INTERNATIONAL JOINT COMMISSION, UNITED STATES AND CANADA

UNITED STATES SECTION

1717 H Street, NW., Suite 835, 20006

phone (202) 736–9000, fax 632–2006, http://www.ijc.org

Chair.—Lana B. Pollack.
Commissioner.—Richard Moy.
Secretary.—Charles A. Lawson.
Legal Advisor.—Susan Daniel.
Engineering Advisors: Mark Colosimo, Mark Gabriel.
Public Information Officer.—Frank Bevacqua.
Ecologist.—Victor Serveiss.
GIS Coordinator.—Michael Laitta.
Senior Advisor.—David Hermann.

CANADIAN SECTION

234 Laurier Avenue West, Ottawa, ON, Canada K1P 6K6

phone (613) 995–2984, fax 993–5583

Chairman.—Gordon Walker.
Commissioners: Benoit Bouchard, Richard Morgan.
Secretary.—Camille Mageau.
Legal Advisor.—Shane Zurbrigg.
Public Affairs Advisor.—Sarah Lobrichon.
Director, Science and Engineering.—Pierre Yves Caux.
Engineering Advisors: David Fay, Wayne Jenkinson.
Ecosystem Advisor.—Glenn Benoy.
Director, Policy and Programs.—Paul Allen.

Policy Advisor.—Cindy Warwick.
Senior Advisor.—Nick Heisler.

GREAT LAKES REGIONAL OFFICE

100 Ouellette Avenue, 8th Floor, Windsor, ON, Canada N9A 6T3

phone (519) 257–6700 (Canada), (313) 226–2170 (U.S.)

Director.—Patricia Morris.
Public Affairs Officer.—Sally Cole-Misch.
Physical Scientists: Antonette Arvai, Raj Bejankiwar, Jennifer Boehme, Mark Burrows, Matthew Child, Lizhu Wang, John E. Wilson.

INTERNATIONAL LABOR ORGANIZATION

Headquarters: 4, route des Morillons, CH–1211, Geneva 22, Switzerland

phone 41–22–799–6111, http://www.ilo.org

Washington Office, 1808 I Street, NW., Suite 900, 20006

phone (202) 617–3952, fax 617–3960, http://www.ilo.org/washington

Liaison Office with the United Nations

One Dag Hammarskjöld Plaza, 885 Second Avenue, 30th Floor, New York, NY 10017

phone (212) 697–0150, fax 697–5218, http://www.ilo.org/newyork

International Labor Office (Permanent Secretariat of the Organization)
Headquarters Geneva:
Director-General.—Guy Ryder.
Washington:
Director.—Vacant.
Officer in Charge / Deputy Director.—Erick J. Zeballos.
New York:
Director.—Vinicius Pinheiro.
Deputy Director.—Vacant.

INTERNATIONAL MONETARY FUND

700 19th Street, NW., 20431, phone (202) 623–7000

http://www.imf.org

MANAGEMENT AND SENIOR OFFICERS

Managing Director.—Christine Lagarde.
First Deputy Managing Director.—David Lipton.
Deputy Managing Director and Chief Administrative Officer.—Carla Grasso.
Deputy Managing Directors: Mitsuhiro Furusawa, Tao Zhang.
Economic Counselor.—Maurice Obstfeld.
Financial Counselor.—Tobias Adrian.
Legal Department General Counsel.—Sean Hagan.
Departmental Directors:
African.—Abebe Aemro Selassie.
Asia and Pacific.—Chang Yong Rhee.
Budget and Planning.—Daniel Citrin.
European.—Poul Mathias Thomsen.
Communications.—Gerard T. Rice.
Finance.—Andrew Tweedie.
Fiscal Affairs.—Vitor Gaspar.
Human Resources.—Kalpana Kochhar.
Internal Audit and Inspection.—Clare Brady.
Middle East and Central Asia.—Jihad Azour.
Monetary and Capital Markets.—Tobias Adrian.
Strategy, Policy, and Review.—Martin Muhleisen.
Research.—Maurice Obstfeld.

Secretary.—Jianhai Lin.
Statistics.—Louis Marc Ducharme.
Information Technology.—Susan Helen Swart.
Western Hemisphere.—Alejandro Werner.
Director, Regional Office for Asia and the Pacific.—Chikahisa Sumi.
Director, Europe Offices.—Jeffrey Franks.
Director and Special Representative to the United Nations.—Chris Lane.
Independent Evaluations Office.—Charles Collyns.
Institute for Capacity Development.—Sharmini A. Correy.
Legal and General Counsel.—Sean Hagan.

EXECUTIVE DIRECTORS AND ALTERNATES

Executive Directors:

Hesham Fahad Alogeel, represents Saudi Arabia.

Herve M. Jodon de Villeroche, represents France.

Thomas Ostros, represents Denmark, Estonia, Finland, Iceland, Latvia, Lithuania, Norway, Sweden.

Alexandre Tombini, represents Brazil, Capo Verde, Dominican Republic, Ecuador, Guyana, Haiti, Nicaragua, Panama, Suriname, Timor-Leste, Trinidad and Tobago.

Nancy Gail Horsman, represents Antigua and Barbuda, the Bahamas, Barbados, Belize, Canada, Dominica, Grenada, Ireland, Jamaica, St. Kitts and Nevis, St. Lucia, St. Vincent and the Grenadines.

Maxwell M. Mkwezalamba, represents Angola, Botswana, Burundi, Eritrea, Ethiopia, Gambia, Kenya, Lesotho, Liberia, Malawi, Mozambique, Namibia, Nigeria, Sierra Leone, Somalia, South Africa, South Sudan (Republic of), Swaziland, Tanzania, Uganda, Zambia, Zimbabwe.

Subir Vithal Gokarn, represents Bangladesh, Bhutan, India, Sri Lanka.

Juda Agung, represents Brunei Darussalam, Cambodia, Fiji, Indonesia, Lao People's Democratic Republic, Malaysia, Myanmar, Nepal, Philippines, Singapore, Thailand, Tonga, Vietnam.

Miroslaw Panek, represents Azerbaijan, Kazakhstan, Kyrgyz Republic, Poland, Serbia, Switzerland, Tajikistan, Turkmenistan.

Carlos Hurtado, represents Colombia, Costa Rica, El Salvador, Guatemala, Honduras, Mexico, Spain, Venezuela (Republica Bolivariana de).

Michaela Erbenova, represents Austria, Belarus, Czech Republic, Hungary, Kosovo, Slovak Republic, Slovenia, Turkey.

Daouda Sembene, represents Benin, Burkina Faso, Cameroon, Central African Republic, Chad, Comoros, Congo (Democratic Republic of), Congo (Republic of), Côte d'Ivoire, Djibouti, Equatorial Guinea, Gabon, Guinea, Guinea-Bissau, Madagascar, Mali, Mauritania, Mauritius, Niger, Rwanda, Sao Tomé and Principe, Senegal, Togo.

Alessandro Leipold, represents Albania, Greece, Italy, Malta, Portugal, San Marino.

Sunil Sabharwal, represents United States.

Masaaki Kaizuka, represents Japan.

Jafar Mojarrad, represents Afghanistan (Islamic Republic of), Algeria, Ghana, Iran (Islamic Republic of), Morocco, Pakistan, Tunisia.

Jorge Estrella, represents Argentina, Bolivia, Chile, Paraguay, Peru, Uruguay.

Steffen Meyer, represents Germany.

Hazem Beblawi Elbeblawi, represents Bahrain, Egypt, Iraq, Jordan, Kuwait, Lebanon, Libya, Maldives, Oman, Qatar, Syrian Arab Republic, United Arab Emirates, Yemen (Republic of).

Aleksei V. Mozhin, represents Russian Federation.

Heenam Choi, represents Australia, Kiribati, Korea, Marshall Islands, Micronesia (Federated States of), Mongolia, New Zealand, Palau, Papua New Guinea, Samoa, Seychelles, Solomon Islands, Tuvalu, Uzbekistan, Vanuatu.

Anthony De Lannoy, represents Armenia, Bosnia and Herzegovina, Bulgaria, Croatia, Cyprus, Georgia, Israel, Luxembourg, Macedonia (former Yugoslav Republic of), Moldova, Montenegro Republic, Netherlands, Romania, Ukraine.

Jin Zhongxia, represents China.

Steve Field, represents United Kingdom.

INTERNATIONAL ORGANIZATION FOR MIGRATION

Geneva Headquarters: 17 Route Des Morillons (P.O. Box 71), CH1211

Geneva 19, Switzerland, phone +41.22.798.61.50

Washington Mission: 1752 N Street, NW., Suite 700

Washington, DC 20036, phone (202) 862–1826

New York Mission: 122 East 42nd Street, 48th Floor

New York, NY 10168–1610, phone (212) 681–7000

HEADQUARTERS

Director General.—William Lacy Swing (United States).
Deputy Director General.—Laura Thompson (Costa Rica).
Washington Chief of Mission.—Luca Dalloglio (Italy).
New York Chief of Mission.—Vacant.
Permanent Observer to the United Nations.—Ashraf El Nour (South Sudan).

MEMBER STATES

Afghanistan
Albania
Algeria
Angola
Antigua and Barbuda
Argentina
Armenia
Australia
Austria
Azerbaijan
Bahamas
Bangladesh
Belarus
Belgium
Belize
Benin
Bolivia (Plurinational State of)
Bosnia and Herzegovina
Botswana
Brazil
Bulgaria
Burkina Faso
Burundi
Cambodia
Cameroon
Canada
Cape Verde
Central African Republic
Chad
Chile
Colombia
Comoros
Congo
Costa Rica
Côte d'Ivoire
Croatia
Cyprus
Czech Republic
Democratic Republic of the Congo
Denmark
Djibouti
Dominican Republic
Ecuador
Egypt
El Salvador
Estonia
Ethiopia
Fiji
Finland
France
Gabon
Gambia
Georgia
Germany
Ghana
Greece
Guatemala
Guinea
Guinea-Bissau
Guyana
Haiti
Holy See
Honduras
Hungary
Iceland
India
Iran (Islamic Republic of)
Ireland
Israel
Italy
Jamaica
Japan
Jordan
Kazakhstan
Kenya
Korea (Republic of)
Kyrgyzstan
Latvia
Lesotho
Liberia
Libya
Lithuania
Luxembourg
Madagascar
Malawi
Maldives
Mali
Malta
Marshall Islands
Mauritania
Mauritius
Mexico
Micronesia
Moldova (Republic of)
Mongolia
Montenegro
Morocco
Mozambique
Myanmar
Namibia
Nauru
Netherlands
Nepal
New Zealand
Nicaragua
Niger
Nigeria
Norway
Pakistan
Panama
Papua New Guinea
Paraguay
Peru
Philippines
Poland
Portugal
Romania
Rwanda
Saint Vincent and the Grenadines
Samoa
Senegal
Serbia
Seychelles
Sierra Leone
Slovakia
Slovenia
Somalia
South Africa
South Sudan

Spain
Sri Lanka
Sudan
Suriname
Swaziland
Sweden
Switzerland
Tajikistan
Thailand
The former Yugoslav Republic of Macedonia
Timor-Leste
Togo
Trinidad and Tobago
Tunisia
Turkey
Turkmenistan
Uganda
Ukraine
United Kingdom of Great Britain and Northern Ireland
United Republic of Tanzania
United States of America
Uruguay
Vanuatu
Venezuela (Bolivarian Republic of)
Viet Nam
Yemen
Zambia
Zimbabwe

OBSERVER STATES (10)

Bahrain
Bhutan
China
Cuba
Indonesia
Qatar
Russian Federation
San Marino
Sao Tome and Principe
Saudi Arabia

INTERNATIONAL GOVERNMENTAL AND NON-GOVERNMENTAL ORGANIZATIONS

Organs and Organizations of the United Nations System

United Nations
Economic and Social Commission for Asia and the Pacific (ESCAP)
Economic Commission for Africa (ECA)
Economic Commission for Latin America and the Caribbean (ECLAC)
Food and Agriculture Organization of the United Nations (FAO)
International Labour Organization (ILO)
International Maritime Organization (IMO)
Office for the Coordination of Humanitarian Affairs (OCHA)
Office of the United Nations High Commissioner for Human Rights (OHCHR)
Office of the United Nations High Commissioner for Refugees (UNHCR)
United Nations Children's Fund (UNICEF)
United Nations Conference on Trade and Development (UNCTAD)
United Nations Development Programme (UNDP)
United Nations Educational, Scientific and Cultural Organization (UNESCO)
United Nations Entity for Gender Equality and the Empowerment of Women (UN–WOMEN)
United Nations Environment Programme (UNEP)
United Nations Human Settlements Programme (UN–HABITAT)
United Nations Industrial Development Organization (UNIDO)
United Nations Population Fund (UNFPA)
United Nations Research Institute for Social Development (UNRISD)
Universal Postal Union (UPU)

World Bank
World Food Programme (WFP)
World Health Organization (WHO)
World Intellectual Property Organization (WIPO)
World Meteorological Organization (WMO)
Intergovernmental organizations and other entities

African Union
African, Caribbean and Pacific Group of States (ACP Group)
Asian-African Legal Consultative Organization (AALCO)
Common Market for Eastern and Southern Africa (COMESA)
Community of Portuguese Speaking Countries (CPLP)
Community of Sahel-Saharan States (CEN–SAD)

Council of Europe
East African Community (EAC)
Economic Community of Central African States (ECCAS)
Economic Community of West African States Commission (ECOWAS)

European Union (EU)
Ibero-American General Secretariat (SEGIB)

Inter-American Development Bank (IADB)
Intergovernmental Authority on Development (IGAD)
International Centre for Migration Policy Development (ICMPD)
International Committee of the Red Cross
International Federation of Red Cross and Red Crescent Societies
Islamic Educational, Scientific and Cultural Organization (ISESCO)
Italian-Latin American Institute

League of Arab States
Organisation internationale de la Francophonie
Organization for Economic Co-operation and Development
Organization of American States
Organization of the Islamic Cooperation
Parliamentary Assembly of the Union for the Mediterranean
Sovereign Order of Malta
Southeast European Cooperative Initiative (SECI) - Regional Center for Combating Transborder Crime
Southern African Development Community Secretariat (SADC)
Union du Maghreb Arabe (UMA)

OTHER ORGANIZATIONS WITH OBSERVER STATUS

Africa Humanitarian Action (AHA)
Africa Recruit
African and Black Diaspora Global Network on HIV and AIDS (ABDGN)
African Foundation for Development
American Jewish Joint Distribution Committee (JDC) - Center for International Migration and Integration (CIMI)
Amnesty International
Assistance pédagogique internationale (API)
Australian Catholic Migrant and Refugee Office (ACMRO)
CARAM Asia
CARE International
Caritas Internationalis
Catholic Relief Services
Center for Migration Studies of New York (CMS)
Danish Refugee Council
December 18
Episcopal Migration Ministries
European Youth Forum (YFJ)
Federation of Ethnic Communities' Councils of Australia, Inc.
Femmes Africa Solidarité (FAS)
FOCSIV-Volontari Nel Mondo (Federation of Christian Organizations for International Volunteer Service)
Food for the Hungry International
Friends World Committee for Consultation (FWCC)
Hassan II Foundation for Moroccans Residing Abroad
HIAS, Inc.
Human Rights Watch
Internal Displacement Monitoring Centre
International Catholic Migration Commission
International Council of Voluntary Agencies
International Council on Social Welfare
International Institute of Humanitarian Law (IIHL)
International Islamic Relief Organisation
International Medical Corps
International Organisation of Employers
International Rescue Committee
International Social Service
International Trade Union Confederation (ITUC)
INTERSOS
Islamic Relief
Japan International Friendship and Welfare Foundation
Jesuit Refugee Service (JRS)
"La Caixa" Foundation
Lutheran World Federation
Migrant Help
Migrants Rights International (MRI)
NGO Committee on Migration
Niwano Peace Foundation
Norwegian Refugee Council
Partage avec les enfants du tiers monde
Paulino Torras Doménech Foundation
Qatar Charity
Refugee Council of Australia
Refugee Education Trust (RET)
Sasakawa Peace Foundation
Save the Children
Scalabrini International Migration Network (SIMN)
Solidar
Terre des Hommes International Federation
The Hague Institute for Global Justice
Tolstoy Foundation, Inc.
United Ukrainian American Relief Committee
World Council of Churches
World Vision International

DUTY STATIONS 2015

Afghanistan 2
Herat
Kabul

Albania 1
Tirana

Algeria 1
Algiers

Angola 3
Luanda
Maquela d Zombo
Uige

Argentina 1
Buenos Aires

Armenia 2
Gyumri
Yerevan

Australia 6
Brisbane
Canberra
Darwin
Melbourne
Perth
Sydney

Austria 2
Vienna CO
Vienna RO

Azerbaijan 2
Baku
Mingachevir

Bangladesh 3
Chittagong
Dhaka
Sylhet

Belarus 1
Minsk

Belgium 1
Brussels

Benin 1
Cotonou

Bolivia (Plurinational State of) 1
La Paz

Bosnia and Herzegovina 2
Banja Luka
Sarajevo

Botswana 1
Gaborone

Bulgaria 2
Burgas
Sofia

Burkina Faso 1
Ouagadougou

Burundi 3
Bujumbura
Rutana
Ruyigi

Cabo Verde 1
Praia

Cambodia 1
Phnom Penh

Cameroon 1
Yaounde

Canada 1
Ottawa

Central African Republic 3
Bangui
Boda
Kabo

Chad 8
Abeche
Farchana
Faya
Gore
Mao
Moussoro
N'Djamena
Tissi

Chile 1
Santiago

China 2
Beijing
Hong Kong SAR

Colombia 31
Arauca
Armenia
Barranquilla
Bogota
Bucaramanga
Buenaventura
Cali
Cartagena
Cauca Valley
Cucuta
Florencia
Guajira
Ibagué
Manizales
Medellin
Mitu
Mocoa
Monteria
Nariño
Neiva
Pasto
Pereira
Popayan
Quibdo
Santa Marta
Sincelejo
SJ de Guaviare
Tumaco
Tunja
Valledupar
Villavicencio

Congo 1
Brazzaville

Costa Rica 1
San Jose

Côte d'Ivoire 4
Abidjan
Danane
Tabou
Toulepleu

Croatia 1
Zagreb

Cyprus 1
Nicosia

Czech Republic 1
Prague

Democratic Republic of the Congo (the) 7
Bukavu
Bunia
Goma
Kasindi
Kimpese
Kinshasa
Lubumbashi

Denmark 1
Copenhagen

Djibouti 1
Djibouti

Dominican Republic 1
Santo Domingo

Ecuador 1
Quito

Egypt 1
Cairo

El Salvador 1
San Salvador

Estonia 1
Tallinn

Ethiopia 9
Addis Ababa
Assosa
Dollo Addo
Gambella
Jijiga
Moyale
Semera
Shimelba
Shire Endaselas

Finland 1
Helsinki

France 2
Marseille
Paris

Gabon 1
Libreville

Gambia 1
Banjul

Georgia 5

Batumi
Gori
Kutaisi
Tbilisi
Telavi

Germany 2
Berlin
Nuremberg

Ghana 1
Accra

Greece 1
Athens

Guatemala 1
Guatemala City

Guinea 2
Conakry
Nzerekore

Guyana 1
Georgetown

Haiti 3
Gonaives
Ouanaminthe
Port-au-Prince

Honduras 1
Tegucigalpa

Hungary 1
Budapest

India 1
New Delhi

Indonesia 25
Aceh Selatan
Aceh Timur
Aceh Utara
Ambon
Balikpapan
Banda Aceh
Batam
Bener Meriah
Jakarta
Jayapura
Jimbaran
Kupang
Langsa
Lhokseumawe
Makassar
Medan
Menado
Merauke
Pekanbaru
Pontianak
Semarang
Surabaya
Takengon
Tanjung Pinang
Yogyakarta

Iran 1
Teheran

Iraq 6
Al Basrah
Ar Ramadi
Baghdad
Dohuk
Erbil
Sulaymaniah

Ireland 1
Dublin

Italy 2
Rome
Turin

Jamaica 1
Kingston

Japan 1
Tokyo

Jordan 1
Amman

Kazakhstan 2
Almaty
Astana

Kenya 8
Dadaab
Eldoret
Garissa
Kakuma
Lodwar
Marsabit
Nairobi
Wajir

Korea (Republic of) 1
Seoul

Kuwait 1
Kuwait City

Kyrgyzstan 2
Bishkek
Osh

Lao People's Democratic Republic 1
Vientiane

Latvia 1
Riga

Lebanon 1
Beirut

Lesotho 1
Maseru

Liberia 4
Buchanan
Monrovia
Sinje
Tubmanburg

Libya 2
Benghazi
Tripoli

Lithuania 1
Vilnius

Madagascar 1
Antananarivo

Malawi 1
Lilongwe

Malaysia 1
Kuala Lumpur

Maldives 1
Male

Mali 4
Bamako
Gao
Mopti
Tomboctou

Malta 1
Valletta

Marshall Islands 1
Majuro

Mauritania 1
Nouakchott

Mauritius 1
Port Louis

Mexico 3
Mexico City
Tapachula
Tuxtla

Micronesia (Federated States of) 4
Chuuk
Kosrae
Pohnpei
Yap

Mongolia 1
Ulaanbaatar

Montenegro 1
Podgorica

Morocco 4
Khouribga
Rabat
Tangier
Tetouan

Mozambique 3
Maputo
Quelimane
Xai-Xai

Myanmar 12
Mon
Ayeyarwady Delt
Bogalay
Hpa-an

Loikaw
Mawlamyinegyun
Myawaddy
Myitkyina
Sittwe
Thaton
Yangon
Ye

Namibia 1
Windhoek

Nepal 4
Chautara
Damak
Gorkha
Kathmandu

Netherlands 3
Schiphol Airp.
The Hague
Zwolle

Nicaragua 1
Managua

Niger 4
Arlit
Diffa
Niamey
Zinder

Nigeria 3
Abuja
Lagos
Yola

Norway 1
Oslo

Pakistan 5
Islamabad
Karachi
Lahore
Mirpur
Peshawar

Panama 1
Panama City

Papua New Guinea 6
Buka
Kimbe
Lae
Manus
Popondetta
Port Moresby

Paraguay 1
Asuncion

Peru 1
Lima

Philippines 8
Cebu
Cotabato City
Guiuan
Manila
Ormoc
Roxas
Tacloban
Zamboanga

Poland 1
Warsaw

Portugal 1
Lisbon

Republic of Moldova 1
Chisinau

Romania 1
Bucharest

Russian Federation 2
Krasnodar
Moscow

Rwanda 1
Kigali

Saudi Arabia 1
Riyadh

Senegal 1
Dakar

Serbia 2
Belgrade
Pristina

Sierra Leone 1
Freetown

Slovakia 2
Bratislava
Kosice

Slovenia 1
Ljubljana

Somalia 4
Bossaso
Garowe
Hargeisa-Somali
Mogadishu

South Africa 1
Pretoria

South Sudan 8
Bentiu
Bor
Juba
Maban
Malakal
Malualkon
Renk
Wau

Spain 1
Madrid

Sri Lanka 6
Ampara
Batticaloa
Colombo
Jaffna
Kilinochchi
Vavuniya

Sudan 8
Abyei
El Fasher
El Fula
Geneina
Kadugli
Kassala
Khartoum
Nyala

Switzerland 5
Altstatten
Basel
Bern
Geneva
Kreuzlingen

Syrian Arab Republic 11
Al Hasakah
Aleppo
Damascus
Deirezzor
Dera'a
Homs
Idleb
Latakia
Quneitra
Sweida
Tartus

Tajikistan 1
Dushanbe

Thailand 10
Bangkok
Chanthaburi
Chiang Mai
Chiang Rai
Mae Hong Son
Mae Sariang
Mae Sot
Phang Nga
Ranong
Songkhla

The former Yugoslav Republic of Macedonia 1
Skopje

Timor-Leste 1
Dili

Togo 1
Lome

Trinidad and Tobago 1
Port of Spain

Tunisia 2
Tunis
Zarzis

Turkey 3
Ankara
Gaziantep

Istanbul

Turkmenistan 1
Ashgabad

Uganda 1
Kampala

Ukraine 3
Kharkiv
Kiev
Odessa

United Arab Emirates 1
Dubai

United Kingdom of Great Britain and Northern Ireland 1
London

United Republic of Tanzania 3
Dar-es-Salaam
Kigoma
Moshi

United States of America 10
Chicago
Guantanamo Bay
Irvine
Los Angeles
Miami
New York
New York-JFK
Newark
SLO New York
Washington

UNSC resolution 1244-administered, Kosovo 3
Mitrovica
Peje
Pristina

Uruguay 1
Montevideo

Uzbekistan 1
Tashkent

Vanuatu 1
Port Vila

Venezuela (Bolivarian Republic of) 2
Caracas
San Cristobal

Viet Nam 2
Hanoi
Ho Chi Minh City

Yemen 3
Aden
Harad
Sana'a

Zambia 1
Lusaka

Zimbabwe 3
Beitbridge
Harare
Mutare

Grand Total 401

INTERNATIONAL PACIFIC HALIBUT COMMISSION
UNITED STATES AND CANADA

Headquarters / Mailing address:
2320 West Commodore Way, Suite 300, Seattle, WA 98199–1287
phone (206) 634–1838, fax 632–2983

American Commissioners:
Dr. Jim Balsiger, National Marine Fisheries Service, P.O. Box 21668, Juneau, AK 99802 (907) 586–7221, fax 586–7249.
Robert Alverson, 4005–20th Avenue West, Room 232, Seattle, WA 98199 (206) 283–7735.
Linda Behnken, P.O. Box 1229, Sitka, AK 99835 (907) 747–3400.

Canadian Commissioners:
Paul Ryall, Suite 200, 401 Burrard Street, Vancouver, BC, Canada V6C 3S4 (604) 666–0115.
Ted Assu, 754 Nursery Road, Campbell River, BC, Canada V9H 3P4 (250) 287–8868.
Jake Vanderheide, 2320 West Commodore Way, Suite 300, Seattle, WA 98199–1287 (250) 710–6853.
Director and Secretary (ex officio).—Dr. David Wilson, 2320 West Commodore Way, Suite 300, Seattle, WA 98199–1287.

ORGANIZATION OF AMERICAN STATES

17th Street and Constitution Avenue, NW., 20006
phone (202) 458–3000, fax 458–3967

PERMANENT MISSIONS TO THE OAS

Antigua and Barbuda.—Ambassador Sir Ronald Sanders, Permanent Representative, 3216 New Mexico Avenue, NW., 20016, phone 362–5122 / 5166 / 5211, fax 362–5225.
Argentina.—Ambassador Juan José, Permanent Representative, 1816 Corcoran Street, NW., 20009, phone 387–4142 / 4146 / 4170, fax 328–1591.
The Bahamas.—Chet Neymour, Interim Representative, 2220 Massachusetts Avenue, NW., 20008, phone 319–2660 to 2667, fax 319–2668.
Barbados.—Ambassador Selwin Charles Hart, Permanent Representative, 2144 Wyoming Avenue, NW., 20008, phone 939–9200 / 9201 / 9202, fax 332–7467.

Belize.—Ambassador Francisco Daniel Gutierez, Permanent Representative, 2535 Massachusetts Avenue, NW., 20008–3098, phone 332–9636, ext. 228, fax 332–6888.

Bolivia.—Ambassador Diego Pary, Permanent Representative, 2728 34th Street, NW., 20008, phone 785–0218 / 0219 / 0224, fax 296–0563.

Brazil.—Ambassador Jose Luis Machaco e Costa, Permanent Representative, 2600 Virginia Avenue, NW., Suite 412, 20037, phone 333–4224 / 4225 / 4226, fax 333–6610.

Canada.—Ambassador Jennifer Loten, Permanent Representative, 501 Pennsylvania Avenue, NW., 20001, phone 682–1768, ext. 7724, fax 682–7624.

Chile.—Ambassador Juan Aníbal Barría, Permanent Representative, 2000 L Street, NW., Suite 440, 20036, phone 887–5475 / 5476 / 5477, fax 775–0713.

Colombia.—Ambassador Andrés González Díaz, Permanent Representative, 1609 22nd Street, NW., 20008, phone 332–8003 / 8004, fax 234–9781.

Costa Rica.—Ambassador Rogelio Sotela Muñoz, Permanent Representative, 2112 S Street, NW., Suite 300, 20008, phone 234–9280 / 9281, fax 986–2274.

Dominica.—Ambassador Dr. Vince Henderson, Permanent Representative, 1001 North 19th Street, Suite 1200., Arlington, VA 22209, phone 571–1370, fax 571–384–7916.

Dominican Republic.—Ambassador Gedeón Santos, Permanent Representative, 1715 22nd Street, NW., 20008, phone 332–9142 / 0616 / 0772, fax 232–5038.

Ecuador.—Ambassador Marco Albuja, Permanent Representative, 2600 Virginia Avenue, NW., Suite 212, 20037, phone 234–1494 / 1692 / 8053, fax 667–3482.

El Salvador.—Ambassador Carlos Calles Castillo, Permanent Representative, 2308 California Street, NW., 20008, phone 595–7546 / 7545, fax 232–4806.

Grenada.—Ambassador Angus Friday, Permanent Representative, 1701 New Hampshire Avenue, NW., 20009, phone 265–2561, fax 265–2468.

Guatemala.—Ambassador Gabriel Aguilera Peralta, Permanent Representative, 1507 22nd Street, NW., 20037, phone 833–4015 / 4016 / 4017, fax 833–4011.

Guyana.—Ambassador Dr. Riyad Insanally, Permanent Representative, 2490 Tracy Place, NW., 20008, phone 265–6900 / 6901, fax 232–1297.

Haiti.—Ambassador Leon Charles, Interim Representative, 2311 Massachusetts Avenue, NW., 20008, phone 332–4090 / 4096, fax 518–8742.

Honduras.—Ambassador Leonidas Rosa Bautista, Permanent Representative, 3007 Tilden Street, NW., Suite 4M–400, 20008, phone 244–5430 / 5653 / 5260, no fax.

Jamaica.—Ambassador Audrey Marks, Permanent Representative, 1520 New Hampshire Avenue, NW., 20036, phone 986–0121 / 0123 / 452–0660, fax 452–9395.

Mexico.—Ambassador Luis Alfonso de Alba, Permanent Representative, 2440 Massachusetts Avenue, NW., 20008, phone 332–3663 / 3664 / 3984, fax 234–0602.

Nicaragua.—Ambassador Denis Ronaldo Moncada Colindres, Permanent Representative, 1627 New Hampshire Avenue, NW., 20009, phone 332–1643 / 1644 / 939–6536, fax 745–0710.

Panama.—Ambassador Jesus Sierra Victoria, Permanent Representative, 2201 Wisconsin Avenue, NW., Suite C–100, 20007, phone 965–4826 / 4819, fax 965–4836.

Paraguay.—Ambassador Elisa Ruiz Diaz Bareiro, Permanent Representative, 2022 Connecticut Avenue, NW., 20008, phone 232–8020 / 8021 / 8022, fax 244–3005.

Peru.—Ambassador Ana Rosa Valdivieso, Permanent Representative, 1901 Pennsylvania Avenue, NW., Suite 402, 20006, phone 232–2281 / 2282 / 1973, fax 466–3068.

Saint Kitts and Nevis.—Ambassador Dr. Everson Hull, Permanent Representative, 1001 North 19th Street, Suite 1260, Arlington, VA 22209, phone 686–2636 / (571) 527–1360, fax 686–5740.

Saint Lucia.—Ambassador Anton E. Edmunds, Permanent Representative, 1001 North 19th Street, Suite 1200, Arlington, VA 22209, phone 364–6792 / (571) 527–1375, fax 364–6723 / (571) 384–7930.

Saint Vincent and The Grenadines.— Ambassador Lou-Anne Gaylene Christ, Permanent Representative, 1001 North 19th Street, Suite 1260, Arlington, VA 22209, phone 364–6730, fax 364–6736.

Suriname.—Ambassador Niermala Badrising, Permanent Representative, 3400 International Place, NW., Suite 4L, 20008, phone 629–4402 / 4401 / 4392, fax 629–4769.

Trinidad and Tobago.—Ambassador Anthony Phillips-Spencer, Permanent Representative, 1708 Massachusetts Avenue, NW., 20036–1903, phone 467–6490, fax 785–3130.

United States of America.—Kevin Sullivan, Interim Representative, WHA/USOAS Bureau of Western Hemisphere Affairs, Department of State, Room 5914, 20520–6258, phone 647–9376, fax 647–0911 / 6973.

Uruguay.—Ambassador Hugo Cayrus, Permanent Representative, 1913 I (Eye) Street, NW., 4th Floor, 20006, phone 223–1961, fax 223–1966.

Venezuela.—Ambassador Carmen Velásquez de Visbal, Interim Representative, 1099 30th Street, NW., Second Floor, 20007, phone 342–5837 / 5838 / 5839 / 5840 / 5841, fax 625–5657.

GENERAL SECRETARIAT

Secretary General.—Luis Almagro (202) 370–5000.
Chief of Staff to the Secretary General.—Gonzalo Koncke, 370–0300.
Assistant Secretary General.—Nestor Mendez, 370–0261, fax 458–3011.
Chief of Staff to the Assistant Secretary General.—Ambassador La Celia Prince, 370–0195.
Executive Secretary for—
Integral Development.—Kim Hurtault-Osborne, 370–9014.
Inter-American Commission on Human Rights.—Paulo Abrão, 370–9000.
Secretary for—
Administration and Finance.—Juan José Goldschtein (acting), 370–5401.
Multidimensional Security.—Claudia Paz y Paz, 370–9959.
Strengthening Democracy.—Francisco Guerrero, 370–9962.
Access to Rights and Equity.—Mauricio Rands, 370–0270.
Hemispheric Affairs.—James M. Lambert, 370–4448.
Legal Affairs.—Jean Michel Arrighi, 370–0741.
Director for—
Summits Secretariat.—(Appointment pending), 370–0281.
Press and Communications.—Gonzalo Espariz (acting), 370–5437.

ORGANIZATION FOR ECONOMIC CO-OPERATION AND DEVELOPMENT

Headquarters: Paris, France, www.oecd.org

Washington Center, 1776 Eye Street, NW., Suite 450, 20006, phone (202) 785–6323, fax 785–0350,Washington.contact@oecd.org, www.oecd.org/washington

PARIS HEADQUARTERS

Secretary-General.—Angel Gurría.
Deputy Secretaries-General: Douglas Frantz, Mari Kiviniemi, Masamichi Kono.
Chief Economist.—Catherine Mann.

WASHINGTON CENTER

Head of Center.—Susan Fridy (acting).
Member Countries:

Australia
Austria
Belgium
Canada
Chile
Czech Republic
Denmark
Estonia
Finland
France
Germany
Greece
Hungary
Iceland
Ireland
Israel
Italy
Japan
Korea
Latvia
Luxembourg
Mexico
Netherlands
New Zealand
Norway
Poland
Portugal
Slovak Republic
Slovenia
Spain
Sweden
Switzerland
Turkey
United Kingdom
United States

OECD WASHINGTON CENTER

1776 Eye Street, NW., Suite 450, 20006, phone (202) 785–6323, fax 315–2508

http://www.oecd.org/washington

Head of Center.—Susan Fridy (acting).

PAN AMERICAN HEALTH ORGANIZATION (PAHO)
REGIONAL OFFICE OF THE WORLD HEALTH ORGANIZATION

525 23rd Street, NW., 20037, phone (202) 974–3000

fax 974–3663

Director.—Dr. Carissa F. Etienne, 974–3408.

Deputy Director.—Dr. Isabella Danel, 974–3178.
Assistant Director.—Dr. Francisco Becerra, 974–3404.
Director of Administration.—Gerald Anderson, 974–3412.

PAHO / WHO FIELD OFFICES

OPS / WHO OFICINAS DE LOS REPRESENTANTES EN LOS PAISES

Barbados and Eastern Caribbean Countries (ECC serves the following countries, territories and departments: Antigua and Barbuda, Barbados, Dominica, Grenada, St. Kitts and Nevis, Saint Lucia, St. Vincent and the Grenadines. Overseas Territories (Anguilla, British Virgin Islands, Montserrat).—Dr. Godfrey Xuereb, Dayralls and Navy Garden Roads, Christ Church, (P.O. Box 508), Bridgetown, Barbados, phone (246) 426–3860 / 435–9263, fax 228–5402, e-mail: ECC@ecc.paho.org, http://www.cpc.paho.org.

Caribbean Program Coordination, CPC.—Eng. Adrianus Vlugman, a.i., Caribbean Program Coordinator, Dayralls and Navy Garden Roads, Christ Church, Bridgetown, Barbados (P.O. Box 508), (French Antilles: Guadaloupe, Martinique, St. Martin and St. Bartholomew, French Guiana), phone (246) 426–3860 / 3865 427–9434, fax 436–9779, e-mail: email@cpc.paho.org, http://www.cpc.paho.org.

PAHO/WHO Representatives:

Argentina.—Dr. Maureen Birmingham, Marcelo T. de Alvear 684, 4o. piso, 1058 Buenos Aires, Argentina, phone (54–11) 4319–4200, fax 4319–4201, e-mail: info@ops.org.ar, http://www.ops.org.ar.

Bahamas (Also serves Turks and Caicos).—Dr. Gerarda Eijkemans, 2nd Floor, Grosvenor Medical Centre, Grosvenor Close, Shirley Street, Nassau, Bahamas, phone (242) 326–7299 / 356–4730, fax 326–7012, e-mail: email@bah.paho.org.

Belize.—Dr. Roberto Escoto, 4792 Coney Drive, Coney Drive Business Plaza, 3rd Floor, (P.O. Box 1834), Belize City, Belize, phone (501–2) 2448–85 / 2339–46, fax 2309–17, e-mail: admin@blz.paho.org, http://www.blz.paho.org.

Bolivia.—Dr. Luis Fernando Leanes, Calle 18 No. 8022, Edificio Parque 18 Piso 2 y 3, Zona Calacoto, La Paz, Bolivia, phone (591–2) 297–9730 / fax 297–1146, e-mail: pwrbol@bol.ops-oms.org, http://www.ops.org.bo.

Brazil.—Dr. Joaquin Molina, Setor de Embaixadas Norte, Lote 19, 70800–400, Brasilia, (Caixa Postal 08–629, 70312–970, Brasilia, D.F., Brasil), phone (55–61) 3251–9455 /9549 /9500, fax 3223–0269, e-mail: email@bra.ops-oms.org, http://www.opas.org.br/.

Chile.—Dra. Paloma Cuchi, Av. Dag Hammarskjold 3269, Vitacura, Santiago, Chile. phone (56–2) 2437–4600 / 4605, fax 207–4717, e-mail: email@chi.ops-oms.org, http://www.chi.ops-oms.org.

Colombia.—Dr. Gina Watson, Calle 66 No. 11–50, Piso 6 y 7, Edificio Villorio, Bogota, D.C., Colombia, phone (57–1) 314–4141 /254–7050, fax 254–7070, e-mail: ops-col@latino.net.co, http://www.col.ops-oms.org/.

Costa Rica.—Dra. Lilian Reneau-Vernon, Calle 16, Avenida 6 y 8, Distrito Hospital, (Apartado 3745), San Jose, Costa Rica, phone (506) 2521–7045 / 2258–5810, fax 2258–5830, e-mail: email@cor.ops-oms.org, http://www.cor.ops-oms.org.

Cuba.—Dr. Christian Morales, Calle 4 No. 407, entre 17 y 19 Vedado, (Casilla diplomatica 68), La Habana, Cuba C.P. 10400, phone (53–7) 831–8944 / 837–5808, fax 833–2075/ 66–2075, e-mail: pwr@cub.ops-oms.org or cruzmari@cub.ops-oms.org, http://www.cub.ops-oms.org.

Dominican Republic.—Dr. Alma Morales, Edificio OPS / OMS, y Defensa Civil, Calle Pepillo Salcedo-Recta Final, Plaza de la Salud, Ensanche La Fe, (Apartado Postal 1464), Santo Domingo, Republica Dominicana, phone (809) 562–1519 / 544–3241/542–6177, fax 544–0322, e-mail: email@dor.ops-oms.org, http://www.dor.ops-oms.org.

Ecuador.—Dra. Gina Tambini, Amazonas N. 2889 y Mariana de Jesus, Quito, Ecuador, phone (593–2) 2460–330 / 296 / 215, fax 2460–325, e-mail: email@ecu.ops-oms.org, http://www.opsecu.org.ec.

El Salvador.—Dr. Carlos Garzón, 73 Avenida Sur No. 135, Colonia Escalón, (Apartado Postal 1072, Sucursal Centro), San Salvador, El Salvador, phone (503) 2511–9500/ 9504/ 9501, fax 2511–9555, e-mail: email@els.ops-oms.org, http://www.ops.org.sv/.

Guatemala.—Dr. Guadalupe Verdejo, Diagonal 6, 10–15 zona 10, Edificio Interamericas, torre norte, cuarto nivel, (Apartado Postal 383), Guatemala, Guatemala, phone (502) 2329–4200 / 2336–7426 / 2336–7425, fax 2334–3804, http://www.ops.org.gt.

Guyana.—Dr. William Adu-Know, Lot 8 Brickdam Stabroek, (P.O. Box 10969), Georgetown, Guyana, phone (592) 225–3000 / 227–5159, fax 226–6654 /227–4205, e-mail: email@guy.paho.org.

Haiti.—Dr. Jean Luc Poncelet, No. 295 Avenue John Brown, (Boite Postale 1330), Port-au-Prince, Haiti, phone (509) 2814–3000/ 3001/ 3002/ 3005, fax 2814–3089, e-mail: email@hai.ops-oms.org.

Honduras.—Ing. Ana Solis-Ortega Treasure, Edificio Imperial, 6o.y 7o.piso, Avenida República de Panamá, Frente a la Casa de Naciones Unidas, Tegucigalpa M.D.C., Honduras, phone (504) 2221–6091 / 6098 / 6102, fax 2221–6103, e-mail: pwr@hon.ops-oms.org, http://www.paho-who.hn.

Jamaica (also serves Bermuda and Cayman).—Dr. Noreen Jack, 8 Gibraltar Way, University of the West Indies, Mona Campus, Kingston 7, Jamaica, (P.O. Box 384, Cross Roads, P.O., Kingston 5) phone (876) 970–0016, fax 927–2657, e-mail: email@jam.ops-oms.org.

México.—Dr. Diego Gonzalez, a.i., Horacio No. 1855, 3er. Piso, Of. 305, Colonia Los Morales, Polanco, Del. Miguel Hidalgo, México D.F., 11510, México, phone (52–55) 5980–0880 / 0871, fax 5395–5681, e-mail: e-mail@mex.ops-oms.org, http://www.mex.ops-oms.org.

Nicaragua.—Dr. Socorro Gross Galiano, Complejo Nacional de Salud, Camino a la Sabana, Apartado Postal 1309, Managua, Nicaragua, phone (505) 2289–4200 / 4800, fax 2289–4999, e-mail: email@nic.ops-oms.org, http://www.ops.org.ni.

Panamá.—Dr. Federico Hernandez Pimentel, Ministerio de Salud de Panamá, Ancon, Avenida Gorgas, Edificio 261, 2o piso, (Casilla Postal 0843–3441), Panamá, Panamá, phone (507) 262–0030 / 1996, fax 262–4052, e-mail: email@pan.ops-oms.org, http://opsoms.org.pa.

Paraguay.—Dr. Carlos Castillo Solórzano, Edificio "Faro del Rio" Mcal Lopez 957 Esq. Estados Unidos, (Casilla de Correo 839), Asunción, Paraguay, (Casilla de Correo 839) phone (595–21) 450–495 / 449–864/ fax 450–498, e-mail: email@par.ops-oms.org, http://www.par.ops-oms.org.

Perú.—Dr. Gustavo Vargas, Los Pinos 251, Urbanización Camacho, La Molina, Lima 12, Perú, phone (51–1) 319–5700 / 5781, fax 437–8289, e-mail: email@per.opsoms.org, http://www.per.ops.oms.org.

Puerto Rico.—Dr. Raúl Castellanos Bran, P.O. Box 70184, San Juan, Puerto Rico 00936, phone (787) 274–7608, fax 250–6547 / 767–8341.

Suriname.—Dr. Guillermo Troya, Burenstraat #33, (P.O. Box 1863), Paramaribo, Suriname, phone (597) 471–676 / 425–355, fax 471–568, e-mail: email@sur.paho.org.

Trinidad and Tobago.—Dr. Bernadette Theodore-Gandi, Sweet Briar Place, First Floor, 10–12 Sweet Briar Road, St. Clair, Trinidad, phone (868) 624–7524 / 4376 / 2078 / 625–4492, fax 624–5643, email: email@trt.paho.org.

Uruguay.—Dr. Eduardo Levcovitz, Ave. Brasil 2697, Aptos. 5, 6 y 8, Esquina Coronel Alegre, Codigo Postal 11300, (Casilla de Correo 1821), Montevideo, Uruguay, phone (598–2) 707–3590 / 2589, fax 707–3530, e-mail: pwr@uru.ops-oms.org, http://www.ops.org.uy/.

Venezuela (Also serves Netherlands Antilles).—Dra. Celia Riera, Avenida Sexta entre 5a y 6a, Transversal No. 43, Quinta OPS/OMS, Urbanización Altamira, Caracas 1060, Venezuela, (Apartado 6722 - Carmelitas, Caracas 1010, Venezuela) phone (58–212) 206–5022 / 5000, 265–0403 fax 261–6069, e-mail: email@ven.ops-oms.org, http://www.opsoms.org.ve/.

CENTERS

Caribbean Epidemiology Center (CAREC).—Dr. Beryl Irons, 16–18 Jamaica Boulevard, Federation Park, (P.O. Box 164), Port-of-Spain, Trinidad, phone (1–868) 622–4262, fax 622–2792, e-mail: email@carec.ops-oms.org.

Caribbean Food and Nutrition Institute (CFNI).—Dr. Fitzroy J. Henry, University of the West Indies, (P.O. Box 140–Mona), Kingston 7, Jamaica, phone (1–876), 977–6726 / 1274, fax 927–2657, e-mail: e-mail@cfni.paho.org.

Latin American and Caribbean Center on Health Sciences Information (BIREME).—Mr. Jacobo Finkelman, a.i., Rua Botucatu 862, Vila Clementino, (Caixa Postal 20381), CEP.04023–901, Sao Paulo, SP, Brasil, phone (55–11) 5576–9800 / 5572–3226, fax 575–8868 / 5549–2590, e-mail: email@bireme.ops-oms.org.

Latin American Center for Perinatology and Human Development (CLAP).—Dra. Suzanne Jacob Serruya, Hospital de Clinicas, Piso 16, (Casilla de Correo 627, 11000 Montevideo, Uruguay), 11600 Montevideo, Uruguay, phone (598–2) 487–2929, fax 487–2593, e-mail: postmaster@clap.ops-oms.org.

Pan American Foot-and-Mouth Disease Center (PANAFTOSA).—Dr. Ottorino Cosivi, Governador Leonel de Moura Brizola 7778, (Antiga Avenida Presidente Kennedy), São Bento, Duque de Caxias, 25040–004 Rio de Janeiro, Brasil, (Caixa Postal 589, 11000 Montevideo, Uruguay) phone (55–21) 3661–9000 / 9005 / 9002, fax 3661–9001, e-mail: panaftosa@panaftosa.pos-oms.org.

PAHO Foundation.—Mailing address: P.O. Box 27733, Washington, DC 30038–7733 / Physical address: 1889 F Street, NW., Suite 313, Washington, DC 20006, phone (202) 974–3416, fax 974–3636.

Regional Program on Bioethics.—Dr. Carla Saenz, Bioethics Regional Advisor, Pan American Health Organization, phone (202) 974–3263, fax: 974–3663.
PAHO HIV Caribbean Office.—112–114 Duke Street, Port-of-Spain, Trinidad W.I., phone (868) 624–0400/623–9417, fax 974–8001.
United States-Mexico Border.—This Center closed in 2013.

PERMANENT JOINT BOARD ON DEFENSE, CANADA-UNITED STATES

CANADIAN SECTION

National Defence Headquarters, MG George R. Pearkes Building, Ottawa, ON Canada K1A OK2, phone (613) 992–4423

Members:
Canadian Co-Chairman.—Hon. Laurie Hawn, P.C., C.D., M.P.
Military Policy.—Cmdre Bob Auchterlonie, Director, of General Plans.
Defence Policy.—Gordon Venner, Assistant Deputy, Minister Policy.
Foreign Affairs.—David Drake, DFATD Director General, Security and Intelligence Bureau.
Canada Strategic Joint Staff.—MGen Charles Lamarre, Director of Staff.
NORAD.—LGen Pierre St-Amand, Deputy Commander NORAD.
Public Safety.—Megan Nichols, Director General, Border Policy and International Affairs.
Military Secretary.—LCol Michael Ward, Directorate of Western Hemisphere Policy.
Political Secretary.—Yasemin Heinbecker, DFADT Directorate of International Defence Relations, (613) 867–1234.

UNITED STATES SECTION

JCS, J–5, Western Hemisphere Directorate, Pentagon, Room 2E773, 20318

phone (703) 695–4955

Members:
U.S. Co-Chair.—Elissa Slotkin, Principal Deputy Assistant Secretary of Defense for International Security Affairs.
Military Policy (Joint Staff).—BG Joseph Whitlock, Deputy Director for Western Hemisphere.
Defense Policy (OSD).—Dr. Rebecca Chavez, Deputy Assistant Secretary of Defense for Western Hemisphere.
State Department.—Karen Choe-Fichte, Deputy Director, Office of Canadian Affairs.
National Security Council.—Denison Offutt, Director of North American Affairs.
USNORTHCOM.—RADM Richard P. Snyder, Director of Strategy, Policy, and Plans.
NORAD.—RADM Richard P. Snyder, Director of Strategy, Policy, and Plans.
DHS.—RDML Joanna Nunan, Military Advisor to the Secretary of DHS.
Military Secretary.—Maj. Francis Marino, Canada Desk Officer on the Joint Staff, 695–4955.
Political Secretary.—Keith Gilges, Political Affairs, Office of Canadian Affairs, 202–647–2228.

SECRETARIAT OF THE PACIFIC COMMUNITY

B.P. D5, 98848 Noumea Cedex, New Caledonia, phone (687) 26.20.00, fax 26.38.18

spc@spc.int, http://www.spc.int

Director-General.—Dr. Colin Tukuitonga.
Deputy Director General (Noumea).—Cameron Diver.
Deputy Director General (Suva).—Dr. Audrey Aumua.
Director:
Public Health Division.—Dr. Paula Vivili.
Fisheries, Aquaculture, and Marine Ecosystems Division.—Moses Amos.
Land Resources Division.—Jan Helsen.
Geoscience, Energy and Maritime Division.—Dr. Andrew Jones.
Social Development Programme.—Kuiniselani Toelupe Tago-Elisara.
Regional Rights Resource Team (Human Rights Programme).—Nicol Cave a.i.
Statistics for Development Division.—Dr. Ofa Ketu'u.

Strategic Engagement, Policy and Planning Facility.—Cameron Bowles.
Strategic and Corporate Communications.—Peter Foster.
Human Resources.—Craig Parker.
Finance.—Martin van Weerdenburg.
Climate Change and Environmental Sustainability.—Sylvie Goyet.

U.S. Contact: Bureau of East Asian and Pacific Affairs, Office of Australia, New Zealand and Pacific Island Affairs, Department of State, Washington, DC 20520, phone (202) 736–4741, fax 647–0118

Member Countries and Territories of the SPC:

American Samoa
Australia
Cook Islands
Federated States of Micronesia
Fiji
France
French Polynesia
Guam
Kiribati
Marshall Islands
Nauru
New Caledonia
Niue
New Zealand
Northern Mariana Islands
Palau
Papua New Guinea
Pitcairn Islands
Samoa
Solomon Islands
Tokelau
Tonga
Tuvalu
United States
Vanuatu
Wallis and Futuna

SECRETARIAT OF THE PACIFIC REGIONAL ENVIRONMENTAL PROGRAMME

P.O. Box 240, Apia, Samoa, phone (685) 21929, fax (685) 20231

E-mail: sprep@sprep.org, http://www.sprep.org

Director General.—Kosi Latu.
Deputy Director.—Roger Cornforth.
Director of:
Biodiversity and Ecosystem Management Programme.—Stuart Chape.
Climate Change Programme.—Vacant.
Environmental Monitoring and Governance.—Easter Galuvao.
Waste Management and Pollution Control.—Vicki Hall.

U.S. Contact: Bureau of Oceans and International Environmental and Scientific Affairs, Office of Ocean and Polar Affairs, Department of State, Washington, DC 20520 phone (202) 647–3262

Member Countries and Territories of SPREP:

American Samoa
Australia
Cook Islands
Federated States of Micronesia
Fiji
France
French Polynesia
Guam
Kiribati
Marshall Islands
Nauru
New Caledonia
New Zealand
Niue
Northern Mariana Islands
Palau
Papua New Guinea
Samoa
Solomon Islands
Tokelau
Tonga
Tuvalu
United Kingdom
United States
Vanuatu
Wallis and Futuna

UNITED NATIONS

GENERAL ASSEMBLY

The General Assembly is composed of all 193 United Nations Member States.

SECURITY COUNCIL

The Security Council has 15 members. The United Nations Charter designates five States as permanent members, and the General Assembly elects ten other members for two-year terms. The term of office for each non-permanent member of the Council ends on 31 December of the year indicated in parentheses next to its name.

The five permanent members of the Security Council are China, France, Russian Federation, United Kingdom, and the United States.

The ten non-permanent members of the Council in 2017 are Egypt (2017), Japan (2017), Senegal (2017), Ukraine (2017), Uruguay (2017), Ethiopia (2018), Kazakhstan (2018), Bolivia (2018), Italy (2018), Sweden (2018).

ECONOMIC AND SOCIAL COUNCIL

The Economic and Social Council has 54 members, elected for three-year terms by the General Assembly. The term of office for each member expires on 31 December of the year indicated in parentheses next to its name. Voting in the Council is by simple majority; each member has one vote. In 2017, the Council is composed of the following 54 States:

Algeria (2018)
Afghanistan (2018)
Andorra (2019)
Argentina (2017)
Australia (2018)
Azerbaijan (2019)
Belgium (2018)
Benin (2019)
Bosnia and Herzegovina (2019)
Brazil (2017)
Burkina Faso (2017)
Cameroon (2019)
Chad (2019)
Chile (2018)
China (2019)
Colombia (2019)
Czech Republic (2018)
Estonia (2017)
France (2017)
Germany (2017)
Ghana (2017)
Guyana (2018)
Honduras (2017)
India (2017)
Iraq (2018)
Ireland (2017)
Italy (2018)
Japan (2017)
Lebanon (2018)
Mauritania (2017)
Nigeria (2018)
Norway (2019)
Pakistan (2017)
Peru (2018)
Republic of Korea (2019)
Republic of Moldova (2018)
Russian Federation (2019)
Rwanda (2018)
Saint Vincent and the Grenadines (2019)
Somalia (2018)
South Africa (2018)
Spain (2017)
Swaziland (2019)
Sweden (2019)
Tajikistan (2019)
Trinidad and Tobago (2017)
Turkey (2017)
UAE (2019)
Uganda (2017)
United Kingdom of Great Britain and Northern Ireland (2019)
United States of America (2018)
Venezuela (2019)
Viet Nam (2018)
Zimbabwe (2017)

TRUSTEESHIP COUNCIL

The Trusteeship Council has five members: China, France, Russian Federation, United Kingdom, and the United States. With the independence of Palau, the last remaining United Nations trust territory, the Council formally suspended operation on 1 November 1994. By a resolution adopted on that day, the Council amended its rules of procedure to drop the obligation to meet annually and agreed to meet as occasion required—by its decision or the decision of its President, or at the request of a majority of its members or the General Assembly or the Security Council.

INTERNATIONAL COURT OF JUSTICE

The International Court of Justice has 15 members, elected by both the General Assembly and the Security Council. Judges hold nine-year terms. The term of office for each member expires on February of the year indicated in parentheses next to its name. The current composition of the court is as follows:

Ronny Abraham (France 2018)
Abdulqawi Ahmed Yusuf (Somalia 2018)
Hisashi Owada (Japan 2021)
Joan E. Donoghue (United States 2024)
Peter Tomka (Slovakia 2021)
Giorgio Gaja (Italy 2021)
Mohamed Bennouna (Morocco 2024)
Julia Sebutinde (Uganda 2021)
Antônio Augusto Cançado Trindade (Brazil 2018)
Dalveer Bhandari (India 2018)
Christopher John Greenwood (United Kingdom 2018)
Patrick Lipton Robinson (Jamaica 2024)
Xue Hangin (China 2021)
James Richard Crawford (Australia 2024)
Kirill Gevorgian (Russian Federation 2024)

UNITED NATIONS SECRETARIAT

One United Nations Plaza, New York, NY 10017, (212) 963–1234, http://www.un.org.

Secretary General.—António Guterres (Portugal).
Deputy Secretary.—Amina J. Mohammed (Nigeria).

EXECUTIVE OFFICE OF THE SECRETARY-GENERAL

Chief of Staff.—Maria Luiza Ribeiro Viotti (Brazil).
Spokesman.—Stephane Dujarric.

OFFICE OF INTERNAL OVERSIGHT SERVICES

Under-Secretary-General.—Heidi Mendoza (Philippines).
Assistant Secretary-General.—David Kanja (Kenya).

OFFICE OF LEGAL AFFAIRS

Under-Secretary-General and Legal Counsel.—Miguel de Serpa Soares (Portugal).
Assistant Secretary-General.—Stephen Mathias (United States).

DEPARTMENT OF POLITICAL AFFAIRS

Under-Secretary-General.—Jeffrey Feltman (United States).
Assistant Secretaries-General: Miroslav Jenca (Slovakia), Tayé-Brook Zerihoun (Ethiopia).

DEPARTMENT FOR DISARMAMENT AFFAIRS

Assistant Secretary-General, Acting High Representative for Disarmament Affairs.—Izumi Nakamitsu (Japan).

DEPARTMENT OF PEACE-KEEPING OPERATIONS

Under-Secretary-General.—Jean-Pierre Lacroix (France).
Assistant Secretaries-General: El Ghassim Wane (Mauritania), Alexander Zuev (Russia).
Military Adviser.—Lieutenant General Carlos Humberto Loitey (Uruguay).

DEPARTMENT OF FIELD SUPPORT

Under-Secretary-General.—Atul Khare (India).
Assistant Secretary-General.—Lisa M. Buttenheim (United States).

OFFICE FOR THE COORDINATION OF HUMANITARIAN AFFAIRS

Under-Secretary-General, Humanitarian Affairs and Emergency Relief Coordinator.—Mark Lowcock (United Kingdom).
Assistant Secretary-General/Deputy Emergency Relief Coordinator.—Ursula Mueller (Germany).

DEPARTMENT OF ECONOMIC AND SOCIAL AFFAIRS

Under-Secretary-General.—Liu Zhenmin (China).
Assistant Secretary-General, Policy Coordination and Inter-Agency Affairs.—Thomas Gass (Switzerland).
Assistant Secretary-General, Economic Development.—Vacant.

DEPARTMENT OF GENERAL ASSEMBLY AND CONFERENCE MANAGEMENT

Under-Secretary-General.—Catherine Pollard (Guyana).
Assistant Secretary-General.—Movses Abelian (Armenia).

DEPARTMENT OF PUBLIC INFORMATION

Under-Secretary-General.—Alison Smale (United Kingdom).

DEPARTMENT OF MANAGEMENT

Under-Secretary-General.—Jan Beagle (New Zealand).
Assistant Secretary-General, Controller.—Bettina Tucci Bartsiotas (Uruguay).
Assistant Secretary-General, Human Resources Management.—Martha Helena Lopez (Colombia).
Assistant Secretary-General, Central Support Services.—Stephen Cutts (United Kingdom).
Assistant Secretary-General, Executive Director of the Capital Master Plan.—Michael Adlerstein (United States).

OFFICE OF THE SPECIAL REPRESENTATIVE OF THE SECRETARY-GENERAL FOR CHILDREN AND ARMED CONFLICT

Under-Secretary-General.—Virginia Gamba (Argentina).

UNITED NATIONS OFFICE FOR PARTNERSHIPS

Officer-in-Charge and Chief of Operations.—Ann de la Roche.

UNITED NATIONS AT GENEVA (UNOG)

Palais des Nations, 1211 Geneva 10, Switzerland, phone (41–022) 917–1234

Director-General of UNOG.—Michael Moller (Denmark).

UNITED NATIONS AT VIENNA (UNOV)

Vienna International Centre, P.O. Box 500, 1400 Vienna, Austria, phone (43–1) 26060

Director-General.—Yury Fedotov (Russian Federation).

UNITED NATIONS AT NAIROBI (UNON)

P.O. Box 67578, Nairobi, Kenya 00200, phone: +254 20 7621234

Director-General.—Sahle-Work Zewde (Ethiopia).

UNITED NATIONS INFORMATION CENTRE

1775 K Street, NW., Suite 500, Washington, DC 20006
phone: (202) 331–8670, fax: (202) 331–9191, email: unicdc@unic.org
http://www.unicwash.org

Director.—Robert Skinner (United States).

REGIONAL ECONOMIC COMMISSIONS

Economic Commission for Africa (ECA), Menelik II Ave., P.O. Box 3001, Addis Ababa, Ethiopia, phone 251–11–544 4999, fax 251–11–551–4416.

Executive Secretary.—Vera Songwe (Cameroon).

Economic Commission for Europe (ECE) Palais des Nations, 1211 Geneva 10, Switzerland, phone (41–22) 917–1234 (switchboard).
Executive Secretary.—Olga Algayerova (Slovakia).

Economic Commission for Latin America and the Caribbean (ECLAC), Casilla 179–D, Santiago, Chile, Postal code: 7630412, phone (56–2) 2471 2000, 2210 2000, fax (56–2) 208–0252.
Executive Secretary.—Alicia Bárcena (Mexico).

ECLAC Washington Office: 1825 K Street, NW., Washington, DC, phone (202) 596–3713.
Director.—Inés Bustillo.

Economic and Social Commission for Asia and the Pacific (ESCAP), United Nations Building, Rajadamnern Nok Avenue, Bangkok, Thailand, phone (66–2) 288–1234, fax (66–2) 288–1000.
Executive Secretary.—Dr. Shamshad Akhtar (Pakistan).

Economic and Social Commission for Western Asia (ESCWA), P.O. Box 11–8575, Riad El-Solh Square, Beirut, Lebanon, phone 9611–981301, fax 9611–981510.
Executive Secretary.—Mohamed Ali Alhakim (Iraq).

Regional Commissions, New York Office, (ECE, ESCAP, ECLAC, ECA, ESCWA), phone (212) 963–8088.
Director.—Amr Nour (Egypt).

FUNDS AND PROGRAMS

United Nations High Commissioner for Refugees (UNHCR), Case Postale 2500, CH–1211 Geneve 2 Depot, Switzerland, phone (41–22) 739–8111.
High Commissioner.—Filippo Grandi (Italy).

United Nations High Commissioner for Refugees (UNHCR), Regional Office for the United States and the Caribbean, 1800 Massachusetts Avenue, NW., Suite 500, Washington, DC 20036, phone (202) 296–5191.
Regional Representative.—Matthew Reynolds.

United Nations Children's Fund (UNICEF), UNICEF House, 3 United Nations Plaza, New York, NY 10017, phone (212) 326–7000.
Executive Director.—Anthony Lake (United States).

United Nations Children's Fund (UNICEF), Representation Office, 1775 K Street, NW., Suite 360, Washington, DC 20006, phone (212) 824–6463.
Public Partnerships Manager.—Sean Snyder.

United Nations Conference on Trade and Development (UNCTAD), Palais des Nations, 8–14 Avenue de la Paix, 1211 Geneva 10, Switzerland, phone (41–22) 917–1234.
Secretary General.—Mukhisa Kituyi (Kenya).

International Trade Centre (ITC), Palais des Nations, 1211 Geneva 10, Switzerland, phone (41–22) 730 01 11.

United Nations Development Programme (UNDP), 1 United Nations Plaza, New York, NY 10017, phone (212) 906–5000.
Administrator.—Achim Steiner (Germany).

United Nations Development Programme (UNDP), Representation Office, 1775 K Street, NW., Suite 500, Washington, DC 20006, phone (202) 331–9130.
Director.—Paul Clayman (United States).

UN Women (United Nations Entity for Gender Equality and the Empowerment of Women), 220 East 42nd Street, New York, NY 10017, phone (646) 781–4400.
Director.—Phumzile Mlambo-Ngcuka (South Africa).

United Nations Volunteers Programme (UNV), Postfach 260 111, D–53153 Bonn, Germany, phone (49–228) 815–2000.
Executive Coordinator.—Olivier Adam (France).

United Nations Environment Programme (UNEP), United Nations Avenue, Gigiri, P.O. Box 30552, 00100, Nairobi, Kenya, phone (254–20) 762–1234.
Executive Director.—Erik Solheim (Norway).

United Nations Environment Programme, Regional Office for North America, 900 17th Street, NW., Suite 506, Washington, DC 20006, phone (202) 785–0465.
Director.—Barbara Hendrie.

United Nations Human Settlements Programme (UN-HABITAT), United Nations Office at Nairobi, United Nations Avenue, Gigiri, P.O. Box 30030, Nairobi, 00100, Kenya, phone (254–20) 762–1234.
Executive Director.—Joan Clos (Spain).

United Nations Office on Drugs and Crime (UNODC), Vienna International Centre, P.O. Box 500, A–1400 Vienna, Austria, phone (43–1) 26060.
Executive Director.—Yury Fedotov (Russian Federation).

United Nations Population Fund (UNFPA), 605 Third Avenue, New York, NY 10158, phone (212) 297–5000.
Executive Director.—Natalia Kanem (Panama).

UNFPA Liaison Office, 2121 K Street, NW., Suite 800–A, Washington, DC 20037, phone (202) 653–1155.
Director.—Sarah Craven (United States).

United Nations Relief and Works Agency for Palestine Refugees in the Near East (UNRWA), Headquarters Amman, Bayader Wadi Seer, P.O. Box 140157, Amman 11814, Jordan, phone (+ 962 6) 580–8100. Headquarters Gaza, P.O. Box 338, IL 78100, Ashqelon, Israel, P.O. Box 371 Gaza City, Palestinian Territory, phone (+ 972 8) 288–7701.
Commissioner-General.—Pierre Krähenbühl (Switzerland).

UNRWA Representative Office, 1889 F Street, NW., 3rd Floor, Washington, DC 20006, phone (202) 974–3528.
Director.—Chris McGrath (acting) (United States).

World Food Programme (WFP), Via Cesare Giulio Viola 68, Parco dei Medici, 00148 Rome, Italy, phone (39–6) 65131.
Executive Director.—David Beasley (United States).

WFP U.S. Relations Office, 2121 K Street, NW., Suite 800–A, Washington, DC 20037, phone (202) 653–0010.
Director.—Jon Brause.

OTHER UNITED NATIONS ENTITIES

Office of the United Nations High Commissioner for Human Rights (OHCHR), Palais des Nations, CH–1211 Geneva 10, Switzerland, phone (41–022) 917–9220.
High Commissioner for Human Rights.—Zeid Ra'ad Al Hussein (Jordan).

Office of the United Nations High Commissioner for Human Rights (OHCHR), Washington DC Liaison Office, 2121 K Street, NW., Suite 800–B, Washington, DC 20037, phone (202) 653–2458.
Representative.—Mac Darrow.

United Nations Non-Governmental Liaison Office (NGLS), New York Office, United Nations Building DC1, Room 1106, New York, NY 10017, phone (212) 963–3125; Geneva Office, Room A1–50, Palais des Nations, 1211 Geneva 10, Switzerland, phone (41 22) 917–2076.
Officer-in-Charge, New York.—Susan Alzner.
Officer-in-Charge, Geneva.—Hamish Jenkins.

United Nations Office for Project Services (UNOPS), Marmorvej 51, P.O. Box 2695, 2100 Copenhagen, Denmark, phone (45–4) 533–7500.
Executive Director.—Grete Faremo (Norway).

UNOPS Liaison Office, 1775 K Street, NW., Suite 500, Washington, DC, phone (917) 200–8248.
Head of Office.—Felipe Munevar.

United Nations System Chief Executives Board (CEB) for Coordination, Geneva Office, C–553, Palais des Nations, CH–1211 Genève 10, Switzerland, phone (41–22) 917–3276; New York Office, DC2–0610, 2 United Nations Plaza, New York, NY 10017, phone (212) 963–8138.

United Nations System Staff College (UNSSC), Viale Maestri del Lavoro 10, 10127 Torino, Italy, phone (39 011) 653–5911.
Deputy Director and Head of Programmes.—Claire Messina.

United Nations University (UNU), 5–53–70 Jingumae, Shibuya-ku, Tokyo 150–8925, Japan, phone (81–3) 5467–1212.
Rector.—David Malone (Canada).

International Computing Centre (ICC), Palais des Nations, 1211 Geneva 10, Switzerland, phone (41–22) 929–1444.
Director.—Simon Jones.

Joint United Nations Programme on HIV / AIDS (UNAIDS), 20, Avenue Appia, CH–1211 Geneva 27, Switzerland, phone (41–22) 791–3666.
Executive Director.—Michel Sidibé.

UNAIDS Washington Office, 1889 F Street, NW., 3rd Floor, Washington, DC 20006, phone (202) 223–7611.
Director.—Lisa Carty.

RESEARCH AND TRAINING INSTITUTES

United Nations Institute for Disarmament Research (UNIDIR), Palais des Nations, 1211 Geneva 10, Switzerland, phone (41–22) 917–3186 / 1583.
Director.—Jarmo Sareva (Finland).

United Nations Institute for Training and Research (UNITAR), UNITAR, International Environment House, Chemin des Anémones 11–13, CH–1219 Châtelaine, Geneva-Switzerland, phone (41–22) 917–8400.
Executive Director.—Nikhil Seth (India).

United Nations International Research and Training Institute for the Advancement of Women (INSTRAW), Part of UN Women as July 2010.

United Nations Interregional Crime and Justice Research Institute (UNICRI), Viale Maestri del Lavoro, 10, 10127 Turin, Italy, phone (39–011) 6537–111.
Director.—Cindy J. Smith (United States).

United Nations Research Institute for Social Development (UNRISD), Palais des Nations, 1211 Geneva 10, Switzerland, phone (41–22) 917–3060.
Director.—Paul Ladd.

SPECIALIZED AGENCIES

Food and Agriculture Organization (FAO), Viale delle Terme di Caracalla, 00153 Rome, Italy, phone (39–6) 57051.
Director-General.—José Graziano da Silva (Brazil).

Food and Agriculture Organization, Liaison Office for North America, Suite 800–B, 2121 K Street, NW., Washington, DC 20037, phone (1–202) 653–2400.
Director.—Vimlendra Sharan (India).

International Civil Aviation Organization (ICAO), 999 University Street, Montreal, Quebec H3C 5H7, Canada, phone (1–514) 954–8219.
Secretary-General.—Dr. Fang Liu (China).

International Fund for Agricultural Development (IFAD), Via Paolo di Dono, 44, 00142 Rome, Italy, phone (39–6) 54591.
President.—Gilbert F. Houngbo (Togo).

External Affairs Department, IFAD North American Liaison Office, 1775 K Street, NW., Suite 500, Washington, DC 20006, phone (1–202) 331–9099.
Chief.— Deirdre McGrenra.

International Labour Organization (ILO), 4, Routes des Morillons, CH–1211 Geneva 22, Switzerland, phone (41–22) 799–6111.
Director-General.—Guy Ryder (United Kingdom).

ILO Washington Branch Office, 1801 I Street, NW., 9th Floor, Washington, DC 20006, phone (1–202) 617–3952.
Director.—Erick Zeballos.

International Maritime Organization (IMO), 4 Albert Embankment, London SE1 7SR, United Kingdom, phone (44–20) 7735–7611.
Secretary-General.—Kitack Lim (Republic of Korea).

International Monetary Fund (IMF), 700 19th Street, NW., Washington, DC 20431, phone (1–202) 623–7000.
Managing Director.—Christine Lagarde (France).

International Telecommunications Union (ITU), Palais des Nations, 1211 Geneva 20, Switzerland, phone (41–22) 730–5111.

Secretary-General.—Houlin Zhao (China).

United Nations Educational, Scientific, and Cultural Organization (UNESCO), 7 Place de Fontenoy, 75352 Paris 07 SP, France, phone (33–01) 4568–1000.
Director-General.—Irina Bokova (Bulgaria).

United Nations Industrial Development Organization (UNIDO), Vienna International Centre, Wagramerstr. 5, P.O. Box 300, A–1400 Vienna, Austria, phone (43–1) 26026–0.
Director-General.—Li Yong (China).

Universal Postal Union (UPU), International Bureau, Case Postale 312, 3015 Berne, Switzerland, phone (41–31) 350–3111.
Director-General.—Bishar Abdirahman Hussein (Kenya).

World Bank Group, 1818 H Street, NW., Washington, DC 20433, phone (1–202) 473–1000.
President.—Jim Yong Kim (United States).

World Health Organization (WHO), 20 Avenue Appia, 1211 Geneva 27, Switzerland, phone (41–22) 791–2111.
Director-General.—Tedros Adhanom Ghebreyesus (Ethiopia).

Pan American Health Organization / World Health Organization Regional Office for the Americas (PAHO), 525 23rd Street, NW., Washington, DC 20037, phone (1–202) 974–3000.
Director.—Carissa F. Etienne (Dominica).

World Intellectual Property Organization (WIPO), 34, chemin des Colombettes, CH–1211 Geneva 20, Switzerland, phone (41–22) 338–9111.
Director General.—Francis Gurry (Australia).

World Meteorological Organization (WMO), 7bis, avenue de la Paix, Case Postale 2300, CH–1211 Geneva 2, Switzerland, phone (41–22) 730–8111.
Secretary-General.—Petteri Taalas (Finland).

RELATED BODY

International Atomic Energy Agency (IAEA), Vienna International Centre, P.O. Box 100 A–1400 Vienna, Austria, phone (431) 2600–0.
Director General.—Yukiya Amano (Japan).

IAEA Washington Office, 1629 K Street, NW., Suite 450, Washington, DC 20006, phone (202) 293–8580.
Respresentative.—Andrew Semmel (United States).

(The IAEA is an independent intergovernmental organization under the aegis of the UN).

SPECIAL AND PERSONAL REPRESENTATIVES AND ENVOYS OF THE SECRETARY-GENERAL

AFRICA

Africa:
Special Adviser to the Secretary-General on Africa, OSAA.—Maged Abdelaziz (Egypt).
High Representative for the Least Developed Countries, Landlocked Developing Countries and Small Island Developing States, UN–OHRLLS.—Fekitamoeloa Katoa 'Utoikamanu (Tonga).
Special Adviser to the Secretary-General on Africa, OSAA.—David Mehdi Hamam (acting) (France).

African Union:
Special Representative of the Secretary-General to the African Union, UNOAU.—Haile Menkerios (South Africa).

Central Africa:
Special Representative of the Secretary-General and Head of UNOCA.—François Louncény Fall (Guinea).

Central African Republic:
Acting Special Representative of the Secretary-General and Head of the United Nations Integrated Peacebuilding Office in the Central African Republic.—Parfait Onanga-Anyanga (Gabon).
Deputy Special Representative of the Secretary-General and Deputy Head of Mission, MINUSCA.—Kenneth Gluck (United States).

Deputy Special Representative of the Secretary-General in the Central African Republic and UN Resident Coordinator and Resident Representative, BINUCA.—Najat Rochdi (Morocco).

Cote d'Ivoire:

Special Representative of the Secretary-General for Cote d'Ivoire and Head of UNOCI.—Aïchatou Mindaoudou Souleymane (Niger).

Deputy Special Representative of the Secretary-General for Cote d'Ivoire, UNOCI.—Simon Munzu (Cameroon).

Deputy Special Representative of the Secretary-General, UN Resident Coordinator, Humanitarian Coordinator and UNDP Resident Representative, UNOCI.—M'Baye Babacar Cisse (Senegal).

Democratic Republic of the Congo:

Special Representative of the Secretary-General for the Democratic Republic of the Congo and Head of MONUSCO.—Maman Sambo Sidikou (Niger).

Deputy Special Representative of the Secretary-General for the Democratic Republic of the Congo, Rule of Law, MONUSCO.—David Gressly (United States).

Deputy Special Representative for the United Nations Stabilization Mission in the Democratic Republic of the Congo, MONUSCO.—Mamadou Diallo (Guinea).

Equatorial Guinea and Gabon:

Special Adviser to the Secretary-General and Mediator in the border dispute between Equatorial Guinea and Gabon.—Nicolas Michel (Switzerland).

Great Lakes Region:

Special Representative of the Secretary-General for the Great Lakes Region.—Said Djinnit (Algeria).

Guinea-Bissau:

Special Representative of the Secretary-General and Head of UNOGBIS.—Modibo Touré (Mali).

Deputy Special Representative of the Secretary-General (Political) with UNIOGBIS.—Marco Carmignani (Brazil).

Deputy Special Representative of the Secretary-General in Guinea-Bissau, UN Resident Coordinator and UN Development Programme Resident Representative.—David McLachlan Karr (Australia).

Liberia:

Special Representative of the Secretary-General for Liberia and Head of UNMIL.—Farid Zarif (Afghanistan).

Deputy Special Representative for Rule of Law.—Waldemar Frey (South Africa).

Deputy Special Representative for Recovery and Governance.—Yacoub El Hillo (Sudan).

Libya:

Special Representative of the Secretary-General and Head of the United Nations Support Mission in Libya.—Ghassan Salamé (Lebanon).

Deputy Special Representative of the Secretary-General, Resident Coordinator and Humanitarian Coordinator.—Maria do Valle Ribeiro (Portugal).

Mali:

Special Representative of the Secretary-General and Head of Mission, MINUSMA.—Mahamat Saleh Annadif (Chad).

Deputy Special Representative of the Secretary-General in MINUSMA.—Koen Davidse (Netherlands).

Deputy Special Representative of the Secretary-General in MINUSMA and UN Resident Coordinator, Humanitarian Coordinator and Resident Representative of UNDP.—Mbaranga Gasarabwe (Rwanda).

Sahel:

Special Envoy of the Secretary-General for the Sahel.—Ruby Sandhu-Rojon (United States).

Somalia:

Special Representative of the Secretary-General for Somalia and Head of Mission, UNSOM.—Michael Keating (United Kingdom).

Deputy Special Representative of the Secretary-General for Somalia.—Raisedon Zenenga (Zimbabwe).

Deputy Special Representative, Resident and Humanitarian Coordinator in Somalia.—Peter de Clercq (Netherlands).

Sudan and South Sudan:

Special Envoy of the Secretary-General for Sudan and South Sudan.—Nicholas Haysom (South Africa).

South Sudan:

Special Representative of the Secretary-General and Head of UNMISS.—David Shearer (New Zealand).

Deputy Special Representative of the Secretary-General, UNMISS.—Alain Noudéhou (Benin).

Deputy Special Representative of the Secretary-General, Resident Coordinator, Humanitarian Coordinator and Resident Representative, UNMISS.—Eugene Owusu (Ghana).

Sudan / Abyei:

Head of Mission and Force Commander, UNISFA.—Major General Hassen Ebrahim Mussa (Ethiopia).

Sudan / Darfur:

Joint African Union-United National Special Representative for Darfur, Head of UNAMID and Joint Chief Mediator.—Jeremiah Nyamane Kingsley Mamabolo (South Africa).

Deputy Joint Special Representative-Pillar One, UNAMID.—Abiodun Oluremi Bashua (Nigeria).

Deputy Joint Special Representative-Pillar Two, UNAMID.—Bintou Keita (Guinea).

West Africa:

Special Representative of the Secretary-General and Head of UNOWA.—Mohammed Ibn Chambas (Ghana).

Deputy Special Representative of the United Nations Secretary-General for West Africa and the Sahel.—Ruby Sandhu-Rojon (United States).

Western Sahara:

Special Representative of the Secretary-General for Western Sahara and Head of MINURSO.—Kim Bolduc (Canada).

Personal Envoy of the Secretary-General for Western Sahara.—Horst Köhler (Germany).

THE AMERICAS

Colombia:

Special Representative of the Secretary-General for Colombia and Head of Mission.—Jean Arnault (France).

El Salvador:

Special Envoy to the Secretary-General to Facilitate Dialogue in El Salvador.—Benito Andion (Mexico).

Guyana / Venezuela:

Personal Representative of the Secretary-General on the Border Controversy between Guyana and Venezuela.—Dag Halvor Nylander (Norway).

Haiti:

Special Representative of the Secretary-General and Head of Mission, MINUSTAH.—Sandra Honoré (Trinidad and Tobago).

Deputy Special Representative of the Secretary-General, MINUSTAH.—Susan D. Page (United States).

Deputy Special Representative of the Secretary-General and United Nations Resident Coordinator and Humanitarian Coordinator, MINUSTAH.—M. El-Mostafa Benlamlih (Morocco).

Special Adviser to the Secretary-General for Community-based Medicine and Lessons from Haiti.—Paul Farmer (United States).

Deputy Special Representative of the United Nations Mission for Justice Support in Haiti.—Mamadou Diallo (Guinea).

Special Envoy of the Secretary-General for Haiti.—Josette Sheeran (United States).

ASIA AND THE PACIFIC

Afghanistan:

Special Representative of the Secretary-General for Afghanistan and Head of UNAMA.—Tadamichi Yamamoto (Japan).

Deputy Special Representative of the Secretary-General, UN Resident Coordinator and UN Humanitarian Coordinator for Afghanistan, UNAMA.—Toby Lanzer (United Kingdom).

Deputy Special Representative of the Secretary-General (Political) for UNAMA.—Pernille Dahler Kardel (Denmark).

Central Asia:

Special Representative of the Secretary-General and Head of the UN Regional Centre for Preventive Diplomacy for Central Asia.—Natalia Gherman (Republic of Moldova).

India-Pakistan:

Chief Military Observer and Head of Mission, UNMOGIP.—Major General Per Lodin (Sweden).

Myanmar:

Special Adviser of the Secretary-General for Myanmar.—Vijay Nambiar (India).

Timor Leste:

Special Adviser of the Secretary-General for Timor-Leste.—Noeleen Heyzer (Singapore).

EUROPE

Cyprus:

Special Representative of the Secretary-General and Head of Mission, UNFICYP.—Elizabeth Spehar (Canada).

Special Adviser to the Secretary-General on Cyprus (Interim).—Elizabeth Spehar (Canada).

Former Yugoslav Republic of Macedonia-Greece:

Personal Envoy of the Secretary-General for the Greece-RYROM Talks.—Matthew Nimetz (United States).

Georgia:

Nations Representative.—Antti Turunen (Finland).

Kosovo:

Special Representative of the Secretary-General and Head of Mission, UNMIK.—Zahir Tanin (Afghanistan).

MIDDLE EAST

Middle East:

Special Coordinator for the Middle East Peace Process and Personal Representative of the Secretary-General to the Palestine Liberation Organization and the Palestinian Authority.—Nickolay Mladenov (Bulgaria).

Deputy Special Coordinator for the Middle East Peace Process/United Nations Coordinator for Humanitarian Aid and Development Activities in the Occupied Palestinian Territory.—Robert Piper (Australia).

Special Envoy for the Implementation of Security Council Resolution 1559.—Jeffrey D. Feltman (United States).

Head of Mission and Chief of Staff of UNTSO.—Major General Kristin Lund (Norway).

Afghanistan:

Special Representative of the Secretary-General for Afghanistan and Head of UNAMA.—Tadamichi Yamamoto (Japan).

Deputy Special Representative of the Secretary-General, UN Resident Coordinator and UN Humanitarian Coordinator for Afghanistan, UNAMA.—Toby Lanzer (United Kingdom).

Deputy Special Representative of the Secretary-General (Political) for UNAMA.—Pernille Dahler Kardel (Denmark).

Iraq (UNAMI):

Special Representative of the Secretary-General for Iraq and Head of Mission, UNAMI.—Ján Kubiš (Slovakia).

Deputy Special Representative of the Secretary-General for Political Affairs, UNAMI.—György Busztin (Hungary).

Deputy Special Representative of the Secretary-General (Development and Humanitarian Support) and Resident Coordinator/Humanitarian Coordinator for Iraq, UNAMI.—Lise Grande (United States).

Special Adviser for Relocation of Camp Hurriya Residents Outside of Iraq.—Jane Holl Lute (United States).

Kuwait:

Humanitarian Envoy of the Secretary-General.—Ahmed Al Meraikhi (Qatar).

Lebanon:

Special Coordinator of the Secretary-General for Lebanon.—Sigrid Kaag (Netherlands).

Deputy Special Coordinator of the Secretary-General for Lebanon, UN Resident Coordinator and UNDP Resident Representative.—Philippe Lazzarini (Switzerland).

Head of Mission and Force Commander of UNIFIL.—Major General Michael Beary (Ireland).

Libya:

Special Representative of the Secretary-General and Head of Mission, UNSMIL.—Ghassan Salamé (Lebanon).

Deputy Special Representative and Deputy Head of the United Nations Support Mission in Libya, UNSMIL.—Maria do Valle Ribeiro (Ireland).

Syria:

Special Envoy of the Secretary-General for Syria.—Staffan de Mistura (Italy / Sweden).

Deputy Special Envoy of the Secretary-General for Syria.—Ramzy Ezzeldin Ramzy (Egypt).

Syria Golan Heights:

Head of Mission and Force Commander of the UN Disengagement Observer Force (UNDOF).—Major General Jai Shanker Menon (India).

Yemen:

Special Adviser to the Secretary-General on Yemen.—Ismail Ould Cheikh Ahmed (Mauritania).

OTHER HIGH LEVEL APPOINTMENTS

Special Advisers to the Secretary-General: Joseph V. Reed (United States), Iqbal Riza (Pakistan), Jennifer Welsh (Canada).

Alliance of Civilizations:

High Representative.—Nassir Abdulaziz al-Nasser (Qatar).

Avian and Human Influenza (Bird flu):

Senior United Nations System Coordinator for Avian and Human Influenza.—David Nabarro (United Kingdom).

Children and Armed Conflict:

Special Representative.—Virginia Gamba (Argentina).

Cities and Climate Change:

Special Envoy.—Michael Bloomberg (United States).

Climate Change:

Special Envoys of the Secretary-General on Climate Change: John Kufuor (Ghana), Mary Robinson (Ireland), Jens Stoltenberg (Norway).

Special Adviser to the Secretary-General on Climate Change.—Robert Orr (United States).

Disability and Accessibility:

Special Envoy on Disability and Accessibility.—María Soledad Cisternas Reyes (Chile).

Disaster Reduction:

Special Representative.—Robert Glasser (Australia).

Disaster Risk Reduction and Water:

Special Envoy.—Han Seung-soo (Republic of Korea).

Ebola Virus Disease:

Special Envoy.—David Nabarro (United Kingdom).

Financing for Development:

Special Adviser.—Phillipe Douste-Blazy (France).

Food Security and Nutrition:

Special Representative.—David Nabarro (United Kingdom).

Global Education:

Special Representative.—Gordon Brown (United Kingdom).

HIV / AIDS in Africa:

Special Envoy.—Speciosa Wandira-Kasibwe (Uganda).

HIV / AIDS in Asia and in the Pacific:

Special Envoy.—Prasada Rao V.R. Jonnalagadda (India).

HIV / AIDS in the Caribbean Region:

Special Envoy.—John Edward Green (Gyana).

HIV / AIDS in Eastern Europe and Central Asia:

Special Envoy.—Michel Kazatchkine (France).

Internet Governance Forum:

Chair of the Multi-Stakeholder Advisory Group (MAG).—Lynn St. Amour (United States).

Malaria and Financing of Health-Related Millennium Development Goals:

Special Envoy.—Ray Chambers (United States).

Migration:

Special Representative.—Louise Arbour (Canada).

Millennium Development Goals:

Special Adviser.—Jeffrey D. Sachs (United States).

Prevention of Genocide:

Special Adviser.—Adama Dieng (Senegal).

Post-2015 Development Planning:

Special Adviser.—Amina Mohammed (Nigeria).

Road Safety:

Special Envoy.—Jean Todt (France).

Sexual Violence in Conflict:

Special Representative.—Pramila Patten (Mauritius).

South-South Cooperation:

Special Envoy.—Jorge Chediek (Argentina).

Sport for Development and Peace:

Special Adviser.—Wilfried Lemke (Germany).

Sustainable Energy for All:

Special Representative.—Rachel Kyte (United Kingdom).

Tuberculosis:

Special Envoy.—Eric Goosby (United States).

Nations International School (UNIS):

Special Representative.—Michael Alderstein (United States).

University for Peace:

Special Representative.—Judy Cheng-Hopkins (Malaysia).

Violence Against Children:

Special Representative.—Marta Santos Pais (Portugal).

Youth:

Envoy.—Jayathma Wickramanayake (Sri Lanka).

Youth Refugees and Sport:

Special Envoy.—Jacques Rogge (Belgium).

WORLD BANK GROUP

The World Bank Group comprises five organizations: the International Bank for Reconstruction and Development (IBRD), the International Development Association (IDA), the International Finance Corporation (IFC), the Multilateral Investment Guarantee Agency (MIGA), and the International Centre for the Settlement of Investment Disputes (ICSID).

Headquarters: 1818 H Street, NW., 20433, (202) 473–1000

INTERNATIONAL BANK FOR RECONSTRUCTION AND DEVELOPMENT

President.—Jim Yong Kim.

Managing Director and World Bank Group Chief Administrative Officer.—Shaolin Yang.

Managing Director and World Bank Group Chief Financial Officer.—Joaquim Levy.

Chief Executive Officer.—Kristalina Georgieva.

Chairperson, Inspection Panel.—Gonzalo Castro.

Senior Vice President and World Bank Group General Counsel.—Sandie Okoro.

Senior Vice President, Development Economics, and Chief Economist.—Paul Romer.

Senior Vice President for the 2030 Development Agenda, United Nations Relations, and Partnerships Operations.—Mahmoud Mohieldin.

Vice President, Human Development Vice Presidency.—Keith Hansen.

World Bank Group Vice President Information and Technology Solutions and WBG Chief Information Officer.—Denis Robitaille.

Vice President and World Bank Group Controller.—Bernard Lauwers.

Vice President, Budget, Performance Review and Strategic Planning.—Antonella Bassani.

Vice President and Corporate Secretary.—Yvonne Tsikata.

Vice President and Treasurer.—Arunma Oteh.

Vice President of:

Africa.—Makhtar Diop.

East Asia and Pacific.—Victoria Kwakwa.

South Asia.—Annette Dixon.

Vice President, World Bank Group External and Corporate Relations.—Sheila Redzepi.

North American Affairs (External and Corporate Relations) Special Representative.—William C. Danvers.

Europe (External and Corporate Relations) Special Representative and Director.—Mario Alexander Sander von Torklus.

UN External Affairs, Special Representative.—Bjorn Erik Gillsater.

Japan-External and Corporate Relations, Special Representative.—Masato Miyazaki.

Human Resources.—Sean McGrath.

Latin America and the Caribbean.—Jorge Familiar Calderon.

Middle East and North Africa.—Hafez Ghanem.

Vice President of Europe and Central Asia.—Cyril Muller.

Vice President and Network Head, Operations Policy and Country Services.—Manuela Ferro.

Vice President, Global Themes.—Hartwig Schafer.

Vice President, Equitable Growth, Finance and Institutions.—Jan Walliser.

Vice President, Sustainable Development Vice Presidency.—Laura Tuck.

Vice President, Development Finance.—Axel van Trotsenburg.

Vice President and Bank Group Risk Officer.—Lakshmi Shyam-Sunder.

Vice President, Compliance Advisor/Ombudsman.—Osvaldo Luis Gratacós.

Director-General, Independent Evaluation.—Caroline Heider.

Vice President and Auditor-General.—Hiroshi Naka.

Vice President, Institutional Integrity.—Pascale Hélène Dubois.

Vice President and World Bank Group Chief Ethics Officer.—Ousmane Diagana.

OTHER WORLD BANK OFFICES

London: Millbank Tower, 12th Floor, 21–24 Millbank, London SW1P 4QP.

Geneva: 3, Chemin Louis Dunant, CP 66, CH 1211, Geneva 10, Switzerland.

Paris: 66, Avenue d'Iena, 75116 Paris, France.

Brussels: Avenue Marnix 17, 2nd Floor, 1000 Brussels, Belgium.

Tokyo: Fukoku Seimei Building, 10th Floor, 2–2–2 Uchisawai-cho, Chiyoda-Ku, Tokyo 100, Japan.

Sydney: CML Building Level 19–14, Martin Place, Sydney, NSW 2000, Australia.

Berlin: Reichpietschufer 20, 10785 Berlin, Germany.

BOARD OF EXECUTIVE DIRECTORS

Bahrain, Egypt (Arab Republic of), Iraq, Jordan, Kuwait, Lebanon, Libya, Maldives, Oman, Qatar, United Arab Emirates, Yemen (Republic of).

Executive Director.—Merza H. Hasan (Kuwait).

Alternate.—Ragui El-Etreby (Arab Republic of Egypt).

Saudi Arabia.

Executive Director.—Khalid Alkhudairy.

Alternate.—Turki Almutairi.

Austria, Belarus, Belgium, Czech Republic, Hungary, Kazakhstan, Luxembourg, Slovak Republic, Slovenia, Turkey.

Executive Director.—Franciscus Godts (Belgium).

Alternate.—Guenther Schoenleitner (Austria).

Australia, Cambodia, Kiribati, Korea (Republic of), Marshall Islands, Micronesia (Federated States of), Mongolia, New Zealand, Palau, Papua New Guinea, Samoa, Solomon Islands, Vanuatu.

Executive Director.—Jason Allford (Australia).

Alternate.—Hoe Jeong Kim (Republic of Korea).

Albania, Greece, Italy, Malta, Portugal, San Marino, Timor-Leste.

Executive Director.—Patrizio Pagano (Italy).

Alternate.—Nuno Mota Pinto (Portugal).

United States.

Executive Director.—Karen Mathiasen.

Alternate.—Vacant.

Brazil, Colombia, Dominican Republic, Ecuador, Haiti, Panama, Philippines, Suriname, Trinidad and Tobago.

Executive Director.—Otaviano Canuto (Brazil).

Alternate.—Diana Quintero (Colombia).

Germany.

Executive Director.—Juergen Zattler.

Alternate.—Claus Happe.

Afghanistan, Algeria, Ghana, Iran (Islamic Republic of), Morocco, Pakistan, Tunisia.

Executive Director.—Omar Bougara (Algeria).
Alternate.—Nasir Mahmood Khosa (Pakistan).

France.
Executive Director.—Herve M. Jodon de Villeroche.
Alternate.—Benoit Catzaras.

Benin, Burkina Faso, Cameroon, Cape Verde, Central African Republic, Chad, Comoros, Congo (Democratic Republic of), Congo (Republic of), Cote d'lvoire, Djibouti, Equatorial Guinea, Gabon, Guinea, Guinea-Bissau, Madagascar, Mali, Mauritania, Mauritius, Niger, Rwanda, Sao Tome and Principe, Senegal, Togo.
Executive Director.—Seydou Bouda (Burkina Faso).
Alternate.—Jean-Claude Tchatchouang (Cameroon).

Fiji, Indonesia, Lao People's Democratic Republic, Malaysia, Myanmar, Nepal, Singapore, Thailand, Tonga, Vietnam.
Executive Director.—Andin Hadiyanto (Indonesia).
Alternate.—Mastura Binti Adul Karim (Malaysia).

Denmark, Estonia, Finland, Iceland, Latvia, Lithuania, Norway, Sweden.
Executive Director.—Susan Ulbaek (Finland).
Alternate.—Martin Poder (Estonia).

Russian Federation, Syrian Arab Republic.
Executive Director.—Andrey Lushin.
Alternate.—Eugene Miagkov.

Costa Rica, El Salvador, Guatemala, Honduras, Mexico, Nicaragua, Spain, Venezuela (Republica Bolivariana de).
Executive Director.—Fernando Jimenez (Spain).
Alternate.—Rodrigo Carriedo (Mexico).

Antigua and Barbuda, Bahamas (The), Barbados, Belize, Canada, Dominica, Grenada, Guyana, Ireland, Jamaica, St. Kitts and Nevis, St. Lucia, St. Vincent and the Grenadines.
Executive Director.—Christine Hogan (Canada).
Alternate.—Peteranne Donalson (Jamaica).

Armenia, Bosnia and Herzegovina, Bulgaria, Croatia, Cyprus, Georgia, Israel, Macedonia (former Yugoslav Republic of), Moldova, Netherlands, Romania, Ukraine.
Executive Director.—Frank Heemskerk (Netherlands).
Alternate.—Roman Kachur (Ukraine)

Japan.
Executive Director.—Kazuhiko Koguchi.
Alternate.—Kenichi Nishikata.

Argentina, Bolivia, Chile, Paraguay, Peru, Uruguay.
Executive Director.—Maximo Torero (Peru).
Alternate.—Daniel Pierini (Argentina).

United Kingdom.
Executive Director.—Melanie Robinson.
Alternate.—Clare Roberts.

Angola, Nigeria, South Africa.
Executive Director.—Bongi Kunene (South Africa).
Alternate.—Haruna Mohammed (Nigeria).

Botswana, Burundi, Eritrea, Ethiopia, Gambia (The), Kenya, Lesotho, Liberia, Malawi, Mozambique, Namibia, Seychelles, Sierra Leone, Sudan, Swaziland, Tanzania, Uganda, Zambia, Zimbabwe.
Executive Director.—Andrew N. Bvumbe (Zimbabwe).
Alternate.—Anne Kabagambe (Uganda).

Bangladesh, Bhutan, India, Sri Lanka.
Executive Director.—Aparna Subramani (India).
Alternate.—Muhammad Bhuiyan (Bangladesh).

Azerbaijan, Serbia and Montenegro, Kyrgyz Republic, Poland, Switzerland, Tajikistan, Turkmenistan, Uzbekistan, Yugoslavia (Fed. Rep. of), Switzerland, Yemen, (Republic of).
Executive Director.—Werner Gruber (Switzerland).
Alternate.—Paulina Gomulak (Poland).

China.
Executive Director.—Yingming Yang.
Alternate.—Minwen Zhang.

INTERNATIONAL DEVELOPMENT ASSOCIATION

[The officers, executive directors, and alternates are the same as those of the International Bank for Reconstruction and Development.]

INTERNATIONAL FINANCE CORPORATION

President.—Jim Yong Kim.
Executive Vice President and Chief Executive Officer.—Philippe Le Houérou.
Vice President and Corporate Secretary.—Yvonne Tsikata.
Director-General, Independent Evaluation.—Caroline Heider.
Compliance Advisor/Ombudsman (IFC/ICC and MIGA).—Osvaldo Luis Gratacos.
Vice President and General Counsel.—Ethiopis Tafara.
Vice President:
Human Resource.—Sean McGrath.
Risk Management and Financial Stability.—Mohamed Gould.
Blended Finance and Partnerships.—Snezana Stoiljkovic.
Portfolio Management.—Saran G. Kebet-Koulibaly.
Treasury and Syndications.—Jingdong Hua.
New Business.—Stephanie von Friedeburg.
Economics and Private Sector Development.—Hans Peters Lankes.
Corporate Strategy and Resources.—Lizabeth Bronder (acting).
Communications and Outreach.—Karin Finkelston.
Asset Management Company Services and CEO, IFC Asset Management Company.—Marcos Brujis.
Director, Communications Services.—Bruce Moats.
Director, Office of:
Budget and Business Administration.—Lizabeth Bronder.
Blended Finance.—Martin Spicer.
Climate Business.—Alzbeta Klein.
Development Partner Relations.—Anita Bhatia.
Corporate Strategy.—Aisha Elaine Williams.
Cross Cutting Advisory Solutions.—Mary Porter Peschka.
Information and Technology.—Suzannah Herring Carr.
Legal.—Fady M. Zeidan.
Business Risk and Compliance.—Ceri Wyn Lawley.
Environment, Social and Governance Sustainability Advice and Solutions.—Morgan J. Landy.
Human Resources.—Davide Bonzano.
Financial Institutions Group.—Paulo de Bolle.
Infrastructure and Natural Resources.—Bernard Sheahan.
Portfolio Management.—Deema Fakhoury.
Country Economics and Engagement.—Mona E. Haddad.
Sector Economics and Development Impact.—Issa Faye.
Global Macro and Market Research.—Jean Pierre Lacombe.
Corporate Risk Management.—Tarek S. Himmo.
Investment and Credit Risk.—Khawaja Aftab Ahmed.
Special Operations.—Eric J. Jourdanet.
Manufacturing, Agribusiness and Services.—Sergio Pimenta.
East Asia and the Pacific.—Vivek Pathak.
Sub-Saharan Africa.—Cheikh O. Seydi.
Europe and Central Asia.—Tomasz Telma.
South Asia.—Mengistu Alemayehu.
Middle East and North Africa.—Mouayed Makhlouf.
Latin America and the Caribbean.—Irene Arias.
Telecom, Media, Tech and Venture Investing.—Atul Mehta.
Treasury Market Operations.—Monish Mahurkar.
Treasury Client Solutions.—Keshav Gaur.
Treasury Quantitative Analysis.—Takehisa Eguchi.
Syndications and FCS Mobilizations.—Georgina E. Baker.
Tokyo.—Toshitake Kurosawa.
Western Europe.—Stephanie J. Miller.

MULTILATERAL INVESTMENT GUARANTEE AGENCY

President.—Jim Yong Kim.
Executive Vice President and Chief Executive Officer.—Keiko Honda.

Director and General Counsel, Legal Affairs and Claims Group.—Aradhana Kumar-Capoor.
Compliance Advisor/Ombudsman (IFC/ICC and MIGA).—Osvaldo Luis Gratacos.
Vice President and Chief Operating Officer.—Sarvesh Suri (acting).
Operations Group.—Sarvesh Suri.
Chief Underwriter, Operations Group.—Muhamet Fall.
Director, Economics and Sustainability Group.—Merli Margaret Baroudi.
Director, Corporate Risk.—Santiago Assalini.
Head, MIGA Africa Hub.—Hoda Moustafa.
Head, MIGA Europe Hub.—Christopher Millward (acting).
Head, MIGA North Asia.—Jae Hyung Kwon.
Head, MIGA Singapore Office.—Timothy Histed.

FOREIGN DIPLOMATIC OFFICES IN THE UNITED STATES

AFGHANISTAN

Embassy of Afghanistan
2341 Wyoming Avenue, NW., Washington, DC 20008
phone (202) 483–6410, fax 483–6488
His Excellency Hamdullah Mohib
Ambassador E. and P.
Consular Offices:
California, Los Angeles
New York, New York

AFRICAN UNION

Delegation of the African Union Mission
1640 Wisconsin Avenue, NW., Washington, DC 20007
Embassy of the African Union
phone (202) 342–1100, fax 342–1101
Her Excellency Arikana Chihombori Quao
Ambassador (Head of Delegation)

ALBANIA

Embassy of the Republic of Albania
2100 S Street, NW., Washington, DC 20008
phone (202) 223–4942, fax 628–7342
Her Excellency Floreta Faber
Ambassador E. and P.
Consular Offices:
Connecticut, Greenwich
Georgia, Avondale Estates
Louisiana, New Orleans
Massachusetts, Boston
Michigan, West Bloomfield
Missouri, Blue Springs
New York, New York
North Carolina, Southern Pines
Texas, Houston

ALGERIA

Embassy of the Peoples Democratic Republic of Algeria
2118 Kalorama Road, NW., Washington, DC 20008
phone (202) 265–2800, fax 667–2174
His Excellency Madjid Bougerra
Ambassador E. and P.
Consular Office: New York, New York

ANDORRA

Embassy of Andorra
2 United Nations Plaza, 27th Floor, New York, NY 10017
phone (212) 750–8064, fax 750–6630
Her Excellency Elisenda Vives Balmaña
Ambassador E. and P.
Consular Office: California, La Jolla

ANGOLA

Embassy of the Republic of Angola
2100–2108 16th Street, NW., Washington, DC 20009
phone (202) 785–1156, fax 785–1258
His Excellency Agostinho Tavares da Silva Neto
Ambassador E. and P.
Consular Offices:
California, Los Angeles
New York, New York
Texas, Houston

ANTIGUA AND BARBUDA

Embassy of Antigua and Barbuda
3216 New Mexico Avenue, NW., Washington, DC 20016
phone (202) 362–5122, fax 362–5225
His Excellency Ronald Sanders
Ambassador E. and P.
Consular Offices:
District of Columbia, Washington
Florida, Miami
New York, New York
Puerto Rico, Guaynabo

ARGENTINA

Embassy of the Argentine Republic
1600 New Hampshire Avenue, NW., Washington, DC 20009
phone (202) 238–6400, fax 332–3171
The Honorable Serigo Perez Gunella
Minister (Charge d'Affaires ad Interim)
Consular Offices:
California, Los Angeles
Florida, Miami
Georgia, Atlanta
Illinois, Chicago
New York, New York
Texas, Houston

ARMENIA

Embassy of the Republic of Armenia
2225 R Street, NW., Washington, DC 20008
phone (202) 319–1976, fax 319–2982
His Excellency Grigor Hovhannissian

Ambassador E. and P.
Consular Offices:
California, Glendale
District of Columbia, Washington

AUSTRALIA

Embassy of Australia
1601 Massachusetts Avenue, NW., Washington, DC 20036
phone (202) 797–3000, fax 797–3331
His Excellency Joseph Benedict Hockey
Ambassador E. and P.
Consular Offices:
California, San Francisco
Colorado, Denver
District of Columbia, Washington
Hawaii, Honolulu
Illinois, Chicago
New York, New York
Texas, Houston

AUSTRIA

Embassy of Austria
3524 International Court, NW., Washington, DC 20008–3035
phone (202) 895–6700, fax 895–6773
His Excellency Wolfgang Waldner
Ambassador E. and P.
Consular Offices:
Alaska, Anchorage
Arizona, Scottsdale
California:
Los Angeles
San Francisco
Florida:
Estero
Hollywood
Orlando
Georgia, Atlanta
Hawaii, Honolulu
Louisiana, New Orleans
Massachusetts, Boston
Michigan, Detroit
Minnesota, St. Paul
Missouri:
Kansas City
St. Louis
Nevada, Las Vegas
New York, New York
Ohio, Columbus
Oregon, Portland
Pennsylvania:
Philadelphia
Pittsburgh
Puerto Rico, San Juan
South Carolina, Cowpens
Texas, Houston
Utah, Salt Lake City
Virgin Islands, St. Thomas
Virginia, Richmond

AZERBAIJAN

Embassy of the Republic of Azerbaijan
2741 34th Street, NW., Washington, DC 20008
phone (202) 337–3500, fax 337–5911
His Excellency Elin Emir Oglu Suleymanov
Ambassador E. and P.
Consular Offices:
California, Los Angeles
New Mexico, Santa Fe

BAHAMAS

Embassy of the Commonwealth of The Bahamas
2220 Massachusetts Avenue, NW., Washington, DC 20008
phone (202) 319–2660, fax 319–2668
His Excelleny Eugene Glenwood Newry
Ambassador E. and P.
Consular Offices:
District of Columbia, Washington
Florida, Miami
Georgia, Atlanta
New York, New York

BAHRAIN

Embassy of the Kingdom of Bahrain
3502 International Drive, NW., Washington, DC 20008
phone (202) 342–0741, fax 362–2192
His Excellency Abdulla Bin Rashed Al Khalifa
Ambassador E. and P.
Consular Offices:
California, San Diego
New York, New York

BANGLADESH

Embassy of the People's Republic of Bangladesh
3510 International Drive, NW., Washington, DC 20008
phone (202) 244–0183, fax 244–5366
His Excellency Mohammad Ziauddin
Ambassador E. and P.
Consular Offices:
California, Los Angeles
Louisiana, New Orleans
New York, New York

BARBADOS

Embassy of Barbados
2144 Wyoming Avenue, NW., Washington, DC 20008
phone (202) 939–9200, fax 332–7467
His Excellency Selwin Charles Hart
Ambassador E. and P.
Consular Offices:
California:
Los Angeles

San Francisco
Florida, Miami
Georgia, Atlanta
Illinois, Chicago
Kentucky, Louisville
Louisiana, New Orleans
Michigan, Detroit
New York, New York
Oregon, Portland
South Carolina, Charleston
Texas, Sugar Land

BELARUS

Embassy of the Republic of Belarus
1619 New Hampshire Avenue, NW., Washington, DC 20009
phone (202) 986–1604, fax 986–1805
Mr. Pavel Shidlovsky
Counselor (Charge d'Affaires ad Interim)
Consular Offices:
District of Columbia, Washington
New York, New York

BELGIUM

Embassy of Belgium
3330 Garfield Street, NW., Washington, DC 20008
phone (202) 333–6900, fax 333–3079
His Excellency Dirk Jozef M. Wouters
Ambassador E. and P.
Consular Offices:
Arizona, Phoenix
California:
Los Angeles
San Diego
San Francisco
Colorado, Denver
Connecticut, Greenwich
District of Columbia, Washington
Florida, Miami
Georgia, Atlanta
Hawaii, Honolulu
Illinois:
Chicago
Moline
Kentucky, Louisville
Louisiana, New Orleans
Maryland, Baltimore
Massachusetts, Boston
Michigan, Bloomfield Hills
Minnesota, St. Paul
Missouri, Kansas City
New York, New York
Ohio, Cincinnati
Oregon, Portland
Pennsylvania:
Philadelphia
Pittsburgh
Puerto Rico, San Juan
Texas:
Fort Worth
Houston
San Antonio
Utah, Salt Lake City
Virginia, Virginia Beach
Washington, Seattle
Wisconsin, Milwaukee

BELIZE

Embassy of Belize
2535 Massachusetts Avenue, NW., Washington, DC 20008
phone (202) 332–9636, fax 332–6888
His Excellency Francisco Daniel Gutierez
Ambassador E. and P.
Consular Offices:
California:
Los Angeles
San Francisco
District of Columbia, Washington
Florida, Coral Gables
Georgia, Atlanta
Illinois:
Belleville
Des Plaines
Louisiana, New Orleans
Michigan, Detroit
North Carolina, Wilmington
Ohio, Dayton
Texas:
Dallas
Houston
San Antonio

BENIN

Embassy of the Republic of Benin
2124 Kalorama Road, NW., Washington, DC 2008
phone (202) 232–6656, fax (202) 265–1996
His Excellency Hector Sedozan Ruffin Festus Posset
Ambassador E. and P.

BOLIVIA

Embassy of Bolivia
3014 Massachusetts Avenue, NW., Washington, DC 20008
phone (202) 483–4410, fax 328–3712
Alejandro Roberto Bilbao La Vieja Ruiz
Counselor (Charge d'Affaires ad Interim)
Consular Offices:
California, Los Angeles
District of Columbia, Washington
Florida, Miami
New York, New York
Puerto Rico, San Juan

BOSNIA AND HERZEGOVINA

Embassy of Bosnia and Herzegovina

2109 E Street, NW., Washington, DC 20037
phone (202) 337–1500, fax 337–1502
His Excellency Haris Hrle
Ambassador E. and P.
Consular Office: Illinois, Chicago

BOTSWANA

Embassy of the Republic of Botswana
1531–1533 New Hampshire Avenue, NW., Washington, DC 20036
phone (202) 244–4990, fax 244–4164
His Excellency David John Newman
Ambassador E. and P.
Consular Offices:
- California:
  - San Francisco
  - Santa Monica
- Michigan, Southfield
- Texas, Houston

BRAZIL

Brazilian Embassy
3006 Massachusetts Avenue, NW., Washington, DC 20008
phone (202) 238–2700, fax 238–2827
His Excellency Sergio Silva Do Amaral
Ambassador E. and P.
Consular Offices:
- Arizona, Tempe
- California:
  - La Jolla
  - Los Angeles
  - San Francisco
- Connecticut, Hartford
- District of Columbia, Washington
- Florida, Miami
- Georgia, Atlanta
- Hawaii, Honolulu
- Illinois, Chicago
- Louisiana, New Orleans
- Massachusetts, Boston
- Nevada, Las Vegas
- New York, New York
- Pennsylvania, Philadelphia
- Tennessee, Memphis
- Texas, Houston
- Utah, Salt Lake City
- Virginia, Norfolk
- Washington, Seattle

BRUNEI

Embassy of the State of Brunei Darussalam
3520 International Court, NW., Washington, DC 20008
phone (202) 237–1838, fax 885–0560
His Excellency Serbini Ali
Ambassador E. and P.

BULGARIA

Embassy of the Republic of Bulgaria
1621 22nd Street, NW., Washington, DC 20008
phone (202) 387–0174, fax 234–7973
His Excellency Tihomir Anguelov Stoytchev
Ambassador E. and P.
Consular Offices:
- California:
  - Los Angeles
  - Palm Springs
  - Sacramento
- District of Columbia, Washington
- Florida, Boca Raton
- Illinois, Chicago
- Maine, Portland
- Massachusetts, Newton
- Nevada, Las Vegas
- New York, New York
- Pennsylvania:
  - Media
  - West Homestead
- South Carolina, Columbia

BURKINA FASO

Embassy of Burkina Faso
2340 Massachusetts Avenue, NW., Washington, DC 20008
phone (202) 332–5577, fax 667–1882
His Excellency Seydou Kabore
Ambassador E. and P.
Consular Offices:
- California, Los Angeles
- Louisiana, New Orleans

BURMA

Embassy of the Union of Burma
2300 S Street, NW., Washington, DC 20008
phone (202) 332–3344, fax 332–4351
His Excellency Aung Lynn
Ambassador E. and P.
Consular Office: New York, New York

BURUNDI

Embassy of the Republic of Burundi
2233 Wisconsin Avenue, NW., Suite 408, Washington, DC 20007
phone (202) 342–2574, fax 342–2578
Benjamin Manirakiza
First Counselor (Charge d'Affaires ad Interim)
Consular Office: California, Los Angeles

CABO VERDE

Embassy of the Republic of Cabo Verde
3415 Massachusetts Avenue, NW., Washington, DC 20007
phone (202) 965–6820, fax 965–1207
His Excellency Jose Luis Fialho Rocha
Ambassador E. and P.

CAMBODIA

Royal Embassy of Cambodia
4530 16th Street, NW., Washington, DC 20011
phone (202) 726–7742, fax 726–8381
His Excellency Chum Bun Rong
Ambassador E. and P.
Consular Offices:
California, Long Beach
Massachusetts, Lowell
Pennsylvania, Philadelphia
Washington, Seattle

CAMEROON

Embassy of the Republic of Cameroon
3400 International Drive, NW., Washington, DC 20008
phone (202) 265–8790, fax 387–3826
His Excellency Essomba Etoundi
Ambassador E. and P.
Consular Offices:
California, San Francisco
Texas, Houston

CANADA

Embassy of Canada
501 Pennsylvania Avenue, NW., Washington, DC 20001
phone (202) 682–1740, fax 682–7726
His Excellency David Brookes MacNaughton
Ambassador E. and P.
Consular Offices:
California:
Los Angeles
Palo Alto
San Diego
San Francisco
Colorado, Denver
District of Columbia, Washington
Florida, Miami
Georgia, Atlanta
Illinois, Chicago
Louisiana, New Orleans
Iowa, Des Moines
Louisiana, New Orleans
Massachusetts, Boston
Michigan, Detroit
Minnesota, Minneapolis
Montana, Nashua
New Jersey, Princeton
New York, New York
North Dakota, Bismarck
Oregon, Portland
Pennsylvania, Philadelphia
Puerto Rico, San Juan
Texas:
Dallas
Houston
San Antonio
Virginia, Richmond
Washington, Seattle

CAPE VERDE

Embassy of the Republic of Cape Verde
3415 Massachusetts Avenue, NW., Washington, DC 20007
phone (202) 965–6820, fax 965–1207
His Excellency Carlos Alberto Wahnon De Carvalho Veiga
Ambassador E. and P.
Consular Office: Massachusetts, Boston

CENTRAL AFRICAN REPUBLIC

Embassy of the Central African Republic
2704 Ontario Road, NW., Washington, DC 20009
phone (202) 483–7800, fax 332–9893
Ms. Lydie Flore Magba
Counselor (Charge d'Affaires ad Interim)
Consular Offices:
California, Los Angeles
New York, New York

CHAD

Embassy of the Republic of Chad
2401 Massachusetts Avenue, NW., Washington, DC 20008
phone (202) 652–1312, fax 758–0431
His Excellency Hassane Mahamat Nasser
Ambassador E. and P.

CHILE

Embassy of the Republic of Chile
1732–1736 Massachusetts Avenue, NW., Washington, DC 20036
phone (202) 785–1746, fax 887–5579
His Excellency Juan Gabriel Valdes Soublette
Ambassador E. and P.
Consular Offices:
Arizona, Phoenix
California:
Los Angeles
San Diego
San Francisco
District of Columbia, Washington
Florida:
Miami
Orlando
Georgia, Atlanta
Hawaii, Honolulu
Illinois, Chicago
Louisiana, New Orleans
Massachusetts, Boston
Michigan, Grosse Pointe Park
Missouri, Kansas City
Nevada, Las Vegas
New York, New York
Pennsylvania, Philadelphia
Puerto Rico, San Juan

South Carolina, Charleston
Texas:
Dallas
Houston

CHINA

Embassy of the People's Republic of China
3505 International Place, NW., Washington, DC 20008
phone (202) 495–2000, fax 495–2138
His Excellency Tiankai Cui
Ambassador E. and P.
Consular Offices:
California:
Los Angeles
San Francisco
Illinois, Chicago
New York, New York
Texas, Houston

COLOMBIA

Embassy of the Republic of Colombia
2118 Leroy Place, NW., Washington, DC 20008
phone (202) 387–8338, fax 232–8643
His Excellency Camilo Reyes Rodriguez
Ambassador E. and P.
Consular Offices:
California:
Beverly Hills
San Francisco
District of Columbia, Washington
Florida:
Miami
Orlando
Georgia, Atlanta
Illinois, Chicago
Massachusetts, Boston
New Jersey, Newark
New York, New York
Puerto Rico, San Juan
Texas, Houston

COMOROS

Embassy of the Union of the Comoros
866 United Nations Plaza, Suite 418, New York, NY 10017
phone (212) 750–1637, fax 750–1657
His Excellency Mohamed Soilihi Soilih
Ambassador E. and P.
Consular Office: Illinois, Chicago

CONGO, DEMOCRATIC REPUBLIC OF THE

Embassy of the Democratic Republic of the Congo
1726 M Street, NW., Suite 601, Washington, DC 20036
phone (202) 234–7690, fax 234–2609
His Excellency François Nkuna Balumuene
Ambassador E. and P.
Consular Office: New York, New York

CONGO, REPUBLIC OF THE

Embassy of the Republic of the Congo
1720 16th Street, NW., Washington, DC 20009
phone (202) 726–5500, fax 726–1860
His Excellency Serge Mombouli
Ambassador E. and P.
Consular Office: Louisiana, New Orleans

COSTA RICA

Embassy of the Republic of Costa Rica
2114 S Street, NW., Washington, DC 20008
phone (202) 234–2945, fax 265–4795
His Excellency Roman Macaya Hayes
Ambassador E. and P.
Consular Offices:
Arizona, Tucson
California, Los Angeles
District of Columbia, Washington
Florida, Miami
Georgia, Atlanta
Illinois, Chicago
Minnesota, St. Paul
New York, New York
Puerto Rico, San Juan
Texas, Houston

CÔTE D'IVOIRE

Embassy of the Republic of Côte d'Ivoire
2424 Massachusetts Avenue, NW., Washington, DC 20008
phone (202) 797–0300, fax 462–9444
His Excellency Daouda Diabate
Ambassador E. and P.
Consular Offices:
California, San Francisco
Connecticut, Stamford
Florida, Orlando
Michigan, Detroit
Texas, Houston

CROATIA

Embassy of the Republic of Croatia
2343 Massachusetts Avenue, NW., Washington, DC 20008
phone (202) 588–5899, fax 588–8936
His Excellency Josip Paro
Ambassador E. and P.
Consular Offices:
Alaska, Anchorage
California, Los Angeles
District of Columbia, Washington
Illinois, Chicago
Kansas, Kansas City
Louisiana, New Orleans

New York, New York
Pennsylvania, Pittsburgh
Texas, Houston
Washington, Seattle

CUBA

Embassy of Cuba
2630 16th Street, NW., Washington, DC 20009
phone (202) 797–8518
His Excellency Jose Ramon Cabanas Rodriguez
Ambassador E. and P.

CYPRUS

Embassy of the Republic of Cyprus
2211 R Street, NW., Washington, DC 20008
phone (202) 462–5772, fax 483–6710
His Excellency Leonidas Pantelides
Ambassador E. and P.
Consular Offices:
California:
Los Angeles
San Francisco
District of Columbia, Washington
Georgia, Chamblee
Illinois, Chicago
Louisiana, New Orleans
Michigan, Dearborn
New York, New York
North Carolina, Jacksonville
Oregon, Portland
Texas, Houston
Washington, Seattle

CZECH REPUBLIC

Embassy of the Czech Republic
3900 Spring of Freedom Street, NW., Washington, DC 20008
phone (202) 274–9100, fax 966–8540
His Excellency Hynek Kmonicek
Ambassador E. and P.
Consular Offices:
Alaska, Anchorage
California:
Los Angeles
San Francisco
Colorado, Boulder
Florida:
Ft. Lauderdale
Orlando
Georgia, Atlanta
Hawaii, Honolulu
Illinois, Chicago
Louisiana, New Orleans
Massachusetts, Wellesley
Missouri, Kansas City
Montana, Livingston
New York:
Buffalo
New York
Oregon, Portland
Pennsylvania:
Philadelphia
Pittsburgh
Puerto Rico, San Juan
Texas, Houston
Utah, Salt Lake City
Washington, Seattle

DENMARK

Royal Danish Embassy
3200 Whitehaven Street, NW., Washington, DC 20008
phone (202) 234–4300, fax 328–1470
His Excellency Lars Gert Lose
Ambassador E. and P.
Consular Offices:
Alabama, Mobile
Alaska, Anchorage
Arizona, Scottsdale
California:
Los Angeles
Sacramento
San Diego
Colorado, Denver
Florida:
Hollywood
Jacksonville
Tampa
Georgia, Macon
Hawaii, Honolulu
Illinois, Chicago
Indiana, Indianapolis
Iowa, Des Moines
Kansas, Kansas City
Louisiana, New Orleans
Maryland, Baltimore
Massachusetts, Boston
Michigan, Detroit
Minnesota, Minneapolis
Nebraska, Omaha
New York, New York
Ohio, Cleveland
Oregon, Portland
Pennsylvania:
Philadelphia
Pittsburgh
Puerto Rico, San Juan
South Carolina, Charleston
Texas:
Dallas
Houston
Utah, Salt Lake City
Virgin Islands, St. Thomas
Virginia, Virginia Beach
Washington, Seattle
Wisconsin, Milwaukee

DJIBOUTI

Embassy of the Republic of Djibouti
1156 15th Street, NW., Suite 515, Washington, DC 20005
phone (202) 331–0270, fax 331–0302
His Excellency Mohamed Said Doule
Ambassador E. and P.

DOMINICA

Embassy of the Commonwealth of Dominica
1001 19th Street, North, Suite 1200, Arlington, VA 22209
phone (571) 527–1370, fax 384–7916
His Excellency Vince Henderson
Ambassador E. and P.
Consular Offices:
- New York, New York
- Puerto Rico, Guaynabo

DOMINICAN REPUBLIC

Embassy of the Dominican Republic
1715 22nd Street, NW., Washington, DC 20008
phone (202) 332–6280, fax 265–8057
His Excellency Jose Tomas Perez Vazquez
Ambassador E. and P.
Consular Offices:
- California, Glendale
- Florida, Miami
- Illinois, Chicago
- Louisiana, New Orleans
- Massachusetts, Boston
- New York, New York
- Puerto Rico:
  - Mayaguez
  - San Juan

ECUADOR

Embassy of Ecuador
2535 15th Street, NW., Washington, DC 20009
phone (202) 234–7200, fax 667–3482
His Excellency Francisco Jose Borja Cevallos
Ambassador E. and P.
Consular Offices:
- Arizona, Phoenix
- California:
  - Los Angeles
  - San Francisco
- Connecticut, New Haven
- District of Columbia, Washington
- Florida, Miami
- Georgia, Atlanta
- Illinois, Chicago
- Louisiana, New Orleans
- Massachusetts, Boston
- Minnesota, Minneapolis
- New Jersey, Newark
- New York:
  - New York
  - Woodside
- Puerto Rico, San Juan
- Texas:
  - Dallas
  - Houston

EGYPT

Embassy of the Arab Republic of Egypt
3521 International Court, NW., Washington, DC 20008
phone (202) 895–5400, fax 244–4319
His Excellency Yasser Reda Abdalla Ali Said
Ambassador E. and P.
Consular Offices:
- California, Los Angeles
- Illinois, Chicago
- New York, New York
- Texas, Houston

EL SALVADOR

Embassy of the Republic of El Salvador
1400 16th Street, NW., Suite 100, Washington, DC 20036
phone (202) 265–9671, fax 232–3763
Her Excellency Claudia Ivette Canjura de Centeno
Ambassador E. and P.
Consular Offices:
- Arizona:
  - Fountain Hills
  - Tucson
- California:
  - Chula Vista
  - Costa Mesa
  - Los Angeles
  - Oakland
  - San Francisco
  - Santa Ana
- District of Columbia, Washington
- Florida, Coral Gables
- Georgia, Woodstock
- Illinois, Chicago
- Nevada, Las Vegas
- New Jersey, Elizabeth
- New York:
  - Brentwood
  - New York
- Pennsylvania, Philadelphia
- Texas:
  - Dallas
  - Houston
- Virginia, Woodbridge
- Washington, Seattle

EQUATORIAL GUINEA

Embassy of the Republic of Equatorial Guinea
2020 16th Street, NW., Washington, DC 20009
phone (202) 518–5700, fax 518–5252

His Excellency Miguel Ntutumu Evuna Andeme
Ambassador E. and P.
Consular Office: Texas, Houston

ERITREA

Embassy of the State of Eritrea
1708 New Hampshire Avenue, NW., Washington, DC 20009
phone (202) 319–1991, fax 319–1304
Mr. Berhane Gebrehiwet Solomon
First Secretary (Charge d'Affaires ad Interim)
Consular Office: District of Columbia, Washington

ESTONIA

Embassy of the Republic of Estonia
2131 Massachusetts Avenue, NW., Washington, DC 20008
phone (202) 588–0101, fax 588–0108
Her Excellency Eerik Marmei
Ambassador E. and P.
Consular Offices:
- Arizona, Scottsdale
- California:
  - Los Angeles
  - San Francisco
- Florida:
  - Miami
  - St. Petersburg
- Georgia, Atlanta
- Illinois, Chicago
- Massachusetts, Boston
- Nebraska, Lincoln
- New Hampshire, Portsmouth
- New York, New York
- North Carolina, Huntersville
- South Carolina, Charleston
- Texas, Houston
- Washington, Seattle

ETHIOPIA

Embassy of the Federal Democratic Republic of Ethiopia
3506 International Drive, NW., Washington, DC 20008
phone (202) 364–1200, fax 587–0195
His Excellency Girma Birru Geda
Ambassador E. and P.
Consular Offices:
- California, Los Angeles
- New York, New York
- Texas, Houston
- Washington, Seattle

EUROPEAN UNION

Delegation of the European Union
2175 K Street, NW., Washington, DC 20037
His Excellency David O. Sullivan
Ambassador (Head of Delegation)

FIJI

Embassy of the Republic of the Fiji
1707 L Street, NW., Suite 200, Washington, DC 20036
phone (202) 466–8320, fax 466–8325
His Excellency Ratu Naivakarurubalavu Solo Mara
Ambassador E. and P.
Consular Offices:
- California:
  - El Segundo
  - San Francisco
- Oregon, Portland
- Texas, Dallas

FINLAND

Embassy of the Republic of Finland
3301 Massachusetts Avenue, NW., Washington, DC 20008
phone (202) 298–5800, fax 298–6030
Her Excellency Kirsti Helena Kauppi
Ambassador E. and P.
Consular Offices:
- Alabama, Birmingham
- Alaska, Anchorage
- Arizona, Phoenix
- California:
  - Los Angeles
  - San Diego
  - San Francisco
- Colorado, Highlands Ranch
- Connecticut, Norwich
- Florida:
  - Lake Worth
  - Miami
- Georgia, Atlanta
- Hawaii, Honolulu
- Illinois, Chicago
- Louisiana, New Orleans
- Maryland, Baltimore
- Massachusetts, Boston
- Michigan:
  - Farmington
  - Hancock
- Minnesota:
  - Minneapolis
  - Virginia
- Missouri, Saint Louis
- New Jersey, Newark
- New York, New York
- Pennsylvania, Philadelphia
- Puerto Rico, San Juan
- Texas:
  - Dallas
  - Houston
- Utah, Salt Lake City
- Virginia, Norfolk
- Washington, Seattle

FRANCE

Embassy of the French Republic
4101 Reservoir Road, NW., Washington, DC 20007
phone (202) 944–6000, fax 944–6166
His Excellency Gerard Roger Araud
Ambassador E. and P.
Consular Offices:
- Alaska, Anchorage
- Arizona, Phoenix
- Arkansas, Little Rock
- California:
  - Los Angeles
  - Sacramento
  - San Diego
  - San Francisco
- Colorado, Denver
- District of Columbia, Washington
- Florida:
  - Clearwater
  - Jacksonville
  - Miami
  - Orlando
- Georgia:
  - Atlanta
  - Savannah
- Guam, Tamuning
- Hawaii, Honolulu
- Idaho, Boise
- Illinois, Chicago
- Indiana, Indianapolis
- Iowa, Indianola
- Kentucky, Louisville
- Louisiana:
  - Lafayette
  - New Orleans
  - Shreveport
- Maine, Portland
- Massachusetts, Boston
- Michigan, Southfield
- Minnesota, Minneapolis
- Mississippi, Hattiesburg
- Missouri, St. Louis
- Montana, Hamilton
- Nebraska, Omaha
- Nevada:
  - Las Vegas
  - Reno
- New Jersey, Princeton
- New Mexico, Albuquerque
- New York:
  - Buffalo
  - New York
- North Carolina:
  - Charlotte
  - Raleigh
- Ohio:
  - Cincinnati
  - Cleveland
- Oklahoma, Oklahoma City
- Oregon, Portland
- Pennsylvania:
  - Philadelphia
  - Pittsburgh
- Puerto Rico, San Juan
- Rhode Island, Providence
- South Carolina:
  - Greenville
  - Mount Pleasant
- Tennessee, Nashville
- Texas:
  - Dallas
  - Houston
  - San Antonio
- Utah, Salt Lake City
- Vermont, Burlington
- Virginia, Norfolk
- Washington, Seattle
- Wyoming, Dubois

GABON

Embassy of the Gabonese Republic
2034 20th Street, NW., Washington, DC 20009
phone (202) 797–1000, fax (301) 983–1994
His Excellency Michael Moussa Adamo
Ambassador E. and P.
Consular Office: New York, New York

GAMBIA

Embassy of The Gambia
2233 Wisconsin Avenue, NW., Suite 240, Washington, DC 20007
phone (202) 785–1399, fax 785–1430
Mr. Manneh Hamba
Counselor (Charge d'Affaires ad Interim)
Consular Office: Florida, Miami

GEORGIA

Embassy of the Republic of Georgia
1824–1826 R Street, NW., Washington, DC 20008
phone (202) 387–2390, fax 387–0864
His Excellency David Bakradze
Ambassador E. and P.
Consular Offices:
- California, Orange
- District of Columbia, Washington
- New York, New York
- South Carolina, Charleston

GERMANY

Embassy of the Federal Republic of Germany
4645 Reservoir Road, NW., Washington, DC 20007
phone (202) 298–4000, fax 298–4249
His Excellency Hans Peter Wittig

Ambassador E. and P.
Consular Offices:
- Alabama, Birmingham
- Alaska, Anchorage
- Arizona, Phoenix
- California:
  - Los Angeles
  - San Diego
  - San Francisco
- Colorado, Denver
- Connecticut, Farmington
- District of Columbia, Washington
- Florida:
  - Miami
  - Naples
  - Orlando
- Georgia:
  - Atlanta
  - Savannah
- Hawaii, Honolulu
- Illinois, Chicago
- Indiana, Indianapolis
- Iowa, Indianola
- Kansas, Leawood
- Kentucky, Louisville
- Louisiana, New Orleans
- Maine, Portland
- Massachusetts, Boston
- Michigan, Auburn Hills
- Minnesota, Minneapolis
- Mississippi, Jackson
- Missouri, St. Louis
- Nevada, Las Vegas
- New Mexico, Albuquerque
- New York:
  - Buffalo
  - New York
- North Carolina:
  - Charlotte
  - Raleigh
- Ohio:
  - Cincinnati
  - Cleveland
- Oklahoma, Oklahoma City
- Oregon, Portland
- Pennsylvania:
  - Philadelphia
  - Pittsburgh
- Puerto Rico, San Juan
- South Carolina, Greer
- Tennessee, Nashville
- Texas:
  - Dallas
  - Houston
  - San Antonio
- Utah, Salt Lake City
- Virginia, Virginia Beach
- Washington, Mercer Island

GHANA

Embassy of Ghana
3512 International Drive, NW., Washington, DC 20008
phone (202) 686–4520, fax 686–4527
His Excellency Barfour Adjei-Barwuah
Ambassador E. and P.
Consular Offices:
- New York, New York
- Texas, Houston

GREECE

Embassy of Greece
2217 Massachusetts Avenue, NW., Washington, DC 20008
phone (202) 939–1300, fax 939–1324
His Excellency Theocharis Lalacos
Ambassador E. and P.
Consular Offices:
- California:
  - Los Angeles
  - San Francisco
- Florida, Tampa
- Georgia, Atlanta
- Illinois, Chicago
- Massachusetts, Boston
- New York, New York
- Texas, Houston

GRENADA

Embassy of Grenada
1701 New Hampshire Avenue, NW., Washington, DC 20009
phone (202) 265–2561, fax 265–2468
His Excellency Ethelstan Angus Friday
Ambassador E. and P.
Consular Office: Illinois, Chicago

GUATEMALA

Embassy of Guatemala
2220 R Street, NW., Washington, DC 20008
phone (202) 745–4953, fax 745–1908
Her Excellency Gladys Marithza Ruiz Sanchez
Ambassador E. and P.
Consular Offices:
- Alabama, Montgomery
- Arizona, Phoenix
- California:
  - Los Angeles
  - San Diego
  - San Francisco
- Colorado, Denver
- Florida:
  - Ft. Lauderdale
  - Jupiter
  - Miami

Georgia, Atlanta
Illinois, Chicago
Louisiana: Lafayette
Maryland, Silver Spring
Massachusetts, Newton
Missouri, Kansas City
Nevada, North Las Vegas
New York, New York
North Carolina, Charlotte
Oklahoma, Oklahoma City
Oregon, Portland
Puerto Rico, San Juan
South Carolina, Columbia
Tennessee, Memphis
Texas:
Houston
San Antonio
Washington, Seattle
Wisconsin, Madison

GUINEA

Embassy of the Republic of Guinea
2112 Leroy Place, NW., Washington, DC 20008
phone (202) 986–4300, fax 986–3800
His Excellency Mamady Conde
Ambassador E. and P.
Consular Office: California, Santa Monica

GUYANA

Embassy of Guyana
2490 Tracy Place, NW., Washington, DC 20008
phone (202) 265–6900, fax 232–1297
His Excellency Sheikh Riyad David Insanally
Ambassador E. and P.
Consular Offices:
California, Los Angeles
Florida, Miami
New York, New York

HAITI

Embassy of the Republic of Haiti
2311 Massachusetts Avenue, NW., Washington, DC 20008
phone (202) 332–4090, fax 745–7215
His Excellency Paul Getty Altidor
Ambassador E. and P.
Consular Offices:
California, San Francisco
Florida:
Miami
Orlando
Georgia, Atlanta
Illinois, Chicago
Louisiana, New Orleans
Massachusetts, Boston
New Jersey, Trenton
New York, New York
Pennsylvania:
Philadelphia
Pottsville
Texas, Houston

HOLY SEE

Apostolic Nunciature
3339 Massachusetts Avenue, NW., Washington, DC 20008
phone (202) 333–7121, fax 337–4036
His Excellency Christophe Pierre
Apostolic Nuncio

HONDURAS

Embassy of Honduras
3007 Tilden Street, NW., Suite 4–M, Washington, DC 20008
phone (202) 966–2604, fax 966–9751
His Excellency Marlon Ramsses Tabora Munoz
Ambassador E. and P.
Consular Offices:
California:
Los Angeles
San Diego
San Francisco
Florida:
Miami
Tampa
Georgia, Atlanta
Hawaii, Honolulu
Illinois, Chicago
Louisiana:
Baton Rouge
New Orleans
Maryland, Baltimore
Missouri, St. Louis
Nevada, Reno
New York, New York
Texas, Houston

HUNGARY

Embassy of Hungary
3910 Shoemaker Street, NW., Washington, DC 20008
phone (202) 362–6730, fax 966–8135
The Honorable Zsolt Gabor Hetesy
Minister (Charge d'Affaires ad Interim)
Consular Offices:
California:
Los Angeles
Sacramento
San Francisco
Colorado, Denver
Connecticut, Hamden
District of Columbia, Washington
Florida:
Miami
Sarasota
Georgia, Morrow

Hawaii, Honolulu
Louisiana, Metairie
Massachusetts, Boston
Minnnesota, Minneapolis
Missouri, St. Louis
New York, New York
Ohio, Cleveland
Puerto Rico, Mayaguez
Texas, Houston
Utah, Sandy
Washington, Seattle

ICELAND

Embassy of Iceland
2900 K Street, NW., Suite 509, Washington, DC 20007
phone (202) 265-6653, fax 265-6656
His Excellency Geir Hilmar Haarde
Ambassador E. and P.
Consular Offices:
Alaska, Anchorage
Arizona, Phoenix
California:
Los Angeles
San Francisco
Colorado, Englewood
Florida:
Orlando
Plantation
Georgia, Atlanta
Illinois, Chicago
Kentucky, Louisville
Louisiana, New Orleans
Massachusetts, Boston
Michigan, Detroit
Minnesota, Minneapolis
Missouri, Grandview
New York, New York
North Dakota, Grand Fork
Oregon, Portland
Pennsylvania, Harrisburg
Puerto Rico, Guaynabo
South Carolina, Charleston
Texas:
Dallas
Houston
Utah, Salt Lake City
Virginia, Norfolk
Washington, Seattle
Wisconsin, Madison

INDIA

Embassy of India
2107 Massachusetts Avenue, NW., Washington, DC 20008
phone (202) 939-7000, fax 483-3972
His Excellency Navtej Singh Sarna
Ambassador E. and P.
Consular Offices:
California, San Francisco
District of Columbia, Washington
Georgia, Atlanta
Illinois, Chicago
New York, New York
Texas, Houston

INDONESIA

Embassy of the Republic of Indonesia
2020 Massachusetts Avenue, NW., Washington, DC 20036
phone (202) 775-5200, fax 775-5365
His Excellency Budi Bowoleksono
Ambassador E. and P.
Consular Offices:
California:
Los Angeles
San Francisco
Illinois, Chicago
New York, New York
Texas, Houston

IRAQ

Embassy of the Republic of Iraq
3421 Massachusetts Avenue, NW., Washington, DC 20007
phone (202) 742-1600, fax 462-5066
His Excellency Fareed Mustafa Kamil Yasseen
Ambassador E. and P.
Consular Offices:
California, Los Angeles
Michigan, Southfield

IRELAND

Embassy of Ireland
2234 Massachusetts Avenue, NW., Washington, DC 20008
phone (202) 462-3939, fax 232-5993
Her Excellency Anne Anderson
Ambassador E. and P.
Consular Offices:
California:
Los Angeles
San Francisco
Colorado, Denver
Florida, Orlando
Georgia, Atlanta
Hawaii, Honolulu
Illinois, Chicago
Louisiana, New Orleans
Massachusetts, Boston
Missouri, St. Louis
Nevada, Las Vegas
New York, New York
Pennsylvania, Pittsburgh
Texas, Houston
Washington, Seattle

ISRAEL

Embassy of Israel
3514 International Drive, NW., Washington, DC 20008
phone (202) 364–5500, fax 364–5607
His Excellency Ron Dermer
Ambassador E. and P.
Consular Offices:
California:
Los Angeles
San Francisco
District of Columbia, Washington
Florida, Miami
Georgia, Atlanta
Illinois, Chicago
Massachusetts, Boston
New York, New York
Pennsylvania, Philadelphia
Texas, Houston

ITALY

Embassy of Italy
3000 Whitehaven Street, NW., Washington, DC 20008
phone (202) 612–4400, fax 518–2151
His Excellency Armando Varricchio
Ambassador E. and P.
Consular Offices:
Alaska, Anchorage
Arizona, Scottsdale
California:
Fresno
Los Angeles
San Diego
San Francisco
San Jose
Connecticut, Hartford
Florida:
Miami
Orlando
Georgia, Atlanta
Hawaii, Honolulu
Illinois, Chicago
Indiana, Indianapolis
Kansas, Leawood
Louisiana, New Orleans
Maryland, Baltimore
Massachusetts:
Boston
Worcester
Michigan, Detroit
Mississippi, Hattiesburg
Missouri, St. Louis
Nevada, Las Vegas
New Jersey, Newark
New York:
Buffalo
Mineola
Mt. Vernon
New York
Rochester
North Carolina, Charlotte
Ohio, Cleveland
Oregon, Portland
Pennsylvania:
Philadelphia
Pittsburgh
Puerto Rico, San Juan
Rhode Island, Providence
South Carolina, Charleston
Texas, Houston
Utah, Salt Lake City
Washington, Seattle

JAMAICA

Embassy of Jamaica
1520 New Hampshire Avenue, NW., Washington, DC 20036
phone (202) 452–0660, fax 452–0081
Her Excellency Audrey Patrice Marks
Ambassador E. and P.
Consular Offices:
California:
Los Angeles
San Francisco
District of Columbia, Washington
Florida, Miami
Georgia, Atlanta
Illinois, Chicago
Massachusetts, Boston
New Hampshire, Concord
New York, New York
Pennsylvania, Philadelphia
Texas, Houston
Virginia, Richmond
Washington, Seattle

JAPAN

Embassy of Japan
2520 Massachusetts Avenue, NW., Washington, DC 20008
phone (202) 238–6700, fax 328–2187
His Excellency Kenichiro Sasae
Ambassador E. and P.
Consular Offices:
Alaska, Anchorage
Arizona, Tempe
California:
Los Angeles
San Diego
San Francisco
Colorado, Denver
Connecticut, Simsbury
District of Columbia, Washington

Florida:
Miami
Orlando
Georgia, Atlanta
Guam, Agana
Hawaii:
Hilo
Honolulu
Idaho, Boise
Illinois, Chicago
Indiana, Indianapolis
Kansas, Prairie Village
Kentucky, Lexington
Louisiana, New Orleans
Massachusetts, Boston
Michigan, Detroit
Minnesota, Minneapolis
Missouri, St. Louis
Nebraska, Omaha
Nevada, Las Vegas
New Mexico, Albuquerque
New York:
Buffalo
New York
North Carolina, Durham
Northern Mariana Islands, Mariana Islands
Ohio, Cincinnati
Oklahoma, Oklahoma City
Oregon, Portland
Pennsylvania, Philadelphia
Puerto Rico, San Juan
Tennessee, Nashville
Texas:
Dallas
Houston
Washington, Seattle

JORDAN

Embassy of the Hashemite Kingdom of Jordan
3504 International Drive, NW., Washington, DC 20008
phone (202) 966–2664, fax 966–3110
Her Excellency Dina Kawar
Ambassador E. and P.
Consular Offices:
California, San Francisco
Illinois, Chicago
Michigan, Detroit

KAZAKHSTAN

Embassy of the Republic of Kazakhstan
1401 16th Street, NW., Washington, DC 20036
phone (202) 232–5488, fax 232–5845
His Excellency Erzhan Kazykhanov
Ambassador E. and P.
Consular Offices:
California:
San Francisco
Santa Monica
District of Columbia, Washington
Louisiana, Baton Rouge
New York, New York
North Dakota, Fargo

KENYA

Embassy of the Republic of Kenya
2249 R Street, NW., Washington, DC 20008
phone (202) 387–6101, fax 462–3829
His Excellency Robinson Njeru Githae
Ambassador E. and P.
Consular Offices:
California, Los Angeles
New York, New York

KIRIBATI

Embassy of the Republic of Kiribati
800 Second Avenue, Suite 400A, New York, NY 10017
phone (212) 867–3310, fax 867–3320
Her Excellency Makurita Baaro
Ambassador E. and P.
Consular Office: Hawaii, Honolulu

KOREA, REPUBLIC OF

Embassy of the Republic of Korea
2450 Massachusetts Avenue, NW., Washington, DC 20008
phone (202) 939–5600, fax 387–0250
His Excellency Ho Young Ahn
Ambassador E. and P.
Consular Offices:
Alaska, Anchorage
Arizona, Tucson
California:
Los Angeles
San Francisco
Colorado, Denver
Connecticut, Stamford
District of Columbia, Washington
Florida, Miami
Georgia, Atlanta
Guam, Agana
Hawaii, Honolulu
Illinois, Chicago
Louisiana, New Orleans
Massachusetts, Boston
Michigan, Southfield
Missouri, Saint Louis
Nevada, Reno
New York, New York
Oklahoma, Oklahoma City
Oregon:
Eugene
Portland
Pennsylvania, Philadelphia
Puerto Rico, San Juan

Texas:
Dallas
Houston
Utah, Salt Lake City
Washington, Seattle

KOSOVO

Embassy of the Republic of Kosovo
2175 K Street, NW., Suite 300, Washington, DC 20037
phone (202) 450–2130, fax 735–0609
Her Excellency Vlora Çitaku
Ambassador E. and P.
Consular Office: New York, New York

KUWAIT

Embassy of the State of Kuwait
2940 Tilden Street, NW., Washington, DC 20008
phone (202) 966–0702, fax 966–0517
His Excellency Sheikh Salem Abdullah Al-Jaber Al-Sabah
Ambassador E. and P.
Consular Office: California, Los Angeles

KYRGYZSTAN

Embassy of the Kyrgyz Republic
2360 Massachusetts Avenue, NW., Washington, DC 20008
phone (202) 449–9822, fax 386–7550
His Excellency Kadyr Toktogulov
Ambassador E. and P.
Consular Offices:
District of Columbia, Washington
New York, New York
Washington, Maple Valley

LAOS

Embassy of the Lao Peoples Democratic Republic
2222 S Street, NW., Washington, DC 20008
phone (202) 332–6416, fax 332–4923
His Excellency Mai Sayavongs
Ambassador E. and P.

LATVIA

Embassy of Latvia
2306 Massachusetts Avenue, NW., Washington, DC 20008
phone (202) 328–2840, fax 328–2860
His Excellency Andris Teikmanis
Ambassador E. and P.
Consular Offices:
Alaska, Palmer
California:
Mill Valley
Rancho Santa Margarita
Florida, Ft. Lauderdale
Illinois, Chicago
Massachusetts, Needham
Michigan, West Bloomfield
Minnesota, Minneapolis
New York:
Buffalo
Greenwich
New York
Ohio, Cincinnati
Oregon, Salem
Pennsylvania, Philadelphia
Rhode Island, North Kingstown
Texas, Houston
Washington, Snohomish

LEBANON

Embassy of Lebanon
2560 28th Street, NW., Washington, DC 20008
phone (202) 939–6300, fax 939–6324
Ms. Carla Jazzar
Counselor (Charge d'Affaires ad Interim)
Consular Offices:
California, Los Angeles
Massachusetts, Boston
Michigan, Detroit
New York, New York
North Carolina, Raleigh
Texas, Houston

LESOTHO

Embassy of the Kingdom of Lesotho
2511 Massachusetts Avenue, NW., Washington, DC 20008
phone (202) 797–5533, fax 234–6815
His Excellency Professor Eliachim Molapi Sebatane
Ambassador E. and P.
Consular Offices:
Louisiana, New Orleans
Ohio, Dayton
Texas, Austin

LIBERIA

Embassy of the Republic of Liberia
5201 16th Street, NW., Washington, DC 20011
phone (202) 723–0437, fax 723–0436
The Honorable Jeff Gongoer Dowana
Minister (Charge d'Affaires ad Interim)
Consular Offices:
District of Columbia, Washington
Florida, Tampa
Georgia, Atlanta

LIBYA

Embassy of Libya
2600 Virginia Avenue, NW., Suite 705, 300, 40, Washington, DC 20037
phone (202) 944–9601, fax 944–9606
Ms. Wafa M. T. Bughaighis
Minister (Charge d'Affaires ad Interim)
Ambassador E. and P.
Consular Office: District of Columbia, Washington

LIECHTENSTEIN

Embassy of the Principality of Liechtenstein
2900 K Street, NW., Suite 602B, Washington, DC 20007
phone (202) 331–0590, fax 331–3221
His Excellency Kurt Jaeger
Ambassador E. and P.
Consular Offices:
- California, Los Angeles
- Georgia, Macon
- Illinois, Chicago
- Oregon, Portland

LITHUANIA

Embassy of the Republic of Lithuania
2622 16th Street, NW., Washington, DC 20009
phone (202) 234–5860, fax 328–0466
His Excellency Rolandas Krisciunas
Ambassador E. and P.
Consular Offices:
- Alaska, Anchorage
- Arizona, Phoenix
- California:
  - Lafayette
  - Santa Monica
- Colorado, Aspen
- Florida:
  - Palm Beach
  - St. Petersburg
- Georgia, Marietta
- Illinois, Chicago
- Michigan:
  - Farmington
  - Lansing
- Minnesota, Stillwater
- Nevada, Las Vegas
- New Hampshire, Manchester
- New York:
  - New York
  - Webster
- Ohio, Cleveland
- Oregon, Portland
- Pennsylvania, Philadelphia
- Texas, Houston
- Washington, Seattle

LUXEMBOURG

Embassy of the Grand Duchy of Luxembourg
2200 Massachusetts Avenue, NW., Washington, DC 20008
phone (202) 265–4171, fax 328–8270
Her Excellency Sylvie Lucas
Ambassador E. and P.
Consular Offices:
- Arizona, Scottsdale
- California:
  - San Francisco
  - Woodland Hills
- Colorado, Louisville
- Florida, Estero
- Georgia, Atlanta
- Hawaii, Kapolei
- Illinois, Elburn
- Indiana, Indianapolis
- Louisiana, New Orleans
- Massachusetts, Boston
- Michigan, Auburn Hills
- Minnesota, Edina
- Missouri, Kansas City
- New York, New York
- Ohio, Cleveland
- Oregon, Portland
- Texas, Ft. Worth
- Washington, Seattle
- Wisconsin, Grafton

MACEDONIA

Embassy of the Republic of Macedonia
2129 Wyoming Avenue, NW., Washington, DC 20008
phone (202) 667–0501, fax 667–2131
His Excellency Vasko Naumovski
Ambassador E. and P.
Consular Offices:
- Arizona, Tucson
- California:
  - Ontario
  - San Diego
- Florida:
  - Hollywood
  - Naples
- Illinois, Chicago
- Michigan, Southfield
- New Jersey, Clifton
- New York, New York
- Ohio, Columbus

MADAGASCAR

Embassy of the Republic of Madagascar
2374 Massachusetts Avenue, NW., Washington, DC 20008
phone (202) 265–5525, fax 265–3034
Mrs. Velotiana Rakotoanosy Raobelina
Counselor (Charge d'Affaires ad Interim)
Consular Office: New York, New York

MALAWI

Embassy of Malawi
2408 Massachusetts Avenue, NW., Washington, DC 20008
phone (202) 721–0270, fax 721–0288
His Excellency Edward Sawerengera
Ambassador E. and P.

MALAYSIA

Embassy of Malaysia

3516 International Court, NW., Washington, DC 20008
phone (202) 572–9700, fax 572–9882
His Excellency Zulhasnan Bin Rafique
Ambassador E. and P.
Consular Offices:
- California, Los Angeles
- Hawaii, Honolulu
- New York, New York
- Oregon, Portland

MALDIVES

Embassy of the Republic of Maldives
800 Second Avenue, Suite 400E, New York, NY 10017
phone (212) 599–6195, fax 661–6405
His Excellency Ali Naseer Mohamed
Ambassador E. and P.

MALI

Embassy of the Republic of Mali
2130 R Street, NW., Washington, DC 20008
phone (202) 332–2249, fax 332–6603
The Honorable Mohamed Cisse
Minister / Counselor (Charge d'Affaires ad Interim)
Consular Offices:
- California, Cupertino
- Florida, Ft. Lauderdale
- Georgia, Atlanta
- Louisiana, New Orleans

MALTA

Embassy of Malta
2017 Connecticut Avenue, NW., Washington, DC 20008
phone (202) 462–3611, fax 387–5470
His Excellency Pierre Clive Agius
Ambassador E. and P.
Consular Offices:
- Arizona, Phoenix
- California:
  - Los Angeles
  - San Francisco
- District of Columbia, Washington
- Florida, Miami
- Georgia, Atlanta
- Illinois, Barrington
- Louisiana, Metairie
- Massachusetts, Bellmont
- Michigan:
  - Detroit
  - Taylor
- Minnesota, St. Paul
- New York, New York
- Pennsylvania, Philadelphia
- Tennessee, Kingsport
- Texas:
  - Dallas
  - Houston
- Washington, Seattle

MARSHALL ISLANDS

Embassy of the Republic of the Marshall Islands
2433 Massachusetts Avenue, NW., 1st Floor, Washington, DC 20008
phone (202) 234–5414, fax 232–3236
His Excellency Gerald Zackios
Ambassador E. and P.
Consular Offices:
- Arkansas, Springdale
- Hawaii, Honolulu

MAURITANIA

Embassy of the Islamic Republic of Mauritania
2129 Leroy Place, NW., Washington, DC 20008
phone (202) 232–5700, fax 319–2623
His Excellency Mohamedoun Daddah
Ambassador E. and P.
Consular Office: Pennsylvania, Newtown Square

MAURITIUS

Embassy of the Republic of Mauritius
1709 N Street, NW., Washington, DC 20036
phone (202) 244–1491, fax 966–0983
His Excellency Sooroojdev Phokeer
Ambassador E. and P.
Consular Offices:
- California:
  - Los Angeles
  - San Francisco

MEXICO

Embassy of Mexico
1911 Pennsylvania Avenue, NW., Washington, DC 20006
phone (202) 728–1600, fax 728–1615
His Excellency Geronimo Gutierrez Fernandez
Ambassador E. and P.
Consular Offices:
- Alaska, Anchorage
- Arizona:
  - Douglas
  - Nogales
  - Phoenix
  - Tucson
  - Yuma
- Arkansas, Little Rock
- California:
  - Calexico
  - Fresno
  - Los Angeles
  - Oxnard
  - Sacramento
  - Salinas
  - San Bernardino
  - San Diego

San Francisco
San Jose
Santa Ana
Colorado, Denver
District of Columbia, Washington
Florida:
Jacksonville
Miami
Orlando
Georgia, Atlanta
Hawaii, Honolulu
Idaho, Boise
Illinois, Chicago
Indiana, Indianapolis
Louisiana, New Orleans
Massachusetts, Boston
Michigan, Detroit
Minnesota, St. Paul
Missouri, Kansas City
Nebraska, Omaha
Nevada, Las Vegas
New Mexico, Albuquerque
New York, New York
North Carolina:
Charlotte
Raleigh
Oregon, Portland
Pennsylvania, Philadelphia
Puerto Rico, San Juan
Texas:
Austin
Brownsville
Dallas
Del Rio
Eagle Pass
El Paso
Houston
Laredo
McAllen
Midland
San Antonio
Utah, Salt Lake City
Washington, Seattle
Wisconsin, Madison

MICRONESIA

Embassy of the Federated States of Micronesia
1725 N Street, NW., Washington, DC 20036
phone (202) 223–4383, fax 223–4391
His Excellency Akillino Harris Susaia
Ambassador E. and P.
Consular Offices:
Guam, Tamuning
Hawaii, Honolulu

MOLDOVA

Embassy of the Republic of Moldova
2101 S Street, NW., Washington, DC 20008
phone (202) 667–1130, fax 667–1204
Ms. Tatiana Solomon
Counselor (Charge d'Affaires ad Interim)
Consular Offices:
District of Columbia, Washington
Florida, Miami
New York, New York
North Carolina, Hickory

MONACO

Embassy of Monoco
3400 International Drive, NW., Suite 2K–100, Washington, DC 20008
Her Excellency Maguy Maccario Doyle
Ambassador E. and P.
Consular Offices:
California:
Los Angeles
San Francisco
Florida, Miami
Georgia, Atlanta
Illinois, Chicago
Louisiana, New Orleans
Massachusetts, Boston
Nevada, Las Vegas
New York, New York
Texas, Dallas

MONGOLIA

Embassy of Mongolia
2833 M Street, NW., Washington, DC 20007
phone (202) 333–7117, fax 298–9227
His Excellency Altangerel Bulgaa
Ambassador E. and P.
Consular Offices:
California, San Francisco
Colorado, Denver
District of Columbia, Washington
Georgia, Atlanta
Illinois, Chicago
Montana, Bozeman
New York, New York
South Dakota, Belle Fourche
Texas, Houston

MONTENEGRO

Embassy of the Republic of Montenegro
1610 New Hampshire Avenue, NW., Washington, DC 20009
phone (202) 234–6108, fax 234–6109
His Excellency Nebojsa Kaludjerovic
Ambassador E. and P.
Consular Offices:
Colorado, Denver
New York, New York

MOROCCO

Embassy of the Kingdom of Morocco
1601 21st Street, NW., Washington, DC 20009

phone (202) 462–7980, fax 265–0161
Her Excellency Lalla Joumala Alaoui
Ambassador E. and P.
Consular Offices:
California, Los Angeles
Colorado, Denver
Hawaii, Honolulu
Illinois, Chicago
Kansas, Kansas City
Kentucky, Louisville
Massachusetts, Cambridge
New York, New York
Texas, Dallas
Utah, Bountiful

MOZAMBIQUE

Embassy of the Republic of Mozambique
1525 New Hampshire Avenue, NW., Washington, DC 20036
phone (202) 293–7146, fax 835–0245
His Excellency Carlos Dos Santos
Ambassador E. and P.

NAMIBIA

Embassy of the Republic of Namibia
1605 New Hampshire Avenue, NW., Washington, DC 20009
phone (202) 986–0540, fax 986–0443
His Excellency Martin Andjaba
Ambassador E. and P.
Consular Offices:
California, San Jose
Florida, Orlando
Georgia, Atlanta
Michigan, Detroit
Nevada, Las Vegas
Texas, San Antonio
Virginia, Richmond

NAURU

Embassy of the Republic of Nauru
801 Second Avenue, New York, NY 10017
phone (212) 937–0074, fax 937–0079
Her Excellency Marlene Inemwin Moses
Ambassador E. and P.
Consular Office: Guam, Agana

NEPAL

Embassy of Nepal
2131 Leroy Place, NW., Washington, DC 20008
phone (202) 667–4550, fax 667–5534
His Excellency Arjun Kumar Karki
Ambassador E. and P.
Consular Offices:
California:
Auburn
Los Angeles
San Francisco
Vista
Hawaii, Naalehu
Illinois, Chicago
Maryland, Baltimore
Massachusetts, Boston
New York, New York

NETHERLANDS

Royal Netherlands Embassy
4200 Linnean Avenue, NW., Washington, DC 20008
phone (202) 244–5300, fax 362–3430
His Excellency Hendrik Jan Juriaan Schuwer
Ambassador E. and P.
Consular Offices:
Arizona, Phoenix
California:
Los Angeles
San Francisco
Colorado, Denver
District of Columbia, Washington
Florida:
Jacksonville
Miami
Orlando
Georgia, Atlanta
Hawaii, Honolulu
Illinois, Chicago
Louisiana, New Orleans
Massachusetts, Boston
Michigan:
Grand Rapids
New Baltimore
Minnesota, Minneapolis
Missouri, St. Louis
New York, New York
North Carolina, Raleigh
Oregon, Beaverton
Puerto Rico, Guaynabo
Utah, Salt Lake City
Washington, Bellevue

NEW ZEALAND

Embassy of New Zealand
37 Observatory Circle, NW., Washington, DC 20008
phone (202) 328–4800, fax 667–5227
His Excellency Timothy John Groser
Ambassador E. and P.
Consular Offices:
California:
Burlingame
El Macero
San Diego
Santa Monica
District of Columbia, Washington
Georgia, Atlanta
Guam, Tamuning
Hawaii, Honolulu

Illinois, Chicago
New Hampshire, Boston
New York, New York
Oregon, Portland
Texas, Houston
Utah, Salt Lake City
Vermont, Shelburne
Washington, Seattle

NICARAGUA

Embassy of the Republic of Nicaragua
1627 New Hampshire Avenue, NW., Washington, DC 20009
phone (202) 939–6570, fax 939–6545
His Excellency Francisco Obadiah Campbell Hooker
Ambassador E. and P.
Consular Offices:
California:
Los Angeles
San Francisco
District of Columbia, Washington
Florida, Miami
Georgia, Atlanta
Louisiana, Baton Rouge
Massachusetts, Springfield
New York, New York
North Carolina, Charlotte
Texas, Houston

NIGER

Embassy of the Republic of Niger
2204 R Street, NW., Washington, DC 20008
phone (202) 483–4224, fax 483–3169
His Excellency Hassana Alidou
Ambassador E. and P.

NIGERIA

Embassy of the Federal Republic of Nigeria
3519 International Court, NW., Washington, DC 20008
phone (202) 986–8400, fax 362–6541
The Honorable Hakeem Toyin Balogun
Minister (Charge d'Affaires ad Interim)
Consular Offices:
Georgia, Atlanta
New York, New York

NORWAY

Royal Norwegian Embassy
2720 34th Street, NW., Washington, DC 20008
phone (202) 333–6000, fax 459–3990
His Excellency Kaare Reidar Aas
Ambassador E. and P.
Consular Offices:
Alabama, Mobile
Alaska, Anchorage
Arizona, Glendale
California:
Los Angeles
San Diego
San Francisco
Colorado, Denver
Florida:
Jacksonville
Miami
Tampa
Georgia, Atlanta
Hawaii, Honolulu
Illinois, Chicago
Iowa, Des Moines
Louisiana, New Orleans
Massachusetts, Boston
Michigan, Detroit
Minnesota, Minneapolis
Montana, Billings
Nebraska, Omaha
New York, New York
North Dakota, Fargo
Oklahoma, Tulsa
Oregon, Portland
Pennsylvania, Philadelphia
Puerto Rico:
Ponce
San Juan
South Carolina, Charleston
South Dakota, Sioux Falls
Texas:
Dallas
Houston
Utah, Salt Lake City
Virginia, Norfolk
Washington, Seattle
Wisconsin, Madison

OMAN

Embassy of the Sultanate of Oman
2535 Belmont Road, NW., Washington, DC 20008
phone (202) 387–1980, fax 745–4933
Her Excellency Hunaina Sultan Ahmed Al Mughairy
Ambassador E. and P.
Consular Office: Pennsylvania, Pittsburgh

PAKISTAN

Embassy of Pakistan
3517 International Court, NW., Washington, DC 20008
phone (202) 243–6500, fax 686–1544
His Excellency Aziz Ahmad Chaudhry
Ambassador E. and P.
Consular Office:
California, Los Angeles
Connecticut, Rocky Hill
Illinois, Chicago
Maine, Portland
Massachusetts, Boston
Missouri, St. Louis

New York, New York
Pennsylvania, Philadelphia
Texas, Houston

PALAU

Embassy of the Republic of Palau
1701 Pennsylvania Avenue, NW., Suite 300, Washington, DC 20036
phone (202) 452–6814, fax 452–6281
His Excellency Hersey Kyota
Ambassador E. and P.
Consular Offices:
California:
Carlsbad
La Canada Flintridge
Guam, Tamuning
Illinois, Chicago

PANAMA

Embassy of the Republic of Panama
2862 McGill Terrace, NW., Washington, DC 20007
phone (202) 483–1407, fax 483–8413
His Excellency Emanuel A Gonzalez Revilla Lince
Ambassador E. and P.
Consular Offices:
Arkansas, Fayetteville
California, Long Beach
District of Columbia, Washington
Florida:
Miami
Tampa
Louisiana, New Orleans
New York, New York
Pennsylvania, Philadelphia
Puerto Rico, San Juan
Texas:
Austin
Houston

PAPUA NEW GUINEA

Embassy of Papua New Guinea
1779 Massachusetts Avenue, NW., Suite 805, Washington, DC 20036
phone (202) 745–3680, fax 745–3679
His Excellency Rupa Abraham Mulina
Ambassador E. and P.
Consular Offices:
California, Los Angeles
Texas, Houston

PARAGUAY

Embassy of Paraguay
2400 Massachusetts Avenue, NW., Washington, DC 20008
phone (202) 483–6960, fax 234–4508
His Excellency German Hugo Rojas Irigoyen
Ambassador E. and P.
Consular Offices:
California, Los Angeles
Florida, Miami
New York, New York
Texas, Bellaire

PERU

Embassy of Peru
1700 Massachusetts Avenue, NW., Washington, DC 20036
phone (202) 833–9860, fax 659–8124
His Excellency Carlos Jose Pareja Rios
Ambassador E. and P.
Consular Offices:
Arizona, Mesa
California:
Los Angeles
San Francisco
Colorado, Denver
Connecticut, Hartford
District of Columbia, Washington
Florida:
Miami
Tampa
Georgia, Atlanta
Illinois, Chicago
Massachusetts, Boston
Missouri, St. Louis
New Jersey, Paterson
New York, New York
Oklahoma, Oklahoma City
Puerto Rico, San Juan
Texas:
Dallas
Houston
Utah, Salt Lake City
Washington, Seattle

PHILIPPINES

Embassy of the Republic of the Philippines
1600 Massachusetts Avenue, NW., Washington, DC 20036
phone (202) 467–9300, fax 328–7614
The Honorable Patrick Ang Chuasoto
Minister (Charge d'Affaires ad Interim)
Consular Offices:
Alaska, Juneau
California:
Los Angeles
San Francisco
District of Columbia, Washington
Georgia, Atlanta
Guam, Tamuning
Hawaii, Honolulu
Illinois, Chicago
Michigan, Livonia
New York, New York
Northern Mariana Islands, Saipan
Oregon, Portland

Texas, Dallas
Trust Territories of the Pacific Islands:
Mariana Islands
Virgin Islands, St. Thomas

POLAND

Embassy of the Republic of Poland
2640 16th Street, NW., Washington, DC 20009
phone (202) 234–3800, fax 588–0565
His Excellency Piotr Antoni Wilczek
Ambassador E. and P.
Consular Offices:
Alaska, Anchorage
Arizona, Phoenix
California:
Belmont
Los Angeles
San Francisco
Colorado, Longmont
District of Columbia, Washington
Georgia, Atlanta
Hawaii, Honolulu
Idaho, Ketchum
Illinois, Chicago
Massachusetts, Boston
Missouri, St. Louis
Nevada, Las Vegas
New York, New York
North Carolina, Raleigh
Ohio, Oxford
Pennsylvania:
Philadelphia
Pittsburgh
Puerto Rico, Catano
Tennessee, Knoxville
Texas, Houston

PORTUGAL

Embassy of Portugal
2012 Massachusetts Avenue, NW., Washington, DC 20036
phone (202) 328–8610, fax 462–3726
His Excellency Domingos Teixeira De Abreu Fezas Vital
Ambassador E. and P.
Consular Offices:
California:
Los Angeles
San Francisco
Tulare
Connecticut, Waterbury
Florida:
Miami
Orlando
Hawaii, Honolulu
Illinois, Chicago
Louisiana, New Orleans
Massachusetts:
Boston
New Bedford
New Jersey, Newark
New York, New York
North Carolina, Durham
Pennsylvania, Philadelphia
Puerto Rico, San Juan
Rhode Island, Providence
Texas, Houston

QATAR

Embassy of the State of Qatar
2555 M Street, NW., Suite 200, Washington, DC 20037
phone (202) 274–1600, fax 237–0061
His Excellency Meshal Hamad M.J. Al Thani
Ambassador E. and P.
Consular Office:
New York, New York
Texas, Houston

ROMANIA

Embassy of Romania
1607 23rd Street, NW., Washington, DC 20008
phone (202) 332–4846, fax 232–4748
His Excellency George Cristian Maior
Ambassador E. and P.
Consular Offices:
Arizona, Tempe
California:
Los Angeles
San Francisco
District of Columbia, Washington
Florida:
Cape Coral
Hollywood
Georgia, Atlanta
Illinois, Chicago
Indiana, Indianapolis
Louisiana, New Orleans
Massachusetts, Boston
Michigan, Detroit
Minnesota, Minneapolis
Nevada, Las Vegas
New York, New York
Ohio, Cleveland
Oklahoma, Norman
Oregon, Portland
Pennsylvania, Philadelphia
Texas:
Dallas
Houston
Utah, Salt Lake City

RUSSIA

Embassy of the Russian Federation

2650 Wisconsin Avenue, NW., Washington, DC 20007
phone (202) 298–5700, fax (202) 939–8919
His Excellency Anatoly Ivanovich Antonov
Ambassador E. and P.
Consular Offices:
California:
Fair Oaks
San Francisco
Colorado, Denver
District of Columbia, Washington
Florida, Pinellas Park
Minnesota, Minneapolis
New York, New York
Puerto Rico, San Juan
Texas, Houston
Utah, Salt Lake City
Washington, Seattle

RWANDA

Embassy of the Republic of Rwanda
1875 Connecticut Avenue, NW., Suite 540, Washington, DC 20009
phone (202) 232–2882, fax 232–4544
Her Excellency Mathilde Mukantabana
Ambassador E. and P.
Consular Offices:
Illinois, Geneva
Massachusetts, Boston
Texas, Houston

SAMOA

Embassy of the Independent State of Samoa
800 2nd Avenue, 4th Floor, New York, NY 10017
phone (212) 599–6196, fax 599–0797
His Excellency Feturi Elisaia
Ambassador E. and P.
Consular Offices:
American Samoa, Pago Pago
California, Torrance
Florida, Melbourne
Hawaii, Honolulu

SAN MARINO

Embassy of Republic of San Marino
1711 N Street, NW., 2nd Floor, Washington, DC 20036
phone (202) 223–2418, fax 223–2748
His Excellency Damiano Beleffi
Ambassador E. and P.
Consular Offices:
District of Columbia, Washington
Hawaii, Honolulu
Michigan, Troy
New York, New York

SAO TOME AND PRINCIPE

Embassy of Sao Tome and Principe
675 Third Avenue, Suite 1807 New York, NY 10017
phone (212) 651–8116, fax 651–8117
His Excellency C. Azevedo Agostinho Das Neves
Ambassador E. and P.
Consular Offices:
Georgia, Atlanta
Illinois, Chicago

SAUDI ARABIA

Embassy of Saudi Arabia
601 New Hampshire Avenue, NW., Washington, DC 20037
phone (202) 342–3800, fax (202) 338–6929
His Excellency Khalid bin Salman bin Abdulaziz Al Saud
Ambassador E. and P.
Consular Offices:
California, Los Angeles
District of Columbia, Washington
Illinois, Chicago
New York, New York
Texas, Houston

SENEGAL

Embassy of the Republic of Senegal
2215 M Street, NW., Washington, DC 20037
phone (202) 234–0540, fax 629–2961
His Excellency Babacar Diagne
Ambassador E. and P.
Consular Offices:
California, Burlingame
Florida, Miami
Georgia, Atlanta
Louisiana:
Baton Rouge
New Orleans
Missouri, Clayton
New York, New York
Rhode Island, Providence

SERBIA

Embassy of the Republic of Serbia
2134 Kalorama Road, NW., Washington, DC 20008
phone (202) 332–0333, fax 332–3933
His Excellency Derd Matkovic
Ambassador E. and P.
Consular Offices:
Colorado, Denver
Illinois, Chicago
Louisiana, Metairie
New York, New York
Ohio, Cleveland
Wyoming, Cheyenne

SEYCHELLES

Embassy of the Republic of Seychelles

800 Second Avenue, Suite 400G, New York, NY 10017
Her Excellency Marie Louise Cecile Potter
Ambassador E. and P.
Consular Offices:
Alaska, Anchorage
Arizona, Sun City
New York, New York
Washington, Seattle

SIERRA LEONE

Embassy of Sierra Leone
1701 19th Street, NW., Washington, DC 20009
phone (202) 939–9261, fax 483–1793
His Excellency Bockari Kortu Stevens
Ambassador E. and P.
Consular Office:
Florida, Miami
Georgia, Decatur
Illinois, Chicago
Massachusetts, Boston
Pennsylvania, Philadelphia

SINGAPORE

Embassy of the Republic of Singapore
3501 International Place, NW., Washington, DC 20008
phone (202) 537–3100, fax 537–0876
His Excellency Ashok Kumar
Ambassador E. and P.
Consular Offices:
California, San Francisco
Florida, Miami
Illinois, Chicago
New York, New York

SLOVAK

Embassy of the Slovak Republic
3523 International Court, NW., Washington, DC 20008
phone (202) 237–1054, fax 237–6438
His Excellency Peter Kmec
Ambassador E. and P.
Consular Offices:
California, San Francisco
Colorado, Denver
District of Columbia, Washington
Florida, Miami
Illinois, Chicago
Indiana, Indianapolis
Massachusetts, Weston
Michigan, Detroit
Minnesota, Bloomington
Missouri, Kansas City
New York, New York
Pennsylvania, Pittsburgh
South Carolina, Columbia
Texas, Dallas

SLOVENIA

Embassy of the Republic of Slovenia
2410 California Street, NW., Washington, DC 20008
phone (202) 386–6610, fax 386–6633
His Excellency Stanislav Vidovic
Ambassador E. and P.
Consular Offices:
California, San Francisco
Colorado, Denver
Florida, Miami Beach
Georgia, Atlanta
Hawaii, Honolulu
Illinois, Chicago
Kansas, Mission Hills
Michigan, Dearborn
Minnesota, St. Paul
New York, New York
Ohio, Cleveland
Pennsylvania, Pitsburgh
Tennessee, Knoxville
Texas, Houston

SOLOMON ISLANDS

Embassy of the Solomon Islands
800 Second Avenue, Suite 400L, New York, NY 10017
phone (212) 599–6192, fax 661–8925
His Excellency Robert Sisilo
Ambassador E. and P.

SOMALIA

Embassy of Somalia
1705 Desales Street, Suite 300, Washington, DC 20036
His Excellency Ahmed Isse Awad
Ambassador E. and P.

SOUTH AFRICA

Embassy of the Republic of South Africa
3051 Massachusetts Avenue, NW., Washington, DC 20008
phone (202) 232–4400, fax 265–1607
His Excellency Mninwa Johannes Mahlangu
Ambassador E. and P.
Consular Offices:
California, Los Angeles
Illinois, Chicago
Kansas, Kansas City
Louisiana, New Orleans
Minnesota, Minneapolis
New York, New York
Texas, Dallas
Wisconsin, Milwaukee

SOUTH SUDAN

Embassy of the Republic of South Sudan
1015 31st Street, NW., Floor 3, Washington, DC 20007

His Excellency Garang Diing Akuong
Ambassador

SPAIN

Embassy of Spain
2375 Pennsylvania Avenue, NW., Washington, DC 20037
phone (202) 452–0100, fax 833–5670
His Excellency Pedro Morenes Eulate
Ambassador E. and P.
Consular Offices:
- Alabama, Birmingham
- Alaska, Anchorage
- Arizona, Phoenix
- California:
  - Los Angeles
  - San Diego
  - San Francisco
- Colorado, Englewood
- District of Columbia, Washington
- Florida:
  - Miami
  - Orlando
  - Pensacola
  - Tampa
- Georgia, Atlanta
- Hawaii, Honolulu
- Idaho, Boise
- Illinois, Chicago
- Louisiana, New Orleans
- Massachusetts, Boston
- Michigan, Ann Arbor
- Missouri:
  - Kansas City
  - St. Louis
- New Jersey, Newark
- New Mexico:
  - Albuquerque
  - Santa Fe
- New York, New York
- Oklahoma, Oklahoma City
- Puerto Rico, San Juan
- Texas:
  - Corpus Christi
  - Dallas
  - El Paso
  - Houston
  - San Antonio
- Utah, Salt Lake City
- Washington, Seattle

SRI LANKA

Embassy of the Democratic Socialist Republic of Sri Lanka
2148 Wyoming Avenue, NW., Washington, DC 20008
phone (202) 483–4025, fax 232–7181
His Excellency Prasad Kariyawasam
Ambassador E. and P.
Consular Offices:
- Arizona, Phoenix
- California, Los Angeles
- Hawaii, Honolulu
- New Hampshire, Boston
- New Mexico, Santa Fe
- New York, New York
- Texas, Houston

SAINT KITTS AND NEVIS

Embassy of St. Kitts and Nevis
1627 K Street, NW., Suite 1200, Washington, DC 20006
phone (202) 686–2636
Her Excellency Thelma Phillip-Browne
Ambassador E. and P.
Consular Offices:
- California, Los Angeles
- Florida, Miami
- New York, New York
- Pennsylvania, Philadelphia
- Puerto Rico, Guaynabo
- Virgin Islands, St. Thomas

SAINT LUCIA

Embassy of St. Lucia
1629 K Street, NW., Suite 1250, Washington, DC 20009
phone (202) 364–6792, fax (202) 364–6723
The Honorable Elaine Juliet Mallet Phillip
Minister/Counselor (Charge d'Affaires ad Interim)
Consular Offices:
- California, Los Angeles
- Florida, Coral Gables
- New York, New York

SAINT VINCENT AND THE GRENADINES

Embassy of St. Vincent and the Grenadines
1627 K Street, NW., Suite 1202, Washington, DC 20006
phone (202) 364–6730, fax 364–6736
Her Excellency Lou-Anne Gaylene Gilchrist
Ambassador E. and P.
Consular Offices:
- California, Los Angeles
- Florida, Groveland
- Louisiana, New Orleans
- New York, New York
- Puerto Rico, Guaynabo

SUDAN

Embassy of the Republic of the Sudan
2210 Massachusetts Avenue, NW., Washington, DC 20008
phone (202) 338–8565, fax 667–2406

Mr. Maowia Osman Khalid Mohammed
Counselor (Deputy Chief of Mission)

SURINAME

Embassy of the Republic of Suriname
4301 Connecticut Avenue, NW., Suite 460, Washington, DC 20008
phone (202) 244–7488, fax 244–5878
Her Excellency Niermala Sakoentala Badrising
Ambassador E. and P.
Consular Offices:
- Florida, Miami
- Louisiana, New Orleans

SWAZILAND

Embassy of the Kingdom of Swaziland
1712 New Hampshire Avenue, NW., Washington, DC 20009
phone (202) 234–5002, fax 234–8254
His Excellency Njabuliso Gwebu
Ambassador E. and P.

SWEDEN

Embassy of Sweden
2900 K Street, NW., Washington, DC 20007
phone (202) 467–2600, fax 467–2699
His Excellency Bjoern Olof Lyrvall
Ambassador E. and P.
Consular Offices:
- Alaska, Anchorage
- Arizona, Scottsdale
- California:
  - San Diego
  - San Francisco
- Colorado, Denver
- District of Columbia, Washington
- Florida:
  - Ft. Lauderdale
  - Tampa
- Georgia, Atlanta
- Hawaii, Honolulu
- Illinois, Chicago
- Kansas, Merriam
- Louisiana, New Orleans
- Massachusetts, Boston
- Michigan, Ann Arbor
- Minnesota, Minneapolis
- Missouri, St. Louis
- Nebraska, Omaha
- Nevada, Las Vegas
- New York:
  - Jamestown
  - New York
- North Carolina, Raleigh
- Ohio, Cleveland
- Pennsylvania, Ardmore
- Puerto Rico, San Juan
- Texas:
  - Dallas
  - Houston
- Utah, Salt Lake City
- Virgin Islands, St. Thomas
- Virginia, Norfolk
- Washington, Seattle
- Wisconsin, Milwaukee

SWITZERLAND

Embassy of Switzerland
2900 Cathedral Avenue, NW., Washington, DC 20008
phone (202) 745–7900, fax 387–2564
His Excellency Martin Werner Dahinden
Ambassador E. and P.
Consular Offices:
- Arizona, Scottsdale
- California:
  - Los Angeles
  - San Francisco
- Colorado, Boulder
- District of Columbia, Washington
- Florida:
  - Miami
  - Orlando
- Georgia, Atlanta
- Hawaii, Honolulu
- Illinois, Chicago
- Indiana, Indianapolis
- Louisiana, New Orleans
- Massachusetts, Boston
- Michigan, Dearborn
- Minnesota, Minneapolis
- Missouri, Kansas City
- Nevada, Las Vegas
- New York:
  - New York
  - Williamsville
- North Carolina, Charlotte
- Ohio, Cleveland
- Oklahoma, Edmond
- Pennsylvania:
  - Philadelphia
  - Pittsburgh
- Puerto Rico, San Juan
- Texas:
  - Dallas
  - Houston
- Utah, Sandy
- Washington, Mercer Island

SYRIA

Embassy of the Syrian Arab Republic
2215 Wyoming Avenue, NW., Washington, DC 20008
phone (202) 232–6313, fax 234–9548

TAJIKISTAN

Embassy of the Republic of Tajikistan
1005 New Hampshire Avenue, NW., Washington, DC 20037
phone (202) 223–6090, fax 223–6091
His Excellency Farhod Salim
Ambassador E. and P.
Consular Office: District of Columbia, Washington

TANZANIA

Embassy of the United Republic of Tanzania
1232 22nd Street, NW., Washington, DC 20037
phone (202) 939–6125, fax 797–7408
His Excellency Wilson Mutagaywa Masilingi
Ambassador E. and P.
Consular Offices:
- California, San Rafael
- Georgia, Atlanta
- Illinois, St. Louis
- Louisiana, New Orleans
- Michigan, Grosse Pointe Farms
- Minnesota, Minneapolis
- New Mexico, Albuquerque
- Pennsylvania, Philadelphia

THAILAND

Embassy of Thailand
1024 Wisconsin Avenue, NW., Washington, DC 20007
phone (202) 944–3600, fax 944–3611
His Excellency Pisan Manawapat
Ambassador E. and P.
Consular Offices:
- Alabama, Montgomery
- California, Los Angeles
- Colorado, Denver
- Florida, Coral Gables
- Georgia, Atlanta
- Hawaii, Honolulu
- Illinois, Chicago
- Louisiana, New Orleans
- Massachusetts, Boston
- New York, New York
- Oklahoma, Broken Arrow
- Oregon, Portland
- Puerto Rico, Hato Rey
- Texas:
  - Dallas
  - Houston
- Utah, Salt Lake City

TIMOR LESTE

Embassy of the Democratic Republic of Timor Leste
4201 Connecticut Avenue, NW., Suite 504, Washington, DC 20008
phone (202) 966–3202, fax 966–3205
His Excellency Domingos Sarmento Alves
Ambassador E. and P.

TOGO

Embassy of the Republic of Togo
2208 Massachusetts Avenue, NW., Washington, DC 20008
phone (202) 234–4212, fax 232–3190
His Excellency Frederic Edem Hegbe
Ambassador E. and P.
Consular Offices:
- California, Chatsworth
- Florida, Miami

TONGA

Embassy of the Kingdom of Tonga
250 East 51st Street, New York, NY 10022
phone (917) 369–1025, fax 369–1024
His Excellency Mahe Uliuli Sandhurst Tupouniua
Ambassador E. and P.
Consular Offices:
- California, San Francisco
- Hawaii, Honolulu

TRINIDAD AND TOBAGO

Embassy of the Republic of Trinidad and Tobago
1708 Massachusetts Avenue, NW., Washington, DC 20036
phone (202) 467–6490, fax 785–3130
His Excellency Anthony Wayne Jerome Phillips Spencer
Ambassador E. and P.
Consular Offices:
- Florida, Miami
- New York, New York
- Puerto Rico, San Juan
- Texas, Houston

TUNISIA

Embassy of Tunisia
1515 Massachusetts Avenue, NW., Washington, DC 20005
phone (202) 862–1850, fax 862–1858
His Excellency Faycal Gouia
Ambassador E. and P.
Consular Offices:
- California, San Francisco
- Florida, Miami
- New York, New York
- Texas, Dallas

TURKEY

Embassy of the Republic of Turkey
2525 Massachusetts Avenue, NW., Washington, DC 20008
phone (202) 612–6700, fax 612–6744
His Excellency Serdar Kilic
Ambassador E. and P.
Consular Offices:

California:
Fair Oaks
Los Angeles
Oakland
Florida, Miami
Georgia, Atlanta
Illinois, Chicago
Maryland, Baltimore
Massachusetts, Boston
Michigan, Farmington
Missouri, Kansas City
New York, New York
Texas, Houston
Washington, Seattle

TURKMENISTAN

Embassy of Turkmenistan
2207 Massachusetts Avenue, NW., Washington, DC 20008
phone (202) 588–1500, fax 588–0697
His Excellency Meret Bairamovich Orazov
Ambassador E. and P.

TUVALU

Embassy of Tuvalu
800 Second Avenue, Suite 400D, New York, NY 10017
phone (212) 490–0534
His Excellency Samuelu Laloniu
Ambassador E. and P.

UGANDA

Embassy of the Republic of Uganda
5911 16th Street, NW., Washington, DC 20011
phone (202) 726–0416, fax 726–1727
The Honorable Dickson Ogwang
Minister / Counselor (Charge d'Affaires ad Interim)
Consular Office: California, San Diego

UKRAINE

Embassy of Ukraine
3350 M Street, NW., Washington, DC 20007
phone (202) 349–2920, fax 333–0817
His Excellency Valerii Chalyi
Ambassador E. and P.
Consular Offices:
Alabama, Birmingham
Arizona, Tucson
California, San Francisco
District of Columbia, Washington
Illinois, Chicago
Louisiana, New Orleans
Michigan, Detroit
New York, New York
Ohio, Cleveland
Texas, Houston
Utah, Salt Lake City

UNITED ARAB EMIRATES

Embassy of the United Arab Emirates
3522 International Court, NW., Washington, DC 20008
phone (202) 243–2400, fax 243–2432
His Excellency Yousif Mana Saeed Alotaiba
Ambassador E. and P.
Consular Offices:
California, Beverly Hills

UNITED KINGDOM

British Embassy
3100 Massachusetts Avenue, NW., Washington, DC 20008
phone (202) 588–6500, fax 588–7870
His Excellency Nigel Kim Darroch
Ambassador E. and P.
Consular Offices:
Alaska, Anchorage
Arizona, Phoenix
California:
Los Angeles
San Francisco
Colorado, Denver
District of Columbia, Washington
Florida:
Miami
Orlando
Tallahassee
Georgia, Atlanta
Illinois, Chicago
Louisiana, New Orleans
Massachusetts, Boston
Michigan, Detroit
Minnesota, Minneapolis
Nevada, Las Vegas
New York, New York
North Carolina, Charlotte
Ohio, Cleveland
Oklahoma, Tulsa
Oregon, Portland
Pennsylvania:
Philadelphia
Pittsburgh
Puerto Rico, San Juan
Tennessee, Nashville
Texas:
Dallas
Houston
San Antonio
Utah, Salt Lake City

URUGUAY

Embassy of Uruguay
1913 I Street, NW., Washington, DC 20006
phone (202) 331–1313, fax 331–8142
His Excellency Carlos Alberto Gianelli Derois
Ambassador E. and P.
Consular Offices:
California:
Los Angeles
Sacramento
San Francisco
District of Columbia, Washington
Florida, Miami
Illinois, Chicago
Louisiana, Jefferson
Nevada, Reno
New York, New York
Pennsylvania, Philadelphia
Puerto Rico, San Juan
Texas, Houston
Utah, Salt Lake City

UZBEKISTAN

Embassy of the Republic of Uzbekistan
1746 Massachusetts Avenue, NW., Washington, DC 20036
phone (202) 293–6803, fax 293–6804
Said Rustamov
Counselor (Charge d'Affaires ad Interim)
Consular Offices:
District of Columbia, Washington
Georgia, Greensboro
New York, New York
Washington, Seattle
Ukraine
United Arbo Emirates
United Kingdom
Uzbekistan

VENEZUELA

Embassy of the Bolivarian Republic of Venezuela
1099 30th Street, NW., Washington, DC 20007
phone (202) 342–2214, fax 342–6810
Mr. Carlos Julio Ron Martinez
Counselor (Charge d'Affaires ad Interim)
Consular Offices:
California, San Francisco
Florida, Miami
Illinois, Chicago
Louisiana, New Orleans
Massachusetts, Boston
New York, New York
Puerto Rico:
Hato Rey
San Juan
Texas, Houston

VIETNAM

Embassy of Vietnam
1233 20th Street, NW., Suite 400, Washington, DC 20036
phone (202) 861–0737, fax 861–0917
His Excellency Pham Quang Vinh
Ambassador E. and P.
Consular Offices:
California, San Francisco
New York, New York
Texas, Houston

YEMEN

Embassy of the Republic of Yemen
2319 Wyoming Avenue, NW., Washington, DC 20008
phone (202) 965–4760, fax 337–2017
His Excellency Ahmed Awad Ahmed bin Mubarak
Counselor (Charge d'Affaires ad Interim)
Consular Offices:
California, San Francisco
District of Columbia, Washington
Michigan, Dearborn

ZAMBIA

Embassy of the Republic of Zambia
2419 Massachusetts Avenue, NW., Washington, DC 20008
phone (202) 265–9717, fax 332–0826
The Honorable Joseph Raphael Chilaizya
Minister / Counselor (Charge d'Affaires ad Interim)

ZIMBABWE

Embassy of the Republic of Zimbabwe
1608 New Hampshire Avenue, NW., Washington, DC 20009
phone (202) 332–7100, fax 483–9326
His Excellency Ammon Mutembwa
Ambassador E. and P.

The following is a list of countries with which diplomatic relations have been severed:

After each country, in parenthesis, is the name of the country's protecting power in the United States.

CUBA (Switzerland)
IRAN (Pakistan)
ZIMBABWE

PRESS GALLERIES *

SENATE PRESS GALLERY

The Capitol, Room S–316, phone 224–0241

www.dailypress.senate.gov

Director.—Laura Lytle
Deputy Director.—Christopher Bois

Senior Media Relations Coordinators:
Amy H. Gross
John E. Mulligan III
Kristyn K. Socknat
Media Relations Coordinators:
Laura E. Reed
Samantha J. Yeider

HOUSE PRESS GALLERY

The Capitol, Room H–315, phone 225–3945

https://pressgallery.house.gov

Superintendent.—Annie Tin
Deputy Superintendent.—Justin J. Supon
Assistant Superintendents:
Ric Anderson
Edward Kachinske
Kristine Michalson

STANDING COMMITTEE OF CORRESPONDENTS

Billy House, Bloomberg, Chair
Joseph Morton, Omaha World Herald, Secretary
Karoun Demirjian, Washington Post
Tamar Hallerman, Atlanta Journal Constitution
Deirdre Shesgreen, Gannett

RULES GOVERNING PRESS GALLERIES

1. Administration of the press galleries shall be vested in a Standing Committee of Correspondents elected by accredited members of the Galleries. The Committee shall consist of five persons elected to serve for terms of two years. Provided, however, that at the election in January 1951, the three candidates receiving the highest number of votes shall serve for two years and the remaining two for one year. Thereafter, three members shall be elected in odd-numbered years and two in even-numbered years. Elections shall be held in January. The Committee shall elect its own chairman and secretary. Vacancies on the Committee shall be filled by special election to be called by the Standing Committee.

2. Persons desiring admission to the press galleries of Congress shall make application in accordance with Rule VI of the House of Representatives, subject to the direction and

*Information is based on data furnished and edited by each respective Gallery.

control of the Speaker and Rule 33 of the Senate, which rules shall be interpreted and administered by the Standing Committee of Correspondents, subject to the review and an approval by the Senate Committee on Rules and Administration.

3. The Standing Committee of Correspondents shall limit membership in the press galleries to bone fide correspondents of repute in their profession, under such rules as the Standing Committee of Correspondents shall prescribe.

4. An applicant for press credentials through the Daily Press Galleries must establish to the satisfaction of the Standing Committee of Correspondents that he or she is a fulltime, paid correspondent who requires on-site access to congressional members and staff.

Correspondents must be employed by a news organization:

(a) with General Publication periodicals mailing privileges under U.S. Postal Service rules, and which publishes daily; or

(b) whose principal business is the daily dissemination of original news and opinion of interest to a broad segment of the public, and which has published continuously for 18 months.

The applicant must reside in the Washington, D.C. area, and must not be engaged in any lobbying or paid advocacy, advertising, publicity or promotion work for any individual, political party, corporation, organization, or agency of the U.S. Government, or in prosecuting any claim before Congress or any federal government department, and will not do so while a member of the Daily Press Galleries.

Applicants' publications must be editorially independent of any institution, foundation or interest group that lobbies the federal government, or that is not principally a general news organization.

Failure to provide information to the Standing Committee for this determination, or misrepresenting information, can result in the denial or revocation of credentials.

5. Members of the families of correspondents are not entitled to the privileges of the Galleries.

6. The Standing Committee of Correspondents shall propose no changes in these rules except upon petition in writing signed by not less than 100 accredited members of the galleries. The above rules have been approved by the Committee on Rules and Administration.

PAUL D. RYAN,
Speaker of the House of Representatives.

RICHARD C. SHELBY,
Chair, Senate Committee on Rules and Administration.

MEMBERS ENTITLED TO ADMISSION

PRESS GALLERIES

Abbott, Charles: FERN's Ag Insider
Abdollah, Tamar: Associated Press
Abdul, Shahzad: Agence France-Presse
Abott, Richard: Defense Daily
Abutaleb, Yasmeen: Thomson Reuters
Achenbach, Joel: Washington Post
Ackerman, Andrew: Wall Street Journal / Dow Jones
Ackerman, Spencer: Daily Beast
Adams, Rebecca: CQ Roll Call
Adams, T. Becket: Washington Examiner
Adams-Heard, Rachel: S&P Global
Ahmann, Timothy: Thomson Reuters
Ahmed-Akbar, Shahid: Huffington Post
Aikawa, Haruyuki: Mainichi Shimbun
Albright Nicole Gaudiano: Gannett Washington Bureau
Alcindor, Yamiche: New York Times
Alexander, Charles: Thomson Reuters
Alexander, Keith: Washington Post
Alfaro, Hector: Bloomberg News
Alhendi, Abdulaziz: Saudi Press Agency
Allahverdi, Safvan: Anadolu News Agency
Allen, Nicholas: London Daily Telegraph
Allen, William: USA Today
Allison, William: Bloomberg News
Alonso-Hernan, Martin: EFE News Services
Alonso, Ricardo: Associated Press
Alonso, Nicolas: El Pais
Ampolsk, Sarah: Kyodo News
Andalo, Paula: Kaiser Health News
Anderson, Mark: Wall Street Journal / Dow Jones
Anderson, Nick: Washington Post
Andrews, Natalie: Wall Street Journal / Dow Jones
Aomoto, Riyo: Kyodo News
Appelbaum, Binyamin: New York Times
Appleby, Julie: Kaiser Health News
Arai, Takuya: Kyodo News
Araki, Yumi: Yomiuri Shimbun
Aratani, Lori: Washington Post
Arkin, James: Real Clear Politics
Armour, Stephanie: Wall Street Journal / Dow Jones
Armstrong, Joshua: S&P Global
Armstrong, Annalee: S&P Global
Arnold, Justin: Yomiuri Shimbun
Arnsdorf, Isaac: ProPublica
Arundel, Kara: LRP Publications
Asami, Eiichi: Kyodo News
Ashizuka, Tomoko: Nikkei
Ashworth, Lauran:Associated Press
Asseo, Laurie: Bloomberg News
Atkins, Kimberly: Boston Herald
Aukofer, Frank: Artists & Writers Syndicate
Babbage, Sarah: Bloomberg News
Bacon, Erin: CQ Roll Call
Bain, Benjamin: Bloomberg News
Baker, Peter: New York Times
Balcerzak, Ashley: Center for Public Integrity
Baldor, Lolita: Associated Press
Ball, Michael: Argus Media
Ballhaus, Rebecca: Wall Street Journal / Dow Jones
Balz, Daniel: Washington Post
Banks, Adelle: Religion News Service
Baradat, Eric: Agence France-Presse
Barakat, Matthew: Associated Press
Barbeta Sanchez, Jordi: La Vanguardia
Barderas, Sara: German Press Agency—DPA
Barker, Jeffrey: Baltimore Sun
Barnes, Robert: Washington Post
Baron, Martin: Washington Post
Barone, Michael: Washington Examiner
Barr, Cameron: Washington Post
Barrera, Ruben: Notimex Mexican News Agency
Barrett, Barbara: McClatchy
Barrett, John: Washington Post
Bartash, Jeffry: MarketWatch
Barthelemy, Laurent: Agence France-Presse
Barthelemy, Anne: Agence France-Presse
Bartz, Diane: Thomson Reuters
Barwick, John: Center for Public Integrity
Basen, Ryan: MedPage Today
Bassett, Laura: Huffington Post
Bastasch, Michael: Daily Caller
Baudoux, Marc-Antoine: Agence France-Presse
Bauer-Wolf, Jeremy: Inside Higher Ed
Baumann, Nicholas: Huffington Post
Baumgaertner, Emily: New York Times
Beachum, Lateshia: Center for Public Integrity
Beattie, Jeff: Energy Daily
Beattie, Anita: Agence France-Presse
Beatty, Andrew: Agence France-Presse
Becker, Amanda: Thomson Reuters
Beckett, Paul: Wall Street Journal / Dow Jones
Beckett, Lois: Guardian US
Bedard, Paul: Washington Examiner
Bedford, Christopher: Daily Caller
Beech, Eric: Thomson Reuters
Beene, Ryan: Bloomberg News
Bell, Alistair: Thomson Reuters
Bell, Jarrett: USA Today
Bendavid, Naftali: Wall Street Journal / Dow Jones

MEMBERS ENTITLED TO ADMISSION—Continued

Bender, Mike: Wall Street Journal / Dow Jones
Bendery, Jennifer: Huffington Post
Benjaminson, Wendy: USA Today
Benkelman, Susan: Wall Street Journal / Dow Jones
Bennett, Brian: Los Angeles Times
Bennett, John: CQ Roll Call
Bennett, Jared: Center for Public Integrity
Benning, Tom: Dallas Morning News
Berg, Rebecca: Real Clear Politics
Bergengruen, Vera: Buzzfeed
Berkowitz, Steve: USA Today
Berley, Max: Bloomberg News
Berry, Deborah: Gannett Washington Bureau
Berry, Lynn: Associated Press
Bialecki, Martin: German Press Agency—DPA
Bierman, Noah: Los Angeles Times
Biesecker, Michael: Associated Press
Billinson, Joshua: Independent Journal Review
Bilski, Christina: Nikkei
Bjerga, Alan: Bloomberg News
Blakely, Rhys: Times of London
Blanc, Sebastien: Agence France-Presse
Bland, Melissa: Thomson Reuters
Blum, Justin: Bloomberg News
Blumenthal, Paul: Huffington Post
Bluth, Rachel: Kaiser Health News
Boak, Joshua: Associated Press
Bobic, Igor: Huffington Post
Bocchetti, Mark: MLEX US
Bochinin, Anatoly: Itar-Tass News Agency
Bohan, Caren: Thomson Reuters
Booker, Janet: Wall Street Journal / Dow Jones
Bordelon, Brendan: National Journal
Borenstein, Seth: Associated Press
Borger, Julian: Guardian US
Boshart, Glen: S&P Global
Bouchard, Mikayla: New York Times
Bowers, Jeremy: New York Times
Bowers, Rebecca: Wall Street Journal / Dow Jones
Boyer, David: Washington Times
Boylan, Daniel: Washington Times
Bradley, Brian: International Trade Today
Brady, Erik: USA Today
Braun, Stephen: Associated Press
Bravin, Jess: Wall Street Journal / Dow Jones
Britton, Kathryn: Bloomberg News
Brock, Samuel: Argus Media
Brodbeck, Scott: LocalNews Now
Brodey, Sam: MinnPost
Brooks, David: La Jornada
Brooks, Jennifer: Minneapolis Star Tribune
Brown, Emily: LRP Publications
Brown, Emma: Washington Post
Brufke, Julia Grace: Daily Caller
Brumfield, Sarah: Associated Press
Brune, Thomas: Newsday
Brusoe, Peter: Bloomberg News
Bull, Alister: Bloomberg News
Bumiller, Elisabeth: New York Times
Burgues, Miriam: EFE News Services
Burke, Melissa: Detroit News
Burley, Tahirah: New York Times
Burns, Robert: Associated Press
Burr, Thomas: Salt Lake Tribune
Burton, Thomas: Wall Street Journal / Dow Jones
Buskirk, Howard: Communications Daily
Butler, Desmond: Associated Press
Butler, Adam: Buzzfeed
Bykowicz, Julie: Associated Press
Byler, David: Real Clear Politics
Byrd, Haley: Independent Journal Review
Cahlink, Mary Clare Jalonick: Associated Press
Cahn, Dianna: Stars and Stripes
Cahn, Morgan: CQ Roll Call
Caldwell, Alicia: Wall Street Journal / Dow Jones
Cannon, Carl: Real Clear Politics
Capaccio, Anthony: Bloomberg News
Caplan, Abby: Argus Media
Cardine, Kyle: Buzzfeed
Carey, Dominic: Bloomberg News
Carey, Mary-Agnes: Kaiser Health News
Carney, Timothy: Washington Examiner
Carrasquillo, Adrian: Buzzfeed
Carroll, Lauren: Tampa Bay Times
Carter, Charlene: CQ Roll Call
Carter, John: Market News International
Carter, Zachary: Huffington Post
Cartillier, Jerome: Agence France-Presse
Casado, Cristina Garcia: EFE News Services
Casey, John: Bond Buyer
Cassata, Donna: Associated Press
Celik, Can: MLEX US
Cerbin, Carolyn: USA Today
Chae, Byunggun: Joongang Ilbo
Chaffee, Conrad: Tokyo Chunichi Shimbun
Chambers, Francesca: Daily Mail (UK)
Chandra, Shobhana: Bloomberg News
Chaney, Sarah: Wall Street Journal / Dow Jones
Chang, Chia: United Daily News
Charlton, Emma: Agence France-Presse
Chen, Hui-Min: World Journal
Chen, Lidan: China People's Daily
Cheng, Tsung-Shen: Taiwan Central News Agency
Cheung, Brian: S&P Global
Chiacu, Doina: Thomson Reuters
Chinni, Dante: Wall Street Journal / Dow Jones
Cho, Cheolwhan: Korea Times
Chon, Gina: Thomson Reuters
Chong, Christina: Korea Times
Christensen, Michael: CQ Roll Call
Christian, Molly-Kathleen: S&P Global
Christian, Rodney: Wall Street Journal / Dow Jones
Chudakov, Anton: Itar-Tass News Agency
Cirilli, Kevin: Bloomberg News

MEMBERS ENTITLED TO ADMISSION—Continued

Clark, Davd: Agence France-Presse
Clark, Lenora: Wall Street Journal / Dow Jones
Clark, Lesley: McClatchy
Clarke, Toni: Thomson Reuters
Clason, Lauren: CQ Roll Call
Clearfield, Alexander: National Journal
Clift, Eleanor: Daily Beast
Cloud, David: Los Angeles Times
Clozel, Lalita: American Banker
Coats, Christopher: S&P Global
Codrea, George: CQ Roll Call
Coglianese, Vincent: Daily Caller
Cohen, Kelly: Washington Examiner
Cohen, Kristin: Bloomberg News
Colman, Michael: Albuquerque Journal
Collins, Brian: American Banker
Collins, Eliza: USA Today
Collins, Michael: Gannett Washington Bureau
Colvin, Ross: Thomson Reuters
Colvin, Jill: Associated Press
Condon, Christopher: Bloomberg News
Condon, George: National Journal
Conlon, Charles: CQ Roll Call
Cook, David: Christian Science Monitor
Cooney, Peter: Thomson Reuters
Copley, Michael: S&P Global
Copur, Hakan: Anadolu News Agency
Corchado, Alfredo: Dallas Morning News
Cornwell, Susan: Thomson Reuters
Costa, Robert: Washington Post
Couronne, Ivan: Agence France-Presse
Cowan, Richard: Thomson Reuters
Cox, Matthew: Military.com
Crane, Marcy: S&P Global
Crilley, Margaret: Daily Caller
Crutsinger, Martin: Associated Press
Cullison, Alan: Wall Street Journal / Dow Jones
Cunningham, Paige: Washington Post
Curran, Timothy: Washington Post
Curry, Thomas: CQ Roll Call
Curtis, Laura: Bloomberg News
Custer, Anne: German Press Agency—DPA
Cuzin, Elodie: Agence France-Presse
Dale, Daniel: Toronto Star
Daley, Kevin: Daily Caller
Daly, Matthew: Associated Press
D'Amico, Esther: Merger Market Group
Daniel, Douglass: Associated Press
Danilova, Mariya: Associated Press
Date, Shirish: Huffington Post
Datoc, Christian: Daily Caller
Daugherty, Alex: McClatchy
Davenport, Coral: New York Times
Davidson, Joe: Washington Post
Davidson, Julie: LRP Publications
Davidson-Choma, Katherine: Wall Street Journal / Dow Jones
Davis, Julie: New York Times
Davis, Robert: Wall Street Journal / Dow Jones
Davis, Aaron: Washington Post
Day, Chad: Associated Press
Day, Jim: Energy Daily
DE-Freytas, Mariko: Kyodo News
DeBonis, Michael: Washington Post
DeChiaro, Dean: CQ Roll Call
Decker, Susan: Bloomberg News
Decker, Cathleen: Los Angeles Times
DeFrank, Thomas: National Journal
Dei, Ryota: Jiji Press
Delaney, Arthur: Huffington Post
Delgado-Robles, Jose: El Nuevo Dia
DelReal-Perez, Jose: New York Times
Demirjian, Karoun: Washington Post
Deng, Boer: Times of London
Dennis, Brady: Washington Post
Dennis, Steven: Bloomberg News
Desiderio, Andrew: Daily Beast
Dexheimer, Elizabeth: Bloomberg News
DeYoung, Karen: Washington Post
Diaz, Kevin: Houston Chronicle
Diaz-Briseno, Jose: Reforma Newspaper
Dieste Markl, Alina: Agence France-Presse
Dillon, Jeremy: CQ Roll Call
Dinan, Stephen: Washington Times
Dlouhy, Jennifer: Bloomberg News
Dobrik, Joseph: Global Investigations Review
Dolan, Christopher: Washington Times
Dolinger, David: Wall Street Journal / Dow Jones
Donachie, Robert: Daily Caller
Donaldson, Margaret: Agence France-Presse
Donhauser, Michael: German Press Agency—DPA
Donnan, Shawn: Financial Times
Donnelly, John: CQ Roll Call
Dopp, Terrence: Bloomberg News
Dorell, Oren: USA Today
Dorning, Michael: Bloomberg News
Doublet, Jean-Louis: Agence France-Presse
Douglas, Anna: McClatchy
Douglas, William: McClatchy
Dowd, Maureen: New York Times
Downey, Kirstin: Honolulu Civil Beat
Downing, James: Power Markets Today
Dozier, Kimberly: Daily Beast
Drabold, David: Mic
Drajem, Mark: Bloomberg News
Draper, Robert: New York Times
Drawbaugh, Kevin: Thomson Reuters
Drinkard, James: Associated Press
Drogin, Robert: Los Angeles Times
Drucker, David: Washington Examiner
Drusch, Andrea: Fort-Worth Star Telegram
du Lac, Joshua Freedom: Washington Post
Duggan, Loren: Bloomberg News
Duggan, Paul: Washington Post
Dumain, Emma: McClatchy

MEMBERS ENTITLED TO ADMISSION—Continued

Dunham, Will: Thomson Reuters
Dunsmuir, Lindsay: Thomson Reuters
Durkin, Erin: National Journal
Dusseau, Brigitte: Agence France-Presse
Earle, Geoffrey: Daily Mail (UK)
Eaton, Sabrina: Cleveland Plain Dealer
Eborn, Katrice: Bloomberg News
Edgerton, Anna: Bloomberg News
Edney, Anna: Bloomberg News
Edsall, Thomas: New York Times
Edwards-Levy, Ariel: Huffington Post
Eichelberger, Curtis: MLEX US
Eidelson, Joshua: Bloomberg News
Eilperin, Juliet: Washington Post
Eisler, Peter: Thomson Reuters
El Hamti, Maribel: EFE News Services
Elkins, Donald: Associated Press
Ellis, Kristi: S&P Global
Emmons, Alexander: The Intercept
Endo, Seiji: Akahata
Engblom, Andrew: S&P Global
Enjeti, Saagar: Daily Caller
Epstein, Edward: Argus Media
Epstein, Jennifer: Bloomberg News
Epstein, Reid: Wall Street Journal / Dow Jones
Epstein, Kayla: Washington Post
Estepa, Jessica: USA Today
Esther, Touitou: Agence France-Presse
Facher, Lev: STAT
Fahrenthold, David: Washington Post
Fallor, Evan: S&P Global
Fandos, Nicholas: New York Times
Faries, William: Bloomberg News
Faus, Catasus Joan: El Pais
Fears, Darryl: Washington Post
Feder, Joseph Lester, Buzzfeed
Feldman, Carole: Associated Press
Feldmann, Linda: Christian Science Monitor
Feldscher, Kyle: Washington Examiner
Felker, Edward: CQ Roll Call
Feltman, Peter: CQ Roll Call
Ferguson, Ellyn: CQ Roll Call
Fernandez, Pedro: EFE News Services
Fernandez-Pereda,Christina: El Pais
Ferragutcasas, Nuria: Ara
Ferriss, Susan: Center for Public Integrity
Festa, Elizabeth: S&P Global
Fineman, Howard: Huffington Post
Finn, Peter: Washington Post
Firth, Shannon: MedPage Today
Fischler, Jaco: CQ Roll Call
Fiscus, Amy: New York Times
Fisher, Marc: Washington Post
FitzGerald, Andrew: Wall Street Journal / Dow Jones
Flaherty, Anne: Associated Press
Flaherty, Mary: Washington Post
Flavelle, Christopher: Bloomberg News
Fleck-Bundchen, Isabel: Folha de Sao Paulo
Fleeson, William: Argus Media
Flegenheimer, Matthew: New York Times
Fleming, Sam: Financial Times
Foley, Elise: Huffington Post
Fontemaggi, Francesco: Agence France-Presse
Forden, Sara: Bloomberg News
Forrest, Brett: Wall Street Journal / Dow Jones
Fortes, Flavia: MLEX US
Fram, Alan: Associated Press
Francis, Theodore: Wall Street Journal / Dow Jones
Franke-Ruta, Garance: Yahoo News
Frappolli, Amelia: CQ Roll Call
Frates, Katherine: Daily Caller
Freedman, Daniel: Hearst Newspapers
Freking, Kevin: Associated Press
Friedman, Lisa: New York Times
Fritze, John: Baltimore Sun
Fuchino, Shinichi: Kyodo News
Fuhrig, Frank: German Press Agency—DPA
Fuller, Matthew: Huffington Post
Fullwood, Adrian: Associated Press
Funahashi, Eiichiro: Kyodo News
Fung, Brian: Washington Post
Fuog, Karin: CQ Roll Call
Furlow, Robert: Associated Press
Galewitz, Phil: Kaiser Health News
Gallu, Joshua: Bloomberg News
Gambino, Lauren: Guardian US
Gamboa, Aldo: Agence France-Presse
Gangitano, Alexandra: CQ Roll Call
Gao, Shi: China People's Daily
Gardner, Amy: Washington Post
Gardner, Tim: Thomson Reuters
Gates-Davis, Marilyn: CQ Roll Call
Gearan, Anne: Washington Post
Gehrke, Joel: Washington Examiner
Geidner, Christopher: Buzzfeed
Geier, Peter: Merger Market Group
Gelie, Philippe: Le Figaro
Germain, Daniel: CQ Roll Call
Ghani, Saleha: Bloomberg News
Ghosh, Nirmal: Singapore Straits Times
Gibney, James: Bloomberg News
Gibson, Virginia: Thomson Reuters
Gilbert, Craig: Milwaukee Journal Sentinel
Gilbert, Jessica: McClatchy
Gillison, Douglas: Agence France-Presse
Gillman, Todd: Dallas Morning News
Gillum, Jack: Washington Post
Ginsberg, Steven: Washington Post
Giroux, Gregory: Bloomberg News
Given, Margaret: Washington Examiner
Given, David: Argus Media
Glass, Pamela: Le Mauricien
Glueck, Katharine: McClatchy
Gnoffo, Anthony: CQ Roll Call

MEMBERS ENTITLED TO ADMISSION—Continued

Godos de la Puente, Raquel: EFE News Services
Gold, Matea: Washington Post
Golden, Rodrek: Thomson Reuters
Goldhamer, Sherry Marisha: Agence France-Presse
Goldman, Adam: New York Times
Goldstein, David: McClatchy
Goldstein, Steven: MarketWatch
Goldstein, Amy: Washington Post
Golle, Vince: Bloomberg News
Gomez, Sergio: El Tiempo
Good, Allison: S&P Global
Goodin, Emily: Real Clear Politics
Goodman, Alana: Daily Mail (UK)
Goodwin, Eric: McClatchy
Goodwin, Liz: Yahoo News
Gordon, D: Bloomberg News
Gordon, Gregory: McClatchy
Gordon, Marcy: Associated Press
Gordon, Michael: New York Times
Goto, Takayoshi: Tokyo Chunichi Shimbun
Gourdin, Michael: Bloomberg News
Grady, Anne: CQ Roll Call
Grandoni, Dino: Washington Post
Graves, Lucia: Guardian US
Greenberg, Jonathan: Tampa Bay Times
Greenwood, Calvin: Bloomberg News
Gresko, Jessica: Associated Press
Griffith, Stephanie: Agence France-Presse
Grim, Ryan: The Intercept
Grimaldi, James: Wall Street Journal / Dow Jones
Grisales, Claudia: Stars and Stripes
Groppe, Maureen: Gannett Washington Bureau
Guevara, Tomas: El Diario de Hoy
Gugarats, Haik: Argus Media
Guggenheim, Kenneth: Associated Press
Gurman, Sadie: Associated Press
Haas, Brandon: CQ Roll Call
Hackman, Michelle: Wall Street Journal / Dow Jones
Hager, George: USA Today
Haggerty, Neil: MLEX US
Hahn, Dorothea: Die Tageszeitung
Haire, Sara: Market News International
Hall, Eileen: Buzzfeed
Hall, Kevin: McClatchy
Hallerman, Tamar: Atlanta Journal Constitution
Halper, Evan: Los Angeles Times
Halsey, Ashley: Washington Post
Hamann, Carlos: Agence France-Presse
Hamburger, Thomas: Washington Post
Hamby, Christopher: Buzzfeed
Hamilton, Jesse: Bloomberg News
Hamilton-Martin, Roger: Global Investigations Review
Hammerman, Lucas: Real Clear Politics
Hammesfahr, Eric: CQ Roll Call
Hampton, Olivia: Agence France-Presse
Hancock, James: Kaiser Health News
Handley, Paul: Agence France-Presse
Hanrahan, Timothy: Wall Street Journal / Dow Jones
Harper, Jennifer: Washington Times
Harras, Steven: CQ Roll Call
Harrell, Donovan: McClatchy
Harris, Andrew: Bloomberg News
Harris, Bryant: Yomiuri Shimbun
Harris, Gardiner: New York Times
Harris, Shane: Wall Street Journal / Dow Jones
Harrison, David: Wall Street Journal / Dow Jones
Hart, Dan: Bloomberg News
Harte, Julia: Thomson Reuters
Hartson, Merrill: Associated Press
Harwell, Andrew: Washington Post
Hatch, David: Merger Market Group
Hayashi, Yuka: Wall Street Journal / Dow Jones
Heath, Bradford: USA Today
Heavey, Susan: Thomson Reuters
Heim, Joseph: Washington Post
Helderman, Rosalind: Washington Post
Heltman, John: American Banker
Henderson, Celia: Wall Street Journal / Dow Jones
Hennemuth, Maren: German Press Agency—DPA
Hennessey-Carroll, Kathleen: Associated Press
Hennigan, William: Los Angeles Times
Henriksson, Karin: Svenska Dagbladet
Hensley-Clancy, Molly: Buzzfeed
Heredia Rodriguez, Carmen: Kaiser Health News
Hermann, Peter: Washington Post
Hernadi, Elizabeth: Kaiser Health News
Hernandez, Arelis: Washington Post
Hernandez, Michael: Anadolu News Agency
Herndon, Astead: Boston Globe
Herrmann, Frank: Rheinische Post
Hewitt, Elizabeth: Vermont Digger
Higgins, Sean: Washington Examiner
Hirano, Ko: Kyodo News
Hitchcock, James: Real Clear Politics
Hnatyshyn, Zenon: Baltimore Sun
Hohmann, James: Washington Post
Holan, Clara: Tampa Bay Times
Holden, Dominic: Buzzfeed
Holland, Benjamin: Bloomberg News
Holland, Jesse: Associated Press
Holland, William: S&P Global
Holly, Christopher: Energy Daily
Holmes, Allan: Center for Public Integrity
Holzman, Jacob: CQ Roll Call
Hood, David: S&P Global
Hook, Janet: Wall Street Journal / Dow Jones
Hopkins, Jamie: Center for Public Integrity
Horikoshi, Toyohiro: Kyodo News
Horwitz, Jeffrey: Associated Press
Horwitz, Sari: Washington Post
Hosenball, Mark: Thomson Reuters
Host, Patrick: Defense Daily
House, Billy: Bloomberg News
Howard, Megan: Bloomberg News

MEMBERS ENTITLED TO ADMISSION—Continued

Howe, Colleen: Argus Media
Howell, Thomas: Washington Times
Hsu, Spencer: Washington Post
Hudson, John: Buzzfeed
Huetteman, Emmarie: New York Times
Huey-Burns, Caitlin: Real Clear Politics
Hughes, John: Bloomberg News
Hughes, Siobhan: Wall Street Journal / Dow Jones
Hulse, Carl: New York Times
Hume, Rebecca Lynn: Bond Buyer
Hunt, Albert: Bloomberg News
Hunter, John: CQ Roll Call
Hurley, Lawrence: Thomson Reuters
Hurt, Charles: Washington Times
Igarashi, Daisuke: Asahi Shimbun
Ikeda, Susumu: Akahata
Ileri, Kasim: Anadolu News Agency
Ip, Gregory: Wall Street Journal / Dow Jones
Irby, Katherine: McClatchy
Ishikawa, Tomonori: Tokyo Chunichi Shimbun
Isikoff, Michael: Yahoo News
Ito, Hitoshi: Kyodo News
Ivanovich, David: Argus Media
Iwaki, Yoshiyuki: Sekai Nippo
Jackson, David: USA Today
Jackson, Herbert: Record (Bergen County, NJ)
Jacobs, Benjamin: Guardian US
Jacobs, Jennifer: Bloomberg News
Jacobson, Louis: Tampa Bay Times
Jahn, Daniel: Agence France-Presse
Jameel, Maryam: Center for Public Integrity
Jamerson, Joshua: Wall Street Journal / Dow Jones
Jamieson, Dave: Huffington Post
Jamrisko, Michelle: Bloomberg News
Jan, Tracy: Washington Post
Jansen, Bart: USA Today
Jenks, Paul: CQ Roll Call
Jha, Lalit: India Press Trust
Jilani, Zaid: The Intercept
John, Arit: Bloomberg News
Johnson, Benjamin: Independent Journal Review
Johnson, Kevin: USA Today
Johnson, Timothy: McClatchy
Johnston, Margret: German Press Agency—DPA
Jopson, Barney: Financial Times
Julien, Cyril: Agence France-Presse
Kakan, Atheer: Anadolu News Agency
Kampeas, Ronald: Jewish Telegraphic Agency
Kane, Paul: Washington Post
Kang, Cecilia: New York Times
Kang, Jin Woo: Korea Times
Kang, Insun: Chosun Ilbo
Kano, Hiroyuki: Sankei Shimbun
Kaplan, Thomas: New York Times
Kapur, Sahil: Bloomberg News
Karam, Joyce: Al-Hayat
Kastner, Kevin: Market News International
Katori, Keisuke: Asahi Shimbun
Kawachi, Motoko: Nikkei
Kawai, Tomoyuki: Nikkei
Kawanami, Takeshi: Nikkei
Keating, Daniel: Washington Post
Keefe, Stephen: Nikkei
Kehoe, John: Austrailian Financial Review
Kell, Amanda: Associated Press
Kelley, Patrick: CQ Roll Call
Kellman Blazar, Laurie: Associated Press
Kelly, Christopher: Tokyo Chunichi Shimbun
Kelly, Erin: USA Today
Kelly, Kimbriell: Washington Post
Kelly, Ryan: CQ Roll Call
Kelly, Laura: Washington Times
Kenasari, Muhammed: Anadolu News Agency
Kendall, Brent: Wall Street Journal / Dow Jones
Kepler, Debra: Associated Press
Kerr, Jennifer: Associated Press
Kertes, Noella: CQ Roll Call
Kesling, Benjamin: Wall Street Journal / Dow Jones
Kessler, Glenn: Washington Post
Kiefer, Francine: Christian Science Monitor
Kim, Anne: CQ Roll Call
Kindy, Kimberly: Washington Post
King, Ledyard: Gannett Washington Bureau
King, Robert: Washington Examiner
Kinoshita, Hideomi: Kyodo News
Kipling, Bogdan: Kipling News Service
Kirsanov, Dmitry: Itar-Tass News Agency
Kittross, David: LRP Publications
Klapper, Bradley: Associated Press
Klein, Philip: Washington Examiner
Klimasinska, Katarzyna: Bloomberg News
Klimek, Eric: Associated Press
Knight, Christopher: Argus Media
Kobayashi, Tetsu: Asahi Shimbun
Kocsis, John: Daily Caller
Koff, Stephen: Cleveland Plain Dealer
Koffler, Keith: White House Dossier
Koh, Elizabeth: McClatchy
Kohda, Satoru: Jiji Press
Kokumo, Norio: Sankei Shimbun
Komarow, Steven: CQ Roll Call
Komori, Yoshihisa: Sankei Shimbun
Kondo, Masaki: Jiji Press
Konishi, Jiro: Jiji Press
Kopp, Emily: Kaiser Health News
Korte, Gregory: USA Today
Kosova, Weston: Bloomberg News
Kotake, Hiroyuki: Nikkei
Kovacheva, Iva: Mainichi Shimbun
Krasny, Rosalind: Bloomberg News
Krawczak, Paul: CQ Roll Call
Krebs, Robert: CQ Roll Call
Kreighbaum, Andrew: Inside Higher Ed
Kucinich, Jacqueline: Daily Beast

MEMBERS ENTITLED TO ADMISSION—Continued

Kumar, Anita: McClatchy
Kumar, Arun: Indo-Asian News Service
Kurihara, Kazuhiro: Kyodo News
Kuromi, Shuhei: Yomiuri Shimbun
Kurose, Yoshinari: Sankei Shimbun
Kussin-Shoptaw, Samuel: Bloomberg News
Kwon, Sangchool: Korea Times
Lacerda-Trevisan, Claudia: O Estado De S. Paulo
Lackey, Katharine: USA Today
LaFranchi, Howard: Christian Science Monitor
LaFraniere, Sharon: New York Times
Laing, Keith: Detroit News
Lake, Eli: Bloomberg News
Lakshmanan, Indira: Boston Globe
Lambert, Lisa: Thomson Reuters
Lambrecht, William: Hearst Newspapers
Lambro, Donald: Universal UClick Syndicate
Landay, Jonathan: Thomson Reuters
Landler, Mark: New York Times
Langan, Michael: Agence France-Presse
Lange, Jason: Thomson Reuters
Lanman, Scott: Bloomberg News
Lardner, Richard: Associated Press
Larimer, Sarah: Washington Post
Laris, Michael: Washington Post
Lauter, David: Los Angeles Times
Lavelle, Marianne: Inside Climate News
Lawder, David: Thomson Reuters
Lawler, Joseph: Washington Examiner
Lawrence, Jill: USA Today
Layton, Lyndsey: Washington Post
Leal Martinez, Bujanda Lucia: EFE News Services
Learn, Joshua: S&P Global
Leary, Alex: Tampa Bay Times
Leavenworth, Stuart: McClatchy
Lebhour, Karim: Agence France-Presse
Lederman, Joshua: Associated Press
Lee, Hinton: Associated Press
Lee, Chang Yul: Korea Times
Lee, Dong: Los Angeles Times
Lee, Jeeah: Asahi Shimbun
Lee, Jong Kook: Korea Times
Lee, Matthew: Associated Press
Lee, Yongil: McClatchy
Lee, Michelle: Washington Post
Lee, Haye-Ah: Yonhap News Agency
Lefkow, David: Agence France-Presse
Leger, Donna Claire: USA Today
Leibovich, Mark: New York Times
Lemus, Katherina: Thomson Reuters
Leonard, Randall: CQ Roll Call
Leondis, Alexis: Bloomberg News
Lerer, Lisa: Associated Press
Lerman, David: CQ Roll Call
Leslie, Katie: Dallas Morning News
Lester, William: Associated Press
Leubsdorf, Benjamin: Wall Street Journal / Dow Jones
Leubsdorf, Carl: Dallas Morning News
Lever, Robert: Agence France-Presse
Levey, Noam: Los Angeles Times
Levin, Alan: Bloomberg News
Levine, Sam: Huffington Post
Levinson, Alexis: Buzzfeed
Levinthal, David: Center for Public Integrity
Lewis, Herbert: CQ Roll Call
Lewis, Philip: Huffington Post
Lewis, Matthew: Daily Beast
Liao, Han Yuan: Taiwan Central News Agency
Liebelson, Dana: Huffington Post
Liebert, Larry: Bloomberg News
Lightman, David: McClatchy
Lindeman, Eric: Energy Daily
Linke, Maureen: Associated Press
Linskey, Anne: Boston Globe
Liptak, Adam: New York Times
Lipton, Eric: New York Times
Lira-Guerra, Alvin: Bloomberg News
Little, Walter: Bloomberg News
Livingston, Rebecca: Texas Tribune
Lobsenz, George: Energy Daily
Lochhead, Carolyn: San Francisco Chronicle
Locker, Raymond: USA Today
Lockwood, Frank: Arkansas Democrat-Gazette
Londres, Eduardo: Bloomberg News
Loop, Emma: Buzzfeed
Lopez, Jose: Notimex Mexican News Agency
Lovelace, Ryan: Washington Examiner
Lowery, Wesley: Washington Post
Lowy, Joan: Associated Press
Lu, Zhenhua: 21st Century Business Herald
Lubold, Gordon: Wall Street Journal / Dow Jones
Lucas, Elizabeth: Kaiser Health News
Lucas, Tammy: CQ Roll Call
Lugo, Luis: Associated Press
Lugones, Paula: Clarin
Luo, Xiaoyuan: World Journal
Lupkin, Sydney: Kaiser Health News
Lustig, Michael: S&P Global
Luthra, Shefali: Kaiser Health News
Lynch, David: Financial Times
Lynch, Sarah: Thomson Reuters
Lynch, Suzanne: Irish Times
MacGillis, Stefan: ProPublica
Macias, Beatriz: EFE News Services
Magner, Michael: CQ Roll Call
Mak, Timothy: Daily Beast
Makarov, Boris: Itar-Tass News Agency
Make, Jonathan: Communications Daily
Maler, Sandra: Thomson Reuters
Malone, Patrick: Center for Public Integrity
Mandato, Brian: McClatchy
Mandel, Susan: Merger Market Group
Mann, Edward: Wall Street Journal / Dow Jones
Mannion, James: Agence France-Presse

MEMBERS ENTITLED TO ADMISSION—Continued

Manson, Katrina: Financial Times
Marans, Daniel: Huffington Post
Marfil, Jude: Wall Street Journal / Dow Jones
Marino, Kim Ben: Financial Times
Markay, Lachlan: Daily Beast
Markoe-Kolko, Lauren: Religion News Service
Marolo, Mariuccia: WolfNews
Marte, Jonnelle: Washington Post
Martin, Jonathan: New York Times
Martin, Gary: Las Vegas Review-Journal
Martin, Lawrence: Globe and Mail
Martinez-Ahrens, Juan: El Pais
Martinson, Erica: Alaska Dispatch News
Martosko, David: Daily Mail (UK)
Mascaro, Lisa: Los Angeles Times
Mason, Jeffrey: Thomson Reuters
Masterson, Lauren: Argus Media
Mastio, David: USA Today
Mathes, Michael: Agence France-Presse
Mathus Ruiz, Rafael: La Nacion
Matsuo, Terrence: Asahi Shimbun
Matthews, Mark: Denver Post
Mauldin, William: Wall Street Journal / Dow Jones
Mauriello, Tracie: Pittsburgh Post-Gazette
Mayeda, Andrew: Bloomberg News
Mazein, Elodie: Agence France-Presse
McCartney, Robert: Washington Post
McConnell, William: Daily Deal
McCrimmon, Ryan: CQ Roll Call
McGarry, Brendan: Military.com
McGill, Brian: Wall Street Journal / Dow Jones
McGinley, Mary: Washington Post
McGough, Michael: Los Angeles Times
McGrady, Clyde: CQ Roll Call
McGrane, Victoria: Boston Globe
McGregor, Sarah: Bloomberg News
McInnes, Maren: National Journal
McIntire, Mary Ellen: CQ Roll Call
McIntyre, Michelle: Washington Post
McKelway, Susan: Washington Examiner
McKendry, Ian: American Banker
McKinnon, John: Wall Street Journal / Dow Jones
McLaughlin, David: Bloomberg News
McLaughlin, Seth: Washington Times
McLeod, Paul: Buzzfeed
McManus, Doyle: Los Angeles Times
McMinn, Sean: CQ Roll Call
McPherson, Lindsey: CQ Roll Call
McPike, Erin: Independent Journal Review
Meadows, Clifton: New York Times
Meckler, Laura: Wall Street Journal / Dow Jones
Meehan, Brian: Bloomberg News
Mehall, Craig: CQ Roll Call
Mejdrich, Kellie: CQ Roll Call
Mellnik, Ted: Washington Post
Mercer, Marsha: Mercer Media
Merrion, Paul: MLEX US
Mershon, Erin: STAT
Meszoly, Robin: Bloomberg News
Michaels, James: USA Today
Michaels, Dave: Wall Street Journal / Dow Jones
Middleton, Chris: Bloomberg News
Milani, Kate: Wall Street Journal / Dow Jones
Milbank, Dana: Washington Post
Miller, Gregory: Washington Post
Miller, Jonathan: CQ Roll Call
Miller, Kathleen: Bloomberg News
Miller, Richard: Bloomberg News
Miller, Steven: Washington Times
Millikin, David: Agence France-Presse
Mills, Mark: Real Clear Politics
Mimms, Sarah: Buzzfeed
Minemura, Kenji: Asahi Shimbun
Minkoff, Michelle: Associated Press
Mir de Francia, Ricardo: El Periodico
Mishak, Michael: Center for Public Integrity
Mitsui, Makoto: Yomiuri Shimbun
Mizumoto, Yoko: Jiji Press
Mizumoto, Tatsuya: Jiji Press
Moday, Todd: Bloomberg News
Mohammed, Arshad: Thomson Reuters
Mojonnier, Laura: Argus Media
Molotsky, Irvin: Washington Dupont Circle News
Monroe, Sylvester: Washington Post
Montet, Virginie: Agence France-Presse
Montgomery, David: Washington Post
Montgomery, Lori: Washington Post
Monyak, Frederick: Associated Press
Moody, Sean: Daily Caller
Moos, Julie: McClatchy
Morath, Eric: Wall Street Journal / Dow Jones
Morello, Carol: Washington Post
Morgan, David: Thomson Reuters
Morgan, Jon: Bloomberg News
Morgenstern, Madeleine: Washington Examiner
Morris, James: Center for Public Integrity
Morrongiello, Gabriella: Washington Examiner
Morrow, Adrian: Globe and Mail
Morton, Joseph: Omaha World-Herald
Mosqueda-Fernandez, Sara: S&P Global
Moss, Daniel: Bloomberg News
Mott, Gregory: Bloomberg News
Mufson, Steven: Washington Post
Mullaney, Tomoko: Associated Press
Mullins, Brody: Wall Street Journal / Dow Jones
Munoz, Carlo: Washington Times
Murakami, Kery: Community Newspaper Holdings
Murray, Brendan: Bloomberg News
Mutikani, Lucia: Thomson Reuters
Myers, Marcia: CQ Roll Call
Myers, Jim: GateHouse Media
Naganuma, Aki: Nikkei
Nagasawa, Tsuyoshi: Nikkei
Nakamura, David: Washington Post

MEMBERS ENTITLED TO ADMISSION—Continued

Nakashima, Ellen: Washington Post
Nasaw, Daniel: Wall Street Journal / Dow Jones
Natter, Ari: Bloomberg News
Nawaguna, Elvina: CQ Roll Call
Nelson, Eliot: Huffington Post
Nelson, Christopher: Asahi Shimbun
Nerbovig, Ariel: Bloomberg News
Newhauser, Daniel: National Journal
Newmyer, Arthur: Washington Post
Ngo, Emily: Newsday
Nguyen, Antonia: Merger Market Group
Nicholas, Peter: Wall Street Journal / Dow Jones
Nieves, Nathalie: New York Times
Nikoloff, Angelina: Bloomberg News
Nippert, Carol: McClatchy
Nishida, Shinichiro: Mainichi Shimbun
Nishigaki, Yuichiro: Jiji Press
Nissenbaum, Dion: Wall Street Journal / Dow Jones
Nista, Julia: Daily Caller
Niwa, Yuji: Kyodo News
Nixon, Ronnie: New York Times
Noble, Andrea: Washington Times
Nocera, Katherine: Buzzfeed
Novak, Viveca: McClatchy
Nuckols, Benjamin: Associated Press
Nunn, Sharon: Wall Street Journal / Dow Jones
Nutt, Amy: Washington Post
Nylen, Leah: MLEX US
O'Connor, Emma: Buzzfeed
O'Harrow, Robert: Washington Post
O'Keefe, Edward: Washington Post
O'Keeffe, Kathryn: Wall Street Journal / Dow Jones
O'Reilly II, Joseph: Bloomberg News
Ogawa, Satoshi: Yomiuri Shimbun
Ohlemacher, Stephen: Associated Press
Ohlheiser, Abigail: Washington Post
Oki, Seima: Yomiuri Shimbun
Olchowy, Mark: Associated Press
Oliphant, James: Thomson Reuters
Olorunnipa, Toluse: Bloomberg News
Olson, Laura: Allentown Morning Call
Orden, Erica: Wall Street Journal / Dow Jones
Ordonez, Francisco: McClatchy
Ornitz, Jill: S&P Global
Orol, Ronald: Daily Deal
Orya, Ahmad: Associated Press
Osborne, James: Houston Chronicle
Oswald, Rachel: CQ Roll Call
Ota, Alan: CQ Roll Call
Ott, Matthew: Associated Press
Ourlian, Robert: Wall Street Journal / Dow Jones
Overberg, Paul: Wall Street Journal / Dow Jones
Ozeki, Koya: Yomiuri Shimbun
Pace, Julie: Associated Press
Page, Clarence: Chicago Tribune
Page, Paul: Wall Street Journal / Dow Jones
Page, Susan: USA Today
Paletta, Damian: Washington Post
Pandi, Nicolas: Jiji Press
Panetta, Alexander: Canadian Press
Parent, Charyssa: Washington Examiner
Park, Kwang Duck: Korea Times
Park, Younghwan: Kyunghyang Daily News
Parker, Ashley: Washington Post
Parlapiano, Alicia: New York Times
Parschalk, William: Jiji Press
Parsons, Christi: Chicago Tribune
Parsons, James: Defense Daily
Parti, Tarini: Buzzfeed
Pawlyk, Oriana: Military.com
Peake, Daniel: CQ Roll Call
Pear, Robert: New York Times
Pearl, Levine: Center for Public Integrity
Pena, Maria: La Opinion
Pennington, Matthew: Associated Press
Pennix, Timothy: Bloomberg News
Pergam, Andrew: McClatchy
Perlberg, Heather: Bloomberg News
Pershing, Benjamin: National Journal
Persons, Sally: Washington Times
Pesce, Edward: CQ Roll Call
Peters, Jeremy: New York Times
Peterson, Kristina: Wall Street Journal / Dow Jones
Peterson, Josephine: Durango Herald
Pettypiece, Shannon: Bloomberg News
Pfeiffer, Alexander: Daily Caller
Phillip, Abigail: Washington Post
Phillips, Amber: Washington Post
Phillips, James: Warren Communications News
Phillips, Michael: Wall Street Journal / Dow Jones
Philpott, Thomas: Military Update
Phippen, Thomas: Daily Caller
Pisani Bolla, Silvia: La Nacion
Pollard, Sonya: Bloomberg News
Pollock, Richard: Daily Caller
Portnoy, Jenna: Washington Post
Postell, Elliot: Washington Post
Powers, Martine: Washington Post
Preciphs, Joi: Bloomberg News
Przybyla, Heidi: USA Today
Puente, Maria: USA Today
Pugh, Anthony: McClatchy
Purce, Melinda: Associated Press
Putman, Peggy: Associated Press
Puzzanghera, James: Los Angeles Times
Qiu, Yiqing: New York Times
Qureshi, Hira: CQ Roll Call
Raasch, Charles: St. Louis Post-Dispatch
Radelat, Ana: Connecticut Mirror
Radnofsky, Louise: Wall Street Journal / Dow Jones
Rajghatta, Chidanand: Times of India
Raman, Sandhya: CQ Roll Call
Rampton, Roberta: Thomson Reuters
Rao, Maya: Minneapolis Star Tribune

MEMBERS ENTITLED TO ADMISSION—Continued

Rappeport, Alan: New York Times
Ratcliff, Summer: Independent Journal Review
Ratnam, Gopal: CQ Roll Call
Rau, Jordan: Kaiser Health News
Regalado, Francesca Rose: Yomiuri Shimbun
Reilly, Ryan: Huffington Post
Rein, Lisa: Washington Post
Reinhard, Beth: Washington Post
Reosti, John: American Banker
Revise, Nicolas: Agence France-Presse
Ricci, Andrea: Thomson Reuters
Rice, Carter: Asahi Shimbun
Rich, Gillian: Investor's Business Daily
Richardson, Bradford: Washington Times
Richey, Warren: Christian Science Monitor
Rigby, Laura Litvan: Bloomberg News
Riley, Michael: Bloomberg News
Rizzo, Katherine: Bloomberg News
Roarty, Alexander: McClatchy
Robb, Gregory: MarketWatch
Roberts, Catalina: CQ Roll Call
Roberts, Gillian: CQ Roll Call
Robertson, Jordan: Bloomberg News
Robertson, Reiko: Kumamoto Nichinichi Shimbun
Robinson, Abraham: Asahi Shimbun
Robinson, Eugene: Washington Post
Rodgers, Henry: Daily Caller
Rogers, Kathryn: New York Times
Rogin, Joshua: Washington Post
Roig-Franzia, Manuel: Washington Post
Roland Neil: MLEX US
Rosenberg, Matthew: New York Times
Rosenthal, Joyce: MedPage Today
Rosenwald, Michael: Washington Post
Rosiak, Luke: Daily Caller
Ross, Andreas: Frankfurter Allgemeine Zeitung
Ross, Janell: Washington Post
Ross, Sonya: Associated Press
Roston, Aram: Buzzfeed
Rotella, Sebastian: ProPublica
Roth, Bennett: Bloomberg News
Rothstein, Betsy: Daily Caller
Rouach, Herve: Agence France-Presse
Rovner, Julie: Kaiser Health News
Rowinsky, Catarina: Bloomberg News
Rowland, Christopher: Boston Globe
Rowley, James: Bloomberg News
Rubin, Richard: Wall Street Journal / Dow Jones
Rubin, Gabriel: Wall Street Journal / Dow Jones
Rucker, Patrick: Thomson Reuters
Rucker, Philip: Washington Post
Ruf, Renzo: Aargauer Zeitung
Rugaber, Chris: Associated Press
Ruger, Todd: CQ Roll Call
Ruiz, Rebecca: New York Times
Rund, Jacob: CQ Roll Call
Russell, Jason: Washington Examiner
Ryan, Timothy: Thomson Reuters
Saarikoski, Laura: Helsingin Sanomat
Sahmkow, Ramon: Agence France-Presse
Saintsing, Matthew: Asahi Shimbun
Sakamoto, Yasuyiki: Kyodo News
Salant, Jonathan: NJ Advance Media
Salcedo, Michele: Associated Press
Salfeety, Stephen: CQ Roll Call
Salmeron, Marvin: Bloomberg News
Salvalaggio, Claudio: ANSA
Samuels, Robert: Washington Post
Sanchez, Alfonso: EFE News Services
Sancho-Lacalle, Victor: El Universal
Sanders, Edmund: Los Angeles Times
Sands, Darren: Buzzfeed
Sands, David: Washington Times
Sanger, David: New York Times
Sanger-Katz, Margot: New York Times
Santini, Jean-Louis: Agence France-Presse
Sargent, Ann: Washington Post
Sarkar, Dibya: Communications Daily
Sato, Taketsugu: Asahi Shimbun
Saunders, Debra: Las Vegas Review-Journal
Savage, David: Los Angeles Times
Sawamura, Wataru: Asahi Shimbun
Scally, William: William Scally Reports
Scarborough, Rowan: Washington Times
Schank, Adam: Bloomberg News
Schectman, Joel: Thomson Reuters
Scheuble, Kristy: Bloomberg News
Schlesinger, Jacob: Wall Street Journal / Dow Jones
Schlisserman, Courtney: Argus Media
Schmidt, Michael: New York Times
Schmidt, Robert: Bloomberg News
Schmitt, Eric: New York Times
Schneider, Howard: Thomson Reuters
Schoenberg, Thomas: Bloomberg News
Schofield, Matthew: McClatchy
Schouten, Fredreka: USA Today
Schram, Martin: Tribune Content Agency
Schroeder, Robert: MarketWatch
Schroeder, Peter: Thomson Reuters
Schulberg, Jessica: Huffington Post
Schulte, Fred: Kaiser Health News
Schultz, Marisa: New York Post
Schutt, Bryan: S&P Global
Schwab, Nicole: Daily Mail (UK)
Schwartz, Felicia: Wall Street Journal / Dow Jones
Schwartz, Matt: The Intercept
Scott, David: Associated Press
Scott, Katherine: Bloomberg News
Scott-Molleda, Heather: Agence France-Presse
Scully, Megan: CQ Roll Call
Seck, Hope: Military.com
Seib, Gerald: Wall Street Journal / Dow Jones
Seibel, Mark: Buzzfeed
Selinger, Marc: Defense Daily

MEMBERS ENTITLED TO ADMISSION—Continued

Seltzer, Frederick: Inside Higher Ed
Selway, William: Bloomberg News
Sevastopulo, Demetrius: Financial Times
Shaban, Hamza: Buzzfeed
Shanker, Thomas: New York Times
Shaw, Michael: CQ Roll Call
Shear, Michael: New York Times
Shepard, Michael: Bloomberg News
Shepardson, David: Thomson Reuters
Shepherd, Todd: Washington Examiner
Sheppard, Kathleen: Huffington Post
Sherfinski, David: Washington Times
Sherman, Mark: Associated Press
Sherry, Marisha: Agence France-Presse
Sherwood, Zach: Bloomberg News
Sherzai, Magan: Associated Press
Shesgreen, Deirdre: Gannett Washington Bureau
Shields, Mark: Creators Syndicate
Shields, Todd: Bloomberg News
Shiffman, John: Thomson Reuters
Shimizu, Kenji: Mainichi Shimbun
Shimizu, Takayoshi: Kyodo News
Shorey, Rachel: New York Times
Shutt, Jennifer: CQ Roll Call
Siciliano, John: Washington Examiner
Siddiqui, Sabrina: Guardian US
Siddons, Andrew: CQ Roll Call
Sigal, Adam: MLEX US
Simao, Paul: Thomson Reuters
Simendinger, Alexis: Real Clear Politics
Simpson, Ian: Thomson Reuters
Singer, Paul: USA Today
Sink, Justin: Bloomberg News
Sipkin, Samuel: CQ Roll Call
Sisk, Richard: Military.com
Sitov, Andrei: Itar-Tass News Agency
Skarzenski, Ronald: New York Times
Skiba, Katherine: Chicago Tribune
Slack, Donovan: USA Today
Slater, James: Agence France-Presse
Smallberg, Michael: Bloomberg News
Smialek, Jeanna: Bloomberg News
Smith, Andrew: S&P Global
Smith, David: Guardian US
Smith, Jeffrey: Center for Public Integrity
Smith, Sarah: S&P Global
Smith, Agnes: Agence France-Presse
Smith, Ashley: Inside Higher Ed
Snell, Kelsey: Washington Post
Snyder, James: Argus Media
Sobczyk, Joseph: Bloomberg News
Socolovsky, Jerome: Religion News Service
Somashekhar, Sandhya: Washington Post
Sonne, Paul: Wall Street Journal / Dow Jones
Sorcher, Sara: Christian Science Monitor
Spang, Thomas: US-Report (Germany)
Spangler, Todd: Detroit Free Press
Sparshott, Jeffrey: Wall Street Journal / Dow Jones
Spencer, Jim: Minneapolis Star Tribune
Spetalnick, Matthew: Thomson Reuters
Springer, Buford: Daily Caller
Stanfield, Jeff: S&P Global
Stanton, John: Buzzfeed
Stapleton, Stephanie: Kaiser Health News
Steel, Susan: Fairchild Publications
Stein, Samuel: Daily Beast
Steinhauer, Jennifer: New York Times
Sternberg, William: USA Today
Stewart, Bruce: Sankei Shimbun
Stewart, Phillip: Thomson Reuters
Stewart, Cameron: Australian Newspaper
Stoddard, Alexandra: Real Clear Politics
Stohr, Greg: Bloomberg News
Stokes, Holly: Market News International
Stolberg, Sheryl: New York Times
Stole, Bryn: Baton Rouge Advocate
Stoltzfoos, Rachel: Daily Caller
Stone, Michael: Thomson Reuters
Stricherz, Mark: CQ Roll Call
Strobel, Warren: Thomson Reuters
Strohm, Chris: Bloomberg News
Strong, Thomas: Associated Press
Stucky, Phillip: Daily Caller
Stumme, Susan: Agence France-Presse
Subbaraman, Nidhi: Buzzfeed
Suebsaeng, Asawin: Daily Beast
Sugiyama, Tadashi: Asahi Shimbun
Sullivan, Andy: Thomson Reuters
Sullivan, Bartholomew: Gannett Washington Bureau
Sullivan, Eileen: New York Times
Sullivan, Gregory: Bloomberg News
Sullivan, Kevin: Washington Post
Sullivan, Patricia: Washington Post
Sullivan, Sean: Washington Post
Sullivan, Sean: S&P Global
Sun, Lena: Washington Post
Superville, Darlene: Associated Press
Sweeney, Jeanne: LRP Publications
Sweet, Lynn: Chicago Sun-Times
Swetlitz, Isaac: STAT
Sword, Stephen: CQ Roll Call
Swoyer, Alexandria: Washington Times
Syeed, Nafeesa: Bloomberg News
Szabados, Linda: Merger Market Group
Szep, Jason: Thomson Reuters
Tabir, Aymen: Saudi Press Agency
Tackett, Michael: New York Times
Takamoto, Kota: Mainichi Shimbun
Takei, Toru: Kyodo News
Talev, Margaret: Bloomberg News
Talley, Ian: Wall Street Journal / Dow Jones
Tamari, Jonathan: Philadelphia Inquirer
Tanaka, Yukiko: Kyodo News
Tanaka, Nobuyuki: Nishi-Nippon Shimbun

MEMBERS ENTITLED TO ADMISSION—Continued

Tanfani, Joseph: Los Angeles Times
Tanzi, Alexandre: Bloomberg News
Tapscott, Stanley: Daily Caller
Tatsubo, Mutsumi: Jiji Press
Tau, Byron: Wall Street Journal / Dow Jones
Tayloe, William: Communications Daily
Taylor, Adam: Bloomberg News
Taylor, Andrew: Associated Press
Taylor, Guy: Washington Times
Taylor, Marisa: Kaiser Health News
Teale, Christopher: LocalNews Now
Teinowitz, Ira: MLEX US
Teitelbaum, Michael: CQ Roll Call
Tenerella-Brody, Benjamin: Bloomberg News
Terkel, Amanda: Huffington Post
Terris, Benjamin: Washington Post
Tharoor, Ishaan: Washington Post
Theobald, William: Gannett Washington Bureau
Thomas, Kenneth: Associated Press
Thomas, Richard: Voterama in Congress
Thomason, Robert: MLEX US
Thompson, Marilyn: Kaiser Health News
Thomson, Jason: Christian Science Monitor
Thrush, Glenn: New York Times
Tillman, Zoe: Buzzfeed
Timiraos, Nicolas: Wall Street Journal / Dow Jones
Timmons, Heather: Quartz
Tiron, Roxana: Bloomberg News
Toiyama, Sakae: Ryukyu Shimpo
Tokar, Dylan: Global Investigations Review
Tokito, Mineko: Yomiuri Shimbun
Tomasky, Michael: Daily Beast
Tomkin, Robert: CQ Roll Call
Toppo, Gregory: USA Today
Torbati, Yeganeh: Thomson Reuters
Toren Bjorling, Ingrid Sanna Katarina: Dagens Nyheter
Torres, Craig: Bloomberg News
Torry, Harriet: Wall Street Journal / Dow Jones
Torry, John: Columbus Dispatch
Tosa, Shigeki: Asahi Shimbun
Toth, Jacqueline: CQ Roll Call
Tourial, Gregory: CQ Roll Call
Tracy, Ryan: Wall Street Journal / Dow Jones
Tracy, Matthew: MLEX US
Traywick, Catherine: Bloomberg News
Tribble, Sarah: Kaiser Health News
Trice, Ayesha: Thomson Reuters
Tritten, Travis: Washington Examiner
Trott, William: Thomson Reuters
Trumbull, Mark: Christian Science Monitor
Tsao, Yu-Fen: Liberty Times
Tsao, Stephanie: S&P Global
Tsuchiya, Konomi: Kyodo News
Tucker, Eric: Associated Press
Tully, Sarah: Bloomberg News
Tully-McManus, Katherine: CQ Roll Call
Tumulty, Karen: Washington Post
Tumulty, Brian: Bond Buyer
Urano, Eri: Tokyo Chunichi Shimbun
Valk, August: Handelsblad
Van Wye, Andrew: CQ Roll Call
Vanden Brook, Thomas: USA Today
Varley, Kevin: Bloomberg News
Vazquez, Maegan: Independent Journal Review
Vergano, Daniel: Buzzfeed
Viebeck, Elise: Washington Post
Viesselman, Kristine: CQ Roll Call
Villa Huerta, Lissandra: Buzzfeed
Vineys, Kevin: Associated Press
Viser, Matthew: Boston Globe
Viswanatha, Aruna: Wall Street Journal / Dow Jones
Vlahou, Toula: CQ Roll Call
Vogt, Patrick: Agence France-Presse
Vogt, Heidi: Wall Street Journal / Dow Jones
Volcovici, Valerie: Thomson Reuters
Volz, Dustin: Thomson Reuters
Wadhams, Nicholas: Bloomberg News
Wagman, Robert: Newspaper Enterprise
Wagner, Daniel: Buzzfeed
Wagner, John: Washington Post
Waldron, Travis: Huffington Post
Walerius, Randolph: CQ Roll Call
Walker, Hunter: Yahoo News
Wallbank, Derek: Bloomberg News
Wallsten, Peter: Washington Post
Walsh, Eric: Thomson Reuters
Walsh, Stephen: CQ Roll Call
Walton, Parker: Asahi Shimbun
Wang, Rujun: China People's Daily
Ward, Jonathan: Yahoo News
Warrick, Joby: Washington Post
Wasserman, Elizabeth: Bloomberg News
Wasson, Erik: Bloomberg News
Watanabe, Kensaku: Jiji Press
Watkins, Thomas: Agence France-Presse
Wax, Emily: Washington Post
Wayne, Alexander: Bloomberg News
Wayne, Kimberly: Bloomberg News
Weaver, Allen: Washington Examiner
Weaver, Courtney: Financial Times
Webb, Kayla: Bloomberg News
Weber, Lauren: Huffington Post
Weekes, Michael: Thomson Reuters
Wehrman, Jessica: Columbus Dispatch
Weickgenant, Joel: Real Clear Politics
Weigel, David: Washington Post
Weil, Martin: Washington Post
Weiland, Noah: New York Times
Weiner, Mark: Syracuse Post-Standard
Weiner, Rachel: Washington Post
Weir, Kytja: Center for Public Integrity
Weisman, Jonathan: New York Times
Weiss, Miles: Bloomberg News
Weiss, William: CQ Roll Call

MEMBERS ENTITLED TO ADMISSION—Continued

Welsh, Teresa: McClatchy
Wentling, Nicole: Stars and Stripes
Werner, Erica: Associated Press
Westbrook, Jesse: Bloomberg News
Westwood, Sarah: Washington Examiner
White, Dina: Chicago Tribune
White, Gordon: Washington Telecommunications Services
White, Keith: CQ Roll Call
Whiteaker, Chloe: Bloomberg News
Whitelaw, Kevin: Bloomberg News
Whitesides, John: Thomson Reuters
Whitlock, Craig: Washington Post
Whoriskey, Peter: Washington Post
Whyte, Elizabeth: Center for Public Integrity
Wieder, Benjamin: McClatchy
Wilber, Delbert: Washington Post
Wilkins, Emily: CQ Roll Call
Wilkinson, Tracy: Los Angeles Times
Williams, Clarence: Washington Post
Williams, Vanessa: Washington Post
Williams, Joseph: CQ Roll Call
Willman, David: Los Angeles Times
Wilson, Scott: Washington Post
Wilson, Trish: Associated Press
Wingfield, Brian: Bloomberg News
Wire, Sarah: Los Angeles Times
Wise, Lindsay: McClatchy
Wiseman, Paul: Associated Press
Witcover, Jules: Tribune Content Agency
Witkin, Gordon: Center for Public Integrit
Witkowski, Nancy: Associated Press
Wolf, Richard: USA Today
Wolfe, Frank: LRP Publications
Wolfgang, Benjamin: Washington Times
Wollner, Adam: National Journal
Woodruff, Betsy: Daily Beast
Woods, Randall: Bloomberg News
Woodward, Robert: Washington Post
Woodward, Calvin: Associated Press
Woolls, Daniel: Agence France-Presse
Wooten, Casey: National Journal
Wright, Christopher: CQ Roll Call
Wroughton, Lesley: Thomson Reuters
Wu, Lejun: China People's Daily
Yadoo, Jordan: Bloomberg News
Yamahiro, Tsaneo: Bloomberg News
Yamamoto, Takanori: Yomiuri Shimbun
Yamawaki, Takeshi: Asahi Shimbun
Yen, Hope: Associated Press
Yerkey, Gary: Svenska Dagbladet
Yildirim, Gulbin: Anadolu News Agency
Yoder, Eric: Washington Post
Yoo, Hyun Ji: Yonhap News Agency
York, Byron: Washington Examiner
Young, Alison: USA Today
Young, Jeffrey: Huffington Post
Young, Kerry Dooley: CQ Roll Call
Young, Donna: S&P Global
Yu, Donghui: China Review News Agency
Yung, Jean: Market News International
Zaha, Yukiyo: Ryukyu Shimpo
Zapotosky, Matthew: Washington Post
Zargham, Mohammad: Thomson Reuters
Zeller, Katherine-Ackley: CQ Roll Call
Zeller, Shawn: CQ Roll Call
Zengerle, Patricia: Thomson Reuters
Zezima, Katherine: Washington Post
Zhang, Niansheng: China People's Daily
Zhang, Penghui: China People's Daily
Zimmermann, Kourtney: Asahi Shimbun
Zitner, Aaron: Wall Street Journal / Dow Jones
Zoroya, Gregg: USA Today
Zou, Jie: Center for Public Integrity
Zoupaniotis, Apostolos: Cyprus News Agency
Zremski, Jerry: Buffalo News
Zumbrun, Joshua: Wall Street Journal / Dow Jones

NEWSPAPERS REPRESENTED IN PRESS GALLERIES

House Gallery 225–3945, 225–6722 Senate Gallery 224–0241

21ST CENTURY BUSINESS HERALD—(202) 664–7670, 4201 Massachusetts Avenue, NW., Washington, DC 20016: Zhen-Hua Lu.

AARGAUER ZEITUNG—(202) 403–7115: Woodfield Estates Drive, Alexandria, VA: Renzo Ruf.

AGENCE FRANCE-PRESSE—(202) 289–0700; 1500 K Street, NW., Suite 600, Washington, DC 20005: Shahzad Abdul, Eric Baradat, Laurent Barthelemy, Anne Barthelemy, Marc-Antoine Baudoux, Anita Beattie, Andrew Beatty, Sebastien Blanc, Jerome Cartillier, Emma Charlton, David Clark, Ivan Couronne, Elodie Cuzin, Alina Dieste Markl, Margaret Donaldson, Jean-Louis Doublet, Brigitte Dusseau, Touitou Esther, Francesco Fontemaggi, Aldo Gamboa, Douglas Gillison, Marisha Goldhamer Sherry, Stephanie Griffith, Carlos Hamann, Olivia Hampton, Paul Handley, Daniel Jahn, Cyril Julien, Michael L Langan, Karim Lebhour, David Lefkow, Robert Lever, James Mannion, Michael Mathes, Elodie Mazein, David Millikin, Virginie Montet, Nicolas Revise, Herve Rouach, Ramon Eduardo Sahmkow Romero, Jean-Louis Santini, Heather Scott-Molleda, Marisha Sherry, James Slater, Agnes Smith, Susan Stumme, Patrick Vogt, Thomas Watkins, Daniel Woolls.

AKAHATA—(202) 393–5238; 978 National Press Building, Washington, DC 20045: Seigi Endo, Susumu Ikeda.

ALASKA DISPATCH NEWS—(202) 436–4234 300 West 31st Street, Anchorage, AK 99503: Erika Martinson.

ALBUQUERQUE JOURNAL—(202) 329–4743; 7777 Jefferson Street, NE., Albuquerque, NM 87109: Michael Coleman.

AL-HAYAT—(202) 248–8525; P.O. Box 73522, Washington, DC 20056: Joyce Karam.

ALLENTOWN MORNING CALL—(202) 824–8216; 1090 Vermont Avenue, NW., Suite 1000, Washington, DC 20005: Laura Olson.

AMERICAN BANKER—(571) 403–3837; 1401 Wilson Boulevard, Suite 1002, Arlington, VA 22209: Lalita Clozel, Brian Collins, John Heltman, Ian McKendry, John Reosti.

ANADOLU NEWS AGENCY—(202) 662–7435; 529 14th Street, NW., Suite 1131, Washington, DC 20045: Safvan Allahverdi, Hakan Copur, Michael Hernandez, Kasim Ileri, Atheer Kakan, Muhammad Kensari, Gulbin Yildirim.

ANSA—(202) 662–7195; 529 14th Street, NW., Suite 1200, Washington, DC 20045: Claudio Salvaggio.

ARA—(914) 954–5521; Massachusetts Avenue, SE., Washington, DC: Nuria Ferragutcasas.

ARGUS MEDIA—(202) 775–0240; 1012 14th Street, NW., Suite 1500, Washington, DC 20005: Michael Ball, Samuel Brock, Abby Caplan, Edward Epstein, William Fleeson, David Givens, Haik Gugarats, Coleen Howe, David Ivanovich, Chris Knight, Lauren Masterson, Laura Mojonnier, Courtney Schlisserman, James Snyder.

ARKANSAS DEMOCRAT-GAZETTE—(202) 662–7690; 960-A National Press Building, Washington, DC 20045: Frank Lockwood.

ARTISTS & WRITERS SYNDICATE—(703) 820–4232; South Jefferson Street, Falls Church, VA: Frank Aukofer.

ASAHI SHIMBUN—(202) 783–1000; 1022 National Press Building, Washington, DC 20045: Daisuke Igarashi, Keisuke Katori, Tetsu Kobayashi, Jeeah Lee, Terrence Matsuo, Kenji Minemura, Christopher Nelson, Carter Rice, Abraham Robinson, Matthew Saintsing, Taketsugu Sato, Wataru Sawamura, Tadashi Sugiyama, Shigeki Tosa, Parker Walton, Takeshi Yamawaki, Kourtney Zimmerman.

ASSOCIATED PRESS—(202) 641–9000; 1100 13th Street, NW., 5th Floor, Washington, DC 20005: Tamar Abdollah, Ricardo Alonso-Zaldivar, Lauran Ashworth, Lolita Baldor, Matthew Barakat, Lynn Berry, Michael Biesecker, Josh Boak, Seth Borenstein, Stephen Braun, Sarah Brumfield, Robert Burns, Desmond Butler, Julie Bykowicz, Alicia Caldwell, Connie Cass, Donna Cassata, Jill Colvin, Martin Crutsinger, Matthew Daly, Douglass Daniel, Mariya Danilova, Chad Day, Jim Drinkard, Donald Elkins, Carole Feldman, Anne Flaherty, Alan Fram, Kevin Freking, Adrian Fullwood, Robert Furlow, Marcy Gordon, Jessica Gresko, Ken Guggenheim, Sadie Gurman, Merrill Hartson, Kathleen Hennessey, Jesse Holland, Jeffrey Horwitz, Mary Clare Jalonick, Laurie Kellman Blazar, Amanda Kell, Jennifer Kerr, Bradley Klapper, Eric Klimek, Richard Lardner, Josh Lederman, Hinton Lee, Matthew Lee, Lisa Lerer, William Lester, Maureen Linke, Joan Lowy, Luis Lugo, Michelle Minkoff, Frederick Monyak, Tomoko Mulaney, Ben Nuckols, Stephen Ohlemacher, Mark Olchowy, Ahmed Orya, Matthew Ott, Julie Pace, Matthew Pennington, Melinda Purce, Eileen Putman, Debra Riechmann-Kepler, Sonya Ross, Chris Rugaber, Michele Salcedo, David Scott, Mark Sherman, Thomas Strong, Darlene Superville, Andrew Taylor, Ken Thomas, Eric Tucker, Kevin Vineys, Erica Werner, Trish Wilson, Paul Wiseman, Nancy Witkowski, Calvin Woodward, Hope Yen.

NEWSPAPERS REPRESENTED—Continued

ATLANTA JOURNAL CONSTITUTION—(202) 777–7033; 400 North Capitol Street, NW., Suite 750, Washington, DC 20001: Tamar Hallerman.

AUSTRALIAN FINANCIAL REVIEW—(202) 285–9000; 1310 G Street, NW., Suite 750, Washington, DC 20005: John Kehoe.

AUSTRALIAN NEWSPAPER—(202) 710–1006; 1025 Connecticut Avenue, NW., Suite 800, Washington, DC 20015: Cameron Stewart.

BALTIMORE SUN—(410) 979–2052; 1090 Vermont Avenue, NW., Suite 1000, Washington, DC 20005: Jeffrey Barker, John Fritze, Zenon Hnatyshyn.

BATON ROUGE ADVOCATE—(225) 200–4810; 7290 Bluebonnet Boulevard, Baton Rouge, LA 70810: Bryn Stole.

BLOOMBERG NEWS—(202) 624–1820; 1101 New York Avenue, NW., 9th Floor Washington, DC 20005: Hector Alfaro, William Allison, Laurie Asseo, Sarah Babbage, Benjamin Bain, Ryan Beene, Alan Bjerga, Justin Blum, Kathryn Britton, Peter Brusoe, Alister Bull, Anthony Capaccio, Dominic Carey, Shobhana Chandra, Kevin Cirilli, Kristin Cohen, Christopher Condon, Laura Curtis, Susan Decker, Steven Dennis, Elizabeth Dexheimer, Jennifer Dlouhy, Terrence Dopp, Mike Dorning, Mark Drajem, Loren Duggan, Katrice Eborn, Anna Edgerton, Anna Edney, Joshua Eidelson, Jennifer Epstein, William Faries, Christopher Flavelle, Sara Forden, Joshua Gallu, Saleha Ghani, James Gibney, Gregory Giroux, Vince Golle, D Craig Gordon, Michael Goudin, Rick Greenwood, Jesse Hamilton, Andrew Harris, Dan Hart, Benjamin Holland, Billy House, Megan Howard, John Hughes, Albert Hunt, Jennifer Jacobs, Michelle Jamrisko, Arit John, Sahil Kapur, Katarzyna Klimasinska, Weston Kosova, Rosalind Krasney, Samuel Kussin-Shoptaw, Eli Lake, Scott Lanman, Alxis Leondis, Alan Levin, Larry Liebert, Alvin Lira-Guerra, Walter Little, Laura Litvan, Eduardo Londres, Andrew Mayeda, Sarah McGregor, David McLaughlin, Brian Meehan, Robin Meszoly, Chris Middleton, Kathleen Miller, Richard Miller, Todd Moday, Jon Morgan, Daniel Moss, Gregory Mott, Brendan Murray, Ari Natter, Ariel Nerbovig, Angelina Nikoloff, Toluse Olorunnipa, Joseph O'Reilly II, Timothy Pennix, Heather Perlberg, Shannon Pettypiece, Sonya Pollard, Joi Preciphs, Michael Riley, Katherine Rizzo, Jordan Robertson, Bennett Roth, Catarina Rowinsky, James Rowley, Marvin Salmeron, Adam Schank, Kristy Scheuble, Robert Schmidt, Tom Schoenberg, Katherine Scott, William Selway, Michael Shepard, Zach Sherwood, Todd Shields, Justin Sink, Michael Smallberg, Jeanna Smialek, Joseph Sobczyk, Greg Stohr, Chris Strohm, Gregory Sullivan, Nafeesa Syeed, Margaret Talev, Alexandre Tanzi, Benjamin Tenerella-Brody, Roxana Tiron, Craig Torres, Catherine Traywick, Sarah Tully, Kevin Varley, Nicholas Wadhams, Derek Wallbank, Elizabeth Wasserman, Erik Wasson, Alexander Wayne, Kimberly Wayne, Kayla Webb, Miles Weiss, Jesse Westbrook, Chloe Whiteaker, Kevin Whitelaw, Brian Wingfield, Randall Woods, Jordan Yadoo, Tsaneo Yamahiro.

BOND BUYER—(571) 403–3843; 1401 Wilson Boulevard, Suite 1002, Arlington, VA 22209: John Casey, Lynn Hume, Brian Tumulty.

BOSTON GLOBE—(202) 857–5050; 1130 Connecticut Avenue, NW., Suite 725, Washington, DC 20036: Astead Herndon, Indira Lakshman, Annie Linskey, Victoria McGrane, Christopher Rowland, Matthew Viser.

BOSTON HERALD—(617) 426–3000; 70 Fargo Street, Boston, MA 02210: Kimberly Atkins.

BUFFALO NEWS—(202) 234–3188; National Press Building, #841, Washington, DC 20045: Jerry Zremski.

BUZZFEED.COM—1630 Connecticut Avenue, NW., Suite 700, Washington, DC 20009: Vera Bergengruen, Adam Butler, Kyle Cardine, Adrian Carrasquillo, Joseph Feder, Christopher Geidner, Eileen Hall, Christopher Hamby, Molly Hensley-Clancy, Dominic Holden, John Hudson, Alexis Levinson, Emma Loop, Paul McLeod, Sarah Mimms, Katherine Nocera, Emma O'Connor, Tarini Parti, Aram Roston, Darren Sands, Mark Seibel, Hamza Shaban, John Stanton, Nidhi Subbaraman, Zoe Tillman, Daniel Vergano, Lissandra Villa Huerta, Daniel Wagner.

CANADIAN PRESS—(202) 641–9734; 1100 13th Street, NW., Washington, DC 20045: Alexander Panetta.

CENTER FOR PUBLIC INTEGRITY—(202) 466–1300; 910 17th Street, NW., 7th Floor Washington, DC 20006: Ashley Balcerzak, John Barwick, Lateshia Beachum, Jared Bennett, Susan Ferriss, Allan Holmes, Jamie Hopkins, Maryam Jameel, David Levinthal, Patrick Malone, Michael Mishak, James Morris, Levine Pearl, Jeffrey Smith, Kytja Weir, Elizabeth Whyte, Gordon Witkin, Jie Zou.

CHICAGO SUN-TIMES—(202) 320–6044; 350 North Orleans Street, 10th Floor, Chicago, IL 60654: Lynn Sweet.

CHICAGO TRIBUNE—(202) 824–8306; 1100 Vermont Avenue, NW., Suite 900, Washington, DC 20005: Clarence Page, Christi Parsons, Katherine Skiba, Dina White.

CHINA PEOPLE'S DAILY—(703) 698–1298; 529 14th Street, NW., Suite 450, Washington, DC 20045: Lidan Chen, Shi Gao, Rujan Wang, Lejun Wu, Niansheng Zhang, Penghui Zhang.

CHINA REVIEW NEWS AGENCY—(703) 725–0720; Brooks Square Place, Falls Church, VA: Donghui Yu.

CHOSUN ILBO—(703) 865–8310; 1291 National Press Building, Washington, DC 20045: Insun Kang.

CHRISTIAN SCIENCE MONITOR—(202) 481–6680; 1615 L Street, NW., Suite 800, Washington, DC 20036: David Cook, Linda Feldmann, Francine Kiefer, Howard LaFranchi, Warren Richey, Sara Sorcher, Jason Thomson, Mark Trumbull.

NEWSPAPERS REPRESENTED—Continued

CLARIN—(202) 476–0920; 988 National Press Building, Washington, DC 20045: Paula Mercedes Lugones.

CLEVELAND PLAIN DEALER—(202) 638–1366; 930 National Press Building, Washington, DC 20045: Sabrina Eaton, Stephen Koff.

COLUMBUS DISPATCH—(202) 777–7015; 400 North Capitol Street, Suite 850, Washington, DC 20001: Jack Torry, Jessica Wehrman.

COMMUNICATIONS DAILY—(202) 872–9202; 2115 Ward Court, NW., Washington, DC 20037: Howard Buskirk, Jonathan Make, Dibya Sarkar, William Tayloe.

COMMUNITY NEWSPAPER HOLDINGS—(202) 383–6032; 700 12th Street, NW., Suite 1000, Washington, DC 20005: Kery Murakami.

CONNECTICUT MIRROR—(301) 949–7007; 63 Russ Street, Hartford, CT 06106: Ana Radelat.

CQ ROLL CALL—(202) 650–6500; 1625 EYE Street, NW., Washington, DC 20002: Kate Ackley, Rebecca Adams, Erin Bacon, John Bennett, Morgan Cahn, Charlene Carter, Mike Christensen, Lauren Clason, George Codrea, Charles Conlon, Thomas Curry, Dean DeChiaro, Jeremy Dillon, John Donnelly, Edward Felker, Peter Feltman, Ellyn Ferguson, Jaco Fischler, Amelia Frappolli, Karin Fuog, Alexandra Gangitano, Marilyn Gates-Davis, Daniel Germain, Anthony Gnoffo, Anne Grady, Brandon Haas, Eric Hammesfahr, Steven Harras, Jacob Holzman, John Hunter, Paul Jenks, Patrick Kelley, Ryan Kelly, Noella Kertes, Anne Kim, Steven Komarow, Paul Krawzak, Robert Krebs, Randall Leonard, David Lerman, Finlay Lewis, Ryan Lucas, Tammy Lucas, Mike Magner, Ryan McCrimmon, Clyde McGrady, Mary Ellen McIntire, Sean McMinn, Lindsey McPherson, Craig Mehall, Kellie Mejdrich, Jonathan Miller, Marcia Myers, Elvina Nawaguna, Rachel Oswald, Alan Ota, Daniel Peake, Edward Pesce, Hira Qureshi, Sandhya Raman, Gopal Ratnam, Catalina Roberts, Gillian Roberts, Todd Ruger, Jacob Rund, Stephen Salfeety, Megan Scully, Michael Shaw, Jennifer Shutt, Andrew Siddons, Samuel Sipkin, Mark Stricherz, Stephen Sword, Michael Teitelbaum, Robert Tomkin, Jacqueline Toth, Gregory Tourial, Katherine Tully-McManus, Andrew Van Wye, Kristine Viesselman, Toula Vlahou, Randolph Walerius, Stephen Walsh, William Weiss, Keith White, Emily Wilkins, Joseph Williams, Christopher Wright, Kerry Dooley Young, Katherine Ackley Zeller, Shawn Zeller.

CREATORS SYNDICATE—(202) 662–1255; 5777 West Century Boulevard, Suite 700; Los Angeles, CA 90045: Mark Shields.

CYPRUS NEWS AGENCY—(202) 462–5772; 2211 R Street, NW., Washington, DC 20008: Apostolos Zoupaniotis.

DAGENS NYHETER—(202) 288–3718: Cambridge Place, NW., Washington, DC: Ingrid Sanna Katarina Toren Bjorling.

DAILY BEAST—(202) 626–2030; 1825 Connecticut Avenue, Suite 620, Washington, DC 20009: Spencer Ackerman, Eleanor Clift, Andrew Desiderio, Kimberly Dozier, Jacqueline Kucinich, Matthew Lewis, Tim Mak, Lachlan Markay, Sam Stein, Asawin Suebsaeng, Michael Tomasky, Betsy Woodruff.

DAILY CALLER—(202) 506–2027; 1050 17th Street, NW., Suite 900, Washington, DC 20036: Michael Bastasch, Christopher Bedford, Julia Grace Brufke, Vincent Coglianese, Margaret Crilley, Kevin Daley, Christian Datoc, Robert Donachie, Saagar Enjeti, Katherine Frates, John Kocsis, Sean Moody, Julia Nista, Alexander Pfeiffer, Thomas Phippen, Richard Pollock, Henry Rodgers, Luke Rosiak, Betsy Rothstein, Buford Springer, Rachel Stoltzfoos, Phillip Stucky, Stanley Tapscott.

DAILY DEAL—(202) 429–2991; 444 North Capitol Street, NW., Suute 413, Washington, DC 20001: William McConnell, Ron Orol.

DAILY DOT—(301) 787–6847; 112 Windsor Road, Suite A391, Austin, TX 78703: Eric Geller.

DAILY MAIL (UK)—(646) 885–5105; 51 Astor Place, 9th Floor, New York, NY 10003: Francesca Chambers, Geoffrey Earle, Alana Goodman, David Martosko, Nocole Schwab.

DALLAS MORNING NEWS—(202) 661–8421; National Press Building, 529 14th Street, NW., Suite 930, Washington, DC 20045: Tom Benning, Alfredo Corchado, Todd Gillman, Katie Leslie, Carl Leubsdorf.

DEFENSE DAILY—(703) 522–6686; 1911 Fort Meyer Drive, Suite 310, Arlington, VA 22209: Richard Abott, Patrick Host, James Parsons, Marc Selinger.

DENVER POST—(202) 662–8907; 969 National Press Building, 529 14th Street, NW., Washington, DC 20045: Mark Matthews.

DER TAGESSPIEGEL—Patterson Street, NW., Washington, DC 20015: Christopher Von Marschall.

DETROIT FREE PRESS—(703) 854–8942; 1575 Eye Street, NW., Suite 350, Washington, DC 20005: Todd Spangler.

DETROIT NEWS—(202) 662–8736; 969 National Press Building, 529 14th Street, NW., Washington, DC 20045: Melissa Burke, Keith Laing.

DIE TAGESZEITUNG—(202) 569–5369; N Street, SW., Washington, DC: Dorothea Hahn.

EFE NEWS SERVICES—(202) 745–7692; 1220 National Press Building, 529 14th Street, NW., Washington, DC 20045: Hernan Martin Alonso, Miriam Burgues, Christina Garcia Casado, Maribel El Hamti, Pedro Fernandez, Raquel Godos de la Puente, Lucia Leal, Beatriz Macias, Alfonso Sanchez.

EL DIARIO DE HOY—(703) 845–4962; 4600 South Four Mile Run Drive, Arlington, VA 22204: Tomas Guevara.

EL NUEVO DIA—(202) 662–7360; 960d National Press Building, 529 14th Street, NW., Washington, DC 20045: Jose Delgado.

NEWSPAPERS REPRESENTED—Continued

EL PAIS—(202) 638–1533; 1134 National Press Building, 529 14th Street, NW., Washington, DC 20045: Nicolas Alonso, Joan Faus Catasus, Christina Fernandez Pereda, Juan Martinez Ahrens.

EL PERIODICO—(202) 679–8656; D Street, NE., Washington, DC 20002: Ricardo Mir De Francia.

EL TIEMPO—(202) 607–5929: Split Creek Lane, Alexandria, VA: Sergio Gomez.

EL UNIVERSAL—(202) 662–7190; 1193 National Press Building, 529 14th Street, NW., Washington, DC 20045: Victor Sancho Lacalle.

ENERGY DAILY—(703) 236–2405; 110 North Royal Street, Suite 200, Alexandria, VA 22314–3240: Jeff Beattie, Jim Day, Christopher Holly, Eric Lindeman, George Lobsenz.

ETHNOS GREECE—(202) 361–7843; 1133 14th Street, NW., Washington, DC 20005: Michail Ignatiou.

FAIRCHILD PUBLICATIONS—(202) 955–0966; 1730 Rhode Island Avenue, NW., Suite 603, Washington, DC 20036: Susan Watters.

FERN'S AG INSIDER BY CHARLES ABBOTT—(202) 841–4004; N Kenilworth Street, Arlington, VA: Charles Abbott.

FINANCIAL TIMES—(202) 434–0986; 1023 15th Street, NW., Suite 700, Washington, DC 20005: Shawn Donnan, Sam Fleming, Barney Jopson, David Lynch, Katrina Manson, Kim Ben Marino, Demetri Sevastopulo, Courtney Weaver.

FOLHA de SAO PAULO—(202) 492–3963; Cecil Place, NW., Washington, DC: Isabel Fleck.

FRANKFURTER ALLGEMEINE ZEITUNG—(202) 248–0980; 2100 Connecticut Avenue, NW., Suite 502, Washington, DC 20016: Andreas Ross.

GANNETT WASHINGTON BUREAU—(202) 854–8900; 7950 Jones Brance Drive, McLean, VA 22108; Washington, DC 20005: Deborah Berry, Michael Collins, Nicole Gaudiano Albright, Maureen Groppe, Ledyard King, Deirdre Shesgreen, Bartholomew Sullivan, William Theobald.

GATEHOUSE MEDIA—(703) 623–4397; 175 Sully's Trail; 3rd Floor; Corporate Crossings Office Park, Pittsford, NY 14354: Jim Myers.

GERMAN PRESS AGENCY—DPA—(202) 662–1220; 1112 National Press Building, 529 14th Street, NW., Washington, DC 20045: Sara Barderas, Martin Bialecki, Anne Custer, Michael Donhauser, Frank Fuhrig, Maren Hennemuth, Margaret Johnston.

GLOBAL INVESTIGATIONS REVIEW—(202) 831–4652; 2121 P Street, NW., Suite 201, Washington, DC 20037: Joseph Dobrik, Roger Hamilton-M, Dylan Tokar.

GLOBE AND MAIL—(202) 662–7167; 2000 M Street, NW., Suite 330, Washington, DC 20036: Lawrence Martin, Adrian Morrow.

GUARDIAN US—(202) 223–2486; 900 17th Street, NW., Suite 250, Washington, DC 20006: Lois Beckett, Julian Borger, Lauren Gambino, Lucia Graves, Ben Jacobs, Sabrina Siddiqui, David Smith.

HANDELSBLAD—(202) 957–6115; Cathedral Avenue, Washington, DC: August Valk.

HANKYOREH DAILY—(703) 989–0723; 821 National Press Building, Washington, DC 20045: Jong Park.

HEARST NEWSPAPERS—(202) 263–6400; 1331 H Street, NW., Suite 1101, Washington, DC 20005: Dan Freedman, William Lambrecht.

HELSINGIN SANOMAT—(301) 907–0080; Vilhonvuorenkatu 11 B, Helsinki, Finland 500: Laura Saarikoski.

HONOLULU CIVIL BEAT—(202) 680–3326; 3465 Waialae Avenue, Site 200; Honolulu, HI 96816: Kristen Downey.

HOUSTON CHRONICLE—(202) 263–6411; 700 12th Street, NW., Suite 1000, Washington, DC 20005: Kevin Diaz, James Osborne.

HUFFINGTON POST—(202) 567–2634; 1750 Pennsylvania Avenue, NW., #600, Washington, DC 20006: Akbar Shahid Ahmed, Laura Bassett, Nicholas Baumann, Jennifer Bendery, Mark Blumenthal, Igor Bobic, Zachary Carter, Shirish Date, Arthur Delaney, Ariel Edwards-Levy, Howard Fineman, Elise Foley, Matthew Fuller, Dave Jamieson, Sam Levine, Phillip Lewis, Dana Liebelson, Daniel Marans, Eliot Nelson, Ryan Reilly, Jessica Schulberg, Kate Sheppard, Amanda Terkel, Travis Waldron, Lauren Weber, Jeffrey Young.

INDEPENDENT JOURNAL REVIEW—(202) 550–2853; 108 South Washington Street, Alexandria, VA 22314: Joshua Billinson, Haley Byrd, Benjamin Johnson, Erin McPike, Summer Ratcliff, Maegan Vazquez.

INDIA PRESS TRUST—(301) 881–2963; Rockhurst Road, Bethesda, MD: Lalit Jha.

INDO-ASIAN NEWS SERVICE—(703) 664–0037; Alexandria, VA 22304: Arun Kumar.

INSIDE CLIMATE NEWS—(718) 624–4587; 16 Court Street, Suite 2307, Brooklykn, NY 11241: Marianne Lavelle.

INSIDE HIGHER ED—(202) 448–6116; 1015 18th Street, NW., Washington, DC 20007: Jeremy Bauer-Wolf, Andrew Kreighbaun, Frederick Seltzer, Ashley Smith.

THE INTERCEPT—(202) 368–0859; 1717 K Street, NW., Suite 900, Washington, DC 20006: Alexander Emmons, Ryan Grim, Zaid Jilani, Matt Schwartz.

INTERNATIONAL TRADE TODAY—(202) 872–9202; 2127 Ward Court, NW., Washington, DC 20037: Brian Dabbs.

INVESTOR'S BUSINESS DAILY—(202) 728–2154; 1001 Connecticut Avenue, Suite 415, Washington, DC 20036: Gillian Rich.

IRISH TIMES—(202) 436–6223: Independence Avenue, SE., Washington, DC: Suzanne Lynch.

NEWSPAPERS REPRESENTED—Continued

ITAR-TASS NEWS AGENCY—(202) 662–7080; 1004 National Press Building, Washington, DC 20045: Anatoly Bochinin, Anton Chudakov, Dmitry Kirsanov, Boris Makarov, Andrei Sitov.

JEWISH TELEGRAPHIC AGENCY—(646) 778–5536; Military Road, Arlington, VA: Ron Kampeas.

JIJI PRESS—(202) 783–4330; 550 National Press Building, NW., Washington, DC 20045: Ryota Dei, Satoru Kohda, Masaki Kondo, Jiro Konishi, Yoko Mizumoto, Tatsuya Mizumoto, Yuichiro Nishigaki, Nicolas Pandi, William Parschalk, Mutsumi Tatsubo, Kensaku Watanabe.

JOONGANG ILBO—(202) 347–0122; 997 National Press Building, Washington, DC 20045: Byunggun Chae.

KAISER HEALTH NEWS—(202) 347–5270; 1330 G Street, NW., Washington, DC 20005: Paula Andalo, Julie Appleby, Rachel Bluth, Mary Agnes Carey, Phil Galewitz, James Hancock, Carmen Heredia Rodriguez, Elizabeth Hernadi, Emily Kopp, Elizabeth Lucas, Sydney Lupkin, Shefali Luthra, Jordan Rau, Julie Rovner, Fred Schulte, Stephanie Stapleton, Marisa Taylor, Marilyn Thompson, Sarah Tribble.

KIPLING NEWS SERVICE—(202) 686–6388: Farnell Drive, Silver Spring, MD: Bogdan Kipling.

KOREA TIMES—(703) 941–8001; 7601 Little River Turnpike, Annandale, VA 22003: Cheolwhan Cho, Christina Chong, Jin Woo Kang, Sangchool Kwon, Chang Yul Lee, Jong Kook Lee, Kwang Duck Park.

KUMAMOTO NICHINICHI SHIMBUN—(301) 299–3775; Rock Run Drive, Potomac, MD: Reiko Robertson.

KUWAIT NEWS AGENCY—(202) 347–5554; 906 National Press Building, Washington, DC 20045: Sherouq Sadeqi.

KYODO NEWS—(202) 347–5767; 400 National Press Building, 529 14th Street, NW., Washington, DC 20045: Sarah Ampolsk, Riyo Aomoto, Takuya Arai, Eiichi Asami, Mariko de Freytas, Shinichi Fuchino, Eiichiro Funahashi, Ko Hirano, Toyohiro Horikoshi, Hitoshi Ito, Hideomi Kinoshita, Kazuhiro Kurihara, Yuji Niwa, Yasuyiki Sakamoto, Takayoshi Shimizu, Toru Takei, Yukiko Tanaka, Konomi Tsuchiya.

KYUNGHYANG DAILY NEWS—(703) 624–3031; Ivy Hill Drive, McLean, VA: Younghwan Park.

LA JORNADA—(202) 669–7760; Fourth Street, NE., Washington, DC: David Brooks.

LA NACION—(202) 744–7737; 1292 National Press Building, Washington, DC 20045: Rafael Mathus Ruiz, Silvia Pisani.

LA OPINION—(301) 325–4980; Silver Leaf Drive, Gaithersburg, MD: Maria Pena.

LA VANGUARDIA—(202) 999–0122; M Street, NW., Washington, DC: Jordi Barbeta Sanchez.

LAS VEGAS REVIEW JOURNAL—1111 West Bonanza Road, Las Vegs, NV 89106: Gary Martin, Debra Saunders.

LE FIGARO—(202) 846–7774; 14 Haussmann Boulevard, Paris, France: Philippe Gelie.

LE MAURICIEN—(301) 728–7442; Pipesteam Place, Potomac, MD: Pamela Glass.

LIBERTY TIMES—(202) 879–6765; 1294 National Press Building, Washington, DC 20045: Nadia Tsao.

LOCAL NEWS NOW—(703) 348–0583; 1200 18th Street, NW., Washington, DC 20036: Scott Brodbeck, Christopher Teale.

LONDON DAILY TELEGRAPH—(202) 247–8047; 1310 G Street, NW., Suite 750, Washington, DC 20005: Nicholas Allen.

LOS ANGELES TIMES—(202) 824–8368; 1090 Vermont Avenue, NW., Suite 1000, Washington, DC 20005: Brian Bennett, Noah Bierman, David Cloud, Cathleen Decker, Robert Drogin, Evan Halper, David Lauter, Dong Lee, Noam Levey, Lisa Mascaro, Michael McGough, Doyle McManus, James Puzzanghera, Edmund Sanders, David Savage, Joseph Tanfani, Tracy Wilkinson, David Willman, Sarah Wire.

LRP PUBLICATIONS—(703) 350–2198; 1901 North Moore Street, Suite 1106, Arlington, VA 22209: Kara Arundel, Emily Brown, Julie Davidson, David Kittross, Jeanne Sweeney, Frank Wolfe.

MAINICHI SHIMBUN—(202) 737–2817; 340 National Press Building, 529 14th Street, NW., Washington, DC 20045: Haruyuki Aikawa, Iva Kovacheva, Shinichiro Nishida, Kenji Shimizu, Kota Takamoto.

MALAYA—(703) 715–8879; 10724 Midsummer Drive, Reston, VA 20191: Josefina Ilustre.

MARKET NEWS INTERNATIONAL—(202) 371–2121; 1100 National Press Building, 529 14th Street, NW., Washington, DC 20045: John Carter, Kevin Kastner, Holly Stokes, Jean Yung.

MARKETWATCH—(202) 824–0548; 1025 Connecticut Avenue, NW., Washington, DC 20036: Jeffry Bartash, Steven Goldstein, Gregory Robb, Robert Schroeder.

MCCLATCHY NEWSPAPERS—(202) 383–6000; 700 12th Street, NW., Suite 1000, Washington, DC 20005: Barbara Barrett, Lesley Clark, Alex Daugherty, Anna Douglas, William Douglas, Andrea Drusch, Emma Dumain, Jessica Gilbert, Katharine Gleuck, David Goldstein, Eric Goodwin, Greg Gordon, Kevin Hall, Donovan Harrell, Katherine Irby, Timothy Johnson, Elizabeth Koh, Anita Kumar, Stuart Leavenworth, Yongil Lee, David Lightman, Brian Mandato, Julie Moos, Carol Nippert, Viveca Novak, Francisco Ordonez, Andrew Pergram, Anthony Pugh, Alexander Roarty, Matthew Schofield, Teresa Welsh, Benjamin Wieder, Lindsay Wise.

MEDPAGE TODAY—(866) 348–9885; 345 Hudson Street, 16th Floor, New York, NY 10014: Ryan Basen, Shannon Firth, Joyce Rosenthal.

MERGER MARKET OF FINANCIAL TIMES—(202) 434–1075; 1012 14th Street, NW., Suite 915, Washington, DC 20005: Esther D'Amico, Peter Geier, David Hatch, Susan Mandel, Antonia Nguyen, Linda Szabados.

NEWSPAPERS REPRESENTED—Continued

MIC—285 Fulton Street, 81st Floor, New York, NY 10007: David Drabold.

MILITARY UPDATE—(703) 830–6893; P.O. Box 23111, Centerville, VA 20120: Thomas Philpott.

MILITARY.COM—(301) 908–4117; 5505 Connecticut Avenue, NW., Suite 262, Washington, DC 20015: Matthew Cox, Brendan McGarry, Oriana Pawlyk, Hope Seck, Richard Sisk.

MILWAUKEE JOURNAL SENTINEL—1575 Eye Street, NW., Suite 350, Washington, DC 20005: Craig Gilbert.

MINNEAPOLIS STAR TRIBUNE—(202) 383–6120; 1090 Vermont Avenue, NW., Suite 1000, Washington, DC 20005: Jennifer Brooks, Maya Rao, Jim Spencer.

MINNPOST—(612) 455–6950; 900 Sixth Avenue, SE., Suite 220, Minneapolis, MN 55414: Sam Brodey.

MLEX US—(202) 909–1238; 1776 I Street, NW., Washington, DC 20006: Mark Bocchetti, Can Celik, Curtis Eichelberger, Flavia Fortes, Neil Haggerty, Paul Merrion, Leah Nylen, Neil Roland, Adam Sigal, Ira Teinowitz, Robert Thomason, Matthew Tracy.

NATIONAL JOURNAL—(202) 739–8400; 600 New Hampshire Avenue, NW., Washington, DC 20037: Brendan Bordelon, Alexander Clearfield, George Condon, Jr., Thomas DeFrank, Erin Durkin, Maren McInnes, Daniel Newhauser, Benjamin Pershing, Adam Wollner, Casey Wooten.

NEW YORK POST—(202) 393–1787; 1114 National Press Building, Washington, DC 20045: Geoff Earle, Marisa Schultz.

NEW YORK TIMES—(202) 862–0300; 1627 I Street, NW., Suite 700, Washington, DC 20006: Yamiche Alcindor, Binyamin Appelbaum, Peter Baker, Emily Baumgaertner, Mikayla Bouchard, Jeremy Bowers, Elisabeth Bumiller, Tahirah Burley, Coral Davenport, Julie Davis, Jose DelReal-Perez, Maureen Dowd, Robert Draper, Thomas Edall, Nicholas Fandos, Amy Fiscus, Mattew Flegenheimer, Lisa Friedman, Adam Goldman, Michael Gordon, Gardiner Harris, Emmarie Huetteman, Carl Hulse, Cecilia Kang, Thomas Kaplan, Sharon LaFraniere, Mark Landler, Mark Leibovich, Adam Liptak, Eric Lipton, Jonathan Martin, Clifton Meadows, Nathalie Nieves, Ronnie Nixon, Alicia Parlapiano, Robert Pear, Jeremy Peters, Yiqing Qiu, Alan Rappeport, Matthew Rosenberg, Rebecca Ruiz, David Sanger, Margot Sanger-Katz, Michael Schmidt, Eric Schmitt, Thomas Shanker, Michael Shear, Rachel Shorey, Ronald Skarzenski, Jennifer Steinhauer, Sheryl Stolberg, R. Michael Tackett, Glenn Thrush, Noah Weiland, Jonathan Weisman.

NEWSDAY—(202) 408–2715; 1090 Vermont Avenue, NW., Washington, DC 20005: Tom Brune, Emily Ngo.

NEWSPAPER ENTERPRISE—(301) 320–5559; Osceola Road, Bethesda, MD: Robert Wagman.

NIKKEI—(202) 393–1388; 815 Connecticut Avenue, NW., Suite 310, Washington, DC 20006: Tomoko Ashizuka, Christina Bilski, Motoko Kawachi, Tomoyuki Kawai, Takeshi Kawanami, Stephen Keefe, Hiroyuki Kotake, Aki Naganuma, Tsuyoshi Nagasawa.

NISHI-NIPPON SHIMBUN—(202) 393–5812; 1012 National Press Building, Washington, DC 20045: Takeshi Yamasaki.

NJ ADVANCE MEDIA—(301) 802–6692; 1101 Connecticut Avenue, NW., Suite 300, Washington, DC 20036: Jonathan Salant.

NOTIMEX MEXICAN NEWS AGENCY—(202) 347–5227; 975 National Press Building, Washington, DC 20045: Ruben Barrera, Jose Lopez Zamorano.

O ESTADO DE S. PAULO—(202) 248–0280; 700 13th Street, Suite 555, Washington, DC 20005: Claudia Trevisan.

OMAHA WORLD-HERALD—(202) 997–9787; 836 National Press Building, Washington, DC 20045: Joseph Morton.

PHILADELPHIA INQUIRER—(609) 217–8320; 400 North Broad Street, Philadelphia, PA 19130: Jonathan Tamari.

PITTSBURGH POST-GAZETTE—(703) 996–9292; 358 North Shore Drive, Pittsburgh, PA 15212: Tracie Mauriello.

POWER MARKETS TODAY—(301) 769–6903; 4908 Hornbeam Drive, Rockville, MD 20853: James Downing.

PRO PUBLICA—(301) 718–4436; 155 Avenue of the Americas, 13th Floor, New York, NY 10013: Isaac Arnsdorf, Stefan Macgills, Sebastian Rotella.

QUARTZ—675 Avenue of the Americans, Suite 410, New York, NY 10011: Heather Timmons.

REAL CLEAR POLITICS—1667 K Street, NW., Suite 1150, Washington, DC 20006: James Arkin, Rebecca Berg, David Byler, Carl Cannon, Emily Goodin, Lucas Hammerman, James Hitchcock, Caitlin Huey-Burns, Mark Mills, Alexis Simendinger, Alexandra Stoddard, Joel Weichgenant.

RECORD (BERGEN COUNTY, NJ)—(202) 249–2160; 1 Garret Mountain Plaza, Woodland Park, NJ 07424: Herbert Jackson.

REFORMA NEWSPAPER—(202) 341–3255: Jose Diaz Briseno.

RELIGION NEWS SERVICE—(202) 463–8777; 529 14th Street, NW., Suite 425, Washington, DC 20045: Adelle Banks, Lauren Markoe-Kolko, Jerome Socolovsky.

RHEINISCHE POST—(202) 966–2393; Chevy Chase Parkway, NW., Washington, DC: Frank Herrmann.

RYUKYU SHIMPO—905 Ameku, Naha Okinawa, Japan: Sakae Toiyama, Yukiyo Zaha.

S&P GLOBAL—(434) 977–1600; One SNL Plaza, Charlottesville, VA 22902: Rachel Adams-Heard, Annalee Armstrong, Joshua Armstrong, Glen Boshant, Brian Cheung, Molly Kathleen Christian, Christopher

NEWSPAPERS REPRESENTED—Continued

Coats, Michael Copley, Marcy Crane, Kristi Ellis, Andrew Engblom, Evan Fallor, Elizabeth Festa, Allison Good, William Holland, David Hood, Michael Lustig, Ximena Mosqueda-Fernandez, Jill Ornitz, Bryan Schutt, Andrew Smith, Sarah Smith, Jeff Stanfield, Sean Sullivan, Stephanie Tsao, Donna Young.

SALT LAKE TRIBUNE—(202) 662–8732; 969 National Press Building, Washington, DC 20045: Thomas Burr.

SAN FRANCISCO CHRONICLE—(202) 263–6573; 700 12th Street, NW., Suite 1000, Washington, DC 20005: Carolyn Lochhead.

SANKEI SHIMBUN—(202) 347–2842; 330 National Press Building, Washington, DC 20045: Hiroyuki Kano, Norio Kokumo, Yoshihisa Komori, Yoshinari Kurose, Bruce Stewart.

SAUDI PRESS AGENCY—(202) 944–3890; 601 New Hampshire Avenue, NW., Washington, DC 20037: Abdulaziz Alhendi, Aymen Tabir.

SEKAI NIPPO—(703) 272–8772; 1133 19th Street, NW., 8th Floor, Washington, DC 20036: Yoshiyuki Iwaki.

SINGAPORE STRAITS TIMES—(202) 680–3303; 916 National Press Building, Washington, DC 20045: Nirmal Ghosh.

ST. LOUIS POST-DISPATCH—(202) 298–6880; 1025 Connecticut Avenue, Suite 1102, Washington, DC 20036: Charles Raasch.

STARS AND STRIPES—(202) 761–0900; 529 14th Street, NW., Suite 350, Washington, DC 20045: Dianna Cahn, Claudia Grisales, Nicole Wentling.

STAT—(617) 929–7235; 1130 Connecticut Avenue, NW., Washington, DC 20036; Lev Facher, Erin Mershon, Isaac Swetlitz.

SVENSKA DAGBLADET—(202) 362–8253; Connecticut Avenue, NW., Washington, DC: Karin Henriksson, Gary Yerkey.

SYRACUSE POST-STANDARD—(571) 970–3751; 220 South Warren Street, Syracuse, NY 13202: Mark Weiner.

TAIWAN CENTRAL NEWS AGENCY—(202) 628–2378; 1173 National Press Building, Washington, DC 20045: Tsung-Shen Cheng, Han Yuan Liao.

TAMPA BAY TIMES—(202) 463–0571; 1100 Connecticut Avenue, NW., 4th Floor, Washington, DC 20036: Lauren Carroll, Jonathan Greenberg, Angie Drobnic Holan, Louis Jacobson, Alex Leary.

THE TEXAS TRIBUNE—(512) 716–8600; 823 Congress Avenue, Suite 1400, Austin, TX 78701: Rebecca Livingston.

THOMSON REUTERS—(202) 898–8300; 1333 H Street, Suite 500, Washington, DC 20005: Yasmeen Abutaleb, Timothy Ahmann, Charles Alexander, Diane Bartz, Amanda Becker, Eric Beech, Alistair Bell, Melissa Bland, Caren Bohan, Doina Chiacu, Gina Chon, Toni Clarke, Ross Colvin, Peter Cooney, Susan Cornwell, Richard Cowan, Kevin Drawbaugh, Will Dunham, Lindsay Dunsmuir, Peter Eisler, Tim Gardner, Virginia Gibson, Rodrek Golden, Julia Harte, Susan Heavey, Mark Hosenball, Lawrence Hurley, Lisa Lambert, Jonathan Landay, Jason Lange, David Lawder, Katherina Lemus, Sarah Lynch, Sandra Maler, Jeffrey Mason, Arshad Mohammed, David Morgan, Lucia Mutikani, James Oliphant, Roberta Rampton, Andrea Ricci, Patrick Rucker, Timothy Ryan, Joel Schechman, Howard Schneider, Peter Schroeder, David Shepardson, John Shiffman, Paul Simao, Ian Simpson, Matthew Spetalnick, Phillip Stewart, Michael Stone, Warren Strobel, Andy Sullivan, Jason Szep, Yeganeh Torbati, Ayesha Trice, William Trott, Valerie Volcovici, Dustin Volz, Eric Walsh, Michael Weekes, Jr., John Whitesides, Lesley Wroughton, Mohammad Zargham, Patricia Zengerle.

TIMES OF INDIA—(301) 695–9348: Alfred Drive, Silver Spring, MD: Chidanand Rajghatta.

TIMES OF LONDON—(202) 530–9901; 1101 17th Street, NW., Suite 601, Washington, DC 20045: Rhys Blakely, Boer Deng.

TOKYO CHUNICHI SHIMBUN—(202) 783–9479; 1012 National Press Building, NW., Washington, DC 20045: Conrad Chaffee, Takayoshi Goto, Tomonori Ishikawa, Chrishopher Kelly, Eri Urano.

TORONTO STAR—(202) 870–0649; 982 National Press Building, Washington, DC 20045: Daniel Dale.

TRIBUNE CONTENT AGENCY—(202) 298–8359; 435 North Michigan Avenue, Chicago, IL 60611: Jules Witcover.

UNITED DAILY NEWS—(240) 428–1164; 954 National Press Building, 529 14th Street, NW., Washington, DC 20045: Chia Chang.

UNIVERSAL UCLICK SYNDICATE—(703) 690–8095; 3600 New York Avenue, NE., Washington, DC 20002: Donald Lambro.

USA TODAY—(703) 854–3400; 7950 Jones Brance Drive, McLean, VA 22108: William Allen, Jarrett Bell, Wendy Benjaminson, Steve Berkowitz, Erik Brady, Carolyn Cerbin, Eliza Collins, Oren Dorell, Jessica Estepa, George Hager, Brad Heath, David Jackson, Bart Jansen, Kevin Johnson, Erin Kelly, Gregory Korte, Katharine Lackey, Jill Lawrence, Donna Leinwand Leger, Ray Locker, David Mastio, Jim Michaels, Susan Page, Heidi Przybyla, Maria Puente, Fredreka Schouten, Paul Singer, Donovan Slack, William Sternberg, Gregory Toppo, Tom Vanden Brook, Richard Wolf, Alison Young, Gregg Zoroya.

US-REPORT (GERMANY)—(301) 299–5777; 10201 Windsor View Drive, Potomac, MD 20854: Thomas Spang.

NEWSPAPERS REPRESENTED—Continued

VERMONT DIGGER—(802) 225–6224; 26 State Street, Suite 8, Montpelier, VT 05602: Elizabeth Hewitt.

VICE NEWS—90 N 11th Street, Brooklyn, NY 11249: David Enders, Ryan Faith.

VOTERAMA IN CONGRESS—(202) 332–0857; 1822 Corcoran Street, NW., Washington, DC 20009: Richard Thomas.

WALL STREET JOURNAL / DOW JONES—(202) 862–9200; 1025 Connecticut Avenue, NW., Suite 800, Washington, DC 20036: Andrew Ackerman, Mark Anderson, Natalie Andrews, Stephanie Armour, Rebecca Ballhaus, Paul Beckett, Neftali Bendavid, Mike Bender, Susan Benkelman, Janet Booker, Rebecca Bowers, Jess Bravin, Thomas Burton, Alicia Caldwell, Sarah Chaney, Dante Chinni, Rodney Christian, Lenora Clark, Alan Cullison, Kate Davidson-Choma, Robert Davis, David Allen Dolinger, Reid Epstein, Andrew Fitzgerald, Brett Forest, Theodore Francis, James Grimaldi, Michelle Hackman, Timothy Hanrahan, Shane Harris, David Harrison, Yuka Hayashi, Celia Henderson, Janet Hook, Siobhan Hughes, Greg Ip, Joshua Jamerson, Brent Kendall, Benjamin Kesling, Ben Leubsdorf, Gordon Lubold, Edward Mann, Jude Marfil, William Maudlin, Brian McGill, John McKinnon, Laura Meckler, Dave Michaels, Kate Milani, Eric Morath, Brody Mullins, Daniel Nasaw, Peter Nicholas, Dion Nissenbaum, Sharon Nunn, Kathryn O'Keefe, Erica Orden, Robert Ourlian, Paul Overberg, Paul Page, Kristina Peterson, Michael Phillips, Louise Radnofsky, Richard Rubin, Gabriel Rubin, Matthew Rose, Jacob Schlesinger, Felicia Schwartz, Gerald Seib, Paul Sonne, Jeffrey Sparshott, Ian Talley, Byron Tau, Nick Timiraos, Harriet Torry, Ryan Tracy, Aruna Viswanatha, Heidi Vogt, Aaron Zitner, Joshua Zumbrun.

WARREN COMMUNICATIONS NEWS—(202) 872–9202; 2115 Ward Court, NW., Washington, DC 20037: James Phillips.

WASHINGTON DUPONT CIRCLE NEWS—(202) 328–1121; T Street, NW., Washington DC: Irvin Molotsky.

WASHINGTON EXAMINER—(202) 903–2000; 1015 15th Street, NW., Suite 500, Washington, DC 20005: T Becket Adams, Michael Barone, Paul Bedard, Timothy Carney, Kelly Cohen, David Drucker, Susan Ferrechio, Kyle Feldscher, Joel Gehrke, Margaret Given, Sean Higgins, Robert King, Philip Klein, Joseph Lawler, Ryan Lovelace, Madeleine Morgenstern, Gabriella Morrongiello, Charyssa Parent, Jason Russell, Todd Shepard, John Siciliano, Travis Tritten, Sarah Westwood, Byron York.

WASHINGTON POST—(202) 334–6000; 1301 K Street, NW., Washington, DC 20071: Joel Achenbach, Keith Alexander, Nick Anderson, Lori Aratani, Daniel Balz, Robert Barnes, Martin Baron, Cameron Barr, John Barrett, Emma Brown, Robert Costa, Paige Cunningham, Timothy Curran, Joe Davidson, Aaron Davis, Mike DeBonis, Karoun Demirjian, Brady Dennis, Karen DeYoung, Joshua Freedom du Lac, Paul Duggan, Juliet Eilperin, Kayla Epstein, David Fahrenthold, Darryl Fears, Peter Finn, Marc Fisher, Mary Pat Flaherty, Brian Fung, Amy Gardner, Anne Gearen, Jack Gillum, Steven Ginsburg, Matea Gold, Amy Goldstein, Dino Grandoni, Ashley Halsey, Thomas Hamburger, Andrew Harwell, Joseph Heim, Rosalind Helderman, Peter Hermann, Arelis Hernandez, James Hohmann, Sari Horwitz, Spencer Hsu, Colby Itkowitz, Tracy Jan, Paul Kane, Dan Keating, Kimbriell Kelly, Glenn Kessler, Kimberly Kindy, Sarah Larimer, Michael Laris, Lyndsey Layton, Michelle Lee, Wesley Lowery, Jonnelle Marte, Robert McCartney, Mary McGinley, Michelle McIntyre, Ted Mellnik, Dana Milbank, Gregory Miller, Sylvester Monroe, David Montgomery, Lori Montgomery, Carol Morello, Sarah Mufson, David Nakamura, Ellen Nakashima, Arthur Newmyer, Amy Nutt, Robert O'Harrow, Edward O'Keefe, Abigail Ohlheiser, Damien Paletta, Ashley Parker, Abigail Phillip, Amber Phillips, Jenna Portnoy, Elliot Postell, Martine Powers, Lisa Rein, Beth Reinhard, Eugene Robinson, Joshua Rogin, Manuel Roig-Franz, Michael Rosenwald, Janell Ross, Phillip Rucker, Robert Samuels, Ann Sargent, Kelsey Snell, Sandhya Somashekhar, Kevin Sullivan, Patricia Sullivan, Sean Sullivan, Lena Sun, Benjamin Terris, Ishaan Tharoor, Karen Tumulty, Elise Viebeck, John Wagner, Peter Wallsten, Joby Warrick, Emily Wax, David Weigel, Martin Weil, Rachel Weiner, Craig Whitlock, Peter Whoriskey, Delbert Wilber, Clarence Williams, Vanessa Williams, Scott Wilson, Bob Woodward, Eric Yoder, Matt Zapotosky, Katherine Zezima.

WASHINGTON TELECOMMUNICATIONS SERVICES—(804) 695–4648; 1006 Harrison Circle, Alexandria, VA 22304: Gordon White.

WASHINGTON TIMES—(202) 636–3000; 3600 New York Avenue, NE., Washington, DC 20002: David Boyer, Daniel Boylan, Stephen Dinan, Christopher Dolan, Jennifer Harper, Thomas Howell, Charles Hurt, Laura Kelly, Seth McLaughlin, Steven Miller, Carlos Munoz, Andrea Noble, Sally Persons, Bradford Richardson, David Sands, Rowan Scarborough, David Sherfinski, Aleandria Swoyer, Guy Taylor, Benjamin Wolfgang.

WHITE HOUSE DOSSIER—(202) 277–5416; Hull Road, Vienna, VA: Keith Koffler.

WILLIAM SCALLY REPORTS—(202) 362–2382; Legation Street, NW., Washington, DC: William Scally.

WOLFNEWS—(202) 237–1019; Arizona Terrace, NW., Washington, DC: Mariuccia Chiantaretto.

WORLD JOURNAL—(202) 751–9023; 954 National Press Building, 529 14th Street, NW., Washington, DC 20045: Hui-Min Chen, Xiaoyuan Luo.

XINHUA NEWS AGENCY—(703) 647–1598; 1740 North 14th Street, Arlington, VA 22209: Mu Dong, Pan Gao, Xiangwen Ge, Yujuan Jiang, Guan Jianwu, Jie Liu, Jie Liu BC, Jiafei Lu, Lin Xiaochun, Qihang Zheng, Linfei Zhi.

NEWSPAPERS REPRESENTED—Continued

YAHOO NEWS—(202) 669–4950; 1500 K Street, NW., Suite 600, Washington, DC 20005: Garance Franke-Ruta, Liz Goodwin, Olivier Knox, Hunter Walker, Jonathan Ward.

YOMIURI SHIMBUN—(202) 783–0363; 802 National Press Building, Washington, DC 20045: Yumi Araki, Justin Arnold, Bryant Harris, Shuhei Kuromi, Makoto Mitsui, Satoshi Ogawa, Seimi Oki, Koya Ozeki, Francesca Rose Regalado, Mineko Tokito, Takanori Yamamoto.

YONHAP NEWS AGENCY—(202) 783–5539; 914 National Press Building, 529 14th Street, NW., Washington, DC 20045: Haye-Ah Lee, Hyun Ji Yoo.

PRESS PHOTOGRAPHERS' GALLERY*

The Capitol, Room S–317, 224–6548

www.pressphotographers.senate.gov

Director.—Jeffrey S. Kent.
Deputy Director.—Mark A. Abraham.
Senior Assistant Director.—Tricia Munro.
Assistant Director.—Matthew Grant.

STANDING COMMITTEE OF PRESS PHOTOGRAPHERS

J. Scott Applewhite, *Chair,* Associated Press
Win McNamee, *Secretary-Treasurer,* Getty Images
Jim Bourg, Reuters News Pictures
Tom Williams, CQ / Roll Call
Stephen Crowley, New York Times
Ronald Sachs, Consolidated News Pictures

RULES GOVERNING PRESS PHOTOGRAPHERS' GALLERY

1. (a) Administration of the Press Photographers' Gallery is vested in a Standing Committee of Press Photographers consisting of six persons elected by accredited members of the Gallery. The Committee shall be composed of one member each from Associated Press Photos; Reuters News Pictures or AFP Photos; magazine media; local newspapers; agency or freelance member; and one at-large member. The at-large member may be, but need not be, selected from media otherwise represented on the Committee; however no organization may have more than one representative on the Committee.

(b) Elections shall be held as early as practicable in each year, and in no case later than March 31. A vacancy in the membership of the Committee occurring prior to the expiration of a term shall be filled by a special election called for that purpose by the Committee.

(c) The Standing Committee of the Press Photographers' Gallery shall propose no change or changes in these rules except upon petition in writing signed by not less than 25 accredited members of the Gallery.

2. Persons desiring admission to the Press Photographers' Gallery of the Senate shall make application in accordance with Rule 33 of the Senate, which rule shall be interpreted and administered by the Standing Committee of Press Photographers subject to the review and approval of the Senate Committee on Rules and Administration.

3. The Standing Committee of Press photographers shall limit membership in the photographers' gallery to bona fide news photographers of repute in their profession and Heads of Photographic Bureaus under such rules as the Standing Committee of Press Photographers shall prescribe.

4. Provided, however, that the Standing Committee of Press Photographers shall admit to the Gallery no person who does not establish to the satisfaction of the Committee all of the following:

(a) That any member is not engaged in paid publicity or promotion work or in prosecuting any claim before Congress or before any department of the Government, and will not become so engaged while a member of the Gallery.

---

*Information is based on data furnished and edited by each respective Gallery.

(b) That he or she is not engaged in any lobbying activity and will not become so engaged while a member of the Gallery.

The above rules have been approved by the Committee on Rules and Administration.

PAUL D. RYAN,
Speaker, House of Representatives.

RICHARD C. SHELBY,
Chair, Senate Committee on Rules and Administration.

MEMBERS ENTITLED FOR ADMISSION

PRESS PHOTOGRAPHERS' GALLERY

Abramson, Mark: Freelance
Ake, David: Associated Press
Andrews, Scott: Canon, USA
Angerer, Drew: Getty Images
Applewhite, J. Scott: Associated Press
Archambault, Charles: Freelance
Ashley, Douglas: Suburban Communications
Augustino, Jocelyn: Freelance
Auth, William: Prensa International
Bao, Dandan: Xinhua News Agency
Baratz, David: USA Today
Barouh, Stan: Freelance
Barrett, Stephen: Freelance
Barria, Carlos: Reuters News Pictures
Barrick, Matthew: Freelance
Benic, Patrick: United Press International
Berglie, James: Zuma Press
Bernstein, Aaron: Freelance
Biddle, Susan: Washington Post
Binks, Porter: Sports Illustrated
Bivera, Johnny: Freelance
Bloom, Richard: National Journal
Boal, John: Freelance
Bongioanni, Carlos: Stars and Stripes
Bourg, Jim: Reuters News Pictures
Bowe, Christy: ImageCatcher News
Bowler, Dana: Freelance
Brack, William: Black Star
Brandon, Alex: Associated Press Photos
Burke, Lauren: Freelance
Burnett, David: Contact Press Images
Caballero-Reynolds, Andrew: Agence France-Presse
Cabrera, Mario: Vision Fotos
Calvert, Mary: Freelance
Campbell, Matt: European Pressphoto Agency
Carioti, Richard: Washington Post
Cedeno, Ken: Freelance
Ceneta, Manuel: Associated Press Photos
Chebbine, Line: US News and World Report
Chikwendiu, Jahi: Washington Post
Christian, Douglas: Freelance
Chung, Andre: Freelance
Clark, Bill: CQ / Roll Call
Cohen, Marshall: Bigmarsh News Photos
Coleman, Chloe: Washington Post
Connor, Kristopher: Freelance
Contreras-Cruz, Oliver: Freelance
Coppage, Gary: Photo Press International
Corum, Samuel: Anadolu Agency
Crowley, Stephen: New York Times
Davidson, Linda: Washington Post
Demczuk, Gabriella: Freelance
Deng, Min: China News Service
Diao, Haiyang: China News Service
Dietsch, Kevin: United Press International
Dougherty, Sean: USA / Today
Douliery, Olivier: Abaca USA
Drago, Al: Freelance
Duggan, James: Freelance
Edelman, Alex: Freelance
Eile, Evan: USA / Today
Elfers, Stephen: USA / Today
Ellsworth, Katie: Politico
Elswick, Jon: Associated Press Photos
Ernst, Jonathan: Reuters News Pictures
Falk, Steven: Philadelphia Inquirer
Frey, Katherine: Washington Post
Gail, Carl: Washington Post
Galietta, Wendy: Washington Post
Gandhi, Pareshkumar: Rediff.com / India Abroad
Garcia, Mannie: Freelance
Gibson, Zach: Freelance
Golon, MaryAnne: Washington Post
Gripas, Yuri: Freelance
Gromelski, Joseph: Stars and Stripes
Gruber, Jack: USA / Today
Guerrucci, Aude: Polaris Images
Gupta, Avijit: US News and World Report
Gurbuz, Sait: Freelance
Guzy, Carol: Freelance
Hambach, Eva: Agence France-Presse
Hamburg, Harry: Freelance
Harnik, Andrew: Associated Press Photos
Harrer, Andrew: Bloomberg
Harrington, John: Black Star
Helber, Stephen: Associated Press Photos
Hill, Robb: Freelance
Hockstein, Evelyn: Polaris Images
Jennings, Graeme: Washington Examiner
Joachim, Jade-Snow: Washington Post
Jones, Leah: Freelance
Joseph, Marvin: Washington Post
Kahn, Greg: Freelance
Kahn, Nikki: Washington Post
Kamm, Nicholas: Agence France-Presse
Kaster, Carolyn: Associated Press Photos
Katopodis, Anastasios: Freelance
Katz, Martin: Chesapeake News Service
Kendall-Ball, Gregory: Freelance
Key, Michael: Washington Blade
Kirkpatrick, T.J.: Freelance
Kirkpatrick, Nick: Washington Post

MEMBERS ENTITLED FOR ADMISSION—Continued

Kittner, Sam: Freelance
Kleponis, Chris: Freelance
Lamarque, Kevin: Reuters News Pictures
Lamkey, Jr., Rod: Freelance
Lane, Keith: Freelance
Lanham, Yuko: Asahi Shimbun
LaVor, Marty: Freelance
Lawidjaja, Rudy: Freelance
Lessig, Alan: Sightlight Media Group
Lewis, Roy: Washington Informer
Lizik, Ronald: Associated Press Photos
Loeb, Saul: Agence France-Presse
Loehrke, Tim: USA / Today
LoScalzo, Jim: European Pressphoto Agency
Lynch, Liz: National Journal
Lynch, Patricia: Freelance
Maddaloni, Chris: Nature
Magana, Jose Luis: Freelance
Mages, Evy: Freelance
Mahaskey, M. Scott: Politico
Malet, Jeff: Freelance
Mallin, Jay: Freelance
Mara, Melina: Washington Post
Markel, Brad: Capri
Marovich, Pete: Freelance
Martinez Monsivais, Pablo: Associated Press
Martin, Jacquelyn: Associated Press Photos
Mathieson, Greg: MAI Photo Agency
May, Cheriss: Freelance
McClain, Matt: Washington Post
McDonnell, John: Washington Post
McNamee, Win: Getty Images
Meyer, Cheryl: McClatchy Washington Bureau
Milbrett, Jennifer: Sightline Media Group
Miller, Mark: Washington Post
Miller, Robert: Washington Post
Mills, Douglas: New York Times
Mohammed, Eman: Freelance
Morigi, Paul: Freelance
Morones, Mike: The Freelance-Star
Mount, Bonnie: Washington Post
Nash, Gregory: The Hill
Newton, Jonathan: Washington Post
Ngan, Mandel: Agence France-Presse
Nipp, Lisa: Freelance
Nolly Araujo, Angel: Notimex
Nordby, Leslie: Freelance
O'Leary, William: Washington Post
Owen, Clifford: Freelance
Panagos, Dimitrios: Greek American News
Partlow, Wayne: Associated Press Photos
Patterson, Kathryn: Freelance
Petros, Bill: Freelance
Poetker, Mark: Montgomery Sentinel
Powers, Christopher: USA / Today
Purcell, Steven: Freelance
Radzinschi, Diego: National Law Journal
Reinhard, Rick: Impact Digitals
Reynolds, Michael: European Pressphoto Agency
Ricardel, Vincent: Freelance
Richards, Paul: Agence France-Presse
Riecken, Astrid: Freelance
Riley, Molly: Freelance
Roberts, Joshua: Freelance
Robinson-Chavez, Michael: Washington Post
Rolfe, Judy: Freelance
Ryan, Patrick: Freelance
Sachs, Ronald: Consolidated News Pictures
Sadof, Karly: Washington Post
Sandys, Toni: Washington Post
Savi, Riccardo: Freelance
Schaeffer-Hopkins, Sandra: MAI Photo Agency
Schaff, Erin: Georgetowner
Schmalz, Julia: Chronicle of Higher Education
Scott, Andrew: USA / Today
Shelley, Allison: Freelance
Shen, Ting: Freelance
Shinkle, John: Politico
Shipman-Singleton, Paulette: Freelance
Simonetti, Thomas: Washington Post
Simon, Martin: Corbis
Slim, Daniel: Agence France-Presse
Smialowski, Brendan: Agence France-Presse
Somodevilla, Kenneth: Getty Images
Squires, Derek: Tax Analysts'
Sullivan, Justin: Getty Images
Susslin, Chet: National Journal
Swall, Lexey: Freelance
Sweets, Fredric: St. Louis American
Sykes, Jack: Professional Pilot Magazine
Tatlow, Dermot: Panos Pictures
Thayer, Eric: Freelance
Theiler, Michael: Freelance
Thew, Shawn: European Pressphoto Agency
Tripplaar, Kristoffer: Sipa Press
Varias, Stelios: Reuters News Pictures
Vick, Vanessa: Freelance
Vogel, Leigh: Freelance
Voisard, Amanda: Freelance
Voisin, Sarah: Washington Post
Voss, Stephen: Freelance
Vucci, Evan: Associated Press Photos
Walsh, Susan: Associated Press Photos
Watkins, Fred: Freelance
Watson, James: Agence France-Presse
Wells, Jonathan: Sipa Press
Wiegold, David: 1105 Media
Williamson, Michael: Washington Post
Williams, Tom: CQ / Roll Call
Wilson, Mark: Getty Images
Wolf, Kevin: Freelance
Wolf, Lloyd: Freelance
Wong, Alex: Getty Images
Woolfolk, Daniel: Sightline Media Group

MEMBERS ENTITLED FOR ADMISSION—Continued

Yim, Heesoon: Hana
Yin, Bogu: Xinhua News Agency
Ziegler, Brett: US News and World Report

SERVICES REPRESENTED

(Service and telephone number, office address, and name of representative)

1105 MEDIA—8609 Westwood Center Drive, Vienna, VA 22182–2215: Wiegold, David.

ABACA USA—989 6th Avenue, New York City, NY 10018: Douliery, Oliver.

AGENCE FRANCE PRESSE—(202) 289–0700; 1500 K Street, NW., Suite 600, Washington, DC 20005: Cahellero-Reynolds, Andrew; Hambach, Eva; Kamm, Nicholas; Loeb, Saul; Ngan, Mandel; Richards, Paul; Slim, Daniel; Smialowski, Brendan; Watson, James.

ANADOLU—1131 National Press Building, Washington, DC 20045: Corum, Samuel.

ASAHI SHIMBUN—(202) 783–1000; 529 14th Street, NW., Suite 1022, Washington, DC 20045: Lanham, Yuko.

ASSOCIATED PRESS PHOTOS—(202) 641–9520; 1100 13th Street, NW., Suite 700, Washington, DC 20005: Ake, David; Applewhite, J. Scott; Brandon, James Alex; Ceneta, Manuel B.; Elswick, Jon; Harnik, Andrew; Helber, Stephen; Kaster, Carolyn; Lizik, Ron; Martin, Jacquelyn; Martinez Monsivas, Pablo; Partlow, Wayne; Vucci, Evan; Walsh, Susan.

BIGMARSH NEWS PHOTOS—(202) 364–8332; 5131 52nd Street, NW., Washington, DC 20016: Cohen, Marshall.

BLACK STAR—(703) 547–1176; 7704 Tauxemont Road, Alexandria, VA 22308: Brack, William; Harrington, John.

BLOOMBERG GOVERNMENT—(202) 654–7300; 1801 South Bell Street, Arlington, VA 22202: Harrer, Andrew.

CAPRI—Markel, Bradley.

CHESAPEAKE NEWS SERVICE—(410) 484–3500; 619 Oakwood Drive, Seven Valleys, PA 17360: Katz, Marty.

CHINA NEWS SERVICE—(703) 536–3657: Deng, Min; Diao, Haiyang.

CHRONICLE OF HIGHER EDUCATION—(202) 466–1728; 1255 23rd Street, NW., Suite 700, Washington, DC 20037: Schmaltz, Julia.

CONSOLIDATED NEWS PICTURES—(202) 543–3203; 10305 Leslie Street, Silver Spring, MD 20902–4857: Sachs, Ronald.

CONTACT PRESS IMAGES—341 West 38th Street, New York City, NY 10018: Burnett, David.

CORBIS—710 2nd Avenue, Suite 200, Seattle, WA 98104: Simon, Martin.

CQ/Roll Call—(202) 650–6500; 1625 Eye Street, NW., Washington, DC 20006: Clark, Bill; Williams, Tom.

EUROPEAN PRESS PHOTO—(202) 347–4694; 529 14th Street, NW., Suite 1122, Washington, DC 20045: Campbell, Matt; LoScalzo, Jim; Reynolds, Michael; Thew, Shawn.

GETTY IMAGES—(202) 347–2050; National Press Building, 529 14th Street, NW., Suite 1125, Washington, DC 20045: Angerer, Drew; McNamee, Win; Somodevilla, Kenneth; Sullivan, Justing; Wilson, Mark L.; Wong, Alex.

GREEK AMERICAN NEWS AGENCY—(516) 931–2333; 35–0723 Avenue, Astoria, NY 11105: Panagos, Dimitrios.

HANA—(202) 262–4541; 3505 International Place, NW., Washington, DC 20008: Yim, Heesoon.

IMAGE CATCHER NEWS—(301) 652–2774; 4911 Hampden Lane, Bethesda, MD 20815: Bowe, Christy.

IMPACT DIGITALS—(212) 614–8406; 32 6th Avenue, New York City, NY 10013: Reinhard, Rick.

MAI PHOTO AGENCY—(703) 968–0030; 10856 Caraway Circle, Manassas, VA 20109: Mathieson, Greg; Schaeffer-Hopkins, Sandra.

MCCLATCHY WASHINGTON BUREAU—(202) 383–6126; 700 12th Street, NW., Suite 1000, Washington, DC 20005: Meyer, Cheryl.

NATIONAL JOURNAL—(202) 739–8400; 600 New Hampshire Avenue, NW., Washington, DC 20037: Bloom, Richard; Lynch, Liz; Susslin, Chet.

NATIONAL LAW JOURNAL—(202) 828–0336; 1100 M Street, NW., Washington, DC 20036: Radzinschi, Diego.

NATURE—(202) 626–0287; 968 National Press Building, 529 14th Street, NW., Washington, DC 20045: Maddaloni, Chris.

NOTIMEX—(202) 347–5227; 529 14th Street, NW., Suite 425, Washington, DC 20045–1401: Araju, Angel Nolly.

PANOS—(617) 710–7413; Unit K, Reliance Wharf, Hertford Road, London, N15EW, UK: Tatlow, Dermott.

PHILADELPHIA INQUIRER—400 N Broad Street, Philadelphia, PA 19130: Falk, Stephen.

PHOTO PRESS INTERNATIONAL—(540) 286–1045; P.O. Box 190, Goldvein, VA 22720: Coppage, Gary.

SERVICES REPRESENTED—Continued

POLARIS IMAGES—259 West 30th Street, 13th Floor, New York, NY 10001: Guerrucci, Aude; Hockstein, Evelyn.

POLITICO—(703) 647–7694: 1100 Wilson Boulevard, 6th Floor, Arlington, VA: Ellsworth, Katie; Mahasky, Scott; Shinkle, John.

PRENSA INTERNATIONAL—3501 West 6th Street, Los Angeles, CA 90020: Auth, William.

PROFESSIONAL PILOT MAGAZINE—30 South Quaker Lane, Unit 300, Alexandira, VA 22314: Sykes, Jack.

REDIFF.COM / INDIA ABROAD PUB.—(646) 432–6054; 42 Broadway, Suite 1836, New York City, NY 10004: Gandhi, Pareshkumar.

REUTERS NEWS PICTURES—(202) 898–8333; 1333 H Street, NW., Suite 500, Washington, DC 20005: Barria, Carlos; Bourg, Jim; Ernst, Jonathan; Lamarque, Kevin; Varias, Stelios.

SAINT LOUIS AMERICAN—(314) 533–8000; 2315 Pine Street, St. Louis, MO 63103: Sweets, Frederic.

SENTINEL NEWSPAPERS—MONTGOMERY SENTINEL—3824 Chesterwood Drive, Silver Spring, MD 20906: Poetker, Mark.

SIGHTLINE MEDIA GROUP—6883 Commercial Drive Springfield, VA 22151: Lessig, Claude; Milbrett, Jennifer; Woolfolk, Daniel.

SIPA PRESS—(212) 463–0150; 307 7th Avenue, Suite 807, New York, NY 10001: Triplar, Kristoffer; Wells, Jonathan.

SPORTS ILLUSTRATED—135 West 50th Street, New York City, NY 10020: Binks, Porter.

STARS AND STRIPES—529 14th Street, NW., Suite 350, Washington, DC 20045: Bongioanni, Carlos; Gromelski, Joseph.

SUBURBAN COMMUNICATIONS CORP.—(248) 568–0006; 331 East Bell Street, Camden, MI 44232: Ashley, Douglas.

TAX ANALYSTS'—(703) 533–4476; 400 South Maple Avenue, Suite 400, Falls Church, VA 22046: Squires, Derek.

THE FREELANCE-STAR—(540) 368–5053; Morones, Mike.

THE GEORGETOWNER—2801 M Street, NW., Washington, DC 20007: Schaff, Erin.

THE HILL—(202) 628–8525; 1625 K Street, Suite 900, Washington, DC 20006: Nash, Greg.

THE NEW YORK TIMES—1627 Eye Street, NW., Washington, DC 20005: Crowley, Stephen; Mills, Doug.

THE WASHINGTON BLADE—1712 14th Street, NW., Washington, DC 20009: Key, Michael.

THE WASHINGTON EXAMINER—(202) 903–2000; 1015 15th Street, NW., Suite 500, Washington, DC 20005: Jennings, Graeme.

THE WASHINGTON INFORMER—(202) 561–4100; 3117 Martin L. King Avenue, SE., Washington, DC 20032: Lewis, Roy.

THE WASHINGTON POST—(202) 334–7380; 1150 17th Street, NW., Washington, DC 20071: Biddle, Susan; Carioti, Richard; Chikwendiu, Jahi; Coleman, Chloe; Davidson, Linda; Frey, Katherine; Gail, Carl; Galieta, Wendy; Golon, MaryAnne; Joachim, Jade-Snow; Joseph, Marvin; Kahn, Nikki; Kirkpatrick, Nick; Mara, Melina; McClain, Matt; McDonnell, John; Miller, Mark; Miller, Robert; Mount, Bonnie; Newton, Jonathan; O'Leary, William; Robinson-Chavez, Michael; Sadof, Karly; Sandys, Toni; Simonetti, Thomas; Voisin, Sarah; Williamson, Michael.

UNITED PRESS INTERNATIONAL—(202) 898–8071; 1133 19th Street, Suite 800, Washington, DC 20036: Benic, Patrick T.; Dietsch, Kevin.

US NEWS AND WORLD REPORT—(202) 955–2000; 1050 Thomas Jefferson Street, NW., Washington, DC 20007: Gupta, Avijit; Ziegler, Brett.

USA / TODAY—(703) 854–5216; 1575 Eye Street, NW., Washington, DC 20005: Baratz, David; Dougherty, Sean; Eile, Evan; Elfers, Stephen; Gruber, Jack; Loehrke, Tim; Powers, Chris; Scott, Andrew.

VISION FOTOS—9708 Hale Drive, Clinton, MD 20735: Cabrera, Mario.

XINHUA NEWS AGENCY—(703) 875–0082; 1740N 14th Street, Arlington, VA 22209: Bao, Dandan; Yin, Bogu.

ZUMA PRESS—408 North El Camino Road, San Clemente, CA 92672: Berglie, James.

FREELANCE

Freelance—Abramson, Mark; Andrews, Scott; Archambault, Charles; Augustino, Jocelyn; Barouh, Stan; Barrett, Stephen; Barrick, Matthew; Bernstein, Aaron; Bivera, Johnny; Boal, John; Bowler, Dana; Burke, Lauren; Calvert, Mary; Cedeno, Ken; Christian, Douglas; Chung, Andre; Connor, Kristopher; Contreras, Oliver; Demczuk, Gabriella; Drago, Al; Duggan, James; Edelman, Alex; Garcia, Mannie; Gibson, Zach; Gripas, Yuri; Gurbuz, Sait; Guzy, Carol; Hamburg, Harry; Hill, Robb; Jones, Leah; Kahn; Katopodis, Anastasios; Kendall-Ball, Gregory; Kirkpatrick, T.J.; Kittner, Sam; Kleponis, Chris; Lamkey, Jr., Rod; Lane, Keith; LaVor, Marty; Lawidjaja, Rudy; Lynch, Patricia; Magana, Jose Luis; Mages, Evy; Malet, Jeff; Mallin, Jay; Marovich, Pete; May, Cheriss; Mohammed, Eman; Morigi, Paul; Nipp, Lisa; Nordby, Leslie; Owen, Clifford; Patterson, Kathryn; Petros, Bill; Purcell, Steven; Ricardel, Vincent; Riecken, Astrid; Riley, Molly; Roberts, Joshua; Rolfe, Judy; Ryan, Patrick; Savi,

SERVICES REPRESENTED—Continued

Riccardo; Shelley, Allison; Shen, Ting; Shipman-Singleton, Paulette; Swall, Lexey; Thayer, Eric; Theiler, Michael; Vick, Vanessa; Vogel, Leigh; Voisard, Amanda; Voss, Stephen; Watkins, Fred; Wolf, Kevin; Wolf, Lloyd.

WHITE HOUSE NEWS PHOTOGRAPHERS' ASSOCIATION

P.O. Box 7119, Ben Franklin Station, Washington, DC 20044–7119

www.whnpa.org

OFFICERS

Whitney Shefte, WTTG–TV, *President*
Jim Bourg, Reuters, *Vice President*
Jessica Koscielniak, McClatchy, *Secretary*
Jonathan Elswick, Associated Press, *Treasurer*

EXECUTIVE BOARD

Jonathan Ernst (Reuters)
Pablo Martinez Monsivais (Associated Press)
Carol Guzy (Freelance)
Janet Weinstein (ABC News)
David Postovit (Hearst TV)
Whitney Leaming (The Washington Post)
Andrew Harnik, Contest Chair, Still (The Associated Press)
Pege Gilgannon, Contest Co-Chair, Video (WJLA-TV (Ret.))
Doug Wilkes, Contest Co-Chair, Video (WTTG-TV)
Jessica Koscielniak, Contest Chair, Multimedia (Freelance)
Al Drago, Contest Chair, Student (Freelance)
Bethany Swain, Contest Co-Chair, Student (University of Maryland)
Pablo Martinez Monsivais, Education Chair (Associated Press)

MEMBERS REPRESENTED

Abdallah, Khalil: CNN
Abraham, Mark: Freelance
Adlerblum, Robin: Freelance
Ake, J. David: Associated Press
Al-Jamea, Sohail: McClatchy
Albert, Christopher: CBS News, Freelance
Alberter, Jr., William: CNN
Allard, Marc: Freelance
Allen, Tom: Washington Post, Retired
Amarai, Kainaz: NPR
Anderson, Kristina: AWPS News
Angerer, Drew:
Applewhite, J. Scott: Associated Press
Apt Johnson, Roslyn: CBS News
Ashley, Douglas: Surburban News Group & ABC TV
Assaf, Christopher: Freelance
Auth, William: Freelance
Bahler, Barry: Dept. of Homeland Security
Bahruth, William: NBC, Retired
Barria, Carlos: Reuters
Barrick, Matthew: Freelance
Baysden, III, Earl: WTTG-TV
Beatie, Sam: Freelance
Beiser, H. Darr: USA Today, Retired
Bena, John: CNN
Benic, Patrick: UPI
Bennett, Ronald T.: Executive Branch, Retired
Bennett, Donald: Washington Post
Berglie, James: Zuma Press
Berkman, Eliezer: Freelance
Bernstein, Aaron: Freelance
Biddle, Susan: Washington Post, Retired
Bing, Bonita: Freelance
Binks, Porter: Freelance
Bivera, Johnny: Freelance
Blair, Adam: ITN
Boal, John: Freelance
Bodnar, John: CNN
Botsford, Jabin: Washington Post
Bourg, James: Reuters
Bowe, Christy: ImageCatcher News
Bowler, Dana Rene: Freelance
Brack, Dennis: Black Star
Brandon, Alex: Associated Press
Brantley, James R.: Freelance

MEMBERS REPRESENTED—Continued

Brown, Stephen: Freelance
Brown, Randall: NBC News
Brown, Beth: Hearst Television
Brown, Sr., Henry: ABC, Retired
Brusk, Steven: CNN
Bryan, Beverly: Freelance, Retired
Buell, Hal: AP, Retired
Burgess, Robert: Freelance
Burke, Jr., William C.: Retired
Burnett, David: Contact Press Images
Calvert, Mary: Freelance, ZUMA Press
Capachi, Casey: CNN
Carioti, Ricky: Washington Post
Carlson, David: Canon
Carlson, Kathryn Louise: National Geographic
Carter, David: NBC4 WRC-TV
Cedeno, Ken: Freelance
Ceneta, Manuel: Associated Press
Chavar, Anthony: Washington Post
Chikwendiu, Jahi: Washington Post
Christian, George: CBS News
Chung, Andre: Baltimore Sun
Cirace, Robert: CNN, Retired
Clark, Bill: Roll Call
Clarkson, Rich: Freelance
Cohen, Marshall H.: Big Marsh News Photos
Cohen, Stuart: Freelance
Colburn, James: Freelance
Cole, Adam: NPR
Collins, Maxine: BBC TV
Conner, Eric: Fox News Network
Contreras, Oliver: Freelance
Cook, Dennis: Associated Press, Retired
Costello II, Thomas: Asbury Park Press
Courtney, Eric: Freelance
Curran, Patrick: WTTG-TV
Cvetnic, Nicole: McClatchy
Czarnecki, Forrest: Student
D'Agostino, Matthew: 740 Jackson Place
Darkhalil, Eman: Freelance
Daugherty, Bob: Associated Press, Retired
Davidson, Linda: Washington Post
Davis, Amy: Baltimore Sun
de la Cruz, Benedict: Washingtonpost.com
Delaney, Danita: The Washington Afro
Demczuk, Gabriella:
Desfor, Max: AP, Retired
Devorah, Carrie: Freelance, Retired
Diaz Meyer, Cheryl: McClatchy
DiBartolo, Melissa: Nikon
Dietsch, Kevin: UPI
Doane, Martin: WJLA-TV
Dorwin, Harold: Smithsonian Institution / Harold Dorwin Photography
Douliery, Oliver: Abaca Press
Downing, Larry: Reuters, Retired
Drago, Al: Roll Call
Drapkin, Arnold: TIME Magazine
Drennen, Kevin: WJLA-TV
Druce, Ian: BBC
Dukehart, Coburn: National Geographic
Dukehart, Jr., Thomas: WUSA-TV, Retired
Dunmire, John: WTTG-TV, Retired
Eaves, Ed: NBC News
Edmonds, Ron: Associated Press
Edrington, Michael: Freelance
Elfers, Stephen: USA
Elswick, Jonathan: Associated Press
Epstein, Linda: IIPP, Department of State
Ernst, Jonathan: Freelance
Ewen, McKenna: Washington Post
Ewing, David: DE Media
Falk, Steven: Philadelphia Inquirer
Farmer, Sharon: Freelance
Feldman, Randy: Viewpoint Communications Inc.
Fertig, Natalie: McClatchy
Fielman, Sheldon: NBC News
Fine, Paul: Fine Films
Fine, Holly: Fine Films
Folwell, Frank: Freelance
Fookes, Gary: Freelance, Retired
Ford, Nancy: IFPO / American International News
Forrest, James: WRC, Retired
Forte, BJ: NBC4 WRC-TV
Foss, Philip: Speed Graphic
Foster, William: Freelance
Frame, John: WTTG-TV
Frey, Katherine: Washington Post
Fridrich, George: Brighter Images Productions LLC
Friedman, David: Freelance
Fulton, Bradley: CTV
Gail, Mark: Freelance
Garcia, Mannie: Freelance
Garcia-Pardo, Gabriella: National Geographic
Geissinger, Michael: Freelance
Gentilo, Richard: Associated Press
Gilgannon, Pege: WJLA, Retired
Gmiter, Bernard: ABC News / Freelance, Retired
Goldman, Judy-Anne: Freelance
Goldman, Mark: Goldman Photos
Goodman, Jeffrey: NBC / Freelance
Gorman, James: Associated Press
Goyal, Raghubir: Asia Today & India Globe / ATN News
Graham, Joshua: NBC News
Grant, Kelli: Yahoo! News
Greenblatt, William: United Press International
Gripas, Yuri: Reuters
Guzy, Carol: Freelance
Haefeli, Brian: ABC
Halstead, Dirck: The Digital Journalist
Harlan, Jeremy: CNN
Harmatz, Ben: Student
Harnik, Andrew: The AP
Harrer, Andrew: Bloomberg
Harrington, John: Freelance

MEMBERS REPRESENTED—Continued

Harrity, Chick: Whimsy Works
Heikes, Darryl: Freelance
Heilemann, Tami: Department of Interior
Hill, Robert: Australian Broadcasting Corp.
Hillian, Vanessa: Washington Post, Retired
Hinds, Hugh: WRC / NBC
Hopkins, Brian: WJLA-TV
Horan, Michael: WTTG-TV
Hoyt, Michael: Catholic Standard
Huff, Daniel: Associated Press
Imai, Kesaharu: World Photo Press
Ing, Lance: WTTG-TV
Ingalls, Bill: NASA e Management
Janney, Oliver: CNN America
Jenkins, David: CNN
Jennings, Graeme: Washington Examiner
Jette, Patricia: CBC
Johnson, Kenneth: ABC-TV
Johnston, Frank: Washington Post
Jones, Nelson: WTTG-TV
Jones, Donnamarie: DCTV
Joplin, Ashleigh: Washington Post
Joseph, Marvin: Washington Post
Judge, Michel: NBC News / Comcast
Kahn, Nikki: Washington Post
Kanicka, Stephen: Fox News Network
Kapustin, Doug: Freelance
Kaster, Carolyn: Associated Press
Katopodis, Anastasios:
Kattar, Pierre: Freelance
Katz, Marty: Chesapeake News Service
Kavanagh, Peter: CNN
Kennerly, David Hume: Eagles Roar Inc.
Kent, Jeffrey: Press Photographers' Gallery
Kerchner, Eric: CBS News
Khan, Mariam: ABC News
Kirkpatrick, TJ: Freelance
Kittner, Sam: Freelance
Kleber, David: Retired
Koppelman, Mitch: Reuters Television
Koscielniak, Jessica: McClatchy
Kossoff-Nordby, Leslie: LK Photos
Kraft, Brooks: Time Magazine
Lamarque, Kevin: Reuters
Lambert, H.M.: Freelance, Retired
Lamkey Jr., Rod: Freelance
Landy, John: BBC
Larsen, Gregory: Freelance
Lavies, Bianca: Freelance
LaVor, Marty: Freelance
Lawrence, Jeffrey: National Geographic
Leaming, Whitney: Washington Post
Lee, Donald: CBS News
Lee, Alexander Stephen: CNN
Levine, Lewis: Costal News Service
Levy, Glenn Ann: Freelance
Li, Alice: Washington Post
Lizik, Ronald: Associated Press
Lockhart, June:
Loeb, Saul: AFP
Long, James: NBC News
LoScalzo, James: EPA
Love, Diane: Tribal Cultures Productions
Luna, Nathan: ABC News
Lutzky, Juana: Freelance
Lynaugh, Mike: Freelance
Lynch, Patricia: Freelance
Lyons, Paul: NET, Retired
MacDonald, Charles: CMacFido Productions
Magana, Jose Luis: Freelance / AP
Mager, Dickon: Sky News
Mahaskey, Michael Scott: Politico
Mallin, Jay: Freelance
Mara, Melina: Washington Post
Markel, Harry: MorePhotos
Marovich, Jr., Peter: Freelance / Corbis
Martin, Gina: National Geographic
Martin, Jacquelin: AP
Martin, Ben: ITN
Martineau, Gerald: Washington Post, Retired
Martinez Monsivais, Pablo: Associated Press
Mason, Thomas: WTTG-TV, Retired
Mathieson, Greg: MAI Photo News Agency, Inc.
Mazariegos, Mark: CBS News
Maze, Stephanie: Moonstone Press LLC
Mazer Field, Joni: Freelance
Mazzatenta, O. Louis: Freelance
McCarthy III, Edward: Hudson Valley Black Press / Hudson Valley Press / Hudson Valley News & Entertainment Network
McCarty, Dennis Page: CBS News
McClain, Matthew: Washington Post
McDermott, Richard: NBC Universal
McDonnell, John: Washington Post
McGreevy, Allen: Freelance
McKenna, William: BBC World News America
McKiernan, Scott: Zuma Press
McKinless, Thomas: CQ Roll Call
McNamee, Wallace: Freelance
McNamee, Win: Getty Images
McNay, James: Senior Editor KobreGuide
McNeeley, Chad: Nikon
Mees, John: CTV
Mills, Doug: New York Times
Millsap, Spencer Hall: National Geographic
Mole, Robert: NBC, Retired
Moorhead, Jeremy: CNN
Morones, Michael: The Free Lance Star
Morris, Larry: Washington Post, Retired
Morris, Peter: CNN
Moulton, Paul: Retired
Mount, Bonnie Jo: Washington Post
Mounts, Ronald: WJLA-TV
Mummert, John: USGA
Murphy, John: Freelance

MEMBERS REPRESENTED—Continued

Murphy, Zoeann: Washington Post
Murtaugh, Peter: Murtaugh Productions, LLC
Natoli, Sharon: Freelance
Negron, Julio: Washington Post
Newton, Jonathan: Washington Post
Nguyen, Phi: U.S. House of Representatives
Nighswander, Marcia: Ohio University
Nikpour, Javad: Metropole Photo
Nolan, David: Nolan & Company
Norling, Richard: Freelance
O'Leary, William: Washington Post
O'Molloy, Colm: Freelance / BBC
Palu, Louie: Zuma Press
Panzer, Chester: NBC-WRC
Parcell, James: Washington Post, Retired
Partlow, Wayne: Associated Press
Perkins, Lucian: Freelance
Perna, Algerina: Baltimore Sun
Peterson, Brittany: McClatchy
Petros, Bill: Freelance
Pinczuk, Murray: Freelance
Pinczuk, Samuel: Student
Plowman, William: Freelance
Polich, John: Retired
Poole, John: NPR
Popper, Andrew:
Postovit, David: Hearst Television WNB
Potasznik, David: Point of View Production Services Inc.
Powell, Lee: Washington Post
Powell Jr., William: NBC, Retired
Powers, Carol: Freelance, Retiired
Premack, Jay: Freelance
Ratner, Moriah: Student
Rensberger, Scott: Freelance
Reynolds, Michael: European Pressphoto Agency
Ribas, Jorge Luis: Washington Post
Ribeiro, Luiz: Freelance
Richards, Paul: AFP
Richardson, Charlotte: Freelance
Riecken, Astrid: Freelance
Riley, Molly: Freelance
Rizvi, Ali: McClatchy
Roberts, Joshua: Freelance
Robinson, Sr., Clyde: Retired
Robinson-Chavez, Michael: Washington Post
Rosen, Alexander: CNN
Roth, Jr., Johnie: NBC, Retired
Russek, II, Ronald: UPI
Ruwe, Renee Lyn: Hudson Valley News & Entertainment
Sachs, Ronald: Consolidated News Photos
Samad, Jewel: AFP
Sanders, Shannon: National Geographic
Sandys, Toni: Washington Post
Sardari, Kaveh: Sardari Group, Inc.
Savi, Riccardo: Freelance
Schaff, Erin: Freelance
Schmick, Paul: Freelance, Retired
Schneider, Jack: NBC-TV
Schwartz, Herb: CBS News
Sharp, Duncan: SKY News
Shefte, Whitney: Washington Post
Shelley, Allison: Freelance
Shepherd, Ray: Defense Media Activity
Sheras, Michael: Canon USA, Inc., Retired
Shinkle, John: Politico
Shlemon, Christopher: Independent TV News
Sierra, Joann: CNN
Sikes, Laura: Laura Sikes Photography
Silverberg, James: The Intellectual Property Group, PLLC
Silverman, Gabriel: Washington Post
Simon, Jeff: CNN
Sisco, Paul: Retired
Skeans, Jr., Ronald: BBC
Smialowski, Brendan: Freelance
Smith, Andrew: CCTV
Smith, Jason: WTTG-TV
Smith, Patrick: Getty Images
Smyth, Christpher: Hearst
Sommer, Emilie: Freelance Emilie Inc. Photography
Somodevilla, Kenneth: Getty Images
Spight Flucker, Benita: Houghton Mifflin Harcourt
Spodak, Cassandra: CNN
Stein, Norman: Freelance
Stein III, Arthur: Freelance
Stewart, Jr., Charles: Hudson Valley Press
Stoddard, Mark: Freelance
Stolz, Peter: CNN
Strasser, Franz: BBC News
Suban, Mark: NIKON
Suddeth, Rick: Freelance
Swain, Bethany Anne:
Swenson, Gordon: ABC, Retired
Sykes, Jack: Harris Corp.
Tessmer, Joseph: Freelance
Thomas, Margaret: Retired
Tiffen, Steve: The Tiffen Company
Tolbert IV, George Dalton: Freelance, U.S. Senate, Retired
Trippett, Robert: Freelance, Retired
Turner, Rob: ITN
Turner, Christopher: CNN
Uhl, Kim: CNN
Usher, Chris: Freelance
Valeri, Charlene: National Geographic
Varias, Stelios: Reuters
Vineys, Kevin: Associated Press
Voisin, Sarah: Washington Post
Voss, Stephen: Freelance
Vucci, Evan: Associated Press
Vurnis, Ambrose: NBC News / WRC-TV
Walker, Diana: Freelance
Wallace, Jim: Smithsonian Institution, Retired
Walsh, Susan: Associated Press

MEMBERS REPRESENTED—Continued

Walz, Mark: CNN
Watkins, Duane: Media Links CCTV
Watrud, Donald: WTTG-TV
Watson, James: AFP
Weinstein, Janet: ABC News
Wiegman, Jr., Dave: NBC, Retired
Wilkes, Douglas: WTTG-TV
Williams, Robert: NBC News
Williams, Milton: Freelance, Retired
Williams, Thomas: Roll Call Newspaper
Williams, Brenna: CNN
Williams Babic, Indira: Newseum
Williamson, Michael: Washington Post
Wilson, Jim: New York Times Photo
Wilson, Mark: Getty Images
Witte, Joel: CCTV
Wong, Alex: Getty Images
Woolfolk, Daniel: Sightline Media Group
Wuls, Jakub: CCTV America
Yarmuth, Floyd: CNN
Yokoyama, Taka: CNN
Zervos, Stratis: Zervos Video Productions, LLC, Freelance

RADIO AND TELEVISION CORRESPONDENTS' GALLERIES*

SENATE RADIO AND TELEVISION GALLERY

The Capitol, Room S–325, 224–6421

Director.—Michael J. Mastrian
Deputy Director.— Ellen Eckert
Senior Media Coordinators: Michael Lawrence, Erin Yeatman
Media Coordinators: Jason Botelho, Charles Moxley

HOUSE RADIO AND TELEVISION GALLERY

The Capitol, Room H–320, 225–5214

Director.— Olga Ramirez Kornacki
Deputy Director.—Andy Elias
Senior Media Logistics Coordinator.—Kim Oates
Media Logistics Coordinators: Ryan Dahl, Kinsey Harvey, Leah Kaplan, Chris Carpenter

EXECUTIVE COMMITTEE OF THE RADIO AND TELEVISION CORRESPONDENTS' GALLERIES

Craig Caplan, C–SPAN, *Chair*
Walt Cronkite, CBS, *Vice Chair*
Abigail Robertson, CBN, *Treasurer*
Paul Courson, Sinclair Broadcasting
Mariam Khan, ABC
Jacqueline Policastro, Gray TV

RULES GOVERNING RADIO AND TELEVISION CORRESPONDENTS' GALLERIES

1. Persons desiring admission to the Radio and Television Galleries of Congress shall make application to the Speaker, as required by Rule 34 of the House of Representatives, as amended, and to the Committee on Rules and Administration of the Senate, as required by Rule 33, as amended, for the regulation of the Senate wing of the Capitol. Applicants shall state in writing the names of all radio stations, television stations, systems, or newsgathering organizations by which they are employed and what other occupation or employment they may have, if any. Applicants shall further declare that they are not engaged in the prosecution of claims or the promotion of legislation pending before Congress, the Departments, or the independent agencies, and that they will not become so employed without resigning from the Galleries. They shall further declare that they are not employed in any legislative or executive department or independent agency of the Government, or by any foreign government or representative thereof; that they are not engaged in any lobbying activities; that they do not and will not, directly or indirectly, furnish special information

*Information is based on data furnished and edited by each respective Gallery.

to any organization, individual, or group of individuals for the influencing of prices on any commodity or stock exchange; that they will not do so during the time they retain membership in the Galleries. Holders of visitors' cards who may be allowed temporary admission to the Galleries must conform to all the restrictions of this paragraph.

2. It shall be a prerequisite to membership that the radio station, television station, system, or news-gathering agency which the applicant represents shall certify in writing to the Radio and Television Correspondents' Galleries that the applicant conforms to the foregoing regulations.

3. The applications required by the above rule shall be authenticated in a manner that shall be satisfactory to the Executive Committee of the Radio and Television Correspondents' Galleries who shall see that the occupation of the Galleries is confined to bona fide news gatherers and/or reporters of reputable standing in their business who represent radio stations, television stations, systems, or news-gathering agencies engaged primarily in serving radio stations, television stations, or systems. It shall be the duty of the Executive Committee of the Radio and Television Correspondents' Galleries to report, at its discretion, violation of the privileges of the Galleries to the Speaker or to the Senate Committee on Rules and Administration, and pending action thereon, the offending individual may be suspended.

4. Persons engaged in other occupations, whose chief attention is not given to—or more than one-half of their earned income is not derived from—the gathering or reporting of news for radio stations, television stations, systems, or news-gathering agencies primarily serving radio stations or systems, shall not be entitled to admission to the Radio and Television Galleries. The Radio and Television Correspondents' List in the Congressional Directory shall be a list only of persons whose chief attention is given to or more than one-half of their earned income is derived from the gathering and reporting of news for radio stations, television stations, and systems engaged in the daily dissemination of news, and of representatives of news-gathering agencies engaged in the daily service of news to such radio stations, television stations, or systems.

5. Members of the families of correspondents are not entitled to the privileges of the Galleries.

6. The Radio and Television Galleries shall be under the control of the Executive Committee of the Radio and Television Correspondents' Galleries, subject to the approval and supervision of the Speaker of the House of Representatives and the Senate Committee on Rules and Administration.

Approved.

PAUL D. RYAN,
Speaker, House of Representatives.

MEMBERS ENTITLED TO ADMISSION

RADIO AND TELEVISION CORRESPONDENTS' GALLERIES

Aaron, John: WTOP Radio
Abbott, Stacey: National Public Radio
Abdalla, Hebah: German TV ZDF
Abdallah, Khalil: CNN
Abdalwahab, Yamen: TIMA
Abdu, Grace: Voice of America
Abdulgawad, Atef: AP–Broadcast
Abdulkareem, Akram: APTVS–American Press & TV Services
Abdullah, Halimah: NBC News
Abdulrazzaq, Ahmed: Aljazeera Satellite Channel (Peninsula)
Abe, Takaaki: Nippon TV Network
Abed, Morad: Aljazeera Satellite Channel (Peninsula)
Abe, Carrie: CBS News
Abeshouse, Robert: Aljazeera English
Abo-Issa, Abdul Hadi: Aljazeera English
Aboud, Abdushakur: Voice of America
Abtar, Rana: Middle East Broadcasting Networks (MBN)
Abu Akleh, Shireen: Aljazeera Satellite Channel (Peninsula)
Abu Diab, Naser: AP–Broadcast
Abu-Kwaik, Biesan: Aljazeera Satellite Channel (Peninsula)
Aburahma, Eyad: Aljazeera English
Abusafia, Jayyab: Sky News Arabia
Accame, Gonzalo: EWTN
Acevedo, Enrique: Univision
Ackerman, Tom: Aljazeera English
Ackland, Matthew: WTTG–Fox Television
Acle, Elizabeth: National Public Radio
Acosta, Abilo: CNN
Adam, Elrashidi: Aljazeera English
Adams, Angelyn: Al Arabiya TV
Adams, Douglas A.: NBC News
Adams, Rebecca: WAMU
Ade, David: Gray Television
Adkins, Candice: WHUR
Adkinson, Jeffrey: AP–Broadcast
Adkison, Janet: Rural TV News
Adler, Shelley: AP–Broadcast
Adlerblum, Robin: NBC News
Adrain, Stephen: BBC
Adridge, Dawin: Morningside Partners, LLC
Agredo, Jose: Caracol Television
Ahmad Serna, Adriana: CMI TV (Colombia)
Ahmed, Ali: Middle East Broadcasting Networks (MBN)
Ahmed, Aziz: AP–Broadcast
Ahmed, Ibrahim: Voice of America
Ahmed, Lukman: BBC
Ahn, Katherine: Korean Broadcasting Systems
Aich, Atirath: CGTN America
Aiello, Augustine: National Public Radio
Aigner-Treworgy, Adam: CBS News
Ake, Gabrielle: CBS News
Akhtar, Monica: Washingtonpost.com
Akkad, Reem: Washingtonpost.com
Akuffo, Rachelle: CGTN America
Al Badry, Rami: CNN
Al Hmoud, Mounira: i24 News
Al Juboori, Haitham: Aljazeera Satellite Channel (Peninsula)
Al Rawi, Khalid: TIMA
Al-Shaib, Zeina: CGTN America
Alallak, Firas: One America
Alami, Mohammed: Aljazeera Satellite Channel (Peninsula)
Alamiri, Yasmeen: CGTN America
Alarian, Laila: Aljazeera English
Alba, Carmen: NBC News
Albano, Thomas: CBS News
Albert, Chris: CBS News
Alberter, William: CNN
Aldag, Jason: Washingtonpost.com
Alderman, Ashley: Fox News
Alegret, Gustau: NTN24
Aleman, Rita: Hearst Television Inc.
Alemany, Jacqueline: CBS News
Alesse, Elizabeth: ABC News
Alexander, Clinton N.: CBS NEWS
Alexander, George: CGTN America
Alexander, Kenneth: C–SPAN
Alexander, Peter: NBC News
Alexandre, Lee: Hearst Television Inc.
Alfarone, Debra: WUSA–TV
Alhuraimi, Nadia: BBC
Ali, Mohammad: WETA
Ali, Omar: Sky News Arabia
Aliaga, Julio: CGTN America
Alipour, Damien: Voice of America
Aljasheme, Mohaimen: Sky News Arabia
Alkadiri, Faisal: ABC News
Allard, John: ABC News
Allbritton, David: CNN
Alldredge, Thomas: C–SPAN
Allen, Brian: Voice of America
Allen, Darrell: Voice of America
Allen, Vadim: Voice of America
Allman, Bryan: NBC News

MEMBERS ENTITLED TO ADMISSION—Continued

Allman, Mark: CNN
Allman, Robert: CBN News
Allmond, Scott: ABC News
Alnwick, Melanie: WTTG–Fox Television
Alowais, Abdulaziz: APTVS–American Press & TV Services
Alqarni, Ahmed: APTVS–American Press & TV Services
Alrawi, Khaldoun: AP–Broadcast
Alvarenga, Adan: Agence France Presse (AFP–TV)
Alvarez, Alejandro: News2Share
Alvey, Peter: WDCW
Amirault-Michel, Theresa: C–SPAN
Amling, Alicia: CBS News
Ammerman, Stuart: CBS News
Amon, Whitney: WUSA–TV
Amos, George: WJLA–TV / Newschannel 8
Anastasi, Patrick: CNBC
Anderson, Charles: WETA
Anderson, Patrick: Swiss Broadcasting
Anderson, Tetiana: TRT World
Anderson, William: Sinclair Broadcast Group
Andree, Eric: AP–Broadcast
Andress, Jeannie: AP–Broadcast
Aneiva, Roberto: NBC News
Angrum, Khadija: Sinclair Broadcast Group
Angulo-Hinkson, Natalia: Sinclair Broadcast Group
Ansari, Azadeh: TRT World
Ansell, Anna: Fox News
Anthony, Tony: Morningside Partners, LLC
Anwar, Sohail: National Public Radio
Anyse, Alana: CBS News
Anzur, Matthew: Scripps News
Ao, Siqiao: Voice of America
Applegate, Van: WTTG–Fox Television
Arabasadi, Arash: Voice of America
Arbogast, Vincent: Fox News
Ard, Alexa: McClatchy
Arena, Bruno: AP–Broadcast
Arenander, Karin: Swedish Broadcasting
Arenas, Andrea: Feature Story News
Arensberg, Chloe: CBS News
Argyri, Eleni: Hellenic Public TV
Arias, Rafael: Aljazeera English
Armah, Omega: CNN
Armstrong, Patricia: NBC News
Armstrong, Thomas: ABC News
Armwood, Adrian: CBS News
Arroyo, Raymond: EWTN
Art, Jeremiah: C–SPAN
Arter, Melanie: CNSNews.com
Aretsona, Eva: BBC
Arthur, Michael: Aljazeera English
Aryankalavil, Babu: Middle East Broadcasting Networks (MBN)
Arzoumanov, Abigail: CNN
Asher, Julie: TF1–French TV
Ashworth, Sara: Aljazeera Satellite Channel (Peninsula)
Asmael, Hussein: AP–Broadcast
Assmann, Karin: Spiegel German TV
Attkisson, Sharyl: Sinclair Broadcast Group
Augenstein, Neal: WTOP Radio
Augustus, Shannon: C–SPAN
Aulenkamp, Jan: German TV ARD
Auresto, John: AP–Broadcast
Austermuhle, Martin: WAMU
Austin, Alana: Gray Television
Austin, Gail: Hearst Television Inc.
Austin, Jonathan: CTV Canadian TV
Austin, Kenneth: NBC News
Austin, Mark: Sky News
Avila-Lindo, Martha: NTN24
Avner, Philip: AP–Broadcast
Avrutine, Matthew: CNN
Awada, Adam: Sky News Arabia
Ayala, Jorge: Telesur
Ayaz, Faruk: TRT
Ayers, Judith: WTTG–Fox Television
Azais, Jean-Pascal: Swiss Broadcasting
B. Fischer, Andrew: News2Share
Babb, Carla: Voice of America
Baca. Nathan: WJLA–TV / NewsChannel 8
Baghi, Baubak: Aljazeera English
Bagnall, Thomas: Voice of America
Baharaeen, Renee: CNN
Bai, Fan: CGTN America
Baier, William: Fox News
Bailey, Blayne: NBC NewsChannel
Bailor, Michelle: C–SPAN
Bainer, Rebecca: Hearst Television Inc
Baker, Elizabeth: National Public Radio
Baker, Leslie: Fox News
Baker, Nancy: Yahoo News
Baker, Sarah: NBC News
Baldwin, Travis Renee: ABC News
Balinovic, Daniel: Reuters Radio & TV
Ball, George: WJLA–TV / NewsChannel 8
Ballard, Hitomi: NHK
Ballou, Jeff: Aljazeera English
Banks, Allyson: WUSA–TV
Banks, David: CQ / Roll Call
Banks, Erik: CNN
Banks, Joshua: Fox News
Banks, Laquasha: Sinclair Broadcast Group
Banks, Laquasha: Fox Business Network
Banks, Mark: ABC News
Banks, Morris: CBS News
Bannigan, Michael: Fox Business Network
Bannister, Craig: CNSNews.com
Banoub, Christina: TV Asahi
Baragona, Steve: Voice of America
Barajas, Angela: CNN
Barat, Andrew: NBC News
Baratta, Christine: Bloomberg Radio & TV

MEMBERS ENTITLED TO ADMISSION—Continued

Barber, Ellison: Fox News
Barber, Paul: CGTN America
Barber, Timothy: WJLA–TV / NewsChannel 8
Barker, Edward: AP–Broadcast
Barlow, Joshua: CGTN America
Barnard, Bob: WTTG–Fox Television
Barnes, David: CTV–Community TV of PG County
Barnett, James: CGTN America
Barnett, Michael: CBS News
Barondess, Rose: NBC News
Barr, Bryan: Sinclair Broadcast Group
Barr, Luke: ABC News
Barrett, Calvin: Fox News
Barrett, Edward: CNN
Barringer, Reginald: CBS News
Barros, Aline: Voice of America
Barss, Kyle: Washingtonpost.com
Barua, Satarupa: Voice of America
Basch, Michelle: WTOP Radio
Bash, Dana: CNN
Bash, David: WETA
Basinger, Stuart: Fox News
Baskerville, Kia: CBS News
Basturk, Tevhid Nazmi: TRT World
Bat, John: CBS News
Bates, Jeffrey: WETA
Batten, Rodney: NBC News
Battistella, Marilisa: CBS News
Baumel, Susan: Voyage Productions
Bautista, Mark: CBN News
Bays, James: Aljazeera English
Baysden III, Earl T.: WTTG–Fox Television
Beahn, James: WTTG–Fox Television
Beal, Robin: Fox News
Bear, Christian: CNN
Bearne, Adam: Eurovision Americas, Inc.
Beattie, Sam: BBC
Beccio, Sarah: Native American TV (NATV)
Becker, Bruce: Fox Business Network
Becker, Christopher: Fox News
Becker, Edward: Free Speech Radio News
Becker, Farrel: CBS News
Becker, Frank: WJLA–TV / NewsChannel 8
Beckett, Paul: Wall Street Journal
Beckner, Steven: National Public Radio
Beitsch, Rebecca: Stateline.org
Bejarano, Mark: National Public Radio
Belgraver, Jet: Aljazeera English
Belha, Nickouszha: Small House Productions
Belizaire, Jacquelin: Voice of America
Bell, Benjamin: ABC News
Bell, Bradley: WJLA–TV / NewsChannel 8
Bellis, Michael: ABC News
Bena, John: CNN
Bender, Jason: C–SPAN
Benetato, Michael: NBC News
Benincasa, Robert: National Public Radio
Bennett, Dalton: Washingtonpost.com
Bennett, Damon: Eurovision Americas, Inc.
Bennett, Geoffrey: National Public Radio
Bennett, Justin: NBC News
Bennett, Kate: CNN
Bennett, Mark: CBS News
Bennewitz, Alexa: CNN
Bensen, Jackie: WRC–TV / NBC–4
Bentouila, Elkheir: Middle East Broadcasting Networks (MBN)
Bentz, Leslie: CNN
Berdiel, Daniel: Sirius XM Satellite Radio
Bergal, Jenni: Stateline.org
Berger, Catherine: German TV ZDF
Berger, Judson: Fox News
Bergfeldt, Barbro: Swedish Broadcasting
Berman, Daniel: CNN
Bernal, Richard: CNN
Bernardini, Laura: CNN
Bernknopf, David: Sinclair Broadcast Group
Bernstein, Howard: WUSA–TV
Bernstein, Leandra: Sinclair Broadcast Group
Bernstein, Matthew: Sinclair Broadcast Group
Betsill, Brett: C–SPAN
Bevington, Ben: BBC
Bevir, John: Feature Story News
Beyer, William: WTTG–Fox Television
Bharania, Anoo: Reuters Radio & TV
Bhatti, Ahad: Aljazeera English
Bicker, Laura: BBC
Bidar, Musadiq: CBS News
Biello, Mark: CNN
Bilal, Sadiq: AP–Broadcast
Bills, Lindzie: CNN
Binswanger, Joshua: Morningside Partners, LLC
Bintrim, Tim: WETA
Biskupic, Joan: CNN
Bivona, Frank: CNN
Bjoergaas, Tove: Norwegian Broadcasting
Black, Jamie: EWTN
Black, Phillip: ABC News
Blackman, Jay: NBC News
Blackman, John: NBC News
Blackwill, Sarah: NBC News
Blair, Adam: Independent Television News (ITN)
Blakey, Leona: C–SPAN
Blakley, Kevin: CNN
Blanchard, Lauren: Fox News
Blanco, Hugo: AP–Broadcast
Blitzer, Wolf: CNN
Bloch, Hannah: National Public Radio
Block, Eliana: WUSA–TV
Block, Melissa: National Public Radio
Blooston, Victoria: NBC News
Blum-Dostie, Jacqueline: AP–Broadcast
Boag, Keith: Canadian Broadcasting Corporation (CBC)
Bodenhorst, Michael: AP–Broadcast

MEMBERS ENTITLED TO ADMISSION—Continued

Bodnar, John: CNN
Boerma, Lindsey: CBS News
Boesche, Jan: German Public Radio (ARD)
Bogle, Emily: National Public Radio
Bogley, John: Metro Teleproductions
Bohannon, Joseph: NBC News
Bohn, Kevin: CNN
Bolden, Warren: Bloomberg Radio & TV
Bolivar, Alexis: FedNet
Bond, Larry: Voice of America
Bonewald, Jason: Fox News Radio
Booker, Brakkton: National Public Radio
Booker, Cory: NBC News
Borak, Donna: CNN
Borger, Gloria: CNN
Borland, Karen: Fox News
Bos, Albertus: Dutch TV & Radio (NOS)
Bos, Emiliano: Swiss Broadcasting
Bossone, Andrew: The Newshour with Jim Lehrer
Bost, Mark: WUSA–TV
Boston, Tyrone: CNN
Boswell, Leonard: CBS News
Boughton, Bryan: Fox News
Bourar, Hicham: Middle East Broadcasting Networks (MBN)
Bowen, Timothy: WETA
Bowman, Jennifer: Fox News
Bowman, Michael: Voice of America
Boxer, Sarah: Yahoo News
Boyd, Wayne: ABC News
Bozek, Walter: CBN News
Brablec, Radek: National Public Radio
Bradner, Eric: CNN
Bragale, Charles: WRC–TV / NBC–4
Brailsford Cato, Grace: Yahoo News
Brain, Jonathan: TRT World
Brangham, William: The Newshour with Jim Lehrer
Brannon, Timothy: Voice of America
Bransford, Neill: Fox News
Brascia, Lorenza: CNN
Brauer, Alexander: Sinclair Broadcast Group
Braun, Joshua: CNN
Brawner, Donald: WETA
Brawner, Greta: C–SPAN
Bream, Shannon: Fox News
Breiterman, Charles: ABC News
Breitman, Kendall: NBC News
Bremer, Brittany: NBC News
Brennan, Allison: CNN
Brennan, Margaret: CBS News
Breuer, Jennifer: AP–Broadcast
Brevner, Michael: CNN
Brewer, Georgina: Independent Television News (ITN)
Brickhouse, Ayana: Aljazeera English
Brieger, Annette: German TV ZDF
Briggs, Philip: CBS DC
Bright, Whitney: CBS News
Britch, Raymond: CNN
Brock, Robert: Aljazeera English
Brockell, Gillian: Washingtonpost.com
Brody, David: CBN News
Broffman, Craig: AP–Broadcast
Brogan, Pat: WAMU
Broleman, Michael: NBC NewsChannel
Bronstein, Scott: CNN
Bronston, Sally: NBC News
Brooke, Sarah: NBC News
Brooks, David: CNN
Brooks, Kurt: WUSA–TV
Brooks, Sarah: Time Warner Cable
Broom, William: WUSA–TV
Browder, Jenna: CBN News
Brower, Brooke: CNN
Brown, Ashley: WRC–TV / NBC–4
Brown, Beth: WRC–TV / NBC–4
Brown, Donald: C–SPAN
Brown, Elizabeth: Fox News
Brown, Kimberly: The Real News Network
Brown, Kristin: Fox News
Brown, Malcolm: Feature Story News
Brown, Pamela: CNN
Brown, Paul: C–SPAN
Brown, Taylor: BBC
Brown, Tracy: AP–Broadcast
Brown-Kaiser, Elizabeth: WUSA–TV
Browne, Ryan: CNN
Browning, Robert: C–SPAN
Bruce, Mary: ABC News
Bruce, Susan: EWTN
Bruggeman, Lucien: ABC News
Brumbaugh, Kathleen: AP–Broadcast
Brumfiel, Geoff: National Public Radio
Bruns, David: Washingtonpost.com
Brusk, Steven: CNN
Bryan, Ellen: WUSA–TV
Bryant, Nicholas: BBC
Bryant, Rodney: Gannett Government Media Corp
Bua, Jon-Christopher: Talk Media News
Bubaris, Philomena: CBS News
Buchholz, Jenny: Fox News
Buchmann, Arielle: WUSA–TV
Buckenmaier, Claudia: German TV ARD
Buckhorn, Burke: CNN
Buckley, Daniel: WRC–TV / NBC–4
Buddenhagen, Kristina: C–SPAN
Buenten, Verena: German TV ARD
Buesing, Patrick: Ventana Productions
Bullard, Gabriel: WAMU
Bullard, John: ABC News
Bullard Harmon, Susan: CBS News
Bullock, Peter: Reuters Radio & TV
Bullock, Tiffany: CNN
Bumsted, Robert: AP–Broadcast
Bundock, Susan: C–SPAN

MEMBERS ENTITLED TO ADMISSION—Continued

Bunson, Matthew: EWTN
Burch, Brian: CNN
Burdick, Leslie: C–SPAN
Burgard, Jan Philipp: German TV ARD
Burger, Todd: EWTN
Burgess, David: CNN
Burk, Penny: NBC News
Burke, Kathleen: EWTN
Burke, Michael: Voice of America
Burkhard, Elizabeth: Fox News
Burles, Jason: Canadian Broadcasting Corporation (CBC)
Burlij, Terence: CNN
Burman, Blake: Fox Business Network
Burnett, Gordon: Radio Free Asia
Burney, Tayla: WAMU
Burns, Mary: Cox Broadcasting
Burton, Matthew: ABC News
Bush, Daniel: The Newshour with Jim Lehrer
Butler, James: Diversified Communications, Inc. (DCI)
Butler, Norman: NBC News
Buttler, Martina: German Public Radio (ARD)
Byrnes, Dennis: National Public Radio
Cabral Pichardo, Juan: CNN
Cades, Michael: CQ / Roll Call
Cadigan, William: CNN
Cahill, Kathy: C–SPAN
Caifa, Karin: CNN
Cala, Ivonne: National Public Radio
Caldwell, Leigh Ann: NBC News
Calfat, Marcel: Canadian Broadcasting Corporation (CBC)
Callahan, Michael: CNN
Callebs, Sean: CGTN America
Calvi, Jason: EWTN
Camah, Malik: Aljazeera English
Camarda, Tim: Eye-To-Eye Video
Cameron, Christina: Fox News
Campbell, Eleanor Jane: Fox News
Candia, Kirsten: German TV ZDF
Cannon, Catherine: CBS News
Cao, Qingyun: CGTN America
Caperton, Katherine: Sirius XM Satellite Radio
Capion, Toby: EWTN
Caplan, Craig: C–SPAN
Capomaccio-Even, Anne-Marie: Radio France Internationale
Capra, Anthony: NBC News
Carbonne, Frederic: Radio France Internationale
Cardine, Kyle: Fuji TV Japan
Cardoze, Jacques: France 2 Television
Carey, Julie: WRC–TV / NBC–4
Carlson, Brett: Global TV Canada
Carlson, Christopher: ABC News
Carlson, Frank: The Newshour with Jim Lehrer
Carlson, Stephen: Fox News
Carlson, Tucker: Fox News
Carmean, Kyle: WTTG–Fox Television
Carney, Keith: FedNet
Carpeaux, Emily: The Newshour with Jim Lehrer
Carpel, Michael: Fox News
Carr, Evan: WRC–TV / NBC–4
Carr, Martin: WETA
Carrick, Kenneth: C–SPAN
Carro, Jessica: AOL Huffington Post
Carson, Chris: FedNet
Carswell, Diana: ABC News
Carter, Christopher: One America
Carter, Dave: WRC–TV / NBC–4
Carter, Jr., Walter: Fox News
Carter-Conneen, Michael: WJLA–TV / NewsChannel 8
Cartwright, Joshua: CBS News
Casenco, Anatolie: Voice of America
Casey, Elizabeth: Washingtonpost.com
Casey, Sean: WRC–TV / NBC–4
Cassano, Joseph: WRC–TV / NBC–4
Castaneda, Gabriel: WFDC–TV Univision
Castaneda-Molina, Diana: NTN24
Castano, Christopher: Sinclair Broadcast Group
Castiel, Carol: Voice of America
Castillo, Rolando: National Public Radio
Castro, Pablo: Hispanic Communications Network
Catrett, David: CNN
Causey, Mike: Federal News Radio 1500 AM
Cecchini, Reginald: Global TV Canada
Cetta, Denise: CBS News
Cevahiroglu, Cengizhan: TRT
Chadha-Kaye, Stephanie: C–SPAN
Chaggaris, Steven: CBS News
Chakraborty, Barnini: Fox News
Chalian, David: CNN
Chamberlain, Jared: WDCW
Chamberlain, Richard: WJLA–TV / NewsChannel 8
Chan, Enoch: WETA
Chance, Bradleigh: NBC News
Chandra, Emma: Bloomberg Radio & TV
Chang, Ailsa: National Public Radio
Chang, Ching-Yi: AP–Broadcast
Chang, Darzen: WETA
Chang, Peggy: Voice of America
Chapman, Irwin: Bloomberg Radio & TV
Chapman, Michael: CNSNews.com
Chappell, Jill: CNN
Charles, Daniel: National Public Radio
Charley, Peter: Aljazeera English
Charpa, Silvia: Austrian Radio & TV (ORF)
Charters-Bilbassy, Nadia: Al Arabiya TV
Chase, David: Cox Broadcasting
Chatelain, Gabrielle: Agence France Presse (AFP–TV)
Chattman, Tanya: C–SPAN
Chavar, Anthony: The New York Times
Chavez, Paola: ABC News
Chaytor, David: Aljazeera English

MEMBERS ENTITLED TO ADMISSION—Continued

Chekuru, Kavitha: Aljazeera English
Chen, Nancy: WJLA–TV / NewsChannel 8
Chen, Natasha: CNN
Chen, Qingwei: Hong Kong Phoenix Satellite Television
Chen, Teng: New Tang Dynasty TV
Chen, Yi Qiu: Hong Kong Phoenix Satellite Television
Chen, Zheng: Shenzhen Media Group (SZMG)
Chenevey, Steve: WTTG–Fox Television
Cheng, He: CGTN America
Cherneff, Elizabeth: Voice of America
Cherouny, Robert: Aljazeera English
Chester, Chris: WAMU
Cheung, Jessica: National Public Radio
Chevez, Carlos: National Public Radio
Chhour, David: National Public Radio
Chick, Jane: CBS News
Childs, Lete: NBC News
Chimoy, Carolina: Deutsche Welle TV
Chipak, John: EWTN
Chirinos, Isabel: Newhouse School / Syracuse University
Chiu, Lisa: CGTN America
Cho, Aimee: WRC–TV / NBC–4
Cho, Eunjung: Voice of America
Cho, Hans: JTBC
Chocola, Joseph: The Hill
Chodl, Stephanie: Live Squawk
Choe, Jaywon: The Newshour with Jim Lehrer
Choedron, Trinlae: Voice of America
Choi, Hannah: JTBC
Chophel, Lobsang: Radio Free Asia
Choto, Raymond: Voice of America
Chowdhury, Maureen: McClatchy
Christian, Douglas: Talk Media News
Christian, George: CBS News
Christian, Nancy: C–SPAN
Chung, E-Ting: CTI–TV (Taiwan)
Chung, Hasuk: Seoul Broadcasting System (SBS)
Chunko, April: WJLA–TV / NewsChannel 8
Cilesizoglu, Ali: TRT
Cinque, Vicente: TV Globo International
Ciridon, Robert: NBC News
Cirilli, Kevin: Bloomberg Radio & TV
Claar, Matthew: C–SPAN
Claiborn, Lindsay: McClatchy
Clancy, Kevin: Scripps News
Clarenne, Gilles: Agence France Presse (AFP–TV)
Clark, James: C–SPAN
Clark, Stuart: CNN
Clarke, John: Feature Story News
Clary, Gregory: CNN
Clash, Shannon: NBC News
Claudet, Marie: Canadian Broadcasting Corporation (CBC)
Cleary, Ronica: WTTG–Fox Television
Clemons, Bobby: CNN
Cloherty, Megan: WTOP Radio
Clottey, Peter: Voice of America
Clugston, Gregory: SRN News (Salem)
Coates, Avron: CNN
Coburn, Davin: McClatchy
Cockerham, Richard: Fox News
Cockey, William: WUSA–TV
Cofske, Harvey: Diversified Communications, Inc. (DCI)
Cohan, Stacey: CNN
Cohen, Marshall: CNN
Cohen, Samantha: NBC News
Cohen, Zachary: CNN
Cohencious, Rebecca: Native American TV (NATV)
Cohencious, Robert: Native American TV (NATV)
Coil, Holley: NBC NewsChannel
Coker, Edward: WJLA–TV / NewsChannel 8
Cole, Bryan: Fox News
Coleau, Manel: WRC–TV / NBC–4
Colella, Anthony: WTTG–Fox Television
Coleman, Thomas: NBC News
Coleman, Youman: CNN
Coleman, Zachary: National Public Radio
Coles, David: The Newshour with Jim Lehrer
Colimore, Eric: Fox News
Coll, Dennis: National Public Radio
Colli, George: Cox Broadcasting
Collins, Bruce: C–SPAN
Collins, Kaitlan: CNN
Collins, Maxine: BBC
Collins, Pat: WRC–TV / NBC–4
Collinson, Stephen: CNN
Colombo-Abdullah, Andrea: AP–Broadcast
Colt, Jasper: USA Today
Colvin, Rhonda: Washingtonpost.com
Conant, Caitlin: CBS News
Concaugh, Jr., Joseph: Diversified Communications, Inc. (DCI)
Coney, Carol: CBS News
Conlin, Sheila: NBC NewsChannel
Connelly, Phoebe: Washingtonpost.com
Conner, Eric: Fox News
Connors, Benjamin: McClatchy
Conte, Michael: ABC News
Contreras, Glenda: Telemundo Network
Contreras, Jorge: Univision
Conway, Marshall: The Real News Network
Cook, James: BBC
Cook, James: C–SPAN
Cook, Jeffery: ABC News
Cook, Malcolm: Washingtonpost.com
Cook, Sara: NHK
Coon, Janice: WUSA–TV
Coonce, Stephen: Aljazeera English
Cooney, Daniel: The Newshour with Jim Lehrer
Cooper, Kyle: WTOP Radio
Cooper, Ralph: CGTN America
Cooper, Jr., Nero: NBC News

MEMBERS ENTITLED TO ADMISSION—Continued

Cordes, Nancy: CBS News
Corke, Kevin: Fox News
Corner, Howard: C–SPAN
Cornish Emery, Audie: National Public Radio
Corpet, Anne: Radio France Internationale
Correa, Pedro: AP–Broadcast
Correa, Pedro: Telemundo Network
Cortes, William: Telesur
Costantini, Bob: Westwood One
Costello, Cheryl: WJLA–TV / NewsChannel 8
Costello, Thomas: NBC News
Cote, Timothy: NBC News
Cotterill, Rebecca: Independent Television News (ITN)
Couger, Charles: Fox News
Coughlan, Victoria: CBS News
Couric, Katherine: Yahoo News
Courson III, Paul: Sinclair Broadcast Group
Courtney, Eric: Diversified Communications, Inc. (DCI)
Cousins, Bria: CNBC
Couture, Denise: WAMU
Cowman, Chris: CGTN America
Cox, Jerry: This Is America with Dennis Wholey
Craca, Thomas: NBC News
Craig, John: Diversified Communications, Inc. (DCI)
Craig, Nathan: C–SPAN
Craig, William: National Public Radio
Crane, Stephen: Cronkite News Service
Crawford, James: CNN
Crawford, Woody: Voice of America
Crawley, Plummer: CNBC
Criales, Ricardo: Agence France Presse (AFP–TV)
Cridland, Jeffrey: WRC–TV / NBC–4
Cridland, Jeffrey: WUSA–TV
Crim, Lorraine: Fox News
Crombe, Laura: CBN News
Cronkite IV, Walter: CBS News
Crookshank, Nate: FedNet
Crosdale, Natalia: CNN
Cross, Christopher: CNN
Crossling, Robert: WTOP Radio
Crouch, Alice: Fox News
Crowder, Anja: ABC News
Crowley, Robert: CNN
Crowther, Philip: AP–Broadcast
Crum, John: CBS News
Crupi, Nicolas: Voice of America
Crutchfield, Curtis: CTV–Community TV of PG County
Cruz, Cara: Canadian Broadcasting Corporation (CBC)
Cruz, Johnny: Wall Street Journal
Csapo, Jonathan: BBC
Cucchiara, Natalie: NBC News
Cuddy, Matthew: CNBC
Cuesta-Roca, Carmen: Agence France Presse (AFP–TV)
Cui, Han: Sinovision
Cui, Lingnan: CGTN America
Culhane, Patricia: Aljazeera English
Cullen, Michael: National Public Radio
Culver, David: WRC–TV / NBC–4
Cumber, Erika: CTV–Community TV of PG County
Cunha, John: CNN
Curameng, Asuka: Nippon TV Network
Curran, Patrick: WTTG–Fox Television
Currier, Liam: C–SPAN
Curtis, Alexander: C–SPAN
Curtis, Jodie: Fox News
Cvetnic, Nicole: McClatchy
Czaplinski, Michael: National Public Radio
Czys, Janet: National Public Radio
Czzowitz, Gregory: C–SPAN
Dailey, Kathleen: BBC
Dakin, Carla: NBC News
Daley, James: The Real News Network
Daley, Kitty Felde: KQED
Dalgetty, Audrey: ABC News
Dalton, Benjamin: TV Tokyo
Daly, John: CBS News
Damdul, Dorjee: Radio Free Asia
Danahar, Paul: BBC
Daniel, Zoe: Australian Broadcasting Corporation
Daniels, Eugene: Scripps News
Daniels, Peter: C–SPAN
Danielski, Marvin: Sinclair Broadcast Group
Danilko, Derek: AP–Broadcast
Dann, Caroline: NBC News
Danzig, Abbigail: NBC News
Dao, Thao: VIETV Network
Dargakis, Minas: Voice of America
Darling, Addie: EWTN
Daschle, Kelly: AP–Broadcast
Dasgupta, Sonia: WUSA–TV
Dashevsky, Arik: Aljazeera English
Date, Ajinkya: ABC News
Dauchess, Matthew: C–SPAN
Daugherty, Jeffery: Voice of America
Davey, Mark: Independent Television News (ITN)
Davidson, Tracy: WRC–TV / NBC–4
Davies, Deborah: Aljazeera English
Davila Castillo, Jaime: CNN
Davis, Barbara: Voice of America
Davis, Clinton: WTTG–Fox Television
Davis, Edward: CNN
Davis, Jennifer: Hearst Television Inc.
Davis, Mitchell: Fox News Radio
Davis, NaKeya: Fox News
Davis, Patrick: CNN
Davis, Ray: NBC NewsChannel
Davis, Susan: National Public Radio
Dawood, Mohammed: APTVS–American Press & TV Services

MEMBERS ENTITLED TO ADMISSION—Continued

Dawson, Wendy: Fox News
Day, Kara: CNN
De Chagas, Bridget: National Public Radio
de Diego, Javier: CNN
de Franceschi, Jela: Voice of America
de La Cuetara, Ines: Global TV Canada
de Schaetzen, Emilie: Eurovision Americas, Inc.
de Vogue, Ariane: CNN
Deahl, Jessica: National Public Radio
Dealgetty, Audrey: ABC News
Dean, Matthew: Fox News
DeChalus, Camila: CNN
Decker, Jonathan: Fox News Radio
DeFeo, Joseph: WJLA–TV / NewsChannel 8
DeFrank, Debra: Fox News
DeFrank, Joseph: Fox News
Dehm, Eric: CBS DC
del Pino, Javier: Cadena SER
del Vado, Marta: Càdena SER
DeLany, Kevin: Westwood One
Delawala, Imtiyaz: ABC News
Delshad, Carmel: WAMU
DeLuca, Ashleigh: Gray Television
Deluca, Joan: Voice of America
DeMarco, Lauren: WTTG–Fox Television
DeMarco, Nicki: Washingtonpost.com
Demarest, Sarah: NBC News
Demaria, Edward: NBC News
Demark, Michael: Fox News
Demas, William: ABC News
DeMilio, Paul: Sirius XM Satellite Radio
DeMillo, Christopher: The Real News Network
DeMoss, Gary: CBS News
Dennert, Mary: Fox News
Dermody, Kevin: Nexstar Media Group
DeRosa, Adam: The Hill
Derrien, Mathieu: TF1–French TV
Desbois, Laurent: France 2 Television
Desjardins, Lisa: The Newshour with Jim Lehrer
Detrow, Scott: National Public Radio
Dewast, Louise: France 2 Television
Dezell, Maureen: Washington Bureau News Service
Dhue, Stephanie: CNBC
Di Caro, Martin: WAMU
Di Marzo, Marina: NBC News
Diab, Ahmed: Aljazeera Satellite Channel (Peninsula)
Diamond, Jeremy: CNN
Diaz, Aixa: Hearst Television Inc.
Diaz, Daniella: CNN
Diaz, Juan Carlos: Small House Productions
Diaz, Robert: CBS News
Diaz Waldman, Illeana: WUSA–TV
DiBella, Richard: Fox News
DiCarlo, Patricia: CNN
Dickerson, John: CBS News
Diggs, Bridget: C–SPAN
Dilanian, Kenneth: NBC News
Dill, Danny: C–SPAN
Dillard, Juanita: ABC News
Ding-Everson, William: TV Asahi
DiPietro, AnnaMaria: WJLA–TV / NewsChannel 8
Diviney, Susan: WTTG–Fox Television
Dixon, Evan: NBC News
Dixon, Gregory: National Public Radio
Dixson, Charles H.: CBS News
Doane, Martin C.: WJLA–TV / NewsChannel 8
Dobal, Michael: NBC NewsChannel
Dockett, Sakina: CTV–Community TV of PG County
Doell, Michelle: C–SPAN
Doerer, Kristen: The Newshour with Jim Lehrer
Doernen, Daniel: German TV ARD
Doherty, Brian: Fox News
Doherty, Peter: ABC News
Doherty, Sue: Middle East Broadcasting Networks (MBN)
Dolce, Stephen: CNN
Dolge, Michelle: CBS DC
Dolma, Rigdhen: Radio Free Asia
Domen, John: WTOP Radio
Dominguez, Jose: WDCW
Dominick, Katie: CBS News
Donaghy, Nina: i24 News
Donahue, Edward: AP–Broadcast
Donald, William: Eye-To-Eye Video
Donaldson, Alice: CNN
Donangmaye, Timothee: Voice of America
Donevan, Connor: National Public Radio
Donnelly, Kristin: NBC News
Donner, Jason: Fox News
Donovan, Maria: Fox News Radio
Doocy, Peter: Fox News
Doody, Sean: C–SPAN
Dooley, Erin: ABC News
Dooley, Rachel: CNN
Dore, Margaret: CBS News
Dorf-Dolce, Heather: German TV ARD
Dorn, Jason: AP–Broadcast
Dorsey, Steve: CBS News
Doty, Mitchell: Aljazeera English
Dougherty, Paul: ABC News
Douglas, Denise: CTV–Community TV of PG County
Douglas, Mark: Aljazeera English
Dove, Nicholas: Aljazeera English
Dowhaluk, Sonya: CNN
Doyle, Geoffrey: Fox News
Doyle, John: C–SPAN
Drabo, Aboubacar: National Public Radio
Dragsted, Stine: Danish Broadcasting Corporation
Drennen, Kevin: WJLA–TV / NewsChannel 8
Drewenskus, Alex: WAMU
Dridi, Sonia: AP–Broadcast
Dries, Robert: CBS News
Dries, William: CBS News

MEMBERS ENTITLED TO ADMISSION—Continued

Druce, Ian: BBC
Drummond, Mallory: C–SPAN
Du, Haipeng: New Tang Dynasty TV
Du, Yubin: CGTN America
Duarte, Alfredo: WFDC–TV Univision
Duarte, Alina: Telesur
Dubert, Michelle: NBC News
DuBose, Kadesh: Diversified Communications, Inc. (DCI)
DuBose, Michael: EWTN
Duckham, Justin: Talk Media News
Dueffert, Lauren: EWTN
Duffy, Conor: Australian Broadcasting Corporation
Dufresne, Louise: CBS News
Dugan, William: CTV Canadian TV
Duggeli, Peter: Swiss Broadcasting
Dukakis, Alexandra: ABC News
Dumont Baron, Yanik: Canadian Broadcasting Corporation (CBC)
Duncan, Victoria: NBC News
Duncombe, Lyndsay: Canadian Broadcasting Corporation (CBC)
Dunkin, John: ABC News
Dunlop, William: Eurovision Americas, Inc.
Dunne, Samantha: WRC–TV / NBC–4
Dupree, James: Cox Broadcasting
Durham, Deborah: Univision
Durkin, Edward: WRC–TV / NBC–4
Duster, Chandelis: NBC News
Dwyer, Devin: ABC News
Dwyer-Shapiro, Lisa: AP–Broadcast
Dyer, Lois: CBS News
Eastin, Yi-Pe: C–SPAN
Ebbs, Stephanie: ABC News
Ebel, Thomas: CNN
Ebersohl, Kevin: WTTG–Fox Television
Ebrahimi, Mehrnoosh: BBC
Echevarria, Pedro: C–SPAN
Echols, Jerry: Fox News
Eck, Christina: German Press Agency
Edem, Ariel: To the Contrary (Persephone Productions)
Edmondson, William: Fox News
Edson, Richard: Fox News
Edwards, Brian: CBN News
Edwards, Christopher: EWTN
Edwards, William: Agence France Presse (AFP–TV)
Edwards, Windsor: National Public Radio
Ehrichs, Matthew: The Newshour with Jim Lehrer
Eicher, Andrew: CNSNews.com
Einarsen, Jonathan: NBC NewsChannel
Eiras, Arlene: Reuters Radio & TV
Ejedepang-Koge, Nkwenten: Middle East Broadcasting Networks (MBN)
El-Hamalawy, Mahmoud: Aljazeera Satellite Channel (Peninsula)
El-khamissi, Elian: APTVS–American Press & TV Services
Elahmed, Mouhamed: Aljazeera Satellite Channel (Peninsula)
Eldridge, Michael: Morningside Partners, LLC
Elfers, Stephen: USA Today
Elgazar, Hosny: AP–Broadcast
Elgin, John: Middle East Broadcasting Networks (MBN)
Elias, Jonathon: WJLA–TV / NewsChannel 8
Elizondo, Gabriel: Aljazeera English
Elker, Jonathan: Washingtonpost.com
Elkhatib, Bian: CQ / Roll Call
Elkomy, Dalia: AP–Broadcast
Ellard, Nancy: NBC NewsChannel
Ellenwood, Gary: C–SPAN
Elving, Ronald: National Public Radio
Elvington, Daniel Glenn: ABC News
Emanuel, Michael: Fox News
Emanuele, Francesca: Telesur
Emily, Gaffney: CNBC
Enda, Jodi: CNN
Engel, Mariam: Aljazeera English
Engel, Seth: C–SPAN
Ensign, Ernie: WJLA–TV / NewsChannel 8
Epatko, Larisa: The Newshour with Jim Lehrer
Epstein, Steven: CBS News
Erbe-Leckar, Bonnie: To the Contrary (Persephone Productions)
Erickson, Bo: CBS News
Ernst, Manuel: German TV ARD
Esfahani, Lara: German TV ZDF
Espinasa-Carvajal, Fernanda: NTN24
Esquivel, Patricia: C–SPAN
Essamuah, Zinhle: Now This News
Estrada, Rodolfo: AP–Broadcast
Estupinan, Andrea: WFDC–TV Univision
Ettrich, Daniela: Austrian Radio & TV (ORF)
Evans, Tyler: Fox News
Evans-Pittman, Olivia: CNN
Ewen, McKenna: Washingtonpost.com
Fabian, Geoffrey: Voice of America
Fabian, Kathleen: Aljazeera English
Fabic, Gregory: C–SPAN
Facal, Luis: Voice of America
Fadoul, Jennifer: The Newshour with Jim Lehrer
Fagen, Joel: Fox News
Fahey, Mark: Scripps News
Fairclough, Owen: CGTN America
Faison, Alfred: EWTN
Fancy, Stephen: ABC News
Fang, Wenwei: CGTN America
Fantacone, John: CBS News
Fantis, Manny: Sinclair Broadcast Group
Farhi, Arden: CBS News
Farkas, Daniel: Middle East Broadcasting Networks (MBN)
Farkas, Mark: C–SPAN
Farley, Tim: Sirius XM Satellite Radio

MEMBERS ENTITLED TO ADMISSION—Continued

Farmer, Christopher: Environment & Energy Publishing, LLC
Farrell, Kathryn: BBC
Farzaneh, Sam: BBC
Fastenberg, Dan: Reuters Radio & TV
Fattahi, Kambiz: BBC
Fatzick, Joshua: Voice of America
Faulders, Katherine: ABC News
Fauqueux-Veit, Hannelore: Austrian Radio & TV (ORF)
Fauria, Krysta: AP–Broadcast
Feeney, Joseph: C–SPAN
Feezer, Cory: EWTN
Feinstein, Jared: ABC News
Feist, Samuel: CNN
Fekadu, Salem: Voice of America
Feldman, Kiera: Voice of America
Feldman, Randy: Viewpoint Communications
Felix, Tsitsiki: WFDC–TV Univision
Fell, Jacqueline: Cox Broadcasting
Feltz, Maureen: WRC–TV / NBC–4
Fendrick, Anne-Marie: NHK
Fenghua, Wang: CGTN America
Fenston, Jacob: WAMU
Fente, Henok: Voice of America
Fenton, Amy: Fox News
Ferder, Bruce: Voice of America
Ferguson, Patrick: Canadian Broadcasting Corporation (CBC)
Feria, Liza: Reuters Radio & TV
Ferrise, Patrick: Sirius XM Satellite Radio
Fertig, Natalie: McClatchy
Fessler, Pamela: National Public Radio
Fetzer, Robert: Diversified Communications, Inc. (DCI)
Fiegel, Eric: CNN
Field, Andy: ABC News
Fifield, Paul: EWTN
Finch, Justin: WRC–TV / NBC–4
Finch, Mark: Fox News
Fingar, Craig: CNN
Finkel, Benjamin: Viewpoint Communications
Finnegan, Conor: ABC News
Finnerty, Deirdre: BBC
Finney, Richard: Radio Free Asia
Finney, Shannon: WTOP Radio
Fioraliso, Theodore: Gray Television
Fischer, Tanya: Eurovision Americas, Inc.
Fischoff, Michael: WTTG–Fox Television
Fishel, Justin: ABC News
Fisher, Harold: WHUR
Fisher, Kathryn: Feature Story News
Fisher, Siobhan: ABC News
Fisher, Thomas: Aljazeera English
Fitzgerald, Meagan: WRC–TV / NBC–4
Fitzgerald, Tom: WTTG–Fox Television
Flack, Eric: WUSA–TV
Flagg, Alexandra: CNN
Fleeson, Richard: C–SPAN
Fleischer, Jodie: WRC–TV / NBC–4
Fleischer Belmar, Heidi: German TV ZDF
Fleishman, Adam: Sinclair Broadcast Group
Fletcher, Lisa: WJLA–TV / NewsChannel 8
Flood, Randolph: Native American TV (NATV)
Florance, Benjamin: Fox News
Flores, Cesar: WFDC–TV Univision
Flores, Cesar: Fox News
Flowers, Alexandra: NBC News
Flynn, Robert: Feature Story News
Foellmer, Kristin: German TV ZDF
Fogarty, Kevin: Reuters Radio & TV
Foley, Dennis: WTOP Radio
Foley, Rita: AP–Broadcast
Forbes, Latoya: CNN
Forcier, Vincent: WETA
Ford, Patrick: CNN
Ford, Sam: WJLA–TV / NewsChannel 8
Forehand, Kristin: Fox News
Foreman, Thomas: CNN
Forgotson, Edward: CBS News
Forman, David: NBC News
Fornicola, Jason: Federal News Radio 1500 AM
Forsythe, Jonathan: McClatchy
Forte, Bernard: WRC–TV / NBC–4
Fortner, Amanda: C–SPAN
Fortney, Daniel: Voice of America
Forward, Kendall: One America
Forzato, Jamie: WTOP Radio
Foster, Carl: C–SPAN
Foster, Rebecca: Feature Story News
Foster, Scott: NBC News
Foster Mathewson, Lesli: WUSA–TV
Foty, Thomas: CBS News
Foukara, Abderrahim: Aljazeera Satellite Channel (Peninsula)
Fouladvand, Hida: Aljazeera English
Fox, Darren: Voice of America
Fox, Lauren: CNN
Fox, Margaret: NBC News
Fox, Matthew: ABC News
Fox, Michael: Aljazeera English
Fox, Peggy: WUSA–TV
Foxwell, Stacey: National Public Radio
Frado, John: CBS News
Frail, Marie: Reuters Radio & TV
Fraley, Jason: WTOP Radio
Frame, John: WTTG–Fox Television
France Wilson, Kim: CGTN America
Frandino, Nathan: Reuters Radio & TV
Franganillo Hernandez, Carlos: TVE–Spanish Public Television
Frank, Noah: WTOP Radio
Frank, William: CNN
Frankel, Bruce: TF1–French TV
Frankel, Melissa: NBC News
Frasier, Jordan: NBC News

MEMBERS ENTITLED TO ADMISSION—Continued

Frasier, Jordan: Washingtonpost.com
Frazier, Leslie: C–SPAN
Frazier, Robert: Feature Story News
Frazier, William: C–SPAN
Fredrickson, Drew: NBC News
Freeland, Charla: Sirius XM Satellite Radio
Freeman, Leah: CNN
Freitag-Schmitt, Christina: German TV ARD
French, Francis: ABC News
Friberg, Mattie: FedNet
Friedman, David: Fox News
Friedman, Mathew: AP–Broadcast
Friedman Winston, Natalie: National Public Radio
Fritz, Michael: The Newshour with Jim Lehrer
Froom, LeRoy: SRN News (Salem)
Fry, James: Voice of America
Fu, Peng: CGTN America
Fuhr, Michael: WUSA–TV
Fulton, Bradley: Australian Broadcasting Corporation
Furlong, Tim: WRC–TV / NBC–4
Furlow, Tony: CBS News
Furman, Hal: CBS News
Fuss, Brian: CBS News
Futrowsky, David: Voice of America
Gabriel, Oscar: AP–Broadcast
Gaetano, Lawrence: NBC News
Gaffney, Dennis: NBC News
Gaffney, John: NBC News
Gaffney, Morgan: NBC News
Gailhard, Stephanie: WUSA–TV
Gains, Mosheh: NBC News
Galdabini, Christian: Fox News
Galey, Travis: CBS News
Gallacher, Andy: Aljazeera English
Gallagher, Dianne: CNN
Gallagher, John: C–SPAN
Gallagher, Tim: Sky News
Gallagher, William: C–SPAN
Gallasch, Hillery: German TV ARD
Gallo, William: Voice of America
Galowin, Craig: C–SPAN
Gamboa, Suzanne: NBC News
Gangel, Jamie: CNN
Ganim, Sara: CNN
Ganslmeier, Martin: German Public Radio (ARD)
Gao, Qi: CGTN America
Gaouette, Katherine: CNN
Garay, Gavino: Reuters Radio & TV
Garber, Scott: CNN
Garbitt, Devin: CNN
Garcia, Danelle: CNN
Garcia, Jon: ABC News
Garcia, Juan: CBN News
Garcia, July: CBS News
Gardella, Richard: NBC News
Gardener, Rupert: WAMU
Gardinier, Elizabeth: The Newshour with Jim Lehrer
Gardinier, Kurt: CGTN America
Gardner, Evan: Fox News
Garg, Maya: Aljazeera English
Garifo, Stephen: WUSA–TV
Garland, Eric: McClatchy
Garlock, Tracy: C–SPAN
Garner, Dave: WTOP Radio
Garner, Melodie: CNN
Garner, Terry: Verizon
Garofalo, Elise: CNN
Garratt, Jonathan: Aljazeera English
Garraty, Timothy: CNN
Garrett, Christopher: CNN
Garrett, Major: CBS News
Garrett Scott, Amina: CNN
Garrison, Lynsea: BBC
Garrott, Jennifer: C–SPAN
Gary, Garney: C–SPAN
Garza, Jose: WFDC–TV Univision
Garzone, Christian: Gannett Government Media Corp
Gaskin, Keith: NBC News
Gasparello, Linda: White House Chronicle
Gassot, Philippe: ARTE TV
Gately, Gary: Talk Media News
Gato, Pablo: Univision
Gatza, Fabian: German TV ZDF
Gaughan, Timothy: CBS News
Gaur, Girish: One America
Gavin, Patrick: Talk Media News
Gayle, Anna-Lysa: WJLA–TV / NewsChannel 8
Gebremariam, Solomon: Voice of America
Geewax, Marilyn: National Public Radio
Gelevska, Irina: Macedonia Radio Television (MRTV)
Gelles, David: CNN
Gelman, Micah: Washingtonpost.com
Gembara, Deborah: Reuters Radio & TV
Gentilo, Richard: AP–Broadcast
Gentry, Robert: TV Asahi
Geoghegan, Thomas: BBC
George, Pavithra: Reuters Radio & TV
Georges, Marc: Scripps News
Gerberg, Jonathan: The Newshour with Jim Lehrer
Gerhiser, James: National Public Radio
Gesing, Lars: German TV ARD
Gestoso, Jorge: Telesur
Geyelin, Philip: CBS News
Ghandour, Michel: Middle East Broadcasting Networks (MBN)
Ghanem, Pierre: Al Arabiya TV
Ghattas, Kim: BBC
Ghildial, Pratiksha: BBC
Ghosh, Srabony: AP–Broadcast
Giaimo, Melissa: CNN
Giammetta, Max: WTTG–Fox Television
Giannakopoulos, Sarah: CNN
Gibson, Giles: Feature Story News

MEMBERS ENTITLED TO ADMISSION—Continued

Gibson, Jake: Fox News
Gibson, Jenna: CBS News
Gibson, Sheri Lynn: NBC NewsChannel
Gilbert, Jennifer: CBN News
Gilchrist, Aaron: WRC–TV / NBC–4
Gile, Charles: NBC News
Gillam, Katharyn: Agence France Presse (AFP–TV)
Gillece, Shannon: CNN
Gillis, Gary: Fox News
Gilmore, John: CGTN America
Ginebra, Nelson: NBC NewsChannel
Ginsberg, Franklyn: Aljazeera English
Ginsburg, Benson: CBS News
Giraldo, Edwin: Caracol Television
Girard, David: ABC News
Gittlen, Jason: WRC–TV / NBC–4
Gladden, Dwayne: The Real News Network
Glasberg, Rachel: CNN
Glass, Kathryn: Bloomberg Radio & TV
Glassman, Matt: WRC–TV / NBC–4
Glaude, Victoria: C–SPAN
Glennon, John: ABC News
Glover, Aronica: CBN News
Gnaizda, Matthew: New Tang Dynasty TV
Gobel, Brandon: Cox Broadcasting
Gobet, Pierre: Swiss Broadcasting
Goddard, Andre: CNN
Godfrey, Autria: WJLA–TV / NewsChannel 8
Godin, Jake: Scripps News
Godinho, Joanna: CGTN America
Godsick, Andrew L.: NBC NewsChannel
Gold, Avra: NBC News
Gold, Emily: NBC News
Gold, Lawrence: AP–Broadcast
Gold, Peter: Fuji TV Japan
Goldberg, Jeffery: WJLA–TV / NewsChannel 8
Goldgeier, Katherine: WAMU
Goldman, Julianna: CBS News
Goldrick, Michael: WRC–TV / NBC–4
Goldsmith, Brian: Yahoo News
Goldstein, David: Metro Teleproductions
Goll, Henning: Deutsche Welle TV
Gomez, Joseph: NBC News Radio
Gomez, Serafin: Fox News
Goncalves Perry, Delia: WUSA–TV
Goncalves-de-Oliveira, Alexandra: The Hill
Gong, Sasha: Voice of America
Gongadze, Myroslava: Voice of America
Gonsar, Dhondup: Radio Free Asia
Gonyea, Donald: National Public Radio
Gonzales-Paul, Andrea: CNN
Gonzalez, Cesar: NBC News
Gonzalez, Dennis: Fox News
Gonzalez, John: WJLA–TV / NewsChannel 8
Gonzalez, Jorge: WRC–TV / NBC–4
Gonzalez, Liliana: WFDC–TV Univision
Gonzalez, Mario: NTN24
Gonzalez, Mario: CBN News
Goodall, Sam: CBS News
Goodknight, Charles A: WRC–TV / NBC–4
Goodman, David: Bloomberg Radio & TV
Goodman, Jeffrey: NBC News
Goolsby, Wyatt: EWTN
Gorap, Pema: Voice of America
Gordemer, Barry: National Public Radio
Gordon, Herbert: WRC–TV / NBC–4
Gordon, Robert: ABC News
Gordon, Tamara: National Public Radio
Gorham, Glenn: ABC News
Gorman, James: AP–Broadcast
Gottlieb, Brian: CBS News
Gould, Robert: C–SPAN
Gracey, David: CNN
Gracia, Michael: AP–Broadcast
Gradison, Robin: NBC News
Graef, Aileen: CNN
Graham, Michael: Washington Examiner
Graham, Taya: The Real News Network
Granadino, Cameron: The Real News Network
Grand, Raphael: Swiss Broadcasting
Granda-Murillo, Marco: NTN24
Granville, Samantha: BBC
Grasso, Neil: CBS News
Graumann, Eva: German Public Radio (ARD)
Graves, Lindsay: NBC News
Gray, Justin: Cox Broadcasting
Gray, Noah: CNN
Graydon, James: CNN
Green, Clayton: CNN
Green, Jessie J.: WTOP Radio
Green, Miranda: CNN
Green, Molette: WRC–TV / NBC–4
Green, Myra: ABC News
Green, Richard: Voice of America
Green, Shannon: USA Today
Greenbaum, Adamson: Voice of America
Greenblatt, Larry: Viewpoint Communications
Greenblatt, Mark: Scripps News
Greenburg, Jan: CBS News
Greene, Gus: CNN
Greene, James: NBC News
Greene, Matty: Now This News
Greene, Trevor: Fox News
Greenfieldboyce, Nell: National Public Radio
Greiner, Nicholas: ABC News
Griffin, Andrew: CNN
Griffin, Jennifer: Fox News
Griffin, Kevin: NBC News
Griffitts, William: Mobile Video Services, Ltd.
Griggs, Kendall: WJLA–TV / NewsChannel 8
Grigsby, Lee: Eurovision Americas, Inc.
Grimaldi, Angelica: CNN
Gringlas, Samuel: National Public Radio
Grobe, Stefan: EuroNews

MEMBERS ENTITLED TO ADMISSION—Continued

Gross, Andrew: NBC News
Gross, David: CBS News
Gross, Eddie: CNN
Gross, Josh: CBS News
Grossman, Andrew: ABC News
Grudovich, Daniel: WTTG–Fox Television
Grumke, Kathryn: Scripps News
Grunberger, Alessia: CNN
Guastadisegni, Richard: WJLA–TV / NewsChannel 8
Guerouani, Fayrouz: AP–Broadcast
Guevara Medrano, Paul: WFDC–TV Univision
Guez, Bertrand: TF1–French TV
Guild, Blair: CBS News
Guise, Gregory: Aljazeera English
Guo, Chun: CGTN America
Guo, Yina: Xinhua
Gura, David: Bloomberg Radio & TV
Guray, Geoffrey Lou: The Newshour with Jim Lehrer
Gutmann, Hanna: Washington Radio and Press Service
Guzman, Armando: Azteca America
Guzman, Wilbert: Telemundo Network
Gypson, Katherine: Voice of America
Ha, Gwen: Radio Free Asia
Haake, Garrett: NBC News
Habe-Evans, Mito: National Public Radio
Habib, Elias: Al Arabiya TV
Habib, Muna: TRT World
Haddad, Karim: Aljazeera English
Haddad, Tamara: Feature Story News
Hadro, Matthew: EWTN
Haefeli, Brian: ABC News
Hagedorn, Elizabeth: Sinclair Broadcast Group
Hager, Mary: CBS News
Hager, Nathan: Bloomberg Radio & TV
Haggerty, Patrick: This Week in Agribusiness
Hahn, Jay: Eurovision Americas, Inc.
Haider, Zahra: Now This News
Haiqing, Zhu: CGTN America
Haji Kakol, Aso: AP–Broadcast
Halkett, Kimberly: Aljazeera English
Hall, Alegra: CBN News
Hall, Andrew: Sinclair Broadcast Group
Hall, Ashley: CBN News
Hall, Kurt: Reuters Radio & TV
Hall, Richard: C–SPAN
Hall, Sylvia: Fox Business Network
Haller, Thomas: EWTN
Hallman, James: WUSA–TV
Halpern, Jared: Fox News Radio
Halpern, Lacey: Fox News
Hamberg, Steven: Viewpoint Communications
Hamedy, Saba Avatar: CNN
Hamilton, Caleb: FedNet
Hamilton, James: Aljazeera English
Hamilton, Lawan: Scripps News
Hammar, Nickolai: National Public Radio
Hammond, Joe: WTTG–Fox Television
Hampton, Brian: CNN
Han, Jiyuan: CGTN America
Hannah, Daniel: ABC News
Hanson, Christopher: C–SPAN
Hanson, David: NBC News
Harada, Katie: Nippon TV Network
Harbage, Claire: National Public Radio
Hardesty, Nicole: WUSA–TV
Harding, Bill: CBS News
Harding, Tomas: Diversified Communications, Inc. (DCI)
Hardwick, Claire: One America
Harkness, Stephen: C–SPAN
Harlan, Jeremy: CNN
Harleston, Robert: C–SPAN
Harmon, Trevor: WRC–TV / NBC–4
Harper, Steven: CBS News
Harrington, Candice: NBC News
Harrington, Joshua: WJLA–TV / NewsChannel 8
Harris, Amelia: CNN
Harris, Hamil: CTV—Community TV of PG County
Harris, Heather: WETA
Harris, Kasey: C–SPAN
Harris, Richard: National Public Radio
Harris, Rodney: EWTN
Harris, Roy: Diversified Communications, Inc. (DCI)
Harrison, Byron: CTV–Community TV of PG County
Hartfield, Elizabeth: CNN
Hartman, Christopher: NBC News
Harton, Marcus: Voice of America
Hartsell, Collin: WUSA–TV
Hartwig, Ralf: German TV ZDF
Hartzenbusch, Jacqueline: BBC
Harwood, John: CNBC
Haselton, Brennan: WTOP Radio
Hash, James: WUSA–TV
Hassan, Sara: Aljazeera Satellite Channel (Peninsula)
Hassanein, Gamal: APTVS–American Press & TV Services
Hatch, Edmund: NBC News
Hawkins, Shonty: WJLA–TV / NewsChannel 8
Hayes, Monique: WRC–TV / NBC–4
Haynes, Maurice: C–SPAN
Haynes, Oscar: Voice of America
Hays, Guerin: Fox News
Haywood, Barry: German TV ZDF
Haywood, Barry: ABC News
He, Alan: CBS News
He, Wenjin: CGTN America
Headington, Brady: Hearst Television Inc.
Healey, Sean: CBS News
Hebden, David: The Real News Network
Hecht, Barry: Diversified Communications, Inc. (DCI)

MEMBERS ENTITLED TO ADMISSION—Continued

Heckels, Dominique: Independent Television News (ITN)
Hecker, Jenna: Sirius XM Satellite Radio
Heckman, Jory: Federal News Radio 1500 AM
Hedges, Thomas: The Real News Network
Heffley, William: C–SPAN
Heimen, Daniela: German TV ZDF
Heina, Martin: Fox News
Heinbaugh, Jack: WRC–TV / NBC–4
Heiner, Stephen: Middle East Broadcasting Networks (MBN)
Heller, Alana: NBC News
Hempen, Michael: AP–Broadcast
Henderson, Jarrad: USA Today
Henderson, Nia-Malika: CNN
Henderson, Susan: AP–Broadcast
Hendren, John: Aljazeera English
Hendry, Erica: The Newshour with Jim Lehrer
Henneberg, Mary Janne: Fox News
Henning, Daniel: Sirius XM Satellite Radio
Henry, Charles: CBS DC
Henry, Charles: Westwood One
Henry, Edward: Fox News
Henry, John: WUSA–TV
Henry, Jonelle: C–SPAN
Henry, Kelvin: CNN
Henry, Robert: Sirius XM Satellite Radio
Henry, Shirley: National Public Radio
Hentunen, Mika: Finnish Broadcasting Company (YLE)
Herb, Jeremy: CNN
Herbas, Francis: C–SPAN
Herbert, Andrew: BBC
Heresh, Jumana: CGTN America
Heritage, Robert: NBC News
Herkner, Michael: CNN
Herman, Cliff: i24 News
Hermelijn, Ryan: Dutch TV & Radio (NOS)
Hernandez, Angel: Univision
Hernandez, Carime: WFDC–TV Univision
Hernandez, Linda: Washington Examiner
Hernon, Louise: NBC News
Herrera, Francisco-Ruben: German TV ZDF
Herridge, Catherine: Fox News
Herring, Charles: One America
Herring, Dawn: One America
Hersh, Joshua: Vice News
Hess, Ione: CNN
Hickman, Stacy: Fox News
Higgins, Ricardo: WRC–TV / NBC–4
Hilk, Matthew: CNN
Hill, Angela: Scripps News
Hill, Anne: Sky News
Hill, Ashley: C–SPAN
Hill, Dallas: C–SPAN
Hill, Jonquilyn: WAMU
Hill, Martin: Fox News
Hillyard, Caitlin: C–SPAN
Hillyard, Vaughn: NBC News
Hindes, Walter: SRN News (Salem)
Hines, Andrea: ABC News
Hines, John: One America
Hinman, Katherine: CNN
Hinson, Elizabeth: CBS News
Hirouchi, Hitoshi: NHK
Hirten, Kevin: Aljazeera English
Hishchynsky, James: NBC News
Ho, King: Radio Free Asia
Hoang, Chan Nhu: Radio Free Asia
Hochmuth, Colby: WJLA–TV / NewsChannel 8
Hodge, Darnley: Imagination Media
Hodge, Darnley: NBC NewsChannel
Hodge, Doreen: Imagination Media
Hodge, Justin: CBS DC
Hoffman, Brian: AP–Broadcast
Hoffman, Charles: NBC News
Hoffman, Jason: CNN
Hogan, Susan: WRC–TV / NBC–4
Hoja, Gulchehra: Radio Free Asia
Holbert, William: CNN
Holland, Faith: CNN
Holland, John: NBC News
Hollenbeck, Paul: BT Video Productions
Holm, Gro: Norwegian Broadcasting
Holmes, Andrew: Environment & Energy Publishing, LLC
Holmes, Horace: WJLA–TV / NewsChannel 8
Holmes, Kristen: CNN
Holmes, Regina: Talk Media News
Hooper, Molly: The Hill
Hopkins, Adrienne Moira: Fox News
Hopkins, Brian: WJLA–TV / NewsChannel 8
Hopkins, Michael: CBS News
Hopper, David: BBC
Horacek, Eric: C–SPAN
Horan, Michael: WTTG–Fox Television
Horie, Tomoko: Nippon TV Network
Hormuth, Thomas: WJLA–TV / NewsChannel 8
Horn, Caroline: CBS News
Horn, Charles: Viewpoint Communications
Horrigan, Derek: CNN
Horsley, Scott: National Public Radio
Horton, Harry: Feature Story News
Horton, Robert: ABC News
Hosford, Matthew Alan: ABC News
Hoshi, Mariko: Nippon TV Network
Hossain, Selim: Voice of America
Hotta, Takashi: TV Asahi
Houston, Carlton: WUSA–TV
Hovell, Dean: ABC News
Howard, Charles: NBC News
Howard, Kevin: ABC News
Howell, Diyana: NBC News
Howell, Emily: CNN
Howell, Kellan: Sinclair Broadcast Group
Hoye, Matthew: CNN

MEMBERS ENTITLED TO ADMISSION—Continued

Hristova, Rozalia: BBC
Hssaini, Nasreddine: Aljazeera Satellite Channel (Peninsula)
Hsu, Andrea: National Public Radio
Hu, Yousong: Xinhua
Huang, Zhuo: Hong Kong Phoenix Satellite Television
Hubert, Jason: ABC News
Hubert-Hogg, Aja: CGTN America
Huchet, Josselin: TF1–French TV
Hudock, Richard: CNN
Huether, Andrew: National Public Radio
Huff, Daniel: AP–Broadcast
Huff, Priscilla: Feature Story News
Hughes, Gregory: ABC News
Hughes, Jacob: CBS DC
Hughes, James: NBC News
Hughes, Jillian: CBS News
Hughes, Katherine: C–SPAN
Hughes, Mallory: WUSA–TV
Hughes Hemmerlein, Megan: ABC News
Hughes, Ryan: WJLA–TV / NewsChannel 8
Hume, Alexander: Fox News
Humeau, Thierry: Aljazeera English
Hummelsheim, Scott: C–SPAN
Hunt, Kasie: NBC News
Hunter, Paul: Canadian Broadcasting Corporation (CBC)
Hunter, Tracy: C–SPAN
Hurst, Nathan: C–SPAN
Hurst, Whitney: Aljazeera English
Hurt, James: NBC NewsChannel
Hussain, Iftikhar: Voice of America
Hussein, Omar: AP–Broadcast
Hussin, Utami: Voice of America
Hutcherson, Trudy: Aljazeera English
Hutchinson, Heather: WRC–TV / NBC–4
Hyberg, Constance: McClatchy
Hydeck, Michael: WUSA–TV
Hyman, Mark: Sinclair Broadcast Group
Hymes, Clare: CBS News
Hynds, Margaret: CBS News
Hyun, Won Sup: MBC–TV Korea (Munhwa)
Iacone, Amanda: WTOP Radio
Iacone, Michael: NBC News
Iannelli, Nick: WTOP Radio
Ibarra, Adolfo: CNN
Ibrahim, Mohamed: German TV ZDF
Ibrahim, Zena: AP–Broadcast
Ide, Charles: WETA
Ikushima, Shinichiro: Tokyo Broadcasting System
Ing, Lance: WRC–TV / NBC–4
Ing, Nina: CGTN America
Ingle, Cynthia: C–SPAN
Inoue, Yukimasa: Nippon TV Network
Inskeep, Steven: National Public Radio
Inzaurralde, Bastien: Washingtonpost.com
Irons, Mark: EWTN
Irwin, Sarah: Reuters Radio & TV
Isdale, Danielle: Independent Television News (ITN)
Isella, Elena: EWTN
Isgro, Ernest: WJLA–TV / NewsChannel 8
Isham, Christopher: CBS News
Ishiyama, Kenkichi: NHK
Italiano, Michael: CGTN America
Ivey, Michael: Voice of America
Izant, Kayla: CNBC
Jaakson, Uelle-Mall: Austrian Radio & TV (ORF)
Jackson, Andreia: Nexstar Media Group
Jackson, Clif: Rural TV News
Jackson, Ezekiel: The Real News Network
Jackson, George: WJLA–TV / NewsChannel 8
Jackson, Hallie: NBC News
Jackson, Jerry: CBS News
Jackson, Jill: CBS News
Jackson, Katharine: Reuters Radio & TV
Jackson, Kaylah: CBS DC
Jackson, Roberta: C–SPAN
Jackson, Ryan: Fox News
Jackson, Samuel: WJLA–TV / NewsChannel 8
Jacobi, Isabelle: Swiss Broadcasting
Jacobi, Steven: CBN News
Jacobs, Adia: CNN
Jaffe, Alexandra: Vice News
Jaffe, Gary: Voice of America
Jamison, Dennis: CBS News
Jamshidi, Kaveh: Voice of America
Janis, Stephen: The Real News Network
Janney, Oliver: CNN
Janney, Renata: TV Asahi
Jansen, Eric: WUSA–TV
Jansen, Lesa: Fox News
Japaridze, Nunu: Fox News
Jarboe, Brian: National Public Radio
Jarrett, Laura: CNN
Jarrett, Ricky: National Public Radio
Jarrett, Tracy: Vice News
Jarvis, Julie: NBC NewsChannel
Jaskot, Sheila: Hearst Television Inc.
Javers, Eamon: CNBC
Jay, Paul: The Real News Network
Jeffcoat, Jan: WUSA–TV
Jefferson, Ricky: CBS News
Jeffrey, Terence: CNSNews.com
Jenkins, David: CNN
Jenkins, Gene: CBN News
Jenkins, Lee: Sinclair Broadcast Group
Jenkins, William: Fox News
Jennings, Alicia: NBC News
Jennings, Natalie: Washingtonpost.com
Jennings, Jr., Edward: ABC News
Jensen, Heidi: ABC News
Jentile, Catherine: TF1–French TV
Jermin, Ede: WRC–TV / NBC–4
Jessen, Peder: TV2–Denmark

MEMBERS ENTITLED TO ADMISSION—Continued

Jessup, John: CBN News
Jette, Patricia: Canadian Broadcasting Corporation (CBC)
Jewsevskyj, George: Fox News
Jia, Elizabeth: WUSA–TV
Jia, Li: CGTN America
Jiang, Weijia: CBS News
Jiang, Xin: CGTN America
Jimenez, Cecilia: ABC News
Jimenez, Christopher: NBC News
Jimenez, Claritza: Washingtonpost.com
Jimenez, Martin: Fox Business Network
Joannides, Jihan: Agence France Presse (AFP–TV)
Jobe, Clarence: CNN
Joehnk, Astrid: German Public Radio (ARD)
Johns, David: Cox Broadcasting
Johns, Joseph: CNN
Johnson, Aidan: BBC
Johnson, Carrie: National Public Radio
Johnson, Chester: WUSA–TV
Johnson, Jennifer: NBC NewsChannel
Johnson, Jesse: WAMU
Johnson, Joshua: WAMU
Johnson, Kevin: Cox Broadcasting
Johnson, Kia: Reuters Radio & TV
Johnson, Mansa: Imagination Media
Johnson, Martha: AP–Broadcast
Johnson, Rich: WTOP Radio
Johnson, Shanica: CBS News
Johnson, Thomas: Washingtonpost.com
Johnston, Jeffrey: CBS News
Johnston, Vanessa: Reuters Radio & TV
Jonas, Gerald: Agence France Presse (AFP–TV)
Jones, Alvin: FedNet
Jones, Anne: Talk Media News
Jones, Athena: CNN
Jones, Douglas: CNN
Jones, Gwyneth: NBC News
Jones, Joyce: BET Nightly News
Jones, Katerra: CTV–Community TV of PG County
Jones, Keith: WRC–TV / NBC–4
Jones, Kenneth: WETA
Jones, Lorna: CBS News
Jones, Lyrone: WRC–TV / NBC–4
Jones, Nelson: WTTG–Fox Television
Jones, Phelix: C–SPAN
Jones, Stephen: Fox News
Jones, Torrance: Fox News
Joost, Nathalie: Fox News
Joplin, Ashleigh: Washingtonpost.com
Jordan, Rosiland: Aljazeera English
Joseph, Akilah: Aljazeera English
Joslyn, James: WJLA–TV / NewsChannel 8
Joy, Richard: Ventana Productions
Joyner, Arcelious: Middle East Broadcasting Networks (MBN)
Jubar, Muriel: Aljazeera English
Judd, Donald: CNN
Juergens, Hans: CBS News
Jun, Jongchul: Korean Broadcasting Systems
Jussim, Roderick: AP–Broadcast
Kades, Cathy: NBC News
Kahwash, Sarah: National Public Radio
Kalman, Nicholas: Fox News
Kamal, Hufsa: Fox News
Kan, Emily: National Public Radio
Kane, Jason: The Newshour with Jim Lehrer
Kang, Yang Woo: MBC–TV Korea (Munhwa)
Kanicka, Stephen: Fox News
Kanneth, Polson: CNN
Kaplan, Rebecca: CBS News
Kapp, Bonney: CNN
Karamehmedovic, Almin: ABC News
Karl, Jonathan: ABC News
Karlsson, Bjorn: Swedish Broadcasting
Karlsson, Lisa: Swedish Broadcasting
Karson, Kendall: ABC News
Kashfi, Monna: CGTN America
Kashgary, Jilil: Radio Free Asia
Kastens, Katharine: ABC News
Kato, Atsushi: NHK
Katz, Craig: CBS News
Katz, Drew: CBS News
Kaupanger, Jonathan: CBS DC
Kavanagh, Peter: CNN
Kay Katharine: BBC
Kaye, Matthew: The Berns Bureau, Inc.
Keane, Patricia: CGTN America
Kearns, Cailin: Fox News
Keator, John: National Public Radio
Keedy, Matthew: CBN News
Keene, Jeffrey: WJLA–TV / NewsChannel 8
Kehoe, Steven: C–SPAN
Kehs, Robert: NBC News
Kelemen, Michele: National Public Radio
Kellerman, Mike: Xinhua
Kelley, Colleen: Fox News
Kelley, Jonathan: C–SPAN
Kelly, Cristina: EWTN
Kelly, Mary: National Public Radio
Kelly, Terence: NBC News
Kennedy, Andrew: Radio Free Asia
Kennedy, Benjamin: CBN News
Kennedy, Miranda: National Public Radio
Kenney, Caitlin: CBS DC
Kenney, Colleen: CGTN America
Kenney, Colleen: Fox News
Kent, Peter: NBC News
Kenyon, Linda: SRN News (Salem)
Keppler, Kristin: CNN
Kerchner, Eric: CBS News
Kerley, Paul: ABC News
Kernmayer, Ernst: Austrian Radio & TV (ORF)
Kerr, Roxane: C–SPAN
Kessler, Aaron: CNN

MEMBERS ENTITLED TO ADMISSION—Continued

Kessler, Jonathan: CBS News
Kettlewell, Christian: AP–Broadcast
Keyes, Allison: CBS News
Khairy, Khaled: AP–Broadcast
Khakiyev, Arslan: Radio Free Asia
Khalaf, Lina: Aljazeera Satellite Channel (Peninsula)
Khaleefah, Basheer: AP–Broadcast
Khamidov, Sandzhar: Voice of America
Khan, Javaria: Washingtonpost.com
Khan, Mariam: ABC News
Khananayev, Grigory: Fox News
Kharel, Nilu: Sagarmatha Television
Kharel, Ram C.: Sagarmatha Television
Khdr, Kawa: AP–Broadcast
Khristenko, Alexander: Russian State TV and Radio (RTR)
Kianpour, Suzanne: BBC
Kidd, Sally F.: Hearst Television Inc.
Kieffer, Vivian: Radio Free Asia
Kiernan, Ryan: NBC News
KIll, Adrian: CBS News
Killion, Nikole: Hearst Television Inc.
Killough, Ashley: CNN
Kilstein, Marc: WAMU
Kim, Ellis: The Newshour with Jim Lehrer
Kim, Hyunki: JTBC
Kim, Rosa: CBS News
Kim, William: Voice of America
Kim, Woo Sik: Seoul Broadcasting System (SBS)
Kim, Yeong Seon: Korean Broadcasting Systems
Kimani, Julia: CBS News
Kimura, Shinjiro: Nippon TV Network
King, Elizabeth: ABC News
King, Erica: ABC News
King, Jennifer: AP–Broadcast
King, John: CNN
King, Karl: CBN News
King, Kevin: Aljazeera English
King, Kevin: C–SPAN
King, Llewellyn: White House Chronicle
King, Nathan: CGTN America
King Lilleston, Kristi: WTOP Radio
Kinjaram, Prashanth: National Public Radio
Kirby, Kevin: Fox News
Kirby, Michael: FedNet
Kirkland, Pamela: The Newshour with Jim Lehrer
Kitchener, Jillian: Reuters Radio & TV
Kitt, Christine: Fox News
Klayman, Elliot: Eye-To-Eye Video
Kleim, Peter: N–TV German News Channel
Klein, Alexander: N–TV German News Channel
Klein, Kent: Sirius XM Satellite Radio
Klein, Mary: CNN
Klein, Richard: ABC News
Kleinman, Avery: WAMU
Klenk, Ann: NBC News
Klien, Robert: Metro Teleproductions
Klopp, Felicitas: German TV ARD
Klos, Daniel: CBS News
Knapp, Timothy: Mobile Video Services, Ltd.
Knier, Rebecca: WUSA–TV
Knier, Thomas: Ventana Productions
Knigge, Michael: Deutsche Welle TV
Knight, Danielle: WAMU
Knight, Graham: WDCW
Knighton, David: C–SPAN
Knoller, Mark: CBS News
Koblitz-Niemann, Anna: German TV ZDF
Kodjak, Alison: National Public Radio
Koenig, Paul: Aljazeera English
Koerber, Ashley: Fox News
Kolinovsky, Sarah: ABC News
Kono, Torao: NHK
Konsmo, Sarah: WUSA–TV
Konte, Hawa: WUSA–TV
Koolhof, Vanessa M.: WJLA–TV / NewsChannel 8
Kopan, Tal: CNN
Koprowicz, Tatiana: Voice of America
Koran, Laura: CNN
Korff, Jay: WJLA–TV / NewsChannel 8
Korte, Caraline: CBS News
Kos, Martin: BT Video Productions
Koscielniak, Jessica: McClatchy
Kosinski, Michelle: CNN
Koskin, Nikolay: Russian State TV and Radio (RTR)
Koslof, Evan: WUSA–TV
Kosnar, Michael: NBC News
Koster, Jesse: Voice of America
Kotke, Wolfgang: German TV ZDF
Kotuby, Stephanie: The Newshour with Jim Lehrer
Koura, Bagassi: Voice of America
Kramer, Kent: Radio One
Kreinbihl, Mary: Fox Business Network
Kretz, Lillian: Danish Broadcasting Corporation
Kretz, Steffen: Danish Broadcasting Corporation
Krieg, Gregory: CNN
Kroener, Justin: FedNet
Krohn, Tina-Jane: Storyhouse Productions
Kroker, Florian: Deutsche Welle TV
Kroker, Florian: German TV ARD
Kroll, Donald Eugene: ABC News
Krolowitz, Benjamin: CNN
Kruger, Chad: CTV Canadian TV
Krupin, David: EWTN
Krupnik, Kathryn: Fox News
Kube, Courtney: NBC News
Kulkarni, Shefali: BBC
Kunitz, Danielle: Washingtonpost.com
Kunz, Carmen: Deutsche Welle TV
Kuo, Frances: CGTN America
Kurtis, Jason: ABC News
Kurtz, Howard: Fox News
Kurtzleben, Danielle: National Public Radio
Kwan, Chi Hai: Shenzhen Media Group (SZMG)

MEMBERS ENTITLED TO ADMISSION—Continued

Kwong, Matthew: Canadian Broadcasting Corporation (CBC)
Kyaw, Nayrein: Radio Free Asia
LaBella, Michael: Aljazeera English
Labott, Elise: CNN
Laboy, Felix: C–SPAN
Lace-Evans, Olivia: BBC
Lacey, Donna: Fox News
Lai, Daniel: Hong Kong Phoenix Satellite Television
Lai, Yunhe: CGTN America
Lak, Daniel: Aljazeera English
Lamb, Brian: C–SPAN
Lamb, Deborah: C–SPAN
Lamb-Atkinson, Grace: CBS News
Lamberg-Karlovsky, Karl: Fox News
Lamonica, Ely: Voyage Productions
Lamonica, John: CBS News
Landau, Simon: WJLA–TV / NewsChannel 8
Landers, Elizabeth: CNN
Landy, Ekaterina: Aljazeera English
Landy, John: BBC
Lane, Christopher: WETA
Lane, Samuel: The Newshour with Jim Lehrer
Langkilde, Johannes: Danish Broadcasting Corporation
Langley, Kevin: National Public Radio
Lanningham, Kyle: Eurovision Americas, Inc.
Lanningham, Sarah: Eurovision Americas, Inc.
Lantigua Williams, Juleyka: National Public Radio
Lanzendoerfer, Nancy: N24 German TV
Larade, Darren: C–SPAN
LaRosa, Michael: NBC News
Larsen, Greg: CBS News
Larson, Benjamin: CBS News
Larson, Lauren: Federal News Radio 1500 AM
Lascaris, Alexander: The Real News Network
Laslo, Matt: Laslo Congressional Bureau
Latendresse, Richard: Groupe TVA
Latreille, Christian: Canadian Broadcasting Corporation (CBC)
Latremoliere, France: NBC News
Laudiero, Anna: EWTN
Laughlin, Ara: CTV–Community TV of PG County
Lautenbach, Barbara: German TV ARD
Laville, Molly: C–SPAN
Lawrence, Chris: WRC–TV / NBC–4
Lazar, Robert: C–SPAN
Lazarev, Anatoly: Channel One Russian TV
Lazernik, Ira: CGTN America
Le, Yen Phuong: VIETV Network
Le Dem, Gaspard: Real Clear Politics
Leahigh, Pamela: WRC–TV / NBC–4
Leake, Lindsey: Sinclair Broadcast Group
Leake, Myron: ABC News
Leaming, Whitney: Washingtonpost.com
LeCroy, Lillian: Fox News
LeCroy, Philip: Fox News
Leddon, Jerome: C–SPAN
Lee, Alexander: CNN
Lee, Donald: CBS News
Lee, Edward: WETA
Lee, Erik: WUSA–TV
Lee, Jae Won: Korean Broadcasting Systems
Lee, Jennifer: NBC News
Lee, Ji: CNN
Lee, Joseph: JTBC
Lee, Min: CNN
Lee, YiHua: Voice of America
Lefrak, Mikaela: WAMU
Legro, Tom: Washingtonpost.com
Leidelmeyer, Ronald: WRC–TV / NBC–4
Leidsmar, George: Small House Productions
Leimbach, Nicholas: WUSA–TV
Lenghi, Abdul-Mola: CBS News
Lent, David: GPI TV
Leon, Erika: WRC–TV / NBC–4
Leong, Dexter: CBS News
Leong, Hsiu: WJLA–TV / NewsChannel 8
Leroy, Jean-Pierre: Voice of America
Leshan, Bruce: WUSA–TV
Lesser, Howard: Washington Radio and Press Service
Lester, Michael: Now This News
Lester, Paul: WTTG–Fox Television
Lettenberger, Becky: National Public Radio
Levin, Hilary: WUSA–TV
Levine, Adam: CNN
LeVine, Indira: WTTG–Fox Television
Levine, Michael: ABC News
Levitt, Ross: CNN
Levkovich, Denis: Feature Story News
Levy, Adam: CNN
Lewis, Darrell: CBS News
Lewis, Edward: Fox News
Lewis, John B.: WJLA–TV / NewsChannel 8
Lewis, Kevin: WJLA–TV / NewsChannel 8
Lewis, Latavia: CNN
Lewis, Loretta: Talk Media News
Lewis, Misha: CNN
Lewis, Tisha: WTTG–Fox Television
Lewnes, Lisa: Reuters Radio & TV
Lewthwaite, Sarah: BBC
Li, Alice: Washingtonpost.com
Li, Anne: Washingtonpost.com
Li, Jiangning: Shenzhen Media Group (SZMG)
Li, Meng: CGTN America
Li, Qingqing: CGTN America
Li, Zhujun: CGTN America
Liasson, Mara: National Public Radio
Liberto, Jennifer: National Public Radio
Libin, Louis: Sinclair Broadcast Group
Lien, Arthur: NBC News
Lien, Jonathan: CBS News
Liesegang, Albert: Diversified Communications, Inc. (DCI)
Liffiton, Bruce: CBS News

MEMBERS ENTITLED TO ADMISSION—Continued

Lilling, Dave: Metro Teleproductions
Lim, Dongsoo: Korean Broadcasting Systems
Lim, Jaehak: Radio Free Asia
Lim, Lister: Aljazeera English
Lim, Sang: MBC–TV Korea (Munhwa)
Limon, Alexandra: Nexstar Media Group
Limon-Parresol, Alexandra: WTTG–Fox Television
Lin, Chuan: New Tang Dynasty TV
Lin, Hui: CGTN America
Lindeboom, Aaltje: German TV ZDF
Lindsey, Melvin: ABC News
Liptak, Kevin: CNN
Lisko, Lisa: Sinclair Broadcast Group
Little, Craig: WTTG–Fox Television
Littleton, Philip: CNN
Litzinger, Sam: CBS News
Liu, Libo: Voice of America
Liu, Shuai: Xinhua
Liu, Xiyang: CGTN America
Lloyd, Brian: C–SPAN
Lloyd, Whitney: ABC News
LoBianco, Thomas: CNN
Lockhart, Kathleen: NBC News
Lodoe, Kalden: Radio Free Asia
Loebach, Joseph: NBC News
Loeschke, Paul: C–SPAN
Logan, Charles: C–SPAN
Logan, Lara: CBS News
Lohr, Christopher: Washington Examiner
Loiaconi, Stephen: Sinclair Broadcast Group
Lokay, James: WTTG–Fox Television
Loker, Jessica: Fox News
Long, James: NBC News
Longhi, Valeria: EWTN
Longo, Adam: WUSA–TV
Lopez Reyes, Edwing: Telemundo Network
Lopez Ruiz, Juan Carlos: CNN
Lora, Edwin: CNN
Lorenz, Taylor: The Hill
Lorenzen, Elizabeth: Native American TV (NATV)
Lorenzen, Jacob: Danish Broadcasting Corporation
Lormand, John: SRN News (Salem)
Loukinykh, Lidiya: New Tang Dynasty TV
Low, Harry: BBC
Lowman, Wayne: Fox News
Lowther, Jason: Canadian Broadcasting Corporation (CBC)
Lozano Villo, Maria: Catalunya Radio
Lu, Tao: Hong Kong Phoenix Satellite Television
Lucas, David: WJLA–TV / NewsChannel 8
Lucas, Mary: Vice News
Lucas, Radicella: Aljazeera English
Lucchini, Maria: Univision
Lucero Lopez, Ivette: C–SPAN
Lujan, Brianna: CNN
Lukas, Jayne: Global TV Canada
Luke, Colette: Reuters Radio & TV
Luna, Nathan: ABC News
Lussenhop, Jessica: BBC
Lutterbeck, Deborah: Reuters Radio & TV
Luzader, Doug: Fox News
Luzi, Iacopo: FedNet
Luzquinos, Julio: NBC News
Lydick, Sarah: WUSA–TV
Lynch, Cordelia: Sky News
Lynn, Emily: Fox News
Lynn, Gary: NBC News
Lynn, Kellye: WJLA–TV / NewsChannel 8
Ma, Jing: CGTN America
Ma, Moqiu: TV Tokyo
Macaluso, Michelle: CBS News
Macaya, Melissa: CNN
Macchi, Victoria: Voice of America
MacFarlane, Scott: WRC–TV / NBC–4
MacGillivray, Graham: C–SPAN
Machles, Maren: Scripps News
Macholz, Wolfgang: German TV ZDF
Macias, Amanda: CBS DC
Macias, Mitzi: Voice of America
Maciulis, Anthony: Yahoo News
Mackereth, Samara: AOL Huffington Post
MacNeil, Lachlan Murdoch: ABC News
Madan, Richard: CTV Canadian TV
Madden, James Patrick: WAMU
Madigan, Tracey: Groupe TVA
Mager, Dickon: Sky News
Magnus, Anders: Norwegian Broadcasting
Mague, Anthony: WRC–TV / NBC–4
Mahdi, Ahmed: AP–Broadcast
Mahdi, Ali: Middle East Broadcasting Networks (MBN)
Maier, Timothy: Talk Media News
Maisler, Aaron: Fuji TV Japan
Majeed, Alicia: NBC News
Makori, Vincent: Voice of America
Malbon, Joy: CTV Canadian TV
Malik, Osman: Washingtonpost.com
Malika, Bilal: Aljazeera English
Mallin, Alexander: ABC News
Mallonee, Mary: CNN
Malloy, Allison: CNN
Malone, James: Voice of America
Maltas, Michael: Fox News
Malveaux, Suzanne: CNN
Mamonov, Roman: Voice of America
Mandelson, Adam: Eurovision Americas, Inc.
Manduley, Christina: CNN
Mangal, Dhanraj: ABC News
Mann, Jonathon: WJLA–TV / NewsChannel 8
Mansour, Fadi: Aljazeera Satellite Channel (Peninsula)
Manzarpour, Mohammad: Voice of America
Maqbool, Aleem: BBC
Marantz, Michael: WTTG–Fox Television
Marcello, Michele: NBC News

MEMBERS ENTITLED TO ADMISSION—Continued

March, Stephanie: Australian Broadcasting Corporation
Marchione, Mark: CNN
Marchitto, John: National Public Radio
Marcucci, John: WRC–TV / NBC–4
Marcum, James: WJLA–TV / NewsChannel 8
Marfil, Judy Grace: Wall Street Journal
Marion, Marvin: Voice of America
Marks, Benjamin: NHK
Marks, Simon: Feature Story News
Marques, Antonio: German TV ARD
Marquez, Maria: Aljazeera English
Marquis, Melissa: National Public Radio
Marraco, Marina: WTTG–Fox Television
Marrapodi, Eric: NBC News
Marriott, Marc: NBC News
Marsh, Michelle: WJLA–TV / NewsChannel 8
Marsh, Rene: CNN
Marshall, Colin: National Public Radio
Marshall, Madeline: Wall Street Journal
Marshall, Serena: ABC News
Marshall, Steven: CBS News
Marshall-Genzer, Nancy: Marketplace Radio
Martin, Ben: Independent Television News (ITN)
Martin, Bianca: WAMU
Martin, David: CBS News
Martin, Greg: NBC News
Martin, Jon: ABC News
Martin, Joseph: NBC News
Martin, Michel: National Public Radio
Martin, Patrick: Washingtonpost.com
Martin, Wisdom: WTTG–Fox Television
Martin Ewing, Samara: WUSA–TV
Martinez, Carlos: WRC–TV / NBC–4
Martinez, Luis: ABC News
Martinez, Mercedes: Aljazeera English
Martinez Fierro, Juan: COPE Radio (Spain)
Martino, Jeff: Canadian Broadcasting Corporation (CBC)
Martone, James: Sky News Arabia
Masecchia, Mark: WRC–TV / NBC–4
Mason, Julie: Sirius XM Satellite Radio
Mason, Suzanne: WJLA–TV / NewsChannel 8
Massey, Emily: CNN
Massini, Regis: France 2 Television
Mate, Aaron: The Real News Network
Matera, Kevin: National Public Radio
Mathew, Priya: Washingtonpost.com
Mathis, James: NBC NewsChannel
Matkosky, Timothy: Cox Broadcasting
Matsumoto, Gary: CGTN America
Matsuyama, Toshiyuki: Fuji TV Japan
Matthews, Andre: CTV–Community TV of PG County
Matthews, Christopher: NBC News
Matthews, Shawn: CBS News
Matthews, Valerie: C–SPAN
Mattingly, Philip: CNN
Matza, Max: BBC
Matzka, Jeffrey: SRN News (Salem)
Maucione, Scott: Federal News Radio 1500 AM
Mauro, Ellen: Canadian Broadcasting Corporation (CBC)
Mayfield, Rosalind: BBC
Mayk, Lauren: WRC–TV / NBC–4
Mazariegos, Luis: To the Contrary (Persephone Productions)
Mazariegos, Mark: CBS News
Mazrieva, Eva: Voice of America
Mazza, Mathieu: German TV ZDF
Mba, Achu: C–SPAN
McAleese, Kevin: Feature Story News
McArdle, John: C–SPAN
McCabe, Valerie: NBC News
McCagg, David: NHK
McCann, Michael: C–SPAN
McCann, Sean: C–SPAN
McCarren, Andrea: WUSA–TV
McCarty, D. Page: CBS News
McCarty, Donald: CBS News
McClam, Kevin: Fox News
McClellan, Max: CBS News
McClelland, Brianna: Fox News
McCleskey, Matthew: WAMU
McCloskey, George: Fox News
McClure, Tipp: German TV ZDF
McConnell, Brianne: WJLA–TV / NewsChannel 8
McConnell, Dave: WTOP Radio
McConnell, Dugald: CNN
McCoo, Cynthia: ABC News
MCray, Qwesi: WJLA–TV / NewsChannel 8
McCray, Ronnie: WTTG–Fox Television
McCrone, Brian: WRC–TV / NBC–4
McCulloch, Lauren: NBC News
McCullough, Colin: CNN
McDevitt, Lauren: Bloomberg Radio & TV
McDevitt, Lauren: Hearst Television Inc.
McDonald, Joel: WUSA–TV
McDonnell, Brigid Mary: Fox News
McDonough, Constance: Fox News
McDougall, Ian: NBC News
McEachern, Cherie: Fox News
McEachern, Terrance: Fox News
McEntee, Anna: Fox News
McGarrity, Gerard: C–SPAN
McGibbon, Adrienne: C–SPAN
McGinniss, Richard: The Daily Caller
McGonagle, Paul: WTTG–Fox Television
McGrath, Megan: WRC–TV / NBC–4
McGraw, Meridith: ABC News
McGreevy, Allen: BBC
McGuire, Gitte: Danish Broadcasting Corporation
McHenry, Robert: ABC News
McIntyre, Colin: Aljazeera English
McKee, Caroline: Sinclair Broadcast Group
McKee, Michael: Bloomberg Radio & TV

MEMBERS ENTITLED TO ADMISSION—Continued

McKellogg, Julie: McClatchy
McKelvey, Tara: BBC
McKelway, Douglas: Fox News
McKenna, Duncan: CBS News
McKenna, Ian: Now This News
McKernan, Elizabeth: Sinclair Broadcast Group
McKinless, Thomas: CQ / Roll Call
McKinley, Douglas: CNN
McKinley, Robert: CBS News
McKinney, Lee: NBC News
McLaughlin, Elizabeth: ABC News
McLean, Scott: CNN
McLellan, Daniel: CBS News
McLellan, Jennifer: Sirius XM Satellite Radio
McManus, Nicole: NBC NewsChannel
McMenamin, Angelique: ABC News
McMichael, Samuel: CNN
McMillin-Lobo, Sabrina: RealClearPolitics
McMinn, Nan Hee: AP–Broadcast
McMorris-Santoro, Evan: Vice News
McNair, Erik: ABC News
McNair, Romaine: WHUR
McNamara, Cassie: NBC News
McNary, Kirstin: Fox News Radio
McNeil, Tiffany: AOL Huffington Post
McPherson, Cecile: Eurovision Americas, Inc.
McShane, Connell: Fox Business Network
McWhinney, David: Aljazeera English
Mears, William: Fox News
Mebane, Martinez: ABC News
Meech, James: CNN
Meek, James: ABC News
Mees, John: CTV Canadian TV
Mees, John: Australian Broadcasting Corporation
Meghani, Sagar: AP–Broadcast
Mehdi, Hasan: Aljazeera English
Mehr, Benjamin: FedNet
Mei, Yan: CGTN America
Meier, Lauren: CNN
Meier, Markus: Austrian Radio & TV (ORF)
Mekonnen, Nehemiah: ABC News
Melhem, Richard: Al Arabiya TV
Meluza, Lourdes: Univision
Memoli, Michael: NBC News
Men, Kimseng: Voice of America
Meredith, Mark: Nexstar Media Group
Merica, Daniel: CNN
Meriwether, Brooks: WRC–TV / NBC–4
Metcalfe, Rhoda: Canadian Broadcasting Corporation (CBC)
Metjian, Julia: CNN
Metzger, Justin: C–SPAN
Metzger, Rochelle: CTV–Community TV of PG County
Metzler, Rebekah: CNN
Meyer, Kellie: Lilly Broadcasting
Meyer, Kerry: Diversified Communications, Inc. (DCI)
Meyer, Richard: Scripps News
Meza-Martinez, Cecily: National Public Radio
Mi, Tra: Voice of America
Mich, Daniel: Washingtonpost.com
Michael, Nicholas: National Public Radio
Michaud, Robert: Aljazeera English
Michell, Erenia: Fox News
Midura, Kyle: Gray Television
Mikols, Glenn: Eurovision Americas, Inc.
Mikutsky, David: NBC News
Milam, Greg: Sky News
Milford, Robert: N24 German TV
Millan Talavera, Alejandro: TVE–Spanish Public Television
Millar, Christopher: NBC News
Miller, Alexandra: Gray Television
Miller, Alexandra: Scripps News
Miller, Andrew: C–SPAN
Miller, Anna: CNN
Miller, Avery: ABC News
Miller, Charles: German TV ARD
Miller, Jason: Federal News Radio 1500 AM
Miller, Larry: WUSA–TV
Miller, Lawrence: European Pressphoto Agency
Miller, Mitchell: WTOP Radio
Miller, Paul: CNN
Miller, Tim: Middle East Broadcasting Networks (MBN)
Miller, William: CBS News
Millington, Takiha: NBC News
Mills, Christopher: Fox Business Network
Mills, Joseph: National Public Radio
Mills, Katherine: C–SPAN
Millward, Craig: CNSNews.com
Milstein, Jeff: CGTN America
Milton, Patricia: CBS News
Minas, Marina: Fox News
Minner, Richard: NBC News
Minott, Gloria: WPFW–FM
Miran, Alec: CNN
Miranda, Alexa: CNN
Miranda, Alfredo: Estrella TV
Mirsaeedi, Guita: Voice of America
Mishev, Riste: Macedonia Radio Television (MRTV)
Mitchell, Adrienne: Bloomberg Radio & TV
Mitchell, Andrea: NBC News
Mitchell, Justin: Reuters Radio & TV
Mitchell, Min: Radio Free Asia
Mitnick, Steven: NBC News
Mizell, Shannon: NBC News
Mizukami, Takashi: NHK
Mock, Sarah: Rural TV News
Modarressy-Tehrani, Caroline: Vice News
Mogor, John: WUSA–TV
Moise, Joseph: WJLA–TV / NewsChannel 8
Mok, Jet: Dutch TV & Radio (NOS)
Molina, Emiliana: WFDC–TV Univision

MEMBERS ENTITLED TO ADMISSION—Continued

Molina Salazar, Maria: Caracol Radio
Moller, Jeffrey: CNN
Monack, David: C–SPAN
Monange, Arielle: France 2 Television
Mondora, William: Nexstar Media Group
Monfort, Ismael: TV3–Televisio De Catalunya
Monnier, Axel: TF1–French TV
Monsalve, Lizeth Juliana: Telemundo Network
Montague, William: Norwegian Broadcasting
Montanaro, Domenico: National Public Radio
Montenegro, Lori: Telemundo Network
Montgomery, Alicia: WAMU
Montgomery, Tamara: Fox News
Montoro, Victor: C–SPAN
Mooar, Brian: NBC NewsChannel
Moore, Garrett: C–SPAN
Moore, Jacob: CBN News
Moore, Linwood: C–SPAN
Moore, Oddessey: Fox News
Moore, Richard: Voice of America
Moore, Robert: Independent Television News (ITN)
Moore, Terrence: NBC News Radio
Moore, W. Harrison: Middle East Broadcasting Networks (MBN)
Moorer, Willie: Voice of America
Moorhead, Jeremy: CNN
Morada, Raymond: NBC News
Morales, Isabel: CNN
Moran, Jane: BBC
Morano, Edward: CBN News
Moreno, Jaime: CMI TV (Colombia)
Moreno-Vargas, Julio: NTN24
Morgan, Donald: CBS News
Morgan, Kuren: C–SPAN
Morgan, Nancy: WETA
Morris, Amy: Bloomberg Radio & TV
Morris, Holly: WTTG–Fox Television
Morris, Jennifer Regan: BBC
Morris, Kylie: Independent Television News (ITN)
Morris, Michael: CNSNews.com
Morris, Peter: CNN
Morrisette, Roland: Bloomberg Radio & TV
Morrison, Donald: BBC
Morrison, Vaughn: AP–Broadcast
Morrissey, John: AP–Broadcast
Morrow, Sean: Now This News
Morse, Richard: Fox News
Mortman, Howard: C–SPAN
Morton, Daniel: C–SPAN
Mortreux, Vincent: TF1–French TV
Mosk, Matthew: ABC News
Mosley, Matthew: Fuji TV Japan
Moton, Kenneth: ABC News
Moutsatsos Morales, Basilio: Televisa News Network (ECO)
Movit, Lisa: The Hill
Mozaffari, Shaheen: NBC News
Mozgovaya, Natalia: Voice of America
Mrad, Danielle: Middle East Broadcasting Networks (MBN)
Mucha, Sarah: CNN
Muhammad, Alverda: National Scene News
Muhammad, Askia: National Scene News
Muhammad, Seleena: Fox News
Mui McClintock, Ylan: CNBC
Muir, David: ABC News
Mullen, Christopher: WUSA–TV
Mullon, Tiffany: Fox News
Munford, Corey: Radio Free Asia
Munoz, Luis: Middle East Broadcasting Networks (MBN)
Muntean, Peter: WUSA–TV
Murillo, Mike: WTOP Radio
Murphy, James: One America
Murphy, John: CBS News
Murphy, Rich: CGTN America
Murphy, Terence: C–SPAN
Murphy, Zoeann: Washingtonpost.com
Murray, Benjamin: Gannett Government Media Corp.
Murray, Mark: NBC News
Murray, Megan: Fox News
Murray, Sara: CNN
Murray, Timothy K.: Ventana Productions
Murtaugh, Peter: BBC
Muskat, Steven: NBC NewsChannel
Myers, Dwayne: WJLA–TV / NewsChannel 8
Mylroie, Laurie: AP–Broadcast
Nado, Jill: Fox News Radio
Naeem, Tabinda: Voice of America
Nagle, Molly: ABC News
Nagy, Ashraf: Aljazeera Satellite Channel (Peninsula)
Naidoo, Anand: CGTN America
Naing, Thet: Voice of America
Najarian, Sarkis: Radio Free Asia
Najjar, Ruqaiyah: CGTN America
Nakai, Yoshihiko: NHK
Namdar, Asieh: CGTN America
Nania, Rachel: WTOP Radio
Nannes, Steven: CNN
Narahari, Priya: Eurovision Americas, Inc.
Narayan, Vivek: Scripps News
Narisi, Stephen: N24 German TV
Nasir, Labib: Reuters Radio & TV
Nasir, Noreen: AP–Broadcast
Nason, Andrew: C–SPAN
Nasr, Hiba: Sky News Arabia
Nasser, Mohamed: AP–Broadcast
Natour, Rhana: The Newshour with Jim Lehrer
Naylor, Brian: National Public Radio
Naylor, Robert: Voice of America
Ndiho, Paul: Voice of America
Neal, Jason: NBC News
Neal, Michelle: NBC News
Neary, Sean: Voice of America

MEMBERS ENTITLED TO ADMISSION—Continued

Neel, Joe: National Public Radio
Neely, Brett: National Public Radio
Neff, Blake: Fox News
Negron, Julio: Washingtonpost.com
Neill, Tara: BBC
Nelson, Christopher: National Public Radio
Nelson, James: Fox News
Nelson, Joseph: Washington Bureau News Service
Nerska, Alexander: NBC News
Neto, Joaquim: WJLA–TV / NewsChannel 8
Nettles, Meredith: ABC News
Nevel, Paul: WETA
Nevins, Elizabeth: NBC News
Newton, Jason: Nexstar Media Group
Newton, Laura: Caracol Televisiòn
Newton, Robin: C–SPAN
Nezu, Hirohito: NHK
Nguyen, Anh: Fox News
Nguyen, Anh: Radio Free Asia
Nguyen, Thao: Voice of America
Nguyen, Trung: Voice of America
Nguyen, Vi: VIETV Network
Nha, Kevin: Korean Broadcasting Systems
Ni, Chia-Hui: TVBS
Nicci, Nicholette: CNN
Nichols, Hans: NBC News
Nicolaidis, Virginia: Fox News
Niemann, Stefan: German TV ARD
Nikuradze, David: Rustavi 2 Broadcasting Company
Niliahmadabadi, Hadi: BBC
Nilsson, Mari: Norwegian Broadcasting
Ninh, Trang: C–SPAN
Nishikawa, Atsutoshi: NHK
Nishimoto, Momoca: NHK
Niu, Qiyang: Shenzhen Media Group (SZMG)
Nixon, Adam: Middle East Broadcasting Networks (MBN)
Nixon, William: WDCW
Niyazi, Kuerban: Radio Free Asia
Nneji, Nkechi: NBC News
Nobles, Ryan: CNN
Nolan, Bridget: CNN
Nolen, John: CBS News
Noor, Dharna: The Real News Network
Noor, Jaisal: The Real News Network
Norins, Jamie: Diversified Communications, Inc. (DCI)
Norling, Richard: ABC News
Norman, Janai: ABC News
Norman, Jeffrey: CNN
Norris, Donna: C–SPAN
Norris, Elise: Fox News
Norris, James: Middle East Broadcasting Networks (MBN)
Northam, Jackie: National Public Radio
Norwood-Dioulo, Jasmine: WDCW
Novikova, Olga: Voice of America
Nunez, Jorge: One America
Nunez, Shoshannah: CBN News
Nur, Ibrahim: Aljazeera English
O'Berry, Donald: Fox News
O'Brien, Benen: C–SPAN
O'Brien, David: NBC News
O'Brien, Marjorie: ABC News
O'Brien-Hosein, Alexi-Noelle: TRT World
O'Connell, Benjamin: C–SPAN
O'Connell, Michael: Federal News Radio 1500 AM
O'Connell, Mike: NBC NewsChannel
O'Connell, Rosalie: Voice of America
O'Connor, Erin: Washingtonpost.com
O'Connor, John: WNYC
O'Day, Andrew: Bloomberg Radio & TV
O'Donnell, Kelly: NBC News
O'Donnell, Norah: CBS News
O'Donnell, Patrick: Eye-To-Eye Video
O'Donoghue, Gary: BBC
O'Gara, Patrick: ABC News
O'Grady, Andrea: Fox News
O'Hara, Jessica: Fox News
O'Leary, William: National Public Radio
O'Molloy, Colm: RTE–Irish Radio & TV
O'Neill, Claire: National Public Radio
O'Regan, Deirdre: Washingtonpost.com
O'Shea, Daniel: ABC News
O'Sullivan, Michael: ABC News
Oat, Michael: CNN
Obasi, Ndidi: C–SPAN
Oberti, Ralf: NHK
Oblaender, Carsten: Storyhouse Productions
Ochsenschlager, Emily: National Public Radio
Oday, Elizabeth: Fox News
Odendahl, Eric: CNN
Odom, Quillie: Fox News
Offermann, Claudia: German TV ZDF
Ogata, Makoto: Tokyo Broadcasting System
Ogrysko, Nicole: Federal News Radio 1500 AM
Oinounou, Mosheh: CBS News
Okada, Takamori: TV Asahi
Oke, Femi: Aljazeera English
Olabanji, Olajumoke: WJLA–TV / NewsChannel 8
Olazagasti, Carlos: Hearst Television Inc.
Olesker, Michael: Talk Media News
Olick, Diana: CNBC
Oliger, Brian: WTOP Radio
Olkhovskaia, Iuliia: Channel One Russian TV
Olmos, Dolores: WUSA–TV
Olmstead, Charles: ABC News
Olmstead, Craig: Aljazeera English
Olmsted, Alan: C–SPAN
Olson, Christopher: Vice News
Oni, Jesusemen: Voice of America
Oo, Thar: Voice of America
Oo, Thein: Voice of America
Opoku, Stacy: CBN News
Orchard, Mark: Sinclair Broadcast Group

MEMBERS ENTITLED TO ADMISSION—Continued

Orellana, Ernesto: Azteca America
Orenstein, Jayne: Washingtonpost.com
Orgel, Paul: C–SPAN
Ortiz, Idaliz: WFDC–TV Univision
Os, Lars: Norwegian Broadcasting
Osagie-Erese, Precious: Hearst Television Inc.
Osman, James: Nexstar Media Group
Ouafi, Mohamed Said: AP–Broadcast
Overby, Peter: National Public Radio
Overzat, Gregory: CNN
Owen, Andrea: ABC News
Owen, Quinton: ABC News
Ozol, Bernard: CBS News
Ozsancak, Hakan: CGTN America
Ozturk, Yasin: Anadolu Agency
Ozug, Matthew: National Public Radio
Pacheco, Antonio: WETA
Pacuraru, Denis: CBN News
Padavick, Robert: USA Today
Padilla-Cirino, Mercy: Hispanic Communications Network
Pagan, Louis: AP–Broadcast
Page, David: CBN News
Page, Paige: Fox News
Page, Steven: CNN
Pajooh, Fariba: FedNet
Palca, Joseph: National Public Radio
Palmer, Hope: NBC News
Palombo, Russell: WPLG–TV10
Pande, Arunima: Voice of America
Panzer, Chester: WRC–TV / NBC–4
Papinashvili, Aleksandre: Rustavi 2 Broadcasting Company
Pappas, Alex: Fox News
Paquette, Cherie: Fox News
Parangot, Ann: CNN
Parent, Charyssa: Fox News
Parenti, Alisa: Bloomberg Radio & TV
Park, Calvin: National Public Radio
Park, Edward: Seoul Broadcasting System (SBS)
Park, Jihee: Eurovision Americas, Inc.
Park, Jung-Woo: Radio Free Asia
Park, Seung Jin: MBC–TV Korea (Munhwa)
Park, Yoo Han: Korean Broadcasting Systems
Parker, Andre: CNN
Parker, Glenn: Canadian Broadcasting Corporation (CBC)
Parker, Marley: CTV Canadian TV
Parker, Robert: CNN
Parkinson, John: ABC News
Parks, Chanlee: CGTN America
Parks, John: BBC
Parks, MaryAlice: ABC News
Parks, Melanie: CNN
Parnass, Sarah: Washingtonpost.com
Parsell, Robert: Voice of America
Pasha, Firoze: National Public Radio
Pathammavong, Kingsavanh: Voice of America
Patience, Keenan: Verizon
Patruznick, Michael: C–SPAN
Patsko, Daniel: ABC News
Patterson, Jay: CBS News
Patterson, Stephen: CNN
Paul, Abowd: Aljazeera English
Paxton, Bradford: Fox News
Payam, Amir: BBC
Paylor, Eddie: NBC News
Paylor, Eddie: CNN
Payson-Denney, Wade: CNN
Paz-Goldenheart, Benny: Hispance Communications Network
Peaches, Sandra: CTV–Community TV of PG County
Peacock, Grant: EUroNews
Peacock, Grant: GPI TV
Peaks, Gershon: Reuters Radio & TV
Pearson, Hampton: CNBC
Peebles, Daniel: CBS News
Pegues, Jeffrey: CBS News
Peligri, Justin: NBC News
Peltier, Anthony: CBN News
Pelzer, Sharnett: Fox News
Pence, Courtney: Time Warner Cable
Pennell, Elizabeth: Morningside Partners, LLC
Pennington, Craig: Aljazeera English
Pentelovitch, Taylor: C–SPAN
Pepino, Jason: Aljazeera English
Percha, Julie: The Newshour with Jim Lehrer
Perez, Evan: CNN
Perez, Simone: Vice News
Pergram, Chad: Fox News
Peries, Sharmini: The Real News Network
Perkins, Anthony: WTTG–Fox Television
Perkins, Douglas: CBN News
Perkins, Douglas: Fox News
Perkins, Vernon: C–SPAN
Perl, Drora: Galei-Tzahal (Israel Army Radio)
Perlmutter-Gumbiner, Elyse: NBC News
Perlow, Rebecca: ABC News
Perrell, Thomas: WJLA–TV / NewsChannel 8
Perry, Caitriona: RTE–Irish Radio & TV
Perry, Christina: C–SPAN
Perry, Clayton: CNN
Perry, Jessica: Nexstar Media Group
Perry, Timothy: CBS News
Persinko, Timothy: Viewpoint Communications
Persons, Sally: Fox News
Pessin, Don: Reuters Radio & TV
Peterson, Brittany: McClatchy
Peterson, Robert: CBS News
Petitte, Patti: WRC–TV / NBC–4
Petraitis, Gerald: AP–Broadcast
Petrilli, Daniel: Fox News
Petrimoulx, Drew: Nexstar Media Group
Petroka, Katelyn: CNN
Pettingell, Dolia: Proyecto Puente

MEMBERS ENTITLED TO ADMISSION—Continued

Pettit, Debra: NBC News
Pexton, Ken: Ventana Productions
Peyton, Michael: CBS News
Pham, Jacqueline: Fox News
Phelps, Jordyn: ABC News
Philipps, Gregory: Radio France
Phillip, Abigail: CNN
Phrommayon, Annie: BBC
Phuong, Ngyuen: CNSNews.com
Piacente (fka Portnoy), Ellen: Morningside Partners, LLC
Picket, Kerry: Sirius XM Satellite Radio
Pickup, Michael: ABC News
Pimienta, Alberto: Time Warner Cable
Pinault, Nicolas: Voice of America
Pinczuk, Murray: Feature Story News
Ping, Sun: CGTN America
Pinto, Susanna: EWTN
Pinzon, Wingel: Small House Productions
Piper, Allan: Now This News
Piper, Jeff: WRC–TV / NBC–4
Pipkin, Chase: Hearst Television Inc.
Pisczek, Scott: CNN
Pisnia-Bystriakova, Nataliia: BBC
Pitney, Nico: Now This News
Pitocco, Nickolas: C–SPAN
Pitti, Edwin: WFDC–TV Univision
Pizarro, Fernando: Univision
Plater, Christopher: WRC–TV / NBC–4
Player, Dani: Washingtonpost.com
Pliszak, Kevin: ABC News
Pluto, Liza: CNN
Poarch, David: CNN
Poch, Reasey: Voice of America
Poentinen, Pirkko: Finnish Broadcasting Company (YLE)
Polantz, Katelyn: CNN
Poley, Michelle: CNN
Policastro, Jacqueline: Gray Television
Pollock, Ryan: CNN
Polmer, Brendan: Bloomberg Radio & TV
Ponnudurai, Parameswaran: Radio Free Asia
Pontzen, Daniel: German TV ZDF
Poole, John: National Public Radio
Pope, Michael: Virginia Public Radio
Porsella, Claude L.: Radio France Internationale
Porter, Almon: C–SPAN
Portnoy, Steve: CBS News
Postovit, David: Hearst Television Inc.
Potts, Nina-Maria: Feature Story News
Potts, Tracie: NBC NewsChannel
Pouladi Najafabadi, Farhad: Voice of America
Pourshariati, Shapoor: ABC News
Pov Sok, Khemara: Voice of America
Powell, Brian William: Radio Free Asia
Powell, Kashon: Radio One
Powell, Lee: Washingtonpost.com
Pratapas, Lauren: CNN
Pratz, Megan: CGTN America
Preloh, Anne: C–SPAN
Preston, Christopher: Vice News
Preston, Mark: CNN
Presutti, Carolyn: Voice of America
Pries, David: C–SPAN
Prifti, Ilir: Aljazeera English
Prokupecz, Shimon: CNN
Pronko, Anthony: C–SPAN
Proskow, Jackson: Global TV Canada
Proud, Kelsey: WAMU
Pruitt, Claude: Scripps News
Pugliese, Pat: CNBC
Puljic, Ivica: Aljazeera English
Pumo, John: CBS News
Purbaugh, Michael: ABC News
Purser, Emily: Sky News
Puryear, Meghan: CNN
Pyatt, Kyle: Scripps News
Qin, Qi: CGTN America
Quadrani, Federico: CNN
Quan, Xiangqin: CGTN America
Quander, Michael: WUSA–TV
Quarry, Ralph: CBS News
Querolo, Jon: NHK
Quijano, Jackeline: WFDC–TV Univision
Quinn, Diana: CBS News
Quinn, Jason: NBC News
Quinn, John: Voice of America
Quinn, Mary: ABC News
Quinnette, John: NBC News
Quinonez, Omar: NBC News
Quiooga, Juan: GPI TV
Rabiee, Mana: Reuters Radio & TV
Rabin, Mark: CBS News
Rad, Ali: Fox News
Radke, Jason: ABC News
Raffa, Alessandra: Fox News
Raffaele, Robert: Voice of America
Rafferty, Meghan: CNN
Rager, Bryan: CNBC
Rahn, Richard: CBS News
Raider, Ira: ABC News
Raju, Manu: CNN
Rama, Padmananda: AP–Broadcast
Ramani, Nithya: CGTN America
Ramirez, Edwin: Small House Productions
Ramirez, Roselena: CGTN America
Ramirez, Stephanie: WUSA–TV
Ramon, Fausto: Reuters Radio & TV
Ramon, Henry: Radio Free Asia
Ramos, Raul: WFDC–TV Univision
Randev, Sonia: CTV–Community TV of PG County
Randle, James: Voice of America
Rangel, Corey: Scripps News
Rankin, James: CNN
Rashid, Kutaba: Aljazeera English

MEMBERS ENTITLED TO ADMISSION—Continued

Rashidi, Rahim: AP–Broadcast
Rathner, Jeffrey: WETA
Ratliff, Walter: AP–Broadcast
Ratner, Ellen: Talk Media News
Rattansi, Shihab: Aljazeera English
Ratzow, Sandra: German TV ARD
Raval, Nikhil: C–SPAN
Raviv, Daniel: i24 News
Ray, Alonzo: NBC News
Ray, Douglas: Fox News
Rayas, Cristina: McClatchy
Raymond, Juan: Aljazeera English
Reber, James: BBC
Reddy, Pallavi: CNN
Redpath, Julia: National Public Radio
Reeve, Richard: WJLA–TV / NewsChannel 8
Reeves, Alea: Aljazeera English
Reeves, Austin: WTTG–Fox Television
Reffes, Melanie: NHK
Rego, Alexandra: Fox News
Rehkopf, George: CBS News
Reid, Charles: CBS News
Reid, John: CBN News
Reid, Paula: CBS News
Reilly, Robert: C–SPAN
Reinsel, Edward: Fox News
Remillard, Michele: C–SPAN
Ren, Meixing: AP–Broadcast
Renbaum, Bryan: Talk Media News
Renfro, Owen: Fox News
Renken, David: Fox News
Rensberger, Scott: Cox Broadcasting
Reston, Maeve: CNN
Reuter, Cynthia: C–SPAN
Revaz, Philippe: Swiss Broadcasting
Reverter Baquer, Fracesc: Catalunya Radio
Reyes, Elaine: CGTN America
Reyes, Joel: Reuters Radio & TV
Reyes, Samantha: CNN
Reyes, Victor: Telemundo Network
Reynolds, Catherine: CBS News
Reynolds, Gioconda: Voice of America
Reynolds, Robert: Aljazeera English
Reynolds, Talesha: NBC News
Rhoades, Alex: i24 News
Rhodes, Elizabeth: Fox News
Ribas, Jorge: Washingtonpost.com
Ricalde, Katheryn: Fox News
Rice, John: WJLA–TV / NewsChannel 8
Rice, Kelly: CGTN America
Rice, Shannon: C–SPAN
Rice, Jr., Rodney: Verizon
Richard, Sylvain: Canadian Broadcasting Corporation (CBC)
Richards, Kristin: TIMA
Richardson, Young: One America
Rickard, Michael: WTTG–Fox Television
Riddle, Casey: CNN
Rieger, John: AOL Huffington Post
Riess, Steffanie: German TV ZDF
Riggs, Beth: WTTG–Fox Television
Riggs, James: NBC News
Rigney, Paul: NBC News
Riha, Anne Marie: Fox News
Riley, Justin: Voice of America
Rios, Delia: C–SPAN
Rios, Paulina: CNN
Rios, Victor: Fox News
Rios-Hernandez, Raul: CNN
Ritchie, Thomas: AP–Broadcast
Ritter, Dana: CBN News
Rivara, Kayla: The Real News Network
Rivas, Ivan: Agence France Presse (AFP–TV)
Rivas-Vazquez, A. Victoria: Telemundo Network
Rivera, Matthew: NBC News
Rivera, Michelle: WRC–TV / NBC–4
Rizvi, Ali: McClatchy
Rizzi, Jared: Sirius XM Satellite Radio
Rizzo, Jennifer: CNN
Rizzo, John: AP–Broadcast
Roane Skehan, Andrea: WUSA–TV
Robbins, Christina: Fox News
Robbins, Diana: German Public Radio (ARD)
Robbins, Francisco: CBS News
Robbins, Michael: Fox News
Robert, Olivier: Eye-To-Eye Video
Roberton, Jamie: Independent Television News (ITN)
Roberts, Bryan: WTTG–Fox Television
Roberts, Corinne: ABC News
Roberts, Jean Pierre: Eurovision Americas, Inc.
Roberts, John: C–SPAN
Roberts, Kristina: CNN
Roberts, Leon: Nippon TV Network
Robertson, Abigail: CBN News
Robertson, Gregory: CNN
Robertson, John: Fox News
Robinson, David: CNN
Robinson, Emerald: One America
Robinson, John: CNN
Robinson, Kelvin: WRC–TV / NBC–4
Robinson, Khalea: CBS News
Robinson, Laura: CNN
Robinson, Ralph: Voice of America
Roca, Xavier: Swiss Broadcasting
Rocha, Juan: Ventana Productions
Rocha-Garzin, Samuel: RCN Television
Rockell, Kira: Aljazeera English
Rocque, Tiffany: C–SPAN
Rodeffer, Mark: C–SPAN
Rodgers, Henry: Fox News
Rodriguez, Eduardo: AP–Broadcast
Rodriguez, Janet: CGTN America
Rodriguez, Marcela: WFDC–TV Univision
Rodriguez, Martine: C–SPAN
Rodriguez, Valdemar: NTN24

MEMBERS ENTITLED TO ADMISSION—Continued

Roeller, Ulf-Jensen: German TV ZDF
Rogers, Rhonda: NBC News
Rogin, Ali: ABC News
Rohemae, Maria-Ann: Estonian Public Broadcasting
Rohrbaugh, Randolph: C–SPAN
Rohrbeck, Douglas: Fox News
Rojas, Jaime: AP–Broadcast
Rokus, Brian: CNN
Romano, Christina: WRC–TV / NBC–4
Romo, Christine: ABC News
Roof, Peter: NBC NewsChannel
Root, Sean: The Hill
Root, Thomas: Fox News Radio
Rosales, Erik: CBN News
Rosario, Eduardo: Eurovision Americas, Inc.
Rosche, Jedd: CNN
Rose, Alicia: NHK
Rose, Art: WTOP Radio
Rose, Bashi: The Real News Network
Rosen, Ira: CBS News
Rosen, James: Fox News
Rosen, Shari: CNBC
Rosenberg, Gary: ABC News
Rosenberg, Howard: CBS News
Rosenfield, Jim: WRC–TV / NBC–4
Ross Taylor, Allyson: CBS News
Rossetti-Meyer, Misaele: Diversified Communications, Inc. (DCI)
Roth, Samantha-Jo: Gray Television
Roth, Samantha-Jo: Time Warner Cable
Roth, Theodore: ABC News
Roussey, Thomas: WJLA–TV / NewsChannel 8
Rowe, Tom: Reuters Radio & TV
Rowland, Kara: Fox News
Roy, D'Annette: CTV–Community TV of PG County
Royce-Bartlett, Lindy: CNN
Royster, Meredith: WRC–TV / NBC–4
Ruck, Ina-Maria: German TV ARD
Rudd, Michael: WJLA–TV / NewsChannel 8
Rudman, Kristin: Fox Business Network
Ruff, Jennifer: C–SPAN
Ruffini, Christina: CBS News
Ruffini, Joseph: CBS News
Ruggiero, Diane: CNN
Rulli, Margaret: ABC News
Rushing, Ian: CBN News
Rushing, Joshua: Aljazeera English
Ruskin, Elizabeth: Alaska Public Radio Network / Alaska Public Media
Russell, Eugene: WTTG–Fox Television
Russell, Lauren: National Public Radio
Ruttenberg, Roee: CGTN America
Rwema, Edward: Voice of America
Ryan, Bruce: WRC–TV / NBC–4
Ryan, Kate: WTOP Radio
Rydell, Mary Kate: CBS News
Ryntjes, Daniel: Feature Story News
Rysak, F. David: WTTG–Fox Television
Saakov, Rafael: Voice of America
Sacks, Michael: Scripps News
Sadighi, Nader: Radio Free Europe
Sadighi, Shahla: Voice of America
Saenz, Katherine: ABC News
Sagalyn, Daniel: The Newshour with Jim Lehrer
Saine-Spang, Cynthia: Voice of America
Saintsing, Matthew: CBS DC
Sakwa, Jenna: CBS News
Salim, Yuni: Voice of America
Salinas, Mary: Voice of America
Salman, Sara: CGTN America
Saloomey, Kristen: Aljazeera English
Sammon, William: Fox News
Sampaio, Frederico: C–SPAN
Sampson, Thomas: AP–Broadcast
Sampy, David: Independent Television News (ITN)
Samuel, Charles: Verizon
Samuel, Stacey: National Public Radio
Samuels, Elyse: Washingtonpost.com
Sanchez, Boris: CNN
Sanchez, George: ABC News
Sanchez, Pablo: Univision
Sanchez, Robert: CBS DC
Sanchez Cruz, Rafael: WFDC–TV Univision
Sanders, Molly: C–SPAN
Sanders-Smith, Sherry: C–SPAN
Sandiford, Michelle: C–SPAN
Sands, Haley: C–SPAN
Sands-Sadowitz, Geneva: ABC News
Sanfuentes, Jose: CNN
Sanfuentes, Lisa: Fox News
Sanli, Tuna: TRT
Sans, Raquel: TV3–Televisio De Catalunya
Sansone, Amanda: CNN
Santa-Rita, Joad: Voice of America
Santayana, Michelle: CNN
Santhuff, Bruce: ABC News
Santucci, John: ABC News
Sarfean, Maysam: TIMA
Sargeant, Nancy: Bloomberg Radio & TV
Sargent, Mark: WTTG–Fox Television
Sarlin, Benjamin: NBC News
Sarshar, Sahar: CGTN America
Sarstedt, Jessica: CGTN America
Sasaki, Tomoaki: ABC News
Sassenberg, Thomas: Storyhouse Productions
Satchell, David: WUSA–TV
Sato, Shota: Tokyo Broadcasting System
Satterfield, John: WETA
Saunders, John: Eurovision Americas, Inc.
Savage, Craig: Fox News
Savage, Ziris: CNN
Savchenko, Yulia: Voice of America
Say, Mony: Voice of America
Sayed, Amr: Middle East Broadcasting Networks (MBN)

MEMBERS ENTITLED TO ADMISSION—Continued

Sayilgan, Barbaros: TRT World
Scanlan, Quinn: ABC News
Scanlan, William: C–SPAN
Scanlon, Bridget: C–SPAN
Scannell, Kara: CNN
Scarnato, David: WUSA–TV
Schantz, Douglas: CNN
Schantz, Kristine: Scripps News
Scharf, Jason: Eurovision Americas, Inc.
Schatzker, Erik: Bloomberg Radio & TV
Scheimer, Dorey: Cox Broadcasting
Scheuer, John: CNN
Schieffer, Bob: CBS News
Schiff, Brian: Voice of America
Schiffner, Christine: CGTN America
Schlegel, Barry: ABC News
Schleifer, Theodore: CNN
Schlenker, Aungthu: Radio Free Asia
Schles, Robert: ABC News
Schloemer, Hans-Peter: German TV ZDF
Schmerling, Stacey: NBC News
Schmitz, Leonard: CBS News
Schneider, Amy: WJLA–TV / NewsChannel 8
Schneider, Edward: Voice of America
Schneider, Fred: CBS News
Schneider, James: WETA
Schneider, Jessica: CNN
Schoenholtz, Howard: ABC News
Schoenmann, Donald: Eye-To-Eye Video
Scholer, Mee: ABC News
Schonberger, Jennifer: Fox Business Network
Schott, Sonia: Radio Valera Venezuela
Schottle, John: WETA
Schrobsdorff, Ingalisa: WAMU
Schubauer, Katharine: Agence France Presse (AFP–TV)
Schultheis, Emily: CBS News
Schultze, Emily: ABC News
Schultze, Franco: WFDC–TV Univision
Schuster, Mark: CBS News
Schwarz, Daniel: CNN
Schwarzkopf, Steffen: N24 German TV
Schweiger, Ellen: C–SPAN
Schweitzer, Ally: WAMU
Schweitzer, Margaret: CBS DC
Schwetje, Lars: Gannett Government Media Corp
Sciacca, Joseph: Fox News
Scialla, Mark: The Newshour with Jim Lehrer
Sciutto, James: CNN
Scott, Andrew: USA Today
Scott, Gurnal: Fox News Radio
Scott, James: WJLA–TV / NewsChannel 8
Scott, Raquel: CNN
Scritchfield, Andrew: NBC News
Scruggs, Wesley: NBC News
Scuiletti, Justin: The Newshour with Jim Lehrer
Scully, Steven: C–SPAN
Seabrook, Willliam: WETA
Seaby, Gregory: CNN
Seales, Chance: Nexstar Media Group
Seales, Chance: Scripps News
Sears, Carl: NBC News
Seem, Thomas H.: CBS News
Segears, Leon: EWTN
Segraves, Mark: WRC–TV / NBC–4
Seib, Gerald: Wall Street Journal
Seidman, Jesse: Vice News
Seidman, Joel: NBC News
Seifert, Jan: German TV ZDF
Seipel, Arnold: National Public Radio
Seitz-Wald, Alexander: NBC News
Seium, Michael: Small House Productions
Sejima, Ryutaro: Fuji TV Japan
Seldin, Jeffrey: Voice of America
Selsky, Lauren: Sinclair Broadcast Group
Selyukh Pickeral, Alina: National Public Radio
Semenova, Anna: Russian State TV and Radio (RTR)
Semler, Ashley: BBC
Sen, Shreya: TRT World
Sens, Eleonore: Agence France Presse (AFP–TV)
Seo, Ja Ryen: Korean Broadcasting Systems
Serbu, Jared: Federal News Radio 1500 AM
Serfaty, Sunlen: CNN
Serrano, Randy: Telemundo Network
Serrano Quintero, Monica: CNN
Setsang, Pema: Voice of America
Sevilla Garcia, Francisco: TVE–Spanish Public Television
Sganga, Nicole: CBS News
Shabad, Rebecca: CBS News
Shaffir, Gregory: CBS News
Shaffir, Kim: CBS News
Shalhoup, Joseph: NBC News
Shammo, Hakim: Voice of America
Shannon, Dennis: CBS News
Shannon, Michael: ABC News
Shapiro, Adam: Fox Business Network
Shapiro, Ari: National Public Radio
Shapiro, Chaya: Aljazeera English
Sharief, Dania: Aljazeera English
Sharma, Versha: Now This News
Sharp, Duncan: Sky News
Sharpe, Abigail: CNN
Shaw, David: Scripps News
Shaw, Joseph: Reuters Radio & TV
Shaw, Katherine: ABC News
Shaw, Lawrence: ABC News
Shaylor, John: CNN
Sheerin, Jude: BBC
Shefte, Whitney: Washingtonpost.com
Sheikh, Ayan: Al Arabiya TV
Shelton, Nina: C–SPAN
Shelton, Steve: Fox News
Sheppard, Holly: CGTN America
Sheridan, Chris: Aljazeera English

MEMBERS ENTITLED TO ADMISSION—Continued

Sherman, Justin: Sinclair Broadcast Group
Sherman, Roger: Voice of America
Sherman, William: NBC News
Sherwood, Tom: WRC–TV / NBC–4
Shi, Yingshan: Xinhua
Shi, Yulin: New Tang Dynasty TV
Shibaki, Tomokazu: Fuji TV Japan
Shields, Daniel: Fox News Radio
Shields, Michael: Voice of America
Shikaki, Muna: Al Arabiya TV
Shimabukuro, Albert: WTOP Radio
Shimizu, Jumpei: Nippon TV Network
Shire, Robert: German TV ZDF
Shirley, Matt: CGTN America
Shlemon, Christopher: Independent Television News (ITN)
Shoffner, Harry: NHK
Shon, Robert: WTTG–Fox Television
Shore, Zach: WTOP Radio
Shortell, David: CNN
Showell, Andre: BET Nightly News
Shull, Roger: Reuters Radio & TV
Shure, Michael: i24 News
Shutt, Charles: WUSA–TV
Shwayder, Maya: Deutsche Welle TV
Siaden-Pena, Christian: CGTN America
Sibert, Brandon: NBC News
Sicile, James: ABC News
Sieg, Setareh: Voice of America
Siegel, Benjamin: ABC News
Siegel, David: CNN
Siegel, Robert C.: National Public Radio
Siegfriedt, Anita: Fox News
Sills, Cecil John: NBC NewsChannel
Silva, Juan: TRT World
Silva-Pinto, Daniel: TV Globo International
Silva-Pinto, Luis: TV Globo International
Silver, Quentin: NBC News
Silverman, Arthur: National Public Radio
Simkins, George: Voice of America
Simmons, Sarah: WTTG–Fox Television
Simmons-Duffin, Selena: National Public Radio
Simms, Jeffery: CNN
Simon, Jeff: CNN
Simon, Matthew: CGTN America
Simons, Stefan: TRT World
Simpson, Janet: ABC News
Simpson, Jennifer: CNN
Sinn, Rebecca: WJLA–TV / NewsChannel 8
Sipos, Joseph: Voice of America
Sistrunk, Jocelyn: Sinclair Broadcast Group
Skeans, Ronald: BBC
Skeele, Erin: Hearst Television Inc.
Skinski, Kathleen: CNN
Skokowski, Christopher: NBC NewsChannel
Skomal, Paul: Eurovision Americas, Inc.
Slansky, Heike: German TV ZDF
Slavica, Branka: HRT / Croatian Radio Television
Slen, Peter: C–SPAN
Slie, Charles: NBC News
Sloan, Karen: CNBC
Sloan, Steven: CNN
Sloane, Ward C.: CBS News
Small, Matthew: AP–Broadcast
Smith, Andrew: CGTN America
Smith, Anthony: Diversified Communications, Inc. (DCI)
Smith, Brian: WETA
Smith, Christie: NBC NewsChannel
Smith, Cindy: ABC News
Smith, Cynthia: Fox News
Smith, Felicia: AP–Broadcast
Smith, James: ABC News
Smith, Janet: Univision
Smith, Jason H.: Fox News
Smith, Kristin: Sinclair Broadcast Group
Smith, Lindley: C–SPAN
Smith, Max: WTOP Radio
Smith, Megan: Scripps News
Smith, Michael: WETA
Smith, Phillip: Diversified Communications, Inc. (DCI)
Smith, Randy: Washingtonpost.com
Smith, Shirley: AP–Broadcast
Smith, Tyler: One America
Smith, William: Cox Broadcasting
Smolkin, Rachel: CNN
Smoot, Kelly: CNN
Smysom, Osamah: Sky News Arabia
Smyth, Chris: Hearst Television Inc.
Sneed, Kimberly: NBC News
So, Linda: Reuters Radio & TV
Soe, Khin Maung: Radio Free Asia
Soete, Koen: Dutch TV & Radio (NOS)
Sohn, Seokmin: Seoul Broadcasting System (SBS)
Sokolov, Sergey: Voice of America
Sokolova, Elena: Russian State TV and Radio (RTR)
Solorzano, Gilbert: NBC News
Soltermann, Beat: Swiss Broadcasting
Somers, Meredith: Federal News Radio 1500 AM
Song, Jiwon: Seoul Broadcasting System (SBS)
Sonnheim, Jon: Cox Broadcasting
Sopel, Jonathan: BBC
Sorenson, Benjamin: C–SPAN
Soric, Miodrag: Deutsche Welle TV
Sotomayor, Marianna: NBC News
Soucy, Peggy: Eurovision Americas, Inc.
Southee, Haley: C–SPAN
Spangenberg, Andrew: EWTN
Spears, John: FedNet
Speck, Bruce: C–SPAN
Spector, Teresa: Fox News
Speer, John: National Public Radio
Spellman, James: CGTN America
Spence, Robert: C–SPAN

MEMBERS ENTITLED TO ADMISSION—Continued

Spevak, Joe: WTTG–Fox Television
Spiegler, Theodore: CBS News
Spodak, Cassandra: CNN
Sprunt, Barbara: National Public Radio
Spurrier, Sharon: NBC News
Sreng, Leakhena: Voice of America
Sriri, Amina: Sky News Arabia
St. James, Greg: C–SPAN
St. Jean, Johnny: C–SPAN
St. John, Jonathan: Fox Business Network
St. Onge, Derek: CNN
Stancik, Lisa: Voice of America
Stansfield, John: Sinclair Broadcast Group
Stanton, Jessica: CNN
Starddard, Donna: AP–Broadcast
Starikoff, Gary: C–SPAN
Stark, Elizabeth: CNN
Starr, Barbara: CNN
Starrs, Jenny: Washingtonpost.com
Statler, James: C–SPAN
Staton, Thomas: ABC News
Stay, Daniel: Fox News
Stead, Scott: CNN
Stein, Cari: To the Contrary (Persephone Productions)
Stein, Rob: National Public Radio
Steinberger, Daniel: ABC News
Steinmetz, Jesper: TV2–Denmark
Stephens, Mark: WRC–TV / NBC–4
Stevens, Seneca: Fox News
Stevenson, Carrie: CNN
Stevenson, John: CNN
Stevenson, Peter: Washingtonpost.com
Stewart, Andrew: SRN News (Salem)
Stewart, Kathy: WTOP Radio
Stewart, Robin: Ventana Productions
Stiles, Victoria: EWTN
Stirewalt, Christopher: Fox News
Stix, Gabriel: CBS News
Stoddard, Mark: ABC News
Stoddard, Richard: C–SPAN
Stolz, Peter: CGTN America
Stone, Evie: National Public Radio
Stone, Jessica: CGTN America
Storkel, Scott: Voice of America
Storms, Leslie: NBC News
Stout, Matthew: Fox News
Stoviak, Morgan: CNN
Stracqualursi, Veronica: ABC News
Strain, Eric: Fox News
Strand, Paul: CBN News
Strasser, Franz: BBC
Streeter, Rodney: ABC News
Streitfeld, Rachel: CNN
Strickland, Kenneth: NBC News
Strickler, Laura: CBS News
Stringer, Ashley: CNBC
Strong, Amber: CBN News
Strong, David: CBS News
Stuard, Christopher: WJLA–TV / NewsChannel 8
Stubblefield, Abraham: WDCW
Stubbs, James: NBC News
Stuhlmacher, Steven: WJLA–TV / NewsChannel 8
Su, Xiaoxiao: CGTN America
Suarez, Fernando: CBS News
Suarez, Sara: WFDC–TV Univision
Subramanian, Courtney: BBC
Sucher, Caroline: Fox News
Suddeth, James: Fox News
Suddeth, Richard: Fox News
Sugg, Anna: CBS News
Sughroue, Jon: NBC News
Suiters, Kimberly: WJLA–TV / NewsChannel 8
Sullivan, Katherine: CNN
Sullivan, Rebecca: National Public Radio
Summers, Juana: CNN
Summers, Kelly: Fox News
Summers, Patrick: Fox News
Sun, Qingzhao: CGTN America
Sutherland, Rachel: Fox News Radio
Suto, Ena: TV Asahi
Suzara, Jennifer: Fox News
Svoboda, Sarah: BBC
Swagler, Craig: CBS News
Swain, Bethany: Mobile Video Services, Ltd.
Swain, Susan: C–SPAN
Swain, Todd: Mobile Video Services, Ltd.
Swalec, Andrea: WRC–TV / NBC–4
Swanson, Carl: Voice of America
Sway, Aung: Voice of America
Sweeney, Robert: WRC–TV / NBC–4
Sweeney, Sam: WJLA–TV / NewsChannel 8
Sweet, David: Fox News
Swezey, Christian: EWTN
Swicord, Jeffrey: Voice of America
Sylvester, John: Fox News Radio
Symanski, Mary: C–SPAN
Szajkowski, Vara: BBC
Szeltner, Catherine: EWTN
Szypulski, Tom: Aljazeera English
Tabet, Joseph: Middle East Broadcasting Networks (MBN)
Tadelman, Samantha: WUSA–TV
Taguchi, Mai: Nippon TV Network
Taing, Sarada: Radio Free Asia
Taira, So: Tokyo Broadcasting System
Tait, Edward: BBC
Takaba, Yusuke: TV Asahi
Takagane, Yuka: NHK
Takahashi, Yoshiyuki: TV Tokyo
Talbot, Haley: NBC News
Tam, Ruth: WAMU
Tamary, Gil: Channel 10 Israel
Tamerlani, George: Reuters Radio & TV
Tanaka, Kenichi: NHK
Tanaka, Kentaro: NHK

MEMBERS ENTITLED TO ADMISSION—Continued

Tanaka, Masayoshi: NHK
Tanner, Dustin: CNN
Tanno, Kiyoshi: NHK
Tapper, Jacob: CNN
Tartaglia, Louis: Fox News
Tashi, Lumbum: Radio Free Asía
Tashi, Yeshi: Radio Free Asia
Tate, Simon: Aljazeera English
Tate, Tiffany: BET Nightly News
Tatum, Samuel: Radio One
Tatum, Sophia: CNN
Tavcar, Erik: Reuters Radio & TV
Tawfik, Nada: BBC
Taylor, Christina: C–SPAN
Taylor, Daron: Washingtonpost.com
Taylor, Jacqueline: Fox News
Taylor, Jessica: National Public Radio
Taylor, Kimberly: CBN News
Taylor, Rayquan: ABC News
Taylor, Russell: C–SPAN
Taylor, Scott: WJLA–TV / NewsChannel 8
Tea, Brandon: CBS News
Teasdale, Millicent: Independent Television News (ITN)
Teeples, Joseph: C–SPAN
Tejera, Richard: ABC News
Tejerina, Pilar: Aljazeera English
Temin, Thomas: Federal News Radio 1500 AM
Tenney, Garrett: Fox News
Terhar, John: WDCW
Terpstra, Patrick: Scripps News
Terpstra, Patrick: Cox Broadcasting
Tessler, Barton: Westwood One
Test1, Makeup: ABC News
Tevault, Neil David: National Public Radio
Tha, Kyaw: Voice of America
Thacker, Erin: WUSA–TV
Thalman, Mark: Ventana Productions
Thein, Kyaw: Voice of America
Theisen, Michael: Voice of America
Theodorou, Christine: TRT World
Thoman, Eric: C–SPAN
Thomas, Amy: ABC News
Thomas, Bert: NBC News
Thomas, Christopher: CTV–Community TV of PG County
Thomas, James: CBS News
Thomas, Lindsay: WAMU
Thomas, Pierre: ABC News
Thomas, Sharahn: National Public Radio
Thomas, Shari: ABC News
Thomas, Shawna: Vice News
Thomas, Stephanie: Federal News Radio 1500 AM
Thompson, Alexander: Vice News
Thompson, Cameron: WDCW
Thompson, Joseph: WETA
Thompson, Mallory: CNN
Thompson, Ron: Radio One
Thorne, Clifford: Washington Bureau News Service
Thornes, Troy: CBS News
Thornton, David: Federal News Radio 1500 AM
Thornton, Ronald: NBC News
Thorp, Frank: NBC News
Thorp, Tamara: CNN
Thueringer, Tamara: C–SPAN
Thuman, Scott: WJLA–TV / NewsChannel 8
Tichawonna, Sowande: Imagination Media
Tienabeso, Seniboye: ABC News
Tiller, Arthur: C–SPAN
Tillett, Emily: AP–Broadcast
Tillett, Emily: CBS News
Tillman, Rachel: ABC News
Tilman, Brandon: C–SPAN
Tinaz, Baybora: TRT
Titus, Rhea: WUSA–TV
Tiyansan, Ediz: TRT World
Tobia, Peter: The Newshour with Jim Lehrer
Tobianski, Sarah: Fox News
Tobias Delgado, Gessel: Voice of America
Todd, Brian: CNN
Todd, Charles: NBC News
Tolliver, Terri: WTTG–Fox Television
Tomasello, Andrew: WRC–TV / NBC–4
Tomeoni, Stephanie: ABC News
Tomlinson, Lucas: Fox News
Toombs, Zachary: Scripps News
Torpey, Robert: Fox News
Toso, Nicolas: CNN
Totenberg, Nina: National Public Radio
Touhey, Noel: C–SPAN
Tracey, Bree: Fox News
Trail, Michael: CNN
Trainor, Kevin: ABC News
Trainor, Thomas: Eurovision Americas, Inc.
Tram, Thanh: CNN
Trammell, Michael: WUSA–TV
Trams, Ines: German TV ZDF
Tran, Hoa Ai: Radio Free Asia
Trauzzi, Monica: Environment & Energy Publishing, LLC
Travers, Karen: ABC News
Traynham, Peter: CBS News
Trevelyan, Laura: BBC
Trevino, Nairka: FedNet
Treyz, Catherine: CNN
Triay, Andres P.: CBS News
Trosclair, Clayton: Eurovision Americas, Inc.
Trull, Armando: WAMU
Truong, Cynthia: VIETV Network
Tschida, Stephen: WJLA–TV / NewsChannel 8
Tserenbaljid, Uyanga: German TV ZDF
Tsurumi, Michiko: NHK
Tsuyuki, Sho: TV Asahi
Tuan, Shih-Yuan: TVBS
Tucker, Caroline: WRC–TV / NBC–4
Tucker, Elke: German TV ZDF

MEMBERS ENTITLED TO ADMISSION—Continued

Tulachom, Pinitkarn: Voice of America
Tuohey, Kenneth: CNN
Turman, Jack: CBS News
Turner, Christopher: CNN
Turner, Geoff: CBS News
Turner, Hayley: Fox News
Turner, James: AP–Broadcast
Turner, Melanie: NBC News
Turner, Mikea: WUSA–TV
Turner, Patricia: ABC News
Turner, Robert: Independent Television News (ITN)
Turner, Taylor: Washingtonpost.com
Turrell, Elizabeth: CNN
Tuss, Adam: WRC–TV / NBC–4
Tutman, Dan: CBS News
Tweed, Robert: CNN
Tyler, Brett: CNN
Tyler, Thomas: Diversified Communications, Inc. (DCI)
Tyson, Robin: CBN News
Ubeda-Carulla, Anna Maria: TVE–Spanish Public Television
Uceda, Claudia: Univision
Uchida, Koudai: TV Tokyo
Uchimiya, Ellen: CBS News
Uhl, Kim: CNN
Uitz-Dallinger, Robert: Austrian Radio & TV (ORF)
Ulbrich-Strothe, Sabine: N24 German TV
Uliano, Dick: WTOP Radio
Ulloa Ramirez, Victor: CBS News
Umeh, Maureen: WTTG–Fox Television
Umrani, Anthony: CNN
Upadhyay, Brajesh: BBC
Uprety, Sharmila: Sagarmatha Television
Upton, Emily: Sky News
Urbina, Luis: WJLA–TV / NewsChannel 8
Ure, Laurie: CNN
Uribe, Juvenal: Morningside Partners, LLC
Usero, Adriana: Washingtonpost.com
Usher, Barbara: BBC
Vaeth-Levin, Benjamin: Viewpoint Communications
Vaidyanathan, Rajini: BBC
Valerio, Michael: WUSA–TV
Van Cleave, Kristopher: CBS News
Van der Bellen, Erin: WUSA–TV
van der Horst, Arjen: Dutch TV & Radio (NOS)
Van Susteren, Greta: Voice of America
Vance, Denise: AP–Broadcast
Vandercook, Rebecca: CBS News
VanderVeen, Lawrence: Mobile Video Services, Ltd.
VanderVeen, Paul: WETA
Vargas, Carlos: AP–Broadcast
Vargas, Julia: Univision
Vasa, Sampath: CGTN America
Vasquez, Jennifer: WRC–TV / NBC–4
Vasquez Ramirez, Cristobal: Caracol Radio
Vaughan, Scott: Reuters Radio & TV
Vaughn, Michael: WJLA–TV / NewsChannel 8
Vazquez, Maegan: CNN
Velasquez, Jose: CGTN America
Vera, Jaime: Telesur
Verhovek, John: ABC News
Vermaak, Dawid: CNN
Vichi, Thomas: Radio Free Asia
Vieira, Andrea: CGTN America
Viers, Dana: ABC News
Viers, Meta: McClatchy
Vigil, Marcos: ABC News
Vilas Delgado, Carlos: European Pressphoto Agency
Vilen, Paula: Finnish Broadcasting Company (YLE)
Villegas, Catalina: WFDC–TV Univision
Villone Garcia, Patricia: CTV–Community TV of PG County
Vinette, Nicole: Fox News
Vingaard, Andreas: Danish Broadcasting Corporation
Vinson, Bryce: Fox News
Virji, Anar: Aljazeera English
Vishnevoy, Dmitry: Channel One Russian TV
Visioli, Christopher: Fox News
Visley, Andrew: AP–Broadcast
Vitale, Joseph: Voice of America
Vitali, Alexandra: NBC News
Vitorovich, Susan: NBC News
Vittert, Leland: Fox News
Vizcarra, Mario: Univision
Vogel, Philip: Fox News
Vohra, Sweta: Aljazeera English
Vollmer, Charles: Bloomberg Radio & TV
von Bonsdorff, Juri: Eurovision Americas, Inc.
von Nahmen, Alexandra: Deutsche Welle TV
von Nahmen, Carsten: Deutsche Welle TV
Vosloh, Allison: NTN24
Vossekuil, Matthew: CNN
Vosti, Andrea: Swiss Broadcasting
Voth, Charles: WETA
Vu, Doanh: VIETV Network
Vu, Tu: CNN
Vuokko, Mikko: Diversified Communications, Inc. (DCI)
Vurnis, Ambrose: WRC–TV / NBC–4
Wagner, Paul: WTTG–Fox Television
Wahl, Elizabeth: Scripps News
Wait, Kevin: National Public Radio
Waldman, Elliot: Tokyo Broadcasting System
Waldman, Joel: Fox News
Walker, Amanda: Sky News
Walker, Hayley: ABC News
Walker, Jackie Lyn: ABC News
Walker, James: WJLA–TV / NewsChannel 8
Walker, Nicole: National Public Radio
Walker, Victoria: Washingtonpost.com
Walker, William: CBS News
Wallace, Christopher: Fox News
Wallace, Elliott: CGTN America

MEMBERS ENTITLED TO ADMISSION—Continued

Wallace, Gregory: CNN
Wallace, John: Fox News
Wallace, Neil: Fox News
Walsh, Daisy: BBC
Walsh, Deirdre: CNN
Walsh, Mary: CBS News
Walter, Jonathan: Fox News
Walters, Amy: Center for Investigative Reporting
Walz, Julia: N24 German TV
Walz, Mark: CNN
Wang, Bingru: Hong Kong Phoenix Satellite Television
Wang, Erdan: CGTN America
Wang, Guan: CGTN America
Wang, Meng: CGTN America
Wang, Min: CGTN America
Wang, Taofeng: AP–Broadcast
Wang, Tianyi: Hong Kong Phoenix Satellite Television
Wang, Wei: CGTN America
Wang, Xiaoquan: Radio Free Asia
Wang, Xin: CGTN America
Wang, Yang: New Tang Dynasty TV
Wang, Youyou: Hong Kong Phoenix Satellite Television
Waqfi, Wajd: Aljazeera Satellite Channel (Peninsula)
Ward, Derrick: WRC–TV / NBC–4
Ward, Donald: Fox News
Ward, Melissa: WUSA–TV
Warfield, Marcel: WUSA–TV
Warfield, RT: CGTN America
Warner, Michael: One America
Warner, Tarik: WRC–TV / NBC–4
Warren-Bey Davis, Jamahn: C–SPAN
Washburn, Kevin: C–SPAN
Washington, Erick: CBS News
Washington, Ervin: Canadian Broadcasting Corporation (CBC)
Washington, Ervin: CNBC
Washington, Travis: WPLG–TV10
Washington-Anderson, Robert: WJLA–TV / NewsChannel 8
Watkins, Duane: CGTN America
Watkins, Eli: CNN
Watkins, Nicholas: Tokyo Broadcasting System
Watrud, Don: WTTG–Fox Television
Watson, Jarid: CBS DC
Watson, Kathryn: CBS News
Watson, Warren: GPI TV
Watters, Gemma: National Public Radio
Watts, Lindsay: WTTG–Fox Television
Weber, Joseph: Fox News
Weber, Ralph: German Public Radio (ARD)
Webster, Aaron: Fox News
Wee, Misha: ABC News
Wehinger, Amy: Fox News
Wei, Xuejiao: CGTN America
Weidenbosch, Glenn: CGTN America
Weinbloom, Henry: Fox News Radio
Weiner, Cydney: NBC News
Weinstein, Richard: C–SPAN
Weinstock, Roy: WRC–TV / NBC–4
Weiss, Ellen: Scripps News
Welker, Kristen: NBC News
Weller, George: NBC News
Wellford, Rachel: The Newshour with Jim Lehrer
Wellons, Mary: CNBC
Welna, David: National Public Radio
Welsh, Meghan: Fox News
Wenzlaff, Rachel: ABC News
Werner, Katharina: BBC
Werner, Michaela: German TV ARD
Werschkul, Benjamin: CNN
West, Caroline: Aljazeera English
West, Janea: C–SPAN
Westin, David: Bloomberg Radio & TV
Westphalen, Gary: ABC News
Whalan, Roscoe: Australian Broadcasting Corporation
Wheeler, Brian: Vice News
Wheeler, Frederick: WJLA–TV / NewsChannel 8
White, Christopher: Washingtonpost.com
White, Douglas: ABC News
White, Eric: Federal News Radio 1500 AM
White, Kevin: CGTN America
White, Mark: CBS News
Whiteman, Caroline: Fox News
Whitley, Walter: Fox News
Whitmire, Sarah: McClatchy
Whitney, Michael: Washington Bureau News Service
Whitson, Ricardo: CBS News
Whitson, William: Fox News
Whittington, Christopher: NBC News
Wholey, Dennis: This Is America with Dennis Wholey
Whyte, Scarlette: CNN
Widmer, Chris: CBS News
Widmer, Christopher: CBS News
Wiedeking, Lara: German TV ZDF
Wienecke, Dennis: German TV ARD
Wiener, Jamie: CNN
Wiernicki, Anna: Nexstar Media Group
Wiersema, Alisa: ABC News
Wiggins, Christopher: NBC NewsChannel
Wiggins, Dion: WUSA–TV
Wik, Snorre: Swedish Broadcasting
Wilde, Winston: NBC News
Wilk, Wendy: Hearst Television Inc.
Wilkes, Douglas H.: WTTG–Fox Television
Wilkes, Malini: Fox News Radio
Wilkie, Christina: CNBC
Williams, Abigail: NBC News
Williams, Andreane: France 2 Television
Williams, Brenna: CNN

MEMBERS ENTITLED TO ADMISSION—Continued

Williams, David: Fox News
Williams, Glenn: Yahoo News
Williams, James: Scripps News
Williams, Jeffrey L.: Cox Broadcasting
Williams, John: Fox News
Williams, Kenneth E.: CBS News
Williams, Louis: NBC News
Williams, Raphael: Sinclair Broadcast Group
Williams, Robert: NBC News
Williams, Roxanne: NBC News
Williams, Steven: WTTG–Fox Television
Williams, Tom: Aljazeera English
Williams, Tonya: Fox News Radio
Williams Vyas, Colleen: Fox News
Williamson, Calum: NBC News
Williamson, Christopher: NBC News
Willis, Anne Marie: Fox News
Willis, David: BBC
Wilson, Jeffrey: Radio One
Wilson, Jonathan: WAMU
Wilson, Mark: CBS News
Wilson, Stephanie: WUSA–TV
Winborn, Tracy: CBN News
Windham, Ronald: WJLA–TV / NewsChannel 8
Wing, Terry: Federal News Radio 1500 AM
Winston, Adrienne: CNN
Winterhalter, Ruthann: C–SPAN
Winters, LaTonya: CBS News
Winters, Ronald: CBS News
Winthrop, Anthony: Metro Teleproductions
Wiseman, Frederick: CNN
Wishingrad, Emily: Hearst Television Inc.
Witkin, Rachel: NBC News
Witte, Joel: CGTN America
Wittwer Soltermann, Ruth: Swiss Broadcasting
Wolf, Zachary: CNN
Wolfe, Lisa: Federal News Radio 1500 AM
Wood, Christopher: C–SPAN
Wood, Owen: WETA
Wood, Rachael: One America
Wood, Ryan: WUSA–TV
Wood, Zachary: Vice News
Woodall, Crystal: CBN News
Woods, Mike: CBS News
Woodsome, Kate: Aljazeera English
Woolbright, Melinda: WRC–TV / NBC–4
Worthington, Barry: White House Chronicle
Wotshela, Sicelo: BBC
Wright, Dale: WJLA–TV / NewsChannel 8
Wright, David: ABC News
Wright, David: CNN
Wright, Jasmine: The Newshour with Jim Lehrer
Wright Kerwin, Kristin: WRC–TV / NBC–4
Wu, Wei: New Tang Dynasty TV
Wuls, Jakub: CGTN America
Wylie, Brooke: Australian Broadcasting Corporation
Xiao, Hejia: CGTN America
Xie, Chenguang: CGTN America
Yager, Joshua: CBS News
Yaklyvich, Brian: ABC News
Yamasaki, Takeshi: NHK
Yamashita, Tatsuya: TV Asahi
Yancy, Shawn: WTTG–Fox Television
Yanevsky, Oleksandr: Voice of America
Yang, Chun: CGTN America
Yang, Daniel: The Newshour with Jim Lehrer
Yang, Guofu: Voice of America
Yang, Hee: Radio Free Asia
Yang, John: The Newshour with Jim Lehrer
Yang, Lianhua: American Chinese Television (ACT)
Yang, Lixin: New Tang Dynasty TV
Yang, Sungwon: Radio Free Asia
Yaqub, Nadeem: Voice of America
Yarborough, Rick: WRC–TV / NBC–4
Yarmuth, Floyd: CNN
Yates, Mark: Swiss Broadcasting
Yee Gaffney, Suzanne: AP–Broadcast
Yeshi, Lobsang: Radio Free Asia
Yeung Yam, Raymond: Voice of America
Yianopoulos, Karen: Middle East Broadcasting Networks (MBN)
Yilmaz, Huseyin: TRT World
Ying, Francis: Kaiser Health News
Yingst, Gerald: One America
Yoder, Alex: Gray Television
Yokoyama, Takahisa: CNN
Yoon, Robert: CNN
Yoshikawa, Junichi: TV Asahi
Young, Jeremy: Aljazeera English
Young, Melissa: ABC News
Young, Robert: C–SPAN
Young, Victor: NBC News
Young, Jr., Jerome: CBN News
Yu, Annie: WTTG–Fox Television
Yu, James: Korean Broadcasting Systems
Yu, Mallory: National Public Radio
Yui, Hideki: NHK
Yun, Samean: Radio Free Asia
Yunjin, Li: American Chinese Television (ACT)
Yurtseven, Aydin: TRT World
Yurus, Matthew: WUSA–TV
Zaatar, Marwan: Middle East Broadcasting Networks (MBN)
Zada, Naskah: CGTN America
Zager, Eric: Sinclair Broadcast Group
Zajko, Robert: Diversified Communications, Inc. (DCI)
Zak, Lana: ABC News
Zaman, Pias: National Public Radio
Zambelich, Ariel: National Public Radio
Zampa, Peter: Gray Television
Zang, Guohua: CTI–TV (Taiwan)
Zarinko, Joseph: CGTN America
Zayas, Ramon: WRC–TV / NBC–4
Zechar, David: ABC News

MEMBERS ENTITLED TO ADMISSION—Continued

Zeffler, Markus: BBC
Zeleny, Jeffrey: CNN
Zeliger, Robert: NBC News
Zeng, Jin: CGTN America
Zenke, Masaru: NHK
Zervos, Stratis: Eurovision Americas, Inc.
Zervos, Stratis: ABC News
Zhang, Adrianna: Voice of America
Zhang, Xiaoyan: Voice of America
Zhang, Xin: CGTN America
Zhao, Peng: CGTN America
Zhao, Xiaoyan: CGTN America
Zhao, Yunjie: CGTN America
Zheng, Ren: WTOP Radio
Ziegenbein, Darren: WRC–TV / NBC–4
Zients, Sasha: CNN
Zimerman, Ariel: AP–Broadcast
Zosso, Elizabeth: Middle East Broadcasting Networks (MBN)
Zschieschang, Marion: German TV ARD
Zucconi, Anthony: Fox News
Zuckerman, Alexandra: CBS News
Zuker, Karen: CNN
Zulu, Blessing: Voice of America
Zumbado, Joaquin: NBC News
Zurcher, Anthony: BBC
Zwart, Wouter: Dutch TV & Radio (NOS)
Zwillich, Todd: WNYC

NETWORKS, STATIONS, AND SERVICES REPRESENTED

Senate Gallery 224–6421   House Gallery 225–5214

ABC NEWS—(202) 222–7700; 1717 DeSales Street, NW., Washington, DC 20036: Audrey Dalgetty, Imtiyaz Delawala, Megan Hughes Hemmerlein, Jason Kurtis, Whitney Lloyd, Nehemiah Mekonnen, Elizabeth Alesse, Faisal Alkadiri, John Allard, Scott Allmond, Thomas Armstrong, Travis Renee Baldwin, Mark Banks, Luke Barr, Benjamin Bell, Michael Bellis, Phillip Black, Wayne Boyd, Charles Breiterman, Mary Bruce, Lucien Bruggeman, John Bullard, Matthew Burton, Christopher Carlson, Diana Carswell, Paola Chavez, Michael Conte, Jeffery Cook, Anja Crowder, Ajinkya Date, Audrey Dealgetty, William Demas, Peter Doherty, Erin Dooley, Alexandra Dukakis, John Dunkin, Devin Dwyer, Stephanie Ebbs, Daniel Glenn Elvington, Katherine Faulders, Conor Finnegan, Justin Fishel, Siobhan Fisher, Jon Garcia, Myra Green, Brian Haefeli, Daniel Hannah, Robert Horton, Matthew Alan Hosford, Gregory Hughes, Heidi Jensen, Cecilia Jimenez, Almin Karamehmedovic, Jonathan Karl, Katharine Kastens, Paul Kerley, Mariam Khan, Erica King, Elizabeth King, Richard Klein, Sarah Kolinovsky, Donald Eugene Kroll, Michael Levine, Nathan Luna, Lachlan Murdoch MacNeil, Dhanraj Mangal, Serena Marshall, Luis Martinez, Meridith McGraw, Elizabeth McLaughlin, Angelique McMenamin, Erik McNair, James Meek, Avery Miller, Matthew Mosk, Kenneth Moton, David Muir, Molly Nagle, Meredith Nettles, Janai Norman, Marjorie O'Brien, Patrick O'Gara, Andrea Owen, John Parkinson, MaryAlice Parks, Rebecca Perlow, Jordyn Phelps, Michael Pickup, Kevin Pliszak, Mary Quinn, Jason Radke, Corinne Roberts, Ali Rogin, Christine Romo, Margaret Rulli, Katherine Saenz, George Sanchez, Geneva Sands-Sadowitz, John Santucci, Robert Schles, Howard Schoenholtz, Mee Scholer, Lawrence Shaw, Benjamin Siegel, Janet Simpson, James Smith, Cindy Smith, Daniel Steinberger, Veronica Stracqualursi, Rayquan Taylor, Richard Tejera, Amy Thomas, Pierre Thomas, Seniboye Tienabeso, Stephanie Tomeoni, Karen Travers, Patricia Turner, John Verhovek, Dana Viers, Hayley Walker, Misha Wee, Rachel Wenzlaff, Gary Westphalen, Douglas White, Alisa Wiersema, David Wright, Melissa Young, Lana Zak.

AGENCE FRANCE PRESSE (AFP-TV)—1500 K Street, NW., Washington, DC 20005: Adan Alvarenga, Gabrielle Chatelain, Ricardo Criales, Carmen Cuesta-Roca, William Edwards, Katharyn Gillam, Jihan Joannides, Gerald Jonas, Ivan Rivas, Katharine Schubauer, Eleonore Sens.

AL ARABIYA TV—(202) 355–6614; 1620 I Street, NW., 10th Floor, Washington, DC 20006: Angelyn Adams, Nadia Charters-Bilbassy, Pierre Ghanem, Elias Habib, Richard Melhem, Ayan Sheikh, Muna Shikaki.

ALASKA PUBLIC RADIO NETWORK/ALASKA PUBLIC MEDIA—140 13th Street, SE., Washington, DC 20003: Elizabeth Ruskin.

ALJAZEERA ENGLISH—1200 New Hampshire Avenue, NW., 2nd Floor, Washington, DC 20036: Robert Abeshouse, Abdul Hadi Abo-Issa, Eyad Aburahma, Tom Ackerman, Elrashidi Adam, Laila Alarian, Rafael Arias, Baubak Baghi, Jeff Ballou, James Bays, Jet Belgraver, Ahad Bhatti, Ayana Brickhouse, Robert Brock, Malik Camah, Peter Charley, Kavitha Chekuru, Stephen Coonce, Patricia Culhane, Deborah Davies, Mitchell Doty, Mark Douglas, Nicholas Dove, Gabriel Elizondo, Mariam Engel, Kathleen Fabian, Thomas Fisher, Hida Fouladvand, Michael Fox, Andy Gallacher, Maya Garg, Jonathan Garratt, Franklyn Ginsberg, Gregory Guise, Karim Haddad, Kimberly Halkett, James Hamilton, John Hendren, Kevin Hirten, Whitney Hurst, Rosiland Jordan, Akilah Joseph, Muriel Jubar, Kevin King, Paul Koenig, Michael LaBella, Daniel Lak, Ekaterina Landy, Lister Lim, Radicella Lucas, Bilal Malika, Maria Marquez, Mercedes Martinez, Colin McIntyre, David McWhinney, Hasan Mehdi, Robert Michaud, Ibrahim Nur, Femi Oke, Craig Olmstead, Craig Pennington, Jason Pepino, Ilir Prifti, Ivica Puljic, Shihab Rattansi, Juan Raymond, Alea Reeves, Robert Reynolds, Kira Rockell, Joshua Rushing, Kristen Saloomey, Chaya Shapiro, Dania Sharief, Chris Sheridan, Tom Szypulski, Simon Tate, Pilar Tejerina, Anar Virji, Sweta Vohra, Caroline West, Tom Williams, Kate Woodsome, Jeremy Young.

ALJAZEERA SATELLITE CHANNEL (PENINSULA)—1200 New Hampshire Avenue, NW., 2nd Floor, Washington, DC 20036: Ahmed Abdulrazzaq, Morad Abed, Shireen Abu Akleh, Biesan Abu-Kwaik, Haitham Al Juboori, Mohammed Alami, Sara Ashworth, Ahmed Diab, Mahmoud El-Hamalawy, Mouhamed Elahmed, Abderrahim Foukara, Sara Hassan, Nasreddine Hssaini, Lina Khalaf, Fadi Mansour, Ashraf Nagy, Wajd Waqfi.

AMERICAN CHINESE TELEVISION (ACT)—(240) 988–4660; 722 Ridgemont Avenue, Rockville, MD 20850: Lianhua Yang, Li Yunjin.

ANADOLU AGENCY—(202) 662–7435; 529 14th Street, NW., #1131, Washington, DC 20045: Yasin Ozturk.

AOL HUFFINGTON POST—(202) 624–9300; 1750 Pennsylvania Avenue, NW., Suite 600, Washington, DC 20006: Samara Mackereth, John Rieger.

NETWORKS, STATIONS, AND SERVICES REPRESENTED—Continued

AP-BROADCAST—(202) 641–9000; 1100 13th Street, NW., Suite 500, Washington, DC 20005: Jeffrey Adkinson, Shelley Adler, Khaldoun Alrawi, Eric Andree, Jeannie Andress, John Auresto, Philip Avner, Edward Barker, Hugo Blanco, Jacqueline Blum-Dostie, Michael Bodenhorst, Jennifer Breuer, Craig Broffman, Tracy Brown, Kathleen Brumbaugh, Robert Bumsted, Andrea Colombo-Abdullah, Derek Danilko, Kelly Daschle, Edward Donahue, Jason Dorn, Lisa Dwyer-Shapiro, Krysta Fauria, Rita Foley, Mathew Friedman, Oscar Gabriel, Richard Gentilo, Srabony Ghosh, Lawrence Gold, James Gorman, Michael Gracia, Michael Hempen, Susan Henderson, Brian Hoffman, Daniel Huff, Roderick Jussim, Christian Kettlewell, Jennifer King, Nan Hee McMinn, Sagar Meghani, Vaughn Morrison, John Morrissey, Noreen Nasir, Louis Pagan, Gerald Petraitis, Padmananda Rama, Walter Ratliff, Thomas Ritchie, John Rizzo, Matthew Small, Felicia Smith, Shirley Smith, Donna Starddard, Emily Tillett, James Turner, Denise Vance, Carlos Vargas, Andrew Visley, Suzanne Yee Gaffney.

APTVS–AMERICAN PRESS & TV SERVICES—(202) 601–2284; 1445 New York Avenue, NW., Suite 500, Washington, DC 20005: Akram Abdulkareem, Abdulaziz Alowais, Ahmed Alqarni, Mohammed Dawood, Elian El-khamissi, Gamal Hassanein.

ARTE TV—2000 M Street, NW., Washington, DC 20036: Philippe Gassot.

AUSTRALIAN BROADCASTING CORPORATION—(202) 466–8575; 2000 M Street, NW., Suite 660, Washington, DC 20036: Zoe Daniel, Conor Duffy, Bradley Fulton, Stephanie March, John Mees, Roscoe Whalan, Brooke Wylie.

AUSTRIAN RADIO & TV (ORF)—1206 Eton Court, NW., Washington, DC 20007: Silvia Charpa, Daniela Ettrich, Hannelore Fauqueux-Veit, Uelle-Mall Jaakson, Ernst Kernmayer, Markus Meier, Robert Uitz-Dallinger.

AZTECA AMERICA—400 North Capitol Street, NW., Suite 361, Washington, DC 20001: Armando Guzman, Ernesto Orellana.

BBC—(202) 223–2050; 2000 M Street, NW., #800, Washington, DC 20009: Stephen Adrain, Lukman Ahmed, Nadia Alhuraimi, Ben Bevington, Laura Bicker, Taylor Brown, Nicholas Bryant, Maxine Collins, James Cook, Jonathan Csapo, Kathleen Dailey, Paul Danahar, Ian Druce, Mehrnoosh Ebrahimi, Kathryn Farrell, Sam Farzaneh, Kambiz Fattahi, Deirdre Finnerty, Lynsea Garrison, Thomas Geoghegan, Kim Ghattas, Pratiksha Ghildial, Samantha Granville, Andrew Herbert, Rozalia Hristova, Katharine Kay, Suzanne Kianpour, Shefali Kulkarni, Olivia Lace-Evans, John Landy, Sarah Lewthwaite, Harry Low, Jessica Lussenhop, Aleem Maqbool, Max Matza, Rosalind Mayfield, Tara McKelvey, Jennifer Regan Morris, Donald Morrison, Tare Neill, Hadi Niliahmadabadi, Gary O'Donoghue, John Parks, Amir Payam, Annie Phrommayon, Nataliia Pisnia-Bystriakova, James Reber, Ashley Semler, Jude Sheerin, Ronald Skeans, Jonathan Sopel, Franz Strasser, Courtney Subramanian, Sarah Svoboda, Vara Szajkowski, Edward Tait, Nada Tawfik, Laura Trevelyan, Brajesh Upadhyay, Barbara Usher, Rajini Vaidyanathan, Daisy Walsy, Anthony Zurcher.

BET NIGHTLY NEWS—(202) 824–6500; 12510 Lanham Severn Road, Bowie, MD 20720: Joyce Jones, Andre Showell, Tiffany Tate.

BLOOMBERG RADIO & TV—1399 New York Avenue, NW., 11th Floor, Washington, DC 20005: Christine Baratta, Emma Chandra, Kevin Cirilli, Kathryn Glass, David Goodman, David Gura, Nathan Hager, Lauren McDevitt, Michael McKee, Adrienne Mitchell, Amy Morris, Roland Morrisette, Andrew O'Day, Alisa Parenti, Brendan Polmer, Nancy Sargeant, Erik Schatzker, Charles Vollmer, David Westin.

BT VIDEO PRODUCTIONS—7117 Wolftree Lane, Rockville, MD 20852: Paul Hollenbeck, Martin Kos.

C-SPAN—(202) 737–3220; 400 North Capitol Street, NW., #650, Washington, DC 20001: Kenneth Alexander, Thomas Alldredge, Theresa Amirault-Michel, Jeremiah Art, Shannon Augustus, Michelle Bailor, Jason Bender, Brett Betsill, Leona Blakey, Greta Brawner, Donald Brown, Paul Brown, Robert Browning, Kristina Buddenhagen, Susan Bundock, Leslie Burdick, Kathy Cahill, Craig Caplan, Kenneth Carrick, Stephanie Chadha-Kaye, Tanya Chattman, Nancy Christian, Matthew Claar, James Clark, Bruce Collins, James Cook, Howard Corner, Nathan Craig, Liam Currier, Alexander Curtis, Gregory Czzowitz, Peter Daniels, Matthew Dauchess, Bridget Diggs, Danny Dill, Michelle Doell, Sean Doody, John Doyle, Mallory Drummond, Yi-Pe Eastin, Pedro Echevarria, Gary Ellenwood, Seth Engel, Patricia Esquivel, Gregory Fabic, Mark Farkas, Joseph Feeney, Richard Fleeson, Amanda Fortner, Carl Foster, William Frazier, Leslie Frazier, William Gallagher, John Gallagher, Craig Galowin, Tracy Garlock, Jennifer Garrott, Garney Gary, Victoria Glaude, Robert Gould, Richard Hall, Christopher Hanson, Stephen Harkness, Robert Harleston, Kasey Harris, Maurice Haynes, William Heffley, Jonelle Henry, Francis Herbas, Dallas Hill, Ashley Hill, Caitlin Hillyard, Eric Horacek, Katherine Hughes, Scott Hummelsheim, Tracy Hunter, Nathan Hurst, Cynthia Ingle, Roberta Jackson, Phelix Jones, Steven Kehoe, Jonathan Kelley, Roxane Kerr, Kevin King, David Knighton, Felix Laboy, Brian Lamb, Deborah Lamb, Darren Larade, Molly Laville, Robert Lazar, Jerome Leddon, Brian Lloyd, Paul Loeschke, Charles Logan, Ivette Lucero Lopez, Graham MacGillivray, Valerie Matthews, Achu Mba, John McArdle, Michael McCann, Sean McCann, Gerard McGarrity, Adrienne McGibbon, Justin Metzger, Andrew Miller, Katherine Mills, David Monack, Victor Montoro, Garrett Moore, Linwood Moore, Kuren Morgan, Howard Mortman, Daniel Morton, Terence Murphy, Andrew Nason, Robin Newton, Trang Ninh, Donna Norris, Benen O'Brien, Benjamin O'Connell, Ndidi Obasi, Alan Olmsted, Paul Orgel, Michael Patruznick, Taylor Pentelovitch, Vernon Perkins, Christina Perry, Nickolas Pitocco, Almon Porter, Anne Preloh,

NETWORKS, STATIONS, AND SERVICES REPRESENTED—Continued

David Pries, Anthony Pronko, Nikhil Raval, Robert Reilly, Michele Remillard, Cynthia Reuter, Shannon Rice, Delia Rios, John Roberts, Tiffany Rocque, Mark Rodeffer, Martine Rodriguez, Randolph Rohrbaugh, Jennifer Ruff, Frederico Sampaio, Molly Sanders, Sherry Sanders-Smith, Michelle Sandiford, Haley Sands, William Scanlan, Bridget Scanlon, Ellen Schweiger, Steven Scully, Nina Shelton, Peter Slen, Lindley Smith, Benjamin Sorenson, Haley Southee, Bruce Speck, Robert Spence, Greg St. James, Johnny St. Jean, Gary Starikoff, James Statler, Richard Stoddard, Susan Swain, Mary Symanski, Christina Taylor, Russell Taylor, Joseph Teeples, Eric Thoman, Tamara Thueringer, Arthur Tiller, Brandon Tilman, Noel Touhey, Jamahn Warren-Bey Davis, Kevin Washburn, Richard Weinstein, Janea West, Ruthann Winterhalter, Christopher Wood, Robert Young.

CADENA SER—(202) 596–6969; 4520 Cumberland Avenue, Chevy Chase, MD 20815: Javier del Pino, Marta del Vado.

CANADIAN BROADCASTING CORPORATION (CBC)—(202) 383–2900; National Press Building 529 14th Street, NW., Suite 510, Washington, DC 20045: Keith Boag, Jason Burles, Marcel Calfat, Marie Claudet, Cara Cruz, Yanik Dumont Baron, Lyndsay Duncombe, Patrick Ferguson, Paul Hunter, Patricia Jette, Matthew Kwong, Christian Latreille, Jason Lowther, Ellen Mauro, Glenn Parker, Sylvain Richard.

CARACOL RADIO—1320 Fairmont Street, #103, Washington, DC 20009: Maria Molina Salazar, Cristobal Vasquez Ramirez.

CARACOL TELEVISION—(202) 615–3899; 400 North Capitol Street, NW., Suite 361, Washington, DC 20001: Jose Agredo, Edwin Giraldo, Laura Newton.

CATALUNYA RADIO—(301) 204–9062; 4608 Cooper Lane, Bethesda, MD 20816: Maria Lozano Villo, Fracesc Reverter Baquer.

CBN NEWS—(202) 833–2707; 1919 M Street, NW., Suite 100, Washington, DC 20036: Robert Allman, Mark Bautista, Walter Bozek, David Brody, Jenna Browder, Laura Crombe, Brian Edwards, Juan Garcia, Jennifer Gilbert, Aronica Glover, Mario Gonzalez, Alegra Hall, Ashley Hall, Steven Jacobi, Gene Jenkins, John Jessup, Matthew Keedy, Benjamin Kennedy, Jacob Moore, Edward Morano, Shoshannah Nunez, Stacy Opoku, Denis Pacuraru, David Page, Anthony Peltier, John Reid, Dana Ritter, Abigail Robertson, Erik Rosales, Ian Rushing, Paul Strand, Amber Strong, Kimberly Taylor, Robin Tyson, Tracy Winborn, Crystal Woodall, Jerome Young, Jr.

CBS DC—(202) 479–0829; 1015 Half Street, SE., Suite 200, Washington, DC 20003: Philip Briggs, Eric Dehm, Michelle Dolge, Charles Henry, Justin Hodge, Jacob Hughes, Kaylah Jackson, Jonathan Kaupanger, Caitlin Kenney, Amanda Macias, Matthew Saintsing, Robert Sanchez, Margaret Schweitzer, Jarid Watson.

CBS NEWS—(202) 457–4444; 2020 M Street, NW., Washington, DC 20036: Abdul-Mola Lenghi, Carrie Aber, Adam Aigner-Treworgy, Gabrielle Ake, Thomas Albano, Jacqueline Alemany, Clinton N. Alexander, Alicia Amling, Alana Anyse, Chloe Arensberg, Morris Banks, Michael Barnett, Kia Baskerville, John Bat, Farrel Becker, Mark Bennett, Musadiq Bidar, Lindsey Boerma, Leonard Boswell, Margaret Brennan, Whitney Bright, Philomena Bubaris, Susan Bullard Harmon, Catherine Cannon, Joshua Cartwright, Denise Cetta, Steven Chaggaris, Jane Chick, George Christian, Caitlin Conant, Carol Coney, Nancy Cordes, Victoria Coughlan, Walter Cronkite IV, John Crum, John Daly, Robert Diaz, John Dickerson, Charles H. Dixson, Katie Dominick, Margaret Dore, Steve Dorsey, Robert Dries, Louise Dufresne, Lois Dyer, Bo Erickson, John Fantacone, Arden Farhi, Edward Forgotson, Thomas Foty, John Frado, Tony Furlow, Hal Furman, Brian Fuss, Travis Galey, July Garcia, Major Garrett, Timothy Gaughan, Jenna Gibson, Benson Ginsburg, Julianna Goldman, Brian Gottlieb, Neil Grasso, Jan Greenburg, David Gross, Josh Gross, Blair Guild, Mary Hager, Bill Harding, Alan He, Elizabeth Hinson, Michael Hopkins, Caroline Horn, Jillian Hughes, Clare Hymes, Margaret Hynds, Christopher Isham, Jill Jackson, Dennis Jamison, Ricky Jefferson, Weijia Jiang, Shanica Johnson, Jeffrey Johnston, Lorna Jones, Rebecca Kaplan, Craig Katz, Eric Kerchner, Jonathan Kessler, Allison Keyes, Adrian KIll, Rosa Kim, Julia Kimani, Daniel Klos, Mark Knoller, Caraline Korte, Grace Lamb-Atkinson, John Lamonica, Benjamin Larson, Donald Lee, Jonathan Lien, Sam Litzinger, Lara Logan, Michelle Macaluso, Steven Marshall, David Martin, Shawn Matthews, Mark Mazariegos, Donald McCarty, D. Page McCarty, Max McClellan, Duncan McKenna, Robert McKinley, William Miller, Patricia Milton, Donald Morgan, John Murphy, John Nolen, Norah O'Donnell, Mosheh Oinounou, Jeffrey Pegues, Timothy Perry, Michael Peyton, Steve Portnoy, John Pumo, Diana Quinn, Richard Rahn, George Rehkopf, Charles Reid, Paula Reid, Catherine Reynolds, Francisco Robbins, Khalea Robinson, Ira Rosen, Howard Rosenberg, Allyson Ross Taylor, Christina Ruffini, Mary Kate Rydell, Jenna Sakwa, Bob Schieffer, Fred Schneider, Emily Schultheis, Mark Schuster, Thomas H. Seem, Nicole Sganga, Rebecca Shabad, Gregory Shaffir, Kim Shaffir, Dennis Shannon, Ward C. Sloane, Gabriel Stix, Laura Strickler, Fernando Suarez, Anna Sugg, Craig Swagler, Troy Thornes, Emily Tillett, Peter Traynham, Andres P. Triay, Jack Turman, Geoff Turner, Dan Tutman, Ellen Uchimiya, Victor Ulloa Ramirez, Kristopher Van Cleave, Rebecca Vandercook, William Walker, Mary Walsh, Erick Washington, Kathryn Watson, Mark White, Ricardo Whitson, Chris Widmer, Christopher Widmer, Kenneth E. Williams, Ronald Winters, LaTonya Winters, Joshua Yager, Alexandra Zuckerman.

CENTER FOR INVESTIGATIVE REPORTING—(510) 809–3160; c/o The Center for Public Integrity, 910 17th Street, NW., Suite 700, Washington, DC 20006: Amy Walters.

NETWORKS, STATIONS, AND SERVICES REPRESENTED—Continued

CGTN AMERICA—(202) 639–4800; 1099 New York Avenue, NW., Washington, DC 20001: Atirath Aich, Rachelle Akuffo, Zeina Al-Shaib, Yasmeen Alamiri, George Alexander, Julio Aliaga, Fan Bai, Paul Barber, Joshua Barlow, James Barnett, Sean Callebs, Qingyun Cao, He Cheng, Lisa Chiu, Ralph Cooper, Chris Cowman, Lingnan Cui, Yubin Du, Owen Fairclough, Wenwei Fang, Wang Fenghua, Kim France Wilson, Peng Fu, Qi Gao, Kurt Gardinier, John Gilmore, Joanna Godinho, Chun Guo, Zhu Haiqing, Jiyuan Han, Wenjin He, Jumana Heresh, Aja Hubert-Hogg, Nina Ing, Michael Italiano, Li Jia, Xin Jiang, Monna Kashfi, Patricia Keane, Colleen Kenney, Nathan King, Frances Kuo, Yunhe Lai, Ira Lazernik, Meng Li, Zhujun Li, Qingqing Li, Hui Lin, Xiyang Liu, Jing Ma, Gary Matsumoto, Yan Mei, Jeff Milstein, Rich Murphy, Anand Naidoo, Ruqaiyah Najjar, Asieh Namdar, Hakan Ozsancak, Chanlee Parks, Sun Ping, Megan Pratz, Qi Qin, Xiangqin Quan, Nithya Ramani, Roselena Ramirez, Elaine Reyes, Kelly Rice, Janet Rodriguez, Roee Ruttenberg, Sara Salman, Sahar Sarshar, Jessica Sarstedt, Christine Schiffner, Holly Sheppard, Matt Shirley, Christian Siaden-Pena, Matthew Simon, Andrew Smith, James Spellman, Peter Stolz, Jessica Stone, Xiaoxiao Su, Qingzhao Sun, Sampath Vasa, Jose Velasquez, Andrea Vieira, Elliott Wallace, Guan Wang, Meng Wang, Wei Wang, Erdan Wang, Xin Wang, Min Wang, RT Warfield, Duane Watkins, Xuejiao Wei, Glenn Weidenbosch, Kevin White, Joel Witte, Jakub Wuls, Hejia Xiao, Chenguang Xie, Chun Yang, Naskah Zada, Joseph Zarinko, Jin Zeng, Xin Zhang, Peng Zhao, Xiaoyan Zhao, Yunjie Zhao.

CHANNEL 10 ISRAEL—(202) 460–0223; 195 Hardy Place, Rockville, MD 20852: Gil Tamary.

CHANNEL ONE RUSSIAN TV—1100 13th Street, NW., Suite 400, Washington, DC 20005: Anatoly Lazarev, Iuliia Olkhovskaia, Dmitry Vishnevoy.

CMI TV (COLOMBIA)—5753 Governor's Pond Circle, Alexandria, VA 22310: Adriana Ahmad Serna, Jaime Moreno.

CNBC—(202) 776–7405; 400 North Capitol Street, NW., Suite 850, Washington, DC 20001: Patrick Anastasi, Bria Cousins, Plummer Crawley, Matthew Cuddy, Stephanie Dhue, Gaffney Emily, John Harwood, Kayla Izant, Eamon Javers, Ylan Mui McClintock, Diana Olick, Hampton Pearson, Pat Pugliese, Shari Rosen, Karen Sloan, Ashley Stringer, Ervin Washington, Mary Wellons, Christina Wilkie.

CNN—(202) 898–7900; 820 1st Street, NE., Washington, DC 20002: Khalil Abdallah, Abilo Acosta, Rami Al Badry, William Alberter, David Allbritton, Mark Allman, Omega Armah, Abigail Arzoumanov, Matthew Avrutine, Renee Baharaeen, Erik Banks, Angela Barajas, Edward Barrett, Dana Bash, Christian Bear, John Bena, Kate Bennett, Alexa Bennewitz, Leslie Bentz, Daniel Berman, Richard Bernal, Laura Bernardini, Mark Biello, Lindzie Bills, Joan Biskupic, Frank Bivona, Kevin Blakley, Wolf Blitzer, John Bodnar, Kevin Bohn, Donna Borak, Gloria Borger, Tyrone Boston, Eric Bradner, Lorenza Brascia, Joshua Braun, Allison Brennan, Michael Brevner, Raymond Britch, Scott Bronstein, David Brooks, Pamela Brown, Ryan Browne, Steven Brusk, Burke Buckhorn, Tiffany Bullock, Brian Burch, David Burgess, Terence Burlij, Juan Cabral Pichardo, William Cadigan, Karin Caifa, Michael Callahan, David Catrett, David Chalian, Jill Chappell, Natasha Chen, Stuart Clark, Gregory Clary, Bobby Clemons, Avron Coates, Marshall Cohen, Zachary Cohen, Youman Coleman, Kaitlan Collins, Stephen Collinson, James Crawford, Natalia Crosdale, Christopher Cross, Robert Crowley, John Cunha, Jaime Davila Castillo, Patrick Davis, Edward Davis, Kara Day, Javier de Diego, Ariane de Vogue, Camila DeChalus, Jeremy Diamond, Daniella Diaz, Patricia DiCarlo, Stephen Dolce, Alice Donaldson, Rachel Dooley, Sonya Dowhaluk, Thomas Ebel, Jodi Enda, Olivia Evans-Pittman, Samuel Feist, Eric Fiegel, Craig Fingar, Alexandra Flagg, Latoya Forbes, Patrick Ford, Thomas Foreman, Lauren Fox, William Frank, Leah Freeman, Dianne Gallagher, Jamie Gangel, Sara Ganim, Katherine Gaouette, Devin Garbitt, Danelle Garcia, Melodie Garner, Elise Garofalo, Timothy Garraty, Christopher Garrett, Amina Garrett Scott, David Gelles, Melissa Giaimo, Sarah Giannakopoulos, Shannon Gillece, Rachel Glasberg, Andre Goddard, Andrea Gonzales-Paul, David Gracey, Aileen Graef, Noah Gray, James Graydon, Clayton Green, Miranda Green, Gus Greene, Andrew Griffin, Angelica Grimaldi, Eddie Gross, Alessia Grunberger, Saba Avatar Hamedy, Brian Hampton, Jeremy Harlan, Amelia Harris, Elizabeth Hartfield, Nia-Malika Henderson, Kelvin Henry, Jeremy Herb, Michael Herkner, Ione Hess, Matthew Hilk, Katherine Hinman, Jason Hoffman, William Holbert, Faith Holland, Kristen Holmes, Derek Horrigan, Emily Howell, Matthew Hoye, Richard Hudock, Adolfo Ibarra, Adia Jacobs, Oliver Janney, Laura Jarrett, David Jenkins, Clarence Jobe, Joseph Johns, Athena Jones, Douglas Jones, Donald Judd, Polson Kanneth, Bonney Kapp, Peter Kavanagh, Kristin Keppler, Aaron Kessler, Ashley Killough, John King, Mary Klein, Tal Kopan, Laura Koran, Michelle Kosinski, Gregory Krieg, Benjamin Krolowitz, Elise Labott, Elizabeth Landers, Min Lee, Alexander Lee, Ji Lee, Adam Levine, Ross Levitt, Adam Levy, Misha Lewis, Latavia Lewis, Kevin Liptak, Philip Littleton, Thomas LoBianco, Juan Carlos Lopez Ruiz, Edwin Lora, Brianna Lujan, Melissa Macaya, Mary Mallonee, Allison Malloy, Suzanne Malveaux, Christina Manduley, Mark Marchione, Rene Marsh, Philip Mattingly, Dugald McConnell, Colin McCullough, Douglas McKinley, Scott McLean, Samuel McMichael, James Meech, Daniel Merica, Julia Metjian, Rebekah Metzler, Paul Miller, Anna Miller, Alec Miran, Alexa Miranda, Jeffrey Moller, Jeremy Moorhead, Isabel Morales, Peter Morris, Sarah Mucha, Sara Murray, Steven Nannes, Nicholette Nicci, Ryan Nobles, Bridget Nolan, Jeffrey Norman, Michael Oat, Eric Odendahl, Gregory Overzat, Steven Page, Ann Parangot, Andre Parker, Robert Parker, Melanie Parks, Stephen Patterson, Eddie

NETWORKS, STATIONS, AND SERVICES REPRESENTED—Continued

Paylor, Wade Payson-Denney, Evan Perez, Clayton Perry, Katelyn Petroka, Abigail Phillip, Scott Pisczek, Liza Pluto, David Poarch, Katelyn Polantz, Michelle Poley, Ryan Pollock, Lauren Pratapas, Mark Preston, Shimon Prokupecz, Meghan Puryear, Federico Quadrani, Meghan Rafferty, Manu Raju, James Rankin, Pallavi Reddy, Maeve Reston, Samantha Reyes, Casey Riddle, Paulina Rios, Raul Rios-Hernandez, Jennifer Rizzo, Kristina Roberts, Gregory Robertson, David Robinson, John Robinson, Brian Rokus, Jedd Rosche, Lindy Royce-Bartlett, Diane Ruggiero, Boris Sanchez, Jose Sanfuentes, Amanda Sansone, Michelle Santayana, Ziris Savage, Kara Scannell, Douglas Schantz, John Scheuer, Theodore Schleifer, Jessica Schneider, Daniel Schwarz, James Sciutto, Raquel Scott, Gregory Seaby, Sunlen Serfaty, Monica Serrano Quintero, Abigail Sharpe, John Shaylor, David Shortell, David Siegel, Jeffery Simms, Jeff Simon, Jennifer Simpson, Kathleen Skinski, Steven Sloan, Rachel Smolkin, Kelly Smoot, Cassandra Spodak, Derek St. Onge, Jessica Stanton, Elizabeth Stark, Barbara Starr, Scott Stead, John Stevenson, Carrie Stevenson, Morgan Stoviak, Rachel Streitfeld, Katherine Sullivan, Juana Summers, Dustin Tanner, Jacob Tapper, Sophia Tatum, Mallory Thompson, Tamara Thorp, Brian Todd, Nicolas Toso, Michael Trail, Thanh Tram, Catherine Treyz, Kenneth Tuohey, Christopher Turner, Elizabeth Turrell, Robert Tweed, Brett Tyler, Kim Uhl, Anthony Umrani, Maegan Vazquez, Dawid Vermaak, Tu Vu, Gregory Wallace, Deirdre Walsh, Mark Walz, Eli Watkins, Benjamin Werschkul, Scarlette Whyte, Jamie Wiener, Brenna Williams, Adrienne Winston, Frederick Wiseman, Zachary Wolf, David Wright, Floyd Yarmuth, Takahisa Yokoyama, Robert Yoon, Jeffrey Zeleny, Sasha Zients, Karen Zuker.

CNSNEWS.COM—(571) 267–3500; 325 South Patrick Street, Alexandria, VA 22314: Melanie Arter, Craig Bannister, Michael Chapman, Andrew Eicher, Terence Jeffrey, Craig Millward, Michael Morris, Ngyuen Phuong.

COPE RADIO (SPAIN)—4904 Bett Road, NW., Washington, DC 20016: Juan Martinez Fierro.

COX BROADCASTING—(202) 777–7000; 400 North Capitol Street, NW., #750, Washington, DC 20001: David Chase, George Colli, James Dupree, Jacqueline Fell, Justin Gray, David Johns, Kevin Johnson, Dorey Scheimer, Jon Sonnheim, Patrick Terpstra, Jeffrey L. Williams.

CQ/ROLL CALL—(202) 650–6500; 77 K Street, NE., 8th Floor, Washington, DC 20002–4681: David Banks, Michael Cades, Bian Elkhatib, Thomas McKinless.

CRONKITE NEWS SERVICE—(202) 684–2400; 1834 Connecticut Avenue, NW., Washington, DC 20009: Stephen Crane.

CTI–TV (TAIWAN)—(301) 792–8883; 7 Monona Court, Derwood, MD 20855: E-Ting Chung, Guohua Zang.

CTV CANADIAN TV—(202) 775–0356; 1717 DeSales Street, NW., Suite 354, Washington, DC 20036: Jonathan Austin, William Dugan, Chad Kruger, Richard Madan, Joy Malbon, John Mees, Marley Parker.

CTV–COMMUNITY TV OF PG COUNTY—(202) 383–6061; 9475 Lottsford Road, Largo, MD 20774: David Barnes, Curtis Crutchfield, Ara Laughlin, Rochelle Metzger, Sandra Peaches, Sonia Randev, Christopher Thomas, Patricia Villone Garcia.

DANISH BROADCASTING CORPORATION—(202) 785–1957; 2000 M Street, NW., Suite 890, Washington, DC 20036: Stine Dragsted, Steffen Kretz, Lillian Kretz, Johannes Langkilde, Jacob Lorenzen.

DEUTSCHE WELLE TV—(202) 785–5730; 2000 M Street, NW., Suite 335, Washington, DC 20036: Carolina Chimoy, Henning Goll, Michael Knigge, Florian Kroker, Carmen Kunz, Maya Shwayder, Miodrag Soric, Alexandra von Nahmen, Carsten von Nahmen.

DIVERSIFIED COMMUNICATIONS, INC. (DCI)—2000 M Street, NW., 3rd Floor, Washington, DC 20036: James Butler, Harvey Cofske, Joseph Concaugh, Jr., Ed Courtney, John Craig, Kadesh DuBose, Robert Fetzer, Tomas Harding, Roy Harris, Barry Hecht, Albert Liesegang, Kerry Meyer, Jamie Norins, Misaele Rossetti-Meyer, Anthony Smith, Phillip Smith, Thomas Tyler, Mikko Vuokko, Robert Zajko.

DUTCH TV & RADIO (NOS)—2000 M Street, NW., #365, Washington, DC 20036: Albertus Bos, Jet Mok, Arjen van der Horst, Wouter Zwart.

ENVIRONMENT & ENERGY PUBLISHING, LLC—(202) 628–6500; 122 C Street, NW., Suite 722, Washington, DC 20001: Christopher Farmer, Andrew Holmes, Monica Trauzzi.

ESTONIAN PUBLIC BROADCASTING—(202) 910–8644; 400 Massachusetts Avenue, #1210, Washington, DC 20001: Maria-Ann Rohemae.

EURONEWS—(202) 420–9852; 1100 13th Street, NW., Washington, DC 20005: Stefan Grobe.

EUROPEAN PRESSPHOTO AGENCY—(202) 347–4694; 1122 National Press Building, Washington, DC 20045: Lawrence Miller, Carlos Vilas Delgado.

EUROVISION AMERICAS, INC.—2000 M Street, NW., Suite 300, Washington, DC 20036: Adam Bearne, Damon Bennett, Emilie de Schaetzen, William Dunlop, Tanya Fischer, Lee Grigsby, Jay Hahn, Sarah Lanningham, Adam Mandelson, Glenn Mikols, Priya Narahari, Jihee Park, Jean Pierre Roberts, Eduardo Rosario, John Saunders, Jason Scharf, Peggy Soucy, Thomas Trainor, Clayton Trosclair, Juri von Bonsdorff.

EWTN—(202) 909–2900; 750 First Street, NE., Suite 1115, Washington, DC 20002: Gonzalo Accame, Raymond Arroyo, Jamie Black, Susan Bruce, Matthew Bunson, Todd Burger, Kathleen Burke, Jason Calvi, Toby Capion, John Chipak, Addie Darling, Michael DuBose, Lauren Dueffert, Christopher

NETWORKS, STATIONS, AND SERVICES REPRESENTED—Continued

Edwards, Alfred Faison, Cory Feezer, Paul Fifield, Wyatt Goolsby, Matthew Hadro, Thomas Haller, Rodney Harris, Mark Irons, Elena Isella, Cristina Kelly, Anna Laudiero, Valeria Longhi, Susanna Pinto, Leon Segears, Victoria Stiles, Christian Swezey, Catherine Szeltner.

EYE-TO-EYE VIDEO—4614 Chevy Chase Boulevard, Chevy Chase, MD 20815; Elliot Klayman, Patrick O'Donnell.

FEATURE STORY NEWS—(202) 296–9012; 1730 Rhode Island Avenue, Suite 405, Washington, DC 20036: Andrea Arenas, John Bevir, Malcolm Brown, John Clarke, Kathryn Fisher, Robert Flynn, Rebecca Foster, Robert Frazier, Giles Gibson, Tamara Haddad, Harry Horton, Priscilla Huff, Denis Levkovich, Simon Marks, Kevin McAleese, Murray Pinczuk, Nina-Maria Potts, Daniel Ryntjes.

FEDERAL NEWS RADIO 1500 AM—3400 Idaho Avenue, NW., Washington, DC 20016: Mike Causey, Jason Fornicola, Jory Heckman, Lauren Larson, Scott Maucione, Jason Miller, Michael O'Connell, Nicole Ogrysko, Jared Serbu, Meredith Somers, Thomas Temin, Stephanie Thomas, David Thornton, Terry Wing, Lisa Wolfe.

FEDNET—50 F Street, NW., Suite 1C, Washington, DC 20001: Alexis Bolivar, Keith Carney, Chris Carson, Nate Crookshank, Mattie Friberg, Caleb Hamilton, Alvin Jones, Michael Kirby, Justin Kroener, Iacopo Luzi, Benjamin Mehr, Fariba Pajooh, John Spears, Nairka Trevino.

FINNISH BROADCASTING COMPANY (YLE)—2000 M Street, NW., Suite 890, Washington, DC 20036: Mika Hentunen, Pirkko Poentinen, Paula Vilen.

FOX BUSINESS NETWORK—(202) 684–4000; 400 North Capitol Street, NW., Washington, DC 20001: Laquasha Banks, Michael Bannigan, Bruce Becker, Blake Burman, Sylvia Hall, Martin Jimenez, Mary Kreinbihl, Connell McShane, Christopher Mills, Kristin Rudman, Jennifer Schonberger, Adam Shapiro, Jonathan St. John.

FOX NEWS—(202) 824–6300; 400 North Capitol Street, NW., Washington, DC 20001: Ashley Alderman, Anna Ansell, Vincent Arbogast, William Baier, Leslie Baker, Joshua Banks, Ellison Barber, Calvin Barrett, Stuart Basinger, Robin Beal, Christopher Becker, Judson Berger, Lauren Blanchard, Bryan Boughton, Jennifer Bowman, Neill Bransford, Shannon Bream, Kristin Brown, Jenny Buchholz, Elizabeth Burkhard, Eleanor Jane Campbell, Stephen Carlson, Tucker Carlson, Michael Carpel, Walter Carter, Jr., Barnini Chakraborty, Richard Cockerham, Bryan Cole, Eric Colimore, Eric Conner, Kevin Corke, Charles Couger, Lorraine Crim, Jodie Curtis, NaKeya Davis, Wendy Dawson, Matthew Dean, Debra DeFrank, Joseph DeFrank, Michael Demark, Mary Dennert, Richard DiBella, Brian Doherty, Jason Donner, Peter Doocy, Jerry Echols, William Edmondson, Richard Edson, Michael Emanuel, Tyler Evans, Joel Fagen, Amy Fenton, Mark Finch, Benjamin Florance, Kristin Forehand, Evan Gardner, Jake Gibson, Gary Gillis, Serafin Gomez, Dennis Gonzalez, Trevor Greene, Jennifer Griffin, Lacey Halpern, Guerin Hays, Edward Henry, Catherine Herridge, Stacy Hickman, Martin Hill, Alexander Hume, Lesa Jansen, Nunu Japaridze, William Jenkins, George Jewsevskyj, Torrance Jones, Stephen Jones, Nathalie Joost, Nicholas Kalman, Hufsa Kamal, Stephen Kanicka, Cailin Kearns, Colleen Kenney, Grigory Khananayev, Kevin Kirby, Christine Kitt, Ashley Koerber, Kathryn Krupnik, Howard Kurtz, Donna Lacey, Karl Lamberg-Karlovsky, Philip LeCroy, Lillian LeCroy, Edward Lewis, Jessica Loker, Wayne Lowman, Doug Luzader, Emily Lynn, Michael Maltas, Kevin McClam, George McCloskey, Brigid Mary McDonnell, Brigid Mary McDonnell, Constance McDonough, Cherie McEachern, Douglas McKelway, Erenia Michell, Marina Minas, Tamara Montgomery, Oddessey Moore, Richard Morse, Seleena Muhammad, Tiffany Mullon, Blake Neff, James Nelson, Elise Norris, Andrea O'Grady, Jessica O'Hara, Elizabeth Oday, Quillie Odom, Paige Page, Alex Pappas, Cherie Paquette, Charyssa Parent, Bradford Paxton, Chad Pergram, Sally Persons, Daniel Petrilli, Jacqueline Pham, Alessandra Raffa, Owen Renfro, David Renken, Elizabeth Rhodes, Katheryn Ricalde, Anne Marie Riha, Victor Rios, Christina Robbins, Michael Robbins, John Robertson, Henry Rodgers, Douglas Rohrbeck, James Rosen, Kara Rowland, William Sammon, Lisa Sanfuentes, Craig Savage, Joseph Sciacca, Steve Shelton, Anita Siegfriedt, Jason H. Smith, Teresa Spector, Daniel Stay, Seneca Stevens, Christopher Stirewalt, Matthew Stout, Eric Strain, James Suddeth, Kelly Summers, Patrick Summers, Jennifer Suzara, Louis Tartaglia, Garrett Tenney, Sarah Tobianski, Lucas Tomlinson, Robert Torpey, Bree Tracey, Hayley Turner, Nicole Vinette, Bryce Vinson, Christopher Visioli, Leland Vittert, Philip Vogel, Joel Waldman, Christopher Wallace, John Wallace, Neil Wallace, Jonathan Walter, Donald Ward, Joseph Weber, Amy Wehinger, Meghan Welsh, Caroline Whiteman, Walter Whitley, William Whitson, John Williams, Colleen Williams Vyas, Anne Marie Willis, Anthony Zucconi.

FOX NEWS RADIO—(212) 301–5800; 400 North Capitol Street, NW., Washington, DC 20001: Jason Bonewald, Mitchell Davis, Jonathan Decker, Maria Donovan, Jared Halpern, Kirstin McNary, Jill Nado, Thomas Root, Gurnal Scott, Daniel Shields, Rachel Sutherland, John Sylvester, Henry Weinbloom, Tonya Williams.

FRANCE 2 TELEVISION—(202) 833–1818; 2000 M Street, NW., Suite 320, Washington, DC 20036: Jacques Cardoze, Jacques Cardoze, Laurent Desbois, Louise Dewast, Regis Massini, Arielle Monange, Andreane Williams.

FREE SPEECH RADIO NEWS—2390 Champlain Street, NW., Washington, DC 20009: Edward Becker.

NETWORKS, STATIONS, AND SERVICES REPRESENTED—Continued

FUJI TV JAPAN—(202) 347–1600; 529 14th Street, NW., Suite 330, Washington, DC 20045: Kyle Cardine, Peter Gold, Aaron Maisler, Toshiyuki Matsuyama, Matthew Mosley, Ryutaro Sejima, Tomokazu Shibaki.

GALEI-TZAHAL (ISRAEL ARMY RADIO)—(301) 520–2503; 112 Shaw Avenue, Silver Spring, MD 20904: Drora Perl.

GANNETT GOVERNMENT MEDIA CORP—(703) 750–7479; 1919 Gallows Road, Vienna, VA 22182: Rodney Bryant, Christian Garzone, Benjamin Murray, Lars Schwetje.

GERMAN PRESS AGENCY—(202) 662–1220; 1112 National Press Building, Washington, DC 20045: Christina Eck.

GERMAN PUBLIC RADIO (ARD)—(202) 342–1730; 3132 M Street, NW., Washington, DC 20007: Jan Boesche, Martina Buttler, Martin Ganslmeier, Eva Graumann, Astrid Joehnk, Diana Robbins, Ralph Weber.

GERMAN TV ARD—(202) 298–6535; 3132 M. Street, NW., Washington, DC 20007: Jan Aulenkamp, Claudia Buckenmaier, Verena Buenten, Jan Philipp Burgard, Daniel Doernen, Christina Freitag-Schmitt, Hillery Gallasch, Lars Gesing, Felicitas Klopp, Florian Kroker, Barbara Lautenbach, Stefan Niemann, Sandra Ratzow, Ina-Maria Ruck, Michaela Werner, Marion Zschieschang.

GERMAN TV ZDF—(202) 333–3909; 1077 31st Street, NW., Washington, DC 20007: Hebah Abdalla, Annette Brieger, Kirsten Candia, Lara Esfahani, Heidi Fleischer Belmar, Fabian Gatza, Ralf Hartwig, Barry Haywood, Daniela Heimen, Francisco-Ruben Herrera, Wolfgang Kotke, Wolfgang Macholz, Claudia Offermann, Daniel Pontzen, Steffanie Riess, Ulf-Jensen Roeller, Hans-Peter Schloemer, Jan Seifert, Heike Slansky, Ines Trams, Uyanga Tserenbaljid, Elke Tucker, Lara Wiedeking.

GLOBAL TV CANADA—(202) 824–6771; 400 North Capitol Street, NW., # 850, Washington, DC 20001: Ines de La Cuetara, Jackson Proskow.

GPI TV—P.O. Box 218, Garrett Park, MD 20896: David Lent, Grant Peacock.

GRAY TELEVISION—(202) 910–8644; 400 North Capitol Street, NW., Suite 850, Washington, DC 20001: David Ade, Alana Austin, Ashleigh DeLuca, Theodore Fioraliso, Kyle Midura, Alexandra Miller, Jacqueline Policastro, Samantha-Jo Roth, Alex Yoder, Peter Zampa.

GROUPE TVA—(202) 822–4588; 820 1st Street, NE., Washington, DC 20002: Richard Latendresse.

HEARST TELEVISION INC.—(202) 457–0220; 1100 13th Street, NW., #425, Washington, DC 20005: Rita Aleman, Lee Alexandre, Gail Austin, Rebecca Bainer, Aixa Diaz, Brady Headington, Sheila Jaskot, Sally F. Kidd, Nikole Killion, Lauren McDevitt, Carlos Olazagasti, Precious Osagie-Erese, Chase Pipkin, David Postovit, Erin Skeele, Chris Smyth, Wendy Wilk, Emily Wishingrad.

HELLENIC PUBLIC TV—(202) 413–9219; 2742 Thornbrook Court, Odenton, MD 21113: Eleni Argyri.

HISPANIC COMMUNICATIONS NETWORK—(202) 360–4112; 50 F Street, NW., 8th Floor, Washington, DC 20001: Pablo Castro, Mercy Padilla-Cirino, Benny Paz-Goldenheart.

HONG KONG PHOENIX SATELLITE TELEVISION—101 Constitution Avenue, NW., #920 East, Washington, DC 20001: Yi Qiu Chen, Qingwei Chen, Zhuo Huang, Daniel Lai, Tao Lu, Bingru Wang, Youyou Wang, Tianyi Wang.

HRT/CROATIAN RADIO TELEVISION—1230 23rd Street, Washington, DC 20037: Branka Slavica.

I24 NEWS—(202) 641–9289; 1100 13th Street, NW., Suite 400, Washington, DC 20005: Mounira Al Hmoud, Nina Donaghy, Cliff Herman, Daniel Raviv, Alex Rhoades, Michael Shure.

IMAGINATION MEDIA—(301) 567–2222; 810 Broderick Drive, Oxon Hill, MD 20745: Darnley Hodge, Doreen Hodge, Mansa Johnson, Sowande Tichawonna.

INDEPENDENT TELEVISION NEWS (ITN)—400 North Capitol Street, NW., #899, Washington, DC 20008: Adam Blair, Georgina Brewer, Rebecca Cotterill, Mark Davey, Dominique Heckels, Danielle Isdale, Ben Martin, Robert Moore, Kylie Morris, Jamie Roberton, David Sampy, Christopher Shlemon, Millicent Teasdale, Robert Turner.

JTBC—529 14th Street, NW., Suite 997, Washington, DC 20045: Hans Cho, Hannah Choi, Hyunki Kim, Joseph Lee.

KAISER HEALTH NEWS—(202) 654–1466; 1330 G Street, NW., Washington, DC 20005: Francis Ying.

KOREAN BROADCASTING SYSTEMS—(202) 662–7345; 529 14th Street, NW., Suite 1055, Washington, DC 20045: Katherine Ahn, Jongchul Jun,Yeong Seon Kim, Jae Won Lee, Dongsoo Lim, Kevin Nha, Yoo Han Park, Ja Ryen Seo, James Yu.

KQED—Kitty Felde Daley.

LASLO CONGRESSIONAL BUREAU—(202) 510–4331; 1705 East West Highway, #519, Silver Spring, MD 20910: Matt Laslo.

LILLY BROADCASTING—(202) 440–3831; 400 North Capitol Street, NW., Washington, DC 22201: Kellie Meyer.

LIVE SQUAWK—(848) 218–2497; 8308 Beech Tree Road, Bethesda, MD 20817: Stephanie Chodl.

MACEDONIA RADIO TELEVISION (MRTV)—(202) 286–5252; 1500 Massachusetts Avenue, NW., Washington, DC 20005: Irina Gelevska, Riste Mishev.

MARKETPLACE RADIO—(202) 263–0204; 1150 Connecticut Avenue, #525, Washington, DC 20036: Nancy Marshall-Genzer.

MBC-TV KOREA (MUNHWA)—529 14th Street, NW., #1131, Washington, DC 20045: Won Sup Hyun, Yang Woo Kang, Sang Lim, Seung Jin Park.

NETWORKS, STATIONS, AND SERVICES REPRESENTED—Continued

MCCLATCHY—(202) 383–6061; 1025 Connecticut Avenue, NW., Suite 1100, Washington, DC 20036: Alexa Ard, Maureen Chowdhury, Lindsay Claiborn, Davin Coburn, Benjamin Connors, Nicole Cvetnic, Natalie Fertig, Jonathan Forsythe, Eric Garland, Constance Hyberg, Jessica Koscielniak, Julie McKellogg, Brittany Peterson, Cristina Rayas, Ali Rizvi, Meta Viers, Sarah Whitmire.

METRO TELEPRODUCTIONS—(301) 608–9077; 2500 Virginia Avenue, NW., 416S, Washington, DC 20037: Dave Lilling.

MIDDLE EAST BROADCASTING NETWORKS (MBN)—7600–D Boston Boulevard, Springfield, VA 22153: Rana Abtar, Ali Ahmed, Babu Aryankalavil, Elkheir Bentouila, Hicham Bourar, Sue Doherty, Nkwenten Ejedepang-Koge, John Elgin, Daniel Farkas, Michel Ghandour, Stephen Heiner, Arcelious Joyner, Ali Mahdi, Tim Miller, W. Harrison Moore, Danielle Mrad, Luis Munoz, Adam Nixon, James Norris, Amr Sayed, Joseph Tabet, Karen Yianopoulos, Marwan Zaatar, Elizabeth Zosso.

MOBILE VIDEO SERVICES, LTD.—1620 I Street, NW., #1000, Washington, DC 20006: William Griffitts, Timothy Knapp, Todd Swain, Lawrence VanderVeen.

MORNINGSIDE PARTNERS, LLC—4200 Forbes Road, Suite 200, Lanham, MD 20706: Dawin Adridge, Tony Anthony, Joshua Binswanger, Elizabeth Pennell, Ellen Piacente (fka Portnoy), Juvenal Uribe.

N–TV GERMAN NEWS CHANNEL—1100 13th Street. NW., Suite 400, Washington, DC 20005: Peter Kleim, Alexander Klein.

N24 GERMAN TV—1620 I Street, NW., Suite 1000, Washington, DC 20006: Robert Milford, Steffen Schwarzkopf, Sabine Ulbrich-Strothe.

NATIONAL PUBLIC RADIO—(202) 513–2073; 1111 North Capitol Street, NE., Washington, DC 20002: Stacey Abbott, Elizabeth Acle, Augustine Aiello, Sohail Anwar, Elizabeth Baker, Mark Bejarano, Robert Benincasa, Geoffrey Bennett, Hannah Bloch, Melissa Block, Emily Bogle, Brakkton Booker, Radek Brablec, Geoff Brumfiel, Dennis Byrnes, Ivonne Cala, Rolando Castillo, Ailsa Chang, Daniel Charles, Jessica Cheung, Carlos Chevez, David Chhour, Zachary Coleman, Dennis Coll, Audie Cornish Emery, William Craig, Michael Cullen, Michael Czaplinski, Janet Czys, Susan Davis, Bridget De Chagas, Jessica Deahl, Scott Detrow, Gregory Dixon, Connor Donevan, Aboubacar Drabo, Windsor Edwards, Ronald Elving, Pamela Fessler, Stacey Foxwell, Natalie Friedman Winston, Marilyn Geewax, James Gerhiser, Donald Gonyea, Barry Gordemer, Tamara Gordon, Nell Greenfieldboyce, Samuel Gringlas, Mito Habe-Evans, Nickolai Hammar, Claire Harbage, Richard Harris, Shirley Henry, Scott Horsley, Andrea Hsu, Andrew Huether, Steven Inskeep, Brian Jarboe, Ricky Jarrett, Carrie Johnson, Sarah Kahwash, Emily Kan, John Keator, Michele Kelemen, Mary Kelly, Miranda Kennedy, Prashanth Kinjaram, Alison Kodjak, Danielle Kurtzleben, Kevin Langley, Juleyka Lantigua Williams, Becky Lettenberger, Mara Liasson, Jennifer Liberto, John Marchitto, Melissa Marquis, Colin Marshall, Michel Martin, Kevin Matera, Cecily Meza-Martinez, Nicholas Michael, Joseph Mills, Domenico Montanaro, Brian Naylor, Joe Neel, Brett Neely, Christopher Nelson, Jackie Northam, William O'Leary, Claire O'Neill, Emily Ochsenschlager, Peter Overby, Matthew Ozug, Joseph Palca, Calvin Park, Firoze Pasha, John Poole, Julia Redpath, Lauren Russell, Stacey Samuel, Arnold Seipel, Alina Selyukh Pickeral, Ari Shapiro, Robert C. Siegel, Arthur Silverman, Selena Simmons-Duffin, John Speer, Barbara Sprunt, Rob Stein, Evie Stone, Rebecca Sullivan, Jessica Taylor, Neil David Tevault, Sharahn Thomas, Nina Totenberg, Kevin Wait, Nicole Walker, Gemma Watters, David Welna, Mallory Yu, Pias Zaman, Ariel Zambelich.

NATIONAL SCENE NEWS—1718 M Street, NW., #333, Washington, DC 20036: Alverda Muhammad, Askia Muhammad.

NATIVE AMERICAN TV (NATV)—17690 Old Waterford Road, Leesburg, VA 20176: Sarah Beccio, Robert Cohencious, Rebecca Cohencious, Randolph Flood, Elizabeth Lorenzen.

NBC NEWS—(202) 885–4200; 4001 Nebraska Avenue, NW., Washington, DC 20016: Halimah Abdullah, Douglas A. Adams, Robin Adlerblum, Carmen Alba, Peter Alexander, Bryan Allman, Roberto Aneiva, Patricia Armstrong, Kenneth Austin, Sarah Baker, Andrew Barat, Rodney Batten, Justin Bennett, Jay Blackman, John Blackman, Sarah Blackwill, Victoria Blooston, Joseph Bohannon, Cory Booker, Kendall Breitman, Brittany Bremer, Sally Bronston, Sarah Brooke, Norman Butler, Leigh Ann Caldwell, Anthony Capra, Bradleigh Chance, Lete Childs, Robert Ciridon, Shannon Clash, Samantha Cohen, Nero Cooper, Jr., Thomas Costello, Natalie Cucchiara, Caroline Dann, Abbigail Danzig, Sarah Demarest, Edward Demaria, Marina Di Marzo, Kenneth Dilanian, Evan Dixon, Kristin Donnelly, Michelle Dubert, Victoria Duncan, Chandelis Duster, Alexandra Flowers, David Forman, Scott Foster, Margaret Fox, Melissa Frankel, Jordan Frasier, Drew Fredrickson, Lawrence Gaetano, Dennis Gaffney, John Gaffney, Morgan Gaffney, Mosheh Gains, Suzanne Gamboa, Richard Gardella, Keith Gaskin, Charles Gile, Emily Gold, Avra Gold, Cesar Gonzalez, Robin Gradison, James Greene, Andrew Gross, Garrett Haake, David Hanson, Candice Harrington, Christopher Hartman, Edmund Hatch, Alana Heller, Robert Heritage, Vaughn Hillyard, Charles Hoffman, John Holland, Charles Howard, Diyana Howell, James Hughes, Kasie Hunt, Michael Iacone, Hallie Jackson, Alicia Jennings, Christopher Jimenez, Gwyneth Jones, Robert Kehs, Terence Kelly, Ryan Kiernan, Ann Klenk, Michael Kosnar, Courtney Kube, Michael LaRosa, Jennifer Lee, Arthur Lien, Kathleen Lockhart, Joseph Loebach, James Long, Gary Lynn, Eric Marrapodi, Marc Marriott, Greg Martin, Joseph Martin, Christopher Matthews, Valerie McCabe, Lauren McCulloch, Lee McKinney, Cassie McNamara, Michael Memoli, Christopher Millar, Richard

NETWORKS, STATIONS, AND SERVICES REPRESENTED—Continued

Minner, Andrea Mitchell, Steven Mitnick, Raymond Morada, Shaheen Mozaffari, Mark Murray, Jason Neal, Michelle Neal, Alexander Nerska, Elizabeth Nevins, Hans Nichols, Nkechi Nneji, David O'Brien, Kelly O'Donnell, Hope Palmer, Eddie Paylor, Justin Peligri, Elyse Perlmutter-Gumbiner, Debra Pettit, John Quinnette, Alonzo Ray, Talesha Reynolds, Paul Rigney, Matthew Rivera, Rhonda Rogers, Benjamin Sarlin, Stacey Schmerling, Andrew Scritchfield, Wesley Scruggs, Carl Sears, Joel Seidman, Alexander Seitz-Wald, Joseph Shalhoup, William Sherman, Brandon Sibert, Kimberly Sneed, Gilbert Solorzano, Marianna Sotomayor, Sharon Spurrier, Kenneth Strickland, Jon Sughroue, Haley Talbot, Ronald Thornton, Frank Thorp, Charles Todd, Melanie Turner, Alexandra Vitali, Susan Vitorovich, Cydney Weiner, Kristen Welker, Christopher Whittington, Winston Wilde, Abigail Williams, Louis Williams, Robert Williams, Christopher Williamson, Calum Williamson, Rachel Witkin, Victor Young, Robert Zeliger, Joaquin Zumbado.

NBC NEWS RADIO—(602) 374–6100; 1801 Rockville Pike, 5th Floor, Rockville, MD 20852: Joseph Gomez, Terrence Moore.

NBC NEWSCHANNEL—(202) 783–2615; 400 North Capitol Street, Suite 850, Washington, DC 20001: Blayne Bailey, Sheila Conlin, Ray Davis, Michael Dobal, Jonathan Einarsen, Nancy Ellard, Sheri Lynn Gibson, Nelson Ginebra, Andrew L. Godsick, James Hurt, Julie Jarvis, Jennifer Johnson, Nicole McManus, Brian Mooar, Steven Muskat, Mike O'Connell, Tracie Potts, Cecil John Sills, Christopher Skokowski, Christopher Wiggins.

NEW TANG DYNASTY TV—(202) 449–9480; 8927 Shady Grove Court, Gaithersburg, MD 20877: Teng Chen, Haipeng Du, Matthew Gnaizda, Chuan Lin, Lidiya Loukinykh, Yulin Shi, Yang Wang, Wei Wu, Lixin Yang.

NEWHOUSE SCHOOL/SYRACUSE UNIVERSITY—Syracuse University, 215 University Place, Syracuse, NY 13244: Isabel Chirinos.

NEWS2SHARE—5453 30th Place, NE., Washington, DC 20015: Alejandro Alvarez, Andrew B. Fischer.

NEXSTAR MEDIA GROUP—(202) 570–5610; 400 North Capitol Street, NW., Washington, DC 20001: Kevin Dermody, Andreia Jackson, Alexandra Limon, Mark Meredith, William Mondora, Jason Newton, James Osman, Jessica Perry, Drew Petrimoulx, Chance Seales, Anna Wiernicki.

NHK—(202) 828–5180; 2030 M Street, NW., #706, Washington, DC 20006: Hitomi Ballard, Sara Cook, Hitoshi Hirouchi, Kenkichi Ishiyama, Torao Kono, Benjamin Marks, David McCagg, Yoshihiko Nakai, Hirohito Nezu, Atsutoshi Nishikawa, Momoca Nishimoto, Jon Querolo, Alicia Rose, Yuka Takagane, Masayoshi Tanaka, Kentaro Tanaka, Kenichi Tanaka, Michiko Tsurumi, Takeshi Yamasaki, Hideki Yui, Masaru Zenke.

NIPPON TV NETWORK—(202) 638–0890; 529 14th Street, NW., #1036, Washington, DC 20045: Takaaki Abe, Asuka Curameng, Katie Harada, Tomoko Horie, Mariko Hoshi, Yukimasa Inoue, Shinjiro Kimura, Leon Roberts, Jumpei Shimizu, Mai Taguchi.

NORWEGIAN BROADCASTING—(202) 785–1460; 2000 M Street, NW., #890, Washington, DC 20036: Tove Bjoergaas, Gro Holm, Anders Magnus, Mari Nilsson.

NOW THIS NEWS—Discovery Networks c/o NowThis, One Discovery Place, Silver Spring, MD 20910: Zinhle Essamuah, Matty Greene, Zahra Haider, Michael Lester, Ian McKenna, Sean Morrow, Allan Piper, Nico Pitney, Versha Sharma.

NTN24—1333 H. Street, NW., Washington, DC 20005: Gustau Alegret, Martha Avila-Lindo, Diana Castaneda-Molina, Fernanda Espinasa-Carvajal, Mario Gonzalez, Marco Granda-Murillo, Julio Moreno-Vargas, Valdemar Rodriguez, Allison Vosloh.

ONE AMERICA—(858) 270–690; 101 Constitution Avenue, NW., Washington, DC 20001: Firas Alallak, Christopher Carter, Kendall Forward, Girish Gaur, Claire Hardwick, Charles Herring, Dawn Herring, John Hines, James Murphy, Jorge Nunez, Young Richardson, Emerald Robinson, Tyler Smith, Michael Warner, Rachael Wood, Gerald Yingst.

PROYECTO PUENTE—2300 Darius Lane, Reston, VA 20191: Dolia Pettingell.

RADIO FRANCE—3126 Dumbarton Street, NW., Washington, DC 20007: Gregory Philipps.

RADIO FRANCE INTERNATIONALE—4509 Ellicott Street, NW., Washington, DC 20016: Anne-Marie Capomaccio-Even, Frederic Carbonne, Anne Corpet, Claude L. Porsella.

RADIO FREE ASIA—(202) 530–4900; 2025 M Street, NW., #300, Washington, DC 20036: Gordon Burnett, Lobsang Chophel, Dorjee Damdul, Rigdhen Dolma, Richard Finney, Dhondup Gonsar, Gwen Ha, King Ho, Chan Nhu Hoang, Gulchehra Hoja, Jilil Kashgary, Andrew Kennedy, Arslan Khakiyev, Vivian Kieffer, Nayrein Kyaw, Jaehak Lim, Kalden Lodoe, Min Mitchell, Corey Munford, Sarkis Najarian, Anh Nguyen, Kuerban Niyazi, Jung-Woo Park, Parameswaran Ponnudurai, Brian William Powell, Henry Ramon, Aungthu Schlenker, Khin Maung Soe, Sarada Taing, Lumbum Tashi, Yeshi Tashi, Hoa Ai Tran, Thomas Vichi, Xiaoquan Wang, Sungwon Yang, Hee Yang, Lobsang Yeshi, Samean Yun.

RADIO FREE EUROPE—(202) 457–6900; 1201 Connecticut Avenue, NW., Washington, DC 20036: Nader Sadighi.

RADIO ONE—(301) 565–8182; 8515 Georgia Avenue, Silver Spring, MD 20910: Kent Kramer, Kashon Powell, Samuel Tatum, Ron Thompson, Jeffrey Wilson.

RADIO VALERA VENEZUELA—529 14th Street, NW., 8th Floor, Washington, DC 20045: Sonia Schott.

NETWORKS, STATIONS, AND SERVICES REPRESENTED—Continued

RCN TELEVISION—(202) 408–5429; 1333 H Street, NW., Washington, DC 20005: Martha Avilo-Lindo, Samuel Rocha-Garzin.

REAL CLEAR POLITICS—(202) 644–8781; 1725 DeSales Street, NW., Suite 700, Washington, DC 20036: Gaspard Le Dem, Sabrina McMillin-Lobo.

REUTERS RADIO & TV—(202) 898–0056; 1333 H Street, NW., 6th Floor, Washington, DC 20005: Daniel Balinovic, Anoo Bharania, Peter Bullock, Arlene Eiras, Dan Fastenberg, Liza Feria, Kevin Fogarty, Marie Frail, Nathan Frandino, Deborah Gembara, Pavithra George, Kurt Hall, Sarah Irwin, Katharine Jackson, Kia Johnson, Vanessa Johnston, Jillian Kitchener, Lisa Lewnes, Deborah Lutterbeck, Labib Nasir, Gershon Peaks, Don Pessin, Mana Rabiee, Fausto Ramon, Joel Reyes, Tom Rowe, Joseph Shaw, Roger Shull, Linda So, George Tamerlani, Erik Tavcar, Scott Vaughan.

RTE–IRISH RADIO & TV—(202) 467–5933; 2000 M Street, NW., #315, Washington, DC 20036: Caitriona Perry.

RURAL TV NEWS—(202) 554–0514; 611 Pennsylvania Avenue, SE., Suite 397, Washington, DC 20003: Janet Adkison, Clif Jackson, Sarah Mock.

RUSSIAN STATE TV AND RADIO (RTR)—(202) 262–2595; 2000 N Street, NW., Suite 810, Washington, DC 20007: Alexander Khristenko, Nikolay Koskin, Anna Semenova, Elena Sokolova.

RUSTAVI 2 BROADCASTING COMPANY—1111 Army Navy Drive, Unit 127, Arlington, VA 22202: David Nikuradze, Aleksandre Papinashvili.

SAGARMATHA TELEVISION—(703) 926–9530; 9655 Hawkshead Drive, Lorton, VA 22079: Nilu Kharel, Ram C. Kharel, Sharmila Uprety.

SCRIPPS NEWS—1100 13th Street, NW., Suite 450, Washington, DC 20005: Matthew Anzur, Kevin Clancy, Eugene Daniels, Mark Fahey, Marc Georges, Jake Godin, Mark Greenblatt, Kathryn Grumke, Lawan Hamilton, Angela Hill, Maren Machles, Richard Meyer, Alexandra Miller, Vivek Narayan, Claude Pruitt, Kyle Pyatt, Corey Rangel, Michael Sacks, Kristine Schantz, Chance Seales, David Shaw, Megan Smith, Patrick Terpstra, Zachary Toombs, Elizabeth Wahl, Ellen Weiss, James Williams.

SEOUL BROADCASTING SYSTEM (SBS)—(202) 637–9850; 529 14th Street, NW., #979, Washington, DC 20045: Hasuk Chung, Woo Sik Kim, Edward Park, Seokmin Sohn, Jiwon Song.

SHENZHEN MEDIA GROUP (SZMG)—(202) 815–6463; 1330S Fair Street, Apartment 1101, Arlington, VA 22202: Zheng Chen, Chi Hai Kwan, Jiangning Li, Qiyang Niu.

SINCLAIR BROADCAST GROUP—(410) 568–1500; 10706 Beaver Dam Road, Cockeysville, MD 21030: Khadija Angrum, William Anderson, Natalia Angulo-Hinkson, Sharyl Attkisson, Laquasha Banks, Bryan Barr, David Bernknopf, Matthew Bernstein, Leandra Bernstein, Alexander Brauer, Christopher Castano, Paul Courson III, Marvin Danielski, Manny Fantis, Adam Fleishman, Elizabeth Hagedorn, Andrew Hall, Kellan Howell, Mark Hyman, Lee Jenkins, Lindsey Leake, Louis Libin, Lisa Lisko, Stephen Loiaconi, Caroline McKee, Elizabeth McKernan, Mark Orchard, Lauren Selsky, Justin Sherman, Jocelyn Sistrunk, Kristin Smith, John Stansfield, Raphael Williams, Eric Zager.

SINOVISION—2111 Jefferson Davis Highway, #202N, Arlington, VA 22202: Han Cui.

SIRIUS XM SATELLITE RADIO—(202) 380–4000; 1500 Eckington Place, NE., Washington, DC 20002: Daniel Berdiel, Katherine Caperton, Paul DeMilio, Tim Farley, Patrick Ferrise, Charla Freeland, Jenna Hecker, Daniel Henning, Robert Henry, Julie Mason, Jennifer McLellan, Jared Rizzi.

SKY NEWS—400 North Capitol Street, NW., #550, Washington, DC 20001: Mark Austin, Tim Gallagher, Anne Hill, Cordelia Lynch, Dickon Mager, Greg Milam, Emily Purser, Duncan Sharp, Emily Upton, Amanda Walker.

SKY NEWS ARABIA—400 North Capitol Street, Suite 770, Washington, DC 20001: Jayyab Abusafia, Mohaimen Aljasheme, Adam Awada, James Martone, Hiba Nasr, Osamah Smysom, Amina Sriri.

SMALL HOUSE PRODUCTIONS—10304 Royal Woods Court, Montgomery Village, MD 20886: Nickouszha Belha, Juan Carlos Diaz, George Leidsmar, Wingel Pinzon, Edwin Ramirez.

SPIEGEL GERMAN TV—(202) 347–1735; 1202 National Press Building, Washington, DC 20045: Karin Assmann.

SRN NEWS (SALEM)—(703) 528–6213; 1901 North Moore Street, #201, Arlington, VA 22209: Gregory Clugston, LeRoy Froom, Walter Hindes, Linda Kenyon, John Lormand, Jeffrey Matzka, Andrew Stewart.

STATELINE.ORG—(202) 552–2188; 901 E Street, NW., Suite 700, Washington, DC 20004: Rebecca Beitsch, Jenni Bergal.

STORYHOUSE PRODUCTIONS—2233 Wisconsin Avenue, NW., #420, Washington, DC 20007: Tina-Jane Krohn, Carsten Oblaender, Thomas Sassenberg.

SWEDISH BROADCASTING—(202) 785–1727; 2000 M Street, NW., Suite 890, Washington, DC 20036: Karin Arenander, Barbro Bergfeldt, Lisa Karlsson.

SWISS BROADCASTING—(202) 429–9668; 2000 M Street, NW., Suite 370, Washington, DC 20036: Emiliano Bos, Peter Duggeli, Pierre Gobet, Raphael Grand, Isabelle Jacobi, Philippe Revaz, Beat Soltermann, Andrea Vosti, Mark Yates.

TALK MEDIA NEWS—(202) 337–5322; 20 F Street, NW., Suite 700, Washington, DC 20001: Michael Olesker, Douglas Christian, Justin Duckham, Gary Gately, Patrick Gavin, Regina Holmes, Anne Jones, Loretta Lewis, Timothy Maier, Ellen Ratner, Bryan Renbaum.

NETWORKS, STATIONS, AND SERVICES REPRESENTED—Continued

TELEMUNDO NETWORK—400 North Capitol Street, NW., Suite 850, Washington, DC 20001: Glenda Contreras, Wilbert Guzman, Edwing Lopez Reyes, Lizeth Juliana Monsalve, Lori Montenegro, Victor Reyes, A. Victoria Rivas-Vazquez, Randy Serrano.

TELESUR—(202) 420–5560; 1100 13th Street, NW., Washington, DC 20005: Jorge Ayala, William Cortes, Alina Duarte, Francesca Emanuele, Jorge Gestoso, Jaime Vera.

TELEVISA NEWS NETWORK (ECO)—1730 Rhode Island Avenue, NW., Suite 405, Washington, DC 20036: Basilio Moutsatsos Morales.

TF1–FRENCH TV—2000 M Street, NW., Suite 870, Washington, DC 20036: Julie Asher, Mathieu Derrien, Bruce Frankel, Bertrand Guez, Josselin Huchet, Catherine Jentile, Axel Monnier, Vincent Mortreux.

THE BERNS BUREAU, INC.—SDG 40, Washington, DC 20510: Matthew Kaye.

THE DAILY CALLER—(202) 506–2003; 1050 17th Street, NW., Suite 900, Washington, DC 20036: Richard McGinniss.

THE HILL—1625 K Street, NE., Suite 900, Washington, DC 20006: Joseph Chocola, Adam DeRosa, Alexandra Goncalves-de-Oliveira, Molly Hooper, Taylor Lorenz, Lisa Movit, Sean Root.

THE NEW YORK TIMES—1627 I Street, NW., Suite 700, Washington, DC 20006: Anthony Chavar.

THE NEWSHOUR WITH JIM LEHRER—3620 S. 27th Street, Arlington, VA 22206: Andrew Bossone, William Brangham, Daniel Bush, Frank Carlson, Emily Carpeaux, Jaywon Choe, David Coles, Daniel Cooney, Lisa Desjardins, Kristen Doerer, Matthew Ehrichs, Larisa Epatko, Jennifer Fadoul, Michael Fritz, Elizabeth Gardinier, Jonathan Gerberg, Geoffrey Lou Guray, Erica Hendry, Jason Kane, Ellis Kim, Pamela Kirkland, Stephanie Kotuby, Samuel Lane, Rhana Natour, Julie Percha, Daniel Sagalyn, Mark Scialla, Justin Scuiletti, Peter Tobia, Rachel Wellford, Jasmine Wright, Daniel Yang, John Yang.

THE REAL NEWS NETWORK—(410) 500–5235; 231 Holliday Street, Baltimore, MD 21202: Kimberly Brown, Marshall Conway, James Daley, Christopher DeMillo, Dwayne Gladden, Taya Graham, Cameron Granadino, David Hebden, Thomas Hedges, Ezekiel Jackson, Stephen Janis, Paul Jay, Alexander Lascaris, Aaron Mate, Dharna Noor, Jaisal Noor, Sharmini Peries, Kayla Rivara, Bashi Rose.

THIS IS AMERICA WITH DENNIS WHOLEY—1333 H Street, NW., Washington, DC 20005: Jerry Cox, Dennis Wholey.

THIS WEEK IN AGRIBUSINESS—(301) 466–7403; 9915 Hillridge Drive, Kensington, MD 20895: Patrick Haggerty.

TIMA—(202) 304–5110; 1620 I Street, NW., Suite 1000, Washington, DC 20006: Yamen Abdalwahab, Khalid Al Rawi, Kristin Richards, Maysam Sarfean.

TIME WARNER CABLE—(202) 783–0565; 400 North Capitol Street, NW., Suite G–95, Washington, DC 20001: Sarah Brooks, Courtney Pence, Alberto Pimienta, Samantha-Jo Roth.

TO THE CONTRARY (PERSEPHONE PRODUCTIONS)—1819 L Street, NW., 7th Floor, Washington, DC 20036: Ariel Edem, Bonnie Erbe-Leckar, Luis Mazariegos, Cari Stein.

TOKYO BROADCASTING SYSTEM—1088 National Press Building, Washington, DC 20045: Shinichiro Ikushima, Makoto Ogata, Shota Sato, So Taira, Elliot Waldman, Nicholas Watkins.

TRT—(703) 401–6482; 529 14th Street, NW., #1085, Washington, DC 20045: Faruk Ayaz, Cengizhan Cevahiroglu, Ali Cilesizoglu, Tuna Sanli, Baybora Tinaz.

TRT WORLD—(202) 800–5734; 1620 Eye Street, NW., Suite 1000, Washington, DC 20006: Tetiana Anderson, Tevhid Nazmi Basturk, Jonathan Brain, Muna Habib, Alexi-Noelle O'Brien-Hosein, Barbaros Sayilgan, Shreya Sen, Juan Silva, Christine Theodorou, Ediz Tiyansan, Huseyin Yilmaz, Aydin Yurtseven.

TV ASAHI—529 14th Street, NW., #1280, Washington, DC 20045: Christina Banoub, William Ding-Everson, Robert Gentry, Takashi Hotta, Renata Janney, Takamori Okada, Ena Suto, Yusuke Takaba, Sho Tsuyuki, Tatsuya Yamashita, Junichi Yoshikawa.

TV GLOBO INTERNATIONAL—(202) 429–2525; 2141 Wisconsin Avenue, NW., Suite L, Washington, DC 20007: Vicente Cinque, Daniel Silva-Pinto, Luis Silva-Pinto.

TV TOKYO—1333 H Street, NW., 5th Floor, Washington, DC 20005: Benjamin Dalton, Moqiu Ma, Yoshiyuki Takahashi, Koudai Uchida.

TV2–DENMARK—2000 M Street, NW., Suite 375, Washington, DC 20036: Peder Jessen, Jesper Steinmetz.

TV3–TELEVISIO DE CATALUNYA—(202) 785–0580; 2000 M Street, NW., Suite 830, Washington, DC 20036: Ismael Monfort, Raquel Sans.

TVBS—2500 Wisconsin Avenue, Washington, DC 20007: Chia-Hui Ni, Shih-Yuan Tuan.

TVE–SPANISH PUBLIC TELEVISION—(202) 785–1813; 2000 M Street, NW., #325, Washington, DC 20036: Carlos Franganillo Hernandez, Alejandro Millan Talavera, Francisco Sevilla Garcia, Anna Maria Ubeda-Carulla.

UNIVISION—(202) 682–6160; 101 Constitution Avenue, NW., Suite 810E, Washington, DC 20001: Enrique Acevedo, Jorge Contreras, Deborah Durham, Pablo Gato, Angel Hernandez, Lourdes Meluza, Fernando Pizarro, Pablo Sanchez, Janet Smith, Claudia Uceda, Julia Vargas, Mario Vizcarra.

USA TODAY—7950 Jones Branch Drive, McLean, VA 22107: Jasper Colt, Stephen Elfers, Shannon Green, Jarrad Henderson, Robert Padavick, Andrew Scott.

VENTANA PRODUCTIONS—(202) 785–5112; 1819 L Street, NW., Washington, DC 20036: Richard Joy, Thomas Knier, Timothy K. Murray, Juan Rocha, Robin Stewart, Mark Thalman.

NETWORKS, STATIONS, AND SERVICES REPRESENTED—Continued

VICE NEWS—U.S. Capitol, Room S–325, Washington, DC 20510: Joshua Hersh, Alexandra Jaffe, Tracy Jarrett, Mary Lucas, Evan McMorris-Santoro, Caroline Modarressy-Tehrani, Christopher Olson, Simone Perez, Christopher Preston, Jesse Seidman, Shawna Thomas, Alexander Thompson, Brian Wheeler, Zachary Wood.

VIETV NETWORK—(215) 883–9738; 1604 Spring Hill Road, Suite 150, Vienna, VA 22182: Thao Dao, Yen Phuong Le, Vi Nguyen, Cynthia Truong, Doanh Vu.

VIEWPOINT COMMUNICATIONS—(301) 565–1650; 8607 2nd Avenue, Suite 402, Silver Spring, MD 20910: Randy Feldman, Benjamin Finkel, Larry Greenblatt, Steven Hamberg, Charles Horn.

VIRGINIA PUBLIC RADIO—703 South Royal Street, Alexandria, VA 22314: Michael Pope.

VOICE OF AMERICA—330 Independence Avenue, SW., Washington, DC 20237: Grace Abdu, Abdushakur Aboud, Ibrahim Ahmed, Brian Allen, Darrell Allen, Vadim Allen, Arash Arabasadi, Carla Babb, Thomas Bagnall, Steve Baragona, Aline Barros, Jacquelin Belizaire, Larry Bond, Michael Bowman, Timothy Brannon, Michael Burke, Carol Castiel, Peggy Chang, Elizabeth Cherneff, Eunjung Cho, Trinlae Choedron, Raymond Choto, Peter Clottey, Woody Crawford, Nicolas Crupi, Minas Dargakis, Jeffery Daugherty, Barbara Davis, Jela de Franceschi, Joan Deluca, Timothee Donangmaye, Geoffrey Fabian, Luis Facal, Joshua Fatzick, Salem Fekadu, Kiera Feldman, Henok Fente, Bruce Ferder, Darren Fox, James Fry, David Futrowsky, William Gallo, Solomon Gebremariam, Sasha Gong, Myroslava Gongadze, Pema Gorap, Richard Green, Adamson Greenbaum, Katherine Gypson, Marcus Harton, Selim Hossain, Iftikhar Hussain, Utami Hussin, Michael Ivey, Gary Jaffe, Kaveh Jamshidi, William Kim, Tatiana Koprowicz, Jesse Koster, Bagassi Koura, Jean-Pierre Leroy, Libo Liu, Victoria Macchi, Mitzi Macias, Vincent Makori, James Malone, Mohammad Manzarpour, Marvin Marion, Eva Mazrieva, Kimseng Men, Tra Mi, Guita Mirsaeedi, Richard Moore, Natalia Mozgovaya, Tabinda Naeem, Thet Naing, Robert Naylor, Paul Ndiho, Sean Neary, Thao Nguyen, Trung Nguyen, Olga Novikova, Rosalie O'Connell, Jesusemen Oni, Thein Oo, Thar Oo, Arunima Pande, Robert Parsell, Nicolas Pinault, Reasey Poch, Farhad Pouladi Najafabadi, Khemara Pov Sok, Carolyn Presutti, John Quinn, Robert Raffaele, James Randle, Gioconda Reynolds, Justin Riley, Ralph Robinson, Edward Rwema, Shahla Sadighi, Cynthia Saine-Spang, Yuni Salim, Mary Salinas, Joad Santa-Rita, Yulia Savchenko, Mony Say, Brian Schiff, Edward Schneider, Jeffrey Seldin, Pema Setsang, Roger Sherman, Michael Shields, Setareh Sieg, George Simkins, Joseph Sipos, Leakhena Sreng, Lisa Stancik, Scott Storkel, Carl Swanson, Aung Sway, Jeffrey Swicord, Kyaw Tha, Kyaw Thein, Michael Theisen, Pinitkarn Tulachom, Greta Van Susteren, Joseph Vitale, Oleksandr Yanevsky, Guofu Yang, Raymond Yeung Yam, Xiaoyan Zhang.

VOYAGE PRODUCTIONS—(202) 276–2848; 565 Pennsylvania Avenue, NW., #302, Washington, DC 20001: Susan Baumel, Ely Lamonica.

WALL STREET JOURNAL—1025 Connecticut Avenue, Washington, DC 20036: Paul Beckett, Johnny Cruz, Judy Grace Marfil, Madeline Marshall, Gerald Seib.

WAMU—4000 Brandywine Street, NW., Washington, DC 20016: Rebecca Adams, Martin Austermuhle, Pat Brogan, Gabriel Bullard, Tayla Burney, Chris Chester, Denise Couture, Carmel Delshad, Martin Di Caro, Alex Drewenskus, Jacob Fenston, Rupert Gardener, Katherine Goldgeier, Jonquilyn Hill, Joshua Johnson, Jesse Johnson, Marc Kilstein, Avery Kleinman, Danielle Knight, Mikaela Lefrak, James Patrick Madden, Bianca Martin, Matthew McCleskey, Alicia Montgomery, Kelsey Proud, Ingalisa Schrobsdorff, Ally Schweitzer, Ruth Tam, Lindsay Thomas, Armando Trull, Jonathan Wilson.

WASHINGTON BUREAU NEWS SERVICE—7425 Savan Point Way, Columbia, MD 21045: Maureen Dezell, Joseph Nelson, Clifford Thorne, Michael Whitney.

WASHINGTON EXAMINER—(202) 459–4943; 1152 15th Street, NW., Suite 200, Washington, DC 20005: Linda Hernandez, Michael Graham, Christopher Lohr.

WASHINGTON RADIO AND PRESS SERVICE—(301) 229–2576; 6702 Pawtucket Road, Bethesda, MD 20817: Hanna Gutmann, Howard Lesser.

WASHINGTONPOST.COM—1150 15th Street, NW., Washington, DC 20071: Monica Akhtar, Reem Akkad, Jason Aldag, Kyle Barss, Dalton Bennett, Gillian Brockell, David Bruns, Elizabeth Casey, Rhonda Colvin, Phoebe Connelly, Malcolm Cook, Nicki DeMarco, Jonathan Elker, McKenna Ewen, Jordan Frasier, Micah Gelman, Bastien Inzaurralde, Natalie Jennings, Claritza Jimenez, Thomas Johnson, Ashleigh Joplin, Javaria Khan, Danielle Kunitz, Whitney Leaming, Tom Legro, Anne Li, Alice Li, Osman Malik, Patrick Martin, Priya Mathew, Daniel Mich, Zoeann Murphy, Julio Negron, Erin O'Connor, Deirdre O'Regan, Jayne Orenstein, Sarah Parnass, Dani Player, Lee Powell, Jorge Ribas, Elyse Samuels, Whitney Shefte, Randy Smith, Jenny Starrs, Peter Stevenson, Daron Taylor, Taylor Turner, Adriana Usero, Victoria Walker, Christopher White.

WDCW—2121 Wisconsin Avenue, NW., Washington, DC 20007: Peter Alvey, Jared Chamberlain, Jose Dominguez, Graham Knight, William Nixon, Jasmine Norwood-Dioulo, Abraham Stubblefield, John Terhar, Cameron Thompson.

WESTWOOD ONE—(202) 457–7991; 2020 M Street, NW., Washington, DC 20036: Bob Costantini, Kevin DeLany, Charles Henry, Barton Tessler.

WETA—(703) 998–1800; 3939 Campbell Avenue, Arlington, VA 22206: Mohammad Ali, Charles Anderson, David Bash, Jeffrey Bates, Timothy Bowen, Donald Brawner, Martin Carr, Enoch Chan, Darzen

NETWORKS, STATIONS, AND SERVICES REPRESENTED—Continued

Chang, Vincent Forcier, Heather Harris, Charles Ide, Kenneth Jones, Christopher Lane, Edward Lee, Nancy Morgan, Paul Nevel, Antonio Pacheco, Jeffrey Rathner, John Satterfield, James Schneider, John Schottle, Willliam Seabrook, Brian Smith, Michael Smith, Paul VanderVeen, Charles Voth, Owen Wood.

WFDC–TV UNIVISION—101 Constitution Avenue, NW., Suite L–100, Washington, DC 20001: Gabriel Castaneda, Alfredo Duarte, Andrea Estupinan, Tsitsiki Felix, Cesar Flores, Jose Garza, Liliana Gonzalez, Paul Guevara Medrano, Carime Hernandez, Emiliana Molina, Idaliz Ortiz, Edwin Pitti, Jackeline Quijano, Raul Ramos, Marcela Rodriguez, Rafael Sanchez Cruz, Franco Schultze, Sara Suarez, Catalina Villegas.

WHITE HOUSE CHRONICLE—1042 Wisconsin Avenue, NW., Washington, DC 20007: Linda Gasparello, Llewellyn King, Barry Worthington.

WHUR—529 Bryant Street, NW., Washington, DC 20059: Candice Adkins, Harold Fisher, Romaine McNair.

WJLA–TV/NEWSCHANNEL 8—(703) 239–9480; 1100 Wilson Boulevard, Arlington, VA 22209: Joaquim Neto, George Amos, Nathan Baca, George Ball, Timothy Barber, Frank Becker, Bradley Bell, Michael Carter-Conneen, Richard Chamberlain, Nancy Chen, April Chunko, Edward Coker, Cheryl Costello, Joseph Defeo, Annamaria Dipietro, Martin C. Doane, Kevin Drennen, Jonathon Elias, Ernie Ensign, Lisa Fletcher, Sam Ford, Anna-Lysa Gayle, Autria Godfrey, Jeffery Goldberg, John Gonzalez, Kendall Griggs, Richard Guastadisegni, Joshua Harrington, Shonty Hawkins, Colby Hochmuth, Horace Holmes, Brian Hopkins, Thomas Hormuth, Ryan Hughes, Ernest Isgro, Samuel Jackson, George Jackson, James Joslyn, Jeffrey Keene, Vanessa M. Koolhof, Jay Korff, Simon Landau, Hsiu Leong, Kevin Lewis, John B. Lewis, David Lucas, Kellye Lynn, Jonathon Mann, James Marcum, Michelle Marsh, Suzanne Mason, Brianne Mcconnell, Qwesi Mccray, Joseph Moise, Dwayne Myers, Olajumoke Olabanji, Thomas Perrell, Richard Reeve, John Rice, Thomas Roussey, Michael Rudd, Amy Schneider, James Scott, Rebecca Sinn, Christopher Stuard, Steven Stuhlmacher, Kimberly Suiters, Sam Sweeney, Scott Taylor, Scott Thuman, Stephen Tschida, Luis Urbina, Michael Vaughn, James Walker, Robert Washington-Anderson, Frederick Wheeler, Ronald Windham, Dale Wright.

WNYC—1642 C Beekman Place, Washington, DC 20009: John O'Connor, Todd Zwillich.

WPFW–FM—(202) 588–0999; 1990 K Street, NW., Washington, DC 20008: Gloria Minott, Gloria Minott.

WPLG–TV10—1717 DeSales Street, Washington, DC 20036: Russell Palombo, Travis Washington.

WRC–TV/NBC–4—40010 Nebraska Avenue, NW., Washington, DC 20005: Jackie Bensen, Charles Bragale, Ashley Brown, Beth Brown, Daniel Buckley, Julie Carey, Evan Carr, Dave Carter, Sean Casey, Joseph Cassano, Aimee Cho, Manel Coleau, Pat Collins, Jeffrey Cridland, David Culver, Tracy Davidson, Samantha Dunne, Edward Durkin, Maureen Feltz, Justin Finch, Meagan Fitzgerald, Jodie Fleischer, Bernard Forte, Tim Furlong, Aaron Gilchrist, Jason Gittlen, Matt Glassman, Michael Goldrick, Jorge Gonzalez, Charles A. Goodknight, Herbert Gordon, Molette Green, Trevor Harmon, Monique Hayes, Jack Heinbaugh, Ricardo Higgins, Susan Hogan, Heather Hutchinson, Lance Ing, Ede Jermin, Lyrone Jones, Keith Jones, Chris Lawrence, Pamela Leahigh, Ronald Leidelmeyer, Erika Leon, Scott MacFarlane, Anthony Mague, John Marcucci, Carlos Martinez, Mark Masecchia, Lauren Mayk, Brian McCrone, Megan McGrath, Brooks Meriwether, Chester Panzer, Patti Petitte, Jeff Piper, Christopher Plater, Michelle Rivera, Kelvin Robinson, Christina Romano, Jim Rosenfield, Meredith Royster, Bruce Ryan, Mark Segraves, Tom Sherwood, Mark Stephens, Andrea Swalec, Robert Sweeney, Andrew Tomasello, Caroline Tucker, Adam Tuss, Jennifer Vasquez, Ambrose Vurnis, Derrick Ward, Tarik Warner, Roy Weinstock, Melinda Woolbright, Kristin Wright Kerwin, Rick Yarborough, Ramon Zayas, Darren Ziegenbein.

WTOP RADIO—3400 Idaho Avenue, NW., Washington, DC 20016: John Aaron, Neal Augenstein, Michelle Basch, Megan Cloherty, Robert Crossling, John Domen, Dennis Foley, Jamie Forzato, Jason Fraley, Noah Frank, Dave Garner, Jessie J. Green, Brennan Haselton, Amanda Iacone, Nick Iannelli, Rich Johnson, Kristi King Lilleston, Dave McConnell, Mitchell Miller, Mike Murillo, Rachel Nania, Brian Oliger, Art Rose, Kate Ryan, Albert Shimabukuro, Zach Shore, Max Smith, Dick Uliano, Ren Zheng.

WTTG–FOX TELEVISION—5151 Wisconsin Avenue, NW., Washington, DC 20016: Matthew Ackland, Melanie Alnwick, Van Applegate, Judith Ayers, Bob Barnard, Earl T. Baysden III, James Beahn, William Beyer, Kyle Carmean, Steve Chenevey, Ronica Cleary, Anthony Colella, Lauren DeMarco, Susan Diviney, Kevin Ebersohl, Michael Fischoff, Tom Fitzgerald, John Frame, Max Giammetta, Daniel Grudovich, Joe Hammond, Michael Horan, Nelson Jones, Paul Lester, Indira LeVine, Tisha Lewis, Alexandra Limon-Parresol, Craig Little, James Lokay, Michael Marantz, Marina Marraco, Wisdom Martin, Ronnie McCray, Paul McGonagle, Holly Morris, Anthony Perkins, Michael Rickard, Beth Riggs, Bryan Roberts, Eugene Russell, F. David Rysak, Mark Sargent, Robert Shon, Sarah Simmons, Joe Spevak, Terri Tolliver, Maureen Umeh, Paul Wagner, Don Watrud, Lindsay Watts, Douglas H. Wilkes, Steven Williams, Shawn Yancy, Annie Yu.

WUSA–TV—(202) 895–5588; 4100 Wisconsin Avenue, NW., Washington, DC 20016: Debra Alfarone, Whitney Amon, Allyson Banks, Howard Bernstein, Eliana Block, Mark Bost, Kurt Brooks, William Broom, Elizabeth Brown-Kaiser, Ellen Bryan, Arielle Buchmann, William Cockey, Janice Coon, Jeffrey Cridland, Sonia Dasgupta, Illeana Diaz Waldman, Eric Flack, Lesli Foster Mathewson, Peggy Fox, Michael Fuhr, Stephanie Gailhard, Stephen Garifo, Delia Goncalves Perry, James Hallman, Nicole Hardesty, Collin Hartsell, James Hash, John Henry, Carlton Houston, Mallory Hughes, Michael Hydeck,

NETWORKS, STATIONS, AND SERVICES REPRESENTED—Continued

Eric Jansen, Jan Jeffcoat, Elizabeth Jia, Chester Johnson, Rebecca Knier, Sarah Konsmo, Hawa Konte, Evan Koslof, Erik Lee, Nicholas Leimbach, Bruce Leshan, Hilary Levin, Adam Longo, Sarah Lydick, Samara Martin Ewing, Andrea McCarren, Joel McDonald, Larry Miller, John Mogor, Christopher Mullen, Peter Muntean, Dolores Olmos, Michael Quander, Stephanie Ramirez, Andrea Roane Skehan, David Satchell, David Scarnato, Charles Shutt, Samantha Tadelman, Erin Thacker, Rhea Titus, Michael Trammell, Mikea Turner, Michael Valerio, Erin Van der Bellen, Melissa Ward, Marcel Warfield, Dion Wiggins, Stephanie Wilson, Ryan Wood, Matthew Yurus.

XINHUA—1740 North 14th Street, Arlington, VA 22209: Yina Guo, Yousong Hu, Shuai Liu, Yingshan Shi.

YAHOO NEWS—1717 DeSales Street, NW., 3rd Floor, Washington, DC 20036: Nancy Baker, Sarah Boxer, Grace Brailsford Cato, Katherine Couric, Brian Goldsmith, Anthony Maciulis, Glenn Williams.

FREELANCE

Freelancers: Reginald Cecchini, Atef Abdulgawad, Mark Abramson, Naser Abu Diab, Aziz Ahmed, Chris Albert, Omar Ali, Damien Alipour, Stuart Ammerman, Patrick Anderson, Scott Andrews, Azadeh Ansari, Siqiao Ao, Bruno Arena, Thomas Armstrong, Adrian Armwood, Eva Artesona, Michael Arthur, Hussein Asmael, Jocelyn Augustino, Jean-Pascal Azais, Travis Renee Baldwin, Mark Banks, Rose Barondess, Stephen Barrett, Matthew Barrick, Reginald Barringer, Satarupa Barua, Marilisa Battistella, Sam Beattie, Steven Beckner, Michael Bellis, Michael Benetato, Catherine Berger, Aaron Bernstein, Sadiq Bilal, Tim Bintrim, John Boal, John Bogley, Warren Bolden, Karen Borland, Wayne Boyd, Charles Breiterman, Michael Broleman, Brooke Brower, Elizabeth Brown, Jon-Christopher Bua, Patrick Buesing, John Bullard, Penny Burk, Mary Burns, Matthew Burton, David Butow, Andrew Caballero-Reynolds, Mary Calvert, Tim Camarda, Christina Cameron, Brett Carlson, Evan Carr, Jessica Carro, Anatolie Casenco, Ching-Yi Chang, Irwin Chapman, David Chaytor, Robert Cherouny, Douglas Christian, Gilles Clarenne, Harvey Cofske, Harvey Cofske, Stacey Cohan, Holley Coil, Manel Coleau, Thomas Coleman, Oliver Contreras Cruz, Kyle Cooper, Pedro Correa, Timothy Cote, Eric Courtney, Thomas Craca, John Craig, Jeffrey Cridland, Alice Crouch, Philip Crowther, Erika Cumber, Patrick Curran, Carla Dakin, Arik Dashevsky, Jennifer Davis, Clinton Davis, William Demas, Gabriella Demczuk, Gary DeMoss, Juanita Dillard, Sakina Dockett, William Donald, Heather Dorf-Dolce, Paul Dougherty, Denise Douglas, Geoffrey Doyle, Alexander Drago, Sonia Dridi, William Dries, Kadesh DuBose, James Duggan, John Dunkin, Stephanie Ebbs, Alexander Edelman, Michael Eldridge, Hosny Elgazar, Dalia Elkomy, Steven Epstein, Manuel Ernst, Rodolfo Estrada, Stephen Fancy, Jared Feinstein, Anne-Marie Fendrick, Andy Field, Shannon Finney, Cesar Flores, Kristin Foellmer, Daniel Fortney, Matthew Fox, Francis French, David Friedman, Christian Galdabini, Gavino Garay, Scott Garber, Mannie Garcia, Philip Geyelin, Zach Gibson, David Girard, John Glennon, Brandon Gobel, David Goldstein, Sam Goodall, Jeffrey Goodman, Robert Gordon, Glenn Gorham, Matthew Grant, Lindsay Graves, Nicholas Greiner, Kevin Griffin, Yuri Gripas, Andrew Grossman, Fayrouz Guerouani, Sait Gurbuz, Carol Guzy, Aso Haji Kakol, Harry Hamburg, Tomas Harding, Steven Harper, Roy Harris, Hamil Harris, Byron Harrison, Jacqueline Hartzenbusch, Oscar Haynes, Barry Haywood, Sean Healey, Barry Hecht, Martin Heina, Mary Janne Henneberg, Ryan Hermelijn, Louise Hernon, Andrea Hines, James Hishchynsky, Adrienne Moira Hopkins, David Hopper, Dean Hovell, Kevin Howard, Jason Hubert, Thierry Humeau, Omar Hussein, Trudy Hutcherson, Heather Hutchinson, Zena Ibrahim, Mohamed Ibrahim, Jerry Jackson, Ryan Jackson, Edward Jennings, Jr., Martha Johnson, Aidan Johnson, Katerra Jones, Hans Juergens, Cathy Kades, Bjorn Karlsson, Kendall Karson, Atsushi Kato, Anastasios Katopodis, Drew Katz, Mike Kellerman, Gregory Kendall-Ball, Peter Kent, Khaled Khairy, Basheer Khaleefah, Sandzhar Khamidov, Kawa Khdr, Karl King, Thomas Jay Kirkpatrick, Samuel Kittner, Kent Klein, Robert Klien, Anna Koblitz-Niemann, David Krupin, Kyle Lanningham, Nancy Lanzendoerfer, Greg Larsen, France Latremoliere, Martin LaVor, Rudy Lawidjaja, Pamela Leahigh, Myron Leake, YiHua Lee, Dexter Leong, Darrell Lewis, Albert Liesegang, Bruce Liffiton, Aaltje Lindeboom, Melvin Lindsey, Maria Lucchini, Jayne Lukas, Colette Luke, Julio Luzquinos, Mary Lynch, Tracey Madigan, Jose Luis Magana, Evy Mages, Ahmed Mahdi, Alicia Majeed, Jeffrey Malet, Jay Mallin, Alexander Mallin, Roman Mamonov, Michele Marcello, Antonio Marques, Jon Martin, Jeff Martino, Emily Massey, James Mathis, Timothy Matkosky, Andre Matthews, Cheriss May, Mathieu Mazza, Brianna McClelland, Tipp McClure, Cynthia McCoo, Ian McDougall, Terrance McEachern, Anna McEntee, Allen McGreevy, Gitte McGuire, Robert McHenry, Daniel McLellan, Tiffany McNeil, Cecile McPherson, William Mears, Martinez Mebane, Lauren Meier, Brooks Meriwether, Rhoda Metcalfe, Kerry Meyer, David Mikutsky, Charles Miller, Takiha Millington, Alfredo Miranda, Justin Mitchell, Shannon Mizell, Takashi Mizukami, Eman Mohammed, William Montague, Willie Moorer, Jane Moran, Paul Morigi, Megan Murray, Peter Murtaugh, Laurie Mylroie, Stephen Narisi, Mohamed Nasser, Anh Nguyen, Virginia Nicolaidis, Lisa Nipp, Leslie Nordby, Richard Norling, Donald O'Berry, Colm O'Molloy, Daniel O'Shea, Michael O'Sullivan, Ralf Oberti, Charles Olmstead, Lars Os, Mohamed Said Ouafi, Quinton Owen, Bernard Ozol, Kingsavanh Pathammavong, Daniel Patsko, Kathryn Patterson, Jay Patterson, Abowd Paul, Grant Peacock, Daniel Peebles, Sharnett Pelzer, Douglas Perkins, Timothy Persinko, Robert Peterson, Vasilios

NETWORKS, STATIONS, AND SERVICES REPRESENTED—Continued

Petros, Ken Pexton, Kerry Picket, Christopher Plater, Shapoor Pourshariati, Michael Purbaugh, Steven Purcell, Ralph Quarry, Jason Quinn, Omar Quinonez, Juan Quiooga, Mark Rabin, Ali Rad, Bryan Rager, Ira Raider, Kutaba Rashid, Rahim Rashidi, Douglas Ray, Austin Reeves, Melanie Reffes, Alexandra Rego, Edward Reinsel, Meixing Ren, Scott Rensberger, Astrid Riecken, James Riggs, Maureen Riley, Olivier Robert, Joshua Roberts, Laura Robinson, Xavier Roca, Eduardo Rodriguez, Jaime Rojas, Peter Roof, Gary Rosenberg, Misaele Rossetti-Meyer, Theodore Roth, D'Annette Roy, Joseph Ruffini, Patrick Ryan, Rafael Saakov, Thomas Sampson, Bruce Santhuff, Tomoaki Sasaki, Quinn Scanlan, Barry Schlegel, Leonard Schmitz, Donald Schoenmann, Emily Schultze, Michael Seium, Hakim Shammo, Michael Shannon, Katherine Shaw, Allison Shelley, Ting Shen, Paulette Shipman-Singleton, Robert Shire, Harry Shoffner, James Sicile, Quentin Silver, Stefan Simons, Paul Skomal, Charles Slie, Anthony Smith, Christie Smith, Cynthia Smith, William Smith, Phillip Smith, Koen Soete, Sergey Sokolov, Andrew Spangenberg, Theodore Spiegler, Thomas Staton, Kathy Stewart, Mark Stoddard, Leslie Storms, Rodney Streeter, David Strong, James Stubbs, Caroline Sucher, Richard Suddeth, Bethany Swain, Robert Sweeney, David Sweet, Kiyoshi Tanno, Jacqueline Taylor, Brandon Tea, Eric Thayer, Michael Theiler, Bert Thomas, Shari Thomas, James Thomas, Joseph Thompson, Rachel Tillman, Gessel Tobias Delgado, Kevin Trainor, Thomas Tyler, Laurie Ure, Benjamin Vaeth-Levin, Marcos Vigil, Andreas Vingaard, Amanda Voisard, Matthew Vossekuil, Mikko Vuokko, Jackie Lyn Walker, Julia Walz, Taofeng Wang, Derrick Ward, Tarik Warner, Ervin Washington, Warren Watson, Aaron Webster, George Weller, Kathrina Werner, Eric White, Dennis Wienecke, Snorre Wik, Malini Wilkes, Roxanne Williams, David Williams, David Willis, Mark Wilson, Anthony Winthrop, Ruth Wittwer Soltermann, Mike Woods, Sicelo Wotshela, Brian Yaklyvich, Nadeem Yaqub, David Zechar, Markus Zeffler, Stratis Zervos, Stratis Zervos, Adrianna Zhang, Ariel Zimerman, Blessing Zulu.

PERIODICAL PRESS GALLERIES*

HOUSE PERIODICAL PRESS GALLERY

The Capitol, H–304, 225–2941

Director.—Robert M. Zatkowski
Deputy Director.—Gerald Rupert, Jr.
Assistant Directors: Jenn Walters, Ryan Hamel

SENATE PERIODICAL PRESS GALLERY

The Capitol, S–320, 224–0265

Director.—Justin Wilson
Deputy Director.—Shawna Blair
Assistant Director.—Nick Mead

EXECUTIVE COMMITTEE OF CORRESPONDENTS

Leo Shane III, Sightline Media Group, *Chairman*
Stephen Cooper, Tax Notes, *Secretary*
Alexander Bolton, The Hill, *Treasurer*
Jason Dick, Roll Call
Anna Palmer, Politico
Philip Elliott, Time Magazine
Tyrone Richardson, BNA News

RULES GOVERNING PERIODICAL PRESS GALLERIES

1. Persons eligible for admission to the Periodical Press Galleries must be bona fide resident correspondents of reputable standing, giving their chief attention to the gathering and reporting of news. They shall state in writing the names of their employers and their additional sources of earned income; and they shall declare that, while a member of the Galleries, they will not act as an agent in the prosecution of claims, and will not become engaged or assist, directly or indirectly, in any lobbying, promotion, advertising, or publicity activity intended to influence legislation or any other action of the Congress, nor any matter before any independent agency, or any department or other instrumentality of the Executive Branch; and that they will not act as an agent for, or be employed by the Federal, or any State, local or foreign government or representatives thereof; and that they will not, directly or indirectly, furnish special or "insider" information intended to influence prices or for the purpose of trading on any commodity or stock exchange; and that they will not become employed, directly or indirectly, by any stock exchange, board of trade or other organization or member thereof, or brokerage house or broker engaged in the buying and selling of any security or commodity. Applications shall be submitted to the Executive Committee of the Periodical Correspondents' Association and shall be authenticated in a manner satisfactory to the Executive Committee.

2. Applicants must be employed by periodicals that regularly publish a substantial volume of news material of either general, economic, industrial, technical, cultural, or trade character. The periodical must require such Washington coverage on a continuing basis and must be owned and operated independently of any government, industry, institution, association, or lobbying organization. Applicants must also be employed by a periodical that is published for profit and is supported chiefly by advertising or by subscription, or by a periodical meeting the conditions in this paragraph but published by a nonprofit organization that, first, operates independently of any government, industry, or institution and, second, does

*Information is based on data furnished and edited by each respective Gallery.

not engage, directly or indirectly, in any lobbying or other activity intended to influence any matter before Congress or before any independent agency or any department or other instrumentality of the Executive Branch. House organs are not eligible.

3. Members of the families of correspondents are not entitled to the privileges of the Galleries.

4. The Executive Committee may issue temporary credentials permitting the privileges of the Galleries to individuals who meet the rules of eligibility but who may be on short-term assignment or temporarily residing in Washington.

5. Under the authority of Rule 6 of the House of Representatives and of Rule 33 of the Senate, the Periodical Galleries shall be under the control of the Executive Committee, subject to the approval and supervision of the Speaker of the House of Representatives and the Senate Committee on Rules and Administration. It shall be the duty of the Executive Committee, at its discretion, to report violations of the privileges of the Galleries to the Speaker or the Senate Committee on Rules and Administration, and pending action thereon, the offending correspondent may be suspended. The committee shall be elected at the start of each Congress by members of the Periodical Correspondents' Association and shall consist of seven members with no more than one member from any one publishing organization. The committee shall elect its own officers and a majority of the committee may fill vacancies on the committee. The list in the Congressional Directory shall be a list only of members of the Periodical Correspondents' Association.

PAUL D. RYAN,
Speaker, House of Representatives.

RICHARD D. SHELBY,
Chair, Senate Committee on Rules and Administration.

MEMBERS ENTITLED TO ADMISSION

PERIODICAL PRESS GALLERIES

Abbott, Ryan: Court House News Service
Abdul-Alim, Jamaal: Diverse Issues in Higher Education
Abel, Allen: Maclean's
Abrahams-Gray, Rosalie: Atlantic Monthly
Adragna, Anthony: Politico
Aftab, Mirza: BNA News
Akin, Stephanie: Roll Call
Albergo, Paul: BNA News
Alberta, Timothy: Politico
Albon, Courtney: Inside Washington Publishers
Alder, Madison: BNA News
Aleem, Zeeshan: Vox Media
Alexander, Parker: BNA News
Alexis, Alexei: BNA News
Al-Faruque, Ferdous: Informa
Allen, Arthur: Politico
Allen, Jonathan: Roll Call
Allmayer, Joshua: Capitol Forum
Allsup, Maeve: BNA News
Alphonse, Lylah: U.S. News & World Report
Altman, Alexander: Time Magazine
Altman, George: Sightline Media Group
Altscher, Judy: The Hill
Alvarez, Priscilla: Atlantic Monthly
Ambrosio, Patrick: BNA News
Anselmo, Joseph: Aviation Week
Antoine, LaTrina: Afro-American Newspapers
Antonides, David: Tax Notes
Aplin, Donald, III: BNA News
Appelbaum, Yonatan: Atlantic Monthly
Apter, Melissa: Gilston-Kalin Communications
Aquino, John: BNA News
Arnsdorf, Isaac: Politico
Ashworth, Jerry: Thompson Information Services
Askarinam, Leah: Inside Elections
Astill, James: Economist
Atkins, Pamela: BNA News
Atwood, John: CCH Inc.
August, Melissa: Time Magazine
Aulino, Margaret: BNA News
Avent, Ryan: Economist
Ayala, Christine: The Hill
Bachai, Sabrina: The Hill
Bade, Rachel: Politico
Baker, Samuel: National Journal
Baksh, Mariam: Morning Consult
Ball, Emily: Atlantic Monthly
Bancroft, John: Inside Mortgage Finance
Barash, Martina: BNA News
Barber, Charles: National Law Journal
Barnes, Denise: Washington Informer
Barnes, Frederic, Jr.: Weekly Standard
Baron, Kevin: Defense One
Barry, Theresa: BNA News
Bartley, Robert: Capitol Forum
Basken, Paul: Chronicle of Higher Education
Basu, Kaustuv: BNA News
Basu, Sandra: U.S. Medicine
Bater, Jeffrey: BNA News
Baumann, Jeannie: BNA News
Beasley, Stephanie: Politico
Beauchamp, Zachary: Vox Media
Beaven, Lara: Inside Washington Publishers
Beavers, Olivia: The Hill
Becker, Bernard, II: Politico
Beckman, Katie: Environment & Energy Publishing
Beddingfield, Matthew: BNA News
Behr, Peter: Environment & Energy Publishing
Behsudi, Adam: Politico
Bell, Kevin: BNA News
Belles, Carina: Atlantic Information Services
Belz, Emily: World Magazine
Bennett, Alison: BNA News
Bennett, Cory: Politico
Benson, Guy: Townhall
Benton, Nicholas: Falls Church News Press
Berenson, Tessa: Time Magazine
Berger, James: Washington Trade Daily
Berger, Mary: Washington Trade Daily
Berman, Russell: Atlantic Monthly
Berman-Gorvine, Martin: BNA News
Bernal, Rafael: The Hill
Bernstein, Danielle: Hotline
Bertuca, Anthony: Inside Washington Publishers
Beutler, Brian: New Republic
Beyoud, Lydia: BNA News
Blackner, Emily: Prince George's Sentinel
Blad, Evie: Education Week
Bliss, Jeffrey: Capitol Forum
Blotner, David: Capitol Forum
Blumenstyk, Goldie: Chronicle of Higher Education
Bogardus, Kevin: Environment & Energy Publishing
Bolstad, Erika: Environment & Energy Publishing
Bolton, Alexander: The Hill
Bomster, Mark: Education Week
Bonaquist, Maria: Tax Notes
Bordelon, Brendan: National Journal
Bottemiller Evich, Helena: Politico
Botterbusch, Lauren: Informa
Boudreau, Catherine: Politico

MEMBERS ENTITLED TO ADMISSION, PERIODICAL PRESS GALLERIES—Continued

Bowman, Bridget: Roll Call
Boyd, Aaron: Sightline Media Group
Boyles, William: Health Market Survey
Bracken, Leonard: BNA News
Bradford, Hazel: Crain Communications
Brandolph, David: BNA News
Brasher, Philip: Agri-Pulse
Bravender, Robin: Environment & Energy Publishing
Breland, Ali: The Hill
Bresnahan, John: Politico
Brevetti, Rossella: BNA News
Britton, Kathryn: BNA News
Brody, Rachel: U.S. News & World Report
Brooks, Michael: RTO Insider
Brostoff, Tera: BNA News
Brown, Dylan: Environment & Energy Publishing
Brownstein, Ronald: National Journal
Bruce, Robert: BNA News
Bruenig, Matthew: Capitol Forum
Bruggeman, Karyn: Hotline
Bruninga, Susan: BNA News
Bruno, Michael: Aviation Week
Brusoe, Peter: BNA News
Bryant, Lori: CEO Update
Buchman, Brandi: Court House News Service
Burton, Kaitlyn: Politico
Byers, Alexander: Politico
Byrnes, Jesse: The Hill
Cahlink, George: Environment & Energy Publishing
Calabresi, Massimo: Time Magazine
Caldwell, Christopher: Weekly Standard
Callahan, Madelyn: BNA News
Cama, Timothy: The Hill
Camera, Lauren: U.S. News & World Report
Campbell, Alexia: Vox Media
Cancryn, Adam: Politico
Caporal, Jack: Inside Washington Publishers
Capps, Kriston: Atlantic Monthly
Carberry, Sean: FCW
Cardoza, Kavitha: Education Week
Carey, William, Jr.: Aviation International News
Carignan, Sylvia: BNA News
Carlile, Amy: Environment & Energy Publishing
Carlson, Jeffrey: Research Institute of America Group
Carney, Jordain: The Hill
Carpenter, Zoe: Nation
Carr, Jennifer: Tax Notes
Casabona, Elizabeth: Thompson Information Services
Cassella, Megan: Politico
Casuga, Jay-Anne: BNA News
Catanese, David: U.S. News & World Report
Cavanagh, Sean: Education Week
Cavas, Christopher: Sightline Media Group
Caygle, Heather: Politico
Chacko, Sarah: The Hill
Chalfant, Morgan: The Hill
Chang, Alvin: Vox Media
Chang, Ashley: Capitol Forum
Chase, Spencer: Agri-Pulse
Chemnick, Jean: Environment & Energy Publishing
Cheney, Kyle: Politico
Chibbaro, Louis, Jr.: Washington Blade
Childers, Andrew: BNA News
Chile, Patricio: BNA News
Chronister, Gregory: Education Week
Cinquegrani, Gayle: BNA News
Cipriano, Michael: Informa
Clark, Charles: Government Executive
Clason, Lauren: The Hill
Clemons, Steven: Atlantic Monthly
Clevenger, Andrew: BNA News
Coffin, James: Public Lands News
Cohen, Ariel: Inside Washington Publishers
Cohen, Jane: BNA News
Cohen, Richard: FCW
Cohen, Zachary: Hotline
Cohn, Alicia: The Hill
Cohn, Amelia: Government Executive
Colman, Zachary: Environment & Energy Publishing
Conetta, Christine: Vox Media
Connolly, Paul: BNA News
Cook, Charles, Jr.: Cook Political Report
Cook, Nancy: Politico
Cook, Steven: BNA News
Cooke, Stephanie: Energy Intelligence
Cooper, Perry: BNA News
Cooper, Stephen: Tax Notes
Coppins, McKay: Atlantic Monthly
Cordell, William, III: Sightline Media Group
Corrigan, John: Government Executive
Cottle, Meredith: Atlantic Monthly
Courtney, Shaun: BNA News
Crampton, Elizabeth: BNA News
Craver, Martha: Kiplinger Washington Editors
Crider, Richie: Thompson Information Services
Crockett, Emily: Vox Media
Crowley, Michael: Politico
Cumings, Stephanie: Tax Notes
Curr, Henry: Economist
Curry, Jonathan: Tax Notes
Cusack, Robert: The Hill
Dabbs, Brian: BNA News
Daly, Kyle: BNA News
Darcey, Susan: Informa
DaSilva, Jessica: BNA News
Datlowe, Nicholas: BNA News
Davenport, Lydia: The Hill
Davidson, Mark: Energy Intelligence
Davies, Stephen: Agri-Pulse
Davis, Sylvia: BNA News
Davison, Laura: BNA News
Debenedetti, Gabriel: Politico

MEMBERS ENTITLED TO ADMISSION, PERIODICAL PRESS GALLERIES—Continued

Demko, Paul: Politico
Derrick, Joshua: World Magazine
Devaney, Timothy: The Hill
Diamond, Daniel: Politico
Diamond, Phyllis: BNA News
Dias, Elizabeth: Time Magazine
Diaz, Jaclyn: BNA News
DiBiagio, Marcia: National Law Journal
Dick, Jason: Roll Call
Dickson, Virgil: Crain Communications
DiCosmo, Bridget: Energy Intelligence
DiMascio, Jennifer: Aviation Week
DiSciullo, Joseph: Tax Notes
Divis, Dee: Inside GNSS
Dixon, Darius: Politico
Dixon, Kim: The Hill
Domone, Dana: BNA News
Dong, Zhaoxia: Epoch Times
Donlan, Thomas: Barron's
Dorrian, Patrick: BNA News
Doubleday, Justin: Inside Washington Publishers
Douglas, Genevieve: BNA News
Dovere, Edward Isaac, Politico
Downey, Theodore: Capitol Forum
Doyle, Kenneth: BNA News
Doyle, Susan: BNA News
Drew, Russell: Aviation Week
Drusch, Andrea: National Journal
Dube, Lawrence, Jr.: BNA News
Duffy, Jennifer: Cook Political Report
Dutra, Antonio: BNA News
Eakin, Britain: Court House News Service
Easley, Cameron: Morning Consult
Easley, Jonathan: The Hill
Ebersole, Jenna: Law360
Eckert, Toby: Politico
Edmonson, Robert: Trains Magazine
Edney, Hazel: Trice Edney Newswire
Edwards, Haley: Time Magazine
Ege, Konrad: Freitag
Egger, Andrew: Weekly Standard
Eggerton, John: Broadcasting & Cable
Ehart, William: CEO Update
Ehley, Brianna: Politico
Eisele, Albert: The Hill
Elfin, Dana: BNA News
Elgatian, Tawny: BNA News
Elis, Niv: The Hill
Elliott, Philip, III: Time Magazine
Ellis, Isobel: National Journal
Emma, Caitlin: Politico
Engelhardt, Courtney: Inside Washington Publishers
Engleman, Eric: Politico
Enoch, Daniel: Agri-Pulse
Ertel, Karen: BNA News
Esquivel, Jesus: Proceso
Everett, John: Politico
Everett, Reynolds: Inside Washington Publishers
Fabian, Jordan: The Hill
Fakile, Oluwatosin: Montgomery County Sentinel
Faler, Brian: Politico
Fasman, Jonathan: Economist
Feinberg, Andrew: Broadband Census
Ferguson, Andrew: Weekly Standard
Ferguson, Brett: FTC: Watch
Ferguson, Hugh: Politico
Ferris, Sarah: Politico
Ferullo, Michael: BNA News
Feuerberg, Gary: Epoch Times
Finn, Teaganne: BNA News
Fitzpatrick, John: BNA News
Flood, Brian: BNA News
Flook, William: Research Institute of America Group
Florko, Nicholas: Inside Washington Publishers
Foran, Clare: Atlantic Monthly
Forbes, Sean: BNA News
Fortnam, Brett: Inside Washington Publishers
Foster, Emily: Tax Notes
Foust, Jeffrey: Space News
Francis, Laura: BNA News
Fribush, Rebecca: BNA News
Frizell, Samuel: Time Magazine
Frostenson, Sarah: Vox Media
Garcia, Eric: Roll Call
Gardner, Lauren: Politico
Garofalo, Patrick: U.S. News & World Report
Gartrell, Antoinette: BNA News
Gaskell, Stephanie: Sightline Media Group
Gattoni-Celli, Luca: Tax Notes
Gatz, Nicholas: Falls Church News Press
Gee, Taylor: Politico
Geller, Eric: Politico
Gerstein, Joshua: Politico
Gewertz, Catherine: Education Week
Gheorghiu, Iulia: Morning Consult
Gibb, Steven: BNA News
Gibson, Stuart: Tax Notes
Gill, Daniel: BNA News
Gilmer, Ellen: Environment & Energy Publishing
Gilpin-Green, Justice: National Journal
Gilston, Meredith: Gilston-Kalin Communications
Gingery, Derrick: Informa
Gizzi, John: NewsMax
Glass, Andrew: Politico
Glatter, Hayley: Atlantic Monthly
Glover, Asha: Tax Notes
Godfrey, Elaine: Atlantic Monthly
Goindi, Geeta: Express India
Gold, Ashley: Politico
Gold, Hadas: Politico
Goldmacher, Shane: Politico
Golshan, Tara: Vox Media
Gonzales, Nathan: Inside Elections
Goslin, JoAnn: BNA News

MEMBERS ENTITLED TO ADMISSION, PERIODICAL PRESS GALLERIES—Continued

Gould, Joseph: Sightline Media Group
Goyal, Raghubir: Asia Today
Graham, David: Atlantic Monthly
Graham, Edward: Morning Consult
Graham, Victoria: BNA News
Gramer, Robert: Foreign Policy
Grandonico, Elizabeth: Crain Communications
Gray, William: Synopsis
Green, Emma: Atlantic Monthly
Green, Kelly: Chronicle of Higher Education
Greene, Michael: BNA News
Gregory, Patrick: BNA News
Gregory, Stephen: Epoch Times
Greiling Keane, Angela: Politico
Grena Manley, Mary Ann: BNA News
Griffiths, Brent: Politico
Groll, Elias: Foreign Policy
Gronewold, Anna: Morning Consult
Guida, Victoria: Politico
Guillen, Alexander: Politico
Guniganti, Pallavi: Global Competition Review
Gunter, William: FCW
Gurciullo, Brianna: Politico
Haberkorn, Jennifer: Politico
Hagen, Lisa: The Hill
Hagstrom, Jerry: National Journal
Hale, Conor: Washington Business Information
Halvorsen, Morgan: Morning Consult
Hamilton, Amy: Tax Notes
Hamrick, Mark: Bankrate.com
Hanna, Andrew: Politico
Hansard, Sara: BNA News
Harbrecht, Douglas: Kiplinger Washington Editors
Harper, Casey: The Hill
Harris, Adam: Chronicle of Higher Education
Harris, Hamil: Afro-American Newspapers
Harris, John: Politico
Haseley, Donna: Inside Washington Publishers
Hawkings, David, Jr.: Roll Call
Hayes, Peter: BNA News
Hedberg, Lars-Eric: BNA News
Hefling, Kimberly: Politico
Hegstad, Maria: Inside Washington Publishers
Heidorn, Richard, Jr.: RTO Insider
Heikkinen, Niina: Environment & Energy Publishing
Helbling, Laura: Informa
Heller, Marc: Environment & Energy Publishing
Hellman, Gregory: Politico
Hellmann, Jessie: The Hill
Hendel, John: Politico
Hendin, Robert: Atlantic Monthly
Hendrie, Paul: BNA News
Henry, Devin: The Hill
Herckis, Mitchel: Government Executive
Hess, Hannah: Environment & Energy Publishing
Hess, Ryan: MII Publications
Hesson, Theodore, III: Politico
Hiar, Corbin: Environment & Energy Publishing
Higgins, Joshua: Inside Washington Publishers
Hill, Keith: BNA News
Hill, Richard: BNA News
Hillman, G.: Politico
Hines, Timoteo: Broadband Census
Hinkes-Jones, Llewellyn: BNA News
Ho, Soyoung: Research Institute of America Group
Hoagland, Isabelle: Inside Washington Publishers
Hoefer, Hayley: U.S. News & World Report
Hoffman, Rebecca: BNA News
Hoffman, William, III: Tax Notes
Holcomb, Justin: Townhall
Holden, Emily: Environment & Energy Publishing
Homan, Timothy: Morning Consult
Hoover, James: Law360
Hopkins, Tatyana: Washington Informer
Hopkinson, Jenny: Politico
Horn, Marissa: BNA News
Horowitz, Jay: BNA News
Horwood, Rachel: Economist
Hotakainen, Robert: Environment & Energy Publishing
Houck, Caroline: Defense One
Housaiux, Matthew: Kiplinger Washington Editors
Howard, Megan: BNA News
Huang, Pochang: Epoch Times
Hudson, Elizabeth: Inside Washington Publishers
Huey, Aisha: FCW
Hujer, Marc: Der Spiegel
Hulac, Benjamin: Environment & Energy Publishing
Hyland, Terence: BNA News
Ichniowski, Thomas: Engineering News-Record
Illing, Sean: Vox Media
Insinna, Valerie: Sightline Media Group
Irfan, Umair: Environment & Energy Publishing
Jagoda, Naomi: The Hill
Janifer, Salina: Research Institute of America Group
Jaworski, Thomas: Tax Notes
Jeane, Jessica: CCH Inc.
Jeffries, Tara: BNA News
Jenkins, Pembroke Nash, Jr.: Time Magazine
Jewell, Randolph, Jr.: BNA News
Jin, Yan: Caijing Magazine
Jing, Hui: Epoch Times
Johnson, Alisa: BNA News
Johnson, Christopher: Washington Blade
Johnson, Clarion: Capitol Forum
Johnson, Derek: FCW
Johnson, Eliana: Politico
Johnson, Fawn: BNA News
Jones, George: CCH Inc.
Jones, Paige: Tax Notes
Joseph, George: Atlantic Monthly
Jost, Kenneth: CQ Researcher
Jowers, Karen: Sightline Media Group
Judson, Jennifer: Sightline Media Group
Juliano, Nicholas: Politico

MEMBERS ENTITLED TO ADMISSION, PERIODICAL PRESS GALLERIES—Continued

Kalish, Brian: Employee Benefit Adviser
Kamens, Jessie: BNA News
Kamisar, Benjamin: The Hill
Kanu, Hassan: BNA News
Karas, Rachel: Inside Washington Publishers
Karem, Brian: Montgomery County Sentinel
Karlin-Smith, Sarah: Politico
Kash, Wyatt: FedScoop
Kasprzak, Thomas: Tax Notes
Katz, Daniel: Aviation Week
Katz, Eric: Government Executive
Katz, Justin: Inside Washington Publishers
Kaufman, Bruce: BNA News
Kelly, Lauren: Atlantic Information Services
Kenen, Joanne: Politico
Kern, Rebecca: BNA News
Kessler, Martha: BNA News
Kettler, Jill: Atlantic Information Services
Khan, Altaf: BNA News
Kheel, Rebecca: The Hill
Kim, Seung Min: Politico
King, Pamela: Environment & Energy Publishing
King, Peter: Politico
King, Robert, Jr.: Politico
Kirby, Paul: Telecommunications Reports
Kirkland, Joel: Environment & Energy Publishing
Klein, Alyson: Education Week
Kliff, Sarah: Vox Media
Klimas, Jacqueline: Politico
Klingst, Ernst: Die Zeit
Knebel, Kristen: BNA News
Knox, Ron: Global Competition Review
Koenig, Bryan: Law360
Koenig, Rebecca: Chronicle of Higher Education
Kohnert-Gross, Natalie: Sightline Media Group
Koo, Jimmy: BNA News
Koren, Marina: Atlantic Monthly
Koss, Geoffrey: Environment & Energy Publishing
Kovach, Kaitlin: Morning Consult
Kovski, Alan: BNA News
Kramer, Alexis: BNA News
Kraushaar, Joshua: National Journal
Krishan, Nihal: Global Competition Review
Kruse, Michael: Politico
Kubetin, William: BNA News
Kuckro, Rod: Environment & Energy Publishing
Kullgren, Ian: Politico
Kumar, Vikas: Capitol Forum
Kurtz, David: Talking Points Memo
Kurtz, Joshua: Environment & Energy Publishing
Kushin, Philip: BNA News
Kussin-Shoptaw, Samuel: BNA News
LaBrecque, Louis: BNA News
Lacey, Anthony: Inside Washington Publishers
Lane, Sylvan: The Hill
LaRoss, David: Inside Washington Publishers
Larsen, Kathryn: BNA News
Larson, Cathleen: BNA News
Larter, David: Sightline Media Group
Lassiter, Shevry: Washington Informer
Last, Jonathan: Weekly Standard
Lavers, Michael: Washington Blade
Leatherman, Jacquelyn: CCH Inc.
Lebo, Diane: BNA News
Lee, Brandon: BNA News
Lee, Constance: Inside Washington Publishers
Lee, Jane: Nature
Lee, Mara: Crain Communications
Lee, Mary: Politico
Lee, Steve: BNA News
Lee, Timothy: Vox Media
Lefebvre, Benjamin: Politico
Lehmann, Evan: Environment & Energy Publishing
Leins, Casey: U.S. News & World Report
Lengell, Sean: Kiplinger Washington Editors
Leonard, Jennifer: Inside Washington Publishers
Leonard, Kimberly: U.S. News & World Report
Leonard, Matthew: FCW
Leone, Daniel: Exchange Monitor Publications
Leonor, Melhor: Politico
Lesesne, William: Research Institute of America Group
Lesniewski, Niels: Roll Call
Leven, Rachel: BNA News
LeVine, Marianne: Politico
LeVines, George: Roll Call
Levy, Gabrielle: U.S. News & World Report
Lewis, Alexander: Tax Notes
Liang, Juan: Inside Washington Publishers
Libson, Elizabeth: Government Executive
Lifhits, Jenna: Weekly Standard
Lillis, Michael: The Hill
Lim, David: Inside Washington Publishers
Lind, Dara: Vox Media
Lippman, Daniel: Politico
Littleton, Julia: Environment & Energy Publishing
Lloyd, Alice: Weekly Standard
Lloyd, Richard: IAM Magazine
Logan, Lee: Inside Washington Publishers
Lorenz, Taylor: The Hill
Lorenzo, Aaron: Politico
Loricchio, Lauren: Tax Notes
Losey, Stephen: Sightline Media Group
Loughran, Matthew: BNA News
Lubell, Karina: Capitol Forum
Luccioli, Colleen: Environment & Energy Publishing
Lucero, Kathryn-Jane, BNA News
Lucia, William: Government Executive
Luety, Allison: Agri-Pulse
Lunney, Kellie: Environment & Energy Publishing
Lustig, Joseph: BNA News
Luthi, Susannah: Inside Washington Publishers
Lynch, George: BNA News
Lynch, Kerry: Aviation International News

MEMBERS ENTITLED TO ADMISSION, PERIODICAL PRESS GALLERIES—Continued

Maas, Angela: Atlantic Information Services
Macagnone, Michael: Law360
Macaluso, Nora: BNA News
MacNeal, Caitlin: Talking Points Memo
Madara, Matthew: Tax Notes
Mahtesian, Charles: Politico
Mandel, Jennifer: Environment & Energy Publishing
Marcos, Cristina: The Hill
Marks, Joseph: Government Executive
Maron, Dina: Scientific American
Marshall, Christa: Environment & Energy Publishing
Martel, Catherine: The Hill
Marx, Claude: FTC:Watch
Matishak, Martin: Politico
Matthews, Dylan: Vox Media
Mauro, Anthony: National Law Journal
Mazmanian, Adam: FCW
Mazumdar, Anandashankar, BNA News
McAllister, William, III: Amos Press
McCaffery, Gregory: BNA News
McCarthy, Meghan: Morning Consult
McCaskill, Nolan: Politico
McCleskey, Ellen: BNA News
McConnell, Charles: Global Competition Review
McCormack, John: Weekly Standard
McCormally, Kevin: Kiplinger Washington Editors
McCutcheon, Charles: BNA News
McDonald, Natashka: Hispanic Link News Service
McGill, Margaret: Politico
McGowan, Kevin: BNA News
McInerney, Susan: BNA News
McIntire, Mary Ellen: Morning Consult
McKnight, Patricia: Frontline Medical Communications
McLaughlin, Jenna: Foreign Policy
McLoughlin, Jennifer: BNA News
McManus, Erin: BNA News
McTague, James: Barron's
Medick, Veit: Der Spiegel
Mehta, Aaron: Sightline Media Group
Mellen, Ruby: Foreign Policy
Menezes, Andrew: Roll Call
Meredith, Emily: Energy Intelligence
Merken, Sara: BNA News
Merolli, Paul: Energy Intelligence
Meyer, Theodoric: Politico
Meyers, David: Roll Call
Mezo, Ingrid: Food Chemical News
Miley, John: Kiplinger Washington Editors
Milhiser, Ellen: Synopsis
Miller, Margaret: Inside Washington Publishers
Miller, Zeke: Time Magazine
Milligan, Susan: U.S. News & World Report
Millman, Jason: Politico
Mitchell, Charles: Inside Washington Publishers
Mitchell, Ellen: The Hill
Mitchell, William, III: FedScoop
Mixter, Bronwyn: BNA News
Mokhiber, Russell: Corporate Crime Reporter
Molnar, Michele: Education Week
Monastersky, Richard: Nature
Montellaro, Zachary: Politico
Moore, Carrie: Telecommunications Reports
Moore, Miles: Crain Communications
Morales, Cecilio: MII Publications
Morello, Lauren: Nature
Moroses, Dylan: Tax Notes
Morring, Thomas, Jr.: Aviation Week
Morris, Catherine: Diverse: Issues in Higher Education
Mulvaney, Erin: National Law Journal
Munoz, Amanda: Townhall
Murphy, Colleen: BNA News
Murphy, Joan: Food Chemical News
Murphy, Patricia: Roll Call
Mutnick, Allison: Hotline
Myers, Meghann: Sightline Media Group
Nasr, Amir: Morning Consult
Nayak, Malathi: BNA News
Needham, Victoria: The Hill
Neidig, Harper: The Hill
Nelles, Roland: Der Spiegel
Nelson, Jill: Pharmaceutical Executive
Nelson, Steven: U.S. News & World Report
Nerbovig, Ariel: BNA News
Neuhauser, Alan: U.S. News & World Report
Neumeyer, Benjamin: Capitol Forum
Newell, James: Slate
Newkirk, Vann, II: Atlantic Monthly
Nicholson, Jonathan: BNA News
Noah, Timothy: Politico
Norman, Brett: Politico
Northey, Hannah: Environment & Energy Publishing
Nussbaum, Matthew: Politico
Nwanevu, Ositadinma: Slate
Obey, Douglas: Inside Washington Publishers
O'Brien, Connor: Politico
O'Brien, Cortney: Townhall
O'Donnell, Katherine: Politico
Ognanovich, Nancy: BNA News
Oh, Soo-Jin: Vox Media
Ollstein, Alice: Talking Points Memo
O'Mahony, Olivier: Paris Match
O'Neil, Megan: Chronicle of Higher Education
Opfer, Christopher: BNA News
Orchowski, Margaret: Hispanic Outlook
Orr, Elizabeth: Informa
Orth, Maureen: Vanity Fair
Otto, Gregory: FedScoop
Packer-Tursman, Judith: Atlantic Information Services
Pak, Kum: USA Journal
Palmer, Anna: Politico
Palmer, Douglas: Politico

MEMBERS ENTITLED TO ADMISSION, PERIODICAL PRESS GALLERIES—Continued

Palmeri, Tara: Politico
Panzino, Charlsy: Sightline Media Group
Parker, Stuart: Inside Washington Publishers
Paschal, Mack: BNA News
Pathe, Simone: Roll Call
Patterson, Brittany: Environment & Energy Publishing
Patterson, James: Kiplinger Washington Editors
Pazanowski, Bernard: BNA News
Pazanowski, Mary Anne: BNA News
Pearson, Samuel: BNA News
Pekow, Charles: American Brewer Media
Pelham, Victoria: BNA News
Penn, Benjamin: BNA News
Perine, Keith: BNA News
Perks, Ashley: The Hill
Phillips, Bergrek: Tax Notes
Pittman, David: Politico
Plautz, Jason: National Journal
Plotkin, Mark: Georgetowner
Polantz, Katelyn: National Law Journal
Pollak, Suzanne: Montgomery County Sentinel
Pomerleau, Mark: Sightline Media Group
Ponnuru, Ramesh: National Review
Pradhan, Rachana: Politico
Prete, Ryan: BNA News
Prokop, Andrew: Vox Media
Pulfrey, Christine: BNA News
Pulsford, Brendan: Capitol Forum
Quinn, Mattie: Governing
Quinones, Manuel: Environment & Energy Publishing
Railey, Kimberly: National Journal
Rainey, Ryan: Morning Consult
Raman, Sandhya: Politico
Ramonas, Andrew: BNA News
Raycheva, Margarita: Food Chemical News
Reardon, Sarah: Nature
Reeves, Dawn: Inside Washington Publishers
Reid, Jonathan, Sr.: Morning Consult
Reilly, Amanda: Environment & Energy Publishing
Reilly, Caitlin: BNA News
Reilly, Sean: Environment & Energy Publishing
Reishus, Mark: Thompson Information Services
Rennie, David: Economist
Ressler, Thomas: Inside Mortgage Finance
Rhodan, Maya: Time Magazine
Rich, Elizabeth: Education Week
Richardson, Tyrone: BNA News
Richman, Nathan: Tax Notes
Ridge, Marian: Economist
Riley, John: Metro Weekly
Rizzuto, Denise: BNA News
Roberts, Edward: CTFN
Roberts, Gregory: BNA News
Robinson, Kimberly: BNA News
Robinson, Melissa: BNA News
Rochkind, Gillian: Capitol Forum
Rogers, Alexander: National Journal
Rogers, David: Politico
Romm, Anthony: Vox Media
Ross, Brandon: BNA News
Ross, Michaela: BNA News
Rothenberg, Stuart: Inside Elections
Rothman, Heather: BNA News
Roubein, Rachel: The Hill
Rousselle, Christine: Townhall
Rubin, Jordan: BNA News
Ruoff, Alexander: BNA News
Ryan, Timothy: Court House News Service
Saenz, Cheryl: BNA News
Sagalow, Zoe: Tax Notes
Saiyid, Amena: BNA News
Salisbury, Melanie: BNA News
Salzano, Carlo: Waterways Journal
Sama, Anita: CEO Update
Samuelsohn, Darren: Politico
Sanchez, Luis, Sr.: Politico
Sarnowski, Jessica: BNA News
Saunders, Karen: BNA News
Savoie, Andre: Aviation Week
Scanlon, Katherine: TheBlaze
Schere, Daniel: Washington Jewish Week
Scherman, Robert: Satellite Business News
Scheuermann, Christoph: Der Spiegel
Schlesinger, Robert: U.S. News & World Report
Schneider, Elena: Politico
Schneier, Cogan: National Law Journal
Schoeff, Mark, Jr.: Crain Communications
Schogol, Jeffrey: Sightline Media Group
Scholtes, Jennifer: Politico
Schomisch, Jeffrey: Thompson Information Services
Schoof, Renee: BNA News
Schor, Elana: Politico
Schreckinger, Benjamin: Politico
Schultz, David: BNA News
Schwartz, David: BNA News
Schwartz, Paul: Montgomery County Sentinel
Scola, Nancy: Politico
Scott, Dean: BNA News
Scott, Dylan: Vox Media
Scott, Katherine: BNA News
Seiden, Daniel: BNA News
Seligman, Lara: Aviation Week
Sellers, Steven: BNA News
Severns-O'Neill, Maggie: Politico
Shafer, Jack: Politico
Shane, Leo, III: Sightline Media Group
Shapiro, Walter: Roll Call
Sheets, Scott: Tax Notes
Shepard, Steven: Politico
Sherman, Jacob: Politico
Shinkman, Paul: U.S. News & World Report
Shreve, Margaret: BNA News
Simmons, Quintin: Tax Notes

MEMBERS ENTITLED TO ADMISSION, PERIODICAL PRESS GALLERIES—Continued

Simon, Vincent: U.S. News & World Report
Siripurapu, Anshuman: Inside Washington Publishers
Skibell, Arianna: Environment & Energy Publishing
Skolnik, Samuel: BNA News
Smelson, Cheryl: BNA News
Smith, Abigail: BNA News
Smith, Brandon: Capitol Forum
Smith, Rhonda: BNA News
Smith-Schoenwalder, Cecelia: Environment & Energy Publishing
Sneed, Tierney: Talking Points Memo
Snider, Ann: Politico
Snow, Nicholas: Oil & Gas Journal
Snow, Shawn: Sightline Media Group
Snyder, Katharine: Mine Safety and Health News
Snyder, Tanya: Politico
Sobczak, Blake: Environment & Energy Publishing
Sodergreen, John: Scudder Publishing
Soderstrom, Nathan: Capitol Forum
Soergel, Andrew: U.S. News & World Report
Somerville, Glenn: Kiplinger Washington Editors
Soraghan, Mike: Environment & Energy Publishing
Spicer, Malcolm: Informa
Sprackland, Teri: Tax Notes
Sprague, John: Budget & Program
Sprenger, Sebastian: Sightline Media Group
Stam, John: BNA News
Stanage, Niall: The Hill
Stanley, Charles: Law360
Stanton, Lynn: Telecommunications Reports
Stanzione, Melissa: BNA News
Stark, Lisa: Education Week
Starks, Timothy, II: Politico
Stecker, Tiffany: BNA News
Stein, Jeffrey: Vox Media
Stein, Michelle: Inside Washington Publishers
Steinberg, Julie: BNA News
Steingart, Jonathan: BNA News
Stern, Mark: Slate
Stiehm, Jamie: U.S. News & World Report
Stiffman, Eden: Chronicle of Higher Education
Stokeld, Frederick: Tax Notes
Stokols, Eli: Politico
Stoller, Daniel: BNA News
Storrow, Benjamin: Environment & Energy Publishing
Stratford, Michael: Politico
Straub, Noelle: Environment & Energy Publishing
Strauss, Daniel: Politico
Street, Jonathan: TheBlaze
Sturges, Peyton: BNA News
Sullivan, Peter: The Hill
Surana, Kavitha: Foreign Policy
Sutter, Susan: Informa
Swann, Deborah: BNA News
Swann, James: BNA News
Swanson, Ian: The Hill
Swarts, Phillip: Space News
Swift, James: Weekly Standard
Swisher, Lawrence: BNA News
Szakonyi, Mark: Journal of Commerce
Tabirian, Alissa: Exchange Monitor Publications
Tahir, Darius: Politico
Takala, Rudy: The Hill
Tamborrino, Kelsey: Politico
Tamkin, Emily: Foreign Policy
Tan, Anjelica: The Hill
Tan, Michelle: Sightline Media Group
Tang, Chiachieh: Sina News
Tankersley, James: Vox Media
Taylor, Thomas: BNA News
Thibodeau, Patrick: IDG Communications
Thompson, Wenoka: DC Spotlight Newspaper
Timms, Edward: Roll Call
Toloken, Steven: Crain Communications
Tomson, William, Jr.: Agri-Pulse
Toobin, Jeffrey: New Yorker
Toosi, Nahal: Politico
Topor, Eric: BNA News
Tosh, Dennis: Thompson Information Services
Tricchinelli, Robert: BNA News
Trimarchi, Michael: BNA News
Trudo, Hanna: Hotline
Trygstad, Kyle: Hotline
Tucker, Charlotte: BNA News
Tully, Sarah: BNA News
Twachtman, Gregory: Frontline Medical Communications
Tyler, Eleanor: BNA News
Tynes, Tyler: Vox Media
Uchill, Joseph: The Hill
Ujifusa, Andrew: Education Week
Unglesbee, Benjamin: Capitol Forum
Unglesbee, Emily: DTN Progressive Farmer
van den Berg, David: Tax Notes
Velarde, Andrew: Tax Notes
Velgot, Stephen: CTFN
Versprille, Allyson: BNA News
Vespa, Matthew: Townhall
Viadero-Rogers, Debra: Education Week
Victor, Kirk: FTC:Watch
Vinik, Daniel: Politico
Vissiere, Helene: Le Point
Vittorio, Andrea: BNA News
Vock, Daniel: Governing
Vogel, Kenneth: Politico
Volpe, Mary Beth: Crain Communications
von Kaenel, Camille: Environment & Energy Publishing
Vyse, Graham: New Republic
Waddell Diab, Melanie: Investment Advisor Magazine
Waggoner, John: Crain Communications
Wagner, Erich: Government Executive
Waldman, Scott: Environment & Energy Publishing

MEMBERS ENTITLED TO ADMISSION, PERIODICAL PRESS GALLERIES—Continued

Walsh, Kenneth: U.S. News & World Report
Walsh, Mark: Education Week
Wang, Beth: Inside Washington Publishers
Wang, Shanshan: Sina News
Ward, Alexander: Vox Media
Warmbrodt, Zachary: Politico
Warminsky, Joseph, III: FedScoop
Warren, Michael: Weekly Standard
Weatherhead, Timothy: The Hill
Weaver, Aubree: Politico
Weaver, Dustin: The Hill
Webb, Kayla: BNA News
Weber, Ricky: Inside Washington Publishers
Webster, James: Agri-Pulse
Weisgerber, Marcus: Defense One
Weixel, Nathaniel: The Hill
Wermund, Benjamin: Politico
Westfall, Sandra: People Magazine
Weyl, Benjamin: Politico
Whieldon, Esther: Politico
Whitaker, Joel: Whitaker Newsletters
White, Molly: Oil Price Information Service
Whiteman, Mauro: The Hill
Wilczek, Yin: BNA News
Wildman, Sarah: Vox Media
Wilhelm, Colin: Politico
Wilhelm, Rebecca: BNA News
Wilkerson, John: Inside Washington Publishers
Wille, Jacklyn: BNA News
Williams, Fred: Bankrate.com
Williams, John: Capitol Forum
Williams, Katherine: The Hill
Williams, Lauren: FCW
Williams, Mark: BNA News
Williams, Michael: Capitol Forum
Williams, Walter: CEO Update
Williams, Joseph, Jr.: U.S. News & World Report
Wilson, Megan: The Hill
Wilson, Reid: The Hill
Wilson, Stanley: Fund Action
Wilt, Evan: World Magazine
Windsor, Joseph: Government Contractor
Winters, Conor: Capitol Forum
Wittenberg, Ariel: Environment & Energy Publishing
Woellert, Lorraine: Politico
Wogan, John: Governing
Wolfe, Kathryn: Politico
Wolff, Eric: Politico
Wong, Scott: The Hill
Woods, John, Jr.: Washington City Paper
Wright, Austin: Politico
Wright, James, Jr.: Afro-American Newspapers
Wyant Johnson, Sara: Agri-Pulse
Yachnin, Jennifer: Environment & Energy Publishing
Yaksick, George, Jr.: CCH Inc.
Yamazaki, Kazutami: Washington Watch
Yang, Bettina: Duowei Times
Yehle, Emily: Environment & Energy Publishing
Yochelson, Mindy: BNA News
Yohannan, Suzanne: Inside Washington Publishers
Yokley, Eli: Morning Consult
Yuill, Barbara: BNA News
Yukhananov, Anna: Morning Consult
Yurkovic, Janet: BNA News
Zaneski, Cyril: Environment & Energy Publishing
Zanona, Melanie: The Hill
Zellweger, Corina: Der Spiegel
Ziezulewicz, Geoffrey: Sightline Media Group
Zimmerman, Eli: Frontline Medical Communications
Zornick, George, III: Nation

PERIODICALS REPRESENTED IN PRESS GALLERIES

House Gallery 225–2941, Senate Gallery 224–0265

AFRO-AMERICAN NEWSPAPERS—(202) 332–0080; 1816 12th Street, NW., Washington, DC 20009: LaTrina Antoine, Hamil Harris, James Wright, Jr.

AGRI-PULSE—(202) 488–0185; 1400 Independence Avenue, SW., Suite 1639, Washington, DC 20250: Philip Brasher, Spencer Chase, Stephen Davies, Daniel Enoch, Allison Luety, William Tomson, Jr., James Webster, Sara Wyant-Johnson.

AMERICAN BREWER MEDIA—(301) 493–6926; 5225 Pooks Hill Road, #1118N, Bethesda, MD 20814: Charles Pekow.

AMOS PRESS—(703) 385–6996; 10121 Ratcliffe Manor Drive, Fairfax, VA 22030: William McAllister III.

ASIA TODAY—(202) 271–1100; 27025 McPherson Square Street, Washington, DC 20038: Raghubir Goyal.

ATLANTIC INFORMATION SERVICES—(202) 775–9008; 1100 17th Street, NW., Suite 300, Washington, DC 20036: Carina Belles, Lauren Kelly, Jill Kettler, Angela Maas, Judith Packer-Tursman.

ATLANTIC MONTHLY—(202) 266–6000; 600 New Hampshire Avenue, NW., Washington, DC 20037: Rosalie Abrahams-Gray, Priscilla Alvarez, Yonatan Appelbaum, Emily Ball, Russell Berman, Kriston Capps, Steven Clemons, McKay Coppins, Meredith Cottle, Clare Foran, Hayley Glatter, Elaine Godfrey, David Graham, Emma Green, Robert Hendin, George Joseph, Marina Koren, Vann Newkirk II.

AVIATION INTERNATIONAL NEWS—(202) 560–5672; 3901 Cathedral Avenue, NW., Washington, DC 20016: William Carey, Jr., Kerry Lynch.

AVIATION WEEK—(703) 997–0234; 1911 North Fort Myer Drive, Suite 600, Arlington, VA 22209: Joseph Anselmo, Michael Bruno, Jennifer DiMascio, Russell Drew, Daniel Katz, Thomas Morring, Jr., Andre Savoie, Lara Seligman.

BANKRATE.COM—(202) 450–4465; National Press Building, Suite 841, Washington, DC 20045: Mark Hamrick, Fred Williams.

BARRON'S—(202) 862–6606; 1025 Connecticut Avenue, NW., Suite 800, Washington, DC 20036: Thomas Donlan, James McTague.

BNA News—(703) 341–3000; 1801 South Bell Street, Arlington, VA 22202: Mirza Aftab, Paul Albergo, Madison Alder, Parker Alexander, Alexei Alexis, Maeve Allsup, Patrick Ambrosio, Donald Aplin III, John Aquino, Pamela Atkins, Margaret Aulino, Martina Barash, Theresa Barry, Kaustuv Basu, Jeffrey Bater, Jeannie Baumann, Matthew Beddingfield, Kevin Bell, Alison Bennett, Martin Berman-Gorvine, Lydia Beyoud, Leonard Bracken, David Brandolph, Rossella Brevetti, Kathryn Britton, Tera Brostoff, Robert Bruce, Susan Bruninga, Peter Brusoe, Madelyn Callahan, Sylvia Carignan, Jay-Anne Casuga, Andrew Childers, Patricio Chile, Gayle Cinquegrani, Andrew Clevenger, Jane Cohen, Paul Connolly, Steven Cook, Perry Cooper, Shaun Courtney, Elizabeth Crampton, Brian Dabbs, Kyle Daly, Jessica DaSilva, Nicholas Datlowe, Sylvia Davis, Laura Davison, Phyllis Diamond, Jaclyn Diaz, Dana Domone, Patrick Dorrian, Genevieve Douglas, Kenneth Doyle, Susan Doyle, Lawrence Dube, Jr., Antonio Dutra, Dana Elfin, Tawny Elgatian, Karen Ertel, Michael Ferullo, Teaganne Finn, John Fitzpatrick, Brian Flood, Sean Forbes, Laura Francis, Rebecca Fribush, Antoinette Gartrell, Steven Gibb, Daniel Gill, JoAnn Goslin, Victoria Graham, Michael Greene, Patrick Gregory, Mary Ann Grena Manley, Sara Hansard, Peter Hayes, Lars-Eric Hedberg, Paul Hendrie, Keith Hill, Richard Hill, Llewellyn Hinkes-Jones, Rebecca Hoffman, Marissa Horn, Jay Horowitz, Megan Howard, Terence Hyland, Tara Jeffries, Randolph Jewell, Jr., Alisa Johnson, Fawn Johnson, Jessie Kamens, Hassan Kanu, Bruce Kaufman, Rebecca Kern, Martha Kessler, Altaf Khan, Kristen Knebel, Jimmy Koo, Alan Kovski, Alexis Kramer, William Kubetin, Philip Kushin, Samuel Kussin-Shoptaw, Louis LaBrecque, Kathryn Larsen, Cathleen Larson, Diane Lebo, Brandon Lee, Steve Lee, Rachel Leven, Matthew Loughran, Kathryn-Jane Lucero, Joseph Lustig, George Lynch, Nora Macaluso, Anandashankar Mazumdar, Gregory McCaffery, Ellen McCleskey, Charles McCutcheon, Kevin McGowan, Susan McInerney, Jennifer McLoughlin, Erin McManus, Sara Merken, Bronwyn Mixter, Colleen Murphy, Malathi Nayak, Ariel Nerbovig, Jonathan Nicholson, Nancy Ognanovich, Christopher Opfer, Mack Paschal, Bernard Pazanowski, Mary Anne Pazanowski, Samuel Pearson, Victoria Pelham, Benjamin Penn, Keith Perine, Ryan Prete, Christine Pulfrey, Andrew Ramonas, Caitlin Reilly, Tyrone Richardson, Denise Rizzuto, Gregory Roberts, Kimberly Robinson, Melissa Robinson, Brandon Ross, Michaela Ross, Heather Rothman, Jordan Rubin, Alexander Ruoff, Cheryl Saenz, Amena Saiyid, Melanie Salisbury, Jessica Sarnowski, Karen Saunders, Renee Schoof, David Schultz, David Schwartz, Dean Scott, Katherine Scott, Daniel Seiden, Steven Sellers, Margaret Shreve, Samuel Skolnik, Cheryl Smelson, Abigail Smith, Rhonda Smith, John Stam, Melissa Stanzione, Tiffany Stecker, Julie Steinberg, Jonathan Steingart, Daniel Stoller, Peyton Sturges, Deborah Swann, James Swann, Lawrence Swisher, Thomas Taylor, Eric Topor, Robert Tricchinelli, Michael Trimarchi, Charlotte Tucker, Sarah Tully, Eleanor Tyler, Allyson Versprille, Andrea Vittorio, Kayla Webb, Yin Wilczek, Rebecca Wilhelm, Jacklyn Wille, Mark Williams, Mindy Yochelson, Barbara Yuill, Janet Yurkovic.

BROADBAND CENSUS—(202) 329–9517; 1750 K Street, NW., Suite 1200, Washington, DC 20006: Andrew Feinberg, Timoteo Hines.

BROADCASTING & CABLE—(571) 830–6440; John Eggerton.

BUDGET & PROGRAM—(202) 328–3860; P.O. Box 6269, Washington, DC 20015: John Sprague.

PERIODICALS REPRESENTED IN PRESS GALLERIES—Continued

CAIJING MAGAZINE—(202) 525–2117; 3133 Connecticut Avenue, NW., 110A, Washington, DC 20008: Yan Jin.

CAPITOL FORUM—(202) 601–2300; 1233 20th Street, NW., Suite 301, Washington, DC 20036: Joshua Allmayer, Robert Bartley, Jeffrey Bliss, David Blotner, Matthew Bruenig, Ashley Chang, Theodore Downey, Clarion Johnson, Vikas Kumar, Karina Lubell, Benjamin Neumeyer, Brendan Pulsford, Gillian Rochkind, Brandon Smith, Nathan Soderstrom, Benjamin Unglesbee, John Williams, Michael Williams, Conor Winters.

CCH INC.—(202) 842–7375; 1015 15th Street, NW., 10th Floor, Washington, DC 20005: John Atwood, Jessica Jeane, George Jones, Jacquelyn Leatherman, George Yaksick, Jr.

CEO UPDATE—(202) 721–7656; 1725 I Street, NW., Suite 200, Washington, DC 20006: Lori Bryant, William Ehart, Anita Sama, Walter Williams.

CHRONICLE OF HIGHER EDUCATION—(202) 466–1000; 1255 23rd Street, NW., Suite 700, Washington, DC 20037: Paul Basken, Goldie Blumenstyk, Kelly Green, Adam Harris, Rebecca Koenig, Megan O'Neil, Eden Stiffman.

COOK POLITICAL REPORT—(202) 739–8525; 600 New Hampshire Avenue, NW., Suite 400, Washington, DC 20037: Charles Cook, Jr., Jennifer Duffy.

CORPORATE CRIME REPORTER—(202) 737–1680; 1209 National Press Building, Washington, DC 20045: Russell Mokhiber.

COURT HOUSE NEWS SERVICE—(443) 783–1463; 125 Chester Avenue, Annapolis, MD 21403: Ryan Abbott, Brandi Buchman, Britain Eakin, Timothy Ryan.

CQ RESEARCHER—(202) 729–1800; 2600 Virginia Avenue, NW., Suite 600, Washington, DC 20037: Kenneth Jost.

CRAIN COMMUNICATIONS—(202) 434–8467; 1200 G Street, NW., Suite 800, Washington, DC 20005: Hazel Bradford, Virgil Dickson, Elizabeth Grandonico, Mara Lee, Miles Moore, Mark Schoeff, Jr., Steven Toloken, Mary Beth Volpe, John Waggoner.

CTFN—(202) 243–8714; 7905 Bounding Bend Court, Rockville, MD 20855: Edward Roberts, Stephen Velgot.

DC SPOTLIGHT NEWSPAPER—(301) 288–7997; P.O. Box 3121, Gaithersburg, MD 20885: Wenoka Thompson.

DEFENSE ONE—(202) 739–8501; 600 New Hampshire Avenue, NW., Washington, DC 20037: Kevin Baron, Caroline Houck, Marcus Weisgerber.

DER SPIEGEL—(202) 347–5222; 1202 National Press Building, Washington, DC 20045: Marc Hujer, Veit Medick, Roland Nelles, Christoph Scheuermann, Corina Zellweger.

DIE ZEIT—(301) 312–8453; 4701 Willard Avenue, #1214, Chevy Chase, MD 20815: Ernst Klingst.

DIVERSE: ISSUES IN HIGHER EDUCATION—(703) 385–2981; 10520 Warwick Avenue, Suite B–8, Fairfax, VA 22030: Jamaal Abdul-Alim, Catherine Morris.

DTN/PROGRESSIVE FARMER—(402) 390–2328; Emily Unglesbee.

DUOWEI TIMES—(301) 658–6808; P.O. Box 3353, Gaithersburg, MD 20885: Bettina Yang.

ECONOMIST—(202) 429–0890; 1730 Rhode Island Avenue, Suite 1210, Washington, DC 20036: James Astill, Ryan Avent, Henry Curr, Jonathan Fasman, Rachel Horwood, David Rennie, Marian Ridge.

EDUCATION WEEK—(301) 280–3100; 6935 Arlington Road, Suite 100, Bethesda, MD 20814: Evie Blad, Mark Bomster, Kavitha Cardoza, Sean Cavanagh, Gregory Chronister, Catherine Gewertz, Alyson Klein, Michele Molnar, Elizabeth Rich, Lisa Stark, Andrew Ujifusa, Debra Viadero-Rogers, Mark Walsh.

EMPLOYEE BENEFIT ADVISER—(571) 403–3835; 1401 Wilson Boulevard, Suite 1002, Arlington, VA 22209: Brian Kalish.

ENERGY INTELLIGENCE—(202) 662–0700; 1401 K Street, NW., Suite 1000, Washington, DC 20005: Stephanie Cooke, Mark Davidson, Bridget DiCosmo, Emily Meredith, Paul Merolli.

ENGINEERING NEWS-RECORD—(301) 649–3508; 10408 Huntley Avenue, Silver Spring, MD 20902: Thomas Ichniowski.

ENVIRONMENT & ENERGY PUBLISHING—(202) 628–6500; 122 C Street, NW., Suite 722, Washington, DC 20001: Katie Beckman, Peter Behr, Kevin Bogardus, Erika Bolstad, Robin Bravender, Dylan Brown, George Cahlink, Amy Carlile, Jean Chemnick, Zachary Colman, Ellen Gilmer, Niina Heikkinen, Marc Heller, Hannah Hess, Corbin Hiar, Emily Holden, Robert Hotakainen, Benjamin Hulac, Umair Irfan, Pamela King, Joel Kirkland, Geoffrey Koss, Rod Kuckro, Joshua Kurtz, Evan Lehmann, Julia Littleton, Colleen Luccioli, Kellie Lunney, Jennifer Mandel, Christa Marshall, Hannah Northey, Brittany Patterson, Manuel Quinones, Amanda Reilly, Sean Reilly, Arianna Skibell, Cecelia Smith-Schoenwalder, Blake Sobczak, Mike Soraghan, Benjamin Storrow, Noelle Straub, Camille von Kaenel, Scott Waldman, Ariel Wittenberg, Jennifer Yachnin, Emily Yehle, Cyril Zaneski.

EPOCH TIMES—(202) 341–9011; 7529 Standish Place, Suite 260, Rockville, MD 20855: Zhaoxia Dong, Gary Feuerberg, Stephen Gregory, Pochang Huang, Hui Jing.

EXCHANGE MONITOR PUBLICATIONS—(571) 527–1402; 1911 North Fort Myer Drive, Suite 310, Arlington, VA 22209: Daniel Leone, Alissa Tabirian.

EXPRESS INDIA—(301) 917–4800; 1541 Wellingham Court, Vienna, VA 22182: Geeta Goindi.

PERIODICALS REPRESENTED IN PRESS GALLERIES—Continued

FALLS CHURCH NEWS PRESS—(703) 532–3267; 200 Little Falls Street, Suite 508, Falls Church, VA 22046: Nicholas Benton, Nicholas Gatz.

FCW—(703) 876–5100; 8521 Greensboro Drive, Suite 510, McLean, VA 22102: Sean Carberry, Richard Cohen, William Gunter, Aisha Huey, Derek Johnson, Matthew Leonard, Adam Mazmanian, Lauren Williams.

FEDSCOOP—(202) 887–8001; 1150 18th Street, NW., Washington, DC 20036: Wyatt Kash, William Mitchell III, Gregory Otto, Joseph Warminsky III.

FOOD CHEMICAL NEWS—(410) 793–5308; 2121 K Street, NW., Suite 300, Washington, DC 20037: Ingrid Mezo, Joan Murphy, Margarita Raycheva.

FOREIGN POLICY—(202) 728–7300; 11 Dupont Circle, NW., Suite 600, Washington, DC 20036: Robert Gramer, Elias Groll, Jenna McLaughlin, Ruby Mellen, Kavitha Surana, Emily Tamkin.

FREITAG—(301) 699–3908; 4506 32nd Street, Mt. Rainier, MD 20712: Konrad Ege.

FRONTLINE MEDICAL COMMUNICATIONS—(240) 221–2400; 2275 Research Boulevard, Suite 400, Rockville, MD 20850: Patricia McKnight, Gregory Twachtman, Eli Zimmerman.

FTC: WATCH—(202) 909–2156; 1776 I Street, NW., Suite 260, Washington, DC 20006: Brett Ferguson, Claude Marx, Kirk Victor.

FUND ACTION—(703) 768–6793; Stanley Wilson.

GEORGETOWNER—(202) 338–4833; 1050 30th Street, NW., Washington, DC 20007: Mark Plotkin.

GILSTON-KALIN COMMUNICATIONS—(301) 460–3060; P.O. Box 5325 Rockville, MD 20848: Melissa Apter, Meredith Gilston.

GLOBAL COMPETITION REVIEW—(202) 831–4660 2122 P Street, NW., Suite 201, Washington, DC 20037: Pallavi Guniganti, Ron Knox, Nihal Krishan, Charles McConnell.

GOVERNING—(202) 862–8802; 1100 Connecticut Avenue, NW., Suite 1300, Washington, DC 20036: Mattie Quinn, Daniel Vock, John Wogan.

GOVERNMENT CONTRACTOR—(202) 377–6201; 1333 H Street, NW., Suite 700, Washington, DC 20005: Joseph Windsor.

GOVERNMENT EXECUTIVE—(202) 739–8501; 600 New Hampshire Avenue, NW., Washington, DC 20037: Charles Clark, Amelia Cohn, John Corrigan, Mitchel Herckis, Eric Katz, Elizabeth Libson, William Lucia, Joseph Marks, Erich Wagner.

HEALTH MARKET SURVEY—(202) 277–1994; P.O. Box 6226, Washington, DC 20016: William Boyles.

THE HILL—(202) 628–8500; 1625 K Street, NW., Suite 900, Washington, DC 20006: Judy Altscher, Christine Ayala, Sabrina Bachai, Olivia Beavers, Rafael Bernal, Alexander Bolton, Ali Breland, Jesse Byrnes, Timothy Cama, Jordain Carney, Sarah Chacko, Morgan Chalfant, Lauren Clason, Alicia Cohn, Robert Cusack, Lydia Davenport, Timothy Devaney, Kim Dixon, Jonathan Easley, Albert Eisele, Niv Elis, Jordan Fabian, Lisa Hagen, Casey Harper, Jessie Hellmann, Devin Henry, Naomi Jagoda, Benjamin Kamisar, Rebecca Kheel, Sylvan Lane, Michael Lillis, Taylor Lorenz, Kathryn-Jane Lucero, Cristina Marcos, Catherine Martel, Ellen Mitchell, Victoria Needham, Harper Neidig, Ashley Perks, Rachel Roubein, Niall Stanage, Peter Sullivan, Ian Swanson, Rudy Takala, Anjelica Tan, Joseph Uchill, Timothy Weatherhead, Dustin Weaver, Nathaniel Weixel, Mauro Whiteman, Katherine Williams, Megan Wilson, Reid Wilson, Scott Wong, Melanie Zanona.

HISPANIC LINK NEWS SERVICE—(202) 234–0280; 1420 N Street, NW., Washington, DC 20005: Natashka McDonald.

HISPANIC OUTLOOK—(202) 236–5595; 2627 O Street, NW., Washington, DC 20007: Margaret Orchowski.

HOTLINE—(202) 266–7900; 600 New Hampshire Avenue, NW., Washington, DC 20037: Danielle Bernstein, Karyn Bruggeman, Zachary Cohen, Allison Mutnick, Hanna Trudo, Kyle Trygstad.

IAM MAGAZINE—(202) 316–4965; 1346 Rittenhouse Street, NW., Washington, DC 20011: Richard Lloyd.

IDG COMMUNICATIONS—(202) 361–2011; 2630 Adams Mill Road, NW., #304, Washington, DC 20009: Patrick Thibodeau.

INFORMA—(202) 899–6900; 2121 K Street, NW., Suite 300, Washington, DC 20037: Ferdous Al-Faruque, Lauren Botterbusch, Michael Cipriano, Susan Darcey, Derrick Gingery, Laura Helbling, Elizabeth Orr, Malcolm Spicer, Susan Sutter.

INSIDE ELECTIONS—(202) 546–2822; 840 First Street, NE., 3rd Floor, Washington, DC 20002: Leah Askarinam, Nathan Gonzales, Stuart Rothenberg.

INSIDE GNSS—(703) 920–9041; 1014 17th Street, South, Arlington, VA 22202: Dee Divis.

INSIDE MORTGAGE FINANCE—(301) 951–1240; 7910 Woodmont Avenue, Suite 1000, Bethesda, MD 20814: John Bancroft, Thomas Ressler.

INSIDE WASHINGTON PUBLISHERS—(703) 416–8500; 1919 South Eads Street, Suite 201, Arlington, VA 22202: Courtney Albon, Lara Beaven, Anthony Bertuca, Jack Caporal, Ariel Cohen, Justin Doubleday, Courtney Engelhardt, Reynolds Everett, Nicholas Florko, Brett Fortnam, Donna Haseley, Maria Hegstad, Joshua Higgins, Isabelle Hoagland, Elizabeth Hudson, Rachel Karas, Justin Katz, Anthony Lacey, David LaRoss, Constance Lee, Jennifer Leonard, Juan Liang, David Lim, Lee Logan, Susannah Luthi, Margaret Miller, Charles Mitchell, Douglas Obey, Stuart Parker, Dawn Reeves, Anshuman Siripurapu, Michelle Stein, Beth Wang, Ricky Weber, John Wilkerson, Suzanne Yohannan.

INVESTMENT ADVISOR MAGAZINE—(202) 370–4810; 1301 Connecticut Avenue, NW., Suite 300, Washington, DC 20036: Melanie Waddell Diab.

PERIODICALS REPRESENTED IN PRESS GALLERIES—Continued

JOURNAL OF COMMERCE—(202) 872–1234; 1300 Connecticut Avenue, NW., Washington, DC 20036: Mark Szakonyi.

KIPLINGER WASHINGTON EDITORS—(202) 887–6400; 1100 13th Street, NW., Suite 750, Washington, DC 20005: Martha Craver, Douglas Harbrecht, Matthew Housaiux, Sean Lengell, Kevin McCormally, John Miley, James Patterson, Glenn Somerville.

LAW360—(646) 783–7100; 1150 18th Street, NW., Suite 600, Washington, DC 20036: Jenna Ebersole, James Hoover, Bryan Koenig, Michael Macagnone, Charles Stanley.

LE POINT—(202) 244–6656; 3234 McKinley Street, NW., Washington, DC 20015: Helen Vissiere.

MACLEAN'S—(301) 233–8479; 2714 Meadowland Court, Olney, MD 20832: Allen Abel.

METRO WEEKLY—(202) 638–6830; 75 I Street, NW., Suite 1150, Washington, DC 20006: John Riley.

MII PUBLICATIONS—(202) 495–1879; 1029 Vermont Avenue, NW., Suite 501, Washington, DC 20005: Ryan Hess, Cecilio Morales.

MINE SAFETY AND HEALTH NEWS—(703) 217–8270; 5935 4th Street, North, Arlington, VA 22203: Katharine Snyder.

MONTGOMERY COUNTY SENTINEL—(301) 838–0788; 22 West Jefferson Street, Suite 309, Rockville, MD 20850: Oluwatosin Fakile, Brian Karem, Suzanne Pollak, Paul Schwartz.

MORNING CONSULT—(202) 506–1957; 729 15th Street, NW., Suite 100, Washington, DC 20005: Mariam Baksh, Cameron Easley, Iulia Gheorghiu, Edward Graham, Anna Gronewold, Morgan Halvorsen, Timothy Homan, Kaitlin Kovach, Meghan McCarthy, Mary Ellen McIntire, Amir Nasr, Ryan Rainey, Jonathan Reid, Sr., Eli Yokley, Anna Yukhananov.

NATION—(202) 546–2239; 110 Maryland Avenue, NE., Suite 308, Washington, DC 20002: Zoe Carpenter, George Zornick III.

NATIONAL JOURNAL—(202) 266–7900; 600 New Hampshire Avenue, NW., Washington, DC 20037: Samuel Baker, Brendan Bordelon, Ronald Brownstein, Andrea Drusch, Isobel Ellis, Justice Gilpin-Green, Jerry Hagstrom, Joshua Kraushaar, Jason Plautz, Kimberly Railey, Alexander Rogers.

NATIONAL LAW JOURNAL—(202) 457–0686; 1100 G Street, NW., Suite 900, Washington, DC 20005: Charles Barber, Marcia DiBiagio, Anthony Mauro, Erin Mulvaney, Katelyn Polantz, Cogan Schneier.

NATIONAL REVIEW—(202) 862–7150; 2221 South Clark Street, Arlington, VA 22202: Ramesh Ponnuru.

NATURE—(202) 737–2355; 968 National Press Building, Washington, DC 20045: Jane Lee, Richard Monastersky, Lauren Morello, Sarah Reardon.

NEW REPUBLIC—(202) 508–4444; 1620 L Street, NW., Suite 300C, Washington, DC 20036: Brian Beutler, Graham Vyse.

NEW YORKER—(212) 286–2860; 1730 Rhode Island Avenue, NW., Suite 603, Washington, DC 20036: Jeffrey Toobin.

NEWSMAX—(202) 315–6632; 1730 Rhode Island Avenue, NW., #405, Washington, DC 20036: John Gizzi.

OIL & GAS JOURNAL—(703) 533–1552; 7013 Jefferson Avenue, Falls Church, VA 22042: Nicholas Snow.

OIL PRICE INFORMATION SERVICE—(301) 284–2000; 9737 Washingtonian Boulevard, Suite 200, Gaithersburg, MD 20878: Molly White.

PARIS MATCH—(202) 721–9571; 5335 Wisconsin Avenue, NW., Suite 850, Washington, DC 20015: Olivier O'Mahony.

PEOPLE MAGAZINE—(202) 861–4000; 1130 Connecticut Avenue, NW., Suite 900, Washington, DC 20036: Sandra Westfall.

PHARMACEUTICAL EXECUTIVE—(301) 656–3339; 7715 Rocton Avenue, Chevy Chase, MD 20815: Jill Nelson.

POLITICO—(703) 647–7999; 1000 Wilson Boulevard, 8th Floor, Arlington, VA 22209: Anthony Adragna, Timothy Alberta, Arthur Allen, Isaac Arnsdorf, Rachel Bade, Stephanie Beasley, Bernard Becker II, Adam Behsudi, Cory Bennett, Helena Bottemiller Evich, Catherine Boudreau, John Bresnahan, Kaitlyn Burton, Alexander Byers, Adam Cancryn, Megan Cassella, Heather Caygle, Kyle Cheney, Nancy Cook, Michael Crowley, Gabriel Debenedetti, Paul Demko, Daniel Diamond, Darius Dixon, Edward Isaac Dovere, Toby Eckert, Brianna Ehley, Caitlin Emma, Eric Engleman, John Everett, Brian Faler, Hugh Ferguson, Sarah Ferris, Lauren Gardner, Taylor Gee, Eric Geller, Joshua Gerstein, Andrew Glass, Ashley Gold, Hadas Gold, Shane Goldmacher, Angela Greiling Keane, Brent Griffiths, Victoria Guida, Alexander Guillen, Brianna Gurciullo, Jennifer Haberkorn, Andrew Hanna, John Harris, Kimberly Hefling, Gregory Hellman, John Hendel, Theodore Hesson III, G. Hillman, Jenny Hopkinson, Eliana Johnson, Nicholas Juliano, Sarah Karlin-Smith, Joanne Kenen, Seung Min Kim, Peter King, Robert King, Jr., Jacqueline Klimas, Michael Kruse, Ian Kullgren, Mary Lee, Benjamin Lefebvre, Melhor Leonor, Marianne LeVine, Daniel Lippman, Aaron Lorenzo, Charles Mahtesian, Martin Matishak, Nolan McCaskill, Margaret McGill, Theodoric Meyer, Jason Millman, Zachary Montellaro, Timothy Noah, Brett Norman, Matthew Nussbaum, Connor O'Brien, Katherine O'Donnell, Anna Palmer, Douglas Palmer, Tara Palmeri, David Pittman, Rachana Pradhan, Sandhya Raman, David Rogers, Darren Samuelsohn, Luis Sanchez, Sr., Elena Schneider, Jennifer Scholtes, Elana Schor, Benjamin Schreckinger, Nancy Scola, Maggie Severns-O'Neill, Jack Shafer, Steven Shepard, Jacob Sherman, Ann Snider,

PERIODICALS REPRESENTED IN PRESS GALLERIES—Continued

Tanya Snyder, Timothy Starks II, Eli Stokols, Michael Stratford, Daniel Strauss, Darius Tahir, Kelsey Tamborrino, Nahal Toosi, Daniel Vinik, Kenneth Vogel, Zachary Warmbrodt, Aubree Weaver, Benjamin Wermund, Benjamin Weyl, Esther Whieldon, Colin Wilhelm, Lorraine Woellert, Kathryn Wolfe, Eric Wolff, Austin Wright.

PRINCE GEORGE'S SENTINEL—(301) 306–9500; 9400 Lanham-Severn Road, Lanham, MD 20706: Emily Blackner.

PROCESO—(202) 737–1538; 529 14th Street, NW., Suite 1117, Washington, DC 20045: Jesus Esquivel.

PUBLIC LANDS NEWS—(703) 553–0552; 133 South Buchanan Street, Arlington, VA 22204: James Coffin.

RESEARCH INSTITUTE OF AMERICA GROUP—(202) 842–1240; 1333 H Street, NW., Suite 7E, Washington, DC 20005: Jeffrey Carlson, William Flook, Soyoung Ho, Salina Janifer, William Lesesne.

ROLL CALL—(202) 650–6500; 1625 I Street, Suite 200, Washington, DC 20006: Stephanie Akin, Jonathan Allen, Bridget Bowman, Jason Dick, Eric Garcia, David Hawkings, Jr., Niels Lesniewski, George LeVines, Andrew Menezes, David Meyers, Patricia Murphy, Simone Pathe, Walter Shapiro, Edward Timms.

RTO INSIDER—(301) 983–0375; 10837 Deborah Drive, Potomac, MD 20854: Michael Brooks, Richard Heidorn, Jr.

SATELLITE BUSINESS NEWS—(202) 785–0505; 5614 Connecticut Avenue, NW., #300, Washington, DC 20015: Robert Scherman.

SCIENTIFIC AMERICAN—(202) 626–2532; 968 National Press Building, Washington, DC 20045: Dina Maron.

SCUDDER PUBLISHING—(410) 923–0688; 1145 Generals Highway, Crownsville, MD 21032: John Sodergreen.

SIGHTLINE MEDIA GROUP—(703) 750–7400; 1919 Gallows Road, Suite 400, Vienna, VA 22182: George Altman, Aaron Boyd, Christopher Cavas, William Cordell III, Stephanie Gaskell, Joseph Gould, Valerie Insinna, Karen Jowers, Jennifer Judson, Natalie Kohnert-Gross, David Larter, Stephen Losey, Aaron Mehta, Meghann Myers, Charlsy Panzino, Mark Pomerleau, Jeffrey Schogol, Leo Shane III, Shawn Snow, Sebastian Sprenger, Michelle Tan, Geoffrey Ziezulewicz.

SINA NEWS—(347) 659–9327; 1415 North Oak Street, Arlington, VA 22209: Chiachieh Tang, Shanshan Wang.

SLATE—(202) 261–1359; 1707 L Street, NW., Suite 800, Washington, DC 20036: James Newell, Ositadinma Nwanevu, Mark Stern.

SPACE NEWS—(571) 421–2300; 1414 Prince Street, Suite 300, Alexandria, VA 22314: Jeffrey Foust, Phillip Swarts.

SYNOPSIS—(301) 728–4988; 20312 Aspenwood Lane, Montgomery Village, MD 20886: William Gray, Ellen Milhiser.

TALKING POINTS MEMO—(202) 758–3048; 1615 L Street, NW., Suite 310, Washington, DC 20036: David Kurtz, Caitlin MacNeal, Alice Ollstein, Tierney Sneed.

TAX NOTES—(703) 533–4400; 400 South Maple Avenue, Suite 400, Falls Church, VA 22046: David Antonides, Maria Bonaquist, Jennifer Carr, Stephen Cooper, Stephanie Cumings, Jonathan Curry, Joseph DiSciullo, Emily Foster, Luca Gattoni-Celli, Stuart Gibson, Asha Glover, Amy Hamilton, William Hoffman III, Thomas Jaworski, Paige Jones, Thomas Kasprzak, Alexander Lewis, Lauren Loricchio, Matthew Madara, Dylan Moroses, Bergrek Phillips, Nathan Richman, Zoe Sagalow, Scott Sheets, Quintin Simmons, Teri Sprackland, Frederick Stokeld, David van den Berg, Andrew Velarde.

TELECOMMUNICATIONS REPORTS —(202) 842–8920; 1015 15th Street, NW., Suite 1000, Washington, DC 20005: Paul Kirby, Carrie Moore, Lynn Stanton.

THEBLAZE—(888) 822–5293; 400 North Capitol Street, NW., Suite 790, Washington, DC 20001: Katherine Scanlon, Jonathan Street.

THOMPSON INFORMATION SERVICES—(202) 872–4000; 4340 East-West Highway, Suite 300, Bethesda, MD, 20814: Jerry Ashworth, Elizabeth Casabona, Richie Crider, Mark Reishus, Jeffrey Schomisch, Dennis Tosh.

TIME MAGAZINE—(202) 861–4000; 1130 Connecticut Avenue, NW., Suite 900, Washington, DC 20036: Alexander Altman, Melissa August, Tessa Berenson, Massimo Calabresi, Elizabeth Dias, Haley Edwards, Philip Elliott III, Samuel Frizell, Pembroke Jenkins, Jr., Zeke Miller, Maya Rhodan.

TOWNHALL—(703) 236–1323; 1735 North Lynn Street, Suite 510, Arlington, VA 22209: Guy Benson, Justin Holcomb, Amanda Munoz, Cortney O'Brien, Christine Rousselle, Matthew Vespa.

TRAINS MAGAZINE—(202) 664–4253; Robert Edmonson.

TRICE EDNEY NEWSWIRE—(202) 291–9310; 6817 Georgia Avenue, NW., Suite 218, Washington, DC 20012: Hazel Edney.

U.S. MEDICINE—(202) 488–0611; Sandra Basu.

U.S. NEWS & WORLD REPORT—(202) 955–2000; 1050 Thomas Jefferson Street, NW., Washington, DC 20007: Lylah Alphonse, Rachel Brody, Lauren Camera, David Catanese, Patrick Garofalo, Hayley Hoefer, Casey Leins, Kimberly Leonard, Gabrielle Levy, Susan Milligan, Steven Nelson, Alan Neuhauser, Robert Schlesinger, Paul Shinkman, Vincent Simon, Andrew Soergel, Jamie Stiehm, Kenneth Walsh, Joseph Williams, Jr.

PERIODICALS REPRESENTED IN PRESS GALLERIES—Continued

USA JOURNAL—(202) 714–7330; P.O. Box 714, Washington, DC 20044: Kum Pak.

VANITY FAIR—(202) 363–5557; 4907 Rockwood Parkway, NW., Washington, DC 20016: Maureen Orth.

VOX MEDIA—(202) 591–1170; 1201 Connecticut Avenue, NW., Suite 1100, Washington, DC 20036: Zeeshan Aleem, Zachary Beauchamp, Alexia Campbell, Alvin Chang, Christine Conetta, Emily Crockett, Sarah Frostenson, Tara Golshan, Sean Illing, Sarah Kliff, Timothy Lee, Dara Lind, Dylan Matthews, Soo-Jin Oh, Andrew Prokop, Anthony Romm, Dylan Scott, Jeffrey Stein, James Tankersley, Tyler Tynes, Alexander Ward, Sarah Wildman.

WASHINGTON BLADE—(202) 747–2077; 1712 14th Street, NW., Washington, DC 20009: Louis Chibbaro, Jr., Christopher Johnson, Michael Lavers.

WASHINGTON BUSINESS INFORMATION—(703) 538–7600; 300 North Washington Street, Suite 200, Falls Church, VA 22046: Conor Hale.

WASHINGTON CITY PAPER—(202) 650–6939; 734 15th Street, NW., Suite 400, Washington, DC 20005: John Woods, Jr.

WASHINGTON INFORMER—(202) 561–4100; 3117 Martin Luther King Jr. Avenue, SE., Washington, DC 20032: Denise Barnes, Tatyana Hopkins, Shevry Lassiter.

WASHINGTON JEWISH WEEK—(301) 230–2222; 11900 Parklawn Drive, Suite 300, Rockville, MD 20852: Daniel Schere.

WASHINGTON TRADE DAILY—(301) 946–0817; P.O. Box 1802, Wheaton, MD 20915: James Berger, Mary Berger.

WASHINGTON WATCH—(301) 263–9023; 5923 Onondaga Road, Bethesda, MD 20816: Kazutami Yamazaki.

WATERWAYS JOURNAL—(703) 524–2490; 5220 North Carlin Springs Road, Arlington, VA 22203: Carlo Salzano.

WEEKLY STANDARD—(202) 293–4900; 1152 15th Street, NW., Suite 200, Washington, DC 20005: Frederic Barnes, Jr., Christopher Caldwell, Andrew Egger, Andrew Ferguson, Jonathan Last, Jenna Lifhits, Alice Lloyd, John McCormack, James Swift, Michael Warren.

WHITAKER NEWSLETTERS—(301) 384–1573; P.O. Box 224, Spencerville, MD 20868: Joel Whitaker.

WORLD MAGAZINE—(202) 744–8987; 4634–C 28th Road South, Arlington, VA 22206: Emily Belz, Joshua Derrick, Evan Wilt.

CONGRESSIONAL DISTRICT MAPS

ALABAMA—Congressional Districts—(7 Districts)

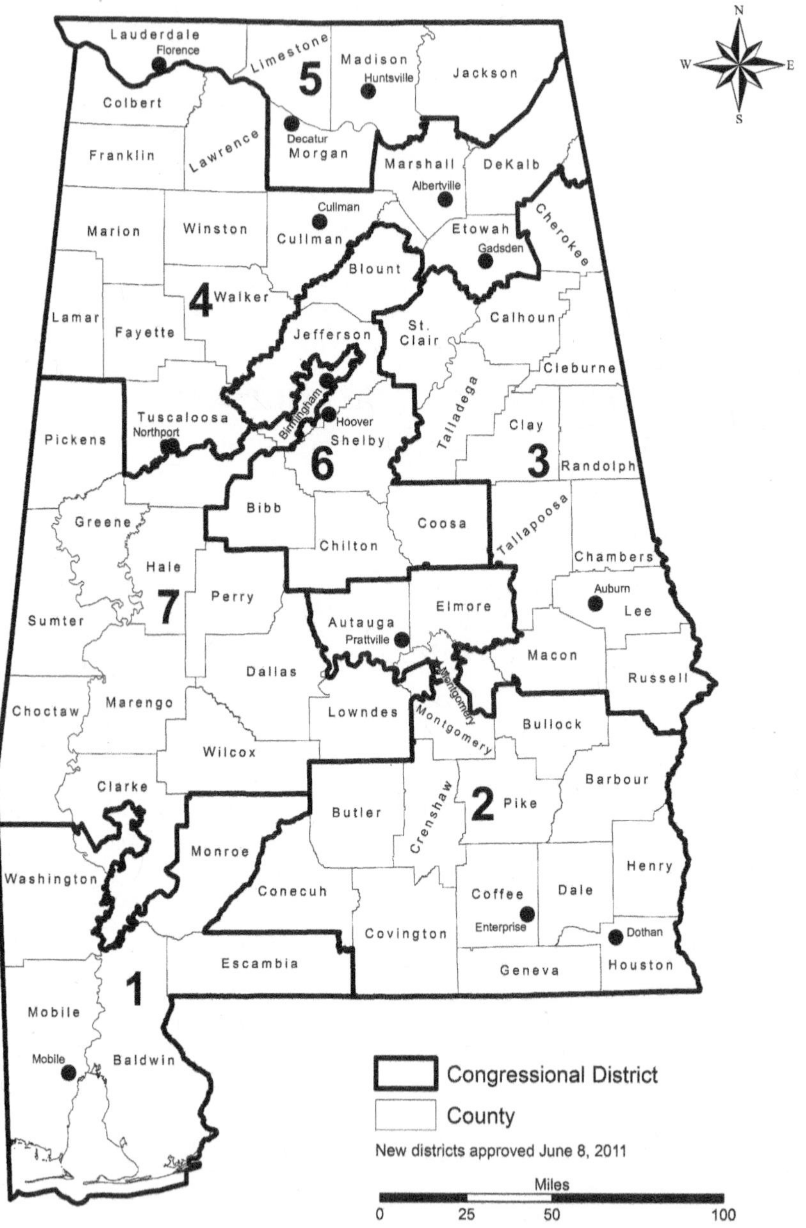

ALASKA—Congressional District—(1 District At Large)

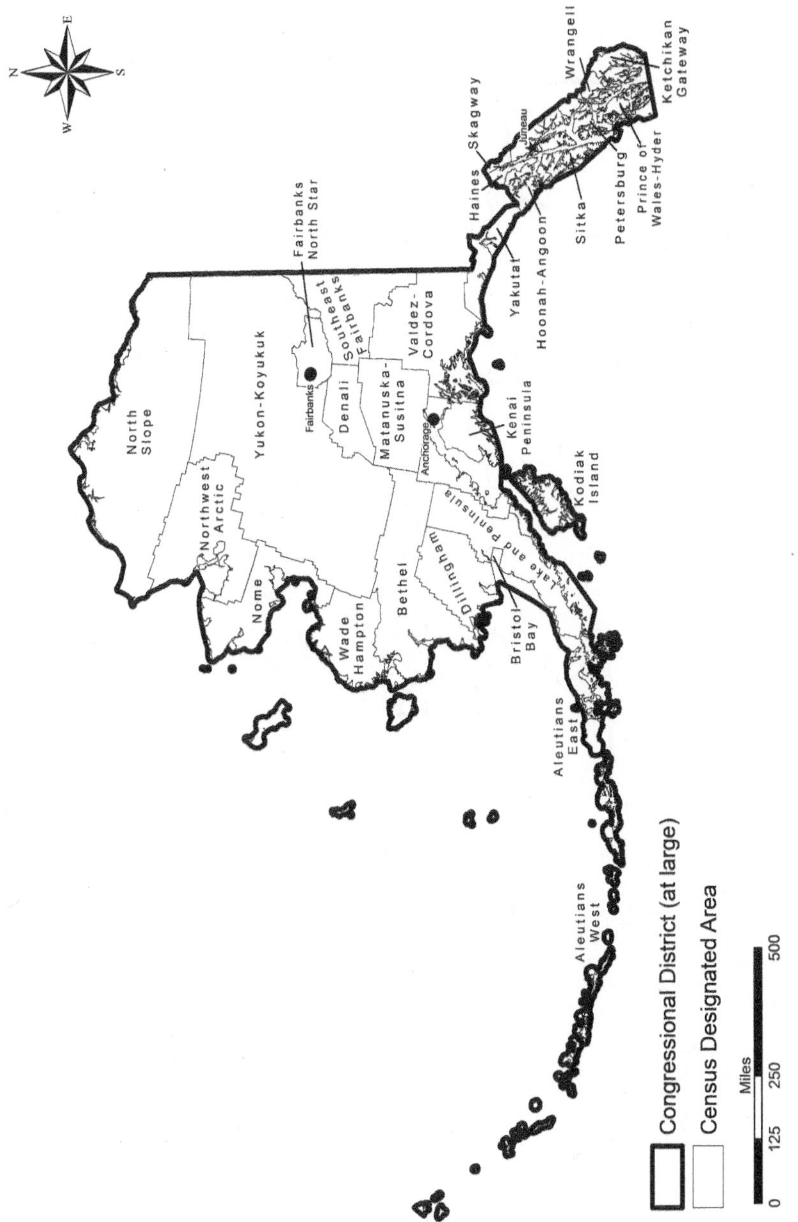

ARIZONA—Congressional Districts—(9 Districts)

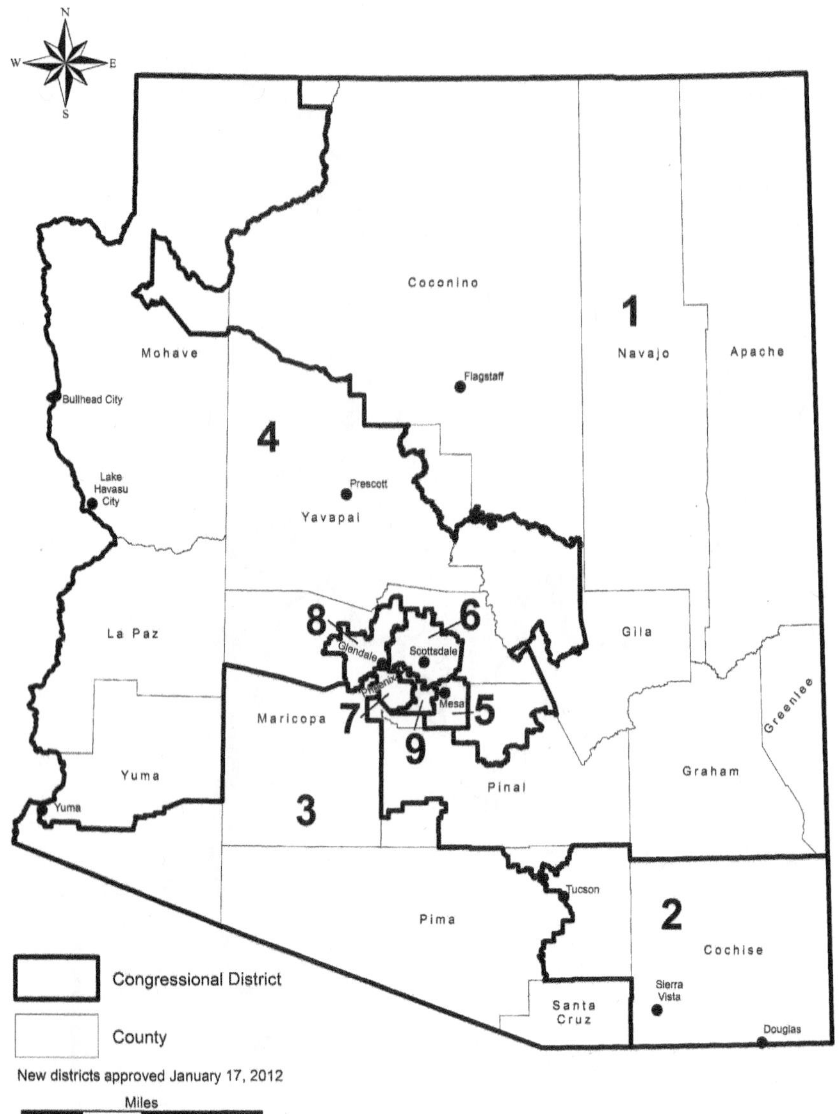

ARKANSAS—Congressional Districts—(4 Districts)

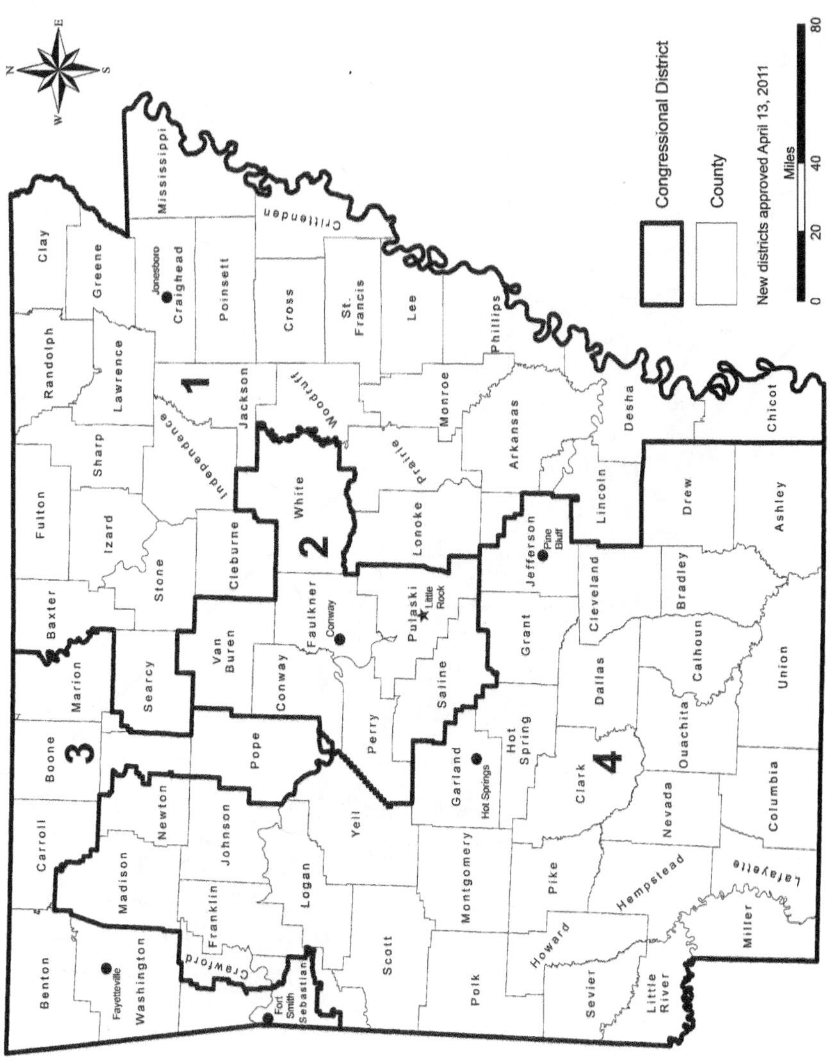

CALIFORNIA—Congressional Districts—(53 Districts)

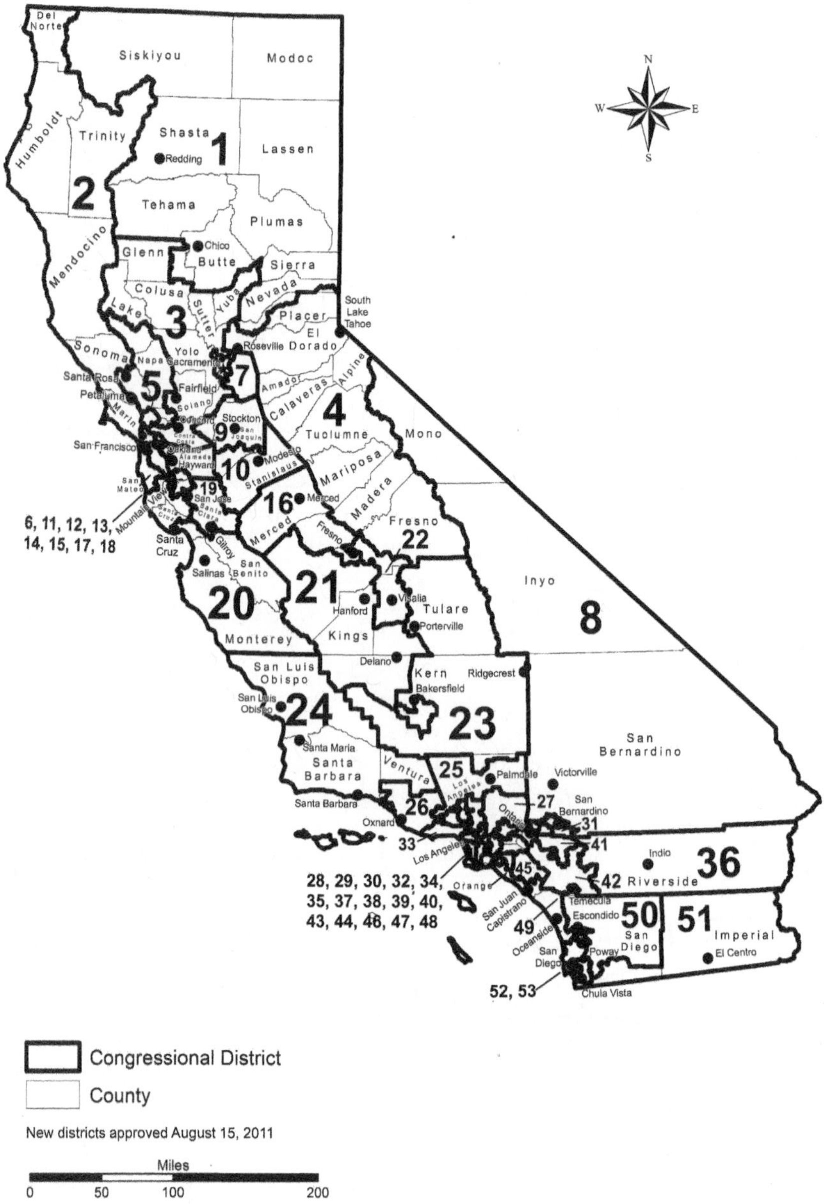

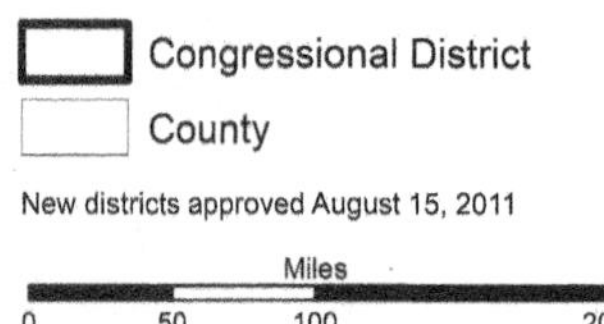

New districts approved August 15, 2011

Miles
0 50 100 200

COLORADO—Congressional Districts—(7 Districts)

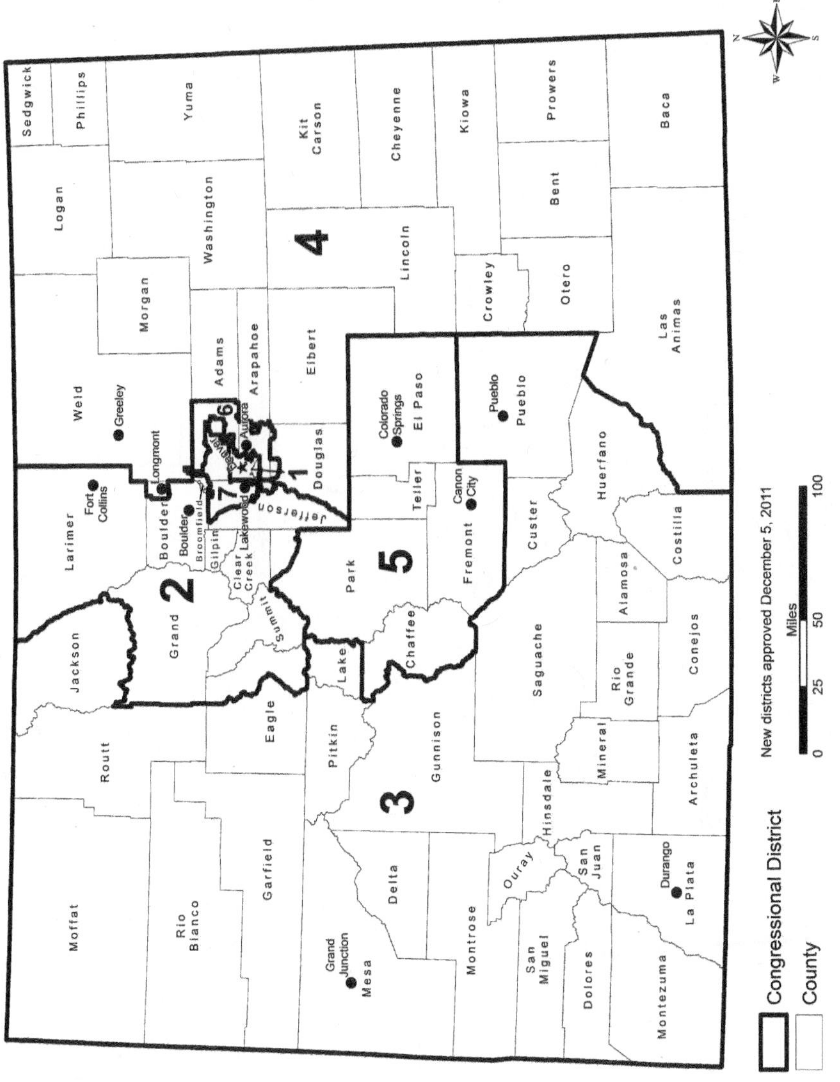

CONNECTICUT—Congressional Districts—(5 Districts)

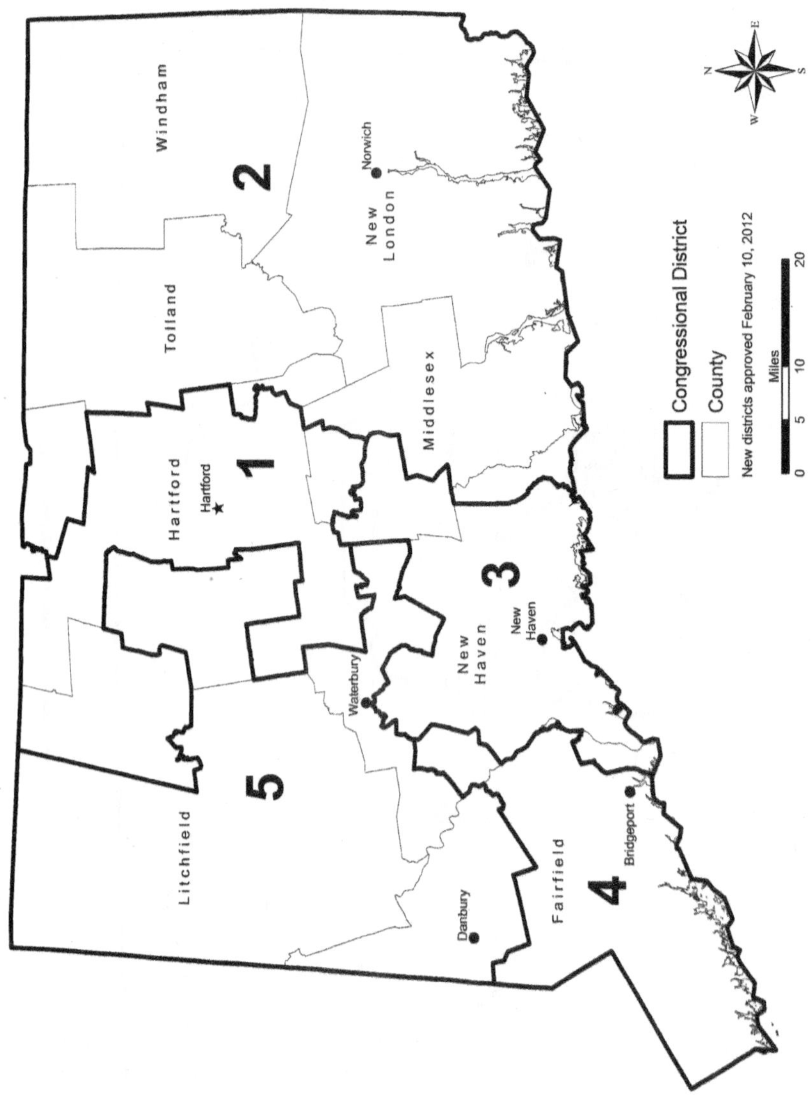

DELAWARE—Congressional District—(1 District At Large)

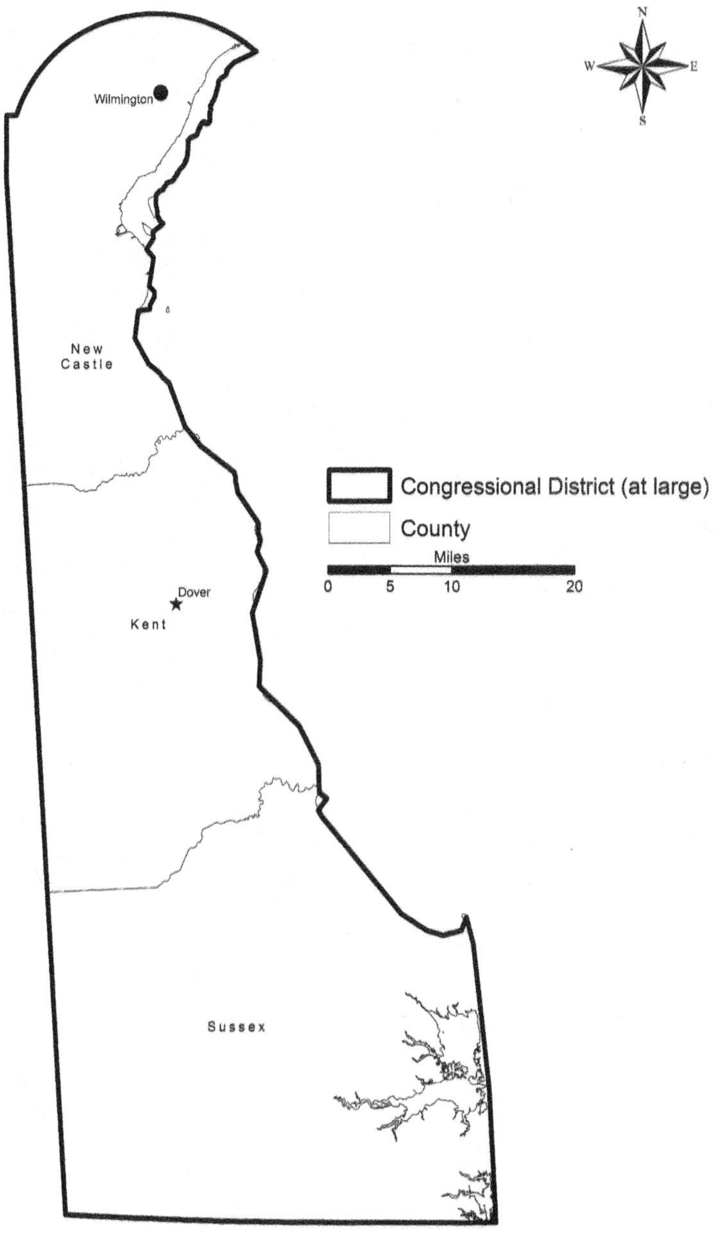

FLORIDA—Congressional Districts—(27 Districts)

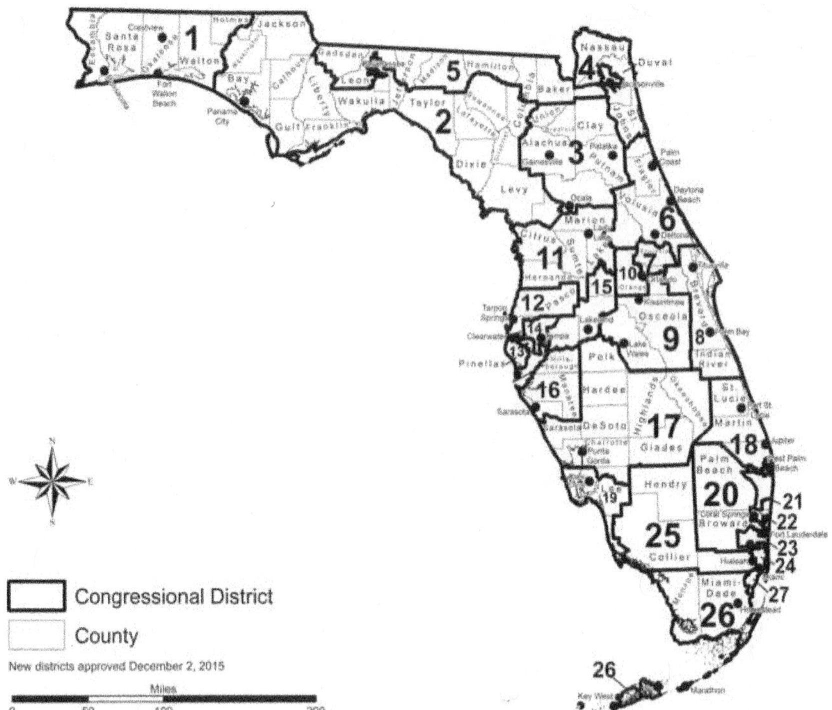

GEORGIA—Congressional Districts—(14 Districts)

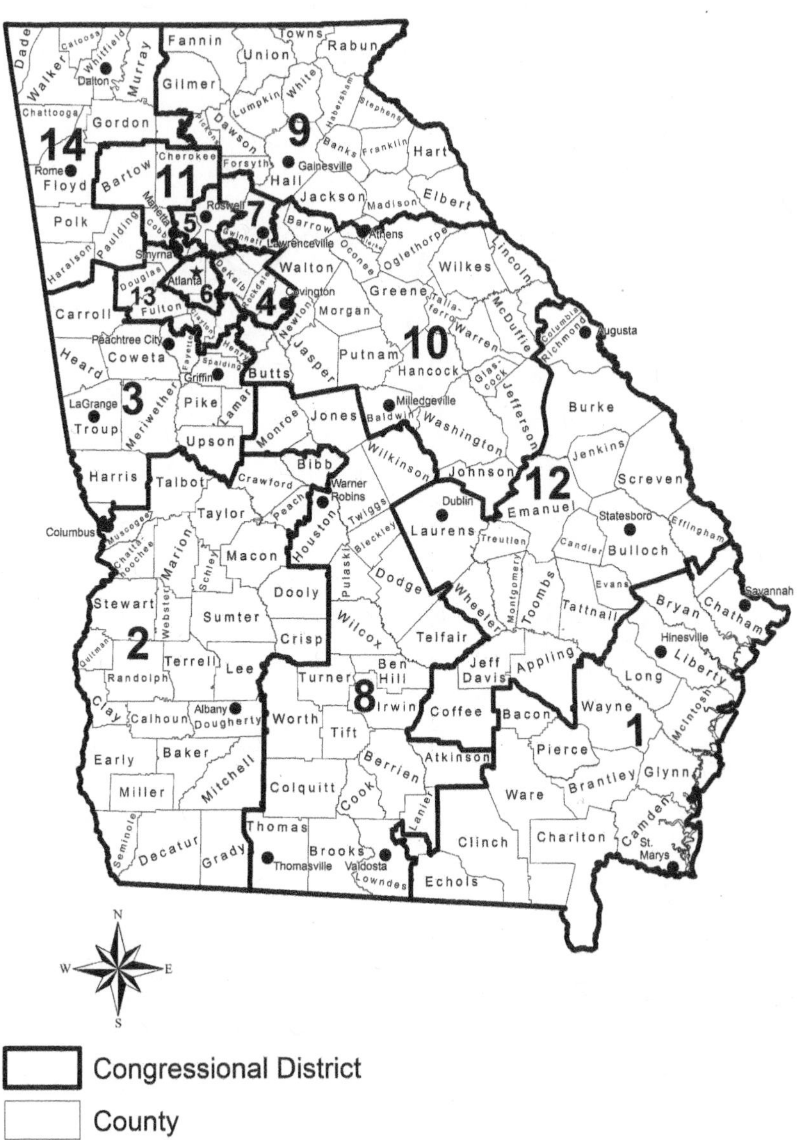

Congressional District

County

New districts approved September 6, 2011

Miles

0 30 60 120

HAWAII—Congressional Districts—(2 Districts)

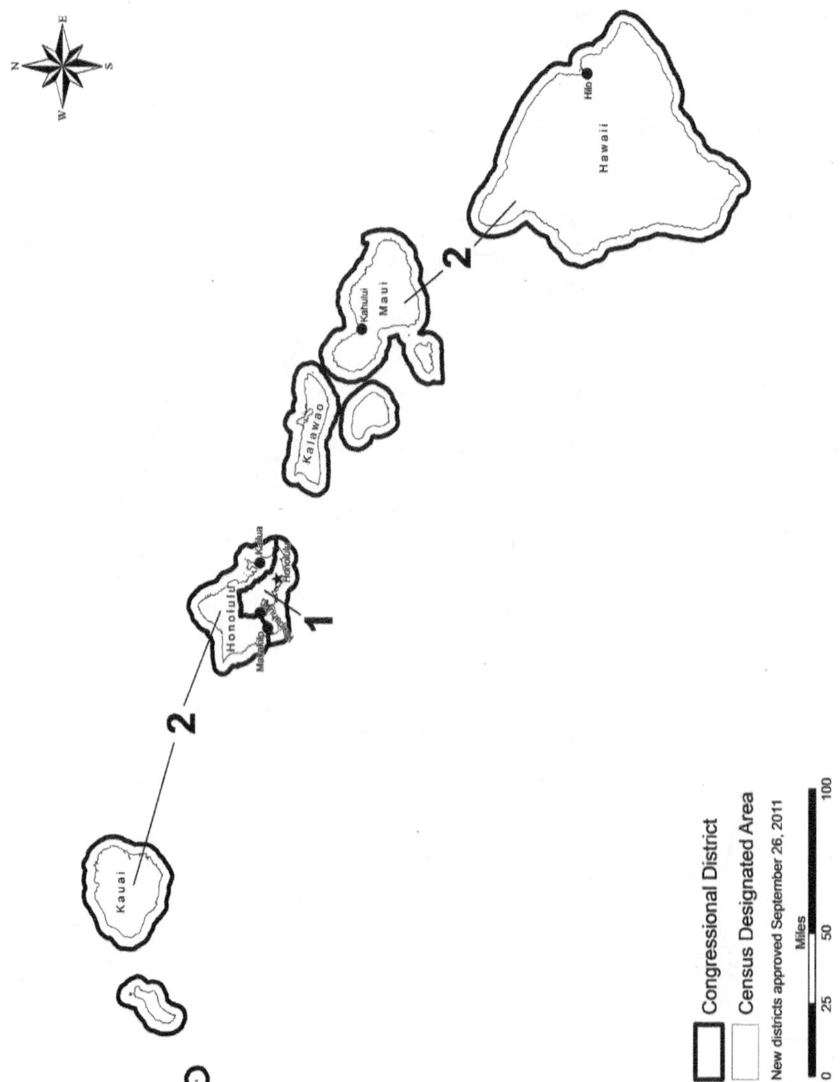

IDAHO—Congressional Districts—(2 Districts)

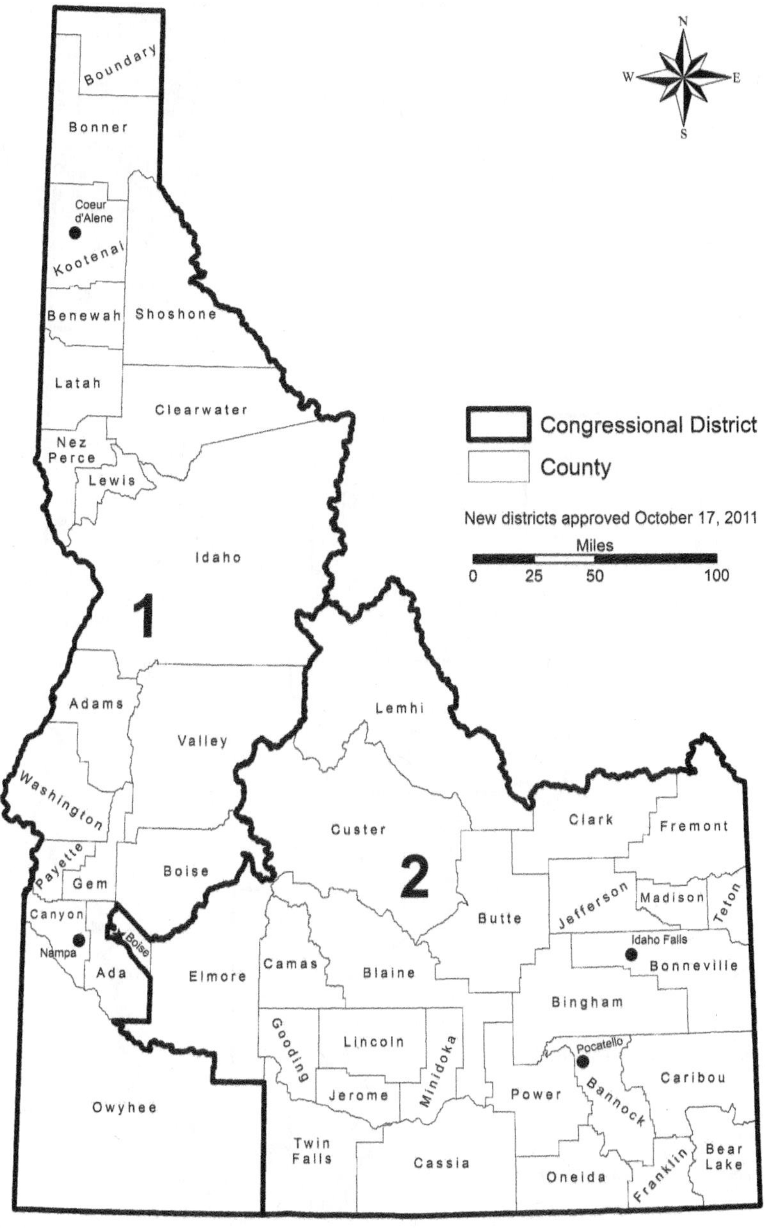

ILLINOIS—Congressional Districts—(18 Districts)

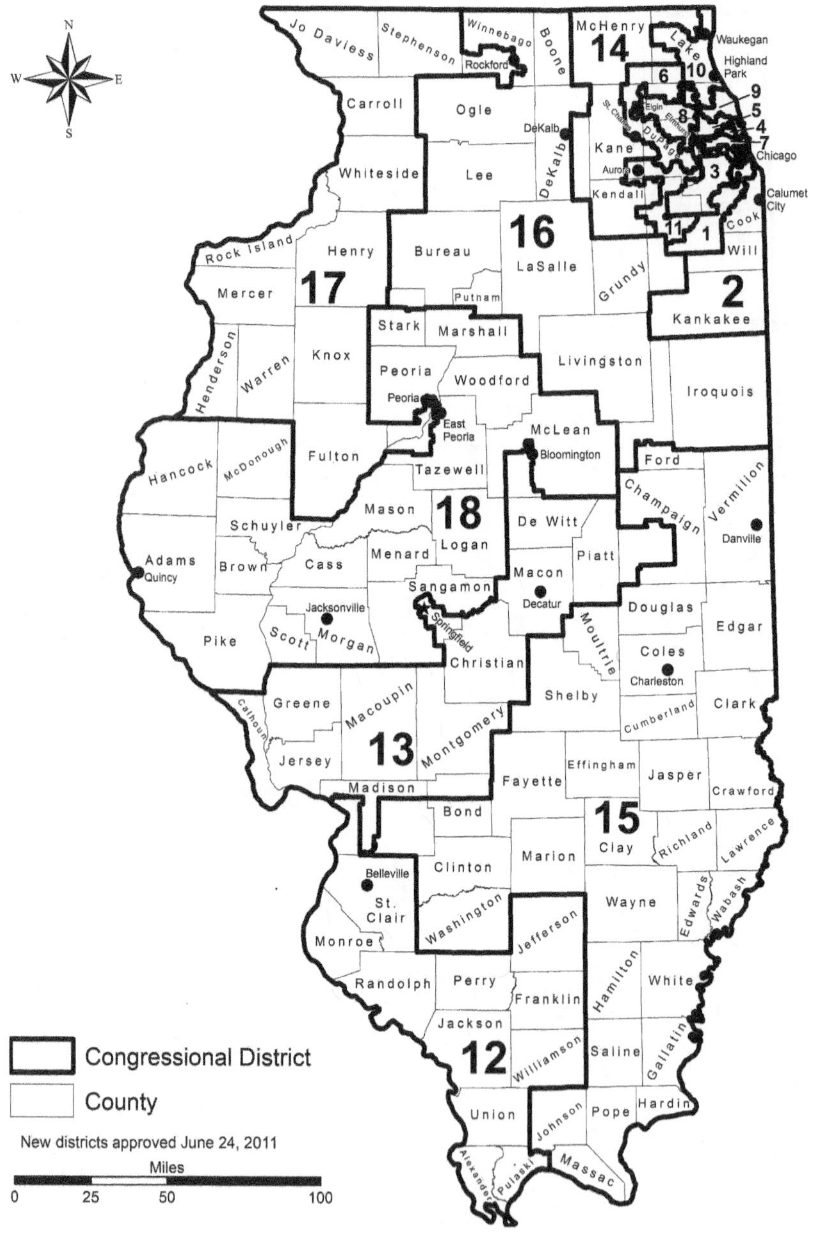

INDIANA—Congressional Districts—(9 Districts)

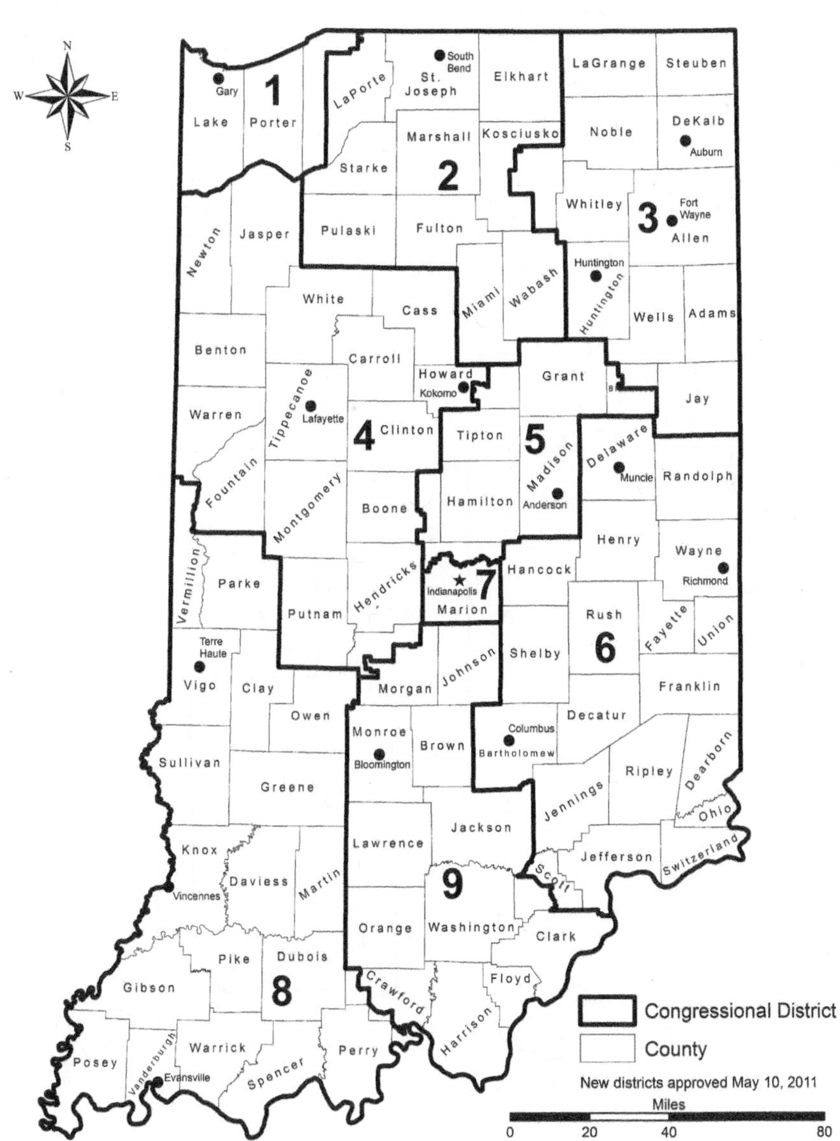

IOWA—Congressional Districts—(4 Districts)

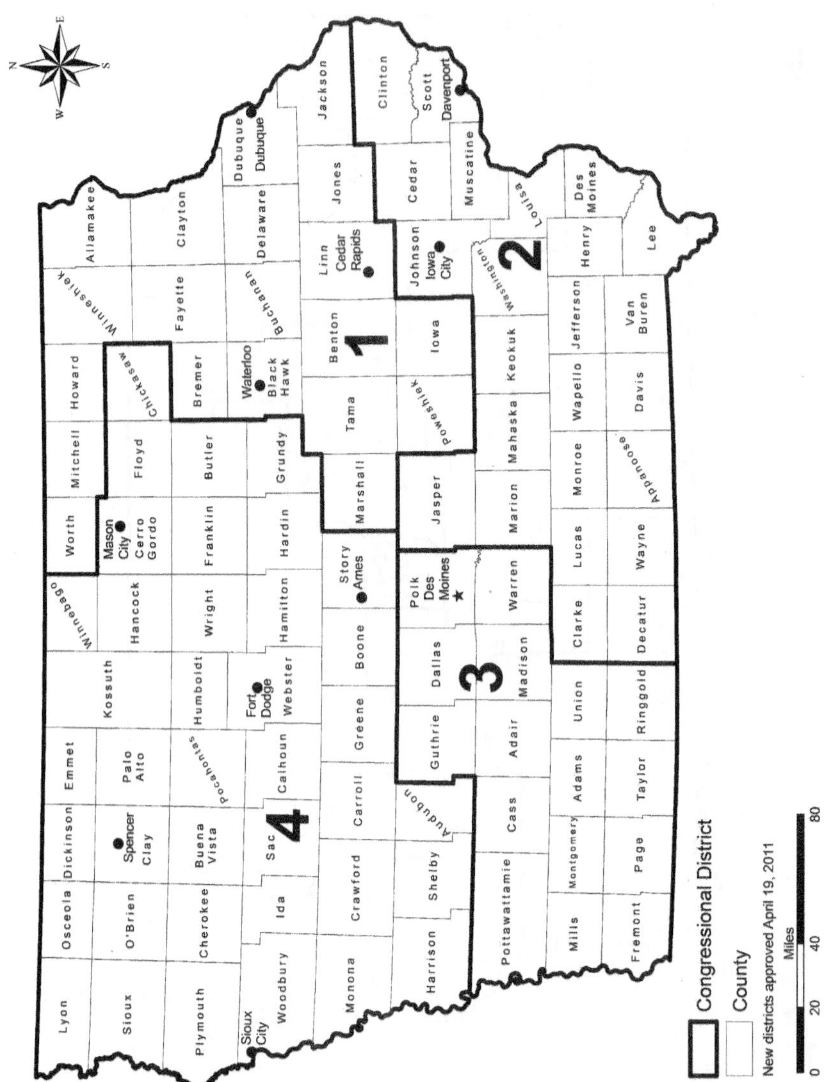

KANSAS—Congressional Districts—(4 Districts)

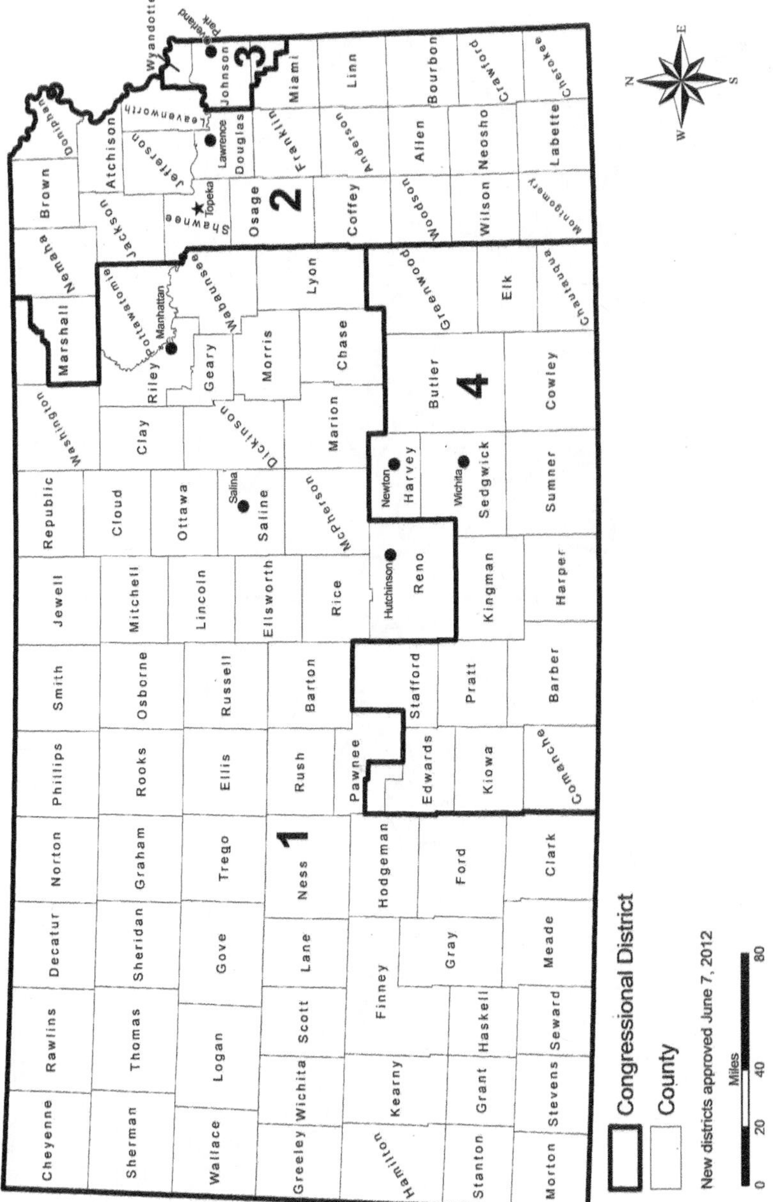

KENTUCKY—Congressional Districts—(6 Districts)

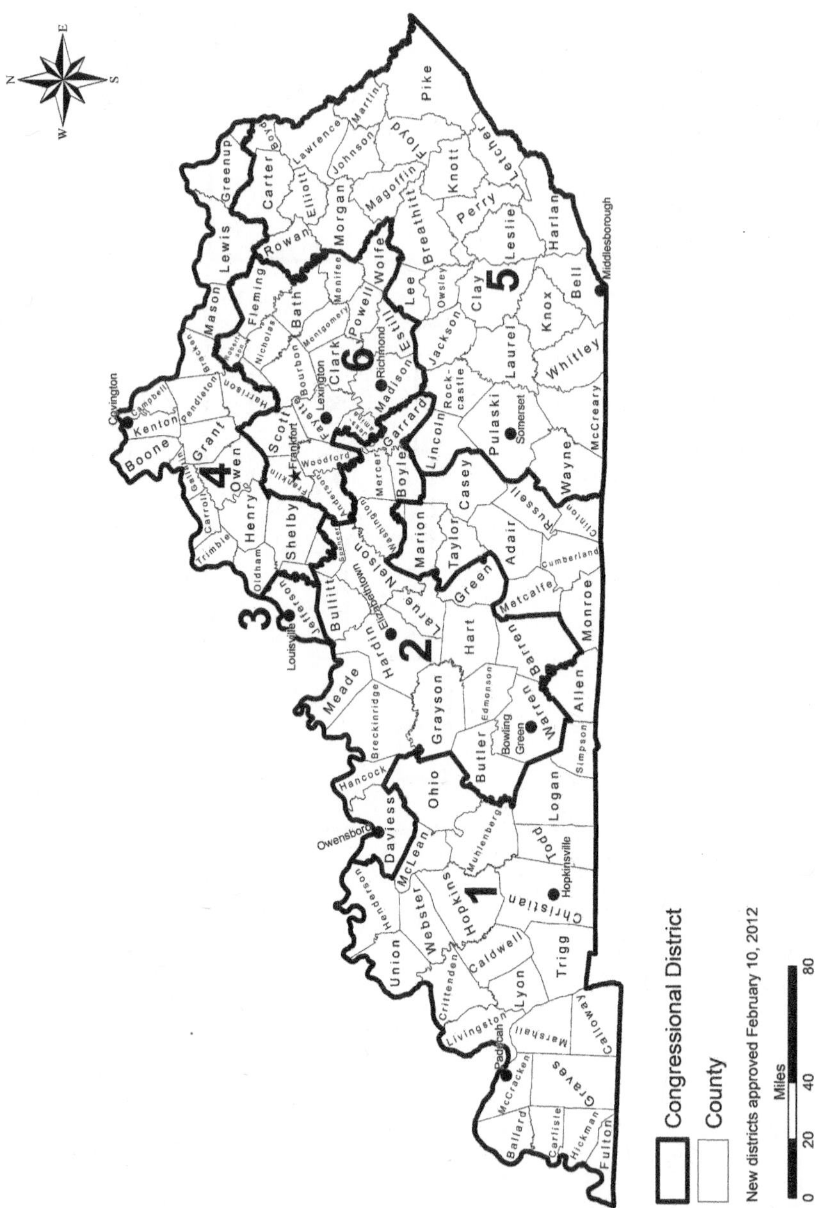

LOUISIANA—Congressional Districts—(6 Districts)

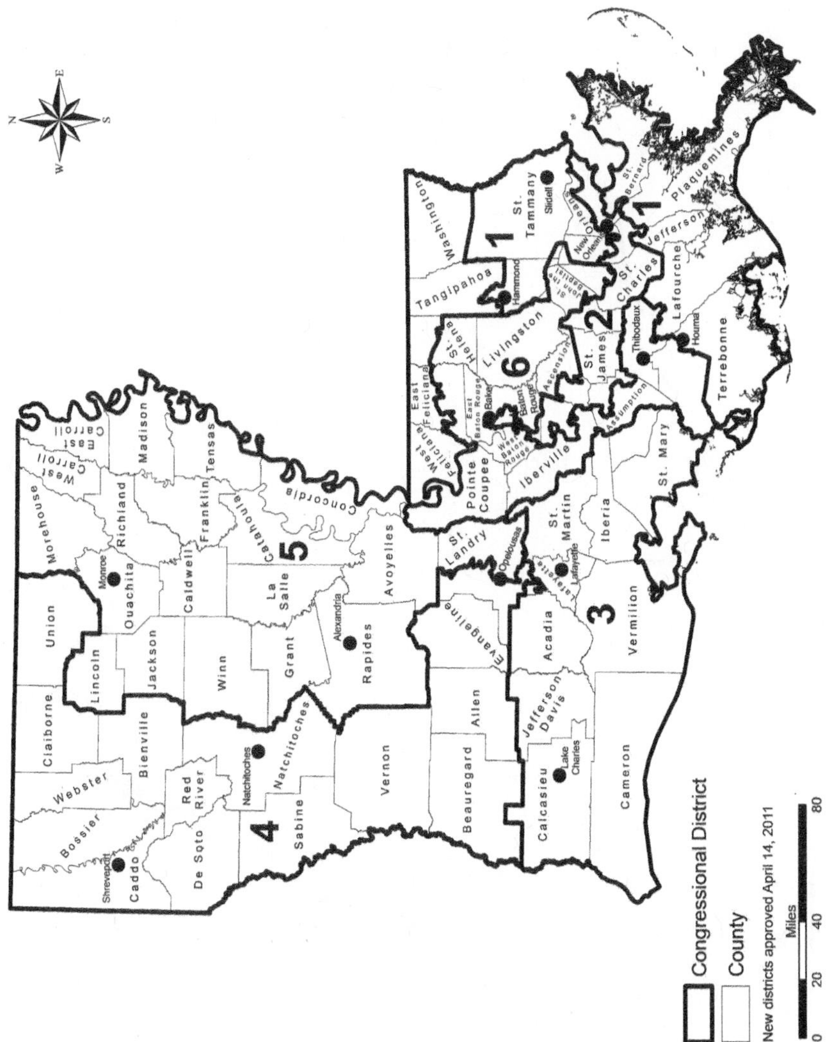

MAINE—Congressional Districts—(2 Districts)

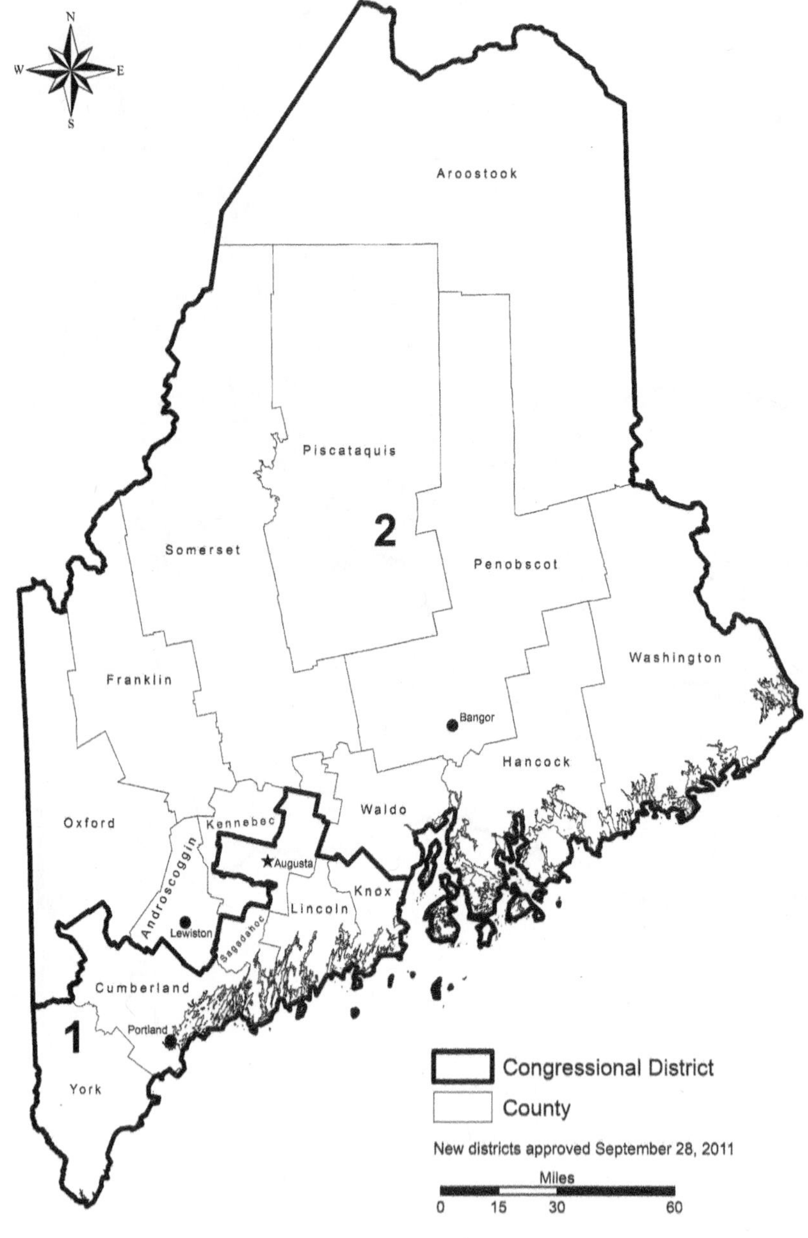

MARYLAND—Congressional Districts—(8 Districts)

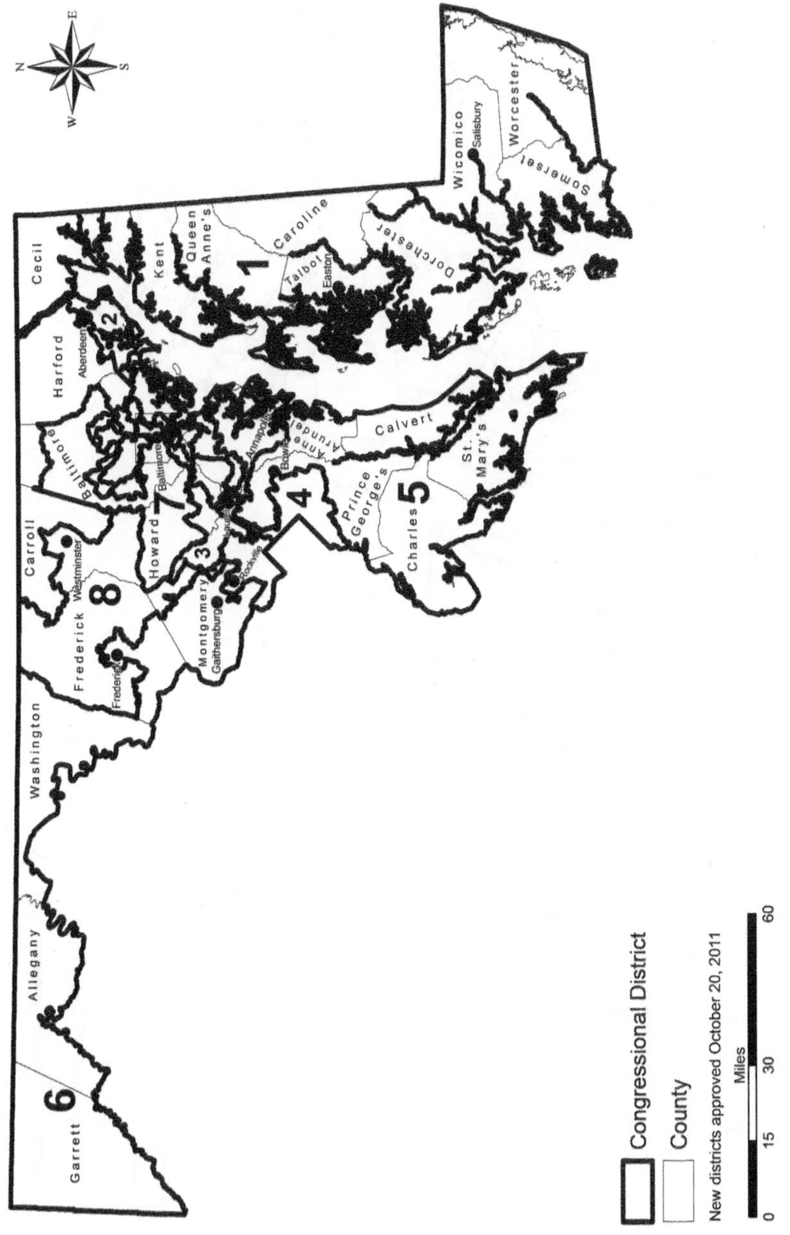

MASSACHUSETTS—Congressional Districts—(9 Districts)

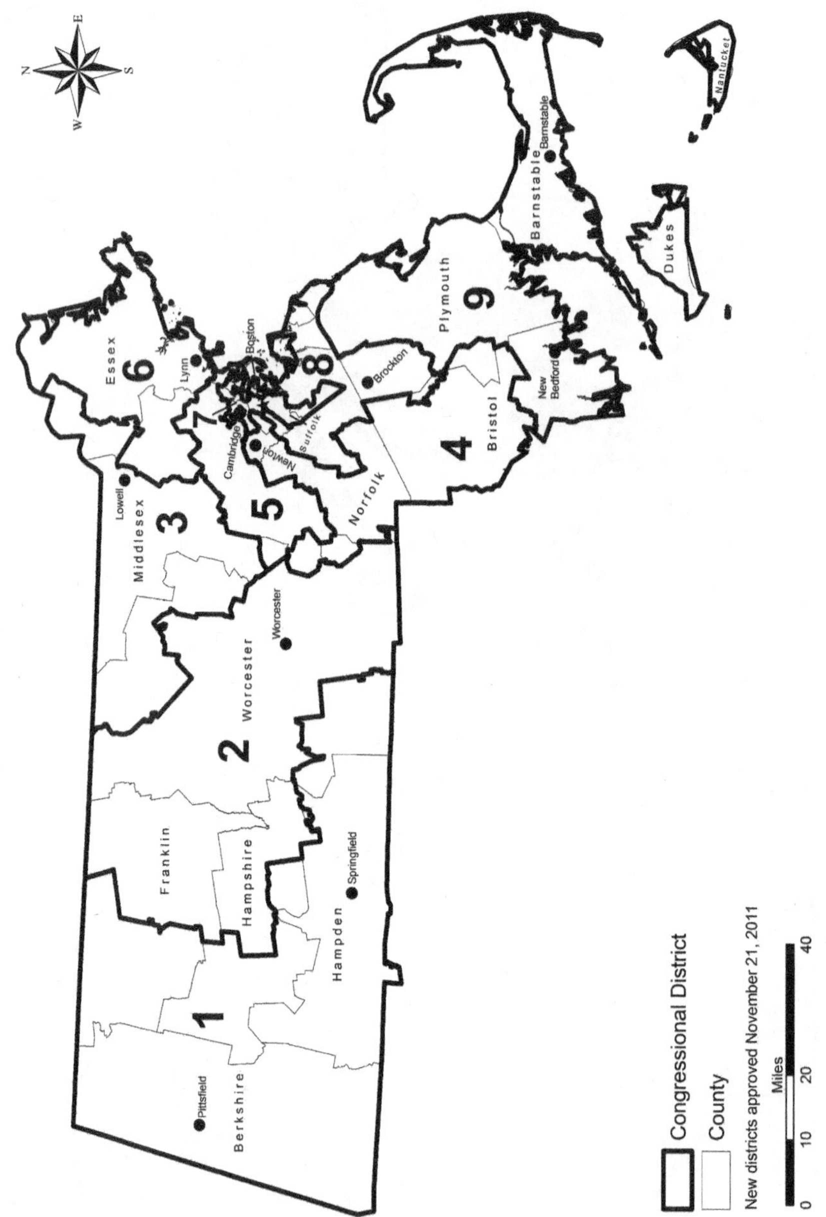

MICHIGAN—Congressional Districts—(14 Districts)

MINNESOTA—Congressional Districts—(8 Districts)

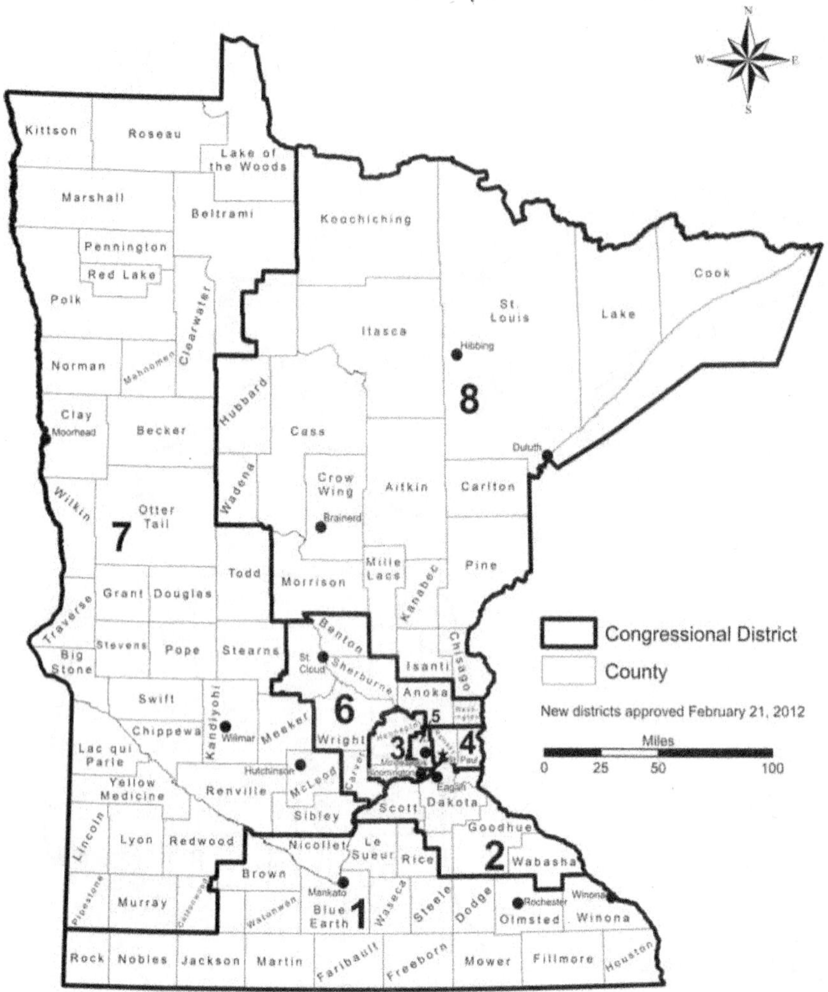

MISSISSIPPI—Congressional Districts—(4 Districts)

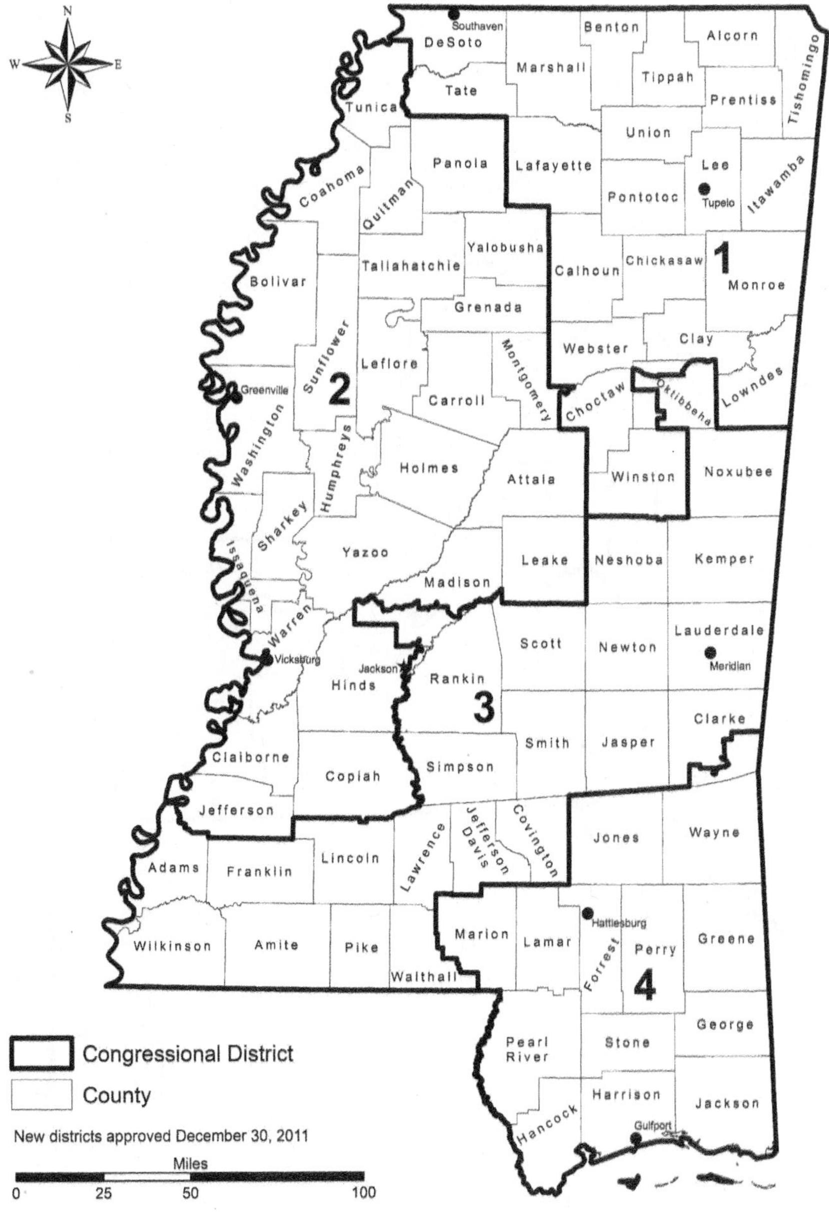

MISSOURI—Congressional Districts—(8 Districts)

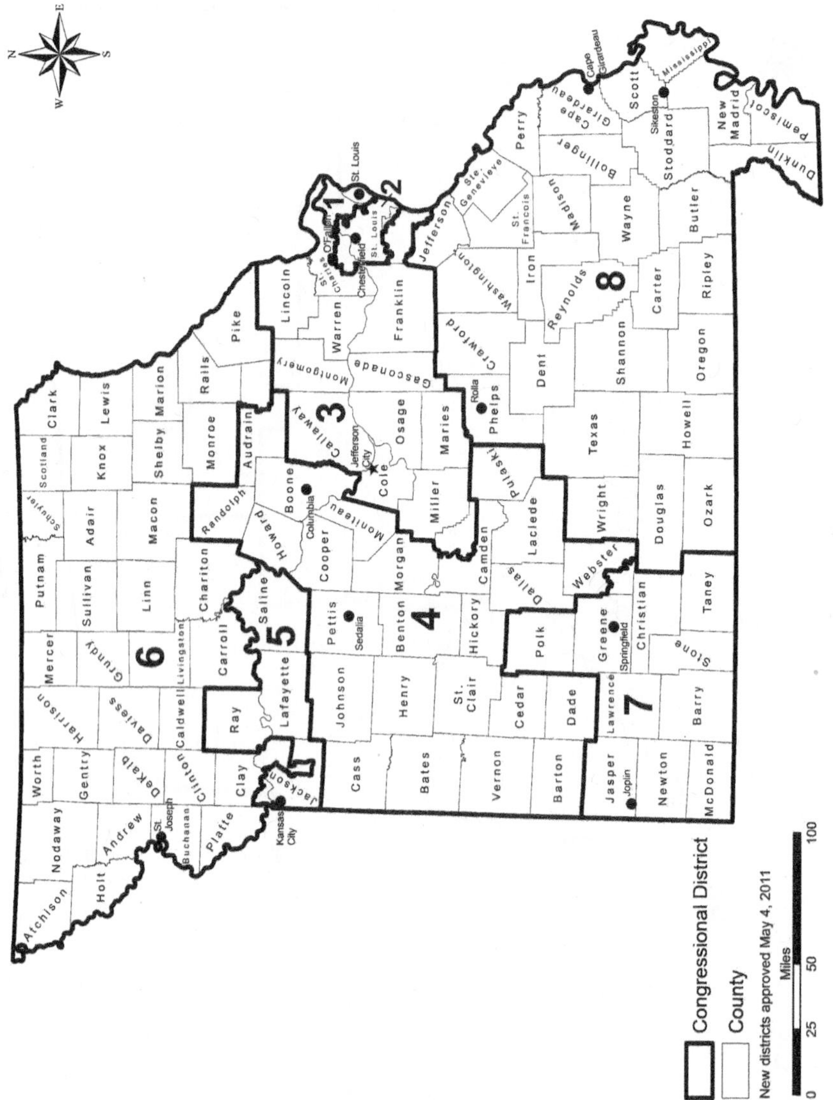

MONTANA—Congressional District—(1 District At Large)

NEBRASKA—Congressional Districts—(3 Districts)

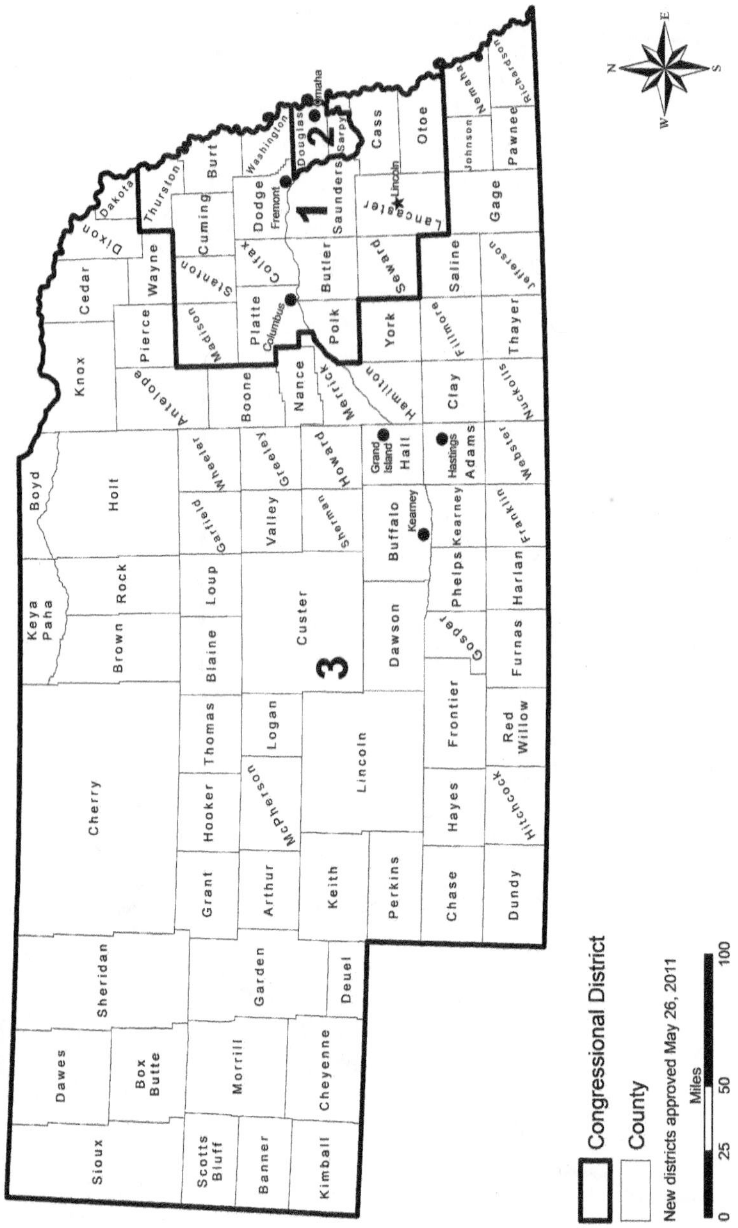

NEVADA—Congressional Districts—(4 Districts)

NEW HAMPSHIRE—Congressional Districts—(2 Districts)

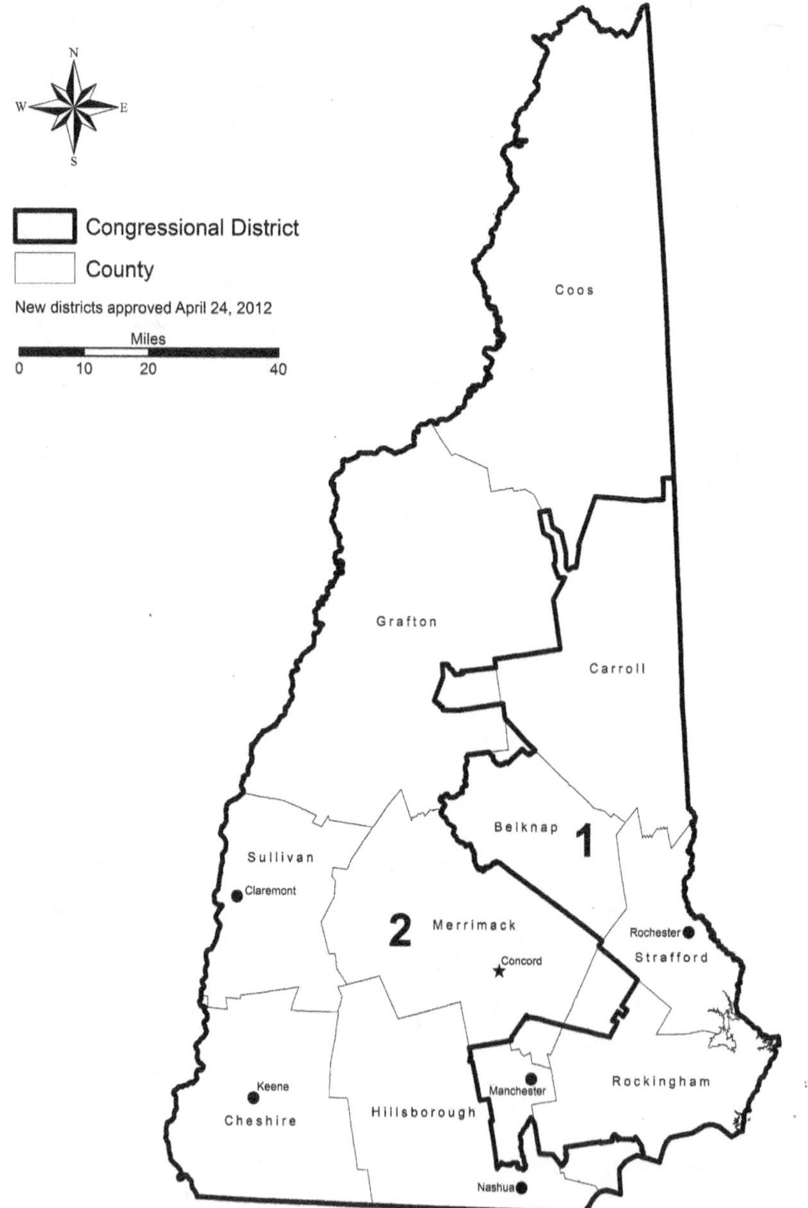

NEW JERSEY—Congressional Districts—(12 Districts)

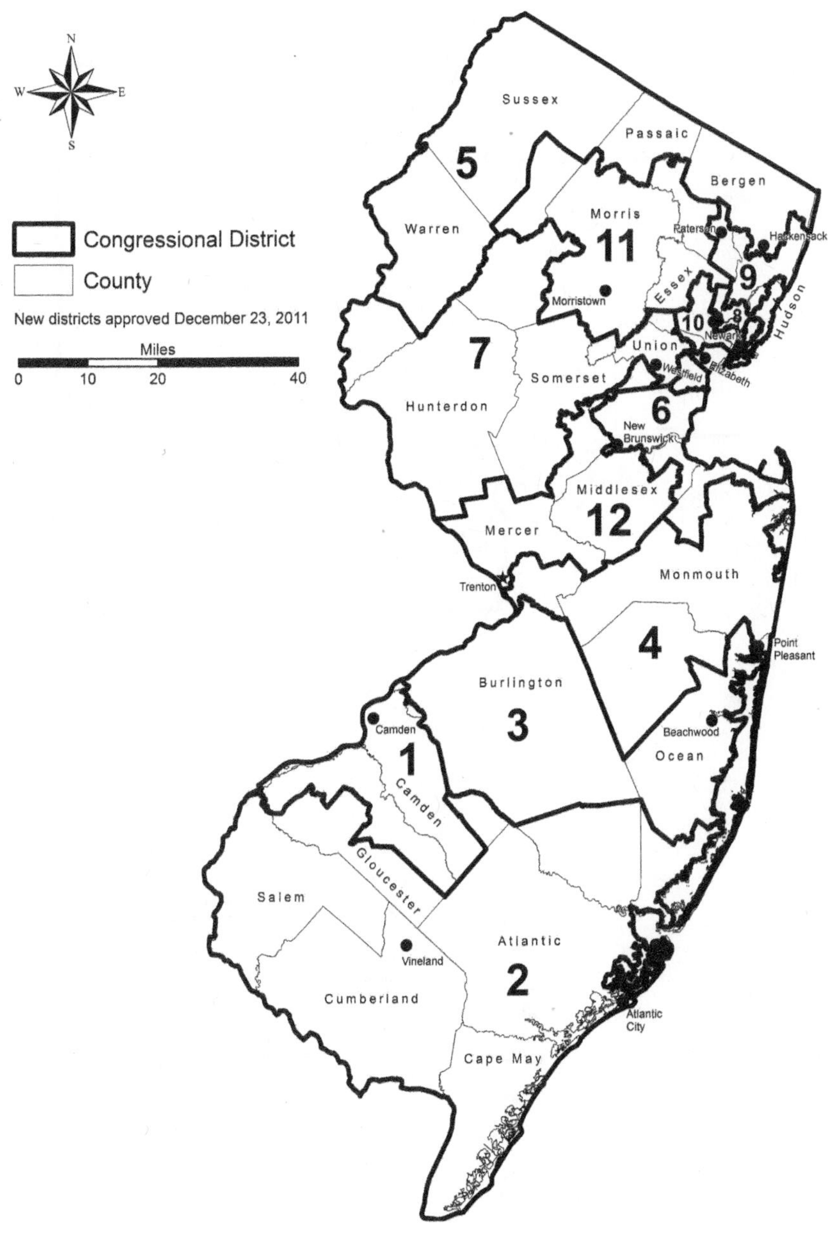

NEW MEXICO—Congressional Districts—(3 Districts)

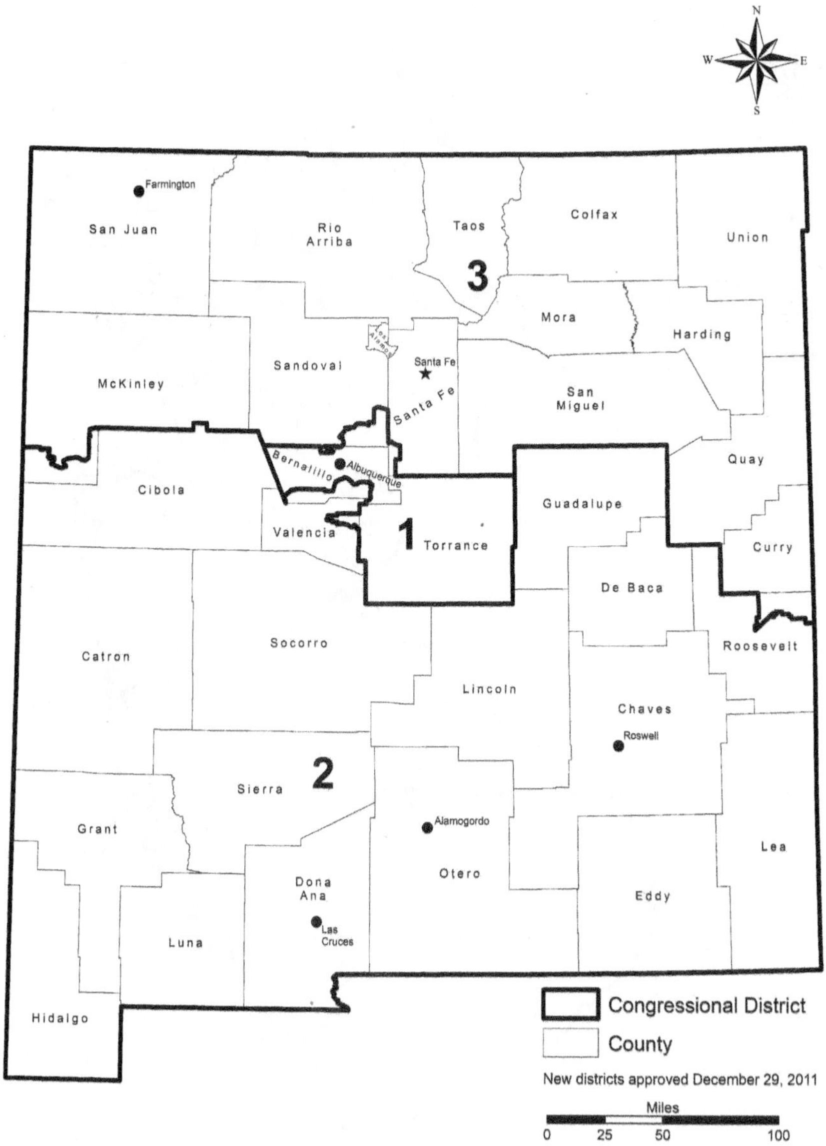

Farmington
San Juan
Rio Arriba
Taos
Colfax
Union
3
Mora
Harding
Los Alamos
Sandoval
Santa Fe
McKinley
Santa Fe
San Miguel
Quay
Bernalillo
Albuquerque
Cibola
Guadalupe
Valencia
1
Torrance
Curry
De Baca
Catron
Socorro
Roosevelt
Lincoln
Chaves
Roswell
Sierra
2
Grant
Alamogordo
Lea
Otero
Dona Ana
Eddy
Las Cruces
Luna
Hidalgo

Congressional District
County
New districts approved December 29, 2011
Miles
0 25 50 100

NEW YORK—Congressional Districts—(27 Districts)

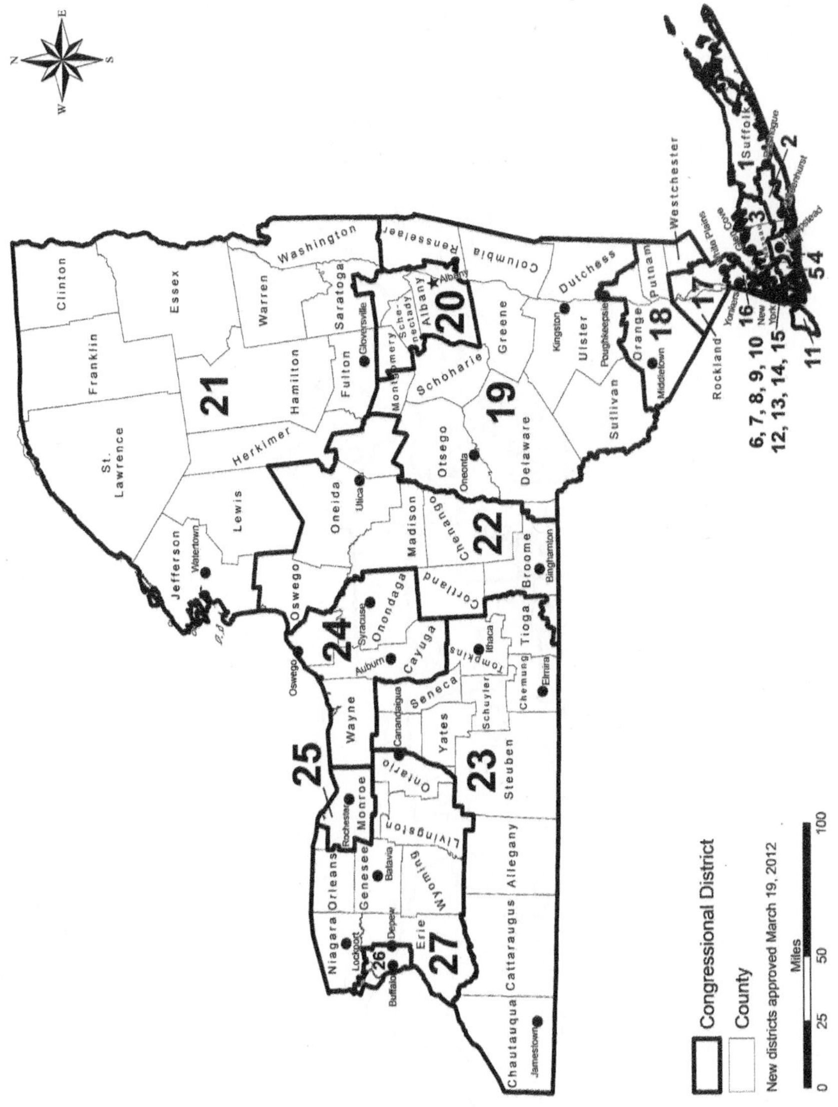

NORTH CAROLINA—Congressional Districts—(13 Districts)

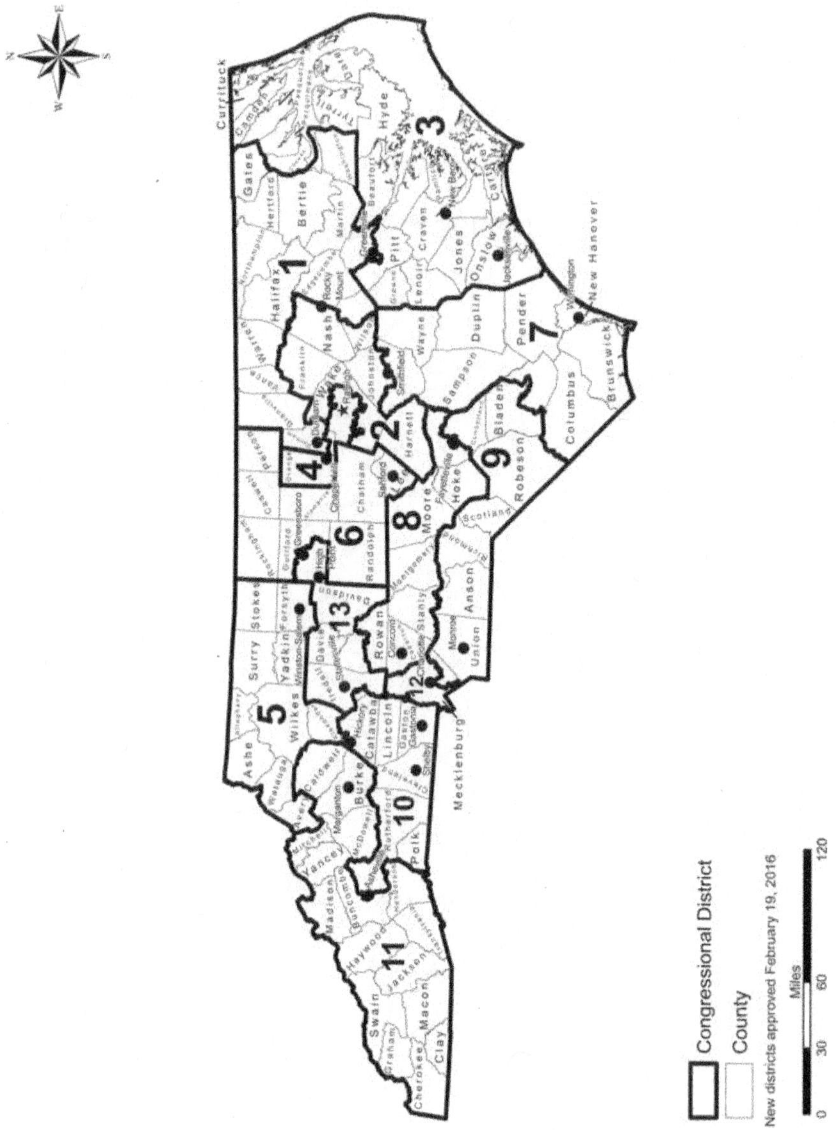

Congressional District

County

New districts approved February 19, 2016

Miles

0 30 60 120

NORTH DAKOTA—Congressional District—(1 District At Large)

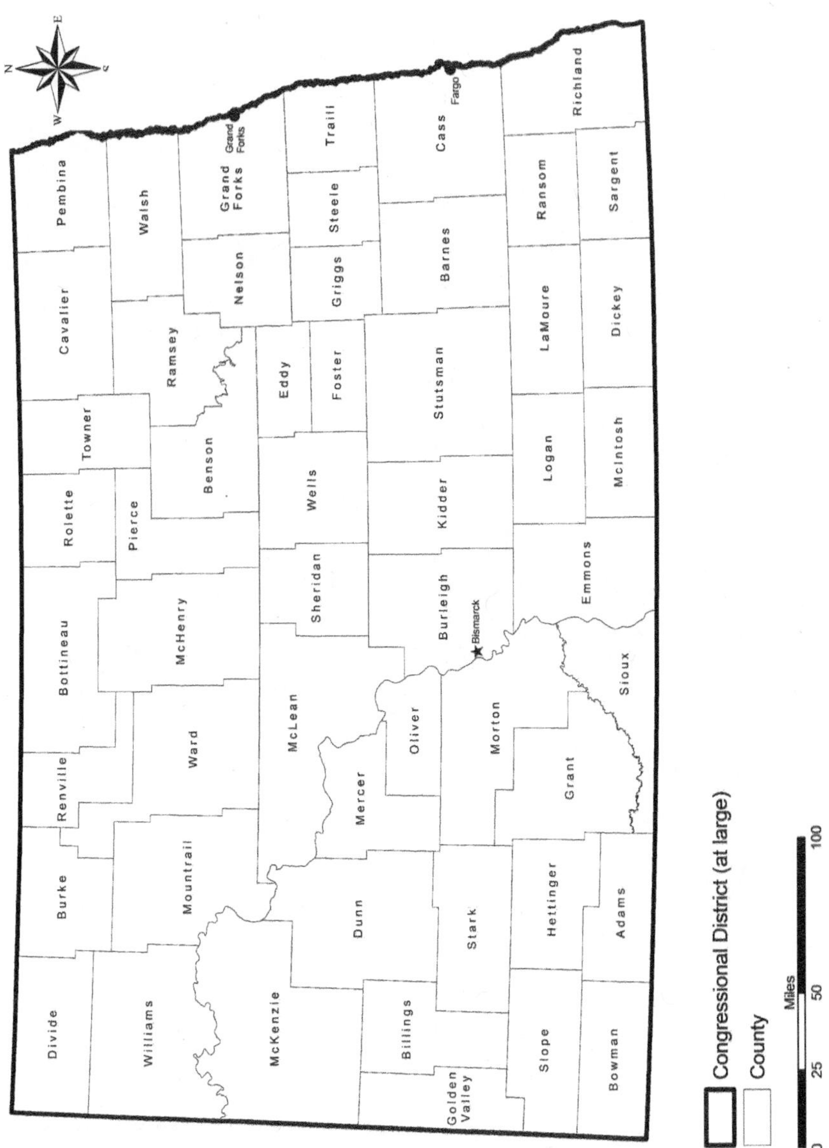

OHIO—Congressional Districts—(16 Districts)

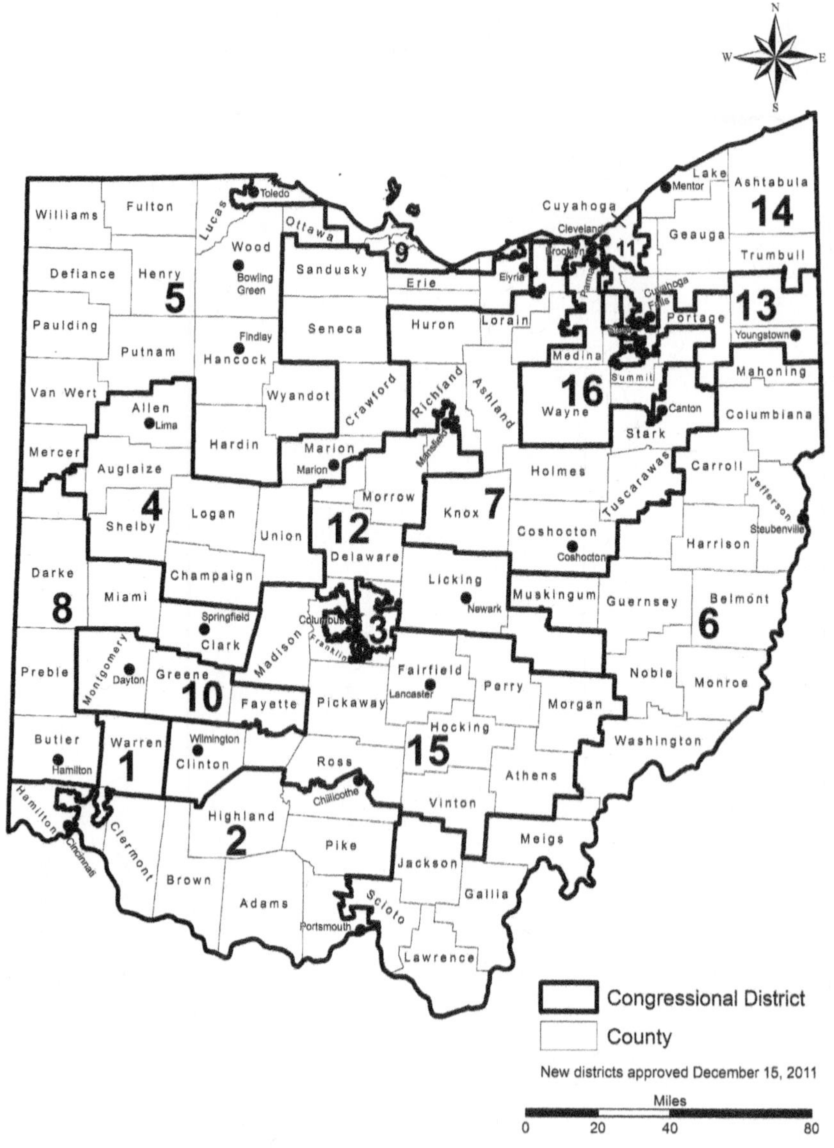

OKLAHOMA—Congressional Districts—(5 Districts)

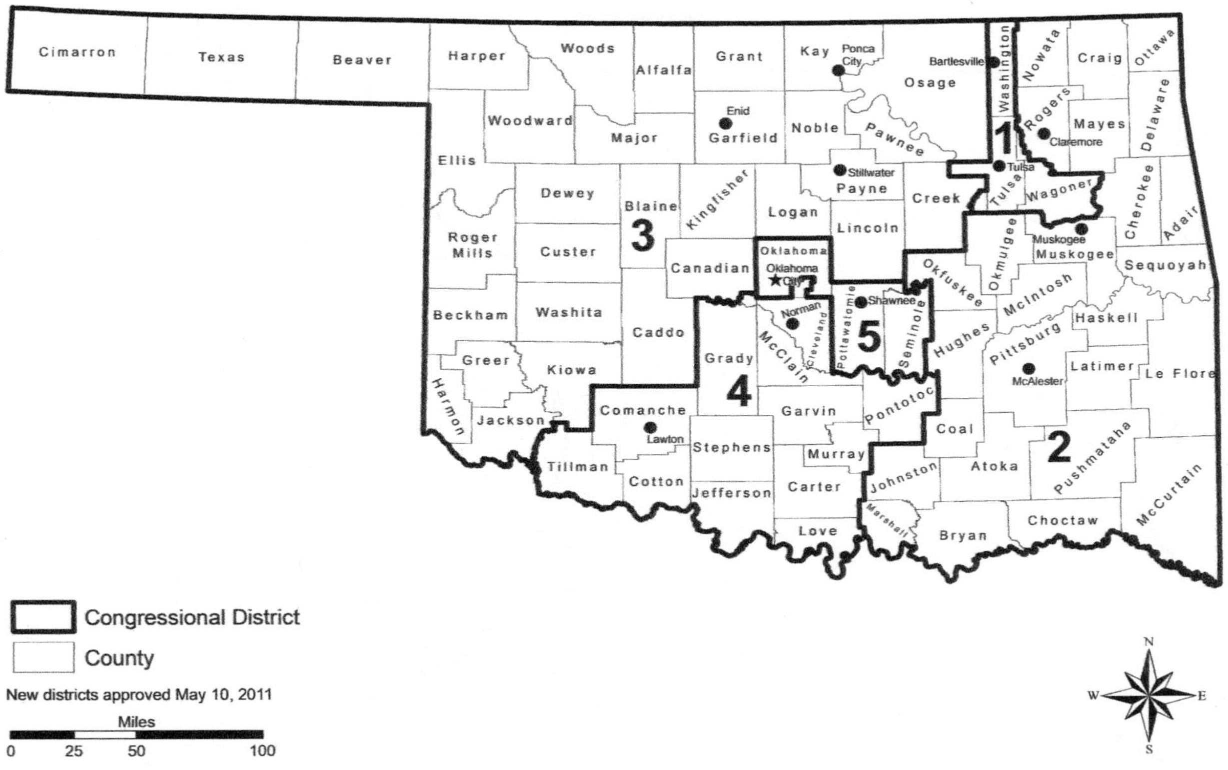

OREGON—Congressional Districts—(5 Districts)

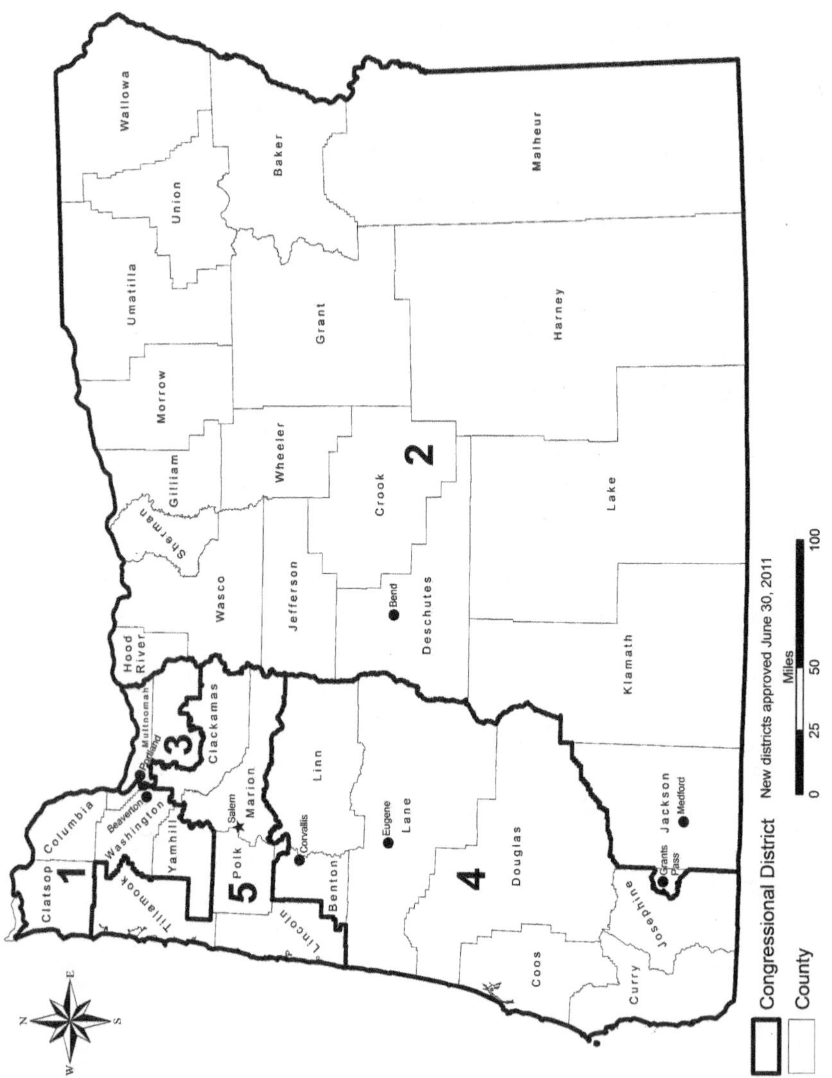

PENNSYLVANIA—Congressional Districts—(18 Districts)

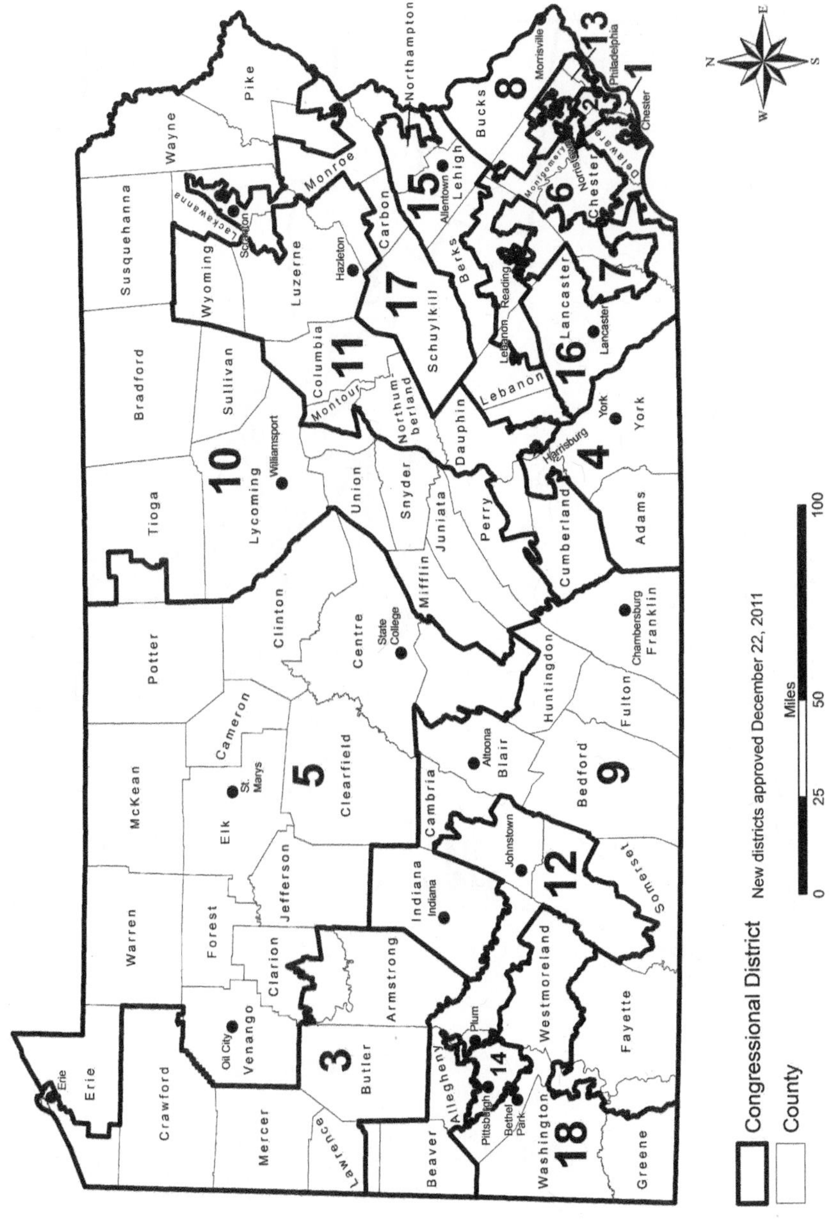

RHODE ISLAND—Congressional Districts—(2 Districts)

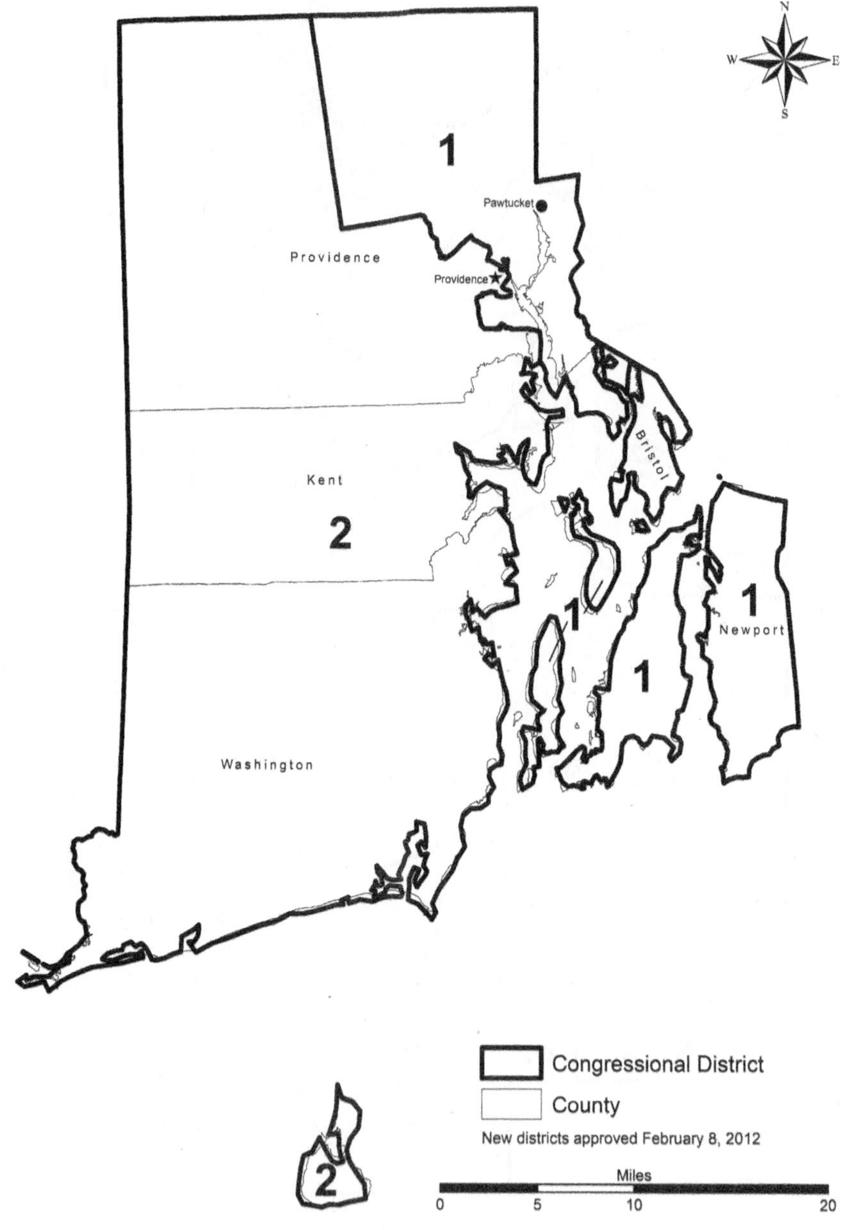

SOUTH CAROLINA—Congressional Districts—(7 Districts)

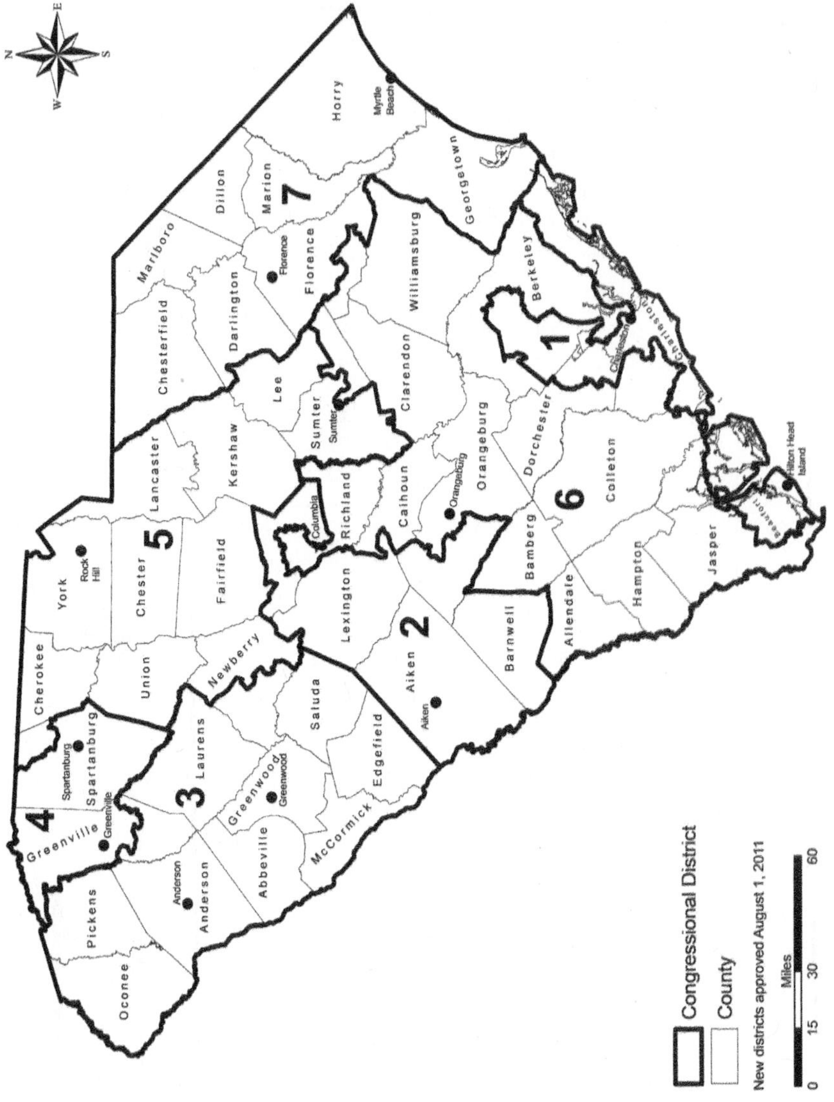

SOUTH DAKOTA—Congressional District—(1 District At Large)

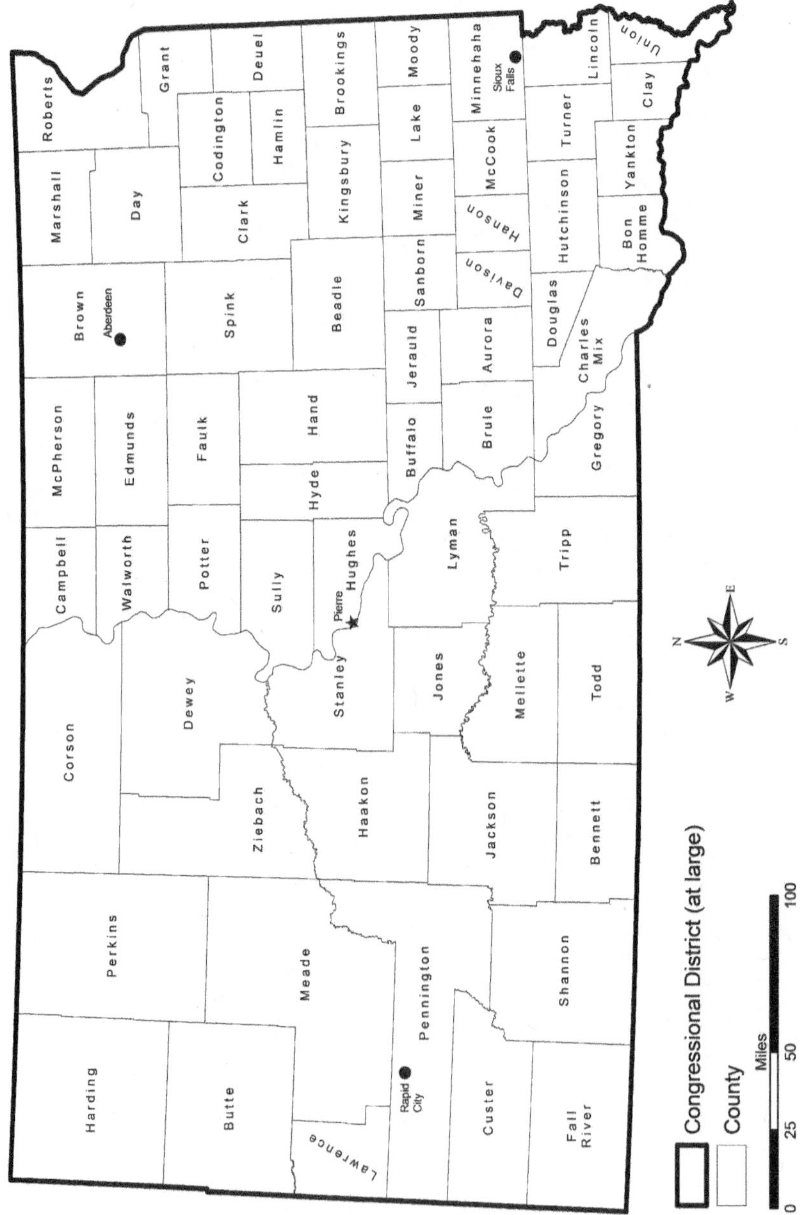

TENNESSEE—Congressional Districts—(9 Districts)

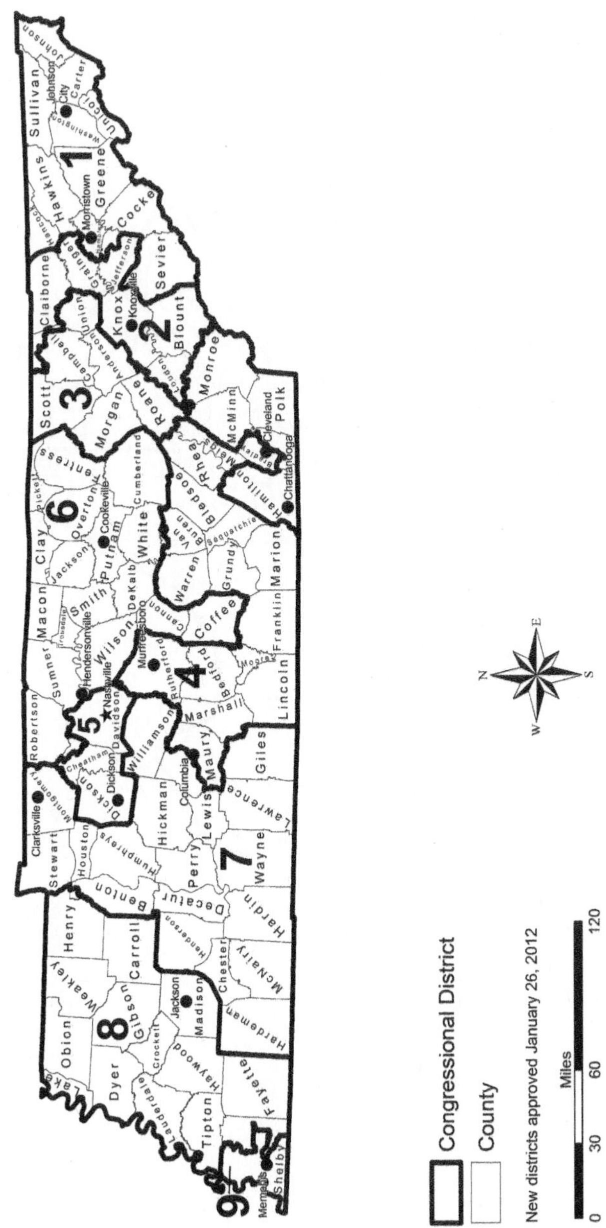

TEXAS—Congressional Districts—(36 Districts)

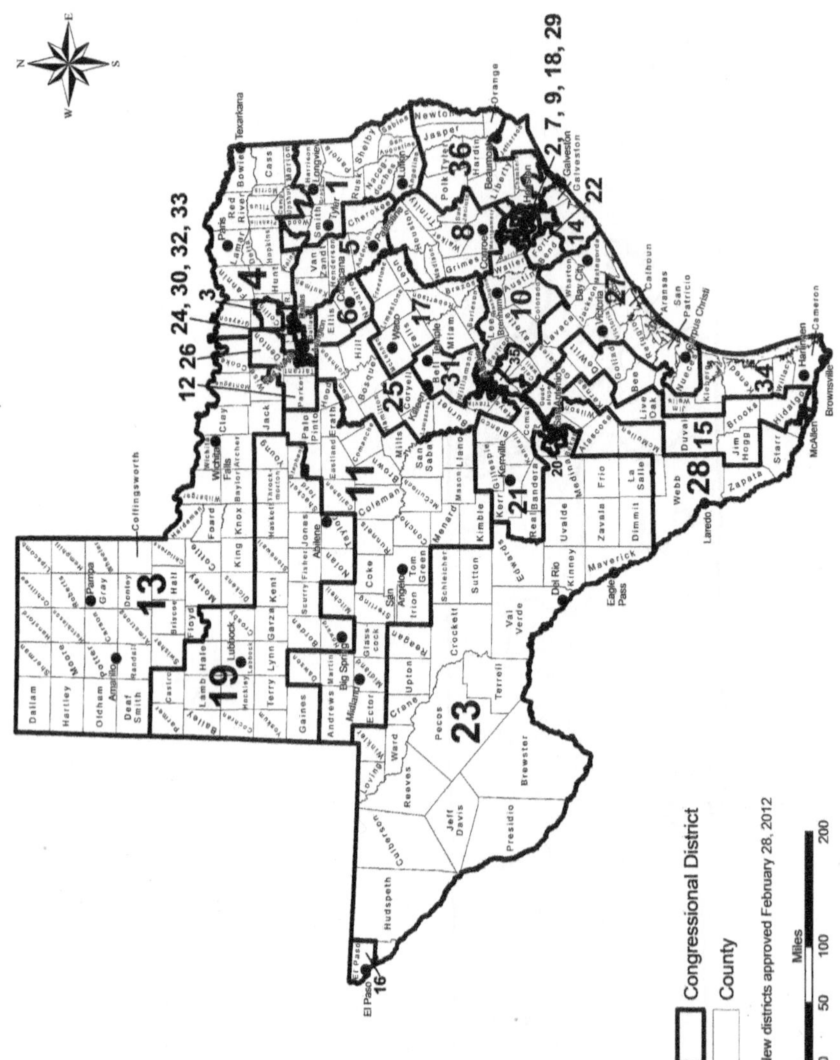

UTAH—Congressional Districts—(4 Districts)

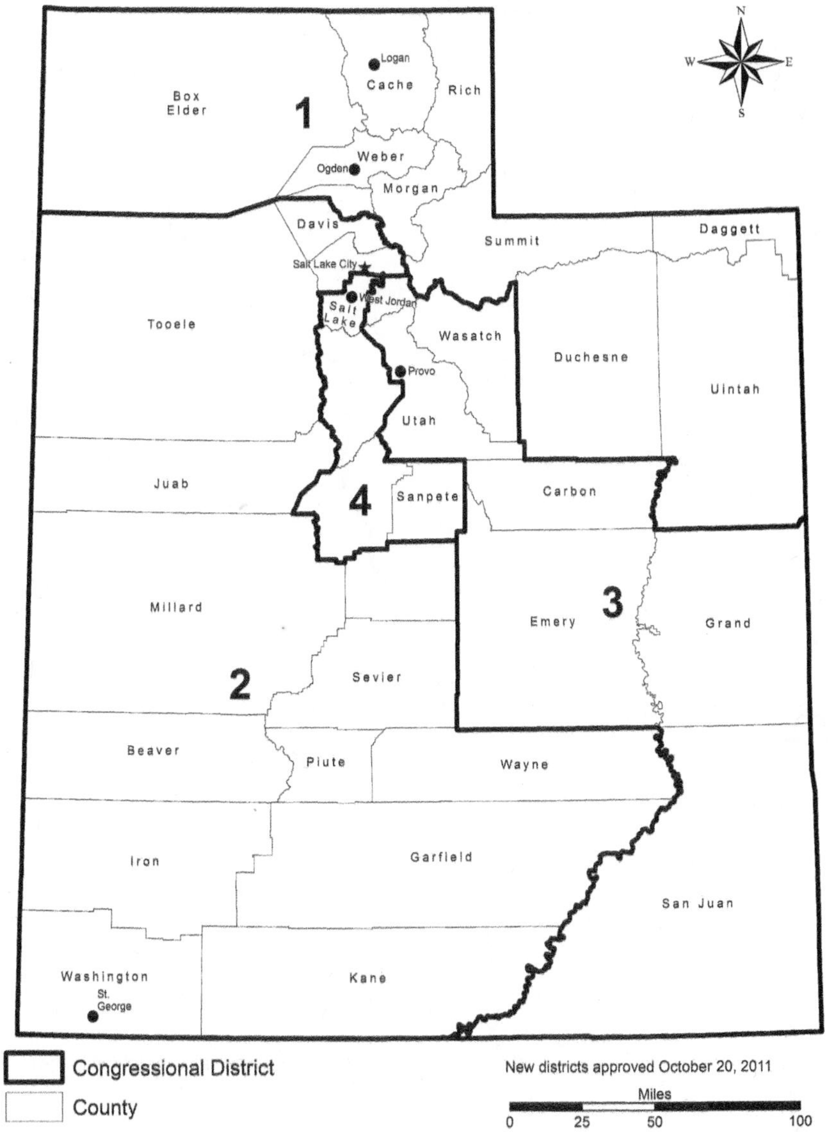

VERMONT—Congressional District—(1 District At Large)

VIRGINIA—Congressional Districts—(11 Districts)

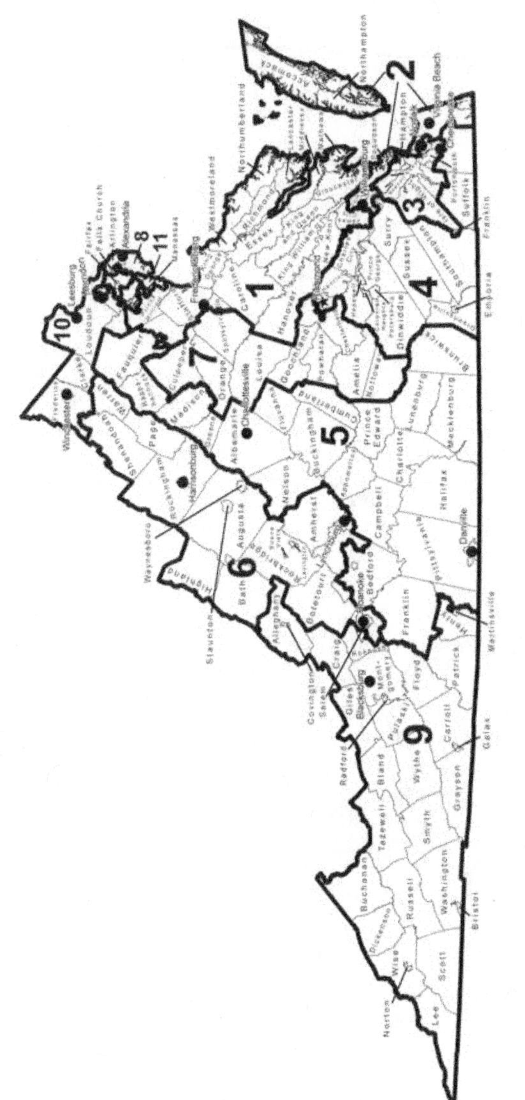

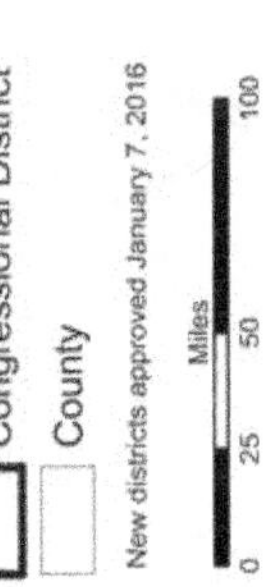

WASHINGTON—Congressional Districts—(10 Districts)

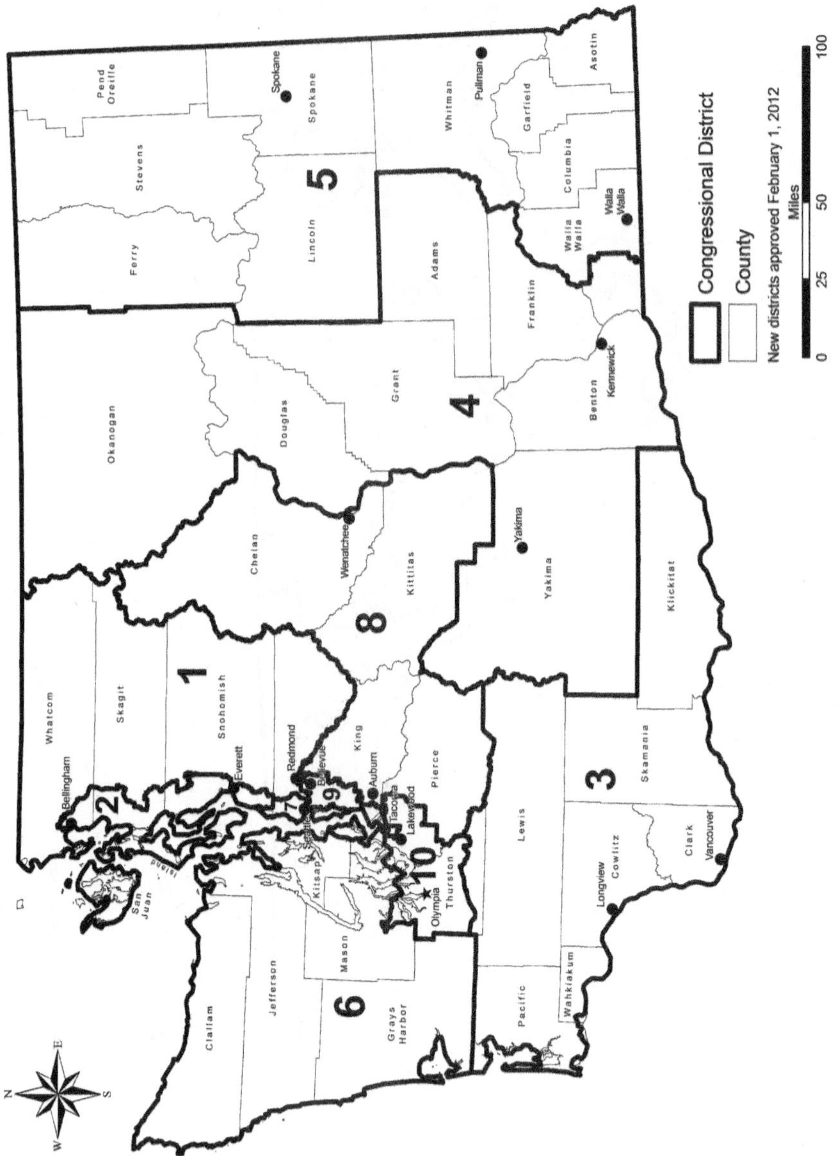

WEST VIRGINIA—Congressional Districts—(3 Districts)

Congressional District

County

New districts approved January 20, 2012

Miles

0 20 40 80

WISCONSIN—Congressional Districts—(8 Districts)

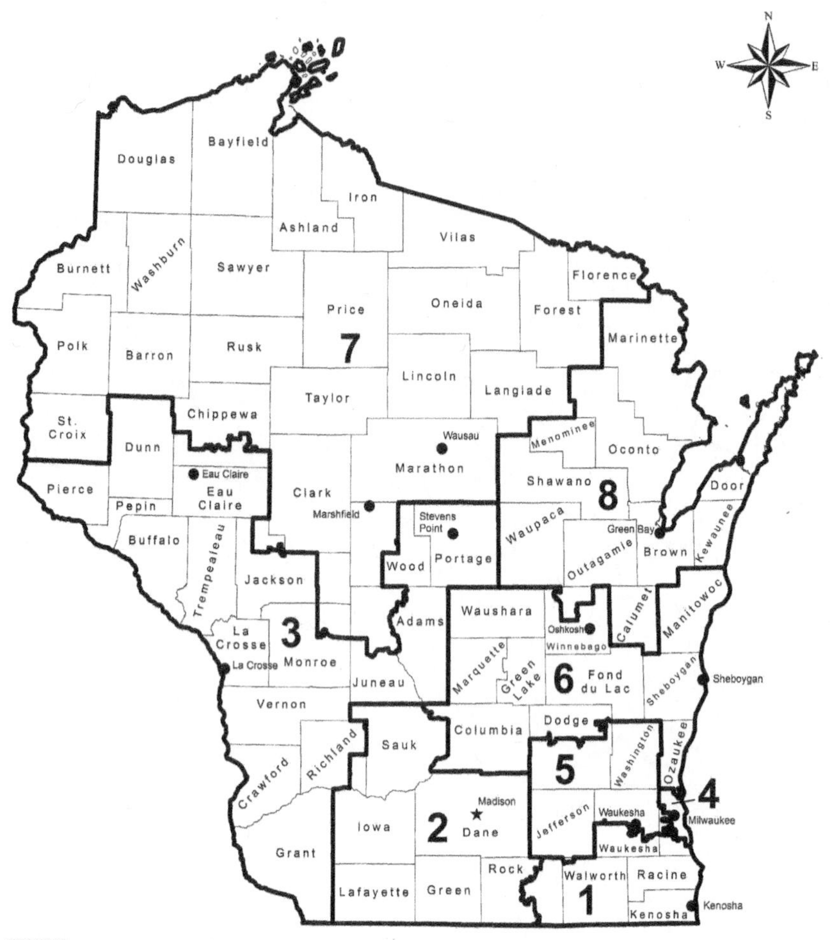

Congressional District

County

New districts approved August 9, 2011

Miles

0 25 50 100

WYOMING—Congressional District—(1 District At Large)

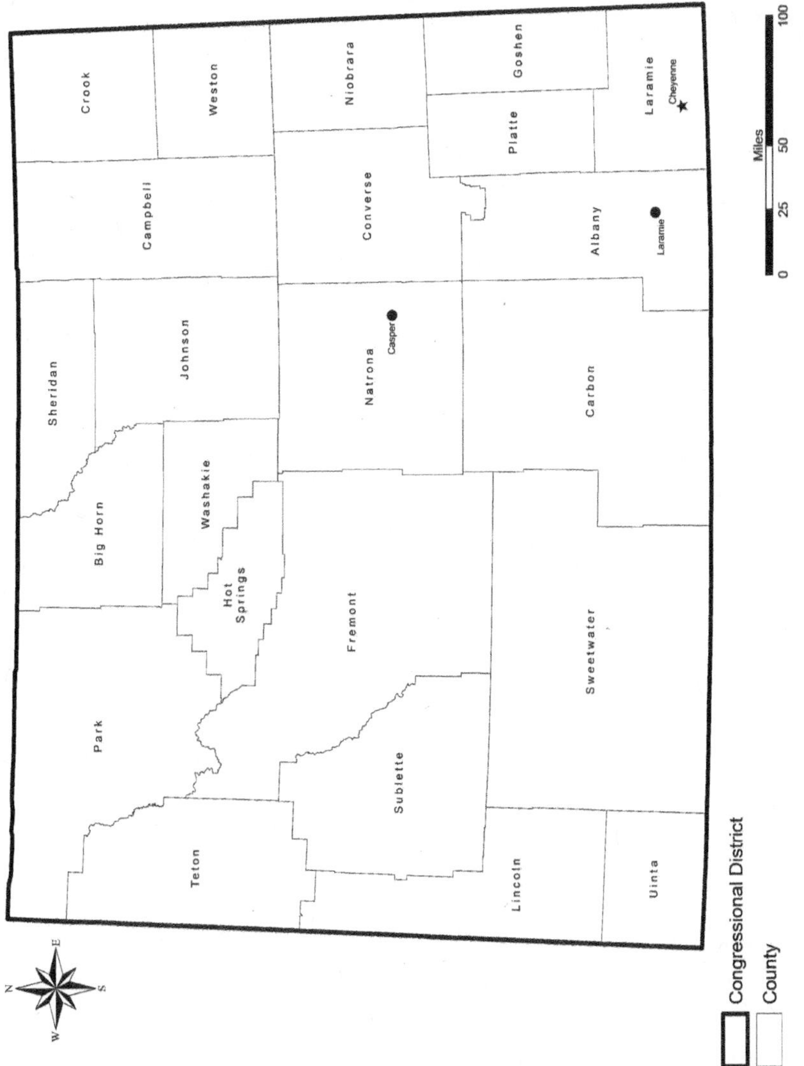

AMERICAN SAMOA—(1 Delegate At Large)

Swains Island

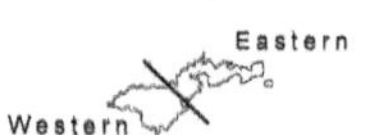

Rose Island

Islands

Miles

0 20 40 80

DISTRICT OF COLUMBIA—(1 Delegate At Large)

N
W E
S

District of Columbia

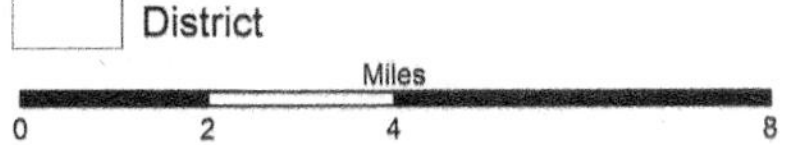

GUAM—(1 Delegate At Large)

NORTHERN MARIANA ISLANDS—(1 Delegate At Large)

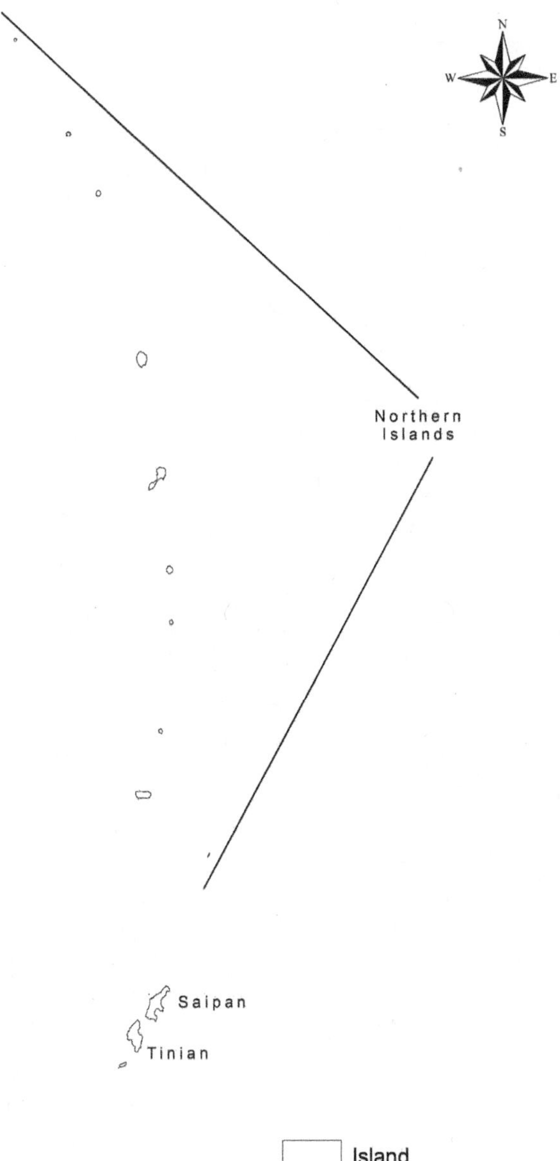

PUERTO RICO—(1 Resident Commissioner At Large)

THE VIRGIN ISLANDS OF THE UNITED STATES—(1 Delegate At Large)

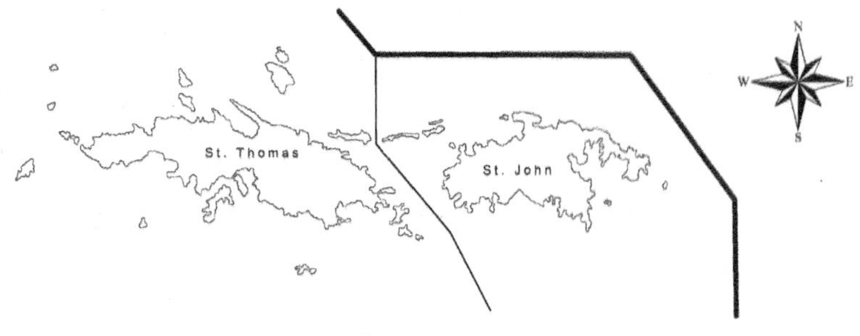

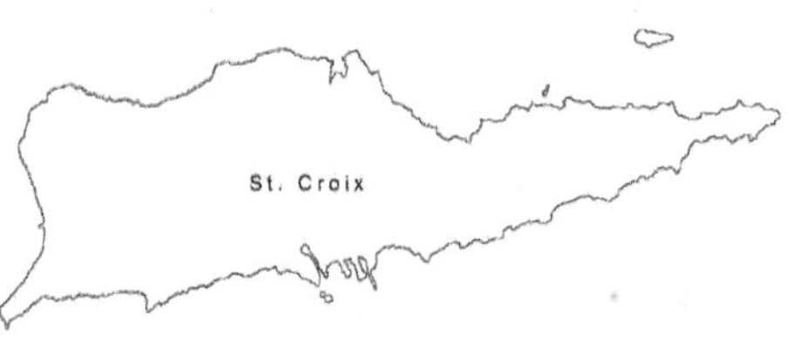

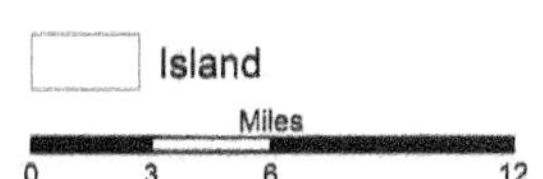

NAME INDEX

Page

A

Aaronson, Stephanie ... 785
Abaroa, Patricia ... 711
Abawi, Alex ... 613
Abbate, Paul D ... 673
Abbott, James T ... 799
Abbott, Jim ... 465
Abbott, Linda C ... 693
Abbott, Steve ... 121
Abboud, Khalil ... 427, 468, 504
Abdelaziz, Maged ... 944
Abegg, John ... 392
Abel, Sidney W ... 706
Abelev, Melissa ... 701
Abelian, Movses ... 940
Abello, Marta ... 916
Abernathy, Robert V ... 650
Abeyta, Diane L ... 586
Abouchar, Keith ... 461
Abow, Steven E ... 825
Abowd, John M ... 711
Abraham, Julie ... 747
Abraham, Ralph Lee ... 119, 308, 340, 399, 400, 406, 407, 438, 439, 483
Abraham, Ryan ... 370
Abram, Anna ... 738
Abramczyk, Nicholas ... 767
Abrames, Katie ... 198
Abrams, Mac ... 164
Abrams, Robert B ... 649
Abrams, Scott ... 34
Abrao, Paulo ... 933
Abruzzo, Jennifer A ... 818
Aburvasamy, Prem ... 818
Acevedo, Eddy ... 423
Achtenberg, Roberta ... 843
Ackerman, Bootsie ... 17
Ackiewicz, Mark ... 594
Acosta, Luis ... 589
Acosta, Marcel C ... 814
Acosta, R. Alexander ... 591, 721, 816, 830, 847
Acton, Dana ... 189
Acton, Mark ... 830
Acuna, Jennifer ... 370
Adaki, Oren ... 423
Adam, Olivier ... 941
Adame, Mariana ... 269
Adami, Blake ... 265
Adamoli, Joseph ... 617
Adams, Alma S ... 201, 311, 339, 399, 401, 410, 411, 441, 442, 467, 483
Adams, Beverly ... 393
Adams, Christopher ... 614
Adams, Eugene ... 909
Adams, Jerome M ... 735
Adams, John S ... 674
Adams, Jon ... 389
Adams, Julie E ... 393, 511, 816
Adams, Lily ... 19
Adams, Lisha H ... 650
Adams, Millie ... 858
Adams, Susan ... 405
Adams, Tasha ... 517
Adams, Todd ... 236
Adams, William ... 812
Adams-Allen, Paloma ... 806
Adamson, Reed ... 37
Adcock, Alley ... 429
Addison, Christopher ... 851
Addison, Stephanie ... 401
Adelfio, Giulia ... 590

Page

Adelman, Frederica ... 836
Aderholt, Robert B ... 4, 305, 334, 402, 403, 483, 504
Adesina, Kellie ... 401
Adkerson, Robert ... 81
Adkins, David ... 350
Adkins, Patricia ... 788
Adkins, Rick ... 239
Adkins-Blanch, Charles ... 669
Adler, Doug ... 793
Adler, Robert "Bob" ... 788
Adlerstein, Michael ... 940
Adorno, Rolena K ... 815
Adrian, Tobias ... 923
Adriance, Ned ... 177
Adu-Know, William ... 934
Agans, Bob ... 642
Agee, G. Steven ... 857
Agen, Jarrod ... 1, 391, 593
Ager, Julia ... 456
Agnello, Gino J ... 858
Agnew, Ann ... 733
Agnew, Lucas ... 350, 351
Agramonte, Tinisha ... 710
Agrella, Austin ... 262
Aguerre, Jose Agustin ... 917
Aguilar, Laura ... 376
Aguilar, Pete ... 34, 306, 340, 402, 403, 404, 483
Aguliera, Ricardo A ... 785
Agung, Juda ... 924
Agurkis, George ... 437
Ahern, Kara ... 299
Ahern, Paul ... 611
Ahern, Paul T ... 849
Ahlstrand, Amanda ... 726
Ahluwalia, Gundeep ... 722
Ahmed, Daanish ... 664
Ahmed, Ismail ... 781
Ahmed, Ismail Ould Cheikh ... 948
Ahmed, Khawaja Aftab ... 952
Ahmed, Ruby ... 387
Ahmed, Sajeel ... 624, 813
Ahmed, Shaghil ... 784
Ahn, Justin ... 43
Ahn, Meeran ... 364
Ahuja, Jay ... 801
Ahumada, Sergio ... 916
Aiken, Claude ... 794
Aiken, James ... 653
Aiken, Mary ... 783
Aimable, Peter ... 701
Aiyer, Vikrum ... 717
Aizcorbe, Christina ... 436
Akhtar, Shamshad ... 941
Akin, Isaiah ... 219, 370
Akiyama, Cliff ... 505
Akowuah, Emmanuel ... 464
al-Nasser, Nassir Abdulaziz ... 948
Alameddin, Salim ... 262
Alasia, Madeline ... 380
Albanese, Eileen M ... 712
Albanese, John ... 624
Albares, Mike ... 3
Alben, Elissa ... 371
Albence, Matthew T ... 779
Albert, Helen ... 95, 745
Albert, Janet ... 905
Alberts, Marc ... 433
Albornoz, Laura ... 846
Alboum, Jonathan ... 693
Albrecht-Taylor, Kimberly D ... 397
Albright, Leslie ... 405
Albright, Madeleine K ... 806
Albright, Richard ... 603

	Page
Albuja, Marco	932
Albuquerque, Jose	795
Alburger, Anna	213
Alcalde, Nancy T	756
Alcock, Charles	837
Alderstein, Michael	949
Alejandro, Vilma	702
Alemayehu, Mengistu	952
Alery, Becky	147
Alety, Saathvik	360
Alexander, Amanda	807
Alexander, Bruce C	701
Alexander, Craig	669
Alexander, Fiona	720
Alexander, Lamar	244, 312, 328, 330, 347, 348, 349, 365, 374, 382, 470, 473
Alexander, LaVerne	175
Alexander, Sheila	724
Alexander, Shirley	423
Alexander, Thomas	422
Alexander-Reid, Sheila	910
Alexiou, Lori	794
Alfonso-Royals, Angelica	780
Alford, Roger	658
Alford, Tim	213
Algayerova, Olga	941
Alhakim, Mohamed Ali	941
Alicandri, Beth	751
Alioto, Nicole Damasco	24
Alire, Camila A	815
Alito, Phil	381
Alito, Samuel Anthony, Jr	854
Alkhudairy, Khalid	950
Alldredge, Kimberly A	807
Allegra, Theodore	609
Allen, Andrew	724
Allen, Barbara	220
Allen, Bill	397, 706
Allen, Brad	405
Allen, Charles	629, 907
Allen, Charles A	625
Allen, Courtney	377
Allen, Craig	606
Allen, Derrick	797
Allen, John, Jr	515
Allen, Joseph J	659
Allen, Joyce	700
Allen, Kenneth E	842
Allen, Kirsten	176
Allen, Laura	390
Allen, Lauren	61
Allen, Mark	750
Allen, Matthew	779
Allen, Michael H	677
Allen, Paul	922
Allen, Reginald	676
Allen, Reginald E	790
Allen, Rick W	81, 307, 340, 399, 400, 410, 411, 483
Allen, Scott	727
Allen, Valerie F	849
Allen, Walter Ray	844
Allen-Brown, Charlotta	682
Allen-Gifford, Patrice	740
Allender-Smith, Michelle	739
Alles, Randolph D	780
Allford, Jason	950
Alli, Tylease	411
Allison, Roderick	778
Allison, Terisa L	420
Allison, Will	409
Allman, Timothy J	826
Allred, Hanna	264
Almagro, Luis	933
Almanza, Margarita	725
Almanza, Margie	291
Almanza, Paul	721
Almond, Kojuan L	840
Almutairi, Turki	950
Alogeel, Hesham Fahad	924
Alonso, C.B	700
Alpert, Matthew	188
Alphin, Bryan	429
Alprin, Geoffrey M	905
Alston, Michael	679
Alston, Michael A	699
Alsup, Carolyn	607
Alt, Curt	699
Altenburg, Bridget	502
Althen, William I	801
Althouse, Joshua	459
Altman, Clara	904
Altman, Michelle	215
Altom, Billy	814
Alva, Alisa	24
Alvarado, Carmen	616
Alvarado, Clelia	405
Alvares, Christopher	703
Alvarez, A. Eric	508
Alvarez, Chris	677
Alvarez, Vincent	730
Alverson, Robert	931
Alvin, David	635
Alvord, Dennis	712
Alzner, Susan	942
Amador, Paola	188
Amano, Yukiya	944
Amaral, Annmarie	517, 770
Amash, Justin	137, 309, 337, 434, 435, 483
Amato, Michael J	848
Ambro, Thomas L	857
Ambrose, Sandra	753
Amchan, Arthur	818
Ament, Douglas P	588
Amereihn, Tina	749
Ames, Fred	596
Amidon, Eric	181
Amin, Kirit	710
Amin, Vishal	430
Ammen, Faith	100
Ammon, Matthew	746
Amodei, Mark E	165, 310, 337, 402, 403, 404, 483
Amodeo, Francesca	34
Amor, Gloria	73
Amos, Lori H	827
Amos, Moses	936
Amour, Lynn St	948
Amparo, Alex	778
Amrhein, Ann	841
Anand, Supreet	765
Anaya-Ortiz, Jeronimo	93
Andalon, Elizabeth	33
Andersen, John	713
Anderson, Ashley	464
Anderson, Blake	168
Anderson, Brandt	101
Anderson, Brian R	420
Anderson, Byron	725
Anderson, Cheryl	843
Anderson, Craig	79
Anderson, David	683
Anderson, David A	897
Anderson, Doug	422, 613
Anderson, Elijah	826
Anderson, Elise	409
Anderson, Elyse	506
Anderson, Erik	707
Anderson, Gerald	934
Anderson, Griffin	449
Anderson, Heath	519
Anderson, James	740
Anderson, James G	688
Anderson, Jean C	785
Anderson, Jeff	148
Anderson, Jennifer M	904
Anderson, Jessica	595
Anderson, John L	820
Anderson, Joseph	647
Anderson, Karen	464
Anderson, Keith	909
Anderson, Kem	517
Anderson, Laura	699
Anderson, Lawrence L	825
Anderson, Lynette	395
Anderson, Margo	766
Anderson, Mark A	826
Anderson, Mary E	823
Anderson, Matthew	405
Anderson, Mike	25
Anderson, Olga M. "Marie"	645
Anderson, Paul Benjamin, Jr	857
Anderson, Philip O	821
Anderson, R. Lanier III	858
Anderson, Scott	804
Anderson, Steven J	780
Anderson, Truman	9
Anderson, Wendy	63

Page

Anderson, William 584
Andion, Benito 946
Andisco, Agustina 48
Andre, Larry 607
Andreae, Taylor 239
Andres, Bobby 370
Andres, Don 267
Andres, Doug 459
Andrews, Anne 720
Andrews, Annie 750
Andrews, Betty 718
Andrews, Bruce H 709
Andrews, Diana 841
Andrews, Hannah 192
Andrews, Jessica 80
Andrews, Kelli 680
Andrews, Mike 385
Andrews, Naomi 168
Andrews, Patrick 916
Andrews, Steve 506
Andrews, Tom 459
Andrucyk, Dennis 810
Angeli, Tony 430
Angelis, Harrison 63
Angelle, Scott A 688
Angelson, Alexander 597
Anger, Amanda 427
Angle, Richard E 650
Angotti, Steven 65
Angres, Leigh 583
Angrisani, Chris 390
Angulo, Jessica 25
Angus, Barbara 451
Annadif, Mahamat Saleh 945
Annerino, Joanna 95
Annino, Angelica 2
Anosike, Dennis 850
Ansley, Judith A 845
Anstine, Paul 425
Antell, Geoff 459
Anthony, Edward D 800
Anthony, Perry Edward "Ed" 787
Anthony, Steven J 848
Anthony, Telisha D 585
Antista, Jonathan 409
Antoskiewicz, Ashley 98
Anzalone, Ronald D 781
Anzur, Jon 229
Apelbaum, Perry 430
Apol, David J 823
Apostol, Amy W 825
Apostolides, Nik 513
App, Steve 797
Appel, Brian 46
Appel, Erika 409
Applegate, David 689
Applegate, Tim 624
Appleton, Rachel 380
Appleton, Seth 155, 743
Aquilino, Thomas J., Jr 881
Aquino, Mariano 826
Aramanda, Alec 733
Arbeit, Ellie 182
Arbeit, Jeffrey 469
Arberg, Kathleen L 856
Arbes, Sarah 733
Arbour, Louise 948
Arcangeli, Paul 408
Archer, Jacques "Don" 516
Archer, Reyn 162
Archeval, Anthony 739
Arel, Tim 750
Arenas, Maria Paula 918
Arends, Ross 660
Arenson, Steve 632
Argo, Mike 685
Arguello, Hector 73
Arias, Irene 952
Arkin, Sarah 373
Armen, Robert N., Jr 893
Armenta, Carina 32
Armijo, Natalie 178
Armington, Beth 658
Armor, John 715
Armstrong, Alexa 435
Armstrong, Charles E 397
Armstrong, Christopher 370
Armstrong, Hedy 699

Page

Armstrong, Jen 350
Armstrong, Jessica 645
Armstrong, Lynden 395
Armstrong, Richard, Jr 517
Armstrong, Thomas A 583
Arnakis, Adrian 363
Arnault, Jean 946
Arner, Shawn 701
Arneson, Christopher 370
Arness, Patrick 24
Arnold, Bob 751
Arnold, James 16
Arnold, Josephine 714
Arnold, Kenneth 677
Arnold, Michael 704
Arnold, Morris S 858
Arnold, Ralph "Brian" 633
Arnold, Sharon B 737
Aron, Leon 786
Aronhalt, Bethany 411
Aronson, Lauren 452
Arratia, Juan 826
Arreaga, Luis E 607
Arrighi, Jean Michel 933
Arrighi, T.W 41
Arrington, Jodey C 260, 313, 341, 399, 400, 401, 409, 448, 470, 483
Arrington, Sheryl 360
Arriola, Carlos Francisco Marin 919
Arriola, Eddy 806
Arrojo, David 417
Arsht, Adrienne 807
Arthur, Errol 905
Artis, Wanda L 643
Artist, Mike 750
Artista-Cuchna, Maria 838
Artz, Cyrus 198
Arvai, Antonette 923
Arviso, Emily 687
Ary, Vaughn 663
Asandas, Nash D 800
Ascencio, Juan Bosco Marti 917
Ascik, Mary Katherine 390
Asgedom, Surafeal 770
Ash, Darren 698
Ash, Michelle 416
Ash, Ned 515
Ashbery, Wayne 605
Ashby, Bryan A 789
Ashby, Hazeen 363
Ashenden, Nicholas 825
Asher, Nathalie R 779
Asher, Nita 469
Ashford, Jeff 405
Ashford, Tamara W 890
Ashley, Brandon 385
Ashley, Carol 764
Ashley, John 384
Ashley, John H 589
Ashley, Robert P 646
Ashman, Robert 783
Ashton, Kelli 397
Ashton, Richard M 785
Ashton, Robin C 681
Ashworth, Brett 639
Ashworth, Dan 80
Askew, Melissa 794
Asmus, Mike 261
Assalini, Santiago 953
Assim, Anisah 456
Assu, Ted 931
Asuncion, Anthony 680
Atkins, Paige R 720
Atkins, Valerie J 780
Atkinson, Carleton 123
Atkinson, Leslie 739
Atkinson, Mary Collins 350
Atlas, Robert 716
Atsatt, Mikki 679
Atterman, Jason 70
Attridge, Richard M 396
Attwood, Cynthia L 822
Atuatasi, Mary 653
Auchterlonie, Bob 936
Aucott, John 692
Audette, Rose Marie L 728
Auer, Daniel W 780
Auerbach, Andrew 730

Page
Auerbach, Gerald M 682
Auger, Daniel 203
Augustine, Patrick B 822
Aultman, Dale L 793
Aumann, Mark 295
Aumua, Audrey 936
Ausby, Janice 745
Ausiello, David 670
Austin, Brad 736
Austin, Christopher 741
Austin, Donna 226
Austin, Stan 687
Austin, Stephen D 644
Austin, Teresa 686
Autrey, Geno 652
Avakian, Stephanie 833
Avant, Lanier 151
Averill, Mark F 644
Avery, Cole 120
Avery, John 832
Aviles, Danielle 461
Avula, Deepa 741
Axson, Robert 271
Ayala, Michael 303
Ayers, Johana 583
Ayers, Nick 1, 391, 593
Ayers, Stephen T 510, 513, 518, 590, 781
Aylward, Anne 756
Ayres, Thomas E 637
Azar, Alex 591
Azar, Alex II 807
Azar, Alex M. II 733, 851
Azevedo, Allison 803
Azour, Jihad 923
Azzam, Stephen G 666

B

Baack, Korry 100
Babayan, Julie 416
Babb, Peter 350
Babb-Brott, Deerin 596
Babbitt, Paul 10
Babcock, Craig 682
Babcock, Robert 805
Babers, Beverly 616
Babers, Lucinda M 909
Babiarz, Paul 515
Babin, Brian 270, 313, 340, 438, 439, 443, 445, 446, 483
Babington, Sean 346
Bacchus, James E 683
Bacharach, Robert E 858
Bachman, Robin J 712
Bachmann, Peter 694
Back, Michelle A 659
Backes, Ronald 588
Baco, Luis 302
Bacon, Antoinette 657
Bacon, David R 840
Bacon, Don 162, 310, 341, 399, 400, 406, 407, 408, 424, 483
Badame, Meghan 44
Bader, Chris 17
Badger, Hilary 54
Badin, Joseph 700
Badorrek, Gerard 803
Badrising, Niermala 932
Baer, Lawrence M 844
Baessler, Sarah 220
Baggaley, John W 397
Baggett, Josh 96
Bagley, Kurt 456
Bagwell, Eric 429
Bahar, Daniel 596
Bahar, Michael 454
Bahar, Mojdeh 704
Baharu, Tegene 909
Bahr, Dorothy 661
Bahrami, Ali 751
Bailey, Angela 777
Bailey, Bill R 619
Bailey, Bradley 616
Bailey, Cheryl R 904
Bailey, Gladys 722, 727
Bailey, Jennifer 782
Bailey, Katie 814
Bailey, Kelsey Stroud 386
Bailey, Kevin 346

Page
Bailey, Megan 749
Bailey, Melissa 706
Bailey, Patrick 377, 813
Bailey, Ronnette 464
Bailey, William 631
Baily, David 187
Baily, Jess L 608
Bainwol, Mitch 510
Baird, Edmund 729
Baird, Edward 451
Baird, Kevin 282, 649
Baird, Mark 630
Baird, Michael 718
Baird, William R 397
Bajic, Irina 350
Bajkowski, Sean G 728
Bakalov, Kalina 88
Baker, Ashley 268
Baker, Barb 98
Baker, Brett 370
Baker, David 396
Baker, Dorenda 751
Baker, Elizabeth 755
Baker, Eric 107
Baker, Georgina E 952
Baker, Greg 111
Baker, Gregory R 798
Baker, Jake 375
Baker, James A 673
Baker, James E 897
Baker, Michael K 451
Baker, Pamela R 822
Baker, Paxton K 505
Baker, Samantha 296
Baker, Stacy 435
Baker, Tim 81
Baker, Todd M 632
Balaguer, James "Jim" 795
Balash, Joseph 687
Baldock, Bobby R 858
Baldovich, Patricia 779
Baldwin, Tammy 293, 314, 327, 331, 347, 348, 349, 362, 363, 374, 388, 473, 815
Baldwin, Valerie 405
Balentine, Brooke 153
Bales, Anita F 625
Balis, Ellen J 409
Ball, Daniel 364
Ball, Deborah L 820
Ball, Peggy S 822
Ball, William 433
Balladares, Francisco Jose Mayorga 917
Balland, David 770
Ballard, Christopher S 647
Ballard, Leonard L 800
Ballard, Tina 787
Ballenger, David 770
Ballman, Luke 616
Ballou, Ernest Wade 464
Balsiger, Jim 931
Baltimore, Jason 513
Balton, David A 605
Balzano, Paul 401
Balzano, Richard A 753
Bamiduro, Portia 378
Banducci, Andrew 411
Banducci, Andy 375
Baney, Drew 436
Banga, Ajay 782
Banister, Simeon 505
Bankovic, Marko Marcelo Machicao 917
Banks, Alvert "Al" 589, 590
Banks, Carole 616
Banks, Christopher 750
Banks, Dennis 692
Banks, Derris 717
Banks, George 749
Banks, Jim 100, 307, 341, 406, 407, 408, 410, 411, 448, 483
Banks, Marnee 159
Banks, Sylvia 56
Banner, Timothy 908
Bannerman, Doug 773
Bansemer, John 626
Baptiste-Jones, Lorna 585
Baran, Jeff 821
Barankin, Nathan 19
Barber, Beth 270

Page
Barber, Craig 417
Barber, Jackie 382, 401
Barber, Sara 440
Barbic, Kenneth Steven 693
Barblan, Jennifer 415
Barbour, Mike 665
Barcena, Alicia 941
Barclay, Eric M 603
Bardin, Sara Benjamin 910
Bardis, John 733
Bardorf, Tracey 779
Bardwell, Shawn 830
Bareiro, Elisa Ruiz Diaz 932
Barfield, Sheila 910
Barger, Norah M 784
Barham, Rochele A 793
Barker, Adam 353, 354, 355, 356
Barker, Erica 80
Barker, Mary Katherine 16
Barker, Nathan 80
Barkley, Chris 389
Barkley, Rachel 455
Barkley, Timothy 752
Barko, Peter 653
Barkow, Rachel E 849
Barksdale, Antoinette 662
Barksdale, Jameill 634
Barksdale, Marshall 464
Barksdale, Rhesa H 857
Barksdale, Sybil N 683
Barlerin, Peter 606
Barletta, Lou 229, 312, 337, 410, 411, 424, 443, 444, 445, 483
Barloon, Linus 395
Barlotta, Allison 681
Barlow, Amanda 736
Barlow, Kate 38
Barminski, Joan 688
Barna, Stephanie A 622
Barnabae, Monica 514
Barnao, Catherine 423
Barnard, Brian 292
Barnes, David 618
Barnes, Elmer 351
Barnes, Janet L 824
Barnes, Kevin 705
Barnes, Kim Canady 195
Barnes, Michael A 587
Barnes, Sandra D 676
Barnett, Bee 510
Barnett, Brynn 843
Barnett, Gary 833
Barnett, Mark A 879
Barnett, Robert 808
Barnhart, Devon 364
Barnhart, Greg 630
Barnicle, Keith 130
Barnwell, Patrick H 900
Baron, Dena 405
Baron, Ira 679
Baron, Kelsey 449
Barone, John 824
Baroudi, Merli Margaret 953
Barr, Andy 115, 308, 339, 418, 419, 483
Barr, Ann Calvaresi 843
Barr, Chris 373
Barr, Delia 442
Barr, G. Stephen 727
Barr, Gary 663
Barr, Lawrence 513
Barr, Meg 430
Barragan, Nanette Diaz 40, 306, 318, 341, 424, 425, 431, 432, 483
Barranca, Alexis 4
Barranti, Michael 677
Barras, Kerry 749
Barrasso, John 298, 314, 327, 330, 365, 366, 367, 372, 385, 389, 473, 808
Barrera, Amy 46
Barrera, Maria Soledad 917
Barrera, Marissa 361
Barrera, Staci 779
Barrera, Virgilio 177
Barrett, Amy Coney 858
Barrett, Barbara M 836
Barrett, Christopher 841
Barrett, Jasmine 648
Barrett, Joan 724
Barrett, Joanna 33
Barrett, Ko 716
Barrett, Todd 692
Barrett, Walker 241
Barria, Juan Anibal 932
Barrick, Carl 405
Barringer, Hailey 202
Barringer, Scott 701
Barrio, Alex 62
Barron, David J 857
Barrows, Walter A 848
Barry, Ashleigh 769
Barry, Dan 735
Barry, Giselle 129
Barry, Mary Nguyen 376
Barry, Maryanne Trump 857
Barry, Randall 589
Barry-Perez, Naomi 722
Barsa, John 776
Barsky, Seth 669
Barstow, Kevin 387
Barth, Stephen G 642
Barth, Zack 264
Barthold, Thomas 469
Bartholomew, Carolyn 508
Bartlett, Anna 240
Bartlett, Blaire 186
Bartlett, Chip 16
Bartlett, Jessica 799
Bartlett, Matthew 637
Bartlett, Patricia 836
Bartlett, Sarah 386
Bartlett, Sean 383
Bartley, Catherine 245
Bartley, Margaret 899
Bartnoff, Judith 904
Bartolomeo, Liz 28
Barton, Joe 253, 313, 333, 413, 414, 415, 483
Barton, Lisa 846
Barton, Mike 815
Barton, Ryan 229
Barton, Stacy Palmer 206
Barton, Victoria 743
Bartsiotas, Bettina Tucci 940
Barz, Chloe 397
Barzilay, Judith M 882
Basanes, Federico 916, 917
Basheerud-Deen, Hakeem 827
Bashford, Janice 37
Bashua, Abiodun Oluremi 946
Basinger, Christina 368
Baskin, Steven 92
Bass, Deana 743
Bass, John R 606
Bass, Karen 37, 306, 338, 421, 428, 429, 483
Bass, Pam 682
Bassani, Antonella 949
Bassermann, Jacqueline G 782
Bassett, Matthew 733
Bassett, William 785
Basso, John 770
Basso, Peter 749
Bastarache, Danielle 744
Bastin, Jennifer 351
Bastomski, Gabriel 218
Basu, Anand 713
Batchelder, Alice M 857
Bates, Christopher 381
Bates, Jim 409
Bates, John D 877
Bates, Keith F 785
Bath, Nick 375
Batista, Aneiry 187
Batista, Michael 65
Batory, Ronald 752
Battle, Karen 712
Battle, Pauletta 612
Battle, Sandra 764
Battles, Thomas 662
Bauer, Ursula 737
Bauer, William J 858
Bauer, Zach 1, 391, 593
Baugh, Patrick 429
Baugher, James R 903
Bauguess, Scott 832
Bauhs, Kimberlyn 715
Baukol, Andy 614
Bauld, Denise 237

	Page
Baum, Kristina	439
Baumann, Caroline	836
Baumann, Theresa	380
Baumerich, Carol A	822
Baumes, Harry	693
Bauserman, Trent	461
Bautista, Joske	378, 828
Bautista, Leonidas Rosa	932
Baxter, Derek	728
Bayard, Rochelle S	824
Bayer, Jake	461
Baylor, Ginger	212
Bayly, John H	905
Baysinger, Betsy	698
Bayu, Meron	164
Bazemore, Bruce	76
Bazydlo, Emily	193
Bazzoni, Stefania Antonella	917
Bea, Carlos T	858
Beach, Anselm	779
Beachy, Roger	820
Beadle, Mirtha R	741
Beagle, Jan	940
Beagle, Milford H	641
Beal, Krista	395
Beal, Lonny	585
Beal, Mary Dee	77
Beall, Brandon	360
Beam, C. Arlen	858
Bean, Brian	395
Bean, Michael J	686
Bean, W.L. Scott III	673
Beard, Douglas	689
Beard, Hillary	6
Beardsley, Erica S	805
Beary, Michael	947
Beasley, David	942
Beasley, Joy	686
Beasley, Roger	660
Beason, Elizabeth L	728
Beatty, Joyce	207, 311, 339, 418, 419, 483
Beatty, Paige	514
Beatty, Paul C	711
Beaubian, Traci	462
Beaudreault, B.D	656
Beaumont, Amanda	376
Beausoleil, Geoffrey	760
Beaver, Sam	392
Becerra, Francisco	934
Bech, Rebecca	706
Bechtel, Peter B	647
Bechtol, Nancy	836
Beck, Amber Busby	350
Beck, Gary	409
Beck, Lucille	772
Beck, Ronna L	904
Beck, Vic M	651
Beckelman, Yuri	39
Beckenbaugh, Scot L	801
Becker, Anton	172
Becker, Daniel J	841
Becker, Deborah	724
Becker, Jacqueline M	785
Becker, Julie	904
Becker, Kelsey	88
Becker, Robert	200
Becker, Sylvia M	676
Beckford, Monique	396
Beckhard, Dan C	676
Beckwith, Corinne	904
Beco, Marlene Olivia L	917
Bedell, Anthony	748
Bednar, Mark	296
Bednarczyk, Philip	423
Beebe, Carol	513
Beebe, John	783
Beeman, Michael	596
Beene, Eric	636
Begeman, Ann	756
Behm, Mitch	748
Behnam, Rostin	787
Behnke, Katie	389
Behnken, Linda	931
Behrends, Paul	423
Behringer, Caroline	460
Beil, Jennifer	113
Beinecke, Frederick W	817
Bejankiwar, Raj	923
Bekkering, Michelle	843
Belair, Brendan	80
Belcher, Robert E	464
Belfield, Ann	633
Belford, Remmington	260
Belknap, Eric	518
Bell, Allyson	271
Bell, Andrew	202
Bell, Beth	383
Bell, Colleen	51
Bell, Douglas	614
Bell, Gloria	686
Bell, Hubert T	821
Bell, Jacqueline	229
Bell, Josh	111
Bell, Keith E	822
Bell, Lisa	784
Bell, March	734
Bell, Megan O'Donnell	115
Bell, Michael	627
Bell, Morgan	132
Bell, Suzanne L	670
Bell, Vonda K	712
Bellis, Douglass	464
Bello, Tiwalade	752
Belsky, Eric S	784
Belson, James A	904
Belt, Rabia	814
Belur, Pradeep	849
Bembo, Dinah	735
Ben'Ary, Michael P	663
Ben-Israel, Joseph	700
Benavides, Fortunato P	857
Benchoff, Peter N	641
Benda, Leigh	679
Bender, Amy	794
Bender, Avi	720
Bender, Rachael	794
Bender, Renee	383
Bender, William J. "Bill"	634
Benecke, Michelle	378
Benedict, Daniel	676
Benenati, Paul M	649
Benevento, Doug	792
Benge, Shawn	686
Benishek, Dan	338
Benishek, Judy	505
Benison, John P	746
Benitez, Rey	164
Benjamin, Billy	459
Benjamin, Chaun	802
Benjamin, Daniel	844
Benjamin, Darren	405
Benjamin-Sirmons, Denise	790
Benlamlih, M. El-Mostafa	946
Benn, Eric	677
Benner, Derek N	779
Bennet, Michael F	46, 306, 329, 330, 345, 346, 369, 370, 373, 374, 470, 473
Bennett, A. Brooke	16
Bennett, Amanda	786
Bennett, Cheryl	245
Bennett, Chris	449
Bennett, Cynthia	840
Bennett, Douglas M	636
Bennett, Edgar	830
Bennett, James F	688
Bennett, Jody L	356, 357, 358
Bennett, Lee Ann	903
Bennett, Megan	660
Bennett, Nathan	103
Bennett, Tate	790
Bennett, Toby	719
Bennett, Virginia	605
Bennett, Wells	454
Benor, David E	735
Benoy, Glenn	922
Benthall, Edward	820
Bentley, Chris	704
Benton, Charles	456
Benton, Donald M	835
Benton, Duane	858
Bentsen, Kenneth E., Jr	510
Bentz, Joseph P	642
Benway, Kathleen	364
Benz, Frank J	811
Benzing, Sarah	205
Bera, Ami	23, 305, 339, 421, 438, 439, 483

Page

Beran, Matthew 652
Berardi, Chris 68
Berg, Alyssa 144
Berger, Adi 830
Berger, Carol 95
Berger, Daniel 736
Berger, Joseph 649
Berger, Luzviminda Peredo 779
Berger, Sherri A 737
Bergersen, Benjamin 850
Bergerson, Kristien T 508
Bergeson, Thomas W 638
Bergh, Katie 346
Bergin, Moira 425
Bergman, Carol 808
Bergman, Jack 136, 309, 341, 409, 431, 432, 448, 483
Bergreen, Timothy 454
Bergren, Eric 113
Bergwin, Diana 425
Berick, Dave 371
Berk, Steven 904
Berko, Julie 740
Berkowitz, Barry 710
Berman, Francine 815
Bernal, Dan 26
Bernal, Elizabeth 380
Bernard, Stephen J 786
Berner, Alaina 456
Berner, Hannah 378
Bernhardt, David 685
Bernhardt, Lisa 351
Bernhart, Christy 825
Bernicat, Marcia Stephens Bloom 606
Berns, Kim M 696
Bernstein, Tom A 844, 845
Berntsen, Laura 371
Berny, Colleen 378
Berquam, Taunja 405
Berret, Emily 460
Berrick, Cathleen A 583
Berrios, Roberto 378
Berry, A. Paulette 826
Berry, Ann 274
Berry, David 689
Berry, David P 818
Berry, Gregory 260
Berry, Jake 168
Berry, Jessica 350
Berry, John W 834
Berry, Lisa 698
Berry, Matthew 794
Berry, Michael 751
Bersani, Kurt 713
Bertalotto, Josh 385
Bertaut, Carol 784
Bertocci, Timothy 144
Bertoni, Dan 583
Bertoni, Malcolm 739
Bertram, Paul 363
Bertrand, Charlotte 791
Bertsch, Charles 699
Bertsch, Kevin M 783
Berzon, Marsha L 858
Beschloss, Afsaneh M 782
Beshar, Peter J 851
Beshore, Alan 756
Beshouri, Joseph E 905
Bess, Garret 437
Bess, Garrett 48
Best, Jean 470
Bethea, Deborah 417
Betka, Sue 767
Betourney, Chanda 350
Bettis, Elizabeth 101
Betts, Susan 744
Bettwy, Greg 836
Betz, Kimberly 427
Beuse, Nathaniel 754
Bevacqua, Frank 922
Beveridge, Albert J. III 815
Beydoun, Ali 728
Beyer, Donald S., Jr 281, 313, 340, 431, 432, 438, 439, 467, 483
Beyler, Juliet 653
Bezio, Brian 751
Bezruki, Steffanie 97
Bhartiya, Jennifer 649
Bharwani, Raj 440

Page

Bhatia, Anita 952
Bhatnagar, Saurabha 772
Bhattacharyya, Rupa 661
Bhuiyan, Muhammad 951
Biagi, Marguerite 23
Bialek, Mark 785
Bianchi, Diana W 740
Bianchi, Dominic 846
Bias, Lori 405
Bibas, Stephanos 857
Bibo, David 778
Bickerstaff, Kier 728
Biddick, Dennis 653
Bidelman, Kiley 435
Bien, Chris 459
Bienenstock, Arthur 820
Bierman, Brock 843
Bierworth, Ashlee 10
Bigelow, Chris 405
Bigesby, Tracey 745
Biggins, James 789
Biggio, Terry 750
Biggs, Andy 12, 305, 341, 428, 429, 438, 439, 484
Biggs, Paul 650
Bighorn, Spike 687
Bigsby, Sandra 718
Bildner, Elisa Spungen 844
Bilirakis, Gus M 64, 306, 336, 413, 414, 415, 448, 484
Bill, Aaron 245
Billerbeck, Peter 132
Billingslea, Marshall S 615
Billman, Jeff 507
Bills, Shawn 284
Billy, Stephen 200, 823
Bilyeu, Dana K 801
Bina, Betsy 405
Bingen, Kari 408
Binger, Sharon B 835
Binkley, Steve 760
Binns, Joseph 702
Binns-Berkey, Augusta 353, 354, 355
Binsted, Anne 462
Binstock, Seth P 839
Birch, Debra 464
Birch, Joseph 464
Bird, Jennifer 408
Birdsong, Betty 619
Birdwell, Stephanie 770
Biribo, Naomi 919
Birman, Igor 22
Birmingham, Maureen 934
Birnbaum, Linda S 741
Birney, William J 681
Biro, Susan 790
Biron, Christine 62
Birx, Deborah 602
Bisacre, Brian R 648
Biscone, Gregory A 637
Bishop, Cameron 79
Bishop, Cherae L 782
Bishop, Deirdre Dalpiaz 712
Bishop, Kevin 237
Bishop, Leslie 718
Bishop, Mike 139, 309, 340, 450, 451, 484
Bishop, Rob 272, 313, 335, 406, 407, 408, 431, 484
Bishop, Sanford D., Jr 76, 307, 334, 402, 403, 404, 484
Bisille, Jacqueline 385
Bisogno, Marcelo 917
Bissell, Katherine 727
Bitar, Maher 454
Bitol, Gabriel 798
Bitter, Rena 608
Bittner, Mamie 513
Bivins, Michelle 850
Black, Barry C 394
Black, Casey 249
Black, Diane 247, 312, 338, 409, 450, 484
Black, Elliott 751
Black, Frederick H., Sr 502
Black, Jonathan 76
Black, Kate 794
Black, Lindsay 280
Black, Michael 687
Black, Renae 363
Black, Steve 759
Black, Susan H 858
Black, Tanner 430
Black, Tori Beth 107

Page

Blackburn, Marsha............ 248, 312, 335, 413, 414, 415, 484
Blackburne-Rigsby, Anna 904
Blackmon, Francine C........ 643
Blacksberg, Aaron........ 127, 436
Blackwell, Edith R 735
Blackwell, Jim 636
Blackwell, Juliana........ 715
Blackwell, Victoria........ 262
Blackwood, R. Duke 812
Bladow, Cassie 203
Blaha, Lydia........ 770
Blair, David 693
Blair, Jeffrey C 839
Blair, Mark........ 371
Blair, Rob 595
Blair, Robert M 799
Blake, Carly........ 454
Blake, Carol........ 704
Blake, Casey........ 630
Blake, Daniel A 638
Blake, Kathleen 821
Blake, Kristene 459
Blake, Nathan 437
Blake, Sebrina........ 736
Blake, Shelly........ 161
Blakely, Allison........ 815
Blakely, Cheryle 706
Blakey, Darryl 401
Blanco, Kenneth A........ 615, 663
Bland, Megan........ 449
Bland, Toney 617
Blando, Tony 293
Blaney, Gregory D 811
Blank, Thomas........ 779
Blankenberger, L.J........ 814
Blankenship, April 446, 451
Blankenship, Ronald E........ 903
Blansitt, Ed 505
Blase, Marcia........ 787
Blaszko, Gregory F 826
Blaydes, Carolyn 449
Bleiweis, Seth........ 614
Blier, William 676
Blim, Larry 702
Blocher, Sarah 422
Block, Gregory O 900
Block, Molly........ 433
Blockwood, James-Christian 584
Blodgett, Tim........ 465
Blom, Dominique G 744
Blome, Donald........ 607
Bloodgood, Laura........ 846
Bloom, David 790
Bloom, Eric........ 646
Bloomberg, Michael 948
Bloomfield, Sara J 844
Bloomquist, Michael 415
Blount, Elonda........ 464
Blount, Emilee........ 695
Blount, Willie 464
Bloxson, Darrin 518
Bloyer, Kelly 840
Blue, Darren........ 804
Blue, Matthew 680
Bluestone, Ronald S 590
Blum, Daniel........ 364
Blum, Jonathan M 420
Blum, Rod........ 105, 308, 340, 434, 441, 442, 484
Blum-Evitts, Lyron........ 456
Blume, Joshua........ 370
Blumenauer, Earl 221, 312, 334, 450, 451, 484
Blumenthal, Richard.......... 51, 306, 329, 330, 352, 353, 362, 363, 379, 380, 384, 387, 473, 502
Blumerman, Lisa M........ 711
Blunt Rochester, Lisa......... 55, 306, 341, 399, 400, 410, 411, 484
Blunt, Roy........ 153, 309, 329, 330, 347, 348, 349, 362, 363, 382, 386, 390, 468, 470, 473, 509, 510, 806, 808
Boasberg, James E........ 872
Bock, Joe 736
Bock, Tonia 769
Bock-Valotta, Claudia 917
Bodenheimer, Laurie 827
Bodine, Susan........ 790
Boehm, Martin........ 830
Boehme, Jennifer........ 923
Boerste, Jerome 519
Boesch, William L., Jr 585

Page

Boffelli, Gabriella........ 74
Bogeljic, Tia 50
Boggs, Clay 36
Boggs, Mara........ 290
Bogle, Darlyanda K........ 837
Bohan, Ravenna........ 696
Bohigian, David........ 847
Bohl, Eric........ 158
Bohman, Mary........ 705
Bohnett, David C........ 807
Bohnsack, Frances 754
Boizelle, Ashley........ 795
Bojes, Gary A........ 701
Bokova, Irina 944
Boland, Patrick 33, 454
Boland, Robert........ 147
Bolden, Christian........ 425
Bolduc, Kim 946
Bolen, Jacquelyn........ 416
Bolen, John O........ 682
Boliek, Sarah 351
Boling, Edward "Ted" 594
Boling, Melinda........ 908
Bolinger, Kimberlie 518
Bolitho, Zachary 657
Bolitho, Zachary C 849
Boll, Theodore 467
Bolten, Joshua B 844, 845
Bolton, John R........ 594
Boman, Josiah........ 155
Bomar, Martin 698
Bomba, Margaret A........ 397
Bombach, Brent........ 378
Bombassaro, Bryan........ 370
Bomersheim, William........ 699
Bomersheim-Wedderburn, Yvette........ 699
Bomfim, Antulio........ 784
Bonamici, Suzanne........... 219, 311, 338, 410, 438, 439, 484
Bonander, Kathryne M........ 397
Bonar, Donna........ 736
Bond, Chris........ 118, 460
Bond, David........ 132
Bond, Rebecca........ 661, 821
Bonds, Anita 907
Bone, Austin 175
Bone, Shawn........ 364
Boness, Christopher........ 378
Boney, Virginia 597
Bonilla, Gerardo 467
Bonilla, Juan Pablo........ 917
Bonine, David........ 51
Bonini, Kyle 141
Bonjorni, Jessica........ 772
Bonner, Bob........ 405
Bonner, Peter 694
Bonner, Rebecca........ 366
Bonnet, Odette........ 718
Bono, Raquel C 625
Bonome, Tomas........ 733
Bonvechio, Kate 425
Bonyun, Sean........ 596
Bonzano, Davide 952
Bonzanto, Tamara........ 449
Booker, Cory A........ 169, 310, 328, 331, 367, 368, 372, 373, 379, 383, 388, 473
Bookstein, Monique 673
Boone, Nichelle 764
Booth, Austin........ 17
Booth, William 623
Boothe, Caroline........ 268, 437
Boots, Sherita 848
Boozman, John 15, 305, 329, 330, 345, 346, 347, 348, 349, 361, 367, 368, 384, 473, 504, 508, 835
Bope, Heath R 408
Borchard, Lauren........ 510
Borck, Thomas........ 361
Bordallo, Madeleine Z....... 301, 314, 343, 406, 407, 431, 432
Bordallo, Madeline Z 484
Bordeaux, JoAnn J 661
Borden, Rob........ 435
Borden, Robert........ 802
Borden, Vera Bostick 839
Bordewich, Jean P 510
Borio, Luciana 738
Borjon, Jose 258
Borkowski, Mark........ 779
Borland, Jim 838
Borlik, Bryan........ 713

Page
Borman, Matthew 712
Bornstein, Jake 273
Bornstein, Rachael 220
Borowicz, Kim 722
Borrelli, Bridget 802
Borro, R 651
Bortnick, David 405
Bortz, Ashton 137
Bos, Amy 296
Bosanko, William J 811
Bosco, Paul 759
Bose, Gira 133
Bose, Kimberly 761
Bosier, Tanya Jones 905
Bosley, Dale 870
Bosse, Natalie S 641
Bosserman, Dylan 451
Bossi, Joseph W 903
Bost, Mike 94, 307, 340, 399, 400, 443, 444, 445, 446, 448, 484
Boston, Sean 840
Bosworth, Michael S 844
Bouchard, Barbara J 783
Bouchard, Benoit 922
Bouchard, Robert 753
Bouchet, Rahkel 905
Bouda, Seydou 951
Boudin, Michael 857
Bougara, Omar 951
Boughton, Marty 411
Boujoukos, G. Jeffrey 835
Boulden, Laurie 777
Boulden, William L 846
Boulton, Caroline 685
Bouman, Rachel 588
Bounds, Lorissa 220, 415
Bourbon, Robert Allen 677
Bourdon, Christy 27
Bourke, Jaron 436
Bourne, Alma 517
Bourne-Goldring, Kimberly R 397
Boutwell, Debra 151
Bouvion, Renee 736
Bouzis, Evangelia "Lea" 614
Bovbjerg, Barbara D 583
Bowan, David 78
Bowden, Alford 605
Bowden, Andrew 832
Bowden, Gary A 903
Bowden, Jamitress 279
Bowdich, David 673
Bowen, Jonathan 364
Bowen, Lindsey 196
Bowen, Melanie 271
Bowen, Timothy 518
Bower, Kaitlyn 516
Bower, Matthew 405
Bower, Michelle 665
Bower, Taylor 22
Bowers, Jamie 200
Bowers, Mandy 425
Bowers, Pamela S 793
Bowers, Tonya 739
Bowersox, Lynn 850
Bowery, Charles R., Jr 644
Bowie, Maria 217
Bowlen, Joshua 197
Bowles, Cameron 937
Bowles, David 811
Bowling, Kenneth 510
Bowling, Tim 584
Bowman, Bertie 373
Bowman, Casey 286
Bowman, David H 784
Bowman, Liz 105, 790
Bowman, Matthew S 734
Bowman, Pasco M. II 858
Bowman, Quinn 389
Bowman, Thomas G 769
Bowron, Jessica 687
Bowser, Katrina 830
Bowser, Muriel E 807, 814, 907
Boyce, Don 734
Boyd, Anna Alvarez 784
Boyd, Katie 153
Boyd, Kenneth R 711
Boyd, Krista 436
Boyd, Lisa M 801
Page
Boyd, R. Dean 786
Boyd, Stephen E 680
Boyd, Theresa 772
Boyd, Tona 381
Boyer, Brooke 405
Boyer, Janet L 894
Boyer, Jennifer 375
Boyer, Kelly 167
Boyer, Lucretia M 783
Boyington, Will 286
Boyken, Lori 155
Boykin, Lisa T 660
Boyl, Molly 439
Boyle, Brendan F 230, 312, 340, 409, 421, 422, 484
Boyle, Coleen 737
Boyle, Garrett 7
Boyle, Mary 788
Boyne, Trinda 613
Boynton, Katelynn 387
Braccio, Dominic D 780
Brachman, Ellis 590
Bradbury, Steven G 748
Braddock, Richard 518
Braden, Parish 433
Braden, Susan G 883
Bradfield, Patrick 766
Bradford, Aryele 436
Bradford, Courtney 351
Bradford, Frank 425
Bradford, Stephen 144
Bradford, Steve 750
Bradley, Katelynn 420
Bradley, Kim 849
Bradley, Mark 812
Brady, Clare 923
Brady, Gable 254
Brady, Janae 346
Brady, Kelly D 660
Brady, Kevin 254, 313, 334, 450, 469, 484
Brady, Michael P 646
Brady, Robert A 224, 312, 334, 406, 407, 427, 468, 484, 510, 511, 623
Brady, Thomas M 623
Bragato, Brandon 433
Bragg, David 637
Brahimi, Samia 425
Brain, Michael 447
Brainard, Colin 110, 467
Brainard, Lael 783, 821
Braithwaite, Kenneth J 608
Bralish, Jessica 47
Bramblett, Jimmy 696
Brammer, Steven 694
Bramwell, Austin 617
Bran, Raul Castellanos 935
Brancaccio, Ivana 166
Branch, Doug 467
Branch, Elliott 654
Branch, Jeff 63
Branch-James, Aquila 722
Brand, Jennifer S 728
Brand, Lauren K 753
Brand, Norman 469
Brandenberger, Mary 664
Brandolini, Gillie 17
Brandon, Andrea 734
Brandon, Thomas E 659
Brandon-Arnold, Cynthia 900
Brandt, Daniel 223, 616
Brandt, Kim 370
Brandt, Rainey R 905
Brangman, H. Alan 787
Branham, James M 783
Branscome, John 364
Branstad, Terry 606
Branz, Danielle 122
Brashares, Edith 617
Brat, Dave 280, 313, 339, 409, 410, 411, 441, 442, 484
Bratahwaite, Jane 916
Bratt, Jay 680
Brauer, Randy 738
Braun, Bertram 601
Brause, Jon 942
Bravacos, John 743
Bravo, Gabriel 302
Bravo, Jesus Ponce 920
Bravo, Matt 460
Brazauskas, Joe 440

Page

Brazel, Susan M 849
Brazelton, Hallet 464
Brebbia, Sean 436
Bredenkamp, Trevor 645
Breeding, Beth 280
Breen, Barry 791
Breene, Sam 225
Bregon, Nelson 744
Breidenbach, Carrie 452
Breitenbach, Ryan 430
Brekhus, Keith 10
Bremberg, Andrew 597
Brenna, Bridget 37
Brennan, Anne 651
Brennan, Anne M 651
Brennan, Deborah 705
Brennan, Dennis 754
Brennan, Elena 416
Brennan, Elizabeth 382
Brennan, Matthew 226
Brennan, Megan J 847
Brennan, Patricia F 741
Brennan, Ryan 847
Brennan, Tim 378
Brennan, Tim P 632
Brennan, Whitney 180
Brennan, William 757
Brenneman, Diane M 905
Brenner, Brett 792
Brenner, Claudine 378
Brenner, Joseph 833
Brenner, Lawrence 908
Brent, James 692
Brereton, Peter 798
Bresler, Jason 456
Breslow, Julie 905
Bresnahan, James 745
Bressack, Leah 657
Bressler, Shellie 422
Bresso, Gineen M 595
Brest, Phil 380
Brett, James 814
Breuer, Nancy Robinson 817
Brewer, David 377
Brewer, David V 841
Brewer, Janet J 842
Brewer, Lawrence 811
Brewer, Leah 353
Brewer, Maria 609
Brewster, Christopher 462
Brewster, Ryan 698
Breyer, Charles R 849, 901
Breyer, Stephen G 854
Breysse, Patrick 737
Briante, Lesley 804
Briatico, Anna 695
Brickell, Missye 364
Bricker, Wesley R 831
Bridenstine, Jim 808
Bridgeman, Peter E 704
Bridges, Claire 121
Bridges, Tim 635
Bridgforth, Henry Turner 694
Brienza, Elizabeth 515
Brierley, Corale L 819
Brigati, Allison F 802, 803
Briggs, Alex 209
Briggs, Anderson 249
Bright, Andrea J 826
Bright, Christopher J 408
Bright, Kathleen 692
Bright, Michael 744
Bright, Rick 734
Brignola, Jodi 408
Brill, Richard 632
Brinck, Casey 300
Brindle, Robert 396
Brink, Bridget 602
Brink, Patricia A 658
Brinson, Chris 4
Briscoe, Johanna 691
Briscoe, Mary Beck 858
Bristol, Teri 750
Britt, Clinton 191
Britt, Katie 2
Britt, Kerry D 631
Britton, Brennen 108
Britton, Joe 177
Britton, Ryan 630
Brizzi, Giancarlo 803
Broady, Marc 127, 436
Brock, Thad 265
Brock, Thomas 767
Brock, Thomas W 767
Brockelman, Stephen 803
Brockett, Del 720
Broderick, Patricia A 904
Brody, Perry 269
Brogan, Frank 767
Bronder, Lizabeth 952
Bronson, Karen 463
Brooks, Brian K 674
Brooks, David 366
Brooks, Ethel C 844
Brooks, Frank E 590
Brooks, Leon 697
Brooks, Martha 506
Brooks, Mo 5, 305, 338, 406, 407, 408, 421, 422, 438, 439, 484
Brooks, Susan W 102, 307, 339, 413, 415, 417, 484
Brooks, Towanda 746
Brooks, Wes 68
Broom, J. Slade 714
Broome, Michael 378
Brose, Chris 353
Brosnan, Kyle 377
Brotherton, Andrea 651
Brouillette, Dan 759
Broussard, John 700
Broussard, Meryl 705
Brower, Gregory A 673
Brown, Alicia 364
Brown, Amy 745
Brown, Anthony G 125, 308, 341, 406, 407, 408, 417, 431, 432, 484
Brown, Baillee 45
Brown, Barbara A 671
Brown, Brandy 226
Brown, Bruce 633
Brown, Catherine 602
Brown, Catrell 793
Brown, Chandra 714
Brown, Chris 155, 750
Brown, Cindi 397
Brown, Cindy 64
Brown, Dama J 802
Brown, Dan 442
Brown, Daniel 805
Brown, Danielle 430
Brown, Dayna 718
Brown, Desmond 826
Brown, Douglas E 623
Brown, Dustin 595
Brown, Dwayne 833
Brown, E. Cooper 721
Brown, Edsel 849
Brown, Elena 725
Brown, Elizabeth 65
Brown, Frederick D 822
Brown, Gordon 948
Brown, Gregory 712
Brown, Janice 751
Brown, Janice Rogers 860
Brown, Jason 615, 646
Brown, Jennifer 439
Brown, Jereon M 744
Brown, Jocelyn 698
Brown, Katherine 843
Brown, Kelly 351
Brown, Kendra 224
Brown, Kevin 724
Brown, Laura 690, 750
Brown, Margo 132
Brown, Mark 602
Brown, Matthew 907
Brown, Melissa 202
Brown, Melissa D 826
Brown, Michael C 779
Brown, Michelle 632
Brown, Mike 396
Brown, Natalie 607
Brown, Natasha 724
Brown, Nicholas R 80
Brown, Nikki 517
Brown, Nonie 5
Brown, Orice Williams 583

Page
Brown, Rebecca ... 436
Brown, Reginald M ... 825
Brown, Romero ... 505
Brown, Ryan ... 57
Brown, Sandra ... 202
Brown, Scott P ... 608
Brown, Shannon ... 682
Brown, Sherrod ... 205, 311, 327, 330, 345, 346, 359, 369, 370, 384, 470, 473
Brown, Taryn ... 148
Brown, Thomas Christian ... 420
Brown, Tim ... 52
Brown, Valerie ... 699
Brown, William Y ... 688
Brown-Ghee, Beth ... 683
Brown-Shaklee, Sally ... 393
Brownell, Susan M ... 848
Brownley, Julia ... 32, 306, 339, 443, 444, 445, 446, 448, 484
Brownlie, Michael ... 14
Brubaker, Joel ... 290
Brubaker, Marcus ... 62
Bruce, Anne Oswalt ... 505
Bruce, Bonnie ... 447
Bruce, Douglas B ... 677
Bruce, Sandra D ... 766
Brudzinski, Walter ... 780
Bruffy, Robert ... 681
Bruggink, Eric G ... 885
Brujis, Marcos ... 952
Brukman, Becca ... 224
Bruley, Callie ... 141
Brumback, Gordon ... 833
Brummette, Rosalyn ... 346
Brune, Sean ... 839
Brunjes, David H ... 780
Brunner, Ilana ... 412
Bruno, Grace ... 361
Bruno, Richard ... 260
Brunson, Barbre A ... 515
Brusberg, Mark ... 693
Brusoe, Peter ... 908
Bryan, Patricia Mack ... 398
Bryan, Patrick M ... 785
Bryan, William ... 776, 777
Bryan-Johnson, Hellen ... 718
Bryan-Wade, Katona ... 800
Bryant, Arthur ... 695
Bryant, Errical ... 657
Bryant, G. Keith ... 778
Bryant, L. Preston, Jr ... 813
Bryant, Michael ... 76
Bryant, Rebecca ... 289
Bryon, Jemine ... 743
Bryson, Jeffrey T ... 821
Bryson, Sharon ... 820
Bryson, William C ... 869
Brzozowski, Christa ... 777
Buch, Ronald L ... 889
Buchan, Richard Duke III ... 606, 609
Buchanan, Avis ... 911
Buchanan, Chris ... 739
Buchanan, Kelly ... 589
Buchanan, Maurice "Buck" ... 729
Buchanan, Natalie ... 459
Buchanan, Vern ... 66, 307, 336, 450, 451, 471, 484, 507
Buchanan-Smith, Henrika ... 753
Buchholz, David E ... 784
Bucio, Luis Rodriguez ... 915
Buck, Brendan ... 459
Buck, Ken ... 48, 306, 340, 428, 429, 437, 454, 484
Buckalew, Adam ... 415
Buckberg, Elaine ... 615
Buckingham, Ann ... 785
Buckingham, Tammy ... 395
Buckler, Tina ... 893
Buckles, Kyle ... 155
Buckley, Joseph ... 516
Buckley, Teresa ... 103
Buckner, Charlene ... 694
Buckner, Jeffrey ... 838
Buckner, Stephen L ... 711
Bucshon, Larry ... 103, 307, 338, 413, 414, 415, 484
Budd, Ted ... 202, 311, 341, 418, 419, 420, 485
Budde, Nic ... 390
Budoff, Jennifer ... 907
Buechner, Jack ... 509
Buehler, Rose Mary ... 840
Page
Bueno, Virgina ... 705
Buerkle, Ann Marie ... 788
Buford, Charlotte ... 833
Bugg, Kimberley ... 589
Buhl, Cindy ... 130, 437
Buie, John ... 718
Bulatao, Brian ... 786
Bulger, Chip ... 633
Bull, Brittany ... 764
Bull, Jonca ... 739
Bull, Leslie ... 373
Bull, Nicholas ... 469
Buller, Kathy ... 829
Bullock, Kathleen M ... 823
Bulls, Herman E ... 782
Bumatay, Patrick ... 657
Bumbary-Langston, Inga ... 694
Bumgardner, Hayden ... 200
Bumpus, Jeanne ... 802
Bunch, Arnold ... 630, 639
Bunch, Lonnie ... 836
Bunning, Eric ... 116
Bunting, Luke ... 98
Buono, Donna ... 515
Burack, Bryan ... 423
Burba, Deron ... 836
Burch, Grace ... 248
Burchfield, James ... 442
Burchuk, Hilary ... 795
Burckman, James ... 687
Burd, Dan ... 370
Burdian, JoAnn ... 515
Burdick, Ruth E ... 818
Burgee, Kirk ... 796
Burger, Carol S ... 664
Burger, Eric ... 796
Burgeson, Eric ... 228
Burgess, A. Franklin ... 905
Burgess, Edward Chase ... 420
Burgess, Jami ... 289
Burgess, Michael C ... 264, 313, 335, 413, 414, 415, 437, 485, 504
Burgess, Rob ... 104
Burghoff, Claire ... 17
Burke, Amy ... 102
Burke, Brad ... 710
Burke, Brendan ... 132
Burke, Caitlin ... 411
Burke, Gregory ... 750
Burke, Kyndra ... 787
Burke, Leacey ... 215
Burke, Leacy ... 239
Burke, Luke ... 425
Burke, Robert ... 654
Burke, Stoney ... 262
Burke, Virginia ... 829
Burke, Warren ... 464
Burkes, Karen ... 616
Burkett, Alex ... 447
Burkett, Britton ... 408
Burkett, Robert ... 725
Burkey, Joy ... 364
Burkhauser, Richard ... 593
Burklow, John T ... 740
Burks, Jonathan ... 459
Burleson, Alyssa ... 271
Burleson, Carl ... 750
Burleson, Roman ... 452
Burlew, Thais ... 793
Burman, Brenda ... 690
Burne, Christopher F ... 638
Burner, Gary ... 612
Burnett, Andrew ... 375
Burnett, Bryan ... 792
Burnett, Douglas ... 753
Burnham, Heather L ... 397
Burnham, Kristen ... 750
Burns, Amelia ... 136
Burns, Andrew ... 465
Burns, Christopher ... 648
Burns, Emily ... 21
Burns, Gerard ... 595
Burns, Jennifer ... 783
Burns, Julie ... 828
Burns, Stephen G ... 821
Burns, Stuart ... 270, 803
Burns-Sulltrop, Judy ... 10
Burnszynski, Jennifer ... 734

Page

Burr, Amy 784
Burr, David 702
Burr, Geoffrey 747
Burr, Richard 195, 311, 329, 330, 369, 370, 374, 386, 387, 473, 501
Burrier, Edward A 422, 847
Burris, Kevin 420
Burris, Larry 649
Burrows, Charlotte A 792
Burrows, James G 793
Burrows, Mark 923
Burrus, Carl 749
Bursch, Eric 378
Burt, Mackenzie 15
Burthey, Grover 748
Burton, Amy Elizabeth 511
Burton, Eldon 279
Burton, Larry 7
Burton, Spence 710
Burwell, Carter 381
Busch, Andrew 787
Buschick, Jennifer 740
Buschor, Laura 613
Bush, Cort 364
Bush, Douglas 408
Bush, George 807
Bush, John Kenneth 857
Bush, Laina 734
Bush, Laura 807
Bush, Lynn J 885
Bush, Nick 213
Bush, Pamela M 789
Bush, Patrick 702
Bush, Zoe 904
Bush-Butler, Deborah 696
Busovsky, John 226
Bussey, Brian 833
Bussman, Susan 840
Bustillo, Eric 834
Bustillo, Ines 941
Bustos, Cheri 97, 307, 339, 399, 400, 443, 444, 445, 446, 485
Busztin, Gyorgy 947
Butcher, Courtney 411
Butler, Aniela 433
Butler, Charles 746
Butler, Cindy 827
Butler, Dwayne 826
Butler, James 716
Butler, Jeff 201
Butler, Jerry Christopher 917
Butler, Mannone 911
Butler, Morgan 468
Butler, Robert 722
Butler, Robin 436
Butler, Sarah 129
Butler, Sydney G 393
Butler, Tanya 469
Butler, Tia N 825
Butler, Tim 225
Butler, Tom 833
Buttenheim, Lisa M 939
Butterfield, G. K 195, 311, 335, 413, 414, 415, 485
Butterworth, James 699
Buzby, Mark H 753
Buzzi, Frank J 849
Bvumbe, Andrew N 951
Byard, Jeff 778
Bybee, Jay S 858
Bycel, Lee T 844
Byerly, Cassie 384
Byerly, Michael 110
Byers, John 173
Bylund, Jeremy 658
Bynum, V. Nicole 784
Bynum-Frazier, Tanisha 722
Byrd, Harry F., Jr 851
Byrd-Chichester, Janell 798
Byrne, Bradley 3, 305, 339, 406, 407, 410, 411, 437, 485
Byrne, Jim 769
Byrne, Michael 778
Byrnes, Andrew 717
Byrnes, Noni 741
Bzik, Lara 516

C

Caballero, Thomas E 398
Cabana, Robert 811

Page

Cabeca, John 718
Cable, Sarah 681
Cabranes, Jose A 857
Cabrejos, Jose 915
Cabrol, Marcelo 917
Cadin, Marc 510
Caesar, Angela D 878
Cafritz, Buffy 808
Cafritz, Zach 281
Cahill, Ellen 9
Cahill, Jessica T 240
Cahill, Jim 405
Cahill, Tom 229
Cahill, William H 754
Cain, Arnetta 619
Cain, Lisa 396
Cain, Terry A 903
Caine, Alex J 753
Caison, John 200
Calabresi, Giudo 857
Calamari, Andrew 835
Calascione, Joseph 797
Calaway, Lee Ann 270
Calbom, Linda 584
Calbos, Philip T 760
Calcagni, Mike 515
Calce, Christina 380
Calderon, Jorge Familiar 950
Caldwell, Anne 2
Caldwell, Carol V 712
Caldwell, James 654, 760
Caldwell, Kathryn 839
Caldwell, Rhonda L 669
Cale, Tabitha 594
Calhoun, K 651
Calhoun, Larry 59
Calhoun, Michelle 698
Calhoun, Sharon D 822
Calio, Nicholas E 510
Calkins, Aaron 86
Callahan, Andrew 67
Callahan, Brian 710
Callahan, Consuelo M 858
Callahan, Daniel F 839
Callahan, Thomas 373
Callahan, Timothy 717
Callahan, William J 780
Callanan, Brian 611
Callas, George 459
Callaway, Jeannine 21
Callear, Mildred 847
Callen, Ashley 440
Callen, Paul 464
Callender, Russell 715
Callicutt, Pamela D 648
Callinicos, Sean 510
Calloway, Joseph 646
Calogero, Chris 724
Calvert, Donna 838
Calvert, Ken 39, 306, 334, 402, 403, 485
Calvo, Karl 779
Calvo, Manuel 919
Calvosa, Christine 795
Cama, Jennifer 405
Camacho, Robert 264
Cameron, Jon 619
Cameron, Scott J 689
Cammack, Kat 59
Camp, Terry 433
Campbell, Caitlin E 508
Campbell, Carl V 722
Campbell, Caroline 425
Campbell, Chelsey 454
Campbell, Christopher 612
Campbell, Cindy 782
Campbell, Doug 423
Campbell, John G 150
Campbell, John M 904
Campbell, Joshua L 643
Campbell, Leslie 384
Campbell, Neil 235
Campbell, Rachel 756
Campbell, Sean 783
Campbell, Sharon 121
Campbell, Will 375
Campbell-Smith, Patricia E 884
Campfield, Chad 647
Campione, Jeff 785

Page

Campos, Leah 423
Campos, Roel 501
Camus, Timothy P 618
Canan, Russell F 904
Canary, Joseph 725
Canby, William C., Jr 858
Candela, Nicholas V 677
Candisky, Caryn 205
Canfield, Ryan 115
Canino, Carlos 659
Cannady, Jim 588
Cannan, Judith 589
Canning, Madeline 368
Cannon, Kate 273
Cannon, Nick 505
Cano, Luis J 711
Cantos, Olegario "Ollie" 764
Cantrell, Gary L 735
Cantwell, Kathleen 738
Cantwell, Maria 284, 313, 327, 330, 362, 363, 365, 369, 370, 383, 385, 473, 502
Cantwell, Mike 206
Cantwell, Patrick 711
Canty, Joe 763
Canuto, Otaviano 950
Capel, Paul 589
Capener, Kami 203
Capito, Shelley Moore 290, 313, 328, 331, 347, 348, 349, 362, 363, 365, 366, 367, 368, 382, 474
Caplan, Josh 361
Capolongo, Mabel 725
Cappello, Joe 590
Capron, Margaret 460
Capuano, Michael E 132, 309, 335, 418, 419, 443, 444, 445, 485
Caputa, Anthony 718
Carabine, Katherine 364
Caram, George 31
Carapiet, Joseph 360
Carara, Ronald 186
Carasso, Adam 370
Caraway, John F 675
Carbajal, Salud O 31, 306, 341, 406, 407, 408, 409, 485
Carbullido, Adam 301
Cardenas, Gladys 920
Cardenas, Tony 33, 306, 339, 413, 414, 415, 485
Cardillo, Robert 626
Cardin, Benjamin L 123, 308, 327, 330, 367, 368, 369, 370, 372, 383, 474, 502, 504, 509, 807
Cardin, Courtney 378
Cardinali, Janae 68
Cardoso, Javier 918
Carey, Brittany 616
Carey, Curtis 792
Carey, Laura 373
Carey, Mark S 784
Carey, Michelle 795
Carey, Ryan 371
Carl, Leon 689
Carl-Yoder, Samantha 602
Carlberg, Kenneth 796
Carle, David 274
Carlile, Joe 405
Carlile, Saesha 616
Carlisle, Homer 360
Carlough, Chad 3
Carlson, Curtis 617
Carlson, Donald G 509, 510
Carlson, Kris 425
Carlson, Terence W 748
Carlton, Peter J 817
Carluzzo, Lewis R 893
Carmack, Dustin 61
Carmack, Terry 112
Carman, Gregory W 880
Carmignani, Marco 945
Carnahan, David L 17
Carnegie, Ruth 392
Carnes, Alex 351
Carnes, Alexandra 425
Carnes, Ed 858
Carnes, Julie E 858
Carnes, Tom 69
Carney, John C 789
Carney, Ryan 171
Carney, Susan L 857
Carnucci, Joe 371
Carone, Mauricio Claver 614

Page

Carowitz, Michael 794
Carpenter, Christopher 395
Carpenter, Cynthia A 822
Carpenter, Mary 76
Carpenter, Scott 760
Carper, Thomas R 55, 306, 327, 330, 367, 369, 370, 377, 474, 808
Carr, Brendan 794
Carr, Colin 81
Carr, Debra A 731
Carr, Florence A 800
Carr, Fredrick E 631
Carr, Julie 114
Carr, Laura 260
Carr, Machalagh 452
Carr, Paul J 825
Carr, Peggy 767
Carr, Suzannah Herring 952
Carr, Ytta B 515
Carraco, Will 160
Carradini, Rosemary 679
Carranza, Jovita 618
Carriedo, Rodrigo 951
Carrier, Amber 456
Carrillo, Manuel Joe 456
Carroll, Alan 425
Carroll, Carol 810
Carroll, Chad 692
Carroll, Conn 271
Carroll, Conner 216
Carroll, Constance M 815
Carroll, Deborah 908
Carroll, James 595, 639
Carroll, Jeff 416
Carroll, Jim 595
Carroll, Kurt 589
Carroll, Nora 728
Carroll, Patrick 350
Carroll, Timothy 174
Carroll, Tom 513
Carrow, Courtney 191
Carson, Andre 103, 307, 336, 443, 444, 445, 453, 485
Carson, Barbara E 850
Carson, Benjamin S., Sr 591, 743, 781, 816
Carson, Chester 366
Carson, Horace 633
Carstensen, James D 107
Cartagena, Ednel 303
Carter, Bruce 815
Carter, Catherine P 728
Carter, Chris 200
Carter, Cyntoria 678
Carter, David W 793
Carter, Denise L 764
Carter, Earl L. "Buddy" 75, 307, 340, 413, 414, 415, 485
Carter, Hall 149
Carter, Jessica 68
Carter, Jimmy 807
Carter, John R 267, 313, 335, 402, 403, 404, 485
Carter, Lisa 612
Carter, Margaret 857
Carter, Mark A 799
Carter, Mary Anne 815
Carter, Michael C 753
Carter, Mickeala 269
Carter, Robert 804
Carter, Scott A 701, 702
Carter, Walter E. "Ted", Jr 655
Carter, Zelia M 683
Cartwright, Heather 680
Cartwright, Matt 232, 312, 339, 402, 403, 434, 435, 485
Carty, Jill 830
Carty, Lisa 943
Caruso, Michael 837
Carvajal, Michael 675
Carvalho, George 235
Carwell, Emily 135
Carwile, P. Kevin 663
Cary, Steven 65
Casados, Joe 179
Casamassa, Glenn 695
Casas, Efren 516
Casaus, Carlos 692
Casciaro, Elizabeth L 644
Case, David T 769
Case, Edward J 625, 626
Case, Marcia 624

	Page
Case, Steve	836
Casey, Bob	510
Casey, Brandon	452
Casey, Kevin	456
Casey, Michael	386
Casey, Robert P., Jr	223, 312, 327, 330, 345, 346, 369, 370, 374, 387, 388, 474, 509
Casey, Sharon	435
Casey, Tome	513
Cash, Caroline	113
Cash, Evan	814
Cashour, Curt	770
Cashwell, Anna	200
Casias, Lisa	710
Caslen, Robert L., Jr	641
Casler, Jeffrey	652
Cason, Jim	685
Cason, Monte A	677
Casper, Anne	606
Casper, Rob	590
Cassidy, Benjamin	776
Cassidy, Bill	117, 308, 328, 331, 365, 366, 369, 370, 374, 384, 467, 474
Cassidy, Jeremiah	846
Cassidy, Keith	831
Cassidy, Patrick	249
Cassidy, Thomas	464
Cassil, Dan	513
Castagna, Charles	73
Castella, Francesco Antonio	420
Castello, Roberto F. Salmon	921
Castelveter, David	821
Castiglione-Cataldo, Ann	642
Castillo, Andeliz	1, 391, 593
Castillo, Carlos Calles	932
Castillo, Julio	904
Castillo, Lisa	464
Castillo, Victor G	39
Castine, Peter	459
Castle, William S	621
Castleman, Patrick	821
Castor, Kathy	65, 306, 336, 413, 414, 415, 485
Castor, Steve	435
Castro, Andre	259
Castro, George	350
Castro, Gonzalo	949
Castro, Jeyben	370
Castro, Joaquin	261, 313, 339, 421, 422, 453, 485
Castro, Laura	703
Castro, Lisset	828
Catalan, Sara	38
Cate, Devin L	640
Catechis, Jennifer	179
Cathrell, Vance	834
Catiaro, Elizabeth	644
Catino, Nick	360
Catlin, Michelle	704
Cato, Van	237
Catron, Marsha	41
Catzaras, Benoit	951
Caux, Pierre Yves	922
Cavallini, Luis Felipe Arauz	918
Cavanagh, Richard	720
Cavanaugh, Amy	700
Cavazos, Andrew	460
Cave, Nicol	936
Cave, Tonda S	590
Cavendish, Betsy	907
Cayce, Lyle W	857
Cayea, Devan	143
Cayrus, Hugo	932
Cazamias, Peter J	850
Cecala, George	62
Cecil, Billy	639
Cedeno, Rossy Yesenia Chumbe	920
Cefkin, Judith Beth	607
Cekuta, Robert F	606
Celata, John	688
Censky, Stephen	691
Centanni, Amy	449
Centeno, Elizabeth	303
Center, Charles	799
Ceresney, Andrew	833
Cerf, Vinton G	820
Cerga, Vlad	423
Ceruti, Monique	782
Cervenak, Jason	430
Cerveny, John X	823
Cervone, Michael B	647
Cevasco, Marc	35
Chabolla, Tom	821
Chabot, Erica	274
Chabot, Steve	206, 311, 335, 421, 422, 428, 429, 441, 485
Chacon, Ashlie	629
Chadrick, Kent	636
Chadwick, Kyle E	805
Chaffee, Marta	784
Chafin, Claude	408
Chagares, Michael A	857
Chahil, Gary	27
Chakmak, Kathryn	451
Chalk, Steven	760
Chambas, Mohammed Ibn	946
Chamberlain, Paul A	642
Chamberlain, Ryan	516
Chamberlayne, Edward P	842
Chambers, Micah	685
Chambers, Ray	948
Champoux, Mark	679
Chan, Jensen	830
Chance, Michael	730
Chand, Robin	77
Chandler, Chammy	670
Chandler, Larry	705
Chandler, Michael L	396
Chandler, Peter	141
Chandler, Shana	289
Chandler, Vicki	820
Chandy, Sunu	734
Chaney, Kimberlin C	824
Chang, Anthony E	420
Chang, Jennifer	784
Chang, John C	903
Chang, Lena	436
Chang, Lisa	764
Chang, Winnie	405
Chao, Daniel	35
Chao, Elaine L	591, 747, 781, 816
Chao, Yao-Chin	785
Chape, Stuart	937
Chapman, Karen	28
Chapman, Kristin	725
Chapman, Stephen	368
Chapman, Todd	607
Chapman, Tom	364
Chapotin, Sahara Moon	513
Chappell, D. Michael	802
Chapuis, Jonathan	392
Chapuis, Suzanne	394
Charboneau, Thomas	726
Charles, Leon	932
Charlier, Lou	723
Charlton, John W	641
Charlton, Jonathan	440
Charow, Alex	390
Charrow, Robert P	734
Chartan, Steve	250
Chase, Cord	824
Chase, Dave	166
Chase, Elvis	826
Chase, Karen DeLaBarre	613
Chasnoff, Megan	464
Chatterjee, Neil	761
Chavez, Rebecca	936
Cheatham, A	651
Cheatham, Micah	811
Checca, Rocky	516
Chediek, Jorge	949
Cheek, Gary H	641, 648
Cheek, Jacquelyn	687
Cheever, Laura	739
Cheh, Mary M	907
Chen, Mingzhi	506
Chen, Paul	469
Chen, Raymond T	868
Cheney, Carole	94
Cheney, Craig	389
Cheney, Liz	299, 314, 341, 406, 407, 431, 432, 437, 485
Cheney, Megan	360
Cheng, Becky	33
Cheng, James K	677
Cheng, Mary	669
Cheng, May T	825
Cheng-Hopkins, Judy	949
Cherry, Arnez	76

Page

Cherry, Daniel ... 730
Cherry, Katrina ... 791
Cherry, Stephanie ... 461
Cherundolo, Gregory J ... 664, 666
Cheshire, Jaime ... 786
Chester, Bronwyn Lance ... 298, 389
Chester, Kemp ... 595
Chevalier, Jacque ... 412
Chew, Debra ... 740
Chew, Michael ... 764
Chiappardi, Frances ... 462
Chiappe, Cristina ... 702
Chiarello, Debbie ... 353
Chiechi, Carolyn P ... 892
Chiedi, Joanne M ... 735
Child, Matthew ... 923
Chiles, Anthony "Tony" ... 719
Chin, Denny ... 857
Chion, Antonia ... 833
Chiotti, Miles ... 94
Chism, Monique ... 765
Chitnis, Parag ... 705
Chitwood, Mitchell ... 839
Chiu, Melissa ... 836
Cho, Austin ... 427, 504
Cho, Jay ... 89
Cho, Jim ... 69
Choe-Fichte, Karen ... 936
Choi, Heenam ... 924
Choi, Jina L ... 835
Choi, Joanne ... 771
Choi, Melissa ... 639
Choksi, Rachit ... 368
Choksy, Jamsheed K ... 815
Chon, Katherine ... 736
Chou, Wesley ... 723
Choudhury, Sayeed ... 816
Chow, James ... 639
Chrappah, Ernest ... 911
Chriss, Sherry L ... 464
Christ, Katelyn E ... 420
Christ, Lou-Anne Gaylene ... 932
Christen, Morgan ... 858
Christensen, Brick ... 436
Christensen, Karen ... 604
Christensen, Keeley ... 178
Christensen, Thomas ... 696
Christensen, Thomas M.P ... 754
Christian, Erik P ... 904
Christian, Karen ... 415
Christian, Kaye R ... 905
Christiansen, Elita ... 618
Christiansen, Vicki ... 695, 696
Christianson, Andrew ... 243
Christie, John ... 36
Christopher, Dale A ... 823
Christopher, David J ... 588
Christopher, Nancy ... 745
Christrup, Henry ... 464
Christus, Nicole ... 447
Christy, Phillip "Phil" ... 770
Chu, Jane ... 507, 815, 816
Chu, Judy ... 32, 306, 337, 441, 450, 485
Chu, Keith ... 371
Chuhta, Carolyn A ... 356, 357
Chung, HyeSook ... 907
Chung, Jason ... 616
Church, Ann ... 740
Church, Christopher ... 698
Church, Joel K ... 515
Churchill, Adrielle ... 17
Churchwell, Leslie ... 152
Chutkan, Tanya S ... 873
Ciarlante, Nick ... 454
Ciccone, Joseph ... 35
Cicilline, David N ... 235, 312, 338, 421, 422, 428, 429, 485
Cigno, Margaret ... 831
Cikanek, Harry ... 716
Ciliberti, Nancy A ... 894
Cilke, James ... 469
Cintron, Carmen A ... 761
Cintron, Robert ... 848
Ciotti, Nick ... 68
Cisneros, Alex ... 73
Cisneros, Juan P ... 652
Cisneros, Raul ... 710, 711
Cisse, M'Baye Babacar ... 945

Page

Cissna, L. Francis ... 780
Citrin, Daniel ... 923
Claffey, Jon ... 701
Claggett, Karyn Temple ... 588
Clair, Troy ... 196
Clancy, Carolyn ... 772
Clanton, Michael ... 693
Clapp, Doug ... 350
Clardy, Herman S ... 622
Clark, Alesia ... 631
Clark, Annie ... 121
Clark, Brooke P ... 821
Clark, Carson ... 4
Clark, Cynthia ... 130
Clark, Donald S ... 802
Clark, Ellen ... 714
Clark, Fred ... 346, 696
Clark, Garth ... 693
Clark, Geraldine L ... 848
Clark, Jacque ... 124
Clark, James ... 634
Clark, Jeanette ... 904
Clark, Jon ... 449
Clark, Jonathan D ... 356, 357
Clark, Joseph R ... 420, 611
Clark, Katherine M ... 131, 309, 339, 402, 404, 485
Clark, Major L. III ... 849
Clark, Michell C ... 785
Clark, Rebecca Brasington ... 590
Clark, Robert ... 812
Clark, Roger ... 712
Clark, Samantha ... 353, 354, 355, 356
Clark, Sheila ... 785
Clark, Thomas ... 636
Clark, Tillena G ... 784
Clark, Tom ... 782
Clark, Virginia ... 836
Clark, Willie ... 772
Clarke, Cait T ... 903
Clarke, Carlisle ... 350
Clarke, R. Scott ... 681
Clarke, Randy ... 364
Clarke, Richard D ... 624, 916
Clarke, Sheria ... 435
Clarke, Stanley ... 638
Clarke, Yvette D ... 185, 310, 336, 413, 414, 415, 417, 441, 485
Clausen, Taylor ... 423
Clauson, Ilene ... 432
Claussen, Roger R ... 653
Clay, Eric Lee ... 857
Clay, Gordon ... 469
Clay, Layton F ... 585
Clay, Wm. Lacy ... 154, 309, 335, 418, 419, 431, 432, 434, 435, 485
Clayborne, Alfred ... 689
Clayman, Paul ... 941
Clayton, Janine ... 740
Clayton, Jay ... 831
Clayton, Justin ... 267
Clayton, Marla ... 675
Clayton, Sean ... 811
Cleary, David ... 244
Cleary, David P ... 375
Cleary, Kelly M ... 734
Cleaver, Emanuel ... 156, 309, 336, 418, 419, 485
Clement, Edith Brown ... 857
Clementi, Mike ... 350
Clemmensen, Craig ... 745
Clemmons, Gina ... 839
Clemons, Nick ... 131
Clendenin, Cletis ... 303
Cleveland, Robin ... 508
Cleveland-Leggett, Denise ... 746
Clevenger, Raymond C. III ... 869
Clifford, Brian ... 368
Clifford, Richard B., Jr ... 637
Clift, Douglas ... 712
Clifton, Jill S ... 691
Clifton, Richard R ... 858
Cline, Donald ... 689
Cline, Meghan ... 346
Clinton, Hillary Rodham ... 807
Clinton, Jonathan ... 803
Clinton, William ... 652
Clipper, Cherry ... 519
Clocker, John ... 462
Clos, Joan ... 942

Page

Close, Nalini 726
Closter, Harold 836
Cloud, Braye 721
Cloud, Michael 264, 313, 434, 435, 438, 439, 485
Clouse, James A 784
Clowers, Angela (Nikki) 583
Cluthe, Sally 709
Clyburn, James E 240, 312, 334, 461, 485
Clyburn, Mignon 794
Clyburn, Vera 589
Clyde Terry, Concord 814
Coale, Dana 706
Coates, Renee 750
Coates, Rosalyn L 846
Coats, Daniel 591, 594
Coats, Derek 153
Cobau, John 713
Cobb, Ty 599
Cobert, Robert 719
Coburn, David C 642
Coburn, Melissa A 639
Coca, Denise 795
Coccaro, Alejandro Salaberry 916
Cochran, Carrie 739
Cochran, Norris 734
Cochrane, Anna V 761
Cochrane, Jim 848
Cocke, Perry 840
Coddington, Traci 801
Coe, Charles 766
Coen, Jon 384
Coffey, Ann 695
Coffield, Mark 272
Coffman, Callie 904
Coffman, Mike 49, 306, 337, 406, 407, 448, 485
Cogan, Amanda 58
Cogan, Robert 409
Cogar, Chuck 237
Cogdill, David 764
Coggins, Colleen 754
Coggins, Wynn 719
Cogswell, Patricia 779
Cohen, Andrew 785
Cohen, Clifford T 588
Cohen, Dara Postar 36
Cohen, David M 660
Cohen, Edward 505
Cohen, Gerald 615
Cohen, Ira 92
Cohen, Jacqueline 416
Cohen, Joel 373
Cohen, Jonathan 602
Cohen, Joseph 464
Cohen, Kenneth P 849
Cohen, Linda 454
Cohen, Lisa B 47
Cohen, Mark 605
Cohen, Mary Ann 891
Cohen, Michele 513
Cohen, Miriam L 822
Cohen, Nicole 456
Cohen, Rachel 276
Cohen, Robert 801
Cohen, Rochelle 796
Cohen, Rosaline 425
Cohen, Scott 658
Cohen, Steve 249, 312, 336, 417, 428, 443, 444, 445, 485, 504, 833
Cohen, Steven H 806
Cohen, Tracey 911
Coit, Sean 55
Colantino, Alison 830
Colarulli, Dana 718
Colasurdo, Dianna 390
Colbert, Julian 798
Colborn, Paul P 679
Colburn, Jill 664
Colby, Paul 681
Colder, Karl C 666
Cole, Bruce 652
Cole, Lorraine 616
Cole, R. Guy, Jr 857
Cole, Thomas E 397
Cole, Tom 217, 311, 335, 402, 403, 404, 409, 437, 485, 835
Cole, William T 800
Cole-Misch, Sally 923
Coleman, Betty L 659
Coleman, Corey 778
Coleman, Dennis D 823
Coleman, Douglas W 666
Coleman, Everett 408
Coleman, John 429
Coleman, Jonathan 846
Coleman, Joycelyn 433
Coleman, Kelvin 751
Coleman, Rose McManus 821
Coleman, S. Robert 793
Coleman, Sam 2, 791
Coleman, Thomas 384
Coleman, Watson 499
Coleman, William S 822
Colindres, Denis Ronaldo Moncada 932
Collazo, Apolonio J., Jr 665
Coller-Monarez, Susan 777
Collett, Johnny W 767
Colley, Steve 384
Colliatie, Drew 440
Collier, Andrew 669
Collier, Craig 408
Collins, Anne L 752
Collins, Chris 193, 311, 339, 413, 415, 486
Collins, Doug 79, 307, 339, 428, 429, 437, 455, 486
Collins, Eugene 643
Collins, Francis S 740
Collins, Jessica 429
Collins, Jessica M 647
Collins, Kelly 416
Collins, Michael 78
Collins, Susan E 842
Collins, Susan M 90, 121, 308, 328, 330, 347, 348, 349, 374, 386, 387, 474
Collins-Mandeville, Aimee 63
Collinsworth, Melanie 136
Colloton, Steven M 858
Collver, Geoffrey 207
Collyer, Rosemary M 877
Collyns, Charles 924
Colman, Mike 729
Colon-Marrero, Laura 678
Colosimo, Mark 922
Colvin, John O 892
Colwell, John F 817
Colwell, William S 721
Comans, Mary 778
Combelic, Alexa 52
Combs, Leslie 93
Combs, Steven C 633
Combs-Greene, Natalia 905
Come, Joseph 748
Comeau, Lauren 350
Comer, James 112, 308, 340, 399, 400, 401, 434, 435, 441, 486
Comer, Michael 411
Comfort, Karen 706
Comins, Brittany 243
Comis, Adam M 425
Commodore, LaKeisha 465
Compean, Guillermo A 917
Compton, Caryn 274
Compton, J. Paul, Jr 745
Compton, Megan 201
Compton, Shane 686
Comstock, Barbara 282, 313, 340, 427, 438, 439, 443, 444, 445, 467, 486, 503, 510, 808
Comstock, Peter 16
Conaway, K. Michael 256, 313, 336, 399, 406, 407, 453, 454, 501
Conaway, Michael K 486
Conchuratt, Sam 370
Condeluci, Laura 513
Condes, Al 809
Condon, Joan 422
Condon, Katherine 137
Conejo, Jose 585
Conesa, Lee 632
Coney, Lillie 260
Conley, Brendan 122
Conley, Michael 832
Conley, Mike 782
Conley, Sheila 734
Connaughton, Kenneth R., Jr 677
Connell, Jamie 688
Connell, John 99
Connell, Sindi 515
Connelly, Chris 155

Page
Connelly, Henry 461
Conner, Dawniel C 640
Conner, Katelyn 112
Conner, Meredith 427, 504
Conner, Misty 514
Connery, Joyce 789
Conniff, Brian 786
Connolly, Brenda 183
Connolly, Douglas 388
Connolly, Elizabeth 56
Connolly, Gerald E 282, 313, 337, 421, 422, 434, 435, 486, 507
Connolly, Jesse 122
Connolly, Josh 26
Connolly, Marjorie 168
Connolly, Robert 677
Connor, Cameron 436
Connor, Deborah 663
Connor, Kathleen 128
Connor, Mark 725
Connor, Patricia S 857
Connors, Thomas A 784
Conoboy, Eileen 788
Cononi, Rachel 615
Conrad, Elizabeth 408
Conrad, Jessica 436
Conrath, Kristine 612, 613
Conroy, Glenda 740
Conroy, Patrick J 463
Conru, Paula 8
Consaul, Ryan 425
Consolvo, Brandon 459
Constantine, Peter 746
Conte, Stephen P 839
Conterno, Enrique A 782
Contreni, Maureen C 397
Contreras, Manuel 376
Contreras, Robert 702
Contreras, Rudolph 873
Contreras, Tomas 464
Conway, Kellyanne 598
Conway, Patrick 738
Cook, Chris 350
Cook, Deborah L 857
Cook, Donnie 396
Cook, Fay L 820
Cook, John 831
Cook, Julia C 464
Cook, Kathleen 638
Cook, Mary Catherine 375
Cook, Michael C 712
Cook, Nerissa J 603
Cook, Paul 23, 305, 339, 406, 407, 408, 421, 422, 431, 432, 486
Cook, Reed 364
Cook, Rob 803
Cook, Steven 657
Cooke, Catherine 462
Cooke, Corey 805
Cooke, Dave 389
Cooke, Jason 199
Cooke, John 805
Cooke, John S 903, 904
Cooke, Kevin R., Jr 745
Cooksey, Katharine 452
Cooksey, Rick 696
Cooling, N.L 656
Coon, Simon 384
Coons, Christopher A 55, 306, 328, 330, 347, 348, 349, 372, 373, 379, 380, 383, 386, 388, 474
Coop, Adam J 835
Cooper, Andrew 405
Cooper, Beth 360
Cooper, Charles 795
Cooper, Chris 213
Cooper, Christine 718
Cooper, Christopher R 873
Cooper, Donna 719
Cooper, Iris 616
Cooper, Jennifer 740
Cooper, Jim 247, 312, 334, 406, 407, 408, 434, 486
Cooper, John B 635
Cooper, Judith 741
Cooper, Steve 710
Cooper-Jones, Barbara 745
Cooperstein, Ted M 825
Copeland, Michael 805
Copenhaver, David 613
Page
Copley, Robert 607
Coppedge, Michelle 750
Coppolino, Tony 661
Coraggio, Mary-Deirdre 720
Corbett, Derick 79
Corbett, Janice 713
Corbett, Joseph 848
Corbin, Kenneth 618
Corbin, Kim 467
Corbin, Robert 760
Corcoran, Gladys 717
Corcoran, Kathleen 52
Corcoran, Sean 416
Cordero, Laura 806
Cordero, Laura A 904
Cordish, Reed 597
Cordon, Byron Omar Acevedo 919
Cordova, Douglas P 638
Cordova, France A 816, 819
Cordray, Richard 797
Corker, Bob 244, 312, 327, 330, 359, 360, 361, 372, 387, 474, 509
Corley, Tim 370, 371
Cormack, Maureen 606
Cormier, Ward 119
Cornell, Becky 34
Cornell, Kevin 464
Cornett, Chelsea 147
Cornett, Jake 375
Cornforth, Roger 937
Cornibert, Agnes 302
Cornish, Dianna 723
Cornyn, John 250, 312, 328, 330, 369, 370, 379, 386, 392, 474, 807
Correa, J. Luis 41, 306, 341, 424, 425, 448, 486
Correa, Soraya 777
Correll, Mark A 632
Correy, Sharmini A 924
Corrigan, Dara 738
Corsi, Robert E., Jr 635
Corsiglia, Nancy 746
Cortez Masto, Catherine 164, 310, 329, 331, 359, 360, 362, 363, 365, 366, 382, 385, 387, 474
Cortez, Marcella 36
Cortez, Marisela 269
Cortina, Joseph 461
Cortinas, John 716
Cosentino, Tom 627
Cosivi, Ottorino 935
Costa, Anthony E 813
Costa, Gregg J 857
Costa, Hope 190
Costa, Jim 27, 306, 336, 399, 400, 431, 432, 486
Costa, Jose Luis Machaco e 932
Costain, Jorge 918
Costakos, Catherine 81
Costantino, Joseph 632
Costanza, Jen 709
Costello, Chance 364
Costello, Darlene 630
Costello, Ryan A 227, 312, 340, 413, 414, 415, 454, 486
Costin, Dondi E 637
Cote, Stephen 437
Cotner, Kelly 256
Cotten, Samantha 192
Cotter, Daniel 777
Cotter, Stephen 616
Cottingham, John 718
Cottingham-Streater, Paige 507
Cotton, Amy 719
Cotton, Katina P 823
Cotton, Tom 15, 305, 328, 331, 352, 353, 359, 361, 386, 467, 474, 506
Cottone, Alisa 830
Cottrell, Amelia A 835
Cottrell, David 699
Cottrell, Guy J 848
Cottrell, Jackie 108
Coughlan, Tony 370
Couglas, Fletcher 676
Couhig, Ben 270
Coulson, Carla K 644
Coulter, Kathryn 776
Coulter, Margaret 375
Couri, Gerald 415
Courtney, Jim 801
Courtney, Joe 52, 306, 336, 406, 407, 410, 411, 486
Courtney, Mike 688

Page

Cousimano, Jonathan ... 41
Cousins, Lynn E ... 848
Coutts, Doug ... 15
Couture, Traci ... 287
Covelli-Ingwell, Carmen ... 815
Covert, Kevin ... 609
Covey, Jason ... 380
Covey, William ... 717
Covey-Brandt, Alexis ... 126, 461
Covitz, Daniel ... 785
Cowan, Chad ... 745
Cowan, Selma ... 696
Cowen, Robert E ... 857
Cox, Debra ... 777
Cox, Emmett R ... 858
Cox, Gerard ... 772
Cox, Gregg ... 640
Cox, Gregory D ... 673
Cox, Jennifer ... 138
Cox, Kenneth ... 464
Cox, Ramsey ... 285
Cox, Samuel D ... 635
Cox, Stephen ... 658, 806
Cox, Walter Thompson III ... 896
Cox-Roush, Deborah ... 788
Coyle, Sarah ... 459
Coyne, Tom ... 462
Cozad, Kyle ... 654
Crabb, Gregory ... 848
Craft, Kelly ... 606
Craig, Jack, Jr ... 760
Craig, James ... 729
Craig, Lisa ... 634
Craig, Thomas ... 368
Craig, Tim ... 395
Craige, Christopher ... 635
Craigshead, Kelly ... 714
Crain, Alicia ... 828
Crain, William F ... 648
Cramer, Kevin ... 204, 311, 339, 413, 414, 486
Cramer, Paul D ... 643
Crandall, Douglas ... 695
Crane, Joanne Buenzli ... 711
Cranston, Seana ... 114
Crapo, Mike ... 85, 307, 329, 330, 359, 361, 369, 370, 379, 380, 385, 469, 470, 474
Craven, Mariane ... 604
Craven, Sarah ... 942
Cravens, Michael ... 151
Cravins, Yvette P ... 154
Crawford, Chris ... 76
Crawford, Eric A. "Rick" ... 305, 338, 399, 400, 401, 443, 444, 445, 446, 453, 486
Crawford, Gail E ... 637
Crawford, James W. III ... 652, 654
Crawford, John W ... 586
Crawford, Rick ... 15
Crawford, Susan J ... 896
Crawley, Allen R., Jr ... 710
Creamer, John ... 603
Creamer, Patrick ... 15
Crean, Sean ... 850
Creasy, Stephanie ... 683
Creel, Robert ... 729
Cregan, Gary ... 650
Cremins, Thomas E ... 808
Crerand, Emily ... 456
Cress, Zach ... 364
Creviston, Rachel ... 393
Crews, John ... 360
Cribbs, Carol ... 777
Cribley, Bud ... 686
Crick, Cindy ... 240
Crisci, Emma ... 28
Criscuolo, Alicia ... 439
Crist, Charlie ... 64, 306, 342, 418, 419, 438, 439, 486
Cristaudo, Frank ... 837
Cristinzio, Dayle ... 739
Cristofaro, Joseph ... 712
Critchfield, Amanda ... 360
Crites, Randy ... 653
Crocker, Nick ... 455
Crocker, Ryan ... 786
Croft, David ... 619
Croft, Ryan ... 296
Croke, Kenneth ... 659
Cronin, Linda ... 694
Cronin, Maggie ... 296

Page

Cronkhite, Isaac ... 848
Cropper, Elizabeth ... 817
Cross, Gina ... 788
Cross, Jesse ... 464
Crosswhite, Caleb ... 401
Crotty, James ... 162
Crouch, Drew ... 370
Crouch, Matt ... 753
Croushorn, Ronald ... 698
Crowards, Tom Matthew ... 917
Crowder, Susan ... 801
Crowell, Heather ... 425
Crowell, James A. IV ... 657
Crowell, Jim ... 360
Crowell, Michaeleen ... 274
Crowley, Joseph ... 187, 311, 335, 450, 451, 456, 486
Crowley, Raquel ... 284
Crowley, Sheila ... 827
Crowley, Timothy ... 729
Crowner, Quasette ... 765
Cruciani, Linda M ... 745
Cruickshank, Walter D ... 688
Crumbly, Angelique ... 843
Crumley, Demetrice ... 665
Crump, Regan ... 772
Cruse, James C ... 792
Cruz, Jeff ... 361
Cruz, Lenin Dario Gonzalez ... 916
Cruz, Mark ... 101
Cruz, Mary Campbell ... 170
Cruz, Ted ... 250, 312, 327, 331, 352, 353, 362, 363, 379, 382, 467, 475
Crytzer, Katherine ... 680
Cuaderes, John ... 378
Cubero, Linda ... 501
Cuchi, Paloma ... 934
Cucurullo, Karen ... 850
Cuebas, Eric ... 632
Cuellar, Henry ... 265, 313, 336, 402, 403, 486
Cuff, Patrick ... 178, 420
Cuffee-Graves, Cassandra ... 764
Culberson, John Abney ... 254, 313, 335, 402, 403, 404, 486
Cullen, Cate ... 5
Cullinane, Scott ... 423
Culp, Rita ... 405
Culpepper, James R ... 631
Culton, John ... 284
Culver, Jared ... 107
Cummings, Aaron ... 380
Cummings, Ann ... 811
Cummings, Anthony ... 745
Cummings, Elijah E ... 127, 308, 334, 434, 443, 444, 445, 486, 502
Cummings, Nick ... 364
Cunfer, James ... 682
Cunha, Rolemberg Ferreira da ... 916
Cunningham, Daniel A ... 903
Cunningham, Elizabeth ... 423
Cunningham, Jameson ... 95
Cunningham, Lucy ... 722
Cunningham, Michael ... 639
Cunningham, Scott ... 263
Cunningham, Terence ... 639
Cunningham, William ... 436
Cunnington, Mike ... 86
Cuomo, Andrew M ... 789
Curbelo, Carlos ... 73, 307, 340, 450, 451, 486
Curcuru, Stephanie ... 784
Curlett, Ed ... 707
Curley, Andrew ... 243
Curley, Peter ... 833
Curran, Kenny ... 51
Curry, Kim ... 755
Curry, Tim F ... 827
Curtin, Bonnie ... 670
Curtin, Teri ... 350, 351
Curtis, Brian ... 820
Curtis, Christopher ... 798
Curtis, John R ... 273, 313, 342, 421, 422, 431, 432, 441, 442, 486
Curtis, Linda ... 623
Curtis, Margarida ... 394
Curtis, Sarah ... 131
Curtsinger, Joe ... 373
Cushenberry, Harold ... 905
Cushing, Amy ... 405
Cushing, Michael ... 792
Cushwa, Patricia K ... 683

Page

Cusick, Michael ... 634
Cutler, Allen ... 350
Cutler, Dawn E ... 651
Cutlip-Mason, Rena E ... 669
Cutrona, Danielle ... 657
Cutrona, Dante ... 227
Cutshall, Mary K ... 703
Cutts, Kenneth ... 76
Cutts, Stephen ... 940
Cuvelier, Charles ... 686
Cylke, Laura ... 405
Cyr, Ned ... 715
Czajkowski, Julie ... 740
Czarnecki, Tammy ... 772
Czarnopys, Greg ... 660
Czin, Michael ... 909
Czwartacki, John "CZ" ... 595

D

D'Alesandro, Paul ... 231
D'Amato, Paul ... 842
D'Andrea, Michael ... 791
D'Angelo, Caroline ... 594
D'Aquino, Michael ... 727
D'Arcy, Meaghan ... 167
D'Elia, John ... 375
D'Onofrio, Max ... 298
Dabbar, Paul M ... 760
Daboya, Iesha ... 389
Dacey, Ted ... 291
Dacus, Eugene ... 821
Dadzie, Louisa McCarter ... 670
Daehn, Jennifer ... 436
Dagul, Reid ... 385
Dagusch, Will ... 378
Dahdouh, Tom ... 802
Daher, Philip ... 785
Dahl, James A ... 784
Dahl, Kateri ... 373
Dahl, Kenneth R ... 644
Dahl, Scott S ... 726
Dahle, Kristen N ... 789
Daigle, J. Jeff ... 604
Daigle, Nicole ... 366
Daigle, Robert ... 408
Daigle, Veronica B ... 622
Dailey, Daniel A ... 641
Dailey, David ... 278
Dailey, Grace ... 617
Dailey, Jack ... 836
Daily, Marjorie ... 104
Daimler-Nothdurft, Kristen ... 7
Daines, Steve ... 159, 309, 328, 331, 345, 346, 347, 348, 349, 365, 377, 385, 475, 506
Dale, Robin ... 816
Dalessandro, Robert J ... 782
Dalfonso, JD ... 98
Dalke, Kathryn ... 264
Dalloglio, Luca ... 925
Dalton, Carol ... 904
Dalton, David ... 663
Dalton, Patricia ... 583
Dalton-Kumins, Selene ... 753
Daly, Cecilia ... 449
Daly, Edward M ... 650
Daly, James ... 832
Daly, Katy ... 417
Daly, Lisa ... 464
Daly, Megan ... 393, 394
Daly, Timothy ... 54
Damiani, Todd ... 749
Damich, Edward J ... 886
Damle, Sarang (Sy) ... 588
Dammons, Cheryl ... 739
Damron, David ... 70
Damschen, Rob ... 263
Dana, M.G ... 656
Dandridge, Sylvia L ... 507
Danel, Isabella ... 934
Daner, Brian ... 350
Danford, Christa ... 261
Danford, James ... 439
Daniel, Edwin ... 623
Daniel, Jean ... 694
Daniel, Katherine Lyon ... 737
Daniel, Susan ... 922
Daniel, Ted ... 465

Page

Daniell, Kelsi ... 15
Daniels, Grafton J ... 515
Daniels, Jody ... 649
Daniels, John J ... 642
Daniels, Lisa ... 842
Daniels, Marguerite V ... 848
Daniels, Mark ... 753
Daniels, McKay ... 297
Daniels, Tim ... 124
Danielson, Jack ... 754
Danielson, Shane ... 699
Danies, Joel ... 607, 609
Danis, Jody ... 662
Danis, Michael R ... 508
Danker, Richard ... 787
Dankler, Mike ... 100
Dankowitz, Beverly ... 728
Danly, James ... 761
Danowski, Tim ... 371
Danvers, William C ... 950
Danylak, Mike ... 368
Dapas, Marc L ... 822
Darby, Brooke ... 603
Darby, Reginald ... 277
Darden, Bill ... 245
Darden, Karen ... 699
Darden, Silas V. III ... 679
Darehshori, Sara ... 844
Dareshori, Zachary ... 416
Darling, Bruce B ... 819
Darling, Nedra ... 687
Darnall, Elizabeth ... 186
Darrow, Mac ... 942
Dart, Lauren ... 23
Das, Himamauli "Him" ... 611
Dash, Aliyah ... 69
Dattilo, Ryan ... 380
Daugherty, Becky ... 395
Daugherty, John T ... 745
Daughtrey, Erica ... 173
Daughtrey, Martha Craig ... 857
Daulby, Jen ... 94
Daum, Margaret ... 378
Dauphin, Dennis ... 677
Davalos, Antonella ... 423
Davenport, Collin ... 283
Davenport, David S., Sr ... 649
Davenport, Shari ... 759
Davey, Sarah ... 29
David, Ruth ... 820
David, Ruth A ... 819
Davidse, Koen ... 945
Davidson, Deborah ... 634
Davidson, Jeanne ... 660
Davidson, Jonathan ... 46
Davidson, Maddie ... 370
Davidson, Mark ... 707
Davidson, Matthew ... 629
Davidson, Michael L ... 645
Davidson, Michelle ... 14
Davidson, Patricia ... 730
Davidson, Peter ... 759
Davidson, Peter B ... 709
Davidson, Raymond ... 908
Davidson, W.R ... 656
Davidson, Warren ... 210, 311, 340, 418, 419, 420, 486
Davie, Mary ... 803
Davies, Glyn T ... 609
Davies, Lauren ... 375
Davies, Sally M ... 784
Davies, Scott ... 753, 754
Davin, Jerome ... 693
Davis, Alec ... 437
Davis, Alysa ... 49
Davis, Andrew ... 730
Davis, Audrey Y ... 625
Davis, Carlton ... 435
Davis, Chip ... 10
Davis, Chris ... 436
Davis, Daniel ... 788
Davis, Danny K ... 92, 307, 334, 450, 451, 486
Davis, Darlene ... 433
Davis, David ... 255
Davis, Delia P ... 753
Davis, Eddie D ... 676
Davis, Emily ... 240
Davis, Eric ... 409
Davis, Ethan ... 661

	Page
Davis, Jeffrey S	734
Davis, John	287
Davis, Jordan	415
Davis, Keirsten	645
Davis, Kenneth	515
Davis, Kevin M	397
Davis, Kimaya	426
Davis, Kolan	380
Davis, Laura M.H	815
Davis, Lauren	353, 354, 355
Davis, Lester	98
Davis, Linda Kay	905
Davis, Mark S	649
Davis, Melinda M	826
Davis, Mike	380
Davis, Nida	783
Davis, Patrick	380
Davis, Ralph F	636
Davis, Rhonda J	820
Davis, Richard A	700
Davis, Richard G	584
Davis, Richard K	782
Davis, Robert	679, 898
Davis, Robyn	694
Davis, Rodney	94, 307, 339, 399, 400, 401, 427, 443, 444, 445, 446, 454, 468, 486, 503
Davis, Rose Marie	687
Davis, Susan A	45, 306, 335, 406, 407, 410, 411, 486, 503, 507
Davis, Susey	103
Davis, Teresa	217
Davis, Traci	839
Davis, Vera G	505
Davis, W. Eugene	857
Davis, Wanda	764
Davy, Monica	814
Dawe, Kathleen Connery	121
Dawkins, Laura	723
Dawkins, Tahara	715
Dawson, Greg	619
Dawson, Kevin	225
Dawson, Liz	405
Dawson, Mark	4
Dawson, Patrick	639
Dawson, Todd	630
Day, Chris	363
Day, Christopher L	650
Day, Jonathan	239
Day, M. Kendall	663
Day, Muffy	78, 273
Day, Pamela	8
Day, Patrick	380
Day, Robert	918
Day, Sharon	607
Day, Tamika	461
Dayal, Tushar	389
Dayan, Elizabeth	750
Dayson, Danya A	904
de Alba, Luis Alfonso	932
de Bolle, Paulo	952
de Clercq, Peter	945
de Gamboa, Nancy Ruiz	723
de Harro, Connie Tsofie	385
de Jesus Luevano Grano, Jose	921
de la Cruz, Rafael	916
de la Roche, Ann	940
de la Vega, Juan	63
de La Vina de Foley, Lydia	506
De Lannoy, Anthony	924
de Leon, Fernando Ernesto	917
De Leon, Maria Lopez	815
De Los Santos, Karen	269
De Lude, Bethany	903
de Marcelus, Roland	603
de Marty, Idalia Dominguez	188
de Mers Raney, Jena	730
de Mistura, Staffan	948
De Rosa, Gustavo	917
de Rueda, Omar Ricardo Rios Bravo	920
de Serpa Soares, Miguel	939
de Villeroche, Herve M. Jodon	924, 951
de Visbal, Carmen Velasquez	932
de Vreeze, Maximilian	63
Deal, Rocky	22
Dean, Gregory	908
Dean, Margaret	408
Dean, Michael	765
Dean, Ted	714
Dean, Telora	702
Dean, Tim	395
Dearborn, Rick	596
Deardorff, Kevin E	712
Dearman, Tony	687
Deasy, Dana	623
Deavers, Leslie	696
DeBoer, Margaret	784
DeBrosse, Frank	211
Debus-Lopez, Karl	589
DeCant, Kyle	412
DeCasper, Jennifer	237
Decato, John	691
deCervens, Jeanne	510
DeCesaro, Anne	452
Deci, Jen	360
Deck, Wiley	446, 752
Decker, Cynthia	716
Decker, James	264, 437
Decker, Lauren	260
Decker, Nelly	268, 276
Decosi, Garnett	375
DeCourcy, Susan	755
Dedrick, Katherine W	446
Deeb, Mary Jane	589
Deeley, Kevin	798
DeFazio, Peter A	221, 312, 333, 443, 486, 808
DeFelice, Joseph J	746
DeFilippo, Catherine	846
DeFillippi, Gwendolyn	750
Defillo, Marquette	691
DeFrancis, Suzanne	782
DeFreitas, Matthew	427, 504
Degani, Nicholas	794
Degenfelder, Ken	433
DeGette, Diana	47, 306, 334, 413, 414, 415, 487
DeGraff, Kenneth	460
DeHarde, Edward	827
Dehlinger, Nancy	300
Dehmlow, Marta	404
Dehoff, Andrew D	842
Deitz, Alexandria	380
Deitz, Patrick	62
Delaney, April McClain	505
Delaney, Eric	126
Delaney, John K	126, 308, 339, 418, 419, 420, 467, 487
Delaney, Lacorie	516
Delaney, Michael J	596
Delaney, William	682
Delanio, Paul	515
DeLauro, Rosa L	52, 306, 333, 402, 404, 456, 487
Delawie, Greg	607
Delay, Debra	713
Delbanco, Dawn H	815
DelBene, Suzan K	284, 313, 338, 409, 450, 451, 487
DelCotto, Ellen	115
Delgado, Glenn A	809
Delgado, Michael A	618
Delgado, Raul	920
Delisi, John	820
Delisle, Deb	765
Dell'Oliver, Max	10
DellaCorte, Michael T	665
Delmar, Richard	612
DelNegro, Elizabeth	804
Delrahim, Makan	658
DeLuca, Andrew	29
DeMar, Gretchen	518
DeMarco, David	433, 464
DeMella, Adam	350
Demeo, Marisa	905
Demers, James	847
Demers, John C	680
Demery, Destinae	417
Deming, Jefferson	18
Demings, Val Butler	63, 306, 342, 424, 428, 429
Demos, Lynn	99
DeMoss, Joyce	765
Dempsey, Erin	370
Demske, Gregory E	735
Denham, Jeff	24, 306, 338, 399, 400, 431, 432, 443, 444, 445, 487
Denison, Mary Boney	718
Dennis, Irving L	745
Dennis, James L	857
Dennis, Matt	405
Dennis-Morial, Kemah	118
Dennison, William K	784

Page

Denoncourt, Jason 132
Densel, Brock 694
Dent, Elizabeth 350
Denton, Ivan 729
Denzel, Kris 196
Deo, Ravindra 801
Deoudes, John 263
DePriest, Trish 76
Dermody, John 751
Derr, April Paris 238
Desai, Anuj C 676
Desai, Sonali 33
DeSantis, Ron 60, 306, 339, 421, 422, 428, 434, 435, 487, 502
DeSaulnier, Mark 25, 306, 340, 410, 411, 434, 435, 443, 445, 487
Desbois, Michel 705
Deschene, Christopher 760
DesJarlais, Scott 246, 312, 338, 399, 400, 401, 406, 407, 434, 487
DeSpain, Mike 177
Desrocher, John 606
DeStefano, John 598
Deters, Allison 405
Dethloff, Lisa 108
Detmers, Deb 96
DeTora, Tony 43
Dettelbach, Brian A 748
Detter, Laura 226
Deubler, John 513
Deutch, Theodore E 70, 307, 337, 417, 421, 422, 428, 487, 806, 845
Deutsch, Jeremy 455
Deutsch-Feldman, Ezra 389
Devaris, Aimee 690
Deveny, Adrian 219
DeVille, Curt 705
Devito, Danny 713
DeVito, Vincent 685
Devlin, Margarita 772
Devlin, Patrick 461
DeVooght, Joe 100
DeVos, Betsy 591, 763, 781, 806, 807, 816, 851
DeVries, Esther 904
DeWeese, Barry 748
Dewey, Samuel Everett 420
Dewhirst, Diane 460
DeWitt, Brett 425
DeWitt, Jeffrey 909
DeWitt, Tyrona 905
DeWitte, Jon 136
Dews, Elizabeth 202
Dexter, Barry 467
Dey, Anita 794
Dhillon, Uttam 599
Diagana, Ousmane 950
Diallo, Mamadou 945, 946
Diamond, Clint 260
Diamonstein-Spielvogel, Barbaralee 782
Diaz, Albert 857
Diaz, Andres Gonzalez 932
Diaz, Eduardo 836
Diaz-Balart, Mario 72, 307, 335, 402, 403, 404, 409, 487
Diaz-Rosillo, Carlos 597
Dibattista, Patrick 516
Dibblee, Christian 216
Dichner, Ellen 817
Dickey, Derrick 75
Dickey, Olivia 249
Dickinson, Hillary 449
Dickinson, Lisa 682
Dickinson, Liz 738
Dickman, Martin J 848
Dickon, Rachel E 799
Dickson, Lane 366
Dickson, Peter 728
Didawick, Kathy 505
Didier, Elaine K 812
Didiuk, Monica 163
Dieng, Adama 949
Dierman, Constance 605
Dieter, Kristen 833
Dietrich, Ross 364
Dietz, Michael 586
Dietz, Polly 616
DiFolco, Francois A 588
Diggs, James 783
diGiacomantonio, William G 510

Page

DiGiantommaso, Jennifer 724
Dill, Barron 514
Dillard, Jeremy 517
Dillard, Stephen 769
Dillen, Jeff 714
Diller, Matt 437
Dilley, Jared 207
Dillihay, Marilyn 249
Dillingham, Steven 828
Dillingham, Steven D 825
Dillon, Sean 264
Dillon, Thomas 464
Dilly, Terri L 637
DiMarco, Brandy 645
DiMartini, Traci 792
Dimenstein, Katherina 12
Dimeo, Robert 720
Dimock, Jonathan 808
Dimunation, Mark G 590
diNanno, Thomas 778
DiNenna, Chris 631
Dingell, Debbie 141, 309, 340, 413, 414, 471, 487, 505
Dingman, Lacey 834
Dingwall, Ian 725
Dinh, Mai 694
Dinh, Uyen 776
Dinh-Zarr, T. Bella 820
Dinnie, Erika 804
Dinwoodie, Jeffrey 831
Diop, Makhtar 949
DiPaolo, Nancy 690
Dirks, Hannah 218
DiSanto, Dino 213
DiSanto, Emilia 602
Discigil, Justin 220
DiSiena, Jennifer 181
DiSilvestro, Michael P 393
Disman, Beatrice 837
Disrud, Doug 405
Distefano, Nichole 153
Ditch, David 361
DiToro, Jennifer A 905
Ditto, Jessica 597
Ditton, Peter 688
Diver, Cameron 936
Dixit, Praveen 714
Dixon, Annette 949
Dixon, Arrington 813
Dixon, Evan 375
Dixon, Herbert B 905
Dixon, Kelly 459
Dixon, Miranda 21
Dixon, Pam 803
Dixon, Sherry 697
Diz, Carlos 516, 584
DiZinno, Richard 380
Diznoff, Robert 167
Djinnit, Said 945
Do, David 909
Doak, Patrick 121
Doane, Margaret M 821
Dobak, Carol L 767
Dobson, Logan 389
Dobson, Waynna 56
Dobyan, Bridget 141
Dockery, Derrick 459
Dockery, Megan 395
Dockham, Andrew 378
Dodaro, Gene L 583
Dodin, Reema 393
Dodman, Michael 603
Dodman, Michael J 608
Dodszuweit, Patricia S 857
Doerner, Richard L 511
Doffermyre, William 847
Dogerty, Clare 351
Doggett, Libby 765
Doggett, Lloyd 269, 313, 334, 450, 451, 487
Doggette, James 260
Dogu, Laura F 608
Dohanic, David 815
Doherty, Clare C 446
Doherty, Jane H 703
Doherty, Kathleen A 607
Doherty, Mary 133
Doherty, Owen 754
Doherty, Patrick 635
Dohner, Robert 614

	Page
Dohr, Bob	465
Dolan, John L	624
Dolan, Meredith	209
Dolliff, Phillip	603
Domenech, Emily	439
Dominguez, Julian	650
Dominguez, Michelle	384
Donahue, Kathryn	417
Donahue, Kevin	907
Donahue, Kristen B	464
Donald, Bernice Bouie	857
Donald, Brenda	909
Donaldson, Ann	598
Donaldson, Lisa Endy	711
Donaldson, Milford Wayne	781
Donaldson, Polly	908
Donaldson, Stephen	639
Donaldson, Steve	392
Donalson, Peteranne	951
Donat, Joseph	189
Donches, Michelle	260
Donegan, Ian M	590
Donegan, Kevin	654
Donenberg, Jon	129
Doney, Lauren	128
Doninger, Chris	718
Donius, Susan K	811, 812
Donkar, Eli N	837
Donlon, Jessica	442
Donlon, Sara	213
Donnell, Katie	294
Donnellon, James	715
Donnelly, Joe	99, 307, 327, 331, 345, 346, 352, 353, 359, 387, 475
Donnelly, John	82
Donnelly, John B	388
Donnelly, Kellie	366
Donoghue, Joseph	9
Donohue, Haley	346
Donohue, Jennifer	205
Donohue, Sean	515
Donovan, Annie	612
Donovan, Colleen	749
Donovan, Daniel M., Jr	186, 311, 340, 421, 422, 424, 487
Donovan, Garrett	134, 423
Donovan, John	693
Donovan, Joseph	664, 665
Donovan, Joseph, Jr	607
Donovan, Matthew	629
Donovan, Raymond P	665, 666
Donzell, Keith	745
Doocey, Sean	598
Doocy, Mary	436
Dooley, Joseph W	510
Doomes, Elliot	447
Doone, Alison	759
Dorame, Thomas	645
Doran, Dawn	679
Dore, Vernita	700
Doremus, Paul	714
Dorey, David	727
Dorfman, Cynthia	765
Dorgan, Byron L	508
Dorgan, Darrell	782
Dorko, Jeffrey	778
Dorman, Caitlin	159
Dorman, Daniel	822
Dorman, Lisha	702
Dormsjo, Leif	909
Dorn, Georgette M	589
Dorn, Linda M	841
Dorn, Terry	584
Dornell, Izella	710
Dorosin, Joshua	602
Dorothy, Michelle	45
Dorrer, Jennifer	364
Dorris, Edward	814
Dorsey, Joshua	517
Dortch, Marlene	795
Dorval, Haley	79
Doss, Christopher Todd	674
Dotson, Bernadine	449
Doty, Art	665
Doty, Erin	37
Doty, John	185
Doud, Gregg	596
Dougherty, Dorothy	727
Dougherty, Ellen	698
Dougherty, Michael	777
Douglas, James	836
Douglas, Nicholas	695
Douglas, Walter	602
Douglass, Heather	433
Douste-Blazy, Phillipe	948
Dove, Laura C	397
Dovilla, Michael D	823
Dowd, John P	274
Dowd, Thomas	726
Dowd, Thomas M	730
Dowd, Tim	469
Dowdy, Alan	707
Dowdy, Tracy	76
Dowell, Greg	248
Dowling, Kevin	181
Dowling, Michael J	625
Downey, Brian	377
Downing, David J	666
Downing, Richard W	663
Doyle, Bonnie L	840
Doyle, Brian M	784
Doyle, Michael F	231, 312, 334, 413, 414, 487
Doyle, Peter	796
Doyle, William	181, 767
Draheim, Justin	617
Draizin, Mitch	505
Drake, David	936
Drake, Johnny	796
Drane, LaDavia S	185
Dravis, Samantha	790
Drayne, Michael R	745
Dreeben, Linda J	818
Dreiling, Mark	162
Drelick, Donna	695
Drenkard, Molly	455
Dressler, Jeff	459, 503
Drew, Benjamin	501
Drewes, Jeanne	590
Driano, Susan	614
Dries, Mark	698
Driscoll, Derrick	682
Driscoll, John	21
Driscoll, Steven J	824
Drisko, Melissa A	625
Dronberger, Hal	652
Droney, Christopher F	857
Drouet, Katuska	918
Drouet, Suzanne	681
Drummer, Donald	750
Drummond, Jerome M	805
Drummond, LaDedra	260
Drummond, Melissa	697
Drummond, Michael	594
Drusina, Edward	921
Drzewicki, John	226
Dubensky, Joshua	387
Duberstein, Kenneth M	808
DuBester, Ernest	799
Dubina, Joel F	858
Dubler, Grant	166
Dubois, Ann	729
Dubois, Pascale Helene	950
Dubose, Avis	385
DuBose, Danielle	452
DuBray, Daniel J	690
Ducharme, Louis Marc	924
Duchesne, Matthew	794
Duck, Jennifer	380
Duckworth, Tammy	88, 307, 329, 331, 362, 363, 365, 366, 367, 368, 383, 475, 509
Dudley, Drenan A	350
Dudley, Lauren	378
Duerst, Cate	110
Dufau-Richet, Marie-Sophie	919
Duff, James C	903
Duffy, Paula B	815
Duffy, Sean P	296, 314, 338, 418, 419, 487, 503
Duffy, Thomas	609
Dugan, John	834
Duggal, Shefali Razdan	844
Duggin, Thelma	851
Duggins, Cori	124
Duhe, John M., Jr	857
Duhovny, Emily	191
Dujarric, Stephane	939
Duke, Andrew	253

Page
Duke, Elaine C 775
Duke, Laura 771
Dulabahn, Beth 590
Duma, David W 621
Dumais, Theresa 420
Dumm, Kenneth 635
Dumont, Michael J 624
Dumser, Rachel 841
Dunbar, Angela 675
Duncan, Allyson K 857
Duncan, Brian A 822
Duncan, Christiana 31
Duncan, Jeff 239, 312, 338, 413, 414, 487, 726
Duncan, John J., Jr 245, 312, 333, 434, 435, 443, 444, 445, 487, 751
Duncan, Kirsten 425
Duncan, Lesley 806
Duncan, Robert 397
Duncan, Thomasenia P 901
Duncan-Peters, Stephanie 905
Dundee, Mark 725
Dunfee, John 787
Dunford, Joseph F., Jr 594, 624
Dunham, Nancy J 903
Dunham, Will 459
Dunigan, Lynn 397
Dunklin, Kristina 30
Dunlap, James 678
Dunlap, MaryAnne 505
Dunlap, Susan 754
Dunleavy, John F 649
Dunn, Neal P 58, 306, 342, 399, 400, 438, 439, 448, 487
Dunn, Sylvia B 770
Dunne, Julie 436
Dunson, Edward D., Jr 787
Dupert, Diane 796
Duque, Clarisol 88
Duran, Mishaela 736
Durand, Adam 147
Durant, Andrew 510
DuRant, Ryann 79
Durbin, Richard J 88, 307, 328, 330, 347, 348, 349, 379, 382, 388, 392, 475, 509, 510
Durham-Aguilera, Karen L 644
Duross, Eben 387
Durrer, Austin 65
Durst, Garrett 21
Dutton, John 124, 373
Duval, Claire 425
Duval, Ed 700
Duvall, Amanda 240
Duygan-Bump, Burcu 785
Dwight, Helen 102
Dworkin, Aaron 815
Dwyer, Anne 371
Dwyer, Jack 144
Dwyer, Julie 153
Dwyer, Molly C 858
Dwyer, Steve 461
Dybas, Samantha 98
Dyck, Joyce Russell 894
Dye, Charlotte A 799
Dye, Rebecca F 799
Dyk, Timothy B 866
Dykema, Rick 43
Dynan, Karen 615
Dyson, Pamela 834
Dzau, Victor J 819
Dziak, Doug 298
Dziedzic, Jeffrey 697

E

Eads, Jeff 783
Eager, Thomas 454
Eaglin, James B 904
Eakins, Carol R 719
Eannello, Joe 110
Earley, Keith B 848
Early, Gerald L 816
Early, Michelle Gilder 825
Earnest, Darryl 706
Easby-Smith, Seton 459
Easley, Stephanie 397
Easter, Abbi 279
Easter, Alberta 380
Easterbrook, Frank H 858

Page
Easterling, William E 820
Easterly, Catharine F 904
Eastman, Kevin 20
Easton, Anne 827
Eaton, Chuck 193
Eaton, Jackson 378
Eaton, Richard K 882
Ebel, David M 858
Ebert-Gray, Catherine 608, 609, 610
Eblen, Alex 373
Ebong, Enoh T 850
Eby, Natasha 429
Echavarria, Lorraine 834
Echeto, Nicole 166
Echols, Debi 5
Echols, Lamar 415
Eck, Andrew Quinn 420
Eckerson, Mary Elisabeth 290
Eckert, Joe 395
Eckert, Marti 841
Eckstein, Mathew 464
Ecoffey, Stacey 736
Edattel, Paul 415
Eddings, Richard 153
Eddy, David S. III 799
Eddy, Julie 23
Edelberg, Wendy 583
Edelblute, Jason 637
Edelman, Eric E 845
Edelman, Robert 299
Edelson, Todd E 905
Edelstein, Rachel 704
Eden, Kathryn 383
Edens, Amanda 727
Ederle, Meghan 646
Edgar, Jennifer 723
Edgar, Kevin R 420
Edge, Elizabeth 777
Edge, Peter 779
Edge, Rochelle M 785
Edgerton, Vic 433
Ediger, Mark 639
Edlow, Joseph 430
Edmondson, J. L 858
Edmondson, Laurel 223
Edmondson, Robert 26
Edmonson, Robert 460
Edmunds, Anton E 932
Edwards, Allen 353, 354, 355
Edwards, Cathy 405
Edwards, Deanna E 397
Edwards, Harry T 861
Edwards, Isaac 366
Edwards, Joseph 183
Edwards, Molly 459
Edwards, Ron 792
Edwards, Yul 92
Edwin, Yeshvanth 917
Edwing, Richard 715
Effron, Andrew S 897
Efron, William 802
Efros, Ellen 907
Egan, Gerald 586
Egan, Kyle 44
Egorin, Melanie 452
Egred, Melissa 378
Eguchi, Takehisa 952
Ehl, Kathlyn 411
Ehly, Ryan 265, 467
Ehrenkrantz, Joe 430
Ehrenstamm, Faye 663
Eichhorn, Jared 459
Eichinger, Kevin 436
Eichner, Matthew J 784
Eid, Allison H 858
Eijkemans, Gerarda 934
Eilperin, Stephen F 905
Eisele, Brooke 373
Eiselsberg, David 252
Eisen, Jean Toal 350
Eisen, Norman L 844
Eisenbach, George 771
Eisenberg, John 599
Eisenberg, Lewis 607, 609
Eisenmann, James M 846
Eisenstatt, Michael 249
Eismeier, Jim 385
Eissenstat, Everett 598

	Page
Ekins, Gavin	467
El-Etreby, Ragui	950
El-Hindi, Jamal	615
El-Lissy, Osama	707
Elam, Erik	7
Elbeblawi, Hazem Beblawi	924
Elder, Christine	608
Elder, Fitzhugh IV	382
Eldred, Joseph	652
Eldridge, Curtis	785
Eldridge, Duane	723
Eldridge, Joseph T	845
Eldridge, Lucy	723
Elias, Adam	94
Elias, Carlos	350, 351
Elias, Mark	387
Elieson, Dayle	670
Eligan, Veronica	430
Elizalde, Rafael	39
Elkins, Arthur, Jr	791
Ellard, Angela	452
Ellertson, Wyatt	416
Ellig, Jerry	796
Ellington, Robert	753
Elliot, Allan W	650
Elliot, Cameron	833
Elliott, Clair	114
Elliott, Farar	462
Elliott, George	718
Elliott, Howard "Skip"	755
Elliott, James	700
Elliott, Jerry	704
Elliott, Joel	99
Elliott, Ramona D	671
Ellis, Blair	415
Ellis, Kathryn	766
Ellis, Larry R	782
Ellis, Shirley	295
Ellison, Annie	23
Ellison, David R	626
Ellison, Eugenia D	804
Ellison, Keith	146, 309, 336, 418, 419, 487, 507
Ellison, Kyle	516
Ellison, Michele	795
Ellzey, Michael	812
Elmer, Todd	717
Elnabraway, Tamir	147
Eloshway, Chuck	718
Elrod, Jennifer Walker	857
Elshami, Nadeam	460
Eltinge, John L	711
Eltsefon, Larissa	397
Elul, Gabrielle	467
Elwell, Daniel	749
Elwood, Courtney S	786
Ely, Kay	803
Emanuel, Jacqueline	695
Emanuel, William J	817
Embree, Tim	517
Emelee, Christophe	921
Emerick, Amy	11
Emerson, Catherine E	661
Emerson, Jeff	596
Emerson, Jeffrey Wade	420
Emerson, W. Eric	813
Emery, Christine	851
Emery, Marshall	836
Emery, Rodney	770
Emhof, Jaryn	63
Emmer, Tom	146, 309, 340, 418, 419, 420, 454, 487
Emmons, Julie Scott	198
Emrich, Matthew	780
Encina, Roswell	588
Endicott, Gary L	397
Engall, Andrew	287
Engel, Eliot L	188, 311, 333, 413, 415, 421, 487
Engel, Gary	583
Engel, Lauren	829
Engel, Steven A	679
Engelhardt, Sue A	643
Engelhardt, Tim	738
Engen, Eric M	785
England, Gordon R	819
England, Rich	262
Engle, Tricia	397
Engling, Max	427, 503
English, Brystol	440
English, Cachavious	6
English, Cathleen	519
English, Grant	375
Englund, Mary Sue	427
Engram, Wayne	670
Engstrom, Eric	785
Engstron, Eric C	784
Ennis, Eileen	748
Eno, Mary	588
Enomoto, Kana	741
Enos, Katie	131
Enriquez, Melissa	366
Entenman, Debra	289
Enzi, Michael B	298, 314, 328, 330, 361, 369, 370, 374, 377, 383, 475
Enzinna, James B	589
Epley, Mark	459
Epley, Paul D	585
Epperson, Jennifer	795
Eppes, Lesya	382
Epstein, Anthony	905
Epstein, Jonathan S	356, 357
Erb, Chris	437
Erbenova, Michaela	924
Erceg, Christopher J	784
Erdmann, Charles E	897
Erdos, Lori	837
Erichs, Alysa	779
Erickson, Janet	447
Erickson, John	651
Erickson, Kristofor	420
Erickson, Mary C	716
Erickson, Matthew	346
Erickson, Ralph R	858
Erickson, Robert C	805
Erickson, Terrell	697
Ericson, Brooke	794
Ericson, Raellen	698
Ernest, Matt	638
Ernst, Joni	105, 308, 328, 331, 345, 346, 352, 353, 367, 368, 383, 470, 475
Ernst, Ruth Ann	397
Erny, Margo	698
Erskine, Tim	722
Ertel, Elizabeth	416
Erwin, Deanne	794
Esau, Laurie	145
Escalona, Prim	680
Esch, Michele	704
Escobar, Jacqueline	648
Escoto, Roberto	934
Eshelman, Sharon	436
Eshoo, Anna G	28, 306, 334, 413, 415, 487
Eskandani, Rebekah	440
Eskow, Glenn S	784
Eskra, Jennifer	350
Eskridge, Robert	417
Espaillat, Adriano	187, 311, 342, 410, 411, 421, 422, 441, 442, 487
Esper, Mark T	641
Espinosa, Diana	739
Espinosa, Sergio	266
Espinosa-Salcedo, Gina	755
Espinoza, Armando Segura	920
Espinoza, Daniel	260
Esquith, David	765
Esser, Michael R	826
Estabrook, David	833
Estep, Gregory E	586
Estep, Lorna	635
Estes, Maia	126, 910
Estes, Ron	110, 308, 342, 410, 411, 424, 425, 487
Estevadeorval, Antoni	917
Estrella, Jorge	924
Esty, Elizabeth H	53, 306, 339, 438, 439, 443, 445, 446, 448, 488
Etchen, Alex	447
Etchingham, Gerald	818
Etheridge, Arrie	830
Ethington, Ryan	268
Ethridge, Max	689
Etienne, Ashley	460
Etienne, Carissa F	933, 944
Etka, Patrick	275
Ettenger, Elijah	31
Etter, Robert	361
Etue, John	264
Etzel, Ruth	790
Etzinger, Michael E	741

	Page
Eugene, Theresa	363
Eugenio, Marcia	724
Eure, Philip K	911
Eusman, Elmer	590
Evalle, John	21
Evangelista, Stephen	839
Evanoff, Michael T	604
Evans, Carol A	784
Evans, Dwight	224, 312, 340, 399, 400, 401, 441, 488
Evans, Gary W	586
Evans, Gregory L	784
Evans, Jack	907
Evans, Jason T	646
Evans, Joseph E., Jr	583
Evans, Kent	701
Evans, Leonard	681
Evans, Michelle	464
Evans, Mike	370
Evans, Nicole K	824
Evans, Robin	718
Evans, Robyn	717
Evans, Stuart	680
Evans, Tracee	255
Evans, Vincent	60
Evans-Vilent, Janan	364
Everett, Jason	430
Everett, Max	759
Everett, Sheila	841
Everett, Tom	751
Everette, Westley	724
Everling, Jennifer	846
Everly, George	361
Everton, Alli	61
Evich, Jordan	286
Ewell, Austin	689
Ewell-Madison, Angela	713
Ewers, J.A	656
Ewy, Michelle	639
Eychaner, Fred	807
Eyler, Gustav	657
Eyler, Yvonne	717
Eynard, Nicole	456
Eyre, Cheryl	814

F

	Page
Faas, John	456
Facchiano, Greg	232
Facchiano, Kathee	119
Fadden, Daniel J	849
Fado, Kelly	394
Fagan, Carey	750
Fagan, John	614
Fahey, David	716
Fahey, John	836
Fahey, Kaitlin	88
Fahey, Kevin	622
Fahey, Patricia Dugan	671
Fahrenkopf, Amy	772
Faiella, Matt	764
Faile, Andrew	717
Failla, Christopher	513
Fairchild, Sarah	244
Fairchild, Scott	164
Fairhurst, Deborah	60
Faison, C. Forrest	654
Faison, Clinton III	654
Faith, Kimberly	464
Faith, Ryan	440
Fakhoury, Deema	952
Falaschetti, Dino D	420
Falcicchio, John	907
Falcone, Elizabeth	276
Falconer, Susan	282
Falconer, TJ Adams	22
Falk, Andrew E	793
Falk, David	505
Falk, Scott	778
Falkowski, Ben	100
Fall, Francois Lounceny	944
Fall, Muhamet	953
Fallon, Christine L	856
Fallon, William	780
Familant, Norman	658
Fan, Queena	370
Fangmeyer, Robert	720
Fanning, Sunny Lee	751
Fannon, Molly	836
Fantini, Michael	630
Farah, Alyssa	1, 201, 391, 593
Farar, Sim	843
Fare, John	765
Farello, Paul	710
Faremo, Grete	942
Fargo, John N	660
Farhadian, Sarah	70
Farias, Anna Maria	744
Farley, Audrey	756
Farley, Evan	803
Farley, John M	615
Farmer, Paul	946
Farnsworth, Jerry	644
Farooq, Madge	55
Farooque, Omer	288
Farr, Scott	652
Farraj-Feijoo, Ricardo	588, 710
Farrar, Elizabeth	381
Farrell, Michael W	904
Farrell, Sonja	702
Farris, J. Jerome	858
Faso, John J	190, 311, 342, 399, 400, 401, 409, 443, 444, 445, 488
Fasolka, Mike	720
Fassler, Jess	180
Fauci, Anthony S	740
Faulkner, Charles	602
Faulkner, Don	750
Faulkner, Gershom	65
Faust, Leona	393
Faust, Thomas	908
Fauth, Gerald W. III	819
Fawell, Joe	91
Fawole, Omolola A	631
Fay, David	922
Fay, Peter T	858
Faye, Issa	952
Fayne, Vincent	704
Faz-Huppert, Marina	88
Fazio, Larry	814
Fearns, Sean	664
Featherson, Wendy	63
Fedder, Judith	501
Fedotov, Yury	940, 942
Fedrigo, John A	633
Feeley, Thomas E	779
Feinstein, Dianne	19, 305, 327, 330, 347, 348, 349, 379, 382, 386, 475, 506, 508
Feinstein, Lee A	844
Feirson, Mary Kay Langan	748
Feit, Y. David	595
Fekete, Stephanie	442
Feldblum, Bryan J	464
Feldblum, Chai	792
Felder, Cole	427
Felder, Emily	738
Feldgus, Steve	433
Feldman, Eric	135
Feldman, Jill	823
Feldman, Peter	364
Feldman, Sarah	153
Feldstein, Karen	809
Feldt, Dennis	678
Fellona, Tom	841
Feltman, Jeffrey	939
Feltman, Jeffrey D	947
Fender, Steven	753
Fennell, Michele T	785
Fenneman, Rebecca A	800
Fenske, Taryn	59
Fenstermacher, Karen	653
Fentress, Allison	900
Fentress, Tara	905
Ferguson, A. Drew IV	77, 307, 342, 409, 410, 411, 443, 444, 445, 446, 488
Ferguson, Carolyn	245
Ferguson, Elliot	912
Ferguson, John H	818
Ferguson, Michael J	666
Ferguson, Theresa	692
Ferguson-Russ, Robynn	659
Ferland, John	106
Fernandes, Fernando Bartholomeu	915
Fernandez, Bruce	133
Fernandez, Claudette	700, 701
Fernandez, Ferdinand F	858
Fernandez, Giselle	807

Page
Fernandez, Keith 74
Fernandez, Magdalena 730
Ferracci, James 805
Ferrao, Joaquin 829
Ferrari, John G 648
Ferreira, Orlando 917
Ferrell, Monique 646
Ferren, John M 904
Ferrer, Lilmarie 303
Ferrero, Rich 689
Ferrier, Antonia 392
Ferriero, David 811, 813, 812, 816, 851
Ferrini-Mundy, Joan 819
Ferriter, Olivia 689
Ferro, Jon 80
Ferro, Manuela 950
Ferro, Segundo 303
Ferseter, Linda 200
Fery, Matthew 193
Fesmire, Anne H 647
Fesmire, Mark 688
Feyerherm, Alan 162
Fiedler, Anna 145
Field, Ian 287
Field, Lesley 595
Field, Steve 924
Fielden, Don 634
Fields, Alexandra "Ally" 97
Fields, Brent J 831
Fields, Christine M 786
Fields, Mallory 155
Fields, Pamela L 507
Fields, Summer 200
Fields, Yvette 753
Fienga, Edward A 632
Figel, Claire 423
Figley, Paul F 661
Figueroa, Ana 39
Figueroa, Blanca 31
Figura, J. Andrew 785
Fila, Stephanie 743
Filip, Allan 139
Filler, Diane E 664
Finch, Andrew C 658
Finch, Warren 812
Findley, Madeleine 796
Fine, Lauren 460
Fine, Steven 790
Finger, Christopher 783
Fink, Katherine 701
Finkelman, Jacobo 935
Finkelston, Karin 952
Finks, LaVern 368
Finlayson, Shelley K 823
Finley, Catie 351
Finnelle, Christine 683
Fioravante, Christopher P 508
Fiorenzo, Les 752
Fiorill, Mark 517
Fiotes, Stella S 770
Firestone, Nancy B 886
Firko, Michael J 706
Firschein, Joseph 784
Fischer, Amanda 360
Fischer, Bart 401
Fischer, Deb 161, 310, 327, 331, 345, 346, 352, 353, 362, 363, 367, 368, 382, 387, 475
Fischer, Laura Lee 589
Fischmann, Elizabeth J 735
Fisenne, Susan 794
Fish, Dasan 385
Fish, Dennis 722
Fish, J.P 788
Fishbein, Allen J 784
Fisher, Ann 831
Fisher, Christopher 65
Fisher, D. Michael 857
Fisher, Gerald I 905
Fisher, John R 904
Fisher, Maia 727
Fisher, Michael 772
Fisher, Raymond C 858
Fisher, Robert 832
Fisher, Ryan A 642
Fisher, Sakurako 807
Fisher, Todd 847
Fisher-Colwill, Andrew 803
Fishman, George 430
Fishman, Robert 798
Fishman, Xan 127
Fitchitt, David 772
Fite, David 373
Fite, Nina Maria 606
Fitts, Catherine E 856
Fitts, Lida 850
Fitzella, James 437
Fitzgerald, Douglas 730
Fitzgerald, Douglas C 730
Fitzgerald, Ted 727
FitzGibbon, Tanga S 800
Fitzgibbons, Patricia J 903
Fitzhugh, Janel 824
Fitzpatrick, Brian K 227, 312, 342, 421, 422, 424, 425, 441, 442, 488
Fitzpatrick, Casey 41
Fitzpatrick, Collins T 858
Fitzpatrick, Kathleen 602
Fitzpatrick, Kathleen M 609
Fitzpatrick, Kevin 442
Fitzpatrick, Michael 603
Fitzpatrick, Paul 201
Fitzpatrick, Robert 465
FitzSimmons, David 147
Fitzsimmons, Elizabeth 601
Fixler, Dennis 710
Fjeld, Christian Tamotsu 364
Flagg, Ronald 808
Flaherty, Eddie 427
Flaherty, Eileen 787
Flake, Jeff 9, 305, 327, 331, 365, 366, 372, 373, 379, 380, 387, 475
Flanagan, Eugene 590
Flanagan, Patrick 697, 778
Flanagan, Steven 10
Flanagin, Tom 191
Flanders, Moira 769
Flanery, Hayden 409
Flanigan, William 454
Flannery, Mark J 832
Flannery, Todd 516
Flanz, Ken 85, 381
Flarida, Joe 440
Flaum, Joel M 858
Fleet, Jamie 427
Fleetwood, Maria A 793
Fleischer, Luis 920
Fleischmann, Charles J. "Chuck" 312, 338, 402, 403, 404, 488
Fleischmann, Chuck 246
Fleishman, Susan 464
Fleming, Julie 688
Fleming, Parker 437
Fleming, Rick 833
Flemings, JonAnn 699
Flemming, Denise 382
Flentje, August 661
Fleshman, Mark 670
Fletcher, Catherine 720
Fletcher, Kenyatta 619
Fletcher, William A 858
Fleury, Nicolle 751
Flick, Andy 132
Flick, Heather 734
Flinn, Shawn 670
Flint, Charles 416
Flint, Chuck 248
Flipse, Scott 506
Flood, Scott 682
Flora, Jeffrey C 824
Flores, Bill 313, 338, 413, 414, 507, 488
Flores, Daniel 430
Flores, Eliezer 262
Flores, Hugo Alexander 919
Flores, Sarah Isgur 681
Flores, William H. "Bill" 259
Florio, Drew 459
Florio, Mike 182
Flournoy, Richard 700
Flowers, Karen I 666
Floyd, Henry F 857
Fluhr, Chris 433
Fluker, Megan 506
Flumignan, Jeffrey 754
Flunker, Matthew 435
Flynn, Christopher 815
Flynn, Diana K 662

Page

Flynn, Heather 373
Flynn, Joseph 714
Flynn, Katy Crooks 425
Flynn, Timothy 409
Flynn-Brown, Josh 380
Foelak, Carol Fox 833
Fogarty, Kevin 181
Fogel, Jeremy D 813, 903
Fogels, Avery 7
Fogle, Loretta 614
Foley, Brian P 644
Foley, Martha 405
Foley, Maurice B 887
Foley, Susan V 784
Folger, Neil C 851
Follette, Glenn 785
Folmsbee, Paul A 608
Foltz, Nicole 459
Foltz, Rhonda 719
Fonda, Clark 200
Fong, Phyllis K 694
Fonnesbeck, Leif 350
Fontaine, Paul 750
Fontana, Elaine 665
Fontenote, Albert E 711, 712
Foote, Daniel L 610
Foote, Gina 251
Foran, Shelia 662
Forbes, Andrew 215
Forbes, Donna 811
Ford, Christopher A 603
Ford, David H 586
Ford, Delorice Price 849
Ford, Gilbert 798
Ford, Jerome 686
Ford, Kelli 139
Ford, Melinda 586
Ford, Robert 518
Ford, Taylor 80
Foreman, Lorraine 465
Foresman, Hank 650
Forester, James 411
Forino, Nini 603
Forman, Alfred J., Jr 420
Formby, Michael D 84
Forrest, Jenny 220
Forrester, Althea 745
Forrester, Robert 516
Forrester, Robert J 840
Forsgren, Lee 791
Forsman, Leonard A 781
Forst, Matthew D 800
Forstein, Samuel 832
Forster, Michael 851
Forster, Zach 383
Forsyth, Bart 296
Forte-Mackay, Jackie 456
Fortenberry, Jeff 162, 310, 336, 402, 403, 404, 488, 507
Forti, Olga Madruga 795
Fortier, Brittany 292
Fortier, Evelyn 380
Fortson, Kyle 819
Fossum, Camelnita 692
Foster, Alye S 785
Foster, Bill 93, 307, 337, 418, 419, 420, 438, 439, 488
Foster, Connie 467
Foster, Crystal 764
Foster, Ed 654
Foster, Janet 17
Foster, Jason 380
Foster, Jason C 825
Foster, John 65
Foster, Lucia S 711
Foster, Michele 770
Foster, Peter 937
Foster, Robert U 814
Foster, Robin Lake 31
Foster, Sandra 726
Foti, Anthony 66
Foti, Leslie 11
Foti, Scott 842
Foushee, H. Clayton 749
Foushee, Jan 840
Fowler, Elizabeth 739
Fowler, Jennifer 615
Fowler, John M 781
Fowler, Sam 366
Fowlke, Lorie 273

Page

Fowlkes, A. Jerome 793
Fowlkes, Lisa M 796
Fox, Alexandra 25
Fox, Elizabeth 447
Fox, Kathleen 778
Fox, Lynn Fischer 713
Fox, Michelle 728
Fox, Nancy 404
Fox, Raquel 831
Fox, Virginia 510
Fox, William 920
Foxx, Rhonda 202
Foxx, Virginia 198, 311, 336, 410, 434, 435, 471, 488
Foy, Sue 288
Foy, Taylor 380
Fraase, Mark G 681
Fragoso, Michael 679
Framer, Isabel 841
Francart, William 726
France, Fenella 590
Francis, Cheryl 701
Francis, David 648
Francis, Lina 420
Francisco, Noel 658
Franco, Arnulfo 920
Franco, Gabriel Hermano Pinilla 915
Franco, Miguel 34
Francois, Michael 916
Frande, Francis H 659
Frank, Evan H 397
Frank, Michael 657
Frank, Stuart 708
Franke, Andy 145
Frankel, Lois 69, 307, 339, 421, 422, 443, 445, 446, 488
Frankel, Morgan J 398
Frankfurt, Tom 651
Franklin, Kevin 824
Franklin, Margaret 60
Franklin, Reno Keoni 781
Franks, Jeffrey 924
Frantz, Douglas 933
Frantz, Ronald 699
Fraser, Beverly Britton 848
Fraser, Bobby 748
Fraser, Tracey 837
Frasier, Diane 740
Frasz, Russell 635
Frayer, Corey 360
Frazee, Christiana 243
Frazer, Gary 686
Frazier, A. D 842
Frazier, Francis 740
Frazier, Geofrey 750
Frechette, Heidi 744
Fredericksen, Greg T 755
Fredrickson, David 832
Freebairn, Spencer 264
Freedhoff, Michal 368
Freedman-Gurspan, Raffi M 844
Freeman, Karen 843
Freeman, Michael P 848
Freeman, Mishawn 411
Freeman, Peter 38
Freiman, Shaun 452
Freire, J.P 467
Freitas, Bruno 129
Frelinghuysen, Rodney P 175, 310, 334, 402, 404, 488
French, Chris 695
French, Courtney 436
French, Jennifer 690
French, Lauren 456
French, Miranda 97
French, Sam 368
Fretz, Abbey 694
Fretz, Shawn 397
Frey, Bridgett 124
Frey, Lou 509
Frey, Waldemar 945
Freyre, Angela M 792
Frias, Carmen 288
Friday, Angus 932
Fridy, Susan 933
Friedeburg, Stephanie von 952
Friedel, Laura A 350
Frieden, Paul L 728
Friedhoff, Andrea 276
Friedl, Sophie 384
Friedland, Michelle T 858

Page

Friedlander, Liz ... 401
Friedman, Aharon ... 451
Friedman, Benjamin ... 714
Friedman, Christopher ... 834
Friedman, David ... 607, 723
Friedman, Paul L ... 875
Friedman, Susan ... 614
Friedrich, Dabney L ... 874
Friedt, Anita ... 604
Friel, Greg ... 661
Friel, Michael ... 779
Friendship, Stanley C ... 841
Frierson, Heather ... 156
Friestad, Scott ... 833
Frischknecht, Daryn ... 272
Frison, Teresa ... 24
Fristedt, Andi ... 375
Fritsch, Benjamin ... 301
Fritz, Cory ... 422
Froeb, Luke ... 658
Froelich, Melissa ... 415
Frohboese, Robinsue ... 734
Froman, Eric ... 611
Fromm, Adam ... 415
Frone, Jamilia ... 677
Front, Mitchell ... 718
Frost, Bert ... 687
Frost, Dylan ... 16
Frost, Martin ... 509
Frost, Patricia A ... 647
Frucht, Craig ... 54
Fruci, Jean ... 416
Frueh, Michael J ... 772
Frushone, Joel ... 828
Fry, Courtney ... 461
Fry, Michele K ... 641
Frye, Jan ... 770, 787
Frye, Stephen ... 638
Fu, Stephenie ... 703
Fuchs, Patrick ... 364
Fuchs, W. Kent ... 820
Fudge, Marcia L ... 211, 311, 336, 399, 400, 401, 410, 488
Fuehrmeyer, Matt ... 456
Fuentes, Julio M ... 857
Fuentes, Pablo Roberto Arenas ... 920
Fulford, Haley ... 91
Fulghum, Chip ... 777
Fulkert, Marc ... 670
Fuller, Janice ... 172
Fuller, Kim ... 183
Fuller, Thomas ... 361
Fuller, Timothy R ... 642
Fullerton, Laura ... 425
Fulmer, Brendan ... 225
Fulmer, Jack ... 385
Fulop, Lesley ... 264
Fulp, Terrance ... 690
Fulton, Austin ... 273
Fulton, Brenda Sue ... 501
Fulton, Catherine ... 698
Fulton, Finch ... 748
Fulton, Heide ... 607
Fung, Inez ... 820
Funger, Norma Lee ... 807
Funk, Jennifer ... 748
Funston, Robin ... 677
Furey, Frank J ... 764
Furgione, Laura K ... 711
Furr, David ... 166
Furst, Robert ... 729
Furstenau, Raymond ... 760
Furth, David ... 796
Furusawa, Mitsuhiro ... 923
Furuta-Toy, Julie ... 607
Fusick, Elizabeth ... 61

G

Gabbard, Tulsi ... 84, 307, 339, 406, 407, 421, 422, 488
Gabello, Dominic ... 178
Gabriel, Edward ... 734
Gabriel, Mark ... 760, 922
Gadbois, Stephanie ... 429
Gadd, Jacob B ... 769
Gade, Daniel ... 814
Gaedecke, David ... 635
Gaetz, Matt ... 58, 306, 342, 406, 407, 408, 409, 428, 429, 454, 488
Gaffigan, Mark ... 583
Gage, Paul ... 222
Gagliardi, Adele ... 726
Gagnon, Jason ... 40
Gagnon, Jean ... 922
Gahun, Jamie ... 254
Gaiani, Vincent J ... 397
Gail, Jessica ... 103
Gaines, Ralph ... 743
Galanes, Jason ... 170
Galassi, Thomas ... 727
Galazin, Jared ... 650
Galdiz, Isabel ... 793
Gale, Joseph H ... 888
Galeota, Stephanie ... 829
Galiano, Socorro Gross ... 935
Galik, Daniel ... 764
Galinas, William ... 655
Galizia, Federico ... 916
Gallagher, Brendan ... 464
Gallagher, Jennifer C ... 783
Gallagher, Kevin ... 689
Gallagher, Mark A ... 636
Gallagher, Meghan ... 423
Gallagher, Mike ... 297, 314, 342, 406, 407, 424, 443, 444, 445, 488, 502
Gallagher, Peter ... 433
Gallagher, Rosemary ... 464
Gallant, Robin ... 396
Gallas, Thomas ... 813
Gallaudent, Tim ... 654
Gallaudet, Timothy ... 714
Gallego, Ruben ... 12, 305, 340, 406, 407, 408, 431, 432, 488
Gallegos, Andres ... 814
Galli, Thomas ... 645
Gallin, John I ... 740
Gallin, Joshua H ... 785
Gallivan, Maeve ... 409
Galloway, Randy ... 811
Galt, Jennifer Zimdahl ... 604, 816
Galuvao, Easter ... 937
Galvan, Gualberto Ramon Marino ... 916
Galvan, Joseph P ... 746
Galvin, James ... 622
Gamache, Stephanie ... 364
Gamba, Virginia ... 940, 948
Gambarrotti, Nury ... 373
Gambo, Angela S ... 420
Gambo, Theresa ... 416
Gamboa, Javier ... 41
Gambrel, Diana ... 47
Gamel-McCormick, Michael ... 387
Gamela, Renee ... 226
Gammello, Joseph A ... 420
Gancio, Michael ... 408
Gandhi, Ricky ... 467
Gandhi, Sajit ... 423
Gandia, Natalia ... 302
Gandy, Marshall ... 834
Gangloff, Joe ... 840
Gangopadhyay, Paula ... 816
Gannon, Curtis ... 679
Gans, Michael E ... 858
Gans, Svetlana ... 802
Gantt, Angela Noel ... 679
Ganz, Julian, Jr ... 817
Ganzer, Ann ... 603
Gao, Fang H ... 587
Gaona, Cynthia ... 265
Garamendi, John ... 21, 305, 337, 406, 407, 443, 444, 445, 446, 488
Garamendi, Patricia ... 505
Garbars, Kurt ... 804
Garber, Judith ... 605
Garber, Wendy ... 717
Garcia, Cheryl ... 726
Garcia, Chris ... 179
Garcia, Christopher ... 714
Garcia, David A ... 824
Garcia, George H ... 793
Garcia, Ileana M ... 393
Garcia, Matt ... 268
Garcia, Mory ... 442
Garcia, Sarah ... 378
Garcia, Yatzi ... 226
Garcia, Yvonne ... 676
Gard, Sean ... 295

Page
Gardei, Dean A 584
Gardella, Ronald 677
Gardenhour, Benjamin 409
Gardineer, Grovetta 821
Gardner, Adrian R 778
Gardner, Cory 46, 306, 328, 331, 361, 362, 363, 365, 372, 373, 389, 475, 501, 504
Gardner, Olivia 417
Gardner, Phil 289
Gardner, Wendell P., Jr 905
Gardy, Laura 787
Garfinkel, Simson 711
Garland, Donna 803
Garland, Jonas M 839
Garland, Merrick Brian 859
Garliauskas, Lucy 753
Garmisa, Ben 88
Garner, Brian 697
Garner, Jackie 738
Garner, Terri 812
Garnett, Karen 832
Garrahan, MaryAnn 727
Garraway, Kendall 160
Garrett, Brian 408
Garrett, Debbie 280
Garrett, Denise 589
Garrett, Judi Simon 675
Garrett, Teri 17
Garrett, Thomas A., Jr 279, 313, 342, 410, 411, 421, 422, 424, 425, 488
Garrity, Michael 834
Garry, Corey 168
Garry, Eileen 678
Gartin, Randy 451
Gartlan, Jennifer M 800
Gartrell, Peter 371
Garvey, Sandy 5
Garvin, Shawn M 789
Gary, Arthur 677
Garza, Gina 618
Garza, Jesse 296
Garzon, Carlos 934
Gasarabwe, Mbaranga 945
Gaschke, David J 676
Gaskins, Kia 724
Gaspar, Chris 509
Gaspar, Orlando Maneiro 921
Gaspar, Vitor 923
Gass, Thomas 940
Gassaway, Brandon 118
Gasser, Brandi 510
Gassie, Lillian W 588
Gaston, Beth 706
Gately, Nathan 423
Gately, Stephen 66
Gates, Angie 909, 910
Gates, Kevin 408
Gatesman, Valerie 725
Gatewood, Catherine 96
Gathers, Shirley E 611
Gatto, John B 823
Gaudet, Tracy 773
Gaudiosi, Eric 603
Gauhar, Tashina 657
Gaur, Keshav 952
Gautreaux, Cathy F 752
Gavin, Andrew G 842
Gavin, Patrick 62
Gavin, Victor 654
Gavrish, Eva 32
Gawrilow, Hilary 47
Gay, Sebastian 583
Gaydos, Colleen 350
Gaydos, Lauren 113
Gaylor, Arlene 673
Gaynor, Amy E 397
Geale, Nicholas 727
Gean, Lissette 730
Gee, James 176
Gee, Jeffrey 795
Geeslin, Chris 626
Geffert, Rebekah 111
Geiderman, Joel M 845
Geier, Paul M 748
Geiger, Teri 205
Geise, John 657
Geise, John "Jack" 681
Geisler, Linda 589
Page
Gelb, Lisa 794
Gelber, Bruce 669
Gelber, Michael 802
Geldart, Chris 910
Geldon, Dan 129
Gelineau, Caridad "Carie" 645
Geller, David 65
Geller, Jamie 423
Gelman, Peter 125
Gendell, Bill 361
Genrty, Elizabeth 80
Gentile, John 734
Gentile, Kristen 223
Gentile, Michael 351
Gentile, Rachel 42
Gentry, Jean A 619
George, Catherine 167
George, Emerson 151
George, J. Russell 618
George, Janelle 736
George, John A 648
George, Natalie 468
George, Tim 670
Georgieva, Kristalina 949
Geraci, Michael N 755
Gerber, Dallas 209
Gerber, Joel 891
Gerber, Kate Jennings 97
Gerecke, Sarah 744
Gerhardstein, Cassie 392
German, Karen St 715, 716
Gerrish, Jeff 596
Gershon, Emily 386
Gerson, Susan 670
Gerstenlauer, James P 858
Gerstenmaier, William H 809
Gertsema, Jay 165
Gervais, Pierre 647
Gerzof, Devin 460
Getchis, John F 745
Getz, Kara 452
Geurts, James F 653
Geyer, Mark 809
Ghanem, Hafez 950
Ghattas, Carl 674
Ghebreyesus, Tedros Adhanom 944
Ghee, Hailey 286
Ghent, Bill 55
Gherman, Natalia 946
Giachetti, David 408
Giaier, Steven 425
Giambastiani, E. Peter III 623
Giancarlo, Angie 405
Giancarlo, J. Christopher 787
Gianforte, Greg 160, 309, 342, 431, 432, 434, 435, 488
Giannangeli, Giulia 416
Giannasi, Robert A 818
Gianturco, Elizabeth Jordan 734
Giardina, Lane 380
Gibbens, Lisa 204
Gibbins, Walt 632
Gibbons, Fern 364
Gibbons, Gary 740
Gibbons, Julia Smith 857
Gibbons, Justin 405
Gibbs, Bob 311, 338, 399, 400, 443, 444, 445, 446, 488, 759
Gibbs, Debbi 21
Gibbs, Erin 829
Gibbs, Michael 780
Gibbs, Pamela 831
Gibbs, Robert 810
Gibbs, Robert B 209
Gibert, Mary D 813
Giblin, Thomas G 728
Gibney, Brien 826
Gibson, Caleb 235
Gibson, Calvin 752
Gibson, Chase 469
Gibson, Dylan 461
Gibson, Elizabeth 375
Gibson, Glena G 632
Gibson, John H. II 623
Gibson, Levi 254
Gibson, Loureatha 694
Gibson, Michael S 783
Gibson, Patricia 849
Gibson, Tatum 200

Page

Gibson, Ventris 910
Gidner, Courtney 456
Gidner, Jerold 690
Gieron, Kate 125
Giertz, Jeff 169
Gilbert, Curtis W 659
Gilbert, Evan 416
Gilbert, Gay 726
Gilbert, Liza 787
Gilbert, Mary 804
Gilbert, Melanie F 903
Gilbert, Richard W 586, 587
Gilbreath, Jen 446
Gilbrech, Richard 811
Gilchrist, Barbara 713
Gildenhorn, Alma 808
Gildner, Leigh Anna 17
Giles, Misty 694
Gilges, Keith 936
Gill, Hannah 437
Gill, Michael 787
Gill, Rhonda 636
Gillam, Laura Haynes 368
Gillam, Natalie 227
Gillaspie, Molly 102, 455
Gillerman, Gordon 720
Gillers, David 366
Gilles, Jean 514
Gillespie, Jamie 459
Gillespie, Linda 254
Gillette, Connie 688
Gillette, Daniel 664
Gillette, Robert 617
Gillfillan, Ross 596
Gilliard, Kevin L 649
Gillibrand, Kirsten E 180, 310, 327, 330, 345, 346, 352, 353, 367, 368, 387, 388, 475, 501
Gillies, David C 350
Gilliland, Betty Lou 705
Gillis, Jordan 643
Gillis, Ursula 618
Gillispie, Elaine 76
Gillsater, Bjorn Erik 950
Gilman, James 741
Gilman, Ronald Lee 857
Gilmartin, Jaimee 176
Gilmore, Keith 703
Gilmore, Michael 98
Gilmore, Shaun P 782
Gilmour, David 609
Gilyard, Beverly 505
Gimont, Stanley 743
Gingerich, Steve 383
Gingrey, Billie 505
Gingrich, Callista L 607
Ginieczki, Boyce 737
Ginsburg, Douglas Howard 862
Ginsburg, Mindy 795
Ginsburg, Ruth Bader 853
Gioeli, Joseph 619
Giordano, Arielle 447
Giordano, Steven 654
Giorgio, Luis 916
Giosa, Chris 469
Girard, Stephanie 670
Giraud, Roger S 649
Giroir, Brett P 735
Girouard, Caitlin 143, 189
Giroux, Matthew 361
Giuda, Michelle S 604
Giuseppe, Jeffrey 754
Given, Andrews 700
Glabe, Scott 454
Glading, Laura 750
Glancey, Tess 425
Glancy, Jake 429
Glaser, David P 648
Glaser, Karen 102
Glaspy, William R 666
Glass, George 608
Glass, Roger I 741
Glasscock, Stacey 216
Glasser, Robert 948
Glawe, David J 776
Glazer, Adam 831
Gleason, Carolyn M 631
Gleason, Jamila 727
Gleason, Jason 125

Page

Gleason, John 423
Gleason, Robert C 664
Glekas, Pamela 744
Glenn, Karen P 837
Glenn, Kyle 66
Glenn, Richard 603
Glenn, Trey 791
Glenn, William 196
Gleysteen, Michael 659
Glick, Richard 761
Glickman, Stephen H 904
Glimcher, Susan A 781
Glissman, Todd A 785
Glockner, David 834
Glomb, Steve 689
Glover, Cathy 700
Glover, Chester 63
Glover, Shad 636
Glover, Victoria 451
Gluck, Kenneth 944
Glueck, James 346
Glynn, J. Patrick 661
Glynn, Melissa S 770
Goddette, Timothy G 642
Godec, Robert F 607
Godfrey, Christopher James 725
Godfrey, Cooper 613
Godinez, Christine 412
Godlove, Timothy 771
Godts, Franciscus 950
Goeas, Lisa 105
Goedke, Jennifer 22
Goek, Joseph Robert 888
Goering, Sienna 822
Goetcheus, John A 397
Goethe, Gisile 801
Goetz, Joseph C. II 642
Goff, Emily 389, 409
Goff, Hans 456
Goff, Shuwanza 461
Goggin, Wendy H 664
Gohmert, Louie 250, 312, 336, 428, 429, 431, 432, 488
Gohringer, Jeff 437
Goins, Hope 425
Gokarn, Subir Vithal 924
Gokcigdem, Murat 267
Golan, Elise 693
Gold, Andrea 702
Gold, Celeste 9, 391
Gold, Victoria 660
Goldammer, Ted 698
Goldberg, Marc 167
Goldberg, Philip S 607
Goldberg, Richard W 882
Goldberg, Stuart M 681
Goldberg, Susan J 857
Goldberger, Thomas 607
Goldblatt, Roger 794
Golden, Alexandra 436
Golden, Brett 718
Golden, Kevin 189
Goldenstein, Jim 113
Goldentyer, Elizabeth 706
Goldes, Jordan 184
Goldfarb, David 230
Goldfein, David 629
Goldfinch, Colin 375
Goldfrank, Andrew 669
Goldhaber, Ben 736
Goldman, David 416, 704
Goldman, John 807
Goldman, Jon 409
Goldman, Jonathan 409
Goldman, Lisa 416
Goldoust, Carah 459
Goldsholle, Gary 833
Goldsmith, Andrew D 657
Goldstein, Dawn 818
Goldstein, Felicia 69
Goldstein, Miriam 26
Goldstein, Naomi 736
Goldstein, Zachary 715
Goldthorp, Jeffery 796
Golley, Jerald 793
Golonka, Susan 736
Golya, Lori A 643
Gomez, Darren 805
Gomez, Jimmy 36, 306, 342, 431, 432, 434, 435, 488

Page

Gomez, Jose Juan Ruiz 916
Gomez, Travis 630
Gomulak, Paulina 951
Goncher, Beth 95
Gongola, Janet 717
Goniprow, Alex 765
Gonzales, Anna 736
Gonzales, Bridget 714
Gonzales, Elena 689
Gonzales, Kate 14
Gonzales, Rebecca E 608
Gonzales, Walter 124
Gonzales-Schreiner, Roseann 689
Gonzalez, Anna 36
Gonzalez, Barbara 779
Gonzalez, Cesar A 73
Gonzalez, David 652
Gonzalez, Diego 935
Gonzalez, Efrain 714
Gonzalez, Gregory 681
Gonzalez, Maria "Malule" 786
Gonzalez, Marlies 749
Gonzalez, Patricio 388
Gonzalez, Samantha 449
Gonzalez, Steven 409
Gonzalez, Vicente 258, 313, 342, 418, 419, 488
Gonzalez-Colon, Jenniffer 302, 314, 342, 431, 432, 441, 442, 448, 488
Gonzalez-Rothi, Sara 364
Gooch, Anne D 464
Gooch, Lucinda 616
Good-Cohn, Meredith 375
Goode, Elizabeth "Kelly" 663
Goode, James M 851
Goodenow, Maureen M 740
Goodlatte, Bob 280, 313, 334, 399, 400, 428, 489
Goodman, Allan H 805
Goodman, Eliana 249
Goodman, Jordan T 844
Goodman, Kevin 832
Goodman, Lee E 797
Goodman, Lucas 470
Goodman, Max 67
Goodman, Mike 295
Goodman, Rick 739
Goodnight, Chase 385
Goodrich, Kate 738
Goodrick, Gordon S 894
Goodstein, Sam 235
Goodwill, Rosanne 755
Goodwin, Alfred T 858
Goodwin, Carte P 508
Goodwin, Charlene 658
Goodwin, Mike 805
Goosby, Eric 949
Gor, Sergio 112
Gorcowski, Susan 754
Gordon, Glenn S 834
Gordon, Jim 728
Gordon, Joshua 741
Gordon, Leo M 879
Gordon, Samuel N 844
Gordon, Susan 626
Gordon, T.J 656
Gordon, Vincent R 711
Gordon, Waverly 416
Gordon, Whitney 31
Gordon-Hagerty, Lisa E 760
Gore, John 661
Gorecki, Mary 662
Gorham, Jennifer 394
Gorman, Elizabeth 375
Gorman, Matt 455
Gorney, Anne L 631
Gorry, Thomas A 627
Gorski, Jenny 425
Gorsuch, Neil M 854
Gosar, Palak 268
Gosar, Paul A 11, 305, 338, 431, 432, 434, 435, 489
Goshi, Allen K 728
Goshorn, Dan 371
Goshorn, Rebekah 614
Goshorn, Rebekah E 420
Gosnell, Ellen 118, 460
Goss, Justin 516, 652
Goss, Lucy Wolfe 464
Goss, Stephen C 837
Gosselin, Geoff 446, 447

Page

Gossett, David 795
Gossum, Michael 113
Goto, Meinan 452
Gottardi, Larry D 646
Gottesman, Aaron 378
Gottesman, Michael M 740
Gottheimer, Josh 172, 310, 342, 418, 419, 420, 489
Gottlich, Vicki 736
Gottlieb, Michael 595
Gottlieb, Scott 738
Gottshall, Samantha 64
Gotwald, Robert 469
Goulart, Frank 619
Gould, George B 505
Gould, Greg 689
Gould, Jonathan 360
Gould, Mohamed 952
Gould, Ronald M 858
Gould, Tessa 203
Goulet, Ryan 515
Gourdikian, Alexandra 31, 459
Gourley, Craig N 637
Gover, Kevin 836
Gowdy, Trey 239, 312, 338, 428, 429, 434, 453, 454, 489, 813
Goyet, Sylvie 937
Graber, Susan P 858
Grabert, Lisa 452
Grace, Andrea 32
Grace, Ed 686
Grady, Claire M 777
Grady, Patricia A 741
Graessle, Marc 632
Graf, Fred 921
Graff, Caleb 415
Graffeo, Jonathan 349
Gragg, Michael L 649
Graham, Amy 99
Graham, Andrew R 659
Graham, Fred 798
Graham, Jacquelyn E 683
Graham, John R 734
Graham, Kimberly 697
Graham, Lindsey 237, 312, 328, 330, 347, 348, 349, 352, 353, 361, 379, 475, 509
Graham, William H 789, 842
Grahn, David P 694
Granados, Sergio Diaz 917
Grancorvitz, Teresa 820
Grande, Lise 947
Grandi, Filippo 941
Grange, Robyn Wheeler 89
Granger, Kay 257, 313, 334, 402, 403, 404, 489
Grannis, David 19, 776
Granston, Michael 660
Grant, Ayanti 52
Grant, Cedric 184
Grant, David 778
Grant, Heidi H 629
Grant, Katie 461
Grant, Lisa 462
Grantz, Brad 223
Grass, Frank G 638
Grassie, Jason 102
Grassley, Chuck 105, 308, 329, 330, 345, 346, 361, 369, 370, 379, 380, 469, 476
Grassmeyer, Tyler 161
Grasso, Carla 923
Gratacos, Osvaldo Luis 950, 952, 953
Graupensperger, Joe 430
Graves, Garret 120, 308, 340, 431, 432, 443, 444, 445, 446, 489
Graves, James E., Jr 857
Graves, Margaret 595
Graves, Meredith 442
Graves, Robert 635
Graves, Sam 156, 309, 335, 406, 407, 408, 443, 444, 445, 489
Graves, Tom 82, 307, 337, 402, 403, 404, 489
Gray, Betty B 408
Gray, Cheryl 916
Gray, David 694
Gray, David W 791
Gray, Jason 405
Gray, Jason K 763
Gray, John 595
Gray, John L 836
Gray, Jonathan 216

Page
Gray, Lisa 13
Gray, Lorri 690
Gray, Spencer 366
Gray, Vincent C 907
Gray-Broughton, Linda 801
Grayson, Win 395
Graziano, Thomas 716
Greaves, Holly 790
Greaves, Samuel A 624
Greaves, Travis A 681
Greco, Kristie 221
Green, Al 255, 313, 336, 418, 419, 489
Green, Alexa 86
Green, Bernadette 296
Green, Christopher 766
Green, Eric 740
Green, Gene 266, 313, 334, 413, 414, 415, 489
Green, Heidi 691
Green, Helen 505
Green, Jim 808
Green, John Edward 948
Green, Jonathan D 356, 357
Green, Joshua 48
Green, Lawrence 505
Green, Lori 70
Green, Lyle L 585
Green, Marilyn 510
Green, Mark 847
Green, Mark A 843
Green, Mary 594
Green, Meghan 436
Green, Patricia 630
Green, R.L 656
Green, Rashage 387
Green, Rob 411
Green, Robert 759
Green, Sam 63
Green, Tim 635, 729
Green, Tom 795
Green, Wade 710
Greenaugh, Cheryle 723
Greenaway, Joseph A., Jr 857
Greenbaum, Elie S 420
Greenberg, Irving 845
Greenberg, Morton I 857
Greenberg, William S 899
Greenblatt, Jason 597
Greenblatt, Mark 710
Greene, Bryan 744
Greene, Christopher 765
Greene, Craig 408
Greene, Creighton 356, 357, 358
Greene, Henry F 905
Greene, Jim 373
Greene, Lisa 606
Greene, Nathan 86
Greene, Nick 294
Greene, Nicole 735
Greener, April 461
Greenfeld, Helaine 381
Greengrass, David 430
Greenhow, KaSandra 465
Greenleaf, Brandi 697
Greenstein, Ira 597
Greenwell, Amanda Hallberg 820
Greenwood, Lee 815
Greenwood, Lisa 702
Greer, Brian 408
Greer, James 677
Greer, Jamieson L 596
Greeson, Autum 98
Gregg, Caroline 776
Gregg, Ingrid 806
Gregg, Larry 805
Gregoire, Michael 706
Gregor, Chapin 364
Gregorius, James R 780
Gregory, Karen V 800
Gregory, Roger L 857
Gregus, Daniel 834
Greiner, Marty 613
Gremban, Keith 720
Grenell, Richard A 607
Gresham, Dana 2
Gresser, Edward 596
Gressly, David 945
Grewal, Steve 804
Grey, Anne 714
Grey, Robert J., Jr 808
Gribben, Tim 849
Griffin, Andrew 279
Griffin, Antwaun 713
Griffin, Claire 807
Griffin, Diane E 819
Griffin, Mike 815
Griffin, Pat 611
Griffin, Richard Allen 857
Griffin, Taylor 461
Griffin, Toni L 787
Griffin, Vanessa 716
Griffin, Ward 346
Griffis, Geoffrey 813
Griffith, Brian 206
Griffith, H. Morgan 281, 313, 338, 413, 414, 415, 489
Griffith, L. Christina 675
Griffith, Thomas B 860
Griffiths, John 661
Griffitts, Bob 246
Griggsby, Lydia Kay 885
Grigoryan, Juliya 440
Grijalva, Raul M 11, 305, 335, 410, 411, 431, 489
Grilli, Kathleen C 849
Grim, David 832
Grimes, Benjamin K 681
Grimes, James 833
Grimes, Joe Patrick 842
Grimes, Nick 254
Grimes, Ron 212
Grimm, Drew M 826
Grimm, Tyler 43
Grinston, Michael 649
Grippando, Gina K 798
Grippo, Gary 612
Griscavage, Stanley 682
Grishaw, Letitia J 669
Griswold, Nancy J 735
Griswold, Sarah 380
Grocki, Steve 663
Groenke, Jeff 206
Grogan, Joe 595
Grohovsky, Alex 614
Grooms, Susanne Sachsman 436
Gropper, Adam 469
Groski, Abigail 12
Grosklags, Paul 655
Gross, Bradley T 675
Gross, Charles R 659
Gross, Hillary 209
Gross, Joshua 239
Gross, Justin 464
Gross, Karas 437
Grossi, Anthony 430
Grossman, Andrew 469
Grossman, David 794
Grossman, Edward 464
Grossman, James 464
Grossman, Luke 848
Grossnickle, Janet 832
Grosso, David 907
Grosvenor, Gilbert M 851
Grothman, Glenn 296, 314, 340, 409, 410, 411, 434, 435, 489
Grout, Penny 805
Grove, John 17
Grove, Paul 351
Grover, CJ 110
Grover, Greg 703
Grover, Jason 729
Groves, Brendan 657
Groves, Robert M 820
Grubbs, Ken 43
Grubbs, Preston 665
Grubbs, Preston L 663
Gruber, Corey 778
Gruber, Henry W 789
Gruber, Joseph W 784
Gruber, Theresa 838
Gruber, Werner 951
Grudzinskas, Walter 637
Gruenberg, Martin J 797
Gruender, Raymond W 858
Gruenspecht, Howard 759
Gruman, Mark 204
Grumbine, Megan 801
Grumbles, Ben 842
Grunder, Alyson L 604

Page

Gruters, Sydney 67
Grzymski, Tom 841
Guaglianone, Paul 452
Guagliardo, Karen 708
Guajardo, Anissa 269
Guarascio, Tiffany 416
Guardado-Gallegos, Theodora 516
Guci, Ledia 711
Gudeman, Rebekah 98
Guen-Murray, Terry 781
Guendelsberger, Nese 796
Guenther, Mary 363
Guenther, Megan E 728
Guerra, Liana 62
Guerrero, Bertha 433
Guerrero, Bertha Alisia 36
Guerrero, Francisco 933
Guerrero, Roberto I 633
Guerrieri, Luca 785
Guertin, Steve 686
Guevara, Julio Cesar 920
Guidry, Jim 839
Guiliamo, James 360
Guillamon, Bernardo 916
Guillen, Jose 409
Guillory, Emmanual 411
Guimond, Christopher L 756
Guise, Amy M 842
Guitchounts, Andrei 922
Guith, Kathleen M 798
Gulley, Bryan 363
Gulliford, Jim 791
Gullo, Theresa 583
Gulshen, Jay 416
Gulvas, Gregory 100
Gum, Rhett 263
Gunasekara, Surya 214
Gundersen, Angela 639
Gunderson-Schwarz, Abby 13, 261
Gunn, Imani 426
Gunnels, Maggi 754
Gunnels, Warren 361
Gunther, Jeffery W 783
Guo, Ruihong 706
Gupta, Deepa 815
Gupta, Pronita 729
Gupton, Judy A 642
Gur-Arie, Mira 904
Gurewitz, Heather 21
Gurgo, Michael 803
Guries, Darin 346
Gurowitz, Leah 904
Gurria, Angel 933
Guse, Brian 698
Gust, Christopher 784
Gustafson, David 889
Gustafson, Kristen 714
Gustafson, Peggy E 710
Guterres, Antonio 939
Guthridge, Clay G 800
Guthrie, Brett 113, 308, 337, 410, 411, 413, 414, 415, 489
Guthrie, Jason W 800
Gutierez, Francisco Daniel 932
Gutierrez, Diego 717
Gutierrez, Luis V 90, 307, 334, 428, 429, 489
Gutierrez, Rosemary 284
Gutro, Doug 791
Guttmann, Nicholas 470
Guven, Cynthia 699
Guy, Daniel A 893
Guy, Jacci 178
Guy, Ralph B 857
Guynn, Michelle 749
Guyselman, Kelsey 415
Guzelsu, Ozge 356, 357
Gwinn, Nancy 836
Gwyn, Nick 140
Gyorda, Lisa 740

H

Haaga, Owen 467
Haas, Greg 31
Haas, Joyce C 805
Haas, Karen L 462
Haas, Peter 603
Haase, Molly 110

Page

Habenstreit, David 818
Haberman, Caitlin 416
Hack, Joe 161
Hackbarth, Craig 630
Hackbarth, David E 712
Hackbarth, Sean 779
Hackmaster, Nelson 682
Haddad, Mona E 952
Hadden, Carlton 792
Haddox, John 68
Hadijski, George 427
Hadiyanto, Andin 951
Hadley, Mark P 583
Hadley, Nancy 284
Hadley, Stephen J 845
Haensel, Curt 464
Haeuptle, Andrew 651
Hafeez, Syed 726
Hafiz, Tariq 717
Hagan, Anne 268
Hagan, Katy 350
Hagan, Sean 923, 924
Hagen, Jim 814
Hagenbuch, Stephen 464
Hagerty, William 607
Hagerup, Loni 296
Haggard, Vence 752
Hagin, Joseph 596
Hagler, John A. "Art" 647
Haglund, Gary 409
Hagnauer, Karl 464
Haidet, Michael 598
Hail, Michael W 806
Haile, Graham 201
Haines, Christian 412
Hair, Connie 251
Hair, John 420
Hairfield, James 763
Hairston, Joseph E 711
Haiwen, Sun 918
Hajec, Don 717
Halataei, Allison 451
Haldar, Swarnali 811
Haldiman, Sylviane 841
Hale, Colby 264
Hale, David 608
Halek, Matthew 380
Halen, Sean 630
Haley, Nikki 606, 610
Haley, Nikki R 591
Haley, Richard II 673
Haley, Vincent 597
Hall, Amy 452
Hall, Anne 608
Hall, Betty Jean 723
Hall, Bill 734
Hall, Charles J 792
Hall, Chris 350
Hall, Christopher 779
Hall, Cindy 153
Hall, Debra A 823
Hall, Galon 697
Hall, Gregory 670
Hall, Hunter 76
Hall, Jeffery S 793
Hall, Jeffrey 658
Hall, Katrina 749
Hall, Katrina M 464
Hall, Keith 446, 583
Hall, Laurie Beyer 584, 587
Hall, Lyssa 725
Hall, Mikayla 455
Hall, Peter W 857
Hall, Robert 820
Hall, Stephanie 378, 837
Hall, Tracy 670
Hall, Travis 160
Hall, Trinity 55
Hall, Vicki 937
Hall-Rivera, Jaelith 696
Hallett, Adrienne 740
Hallett, Lisa 782
Hallman, Janet M 848
Hallman, Wesley 638
Halper, Neal 713
Halpern, Hugh 459
Halpern, James S 892
Halpern, Jonathan 76

Page

Halstead, TJ 588
Ham, Thomas B 649
Ham-Warren, Heather 58
Hamam, David Mehdi 944
Hambleton, Ryan 436
Hamburg, Margaret 819
Hamby, Janice M 627
Hamer, Hubert 705
Hamill, Bobby 282
Hamill, Johnathan T 636
Hamilton, Amanda 252
Hamilton, Bruce 789
Hamilton, Clyde H 857
Hamilton, David F 858
Hamilton, Diana Gourlay 350
Hamilton, Ellen 33
Hamilton, John O 812
Hamilton, Lasharn 818
Hamilton, Michael 718
Hamilton, Mike 291
Hamilton, Ryan 263
Hamilton, Samantha 373
Hamilton, Scott T 783
Hamilton, Wendy 288
Hamlett, Joyce 465
Hamley, Jeffrey 687
Hamm, Shannon 707
Hammer, Sarah 612
Hammer, Viva 469
Hammill, Drew 460
Hammond, Alex 427
Hammond, Donald V 785
Hammond, Tom 440
Hammond, Tony 830
Hamner, Caryn 80
Hampsten, Emily 88, 393
Hampton, Matthew 748
Hamrick, Mary Moore 510
Hanabusa, Colleen 83, 307, 339, 406, 407, 431, 432, 438, 489
Hanagan, Tony 397
Hancock, Diana 785
Hancock, Mark 229
Hancock, Tracy 696
Hand, Bob 504
Hand, Carrol P 799
Handal, Megan 408
Handel, Karen C 78, 307, 342, 410, 411, 428, 429, 467, 489
Haney, Catherine 822
Hankerson, Derek 68
Hankey, Mary Blanche 657, 680
Hankins, Dennis 607
Hankins, Rebecca 813
Hanley, Karen 594
Hanley, Paul 653
Hanley, Sharon 730
Hanlon, Brian 717, 718
Hanlon, Tim 903
Hanly, Garnet 796
Hanna, Christopher 370
Hannah, Lisle 719
Hannah, Tom 700
Hannan, John L 585
Hannink, John 652
Hanrahan, Peggi 657
Hanretta, Kevin T 770
Hansberry, Donna 618
Hansell, Chris 175
Hansen, Chris 389
Hansen, Deborah 144
Hansen, Donald 920
Hansen, Erik 699, 840
Hansen, Karl 800
Hansen, Keith 949
Hansen, Richard 646
Hanson, Alan R 678
Hanson, Anita 771
Hanson, Bobbi 260
Hanson, Chris 350
Hanson, Harold 779
Hanson, Marc 36
Hanson, Sarah 65, 699
Hanson, Stephen 614
Hanson, Tracey 695
Happe, Claus 950
Harary, Howard 720
Harbison, Diana 850

Page

Harbour, Wendy 814
Harclerode, Justin 446
Hardaway, Jay 260
Hardaway, Michael 184
Hardecke, Laura 155
Harden, Blake 452
Harden, Gil 694
Harder, Dan 139
Hardgrove, Stephen 690
Hardiman, Thomas M 857
Hardimon, Madison 411
Harding, Andrew 368
Harding, Elliott 279
Harding, Frances M 741
Hardison, Brooke 703
Hardy, Dennis 827
Hardy, Johanna 447
Hardy, Joseph L., Jr 894
Hardy, Liam 679
Hardy, Lyn 681
Hardy, Melinda 832
Hardy, Shawanda 792
Hardy, Sherida 692
Hardy, Thomas R 850
Hare, Helen 375
Harencak, Garrett 636
Hargan, Eric D 733
Harjo, Rhonda 385
Harker, Deborah 612
Harker, Thomas W 653
Harkins, Donna 436
Harkins, Gregory S 650
Harkins, Michael 594
Harkless, Gresham 585
Harkrader, Trent 796
Harley, Derek 206
Harlow, David L 682
Harman, Callie 411
Harman, Heather 469
Harman, Jane 851
Harmann, Jean 464
Harmon, Cody 652
Harmon, Florence 834
Harney, Janet 804
Harney, Mike 276
Harold, Rosemary 794
Harper, Bill 146
Harper, Chuck 373
Harper, Gregg 151, 309, 337, 413, 414, 415, 427, 468, 489, 510
Harper, Jewel 371
Harper, Molly 195
Harper, Robert 695
Harra, Scott 650
Harrell, Delicia T 823
Harrell, Jamie 446
Harrell, Mary Beth 833
Harrelson, Jill 361
Harrigan-Farrelly, Joan 729
Harrington, Ellen 383
Harrington, Jeffrey 829
Harrington, Molly 140
Harrington, Mona 870
Harris, Andy 124, 308, 338, 402, 403, 404, 489
Harris, Antonia T 804
Harris, Brian 386
Harris, Claire 740
Harris, Dan 713
Harris, Deborah 669
Harris, Grant 589
Harris, Grant T 844
Harris, Jerry 635
Harris, Jocelyn 409
Harris, Jodie 612
Harris, Joyce 613
Harris, Kamala D 19, 305, 329, 331, 361, 377, 379, 380, 386, 476
Harris, Kevin 907
Harris, Lance 827
Harris, Ondray T 730
Harris, Pamela A 857
Harris, Robert 395
Harris, Ron 696
Harris, Rosa 516, 584
Harris, Sarah 679, 719
Harris, Scott 6
Harris, Scott S 856
Harris, Steven 776

Page

Harris-Berry, Gail 618
Harrison, Brian 733
Harrison, Kenneth R 712
Harrison, Lorenzo 730
Harrity, David 804
Harry, Jody A 588
Harry, Sharntay 691
Harsha, Christen 433, 436
Hart, Brian 796
Hart, Christopher 820
Hart, J. Steven 505
Hart, Patricia Maria Miloslavich 917
Hart, Philip C 515
Hart, Reeve 350
Hart, Rosemary 679, 812
Hart, Selwin Charles 931
Harter, L. "Chip" 617
Hartford, Rachael 205
Harthill, Susan 727
Hartley, Brent 609
Hartley, Richard 635
Hartley, Richard K 632
Hartline, Chris 409
Hartman, Kristen 275
Hartman, Laura 107
Hartman, Tim 828
Hartmann, George 380
Hartobey, Patrick 436, 814
Hartwich, Alison 464
Hartz, Gary 740
Hartz, Harris L 858
Hartz, Jerry 461
Hartz, Joe 442
Hartzler, Vicky 155, 309, 338, 399, 400, 401, 406, 407, 489
Harvell, Thea III 641
Harvey, Ana 909
Harvey, G. Michael 878
Harvey, Jack 717
Harvey, Krista P 425
Harvey, Mariam 616
Harvey, Robert 469
Harvey, Taylor 371
Harvey, Todd 622
Harwell, Phyllis L 784
Harwood, Charles 802
Harwood, Joy 697
Hasan, Merza H 950
Hasan, Rasheedah 449
Hasenberg, Amy 101
Hasenfus, Julie A 586
Hasiak, Cindy 395
Hasier, Paulette 589
Haskell, Alex 380
Haskell, John 590
Haskell, Todd 607
Haskins, Matthew 262
Hasler, Kirsten 230
Haslett, Brighton 415, 452
Haspel, Gina C 786
Hassan, Amira 388
Hassan, Maggie 331
Hassan, Margaret Wood 167, 310, 329, 362, 363, 374, 377, 467, 476
Hassebrock, Douglas 712
Hassell, Bayly 197
Hassenboehler, Thomas 415
Hassett, Kevin 593
Hastings, Alcee L 68, 307, 334, 437, 489, 504
Hastings, Jimmy 687
Hatalsky, Laura 164
Hatch, Erin 261
Hatch, Orrin G 271, 313, 327, 330, 369, 374, 379, 380, 387, 391, 469, 470, 476, 510, 511, 845
Hatcher, Allen 691
Hatcher, Arthur "AG" 634
Hatcher, Gary 839
Hatcher, Nick 353, 354
Hatfield, Jenn 375
Hatfield, Jonathan 800
Hatfield, Melissa S 584
Hatfield, Yvette 818
Hatheway, Gayle A 618
Hatmaker, Justin 700
Hatter, John 102
Hattix, Larry 617
Hauck, David 515
Hauck, Kara 455
Haueter, Bob 265
Haueter, Lynn 111
Haughton, Robert 698
Haugrud, K. Jack 690
Haun-Mohamed, Robin L 587
Hauptmann, David 392
Haurek, Alex 184, 442
Hauser, Ann Marie 390
Hauser, Timothy 725
Hauser, Valerie 781
Hauttman, Kyle 360
Haven, Jackie 703
Havenner, Sheila 412
Havens, Brittany 415
Haverly, Jordan 416
Haverly, Tiffany 449
Haverstock, Christopher 671
Haverstock, John 396
Haw, Kate 836
Hawatmeh, Nick 381, 427, 504
Hawbecker, Karen 690
Hawes, Matthew 112
Hawkens, E. Roy 822
Hawkins, Alicia 368
Hawkins, David 515
Hawkins, Felicia 378
Hawkins, Garrett 82
Hawkins, George S 912
Hawkins, Jennifer L 782
Hawkins, Michael D 858
Hawkins, Robert 515
Hawkins, Robert J 856
Hawkins, Tom 392
Hawley, Thomas 408
Hawn, Laurie 936
Hawney, Wayne 677
Hawrylak, Egon F 650
Hawthorne, Margaret 607
Hawthorne, Sandra L 826
Hayash, Susan 718
Hayba, Daniel 689
Hayden, Carla 508, 588, 807, 816
Hayden, Carla D 851
Hayes, Bradley 779
Hayes, Carmen 755
Hayes, Colin 17
Hayes, Jeremy 389
Hayes, John 263, 632
Hayes, Mark L 676
Hayes, Pat 290
Hayes, Sean 733
Hayes-Byrd, Jacquelyn 769
Haynes, Catharina 857
Haynes, Hayden 119
Haynes, Wil 460
Haysom, Nicholas 945
Hayward, Matt 93
Hazlett, Anne 346
Hazlett, Kathleen 175
Hazlett, Stuart A 642
Head, Dan 237
Head, Mary S 831
Healey, Burke 707
Healton, Kelly 189
Healy, Colleen 467
Heard, Jenna 77
Hearn, Candy R 654
Hearne, Walter 405
Hearron, Marc 380
Heasley, Laura 37
Heaslip, Sean 368
Heath, Becki 696
Heath, Josh 371
Heath, Linda 696
Hebert, Ashley 427
Hechavarria, Adam 99
Heck, Denny 289, 313, 339, 418, 419, 453, 489
Heck, Thomas 654
Heckenberg, Loraine 405
Heckscher, Fiona 464
Hecox, Doug 751
Hedberg, Brian 747
Hedge, Brook 905
Heemskerk, Frank 951
Heemskerk, Jill 741
Heerschap, Julianna 281
Heffern, John 602
Heflin, Donald L 606

Page

Hefner, Keith 811
Hegg, Dabney 351
Heggem, Christine 401
Heiden, Helen 9
Heider, Caroline 950, 952
Heidt, William A 606
Heighberger, Eric 777
Heiles, Holli N 420
Heilman, Chandra 836
Heiman, Andy 371
Heinbecker, Yasemin 936
Heinrich, Lauren 260
Heinrich, Martin 177, 310, 327, 331, 352, 353, 365, 386, 467, 476, 508
Heisler, Nick 923
Heist, Melissa 785
Heitfield, Erik 785
Heitkamp, Heidi 203, 311, 327, 331, 345, 346, 359, 377, 383, 385, 470, 476, 509
Hekhuis, Jeremy 205
Helgen, Brigit 143
Helis, James 754
Heller, David 754
Heller, Dean 164, 310, 327, 331, 359, 360, 362, 363, 369, 370, 384, 476
Heller, Martha 796
Heller, Michelle 380
Helm, Cathy 836
Helms, Lucas 516
Helsen, Jan 936
Helton, Clay 99
Helton, Josh 248
Helwig, Janice 504
Hemingway, Jennifer 459
Hencinski, Mia 516
Henderschedt, John 715
Henderson, Adam 378
Henderson, Chelsea 764
Henderson, James 806
Henderson, John A 397
Henderson, John W 632
Henderson, Karen LeCraft 859
Henderson, Katherine C 601
Henderson, Kaya 911
Henderson, Veleda T 903
Henderson, Vince 932
Henderson, William 112
Hendrickson, Eric 655
Hendrie, Barbara 941
Hendriksson, Marla 741
Hendrix, Holly 246
Hendrixson, Luke 396
Hendrixson-White, Jennifer 423
Heneghan, John 755
Heneghan, Philip M 846
Heng, Elizabeth 423
Henick, Jonathan 604
Henke, Robert 384
Henke, Tracy 153
Henle, Drake 112
Henley, Adrija 590
Henley, Stephen R 721
Henline, Robert 427
Henn, Jay 810
Henneberg, Maureen 678
Henney, Jane E 819
Henry, Charles 118
Henry, D 656
Henry, Dalton 109
Henry, Fitzroy J 935
Henry, Mike 276
Henry, Wayne 662
Hensarling, Jeb 253, 313, 335, 418, 489
Henseler, Timothy 831
Henshaw, Emilee 86
Henshaw, Marijane 435
Henshaw, Simon 605
Henson, Christopher 31
Henson, Mark 53
Hentz, Andre 776
Heppard, Scott 231
Heppner, Virginia 375
Herb, Martha 916
Herbert, Ashley 504
Herbert, Donna 417
Herbert, Jason 437
Herbert, Noller 697
Herbert, Torwanna D 647

Page

Herbolsheimer, Nancy 828
Herbst, Andrew 649
Herbst, Ellen 709
Herbst, Lars T 688
Heredia, Luis 13
Herencia, Roberto 847
Heriot, Gail 843
Herlihy, Thomas W 748
Herman, Nathalie S 793
Herman, Steven J 589
Hermann, David 922
Hermann, Robert 584
Hernandez, Aaron 788
Hernandez, Diana Elizabeth Barahona 918
Hernandez, Elena 64
Hernandez, Elias 849
Hernandez, Gilberto Elizalde 921
Hernandez, Gladys M 618
Hernandez, Juan 696
Hernandez, Martha 260
Hernandez, Perla 35
Hernandez, Tyler 290
Herndon, Benjamin 618
Herndon, Charles C 595
Herren, Chris 662
Herrera Beutler, Jaime 285, 313, 338, 402, 403, 404, 489
Herrera, Frederick 519
Herrera, Luis 816
Herrgott, Alexander "Alex" 594
Herring, Albert 681
Herrle, Cindy 459
Herrle, Patrick 518
Herrmann, Heide 905
Herrmann, Matthew 301
Herrock, Emma 120
Herron, Kayla 273
Hersey, Eric 420
Hershey, Michael 849
Hershkowitz, Meryl 718
Hertel, Dennis 509
Hertz, David M 816
Herve, Patrick Jean 917
Herwig, Meghan 614
Herwitt, Allison 51
Herz, Jim 595
Heslington, Rory 370
Heslop, Jeff 831
Hess, Christopher 752
Hess, David 776
Hess, James 690
Hess, Tim 751
Hester, Thomas 256
Heuer, Kathleen 795
Hewes, Taylor R 420
Hewitt, Bart 705
Hewko, Anna L 783
Heyse, Erica Wheelan 505
Heywood, Thomas B 397
Heyworth, Charlotte 124
Hiatt, Christina 646
Hibbert, Farhanna 85
Hibbert, Garth 850
Hice, Jody B 80, 307, 341, 406, 407, 431, 432, 434, 435, 489
Hickey, Adam 680
Hickey, James 353, 355, 356
Hickey, Jim 356
Hickey, John 751
Hickman, Darren 697
Hickman, Kate 683, 839
Hickman, Natasha 195
Hickman, Stephen 823
Hicks, Eva 165
Hicks, Greg 654
Hicks, Gregory L 651
Hicks, Hope 597
Hicks, Otis 632
Hicks, Thomas 844
Hicks, Tom 653
Hicks, Trey 373
Hicks, William P 834
Higby, Patrick 634
Higginbotham, Keith 42
Higginbotham, Patrick E 857
Higgins, Brian 193, 311, 336, 409, 450, 451, 489
Higgins, Casey 459
Higgins, Clay 118, 308, 342, 424, 425, 438, 439, 448, 489

Page

Higgins, Craig ... 405
Higgins, Heather ... 729
Higgins, Holly ... 698
Higgins, Jeanne ... 695
Higgins, Jennifer ... 780
Higgins, Keith ... 832
Higgins, Rebecca ... 368
Higgins, Toni-Marie ... 15
Higgins, Wayne ... 716
Higginson, Stephen A ... 857
High, Mark ... 469
Hildebrand, Asher ... 197
Hildebrand, John ... 819
Hildebrand, Ralita ... 653
Hildebrandt, Betsy ... 689
Hildreth, Shari ... 286
Hiler, Jonathan ... 1, 391, 593
Hill, Amanda ... 378
Hill, Ben ... 143
Hill, Bill ... 395
Hill, Christine ... 449
Hill, Daniel O ... 712
Hill, Farris "Carlos" ... 638
Hill, Frederick ... 363
Hill, G. Kathleen ... 608
Hill, Gary W ... 665, 666
Hill, Harry A ... 507
Hill, J. French ... 16, 305, 341, 418, 419, 420, 490
Hill, James C ... 858
Hill, Janet ... 807
Hill, Jeffrey ... 723
Hill, Jesse ... 505
Hill, Joann ... 714
Hill, John ... 613, 657
Hill, Jon A ... 624
Hill, Kathryn ... 693
Hill, Kristi ... 736
Hill, Lesley ... 16
Hill, Liz ... 253, 446, 447
Hill, Marcus L ... 780
Hill, Preston ... 460
Hill, Ruby ... 636
Hill, Shavonda ... 76
Hill, Thomas ... 423
Hill, Walter B., Jr ... 793
Hillebrands, Joan ... 138
Hiller, Aaron ... 430
Hillesheim, Chris ... 168
Hillo, Yacoub El ... 945
Hilmer, Rosie ... 69, 168
Hilton, Cheryl L ... 805
Himebaugh, Nicholas ... 231
Himes, James A ... 53, 306, 337, 418, 420, 453, 454, 490
Himmo, Tarek S ... 952
Hinckley, Linda ... 170
Hines, Anson ... 837
Hines, Charon ... 907, 909
Hines, Kalila ... 56
Hines, Shannon ... 349
Hing, Jennifer ... 404
Hingeley, Anne ... 845
Hinkle, Mark ... 838
Hinkle, Scott ... 44
Hinkle-Bowles, Paige ... 653
Hinman, Alyssa ... 427
Hinojosa, Juan ... 91
Hinton, Michael ... 698
Hipolit, Richard ... 769
Hippe, Jim ... 246
Hipsley, Kyle K ... 921
Hipsley, Megan ... 511
Hirami, Patti ... 696
Hirayama, Tatsuo ... 919
Hirono, Mazie K ... 83, 307, 327, 331, 352, 353, 365, 379, 380, 383, 384, 470, 476, 501
Hirsch, Harold ... 469
Hirschberg, Paul ... 716
Hirshfeld, Andrew ... 717
Hirte, Jonathan ... 139
Histed, Timothy ... 953
Hitch, Kathryn ... 85
Hitchcock, Kelly ... 405
Hiteshew, Kent ... 612
Hitt, H. Lucas ... 710
Hittle, Matthew ... 243
Hittos, Elizabeth ... 64
Hixon, Chris ... 377
Hixson, Jana ... 259

Page

Hixson, Tiffany ... 805
Hixson, Tiffany T ... 803
Ho, Christina ... 612, 613
Ho, James C ... 857
Ho, Scarlett ... 378
Hoadley, Michael ... 644
Hoag, Aaron ... 658
Hoang, Mary T ... 799
Hoburg, Maddie ... 251
Hoch, Richard W ... 786
Hock, Jim ... 709
Hodes, Paul ... 815
Hodes, Richard J ... 740
Hodgdon, Dave ... 390
Hodge, Caroline ... 373
Hodge, Jennifer ... 663
Hodge, Olivia ... 69
Hodges, Andrea L ... 632
Hodges, David ... 284
Hodges, Josh ... 736
Hodges, Joshua ... 119
Hodges, Marcia ... 777
Hodgkins, Gerald ... 833
Hodgkins, Shelby ... 58
Hodgson, Chris ... 1, 391, 460, 593
Hodnette, Jon ... 449
Hodson, Nate ... 455
Hoecker, Carl ... 833
Hoefler, Annie ... 366
Hoefly, Christian ... 797
Hoehne, Jena ... 163
Hoehne, John ... 85
Hoekstra, Peter ... 608
Hoelscher, Douglas Lynn ... 598
Hoelz, Joe ... 652
Hoenig, Thomas ... 821
Hoenig, Thomas M ... 797
Hoenle, Darin ... 631
Hoeven, John ... 203, 311, 329, 330, 345, 346, 347, 348, 349, 365, 377, 385, 476, 510
Hoff, Joane ... 351
Hoff, Joanne ... 739
Hoff, Rachel ... 353
Hoffman, Denise ... 728
Hoffman, Eileen ... 801
Hoffman, Elizabeth ... 425
Hoffman, Janice L ... 734
Hoffman, Jeffrey L ... 789
Hoffman, Jonathan Rath ... 776
Hoffman, Josh ... 433
Hoffman, Lisa Funderburke ... 816
Hoffman, Mary T ... 784
Hoffman, Matt ... 459
Hoffman, Patricia ... 760
Hoffman, Thomas ... 692
Hoffman, William J ... 793
Hogan, Christine ... 951
Hogan, Derek ... 601
Hogan, Michael R ... 769
Hogan, Thomas F ... 875
Hogberg, Edward ... 692
Hogg, Dorothy ... 639
Hogge, James ... 136
Hogin, Andrew ... 249
Hohenstein, William ... 693
Hokanson, Daniel R ... 645
Hokenson, Andrew ... 829
Holahan, Patricia ... 822
Holbein, James ... 846
Holcomb, Jenn ... 146
Holden, Caroline ... 76
Holden, Kimberly ... 827
Holder, Edward W ... 797
Holder, Natalie ... 519
Holderness, Skiffington ... 383
Holding, George ... 196, 311, 339, 450, 451, 490
Holeman, Brian ... 905
Holian, Brian ... 822
Holifield, Freeman ... 632
Hollabaugh, Allison B ... 504
Holland, Brendan ... 796
Holland, Jennifer ... 141
Holland, Luke ... 215
Holland, Rachel ... 262
Holland, Ralph ... 760
Holland, Robert ... 705
Hollander, Evan ... 146
Hollatz, Beth ... 243

	Page
Holler, Mark	648
Hollett, Douglas	760
Holley, Leta L	798
Hollingshead, Megan	133
Hollingsworth, Kimo	624
Hollingsworth, Trey	104, 307, 342, 418, 419, 490
Hollis, Kate	3
Hollis, Liz	411
Hollis, Patricia	612
Holloway, Jerome	713
Holloway, Perry	607
Hollowell, Christian	417
Hollrah, Jennifer	405
Holman, Richard	692
Holman, Tim	515
Holman, Timothy	645
Holman, Victor	649
Holmberg, Garrison	382
Holmes, James M	635
Holmes, Jerome A	858
Holmes, Kevin	794
Holmes, Lee	381
Holmes, Mark V	888
Holmes, Nathaniel	460
Holmes, Virgil R	789
Holohan, Maureen	405
Holsman, Marianne	792
Holt, Allan M	844
Holt, Keith	634
Holt, Sharita	513
Holtan, Elizabeth	816
Holtmann, Thomas	469
Holtz, Cliff	782
Holtzman, Joshua	750
Holyfield, Ainsley	119
Homa, Cherie	229
Homan, Anthony	800
Homan, Thomas	779
Homan, Todd	747
Homendy, Jennifer	447
Hommel, Scott	685
Honda, Keiko	952
Honda, Keith	828
Hone, Lisa	796
Honeycutt, Christopher	634
Hongwon, Kim	919
Honore, Sandra	946
Hood, Robert R	623
Hooghan, Priyanka	440
Hook, Brian	602
Hook, Erynn	194
Hook, Michael	194
Hooke, Kathleen	602
Hooper, Bryan	700
Hooper, Cheryl	664
Hooper, Shawn	722
Hootsman, Dominic	639
Hoover, Patty	230
Hope, Durell	664
Hope, Karin	467
Hope, Nia A	623
Hopkins, Jamie	226
Hopkins, Lara	65
Hopkins, Mark	510
Hoppin, Soudarak	501
Horan, Thomas	795
Horlander, Thomas A	642
Horn, Brian	664
Horn, Donald H	748
Horn, Marian Blank	883
Hornbuckle, Wyn	681
Horne, Jennifer	838
Horne, John	1, 391, 593
Horne, Mary	840
Horne, Timothy	805
Horner, Elizabeth	368
Horner, Gerard	712
Horner, John P	626
Horowith, Michael E	676
Horrell, Abby Curran	168
Horrigan, Michael	723
Horsey, Outerbridge	850, 851
Horsford, Sonya	506
Horsley, Constance M	783
Horsman, Nancy Gail	924
Horta, Christofer	456
Hortin, Steve	702
Horton, Brett	118, 460
Horton, Cory	151, 425
Horton, Edward	715
Horton, Elizabeth "Beth"	611
Horvath, Albert G	836
Hoskins, David	686
Hoskins, Isaac Borden	420
Hostelley, Stephen	214
Houerou, Philippe Le	952
Hough, Michael	291
Houghton, Dianne	588
Houlihan, Bill	88
Houlihan, Ryan	146
Houngbo, Gilbert F	943
Hourigan, Brendan	719
Houry, Debra	737
House, Andrew	454
House, Matt	180, 392
House, Michael	713
House, Missy	240
House, Trisha	121
Housel, Paul	4
Houser, Danielle	58
Houser, Elaina	174
Houser, Melani	469
Houser, Sheila	245
Housley, Ashley A	631
Houston, Brad	772
Houton, Brigid	350
Hovakiman, Patrick	658
Hoven, Christopher	33
Hovland, Benjamin	382
Howard, Adam	211
Howard, Brad	61
Howard, Gary	353
Howard, Jasper C	633
Howard, Jeffrey R	857
Howard, John	737
Howard, Kate	750
Howard, Michael	464
Howard, Michael L	641, 650
Howard, Patrick	766
Howard, Stanley Ed	713
Howard, Tom	771
Howder, Tom	803
Howell, Beryl A	871
Howell, Brady	423
Howell, J. Brady	616
Howell, Kimberly A	822
Howell, Patrick	292
Howell, Paul	150
Howell, Tomas	718
Howell, Zach	193
Howells, Tom	711
Howie, Leonard	729
Howorth, Richard C	842
Hoyer, Steny H	126, 308, 333, 461, 490
Hoyle, Nicholas E	826
Hoyos, Luis G	781
Hrkman, Lou	291
Hromada, Erin M	463
Hruska, Courtney	211
Hsu, Josh	381
Hsu, Mike	783
Hsueh, Wally	159
Hua, Jingdong	952
Huang, Hong-Yen	920
Huang, Larke	741
Hubbard, Eugene F	727
Hubbard, Glenn	508
Hubbard, Jacqueline	375
Hubbard, Kevin	437
Hubbard, Roderick R	835
Hubbert, David A	681
Huber, Valerie	735
Huckleberry, Chris	222
Hudak, Kelley	460
Huddelston, Charli	435
Hudgins, Cathaee	908
Hudson, Dane	166
Hudson, Hope Renee	598
Hudson, Larry	797
Hudson, Richard	199, 311, 339, 413, 414, 415, 490, 504, 505
Huff, Dan	430
Huffman, Jared	305, 339, 431, 432, 443, 444, 445, 446, 490
Huffman, Jared W	20
Hughes, Andrew	743

Page

Hughes, Bill 460
Hughes, Brian 366
Hughes, Carrie 412
Hughes, Hannah 68
Hughes, Kai 922
Hughes, Ronald 651
Hughes, Scott 299
Hughes, Tammy 405
Hughes, Todd M 868
Hughes, William C 595
Hugler, Edward C 721
Huizenga, Bill 136, 309, 338, 418, 419, 490, 503
Huizenga, David 760
Huizinga, Madeleine 767
Hulihan, Siobhan 405
Hull, Aline A 800
Hull, Cordell 436
Hull, Everson 916, 932
Hull, Frank M 858
Hull, Leslie 614
Hull, ZJ 427
Hulse, Bill 95
Hulser, Raymond N 663
Hultgren, Randy 95, 307, 338, 418, 419, 438, 439, 490, 504, 506
Hultin, Jerry 782
Humbert, Harry 689
Hume, Chuck 772
Humes, Richard M 832
Hummer, John 754
Humphrey, Cameron 447
Humphries, Terri 588
Hungate, Joseph 745
Hunley, Chance 346
Hunstman, Jon M., Jr 608
Hunt, Alison 192
Hunt, David L 795
Hunt, David W 505
Hunt, Deborah 857
Hunt, James J 666
Hunt, Jennifer 615
Hunt, Joseph H 657, 661
Hunt, Katie 95
Hunt, Ryan 350
Hunt, Scott 814
Hunt, Ted 657
Hunt, Thomas 587
Hunter, Aaron 45
Hunter, Andrew 808
Hunter, Caroline C 797
Hunter, Christine 827
Hunter, Dan 718
Hunter, Dean 824, 826
Hunter, Debbie B 463
Hunter, Duncan 43, 306, 337, 406, 407, 410, 411, 443, 444, 445, 490
Hunter, James 197
Hunter, Jordan 257
Hunter, Karen 704
Hunter, Katie 81
Hunter, Maryann F 783
Hunter, Mathew F 744
Hunter, Peter 118
Hunter, Ryan 141
Hunter, Zachary 415
Hunter-Williams, Jill 92
Huon-Dumentat, Audrey 601
Hupart, Sherri 161
Hur, Robert K 657
Hurckes, Jerry 90
Hurd, Will 262, 313, 341, 424, 434, 435, 453, 454, 490
Hurdle, Lana 748
Hurlbert, Jeffrey 638
Hurley, Paul K 645
Hurley, Raymond C. "Neil" 681
Hurndon, Roy 771
Hurst, Melissa 782
Hurt, Jay 765
Hurtado, Carlos 924
Hurtault-Osborne, Kim 933
Hurwit, Cathy 93
Hurwitz, Andrew D 858
Hurwitz, Sarah K 844
Husband, Shelley 429
Hushek, Thomas 601
Hushek, Thomas J 609
Husk, Stephen J 683
Hussain, Nazrul 916

Page

Hussein, Bishar Abdirahman 944
Hussein, Zeid Ra'ad Al 942
Hussey, Thomas W 661
Huston, John 455
Huston, Partrick R 649
Hutchinson, Darlene L 678
Hutchinson, Lytwaive 624
Hutchinson, Matt 229
Hutchinson, Nzinga 425
Hutchison, Kay Bailey 608, 610
Hutchison, Steven 777
Hutkin, Alex 218
Hutson, James H 508, 589
Hutson, Janet 634
Hutson, Matt 122
Huttenlocker, Robert J 707
Hutton, James 770
Hutton, Susan 729
Hutton, Valerie A 351
Huus, Amber 397
Huus, Bryan 395
Huvelle, Ellen Segal 876, 901
Huwa, Kyle 48
Huweart, Eric 771
Huxley-Cohen, Rachel 69
Huynh, Hoa 699
Huyssen, Brynn 830
Hyatt, Amy J 608
Hyatt, Catherine B 806
Hyatt, Ken 713
Hybl, William J 843
Hyde, Janice 589
Hyde, Ken 675
Hyde, Kurt 590
Hyde-Smith, Cindy 149, 309, 328, 331, 345, 346, 347, 348, 349, 382, 476
Hyduke, Barbara 772
Hyers, Elizabeth 229
Hyland, James 783
Hylton, Roberto L 777
Hyndman, Mervin 618
Hynes, Jordan 375
Hynes, Shaylyn 251
Hyppolite, Marven 132
Hysom, Tim 42
Hyun, Peter 380

I

Iacaruso, Chris 147
Iacono, Suzanne 820
Iacoviello, Matteo 784
Iademarco, Michael F 737
Iancu, Andrei 717
Ibach, Greg 705
Ibarra, Robert 699, 700
Ibrahim, Anitha 663
Ierardi, Anthony R 624
Ieronimo, Anthony 614
Igasaki, Paul M 721
Iger, Michael 186
Ihrig, Jane E 784
Iiams, K.M 656
Ikeda, Robin 737
Ikene, Eunice 412
Ikuta, Sandra S 858
Immler, Michael E 640
Inacay, Michael 83
Inch, Mark S 675
Inclan, Javier 702
Inderfurth, Alison 50
Indovina, Ana 670
Inglee, Corey 254
Ingold, Bernard P 645
Ingram, Caroline 440
Ingram, Conner 246
Ingram, Daria 804
Ingram, Judith 797
Inhofe, James M 215, 311, 328, 330, 352, 353, 362, 363, 367, 368, 383, 476, 509
Inman, Celina 364
Inman, J. Todd 747
Insanally, Riyad 932
Insinga, David 803
Intrieri, Alana 907
Inzeo, Nicholas 792
Iodice, Carolyn 137
Iozzi, Mark 423

Page

Irazola, Seri 678
Ireland, Lynne M 816
Irons, Beryl 935
Irvine, Darren 624
Irvine, Thomas B 809
Irving, Alfred S 905
Irving, Paul D 465, 517
Irwin, Molly 723
Isakovic, Jason 208
Isakowitz, Mark 205
Isakson, Johnny 75, 307, 329, 330, 369, 370, 372, 373, 374, 384, 386, 476, 505
Iscoe, Craig 905
Iselin, Steven R 653
Isenberg, Erin 212
Ishakian, Michel M 903
Ishida, James N 857
Iskikian, Anna 33
Islam, Frank F 807
Ismail, Lori 437
Isom, Pamela 719
Issa, Darrell E 43, 306, 335, 421, 422, 428, 429, 434, 435, 490
Issaacson, Kendra 375
Itnyre, Anita 291
Iturregui, Juan Carlos 806
Ivanauskas, Robert 366
Iverson, David 629
Iverson, George Chris 696
Ivy, Angela 664
Ivy, James 706
Iyengar, Sunil 815

J

Jablonski, Edward R 588
Jack, Catherine 785
Jack, Noreen 935
Jackman, Michael 134
Jackson Lee, Sheila 259, 313, 334, 409, 424, 428, 429, 504, 505
Jackson, Amy Berman 872
Jackson, Barry S 851
Jackson, Ben 266
Jackson, Bill 596
Jackson, Candice 764
Jackson, Christopher 596
Jackson, David 62
Jackson, Deb 700
Jackson, Donald E 648
Jackson, Edward 920
Jackson, Eric 405
Jackson, Frederick R 770
Jackson, Gregory 905
Jackson, Herbert H., Jr 584, 585, 586, 812
Jackson, Jack 10
Jackson, James F 639
Jackson, James S 618, 820
Jackson, Jeffrey W 712
Jackson, Joseph 299, 713
Jackson, Josh 163
Jackson, Karen 738
Jackson, Kateland 381
Jackson, Ketanji Brown 873
Jackson, Kimberly R 702
Jackson, Kyle 253
Jackson, Maria Rosario 815
Jackson, Nancy I 605
Jackson, Nicole 634
Jackson, Rhonda 266
Jackson, Robert J., Jr 831
Jackson, Robert P 607
Jackson, Ronald A 748
Jackson, Rosalind 430
Jackson, Ryan 790
Jackson, Shirley Ann 836
Jackson, Tamika 794
Jackson, Tasia 184
Jackson, Timothy 5
Jackson, Tracy 636
Jackson, William M 905
Jackson, Yvette 702
Jacksta, Linda 778
Jacob, Fred B 798
Jacobs, Aaron 167
Jacobs, Daniel 125
Jacobs, Dennis 857
Jacobs, Elizabeth 833

Page

Jacobs, Joanna M 663
Jacobs, Julian I 891
Jacobs, Kyle 245
Jacobs, Phillip 664
Jacobs, Rachel 104
Jacobs, Robert 809
Jacobs, Sam 397
Jacobs-Simmons, Lenita 726
Jacobs-Young, Chavonda 704
Jacobson, David C 851
Jacobson, James 632
Jacobson, Roberta 608
Jacobstein, Eric 423
Jacquet, Christina N 397
Jacquez, Alex 388
Jadallah, Diala 26
Jadotte, Marcus 714
Jafari, Beth 250
Jaffe, David 663
Jaffe, Holli Beckerman 740
Jaffee, Bill 232
Jagdish, Nitin 840
Jagusch, Sybille A 589
Jaimefranco, Jovanka 516
Jakious, Rick 132
James, Alice 237
James, Bill 771
James, Cara 738
James, Charles 747
James, Charles F 729
James, Deirdre 469
James, Elizabeth 772
James, Gabrielle 703
James, Kathleen 710
James, R.D 642
Jamison, Brooke 180
Jamry, Pauline 154
Jandrlich, Robert 838
Janicke, Jean 714
Janin, Al 652
Jankovich, Laura N 637
Jankus, Ed 395
Jansen, Dave 447
Jansen, Karl 646
Janson, Michael 796
Janushkowsky, Steve 270
Japson, Saul 803
Jaquette, Scott 617
Jaramillo, Johnny J 651
Jaramillo, Mario Fernando 916
Jarcho, Jane 832
Jarmin, Ron S 711
Jarmon, Gloria L 735
Jarnagin, Angie 245
Jaross, Maria Barrera 269
Jarrell, Dan 427
Jarrell, Phil 699
Jarrett, Bryan 730
Jarrett, Chelsea 115
Jarrett, Ebony 800
Jarrett, Valerie 807
Jarsulic, Laura 832
Jasien, William 801
Jason, Meredith 818
Jativa, Danny 63
Javed, Umair 794
Jayapal, Pramila 288, 313, 342, 409, 428, 429, 490
Jayaram, Sanchitha 680
Jayme, Frederico Gonzaga, Jr 917
Jean-Pierre, Daphne 72
Jedlicka, Damion 469
Jeffers, Erika 420
Jeffress, Justin 824
Jeffries, Hakeem S 184, 310, 339, 409, 428, 429, 490
Jelnicky, Michelle 136
Jen, Sophie 506
Jenca, Miroslav 939
Jenkins, Alexandra 392
Jenkins, Ashley 78
Jenkins, Evan H 292, 313, 341, 402, 403, 404, 490
Jenkins, George 720
Jenkins, Hamish 942
Jenkins, Lloyd A 464
Jenkins, Lynn 109, 308, 337, 450, 451, 490
Jenkins, Mark A 680
Jenkins, Michelle 282
Jenkins, William 644
Jenkinson, Wayne 922

Page
Jennnings, Lynn 808
Jensen, Craig 653
Jensen, Danielle 162
Jensen, Matt 271
Jensen, Michael 594
Jensen, Nathaniel 777
Jensen, Susan 430
Jenson, William G 691
Jeong, Il Jeong 919
Jepson, Kristin 454
Jerger, Michael 816
Jermolowizc, Andy 700
Jeronimides, H. Rosemary 917
Jeronimo, Jose M 779
Jett, Jen 255
Jette, Bruce D 642
Jewell, John 395
Jewett, Libby 716
Ji, Ming 716
Jimenez, Arturo Javier Gonzalez 916
Jimenez, Blanca 40
Jimenez, Fernando 951
Jimenez, Sonia 706
Jiminez, M. Andy 797
Jin, Ginger Z 802
Jiron, Dan 695
Jiron, Richard 692
Joa, Elena 517
Jochum, Rita Lari 380
Joe, Niharika C 507
Johanson, David S 845
Johanson, Elaine 738
Johansson, Robert 693, 697
John, Jack St 804
Johnsen, Kristen 289
Johnson, A Wayne 765
Johnson, Aisha 387
Johnson, Alfred C 740
Johnson, Alfreda 724
Johnson, Andrew 145
Johnson, Anita L 420
Johnson, Ben 178
Johnson, Bill 311, 338, 409, 413, 414, 454, 490
Johnson, Blake 411
Johnson, Brian 420
Johnson, Bruce 408
Johnson, Bruce II 420
Johnson, Calvin C 744
Johnson, Carol 701
Johnson, Charles 583
Johnson, Charles W. III 464
Johnson, Charlie 107
Johnson, Cherish 715
Johnson, Clifford R 800
Johnson, Cynthia 103
Johnson, David 654
Johnson, Debra 89
Johnson, Dennis 722
Johnson, Drema 794
Johnson, Eddie Bernice 266, 313, 334, 438, 443, 444, 445, 446, 490
Johnson, Elizabeth 100
Johnson, Ellen 409
Johnson, Eric 676
Johnson, Glen 605
Johnson, Glenn 770
Johnson, Gregory E 634
Johnson, Harvey 771
Johnson, Henry C. "Hank", Jr 77, 307, 336, 428, 429, 443, 444, 445, 490
Johnson, J. Ramsey 905
Johnson, James A 808
Johnson, Jay 705
Johnson, Jeff 723, 848
Johnson, Jeffrey 760
Johnson, Jessica Furst 389
Johnson, John N 408
Johnson, Joseph E 626
Johnson, Julian 76
Johnson, Karis 260
Johnson, Kathleen 463, 783
Johnson, Kenneth 834
Johnson, Kimberly 741
Johnson, Kirk 836
Johnson, Kristen 102
Johnson, Kristine 360
Johnson, Lisa 608
Johnson, Lonnie 405
Johnson, Lyndon 770
Johnson, Mark 242
Johnson, Mary L 819
Johnson, Micah 244, 373
Johnson, Michael R 822
Johnson, Mike 119, 308, 342, 428, 429, 431, 432, 490, 516
Johnson, Noel 905
Johnson, Patrice N 642
Johnson, Paul 635
Johnson, Phillip F 645
Johnson, Robert Wood IV 609
Johnson, Ron 293, 314, 329, 330, 361, 362, 363, 372, 373, 377, 476, 813
Johnson, Sam 251, 312, 333, 450, 451, 469, 490, 835
Johnson, Samantha 648
Johnson, Scott 430
Johnson, Stanton 440
Johnson, Stefanie 798
Johnson, Steve 148
Johnson, Steven 463
Johnson, Tae D 779
Johnson, Tallman 420
Johnson, Ted A 711
Johnson, Teresa 465
Johnson, Thomas 619
Johnson, Thomas, Jr 795
Johnson, Tonya R 824
Johnson, Will 86
Johnson, William D 842
Johnson, William L. "Bill" 208
Johnson, William S 408
Johnson, Yalanda 584
Johnson-Kutch, Danielle 613
Johnson-Obey, Kirsten 821
Johnston, Ann 415
Johnston, Ashton 401
Johnston, Joseph 514
Johnston, Kimberly 285
Johnston, Moira 702
Johnston, Theodore 709
Jolly, E. Grady 857
Jolly, Ernie 183
Jonas, Patricia 839
Jones, Amy 411
Jones, Andrew 936
Jones, Asha 166
Jones, Ashley 93
Jones, Autumn 804
Jones, Bethany 706
Jones, Brenda 78
Jones, Brian R 719
Jones, Carl 636
Jones, Carol 103
Jones, Chris 16
Jones, Chyrl Y 678
Jones, Clinton Columbus III 420
Jones, David A 801
Jones, Deborah E 463
Jones, Dennis 820
Jones, Denzel 279
Jones, Diem-Linh 692
Jones, Doug 2, 305, 328, 331, 359, 360, 374, 377, 387, 477, 801
Jones, Edith H 857
Jones, Eric C 776
Jones, Erik 840
Jones, Gary 718
Jones, Jarrod 698
Jones, Jennifer E 515
Jones, John 156
Jones, Joyce 72
Jones, Kacie 382
Jones, Keira 823
Jones, Keith 401
Jones, Kevin 679
Jones, Kyle T 464
Jones, Lenzie 76
Jones, Linda 696
Jones, Mary Suit 393
Jones, Matt 360
Jones, Mike 361
Jones, Morgan 170
Jones, Omar J. IV 646
Jones, Pam 63
Jones, Paul W 608
Jones, Randall 707, 708
Jones, Reginald E 584

	Page
Jones, Rendell	814
Jones, Richard S	799
Jones, Robert Allen	674
Jones, Roscoe	19
Jones, Samantha T	819
Jones, Samuel C	711
Jones, Shary	736
Jones, Shawn	744
Jones, Shonneice	787
Jones, Simon	943
Jones, Tiffany	704
Jones, Walter B	196, 311, 334, 406, 407, 408, 490
Jones, Wanda	735
Jones, Whitney	389
Jonnalagadda, Prasada Rao V.R	948
Joost, Cameron	88
Jordan, Aaron	766
Jordan, Adalberto	858
Jordan, Anthony	188
Jordan, Catherine	197
Jordan, Darrell "DJ"	215
Jordan, Debra	796
Jordan, Everette	615
Jordan, James	753
Jordan, Jennifer Dukes	849
Jordan, Jim	207, 311, 336, 428, 429, 434, 490
Jordan, Kent A	857
Jordan, Kyle	151
Jordan, Leonard	696
Jordan, Maria	722
Jordan, Mary	801
Jordan, Suzette	240
Jordan, Taylor	440
Jorde, Adam	204
Jorgenson, Sarah	440
Jorjani, Daniel H	690
Jortland, Brett	752
Jose, Juan	931, 933
Joseph, Arthur	846
Joseph, Donna	612
Joseph, Guilliam Ingrid	915
Joseph, Jeremy	132
Joseph, Ken	835
Joseph, Meg	14
Joseph, Richard J	639
Josey-Herring, Anita	905
Jospin, Walter	834
Joss, Laura	687
Jourdanet, Eric J	952
Joy, Roy M	921
Joyce, David P	212, 311, 339, 402, 403, 404, 490
Joyce, Kathleen	465
Joyce, Morgan	82
Joyner, Christopher A	386
Joyner, Miekl	464
Joyner, Tony	639
Joys, Heather A	823
Juarez, Anthony	389
Juarez, Bernadette	706
Juarez, Nancy	31
Judd, Montana	219
Juelis, Kate	433
Juengst, Phillip	763
Juliano, Robin	405
Julius, Nicole	142
Jumde, Anushree	17
Jung, Melissa	442
Junge, Aaron	451
Jurczyk, Steve	808
Jurinka, Elizabeth	371
Jurkovich, Evan	401
Juster, Kenneth I	607

K

	Page
Ka'ai, Krystal	33
Kaag, Sigrid	947
Kabagambe, Anne	951
Kachur, Roman	951
Kadavy, Timothy J	638, 645
Kade, Daryl	741
Kader, Gabe	380
Kadesch, Kim	777
Kadlec, Robert	734
Kaelin, Jim	465
Kagan, Elena	854
Kagan, Joshua	724
Kaguyutan, Janice	423
Kahler, Rachel	405
Kahn, Tammie	816
Kahng, Esther	420
Kaidanow, Tina	604
Kaido, Matt	467
Kaine, Tim	276, 313, 327, 331, 352, 353, 361, 372, 373, 374, 477
Kaiser, Javaid	731
Kaiser, Michael M	808
Kaizuka, Masaaki	924
Kalavritinos, Jack	733, 738
Kaldahl, Rachel	452
Kaleta, Judith S	748
Kalinowski, Doug	727
Kalla, Hari	751
Kalluri, Atri	711
Kalmin, Joseph	186
Kalyanam, Aruna	452
Kamal, Najy	409
Kaman, Andrea	515
Kamin, Steve B	784
Kaminski, Scott	826
Kammerer, Jack	772
Kammler, Albert	425
Kamphaus, Natalie	288
Kampschroer, Kevin	803
Kan, Derek	747, 748
Kane, Betty Ann	911
Kane, John	368
Kane, Robert F	817
Kaneer, Kirk	378
Kanem, Natalia	942
Kang, Eliott	603
Kang, Emil J	815
Kang, Hanseul	910
Kaniewski, Dan	777
Kanja, David	939
Kann, Curtis Von	905
Kanne, Michael S	858
Kannenberg, Dave	752
Kannenberg, Loren	295
Kanter, Eric	132
Kantorosinski, Zbigniew	589
Kaplan, Elaine D	885
Kaplan, Gilbert B	713
Kaplan, Jennifer E	683
Kaplan, Jeremy	142
Kaplan, Lewis A	901
Kaplan, Marvin E	817
Kaplan, Michael	614
Kaplan, Peter	802
Kaplan, Robert	791
Kaplan, Sam	776
Kaplan, Zoya	730
Kappeler, Evelyn	735
Kappes, Steven	704
Kaproth, Robert	614
Kapsner, Allison	117
Kaptur, Marcy	210, 311, 333, 402, 403, 491, 506, 510
Karaccusian, Maral	37
Karafotas, Peter	236
Karcher, Victor A., Jr	825
Kardel, Pernille Dahler	946, 947
Kardian, Gary G	800
Karem, Jordan	593
Karem, Robert	622
Karesh, Lewis	596
Karetny, Josh	235
Karim, Mastura Binti Adul	951
Karlinchak, Karen	719
Karmen, Brad	697
Karr, Barrett	459
Karr, David McLachlan	945
Karsh, Aaron	818
Karvelas, Dave	67
Karvelas, Matt	16
Karvonides, Mia	764
Kasior, Anna	764
Kasomo, Lukogho	188
Kasper, Joe	44
Kasper, Maren	745
Kasraei, Saeid	842
Kasunic, Robert J	588
Katich, Steve	211
Katko, John	192, 311, 341, 424, 425, 443, 445, 446, 454, 491
Kato, Ken	463
Katt, Otto	245

Page

Katz, Jeremy 598
Katz, Ruth 734
Katz, Stephen I 741
Katzman, Julie T 916
Katzmann, Robert A 857
Kaufer, Kate 350
Kauffman, Caryn 834
Kaufman, Emily 131
Kaufman, Kathryn C 847
Kaumo, Chris 433
Kautter, David J 617
Kavalec, Kathleen 602
Kavanaugh, Brett M 860
Kavanaugh, Lindsay 408
Kavandi, Janet L 810
Kaveney, Brian 59
Kay, Leo 727
Kay, Wendy 636
Kaya, Briana 824
Kayatta, William J., Jr 857
Kaye, Elliot 788
Kayea, David 396
Kayne, Jonathan 910
Kayon, Michelle 514
Kayser, Richard 720
Kazan, Matt 371
Kazan, Rachael 797
Kazatchkine, Michel 948
Kazazian, Michael 718
Kea, Charlotte 828
Keable, Ed 690
Kearney, Mark 423
Kearney, Virginia 842
Kearns, Jason 452, 845
Kearns, Michael 681
Kearse, Amalya L 857
Keary, Ann O'Regan 905
Keating, Kate Winkler 187, 456
Keating, Michael 945
Keating, Walter F 793
Keating, William R 133, 309, 338, 421, 422, 424, 425, 491
Keats, Craig 756
Kebet-Koulibaly, Saran G 952
Keckler, Charles N.W 808
Keech, Rosemary E 420
Keefe, Maura 167
Keefer, Brooks 467
Keegan, Patricia 189
Keeler, Ben 209
Keeley, Joe 429
Keeling, Synta 818
Keen, Ruth 806
Keenan, Barbara Milano 857
Keenan, Catrina Pavlik 779
Keenan, Molly 285
Keene, Jim R 646
Keene, Scott 752
Keener, Donald E 661
Keener, Emily 256
Keeney, Ronald J 586
Keeter, Brett 201
Keeter, Lisa 693
Keeys, Mia 89
Kehoe, Allyson 170
Kehoe, Wayne 513
Keiderling, Kelly 610
Keightley, Rebecca 40
Keiser, Rebecca L 820
Keita, Bintou 946
Keita, Kamilah 460
Keith, Damon J 857
Keith, Gregory A 745
Keith, Robert 735
Keith, Steve 454
Keith, Susan 346
Kelaher, Marjorie "Gigi" 462
Kelch, Jessica 423
Kelleher, Kevin 716
Keller, Catherine Bellah 598
Keller, Charlie 280
Keller, David 101
Keller, Jeff 675
Keller, Karen 836
Keller, Keenan 430
Keller, MaryBeth 669
Keller, Terri 393
Keller-Goodridge, Marcella 766
Kelley, Anne-Marie 831
Kelley, Beth 661
Kelley, Frank 654
Kelley, Karen Dunn 710
Kelley, Katharine "Kate" 644
Kelley, Kendall 58
Kelley, Kevin 387
Kelley, Lizanne D 588
Kelley, Marcy 806
Kelley, Michael 743
Kelley, Nathan 719
Kelley, Ray 449
Kelley, Russ 446
Kelliher, Michael 819
Kellogg, Allan G 646
Kellogg, Keith 1, 391, 593
Kellogg, Matthew 616
Kelly, Amanda 346
Kelly, Brian 635
Kelly, Brie 237
Kelly, Cari 5
Kelly, Claire R 880
Kelly, Dale 712
Kelly, David A 818
Kelly, Dennis 836
Kelly, Franklin 817
Kelly, Ian C 607
Kelly, Jane L 858
Kelly, John 596
Kelly, John F 591, 594
Kelly, John V 775
Kelly, Karen 115
Kelly, Karlease 691
Kelly, Lindy Birch 241
Kelly, Marcia Lee 595, 597
Kelly, Mark 281
Kelly, Melissa 262
Kelly, Meredith 456
Kelly, Michael 751
Kelly, Mike 225, 312, 338, 450, 451, 491
Kelly, Nate 717
Kelly, Pamela 711
Kelly, Patricia 830
Kelly, Paul J., Jr 858
Kelly, Robert 169
Kelly, Robert T., Jr 787
Kelly, Robin L 89, 307, 339, 421, 422, 434, 435, 491
Kelly, Shay 290
Kelly, Taylor 405
Kelly, Thomas E 641
Kelly, Timothy J 874
Kelly, Tom 47
Kelly, Trent 150, 309, 341, 399, 400, 406, 407, 408, 441, 442, 491
Kelsey, Joel 51
Kem, John S 641
Kemper, Craig 230
Kemper, Laura 733
Kempf, Donald 658
Kempner, Michael 786
Kendall, James J., Jr 688
Kendall, Mary 690
Kendler, Owen 658
Kendrick, Shannon 828
Kendrick, Will 58
Kenebrew, Delora 662
Keninger, Karen 590
Keniry, Dan 409, 470
Kenna, Lisa 601
Kennedy, Anthony M 853
Kennedy, Arthur W 69
Kennedy, Carolyn 679
Kennedy, Clayton 829
Kennedy, Deborah 632
Kennedy, James H 638
Kennedy, John 117, 308, 329, 331, 347, 348, 349, 359, 361, 379, 380, 383, 477, 491
Kennedy, Joseph P., III 131, 309, 339, 413, 414, 415, 808
Kennedy, Joseph S 825
Kennedy, Kerry 845
Kennedy, Kreg 4
Kennedy, Kriss M 822
Kennedy, Marilyn 691
Kennedy, Matthew Maxwell Taylor 847
Kennedy, Michael 801
Kennedy, Theresa 193
Kennedy, Travis 121

	Page
Kennedy, Victoria Reggie	807
Kennelly, Barbara	509
Kenner, Brian	907
Kennett, Dave	40
Kenny, Andrew	664
Kenny, Michael	65
Kenny, MJ	393
Kenny, Peter	378
Kenny, Steve	380
Kensinger-Clark, Sheila M	644
Kent, Jeff	395
Kent, John C	643
Kent, Ronda	613
Kent, Tom	786
Kenyon, Geoffrey	724
Ker, Michelle	508
Kerber, Jackie	353, 354, 355
Kerestes, Daniel	705
Kermott, Julia	42
Kerner, Henry	827
Kerr, James T	738
Kerr, Kim	454
Kerr, Lindsey	382
Kerrigan, Kathleen	889
Kerscher, George	816
Kersten, Maria C	807
Kersten, Pricilla Levine	844
Keshap, Atul	609
Keshian, Jaclyn	364
Kessler, Charlotte	815
Kessler, Gladys	908
Kessler, Matt	449
Kessler, Rick	416
Kessler, Tamara	662
Kesteloot, James M	787
Ketcham, Lori	818
Kethledge, Raymond M	857
Ketterer, Jeremy	155
Ketu'u, Ofa	936
Keveney, Sean	661
Keylin, Daniel	195
Keys, Chelsie	346
Keys, Elizabeth	361
Keys, Mirta-Marie M	720
Keys, Ross	203
Keysor, Debbie	589
Kezer, Gail	121
Khabbaz, Rima	737
Khan, Atyia	703
Khan, Ikram U	845
Khan, Sadaf	423
Khanna, Ro	28, 306, 342, 406, 407, 409, 491
Khare, Atul	939
Khasawinah, Sarah	387
Khosa, Nasir Mahmood	951
Khosla, Jay	392
Khouri, Michael A	799
Kiamos, Paul C	652
Kiandoli, Cietta	392
Kiang, Agnes	897
Kibben, Margaret	654
Kidd, Richard E	643
Kidder, Rolland	782
Kiddoo, Jean	796
Kiecker, Paul	703
Kiedrowicz, Melissa	38, 457
Kieffer, Charles E	350
Kielceski, Kate	378
Kielty, Peter	415
Kihuen, Ruben J	166, 310, 342, 418, 419, 420, 491
Kiko, Colleen	798
Kiko, Philip	462
Kilbourne, James C	669
Kilbride, Laura W	377
Kildee, Daniel T	138, 309, 339, 418, 419, 420, 491
Kile, Joseph	583
Kiley, Charlotte "Charli"	515
Kiley, Michael T	785
Kilgallon, John	682
Kilkelly, Marge	121
Killeen, Sarah	103
Killen, Edward	618
Killian, Suzanne G	784
Killion, David T	504
Killius, Anna	125
Killoran, Beth Anne	733
Kilmer, Derek	287, 313, 339, 402, 403, 470, 491
Kilpatrick, Elizabeth	818
Kilroe, Deborah	583
Kilroy, Jaclyn	405
Kilroy, Katherine	397
Kilvington, John	378
Kim, Ann	763
Kim, Chris	718
Kim, Don	784
Kim, Grace	841
Kim, Hoe Jeong	950
Kim, Janet	436
Kim, Jim Yong	944, 949, 952
Kim, MiYong	712
Kim, Moses	612
Kim, Scott	462
Kim, Sung	608
Kimball, Kevin	720
Kimble, Tina Potuto	882
Kimmel, Allie	375
Kincaid, Mike	809
Kind, Bonnie	839
Kind, Ron	294, 314, 334, 450, 451, 491
King, Angus S., Jr	121, 308, 327, 331, 352, 353, 361, 365, 382, 386, 477, 506
King, Carolyn	277
King, Carolyn Dineen	857
King, Christina	467
King, Christopher J	819
King, Elizabeth	405
King, Elizabeth Aldridge	397
King, Elizabeth L	356
King, Emily	287, 455
King, Greg	72
King, Heidi R	754
King, Hunter	107
King, Jean C	669
King, Larry	730
King, Louis	748
King, Matthew	777
King, Melissa	750
King, Melvin D., Jr	659
King, Michelle A	839
King, Peter J	800
King, Peter T	181, 310, 334, 418, 419, 424, 453, 491
King, Robert B	857
King, Rufus G. III	905
King, Stephen B	607
King, Steve	107, 308, 335, 399, 400, 401, 428, 429, 441, 491
King, Tatum	779
Kingsbury, Nancy	583
Kinirons, Kerry	425
Kinkoph, Douglas	720
Kinneen, Kelly	595
Kinney, Angela	589
Kinney, Ryann	53
Kinsinger, Anne	689
Kinsley, Kody	616
Kinsman, Art	754
Kinzel, Marcie	159
Kinzinger, Adam	96, 307, 338, 413, 414, 421, 422, 491
Kinzler, David	244
Kirby, Carolyn	516, 584
Kirchhoefer, Amber	108
Kirchner, Joan	75
Kirchner, Julie	775
Kirk, Andrew	806
Kirkland, Billy	1, 391, 593
Kirkland, Donald	635
Kirkland, Jeremy	745
Kirkland, Steve	380
Kirkpatrick, Chris	788
Kirkpatrick, Paul	514
Kirsanow, Peter N	843
Kirwan, Pat	713
Kiser, Elizabeth K	785
Kiser, Scott	630
Kishiyama, Lonnie T	753
Kisliuk, Bruce	717
Kissel, Adam	767
Kissel, Angela	828
Kitay, Steve	408
Kituyi, Mukhisa	941
Kiviniemi, Mari	933
Kiyokawa, Guy T	625
Kizzier, Kyle	140
Kladney, David	843
Klaiman, Seth	236
Klapper, Matt	169

Page

Klass, Richard L 782
Klee, Elizabeth 784
Kleiman, Andrew 417
Klein, Alzbeta 952
Klein, Jeffrey 611
Klein, Josh 373
Klein, Julie 378
Klein, Kyle 425
Klein, Mark F 652
Klein, Matthew 779
Klein, Timothy 756
Kleinfeld, Andrew J 858
Kleinman, Joan 124
Klem, Lisa J 878
Klemm, Hans 608
Klima, Jaime 831
Klimavicz, Joseph 678
Kline, John D 647
Kline, Mary Ellen 683
Kling, Jeffrey 583
Klinger, Patricia 755
Klippstein, Daniel M 647
Klobuchar, Amy 143, 309, 327, 330, 345, 346, 362, 363, 379, 380, 382, 388, 467, 468, 477, 510, 511
Klokis, Philip 804
Klopack, Diane 614
Klopp, Jacki B 779
Klopp, Robert 841
Klopp, Stephen 396
Kloster, Andrew R 748
Klotz, Mark 789
Klouda, Tom 371
Klump, Allen 239
Klumpp, Lee 505
Klutts, Mary 588
Kluttz, Lawrence 197
Knackstedt, Kimberly 412
Knapke, Anne 143
Knapp, Beverly 646
Knapp, John 276
Knapp, Julius P 795
Knapper, Marc 609
Knauer, Chris 416
Kneeland, Jason 102
Knell, Scott 829
Knierim, Paul 665
Knigge, Mary 401
Knight, Anna 373
Knight, Anthony 717
Knight, Kelsey 214
Knight, Kristal 908
Knight, Natali 63
Knight, Shahira 597
Knight, Stephen 306, 341, 406, 407, 408, 438, 439, 441, 491, 507
Knight, Steve 31
Knight, Steven, Jr 838
Knoblock, Cherie 659
Knoll, Kirk D 586
Knopp, Martin 751
Knott, Tucker 196
Knouse, Mike 229
Knouse, Ruth 747
Knowles, Bryan 691
Knowles, Joseph 228
Knowles, Kimberley S 905
Knox, Jason 432
Knox, Matthew 24
Knudsen, Patrick Louis 409
Knudson, Kate 460
Ko, Denny 670
Kobelja, Mark A 655
Koch, Louisa 714
Koch, Nora 839
Koch, Robin 749
Koch, Steve 716
Kochhar, Kalpana 923
Kochman, Ben 257
Kocur, Ana M 669, 848
Kodis, Marty 686
Koeberlein, Teresa 248
Koed, Betty K 393
Koehler, Erv 803
Koehler, Samantha 387
Koehn, Steve 696
Koek, Irene 843
Koenig, Andy 597
Koenig, Jennifer 633

Page

Koeppel, David 728
Koeppel, Dennis 766
Koestler, Robert 837
Koffsky, Daniel 679
Koffsky, Paul S 625
Kogan, Bobby 361
Kogod, Robert P 836
Koguchi, Kazuhiko 951
Kohler, Horst 946
Kohlman, Kevin 753
Kohns, Carrie 37
Kohnstamm, Paul 88
Kohorst, W. Robert 607
Kolasky, Robert 776
Kolb, Ingrid 759
Kolbe, Kathryn 779
Koleski, Katherine E 508
Kollar-Kotelly, Colleen 872
Kolodjeski, Erin 405
Kolovson, David 294
Kolpien, Tim 192
Konar, Howard 844
Koncar, Steve 63
Koncke, Gonzalo 933
Kong, Stephen 712
Kono, Masamichi 933
Konolige, Rebecca 433
Konsella, Laurie 736
Kontanis, Elias 820
Kontos, Chloe 596
Konya, John 401
Koob, George 740
Koohmaraie, Bijan 415
Koonce, Murphie Barrett 447
Koontz, Cara 437
Koontz, Thomas 718
Kopan, Walter G 720
Kopshever, Kristin 440
Korell, Scott 629
Koren, Michael 417, 436
Korkor, Julie 754
Korkor, Samer 663
Korman, Shai 845
Kornbluh, Karen 786
Kornegay, Emily 745
Koroshetz, Walter 741
Korrell, Harry 808
Kortan, Michael 673
Koses, Jeff 803
Kosinski, Dorothy M 816
Kosinski, Kenneth 789
Koski, John 632
Koskinen, John 618
Koslov, Tara Isa 802
Kosnett, Philip 609
Kossow, Todd 802
Kossoy, Joshua 830
Kostel, Claudia A 393
Koster, Julia A 814
Kostka, Gregory M 464
Koszela, Kaylan 173
Kotiswaran, Prasad 801
Kotman, Dan 139
Kotschwar, Nichole 382
Kott, Jonathan 290
Kouri, Joey 98
Koutsis, Steven 609
Kouzoukas, Demetrios 738
Kovatch, George E 780
Kowalczyk, Daniel 632
Kowalski, Heather 825
Kowalsky, Theodore 612
Kozanas, Dena 425
Kozeny, Jill 105
Kozubski, Susan 463
Krabbe, Carla A 839
Kracker, Michael 194
Kraemer, Michael J 785
Krafts, Andrew J 817
Krahenbuhl, Pierre 942
Kraistol, Joe 15
Kral, Christine 650
Kramer, Donna 730
Kramer, James 717
Kramer, Martin 739
Kramer, Mike 841
Kraninger, Kathy 595
Kranthi, Keshava Raj 922

Page

Krapels, Helen H 683
Krapf, Alan 700
Krasner, Stephen D 845
Kratovil, Lindley 191
Kratsios, Michael 596
Kratz, Jeff 162
Kraus, John 293
Krause, Cheryl Ann 857
Krause, Scott 775
Krauthamer, Peter 905
Kravetz, Lauren 796
Kravitch, Phyllis A 858
Kravitz, Neal E 905
Kreamer, Christine 836
Krebs, Brian 456
Krebs, Christopher C 776
Krebs, Robert 382
Kreisman, Barbara A 796
Kreitz, Jon 654
Krejci, Aaron 725
Kremer, Kyle J 624
Kress, Carl B 850
Kresse, Carol 25
Krieger, Alex 787
Krieger, Mark 719
Krings, Natalie 242
Krishnamoorthi, Raja 92, 307, 342, 410, 411, 434, 435, 491
Krislov, Marvin 816
Kritenbrink, Daniel J 610
Kriviski, Diane M 703
Krizay, Glen 648
Kroese, Daniel 252
Kroft, Meredith 20
Krol, George A 607
Kronforst, Mark 832
Krongaus, McKinley 23
Kronheim, Jonathan M 728
Kronopolus, Cathy 830
Krovi, Varun 142
Krueger, Dan 515
Kruger, Mary 778
Krull, Kelsey 205
Kruntz, Jennifer 114
Kryger, Rick 723
Krysa, Thomas J 834
Kryzak, Lindsay 389
Kubacki, MelaJo 745
Kubena, Kellie McGuiness 701
Kubis, Jan 947
Kubista-Hovis, Kristi 700
Kuchno, Ken 701
Kuchta, Jordan 380
Kuckro, Melissa 687
Kuczynski, Chris 792
Kudler, Harold 772
Kudlow, Larry 594, 598
Kuepper, Andrew 777
Kuester, Michele A 792
Kueter, Dean 660
Kufuor, John 948
Kuhlman, Robert 111
Kuhn, Elena 461
Kulikowski, Jim 404
Kullberg, Harold C 806
Kulnis, Dan 393
Kumar-Capoor, Aradhana 953
Kumpf, Roger 201
Kundanis, George 456, 460
Kunene, Bongi 951
Kungel, Wes 290
Kunkel, Thomas 515
Kunkle, Sonya 368
Kunse, Suzanne 222
Kunsman, Dan 298, 389
Kupers, Larry 681
Kupka, Nathan K 822
Kupperman, Jonathan 44
Kurfehs, Bill 754
Kurien, Alexander 803
Kurin, Richard 836
Kurland, Kevin 712
Kurosawa, Toshitake 952
Kurose, James F 820
Kurth, Jim 686
Kurth, Timothy 415
Kurtz, Olivia 121
Kushmerick, James 720

Page

Kushner, Jared 597
Kuskowski, Jennifer 370
Kuster, Ann M 168, 310, 339, 399, 400, 448, 491
Kustin, Casey 423
Kustoff, David 248, 312, 342, 418, 419, 420, 491, 845
Kusumoto, Sandra K 800
Kutchey, John 814
Kutz, Greg D 618
Kutz, Thomas 451
Kuwabara, Gary 624
Kux, Leslie 739
Kvetko, Lance 665
Kwak, Sally 469
Kwakwa, Victoria 949
Kwiecinski, Jeff 828
Kwok, Alfred 729
Kwon, Jae Hyung 953
Kwon, Jean 350, 351
Kyte, Rachel 949

L

L'Esperance, Nicole 221
Laba, Sherianne 838
LaBotte, Ellie 97
Laboueuf, Beila 467
Labrador, Raul R 86, 307, 338, 428, 429, 431, 432, 491
LaCanfora, Marianna 838
LaCapra, Quin 45
LaCasse, Andrew 375
Lacey, Clinton 909
Lacey, Michael 643
Lackey, Jennifer 437
Lacombe, Jean Pierre 952
LaCour, Alice 657
Lacroix, Jean-Pierre 939
Lacroix, Stephen Michel 915
Ladak, Nawaid 267
Ladd, Chelsey 108
Ladd, John 726
Ladd, Paul 943
Ladowicz, John P 778
Lafargue, Sophia 183
Lafferty, Annette 844
LaFleur, Cheryl A 761
LaFond, Daniel 730
LaFrancois, Jeremy R 676
Lagarde, Christine 923, 943
Lagasse, Carol 645
Lagemann, Paul 101
Lager, James 583
LaGuarda, Wendy 793
Lahasky, Rosemary 452, 726
LaHood, Darin 97, 307, 341, 450, 451, 467, 491
Lahr, Matt 101
Lai, Joseph 597
Laihow, Amanda Wood 822
Laird, Carolyn 389
Laird, Melvin R 808
Laisch, Mark 351
Laitta, Michael 922
Lake, Anthony 941
Lakhdhir, Kamala 608
Laliberte, Cody 41
Lalle, Stephanie 412
Lalumiere, Frank 850
Lam, Livia 284
LaMalfa, Doug 20, 305, 339, 399, 400, 431, 432, 443, 444, 445, 446, 491
LaManna, Nancy A 618
Lamarre, Charles 936
Lamary, Mary 678
Lamas, Enrique 711
Lamb, Coleman 182
Lamb, Conor 233, 312, 342, 438, 439, 448, 491
Lamb, Jennifer 53
Lamb, Vanessa 795
Lambert, James M 933
Lambert, Mark W 824
Lambert, Michael J 784
Lambert, Tammi 910
Lambert, Terry 904
Lamberth, Royce C 875
Lamborn, Doug 49, 306, 336, 406, 407, 431, 432, 491, 501
Lamont, Thomas R 782
LaMothe, Cicely 832
Lamoureux, Randall 653

Page
Lampert, Matt 353, 355, 356
Lan, Iris 657
Lancaster, Elise 135
Lancaster, John A 845
Lance, Leonard 173, 310, 337, 413, 414, 415, 417, 491
Lanctin, Johnathan 296
Land, Guy 783
Lande, Emily 433
Landefeld, Paul 469
Landfried, Phillip A 778
Landis, Dean 838
Landon, Jim 715
Landow, Mindy 818
Landy, Morgan J 952
Lane, Alan 838
Lane, Ca Asia 517
Lane, Chris 924
Lane, D.A 656
Lane, Jordan 119
Lane, Katherine L 464
Lane, Michelle 366
Lane, Stewart 585
Lang, Kate 750
Lang, Michael 663
Lange, Bill 696
Langenderfer, James 68
Langenderfer, Lisa 206
Langenwalter, Corey R 650
Langer, Jack 30, 454
Langer, Mark J 864
Langevin, James R 236, 312, 335, 406, 407, 408, 424, 491
Langley, Nanci 830
LaNier, Elisa 436
Lankes, Hans Peters 952
Lankford, Breanna 633
Lankford, David 740
Lankford, James 215, 311, 329, 331, 347, 348, 349, 377, 385, 386, 470, 477, 502, 506
Lanphear, Thomas J 846
Lanpher, Laurie 515
Lansford, Nicole 264
Lansing, John F 786
Lanum, Scott F 779
Lanza, Valerie 918
Lanzer, Toby 946, 947
Lanzillotta, Mary Katherine 787
LaPalme, Joe 395
Lapenn, Jessica 609
Lapenta, William 716
Lapiana, John 836
Lapitino, Mary 670
Lapointe, Paul 467
LaPorte, Gerald 678
LaPuz, Miguel 772
Lara, Ashley 286
Lara, Frank 675
Lara, Sally 269
Laragy, Scott 670
Large, Alex 449
Large, Patrick 152
Larkin, Brendan 191
Larkin, Pete 280
Laro, David 893
LaRocco, Larry 509
Larrabee, Jason 25
Larsen, Joan Louise 857
Larsen, Jonathan C 644
Larsen, Leif 653
Larsen, Lewis F 807
Larsen, Matt 837
Larsen, Rick 285, 313, 335, 406, 407, 443, 444, 492
Larson, Bess 439, 440
Larson, John B 51, 306, 335, 450, 451, 492, 510
Larson, Sally Rose 80, 437
Larson, Susan 139
LaSane, Karlos 505
Laslovich, Dylan 159
Lasseter, David 680
Lassiter, Nicole 827
Lasure, Sara 15
Latham, Dawn P 783
Lathbury, Donald 21
Latta, Robert E 208, 311, 336, 413, 414, 415, 492, 503
Latta, Sandra 652
Lattanner, Andrew 99
Lattin, Grant 652
Latu, Kosi 937
Page
Lau, Jeff 805
Lau, Sam 409
Laub, Danny 273
Laubach, Thomas 784
Lauber, Albert G 889
Lauby, Robert 752
Lauer, Ethan B 464
Lauer, Michael S 740
Laufer, John 61
Laug, Connie 205
Laughery, Jessica 287
Laughlin, Alexander M 817
Laughlin, Brian 172
Laughlin, Rose 437
Laughton, Steven 611
Laukitis, R.J 139
Laura Profeta, ai 916
Laurent-Monpetit, Christiane 919
Lauria, Jolene 677
Lauritsen, Sharon Bomer 596
Lausten, Eric 90
Lautner, Beth 707
Lauwers, Bernard 949
Lavallee, Aaron 704
Laver, Michelle 759
Lavigne, Carrie Mann 756
Lavigne, Thomas A 756
Lavik, A. Roy 788
Lavin, Pat 850
Lavine, Jonathan S 844
Lavinsky, John S 676
Lavizzo-Mourey, Risa J 836
Lavoy, Donald J 744
Law, Kathryn 701
Law, Ryan 616
Law, Tyler 456
Lawkowski, Gary 685
Lawler, Brian 617
Lawler, Sean P 601
Lawless, Julia 370
Lawless, Martha 846
Lawley, Ceri Wyn 952
Lawrence, Amy 216
Lawrence, Andrew 718
Lawrence, Brenda L 142, 309, 341, 434, 443, 444, 445, 446, 492
Lawrence, Courtney 733
Lawrence, Daryl 634
Lawrence, Gavin A 647
Lawrence, Jeffrey 612
Lawrence, Katie 196
Lawrence, Matt 387
Lawrence, Tamara D 651
Lawrence, Tanya 790
Lawson, Al, Jr 60, 306, 342, 399, 400, 401, 441, 442, 492
Lawson, Charles A 922
Lawson, Chris 4
Lawson, Michael 51
Lawson, Michael J 515, 645
Lawson, Mike 510
Lawson, Rona 840
Lay, DeLisa 380
Layden, Will 433
Layfield, Patricia 844
Layne, Michele 834
Layng, John 723
Layton, Chip 119
Lazare, Mary 736
Lazarus, Allison 353, 354, 355, 356
Lazarus, Edward P 844
Lazowski, Alan B 844
Lazzarini, Philippe 947
Lazzeri, Michael 730
Le, Huy 825
Le, Margaret 718
Le, Nancy 717
Le, Ricky 27
Lea, Robyn 460
Leach, David J 642
Leach-Carlos, Renee 691
Leader, Joe 850
Leahy, Jeremy J 824
Leahy, Patrick J 274, 313, 329, 330, 345, 346, 347, 348, 349, 379, 380, 382, 388, 468, 477, 502, 835
Leahy, Robert M 824
Leahy, Terry 464
Leal, Lotus 644

Page

Leamer, Nathan 794
Leanes, Luis Fernando 934
Lear, Monica M 696
Leasure, Matt 221
Leavandosky, Stacey 29
Leavitt, Andy 138
Leavitt, Ryan 273
Leavitt, Tristan 827
Leavy, Edward 858
LeBlanc, Stephen G 586
LeBoeuf, Nicole 715
LeBold, Sandra 799
Lebow, David E 785
Lebryk, Dave A 612
Lebryk, David 812
Lebryk, David A 613
Lebryk, Kristen 94
LeCates, Joseph 469
Lecce, Dan 652
LeCompte, Theodore 709
Leddy, Carolyn 373
Ledeen, Barbara 380
Leder, Paul A 833
Lederer, Calvin 780
Ledford, Janine 781
Ledgett, Richard H., Jr 626
LeDuc, Mark 387
Ledvina, Thomas 651
Lee, Andrea 151
Lee, Barbara 26, 306, 334, 402, 404, 409, 492
Lee, Brian 179
Lee, Christian 350
Lee, Cindy 33
Lee, Collin 405
Lee, Deborah H 716
Lee, Doug 91
Lee, Ebony 763
Lee, Evan 58
Lee, Garry 696
Lee, Jackson 490
Lee, James 792
Lee, Jane 392
Lee, Jennifer 21
Lee, Jessica 203
Lee, John J 839
Lee, Joy 461
Lee, Kimya 827
Lee, Lisa 735
Lee, Luther 10
Lee, Mark 803
Lee, Mike 271, 313, 329, 331, 362, 363, 365, 366, 379, 380, 467, 477
Lee, Milton C 905
Lee, Patricia 850
Lee, Paula 707
Lee, Rebecca L 809
Lee, Rene R 676
Lee, Richard 147
Lee, Una 416
Lee, Unjin 169
Leeling, Gerald J 356, 357
Leen, Craig 730
LeFebvre, Brian 516
Lefkowitz, Edward 717
Leganski, John 459
Legarza, Shawna 696
Legg, Kenneth 760
Legg, Mike 446
Leggett, Matt 368
Leggieri, Rebecca 405
Legum, Radine 728
LeGuyader, John 717
Lehman, John 353, 354, 356
Lehman, Patrick 161
Lehman, Ryan 189
Lehman, Ted 195
Lehn, Andrea 632
Lehnert, Andreas W 785
Lehrer, Mia 787
Lehver, Misha 51
Leibowitz, Lynn 905
Leibtag, Ephraim 705
Leieritz, Jeff 803
Leighton, Stephen 68
Leighton, Wayne 796
Leiner, Frederick 681
Leipold, Alessandro 924
Leiserson, Nick 236

Page

Leith, William 689, 765
Leiton, Rachel 730
Leland, Arlean 694
Lemke, Wilfried 949
Lemma, Anthony 184
Lemmon, Rick 772
Lemon, Greg 277
Lemons, Terry 618
Lempert, Yael 603
Lenderking, Timothy 603
Leney, Tom 769
Lenfert, Winsome 751
Lengyel, Joseph L 638, 645
Lenicheck, Jon 133
Lennie, Rachel G 817
Lennon, Jaime 124
Lennon, Jared 378
Lensch, Nyree D 631
Lenter, David 469
Lentz, Connor 104
Lenz, Joseph 386
Leon, Charles 916
Leon, Michel Dreyfus 920
Leon, Richard J 877
Leonard, Andrew 786
Leonard, Christine M 849
Leonard, Fran L 801
Leonard, Judith 836
Leonard, Kenneth M 756
Leonard, Lauren 709
Leonard, Mary Beth 609, 610
Leonard, Rachael 596
Leonardi, Alan 716
Leong, Wayne 753
Leonova, Sofya 90
Leopold, Matthew Z 790
Leopold, Pat 110
LePage, G. Peter 820
Lepley, Diane 905
Lepore, Mary Beth 695
Lepre, Janet L 821
Lerda, Jillian 396
Lerma, Eduardo 388
Lerman, Miles 845
Lerner, Allison C 820
Lerner, Jon 606
Lescher, Bill 654
Leschke, Julie 293
Leshner, Alan I 820
Lesko, Debbie 13, 305, 342, 424, 425, 438, 439, 492
Leslie, Althea Coetzee 849
Lesnick, Robert J 801
Lesofski, Emy 350
Lesser, William C 728
Lessley, Lucinda 436
LesStrang, Dave 405
Lester, Dean 401
Lester, Harold D. "Harv", Jr 806
Letlow, Luke 120
Letsch, Andrew 459
Lett, Gloria 462
Letter, Douglas 660
Letter, Lizzy 376
Lettow, Charles F 883
Letz, Deborah 464
Leuders, Amy 686
Leuschen, James 461
Leval, Gerard 845
Leval, Pierre N 857
LeVasseur, Josh 371
Levcovitz, Eduardo 935
Levenson, Paul 834
Leverette, Mitch 688
Leverich, Gerald 416
Leverone, Susan 818
Leverrier, Laurel 701
Levesque, Ashley 707
Levey, Stuart A 844
Levi, John G 808
Levi, Michael 723
Levie, Richard A 905
Levin, Don 718
Levin, Matthew 724
Levin, Sander M 140, 309, 333, 450, 451, 492
Levin, Sarah 452
LeVine, Eric A 844
Levine, Sharron 798
Levine, Steven 834

Page
Levine, Susan G 844
Leviner, Emily 161, 252
Levy, Joaquim 949
Levy, Santiago 916
Levy, Will III 617
Lewis, Alvin 4
Lewis, Andrew 654
Lewis, Anil 787
Lewis, Ashley 360
Lewis, Carol L 397
Lewis, Chasseny 6, 72
Lewis, Christy 389
Lewis, Dale 286
Lewis, David 516, 584
Lewis, Donald R 780
Lewis, Elliot P 726
Lewis, Emily 433
Lewis, Holly 3
Lewis, James 89
Lewis, Jason 144, 309, 342, 409, 410, 411, 443, 444, 445, 492
Lewis, Jeff 364
Lewis, Jessica 373
Lewis, John 78, 307, 333, 450, 451, 469, 492
Lewis, Jourdan 416
Lewis, Karen J 588
Lewis, Kendrick 65
Lewis, Maurice 455
Lewis, Mike 616
Lewis, Miller 460
Lewis, Rodney 629
Lewis, Terry 847
Lewis, Tracey 387
Lewis, Tyler 629
Lewis, William "Jim" 820
Ley, Jennifer 778
Leyden, Diana L 893
Lezell, Mira 229
Lhamon, Catherine E 843
Li, Allen 440
Li, Zhao 724
Liburd, Leandris 737
Lichtenfels, Marvin 726
Lichter, Ann 730
Lichtman, Miles 416
Liddell, Chris 597
Lieber, Sheila M 661
Lieberman, Ben 415
Lieberman, Eve 47
Lieberman, Steve 772
Liebes, Cindy A 802
Liedel, Chris 837
Lieu, Ben 662
Lieu, Stephanie 364
Lieu, Ted 35, 306, 341, 421, 422, 428, 429, 492, 506, 507
Lighthizer, Robert 591, 596, 847
Ligon, Keith 783
Like, George 829
Liley, Terence 394
Liling, Zhao 918
Lillie, Juliette 685
Lillis, Joe 157
Lilly, Greg 353
Lim, Kitack 943
Limardo, Rick 452
Limarzi, Kristen 658
Limerick, Patricia Nelson 816
Lin, Alice 468
Lin, Irene 700
Lin, Jianhai 924
Lin, Kakuti 464
Lin, Matthew Y.C 735
Lincoln, Amanda 375
Lincoln, Edward 507
Lincoln, Larry 791
Lincoski, John 718
Lindblad, Joseph 378
Lindbo, David 697
Lindborg, Nancy 845
Linde, Jonas 411
Linde, Sarah 739
Lindeman, Joel 625
Linden, Ralph 694
Linder, Mike 613
Lindler, Melissa 241
Lindner, Dan 11
Lindo, Arthur W 783
Lindquist, Douglas E 674
Lindsey, Adrian 694
Lindsey, Brian 464
Lindsey, Yancy 653
Lindstrom, Frederick J 787
Lindwall, David 609
Lineberger, W. Carl 820
Linehan, Ann 736
Ling, Vivian 442
Linick, Steve 602
Link, Craig 461
Link, Frank 636
Link, Kendra 850
Linn, Richard 869
Linscott, Mark 596
Linsk, Reed 44
Linsmayer, Lauren 364
Lintz, Gilda 108
Linzie, Oliver 825
Lipcaman, Suzanne B 637
Lipez, Kermit V 857
Lipinski, Daniel 90, 307, 336, 438, 439, 443, 444, 445, 492
Lipnic, Victoria 792
Lippert, Dorothy 781
Lippman, Jonathan 841
Lipps, Brandon 701
Lips, Dan 377
Lipscomb, Laura 784
Lipsich, Wendi 70
Lipsky, Abbott "Tad" 802
Lipsky, Faye 840
Lipsky, Kim 363
Lipton, David 923
Lis, Tony 136
Liscovitz, Matt 121
Lisman, Sarah 136
Liszewski, S 651
Litman, Travis 794
Litras, Marika 731
Little, Cathy 405
Little, Jeffrey 744
Little, Kevin 718
Little, Sarah 108
Littlejohn, Sabrina 619
Littleton, Rachel 350
Littleton, Thomas 753
Littman, Kristina 831
Litvack, Neal 782
Litwak, Robert S 851
Litzow, Elizabeth 256
Liu, Chi-Chao 920
Liu, Fang 943
Liu, Libby 786
Liu, Lirio 751
Liu, Simon 704
Livengood, Steve 510
Livingston, Christopher 26
Livingston, Debra A 857
Livingston, JoAnne 766
Livornese, John 831
Lizarraga, Jaime 460
Lloyd, Brenda M 780
Lloyd, Karen 589
Lloyd, Scott 736
Loach, Eric 464
LoBiondo, Frank A 170, 310, 334, 406, 408, 443, 444, 445, 453, 492
Lobrano, Wyatt 120
Lobrichon, Sarah 922
Lobue, Christian 132
LoBurgio, Nicholas J 838
Locey, Kimberly A 727
Locke, Nancy 411
Lockwood, Andrea 759
Loddo, Joseph P 849
Lodge, Virginia S 842
Lodin, Per 947
Loeblein, Jim 652, 654
Loebsack, David 106, 308, 336, 413, 414, 492
Loewenstein, Roy 189
Loewentritt, Lennard S 804
Lofgren, Zoe 29, 306, 334, 427, 428, 429, 438, 439, 468, 492, 511
Lofthus, Lee J 677
Loftin, Melinda 690
Logan, Catherine 635
Logan, Robert 736

Page

Logann, Susan G ... 825
Loggie, Matthew ... 464
Lohier, Raymond J., Jr ... 857
Lohr, Christopher ... 630
Loitey, Carlos Humberto ... 939
Loken, James B ... 858
Lolli, Tim ... 213
Lombard, Charles ... 810
Lombardi, Kyle ... 31
Lombardo, Michael ... 807
Lombardo, Regina ... 659
Lomonaco, Jeff ... 143
London, Jeffrey ... 772
Long, Billy ... 157, 309, 338, 413, 414, 415, 492
Long, Brock ... 777
Long, Cheryl M ... 905
Long, Cindy ... 703
Long, Graham ... 200
Long, Jamie ... 146
Long, Karyn ... 154
Long, Kerry ... 749
Long, Kristy ... 513
Long, Michael ... 456, 460
Long, Michelle ... 704
Long, Rachel ... 22
Long, Shannon ... 662
Longani, Kapil ... 436
Longi, Maria ... 843
Longo, David ... 753
Lonsberry, Lee ... 272
Looney, Jack ... 465
Looney, Rita S ... 633
Loos, Glenn M ... 729
Loper, Brett ... 510
Lopes, Alexander ... 712
Lopes, Mark Edward ... 917
Lopez, Andres W ... 807
Lopez, Brenda ... 269
Lopez, Eva X ... 826
Lopez, Joe ... 837
Lopez, Jose M ... 905
Lopez, Juan ... 27
Lopez, Kenia Seoane ... 905
Lopez, Kenneth ... 588
Lopez, Leonardo Jose Longa ... 916
Lopez, Mark ... 100, 614
Lopez, Martha Helena ... 940
Lopez, Pete ... 791
Lopez-Salido, David ... 784
Lopez-Sandoval, Elizabeth ... 456
Lorber, Howard M ... 844
Lord, Ellen M ... 622
Lord, Mark ... 113
Lord, Ronald ... 699
Lordos, Ryan ... 783
Loren, Donald P ... 770
Lorengo, Jerry ... 717
Lorentzen, Ronald ... 713
Lorenzen, Barbara ... 832
Lorenzo, Robert ... 718
Lorsch, Jon ... 741
Loser, Eva ... 652
Loten, Jennifer ... 932
Lothian, Milly ... 226
Lott, Alfred ... 765
Lott, Everett ... 755
Loud, Marc D., Sr ... 912
Loudermilk, Barry ... 80, 307, 341, 418, 419, 427, 438, 439, 468, 492, 511
Loudermilk, Weldon ... 687
Lough, Sunita ... 618
Louis, Henry ... 617
Louis-Charles, Nadgey ... 80
Lourd, Bryan ... 807
Lourie, Alan D ... 865
Lourie, Alexander "Sasha" ... 511
Loutsenhizer, Nicole ... 464
Love, Elena ... 378
Love, Mia B ... 273, 313, 341, 418, 419, 420, 492
Love, Monique ... 725
Love-Holmon, Shana ... 770
Lovelace, Joel ... 725
Loveland, Daniel ... 657
Lovern, Marie ... 716
Lovett, Hamilton ... 200
Loving, Andrea ... 430
Lovinger, Dvora ... 125
Low, Claire ... 456

Page

Lowcock, Mark ... 939
Lowder, Michael ... 747
Lowe, Alan ... 812
Lowe, Christopher ... 693
Lowe, Jonathan ... 206
Lowe, Rick ... 815
Lowe, Shelly C ... 816
Lowe, Tyler ... 425
Lowell, Heather A ... 397
Lowenberg, Susan E ... 844
Lowenberg, William J ... 845
Lowenstein, Jeff ... 33
Lowenthal, Alan S ... 42, 306, 339, 431, 432, 443, 444, 445, 446, 492
Lowery, John ... 654
LoweSolis, Michelle ... 635
Lowey, Nita M ... 189, 311, 333, 402, 404, 470, 492
Lowry, John ... 380
Loyd, Thomas ... 518
Loyola, Mario ... 594
Lu, Donald ... 606
Lu, Michael ... 739
Lu, Natalie ... 839
Lubing, Lael ... 702
Lucas, Daniel ... 907
Lucas, David ... 231
Lucas, Frank D ... 216, 311, 334, 399, 400, 418, 419, 438, 439, 492
Lucas, John ... 759
Lucas, Rich ... 701
Luce, Mark ... 720
Lucero, Amy ... 751
Lucero, Carl ... 696
Lucero, Carlos F ... 858
Luchette, Richard ... 236
Lucier, Jennifer A ... 784
Lucio, John ... 350
Luckett, David ... 652
Luckey, Charles D ... 644
Luczak, Ronald ... 764
Ludwig, Stacy M ... 681
Lue, Bert ... 469
Luebke, Thomas ... 787
Luecke, Matthew M ... 784
Lueptow, Michael ... 378
Luetkemeyer, Blaine ... 154, 309, 337, 418, 419, 441, 442, 492
Luginbill, Scott ... 198
Lujan, Ben Ray ... 178, 310, 337, 413, 414, 415, 455, 492
Lujan Grisham, Michelle ... 177, 310, 319, 339, 399, 400, 401, 409, 492
Luke, Sean ... 793
Lukens, Jennifer ... 715
Lukoff, Roger ... 744
Lukow, Gregory ... 590
Lukso, Michael ... 172
LumHo, Kekoa ... 669
Lumia, Jason ... 247
Lumpkin, Travis ... 284
Luna, Frank ... 171
Lund, Kristin ... 947
Lund, Kurt ... 665
Luparello, Stephen ... 833
Lupo, Andrea ... 850
Lupo, Jose Luis ... 916
Lurie, Peter ... 739
Lusby, Jane ... 516
Lushin, Andrey ... 951
Lusi, Rose ... 733
Lussenhop, Matthew ... 606
Lussier, Philippe ... 605
Lute, Jane Holl ... 502, 947
Luthi, Jeffery N ... 901
Lutz, Julie K ... 834
Lutz, Miranda ... 423
Lyles, Anne ... 395
Lyles, Latifa ... 729
Lyles, Sylvia ... 765
Lyman, April ... 206
Lyn, Jessica ... 728
Lynch, Brittany ... 426
Lynch, Chris ... 123
Lynch, David ... 783
Lynch, Gerard E ... 857
Lynch, James G ... 649
Lynch, John ... 663
Lynch, LaFondra ... 802
Lynch, Liza ... 269

Page

Lynch, Mary Kay 790
Lynch, Meaghan 196
Lynch, Mike 180, 392, 633
Lynch, Philip B 397
Lynch, Sandra L 857
Lynch, Sarah-Ann 843
Lynch, Stephen F 133, 309, 335, 418, 420, 434, 435, 492
Lynch, Tim 436
Lynn, Alison 408
Lynn, Mairead 375
Lynton, Michael M 836
Lyon, Shonnie 776
Lyons, Derek 598
Lyons, Emel 699
Lyons, Holly E. Woodruff 446
Lyons, Lynn 505
Lyons, Maggie 701
Lyons, S. Robert "Bob" 681
Lyons, Stephen R 624
Lyons, Troy 790
Lyskowski, Kevin 727
Lytle, Laura 395
Lytle, Marshall B. III 624

M

Maas, Timothy W 784
Mabry, Brian 693
Mabry, Elizabeth 368
Mabry, Scott 688
MacAfee, Jeffrey D 586
MacAfee, Sandra K 586
Macaluso, Judith N 905
MacArthur, Thomas 171, 310, 341, 418, 419, 492
MacArthur, Tom 808
MacBride, Marsha 720
Macchiaroli, Michael 833
MacDonald, Alexander 716
MacDonald, Andrew 631
MacDonald, Char 461
MacDonald, Don 34, 423
MacDonald, Ian Christopher 917
MacDonough, Elizabeth C 394
MacDougall, Heather L 822
MacFarlane, Alex 37
MacGregor, Katharine 687
MacGregor, Rob 178
Machelski, Jeffrey S 696
Macias, Rene 451
Mack, Carolyn 368
Mack, Lizbeth 750
Mack, Paris M 729
Mack, Vandetta 691
Mack-Abney, Regina 770
Macke, Robert 699
MacKenzie, Christopher 6
MacKenzie, Matthew 401
Mackey, Tonya 759
Mackie, James 617
Mackie, Kathleen T 469
Mackin, Michele 583
Macklin, Jay 670
Maclachlan, Patricia 507
MacLeay, Geoffrey 411
MacLellan, Jennifer 167
MacNaughton, Phil 408
MacPherson, Rebecca 749
Macrae, James 739
MacRae, Scott 813
MacTaggart, Elizabeth Schneider 121
Mactaggart, Stacy 517
Madan, Rafael A 679
Madden, Chris 652
Madden, Molly 688
Madden, Robert 770
Maddox, Cheryl 505
Maddox, Clarence 857
Maddox, Victor B 808
Madigan, Brian 784
Madigan, Thomas J 519
Madison, Joseph E 782
Madison, Kirsten Dawn 603
Madni, Brittany 409
Madyun, Zarifa 589
Maenle, Nathan 771
Maffei, Daniel B 799
Magallanes, Downey 685
Magary, Adam 49

Page

Magdaleno, Raul 505
Mageau, Camille 922
Maggard, R. Print 669
Magnasco, Dennis 132
Magnus, Katie 353, 354
Magnus, Vicki 588
Magnuson, Patrick 351
Mahaffie, Lynn 767
Mahaffie, Robert 616
Mahaley, Joseph 810
Mahalingappa, Jessica 706
Mahan, Erin 813
Mahan, Owen 387
Mahan, Roger 459
Mahar, Harry 604
Mahar, Molly 783
Mahar-Piersma, Auke Merrill 447
Mahoney, Amalia Perea 807
Mahoney, C.J 596
Mahoney, Christina 156
Mahoney, James A 793
Mahoney, Kevin 710
Mahoney, Kristen 678
Mahr, Tom 461
Mahr, Wesley 518
Mahurkar, Monish 952
Maik, Inga 753
Main, Jennifer 738
Mainzer, Elliott 760
Mairella, Rachel 378
Maitland, Michael J 170
Maizel, Donna C 660
Majauskas, Richard 712
Majeed, Sameena Shina 662
Major, Christine 733
Major, Lisa 454
Majower, Nancy 715
Majure, W. Robert 658
Makhlouf, Mouayed 952
Makin, Sarah 1, 391, 593
Malac, Deborah 609
Malague, Katie 616
Malanum, Theresa 511
Malawer, Hilary 766
Malcolm, India 795
Malcomson, Dennis 739
Maldonado, Ferdinand 632
Malecki, Eva 518
Malek, Frederic V 851
Malek, John 517
Malen, Chris 262
Mallard, Kris 405
Mallin, Blair 143
Mallison, Bill 449
Mallon, Carmen L 676
Malloy, Matthew 614
Malmstrom, Jason R 676
Malone, David 942
Maloney, Andrew K 615
Maloney, Carolyn B 186, 311, 334, 418, 419, 420, 434, 467, 493
Maloney, Michael 833
Maloney, Sean Patrick 189, 311, 339, 399, 400, 401, 443, 444, 445, 446, 493, 501
Malpass, David 613
Malpass, David R 847
Malvaney, Scot 151
Malvirlani, Dimitri 921
Mamabolo, Jeremiah Nyamane Kingsley 946
Mamaux, Lale 437
Mamish, Nader L 821
Manasco, James 4
Manchin, Joe III 290, 313, 327, 330, 347, 348, 349, 365, 366, 384, 386, 388, 470, 477, 505
Mancini, Nadine N 823
Mandavilli, Neel 197
Mandel, David 590
Mandel, Ruth B 845
Mandelker, Sigal P 615
Mandt, Greg 716
Mandzia, Lesia 770
Manecke, Dominic 207
Manes, Jean 607
Maness, Ted 150
Maneval, Christopher 147
Manfra, Jeanette 776
Manger, Charles 804
Manger, William 849

	Page
Mangum, Lance	505
Manilow, Barbara Goodman	807
Manion, Daniel A	858
Maniscalco, John	61
Manker, James E., Jr	772
Manley, Allyson	255
Mann, Catherine	933
Mann, CJ	346
Mann, James C	663
Mann, Liz	273
Mannering, Amy	392
Manning, Emily	373
Manning, Glenda	724
Manning, James	763
Manning, John	429, 644, 676
Manning, Monica	810
Manning, Steve	613
Manning, Tonya	723
Mannix, Aileen	699
Manno, Claudio	750
Manosalvas, Marcos F	420
Mansaray, Saibatu	1, 391, 593
Mansbach, Shana	461
Mansker, Rodger W	650
Manson, Lindsay	288
Mansour, Michael	282
Mantel, Brad J	728
Manzano, Heather	699
Manzelli, Brianna	363
Maples, Gus	351
Mara, Shannon	514
Marazzani, Maria Claudia Vasquez	918
Marca, Danny	423
Marchand, Becki	725
Marchant, Kenny	263, 313, 336, 417, 450, 451, 493
Marchese, April	594
Marchese, Steve	405
Marchick, David M	844
Marchione, Kara	375
Marciel, Scot	606
Marcott, Stacy	777
Marcum, Deanna	507
Marcus, Anthony	614
Marcus, Jeremy	233, 795
Marcus, Stanley	858
Marella, Daniel K	823
Maresh, Annette B	793
Margary, Maria A	643
Margolis, Andrew	800
Margolis, Jonathan	605
Margolis, Sara	461
Margowsky, Miranda	388
Marianetti, Jadon	766
Mariani, Patricia	897
Mariani, Tom	669
Marietta-Westberg, Jennifer	832
Marigliano, Richard	654
Marin, Mark	439
Marin, Paul A	850
Marine, Noah	50
Marinec, Matthew A	823
Marino, Francis	936
Marino, Tom	228, 312, 338, 421, 422, 428, 429, 493
Marion, Robert L	642
Marion, William E. "Bill"	634
Markey, Edward J	129, 309, 328, 331, 362, 363, 367, 368, 372, 383, 477
Markey, Timothy E	785
Markey, Vincent	772
Markle, Lindsay	353, 354
Marklund, Chris	433
Markon, Jerry	377
Markowitz, David	647
Marks, Audrey	932
Marks, Peter	739
Marks, Tommy L	648
Marksteiner, Peter R	870
Marmolejos, Poli	759
Marohl, Chris	204
Marois, Alyssa	14
Maroney, Chris	636
Maroni, Alice	830
Marquardt, Jeffrey C	784
Marquardt, Kristen	423
Marques, Javier	781
Marquette, Margaret	613
Marquez, Gabriela	34
Marquis, Ashley	598
Marquis, Michael	734
Marr, Becky	390
Marr, Betsy Arnold	25
Marrero, Jose Diaz	303
Marrs, James R	624
Marrs, Richard L	810
Marrs, Vicki	783
Mars, Jacqueline Badger	807
Marseilles, Dawn	665
Marsh, Christian	713
Marsh, James	225
Marsh, Molly	350
Marsh, Sharon	718
Marshall, Charles	395
Marshall, Duron	142
Marshall, Era	836
Marshall, Hazen	392
Marshall, Heather C.D	638
Marshall, Jerome	612
Marshall, John	416
Marshall, Kamau	255
Marshall, Lane	390
Marshall, Lydia	840
Marshall, Lynda	658
Marshall, Maria Day	911
Marshall, Maureen	647
Marshall, Misty	375
Marshall, Roger W	109, 308, 342, 399, 400, 401, 438, 439, 441, 442, 493
Marshall, Samantha	85
Marshall, Thomas	848
Marshall, Zack	114
Marsteller, William A	793
Martein, Robert M	586
Martello, Ben	131
Martens, John	405
Marter, Jean	423
Martin, Allison	244
Martin, Andrea	103
Martin, Beverly B	858
Martin, Caric	81
Martin, Clarene Phyllis	911
Martin, Dana	660
Martin, Dennis	698
Martin, Glen	750
Martin, Greg	750
Martin, James	724
Martin, James F	631
Martin, Jeffrey	785
Martin, John J	666
Martin, Joseph	777
Martin, Josh	257
Martin, Katie	389
Martin, Kenneth	368
Martin, Lee	618
Martin, Michiko	696
Martin, Paul K	809
Martin, Ray	385
Martin, Rebecca	737
Martin, Russell	618
Martin, Ryan	370, 452
Martin, Shayne	252
Martin, Stephanie	785
Martin, Theodore D	649
Martin, Tod	153
Martin, Todd	263
Martin, Zach	147
Martinez, Alvin Delgado	921
Martinez, Andrea Ramirez	918
Martinez, Anthony	456
Martinez, Cynthia	686
Martinez, Eric A	644
Martinez, Ismael	812
Martinez, Jessica	416
Martinez, Karen L	835
Martinez, Luis	653
Martinez, Raymond P	751
Martinez, Vincente	833
Martinez, Wilfredo	841
Martinez, William	841
Martini, Angela	919
Martino, Jeffrey	659
Martins, Jorge Cardoso	916
Martorony, Gene	173
Marum, Victoria	516
Marvel, L. Paige	887
Marvin, Lucille	757
Marx, Michele C	595

Page
Marx, Natasha L 848
Marx, William 435
Maschino, Karl 583
Mascioli, William 818
Mashagbeh, Wassel 714
Mashburn, John 724
Masica, Sue 687
Masling, Mark 681
Maslow, Linda 856
Mason, Cheryl L 769
Mason, Graham 179
Mason, McKinley 393
Mason, Michael 615, 836
Mason, Rosanna 904
Mason, William 652
Massaro, A. Paul III 504
Massarone, Charles T 683
Massey, Marsha 833
Massie, Thomas 114, 308, 338, 434, 435, 438, 439, 443, 444, 445, 446, 493
Massoudi, Mehran S 736
Mast, Brian J 67, 307, 342, 421, 422, 443, 444, 446, 448, 493
Masterson, John 712
Masterson, Matthew 844
Mastman, Katy 724
Mastrandea, Linda 778
Mastrangelo, David 191
Mastrian, Michael 395
Mastrogianis, Helena 231
Mastromonaco, Alyssa 807
Masumoto, David "Mas" 815
Matalon, Kali 351
Mate, E 651
Matecki, Katherine 717
Matese, Jamie 181
Matesic, Hannah 446
Matheson, Scott M., Jr 858
Mathew, Ann 126
Mathews, Daniel W 447
Mathews, Lance E 638
Mathias, Charles 796
Mathias, Karl 683
Mathias, Stephen 939
Mathiasen, Karen 614, 950
Mathis, Josh 216
Mathur, Rajat 351
Matias, Jerson 824
Matic, Jelena 137
Matini, Shana Frost 905
Matlock, Patrick E 647
Matoff-Stepp, Sabrina 739
Matos, Angela 594
Matous, Kyle 268
Matous, Torrie 3
Matson, Natalie 425
Matsui, Doris O 22, 305, 336, 413, 414, 415, 493, 835
Mattavous-Frye, Sandra 911
Matteri, Robert 705
Matthes, Rachel 516
Matthew, Kathryn K 816
Matthews, Dan 802
Matthews, Daniel 816
Matthews, Earl G 643
Matthews, Heidi 214
Matthews, Kameron 772
Matthews, Linda 212
Matthews, Macey 14
Matthews, Madeline 425
Matthews, Matrina 680
Matthews, Matt 602
Matthews, Sarah 425
Mattiello, Jonathan D 842
Mattimore, John C 835
Mattis, James 591, 594, 781
Mattis, James N 621
Mattis, Jim 813, 845
Mattlet, Anne-France 919
Mattos, Kim 794
Matzelle, J 651
Maulding, Davis H 631
Maurin, Fred 841
Maxfield, Julie Hatch 723
Maxson, Phil 112
Maxwell, Chloe 17
Maxwell, David O 817
Maxwell, Gray 123
Maxwell, Josh 401
Maxwell, Richard E 17
May, Peter 813
May, Rick 685
May, Todd A 811
Mayayeva, Yana 69
Mayberry, Alan 755
Mayberry, Anne 701
Mayberry, Karen E 638
Maye, Gerald 785
Mayer, Deborah Sue 386
Mayer, Haldane Robert 868
Mayes, Carl A 704
Mayne, Susan 739
Mayo, Gary 704
Mayo, Milton 792
Mayo, Steven L 820
Mazanec, Mary B 588
Mazer, Roslyn A 802
Mazina, Dina 371
Mazyck, Veleter 212
Mazzei, Mark 664
Mazzi, Ana 824
Mazzone, Mark L 397
McAdams, Callie 401
McAdams, Kate 709
McAdams, Kevin 848
McAfee, Karen 452
McAleenan, Kevin 778
McAleer, Laura P 623
McAllister, Ryan 190
McAloon, Kevin 416
McArdle, Dawn 58
McArthur, Eric 658
McAuliffe, Jane 590
McBrayer, Kate 260
McBride, Caitlin 68
McBride, David 810
McBride, Jessica 242
McBride, Kathleen 518
McBride, Stacy 153
McCabe, Andrew 673
McCabe, Catherine R 789
McCabe, John 905
McCabe, Patrick 785
McCabe, William 733
McCaffery, Thomas 622
McCain, Amy 630
McCain, John 9, 305, 329, 330, 352, 377, 385, 386, 477, 509
McCall, Drew 743
McCall, Tiana 97
McCallum, Dana 393
McCallum, Daniel F 643
McCallum, Sally H 589
McCament, James W 780
McCance-Katz, Elinore F 741
McCane, Bobby 778
McCane, Chris 114
McCann, Robert 632
McCann, Ted 459
McCarragher, Ward 446
McCarroll, Kate 276
McCarron, Jess 346
McCarry, Caleb 373
McCarter, John W 836
McCarthy, Dan 293
McCarthy, Ed 632
McCarthy, Jennifer 679
McCarthy, John 231
McCarthy, Kevin 30, 306, 336, 455, 459, 493, 507, 510
McCarthy, Margaret 23
McCarthy, Michael T 793
McCarthy, Ryan D 641
McCartin, Jude 167
McCartin, Terrence J 596
McCartney, Bobbie J 691
McCartney, Daniel 517
McCarty, Anthony 515
McCarty, Lauren 415
McCarty, Margaret 681
McCarty, Molly 417
McCarty, Robert 788
McCaskill, Claire 153, 309, 327, 330, 352, 353, 369, 370, 377, 477, 806
McCaul, Michael T 256, 313, 336, 421, 422, 424, 493, 503
McCauley, Brian 615
McClain, Joseph 101

Page

McClain, Lauren ... 425
McClain, Tony ... 384
McClain, Tyrone ... 53
McCleery, Rachel ... 371
McClelland, Cody ... 279
McClelland, John ... 583
McClelland, Joseph ... 761
McClelland, Katherine ... 376
McClelland, Kyle ... 645
McClelland, Teri ... 772
McClenny, Lee ... 608
McClintock, Tom ... 21, 305, 337, 409, 431, 432, 493
McCloskey, John ... 821
McCloud, Edith ... 714
McClure, Sam ... 812
McClure, Stacey ... 15
McClure, William W ... 817
McCluskey, Brian ... 707
McCollum, Betty ... 145, 309, 335, 402, 403, 404, 493
McCollum, Kelly Lungren ... 282
McCollum, Kyle ... 380
McCollum, Luke ... 654
McComb, Rich ... 777
McCombs, Kevin ... 826
McConaghy, Ryan ... 397
McConnell, David M ... 661
McConnell, James J ... 760
McConnell, Linda ... 772
McConnell, Mitch ... 112, 308, 328, 330, 345, 346, 347, 348, 349, 382, 386, 391, 477, 508, 510, 511, 808
McConnell, Sheila ... 726
McConnell, Thomas K ... 356, 357, 358
McConville, James C ... 641, 646
McCord, Ariel ... 257
McCord, Michael ... 801
McCord, Morgan ... 378
McCormack, Brian ... 759
McCormick, Christy ... 844
McCormick, Jamie ... 422
McCormick, Kelly ... 380
McCormick, Patrick ... 366
McCormick, Rich ... 749
McCourt, Jamie D ... 607, 608
McCoy, Jeffrey ... 646
McCoy, Kim ... 613
McCoy, Kimberly A ... 613
McCoy, Moyer ... 452
McCoy, Nona ... 350
McCracken, Erin ... 427
McCrary, Daryl R ... 659
McCrary, David ... 201
McCrary, Francesca ... 436
McCrary, Victor R ... 820
McCray, Jason ... 807
McCray, Ronald D ... 801
McCrea, Daniel ... 678
McCree, Victor M ... 822
McCubbin, Bruce J ... 589
McCubbin, Janet ... 617
McCulloch, Nicholas ... 436
McCullough, Aisa K ... 746
McCullough, Matt ... 94
McCullough, Noah ... 392
McCully, Shannon ... 778
McCune, Collin ... 446
McCusker, Elaine A ... 622
McDade, Joseph M ... 637
McDaniel, Charles ... 633
McDaniel, Corvelli ... 613
McDaniel, Deirdre M ... 683
McDaniel, Eileen ... 735
McDaniel, James ... 669
McDermond, James E ... 660
McDermott, Kevin ... 412
McDermott, Patricia ... 469
McDermott, Susan ... 747
McDermott, Thomas ... 777
McDermott, William "Tim" ... 664
McDonagh, Anne ... 713
McDonald, Douglas ... 753
McDonald, Jamie ... 787
McDonald, Michael ... 815
McDonald, Shane ... 452
McDonald, Thea ... 439
McDonald, W. Larry ... 614
McDonald, Walter ... 764
McDonnell, James F ... 778
McDonnell, Patrick ... 790, 842

Page

McDonough, Benjamin ... 785
McDowall, Lena ... 686
McDowell, Drew ... 157, 416
McDowell, Sheila A ... 409
McDuffie, Kenyan ... 907
McEachin, A. Donald ... 278, 313, 342, 406, 407, 431, 432, 493, 503
McElroy, Marianne ... 699
McElveen-Hunter, Bonnie ... 782
McElvein, Elizabeth ... 430
McElwain, Lorena ... 788
McElwain, Maria ... 51
McEnery, Rosemary ... 795
McEvoy, Jeff ... 397
McEvoy, Miles ... 706
McEvoy, Trecia ... 159
McFadden, Elizabeth ... 766
McFadden, Trevor N ... 663, 874
McFarland, Kyle ... 425
McFarland, William ... 465
McFeeters, Brian ... 603
McFerran, Lauren McGarity ... 817
McGahn, Donald ... 598
McGahn, Donald F ... 594
McGarvey, Carla ... 57
McGary, Robert ... 698
McGee, Nick ... 103
McGehee, Jason ... 18
McGeorge, Audra ... 422
McGettigan, Kathleen ... 823
McGhie, Lisa ... 206
McGhie, Matthew D ... 397
McGilvray, Andrew ... 713, 802
McGilvray, Laurie ... 613
McGinley, James ... 905
McGinley, William ... 596
McGinn, John ... 622
McGinnis, Colin ... 360
McGinnis, Colleen ... 765
McGinnis, J. Michael ... 819
McGinnis, Nicole ... 796
McGinty, Brian ... 396
McGlinchey, Daniel P ... 420
McGlynn, A. Daniel ... 615
McGoings, Michael C ... 669
McGovern, Clement ... 680
McGovern, Gail J ... 782
McGovern, James P ... 130, 309, 334, 399, 400, 401, 437, 493
McGowan, Gerald ... 502
McGowan, Matt ... 468
McGowen, Misty ... 446
McGrath, Brian ... 679
McGrath, Chase ... 698
McGrath, Chris ... 942
McGrath, Erin ... 794
McGrath, Kelly E ... 420
McGrath, Sean ... 950, 952
McGrath, T.J ... 583
McGraw, Deven ... 734
McGruder, Shawn ... 694
McGuigan, Patrick ... 384
McGuire, James ... 469
McGuire, Katherine ... 95, 724
McGuire, Peter ... 510
McGunagle, Mark M ... 397
McHale, Mark ... 803
McHenry, Christina ... 821
McHenry, Patrick T ... 200, 311, 336, 418, 419, 460, 493
McHenry, Teresa ... 663
McHugh, Carolyn B ... 858
McHugh, Matt ... 509
McHugh-Polley, Susan ... 771
McIlveen, John ... 393
McInerney, John D ... 713
McInerney, Marianne ... 749
McIntire, John ... 830
McIntosh, Brent ... 611
McIntosh, Garvey ... 811
McIntosh, Lynn ... 728
McIntosh, Troy D ... 634
McIntyre, Jason ... 514
McIntyre, Jennifer ... 604
McIntyre, John ... 609
McIntyre, Kevin ... 760
McIver, Kevin ... 618
McKay, Aaron ... 105
McKay, Dominique ... 390

	Page
McKay, Michael	830
McKay, Monroe G	858
McKay, Teresa A	625
McKeague, David W	857
McKeague, Kelly K	626
McKee, Brandon	95
McKee, Scott	366
McKee, Theodore A	857
McKeehan, Ann	784
McKenna, John	730
McKenna, Juliet J	905
McKenna, Liam	435
McKenna, Michael	814
McKenney, Michael E	618
McKenzie, Dean	727
McKenzie, Kenneth F	624
McKeogh, Katie	415
McKeon, Ashley	346
McKeown, A. J	467
McKeown, Joe	238
McKeown, M. Margaret	858
McKessey, Sean	833
McKew, Sean	516, 824
McKibben, Bryce	376
McKiernan, Neil	52
McKinley, David B	290, 313, 338, 413, 414, 493
McKinley, Michael	606
McKinnell, Cathy	699
McKinney, Matthew	827
McKinney, Nikki	375
McKinney, Ted	697
McKinnon, Don	405
McKinstry, Jonathan	429
McKittrick, J. Kevin	515
McKnight, Brian	664
McLanahan, Elizabeth	714
McLaren, Ellen	70
McLaren, Nicole	62
McLaughlin, Dena	805
McLaughlin, Janet	750
McLaughlin, Joan	767
McLaughlin, Maureen	766
McLaughlin, Paul	469
McLaughlin, Tricia	611
McLaurin, Juschelle	594
McLean, Christopher	700
McLean, Craig	714, 716
McLeese, Roy W	904
McLenachen, David	772
McLeod, Josh	378, 813
McLeod, Kimberly P	771
McLeod, Marie	829
McLerran, Elissa	260
McMahon, Jason	351
McMahon, Linda	849
McMahon, Linda E	591
McMahon, Robert H	622
McManaman, Kathleen	771
McManus, Katherine	602
McManus, Marliss	136
McManus, Marliss A	420
McMaster, Jack	782
McMaster, Sean	748
McMichael, Chara	258
McMichael, Stanley	693
McMillan, Howard "Mac"	755
McMillan, Jon	652
McMillin, Bobby	375
McMorris Rodgers, Cathy	286, 313, 336, 413, 415, 455, 493
McMorris, Jeffrey	746
McMullan, Pace	10
McMullan, William	659
McMullen, Debra	470
McMullen, Edward, Jr	608, 609
McMullen, Neval	470
McMullen, Patrick	417
McMurray, Matt	89
McMurray, Matthew	28
McMurray, Tom	809
McMurtrey, Shannon	703
McNabb, Kelley	411
McNall, Patricia	750
McNally, Dan	387
McNally, Elizabeth	502
McNally, Kristie	619
McNally, P	651
McNamara, Mariah K	356, 357
McNamara, Nancy	673
McNamee, Chris	449
McNaught, Becky	383
McNeal, Michael	772
McNeil, Jena	105
McNeil, Sue	796
McNeill, Greg	378
McNeill, Ha Nguyen	778
McNeillie, Nancy	464
McNerney, Jerry	24, 306, 336, 413, 414, 438, 439, 493
McNerney, Maura	848
McNerney, W. James, Jr	807
McNichols, Jim	155
McNutt, Marcia	819
McPadden, Christopher	647
McPeak, Merrill A. "Tony"	781
McPherson, James	825
McPherson, James E	643
McPike, Richard Kirk	39
McQuade, Katherine	455
McQuade, Kathryn	392
McQuay, Katherine	662
McRae, Clarence F	632
McRory, Kevin "Scott"	664, 666
McSally, Martha	10, 305, 341, 406, 407, 408, 424, 493, 501
McShane, Kathleen	850
McSwain, Robert	740
McSweeny, Terrell	802
McVicker, Grant	631
McVicker, Michelle	748
McWatters, J. Mark	814, 821
McWhorter, Elizabeth	378
Meachum, Pete	296
Meade, Ellen	784
Meade, Joe	695
Meade, Jordan	286
Meadows, Carrie	286
Meadows, Mark	3201, 11, 339, 421, 422, 434, 443, 444, 445, 493, 813
Meale, David	603
Means, Kristine	470
Mears, Mary	791
Mebane, Reginald R	737
Mecher, Greg	131
Medders, Sherry	639
Medema, Tom	686
Medina, Amelia	657
Medina, Francisco	420
Medina, Rob	62
Medina, Yvonne	747
Medve, John	770
Medzhibovsky, Boris	34
Meehan, Jack	446
Meeker, Shelee	66
Meeks, Brett	375
Meeks, Gregory W	183, 310, 334, 418, 419, 421, 422, 493
Meeks, Kevin	739
Meeks, Simone Marie	506
Megahan, Patrick	423
Mehler, Lauren	380
Mehra, Pritha	848
Mehrabi, Emma	26
Mehrens, Nathan	723
Mehringer, Holly	636
Mehta, Amit	874
Mehta, Atul	952
Mehta, Bobby	346
Meick, Ethan S	508
Meier, Sarah	437
Meilinger, Frank	727
Meiners, Molly	616
Meisel, Jeffrey	711
Meissner, Dennis	813
Mejia, Marcia	65
Meland, Deborah S	681
Melendez, Aida	905
Melendez, Alex	68
Melendez, Carmelo	759
Melendrez, Dahlia	384
Melius, Thomas	686
Melle, John M	596
Melloy, Michael J	858
Melton, Tracy	663
Meltzer, Alan	608
Meltzer, David B	782
Meltzer, Dick	460

	Page
Meltzer, Richard	456
Melville, James	607
Melvin, Justin	249
Melvin, Valerie	583
Memmott, Justin	368
Memon, Sean	831
Menashi, Steven J	766
Menchaca-Gendron, Adriana	850
Mencher, Bruce S	905
Mende, Carl D	849
Mendelson, David E	649
Mendelson, Lisa	686
Mendelson, Phil	814, 907
Mendenhall, Bradley "Grant"	674
Mendes, Justin	30
Mendez, Nestor	933
Mendez-Sanchez, Katherinne	516
Mendoza, Heidi	939
Mendoza, Juanita	687
Mendoza, L. Antonio Rascon	921
Mendoza, Martin, Jr	707
Mendoza, Miguel	73
Mendoza, Nikko	129
Mendoza, Rosa	456
Menendez, Robert	169, 310, 327, 330, 359, 360, 369, 370, 372, 373, 388, 478, 509
Meneses, Gustavo	918
Menezes, Mark	759
Meng, Grace	183, 310, 339, 402, 404, 493
Menikoff, Jerry	735
Menkerios, Haile	944
Mennes, Brian J	647
Meno, Rosanne	301
Menon, Jai Shanker	948
Menorca, Doug	102
Mensah, Lisa	700
Mentkowski, Anne C	849
Mentzer, Tom	19
Menzler, Tyler	447
Meraikhi, Ahmed Al	947
Merberg, Elinor	818
Merberg, Julie	269
Mercado, Belle	240
Mercandante, Vincent	755
Mercer, Christy	153
Mercer, Edward	237
Mercer, Megan	397
Mercer, Ted, Jr	750
Merchant, Kusai	368
Merdon, Christine	513
Meredith, Diana	409
Meriweather, Robin M	878
Merkle, Phillip K	679
Merkley, Jeff	219, 311, 328, 330, 347, 348, 349, 361, 367, 368, 372, 478, 506
Merlino, John J	394
Mermin, Jonathan	737
Merrell, Jonathan	739
Merriett, Steve	783
Merrill, Christopher	816
Merrill, Debbie	29
Merrill, Stuart	715
Merritt, Gilbert S	857
Merritt, Heather	603
Merryman, Brad	829
Merten, Kenneth	603
Meryweather, Kelly	464
Meryweather, Tom	464
Merz, Bill	654
Mesch, Anne	805
Messer, Jennifer	505
Messer, Luke	102, 307, 339, 410, 411, 418, 419, 420, 455, 493
Messersmith, Cynthia	681
Messina, Claire	942
Messonnier, Nancy	737
Metcalf, Kevin G	712
Metheny, Bill	729
Methfessel, "Bucky"	766
Metsger, Rick	814
Mettler, Erik	738, 739
Metzler, Chad	121
Meuli, Marlo	293
Mevis, Kate	387
Mewbourne, Dee L	654
Mewhirter, Erin	803
Meyer, Caitlin	380
Meyer, Elizabeth K	787
Meyer, Eric	614
Meyer, Heather	636
Meyer, Joyce	597
Meyer, Katie	459
Meyer, Matt	245, 449
Meyer, Seth	693
Meyer, Steffen	924
Meyer, Stephen A	784
Meyer-Pietruszka, Deanna P	688
Meyerhoff, Harvey M	845
Meyerriecks, Dawn C	786
Meyers, Leslie	844
Meyers, William E	903
Meza, Danny	261
Mezainis, Valdis E	695
Miagkov, Eugene	951
Mica, Carl	250
Michael, Jeff	754
Michael, Matthew	703
Michaelis, Patrick R	641
Michaels, James A	784
Michalek, E.H. "Ned"	188
Michalic, Mark E	657
Michalic, Vivian B	659
Michalski, Lori	743
Michel, Charles D	780
Michel, Nicolas	945
Michels, Jeff	219
Middlebrook, Craig H	756
Middlebrooks, Jake	411
Middleton, Brandon M	669
Middleton, Carson	198
Middleton, Joeana	153
Mielke, Dan M	585
Miguel, Melinda M	584
Mihalic, Dave	685
Mihm, J. Christopher	583
Mikkelsen, Alan	690
Mikkelson, Kathleen R	637
Mikula, Nick	408
Mikva, Laurie I	808
Milam, Megan	405
Milby, Michael	903
Mildrew, Sean	778
Miles, Adam	676
Miles, Chris	73
Miles, George A	813
Miles, Jack	102
Miles, Penny	351
Millan, Juan A	596
Millard, Rachel	401
Miller, Addison	209
Miller, Alex	415
Miller, Benjamin	21
Miller, Brandon	433
Miller, Brianne	366
Miller, Brooke	76
Miller, Bruce	165
Miller, Dan	416
Miller, Deb	756
Miller, Dennis	630
Miller, Derek	223
Miller, Earl	606
Miller, Eli	611
Miller, Elizabeth	814
Miller, Emily	163
Miller, Essye B	623
Miller, Fred	446
Miller, Gabrielle	72
Miller, Gail	776
Miller, Garth	772
Miller, Gwendolyn	683
Miller, Jamie	277
Miller, Jay	518
Miller, Jennifer	405, 632
Miller, Jodi	827
Miller, Joel	113
Miller, John	630
Miller, Jonas	267
Miller, Kathleen S	647
Miller, Katie	395
Miller, Keith	387
Miller, Kerry L	584
Miller, Lorraine	510
Miller, Mary	622
Miller, Maryanne	639
Miller, Matt	613
Miller, Matthew M	729

Page
Miller, Megan 118
Miller, Michelle 746
Miller, Miles 515
Miller, Morna 452
Miller, Palmer 10
Miller, Pam 405
Miller, Philip T 779
Miller, Rebecca 766
Miller, Richard 412
Miller, Sarah 68
Miller, Shea 4
Miller, Stephanie J 952
Miller, Stephen 597
Miller, Susie 263
Miller, Virgil 118
Miller, Wesley C 642
Miller, Will 459
Miller-Lewis, Josh 274
Millett, Patricia A 860
Milley, Mark A 641
Milliman, Jim 112
Mills, David C 784
Mills, Emily 168
Mills, Krista 744
Mills, Richard M., Jr 606
Mills, Waples 636
Millward, Christopher 953
Milner, Michael S 780
Milnes, Lauren 184
Milosch, Mark 504
Milstead, Jimmy 270
Milteer, Jessica 702
Milton, Karen Greve 857
Min, James 31, 459
Min, Royce 840
Minami, Kristine 764
Minchew, Kaye Lanning 813
Minear, Jeffrey P 856
Minehardt, Adam 184, 442
Minehart, Robert 454
Mineiro, Mike 440
Minelli, Tim 516, 584
Miner, Chris 604
Mineta, Norm 509
Miniace, Joseph N 749
Minkel, Sarah 194
Minkler, Annie 437
Minnix, Carlos 794
Minoli, Kevin 790
Minor, Jack 198
Minor, Laura C 903
Minor, Robin 765
Minow, Martha L 808
Minow, Mary 816
Minthorn, Cisco 709
Minton, Jeff 832
Minton, Kaylin 86
Minton, Shira 832
Mintz, Eric O 800
Mintz, Tom 189
Minutillo, Maryann 827
Mir, Aimen 614
Miranda, Christine E 397
Miranda, Norma 303
Miranda, Steven 785
Miras, Floyd 754
Mirfakhrai, Samine 371
Mirza, Anum 511
Mirza, Omair 103
Misback, Ann E 785
Miscimarra, Philip A 817
Mish, Stephen 846
Mishkin, Kelsey 11
Missal, Michael 769
Mitchell, A. Wess 602
Mitchell, Anthony "Tony" 642
Mitchell, Cindy G 649
Mitchell, Darphaus 636
Mitchell, Jodi 515
Mitchell, John 389
Mitchell, Linda 505
Mitchell, M. Delores 646
Mitchell, Mary 675
Mitchell, MaryKay 795
Mitchell, Maureen 459
Mitchell, Meredith 832
Mitchell, Paul 140, 309, 342, 406, 407, 434, 435, 443, 444, 445, 493

Page
Mitchell, Robert E 587
Mitchell, Roger 909
Mitchell, Sean 664
Mitchell, Todd 173
Mitchell, Will 148
Mitchell-Rankin, Zinora 905
Mitnick, John 775
Mitrano, Catherine 769
Mitsui, Mark 765
Mittal, Anang 392
Mittelhauser, Mark 724
Mittelstaedt, Oliver 380
Mitten, Ray, Jr 728
Mitterhoff, Mary Louise 903
Mittler, Michelle 392
Mitton, Chris 748
Mixon, Clint J 586
Miyasato, Diane 83
Miyazaki, Masato 950
Mize, Gregory E 905
Mize, Lawrence 784
Mizelle, Chad 657
Mkwezalamba, Maxwell M 924
Mladenov, Nickolay 947
Mlambo-Ngcuka, Phumzile 941
Mnuchin, Steven T 591, 594, 611, 802, 817, 830
Moakley, John Joseph 857
Moaney, Lynn 693
Moar, Ian 729
Moats, Bruce 952
Modari, Gordon 651
Modder, Don 695
Modeste, Brian 433
Modly, Thomas B 651, 654
Modrow, Eric 688
Modzelewski, James 660
Moe, Kari 146
Moebius-Clune, Bianca 697
Moeglein, Vivian 18
Moffatt, Kyle 832
Moffet, Erin 65
Moffitt, Melissa 465
Moffitt, Steve 218
Moger, Daniel 615
Moghtader, Lailee 614
Mohamed, Mohamed 910
Mohammed, Amina 949
Mohammed, Amina J 939
Mohammed, Haruna 951
Mohan, Katherine 683
Mohieldin, Mahmoud 949
Mohler, Hallock N., Jr 621
Mohler, Stefanie 75
Mohorovic, Joseph 788
Mohr, Jason 746
Mojarrad, Jafar 924
Molander, Chris 839
Moley, Kevin Edward 603
Molina, Joaquin 934
Molledo, Luis 919
Moller, Michael 940
Moller, Robert 714
Mollet, Kristin 46
Molloy, Marjorie 515
Molloy, Paula 847
Molloy, Robert 820
Molnar, Mike 720
Molofsky, Josh 392
Molpus, Anna 799
Molt, Alicia 294
Momber, Any 638
Monaco, Kristen 723
Monahan, Brian P 463
Monahan, Edward J 638
Monahan, Tim 405
Monahan, William G.P 356, 357
Mondl, Rachel 411
Monge, Katherine 460
Monger, Jon 416
Monica, Jeff 785
Monico, Tim Del 169
Monie, Alex 370
Monje, Carlos 423
Monogue, Sean 639
Monroe, Christina 351
Monroe, David 612
Monroe, Johnathan 701, 736
Montanio, Pat 715, 716

Page

Montano, Alfonso, Jr 820
Montano, Trevor 613
Monteith, Kris 796
Monteith, Steve 848
Montemarano, Anthony 625
Montero, Jose T 737
Montgomery, Christa 155
Montgomery, Clay 115
Montgomery, Cynthia 705
Montgomery, Mark 353, 354, 355
Montgomery, Sharnell 724
Montiel, Gina 916
Montoya, Ruth 271
Montoya-Picazo, Ricardo 97
Montz, Robert 649
Moodie, Michael L 588
Moody, Mary 270
Moody, Vanessa 15
Moolenaar, John R 137, 309, 341, 402, 403, 404, 493
Moomau, Pamela 469
Moon, Amber 135
Moon, Danielle 261
Mooney, Alexander X 291, 313, 341, 418, 419, 494
Mooney, Andrew 95
Mooney, Brandon 415
Mooney, Michael P 586
Mooney, Richard 639
Mooppan, Hashim 660
Moore, Allison 749
Moore, Brad 225
Moore, C. Maggie 427
Moore, Caleb 75
Moore, Calvin 43
Moore, Camlin 262
Moore, Camline 384
Moore, Carrie 617
Moore, Caryn 447
Moore, Cheryl 62
Moore, David H 843
Moore, Eugene 636
Moore, Gerald 750
Moore, Gerard 701
Moore, Gwen 295, 314, 336, 418, 419, 494, 504, 507
Moore, Jay 395
Moore, Jessica 67
Moore, Joanne 643
Moore, John D 870
Moore, John T., Jr 921
Moore, Jonathan 452
Moore, Joseph 780
Moore, Julie S 847
Moore, Karen 393
Moore, Karen Nelson 857
Moore, Katie 109
Moore, Kimberly A 866
Moore, Kimberly P 712
Moore, Maggie 442
Moore, Mark 371
Moore, Megan 798
Moore, Michelle 699
Moore, Patricia 691
Moore, Rachel 469
Moore, Sean 383
Moore, Shannice 510
Moore, Sherriann C 683
Moore, Taurus 395
Moore, Wayne 693
Moore, William F 647
Moosally, Fred 910
Moose, George E 845
Moossy, Robert 661
Mora, Steve 675
Moragne, Jeffrey 769
Morales, Alma 934
Morales, Christian 934
Morales, Mauro A 843
Morales, Ritzy 174
Moran, Bill 654
Moran, Catherine A 464
Moran, Emilio F 820
Moran, Guillermo 918
Moran, Janet 795
Moran, Jerry 108, 308, 329, 331, 347, 348, 349, 359, 360, 362, 363, 367, 368, 384, 385, 478, 501
Moran, John A 799
Moran, Kelsey 69
Moran, Mike 240
Moran, Robert 375

Page

Moran, Sean 427, 468
Moravec, Charles 614
Moreau-Lafleur, Shirlee 72
Morehouse, Mark 408
Morella, Constance ''Connie'' 509, 782
Moreno, Luis Alberto 916
Morenz, John 841
Moretti, Scott 605
Morfitt, Mary 636
Morgan, Aaron 838
Morgan, Andrew S 642
Morgan, Ashley 368
Morgan, Christian 154
Morgan, Debra 514
Morgan, Earl 764
Morgan, Hallee Katherine 420
Morgan, Jeff 191
Morgan, Keith 794
Morgan, Matt 1, 391, 430, 593
Morgan, Morris 617
Morgan, Regina 754
Morgan, Richard 922
Morgan, Sarah 389
Morgan, Ted 711
Morgan, Teri 427
Morhard, James W 394
Moriarty, Maureen 52
Morin, Normin 785
Morin, Robert A 792
Morin, Robert E 904
Moritz, Nancy L 858
Mork, David 91
Mork, Kirsten J 420
Morley, Andrew 411
Morley, Frank D 654
Morley, Katie 17
Morris, Booker 260
Morris, Charisa 686
Morris, Craig 706
Morris, David 766
Morris, Doug 688
Morris, Erin 706
Morris, John B., Jr 720
Morris, Karen 830
Morris, Patricia 923
Morris, Tom 739
Morris, Tracy 921
Morris, Willis 747
Morris-Skeete, Cheryl Anita 917
Morrison, James W 847
Morrison, Jeffry 807
Morrison, Jonathan 754
Morrison, Lale 69
Morrison, Liz 588
Morrison, Richard T 889
Morrison, Timothy 408
Morrison, Truman A. III 905
Morrissey, Brian 657
Morrissey, Jack 100
Morrissey, Molly 143
Morrow, Brett 146
Morrow, Dixie 633
Morrow, George W 810
Morrow, Jennifer 30
Morrow, Seth 3
Morrow, William S., Jr 908
Morse, Anne Nishimura 507
Morse, Chandler 9
Morse, Robert D 903
Morse, Sara 733
Morton, Andy 409
Morton, Keith 815
Moschetto, Thomas 823
Moschkin, Lydia 753
Mosebey, Tracy G 446
Moseley, Kimberly 798, 799
Moser, William 605
Moses, Charles T. III 679
Mosher, David E 583
Moskowitz, Charlie 378
Moskowitz, Lucas 831
Moss, Jonathan P 748
Moss, Randolph D 874
Mote, C.D. ''Dan'', Jr 819
Motl, David 619
Motley, Thomas J 905
Mott, John M 905
Motta, Wendy 31

Page
Motyka, Susan 783
Motz, Diana Gribbon 857
Moughalian, Jen 734
Moulton, Lisa 32
Moulton, Seth 132, 309, 341, 406, 407, 409, 494
Mouritsen, Karen 688
Moury, Matthew 759
Mousa, Jay 723
Moustafa, Hoda 953
Mowry, Sharon L 784
Moxley, Kim 385
Moxley, Sarah 436
Moy, Richard 922
Moya, Rafael 839
Moyer, Brian 710
Moyer, Jensine 108
Moyerman, Amber 298
Moylan, Christopher 28
Moynihan, Timothy 779
Mozden, Mike 388
Mozhin, Aleksei V 924
Mucchetti, Michael J 270
Mucchetti, Peter J 658
Muchmoore, Tim 648
Muchow, Dan 378
Muchow, Stefanie 392
Mueller, Thomas 804
Mueller, Ursula 939
Muglia, Lauren 226
Muhleisen, Martin 923
Muilenburg, Bret 655
Muir, Lawrence L 595
Muir, Linda 405
Muirragui-Villagomez, Matthew 433
Mulach, Ronald 694
Mulcahy, Ryan 10
Mulcahy, Valerie 670
Mulder, Matt 201
Mulder, Matthew Kinley 420
Mulka, Stephanie 140
Mulkerrin, Margaret 461
Mulkey, Shelly A 905
Mulkins, Chris 378
Mull, Keigan 452
Mullaney, L. Daniel 596
Mullaney, Michael J 680
Mullarkey, D. Patrick 681
Mullarkey, Daniel 697
Mullen, Elise 368
Mullen, Timothy 785
Mullen-Roth, Barbara A 823
Muller, Cyril 950
Mulligan, Avery 368
Mulligan, Edward T 464
Mulligan, Kasia 223
Mullin, Markwayne 216, 311, 340, 413, 414, 415, 494
Mullinax, Cooper 80
Mullins, Billy 636
Mullins, Carol 723
Mullins, Grant 373
Mulrooney, John 664
Mulrow, Jeri M 678
Mulvaney, Mick 591, 595
Mulvey, Tim 423
Mumaw, Elizabeth 794
Mumford, Cara 353, 354
Mummaw, Karen 605
Munday, Merrick 459, 469
Munevar, Felipe 942
Munisamy, Gopinath "Gopi" 705
Munisteri, Stephen 598
Munoz, Brigitte A 848
Munoz, Charles 790
Munoz, Rene 425
Munoz, Rogelio Sotela 932
Munshi, Kaizad 780
Munzu, Simon 945
Murat, Bill 293, 388
Murfitt, Lucy 366
Murguia, Mary H 858
Murillo, David 690
Murkowski, Lisa 7, 305, 329, 330, 347, 348, 349, 365, 374, 385, 478, 507
Murphy, Aaron 159
Murphy, Amy 254
Murphy, Beth 772
Murphy, Carol 404
Murphy, Chris 755

Page
Murphy, Christopher 51, 306, 327, 331, 347, 349, 372, 373, 374, 388, 478, 494, 501
Murphy, Colleen 811
Murphy, Damian 373
Murphy, Daniel 514
Murphy, Darren 749
Murphy, Diana E 858
Murphy, Elizabeth 194, 832
Murphy, Emily W 781, 802, 813, 816
Murphy, Frank 719
Murphy, James R 817
Murphy, Jason 82
Murphy, Jim 683
Murphy, Jolyn 40
Murphy, Kathy 617
Murphy, Katie 455
Murphy, Marcia 657
Murphy, Marietta 784
Murphy, Mary Beth 618, 795
Murphy, Meg 373
Murphy, Melissa 199
Murphy, Michael R 858
Murphy, Patrick 602
Murphy, Phil 231
Murphy, Philip D 789
Murphy, Richard 635
Murphy, Sheila A 894
Murphy, Stephanie N 61, 306, 342, 406, 407, 441, 501
Murphy, Thomas J 631, 772
Murphy, Westbrook 806
Murray, Alexis 411
Murray, Brenda 833
Murray, Carol 449
Murray, Christopher 654
Murray, Christopher D 786
Murray, DaNita 346
Murray, Darlene 188
Murray, David 740
Murray, Ed 516
Murray, Edward 653, 771
Murray, Ellen 350
Murray, James 701
Murray, Jerome 303
Murray, John M 647
Murray, Kathy 5
Murray, Michael 657
Murray, Patty 284, 313, 329, 330, 347, 348, 349, 361, 374, 384, 393, 478
Murray, Renard 738
Murray, Rob 149
Murrin, Suzanne 735
Murry, Emily 452
Murry, Luke 459
Murtaugh, Tim 693
Murtha, Laura 64
Murthy, Ram 849
Murthy, Veena 469
Muscolini, John 257
Musel, David 682
Musgrave, R. Kenton 881
Musgrove, Rebekah J 397
Mushingi, Tuli Salama 607
Mushingi, Tulinabo Salama 609
Muskovitz, Benjamin 698
Mussa, Hassen Ebrahim 946
Musselman, Patricia T 712
Mustard, Allan Phillip 609
Mutter, Andrew 623, 792
Muzeroll, Kim 93
Myers, Amanda 630
Myers, Baylor 611
Myers, Christina 707
Myers, Dean 195
Myers, Jacqueline 703
Myers, Justus 467
Myers, Kenneth A. III 626
Myers, Lewis 212
Myers, Matt 921
Myers, Mindy 387
Myers, N. Lenette 89
Myers, Ryan 375
Myers-Mutschall, Sarah 417
Myhre, Allison 147
Mylott, Lauren 70
Myrick, Bismarck 719
Myrick, Gary 397

N

Page

Nabarro, David 948
Nachtigal, Gayle A 841
Nada, Basmah 389
Nadal, Jacob 590
Nadeau, Brianne 907
Nadler, Jerrold 185, 310, 333, 428, 494
Naessens, Katie 346
Naficy, Homa 816
Naft, Mike 165
Nagle, Cathy 235
Nagle, Patrick 838
Nagle, Paul 415
Nahom, David 629
Naik, Nitin S 711
Najieb-Locke, Halimah 442
Naka, Hiroshi 950
Nakamitsu, Izumi 939
Nakamura, Keisuke 917
Nakazawa, Zenji 794
Nalbandian, John B 841
Nalepa, Jessica 256, 778
Nalls, Dennis 460
Nambiar, Vijay 947
Nance, Laura 695
Nance, Robert 241
Nance, Scott 350
Naniole, Ainoa 84
Napier, Ben 460
Napolitano, Grace F 35, 306, 335, 431, 432, 443, 444, 445, 446, 494
Narasaki, Karen 843
Narode, Dane M 745
Naron, Cameron 753
Nash, Douglas 693
Nassif, Marybeth 405
Nation, Kayla 260
Natonski, Dave 110
Natsuhara, Roger 653
Nauert, Heather 604
Navaro, Ann 690
Navarro, Erica 767
Navarro, Peter 598
Navia, Daniela A 397
Nawrocki, Jenifer 59
Naylor, Chris 111
Naylor, Mary 276
Naylor, Richard A 783
Ndikum, Alex 156
Neal, Andrew S 464
Neal, Arthur 706
Neal, Brian 630
Neal, David L 669
Neal, Kristina 670
Neal, Nicole L 636
Neal, Rebecca 292
Neal, Richard E 129, 309, 333, 450, 469, 471, 494
Neale, Brian 738
Nealon, James D 777
Neary, William T 671
Nebeker, Frank Q 904
Nedd, Mike 688
Nedzar, Tamar 417
Needham, Michael 57
Neely, Amanda 378
Neely, Andrew 364
Nega, Daniel L 654
Nega, Joseph W 890
Negrete, Juan 392
Negron, Juan 207
Neiderhiser, Patricia 826
Neidorff, Michael F 807
Neill, Andrew 287
Neill, Jim 392
Neill, Samuel 629
Neilson, Nicole 245
Neis, Robert 617
Neller, R.B 656
Nellor, Dianne 350
Nelson, April 728
Nelson, Bill 57, 306, 327, 330, 352, 362, 369, 370, 387, 388, 478, 509
Nelson, Damon 454
Nelson, David J 822
Nelson, Dorothy W 858
Nelson, Edward 784
Nelson, Elizabeth 707
Nelson, Emma 455

Page

Nelson, John D 650
Nelson, Kathleen A 644
Nelson, Keith 747, 748
Nelson, Naomi 813
Nelson, Poppy 137
Nelson, Reid J 781
Nelson, Richard 697
Nelson, Ryan 242
Nelson, Samantha 350
Nelson, Samuel David 640
Nelson, Sarah 740
Nemeth, Alison 794
Nenon, Sharynne 698
Nersesian, Mallory 378
Nesbitt, LaQuandra 908
Nesbitt, Wanda 605, 627
Nesmeyer, Diane E 397
Nesmith, Travis 784
Nesseler, Kerry 739
Nester, John 833
Nesvet, Jeffrey L 728
Neubauer, Ellen 613
Neubauer, Kurt 637
Neubert, Michael 589
Neuendorf, Michele L 848
Neufeld, Donald 780
Neufeld, Michael 615
Neufville, Nadine M 683
Neumayr, Mary 594
Neunlist, Ed 670
Neustadt, Marla 826
Nevarez, Rafael 766
New, Nancy 698
Newberger, Tamar 844
Newby, Brian 844
Newby, Darek 405
Newell, Rob 652
Newell, Russell 685
Newhouse, Dan 286, 313, 341, 402, 403, 404, 437, 494
Newman, Emily 739
Newman, Jacqui 456
Newman, Jon O 857
Newman, Pauline 865
Newman, Phillip 748
Newman, Theodore R., Jr 904
Newsham, Peter 909
Newstead, Jennifer Gillian 602
Newton, Andrew 350, 616
Newton, Jonathan 469
Newton, Patrick 246
Neymour, Chet 931
Nguyen, Alex 38, 457
Nguyen, Hong 350
Nguyen, Jacqueline H 858
Nguyen, Lynn 847
Nguyen, Tom 784
Nguyen, Tommy 375
Nguyen, Tony 686
Niceta, Rickie 597
Nichola, Mike 62
Nicholls, Richard 736
Nichols, Ashley 115, 433
Nichols, Kristine 178
Nichols, Marc 755
Nichols, Megan 936
Nichols, Nils 761
Nichols, Nina 798
Nicholson, Ian 371
Nickel, Ryan 167
Nickerson, Joe 804
Nickerson, Valerie A 666
Nickson, Julie 26
Niederee, Katie 108, 370
Nield, George C 751
Nielsen, Kirstjen M 591, 775, 781
Niemeyer, Lucian 622
Niemeyer, Paul V 857
Nierle, James 653
Nies-Vogel, Karen 712
Nieves-Lee, Lila 452
Nifosi, Dana 753
Nigaglioni, Angel 188
Nigam, Nita 745
Nigro, Bernard 658
Nikas, Katherine 380
Niles, Jennifer 907
Nilsson, Brian 604
Nimetz, Matthew 947

Page

Ninichuk, Martha 814
Nintemann, Terri 703
Nishida, Jane 791
Nishikata, Kenichi 951
Nishiura, Katherine 699
Nissenbaum, Paul 752
Niu, Steve 827
Nixon, Kathleen 817
Nixon, Natalie 437
Noack, Sarah 258
Noblet, Michael J 356, 357
Noel, Roger 796
Noel, Tiffany 5
Noelker, Tim 788
Noem, Kristi L 242, 312, 338, 450, 451, 494
Noh, Andrew 36
Nolan, Edwin 609
Nolan, Emmitt 76
Nolan, Lloyd U 905
Nolan, Matthew 467
Nolan, Richard M 147, 309, 337, 399, 400, 443, 444, 445, 494
Nolt, Dorie 765
Nolta, Christy 638
Nolte, Timothy 634
Noonan, Bob 803
Noonan, Mary McDermott 171
Nooter, William 905
Norby, Stephanie L 836
Norcom, Henry 705
Norcross, Donald 169, 310, 340, 406, 407, 410, 411, 471, 494
Nordquist, DJ 593
Nordquist, Jeremy 10
Noreika, Keith 797
Norfleet, Jessica 59
Norman, Corey 273
Norman, Kim 505
Norman, Ralph 240, 312, 342, 438, 439, 441, 442, 494
Norman, Russell 440
Norment, Lucy 282
Noronha, Gabriel 353
Norquist, David 622
Norris, Alan E 857
Norris, Andrea T 740, 741
Norris, Jane 738
Norris, Trevor 616
Norsworthy, Levator, Jr 643
North, Tracey A 673
Northcross, Chris 389
Northern, Jayne 470
Northey, William 697
Northrop, Alison B 425
Norton, Eleanor Holmes 300, 314, 343, 434, 443, 444, 445, 494
Norton, Nancy 625
Noruk, Alexa 378
Nosal, Tim 782
Nothern, Lindsay 85
Noti, Adrienne 905
Notter, Jim 126
Noudehou, Alain 946
Nour, Amr 941
Nour, Ashraf El 925
Novak, Christian 917
Novak, Sheila 694
Novoa, Raul 917
Novy, Ari E 590
Novy, Davy B 632
Novy, Steve 734
Nowakowski, Judy 689
Nowland, Mark 635
Nuebel-Kovarik, Kathy 780
Nunan, Joanna 936
Nunan, Joanna M 780
Nunes, Devin 30, 306, 335, 450, 451, 453, 469, 494
Nunez, Christina 270
Nunez, Jose 921
Nunez, Manuel 806
Nunn, Tey Marianna 816
Nussbaumer, James A 800
Nuttall, Robert 6
Nutter, Olivia 383
Nuzzi, Rebecca 378
Nygaard, Richard L 857
Nylander, Dag Halvor 946
Nysted, Tina 749

O

Page

O'Boyle, Nicholas 111
O'Brien, Abigail 13
O'Brien, Bill 815
O'Brien, Corenna 122
O'Brien, Dan 713
O'Brien, Holley 683
O'Brien, John 734
O'Brien, Mark 644
O'Brien, Melissa 470
O'Brien, Patrick J 623
O'Brien, Terrence L 858
O'Brien, Tom 405
O'Connell, Charles 637
O'Connell, Richie 433
O'Connor, Carolyn 693
O'Connor, Christopher E 770
O'Connor, Dennis 619
O'Connor, Erin 695
O'Connor, George 94
O'Connor, Jennifer 452
O'Connor, Julia 287
O'Connor, Kevin 680
O'Connor, Sandra Day 855
O'Connor, Sean 508
O'Dell, Greg 911
O'Donnell, Carol 836
O'Donnell, David 636
O'Donnell, Denise E 678
O'Donnell, Douglas 618
O'Donnell, Jerry 35
O'Donnell, Michael 751
O'Donnell, Shawn 702
O'Halleran, Tom 9, 305, 342, 399, 400, 406, 407, 408, 494
O'Hanlon, Ann 281
O'Hara, Amy 711
O'Hara, John 360
O'Hara, Tracie 245
O'Harra, Michael 750
O'Hearn, Donald P 682
O'Herin, Zoe 281
O'Kane, Edward 903
O'Keefe, Gerald B 644
O'Keefe, Kevin 604
O'Keefe, Michael R 905
O'Keefe, Sean 353, 354, 355
O'Keefe, Shannon 404
O'Laughlin, Margaret 846
O'Leary, Karin 903
O'Leary, Katie 393
O'Malley, Adam 714
O'Malley, Kathleen M 866
O'Malley, Kevin P 756
O'Mara, Raymond 125
O'Neal, David 240
O'Neil, Christopher 820
O'Neil, Jaclyn 215
O'Neil, Kathleen S 658
O'Neill, Barbara 818
O'Neill, Kristen 266
O'Neill, Stephen 707
O'Quinn, Erin 23
O'Quinn, Robert 451
O'Rielly, Michael P 794
O'Rourke, Beto 258, 313, 340, 406, 407, 448
O'Rourke, Kathleen J 806
O'Rourke, Marie 670
O'Scannlain, Diarmuid F 858
O'Scannlain, Kate 727
O'Sullivan, Dylan 132
O'Toole, Ryan 459
Obama, Michelle 807
Oberleitner, Robert 717
Obermann, Richard 440
Obermiller, Chad 23
Obernesser, Rick 687
Obscura, Julio 461
Obstfeld, Maurice 923
Ocampo, Roger 722
Ochoa, Carol F 805
Ochoa, Christine C 39
Ochoa, Ellen 811, 820
Ochylski, Daniel 452
Odegaard, J 651
Odegard, Kirk 783
Odom, Anita J 642
Odom, Clint 19

Page
Odom, Jefferson 226
Oehmen, Jon 259
Oestfield, Marc 605
Oetker, Mike 686
Offutt, Brett 708
Offutt, Denison 936
Ofosu, Asi 185
Ogden, J. Anthony 785
Oglesby, Ted L 811
Ogunyipe, Benro 814
Oh, Sam 41
Ohlhausen, Maureen K 801
Ohlson, Kevin A 895
Ohly, John 415
Ohm, Angela 405
Ohman, Mynda 634
Ohr, Bruce G 657
Ohri, Mukta 590
Okamoto, Geoffrey "Geoff" 614
Okolo, Osaremen 375
Okoro, Sandie 949
Okun, Robert D 905
Okuyiga, Andrew 447
Old Crow, Alexa 446, 447
Oldham-Moore, Charlotte 373
Olds, James L 820
Olechowski, Mark 784
Oleskowicz, John F 676
Olijar, Leonard R 617
Olin, Jason 425
Oliva, Judith B 632
Oliva, Tomas 44
Oliver, Chris 715
Oliver, Jan 442
Oliver, Linzie T 825
Oliver, Ramona 728
Oliver, Stacie 373
Oliver, Stephen "Steve" 629
Ollen-Smith, James L 397
Olmstead, Megan 433
Olsavsky, Patricia H 397
Olsen, Elizabeth 368
Olsen, Erika 796
Olsen, Jody 827
Olsen, Susan 15
Olson, Andy 373
Olson, Eric 616
Olson, James C 595
Olson, Kathryn 452
Olson, Lyndon, Jr 843
Olson, Maria 387
Olson, Nina E 618
Olson, Pete 262, 313, 337, 413, 414, 494
Olson, Timothy P 711
Olszewski, Robert 717
Olthoff, Jim 720
Oman, Eric 370
Omer, Angela 237
Onanga-Anyanga, Parfait 944
Onusko, James C 824
Onwubiko, Udochi 412
Onyeije, Karen 795
Ophaso, Farouk 409
Oppenheim, Peter 767
Oppenheimer, Deborah A 844
Ordaz, Vonna 822
Orlando, Jason 614
Orme-Zavaleta, Jennifer 791
Orner, Jeffery 777
Orozco, Sylvia 816
Orr, Derek 720
Orr, Jen 842
Orr, Jennifer 790
Orr, L. Renee 688
Orr, Martha 771
Orr, Robert 948
Orrock, Patricia C 797
Orsini, Nick 711
Ortega, Dennis 469
Ortega, Ronald 586
Ortiz, Alex 8
Ortiz, Hankie 687
Ortiz, Kevin 436
Ortiz, Luis 303
Ortiz, Mauricio 711
Ortiz, Melissa 736
Ortiz, Raho 740
Ortner, Charles B 807
Ortner, Eric P 844
Orzechowski, Jeff 427
Osborne, Christopher 464
Osborne, Janine 198
Osborne, Jason 670
Osborne, Nate 636
Osborne, Renn 425
Osbourne, Sheila 807
Osmond, Kari 176
Osterberg, Gayle 588
Ostro, Zachary 89
Ostros, Thomas 924
Ostrowski, John 516
Ostrowski, Paul A 642
Osuna, Juan P 669
Oswald, Justin 183
Oteh, Arunma 949
Otero, Carin 771
Otero, Jose 230
Otero, Miguel 73
Ott, Alan 296
Ott, Kathleen G 588
Otte, Jill M 729
Otten, Brad 243
Ottignon, D.A 656
Otting, Joseph M 617
Otto, Allison M 397
Otto, Robert 634
Oubichon, Michon 706
Ouertatani, Charla 420
Oulton, Scott 665
Oursler, Leonard 618
Oursler, Tara 124
Outterson, Sara 131
Overbeek, Kimberly 409
Overend, Christopher 469
Owen, Gary 664
Owen, John 840
Owen, Matt 378
Owen, Priscilla R 857
Owen, Suzanne 127, 436
Owen, Todd 778
Owendoff, James 759
Owens, Andrea 787
Owens, Annie 380
Owens, Frances 517
Owens, Glenda H 689
Owens, James C., Jr 748
Owens, John B 858
Owens, John B. II 719
Owens, Robert 735
Owens, Sharon 848
Owens, Tyler 350
Owusu, Eugene 946
Ozdinec, Milan 744

P

Paape, William 753
Pace, Davis 260
Pacheco, Lucas 920
Pachon, Juan 373
Paciello, Nicole 181
Pack, Nancy 262
Packer, Shawn 727
Packnett, Patrick 699
Pacula, Anna 665
Padilla, Diane 433
Padilla, Edwin Oswaldo Vides 916
Padilla, Frederick 626
Padilla, Luis 739
Padilla, Nicolas 745
Padro-Raldiris, Marieli 302
Padron, Enrique 73
Paese, Mark 715, 716
Paez, Richard A 858
Paffenback, Jean 446
Pagano, Patrizio 950
Page, Snider 659
Page, Susan D 946
Paguni, Rosemary E 681
Pahl, Thomas B 802
Pahls, Eric 109
Pai, Ajit 794
Paige, Dana 678
Paige, Thomas A 728
Paine, Stuart 380
Painter-Jacquess, Karen 702

Page

Pairis, Janine ... 44
Pais, Marta Santos ... 949
Paiva, Joe ... 713
Palacio, Monica ... 910
Palafox, Rocio ... 917
Palasits, Sara ... 440
Palazzo, Steven M ... 152, 309, 338, 402, 403, 494
Palensky, Michael L ... 711
Palian, Robert ... 590
Palisi, Alyssa ... 452
Pallone, Frank, Jr ... 172, 310, 333, 413, 494
Palmen, Brynn ... 164
Palmer, Ashley ... 351, 733
Palmer, Ashli ... 461
Palmer, Carrie ... 267
Palmer, D. Alec ... 797
Palmer, Gary J ... 5, 305, 341, 409, 434, 435, 438, 494
Palmer, Scott ... 719
Palmer, Virginia E ... 608
Palmer, Wayne ... 726
Palmieri, Francisco ... 603
Palumbo, David ... 690
Palumbo, Michael G ... 785
Paluskiewicz, JP ... 415
Palya, Theresa C ... 784
Pan, Eric ... 788
Pan, Florence Y ... 905
Pananon, Israporn ... 686
Panchanathan, Sethuraman ... 820
Pandolfe, Frank C ... 624
Pandya, Nishith ... 89
Pane, Karen W ... 779
Panek, Miroslaw ... 924
Panetta, Jimmy ... 29, 306, 342, 399, 400, 401, 406, 407, 408, 494
Pannel, Madeleine ... 375
Pannocchia, Orlando J ... 729
Pannozzo, John R., Jr ... 799
Panone, Jennifer ... 405
Panuccio, Jesse M ... 658
Panuthos, Peter J ... 893
Pao, Jean Lin ... 746
Paoli, Jim ... 55
Paone, Stephanie ... 397
Pape, Lisa ... 772
Papian, Anthony ... 378
Papirmeister, Charles ... 380
Pappas, George ... 454
Pappas, Zannis ... 636
Paquin, Krista ... 808
Paras, Mark A. "Tony" ... 584, 585
Pardue, Liz ... 437
Parekh, Deven ... 847
Parekh, Mehul ... 818
Parella, Courtney ... 427
Parente, Laurent ... 921
Paret, Betsy ... 864
Parets, Brendan ... 389
Paretzky, Kenneth I ... 464
Parham-Hopson, Deborah ... 739
Paris, Elizabeth Crewson ... 889
Paris-Behr, Caroline ... 416
Parisi, Thomas ... 797
Park, Charles ... 432
Park, James ... 430
Park, Jeongseok ... 919
Park, Joon ... 704
Park, Laurie ... 771
Park, Victoria ... 468
Parker, Amy L ... 771
Parker, Barrington D., Jr ... 857
Parker, Basil ... 823
Parker, Chad ... 700, 701
Parker, Craig ... 937
Parker, Cynthia ... 754
Parker, Daniel ... 380
Parker, Darren ... 86
Parker, Elkin ... 708
Parker, Eloise K ... 711
Parker, Fred ... 633
Parker, Gregory ... 632
Parker, Irene ... 715
Parker, Jason ... 360
Parker, Kathleen M ... 398
Parker, Kevin ... 452
Parker, Kyle ... 423
Parker, Lewis F ... 826
Parker, Lindsey ... 907

Page

Parker, Rachel K ... 658
Parker, Sabrina ... 217
Parker, Sarah ... 433
Parker, Wyndee ... 460
Parkinson, Larry R ... 761
Parkinson, N. Roy ... 824
Parks, Bryan ... 664
Parks, Elizabeth ... 150
Parks, J. Gregory ... 805
Parks, Stephanie ... 452
Parlave, Valerie ... 674
Parmiter, Bobby ... 430
Parnell, Howard ... 794
Paroutsas, Aspasia ... 795
Parr, Steven ... 432
Parr, Ted L ... 719
Parratt, Shelley E ... 832
Parrish, Michael ... 728
Parrott, Charles ... 706
Parrott, Michael ... 433
Parry, Dan ... 841
Parry, Stephanie ... 633
Parsons, Jason ... 515
Parsons, Joe ... 705
Partee, Erin ... 208
Parthasarathy, Kalyani ... 464
Pary, Diego ... 932
Pasch, David ... 91
Pascocello, Dain ... 190
Pascoe, Cheri ... 364
Pascoe, Oral ... 916
Pascrell, Bill, Jr ... 174, 310, 334, 450, 451, 494
Pasi, Geeta ... 606
Pasichow, Heidi ... 905
Pasqualino, Donna L ... 397
Passalacqua, Lauren ... 387
Passantino, Stefan ... 599
Passino, John ... 699
Passmore, S. Wayne ... 785
Pasternak, Doug ... 440
Pataki, Timothy ... 597
Patankar-Stoll, Anita ... 796
Patchen, Elieka Kate ... 658
Pate, Randolph ... 738
Patel, Kash ... 454
Patel, Nirali ... 794
Patel, Rina ... 378
Patel, Saad ... 464
Patel-Weynand, Toral ... 696
Patella, Michael ... 594
Patenaude, Meghan ... 1, 391, 593
Patenaude, Pamela Hughes ... 743, 821
Pathak, Vivek ... 952
Patil, Jason S ... 833
Patinella, Ralph ... 840
Patout, Brad ... 353, 354, 355
Patriarca, Carmen ... 752
Patrick, Brian ... 136
Patrick, Dibattista ... 584
Patrick, Michelle ... 49
Patrick, Steven L ... 838
Patru, Katie ... 427
Patten, Pramila ... 949
Patterson, Clara ... 595
Patterson, Inmi ... 609
Patterson, L. Eric ... 776
Patterson, Mark ... 392
Patterson, Robert W ... 663
Pattison, Brian ... 746
Patton, Cynthia ... 45
Patton, Lynne M ... 746
Patton, Roderick ... 110
Patton, Sean ... 518
Paul, Rand ... 112, 308, 329, 331, 372, 373, 374, 377, 383, 478
Paul, Sarah Timoney ... 164
Paul, William ... 618
Paul-Bryant, Towanda ... 912
Paull, Douglas ... 773
Paulsen, Erik ... 145, 309, 337, 450, 451, 467, 494
Pausch, Patricia ... 750
Pavlick, Stephen ... 616
Pavlik, Ronald ... 850
Pavlock, Cara ... 53
Pawlak, Brian ... 715
Pawlak, Micheal T ... 849
Pawlow, Jonathan R ... 447
Pawlowski, Michael ... 7

Page

Paxman, Dalton G ... 736
Payne, Alexander ... 412
Payne, Avis ... 838
Payne, Chelsey ... 263
Payne, Donald M., Jr ... 174, 310, 338, 424, 425, 443, 444, 445, 494
Payne, Grayford ... 690
Payne, James O., Jr ... 719
Payne, Jeff ... 715
Payne, John ... 637
Payne, Michael D ... 635
Payne, Nina M ... 639
Payne, Suzanne ... 840
Payne, William ... 381
Payton, Rayshon ... 388
Paz y Paz, Claudia ... 933
Peacock, Penne K ... 843
Pearce, Drue ... 755
Pearce, Krisann ... 411
Pearce, Mark Gaston ... 817
Pearce, Stevan ... 178, 310, 336, 418, 419, 420, 431, 432, 494
Pearlstein, Arthur ... 801
Pearson, Charles A ... 717, 718
Pearson, Christa ... 64
Pearson, Cyrus ... 390
Pearson, Ervin ... 772
Pearson, Lisa ... 805
Pearson, Margaret P ... 824
Pearson, Nick ... 842
Pearson, Scott ... 911
Pearson, Stephen ... 785
Pearson, Tim ... 429
Pearson, Tina ... 513
Pearson, Trevor ... 11
Pearson, Victoria ... 826
Pease, Edward A ... 510
Peaster, Josh ... 392
Peavler, David ... 834
Peccia, James D ... 631
Peck, Sarah ... 276
Pecoraro, Brandon ... 469
Pede, Charles N ... 649
Pedersen, Chris ... 718
Pederson, Cynthia ... 822
Peede, Jon Parrish ... 815, 816, 851
Peede, Robert ... 598
Peifer, Ann ... 33
Peiper, Pam ... 286
Peirce, Hester M ... 831
Peirce, Jeffret R ... 786
Peisch, Greta ... 371
Pekkala, Jonathan ... 65
Pekoske, David P ... 778
Pekrul, Mark R ... 824
Pelczar, Alex ... 121
Pelgro, Michael ... 839
Pelitere, Tara Tinsley ... 785
Pell, Susan K ... 590
Pellecchia, Anna ... 173
Pellegrino, Amy ... 387
Pelletier, Jonathan ... 670
Pelletier, Justin ... 184
Pelletier, Nina ... 676
Pelletier, Pat ... 140
Pellettiere, Christopher A ... 659
Pelosi, Nancy ... 25, 306, 333, 455, 456, 460, 494, 507, 510, 807
Pelter, Jeremy ... 710
Peltz-Strauss, Karen ... 794
Peluso, Elizabeth ... 382
Pempel, T.J ... 507
Penaroza, Kainoa ... 84
Pence, Karen M ... 785
Pence, Michael R ... 591
Pence, Mike ... 1, 391, 593, 594, 835
Pence, Robert F ... 607
Pendle, David ... 381
Penland, Michael ... 633
Penn, Damon ... 778
Penna, Alyssa ... 174
Pennington, Amy ... 286
Pennington, Rebecca ... 752
Pennock, Jonathan ... 716
Peoples, Dovarius L ... 824, 825
Pepin, Andrew J ... 767
Peraertz, Louis ... 794
Peralta, Gabriel Aguilera ... 932

Page

Perbohner, Robert M ... 848
Percival, Barrett ... 378
Percival, Emily ... 63
Percival, James ... 658
Perdue, David ... 75, 307, 328, 331, 345, 346, 352, 353, 359, 361, 470, 478, 835
Perdue, Kathy ... 829
Perdue, Sonny ... 508, 591, 691
Perea, Omar ... 515
Pereida, Jose ... 269
Pereira, Ariel ... 745
Peres, Flavio ... 803
Peretti, Brian ... 612
Pereyra-Vera, Maria ... 378
Perez, Alex ... 433
Perez, Amanda ... 388
Perez, Carol ... 606
Perez, Jazmin ... 262
Perez, Jerome ... 688
Perez, Julio Ernesto Florian ... 916
Perez, Megan ... 287
Perez, Michele ... 847
Perez, Paloma ... 268
Perez, Robert ... 778
Perez, Simon ... 364
Perez, Simone ... 446
Perez-Acosta, Mehgan ... 170
Perez-Davis, Marla E ... 810
Perez-Grines, Katherine ... 785
Perez-Stable, Eliseo J ... 741
Perkins, Brian ... 26
Perkins, Michael ... 380
Perkins, Trudy ... 127
Perlak, Joseph R ... 897
Perlman, Dana M ... 844
Perlman, Helaine ... 669
Perlmutter, Ed ... 49, 306, 336, 418, 420, 438, 439, 494
Perlmutter, Shira ... 718
Perlow, Jarrett B ... 870
Perna, Gustave "Gus" ... 650
Perriello, Tami ... 755
Perrine, Erin ... 459
Perrino, Jenny ... 211
Perro, Catherine ... 629
Perry, Anna ... 28
Perry, Beverly ... 907
Perry, Bill ... 727
Perry, Catherine D ... 901
Perry, James Richard ... 591
Perry, James Richard "Rick" ... 759
Perry, Michael ... 229
Perry, Richard ... 237
Perry, Robert ... 697
Perry, Ryan ... 652
Perry, Scott ... 225, 312, 340, 421, 422, 424, 425, 443, 444, 445, 495
Perry, Tracy ... 695
Perryman, Sean ... 436
Persaud, Clifton ... 464
Perselay, Lee ... 722
Persico, Timothy ... 189
Pesante, Kiara ... 411
Peschka, Mary Porter ... 952
Peska, Kevin ... 718
Pete, Darren ... 687
Peters, David J ... 711
Peters, Gary C ... 135, 309, 328, 331, 352, 353, 362, 363, 377, 467, 478, 506
Peters, Gregory T ... 676
Peters, Jacob ... 45
Peters, Joseph R., Jr ... 903
Peters, Morgan ... 396
Peters, Scott H ... 44, 306, 340, 413, 414, 415, 448, 495
Petersen, Alana ... 143
Petersen, Matthew S ... 797
Petersen, Michael D ... 637
Petersen, Molly ... 767
Petersen, Scott ... 27
Petersen, Steve ... 272
Petersen, Steven ... 716
Peterson, Andrew ... 408
Peterson, Collin C ... 147, 309, 333, 399, 495
Peterson, Elizabeth ... 589
Peterson, Erik ... 425
Peterson, G.P. "Bud" ... 820
Peterson, Jacob ... 296
Peterson, Jill ... 831
Peterson, Lisa ... 609

Page

Peterson, Mark 396
Peterson, Mike 396
Peterson, Sage 409
Peterson, Steven J 697
Peterson, Ted 455
Peterson, Thurman 664
Petit, Bryan 366
Peto, Lisa 420
Petracca, Ron 766
Petrella, Gerry 392
Petri, Tim 509
Petrick, David 506
Petrizzi, Maribeth 658
Petrosino-Wolverton, Marie 747
Petteway, Lance 702
Pettit, James D 608
Pettit, Nancy Bikoff 608
Pettitt, Mark 5
Petty, Randi 278
Petty, Timothy R 689
Petty, Ty 262
Petyo, Briana 777
Pew, Penny 11
Pfeifer, Joe 670
Pfeiffer, Amy Miller 461
Pfrang, Steven 98
Phalen, Charles S., Jr 824
Phalen, Susan 425, 778
Pham, Darwin 32
Phan, Michael 633
Phaup, Elliott 124
Phee, Molly 603
Phelan, Lisa M 658
Phelan, Michael 373
Phelan, Regis 778
Phelps, Ashley 94
Phelps, Jason 287
Phelps, Michael 710
Pheto, Beverly 53
Phifer, Kierra 284
Philcox, Crystal 618
Philips, Mariah 131
Philipson, Tomas 593
Phillip, Pam 701
Phillips, Clay 65
Phillips, Dennis L 823
Phillips, Elise 426
Phillips, Gregory A 858
Phillips, Heather 729
Phillips, John 839
Phillips, John L 612
Phillips, Julia M 819, 820
Phillips, Madolyn C 792, 793
Phillips, Marjorie 605
Phillips, Mary B 447
Phillips, Meg 812
Phillips, Sally 612, 734
Phillips, Todd 127, 436
Phillips, Troy 401
Phillips-Spencer, Anthony 932
Philpot, Christine 782
Philson, Christopher 653
Phipps, Jane 268
Phipps, Rae Ann 368
Piacentini, Joseph 725
Piatt, Jenn 380
Piazza, John 440
Pica, Joseph 716
Picanso, Renee 705
Picard, Michelle 719
Piccioli, Laura 97
Piche, Catherine 783
Pickel, Toni 76
Pickelsimer, Corey 699
Pickering, Jane 816
Pickett, Jeffrey 518
Picolla, Joseph C 464
Picozzi, Joe 460
Piehota, Christopher M 674
Pierce, Ann 425
Pierini, Daniel 951
Pierre, Cynthia 792
Pietrangeli, Fred 612
Pietrzyk, Joseph Pius 808
Piggee, Aundre F 647
Pilat, Jennifer 713
Pilato, Anna 736
Pilchen, Zach 368
Pile, Mathew 839
Pileggi, Anthony 191
Pileggi, Joe 455
Pilkerton, Chris 849
Pillard, Cornelia T.L 860
Pimenta, Sergio 952
Pimentel, Federico Hernandez 935
Pina, Oriana 62
Pincus, David I 681
Pinder, Anita 738
Pinder, Joe 420
Pineiro, Marlen 779
Pingree, Chellie 122, 308, 337, 402, 403, 495, 815
Pinheiro, Vinicius 923
Pinkard, Delice 918
Pinkerton, Michael 371
Pinkney, India 815
Pinkos, Steve 1, 391, 593
Pinkston, Brian 634
Pino, John 395
Pinson, Alex 115
Pintado, Oscar H 643
Pintar, MaryAnne 45
Pinto, Consuela 728
Pinto, John 801
Pinto, Nuno Mota 950
Pinzon, Zuleika 920
Piorkowski, Jennifer 219
Piper, Danielle Radovich 50
Piper, Robert 947
Piquado, Paul 713
Piraino, Janet 293
Piro, George 673
Pirzadeh, Michelle 792
Pittenger, Robert 200, 311, 340, 418, 419, 420, 495, 506
Pittman, Dean 608
Pittman, Heather 632
Pittman, Lisa 432
Pittman, Yogananda 518
Pitts, Floyd 782
Pitts, Kara 392
Piwowar, Michael S 831
Plack, Brendon 242, 390
Plager, S. Jay 869
Plaisier, Melinda 739
Plake, Lindsay 33
Planchet, Elise 385
Plancon, Timothy J 666
Plank, Jilian 30
Planning, David 460
Plante, Jeanette 677
Plasencia, Paul 722
Plaskett, Stacey E 303, 314, 343, 399, 400, 434, 435, 443, 444, 495
Plaster, Matthew 364
Plater, Angelina 464
Platt, Deana 777
Platt, Joel 710
Platt, Michael, Jr 709
Platt, Mike 248
Platt, Nancy 818
Plaus, Marianne 708
Pleffner, Mary 710
Plemmons, Beth 513
Plemmons, Ramona 624
Pletcher, Mary 689
Plick, Joseph J 728
Plumb, Thomas 810
Plummer, Charles L 638
Plummer, Melissa 285
Plunkett, Vickie 408
Pluviose, Veronique 411
Po, Rosa 143
Poblete, Yleem D.S 604
Pocan, Mark 294, 314, 340, 402, 404, 495
Pochet, German 918
Poder, Martin 951
Podewell, Stephanie 54
Podgorski, Elizabeth 411
Podonsky, Glenn 759
Poe, Ted 251, 312, 336, 421, 422, 428, 429, 495, 503
Poe, Virginia 65
Pogue, Donald C 882
Pohlad, Rebecca 807
Pohlmeier, Mark 632
Poindexter, Tonya 907
Pointer, Katie 459
Poirot, Debra 79

	Page
Polan, James	847
Polanco, Jose	915
Polanowicz, Kathleen	130
Polefko, Emma	258
Polen, Chris	724
Polesovsky, Andrew	378
Poling, Ashley	378
Poling, Parker	460
Poling, Susan A	583
Poliquin, Bruce	122, 308, 341, 418, 420, 448, 495
Poliquin, Gerard	814
Polis, Jared	47, 306, 337, 410, 411, 417, 437, 456, 495, 501
Polisar, Evan	69
Polise, John	832
Polk, Ferris B	676
Polk, James	808
Polk, Michelle	629
Pollack, Lana B	922
Pollack, Leslie	825
Pollard, Alfred	798
Pollard, Catherine	940
Pollas, Yardly	89
Pollock, John	393
Pollock, Karol	834
Polsky, Michael P	844
Polumbo, Robert	635
Polzin, Savannah	460
Pompelli, Greg	705
Pompeo, Mike	591, 594, 601, 786, 807, 817
Poms, Douglas	617
Pon, Jeff T.H	823
Poncelet, Jean Luc	934
Ponds, Loren	451
Ponseti, Caroline	449
Ponton, Wendy	739
Pool, Maria	699
Poole, Douglas W	664
Poole, Jessica	45
Poole, Julie	463
Pooler, Rosemary S	857
Poorman, Emma	709
Popadiuk, Mary	409
Pope, Madeleine C	822
Pope, Tameika	785
Popp, David	392
Popp, Monica	392
Porch, Susanne	720
Porfilio, John C	858
Porta, Ann Della	590
Porter, Amy	38, 422
Porter, Anton C	761
Porter, Gail J	720
Porter, Mark	702
Porter, Whitney	150
Portillo, Gustavo Antonio	919
Portman, Rob	205, 311, 329, 331, 365, 366, 369, 370, 372, 373, 377, 467, 470, 478
Posegay, Andrew	393
Posey, Bill	61, 306, 337, 418, 419, 438, 439, 495
Posey, DeBorah	69
Posner, Michael H	844
Post, Jeffrey	814
Post, Lawrence	812
Postell, Joyce	72
Posten, Ryan	754
Pothier, Bonnie	121
Potter, Charles	639
Potter, Jason	353, 354, 355, 356
Potter, Lee Ann	590
Potter, Robert A	658
Potter, Whitney	177
Potts, Brian	350
Potts, John	716
Potts, Millicent B	745
Potts, Oliver A	812
Potts, Robert	850
Pough, Graham	386
Pough, Tracie	70
Poulios, Allison	208
Pouliott, David	748
Poulson, Mike	287
Powalski, Lynn	831
Powden, Mark	360
Powell, Amy	821
Powell, Debbie	736
Powell, Earl A. III	787, 807, 816, 817
Powell, Eric	771
Powell, Erica	103
Powell, Jared	287
Powell, Jason	40, 420
Powell, Jerome H	783
Powell, Jessica	17
Powell, Lewis F., Jr	857
Powell, Linda L	616
Powell, Mark	717
Powell, Matthew	229
Powelson, Robert F	761
Power, Thomas	64
Powers, Glenn	771
Powers, Michael T	642
Powers, Robert	653
Powers, Victor E	713
Powers, William	130, 846
Poyer, Davide	366
Prado, Edward C	606, 857
Prager, Brittany	386
Prager, Robin	785
Prandoni, Christopher "Chris"	594
Prater, Bret	58
Prater, Lori	225
Pratt, Kris	221
Pratt, Lashion	794
Pray, Keith	463
Predmore, Tom	710
Preim-Siddon, Whitlee	222
Preiss, Robert	805
Prescott, Jennifer Y	596
Prescott, Willa	10
Presley, Doug	454
Presley, Jessica	436
Prespare, Deborah	784
Press, Jacob	351
Press, William H	819
Pressman, Debbie	696
Prest, Josh	205
Presta, Tony	89
Presti, Thomas Hunter	446
Preston, Robert J	638
Preston, Shanelle Scales	25
Preston, Tawanna	745
Preston, Warren	693
Prey, Barbara Ernst	815
Price, David E	197, 311, 333, 402, 403, 404, 495, 506
Price, Everett	504
Price, Laurel	273
Price, Marvin N., Jr	658
Price, Matt	69
Price, MC	825
Price, Michael	826
Price, Reva	460
Price, Richard S	844
Price, Samuel T. II	595
Price, Wendi	215
Price-Butler, Kimberly A	848
Prichard, Ji	452
Priebe, Teddy J	586
Priehs, Kayla	216
Priest, Laurie	783
Priestap, E.W	674
Prillman, Renaldo	665
Primus, Robert	133
Primus, Wendell	460
Prince, La Celia	933
Prince-Wheeler, Latriece	771
Prior, Ian	681
Probst, Scott	464
Proby, Tera	184
Prochaska, George	805
Proctor, Kim	361
Proctor, R. David	901
Propis, Ryan	425
Propp, Rebeccah	1, 391, 593
Proseus, Greg	375
Prosperie, Terri	515
Prost, Sharon	865
Protic, Paul B	506
Prout, Gabriel	366
Provancha, Bradley	813
Provencher, Richard	760
Provenzano, Nick	95
Provost, Carla	779
Prusacki, Joseph	705
Pryor, Jill A	858
Pryor, Rachel	416
Pryor, William C	904

Page

Pryor, William H., Jr 849, 858
Ptasienski, Michael T 463
Puccerella, Ed 427
Puccini, Brianna 161
Puccio, Joseph 589
Puchala, Linda 819
Puckett, Phil 722
Puente, Joseph 266
Puerini, James 220
Puerzer, Thomas O 676
Pugh, Adam 22
Pugh, Cary Douglas 890
Pugh, Elizabeth 588
Pugh, J. Duane 797
Puig-Lugo, Hiram E 905
Pulido, Mark 42
Pulju, Thomas 389
Pulliam, Joel 611
Pulz, Jessica 703
Purdue, Sonny 781
Purekal, Jim 516
Purifoy, Felicia 746
Purser, Craig 510
Purucker, Katherine 1, 391, 593
Purucker, Roxanne E 760
Pusateri, Drew 378
Pustay, Melanie Ann 676
Putnam, Robert W 349
Putnam, Thomas 812
Putz, Scott 446
Pyatt, Geoffrey 607
Pyatt, Jon 97

Q

Quaglino, Christopher 664
Qualley, Cindy 382
Qualtere, Tom 225
Quander, Mark 646
Quantius, Sue 405
Quarles, Randal K 783
Quick, Bryce 698
Quickel, Mike 360
Quickle, Kelly 715
Quigley, Janet 652
Quigley, Lisa 247
Quigley, Mike 91, 307, 337, 402, 403, 404, 453, 454, 495
Quinn, Andrew 392
Quinn, Cameron 775
Quinn, J. Arnold 761
Quinn, James 117
Quinn, John 753
Quinn, Katy 408
Quinn, Maura 665
Quinn, Susie Perez 57
Quinn, Timothy 779
Quinn, Will 353, 354, 355
Quint, Lara 381
Quintana, Gabrielle 386
Quintana, German 916
Quintenz, Brian D 787
Quintero, Diana 950
Quirk, John H. V 356, 357, 358
Quirk, Sherry A 842
Quiroz, Gilberto Rene Glen 916
Quittman, Louisa 612
Qureshi, Farah 818
Qureshi, Muquarrab 705

R

Ra'anan, Gabriella 423
Raab, Scott 392
Rabiteau, Marsha J 841
Rabkin, Jeremy A 845
Raby, Jon 688
Raby, Julian 836
Racalto, Joseph 39
Racine, Karl 909
Rackleff, Neal J 743
Radcliffe, Craig 360
Radesky, Robert 629
Radewagen, Aumua Amata Coleman 300, 314, 343, 431, 432, 441, 442, 448, 495
Radford, Julie 597
Radintz, Jim 698
Rae, Kerry 689

Page

Rae, Michael 830
Raffel, Joshua 597
Rafferty, John L 648
Raffinan, Maribeth 905
Rager, Jessica M 514
Raggi, Reena 857
Rahilly, Lyn 779
Rahman, Rezaur 781
Raimo, Bernie 460
Rain, McKenna 589
Raish, Anne 662
Rales, Mitchell P 817
Ralph, Eric 796
Ralston, Jill 688
Ralston, Robert 650
Ramamurti, Bharat 360
Raman, Sujit 657
Ramanathan, Sue 378
Ramaswamy, Ranee 815
Ramaswamy, Sonny 705
Ramaswamy, Venkatachalam 716
Ramirez, Angela 179
Ramirez, Lisa 765
Ramirez, Nestor 717
Ramirez, Rosa 629
Ramker, Gerard 678
Ramoni, Rachel 772
Ramos, Tee 801
Ramos, William 709
Ramotowski, Edward 604
Ramsay, Adrienne 405
Ramsey, Barry 700
Ramsey, Ryan 588
Ramsingh, Omyra 728
Ramzy, Ramzy Ezzeldin 948
Rand, Kay 121
Randal, Allison 683
Randall, Brittany 94
Randle, Chris 184
Randolph, A. Raymond 863
Randolph, Jesica 389
Randolph, Stephen P 813
Randon, Diane M 643
Rands, Mauricio 933
Range, Cheyenne 72
Rankin, Carrie 132
Rankin, Michael L 905
Ranstrom, Tim 130
Ranz, David 603
Rao, Naveen 446
Rao, Neomi 595
Rao, Seema 717
Rapallo, Dave 436
Rapanos, Nicole 73
Raphael, Victor 602
Rapp, Jeffrey N 646
Rapp, John 695
Rapuano, Kenneth 622
Rardin, David 209
Rasetti, Lorenzo 613
Raskin, Jamie 128, 308, 342, 427, 428, 429, 434, 435, 468, 495
Raskin, Max 616
Rasmussen, Mark 699
Rasmussen, Sonja 737
Ratchford, Lewis, Jr 770
Ratcliff, Sara B 823
Ratcliffe, John 252, 312, 341, 417, 424, 425, 428, 429, 495
Ratekin, Anthony 30
Rater, Barbara 705
Rathgeb, Collen 736
Ratliff, Dawn 360
Ratliff, Gerri 662
Ratliff, John 709
Ratliff, Ronnie 516
Ratliff, Sara 440
Ratner, Alexander 416
Ratner, Mark 416
Ratner, Ronald 844
Ratney, Michael 603
Ratto, Mark 94
Rauch, John 634
Rauch, Paul 686
Rauch, Sam 714
Rauch, Samuel 715
Rauland, Scott 504
Rausch, Scott 291

Page

Rauscher, Carl ... 808
Raut, Anant ... 380
Raven, Erik ... 350
Ravenel, Henry, Jr ... 850, 851
Rawlinson, Johnnie B ... 858
Rawls, Charles R ... 793
Rawls, Cheryl ... 772
Rawls, Katrina M ... 632
Rawson, Dairel L ... 826
Rawson, Greg ... 59
Ray, Charles W ... 780
Ray, DeWane ... 788
Ray, Elizabeth G ... 807
Rayes, Nathalie ... 851
Rayfield, John C ... 447
Raymond, Christine ... 132
Raymond, John ... 678
Raymond, Renee ... 905
Raynor, Michael Arthur ... 607
Rea, Laurie ... 793
Read, Jennifer ... 420
Readler, Chad A ... 660
Reagan, Ronald ... 807
Reamy, Lauren ... 57
Reardon, Anthony P ... 629
Reardon, Leigh ... 818
Reavis, Brandon ... 378
Reavley, Thomas M ... 857
Rebarich, Rebecca ... 651
Reblin, Gary C ... 848
Rebollo, Diane ... 800
Record, Art ... 652
Rector, Chris ... 121
Reczek, Jeff ... 351
Redd, Dillon ... 273
Redd, Stephen C ... 737
Reddick-Smith, Shadawn ... 430
Redfield, James ... 420
Redl, David ... 415, 720
Redmann, Steven J ... 648
Redmiles, Mark ... 670
Redmond, Marilyn ... 633
Redmond, Peter ... 828
Redstone, James ... 411
Redzepi, Sheila ... 949
Reece, Adam ... 384
Reece, David ... 834
Reece, Kathy ... 515
Reed, Carla ... 764
Reed, J.R ... 114
Reed, Jack ... 235, 312, 328, 330, 347, 348, 349, 352, 359, 360, 386, 478, 508
Reed, Joseph V ... 948
Reed, Julia Hart ... 503
Reed, Keenan Austin ... 279
Reed, Mark ... 513
Reed, Michael ... 76, 176
Reed, Michele E ... 903
Reed, Shirley L ... 631
Reed, Tom ... 192, 311, 337, 450, 451, 495
Reeder, Raven ... 301
Reeder, Tom ... 830
Reedholm, Carly ... 401
Reel, Matt ... 449
Rees, Gareth ... 685
Rees, Jonathan T ... 728
Rees, Raymond F. "Fred" ... 643
Rees, Stephen P ... 673
Reese, Sarah ... 270
Reese, William ... 637
Reeser, John D ... 653
Reeve, Trevor A ... 783
Reeves, Amy M ... 643
Reeves, Danny C ... 849
Reeves, Randy C ... 771
Reeves, Robert F ... 462
Regan, Kate ... 69
Reger, Amy ... 506
Reger, Mark ... 595
Register, Jeffrey ... 623
Register, Kathy ... 77
Rego, Jarred ... 49
Reheuser, Michael ... 646
Reich, David ... 470
Reichert, David G ... 288, 313, 336, 450, 451, 495
Reid, Ann Carroll ... 681
Reid, Inez Smith ... 904
Reid, Marisa A ... 784

Page

Reidenbach, Gary ... 653
Reidy, Maura ... 836
Reidy, Taylor ... 237
Reifsnyder, Daniel ... 605
Reilly, Bob ... 226
Reilly, Byron ... 708
Reilly, Nanette Foster ... 738
Reilly, Nell ... 182
Reilly, Tom ... 595
Reimer, David ... 608, 609
Reimold, Dorothy ... 751
Reimschussel, Lindsay ... 386
Reinbold, Jeffrey ... 687
Reinhalter, Mark A ... 728
Reinhold, David S ... 707
Reinhold, Kent ... 516
Reinhold, Mark ... 827
Reinke, Benjamin ... 366
Reinke, Judy ... 713
Reinshuttle, Michelle ... 67
Reiser, Marty ... 460
Reising, Bart ... 460
Reiskin, Julie A ... 808
Reisling, Grace M ... 659
Reitz, Tim ... 80
Relfe, Mitch ... 437
Rell, Brian ... 4
Relyea, William ... 624
Remington, Danny ... 386
Renacci, James B ... 213, 311, 338, 409, 450, 451, 495
Rendell, Marjorie O ... 857, 901
Reneau-Vernon, Lilian ... 934
Renner, Elinor ... 685
Reno, Tammy ... 670
Renteria, Alejandro ... 42
Renz, Brandon ... 411
Renzi, Patrick ... 394
Repair, Kelly ... 516
Repass, Todd ... 692
Repko, Mary Frances ... 368
Resch, David T ... 674
Resnick, Mira ... 423
Restani, Jane A ... 880
Restrepo, L. Felipe ... 857
Retchin, Judith E ... 905
Reuschel, Claire ... 88, 393
Reuschel, Trevor ... 97
Reusser, Lindsay ... 226
Reuter, James ... 810
Revana, Arun ... 83
Revell, Sara ... 675
Revels, Stacy ... 401
Revesz, Marietta ... 436
Rexrode, Kathryn ... 429
Rey, Jeth B ... 645
Rey, Yasmin ... 401
Reyes, Alejandro ... 764
Reyes, Christina ... 44
Reyes, Erica ... 31
Reyes, Juan III ... 752
Reyes, Maria Soledad Cisternas ... 948
Reyes, Tina ... 138
Reyes-Gavilan, Richard ... 911
Reyes-Yanes, Jackie ... 910
Reyna, Jimmie V ... 867
Reynolds, Bruce ... 700
Reynolds, Chip ... 151
Reynolds, Glenn ... 720
Reynolds, John W ... 647
Reynolds, Kevin ... 279
Reynolds, Lee ... 396
Reynolds, Lindsay ... 597
Reynolds, Matthew ... 941
Reynolds, Michael ... 813
Reynolds, Michael T ... 686
Reynolds, Mike ... 364
Reynolds, Parker ... 101
Reynolds, Robert ... 772
Rezaee-Rod, Paniz ... 420
Rezendes, Andrew ... 346
Rhames, Samuel ... 722
Rhea, Daniel ... 254
Rhed, Martene ... 516, 584
Rhee, Chang Yong ... 923
Rhee, Peter ... 693
Rhees, Brent ... 690
Rhimes, Shonda L ... 807
Rhine, Russell ... 467

Page
Rhoa, Brian J 782
Rhoad, Erica 433
Rhodes, Benjamin J 844
Rhodes, Michael L 813
Rhodeside, Ben 88
Rhue, Phanalphie 202
Ribeiro, Maria do Valle 945, 948
Ricardel, Mira Radielovic 712
Ricchetti, Daniel 373
Ricci, Alex 411
Ricci, Carrie 694
Ricci, Mike 459
Riccuiti, Anne 767
Rice, Charles L 627
Rice, Cheryl 182
Rice, Edmund 423
Rice, Edward 501
Rice, Gerard T 923
Rice, James 105
Rice, Jon E 595
Rice, Kathleen M 182, 310, 341, 424, 425, 448, 495
Rice, L. Scott 645
Rice, Matt 94
Rice, Susan 807
Rice, Tom 241, 312, 340, 450, 451, 495, 507
Rich, Andrew 806
Rich, Ben 174
Rich, Elizabeth A 586
Rich, Michawn 693
Rich, Stacy 393
Richard, Alex 109
Richard, Elizabeth 608
Richard, Gregg 360
Richards, Anne L 644
Richards, Chelsey 737
Richards, Thomas 378
Richards, Tina 415
Richards, Zachary 469
Richardson, David L 808
Richardson, Debra 617
Richardson, Dorothy 59
Richardson, Emily 261
Richardson, Erica Elliott 788
Richardson, John 654
Richardson, Kevin 707
Richardson, Laura 649
Richardson, Marvin G 659
Richardson, Mary Ellen 98
Richardson, Michelle Barlow 149
Richardson, Robin M 826
Richardson, Samara 839
Richardson, Scott 373
Richardson, Stephanie L 842
Richardson, Stephen E 673
Richardson, Susan 850
Richardson, Todd M 744
Richardson-Crooks, Cynthia 733
Richetts, Jennifer D 661
Richey, Hobart 67
Richey, Kimberly M 767
Richmond, Carol 267
Richmond, Cedric L 118, 308, 338, 424, 428, 429, 495
Richmond, Geraldine 820
Richmond, Kristin 405
Richo, Stephanie 797
Richter, Robert I 905
Richter, Shanon 378
Rickard, David 749
Ricker, Cameron 360
Rickert, Annelise 415
Ricketts, Laura 807
Rickman, Gregg 242
Ricks, Sharon 736
Rico, Irene 751
Rico, Martha P. "Pat" 848
Riddle, Paul 766
Rideaux, Chauntra 727
Rider, Andrew 724
Rides, Roylene 697
Ridgeway, Grace 396
Ridgway, Delissa A 879
Ridgway, Hunter 233
Riedel, Joel 260
Riedel, Michael 699
Rieg, Kevin 447
Riehl, Jeffrey 653
Rieman, Heather 765
Riera, Celia 935
Ries, Lora 780
Rieser, Tim 351
Riesterer, Angela 286
Rigas, Laura 685
Rigas, Michael J 823
Riggs, Helen 687
Riggs, Jennifer 124
Riggs, Tami 752
Righter, John 375
Rigsby, Robert 905
Rihane, Colette 703
Rikkers, Sam 700
Rile, Rebecca 373
Riley, Kelly C 823
Riley, Patsy 719
Riley, Robert A 608
Riley, Robert J 606
Riley, Sean 293
Riley, Tim 605
Riley, William T 740
Rimkunas, Mathew 237
Rinaldi, Rada 717
Rinat, Ory 597
Rindone, Michelle 658
Ringel, Aaron 200
Ringel, Noelle Busk 397
Riojas, Francisco 616
Riordan, Daniel 618
Riordan, Maureen 661
Ripchensky, Darla 366
Riplinger, Scott 360
Ripple, Kenneth F 858
Risch, Carl 604
Risch, James E 85, 307, 328, 330, 365, 366, 372, 373, 383, 386, 478, 508
Risch, Stewart W 649
Risenhoover, Alan 715
Rishchynski, Guillermo Enrique 917
Ritchey, George 423
Ritchie, Branden 429
Ritchie, Jondell 652
Ritman, Allison 749
Ritter, James 820
Ritz, Angela K 644
Rivard, Mitchell 138
Rivelli, Donna 715
Rivera, James 849
Rivera, Martin 62
Rivera-Journier, Alberto 785
Rivero, Marita 781
Rives, Mark 740
Rivlin, Douglas 90
Rixey, Joseph W 626
Riza, Iqbal 948
Rize, Greg 722
Rizzo, John 223
Rizzo, Michael J 849
Roach, Barbra M 665
Roach, Bob 360
Roach, Elizabeth 394
Roach, Reginald V 785
Roane, Gerald A 912
Roark, Robin 714
Roat, Maria 849
Rob, Brian 665
Robare, David J 586
Robb, Karen 124
Robb, Peter B 818
Robbins, David B 802
Robbins, Mark A 846
Roberson, Ed 688
Roberson, Jessie 789
Robert, Marilyn 678
Roberts, Brenda 827
Roberts, Clare 951
Roberts, Cokie 510
Roberts, Craig 96
Roberts, Deborah 665
Roberts, Dennis 750
Roberts, Gerald 674
Roberts, Gregory 464
Roberts, Guy B 622
Roberts, John G., Jr 817, 835, 853
Roberts, John M 785
Roberts, Jordan 391
Roberts, Julie 714
Roberts, Karen 828
Roberts, Keith 897

Page
Roberts, Pat...... 108, 308, 328, 330, 345, 369, 370, 374, 382, 386, 468, 478
Roberts, Philip T 799
Roberts, Samantha 303
Roberts, Sara 433
Roberts, Steven 505
Roberts, William 128
Roberts, William J 588
Robertson, Brent 109
Robertson, Dave 911
Robertson, Jim 383
Robertson, Kenneth 723
Robertson, Lance Allen 736, 816
Robertson, Laura 396
Robertson, Linda L 783
Robertson, Marie 904
Robertson, Ritika 48
Robertson, Summer 64
Robins, Douglas 721
Robinson, Barry 710
Robinson, Brent 277
Robinson, Brian 635
Robinson, Courtney 420
Robinson, Deborah A 878
Robinson, India K 797
Robinson, J. Randall 643
Robinson, Janice 463
Robinson, Jozetta 823
Robinson, Lesley 160
Robinson, Marietta 788
Robinson, Mary 948
Robinson, Melanie 951
Robinson, Michael D 840
Robinson, Nathan 351
Robinson, Preston 117
Robinson, Robert 918
Robinson, Roberto 682
Robinson, Thomas D 787
Robinson, Timothy 416
Robinson-Burnette, Jackie 850
Robison, Charles 159, 160
Robison, Greg 764
Robison, Timothy 815
Robitaille, Denis 949
Robles, Clarissa 269
Robles, Enrique 33
Robreno, Andrew 232
Roby, Martha 3, 305, 338, 402, 403, 404, 428, 429, 495
Rocca, Andrew 452
Rocco, M.A 656
Rochdi, Najat 945
Roche, Shannon 714
Rocheleau, Chris 750
Rochford, Kent 720
Rock, Cecily 469
Rock, Charles "Chip" 650, 655
Rockaway, Stacie 114
Rocke, Sidney 617
Rockefeller, Sharon Percy 817
Rockwell, Jeffrey A 638
Rockwood, Bill 62
Rodan, Bruce 791
Rodden, Grace 449
Roddy, Katherine 623
Roddy, Rusty 685
Rodgers, Carlos 631
Rodgers, Golan 423
Rodgers, Griffin P 741
Rodgers, Jon 652
Rodgers, Meghan 67, 693
Rodgers, Twanda 702
Rodman, Danica 397
Rodman, Scott 392
Rodriguez, Alta 831
Rodriguez, Brenda 696
Rodriguez, Diane 815
Rodriguez, Edgar D 36
Rodriguez, Emma 393
Rodriguez, Ernesto 468
Rodriguez, Estefania 302
Rodriguez, Herbert Alexandre Lopez 916
Rodriguez, Janille 302
Rodriguez, Joanna 73
Rodriguez, Lara 814
Rodriguez, Rachael 255
Rodriguez, Vivian 62
Rodriguez-Arroyo, Allison 303
Rodriguez-Franco, Carlos 696

Page
Rodriguez-Ortiz, Ana Maria 917
Rodriquez, Nicolas 35
Roe, David P 245, 312, 337, 410, 448, 471, 495
Roe, Ralph 808
Roebuck, Roselyn 692
Roegge, Fritz 845
Roerink, Kyle 165
Roesch, Kraig J 708
Roessner, Joel J 659
Roetter, Karen 85
Rogan, Bob 275
Rogero, Joel 805
Rogers, Andrew 368
Rogers, Chase T 841
Rogers, Cindy 182
Rogers, Fredinal 518
Rogers, Gerard 717
Rogers, Harold 115, 308, 333, 402, 403, 404, 495
Rogers, John 454, 788
Rogers, John H 784
Rogers, John M 857
Rogers, Judith W 859
Rogers, Karen L 740
Rogers, Lucia 470
Rogers, Melinda 678
Rogers, Melissa 844
Rogers, Michael S 626
Rogers, Mike 4, 305, 335, 399, 400, 406, 407, 424, 425, 495
Rogers, Natalie 46
Rogers, Sara 229
Rogers, Sarah 455
Rogers, Wanda 613
Roget, Gisele 744
Rogge, Jacques 949
Rogin, Joshua 70
Rohlf, John 751
Rohlfing, Eric A 759
Rohrabacher, Dana 42, 306, 333, 421, 422, 438, 439, 496
Roig, Kevin 120
Roisman, Elad 360
Rojas, Armando Jose Leon 917
Rojewski, Cole 30
Rokita, Todd 101, 307, 338, 409, 410, 443, 444, 445, 446, 496
Roland, Renee 796
Rolfe, Leslie 392
Rollins, Blake 694
Rollins, Deborah 254
Rollins, Glenda A 664
Rollins, Monique 612
Rollins, Sheri 4
Rolon, Juan C. Garcia 825
Rolph, John 838
Rolwes, Edward 155
Romaniello, Cathy 229
Romano, Neil 814
Romanowski, Alina 601
Romanowski, Michael 751
Romberg, Jennifer 510
Rome, Kecia S 840
Romer, Paul 949
Romero, Eladia 130
Romero, Jennifer 385
Romero, Kristin K 397
Romero, Raymond 784
Romick, Brian 461
Romig, Alton D 819
Romig, Christopher 405
Romine, Charles 720
Romito, Jonathan 409
Roncone, Stephen 779
Rondo, Marla 141
Rood, John C 622
Rook, Mary Grace 905
Rooney, Covette 823
Rooney, Dana 798
Rooney, Dawn C 652
Rooney, Francis 68, 307, 342, 410, 411, 421, 422, 454, 467, 496
Rooney, Ken 385
Rooney, Nancy 721, 726
Rooney, Patrick 190
Rooney, Thomas J...... 67, 307, 337, 402, 404, 453, 454, 496, 501
Root, Michelle 750
Ropelewski, James L 826
Roper, Andrea 287

Page

Roper, Cassie 44
Roper, Will 630
Ros, Vanessa 804
Ros-Lehtinen, Ileana 74, 307, 333, 421, 422, 453, 454, 496, 845
Rosa, Alexandre Meira da 916
Rosa, Allison 30
Rosa, Francine R. "Renee" 586
Rosa, Richard 665
Rosa, Yasmin A 826
Rosado, Mary 116
Rosado, Robert 346
Rosado, Tim 713
Rosales, Adilene 76
Rosario, Kate 230
Rosario, Miguel 515
Rosario, Peter 833
Rosario, Phillip 794
Rosaro, Luis 513
Rosato, Joanna 805
Roscoe, Jared 360
Rose, Ashley 73
Rose, Carol 712
Rose, Gamaliel 664
Rose, Margaret A 397
Rose, Rebecca M 793
Rose, Ryan 515
Rose, Stu 236
Rose, Sydney 722
Roseboro, Germaine 792
Roseme, Jean 72
Rosen, Aimee 17
Rosen, Alex 425
Rosen, Daniel J 844
Rosen, Jacky 165, 310, 342, 406, 407, 408, 438, 439, 496
Rosen, Jacob "Izzy" 121
Rosen, Jeff 747
Rosen, Max 446
Rosen, Zach 224
Rosenbaum, David 165
Rosenbaum, Robin S 858
Rosenbaum, Steven 662
Rosenberg, Adam 440
Rosenberg, Ron 780
Rosenberg, Steven 796
Rosenblum, Daniel 603
Rosenblum, Jeffrey 832
Rosenblum, Marc 777
Rosenfarb, Charles 605
Rosenfeld, Anne 181
Rosenfeld, Arthur 727
Rosenfeld, Betsy 735
Rosenfeld, David 835
Rosenfelt, Philip H 766, 845
Rosenkranz, Ethan 361
Rosensaft, Menachem Z 844
Rosenstein, Rod J 657
Rosenthal, Ann S 729
Rosenthall, Krista 254
Rosenworcel, Jessica 794
Roskam, Peter J 91, 307, 336, 450, 451, 496, 506
Roskey, Joanne 729
Rosner, Lara 452
Ross, Alexis L 408, 642
Ross, Amena 255
Ross, Bob 350
Ross, Dave 791
Ross, Dennis A 65, 307, 338, 418, 419, 434, 435, 496
Ross, Hadley 464
Ross, Jason 252
Ross, Jed 910
Ross, John 439
Ross, Kimberly 207
Ross, Maurice 905
Ross, Michael P 844
Ross, Rebecca A 408
Ross, Susan 405
Ross, Susannah 266
Ross, Taisha 629
Ross, Thomas 829
Ross, Tim 210
Ross, Wilbur L., Jr 591, 709, 802, 816, 830, 847
Ross, Zeke 417
Rossi, Janet 79, 437
Rossi, Nick 363
Roth, Arielle 797
Roth, David 405

Page

Roth, Jane R 857
Roth, John P 631
Roth, Justin 10
Roth, Kristine 469
Roth, Linda 851
Roth, Michael 771
Rothblum, Michelle 19
Rothchild, Roxanne 817
Rothenberg, Gilbert S 681
Rother, Mary Catherine 436
Rothfus, Keith J 230, 312, 340, 418, 419, 420, 428, 429, 454, 496
Rothfus, Mimi 61
Rothman, Tim 815
Rothmier, Kevin 805
Rothschild, Sarah 99
Rothwell, Charles J 737
Rotondo, Glenn 804
Rottenberg, Carmen 703
Roudik, Peter 589
Rouiller, Donald 518
Rounds, Emory A 823
Rounds, Mike 242, 312, 328, 331, 352, 353, 359, 360, 367, 383, 384, 479
Rountree, Tara 279
Roush, Jennifer 785
Rouson, Herb 904
Rousseau, Maggie 220
Rouzer, David 199, 311, 341, 399, 400, 401, 443, 444, 445, 446, 496
Rovner, Ilana Diamond 858
Rowan, Anne 791
Rowan, Jasmine 212
Rowe, Audrey 701
Rowe, Deborah 461
Rowe, William 797
Rowland, Caroline 63
Rowland, Matthew 903
Rowland, Yvette 237
Rowley, Allen 695
Rowley, Kalene 68
Rowley, Kris 804
Rowse, Mark 699
Roxburgh, Jessica 43
Roy, Robert F.X., Jr 793
Roybal-Allard, Lucille 38, 306, 334, 402, 403, 404, 470, 496, 507
Royce, Edward R 38, 306, 334, 418, 419, 421, 496, 503
Royce, Marie Therese 604
Royce, Shannon O 737
Royer, Matthew 707
Royer, Rebecca 784
Royse, Zak 10
Royster, Cecelia 720
Royster, Tanya 909
Rozdzielski, Debra L 586
Rozier, Sarah 420
Rubenstein, David M 807, 817, 836
Rubeor, James 637
Rubin, Dan 452
Rubin, Eric 606
Rubinger, Katie 388
Rubino, Michael 715
Rubinovitz, Robert 710
Rubinstein, Daniel 609
Rubio, Luis Miguel Castilla 916
Rubio, Marco 57, 306, 329, 331, 347, 348, 349, 372, 373, 383, 386, 387, 479, 504, 506, 509, 845
Ruble, Stacy 831
Ruby, Lauren 697
Rucker, Cliff 848
Rucker, Donald W 735
Rucker, Mark A 698
Rucker, Nicci 629
Rudd, Alexis 364
Rudd, Jeremy 785
Rudd, Phil 360
Rudd, Richard 518
Rudder, S 656
Ruddy, Jack 157
Rude, Laura 97
Ruder, Will 108
Rudolph, Kim 103
Rudolph, Lawrence 819
Rudwell, Mary Jo 688
Ruggieri, Fig 893
Ruisanchez, Alberto 661
Ruiz, Adele 639

Page
Ruiz, Alex 516
Ruiz, Kristin 702
Ruiz, Lorena 922
Ruiz, Raul 37, 306, 340, 413, 414, 415, 496
Ruiz, Vanessa 904
Ruiz, Xenia 10
Ruiz-Martinez, Martha 108
Rumsfeld, Kurt 799
Runge, Sarah 615
Runk, Michelle 214
Ruoff, Beth Ann 505
Rupert, Clarke D 789
Ruppersberger, C. A. Dutch 124, 308, 335, 402, 403, 404, 496, 502
Rusbuldt, Ryan 192
Rusche, Linda 850
Rush, Anthony W 641
Rush, Bobby L 88, 307, 334, 413, 414, 496
Rush, Carly 376
Rush, Laura 435
Rushing, Glenn 260
Rusk, Justin 228
Rusk, Richard S 638
Ruskowsky, Dianna 411
Rusnak, Allison 594
Russell, Beverly M 806
Russell, Corinne 798
Russell, David 137
Russell, Jacqui 350
Russell, Lisa 669
Russell, Margaret 807
Russell, Matt 452
Russell, Matthew 256
Russell, Nancy V 848
Russell, Richard 368
Russell, Rucks 260
Russell, Scott R 409
Russell, Steve 217, 311, 341, 406, 407, 434, 435, 496
Russell, Susan 95
Russell, Terri 584
Russell, Thomas P 642
Russell, Tracey 405
Russell, Tricia 172
Russell, Tyler 58
Russo, Carol 662
Russo, Joe 429
Russo, Karl 469
Russo, Mark 739
Rust, Erik R 420
Rust, Rebecca 723
Rust, Stephanie 829
Rust, Tom 417
Rutherford, John H 59, 306, 342, 402, 404, 428, 429, 496
Rutherford, Kati 289
Rutkin, Amy 185
Rutledge, John E 588
Rutledge, Michael J 727
Rutledge, Preston 725
Ruto, Kenneshia D 664
Rutson, Victoria 757
Rutter, Deborah F 807
Ruwe, Robert Paul 892
Ruwwe, Mary 805
Ryall, Paul 931
Ryan, Barbara 797
Ryan, Cathleen 712
Ryan, John 205, 373
Ryan, Joseph A 641
Ryan, Katie 427
Ryan, Kevin 133
Ryan, Magen 93
Ryan, Margaret A 895
Ryan, Melissa McKenney 864
Ryan, Michael J 690, 905
Ryan, Patrick 186
Ryan, Patrick N 397
Ryan, Paul D 293, 314, 335, 455, 459, 496, 507, 510, 807
Ryan, Tim 212, 311, 335, 402, 403, 404, 496
Rybicki, James 673
Rychalski, Jon J 771
Ryder, David J 619
Ryder, Guy 923, 943
Ryder, Neil 677
Ryder, Ruth 767
Rymer, Jon T 622
Rynearson, Marcia E 842
Ryu, Lisa H 783

S

Page
Saab, Al David 249
Saba, Kevin 604
Sabag, Terra 285
Sabatino, Robin 840
Sabelhaus, John 785
Sabharwal, Sunil 614, 924
Sabia, Jay 636
Sabine, Chris 716
Sablan, Gregorio Kilili Camacho 302, 314, 343, 410, 411, 431, 432, 496
Sabol, Teresa S 712
Sacchetti, Dylan 724
Saccoccia, Kenneth J 625
Sachs, Jeffrey D 949
Sachse, Andrew 456
Sachtjen, Alex 364
Sack, Robert D 857
Sacristan, Gema 917
Saddler, Fern Flanagan 905
Sadeghzadeh, Kaveh 696
Sadler, Hailey 206
Sadler, Robert M 729
Sadlosky, Dan 460
Saegesser, Jodi 254
Saenz, Carla 936
Saez, Mariel 461
Safaie, Farhad K 903
Safian, Janet 694
Sagul, Peggy 76
Sahibzada, Nadeem 585
Sahr, Dan 33
Sajadian, Mort 816
Sajet, Kim 836
Sakai, Laurel 375
Sakwa, Jenna 459
Salad, Bruce 681
Salame, Ghassan 945, 948
Salamone, John 462
Salas, Stephen 179
Salazar, Julio 179
Salazar, Miguel 166
Salazar, Ray 461
Salazar, Roberto 589
Saldivar, Ramon 816
Sale, Dominic 803
Salem, David 396
Salen, Jen 506
Salerno, Lillian 700
Salerno, Robert 905
Sales, Nathan 601
Salidjanova, Nargiza 508
Sallay, Roderick 847
Sallenave, Michel 919
Salles, Marcello 650
Salley, Kevin 797
Salmi, Molly 411
Salmoiraghi, Jessica 803
Salmon, Adam 378
Salmon, Diem 353, 354, 355
Salmon, Kathryn 405
Salmon, Paul 718
Salo, Donald G 643
Salopek, Michael 639
Salotti, Chris 685
Salotto, John 718
Salpeter, Joshua 74
Salter, Daniel R 665
Saltzman, Bradley 635
Salvatori, John 636
Salzer, Kristin 696
Salzgaber, Wayne H 677
Salzmann, Kelly 838
Samant, Sagar 804
Sample, Allen 733
Sample, James 632
Samples, Colin 405
Sampson, D.W 656
Samra, Tom A 848
Samuel, Twaun 40
Samuels, Scott 682
Sanborn, Benjamin C 665
Sanborn, Scott M 394
Sanchez, Alma 260
Sanchez, Carlos 456
Sanchez, Felipe 696
Sanchez, Francisco 714
Sanchez, Ivan 260

Page

Sanchez, Jacqueline 261
Sanchez, Jane 589
Sanchez, Linda T 38, 306, 335, 450, 451, 456, 496
Sanchez, Mario Aguilar 920
Sancken, Isaac 90
Sandell, John 451
Sanders, Bernard 274, 313, 327, 330, 361, 365, 366, 367, 368, 374, 384, 479, 845
Sanders, Douglas D 637
Sanders, Mark 79
Sanders, Ronald 931
Sanders, Sarah Huckabee 597
Sanders, Stacy 387
Sandgren, Matt 271, 391
Sandhu-Rojon, Ruby 945, 946
Sandler, Risa D 729
Sandlin, Erin 31
Sandman, James J 808
Sandoval, Camilo J 771
Sandoval, Valeria 42
Sandretti, David 700
Sands, Carla 607
Sands, Jeffrey 790
Sandy, Bayley 446
Sandy, John 86
Sanford, Jim 596
Sanford, Mark 238, 312, 337, 409, 434, 435, 443, 444, 445, 446, 496
Sanianwala, Umesh 150
Sant, Victoria P 817
Santabar, Lauren 127
Santamaria, Alicia Montalvo 917
Santamorena, Lori 613
Santangelo, Mari 677
Santiago, Claudia 27
Santini, Chris 433
Santos, Daniel 789
Santos, Derek 637
Santos, Gedeon 932
Santos, Jennifer S 350
Santos, Lucas 132
Santos, Nelson 665
Santos, Sherie Lou 375
Sanz, Maytee 74
Sanz-Rexach, Gabrielle 680
Saparow, Bobby 77
Sapir, Zev 730
Sapong, Kofi 784
Sarar, Ariana 405
Sarasin, Ron 509, 510
Sarbanes, John P 125, 308, 336, 413, 414, 415, 434, 496
Sarcone, John A. III 805
Sareva, Jarmo 943
Sargent, Annelia 820
Sargent, Marilyn R 864
Sargrad, Scott 765
Sarmiento, Victor 447
Saroff, Laurie 42
Sartori, Joan 514
Sarvana, Adam 433
Sasajima, Kim 722
Sasaki, Lisa 836
Sass, Paul J 157
Sass, Raymond 161
Sasse, Ben 161, 310, 328, 331, 352, 353, 359, 360, 379, 380, 467, 479, 509
Sasser, Brandie 724
Sasser, Tracey 766
Sastry, Hari 606
Satalin, Patrick 275
Satchell, Samantha 416
Satterfield, Lee F 905, 911
Satz, Eric M 842
Saul, Andrew M 817
Saulnier, Steve 701
Sauls, Karen 633
Saunders, Ian 779
Saunders, Joan Parks 838
Saunders, Michael 733
Saunders, Sharyn 646
Saundry, Claire M 720
Sauvajot, Ray 686
Savage, Hank 464
Savage, John 729
Savage, Megan 102, 417
Savoy, Marie S 785
Sawyer, Heather 380
Sawyer, Paul 120

Page

Saxman, Dianna M 825
Sayegh, Tony 616
Sayles, Andre 759
Saylor, Jeffrey 664
Saylor, Nicole 813
Saylor, Ryan 18
Scaggs, Janice 17
Scalise, Steve 117, 308, 336, 413, 460, 496
Scandurra, Laura 698
Scanlon, Kelley 701
Scannell, Brooke 132
Scarbrough, Marvida 764
Scardino, Anthony 719
Scavalla, Erica 772
Scavino, Daniel 597
Schadler, Nevada 408
Schaeffer, Cathy 287
Schaeffer, Steve 840
Schaeffer, Timothy D 790
Schaeffer, Tracey 725
Schafer, Hartwig 950
Schaff, Tom 366
Schaffer, Laurie S 785
Schafle, Matt 432
Schaick, Steven A 637
Schakowsky, Janice D 92, 307, 335, 409, 413, 414, 415, 496
Schall, Alvin A 869
Schantz, Adam 84
Schanz, Jeffrey E 808
Scharf, Jeffrey W 756
Schartner, Anna 286
Schatz, Brian 83, 307, 329, 331, 347, 348, 349, 359, 362, 363, 385, 386, 388, 470, 479
Schatz, Evan 375
Schatz, Rebecca 360
Schauerte, Mark 92
Schaumburg, Amanda 411
Scheele, Scott A 658
Scheffler, Elizabeth 588
Scheidhauer, Gregory 645
Scheidler, Adam 390
Scheidler, Adam J 420
Scheidt, Douglas J 832
Scheinost, Emily 59
Scheirman, Shadrack 800
Schelble, Nathan 178
Schemmel, Nick 76
Schenning, Sarah 124
Scher, Deborah 769
Scherer, Jennifer 678
Scherer, Robert 830
Schertz, Matt 401
Schiappa, David 505
Schibi, Kelly 10
Schibuola, Alexander 467
Schiemeyer, Corry 267
Schiess, Doug 629
Schiff, Adam B 33, 306, 335, 453, 496
Schiffer, Michael 373
Schiller, Aschley 405
Schiller, Laura 388
Schiller, Susannah 720
Schilling, Patrick 226
Schindler, John 785
Schlagenhauf, Jeff 595
Schlager, Erika B 504
Schlapp, Mercedes 597
Schleffer, Jonathan 664
Schlendorf, David W 674
Schleuning, Amber 770
Schlichting, Jim 795
Schlientz, Steven 695
Schloegel, Scott P 792
Schloesser, Chris 28
Schlossberg, Rose Kennedy 807
Schmauder, Craig R 643
Schmid, Jason 408
Schmidt, Aaron 285
Schmidt, Brynna 143
Schmidt, Diana 828
Schmidt, Gavin A 810
Schmidt, Hannah 442
Schmidt, Mike 346
Schmidt, Robin 625
Schmidt, Terri 740
Schmidtlein, Rhonda K 845
Schmitt, Glenn R 849

Page

Schmitz, Sarah 364
Schmoke, Julian 766
Schmoyer, Michael 733
Schneider, Anna 510
Schneider, Bob 131
Schneider, Bradley Scott.... 93, 307, 341, 421, 422, 428, 429, 441, 496, 845
Schneider, Dan 415
Schneider, Donald 451
Schneider, Erin 835
Schneider, Jacqlyn 346
Schneider, Margaret N 688
Schneider, Mary 254
Schock, Lori J 831
Schoelen, Mary J 898
Schoenecker, John 451
Schoenleitner, Guenther 950
Schoettler, Katie 433
Schonfeld, Toby 773
Schonhoff, Tara 383
School, Page 394
Schools, Scott 657
Schoone-Jongen, Terence 818
Schoonmaker, Jan 510
Schoonover, William 755
Schopp, Carolyn 793
Schoppa, Leonard J., Jr 507
Schorr, Jonathan 765
Schorr, Stephen 778
Schothorst, Lauryn Bernier 227
Schott, Joseph 633
Schoultz, Nichelle 126
Schrader, Kurt 221, 312, 337, 413, 414, 415, 497
Schrage, Elliot J 844
Schram, Zachary 378
Schramek, Jeff 613
Schramm, Heidi 469
Schregardus, D 653
Schritz, Athena 371
Schriver, Alex 3
Schriver, Randall 622
Schrodt, Adrienne 158
Schrodt, Corey 68
Schroeder, Alyssa 425
Schroeder, Amber 516
Schroeder, Jeannine 798
Schroeder, Kurt 794
Schroeder, Mary M 858
Schroeder, Meghan 228
Schroeder, Michele 846
Schroeder, Rachelle 382
Schubert, Brian 58
Schuchat, Anne 737
Schufreider, Jim 720
Schuham, Aaron 735
Schuldt, Patrick 637
Schuler, Christopher 114
Schuler, Jack 408
Schulken, Chad 351
Schulken, Jessica Arden 350
Schulman, Andrew 408
Schulman, Maureen 844
Schult, Deborah G 675
Schultheis, Roy 73
Schultz, Erich 389
Schultz, Eva Weigold 601
Schultz, Karl 780
Schultz, Lisa 394
Schultz, Mary Beth 346
Schultz, Stephen L 825
Schulz, William 714
Schumacher, Joe 277
Schumacher, John H 823
Schumacher, Matt 416
Schumann, Holly 827
Schumann, Stacy 821
Schumate, Brett A 661
Schumer, Charles E 180, 310, 329, 330, 382, 386, 387, 388, 389, 392, 479, 508, 510, 511, 808
Schumm, Sandra 394
Schurman, Christian 605
Schutte, Tanner 98
Schutter, George 910
Schutz, Kenneth J 816
Schuyler, Anne R 814
Schwab, Justin 790
Schwab, Oliver 12
Schwager, Dan 393

Page

Schwalbach, Robert J 302
Schwartz, Larry 603
Schwartz, Lowell 373
Schwartz, Mark 780
Schwartz, Neil 393
Schwartz, Thomas 812
Schwartzman, Sara 393
Schwarz, Jay 794
Schwarzbach, Kirk 420
Schwarzman, Stephen A 808
Schweickhardt, Reynold 427
Schweikert, David 12, 305, 338, 450, 451, 454, 467, 471, 497
Schweizer, Diane 725
Schwenk, Heather 827
Schwenke, Pamela C 631
Sciascia, Anthony 464
Scibetta, Andrew 42
Scinto, Blaise 796
Sciortino, John 681
Sciretta, Scott 516, 653
Scirica, Anthony J 857
Scodellaro, Matthew 679
Scofield, Meg 695
Scolese, Christopher J 810
Score, David 715
Scott, Austin 79, 307, 338, 399, 400, 406, 407, 497
Scott, B.W 656
Scott, Charles C. II 72
Scott, David 82, 307, 335, 399, 400, 418, 419, 497
Scott, Deirdre 590
Scott, Denise 420
Scott, George A 583
Scott, Greg J 797
Scott, Jimmy 745
Scott, John 917
Scott, Kevin D 624
Scott, Kyle R 609
Scott, Nancy C 756
Scott, Nicole 401
Scott, Robert C. "Bobby" 278, 313, 334, 410, 471, 497
Scott, Tim 237, 312, 329, 331, 352, 353, 359, 360, 369, 370, 374, 383, 387, 479, 845
Scott, Vince 510
Scott, William 729
Scovel, Calvin L. III 748
Screen, Gina 773
Scriven, James P 917
Scullin, Caroline L 792
Scully, Bethany 597
Scully, John 680
Scully, Kelly 368
Scurlock, Aaron 804
Seaborn, Dianna 849
Seabott, Ann 284
Seagle, Christopher 735
Seale, John 118
Seale, Viktoria 594
Seaman, Dara 613
Sears, David 700
Sears, George 695
Sears, Glen 420
Seastrom, Mark 772
Seaton, Fabion 436
Seats, C. Lamar 744
Seaver, Kristin 848
Seay, Doug 422
Seckar, Daryle "Mike" 804
Secreto, Jim 388
Sedighi, Gohar 143
Sedillo, Anthony 385
See, Jordan 76
Seeger, Mark R 650
Seelamneni, Gopala 826
Seely, W.H. III 656
Seep, Ralph V 464
Seese, Amanda 748
Segal, Berry 804
Segal, Susanna 371
Seggos, Basil 789, 842
Segovia, Theresa 662
Seguin, Debbie 779
Sehgal, Tanya 427
Seidel, Heather 833
Seidel, Richard 717
Seidl, Zach 37
Seidlitz, Aden 688
Seidman, Lindsey 375

	Page
Seifert, Jeffrey W	588
Seigel, Benjamin	726
Seiger, Ryan	447
Seigle, Jean	828
Seitz, Sarah	215
Selassie, Abebe Aemro	923
Selde, Jennifer	378
Selesnick, Kelly	386
Seligman, Meyer	350
Seligmann-Silva, Jose Jorge	916
Seller, Mark	715
Sellers, David A	903
Sellers, Douglas	847
Selva, Paul J	624
Selweski, Mark	677
Selya, Bruce M	857
Sembene, Daouda	924
Semmel, Andrew	944
Semmer, Stephanie	722
Semo, Alina	812
Semonite, Todd T	646
Sena, Dan	456
Sena, David M	792
Sendak, Catherine	408
Sennott, Daniel	408
Sense, Rick	297
Sensenbrenner, Bob	427
Sensenbrenner, F. James, Jr	295, 314, 333, 421, 422, 428, 429, 497
Sentelle, David Bryan	863
Sepp, Stephen	404
Sequeira, Ronald	707
Seraphin, Arun A	356, 357
Serrano, Jose E	187, 311, 333, 402, 403, 497
Serrano, Lenin	916
Serrano, Sheldon	651
Serruya, Suzanne Jacob	935
Servais, Shaun	783
Serveiss, Victor	922
Servidio, Cosmo	791
Servoss, Stephanie A	893
Sessa, Matthew	765
Sessamen, Berry F	711
Sessions, Jeff	497, 591, 657
Sessions, Lewe F	677
Sessions, Pete	267, 313, 334, 437, 470
Seth, Nikhil	943
Setia, Parveen	707
Settles, Clark	779
Seung-soo, Han	948
Severens, C. Alex	614
Severino, Roger	734
Severs, Sara	449
Sevier, Adrian	778
Sewell, Briana	283
Sewell, Terri A	6, 305, 338, 450, 453, 454, 497
Sewmaker, Lillian	785
Sexton, Geno	37
Seydi, Cheikh O	952
Seymour, Jud	76
Seymour, Stephanie K	858
Sferlazzo, Julia	442
Shackelford, Lindsey	201
Shackleford, Dawn	596
Shaefer, Christopher C	660
Shafernich, Mark	665
Shaffer, Dana	796
Shaffer, Shasta	62
Shah, Pre	250
Shah, Raj	597
Shahbaz, Donna	405
Shaheen, Jeanne	167, 310, 328, 330, 347, 348, 349, 352, 353, 372, 373, 383, 386, 388, 479, 502, 504
Shaheen, Patrick	766
Shahin, Jessica	702
Shahinian, Yvette	38
Shahoulian, David	430
Shalhoub, Donald G	822
Shampaine, Nicole	609
Shanahan, Patrick M	621
Shanks, Margaret M	785
Shanks, Robert	828
Shannon, Caitlin	30
Shannon, Cliff	440
Shannon, Michael D	740
Shannon, Thomas	602
Shantz, Joseph	375
Shao, Dongfang	589
Shapell, Irvin N	844
Shapiro, Arin	393
Shapiro, Gary E	847
Shapiro, Jessica	464
Shapiro, Michael	459, 718
Shapiro, Neil	740
Shappert, Gretchen C	670
Shaqir, Ibrahim M	706
Sharan, Vimlendra	943
Share, Alison	138
Sharek, Rebecca	833
Sharma, Khem	850
Sharp, Gary	652
Sharp, Phillip	698
Sharp, Robert D	655
Sharpe, Steven A	785
Sharpless, Norman E. "Ned"	740
Sharshar, Farah	639
Shattuck, Sarah	594
Shatynski, Kristen	415
Shatz, Eileen M	681
Shatzer, W.A. "Bud"	782
Shavers, Michael	664
Shaw, Betsy	790
Shaw, Charles	378
Shaw, Cindy	677
Shaw, Dalbert	630
Shaw, Emily	260
Shaw, Eric	814, 910
Shaw, Kelly Ann	452
Shaw, Rebecca	104
Shaw, Tara	298
Shaw, Wes	157
Shay, Matthew	510
Shea, Dana A	588
Shea, Dennis	596
Shea, Dennis C	508
Shea, Hannah	17
Shea, Josephine	511
Shea-Porter, Carol	167, 310, 339, 406, 407, 410, 411, 497
Sheahan, Bernard	952
Shearer, David	946
Shearman, David	384
Shedd, Dennis W	857
Shedd, Steven T	584, 585
Sheehan, Brian	630
Sheehan, Charles	791
Sheehan, Denise	686
Sheehan, Gregory	686
Sheehan, John "Jack"	682
Sheehan, Mark	633
Sheehan, Matthew	657
Sheehey, Kathryn D	669
Sheehey, Matthew	828
Sheehy, Jennifer	725
Sheehy, Joe	35
Sheehy, Thomas P	422
Sheenan, Patricia	805
Sheeran, Josette	946
Sheeren, David M	676
Sheffer, Rudy	629
Sheffey, TreShonda	267
Sheffield, Rachel	467
Sheinkman, Joshua	370
Shelat, Neilesh	843
Shelby, Peter J	771
Shelby, Richard C	2, 305, 329, 330, 347, 348, 349, 359, 360, 367, 368, 382, 468, 479, 510, 511
Sheldon, Terry	754
Shell, Jeffrey	786
Shellabarger, Nan	750
Shelleby, Ed	143
Shellenberger, J.S	729
Shellenberger, Sam	730
Shelley, Clyde E., Jr	665
Shelly, Kasey	382
Shelton, Jeffery R	636
Shelton, Lisa	401
Shen, Valerie	436
Shepard, Eric	437, 690
Shepard, Joseph	849
Shepard, Robert B	724
Shepherd, Bobby E	858
Shepherd, Gloria	751
Shepherd, Meagan	9
Shepherd, Ray B	623
Sheppard, Christal	718
Sher, Susan S	807

	Page
Shere, Jack	707
Sherer, Dustin	48
Sheridan, Blaise	350
Sheridan, Patricia J	806
Sheridan, Peter	785
Sheriff-Parker, Jennifer	763, 764
Sherlund, Shane M	785
Sherman, Amanda	295
Sherman, Andrew M	584, 585, 812
Sherman, Brad	34, 306, 334, 418, 419, 421, 422, 497, 503
Sherman, Brandon	764
Sherman, Floyd	749
Sherman, Jennifer	415
Sherman, Lisa	45
Sherman, Max	806
Sherman, Michael A	814
Sherman, Rachel	738
Sherman, William R	666
Sherwin, Mark P	824
Sherwin, Martin B	819
Shetty, Rohan	468
Shield, Will	801
Shields, Brendan P	425
Shields, Daniel	610
Shiffer, Jeannie	750
Shih, Stephen T	809
Shillman, David	833
Shim, Linda	33
Shima, Frank	469
Shimabukuro, Jorge M	824
Shimkus, John	96, 307, 334, 413, 414, 415, 497
Shin, Diana	162
Shin, Jaiwon	809
Shinners, Gary W	817
Shipp, Paula	766
Shire, Gavin	686
Shirven, Michael	514
Shive, David	804
Shively, Alex	230
Shivers-Barclay, Sambia	766
Shockey, Joni	66
Shoemaker, Douglas	749
Shoemaker, Joe	179
Shogan, Colleen	590
Sholly, Cam	687
Shonka, David	802
Shoop, Doug	760
Shoop, Gregory	688
Shope, Thomas D	689
Shores, Michael	769
Shores, Sarah J	751
Short, Lani	245
Short, Lynne	691
Short, Tracy	779
Shorter, Chris	909
Shorter, Malcom A	691, 695
Shortino, Elizabeth	614
Shotwell, Patty	642
Shoulders, Meco	151
Shoults, Michael	636
Showers, Carole	713
Showman, John	790
Showman, Tracey	778
Shpak, Anna	464
Shrestha, Laura B	588
Shrier, Jonathan	784
Shrieves, Glenn	670
Shrive, Tyler	375
Shroba, James P	666
Shuart, Amy	452
Shub, Adam	607
Shubert, Thomas	633
Shuker, Nan R	905
Shull, Thomas C	640
Shultz, Joe	346
Shumaker, Betsy	858
Shumate, Jonah	16
Shuren, Jeffrey	739
Shurtleff, David	741
Shust, Diane	182
Shuster, Bill	228, 312, 335, 406, 443, 497, 502, 807
Shwartz, Patty	857
Shwedo, Eric P	641
Shyam-Sunder, Lakshmi	950
Shyamsunder, Srividhya	830
Shylkofski, Stephen	63
Siberell, Justin	606
Sibley, Kenneth	633, 634
Sibley, Shirl	825
Siciliano, Alex	46
Sidari, David P	784
Siddiqui, Faisal	401
Sidibe, Michel	943
Sidikou, Maman Sambo	945
Sidney, Arthur D	77
Sidrak, Hany	703
Siegel, Bernice ''Dee''	594
Siegel, Jennifer E	893
Siegel, Mike	16
Siegel, Susan	588
Sieger, Edward	727
Siegfried, Kristin	722
Siekaniec, Greg	686
Sienicki, David	408
Sierra, Cristina	303
Sierra, Teresa V	590
Sievers, Bruce R	816
Sievers, Marc J	608
Sieving, Paul A	740
Sifford, Mary Ann	396
Sigg, James	738
Siggerud, Katherine	516, 584
Sigmon, Kelly	848
Sikora, Rebecca	286
Silberberg, David	33
Silberman, Laurence Hirsch	862
Silbermann, Lizbeth	702
Siler, Eugene E., Jr	857
Silk, Mitchell (Mitch)	614
Silliman, Douglas	607
Silva, Jorge Da	916
Silva, Jose Graziano da	943
Silva, Jose Mauricio	917
Silveira, Antonio Hernique Pinheiro	917
Silver, Robert F	397
Silverberg, Daniel	461
Silverman, Barry G	858
Silverman, David	460
Silverman, Elissa	907
Silverman, Lawrence	607
Silverman, Steven C	695
Silverstein, Leonard L	808
Silverthorne, Joyce	765
Silvey, Patricia W	726
Silvis, Lauren	738
Silvis, Randy M	618
Simermeyer, John	385, 841
Simkin, Brian M	676
Simler, Jenness	408
Simmons, Anne	401
Simmons, Anthony	396
Simmons, Chris	470
Simmons, Dougie	763
Simmons, Jason	849
Simmons, Maalik	397
Simmons, Machelle	697
Simmons, Michele	704
Simmons, Rachel L	848
Simmons, Robert	183
Simmons, Shelvin	360
Simms, Cynthia	597
Simms, Douglas A	647
Simms, Eleanor	728
Simms, Elena J	903
Simms, Martha	425
Simms, Vernon	127
Simon, Ammon	360
Simon, David	72
Simon, Gottlieb	910
Simon, Harvey	790
Simon, Katherine Hord	903
Simon, Matt	13
Simon, Nigel	791
Simon, Noah	281
Simon, Sam	381
Simon, Samantha	708
Simone, Raymond	235
Simons, Shaheena	662
Simonsen, Brian	380
Simpkins, Gregory	423
Simpson, Gary	675
Simpson, Hilery	723
Simpson, Kelly	59
Simpson, Kevin M	745
Simpson, Lexie	373

Page
Simpson, Michael K 86, 307, 335, 402, 403, 404, 497
Simpson, Sandy 113
Simpson, Susan 463
Simpson, Todd 738
Sims, Aislan 427, 504
Sims, Jill 163, 288
Sims, Lionel 910
Sims, Megan 103
Sims, Stanley L 626
Simson, Kate 121
Sinclair, Francine 765
Sinema, Kyrsten 13, 305, 340, 418, 420, 497
Singdahlsen, Jeffrey 679
Singer, Gabrielle D'Adamo 377
Singer, Jenilee Keefe 709
Singerman, Phillip 720
Singh, Harry 617
Singh, Manisha 603
Singletary, Tajuanda L 800
Singleton, Suzanne 794
Sinko, Adam 800
Siomacco, Edward M 647
Sippel, Richard L 794
Sires, Albio 173, 310, 336, 421, 422, 443, 444, 445, 497
Sisk, Christinia K 664
Sisk, Susan 513
Sisk, William 787
Sisneros, Steve 456
Sison, Michele Jeanne 607
Sisson, Don 437
Sisto, Brett A 420
Sitcovsky, David 52
Sivulich, Jay 405
Sixbey, Mary 180
Skaggs, Marissa 454
Skaggs, Michael D 842
Skala, Edward G 420
Skarlatos, Tony 396
Skarvelis, Michele K 464
Skeen, Tanya M 640
Skidmore, David W 783
Skillman, David 221
Skinner, Robert 940
Skjodt, Cindy Simon 844
Skjonsberg, Rob 242
Skladany, Jonathan 435
Sklar, Cary P 900
Sklar, Glenn 789, 839
Sklerov, Matt 652
Skoczenski, Eric 516
Skorton, David J 807, 816, 817, 836, 851
Skouras, Lindsey 464
Skretny, Brian 188, 423
Skud, Timothy 617
Skule, Joshua 674
Slabach, Frederick 806
Slack, Emily 411
Slagell, Alison 216
Slane, Daniel M 508
Slater, Bryan 721
Slater, Lee 452
Slater, Lindsay 86
Slater, Rodney E 505
Slater, Samantha 46
Slates, SueAnn 658
Slattery, Jim 509
Slaydon, David 638
Slayton, April 687
Sledzik, Paul 820
Sleeper, Kerry 673
Slemrod, Jonny 595
Slifer, Russell 717
Slikker, William, Jr 739
Slingsby, Julia 459
Sloan, Mary Ann 839
Sloane, Al 722
Sloans, Tonya 417
Slobodin, Alan 415
Slotkin, Elissa 936
Slough, Andria L 651
Slupek, Mark 699
Slusher, Michelle 670
Sly, Mary 516
Smale, Alison 940
Small, Ann K 832
Small, Kristie 427
Small, Lee III 515
Smallen, David 756
Page
Smalls, Dontai 510
Smalls, Perre 154
Smar, Larry 376
Smeda, Elisabeth 749
Smentek, David 455
Smeraglia, Domenic 639
Smith, Adam 289, 313, 335, 406, 497
Smith, Adrian 163, 310, 336, 427, 450, 497, 502, 507
Smith, Alicia 425
Smith, Allison 220
Smith, Amy 144, 384
Smith, Angel 454
Smith, Annette Evans 816
Smith, Anthony Donovan 587
Smith, Ashley 82, 439
Smith, Barry 68
Smith, Barry F 818
Smith, Benjamin 739
Smith, Bradley 611
Smith, Brandon 454
Smith, Brenda 779
Smith, Brian 612
Smith, Brittany 228
Smith, Cabrina S 799
Smith, Caleb 459
Smith, Chandler 390
Smith, Christopher H 171, 310, 333, 421, 422, 497, 504, 506
Smith, Cindy J 943
Smith, Colleen V 644
Smith, Craig A 637
Smith, D. Brooks 857
Smith, Dan 807
Smith, Daniel B 602
Smith, David 670, 697
Smith, David J 858
Smith, DeeAnn 794
Smith, Dixon 654
Smith, Donald Malcolm 849
Smith, Edie 121
Smith, Elissa 652
Smith, Eliza 371
Smith, Elizabeth A 858
Smith, Enix 118
Smith, Eric 760
Smith, Faye 401
Smith, Fred 665
Smith, George 765
Smith, Gladys Morales 63
Smith, Glen R 793
Smith, Greg 695
Smith, Gregory B 601
Smith, Hal 98
Smith, Hannah 141, 157
Smith, Jackie 59
Smith, James Donald 717
Smith, Jamie 283
Smith, Jared S 97
Smith, Jason 157, 309, 340, 364, 409, 450, 451, 455, 497
Smith, Jason A 464
Smith, Jean 824
Smith, Jean Kennedy 808
Smith, Jeff W 842
Smith, Jennifer 680
Smith, Jenny H 398
Smith, Jerry E 857
Smith, Jimmy 654
Smith, John 615, 627, 629, 632
Smith, Jonathan 287
Smith, Josh 361
Smith, Joy 670
Smith, Judd 229
Smith, Judith 905
Smith, Julie 703
Smith, Katherine 594, 846
Smith, Kathleen 767
Smith, Kathy 720
Smith, Katie 361
Smith, Kelley J 730
Smith, Kelsey 460
Smith, Kevin 205, 677, 708, 719
Smith, Kevin B 711
Smith, Lamar 261, 313, 333, 424, 428, 429, 438, 497
Smith, LaShawnda 350, 351
Smith, Laura 5
Smith, Lavenski R 858
Smith, Leslie C 648
Smith, Marc 690

Page

Smith, Matt 405
Smith, Maureen 714
Smith, Max 748
Smith, Melinda K 393, 511
Smith, Michael 718
Smith, Michelle A 783
Smith, Mike 397, 456
Smith, Milan D., Jr 858
Smith, N. Randy 858
Smith, Nicholas 263
Smith, Nyasha 907
Smith, Paul 106, 785
Smith, Phyllis 841
Smith, Regina B 839
Smith, Richard 764
Smith, Scott 635
Smith, Scott S 673
Smith, Sean 237
Smith, Shane T 456
Smith, Shannon 230
Smith, Sheila 507
Smith, Shep 715
Smith, Stephen G 793
Smith, Steven D 38
Smith, Tadgh 779
Smith, Tiffany 370
Smith, Tina 143, 309, 328, 331, 345, 346, 365, 366, 374, 385, 470, 479
Smith, Tonia 417
Smith, Traci 721
Smith, Urula 652
Smith, Wendy 417
Smith, Wilbert 636
Smith, William 5
Smith, William "Bill" 700
Smith, William C 703
Smith, Willie 221, 747
Smith, Zachary L 637
Smith-Hawkins, Loretta 692
Smith-Heimborck, Sydney 825
Smith-Hirak, April 735
Smithson, Austin 251
Smolinsky, Frank 632
Smolinsky, Steve 423
Smoot, J. Patricia Wilson 683, 849
Smothers, Georgia 629
Smotkin, Danielle Adams 199
Smucker, Lloyd 232, 312, 342, 409, 410, 411, 443, 444, 445, 497
Smullen, Mike 209
Smyth, Reece 607
Smyth, Timothy 744
Smythe, Austin 459
Snead, Josh 452
Sneider, David 507
Snell, Scott 677
Snelson, William 682
Snipes, Steve 753
Snodderly, Tony 85
Snodgrass, Charles 375
Snoeyenbos, Douglas W 893
Snow, Jeff 389
Snow, Lacresha D 646
Snowden, Courtney 907
Snyder, Alexis 72
Snyder, Amiee 229
Snyder, Howard 678
Snyder, Kristin A 835
Snyder, Mark 166
Snyder, Matthew 508
Snyder, Richard P 936
Snyder, Sara 846
Snyder, Sean 941
Sobczak, Mary 91
Sobel, John 24
Sobel, Sylvan A 904
Socha, Chris 509
Socks, Barry S 814
Soderstrom, Sharon 391
Sogge, Mark 690
Sokolov, Anne 212
Sokolov, Dahlia 440
Solberg, Kristina 27
Sole, Tom 782
Solem, Rebekah 147
Solheim, Erik 941
Solhjem, Thomas L 645
Solie, Sean 366

Page

Sollazzo, Amanda 157
Sollazzo, Robert A 835
Solomon, Doreen 671
Solomon, Jennifer 749
Solomon, Karen 617
Solomon, Michael 783
Solomon, Russell 422
Solomon, Steven 739
Solorzano, Carlos Castillo 935
Soltani, Lauren 285
Soltis, Tim 763
Soltys, Darlene M 905
Solyan, Bradley 69
Somerman, Martha 741
Somers, Jeri K 805
Somers, Zachary 429
Somerset, Gary G 584
Sommer, Michael J 586
Sonderling, Keith 730
Sonfield, Brian 611
Songer, Erica 381
Songwe, Vera 941
Sonneborn, Matt 191
Soper, Kristen 516, 824
Soper, Martha 633
Sophir, Jayme 818
Sorensen, David 594
Soreth, Janice M 739
Sorrendino, Abbie 382
Sosebee, Carl 827
Sotaski, Frank 841
Sotirin, Barbara 647
Soto, Darren 62, 306, 342, 399, 400, 401, 431, 432, 497
Soto, Isabel 765
Soto, Rudy 36
Soto, Sandra 29
Sotomayor, Sonia 854
Souders, Pat 393
Souders, Patrick 88
Souleymane, Aichatou Mindaoudou 945
Sours, David 80
Sourth, Thomas 826
Souter, David H 855
Southerland, Matthew O 508
Southwick, Leslie H 857
Souvaine, Diane L 820
Souvall, Andrew 416
Souza, Allen 454
Souza, Paul 686
Spacy, William 633
Spadavecchia, Dominique 260
Spahn, Mike 284, 393
Spain, Emily 55
Spangler, C.E 656
Spannagel, Mark 20
Sparber, Madison 353
Sparks, John E 896
Sparks, Matt 31, 459
Sparrow, Mary 718
Spath, Vance H 638
Spealman, Jenna 409
Spear, Chris 505
Spear, Marie 423
Spear, Susan 696
Spector, Adam 679
Spector, Samuel 416
Spehar, Elizabeth 947
Speier, Jackie 26, 306, 336, 406, 407, 453, 454, 497
Speight, Donna Childs 722
Spell, Carmen F 818
Spellman, Chester 788
Spence, Gabriela 116
Spencer, Dion 798
Spencer, Michael 797
Spencer, Paul 699
Spencer, Peter 415
Spencer, Richard 651
Spencer, Sally 921
Spencer, Shalonda 151, 426
Sperin, Siobhan 670
Sperry, Stuart E 784
Speth, Andy 459
Spicer, Kevin 100
Spicer, Martin 952
Spickler, David C 769
Spielman, Alan P 827
Spiers, David 586
Spilman, Lena 221

Page
Spino, Daniel ... 378
Spira, Howard ... 792
Spiridon, Kristin Nelson ... 375
Spiro, Pete ... 28
Spisak, Craig ... 642
Spitalnic, Paul ... 738
Spitzer, Bob ... 699
Spitzer, Max A ... 464
Spivak, Howard ... 678
Splinter, David ... 469
Spochart, Michael ... 518
Spoerer, Katie ... 236
Spraggins-Scott, Jody ... 394
Sprague, Brenda ... 604
Spratlen, Pamela L ... 610
Spriggs, Deborah ... 405
Spriggs, Sean ... 634
Springfield, Robert ... 724
Springs, James ... 812
Springuel, Myriam ... 836
Spurrier, Mark ... 720
Spurry, Steve ... 783
Srinivasa, Veena ... 464
Srinivasan, Sayee ... 788
Srinivasan, Sri ... 860
St-Amand, Pierre ... 936
Staal, Tom ... 843
Stabenow, Debbie ... 135, 309, 327, 330, 345, 361, 365, 369, 370, 388, 469, 479
Stachel, Deborah ... 839
Stacy, Todd ... 3
Stadius, Stephen ... 364
Stafford, Bob ... 804
Stafford, Dillion ... 65
Stafford, Earl W ... 851
Stagner, Laura ... 802
Stahl, Norman H ... 857
Stahler, Jonathan ... 55
Stalzer, Jennifer Renee ... 420
Stanceu, Timothy C ... 879
Stanchfield, Eric ... 911
Stanek, Jason ... 415
Stanfill, Michael ... 664
Stanford, Gregory ... 604
Stanley, Elizabeth ... 189
Stanley, Jeff ... 630
Stanley, R. Christopher ... 780
Stanley, Rory ... 366
Stanski, Anne ... 135
Stanton, Alexandra C ... 807
Stanton, Joan ... 192
Stanton, Laura ... 803
Stanton, Robert G ... 781
Stanwich, Maria ... 811
Staples, Sean ... 905
Stapleton, John ... 291
Stapleton, Walter K ... 857
Starinsky, Melissa ... 738
Stark, Sharon ... 283
Starkey, John ... 366
Starks, Geoffrey ... 795
Starr, Dawn ... 801
Starr, Judith ... 830
Starzynski, Neil ... 724
Staton, Darrell ... 518
Stauffer, Lawrence ... 798
Staunton, Kathleen ... 43
Stayanovich, Jason E ... 744
Steacy, Zach ... 408
Steadman, John M ... 904
Stearman, Gary K ... 728
Stearns, Cliff ... 509
Stebich, Stephanie ... 836
Steckler, Frederick ... 719
Steed, Brian ... 272, 688
Steele, Danielle ... 416
Steele, Gloria ... 843
Steele, Kelly ... 511
Steele, Marvin ... 783
Steere, J. Douglas ... 870
Stefanik, Elise M ... 191, 311, 341, 406, 407, 410, 411, 453, 454, 497
Stefanki, Sam ... 23
Stefanski, Daniel ... 12
Stefany, Frederick J ... 654
Stehouwer, Peter ... 157
Steiger, Jon M ... 802
Steigleder, Stephen ... 405
Steil, Allison ... 294
Stein, Ben ... 49
Stein, Beth ... 376
Stein, Kara M ... 831
Stein, Steve ... 717, 718
Steinbaum, Jason ... 423
Steinberg, Gary ... 730
Steiner, Achim ... 941
Steingass, Henry ... 850
Steingasser, Jennifer ... 814
Steininger, Michael ... 700
Steinrauf, Robert ... 646
Steitz, Danielle ... 408
Stemler, Patty M ... 663
Stempowski, Deborah M ... 711
Stenger, Michael C ... 394, 517
Stephanou, Scott ... 52
Stephens, Andrew ... 699
Stephens, Bart ... 687
Stephens, David E ... 631
Stephens, Deborah ... 717
Stephens, Fred ... 710
Stephens, Garrett ... 2
Stephens, Mark ... 795
Stephens, Todd ... 255
Stephenson, April ... 759
Stephenson, Beth ... 409
Stephenson, Mark ... 436
Stephenson, Robert ... 697
Stepien, William ... 598
Stepp, Laura McCulty ... 510
Sterkx, Craig ... 464
Sterling, Adam ... 609
Stern, Andrew ... 716
Stern, Brian ... 805
Stern, Gary M ... 812
Stern, Keith ... 460
Stern, Matt ... 375
Stern, Richard ... 22
Stern, Terri ... 629
Stessel, Dan ... 850
Stetson, Jane Watson ... 851
Steurer, Robert ... 112
Stevens, Amanda ... 264
Stevens, John J ... 785
Stevens, John Paul ... 855
Stevens, Kim ... 427
Stevens, Kimberly ... 504
Stevens, Michael ... 813
Stevens, Molly ... 154
Stevens, Richard L ... 646
Stevens, Roger L ... 808
Stevens, Sarah ... 107
Stevenson, Christen ... 463
Stevenson, Lisa J ... 797, 798
Stevenson, Susan ... 604
Stevenson, Todd A ... 788
Steward, Bryan ... 396
Steward, Lindsay ... 452
Stewart, Adam ... 272
Stewart, Al ... 721
Stewart, Alexander ... 464
Stewart, Barbara ... 788
Stewart, Brad ... 68
Stewart, Bryn ... 298
Stewart, Carl E ... 857
Stewart, Chris ... 272, 313, 340, 402, 403, 404, 453, 497
Stewart, David ... 451
Stewart, Don ... 392
Stewart, Geoff ... 648
Stewart, Karen ... 608
Stewart, Mark ... 454
Stewart, Nick ... 192
Stewart, Ronda ... 396
Stewart, Stephen ... 651
Stewart, Vincent R ... 625
Sthanki, Maunica ... 430
Stiles, Samantha ... 259
Stiller, Allison ... 654
Stillman, Jacob ... 832
Stimson, Brian R ... 734
Stipicevic, Kristin ... 459
Stith, Lori ... 72
Stith, Ronald ... 815
Stivers, Jonathan N ... 508
Stivers, Steve ... 213, 311, 338, 418, 419, 454, 455, 497
Stock, Troy ... 436
Stockdale, Donald ... 796

	Page
Stoddard, Alex	382, 409
Stoiljkovic, Snezana	952
Stokely, David	153
Stokes, Gilbert	692
Stokes, Michael	653
Stokes, Steven	789
Stokke, Michael A	793
Stole, Scott	586
Stoliker, Patrick	810
Stolitzka, Anna	132
Stoll, Kara Farnandez	868
Stoltenberg, Jens	948
Stomski, Laura	831
Stone, Gale Stallworth	840
Stone, Jacqueline	717
Stone, John	415
Stone, Jordan	350, 351
Stone, Judd	381
Stone, Laura	602
Stone, Mark	794
Stone, Sarah	373
Stonebraker, Miriam	154
Stoneking, Tricia	294
Stoner, Kristina	652
Stopp, Mike	216
Storch, Robert P	676
Storella, Mark	605
Storelli, Dominic A	518
Storey, Simon	848
Storipan, Jennifer	207
Storm, Amy	634
Stoskopf, Wayne	346
Stosz, Sandra L	780
Stotler, Brad	98
Stottmann, Chris	451
Stouder, Janice	700
Stout, Bo	638
Stout, Jeffrey	612
Stout, Michael	682
Stower, Elizabeth	295
Stowers, Jim	709
Strachan, Timothy	795
Stracner, Jimmy	746
Stradtman, Terry M	841
Straka, Joshua	146
Stranch, Jane B	857
Stranz, Mike	401
Strassner, Erich	710
Stratienko, Maria	363, 364
Stratman-Krusemark, Karen	765
Straub, Chester J	857
Straughn, Patricia	401
Straus, Scott	844
Strauss, Alexis	792
Strauss, Herb	841
Strauss, Michael	615
Strawcutter, Alissa	449
Strayer, Robert L	603
Street, Casey	152
Streeter, Pamela	360
Strelsky, Felix	644
Stretton, Tim	387
Strickland, Brenda	57
Strickland, Kelle	264
Strickler, Matt	433
Stricklin, Kevin	726
Strimer, Luke	447
Stringer, Mark	716
Stringfield, LaVerne Y	740
Strock, Callie	262
Stroia, Matthew	225
Stroker, Kathy	827
Strom, Cordia A	903
Stroman, Ronald A	847
Strombom, Emily	42
Strong, AshLee	459
Strong, Karl	653
Strong, Kim	753
Strong, Scott M	511
Strother, Channing D	691
Stroul, Dana	373
Strupp, Hunter	423
Stuart, Keri	155
Stuart, Shannon	454
Stubblefield, Angela	750
Stubblefield, Larry	849
Stucky, Scott W	895
Studds, Stephanie I	711
Stuntz, Grace	375
Stuntz, Lori	469
Sturges, Mathew	752
Sturges, Mathew M	446
Sturgis, Antonio	653
Stute, Will	505
Stutman, Robin M	669
Stygles, Anne P	900
Styles, Kathleen	764
Su, Nien	423
Su, Sahra	255
Su, Shelley	423
Suarato, Ben	33
Suares, Erica	392
Suazo, Raymond	688
Subbio, Richard	427
Subich, Brian	230
Subramani, Aparna	951
Subramani, Gauri	615
Sudbay, Karen	122
Suddes, Paul	670
Sueppel, Rob	106
Sugar-Carlsgaard, Jordan	461
Suhol, Dmitry	717
Suhrheinrich, Richard F	857
Sujoy, Jaime	917
Sukach, Christina	639
Sukol, Robert M	464
Sulfab, Elmamoun	392
Sulivan, Dan	331
Sulkala, Lea	38, 457
Sullenberger, Keith	464
Sullivan, Adam	351, 748
Sullivan, Chris	200
Sullivan, Dan	7, 305, 328, 352, 353, 362, 363, 367, 368, 384, 480, 502
Sullivan, Daniel	813
Sullivan, David	611
Sullivan, Diane	814
Sullivan, Emmet G	871, 908
Sullivan, Eugene R	896
Sullivan, Francis	903
Sullivan, Frederick J	905
Sullivan, Georgeanna	392
Sullivan, James J	822
Sullivan, Jim	771
Sullivan, Joan A	818
Sullivan, John	425, 601, 851
Sullivan, John F	408
Sullivan, John J	845, 847
Sullivan, John P	647
Sullivan, Kevin	932
Sullivan, Marian E	806
Sullivan, Matthew	408, 771
Sullivan, Michael	617
Sullivan, Regina	850
Sullivan, Robert	730
Sullivan, Sean	788
Sullivan, Susan	770
Sullivan, Thomas	783
Sullivan, Thomas P	795
Sullivan, Tim	427, 504, 799
Sumi, Chikahisa	924
Summer, Barry	832
Summers, Bruce	706
Summers, Kate	396
Summers, Thomas	636
Summit, Monica	788
Sumwalt, Robert L. III	820
Sun, Howard	594
Sund, Steven	518
Sundstrand, Jacquelyn K	816
Sunga, Andres Fernando Aguirre O	916
Sunstrum, Greg	141
Suomi, David	749
Suozzi, Thomas R	181, 310, 342, 406, 407, 408, 421, 422, 498
Supinka, Tom	447
Sur, Christine	433
Suranno, Lauren	396
Surash, John E	643
Surber, Keith	745
Surgeon, Bina	460
Suri, Sarvesh	953
Suruma, Askia	268
Susman, Louis	851
Sussan, Ibrahim N. ''Abe''	586
Sussell, Nasim	370

Page
Susskind, Jamie 794
Sussman, Ron 718
Sutch, Zina B 826, 827
Sutphin, Holly 226
Sutton, Jeffrey 664
Sutton, Jeffrey S 857
Sutton, Peter A 799
Sutton, Tracee 203
Svinicki, Kristine L 821
Swafford, Susan 846
Swager, Curtis 46
Swain, Donald 775
Swain, Robert W 729
Swallow, Bill 749
Swalwell, Eric 27, 306, 340, 428, 429, 453, 456, 498
Swanner, Bob 395
Swanson, Dayna 159
Swanson, Debra R 637
Swanson, Eric 514
Swanson, James 657
Swart, Susan Helen 924
Swarttz, Richard 829
Swartz, Bruce C 663
Swatzfager, Philip 122
Sweda, Emily 233, 392
Swee, Alexandra 346
Sweeney, Bill 388
Sweeney, Margaret M 884
Sweeney, Mark 588
Sweezy, Benjamin 816
Swick, Anna 101
Swietlik, Dariusz 705
Swift, Heather 685
Swims, Breanna 82
Swing, Lauren 81
Swing, William Lacy 925
Swinnerton, Kenneth 724
Swinton, Maurice 783
Swirsky, Stephanie 723
Swiss, Kathryn 464
Swonger, Amy 597
Sybenga, Kata 378
Syed, Mohsin 364
Sykes, Angela 717
Sykes, Diane S 858
Sylvester, Ashley 12
Sylvester, Marco 200
Symington, James W 851
Symington, Stuart 608
Symons, Craig 780
Synnes, Mark 464
Sypolt, Jennifer 90
Syptak-Ramnath, Stephanie 609
Syrek, Christopher 770
Syrjamaki, Josh 144
Szakal, Keith 747
Szapiro, Miriam 818
Szaro, Deb 791
Szpindor, Catherine 462
Szwec, Peter 464

T

Ta, Minh 56
Taalas, Petteri 944
Tabache, Micheline 915
Tabak, Lawrence A 740
Tablante, Nancy 921
Tabler, Caroline 15
Tachau, Katherine H 816
Tafara, Ethiopis 952
Tagen, Julie 128, 427
Taggart, Rob 427, 468
Taglialatela, Linda 606
Tago-Elisara, Kuiniselani Toelupe 936
Tahir, Veronica 766
Tahirkheli, Sylvia 464
Tai, Katherine 452
Taira, Meghan 180, 392
Takai, Ricky 767
Takano, Mark 39, 306, 340, 410, 411, 438, 448, 498, 507
Takekawa, Beth 816
Talaga, Emily 796
Talbot, Eric 595
Talbott, David 717
Talent, James M 508
Talisman, Mark E 845
Talkin, Pamela 856
Page
Tallent, Terry 632
Talley, Amber 387
Talley, Brett 679
Tallman, Gary C 770
Tallman, Richard C 858
Talvitie, Travis 382
Tamber, Kimberly A 397
Tambini, Gina 934
Tambini, Steven J 789
Tame, Jacqueline 454
Tamlyn, Lucy 606
Tanaka, Kengo 919
Tandy, Carolyn 114
Tanga, Aketa 919
Tanin, Zahir 947
Tannenbaum, Jordan E 781
Tanner, George 772
Tanner, John 685
Tanner, Troy 795
Tao, Leonard 761
Tarallo, Julie 9
Taranto, Richard G 867
Taraszka, Carol S 676
Tarbert, Heath P 614
Tarcza, Ken 760
Tardif, Abigale 368
Tardif, Nicole 297
Tarrant, Ryan 137
Tarwid, Caroline 245
Tash, Nathan 749
Tashima, A. Wallace 858
Tasova, Erin 800
Tate, Edward 75
Tate, Frank W 647
Tatel, David S 859
Tatum, Cliff 844, 911
Tatum, Leslie 411
Taub, Robert 830
Taubenblatt, Joel 796
Tausend, Stephen 250
Tavernier, Delice 396
Tawadrous, Armia 703
Tawney, Timothy 811
Taylor, Andrew 423
Taylor, Blair 2, 350
Taylor, Craig R 589
Taylor, Dan 417
Taylor, Deborah 816
Taylor, Dominic 366
Taylor, Houston 804
Taylor, Jennifer 4
Taylor, Kawan 616
Taylor, Kelly 739
Taylor, Kenneth 686
Taylor, Margaret 373
Taylor, Mary 597
Taylor, Matthew 238
Taylor, Megan 164
Taylor, Michele 844
Taylor, Mona 215
Taylor, Paul 429
Taylor, Rachael 350
Taylor, Rhonda 254
Taylor, Robin 776
Taylor, Scott 277, 313, 342, 402, 403, 404, 498
Taylor, Stephen 909
Taylor, Synthia 662
Taylor, Terri 397
Taylor, William B 845
Taylor, William II 681
Taylor-Mackey, Sylvia 517
Tchatchouang, Jean-Claude 951
Teague, Cornell 405
Teague, John Abe 245
Teague, Larry 918
Tecklenburg, Michael 460
Teebi, Noor 191
Teel, S. Martin, Jr 878
Teel, Vance N 839
Tehrani, Michael 79
Teitelbaum, Josh 713
Tekach, Mara 603
Tekleberhan, Karen 724
Teleky, Katie 436
Telle, Adam 350
Teller, Paul 597
Tellez, Corey 88
Telliga, Mike 137

Page

Tellis, Arthur 353, 354
Telma, Tomasz 952
Tempel, Tanner 111
Temple, Tom 515
Tencher, Paul 129
Tenhet, Robert D 649
Tenney, Claudia 191, 311, 342, 418, 419, 498
Tenney, Daniel J 810
Tennyson, Mike 669
Tenorio, Mike 302
Tenpenny, Chad 108
Teplitz, Alaina 608
Terra, Judith F 908
Terrell, Brandye 772
Terrell, Tina 695
Terrier, Douglas 808
Terry, D'wana 796
Terry, John A 904
Terry, Lisa V 792
Terry, Neva 702
Terry, Paul 405
Terwilliger, G. Zachary 657
Teskey, Mark S 633, 639
Tessema, Yonas 821
Tester, Jon 159, 309, 327, 330, 347, 348, 349, 359, 360, 362, 384, 385, 388, 480
Teti, Catherine 734
Tetlow, Robert 784
Tetreault, Suzanne 796
Tevlin, Stacey M 785
Tewoldeberhan, Alem 77
Tezak, Joseph E 779
Thacker, Darin 159
Thacker, Jeff 17
Thacker, Stephanie D 857
Thallam, Satya 377
Thames, Beth 205
Thames, Karin 351
Thames, Madison 216
Thedford, Hunter 254
Theodore-Gandi, Bernadette 935
Theriot, Luke 269
Therit, Tracy 771
Thielman, Jason 159
Thiemann, Robyn 679
Thieme, Michael T 711
Thierauf, Linda 630
Thiessen, Pam 205
Thom, Barry 920
Thomas, Alan 803
Thomas, Annette 670
Thomas, Ben 261
Thomas, Bits 138
Thomas, Brad 411
Thomas, Brendan 247
Thomas, Brian 263
Thomas, Carroll 720
Thomas, Chad 518
Thomas, Charles 200
Thomas, Charles P 784
Thomas, Clarence 853
Thomas, Dave 841
Thomas, David A 782
Thomas, David M 724
Thomas, Doug 95
Thomas, Evan 256
Thomas, G.L 656
Thomas, Harry K., Jr 610
Thomas, J. Michael 616
Thomas, James 49
Thomas, Jeffrey 715
Thomas, John 277
Thomas, John M. III 842
Thomas, Joseph 717
Thomas, Katherine 346
Thomas, Kenneth 464
Thomas, Kyra 62
Thomas, Lisa 839
Thomas, Marilyn M 631
Thomas, Michael 616
Thomas, Ronald Dale 462
Thomas, Sidney R 858
Thomas, Teresa 730
Thomas, Theresa 237
Thomas, Tim 783
Thomas, Tyshawn J 826
Thomas, William G. III 813
Thomasson, Russell 260

Page

Thompson, Amy 744
Thompson, Andrea L 603
Thompson, Anthony C 788
Thompson, Bennie G 150, 309, 334, 424, 498
Thompson, Billy D 638
Thompson, Caitlin 744
Thompson, Carrie 665
Thompson, Christen 298
Thompson, Christy 76
Thompson, Damon 704
Thompson, Delores 726
Thompson, George 396
Thompson, Gerald 393
Thompson, Glenn 226, 312, 337, 399, 400, 401, 410, 411, 431, 432, 498
Thompson, Hart 76
Thompson, James 719
Thompson, James R. III 842
Thompson, Jamila 78
Thompson, Jason 687
Thompson, Jett 252
Thompson, John H 711
Thompson, Joy G 835
Thompson, Kathryn 408
Thompson, Katie 273
Thompson, Katrina 696
Thompson, Kristi 375, 795
Thompson, Laura 925
Thompson, Marcia 515, 586
Thompson, Matt 155
Thompson, Mike 22, 305, 335, 450, 451, 498, 508
Thompson, Mischa 504
Thompson, Monica 464
Thompson, Nikita 517
Thompson, O. Rogeriee 857
Thompson, Paul 516, 584
Thompson, Phyllis D 904
Thompson, Ron 705
Thompson, Ryan 254
Thompson, Sally 710
Thompson, Sandra 798
Thompson, Sara 651
Thompson, Scott J 631
Thompson, Sherry 838
Thompson, Stacey 723
Thompson, Tola 60
Thompson, William W. II 726
Thompson-King, Sumara 809
Thompson-Smith, Arminta 825
Thomsen, Poul Mathias 923
Thomson, Mark L 848
Thorin, Suzanne 816
Thorlin, Jack 389
Thorlin, John 436
Thornberry, Mac 257, 313, 334, 406, 498
Thornburg, Kelly M 397
Thornton, Charlie 788
Thornton, Christopher G 669
Thornton, Michael B 888
Thornton, Susan 602, 630, 780
Thorpe, Amanda Rogers 454
Thorson, Eric 612
Thorson, Robyn 686
Threadgill, Tyler 249
Threatt, Martha 830
Thrift, Laura 221
Thro, Alison M 785
Thummalapally, Vinay 713
Thune, John 242, 312, 329, 330, 345, 346, 362, 369, 370, 390, 480
Thur, Steve 715
Thurber, James A 510
Thurber, James C 798
Thurman, Karen 509
Tibbetts, Sally 67
Tidwell, Daniel 246
Tieman, Nicole 296
Tien, Michael 447
Tierney, James M 842
Tiersky, Alex 504
Tighe, David 858
Tighe, Jan 654
Tighe, Kathleen 766
Tigner, Susan D 644
Tignor, Robert S 905
Tilden, Jay A 760
Tilford, Catherine 783
Tillbury, Dawn 820

Page
Tille, David E ... 746
Tiller, Jennifer ... 401
Tillery, George ... 678
Tillery, J.R ... 643
Tillett, Essence ... 594
Tillis, Thom ... 195, 311, 328, 331, 352, 353, 359, 360, 379, 380, 384, 387, 389, 480, 504
Tillman, James E., Sr ... 696
Tillotson, David III ... 623
Tills, Thom ... 380
Tilman, Justin ... 811
Tilton, Jay ... 350
Tilton, Lee ... 688
Timm, Andrew ... 364
Timm, Lane ... 695
Timmerman, Amy ... 77
Timmons, Mollie ... 658
Timmons-Goodson, Patricia ... 843
Tingle, Carlos ... 516
Tingle, Carlos E ... 824
Tino, Elizabeth ... 840
Tinsley, Daniel ... 397
Tinsley, Kenneth M ... 793
Tipton, Connie ... 509, 510
Tipton, Scott R ... 47, 306, 338, 418, 419, 420, 431, 432, 498
Tirol, AnnaLou ... 663
Tisdale, Leslie A ... 508
Tisdale, Nichole ... 425
Tittle, Jeremy ... 31
Titus, Dina ... 164, 310, 339, 421, 422, 443, 444, 445, 446, 498, 507
Tjelmeland, Brenan ... 257
Tjoflat, Gerald Bard ... 858
Tkachuk, Jonathan ... 114
Tkacz, Kailee ... 694
Tobey, William R ... 799
Tobias, Constance B ... 733
Tobin, Katherine C ... 508
Tobin, Sean ... 231
Tochen, David ... 820
Todd, Brandon T ... 907
Todd, Will ... 350
Todd, William ... 605
Todman, Adrianne ... 911
Todt, Jean ... 949
Toedt, Michael ... 739
Toeppe, Myra ... 815
Tohamy, Soumaya ... 703
Tokarski, Kevin M ... 754
Tolentino, Anaisy ... 164
Tollefson, Elise ... 95
Tolleson, Jesse D ... 408
Tomassi, Chris ... 350
Tombini, Alexandre ... 924
Tombs-Souvey, Barbara ... 911
Tomchick, George J ... 745
Tomero, Leonor ... 408
Tomlinson, Adam ... 290
Tompkins, Clifford R ... 634
Tompkins, Michael P ... 677
Tompkins, Stefanie ... 624
Toner, Jana ... 1, 391, 593
Toney, Lisa Richards ... 908
Tong, Chiling ... 505
Tong, Kurt W ... 607
Tonguch-Murray, Inci ... 793
Tonko, Paul ... 190, 311, 337, 413, 414, 415, 438, 498
Tonnessen, Kayla ... 595
Tonsager, Dallas P ... 793
Toomey, Kathleen ... 661
Toomey, Patrick J ... 223, 312, 329, 331, 359, 360, 361, 369, 370, 480
Topper, Adam ... 169
Topper, David ... 464
Toppings, Christopher ... 195
Torero, Maximo ... 951
Torian, Gabriela ... 516
Torkelson, Jodie ... 148
Torklus, Mario Alexander Sander von ... 950
Tornow, Joanne S ... 820
Toro, Angie ... 166
Torppey, Brad ... 364
Torre, Karen ... 730
Torrence, Gerald ... 782
Torres, Alec ... 459
Torres, Angela ... 701
Torres, Narel Colon ... 303
Page
Torres, Norma J ... 36, 306, 341, 421, 422, 437, 498, 507
Torres, Rachel ... 730
Torres, Rosanna ... 442
Torres, Zoraida ... 393
Torrey, Ethan V ... 856
Torrez, Daniel ... 433
Torrez, Martha ... 700
Torruella, Juan R ... 857
Toscano, Richard ... 678
Toscas, George ... 680
Tosi, Greg ... 302
Tosick, William ... 798
Tosini, Suzanne ... 801
Tossas, Nydia ... 303
Tosten, Timothy ... 740
Toth, William ... 803
Touhey, James ... 661
Toure, Modibo ... 945
Tousman, Carlee ... 429
Touzinsky, Timothy C ... 650
Tovo, Kenneth E ... 650
Towers, Jon ... 449
Towle, Jacob ... 387
Townsend, Brian ... 664
Townsend, Da Shawnna ... 828
Townsend-Treleaven, Regena L ... 642
Townshend, Stephen J ... 649
Tozzi, Piero ... 423
Trachman, William E ... 764
Trachtenberg, David ... 622
Tracy, Collin ... 287
Tracy, June ... 740
Trafford, Sherry ... 905
Trager, Eric ... 373
Train, Laura ... 840
Traina, Trevor D ... 606
Trainer, Jay ... 811
Tran, Dat P ... 770
Tranghese, William ... 130
Tratos, Elizabeth ... 394, 514
Traubert, Bryan ... 807
Trautman, Tracey ... 678
Traver, Andrew ... 654, 655
Travis, Thomas ... 639
Travnicek, Andrea ... 689
Traxler, William B., Jr ... 857
Traylor, Patrick ... 790
Traynham, Eleanor ... 296
Treacy, William F ... 784
Treasure, Ana Solis-Ortega ... 935
Treat, James B ... 711
Treene, Eric ... 661
Treese, Linda ... 698
Trehan, Ranvir ... 807
Treichel, Mark ... 814
Tremblay, Carlene ... 121
Tremmel, Danyell ... 294
Tremols, Joaquin ... 700
Trent, Josh ... 415
Trent, Joshua ... 415
Trentacoste, Michael F ... 751
Trenti, Beth ... 368
Trevino, Andrea ... 265
Trevino, Anthony ... 44
Trew, Heather ... 611
Tribble, Conrad ... 602
Tribiano, Jeffrey ... 618
Trier, Dana L ... 617
Trigg, Brent ... 469
Trim, Arika ... 411
Trimble, Kim ... 420
Trimble, Theresa A ... 785
Trippe, Charlie ... 750
Tripplaar, Maria ... 449
Trissell, David ... 831
Trister, Sarah ... 236
Tritell, Randolph W ... 802
Trocchio, Clint ... 350
Troester, Robert ... 657
Troiano, Brian L ... 800
Trokey, Claire ... 155
Trost, Tami ... 694
Trott, Brian ... 396
Trott, David A ... 141, 309, 341, 418, 419, 498
Trott, Stephen S ... 858
Trott, Taylor ... 452
Trotter, Mocile ... 693
Troutman, Mary ... 114

Page

Troya, Guillermo 935
Truax, Parker 286
Truding, Bradley 301
True, Peter 366
Truelove, William S 916
Trugman, Kristan 397
Trujillo, Aaron 456
Trujillo, Carlos 608, 610
Trujillo, Cecilia M 595
Trump, Donald J 593, 594, 782, 850
Trump, Ivanka 597
Trump, Melania 807
Trupo, Mary 713
Trupo, Paul 699
Trzeciak, Adam 584
Trzeciak, Kimberlee 416
Tsaganos, Vasiliki 755
Tsai, Sabrina 506
Tsai, Ted Tien-Hsiang 920
Tsentas, Jonathan 373
Tsikata, Yvonne 949, 952
Tsiros, Alexandra 728
Tso, Roselyn 740
Tso, Thomas 729
Tsongas, Niki 131, 309, 336, 406, 407, 408, 431, 432, 498
Tsoucalas, Nicholas 881
Tu, Eugene 810
Tuccillo, Robert 753
Tuchband, Matthew 611
Tuck, Chris 397
Tuck, Laura 950
Tucker, Allison 197
Tucker, Ben 121
Tucker, Brooks D 770
Tucker, Cheryle 405
Tucker, David M 815
Tucker, Douglas 632
Tucker, Kaprice 690
Tucker, Maureen 603
Tucker, Natalie 469
Tucker, Rachael 657
Tucker, Tom 29
Tucker-Sorini, Desiree 788
Tudor, Chris 22
Tueller, Matthew H 610
Tufts, Clayton 240
Tufts, Suzanne Israel 743
Tuggle, Benjamin 686
Tuggle, Gary 666
Tuku, Elisha 360
Tukuitonga, Colin 936
Tulino, Douglas A 848
Tulloch, Rebecca 186
Tullos, Andrea 635
Tully, Chris 172
Tully, Crystal 364
Tulou, Christophe 368
Tumolo, Ann 140
Tuohey, Mark 907
Tupas, Luis 705
Tupper, Michael 689
Turgal, James L., Jr 673
Turk, Allison 226
Turk, Rod 710
Turk, Ronald B 659
Turkel, Allison 678
Turley, Geoff 386
Turley, Sheldon O., Jr 728
Turley, Victoria 693
Turman, Kathryn M 673
Turnbull, Michael G 513
Turnbull, Mike 752
Turner, Amy 725
Turner, Bruce 604
Turner, Calvin 693
Turner, Carolyn 272
Turner, Derrell 751
Turner, Eric 784
Turner, Fred L 169
Turner, Jeffrey 587
Turner, Johnny 5
Turner, Kam 240
Turner, Kimberly 224
Turner, Larry D 726
Turner, LaTonya 677
Turner, Linda D 905
Turner, Marella 724

Page

Turner, Matthew 615
Turner, Maurice 378
Turner, Michael R 211, 311, 335, 406, 407, 408, 453, 454, 498, 503
Turner, Reginald 904
Turner, Roslyne 380
Turner, Vaughn 750
Turner-Jones, Tamara 838
Turner-Jones, Therese 916
Turpin, Terry 761
Tursell, Beth 818
Turunen, Antti 947
Tuttle, Christopher 373
Tuwafie, Abele 389
Tvrdy, Joe 155
Tweedie, Andrew 923
Twigg, George 275
Twinchek, Michael S 425
Tyler, James 738
Tyler, Jason 162
Tyler, Jeff 682
Tyler, Jenn 515
Tyler, Maggie 433
Tyler, Millie 665
Tyler, Norris 726
Tyler, Sharon 730
Tyler, Tina M 782
Tyllas, Michael A 848
Tymkovich, Timothy M 858
Tyrrell, Abigail 63
Tyson, Jill C 680
Tyson, Patricia "Tish" 771
Tzamaras, Takis 513

U

Uccellini, Louis W 716
Udall, Tom 177, 310, 328, 330, 347, 348, 349, 362, 363, 372, 373, 382, 385, 468, 480, 501, 504
Uddyback-Fortson, Leni 727
Udochi, Frederick 821
Uehlecke, Nick 452
Ueland, Eric 361
Uhing, Cody 10
Uhlmann, Peter 832
Ulbaek, Susan 951
Ulloa, Walter F 807
Ullom, Tom 749
Ullrich, Tom 430
Ullyot, John 770
Ulmer, Daniel 150
Ulrich, Rebecca 423
Ulvestad, James S 820
Underhill, Robert 661
Undersander, Roy 655
Underwood, Charlotte 386
Unger, Howard D 844
Unger, Seth 616
Ungerecht, Todd 432
Ungerman, Ben 162
Unruh, Chip 235
Unsworth, John M 816
Untermeyer, Emily 828
Upchurch, Sara 594
Updegrove, Mark 812
Upshur, R. Terry 463
Upton, Fred 138, 309, 333, 413, 414, 415, 498
Upwright, Samantha 616
Urbanchuk, Jeff 446
Urbanowicz, Peter 733
Urcuyo, Miguel Marenco 920
Urisko, James 756
Urquhart, Celia 237
Urrabazo, Claudia 461
Urrutia-Varhall, Linda 634
Urs, Krishna R 608
Usowski, Kurt G 744
Usyk, Jacqueline 34
Utoikamanu, Fekitamoeloa Katoa 944
Utz, Sharon 442
Uvin, Johan 765
Uyeda, Mark 831
Uyehara, Margaret Ann 608

V

V, Arun 713
Vaccaro, Michael 712

Page
Vachon, Heather 384
Vaden, Stephen Alexander 694
Vaeth, Matthew 595
Vajda, Thomas 603
Valadao, David G 29, 306, 340, 402, 404, 498
Valceanu, John 812
Valder, Zach 366
Valdes, Vincent 753
Valdez, Mary Lou 739
Valdez, Roberto 61
Valdez, Teresa 34
Valdez, Victor 833
Valdivieso, Ana Rosa 932
Valencia, Stephanie 709
Valencia-Weber, Gloria 808
Vales, Tara 91
Valett, Lawrence 785
Vallabhaneni, Krishna 617
Vallario, John 634
Valle, Katherine 412
Valtos, Nicole M 793
Valverde, Madhura 709
Vamvakas, Andriana 730
Van Alstyne, Christian 662
Van Beek, Jason 363, 364
Van Camp, Anne 836
Van Cleve, Brie 366
Van den Heuvel, Skander 785
Van Der Weide, Mark 785
Van Doren, Terry 392
Van Duyne, Beth A 746
Van Flein, Thomas 11
Van Heest, Deborah L 648
Van Hollen, Chris 123, 308, 329, 331, 347, 348, 349, 359, 360, 361, 367, 387, 480
Van Keuren, Tammy 750
Van Lee, Reginald 807
Van Lieshout, Martha 201
Van Mersbergen, Rachael 209
Van Meter, Gary K 793
Van Orden, Tricia 714
Van Oudenaren, John 590
Van Ovost, Jacqueline 629
Van Pelt, Jason 505
Van Steenburg, John 752
Van Tassell, Melanie Rhinehart 22
van Trotsenburg, Axel 950
Van Valkenburg, Denise 279
van Weerdenburg, Martin 937
Van Woerkom, Greg 136
Vanaskie, Thomas I 857
Vance, Sarah 436
Vance, Sarah S 901
VandeHey, Vanessa 459
VanderBrink, Keith M 719
Vandergiff, Kristin 257
Vanderheide, Jake 931
Vanderslice, Jeff 43
Vanek, Michelle 464
VanHecke, Lucie 97
VanKuiken, Matt 135
Vanlandingham, Andy 350
VanMeter, Rick 116
VanMetter, Rick 149
Vann, Curtis 375
Vanonese, Dan 718
Vanoy, Lee 4
VanVranken, Howard 603
Varela, Blanca 10
Varese, Dane 294
Vargas, David 827
Vargas, Gustavo 935
Vargas, Juan 44, 306, 340, 418, 419, 420, 498
Vargason, James 681
Vargo, Alex 202
Varhegyi, Wendy 639
Variyam, Jay 705
Varn, Richard 716
Varnado, Martina 738
Varnasidis, Sophia 432
Varner, Kyle 346
Varner, Nicole 268
Varnes, Nicole 605
Varnon, Winona 785
Varnum, Steven 803
Vasiades, Mark 735
Vasquez, Adriano 698
Vasquez, Juan F 887
Page
Vassallo, Karen 786
Vassar, Banyon 430
Vaswani, Rita 505
Vaughan, Dusty 161
Vaughn, Erin Sager 180, 392
Vaughn, Lauren 907
Vaughn, Richard 247
Vaughn, Skip 720
Vaughn, Stephen 596
Vavasour, Daniel 613
Vayo, Elizabeth 669
Veal, Latoya 468
Veasey, Marc A 268, 313, 340, 406, 408, 438, 439, 498
Veatch, Courtney 58
Veatch, John E 778
Vecchio, Paolo del 741
Vecera, Andrew 433
Vega, Robert 263
Vehe, Robert 776
Veil, Andrea 822
Vela, Filemon 268, 313, 340, 399, 400, 424, 498
Velasco, Robert 695
Velasquez, Carlos Alejandro Tejeda 919
Velazco, Maurice 63
Velazquez, Nydia M 184, 310, 334, 418, 419, 431, 432, 441, 498
Velde, Rachel Ver 296
Velez, Frederick 188
Veliz, MaryEllen 270
Velkoff, Victoria A 711
Vella-Marrone, Fran 186
Veltri, Joanne 614
Vembar, Navin 804
Venable, Joshua 763
Venner, Gordon 936
Vera, Hernan D 841
Vera, Mauricio 843
Verastigui, Ruben 467
Verdejo, Guadalupe 934
Verderosa, Matthew 518
Verett, Whitney 4
Vergara, Luis Humberto Guzman 918
Verghese, Matthew 126
Vergilio, Joseph A 806
Verma, Seema 738
Vermilyea, Todd 783
Vernasco, Lucy 371
Verneuille, Danny 618
Vernon, LaMont R 585
Verrill, Ted 120
Verschoor, Thayer 770
Versi, Jannine 713
Vert, Alyson 777
Vesta, Michael L 780
Vey, Madeline 416
Viana, Jose 765
Viau, Evan 416
Victoria, Jesus Sierra 932
Vidal, Carlos Augusto Pared 917
Vidal, Gustavo Javier 915
Vidoli, Marino F 660
Vidovich, Greg 717
Vieson, Chris 446
Vietti-Cook, Annette L 821
Vietzke, Gay 687
Vieweger, Taryn 209
Viggiano, Jessica 845
Vila, Nuria Simo 917
Vilca, Julianne 630
Villa, Cristina 11, 433
Villa, Rick 465
Villafane, Jacqueline 782
Villalobos, Stephanie 383
Villalobos, Veronica 827
Villano, Peter 408
Villanueva, Raymond 779
Villarreal, Robert 258
Villegas, Dan 670
Vince, David 437
Vincent, Laura 112, 392
Vincent, Terri 588
Vincentz, Katie 141
Vinik, Grant R 398
Vint, Norbert E 825
Vint, Norbet E 825
Vinyard, Ashlee 261
Violette, Leslie 697
Viotti, Maria Luiza Ribeiro 939

	Page
Virga, Elizabeth	127
Virtue, Timothy	682
Visclosky, Peter J	99, 307, 333, 402, 403, 498
Viso, Olga	815
Vita, Susan H	590
Vitale, Heather	728
Vitiello, Ronald D	778
Vivili, Paula	936
Vizian, Donna	790
Vlasaty, Andrew	346
Vleek, Tomas	718
Vlugman, Adrianus	934
Voelkel, Ben	293
Voelker, Ron	617
Vogel, Ann	155
Vogel, Bob	686
Vogel, James K	638
Vogel, Karl J	637
Vogel, Robert	851
Vogel, Robert "Bob"	813
Vogt, Andy	375
Vogt, Anthony J	780
Vogt, Justin	36
Voight, Amanda R	664
Vojta, Christopher	772
Volkow, Nora D	741
Volz, Stephen M	714, 715
Vona, Russ	650
Vondrak, Frank J	658
Voorhees, John	843
Vorbach, Dylan	392
Voslow, Olivia	411
Vowell, Joel Bryant "JB"	641
Vrabel, Dr. Beth	371
Vrana, Eva	137
Vreeburg, Jake	455
Vrooman, Peter	609
Vu, Jessica	380
Vu, Victor T	701

W

Wackler, Ted	596
Wackowski, Steve	685
Waddell, Rick	594
Waddell, Ricky L	627
Waddell, Tina	840
Waddington, David G	712
Wade, Anne-Berry	689
Wade, Dana	744
Wade, Hamlin	415
Wade, Melissa	207
Wade, Sanura	630
Wade, Tonji	806
Wadhams, Unabyrd	744
Wadhwa, Sanjay	835
Wadhwani, Romesh	807
Waechter, Joseph M	848
Waelder, Ada	366
Wagener, Sharon	32
Wagner, Ann	154, 309, 340, 418, 419, 421, 422, 498
Wagner, Candace	408
Wagner, Charles	679
Wagner, Jeffrey	824, 825
Wagner, John "Wolf"	770
Wagner, John F., Jr	464
Wagner, Mary Louise	366
Wagner, Meg	216
Wagner, Roberta	703
Wagoner, Douglas	285
Waide, Cheryl R	72
Waidelich, Walter "Butch"	751
Wailes, Diana E	510
Wainman, Barbara	686
Wainstein, Richard	818
Wainwright, Ben	653
Wakabayashi, Ronald	662
Wakim, Joanne	783
Walberg, Tim	139, 309, 337, 410, 413, 414, 415, 498
Wald, Conrad Von	638
Walden, Elliott	378
Walden, Greg	220, 312, 335, 413, 498
Walden, Paul	692
Walden, Randall	631
Waldock, Andrea Niethold	229
Waldon, Samuel	833
Waldow, Eric	518
Waldron, Erin	63
Waldrop, PJ	75
Waldstreicher, Marcia	691
Walgren, Chip	350
Walitsky, Sue	123
Walker, Algie	634
Walker, Antoine	452
Walker, Beau	17
Walker, Bryan J	645
Walker, Cheryl	751
Walker, Darcelle	691
Walker, Don	246
Walker, Dustin	353, 354, 355
Walker, Eddie	436
Walker, Edward	416
Walker, Edwin L	736
Walker, Gordon	922
Walker, J.R, III	383
Walker, Janet	840
Walker, Janice	848
Walker, Jeffrey D	784
Walker, John M., Jr	857
Walker, Kirt A	782
Walker, Marcus	682
Walker, Mark	198, 311, 341, 427, 434, 435, 468, 498
Walker, Melinda	462
Walker, Ovonda	794
Walker, Polly	195
Walker, Reginald	585
Walker, Ryan	198
Walker, Sally	464
Walker, Steven	624, 909
Walker, Wanda	717
Walker, William M	912
Walkinshaw, James	283
Walkowiak, William	632
Wall, Debra S	811
Wall, Erin	80
Wall, Jeffrey	658
Wall, Kelsey	436
Wall, Virginia M	784
Wallace, Andrew	177
Wallace, Campbell	368
Wallace, Christopher	820
Wallace, Gordon T	642
Wallace, J. Clifford	858
Wallace, Jane M	515
Wallace, Lyvette	585
Wallace, Nikki	86
Wallace, Patricia	772
Wallace, Rachel	719
Wallace, Roy A	646
Wallace, Tyra	226
Wallace, Valencia Martin	717
Wallach, Evan J	867
Waller, Lorraine	827
Walliser, Jan	950
Walls, Jesse	455
Walorski, Jackie	100, 307, 340, 450, 451, 499, 507
Walser, Carolyn	293
Walsh, Amanda	182
Walsh, Bonnie	96
Walsh, Elizabeth Erin	713
Walsh, Helene S	793
Walsh, James	59
Walsh, James A	603
Walsh, Joel	378
Walsh, Kevin	361
Walsh, Michael J	709
Walsh, Noreen	686
Walsh, Sally	393
Walsh, Tim	44
Walt, Grace	281
Waltemeyer, Robert	772
Walter, Andrew T	408
Walter, Ronald A	842
Walter, Sheryl L	903
Walter, Terry	632
Walters, Barry	831
Walters, G.M	656
Walters, Gregory Martin	596
Walters, Jane A	815
Walters, Kirsten	665
Walters, Mimi	41, 306, 341, 413, 414, 415, 417, 454, 499
Walters, Ronald E	771
Walters, Sandi	712
Walters, Sarah	389, 687
Walters, Thomas J	780

Page

Walther, Steven T ... 797
Walton, Reggie B ... 876
Walz, Timothy J ... 144, 309, 337, 399, 400, 448, 499, 506
Wamariya, Clemantine ... 844
Wambold, Adam ... 417
Wandira-Kasibwe, Speciosa ... 948
Wane, El Ghassim ... 939
Wang, Alton ... 33
Wang, Andrew ... 717
Wang, Edgar ... 784
Wang, Gary ... 645
Wang, Lizhu ... 923
Wang, Phoenix Chi ... 72
Want, Stephen D ... 589
Ward, Aaron ... 78
Ward, Barbara ... 681, 769
Ward, Bradford ... 596
Ward, Diane ... 724
Ward, Joyce ... 378
Ward, Justin ... 803
Ward, Lisa ... 669
Ward, Mary Beth ... 790
Ward, Michael ... 936
Ward, Richard R ... 681
Ward, Ron ... 702
Ward, Ruth ... 119
Ward, Sam ... 106
Ward, Tracy ... 634
Wardell, Hannah ... 392
Wardlaw, Kim McLane ... 858
Wardlaw, Van M ... 842
Wardzinski, Karen ... 669
Ware, Fannie ... 151
Ware, Hannibal "Mike" ... 849
Ware, Jamal ... 425
Warlick, Jordan ... 504
Warner, Caitlin ... 378
Warner, Cameron ... 208
Warner, Lesley ... 423
Warner, Mark R ... 276, 313, 328, 330, 359, 360, 361, 369, 370, 382, 386, 480, 808
Warnke, Kevin R ... 792, 793
Warren, Andrew ... 408
Warren, Christopher ... 907
Warren, Debbie ... 63
Warren, Elizabeth ... 129, 309, 327, 331, 352, 353, 359, 360, 374, 387, 480
Warren, Michael J ... 847
Warren, Shane ... 370
Warren, Sheryl L ... 784
Warren, Stephen W ... 617
Warren, Timothy L ... 834
Warrington, Karen ... 224
Warwick, Cindy ... 923
Wascher, William L. III ... 785
Wasem, Stephen ... 665
Washburne, Ray W ... 847
Washington, Cynthia ... 801
Washington, Eric T ... 904, 911
Washington, Gerald ... 76
Washington, Harold L ... 712
Washington, Jacqueline ... 364
Washington, John A ... 851
Washington, Karinda L ... 776
Washington, Keith ... 747
Washington, Matt ... 405
Washington, Russell ... 662
Wasilewski, James ... 720
Waske, Michael ... 376
Waskiewicz, Steve ... 409
Wasniewski, Matthew ... 463
Wason, John ... 408
Wasserman, Aaron ... 287
Wasserman Schultz, Debbie ... 70, 307, 336, 402, 403, 404, 409, 499
Wasshausen, David ... 711
Wassmer, Victoria ... 749
Wasson, Lou ... 182
Waterfield, Anna ... 408
Waters, Bridgette ... 514
Waters, Mary K ... 602
Waters, Maxine ... 40, 306, 333, 418, 499
Watford, Paul J ... 858
Watkins, David ... 433
Watkins, Marcus ... 810, 811
Watkins, Michael M ... 810
Watkins, Roland ... 819
Watkins, Timothy ... 726
Watkins, Yelberton ... 241
Watkins, Yelberton R ... 461
Watson Coleman, Bonnie ... 176, 310, 341, 424, 425, 434
Watson, Brad ... 409
Watson, Crandall ... 692
Watson, Gina ... 934
Watson, Jennifer ... 241
Watson, John Paul ... 392
Watson, Kathy ... 15
Watson, Laura P ... 726
Watson, Michael ... 436, 706, 707
Watson, Sheridan ... 198
Watson, Terry ... 646
Watson, Todd ... 630
Watt, Brad ... 397
Watt, Matthew ... 803
Watt, Melvin L ... 798
Watts, Brad ... 381
Watts, Kathryn ... 821
Watts, Michael G ... 704
Watts, Sharon ... 470
Watts-Massenburg, Avis ... 698
Wavrunek, Glenn ... 294
Way, Elizabeth ... 721
Way, Kashi ... 469
Wayman, Carol ... 146
Wayne, Drew ... 192
Wayne, Spencer ... 389
Weahkee, Michael D ... 739
Weatherford, Austin ... 96
Weaver, Andrew ... 634
Weaver, Christopher ... 612
Weaver, David ... 583
Weaver, Kiel ... 459
Weaver, Kimberly ... 801
Weaver, Kyle ... 17
Weaver, Rachel ... 435
Webb, Brandon ... 89
Webb, Courtney ... 286
Webb, Donna ... 783
Webb, Glennis ... 514
Webb, Jim ... 378
Webb, Kevin ... 787
Webb, Nancy ... 838
Webb, Robert ... 716
Webb, Tracey ... 847
Weber, Dave ... 229
Weber, James ... 738
Weber, John ... 401
Weber, Josh ... 912
Weber, Mark ... 734
Weber, Michael F ... 822
Weber, Randy K., Sr ... 258, 313, 340, 438, 443, 444, 445, 446, 499
Weber, Richard ... 618
Weber, Wendi ... 686
Webre, Patrick ... 794
Webster, Crystal ... 255
Webster, Daniel ... 63, 306, 338, 431, 432, 438, 439, 443, 444, 445, 446, 499
Webster, Douglas ... 763
Webster, Gary ... 272
Weddle, Pam ... 396
Wedge, Ellen ... 516
Wedgeworth, Robert ... 816
Wedig, Mykel ... 401
Wedner, Anne Terman ... 843
Weech, Paul ... 821
Weeda, Jonathan ... 616
Weeden, Kathryn ... 505
Weeden, Kathryn S ... 393, 517
Weeks, Andria ... 695
Weeks, Cole ... 736
Weeks, John ... 614
Weener, Earl ... 820
Weerasinghe, Pamitha ... 440
Weger, Kristina ... 155
Weglein, Michael ... 68
Wehde, Anne ... 754
Wehrum, Bill ... 790
Wei, Min ... 784
Weichlein, Peter M ... 509
Weidemeyer, William M ... 514
Weidinger, Matt ... 451
Weigel, Deborah ... 12
Weil, Lynne ... 47
Wein, Justin ... 197, 507
Weinbach, Gretchen C ... 784

Page

Weinberg, Bill ... 779
Weinberg, David ... 135
Weinberg, Marca ... 705
Weinberg, Martha W ... 816
Weinfeld, Carrie B ... 671
Weinhagen, Robert ... 464
Weinsheimer, G. Bradley ... 680, 681
Weinstein, Andrew J ... 845
Weinstein, Erin ... 709
Weinstein, Jeremy M ... 845
Weinstein, Kenneth ... 786
Weinstein, Sarah ... 34, 167
Weinstock, Britt ... 376
Weinstock, Susan ... 612
Weintrab, Liz ... 387
Weintraub, Ellen L ... 797
Weir, Matthew A ... 618
Weirich, Jeremy ... 350
Weis, Keith R ... 666
Weis, Tristan ... 689
Weisberg, Frederick H ... 905
Weiser, Carol ... 617
Weisman, Matt ... 249
Weismuller, Jay ... 370
Weiss, Brian ... 383
Weiss, Daniel G ... 845
Weiss, Katie ... 43
Weiss, Nancy ... 816
Weissenbach, Karl ... 812
Weissman, Andrew ... 663
Weissman, Edward ... 921
Weissmann, Adam ... 461
Weitz, William F ... 188
Welch, Peter ... 274, 313, 337, 413, 414, 434, 435, 499
Weldon, Leslie A.C ... 695
Weldon, Scott ... 277
Wellner, Steven ... 905
Wells, Alice ... 603
Wells, G. Shawn ... 643
Wells, Jennifer ... 76
Wells, Kim ... 827
Wells, Reginald F ... 839
Wells, Thomas B ... 891
Wells, Tommy ... 908
Wells, Willard B. "Bond", Jr ... 665
Welsh, Jennifer ... 948
Welsh, Kevin ... 750
Welsh-Simpson, Kristin ... 394
Welters, Anthony ... 807
Wenberg, Michelle ... 707
Wenstrup, Brad R ... 206, 311, 340, 450, 451, 453, 499
Wentzel, Josh ... 201
Werkheiser, William H ... 689
Werling, Jeffrey ... 583
Werner, Alejandro ... 924
Werner, Darren ... 647
Werner, Francisco ... 715
Werner, Jennifer ... 436
Wertheim, Bianca Ortiz ... 177
Wertheim, Ronald P ... 905
Wertheimer, Laura S ... 798
Wesley, Kortney ... 60
Wesley, Richard C ... 857
Wessel, Michael R ... 508
Wessels, John ... 782
Wessler, Susan R ... 819
West, J. Robinson ... 845
West, Julius ... 460
West, Justin ... 373
West, K. Steven ... 822
West, Lucas ... 155
West, Madison ... 387
West, Meredith ... 383
West, Nadja Y ... 649
West, Owen ... 622
West, Thomas ... 617
West, Timothy J ... 689
Westcott, Lauren R ... 824
Wester, Paul ... 704
Westerholm, Dave ... 715
Westerhout, Madeleine ... 593
Westerman, Bruce ... 17, 305, 341, 409, 431, 432, 443, 444, 445, 499
Westine, Lezlee ... 843
Westley, Marian ... 715
Westmoreland, Grayson ... 449
Wexler, Robert ... 766
Weyeneth, Taylor P ... 595

Page

Weyers, Holly ... 689
Whalen, Laurence J ... 892
Wharton, April ... 646
Wharton, Melinda ... 735
Whatley, Kim M ... 908
Wheatley, Ellen C ... 736
Wheatley, Katherine H ... 785
Wheeland, Daniel ... 740
Wheeler, Andrew ... 508, 790
Wheeler, Jillian ... 271
Wheeler, Joe ... 411
Wheeler, Kevin ... 383
Wheeler, Susan ... 85
Wheeler, Thomas C ... 884
Wheeler, Thomas E. II ... 661
Wheelock, Jason ... 351
Wheelock, Jennifer ... 405
Whelan, Dan ... 221
Whelan, Holmes ... 385
Whelan, Michael ... 793
Wherry, Robert A., Jr ... 893
Whetsell, Walter ... 240
Whetstone, Courtney ... 213
Whippey, Peter ... 29
Whipple, Kathie Ann ... 825
Whitaker, Eric ... 608
Whitaker, Heather ... 1, 391, 593
Whitaker, Henry ... 679
Whitaker, Jacqueline ... 519
Whitaker, Kevin ... 606
White, Aaron ... 295
White, Abraham ... 130
White, Beth ... 813
White, Bob ... 246
White, Brad ... 150
White, Bradford J ... 781
White, Carol E ... 639
White, Carolyn ... 637
White, Clifford J. III ... 671
White, Dana W ... 623
White, Darrell ... 682
White, Doug ... 396
White, Elizabeth ... 790
White, Frances ... 151
White, Germaine ... 267
White, Helene N ... 857
White, Jayme ... 371
White, Jeffrey S ... 642
White, Jerry ... 287, 455
White, Joyce ... 75
White, Randy E ... 649
White, Robert ... 712
White, Robert J., Jr ... 907
White, Robin ... 706
White, Sonja ... 63
White, Stan ... 224
White, Stanley ... 427
White, Steve ... 205
White, Tania ... 714
White, Tim ... 510
White, Trayvon, Sr ... 907
White, Trevor ... 401
White, Victoria ... 64
White, William (Bill) ... 584
White-Dunston, Erica ... 792
White-Olson, B.J ... 654
Whitehead, Elizabeth ... 815
Whitehouse, Sheldon ... 235, 312, 327, 330, 361, 367, 368, 369, 370, 379, 380, 470, 480, 504
Whitehurst, Roland ... 587
Whiteley, Everett G ... 711
Whiteman, Aimee ... 803
Whitener, Bryan ... 844
Whitener, Jeanette ... 32
Whiteside, Fred ... 723
Whitfield, Emily ... 108
Whitley, Daniel ... 698, 699
Whitley, Pamela ... 750
Whitlock, Joseph ... 936
Whitlock, Matt ... 271
Whitlock, Steven ... 618
Whitman, Lloyd ... 596
Whitman, Shawn ... 505
Whitmore, Faith ... 23
Whitney, Jim ... 467
Whitney, Pam ... 440
Whitney, Robyn ... 694
Whittaker, Larry ... 446

Page
Whittemore, Megan 75
Whittet, Kimberly 705
Whittlesey, Tess 31
Wiatrowski, William 723
Wiberg, Madison 297
Wichern, Dennis A 665
Wichlin, Mark 724
Wicker, Roger F 149, 309, 327, 330, 352, 353, 362, 363, 367, 368, 382, 468, 480, 502, 504
Wickham, Thomas J., Jr 464
Wickiser, Tory 459
Wickramanayake, Jayathma 949
Wickre, Jenn 440
Wicks, Anne B 904
Widner, Mary Frances 516, 584
Widor, Sarah 703
Wieand, Jeff 229, 460
Wiedefeld, Paul J 850
Wiegand, Margaret A 857
Wiegmann, Brad 680
Wielobob, Kirsten 618
Wiener, Jacques L., Jr 857
Wiener, Margaret 796
Wiese, Eric 257
Wiese, John Paul 885
Wiesel, Elie 845
Wiest, Carol 226
Wieting, Donna 715
Wigfield, Mark 796
Wiggins, Beacher 589
Wiggins, Frontis 605
Wiggins, Marsha A 691
Wilbourn, Anna 16
Wilcox, Brodrick 692
Wilcox, Chris 63
Wilcox, David 784
Wilcutt, Terrence 808
Wilder, Christy K 824
Wilder, Renee 801
Wiles, Martie 113
Wiley, David 717
Wiley, Jennifer 380
Wilhelm, Melanie 828
Wilken, Mollie 401
Wilkerson, Courtney 750
Wilkerson, Jessica 415
Wilkerson, Patrick 688
Wilkes, Christina 461
Wilkie, Robert 622, 769, 781, 816
Wilkins, Ann Marie 807
Wilkins, Richard 247
Wilkins, Robert L 861
Wilkinson, J. Harvie III 857
Wilkinson, Monty 670
Wilkinson, Porter 836
Will, Candice M 673
Willbrand, Zhulieta 697
Willcutts, Kevin 724
Willens, Todd 178, 685
Willertz, Stephen 730
Willett, Don R 857
Willett, J.L 704
Willey, Katharine 380
William G. Sutton, CAE 510
Williams, Aaron P 585
Williams, Aisha Elaine 952
Williams, Amy 812
Williams, Anthony D 665
Williams, Barbara 660
Williams, Beth A 679
Williams, Beverly J 585
Williams, Calvin F 810
Williams, Cary K 785
Williams, Charlene 617
Williams, Clifton 212
Williams, Connie 707
Williams, David 847
Williams, Dean 378
Williams, Duane 692
Williams, Dwight 199, 778
Williams, Hallie 244
Williams, Harry B 645
Williams, Herman "Tracy" III 648
Williams, Howard, Jr 584
Williams, Jean 669
Williams, Jessica 101
Williams, Jessie 346
Williams, John S 719
Page
Williams, Josiah 97
Williams, K. Jane 753
Williams, Kathleen 812, 813
Williams, Kayla M 769
Williams, Kevin E 635
Williams, Lance 239
Williams, LaShonne 824
Williams, Lauren 212, 411
Williams, Lisa 747
Williams, Lisa L 587
Williams, Marcus 682
Williams, Mark 256
Williams, Marshall M 643
Williams, Mary Anne 395
Williams, Mary Ellen Coster 884
Williams, Mele 395
Williams, Mike 97
Williams, Natasha S 645
Williams, Pamela 469
Williams, Pamela S 447
Williams, Parker 20
Williams, Patricia 513
Williams, Phelemon T 631
Williams, Raphael 744
Williams, Richard 787
Williams, Rise 808
Williams, Roger 263, 313, 340, 418, 419, 420, 499
Williams, Sanford 794
Williams, Sharon J 679
Williams, Sheenia T 632
Williams, Sheri 510
Williams, Stephen F 862
Williams, Susan 678
Williams, Suzanne L 783
Williams, Teresa F 823
Williams, Thomas 726
Williams, Tina 829
Williams, Tony 705
Williams, Tonya 260
Williams, Vanester 754
Williams, Wayne A 756
Williams, Yvonne 905
Williamson, Ben 201
Williamson, Bruce 605
Williamson, Jeffrey 848
Willingham, Keith 824
Willingham, Kimberly 251
Willis, Kevin 751
Willis, Mary-Langston 240
Willis, Susan 514
Wills, Randolph 764
Willson, Darrell R 817
Wilmer, Jack 596
Wilmerding, John 817
Wilmot, Ron 179
Wilochka, Nancy 756
Wilschke, Susan 839
Wilson, Amelia 113
Wilson, Angela 718
Wilson, Audra 89
Wilson, Bernadette 792
Wilson, Beth Anne 784
Wilson, Charles R 858
Wilson, David 931
Wilson, Elizabeth F 643
Wilson, Frederica S 71, 307, 338, 410, 443, 445, 446, 499
Wilson, Gregory 632
Wilson, Heather 629
Wilson, James 368
Wilson, Jeanne Klinefelter 725
Wilson, Jeffrey 211
Wilson, Joe 238, 312, 335, 406, 407, 410, 411, 421, 422, 499
Wilson, John E 923
Wilson, Jordan 508
Wilson, Justin 395
Wilson, Kathleen 508
Wilson, Keith 765
Wilson, Kim 611
Wilson, Lawyer, Jr 665
Wilson, Luconda 650
Wilson, Mike 396
Wilson, Raquel K 849
Wilson, Reed 96
Wilson, Stephen 629
Wilson, Steve 175
Wilson, Susan 744

Page

Wilson-Coleman, Stephanie 804
Wilt, Aaron N 632
Wiltz, Jeremy M 673
Wimberly, Geisela 517
Wimbush, Tameka 76
Windhause, Jake 378
Winer, Andrew 83
Winfield, Susan R 905
Wingate, Mark 594
Wingfield, Dee 652
Wingo, Elizabeth 905
Wingo, Latrice 517
Winkelman, Chris 454
Winkler, Jenny 350
Winkler, Kevin 798
Winkler, Peter 226
Winnick, Everett 416
Winseck, Brian 55
Winship, Scott 467
Winski, Brian E 645
Winston, Melanie 767
Winston, Rhonda Reid 905
Winter, Mark 121
Winter, Mathias W 622
Winter, Ralph K 857
Winter, Theodore 830
Winters, Virna L 787
Winzenberg, Karen 670
Wirkkala, Rheanne 454
Wirth, Erin M 800
Wirtz, Denny 228
Wisch, Samuel 436
Wisdom, John Minor 857
Wise, Daryl 839
Wise, Katie 67
Wise, Louise 791
Wisecup, James P 651
Wiser, Devin 272
Wishnia, Andrew 368
Wisner, Peter 614
Wissmann, Yvette 41
Witherspoon, John 245
Witherspoon, Melony 516
Witkin, Maxanne R 769
Witmer, Andrew 216
Witte, Eric 106
Wittman, Robert J 277, 313, 337, 406, 407, 408, 431, 432, 499, 502, 508
Wittmann, Scott 378
Wixson, Jessica 286
Woerner, Johann-Dietrich 915
Woeste, Michael 411
Wofford, Denise 588
Wofsy, Noah 464
Wohl, Devon 177
Wohlgemuth, Mary 716
Wojahn, Nicole 395
Wolcott, Clinton 728
Wolf, Adam 73
Wolf, Chad F 775
Wolf, Derick 630
Wolf, Michael 798
Wolf, Patricia A 793
Wolf, Peter H 905
Wolf, Todd 650
Wolf, Tom 789
Wolfe, Catherine O'Hagan 857
Wolfe, Kaity 113
Wolfe, Mark 781
Wolfe, Mitchell 735, 737
Wolfensohn, James D 808
Wolff, Ben 126
Wolfgang, Donna 464
Wolford, Judi 173
Wolfson, Len 743
Wolfteich, Paul 613
Wolgemuth, Liz 244
Wolinetz, Carrie 740
Wolitski, Richard 735
Wolking, Matt 117
Woll, David, Jr 745
Wollman, Roger L 858
Woloshen, Amanda 173
Wolski, Victor John 884
Woltornist, Alexei 210
Wolverton, Tim 150
Womack, Kevin 756
Womack, Steve 17, 305, 338, 402, 403, 404, 409, 470, 499, 501, 507

Page

Womack, Todd 244, 373
Womble, Matt 350
Womeldorf, Rebecca 903
Wong, Andy 506
Wong, Bryson 433
Wong, Carolyn 771
Wong, Emily 401
Wong, John 796
Wong, Jordan 378
Wong, Norman 670
Wong, Robb 850
Wong, Vanessa 639
Wong, Veronica 43
Wong-Pietsch, Coral 898
Wonnenberg, David 776
Wonnenberg, Isaiah 364
Woo, Jaimie 270
Wood, Alden 611
Wood, Angela 683
Wood, Bryan Alexander 420
Wood, Diane P 858
Wood, Gary 763
Wood, Jeffrey H 669
Wood, Paul 784
Wood, Rebecca K 735
Wood, Roy L 626
Wood, Sandra 698
Wood, Tyler J 800
Wood, William 514
Woodall, George 361
Woodall, Rob 78, 307, 338, 409, 437, 443, 444, 445, 446, 470, 499, 507
Woodall, Roy 613
Woodard, Andrea 430
Woodard, Dean 730
Woodbury, Brendan 289
Woodcock, Carol 121
Woodcock, David 834
Woodcock, Janet 739
Wooden-Aguilar, Helena 790
Woodland, LaShonn M 826
Woodle, Sherri 664
Woodrow, Jean 433
Woodruff, Christy 271
Woodrum, Jeremy 187
Woods, Erica 425
Woods, Fran 245
Woods, Lillian 697
Woods, Michelle 378
Woods, R 651
Woods, Ranae P 631
Woods, Robert L 653
Woods, Tamara 108
Woods, Tonya 707
Woods, Velicia 714
Woods, Whitney 76
Woodside, Dennis M 782
Woodward, Gary 82
Woody, Thaddeus 268
Woolcock, Wendy 664
Wooldridge, Charles 715
Woolf, Aaron 259
Woolley, Mark 181
Woolsey, James P 626
Woolwine, Gwyneth 353, 354, 355, 356
Woolwine, Jason 351
Worden, Jeanine 745
Workie, Blane A 748
Workman, Jillian 384
Worley, Cheyne 110
Worley, Robert 772
Woronka, Ted 689
Woronoff, Arielle 371
Worrell, Nicholas 820
Wortham, Carly 48
Wortham, Micah 346
Worthy, Sharon 752
Wortzel, Larry M 508
Wrase, Jeff 370
Wrasse, Ryan 242
Wrasse, Suzanne 383
Wray, Christopher A 673
Wright, Adolphus P 666
Wright, B.G 405
Wright, Don 735
Wright, Jody 392
Wright, Judy 506
Wright, Kaleth 629

Page

Wright, Kathy 392
Wright, Kimberly 771
Wright, Mark 624
Wright, Melvin R 905
Wright, Mina 813
Wright, Pamela 811
Wright, Roy E 778
Wright, Sangina 439
Wright, Sharon 794
Wright, Sheila 746
Wright, Tommy 711
Wright, Tuley 416
Writer, John A 631
Wrobel, William 811
Wroblewski, Jonathan 663
Wroe, Elizabeth 375
Wszalek, Larry J 681
Wu, Jason 784
Wulfhorst, Kevin C 647
Wun, Ivan 784
Wyatt, Arthur 663
Wyatt, Marc 832
Wyatt, Nick 370
Wycinsky, David 726
Wyden, Ron 219, 311, 329, 330, 361, 365, 366, 369, 386, 469, 480
Wydler, Chris 439
Wyke, Darnley Eddison 916
Wyler, Russell 636
Wylie, Maureen 821
Wynn, DeAnna 619
Wynn, Elaine 807
Wynn, James A., Jr 857
Wynn, Patricia A 905
Wynn, Renee 808
Wynn, Todd 685
Wysocki, Kevin D 420
Wysong, David 259

X

Xenakis, Nick 380
Xu, Mark 697
Xuereb, Godfrey 934

Y

Yaakoub, Sara 103
Yaeger, John 627
Yahn, Leafaina O 300
Yak, Shelley 750
Yaki, Michael 843
Yakimov, Gary 903
Yamada, Debbie 123
Yamada, Richard 440
Yamada, Richard (Yujiro) 791
Yamagata, Les 805
Yamamoto, Alan 83
Yamamoto, Tadamichi 946, 947
Yamashita, Jun 919
Yamate, Robert T 606, 608
Yancey, Valerie Hall 658
Yang, Jenny 792
Yang, Shaolin 949
Yang, Sharon 614
Yang, Victor 65
Yang, Yingming 951
Yantko, Dominique 455
Yarmuth, John A 114, 308, 337, 409, 470, 499
Yarnall, Richard 589
Yarnell, Michaela 376
Yarrington, Michael 754
Yarrish, Lori 836
Yarwood, Susan 624
Yasner, Jason 590
Yasui, Toshiyuki 917
Yates, Kimberly 633
Yates, Perry 405
Yatrousis, Mary 52
Yavor, Robert 442
Yaworske, Jason 210
Yazdgerdi, Thomas K 845
Yeakel, Robert 409
Yee, Hoyt 602
Yelinski, Chad 201
Yelisetty, Rajasekhar R 784
Yerxa, Christopher 721
Yetishefsky, Matthew H 638

Page

Yezerski, Adam 351
Yglesias, Tara 806
Yi, Sang 433
Yingling, Shannon 516
Yingst, Bambi 36
Yoder, Brandon 373
Yoder, Kevin 110, 308, 338, 402, 403, 454, 468, 499, 511
Yoder, Ronnie A 747
Yoghourtdjian, Sarkis D 784
Yoho, Ted S 59, 306, 340, 399, 400, 401, 421, 422, 499
Yong, Li 944
Yonkura, Ray 207
Yoon, Bruce 724
York, Amy 397
Yost, Paul A., Jr 807
Young, Adrienne E 726
Young, Andrew 606
Young, Benjamin 694
Young, Brady 464
Young, Charles "Chuck" 584
Young, Charles B 784
Young, CJ 416
Young, David 106, 308, 341, 402, 403, 404, 499
Young, Deborah B 814
Young, Don 8, 305, 333, 431, 432, 443, 444, 445, 499
Young, Edward 778
Young, Ellen 231
Young, Jaunae 724
Young, Joby 79, 694
Young, Joshua 423
Young, Karen 717
Young, Lenny 32
Young, Linda 705
Young, Michael 801
Young, Patricia M 624
Young, Patrick 828
Young, Rashad 907, 908
Young, Richard 698
Young, Sarah 405
Young, Shalanda 405
Young, Sherry 405
Young, Steve W 772
Young, Todd 99, 307, 329, 331, 362, 363, 372, 373, 374, 383, 481, 506
Young, Torlanda 823
Younge, Nathan 850
Youngen, Angie 205
YoungSmith, Barron 408
Younkin, Nora 389
Yount, Dean 635
Yovanovitch, Marie 609
Yow, Mark 772
Yucel, Remy 717
Yuen, Jon 655
Yuen, Jonathan A 787
Yuengert, Mary 386
Yun, Joseph 602
Yuzon, Florencio 652

Z

Zabarsky, Mark 710
Zaccaro, Ray 219
Zach, Andy 415
Zagame, Monica L 420
Zagurski, T.J 656
Zaheer, Sara 375
Zaid, S. Ali 36
Zaidi, Amir 788
Zakarka, Christine 707
Zakel, Anthony 748
Zakrajsek, Egon 784
Zakriski, Jennifer N 626
Zamore, Michael 219
Zamrzla, Mike 109
Zams, Kelly 5
Zangardi, John A 777
Zaragoza, Zach 164
Zarba, Christopher 790
Zarco, Alvaro 388
Zarif, Farid 945
Zarodkiewicz, Patricia J 636
Zarrelli, Mike 510
Zaso, Andrew M 903
Zatezalo, David G 726
Zattler, Juergen 950
Zawatsky, Judith 803

Page
Zawitoski, Daniel ... 45
Zawodny, Kenneth J., Jr ... 825
Zeballos, Erick ... 943
Zeballos, Erick J ... 923
Zegers, Ted E ... 409
Zehren, Christopher ... 692
Zeidan, Fady M ... 952
Zeidman, Fred S ... 845
Zeilinger, Laura ... 908
Zeldin, Lee M ... 181, 310, 341, 418, 419, 420, 421, 422, 454, 499, 845
Zeldon, Joan ... 905
Zeleny, Diane ... 845
Zeller, Mitch ... 739
Zelman, Allison ... 721
Zenenga, Raisedon ... 945
Zerihoun, Taye-Brook ... 939
Zewde, Sahle-Work ... 940
Zhang, Minwen ... 951
Zhang, Tao ... 923
Zhao, Houlin ... 944
Zhenmin, Liu ... 940
Zhongxia, Jin ... 924
Ziaya, David R ... 711
Zick, Lara ... 817
Zickler, Joyce K ... 784
Ziebarth, Elizabeth ... 836
Ziegler, Emily ... 211
Ziegler, Mary ... 730
Ziehmann, Lisa ... 803
Zielinski, Paul ... 720

Page
Ziff, Benjamin ... 602
Ziff, Laura ... 748
Zimmerman, Ari ... 408
Zimmerman, Matthew ... 650
Zimmerman, Melissa ... 350, 351
Zimmerman, Paul ... 806
Zimmerman, Scott ... 757
Zinke, Ryan ... 507, 591, 685, 781, 813
Zinkham, Helena ... 589, 590
Zirkin, Nancy M ... 845
Zischkau, Jonathan D ... 806
Zito, Bill ... 262
Zito, Kelly ... 792
Zito, Vince ... 264
Zittrain, Jonathan L ... 816
Ziv, Blanche ... 713
Zobeck, Terry W ... 595
Zogby, Joseph ... 381
Zoks, Gita ... 719
Zorn, Jason ... 821
Zschiesche, Joe ... 749
Zuber, Maria T ... 820
Zuev, Alexander ... 939
Zupnick, Eli ... 284, 393
Zurbrigg, Shane ... 922
Zurbuchen, Thomas H ... 809
Zvenyach, Dave ... 803
Zwaard, Katherine ... 590
Zweig, Matthew ... 422
Zyblikewycz, Helena ... 447